Digest of Education Statistics 2019

55th Edition

February 2021

Cristobal de Brey
Thomas D. Snyder (retired)
National Center for Education

Anlan Zhang
Sally A. Dillow (retired)
American Institutes for Research

U.S. Department of Education
Phil Rosenfelt
Acting Secretary

Institute of Education Sciences
Mark Schneider
Director

National Center for Education Statistics
James L. Woodworth
Commissioner

The National Center for Education Statistics (NCES) is the primary federal entity for collecting, analyzing, and reporting data related to education in the United States and other nations. It fulfills a congressional mandate to collect, collate, analyze, and report full and complete statistics on the condition of education in the United States; conduct and publish reports and specialized analyses of the meaning and significance of such statistics; assist state and local education agencies in improving their statistical systems; and review and report on education activities in foreign countries. NCES activities are designed to address high-priority education data needs; provide consistent, reliable, complete, and accurate indicators of education status and trends; and report timely, useful, and high-quality data to the U.S. Department of Education, Congress, the states, other education policymakers, practitioners, data users, and the general public. Unless specifically noted, all information contained herein is in the public domain.

This report was prepared for the National Center for Education Statistics under Contract No. ED-IES-12-D-0002 with American Institutes for Research. Mention of trade names, commercial products, or organizations does not imply endorsement by the U.S. Government.

Suggested Citation
De Brey, C., Snyder, T.D., Zhang, A., and Dillow, S.A. (2021). *Digest of Education Statistics 2019* (NCES 2021-009). National Center for Education Statistics, Institute of Education Sciences, U.S. Department of Education. Washington, DC

ISBN: 978-1-63671-011-2

FOREWORD

The 2019 edition of the *Digest of Education Statistics* is the 55th in a series of publications initiated in 1962. The *Digest* has been issued annually except for combined editions for the years 1977–78, 1983–84, and 1985–86. Its primary purpose is to provide a compilation of statistical information covering the broad field of American education from prekindergarten through graduate school. The *Digest* includes a selection of data from many sources, both government and private, and draws especially on the results of surveys and activities carried out by the National Center for Education Statistics (NCES). To qualify for inclusion in the *Digest*, material must be nationwide in scope and of current interest and value. The publication contains information on a variety of subjects in the field of education statistics, including the number of schools and colleges, teachers, enrollments, and graduates, in addition to data on educational attainment, finances, federal funds for education, libraries, and international comparisons. Supplemental information on population trends, attitudes on education, education characteristics of the labor force, government finances, and economic trends provides background for evaluating education data. Although the *Digest* contains important information on federal education funding, more detailed information on federal activities is available from federal education program offices

The *Digest* contains seven chapters: All Levels of Education, Elementary and Secondary Education, Postsecondary Education, Federal Funds for Education and Related Activities, Outcomes of Education, International Comparisons of Education, and Libraries and Use of Technology. Each chapter is divided into a number of topical subsections. Preceding the seven chapters is an Introduction that provides a brief overview of current trends in American education, which supplements the tabular materials in chapters 1 through 7. The *Digest* concludes with two appendixes. The first appendix, Guide to Sources, provides a brief synopsis of the surveys used to generate the *Digest* tables; the second, Definitions, is included to help readers understand terms used in the *Digest*.

The *Digest* can be accessed from https://nces.ed.gov/programs/digest. Tables from each *Digest* edition since 1995 can be viewed by selecting the edition year from a drop-down menu. All tables that appear in the print version of the *Digest* are also included in the online version. In addition, the online version of recent editions includes a number of supplemental "web-only" tables. (Web-only tables are identified as such in the print version's comprehensive List of Reference Tables.) In the online version, *Digest* tables are available both in HTML format and as downloadable Excel files. The most current versions of *Digest* tables are posted to the NCES website on a rolling basis before the entire edition of the report has been completed. The "Most Current Digest Tables" page provides access to the most recent versions of all tables, including any tables already completed for an edition currently in progress.

In addition to providing updated versions of many statistics that have appeared in previous years, this edition incorporates new material on the following topics:

- Enrollment in public elementary and secondary schools, by level, grade, and race/ethnicity (table 203.65)
- Percentage distribution of teachers in public elementary and secondary schools, by school locale and selected teacher characteristics (*web-only table 209.26*)
- Unadjusted and geographically adjusted average base salary for full-time teachers in public elementary and secondary schools, by highest degree earned and school locale (*web-only table 211.45*)
- Percentage of fall 2010 first-time kindergartners whose school administrator in fifth grade reported that selected problems occurred at the school at least once a month or were a problem in the school's neighborhood, by selected child, family, and school characteristics in spring of fifth grade (*web-only table 220.65a*)
- Percentage distribution of fall 2010 first-time kindergartners in spring of fifth grade and fifth-grade scores on and standard deviations of various academic, social, and emotional scales, by frequency or extent of selected school or neighborhood problems reported by the school administrator (*web-only table 220.65b*)
- Percentage of fall 2010 first-time kindergartners who reported consistent positive feelings about school in fifth grade and percentage whose parents reported frequent avoidance of school by their child, by frequency or extent of selected school or neighborhood problems reported by school administrator (*web-only table 220.65c*)

- Average National Assessment of Educational Progress (NAEP) mathematics scale score and standard deviation, by selected student characteristics, percentile, and grade (*web-only table 222.77*)
- Number of casualties from shootings at elementary and secondary schools and number of school shootings, by type of casualty and level of school (*web-only table 228.12*)
- Number of school shootings at public and private elementary and secondary schools, by type of situation associated with shooting (*web-only table 228.13*)
- Number of hate crimes occurring at public schools, percentage of schools reporting any hate crimes, and percentage reporting hate crimes motivated by specific types of bias, by school level (*web-only table 229.70*)
- Percentage of lower secondary teachers in public schools who reported being able to manage various aspects of student behavior "quite a bit" or "a lot," by selected teacher and school characteristics (*web-only table 230.94*)
- Number and percentage of public schools providing diagnostic mental health assessments and treatment to students and, among schools providing these services, percentage providing them at school and outside of school, by selected school characteristics (*web-only table 233.69a*)
- Percentage of public schools reporting that various factors limited in a major way their efforts to provide mental health services to students, by selected school characteristics (*web-only table 233.69b*)

- Number and percentage distribution of 25- to 64-year-old bachelor's degree holders, percentage of degree holders among all 25- to 64-year-olds, and unemployment rates and median annual earnings of 25- to 64-year-old bachelor's degree holders, by age group, field of study, and science, technology, engineering, or mathematics (STEM) status of field (*web-only table 505.06*)
- Percentage of lower secondary teachers in public schools who reported being able to manage various aspects of student behavior "quite a bit" or "a lot," by country or other education system (*web-only table 602.93*)
- Percentage distribution of children ages 3 to 18, by whether they have home internet access, whether they have access through computer or only smartphone, and selected child and family characteristics (*web-only table 702.12*)

Cristobal de Brey
Supervisor
Annual Reports and Information Staff

CONTENTS

List of Figures

Figure   **Page**

List of Text Tables

List of Reference Tables

Summary of Enrollment, Teachers, and Schools

Summary of Finances

Chapter 2. Elementary and Secondary Education

Historical

Enrollment Status and Child Care Arrangements of Young Children

Private School Education

Teachers and Pupil/Teacher Ratios

Teacher Characteristics, Class Sizes, and Assignments

Teacher Attitudes and Teacher Mobility

Skills of Young Children

Achievement in Other Subjects

Student Activities, Homework, and Attendance

School Crime Victims

Alcohol, Illicit Drugs, and Cigarettes

Discipline, Safety, and Security Measures

Large Institutions and Institutions Serving Specific Groups

Summary of Degrees Conferred

Degrees Conferred—State-Level

Certificates Below the Associate's Degree Level

Associate's Degrees

Student Charges

Financial Aid for Undergraduates

Chapter 6. International Comparisons of Education

Population, Enrollment, and Teachers

Achievement, Instruction, and School Environment

Attainment, Degrees, and Outcomes

Computer and Internet Use

READER'S GUIDE

Data Sources

The data in this edition of the *Digest of Education Statistics* were obtained from many different sources—including students and teachers, state education agencies, local elementary and secondary schools, and colleges and universities—using surveys and compilations of administrative records. Users should be cautious when comparing data from different sources. Differences in aspects such as procedures, timing, question phrasing, and interviewer training can affect the comparability of results across data sources.

Most of the tables present data from surveys conducted by the National Center for Education Statistics (NCES) or conducted by other agencies and organizations with support from NCES. Some tables also include other data published by federal and state agencies, private research organizations, or professional organizations. Totals reported in the *Digest* are for the 50 states and the District of Columbia unless otherwise noted. Brief descriptions of the surveys and other data sources used in this volume can be found in Appendix A: Guide to Sources. For each NCES and non-NCES data source, the Guide to Sources also provides information on where to obtain further details about that source.

Data are obtained primarily from two types of surveys: universe surveys and sample surveys. In universe surveys, information is collected from every member of the population. For example, in a survey regarding certain expenditures of public elementary and secondary schools, data would be obtained from each school district in the United States. When data from an entire population are available, estimates of the total population or a subpopulation are made by simply summing the units in the population or subpopulation. As a result, there is no sampling error, and observed differences are reported as true.

Since universe surveys are often expensive and time consuming, many surveys collect data from a sample of the population of interest (sample surveys). For example, the National Assessment of Educational Progress (NAEP) assesses a representative sample of students rather than the entire population of students. When a sample survey is used, statistical uncertainty is introduced, because the data come from only a portion of the entire population. This statistical uncertainty must be considered when reporting estimates and making comparisons. For information about how NCES accounts for statistical uncertainty when reporting sample survey results, see "Data Analysis and Interpretation," later in this Reader's Guide.

Common Measures and Indexes

Various types of statistics derived from universe and sample surveys are reported. Many tables report the size of a population or a subpopulation, and often the size of a subpopulation is expressed as a percentage of the total population.

In addition, the average (or *mean*) value of some characteristic of the population or subpopulation may be reported. The average is obtained by summing the values for all members of the population and dividing the sum by the size of the population. An example is the average annual salary of full-time instructional faculty at degree-granting postsecondary institutions. Another measure that is sometimes used is the *median*. The median is the midpoint value of a characteristic at or above which 50 percent of the population is estimated to fall, and at or below which 50 percent of the population is estimated to fall. An example is the median annual earnings of young adults who are full-time year-round workers. Some tables also present an *average per capita*, or per person, which represents an average computed for every person in a specified group or population. It is derived by dividing the total for an item (such as income or expenditures) by the number of persons in the specified population. An example is the per capita expenditure on education in each state.

Many tables report financial data in dollar amounts. Unless otherwise noted, all financial data are in *current dollars*, meaning not adjusted for changes in the purchasing power of the dollar over time due to ination. or example, 1996–97 teacher salaries in current dollars are the amounts that the teachers earned in 1996–97, without any adjustments to account for ination. *Constant dollar* adjustments attempt to remove the effects of price changes (ination) from statistical series reported in dollars. For example, if teacher salaries over a 20-year period are adjusted to constant 2018–19 dollars, the salaries for all years are adjusted to the dollar values that presumably would exist if prices in each year were the same as in 2018–19 (in other words, as if the dollar had constant purchasing power over the entire period). Any changes in the constant dollar amounts would reect only changes in real values. Constant dollar amounts are computed using *price indexes*. Price indexes for ination adjustments can be found in *web-only table 106.70*. Each table that presents constant dollars includes a note indicating which index was used for the ination adjustments; in most cases, the Consumer Price Index was used.

When presenting data for a time series, some tables include both *actual* and *projected* data. Actual data are data that have already been collected. Projected data can be used when data for a recent or future year are not yet available. Projections are estimates that are based on recent trends in relevant statistics and patterns associated with correlated variables. Unless otherwise noted, all data in this volume are actual.

Standard Errors

Using estimates calculated from data based on a sample of the population requires consideration of several factors before the estimates can be interpreted. When using data from a sample, some margin of error will always be present in estimations of characteristics of the total population or subpopulation because the data are available from only a portion of the total population. Consequently, data from samples can provide only an approximation of the true or actual value. The margin of error of an estimate, or the range of potential true or actual values, depends on several factors such as the amount of variation in the responses, the size and representativeness of the sample, and the size of the subgroup for which the estimate is computed. The magnitude of this margin of error is measured by what statisticians call the *standard error* of an estimate.

When data from sample surveys are reported, the standard error is calculated for each estimate. In the tables, the standard error for each estimate generally appears in parentheses next to the estimate to which it applies. In order to caution the reader when interpreting findings, estimates from sample surveys are flagged with a "!" when the standard error is between 30 and 50 percent of the estimate and suppressed with a "‡" when the standard error is 50 percent of the estimate or greater. The term *coefficient of variation* (CV) refers to the ratio of the standard error to the estimate; for example, if an estimate has a CV of 30 percent, this means that the standard error is equal to 30 percent of the value of the estimate.

Nonsampling Errors

In addition to standard errors, which apply only to sample surveys, all surveys are subject to nonsampling errors. Nonsampling errors may arise when individual respondents or interviewers interpret questions differently; when respondents must estimate values, or when coders, keyers, and other processors handle answers differently; when people who should be included in the universe are not; or when people fail to respond, either totally or partially. Total nonresponse means that people do not respond to the survey at all, while partial nonresponse (or item nonresponse) means that people fail to respond to specific survey items. To compensate for nonresponse, adjustments are often made. For universe surveys, an adjustment made for either type of nonresponse, total or partial, is often referred to as an *imputation*, which is often

a substitution of the "average" questionnaire response for the nonresponse. For universe surveys, imputations are usually made separately within various groups of sample members that have similar survey characteristics. For sample surveys, total nonresponse is handled through nonresponse adjustments to the sample weights. For sample surveys, imputation for item nonresponse is usually made by substituting for a missing item the response to that item of a respondent having characteristics that are similar to those of the nonrespondent. For additional general information about imputations, see the *NCES Statistical Standards* (NCES 2014-097). Standard 4-1 provides information about imputation for item nonresponse. Appendix A: Guide to Sources includes some information about specific surveys' response rates, nonresponse adjustments, and other efforts to reduce nonsampling error. Although the magnitude of nonsampling error is frequently unknown, idiosyncrasies that have been identified are noted in the appropriate tables.

Data Analysis and Interpretation

When estimates are from a sample, caution is warranted when drawing conclusions about one estimate in comparison to another or about whether a time series of estimates is increasing, decreasing, or staying the same. Although one estimate may appear to be larger than another, a statistical test may find that the apparent difference between them is not reliably measurable due to the uncertainty around the estimates. In this case, the estimates will be described as having "no measurable difference," meaning that the difference between them is not statistically significant.

Whether differences in means or percentages are statistically significant can be determined using the standard errors of the estimates. In reports produced by NCES, when differences are statistically significant, the probability that the difference occurred by chance is less than 5 percent, according to NCES standards.

Data presented in the text do not investigate more complex hypotheses, account for interrelationships among variables, or support causal inferences. We encourage readers who are interested in more complex questions and in-depth analysis to explore other NCES resources, including publications, online data tools, and public- and restricted-use datasets at https://nces.ed.gov.

In text that reports estimates based on samples, differences between estimates (including increases and decreases) are stated only when they are statistically significant. To determine whether differences reported are statistically significant, two-tailed *t* tests at the .05 level are typically used. The *t* test formula for determining statistical significance is adjusted when the samples being compared are dependent. The *t* test formula is not adjusted for multiple comparisons, with the exception of statistical tests conducted using the NAEP Data Explorer (https://nces.ed.gov/nationsreportcard/data/). When the variables to be tested are postulated to form a trend, the relationship may be tested using linear regression, logistic regression, or ANOVA trend analysis instead of a series of *t* tests. These alternate methods of analysis test for specific relationships (e.g., linear, quadratic, or cubic) among variables. For more information on data analysis, please see the NCES Statistical Standards, Standard 5-1, available at https://nces.ed.gov/statprog/2012/pdf/Chapter5.pdf.

A number of considerations inuence the ultimate selection of the data years to include in the tables and to feature in the text. To make analyses as timely as possible, the latest year of available data is shown. The choice of comparison years is often also based on the need to show the earliest available survey year, as in the case of NAEP and the international assessment surveys. The text typically compares the most current year's data with those from the initial year and then with those from a more recent year. In the case of surveys with long time frames, such as surveys measuring enrollment, changes over the course of a decade may be noted in the text. Where applicable, the text may also note years in which the data begin to diverge from previous trends. In figures and tables, intervening years are selected in increments in order to show the general trend.

Rounding and Other Considerations

All calculations are based on unrounded estimates. Therefore, the reader may find that a calculation, such as a difference or a percentage change, cited in the text or a figure may not be identical to the calculation obtained by using the rounded values shown in the accompanying tables. Although values reported in the tables are generally rounded to one decimal place (e.g., 76.5 percent), values reported in the text are generally rounded to whole numbers (with any value of 0.50 or above rounded to the next highest whole number). Due to rounding, cumulative percentages may sometimes equal 99 or 101 percent rather than 100 percent.

Race and Ethnicity

The Office of Management and udget (OM) is responsible for the standards that govern the categories used to collect and present federal data on race and ethnicity. The OMB revised the guidelines on racial/ethnic categories used by the federal government in October 1997, with a January 2003 deadline for implementation. The revised standards reuire a minimum of these five categories for data on race: American Indian or Alaska Native, Asian, Black or African American, Native Hawaiian or Other Pacific Islander, and hite. The standards also reuire the collection of data on the ethnicity categories Hispanic or Latino and Not Hispanic or Latino. It is important to note that Hispanic origin is an ethnicity rather than a race, and therefore persons of Hispanic origin may be of any race.

Origin can be viewed as the heritage, nationality group, lineage, or country of birth of the person or the person's parents or ancestors before their arrival in the United States. The race categories White, Black, Asian, Native Hawaiian or Other Pacific Islander, and American Indian or Alaska Native exclude persons of Hispanic origin unless otherwise noted.

For a description of each racial/ethnic category, please see the "Racial/ethnic group" entry in Appendix : Definitions. Some of the category labels are shortened for more concise presentation in text, tables, and figures. American Indian or Alaska Native is denoted as American Indian/Alaska Native (except when separate estimates are available for American Indians alone or Alaska Natives alone); lack or African American is shortened to lack; and Hispanic or Latino is shortened to Hispanic. When discussed separately from Asian estimates, Native Hawaiian or Other Pacific Islander is shortened to Pacific Islander

Many of the data sources used for this volume are federal surveys that collect data using the OMB standards for racialethnic classification described above; however, some sources have not fully adopted the standards, and some tables include historical data collected prior to the adoption of the OM standards. Asians and Pacific Islanders are combined into a single category for years in which the data were not collected separately for the two groups. The combined category can sometimes mask significant differences between the two subgroups. For example, prior to 2011, NAEP collected data that did not allow for separate reporting of estimates for Asians and Pacific Islanders. The population counts presented in table 101.20, based on the U.S. Census Bureau's Current Population Reports, indicate that 6 percent of all AsianPacific Islander 5- to 17-year-olds were Asian in 2010. Thus, the combined category for AsiansPacific Islanders is more representative of Asians than of Pacific Islanders.

Some surveys give respondents the option of selecting more than one race category, an "other" race category, or a "Two or more races" or "more than one race" category. Where possible, tables present data on the "Two or more races" category; however, in some cases this category may not be separately shown because the information was not collected or due to other data issues. Some tables include the "other" category. Any comparisons made between persons of one racial/ethnic group and persons of "all other racial/ethnic groups" include only the racial/ethnic groups shown in the reference table. In some surveys, respondents are not given the option to select more than one race category and also are not given an option such as "other" or "more than one race." In these surveys, respondents of Two or more races must select a single race category. Any comparisons between data from surveys that give the option to select more than one race and surveys that do not offer such an option should take into account the fact that there is a potential for bias if members of one racial group are more likely than members of the others to identify themselves as

"Two or more races."[1] For postsecondary data, foreign students are counted separately and are therefore not included in any racial/ethnic category.

In addition to the major racial/ethnic categories, several tables include Hispanic ancestry subgroups (such as Mexican, Puerto Rican, Cuban, Dominican, Salvadoran, Other Central American, and South American) and Asian ancestry subgroups (such as Asian Indian, Chinese, Filipino, Japanese, Korean, and Vietnamese). In addition, selected tables include "Two or more races" subgroups (such as White and Black, White and Asian, and White and American Indian/Alaska Native).

Limitations of the Data

Due to large standard errors, some differences that seem substantial are not statistically significant and, therefore, are not cited in the text. This situation often applies to estimates involving American Indians/Alaska Natives and Pacific Islanders. The relatively small sies' of these populations pose many measurement difficulties when conducting statistical analysis. Even in larger surveys, the numbers of American IndiansAlaska' Natives and Pacific Islanders included in a sample are often small. Researchers studying data on these two populations often face small sample sizes that increase the size of standard errors and reduce the reliability of results. Readers should keep these limitations in mind when comparing estimates presented in the tables.

As mentioned, caution should be exercised when comparing data from different sources. Differences in sampling, data collection procedures, coverage of target population, timing, phrasing of questions, scope of nonresponse, interviewer training, and data processing and coding mean that results from different sources may not be strictly comparable. For example, the racial/ethnic categories presented to a respondent, and the way in which the uestion` is asked, can inuence` the response, especially for individuals who consider themselves of more than one race or ethnicity. In addition, data on American Indians/Alaska Natives are often subject to inaccuracies that can result from respondents self-identifying their race/ethnicity. Research on the collection of race/ethnicity data suggests that the categorization of American Indian and Alaska Native is the least stable self-identification (for example, the same individual may identify as American Indian when responding to one survey but may not do so on a subsequent survey).[2]

---

[1] For discussion of such bias in responses to the 2000 Census, see Parker, J., et al. (2004). Bridging Between Two Standards for Collecting Information on Race and Ethnicity: An Application to Census 2000 and Vital Rates. *Public Health Reports, 119*(2): 192–205. Available at https://www.ncbi.nlm.nih.gov/pmc/articles/PMC1497618/.

[2] See U.S. Department of Labor, Bureau of Labor Statistics (1995). *A Test of Methods for Collecting Racial and Ethnic Information* (USDL 95-428). Washington DC: Author. Available at https://www.bls.gov/news.release/history/ethnic_102795.txt.

INTRODUCTION

The Introduction provides a brief overview of current trends in American education, highlighting key data that are presented in more detail later in this volume. Topics outlined include the participation of students, teachers, and faculty in U.S. educational institutions; the performance of U.S. elementary/secondary students overall and in comparison to students in other countries; the numbers of high school graduates and postsecondary degrees; and the amounts of expenditures on education at the elementary/secondary and postsecondary levels. Data on enrollments, teachers, and faculty are for fall of the given year.

In fall 2019, about 76.1 million people were enrolled in American schools and colleges (table 105.10). About 4.7 million people were employed as elementary and secondary school teachers or as college faculty, in full-time equivalents (FTE). Other professional, administrative, and support staff at educational institutions totaled 5.7 million FTE employees. All data for 2019 in this Introduction are projected, except for data on student performance and educational attainment. Some data for other years are projected or estimated as noted. All projections were estimated prior to the coronavirus pandemic. In discussions of historical trends, different time periods and specific years are cited, depending on the timing of important changes as well as the availability of relevant data.

Elementary/Secondary Education

Enrollment

Overall, public school enrollment rose 28 percent, from 39.4 million to 50.6 million, between 1985 and 2019. This reects` a pattern of annual increases in total public elementary and secondary school enrollment, which began in 1985, but stalled at 49.3 million between 2006 and 2008, before beginning to increase again (table 105.30). Private school enrollment uctuated` during this period, with the fall 2019 enrollment of 5.7 million being 3 percent higher than the fall 1985 enrollment of 5.6 million. About 10 percent of elementary and secondary school students were enrolled in private schools in 201,` reecting` a decrease from 12 percent in 1985.

In public schools between 1985 and 2019, there was a 31 percent increase in elementary enrollment (prekindergarten through grade 8), compared with a 23 percent increase in secondary enrollment (grades 9 through 12;

table 105.30). Part of the higher growth in public elementary school enrollment resulted from the expansion of prekindergarten enrollment. Between 1985 and 2019, enrollment in prekindergarten increased 880 percent, while enrollment in other elementary grades (including kindergarten through grade 8 and ungraded elementary programs) increased 26 percent (table 203.10). The number of children enrolled in prekindergarten increased from 0.2 million in 1985 to 1.5 million in 2019, and the number enrolled in other elementary grades increased from 26.9 million to 33.9 million. Public secondary school enrollment declined 8 percent from 1985 to 1990 but then increased 33 percent from 1990 to 2007. Over the most recent 10-year period (between 2009 and 2019), public school enrollment rose 3 percent. Elementary school enrollment increased 3 percent between 2009 and 2019, while secondary school enrollment increased 2 percent.

Since the enrollment rates of 5- and 6-year-olds (typical ages for preprimary grades) and 7- to 13-year-olds (typical ages for elementary grades) decreased by fewer than 5 percentage points from 1985 to 2018 and the enrollment rate for 14- to 17-year-olds (typical ages for secondary grades) in 2018 was not measurably different from the rate in 1985, overall increases in public school enrollment primarily reect` increases in the number of children in these age groups (tables 101.10 and 103.20). For example, the enrollment rate of 7- to 13-year-olds decreased from 99 to 98 percent between 1985 and 2018, but the number of 7- to 13-year-olds increased 26 percent. Similarly, increases in public secondary school enrollment are more reective` of the 12 percent increase in the 14- to 17-year-old population between 1985 and 2018 than of the enrollment rates for these years, which were not measurably different (about 95 percent for both years). Increases in the enrollment rate of prekindergarten-age children (ages 3 and 4), from 39 percent in 1985 to 54 percent in 2018, and in the number of 3- and 4-year-olds, from 7.1 million to 8.1 million, also contributed to overall increases in prekindergarten through grade 12 enrollment.

Before the coronavirus pandemic, the National Center for Education Statistics (NCES) projected near record levels of total public elementary and secondary school enrollment from 2019 (50.6 million) through 2029 (51.1 million; table 105.30). Public elementary school enrollment was projected to increase 2 percent between 2019 and 2029, while public secondary school enrollment was projected to be about 1 percent lower in 2029 than in

2019. Overall, total public school enrollment was projected to increase 1 percent between 2019 and 2029. However, as the impact of the coronavirus pandemic remains unknown, these projections are subject to revision.

Teachers

A projected 3.7 million full-time-equivalent (FTE) elementary and secondary school teachers were engaged in classroom instruction in fall 2019, which was less than 1 percent higher than the number of FTE teachers in fall 2009 (table 105.40). Of these 3.7 million FTE elementary and secondary school teachers in 2019, about 3.2 million taught in public schools and 0.5 million taught in private schools.

Public school enrollment was 3 percent higher in 2019 than in 2009, while the number of public school teachers was 1 percent lower (table 208.20). The number of public school pupils per teacher was higher in 2019 (15.9) than in 2009 (15.4).

The average salary for public school teachers in 2018–19 was $61,730 (table 211.50). In constant (i.e., inflation-adjusted) dollars, the average teacher salary was 1 percent lower in 2018–19 than in 1990–91.

Student Performance

National Comparisons

Much of the student performance data in the *Digest* are drawn from the National Assessment of Educational Progress (NAEP). The NAEP assessments have been conducted using three basic designs: the national main NAEP, state NAEP, and long-term trend NAEP. The national main NAEP and state NAEP provide current information about student performance in subjects including reading, mathematics, science, and writing, while long-term trend NAEP provides information on performance since the early 1970s in reading and mathematics only. Results from long-term trend NAEP are included in the discussion in chapter 2 of the *Digest*, while the information in this Introduction includes only selected results from the national main NAEP. Readers should keep in mind that comparisons of NAEP scores in the text (like all comparisons of estimates in the *Digest*) are based on statistical testing of unrounded values.

The main NAEP reports current information for the nation and specific geographic regions of the country. The assessment program includes students drawn from both public and private schools and reports results for student achievement at grades 4, 8, and 12. The main NAEP assessments follow the frameworks developed by the National Assessment Governing Board and use the latest advances in assessment methodology. The state NAEP is identical in content to the national main NAEP, but the state NAEP reports information only for public school students. Chapter 2 presents more information on the NAEP designs and methodology, and additional details appear in Appendix A: Guide to Sources.

NAEP Reading

The main NAEP reading assessment data are reported on a scale of 0 to 500. For 4th-grade students, the average reading score in 2019 (220) was lower than the score in 2017 (222) but was higher than the 1992 score (217; table 221.10). This pattern held for certain racial/ethnic groups (White and Black students), but not for others (Hispanic, AsianPacific Islander, and American IndianAlaska` Native students). Specifically, at grade 4, the 201` reading scores for White (230) and Black (204) students were lower than the corresponding scores in 2017 (232 and 206, respectively), but higher than 1992 (224 and 192, respectively). In contrast, the 4th-grade reading scores for Hispanic (209) and AsianPacific Islander (237) students were not measurably different in 2019 than in 2017, but the scores for both groups were higher in 2019 than in 1992 (197 and 216, respectively). For American Indian/Alaska Native students, the average 4th-grade reading score in 2019 (204) was not measurably different from the scores in either 2017 or 1994 (1994 was the first year data were available for 4th-grade American Indian/Alaska Native students).

From 1992 through 2019, the average reading scores for White 4th-graders were higher than those for their Black and Hispanic peers. Although the White-Black achievement gap did not change measurably from 2017 to 2019, the achievement gap narrowed from 32 points in 1992 to 27 points in 2019. The White-Hispanic achievement gap in 2019 (21 points) was smaller than the achievement gap in 2017 (23 points), but it was not measurably different from the achievement gap in 1992.

At grade 8, the average reading score in 2019 (263) was lower than the score in 2017 (267), but it was higher than the score in 1992 (260). The reading scores for White (272), Black (244), and Hispanic (252) 8th-grade students in 2019 were lower than the corresponding scores in 2017 (275, 249, and 255, respectively), but the score for each group was higher in 2019 than in 1992 (267, 237, and 241, respectively). The reading score for th-grade` AsianPacific Islander students in 2019 (281) was not measurably different from the score in 2017, but it was higher than the score in 1992 (268). The reading score for 8th-grade American Indian/Alaska Native students in 2019 (248) was lower than the score in 2017 (253), but it was not measurably different from the score in 1994 (1994 was the first year data were available for 8th-grade American Indian/Alaska Native students).

From 1992 through 2019, the average reading score for White 8th-graders was higher than the scores for their Black and Hispanic peers. The White-Black achievement gap in 2019 (28 points) was larger than the White-Black achievement gap in 2017 (25 points), but it was not measurably different from the achievement gap in 1992. Although the White-Hispanic achievement gap at grade 8 did not change measurably from 2017 to 2019, the achievement gap narrowed from 26 points in 1992 to 20 points in 2019.

For 12th-grade students, the most recent scores available are from 2015. The average reading score for 12th-grade students in 2015 (287) was not measurably different from the score in 2013, but it was lower than the score in 1992 (292). At grade 12, the reading scores in 2015 for White (25), Hispanic (26), and AsianPacific Islander (297) students were not measurably different from the scores in 2013 and 1992. For Black students, the 2015 reading score (266) was lower than the 1992 score (273), but it was not measurably different from the 2013 score. The reading score for American Indian/Alaska Native students in 2015 (279) was not measurably different from the scores in 2013 and 1994 (1994 was the first year data were available for 12th-grade American Indian/Alaska Native students).

The White-Black achievement gap for 12th-grade students was larger in 2015 (30 points) than in 1992 (24 points), while the White-Hispanic achievement gap in 2015 (20 points) was not measurably different from the achievement gap in any previous assessment year.

NAEP Mathematics

The main NAEP mathematics assessment data for 4th- and 8th-graders are reported on a scale of 0 to 500. The average mathematics score for 4th-grade students in 2019 (241) was higher than the scores in both 2017 (240) and 1990 (213; table 222.10). At grade 4, the average mathematics scores in 201 for AsianPacific Islander (260), White (249), and Black (224) students were not measurably different from the corresponding scores in 2017, but the mathematics score for each group was higher in 2019 than in 1990 (225, 220, and 188, respectively). The 2019 mathematics score for 4th-grade Hispanic students (231) was higher than the scores in both 2017 (229) and 1990 (200). The 2019 mathematics score for 4th-grade American Indian/Alaska Native students (227) was not measurably different from the scores in 2017 and 1996 (1996 was the first year data were available for 4th-grade American Indian/Alaska Native students).

In 2019 and in all assessment years since 1990, the average mathematics scores for White students in grade 4 have been higher than those of their Black and Hispanic peers. Although the White-Black and White-Hispanic achievement gaps at grade 4 did not change measurably from 2017 to 2019, the White-Black achievement gap narrowed from 32 points in 1990 to 25 points in 2019. The 4th-grade White-Hispanic achievement gap in 2019 (18 points) was not measurably different from the gap in 1990.

For 8th-grade students, the average mathematics score in 2019 (282) was lower than the score in 2017 (283), but it was higher than the score in 1990 (263). At grade 8, the mathematics scores for AsianPacific Islander (10), hite (292), Hispanic (268), and Black (260) students in 2019 were not measurably different from the corresponding scores in 2017, but the score for each group was higher in 2019 than in 1990 (275, 270, 246, and 237, respectively). The mathematics score for 8th-grade American Indian/Alaska Native students in 2019 (262) was lower than the

score in 2017 (267), but it was not measurably different from the score in 2000 (2000 was the first year data were available for 8th-grade American Indian/Alaska Native students).

In 2019 and in all assessment years since 1990, the average mathematics scores for White students in grade 8 have been higher than the scores for their Black and Hispanic peers. At grade 8, the White-Black (32 points) and White-Hispanic (24 points) achievement gaps in 2019 were not measurably different from the corresponding gaps in 2017 and 1990.

For 12th-grade students, the average mathematics score in 2015 (152) was lower than the score in 2013 (153), but it was not measurably different from the score in 2005, the earliest year with comparable data. At grade 12, the mathematics scores for AsianPacific Islander (10), hite (160), Hispanic (139), and Black (130) students in 2015 were not measurably different from the scores in 2013, but the score for each group was higher in 2015 than in 2005 (163, 157, 133, and 127, respectively). The mathematics score for American Indian/Alaska Native students in 2015 (138) was not measurably different from the scores in 2013 and 2005.

In 2015, the mathematics score for White 12th-grade students was 30 points higher than the score for their Black peers and 22 points higher than the score for their Hispanic peers. The White-Black and White-Hispanic gaps in 2015 were not measurably different from the corresponding gaps in 2005 and 2013.

NAEP Science

NAEP has assessed the science abilities of students in grades 4, 8, and 12 in both public and private schools since 1996. As of 2009, however, NAEP science assessments are based on a new framework, so results from these assessments cannot be compared to results from earlier science assessments. Scores are based on a scale ranging from 0 to 300 (table 223.10). In 2015, the average 4th-grade science score (154) was higher than the score in 2009 (150). The 8th-grade science score in 2015 (154) was higher than the scores in 2009 (150) and in 2011 (152). The 12th-grade science score in 2015 (150) was not measurably different from the score in 2009.

While the scores for White 4th- and 8th-grade students remained higher than those for their Black and Hispanic peers in 2015, racial/ethnic achievement gaps in 2015 were smaller than in 2009. For example, at grade 4, the White-Black achievement gap was 36 points in 2009 and 33 points in 2015, and the White-Hispanic achievement gap was 32 points in 2009 and 27 points in 2015. For 12th-grade students, in contrast, science scores for White students remained higher than those for their Black and Hispanic peers in 2015, and these racial/ethnic achievement gaps were not measurably different from 2009. In addition, the 5-point gender gap, which favored male 12th-graders, in 2015 was not measurably different from the gap in 2009.

International Comparisons

Trends in International Mathematics and Science Study (TIMSS)

The 2015 Trends in International Mathematics and Science Study (TIMSS) assessed students' mathematics and science performance at grades 4 and 8. Mathematics performance was assessed in 43 countries at grade 4 and in 34 countries at grade 8. Science performance was assessed in 42 countries at grade 4 and in 34 countries at grade 8. In addition, TIMSS Advanced data were collected by ` countries from students in their final year of secondary school (grade 12 in the United States). At grades 4 and 8, several subnational entities also participated in TIMSS as separate education systems (e.g., Hong Kong, the U.S. state of Florida, England and Northern Ireland within the United Kingdom). However, the following paragraphs include results only from countries, not from subnational entities. At all three grades, TIMSS scores are reported on a scale of 0 to 1,000, with a fixed scale centerpoint of 500. The scale centerpoint represents the mean of the overall achievement distribution in 1995. The TIMSS scale is the same in each administration; thus, a value of 500 in 2015 equals 500 in 1995.

In 2015, the average mathematics scores of U.S. 4th-graders (539) and 8th-graders (518) were higher than the TIMSS centerpoint of 500 (tables 602.20 and 602.30). At grade 4, the average U.S. mathematics score was higher than the average score in 30 of the 42 other countries participating, lower than the average score in 6 countries, and not measurably different from the average score in the remaining 6 countries (table 602.20). The 6 countries that outperformed the United States in 4th-grade mathematics were Ireland, Japan, the Republic of Korea, Norway, the Russian Federation, and Singapore. At grade 8, the average U.S. mathematics score was higher than the average score in 21 of the 33 other participating countries, lower than the average score in 5 countries, and not measurably different from the average score in the remaining 7 countries (table 602.30). The 5 countries that outperformed the United States in eighth-grade mathematics were Canada, Japan, the Republic of Korea, the Russian Federation, and Singapore.

In science, the average scores of both U.S. 4th-graders (546) and U.S. 8th-graders (530) were higher than the TIMSS scale centerpoint of 500 in 2015 (tables 602.20 and 602.30). The average U.S. fourth-grade science score was higher than the average score in 30 of the 41 other countries participating in the science assessment at grade 4, lower than the average score in 5 countries, and not measurably different from the average score in the remaining 6 countries (table 602.20). The 5 countries that outperformed the United States in 4th-grade science were Finland, Japan, the Republic of Korea, the Russian Federation, and Singapore. At grade 8, the average U.S. science score was higher than

the average score in 23 of the 33 other participating countries in 2015, lower than the average score in 5 countries, and not measurably different from the average score in the remaining 5 countries (table 602.30). The 5 countries that outperformed the United States in 8th-grade science were Japan, the Republic of Korea, the Russian Federation, Singapore, and Slovenia.

The TIMSS Advanced assessment measures the advanced mathematics and physics achievement of students in their final year of secondary school who are taking or have taken advanced courses in those two subjects (table 602.35). On TIMSS Advanced, the U.S. average advanced mathematics score (485) and physics score (437) in 2015 were lower than the TIMSS Advanced scale centerpoint of 500. However, the U.S. average scores in advanced mathematics and physics were not measurably different from the U.S. average scores in those subjects in 1995. No education systems had higher average advanced mathematics or physics scores in 2015 than in 1995, but three education systems (France, Italy, and Sweden) had lower average scores in advanced mathematics and four (France, Norway, Russian Federation, and Sweden) had lower average physics scores.

Program for International Student Assessment (PISA)

The Program for International Student Assessment (PISA) assesses 15-year-old students' application of reading, mathematics, and science literacy to problems within a real-life context. In 2018, PISA assessed students in all 37 Organization for Economic Cooperation and Development (OECD) countries as well as more than 40 other education systems. While data on mathematics literacy and science literacy were reported for all OECD countries, data on reading literacy were reported for only 36 countries due to data quality concerns. PISA scores are reported on a scale of 0 to 1,000.

On the 2018 PISA assessment, U.S. 15-year-olds' average score in reading literacy was 505, which was higher than the OECD average score of 487 (table 602.50). The average reading literacy score in the United States was lower than the average score in 4 other OECD countries, higher than the average score in 21 OECD countries, and not measurably different from the average score in 10 OECD countries. In all participating education systems, females outperformed males in reading literacy (table 602.40). The U.S. gender gap in reading (24 points) was not measurably different from the OECD average gap but was smaller than the gaps in 12 other OECD countries, larger than the gaps in 2 OECD countries, and not measurably different from the gaps in 21 other OECD countries.

In mathematics literacy, U.S. 15-year-olds' average score of 478 on the 2018 PISA assessment was lower than the OECD average score of 489 (table 602.60). The average mathematics literacy score in the United States was lower than the average score in 24 other OECD countries, higher than the average score in 6 OECD countries, and not measurably different from the average score in 6 OECD countries. In 21 OECD countries, including the United States, males outperformed females in mathematics literacy; in 3 countries, females outperformed males in mathematics (table 602.40).

In science literacy, U.S. 15-year-olds' average score of 502 on the 2018 PISA assessment was higher than the OECD average score of 489 (table 602.70). The average science literacy score in the United States was lower than the average score in 6 other OECD countries, higher than the average score in 19 OECD countries, and not measurably different from the average score in 11 OECD countries. On average across OECD countries, females outperformed male students in science by 2 points. There was no measurable difference in the average science literacy scores for males and females in 22 OECD countries, including the United States. In 13 OECD countries, females outperformed males in science literacy; in 2 countries, males outperformed females in science literacy.

Progress in International Reading Literacy Study (PIRLS)

The Progress in International Reading Literacy Study (PIRLS) measures the reading knowledge and skills of 4th-graders over time. PIRLS scores are reported on a scale from 0 to 1,000, with the scale centerpoint set at 500. On the 2016 PIRLS, U.S. 4th-graders had an average reading literacy score of 549 (table 602.10). The U.S. average score in 2016 was 7 points lower than in 2011 but 10 points higher than in 2006. In all 4 assessment years, the U.S. average score was higher than the PIRLS scale centerpoint. The average reading literacy score of 4th-graders in the United States was higher than the average score in 24 of the 42 other countries participating in 2016, lower than the average score in 7 countries, and not measurably different from the average score in the remaining 11 countries.

High School Graduates and Dropouts

About 3,663,000 high school students were projected to graduate during the 2020–21 school year (based on pre-pandemic data), including 3,302,000 public school graduates and 360,000 private school graduates (table 219.10). High school graduates include only recipients of diplomas, not recipients of equivalency credentials. The 2020–21 projection of high school graduates is slightly lower than the prior record-high projection of 3,674,000 graduates in 2018–19, but it exceeds the baby boom era's high point in 1975–76, when 3,142,000 students earned diplomas. In 2017–18, about 85 percent of public high school students graduated with a regular diploma within 4 years of first starting 9th grade, which reects an increase since 201011 (79 percent; table 219.46). This rate is known as the 4-year adjusted cohort graduation rate (ACGR).

The status dropout rate has decreased since 2000. The status dropout rate is the percentage of the civilian noninstitutionalized 16- to 24-year-old population who are not enrolled in school and who have not completed a high school program, regardless of when they left school. (People who left school but went on to receive a GED credential are not treated as dropouts.) Between 2000 and 2018, the status dropout rate declined from 10.9 to 5.7 percent (table 219.70). During this period, the status dropout rate for Black 16- to 24-year-olds declined from 13.1 to 5.8 percent, and the rate for Hispanic 16- to 24-year-olds declined from 27.8 to 9.0 percent. In 2018, the status dropout rate for White 16- to 24-year-olds (4.5 percent) was lower than the rate for Hispanic 16- to 24-year-olds, but it was not measurably different from the rate for Black 16- to 24-year-olds.

Postsecondary Education

Enrollment in Degree-Granting Institutions

College enrollment was 19.6 million in fall 2018, reecting a percent decrease from the record enrollment of 21.0 million in fall 2010 (table 105.30). College enrollment is expected to remain below the 2010 record through fall 2029, the last year for which NCES enrollment projections have been developed. Based on these pre-pandemic projections, enrollment is expected to increase 2 percent between fall 2018 and fall 2029.

Despite decreases in the size of the traditional college-age population (18 to 24 years old) during the late 1980s and early 1990s, total enrollment increased during this period (tables 101.10 and 105.30). The traditional college-age population was 1 percent higher in 2018 than in 2008, and total college enrollment was 3 percent higher in 2018 than in 2008. The number of full-time students was 2 percent higher in 2018 than in 2008, while the number of part-time students was 4 percent higher (table 303.10). Postsecondary enrollment was 3 percent higher in 2018 than in 2008 for both male and female students.

Faculty

In fall 201, degree-granting institutionsdefined as postsecondary institutions that grant an associate's or higher degree and are eligible for Title I federal financial aid programs—employed 1.5 million faculty members, including 0.8 million full-time and 0.7 million part-time faculty (table 314.30). In addition, degree-granting institutions employed 0.4 million graduate assistants.

Degrees

During the 2019–20 academic year, postsecondary degrees conferred were projected to number 981,000 associate's degrees, 1,996,000 bachelor's degrees, 832,000 master's degrees, and 186,000 doctor's degrees (table 318.10). The doctor's degree total includes most degrees that were classified as first-professional prior to 201011, such as M.D.'s, D.D.S.'s, and law degrees. Between 2007–08 and 2017–18 (the last year of actual data), the number of degrees conferred increased at all levels. Between 2007–08 and 2017–18, the number of associate's degrees increased 35 percent, the number of bachelor's degrees increased 27 percent, the number of master's degrees increased 30 percent, and the number of doctor's degrees increased 23 percent.

Between 2007–08 and 2017–18, the number of bachelor's degrees awarded to male students increased 26 percent, while the number of bachelor's degrees awarded to female students increased 27 percent (table 318.10). Female students earned 57 percent of all bachelor's degrees in 2017–18, which was the same as the percentage in 2007–08. Between 2007–08 and 2017–18, the number of bachelor's degrees awarded to White students increased 6 percent, which was smaller than the increases for Black students (28 percent), Hispanic students (118 percent), and Asian/Pacific Islander students (38 percent; table 22.20). The number of bachelor's degrees awarded to American Indian/Alaska Native students decreased 20 percent during this period. In 2017–18, White students earned 63 percent of all bachelor's degrees (compared with 74 percent in 2007–08), Black students earned 10 percent (the same percentage as 2007–08), Hispanic students earned 14 percent (compared with . percent in 2007–08), and Asian/Pacific Islander students earned 8 percent (compared with 7 percent in 2007–08). American Indian/Alaska Native students earned less than 1 percent of all bachelor's degrees in both years. In 2017–18, students of Two or more races earned 4 percent of all bachelor's degrees.

Undergraduate Prices

For the 2018–19 academic year, average annual prices for undergraduate tuition, fees, room, and board were estimated to be $18,383 at public institutions, $47,419 at private nonprofit institutions, and $27,040 at private for-profit institutions (table 330.10). Between 2008–09 and 2018–19, prices for undergraduate tuition, fees, room, and board at public institutions rose 28 percent, and prices at private nonprofit institutions rose 19 percent, after adjustment for inflation. The average price for total tuition, fees, room, and board at private for-profit institutions was 6 percent lower in 2018–19 than in 2008–09.

Educational Attainment

The U.S. Census Bureau collects annual statistics on the educational attainment of the population. Between 2009 and 2019, the percentage of the adult population age 25 and over who had completed at least high school (or an equivalency program) rose from 87 to 90 percent, and the percentage of adults with a bachelor's or higher degree increased from 30 to 36 percent (table 104.10). Among 25- to 29-year-olds, the percentage who had completed at least high school increased from 89 to 94 percent between 2009 and 2019, and the percentage who had completed a bachelor's or higher degree increased from 31 percent to 39 percent (table 104.20). During this same period, the percentage of 25- to 29-year-olds who had completed a master's or higher degree increased from 7 to 9 percent.

Among employed adults age 25 and over 42 percent had a bachelor's or higher degree in 2019, and about half (53 percent) had an associate's or higher degree (table 502.10).

Education Expenditures

U.S. expenditures for public and private education, from prekindergarten through graduate school (excluding postsecondary schools not awarding associate's or higher degrees), were an estimated $1.5 trillion for 2018–19 (table 106.10). Expenditures of elementary and secondary schools totaled an estimated $832 billion, while those of degree-granting postsecondary institutions totaled an estimated $620 billion. Total expenditures for education were an estimated 7.1 percent of the gross domestic product (GDP) in 2018–19. Education spending as a percentage of GDP peaked at 7.6 percent in 2009–10 but declined between 2009–10 and 2014–15 (7.1 percent).

CHAPTER 1
All Levels of Education

This chapter provides a broad overview of education in the United States. It brings together material from pre-primary, elementary, secondary, and postsecondary education, as well as from the general population, to present a composite picture of the American education system. Tables summarize the total number of people enrolled in school, the number of teachers, the number of schools, and the total expenditures for education at all levels. This chapter also includes statistics on education-related topics such as school-age resident populations, characteristics of households with children, and educational attainment. Economic indicators and price indexes have been added to facilitate analyses.

Many of the statistics in this chapter are derived from the statistical activities of the National Center for Education Statistics (NCES). In addition, substantial contributions have been drawn from the work of other groups, both governmental and nongovernmental, as shown in the source notes of the tables. Information on survey methodologies is contained in Appendix A: Guide to Sources and in the publications cited in the table source notes.

The U.S. System of Education

The U.S. system of education can be described generally as having three levels of formal education: elementary, secondary, and postsecondary (figure 1). However, these levels can be defined quite differently across school districts. For example, students may spend 1 to 3 years in preprimary programs (prekindergarten [PK] and kindergarten [K]), which may be offered either in separate schools or in elementary schools that also offer higher grades. (For simplicity, in *Digest of Education Statistics* tables, prekindergarten and kindergarten are generally defined as a part of elementary education, although preprimary schooling is not universally included in the elementary level.) Following kindergarten, students ordinarily spend 6 to 8 years in elementary school. The elementary school program is followed by a 4- to 6-year program in secondary school. Students typically complete the entire program of elementary and secondary schooling by age 18. This formal schooling is provided in a range of institutional settings—including elementary schools (preprimary schools, primary schools, middle schools, and other types of schools offering broader ranges of elementary grades); secondary schools (junior high schools, high schools, and senior high schools); and combined (multi-age, ungraded, and elementary/secondary schools)—that vary in structure from locality to locality.

High school graduates who decide to continue their education may enter a specialized career/technical institution, a 2-year community or junior college, or a 4-year college or university. A 2-year college typically offers the first 2 years of a standard 4-year college curriculum, awarding an associate's degree upon completion of at least 2 years of postsecondary coursework, as well as a selection of terminal career and technical education programs. Academic courses completed at a 2-year college are usually transferable for credit at a 4-year college or university. A career/technical institution offers postsecondary technical training programs of varying lengths that lead to a specific career

A 4-year college or university offers at least a bachelor's degree, which typically requires 4 years of postsecondary coursework, and some offer master's or doctor's degrees. At least 1 year of coursework beyond a bachelor's degree is necessary for a master's degree, while a doctor's degree (which comprises a wide variety of degrees, including doctor of medicine [M.D.], juris doctor [J.D.], and doctor of philosophy [Ph.D.]) usually requires a minimum of 3 or 4 years beyond a bachelor's degree.

Professional schools are pathways to licensed or ordained professions, such as dentistry, law, or ministry. They differ widely in admission requirements and program length. Medical students, for example, generally complete a bachelor's program of premedical studies at a college or university before they can enter the 4-year program at a professional medical school. Law programs typically involve 3 years of coursework beyond a bachelor's degree. Depending on the length of the program and the degree awarded, degrees from professional schools are categorized as either master's or doctor's degrees.

Enrollment: From Preprimary to Postsecondary

Total enrollment in public and private elementary and secondary schools (prekindergarten through grade 12) grew rapidly during the 1950s and 1960s, reaching a peak year in 1971 (table A, table 105.30, and figure 2). This growth in enrollment reflected what is known as the "baby boom," a dramatic increase in births following World War II. Between 1971 and 1984, total elementary and secondary school enrollment decreased every year, reflecting a decline in the size of the school-age population over that period. After these years of decline, enrollment in elementary and secondary schools started increasing in fall 1985, began hitting new record levels in the mid-1990s, and continued to reach new record levels every year through 2006. After declining 1 percent between 2006 and 2011, enrollments in 2019 are projected to have increased 3 percent over 2011 levels. Enrollments since fall 2013 have remained above the fall 2006 enrollment of 55.3 million, the final year of the post "baby boom" record highs. Before the coronavirus pandemic, national changes in school enrollment were projected to remain relatively small through 2029, with annual percentage changes of less than 0.4 percent. However, as the impact of the coronavirus pandemic remains unknown, these projections are subject to revision.

Table A. Total elementary and secondary school enrollment, by overall trends: Selected years, 1949–50 through fall 2029

Trend and year	Number of students (in millions)
"Baby boom" increases	
1949–50 school year	28.5
Fall 1959	40.9
Fall 1969	51.1
Fall 1971 (peak)	51.3
13 years with annual post "baby boom" declines	
Fall 1972 (first year of decline)	50.7
Fall 1984 (final year of decline)	44.9
Annual increases from 1985 to 2006	
Fall 1985	45.0
Fall 1996 (surpasses "baby boom" peak)	51.5
Fall 2006 (final year of post "baby boom" record highs)	55.3
Slight declines or stable enrollment	
Fall 2007	55.2
Fall 2010	54.9
Fall 2011	54.8
Annual increases with new record highs	
Fall 2013	55.4
Fall 2014	55.9
Fall 2015	56.2
Fall 2017	56.4
Fall 2018 (projected)	56.4
Fall 2019 (projected)	56.3
Fall 2029 (projected)	56.8*

*Subject to revision once the impact of the coronavirus pandemic becomes known.
SOURCE: U.S. Department of Education, National Center for Education Statistics, *Biennial Survey of Education in the United States*, 1949–50; *Statistics of Public Elementary and Secondary School Systems*, 1959 through 1972; Common Core of Data (CCD), 1984 through 2017; Private School Universe Survey (PSS), 1997–98 through 2017–18; and National Elementary and Secondary Enrollment Projection Model, 1972 through 2029.

Between 1985 and 2018, the total public and private elementary and secondary school enrollment rate decreased for 5- and 6-year-olds (typical ages for preprimary grades) from 96 to 94 percent, and for 7- to 13-year-olds (typical ages for elementary grades) from 99 to 98 percent (table 103.20). In contrast, the enrollment rate for 14- to 17-year-olds (typical ages for secondary grades) in 2018 (95 percent) was not measurably different from the rate in 1985. As there were no measurable increases in enrollment rates between 1985 and 2018, increases in the total number of enrolled elementary and secondary students primarily reflect the increases in the number of children in these age groups. Between 1985 and 2018, the number of 5- and 6-year-olds increased by 16 percent, the number of 7- to 13-year-olds increased by 26 percent, and the number of 14- to 17-year-olds increased by 12 percent (table 101.10). Increases in the enrollment rate of prekindergarten-age children (ages 3 and 4), from 39 percent in 1985 to

54 percent in 2018, and in the number of 3- and 4-year-olds, from 7.1 million to 8.1 million, also contributed to overall increases in prekindergarten through grade 12 enrollment (tables 101.10 and 103.20).

The vast majority of elementary and secondary students in the United States attend public schools. Considering only these students, enrollment at the elementary level (prekindergarten through grade 8) rose from 29.9 million in fall 1990 to 34.2 million in fall 2003 (table 105.30). Public elementary school enrollment was lower in fall 2004 than in fall 2003 (by less than 1 percent) and then generally increased to a projected total of 35.4 million for fall 2019. From 2019 to 2029, public elementary school enrollment has been projected to increase 2 percent. At the secondary level (grades 9 through 12), public school enrollment rose from 11.3 million in 1990 to 15.1 million in 2007. After a decline of 2 percent to 14.7 million in 2011, public secondary enrollments are projected to have increased 3 percent by 2019.

The percentage of students opting out of public schools in favor of private elementary and secondary schools was lower in 2017 (10.1 percent) than in 2007 (10.7 percent; table 105.30). In fall 2019, an estimated 5.7 million students were enrolled in private schools at the elementary and secondary levels, or 10.1 percent of students.

At the postsecondary level, total enrollment in public and private degree-granting institutions increased 47 percent between 1995 and 2010 (to 21.0 million) but declined 7 percent between 2010 and 2018 (to 19.6 million; table 105.30). Total enrollment is expected to increase 2 percent between fall 2018 and fall 2029, reaching 20.1 million. The percentage of students who attended private institutions (including both for-profit and nonprofit institutions) in fall 2018 (26 percent) was 1 percentage point lower than in 2008. During this period, the percentage of postsecondary students attending private nonprofit institutions increased from 19 to 21 percent and the percentage of students attending for-profit institutions decreased from 8 to 5 percent (table 303.10). In fall 2018, about 5.1 million students attended private institutions, with 4.1 million in nonprofit institutions and 1.0 million in for-profit institutions.

Despite a decrease since 2010, enrollment in postsecondary degree-granting institutions in fall 2018 was 3 percent higher than in fall 2008 (table 105.30). Changes in total enrollment may be affected by changes in enrollment rates, changes in the population, or both. While the postsecondary enrollment rate of 18- and 19-year-olds in 2018 (50 percent) was not measurably different from the percentage in 2008, the overall number of 18- and 19-year-olds in the population decreased 5 percent, from 9.0 million in 2008 to 8.6 million in 2018 (tables 101.10 and 103.20). In contrast, although the enrollment rate of 20- to 24-year-olds in 2018 (39 percent) was also not measurably different from the rate in 2008, the number of 20- to 24-year-olds was 3 percent higher in 2018 (21.9 million) than in 2008 (21.2 million).

Educational Attainment

The percentage of people 25 years old and over who earned a high school degree (or equivalent) or higher has been increasing over the past decade. Between 2009 and 2019, the percentage of people 25 years old and over who had completed at least high school increased from 87 to 90 percent, and the percentage who had completed a bachelor's or higher degree increased from 30 to 36 percent (table 104.10 and figure 3). In 2019, about 10 percent of people 25 years old and over held a master's degree as their highest degree, and 3 percent held a doctor's or first professional degree (table 104.30). Among 25- to 29-year-olds, the percentage who had completed at least high school increased from 89 to 94 percent between 2009 and 2019, and the percentage who had completed a bachelor's or higher degree increased from 31 to 39 percent (table 104.20 and figure 4). Overall, the percentage of 25- to 29-year-olds who held a master's or higher degree rose from 7 percent in 2009 to 9 percent in 2019, including about 2 percent who held a doctor's or first-professiona degree (tables 104.20 and 104.30 and figures 4 and 5)

These changes in the educational attainment of 25- to 29-year-olds over the last decade varied by race/ethnicity. The percentages of Hispanic and White 25- to 29-year-olds who had completed at least high school increased between 2009 and 2019; however, there was no measurable change among Asian and Black 25- to 29-year-olds (table 104.20 and figure 6). The percentage of Hispanic 25- to 29-year-olds who had completed at least high school rose from 69 percent in 2009 to 86 percent in 2019, an increase of 17 percentage points. During the same period, the percentage of White 25- to 29-year-olds who had completed at least high school rose from 95 to 96 percent. Taken together, the gap between the high school completion percentages for these two groups decreased from 26 percentage points in 2009 to 10 percentage points in 2019. In contrast, the gap between the White and Black high school completion percentages in 2019 (5 percentage points) was not measurably different from the gap in 2009. Whereas high school completion rates were higher among White 25- to 29-year-olds than among their Black or Hispanic peers in 2019, they were not measurably different from the high school completion rates of Asian 25- to 29-year-olds (97 percent).

The percentage of bachelor's degree holders also varied among 25- to 29-year-olds of different racial/ethnic groups. Between 2009 and 2019, the percentages who had completed a bachelor's or higher degree showed no measurable change for those who were of Two or more races, Pacific Islander, and American Indian/Alaska Native (34 percent, 22 percent, and 14 percent, respectively, in 2019). In contrast, the percentage who had completed a bachelor's or higher degree increased for Asian, White, Black, and Hispanic 25- to 29-year-olds during this 10-year period. Between 2009 and 2019, the percentages who held a bachelor's or higher degree increased from 60 to 71 percent among Asian 25- to 29-year-olds, from 37 to 45 percent among White 25- to 29-year-olds, from 19 to 29 percent among Black 25- to 29-year-olds, and from 12 to 21 percent among Hispanic 25- to 29-year-olds (table 104.20 and figure 6). The gaps in bachelor's degree attainment percentages between White and Black 25- to 29-year-olds (16 percentage points) and White and Hispanic 25- to 29-year-olds (24 percentage points) in 2019 were not measurably different from these gaps in 2009.

Teachers and Faculty

A projected 3.7 million elementary and secondary school full-time-equivalent (FTE) teachers were engaged in classroom instruction in the fall of 2019, which was less than 1 percent higher than in 2009 (table 105.40). Of these 3.7 million FTE elementary and secondary school teachers in 2019, about 3.2 million taught in public schools and 0.5 million taught in private schools.

FTE faculty at degree-granting postsecondary institutions totaled a projected 1.1 million in 2019, including 0.7 million at public institutions and 0.4 million at private institutions (table 105.10).

Expenditures

Expenditures of educational institutions were an estimated $1.5 trillion for the 2018–19 school year (table 106.20 and figure 2). Elementary and secondary schools spent 57 percent of this total ($832 billion), and degree-granting postsecondary institutions spent the remaining 43 percent ($620 billion). After adjustment for inflation total expenditures of all educational institutions rose by an estimated 13 percent between 2008–09 and 2018–19. Inflation-adjusted expenditures for public elementary and secondary schools increased by an estimated 7 percent during this period, while expenditures of degree-granting postsecondary institutions increased by an estimated 22 percent. In 2018–19, expenditures of educational institutions were an estimated 7.1 percent of the gross domestic product (table 106.10).

Figure 1.   The structure of education in the United States

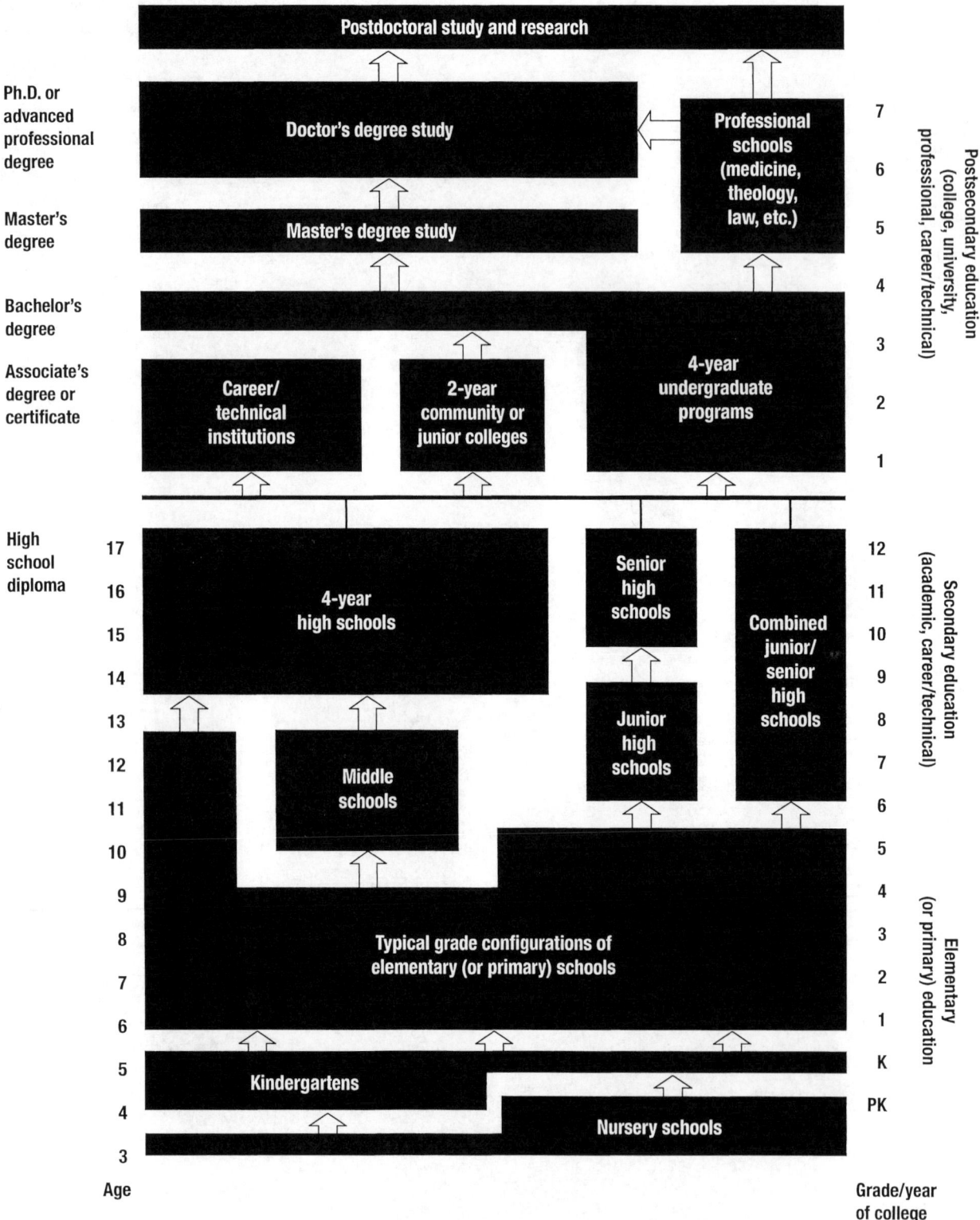

NOTE: Figure is not intended to show relative number of institutions nor relative size of enrollment for the different levels of education. Figure reflects typical patterns of progression rather than all possible variations. Adult education programs, while not separately delineated above, may provide instruction at the adult basic, adult secondary, or postsecondary education levels.
SOURCE: U.S. Department of Education, National Center for Education Statistics, Annual Reports Program.

Figure 2. Fall enrollment, total expenditures, and expenditures as a percentage of the gross domestic product (GDP), by level of education: Selected years, 1965–66 through 2018–19

Enrollment, in millions

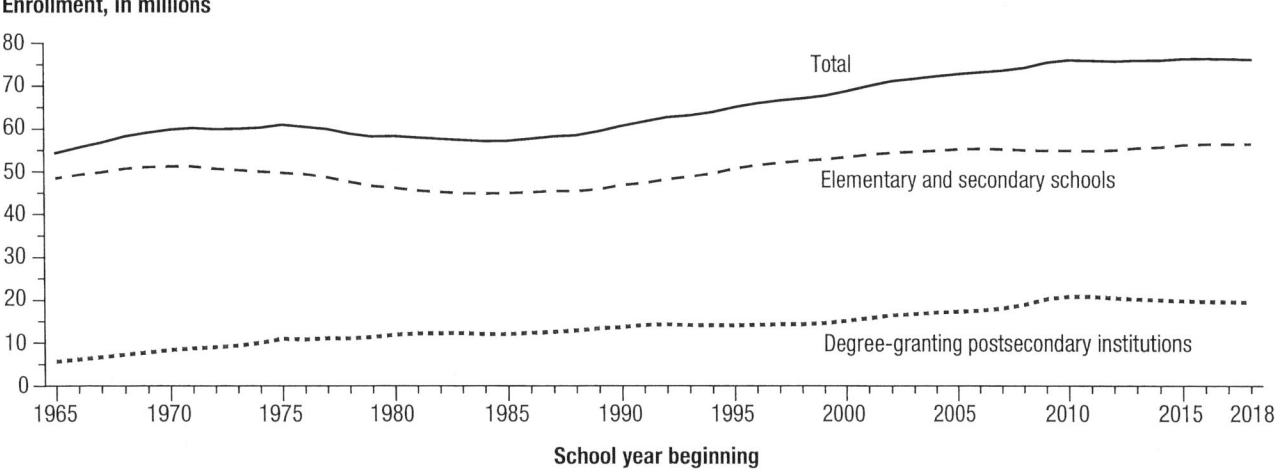

Expenditure, in billions of constant 2018–19 dollars

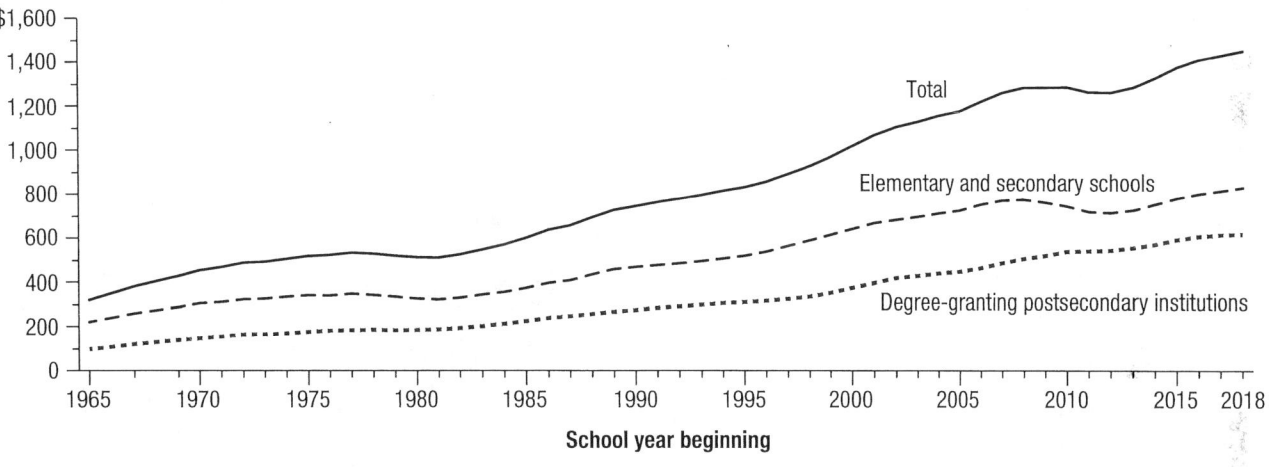

Expenditure as a percent of GDP

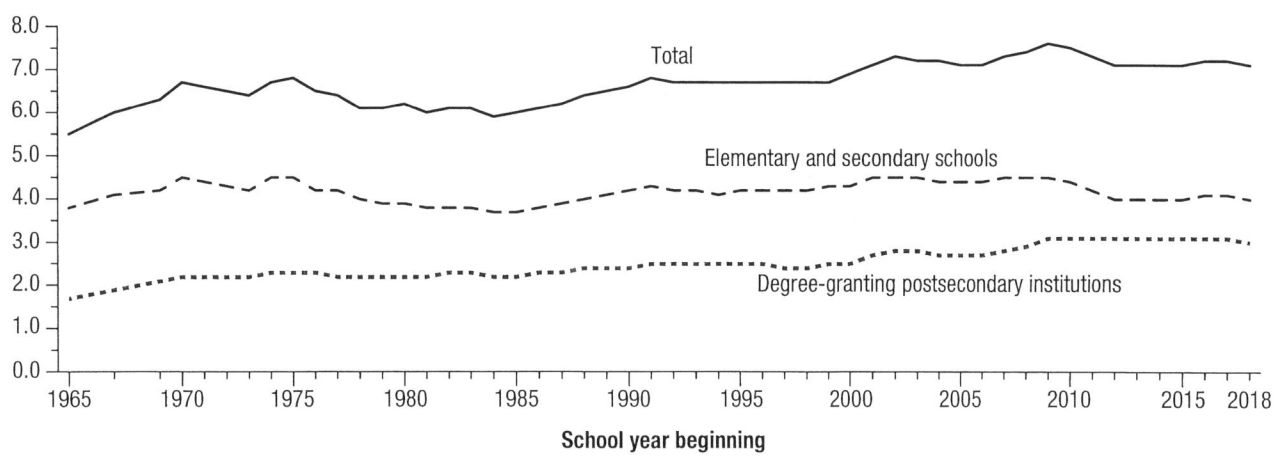

NOTE: Elementary and secondary enrollment data for school year 2018 (2018–19) are projected. Elementary and secondary expenditure data for school years 2017 and 2018 (2017–18 and 2018–19) and postsecondary expenditure data for school year 2018 (2018–19) are estimated based on teacher and enrollment data and actual expenditures for prior years.
SOURCE: U.S. Department of Education, National Center for Education Statistics, *Statistics of State School Systems*, 1965–66 through 1969–70; *Statistics of Public Elementary and Secondary School Systems*, 1965 through 1980; *Revenues and Expenditures for Public Elementary and Secondary Education*, 1970–71 through 1986–87; Common Core of Data (CCD), "State Nonfiscal Survey of Public Elementary and Secondary Education," 1981–82 through 2017–18, and "National Public Education Financial Survey," 1987–88 through 2016–17; Private School Universe Survey (PSS), 1989–90 through 2017–18; National Elementary and Secondary Enrollment Projection Model, 1972 through 2029; Higher Education General Information Survey (HEGIS), "Fall Enrollment in Institutions of Higher Education" and "Financial Statistics of Institutions of Higher Education" surveys, 1965–66 through 1985–86; Integrated Postsecondary Education Data System (IPEDS), "Fall Enrollment Survey" (IPEDS-EF:86–99) and "Finance Survey" (IPEDS-F:FY87–99); and IPEDS Spring 2001 through Spring 2019, Fall Enrollment and Finance components. U.S. Department of Commerce, Bureau of Economic Analysis, National Income and Product Accounts Tables, retrieved December 31, 2019, from https://apps.bea.gov/itable/index.cfm.

Figure 3. Percentage of persons 25 years old and over, by highest level of educational attainment: Selected years, 1940 through 2019

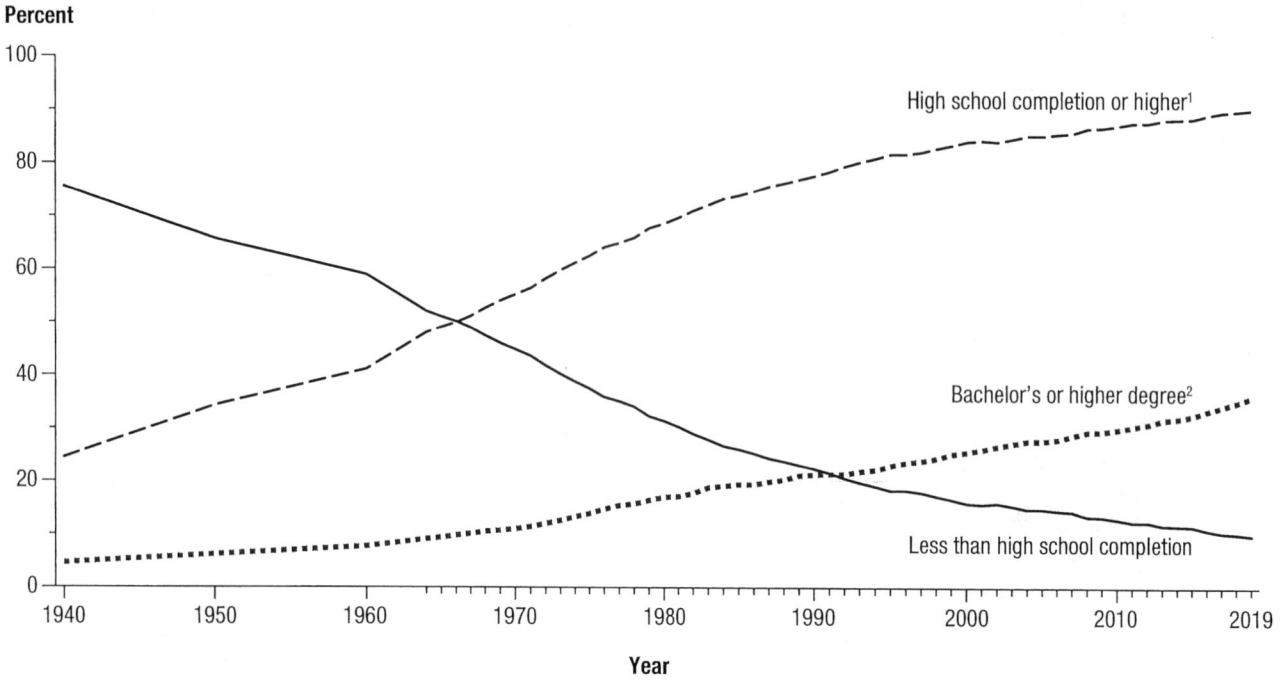

[1]Includes high school completion through equivalency programs, such as a GED program. For years prior to 1993, includes all persons with 4 or more years of high school.
[2]For years prior to 1993, includes all persons with 4 or more years of college.
SOURCE: U.S. Department of Commerce, Census Bureau, *U.S. Census of Population: 1960*, Vol. I, Part 1; J.K. Folger and C.B. Nam, *Education of the American Population* (1960 Census Monograph); Current Population Reports, Series P-20, various years; and Current Population Survey (CPS), Annual Social and Economic Supplement, 1961 through 2019.

Figure 4. Percentage of persons 25 to 29 years old, by highest level of educational attainment: Selected years, 1940 through 2019

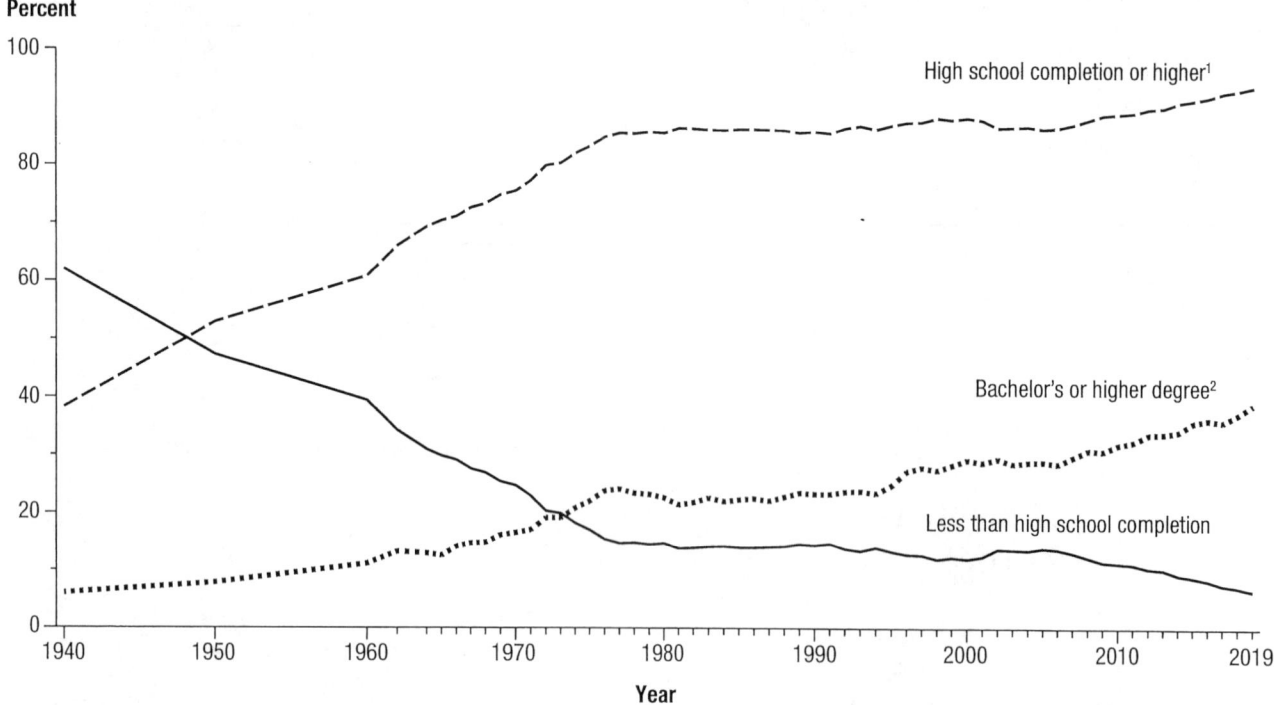

[1]Includes high school completion through equivalency programs, such as a GED program. For years prior to 1993, includes all persons with 4 or more years of high school.
[2]For years prior to 1993, includes all persons with 4 or more years of college.
SOURCE: U.S. Department of Commerce, Census Bureau, *U.S. Census of Population: 1960*, Vol. I, Part 1; J.K. Folger and C.B. Nam, *Education of the American Population* (1960 Census Monograph); Current Population Reports, Series P-20, various years; and Current Population Survey (CPS), Annual Social and Economic Supplement, 1961 through 2019.

Figure 5. Percentage distribution of persons 25 to 29 years old, by highest level of educational attainment: 2019

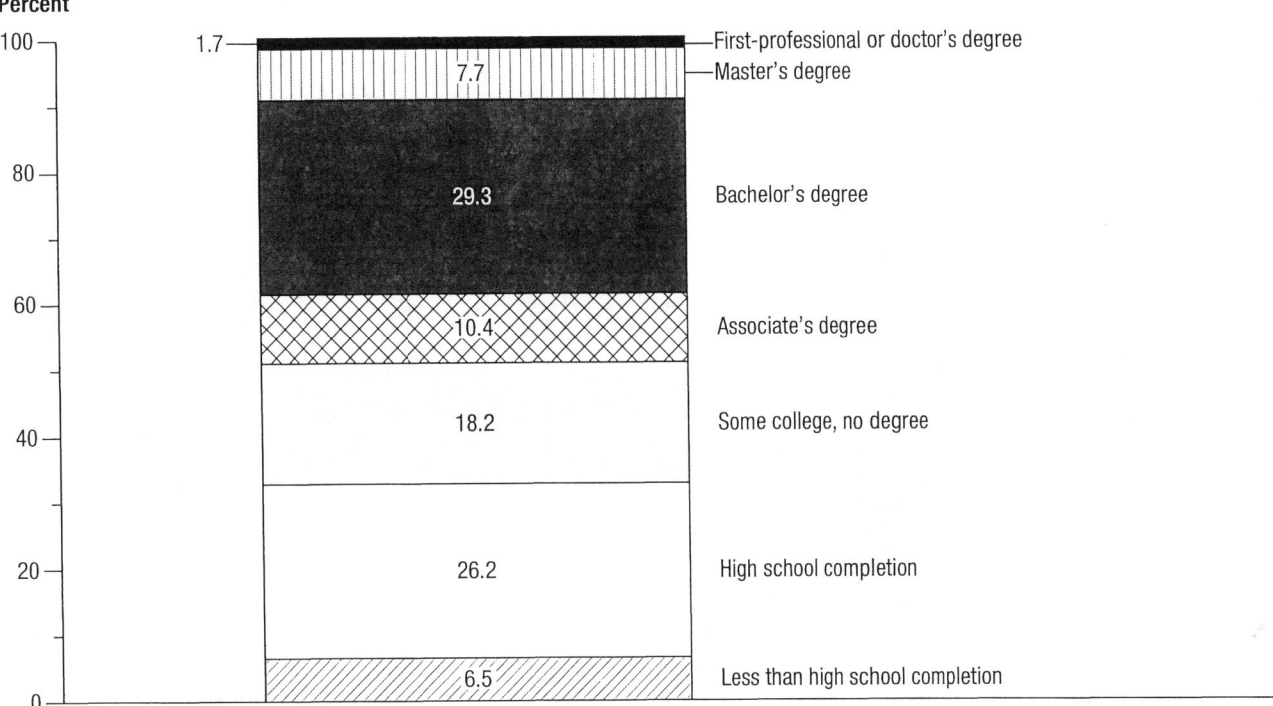

NOTE: High school completion includes equivalency programs, such as a GED program. Graphic display was generated using unrounded data. Detail may not sum to totals because of rounding.
SOURCE: U.S. Department of Commerce, Census Bureau, Current Population Survey (CPS), Annual Social and Economic Supplement, 2019.

Figure 6. Percentage of persons 25 to 29 years old with selected levels of educational attainment, by race/ethnicity: 2009 and 2019

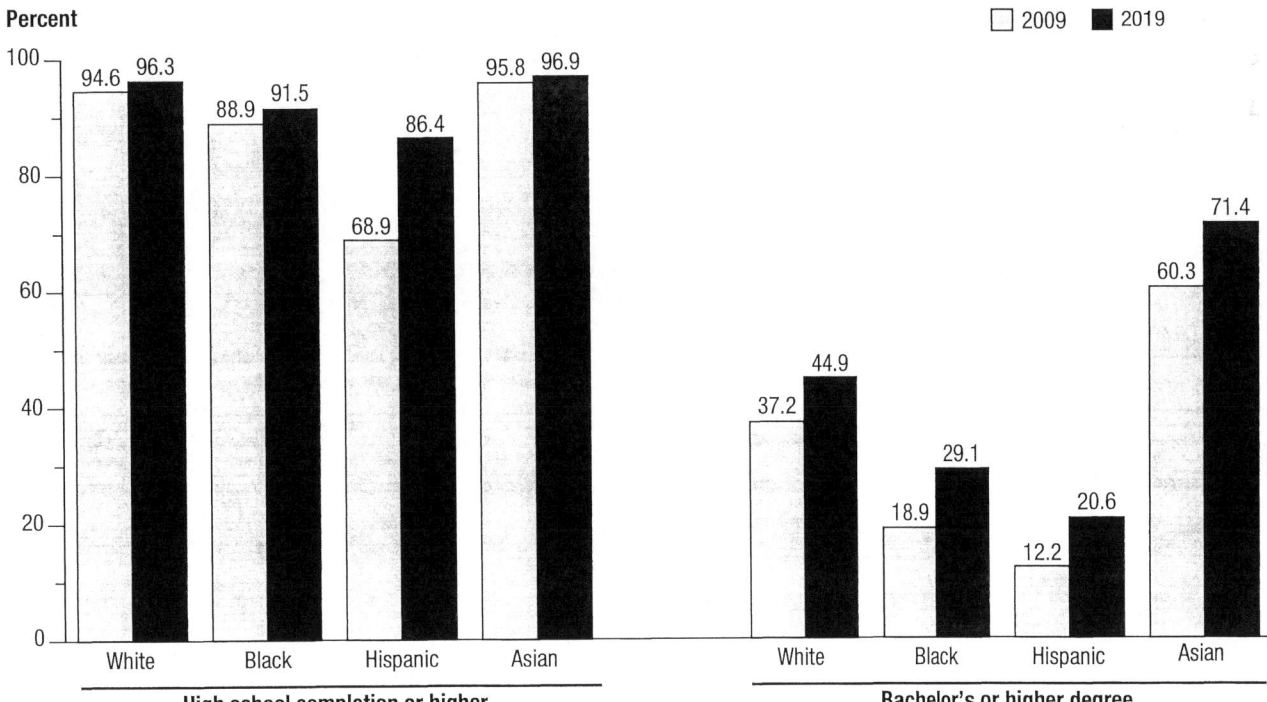

NOTE: High school completion includes equivalency programs, such as a GED program. Graphic display was generated using unrounded data. Race categories exclude persons of Hispanic ethnicity.
SOURCE: U.S. Department of Commerce, Census Bureau, Current Population Survey (CPS), Annual Social and Economic Supplement, 2009 and 2019.

Table 101.10.   Estimates of resident population, by age group: 1970 through 2019

[In thousands]

Year	Total, all ages	Total, 3 to 34 years old	3 and 4 years old	5 and 6 years old	7 to 13 years old	14 to 17 years old	18 and 19 years old	20 and 21 years old	22 to 24 years old	25 to 29 years old	30 to 34 years old
1	2	3	4	5	6	7	8	9	10	11	12
1970	205,052	109,592	6,961	7,703	28,969	15,924	7,510	7,210	9,992	13,736	11,587
1971	207,661	111,202	6,805	7,344	28,892	16,328	7,715	7,350	10,809	14,041	11,917
1972	209,896	112,807	6,789	7,051	28,628	16,639	7,923	7,593	10,560	15,240	12,383
1973	211,909	114,426	6,938	6,888	28,158	16,867	8,114	7,796	10,725	15,786	13,153
1974	213,854	116,075	7,117	6,864	27,600	17,035	8,257	8,003	10,972	16,521	13,704
1975	215,973	117,435	6,912	7,013	26,905	17,128	8,478	8,196	11,331	17,280	14,191
1976	218,035	118,474	6,436	7,195	26,321	17,119	8,659	8,336	11,650	18,274	14,485
1977	220,239	119,261	6,190	6,978	25,877	17,045	8,675	8,550	11,949	18,277	15,721
1978	222,585	119,833	6,208	6,500	25,594	16,946	8,677	8,730	12,216	18,683	16,280
1979	225,055	120,544	6,252	6,256	25,175	16,611	8,751	8,754	12,542	19,178	17,025
1980	227,225	121,132	6,366	6,291	24,800	16,143	8,718	8,669	12,716	19,686	17,743
1981	229,466	121,999	6,535	6,315	24,396	15,609	8,582	8,759	12,903	20,169	18,731
1982	231,664	121,823	6,658	6,407	24,121	15,057	8,480	8,768	12,914	20,704	18,714
1983	233,792	122,302	6,877	6,572	23,709	14,740	8,290	8,652	12,981	21,414	19,067
1984	235,825	122,254	7,045	6,694	23,367	14,725	7,932	8,567	12,962	21,459	19,503
1985	237,924	122,512	7,134	6,916	22,976	14,888	7,637	8,370	12,895	21,671	20,025
1986	240,133	122,688	7,187	7,086	22,992	14,824	7,483	8,024	12,720	21,893	20,479
1987	242,289	122,672	7,132	7,178	23,325	14,502	7,502	7,742	12,450	21,857	20,984
1988	244,499	122,713	7,176	7,238	23,791	14,023	7,701	7,606	12,048	21,739	21,391
1989	246,819	122,655	7,315	7,184	24,228	13,536	7,898	7,651	11,607	21,560	21,676
1990	249,623	122,787	7,359	7,244	24,785	13,329	7,702	7,886	11,264	21,277	21,939
1991	252,981	123,210	7,444	7,393	25,216	13,491	7,208	8,029	11,205	20,923	22,301
1992	256,514	123,722	7,614	7,447	25,752	13,775	6,949	7,797	11,391	20,503	22,494
1993	259,919	124,371	7,887	7,549	26,212	14,096	6,985	7,333	11,657	20,069	22,584
1994	263,126	124,976	8,089	7,725	26,492	14,637	7,047	7,071	11,585	19,740	22,590
1995	266,278	125,478	8,107	8,000	26,825	15,013	7,182	7,103	11,197	19,680	22,372
1996	269,394	125,924	8,022	8,206	27,168	15,443	7,399	7,161	10,715	19,864	21,945
1997	272,647	126,422	7,915	8,232	27,683	15,769	7,569	7,309	10,601	19,899	21,446
1998	275,854	126,939	7,841	8,152	28,302	15,829	7,892	7,520	10,647	19,804	20,953
1999	279,040	127,446	7,772	8,041	28,763	16,007	8,094	7,683	10,908	19,575	20,603
2000	282,162	128,041	7,724	7,972	29,082	16,144	8,199	7,995	11,122	19,280	20,524
2001	284,969	128,467	7,630	7,883	29,210	16,280	8,235	8,290	11,467	18,819	20,652
2002	287,625	128,955	7,617	7,750	29,251	16,506	8,237	8,342	11,902	18,691	20,658
2003	290,108	129,346	7,678	7,661	29,153	16,694	8,325	8,324	12,267	18,772	20,472
2004	292,805	129,965	7,885	7,652	28,806	17,054	8,457	8,312	12,534	19,107	20,160
2005	295,517	130,280	7,973	7,721	28,527	17,358	8,482	8,392	12,568	19,535	19,724
2006	298,380	130,754	7,937	7,942	28,327	17,549	8,567	8,507	12,529	20,110	19,285
2007	301,231	131,417	8,002	8,040	28,256	17,597	8,730	8,500	12,578	20,543	19,171
2008	304,094	132,269	8,033	8,012	28,426	17,395	9,014	8,555	12,626	20,903	19,305
2009	306,772	133,202	8,059	8,088	28,569	17,232	9,146	8,691	12,693	21,078	19,645
2010	309,326	134,095	8,189	8,137	28,729	17,066	9,061	8,955	12,746	21,143	20,068
2011	311,580	134,886	8,223	8,162	28,753	16,870	8,920	9,192	12,968	21,282	20,516
2012	313,874	135,486	8,093	8,228	28,775	16,719	8,786	9,176	13,411	21,387	20,911
2013	316,058	136,040	7,984	8,263	28,808	16,650	8,677	9,027	13,788	21,573	21,271
2014	318,386	136,584	8,010	8,138	28,812	16,743	8,543	8,892	13,985	21,955	21,505
2015	320,743	136,885	7,995	8,035	28,864	16,802	8,463	8,791	13,881	22,415	21,638
2016	323,071	137,263	7,972	8,065	28,893	16,769	8,461	8,661	13,698	22,919	21,825
2017	325,147	137,518	8,003	8,049	28,898	16,745	8,483	8,574	13,492	23,336	21,938
2018	327,167	137,801	8,058	8,025	28,883	16,681	8,583	8,566	13,307	23,562	22,136
2019	329,159	138,091	8,057	8,056	28,825	16,668	8,618	8,589	13,156	23,612	22,510

NOTE: Resident population includes civilian population and armed forces personnel residing within the United States; it excludes armed forces personnel residing overseas. Detail may not sum to totals because of rounding. Population estimates as of July 1 of the indicated reference year. Some data have been revised from previously published figures. SOURCE: U.S. Department of Commerce, Census Bureau, Current Population Reports, Series P-25, Nos. 1000, 1022, 1045, 1057, 1059, 1092, and 1095; 2000 through 2009 Population Estimates, retrieved August 14, 2012, from http://www.census.gov/popest/ data/national/asrh/2011/index.html; and 2010 through 2019 Population Estimates, retrieved November 29, 2019, from https://www.census.gov/data/datasets/time-series/ demo/popest/2010s-national-detail.html#par_textimage_57373479. (This table was prepared November 2019.)

Table 101.20. Estimates of resident population, by race/ethnicity and age group: Selected years, 1980 through 2019

Year and age group	Number (in thousands)								Percentage distribution							
	Total	White	Black	Hispanic	Asian	Pacific Islander	American Indian/ Alaska Native	Two or more races	Total	White	Black	Hispanic	Asian	Pacific Islander	American Indian/ Alaska Native	Two or more races
1	2	3	4	5	6	7	8	9	10	11	12	13	14	15	16	17
Total																
1980	227,225	181,140	26,215	14,869	3,665	(¹)	1,336	—	100.0	79.7	11.5	6.5	1.6	(¹)	0.6	—
1990	249,623	188,725	29,439	22,573	7,092	(¹)	1,793	—	100.0	75.6	11.8	9.0	2.8	(¹)	0.7	—
1995	266,278	194,389	32,500	28,158	9,188	(¹)	2,044	—	100.0	73.0	12.2	10.6	3.5	(¹)	0.8	—
2000²	282,162	195,702	34,406	35,662	10,469	370	2,102	3,452	100.0	69.4	12.2	12.6	3.7	0.1	0.7	1.2
2005²	295,517	196,621	36,147	43,024	12,658	434	2,186	4,447	100.0	66.5	12.2	14.6	4.3	0.1	0.7	1.5
2009²	306,772	197,275	37,657	49,327	14,361	488	2,252	5,411	100.0	64.3	12.3	16.1	4.7	0.2	0.7	1.8
2010²	309,326	197,387	38,014	50,747	14,762	500	2,269	5,647	100.0	63.8	12.3	16.4	4.8	0.2	0.7	1.8
2014²	318,386	197,765	39,497	55,175	16,683	544	2,351	6,371	100.0	62.1	12.4	17.3	5.2	0.2	0.7	2.0
2015²	320,743	197,794	39,873	56,364	17,227	555	2,369	6,561	100.0	61.7	12.4	17.6	5.4	0.2	0.7	2.0
2016²	323,071	197,794	40,243	57,573	17,759	566	2,387	6,750	100.0	61.2	12.5	17.8	5.5	0.2	0.7	2.1
2017²	325,147	197,699	40,580	58,707	18,249	576	2,403	6,933	100.0	60.8	12.5	18.1	5.6	0.2	0.7	2.1
2018²	327,167	197,546	40,902	59,872	18,729	586	2,417	7,115	100.0	60.4	12.5	18.3	5.7	0.2	0.7	2.2
2019²	329,159	197,395	41,222	60,998	19,210	596	2,432	7,305	100.0	60.0	12.5	18.5	5.8	0.2	0.7	2.2
Under 5 years old																
1980	16,451	11,904	2,413	1,677	319	(¹)	137	—	100.0	72.4	14.7	10.2	1.9	(¹)	0.8	—
1990	18,856	12,757	2,825	2,497	593	(¹)	184	—	100.0	67.7	15.0	13.2	3.1	(¹)	1.0	—
1995	19,627	12,415	3,050	3,245	734	(¹)	182	—	100.0	63.3	15.5	16.5	3.7	(¹)	0.9	—
2000²	19,178	11,253	2,753	3,748	686	30	171	538	100.0	58.7	14.4	19.5	3.6	0.2	0.9	2.8
2005²	19,917	10,847	2,706	4,607	839	35	171	712	100.0	54.5	13.6	23.1	4.2	0.2	0.9	3.6
2009²	20,245	10,395	2,776	5,101	890	39	176	868	100.0	51.3	13.7	25.2	4.4	0.2	0.9	4.3
2010²	20,189	10,278	2,780	5,128	891	39	176	898	100.0	50.9	13.8	25.4	4.4	0.2	0.9	4.4
2014²	19,872	9,931	2,736	5,135	931	39	171	931	100.0	50.0	13.8	25.8	4.7	0.2	0.9	4.7
2015²	19,918	9,921	2,744	5,152	955	40	169	937	100.0	49.8	13.8	25.9	4.8	0.2	0.8	4.7
2016²	19,922	9,883	2,745	5,162	979	40	167	946	100.0	49.6	13.8	25.9	4.9	0.2	0.8	4.7
2017²	19,892	9,836	2,738	5,170	992	41	165	951	100.0	49.4	13.8	26.0	5.0	0.2	0.8	4.8
2018²	19,810	9,767	2,724	5,172	992	41	162	952	100.0	49.3	13.8	26.1	5.0	0.2	0.8	4.8
2019²	19,703	9,669	2,704	5,173	996	41	160	960	100.0	49.1	13.7	26.3	5.1	0.2	0.8	4.9
5 to 17 years old																
1980	47,232	35,220	6,840	4,005	790	(¹)	377	—	100.0	74.6	14.5	8.5	1.7	(¹)	0.8	—
1990	45,359	—	—	—	—	—	—	—	—	—	—	—	—	—	—	—
1995	49,838	—	—	—	—	—	—	—	—	—	—	—	—	—	—	—
2000²	53,198	33,008	7,994	8,700	1,829	85	522	1,059	100.0	62.0	15.0	16.4	3.4	0.2	1.0	2.0
2005²	53,606	31,379	7,987	10,207	2,047	92	499	1,396	100.0	58.5	14.9	19.0	3.8	0.2	0.9	2.6
2009²	53,890	29,851	7,726	11,717	2,290	99	478	1,729	100.0	55.4	14.3	21.7	4.2	0.2	0.9	3.2
2010²	53,932	29,496	7,644	12,057	2,350	101	475	1,809	100.0	54.7	14.2	22.4	4.4	0.2	0.9	3.4
2014²	53,693	28,290	7,431	12,818	2,549	104	463	2,037	100.0	52.7	13.8	23.9	4.7	0.2	0.9	3.8
2015²	53,702	28,010	7,410	13,022	2,599	105	461	2,095	100.0	52.2	13.8	24.2	4.8	0.2	0.9	3.9
2016²	53,727	27,748	7,395	13,233	2,643	105	459	2,144	100.0	51.6	13.8	24.6	4.9	0.2	0.9	4.0
2017²	53,691	27,476	7,378	13,395	2,689	106	457	2,190	100.0	51.2	13.7	24.9	5.0	0.2	0.9	4.1
2018²	53,589	27,186	7,346	13,529	2,733	107	454	2,234	100.0	50.7	13.7	25.2	5.1	0.2	0.8	4.2
2019²	53,550	26,953	7,334	13,654	2,769	107	452	2,280	100.0	50.3	13.7	25.5	5.2	0.2	0.8	4.3
18 to 24 years old																
1980	30,103	23,278	3,872	2,284	468	(¹)	201	—	100.0	77.3	12.9	7.6	1.6	(¹)	0.7	—
1990	26,853	—	—	—	—	—	—	—	—	—	—	—	—	—	—	—
1995	25,482	—	—	—	—	—	—	—	—	—	—	—	—	—	—	—
2000²	27,315	16,913	3,780	4,786	1,158	50	239	389	100.0	61.9	13.8	17.5	4.2	0.2	0.9	1.4
2005²	29,442	17,741	4,092	5,406	1,351	57	263	531	100.0	60.3	13.9	18.4	4.6	0.2	0.9	1.8
2009²	30,530	17,705	4,363	6,006	1,481	64	266	645	100.0	58.0	14.3	19.7	4.9	0.2	0.9	2.1
2010²	30,763	17,616	4,436	6,182	1,519	66	266	678	100.0	57.3	14.4	20.1	4.9	0.2	0.9	2.2
2014²	31,420	17,323	4,669	6,598	1,661	64	275	829	100.0	55.1	14.9	21.0	5.3	0.2	0.9	2.6
2015²	31,136	17,025	4,588	6,647	1,682	62	271	860	100.0	54.7	14.7	21.3	5.4	0.2	0.9	2.8
2016²	30,820	16,716	4,495	6,693	1,700	61	266	889	100.0	54.2	14.6	21.7	5.5	0.2	0.9	2.9
2017²	30,549	16,463	4,402	6,731	1,715	60	261	916	100.0	53.9	14.4	22.0	5.6	0.2	0.9	3.0
2018²	30,457	16,295	4,337	6,820	1,743	60	257	944	100.0	53.5	14.2	22.4	5.7	0.2	0.8	3.1
2019²	30,362	16,122	4,274	6,908	1,775	60	255	968	100.0	53.1	14.1	22.8	5.8	0.2	0.8	3.2
25 years old and over																
1980	133,438	110,737	13,091	6,903	2,088	(¹)	620	—	100.0	83.0	9.8	5.2	1.6	(¹)	0.5	—
1990	158,555	125,653	16,322	11,447	4,190	(¹)	944	—	100.0	79.2	10.3	7.2	2.6	(¹)	0.6	—
1995	171,332	131,839	18,250	14,519	5,628	(¹)	1,096	—	100.0	76.9	10.7	8.5	3.3	(¹)	0.6	—
2000²	182,471	134,529	19,879	18,427	6,796	205	1,170	1,465	100.0	73.7	10.9	10.1	3.7	0.1	0.6	0.8
2005²	192,551	136,655	21,361	22,804	8,421	250	1,253	1,808	100.0	71.0	11.1	11.8	4.4	0.1	0.7	0.9
2009²	202,107	139,324	22,792	26,504	9,700	285	1,332	2,170	100.0	68.9	11.3	13.1	4.8	0.1	0.7	1.1
2010²	204,443	139,997	23,154	27,381	10,002	294	1,352	2,262	100.0	68.5	11.3	13.4	4.9	0.1	0.7	1.1
2014²	213,401	142,221	24,662	30,624	11,543	337	1,442	2,574	100.0	66.6	11.6	14.4	5.4	0.2	0.7	1.2
2015²	215,987	142,838	25,131	31,542	11,991	348	1,467	2,669	100.0	66.1	11.6	14.6	5.6	0.2	0.7	1.2
2016²	218,602	143,447	25,609	32,485	12,437	359	1,494	2,771	100.0	65.6	11.7	14.9	5.7	0.2	0.7	1.3
2017²	221,015	143,923	26,062	33,412	12,853	369	1,520	2,877	100.0	65.1	11.8	15.1	5.8	0.2	0.7	1.3
2018²	223,311	144,299	26,496	34,350	13,260	379	1,544	2,984	100.0	64.6	11.9	15.4	5.9	0.2	0.7	1.3
2019²	225,544	144,652	26,910	35,263	13,669	388	1,566	3,096	100.0	64.1	11.9	15.6	6.1	0.2	0.7	1.4

—Not available.

¹Included under Asian.

²Data on persons of Two or more races were collected beginning in 2000. Direct comparability of the data (other than Hispanic) prior to 2000 with the data for 2000 and later years is limited by the extent to which people reporting more than one race in later years had been reported in specific race groups in earlier years.

NOTE: Resident population includes civilian population and armed forces personnel residing within the United States; it excludes armed forces personnel residing overseas. Race categories exclude persons of Hispanic ethnicity. Detail may not sum to totals because of rounding. Some data have been revised from previously published figures. Population estimates as of July 1 of the indicated reference year.

SOURCE: U.S. Department of Commerce, Census Bureau, Current Population Reports, Series P-25, Nos. 1092 and 1095; 2000 through 2009 Population Estimates, retrieved August 14, 2012, from http://www.census.gov/popest/data/national/asrh/2011/index.html; and 2010 through 2019 Population Estimates, retrieved November 29, 2019, from https://www.census.gov/data/datasets/time-series/demo/popest/2010s-national-detail.html#par_textimage_57373479. (This table was prepared November 2019.)

Table 102.10. Number and percentage distribution of family households, by family structure and presence of own children under 18: Selected years, 1970 through 2018

[Standard errors appear in parentheses]

Number (in thousands)

Family structure and presence of own children	1970	1980	1990	2000	2010	2015	2016	2017	2018	Change, 2000 to 2010	Change, 2010 to 2018
1	2	3	4	5	6	7	8	9	10	11	12
										Percent change	
All families	51,456 (257.3)	59,550 (271.4)	66,090 (307.8)	72,025 (311.6)	78,833 (241.0)	81,716 (267.6)	82,184 (268.0)	82,827 (268.6)	83,088 (268.8)	9.5 (0.58)	5.4 (0.47)
Married-couple families	44,728 (243.6)	49,112 (252.7)	52,317 (283.3)	55,311 (289.5)	58,410 (218.6)	60,010 (243.1)	60,251 (243.5)	60,804 (244.2)	61,241 (244.8)	5.6 (0.68)	4.8 (0.57)
Without own children under 18	19,196 (168.7)	24,151 (187.3)	27,780 (218.1)	30,062 (230.5)	33,835 (176.1)	35,970 (199.4)	36,480 (200.6)	37,153 (202.1)	37,430 (202.7)	12.6 (1.04)	10.6 (0.83)
With own children under 18	25,532 (192.0)	24,961 (190.1)	24,537 (206.4)	25,248 (214.1)	24,575 (153.1)	24,040 (167.3)	23,772 (166.5)	23,651 (166.1)	23,812 (166.6)	-2.7! (1.02)	-3.1 (0.91)
One own child under 18	8,045 (112.5)	9,671 (122.0)	9,583 (133.0)	9,402 (136.2)	9,567 (98.5)	9,662 (106.6)	9,581 (106.4)	9,492 (106.8)	9,205 (106.8)	‡ (†)	‡ (†)
Two own children under 18	8,163 (111.7)	9,488 (120.9)	9,784 (134.3)	10,274 (142.1)	9,658 (98.9)	9,662 (109.3)	9,581 (108.9)	9,492 (108.4)	9,397 (107.9)	-6.0 (1.62)	-3.8! (1.49)
Three or more own children under 18	9,325 (119.9)	5,802 (95.3)	5,170 (98.5)	5,572 (105.9)	5,351 (74.3)	5,215 (81.0)	5,061 (79.8)	4,954 (79.0)	5,209 (81.0)	‡ (†)	‡ (†)
Families with male householder, no spouse present	1,228 (44.2)	1,733 (52.5)	2,884 (73.9)	4,028 (90.4)	5,580 (75.8)	6,162 (87.9)	6,310 (88.9)	6,452 (89.9)	6,424 (89.7)	38.5 (3.63)	15.1 (2.24)
Without own children under 18	887 (37.6)	1,117 (42.2)	1,731 (57.4)	2,242 (67.7)	3,356 (59.0)	3,774 (69.1)	3,838 (69.7)	4,057 (71.6)	3,939 (70.6)	49.7 (5.23)	17.4 (2.95)
With own children under 18	341 (23.3)	616 (31.3)	1,153 (46.9)	1,786 (60.5)	2,224 (48.2)	2,388 (55.1)	2,472 (56.1)	2,395 (55.2)	2,484 (56.2)	24.5 (5.01)	11.7 (3.50)
One own child under 18	179 (16.9)	374 (24.4)	723 (37.2)	1,131 (48.2)	1,375 (37.9)	1,453 (42.8)	1,487 (43.6)	1,403 (42.3)	1,339 (41.4)	21.6 (6.17)	‡ (†)
Two own children under 18	87 (11.8)	165 (16.2)	307 (24.2)	483 (31.6)	576 (24.6)	653 (28.9)	663 (29.2)	690 (29.7)	811 (32.2)	19.3! (9.31)	40.8 (8.21)
Three or more own children under 18	75 (10.9)	77 (11.1)	123 (15.3)	171 (18.8)	273 (16.9)	302 (19.7)	322 (20.3)	302 (19.7)	335 (20.7)	59.6! (20.15)	22.7! (10.75)
Families with female householder, no spouse present	5,500 (92.8)	8,705 (116.0)	10,890 (141.4)	12,687 (156.9)	14,843 (121.0)	15,544 (137.0)	15,622 (137.3)	15,572 (137.1)	15,423 (136.5)	17.0 (1.73)	3.9! (1.25)
Without own children under 18	2,642 (64.7)	3,261 (71.8)	4,290 (89.9)	5,116 (101.6)	6,424 (81.2)	6,993 (93.5)	7,097 (94.2)	7,326 (95.6)	7,267 (95.3)	25.6 (2.96)	13.1 (2.06)
With own children under 18	2,858 (67.2)	5,445 (92.3)	6,599 (111.0)	7,571 (122.8)	8,419 (92.6)	8,551 (103.1)	8,525 (102.9)	8,246 (101.3)	8,156 (100.7)	11.2 (2.18)	‡ (†)
One own child under 18	1,008 (40.1)	2,398 (61.6)	3,225 (78.1)	3,777 (87.6)	4,207 (66.0)	4,192 (72.8)	4,173 (72.6)	4,119 (72.2)	4,032 (71.4)	11.4! (3.12)	‡ (†)
Two own children under 18	810 (35.9)	1,817 (53.7)	2,173 (64.2)	2,458 (70.9)	2,714 (53.2)	2,844 (60.1)	2,794 (59.6)	2,620 (57.7)	2,534 (56.8)	10.4! (3.85)	-6.6! (2.78)
Three or more own children under 18	1,040 (40.7)	1,230 (44.2)	1,202 (47.9)	1,336 (52.4)	1,499 (39.6)	1,515 (44.0)	1,557 (44.6)	1,508 (43.9)	1,590 (45.1)	12.2! (5.31)	‡ (†)

Percentage distribution of all families

Family structure and presence of own children	1970	1980	1990	2000	2010	2015	2016	2017	2018	Change, 2000 to 2010	Change, 2010 to 2018
										Change in percentage points	
All families	100.0 (†)	100.0 (†)	100.0 (†)	100.0 (†)	100.0 (†)	100.0 (†)	100.0 (†)	100.0 (†)	100.0 (†)	† (†)	† (†)
Married-couple families	86.9 (0.19)	82.5 (0.20)	79.2 (0.22)	76.8 (0.23)	74.1 (0.16)	73.4 (0.18)	73.3 (0.17)	73.4 (0.17)	73.7 (0.17)	-2.7 (0.28)	† (†)
Without own children under 18	37.3 (0.27)	40.6 (0.25)	42.0 (0.27)	41.7 (0.26)	42.9 (0.18)	44.0 (0.20)	44.4 (0.20)	44.9 (0.20)	45.0 (0.20)	1.2 (0.32)	2.1 (0.27)
With own children under 18	49.6 (0.28)	41.9 (0.26)	37.1 (0.26)	35.1 (0.26)	31.2 (0.17)	29.4 (0.18)	28.9 (0.18)	28.6 (0.18)	28.7 (0.18)	-3.9 (0.31)	-2.5 (0.25)
One own child under 18	15.9 (0.20)	16.2 (0.19)	14.5 (0.19)	13.1 (0.18)	12.1 (0.12)	11.2 (0.13)	11.1 (0.13)	11.1 (0.12)	11.1 (0.12)	-0.9 (0.22)	-1.1 (0.17)
Two own children under 18	15.6 (0.20)	15.9 (0.19)	14.8 (0.19)	14.3 (0.19)	12.3 (0.12)	11.8 (0.13)	11.7 (0.13)	11.5 (0.13)	11.3 (0.12)	-2.0 (0.22)	-0.9 (0.17)
Three or more own children under 18	18.1 (0.21)	9.7 (0.15)	7.8 (0.14)	7.7 (0.14)	6.8 (0.09)	6.4 (0.10)	6.2 (0.10)	6.0 (0.09)	6.3 (0.10)	-0.9 (0.17)	-0.5 (0.13)
Families with male householder, no spouse present	2.4 (0.09)	2.9 (0.09)	4.4 (0.11)	5.6 (0.12)	7.1 (0.09)	7.5 (0.10)	7.7 (0.11)	7.8 (0.11)	7.7 (0.11)	1.5 (0.15)	0.7 (0.14)
Without own children under 18	1.7 (0.07)	1.9 (0.07)	2.6 (0.09)	3.1 (0.09)	4.3 (0.07)	4.6 (0.08)	4.7 (0.08)	4.9 (0.09)	4.7 (0.08)	1.1 (0.12)	0.5 (0.11)
With own children under 18	0.7 (0.05)	1.0 (0.05)	1.7 (0.07)	2.5 (0.08)	2.8 (0.06)	2.9 (0.07)	3.0 (0.07)	2.9 (0.07)	3.0 (0.07)	0.31 (0.10)	‡ (†)
One own child under 18	0.3 (0.03)	0.6 (0.04)	1.1 (0.06)	1.6 (0.07)	1.8 (0.05)	1.8 (0.05)	1.8 (0.05)	1.7 (0.05)	1.6 (0.05)	0.21 (0.08)	‡ (†)
Two own children under 18	0.2 (0.02)	0.3 (0.03)	0.5 (0.04)	0.7 (0.04)	0.7 (0.03)	0.8 (0.04)	0.8 (0.04)	0.8 (0.04)	1.0 (0.04)	‡ (†)	0.2 (0.05)
Three or more own children under 18	0.1 (0.02)	0.1 (0.02)	0.2 (0.02)	0.2 (0.03)	0.3 (0.02)	0.4 (0.02)	0.4 (0.02)	0.4 (0.02)	0.4 (0.02)	0.1! (0.03)	‡ (†)
Families with female householder, no spouse present	10.7 (0.17)	14.6 (0.18)	16.5 (0.20)	17.6 (0.20)	18.8 (0.14)	19.0 (0.16)	19.0 (0.16)	18.8 (0.15)	18.6 (0.15)	1.2 (0.25)	‡ (†)
Without own children under 18	5.1 (0.12)	5.5 (0.12)	6.5 (0.13)	7.1 (0.14)	8.1 (0.10)	8.6 (0.11)	8.6 (0.11)	8.8 (0.11)	8.7 (0.11)	1.0 (0.17)	0.6 (0.15)
With own children under 18	5.6 (0.13)	9.1 (0.15)	10.0 (0.16)	10.5 (0.16)	10.7 (0.11)	10.5 (0.12)	10.4 (0.12)	10.0 (0.12)	9.8 (0.12)	‡ (†)	-0.9 (0.16)
One own child under 18	2.0 (0.08)	4.0 (0.10)	4.9 (0.12)	5.2 (0.12)	5.3 (0.08)	5.1 (0.09)	5.1 (0.09)	5.0 (0.09)	4.9 (0.08)	‡ (†)	-0.5 (0.12)
Two own children under 18	1.6 (0.07)	3.1 (0.09)	3.3 (0.10)	3.4 (0.10)	3.4 (0.07)	3.5 (0.07)	3.4 (0.07)	3.2 (0.07)	3.0 (0.07)	‡ (†)	-0.4 (0.09)
Three or more own children under 18	2.0 (0.08)	2.1 (0.07)	1.8 (0.07)	1.9 (0.07)	1.9 (0.05)	1.9 (0.05)	1.9 (0.05)	1.8 (0.05)	1.9 (0.05)	‡ (†)	‡ (†)

†Not applicable.
!Interpret data with caution. The coefficient of variation (CV) for this estimate is between 30 and 50 percent.
‡Reporting standards not met. The coefficient of variation (CV) for this estimate is 50 percent or greater.
NOTE: A family household consists of two or more people who are related by birth, marriage, or adoption and are residing together. Own children are never-married sons and daughters, including stepchildren and adopted children, of the householder or married couple. Detail may not sum to totals because of rounding.

SOURCE: U.S. Department of Commerce, Census Bureau, Current Population Reports, Series P20, *Household and Family Characteristics*, 1994 and 1995; and Current Population Survey (CPS), Annual Social and Economic Supplement, *America's Families and Living Arrangements* (F table series), 2000 and 2010–2018. 2018 data retrieved May 24, 2019, from https://www.census.gov/content/census/en/data/tables/2018/demo/families/cps-2018.html. (This table was prepared May 2019.)

Table 102.20. Number and percentage distribution of children under age 18 and under age 6, by living arrangements, race/ethnicity, and selected racial/ethnic subgroups: 2018

[Standard errors appear in parentheses]

Age and race/ethnicity	Number of children (in thousands)		Percentage distribution of children		Total		Married-couple household		Female householder, no spouse present		Male householder, no spouse present		All other children[2]	
1	2		3		4		5		6		7		8	
All children under age 18														
Total	73,273	(27.2)	100.0	(†)	100.0	(†)	63.7	(0.12)	26.4	(0.11)	7.9	(0.06)	2.0	(0.03)
White	36,797	(8.0)	50.2	(0.02)	100.0	(†)	73.8	(0.15)	16.8	(0.11)	7.3	(0.10)	2.0	(0.04)
Black	9,784	(32.6)	13.4	(0.04)	100.0	(†)	33.7	(0.35)	55.4	(0.37)	8.3	(0.19)	2.6	(0.09)
Hispanic	18,622	(9.6)	25.4	(0.01)	100.0	(†)	57.3	(0.21)	31.7	(0.21)	9.2	(0.13)	1.8	(0.05)
Cuban	467	(11.5)	0.6	(0.02)	100.0	(†)	59.2	(1.36)	30.6	(1.30)	8.5	(0.61)	1.7	(0.24)
Dominican	613	(14.0)	0.8	(0.02)	100.0	(†)	44.6	(1.27)	46.0	(1.20)	7.8	(0.58)	1.6	(0.25)
Mexican	12,360	(36.7)	16.9	(0.05)	100.0	(†)	59.0	(0.26)	30.2	(0.27)	9.1	(0.17)	1.7	(0.06)
Puerto Rican	1,731	(21.2)	2.4	(0.03)	100.0	(†)	46.0	(0.83)	43.0	(0.75)	9.1	(0.42)	1.9	(0.18)
Spaniard	190	(7.6)	0.3	(0.01)	100.0	(†)	67.4	(1.87)	22.0	(1.52)	9.0	(1.25)	1.6	(0.40)
Central American[3]	1,685	(26.4)	2.3	(0.04)	100.0	(†)	54.1	(0.73)	31.3	(0.70)	12.0	(0.54)	2.6	(0.21)
Costa Rican	38	(3.5)	0.1	(#)	100.0	(†)	73.7	(3.87)	20.2	(3.89)	4.8!	(1.50)	1.3!	(0.65)
Guatemalan	476	(15.4)	0.6	(0.02)	100.0	(†)	55.0	(1.36)	27.2	(1.21)	14.1	(1.06)	3.7	(0.48)
Honduran	338	(13.4)	0.5	(0.02)	100.0	(†)	49.2	(1.81)	36.9	(1.84)	11.5	(1.08)	2.5	(0.43)
Nicaraguan	95	(6.0)	0.1	(0.01)	100.0	(†)	60.1	(2.79)	32.0	(3.15)	6.8	(1.48)	‡	(†)
Panamanian	51	(4.1)	0.1	(0.01)	100.0	(†)	46.5	(4.02)	46.1	(4.48)	6.5	(1.91)	‡	(†)
Salvadoran	671	(16.0)	0.9	(0.02)	100.0	(†)	54.5	(1.23)	30.9	(1.34)	12.4	(0.82)	2.2	(0.23)
South American	881	(18.0)	1.2	(0.02)	100.0	(†)	69.8	(0.96)	22.0	(0.94)	7.0	(0.45)	1.1	(0.14)
Chilean	42	(3.5)	0.1	(#)	100.0	(†)	82.0	(2.61)	12.2	(2.25)	4.0!	(1.51)	‡	(†)
Colombian	268	(10.8)	0.4	(0.01)	100.0	(†)	66.4	(2.08)	25.3	(2.03)	7.3	(0.90)	0.9	(0.24)
Ecuadorian	182	(8.9)	0.2	(0.01)	100.0	(†)	65.2	(1.98)	23.9	(1.87)	9.2	(1.18)	1.6	(0.41)
Peruvian	145	(8.2)	0.2	(0.01)	100.0	(†)	68.3	(2.12)	23.1	(2.05)	7.9	(1.42)	0.7!	(0.21)
Venezuelan	128	(8.1)	0.2	(0.01)	100.0	(†)	77.4	(2.11)	17.9	(1.97)	3.9	(1.03)	0.8!	(0.35)
Other South American	116	(6.3)	0.2	(0.01)	100.0	(†)	74.1	(2.35)	18.0	(2.19)	6.3	(1.17)	1.6!	(0.62)
Other Hispanic	696	(16.9)	0.9	(0.02)	100.0	(†)	53.4	(1.04)	32.8	(1.07)	9.8	(0.64)	4.0	(0.34)
Asian	3,472	(16.8)	4.7	(0.02)	100.0	(†)	84.4	(0.32)	9.9	(0.25)	4.3	(0.22)	1.4	(0.08)
Chinese[4]	718	(11.3)	1.0	(0.02)	100.0	(†)	82.3	(0.77)	11.4	(0.58)	4.2	(0.40)	2.1	(0.25)
Filipino	419	(9.2)	0.6	(0.01)	100.0	(†)	79.1	(1.03)	14.1	(0.79)	5.0	(0.57)	1.8	(0.29)
Japanese	70	(4.2)	0.1	(0.01)	100.0	(†)	85.9	(2.14)	7.4	(1.66)	5.3	(1.46)	1.4!	(0.46)
Korean	222	(7.1)	0.3	(0.01)	100.0	(†)	88.2	(1.07)	7.5	(0.82)	2.9	(0.60)	1.4	(0.33)
South Asian[5]	1,205	(16.1)	1.6	(0.02)	100.0	(†)	92.8	(0.41)	4.6	(0.33)	2.0	(0.22)	0.6	(0.10)
Asian Indian	953	(12.4)	1.3	(0.02)	100.0	(†)	93.9	(0.37)	4.0	(0.31)	1.7	(0.20)	0.5	(0.10)
Bangladeshi	57	(3.9)	0.1	(0.01)	100.0	(†)	85.5	(2.71)	9.1	(1.94)	‡	(†)	‡	(†)
Bhutanese	8	(1.5)	#	(†)	100.0	(†)	88.7	(5.30)	‡	(†)	‡	(†)	‡	(†)
Nepalese	45	(3.8)	0.1	(0.01)	100.0	(†)	88.8	(2.16)	7.5	(1.91)	3.1!	(1.32)	‡	(†)
Pakistani	129	(6.3)	0.2	(0.01)	100.0	(†)	89.9	(1.67)	6.3	(1.20)	3.1!	(1.09)	0.6!	(0.26)
Southeast Asian	632	(13.5)	0.9	(0.02)	100.0	(†)	72.9	(1.03)	16.7	(0.94)	8.5	(0.69)	1.9	(0.26)
Burmese	65	(5.2)	0.1	(0.01)	100.0	(†)	82.0	(3.59)	11.0	(3.00)	6.2!	(2.06)	‡	(†)
Cambodian	44	(3.6)	0.1	(#)	100.0	(†)	56.2	(4.62)	33.6	(4.55)	8.8	(2.06)	‡	(†)
Hmong	97	(5.4)	0.1	(0.01)	100.0	(†)	59.3	(3.33)	20.1	(2.73)	19.4	(2.69)	1.2!	(0.43)
Laotian	31	(3.1)	#	(†)	100.0	(†)	59.7	(5.20)	21.9	(4.10)	15.0	(3.84)	‡	(†)
Thai	29	(3.2)	#	(†)	100.0	(†)	67.8	(4.64)	18.8	(3.95)	‡	(†)	6.7!	(2.56)
Vietnamese	352	(8.3)	0.5	(0.01)	100.0	(†)	78.2	(1.16)	14.3	(1.07)	5.7	(0.69)	1.8	(0.26)
Other Southeast Asian[6]	14	(2.3)	#	(†)	100.0	(†)	86.4	(4.76)	‡	(†)	‡	(†)	‡	(†)
Other Asian	205	(8.0)	0.3	(0.01)	100.0	(†)	83.7	(1.22)	10.1	(1.01)	5.0	(0.85)	1.2	(0.29)
Pacific Islander	125	(5.6)	0.2	(0.01)	100.0	(†)	61.4	(2.59)	27.1	(2.43)	8.0	(1.35)	3.4	(0.88)
American Indian/Alaska Native	545	(6.4)	0.7	(0.01)	100.0	(†)	42.8	(1.09)	38.0	(1.04)	15.1	(0.73)	4.1	(0.32)
Some other race[7]	269	(11.6)	0.4	(0.02)	100.0	(†)	56.7	(1.81)	31.8	(1.62)	8.7	(0.94)	2.8	(0.49)
Two or more races	3,660	(30.2)	5.0	(0.04)	100.0	(†)	59.0	(0.52)	31.5	(0.50)	7.6	(0.26)	1.9	(0.10)
White and Black	1,569	(25.7)	2.1	(0.04)	100.0	(†)	43.1	(0.79)	45.9	(0.78)	8.4	(0.44)	2.7	(0.20)
White and Asian	1,070	(14.9)	1.5	(0.02)	100.0	(†)	81.6	(0.63)	12.5	(0.51)	5.0	(0.35)	0.9	(0.14)
White and American Indian/ Alaska Native	360	(10.1)	0.5	(0.01)	100.0	(†)	63.4	(1.11)	25.2	(1.11)	9.7	(0.70)	1.7	(0.28)
Other Two or more races	661	(12.1)	0.9	(0.02)	100.0	(†)	57.7	(1.04)	31.7	(1.03)	8.8	(0.66)	1.8	(0.23)
Children under age 6														
Total	23,423	(29.5)	100.0	(†)	100.0	(†)	63.9	(0.15)	26.2	(0.15)	8.2	(0.10)	1.7	(0.04)
White	11,616	(13.3)	49.6	(0.06)	100.0	(†)	75.5	(0.22)	15.6	(0.19)	7.2	(0.13)	1.7	(0.06)
Black	3,070	(19.5)	13.1	(0.08)	100.0	(†)	31.4	(0.54)	57.2	(0.54)	9.1	(0.28)	2.3	(0.14)
Hispanic	6,055	(15.7)	25.9	(0.06)	100.0	(†)	55.5	(0.34)	32.8	(0.33)	10.2	(0.22)	1.4	(0.07)
Cuban	171	(7.0)	0.7	(0.03)	100.0	(†)	58.1	(1.88)	31.8	(1.86)	9.4	(1.00)	0.7!	(0.26)
Dominican	213	(6.7)	0.9	(0.03)	100.0	(†)	45.5	(1.91)	45.8	(1.85)	7.4	(0.92)	1.3	(0.35)
Mexican	3,942	(16.9)	16.8	(0.07)	100.0	(†)	56.3	(0.43)	32.3	(0.41)	10.1	(0.26)	1.4	(0.09)
Puerto Rican	567	(10.6)	2.4	(0.04)	100.0	(†)	46.4	(1.25)	42.0	(1.27)	10.0	(0.73)	1.6	(0.29)
Spaniard	58	(3.9)	0.2	(0.02)	100.0	(†)	69.2	(3.26)	20.6	(2.89)	9.6	(2.42)	‡	(†)
Central American[3]	594	(13.5)	2.5	(0.06)	100.0	(†)	53.2	(1.16)	31.6	(1.16)	13.5	(0.72)	1.7	(0.31)
Costa Rican	13	(2.0)	0.1	(0.01)	100.0	(†)	81.1	(5.60)	15.7!	(5.17)	‡	(†)	‡	(†)
Guatemalan	163	(7.7)	0.7	(0.03)	100.0	(†)	53.3	(2.29)	29.8	(2.33)	14.9	(1.60)	2.1	(0.55)
Honduran	130	(7.6)	0.6	(0.03)	100.0	(†)	45.3	(2.46)	38.5	(2.45)	14.0	(1.86)	2.2!	(0.74)
Nicaraguan	30	(3.0)	0.1	(0.01)	100.0	(†)	65.6	(4.39)	25.6	(4.13)	8.0	(2.35)	‡	(†)
Panamanian	15	(2.2)	0.1	(0.01)	100.0	(†)	48.9	(6.94)	42.0	(7.04)	9.1!	(3.22)	‡	(†)
Salvadoran	236	(8.0)	1.0	(0.03)	100.0	(†)	54.4	(1.92)	30.0	(1.90)	14.1	(1.31)	1.5	(0.38)
South American	295	(9.1)	1.3	(0.04)	100.0	(†)	72.1	(1.33)	19.7	(1.24)	7.5	(0.69)	0.7	(0.20)
Chilean	16	(1.8)	0.1	(0.01)	100.0	(†)	81.6	(4.75)	11.5!	(3.95)	‡	(†)	‡	(†)
Colombian	82	(4.7)	0.3	(0.02)	100.0	(†)	70.5	(2.99)	20.4	(2.91)	8.4	(1.52)	‡	(†)
Ecuadorian	68	(4.8)	0.3	(0.02)	100.0	(†)	68.2	(3.23)	22.0	(2.93)	8.5	(1.84)	1.3!	(0.62)
Peruvian	49	(3.9)	0.2	(0.02)	100.0	(†)	68.8	(3.17)	20.3	(2.64)	10.4	(2.50)	‡	(†)
Venezuelan	42	(3.3)	0.2	(0.01)	100.0	(†)	76.9	(3.13)	21.1	(3.19)	2.0!	(0.91)	‡	(†)
Other South American	39	(3.6)	0.2	(0.02)	100.0	(†)	77.3	(3.57)	15.1	(3.12)	7.1!	(2.17)	‡	(†)
Other Hispanic	215	(9.0)	0.9	(0.04)	100.0	(†)	53.2	(1.77)	31.5	(1.67)	12.1	(1.15)	3.1	(0.50)

See notes at end of table.

Table 102.20.   Number and percentage distribution of children under age 18 and under age 6, by living arrangements, race/ethnicity, and selected racial/ethnic subgroups: 2018—Continued

[Standard errors appear in parentheses]

Age and race/ethnicity	Number of children (in thousands)		Percentage distribution of children		Percentage distribution of children, by living arrangements										
					Total		Children living with parent(s) or related to householder[1]						All other children[2]	
							Married-couple household		Female householder, no spouse present		Male householder, no spouse present			
1	2		3		4		5		6		7		8	
Asian	1,074	(9.3)	4.6	(0.04)	100.0	(†)	87.3	(0.44)	7.8	(0.35)	4.1	(0.27)	0.8	(0.11)
Chinese[4]	213	(5.7)	0.9	(0.02)	100.0	(†)	86.3	(0.92)	8.4	(0.78)	4.3	(0.59)	1.0	(0.25)
Filipino	101	(4.2)	0.4	(0.02)	100.0	(†)	78.4	(2.08)	14.7	(1.56)	5.3	(1.09)	1.6!	(0.51)
Japanese	25	(2.1)	0.1	(0.01)	100.0	(†)	94.6	(1.67)	3.9!	(1.64)	‡	(†)	‡	(†)
Korean	59	(3.0)	0.3	(0.01)	100.0	(†)	93.4	(1.32)	3.7	(0.87)	2.2!	(0.74)	‡	(†)
South Asian[5]	425	(8.8)	1.8	(0.04)	100.0	(†)	95.0	(0.53)	3.1	(0.38)	1.5	(0.30)	0.4!	(0.14)
Asian Indian	338	(7.2)	1.4	(0.03)	100.0	(†)	96.0	(0.50)	2.4	(0.34)	1.2	(0.32)	0.4!	(0.17)
Bangladeshi	19	(1.8)	0.1	(0.01)	100.0	(†)	93.4	(3.19)	‡	(†)	‡	(†)	‡	(†)
Bhutanese	‡	(†)	#	(†)	100.0	(†)	‡	(†)	‡	(†)	‡	(†)	‡	(†)
Nepalese	16	(2.2)	0.1	(0.01)	100.0	(†)	86.9	(3.85)	9.4!	(3.59)	‡	(†)	‡	(†)
Pakistani	44	(2.9)	0.2	(0.01)	100.0	(†)	91.2	(1.85)	5.5	(1.56)	2.9!	(1.10)	‡	(†)
Southeast Asian	178	(5.3)	0.8	(0.02)	100.0	(†)	71.7	(1.61)	16.8	(1.29)	10.2	(1.13)	1.4!	(0.54)
Burmese	24	(2.0)	0.1	(0.01)	100.0	(†)	85.8	(4.09)	8.8!	(3.24)	5.0!	(2.39)	‡	(†)
Cambodian	11	(1.2)	#	(†)	100.0	(†)	57.4	(6.06)	33.0	(6.02)	9.4!	(3.30)	‡	(†)
Hmong	33	(2.6)	0.1	(0.01)	100.0	(†)	51.2	(4.55)	23.6	(3.91)	24.0	(3.62)	‡	(†)
Laotian	11	(1.6)	#	(†)	100.0	(†)	48.9	(8.05)	25.2	(6.17)	19.2!	(6.69)	‡	(†)
Thai	7	(1.2)	#	(†)	100.0	(†)	80.4	(6.68)	7.3!	(3.06)	‡	(†)	‡	(†)
Vietnamese	87	(3.7)	0.4	(0.02)	100.0	(†)	78.7	(1.86)	14.5	(1.59)	6.0	(1.13)	0.8!	(0.36)
Other Southeast Asian[6]	‡	(†)	#	(†)	100.0	(†)	‡	(†)	‡	(†)	‡	(†)	‡	(†)
Other Asian	74	(3.4)	0.3	(0.01)	100.0	(†)	87.8	(1.64)	7.1	(1.15)	4.5	(1.27)	‡	(†)
Pacific Islander	39	(2.8)	0.2	(0.01)	100.0	(†)	65.1	(3.30)	23.7	(2.77)	8.0	(1.90)	3.2!	(1.42)
American Indian/Alaska Native	160	(3.7)	0.7	(0.02)	100.0	(†)	41.2	(1.62)	40.0	(1.58)	16.2	(1.41)	2.6	(0.46)
Some other race[7]	97	(5.3)	0.4	(0.02)	100.0	(†)	57.7	(2.64)	29.8	(2.45)	8.9	(1.26)	3.7	(1.04)
Two or more races	1,312	(16.3)	5.6	(0.07)	100.0	(†)	60.1	(0.75)	30.5	(0.69)	7.9	(0.39)	1.5	(0.14)
White and Black	585	(12.8)	2.5	(0.05)	100.0	(†)	41.9	(1.21)	46.5	(1.17)	9.2	(0.68)	2.4	(0.30)
White and Asian	395	(8.1)	1.7	(0.03)	100.0	(†)	87.1	(0.62)	7.7	(0.54)	4.6	(0.45)	0.6	(0.14)
White and American Indian/ Alaska Native	110	(4.4)	0.5	(0.02)	100.0	(†)	62.4	(1.89)	26.3	(1.75)	10.2	(1.17)	1.1!	(0.33)
Other Two or more races	222	(7.5)	0.9	(0.03)	100.0	(†)	58.7	(1.80)	31.0	(1.80)	9.3	(1.21)	1.0	(0.27)

†Not applicable.
#Rounds to zero.
!Interpret data with caution. The coefficient of variation (CV) for this estimate is between 30 and 50 percent.
‡Reporting standards not met. Either there are too few cases for a reliable estimate or the coefficient of variation (CV) is 50 percent or greater.
[1]Includes all children who live either with their parent(s) or with a householder to whom they are related by birth, marriage, or adoption (except a child who is the spouse of the householder). Children are classified by their parents' marital status or, if no parents are present in the household, by the marital status of the householder who is related to the children. Living arrangements with only a "female householder" or "male householder" are those in which the parent or the householder who is related to the child does not have a spouse living in the household. The householder is the person (or one of the people) who owns or rents (maintains) the housing unit.

[2]Includes foster children, children in unrelated subfamilies, children living in group quarters, and children who were reported as the householder or spouse of the householder.
[3]Includes other Central American subgroups not shown separately.
[4]Includes Taiwanese.
[5]In addition to the subgroups shown, also includes Sri Lankan.
[6]Consists of Indonesian and Malaysian.
[7]Respondents who wrote in some other race that was not included as an option on the questionnaire.
NOTE: Data are based on sample surveys of the entire population residing within the United States, including both noninstitutionalized persons (e.g., those living in households, college housing, or military housing located within the United States) and institutionalized persons (e.g., those living in prisons, nursing facilities, or other healthcare facilities). Race categories exclude persons of Hispanic ethnicity. Detail may not sum to totals because of rounding.
SOURCE: U.S. Department of Commerce, Census Bureau, American Community Survey (ACS), 2018. (This table was prepared November 2019.)

Table 102.40. Poverty rates for all persons and poverty status of related children under age 18, by region and state: Selected years, 1990 through 2018

[Standard errors appear in parentheses]

Region and state	Percent of persons in poverty[1]					Poverty status of related children[2] under age 18						
									2015[5]		2018[5]	
	1990[3]	2000[4]	2010[5]	2015[5]	2018[5]	1990,[3] percent in poverty	2000,[4] percent in poverty	2010,[5] percent in poverty	Number in poverty (in thousands)	Percent in poverty	Number in poverty (in thousands)	Percent in poverty
1	2	3	4	5	6	7	8	9	10	11	12	13
United States	**13.1**	**12.4**	**14.9 (0.06)**	**14.3 (0.06)**	**12.7 (0.05)**	**17.9 (0.02)**	**16.1 (0.01)**	**21.1 (0.13)**	**14,652 (109.9)**	**20.3 (0.15)**	**12,575 (92.5)**	**17.5 (0.12)**
Region												
Northeast	10.6	11.4	12.5 (0.09)	12.5 (0.09)	11.4 (0.10)	14.3 (0.54)	14.3 (0.39)	17.4 (0.20)	2,057 (25.4)	17.7 (0.22)	1,772 (25.5)	15.7 (0.22)
Midwest	12.0	10.2	16.5 (0.08)	15.6 (0.09)	14.1 (0.08)	14.9 (0.58)	12.0 (0.37)	23.8 (0.18)	6,291 (58.7)	22.7 (0.21)	5,619 (53.1)	20.1 (0.19)
South	15.7	13.9	14.1 (0.10)	13.5 (0.12)	12.2 (0.10)	20.5 (0.90)	17.6 (0.64)	20.0 (0.24)	2,878 (41.4)	18.8 (0.27)	2,427 (35.8)	16.1 (0.23)
West	12.6	13.0	15.0 (0.09)	14.4 (0.09)	12.1 (0.08)	16.2 (0.79)	16.2 (0.54)	20.6 (0.19)	3,425 (32.6)	19.6 (0.18)	2,758 (32.8)	15.8 (0.18)
Alabama	18.3	16.1	18.6 (0.39)	18.4 (0.37)	16.3 (0.31)	24.0 (0.14)	21.2 (0.10)	27.6 (0.86)	285 (8.7)	26.2 (0.79)	257 (8.2)	24.1 (0.77)
Alaska	9.0	9.4	10.6 (0.75)	9.9 (0.95)	10.4 (0.79)	10.9 (0.24)	11.2 (0.16)	13.5 (1.32)	27 (3.7)	14.7 (2.03)	22 (2.9)	12.5 (1.62)
Arizona	15.7	13.9	17.1 (0.35)	16.9 (0.31)	13.6 (0.27)	21.7 (0.13)	18.8 (0.10)	24.0 (0.74)	381 (10.8)	24.0 (0.67)	313 (10.7)	19.5 (0.66)
Arkansas	19.1	15.8	18.2 (0.41)	18.8 (0.44)	16.9 (0.46)	25.0 (0.17)	21.4 (0.11)	26.6 (1.00)	185 (6.7)	26.9 (0.97)	166 (6.6)	24.2 (0.95)
California	12.5	14.2	15.4 (0.13)	15.0 (0.12)	12.5 (0.12)	17.8 (0.05)	19.0 (0.04)	21.5 (0.28)	1,866 (25.4)	20.9 (0.28)	1,490 (23.8)	16.9 (0.27)
Colorado	11.7	9.3	12.8 (0.33)	11.3 (0.26)	9.5 (0.26)	15.0 (0.11)	10.8 (0.07)	16.6 (0.71)	177 (7.2)	14.3 (0.58)	144 (7.8)	11.6 (0.62)
Connecticut	6.8	7.9	9.6 (0.30)	9.9 (0.33)	10.0 (0.28)	10.4 (0.13)	10.0 (0.09)	12.3 (0.63)	100 (5.6)	13.4 (0.76)	100 (4.9)	13.9 (0.68)
Delaware	8.7	9.2	11.7 (0.73)	13.1 (0.87)	11.5 (0.70)	11.7 (0.23)	11.9 (0.20)	18.2 (1.59)	42 (4.4)	21.0 (2.19)	33 (3.6)	16.9 (1.83)
District of Columbia	16.9	20.2	18.3 (0.87)	15.5 (0.76)	15.8 (0.94)	25.0 (0.49)	31.1 (0.37)	29.3 (2.58)	29 (2.6)	25.4 (2.21)	29 (4.0)	23.3 (3.20)
Florida	12.7	12.5	16.2 (0.16)	15.3 (0.16)	13.1 (0.14)	18.3 (0.09)	17.2 (0.06)	23.2 (0.40)	917 (17.5)	22.9 (0.43)	780 (14.8)	18.9 (0.36)
Georgia	14.7	13.0	17.4 (0.27)	16.6 (0.22)	14.0 (0.22)	19.8 (0.12)	16.7 (0.07)	24.4 (0.46)	590 (12.3)	24.0 (0.50)	491 (12.2)	20.0 (0.49)
Hawaii	8.3	10.7	10.1 (0.50)	10.4 (0.52)	9.0 (0.52)	11.1 (0.21)	13.5 (0.16)	12.5 (1.29)	41 (3.8)	13.4 (1.24)	37 (3.9)	12.3 (1.30)
Idaho	13.3	11.8	15.0 (0.50)	13.8 (0.63)	11.8 (0.55)	15.8 (0.21)	13.8 (0.13)	17.5 (0.96)	66 (4.9)	15.6 (1.16)	62 (5.3)	14.2 (1.22)
Illinois	11.9	10.7	13.6 (0.19)	13.4 (0.21)	11.7 (0.20)	16.8 (0.07)	14.0 (0.04)	19.4 (0.41)	560 (14.7)	19.3 (0.50)	433 (13.1)	15.4 (0.46)
Indiana	10.7	9.5	14.9 (0.28)	14.6 (0.29)	12.7 (0.26)	13.9 (0.09)	11.7 (0.08)	21.7 (0.63)	332 (10.8)	21.6 (0.70)	265 (8.9)	17.4 (0.58)
Iowa	11.5	9.1	12.3 (0.41)	12.5 (0.47)	10.9 (0.35)	14.0 (0.13)	10.5 (0.08)	16.7 (0.94)	111 (7.5)	15.7 (1.07)	95 (6.2)	13.2 (0.86)
Kansas	11.5	9.9	12.7 (0.42)	12.6 (0.40)	11.8 (0.36)	13.9 (0.13)	11.5 (0.09)	17.4 (0.94)	123 (6.2)	17.5 (0.85)	100 (6.0)	14.6 (0.86)
Kentucky	19.0	15.8	18.1 (0.32)	17.6 (0.32)	16.2 (0.32)	24.5 (0.14)	20.4 (0.09)	25.4 (0.76)	245 (7.7)	25.0 (0.77)	215 (7.5)	22.1 (0.75)
Louisiana	23.6	19.6	17.9 (0.31)	18.8 (0.43)	18.1 (0.34)	31.2 (0.16)	26.3 (0.10)	26.9 (0.68)	303 (10.3)	27.6 (0.94)	284 (8.9)	26.3 (0.81)
Maine	10.8	10.9	13.3 (0.58)	12.5 (0.56)	10.8 (0.49)	13.2 (0.18)	13.0 (0.14)	18.3 (1.28)	35 (2.8)	14.3 (1.12)	28 (2.9)	11.7 (1.21)
Maryland	8.3	8.5	9.8 (0.25)	9.8 (0.28)	8.6 (0.25)	10.9 (0.10)	10.3 (0.08)	12.8 (0.51)	173 (8.5)	13.2 (0.64)	141 (7.7)	10.8 (0.58)
Massachusetts	8.9	9.3	11.0 (0.25)	10.9 (0.22)	9.7 (0.20)	12.9 (0.10)	11.6 (0.07)	13.7 (0.55)	194 (7.1)	14.2 (0.52)	158 (6.7)	11.9 (0.50)
Michigan	13.1	10.5	16.2 (0.24)	15.5 (0.28)	13.7 (0.23)	18.2 (0.08)	13.4 (0.05)	22.5 (0.52)	472 (13.3)	22.0 (0.62)	394 (11.5)	18.7 (0.54)
Minnesota	10.2	7.9	11.1 (0.32)	9.7 (0.26)	9.5 (0.29)	12.4 (0.09)	9.2 (0.06)	14.6 (0.72)	153 (7.9)	12.2 (0.62)	143 (9.5)	11.2 (0.74)
Mississippi	25.2	19.9	21.5 (0.51)	21.1 (0.51)	19.3 (0.40)	33.5 (0.18)	26.7 (0.11)	31.7 (1.05)	224 (7.7)	31.2 (1.07)	195 (7.0)	28.2 (0.99)
Missouri	13.3	11.7	15.1 (0.28)	14.2 (0.28)	12.8 (0.26)	17.4 (0.10)	15.3 (0.07)	20.6 (0.59)	266 (10.5)	19.6 (0.77)	235 (8.6)	17.6 (0.64)
Montana	16.1	14.6	14.1 (0.70)	14.2 (0.70)	11.8 (0.52)	19.9 (0.27)	18.4 (0.18)	19.8 (1.43)	41 (3.9)	18.5 (1.74)	28 (3.2)	12.8 (1.44)
Nebraska	11.1	9.7	12.7 (0.56)	12.2 (0.43)	11.2 (0.51)	13.5 (0.16)	11.8 (0.11)	18.2 (1.32)	71 (4.2)	15.4 (0.91)	61 (4.7)	13.3 (1.02)
Nevada	10.2	10.5	14.9 (0.49)	14.7 (0.46)	12.8 (0.35)	12.8 (0.22)	13.5 (0.14)	21.7 (0.97)	136 (7.3)	20.8 (1.11)	115 (5.1)	17.0 (0.78)
New Hampshire	6.4	6.5	8.0 (0.44)	7.7 (0.49)	7.0 (0.39)	7.0 (0.14)	7.3 (0.11)	9.8 (1.09)	26 (3.0)	9.9 (1.16)	23 (3.0)	9.3 (1.19)
New Jersey	7.6	8.5	10.0 (0.22)	10.4 (0.22)	9.2 (0.21)	11.0 (0.08)	10.8 (0.06)	14.0 (0.45)	293 (10.9)	14.9 (0.55)	257 (10.3)	13.4 (0.53)
New Mexico	20.6	18.4	19.9 (0.65)	20.4 (0.66)	19.6 (0.66)	27.5 (0.21)	24.6 (0.15)	29.5 (1.22)	150 (7.0)	30.5 (1.38)	125 (6.4)	26.7 (1.39)
New York	13.0	14.6	14.6 (0.19)	14.8 (0.17)	13.4 (0.17)	18.8 (0.07)	19.6 (0.05)	21.1 (0.36)	879 (17.8)	21.4 (0.43)	743 (17.8)	18.7 (0.44)
North Carolina	13.0	12.3	16.8 (0.24)	16.2 (0.23)	13.6 (0.23)	16.9 (0.09)	15.7 (0.06)	24.1 (0.52)	532 (11.7)	23.7 (0.51)	442 (11.1)	19.7 (0.49)
North Dakota	14.4	11.9	11.8 (0.77)	11.3 (0.57)	9.8 (0.70)	16.9 (0.26)	13.5 (0.15)	14.2 (1.92)	19 (2.2)	11.0 (1.28)	14 (2.1)	8.3 (1.23)
Ohio	12.5	10.6	15.4 (0.21)	14.5 (0.21)	13.5 (0.24)	17.6 (0.07)	14.0 (0.05)	22.9 (0.48)	552 (13.3)	21.5 (0.51)	484 (14.6)	19.1 (0.58)
Oklahoma	16.7	14.7	16.5 (0.39)	15.7 (0.38)	14.9 (0.40)	21.4 (0.14)	19.1 (0.09)	24.9 (0.98)	207 (8.3)	22.1 (0.88)	195 (8.3)	21.0 (0.87)
Oregon	12.4	11.6	15.6 (0.34)	14.8 (0.40)	12.0 (0.35)	15.2 (0.13)	14.0 (0.09)	21.0 (0.77)	165 (7.9)	19.7 (0.95)	124 (7.4)	14.6 (0.86)
Pennsylvania	11.1	11.0	12.8 (0.18)	12.5 (0.21)	11.8 (0.21)	15.4 (0.07)	14.3 (0.05)	18.2 (0.44)	480 (13.2)	18.3 (0.49)	418 (13.0)	16.2 (0.50)
Rhode Island	9.6	11.9	14.0 (0.59)	13.1 (0.61)	12.0 (0.63)	13.5 (0.26)	16.5 (0.22)	19.7 (1.49)	38 (3.3)	18.5 (1.56)	34 (3.3)	17.2 (1.65)
South Carolina	15.4	14.1	17.6 (0.33)	16.0 (0.32)	14.7 (0.32)	20.8 (0.16)	18.5 (0.10)	25.5 (0.73)	245 (7.6)	23.1 (0.70)	235 (9.0)	21.6 (0.82)
South Dakota	15.9	13.2	14.4 (0.89)	12.5 (0.69)	12.8 (0.66)	20.1 (0.28)	16.7 (0.19)	18.7 (1.97)	29 (3.2)	14.0 (1.51)	32 (2.6)	15.3 (1.28)
Tennessee	15.7	13.5	17.2 (0.30)	16.4 (0.31)	15.0 (0.28)	20.7 (0.12)	17.6 (0.09)	25.3 (0.67)	351 (10.9)	24.0 (0.74)	326 (10.7)	22.1 (0.72)
Texas	18.1	15.4	17.3 (0.16)	15.4 (0.17)	14.5 (0.14)	24.0 (0.08)	20.2 (0.05)	25.2 (0.31)	1,591 (25.1)	22.4 (0.35)	1,506 (23.3)	20.7 (0.32)
Utah	11.4	9.4	13.1 (0.46)	11.2 (0.43)	8.6 (0.34)	12.2 (0.14)	9.7 (0.08)	15.8 (0.87)	115 (6.9)	12.8 (0.77)	78 (5.5)	8.5 (0.59)
Vermont	9.9	9.4	11.4 (0.76)	9.2 (0.84)	10.7 (0.71)	11.5 (0.23)	10.7 (0.15)	14.8 (2.12)	14 (2.5)	11.7 (2.16)	10 (1.7)	9.5 (1.58)
Virginia	10.2	9.6	11.0 (0.18)	11.0 (0.22)	10.3 (0.22)	13.0 (0.10)	11.9 (0.07)	15.0 (0.42)	279 (8.7)	15.2 (0.47)	239 (8.4)	13.0 (0.46)
Washington	10.9	10.6	13.2 (0.27)	12.4 (0.25)	10.2 (0.25)	14.0 (0.09)	13.2 (0.08)	17.8 (0.58)	248 (9.8)	15.8 (0.62)	204 (10.8)	12.5 (0.67)
West Virginia	19.7	17.9	17.9 (0.54)	17.3 (0.55)	17.2 (0.59)	25.9 (0.21)	23.9 (0.15)	25.9 (1.37)	93 (5.4)	25.3 (1.44)	84 (5.1)	23.8 (1.44)
Wisconsin	10.7	8.7	12.7 (0.31)	11.3 (0.34)	10.5 (0.28)	14.6 (0.09)	10.8 (0.07)	18.1 (0.76)	191 (10.0)	15.2 (0.79)	172 (8.1)	13.8 (0.64)
Wyoming	11.9	11.4	10.4 (0.80)	9.9 (0.80)	10.8 (0.76)	14.1 (0.30)	13.8 (0.22)	13.4 (1.69)	15 (2.5)	10.9 (1.81)	16 (1.8)	12.7 (1.43)

[1]Data exclude institutionalized persons (e.g., those living in prisons or nursing homes) as well as persons living in most types of noninstitutional group quarters (e.g., college housing or military barracks). Data include noninstitutionalized persons living in households as well as those living in group homes and shelters.

[2]Related children in a family include all children in the household who are related to the householder by birth, marriage, or adoption (except a child who is the spouse of the householder). The householder is the person (or one of the people) who owns or rents (maintains) the housing unit. This table excludes unrelated children and householders who are themselves under the age of 18.

[3]Based on 1989 incomes and family sizes collected in the 1990 census.

[4]Based on 1999 incomes and family sizes collected in the 2000 census.

[5]Based on income and family size data from the American Community Survey (ACS). ACS respondents were interviewed throughout the given year and reported the income they received during the previous 12 months. Data are based on sample surveys of the entire population residing within the United States.

NOTE: Poverty status is determined by the Census Bureau using a set of money income thresholds that vary by family size and composition. For additional information about poverty status, see https://www.census.gov/topics/income-poverty/poverty/guidance/poverty-measures.html. Poverty estimates in this table may differ from table 102.50's official national poverty estimates, which are based on a different data source (the Current Population Survey). Detail may not sum to totals because of rounding.

SOURCE: U.S. Department of Commerce, Census Bureau, 1990 Summary Tape File 3 (STF 3), "Median Household Income in 1989" and "Poverty Status in 1989 by Family Type and Age"; Decennial Census, 1990, *Minority Economic Profiles*, unpublished data; Decennial Census, 2000, *Summary Social, Economic, and Housing Characteristics*; Census 2000 Summary File 4 (SF 4), "Poverty Status in 1999 of Related Children Under 18 Years by Family Type and Age"; and American Community Survey (ACS), 2010, 2015, and 2018. (This table was prepared November 2019.)

Table 102.62. Percentage of children under age 18 living in poverty, by parents' highest level of educational attainment, child's race/ethnicity, and selected racial/ethnic subgroups: 2010 and 2018

[Standard errors appear in parentheses]

Year and race/ethnicity	Percent in poverty, all children under age 18 who resided with at least one parent[1]	Less than high school completion	High school completion[2]	Some college, no degree	Associate's degree	Bachelor's or higher degree — Total	Bachelor's degree	Master's degree	Doctor's degree[3]
1	2	3	4	5	6	7	8	9	10
2010									
Total	20.8 (0.13)	53.4 (0.33)	32.3 (0.25)	23.0 (0.22)	12.7 (0.27)	4.3 (0.08)	5.6 (0.12)	2.8 (0.10)	2.1 (0.13)
White	12.5 (0.12)	48.8 (0.75)	24.6 (0.31)	17.1 (0.25)	8.8 (0.23)	3.2 (0.08)	4.1 (0.13)	2.1 (0.10)	1.5 (0.14)
Black	37.6 (0.39)	72.8 (0.76)	49.0 (0.65)	36.9 (0.72)	23.9 (0.99)	8.0 (0.37)	10.0 (0.51)	4.6 (0.57)	4.7 (1.12)
Hispanic	31.8 (0.23)	50.6 (0.42)	34.1 (0.44)	24.8 (0.50)	16.4 (0.68)	7.9 (0.33)	9.5 (0.45)	4.9 (0.55)	4.9 (0.73)
Cuban	18.6 (1.12)	52.3 (5.24)	27.0 (2.56)	21.9 (2.80)	11.4 (2.21)	6.7 (1.07)	9.5 (1.77)	2.2! (0.99)	3.4! (1.52)
Dominican	33.9 (1.22)	50.9 (3.29)	46.5 (2.73)	32.2 (2.61)	11.1 (2.60)	11.1 (1.91)	14.2 (2.60)	‡ (†)	‡ (†)
Mexican	33.8 (0.28)	50.7 (0.49)	34.4 (0.53)	24.9 (0.62)	15.8 (0.90)	8.1 (0.44)	9.1 (0.58)	5.7 (0.91)	‡ (†)
Puerto Rican	33.3 (0.78)	68.6 (2.06)	38.7 (1.44)	29.0 (1.42)	23.7 (2.50)	7.9 (0.83)	9.9 (1.20)	5.1! (1.58)	5.9 (1.19)
Spaniard	16.9 (1.58)	44.1 (8.89)	30.9 (4.83)	21.6 (3.34)	17.0! (5.73)	3.4! (1.05)	3.9! (1.28)	‡ (†)	‡ (†)
Central American[4]	26.8 (0.79)	40.0 (1.44)	26.8 (1.63)	19.7 (1.62)	10.0 (1.87)	9.5 (1.33)	11.8 (1.86)	4.4! (1.85)	8.1! (3.51)
Costa Rican	18.9 (3.67)	‡ (†)	28.7! (9.73)	29.7 (8.13)	‡ (†)	‡ (†)	‡ (†)	‡ (†)	‡ (†)
Guatemalan	31.2 (1.67)	50.2 (2.44)	27.4 (3.45)	22.4 (3.74)	11.0! (3.37)	8.3 (1.99)	11.5 (3.40)	‡ (†)	‡ (†)
Honduran	33.5 (2.15)	41.0 (3.44)	37.0 (4.44)	25.8 (4.58)	12.4! (5.46)	19.4 (4.59)	24.5 (6.06)	‡ (†)	‡ (†)
Nicaraguan	21.6 (2.96)	51.2 (7.70)	29.2 (5.70)	20.1 (5.13)	‡ (†)	‡ (†)	‡ (†)	‡ (†)	‡ (†)
Panamanian	15.5 (3.54)	‡ (†)	41.9! (17.94)	15.7! (5.31)	‡ (†)	8.9! (3.92)	18.3! (7.25)	‡ (†)	‡ (†)
Salvadoran	23.8 (1.09)	33.6 (2.28)	20.7 (2.13)	15.4 (2.26)	9.9 (2.87)	11.9 (2.65)	11.3 (2.71)	‡ (†)	‡ (†)
South American	17.0 (0.77)	41.7 (3.69)	25.7 (1.99)	18.4 (1.80)	16.5 (2.61)	7.4 (0.82)	9.8 (1.22)	3.6 (0.94)	5.1! (1.58)
Chilean	10.9 (3.02)	‡ (†)	13.2! (5.94)	23.0! (10.50)	‡ (†)	‡ (†)	‡ (†)	‡ (†)	‡ (†)
Colombian	13.8 (1.29)	37.1 (8.57)	24.6 (3.47)	16.3 (2.92)	10.2! (3.53)	6.0 (1.26)	7.5 (1.88)	3.2! (1.45)	‡ (†)
Ecuadorian	24.2 (2.05)	42.4 (4.95)	29.8 (4.40)	21.9 (4.73)	17.2 (4.90)	9.8 (2.85)	11.5! (4.06)	‡ (†)	‡ (†)
Peruvian	17.9 (2.17)	65.0 (11.70)	22.9 (4.15)	17.1 (4.07)	10.5! (4.43)	11.4 (2.43)	13.8 (2.98)	‡ (†)	‡ (†)
Venezuelan	17.1 (3.20)	‡ (†)	37.8! (12.96)	‡ (†)	61.0 (11.07)	7.3 (1.84)	8.3! (2.75)	‡ (†)	‡ (†)
Other South American	14.0 (1.89)	33.0 (8.91)	24.5 (6.93)	20.6 (4.29)	10.8! (5.38)	4.5! (1.40)	8.3! (2.85)	‡ (†)	‡ (†)
Other Hispanic	28.2 (1.18)	52.8 (3.10)	34.7 (2.38)	24.9 (2.09)	18.2 (3.39)	7.5 (1.25)	9.2 (1.79)	6.0! (2.32)	3.6! (1.52)
Asian	12.0 (0.30)	41.7 (1.71)	24.3 (1.26)	15.2 (0.99)	11.0 (1.09)	5.2 (0.27)	7.0 (0.43)	4.1 (0.37)	2.7 (0.35)
Chinese[5]	9.5 (0.53)	32.0 (2.77)	23.5 (2.60)	12.8 (2.11)	9.5 (2.17)	3.8 (0.39)	6.1 (0.92)	3.1 (0.66)	2.4 (0.56)
Filipino	5.2 (0.71)	10.6! (4.73)	12.4 (3.03)	9.1 (1.83)	7.6! (2.61)	2.8 (0.59)	2.9 (0.67)	‡ (†)	‡ (†)
Japanese	4.5 (1.14)	‡ (†)	26.9! (10.91)	‡ (†)	‡ (†)	2.7! (0.91)	3.7! (1.45)	‡ (†)	‡ (†)
Korean	12.9 (0.99)	‡ (†)	16.9 (4.85)	18.2 (5.18)	6.0! (2.17)	11.7 (1.16)	14.9 (1.66)	10.7 (1.70)	6.6 (1.86)
South Asian[6]	9.9 (0.63)	50.7 (4.76)	26.9 (3.38)	22.7 (3.92)	17.7 (3.66)	4.9 (0.49)	8.7 (1.16)	3.2 (0.53)	1.6! (0.50)
Asian Indian	7.6 (0.61)	49.2 (5.88)	25.0 (4.31)	22.9 (4.32)	13.0! (4.52)	3.6 (0.49)	7.4 (1.25)	1.9 (0.42)	0.9! (0.45)
Bangladeshi	30.0 (4.25)	79.5 (9.81)	‡ (†)	‡ (†)	‡ (†)	21.3 (4.96)	24.8! (7.93)	23.5! (8.18)	‡ (†)
Bhutanese	— (†)	— (†)	— (†)	— (†)	— (†)	— (†)	— (†)	— (†)	— (†)
Nepalese	— (†)	— (†)	— (†)	— (†)	— (†)	— (†)	— (†)	— (†)	— (†)
Pakistani	19.2 (2.33)	43.5 (10.91)	33.9 (6.31)	‡ (†)	30.5! (10.37)	11.1 (2.00)	12.2 (3.16)	12.0! (3.80)	‡ (†)
Southeast Asian	21.4 (0.91)	43.0 (2.51)	27.5 (2.04)	16.1 (1.74)	12.1 (2.36)	7.0 (1.07)	8.0 (1.32)	6.0 (1.55)	‡ (†)
Burmese	— (†)	— (†)	— (†)	— (†)	— (†)	— (†)	— (†)	— (†)	— (†)
Cambodian	27.2 (3.09)	57.0 (6.67)	31.3 (7.65)	19.3! (6.53)	‡ (†)	4.7! (2.22)	‡ (†)	‡ (†)	‡ (†)
Hmong	39.5 (3.68)	70.2 (6.78)	39.2 (6.62)	16.5! (5.47)	20.6! (8.76)	13.7! (6.32)	19.3! (8.84)	‡ (†)	‡ (†)
Laotian	19.0 (3.16)	27.7! (8.40)	26.7 (6.08)	14.4 (4.29)	‡ (†)	‡ (†)	‡ (†)	‡ (†)	‡ (†)
Thai	23.2 (6.73)	‡ (†)	‡ (†)	‡ (†)	‡ (†)	‡ (†)	‡ (†)	‡ (†)	‡ (†)
Vietnamese	15.9 (1.01)	28.2 (2.48)	22.9 (2.47)	15.7 (2.27)	10.1 (2.52)	5.2 (0.96)	5.9 (1.07)	‡ (†)	‡ (†)
Other Southeast Asian[7]	22.9 (5.69)	‡ (†)	‡ (†)	‡ (†)	‡ (†)	17.1! (5.22)	15.2! (7.06)	22.8! (8.78)	‡ (†)
Other Asian	15.9 (1.29)	54.3 (6.45)	23.8 (4.15)	21.1 (4.47)	12.1 (3.55)	5.6 (0.96)	6.1 (1.51)	6.3! (2.46)	3.4! (1.54)
Pacific Islander	22.4 (2.29)	68.3 (9.33)	23.6 (3.90)	18.7 (3.45)	21.8 (6.17)	11.7! (5.04)	13.5! (6.66)	‡ (†)	‡ (†)
American Indian/Alaska Native[8]	33.9 (1.16)	65.0 (2.96)	42.0 (2.30)	29.8 (1.88)	20.1 (2.76)	12.6 (2.24)	14.6 (3.03)	6.0! (2.77)	15.2! (5.64)
American Indian	35.4 (1.24)	66.7 (2.92)	44.5 (2.58)	31.1 (2.16)	19.8 (2.96)	12.6 (2.63)	14.5 (3.55)	3.6! (1.81)	22.1! (8.12)
Alaska Native	25.3 (3.55)	61.6 (12.23)	32.1 (5.12)	15.8! (5.45)	‡ (†)	‡ (†)	‡ (†)	‡ (†)	‡ (†)
Some other race[9]	19.3 (1.63)	41.5 (6.50)	30.9 (4.30)	22.9 (4.49)	9.0! (4.28)	6.6! (2.05)	13.8! (4.15)	‡ (†)	‡ (†)
Two or more races	21.0 (0.49)	57.8 (2.04)	35.8 (1.38)	27.1 (0.77)	18.0 (1.38)	5.3 (0.39)	7.2 (0.60)	3.4 (0.45)	1.7! (0.52)
2018									
Total	17.1 (0.13)	46.2 (0.41)	29.9 (0.32)	21.2 (0.20)	12.4 (0.26)	4.1 (0.08)	5.5 (0.12)	2.7 (0.10)	1.8 (0.13)
White	10.0 (0.12)	43.0 (0.78)	23.4 (0.45)	15.6 (0.24)	8.6 (0.25)	2.7 (0.07)	3.8 (0.12)	1.7 (0.09)	1.3 (0.14)
Black	31.7 (0.45)	64.2 (1.18)	45.9 (0.82)	34.2 (0.73)	22.8 (1.14)	8.1 (0.44)	10.2 (0.63)	6.2 (0.63)	2.9 (0.83)
Hispanic	25.1 (0.27)	43.5 (0.60)	29.1 (0.59)	21.6 (0.41)	15.0 (0.68)	7.6 (0.29)	9.4 (0.40)	4.7 (0.41)	3.9 (0.68)
Cuban	16.8 (1.13)	43.1 (5.74)	24.4 (3.19)	23.8 (3.21)	20.2 (4.28)	6.1 (0.90)	8.2 (1.42)	4.3! (1.34)	2.0! (0.96)
Dominican	28.4 (1.19)	52.0 (3.45)	35.6 (2.38)	30.8 (2.78)	10.9 (2.58)	11.5 (1.60)	13.5 (2.13)	5.8! (2.47)	13.1! (5.60)
Mexican	25.9 (0.31)	42.3 (0.69)	28.7 (0.68)	20.4 (0.51)	15.2 (0.82)	7.5 (0.40)	9.0 (0.59)	4.4 (0.63)	5.1 (1.14)
Puerto Rican	28.2 (0.87)	68.9 (2.71)	37.6 (1.77)	27.1 (1.36)	20.1 (2.11)	8.0 (0.81)	10.9 (1.23)	4.3 (1.13)	‡ (†)
Spaniard	10.0 (1.02)	62.3 (11.07)	17.9 (4.47)	18.4 (3.27)	4.9! (1.92)	3.2 (0.89)	5.3! (1.75)	2.2! (0.97)	‡ (†)
Central American[4]	26.6 (0.74)	42.0 (1.48)	23.8 (1.37)	23.5 (1.71)	8.0 (1.59)	8.4 (1.12)	10.3 (1.52)	6.8! (2.08)	‡ (†)
Costa Rican	9.9! (3.63)	‡ (†)	‡ (†)	‡ (†)	‡ (†)	‡ (†)	‡ (†)	‡ (†)	‡ (†)
Guatemalan	34.0 (1.58)	49.7 (2.54)	28.0 (3.04)	24.0 (3.78)	8.5! (3.17)	11.7 (2.73)	16.3 (3.83)	‡ (†)	‡ (†)
Honduran	31.2 (1.87)	44.7 (3.21)	27.3 (3.48)	32.0 (4.00)	‡ (†)	8.8 (2.26)	11.1! (3.50)	‡ (†)	‡ (†)
Nicaraguan	16.0 (2.32)	49.7 (9.22)	13.3! (4.62)	19.0 (4.87)	‡ (†)	8.7! (2.90)	10.9! (3.75)	‡ (†)	‡ (†)
Panamanian	14.3 (2.37)	‡ (†)	22.1! (6.85)	21.7! (6.68)	7.5! (3.47)	5.6! (2.53)	‡ (†)	‡ (†)	‡ (†)
Salvadoran	22.6 (1.02)	32.7 (2.21)	22.2 (2.04)	20.0 (2.59)	9.0! (3.05)	7.2 (1.85)	7.7 (2.03)	‡ (†)	‡ (†)
South American	11.5 (0.64)	21.7 (3.18)	21.4 (2.10)	12.7 (1.67)	10.0 (1.93)	7.2 (0.70)	9.4 (1.20)	4.8 (1.08)	4.6 (1.27)
Chilean	7.0 (1.92)	‡ (†)	38.4! (14.15)	‡ (†)	‡ (†)	‡ (†)	‡ (†)	‡ (†)	‡ (†)
Colombian	9.3 (0.99)	14.0! (5.83)	22.0 (4.78)	12.1 (2.81)	3.2! (1.56)	5.8 (1.02)	7.7 (1.70)	3.2! (1.58)	3.3! (1.41)
Ecuadorian	14.3 (1.96)	24.0 (4.80)	21.2 (4.16)	14.4! (4.62)	14.6! (7.14)	4.8! (1.49)	6.0! (2.19)	‡ (†)	‡ (†)
Peruvian	10.0 (1.48)	‡ (†)	18.7 (4.97)	12.8 (3.56)	9.4! (4.27)	3.8! (1.34)	5.2! (2.30)	‡ (†)	‡ (†)
Venezuelan	19.6 (2.08)	‡ (†)	35.3 (9.93)	20.2! (6.81)	24.1! (7.53)	17.4 (2.16)	21.5 (3.61)	11.6! (4.07)	13.6! (4.94)
Other South American	6.5 (1.37)	‡ (†)	13.7! (5.23)	9.8! (4.53)	‡ (†)	3.0! (0.96)	3.1! (1.55)	‡ (†)	‡ (†)
Other Hispanic	24.7 (1.08)	45.6 (3.75)	32.9 (2.47)	23.0 (2.10)	15.2 (2.42)	7.3 (1.31)	8.7 (1.82)	7.0! (2.59)	‡ (†)

See notes at end of table.

Table 102.62. Percentage of children under age 18 living in poverty, by parents' highest level of educational attainment, child's race/ethnicity, and selected racial/ethnic subgroups: 2010 and 2018—Continued

[Standard errors appear in parentheses]

Year and race/ethnicity	Percent in poverty, all children under age 18 who resided with at least one parent[1]	Percent of children in poverty, by highest level of education attained by any parent residing with child[1]							
		Less than high school completion	High school completion[2]	Some college, no degree	Associate's degree	Bachelor's or higher degree			
						Total	Bachelor's degree	Master's degree	Doctor's degree[3]
1	2	3	4	5	6	7	8	9	10
Asian	9.3 (0.26)	33.7 (2.07)	22.4 (1.44)	14.9 (1.08)	10.5 (1.00)	4.4 (0.24)	6.1 (0.44)	3.7 (0.29)	2.4 (0.30)
Chinese[5]	9.7 (0.49)	26.8 (2.77)	21.8 (2.75)	17.5 (2.26)	8.7 (2.11)	5.1 (0.52)	7.5 (1.10)	4.9 (0.82)	2.9 (0.61)
Filipino	4.3 (0.54)	19.5! (9.23)	10.2! (3.13)	7.5 (1.79)	3.3! (1.50)	2.8 (0.50)	3.1 (0.57)	2.9! (1.01)	‡ (†)
Japanese	7.6 (1.90)	‡ (†)	38.8! (13.66)	‡ (†)	‡ (†)	4.7 (1.29)	3.7! (1.64)	5.0! (2.17)	‡ (†)
Korean	7.8 (0.78)	‡ (†)	22.0! (7.36)	11.9! (3.85)	‡ (†)	6.2 (0.72)	6.7 (1.35)	7.4 (1.43)	4.1 (0.97)
South Asian[6]	7.1 (0.41)	32.5 (3.80)	22.2 (2.81)	19.2 (3.46)	17.4 (3.37)	3.9 (0.36)	7.5 (0.93)	2.7 (0.36)	1.5! (0.46)
Asian Indian	4.2 (0.36)	26.4 (5.00)	20.3 (4.16)	14.0 (3.32)	17.4 (3.63)	2.3 (0.31)	4.3 (0.78)	1.8 (0.32)	0.8! (0.34)
Bangladeshi	21.0 (2.82)	32.6! (12.83)	36.7 (8.52)	‡ (†)	31.4! (15.51)	15.2 (3.07)	17.2 (5.12)	15.1! (5.12)	‡ (†)
Bhutanese	19.6! (8.45)	‡ (†)	‡ (†)	‡ (†)	‡ (†)	‡ (†)	‡ (†)	‡ (†)	‡ (†)
Nepalese	12.3 (2.65)	36.8 (8.63)	‡ (†)	‡ (†)	‡ (†)	‡ (†)	‡ (†)	‡ (†)	‡ (†)
Pakistani	19.7 (2.50)	42.8 (9.73)	28.9 (7.29)	39.8 (9.27)	‡ (†)	15.0 (2.58)	23.1 (4.63)	9.7! (3.42)	5.2! (2.48)
Southeast Asian	17.3 (0.87)	38.1 (3.49)	24.8 (2.84)	15.6 (2.17)	11.5 (2.38)	5.9 (0.87)	6.6 (1.17)	4.8! (1.75)	4.0! (1.61)
Burmese	27.7 (4.45)	46.7 (7.24)	17.7! (7.33)	‡ (†)	‡ (†)	‡ (†)	‡ (†)	‡ (†)	‡ (†)
Cambodian	19.5 (3.29)	35.6 (10.14)	18.3! (6.56)	17.9! (8.78)	‡ (†)	15.6! (5.73)	‡ (†)	‡ (†)	‡ (†)
Hmong	21.3 (2.73)	52.2 (11.53)	26.3 (6.75)	16.4! (5.00)	26.1! (8.83)	‡ (†)	‡ (†)	‡ (†)	‡ (†)
Laotian	26.0 (4.78)	‡ (†)	46.3 (10.38)	33.7 (9.77)	‡ (†)	‡ (†)	‡ (†)	‡ (†)	‡ (†)
Thai	24.5 (4.67)	57.3 (13.51)	‡ (†)	‡ (†)	‡ (†)	16.2! (5.21)	27.3! (8.88)	‡ (†)	‡ (†)
Vietnamese	12.9 (1.09)	27.0 (3.73)	22.5 (3.74)	15.6 (2.77)	8.1 (1.95)	4.9 (0.86)	5.5 (1.13)	4.8! (1.88)	‡ (†)
Other Southeast Asian[7]	‡ (†)	‡ (†)	‡ (†)	‡ (†)	‡ (†)	‡ (†)	‡ (†)	‡ (†)	‡ (†)
Other Asian	9.2 (1.02)	32.0 (7.76)	25.9 (6.37)	21.0 (4.70)	15.3! (7.07)	3.3 (0.76)	4.3 (1.26)	4.4! (1.56)	‡ (†)
Pacific Islander	24.3 (2.32)	66.1 (8.37)	26.3 (4.63)	21.5 (4.64)	19.8! (7.76)	10.5! (3.35)	13.4! (4.63)	‡ (†)	‡ (†)
American Indian/Alaska Native[8]	29.8 (1.06)	60.8 (3.07)	36.2 (2.13)	29.7 (2.01)	19.4 (2.66)	9.3 (1.51)	8.6 (1.82)	13.8 (3.70)	‡ (†)
Amercian Indian	31.0 (1.19)	62.9 (3.59)	37.1 (2.25)	32.1 (2.21)	19.8 (2.76)	10.2 (1.73)	9.0 (2.00)	15.6 (4.36)	‡ (†)
Alaska Native	21.7 (3.03)	44.6 (11.01)	32.5 (5.78)	16.4! (6.07)	‡ (†)	‡ (†)	‡ (†)	‡ (†)	‡ (†)
Some other race[9]	18.2 (1.59)	40.4 (6.52)	28.8 (3.76)	22.0 (4.22)	23.2 (5.80)	4.2 (1.05)	7.0! (2.14)	1.8! (0.85)	‡ (†)
Two or more races	16.4 (0.39)	54.3 (2.32)	33.5 (1.22)	24.5 (1.01)	14.0 (1.04)	4.5 (0.31)	6.3 (0.46)	3.0 (0.46)	2.0 (0.58)

—Not available.
†Not applicable.
!Interpret data with caution. The coefficient of variation (CV) for this estimate is between 30 and 50 percent.
‡Reporting standards not met. Either there are too few cases for a reliable estimate or the coefficient of variation (CV) is 50 percent or greater.
[1]Parents include adoptive and stepparents but exclude parents not residing in the same household as their children.
[2]Includes parents who completed high school through equivalency programs, such as a GED program.
[3]Includes parents with professional degrees.
[4]Includes other Central American subgroups not shown separately.
[5]Includes Taiwanese.
[6]In addition to the subgroups shown, also includes Sri Lankan.
[7]Consists of Indonesian and Malaysian.

[8]Includes persons reporting American Indian alone, persons reporting Alaska Native alone, and persons from American Indian and/or Alaska Native tribes specified or not specified.
[9]Respondents who wrote in some other race that was not included as an option on the questionnaire.
NOTE: Table includes only children under the age of 18 who resided with at least one of their parents (including an adoptive or stepparent). Respondents were interviewed throughout the given year and reported the income they received during the previous 12 months. Data are based on sample surveys of the entire population residing within the United States. Poverty status is determined by the Census Bureau using a set of money income thresholds that vary by family size and composition. For additional information about poverty status, see https://www.census.gov/topics/income-poverty/poverty/guidance/poverty-measures.html. Race categories exclude persons of Hispanic ethnicity.
SOURCE: U.S. Department of Commerce, Census Bureau, American Community Survey (ACS), 2010 and 2018. (This table was prepared December 2019.)

Table 103.10. Percentage of the population 3 to 34 years old enrolled in school, by sex, race/ethnicity, and age group: Selected years, 1980 through 2018

[Standard errors appear in parentheses]

Year and age group	Total				Male				Female			
	Total	White	Black	Hispanic	Total	White	Black	Hispanic	Total	White	Black	Hispanic
1	2	3	4	5	6	7	8	9	10	11	12	13
1980												
Total, 3 to 34 years old	**49.7** (0.21)	**48.8** (0.24)	**54.0** (0.69)	**49.8** (1.40)	**50.0** (0.30)	**50.0** (0.34)	**56.2** (0.99)	**49.9** (2.00)	**47.7** (0.30)	**47.7** (0.34)	**52.1** (0.95)	**49.8** (1.98)
3 and 4 years old	36.7 (0.95)	37.4 (1.12)	38.2 (2.85)	28.5 (5.13)	37.8 (1.34)	39.2 (1.59)	36.4 (3.98)	30.1 (7.03)	35.5 (1.35)	35.5 (1.59)	40.0 (4.08)	26.6 (7.48)
5 and 6 years old	95.7 (0.40)	95.9 (0.46)	95.5 (1.23)	94.5 (2.79)	95.0 (0.61)	95.4 (0.68)	94.1 (1.97)	94.0 (4.21)	96.5 (0.53)	96.5 (0.62)	97.0 (1.45)	94.9 (3.70)
7 to 9 years old	99.1 (0.15)	99.1 (0.18)	99.4 (0.36)	98.4 (1.19)	99.0 (0.22)	99.0 (0.26)	99.5 (0.46)	97.7 (2.05)	99.3 (0.20)	99.2 (0.24)	99.3 (0.55)	99.0 (1.29)
10 to 13 years old	99.4 (0.10)	99.4 (0.12)	99.4 (0.31)	99.7 (0.47)	99.4 (0.14)	99.4 (0.16)	99.4 (0.43)	99.4 (0.86)	99.3 (0.15)	99.2 (0.18)	99.3 (0.46)	99.9 (0.32)
14 and 15 years old	98.2 (0.22)	98.7 (0.22)	97.9 (0.73)	94.3 (2.46)	98.7 (0.27)	98.9 (0.28)	98.4 (0.89)	96.7 (2.74)	98.1 (0.36)	98.5 (0.34)	97.3 (1.16)	92.1 (3.91)
16 and 17 years old	89.0 (0.51)	89.2 (0.57)	90.7 (1.46)	81.8 (4.25)	89.1 (0.71)	89.4 (0.80)	90.7 (2.06)	81.5 (6.15)	89.0 (0.73)	89.0 (0.83)	90.6 (2.06)	82.2 (5.88)
18 and 19 years old	46.4 (0.80)	47.0 (0.91)	45.8 (2.58)	37.8 (5.16)	47.0 (1.15)	48.5 (1.30)	48.5 (3.76)	36.9 (7.12)	45.7 (1.12)	45.7 (1.27)	48.3 (3.55)	38.8 (7.47)
20 and 21 years old	33.0 (0.75)	33.0 (0.86)	23.3 (2.23)	19.5 (4.31)	32.6 (1.09)	34.8 (1.24)	22.8 (3.32)	21.4 (6.39)	31.3 (1.18)	31.3 (1.18)	23.7 (3.02)	17.6! (5.80)
22 to 24 years old	16.8 (0.49)	16.8 (0.56)	13.6 (1.54)	11.7 (2.96)	17.8 (0.73)	18.7 (0.84)	13.4 (2.31)	10.7! (4.11)	14.9 (0.66)	15.0 (0.75)	13.7 (2.07)	12.6! (4.25)
25 to 29 years old	9.3 (0.31)	8.8 (0.35)	8.8 (1.05)	6.9 (1.88)	9.8 (0.46)	9.8 (0.51)	10.6 (1.71)	6.8! (2.70)	8.8 (0.42)	9.1 (0.48)	7.5 (1.31)	6.9! (2.61)
30 to 34 years old	6.4 (0.27)	6.4 (0.30)	6.9 (1.01)	5.1! (1.77)	5.9 (0.38)	5.6 (0.40)	7.2 (1.56)	6.2! (2.72)	7.0 (0.39)	7.2 (0.45)	6.6 (1.33)	‡ (†)
1990												
Total, 3 to 34 years old	**50.2** (0.23)	**49.8** (0.27)	**52.2** (0.71)	**47.2** (1.06)	**50.9** (0.32)	**50.4** (0.38)	**54.3** (1.02)	**46.8** (1.48)	**49.5** (0.32)	**49.2** (0.38)	**50.3** (0.99)	**47.7** (1.52)
3 and 4 years old	44.4 (0.99)	47.2 (1.19)	41.8 (2.97)	30.7 (4.08)	43.9 (1.38)	47.9 (1.66)	38.1 (4.14)	28.0 (5.57)	44.9 (1.41)	46.6 (1.70)	45.5 (4.25)	33.6 (5.95)
5 and 6 years old	96.5 (0.37)	96.7 (0.43)	96.5 (1.05)	94.9 (1.96)	96.5 (0.51)	96.8 (0.59)	96.2 (1.53)	95.8 (2.48)	96.4 (0.53)	96.7 (0.62)	96.9 (1.43)	93.9 (3.05)
7 to 9 years old	99.7 (0.09)	99.7 (0.11)	99.8 (0.19)	99.5 (0.52)	99.7 (0.13)	99.7 (0.16)	99.9 (0.24)	99.5 (0.70)	99.6 (0.14)	99.7 (0.15)	99.8 (0.31)	99.4 (0.79)
10 to 13 years old	99.6 (0.09)	99.7 (0.10)	99.8 (0.15)	99.1 (0.64)	99.6 (0.13)	99.6 (0.14)	99.9 (0.19)	99.1 (0.93)	99.7 (0.12)	99.8 (0.13)	99.8 (0.24)	99.1 (0.87)
14 and 15 years old	99.0 (0.19)	99.0 (0.23)	99.4 (0.46)	99.0 (0.90)	99.1 (0.25)	99.2 (0.30)	99.7 (0.48)	99.1 (1.10)	98.9 (0.29)	98.9 (0.35)	99.1 (0.79)	98.8 (1.47)
16 and 17 years old	92.5 (0.52)	93.5 (0.58)	91.7 (1.59)	85.4 (3.22)	92.6 (0.72)	93.4 (0.82)	93.0 (2.09)	85.5 (4.39)	92.4 (0.74)	93.7 (0.81)	90.5 (2.41)	85.3 (4.73)
18 and 19 years old	57.2 (0.94)	59.1 (1.11)	55.0 (2.83)	44.0 (4.36)	58.2 (1.33)	59.7 (1.56)	60.4 (3.99)	47.7 (6.23)	56.3 (1.32)	58.5 (1.57)	49.8 (3.96)	47.2 (6.08)
20 and 21 years old	39.7 (0.92)	43.1 (1.10)	28.3 (2.56)	27.2 (3.82)	40.3 (1.32)	44.2 (1.59)	31.0 (3.81)	21.7 (4.94)	39.2 (1.28)	42.0 (1.53)	25.8 (3.45)	33.1 (5.79)
22 to 24 years old	21.0 (0.63)	21.9 (0.75)	19.7 (2.01)	9.9 (2.05)	22.3 (0.92)	23.7 (1.11)	19.3 (3.03)	11.2 (2.98)	19.9 (0.86)	20.3 (1.02)	20.0 (2.68)	8.4! (2.77)
25 to 29 years old	9.7 (0.33)	10.4 (0.39)	6.1 (0.87)	6.3 (1.29)	9.2 (0.46)	9.2 (0.55)	4.7 (1.14)	4.6! (1.55)	10.2 (0.47)	10.7 (0.56)	7.3 (1.27)	8.1 (2.05)
30 to 34 years old	5.8 (0.25)	6.2 (0.30)	4.5 (0.75)	3.6 (0.99)	4.8 (0.33)	5.0 (0.38)	2.3! (0.80)	4.0! (1.45)	6.9 (0.38)	7.4 (0.46)	6.3 (1.19)	3.1! (1.32)
2000												
Total, 3 to 34 years old[1]	**55.9** (0.22)	**56.0** (0.27)	**59.3** (0.59)	**51.3** (0.63)	**55.8** (0.31)	**55.8** (0.38)	**59.7** (0.85)	**50.5** (0.88)	**56.0** (0.31)	**56.1** (0.38)	**59.0** (0.83)	**52.2** (0.89)
3 and 4 years old	52.1 (0.93)	54.6 (1.19)	59.8 (2.50)	35.9 (2.36)	50.8 (1.30)	54.1 (1.66)	58.0 (3.53)	31.9 (3.23)	53.4 (1.32)	55.2 (1.70)	61.8 (3.55)	40.0 (3.43)
5 and 6 years old	95.6 (0.38)	95.5 (0.49)	96.7 (0.89)	94.3 (1.13)	95.1 (0.56)	95.1 (0.76)	96.2 (1.38)	95.4 (1.41)	96.1 (0.51)	96.0 (0.63)	97.5 (1.12)	93.1 (1.79)
7 to 9 years old	98.1 (0.20)	98.4 (0.24)	97.5 (0.61)	97.5 (0.65)	98.0 (0.29)	98.1 (0.36)	98.2 (0.72)	96.6 (1.09)	98.2 (0.28)	98.6 (0.32)	96.7 (1.01)	98.4 (0.74)
10 to 13 years old	98.3 (0.17)	98.5 (0.19)	98.5 (0.42)	97.4 (0.59)	98.3 (0.23)	98.2 (0.30)	98.8 (0.52)	98.4 (0.65)	98.3 (0.25)	98.8 (0.32)	98.1 (0.66)	96.4 (1.01)
14 and 15 years old	98.7 (0.20)	98.9 (0.22)	99.6 (0.30)	96.2 (0.99)	98.7 (0.27)	98.8 (0.33)	99.6 (0.42)	96.9 (1.26)	98.6 (0.29)	99.0 (0.31)	99.6 (0.42)	95.4 (1.54)
16 and 17 years old	92.8 (0.45)	94.0 (0.50)	91.7 (1.32)	87.0 (1.77)	92.7 (0.63)	93.3 (0.66)	88.8 (2.09)	85.7 (2.60)	92.9 (0.64)	94.6 (0.76)	94.6 (1.54)	88.3 (2.40)
18 and 19 years old	61.2 (0.84)	63.9 (1.02)	57.2 (2.34)	49.5 (2.47)	58.3 (1.19)	61.2 (1.46)	51.5 (3.45)	48.0 (3.40)	64.2 (1.16)	66.7 (1.42)	62.2 (3.14)	51.1 (3.59)
20 and 21 years old	44.1 (0.88)	49.2 (1.10)	37.4 (2.38)	26.1 (2.22)	41.0 (1.23)	45.8 (1.54)	31.3 (3.42)	24.2 (3.02)	47.3 (1.26)	52.7 (1.58)	42.3 (3.26)	28.1 (3.26)
22 to 24 years old	24.6 (0.63)	24.9 (0.78)	24.0 (1.76)	18.2 (1.64)	23.9 (0.88)	25.0 (1.12)	22.0 (2.46)	15.2 (2.08)	25.3 (0.89)	24.8 (1.09)	25.8 (2.51)	21.6 (2.55)
25 to 29 years old	11.4 (0.37)	11.1 (0.45)	14.5 (1.18)	7.4 (0.88)	10.0 (0.50)	10.5 (0.62)	11.6 (1.63)	5.1 (1.06)	12.7 (0.53)	11.8 (0.65)	16.7 (1.66)	9.5 (1.38)
30 to 34 years old	6.7 (0.27)	6.1 (0.32)	9.9 (0.97)	5.6 (0.75)	5.6 (0.36)	4.7 (0.41)	8.5 (1.34)	5.7 (1.06)	7.7 (0.41)	7.4 (0.50)	11.2 (1.39)	5.5 (1.05)
2005												
Total, 3 to 34 years old[1]	**56.5** (0.20)	**57.6** (0.20)	**58.5** (0.57)	**50.9** (0.53)	**55.8** (0.28)	**57.1** (0.37)	**58.8** (0.82)	**48.4** (0.73)	**57.2** (0.29)	**58.0** (0.37)	**58.1** (0.80)	**53.7** (0.76)
3 and 4 years old[1]	53.6 (0.86)	58.5 (1.14)	52.4 (2.39)	43.0 (2.07)	52.8 (1.21)	56.8 (1.61)	54.8 (3.42)	43.0 (2.91)	54.4 (1.23)	60.3 (1.63)	50.1 (3.32)	43.0 (2.96)
5 and 6 years old	95.4 (0.37)	95.9 (0.47)	95.9 (0.97)	93.8 (1.06)	94.8 (0.54)	95.4 (0.68)	94.8 (1.50)	92.4 (1.62)	96.1 (0.50)	96.3 (0.63)	97.1 (1.18)	95.3 (1.34)
7 to 9 years old	98.6 (0.17)	99.0 (0.19)	98.7 (0.45)	97.4 (0.58)	98.2 (0.27)	98.0 (0.27)	98.0 (0.81)	96.0 (1.00)	99.0 (0.20)	99.0 (0.27)	99.3 (0.41)	98.8 (0.57)
10 to 13 years old	98.6 (0.14)	99.0 (0.16)	98.5 (0.40)	97.9 (0.46)	98.4 (0.22)	98.9 (0.21)	98.0 (0.70)	97.2 (0.72)	98.9 (0.18)	98.8 (0.24)	99.5 (0.33)	98.6 (0.54)
14 and 15 years old	98.0 (0.22)	98.6 (0.24)	96.1 (0.83)	97.3 (0.70)	99.1 (0.34)	99.1 (0.35)	93.3 (1.52)	97.8 (0.90)	98.4 (0.28)	98.7 (0.33)	98.8 (0.66)	96.7 (1.09)
16 and 17 years old	95.1 (0.33)	96.1 (0.38)	93.6 (1.05)	92.6 (1.14)	95.1 (0.47)	95.9 (0.55)	93.6 (1.51)	92.5 (1.61)	95.1 (0.47)	96.3 (0.53)	93.6 (1.47)	92.6 (1.60)
18 and 19 years old	67.6 (0.79)	71.6 (0.95)	62.0 (2.30)	55.0 (1.96)	66.5 (1.11)	69.8 (1.35)	66.9 (3.20)	51.8 (3.22)	68.8 (1.12)	73.5 (1.34)	57.4 (3.27)	57.2 (3.37)
20 and 21 years old	48.7 (0.80)	54.4 (1.01)	37.9 (2.25)	30.0 (1.96)	45.3 (1.11)	50.5 (1.42)	35.5 (3.12)	25.2 (2.56)	52.3 (1.15)	58.5 (1.43)	40.4 (3.23)	35.3 (2.99)
22 to 24 years old	27.3 (0.59)	27.8 (0.76)	28.6 (1.75)	19.5 (1.41)	25.2 (0.83)	26.4 (1.07)	24.0 (2.45)	17.5 (1.85)	29.2 (0.85)	29.1 (1.09)	32.5 (2.45)	21.8 (2.17)
25 to 29 years old	11.9 (0.34)	12.5 (0.45)	11.9 (1.00)	7.8 (0.70)	9.6 (0.43)	10.2 (0.58)	9.1 (1.32)	5.6 (0.82)	14.2 (0.51)	14.7 (0.67)	14.2 (1.47)	10.4 (1.19)
30 to 34 years old	6.9 (0.27)	6.9 (0.34)	9.8 (0.94)	4.2 (0.54)	6.5 (0.35)	6.5 (0.47)	6.3 (1.15)	2.6 (0.58)	7.9 (0.40)	7.4 (0.50)	12.7 (1.42)	6.1 (0.94)

See notes at end of table.

Table 103.10. Percentage of the population 3 to 34 years old enrolled in school, by sex, race/ethnicity, and age group: Selected years, 1980 through 2018—Continued

[Standard errors appear in parentheses]

Year and age group	Total				Male				Female			
	Total	White	Black	Hispanic	Total	White	Black	Hispanic	Total	White	Black	Hispanic
1	2	3	4	5	6	7	8	9	10	11	12	13
2010												
Total, 3 to 34 years old¹	**56.6** (0.17)	**56.1** (0.25)	**58.7** (0.58)	**55.1** (0.35)	**55.9** (0.23)	**55.5** (0.29)	**58.4** (0.78)	**52.9** (0.45)	**57.4** (0.26)	**56.7** (0.36)	**58.9** (0.77)	**57.4** (0.49)
3 and 4 years old¹	53.2 (0.89)	53.2 (1.17)	57.2 (2.78)	44.2 (1.84)	53.0 (1.21)	55.9 (1.64)	57.0 (3.79)	43.3 (2.60)	53.4 (1.27)	56.3 (1.53)	57.4 (3.79)	45.0 (2.68)
5 and 6 years old	94.5 (0.46)	94.2 (0.66)	94.1 (1.12)	94.3 (0.96)	93.7 (0.69)	93.3 (1.04)	93.5 (1.94)	93.4 (1.31)	95.3 (0.54)	95.2 (0.77)	94.7 (1.38)	95.2 (1.20)
7 to 9 years old	97.7 (0.25)	97.4 (0.37)	96.9 (0.77)	98.5 (0.37)	97.6 (0.36)	97.1 (0.54)	97.3 (0.88)	98.1 (0.60)	98.0 (0.35)	97.7 (0.53)	96.5 (1.23)	98.9 (0.40)
10 to 13 years old	98.2 (0.21)	98.0 (0.26)	99.2 (0.41)	97.3 (0.54)	97.9 (0.30)	97.7 (0.42)	99.6 (0.37)	96.9 (0.77)	98.6 (0.26)	98.9 (0.24)	98.8 (0.74)	97.7 (0.61)
14 and 15 years old	98.1 (0.25)	98.0 (0.37)	98.8 (0.58)	97.9 (0.69)	98.0 (0.37)	98.0 (0.52)	98.4 (0.92)	97.5 (0.98)	98.3 (0.34)	98.1 (0.49)	99.3 (0.46)	98.3 (0.85)
16 and 17 years old	96.1 (0.33)	96.2 (0.47)	95.7 (0.82)	95.7 (0.83)	94.9 (0.51)	94.7 (0.74)	93.7 (1.41)	96.0 (1.17)	97.3 (0.38)	97.8 (0.47)	97.6 (0.95)	96.0 (1.10)
18 and 19 years old	69.2 (0.92)	71.0 (1.28)	62.9 (2.42)	66.2 (2.03)	66.9 (1.25)	67.8 (1.63)	62.3 (3.88)	64.9 (3.02)	71.5 (1.38)	74.3 (2.01)	63.4 (3.44)	67.6 (2.78)
20 and 21 years old	52.4 (1.08)	55.5 (1.28)	51.1 (2.93)	37.0 (2.34)	49.2 (1.31)	52.1 (1.76)	45.7 (4.18)	34.0 (3.08)	56.0 (1.47)	59.2 (1.78)	56.0 (3.84)	40.5 (3.36)
22 to 24 years old	28.9 (0.79)	29.1 (1.01)	29.8 (2.13)	23.8 (1.57)	27.0 (1.15)	27.8 (1.44)	29.5 (3.12)	18.6 (2.08)	30.8 (1.10)	30.4 (1.46)	30.0 (2.99)	29.2 (2.16)
25 to 29 years old	14.6 (0.47)	14.6 (0.64)	16.5 (1.34)	11.4 (0.90)	13.5 (0.65)	13.8 (0.84)	13.9 (2.06)	9.6 (1.21)	15.8 (0.66)	15.4 (0.88)	18.8 (1.97)	13.6 (1.44)
30 to 34 years old	8.3 (0.39)	8.5 (0.50)	11.0 (1.14)	5.7 (0.65)	6.7 (0.44)	7.2 (0.62)	6.6 (1.20)	4.9 (0.87)	9.9 (0.58)	9.8 (0.77)	14.8 (1.80)	6.6 (0.95)
2015												
Total, 3 to 34 years old¹	**55.2** (0.20)	**54.4** (0.25)	**55.4** (0.63)	**55.8** (0.38)	**54.9** (0.26)	**54.1** (0.36)	**55.7** (0.75)	**54.4** (0.48)	**55.6** (0.28)	**54.6** (0.35)	**55.0** (0.83)	**57.3** (0.54)
3 and 4 years old¹	52.7 (1.02)	56.0 (1.26)	53.7 (2.90)	44.1 (2.24)	53.6 (1.40)	57.1 (1.75)	52.4 (3.57)	44.3 (2.88)	51.8 (1.55)	54.8 (1.97)	55.3 (4.34)	44.0 (3.08)
5 and 6 years old	94.2 (0.46)	94.1 (0.64)	94.7 (1.41)	93.7 (1.00)	93.5 (0.69)	93.2 (0.92)	93.3 (1.93)	93.6 (1.48)	94.9 (0.64)	95.1 (0.92)	96.1 (1.62)	93.9 (1.38)
7 to 9 years old	97.3 (0.28)	97.5 (0.35)	94.9 (1.16)	97.9 (0.49)	97.5 (0.34)	97.8 (0.42)	95.4 (1.31)	97.5 (0.72)	97.2 (0.41)	97.9 (0.58)	94.4 (1.63)	98.4 (0.59)
10 to 13 years old	98.0 (0.19)	98.1 (0.25)	98.6 (0.47)	97.1 (0.46)	98.3 (0.23)	98.3 (0.29)	100.0² (#)	97.3 (0.67)	97.6 (0.28)	98.4 (0.36)	97.2 (0.94)	96.9 (0.66)
14 and 15 years old	98.0 (0.27)	98.3 (0.32)	98.6 (0.68)	96.7 (0.74)	97.9 (0.37)	98.3 (0.42)	99.5 (0.50)	96.0 (1.17)	98.1 (0.38)	98.4 (0.48)	97.6 (1.30)	97.4 (0.96)
16 and 17 years old	93.7 (0.49)	94.4 (0.61)	95.1 (0.94)	92.6 (1.10)	93.1 (0.71)	93.8 (0.85)	94.1 (1.49)	91.7 (1.66)	94.4 (0.58)	95.0 (0.83)	96.0 (1.24)	93.7 (1.42)
18 and 19 years old	68.5 (0.86)	70.1 (1.05)	64.1 (2.91)	65.2 (2.20)	65.7 (1.39)	67.2 (1.66)	63.3 (4.43)	59.9 (3.30)	71.4 (1.19)	73.1 (1.60)	64.8 (3.86)	70.1 (2.74)
20 and 21 years old	53.3 (1.14)	55.5 (1.46)	43.1 (2.92)	48.8 (2.46)	50.2 (1.61)	53.3 (2.20)	38.0 (3.92)	44.4 (3.13)	56.5 (1.52)	57.7 (1.93)	47.9 (4.26)	53.2 (3.54)
22 to 24 years old	28.8 (0.81)	28.9 (1.02)	27.4 (2.11)	25.2 (1.67)	27.5 (1.07)	26.9 (1.33)	30.5 (3.24)	24.2 (2.51)	30.1 (1.25)	30.9 (1.43)	24.5 (3.07)	26.3 (2.69)
25 to 29 years old	13.2 (0.50)	13.1 (0.60)	13.7 (1.29)	11.2 (1.03)	11.7 (0.67)	12.3 (0.83)	10.9 (1.69)	9.2 (1.25)	14.6 (0.72)	14.0 (0.89)	16.3 (2.02)	13.2 (1.47)
30 to 34 years old	6.6 (0.30)	6.5 (0.35)	8.6 (1.05)	4.6 (0.61)	5.5 (0.39)	5.9 (0.48)	4.8 (1.37)	3.3 (0.77)	7.7 (0.44)	7.1 (0.55)	11.9 (1.57)	5.9 (1.02)
2017												
Total, 3 to 34 years old¹	**54.6** (0.19)	**53.2** (0.26)	**55.0** (0.60)	**56.4** (0.40)	**54.0** (0.28)	**52.8** (0.35)	**54.9** (0.79)	**55.0** (0.51)	**55.2** (0.25)	**53.6** (0.34)	**55.0** (0.77)	**57.8** (0.57)
3 and 4 years old¹	53.8 (1.08)	56.0 (1.41)	59.0 (3.08)	47.9 (2.22)	53.4 (1.39)	54.3 (1.82)	62.3 (3.95)	47.1 (2.70)	54.1 (1.48)	57.8 (2.07)	55.3 (4.06)	48.8 (3.11)
5 and 6 years old	93.5 (0.54)	93.0 (0.78)	91.0 (1.69)	95.0 (1.10)	92.8 (0.71)	92.5 (0.94)	89.4 (2.43)	94.6 (1.45)	94.2 (0.78)	93.5 (1.06)	92.8 (2.19)	95.5 (1.42)
7 to 9 years old	97.1 (0.30)	97.0 (0.40)	96.9 (0.75)	97.0 (0.58)	97.1 (0.43)	97.0 (0.52)	96.3 (1.16)	97.5 (0.75)	97.0 (0.38)	96.8 (0.57)	97.5 (0.64)	97.3 (0.85)
10 to 13 years old	97.8 (0.21)	97.8 (0.29)	98.7 (0.47)	97.3 (0.44)	97.4 (0.28)	97.9 (0.41)	98.7 (0.70)	97.4 (0.59)	98.3 (0.32)	97.6 (0.42)	98.8 (0.64)	97.3 (0.69)
14 and 15 years old	98.2 (0.25)	98.5 (0.33)	96.3 (1.19)	98.4 (0.55)	98.2 (0.40)	98.6 (0.45)	95.1 (1.91)	98.2 (0.90)	98.3 (0.35)	98.4 (0.46)	97.5 (1.30)	98.6 (0.73)
16 and 17 years old	92.9 (0.55)	93.3 (0.65)	90.4 (1.54)	92.7 (1.17)	92.3 (0.73)	92.8 (0.88)	87.9 (2.11)	91.7 (1.68)	93.5 (0.68)	93.8 (0.86)	92.9 (2.11)	93.6 (1.46)
18 and 19 years old	68.2 (1.08)	67.8 (1.42)	67.8 (2.98)	67.2 (2.22)	65.1 (1.40)	65.4 (1.87)	65.3 (4.19)	63.3 (2.91)	71.3 (1.53)	70.3 (1.87)	70.2 (4.04)	71.1 (3.14)
20 and 21 years old	55.0 (1.13)	58.1 (1.53)	47.8 (2.87)	46.0 (2.57)	50.8 (1.63)	54.6 (2.12)	42.4 (4.23)	40.9 (3.39)	59.2 (1.45)	61.8 (2.02)	53.7 (4.16)	50.7 (3.07)
22 to 24 years old	28.4 (0.92)	27.2 (1.19)	28.1 (2.59)	25.9 (1.84)	26.8 (1.15)	25.9 (1.46)	24.7 (3.50)	23.0 (2.43)	30.0 (1.26)	28.4 (1.62)	30.9 (3.45)	29.2 (2.71)
25 to 29 years old	12.1 (0.45)	11.3 (0.57)	13.4 (1.33)	12.3 (0.92)	10.9 (0.64)	10.5 (0.81)	11.8 (2.01)	9.9 (1.28)	13.4 (0.63)	12.1 (0.74)	15.0 (1.87)	14.7 (1.51)
30 to 34 years old	5.9 (0.31)	5.8 (0.38)	7.7 (0.97)	4.8 (0.65)	5.2 (0.40)	5.0 (0.44)	6.3 (1.39)	5.0 (0.95)	6.5 (0.45)	6.6 (0.54)	8.9 (1.44)	4.6 (0.84)
2018												
Total, 3 to 34 years old¹	**54.6** (0.20)	**53.6** (0.27)	**54.8** (0.56)	**55.7** (0.44)	**54.1** (0.28)	**53.2** (0.37)	**54.1** (0.72)	**54.7** (0.58)	**55.1** (0.24)	**53.9** (0.33)	**55.4** (0.83)	**56.9** (0.53)
3 and 4 years old¹	54.0 (1.19)	58.2 (1.79)	54.2 (3.54)	47.9 (2.31)	53.6 (1.66)	58.1 (2.13)	50.4 (4.89)	48.2 (3.52)	54.4 (1.55)	58.2 (2.31)	57.5 (4.49)	47.6 (3.21)
5 and 6 years old	93.5 (0.60)	93.9 (0.68)	92.9 (1.56)	93.5 (1.25)	93.3 (0.84)	94.0 (1.06)	91.6 (2.54)	92.8 (1.91)	93.8 (0.75)	93.8 (1.03)	94.4 (2.12)	94.3 (1.47)
7 to 9 years old	97.0 (0.29)	97.2 (0.45)	97.2 (0.87)	97.1 (0.66)	97.1 (0.38)	96.8 (0.57)	96.9 (0.95)	96.8 (0.89)	96.9 (0.44)	98.5 (0.63)	96.9 (1.38)	96.9 (0.92)
10 to 13 years old	98.2 (0.20)	98.6 (0.26)	98.7 (0.41)	97.8 (0.42)	98.1 (0.29)	98.7 (0.33)	98.5 (0.65)	97.9 (0.62)	98.4 (0.26)	98.5 (0.37)	98.9 (0.52)	97.7 (0.64)
14 and 15 years old	98.6 (0.27)	98.8 (0.30)	97.7 (1.15)	98.1 (0.59)	98.8 (0.26)	99.0 (0.35)	99.3 (0.46)	97.8 (0.83)	98.3 (0.42)	98.5 (0.46)	96.1 (2.03)	98.3 (0.79)
16 and 17 years old	92.3 (0.58)	93.9 (0.71)	88.1 (1.74)	91.7 (1.26)	93.7 (0.61)	93.8 (0.83)	92.2 (1.95)	93.4 (1.32)	90.8 (0.95)	94.0 (1.01)	83.9 (2.95)	90.1 (1.97)
18 and 19 years old	69.1 (1.01)	71.3 (1.20)	65.5 (2.79)	63.5 (2.14)	66.1 (1.39)	68.3 (1.64)	64.6 (4.10)	59.4 (3.05)	72.2 (1.37)	74.3 (1.73)	66.3 (3.86)	67.9 (2.83)
20 and 21 years old	54.6 (1.18)	57.5 (1.58)	52.2 (2.91)	46.0 (2.29)	50.9 (1.69)	53.4 (2.13)	50.3 (4.74)	42.1 (3.07)	58.4 (1.48)	61.8 (2.18)	54.1 (4.52)	50.0 (3.16)
22 to 24 years old	28.0 (0.88)	27.5 (1.12)	27.5 (2.19)	24.8 (1.76)	26.1 (1.17)	26.2 (1.54)	22.9 (2.92)	21.4 (2.15)	29.9 (1.21)	28.9 (1.51)	31.7 (3.42)	28.2 (2.71)
25 to 29 years old	12.7 (0.44)	11.3 (0.56)	15.6 (1.47)	12.0 (0.97)	11.2 (0.59)	9.9 (0.74)	12.9 (1.93)	10.7 (1.37)	14.2 (0.62)	12.8 (0.81)	18.2 (1.92)	13.3 (1.29)
30 to 34 years old	6.3 (0.33)	5.9 (0.36)	8.6 (1.01)	4.9 (0.77)	5.4 (0.47)	5.5 (0.51)	4.5 (1.20)	5.1 (1.16)	7.2 (0.49)	6.6 (0.53)	12.2 (1.55)	4.7 (0.87)

†Not applicable.
#Rounds to zero.
‡Interpret data with caution. The coefficient of variation (CV) for this estimate is between 30 and 50 percent.
‡Reporting standards not met. The coefficient of variation (CV) for this estimate is 50 percent or greater.
¹Beginning in 1994, preprimary enrollment data were collected using new procedures. Data may not be comparable to figures for earlier years.
²Rounds to 100.0.
NOTE: Data are based on sample surveys of the civilian noninstitutionalized population, which excludes persons in the military and persons living in institutions (e.g., prisons or nursing facilities). Includes enrollment in any type of graded public, parochial, or other private schools. Includes nursery schools, preschools, kindergartens, elementary and secondary schools, colleges, universities, and professional schools. Attendance may be on either a full-time or part-time basis and during the day or night. Prior to 2010, standard errors were computed using generalized variance function methodology rather than the more precise replicate weight methodology used in later years. Total includes persons from other racial/ethnic groups not shown separately. Race categories exclude persons of Hispanic ethnicity.
SOURCE: U.S. Department of Commerce, Census Bureau, Current Population Survey (CPS), October, selected years, 1980 through 2018. (This table was prepared November 2019.)

Table 103.20. Percentage of the population 3 to 34 years old enrolled in school, by age group: Selected years, 1940 through 2018

[Standard errors appear in parentheses]

Year	Total, 3 to 34 years old	3 and 4 years old	5 and 6 years old	7 to 13 years old	14 to 17 years old			18 and 19 years old			20 to 24 years old			25 to 29 years old	30 to 34 years old
					Total	14 and 15	16 and 17	Total	In secondary education	In higher education	Total	20 and 21	22 to 24		
1	2	3	4	5	6	7	8	9	10	11	12	13	14	15	16
1940	†	—	†	95.0	79.3	†	—	28.9	†	†	6.6	†	†	—	—
1945	†	—	†	98.1	78.4	†	†	20.7	†	†	3.9	†	†	—	—
1947	†	—	73.8	98.5	79.3	91.6	67.6	24.3	—	—	10.2	—	—	3.0	1.0
1948	†	—	74.7	98.1	81.8	92.7	71.2	26.9	—	—	9.7	—	—	2.6	0.9
1949	†	—	76.2	98.6	81.6	93.5	69.5	25.3	—	—	9.2	—	—	3.8	1.1
1950	†	—	74.4	98.7	83.7	94.7	71.3	29.4	—	—	9.0	—	—	3.0	0.9
1951	†	—	73.6	99.1	85.2	94.8	75.1	26.2	—	—	8.6	—	—	2.5	0.7
1952	†	—	75.2	98.8	85.2	96.2	73.4	28.8	—	—	9.7	—	—	2.6	1.2
1953	†	—	78.6	99.4	85.9	96.5	74.7	31.2	—	—	11.1	—	—	2.9	1.7
1954	†	—	77.3	99.4	87.1	95.8	78.0	32.4	—	—	11.2	—	—	4.1	1.5
1955	†	—	78.1	99.2	86.9	95.9	77.4	31.5	†	†	11.1	†	†	4.2	1.6
1956	†	—	77.6	99.3	88.2	96.9	78.4	35.4	†	†	12.8	†	†	5.1	1.9
1957	†	—	78.6	99.5	89.5	97.1	80.5	34.9	†	†	14.0	†	†	5.5	1.8
1958	†	—	80.4	99.5	89.2	96.9	80.6	37.6	†	†	13.4	†	†	5.7	2.2
1959	†	—	80.0	99.4	90.2	97.5	82.9	36.8	†	†	12.7	18.8	8.6	5.1	2.2
1960	†	—	80.7	99.5	90.3	97.8	82.6	38.4	†	†	13.1	19.4	8.7	4.9	2.4
1961	†	—	81.7	99.3	91.4	97.6	83.6	38.0	†	†	13.7	21.5	8.4	4.4	2.0
1962	†	—	82.2	99.3	92.0	98.0	84.3	41.8	†	†	15.6	23.0	10.3	5.0	2.6
1963	†	—	82.7	99.3	92.9	98.4	87.1	40.9	10.9	29.8	17.3	25.0	11.4	4.9	2.5
1964[1]	†	9.5	83.3	99.0	93.1	98.6	87.7	41.6	11.0	30.6	16.8	26.3	9.9	5.2	2.6
1965	55.5 (0.22)	10.6	84.9	99.4	93.2	98.9	87.4	46.3	11.2	35.0	19.0	27.6	13.2	6.1	3.2
1966	56.1 (0.22)	12.5	85.8	99.3	93.7	98.6	88.5	47.2	10.8	36.3	19.9	29.9	13.2	6.5	2.7
1967	56.6 (0.22)	14.2	87.4	99.3	93.7	98.2	88.8	47.6	11.7	36.0	22.0	33.3	13.6	6.6	4.0
1968	56.7 (0.22)	15.7	87.6	99.1	94.2	98.0	90.2	50.4	12.4	38.0	21.4	31.2	13.8	7.0	3.9
1969	57.0 (0.22)	16.1	88.4	99.2	94.0	98.1	89.7	50.2	11.2	39.0	23.0	34.1	15.4	7.9	4.8
1970	56.4 (0.22)	20.5 (0.74)	89.5 (0.54)	99.2 (0.08)	94.1 (0.27)	98.1 (0.22)	90.0 (0.50)	47.7 (0.87)	10.5 (0.53)	37.3 (0.84)	21.5 (0.48)	31.9 (0.87)	14.9 (0.53)	7.5 (0.33)	4.2 (0.27)
1971	56.2 (0.22)	21.2 (0.76)	91.6 (0.50)	99.1 (0.08)	94.5 (0.26)	98.6 (0.19)	90.2 (0.49)	49.2 (0.85)	11.5 (0.54)	37.7 (0.83)	21.9 (0.47)	32.2 (0.85)	15.4 (0.52)	8.0 (0.33)	4.9 (0.29)
1972	54.9 (0.22)	24.4 (0.81)	91.9 (0.51)	99.2 (0.08)	93.3 (0.28)	97.6 (0.24)	88.9 (0.51)	46.3 (0.84)	10.4 (0.51)	35.9 (0.81)	21.6 (0.46)	31.4 (0.81)	14.8 (0.51)	8.6 (0.34)	4.6 (0.28)
1973	53.5 (0.22)	24.2 (0.80)	92.5 (0.50)	99.2 (0.08)	92.9 (0.29)	97.5 (0.25)	88.3 (0.52)	42.9 (0.82)	10.0 (0.50)	32.9 (0.78)	20.8 (0.44)	30.1 (0.79)	14.5 (0.50)	8.5 (0.33)	4.5 (0.27)
1974	53.6 (0.22)	28.8 (0.85)	94.2 (0.44)	99.3 (0.08)	92.9 (0.29)	97.9 (0.23)	87.9 (0.52)	43.1 (0.81)	9.9 (0.49)	33.2 (0.77)	21.4 (0.45)	30.2 (0.77)	15.1 (0.51)	9.6 (0.34)	5.7 (0.29)
1975	53.7 (0.22)	31.5 (0.89)	94.7 (0.42)	99.3 (0.08)	93.6 (0.27)	98.2 (0.21)	89.0 (0.50)	46.9 (0.81)	10.2 (0.49)	36.7 (0.78)	22.4 (0.45)	31.2 (0.77)	16.2 (0.52)	10.1 (0.34)	6.6 (0.31)
1976	53.1 (0.21)	31.3 (0.91)	95.5 (0.38)	99.2 (0.09)	93.7 (0.27)	98.2 (0.21)	89.1 (0.50)	46.2 (0.80)	10.2 (0.49)	36.0 (0.77)	23.3 (0.45)	32.0 (0.77)	17.1 (0.52)	10.0 (0.33)	6.0 (0.29)
1977	52.5 (0.21)	32.0 (0.94)	95.8 (0.38)	99.4 (0.07)	93.7 (0.28)	98.5 (0.20)	88.9 (0.50)	46.2 (0.80)	10.4 (0.49)	35.7 (0.77)	22.9 (0.44)	31.8 (0.76)	16.5 (0.51)	10.8 (0.34)	6.9 (0.30)
1978	51.2 (0.21)	34.2 (0.95)	95.3 (0.42)	99.1 (0.09)	93.7 (0.28)	98.4 (0.20)	89.1 (0.50)	45.4 (0.80)	9.8 (0.48)	35.6 (0.77)	21.8 (0.43)	29.5 (0.74)	16.3 (0.50)	9.4 (0.32)	6.4 (0.28)
1979	50.3 (0.21)	35.1 (0.95)	95.8 (0.40)	99.2 (0.09)	93.6 (0.28)	98.1 (0.22)	89.2 (0.50)	45.0 (0.80)	10.3 (0.49)	34.6 (0.76)	21.7 (0.43)	30.2 (0.74)	15.8 (0.49)	9.6 (0.32)	6.4 (0.28)
1980	49.7 (0.21)	36.7 (0.95)	95.7 (0.40)	99.3 (0.09)	93.4 (0.29)	98.2 (0.22)	89.0 (0.51)	46.4 (0.80)	10.5 (0.49)	35.9 (0.77)	22.3 (0.43)	31.0 (0.75)	16.3 (0.49)	9.3 (0.31)	6.4 (0.27)
1981	48.9 (0.21)	36.0 (0.93)	94.0 (0.46)	99.2 (0.09)	94.1 (0.28)	98.0 (0.24)	90.6 (0.47)	49.0 (0.81)	11.5 (0.51)	37.5 (0.78)	22.5 (0.42)	31.6 (0.74)	16.5 (0.48)	9.0 (0.30)	6.9 (0.27)
1982	48.6 (0.22)	36.4 (0.97)	95.0 (0.45)	99.2 (0.10)	94.4 (0.29)	98.5 (0.22)	90.6 (0.51)	47.8 (0.86)	11.3 (0.54)	36.5 (0.83)	23.5 (0.45)	34.0 (0.81)	16.8 (0.51)	9.6 (0.32)	6.3 (0.28)
1983	48.4 (0.22)	37.5 (0.96)	95.4 (0.43)	99.2 (0.10)	95.0 (0.28)	98.3 (0.23)	91.7 (0.50)	50.4 (0.87)	12.8 (0.58)	37.6 (0.84)	22.7 (0.45)	32.5 (0.80)	16.6 (0.51)	9.6 (0.32)	6.4 (0.28)
1984	47.9 (0.22)	36.3 (0.94)	94.5 (0.46)	99.2 (0.10)	94.7 (0.29)	97.8 (0.26)	91.5 (0.51)	50.1 (0.89)	11.5 (0.57)	38.6 (0.87)	23.7 (0.46)	33.9 (0.82)	17.3 (0.52)	9.1 (0.30)	6.3 (0.27)
1985	48.3 (0.22)	38.9 (0.95)	96.1 (0.38)	99.2 (0.09)	94.9 (0.28)	98.1 (0.24)	91.7 (0.50)	51.6 (0.91)	11.2 (0.57)	40.4 (0.89)	24.0 (0.47)	35.3 (0.84)	16.9 (0.52)	9.2 (0.31)	6.1 (0.26)
1986	48.2 (0.22)	38.9 (0.95)	95.3 (0.41)	99.2 (0.10)	94.9 (0.28)	97.6 (0.28)	92.3 (0.48)	54.6 (0.91)	13.1 (0.62)	41.5 (0.90)	23.6 (0.47)	33.0 (0.84)	17.9 (0.54)	8.8 (0.30)	6.0 (0.25)
1987	48.6 (0.22)	38.3 (0.95)	95.1 (0.42)	99.5 (0.07)	95.0 (0.28)	98.6 (0.22)	91.7 (0.49)	55.6 (0.90)	13.1 (0.61)	42.5 (0.90)	25.5 (0.49)	38.7 (0.89)	17.5 (0.54)	9.0 (0.30)	5.8 (0.25)
1988	48.7 (0.24)	38.2 (1.02)	96.0 (0.41)	99.7 (0.07)	95.1 (0.31)	98.8 (0.22)	91.6 (0.55)	55.6 (0.98)	13.9 (0.68)	41.8 (0.97)	26.1 (0.54)	39.1 (0.98)	18.2 (0.60)	8.3 (0.32)	5.9 (0.27)
1989	49.0 (0.22)	39.1 (0.97)	95.2 (0.43)	99.3 (0.09)	95.7 (0.28)	98.8 (0.21)	92.7 (0.50)	56.0 (0.92)	14.4 (0.65)	41.6 (0.91)	27.0 (0.53)	38.5 (0.94)	19.0 (0.60)	9.3 (0.32)	5.7 (0.25)
1990	50.2 (0.23)	44.4 (0.99)	96.5 (0.37)	99.6 (0.06)	95.8 (0.28)	99.0 (0.19)	92.5 (0.52)	57.2 (0.94)	14.5 (0.67)	42.7 (0.94)	28.6 (0.54)	39.7 (0.92)	21.0 (0.63)	9.7 (0.33)	5.8 (0.25)
1991	50.7 (0.23)	40.5 (0.96)	95.4 (0.41)	99.6 (0.06)	96.0 (0.27)	98.8 (0.22)	93.3 (0.49)	59.6 (0.96)	15.6 (0.71)	44.0 (0.97)	30.2 (0.55)	42.0 (0.92)	22.2 (0.64)	10.2 (0.34)	6.2 (0.26)
1992	51.4 (0.23)	39.7 (0.95)	95.5 (0.41)	99.4 (0.08)	96.7 (0.25)	98.9 (0.18)	94.1 (0.46)	61.4 (0.96)	17.1 (0.74)	44.3 (0.98)	31.6 (0.56)	44.0 (0.95)	23.7 (0.65)	9.8 (0.34)	6.1 (0.26)
1993	51.8 (0.23)	40.4 (0.93)	95.4 (0.41)	99.5 (0.07)	96.5 (0.25)	98.8 (0.20)	94.0 (0.46)	61.6 (0.95)	17.2 (0.74)	44.4 (0.97)	30.8 (0.56)	42.7 (0.97)	23.6 (0.65)	10.2 (0.35)	5.9 (0.25)
1994	53.3 (0.23)	47.3[2] (0.94)	96.7 (0.34)	99.4 (0.08)	96.6 (0.24)	98.8 (0.20)	94.4 (0.43)	60.2 (0.94)	16.2 (0.70)	43.9 (0.95)	32.0 (0.55)	44.9 (0.95)	24.0 (0.64)	10.8 (0.36)	6.7 (0.27)

See notes at end of table.

Table 103.20. Percentage of the population 3 to 34 years old enrolled in school, by age group: Selected years, 1940 through 2018—Continued

[Standard errors appear in parentheses]

Year	Total, 3 to 34 years old	3 and 4 years old	5 and 6 years old	7 to 13 years old	14 to 17 years old			18 and 19 years old			20 to 24 years old			25 to 29 years old	30 to 34 years old
					Total	14 and 15	16 and 17	Total	In secondary education	In higher education	Total	20 and 21	22 to 24		
1	2	3	4	5	6	7	8	9	10	11	12	13	14	15	16
1995	53.7 (0.21)	48.7[2] (0.87)	96.0 (0.34)	98.9 (0.10)	96.3 (0.23)	98.9 (0.18)	93.6 (0.42)	59.4 (0.86)	16.3 (0.64)	43.1 (0.86)	31.5 (0.52)	44.9 (0.90)	23.2 (0.60)	11.6 (0.34)	5.9 (0.24)
1996	54.1 (0.22)	48.3[2] (0.91)	94.0 (0.43)	97.7 (0.15)	95.4 (0.26)	98.0 (0.24)	92.8 (0.45)	61.5 (0.87)	16.7 (0.67)	44.9 (0.89)	32.5 (0.55)	44.4 (0.93)	24.8 (0.65)	11.9 (0.36)	6.1 (0.25)
1997	55.6 (0.22)	52.6[2] (0.92)	96.5 (0.33)	99.1 (0.09)	96.6 (0.22)	98.9 (0.18)	94.3 (0.40)	61.5 (0.86)	16.7 (0.66)	44.7 (0.88)	34.3 (0.55)	45.9 (0.91)	26.4 (0.66)	11.8 (0.36)	5.7 (0.25)
1998	55.8 (0.22)	52.1[2] (0.92)	95.6 (0.37)	98.9 (0.10)	96.1 (0.24)	98.4 (0.22)	93.9 (0.41)	62.2 (0.84)	15.7 (0.63)	46.4 (0.86)	33.0 (0.54)	44.8 (0.91)	24.9 (0.65)	11.9 (0.36)	6.6 (0.27)
1999	56.0 (0.22)	54.2[2] (0.93)	96.0 (0.36)	98.7 (0.11)	95.8 (0.24)	98.2 (0.23)	93.6 (0.42)	60.6 (0.84)	16.5 (0.64)	44.1 (0.85)	32.8 (0.54)	45.3 (0.90)	24.5 (0.64)	11.1 (0.36)	6.2 (0.27)
2000	55.9 (0.22)	52.1[2] (0.93)	95.6 (0.38)	98.2 (0.13)	95.7 (0.25)	98.7 (0.20)	92.8 (0.45)	61.2 (0.84)	16.5 (0.64)	44.7 (0.85)	32.5 (0.53)	44.1 (0.88)	24.6 (0.63)	11.4 (0.37)	6.7 (0.27)
2001	56.4 (0.20)	52.4[2] (0.88)	95.3 (0.37)	98.3 (0.12)	95.8 (0.23)	98.1 (0.22)	93.4 (0.40)	61.1 (0.79)	17.1 (0.61)	44.0 (0.80)	34.1 (0.50)	46.1 (0.82)	25.5 (0.61)	11.8 (0.36)	6.9 (0.26)
2002	56.2 (0.20)	56.3[2] (0.89)	95.5 (0.37)	98.3 (0.12)	96.4 (0.21)	98.4 (0.20)	94.3 (0.37)	63.3 (0.79)	18.0 (0.63)	45.3 (0.82)	34.4 (0.50)	47.8 (0.83)	25.6 (0.59)	12.1 (0.35)	6.6 (0.25)
2003	56.2 (0.20)	55.1[2] (0.85)	94.5 (0.40)	98.3 (0.12)	96.2 (0.21)	97.5 (0.25)	94.9 (0.34)	64.5 (0.80)	17.9 (0.64)	46.6 (0.84)	35.6 (0.50)	48.3 (0.83)	27.8 (0.59)	11.8 (0.34)	6.8 (0.26)
2004	56.2 (0.20)	54.0[2] (0.85)	95.4 (0.37)	98.4 (0.12)	96.5 (0.21)	98.5 (0.19)	94.5 (0.36)	64.4 (0.80)	16.6 (0.62)	47.8 (0.83)	35.2 (0.49)	48.9 (0.82)	26.3 (0.58)	13.0 (0.35)	6.6 (0.26)
2005	56.5 (0.20)	53.6[2] (0.86)	95.4 (0.37)	98.6 (0.11)	96.5 (0.20)	98.0 (0.22)	95.1 (0.33)	67.6 (0.79)	18.3 (0.65)	49.3 (0.84)	36.1 (0.49)	48.7 (0.80)	27.3 (0.59)	11.9 (0.34)	6.9 (0.27)
2006	56.0 (0.20)	55.7[2] (0.86)	94.6 (0.39)	98.3 (0.12)	96.4 (0.21)	98.3 (0.21)	94.6 (0.36)	65.5 (0.77)	19.3 (0.64)	46.2 (0.81)	35.0 (0.49)	47.5 (0.81)	26.7 (0.58)	11.7 (0.33)	7.2 (0.27)
2007	56.1 (0.20)	54.5[2] (0.86)	94.7 (0.39)	98.4 (0.12)	96.4 (0.21)	98.7 (0.18)	94.3 (0.36)	66.8 (0.75)	17.9 (0.61)	48.9 (0.80)	35.7 (0.49)	48.4 (0.81)	27.3 (0.59)	12.4 (0.33)	7.2 (0.27)
2008	56.2 (0.20)	52.8[2] (0.85)	93.8 (0.42)	98.7 (0.11)	96.8 (0.20)	98.6 (0.19)	95.2 (0.34)	66.0 (0.75)	17.4 (0.60)	48.6 (0.79)	36.9 (0.49)	50.1 (0.81)	28.2 (0.59)	13.2 (0.34)	7.3 (0.27)
2009	56.5 (0.20)	52.4[2] (0.85)	94.1 (0.40)	98.2 (0.12)	96.3 (0.22)	98.0 (0.23)	94.6 (0.36)	68.9 (0.73)	19.1 (0.62)	49.8 (0.79)	38.7 (0.50)	51.7 (0.81)	30.4 (0.60)	13.5 (0.34)	8.1 (0.28)
2010	56.6 (0.17)	53.2[2] (0.89)	94.5 (0.46)	98.0 (0.16)	97.1 (0.21)	98.1 (0.25)	96.1 (0.33)	69.2 (0.92)	18.1 (0.71)	51.2 (1.05)	38.6 (0.71)	52.4 (1.08)	28.9 (0.79)	14.6 (0.47)	8.3 (0.39)
2011	56.8 (0.19)	52.4[2] (0.90)	95.1 (0.43)	98.3 (0.14)	97.1 (0.22)	98.6 (0.21)	95.7 (0.38)	71.1 (0.95)	21.0 (0.78)	50.1 (1.08)	39.9 (0.68)	52.7 (1.05)	31.1 (0.82)	14.8 (0.44)	7.7 (0.32)
2012	56.6 (0.22)	53.5[2] (1.11)	93.2 (0.49)	98.0 (0.17)	97.0 (0.28)	98.2 (0.31)	95.8 (0.40)	69.0 (0.98)	21.7 (0.77)	47.3 (0.96)	40.2 (0.72)	54.0 (1.04)	30.7 (0.84)	14.0 (0.48)	7.5 (0.33)
2013	55.8 (0.18)	54.9[2] (1.00)	93.8 (0.45)	98.1 (0.16)	96.1 (0.28)	98.4 (0.27)	93.7 (0.50)	67.1 (0.97)	20.5 (0.80)	46.6 (1.00)	38.7 (0.76)	52.8 (1.24)	29.7 (0.81)	13.3 (0.44)	6.7 (0.32)
2014	55.2 (0.21)	54.5[2] (0.98)	93.4 (0.53)	97.6 (0.19)	95.4 (0.29)	97.8 (0.26)	92.9 (0.51)	68.4 (0.92)	19.6 (0.79)	48.9 (1.09)	38.0 (0.76)	51.4 (1.24)	29.6 (0.80)	13.1 (0.44)	6.4 (0.31)
2015	55.2 (0.21)	52.7[2] (1.02)	94.2 (0.46)	97.7 (0.17)	95.9 (0.28)	98.0 (0.27)	93.7 (0.49)	68.5 (0.86)	19.8 (0.79)	48.8 (0.98)	38.5 (0.80)	53.3 (1.14)	28.8 (0.81)	13.2 (0.50)	6.6 (0.30)
2016	55.2 (0.21)	53.8[2] (1.04)	93.3 (0.58)	98.2 (0.15)	95.5 (0.30)	98.0 (0.27)	93.0 (0.55)	69.5 (1.05)	19.0 (0.76)	50.5 (1.15)	39.0 (0.78)	55.5 (1.12)	28.8 (0.85)	13.2 (0.46)	6.4 (0.31)
2017	54.6 (0.19)	53.8[2] (1.08)	93.5 (0.54)	97.5 (0.20)	95.5 (0.31)	98.2 (0.25)	92.9 (0.55)	68.2 (1.08)	20.2 (0.85)	48.0 (1.21)	38.8 (0.71)	55.0 (1.13)	28.4 (0.92)	12.1 (0.45)	5.9 (0.31)
2018	54.6 (0.20)	54.0[2] (1.19)	93.5 (0.60)	97.7 (0.19)	95.4 (0.34)	98.6 (0.27)	92.3 (0.58)	69.1 (1.01)	18.6 (0.78)	50.5 (1.09)	38.5 (0.82)	54.6 (1.18)	28.0 (0.88)	12.7 (0.44)	6.3 (0.33)

—Not available.
†Not applicable.
[1]It is not possible to compute a 1964 enrollment percentage for the total 3- to 34-year-old population because, although enrollment percentages are available for each component age group, underlying data on population size are not available for 3- and 4-year-olds.
[2]Beginning in 1994, preprimary enrollment data were collected using new procedures. Data may not be comparable to figures for earlier years.
NOTE: Data for 1940 are for April. Data for all other years are as of October. Data are based on sample surveys of the civilian noninstitutionalized population, which excludes persons in the military and persons living in institutions (e.g., prisons or nursing facilities). Includes enrollment in any type of graded public, parochial, or other private schools. Includes nursery schools, kindergartens, elementary and secondary schools, colleges, universities, and professional schools. Attendance may be on either a full-time or part-time basis and during the day or night. Prior to 2010, standard errors were computed using generalized variance function methodology rather than the more precise replicate weight methodology used in later years.

SOURCE: U.S. Department of Commerce, Census Bureau, *Historical Statistics of the United States, Colonial Times to 1970*; Current Population Reports, Series P-20, various years; CPS Historical Time Series Tables on School Enrollment, retrieved June 6, 2012, from http://www.census.gov/hhes/school/data/cps/historical/index.html; and Current Population Survey (CPS), October, 1970 through 2018. (This table was prepared November 2019.)

Table 104.10.   Rates of high school completion and bachelor's degree attainment among persons age 25 and over, by race/ethnicity and sex: Selected years, 1910 through 2019

[Standard errors appear in parentheses]

Sex, high school or bachelor's degree attainment, and year	Total, percent of all persons age 25 and over	White[1]	Black[1]	Hispanic	Asian/Pacific Islander Total	Asian	Pacific Islander	American Indian/ Alaska Native	Two or more races
1	2	3	4	5	6	7	8	9	10
Total									
High school completion or higher[2]									
1910[3]	13.5 (—)	— (†)	— (†)	— (†)	— (†)	— (†)	— (†)	— (†)	— (†)
1920[3]	16.4 (—)	— (†)	— (†)	— (†)	— (†)	— (†)	— (†)	— (†)	— (†)
1930[3]	19.1 (—)	— (†)	— (†)	— (†)	— (†)	— (†)	— (†)	— (†)	— (†)
1940	24.5 (—)	26.1 (—)	7.7 (—)	— (†)	— (†)	— (†)	— (†)	— (†)	— (†)
1950	34.3 (—)	36.4 (—)	13.7 (—)	— (†)	— (†)	— (†)	— (†)	— (†)	— (†)
1960	41.1 (—)	43.2 (—)	21.7 (—)	— (†)	— (†)	— (†)	— (†)	— (†)	— (†)
1970	55.2 (—)	57.4 (—)	36.1 (—)	— (†)	— (†)	— (†)	— (†)	— (†)	— (†)
1975	62.5 (—)	65.8 (—)	42.6 (—)	38.5 (—)	— (†)	— (†)	— (†)	— (†)	— (†)
1980	68.6 (0.20)	71.9 (0.21)	51.4 (0.81)	44.5 (1.18)	— (†)	— (†)	— (†)	— (†)	— (†)
1985	73.9 (0.18)	77.5 (0.19)	59.9 (0.74)	47.9 (0.99)	— (†)	— (†)	— (†)	— (†)	— (†)
1986	74.7 (0.18)	78.2 (0.19)	62.5 (0.72)	48.5 (0.96)	— (†)	— (†)	— (†)	— (†)	— (†)
1987	75.6 (0.17)	79.0 (0.18)	63.6 (0.71)	50.9 (0.94)	— (†)	— (†)	— (†)	— (†)	— (†)
1988	76.2 (0.17)	79.8 (0.18)	63.5 (0.70)	51.0 (0.92)	— (†)	— (†)	— (†)	— (†)	— (†)
1989	76.9 (0.17)	80.7 (0.18)	64.7 (0.69)	50.9 (0.89)	82.3 (1.17)	— (†)	— (†)	— (†)	— (†)
1990	77.6 (0.17)	81.4 (0.17)	66.2 (0.67)	50.8 (0.88)	84.2 (1.09)	— (†)	— (†)	— (†)	— (†)
1991	78.4 (0.16)	82.4 (0.17)	66.8 (0.66)	51.3 (0.86)	84.2 (1.05)	— (†)	— (†)	— (†)	— (†)
1992	79.4 (0.16)	83.4 (0.16)	67.7 (0.65)	52.6 (0.85)	83.7 (1.02)	— (†)	— (†)	— (†)	— (†)
1993	80.2 (0.16)	84.1 (0.16)	70.5 (0.63)	53.1 (0.83)	84.2 (1.00)	— (†)	— (†)	— (†)	— (†)
1994	80.9 (0.15)	84.9 (0.16)	73.0 (0.61)	53.3 (0.78)	84.8 (0.98)	— (†)	— (†)	— (†)	— (†)
1995	81.7 (0.15)	85.9 (0.16)	73.8 (0.61)	53.4 (0.78)	83.8 (1.06)	— (†)	— (†)	— (†)	— (†)
1996	81.7 (0.16)	86.0 (0.16)	74.6 (0.53)	53.1 (0.68)	83.5 (0.82)	— (†)	— (†)	— (†)	— (†)
1997	82.1 (0.14)	86.3 (0.15)	75.3 (0.52)	54.7 (0.54)	85.2 (0.75)	— (†)	— (†)	— (†)	— (†)
1998	82.8 (0.14)	87.1 (0.14)	76.4 (0.50)	55.5 (0.53)	84.9 (0.74)	— (†)	— (†)	— (†)	— (†)
1999	83.4 (0.14)	87.7 (0.14)	77.4 (0.49)	56.1 (0.52)	84.7 (0.73)	— (†)	— (†)	— (†)	— (†)
2000	84.1 (0.13)	88.4 (0.14)	78.9 (0.48)	57.0 (0.51)	85.7 (0.71)	— (†)	— (†)	— (†)	— (†)
2001	84.3 (0.13)	88.7 (0.13)	79.5 (0.47)	56.5 (0.50)	87.8 (0.60)	— (†)	— (†)	— (†)	— (†)
2002	84.1 (0.09)	88.7 (0.10)	79.2 (0.34)	57.0 (0.34)	87.7 (0.44)	— (†)	— (†)	— (†)	— (†)
2003	84.6 (0.09)	89.4 (0.09)	80.3 (0.33)	57.0 (0.33)	87.8 (0.43)	87.8 (0.44)	88.2 (1.87)	77.2 (1.64)	86.1 (0.97)
2004	85.2 (0.09)	90.0 (0.09)	81.1 (0.32)	58.4 (0.32)	86.9 (0.43)	86.9 (0.44)	88.5 (1.91)	77.8 (1.61)	87.2 (0.91)
2005	85.2 (0.14)	90.1 (0.16)	81.4 (0.44)	58.5 (0.53)	87.8 (0.62)	87.7 (0.62)	90.1 (2.69)	75.6 (2.02)	88.6 (0.83)
2006	85.5 (0.15)	90.5 (0.15)	81.2 (0.43)	59.3 (0.58)	87.5 (0.71)	87.5 (0.71)	85.7 (2.51)	78.5 (2.11)	88.1 (0.90)
2007	85.7 (0.15)	90.6 (0.15)	82.8 (0.39)	60.3 (0.56)	88.0 (0.79)	87.9 (0.81)	88.6 (2.30)	80.3 (2.27)	89.3 (0.87)
2008	86.6 (0.15)	91.5 (0.15)	83.3 (0.40)	62.3 (0.58)	89.0 (0.62)	88.8 (0.64)	94.4 (1.00)	78.4 (2.74)	89.5 (1.12)
2009	86.7 (0.15)	91.6 (0.15)	84.2 (0.44)	61.9 (0.56)	88.4 (0.61)	88.3 (0.63)	90.8 (1.76)	81.5 (1.83)	87.4 (0.96)
2010	87.1 (0.13)	92.1 (0.14)	84.6 (0.41)	62.9 (0.53)	89.1 (0.67)	89.1 (0.68)	90.2 (1.95)	80.8 (1.76)	88.9 (0.90)
2011	87.6 (0.13)	92.4 (0.14)	84.8 (0.41)	64.3 (0.54)	88.8 (0.55)	88.7 (0.57)	90.4 (1.61)	82.3 (1.77)	89.4 (1.00)
2012	87.6 (0.15)	92.5 (0.14)	85.7 (0.40)	65.0 (0.59)	89.1 (0.59)	89.0 (0.61)	91.6 (1.33)	81.8 (1.69)	91.0 (0.89)
2013	88.2 (0.14)	92.9 (0.13)	85.9 (0.42)	66.2 (0.52)	90.2 (0.51)	90.2 (0.53)	89.5 (1.72)	82.2 (1.68)	92.6 (0.75)
2014	88.3 (0.15)	93.1 (0.17)	86.7 (0.45)	66.5 (0.57)	89.5 (0.62)	89.5 (0.64)	88.8 (2.15)	81.0 (2.01)	93.3 (0.88)
2015	88.4 (0.12)	93.3 (0.13)	87.7 (0.37)	66.7 (0.48)	88.9 (0.49)	89.1 (0.51)	85.1 (2.04)	83.8 (1.64)	91.6 (0.87)
2016	89.1 (0.13)	93.8 (0.13)	87.7 (0.34)	68.5 (0.48)	90.7 (0.49)	90.6 (0.51)	93.3 (1.38)	84.7 (1.35)	92.8 (0.83)
2017	89.6 (0.12)	94.1 (0.13)	88.1 (0.37)	70.5 (0.47)	90.9 (0.47)	90.9 (0.49)	89.3 (2.03)	85.3 (1.36)	93.4 (0.71)
2018	89.8 (0.12)	94.3 (0.13)	88.6 (0.33)	71.6 (0.40)	90.6 (0.40)	90.6 (0.41)	90.6 (1.77)	83.6 (1.32)	93.2 (0.61)
2019	90.1 (0.12)	94.6 (0.11)	88.8 (0.38)	71.8 (0.48)	91.3 (0.45)	91.2 (0.46)	93.8 (1.32)	87.9 (1.31)	92.6 (0.84)
Bachelor's or higher degree[4]									
1910[3]	2.7 (—)	— (†)	— (†)	— (†)	— (†)	— (†)	— (†)	— (†)	— (†)
1920[3]	3.3 (—)	— (†)	— (†)	— (†)	— (†)	— (†)	— (†)	— (†)	— (†)
1930[3]	3.9 (—)	— (†)	— (†)	— (†)	— (†)	— (†)	— (†)	— (†)	— (†)
1940	4.6 (—)	4.9 (—)	1.3 (—)	— (†)	— (†)	— (†)	— (†)	— (†)	— (†)
1950	6.2 (—)	6.6 (—)	2.2 (—)	— (†)	— (†)	— (†)	— (†)	— (†)	— (†)
1960	7.7 (—)	8.1 (—)	3.5 (—)	— (†)	— (†)	— (†)	— (†)	— (†)	— (†)
1970	11.0 (—)	11.6 (—)	6.1 (—)	— (†)	— (†)	— (†)	— (†)	— (†)	— (†)
1975	13.9 (—)	14.9 (—)	6.4 (—)	6.6 (—)	— (†)	— (†)	— (†)	— (†)	— (†)
1980	17.0 (0.16)	18.4 (0.18)	7.9 (0.44)	7.6 (0.63)	— (†)	— (†)	— (†)	— (†)	— (†)
1985	19.4 (0.16)	20.8 (0.19)	11.1 (0.47)	8.5 (0.55)	— (†)	— (†)	— (†)	— (†)	— (†)
1986	19.4 (0.16)	20.9 (0.19)	10.9 (0.47)	8.4 (0.53)	— (†)	— (†)	— (†)	— (†)	— (†)
1987	19.9 (0.16)	21.4 (0.19)	10.8 (0.46)	8.6 (0.53)	— (†)	— (†)	— (†)	— (†)	— (†)
1988	20.3 (0.16)	21.8 (0.19)	11.2 (0.46)	10.0 (0.55)	— (†)	— (†)	— (†)	— (†)	— (†)
1989	21.1 (0.16)	22.8 (0.19)	11.7 (0.46)	9.9 (0.53)	41.5 (1.51)	— (†)	— (†)	— (†)	— (†)
1990	21.3 (0.16)	23.1 (0.19)	11.3 (0.46)	9.2 (0.51)	41.7 (1.47)	— (†)	— (†)	— (†)	— (†)
1991	21.4 (0.16)	23.3 (0.19)	11.5 (0.45)	9.7 (0.51)	40.3 (1.42)	— (†)	— (†)	— (†)	— (†)
1992	21.4 (0.16)	23.2 (0.19)	11.9 (0.45)	9.3 (0.49)	39.3 (1.35)	— (†)	— (†)	— (†)	— (†)
1993	21.9 (0.16)	23.8 (0.19)	12.2 (0.45)	9.0 (0.48)	42.1 (1.35)	— (†)	— (†)	— (†)	— (†)
1994	22.2 (0.16)	24.3 (0.19)	12.9 (0.46)	9.1 (0.45)	41.3 (1.34)	— (†)	— (†)	— (†)	— (†)
1995	23.0 (0.16)	25.4 (0.19)	13.3 (0.47)	9.3 (0.45)	38.5 (1.40)	— (†)	— (†)	— (†)	— (†)
1996	23.6 (0.17)	25.9 (0.20)	13.8 (0.42)	9.3 (0.40)	42.3 (1.09)	— (†)	— (†)	— (†)	— (†)
1997	23.9 (0.16)	26.2 (0.19)	13.3 (0.41)	10.3 (0.33)	42.6 (1.04)	— (†)	— (†)	— (†)	— (†)
1998	24.4 (0.16)	26.6 (0.19)	14.8 (0.42)	11.0 (0.33)	42.3 (1.02)	— (†)	— (†)	— (†)	— (†)
1999	25.2 (0.16)	27.7 (0.19)	15.5 (0.43)	10.9 (0.33)	42.4 (1.01)	— (†)	— (†)	— (†)	— (†)
2000	25.6 (0.16)	28.1 (0.19)	16.6 (0.44)	10.6 (0.32)	44.4 (1.00)	— (†)	— (†)	— (†)	— (†)
2001	26.1 (0.16)	28.6 (0.19)	16.1 (0.43)	11.2 (0.32)	48.0 (0.92)	— (†)	— (†)	— (†)	— (†)
2002	26.7 (0.11)	29.4 (0.14)	17.2 (0.31)	11.1 (0.21)	47.7 (0.66)	— (†)	— (†)	— (†)	— (†)
2003	27.2 (0.11)	30.0 (0.14)	17.4 (0.31)	11.4 (0.21)	48.8 (0.65)	50.0 (0.67)	27.0 (2.56)	12.6 (1.30)	22.0 (1.17)
2004	27.7 (0.11)	30.6 (0.14)	17.7 (0.31)	12.1 (0.21)	48.9 (0.64)	49.7 (0.66)	32.4 (2.81)	14.3 (1.36)	21.8 (1.13)
2005	27.7 (0.23)	30.6 (0.29)	17.6 (0.45)	12.0 (0.31)	49.3 (0.91)	50.4 (0.93)	24.6 (3.67)	14.5 (1.51)	23.2 (1.19)

See notes at end of table.

Table 104.10. Rates of high school completion and bachelor's degree attainment among persons age 25 and over, by race/ethnicity and sex: Selected years, 1910 through 2019—Continued

[Standard errors appear in parentheses]

Sex, high school or bachelor's degree attainment, and year	Total, percent of all persons age 25 and over	White[1]	Black[1]	Hispanic	Asian/Pacific Islander Total	Asian	Pacific Islander	American Indian/ Alaska Native	Two or more races
1	2	3	4	5	6	7	8	9	10
2006	28.0 (0.20)	31.0 (0.25)	18.6 (0.47)	12.4 (0.32)	49.1 (1.04)	50.0 (1.06)	26.9 (3.42)	12.9 (1.60)	23.1 (1.28)
2007	28.7 (0.21)	31.8 (0.27)	18.7 (0.51)	12.7 (0.31)	51.2 (1.02)	52.5 (1.03)	23.8 (3.30)	13.1 (1.24)	23.7 (1.30)
2008	29.4 (0.21)	32.6 (0.26)	19.7 (0.51)	13.3 (0.29)	51.9 (0.95)	52.9 (0.97)	28.4 (2.86)	14.9 (1.52)	24.4 (1.36)
2009	29.5 (0.21)	32.9 (0.26)	19.4 (0.45)	13.2 (0.34)	51.6 (0.91)	52.8 (0.95)	28.3 (2.68)	17.5 (2.08)	25.5 (1.34)
2010	29.9 (0.19)	33.2 (0.24)	20.0 (0.51)	13.9 (0.31)	51.6 (1.04)	52.8 (1.09)	25.6 (2.89)	16.0 (1.77)	25.3 (1.30)
2011	30.4 (0.19)	34.0 (0.24)	20.2 (0.50)	14.1 (0.34)	49.5 (0.92)	50.8 (0.96)	22.1 (2.73)	16.1 (1.73)	27.4 (1.27)
2012	30.9 (0.21)	34.5 (0.27)	21.4 (0.53)	14.5 (0.35)	50.7 (0.92)	51.9 (0.94)	24.5 (2.75)	16.7 (1.82)	27.1 (1.34)
2013	31.7 (0.21)	35.2 (0.26)	22.0 (0.49)	15.1 (0.34)	52.5 (0.92)	53.9 (0.93)	25.6 (2.66)	15.4 (1.72)	30.6 (1.35)
2014	32.0 (0.27)	35.6 (0.35)	22.8 (0.66)	15.2 (0.39)	51.3 (1.00)	52.7 (1.02)	22.3 (3.27)	13.8 (1.43)	31.2 (1.81)
2015	32.5 (0.22)	36.2 (0.28)	22.9 (0.52)	15.5 (0.31)	52.9 (0.84)	54.4 (0.87)	22.8 (2.39)	19.8 (1.32)	30.6 (1.52)
2016	33.4 (0.24)	37.3 (0.31)	23.5 (0.46)	16.4 (0.40)	55.1 (0.87)	56.4 (0.89)	27.5 (2.92)	16.8 (1.39)	30.6 (1.52)
2017	34.2 (0.24)	38.1 (0.31)	24.3 (0.49)	17.2 (0.35)	53.9 (0.84)	55.4 (0.88)	25.1 (2.81)	20.5 (1.92)	32.6 (1.39)
2018	35.0 (0.26)	38.8 (0.34)	25.6 (0.53)	18.3 (0.37)	55.6 (0.81)	57.1 (0.80)	24.1 (2.34)	18.8 (1.72)	32.4 (1.40)
2019	36.0 (0.23)	40.1 (0.33)	26.3 (0.51)	18.8 (0.35)	57.3 (0.78)	58.6 (0.79)	28.1 (2.78)	16.8 (1.40)	34.1 (1.38)
Males									
High school completion or higher[2]									
1940	22.7 (—)	24.2 (—)	6.9 (—)	— (†)	— (†)	— (†)	— (†)	— (†)	— (†)
1950	32.6 (—)	34.6 (—)	12.6 (—)	— (†)	— (†)	— (†)	— (†)	— (†)	— (†)
1960	39.5 (—)	41.6 (—)	20.0 (—)	— (†)	— (†)	— (†)	— (†)	— (†)	— (†)
1970	55.0 (—)	57.2 (—)	35.4 (—)	— (†)	— (†)	— (†)	— (†)	— (†)	— (†)
1980	69.2 (0.29)	72.4 (0.31)	51.2 (1.21)	44.9 (1.71)	— (†)	— (†)	— (†)	— (†)	— (†)
1990	77.7 (0.24)	81.6 (0.25)	65.8 (1.01)	50.3 (1.25)	86.0 (1.49)	— (†)	— (†)	— (†)	— (†)
1995	81.7 (0.22)	86.0 (0.22)	73.5 (0.91)	52.9 (1.11)	85.8 (1.46)	— (†)	— (†)	— (†)	— (†)
1996	81.9 (0.23)	86.1 (0.23)	74.6 (0.80)	53.0 (0.97)	86.2 (1.10)	— (†)	— (†)	— (†)	— (†)
1997	82.0 (0.21)	86.3 (0.21)	73.8 (0.79)	54.9 (0.76)	87.5 (1.00)	— (†)	— (†)	— (†)	— (†)
1998	82.8 (0.20)	87.1 (0.21)	75.4 (0.77)	55.7 (0.74)	87.9 (0.98)	— (†)	— (†)	— (†)	— (†)
1999	83.4 (0.20)	87.7 (0.20)	77.2 (0.74)	56.0 (0.75)	86.9 (1.00)	— (†)	— (†)	— (†)	— (†)
2000	84.2 (0.19)	88.5 (0.20)	79.1 (0.72)	56.6 (0.73)	88.4 (0.94)	— (†)	— (†)	— (†)	— (†)
2001	84.4 (0.19)	88.6 (0.19)	80.6 (0.69)	55.6 (0.72)	90.6 (0.78)	— (†)	— (†)	— (†)	— (†)
2002	83.8 (0.14)	88.5 (0.14)	79.0 (0.51)	56.1 (0.48)	89.8 (0.58)	— (†)	— (†)	— (†)	— (†)
2003	84.1 (0.13)	89.0 (0.14)	79.9 (0.50)	56.3 (0.46)	89.8 (0.58)	89.8 (0.59)	89.8 (2.61)	76.5 (2.33)	87.2 (1.36)
2004	84.8 (0.13)	89.9 (0.13)	80.8 (0.49)	57.3 (0.45)	88.8 (0.59)	88.8 (0.60)	88.9 (2.65)	77.1 (2.31)	87.8 (1.29)
2005	84.9 (0.19)	89.9 (0.20)	81.4 (0.60)	57.9 (0.69)	90.4 (0.65)	90.5 (0.66)	88.5 (3.62)	75.6 (2.57)	89.0 (1.19)
2006	85.0 (0.20)	90.2 (0.21)	80.7 (0.63)	58.5 (0.77)	89.5 (0.84)	89.7 (0.86)	85.8 (3.10)	78.1 (2.77)	88.0 (1.36)
2007	85.0 (0.21)	90.2 (0.22)	82.5 (0.55)	58.2 (0.80)	90.0 (0.81)	90.1 (0.82)	88.1 (2.75)	78.3 (3.58)	89.4 (1.28)
2008	85.9 (0.19)	91.1 (0.20)	82.1 (0.61)	60.9 (0.72)	91.0 (0.66)	90.8 (0.69)	95.8 (1.40)	77.3 (3.37)	89.6 (1.21)
2009	86.2 (0.19)	91.4 (0.20)	84.2 (0.60)	60.6 (0.72)	90.8 (0.66)	90.7 (0.68)	92.1 (2.18)	80.0 (2.33)	87.3 (1.26)
2010	86.6 (0.17)	91.8 (0.19)	84.2 (0.57)	61.4 (0.68)	91.4 (0.78)	91.5 (0.79)	89.3 (2.84)	78.9 (2.46)	88.1 (1.36)
2011	87.1 (0.18)	92.0 (0.17)	84.2 (0.55)	63.6 (0.71)	90.6 (0.68)	90.6 (0.69)	91.5 (2.22)	80.6 (2.35)	88.1 (1.40)
2012	87.3 (0.19)	92.2 (0.18)	85.1 (0.56)	64.0 (0.73)	90.6 (0.68)	90.5 (0.70)	93.3 (1.84)	81.8 (2.39)	90.2 (1.45)
2013	87.6 (0.17)	92.7 (0.17)	84.9 (0.62)	64.6 (0.66)	91.6 (0.57)	91.7 (0.57)	89.3 (2.48)	81.0 (2.11)	93.3 (1.03)
2014	87.7 (0.19)	92.5 (0.22)	86.3 (0.58)	65.1 (0.74)	91.8 (0.70)	91.9 (0.72)	90.0 (2.68)	80.2 (2.30)	93.8 (1.08)
2015	88.0 (0.16)	93.0 (0.16)	87.2 (0.48)	65.5 (0.63)	90.9 (0.56)	91.3 (0.58)	84.9 (2.83)	81.9 (2.12)	92.5 (1.23)
2016	88.5 (0.17)	93.4 (0.19)	87.0 (0.51)	67.2 (0.63)	92.3 (0.58)	92.2 (0.60)	94.9 (1.58)	84.1 (2.07)	92.8 (1.15)
2017	89.1 (0.16)	93.7 (0.18)	87.4 (0.53)	69.5 (0.59)	92.5 (0.55)	92.7 (0.55)	89.1 (2.77)	83.0 (1.96)	93.2 (1.15)
2018	89.4 (0.16)	93.9 (0.18)	88.3 (0.48)	70.7 (0.53)	92.8 (0.48)	92.9 (0.49)	92.2 (2.31)	79.3 (1.93)	92.5 (1.02)
2019	89.6 (0.16)	94.2 (0.15)	88.1 (0.54)	70.8 (0.59)	92.8 (0.52)	92.8 (0.54)	93.3 (2.11)	84.1 (1.96)	91.0 (1.17)
Bachelor's or higher degree[4]									
1940	5.5 (—)	5.9 (—)	1.4 (—)	— (†)	— (†)	— (†)	— (†)	— (†)	— (†)
1950	7.3 (—)	7.9 (—)	2.1 (—)	— (†)	— (†)	— (†)	— (†)	— (†)	— (†)
1960	9.7 (—)	10.3 (—)	3.5 (—)	— (†)	— (†)	— (†)	— (†)	— (†)	— (†)
1970	14.1 (—)	15.0 (—)	6.8 (—)	— (†)	— (†)	— (†)	— (†)	— (†)	— (†)
1980	20.9 (0.26)	22.7 (0.29)	7.7 (0.65)	9.2 (0.99)	— (†)	— (†)	— (†)	— (†)	— (†)
1990	24.4 (0.25)	26.7 (0.28)	11.9 (0.69)	9.8 (0.74)	45.9 (2.14)	— (†)	— (†)	— (†)	— (†)
1995	26.0 (0.25)	28.9 (0.29)	13.7 (0.71)	10.1 (0.67)	42.3 (2.06)	— (†)	— (†)	— (†)	— (†)
1996	26.0 (0.26)	28.8 (0.30)	12.5 (0.61)	10.3 (0.59)	46.9 (1.59)	— (†)	— (†)	— (†)	— (†)
1997	26.2 (0.24)	29.0 (0.28)	12.5 (0.60)	10.6 (0.47)	48.0 (1.51)	— (†)	— (†)	— (†)	— (†)
1998	26.5 (0.24)	29.3 (0.28)	14.0 (0.62)	11.1 (0.47)	46.0 (1.50)	— (†)	— (†)	— (†)	— (†)
1999	27.5 (0.24)	30.6 (0.28)	14.3 (0.62)	10.7 (0.46)	46.3 (1.48)	— (†)	— (†)	— (†)	— (†)
2000	27.8 (0.24)	30.8 (0.28)	16.4 (0.65)	10.7 (0.45)	48.1 (1.47)	— (†)	— (†)	— (†)	— (†)
2001	28.0 (0.24)	30.9 (0.28)	15.9 (0.64)	11.1 (0.45)	52.9 (1.33)	— (†)	— (†)	— (†)	— (†)
2002	28.5 (0.17)	31.7 (0.20)	16.5 (0.47)	11.0 (0.30)	51.5 (0.96)	— (†)	— (†)	— (†)	— (†)
2003	28.9 (0.17)	32.3 (0.20)	16.8 (0.47)	11.2 (0.29)	52.8 (0.96)	54.2 (0.98)	25.7 (3.76)	13.1 (1.85)	21.9 (1.69)
2004	29.4 (0.17)	32.9 (0.20)	16.6 (0.46)	11.8 (0.30)	52.9 (0.93)	54.0 (0.95)	31.9 (3.94)	15.6 (1.99)	20.7 (1.60)
2005	28.9 (0.29)	32.4 (0.37)	16.0 (0.64)	11.8 (0.43)	53.0 (1.10)	54.3 (1.13)	25.1 (4.70)	17.0 (2.30)	23.1 (1.67)
2006	29.2 (0.24)	32.8 (0.31)	17.5 (0.63)	11.9 (0.40)	51.9 (1.33)	53.1 (1.35)	26.6 (4.67)	13.7 (2.07)	22.6 (1.75)
2007	29.5 (0.25)	33.2 (0.33)	18.1 (0.62)	11.8 (0.37)	54.2 (1.31)	55.8 (1.32)	19.2 (4.14)	12.7 (1.89)	21.5 (1.81)
2008	30.1 (0.25)	33.8 (0.33)	18.7 (0.67)	12.6 (0.39)	54.9 (1.24)	56.1 (1.24)	27.5 (3.64)	14.6 (2.15)	22.7 (1.62)
2009	30.1 (0.28)	33.9 (0.36)	17.9 (0.57)	12.5 (0.41)	54.8 (1.14)	56.5 (1.17)	23.0 (3.35)	16.1 (2.96)	24.4 (1.92)
2010	30.3 (0.23)	34.2 (0.30)	17.9 (0.59)	12.9 (0.37)	54.6 (1.26)	56.2 (1.30)	18.0 (3.74)	13.5 (2.61)	24.8 (1.86)
2011	30.8 (0.23)	35.0 (0.29)	18.4 (0.64)	13.1 (0.34)	52.4 (1.15)	54.0 (1.21)	19.1 (3.55)	14.1 (1.98)	25.7 (1.91)
2012	31.4 (0.27)	35.5 (0.33)	19.5 (0.62)	13.3 (0.45)	53.0 (1.26)	54.4 (1.29)	24.1 (3.34)	16.1 (2.27)	25.2 (1.85)
2013	32.0 (0.25)	36.0 (0.31)	20.2 (0.64)	13.9 (0.43)	55.1 (1.17)	56.9 (1.20)	23.1 (3.32)	14.0 (2.13)	29.0 (1.78)
2014	31.9 (0.32)	35.9 (0.41)	21.0 (0.88)	14.2 (0.51)	53.7 (1.33)	55.5 (1.34)	16.7 (3.42)	14.8 (2.46)	29.2 (2.56)
2015	32.3 (0.27)	36.3 (0.35)	21.1 (0.63)	14.3 (0.38)	55.6 (1.11)	57.3 (1.16)	24.4 (2.87)	18.1 (2.14)	27.2 (2.14)

See notes at end of table.

Table 104.10.   Rates of high school completion and bachelor's degree attainment among persons age 25 and over, by race/ethnicity and sex: Selected years, 1910 through 2019—Continued

[Standard errors appear in parentheses]

Sex, high school or bachelor's degree attainment, and year	Total, percent of all persons age 25 and over	White[1]	Black[1]	Hispanic	Asian/Pacific Islander Total	Asian	Pacific Islander	American Indian/ Alaska Native	Two or more races
1	2	3	4	5	6	7	8	9	10
2016	33.2 (0.29)	37.2 (0.37)	21.8 (0.62)	15.4 (0.48)	57.7 (1.05)	59.4 (1.10)	22.2 (3.65)	16.5 (1.87)	25.6 (2.06)
2017	33.7 (0.28)	37.8 (0.37)	22.6 (0.61)	15.8 (0.41)	55.7 (1.10)	57.2 (1.14)	26.2 (3.61)	17.7 (1.93)	30.3 (1.87)
2018	34.6 (0.30)	38.9 (0.40)	23.7 (0.73)	16.6 (0.45)	58.5 (1.01)	60.1 (1.02)	23.6 (3.59)	15.4 (1.78)	30.0 (2.05)
2019	35.4 (0.30)	39.9 (0.43)	24.4 (0.72)	16.9 (0.43)	59.4 (1.00)	60.9 (1.01)	24.8 (4.02)	12.9 (1.59)	31.1 (2.11)
Females									
High school completion or higher[2]									
1940	26.3 (—)	28.1 (—)	8.4 (—)	— (†)	— (†)	— (†)	— (†)	— (†)	— (†)
1950	36.0 (—)	38.2 (—)	14.7 (—)	— (†)	— (†)	— (†)	— (†)	— (†)	— (†)
1960	42.5 (—)	44.7 (—)	23.1 (—)	— (†)	— (†)	— (†)	— (†)	— (†)	— (†)
1970	55.4 (—)	57.7 (—)	36.6 (—)	— (†)	— (†)	— (†)	— (†)	— (†)	— (†)
1980	68.1 (0.28)	71.5 (0.30)	51.5 (1.08)	44.2 (1.63)	— (†)	— (†)	— (†)	— (†)	— (†)
1990	77.5 (0.23)	81.3 (0.24)	66.5 (0.90)	51.3 (1.23)	82.5 (1.57)	— (†)	— (†)	— (†)	— (†)
1995	81.6 (0.21)	85.8 (0.22)	74.1 (0.81)	53.8 (1.09)	81.9 (1.54)	— (†)	— (†)	— (†)	— (†)
1996	81.6 (0.22)	85.9 (0.22)	74.6 (0.71)	53.3 (0.97)	81.0 (1.21)	— (†)	— (†)	— (†)	— (†)
1997	82.2 (0.20)	86.3 (0.20)	76.5 (0.68)	54.6 (0.76)	82.9 (1.11)	— (†)	— (†)	— (†)	— (†)
1998	82.9 (0.19)	87.1 (0.20)	77.1 (0.67)	55.3 (0.75)	82.3 (1.09)	— (†)	— (†)	— (†)	— (†)
1999	83.3 (0.19)	87.6 (0.19)	77.5 (0.66)	56.3 (0.73)	82.8 (1.06)	— (†)	— (†)	— (†)	— (†)
2000	84.0 (0.19)	88.4 (0.19)	78.7 (0.64)	57.5 (0.71)	83.4 (1.03)	— (†)	— (†)	— (†)	— (†)
2001	84.2 (0.18)	88.8 (0.19)	78.6 (0.64)	57.4 (0.70)	85.2 (0.91)	— (†)	— (†)	— (†)	— (†)
2002	84.4 (0.13)	88.9 (0.13)	79.4 (0.45)	57.9 (0.48)	85.7 (0.64)	— (†)	— (†)	— (†)	— (†)
2003	85.0 (0.13)	89.7 (0.13)	80.7 (0.44)	57.8 (0.46)	86.1 (0.62)	86.1 (0.64)	86.9 (2.63)	77.9 (2.30)	85.1 (1.38)
2004	85.4 (0.12)	90.1 (0.12)	81.2 (0.43)	59.5 (0.46)	85.3 (0.63)	85.1 (0.64)	88.1 (2.76)	78.6 (2.24)	86.5 (1.29)
2005	85.5 (0.15)	90.3 (0.18)	81.5 (0.53)	59.1 (0.63)	85.4 (0.76)	85.2 (0.78)	91.7 (2.46)	75.6 (2.29)	88.1 (1.12)
2006	85.9 (0.16)	90.8 (0.17)	81.5 (0.51)	60.1 (0.59)	85.6 (0.82)	85.6 (0.81)	85.7 (3.08)	78.9 (2.18)	88.2 (1.11)
2007	86.4 (0.15)	91.0 (0.16)	83.0 (0.49)	62.5 (0.56)	86.1 (0.93)	86.0 (0.97)	89.1 (2.40)	81.9 (1.91)	89.2 (1.22)
2008	87.2 (0.17)	91.8 (0.18)	84.2 (0.49)	63.7 (0.61)	87.2 (0.75)	87.0 (0.78)	93.0 (1.57)	79.2 (2.95)	89.5 (1.53)
2009	87.1 (0.16)	91.9 (0.17)	84.2 (0.48)	63.3 (0.59)	86.4 (0.73)	86.3 (0.75)	89.7 (2.33)	82.7 (1.96)	87.6 (1.16)
2010	87.6 (0.15)	92.3 (0.17)	85.0 (0.46)	64.4 (0.59)	87.2 (0.72)	87.1 (0.75)	90.9 (2.41)	82.5 (1.95)	89.7 (1.13)
2011	88.0 (0.15)	92.8 (0.16)	85.3 (0.50)	65.1 (0.57)	87.1 (0.64)	87.0 (0.66)	89.5 (2.25)	83.8 (2.00)	90.7 (1.22)
2012	88.0 (0.17)	92.7 (0.18)	86.1 (0.46)	66.0 (0.65)	87.9 (0.64)	87.8 (0.66)	90.1 (2.11)	81.8 (1.84)	91.6 (1.13)
2013	88.6 (0.16)	93.2 (0.16)	86.6 (0.46)	67.9 (0.55)	89.0 (0.61)	88.9 (0.63)	89.6 (2.01)	83.1 (2.16)	92.0 (0.95)
2014	88.9 (0.17)	93.7 (0.20)	87.0 (0.55)	67.9 (0.61)	87.4 (0.76)	87.4 (0.77)	87.8 (2.98)	81.6 (2.78)	92.8 (1.28)
2015	88.8 (0.14)	93.5 (0.15)	88.2 (0.43)	67.8 (0.53)	87.1 (0.60)	87.2 (0.62)	85.3 (2.46)	85.6 (2.10)	90.9 (1.14)
2016	89.6 (0.14)	94.3 (0.15)	88.3 (0.39)	69.7 (0.53)	89.3 (0.55)	89.2 (0.56)	91.8 (2.26)	85.2 (1.69)	92.8 (1.07)
2017	90.0 (0.14)	94.5 (0.14)	88.6 (0.43)	71.6 (0.52)	89.4 (0.54)	89.4 (0.56)	89.5 (2.20)	87.2 (1.52)	93.6 (0.92)
2018	90.2 (0.13)	94.7 (0.15)	88.7 (0.41)	72.5 (0.48)	88.6 (0.51)	88.6 (0.52)	89.1 (2.77)	87.4 (1.51)	93.7 (0.86)
2019	90.5 (0.13)	95.0 (0.14)	89.3 (0.43)	72.8 (0.49)	90.0 (0.52)	89.8 (0.54)	94.2 (1.63)	91.3 (1.30)	93.9 (1.02)
Bachelor's or higher degree[4]									
1940	3.8 (—)	4.0 (—)	1.2 (—)	— (†)	— (†)	— (†)	— (†)	— (†)	— (†)
1950	5.2 (—)	5.4 (—)	2.4 (—)	— (†)	— (†)	— (†)	— (†)	— (†)	— (†)
1960	5.8 (—)	6.0 (—)	3.6 (—)	— (†)	— (†)	— (†)	— (†)	— (†)	— (†)
1970	8.2 (—)	8.6 (—)	5.6 (—)	— (†)	— (†)	— (†)	— (†)	— (†)	— (†)
1980	13.6 (0.20)	14.4 (0.23)	8.1 (0.59)	6.2 (0.79)	— (†)	— (†)	— (†)	— (†)	— (†)
1990	18.4 (0.21)	19.8 (0.25)	10.8 (0.59)	8.7 (0.69)	37.8 (2.01)	— (†)	— (†)	— (†)	— (†)
1995	20.2 (0.22)	22.1 (0.26)	13.0 (0.62)	8.4 (0.61)	35.0 (1.90)	— (†)	— (†)	— (†)	— (†)
1996	21.4 (0.23)	23.2 (0.27)	14.8 (0.58)	8.3 (0.53)	38.0 (1.50)	— (†)	— (†)	— (†)	— (†)
1997	21.7 (0.21)	23.7 (0.25)	14.0 (0.56)	10.1 (0.46)	37.4 (1.43)	— (†)	— (†)	— (†)	— (†)
1998	22.4 (0.21)	24.1 (0.25)	15.4 (0.58)	10.9 (0.47)	38.9 (1.39)	— (†)	— (†)	— (†)	— (†)
1999	23.1 (0.22)	25.0 (0.26)	16.5 (0.59)	11.0 (0.46)	39.0 (1.37)	— (†)	— (†)	— (†)	— (†)
2000	23.6 (0.22)	25.5 (0.26)	16.8 (0.59)	10.6 (0.44)	41.0 (1.37)	— (†)	— (†)	— (†)	— (†)
2001	24.3 (0.22)	26.5 (0.26)	16.3 (0.58)	11.3 (0.45)	43.4 (1.26)	— (†)	— (†)	— (†)	— (†)
2002	25.1 (0.15)	27.3 (0.19)	17.7 (0.42)	11.2 (0.31)	44.2 (0.91)	— (†)	— (†)	— (†)	— (†)
2003	25.7 (0.15)	27.9 (0.19)	18.0 (0.43)	11.6 (0.30)	45.3 (0.89)	46.3 (0.92)	28.0 (3.50)	12.2 (1.81)	22.2 (1.61)
2004	26.1 (0.15)	28.4 (0.19)	18.5 (0.43)	12.3 (0.31)	45.2 (0.88)	45.7 (0.90)	32.9 (4.01)	13.1 (1.84)	22.7 (1.59)
2005	26.5 (0.23)	28.9 (0.30)	18.9 (0.51)	12.1 (0.42)	46.0 (1.08)	46.8 (1.10)	24.1 (4.08)	12.2 (2.00)	23.3 (1.43)
2006	26.9 (0.22)	29.3 (0.28)	19.5 (0.55)	12.9 (0.39)	46.6 (1.11)	47.3 (1.15)	27.2 (4.03)	12.3 (1.81)	23.6 (1.70)
2007	28.0 (0.23)	30.6 (0.29)	19.2 (0.59)	13.7 (0.44)	48.6 (1.07)	49.5 (1.10)	27.9 (4.16)	13.4 (1.53)	25.8 (1.58)
2008	28.8 (0.24)	31.5 (0.29)	20.5 (0.58)	14.1 (0.37)	49.3 (0.99)	50.1 (1.02)	29.3 (3.82)	15.1 (1.75)	26.1 (1.92)
2009	29.1 (0.21)	31.9 (0.26)	20.6 (0.56)	14.0 (0.41)	48.8 (0.98)	49.7 (1.02)	32.9 (3.74)	18.8 (1.91)	26.6 (1.67)
2010	29.6 (0.21)	32.4 (0.26)	21.6 (0.63)	14.9 (0.42)	49.1 (1.12)	49.9 (1.19)	32.2 (4.11)	18.2 (1.83)	25.7 (1.59)
2011	30.1 (0.22)	33.1 (0.28)	21.7 (0.60)	15.2 (0.43)	47.0 (1.04)	48.0 (1.07)	24.7 (3.52)	17.9 (2.17)	28.9 (1.70)
2012	30.6 (0.23)	33.5 (0.30)	22.9 (0.61)	15.8 (0.45)	48.6 (0.93)	49.7 (0.94)	24.9 (3.70)	17.2 (2.13)	28.8 (1.88)
2013	31.4 (0.24)	34.4 (0.31)	23.4 (0.61)	16.2 (0.42)	50.2 (0.94)	51.3 (0.96)	28.0 (3.44)	16.6 (2.05)	32.0 (1.89)
2014	32.0 (0.32)	35.3 (0.42)	24.2 (0.75)	16.1 (0.50)	49.3 (1.12)	50.4 (1.15)	27.1 (4.38)	13.1 (1.92)	33.1 (2.08)
2015	32.7 (0.25)	36.1 (0.32)	24.3 (0.60)	16.6 (0.42)	50.4 (0.82)	51.8 (0.85)	21.3 (3.13)	21.3 (1.71)	33.4 (1.96)
2016	33.7 (0.27)	37.3 (0.32)	24.8 (0.54)	17.4 (0.47)	52.9 (0.96)	53.8 (0.97)	32.4 (3.94)	17.0 (1.78)	35.0 (2.17)
2017	34.6 (0.28)	38.3 (0.36)	25.7 (0.59)	18.6 (0.48)	52.3 (0.94)	53.8 (0.97)	24.2 (3.54)	22.9 (2.73)	34.6 (1.87)
2018	35.3 (0.30)	38.8 (0.37)	27.1 (0.63)	20.1 (0.47)	53.1 (0.90)	54.4 (0.88)	24.6 (3.34)	21.7 (2.26)	34.4 (1.84)
2019	36.6 (0.25)	40.3 (0.34)	27.9 (0.61)	20.8 (0.46)	55.4 (0.83)	56.6 (0.82)	30.8 (3.50)	20.2 (1.95)	36.8 (1.98)

—Not available.
†Not applicable.
[1]Includes persons of Hispanic ethnicity for years prior to 1980.
[2]Data for years prior to 1993 are for persons with 4 or more years of high school. Data for later years are for high school completers—i.e., those persons who graduated from high school with a diploma as well as those who completed high school through equivalency programs, such as a GED program.
[3]Estimates based on Census Bureau reverse projection of 1940 census data on education by age.
[4]Data for years prior to 1993 are for persons with 4 or more years of college.

NOTE: Prior to 2005, standard errors were computed using generalized variance function methodology rather than the more precise replicate weight methodology used in later years. For 1960 and prior years, data were collected in April. For later years, data were collected in March. Race categories exclude persons of Hispanic ethnicity except where otherwise noted.
SOURCE: U.S. Department of Commerce, Census Bureau, *U.S. Census of Population: 1960*, Vol. I, Part 1; J.K. Folger and C.B. Nam, *Education of the American Population* (1960 Census Monograph); Current Population Reports, Series P-20, various years; and Current Population Survey (CPS), Annual Social and Economic Supplement, 1970 through 2019. (This table was prepared October 2019.)

Table 104.20. Percentage of persons 25 to 29 years old with selected levels of educational attainment, by race/ethnicity and sex: Selected years, 1920 through 2019

[Standard errors appear in parentheses]

Sex, selected level of educational attainment, and year	Total		White[1]		Black[1]		Hispanic		Asian/Pacific Islander						American Indian/ Alaska Native		Two or more races	
									Total		Asian		Pacific Islander					
1	2		3		4		5		6		7		8		9		10	
Total																		
High school completion or higher[2]																		
1920[3]	—	(†)	22.0	(—)	6.3	(—)	—	(†)	—	(†)	—	(†)	—	(†)	—	(†)	—	(†)
1940	38.1	(—)	41.2	(—)	12.3	(—)	—	(†)	—	(†)	—	(†)	—	(†)	—	(†)	—	(†)
1950	52.8	(—)	56.3	(—)	23.6	(—)	—	(†)	—	(†)	—	(†)	—	(†)	—	(†)	—	(†)
1960	60.7	(—)	63.7	(—)	38.6	(—)	—	(†)	—	(†)	—	(†)	—	(†)	—	(†)	—	(†)
1970	75.4	(—)	77.8	(—)	58.4	(—)	—	(†)	—	(†)	—	(†)	—	(†)	—	(†)	—	(†)
1980	85.4	(0.40)	89.2	(0.40)	76.7	(1.64)	58.0	(2.59)	—	(†)	—	(†)	—	(†)	—	(†)	—	(†)
1990	85.7	(0.38)	90.1	(0.37)	81.7	(1.37)	58.2	(1.94)	91.5	(2.09)	—	(†)	—	(†)	—	(†)	—	(†)
1995	86.8	(0.39)	92.5	(0.36)	86.7	(1.23)	57.1	(1.80)	90.8	(2.26)	—	(†)	—	(†)	81.5	(6.97)	—	(†)
2000	88.1	(0.37)	94.0	(0.33)	86.8	(1.13)	62.8	(1.22)	93.7	(1.27)	—	(†)	—	(†)	79.2	(5.19)	—	(†)
2005	86.2	(0.42)	92.8	(0.39)	87.0	(1.03)	63.3	(1.32)	95.6	(0.88)	95.5	(0.92)	99.5	(0.54)	80.2	(4.77)	91.4	(1.93)
2006	86.4	(0.36)	93.4	(0.35)	86.3	(1.09)	63.2	(1.17)	96.4	(0.88)	96.6	(0.86)	93.4	(3.70)	79.8	(5.19)	89.3	(2.70)
2007	87.0	(0.36)	93.5	(0.33)	87.7	(1.16)	65.0	(1.06)	96.8	(0.91)	97.5	(0.73)	86.2	(7.36)	84.5	(4.41)	90.5	(2.19)
2008	87.8	(0.36)	93.7	(0.38)	87.5	(1.29)	68.3	(1.16)	95.9	(0.86)	95.8	(0.91)	97.5	(2.09)	86.7	(3.36)	94.2	(1.72)
2009	88.6	(0.36)	94.6	(0.33)	88.9	(0.98)	68.9	(1.16)	95.4	(0.91)	95.8	(0.95)	91.6	(3.46)	81.1	(4.26)	88.5	(2.40)
2010	88.8	(0.32)	94.5	(0.31)	89.6	(0.93)	69.4	(1.22)	93.7	(1.18)	94.0	(1.24)	89.7	(5.05)	89.9	(2.98)	88.5	(2.76)
2011	89.0	(0.34)	94.4	(0.34)	88.1	(0.98)	71.5	(1.12)	95.4	(0.87)	95.3	(0.91)	98.3	(1.23)	84.9	(3.95)	90.7	(2.15)
2012	89.7	(0.38)	94.6	(0.37)	88.5	(0.96)	75.0	(1.16)	96.2	(0.73)	96.1	(0.77)	98.6	(0.83)	84.5	(3.94)	92.8	(2.22)
2013	89.9	(0.35)	94.1	(0.35)	90.3	(0.92)	75.8	(1.10)	95.4	(0.77)	95.4	(0.81)	95.5	(2.71)	84.7	(3.47)	97.4	(1.11)
2014	90.8	(0.39)	95.6	(0.41)	91.9	(0.93)	74.7	(1.31)	96.6	(0.76)	96.6	(0.79)	96.0	(2.19)	83.9	(4.67)	96.0	(2.01)
2015	91.2	(0.31)	95.4	(0.32)	92.5	(0.78)	77.1	(1.02)	95.3	(0.92)	95.8	(0.87)	87.2	(6.60)	86.7	(2.65)	94.9	(1.54)
2016	91.7	(0.34)	95.2	(0.33)	91.1	(0.92)	80.6	(1.01)	96.7	(0.68)	96.8	(0.68)	94.0	(3.90)	84.5	(4.13)	94.8	(1.49)
2017	92.5	(0.32)	95.6	(0.30)	92.3	(0.89)	82.7	(0.92)	96.4	(0.76)	96.8	(0.76)	90.1	(4.96)	84.6	(4.34)	94.8	(2.01)
2018	92.9	(0.32)	95.6	(0.37)	92.0	(0.86)	85.2	(0.89)	97.0	(0.70)	97.5	(0.71)	90.7	(3.86)	89.1	(3.06)	93.3	(1.68)
2019	93.5	(0.29)	96.3	(0.32)	91.5	(0.91)	86.4	(0.80)	96.9	(0.71)	96.9	(0.76)	97.3	(2.00)	94.8	(2.27)	95.5	(1.76)
Associate's or higher degree																		
1995	33.0	(0.54)	38.3	(0.67)	22.5	(1.52)	13.0	(1.23)	51.1	(3.91)	—	(†)	—	(†)	11.6!	(5.75)	—	(†)
2000	37.7	(0.55)	43.7	(0.70)	26.0	(1.47)	15.4	(0.91)	60.8	(2.55)	—	(†)	—	(†)	29.7	(5.84)	—	(†)
2005	37.3	(0.56)	43.9	(0.77)	26.5	(1.43)	17.3	(0.91)	66.4	(2.14)	68.7	(2.17)	17.8!	(6.08)	24.4	(4.13)	36.8	(3.99)
2006	37.6	(0.51)	45.1	(0.75)	25.3	(1.48)	16.1	(0.77)	66.7	(2.27)	68.6	(2.33)	33.5	(8.26)	18.2	(5.17)	31.6	(3.67)
2007	38.6	(0.55)	45.8	(0.77)	27.3	(1.36)	18.1	(0.77)	66.2	(2.08)	68.0	(2.11)	37.1	(8.93)	14.6	(4.27)	35.3	(3.80)
2008	39.7	(0.55)	47.6	(0.72)	27.6	(1.39)	18.7	(0.90)	65.1	(2.21)	66.9	(2.19)	35.3	(7.53)	20.9	(3.60)	33.5	(3.84)
2009	39.3	(0.58)	47.1	(0.83)	27.8	(1.43)	18.4	(0.89)	63.0	(2.21)	66.7	(2.23)	20.9	(5.84)	20.8	(4.05)	35.6	(3.76)
2010	41.1	(0.51)	48.9	(0.69)	29.4	(1.41)	20.5	(0.99)	60.5	(2.33)	63.4	(2.45)	22.0!	(7.92)	28.9	(6.19)	36.9	(3.57)
2011	42.1	(0.65)	50.1	(0.85)	29.8	(1.50)	20.6	(0.87)	63.6	(2.36)	64.6	(2.35)	39.7	(9.75)	25.0	(4.52)	42.0	(4.33)
2012	42.8	(0.58)	49.9	(0.80)	31.6	(1.40)	22.7	(1.01)	66.3	(1.96)	68.3	(2.01)	32.4	(6.33)	23.6	(4.32)	47.6	(3.76)
2013	43.2	(0.57)	51.0	(0.79)	29.5	(1.42)	23.1	(0.87)	65.5	(1.93)	67.2	(1.96)	37.3	(7.84)	26.3	(5.70)	44.2	(3.81)
2014	44.1	(0.75)	51.9	(1.01)	32.0	(1.98)	23.4	(1.18)	67.8	(2.35)	70.3	(2.40)	‡	(†)	18.2	(4.23)	40.8	(4.46)
2015	45.7	(0.53)	54.0	(0.78)	31.1	(1.41)	25.7	(1.01)	68.9	(2.09)	71.7	(2.13)	24.9	(6.58)	22.3	(3.65)	38.4	(3.56)
2016	46.1	(0.62)	54.3	(0.82)	31.7	(1.46)	27.0	(1.19)	69.5	(2.07)	71.5	(2.15)	28.6	(8.03)	16.5	(3.47)	41.3	(4.10)
2017	46.1	(0.61)	53.5	(0.83)	32.7	(1.35)	27.7	(1.00)	68.0	(2.11)	69.9	(2.10)	35.8	(8.65)	27.1	(5.97)	45.6	(3.86)
2018	46.7	(0.65)	53.6	(0.89)	32.6	(1.54)	30.5	(1.17)	72.2	(1.90)	75.5	(1.83)	22.6	(5.98)	24.4	(4.14)	41.5	(3.50)
2019	49.1	(0.65)	55.7	(0.87)	39.6	(1.90)	31.3	(1.04)	75.0	(1.67)	77.5	(1.71)	36.5	(7.07)	22.7	(4.34)	44.7	(3.81)
Bachelor's or higher degree[4]																		
1920[3]	—	(†)	4.5	(—)	1.2	(—)	—	(†)	—	(†)	—	(†)	—	(†)	—	(†)	—	(†)
1940	5.9	(—)	6.4	(—)	1.6	(—)	—	(†)	—	(†)	—	(†)	—	(†)	—	(†)	—	(†)
1950	7.7	(—)	8.2	(—)	2.8	(—)	—	(†)	—	(†)	—	(†)	—	(†)	—	(†)	—	(†)
1960	11.0	(—)	11.8	(—)	5.4	(—)	—	(†)	—	(†)	—	(†)	—	(†)	—	(†)	—	(†)
1970	16.4	(—)	17.3	(—)	10.0	(—)	—	(†)	—	(†)	—	(†)	—	(†)	—	(†)	—	(†)
1980	22.5	(0.47)	25.0	(0.55)	11.6	(1.24)	7.7	(1.39)	—	(†)	—	(†)	—	(†)	—	(†)	—	(†)
1990	23.2	(0.46)	26.4	(0.55)	13.4	(1.20)	8.1	(1.07)	43.0	(3.71)	—	(†)	—	(†)	—	(†)	—	(†)
1995	24.7	(0.49)	28.8	(0.62)	15.4	(1.31)	8.9	(1.04)	43.1	(3.87)	—	(†)	—	(†)	‡	(†)	—	(†)
2000	29.1	(0.52)	34.0	(0.67)	17.8	(1.28)	9.7	(0.75)	54.3	(2.60)	—	(†)	—	(†)	15.9	(4.68)	—	(†)
2005	28.8	(0.55)	34.5	(0.78)	17.6	(1.21)	11.2	(0.81)	60.0	(2.20)	62.1	(2.25)	17.0!	(6.01)	16.4	(3.56)	28.0	(3.79)
2006	28.4	(0.52)	34.3	(0.78)	18.7	(1.33)	9.5	(0.66)	59.6	(2.39)	61.9	(2.44)	20.7!	(6.70)	9.5!	(4.26)	23.3	(3.14)
2007	29.6	(0.54)	35.5	(0.75)	19.5	(1.21)	11.6	(0.61)	59.4	(2.24)	61.5	(2.26)	26.5!	(8.25)	6.4!	(2.99)	26.3	(3.44)
2008	30.8	(0.51)	37.1	(0.70)	20.4	(1.35)	12.4	(0.69)	57.9	(2.26)	60.2	(2.32)	20.2!	(6.75)	14.3	(3.17)	26.6	(3.75)
2009	30.6	(0.57)	37.2	(0.85)	18.9	(1.36)	12.2	(0.80)	56.4	(2.25)	60.3	(2.28)	12.5!	(4.44)	15.9	(3.73)	29.7	(3.84)
2010	31.7	(0.51)	38.6	(0.72)	19.4	(1.20)	13.5	(0.80)	52.5	(2.32)	55.8	(2.47)	10.0!	(4.40)	18.6	(4.80)	29.8	(3.22)
2011	32.2	(0.62)	39.2	(0.88)	20.1	(1.25)	12.8	(0.73)	56.0	(2.50)	57.2	(2.52)	28.8!	(9.04)	17.3	(4.45)	32.4	(3.85)
2012	33.5	(0.58)	39.8	(0.78)	23.2	(1.38)	14.8	(0.90)	59.6	(2.17)	61.7	(2.24)	25.5	(6.12)	10.4	(2.87)	32.9	(3.72)
2013	33.6	(0.55)	40.4	(0.77)	20.5	(1.38)	15.7	(0.82)	58.0	(2.16)	60.1	(2.18)	24.7!	(7.54)	16.6	(4.89)	29.6	(3.45)
2014	34.0	(0.75)	40.8	(1.05)	22.4	(1.82)	15.1	(0.97)	60.8	(2.44)	63.2	(2.50)	‡	(†)	5.6!	(2.24)	32.4	(4.12)
2015	35.6	(0.55)	43.0	(0.83)	21.3	(1.33)	16.4	(0.78)	62.8	(2.25)	66.0	(2.27)	11.4!	(4.64)	15.3	(3.21)	29.6	(3.62)
2016	36.1	(0.61)	42.9	(0.87)	22.7	(1.26)	18.7	(1.06)	63.5	(2.11)	65.6	(2.20)	20.4!	(6.62)	10.2	(2.57)	28.3	(3.76)
2017	35.7	(0.63)	42.1	(0.88)	23.8	(1.37)	18.5	(0.82)	60.6	(2.22)	62.7	(2.28)	25.3	(7.04)	16.3!	(5.22)	32.8	(3.84)
2018	37.0	(0.66)	43.5	(0.96)	22.6	(1.39)	20.7	(1.03)	67.1	(2.10)	70.5	(2.08)	15.1	(4.53)	15.5	(3.30)	26.9	(3.01)
2019	38.7	(0.62)	44.9	(0.88)	29.1	(1.64)	20.6	(0.86)	68.3	(1.94)	71.4	(1.96)	21.6	(6.22)	13.6	(3.59)	34.3	(3.68)

See notes at end of table.

Table 104.20. Percentage of persons 25 to 29 years old with selected levels of educational attainment, by race/ethnicity and sex: Selected years, 1920 through 2019—Continued

[Standard errors appear in parentheses]

Sex, selected level of educational attainment, and year	Total		White[1]		Black[1]		Hispanic		Asian/Pacific Islander						American Indian/ Alaska Native		Two or more races	
									Total		Asian		Pacific Islander					
1	2		3		4		5		6		7		8		9		10	
Master's or higher degree																		
1995	4.5	(0.24)	5.3	(0.31)	1.8	(0.48)	1.6	(0.46)	10.9	(2.43)	—	(†)	—	(†)	‡	(†)	—	(†)
2000	5.4	(0.26)	5.8	(0.33)	3.7	(0.63)	2.1	(0.36)	15.5	(1.89)	—	(†)	—	(†)	‡	(†)	—	(†)
2005	6.3	(0.31)	7.5	(0.45)	2.6	(0.44)	2.1	(0.38)	16.9	(1.93)	17.5	(2.01)	‡	(†)	‡	(†)	7.0!	(2.49)
2006	6.4	(0.29)	7.5	(0.42)	3.2	(0.58)	1.5	(0.25)	20.1	(2.00)	21.1	(2.10)	‡	(†)	‡	(†)	7.1	(1.83)
2007	6.3	(0.30)	7.6	(0.42)	3.5	(0.59)	1.5	(0.25)	17.5	(1.84)	18.5	(1.93)	‡	(†)	‡	(†)	6.2!	(2.38)
2008	7.0	(0.28)	8.2	(0.40)	4.4	(0.64)	2.0	(0.28)	19.9	(1.84)	21.0	(1.96)	‡	(†)	‡	(†)	6.9!	(2.57)
2009	7.4	(0.30)	8.9	(0.45)	4.2	(0.54)	1.9	(0.26)	21.1	(1.98)	22.9	(2.16)	‡	(†)	‡	(†)	6.5!	(2.02)
2010	6.8	(0.26)	7.7	(0.38)	4.7	(0.60)	2.5	(0.37)	17.9	(1.87)	19.2	(1.99)	‡	(†)	‡	(†)	5.3!	(1.63)
2011	6.9	(0.32)	8.1	(0.45)	4.0	(0.52)	2.7	(0.37)	16.7	(1.78)	17.5	(1.85)	‡	(†)	‡	(†)	6.1	(1.59)
2012	7.2	(0.35)	8.2	(0.51)	5.1	(0.66)	2.7	(0.36)	17.8	(1.85)	18.9	(1.92)	‡	(†)	2.6!	(1.28)	4.1!	(1.49)
2013	7.4	(0.31)	8.6	(0.50)	3.3	(0.50)	3.0	(0.37)	20.6	(1.73)	21.8	(1.79)	‡	(†)	‡	(†)	4.8!	(1.54)
2014	7.6	(0.41)	9.0	(0.58)	3.9	(0.77)	2.9	(0.43)	17.9	(1.84)	18.8	(1.92)	‡	(†)	‡	(†)	7.1!	(2.32)
2015	8.7	(0.33)	10.1	(0.51)	5.0	(0.60)	3.2	(0.41)	21.6	(1.85)	22.8	(1.97)	‡	(†)	‡	(†)	7.8	(1.79)
2016	9.2	(0.33)	10.5	(0.52)	5.2	(0.69)	4.1	(0.49)	23.8	(1.95)	24.9	(2.01)	‡	(†)	2.1!	(0.85)	5.3!	(1.74)
2017	9.2	(0.34)	10.1	(0.55)	5.5	(0.71)	3.9	(0.40)	24.5	(1.76)	25.6	(1.89)	‡	(†)	‡	(†)	5.0!	(1.72)
2018	9.0	(0.36)	10.1	(0.62)	4.5	(0.65)	3.4	(0.43)	27.5	(1.87)	29.2	(1.98)	‡	(†)	‡	(†)	2.9!	(1.44)
2019	9.4	(0.36)	10.3	(0.52)	6.2	(0.80)	3.4	(0.40)	27.1	(1.79)	28.9	(1.90)	‡	(†)	‡	(†)	10.4	(2.52)
Males																		
High school completion or higher[2]																		
1980	85.4	(0.49)	89.1	(0.48)	74.7	(1.97)	57.0	(3.45)	—	(†)	—	(†)	—	(†)	—	(†)	—	(†)
1990	84.4	(0.56)	88.6	(0.57)	81.4	(2.03)	56.6	(2.69)	95.3	(1.78)	—	(†)	—	(†)	—	(†)	—	(†)
1995	86.3	(0.56)	92.0	(0.53)	88.4	(1.72)	55.7	(2.51)	90.5	(3.11)	—	(†)	—	(†)	83.6	(9.73)	—	(†)
2000	86.7	(0.55)	92.9	(0.51)	87.6	(1.67)	59.2	(1.76)	92.1	(2.03)	—	(†)	—	(†)	68.5	(9.40)	—	(†)
2005	85.0	(0.58)	91.8	(0.53)	86.6	(1.76)	63.2	(1.72)	96.8	(1.09)	96.7	(1.15)	99.1	(0.94)	73.0	(8.43)	89.1	(3.07)
2006	84.4	(0.54)	92.3	(0.52)	84.2	(2.02)	60.5	(1.64)	97.2	(1.01)	97.2	(1.06)	97.8	(1.60)	75.0	(6.34)	89.2	(3.81)
2007	84.9	(0.50)	92.7	(0.48)	87.4	(1.65)	60.5	(1.59)	95.9	(1.13)	96.3	(1.10)	‡	(†)	76.6	(8.90)	92.9	(2.64)
2008	85.8	(0.54)	92.6	(0.58)	85.7	(1.99)	65.6	(1.55)	95.6	(1.23)	95.4	(1.31)	100.0	(0.00)	90.5	(4.04)	92.7	(2.68)
2009	87.5	(0.51)	94.4	(0.46)	88.8	(1.56)	66.2	(1.54)	96.4	(1.17)	96.2	(1.25)	98.2	(1.81)	77.5	(8.59)	92.0	(3.01)
2010	87.4	(0.44)	94.6	(0.42)	87.9	(1.52)	65.7	(1.52)	93.8	(1.83)	93.5	(1.95)	98.2	(1.35)	93.2	(3.47)	87.9	(4.32)
2011	87.5	(0.49)	93.4	(0.48)	88.0	(1.43)	69.2	(1.62)	94.2	(1.30)	93.9	(1.36)	98.5	(1.46)	84.5	(5.28)	86.2	(4.41)
2012	88.4	(0.51)	93.8	(0.50)	86.2	(1.58)	73.3	(1.57)	96.1	(1.04)	96.0	(1.09)	97.3	(1.74)	82.8	(8.27)	91.0	(3.58)
2013	88.3	(0.52)	93.3	(0.53)	87.8	(1.60)	73.1	(1.64)	94.4	(1.12)	94.3	(1.21)	96.3	(3.04)	89.0	(3.25)	96.8	(1.77)
2014	90.1	(0.53)	95.4	(0.60)	93.5	(1.18)	72.4	(1.76)	96.1	(1.10)	96.1	(1.14)	‡	(†)	83.5	(7.17)	96.9	(2.02)
2015	90.5	(0.45)	95.1	(0.45)	91.8	(1.22)	75.7	(1.41)	95.9	(1.23)	97.1	(0.96)	75.8	(12.49)	83.2	(4.73)	98.0	(1.27)
2016	90.9	(0.46)	94.8	(0.44)	91.7	(1.19)	78.3	(1.34)	96.0	(1.06)	96.2	(1.05)	‡	(†)	84.4	(5.70)	98.1	(1.22)
2017	91.5	(0.48)	94.8	(0.46)	92.0	(1.19)	80.7	(1.31)	97.3	(0.77)	97.7	(0.75)	89.3	(6.87)	76.5	(8.11)	95.9	(2.38)
2018	91.9	(0.44)	95.0	(0.53)	90.7	(1.37)	83.4	(1.22)	97.1	(0.92)	97.6	(0.96)	89.3	(6.35)	82.9	(5.67)	92.8	(2.42)
2019	92.7	(0.39)	96.2	(0.42)	89.8	(1.41)	84.6	(1.11)	96.8	(0.98)	96.9	(1.00)	‡	(†)	92.1	(4.18)	93.8	(3.00)
Associate's or higher degree																		
1995	32.1	(0.76)	37.1	(0.94)	23.5	(2.28)	11.6	(1.62)	49.8	(5.30)	—	(†)	—	(†)	‡	(†)	—	(†)
2000	35.3	(0.78)	40.7	(0.98)	24.1	(2.16)	13.0	(1.20)	60.7	(3.68)	—	(†)	—	(†)	17.6!	(7.71)	—	(†)
2005	33.4	(0.74)	39.6	(1.05)	22.7	(1.77)	16.1	(1.12)	64.0	(3.16)	66.7	(3.19)	18.5!	(7.78)	19.9!	(7.06)	31.0	(5.10)
2006	33.8	(0.67)	41.5	(0.97)	21.3	(2.02)	12.8	(1.02)	65.4	(3.32)	67.9	(3.37)	25.6!	(9.90)	18.9!	(6.54)	28.4	(5.26)
2007	34.1	(0.76)	40.8	(1.01)	26.4	(2.06)	13.8	(0.96)	64.5	(3.04)	66.3	(3.12)	‡	(†)	14.9!	(6.39)	30.8	(5.22)
2008	34.7	(0.72)	42.2	(0.98)	24.2	(2.16)	15.2	(1.05)	61.5	(3.23)	62.8	(3.21)	41.3	(11.71)	22.0!	(6.95)	29.9	(4.62)
2009	34.5	(0.66)	41.8	(1.04)	21.9	(1.97)	15.9	(1.16)	63.0	(2.86)	66.6	(2.99)	17.4!	(8.42)	17.1!	(7.26)	31.7	(5.35)
2010	36.1	(0.68)	44.5	(0.98)	22.9	(2.16)	16.0	(1.20)	57.4	(3.12)	61.1	(3.27)	‡	(†)	30.1	(8.14)	31.5	(5.23)
2011	37.0	(0.88)	45.2	(1.17)	25.9	(2.24)	16.1	(1.18)	57.9	(3.40)	58.8	(3.48)	42.9	(12.13)	22.0	(5.29)	38.4	(7.04)
2012	38.2	(0.81)	44.8	(1.11)	25.3	(1.92)	20.6	(1.45)	63.4	(3.00)	65.5	(2.94)	28.8!	(10.22)	15.7!	(5.97)	46.3	(5.90)
2013	38.5	(0.69)	46.0	(1.03)	24.8	(1.76)	20.0	(1.20)	61.2	(2.74)	62.6	(2.80)	39.3	(11.03)	27.5	(7.59)	42.8	(5.00)
2014	39.4	(0.95)	47.4	(1.35)	28.9	(2.66)	18.2	(1.40)	63.5	(3.37)	66.0	(3.41)	‡	(†)	23.7!	(8.06)	33.5	(6.67)
2015	41.3	(0.73)	49.3	(1.15)	24.6	(2.00)	22.7	(1.32)	67.1	(3.01)	69.5	(2.93)	26.0!	(9.45)	17.7!	(5.36)	37.7	(5.16)
2016	41.8	(0.87)	49.9	(1.19)	28.3	(2.21)	23.4	(1.56)	68.2	(2.90)	68.2	(2.90)	‡	(†)	13.7!	(4.53)	27.7	(5.03)
2017	41.3	(0.86)	48.3	(1.22)	29.5	(2.22)	22.0	(1.33)	64.8	(2.85)	66.0	(2.88)	38.6!	(11.88)	19.4!	(7.61)	41.0	(5.82)
2018	42.0	(0.85)	47.8	(1.22)	29.1	(2.36)	27.3	(1.49)	71.2	(2.69)	74.1	(2.67)	21.2!	(8.56)	15.6!	(4.70)	34.9	(5.45)
2019	44.9	(0.86)	50.6	(1.15)	37.6	(2.75)	26.8	(1.41)	73.8	(2.46)	75.6	(2.55)	‡	(†)	16.1!	(5.28)	45.2	(5.46)
Bachelor's or higher degree[4]																		
1980	24.0	(0.59)	26.8	(0.69)	10.5	(1.39)	8.4	(1.94)	—	(†)	—	(†)	—	(†)	—	(†)	—	(†)
1990	23.7	(0.65)	26.6	(0.79)	15.1	(1.87)	7.3	(1.41)	47.6	(4.19)	—	(†)	—	(†)	—	(†)	—	(†)
1995	24.5	(0.70)	28.4	(0.88)	17.4	(2.04)	7.8	(1.35)	42.0	(5.23)	—	(†)	—	(†)	‡	(†)	—	(†)
2000	27.9	(0.73)	32.3	(0.93)	18.4	(1.96)	8.3	(0.98)	55.5	(3.74)	—	(†)	—	(†)	‡	(†)	—	(†)
2005	25.5	(0.68)	30.7	(0.98)	14.2	(1.57)	10.2	(0.99)	58.5	(3.11)	61.0	(3.17)	17.2!	(7.62)	14.5!	(6.14)	24.5	(4.93)
2006	25.3	(0.67)	31.4	(0.98)	15.2	(1.66)	6.9	(0.70)	58.7	(3.46)	60.9	(3.52)	23.3!	(9.77)	‡	(†)	20.8	(4.65)
2007	26.3	(0.72)	31.9	(0.98)	18.9	(1.86)	8.6	(0.71)	58.5	(3.45)	60.4	(3.54)	‡	(†)	‡	(†)	23.3	(4.88)
2008	26.8	(0.64)	32.6	(0.89)	19.0	(1.94)	10.0	(0.86)	54.1	(3.41)	55.8	(3.53)	26.1!	(9.86)	17.7!	(6.67)	25.7	(4.45)
2009	26.6	(0.66)	32.6	(1.04)	14.8	(1.82)	11.0	(1.04)	55.2	(3.07)	59.2	(3.24)	‡	(†)	15.2!	(7.21)	24.6	(5.77)
2010	27.8	(0.68)	34.8	(0.96)	15.0	(1.72)	10.8	(1.06)	49.0	(3.12)	52.3	(3.31)	‡	(†)	18.9!	(7.12)	24.9	(4.91)
2011	28.4	(0.82)	35.5	(1.16)	17.0	(1.83)	9.6	(0.90)	50.8	(3.42)	52.1	(3.55)	28.1!	(11.40)	15.4!	(4.80)	34.1	(6.62)
2012	29.8	(0.82)	36.0	(1.06)	19.1	(1.74)	12.5	(1.20)	55.0	(3.15)	56.9	(3.16)	24.3!	(9.06)	‡	(†)	30.4	(5.43)
2013	30.2	(0.68)	37.1	(1.00)	17.4	(1.63)	13.1	(1.06)	53.0	(3.03)	55.1	(3.13)	19.0!	(9.38)	16.8!	(6.40)	29.3	(4.61)
2014	30.9	(0.93)	37.7	(1.36)	20.8	(2.40)	12.4	(1.22)	56.9	(3.55)	59.0	(3.59)	‡	(†)	‡	(†)	26.4	(6.13)
2015	32.4	(0.74)	39.5	(1.12)	17.6	(1.83)	14.5	(1.04)	60.9	(3.13)	63.8	(3.12)	‡	(†)	‡	(†)	26.7	(5.07)

See notes at end of table.

Table 104.20.   Percentage of persons 25 to 29 years old with selected levels of educational attainment, by race/ethnicity and sex: Selected years, 1920 through 2019—Continued

[Standard errors appear in parentheses]

Sex, selected level of educational attainment, and year	Total	White[1]	Black[1]	Hispanic	Asian/Pacific Islander Total	Asian	Pacific Islander	American Indian/ Alaska Native	Two or more races
1	2	3	4	5	6	7	8	9	10
2016	32.7 (0.80)	39.5 (1.20)	20.4 (1.87)	16.2 (1.31)	59.0 (2.86)	61.4 (2.98)	‡ (†)	7.8! (3.17)	19.7 (4.52)
2017	32.0 (0.81)	37.7 (1.19)	21.7 (1.79)	15.0 (1.13)	57.7 (2.92)	59.2 (3.00)	26.4! (10.58)	‡ (†)	26.1 (5.48)
2018	33.2 (0.85)	38.8 (1.32)	18.7 (1.95)	18.4 (1.34)	66.7 (2.97)	69.6 (2.97)	17.3! (8.00)	8.4! (3.50)	25.1 (4.93)
2019	35.7 (0.83)	40.8 (1.17)	28.3 (2.30)	18.2 (1.23)	67.6 (2.73)	70.1 (2.79)	‡ (†)	6.4! (3.12)	36.7 (5.14)
Master's or higher degree									
1995	4.9 (0.35)	5.6 (0.45)	2.2! (0.80)	2.0! (0.70)	12.6 (3.52)	— (†)	— (†)	‡ (†)	— (†)
2000	4.7 (0.34)	4.9 (0.43)	2.1! (0.72)	1.5 (0.43)	17.2 (2.85)	— (†)	— (†)	‡ (†)	— (†)
2005	5.2 (0.38)	6.2 (0.55)	1.1! (0.43)	1.7 (0.46)	19.7 (3.13)	20.5 (3.30)	‡ (†)	‡ (†)	‡ (†)
2006	5.1 (0.37)	5.8 (0.51)	1.7! (0.52)	1.1 (0.32)	20.5 (2.68)	21.8 (2.83)	‡ (†)	‡ (†)	5.9! (2.66)
2007	5.0 (0.39)	5.7 (0.50)	3.3 (0.99)	0.6! (0.19)	18.4 (2.89)	19.3 (3.00)	‡ (†)	‡ (†)	9.8! (4.28)
2008	5.3 (0.34)	5.9 (0.49)	3.4 (0.90)	1.2 (0.32)	20.9 (2.94)	22.1 (3.07)	‡ (†)	‡ (†)	7.8! (2.85)
2009	6.1 (0.37)	7.4 (0.60)	3.2 (0.73)	1.2 (0.48)	20.4 (2.48)	22.0 (2.69)	‡ (†)	‡ (†)	5.0! (2.38)
2010	5.2 (0.32)	6.3 (0.50)	2.9 (0.69)	1.5 (0.39)	15.0 (2.19)	16.2 (2.36)	‡ (†)	‡ (†)	‡ (†)
2011	5.1 (0.38)	5.9 (0.49)	1.9 (0.54)	1.8 (0.41)	18.0 (2.58)	19.1 (2.71)	‡ (†)	‡ (†)	‡ (†)
2012	5.6 (0.42)	6.3 (0.59)	2.7 (0.72)	2.4 (0.50)	16.2 (2.46)	17.2 (2.60)	‡ (†)	‡ (†)	‡ (†)
2013	5.7 (0.38)	6.3 (0.53)	1.5! (0.56)	2.1 (0.43)	20.8 (2.49)	22.1 (2.60)	‡ (†)	‡ (†)	5.9! (2.47)
2014	5.9 (0.51)	7.0 (0.72)	2.6! (0.82)	2.2 (0.52)	15.9 (2.56)	16.6 (2.65)	‡ (†)	‡ (†)	‡ (†)
2015	7.0 (0.40)	8.2 (0.62)	2.5 (0.75)	2.3 (0.56)	21.1 (2.65)	22.4 (2.78)	‡ (†)	‡ (†)	5.6! (2.37)
2016	7.2 (0.43)	8.7 (0.68)	3.9 (0.87)	2.1 (0.43)	19.7 (2.73)	20.6 (2.85)	‡ (†)	‡ (†)	‡ (†)
2017	7.8 (0.42)	8.5 (0.64)	3.9 (0.89)	2.8 (0.52)	24.3 (2.52)	25.4 (2.63)	‡ (†)	‡ (†)	‡ (†)
2018	7.3 (0.44)	7.7 (0.70)	2.8 (0.74)	3.1 (0.56)	27.0 (2.81)	28.6 (2.95)	‡ (†)	‡ (†)	‡ (†)
2019	7.7 (0.43)	8.0 (0.61)	3.8 (0.90)	2.2 (0.45)	29.1 (2.86)	30.3 (2.96)	‡ (†)	‡ (†)	11.7! (3.59)
Females									
High school completion or higher[2]									
1980	85.5 (0.48)	89.2 (0.48)	78.3 (1.71)	58.9 (3.38)	— (†)	— (†)	— (†)	— (†)	— (†)
1990	87.0 (0.51)	91.7 (0.49)	82.0 (1.85)	59.9 (2.79)	85.1 (2.82)	— (†)	— (†)	— (†)	— (†)
1995	87.4 (0.54)	93.0 (0.50)	85.3 (1.75)	58.7 (2.60)	91.2 (3.28)	— (†)	— (†)	79.6 (9.88)	— (†)
2000	89.4 (0.49)	95.2 (0.43)	86.2 (1.53)	66.4 (1.69)	95.2 (1.55)	— (†)	— (†)	86.3 (5.68)	— (†)
2005	87.4 (0.44)	93.8 (0.47)	87.3 (1.22)	63.4 (1.54)	94.6 (1.36)	94.4 (1.41)	‡ (†)	87.1 (5.12)	94.2 (2.26)
2006	88.5 (0.44)	94.6 (0.41)	88.0 (1.14)	66.6 (1.41)	95.6 (1.44)	96.0 (1.31)	‡ (†)	83.3 (6.55)	89.4 (3.81)
2007	89.1 (0.45)	94.2 (0.44)	87.9 (1.46)	70.7 (1.30)	97.7 (1.05)	98.5 (0.68)	86.0 (8.19)	90.2 (4.49)	87.9 (3.82)
2008	89.9 (0.39)	94.7 (0.44)	89.2 (1.43)	71.9 (1.34)	96.1 (1.12)	96.2 (1.18)	95.2 (4.01)	84.2 (4.68)	95.9 (2.44)
2009	89.8 (0.41)	94.8 (0.44)	89.0 (1.12)	72.5 (1.34)	94.5 (1.20)	95.3 (1.18)	86.2 (5.92)	83.4 (4.81)	84.8 (3.57)
2010	90.2 (0.39)	94.4 (0.42)	91.1 (0.96)	74.1 (1.53)	93.6 (1.25)	94.5 (1.27)	81.2 (9.50)	86.8 (4.80)	89.1 (3.55)
2011	90.7 (0.36)	95.5 (0.42)	88.2 (1.24)	74.3 (1.26)	96.6 (0.89)	96.6 (0.92)	‡ (†)	85.3 (6.02)	94.0 (2.52)
2012	91.1 (0.44)	95.3 (0.46)	90.6 (1.11)	76.9 (1.39)	96.3 (0.98)	96.1 (1.04)	100.0 (0.00)	85.8 (4.53)	94.7 (2.35)
2013	91.5 (0.38)	94.9 (0.43)	92.5 (0.95)	78.8 (1.17)	96.2 (0.96)	96.3 (1.01)	94.8 (2.88)	82.0 (5.40)	98.2 (1.15)
2014	91.5 (0.38)	95.9 (0.46)	90.5 (1.62)	77.4 (1.56)	97.1 (0.96)	97.1 (0.99)	‡ (†)	84.1 (6.05)	95.2 (3.44)
2015	91.8 (0.39)	95.8 (0.41)	93.2 (0.90)	78.6 (1.34)	94.8 (1.18)	94.6 (1.25)	96.7 (1.86)	89.3 (3.52)	91.5 (2.99)
2016	92.5 (0.40)	95.7 (0.41)	90.7 (1.33)	83.2 (1.22)	97.4 (0.76)	97.4 (0.79)	‡ (†)	84.6 (5.34)	91.5 (2.76)
2017	93.4 (0.34)	96.4 (0.39)	92.6 (1.22)	84.8 (1.04)	95.5 (1.10)	95.8 (1.16)	90.7 (4.70)	90.9 (3.70)	94.0 (3.24)
2018	94.0 (0.39)	96.3 (0.44)	93.2 (0.95)	87.2 (1.13)	97.0 (0.91)	97.4 (0.85)	91.8 (6.23)	95.1 (2.18)	93.8 (2.49)
2019	94.3 (0.36)	96.4 (0.41)	93.1 (1.06)	88.4 (0.98)	97.1 (0.95)	96.9 (1.02)	98.9 (1.09)	97.5 (1.87)	97.0 (1.69)
Associate's or higher degree									
1995	34.0 (0.77)	39.5 (0.95)	21.6 (2.03)	14.6 (1.86)	52.6 (5.77)	— (†)	— (†)	‡ (†)	— (†)
2000	40.1 (0.78)	46.6 (1.00)	27.5 (1.99)	17.7 (1.37)	60.8 (3.54)	— (†)	— (†)	37.7 (8.00)	— (†)
2005	41.3 (0.72)	48.2 (0.99)	29.8 (1.81)	18.8 (1.23)	68.5 (2.86)	70.4 (2.90)	‡ (†)	28.7 (6.96)	43.7 (6.04)
2006	41.5 (0.72)	48.8 (1.00)	28.8 (1.91)	20.3 (1.17)	68.0 (2.60)	69.4 (2.65)	‡ (†)	17.6! (6.91)	34.7 (5.09)
2007	43.2 (0.72)	50.8 (1.02)	28.0 (1.61)	23.5 (1.25)	67.7 (2.73)	69.6 (2.88)	42.5 (11.79)	14.5! (5.53)	40.2 (5.87)
2008	44.9 (0.77)	53.0 (1.00)	30.7 (1.79)	23.2 (1.43)	68.5 (2.80)	70.8 (2.82)	29.5! (9.83)	20.2 (4.14)	37.6 (5.73)
2009	44.4 (0.75)	52.5 (1.02)	33.0 (1.79)	21.7 (1.22)	63.0 (3.19)	66.8 (3.13)	23.6! (8.47)	23.3 (5.09)	39.8 (5.19)
2010	46.3 (0.71)	53.5 (0.92)	35.2 (1.77)	26.2 (1.48)	63.3 (2.68)	65.6 (2.80)	31.4! (13.43)	27.7 (8.27)	41.8 (5.08)
2011	47.4 (0.74)	55.2 (1.00)	33.3 (1.92)	26.2 (1.29)	69.1 (2.50)	70.2 (2.48)	‡ (†)	28.7 (7.46)	44.5 (5.08)
2012	47.4 (0.68)	55.0 (0.94)	37.0 (1.80)	25.1 (1.23)	69.1 (2.22)	71.0 (2.29)	36.1 (9.80)	29.2 (6.04)	49.0 (5.15)
2013	47.9 (0.77)	56.1 (0.99)	33.6 (1.99)	26.8 (1.30)	69.2 (2.29)	71.2 (2.33)	35.5 (10.28)	25.6 (7.48)	46.0 (6.22)
2014	48.9 (0.99)	56.5 (1.28)	34.8 (2.77)	29.4 (1.67)	71.5 (3.14)	74.1 (3.18)	‡ (†)	15.7! (5.27)	48.2 (6.06)
2015	50.1 (0.72)	58.7 (0.98)	36.9 (1.78)	29.0 (1.47)	70.7 (2.55)	73.8 (2.61)	24.0! (9.77)	25.8 (4.73)	39.2 (5.20)
2016	50.5 (0.71)	58.7 (0.95)	34.8 (1.73)	31.0 (1.51)	72.6 (2.49)	74.5 (2.56)	‡ (†)	18.9 (4.75)	54.5 (5.59)
2017	51.0 (0.73)	58.8 (1.04)	35.5 (1.69)	33.9 (1.34)	71.2 (2.77)	73.9 (2.71)	34.0! (10.51)	33.1 (7.83)	49.6 (5.82)
2018	51.5 (0.82)	59.6 (1.17)	35.8 (1.86)	34.2 (1.56)	73.1 (2.31)	76.9 (2.21)	23.6! (8.51)	32.8 (6.29)	48.2 (5.45)
2019	53.5 (0.77)	60.9 (1.12)	41.4 (2.20)	36.2 (1.44)	76.1 (2.03)	79.5 (2.12)	38.1 (8.05)	29.2 (6.55)	44.2 (5.30)
Bachelor's or higher degree[4]									
1980	21.0 (0.56)	23.2 (0.65)	12.4 (1.36)	6.9 (1.74)	— (†)	— (†)	— (†)	— (†)	— (†)
1990	22.8 (0.64)	26.2 (0.78)	11.9 (1.56)	9.1 (1.64)	37.4 (3.83)	— (†)	— (†)	— (†)	— (†)
1995	24.9 (0.70)	29.2 (0.89)	13.7 (1.70)	10.1 (1.59)	44.5 (5.74)	— (†)	— (†)	‡ (†)	— (†)
2000	30.1 (0.73)	35.8 (0.96)	17.4 (1.69)	11.0 (1.12)	53.1 (3.62)	— (†)	— (†)	19.1! (6.48)	— (†)
2005	32.2 (0.75)	38.2 (1.00)	20.5 (1.68)	12.4 (1.07)	61.4 (3.06)	63.1 (3.11)	‡ (†)	18.2! (6.43)	32.1 (5.70)
2006	31.6 (0.70)	37.2 (0.99)	21.7 (1.77)	12.8 (1.05)	60.4 (2.76)	62.8 (2.82)	‡ (†)	‡ (†)	25.7 (4.72)
2007	33.0 (0.72)	39.2 (1.03)	20.0 (1.38)	15.4 (1.10)	60.3 (2.83)	62.5 (2.88)	32.1! (11.09)	‡ (†)	29.6 (5.17)
2008	34.9 (0.71)	41.7 (0.98)	21.6 (1.57)	15.5 (1.11)	61.6 (2.67)	64.4 (2.71)	‡ (†)	12.2! (3.69)	27.7 (5.57)
2009	34.8 (0.78)	42.0 (1.12)	22.6 (1.75)	13.8 (1.09)	57.6 (3.00)	61.3 (3.03)	18.2! (6.42)	16.3 (4.42)	35.0 (5.07)
2010	35.7 (0.68)	42.4 (0.96)	23.3 (1.72)	16.8 (1.20)	55.8 (2.93)	58.9 (3.00)	‡ (†)	18.4! (6.68)	34.0 (4.96)

See notes at end of table.

Table 104.20.   Percentage of persons 25 to 29 years old with selected levels of educational attainment, by race/ethnicity and sex: Selected years, 1920 through 2019—Continued

[Standard errors appear in parentheses]

Sex, selected level of educational attainment, and year	Total	White[1]	Black[1]	Hispanic	Asian/Pacific Islander Total	Asian/Pacific Islander Asian	Asian/Pacific Islander Pacific Islander	American Indian/ Alaska Native	Two or more races
1	2	3	4	5	6	7	8	9	10
2011	36.1 (0.71)	43.0 (1.03)	22.9 (1.62)	16.8 (1.10)	61.0 (2.74)	62.0 (2.75)	‡ (†)	19.7! (6.64)	31.2 (4.36)
2012	37.2 (0.69)	43.6 (0.97)	26.7 (1.78)	17.4 (1.10)	64.0 (2.38)	66.2 (2.45)	26.8! (9.73)	14.0! (4.55)	35.5 (5.50)
2013	37.0 (0.71)	43.8 (0.95)	23.2 (2.03)	18.6 (1.10)	62.4 (2.51)	64.3 (2.54)	29.7! (10.58)	16.4! (6.57)	30.0 (5.26)
2014	37.2 (1.00)	43.9 (1.36)	23.8 (2.61)	18.3 (1.40)	64.3 (3.23)	66.9 (3.29)	‡ (†)	‡ (†)	38.4 (5.96)
2015	38.9 (0.74)	46.6 (1.06)	24.6 (1.72)	18.5 (1.21)	64.5 (2.74)	68.1 (2.73)	‡ (†)	21.8 (4.51)	32.9 (5.20)
2016	39.5 (0.75)	46.3 (1.03)	24.9 (1.55)	21.5 (1.44)	67.7 (2.66)	69.6 (2.72)	‡ (†)	12.2! (4.00)	36.8 (5.55)
2017	39.3 (0.78)	46.5 (1.11)	23.8 (1.79)	22.4 (1.16)	63.5 (2.88)	66.3 (2.85)	24.6! (9.17)	18.7! (6.83)	38.5 (5.84)
2018	40.8 (0.84)	48.4 (1.24)	26.2 (1.81)	23.2 (1.43)	67.4 (2.60)	71.5 (2.55)	13.5! (6.42)	22.5 (5.87)	28.7 (4.34)
2019	41.8 (0.76)	49.2 (1.14)	29.8 (1.97)	23.1 (1.26)	69.0 (2.38)	72.7 (2.38)	27.0! (8.25)	20.6! (6.21)	32.1 (4.87)
Master's or higher degree									
1995	4.1 (0.32)	5.0 (0.42)	1.4! (0.59)	1.2! (0.58)	8.9! (3.29)	— (†)	— (†)	‡ (†)	— (†)
2000	6.2 (0.38)	6.7 (0.50)	4.9 (0.96)	2.7 (0.58)	13.9 (2.51)	— (†)	— (†)	‡ (†)	— (†)
2005	7.3 (0.44)	8.8 (0.64)	4.0 (0.70)	2.6 (0.51)	14.4 (2.08)	15.0 (2.15)	‡ (†)	‡ (†)	10.0! (4.26)
2006	7.8 (0.42)	9.2 (0.63)	4.5 (0.93)	2.0 (0.41)	19.7 (2.33)	20.4 (2.44)	‡ (†)	‡ (†)	8.3! (2.89)
2007	7.6 (0.43)	9.4 (0.63)	3.7 (0.66)	2.6 (0.53)	16.5 (2.39)	17.7 (2.54)	‡ (†)	‡ (†)	‡ (†)
2008	8.7 (0.44)	10.4 (0.64)	5.2 (0.87)	2.9 (0.46)	18.9 (2.30)	19.9 (2.44)	‡ (†)	‡ (†)	‡ (†)
2009	8.8 (0.45)	10.4 (0.66)	5.1 (0.80)	2.7 (0.43)	21.7 (2.45)	23.7 (2.70)	‡ (†)	‡ (†)	7.9! (2.84)
2010	8.5 (0.39)	9.2 (0.56)	6.2 (0.94)	3.8 (0.56)	20.6 (2.60)	21.8 (2.75)	‡ (†)	‡ (†)	10.0! (3.06)
2011	8.8 (0.48)	10.4 (0.72)	5.8 (0.85)	3.8 (0.63)	15.4 (1.98)	15.9 (2.03)	‡ (†)	‡ (†)	9.9 (2.61)
2012	8.8 (0.45)	10.0 (0.67)	7.1 (1.00)	3.0 (0.45)	19.3 (2.23)	20.4 (2.31)	‡ (†)	‡ (†)	6.3! (2.49)
2013	9.2 (0.44)	10.8 (0.71)	4.8 (0.74)	4.0 (0.59)	20.4 (1.91)	21.6 (2.00)	‡ (†)	‡ (†)	3.3! (1.56)
2014	9.3 (0.56)	11.1 (0.84)	5.0 (1.17)	3.6 (0.63)	19.7 (2.33)	20.8 (2.47)	‡ (†)	‡ (†)	7.5! (3.00)
2015	10.4 (0.51)	12.0 (0.73)	7.2 (0.98)	4.1 (0.60)	22.0 (2.51)	23.2 (2.67)	‡ (†)	‡ (†)	10.2! (3.20)
2016	11.2 (0.51)	12.3 (0.74)	6.3 (1.02)	6.3 (0.89)	27.5 (2.51)	28.8 (2.58)	‡ (†)	‡ (†)	8.2! (3.17)
2017	10.5 (0.49)	11.8 (0.75)	6.8 (1.06)	5.0 (0.67)	24.8 (2.38)	25.8 (2.54)	‡ (†)	‡ (†)	5.4! (2.45)
2018	10.7 (0.50)	12.6 (0.83)	6.2 (1.02)	3.8 (0.54)	27.9 (2.40)	29.9 (2.56)	‡ (†)	‡ (†)	‡ (†)
2019	11.2 (0.55)	12.6 (0.81)	8.5 (1.23)	4.6 (0.62)	25.2 (2.27)	27.5 (2.47)	‡ (†)	‡ (†)	9.1! (3.32)

—Not available.
†Not applicable.
!Interpret data with caution. The coefficient of variation (CV) for this estimate is between 30 and 50 percent.
‡Reporting standards not met. Either there are too few cases for a reliable estimate or the coefficient of variation (CV) is 50 percent or greater.
[1]Includes persons of Hispanic ethnicity for years prior to 1980.
[2]Data for years prior to 1993 are for persons with 4 or more years of high school. Data for later years are for high school completers—i.e., those persons who graduated from high school with a diploma as well as those who completed high school through equivalency programs, such as a GED program.
[3]Estimates based on Census Bureau reverse projection of 1940 census data on education by age.
[4]Data for years prior to 1993 are for persons with 4 or more years of college.

NOTE: Prior to 2005, standard errors were computed using generalized variance function methodology rather than the more precise replicate weight methodology used in later years. For 1960 and prior years, data were collected in April. For later years, data were collected in March. Data are based on sample surveys of the noninstitutionalized population, which excludes persons living in institutions (e.g., prisons or nursing facilities); data include military personnel who live in households with civilians, but exclude those who live in military barracks. Race categories exclude persons of Hispanic ethnicity except where otherwise noted.
SOURCE: U.S. Department of Commerce, Census Bureau, *U.S. Census of Population: 1960*, Vol. I, Part 1; J.K. Folger and C.B. Nam, *Education of the American Population* (1960 Census Monograph); Current Population Reports, Series P-20, various years; and Current Population Survey (CPS), Annual Social and Economic Supplement, 1970 through 2019. (This table was prepared October 2019.)

Table 104.30. Number of persons age 18 and over, by highest level of educational attainment, sex, race/ethnicity, and age: 2019

[Numbers in thousands. Standard errors appear in parentheses]

Sex, race/ethnicity, and age	Total	Elementary school (kindergarten–8th grade)	High school: 1 to 3 years	High school: 4 years, no completion	Completion[1]	Some college, no degree	Associate's degree	Bachelor's degree	Master's degree	First-professional or doctor's degree
1	2	3	4	5	6	7	8	9	10	11
Total, 18 and over	250,563 (112.1)	8,879 (181.5)	13,976 (200.9)	3,705 (110.2)	70,947 (532.4)	45,028 (382.6)	24,550 (281.7)	53,312 (433.1)	22,459 (248.4)	7,707 (163.9)
18 and 19 years old	7,831 (86.2)	104 (16.5)	2,429 (65.7)	650 (36.7)	2,271 (66.4)	2,235 (70.3)	101 (16.0)	‡ (†)	‡ (†)	‡ (†)
20 to 24 years old	21,254 (30.8)	172 (23.8)	845 (47.6)	385 (34.2)	6,417 (151.0)	8,103 (151.1)	1,711 (71.8)	3,344 (112.1)	234 (27.9)	‡ (†)
25 years old and over	221,478 (50.3)	8,603 (173.6)	10,701 (176.5)	2,671 (91.0)	62,259 (463.1)	34,690 (330.2)	22,738 (265.5)	49,937 (397.8)	22,214 (246.3)	7,665 (160.5)
25 to 29 years old	23,277 (42.7)	357 (34.3)	857 (49.9)	297 (33.7)	6,089 (128.6)	4,243 (111.2)	2,416 (87.3)	6,823 (117.4)	1,803 (75.3)	392 (37.9)
30 to 34 years old	21,932 (39.0)	554 (36.8)	930 (48.1)	269 (26.0)	5,549 (107.6)	3,287 (82.9)	2,323 (76.4)	5,904 (107.1)	2,294 (69.5)	821 (51.2)
35 to 39 years old	21,443 (39.7)	684 (39.6)	1,085 (49.4)	245 (22.7)	5,184 (102.8)	2,984 (64.6)	2,274 (70.0)	5,515 (97.0)	2,643 (73.7)	829 (44.7)
40 to 49 years old	39,929 (54.4)	1,605 (65.0)	1,908 (69.3)	449 (36.8)	10,289 (173.2)	5,737 (110.1)	4,311 (97.5)	9,457 (152.8)	4,590 (108.8)	1,582 (66.3)
50 to 59 years old	41,518 (161.7)	1,571 (66.3)	2,040 (70.4)	607 (42.4)	12,205 (173.1)	6,429 (123.7)	4,521 (120.4)	8,839 (154.9)	3,983 (107.2)	1,323 (64.1)
60 to 64 years old	20,592 (147.3)	812 (44.5)	991 (52.1)	241 (23.4)	6,423 (148.9)	3,223 (92.1)	2,280 (78.2)	4,051 (102.1)	1,887 (71.0)	705 (46.5)
65 years old and over	52,788 (159.2)	3,019 (97.6)	2,890 (81.1)	563 (43.9)	16,519 (207.5)	8,787 (163.3)	4,613 (111.2)	9,348 (175.4)	5,034 (128.7)	2,013 (86.2)
Males, 18 and over	121,301 (98.0)	4,458 (104.8)	7,156 (137.6)	2,003 (80.6)	36,076 (347.6)	21,500 (260.7)	10,758 (163.9)	25,206 (269.8)	9,721 (167.1)	4,423 (111.4)
18 and 19 years old	3,890 (68.2)	50 (10.1)	1,274 (46.0)	367 (26.0)	1,167 (48.6)	976 (48.5)	‡ (†)	‡ (†)	‡ (†)	‡ (†)
20 to 24 years old	10,716 (30.5)	96 (15.9)	502 (33.6)	225 (25.3)	3,651 (101.0)	3,933 (94.5)	783 (44.5)	1,411 (72.2)	93 (17.3)	‡ (†)
25 years old and over	106,695 (50.8)	4,313 (102.3)	5,380 (120.1)	1,412 (65.3)	31,257 (307.9)	16,591 (222.8)	9,936 (159.5)	23,785 (253.9)	9,621 (166.0)	4,400 (110.6)
25 to 29 years old	11,792 (44.0)	210 (24.5)	466 (33.3)	182 (24.7)	3,416 (99.1)	2,227 (83.1)	1,079 (59.7)	3,302 (90.7)	734 (46.6)	176 (25.4)
30 to 34 years old	10,935 (38.9)	316 (26.8)	492 (30.7)	163 (20.4)	3,178 (81.0)	1,632 (61.4)	1,000 (51.1)	2,841 (78.3)	858 (41.3)	454 (39.4)
35 to 39 years old	10,629 (39.5)	373 (29.5)	611 (38.2)	134 (18.3)	2,951 (81.9)	1,512 (56.5)	1,018 (46.6)	2,566 (71.6)	1,068 (50.8)	396 (30.1)
40 to 49 years old	19,621 (54.5)	840 (44.1)	1,042 (53.6)	231 (23.8)	5,680 (117.2)	2,822 (75.6)	2,053 (62.0)	4,206 (93.3)	1,952 (62.6)	796 (42.4)
50 to 59 years old	19,976 (156.9)	838 (45.4)	1,093 (48.8)	329 (29.5)	6,173 (122.9)	2,957 (88.7)	1,935 (75.1)	4,137 (98.0)	1,755 (63.9)	760 (44.1)
60 to 64 years old	9,819 (140.9)	395 (29.6)	464 (36.6)	122 (18.6)	3,171 (100.5)	1,487 (62.9)	972 (48.3)	1,949 (75.2)	817 (49.6)	443 (32.7)
65 years old and over	23,923 (159.2)	1,341 (56.5)	1,213 (51.6)	252 (28.4)	6,689 (124.1)	3,953 (104.3)	1,879 (70.0)	4,783 (116.2)	2,437 (88.4)	1,376 (62.6)
Females, 18 and over	129,262 (62.6)	4,421 (104.7)	6,820 (127.7)	1,702 (61.8)	34,872 (267.4)	23,528 (219.0)	13,792 (195.0)	28,106 (264.8)	12,738 (162.6)	3,284 (95.6)
18 and 19 years old	3,941 (62.5)	‡ (†)	1,155 (46.5)	283 (22.8)	1,104 (43.8)	1,258 (52.3)	61 (12.7)	‡ (†)	‡ (†)	‡ (†)
20 to 24 years old	10,538 (3.5)	76 (16.2)	344 (30.6)	160 (22.5)	2,766 (88.3)	4,171 (96.2)	928 (51.9)	1,934 (73.8)	141 (20.9)	‡ (†)
25 years old and over	114,783 (11.5)	4,290 (98.4)	5,321 (105.7)	1,259 (51.7)	31,002 (246.9)	18,099 (206.8)	12,802 (183.5)	26,151 (245.3)	12,593 (160.2)	3,265 (93.5)
25 to 29 years old	11,485 (7.4)	147 (20.4)	391 (32.4)	116 (18.7)	2,674 (76.6)	2,015 (67.6)	1,337 (59.5)	3,521 (85.4)	1,069 (58.2)	216 (23.9)
30 to 34 years old	10,997 (3.9)	237 (23.5)	439 (32.5)	106 (16.2)	2,372 (62.6)	1,655 (53.0)	1,323 (51.1)	3,063 (69.6)	1,436 (54.0)	367 (28.1)
35 to 39 years old	10,814 (6.1)	312 (23.7)	475 (30.1)	111 (14.6)	2,232 (58.5)	1,472 (41.0)	1,256 (47.3)	2,949 (62.6)	1,574 (51.3)	433 (29.7)
40 to 49 years old	20,307 (4.0)	766 (37.0)	866 (43.6)	217 (24.0)	4,609 (90.6)	2,915 (71.6)	2,258 (73.0)	5,251 (105.8)	2,639 (80.7)	786 (41.6)
50 to 59 years old	21,542 (44.9)	734 (36.9)	947 (37.7)	278 (25.7)	6,032 (104.9)	3,472 (84.3)	2,586 (80.2)	4,702 (102.5)	2,228 (71.1)	563 (35.1)
60 to 64 years old	10,773 (44.9)	417 (26.4)	527 (38.9)	119 (17.7)	3,252 (85.6)	1,736 (60.0)	1,308 (54.5)	2,102 (62.4)	1,050 (53.2)	262 (27.9)
65 years old and over	28,865 (0.8)	1,678 (63.5)	1,678 (58.9)	311 (27.8)	9,830 (138.5)	4,834 (106.2)	2,735 (81.7)	4,565 (106.9)	2,597 (84.5)	637 (48.5)
White, 18 and over	158,197 (130.4)	1,951 (92.5)	6,398 (139.4)	1,528 (51.6)	43,449 (423.1)	28,674 (293.6)	16,743 (244.1)	37,806 (356.7)	16,000 (223.0)	5,647 (152.3)
18 and 19 years old	4,215 (65.2)	58 (13.7)	1,382 (49.7)	289 (13.2)	1,192 (52.9)	1,223 (54.3)	57 (12.3)	‡ (†)	‡ (†)	‡ (†)
20 to 24 years old	11,425 (28.6)	‡ (†)	317 (18.5)	109 (19.4)	3,163 (101.2)	4,533 (106.2)	980 (58.3)	2,150 (81.7)	104 (19.3)	‡ (†)
25 years old and over	142,557 (111.7)	1,856 (87.2)	4,699 (120.5)	1,131 (63.5)	39,094 (386.6)	22,918 (259.9)	15,707 (229.9)	35,642 (337.8)	15,897 (222.8)	5,614 (148.6)
25 to 29 years old	12,558 (40.6)	70 (16.9)	312 (32.2)	84 (16.7)	2,999 (93.0)	2,099 (81.6)	1,350 (66.7)	4,353 (95.2)	1,056 (60.2)	234 (31.1)
30 to 34 years old	12,333 (47.7)	105 (16.6)	311 (32.2)	91 (15.5)	2,688 (79.7)	1,795 (68.2)	1,400 (56.7)	3,902 (90.0)	1,470 (59.5)	572 (43.3)
35 to 39 years old	12,190 (45.1)	99 (16.4)	323 (28.5)	72 (14.4)	2,611 (71.5)	1,662 (52.6)	1,382 (57.3)	3,758 (82.5)	1,740 (64.2)	543 (36.4)
40 to 49 years old	23,196 (55.1)	178 (25.1)	620 (36.0)	144 (21.3)	5,539 (123.0)	3,499 (87.5)	2,884 (72.8)	6,301 (119.0)	2,990 (92.3)	1,040 (55.9)
50 to 59 years old	27,443 (143.3)	252 (28.0)	928 (49.8)	267 (30.0)	7,930 (159.1)	4,396 (101.3)	3,202 (106.3)	6,601 (135.5)	2,909 (88.0)	958 (55.0)
60 to 64 years old	14,620 (131.8)	159 (21.0)	499 (40.5)	151 (21.8)	4,584 (121.5)	2,313 (76.7)	1,788 (76.1)	3,091 (91.0)	1,447 (66.6)	588 (44.8)
65 years old and over	40,218 (152.0)	993 (61.7)	1,706 (66.3)	323 (35.8)	12,743 (183.0)	7,153 (147.4)	3,701 (100.4)	7,636 (165.1)	4,284 (118.0)	1,679 (80.2)
Black, 18 and over	29,618 (83.0)	666 (46.6)	2,180 (76.8)	681 (51.6)	9,912 (163.2)	6,148 (125.3)	2,919 (87.5)	4,610 (112.4)	2,036 (73.5)	467 (37.8)
18 and 19 years old	1,015 (31.7)	‡ (†)	306 (27.1)	98 (13.2)	340 (26.8)	244 (22.9)	‡ (†)	‡ (†)	‡ (†)	‡ (†)
20 to 24 years old	2,875 (28.6)	‡ (†)	130 (18.5)	‡ (†)	1,151 (55.1)	1,010 (52.5)	154 (23.0)	321 (32.7)	‡ (†)	‡ (†)
25 years old and over	25,728 (70.5)	633 (45.0)	1,744 (67.8)	516 (41.7)	8,422 (141.1)	4,894 (108.7)	2,754 (85.0)	4,285 (106.8)	2,015 (72.4)	466 (37.7)
25 to 29 years old	3,322 (27.7)	‡ (†)	185 (24.9)	‡ (†)	964 (54.8)	759 (46.9)	349 (35.7)	758 (45.6)	186 (25.7)	63 (12.4)
30 to 34 years old	2,870 (24.4)	‡ (†)	108 (17.5)	58 (11.8)	962 (45.5)	640 (36.8)	298 (27.4)	531 (36.7)	215 (21.9)	134 (18.6)
35 to 39 years old	2,624 (23.4)	‡ (†)	144 (17.8)	81 (16.1)	778 (42.1)	501 (30.8)	343 (28.7)	472 (33.1)	250 (22.7)	105 (19.9)
40 to 49 years old	4,864 (29.6)	‡ (†)	225 (25.9)	110 (17.5)	1,538 (57.5)	881 (40.7)	519 (35.7)	918 (45.3)	518 (34.9)	‡ (†)
50 to 59 years old	4,999 (56.7)	95 (17.9)	357 (31.8)	‡ (†)	1,685 (56.3)	895 (41.8)	598 (35.0)	761 (43.4)	394 (33.3)	‡ (†)
60 to 64 years old	2,247 (63.7)	52 (14.0)	206 (22.5)	‡ (†)	833 (46.9)	416 (26.9)	232 (21.7)	285 (24.2)	160 (20.3)	‡ (†)
65 years old and over	4,803 (39.2)	343 (28.9)	519 (31.9)	128 (16.3)	1,661 (51.4)	802 (41.7)	415 (27.3)	560 (35.3)	292 (24.8)	84 (14.5)

See notes at end of table.

Table 104.30. Number of persons age 18 and over, by highest level of educational attainment, sex, race/ethnicity, and age: 2019—Continued

[Numbers in thousands. Standard errors appear in parentheses]

Sex, race/ethnicity, and age	Total	Elementary school (kindergarten– 8th grade)	High school 1 to 3 years	High school 4 years, no completion	Completion[1]	Some college, no degree	Postsecondary education Associate's degree	Bachelor's degree	Master's degree	First-professional or doctor's degree
1	2	3	4	5	6	7	8	9	10	11
Hispanic, 18 and over	**41,217** (49.2)	**5,482** (129.1)	**4,461** (114.8)	**1,188** (58.7)	**13,029** (159.4)	**6,915** (111.2)	**3,236** (85.6)	**4,900** (110.6)	**1,555** (57.9)	**452** (30.9)
18 and 19 years old	1,862 (44.1)	‡ (†)	549 (30.3)	196 (22.0)	544 (30.8)	518 (29.4)	‡ (†)	‡ (†)	‡ (†)	‡ (†)
20 to 24 years old	4,780 (8.8)	91 (13.9)	340 (28.9)	169 (20.8)	1,636 (55.0)	1,717 (54.1)	434 (28.8)	371 (31.5)	‡ (†)	‡ (†)
25 years old and over	34,575 (15.1)	5,367 (125.6)	3,572 (101.2)	823 (47.8)	10,848 (137.6)	4,680 (84.5)	2,775 (82.3)	4,527 (107.2)	1,532 (57.6)	452 (30.9)
25 to 29 years old	4,963 (31.3)	223 (25.6)	308 (25.9)	144 (19.8)	1,693 (54.5)	1,042 (46.5)	532 (35.5)	853 (42.5)	131 (17.3)	53 (10.3)
30 to 34 years old	4,421 (30.1)	404 (30.3)	453 (31.2)	112 (16.5)	1,535 (50.1)	602 (32.4)	444 (33.2)	613 (39.2)	205 (23.1)	54 (11.2)
35 to 39 years old	4,480 (36.9)	530 (32.8)	564 (37.2)	91 (15.3)	1,434 (44.1)	585 (34.4)	383 (25.3)	596 (37.4)	244 (22.0)	117 (16.3)
40 to 49 years old	7,931 (51.8)	1,283 (55.5)	952 (50.6)	186 (18.4)	2,491 (70.1)	929 (43.6)	591 (34.1)	1,004 (47.1)	379 (32.6)	70 (11.1)
50 to 59 years old	5,992 (62.2)	1,095 (50.5)	607 (38.1)	185 (22.1)	1,806 (59.7)	757 (35.7)	424 (32.0)	747 (38.7)	301 (22.5)	‡ (†)
60 to 64 years old	2,244 (50.7)	517 (34.4)	218 (21.7)	‡ (†)	630 (34.5)	305 (22.0)	145 (16.0)	264 (22.7)	95 (12.2)	‡ (†)
65 years old and over	4,544 (6.2)	1,314 (51.5)	470 (26.8)	72 (13.1)	1,258 (44.1)	460 (27.9)	255 (23.3)	452 (29.6)	178 (17.9)	85 (11.6)
Asian, 18 and over	**15,400** (105.1)	**679** (44.8)	**517** (40.7)	**186** (21.8)	**2,657** (85.2)	**1,839** (62.2)	**995** (51.3)	**4,994** (106.6)	**2,512** (88.7)	**1,021** (51.3)
18 and 19 years old	390 (23.0)	‡ (†)	92 (13.5)	‡ (†)	93 (14.6)	142 (15.4)	‡ (†)	‡ (†)	‡ (†)	‡ (†)
20 to 24 years old	1,327 (32.4)	‡ (†)	‡ (†)	‡ (†)	178 (21.5)	519 (33.5)	90 (16.3)	397 (35.3)	85 (17.4)	‡ (†)
25 years old and over	13,683 (99.1)	659 (42.6)	410 (38.4)	132 (17.9)	2,386 (80.2)	1,178 (50.9)	899 (47.4)	4,589 (101.6)	2,416 (82.8)	1,014 (51.3)
25 to 29 years old	1,646 (37.8)	‡ (†)	‡ (†)	‡ (†)	162 (22.1)	157 (19.2)	101 (18.3)	699 (37.3)	391 (30.9)	85 (15.4)
30 to 34 years old	1,659 (37.8)	‡ (†)	‡ (†)	‡ (†)	200 (22.1)	120 (17.0)	106 (15.4)	695 (39.5)	365 (29.6)	139 (18.6)
35 to 39 years old	1,596 (35.7)	‡ (†)	‡ (†)	‡ (†)	208 (22.3)	125 (17.5)	98 (14.3)	577 (31.7)	363 (26.7)	150 (18.8)
40 to 49 years old	2,970 (56.5)	87 (14.2)	69 (14.6)	‡ (†)	457 (31.2)	232 (24.1)	197 (22.3)	1,031 (49.3)	598 (36.2)	271 (23.6)
50 to 59 years old	2,255 (50.0)	118 (16.4)	97 (16.5)	‡ (†)	516 (35.3)	210 (21.3)	183 (19.6)	622 (33.1)	313 (27.6)	166 (18.8)
60 to 64 years old	1,115 (42.6)	80 (13.7)	‡ (†)	‡ (†)	242 (23.1)	106 (15.1)	55 (10.8)	373 (30.4)	150 (20.9)	55 (10.1)
65 years old and over	2,443 (37.9)	313 (26.7)	131 (18.1)	‡ (†)	601 (39.0)	229 (23.8)	158 (20.4)	592 (37.3)	235 (24.9)	149 (20.0)

†Not applicable.
‡Reporting standards not met. Either there are too few cases for a reliable estimate or the coefficient of variation (CV) is 50 percent or greater.
[1]Includes completion of high school through equivalency programs, such as a GED program.

NOTE: Total includes other racial/ethnic groups not shown separately. Race categories exclude persons of Hispanic ethnicity. Detail may not sum to totals because of rounding.
SOURCE: U.S. Department of Commerce, Census Bureau, Current Population Survey (CPS), Annual Social and Economic Supplement, 2019. (This table was prepared January 2020.)

Table 104.50. Persons age 25 and over who hold a bachelor's or higher degree, by sex, race/ethnicity, age group, and field of bachelor's degree: 2017

[Standard errors appear in parentheses]

Field of bachelor's degree	Total	Sex: Male	Sex: Female	Race/ethnicity: White	Race/ethnicity: Black	Race/ethnicity: Hispanic	Race/ethnicity: Asian/Pacific Islander	Race/ethnicity: American Indian/Alaska Native	Age: 25 to 29 years old	Age: 30 to 49 years old	Age: 50 years old and over
1	2	3	4	5	6	7	8	9	10	11	12
Total population, 25 and over (in thousands)	221,310 (21.0)	106,905 (24.7)	114,406 (21.0)	143,646 (27.3)	25,835 (9.8)	33,490 (8.9)	13,124 (9.2)	1,342 (1.3)	23,029 (10.1)	84,099 (23.7)	114,182 (19.8)
Percent of population with bachelor's degree	32.0 (0.07)	31.4 (0.08)	32.6 (0.07)	35.8 (0.08)	21.6 (0.12)	16.0 (0.11)	53.2 (0.20)	15.0 (0.36)	34.3 (0.18)	35.9 (0.10)	28.7 (0.06)
Bachelor's degree holders											
Number (in thousands)											
Total	70,854 (164.9)	33,521 (87.4)	37,334 (87.7)	51,378 (110.8)	5,572 (31.1)	5,370 (39.3)	6,984 (27.5)	201 (5.5)	7,890 (42.2)	30,169 (84.5)	32,795 (76.3)
Agriculture	715 (9.7)	468 (7.5)	247 (5.1)	598 (8.7)	24 (2.0)	35 (2.5)	47 (2.8)	‡ (†)	75 (3.5)	274 (6.3)	366 (6.0)
Architecture	507 (8.7)	340 (6.7)	167 (4.7)	339 (6.3)	26 (2.4)	63 (3.2)	68 (2.7)	‡ (†)	54 (3.6)	218 (6.1)	235 (5.8)
Business/management	14,355 (50.2)	7,912 (39.1)	6,443 (30.9)	10,231 (38.5)	1,300 (16.1)	1,225 (16.6)	1,313 (13.3)	41 (3.0)	1,381 (17.4)	6,378 (35.8)	6,596 (26.8)
Communications and communications technologies	2,737 (19.5)	1,129 (12.9)	1,608 (15.2)	2,087 (16.8)	244 (6.6)	213 (6.8)	133 (4.1)	6 (0.9)	427 (7.8)	1,424 (15.6)	886 (9.6)
Computer and information sciences	2,276 (20.1)	1,626 (16.4)	650 (9.4)	1,238 (12.3)	224 (6.6)	165 (5.6)	584 (9.8)	3 (0.6)	318 (8.6)	1,302 (15.6)	656 (9.8)
Criminal justice and fire protection	1,262 (15.1)	745 (10.5)	517 (10.5)	843 (11.6)	203 (6.4)	144 (5.3)	38 (2.5)	6 (0.9)	209 (6.4)	693 (10.9)	361 (6.4)
Education	8,973 (39.1)	2,129 (17.6)	6,844 (30.2)	7,255 (31.7)	677 (11.2)	577 (9.8)	325 (7.1)	35 (2.2)	559 (10.1)	2,775 (22.8)	5,639 (27.1)
Engineering and engineering technologies	6,357 (35.0)	5,359 (30.3)	998 (12.0)	4,076 (26.2)	310 (7.4)	548 (10.7)	1,294 (13.5)	11 (1.2)	705 (10.1)	2,657 (23.7)	2,995 (19.8)
English language and literature	2,254 (17.9)	762 (11.2)	1,492 (12.6)	1,807 (15.1)	124 (4.5)	110 (5.1)	162 (4.5)	4 (0.6)	217 (6.2)	920 (11.3)	1,117 (12.6)
Foreign languages, literatures, and linguistics	736 (10.7)	200 (5.2)	536 (9.9)	535 (9.6)	31 (2.8)	77 (3.5)	75 (2.9)	‡ (†)	75 (2.8)	291 (5.9)	369 (7.5)
Health sciences	5,365 (24.0)	954 (9.8)	4,411 (21.3)	3,792 (18.1)	482 (10.9)	356 (7.3)	622 (9.8)	18 (1.3)	618 (8.2)	2,252 (17.1)	2,496 (16.4)
Liberal arts and humanities	982 (12.7)	388 (7.9)	594 (9.3)	710 (10.1)	71 (3.4)	89 (3.6)	85 (3.7)	4 (0.9)	85 (3.6)	432 (7.8)	465 (7.1)
Mathematics/statistics	1,071 (12.2)	614 (8.3)	456 (8.1)	782 (10.0)	64 (3.1)	51 (3.1)	152 (4.6)	‡ (†)	107 (3.9)	375 (7.5)	589 (9.3)
Natural sciences (biological, environmental, and physical)	5,974 (40.0)	3,339 (25.7)	2,635 (23.0)	4,258 (28.0)	361 (9.3)	369 (7.4)	843 (10.2)	16 (1.5)	791 (13.3)	2,552 (25.9)	2,632 (18.0)
Philosophy/religion/theology	941 (13.5)	646 (10.1)	295 (6.8)	721 (10.4)	80 (3.8)	59 (3.1)	60 (3.0)	3 (0.6)	82 (3.7)	353 (7.6)	506 (7.7)
Psychology	3,403 (22.5)	1,024 (12.3)	2,380 (17.9)	2,462 (17.8)	333 (7.0)	312 (7.5)	201 (5.0)	10 (1.3)	482 (8.9)	1,607 (14.6)	1,314 (13.2)
Social sciences and history	6,638 (35.1)	3,701 (24.7)	2,937 (21.0)	4,990 (27.3)	485 (9.8)	471 (8.9)	528 (9.2)	16 (1.3)	743 (11.6)	2,767 (22.9)	3,129 (20.5)
Social work and public administration	1,005 (11.8)	220 (5.7)	785 (10.7)	652 (8.9)	182 (6.4)	97 (4.0)	48 (2.7)	6 (0.9)	115 (4.3)	437 (8.6)	453 (7.4)
Visual and performing arts	2,914 (21.0)	1,104 (13.8)	1,810 (16.7)	2,239 (18.1)	154 (6.0)	204 (5.9)	243 (6.5)	7 (1.0)	444 (9.7)	1,324 (16.8)	1,146 (11.6)
Other fields[1]	2,389 (18.6)	861 (11.3)	1,528 (13.0)	1,761 (15.2)	196 (6.5)	205 (5.1)	165 (4.9)	9 (1.1)	404 (9.1)	1,139 (14.6)	846 (11.5)
Percentage distribution, by field											
Total	100.0 (†)	100.0 (†)	100.0 (†)	100.0 (†)	100.0 (†)	100.0 (†)	100.0 (†)	100.0 (†)	100.0 (†)	100.0 (†)	100.0 (†)
Agriculture	1.0 (0.01)	1.4 (0.02)	0.7 (0.01)	1.2 (0.02)	0.4 (0.04)	0.7 (0.05)	0.7 (0.04)	0.2! (0.25)	0.9 (0.04)	0.9 (0.02)	1.1 (0.02)
Architecture	0.7 (0.01)	1.0 (0.02)	0.4 (0.01)	0.7 (0.01)	0.5 (0.04)	1.2 (0.06)	1.0 (0.04)	0.4! (0.14)	0.7 (0.05)	0.7 (0.02)	0.7 (0.02)
Business/management	20.3 (0.06)	23.6 (0.10)	17.3 (0.08)	19.9 (0.06)	23.3 (0.26)	22.8 (0.28)	18.8 (0.17)	20.5 (1.30)	17.5 (0.19)	21.1 (0.12)	20.1 (0.07)
Communications and communications technologies	3.9 (0.03)	3.4 (0.04)	4.3 (0.04)	4.1 (0.03)	4.4 (0.12)	4.0 (0.12)	1.9 (0.06)	2.8 (0.45)	5.4 (0.10)	4.7 (0.05)	2.7 (0.03)
Computer and information sciences	3.2 (0.03)	4.9 (0.05)	1.7 (0.03)	2.4 (0.02)	4.0 (0.12)	3.1 (0.11)	8.4 (0.14)	1.7 (0.30)	4.0 (0.11)	4.3 (0.05)	2.0 (0.03)
Criminal justice and fire protection	1.8 (0.02)	2.2 (0.03)	1.4 (0.03)	1.6 (0.02)	3.7 (0.11)	2.7 (0.10)	0.5 (0.04)	3.2 (0.42)	2.6 (0.08)	2.3 (0.04)	1.1 (0.02)
Education	12.7 (0.04)	6.4 (0.05)	18.3 (0.06)	14.1 (0.05)	12.1 (0.20)	10.7 (0.17)	4.6 (0.10)	17.4 (0.97)	7.1 (0.12)	9.2 (0.07)	17.2 (0.06)
Engineering and engineering technologies	9.0 (0.04)	16.0 (0.08)	2.7 (0.03)	7.9 (0.05)	5.6 (0.13)	10.2 (0.18)	18.5 (0.18)	5.4 (0.60)	8.9 (0.12)	8.8 (0.07)	9.1 (0.05)
English language and literature	3.2 (0.02)	2.3 (0.03)	4.0 (0.03)	3.5 (0.03)	2.2 (0.08)	2.0 (0.09)	2.3 (0.06)	1.8 (0.28)	2.8 (0.08)	3.0 (0.04)	3.4 (0.04)
Foreign languages, literatures, and linguistics	1.0 (0.01)	0.6 (0.02)	1.4 (0.03)	1.0 (0.02)	0.6 (0.05)	1.4 (0.06)	1.1 (0.04)	0.7! (0.22)	1.0 (0.04)	1.0 (0.02)	1.1 (0.02)
Health sciences	7.6 (0.03)	2.8 (0.03)	11.8 (0.06)	7.4 (0.03)	8.7 (0.19)	6.6 (0.13)	8.9 (0.13)	9.2 (0.64)	7.8 (0.10)	7.5 (0.06)	7.6 (0.05)
Liberal arts and humanities	1.4 (0.02)	1.2 (0.02)	1.6 (0.02)	1.4 (0.02)	1.3 (0.06)	1.7 (0.07)	1.2 (0.05)	2.1 (0.46)	1.1 (0.05)	1.4 (0.03)	1.4 (0.02)
Mathematics/statistics	1.5 (0.02)	1.8 (0.02)	1.2 (0.02)	1.5 (0.02)	1.1 (0.05)	0.9 (0.06)	2.2 (0.07)	0.9! (0.27)	1.4 (0.05)	1.2 (0.02)	1.8 (0.03)
Natural sciences (biological, environmental, and physical)	8.4 (0.05)	10.0 (0.07)	7.1 (0.06)	8.3 (0.05)	6.5 (0.16)	6.9 (0.13)	12.1 (0.14)	8.0 (0.71)	10.0 (0.15)	8.5 (0.08)	8.0 (0.05)
Philosophy/religion/theology	1.3 (0.02)	1.9 (0.03)	0.8 (0.02)	1.4 (0.02)	1.4 (0.07)	1.1 (0.06)	0.9 (0.05)	1.4 (0.29)	1.0 (0.05)	1.2 (0.03)	1.5 (0.02)
Psychology	4.8 (0.03)	3.1 (0.04)	6.4 (0.04)	4.8 (0.03)	6.0 (0.12)	5.8 (0.13)	2.9 (0.07)	4.9 (0.63)	6.1 (0.11)	5.3 (0.05)	4.0 (0.04)
Social sciences and history	9.4 (0.04)	11.0 (0.07)	7.9 (0.05)	9.7 (0.05)	8.7 (0.17)	8.8 (0.15)	7.6 (0.13)	8.1 (0.64)	9.4 (0.13)	9.2 (0.07)	9.5 (0.06)
Social work and public administration	1.4 (0.02)	0.7 (0.02)	2.1 (0.03)	1.3 (0.02)	3.3 (0.11)	1.8 (0.07)	0.7 (0.04)	2.9 (0.43)	1.5 (0.06)	1.4 (0.03)	1.4 (0.02)
Visual and performing arts	4.1 (0.03)	3.3 (0.04)	4.8 (0.04)	4.4 (0.04)	2.8 (0.11)	3.8 (0.10)	3.5 (0.09)	3.4 (0.51)	5.6 (0.12)	4.4 (0.05)	3.5 (0.03)
Other fields[1]	3.4 (0.02)	2.6 (0.03)	4.1 (0.03)	3.4 (0.03)	3.5 (0.11)	3.8 (0.09)	2.4 (0.07)	4.3 (0.53)	5.1 (0.11)	3.8 (0.05)	2.6 (0.03)

†Not applicable.

!Interpret data with caution. The coefficient of variation (CV) for this estimate is between 30 and 50 percent.

‡Reporting standards not met (too few cases for a reliable estimate).

[1]Includes area, ethnic, and civilization studies; family and consumer sciences; library sciences; military sciences; multi/interdisciplinary studies; physical fitness, parks, recreation and leisure; precision production; transportation technologies; and other fields, not separately classified.

NOTE: Data are based on sample surveys of the entire population age 25 and over residing within the United States, including both noninstitutionalized persons (e.g., those living in households, college housing, or military housing located within the United States) and institutionalized persons (e.g., those living in prisons, nursing facilities, or other healthcare facilities). The first bachelor's degree major reported by respondents was used to classify their field of study, even though they were able to report a second bachelor's degree major and may possess advanced degrees in other fields. Totals include other racial/ethnic groups not separately shown. Race categories exclude persons of Hispanic ethnicity. Detail may not sum to totals because of rounding.

SOURCE: U.S. Department of Commerce, Census Bureau, American Community Survey (ACS), 2017. (This table was prepared May 2019.)

Table 104.80. Percentage of persons 18 to 24 years old and age 25 and over, by educational attainment and state: 2000 and 2018

[Standard errors appear in parentheses]

State	Percent of 18- to 24-year-olds who were high school completers[1]		Percent of population 25 years old and over, by educational attainment										
			2000					2018					
			Less than high school completion	High school completion[1] or higher	Bachelor's or higher degree			Less than high school completion	High school completion[1] or higher		Bachelor's or higher degree		
	2000	2018			Total	Bachelor's degree	Graduate degree		Total	High school only	Total	Bachelor's degree	Graduate degree
1	2	3	4	5	6	7	8	9	10	11	12	13	14
United States	**74.7 (0.02)**	**87.6 (0.08)**	**19.6 (0.01)**	**80.4 (0.01)**	**24.4 (0.01)**	**15.5 (0.01)**	**8.9 (#)**	**11.7 (0.04)**	**88.3 (0.04)**	**26.9 (0.05)**	**32.6 (0.07)**	**20.0 (0.04)**	**12.7 (0.04)**
Alabama	72.2 (0.15)	87.2 (0.70)	24.7 (0.06)	75.3 (0.06)	19.0 (0.05)	12.1 (0.04)	6.9 (0.03)	13.5 (0.28)	86.5 (0.28)	30.8 (0.31)	25.3 (0.34)	15.8 (0.28)	9.5 (0.23)
Alaska	76.9 (0.40)	87.6 (1.67)	11.7 (0.12)	88.3 (0.12)	24.7 (0.16)	16.1 (0.13)	8.6 (0.10)	6.0 (0.52)	94.0 (0.52)	27.9 (0.95)	30.1 (1.13)	18.6 (0.88)	11.4 (0.79)
Arizona	69.2 (0.19)	84.9 (0.71)	19.0 (0.06)	81.0 (0.06)	23.5 (0.07)	15.1 (0.06)	8.4 (0.04)	12.4 (0.17)	87.6 (0.17)	24.1 (0.24)	29.6 (0.26)	18.5 (0.21)	11.1 (0.17)
Arkansas	75.4 (0.19)	88.5 (0.82)	24.7 (0.07)	75.3 (0.07)	16.7 (0.06)	11.0 (0.05)	5.7 (0.04)	12.7 (0.30)	87.3 (0.30)	34.3 (0.47)	23.3 (0.40)	14.8 (0.28)	8.5 (0.26)
California	70.7 (0.07)	89.9 (0.17)	23.2 (0.03)	76.8 (0.03)	26.6 (0.03)	17.1 (0.02)	9.5 (0.02)	16.1 (0.09)	83.9 (0.09)	20.7 (0.09)	34.4 (0.11)	21.4 (0.10)	13.0 (0.09)
Colorado	75.1 (0.15)	87.2 (0.63)	13.1 (0.05)	86.9 (0.05)	32.7 (0.06)	21.6 (0.06)	11.1 (0.04)	7.8 (0.19)	92.2 (0.19)	21.0 (0.34)	42.0 (0.29)	26.1 (0.27)	15.9 (0.22)
Connecticut	78.2 (0.21)	90.3 (0.74)	16.0 (0.06)	84.0 (0.06)	31.4 (0.08)	18.1 (0.07)	13.3 (0.06)	9.2 (0.24)	90.8 (0.24)	27.0 (0.37)	39.7 (0.35)	21.8 (0.27)	17.9 (0.27)
Delaware	77.6 (0.41)	86.2 (1.77)	17.4 (0.14)	82.6 (0.14)	25.0 (0.16)	15.6 (0.14)	9.4 (0.11)	10.4 (0.57)	89.6 (0.57)	32.9 (0.83)	31.2 (0.77)	18.2 (0.64)	13.0 (0.51)
District of Columbia	79.4 (0.40)	90.4 (1.42)	22.2 (0.18)	77.8 (0.18)	39.1 (0.21)	18.1 (0.17)	21.0 (0.18)	8.2 (0.57)	91.8 (0.57)	16.9 (0.67)	60.2 (0.61)	25.4 (0.62)	34.8 (0.62)
Florida	71.7 (0.11)	84.9 (0.37)	20.1 (0.04)	79.9 (0.04)	22.3 (0.04)	14.2 (0.03)	8.1 (0.02)	11.5 (0.09)	88.5 (0.09)	28.5 (0.16)	30.5 (0.15)	19.2 (0.14)	11.3 (0.09)
Georgia	70.0 (0.15)	84.9 (0.42)	21.4 (0.05)	78.6 (0.05)	24.3 (0.05)	16.0 (0.05)	8.3 (0.04)	12.5 (0.18)	87.5 (0.18)	27.7 (0.21)	32.0 (0.21)	19.5 (0.19)	12.5 (0.16)
Hawaii	85.8 (0.25)	90.0 (0.99)	15.4 (0.10)	84.6 (0.10)	26.2 (0.12)	17.8 (0.10)	8.4 (0.08)	8.3 (0.42)	91.7 (0.42)	26.9 (0.63)	33.2 (0.65)	21.7 (0.49)	11.5 (0.40)
Idaho	77.3 (0.25)	84.6 (1.48)	15.3 (0.09)	84.7 (0.09)	21.7 (0.10)	14.9 (0.09)	6.8 (0.06)	9.3 (0.39)	90.7 (0.39)	28.2 (0.63)	27.4 (0.52)	18.4 (0.49)	9.0 (0.41)
Illinois	76.0 (0.09)	88.4 (0.39)	18.6 (0.03)	81.4 (0.03)	26.1 (0.03)	16.6 (0.03)	9.5 (0.02)	10.6 (0.14)	89.4 (0.14)	26.2 (0.21)	35.2 (0.21)	21.1 (0.17)	14.0 (0.15)
Indiana	76.5 (0.15)	84.1 (0.66)	17.9 (0.05)	82.1 (0.05)	19.4 (0.05)	12.2 (0.04)	7.2 (0.04)	11.2 (0.22)	88.8 (0.22)	33.2 (0.28)	26.9 (0.29)	17.2 (0.21)	9.7 (0.19)
Iowa	81.4 (0.16)	88.6 (0.82)	13.9 (0.06)	86.1 (0.06)	21.2 (0.07)	14.7 (0.06)	6.5 (0.04)	7.8 (0.27)	92.2 (0.27)	31.0 (0.42)	28.6 (0.49)	19.4 (0.38)	9.2 (0.35)
Kansas	78.3 (0.18)	88.6 (0.85)	14.0 (0.06)	86.0 (0.06)	25.8 (0.08)	17.1 (0.06)	8.7 (0.05)	9.1 (0.27)	90.9 (0.27)	25.6 (0.38)	33.4 (0.38)	20.9 (0.34)	12.5 (0.30)
Kentucky	74.9 (0.15)	88.5 (0.75)	25.9 (0.06)	74.1 (0.06)	17.1 (0.05)	10.2 (0.04)	6.9 (0.03)	12.9 (0.28)	87.1 (0.28)	32.3 (0.31)	25.2 (0.30)	14.8 (0.23)	10.4 (0.22)
Louisiana	72.3 (0.15)	83.5 (0.81)	25.2 (0.06)	74.8 (0.06)	18.7 (0.05)	12.2 (0.04)	6.5 (0.03)	14.0 (0.33)	86.0 (0.33)	34.6 (0.41)	24.3 (0.31)	15.9 (0.28)	8.4 (0.19)
Maine	78.9 (0.28)	90.1 (1.23)	14.6 (0.08)	85.4 (0.08)	22.9 (0.10)	15.0 (0.09)	7.9 (0.06)	7.2 (0.43)	92.8 (0.43)	31.0 (0.67)	30.6 (0.62)	19.1 (0.48)	11.5 (0.44)
Maryland	79.6 (0.16)	89.7 (0.58)	16.2 (0.05)	83.8 (0.05)	31.4 (0.07)	18.0 (0.06)	13.4 (0.05)	9.5 (0.21)	90.5 (0.21)	24.4 (0.31)	40.7 (0.33)	21.7 (0.26)	19.0 (0.28)
Massachusetts	82.2 (0.13)	89.7 (0.47)	15.2 (0.05)	84.8 (0.05)	33.2 (0.06)	19.5 (0.05)	13.7 (0.04)	9.2 (0.18)	90.8 (0.18)	23.5 (0.28)	44.4 (0.28)	24.4 (0.23)	20.1 (0.22)
Michigan	76.5 (0.10)	87.8 (0.48)	16.6 (0.03)	83.4 (0.03)	21.8 (0.04)	13.7 (0.03)	8.1 (0.02)	9.0 (0.16)	91.0 (0.16)	28.6 (0.22)	29.6 (0.27)	18.1 (0.20)	11.5 (0.16)
Minnesota	79.3 (0.13)	88.5 (0.66)	12.1 (0.04)	87.9 (0.04)	27.4 (0.06)	19.1 (0.05)	8.3 (0.03)	6.6 (0.20)	93.4 (0.20)	24.0 (0.34)	37.2 (0.40)	24.2 (0.36)	13.0 (0.26)
Mississippi	71.3 (0.18)	86.0 (0.94)	27.1 (0.08)	72.9 (0.08)	16.9 (0.06)	11.1 (0.05)	5.8 (0.04)	14.6 (0.34)	85.4 (0.34)	29.6 (0.45)	23.4 (0.43)	14.5 (0.34)	8.9 (0.26)
Missouri	76.5 (0.13)	88.1 (0.60)	18.7 (0.05)	81.3 (0.05)	21.6 (0.05)	14.0 (0.04)	7.6 (0.03)	9.7 (0.22)	90.3 (0.22)	30.0 (0.26)	29.6 (0.26)	17.8 (0.27)	11.7 (0.19)
Montana	78.6 (0.31)	87.5 (1.60)	12.8 (0.10)	87.2 (0.10)	24.4 (0.13)	17.2 (0.11)	7.2 (0.08)	6.6 (0.39)	93.4 (0.39)	28.3 (0.70)	30.4 (0.80)	20.0 (0.72)	10.4 (0.43)
Nebraska	80.0 (0.21)	89.1 (1.04)	13.4 (0.07)	86.6 (0.07)	23.7 (0.09)	16.4 (0.08)	7.3 (0.06)	8.2 (0.24)	91.8 (0.24)	25.4 (0.55)	32.9 (0.53)	21.8 (0.43)	11.1 (0.36)
Nevada	66.7 (0.32)	85.5 (0.97)	19.3 (0.10)	80.7 (0.10)	18.2 (0.10)	12.1 (0.08)	6.1 (0.06)	13.2 (0.29)	86.8 (0.29)	27.7 (0.46)	24.9 (0.41)	16.1 (0.33)	8.8 (0.25)
New Hampshire	77.8 (0.29)	90.5 (1.17)	12.6 (0.08)	87.4 (0.08)	28.7 (0.11)	18.7 (0.10)	10.0 (0.07)	7.1 (0.31)	92.9 (0.31)	27.4 (0.54)	37.2 (0.59)	22.5 (0.52)	14.7 (0.42)
New Jersey	76.3 (0.14)	89.5 (0.45)	17.9 (0.04)	82.1 (0.04)	29.8 (0.05)	18.8 (0.04)	11.0 (0.04)	9.9 (0.17)	90.1 (0.17)	26.3 (0.21)	40.6 (0.24)	24.5 (0.22)	16.1 (0.18)
New Mexico	70.5 (0.24)	82.3 (1.57)	21.1 (0.09)	78.9 (0.09)	23.5 (0.09)	13.7 (0.07)	9.8 (0.06)	14.7 (0.43)	85.3 (0.43)	26.6 (0.52)	27.5 (0.50)	15.8 (0.39)	11.7 (0.34)
New York	76.1 (0.09)	88.9 (0.31)	20.9 (0.03)	79.1 (0.03)	27.4 (0.04)	15.6 (0.03)	11.8 (0.03)	12.8 (0.12)	87.2 (0.12)	25.8 (0.16)	37.3 (0.18)	20.8 (0.15)	16.5 (0.14)
North Carolina	74.2 (0.11)	87.1 (0.52)	21.9 (0.04)	78.1 (0.04)	22.5 (0.04)	15.3 (0.04)	7.2 (0.03)	11.7 (0.17)	88.3 (0.17)	25.4 (0.20)	31.9 (0.23)	20.5 (0.17)	11.4 (0.15)
North Dakota	84.4 (0.24)	93.1 (1.03)	16.1 (0.10)	83.9 (0.10)	22.0 (0.12)	16.5 (0.10)	5.5 (0.06)	7.4 (0.51)	92.6 (0.51)	26.3 (0.80)	28.8 (1.00)	21.2 (0.87)	7.6 (0.40)
Ohio	76.8 (0.09)	87.7 (0.38)	17.0 (0.03)	83.0 (0.03)	21.1 (0.03)	13.7 (0.03)	7.4 (0.02)	9.5 (0.13)	90.5 (0.13)	32.8 (0.21)	28.8 (0.21)	17.6 (0.15)	11.2 (0.16)
Oklahoma	74.8 (0.16)	83.9 (0.91)	19.4 (0.06)	80.6 (0.06)	20.3 (0.06)	13.5 (0.05)	6.8 (0.04)	11.5 (0.28)	88.5 (0.28)	31.5 (0.41)	25.8 (0.38)	16.7 (0.33)	9.2 (0.28)
Oregon	74.2 (0.17)	86.8 (0.76)	14.9 (0.05)	85.1 (0.05)	25.1 (0.06)	16.4 (0.06)	8.7 (0.04)	9.8 (0.26)	90.2 (0.26)	21.9 (0.35)	34.2 (0.38)	21.1 (0.32)	13.1 (0.26)
Pennsylvania	79.8 (0.09)	88.2 (0.44)	18.1 (0.03)	81.9 (0.03)	22.4 (0.03)	14.0 (0.03)	8.4 (0.02)	8.9 (0.15)	91.1 (0.15)	34.9 (0.20)	31.8 (0.22)	19.0 (0.19)	12.9 (0.15)
Rhode Island	81.3 (0.32)	91.3 (1.32)	22.0 (0.13)	78.0 (0.13)	25.6 (0.14)	15.9 (0.12)	9.7 (0.10)	11.2 (0.45)	88.8 (0.45)	28.4 (0.68)	34.5 (0.71)	20.0 (0.50)	14.5 (0.53)
South Carolina	74.3 (0.18)	86.5 (0.70)	23.7 (0.07)	76.3 (0.07)	20.4 (0.07)	13.5 (0.06)	6.9 (0.04)	11.9 (0.25)	88.1 (0.25)	29.9 (0.36)	28.2 (0.31)	17.8 (0.27)	10.5 (0.19)
South Dakota	78.2 (0.33)	83.7 (1.65)	15.4 (0.12)	84.6 (0.12)	21.5 (0.13)	15.5 (0.12)	6.0 (0.08)	7.8 (0.46)	92.2 (0.46)	30.5 (0.97)	28.9 (0.92)	20.1 (0.71)	8.7 (0.60)
Tennessee	75.1 (0.16)	87.5 (0.58)	24.1 (0.06)	75.9 (0.06)	19.6 (0.06)	12.8 (0.05)	6.8 (0.03)	12.2 (0.20)	87.8 (0.20)	32.0 (0.28)	27.4 (0.29)	17.4 (0.20)	10.0 (0.21)
Texas	68.6 (0.08)	85.6 (0.28)	24.3 (0.03)	75.7 (0.03)	23.2 (0.03)	15.6 (0.03)	7.6 (0.02)	16.1 (0.13)	83.9 (0.13)	25.0 (0.14)	30.3 (0.14)	19.6 (0.11)	10.7 (0.10)
Utah	80.3 (0.16)	89.6 (0.70)	12.3 (0.07)	87.7 (0.07)	26.1 (0.09)	17.8 (0.08)	8.3 (0.06)	7.3 (0.33)	92.7 (0.33)	22.8 (0.44)	35.0 (0.51)	22.9 (0.38)	12.2 (0.33)
Vermont	83.0 (0.28)	91.3 (1.85)	13.6 (0.10)	86.4 (0.10)	29.4 (0.13)	18.3 (0.11)	11.1 (0.09)	6.6 (0.61)	93.4 (0.61)	29.0 (0.81)	39.1 (1.00)	23.4 (0.83)	15.7 (0.58)
Virginia	79.4 (0.13)	89.7 (0.46)	18.5 (0.05)	81.5 (0.05)	29.5 (0.06)	17.9 (0.05)	11.6 (0.04)	10.0 (0.17)	90.0 (0.17)	24.0 (0.24)	39.5 (0.29)	22.3 (0.26)	17.2 (0.22)
Washington	75.3 (0.16)	87.2 (0.57)	12.9 (0.05)	87.1 (0.05)	27.7 (0.06)	18.4 (0.05)	9.3 (0.04)	8.4 (0.15)	91.6 (0.15)	21.8 (0.23)	36.7 (0.31)	22.7 (0.24)	13.9 (0.19)
West Virginia	78.2 (0.22)	87.3 (1.26)	24.8 (0.09)	75.2 (0.09)	14.8 (0.07)	8.9 (0.06)	5.9 (0.05)	11.9 (0.39)	88.1 (0.39)	40.1 (0.59)	21.4 (0.56)	12.7 (0.38)	8.6 (0.32)
Wisconsin	78.9 (0.13)	89.2 (0.52)	14.9 (0.04)	85.1 (0.04)	22.4 (0.05)	15.2 (0.04)	7.2 (0.03)	7.7 (0.19)	92.3 (0.19)	30.9 (0.32)	30.2 (0.37)	19.8 (0.28)	10.4 (0.21)
Wyoming	79.0 (0.41)	88.2 (2.02)	12.1 (0.13)	87.9 (0.13)	21.9 (0.16)	14.9 (0.14)	7.0 (0.10)	7.3 (0.60)	92.7 (0.60)	28.9 (1.03)	27.0 (0.83)	17.3 (0.81)	9.7 (0.73)

#Rounds to zero.

[1]High school completers include those graduating from high school with a diploma as well as those completing high school through equivalency programs, such as a GED program.

NOTE: Data for 2018 are based on sample surveys of the entire population in the given age range residing within the United States, including both noninstitutionalized persons (e.g., those living in households, college housing, or military housing located within the United States) and institutionalized persons (e.g., those living in prisons, nursing facilities, or other healthcare facilities), while data for 2000 are based on sample surveys of the population residing in individual housing units only. Caution should be used when comparing data between these two years. Detail may not sum to totals because of rounding.

SOURCE: U.S. Department of Commerce, Census Bureau, Census 2000 Summary File 3, retrieved October 11, 2006, from https://factfinder2.census.gov/faces/tableservices/jsf/pages/productview.xhtml?pid=DEC_00_SF3_QTP20&prodType=table; Census Briefs, *Educational Attainment: 2000*; and American Community Survey (ACS), 2018. (This table was prepared February 2020.)

Table 104.85. Rates of high school completion and bachelor's degree attainment among persons age 25 and over, by race/ethnicity and state: 2018

[Standard errors appear in parentheses]

State	Percent with high school completion[1] or higher — Total[2]	White	Black	Hispanic	Asian	Two or more races	Percent with bachelor's or higher degree — Total[2]	White	Black	Hispanic	Asian	Two or more races
1	2	3	4	5	6	7	8	9	10	11	12	13
United States	88.3 (0.04)	93.1 (0.04)	86.6 (0.09)	69.7 (0.15)	87.7 (0.12)	92.0 (0.22)	32.6 (0.07)	36.3 (0.08)	22.1 (0.14)	17.0 (0.12)	55.3 (0.21)	35.9 (0.39)
Alabama	86.5 (0.28)	88.6 (0.31)	83.4 (0.56)	65.9 (2.38)	84.3 (2.45)	88.2 (2.32)	25.3 (0.34)	28.0 (0.41)	17.2 (0.58)	18.3 (2.13)	52.9 (3.14)	25.6 (2.89)
Alaska	94.0 (0.52)	96.5 (0.48)	98.2 (1.53)	88.5 (4.23)	91.6 (3.68)	95.7 (1.78)	30.1 (1.13)	36.5 (1.39)	23.5 (6.04)	23.1 (4.42)	24.6 (4.05)	24.6 (3.95)
Arizona	87.6 (0.17)	94.6 (0.18)	89.8 (1.02)	71.3 (0.51)	89.3 (1.05)	93.7 (1.04)	29.6 (0.26)	36.0 (0.31)	25.0 (1.33)	13.7 (0.40)	57.7 (1.84)	37.7 (2.76)
Arkansas	87.3 (0.30)	89.5 (0.33)	86.2 (0.79)	59.7 (2.38)	88.7 (3.40)	85.3 (2.59)	23.3 (0.40)	25.0 (0.46)	16.8 (1.02)	11.5 (1.40)	44.3 (3.84)	20.4 (2.72)
California	83.9 (0.09)	95.1 (0.08)	91.0 (0.30)	66.1 (0.23)	88.4 (0.19)	93.4 (0.37)	34.4 (0.11)	44.6 (0.17)	27.0 (0.54)	13.6 (0.19)	53.8 (0.33)	41.9 (0.84)
Colorado	92.2 (0.19)	96.8 (0.14)	90.4 (1.14)	73.7 (0.79)	90.4 (0.98)	95.4 (0.84)	42.0 (0.29)	48.3 (0.32)	28.6 (1.94)	17.0 (0.64)	56.6 (1.54)	44.2 (2.24)
Connecticut	90.8 (0.24)	94.6 (0.23)	88.0 (0.83)	73.9 (1.10)	89.4 (1.04)	89.6 (2.38)	39.7 (0.35)	44.6 (0.43)	22.9 (1.19)	16.9 (0.82)	65.3 (1.70)	45.4 (4.54)
Delaware	89.6 (0.57)	93.2 (0.52)	88.7 (1.15)	61.9 (3.18)	85.3 (4.30)	89.2 (4.91)	31.2 (0.77)	34.2 (0.93)	22.1 (1.65)	17.2 (2.24)	55.2 (4.92)	23.4 (5.21)
District of Columbia	91.8 (0.57)	99.3 (0.23)	87.6 (1.05)	76.0 (3.32)	96.8 (1.72)	96.2 (1.82)	60.2 (0.61)	92.9 (0.62)	27.8 (1.29)	53.9 (3.67)	88.9 (2.61)	70.4 (5.35)
Florida	88.5 (0.09)	93.1 (0.12)	83.7 (0.41)	80.0 (0.28)	87.9 (0.63)	92.2 (0.88)	30.5 (0.15)	34.0 (0.17)	20.0 (0.48)	25.5 (0.29)	50.0 (1.16)	35.0 (1.57)
Georgia	87.5 (0.18)	90.8 (0.20)	87.6 (0.27)	61.8 (1.05)	87.1 (0.88)	92.6 (1.31)	32.0 (0.21)	35.9 (0.26)	24.6 (0.47)	18.1 (0.75)	56.4 (1.17)	39.5 (2.41)
Hawaii	91.7 (0.42)	97.1 (0.42)	95.8 (2.16)	89.1 (1.37)	88.9 (0.78)	95.3 (0.64)	33.2 (0.65)	44.1 (1.56)	30.8 (4.63)	27.2 (2.02)	35.0 (1.01)	26.3 (1.39)
Idaho	90.7 (0.39)	93.8 (0.34)	92.4 (5.30)	64.3 (2.56)	90.2 (3.78)	96.8 (1.73)	27.4 (0.52)	29.3 (0.56)	24.5 (7.26)	11.0 (1.42)	41.5 (5.73)	22.8 (4.37)
Illinois	89.4 (0.14)	94.2 (0.11)	86.7 (0.46)	69.2 (0.70)	90.9 (0.62)	91.5 (1.47)	35.2 (0.21)	39.5 (0.24)	22.1 (0.57)	14.4 (0.43)	66.4 (0.97)	41.0 (2.25)
Indiana	88.8 (0.22)	90.5 (0.21)	86.0 (0.74)	68.6 (1.81)	83.5 (1.94)	88.2 (2.08)	26.9 (0.29)	27.7 (0.33)	18.6 (0.90)	14.0 (1.07)	58.8 (2.45)	31.2 (2.68)
Iowa	92.2 (0.27)	94.3 (0.24)	81.5 (3.21)	62.1 (2.73)	82.3 (2.95)	93.1 (2.23)	28.6 (0.49)	29.4 (0.47)	12.0 (2.22)	14.3 (1.79)	48.0 (3.98)	26.6 (5.26)
Kansas	90.9 (0.27)	94.4 (0.26)	86.5 (1.83)	63.8 (1.68)	87.7 (2.08)	94.2 (1.57)	33.4 (0.38)	35.9 (0.45)	20.3 (2.07)	13.8 (1.29)	58.1 (2.42)	25.4 (3.29)
Kentucky	87.1 (0.28)	87.7 (0.27)	87.0 (0.98)	70.6 (2.65)	82.1 (2.61)	86.4 (2.35)	25.2 (0.31)	25.6 (0.33)	17.0 (1.25)	21.1 (2.30)	50.6 (3.39)	28.5 (3.78)
Louisiana	86.0 (0.33)	89.3 (0.32)	81.5 (0.57)	73.2 (1.90)	83.4 (2.09)	91.1 (2.15)	24.3 (0.31)	28.4 (0.43)	15.3 (0.48)	19.1 (1.61)	44.7 (2.86)	29.8 (2.86)
Maine	92.8 (0.43)	93.0 (0.44)	74.0 (11.31)	92.1 (2.27)	87.0 (4.35)	98.1 (1.24)	30.6 (0.62)	30.7 (0.61)	20.2! (7.30)	41.3 (6.33)	34.8 (6.26)	24.1 (5.34)
Maryland	90.5 (0.21)	94.2 (0.21)	90.0 (0.34)	68.5 (1.15)	89.9 (1.06)	92.4 (1.11)	40.7 (0.33)	46.3 (0.40)	30.0 (0.53)	23.3 (0.99)	64.4 (1.34)	43.2 (2.14)
Massachusetts	90.8 (0.18)	94.3 (0.18)	86.6 (0.83)	70.5 (0.85)	86.6 (0.80)	92.6 (1.57)	44.4 (0.28)	47.8 (0.31)	30.2 (1.07)	21.5 (0.86)	62.7 (1.24)	47.8 (2.63)
Michigan	91.0 (0.16)	92.8 (0.16)	86.2 (0.49)	75.1 (1.28)	89.8 (0.99)	88.2 (1.50)	29.6 (0.27)	30.7 (0.27)	17.8 (0.73)	19.7 (1.15)	65.5 (1.54)	26.8 (1.94)
Minnesota	93.4 (0.16)	96.0 (0.14)	81.7 (1.65)	70.6 (2.42)	84.8 (1.30)	91.7 (2.05)	37.2 (0.40)	38.5 (0.45)	23.0 (1.98)	21.9 (1.61)	48.1 (2.19)	35.3 (3.68)
Mississippi	85.4 (0.34)	88.4 (0.39)	81.4 (0.60)	68.0 (3.11)	88.0 (2.33)	88.1 (3.25)	23.4 (0.43)	27.2 (0.53)	16.7 (0.54)	17.8 (2.69)	47.4 (4.15)	33.5 (5.85)
Missouri	90.3 (0.22)	91.4 (0.21)	86.6 (0.78)	75.6 (1.93)	91.8 (1.32)	89.1 (2.10)	29.6 (0.26)	30.4 (0.33)	19.2 (0.93)	23.1 (1.42)	63.0 (2.72)	26.5 (2.12)
Montana	93.4 (0.39)	94.2 (0.40)	‡ (†)	90.3 (3.20)	80.9 (7.21)	88.8 (4.05)	30.4 (0.80)	31.4 (0.78)	‡ (†)	31.2 (7.44)	40.5 (11.17)	13.8 (3.51)
Nebraska	91.8 (0.24)	95.0 (0.22)	88.6 (2.13)	66.0 (2.15)	80.3 (3.10)	84.3 (4.77)	32.9 (0.53)	35.2 (0.55)	22.6 (3.13)	13.8 (1.65)	44.7 (4.58)	25.4 (4.45)
Nevada	86.8 (0.29)	93.9 (0.27)	89.5 (1.09)	67.3 (0.89)	90.3 (0.88)	91.9 (1.67)	24.9 (0.41)	29.6 (0.59)	17.3 (1.29)	11.6 (0.64)	38.3 (1.54)	28.4 (2.87)
New Hampshire	92.9 (0.31)	94.0 (0.30)	72.8 (5.01)	74.6 (3.34)	87.6 (2.42)	90.2 (4.02)	37.2 (0.59)	37.3 (0.61)	13.8! (4.81)	20.4 (3.30)	62.7 (4.15)	35.0 (5.51)
New Jersey	90.1 (0.17)	94.7 (0.14)	88.0 (0.55)	75.2 (0.63)	92.4 (0.39)	94.1 (0.95)	40.6 (0.24)	44.8 (0.29)	25.6 (0.71)	20.6 (0.52)	70.9 (0.74)	48.9 (2.15)
New Mexico	85.3 (0.43)	95.5 (0.28)	89.1 (3.37)	76.5 (0.84)	87.1 (3.02)	95.3 (1.68)	27.5 (0.50)	42.2 (0.78)	22.6 (3.61)	15.3 (0.64)	56.2 (4.40)	33.7 (4.10)
New York	87.2 (0.12)	93.5 (0.12)	84.7 (0.42)	71.7 (0.44)	80.0 (0.47)	89.9 (0.95)	37.3 (0.18)	43.5 (0.21)	25.0 (0.46)	20.1 (0.42)	48.5 (0.66)	44.8 (1.52)
North Carolina	88.3 (0.17)	91.7 (0.17)	86.6 (0.35)	62.7 (1.16)	85.7 (1.31)	90.2 (1.47)	31.9 (0.23)	35.8 (0.25)	21.4 (0.54)	16.2 (0.88)	58.6 (1.68)	34.2 (2.07)
North Dakota	92.6 (0.51)	94.1 (0.41)	80.4 (7.18)	86.6 (4.34)	67.6 (8.97)	91.0 (5.22)	28.8 (1.00)	29.8 (1.11)	23.3! (8.35)	19.4 (4.75)	38.2 (8.59)	23.2! (7.29)
Ohio	90.5 (0.13)	91.9 (0.13)	85.4 (0.57)	77.4 (1.26)	86.8 (1.18)	89.1 (1.50)	28.8 (0.21)	29.9 (0.21)	17.6 (0.57)	20.3 (1.28)	59.6 (1.67)	27.7 (1.75)
Oklahoma	88.5 (0.28)	91.3 (0.25)	90.6 (0.89)	61.7 (1.67)	86.0 (2.16)	89.3 (1.01)	25.2 (0.38)	28.3 (0.44)	19.4 (1.39)	9.9 (0.98)	53.5 (3.84)	25.2 (1.82)
Oregon	90.2 (0.26)	94.0 (0.22)	88.6 (2.22)	62.5 (1.58)	86.0 (1.29)	90.5 (1.43)	34.2 (0.38)	36.1 (0.42)	27.6 (2.61)	15.9 (0.96)	51.0 (1.36)	30.6 (1.95)
Pennsylvania	91.1 (0.15)	93.2 (0.10)	87.6 (0.59)	71.4 (1.03)	85.5 (1.03)	92.1 (1.25)	31.8 (0.22)	33.3 (0.24)	19.8 (0.79)	16.8 (0.79)	59.2 (1.68)	28.7 (2.17)
Rhode Island	88.8 (0.45)	91.7 (0.40)	80.4 (1.94)	73.6 (2.30)	67.6 (2.81)	88.8 (4.31)	34.5 (0.71)	37.9 (0.81)	23.6 (2.99)	16.1 (1.75)	45.7 (4.23)	35.3 (5.65)
South Carolina	88.1 (0.25)	91.0 (0.28)	83.5 (0.66)	69.2 (1.73)	91.7 (1.83)	90.2 (1.78)	28.2 (0.31)	33.0 (0.40)	15.6 (0.65)	18.3 (1.35)	52.4 (3.04)	31.5 (3.14)
South Dakota	92.2 (0.46)	94.7 (0.39)	76.1 (7.61)	65.0 (6.39)	68.3 (9.62)	83.8 (7.59)	28.9 (0.92)	31.1 (0.99)	12.1! (5.65)	15.0 (4.32)	44.5 (8.72)	25.8! (7.75)
Tennessee	87.6 (0.20)	89.4 (0.19)	85.9 (0.54)	65.0 (1.66)	87.3 (1.66)	90.6 (1.52)	27.4 (0.29)	28.7 (0.31)	20.0 (0.72)	17.4 (1.25)	51.4 (2.45)	25.7 (2.39)
Texas	83.9 (0.13)	94.4 (0.10)	90.0 (0.27)	66.7 (0.28)	87.7 (0.47)	93.7 (0.72)	30.3 (0.14)	39.3 (0.20)	25.1 (0.44)	15.1 (0.21)	59.8 (0.71)	39.6 (1.21)
Utah	92.7 (0.33)	95.7 (0.24)	88.5 (4.08)	73.7 (1.79)	91.4 (1.79)	96.2 (1.74)	35.0 (0.51)	37.8 (0.54)	22.5 (5.57)	16.6 (1.23)	51.1 (3.62)	35.5 (3.63)
Vermont	93.4 (0.61)	93.6 (0.61)	‡ (†)	89.0 (4.72)	89.0 (7.83)	85.6 (6.87)	39.1 (1.00)	38.2 (0.97)	‡ (†)	35.9 (8.92)	80.9 (6.90)	51.8 (10.40)
Virginia	90.0 (0.17)	93.1 (0.15)	86.1 (0.47)	72.0 (1.13)	90.7 (0.52)	92.2 (1.10)	39.5 (0.29)	43.0 (0.32)	24.5 (0.65)	24.9 (0.92)	63.5 (1.01)	39.6 (2.03)
Washington	91.6 (0.15)	95.2 (0.14)	90.0 (1.02)	66.8 (1.58)	86.8 (0.48)	94.0 (0.69)	36.7 (0.31)	37.9 (0.32)	27.3 (1.55)	16.2 (0.63)	55.0 (1.03)	36.7 (1.58)
West Virginia	88.1 (0.39)	88.0 (0.40)	91.4 (1.78)	76.2 (5.27)	98.7 (1.06)	82.0 (4.38)	21.4 (0.56)	21.4 (0.58)	13.4 (1.77)	24.4 (4.66)	61.6 (7.39)	18.3 (4.52)
Wisconsin	92.3 (0.19)	94.3 (0.16)	85.2 (1.10)	71.6 (1.77)	83.0 (2.13)	95.3 (1.65)	30.2 (0.37)	31.6 (0.37)	15.8 (1.45)	16.5 (1.34)	45.8 (2.92)	36.8 (3.72)
Wyoming	92.7 (0.60)	93.8 (0.53)	‡ (†)	81.0 (3.83)	‡ (†)	95.1 (3.64)	28.5 (0.83)	28.5 (0.94)	‡ (†)	10.1 (2.12)	‡ (†)	‡ (†)

†Not applicable.
‡Reporting standards not met. Either there are too few cases for a reliable estimate or the coefficient of variation (CV) is 50 percent or greater.
!Interpret data with caution. The coefficient of variation (CV) for this estimate is between 30 and 50 percent.
[1]Includes completion of high school through equivalency programs, such as a GED program.
[2]Total includes racial/ethnic groups not shown separately.

NOTE: Data are based on sample surveys of the entire population in the given age range residing within the United States, including both noninstitutionalized persons (e.g., those living in households, college housing, or military housing located within the United States) and institutionalized persons (e.g., those living in prisons, nursing facilities, or other healthcare facilities). Race categories exclude persons of Hispanic ethnicity.
SOURCE: U.S. Department of Commerce, Census Bureau, American Community Survey (ACS), 2018 (This table was prepared February 2020.)

Table 105.10.   Projected number of participants in educational institutions, by level and control of institution: Fall 2019

[In millions]

Participants	All levels (elementary, secondary, and degree-granting postsecondary)	Elementary and secondary schools			Degree-granting postsecondary institutions		
		Total	Public	Private	Total	Public	Private
1	2	3	4	5	6	7	8
Total	**86.5**	**63.8**	**57.2**	**6.6**	**22.7**	**16.6**	**6.2**
Enrollment	76.1	56.3	50.6	5.7	19.7	14.6	5.1
Teachers and faculty	4.7	3.7	3.2	0.5	1.1	0.7	0.4
Other professional, administrative, and support staff	5.7	3.8	3.4	0.4	1.9	1.3	0.7

NOTE: Includes enrollments in local public school systems and in most private schools (religiously affiliated and nonsectarian). Excludes federal Bureau of Indian Education schools and Department of Defense Education Activity schools. Excludes private preprimary enrollment in schools that do not offer kindergarten or above. Degree-granting institutions grant associate's or higher degrees and participate in Title IV federal financial aid programs. Data for teachers and other staff in public and private elementary and secondary schools and colleges and universities are reported in terms of full-time equivalents. Detail may not sum to totals because of rounding.

SOURCE: U.S. Department of Education, National Center for Education Statistics, National Elementary and Secondary Enrollment Projection Model, 1972 through 2029; Enrollment in Degree-Granting Institutions Projection Model, 2000 through 2029; Elementary and Secondary Teacher Projection Model, 1973 through 2029; and unpublished projections and estimates. (This table was prepared January 2020.)

Table 105.20. Enrollment in elementary, secondary, and degree-granting postsecondary institutions, by level and control of institution, enrollment level, and attendance status and sex of student: Selected years, fall 1990 through fall 2029

[In thousands]

Level and control of institution, enrollment level, and attendance status and sex of student	Actual				Projected												
	1990	2000	2010	2017	2018	2019	2020	2021	2022	2023	2024	2025	2026	2027	2028	2029
1	2	3	4	5	6	7	8	9	10	11	12	13	14	15	16	17
All levels	60,683	68,685	75,886	76,184[1]	76,013	76,070	76,112	76,122	76,247	76,342	76,386	76,397	76,441	76,538	76,714	76,921
Elementary and secondary schools[2]	46,864	53,373	54,867	56,406[1]	56,367	56,350	56,368	56,343	56,434	56,480	56,460	56,404	56,370	56,439	56,605	56,806
Public	41,217	47,204	49,484	50,686[1]	50,650	50,634	50,654	50,643	50,721	50,768	50,758	50,704	50,672	50,734	50,885	51,068
Private	5,648[3]	6,169[3]	5,382[3]	5,720	5,717	5,716	5,714	5,700	5,713	5,712	5,702	5,700	5,699	5,704	5,720	5,738
Prekindergarten to grade 8	34,388	38,592	38,708	39,748[1]	39,656	39,605	39,476	39,256	39,190	39,196	39,309	39,470	39,676	39,886	40,082	40,268
Public[4]	29,876	33,686	34,625	35,496[1]	35,443	35,402	35,293	35,094	35,019	35,022	35,123	35,267	35,452	35,641	35,818	35,987
Private	4,512[3]	4,906[3]	4,084[3]	4,252	4,213	4,203	4,183	4,161	4,171	4,174	4,187	4,204	4,224	4,245	4,263	4,281
Grades 9 to 12	12,476	14,781	16,159	16,658	16,711	16,745	16,892	17,088	17,245	17,285	17,150	16,934	16,694	16,553	16,523	16,539
Public[4,5]	11,341	13,517	14,860	15,190	15,206	15,232	15,361	15,549	15,703	15,746	15,635	15,438	15,220	15,093	15,067	15,081
Private	1,136[3]	1,264[3]	1,299[3]	1,468	1,504	1,512	1,531	1,539	1,542	1,538	1,515	1,496	1,474	1,460	1,456	1,457
Degree-granting post-secondary institutions	13,819	15,312	21,019	19,778	19,646[6]	19,720	19,744	19,778	19,813	19,862	19,926	19,993	20,070	20,099	20,110	20,115
Undergraduate	11,959	13,155	18,082	16,773	16,610[6]	16,673	16,692	16,721	16,750	16,790	16,845	16,901	16,967	16,991	16,999	17,003
Full-time	6,976	7,923	11,457	10,372	10,267[6]	10,296	10,293	10,292	10,297	10,312	10,341	10,377	10,415	10,419	10,410	10,397
Part-time	4,983	5,232	6,625	6,401	6,343[6]	6,377	6,399	6,428	6,452	6,478	6,504	6,524	6,551	6,572	6,589	6,606
Male	5,380	5,778	7,836	7,351	7,226[6]	7,250	7,254	7,263	7,273	7,288	7,312	7,338	7,367	7,378	7,383	7,385
Female	6,579	7,377	10,246	9,422	9,384[6]	9,423	9,438	9,457	9,477	9,503	9,533	9,564	9,600	9,613	9,616	9,618
2-year	5,240	5,948	7,684	5,953	5,745[6]	5,770	5,783	5,799	5,814	5,832	5,853	5,872	5,895	5,907	5,915	5,922
4-year	6,719	7,207	10,399	10,820	10,865[6]	10,902	10,910	10,921	10,936	10,958	10,992	11,030	11,072	11,083	11,084	11,080
Public	9,710	10,539	13,703	13,113	13,049[6]	13,100	13,118	13,142	13,167	13,201	13,244	13,289	13,340	13,361	13,370	13,375
Private	2,250	2,616	4,379	3,660	3,561[6]	3,573	3,575	3,578	3,582	3,590	3,600	3,613	3,626	3,630	3,629	3,628
Postbaccalaureate	1,860	2,157	2,937	3,005	3,036[6]	3,048	3,052	3,058	3,064	3,071	3,081	3,092	3,104	3,109	3,111	3,112
Full-time	845	1,087	1,630	1,704	1,725[6]	1,729	1,729	1,729	1,730	1,732	1,737	1,743	1,750	1,750	1,749	1,747
Part-time	1,015	1,070	1,307	1,301	1,311[6]	1,318	1,323	1,329	1,334	1,339	1,344	1,349	1,354	1,358	1,362	1,365
Male	904	944	1,209	1,220	1,217[6]	1,221	1,222	1,223	1,225	1,228	1,232	1,236	1,241	1,243	1,244	1,245
Female	955	1,213	1,728	1,785	1,819[6]	1,827	1,830	1,834	1,838	1,844	1,850	1,856	1,863	1,865	1,866	1,867

[1]Includes imputations for public school prekindergarten enrollment in California and Oregon.
[2]Includes enrollments in local public school systems and in most private schools (religiously affiliated and nonsectarian). Excludes homeschooled children who were not also enrolled in public and private schools. Private elementary enrollment includes preprimary students in schools offering kindergarten or higher grades.
[3]Estimated.
[4]Includes prorated proportion of students classified as ungraded. The total ungraded counts of students were prorated to the elementary level (prekindergarten to grade 8) and the secondary level (grades 9 to 12) based on prior reports.
[5]In addition to students in grades 9 to 12 and ungraded secondary students, includes a small number of students reported as being enrolled in grade 13.
[6]Data are actual.

NOTE: Postsecondary data for 1990 are for institutions of higher education, while later data are for degree-granting institutions. Degree-granting institutions grant associate's or higher degrees and participate in Title IV federal financial aid programs. Detail may not sum to totals because of rounding. Some data have been revised from previously published figures. SOURCE: U.S. Department of Education, National Center for Education Statistics, Common Core of Data (CCD), "State Nonfiscal Survey of Public Elementary and Secondary Education," 1990–91 through 2017–18; Private School Universe Survey (PSS), 1995–96 through 2017–18; National Elementary and Secondary Enrollment Projection Model, 1972 through 2029; Integrated Postsecondary Education Data System (IPEDS), "Fall Enrollment Survey" (IPEDS-EF:90–99); IPEDS Spring 2001 through Spring 2019, Fall Enrollment component; and Enrollment in Degree-Granting Institutions Projection Model, 2000 through 2029. (This table was prepared December 2019.)

Table 105.30. Enrollment in elementary, secondary, and degree-granting postsecondary institutions, by level and control of institution: Selected years, 1869–70 through fall 2029

[In thousands]

Year	Total enrollment, all levels	Elementary and secondary, total	Public elementary and secondary schools			Private elementary and secondary schools[1]			Degree-granting postsecondary institutions[2]		
			Total	Prekindergarten through grade 8[3]	Grades 9 through 12[3]	Total	Prekindergarten through grade 8	Grades 9 through 12	Total	Public	Private
1	2	3	4	5	6	7	8	9	10	11	12
1869–70	—	—	6,872	6,792	80	—	—	—	52	—	—
1879–80	—	—	9,868	9,757	110	—	—	—	116	—	—
1889–90	14,491	14,334	12,723	12,520	203	1,611	1,516	95	157	—	—
1899–1900	17,092	16,855	15,503	14,984	519	1,352	1,241	111	238	—	—
1909–10	19,728	19,372	17,814	16,899	915	1,558	1,441	117	355	—	—
1919–20	23,876	23,278	21,578	19,378	2,200	1,699	1,486	214	598	—	—
1929–30	29,430	28,329	25,678	21,279	4,399	2,651	2,310	341	1,101	—	—
1939–40	29,539	28,045	25,434	18,832	6,601	2,611	2,153	458	1,494	797	698
1949–50	31,151	28,492	25,111	19,387	5,725	3,380	2,708	672	2,659	1,355	1,304
Fall 1959	44,497	40,857	35,182	26,911	8,271	5,675	4,640	1,035	3,640	2,181	1,459
Fall 1969	59,055	51,050	45,550	32,513	13,037	5,500[4]	4,200[4]	1,300[4]	8,005	5,897	2,108
Fall 1985	57,226	44,979	39,422	27,034	12,388	5,557	4,195	1,362	12,247	9,479	2,768
Fall 1990	60,683	46,864	41,217	29,876	11,341	5,648[4]	4,512[4]	1,136[4]	13,819	10,845	2,974
Fall 1991	62,087	47,728	42,047	30,503	11,544	5,681	4,550	1,131	14,359	11,310	3,049
Fall 1992	63,181	48,694	42,823	31,086	11,737	5,870[4]	4,746[4]	1,125[4]	14,487	11,385	3,103
Fall 1993	63,837	49,532	43,465	31,502	11,963	6,067	4,950	1,118	14,305	11,189	3,116
Fall 1994	64,385	50,106	44,111	31,896	12,215	5,994[4]	4,856[4]	1,138[4]	14,279	11,134	3,145
Fall 1995	65,020	50,759	44,840	32,338	12,502	5,918	4,756	1,163	14,262	11,092	3,169
Fall 1996	65,911	51,544	45,611	32,762	12,849	5,933[4]	4,755[4]	1,178[4]	14,368	11,120	3,247
Fall 1997	66,574	52,071	46,127	33,071	13,056	5,944	4,759	1,185	14,502	11,196	3,306
Fall 1998	67,033	52,526	46,539	33,344	13,195	5,988[4]	4,776[4]	1,212[4]	14,507	11,138	3,369
Fall 1999	67,725	52,875	46,857	33,486	13,371	6,018	4,789	1,229	14,850	11,376	3,474
Fall 2000	68,685	53,373	47,204	33,686	13,517	6,169[4]	4,906[4]	1,264[4]	15,312	11,753	3,560
Fall 2001	69,920	53,992	47,672	33,936	13,736	6,320	5,023	1,296	15,928	12,233	3,695
Fall 2002	71,015	54,403	48,183	34,114	14,069	6,220[4]	4,915[4]	1,306[4]	16,612	12,752	3,860
Fall 2003	71,551	54,639	48,540	34,201	14,339	6,099	4,788	1,311	16,911	12,859	4,053
Fall 2004	72,154	54,882	48,795	34,178	14,618	6,087[4]	4,756[4]	1,331[4]	17,272	12,980	4,292
Fall 2005	72,674	55,187	49,113	34,204	14,909	6,073	4,724	1,349	17,487	13,022	4,466
Fall 2006	73,061	55,307	49,316	34,235	15,081	5,991[4]	4,631[4]	1,360[4]	17,754	13,175	4,579
Fall 2007	73,459	55,201	49,291	34,204	15,086	5,910	4,546	1,364	18,258	13,501	4,757
Fall 2008	74,055	54,973	49,266	34,286	14,980	5,707[4]	4,365[4]	1,342[4]	19,082	13,971	5,111
Fall 2009	75,163	54,849	49,361	34,409	14,952	5,488	4,179	1,309	20,314	14,811	5,503
Fall 2010	75,886	54,867	49,484	34,625	14,860	5,382[4]	4,084[4]	1,299[4]	21,019	15,142	5,877
Fall 2011	75,800	54,790	49,522	34,773	14,749	5,268	3,977	1,291	21,011	15,116	5,894
Fall 2012	75,748	55,104	49,771	35,018	14,753	5,333[4]	4,031[4]	1,302[4]	20,644	14,885	5,760
Fall 2013	75,817	55,440	50,045	35,251	14,794	5,396	4,084	1,312	20,377	14,747	5,630
Fall 2014	76,097	55,888	50,313	35,370	14,943	5,575[4]	4,202[4]	1,373[4]	20,209	14,655	5,554
Fall 2015	76,177[5]	56,189[5]	50,438[5]	35,388[5]	15,050	5,751	4,304	1,446	19,988	14,573	5,415
Fall 2016	76,216[6]	56,369[6]	50,615[6]	35,477[6]	15,138	5,754[4]	4,272[4]	1,482[4]	19,847	14,586	5,261
Fall 2017	76,184[5]	56,406[5]	50,686[5]	35,496[5]	15,190	5,720	4,252	1,468	19,778	14,572	5,206
Fall 2018[7]	76,013	56,367	50,650	35,443	15,206	5,717	4,213	1,504	19,646	14,529	5,117
Fall 2019[7]	76,070	56,350	50,634	35,402	15,232	5,716	4,203	1,512	19,720	14,586	5,135
Fall 2020[7]	76,112	56,368	50,654	35,293	15,361	5,714	4,183	1,531	19,744	14,605	5,139
Fall 2021[7]	76,122	56,343	50,643	35,094	15,549	5,700	4,161	1,539	19,778	14,633	5,145
Fall 2022[7]	76,247	56,434	50,721	35,019	15,703	5,713	4,171	1,542	19,813	14,661	5,152
Fall 2023[7]	76,342	56,480	50,768	35,022	15,746	5,712	4,174	1,538	19,862	14,698	5,163
Fall 2024[7]	76,386	56,460	50,758	35,123	15,635	5,702	4,187	1,515	19,926	14,747	5,179
Fall 2025[7]	76,397	56,404	50,704	35,267	15,438	5,700	4,204	1,496	19,993	14,796	5,197
Fall 2026[7]	76,441	56,370	50,672	35,452	15,220	5,699	4,224	1,474	20,070	14,854	5,217
Fall 2027[7]	76,538	56,439	50,734	35,641	15,093	5,704	4,245	1,460	20,099	14,877	5,222
Fall 2028[7]	76,714	56,605	50,885	35,818	15,067	5,720	4,263	1,456	20,110	14,887	5,223
Fall 2029[7]	76,921	56,806	51,068	35,987	15,081	5,738	4,281	1,457	20,115	14,893	5,222

—Not available.
[1]Beginning in fall 1985, data include estimates for an expanded universe of private schools. Therefore, direct comparisons with earlier years should be avoided.
[2]Data for 1869–70 through 1949–50 include resident degree-credit students enrolled at any time during the academic year. Beginning in 1959, data include all resident and extension students enrolled at the beginning of the fall term.
[3]Total counts of ungraded students were prorated to prekindergarten through grade 8 and grades 9 through 12 based on prior reports.
[4]Estimated.
[5]Includes imputations for public school prekindergarten enrollment in California and Oregon.
[6]Includes imputations for public school prekindergarten enrollment in California.
[7]Projected data. Fall 2017 data for degree-granting institutions are actual.
NOTE: Data for 1869–70 through 1949–50 reflect enrollment for the entire school year. Elementary and secondary enrollment includes students in local public school systems and in most private schools (religiously affiliated and nonsectarian), but generally excludes homeschooled children and students in subcollegiate departments of colleges and in federal schools. Excludes preprimary students in private schools that do not offer kindergarten or higher grades. Postsecondary data through 1995 are for institutions of

higher education, while later data are for degree-granting institutions. Degree-granting institutions grant associate's or higher degrees and participate in Title IV federal financial aid programs. Some data have been revised from previously published figures. Detail may not sum to totals because of rounding.
SOURCE: U.S. Department of Education, National Center for Education Statistics, *Annual Report of the Commissioner of Education*, 1870 to 1910; *Biennial Survey of Education in the United States*, 1919–20 through 1949–50; *Statistics of Public Elementary and Secondary School Systems*, 1959 through 1979; *Statistics of Nonpublic Elementary and Secondary Schools*, 1959 through 1980; 1985–86 Private School Survey; Common Core of Data (CCD), "State Nonfiscal Survey of Public Elementary and Secondary Education," 1985–86 through 2017–18; Private School Universe Survey (PSS), 1991–92 through 2017–18; National Elementary and Secondary Enrollment Projection Model, 1972 through 2029; Opening (Fall) Enrollment in Higher Education, 1959; Higher Education General Information Survey (HEGIS), "Fall Enrollment in Institutions of Higher Education" surveys, 1969 and 1985; Integrated Postsecondary Education Data System (IPEDS), "Fall Enrollment Survey" (IPEDS-EF:90–99); IPEDS Spring 2001 through Spring 2019, Fall Enrollment component; and Enrollment in Degree-Granting Institutions Projection Model, 2000 through 2029. (This table was prepared December 2019.)

Table 105.40. Number of teachers in elementary and secondary schools, and faculty in degree-granting postsecondary institutions, by control of institution: Selected years, fall 1970 through fall 2029

[In thousands]

Year	All levels			Elementary and secondary teachers[1]			Degree-granting institutions instructional staff[2]		
	Total	Public	Private	Total	Public	Private	Total	Public	Private
1	2	3	4	5	6	7	8	9	10
1970	2,766	2,373	393	2,292	2,059	233	474	314	160
1975	3,081	2,641	440	2,453	2,198	255[3]	628	443	185
1980	3,171	2,679	492	2,485	2,184	301	686[3,4]	495[3,4]	191[3,4]
1981	3,145	2,636	509	2,440	2,127	313[3]	705	509	196
1982	3,168	2,639	529	2,458	2,133	325[3]	710[3,4]	506[3,4]	204[3,4]
1983	3,200	2,651	549	2,476	2,139	337	724	512	212
1984	3,225	2,673	552	2,508	2,168	340[3]	717[3,4]	505[3,4]	212[3,4]
1985	3,264	2,709	555	2,549	2,206	343	715[3,4]	503[3,4]	212[3,4]
1986	3,314	2,754	560	2,592	2,244	348[3]	722[3,4]	510[3,4]	212[3,4]
1987	3,424	2,832	592	2,631	2,279	352	793	553	240
1988	3,472	2,882	590	2,668	2,323	345	804[3]	559[3]	245[3]
1989	3,537	2,934	603	2,713	2,357	356	824	577	247
1990	3,577	2,972	604	2,759	2,398	361[3]	817[3]	574[3]	244[3]
1991	3,623	3,013	610	2,797	2,432	365	826	581	245
1992	3,700	3,080	621	2,823	2,459	364[3]	877[3]	621[3]	257[3]
1993	3,784	3,154	629	2,868	2,504	364	915	650	265
1994	3,846	3,205	640	2,922	2,552	370[3]	923[3]	653[3]	270[3]
1995	3,906	3,255	651	2,974	2,598	376	932	657	275
1996	4,006	3,339	666	3,051	2,667	384[3]	954[3]	672[3]	282[3]
1997	4,127	3,441	687	3,138	2,746	391	990	695	295
1998	4,230	3,527	703	3,230	2,830	400[3]	999[3]	697[3]	303[3]
1999	4,347	3,624	723	3,319	2,911	408	1,028	713	315
2000	4,432	3,683	750	3,366	2,941	424[3]	1,067[3]	741[3]	325[3]
2001	4,554	3,771	783	3,440	3,000	441	1,113	771	342
2002	4,631	3,829	802	3,476	3,034	442[3]	1,155[3]	794[3]	361[3]
2003	4,663	3,840	823	3,490	3,049	441	1,174	792	382
2004	4,773	3,909	863	3,536	3,091	445[3]	1,237[3]	818[3]	418[3]
2005	4,883	3,984	899	3,593	3,143	450	1,290	841	449
2006	4,944	4,020	924	3,622	3,166	456[3]	1,322[3]	853[3]	468[3]
2007	5,028	4,077	951	3,656	3,200	456	1,372	877	495
2008	5,063	4,106	957	3,670	3,222	448[3]	1,393[3]	884[3]	509[3]
2009	5,086	4,123	963	3,647	3,210	437	1,439	914	525
2010	5,022	4,044	978	3,512	3,099	413[3]	1,510[3]	945[3]	565[3]
2011	5,032	4,057	975	3,508	3,103	405	1,524	954	570
2012	5,049	4,067	981	3,517	3,109	408[3]	1,531[3]	958[3]	573[3]
2013	5,101	4,082	1,018	3,555	3,114	441	1,545	969	577
2014	5,146	4,102	1,044	3,594	3,132	461[3]	1,552[3]	970[3]	582[3]
2015	5,185	4,122	1,063	3,633	3,151	482	1,552	971	581
2016	5,199	4,144	1,055	3,653	3,169	483[3]	1,546	974	572
2017	5,198	4,142	1,055	3,652	3,170	482	1,546	973	573
2018[5]	5,182	4,137	1,044	3,639	3,157	482	1,543	981	562
2019[6]	—	—	—	3,661	3,176	485	—	—	—
2020[6]	—	—	—	3,670	3,184	486	—	—	—
2021[6]	—	—	—	3,684	3,197	488	—	—	—
2022[6]	—	—	—	3,708	3,217	491	—	—	—
2023[6]	—	—	—	3,731	3,237	494	—	—	—
2024[6]	—	—	—	3,758	3,260	498	—	—	—
2025[6]	—	—	—	3,786	3,284	502	—	—	—
2026[6]	—	—	—	3,813	3,307	506	—	—	—
2027[6]	—	—	—	3,842	3,332	510	—	—	—
2028[6]	—	—	—	3,880	3,364	516	—	—	—
2029[6]	—	—	—	3,909	3,390	520	—	—	—

—Not available.
[1]Includes teachers in local public school systems and in most private schools (religiously affiliated and nonsectarian). Teachers are reported in terms of full-time equivalents.
[2]Includes full-time and part-time faculty with the rank of instructor or above in colleges, universities, professional schools, and 2-year colleges. Excludes teaching assistants. Headcounts are used to report data for faculty. Data through 1995 are for institutions of higher education, while later data are for degree-granting institutions. Degree-granting institutions grant associate's or higher degrees and participate in Title IV federal financial aid programs. The degree-granting classification is very similar to the earlier higher education classification, but it includes more 2-year colleges and excludes a few higher education institutions that did not grant degrees.
[3]Estimated on the basis of enrollment and staff counts in adjacent years.
[4]Inclusion of institutions is not consistent with surveys for 1987 and later years.
[5]Data for elementary and secondary schools are projected; data for degree-granting institutions are actual.

[6]Projected.
NOTE: Detail may not sum to totals because of rounding. Some data have been revised from previously published figures.
SOURCE: U.S. Department of Education, National Center for Education Statistics, *Statistics of Public Elementary and Secondary Day Schools*, 1970 and 1975; Common Core of Data (CCD), "State Nonfiscal Survey of Public Elementary/Secondary Education," 1980 through 2017; Private School Universe Survey (PSS), 1989–90 through 2017–18; Elementary and Secondary Teacher Projection Model, 1973 through 2029; Higher Education General Information Survey (HEGIS), "Fall Staff" survey, 1970 and 1975; Integrated Postsecondary Education Data System (IPEDS), "Fall Staff Survey" (IPEDS-S:87–99); IPEDS Winter 2001–02 through Winter 2011–12, Human Resources component, Fall Staff section; IPEDS Spring 2014 through Spring 2019, Human Resources component, Fall Staff section; U.S. Equal Opportunity Commission, EEO-6, 1981 and 1983; and unpublished data. (This table was prepared December 2019.)

Table 105.50.   Number of educational institutions, by level and control of institution: Selected years, 1980–81 through 2017–18

Level and control of institution	1980–81	1990–91	1999–2000	2007–08	2008–09	2009–10	2010–11	2011–12	2012–13	2013–14	2014–15	2015–16	2016–17	2017–18
1	2	3	4	5	6	7	8	9	10	11	12	13	14	15
All institutions	—	—	131,414	139,207	—	138,925	—	136,423	—	139,126	—	139,874	—	137,432
Elementary and secondary schools	106,746	109,228	125,007	132,656	—	132,183	—	129,189	—	131,890	—	132,853	—	130,930
Elementary	72,659	74,716	86,433	88,982	—	88,565	—	86,386	—	89,543	—	88,665	—	87,498
Secondary	24,856	23,602	24,903	27,575	—	27,427	—	27,034	—	26,767	—	26,986	—	26,727
Combined	5,202	8,847	12,197	14,837	—	14,895	—	14,799	—	14,599	—	16,511	—	15,804
Other[1]	4,029	2,063	1,474	1,262	—	1,296	—	971	—	981	—	691	—	901
Public schools	85,982	84,538	92,012	98,916	98,706	98,817	98,817	98,328	98,454	98,271	98,176	98,277	98,158	98,469
Elementary	59,326	59,015	64,131	67,112	67,148	67,140	67,086	66,689	66,708	67,034	67,073	66,758	66,837	67,408
Secondary	22,619	21,135	22,365	24,643	24,348	24,651	24,544	24,357	24,294	24,067	24,181	24,040	23,814	23,882
Combined	1,743	2,325	4,042	5,899	5,623	5,730	6,137	6,311	6,329	6,189	6,347	6,788	6,783	6,278
Other[1]	2,294	2,063	1,474	1,262	1,587	1,296	1,050	971	1,123	981	575	691	724	901
Private schools[2]	20,764	24,690	32,995	33,740	—	33,366	—	30,861	—	33,619	—	34,576	—	32,461
Elementary	13,333	15,701	22,302	21,870	—	21,425	—	19,697	—	22,509	—	21,907	—	20,090
Schools with highest grade of kindergarten	†	†	5,952	5,522	—	5,275	—	4,658	—	5,255	—	5,147	—	4,320
Secondary	2,237	2,467	2,538	2,932	—	2,776	—	2,677	—	2,700	—	2,946	—	2,845
Combined	3,459	6,522	8,155	8,938	—	9,165	—	8,488	—	8,410	—	9,723	—	9,526
Other[1]	1,735	(3)	(3)	(3)	—	(3)	—	(3)	—	(3)	—	(3)	—	(3)
Postsecondary Title IV institutions	—	—	6,407	6,551	6,632	6,742	7,021	7,234	7,253	7,236	7,151	7,021	6,606	6,502
Public	—	—	2,078	2,004	1,997	1,989	2,015	2,011	1,981	1,980	1,964	1,965	1,958	1,955
Private	—	—	4,329	4,547	4,635	4,753	5,006	5,223	5,272	5,256	5,187	5,056	4,648	4,547
Nonprofit	—	—	1,936	1,815	1,809	1,809	1,812	1,830	1,820	1,834	1,827	1,859	1,823	1,826
For-profit	—	—	2,393	2,732	2,826	2,944	3,194	3,393	3,452	3,422	3,360	3,197	2,825	2,721
Title IV non-degree-granting institutions	—	—	2,323	2,199	2,223	2,247	2,422	2,528	2,527	2,512	2,524	2,438	2,246	2,189
Public	—	—	396	319	321	317	359	362	358	355	343	345	335	329
Private	—	—	1,927	1,880	1,902	1,930	2,063	2,166	2,169	2,157	2,181	2,093	1,911	1,860
Nonprofit	—	—	255	191	180	185	182	177	168	159	155	158	141	137
For-profit	—	—	1,672	1,689	1,722	1,745	1,881	1,989	2,001	1,998	2,026	1,935	1,770	1,723
Title IV degree-granting institutions	3,231	3,559	4,084	4,352	4,409	4,495	4,599	4,706	4,726	4,724	4,627	4,583	4,360	4,313
2-year colleges	1,274	1,418	1,721	1,677	1,690	1,721	1,729	1,738	1,700	1,685	1,616	1,579	1,528	1,485
Public	945	972	1,068	1,032	1,024	1,000	978	967	934	934	920	910	886	876
Private	329	446	653	645	666	721	751	771	766	751	696	669	642	609
Nonprofit	182	167	150	92	92	85	87	100	97	88	88	107	101	99
For-profit	147	279	503	553	574	636	664	671	669	663	608	562	541	510
4-year colleges	1,957	2,141	2,363	2,675	2,719	2,774	2,870	2,968	3,026	3,039	3,011	3,004	2,832	2,828
Public	552	595	614	653	652	672	678	682	689	691	701	710	737	750
Private	1,405	1,546	1,749	2,022	2,067	2,102	2,192	2,286	2,337	2,348	2,310	2,294	2,095	2,078
Nonprofit	1,387	1,482	1,531	1,532	1,537	1,539	1,543	1,553	1,555	1,587	1,584	1,594	1,581	1,590
For-profit	18	64	218	490	530	563	649	733	782	761	726	700	514	488

—Not available.
†Not applicable.
[1]Includes special education, alternative, and other schools not classified by grade span. Because of changes in survey definitions, figures for "other" schools are not comparable from year to year.
[2]Data for 1980–81 and 1990–91 include schools with first or higher grades. Data for later years include schools with kindergarten or higher grades.
[3]Included in the elementary, secondary, and combined categories.
NOTE: Postsecondary data for 1980–81 and 1990–91 are for institutions of higher education, while later data are for Title IV degree-granting and non-degree-granting institutions. Degree-granting institutions grant associate's or higher degrees and participate in Title IV federal financial aid programs. The degree-granting classification is very similar to the earlier higher education classification, but it includes more 2-year colleges and excludes a few higher education institutions that did not grant degrees.

SOURCE: U.S. Department of Education, National Center for Education Statistics, Common Core of Data (CCD), "Public Elementary/Secondary School Universe Survey," 1989–90 through 2017–18; Private Schools in American Education; Statistics of Public Elementary and Secondary Day Schools, 1980–81; Schools and Staffing Survey (SASS), "Private School Data File," 1990–91; Private School Universe Survey (PSS), 1995–96 through 2017–18; Higher Education General Information Survey (HEGIS), "Institutional Characteristics of Colleges and Universities" survey, 1980–81; Integrated Postsecondary Education Data System (IPEDS), "Institutional Characteristics Survey" (IPEDS-IC:90–99); and IPEDS Fall 2001 through Fall 2017, Institutional Characteristics component. (This table was prepared January 2020.)

Table 106.10. Expenditures of educational institutions related to the gross domestic product, by level of institution: Selected years, 1929–30 through 2018–19

Year	Gross domestic product (GDP) (in billions of current dollars)	School year	Expenditures for education in current dollars					
			All educational institutions		All elementary and secondary schools		All degree-granting postsecondary institutions	
			Amount (in millions)	As a percent of GDP	Amount (in millions)	As a percent of GDP	Amount (in millions)	As a percent of GDP
1	2	3	4	5	6	7	8	9
1929	$104.6	1929–30	—	—	—	—	$632	0.6
1939	93.4	1939–40	—	—	—	—	758	0.8
1949	272.5	1949–50	$8,494	3.1	$6,249	2.3	2,246	0.8
1959	521.7	1959–60	22,314	4.3	16,713	3.2	5,601	1.1
1961	562.2	1961–62	26,828	4.8	19,673	3.5	7,155	1.3
1963	637.5	1963–64	32,003	5.0	22,825	3.6	9,178	1.4
1965	742.3	1965–66	40,558	5.5	28,048	3.8	12,509	1.7
1967	860.0	1967–68	51,558	6.0	35,077	4.1	16,481	1.9
1969	1,017.6	1969–70	64,227	6.3	43,183	4.2	21,043	2.1
1970	1,073.3	1970–71	71,575	6.7	48,200	4.5	23,375	2.2
1971	1,164.9	1971–72	76,510	6.6	50,950	4.4	25,560	2.2
1972	1,279.1	1972–73	82,908	6.5	54,952	4.3	27,956	2.2
1973	1,425.4	1973–74	91,084	6.4	60,370	4.2	30,714	2.2
1974	1,545.2	1974–75	103,903	6.7	68,846	4.5	35,058	2.3
1975	1,684.9	1975–76	114,004	6.8	75,101	4.5	38,903	2.3
1976	1,873.4	1976–77	121,793	6.5	79,194	4.2	42,600	2.3
1977	2,081.8	1977–78	132,515	6.4	86,544	4.2	45,971	2.2
1978	2,351.6	1978–79	143,733	6.1	93,012	4.0	50,721	2.2
1979	2,627.3	1979–80	160,075	6.1	103,162	3.9	56,914	2.2
1980	2,857.3	1980–81	176,378	6.2	112,325	3.9	64,053	2.2
1981	3,207.0	1981–82	190,825	6.0	120,486	3.8	70,339	2.2
1982	3,343.8	1982–83	204,661	6.1	128,725	3.8	75,936	2.3
1983	3,634.0	1983–84	220,993	6.1	139,000	3.8	81,993	2.3
1984	4,037.6	1984–85	239,351	5.9	149,400	3.7	89,951	2.2
1985	4,339.0	1985–86	259,336	6.0	161,800	3.7	97,536	2.2
1986	4,579.6	1986–87	280,964	6.1	175,200	3.8	105,764	2.3
1987	4,855.2	1987–88	301,786	6.2	187,999	3.9	113,787	2.3
1988	5,236.4	1988–89	333,245	6.4	209,377	4.0	123,867	2.4
1989	5,641.6	1989–90	365,825	6.5	231,170	4.1	134,656	2.4
1990	5,963.1	1990–91	395,318	6.6	249,230	4.2	146,088	2.4
1991	6,158.1	1991–92	417,944	6.8	261,755	4.3	156,189	2.5
1992	6,520.3	1992–93	439,676	6.7	274,435	4.2	165,241	2.5
1993	6,858.6	1993–94	460,756	6.7	287,407	4.2	173,351	2.5
1994	7,287.2	1994–95	485,169	6.7	302,200	4.1	182,969	2.5
1995	7,639.7	1995–96	508,523	6.7	318,046	4.2	190,476	2.5
1996	8,073.1	1996–97	538,854	6.7	338,951	4.2	199,903[1]	2.5
1997	8,577.6	1997–98	570,471	6.7	361,615	4.2	208,856[1]	2.4
1998	9,062.8	1998–99	603,847	6.7	384,638	4.2	219,209	2.4
1999	9,630.7	1999–2000	649,322	6.7	412,538	4.3	236,784	2.5
2000	10,252.3	2000–01	705,017	6.9	444,811	4.3	260,206	2.5
2001	10,581.8	2001–02	752,780	7.1	472,064	4.5	280,715	2.7
2002	10,936.4	2002–03	795,691	7.3	492,807	4.5	302,884	2.8
2003	11,458.2	2003–04	830,293	7.2	513,542	4.5	316,751	2.8
2004	12,213.7	2004–05	875,988	7.2	540,969	4.4	335,019	2.7
2005	13,036.6	2005–06	925,249	7.1	571,669	4.4	353,580	2.7
2006	13,814.6	2006–07	984,048	7.1	608,495	4.4	375,553	2.7
2007	14,451.9	2007–08	1,054,901	7.3	646,414	4.5	408,487	2.8
2008	14,712.8	2008–09	1,089,683	7.4	658,926	4.5	430,757	2.9
2009	14,448.9	2009–10	1,100,897	7.6	654,418	4.5	446,479	3.1
2010	14,992.1	2010–11	1,124,352	7.5	652,356	4.4	471,997	3.1
2011	15,542.6	2011–12	1,136,876	7.3	648,794	4.2	488,083	3.1
2012	16,197.0	2012–13	1,153,874	7.1	655,013	4.0	498,861	3.1
2013	16,784.9	2013–14	1,192,886	7.1	675,818	4.0	517,067	3.1
2014	17,527.3	2014–15	1,241,626	7.1	706,135	4.0	535,491	3.1
2015	18,224.8	2015–16	1,296,371	7.1	736,905	4.0	559,466	3.1
2016	18,715.0	2016–17	1,352,976	7.2	769,401	4.1	583,574	3.1
2017	19,519.4	2017–18[2]	1,404,000	7.2	800,000	4.1	604,000	3.1
2018	20,580.2	2018–19[3]	1,453,000	7.1	832,000	4.0	620,000	3.0

—Not available.
[1]Estimated by the National Center for Education Statistics based on enrollment data for the given year and actual expenditures for prior years.
[2]Data for elementary and secondary education are estimated; data for degree-granting institutions are actual.
[3]Estimated by the National Center for Education Statistics based on teacher and enrollment data, and actual expenditures for prior years.
NOTE: Total expenditures for public elementary and secondary schools include current expenditures, interest on school debt, and capital outlay. Data for private elementary and secondary schools are estimated. Expenditures for colleges and universities in 1929–30 and 1939–40 include current-fund expenditures and additions to plant value. Public and private degree-granting institutions data for 1949–50 through 1995–96 are for current-fund expenditures. Data for private degree-granting institutions for 1996–97 and later years are for total expenditures. Data for public degree-granting institutions for 1996–97 through 2000–01 are for current expenditures; data for later years are for total expenditures. Postsecondary data through 1995–96 are for institutions of higher education,

while later data are for degree-granting institutions. Degree-granting institutions grant associate's or higher degrees and participate in Title IV federal financial aid programs. Some data have been revised from previously published figures. Detail may not sum to totals because of rounding.
SOURCE: U.S. Department of Education, National Center for Education Statistics, *Biennial Survey of Education in the United States*, 1929–30 through 1949–50; *Statistics of State School Systems*, 1959–60 through 1969–70; *Revenues and Expenditures for Public Elementary and Secondary Education*, 1970–71 through 1986–87; Common Core of Data (CCD), "National Public Education Financial Survey," 1987–88 through 2016–17; Higher Education General Information Survey (HEGIS), Financial Statistics of Institutions of Higher Education, 1965-66 through 1985-86; Integrated Postsecondary Education Data System (IPEDS), "Finance Survey" (IPEDS-F:FY87–99); and IPEDS Spring 2001 through Spring 2019, Finance component. U.S. Department of Commerce, Bureau of Economic Analysis, National Income and Product Accounts Tables, retrieved December 31, 2019, from https://apps.bea.gov/itable/index.cfm. (This table was prepared December 2019.)

Table 106.20. Expenditures of educational institutions, by level and control of institution: Selected years, 1899–1900 through 2018–19

[In millions]

Year	Current dollars							Constant 2018–19 dollars[1]			
	Total	Elementary and secondary schools			Degree-granting postsecondary institutions			Total	Elementary and secondary schools		Degree-granting postsecondary institutions
		Total	Public	Private[2]	Total	Public	Private		Total	Public	
1	2	3	4	5	6	7	8	9	10	11	12
1899–1900	—	—	$215	—	—	—	—	—	—	—	—
1909–10	—	—	426	—	—	—	—	—	—	—	—
1919–20	—	—	1,036	—	—	—	—	—	—	$13,770	—
1929–30	—	—	2,317	—	$632	$292	$341	—	—	34,280	$9,355
1939–40	—	—	2,344	—	758	392	367	—	—	42,481	13,745
1949–50	$8,494	$6,249	5,838	$411	2,246	1,154	1,092	$90,839	$66,824	62,428	24,015
1959–60	22,314	16,713	15,613	1,100	5,601	3,131	2,470	192,337	144,061	134,579	48,276
1969–70	64,227	43,183	40,683	2,500	21,043	13,250	7,794	430,616	289,530	272,768	141,087
1970–71	71,575	48,200	45,500	2,700	23,375	14,996	8,379	456,329	307,300	290,086	149,029
1971–72	76,510	50,950	48,050	2,900	25,560	16,484	9,075	470,899	313,586	295,738	157,313
1972–73	82,908	54,952	51,852	3,100	27,956	18,204	9,752	490,514	325,118	306,777	165,396
1973–74	91,084	60,370	56,970	3,400	30,714	20,336	10,377	494,770	327,933	309,464	166,837
1974–75	103,903	68,846	64,846	4,000	35,058	23,490	11,568	508,098	336,663	317,103	171,435
1975–76	114,004	75,101	70,601	4,500	38,903	26,184	12,719	520,637	342,973	322,422	177,665
1976–77	121,793	79,194	74,194	5,000	42,600	28,635	13,965	525,564	341,737	320,161	183,827
1977–78	132,515	86,544	80,844	5,700	45,971	30,725	15,246	535,849	349,958	326,909	185,891
1978–79	143,733	93,012	86,712	6,300	50,721	33,733	16,988	531,429	343,896	320,603	187,533
1979–80	160,075	103,162	95,962	7,200	56,914	37,768	19,146	522,225	336,552	313,063	185,673
1980–81	176,378	112,325	104,125	8,200	64,053	42,280	21,773	515,681	328,408	304,433	187,273
1981–82	190,825	120,486	111,186	9,300	70,339	46,219	24,120	513,559	324,258	299,229	189,301
1982–83	204,661	128,725	118,425	10,300	75,936	49,573	26,363	528,110	332,164	305,586	195,946
1983–84	220,993	139,000	127,500	11,500	81,993	53,087	28,907	549,901	345,876	317,260	204,025
1984–85	239,351	149,400	137,000	12,400	89,951	58,315	31,637	573,147	357,751	328,058	215,396
1985–86	259,336	161,800	148,600	13,200	97,536	63,194	34,342	603,595	376,584	345,862	227,011
1986–87	280,964	175,200	160,900	14,300	105,764	67,654	38,110	639,730	398,915	366,355	240,815
1987–88	301,786	187,999	172,699	15,300	113,787	72,641	41,145	659,802	411,026	377,576	248,776
1988–89	333,245	209,377	192,977	16,400	123,867	78,946	44,922	696,417	437,559	403,286	258,859
1989–90	365,825	231,170	212,770	18,400	134,656	85,771	48,885	729,685	461,097	424,396	268,588
1990–91	395,318	249,230	229,430	19,800	146,088	92,961	53,127	747,637	471,351	433,905	276,286
1991–92	417,944	261,755	241,055	20,700	156,189	98,847	57,342	765,888	479,669	441,736	286,219
1992–93	439,676	274,435	252,935	21,500	165,241	104,570	60,671	781,307	487,673	449,467	293,635
1993–94	460,757	287,407	265,307	22,100	173,351	109,310	64,041	798,095	497,828	459,548	300,267
1994–95	485,169	302,200	279,000	23,200	182,969	115,465	67,504	816,963	508,867	469,801	308,096
1995–96	508,523	318,046	293,646	24,400	190,476	119,525	70,952	833,609	521,366	481,367	312,243
1996–97	538,854	338,951	313,151	25,800	199,903[2]	125,978	73,925[2]	858,827	540,221	499,101	318,606[2]
1997–98	570,471	361,615	334,315	27,300	208,856[2]	132,846	76,010[2]	893,287	566,244	523,496	327,043[2]
1998–99	603,847	384,638	355,838	28,800	219,209	140,539	78,670	929,459	592,046	547,716	337,413
1999–2000	649,322	412,538	381,838	30,700	236,784	152,325	84,459	971,414	617,175	571,246	354,239
2000–01	705,017	444,811	410,811	34,000	260,206	170,345	89,861	1,019,796	643,413	594,232	376,384
2001–02	752,780	472,064	435,364	36,700	280,715	183,436	97,280	1,069,941	670,955	618,792	398,987
2002–03	795,691	492,807	454,907	37,900	302,884	197,026	105,858	1,106,613	685,375	632,665	421,239
2003–04	830,293	513,542	474,242	39,300	316,751	205,069	111,682	1,130,014	698,921	645,435	431,093
2004–05	875,988	540,969	499,569	41,400	335,019	215,794	119,225	1,157,376	714,741	660,042	442,635
2005–06	925,249	571,669	528,269	43,400	353,580	226,550	127,030	1,177,615	727,594	672,357	450,021
2006–07	984,048	608,495	562,195	46,300	375,553	238,829	136,724	1,220,879	754,942	697,499	465,938
2007–08	1,054,901	646,414	597,314	49,100	408,487	261,046	147,441	1,262,022	773,332	714,592	488,690
2008–09	1,089,683	658,926	610,326	48,600	430,757	273,019	157,739	1,285,682	777,445	720,104	508,237
2009–10	1,100,897	654,418	607,018	47,400	446,479	281,390	165,088	1,286,465	764,727	709,338	521,737
2010–11	1,124,352	652,356	604,356	48,000	471,997	296,863	175,134	1,288,011	747,312	692,325	540,699
2011–12	1,136,876	648,794	601,994	46,800	488,083	305,538	182,545	1,265,284	722,073	669,988	543,211
2012–13	1,153,874	655,013	606,813	48,200	498,861	311,421	187,439	1,263,180	717,063	664,297	546,118
2013–14	1,192,886	675,818	625,018	50,800	517,067	323,893	193,174	1,285,802	728,459	673,702	557,343
2014–15	1,241,626	706,135	651,135	55,000	535,491	335,630	199,861	1,328,664	755,635	696,780	573,028
2015–16	1,296,371	736,905	677,605	59,300	559,466	354,776	204,690	1,377,954	783,280	720,248	594,674
2016–17	1,352,976	769,401	707,601	61,800	583,574	371,705	211,869	1,412,145	803,049	738,547	609,096
2017–18[3]	1,404,000	800,000	736,000	64,000	604,000	385,000	219,000	1,433,000	817,000	751,000	617,000
2018–19[4]	1,453,000	832,000	765,000	67,000	620,000	395,000	225,000	1,453,000	832,000	765,000	620,000

—Not available.
[1]Constant dollars based on the Consumer Price Index, prepared by the Bureau of Labor Statistics, U.S. Department of Labor, adjusted to a school-year basis.
[2]Estimated by the National Center for Education Statistics based on enrollment data for the given year and actual expenditures for prior years.
[3]Data for elementary and secondary education are estimated; data for degree-granting institutions are actual.
[4]Estimated by the National Center for Education Statistics based on teacher and enrollment data, and actual expenditures for prior years.
NOTE: Total expenditures for public elementary and secondary schools include current expenditures, interest on school debt, and capital outlay. Expenditures for public and private colleges and universities in 1929–30 and 1939–40 include current-fund expenditures and additions to plant value. Public and private degree-granting institutions data for 1949–50 through 1995–96 are for current-fund expenditures. Data for private degree-granting institutions for 1996–97 and later years are for total expenditures. Data for public degree-granting institutions for 1996–97 through 2000–01 are for current expenditures; data for later

years are for total expenditures. Postsecondary data through 1995–96 are for institutions of higher education, while later data are for degree-granting institutions. Degree-granting institutions grant associate's or higher degrees and participate in Title IV federal financial aid programs. Some data have been revised from previously published figures. Detail may not sum to totals because of rounding.
SOURCE: U.S. Department of Education, National Center for Education Statistics, *Annual Report of the Commissioner of Education*, 1899–1900 and 1909–10; *Biennial Survey of Education in the United States*, 1919–20 through 1949–50; *Statistics of State School Systems*, 1959–60 and 1969–70; *Revenues and Expenditures for Public Elementary and Secondary Education*, 1970–71 through 1986–87; Common Core of Data (CCD), "National Public Education Financial Survey," 1987–88 through 2016–17; Higher Education General Information Survey (HEGIS), Financial Statistics of Institutions of Higher Education, 1965–66 through 1985–86; Integrated Postsecondary Education Data System (IPEDS), "Finance Survey," (IPEDS-F:FY87–99); IPEDS Spring 2001 through Spring 2019, Finance component; and unpublished tabulations. (This table was prepared December 2019.)

Table 106.30. Amount and percentage distribution of direct general expenditures of state and local governments, by function: Selected years, 1970–71 through 2016–17

Function	1970–71	1980–81	1990–91	2000–01	2010–11	2011–12	2012–13	2013–14	2014–15	2015–16	2016–17
1	2	3	4	5	6	7	8	9	10	11	12
	Amount (in millions of current dollars)										
Total direct general expenditures	$150,674	$407,449	$908,109	$1,621,757	$2,579,509	$2,589,246	$2,623,305	$2,710,967	$2,839,458	$2,961,032	$3,071,187
Education and public libraries	60,174	147,649	313,744	571,374	872,969	879,294	888,240	916,301	947,318	985,051	1,022,721
Education	59,413	145,784	309,302	563,572	862,271	867,839	877,059	905,213	935,754	973,025	1,010,131
Public libraries	761	1,865	4,442	7,802	10,699	11,455	11,181	11,088	11,564	12,026	12,590
Social services and income maintenance	30,376	92,555	214,919	396,086	729,846	732,663	765,511	805,538	883,060	935,325	973,903
Public welfare	18,226	54,121	130,402	257,380	490,645	484,025	515,296	543,511	614,553	652,514	678,238
Hospitals and health	11,205	36,101	81,110	134,010	233,018	242,684	244,290	256,553	263,420	277,324	290,962
Social insurance administration	945	2,276	3,250	4,359	5,256	5,116	4,901	4,415	4,114	4,107	3,914
Veterans' services	†	57	157	337	927	838	1,024	1,060	973	1,381	789
Transportation[1]	19,819	39,231	75,410	130,422	183,282	188,344	186,324	191,924	198,621	210,140	216,458
Public safety	9,416	31,233	79,932	146,544	225,202	225,666	228,400	235,042	241,787	249,346	257,967
Police and fire protection	7,531	21,283	46,568	84,554	138,147	139,344	141,308	145,952	151,011	157,098	164,961
Correction	1,885	7,393	27,356	52,370	73,243	72,766	73,040	74,943	77,058	77,885	78,733
Protective inspection and regulation	†	2,557	6,008	9,620	13,812	13,556	14,052	14,147	13,718	14,363	14,273
Environment and housing	11,832	35,223	76,167	124,203	200,491	196,193	190,321	190,175	193,912	202,636	211,184
Natural resources, parks, and recreation	5,191	13,239	28,505	50,082	67,053	66,455	65,472	65,544	68,358	72,553	77,037
Housing and community development	2,554	7,086	16,648	27,402	56,284	53,647	50,586	50,244	49,916	49,871	52,401
Sewerage and sanitation	4,087	14,898	31,014	46,718	77,154	76,090	74,263	74,387	75,638	80,213	81,746
Governmental administration	6,703	20,001	48,461	85,910	123,851	123,245	123,580	127,676	130,458	139,139	144,245
Financial administration	2,271	7,230	16,995	30,007	39,351	38,620	39,785	40,501	41,920	44,187	45,508
General control[2]	4,432	12,771	31,466	55,903	84,500	84,624	83,796	87,175	88,538	94,952	98,738
Interest on general debt	5,089	17,131	52,234	73,836	108,478	110,219	108,614	106,940	105,258	105,221	106,323
Other direct general expenditures	7,265	24,426	47,242	93,382	135,388	133,622	132,314	137,371	139,043	134,174	138,387
	Amount (in millions of constant 2018–19 dollars)[3]										
Total direct general expenditures	$960,627	$1,191,270	$1,717,444	$2,345,848	$2,954,977	$2,881,696	$2,871,811	$2,922,130	$3,038,504	$3,147,376	$3,205,499
Education and public libraries	383,641	431,686	593,362	826,484	1,000,037	978,609	972,383	987,673	1,013,725	1,047,042	1,067,448
Education	378,789	426,233	584,962	815,199	987,781	965,860	960,143	975,722	1,001,350	1,034,259	1,054,307
Public libraries	4,852	5,453	8,401	11,286	12,256	12,749	12,240	11,951	12,375	12,783	13,140
Social services and income maintenance	193,663	270,606	406,462	572,932	836,081	815,416	838,028	868,284	944,963	994,187	1,016,494
Public welfare	116,200	158,235	246,620	372,297	562,062	538,695	564,110	585,846	657,633	693,578	707,899
Hospitals and health	71,438	105,550	153,398	193,844	266,936	270,094	267,431	276,536	281,886	294,776	303,687
Social insurance administration	6,025	6,654	6,147	6,305	6,021	5,694	5,365	4,759	4,402	4,366	4,085
Veterans' services	†	167	297	487	1,062	933	1,122	1,142	1,041	1,468	823
Transportation[1]	126,357	114,701	142,618	188,654	209,960	209,617	203,975	206,873	212,544	223,364	225,924
Public safety	60,032	91,317	151,170	211,974	257,982	251,154	250,037	253,350	258,736	265,038	269,248
Police and fire protection	48,014	62,226	88,071	122,307	158,255	155,082	154,694	157,320	161,597	166,985	172,175
Correction	12,018	21,615	51,737	75,753	83,905	80,985	79,959	80,781	82,459	82,786	82,176
Protective inspection and regulation	†	7,476	11,363	13,915	15,822	15,087	15,383	15,249	14,680	15,267	14,897
Environment and housing	75,435	102,982	144,049	179,658	229,674	218,352	208,350	204,988	207,505	215,389	220,420
Natural resources, parks, and recreation	33,095	38,707	53,910	72,444	76,814	73,961	71,674	70,649	73,150	77,119	80,406
Housing and community development	16,283	20,718	31,485	39,637	64,476	59,707	55,378	54,157	53,415	53,009	54,693
Sewerage and sanitation	26,057	43,558	58,655	67,577	88,385	84,685	81,298	80,181	80,940	85,261	85,321
Governmental administration	42,735	58,477	91,651	124,267	141,879	137,165	135,287	137,621	139,604	147,895	150,554
Financial administration	14,479	21,139	32,141	43,405	45,079	42,982	43,553	43,656	44,859	46,967	47,498
General control[2]	28,256	37,339	59,509	80,862	96,800	94,183	91,734	93,965	94,745	100,928	103,056
Interest on general debt	32,445	50,086	98,787	106,803	124,268	122,668	118,903	115,270	112,637	111,843	110,973
Other direct general expenditures	46,318	71,415	89,346	135,076	155,095	148,714	144,848	148,072	148,790	142,617	144,439
	Percentage distribution										
Total direct general expenditures	100.0	100.0	100.0	100.0	100.0	100.0	100.0	100.0	100.0	100.0	100.0
Education and public libraries	39.9	36.2	34.5	35.2	33.8	34.0	33.9	33.8	33.4	33.3	33.3
Education	39.4	35.8	34.1	34.8	33.4	33.5	33.4	33.4	33.0	32.9	32.9
Public libraries	0.5	0.5	0.5	0.5	0.4	0.4	0.4	0.4	0.4	0.4	0.4
Social services and income maintenance	20.2	22.7	23.7	24.4	28.3	28.3	29.2	29.7	31.1	31.6	31.7
Public welfare	12.1	13.3	14.4	15.9	19.0	18.8	19.6	20.0	21.6	22.0	22.1
Hospitals and health	7.4	8.9	8.9	8.3	9.0	9.3	9.3	9.5	9.3	9.4	9.5
Social insurance administration	0.6	0.6	0.4	0.3	0.2	0.2	0.2	0.2	0.1	0.1	0.1
Veterans' services	†	#	#	#	#	#	#	#	#	#	#
Transportation[1]	13.2	9.6	8.3	8.0	7.1	7.3	7.1	7.1	7.0	7.1	7.0
Public safety	6.2	7.7	8.8	9.0	8.7	8.7	8.7	8.7	8.5	8.4	8.4
Police and fire protection	5.0	5.2	5.1	5.2	5.4	5.4	5.4	5.4	5.3	5.3	5.4
Correction	1.3	1.8	3.0	3.2	2.8	2.8	2.8	2.8	2.7	2.6	2.6
Protective inspection and regulation	†	0.6	0.7	0.6	0.5	0.5	0.5	0.5	0.5	0.5	0.5
Environment and housing	7.9	8.6	8.4	7.7	7.8	7.6	7.3	7.0	6.8	6.8	6.9
Natural resources, parks, and recreation	3.4	3.2	3.1	3.1	2.6	2.6	2.5	2.4	2.4	2.5	2.5
Housing and community development	1.7	1.7	1.8	1.7	2.2	2.1	1.9	1.9	1.8	1.7	1.7
Sewerage and sanitation	2.7	3.7	3.4	2.9	3.0	2.9	2.8	2.7	2.7	2.7	2.7

See notes at end of table.

Table 106.30. Amount and percentage distribution of direct general expenditures of state and local governments, by function: Selected years, 1970–71 through 2016–17—Continued

Function	1970–71	1980–81	1990–91	2000–01	2010–11	2011–12	2012–13	2013–14	2014–15	2015–16	2016–17
1	2	3	4	5	6	7	8	9	10	11	12
Governmental administration	4.4	4.9	5.3	5.3	4.8	4.8	4.7	4.7	4.6	4.7	4.7
Financial administration	1.5	1.8	1.9	1.9	1.5	1.5	1.5	1.5	1.5	1.5	1.5
General control[2]	2.9	3.1	3.5	3.4	3.3	3.3	3.2	3.2	3.1	3.2	3.2
Interest on general debt	3.4	4.2	5.8	4.6	4.2	4.3	4.1	3.9	3.7	3.6	3.5
Other direct general expenditures	4.8	6.0	5.2	5.8	5.2	5.2	5.0	5.1	4.9	4.5	4.5

†Not applicable.
#Rounds to zero.
[1]Includes highways, air transportation (airports), parking facilities, and sea and inland port facilities. For 2000–01 and earlier years, also includes transit subsidies.
[2]Includes judicial and legal expenditures, expenditures on general public buildings, and other governmental administration expenditures.
[3]Constant dollars based on the Consumer Price Index, prepared by the Bureau of Labor Statistics, U.S. Department of Labor, adjusted to a school-year basis.

NOTE: Excludes monies paid by states to the federal government. Some data have been revised from previously published figures. Detail may not sum to totals because of rounding.
SOURCE: U.S. Department of Commerce, Census Bureau, Governmental Finances. Retrieved April 15, 2020, from https://www.census.gov/data/datasets/2017/econ/local/public-use-datasets.html. (This table was prepared April 2020.)

Table 106.40. Direct general expenditures of state and local governments for all functions and for education, by level of education and state: 2015–16 and 2016–17

[In millions of current dollars. Standard errors appear in parentheses]

State	Direct general expenditures, 2015–16		Direct general expenditures, 2016–17								
				For education							
						Elementary and secondary education			Colleges and universities			
	Total[1]	For education	Total[1]	Total for education	Total for elementary and secondary	Current expenditure	Capital outlay	Total for colleges and universities	Current expenditure	Capital outlay	Other education[2]
1	2	3	4	5	6	7	8	9	10	11	12
United States	**$2,961,032** (1,480.5)	**$973,025** (389.2)	**$3,071,187**	**$1,010,131**	**$660,443**	**$596,772**	**$63,671**	**$296,452**	**$262,477**	**$33,975**	**$53,236**
Alabama	40,186 (84.4)	13,602 (9.5)	41,515	14,067	7,854	7,218	636	5,112	4,497	615	1,101
Alaska	13,642 (24.6)	3,543 (16.6)	12,723	3,279	2,347	2,177	170	847	692	155	85
Arizona	45,853 (82.5)	14,540 (#)	48,201	15,107	8,244	7,670	574	6,052	5,392	660	811
Arkansas	23,797 (42.8)	8,359 (#)	24,703	8,310	5,132	4,613	519	2,635	2,414	221	542
California	444,897 (934.3)	124,675 (149.6)	455,469	131,236	83,377	75,980	7,397	41,476	37,667	3,809	6,383
Colorado	47,388 (199.0)	16,331 (#)	50,315	17,409	9,950	8,780	1,170	6,452	5,576	876	1,007
Connecticut	34,774 (69.5)	13,639 (57.3)	33,914	13,481	9,358	8,905	453	3,400	2,851	549	723
Delaware	9,939 (#)	3,678 (#)	10,688	3,984	2,052	1,921	131	1,453	1,281	172	479
District of Columbia	12,771 (#)	2,766 (#)	13,255	2,907	2,782	2,360	422	125	125	0	0
Florida	145,405 (290.8)	41,501 (#)	154,092	42,787	28,350	26,055	2,295	11,010	10,262	748	3,427
Georgia	68,700 (158.0)	26,726 (#)	71,554	28,063	19,869	17,920	1,949	6,013	5,207	806	2,181
Hawaii	13,708 (#)	3,390 (30.8)	14,006	3,410	2,069	1,871	198	1,207	1,031	176	134
Idaho	11,009 (#)	3,357 (#)	11,630	3,563	2,205	2,093	111	1,127	1,079	47	232
Illinois	111,475 (345.6)	37,607 (#)	117,229	37,803	26,590	24,704	1,886	9,200	8,616	584	2,013
Indiana	51,842 (124.4)	17,490 (#)	53,022	17,820	10,220	9,171	1,049	6,427	5,672	755	1,173
Iowa	30,565 (103.9)	11,006 (#)	31,010	11,067	6,682	5,875	807	3,868	3,404	464	517
Kansas	25,208 (93.3)	9,391 (#)	26,928	9,811	6,026	5,170	856	3,491	2,845	647	294
Kentucky	38,917 (46.7)	12,550 (#)	39,402	12,876	7,322	6,566	756	4,480	3,872	608	1,074
Louisiana	40,616 (28.4)	12,307 (#)	42,713	12,351	8,085	7,411	674	3,478	3,142	336	788
Maine	11,364 (27.3)	3,418 (15.4)	11,619	3,549	2,561	2,413	148	782	733	50	206
Maryland	58,597 (29.3)	20,041 (#)	60,525	20,807	13,698	12,459	1,239	6,276	5,572	704	833
Massachusetts	75,269 (143.0)	21,962 (107.6)	77,578	23,162	16,240	15,001	1,239	5,542	4,577	965	1,380
Michigan	82,626 (272.7)	29,997 (#)	85,081	30,736	17,434	16,108	1,326	11,861	10,176	1,685	1,441
Minnesota	56,579 (147.1)	18,246 (#)	59,022	19,717	13,005	10,863	2,141	5,693	5,256	437	1,020
Mississippi	25,830 (43.9)	8,273 (#)	26,154	8,180	4,621	4,242	379	3,020	2,653	367	538
Missouri	45,936 (119.4)	15,082 (#)	47,162	15,328	10,434	9,634	799	3,979	3,611	369	915
Montana	8,707 (15.7)	2,880 (#)	9,443	2,942	1,864	1,682	182	972	876	96	106
Nebraska	17,154 (72.0)	7,198 (#)	17,597	7,325	4,708	4,019	689	2,365	2,101	264	252
Nevada	20,279 (137.9)	6,085 (#)	21,947	6,676	4,632	4,169	463	1,498	1,334	164	546
New Hampshire	10,792 (14.0)	4,131 (8.3)	11,098	4,160	2,972	2,828	144	940	830	110	248
New Jersey	92,683 (231.7)	36,311 (39.9)	93,169	36,871	27,266	25,482	1,784	7,457	6,232	1,226	2,147
New Mexico	21,893 (10.9)	6,671 (#)	21,367	6,814	3,714	3,164	550	2,680	2,291	389	420
New York	269,058 (269.1)	82,516 (82.5)	281,743	85,161	68,901	63,617	5,284	14,180	12,526	1,654	2,080
North Carolina	78,824 (228.6)	25,803 (183.2)	80,603	27,126	15,045	13,714	1,330	10,175	9,373	802	1,906
North Dakota	9,487 (17.1)	3,221 (#)	9,698	3,044	1,807	1,521	287	1,113	1,006	107	124
Ohio	103,095 (309.3)	34,100 (112.5)	107,318	35,724	24,341	22,414	1,927	9,866	8,481	1,386	1,517
Oklahoma	29,318 (67.4)	10,556 (#)	29,331	10,474	5,753	5,121	633	4,103	3,524	578	618
Oregon	43,542 (91.4)	13,380 (#)	44,814	13,631	7,582	6,755	827	4,777	4,112	665	1,273
Pennsylvania	122,289 (207.9)	41,545 (4.2)	129,206	43,396	29,533	27,646	1,887	11,091	9,797	1,294	2,771
Rhode Island	10,618 (6.4)	3,340 (#)	10,884	3,451	2,510	2,428	82	692	683	9	248
South Carolina	40,754 (65.2)	14,309 (#)	43,253	15,061	9,018	7,837	1,181	4,444	3,887	556	1,599
South Dakota	6,991 (18.2)	2,454 (#)	7,066	2,424	1,513	1,362	151	749	668	81	162
Tennessee	45,045 (202.7)	13,914 (153.1)	46,413	14,513	9,788	9,011	777	3,752	3,380	372	973
Texas	214,444 (321.7)	83,343 (16.7)	226,090	89,473	56,489	46,657	9,832	30,528	26,623	3,905	2,455
Utah	23,939 (150.8)	9,533 (#)	26,000	9,949	5,123	4,293	830	4,573	4,067	506	253

See notes at end of table.

Table 106.40.   Direct general expenditures of state and local governments for all functions and for education, by level of education and state: 2015–16 and 2016–17—Continued

[In millions of current dollars. Standard errors appear in parentheses]

	Direct general expenditures, 2015–16		Direct general expenditures, 2016–17								
				For education							
					Elementary and secondary education			Colleges and universities			
State	Total[1]	For education	Total[1]	Total for education	Total for elementary and secondary	Current expenditure	Capital outlay	Total for colleges and universities	Current expenditure	Capital outlay	Other education[2]
1	2	3	4	5	6	7	8	9	10	11	12
Vermont	7,232 (12.3)	2,752 (#)	7,353	2,839	1,651	1,595	56	893	785	108	296
Virginia	71,279 (256.6)	25,549 (150.7)	73,689	26,959	17,618	15,994	1,624	8,199	7,259	940	1,141
Washington	70,327 (211.0)	23,368 (39.7)	74,531	24,596	15,749	13,409	2,340	7,464	6,480	984	1,383
West Virginia	16,227 (26.0)	5,359 (#)	16,375	5,394	3,100	2,900	200	1,769	1,583	187	524
Wisconsin	51,084 (122.6)	18,086 (5.4)	53,799	18,251	11,351	10,415	936	6,254	5,659	595	647
Wyoming	9,079 (30.0)	3,149 (#)	8,889	3,066	1,909	1,558	351	911	721	190	246

#Rounds to zero.
[1]Includes state and local government expenditures for education and public libraries, social services and income maintenance, transportation, public safety, environment and housing, governmental administration, interest on general debt, and other direct general expenditures.
[2]Includes assistance and subsidies to individuals, private elementary and secondary schools, and private colleges and universities, as well as miscellaneous education expenditures. Does not include expenditures for public libraries.

NOTE: Current expenditure data in this table differ from figures appearing in other tables because of slightly varying definitions used in the Governmental Finances and Common Core of Data surveys. In 2016–17, a census of state and local governments was conducted; therefore, standard errors are not applicable. Detail may not sum to totals because of rounding. Some data have been revised from previously published figures.
SOURCE: U.S. Department of Commerce, Census Bureau, Governmental Finances. Retrieved April 15, 2020, from https://www.census.gov/data/datasets/2016/econ/local/public-use-datasets.html. (This table was prepared June 2020.)

Table 106.50. Direct general expenditures of state and local governments per capita for all functions and for education, by level of education and state: 2015–16 and 2016–17

[Amounts in current dollars]

	Direct general expenditures, 2015–16			Direct general expenditures, 2016–17								
					For education							
		For education			All education		Elementary and secondary education		Colleges and universities		Other education[2]	
State	Total amount per capita[1]	Amount per capita	As a percent of all functions	Total amount per capita[1]	Amount per capita	As a percent of all functions	Amount per capita	As a percent of all functions	Amount per capita	As a percent of all functions	Amount per capita	As a percent of all functions
1	2	3	4	5	6	7	8	9	10	11	12	13
United States	**$9,169**	**$3,013**	**32.9**	**$9,450**	**$3,108**	**32.9**	**$2,032**	**21.5**	**$912**	**9.7**	**$164**	**1.7**
Alabama	8,263	2,797	33.8	8,517	2,886	33.9	1,611	18.9	1,049	12.3	226	2.7
Alaska	18,400	4,778	26.0	17,200	4,433	25.8	3,173	18.4	1,146	6.7	115	0.7
Arizona	6,606	2,095	31.7	6,843	2,145	31.3	1,170	17.1	859	12.6	115	1.7
Arkansas	7,959	2,796	35.1	8,231	2,769	33.6	1,710	20.8	878	10.7	181	2.2
California	11,359	3,183	28.0	11,572	3,334	28.8	2,118	18.3	1,054	9.1	162	1.4
Colorado	8,555	2,948	34.5	8,966	3,102	34.6	1,773	19.8	1,150	12.8	180	2.0
Connecticut	9,719	3,812	39.2	9,491	3,773	39.8	2,619	27.6	951	10.0	202	2.1
Delaware	10,474	3,876	37.0	11,170	4,164	37.3	2,145	19.2	1,519	13.6	501	4.5
District of Columbia	18,621	4,033	21.7	19,075	4,183	21.9	4,004	21.0	179	0.9	0	0.0
Florida	7,054	2,013	28.5	7,350	2,041	27.8	1,352	18.4	525	7.1	163	2.2
Georgia	6,669	2,594	38.9	6,873	2,696	39.2	1,909	27.8	578	8.4	210	3.0
Hawaii	9,603	2,375	24.7	9,833	2,394	24.3	1,452	14.8	847	8.6	94	1.0
Idaho	6,544	1,995	30.5	6,771	2,074	30.6	1,283	19.0	656	9.7	135	2.0
Illinois	8,695	2,933	33.7	9,174	2,958	32.2	2,081	22.7	720	7.8	158	1.7
Indiana	7,814	2,636	33.7	7,964	2,677	33.6	1,535	19.3	965	12.1	176	2.2
Iowa	9,761	3,515	36.0	9,871	3,523	35.7	2,127	21.5	1,231	12.5	165	1.7
Kansas	8,660	3,226	37.3	9,258	3,373	36.4	2,072	22.4	1,200	13.0	101	1.1
Kentucky	8,769	2,828	32.2	8,850	2,892	32.7	1,645	18.6	1,006	11.4	241	2.7
Louisiana	8,682	2,631	30.3	9,145	2,644	28.9	1,731	18.9	745	8.1	169	1.8
Maine	8,536	2,567	30.1	8,706	2,659	30.5	1,919	22.0	586	6.7	154	1.8
Maryland	9,761	3,338	34.2	10,048	3,454	34.4	2,274	22.6	1,042	10.4	138	1.4
Massachusetts	11,031	3,219	29.2	11,309	3,376	29.9	2,367	20.9	808	7.1	201	1.8
Michigan	8,304	3,015	36.3	8,531	3,082	36.1	1,748	20.5	1,189	13.9	145	1.7
Minnesota	10,245	3,304	32.2	10,604	3,542	33.4	2,336	22.0	1,023	9.6	183	1.7
Mississippi	8,645	2,769	32.0	8,752	2,737	31.3	1,546	17.7	1,011	11.5	180	2.1
Missouri	7,546	2,478	32.8	7,723	2,510	32.5	1,709	22.1	652	8.4	150	1.9
Montana	8,365	2,767	33.1	8,972	2,795	31.2	1,771	19.7	924	10.3	101	1.1
Nebraska	9,002	3,777	42.0	9,184	3,823	41.6	2,457	26.8	1,234	13.4	132	1.4
Nevada	6,951	2,086	30.0	7,390	2,248	30.4	1,560	21.1	505	6.8	184	2.5
New Hampshire	8,040	3,077	38.3	8,228	3,084	37.5	2,203	26.8	697	8.5	184	2.2
New Jersey	10,448	4,093	39.2	10,485	4,150	39.6	3,069	29.3	839	8.0	242	2.3
New Mexico	10,467	3,189	30.5	10,215	3,257	31.9	1,775	17.4	1,281	12.5	201	2.0
New York	13,704	4,203	30.7	14,382	4,347	30.2	3,517	24.5	724	5.0	106	0.7
North Carolina	7,762	2,541	32.7	7,850	2,642	33.7	1,465	18.7	991	12.6	186	2.4
North Dakota	12,576	4,269	34.0	12,846	4,032	31.4	2,394	18.6	1,474	11.5	164	1.3
Ohio	8,861	2,931	33.1	9,204	3,064	33.3	2,088	22.7	846	9.2	130	1.4
Oklahoma	7,467	2,688	36.0	7,461	2,664	35.7	1,463	19.6	1,044	14.0	157	2.1
Oregon	10,646	3,271	30.7	10,815	3,290	30.4	1,830	16.9	1,153	10.7	307	2.8
Pennsylvania	9,567	3,250	34.0	10,104	3,394	33.6	2,310	22.9	867	8.6	217	2.1
Rhode Island	10,048	3,160	31.5	10,310	3,269	31.7	2,378	23.1	656	6.4	235	2.3
South Carolina	8,220	2,886	35.1	8,614	2,999	34.8	1,796	20.9	885	10.3	318	3.7
South Dakota	8,101	2,844	35.1	8,095	2,778	34.3	1,734	21.4	858	10.6	186	2.3
Tennessee	6,778	2,094	30.9	6,918	2,163	31.3	1,459	21.1	559	8.1	145	2.1
Texas	7,682	2,986	38.9	7,990	3,162	39.6	1,996	25.0	1,079	13.5	87	1.1
Utah	7,870	3,134	39.8	8,384	3,208	38.3	1,652	19.7	1,475	17.6	82	1.0
Vermont	11,595	4,413	38.1	11,778	4,548	38.6	2,644	22.5	1,430	12.1	473	4.0
Virginia	8,475	3,038	35.8	8,707	3,185	36.6	2,082	23.9	969	11.1	135	1.5
Washington	9,641	3,203	33.2	10,040	3,313	33.0	2,122	21.1	1,006	10.0	186	1.9
West Virginia	8,862	2,927	33.0	9,012	2,969	32.9	1,706	18.9	974	10.8	288	3.2
Wisconsin	8,849	3,133	35.4	9,291	3,152	33.9	1,960	21.1	1,080	11.6	112	1.2
Wyoming	15,540	5,389	34.7	15,354	5,296	34.5	3,298	21.5	1,574	10.2	424	2.8

[1]Includes state and local government expenditures for education and public libraries, social services and income maintenance, transportation, public safety, environment and housing, governmental administration, interest on general debt, and other direct general expenditures.

[2]Includes assistance and subsidies to individuals, private elementary and secondary schools, and private colleges and universities, as well as miscellaneous education expenditures. Does not include expenditures for public libraries.

NOTE: Per capita amounts for 2016–17 are based on population estimates for July 2017. Per capita amounts for 2015–16 are based on the latest population estimates for July

2016 and have been revised from previously published figures. Detail may not sum to totals because of rounding.

SOURCE: U.S. Department of Commerce, Census Bureau, Governmental Finances, retrieved April 15, 2020, from https://www.census.gov/data/datasets/2016/econ/local/public-use-datasets.html; and Population Estimates, retrieved June 15, 2020, from https://www.census.gov/data/tables/time-series/demo/popest/2010s-state-total.html#par_textimage_1574439295. (This table was prepared June 2020.)

CHAPTER 2
Elementary and Secondary Education

This chapter contains a variety of statistics on public and private elementary and secondary education. Data are presented for enrollments, teachers and other school staff, schools, dropouts, achievement, school violence, and revenues and expenditures. These data are derived from surveys, censuses, and administrative data collections conducted by the National Center for Education Statistics (NCES) and other public and private organizations. The information ranges from counts of students and schools to state graduation requirements. Public school enrollment data are for fall of the given year. Private school data are available only for odd-numbered years. Information on enrollments is also available in Chapter 1. Discussion in this chapter typically focuses on more recent years, although longer trends are available in the tables.

Enrollments

Public Elementary/Secondary

In fall of 2017—the most recent year of data collection—50.7 million students were enrolled in public elementary and secondary schools, an increase of 2 percent from 49.8 million over the preceding 5 years (table 203.10 and figure 7). At the elementary level, public school enrollment increased 1 percent between 2012 and 2017 (from 35.0 million to 35.5 million), while public secondary enrollment increased 3 percent (from 14.8 million to 15.2 million).[1]

Although public school enrollment increased overall between 2012 and 2017, this was not true of all racial/ethnic groups. Increases occurred in Hispanic student enrollment (12 percent), Asian student enrollment (11 percent), and enrollment of students of Two or more races (41 percent; table 203.50). Also, the enrollment of Pacific Islander students was 3 percent higher in 2017 than in 2012. In contrast, the enrollment of American Indian/Alaska Native students decreased 7 percent, the enrollment of White students decreased 5 percent, and the enrollment of Black students decreased 1 percent between these years.

From 2012 to 2017, changes in public elementary and secondary school enrollment also varied from state to state. Thirty-four states and the District of Columbia had higher enrollment in 2017 than in 2012, while 16 states had lower enrollment in 2017 than in 2012 (table 203.20 and figure 8). The largest public school enrollment increases occurred in the District of Columbia (15 percent), North Dakota (11 percent), Nevada (9 percent), and Utah (9 percent). The largest decrease in public school enrollment occurred in New Hampshire (5 percent); decreases of 3 percent or more occurred in 4 other states (West Virginia, Connecticut, Illinois, and Mississippi; table 203.20).

Private Elementary/Secondary

Enrollment in private elementary and secondary schools in 2017 (5.7 million) was 9 percent higher than in 2011 (5.3 million; table 105.30). In 2017, private school students made up 10.1 percent of all elementary and secondary school students, which was 0.5 percentage points higher than in 2011.

Preprimary

Sixty-four percent of 3- to 5-year-olds were enrolled in preprimary education (prekindergarten and kindergarten) in 2018, which was not measurably different from the percentage enrolled in 2008 (table 202.10 and figure 9). However, among 3- to 5-year-olds who were enrolled in preprimary education, the percentage enrolled in full-day programs increased from 58 percent in 2008 to 65 percent in 2018. Among 3- to 5-year-old children not yet enrolled in kindergarten, a higher percentage were cared for primarily in center-based programs (49 percent) than had no regular nonparental care (27 percent) or were cared for primarily in home-based settings by relatives (14 percent) or by non-relatives (8 percent), according to the most recent data from 2016 (table 202.30).

An earlier survey in 2005–06 found that there were differences in the average quality of care 4-year-old children received in these settings. A higher percentage of children in Head Start and other center-based programs (35 percent) received high-quality care than those in home-based relative and nonrelative care (9 percent), according to the ratings of trained observers (*web-only table 202.60*).

Individuals with Disabilities

The Individuals with Disabilities Education Act (IDEA), enacted in 1975, mandates that children and youth ages 3–21 with disabilities be provided a free and appropriate public

---

[1] Public elementary enrollment includes students in prekindergarten through grade 8 as well as elementary ungraded students. Public secondary enrollment includes students in grades 9 through 12 as well as secondary ungraded students and students reported as being enrolled in grade 13.

school education. The overall percentage of students being served by federally supported special education programs was 14.1 percent in 2018–19 (table 204.30). This was slightly higher than in 2004–05 (13.8 percent), but reflected a 5.8 percentage point increase from 8.3 percent in 1976–77, immediately following the passage of IDEA (table 204.30 and *Digest of Education Statistics 2016*, table 204.30). Much of the growth in the percentage of students served in programs for those with disabilities is attributable to concurrent increases in the percentage of students identified as having specific learning disabilities, from 1.8 percent in 1976–77 to 5.7 percent in 2004–05. After 2004–05, the percentage of children identifie as having specific learning disabilities declined from 5.7 percent of total public school enrollment to 4.7 percent in 2018–19. However, there were different patterns of change in the percentages of students served with some specific conditions between 2004–05 and 2018–19. The percentage of children identified as having autism rose from 0.4 to 1.5 percent of total public school enrollment; the percentage identified as having a developmental delay rose from 0.7 to 0.9 percent; and the percentage with other health impairments (limited strength, vitality, or alertness due to chronic or acute health problems such as a heart condition, tuberculosis, rheumatic fever, nephritis, asthma, sickle cell anemia, hemophilia, epilepsy, lead poisoning, leukemia, or diabetes) rose from 1.1 to 2.1 percent. In contrast, the percentage identified as having speech or language impairments decreased from 3.0 to 2.7 percent and the percentage with intellectual disabilities decreased from 1.2 to 0.9 percent.

In fall 2018, some 95 percent of 6- to 21-year-old students with disabilities were served in regular schools; 3 percent were served in a separate school for students with disabilities; 1 percent were placed in regular private schools by their parents; and less than 1 percent each were served in one of the following environments: homebound or in a hospital, in a separate residential facility, or in a correctional facility (*web-only table 204.60*).

Teachers and Other School Staff

Teachers

During the 1970s and early 1980s, public school enrollment decreased while the number of teachers generally increased. For public schools, the number of pupils per teacher—that is, the pupil/teacher ratio[2]—declined from 22.3 in 1970 to 17.9 in 1985 (table 208.20 and figure 7). After enrollment started increasing in 1985, the public school pupil/teacher ratio continued to decline, reaching 17.2 in 1989. After a period of relative stability from the late 1980s through the mid-1990s, the ratio declined from 17.3 in 1995 to 15.3 in 2008, before increasing again to 16.1 in 2013. Following this increase, there was a decrease in the

pupil/teacher ratio to 16.0 in 2017. Because some classrooms have multiple teachers, the pupil/teacher ratio is smaller than average class size. The average class size was 21.2 pupils for public elementary schools and 26.8 pupils for public secondary schools in 2011–12, when the most recent data were obtained (table 209.30).

The demographic composition of public school teachers has changed over the last 20 years. In 2017–18, 76 percent of public school teachers were female, up from 75 percent in 1999–2000 (table 209.10). Over the same period, the percentage of public school teachers who were White decreased from 84 percent to 79 percent. The percentage of public school teachers who were Black was 1 percentage point lower in 2017–18 than in 1999–2000 (7 vs. 8 percent). In contrast, the percentage of Hispanic teachers increased from 6 percent of all teachers to 9 percent of all teachers. In 2017–18, about 2 percent of public school teachers were Asian, 2 percent were of Two or more races, 1 percent were American Indian/Alaska Native, and less than 1 percent were Pacific Islander. Changes in the percentage of teachers from different racial/ethnic backgrounds did not mirror demographic changes among students. For instance, although the percentage of teachers who were White decreased by 5 percentage points between 1999–2000 and 2017–18, White teachers still constituted the vast majority of teachers (79 percent). In contrast, the percentage of students who were White decreased 14 percentage points (from 61 percent in 2000 to 48 percent in 2017).

Teachers acquire skills both during formal training and in the classroom. The majority of public school teachers now have formal training culminating in a postbaccalaureate degree (table 209.10). pecifically, the percentage of public school teachers with a master's or higher degree increased from 47 percent in 1999–2000 to 58 percent in 2017–18. During the same time period, there were shifts in the average experience of public school teachers, with an increase in mid-career teachers. pecifically, the percentage of public school teachers with 10 to 20 years of teaching experience increased from 29 percent in 1999–2000 to 40 percent in 2017–18, while the percentage of teachers with more than 20 years of teaching experience decreased from 32 to 23 percent. The percentage of public school teachers with less than 3 years of teaching experience was lower in 2017–18 (9 percent) than in 1999–2000 (11 percent).

There were differences in the demographics of public and private school teachers in 2017–18. The percentage of private school teachers who were female (74 percent) was lower than the corresponding percentage for public school teachers (76 percent; table 209.10). The percentage of private school teachers who were White (85 percent) was higher than the percentage for public school teachers (79 percent). The percentage of private school teachers with a master's or higher degree (48 percent) was lower than the percentage for public school teachers (58 percent). However, although there are no comparable figures on teacher experience, the percentage of private school teachers who were age 60 and over (15 percent) was higher than the percentage for public school teachers (7 percent) in 2017–18.

---

[2] The pupil/teacher ratio is based on all teachers—including teachers of students with disabilities and other special teachers—and all students enrolled in the fall of the school year. Unlike the pupil/teacher ratio, the average class size excludes students and teachers in classes that are exclusively for special education students. Class size averages are based on surveys of teachers reporting on the counts of students in their classes.

Public school teachers with more years of teaching experience and those with higher levels of education earn higher average salaries than their peers with less experience or lower levels of education. In 2017–18, the average salary among public school teachers who had completed a bachelor's degree as their highest degree was $50,920 (in constant 2018–19 dollars), compared with $64,430 among those who had completed a master's degree, $67,890 among those who had an education specialist degree, and $70,960 among those who had a doctor's degree as their highest degree (table 211.20). Within each level of education, teachers who had more teaching experience had higher salaries than those who had taught for fewer years. For example, average salaries for those who had completed a bachelor's degree ranged from $43,010 for those with 1 year or less of teaching experience to $65,340 for those who had 30 to 34 years of teaching experience.

Average salaries for public school teachers in 2017–18 were lower than in 1999–2000 for teachers overall, and at the bachelor's, master's, and specialist degree levels (after adjusting for inflation in 2018–19 dollars). For example, the average salary for teachers with a master's degree was $64,430 in 2017–18 compared with $66,910 in 1999–2000 (table 211.20). However, this pattern was not consistent across all combinations of experience and educational attainment.

Public School Principals

Public school principals tend to be older and have more advanced credentials than public school teachers. In 2017–18, some 83 percent of public school principals were over age 40, and 98 percent had a master's or higher degree (table 212.08). In comparison, only 57 percent of public school teachers were over age 40, and 58 percent had a master's or higher degree (table 209.10). Relative to the composition of the teacher workforce, principals were also disproportionately male only 54 percent of principals were female, compared with 76 percent of teachers (tables 209.10 and 212.08).

There were changes in the characteristics of public school principals between 1999–2000 and 2017–18. The percentage of principals who were female increased from 44 percent in 1999–2000 to 54 percent in 2017–18 (table 212.08). The percentage of principals who were White decreased from 82 to 78 percent, while the percentage of principals who were Hispanic increased from 5 to 9 percent. The percentage of principals who were under age 40 was higher in 2017–18 (17 percent) than in 1999–2000 (10 percent), and the percentage who were ages 40 to 44 was also higher in 2017–18 (20 percent) than in 1999–2000 (13 percent). In contrast, the percentage who were ages 50 to 54 in 2017–18 (18 percent) was lower than in 1999–2000 (32 percent). The percentage of principals who had 20 or more years of experience as a principal was lower in 2017–18 (4 percent) than in 1999–2000 (11 percent). The percentage of principals with 3 or fewer years of experience as a principal was higher in 2017–18 (37 percent) than in 1999–2000 (30 percent). The average salary for public school principals in 2017–18 was $100,340 (in 2018–19 dollars; *web-only table 212.10*).

School Staff

From 1969–70 to 1980, there was an 8 percent increase in the number of public school teachers, compared with a 48 percent increase in the number of all other public school staff[3] (table B and table 213.10). Consequently, the percentage of staff who were teachers declined from 60 percent in 1969–70 to 52 percent in 1980. From 1980 to 2017, the number of teachers and the number of all other staff grew at more similar rates (45 and 70 percent, respectively) than they did in the 1970s. As a result, the proportion of teachers among total staff was 4 percentage points lower in 2017 than in 1980, in contrast to the decrease of 8 percentage points during the 1970s. The numbers of staff in two categories increased more than 100 percent between 1980 and 2017: the number of instructional aides rose 153 percent, and the number of instruction coordinators rose 366 percent. Taken together, the percentage of staff with direct instructional responsibilities (teachers and instructional aides) was higher in 2017 (61 percent) than in 1980 (60 percent). In 2017, there were 8 pupils per staff member (total staff) at public schools, compared with 10 pupils per staff member in 1980 (table 213.10). At private schools in 2011–12, the number of pupils per staff member was 6 (*web-only table 205.60*).

Table B. Number of public school staff, by selected categories: 1969–70, fall 1980, fall 2010, and fall 2017

[In thousands]

Selected staff category	1969–70	1980	2010	2017
Total	**3,361**	**4,168**	**6,195**	**6,545**
Teachers	2,016	2,184	3,099	3,170
Instructional aides	57	326	732	824
Instruction coordinators	32	21	69	96

SOURCE: U.S. Department of Education, National Center for Education Statistics, *Statistics of State School Systems, 1969–70*; *Statistics of Public Elementary and Secondary Schools, 1980*; and Common Core of Data (CCD), "State Nonfiscal Survey of Public Elementary/Secondary Education," 2010–11 and 2017–18.

In more recent years, the numbers of most types of staff have increased. Overall, the number of public school staff increased 6 percent between fall 2012 and fall 2017 (table 213.10). The number of officials and administrators rose 14 percent during this period, and the number of principals and assistant principals rose 12 percent. Also, the number of instruction coordinators rose 35 percent, the number of instructional aides rose 13 percent, and the number of support staff rose 8 percent. The number of teachers rose 2 percent between fall 2012 and fall 2017, and the number of guidance counselors increased 11 percent. In contrast, the number of librarians decreased by 9 percent during this period.

Schools

Total Schools

Despite an increase in the number of students, the number of public schools declined in the United States, reflecting a trend toward consolidating small schools during

---

[3] "All other public school staff" includes administrative staff, principals, librarians, guidance counselors, secretaries, custodial staff, food service workers, school bus drivers, and other professional and nonprofessional staff.

most of the last century. In 1929–30, there were approximately 248,000 public schools, compared with about 98,500 in 2017–18 (table 214.10). However, the number of public schools has increased in recent decades: Between 1988–89 and 2006–07, there was an increase of approximately 15,600 schools, up to a total of 98,800. Since 2006–07, the number of public schools has remained relatively stable, varying by fewer than 500 schools from year to year.

While the total number of public schools in the country has remained relatively stable in recent years, new schools have opened and some schools have closed. In 2017–18, there were 1,310 school closures (*web-only table 216.95*). The schools that closed had enrolled about 267,000 students in the prior school year (2016–17). Of the schools that closed, 889 were regular schools, 217 were special education schools, 13 were vocational schools, and 191 were alternative schools. Of these closed schools, 247 were classified as charter schools. The number of schools that closed in 2017–18 was higher than the number in 2015–16 (1,160) or 2016–17 (1,098); however, the number of annual school closures fluctuated during the 2000–01 to 2017–18 period, ranging from 1,098 to 2,168. School closures do not necessarily reflect the number of school buildings that have been closed, since a school may share a building with another school, or one school may have multiple buildings.

School Structure

Since the early 1970s, public school systems have been shifting away from junior high schools (schools consisting of either grades 7 and 8 or grades 7–9) and moving toward middle schools (a subset of elementary schools beginning with grade 4, 5, or 6 and ending with grade 6, 7, or 8). The number of all public elementary schools (schools beginning with grade 6 or below and ending with grade 8 or below) increased 5 percent between 1970–71 and 2017–18 (from 64,000 to 67,400), and the number of middle schools increased by 546 percent (from 2,100 in 1970–71 to 13,400 in 2017–18; table 216.10). During the same period, the number of junior high schools declined by 68 percent (from 7,800 in 1970–71 to 2,500 in 2017–18). Compared over more recent years, the number of all elementary schools was less than 1 percent higher in 2017–18 than in 2007–08, while the subset of middle schools rose by 3 percent, from 13,000 to 13,400. During the same period, the number of junior high schools declined by 20 percent, from 3,100 to 2,500. The total number of secondary schools decreased 3 percent, from 24,600 in 2007–08 to 23,900 in 2017–18.

The average number of students in public elementary schools increased from 469 in 2007–08 to 483 in 2017–18 (table 216.45). The average enrollment size of public secondary schools was also higher in 2017–18 (709) than in 2007–08 (704). However, considering only regular public secondary schools—which exclude alternative, special education, and vocational education schools—average enrollment sie` was lower in 2017–18 (804) than in 2007–08 (816).

School Choice

Over the past two decades, the range of options that parents have for the education of their children has expanded. Private schools have been a traditional alternative to public school education, but there are now more options for parents to choose public charter schools, and more parents are also homeschooling their children. Between fall 1999 and fall 2017, enrollment in private elementary and secondary schools decreased from 6.0 million to 5.7 million, a decline of 0.3 million or 5 percent (table 105.30). Although private school enrollment declined through much of this period, it was higher in fall 2017 (5.7 million) than in fall 2011 (5.3 million). From fall 1999 to fall 2017, the percentage of students who were enrolled in private schools declined from 11.4 percent to 10.1 percent. In contrast, enrollment in public charter schools increased between fall 1999 and fall 2017, rising from 0.3 million to 3.1 million, an increase of 2.8 million students or 825 percent (table 216.20). During this period, the percentage of public elementary and secondary school students who were in charter schools increased from 0.7 percent to 6.2 percent. In addition, there has been an increase in the number and percentage of 5- to 17-year-olds who are homeschooled (table 206.10 and *web-only table 206.20*). About 1.7 million children were homeschooled in 2016, compared with 0.9 million in 1999.[4] This also reflects an increase in the percentage of 5- to 17-year-olds who were homeschooled, from 1.7 percent in 1999 to 3.3 percent in 2016.

Today, charter schools are the archetypical form of school choice available to parents within the public education sector; however, there is also opportunity for school choice among traditional public schools. In 2016, the parents of 41 percent of all students in grades 1–12 indicated that public school choice was available to them (*web-only table 206.40*). Also in 2016, some 20 percent of the students in grades 1–12 were enrolled in public schools chosen by their families (*Digest of Education Statistics 2017*, table 206.30). Of the remaining 80 percent of students, 71 percent attended an assigned public school and 9 percent attended a private school. Not all school choice options are equally accessible to all families—private schools require personal financial investments for tuition, while public choice options are more prevalent in urban districts—and there were differences by some characteristics in the percentages of students who attended public schools chosen by their parents and the percentages of students who attended private schools in 2016. The percentage of students attending chosen public schools was

---

[4] The number of homeschooled children in 1999 is from *Homeschooling in the United States: 1999* (NCES 2001-033), available at https://nces.ed.gov/pubsearch/pubsinfo.asp?pubid=2001033. While National Household Education Surveys Program (NHES) administrations prior to 2012 were administered via telephone with an interviewer, NHES:2016 used self-administered paper-and-pencil questionnaires that were mailed to respondents. Measurable differences in estimates between 1999 and 2016 could reflect actual changes in the population, or the changes could be due to the mode change from telephone to mail.

higher for students living in cities (31 percent) than for students in suburban areas (17 percent), towns (14 percent), and rural areas (11 percent). Meanwhile, the percentage of students attending private schools was higher for students whose parents had a bachelor's degree (13 percent) or graduate degree (18 percent) than for students whose parents had less than a high school diploma (5 percent), only a high school diploma (4 percent), or only some college or a vocational degree (6 percent). Conversely, a lower percentage of students whose parents had completed only a bachelor's degree (18 percent) were enrolled in chosen schools, compared with students whose parents had not completed high school (23 percent) or who had only completed high school (21 percent). There were also some differences in the percentage of students in chosen public versus private schools by student race. The percentage of students attending chosen public schools was higher for Black students (32 percent) and Hispanic students (25 percent) than for White students (14 percent). In contrast, the percentage attending private schools was higher for White students (11 percent) than for Black students (8 percent) and Hispanic students (6 percent).

Compared with students in assigned public schools, a higher percentage of students in chosen public schools had parents who were very satisfied with some elements of their children's education in 2016 (web-only table 206.50). pecifically, among students in grades 3 through 12, the percentage of students whose parents were very satisfied with their school was higher for students in chosen schools (60 percent) than for students in assigned schools (54 percent). Similarly, the percentage of students whose parents were very satisfied with their school's academic standards was higher for students in chosen schools (60 percent) than for students in assigned schools (53 percent). Also, higher percentages of students in chosen schools than in assigned schools had parents who were very satisfied with school order and discipline (57 vs. 53 percent) as well as with staff interaction with parents (51 vs. 47 percent). There was no measurable difference in the percentage of students who had parents who were highly satisfied with the teachers in their school, whether assigned or chosen.

High School Graduates and Dropouts

About 3,663,000 high school students were projected to graduate during the 2020–21 school year (based on pre-pandemic data), including 3,302,000 public school graduates and 360,000 private school graduates (table 219.10). High school graduates include only recipients of diplomas, not recipients of equivalency credentials. The 2020–21 projection of high school graduates is slightly lower than the prior record high projection of 3,674,000 graduates for 2018–19, but it exceeds the baby boom era's high point in 1975–76, when 3,142,000 students earned diplomas. In 2017–18, about 85 percent of public high school students graduated with a regular diploma within 4 years of first starting 9th grade, which reflects an increase since 2010–11 (79 percent; table 219.46). This rate is known as the 4-year adjusted cohort graduation rate (ACGR).

The status dropout rate has decreased since 2000. The status dropout rate is the percentage of the civilian noninstitutionalized 16- to 24-year-old population who are not enrolled in school and who have not completed a high school program, regardless of when they left school. (People who left school but went on to receive a GED credential are not treated as dropouts.) Between 2000 and 2018, the status dropout rate declined from 10.9 to 5.7 percent (table 219.70). During this period, the status dropout rate for Black 16- to 24-year-olds declined from 13.1 to 5.8 percent and the rate for Hispanic 16- to 24-year-olds declined from 27.8 to 9.0 percent. In 2018, the status dropout rate for White 16- to 24-year-olds (4.5 percent) was lower than the rate for Hispanic 16- to 24-year-olds, but it was not measurably different from the rate for Black 16- to 24-year-olds.

Achievement

Much of the student performance data in the *Digest* are drawn from the National Assessment of Educational Progress (NAEP). The NAEP assessments have been conducted using three basic designs: the national main NAEP, state NAEP (which includes the Trial Urban District Assessment), and national long-term trend NAEP. The main NAEP reports current information for the nation and specific geographic regions of the country. The assessment program includes students drawn from both public and private schools and reports results for student achievement at grades 4, 8, and 12. The main NAEP assessments follow the frameworks developed by the National Assessment overning Board and use the latest advances in assessment methodology. Because the assessment items reflect curricula associated with specific grade levels, the main NAEP uses samples of students at those grade levels.

ince 1990, NAEP assessments have also been conducted at the state level. Each participating state receives assessment results that report on the performance of students in that state. In its content, the state assessment is identical to the assessment conducted nationally. From 1990 through 2001, the national sample was a subset of the combined sample of students assessed in each participating state along with an additional sample from the states that did not participate in the state assessment. For mathematics, reading, science, and writing assessments since 2002, a combined sample of public schools has been selected for 4th- and 8th-grade national NAEP and state NAEP (including the Trial Urban District Assessment).

NAEP long-term trend assessments are designed to give information on the changes in the basic achievement level of America's youth since the early 1970s. They are administered nationally and report student performance in reading and mathematics at ages 9, 13, and 17. Measuring long-term trends of student achievement requires the precise replication of past procedures. For example, students of specific ages are sampled in order to maintain consistency with the original sample design. Similarly, the long-term trend instrument does not evolve based on changes in curricula or in educational practices. The differences in procedures between the main NAEP and the long-term trend NAEP mean that their results cannot be compared directly.

The following paragraphs discuss results for the national main NAEP, state NAEP, and long-term trend NAEP. eaders` should keep in mind that comparisons of NAEP scores in the text (like all comparisons of estimates in the *Digest*) are based on statistical testing of unrounded values.

Reading

Main NAEP

The main NAEP reading assessment data are reported on a scale of 0 to 500. For 4th-grade students, the average reading score in 2019 (220) was lower than the score in 2017 (222) but was higher than the 1992 score (217; table 221.10). This pattern held for certain racial/ethnic groups (White and Black students), but not for others (Hispanic, Asian/Pacific Islander, and American Indian/ Alaska Native students). pecifically, at grade 4, the 2019 reading scores for White (230) and Black (204) students were lower than the corresponding scores in 2017 (232 and 206, respectively), but higher than in 1992 (224 and 192, respectively). In contrast, the 4th-grade reading scores for Hispanic (209) and Asian/Pacific Islander (237) students were not measurably different in 2019 than in 2017, but the scores for both groups were higher in 2019 than in 1992 (197 and 216, respectively). For American Indian/Alaska Native students, the average 4th-grade reading score in 2019 (204) was not measurably different from the scores in either 2017 or 1994 (1994 was the first year data were available for 4th-grade American Indian/Alaska Native students).

From 1992 through 2019, the average reading scores for White 4th-graders were higher than those for their Black and Hispanic peers. Although the White-Black achievement gap did not change measurably from 2017 to 2019, the achievement gap narrowed from 32 points in 1992 to 27 points in 2019. The White-Hispanic achievement gap in 2019 (21 points) was smaller than the achievement gap in 2017 (23 points), but it was not measurably different from the achievement gap in 1992.

At grade 8, the average reading score in 2019 (263) was lower than the score in 2017 (267), but it was higher than the score in 1992 (260). The reading scores for White (272), Black (244), and Hispanic (252) 8th-grade students in 2019 were lower than the corresponding scores in 2017 (275, 249, and 255, respectively), but the score for each group

was higher in 2019 than in 1992 (267, 237, and 241, respectively). The reading score for 8th-grade Asian/Pacific Islander students in 2019 (281) was not measurably different from the score in 2017, but it was higher than the score in 1992 (268). The reading score for 8th-grade American Indian/Alaska Native students in 2019 (248) was lower than the score in 2017 (253), but it was not measurably different from the score in 1994 (1994 was the first year data were available for 8th-grade American Indian/ Alaska Native students).

From 1992 through 2019, the average reading score for White 8th-graders was higher than the scores for their Black and Hispanic peers. The White-Black achievement gap in 2019 (28 points) was larger than the White-Black achievement gap in 2017 (25 points), but it was not measurably different from the achievement gap in 1992. Although the White-Hispanic achievement gap at grade 8 did not change measurably from 2017 to 2019, the achievement gap narrowed from 26 points in 1992 to 20 points in 2019.

The average reading scores for 4th- and 8th-grade students varied by state. Although 4th-grade reading scores fell nationally from 2017 to 2019, they were higher in 2019 than in 2017 in one state (Mississippi) and showed no measurable change in 32 states and the District of Columbia (table 221.40). In the remaining 17 states, 4th-grade reading scores were lower in 2019 than in 2017. The reading score for 8th-grade students was higher in 2019 than in 2017 in the District of Columbia, but the scores showed no measurable change in 19 states (table 221.60). In the remaining 31 states, the reading scores for 8th-grade students were lower in 2019 than in 2017.

For 12th-grade students, the most recent scores available are from 2015. The reading score for 12th-grade students in 2015 (287) was not measurably different from the score in 2013, but it was lower than the score in 1992 (292; table 221.10). At grade 12, the reading scores in 2015 for White (295), Hispanic (276), and Asian/Pacific Islander (297) students were not measurably different from the scores in 2013 and 1992. For Black students, the 2015 reading score (266) was lower than the 1992 score (273), but it was not measurably different from the 2013 score. The reading score for American Indian/Alaska Native students in 2015 (279) was not measurably different from the scores in 2013 and 1994 (1994 was the first year data were available for 12th-grade American Indian/Alaska Native students).

The White-Black achievement gap for 12th-grade students was larger in 2015 (30 points) than in 1992 (24 points), while the White-Hispanic achievement gap in 2015 (20 points) was not measurably different from the achievement gap in any previous assessment year.

Long-Term NAEP

eported` on a scale of 0 to 500, NAEP long-term trend results in reading are available for 13 assessment years going back to the first in 1971. The average reading score for 9-year-olds was higher in 2012 (221) than in assessment years prior to 2008, increasing 5 points since 2004 and 13 points since 1971 (*web-only table 221.85*). The score for 13-year-olds in 2012 (263) was higher than in all previous assessment years except for 1992. The score for 17-year-olds was higher in 2012 (287) than in 2004 (283), but it was not measurably different from the score in 1971 (285).

White, Black, and Hispanic 9-, 13-, and 17-year-old students all had higher average reading scores in 2012 than they did in the first assessment year (which was 1975 for Hispanic students because separate data for Hispanics were not collected in 1971). The scores were higher in 2012 than in 2004 for White, Black, and Hispanic students at all three ages (*web-only table 221.85*). Reading results for 2012 continued to show gaps in scores between White and Black students (ranging from 23 to 26 points, depending on age) and between White and Hispanic students (about 21 points at all three ages). The White-Black and White-Hispanic achievement gaps were smaller in 2012 than in the first assessment year at all three ages. For example, the White-Black reading gap for 17-year-olds was 53 points in 1971 compared with 26 points in 2012. Similarly, the White-Hispanic gap for 17-year-olds narrowed from 41 points in 1975 to 21 points in 2012.

In 2012, female 9-, 13-, and 17-year-old students continued to have higher average reading scores than male students at all three ages (*web-only table 221.85*). The gap between male and female 9-year-olds was 5 points in 2012; this was narrower than the gap in 1971 (13 points). The 8-point gender gap for 13-year-olds in 2012 was not measurably different from the gap in 1971. At age 17, the 8-point gap between males and females in 2012 was not measurably different from the gap in 1971.

Mathematics

Main NAEP

The main NAEP mathematics assessment data for 4th- and 8th-graders are reported on a scale of 0 to 500. The average mathematics score for 4th-grade students in 2019 (241) was higher than the scores in both 2017 (240) and 1990 (213; table 222.10). At grade 4, the average mathematics scores in 2019 for Asian/Pacific Islander (260), White (249), and Black (224) students were not measurably different from the corresponding scores in 2017, but the mathematics score for each group was higher in 2019 than in 1990 (225, 220, and 188, respectively). The 2019 mathematics score for 4th-grade Hispanic students (231) was higher than the scores in both 2017 (229) and 1990 (200). The 2019 mathematics score for 4th-grade American Indian/Alaska Native students (227) was not measurably different from the scores in 2017 and 1996 (1996 was the first year data were available for 4th-grade American Indian/Alaska Native students).

In 2019 and in all assessment years since 1990, the average mathematics scores for White students in grade 4 have been higher than those of their Black and Hispanic peers. Although the White-Black and White-Hispanic achievement gaps at grade 4 did not change measurably from

2017 to 2019, the White-Black achievement gap narrowed from 32 points in 1990 to 25 points in 2019. The 4th-grade White-Hispanic achievement gap in 2019 (18 points) was not measurably different from the gap in 1990.

For 8th-grade students, the average mathematics score in 2019 (282) was lower than the score in 2017 (283), but it was higher than the score in 1990 (263). At grade 8, the mathematics scores for Asian/Pacific Islander (310), White (292), Hispanic (268), and Black (260) students in 2019 were not measurably different from the corresponding scores in 2017, but the score for each group was higher in 2019 than in 1990 (275, 270, 246, and 237, respectively). The mathematics score for 8th-grade American Indian/Alaska Native students in 2019 (262) was lower than the score in 2017 (267), but it was not measurably different from the score in 2000 (2000 was the first year data were available for 8th-grade American Indian/Alaska Native students).

In 2019 and in all assessment years since 1990, the average mathematics scores for White students in grade 8 have been higher than the scores for their Black and Hispanic peers. At grade 8, the White-Black (32 points) and White-Hispanic (24 points) achievement gaps in 2019 were not measurably different from the corresponding gaps in 2017 and 1990.

For 12th-grade students, the average mathematics score in 2015 (152) was lower than the score in 2013 (153), but it was not measurably different from the score in 2005, the earliest year with comparable data. At grade 12, the mathematics scores for Asian/Pacific Islander (170), White (160), Hispanic (139), and Black (130) students in 2015 were not measurably different from the scores in 2013, but the score for each group was higher in 2015 than in 2005 (163, 157, 133, and 127, respectively). The mathematics score for American Indian/Alaska Native students in 2015 (138) was not measurably different from the scores in 2013 and 2005.

In 2015, the mathematics score for White 12th-grade students was 30 points higher than the score for their Black peers and 22 points higher than the score for their Hispanic peers. The White-Black and White-Hispanic gaps in 2015 were not measurably different from the corresponding gaps in 2005 and 2013.

Long-Term NAEP

NAEP long-term trend mathematics results, reported on a scale of 0 to 500, are available for 12 assessment years, going back to the first in 1973. In 2012, the average mathematics score for 9-year-olds (244) was higher than in all assessment years prior to 2008 (*web-only table 222.85*). The score for 9-year-olds in 2012 was 5 points higher than in 2004 and 25 points higher than in 1973. The score for 13-year-olds in 2012 (285) was higher than in all previous assessment years. For 13-year-olds, the score in 2012 was 6 points higher than in 2004 and 19 points higher than in 1973. In contrast, the score for 17-year-olds in 2012 (306) was not measurably different from the scores in 2004 and in 1973.

White, Black, and Hispanic 9-, 13-, and 17-year-olds all had higher average mathematics scores in 2012 than in 1973 (*web-only table 222.85*). In comparison to 2004, scores were higher in 2012 for White 9- and 13-year-olds; Hispanic 13-year-olds; and Black 13-year-olds. athematics results for 2012 continued to show achievement gaps between White and Hispanic students (ranging from 17 to 21 points [based on unrounded scores], depending on age) and between White and Black students (ranging from 25 to 28 points). For 9-year-olds, the White-Black gap was lower in 2012 than in 1973. For 13- and 17-year-olds, both the White-Black and the White-Hispanic gaps were lower in 2012 than in 1973. For example, among 17-year-olds, the White-Black gap was 40 points in 1973 compared with 26 points in 2012, and the White-Hispanic gap was 33 points in 1973 compared with 19 points in 2012.

While there was no significant difference between the average mathematics scores of male and female 9- and 13-year-olds in 2012, among students still in high school at age 17, male students scored higher than female students (*web-only table 222.85*). At age 17, the 4-point gender score gap in 2012 was smaller than the gap in 1973 (8 points).

Science

Main NAEP

NAEP has assessed the science abilities of students in grades 4, 8, and 12 in both public and private schools since 1996. As of 2009, however, NAEP science assessments are based on a new framework, so results from these assessments cannot be compared with results from earlier science assessments. Scores are based on a scale ranging from 0 to 300 (table 223.10). In 2015, the average 4th-grade science score (154) was higher than the score in 2009 (150). The 8th-grade science score in 2015 (154) was higher than the scores in 2009 (150) and in 2011 (152). The 12th-grade science score in 2015 (150) was not measurably different from the score in 2009.

While the scores for White 4th- and 8th-grade students remained higher than those for their Black and Hispanic peers in 2015, racial/ethnic achievement gaps in 2015 were smaller than in 2009. For example, at grade 4, the White-Black achievement gap was 36 points in 2009 and 33 points in 2015, and the White-Hispanic achievement gap was 32 points in 2009 and 27 points in 2015. For 12th-grade students, in contrast, science scores for White students remained higher than those for their Black and Hispanic peers in 2015, and these racial/ethnic achievement gaps were not measurably different from 2009. In addition, the 5-point gender gap, which favored male 12th-graders, in 2015 was not measurably different from the gap in 2009.

Skills of Young Children

In addition to student performance data available through NAEP, the *Digest* presents data from other surveys to provide additional perspectives on student achievement. Differences among demographic groups in the acquisition of cognitive skills have been demonstrated at relatively early ages in the Early Childhood Longitudinal tudy, indergarten Class of 2010–11 (ECLS-K:2011). Possible scores for the mathematics assessment range from 0 to 159, and possible scores for the reading assessment range from 0 to 167.

Children who enrolled in kindergarten for the first time in 2010–11 showed similar patterns of score differences across racial/ethnic and socioeconomic status (SES) groups for both mathematics and reading. In fall 2010, average mathematics scores were higher for first-tim kindergartners from high-SES families (43) than for those from low-SES families (29). White (39) and Asian (41) first-time kindergartners had higher mathematics scores than their Black (32), Hispanic (31), and American Indian/Alaska Native (33) peers (table 220.40 and *web-only table 220.41*). Similarly, average early reading scores in fall 2010 were higher for White (56) and Asian (59) first-tim kindergartners than for their Black (53), Hispanic (51), and American Indian/Alaska Native (50) peers. High-SES children (61) had higher early reading scores than low-SES children (49).

School Violence

In 2017–18, some 71 percent of public schools reported one or more violent incidents, such as a serious violent incident, a physical attack, or a threat of a physical attack (table 229.10). This 2017–18 percentage was not measurably different from the percentage of schools reporting violent incidents in 1999–2000. erious violent incidents is a subcategory of violent incidents that includes the crimes of rape, sexual assault, robbery, and aggravated assault. The percentage of schools reporting a serious violent incident in 2017–18 (21 percent) also was not measurably different from the percentage reporting a serious violent incident in 1999–2000. The percentage of schools reporting a physical attack or fight without a weapon in 2017–18 (66 percent) was not measurably different from the percentage in 1999–2000; however, the percentage of schools reporting a physical attack or fight with a weapon in 2017–18 (3 percent) was lower than the percentage in 1999–2000 (5 percent). Also, the percentage of schools reporting a threat of a physical attack without a weapon in 2017–18 (41 percent) was lower than the percentage in 1999–2000 (52 percent). One percent of public schools reported that a rape had occurred in 2017–18, which was not measurably different from the percentage in 1999–2000; however, the percentage of schools that reported that some other type of sexual assault had occurred in 2017–18 (5 percent) was higher than the percentage in 1999–2000 (2 percent). The percentage of schools reporting that a theft/larceny had occurred in 2017–18 (33 percent) was lower than in 1999–2000 (46 percent), and also the percentage reporting that vandalism had occurred in 2017–18 (33 percent) was lower than in 1999–2000 (51 percent). Overall, schools reported 20 violent incidents per 1,000 students in 2017–18, which was lower than the 31 violent incidents per 1,000 students reported in 1999–2000 (*web-only table 229.20*).

On the National Crime Victimization urvey,` students ages 12 to 18 reported a decrease in victimizations at school between 2000 and 2018 (*web-only table 228.20*). The total victimization rates for students ages 12 to 18 declined 61 percent, from 85 victimizations per 1,000 students in 2000 to 33 victimizations per 1,000 students in 2018. This pattern of decline in total victimization rates between 2000 and 2018 also held for thefts and violent victimizations overall. Thefts at school declined from a rate of 49 thefts per 1,000 students to 9 thefts per 1,000 students. The rate of violent victimization at school declined overall from 36 victimizations per 1,000 students in 2000 to 24 victimizations per 1,000 students in 2018. The rate of violent victimizations excluding simple assault at school was 6 per 1,000 students in 2018, which was not measurably different from the rate in 2000. The victimization rates for theft declined more rapidly than the victimization rates for violent crimes. In 2000, the victimization rates for theft were higher than the rates for violent crimes, but in 2018 the victimization rates for theft were lower than the rates for violent crimes.

Revenues and Expenditures

After adjustment for inflation, current expenditures per student at public schools (based on fall enrollment) rose during the 1980s but remained stable during the first part of the 1990s. There was an increase of 37 percent from 1980–81 to 1990–91, followed by minor fluctuations from 1990–91 to 1994–95 (table 236.55 and figure 10). Current expenditures per student increased 34 percent from 1994–95 to 2008–09 but declined 5 percent from 2008–09 to 2012–13. Current expenditures per student increased 9 percent between 2012–13 and 2016–17, reaching $12,258 in unadjusted dollars.

The federal share of public school revenues in 2016–17 (8.1 percent) was lower than in 2006–07 (8.5 percent; table 235.10 and figure 11). Also, the state share in 2016–17 (47.0 percent) was lower than in 2006–07 (47.4 percent). The remaining, local, share in 2016–17 (44.9 percent) was higher than in 2006–07 (44.1 percent).

Figure 7. Fall enrollment, number of teachers, pupil/teacher ratio, and expenditures in public elementary and secondary schools: Selected years, 1960–61 through 2017–18

Fall enrollment, in millions

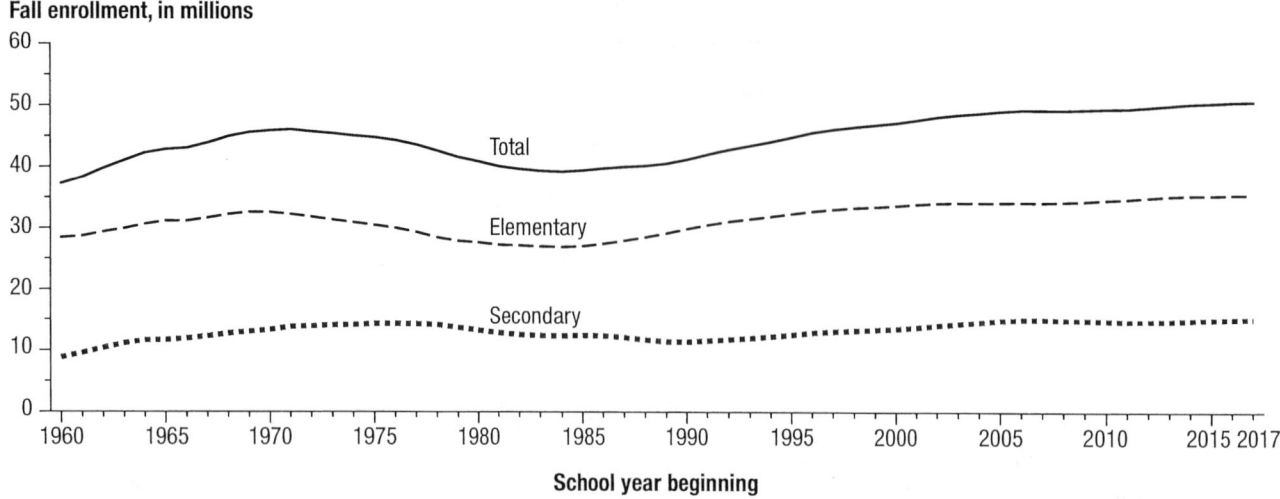

School year beginning

Teachers, in millions

Pupil/teacher ratio

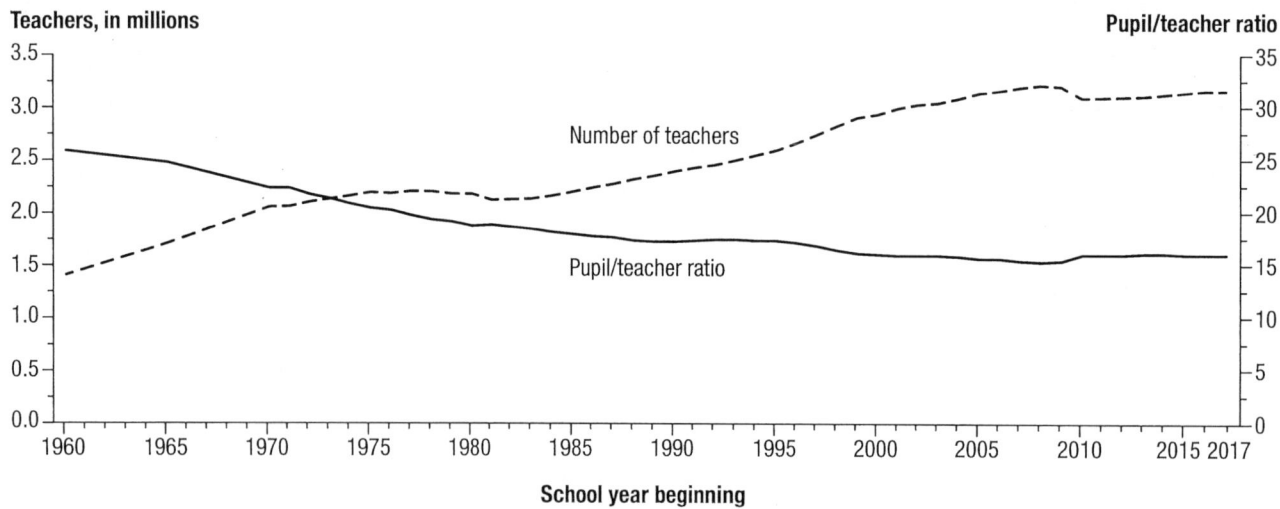

School year beginning

Current expenditures, in billions

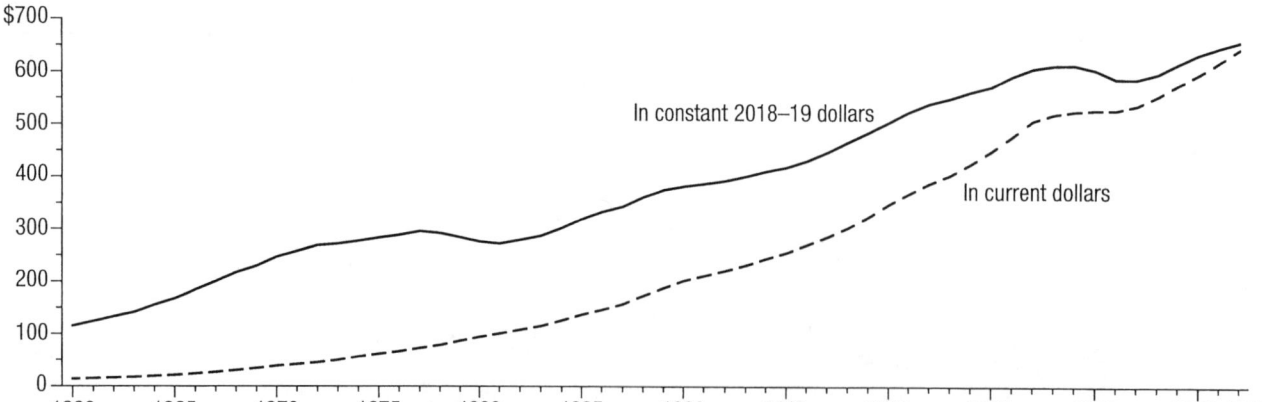

School year beginning

NOTE: Expenditure data for school year 2017 (2017–18) are projected. Constant dollars based on the Consumer Price Index, prepared by the Bureau of Labor Statistics, U.S. Department of Labor, adjusted to a school-year basis.
SOURCE: U.S. Department of Education, National Center for Education Statistics, *Statistics of State School Systems*, 1959–60 through 1969–70; *Statistics of Public Elementary and Secondary Day Schools*, 1959–60 through 1980–81; *Revenues and Expenditures for Public Elementary and Secondary Education*, 1970–71 through 1980–81; and Common Core of Data (CCD), "State Nonfiscal Survey of Public Elementary/Secondary Education," 1981–82 through 2017–18; "National Public Education Financial Survey," 1989–90 through 2016–17; and Public Elementary and Secondary Education Current Expenditure Projection Model, 1973–74 through 2029–30.

Figure 8.   Percentage change in public elementary and secondary enrollment, by state: Fall 2012 to fall 2017

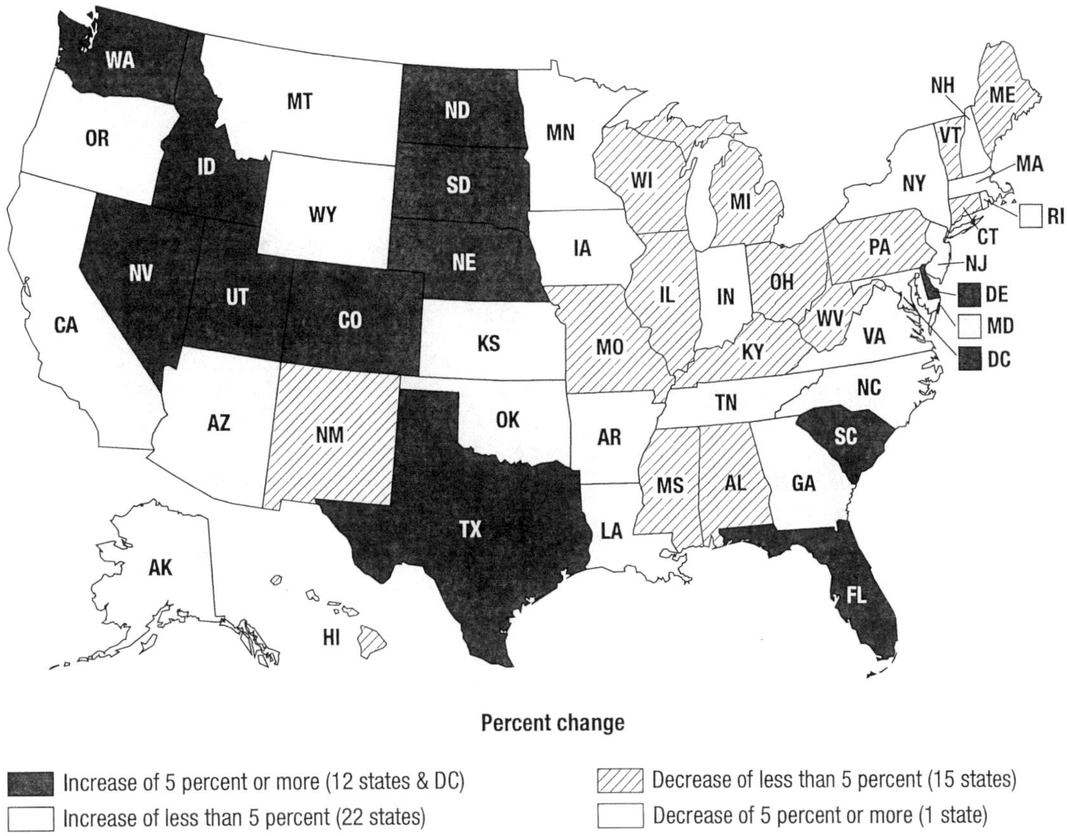

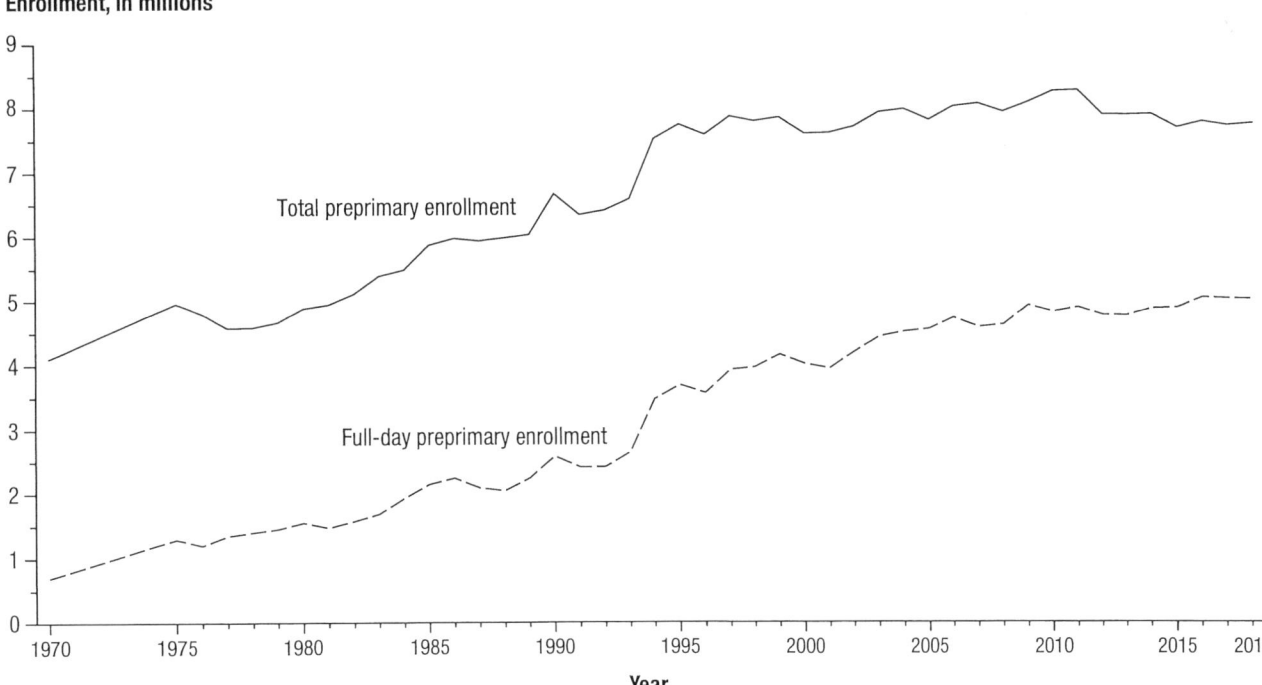

Percent change

■ Increase of 5 percent or more (12 states & DC)	▨ Decrease of less than 5 percent (15 states)
□ Increase of less than 5 percent (22 states)	□ Decrease of 5 percent or more (1 state)

NOTE: Includes imputations for prekindergarten enrollment in California and Oregon. Graphic display was generated using unrounded data.
SOURCE: U.S. Department of Education, National Center for Education Statistics, Common Core of Data (CCD), "State Nonfiscal Survey of Public Elementary/Secondary Education," 2012–13 and 2017–18.

Figure 9.   Total and full-day preprimary enrollment of 3- to 5-year-olds: October 1970 through October 2018

Enrollment, in millions

Total preprimary enrollment

Full-day preprimary enrollment

Year

NOTE: Data prior to 1994 may not be comparable to later years. Preprimary programs include kindergarten and preschool (or nursery school) programs.
SOURCE: U.S. Department of Commerce, Census Bureau, Current Population Survey (CPS), October 1970 through October 2018.

Figure 10. Current expenditure per pupil in fall enrollment in public elementary and secondary schools: 1970–71 through 2016–17

Per pupil expenditure

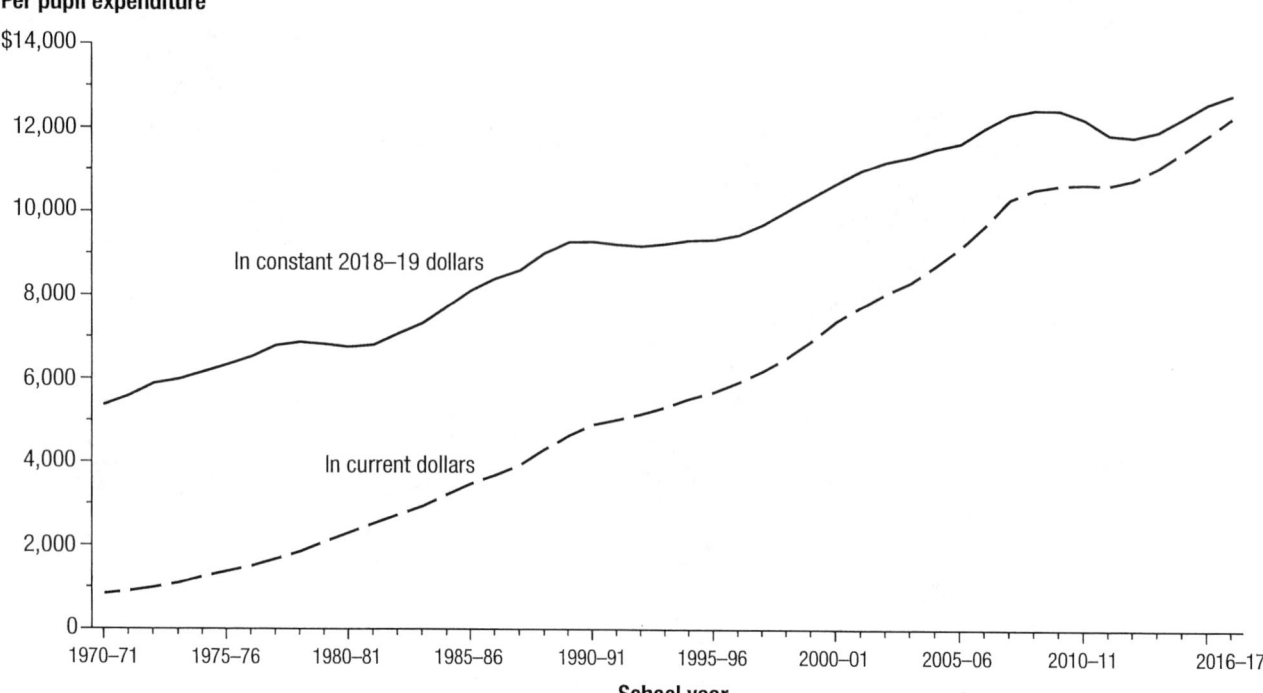

School year

NOTE: Current expenditures include instruction, support services, food services, and enterprise operations. Beginning in 1988–89, extensive changes were made in the data collection procedures. As a result, data collected from 1988–89 onward may not be comparable to earlier data. Constant dollars based on the Consumer Price Index, prepared by the Bureau of Labor Statistics, U.S. Department of Labor, adjusted to a school-year basis.
SOURCE: U.S. Department of Education, National Center for Education Statistics, *Revenues and Expenditures for Public Elementary and Secondary Education*, 1970–71 through 1986–87; and Common Core of Data (CCD), "National Public Education Financial Survey," 1987–88 through 2016–17.

Figure 11. Percentage of revenue for public elementary and secondary schools, by source of funds: 1970–71 through 2016–17

Percent of revenue

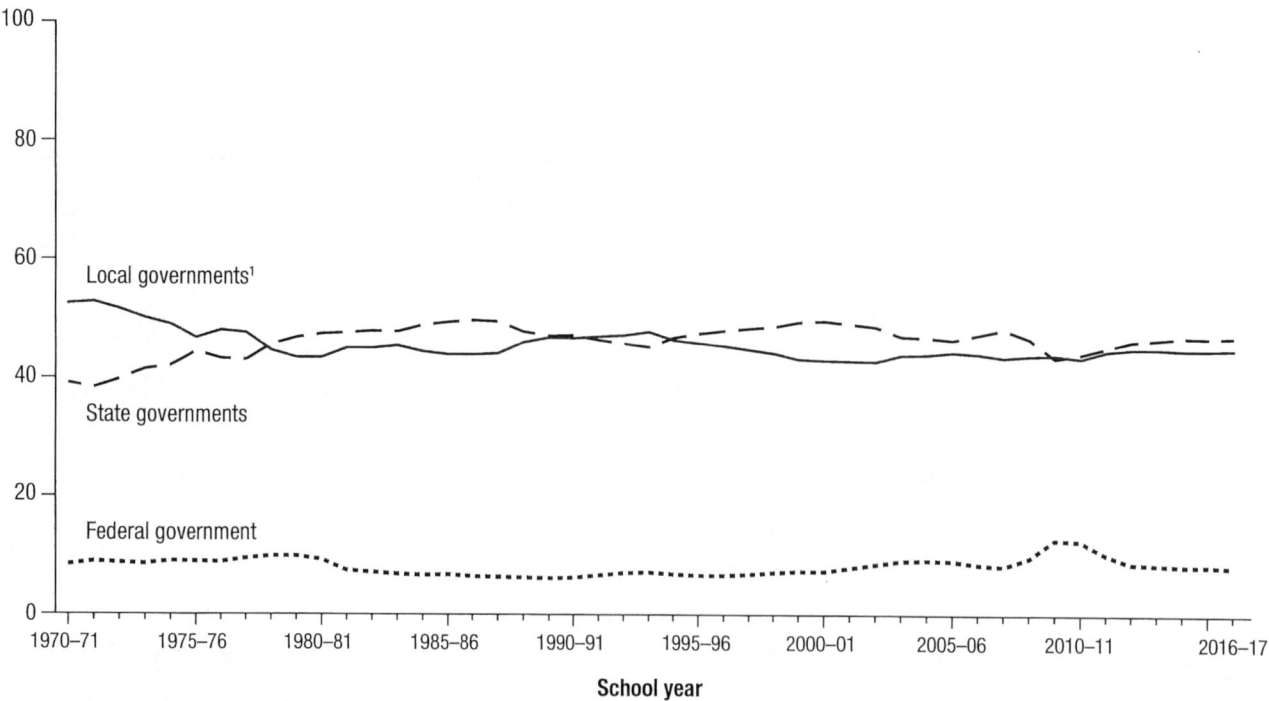

School year

[1]Includes intermediate sources below the state level.
NOTE: Beginning in 1988–89, extensive changes were made in the data collection procedures. As a result, data collected from 1988–89 onward may not be comparable to earlier data.
SOURCE: U.S. Department of Education, National Center for Education Statistics, *Revenues and Expenditures for Public Elementary and Secondary Education*, 1970–71 through 1986–87; and Common Core of Data (CCD), "National Public Education Financial Survey," 1987–88 through 2016–17.

Table 201.10. Historical summary of public elementary and secondary school statistics: Selected years, 1869–70 through 2016–17

Selected characteristic	1869–70	1879–80	1889–90	1899–1900	1909–10	1919–20	1929–30	1939–40	1949–50	1959–60	1969–70	1979–80	1989–90	1999–2000	2009–10	2013–14	2014–15	2015–16	2016–17
1	2	3	4	5	6	7	8	9	10	11	12	13	14	15	16	17	18	19	20
Population, pupils, and instructional staff																			
Total population (in thousands)	38,558	50,156	62,622	75,995	90,490	104,514	121,878	131,028	149,188	177,830	201,385	225,055	246,819	279,040	306,772	316,058	318,386	320,743	323,071
5- to 17-year-olds (in thousands)[1]	11,683	15,066	18,473	21,573	24,011	27,571	31,414	30,151	30,223	43,881	52,386	48,043	44,947	52,811	53,890	53,721	53,693	53,702	53,727
5- to 17-year-olds as a percent of total population	30.3	30.0	29.5	28.4	26.5	26.4	25.8	23.0	20.3	24.7	26.0	21.3	18.2	18.9	17.6	17.0	16.9	16.7	16.6
Total enrollment in elementary and secondary schools (in thousands)[2]	7,562[3]	9,867	12,723	15,503	17,814	21,578	25,678	25,434	25,112	36,087	45,550	41,651	40,543	46,857	49,361	50,045	50,313	50,438	50,615
Prekindergarten through grade 8 (in thousands)	7,481[3]	9,757	12,520	14,984	16,899	19,378	21,279	18,833	19,387	27,602	32,513	28,034	29,152	33,486	34,409	35,251	35,370	35,388	35,477
Grades 9-12 (in thousands)	80[3]	110	203	519	915	2,200	4,399	6,601	5,725	8,485	13,037	13,616	11,390	13,371	14,952	14,794	14,943	15,050	15,138
Enrollment as a percent of total population	19.6[3]	19.7	20.3	20.4	19.7	20.6	21.1	19.4	16.8	20.3	22.6	18.5	16.4	16.8	16.1	15.8	15.8	15.7	15.7
Enrollment as a percent of 5- to 17-year-olds	64.7[3]	65.5	68.9	71.9	74.2	78.3	81.7	84.4	83.1	82.2	87.0	86.7	90.2	88.7	91.6	93.2	93.7	93.9	94.2
Percent of total enrollment in grades 9-12	1.1[3]	1.1	1.6	3.3	5.1	10.2	17.1	26.0	22.8	23.5	28.6	32.7	28.1	28.5	30.3	29.6	29.7	29.8	29.9
High school graduates (in thousands)	—	—	22	62	111	231	592	1,143	1,063	1,627	2,589	2,748	2,320	2,554	3,128	—	—	—	—
Average daily attendance (in thousands)	4,077	6,144	8,154	10,633	12,827	16,150	21,265	22,042	22,284	32,477	41,934	38,289	37,799	43,807	45,919	46,830	47,064	47,248	47,286
Total number of days attended by pupils enrolled (in millions)	539	801	1,098	1,535	2,011	2,615	3,673	3,858	3,964	5,782	7,501	6,835[4]	—	7,858	8,199	8,404	8,434	8,467	8,474
Percent of enrolled pupils attending daily	59.3	62.3	64.1	68.6	72.1	74.8	82.8	86.7	88.7	90.0	90.4	90.1[4]	—	94.3	—	—	—	93.0	—
Average length of school term, in days	132.2	130.3	134.7	144.3	157.5	161.9	172.7	175.0	177.9	178.0	178.9	178.5[4]	—	179.4	178.6	179.5	179.2	179.2	179.2
Average number of days attended per pupil	78.4	81.1	86.3	99.0	113.0	121.2	143.0	151.7	157.9	160.2	161.7	160.8[4]	—	169.2	—	—	—	166.6	—
Total full-time-equivalent (FTE) instructional staff (in thousands)	—	—	—	—	—	678	880	912	963	1,457	2,286	2,406	2,986	3,819	4,279	4,167	4,205	4,250	4,294
Supervisors (in thousands)	—	—	—	—	—	7	7	5	—	—	—	—	—	—	—	—	—	—	—
Principals (in thousands)	—	—	—	—	—	14	31	32	43	64	91	106	126	137	168	168	175	182	184
Teachers, teacher aides, librarians, and guidance counselors (in thousands)[5]	201	287	364	423	523	657	843	875	920	1,393	2,195	2,300	2,860	3,682	4,111	3,999	4,030	4,068	4,111
Males (in thousands)	78	123	126	127	110	93	140	195	196	404[4]	711[4]	782[4]	—	—	—	—	—	—	—
Females (in thousands)	123	164	238	296	413	585	703	681	724	989[4]	1,484[4]	1,518[4]	—	—	—	—	—	—	—
Percent male	38.7	42.8	34.5	29.9	21.1	14.1	16.6	22.2	21.3	29.1	32.4[4]	34.0[4]	—	—	—	—	—	—	—
Total revenues and expenditures _Amounts in current dollars_																			
Total revenue receipts (in millions)	—	—	$143	$220	$433	$970	$2,089	$2,261	$5,437	$14,747	$40,267	$96,881	$208,548	$372,944	$596,391	$623,650	$647,679	$677,219	$705,267
Federal government	—	—	—	—	—	2	7	40	156	652	3,220	9,504	12,701	27,098	75,998	54,506	55,003	55,975	57,311
State governments	—	—	—	—	—	160	354	684	2,166	5,768	16,063	45,349	98,239	184,613	258,864	288,637	301,530	317,660	331,322
Local sources, including intermediate	—	—	—	—	—	808	1,728	1,536	3,116	8,327	20,985	42,029	97,608	161,233	261,529	280,507	291,147	303,583	316,635
Percentage distribution of revenue receipts																			
Federal government	—	—	—	—	—	0.3	0.4	1.8	2.9	4.4	8.0	9.8	6.1	7.3	12.7	8.7	8.5	8.3	8.1
State governments	—	—	—	—	—	16.5	16.9	30.3	39.8	39.1	39.9	46.8	47.1	49.5	43.4	46.3	46.6	46.9	47.0
Local sources, including intermediate	—	—	—	—	—	83.2	82.7	68.0	57.3	56.5	52.1	43.4	46.8	43.2	43.9	45.0	45.0	44.8	44.9
Total expenditures for public schools (in millions)	$63	$78	$141	$215	$426	$1,036	$2,317	$2,344	$5,838	$15,613	$40,683	$95,962	$212,770	$381,838	$607,018	$625,018	$651,135	$677,605	$707,601
Current expenditures[6]	—	—	114	180	356	861	1,844	1,942	4,687	12,329[7]	34,218[7]	86,984[7]	188,229[7]	323,889[7]	524,715[7]	553,501[7]	575,332[7]	596,202[7]	619,165[7]
Capital outlay[8]	—	—	26	35	70	154	371	258	1,014	2,662	4,659	6,506	17,781	43,357	56,715	46,438	50,610	55,989	61,442
Interest on school debt	—	—	—	—	—	18	93	131	101	490	1,171	1,874	3,776	9,135	17,232	17,152	17,479	17,501	18,334
Other current expenditures[9]	—	—	—	—	—	3	10	13	36	133	636	598[10]	2,983	5,457	8,356	7,926	7,714	7,914	8,661
Percentage distribution of total expenditures																			
Current expenditures[6]	—	—	81.3	83.5	83.6	83.1	79.6	82.8	80.3	79.0[7]	84.1[7]	90.6[7]	88.5[7]	84.8[7]	86.4[7]	88.6[7]	88.4[7]	88.0[7]	87.5[7]
Capital outlay[8]	—	—	18.7	16.5	16.4	14.8	16.0	11.0	17.4	17.0	11.5	6.8	8.4	11.4	9.3	7.4	7.8	8.3	8.7
Interest on school debt	—	—	—	—	—	1.8	4.0	5.6	1.7	3.1	2.9	2.0	1.8	2.4	2.8	2.7	2.7	2.6	2.6
Other current expenditures[9]	—	—	—	—	—	0.3	0.4	0.6	0.6	0.8	1.6	0.6[10]	1.4	1.4	1.4	1.3	1.2	1.2	1.2

See notes at end of table.

Table 201.10. Historical summary of public elementary and secondary school statistics: Selected years, 1869–70 through 2016–17—Continued

Selected characteristic	1869–70	1879–80	1889–90	1899–1900	1909–10	1919–20	1929–30	1939–40	1949–50	1959–60	1969–70	1979–80	1989–90	1999–2000	2009–10	2013–14	2014–15	2015–16	2016–17
1	2	3	4	5	6	7	8	9	10	11	12	13	14	15	16	17	18	19	20
Teacher salaries; income and expenditures per pupil and per capita																			
Annual salary of classroom teachers[11]	$189	$195	$252	$325	$485	$871	$1,420	$1,441	$3,010	$4,995	$8,626	$15,970	$31,367	$41,807	$55,370	$56,826	$57,626	$58,316	$59,539
Personal income per member of labor force[1]	—	—	—	—	—	—	1,734	1,333	3,445	5,893	9,913	19,842	37,343	57,416	78,234	91,262	96,149	100,031	101,272
Total school expenditures per capita of total population	2	2	2	3	5	10	19	18	39	88	202	426	862	1,368	1,979	1,978	2,045	2,113	2,190
National income per capita[1]	—	—	—	—	—	—	773	629	1,607	2,580	4,455	9,954	19,286	29,710	39,206	45,861	47,874	49,223	49,691
Current expenditure per pupil in ADA[6,12,13]	—	—	14	17	28	53	87	88	210	375	816	2,272	4,980	7,394	11,427	11,819	12,224	12,619	13,094
Total expenditure per pupil in ADA[13,14]	16	13	17	20	33	64	108	106	260	471	955	2,491	5,547	8,589	13,035	13,174	13,668	14,171	14,778
National income per pupil in ADA[13]	—	—	—	—	—	—	4,430	3,738	10,757	14,127	21,396	58,510	125,931	189,249	261,921	309,519	323,865	334,149	339,501
Current expenditure per day per pupil in ADA[6,13,15]	0.12	0.10	0.10	0.12	0.18	0.33	0.50	0.50	1.17	2.11	4.56	12.73	—	41.22	64.00	65.86	68.22	70.42	73.07
Total expenditure per day per pupil in ADA[13]	—	—	0.13	0.14	0.21	0.40	0.63	0.60	1.46	2.65	5.34	13.95	—	47.90	73.02	73.43	76.29	79.10	82.49
Amounts in constant 2018–19 dollars[16]																			
Total revenues and expenditures																			
Total revenue receipts (in millions)	—	—	—	—	—	$12,892	$30,903	$40,967	$58,144	$127,109	$269,975	$316,063	$415,975	$557,940	$696,919	$672,227	$693,081	$719,837	$736,111
Federal government	—	—	—	—	—	33	109	721	1,667	5,617	21,586	31,004	25,333	40,540	88,808	58,752	58,859	59,498	59,817
State governments	—	—	—	—	—	2,127	5,233	12,403	23,160	49,718	107,695	147,945	195,950	276,189	302,498	311,120	322,667	337,651	345,812
Local sources, including intermediate	—	—	—	—	—	10,732	25,561	27,843	33,317	71,774	140,694	137,114	194,692	241,211	305,612	302,356	311,556	322,688	330,482
Total expenditures for public schools (in millions)	—	—	—	—	—	$13,770	$34,280	$42,481	$62,428	$134,579	$272,768	$313,063	$424,396	$571,246	$709,338	$673,702	$696,780	$720,248	$738,547
Current expenditures[8]	—	—	—	—	—	11,444	27,278	35,191	50,126	106,274[7]	229,418[7]	283,775[7]	375,448[7]	484,551[7]	613,162[7]	596,615[7]	615,662[7]	633,722[7]	646,242[7]
Capital outlay[8]	—	—	—	—	—	2,040	5,488	4,675	10,846	22,943	31,237	21,226	35,467	64,864	66,275	50,056	54,158	59,513	64,129
Interest on school debt	—	—	—	—	—	242	1,369	2,372	1,076	4,219	7,850	6,113	7,532	13,667	20,137	18,489	18,705	18,602	19,136
Other current expenditures[9]	—	—	—	—	—	44	145	242	381	1,143	4,263	1,950[10]	5,949	8,164	9,764	8,544	8,255	8,412	9,040
Teacher salaries; income and expenditures per pupil and per capita																			
Annual salary of classroom teachers[11]	—	—	—	—	—	$11,575	$21,011	$26,115	$32,189	$43,055	$57,834	$52,100	$62,566	$62,545	$64,703	$61,252	$61,666	$61,986	$62,143
Personal income per member of labor force[1]	—	—	—	—	—	—	25,663	24,151	36,836	50,795	66,462	64,733	74,485	85,896	91,421	98,371	102,889	106,326	105,701
Total school expenditures per capita of total population	—	—	—	—	—	132	281	324	418	757	1,354	1,391	1,719	2,047	2,312	2,132	2,188	2,246	2,286
National income per capita[1]	—	—	—	—	—	—	11,436	11,397	17,182	22,238	29,870	32,475	38,468	44,448	45,814	49,433	51,230	52,321	51,864
Current expenditure per pupil in ADA[6,12,13]	—	—	—	—	—	709	1,283	1,597	2,249	3,234	5,471	7,411	9,933	11,061	13,353	12,740	13,081	13,413	13,667
Total expenditure per pupil in ADA[13,14]	—	—	—	—	—	850	1,605	1,916	2,784	4,060	6,403	8,125	11,064	12,849	15,232	14,201	14,626	15,063	15,424
National income per pupil in ADA[13]	—	—	—	—	—	—	65,545	67,749	115,032	121,768	143,449	190,883	251,185	283,125	306,070	333,628	346,568	355,178	354,348
Current expenditure per day per pupil in ADA[6,13,15]	—	—	—	—	—	4.4	7.4	9.1	12.5	18.2	30.6	41.5	—	61.7	74.8	71.0	73.0	74.8	76.3
Total expenditure per day per pupil in ADA[13]	—	—	—	—	—	5.3	9.3	10.9	15.6	22.8	35.8	45.5	—	71.7	85.3	79.1	81.6	84.1	86.1

—Not available.

[1]Data on population and labor force are from the Census Bureau, and data on personal income and national income are from the Bureau of Economic Analysis, U.S. Department of Commerce. Population data through 1900 are based on total population from the decennial census. From 1909–10 to 1959–60, population data are total population, including armed forces overseas, as of July 1. Data for later years are for resident population that excludes population overseas.

[2]Data for 1869–70 through 1959–60 are school year enrollment. Data for later years are fall enrollment. Total counts of ungraded students were prorated to prekindergarten through grade 8 and grades 9 through 12 based on prior reports.

[3]Data for 1870–71.

[4]Estimated by the National Center for Education Statistics.

[5]Prior to 1919–20, data are for the number of different persons employed rather than number of positions.

[6]Prior to 1919–20, includes interest on school debt.

[7]Because of the modification of the scope of "current expenditures for elementary and secondary schools," data for 1959–60 and later years are not entirely comparable with prior years.

[8]Beginning in 1969–70, includes capital outlay by state and local school building authorities.

[9]Includes summer schools, community colleges, and adult education. Beginning in 1959–60, also includes community services, formerly classified with "current expenditures for elementary and secondary schools."

[10]Excludes community colleges and adult education.

[11]Prior to 1959–60, average includes supervisors, principals, teachers, and other nonsupervisory instructional staff. Data for 1959–60 and later years are estimated by the National Education Association.

[12]Excludes current expenditures not allocable to pupil costs.

[13]"ADA" means average daily attendance in elementary and secondary schools.

[14]Expenditure figure is the sum of current expenditures allocable to pupil costs, capital outlay, and interest on school debt.

[15]Per-day rates derived by dividing annual rates by average length of term.

[16]Constant dollars based on the Consumer Price Index, prepared by the Bureau of Labor Statistics, U.S. Department of Labor, adjusted to a school-year basis. No Consumer Price Index data available for years prior to 1919–20.

NOTE: Some data have been revised from previously published figures. Beginning in 1959–60, data include Alaska and Hawaii. Detail may not sum to totals because of rounding.

SOURCE: U.S. Department of Education, National Center for Education Statistics, *Annual Report of the United States Commissioner of Education,* 1869–70 through 1909–10; *Biennial Survey of Education in the United States,* 1919–20 through 1949–50; *Statistics of State School Systems,* 1959–60 and 1969–70; *Statistics of Public Elementary and Secondary School Systems,* 1979–80; *Revenues and Expenditures for Public Elementary and Secondary Education, FY 1980;* Schools and Staffing Survey (SASS), "Public School Questionnaire," 1999–2000, 2007–08, and 2011–12; and Common Core of Data (CCD), "State Nonfiscal Survey of Public Elementary/Secondary Education," 1989–90 through 2017–18; "National Public Education Financial Survey," 1989–90 through 2016–17; and "State Dropout and Completion Data File," 2012–13. U.S. Department of Commerce, Census Bureau, retrieved November 29, 2019, from https://www.census.gov/data/datasets/time-series/demo/popest/2010s-national-detail.html#par_textimage_57373479. U.S. Department of Commerce, Bureau of Economic Analysis, retrieved January 1, 2020, from https://www.bea.gov/itable/. U.S. Department of Labor, Bureau of Labor Statistics, retrieved January 1, 2020, from https://stats.bls.gov/cps/tables.htm#empstat. (This table was prepared January 2020.)

Table 201.20. Enrollment in grades 9 through 12 in public and private schools compared with population 14 to 17 years of age: Selected years, 1889–90 through fall 2019

[In thousands]

Year	All schools	Enrollment, grades 9 to 12 — Public schools — Total	9th grade	10th grade	11th grade	12th grade	Secondary ungraded[1]	Private schools — Total	9th grade	10th grade	11th grade	12th grade	Secondary ungraded	Population 14 to 17 years of age[2]	Enrollment as a ratio of population 14 to 17 years of age[3]
1	2	3	4	5	6	7	8	9	10	11	12	13	14	15	16
1889–90	298	203	—	—	—	—	—	95	—	—	—	—	—	5,355	5.6
1899–1900	630	519	—	—	—	—	—	111	—	—	—	—	—	6,152	10.2
1909–10	1,032	915	—	—	—	—	—	117	—	—	—	—	—	7,220	14.3
1919–20	2,414	2,200	917	576	396	312	0	214	—	—	—	—	—	7,736	31.2
1929–30	4,741	4,399	1,627	1,192	880	701	0	341[4]	—	—	—	—	—	9,341	50.7
1939–40	7,059	6,601	2,011	1,767	1,486	1,282	55	458[5]	—	—	—	—	—	9,720	72.6
1949–50	6,397	5,725	1,761	1,513	1,275	1,134	42	672	—	—	—	—	—	8,405	76.1
Fall 1959	9,306	8,271	—	—	—	—	—	1,035	—	—	—	—	—	11,155	83.4
Fall 1969	14,337	13,037	3,568	3,405	3,047	2,732	285	1,300[6]	—	—	—	—	—	15,549	92.2
Fall 1970	14,647	13,336	3,654	3,458	3,128	2,775	321	1,311	—	—	—	—	—	15,924	92.0
Fall 1971	15,053	13,753	3,781	3,571	3,200	2,864	337	1,300[6]	—	—	—	—	—	16,328	92.2
Fall 1972	15,148	13,848	3,779	3,648	3,248	2,873	299	1,300[6]	—	—	—	—	—	16,639	91.0
Fall 1973	15,344	14,044	3,801	3,650	3,323	2,918	352	1,300[6]	—	—	—	—	—	16,867	91.0
Fall 1974	15,403	14,103	3,832	3,675	3,302	2,955	339	1,300[6]	—	—	—	—	—	17,035	90.4
Fall 1975	15,604	14,304	3,879	3,723	3,354	2,986	362	1,300[6]	—	—	—	—	—	17,128	91.1
Fall 1976	15,656	14,314	3,825	3,738	3,373	3,015	363	1,342	—	—	—	—	—	17,119	91.5
Fall 1977	15,546	14,203	3,779	3,686	3,388	3,026	324	1,343	—	—	—	—	—	17,045	91.2
Fall 1978	15,441	14,088	3,726	3,610	3,312	3,023	416	1,353	—	—	—	—	—	16,946	91.1
Fall 1979	14,916	13,616	3,526	3,532	3,241	2,969	348	1,300[6]	—	—	—	—	—	16,611	89.8
Fall 1980	14,570	13,231	3,377	3,368	3,195	2,925	366	1,339	—	—	—	—	—	16,143	90.3
Fall 1981	14,164	12,764	3,286	3,218	3,039	2,907	314	1,400[6]	—	—	—	—	—	15,609	90.7
Fall 1982	13,805	12,405	3,248	3,137	2,917	2,787	315	1,400[6]	—	—	—	—	—	15,057	91.7
Fall 1983	13,671	12,271	3,330	3,103	2,861	2,678	299	1,400	—	—	—	—	—	14,740	92.7
Fall 1984	13,704	12,304	3,440	3,145	2,819	2,599	300	1,400[6]	—	—	—	—	—	14,725	93.1
Fall 1985	13,750	12,388	3,439	3,230	2,866	2,550	303	1,362	—	—	—	—	—	14,888	92.4
Fall 1986	13,669	12,333	3,256	3,215	2,954	2,601	308	1,336[6]	—	—	—	—	—	14,824	92.2
Fall 1987	13,323	12,076	3,143	3,020	2,936	2,681	296	1,247	—	—	—	—	—	14,502	91.9
Fall 1988	12,893	11,687	3,106	2,895	2,749	2,650	288	1,206[6]	—	—	—	—	—	14,023	91.9
Fall 1989	12,524	11,393	3,141	2,868	2,629	2,473	281	1,131	303	284	267	273	5	13,536	92.5
Fall 1990	12,476	11,341	3,169	2,896	2,612	2,381	284	1,136[6]	—	—	—	—	—	13,329	93.6
Fall 1991	12,675	11,544	3,313	2,915	2,645	2,392	278	1,131	309	286	272	260	4	13,491	94.0
Fall 1992	12,862	11,737	3,352	3,027	2,656	2,431	272	1,125[6]	—	—	—	—	—	13,775	93.4
Fall 1993	13,081	11,963	3,487	3,050	2,751	2,424	250	1,118	312	286	266	249	5	14,096	92.8
Fall 1994	13,354	12,215	3,604	3,131	2,748	2,488	244	1,138[6]	—	—	—	—	—	14,637	91.2
Fall 1995	13,665	12,502	3,704	3,237	2,826	2,487	247	1,163	325	304	276	255	2	15,013	91.0
Fall 1996	14,027	12,849	3,801	3,323	2,930	2,586	208	1,178[6]	—	—	—	—	—	15,443	90.8
Fall 1997	14,241	13,056	3,819	3,376	2,972	2,673	216	1,185	326	306	283	266	4	15,769	90.3
Fall 1998	14,407	13,195	3,856	3,382	3,021	2,722	214	1,212[6]	—	—	—	—	—	15,829	91.0
Fall 1999	14,600	13,371	3,935	3,415	3,034	2,782	205	1,229	336	313	295	280	5	16,007	91.2
Fall 2000	14,781	13,517	3,963	3,491	3,083	2,803	177	1,264[6]	—	—	—	—	—	16,144	91.6
Fall 2001	15,032	13,736	4,012	3,528	3,174	2,863	159	1,296	350	333	316	293	3	16,280	92.3
Fall 2002	15,374	14,069	4,105	3,584	3,229	2,990	161	1,306[6]	—	—	—	—	—	16,506	93.1
Fall 2003	15,651	14,339	4,190	3,675	3,277	3,046	150	1,311	351	334	317	304	5	16,694	93.8
Fall 2004	15,949	14,618	4,281	3,750	3,369	3,094	122	1,331[6]	—	—	—	—	—	17,054	93.5
Fall 2005	16,258	14,909	4,287	3,866	3,454	3,180	121	1,349	356	348	326	315	3	17,358	93.7
Fall 2006	16,441	15,081	4,260	3,882	3,551	3,277	110	1,360[6]	—	—	—	—	—	17,549	93.7
Fall 2007	16,451	15,086	4,200	3,863	3,557	3,375	92	1,364	357	347	334	324	2	17,597	93.5
Fall 2008	16,322	14,980	4,123	3,822	3,548	3,400	87	1,342[6]	—	—	—	—	—	17,395	93.8
Fall 2009	16,261	14,952	4,080	3,809	3,541	3,432	90	1,309	333	330	324	319	3	17,232	94.4
Fall 2010	16,159	14,860	4,008	3,800	3,538	3,472	42	1,299[6]	—	—	—	—	—	17,066	94.7
Fall 2011	16,040	14,749	3,957	3,751	3,546	3,452	43	1,291	330	325	318	315	4	16,870	95.1
Fall 2012	16,055	14,753	3,975	3,730	3,528	3,477	43	1,302[6]	—	—	—	—	—	16,719	96.0
Fall 2013	16,106	14,794	3,980	3,761	3,526	3,476	52	1,312	334	331	325	320	3	16,650	96.7
Fall 2014	16,316	14,943	4,033	3,794	3,568	3,496	52	1,373[6]	—	—	—	—	—	16,743	97.4
Fall 2015	16,496	15,050	4,019	3,846	3,598	3,537	49	1,446	368	367	356	349	6	16,802	98.2
Fall 2016	16,620	15,138	3,986	3,860	3,669	3,571	52	1,482[6]	—	—	—	—	—	16,769	99.1
Fall 2017	16,658	15,190	3,996	3,834	3,677	3,631	52	1,468	374	366	365	359	5	16,745	99.5
Fall 2018[7]	16,711	15,206	4,021	3,843	3,652	3,639	52	1,504	—	—	—	—	—	16,681	100.2
Fall 2019[7]	16,745	15,232	4,038	3,867	3,661	3,615	52	1,512	—	—	—	—	—	16,668	100.5

—Not available.
[1]Includes students reported as being enrolled in grade 13.
[2]Data for 1890 through 1950 are from the decennial censuses of population. Later data are Census Bureau estimates as of July 1 preceding the opening of the school year.
[3]Gross enrollment ratio (GER) based on school enrollment of all ages in grades 9 to 12 divided by the 14- to 17-year-old population. The GER allows for comparisons over time but is not intended to provide a precise measure of enrollment for any single year. Because some high school students are younger than 14 or older than 17, the GER is likely higher than the enrollment rate for the 14- to 17-year-old population. The GER differs from enrollment rates in other tables, which compare the population in a given age group with enrollment of persons in that age group only.
[4]Data are for 1927–28.
[5]Data are for 1940–41.
[6]Estimated.
[7]Projected.
NOTE: Includes enrollment in public schools that are a part of state and local school systems and also in most private schools, both religiously affiliated and nonsectarian. The enrollment for ungraded public school students was estimated based on the secondary proportion of ungraded students in prior years. The enrollment of ungraded private school students was estimated based on the secondary proportion of ungraded students in individual high schools. Some data have been revised from previously published figures. Detail may not sum to totals because of rounding.
SOURCE: U.S. Department of Education, National Center for Education Statistics, *Annual Report of the Commissioner of Education*, 1890 through 1910; *Biennial Survey of Education in the United States*, 1919–20 through 1949–50; *Statistics of State School Systems*, 1951–52 through 1957–58; *Statistics of Public Elementary and Secondary School Systems*, 1959 through 1980; *Statistics of Nonpublic Elementary and Secondary Schools*, 1959 through 1980; Common Core of Data (CCD), "State Nonfiscal Survey of Public Elementary/Secondary Education," 1981–82 through 2017–18; Schools and Staffing Survey, Private School Data File, 1987–88; Private School Universe Survey (PSS), 1989–90 through 2017–18; National Elementary and Secondary Enrollment Projection Model, 1972 through 2029; and unpublished data. U.S. Department of Commerce, Census Bureau, Current Population Reports, Series P–25, Nos. 1000, 1022, 1045, 1057, 1059, 1092, and 1095; 2000 through 2009 Population Estimates, retrieved August 14, 2012, from http://www.census.gov/popest/data/national/asrh/2011/index.html; and 2010 through 2019 Population Estimates, retrieved November 29, 2019, from https://www.census.gov/data/datasets/time-series/demo/popest/2010s-national-detail.html#par_textimage_57373479. (This table was prepared March 2020.)

Table 202.10. Enrollment of 3-, 4-, and 5-year-old children in preprimary programs, by age of child, level of program, control of program, and attendance status: Selected years, 1970 through 2018

[Standard errors appear in parentheses]

Age of child, level and control of program, and attendance status	1970	1980	1990	2000[1]	2003[1]	2005[1]	2010[1]	2015[1]	2016[1]	2017[1]	2018[1]
1	2	3	4	5	6	7	8	9	10	11	12
3 to 5 years old[2]											
Total population (in thousands)	10,949 (131.4)	9,284 (121.0)	11,207 (145.5)	11,858 (155.3)	12,204 (149.6)	12,134 (149.1)	12,949 (80.4)	11,958 (79.8)	12,032 (113.7)	12,001 (133.4)	12,109 (112.5)
Enrollment of 3- to 5-year-olds (in thousands)											
Total	4,104 (78.9)	4,878 (75.0)	6,659 (88.8)	7,592 (86.2)	7,921 (82.6)	7,801 (82.7)	8,246 (107.3)	7,681 (107.3)	7,776 (103.5)	7,716 (117.0)	7,747 (118.5)
Level and attendance status											
Preschool	1,094 (48.9)	1,981 (61.5)	3,379 (83.0)	4,326 (86.5)	4,859 (84.7)	4,529 (83.4)	4,797 (94.5)	4,475 (96.9)	4,701 (116.0)	4,620 (141.8)	4,735 (98.3)
Full-day	291 (26.2)	681 (39.1)	1,150 (54.9)	2,049 (67.9)	2,479 (69.6)	2,275 (67.3)	2,297 (81.4)	2,264 (73.0)	2,544 (91.0)	2,584 (108.0)	2,579 (85.6)
Part-day	803 (42.5)	1,301 (52.1)	2,229 (72.2)	2,277 (70.8)	2,380 (68.5)	2,255 (67.1)	2,500 (75.4)	2,211 (81.3)	2,157 (86.7)	2,036 (90.2)	2,156 (86.2)
Kindergarten	3,010 (72.8)	2,897 (69.6)	3,280 (82.3)	3,266 (80.3)	3,062 (75.0)	3,272 (76.6)	3,449 (75.9)	3,207 (84.3)	3,075 (92.9)	3,097 (90.2)	3,013 (101.4)
Full-day	407 (30.9)	870 (43.8)	1,428 (60.3)	1,959 (66.7)	1,950 (63.4)	2,274 (67.3)	2,516 (69.7)	2,613 (77.3)	2,494 (86.7)	2,438 (83.4)	2,436 (86.0)
Part-day	2,603 (69.4)	2,026 (62.0)	1,853 (67.2)	1,307 (56.3)	1,112 (49.8)	998 (47.4)	932 (53.4)	594 (42.3)	581 (44.8)	659 (48.6)	577 (43.9)
Control											
Public	2,830 (71.4)	3,066 (70.6)	3,971 (86.5)	4,847 (88.3)	5,051 (85.2)	5,213 (85.4)	5,829 (105.5)	5,426 (95.6)	5,586 (98.7)	5,501 (105.4)	5,398 (117.5)
Private	1,274 (52.3)	1,812 (59.5)	2,688 (77.2)	2,745 (75.8)	2,870 (73.4)	2,588 (70.7)	2,417 (77.1)	2,255 (70.5)	2,190 (83.4)	2,216 (100.2)	2,349 (88.6)
Attendance status											
Full-day	698 (39.8)	1,551 (56.0)	2,577 (76.1)	4,008 (85.0)	4,429 (83.2)	4,548 (83.5)	4,813 (98.5)	4,877 (101.5)	5,038 (105.0)	5,022 (109.8)	5,015 (118.0)
Part-day	3,406 (75.5)	3,327 (72.0)	4,082 (87.0)	3,584 (82.5)	3,492 (78.2)	3,253 (76.4)	3,432 (88.5)	2,804 (91.6)	2,738 (87.7)	2,694 (93.9)	2,733 (85.2)
Percent of 3- to 5-year-olds enrolled											
Total	37.5 (0.72)	52.5 (0.81)	59.4 (0.79)	64.0 (0.73)	64.9 (0.68)	64.3 (0.68)	63.7 (0.66)	64.2 (0.79)	64.6 (0.81)	64.3 (0.77)	64.0 (0.98)
Full-day as a percent of total enrollment	17.0 (0.91)	31.8 (1.04)	38.7 (1.02)	52.8 (0.95)	55.9 (0.87)	58.3 (0.87)	58.4 (0.92)	63.5 (1.04)	64.8 (1.03)	65.1 (1.08)	64.7 (1.04)
Full-day preschool as a percent of total preschool enrollment	26.6 (2.08)	34.3 (1.66)	34.0 (1.39)	47.4 (1.25)	51.0 (1.12)	50.2 (1.16)	47.9 (1.31)	50.6 (1.34)	54.1 (1.45)	55.9 (1.51)	54.5 (1.49)
Full-day kindergarten as a percent of total kindergarten enrollment	13.5 (0.97)	30.0 (1.33)	43.5 (1.48)	60.0 (1.41)	63.7 (1.36)	69.5 (1.26)	73.0 (1.38)	81.5 (1.21)	81.1 (1.34)	78.7 (1.42)	80.8 (1.25)
3 and 4 years old											
Total population (in thousands)	7,135 (106.1)	6,215 (99.0)	7,415 (118.3)	7,869 (126.5)	8,336 (123.6)	8,179 (122.4)	8,850 (63.8)	7,971 (80.7)	7,971 (156.9)	8,030 (186.2)	8,138 (175.8)
Age											
3 years old	3,516 (74.4)	3,143 (70.4)	3,692 (83.5)	3,929 (89.4)	4,260 (88.4)	4,151 (87.2)	4,492 (59.4)	3,937 (92.3)	3,978 (71.2)	4,086 (81.1)	3,986 (193.1)
4 years old	3,620 (75.5)	3,072 (69.6)	3,723 (83.8)	3,940 (89.5)	4,076 (86.4)	4,028 (85.9)	4,358 (57.7)	4,034 (76.3)	3,993 (137.5)	3,943 (158.3)	4,152 (77.0)
Enrollment of 3- and 4-year-olds (in thousands)											
Total	1,461 (53.1)	2,280 (59.2)	3,292 (73.1)	4,097 (73.1)	4,590 (71.1)	4,383 (70.6)	4,706 (84.1)	4,203 (91.5)	4,289 (121.2)	4,319 (148.1)	4,393 (103.5)
Age											
3 years old	454 (31.0)	857 (38.9)	1,205 (48.7)	1,541 (50.5)	1,806 (50.5)	1,715 (49.7)	1,718 (59.5)	1,512 (70.2)	1,656 (63.8)	1,641 (76.5)	1,583 (92.9)
4 years old	1,007 (42.0)	1,423 (43.1)	2,087 (51.7)	2,556 (49.4)	2,785 (46.5)	2,668 (47.0)	2,988 (67.2)	2,691 (72.1)	2,633 (87.9)	2,678 (121.9)	2,811 (82.4)
Level and attendance status											
Preschool	1,003 (45.8)	1,889 (56.5)	3,026 (72.3)	3,762 (73.1)	4,198 (71.5)	4,024 (70.8)	4,245 (85.3)	3,855 (88.9)	4,034 (110.7)	3,966 (145.2)	4,065 (98.5)
Full-day	263 (24.8)	649 (37.6)	1,028 (50.8)	1,763 (61.0)	2,135 (62.4)	1,986 (60.7)	2,018 (70.6)	1,914 (70.3)	2,178 (81.4)	2,223 (106.3)	2,215 (82.7)
Part-day	741 (40.1)	1,240 (49.1)	1,998 (65.3)	1,999 (63.7)	2,063 (61.7)	2,038 (61.3)	2,226 (73.0)	1,941 (75.5)	1,856 (80.9)	1,742 (87.8)	1,849 (75.1)
Kindergarten	458 (32.3)	391 (29.8)	266 (27.3)	335 (29.6)	392 (30.3)	359 (29.0)	462 (44.6)	348 (36.5)	254 (32.0)	353 (34.3)	329 (35.6)
Full-day	110 (16.2)	139 (18.2)	135 (19.7)	181 (21.9)	245 (24.1)	247 (24.2)	247 (31.4)	253 (32.2)	202 (26.7)	216 (29.5)	215 (27.4)
Part-day	348 (28.3)	252 (24.2)	131 (19.4)	154 (20.3)	147 (18.8)	112 (16.5)	214 (28.5)	95 (17.4)	‡ (†)	137 (23.4)	114 (22.5)
Control											
Public	617 (37.0)	838 (42.0)	1,211 (54.4)	2,042 (64.2)	2,374 (64.5)	2,341 (64.0)	2,795 (82.2)	2,477 (80.6)	2,532 (86.5)	2,630 (111.8)	2,492 (103.5)
Private	844 (42.5)	1,441 (51.9)	2,081 (66.1)	2,055 (64.3)	2,216 (63.2)	2,042 (61.3)	1,911 (64.0)	1,726 (68.7)	1,757 (80.9)	1,689 (86.4)	1,901 (73.4)
Attendance status											
Full-day	373 (29.3)	788 (40.9)	1,163 (53.5)	1,944 (63.1)	2,380 (64.6)	2,233 (63.1)	2,265 (69.0)	2,167 (75.0)	2,381 (87.8)	2,439 (108.0)	2,430 (87.8)
Part-day	1,088 (47.3)	1,492 (52.5)	2,129 (66.6)	2,153 (65.3)	2,211 (63.1)	2,150 (62.4)	2,441 (76.5)	2,036 (75.3)	1,908 (83.3)	1,879 (91.8)	1,963 (78.9)

See notes at end of table.

Table 202.10. Enrollment of 3-, 4-, and 5-year-old children in preprimary programs, by age of child, level of program, control of program, and attendance status: Selected years, 1970 through 2018—Continued

[Standard errors appear in parentheses]

Age of child, level and control of program, and attendance status	1970	1980	1990	2000[1]	2003[1]	2005[1]	2010[1]	2015[1]	2016[1]	2017[1]	2018[1]
1	2	3	4	5	6	7	8	9	10	11	12
Percent of 3- and 4-year-olds enrolled											
Total	20.5 (1.65)	36.7 (1.57)	44.4 (1.48)	52.1 (1.29)	55.1 (1.15)	53.6 (1.18)	53.2 (0.89)	52.7 (1.02)	53.8 (1.04)	53.8 (1.08)	54.0 (1.19)
Age											
3 years old	12.9 (2.45)	27.3 (2.37)	32.6 (2.31)	39.2 (2.05)	42.4 (1.82)	41.3 (1.86)	38.2 (1.25)	38.4 (1.45)	41.6 (1.49)	40.2 (1.67)	39.7 (1.50)
4 years old	27.8 (2.20)	46.3 (2.06)	56.1 (1.86)	64.9 (1.56)	68.3 (1.38)	66.2 (1.43)	68.6 (1.25)	66.7 (1.32)	65.9 (1.50)	67.9 (1.35)	67.7 (1.43)
Full-day as a percent of total enrollment	25.5 (1.78)	34.5 (1.55)	35.3 (1.42)	47.4 (1.29)	51.8 (1.16)	50.9 (1.18)	48.1 (1.26)	51.6 (1.42)	55.5 (1.42)	56.5 (1.57)	55.3 (1.48)
Full-day preschool as a percent of total preschool enrollment	26.2 (2.16)	34.3 (1.70)	34.0 (1.47)	46.9 (1.34)	50.9 (1.21)	49.3 (1.23)	47.5 (1.36)	49.6 (1.49)	54.0 (1.49)	56.1 (1.64)	54.5 (1.51)
Full-day kindergarten as a percent of total kindergarten enrollment	24.0 (3.11)	35.6 (3.77)	50.8 (5.24)	54.0 (4.49)	62.4 (3.83)	68.8 (3.83)	53.6 (4.30)	72.8 (4.53)	79.6 (5.44)	61.2 (5.69)	65.3 (5.32)
5 years old[2]											
Total population (in thousands)	3,814 (77.5)	3,069 (69.6)	3,792 (84.6)	3,989 (90.1)	3,867 (84.2)	3,955 (85.1)	4,099 (57.9)	3,987 (73.9)	4,061 (90.5)	3,972 (100.6)	3,971 (123.3)
Enrollment of 5-year-olds (in thousands)											
Total	2,643 (44.4)	2,598 (31.1)	3,367 (33.2)	3,495 (34.3)	3,331 (33.7)	3,418 (33.7)	3,540 (56.2)	3,478 (74.8)	3,488 (96.5)	3,398 (90.4)	3,354 (104.9)
Level and attendance status											
Preschool	91 (14.7)	93 (14.8)	352 (30.5)	565 (36.3)	661 (36.7)	505 (32.9)	552 (35.8)	620 (46.1)	667 (45.3)	654 (48.1)	670 (47.9)
Full-day	28 (8.3)	32 (8.8)	122 (18.5)	286 (26.9)	344 (27.7)	289 (25.6)	279 (29.2)	350 (31.8)	366 (36.8)	361 (32.0)	364 (35.8)
Part-day	62 (12.2)	61 (12.0)	231 (25.2)	278 (26.6)	316 (26.7)	216 (22.4)	274 (26.9)	270 (32.1)	301 (31.2)	293 (36.5)	306 (35.7)
Kindergarten	2,552 (45.3)	2,505 (33.4)	3,015 (42.5)	2,931 (46.0)	2,670 (45.0)	2,913 (43.4)	2,987 (59.8)	2,859 (75.1)	2,821 (93.5)	2,744 (88.2)	2,684 (95.0)
Full-day	297 (25.8)	731 (36.8)	1,293 (49.9)	1,778 (51.8)	1,705 (48.4)	2,027 (49.2)	2,269 (60.2)	2,360 (70.9)	2,292 (85.3)	2,222 (77.4)	2,221 (80.8)
Part-day	2,255 (47.3)	1,774 (42.6)	1,722 (52.4)	1,152 (47.2)	965 (42.1)	886 (41.1)	718 (43.0)	499 (39.8)	529 (46.5)	522 (42.7)	463 (40.6)
Control											
Public	2,214 (47.5)	2,228 (38.5)	2,760 (46.8)	2,806 (47.6)	2,677 (45.0)	2,872 (43.9)	3,034 (57.8)	2,950 (70.7)	3,055 (89.2)	2,871 (90.7)	2,906 (99.9)
Private	429 (30.4)	370 (28.1)	607 (38.6)	690 (39.4)	654 (36.5)	546 (34.0)	506 (35.0)	529 (37.6)	433 (37.3)	527 (39.7)	448 (38.1)
Attendance status											
Full-day	326 (26.9)	763 (37.3)	1,414 (50.9)	2,065 (52.1)	2,050 (48.6)	2,316 (48.5)	2,548 (60.1)	2,710 (72.4)	2,657 (87.4)	2,583 (78.4)	2,585 (91.3)
Part-day	2,317 (47.0)	1,835 (42.3)	1,953 (52.6)	1,431 (50.0)	1,281 (45.8)	1,102 (44.2)	992 (44.6)	768 (51.7)	830 (52.5)	815 (56.2)	769 (51.4)
Percent of 5-year-olds enrolled											
Total	69.3 (1.16)	84.7 (1.01)	88.8 (0.88)	87.6 (0.86)	86.1 (0.87)	86.4 (0.85)	86.3 (0.92)	87.2 (0.95)	85.9 (1.05)	85.5 (1.08)	84.5 (1.14)
Full-day as a percent of total enrollment	12.3 (1.00)	29.4 (1.39)	42.0 (1.45)	59.1 (1.37)	61.5 (1.32)	67.7 (1.25)	72.0 (1.20)	77.9 (1.38)	76.2 (1.34)	76.0 (1.42)	77.1 (1.35)
Full-day preschool as a percent of total preschool enrollment	31.3 (7.58)	34.6 (7.70)	34.5 (4.33)	50.7 (3.47)	52.1 (3.04)	57.2 (3.45)	50.5 (3.90)	56.5 (3.60)	54.9 (3.82)	55.2 (3.76)	54.3 (4.00)
Full-day kindergarten as a percent of total kindergarten enrollment	11.6 (0.99)	29.2 (1.42)	42.9 (1.54)	60.7 (1.49)	63.9 (1.46)	69.6 (1.34)	76.0 (1.35)	82.6 (1.30)	81.2 (1.48)	81.0 (1.36)	82.8 (1.31)

†Not applicable.
‡Reporting standards not met. Either there are too few cases for a reliable estimate or the coefficient of variation (CV) is 50 percent or greater.
[1]Beginning in 1994, preprimary enrollment data were collected using new procedures. Data may not be comparable to figures for earlier years.
[2]Enrollment data for 5-year-olds include only those students in preprimary programs and do not include those enrolled in primary programs.

NOTE: Preprimary programs include kindergarten and preschool (or nursery school) programs. "Preschool," which was referred to as "nursery school" in previous versions of this table, is defined as a group or class that is organized to provide educational experiences for children during the year or years preceding kindergarten. Data are based on sample surveys of the civilian noninstitutionalized population, which excludes persons in the military and persons living in institutions (e.g., prisons or nursing facilities). Prior to 2010, standard errors were computed using generalized variance function methodology rather than the more precise replicate weight methodology used in later years. Detail may not sum to totals because of rounding.
SOURCE: U.S. Department of Commerce, Census Bureau, Current Population Survey (CPS), October, 1970 through 2018. (This table was prepared July 2019.)

Table 202.20. Percentage of 3-, 4-, and 5-year-old children enrolled in preprimary programs, by level of program, attendance status, and selected child and family characteristics: 2018

[Standard errors appear in parentheses]

Selected child or family characteristic	Total 3- to 5-year-old population (in thousands)	Total enrollment (in thousands)	Percent of 3- to 5-year-old population enrolled — Total	Preschool — Total	Preschool — Full-day	Preschool — Part-day	Kindergarten — Total	Kindergarten — Full-day	Kindergarten — Part-day	Percentage distribution of enrollment — Full-day	Percentage distribution of enrollment — Part-day
1	2	3	4	5	6	7	8	9	10	11	12
Total	12,109 (112.5)	7,747 (118.5)	64.0 (0.98)	39.1 (0.74)	21.3 (0.71)	17.8 (0.67)	24.9 (0.88)	20.1 (0.74)	4.8 (0.37)	64.7 (1.04)	35.3 (1.04)
Sex											
Male	6,147 (95.1)	3,945 (140.3)	64.2 (1.61)	39.1 (1.08)	21.3 (1.02)	17.8 (1.07)	25.0 (1.62)	20.4 (1.31)	4.7 (0.57)	64.9 (1.76)	35.1 (1.76)
Female	5,962 (138.8)	3,803 (107.6)	63.8 (1.14)	39.1 (1.15)	21.3 (1.06)	17.8 (0.95)	24.7 (0.79)	19.8 (0.76)	4.9 (0.49)	64.5 (1.45)	35.5 (1.45)
Age of child											
3 and 4 years old	8,138 (175.8)	4,393 (103.5)	54.0 (1.19)	49.9 (1.13)	27.2 (1.05)	22.7 (0.83)	4.0 (0.43)	2.6 (0.34)	1.4 (0.27)	55.3 (1.48)	44.7 (1.48)
3 years old	3,986 (193.1)	1,583 (92.9)	39.7 (1.50)	38.0 (1.49)	21.4 (1.32)	16.6 (1.15)	1.7 (0.41)	0.8! (0.28)	0.9! (0.32)	55.9 (2.60)	44.1 (2.60)
4 years old	4,152 (77.0)	2,811 (82.4)	67.7 (1.43)	61.4 (1.51)	32.8 (1.42)	28.6 (1.31)	6.3 (0.72)	4.4 (0.59)	1.9 (0.41)	55.0 (1.75)	45.0 (1.75)
5 years old	3,971 (123.3)	3,354 (104.9)	84.5 (1.14)	16.9 (1.12)	9.2 (0.83)	7.7 (0.92)	67.6 (1.45)	55.9 (1.51)	11.7 (0.92)	22.9 (1.35)	77.1 (1.35)
Race/ethnicity of child											
White	5,915 (109.3)	4,009 (67.6)	67.8 (1.42)	42.9 (1.13)	20.6 (0.97)	22.2 (1.00)	24.9 (1.08)	19.7 (0.92)	5.2 (0.53)	59.5 (1.48)	40.5 (1.48)
Black	1,614 (62.7)	1,011 (55.9)	62.6 (2.50)	37.9 (2.52)	25.7 (2.44)	12.2 (1.81)	24.8 (2.22)	22.5 (2.18)	2.3! (0.78)	76.8 (2.92)	23.2 (2.92)
Hispanic	3,150 (58.8)	1,871 (74.3)	59.4 (2.13)	37.4 (1.72)	25.2 (1.47)	13.2 (1.32)	25.0 (2.04)	19.3 (1.86)	5.7 (0.87)	68.3 (2.51)	31.7 (2.51)
Asian	662 (42.8)	384 (33.2)	57.9 (3.49)	35.9 (3.39)	20.3 (2.88)	15.6 (2.58)	22.0 (2.98)	18.6 (2.74)	3.4! (1.21)	67.1 (4.24)	32.9 (4.24)
Pacific Islander	‡ (†)	‡ (†)	‡ (†)	‡ (†)	‡ (†)	‡ (†)	‡ (†)	‡ (†)	‡ (†)	‡ (†)	‡ (†)
American Indian/Alaska Native	132 (22.4)	71 (15.5)	53.5 (8.53)	38.4 (9.02)	17.4! (6.02)	21.0! (8.25)	15.1! (4.60)	12.3! (4.52)	† (†)	55.5! (12.28)	44.5! (12.28)
Two or more races	590 (45.4)	382 (37.1)	64.8 (3.74)	34.4 (3.91)	18.6 (3.24)	15.8 (3.05)	30.4 (2.89)	25.9 (3.03)	4.5! (1.59)	68.7 (4.78)	31.3 (4.78)
Number of parents or guardians in household											
One parent or guardian	3,320 (110.9)	2,082 (87.5)	62.7 (1.74)	36.1 (1.50)	21.7 (1.49)	14.4 (1.22)	26.7 (1.44)	22.6 (1.40)	4.1 (0.67)	70.6 (2.12)	29.4 (2.12)
Two parents or guardians	8,790 (130.7)	5,665 (109.6)	64.5 (1.13)	40.2 (0.91)	21.2 (0.80)	19.1 (0.82)	24.2 (1.10)	19.2 (0.91)	5.0 (0.45)	62.6 (1.23)	37.4 (1.23)
Mother's current employment status[1]											
Employed	7,499 (147.6)	5,085 (117.8)	67.8 (1.24)	42.6 (0.97)	25.1 (0.99)	17.4 (0.91)	25.3 (1.03)	20.8 (0.92)	4.4 (0.41)	67.8 (1.41)	32.2 (1.41)
Unemployed	258 (33.6)	163 (25.5)	63.3 (5.60)	35.1 (6.22)	18.8 (5.09)	16.4 (4.85)	28.2 (5.87)	20.6 (4.88)	7.6! (3.41)	62.2 (8.37)	37.8 (8.37)
Not in the labor force	3,820 (113.0)	2,162 (92.8)	56.6 (1.66)	33.2 (1.27)	14.0 (1.01)	19.2 (1.19)	23.4 (1.41)	18.1 (1.26)	5.3 (0.70)	56.8 (2.08)	43.2 (2.08)
No mother in household	533 (47.4)	337 (40.7)	63.2 (4.32)	34.6 (3.75)	20.7 (3.08)	13.9 (2.53)	28.6 (4.15)	24.2 (3.67)	4.4! (1.88)	71.0 (4.26)	29.0 (4.26)
Father's current employment status[1]											
Employed	8,517 (137.2)	5,527 (106.3)	64.9 (1.16)	40.6 (0.93)	21.5 (0.83)	19.1 (0.83)	24.3 (1.06)	19.2 (0.90)	5.1 (0.44)	62.7 (1.21)	37.3 (1.21)
Unemployed	233 (37.3)	145 (28.2)	62.1 (6.48)	40.1 (6.95)	21.5 (6.14)	18.6 (5.24)	22.0 (5.29)	18.5 (5.53)	† (†)	64.4 (7.74)	35.6 (7.74)
Not in the labor force	572 (47.8)	330 (36.1)	57.7 (4.32)	30.3 (3.80)	15.7 (3.01)	14.6 (2.84)	27.3 (3.60)	23.3 (3.45)	4.0! (1.55)	67.7 (4.87)	32.3 (4.87)
No father in household	2,787 (99.7)	1,745 (76.7)	62.6 (1.88)	36.3 (1.70)	21.9 (1.64)	14.5 (1.41)	26.3 (1.50)	22.3 (1.50)	4.0 (0.73)	70.5 (2.41)	29.5 (2.41)
Every parent or guardian employed[1]	7,493 (143.9)	5,090 (117.1)	67.9 (1.23)	42.4 (0.95)	25.2 (0.96)	17.2 (0.88)	25.5 (1.04)	21.1 (0.92)	4.4 (0.40)	68.2 (1.35)	31.8 (1.35)
No parent or guardian employed[1]	1,149 (72.6)	603 (48.3)	52.4 (2.98)	31.0 (2.64)	17.0 (2.04)	14.0 (1.86)	21.4 (2.40)	18.1 (2.24)	3.3! (1.02)	67.0 (3.42)	33.0 (3.42)
Highest educational attainment of parents or guardians[1]											
Less than high school	979 (65.7)	566 (48.6)	57.8 (3.24)	30.5 (2.80)	19.5 (2.55)	11.1 (1.73)	27.3 (2.69)	23.5 (2.55)	3.8! (1.28)	74.3 (3.36)	25.7 (3.36)
High school completion[2]	2,683 (101.8)	1,526 (80.0)	56.9 (2.01)	32.7 (1.75)	19.3 (1.65)	13.3 (1.27)	24.2 (1.72)	19.8 (1.53)	4.4 (0.85)	68.8 (2.39)	31.2 (2.39)
Some college, no degree	1,778 (77.5)	1,050 (62.9)	59.0 (2.55)	35.8 (2.29)	19.3 (1.82)	16.4 (1.50)	23.2 (1.87)	18.8 (1.62)	4.5 (0.84)	64.6 (2.44)	35.4 (2.44)
Associate's degree	1,289 (71.9)	821 (56.8)	63.7 (2.85)	37.7 (2.69)	20.5 (2.34)	17.2 (1.86)	26.0 (2.13)	22.7 (2.03)	3.3 (0.89)	67.7 (3.02)	32.3 (3.02)
Bachelor's degree	2,823 (102.6)	1,922 (78.7)	68.1 (1.67)	42.9 (1.77)	21.7 (1.55)	21.2 (1.55)	25.1 (1.55)	19.0 (1.25)	6.2 (0.89)	59.8 (2.11)	40.2 (2.11)
Graduate or professional degree	2,557 (101.7)	1,862 (88.7)	72.8 (1.82)	47.9 (1.83)	25.4 (1.69)	22.5 (1.80)	25.1 (1.87)	20.1 (1.74)	4.9 (0.73)	62.4 (2.59)	37.6 (2.59)

†Not applicable.
!Interpret data with caution. The coefficient of variation (CV) for this estimate is between 30 and 50 percent.
‡Reporting standards not met. Either there are too few cases for a reliable estimate or the coefficient of variation (CV) is 50 percent or greater.
[1]Data pertain only to parents or guardians who live in the household with the child.
[2]Includes completion of high school through equivalency programs, such as a GED program.
NOTE: Preprimary programs include kindergarten and preschool (or nursery school) programs. "Preschool," which was referred to as "nursery school" in previous versions of this table, is defined as a group or class that is organized to provide educational experiences for children during the year or years preceding kindergarten. Enrollment data for 5-year-olds include only those children in preprimary programs and do not include those enrolled in primary programs. Race categories exclude persons of Hispanic ethnicity. Data are based on sample surveys of the civilian noninstitutionalized population, which excludes persons in the military and persons living in institutions (e.g., prisons or nursing facilities). Detail may not sum to totals because of rounding.
SOURCE: U.S. Department of Commerce, Census Bureau, Current Population Survey (CPS), October, 2018. (This table was prepared July 2019.)

Table 202.30. Number of children under 6 years old and not yet enrolled in kindergarten, percentage participating in center-based programs, average weekly hours in nonparental care, and percentage in various types of primary care arrangements, by selected child and family characteristics: 2016

[Standard errors appear in parentheses]

Selected child or family characteristic	Number of children under 6 years old (in thousands)	Percent participating in center-based programs[1]	Average hours per week in nonparental care[2]	Parental care only	Center-based care	Nonrelative home-based care — Total	In another home	In child's home	Relative	Multiple arrangments[4]
1	2	3	4	5	6	7	8	9	10	11
Total children under 6 years old	21,362 (54.2)	35.9 (0.79)	30.6 (0.38)	40.3 (0.94)	29.4 (0.73)	10.0 (0.42)	6.9 (0.37)	3.2 (0.26)	18.5 (0.72)	1.8 (0.21)
Age										
Under 1 year old	4,724 (150.4)	13.2 (1.13)	33.0 (0.60)	52.6 (2.13)	10.7 (0.87)	11.8 (1.08)	8.0 (0.88)	3.7 (0.61)	23.2 (1.90)	1.6 (0.45)
1 to 2 years old	8,552 (176.3)	24.7 (1.18)	30.8 (0.74)	46.0 (1.34)	21.4 (1.16)	11.4 (0.77)	7.9 (0.66)	3.5 (0.45)	19.9 (1.09)	1.3 (0.28)
3 to 5 years old	8,087 (91.1)	60.9 (1.49)	29.5 (0.56)	27.1 (1.47)	48.7 (1.44)	7.6 (0.55)	5.1 (0.46)	2.5 (0.34)	14.4 (1.02)	2.3 (0.32)
Race/ethnicity of child and poverty status of household[5]										
White	10,731 (97.5)	38.5 (0.90)	30.5 (0.47)	37.8 (0.95)	31.4 (0.84)	12.4 (0.67)	8.5 (0.51)	3.9 (0.40)	16.4 (0.89)	2.0 (0.31)
Poor	1,182 (77.7)	23.4 (2.85)	27.4 (1.99)	59.3 (3.49)	19.7 (2.71)	4.7! (1.61)	2.6! (1.29)	2.1! (1.03)	14.8 (2.35)	‡ (†)
Near-poor	1,962 (89.7)	25.5 (2.17)	30.5 (1.53)	51.7 (2.53)	17.8 (1.50)	9.0 (1.51)	7.5 (1.30)	1.5! (0.57)	19.8 (2.31)	1.8! (0.80)
Nonpoor	7,586 (77.6)	44.2 (1.23)	30.7 (0.44)	30.9 (1.30)	36.7 (1.13)	14.5 (0.85)	9.6 (0.65)	4.8 (0.53)	15.8 (0.94)	2.1 (0.30)
Black	2,837 (0.0)	40.3 (3.37)	33.5 (1.29)	32.5 (3.38)	31.6 (3.07)	8.8 (1.70)	6.6 (1.62)	2.2! (0.71)	24.9 (2.54)	2.3! (0.75)
Poor	1,069 (40.7)	35.4 (4.70)	35.1 (2.83)	40.2 (5.63)	22.9 (4.24)	9.4! (3.29)	6.4! (2.99)	‡ (†)	25.1 (4.36)	‡ (†)
Near-poor	725 (47.3)	35.2 (8.13)	31.0 (2.42)	33.2 (6.61)	31.2 (8.12)	5.8! (2.79)	‡ (†)	‡ (†)	29.3 (6.15)	‡ (†)
Nonpoor	1,043 (32.9)	48.7 (4.75)	33.7 (1.81)	24.0 (4.32)	40.8 (4.57)	10.2 (2.76)	8.7! (2.67)	‡ (†)	21.6 (3.97)	3.4! (1.61)
Hispanic	5,418 (1.6)	28.3 (1.60)	28.1 (0.87)	48.5 (2.23)	23.1 (1.54)	7.2 (0.98)	4.9 (0.78)	2.3 (0.55)	19.7 (1.56)	1.5 (0.36)
Poor	1,443 (44.1)	21.8 (3.13)	27.8 (2.14)	60.1 (4.04)	17.1 (2.72)	3.9! (1.53)	3.0! (1.35)	‡ (†)	16.7 (2.88)	2.1! (0.84)
Near-poor	1,800 (91.8)	21.3 (2.63)	26.3 (2.00)	57.8 (4.08)	15.4 (2.12)	4.7 (1.40)	3.4! (1.10)	‡ (†)	20.5 (3.04)	1.6! (0.79)
Nonpoor	2,175 (80.2)	38.4 (2.71)	29.2 (1.06)	33.2 (3.05)	33.4 (2.68)	11.3 (1.89)	7.4 (1.50)	3.9 (1.11)	21.1 (2.37)	1.0! (0.46)
Asian/Pacific Islander	1,009 (69.7)	36.1 (2.75)	30.0 (1.68)	43.2 (3.66)	30.9 (2.60)	5.7 (1.32)	2.3! (0.77)	3.5! (1.15)	19.6 (3.31)	‡ (†)
Asian	995 (69.5)	35.9 (2.70)	30.3 (1.68)	43.1 (3.66)	30.6 (2.53)	5.8 (1.33)	2.3! (0.78)	3.5! (1.17)	19.9 (3.36)	‡ (†)
Pacific Islander	‡ (†)	‡ (†)	‡ (†)	‡ (†)	‡ (†)	‡ (†)	‡ (†)	‡ (†)	‡ (†)	‡ (†)
American Indian/Alaska Native	‡ (†)	‡ (†)	‡ (†)	‡ (†)	‡ (†)	‡ (†)	‡ (†)	‡ (†)	‡ (†)	‡ (†)
Two or more races	1,235 (77.7)	37.3 (3.56)	33.6 (1.40)	39.2 (3.62)	33.7 (3.37)	9.0 (1.68)	6.9 (1.59)	2.1! (0.73)	17.7 (2.43)	‡ (†)
Number of parents in the household[6]										
Two parents	16,428 (149.4)	35.8 (0.87)	29.3 (0.41)	42.9 (1.02)	30.0 (0.83)	9.8 (0.47)	6.5 (0.39)	3.3 (0.31)	15.5 (0.76)	1.8 (0.24)
One parent	4,449 (164.2)	36.5 (2.09)	34.2 (0.82)	32.3 (2.12)	27.5 (1.84)	11.5 (1.29)	8.7 (1.18)	2.8 (0.64)	27.1 (1.97)	1.7 (0.40)
Mother in household										
Yes	20,233 (99.4)	36.1 (0.81)	30.3 (0.36)	40.9 (0.98)	29.7 (0.79)	10.1 (0.45)	6.9 (0.37)	3.2 (0.28)	17.4 (0.74)	1.8 (0.22)
No	1,129 (80.9)	32.3 (3.39)	34.0 (1.85)	28.9 (3.90)	23.2 (2.73)	8.8 (2.50)	6.6! (2.23)	2.2! (0.96)	38.1 (4.13)	‡ (†)
Mother's employment status[7]										
Currently employed	12,154 (179.6)	45.5 (1.11)	33.2 (0.40)	21.1 (1.04)	36.5 (0.97)	15.2 (0.72)	10.9 (0.59)	4.3 (0.43)	24.6 (1.07)	2.6 (0.31)
35 or more hours per week	8,884 (159.5)	49.3 (1.31)	35.9 (0.45)	15.9 (1.08)	39.9 (1.14)	17.5 (0.87)	12.8 (0.71)	4.7 (0.52)	24.2 (1.14)	2.6 (0.36)
Less than 35 hours per week	3,270 (130.0)	35.2 (2.07)	23.6 (0.85)	35.3 (2.14)	27.2 (1.79)	9.1 (0.99)	5.8 (0.92)	3.2 (0.51)	25.9 (2.02)	2.5 (0.60)
Looking for work	795 (66.6)	22.2 (3.89)	22.0 (2.50)	59.9 (4.33)	15.4 (3.08)	5.6! (2.39)	‡ (†)	‡ (†)	16.9 (3.67)	‡ (†)
Not in labor force	7,811 (152.6)	22.7 (1.12)	20.6 (0.87)	69.0 (1.51)	20.4 (1.11)	2.3 (0.41)	0.8 (0.20)	1.5 (0.31)	7.9 (0.91)	0.4! (0.15)
Mother's highest education[7]										
Less than high school	2,716 (88.3)	20.9 (3.66)	27.6 (2.07)	60.4 (4.32)	18.0 (3.61)	5.5 (1.51)	3.9! (1.45)	1.7! (0.72)	15.4 (2.23)	‡ (†)
High school/GED	4,085 (86.0)	25.3 (1.66)	29.4 (1.10)	51.0 (2.40)	18.5 (1.54)	6.1 (1.08)	4.5 (0.90)	1.6! (0.62)	21.8 (2.23)	2.5 (0.61)
Vocational/technical or some college	3,698 (93.1)	33.7 (1.47)	28.8 (0.92)	41.1 (1.52)	27.6 (1.51)	9.2 (1.02)	7.8 (0.97)	1.4! (0.44)	20.9 (1.61)	1.2! (0.42)
Associate's degree	1,752 (94.1)	33.4 (2.49)	33.3 (1.35)	39.0 (2.81)	26.2 (2.02)	10.8 (1.84)	9.5 (1.53)	‡ (†)	22.1 (2.22)	1.9! (0.64)
Bachelor's degree	5,675 (126.7)	45.1 (1.40)	30.3 (0.61)	33.9 (1.52)	38.1 (1.42)	10.9 (0.74)	7.2 (0.69)	3.7 (0.52)	15.4 (1.17)	1.7 (0.35)
Graduate/professional degree	2,835 (49.7)	52.5 (1.71)	33.0 (0.76)	20.5 (1.51)	44.5 (1.61)	18.6 (1.45)	9.5 (0.98)	9.2 (1.03)	14.2 (1.37)	2.2 (0.47)
Language spoken most at home by mother[7]										
English	16,847 (167.2)	37.9 (0.78)	30.9 (0.40)	38.0 (0.91)	31.1 (0.72)	11.0 (0.54)	7.7 (0.44)	3.3 (0.28)	18.1 (0.80)	1.8 (0.25)
Non-English	2,640 (149.9)	26.4 (2.35)	28.0 (1.58)	52.4 (3.52)	22.5 (2.31)	6.7 (1.39)	4.0 (1.12)	2.7! (0.80)	16.6 (2.28)	1.8! (0.62)
English and another language equally	1,273 (85.0)	30.5 (2.97)	26.4 (1.57)	50.6 (3.68)	25.3 (2.82)	3.8! (1.43)	1.4! (0.53)	‡ (†)	19.7 (2.43)	‡ (†)
Mother's age when first became parent[7]										
Less than 18	1,237 (100.9)	26.0 (3.81)	32.2 (1.90)	50.4 (4.78)	20.1 (3.59)	6.5 (1.85)	5.4! (1.66)	‡ (†)	21.6 (3.61)	‡ (†)
18 or 19	2,476 (155.5)	25.7 (3.26)	31.7 (1.67)	47.0 (3.96)	21.0 (3.07)	8.4 (1.66)	6.3 (1.47)	2.1! (0.79)	22.2 (2.36)	1.3! (0.55)
20 or older	16,899 (176.1)	38.3 (0.86)	30.2 (0.39)	38.9 (1.00)	31.7 (0.81)	10.5 (0.50)	7.1 (0.41)	3.4 (0.30)	17.1 (0.81)	1.8 (0.23)
Household income										
$20,000 or less	3,049 (10.3)	30.5 (2.28)	31.3 (1.66)	52.3 (2.48)	22.5 (2.07)	5.7 (1.41)	3.8! (1.22)	1.9! (0.74)	17.4 (1.95)	2.2! (0.66)
$20,001 to $50,000	5,706 (53.6)	26.7 (1.87)	30.0 (0.85)	50.2 (2.03)	21.3 (1.88)	6.5 (0.75)	5.2 (0.67)	1.3 (0.34)	20.8 (1.48)	1.3 (0.31)
$50,001 to $75,000	3,821 (0.0)	27.7 (1.60)	29.1 (0.87)	43.9 (2.18)	21.6 (1.41)	11.6 (1.28)	9.5 (1.20)	2.1 (0.59)	21.0 (1.67)	1.9 (0.57)
$75,001 to $100,000	2,882 (0.0)	38.4 (2.39)	29.9 (0.96)	34.2 (2.16)	31.9 (2.14)	10.4 (1.28)	8.8 (1.23)	1.6 (0.39)	21.8 (2.21)	1.7 (0.42)
Over $100,000	5,904 (4.6)	51.5 (1.58)	31.7 (0.46)	25.3 (1.46)	44.6 (1.52)	14.5 (0.87)	7.4 (0.60)	7.1 (0.76)	13.8 (1.09)	1.9 (0.33)

See notes at end of table.

Table 202.30.   Number of children under 6 years old and not yet enrolled in kindergarten, percentage participating in center-based programs, average weekly hours in nonparental care, and percentage in various types of primary care arrangements, by selected child and family characteristics: 2016—Continued

[Standard errors appear in parentheses]

Selected child or family characteristic	Number of children under 6 years old (in thousands)	Percent participating in center-based programs[1]	Average hours per week in nonparental care[2]	Parental care only	Center-based care	Nonrelative home-based care — Total	In another home	In child's home	Relative	Multiple arrangments[4]
1	2	3	4	5	6	7	8	9	10	11
Poverty status of household[5]										
Poor	4,203 (92.6)	26.8 (1.98)	30.9 (1.27)	54.4 (2.53)	20.3 (1.81)	5.4 (1.10)	3.7 (0.96)	1.7! (0.58)	18.1 (1.93)	1.7 (0.49)
Near-poor	4,997 (156.1)	25.2 (1.82)	29.1 (0.91)	51.3 (2.16)	19.2 (1.74)	6.4 (0.76)	5.0 (0.65)	1.4 (0.38)	21.6 (1.67)	1.4 (0.42)
Nonpoor	12,162 (109.4)	43.4 (0.98)	30.9 (0.40)	30.9 (1.11)	36.7 (0.93)	13.1 (0.64)	8.7 (0.53)	4.4 (0.42)	17.4 (0.86)	1.9 (0.25)
Household size										
2 or 3 persons	5,109 (114.0)	41.1 (1.33)	33.7 (0.75)	32.3 (1.36)	34.5 (1.31)	12.2 (0.93)	8.5 (0.87)	3.7 (0.50)	18.6 (1.38)	2.2 (0.40)
4 persons	7,574 (116.9)	40.8 (1.42)	30.1 (0.55)	37.1 (1.49)	33.6 (1.27)	11.0 (0.92)	7.9 (0.78)	3.0 (0.50)	16.6 (1.00)	1.8 (0.39)
5 persons	4,610 (164.4)	33.3 (1.77)	28.7 (0.89)	44.1 (2.03)	27.0 (1.62)	8.5 (0.93)	5.1 (0.78)	3.4 (0.59)	19.2 (1.60)	1.3 (0.34)
6 or more persons	4,069 (166.3)	23.1 (1.64)	28.6 (1.11)	52.0 (2.60)	17.7 (1.53)	7.3 (1.06)	4.9 (0.97)	2.4 (0.63)	21.3 (2.05)	1.6 (0.44)
Locale										
City	7,246 (180.0)	36.4 (1.35)	30.8 (0.66)	40.2 (1.80)	29.6 (1.24)	9.7 (0.73)	5.9 (0.65)	3.8 (0.54)	18.8 (1.34)	1.7 (0.35)
Suburban	8,733 (203.4)	37.7 (1.30)	29.3 (0.61)	38.4 (1.39)	31.8 (1.18)	9.3 (0.69)	6.2 (0.61)	3.2 (0.42)	18.9 (1.09)	1.5 (0.25)
Town	1,931 (96.0)	31.2 (2.44)	30.3 (1.24)	44.2 (2.87)	24.3 (2.47)	10.5 (1.63)	7.7 (1.38)	2.8! (1.05)	19.0 (2.47)	‡ (†)
Rural	3,452 (141.6)	32.8 (2.02)	33.5 (1.19)	43.2 (2.22)	25.6 (1.81)	12.2 (1.23)	10.1 (1.01)	2.0 (0.49)	16.7 (1.94)	2.3 (0.63)

†Not applicable.

!Interpret data with caution. The coefficient of variation (CV) for this estimate is between 30 and 50 percent.

‡Reporting standards not met. Either there are too few cases for a reliable estimate or the coefficient of variation (CV) is 50 percent or greater.

[1]Center-based arrangements include day care centers, Head Start programs, preschools, prekindergartens, and other early childhood programs.

[2]Mean hours per week per child, among preschool children enrolled in any type of nonparental care arrangement. For children with more than one arrangement, the hours of each weekly arrangement were summed to calculate the total amount of time in child care per week.

[3]A child's primary arrangement is the regular nonparental care arrangement or early childhood education program in which the child spent the most time per week.

[4]Children who spent an equal number of hours per week in multiple nonparental care arrangements.

[5]Poor children are those whose family incomes were below the Census Bureau's poverty threshold in the year prior to data collection; near-poor children are those whose family incomes ranged from the poverty threshold to 199 percent of the poverty threshold; and nonpoor children are those whose family incomes were at or above 200 percent of the poverty threshold. The poverty threshold is a dollar amount that varies depending on a family's size and composition and is updated annually to account for inflation. In 2015, for example, the poverty threshold for a family of four with two children was $24,257. Survey respondents are asked to select the range within which their income falls, rather than giving the exact amount of their income; therefore, the measure of poverty status is an approximation.

[6]Excludes children living apart from their parents.

[7]Excludes children living in households with no mother or female guardian present.

NOTE: For the 2016 administration of the National Household Education Surveys Program (NHES), initial contact with all respondents was by mail, and the majority of respondents received paper-and-pencil questionnaires. However, as an experiment with web use, a small sample of NHES:2016 respondents received mailed invitations to complete the survey online. Race categories exclude persons of Hispanic ethnicity. Detail may not sum to totals because of rounding.

SOURCE: U.S. Department of Education, National Center for Education Statistics, Early Childhood Program Participation Survey of the National Household Education Surveys Program (ECPP-NHES:2016). (This table was prepared December 2017.)

Table 203.10. Enrollment in public elementary and secondary schools, by level and grade: Selected years, fall 1980 through fall 2029

[In thousands]

Year	All grades	Total	Pre-kinder-garten	Kinder-garten	1st grade	2nd grade	3rd grade	4th grade	5th grade	6th grade	7th grade	8th grade	Un-graded	Total	9th grade	10th grade	11th grade	12th grade	Un-graded[1]
1	2	3	4	5	6	7	8	9	10	11	12	13	14	15	16	17	18	19	20
1980	40,877	27,647	96	2,593	2,894	2,800	2,893	3,107	3,130	3,038	3,085	3,086	924	13,231	3,377	3,368	3,195	2,925	366
1985	39,422	27,034	151	3,041	3,239	2,941	2,895	2,771	2,776	2,789	2,938	2,982	511	12,388	3,439	3,230	2,866	2,550	303
1990	41,217	29,876	303	3,306	3,499	3,327	3,297	3,248	3,197	3,110	3,067	2,979	541	11,341	3,169	2,896	2,612	2,381	284
1991	42,047	30,503	375	3,311	3,556	3,360	3,334	3,315	3,268	3,239	3,181	3,020	542	11,544	3,313	2,915	2,645	2,392	278
1992	42,823	31,086	505	3,313	3,542	3,431	3,361	3,342	3,325	3,303	3,299	3,129	536	11,737	3,352	3,027	2,656	2,431	272
1993	43,465	31,502	545	3,377	3,529	3,429	3,437	3,361	3,350	3,356	3,355	3,249	513	11,963	3,487	3,050	2,751	2,424	250
1994	44,111	31,896	603	3,444	3,593	3,440	3,439	3,426	3,372	3,381	3,404	3,302	492	12,215	3,604	3,131	2,748	2,488	244
1995	44,840	32,338	637	3,536	3,671	3,507	3,445	3,431	3,438	3,395	3,422	3,356	500	12,502	3,704	3,237	2,826	2,487	247
1996	45,611	32,762	670	3,532	3,770	3,600	3,524	3,454	3,453	3,494	3,464	3,403	399	12,849	3,801	3,323	2,930	2,586	208
1997	46,127	33,071	695	3,503	3,755	3,689	3,597	3,507	3,458	3,492	3,520	3,415	440	13,056	3,819	3,376	2,972	2,673	216
1998	46,539	33,344	729	3,443	3,727	3,681	3,696	3,592	3,520	3,497	3,530	3,480	449	13,195	3,856	3,382	3,021	2,722	214
1999	46,857	33,486	751	3,397	3,684	3,656	3,691	3,686	3,604	3,564	3,541	3,497	415	13,371	3,935	3,415	3,034	2,782	205
2000	47,204	33,686	776	3,382	3,636	3,634	3,676	3,711	3,707	3,663	3,629	3,538	334	13,517	3,963	3,491	3,083	2,803	177
2001	47,672	33,936	865	3,379	3,614	3,593	3,653	3,695	3,727	3,769	3,720	3,616	304	13,736	4,012	3,528	3,174	2,863	159
2002	48,183	34,114	915	3,434	3,594	3,565	3,623	3,669	3,711	3,788	3,821	3,709	285	14,069	4,105	3,584	3,229	2,990	161
2003	48,540	34,201	950	3,503	3,613	3,544	3,611	3,619	3,685	3,772	3,841	3,809	255	14,339	4,190	3,675	3,277	3,046	150
2004	48,795	34,178	990	3,544	3,663	3,560	3,580	3,612	3,635	3,735	3,818	3,825	215	14,618	4,281	3,750	3,369	3,094	122
2005	49,113	34,204	1,036	3,619	3,691	3,606	3,586	3,578	3,633	3,670	3,777	3,802	205	14,909	4,287	3,866	3,454	3,180	121
2006	49,316	34,235	1,084	3,631	3,751	3,641	3,627	3,586	3,602	3,660	3,716	3,766	170	15,081	4,260	3,882	3,551	3,277	110
2007	49,291	34,204	1,081	3,609	3,750	3,704	3,659	3,624	3,600	3,628	3,700	3,709	139	15,086	4,200	3,863	3,557	3,375	92
2008	49,266	34,286	1,180	3,640	3,708	3,699	3,708	3,647	3,629	3,614	3,653	3,692	117	14,980	4,123	3,822	3,548	3,400	87
2009	49,361	34,409	1,223	3,678	3,729	3,665	3,707	3,701	3,652	3,644	3,641	3,651	119	14,952	4,080	3,809	3,541	3,432	90
2010	49,484	34,625	1,279	3,682	3,754	3,701	3,686	3,711	3,718	3,682	3,676	3,659	77	14,860	4,008	3,800	3,538	3,472	42
2011	49,522	34,773	1,291	3,746	3,773	3,713	3,703	3,672	3,699	3,724	3,696	3,679	77	14,749	3,957	3,751	3,546	3,452	43
2012	49,771	35,018	1,307	3,831	3,824	3,729	3,719	3,690	3,673	3,723	3,746	3,699	76	14,753	3,975	3,730	3,528	3,477	43
2013	50,045	35,251	1,328	3,834	3,885	3,791	3,738	3,708	3,697	3,684	3,748	3,753	85	14,794	3,980	3,761	3,526	3,476	52
2014	50,313	35,370	1,369	3,772	3,863	3,857	3,806	3,719	3,719	3,710	3,710	3,757	87	14,943	4,033	3,794	3,568	3,496	52
2015[2]	50,438	35,388	1,402	3,713	3,768	3,842	3,869	3,793	3,733	3,731	3,732	3,719	87	15,050	4,019	3,846	3,598	3,537	49
2016[3]	50,615	35,477	1,426	3,699	3,694	3,761	3,874	3,858	3,814	3,754	3,761	3,749	88	15,138	3,986	3,860	3,669	3,571	52
2017[2]	50,686	35,496	1,471	3,684	3,667	3,684	3,788	3,859	3,877	3,827	3,777	3,772	89	15,190	3,996	3,834	3,677	3,631	52
								Projected											
2018	50,650	35,443	1,474	3,691	3,639	3,658	3,709	3,777	3,872	3,893	3,852	3,789	89	15,206	4,021	3,843	3,652	3,639	52
2019	50,634	35,402	1,483	3,714	3,645	3,629	3,683	3,699	3,790	3,888	3,919	3,864	89	15,232	4,038	3,867	3,661	3,615	52
2020	50,654	35,293	1,489	3,728	3,665	3,636	3,654	3,672	3,711	3,805	3,914	3,931	88	15,361	4,119	3,884	3,683	3,623	52
2021	50,643	35,094	1,484	3,716	3,679	3,655	3,661	3,644	3,684	3,726	3,830	3,926	88	15,549	4,190	3,961	3,700	3,646	52
2022	50,721	35,019	1,517	3,798	3,667	3,669	3,680	3,650	3,656	3,700	3,750	3,842	88	15,703	4,185	4,030	3,773	3,662	53
2023	50,768	35,022	1,525	3,819	3,749	3,658	3,695	3,670	3,662	3,671	3,724	3,763	89	15,746	4,095	4,025	3,839	3,735	52
2024	50,758	35,123	1,532	3,838	3,769	3,739	3,683	3,684	3,682	3,677	3,695	3,736	89	15,635	4,010	3,939	3,834	3,799	52
2025	50,704	35,267	1,539	3,854	3,787	3,759	3,764	3,672	3,696	3,697	3,701	3,707	89	15,438	3,982	3,857	3,752	3,795	52
2026	50,672	35,452	1,545	3,868	3,804	3,777	3,785	3,753	3,685	3,711	3,721	3,713	90	15,220	3,951	3,829	3,674	3,714	52
2027	50,734	35,641	1,549	3,879	3,817	3,794	3,803	3,774	3,766	3,700	3,735	3,733	90	15,093	3,958	3,800	3,648	3,637	52
2028	50,885	35,818	1,552	3,888	3,828	3,807	3,820	3,792	3,786	3,782	3,724	3,748	91	15,067	3,979	3,806	3,620	3,610	52
2029	51,068	35,987	1,555	3,894	3,837	3,818	3,834	3,809	3,805	3,802	3,806	3,736	91	15,081	3,994	3,827	3,626	3,582	52

[1]Includes students reported as being enrolled in grade 13.
[2]The prekindergarten, elementary total, and "all grades" counts include imputations for prekindergarten enrollment in California and Oregon.
[3]The prekindergarten, elementary total, and "all grades" counts include imputations for prekindergarten enrollment in California.
NOTE: Due to changes in reporting and imputation practices, prekindergarten enrollment for years prior to 1992 represent an undercount compared to later years. The total ungraded counts of students were prorated to the elementary and secondary levels based on prior reports. Detail may not sum to totals because of rounding. Some data have been revised from previously published figures.
SOURCE: U.S. Department of Education, National Center for Education Statistics, *Statistics of Public Elementary and Secondary School Systems, 1980–81*; Common Core of Data (CCD), "State Nonfiscal Survey of Public Elementary/Secondary Education," 1985–86 through 2017–18; and National Elementary and Secondary Enrollment Projection Model, 1972 through 2029. (This table was prepared December 2019.)

Table 203.20. Enrollment in public elementary and secondary schools, by region, state, and jurisdiction: Selected years, fall 1990 through fall 2029

Region, state, and jurisdiction	Fall 1990	Fall 2000	Fall 2007	Fall 2008	Fall 2009	Fall 2010	Fall 2011	Fall 2012	Fall 2013	Fall 2014	Fall 2015[1]	Fall 2016[2]	Fall 2017[1]	Percent change in total enrollment, 2012 to 2017	Fall 2018	Fall 2019	Fall 2020	Fall 2021	Fall 2022	Fall 2029	Percent change in total enrollment, 2017 to 2029
1	2	3	4	5	6	7	8	9	10	11	12	13	14	15	16	17	18	19	20	21	22
United States	41,216,683	47,203,539	49,290,559	49,265,572	49,360,982	49,484,181	49,521,669	49,771,118	50,044,522	50,312,581	50,438,043	50,615,189	50,685,567	1.8	50,649,800	50,634,000	50,654,200	50,643,100	50,721,200	51,068,100	0.8
Region																					
Northeast	7,281,763	8,222,127	8,122,022	8,052,985	8,092,029	8,071,335	7,953,981	7,959,128	7,961,243	7,979,856	7,933,762	7,959,304	7,946,536	-0.2	7,915,600	7,889,500	7,866,800	7,838,300	7,824,100	7,705,000	-3.0
Midwest	9,943,761	10,729,987	10,770,210	10,742,973	10,672,171	10,609,604	10,573,792	10,559,230	10,572,920	10,560,539	10,555,579	10,538,047	10,523,753	-0.3	10,488,200	10,455,400	10,437,400	10,413,800	10,400,300	10,300,900	-2.1
South	14,807,016	17,007,261	18,422,773	18,490,770	18,651,889	18,805,000	18,955,932	19,128,376	19,298,714	19,506,193	19,641,472	19,749,816	19,824,469	3.6	19,849,000	19,878,600	19,926,300	19,975,000	20,065,800	20,519,200	3.5
West	9,184,143	11,244,164	11,975,554	11,978,844	11,944,893	11,998,242	12,037,964	12,124,384	12,211,645	12,265,993	12,307,230	12,367,122	12,390,809	2.2	12,397,100	12,410,500	12,423,700	12,416,000	12,431,000	12,543,100	1.2
State																					
Alabama	721,806	739,992	742,919	745,668	748,889	755,552	744,621	744,637	746,204	744,164	743,789	744,930	742,444	-0.3	737,200	733,500	732,900	733,500	735,200	743,900	0.2
Alaska	113,903	133,356	131,029	130,662	131,661	132,104	131,167	131,489	130,944	131,176	132,477	132,737	132,872	1.1	133,100	133,500	134,100	134,600	135,500	138,100	4.0
Arizona	639,853	877,696	1,087,447	1,087,817	1,077,831	1,071,751	1,080,319	1,089,384	1,102,445	1,111,695	1,109,040	1,123,137	1,110,851	2.0	1,111,000	1,112,600	1,113,200	1,113,400	1,115,400	1,139,300	2.6
Arkansas	436,286	449,959	479,016	478,965	480,559	482,114	483,114	486,157	489,979	490,917	492,132	493,447	493,114	2.0	496,100	496,600	496,900	497,400	499,400	510,900	3.0
California	4,950,474	6,140,814	6,343,471	6,322,528	6,263,438	6,289,578	6,287,834	6,299,451	6,312,623	6,312,161	6,305,347	6,309,138	6,304,266	0.1	6,285,300	6,269,700	6,251,900	6,220,500	6,200,300	6,112,700	-3.0
Colorado	574,213	724,508	801,867	818,443	832,368	843,316	854,265	863,561	876,999	889,006	899,112	905,019	910,280	5.4	912,600	915,000	917,600	918,300	921,800	951,100	4.5
Connecticut	469,123	562,179	570,626	567,198	563,968	560,546	554,437	550,954	546,200	542,678	537,933	535,118	531,288	-3.6	524,300	517,900	511,900	505,600	501,100	478,000	-10.0
Delaware	99,658	114,676	122,574	125,430	126,801	129,403	128,946	129,026	131,687	134,042	134,847	136,264	136,293	5.6	136,900	137,500	138,000	138,200	138,800	138,800	5.6
District of Columbia	80,694	68,925	78,422	68,681	69,433	71,284	73,911	76,140	78,153	80,958	84,024	85,850	87,315	14.7	87,200	89,700	91,800	94,000	96,100	99,800	14.3
Florida	1,861,592	2,434,821	2,666,811	2,631,020	2,634,522	2,643,347	2,668,156	2,692,162	2,720,744	2,756,944	2,792,234	2,816,791	2,832,424	5.2	2,849,400	2,865,200	2,887,200	2,908,600	2,935,700	3,109,900	9.8
Georgia	1,151,687	1,444,937	1,649,589	1,655,792	1,667,685	1,677,067	1,685,016	1,703,332	1,723,909	1,744,437	1,757,237	1,764,346	1,768,642	3.8	1,767,200	1,765,600	1,765,900	1,767,200	1,770,700	1,785,300	0.9
Hawaii	171,708	184,360	179,897	179,478	180,196	179,601	182,706	184,760	186,825	182,384	181,995	181,550	180,837	-2.1	180,600	180,300	179,500	178,500	177,400	168,600	-6.8
Idaho	220,840	245,117	272,119	275,051	276,299	275,859	279,873	284,834	290,476	290,885	292,277	297,200	301,186	5.7	303,500	305,900	308,100	310,300	312,600	326,200	8.3
Illinois	1,821,407	2,048,792	2,112,805	2,119,707	2,104,175	2,091,654	2,083,097	2,072,880	2,066,990	2,050,239	2,041,779	2,026,718	2,005,153	-3.3	2,000,200	1,991,600	1,984,800	1,976,800	1,966,000	1,872,000	-6.6
Indiana	954,525	989,267	1,046,764	1,046,147	1,046,661	1,047,232	1,040,765	1,041,369	1,047,385	1,046,269	1,046,757	1,049,547	1,054,187	1.2	1,053,400	1,050,400	1,050,200	1,051,100	1,052,500	1,065,700	1.1
Iowa	483,652	495,080	485,115	487,559	491,842	495,775	495,870	499,825	502,964	505,311	508,014	509,831	511,850	2.4	511,700	512,600	513,800	514,100	516,400	521,800	1.9
Kansas	437,034	470,610	468,295	471,060	474,489	483,701	486,108	489,043	496,440	497,275	497,088	494,017	497,088	1.6	495,100	493,700	492,400	490,300	489,200	478,900	-3.7
Kentucky	636,401	665,850	666,225	670,030	680,089	673,128	681,987	685,167	677,389	688,640	686,598	684,017	680,978	-0.6	678,900	677,000	676,000	674,800	675,300	683,100	0.3
Louisiana	784,757	743,089	681,038	684,873	690,915	696,558	703,390	710,903	711,491	716,800	718,711	716,293	715,135	0.6	710,600	706,800	703,900	702,800	702,700	700,900	-2.0
Maine	215,149	207,037	196,245	192,935	189,225	189,077	188,969	185,739	183,995	182,470	181,613	180,512	180,473	-2.8	179,200	178,100	177,300	176,700	176,100	174,500	-3.3
Maryland	715,176	852,920	845,700	843,861	848,412	852,211	854,086	859,638	866,169	874,514	879,601	886,221	893,684	4.0	898,800	904,800	908,300	911,000	914,600	910,500	1.9
Massachusetts	834,431	975,150	962,958	958,910	957,053	955,563	953,369	954,773	955,739	955,844	964,026	964,514	964,751	1.0	963,100	960,800	958,400	955,100	953,600	945,400	-2.0
Michigan	1,584,431	1,720,626	1,692,739	1,659,921	1,649,082	1,587,067	1,573,537	1,555,370	1,548,841	1,537,922	1,536,231	1,528,666	1,516,398	-2.5	1,499,800	1,484,200	1,473,200	1,461,600	1,452,300	1,421,500	-6.3
Minnesota	756,374	854,340	837,578	836,048	837,053	838,037	839,738	845,404	850,973	857,235	864,384	875,021	884,944	4.7	892,200	897,400	903,300	907,800	912,200	929,300	5.0
Mississippi	502,417	497,871	494,122	491,962	492,481	490,526	490,619	493,650	492,586	490,484	487,200	483,150	478,321	-3.1	471,400	465,500	460,600	456,400	452,500	427,100	-10.7
Missouri	816,558	912,744	917,188	917,871	917,982	918,710	916,584	917,900	918,288	917,785	919,234	915,040	915,472	-0.3	913,100	911,800	911,700	911,100	912,600	918,100	0.3
Montana	152,974	154,875	142,823	141,899	141,807	141,693	142,349	142,908	144,129	144,532	145,319	146,375	149,474	4.6	150,400	151,500	152,400	153,100	154,100	159,500	6.7
Nebraska	274,081	286,199	291,244	292,590	295,368	298,500	301,296	303,505	307,677	312,635	316,014	319,194	323,766	6.7	325,900	328,300	330,400	331,900	333,800	345,700	6.8
Nevada	201,316	340,706	429,362	433,371	428,947	437,149	439,634	445,707	451,831	459,189	467,527	473,744	485,785	9.0	492,000	499,600	506,200	512,600	519,700	554,000	14.0
New Hampshire	172,785	208,461	200,772	197,934	197,140	194,711	191,900	188,974	186,310	184,670	182,425	180,888	179,433	-5.0	177,900	176,400	174,600	173,000	171,600	166,100	-7.4
New Jersey	1,089,646	1,313,405	1,382,348	1,381,420	1,396,029	1,402,548	1,356,431	1,372,203	1,370,295	1,400,579	1,408,845	1,410,421	1,408,102	2.6	1,402,200	1,396,800	1,392,000	1,385,600	1,381,300	1,353,100	-3.9
New Mexico	301,881	320,306	329,040	330,245	334,419	338,122	337,225	338,220	339,244	340,365	335,694	336,263	334,345	-1.1	330,600	327,200	323,700	320,100	317,000	294,200	-12.0
New York	2,598,337	2,882,188	2,765,435	2,740,592	2,766,052	2,734,955	2,704,718	2,710,703	2,732,770	2,741,185	2,744,934	2,724,776	2,724,663	0.5	2,718,900	2,715,500	2,710,800	2,704,500	2,704,400	2,661,500	-2.3
North Carolina	1,086,871	1,293,638	1,489,492	1,488,645	1,483,397	1,490,605	1,507,864	1,518,465	1,530,857	1,548,686	1,544,934	1,550,062	1,553,513	2.3	1,550,400	1,548,600	1,550,200	1,551,800	1,563,200	1,598,400	2.9
North Dakota	117,825	109,201	95,059	94,728	95,073	96,323	97,646	101,111	103,947	106,586	108,644	109,706	111,920	10.7	111,100	113,000	115,100	117,000	119,000	130,300	16.5
Ohio	1,771,089	1,835,049	1,827,184	1,817,163	1,764,297	1,754,191	1,740,030	1,729,916	1,724,111	1,724,810	1,716,585	1,710,143	1,704,399	-1.5	1,690,900	1,679,900	1,671,100	1,662,400	1,657,200	1,631,400	-4.3
Oklahoma	579,087	623,110	642,065	645,108	654,802	659,911	666,120	673,483	681,848	688,511	692,878	693,903	695,092	3.2	697,400	698,500	699,900	700,100	702,500	709,900	2.1
Oregon	472,394	546,231	565,586	575,393	582,839	570,720	568,208	587,564	593,000	601,318	608,825	606,277	608,014	3.5	610,200	612,600	616,000	619,000	623,000	637,000	4.8
Pennsylvania	1,667,834	1,814,311	1,801,971	1,775,029	1,785,993	1,793,284	1,771,395	1,763,677	1,755,236	1,743,160	1,717,414	1,727,497	1,726,809	-2.1	1,719,900	1,714,700	1,713,800	1,711,000	1,709,800	1,704,500	-1.3
Rhode Island	138,813	157,347	147,629	145,342	145,118	143,793	142,854	142,481	142,008	141,959	142,014	142,150	142,949	0.3	143,200	142,800	142,100	141,600	141,200	139,900	-2.1

See notes at end of table.

Table 203.20. Enrollment in public elementary and secondary schools, by region, state, and jurisdiction: Selected years, fall 1990 through fall 2029—Continued

Region, state, and jurisdiction	Actual total enrollment													Percent change in total enrollment, 2012 to 2017	Projected enrollment						Percent change in total enrollment, 2017 to 2029
	Fall 1990	Fall 2000	Fall 2007	Fall 2008	Fall 2009	Fall 2010	Fall 2011	Fall 2012	Fall 2013	Fall 2014	Fall 2015[1]	Fall 2016[2]	Fall 2017[1]		Fall 2018	Fall 2019	Fall 2020	Fall 2021	Fall 2022	Fall 2029	
1	2	3	4	5	6	7	8	9	10	11	12	13	14	15	16	17	18	19	20	21	22
South Carolina	622,112	677,411	712,317	718,113	723,143	725,838	727,186	735,998	745,657	756,523	763,533	771,250	777,507	5.6	780,200	783,800	787,900	792,500	797,700	812,500	4.5
South Dakota	129,164	128,603	121,606	126,429	123,713	126,128	128,016	130,471	130,890	133,040	134,253	136,302	137,823	5.6	139,000	140,500	142,000	143,200	144,500	149,800	8.7
Tennessee	824,595	909,161	964,259	971,950	972,549	987,422	999,693	993,496	993,556	995,475	1,001,235	1,001,562	1,001,967	0.9	1,000,200	999,000	1,000,200	1,002,000	1,006,800	1,043,600	4.2
Texas	3,382,887	4,059,619	4,674,832	4,752,148	4,850,210	4,935,715	5,000,470	5,077,659	5,153,702	5,233,765	5,301,477	5,360,849	5,401,341	6.4	5,425,200	5,447,000	5,468,000	5,488,000	5,517,300	5,674,500	5.1
Utah	446,652	481,485	576,244	559,778	571,586	585,552	598,832	613,279	625,461	635,577	647,870	659,801	668,274	9.0	675,400	681,700	687,800	692,300	697,700	736,700	10.2
Vermont	95,762	102,049	94,038	93,625	91,451	96,858	89,908	89,624	88,690	87,311	87,866	88,428	88,028	-1.8	87,000	86,500	85,900	85,300	85,000	82,000	-6.9
Virginia	998,601	1,144,915	1,230,857	1,235,795	1,245,340	1,251,440	1,257,883	1,265,419	1,273,825	1,280,381	1,283,590	1,287,026	1,291,462	2.1	1,292,600	1,293,900	1,295,600	1,297,000	1,299,900	1,323,800	2.5
Washington	839,709	1,004,770	1,030,247	1,037,018	1,035,347	1,043,788	1,045,453	1,051,694	1,058,936	1,073,638	1,087,030	1,101,711	1,110,367	5.6	1,118,400	1,127,800	1,139,700	1,150,600	1,163,700	1,234,000	11.1
West Virginia	322,389	286,367	282,535	282,729	282,662	282,879	282,870	283,044	280,958	280,310	277,452	273,855	272,266	-3.8	269,200	265,900	262,500	259,600	257,400	246,200	-9.6
Wisconsin	797,621	879,476	874,633	873,750	872,436	872,286	871,105	872,436	874,414	871,432	867,800	864,432	860,753	-1.3	855,700	852,100	849,500	846,300	844,700	836,200	-2.8
Wyoming	98,226	89,940	86,422	87,161	88,155	89,009	90,099	91,533	92,732	94,067	94,717	94,170	94,258	3.0	93,700	93,400	93,200	92,800	92,700	91,500	-3.0
Jurisdiction																					
Bureau of Indian Education	—	46,938	—	40,927	41,351	41,962	—	—	—	—	—	45,399	46,330	—	—	—	—	—	—	—	—
DoDEA[3]	—	107,755	84,795	84,781	—	—	—	—	—	—	74,970	—	—	—	—	—	—	—	—	—	—
Other jurisdictions																					
American Samoa	12,463	15,702	—	—	—	—	—	—	—	—	—	—	12,620	—	—	—	—	—	—	—	—
Guam	26,391	32,473	—	—	—	31,618	31,243	31,186	33,414	31,144	30,821	30,758	30,112	-3.4	—	—	—	—	—	—	—
Northern Marianas	6,449	10,004	11,299	10,913	10,961	11,105	11,011	10,646	10,638	—	—	—	—	—	—	—	—	—	—	—	—
Puerto Rico	644,734	612,725	526,565	503,635	493,393	473,735	452,740	434,609	423,934	410,950	379,818	365,181	346,096	-20.4	—	—	—	—	—	—	—
U.S. Virgin Islands	21,750	19,459	15,903	15,768	15,493	15,495	15,711	15,192	14,953	14,241	13,805	13,194	10,868	-28.5	—	—	—	—	—	—	—

—Not available.
[1]Includes imputations for prekindergarten enrollment in California and Oregon.
[2]Includes imputations for prekindergarten enrollment in California.
[3]DoDEA = Department of Defense Education Activity. Includes both domestic and overseas schools.

NOTE: Detail may not sum to totals because of rounding. Some data have been revised from previously published figures. SOURCE: U.S. Department of Education, National Center for Education Statistics, Common Core of Data (CCD), "State Nonfiscal Survey of Public Elementary/Secondary Education," 1990–91 through 2017–18; and State Public Elementary and Secondary Enrollment Projection Model, 1980 through 2029. (This table was prepared December 2019.)

Table 203.40. Enrollment in public elementary and secondary schools, by level, grade, and state or jurisdiction: Fall 2017

State or jurisdiction	Total, all grades	Elem. Total	Prekindergarten	Kindergarten	Grade 1	Grade 2	Grade 3	Grade 4	Grade 5	Grade 6	Grade 7	Grade 8	Elementary ungraded	Sec. Total	Grade 9	Grade 10	Grade 11	Grade 12	Secondary ungraded[1]
1	2	3	4	5	6	7	8	9	10	11	12	13	14	15	16	17	18	19	20
United States	50,685,567	35,496,055	1,471,216	3,684,238	3,667,166	3,684,091	3,787,970	3,859,475	3,877,267	3,827,023	3,776,565	3,772,276	88,768	15,189,512	3,995,574	3,833,718	3,676,753	3,631,450	52,017
Alabama	742,444	523,057	15,520	54,985	56,414	55,606	57,526	58,541	57,928	55,711	55,600	55,226	0	219,387	57,301	55,318	53,920	52,848	0
Alaska	132,872	94,618	3,586	10,196	10,243	10,331	10,409	10,398	10,229	10,007	9,741	9,478	0	38,254	9,584	9,285	9,503	9,882	0
Arizona	1,110,851	777,744	14,124	79,520	80,377	81,200	84,933	88,800	88,844	87,512	86,544	86,287	306	333,107	86,236	83,999	78,514	84,330	28
Arkansas	496,085	352,513	16,827	36,942	36,820	36,915	37,797	38,800	38,844	36,305	36,431	36,631	201	143,572	37,758	37,245	35,387	33,097	85
California	6,304,266	4,357,267	83,853[2]	531,725	456,175	455,523	447,253	466,660	472,202	486,261	477,308	474,828	5,479	1,946,999	495,277	483,745	475,696	489,221	3,060
Colorado	910,280	639,875	33,048	63,574	64,967	65,616	67,991	69,784	69,821	69,321	67,899	67,854	0	270,405	70,017	67,140	65,136	68,112	0
Connecticut	531,288	365,546	18,579	36,225	36,783	36,848	38,020	38,873	40,145	39,621	40,142	40,310	0	165,742	43,232	41,092	40,616	40,802	0
Delaware	136,293	95,390	1,802	9,943	10,048	10,327	10,602	10,838	10,754	10,498	10,362	10,216	0	40,903	11,806	10,476	9,521	9,100	0
District of Columbia	87,315	68,142	12,727	7,465	7,222	6,820	6,602	6,339	6,159	5,270	4,971	4,567	0	19,173	6,085	4,725	4,259	4,104	0
Florida	2,832,424	1,980,941	61,241	200,185	207,590	207,609	226,346	220,504	215,793	219,942	210,658	211,073	0	851,483	219,331	216,578	212,640	202,952	0
Georgia	1,768,642	1,246,608	47,726	126,400	128,192	130,015	135,911	138,249	139,160	135,448	132,993	132,514	0	522,034	147,677	135,406	123,273	115,678	0
Hawaii	180,837	130,255	1,582	14,316	14,755	14,981	11,986	15,443	15,308	14,425	13,996	13,226	237	50,582	14,408	13,143	11,766	11,068	197
Idaho	301,186	210,927	2,845	21,111	22,148	22,376	23,146	24,003	24,147	23,732	24,005	23,414	16	90,259	23,599	22,935	22,210	21,512	3
Illinois	2,005,153	1,388,977	83,664	132,075	137,580	139,991	145,553	148,792	151,331	149,568	149,227	151,180	1,604	616,176	159,550	155,612	150,969	150,045	0
Indiana	1,054,187	728,666	19,198	77,944	76,301	76,468	78,722	80,111	80,201	79,338	78,616	80,163	0	325,521	80,535	80,799	83,712	80,475	0
Iowa	511,850	363,718	30,454	38,293	34,934	36,056	36,683	37,980	38,071	37,618	37,138	36,491	0	148,132	37,728	37,111	36,238	37,055	0
Kansas	497,088	353,430	21,281	35,661	35,554	36,462	36,888	37,687	37,715	36,808	36,210	36,269	2,895	143,658	37,510	35,904	34,718	34,437	1,089
Kentucky	680,978	481,962	29,493	44,058	50,518	49,478	51,350	52,328	52,669	51,102	50,249	50,293	423	199,016	53,687	50,822	48,739	45,593	175
Louisiana	715,135	514,159	27,491	53,070	54,585	53,478	55,396	55,835	55,456	53,698	52,928	52,222	0	200,976	56,596	51,715	47,551	45,114	0
Maine	180,473	124,937	5,617	12,586	12,569	12,688	13,246	13,343	13,727	13,513	13,852	13,796	0	55,536	13,814	13,846	13,946	13,930	0
Maryland	893,684	633,791	30,422	64,045	66,082	66,879	68,516	70,330	69,515	67,059	65,571	65,372	0	259,893	71,633	67,738	60,336	60,186	0
Massachusetts	964,791	668,415	30,684	66,122	68,195	68,491	70,416	72,620	73,012	71,892	71,705	72,860	2,418	296,376	77,572	74,170	72,950	71,684	0
Michigan	1,516,398	1,037,784	44,258	116,636	105,819	103,930	105,399	107,959	112,263	112,397	111,842	114,521	2,760	478,614	123,324	121,134	115,646	117,197	1,313
Minnesota	884,944	614,476	22,692	64,111	63,518	64,385	65,710	67,226	67,694	66,560	66,152	66,428	0	270,468	67,007	65,975	66,653	70,833	0
Mississippi	478,321	341,927	5,732	35,988	36,391	36,409	37,952	38,880	38,842	35,783	35,864	35,613	4,473	136,394	35,716	34,365	32,230	30,933	3,150
Missouri	915,472	648,697	33,054	66,010	66,399	67,231	69,041	70,749	71,042	69,214	68,224	67,733	0	266,775	69,398	67,397	65,697	64,283	0
Montana	149,474	106,075	2,321	11,702	11,407	11,144	11,559	11,971	11,721	11,804	11,239	11,207	0	43,399	11,556	11,245	10,667	9,931	0
Nebraska	323,766	228,831	17,513	23,232	22,892	23,559	24,173	24,169	22,553	23,661	23,357	23,722	0	94,935	23,832	23,747	23,007	24,349	28
Nevada	485,785	343,807	8,908	53,083	36,354	36,375	36,959	38,624	39,062	38,004	37,216	36,389	833	141,978	36,452	36,510	35,532	33,456	28
New Hampshire	179,433	122,657	3,907	11,419	12,745	12,514	13,003	13,456	13,694	13,801	13,895	14,223	0	56,776	14,992	14,567	13,779	13,435	3
New Jersey	1,408,102	987,988	64,351	91,077	94,920	95,253	98,425	99,443	100,606	99,986	99,191	100,919	43,817	420,114	103,655	100,781	99,613	98,845	17,220
New Mexico	334,345	235,839	9,689	23,709	24,166	24,309	25,880	26,363	26,248	25,343	25,304	24,828	0	98,506	28,522	25,597	22,814	21,573	0
New York	2,724,663	1,880,208	65,558	193,045	197,155	198,490	200,783	202,149	203,385	199,743	197,715	198,879	23,306	844,455	218,826	212,490	195,169	194,079	23,891
North Carolina	1,553,513	1,080,861	18,734	115,064	115,584	117,037	121,228	122,866	122,997	119,927	117,127	110,297	0	472,652	129,965	120,884	114,820	105,208	1,775
North Dakota	111,920	81,031	2,778	9,273	8,739	8,713	8,876	8,781	8,746	8,575	8,307	8,243	0	30,889	8,199	7,760	7,561	7,369	0
Ohio	1,704,399	1,187,254	38,310	123,036	123,188	123,921	131,207	128,118	130,839	129,831	128,323	130,481	0	517,145	141,280	133,705	120,359	121,801	0
Oklahoma	695,092	503,796	41,727	51,920	52,328	51,834	53,565	52,385	52,257	50,368	47,950	49,462	0	191,296	52,268	49,055	46,439	43,534	0
Oregon	608,014	427,690	27,330[2]	41,884	43,156	43,504	44,827	46,543	46,542	45,378	44,151	44,375	0	180,324	44,819	44,257	44,003	47,245	0
Pennsylvania	1,726,809	1,182,944	8,498	121,043	126,361	126,616	129,812	134,060	134,805	133,628	133,276	134,845	0	543,865	141,407	136,286	133,081	133,091	0
Rhode Island	142,949	98,737	2,477	10,006	10,297	10,434	10,583	11,003	11,119	10,913	10,853	11,052	0	44,212	11,580	11,470	10,867	10,295	0
South Carolina	777,507	553,414	27,006	55,598	57,183	57,012	60,334	60,890	61,389	59,112	57,857	57,033	0	224,093	63,516	57,755	52,722	50,100	0
South Dakota	137,823	99,878	3,393	11,720	10,432	10,494	10,655	10,966	10,921	10,677	10,516	10,104	0	37,945	10,600	9,649	8,913	8,783	0
Tennessee	1,001,967	710,398	28,379	75,482	74,633	74,145	74,844	78,085	78,681	76,941	75,058	74,150	0	291,569	75,784	74,234	72,053	69,498	0
Texas	5,401,341	3,852,952	256,222	371,638	388,650	394,381	409,998	413,843	414,412	402,634	402,512	398,662	0	1,548,389	433,521	397,573	372,052	345,243	0
Utah	668,274	475,107	15,904	47,591	49,791	50,429	51,635	52,970	53,368	51,951	50,841	50,627	0	193,167	50,184	48,968	47,499	46,516	0
Vermont	88,028	63,052	8,818	5,789	5,814	5,871	5,848	6,236	6,265	6,040	6,240	6,131	0	24,976	6,447	6,430	6,192	5,907	0
Virginia	1,291,462	900,027	33,617	91,002	94,312	94,166	96,946	99,305	99,548	97,617	96,633	96,881	0	391,435	103,925	99,531	94,858	93,121	0
Washington	1,110,367	769,992	15,754	80,917	82,843	83,077	85,583	87,366	86,667	83,947	82,040	81,798	0	340,375	83,131	82,138	83,214	91,892	0
West Virginia	272,266	193,961	16,665	19,521	19,402	19,150	19,659	20,069	20,218	19,539	19,780	19,958	0	78,305	21,317	20,164	18,547	18,277	0
Wisconsin	860,753	598,837	55,186	56,832	57,517	58,370	60,783	61,913	62,743	61,551	61,583	62,359	0	261,916	65,980	64,354	64,556	67,026	0
Wyoming	94,258	66,897	671	7,469	7,118	7,179	7,411	7,537	7,604	7,449	7,373	7,086	0	27,361	7,453	6,893	6,610	6,405	0

See notes at end of table.

Table 203.40.   Enrollment in public elementary and secondary schools, by level, grade, and state or jurisdiction: Fall 2017—Continued

State or jurisdiction	Total, all grades	Elementary												Secondary					
		Total	Prekinder-garten	Kinder-garten	Grade 1	Grade 2	Grade 3	Grade 4	Grade 5	Grade 6	Grade 7	Grade 8	Elementary ungraded	Total	Grade 9	Grade 10	Grade 11	Grade 12	Secondary ungraded[1]
1	2	3	4	5	6	7	8	9	10	11	12	13	14	15	16	17	18	19	20
Bureau of Indian Education	46,330	35,064	—	4,601	4,064	3,899	3,931	3,962	3,774	3,756	3,614	3,463	0	11,266	3,315	2,990	2,470	2,491	0
DoDEA[3]	—	—	—	—	—	—	—	—	—	—	—	—	—	—	—	—	—	—	—
Other jurisdictions																			
American Samoa	12,620	8,877	1,128	729	800	817	850	845	855	873	1,010	970	0	3,743	1,007	946	982	808	0
Guam	30,112	20,227	602	1,953	2,153	2,164	2,181	2,327	2,315	2,139	2,159	2,234	0	9,885	2,888	2,834	2,350	1,813	0
Northern Marianas	—	—	—	—	—	—	—	—	—	—	—	—	—	—	—	—	—	—	—
Puerto Rico	346,096	238,807	2,536	22,189	25,701	24,247	25,082	25,360	25,827	25,754	27,494	26,186	8,431	107,289	25,865	26,222	25,627	25,064	4,511
U.S. Virgin Islands	10,868	7,427	—	732	745	780	898	865	833	848	955	771	0	3,441	1,196	875	676	694	0

—Not available.
[1]Includes students reported as being enrolled in grade 13.
[2]Inputed by the National Center for Education Statistics.
[3]DoDEA = Department of Defense Education Activity. Includes both domestic and overseas schools.

NOTE: The total ungraded counts of students were prorated to the elementary and secondary levels based on prior state reports of the percentage of elementary and of secondary ungraded students.
SOURCE: U.S. Department of Education, National Center for Education Statistics, Common Core of Data (CCD), "State Nonfiscal Survey of Public Elementary/Secondary Education," 2017–18. (This table was prepared August 2019.)

Table 203.50.   Enrollment and percentage distribution of enrollment in public elementary and secondary schools, by race/ethnicity and region: Selected years, fall 1995 through fall 2029

Region and year	Enrollment (in thousands)								Percentage distribution							
	Total	White	Black	Hispanic	Asian	Pacific Islander	American Indian/ Alaska Native	Two or more races	Total	White	Black	Hispanic	Asian	Pacific Islander	American Indian/ Alaska Native	Two or more races
1	2	3	4	5	6	7	8	9	10	11	12	13	14	15	16	17
United States																
1995	44,840	29,044	7,551	6,072	1,668[1]	—	505	—	100.0	64.8	16.8	13.5	3.7[1]	—	1.1	—
2000	47,204	28,878	8,100	7,726	1,950[1]	—	550	—	100.0	61.2	17.2	16.4	4.1[1]	—	1.2	—
2001	47,672	28,735	8,177	8,169	2,028[1]	—	564	—	100.0	60.3	17.2	17.1	4.3[1]	—	1.2	—
2002	48,183	28,618	8,299	8,594	2,088[1]	—	583	—	100.0	59.4	17.2	17.8	4.3[1]	—	1.2	—
2003	48,540	28,442	8,349	9,011	2,145[1]	—	593	—	100.0	58.6	17.2	18.6	4.4[1]	—	1.2	—
2004	48,795	28,318	8,386	9,317	2,183[1]	—	591	—	100.0	58.0	17.2	19.1	4.5[1]	—	1.2	—
2005	49,113	28,005	8,445	9,787	2,279[1]	—	598	—	100.0	57.0	17.2	19.9	4.6[1]	—	1.2	—
2006	49,316	27,801	8,422	10,166	2,332[1]	—	595	—	100.0	56.4	17.1	20.6	4.7[1]	—	1.2	—
2007	49,291	27,454	8,392	10,454	2,396[1]	—	594	—	100.0	55.7	17.0	21.2	4.9[1]	—	1.2	—
2008	49,266	27,057	8,358	10,563	2,405	46	589	247[2]	100.0	54.9	17.0	21.4	4.9	0.1	1.2	0.5[2]
2009	49,361	26,702	8,245	10,991	2,435	49	601	338[2]	100.0	54.1	16.7	22.3	4.9	0.1	1.2	0.7[2]
2010	49,484	25,933	7,917	11,439	2,296	171	566	1,164	100.0	52.4	16.0	23.1	4.6	0.3	1.1	2.4
2011	49,522	25,602	7,827	11,759	2,334	179	547	1,272	100.0	51.7	15.8	23.7	4.7	0.4	1.1	2.6
2012	49,771	25,386	7,803	12,104	2,372	180	534	1,393	100.0	51.0	15.7	24.3	4.8	0.4	1.1	2.8
2013	50,045	25,160	7,805	12,452	2,417	176	523	1,511	100.0	50.3	15.6	24.9	4.8	0.4	1.0	3.0
2014	50,313	24,923	7,807	12,805	2,470	176	519	1,612	100.0	49.5	15.5	25.4	4.9	0.3	1.0	3.2
2015[3]	50,438	24,644	7,784	13,080	2,521	177	510	1,723	100.0	48.9	15.4	25.9	5.0	0.4	1.0	3.4
2016[4]	50,615	24,413	7,765	13,329	2,571	184	511	1,842	100.0	48.2	15.3	26.3	5.1	0.4	1.0	3.6
2017[3]	50,686	24,124	7,709	13,571	2,640	185	498	1,959	100.0	47.6	15.2	26.8	5.2	0.4	1.0	3.9
2018[5]	50,650	23,846	7,671	13,704	2,691	187	491	2,060	100.0	47.1	15.1	27.1	5.3	0.4	1.0	4.1
2019[5]	50,634	23,597	7,639	13,831	2,737	188	484	2,160	100.0	46.6	15.1	27.3	5.4	0.4	1.0	4.3
2020[5]	50,654	23,376	7,616	13,952	2,787	189	477	2,257	100.0	46.1	15.0	27.5	5.5	0.4	0.9	4.5
2021[5]	50,643	23,170	7,598	14,044	2,823	190	471	2,347	100.0	45.8	15.0	27.7	5.6	0.4	0.9	4.6
2022[5]	50,721	23,041	7,636	14,070	2,882	189	464	2,439	100.0	45.4	15.1	27.7	5.7	0.4	0.9	4.8
2023[5]	50,768	22,910	7,657	14,082	2,939	187	458	2,535	100.0	45.1	15.1	27.7	5.8	0.4	0.9	5.0
2024[5]	50,758	22,779	7,665	14,057	2,999	186	452	2,619	100.0	44.9	15.1	27.7	5.9	0.4	0.9	5.2
2025[5]	50,704	22,639	7,664	14,016	3,060	186	446	2,694	100.0	44.6	15.1	27.6	6.0	0.4	0.9	5.3
2026[5]	50,672	22,522	7,664	13,975	3,122	185	441	2,762	100.0	44.4	15.1	27.6	6.2	0.4	0.9	5.5
2027[5]	50,734	22,446	7,675	13,967	3,192	186	437	2,832	100.0	44.2	15.1	27.5	6.3	0.4	0.9	5.6
2028[5]	50,885	22,401	7,707	13,995	3,260	186	434	2,901	100.0	44.0	15.1	27.5	6.4	0.4	0.9	5.7
2029[5]	51,068	22,359	7,746	14,049	3,327	186	433	2,967	100.0	43.8	15.2	27.5	6.5	0.4	0.8	5.8
Northeast																
1995	7,894	5,497	1,202	878	295[1]	—	21	—	100.0	69.6	15.2	11.1	3.7[1]	—	0.3	—
2000	8,222	5,545	1,270	1,023	361[1]	—	24	—	100.0	67.4	15.4	12.4	4.4[1]	—	0.3	—
2005	8,240	5,317	1,282	1,189	425[1]	—	27	—	100.0	64.5	15.6	14.4	5.2[1]	—	0.3	—
2010	8,071	4,876	1,208	1,364	494	6	27	96	100.0	60.4	15.0	16.9	6.1	0.1	0.3	1.2
2014	7,980	4,507	1,155	1,566	538	7	28	179	100.0	56.5	14.5	19.6	6.7	0.1	0.4	2.2
2015	7,934	4,409	1,136	1,610	547	7	29	197	100.0	55.6	14.3	20.3	6.9	0.1	0.4	2.5
2016	7,959	4,345	1,132	1,668	558	13	30	214	100.0	54.6	14.2	21.0	7.0	0.2	0.4	2.7
2017	7,947	4,269	1,117	1,714	570	13	30	232	100.0	53.7	14.1	21.6	7.2	0.2	0.4	2.9
Midwest																
1995	10,512	8,335	1,450	438	197[1]	—	92	—	100.0	79.3	13.8	4.2	1.9[1]	—	0.9	—
2000	10,730	8,208	1,581	610	239[1]	—	92	—	100.0	76.5	14.7	5.7	2.2[1]	—	0.9	—
2005	10,819	7,950	1,654	836	283[1]	—	96	—	100.0	73.5	15.3	7.7	2.6[1]	—	0.9	—
2010	10,610	7,327	1,505	1,077	303	9	94	294	100.0	69.1	14.2	10.2	2.9	0.1	0.9	2.8
2014	10,561	7,037	1,459	1,249	338	11	86	380	100.0	66.6	13.8	11.8	3.2	0.1	0.8	3.6
2015	10,556	6,968	1,458	1,284	348	12	84	400	100.0	66.0	13.8	12.2	3.3	0.1	0.8	3.8
2016	10,539	6,893	1,449	1,312	360	12	86	426	100.0	65.4	13.8	12.4	3.4	0.1	0.8	4.0
2017	10,524	6,825	1,446	1,340	372	13	82	447	100.0	64.9	13.7	12.7	3.5	0.1	0.8	4.2
South																
1995	16,118	9,565	4,236	1,890	280[1]	—	148	—	100.0	59.3	26.3	11.7	1.7[1]	—	0.9	—
2000	17,007	9,501	4,516	2,468	352[1]	—	170	—	100.0	55.9	26.6	14.5	2.1[1]	—	1.0	—
2005	18,103	9,381	4,738	3,334	456[1]	—	194	—	100.0	51.8	26.2	18.4	2.5[1]	—	1.1	—
2010	18,805	8,869	4,545	4,206	533	22	207	424	100.0	47.2	24.2	22.4	2.8	0.1	1.1	2.3
2014	19,506	8,681	4,577	4,846	613	28	184	579	100.0	44.5	23.5	24.8	3.1	0.1	0.9	3.0
2015	19,641	8,601	4,583	4,994	637	29	181	615	100.0	43.8	23.3	25.4	3.2	0.1	0.9	3.1
2016	19,750	8,513	4,571	5,142	665	30	177	652	100.0	43.1	23.1	26.0	3.4	0.2	0.9	3.3
2017	19,824	8,439	4,555	5,249	689	32	174	688	100.0	42.6	23.0	26.5	3.5	0.2	0.9	3.5
West																
1995	10,316	5,648	662	2,866	896[1]	—	244	—	100.0	54.7	6.4	27.8	8.7[1]	—	2.4	—
2000	11,244	5,624	733	3,625	998[1]	—	264	—	100.0	50.0	6.5	32.2	8.9[1]	—	2.4	—
2005	11,951	5,356	771	4,428	1,115[1]	—	281	—	100.0	44.8	6.5	37.1	9.3[1]	—	2.4	—
2010	11,998	4,861	659	4,792	966	133	237	349	100.0	40.5	5.5	39.9	8.1	1.1	2.0	2.9
2014	12,266	4,698	616	5,144	982	130	221	475	100.0	38.3	5.0	41.9	8.0	1.1	1.8	3.9
2015[3]	12,307	4,665	606	5,192	988	129	216	511	100.0	37.9	4.9	42.2	8.0	1.1	1.8	4.2
2016[4]	12,367	4,662	612	5,208	989	128	217	550	100.0	37.7	5.0	42.1	8.0	1.0	1.8	4.4
2017[3]	12,391	4,592	592	5,268	1,009	127	211	592	100.0	37.1	4.8	42.5	8.1	1.0	1.7	4.8

—Not available.
[1]Includes Pacific Islanders.
[2]For this year, data on Pacific Islanders and students of Two or more races were reported by only a small number of states. Therefore, the data are not comparable to figures for 2010 and later years.
[3]Includes imputations for prekindergarten enrollment in California and Oregon.
[4]Includes imputations for prekindergarten enrollment in California.
[5]Projected.

NOTE: Race categories exclude persons of Hispanic ethnicity. Enrollment data for students not reported by race/ethnicity were prorated by state and grade to match state totals. Prior to 2008, data on students of Two or more races were not collected. Some data have been revised from previously published figures. Detail may not sum to totals because of rounding.
SOURCE: U.S. Department of Education, National Center for Education Statistics, Common Core of Data (CCD), "State Nonfiscal Survey of Public Elementary and Secondary Education," 1995–96 through 2017–18; and National Elementary and Secondary Enrollment by Race/Ethnicity Projection Model, 1972 through 2029. (This table was prepared December 2019.)

Table 203.60. Enrollment and percentage distribution of enrollment in public elementary and secondary schools, by race/ethnicity and level of education: Fall 1999 through fall 2029

Level of education and year	Enrollment (in thousands)									Percentage distribution								
	Total	White	Black	His-panic	Asian/Pacific Islander			American Indian/ Alaska Native	Two or more races	Total	White	Black	His-panic	Asian/Pacific Islander			American Indian/ Alaska Native	Two or more races
					Total	Asian	Pacific Islander							Total	Asian	Pacific Islander		
1	2	3	4	5	6	7	8	9	10	11	12	13	14	15	16	17	18	19
Total																		
1999	46,857	29,035	8,066	7,327	1,887	—	—	542	—	100.0	62.0	17.2	15.6	4.0	†	†	1.2	†
2000	47,204	28,878	8,100	7,726	1,950	—	—	550	—	100.0	61.2	17.2	16.4	4.1	†	†	1.2	†
2001	47,672	28,735	8,177	8,169	2,028	—	—	564	—	100.0	60.3	17.2	17.1	4.3	†	†	1.2	†
2002	48,183	28,618	8,299	8,594	2,088	—	—	583	—	100.0	59.4	17.2	17.8	4.3	†	†	1.2	†
2003	48,540	28,442	8,349	9,011	2,145	—	—	593	—	100.0	58.6	17.2	18.6	4.4	†	†	1.2	†
2004	48,795	28,318	8,386	9,317	2,183	—	—	591	—	100.0	58.0	17.2	19.1	4.5	†	†	1.2	†
2005	49,113	28,005	8,445	9,787	2,279	—	—	598	—	100.0	57.0	17.2	19.9	4.6	†	†	1.2	†
2006	49,316	27,801	8,422	10,166	2,332	—	—	595	—	100.0	56.4	17.1	20.6	4.7	†	†	1.2	†
2007	49,291	27,454	8,392	10,454	2,396	—	—	594	—	100.0	55.7	17.0	21.2	4.9	†	†	1.2	†
2008	49,266	27,057	8,358	10,563	2,451	2,405	46	589	247[1]	100.0	54.9	17.0	21.4	5.0	4.9	0.1	1.2	0.5[1]
2009	49,361	26,702	8,245	10,991	2,484	2,435	49	601	338[1]	100.0	54.1	16.7	22.3	5.0	4.9	0.1	1.2	0.7[1]
2010	49,484	25,933	7,917	11,439	2,466	2,296	171	566	1,164	100.0	52.4	16.0	23.1	5.0	4.6	0.3	1.1	2.4
2011	49,522	25,602	7,827	11,759	2,513	2,334	179	547	1,272	100.0	51.7	15.8	23.7	5.1	4.7	0.4	1.1	2.6
2012	49,771	25,386	7,803	12,104	2,552	2,372	180	534	1,393	100.0	51.0	15.7	24.3	5.1	4.8	0.4	1.1	2.8
2013	50,045	25,160	7,805	12,452	2,593	2,417	176	523	1,511	100.0	50.3	15.6	24.9	5.2	4.8	0.4	1.0	3.0
2014	50,313	24,923	7,807	12,805	2,646	2,470	176	519	1,612	100.0	49.5	15.5	25.4	5.3	4.9	0.3	1.0	3.2
2015[2]	50,438	24,644	7,784	13,080	2,697	2,521	177	510	1,723	100.0	48.9	15.4	25.9	5.3	5.0	0.4	1.0	3.4
2016[3]	50,615	24,413	7,765	13,329	2,756	2,571	184	511	1,842	100.0	48.2	15.3	26.3	5.4	5.1	0.4	1.0	3.6
2017[2]	50,686	24,124	7,709	13,571	2,825	2,640	185	498	1,959	100.0	47.6	15.2	26.8	5.6	5.2	0.4	1.0	3.9
2018[4]	50,650	23,846	7,671	13,704	2,878	2,691	187	491	2,060	100.0	47.1	15.1	27.1	5.7	5.3	0.4	1.0	4.1
2019[4]	50,634	23,597	7,639	13,831	2,925	2,737	188	484	2,160	100.0	46.6	15.1	27.3	5.8	5.4	0.4	1.0	4.3
2020[4]	50,654	23,376	7,616	13,952	2,976	2,787	189	477	2,257	100.0	46.1	15.0	27.5	5.9	5.5	0.4	0.9	4.5
2021[4]	50,643	23,170	7,598	14,044	3,013	2,823	190	471	2,347	100.0	45.8	15.0	27.7	5.9	5.6	0.4	0.9	4.6
2022[4]	50,721	23,041	7,636	14,070	3,071	2,882	189	464	2,439	100.0	45.4	15.1	27.7	6.1	5.7	0.4	0.9	4.8
2023[4]	50,768	22,910	7,657	14,082	3,126	2,939	187	458	2,535	100.0	45.1	15.1	27.7	6.2	5.8	0.4	0.9	5.0
2024[4]	50,758	22,779	7,665	14,057	3,185	2,999	186	452	2,619	100.0	44.9	15.1	27.7	6.3	5.9	0.4	0.9	5.2
2025[4]	50,704	22,639	7,664	14,016	3,246	3,060	186	446	2,694	100.0	44.6	15.1	27.6	6.4	6.0	0.4	0.9	5.3
2026[4]	50,672	22,522	7,664	13,975	3,307	3,122	185	441	2,762	100.0	44.4	15.1	27.6	6.5	6.2	0.4	0.9	5.5
2027[4]	50,734	22,446	7,675	13,967	3,378	3,192	186	437	2,832	100.0	44.2	15.1	27.5	6.7	6.3	0.4	0.9	5.6
2028[4]	50,885	22,401	7,707	13,995	3,446	3,260	186	434	2,901	100.0	44.0	15.1	27.5	6.8	6.4	0.4	0.9	5.7
2029[4]	51,068	22,359	7,746	14,049	3,514	3,327	186	433	2,967	100.0	43.8	15.2	27.5	6.9	6.5	0.4	0.8	5.8
Prekindergarten through grade 8																		
1999	33,486	20,327	5,952	5,512	1,303	—	—	391	—	100.0	60.7	17.8	16.5	3.9	†	†	1.2	†
2000	33,686	20,130	5,981	5,830	1,349	—	—	397	—	100.0	59.8	17.8	17.3	4.0	†	†	1.2	†
2001	33,936	19,960	6,004	6,159	1,409	—	—	405	—	100.0	58.8	17.7	18.1	4.2	†	†	1.2	†
2002	34,114	19,764	6,042	6,446	1,447	—	—	415	—	100.0	57.9	17.7	18.9	4.2	†	†	1.2	†
2003	34,201	19,558	6,015	6,729	1,483	—	—	415	—	100.0	57.2	17.6	19.7	4.3	†	†	1.2	†
2004	34,178	19,368	5,983	6,909	1,504	—	—	413	—	100.0	56.7	17.5	20.2	4.4	†	†	1.2	†
2005	34,204	19,051	5,954	7,216	1,569	—	—	412	—	100.0	55.7	17.4	21.1	4.6	†	†	1.2	†
2006	34,235	18,863	5,882	7,465	1,611	—	—	414	—	100.0	55.1	17.2	21.8	4.7	†	†	1.2	†
2007	34,204	18,679	5,821	7,632	1,660	—	—	412	—	100.0	54.6	17.0	22.3	4.9	†	†	1.2	†
2008	34,286	18,501	5,793	7,689	1,705	1,674	31	410	187[1]	100.0	54.0	16.9	22.4	5.0	4.9	0.1	1.2	0.5[1]
2009	34,409	18,316	5,713	7,977	1,730	1,697	33	419	254[1]	100.0	53.2	16.6	23.2	5.0	4.9	0.1	1.2	0.7[1]
2010	34,625	17,823	5,495	8,314	1,711	1,589	122	394	887	100.0	51.5	15.9	24.0	4.9	4.6	0.4	1.1	2.6
2011	34,773	17,654	5,470	8,558	1,744	1,616	128	384	963	100.0	50.8	15.7	24.6	5.0	4.6	0.4	1.1	2.8
2012	35,018	17,535	5,473	8,804	1,773	1,644	129	375	1,057	100.0	50.1	15.6	25.1	5.1	4.7	0.4	1.1	3.0
2013	35,251	17,390	5,483	9,054	1,809	1,683	126	367	1,148	100.0	49.3	15.6	25.7	5.1	4.8	0.4	1.0	3.3
2014	35,370	17,193	5,471	9,273	1,842	1,718	124	363	1,227	100.0	48.6	15.5	26.2	5.2	4.9	0.4	1.0	3.5
2015[2]	35,388	16,972	5,448	9,424	1,878	1,754	124	356	1,311	100.0	48.0	15.4	26.6	5.3	5.0	0.4	1.0	3.7
2016[3]	35,477	16,823	5,440	9,544	1,914	1,784	129	358	1,399	100.0	47.4	15.3	26.9	5.4	5.0	0.4	1.0	3.9
2017[2]	35,496	16,623	5,409	9,678	1,956	1,827	129	347	1,482	100.0	46.8	15.2	27.3	5.5	5.1	0.4	1.0	4.2
2018[4]	35,443	16,442	5,401	9,718	1,992	1,862	130	342	1,549	100.0	46.4	15.2	27.4	5.6	5.3	0.4	1.0	4.4
2019[4]	35,402	16,291	5,393	9,748	2,023	1,894	129	336	1,610	100.0	46.0	15.2	27.5	5.7	5.3	0.4	0.9	4.5
2020[4]	35,293	16,130	5,371	9,745	2,060	1,930	130	330	1,658	100.0	45.7	15.2	27.6	5.8	5.5	0.4	0.9	4.7
2021[4]	35,094	15,968	5,324	9,700	2,086	1,956	130	323	1,693	100.0	45.5	15.2	27.6	5.9	5.6	0.4	0.9	4.8
2022[4]	35,019	15,900	5,332	9,603	2,135	2,007	129	318	1,730	100.0	45.4	15.2	27.4	6.1	5.7	0.4	0.9	4.9
2023[4]	35,022	15,856	5,336	9,549	2,187	2,058	129	313	1,780	100.0	45.3	15.2	27.3	6.2	5.9	0.4	0.9	5.1
2024[4]	35,123	15,852	5,365	9,529	2,238	2,109	129	310	1,828	100.0	45.1	15.3	27.1	6.4	6.0	0.4	0.9	5.2
2025[4]	35,267	15,858	5,406	9,531	2,290	2,161	129	309	1,872	100.0	45.0	15.3	27.0	6.5	6.1	0.4	0.9	5.3
2026[4]	35,452	15,868	5,449	9,567	2,338	2,209	129	309	1,922	100.0	44.8	15.4	27.0	6.6	6.2	0.4	0.9	5.4
2027[4]	35,641	15,872	5,493	9,617	2,376	2,248	128	308	1,975	100.0	44.5	15.4	27.0	6.7	6.3	0.4	0.9	5.5
2028[4]	35,818	15,855	5,533	9,672	2,421	2,293	128	308	2,030	100.0	44.3	15.4	27.0	6.8	6.4	0.4	0.9	5.7
2029[4]	35,987	15,832	5,572	9,726	2,462	2,335	127	308	2,087	100.0	44.0	15.5	27.0	6.8	6.5	0.4	0.9	5.8

See notes at end of table.

Table 203.60.   Enrollment and percentage distribution of enrollment in public elementary and secondary schools, by race/ethnicity and level of education: Fall 1999 through fall 2029—Continued

Level of education and year	Enrollment (in thousands)									Percentage distribution								
					Asian/Pacific Islander			American Indian/ Alaska Native	Two or more races					Asian/Pacific Islander			American Indian/ Alaska Native	Two or more races
	Total	White	Black	His-panic	Total	Asian	Pacific Islander			Total	White	Black	His-panic	Total	Asian	Pacific Islander		
1	2	3	4	5	6	7	8	9	10	11	12	13	14	15	16	17	18	19
Grades 9 through 12																		
1999	13,371	8,708	2,114	1,815	584	—	—	151	—	100.0	65.1	15.8	13.6	4.4	†	†	1.1	†
2000	13,517	8,747	2,119	1,896	601	—	—	153	—	100.0	64.7	15.7	14.0	4.4	†	†	1.1	†
2001	13,736	8,774	2,173	2,011	619	—	—	159	—	100.0	63.9	15.8	14.6	4.5	†	†	1.2	†
2002	14,069	8,854	2,257	2,148	642	—	—	168	—	100.0	62.9	16.0	15.3	4.6	†	†	1.2	†
2003	14,339	8,884	2,334	2,282	663	—	—	177	—	100.0	62.0	16.3	15.9	4.6	†	†	1.2	†
2004	14,618	8,950	2,403	2,408	679	—	—	178	—	100.0	61.2	16.4	16.5	4.6	†	†	1.2	†
2005	14,909	8,954	2,490	2,570	709	—	—	186	—	100.0	60.1	16.7	17.2	4.8	†	†	1.2	†
2006	15,081	8,938	2,540	2,701	720	—	—	181	—	100.0	59.3	16.8	17.9	4.8	†	†	1.2	†
2007	15,086	8,775	2,571	2,821	736	—	—	183	—	100.0	58.2	17.0	18.7	4.9	†	†	1.2	†
2008	14,980	8,556	2,565	2,874	746	731	15	179	59[1]	100.0	57.1	17.1	19.2	5.0	4.9	0.1	1.2	0.4[1]
2009	14,952	8,385	2,532	3,014	754	738	16	182	84[1]	100.0	56.1	16.9	20.2	5.0	4.9	0.1	1.2	0.6[1]
2010	14,860	8,109	2,422	3,125	755	707	49	171	277	100.0	54.6	16.3	21.0	5.1	4.8	0.3	1.2	1.9
2011	14,749	7,948	2,357	3,202	769	719	50	163	309	100.0	53.9	16.0	21.7	5.2	4.9	0.3	1.1	2.1
2012	14,753	7,851	2,330	3,300	779	727	51	158	335	100.0	53.2	15.8	22.4	5.3	4.9	0.3	1.1	2.3
2013	14,794	7,770	2,322	3,398	784	733	51	156	363	100.0	52.5	15.7	23.0	5.3	5.0	0.3	1.1	2.5
2014	14,943	7,730	2,336	3,532	804	753	52	156	385	100.0	51.7	15.6	23.6	5.4	5.0	0.3	1.0	2.6
2015[2]	15,050	7,672	2,336	3,656	819	767	52	154	412	100.0	51.0	15.5	24.3	5.4	5.1	0.3	1.0	2.7
2016[3]	15,138	7,590	2,324	3,786	842	787	55	153	443	100.0	50.1	15.4	25.0	5.6	5.2	0.4	1.0	2.9
2017[2]	15,190	7,501	2,300	3,892	869	813	56	150	477	100.0	49.4	15.1	25.6	5.7	5.4	0.4	1.0	3.1
2018[4]	15,206	7,405	2,270	3,986	885	829	57	149	511	100.0	48.7	14.9	26.2	5.8	5.4	0.4	1.0	3.4
2019[4]	15,232	7,305	2,245	4,083	902	843	58	147	550	100.0	48.0	14.7	26.8	5.9	5.5	0.4	1.0	3.6
2020[4]	15,361	7,245	2,245	4,208	916	857	59	147	600	100.0	47.2	14.6	27.4	6.0	5.6	0.4	1.0	3.9
2021[4]	15,549	7,202	2,274	4,345	927	867	60	148	654	100.0	46.3	14.6	27.9	6.0	5.6	0.4	0.9	4.2
2022[4]	15,703	7,142	2,304	4,467	935	875	60	146	709	100.0	45.5	14.7	28.5	6.0	5.6	0.4	0.9	4.5
2023[4]	15,746	7,054	2,321	4,533	939	881	58	145	755	100.0	44.8	14.7	28.8	6.0	5.6	0.4	0.9	4.8
2024[4]	15,635	6,927	2,300	4,528	947	889	58	141	791	100.0	44.3	14.7	29.0	6.1	5.7	0.4	0.9	5.1
2025[4]	15,438	6,781	2,259	4,485	956	899	57	136	821	100.0	43.9	14.6	29.0	6.2	5.8	0.4	0.9	5.3
2026[4]	15,220	6,655	2,214	4,408	970	913	56	132	841	100.0	43.7	14.5	29.0	6.4	6.0	0.4	0.9	5.5
2027[4]	15,093	6,574	2,182	4,349	1,001	944	58	129	858	100.0	43.6	14.5	28.8	6.6	6.3	0.4	0.9	5.7
2028[4]	15,067	6,546	2,173	4,323	1,026	967	58	126	872	100.0	43.4	14.4	28.7	6.8	6.4	0.4	0.8	5.8
2029[4]	15,081	6,527	2,174	4,323	1,052	993	59	125	880	100.0	43.3	14.4	28.7	7.0	6.6	0.4	0.8	5.8

—Not available.
†Not applicable.
[1]For this year, data on students of Two or more races were reported by only a small number of states. Therefore, the data are not comparable to figures for 2010 and later years.
[2]Includes imputations for prekindergarten enrollment in California and Oregon.
[3]Includes imputations for prekindergarten enrollment in California.
[4]Projected.
NOTE: Race categories exclude persons of Hispanic ethnicity. Enrollment data for students not reported by race/ethnicity were prorated by state and grade to match state totals.

Prior to 2008, data on students of Two or more races were not collected. Total counts of ungraded students were prorated to prekindergarten through grade 8 and grades 9 through 12 based on prior reports. Some data have been revised from previously published figures. Detail may not sum to totals because of rounding.
SOURCE: U.S. Department of Education, National Center for Education Statistics, Common Core of Data (CCD), "State Nonfiscal Survey of Public Elementary and Secondary Education," 1998–99 through 2017–18; and National Elementary and Secondary Enrollment by Race/Ethnicity Projection Model, 1972 through 2029. (This table was prepared December 2019.)

Table 203.65. Enrollment in public elementary and secondary schools, by level, grade, and race/ethnicity: Selected years, fall 1999 through fall 2017

[In thousands]

Year	All grades	Elementary													Secondary					
		Total	Pre-kinder-garten	Kinder-garten	1st grade	2nd grade	3rd grade	4th grade	5th grade	6th grade	7th grade	8th grade	Ungraded	Total	9th grade	10th grade	11th grade	12th grade	Ungraded[1]
1	2	3	4	5	6	7	8	9	10	11	12	13	14	15	16	17	18	19	20
1999																			
Total	46,857	33,486	751	3,397	3,684	3,656	3,691	3,686	3,604	3,564	3,541	3,497	415	13,371	3,935	3,415	3,034	2,782	205
White	29,035	20,327	354	2,010	2,159	2,175	2,219	2,261	2,240	2,231	2,243	2,254	183	8,708	2,438	2,214	2,045	1,920	90
Black	8,066	5,952	181	590	679	660	666	644	622	610	595	564	141	2,114	695	537	432	380	70
Hispanic	7,327	5,512	180	627	662	636	620	594	556	538	522	499	79	1,815	598	474	382	321	39
Asian/Pacific Islander	1,887	1,303	27	132	142	142	143	145	143	144	138	138	9	584	156	151	141	131	4
American Indian/Alaska Native	542	391	9	39	43	43	43	43	43	42	43	41	3	151	47	40	33	29	2
2001																			
Total	47,672	33,936	865	3,379	3,614	3,593	3,653	3,695	3,727	3,769	3,720	3,616	304	13,736	4,012	3,528	3,174	2,863	159
White	28,732	19,959	404	1,955	2,073	2,063	2,114	2,178	2,228	2,285	2,282	2,248	129	8,773	2,408	2,247	2,108	1,943	67
Black	8,181	6,006	192	558	630	642	665	661	655	658	646	602	97	2,175	723	555	453	393	51
Hispanic	8,168	6,158	225	683	717	696	680	658	645	627	593	566	68	2,010	667	526	427	354	36
Asian/Pacific Islander	2,027	1,409	33	144	152	152	152	153	153	154	153	155	8	619	165	157	151	142	4
American Indian/Alaska Native	564	405	11	40	42	41	43	44	45	46	46	44	3	159	49	42	35	31	1
2003																			
Total	48,540	34,201	950	3,503	3,613	3,544	3,611	3,619	3,685	3,772	3,841	3,809	255	14,339	4,190	3,675	3,277	3,046	150
White	28,442	19,558	437	1,975	2,022	2,006	2,045	2,069	2,127	2,203	2,271	2,297	107	8,884	2,442	2,255	2,106	2,017	63
Black	8,349	5,954	198	588	619	600	633	641	654	677	681	652	73	2,334	774	600	487	430	43
Hispanic	9,011	7,216	264	748	767	735	730	706	699	686	679	650	65	2,282	740	602	487	414	38
Asian/Pacific Islander	2,145	1,483	38	151	161	162	161	160	160	160	161	162	7	663	178	172	158	150	4
American Indian/Alaska Native	593	415	13	42	44	42	42	43	45	47	48	47	2	177	56	46	39	35	1
2005																			
Total	49,113	34,204	1,036	3,619	3,691	3,606	3,586	3,578	3,633	3,670	3,777	3,802	205	14,909	4,287	3,866	3,454	3,180	121
White	28,005	19,051	465	1,989	2,023	1,992	1,991	2,014	2,051	2,083	2,158	2,212	73	8,954	2,418	2,304	2,153	2,035	43
Black	8,445	5,954	214	603	630	616	612	603	623	649	675	665	64	2,490	803	651	534	464	38
Hispanic	9,787	7,216	301	815	825	788	770	747	747	726	729	708	60	2,570	824	680	552	479	35
Asian/Pacific Islander	2,279	1,569	43	169	168	168	170	171	170	168	168	169	7	709	186	181	173	165	4
American Indian/Alaska Native	598	412	14	43	45	44	42	43	43	45	47	47	2	186	56	49	42	38	1
2007																			
Total	49,291	34,204	1,081	3,609	3,750	3,704	3,659	3,624	3,600	3,628	3,700	3,709	139	15,086	4,200	3,863	3,557	3,375	92
White	27,454	18,679	491	1,944	2,009	2,000	1,996	1,995	1,997	2,028	2,076	2,098	46	8,775	2,291	2,221	2,143	2,091	30
Black	8,392	5,821	224	582	627	623	620	611	600	610	634	642	48	2,571	797	669	564	509	32
Hispanic	10,454	7,632	310	863	886	850	821	797	781	769	769	748	39	2,821	868	739	627	560	26
Asian/Pacific Islander	2,396	1,660	42	169	184	187	177	177	179	178	177	176	5	736	190	186	181	175	3
American Indian/Alaska Native	594	412	14	43	45	44	44	44	43	43	45	45	1	183	52	48	42	40	1
2009																			
Total	49,361	34,409	1,223	3,678	3,729	3,665	3,707	3,701	3,652	3,644	3,641	3,651	119	14,952	4,080	3,809	3,541	3,432	90
White	26,702	18,316	556	1,932	1,952	1,924	1,960	1,978	1,977	1,984	1,995	2,021	35	8,385	2,188	2,116	2,034	2,022	26
Black	8,245	5,713	244	576	600	602	617	617	604	609	604	602	38	2,532	741	656	573	534	29
Hispanic	10,991	7,977	351	903	907	876	867	843	819	802	792	779	39	3,014	882	778	689	636	30
Asian	2,435	1,697	47	184	191	186	185	188	177	176	179	179	5	738	191	187	180	176	5
Pacific Islander	49	33		4	4	4	3	4	4	4	4	4	0	16	4	4	4	4	0
American Indian/Alaska Native	601	419	18	45	45	44	44	44	45	45	44	44	1	182	50	47	42	42	1
Two or more races[2]	338	254	6	34	31	29	29	27	26	24	23	22	0	84	24	21	20	19	0

See notes at end of table.

Table 203.65. Enrollment in public elementary and secondary schools, by level, grade, and race/ethnicity: Selected years, fall 1999 through fall 2017—Continued

[In thousands]

Year	All grades	Elementary													Secondary					
		Total	Pre-kinder-garten	Kinder-garten	1st grade	2nd grade	3rd grade	4th grade	5th grade	6th grade	7th grade	8th grade	Ungraded	Total	9th grade	10th grade	11th grade	12th grade	Ungraded[1]
1	2	3	4	5	6	7	8	9	10	11	12	13	14	15	16	17	18	19	20
2011																			
Total	**49,522**	**34,773**	**1,291**	**3,746**	**3,773**	**3,713**	**3,703**	**3,672**	**3,699**	**3,724**	**3,696**	**3,679**	**77**	**14,749**	**3,957**	**3,751**	**3,546**	**3,452**	**43**
White	25,602	17,654	563	1,845	1,865	1,866	1,875	1,872	1,908	1,933	1,944	1,951	31	7,948	2,049	2,008	1,946	1,928	18
Black	7,827	5,470	247	566	576	563	571	575	579	595	590	586	21	2,357	670	602	547	526	12
Hispanic	11,759	8,558	379	986	981	936	919	896	887	871	850	834	19	3,202	908	823	751	709	11
Asian	2,334	1,616	44	164	176	181	181	176	175	177	168	169	3	719	182	183	179	174	2
Pacific Islander	179	128	3	14	15	14	14	14	13	13	13	13	0	50	14	13	12	11	0
American Indian/Alaska Native	547	384	19	41	40	40	40	40	40	41	42	41	1	163	44	41	39	39	0
Two or more races	1,272	963	37	130	119	112	105	99	96	93	89	84	1	309	90	82	72	65	0
2013[3]																			
Total	**50,045**	**35,251**	**1,328**	**3,834**	**3,885**	**3,791**	**3,738**	**3,708**	**3,697**	**3,684**	**3,748**	**3,753**	**85**	**14,794**	**3,980**	**3,761**	**3,526**	**3,476**	**52**
White	25,160	17,390	577	1,828	1,861	1,832	1,831	1,851	1,863	1,864	1,912	1,934	37	7,770	2,018	1,960	1,884	1,886	22
Black	7,805	5,483	248	587	605	581	571	558	557	573	588	592	22	2,322	665	597	534	513	13
Hispanic	12,452	9,054	392	1,038	1,039	1,008	975	941	927	909	912	892	21	3,398	954	872	792	767	13
Asian	2,417	1,683	47	174	178	180	183	187	187	180	180	183	4	733	181	183	184	184	2
Pacific Islander	176	126	3	14	14	13	14	14	14	13	13	13	0	51	14	13	12	11	0
American Indian/Alaska Native	523	367	17	39	40	39	38	38	38	39	39	40	1	156	43	40	36	36	0
Two or more races	1,511	1,148	44	154	148	137	125	119	112	106	103	99	1	363	105	95	84	79	1
2015[3]																			
Total	**50,438**	**35,388**	**1,402**	**3,713**	**3,768**	**3,842**	**3,869**	**3,793**	**3,733**	**3,731**	**3,732**	**3,719**	**87**	**15,050**	**4,019**	**3,846**	**3,598**	**3,537**	**49**
White	24,644	16,972	600	1,742	1,768	1,804	1,829	1,814	1,816	1,842	1,860	1,863	34	7,672	1,978	1,942	1,872	1,860	20
Black	7,784	5,448	263	556	590	598	600	575	558	558	561	569	22	2,336	656	602	542	525	12
Hispanic	13,080	9,424	413	1,019	1,021	1,043	1,047	1,022	987	961	950	937	24	3,656	1,018	944	854	827	14
Asian	2,521	1,754	54	183	180	189	189	190	191	194	192	188	5	767	195	198	185	187	3
Pacific Islander	177	124	3	13	12	13	14	14	14	14	13	13	0	52	14	14	13	12	0
American Indian/Alaska Native	510	356	16	37	38	38	38	37	37	38	38	38	1	154	41	39	36	36	0
Two or more races	1,723	1,311	52	164	159	158	152	142	130	125	118	111	1	412	117	107	97	91	1
2017[3]																			
Total	**50,686**	**35,496**	**1,471**	**3,684**	**3,667**	**3,684**	**3,788**	**3,859**	**3,877**	**3,827**	**3,777**	**3,772**	**89**	**15,190**	**3,996**	**3,834**	**3,677**	**3,631**	**52**
White	24,124	16,623	627	1,711	1,703	1,708	1,751	1,796	1,821	1,812	1,816	1,843	34	7,501	1,920	1,873	1,840	1,849	20
Black	7,709	5,409	263	539	557	563	592	592	589	576	561	556	21	2,300	622	585	546	536	12
Hispanic	13,571	9,678	439	1,008	996	1,006	1,039	1,059	1,060	1,043	1,012	990	26	3,892	1,058	1,000	930	889	15
Asian	2,640	1,827	62	199	190	191	191	198	197	196	197	201	5	813	206	202	200	202	3
Pacific Islander	185	129	3	13	14	14	13	14	14	14	15	14	0	56	15	14	13	13	0
American Indian/Alaska Native	498	347	17	35	35	36	37	37	38	38	37	38	0	150	40	38	36	36	0
Two or more races	1,959	1,482	59	179	172	167	165	164	158	149	138	131	2	477	135	122	112	107	1

[1]Includes students reported as being enrolled in grade 13.
[2]For 2009, data on students of Two or more races were reported by only a small number of states. Therefore, the data are not comparable to the figures for later years.
[3]Includes imputations for prekindergarten enrollment in California and Oregon.
NOTE: Race categories exclude persons of Hispanic ethnicity. Enrollment data for students not reported by race/ethnicity were prorated by state and grade to match state totals. Prior to 2008, the survey did not yet include separate categories for "Asian" and "Pacific Islander" or a "Two or more races" category; each student could be assigned to only one of the available race categories. The total ungraded counts of students were prorated to the elementary and secondary levels based on prior reports. Detail may not sum to totals because of rounding.
SOURCE: U.S. Department of Education, National Center for Education Statistics, Common Core of Data (CCD), "State Nonfiscal Survey of Public Elementary/Secondary Education," 1999–2000 through 2017–18. (This table was prepared August 2019.)

Table 203.70. Percentage distribution of enrollment in public elementary and secondary schools, by race/ethnicity and state or jurisdiction: Fall 2000 and fall 2017

State or jurisdiction	Percentage distribution, fall 2000						Percentage distribution, fall 2017							
	Total	White	Black	Hispanic	Asian/ Pacific Islander	American Indian/ Alaska Native	Total	White	Black	Hispanic	Asian	Pacific Islander	American Indian/ Alaska Native	Two or more races
1	2	3	4	5	6	7	8	9	10	11	12	13	14	15
United States	**100.0**	**61.2**	**17.2**	**16.3**	**4.1**	**1.2**	**100.0**	**47.6**	**15.2**	**26.7**	**5.2**	**0.4**	**1.0**	**3.9**
Alabama	100.0	60.8	36.5	1.3	0.7	0.7	100.0	54.5	32.8	7.9	1.5	0.1	0.9	2.2
Alaska	100.0	61.5	4.6	3.4	5.5	25.0	100.0	47.6	2.9	6.7	5.9	2.9	22.9	11.1
Arizona	100.0	52.8	4.6	33.9	2.1	6.6	100.0	38.2	5.4	45.5	2.9	0.4	4.5	3.1
Arkansas	100.0	71.7	23.3	3.6	0.9	0.5	100.0	60.8	20.4	13.1	1.6	0.8	0.6	2.6
California	100.0	36.1	8.5	43.4	11.1	0.9	100.0	23.2	5.5	54.3	11.6	0.5	0.5	4.5
Colorado	100.0	68.2	5.7	22.0	2.9	1.2	100.0	53.4	4.6	33.7	3.2	0.3	0.7	4.2
Connecticut	100.0	70.1	13.7	13.1	2.8	0.3	100.0	53.6	12.8	24.8	5.1	0.1	0.3	3.3
Delaware	100.0	60.7	30.8	6.0	2.3	0.3	100.0	44.2	30.3	17.4	3.9	0.1	0.4	3.7
District of Columbia	100.0	4.5	84.6	9.2	1.6	0.1	100.0	11.1	68.5	16.3	1.6	0.1	0.2	2.2
Florida	100.0	53.3	25.2	19.4	1.9	0.3	100.0	38.0	22.1	33.1	2.7	0.2	0.3	3.5
Georgia	100.0	54.7	38.2	4.8	2.2	0.2	100.0	39.7	36.7	15.6	4.1	0.1	0.2	3.7
Hawaii	100.0	20.4	2.3	4.5	72.3	0.4	100.0	12.2	1.7	14.2	28.6	28.6	0.2	14.4
Idaho	100.0	86.0	0.7	10.7	1.2	1.4	100.0	75.4	1.1	18.1	1.2	0.3	1.1	2.7
Illinois	100.0	59.8	21.3	15.4	3.4	0.2	100.0	48.0	16.8	26.2	5.1	0.1	0.3	3.5
Indiana	100.0	83.6	11.7	3.5	1.0	0.2	100.0	67.9	12.6	11.9	2.4	0.1	0.2	4.9
Iowa	100.0	90.2	4.0	3.6	1.7	0.5	100.0	75.9	6.1	10.8	2.5	0.3	0.4	4.0
Kansas	100.0	78.7	8.9	8.9	2.2	1.3	100.0	64.2	6.9	19.8	2.8	0.2	1.0	5.2
Kentucky	100.0	87.5	10.7	1.0	0.6	0.2	100.0	76.8	10.5	6.7	1.8	0.1	0.1	3.9
Louisiana	100.0	48.9	47.8	1.4	1.3	0.6	100.0	44.7	43.6	6.9	1.6	0.1	0.7	2.5
Maine	100.0	96.5	1.2	0.6	1.0	0.7	100.0	89.3	3.6	2.2	1.5	0.1	0.8	2.5
Maryland	100.0	53.4	37.1	4.8	4.4	0.4	100.0	37.3	33.7	17.4	6.6	0.1	0.3	4.6
Massachusetts	100.0	76.1	8.5	10.7	4.4	0.3	100.0	60.2	9.0	20.0	6.8	0.1	0.2	3.6
Michigan	100.0	73.8	19.8	3.5	1.8	1.0	100.0	66.2	18.0	7.9	3.4	0.1	0.6	3.9
Minnesota	100.0	82.9	6.6	3.4	5.1	2.0	100.0	66.5	11.0	9.3	6.8	0.1	1.6	4.7
Mississippi	100.0	47.3	51.1	0.8	0.7	0.1	100.0	44.2	48.5	3.7	1.1	0.1	0.2	2.1
Missouri	100.0	79.3	17.4	1.8	1.2	0.3	100.0	71.1	15.9	6.4	2.0	0.3	0.4	3.9
Montana	100.0	86.2	0.6	1.7	1.0	10.5	100.0	78.3	0.9	4.6	0.8	0.2	11.6	3.6
Nebraska	100.0	83.0	6.7	7.3	1.5	1.5	100.0	66.5	6.7	18.8	2.8	0.1	1.4	3.8
Nevada	100.0	56.7	10.2	25.7	5.7	1.7	100.0	32.5	11.1	42.4	5.5	1.4	0.9	6.2
New Hampshire	100.0	95.5	1.1	1.8	1.3	0.2	100.0	85.5	2.0	5.6	3.3	0.1	0.3	3.3
New Jersey	100.0	60.3	17.9	15.3	6.3	0.2	100.0	43.6	15.3	28.7	10.0	0.2	0.1	2.0
New Mexico	100.0	35.3	2.4	50.2	1.1	11.1	100.0	23.2	1.9	61.7	1.1	0.1	10.0	1.9
New York	100.0	54.9	20.2	18.5	6.0	0.4	100.0	43.2	17.2	27.0	9.3	0.3	0.7	2.4
North Carolina	100.0	61.0	31.3	4.4	1.9	1.5	100.0	48.2	25.3	17.5	3.3	0.1	1.2	4.3
North Dakota	100.0	89.4	1.0	1.2	0.8	7.6	100.0	77.4	4.9	4.9	1.6	0.3	8.5	2.4
Ohio	100.0	80.7	16.3	1.7	1.1	0.1	100.0	69.9	16.6	5.7	2.4	0.1	0.1	5.2
Oklahoma	100.0	64.9	10.8	6.0	1.4	16.9	100.0	48.9	8.6	17.2	2.0	0.4	13.6	9.3
Oregon	100.0	80.4	2.9	10.5	4.0	2.1	100.0	62.4	2.3	23.0	4.0	0.7	1.3	6.1
Pennsylvania	100.0	78.2	15.1	4.5	2.0	0.1	100.0	65.8	14.7	11.4	3.9	0.1	0.2	3.9
Rhode Island	100.0	74.3	7.9	14.0	3.3	0.5	100.0	57.7	8.6	25.3	3.3	0.2	0.7	4.2
South Carolina	100.0	54.9	42.1	1.9	1.0	0.2	100.0	50.8	33.6	9.5	1.6	0.1	0.3	4.1
South Dakota	100.0	86.5	1.2	1.2	0.9	10.1	100.0	73.9	3.2	6.0	1.8	0.1	11.1	4.0
Tennessee	100.0	72.4	24.5	1.8	1.1	0.2	100.0	62.8	21.9	10.3	2.0	0.1	0.2	2.7
Texas	100.0	42.0	14.4	40.6	2.7	0.3	100.0	27.9	12.6	52.4	4.4	0.1	0.4	2.3
Utah	100.0	85.8	1.0	8.9	2.8	1.6	100.0	74.4	1.4	17.1	1.7	1.6	1.1	2.7
Vermont	100.0	96.3	1.1	0.6	1.4	0.6	100.0	90.2	2.1	2.0	2.0	0.1	0.2	3.5
Virginia	100.0	63.6	27.1	4.9	4.1	0.3	100.0	48.9	22.4	15.7	7.0	0.2	0.3	5.5
Washington	100.0	74.4	5.3	10.2	7.3	2.7	100.0	54.4	4.4	23.2	7.7	1.1	1.2	8.0
West Virginia	100.0	94.7	4.3	0.4	0.5	0.1	100.0	90.1	4.3	1.8	0.7	#	0.1	3.1
Wisconsin	100.0	80.7	10.0	4.5	3.3	1.4	100.0	69.9	9.2	12.0	4.0	0.1	1.1	3.8
Wyoming	100.0	87.9	1.2	6.9	0.9	3.1	100.0	77.9	1.1	13.7	0.8	0.1	3.7	2.6
Bureau of Indian Education	100.0	0.0	0.0	0.0	0.0	100.0	100.0	0.0	0.0	0.0	0.0	0.0	100.0	0.0
DoDEA[1]	100.0	56.9	23.1	11.4	7.9	0.8	—	—	—	—	—	—	—	—
Other jurisdictions														
American Samoa	100.0	0.0	0.0	0.0	100.0	0.0	100.0	0.1	#	#	0.4	99.4	#	0.0
Guam	100.0	1.7	0.3	0.2	97.7	0.1	100.0	0.6	0.1	0.1	22.3	74.3	0.1	2.5
Northern Marianas	100.0	0.3	#	0.0	99.7	0.0	—	—	—	—	—	—	—	—
Puerto Rico	100.0	0.0	0.0	100.0	0.0	0.0	100.0	0.1	#	99.8	#	#	0.1	0.0
U.S. Virgin Islands	100.0	0.8	85.8	13.1	0.2	0.1	100.0	1.7	77.0	20.2	0.6	0.1	0.1	0.3

—Not available.
#Rounds to zero.
[1]DoDEA = Department of Defense Education Activity. Includes both domestic and overseas schools.
NOTE: Percentage distribution based on students for whom race/ethnicity was reported, which may be less than the total number of students in the state. Race categories exclude persons of Hispanic ethnicity. Detail may not sum to totals because of rounding.

SOURCE: U.S. Department of Education, National Center for Education Statistics, Common Core of Data (CCD), "State Nonfiscal Survey of Public Elementary/Secondary Education," 2000–01 and 2017–18. (This table was prepared January 2020.)

Table 204.10. Number and percentage of public school students eligible for free or reduced-price lunch, by state: Selected years, 2000–01 through 2017–18

State	Number of students enrolled				Number of students eligible for free/reduced-price lunch				Percent of students eligible for free/reduced-price lunch			
	2000–01	2010–11	2016–17	2017–18	2000–01	2010–11	2016–17	2017–18	2000–01	2010–11	2016–17	2017–18
1	2	3	4	5	6	7	8	9	10	11	12	13
United States	46,579,068[1]	48,941,267	49,944,748	50,044,716	17,839,867[1]	23,544,479	26,113,604[1]	26,341,970[1]	38.3[1]	48.1	52.3[1]	52.6[1]
Alabama	728,351	730,427	744,809	742,437	335,143	402,386	384,199	415,423	46.0	55.1	51.6	56.0
Alaska	105,333	132,104	132,709	132,820	32,468	50,701	60,182	72,080	30.8	38.4	45.3	54.3
Arizona	877,696[2]	1,067,210	993,129	977,571	274,277[2]	482,044	566,549	538,290	31.2[2]	45.2	57.0	55.1
Arkansas	449,959	482,114	492,802	495,773	205,058	291,608	313,314[3]	315,203[3]	45.6	60.5	63.6[3]	63.6[3]
California	6,050,753	6,169,427	6,214,620	6,195,446	2,820,611	3,335,885	3,611,597	3,726,495	46.6	54.1	58.1	60.1
Colorado	724,349	842,864	904,798	910,050	195,148	336,426	381,537	380,318	26.9	39.9	42.2	41.8
Connecticut	562,179[2]	552,919	529,616	519,710	143,030[2]	190,554	188,877	188,482	25.4[2]	34.5	35.7	36.3
Delaware	114,676	128,342	136,217	136,041	37,766	61,564	65,563[4]	47,580[4]	32.9	48.0	48.1[4]	35.0[4]
District of Columbia	68,380	71,263	84,970	86,360	47,839	52,027	64,900[3,4]	65,961[3,4]	70.0	73.0	76.4[3,4]	76.4[3,4]
Florida	2,434,755	2,641,555	2,811,090	2,832,766	1,079,009	1,479,519	1,633,226	1,622,871	44.3	56.0	58.1	57.3
Georgia	1,444,937	1,676,419	1,763,540	1,768,562	624,511	961,954	1,092,777	1,076,613	43.2	57.4	62.0	60.9
Hawaii	184,357	179,601	181,550	180,837	80,657	84,106	86,376	85,219	43.8	46.8	47.6	47.1
Idaho	244,755	275,815	297,118	301,118	85,824	124,104	136,058	132,442	35.1	45.0	45.8	44.0
Illinois	2,048,792[2]	1,973,401	2,009,331	1,992,111	759,973[2]	921,471	1,008,830	983,855	37.1[2]	46.7	50.2	49.4
Indiana	977,219	1,038,817	1,048,952	1,053,841	285,267	485,728	502,844	525,526	29.2	46.8	47.9	49.9
Iowa	492,021	484,856	500,960	502,877	131,553	188,486	204,841	201,627	26.7	38.9	40.9	40.1
Kansas	462,594	479,953	489,706	490,629	154,693	228,852	235,849	233,302	33.4	47.7	48.2	47.6
Kentucky	626,723	673,128	683,844	680,860	298,334	380,773	401,614	406,314	47.6	56.6	58.7	59.7
Louisiana	741,162	695,772	716,248	715,096	433,068	460,546	451,173	387,083	58.4	66.2	63.0	54.1
Maine	198,532	183,477	175,383	175,304	60,162	78,915	79,819	78,522	30.3	43.0	45.5	44.8
Maryland	852,911	852,202	886,187	893,679	255,872	341,557	413,580	415,367	30.0	40.1	46.7	46.5
Massachusetts	979,590	955,301	953,693	953,645	237,871	326,849	380,744[4,5]	380,725[4,5]	24.3	34.2	39.9[4,5]	39.9[4,5]
Michigan	1,703,260	1,551,861	1,477,193	1,471,209	504,044	719,800	675,696	740,066	29.6	46.4	45.7	50.3
Minnesota	854,154	837,930	874,432	884,397	218,867	306,136	329,341	328,701	25.6	36.5	37.7	37.2
Mississippi	497,421	489,462	483,148	478,124	319,670	345,734	362,296	356,365	64.3	70.6	75.0	74.5
Missouri	912,247	902,375	913,838	910,283	315,608	406,358	481,683	478,503	34.6	45.0	52.7	52.6
Montana	154,438	140,497	146,213	146,550	47,415	57,836	66,649	64,961	30.7	41.2	45.6	44.3
Nebraska	286,138	298,276	319,147	323,728	87,045	127,114	142,555	148,540	30.4	42.6	44.7	45.9
Nevada	282,621	436,840	472,790	481,005	92,978	219,904	287,510	282,776	32.9	50.3	60.8	58.8
New Hampshire	206,919	194,001	179,762	178,306	31,212	48,904	49,058	47,169	15.1	25.2	27.3	26.5
New Jersey	1,312,983	1,356,882	1,370,824	1,370,584	357,728	444,735	519,298	519,524	27.2	32.8	37.9	37.9
New Mexico	320,303	335,810	332,184	333,879	174,939	227,077	237,331	245,797	54.6	67.6	71.4	73.6
New York	2,859,927	2,722,761	2,701,730	2,697,327	1,236,945	1,315,564	1,422,290	1,477,753	43.3	48.3	52.6	54.8
North Carolina	1,194,371	1,487,699	1,549,452	1,553,494	470,316	747,978	889,189	868,117	39.4	50.3	57.4	55.9
North Dakota	109,201	94,273	107,460	109,688	31,840	29,929	33,248	33,001	29.2	31.7	30.9	30.1
Ohio	1,745,237	1,747,851	1,707,469	1,701,472	494,829	745,121	757,120	782,651	28.4	42.6	44.3	46.0
Oklahoma	623,110	659,376	693,747	694,932	300,179	398,917	433,509	432,732	48.2	60.5	62.5	62.3
Oregon	535,617	553,468	552,350	553,257	186,203	280,174	279,145	272,748	34.8	50.6	50.5	49.3
Pennsylvania	1,798,977	1,742,608	1,572,026	1,601,823	510,121	686,641	747,388	794,648	28.4	39.4	47.5	49.6
Rhode Island	157,347	142,575	140,469	141,448	52,209	61,127	66,895	66,156	33.2	42.9	47.6	46.8
South Carolina	677,411	722,203	770,800	777,254	320,254	395,033	516,520	514,156	47.3	54.7	67.0	66.2
South Dakota	128,598	125,883	135,762	137,251	37,857	46,718	51,430	51,412	29.4	37.1	37.9	37.5
Tennessee	909,161[2]	987,078	997,148	994,568	436,298[2]	542,953	586,427[3,4]	584,910[3,4]	48.0[2]	55.0	58.8[3,4]	58.8[3,4]
Texas	4,059,353	4,916,401	5,360,055	5,400,720	1,823,029	2,471,212	3,159,896	3,169,088	44.9	50.3	59.0	58.7
Utah	470,265	585,552	645,030	666,841	135,428	223,943	235,042	227,388	28.8	38.2	36.4	34.1
Vermont	102,049	85,144	84,325	84,334	23,986	31,339	32,507	32,171	23.5	36.8	38.5	38.1
Virginia	1,067,710	1,250,206	1,273,127	1,278,044	320,233	458,879	525,022	560,281	30.0	36.7	41.2	43.8
Washington	1,004,770[2]	1,043,466	1,101,514	1,110,163	326,295[2]	418,065	480,171	477,543	32.5[2]	40.1	43.6	43.0
West Virginia	286,285	282,879	273,845	272,253	143,446	145,605	122,257	151,490[4]	50.1	51.5	44.6	55.6[4]
Wisconsin	859,276	872,164	863,557	860,067	219,276	342,660	323,368	319,045	25.5	39.3	37.4	37.1
Wyoming	89,895	88,779	94,079	94,182	43,483	32,968	36,314	34,980	48.4	37.1	38.6	37.1

[1]U.S. total includes imputation for nonreporting states.
[2]Imputation for survey nonresponse. State-level imputations for 2000–01 were based on the reported percentages for 2001–02 applied to the 2000–01 enrollments.
[3]Imputation for survey nonresponse. State-level imputations for 2016–17 and 2017–18 were based on the reported percentages for 2015–16 applied to the 2016–17 and 2017–18 enrollments.
[4]This state reported only the count of students who were eligible based on direct certification. Direct certification is the process by which children are certified for free meals based on household participation in one or more means-tested federal assistance programs—such as the Supplemental Nutrition Assistance Program (SNAP)—without the need for a household application.

[5]Imputation for survey nonresponse. State-level imputations for 2016–17 and 2017–18 were based on the reported percentages for 2014–15 (the most recent year for which percentages were reported) applied to the 2016–17 and 2017–18 enrollments.
NOTE: The National School Lunch Program (NSLP) is a federally assisted meal program. Table reflects counts of students enrolled in all schools for which both enrollment data and free/reduced-price lunch eligibility data were reported. Data for 2016–17 and 2017–18 include students whose NSLP eligibility has been determined through direct certification.
SOURCE: U.S. Department of Education, National Center for Education Statistics, Common Core of Data (CCD), "Public Elementary/Secondary School Universe Survey," 2000–01, 2010–11, 2016–17, and 2017–18. (This table was prepared February 2020.)

Table 204.20. English language learner (ELL) students enrolled in public elementary and secondary schools, by state: Selected years, fall 2000 through fall 2017

State	Number of ELL students							Number of ELL students as a percent of total enrollment						
	2000	2005	2010	2014	2015	2016	2017	2000	2005	2010	2014	2015	2016	2017
1	2	3	4	5	6	7	8	9	10	11	12	13	14	15
United States	3,793,764[1]	4,471,300[1]	4,455,860[1]	4,670,356	4,794,994	4,858,377	4,952,708	8.1[1]	9.2[1]	9.2[1]	9.5	9.8	9.9	10.1
Alabama	7,226	16,550	17,559	18,651	20,228	20,725	25,212	1.0	2.3	2.4	2.5	2.8	2.8	3.5
Alaska	19,337	20,743	14,963	15,089	15,203	14,662	15,623	14.5	15.4	11.3	11.8	11.8	11.3	12.1
Arizona	131,933	174,856	76,320	67,389	67,195	70,546	88,629	15.0	18.2	7.3	6.1	6.1	6.3	8.1
Arkansas	11,850	20,709	31,537	37,799	38,376	41,482	39,836	2.6	4.6	6.8	7.9	8.1	8.7	8.3
California	1,479,819	1,571,463	1,474,250[2]	1,392,295	1,307,804	1,260,672	1,197,296	24.5	25.2	23.3[2]	22.3	21.0	20.2	19.2
Colorado	60,852	99,797	99,804	104,979	104,289	105,810	104,299	8.4	13.3	13.0	12.2	12.0	12.1	11.9
Connecticut	20,499	29,789	30,428	34,855	35,064	36,573	38,089	3.6	5.2	5.3	6.6	6.7	7.1	7.4
Delaware	2,081	5,919	6,858	8,482	9,704	10,831	12,296	1.8	5.1	5.8	6.4	7.3	8.1	9.1
District of Columbia	8,594	5,001	5,261	7,330	6,215	6,574	8,145	12.5	6.6	6.9	10.6	8.7	9.0	10.9
Florida	187,566	221,705	229,758	252,318	268,189	288,921	280,540	7.7	8.7	8.7	9.4	9.8	10.5	10.1
Georgia	54,444	86,615	81,409	97,768	112,006	114,427	113,605	3.8	5.8	5.2	5.8	6.5	6.7	6.6
Hawaii	12,718	18,106	19,092	14,425	13,619	12,658	14,773	6.9	9.8	10.4	8.0	7.5	7.0	8.2
Idaho	18,097	18,184	15,393	12,755	13,492	16,187	17,849	7.4	7.3	6.0	4.4	4.7	5.5	6.0
Illinois	126,475	172,049[3]	174,340	210,221	194,040	197,496	217,790	6.2	8.3[3]	8.3	10.7	9.9	10.2	11.3
Indiana	30,953	56,510	49,573	57,839	50,717	47,676	55,607	3.1	5.6	4.9	5.6	4.9	4.6	5.4
Iowa	11,253	15,156	21,733	25,875	27,300	28,659	29,473	2.3	3.1	4.5	5.4	5.7	6.0	6.1
Kansas	14,878	24,671	39,323	47,209	52,789	54,667	49,238	3.2	5.2	8.4	9.9	11.1	11.5	10.3
Kentucky	4,030	10,138	16,351	20,716	22,067	21,897	25,653	0.6	1.5	2.4	3.1	3.3	3.3	3.9
Louisiana	10,293	12,006	11,698	18,665	23,924	22,843	25,060	1.4	1.6	1.6	2.7	3.5	3.3	3.6
Maine	2,410[3]	3,353	4,792	5,177	5,091	5,295	5,775	1.1[3]	1.6	2.4	2.9	2.9	3.0	3.3
Maryland	24,213	31,416	45,500	60,705	63,349	69,079	79,656	2.8	3.6	5.3	7.2	7.5	8.1	9.2
Massachusetts	49,077	51,618	54,988	75,531	82,779	86,658	93,217	5.0	5.3	5.6	8.1	8.9	9.3	10.0
Michigan	49,279[3]	65,419	56,474	81,678	89,597	94,921	97,837	2.9[3]	3.7	3.2	5.5	6.0	6.4	6.6
Minnesota	44,360	57,831	48,428	66,934	71,162	72,128	73,203	5.2	6.8	5.8	7.9	8.4	8.4	8.5
Mississippi	2,176	2,859	5,620	7,773	9,588	13,042	12,865	0.4	0.6	1.1	1.6	2.0	2.7	2.7
Missouri	10,238	18,745	21,918	29,144	29,690	30,950	33,925	1.1	2.0	2.4	3.3	3.4	3.5	3.8
Montana	7,713[3]	6,711	3,300	3,299	3,202	3,000	3,191	5.0[3]	4.5	2.2	2.3	2.2	2.1	2.2
Nebraska	11,276	17,449	20,077	17,528	20,900	22,507	23,332	3.9	6.1	7.0	5.9	7.0	7.4	7.6
Nevada	38,301[3]	63,856	83,352	75,282	78,416	75,430	81,635	11.2[3]	17.3	20.8	16.6	17.0	16.1	17.1
New Hampshire	2,728	2,876[3]	3,965	3,605	4,116	4,321	4,988	1.3	1.4[3]	1.9	2.0	2.3	2.4	2.8
New Jersey	55,463[3]	50,515	52,771	66,748	68,725	70,941	79,574	4.2[3]	3.7	3.8	5.0	5.1	5.3	5.9
New Mexico	68,679	62,682	52,557	48,906	52,821	44,899	52,892	21.4	19.6	16.1	14.7	16.1	13.7	16.3
New York	230,625	194,123	208,125	187,445	216,378	236,792	243,737	8.0	6.7	7.3	7.0	8.1	8.9	9.2
North Carolina	44,165	73,634	103,249	94,093	102,090	92,388	105,801	3.4	5.5	7.5	6.2	6.7	6.0	6.9
North Dakota	925[3]	2,213[3]	2,788	3,111	3,171	3,198	3,669	0.8[3]	2.1[3]	2.8	3.0	3.0	3.0	3.4
Ohio	25,658[3]	29,804	37,116	46,766	51,441	56,945	53,392	1.4[3]	1.6	2.0	2.8	3.1	3.4	3.2
Oklahoma	38,042	47,381	41,812	49,102	46,831	46,396	52,200	6.1	7.6	6.6	7.6	7.2	7.1	8.0
Oregon	43,416	64,676	58,946	49,485	52,786	56,598	51,036	7.9	11.7	10.7	8.7	9.2	9.8	8.8
Pennsylvania	42,412[3]	42,795[3]	47,014	51,623	52,624	56,454	61,724	2.3[3]	2.4[3]	2.6	3.0	3.1	3.3	3.6
Rhode Island	10,245	7,468	7,655	10,066	10,550	11,057	12,620	6.5	4.7	4.9	7.2	7.6	7.9	9.0
South Carolina	5,121	14,388	36,379	42,480	42,574	44,301	45,574	0.8	2.1	5.2	5.8	5.8	5.9	6.1
South Dakota	4,270	5,110	4,383	4,679	4,598	4,678	5,452	3.3	4.0	3.5	3.6	3.5	3.5	4.1
Tennessee	26,452[3]	28,251[3]	29,681	36,398	40,637	43,277	44,790	3.0[3]	3.1[3]	3.2	3.8	4.2	4.4	4.6
Texas	570,453	711,737	738,663	814,945	892,082	922,012	926,325	14.1	16.7	16.8	16.3	17.6	18.0	18.0
Utah	38,998	49,973	42,804	38,543	42,815	41,339	46,220	8.2	10.3	8.7	6.2	6.8	6.4	7.1
Vermont	942	1,775	1,510	1,439	1,448	1,506	1,770	0.9	1.8	1.5	1.8	1.8	1.9	2.2
Virginia	36,802	72,420	88,033	97,871	109,104	100,814	114,739	3.2	6.2	7.3	7.8	8.7	8.0	9.1
Washington	70,431[3]	75,103	90,282	107,197	112,763	122,408	127,777	7.0[3]	7.4	8.9	10.1	10.5	11.3	11.7
West Virginia	920	1,944	1,788	2,707	2,812	2,546	2,035	0.3	0.7	0.6	1.0	1.1	1.0	0.8
Wisconsin	22,542	30,130	43,638	42,729	45,669	46,342	49,905	2.6	3.4	5.0	5.2	5.6	5.7	6.2
Wyoming	2,534	3,077	2,602	2,707	2,964	2,849	2,839	2.8	3.6	3.1	2.9	3.1	3.0	3.0

[1]U.S. total includes imputation for nonreporting states.

[2]Data are from U.S. Department of Education, National Center for Education Statistics, EDFacts file 046, Data Group 123, extracted October 25, 2017, from the EDFacts Data Warehouse (internal U.S. Department of Education source).

[3]Imputation for survey nonresponse. State-level imputations were based on the percentages reported by the state for other years applied to the enrollment for the given year.

NOTE: Data for 2009 and earlier years may include prekindergarten ELL students. Starting with 2010, states were instructed to exclude prekindergarten ELL students from EDFacts reporting. Data for 2014 and earlier years include only those ELL students who participated in ELL programs. Starting with 2015, data include all ELL students, regardless of program participation. Counts and percentages in this table are aggregated from data collected at the school district level and may differ from those in tables based on data collected at other levels.

SOURCE: U.S. Department of Education, National Center for Education Statistics, Common Core of Data (CCD), "Local Education Agency Universe Survey," 2000–01 through 2017–18. (This table was prepared September 2019.)

Table 204.30.   Children 3 to 21 years old served under Individuals with Disabilities Education Act (IDEA), Part B, by type of disability: Selected years, 1976–77 through 2018–19

Type of disability	1976–77	1980–81	1990–91	2000–01	2008–09[1]	2009–10	2010–11	2011–12	2012–13	2013–14	2014–15	2015–16	2016–17[2,3]	2017–18[3,4]	2018–19[2]
1	2	3	4	5	6	7	8	9	10	11	12	13	14	15	16
	Number of children served (in thousands)														
All disabilities	**3,694**	**4,144**	**4,710**	**6,296**	**6,483**	**6,481**	**6,436**	**6,401**	**6,429**	**6,464**	**6,555**	**6,677**	**6,802**	**6,964**	**7,134**
Autism	—	—	—	93	336	378	417	455	498	538	576	617	661	710	762
Deaf-blindness	—	3	1	1	2	2	2	2	1	1	1	1	1	1	2
Developmental delay	—	—	—	213	354	368	382	393	402	410	419	434	446	461	479
Emotional disturbance	283	347	389	480	420	407	390	373	362	354	349	347	348	353	358
Hearing impairment	88	79	58	77	78	79	78	78	77	77	76	75	75	75	74
Intellectual disability	961	830	534	624	478	463	448	435	430	425	423	425	431	436	439
Multiple disabilities	—	68	96	131	130	131	130	132	133	132	132	131	132	132	133
Orthopedic impairment	87	58	49	82	70	65	63	61	59	56	52	47	42	41	39
Other health impairment[5]	141	98	55	303	659	689	716	743	779	817	862	909	955	1,002	1,049
Preschool disabled[6]	†	†	390	†	†	†	†	†	†	†	†	†	†	†	†
Specific learning disability	796	1,462	2,129	2,860	2,476	2,431	2,361	2,303	2,277	2,264	2,278	2,298	2,318	2,342	2,368
Speech or language impairment	1,302	1,168	985	1,388	1,426	1,416	1,396	1,373	1,356	1,334	1,332	1,337	1,337	1,357	1,378
Traumatic brain injury	—	—	—	16	26	25	26	26	26	26	26	27	27	27	27
Visual impairment	38	31	23	29	29	29	28	28	28	28	28	27	27	27	27
	Percentage distribution of children served														
All disabilities	**100.0**	**100.0**	**100.0**	**100.0**	**100.0**	**100.0**	**100.0**	**100.0**	**100.0**	**100.0**	**100.0**	**100.0**	**100.0**	**100.0**	**100.0**
Autism	—	—	—	1.5	5.2	5.8	6.5	7.1	7.8	8.3	8.8	9.2	9.7	10.2	10.7
Deaf-blindness	—	0.1	#	#	#	#	#	#	#	#	#	#	#	#	#
Developmental delay	—	—	—	3.4	5.5	5.7	5.9	6.1	6.2	6.3	6.4	6.5	6.6	6.6	6.7
Emotional disturbance	7.7	8.4	8.3	7.6	6.5	6.3	6.1	5.8	5.6	5.5	5.3	5.2	5.1	5.1	5.0
Hearing impairment	2.4	1.9	1.2	1.2	1.2	1.2	1.2	1.2	1.2	1.2	1.2	1.1	1.1	1.1	1.0
Intellectual disability	26.0	20.0	11.3	9.9	7.4	7.1	7.0	6.8	6.7	6.6	6.4	6.4	6.3	6.3	6.2
Multiple disabilities	—	1.6	2.0	2.1	2.0	2.0	2.0	2.1	2.1	2.0	2.0	2.0	1.9	1.9	1.9
Orthopedic impairment	2.4	1.4	1.0	1.3	1.1	1.0	1.0	1.0	0.9	0.9	0.8	0.7	0.6	0.6	0.5
Other health impairment[5]	3.8	2.4	1.2	4.8	10.2	10.6	11.1	11.6	12.1	12.6	13.2	13.6	14.0	14.4	14.7
Preschool disabled[6]	†	†	8.3	†	†	†	†	†	†	†	†	†	†	†	†
Specific learning disability	21.5	35.3	45.2	45.4	38.2	37.5	36.7	36.0	35.4	35.0	34.8	34.4	34.1	33.6	33.2
Speech or language impairment	35.2	28.2	20.9	22.0	22.0	21.8	21.7	21.4	21.1	20.6	20.3	20.0	19.7	19.5	19.3
Traumatic brain injury	—	—	—	0.2	0.4	0.4	0.4	0.4	0.4	0.4	0.4	0.4	0.4	0.4	0.4
Visual impairment	1.0	0.7	0.5	0.5	0.4	0.4	0.4	0.4	0.4	0.4	0.4	0.4	0.4	0.4	0.4
	Number of children served as a percent of total enrollment[7]														
All disabilities	**8.3**	**10.1**	**11.4**	**13.3**	**13.2**	**13.1**	**13.0**	**12.9**	**12.9**	**12.9**	**13.0**	**13.2**	**13.4**	**13.7**	**14.1**
Autism	—	—	—	0.2	0.7	0.8	0.8	0.9	1.0	1.1	1.1	1.2	1.3	1.4	1.5
Deaf-blindness	—	#	#	#	#	#	#	#	#	#	#	#	#	#	#
Developmental delay	—	—	—	0.5	0.7	0.7	0.8	0.8	0.8	0.8	0.8	0.9	0.9	0.9	0.9
Emotional disturbance	0.6	0.8	0.9	1.0	0.9	0.8	0.8	0.8	0.7	0.7	0.7	0.7	0.7	0.7	0.7
Hearing impairment	0.2	0.2	0.1	0.2	0.2	0.2	0.2	0.2	0.2	0.2	0.2	0.1	0.1	0.1	0.1
Intellectual disability	2.2	2.0	1.3	1.3	1.0	0.9	0.9	0.9	0.9	0.9	0.8	0.8	0.9	0.9	0.9
Multiple disabilities	—	0.2	0.2	0.3	0.3	0.3	0.3	0.3	0.3	0.3	0.3	0.3	0.3	0.3	0.3
Orthopedic impairment	0.2	0.1	0.1	0.2	0.1	0.1	0.1	0.1	0.1	0.1	0.1	0.1	0.1	0.1	0.1
Other health impairment[5]	0.3	0.2	0.1	0.6	1.3	1.4	1.4	1.5	1.6	1.6	1.7	1.8	1.9	2.0	2.1
Preschool disabled[6]	†	†	0.9	†	†	†	†	†	†	†	†	†	†	†	†
Specific learning disability	1.8	3.6	5.2	6.1	5.0	4.9	4.8	4.7	4.6	4.5	4.5	4.6	4.6	4.6	4.7
Speech or language impairment	2.9	2.9	2.4	2.9	2.9	2.9	2.8	2.8	2.7	2.7	2.6	2.7	2.6	2.7	2.7
Traumatic brain injury	—	—	—	#	0.1	0.1	0.1	0.1	0.1	0.1	0.1	0.1	0.1	0.1	0.1
Visual impairment	0.1	0.1	0.1	0.1	0.1	0.1	0.1	0.1	0.1	0.1	0.1	0.1	0.1	0.1	0.1

—Not available.
†Not applicable.
#Rounds to zero.
[1]Data do not include Vermont, for which 2007–08 and 2008–09 data were not available. In 2006–07, the total number of 3- to 21-year-olds served in Vermont was 14,010.
[2]Data in the 2016–17, 2017–18, and 2018–19 columns include 2015–16 data for 3- to 21-year-olds in Wisconsin because 2016–17, 2017–18, and 2018–19 data were not available for children served in Wisconsin.
[3]Data in the 2016–17 column include 2015–16 data for 3- to 5-year-olds in Nebraska because 2016–17 data were not available for children in that age group served in Nebraska.
[4]Data in the 2017–18 column include 2016–17 data for 3- to 5-year-olds in Minnesota and 6- to 21-year-olds in Maine and Vermont because 2017–18 data were not available for children in those age groups served in those states.
[5]Other health impairments include having limited strength, vitality, or alertness due to chronic or acute health problems such as a heart condition, tuberculosis, rheumatic fever, nephritis, asthma, sickle cell anemia, hemophilia, epilepsy, lead poisoning, leukemia, or diabetes.
[6]For 1990–91, preschool children are not included in the counts by disability condition but are separately reported. For other years, preschool children are included in the counts by disability condition.

[7]Based on total public school enrollment in prekindergarten through grade 12. For total public school enrollment, see table 203.20.
NOTE: Prior to October 1994, children and youth with disabilities were served under Chapter 1 of the Elementary and Secondary Education Act (ESEA) as well as under the Individuals with Disabilities Education Act (IDEA), Part B. Data reported in this table for years prior to 1994–95 include children ages 0–21 served under Chapter 1 of ESEA. Data are for the 50 states and the District of Columbia only. Increases since 1987–88 are due in part to new legislation enacted in fall 1986, which added a mandate for public school special education services for 3- to 5-year-old children with disabilities. Detail may not sum to totals because of rounding.
SOURCE: U.S. Department of Education, Office of Special Education Programs, *Annual Report to Congress on the Implementation of the Individuals with Disabilities Education Act,* selected years, 1979 through 2006; and Individuals with Disabilities Education Act (IDEA) database, retrieved February 20, 2020, from https://www2.ed.gov/programs/osepidea/618-data/state-level-data-files/index.html#bcc. National Center for Education Statistics, *Statistics of Public Elementary and Secondary School Systems,* 1977–78 and 1980–81; Common Core of Data (CCD), "State Nonfiscal Survey of Public Elementary/Secondary Education," 1990–91 through 2018–19; and National Elementary and Secondary Enrollment Projection Model, 1972 through 2029. (This table was prepared February 2020.)

Table 204.40. Children 3 to 21 years old served under Individuals with Disabilities Education Act (IDEA), Part B, by race/ethnicity and age group: 2000–01 through 2018–19

Age group and year	Total	White	Black	Hispanic	Asian	Pacific Islander	American Indian/ Alaska Native	Two or more races
1	2	3	4	5	6	7	8	9
	Number of children served							
3 to 21 years old								
2000–01	6,295,709	3,957,589	1,259,348	877,655	121,044	([1])	80,073	—
2001–02	6,407,417	3,989,528	1,281,803	928,776	123,434	([1])	83,876	—
2002–03	6,522,977	4,014,340	1,311,270	980,590	130,252	([1])	86,525	—
2003–04	6,633,902	4,035,880	1,334,666	1,035,463	137,544	([1])	90,349	—
2004–05	6,718,630	4,044,491	1,355,550	1,081,697	144,339	([1])	92,553	—
2005–06	6,712,614	4,003,865	1,346,177	1,119,140	149,954	([1])	93,478	—
2006–07	6,686,386	3,948,853	1,335,870	1,154,217	153,265	([1])	94,181	—
2007–08[2]	6,574,368	3,833,922	1,307,462	1,181,130	158,623	([1])	93,231	—
2008–09[2]	6,461,938	3,725,896	1,273,996	1,200,290	162,630	([1])	93,672	5,454[3]
2009–10	6,461,226	3,659,194	1,262,799	1,252,493	167,144	([1])	92,646	26,950[3]
2010–11	6,435,141	3,518,169	1,214,849	1,310,031	145,896	19,581	91,258	135,357
2011–12[4]	6,401,238	3,436,105	1,196,679	1,352,435	147,697	19,203	88,665	160,458
2012–13[4]	6,429,331	3,396,135	1,189,148	1,406,540	150,913	20,343	86,884	180,268
2013–14[4]	6,464,096	3,356,261	1,191,817	1,469,282	155,668	19,606	86,307	185,274
2014–15[4]	6,555,291	3,350,084	1,199,743	1,531,923	161,250	20,227	86,226	205,980
2015–16[4]	6,676,974	3,366,701	1,208,510	1,602,140	167,263	20,408	87,870	224,911
2016–17[4,5,6]	6,802,402	3,374,045	1,219,376	1,679,626	174,486	20,525	87,724	247,278
2017–18[4,5,7,8]	6,964,424	3,409,308	1,234,609	1,758,498	184,409	20,807	88,870	268,565
2018–19[4,5]	7,134,248	3,443,719	1,251,038	1,844,017	192,918	20,640	90,489	291,673
3 to 5 years old								
2000–01	592,090	400,650	93,281	78,070	13,203	([1])	6,886	—
2010–11	723,793	416,034	102,097	153,033	23,189	2,159	9,141	18,140
2017–18[4,5,7]	793,039	416,222	104,229	195,242	32,242	1,964	8,775	34,378
2018–19[4,5]	818,575	423,308	106,370	206,795	33,591	2,065	9,554	36,960
6 to 21 years old								
2000–01	5,703,619	3,556,939	1,166,067	799,585	107,841	([1])	73,187	—
2010–11	5,711,348	3,102,135	1,112,752	1,156,998	122,707	17,422	82,117	117,217
2017–18[4,5,8]	6,171,385	2,993,086	1,130,380	1,563,256	152,167	18,843	80,095	234,187
2018–19[4,5]	6,315,673	3,020,411	1,144,668	1,637,222	159,327	18,575	80,935	254,713
	Percentage distribution of children served							
3 to 21 years old								
2000–01	100.0	62.9	20.0	13.9	1.9	([1])	1.3	—
2001–02	100.0	62.3	20.0	14.5	1.9	([1])	1.3	—
2002–03	100.0	61.5	20.1	15.0	2.0	([1])	1.3	—
2003–04	100.0	60.8	20.1	15.6	2.1	([1])	1.4	—
2004–05	100.0	60.2	20.2	16.1	2.1	([1])	1.4	—
2005–06	100.0	59.6	20.1	16.7	2.2	([1])	1.4	—
2006–07	100.0	59.1	20.0	17.3	2.3	([1])	1.4	—
2007–08[2]	100.0	58.3	19.9	18.0	2.4	([1])	1.4	—
2008–09[2]	100.0	57.7	19.7	18.6	2.5	([1])	1.4	0.1[3]
2009–10	100.0	56.6	19.5	19.4	2.6	([1])	1.4	0.4[3]
2010–11	100.0	54.7	18.9	20.4	2.3	0.3	1.4	2.1
2011–12	100.0	53.7	18.7	21.1	2.3	0.3	1.4	2.5
2012–13	100.0	52.8	18.5	21.9	2.3	0.3	1.4	2.8
2013–14	100.0	51.9	18.4	22.7	2.4	0.3	1.3	2.9
2014–15	100.0	51.1	18.3	23.4	2.5	0.3	1.3	3.1
2015–16	100.0	50.4	18.1	24.0	2.5	0.3	1.3	3.4
2016–17[5,6]	100.0	49.6	17.9	24.7	2.6	0.3	1.3	3.6
2017–18[5,7,8]	100.0	49.0	17.7	25.2	2.6	0.3	1.3	3.9
2018–19[5]	100.0	48.3	17.5	25.8	2.7	0.3	1.3	4.1
	Number of children served as a percent of total enrollment[9]							
3 to 21 years old								
2000–01	13.3	13.7	15.5	11.4	6.2	([1])	14.6	—
2001–02	13.4	13.9	15.7	11.4	6.1	([1])	14.9	—
2002–03	13.5	14.0	15.8	11.4	6.2	([1])	14.8	—
2003–04	13.7	14.2	16.0	11.5	6.4	([1])	15.2	—
2004–05	13.8	14.3	16.1	11.5	6.5	([1])	15.7	—
2005–06	13.7	14.3	15.9	11.4	6.6	([1])	15.6	—
2006–07	13.6	14.2	15.9	11.3	6.6	([1])	15.8	—
2007–08[2]	13.3	14.0	15.6	11.3	6.6	([1])	15.7	—
2008–09[2]	13.1	13.8	15.2	11.4	6.6	([1])	15.9	2.2[3]
2009–10	13.1	13.7	15.2	11.5	6.7	([1])	15.6	8.0[3]
2010–11	13.0	13.6	15.4	11.5	6.4	11.5	16.2	11.7
2011–12	12.9	13.4	15.3	11.5	6.4	10.8	16.2	12.6
2012–13	12.9	13.4	15.2	11.7	6.4	11.3	16.3	13.0
2013–14	12.9	13.4	15.3	11.8	6.5	11.2	16.5	12.3
2014–15	13.0	13.4	15.4	12.0	6.5	11.5	16.6	12.8
2015–16	13.2	13.7	15.5	12.2	6.6	11.6	17.2	13.0
2016–17[5,6]	13.4	13.8	15.7	12.6	6.8	11.1	17.2	13.4
2017–18[5,7,8]	13.7	14.1	16.0	13.0	7.1	10.9	17.5	13.8
2018–19[5]	14.1	14.4	16.3	13.5	7.2	11.1	18.4	14.2

—Not available.
[1]Included under Asian.
[2]Data do not include Vermont, for which 2007–08 and 2008–09 data were not available.
[3]For 2008–09 and 2009–10, data on children of Two or more races were reported by only a small number of states. Therefore, these data are not comparable to figures for later years.
[4]For 2011–12 and later years, the total column shows the overall counts of children as reported by the 50 states and the District of Columbia rather than the sum of counts reported for individual racial/ethnic groups. (Due to data limitations, summing the data for the racial/ethnic groups can result in overcounts. For 2017–18, summing these data would result in a total overcount of 13 children in the 3- to 5-year-old age group and 629 children in the 6- to 21-year-old age group. For 2018–19, summing these data would result in a total overcount of 68 children in the 3-to 5-year-old age group and 178 children in the 6- to 21-year-old age group.)
[5]Includes 2015–16 data for children served in Wisconsin. More recent data were not available for children in any age group served in Wisconsin.
[6]Includes 2015–16 data for 3- to 5-year-olds served in Nebraska because 2016–17 data were not available.

[7]Includes 2016–17 data for 3- to 5-year-olds served in Minnesota because 2017–18 data were not available.
[8]Includes 2016–17 data for 6- to 21-year-olds served in Maine and Vermont because 2017–18 data were not available.
[9]Based on total public school enrollment in prekindergarten through grade 12 by race/ethnicity. For total public school enrollment by race/ethnicity, see table 203.60.
NOTE: Data include only those children served for whom race/ethnicity was reported. Race categories exclude persons of Hispanic ethnicity. Detail may not sum to totals because of rounding.
SOURCE: U.S. Department of Education, Office of Special Education Programs, Individuals with Disabilities Education Act (IDEA) database, retrieved February 20, 2020, from https://www2.ed.gov/programs/osepidea/618-data/state-level-data-files/index.html#bcc. National Center for Education Statistics, Common Core of Data (CCD), "State Nonfiscal Survey of Public Elementary and Secondary Education," 2000–01 through 2018–19; and National Elementary and Secondary Enrollment Projection Model, 1972 through 2029. (This table was prepared February 2020.)

Table 204.70. Number and percentage of children served under Individuals with Disabilities Education Act (IDEA), Part B, by age group and state or jurisdiction: Selected years, 1990–91 through 2018–19

State or jurisdiction	3- to 21-year-olds served								3- to 5-year-olds served					
	1990–91	2000–01	2010–11	2015–16	2017–18[1]	2018–19[1]	As a percent of public school enrollment, 2018–19[2]	Percent change in number served, 2000–01 to 2018–19	1990–91	2000–01	2010–11	2015–16	2017–18[1]	2018–19[1]
1	2	3	4	5	6	7	8	9	10	11	12	13	14	15
United States	4,710,089	6,295,816	6,434,916	6,676,974	6,964,424	7,134,248	14.1	13.3	389,751	592,087	723,738	746,499	793,039	818,575
Alabama	94,601	99,828	82,286	84,278	90,319	93,472	12.7	-6.4	7,154	7,554	7,492	7,368	7,827	8,036
Alaska	14,390	17,691	18,048	18,390	19,148	19,479	14.6	10.1	1,458	1,637	2,104	2,115	2,430	2,477
Arizona	56,629	96,442	125,816	132,592	140,702	144,812	13.0	50.2	4,330	9,144	14,756	15,328	16,517	16,746
Arkansas	47,187	62,222	64,881	68,178	72,835	74,863	15.1	20.3	4,626	9,376	13,034	12,981	13,716	13,497
California	468,420	645,287	672,174	727,718	767,562	788,268	12.5	22.2	39,627	57,651	72,404	78,610	83,853	86,456
Colorado	56,336	78,715	84,710	95,101	102,240	105,186	11.5	33.6	4,128	8,202	11,797	12,774	14,293	14,471
Connecticut	63,886	73,886	68,167	75,030	79,758	82,336	15.7	11.4	5,466	7,172	7,933	8,691	9,120	9,785
Delaware	14,208	16,760	18,608	20,742	23,196	24,382	17.8	45.5	1,493	1,652	2,123	2,030	2,616	2,801
District of Columbia	6,290	10,559	11,947	12,258	13,399	14,113	16.2	33.7	411	374	957	1,471	1,789	1,895
Florida	234,509	367,335	368,808	372,476	389,626	405,796	14.2	10.5	14,883	30,660	36,027	39,359	39,862	42,076
Georgia	101,762	171,292	177,544	202,314	214,267	219,111	12.4	27.9	7,098	16,560	15,911	18,201	18,833	18,661
Hawaii	12,705	23,951	19,716	19,223	19,276	19,592	10.8	-18.2	809	1,919	2,398	2,444	2,469	2,555
Idaho	21,703	29,174	27,388	29,718	32,908	34,310	11.3	17.6	2,815	3,591	3,596	3,331	3,733	3,866
Illinois	236,060	297,316	302,830	296,784	295,066	297,960	14.9	0.2	22,997	28,787	36,488	37,878	37,137	38,046
Indiana	112,949	156,320	166,073	171,368	176,104	178,511	16.9	14.2	7,243	15,101	18,725	18,049	18,644	18,914
Iowa	59,787	72,461	68,501	63,822	65,935	67,990	13.3	-6.2	5,421	5,580	7,378	6,226	6,976	7,429
Kansas	44,785	61,267	66,873	70,762	73,729	75,511	15.3	23.2	3,881	7,728	10,604	11,387	11,772	12,105
Kentucky	78,853	94,572	102,370	99,283	104,270	106,158	15.6	12.3	10,440	16,372	17,963	17,044	18,070	18,232
Louisiana	72,825	97,938	82,943	84,221	84,473	86,829	12.2	-11.3	6,703	9,957	10,427	10,430	9,885	10,484
Maine	27,987	35,633	32,261	32,531	33,004[3]	34,382	19.2	-3.5	2,895	3,978	3,824	3,512	3,384	3,642
Maryland	88,017	112,077	103,490	105,440	108,491	110,563	12.3	-1.4	7,163	10,003	12,875	13,473	14,300	14,645
Massachusetts	149,743	162,216	167,526	168,199	173,762	176,627	18.3	8.9	12,141	14,328	16,662	16,802	18,022	18,377
Michigan	166,511	221,456	218,957	197,316	198,751	199,794	13.3	-9.8	14,547	19,937	23,183	20,573	21,624	22,073
Minnesota	79,013	109,880	122,850	128,218	135,386[4]	141,454	15.9	28.7	8,646	11,522	15,076	15,843	16,586[4]	18,353
Mississippi	60,872	62,281	64,038	66,799	69,197	69,433	14.7	11.5	5,642	6,944	10,191	8,660	8,400	8,261
Missouri	101,166	137,381	127,164	126,328	131,114	132,286	14.5	-3.7	4,100	11,307	15,891	17,123	18,400	18,253
Montana	16,955	19,313	16,761	17,387	18,803	19,380	12.9	0.3	1,751	1,635	1,656	1,592	1,660	1,722
Nebraska	32,312	42,793	44,299	47,795	50,415	52,005	16.0	21.5	2,512	3,724	5,050	5,557	6,217	6,551
Nevada	18,099	38,160	48,148	55,452	60,123	60,120	12.2	57.5	1,401	3,676	6,947	8,838	8,984	8,443
New Hampshire	19,049	30,077	29,920	28,806	29,233	29,920	16.8	-0.5	1,468	2,387	3,135	3,335	3,519	3,677
New Jersey	178,870	221,715	232,002	232,401	238,178	241,063	17.2	8.7	14,741	16,361	17,073	18,674	19,846	20,701
New Mexico	36,000	52,256	46,628	49,667	52,838	53,996	16.3	3.3	2,210	4,970	5,224	4,245	4,413	6,607
New York	307,366	441,333	454,542	499,551	522,221	530,702	19.5	20.2	26,266	51,665	64,923	67,067	71,893	73,348
North Carolina	122,942	173,067	185,107	198,808	200,905	201,658	13.0	16.5	10,516	17,361	18,433	19,070	19,899	20,111
North Dakota	12,294	13,652	13,170	13,953	15,153	15,902	14.3	16.5	1,164	1,247	1,714	1,972	2,189	2,343
Ohio	205,440	237,643	259,454	253,896	266,670	271,090	16.0	14.1	12,487	18,664	22,454	21,897	25,247	26,419
Oklahoma	65,457	85,577	97,250	108,459	112,080	115,289	16.5	34.7	5,163	6,393	8,298	9,023	9,751	10,309
Oregon	54,422	75,204	81,050	84,517	87,156	89,125	14.6	18.5	2,854	6,926	9,392	10,374	11,331	11,693
Pennsylvania	214,254	242,655	295,080	303,633	320,817	327,908	19.1	35.1	17,982	21,477	31,072	33,022	36,340	37,012
Rhode Island	20,646	30,727	25,332	23,515	23,748	24,170	16.9	-21.3	1,682	2,614	2,945	3,022	3,168	3,235
South Carolina	77,367	105,922	100,289	101,776	104,698	106,521	13.7	0.6	7,948	11,775	11,083	9,432	9,568	9,792
South Dakota	14,726	16,825	18,026	19,527	21,190	21,712	15.6	29.0	2,105	2,286	2,738	2,627	2,941	2,923
Tennessee	104,853	125,863	120,263	129,386	129,319	130,229	13.0	3.5	7,487	12,866	13,096	12,905	13,950	14,592
Texas	344,529	491,642	442,019	463,238	498,588	532,185	9.8	8.2	24,848	36,442	41,494	43,787	49,681	53,750
Utah	46,606	53,921	70,278	79,932	84,196	86,532	12.8	60.5	3,424	5,785	8,990	10,007	10,731	10,741
Vermont	12,160	13,623	13,936	13,903	14,482[3]	14,911	17.1	9.5	1,097	1,237	1,762	1,774	2,005	2,050
Virginia	112,072	162,212	162,338	164,757	172,370	175,450	13.6	8.2	9,892	14,444	17,081	16,755	18,296	18,807
Washington	83,545	118,851	127,978	135,757	143,498	147,628	13.2	24.2	9,558	11,760	14,275	15,361	16,425	17,140
West Virginia	42,428	50,333	45,007	45,297	46,810	47,183	17.5	-6.3	2,923	5,445	5,607	5,004	5,219	5,245
Wisconsin	85,651	125,358	124,722	120,864	120,864[5]	120,864[5]	14.1	-3.6	10,934	14,383	16,079	16,089	16,089[5]	16,089[5]
Wyoming	10,852	13,154	15,348	15,608	15,551	15,487	16.5	17.7	1,221	1,695	3,398	3,367	3,419	3,419
Bureau of Indian Education	6,997	8,448	6,801	6,309	6,285	6,754	—	-20.1	1,092	338	396	266	250	240
Other jurisdictions	38,986	70,670	131,847	128,268	110,613	107,736	—	52.4	3,892	8,168	14,505	16,743	12,840	12,203
American Samoa	363	697	935	666	636	561	—	-19.5	48	48	142	50	37	56
Guam	1,750	2,267	2,003	2,036	2,015	1,929	—	-14.9	198	205	165	159	167	149
Northern Marianas	411	569	944	886	956	964	—	69.4	211	53	104	93	116	108
Palau	—	131	—	97	74	81	—	-38.2	—	10	—	6	3	1
Puerto Rico	35,129	65,504	126,560	123,376	105,827	103,137	—	57.5	3,345	7,746	13,952	16,303	12,391	11,799
U.S. Virgin Islands	1,333	1,502	1,405	1,207	1,105	1,064	—	-29.2	90	106	142	132	126	90

—Not available.
[1]Includes some data for 2015–16 or 2016–17 due to unavailability of 2017–18 and 2018–19 data for specific states, as noted below.
[2]Based on projected total public school enrollment in prekindergarten through grade 12. For total public school enrollment, see table 203.20.
[3]Data for 6- to 21-year-olds are for 2016–17 instead of 2017–18 because 2017–18 data for this age group were not available for this state.
[4]Data for 3- to 5-year-olds are for 2016–17 instead of 2017–18 because 2017–18 data for this age group were not available for this state.
[5]Data are for 2015–16 because 2017–18 and 2018–19 data were not available for this state.

NOTE: Prior to October 1994, children and youth with disabilities were served under Chapter 1 of the Elementary and Secondary Education Act (ESEA) as well as under the Individuals with Disabilities Education Act (IDEA), Part B. Data reported in this table for 1990–91 include children ages 0–21 served under Chapter 1 of ESEA.
SOURCE: U.S. Department of Education, Office of Special Education Programs, *Annual Report to Congress on the Implementation of the Individuals with Disabilities Education Act,* selected years, 1992 through 2006; and Individuals with Disabilities Education Act (IDEA) database, retrieved February 20, 2020, from https://www2.ed.gov/programs/osepidea/618-data/state-level-data-files/index.html. National Center for Education Statistics, Common Core of Data (CCD), "State Nonfiscal Survey of Public Elementary/Secondary Education," 2018–19; and State Public Elementary and Secondary Enrollment Projection Model, 1980 through 2029. (This table was prepared February 2020.)

Table 204.75a. Homeless students enrolled in public elementary and secondary schools, by grade, primary nighttime residence, and selected student characteristics: 2009–10 through 2016–17

Grade, primary nighttime residence, or selected student characteristic	2009–10	2010–11	2011–12	2012–13	2013–14	2014–15[1]	2015–16	2016–17[2]
1	2	3	4	5	6	7	8	9
Total number of homeless students[3]	910,439	1,047,397	1,128,503	1,216,117	1,285,641	1,260,721	1,301,238	1,351,120
As a percent of total public school enrollment	1.8	2.1	2.3	2.4	2.6	2.5	2.6	2.7
Total number, by grade and nighttime residence								
Grade								
Prekindergarten[4]	28,871	32,966	32,866	38,281	47,976	39,381	42,580	43,333
Kindergarten	82,378	89,589	105,795	115,943	112,343	118,470	109,852	115,653
Grade 1	83,675	92,153	104,554	113,226	121,159	116,464	116,517	115,312
Grade 2	80,437	88,125	96,845	105,311	113,238	111,189	115,054	114,772
Grade 3	77,594	86,253	93,214	99,446	107,574	105,739	110,868	115,200
Grade 4	73,942	82,570	88,809	94,303	99,005	98,221	103,859	108,411
Grade 5	69,605	79,314	85,224	89,769	93,912	91,647	97,068	102,560
Grade 6	65,238	75,867	80,962	86,880	89,965	87,844	90,716	94,806
Grade 7	61,009	71,412	76,481	82,159	86,659	83,924	86,480	89,234
Grade 8	60,186	69,406	73,528	79,516	83,404	82,122	85,327	88,326
Grade 9	66,474	79,897	81,262	90,139	97,129	94,508	95,662	99,880
Grade 10	54,510	68,484	69,396	72,673	77,486	76,951	82,040	85,644
Grade 11	47,835	59,120	63,078	66,519	69,619	68,729	73,881	78,969
Grade 12	54,030	68,532	73,687	79,260	83,671	83,022	88,452	95,723
Ungraded[5]	4,655	3,709	2,802	2,692	2,501	2,510	2,882	3,297
Primary nighttime residence[6]								
Doubled-up or shared housing[7]	648,233	741,460	849,684	917,122	978,463	957,053	983,782	1,022,425
Hotels or motels	45,727	53,499	62,530	69,179	78,767	82,187	84,978	90,013
Shelters, transitional housing, or awaiting foster care placement	172,644	177,028	174,472	173,397	183,653	180,302	185,596	186,141
Unsheltered[8]	38,450	74,044	40,151	39,108	41,738	39,327	43,014	49,864
Number with selected characteristics								
Unaccompanied homeless youth[9]	—	—	—	78,654	88,390	94,800	111,720	118,362
English language learners[10]	—	—	—	174,821	190,256	181,764	201,099	216,245
Migrant students[11]	—	—	—	16,231	18,588	17,748	16,700	16,170
Students with disabilities[12]	—	—	—	190,050	217,048	215,630	232,764	245,130

—Not available.

[1]The decrease in homeless students in 2014–15 was caused in part by changes to California's data collection systems. For more information, see section 1.9.1.1 of California's 2014–15 *Consolidated State Performance Report*, available at https://www2.ed.gov/admins/lead/account/consolidated/sy14-15part1/ca.pdf.

[2]Includes imputed data for Kansas.

[3]The sum of counts by grade.

[4]Homeless children 3 to 5 years old who are not in kindergarten.

[5]Includes students reported as being enrolled in grade 13.

[6]Does not sum to the total number of homeless students because of missing data on primary nighttime residence. (Counts by primary nighttime residence differ from those shown in the total row by less than 2 percent for 2012–13 and less than 1 percent for all other years.)

[7]Refers to temporarily sharing the housing of other persons due to loss of housing, economic hardship, or other reasons (such as domestic violence).

[8]Includes living in cars, parks, campgrounds, temporary trailers—including Federal Emergency Management Agency (FEMA) trailers—or abandoned buildings.

[9]Youth who are not in the physical custody of a parent or guardian. Includes youth living on their own and youth living with a caregiver who is not their legal guardian.

[10]Students who met the definition of limited English proficient students as outlined in the ED*Facts* workbook. For more information, see https://www2.ed.gov/about/inits/ed/edfacts/eden-workbook.html.

[11]Students who met the definition of eligible migrant children as outlined in the ED*Facts* workbook. Such students are either migratory workers or the children or spouses of migratory workers and have moved within the preceding 36 months in order to obtain, or to accompany parents or spouses who moved in order to obtain, temporary or seasonal employment in agricultural or fishing work. For more information, see https://www2.ed.gov/about/inits/ed/edfacts/eden-workbook.html. Connecticut, the District of Columbia, Rhode Island, and West Virginia did not operate a migrant education program during the 2012–13, 2013–14, 2014–15, 2015–16, and 2016–17 school years and therefore had no data to provide on migrant homeless students.

[12]Includes only students with disabilities who were served under the Individuals with Disabilities Education Act (IDEA).

NOTE: Homeless students are defined as children/youth who lack a fixed, regular, and adequate nighttime residence. For more information, see "C118—Homeless Students Enrolled" at https://www2.ed.gov/about/inits/ed/edfacts/sy-16-17-nonxml.html. Data include all homeless students enrolled at any time during the school year. Data exclude Puerto Rico and the Bureau of Indian Education. This table is based on state-level data unless otherwise noted.

SOURCE: U.S. Department of Education, National Center for Education Statistics, ED*Facts* file 118, Data Group 655, extracted June 5, 2019, from the ED*Facts* Data Warehouse (internal U.S. Department of Education Source); and Common Core of Data (CCD), "State Nonfiscal Survey of Public Elementary and Secondary Education," 2009–10 through 2016–17. (This table was prepared June 2019.)

Table 204.90. Percentage of public school students enrolled in gifted and talented programs, by sex, race/ethnicity, and state: Selected years, 2004 through 2013–14

[Standard errors appear in parentheses]

State	2004, total		2006, total		2011–12, total[1]	2013–14[1]								
						Sex		Race/ethnicity						
						Total	Male	Female	White	Black	Hispanic	Asian	Pacific Islander	American Indian/ Alaska Native	Two or more races
1	2		3		4	5	6	7	8	9	10	11	12	13	14
United States	**6.7**	**(0.05)**	**6.7**	**(0.04)**	**6.4**	**6.7**	**6.4**	**7.0**	**7.7**	**4.3**	**4.9**	**13.3**	**4.4**	**5.2**	**6.9**
Alabama	4.8	(0.11)	5.5	(0.06)	8.4	8.4	8.0	8.9	11.2	3.9	4.9	17.6	6.9	11.7	5.7
Alaska	4.1	(0.19)	4.1	(0.19)	4.7	4.9	4.7	5.2	6.8	3.0	4.3	6.3	2.3	0.9	6.5
Arizona	5.9	(0.17)	6.3	(0.11)	5.8	4.8	5.0	4.6	6.6	2.3	3.4	9.9	3.3	1.7	5.5
Arkansas	9.9	(0.65)	9.5	(0.43)	9.8	9.8	8.9	10.9	11.1	8.5	5.5	16.2	2.2	6.2	6.3
California	8.4	(0.18)	8.3	(0.21)	8.2	7.8	7.6	8.1	9.7	4.5	5.8	15.1	8.1	5.3	9.0
Colorado	6.7	(0.11)	6.8	(0.11)	6.5	7.7	7.9	7.5	9.6	4.1	4.4	12.8	6.4	4.3	9.0
Connecticut	3.0	(0.32)	3.8	(0.41)	2.3	2.2	2.0	2.4	2.7	1.1	1.0	4.6	0.5	1.1	2.4
Delaware	4.6[1]	(†)	5.6[1]	(†)	2.0	2.3	2.1	2.5	2.9	1.4	1.2	6.1	0.7–2.0	1.8	2.4
District of Columbia	—	(†)	—	(†)	0.1	#	#	#	0.1	#	#	0.1–0.3	0.0	0.0	0.0
Florida	4.5	(0.06)	4.7	(0.05)	5.4	5.8	5.6	5.9	7.6	2.3	5.3	13.3	4.1	4.3	6.2
Georgia	8.9	(0.30)	9.3	(0.35)	10.4	12.9	12.1	13.8	16.1	10.4	6.5	26.5	9.0	10.5	12.5
Hawaii	5.7	(0.57)	6.2[1]	(†)	1.4	3.0	2.4	3.5	4.4	2.1	1.6	4.2	1.7	4.2	2.5
Idaho	3.9	(0.23)	4.2	(0.20)	3.0	3.6	3.5	3.7	4.1	2.2	1.4	7.1	2.7	1.9	2.9
Illinois	5.4	(0.22)	5.8	(0.24)	3.5	6.8	6.5	7.1	5.7	7.7	6.7	15.4	10.9	6.4	7.1
Indiana	7.1	(0.49)	7.9	(0.40)	12.6	12.1	11.6	12.6	14.0	4.9	6.5	20.8	8.7	9.5	9.8
Iowa	8.5	(0.38)	8.2	(0.26)	9.3	9.4	9.2	9.7	10.5	3.2	4.2	13.9	4.4	4.1	7.9
Kansas	3.3	(0.11)	3.0	(0.12)	2.9	2.7	2.8	2.5	3.2	0.9	0.9	6.8	1.9	1.6	2.5
Kentucky	13.0	(0.54)	14.6	(0.50)	12.7	15.8	14.7	17.0	17.3	7.9	7.5	26.8	14.6	10.9	11.7
Louisiana	3.9	(0.32)	3.4	(0.13)	3.0	4.2	3.7	4.8	5.8	2.3	3.6	14.8	5.2	2.8	4.3
Maine	3.0	(0.36)	3.2	(0.19)	4.6	4.9	4.5	5.3	5.0	2.4	2.6	8.0	3.5	3.1	3.7
Maryland	13.8[1]	(†)	16.1[1]	(†)	15.8	16.0	14.7	17.4	17.5	11.1	14.0	39.4	10.1	10.2	17.2
Massachusetts	0.8	(0.13)	0.7	(0.10)	0.7	0.5	0.4	0.5	0.4	0.6	0.4	1.0	0.4	0.3	0.5
Michigan	3.9	(0.37)	3.4	(0.29)	1.9	1.3	1.2	1.4	1.5	0.7	0.6	3.0	1.6	1.0	0.7
Minnesota	8.1	(0.37)	8.8	(0.28)	8.0	7.2	7.1	7.4	7.2	6.0	4.7	14.9	4.6	2.5	5.8
Mississippi	6.0	(0.19)	6.1	(0.20)	6.7	6.7	6.3	7.1	10.2	3.5	5.7	14.7	10.7	3.3	4.8
Missouri	3.8	(0.12)	3.6	(0.11)	4.0	4.2	4.1	4.3	4.5	2.2	2.7	11.6	2.2	3.0	3.9
Montana	5.6	(0.28)	5.2	(0.20)	4.2	3.8	3.9	3.7	4.2	2.4	2.0	6.5	3.4	1.7	2.5
Nebraska	11.4	(0.31)	11.4	(0.24)	11.8	12.0	11.5	12.6	13.5	8.3	6.9	19.9	8.7	5.6	11.7
Nevada	1.9	(0.01)	1.9[1]	(†)	2.0	3.3	3.3	3.3	5.4	0.9	1.7	5.5	2.0	1.8	4.6
New Hampshire	2.3	(0.55)	2.6	(0.54)	1.4	1.2	1.2	1.2	1.2	0.4	0.3	1.6	0.0	0.7	1.1
New Jersey	6.9	(0.38)	7.0	(0.35)	6.5	5.9	5.4	6.5	7.1	3.1	2.9	11.9	7.5	2.9	4.6
New Mexico	10.7	(0.26)	4.0	(0.14)	4.6	4.5	4.6	4.3	8.2	3.3	3.1	13.4	5.7	2.6	5.8
New York	2.2	(0.18)	2.9	(0.13)	1.5	1.7	1.6	1.9	2.2	0.9	0.6	3.6	1.9	1.1	2.1
North Carolina	10.9	(0.83)	10.8	(0.42)	10.6	10.0	9.8	10.3	14.4	4.0	4.5	18.7	7.9	5.9	9.8
North Dakota	3.1	(0.30)	2.8	(0.18)	3.3	2.3	2.3	2.2	2.2	1.7	0.7	6.2	3.1	3.1	0.1–0.2
Ohio	7.4	(0.40)	7.3	(0.33)	3.7	4.3	4.2	4.3	4.9	1.4	1.9	11.2	1.8	3.5	3.5
Oklahoma	14.0	(0.45)	13.7	(0.39)	13.9	13.7	13.1	14.3	16.5	7.6	7.7	26.5	8.5	13.3	11.1
Oregon	7.1	(0.20)	6.9	(0.16)	6.8	6.5	6.7	6.3	7.4	3.1	2.6	16.6	3.0	2.5	7.6
Pennsylvania	4.8	(0.19)	4.5	(0.17)	3.8	3.7	3.7	3.7	4.4	1.0	1.2	8.8	3.3	2.0	2.7
Rhode Island	1.8	(0.38)	1.4	(0.21)	0.5	0.3	0.3	0.3	0.2	0.5	0.6	0.6	0.0	0.1–0.2	0.1
South Carolina	12.7	(0.98)	11.0	(0.57)	12.0	13.4	12.0	14.9	18.7	6.5	7.2	25.6	14.1	8.2	11.7
South Dakota	2.2	(0.20)	2.7	(0.17)	2.0	2.0	2.0	1.9	2.3	0.8	0.7	4.5	3.0	0.4	1.3
Tennessee	3.3	(0.18)	1.7	(0.10)	2.5	1.6	1.6	1.6	2.0	0.6	0.7	4.0	1.8	1.3	1.5
Texas	8.0	(0.10)	7.6	(0.07)	7.7	7.6	7.4	7.9	10.6	4.0	6.0	18.3	6.6	5.8	8.2
Utah	4.6	(0.29)	5.0	(0.05)	3.9	4.7	4.4	5.0	4.9	3.7	3.4	10.7	5.6	2.2	3.4
Vermont	0.8	(0.17)	0.8	(0.15)	0.3	0.4	0.4	0.4	0.4	0.3	0.1–0.3	0.6	0.9–2.6	0.2–0.6	0.1–0.2
Virginia	12.1	(0.38)	12.6	(0.32)	11.8	12.1	11.6	12.6	14.6	6.0	7.5	22.6	11.3	8.4	13.4
Washington	3.8	(0.10)	3.9	(0.13)	3.5	3.3	3.2	3.4	3.7	1.3	1.9	6.7	1.3	1.2	3.1
West Virginia	2.2	(0.19)	2.2	(0.21)	1.9	2.1	2.1	2.1	2.1	1.3	1.1	10.2	5.4	1.9	1.7
Wisconsin	6.8	(0.47)	6.4	(0.35)	6.0	6.2	6.0	6.4	6.5	5.2	4.7	8.8	3.0	2.1	5.5
Wyoming	3.2!	(1.04)	2.2	(0.35)	3.3	3.6	3.6	3.7	4.2	2.4	1.3	5.6	3.1	0.9	1.8

—Not available.
†Not applicable.
#Rounds to zero.
!Interpret data with caution. The coefficient of variation (CV) for this estimate is between 30 and 50 percent.
[1]Data are based on universe counts of schools and school districts; therefore, these figures do not have standard errors.

NOTE: Race categories exclude persons of Hispanic ethnicity. Percentages based on counts of between 1 and 3 gifted and talented students are displayed as ranges to protect student privacy.
SOURCE: U.S. Department of Education, Office for Civil Rights, Civil Rights Data Collection: 2004, 2006, 2011–12, and 2013–14. (This table was prepared June 2018.)

Table 205.10. Private elementary and secondary school enrollment and private enrollment as a percentage of total enrollment in public and private schools, by region and grade level: Selected years, fall 1995 through fall 2017

[Standard errors appear in parentheses]

Grade level and year	Total private enrollment		Private enrollment, by region							
			Northeast		Midwest		South		West	
	In thousands	Percent of total enrollment	In thousands	Percent of total enrollment in Northeast	In thousands	Percent of total enrollment in Midwest	In thousands	Percent of total enrollment in South	In thousands	Percent of total enrollment in West
1	2	3	4	5	6	7	8	9	10	11
Total, all grades										
1995	5,918 (31.8)	11.7 (0.06)	1,509 (18.8)	16.1 (0.17)	1,525 (14.2)	12.7 (0.10)	1,744 (12.8)	9.8 (0.07)	1,141 (11.5)	10.0 (0.09)
1997	5,944 (18.5)	11.4 (0.03)	1,496 (8.3)	15.6 (0.07)	1,528 (11.6)	12.5 (0.08)	1,804 (11.3)	9.8 (0.06)	1,116 (5.2)	9.4 (0.04)
1999	6,018 (30.2)	11.4 (0.05)	1,507 (7.9)	15.5 (0.07)	1,520 (10.3)	12.4 (0.07)	1,863 (26.7)	10.0 (0.13)	1,127 (5.4)	9.3 (0.04)
2001	6,320 (40.3)	11.7 (0.07)	1,581 (9.5)	16.1 (0.08)	1,556 (22.9)	12.6 (0.16)	1,975 (21.4)	10.3 (0.10)	1,208 (23.4)	9.6 (0.17)
2003	6,099 (41.2)	11.2 (0.07)	1,513 (25.8)	15.4 (0.22)	1,460 (15.1)	11.9 (0.11)	1,944 (21.0)	9.9 (0.10)	1,182 (19.1)	9.2 (0.14)
2005	6,073 (42.4)	11.0 (0.07)	1,430 (7.7)	14.8 (0.07)	1,434 (21.0)	11.7 (0.15)	1,976 (24.7)	9.9 (0.11)	1,234 (26.3)	9.5 (0.18)
2007	5,910 (28.4)	10.8 (0.05)	1,426 (11.0)	15.0 (0.10)	1,352 (8.3)	11.2 (0.06)	1,965 (21.5)	9.7 (0.10)	1,167 (12.3)	9.1 (0.09)
2009	5,488 (35.9)	10.1 (0.06)	1,310 (15.7)	14.1 (0.14)	1,296 (25.9)	10.9 (0.19)	1,842 (17.6)	9.0 (0.08)	1,041 (8.0)	8.1 (0.06)
2011	5,268 (24.9)	9.7 (0.04)	1,252 (18.0)	13.7 (0.17)	1,263 (17.1)	10.7 (0.13)	1,747 (2.6)	8.5 (0.01)	1,006 (0.4)	7.8 (#)
2013	5,396 (50.3)	9.8 (0.08)	1,201 (9.5)	13.2 (0.09)	1,326 (45.2)	11.2 (0.34)	1,840 (8.3)	8.7 (0.04)	1,028 (18.3)	7.8 (0.13)
2015	5,751 (85.7)	10.3 (0.14)	1,314 (37.3)	14.3 (0.35)	1,408 (54.5)	11.9 (0.40)	1,965 (53.2)	9.1 (0.22)	1,062 (12.5)	8.0 (0.09)
2017	5,720 (74.1)	10.2 (0.12)	1,229 (18.4)	13.6 (0.18)	1,378 (45.5)	11.7 (0.34)	2,030 (45.4)	9.3 (0.19)	1,082 (32.0)	8.1 (0.22)
Prekindergarten through grade 8										
1995	4,756 (28.4)	12.8 (0.07)	1,174 (16.8)	17.0 (0.20)	1,238 (13.5)	14.2 (0.13)	1,413 (11.9)	10.8 (0.08)	931 (9.2)	11.2 (0.10)
1997	4,759 (17.3)	12.6 (0.04)	1,165 (8.3)	16.7 (0.10)	1,235 (11.0)	14.1 (0.11)	1,449 (10.0)	10.8 (0.07)	909 (4.4)	10.6 (0.05)
1999	4,789 (23.1)	12.6 (0.05)	1,168 (7.5)	16.5 (0.09)	1,222 (8.4)	14.0 (0.08)	1,487 (19.6)	10.8 (0.13)	913 (4.4)	10.5 (0.04)
2001	5,023 (36.1)	12.9 (0.08)	1,216 (9.4)	17.2 (0.11)	1,253 (21.2)	14.3 (0.21)	1,584 (17.8)	11.3 (0.11)	969 (21.2)	10.8 (0.21)
2003	4,788 (30.3)	12.3 (0.07)	1,131 (7.8)	16.3 (0.09)	1,167 (13.6)	13.5 (0.14)	1,547 (18.6)	10.9 (0.12)	944 (18.1)	10.4 (0.18)
2005	4,724 (33.0)	12.2 (0.07)	1,063 (6.6)	15.8 (0.08)	1,142 (19.3)	13.4 (0.20)	1,551 (21.2)	10.8 (0.13)	969 (15.0)	10.6 (0.15)
2007	4,546 (21.9)	11.8 (0.05)	1,047 (6.3)	15.9 (0.08)	1,065 (7.7)	12.7 (0.08)	1,525 (17.7)	10.5 (0.11)	909 (8.1)	10.2 (0.08)
2009	4,179 (33.2)	10.9 (0.08)	938 (12.6)	14.6 (0.17)	1,016 (25.1)	12.2 (0.26)	1,424 (16.2)	9.7 (0.10)	802 (7.2)	9.0 (0.07)
2011	3,977 (18.2)	10.3 (0.04)	898 (12.8)	14.1 (0.17)	967 (12.8)	11.7 (0.14)	1,337 (1.8)	9.0 (0.01)	774 (0.3)	8.6 (#)
2013	4,084 (42.4)	10.4 (0.10)	859 (8.8)	13.5 (0.12)	1,036 (37.9)	12.4 (0.40)	1,403 (7.9)	9.2 (0.05)	786 (15.0)	8.6 (0.15)
2015	4,304 (69.2)	10.9 (0.16)	932 (27.8)	14.6 (0.37)	1,099 (48.9)	13.1 (0.51)	1,471 (38.4)	9.5 (0.23)	802 (12.2)	8.7 (0.12)
2017	4,252 (69.0)	10.8 (0.16)	860 (18.3)	13.7 (0.25)	1,062 (41.8)	12.8 (0.44)	1,525 (42.4)	9.8 (0.25)	805 (29.9)	8.6 (0.29)
Grades 9 through 12										
1995	1,163 (4.6)	8.6 (0.03)	335 (2.9)	13.4 (0.10)	287 (0.9)	8.6 (0.03)	331 (2.1)	7.1 (0.04)	209 (2.3)	6.9 (0.07)
1997	1,185 (2.4)	8.3 (0.02)	331 (0.5)	12.8 (0.02)	293 (0.7)	8.4 (0.02)	354 (1.7)	7.2 (0.03)	207 (1.2)	6.4 (0.04)
1999	1,229 (8.3)	8.4 (0.05)	340 (1.1)	12.9 (0.04)	299 (2.5)	8.5 (0.07)	376 (7.6)	7.5 (0.14)	215 (1.8)	6.3 (0.05)
2001	1,296 (6.7)	8.6 (0.04)	365 (0.8)	13.3 (0.03)	302 (2.0)	8.5 (0.05)	390 (4.4)	7.6 (0.08)	239 (4.5)	6.8 (0.12)
2003	1,311 (24.7)	8.4 (0.15)	382 (24.0)	13.3 (0.72)	294 (4.1)	8.2 (0.11)	397 (3.0)	7.4 (0.05)	238 (3.5)	6.4 (0.09)
2005	1,349 (18.1)	8.3 (0.10)	367 (1.7)	12.4 (0.05)	292 (5.0)	8.0 (0.13)	425 (7.2)	7.5 (0.12)	265 (15.7)	6.7 (0.37)
2007	1,364 (12.0)	8.3 (0.07)	379 (8.8)	12.8 (0.26)	287 (1.3)	7.8 (0.03)	440 (5.5)	7.6 (0.09)	257 (5.7)	6.6 (0.14)
2009	1,309 (6.5)	8.1 (0.04)	372 (5.7)	13.0 (0.17)	280 (2.2)	7.8 (0.06)	418 (1.7)	7.2 (0.03)	239 (1.1)	6.1 (0.03)
2011	1,291 (15.4)	8.1 (0.09)	353 (5.2)	12.6 (0.16)	295 (14.4)	8.4 (0.38)	411 (1.8)	7.1 (0.03)	232 (0.1)	5.9 (#)
2013	1,312 (14.9)	8.2 (0.09)	342 (0.8)	12.4 (0.03)	291 (13.1)	8.4 (0.35)	437 (1.3)	7.4 (0.02)	242 (7.0)	6.2 (0.17)
2015	1,446 (23.8)	8.8 (0.13)	382 (10.5)	13.7 (0.32)	309 (10.9)	8.8 (0.28)	494 (18.2)	8.0 (0.27)	261 (1.9)	6.6 (0.04)
2017	1,468 (17.4)	8.8 (0.10)	369 (1.3)	13.3 (0.04)	316 (7.5)	9.0 (0.20)	505 (15.2)	8.0 (0.22)	278 (3.4)	6.9 (0.08)

#Rounds to zero.
NOTE: Includes enrollment in prekindergarten through grade 12 in schools that offer kindergarten or higher grade. Ungraded students are prorated into prekindergarten through grade 8 and grades 9 through 12. Detail may not sum to totals because of rounding.

SOURCE: U.S. Department of Education, National Center for Education Statistics, Private School Universe Survey (PSS), 1995–96 through 2017–18; and Common Core of Data (CCD), "Public Elementary/Secondary School Universe Survey," 1995–96 through 2017–18. (This table was prepared August 2019.)

Table 205.15. Private elementary and secondary school enrollment, percentage distribution of private school enrollment, and private school enrollment as a percentage of total enrollment in public and private schools, by school orientation and grade: Selected years, fall 1999 through fall 2017

[Standard errors appear in parentheses]

Grade	1999	2005	2011	2013	2015	2017 Total	Catholic	Other religious	Nonsectarian
1	2	3	4	5	6	7	8	9	10
Enrollment									
Total, all grades	6,018,280 (30,179)	6,073,240 (42,446)	5,268,090 (24,908)	5,395,740 (50,342)	5,750,520 (85,729)	5,719,990 (74,133)	2,137,330 (40,520)	2,188,240 (40,106)	1,394,420 (26,889)
Prekindergarten through grade 8	4,788,990 (23,055)	4,724,310 (33,034)	3,976,960 (18,241)	4,083,860 (42,441)	4,304,470 (69,171)	4,251,960 (69,049)	1,478,040 (37,641)	1,727,280 (36,077)	1,046,640 (24,548)
Prekindergarten	763,790 (6,261)	926,430 (15,701)	773,240 (2,420)	819,320 (10,185)	846,920 (17,898)	821,830 (17,849)	175,660 (4,995)	330,470 (12,883)	315,710 (8,956)
Kindergarten	593,690 (4,053)	547,590 (4,887)	449,820 (2,989)	461,690 (5,429)	466,470 (8,411)	456,880 (7,890)	144,990 (3,694)	186,250 (3,450)	125,630 (3,870)
1st grade	472,110 (2,080)	421,120 (2,826)	348,730 (2,191)	357,860 (4,963)	373,850 (6,901)	361,030 (6,042)	137,970 (3,863)	156,640 (3,214)	66,410 (1,772)
2nd grade	449,090 (2,248)	405,470 (2,659)	340,230 (2,008)	344,520 (4,887)	368,450 (6,625)	352,130 (5,906)	138,210 (3,904)	151,220 (3,217)	62,700 (1,563)
3rd grade	436,730 (1,962)	398,120 (2,462)	336,150 (1,850)	338,840 (4,193)	364,290 (6,479)	354,400 (6,167)	141,640 (4,058)	149,980 (3,217)	62,780 (1,287)
4th grade	425,140 (1,956)	391,530 (2,297)	328,950 (1,921)	337,440 (4,508)	357,820 (6,202)	355,650 (5,831)	142,810 (4,008)	149,900 (3,174)	62,950 (1,294)
5th grade	407,590 (2,019)	389,720 (2,379)	330,390 (1,832)	337,950 (4,192)	354,710 (5,903)	358,720 (5,811)	145,550 (4,032)	146,790 (2,955)	66,380 (1,669)
6th grade	403,110 (2,094)	393,220 (2,280)	341,690 (1,766)	344,960 (4,820)	372,750 (7,276)	374,200 (6,861)	148,490 (4,091)	151,830 (3,558)	73,870 (2,066)
7th grade	384,140 (2,140)	390,550 (4,093)	336,770 (1,684)	343,370 (4,317)	367,920 (6,574)	370,920 (6,791)	147,790 (4,249)	146,020 (3,417)	77,100 (2,028)
8th grade	369,580 (2,285)	387,720 (4,024)	336,670 (1,951)	343,500 (3,717)	363,840 (7,047)	374,210 (6,444)	148,740 (3,812)	145,060 (3,494)	80,410 (2,007)
Elementary ungraded	84,000 (1,267)	72,830 (1,916)	54,300 (672)	54,380 (1,061)	67,440 (11,164)	72,000 (12,109)	6,190 (†)	13,130! (4,668)	52,680 (11,179)
Grades 9 through 12	1,229,290 (8,260)	1,348,930 (18,073)	1,291,130 (15,396)	1,311,880 (14,936)	1,446,060 (23,777)	1,468,020 (17,378)	659,290 (15,189)	460,960 (6,962)	347,780 (4,172)
9th grade	336,220 (2,131)	356,130 (4,333)	329,600 (3,875)	333,610 (3,612)	367,810 (6,279)	373,950 (4,554)	168,010 (3,729)	120,140 (2,073)	85,800 (1,322)
10th grade	313,310 (1,919)	348,190 (5,949)	324,540 (4,161)	330,710 (3,780)	367,250 (6,041)	365,940 (4,257)	165,130 (3,681)	116,280 (1,662)	84,530 (1,060)
11th grade	294,650 (2,193)	326,260 (4,456)	318,310 (3,647)	324,680 (3,850)	356,150 (5,906)	364,600 (4,572)	163,880 (4,110)	113,570 (1,639)	87,150 (1,169)
12th grade	280,380 (1,958)	315,290 (4,850)	314,500 (3,769)	319,720 (3,787)	348,600 (5,652)	359,030 (4,200)	162,050 (3,683)	109,540 (1,778)	87,440 (1,011)
Secondary ungraded	4,720 (1,404)	3,070 (†)	4,180 (92)	3,160 (14)	6,240 (†)	4,500 (†)	210 (†)	1,430 (†)	2,860 (†)
Percentage distribution									
Total, all grades	100.0 (0.06)	100.0 (0.22)	100.0 (0.23)	100.0 (0.22)	100.0 (0.27)	100.0 (0.35)	100.0 (0.73)	100.0 (0.31)	100.0 (0.38)
Prekindergarten through grade 8	77.8 (0.08)	75.5 (0.21)	75.7 (0.08)	75.7 (0.15)	74.9 (0.22)	74.3 (0.22)	69.2 (0.17)	78.9 (0.45)	75.1 (0.49)
Prekindergarten	12.7 (0.08)	15.3 (0.21)	14.7 (0.08)	15.2 (0.15)	14.7 (0.22)	14.4 (0.22)	8.2 (0.17)	15.1 (0.45)	22.6 (0.49)
Kindergarten	9.9 (0.04)	9.0 (0.06)	8.5 (0.04)	8.6 (0.08)	8.1 (0.08)	8.0 (0.06)	6.8 (0.08)	8.5 (0.08)	9.0 (0.16)
1st grade	7.8 (0.02)	6.9 (0.03)	6.6 (0.02)	6.6 (0.05)	6.5 (0.07)	6.3 (0.06)	6.5 (0.09)	7.2 (0.09)	4.8 (0.08)
2nd grade	7.5 (0.01)	6.7 (0.03)	6.5 (0.02)	6.4 (0.05)	6.4 (0.06)	6.2 (0.05)	6.5 (0.09)	6.9 (0.07)	4.5 (0.08)
3rd grade	7.3 (0.02)	6.6 (0.03)	6.4 (0.02)	6.3 (0.04)	6.3 (0.05)	6.2 (0.06)	6.6 (0.10)	6.9 (0.07)	4.5 (0.07)
4th grade	7.1 (0.01)	6.4 (0.03)	6.2 (0.02)	6.3 (0.04)	6.2 (0.05)	6.2 (0.05)	6.7 (0.08)	6.9 (0.07)	4.5 (0.08)
5th grade	6.8 (0.01)	6.4 (0.04)	6.3 (0.02)	6.3 (0.04)	6.2 (0.05)	6.3 (0.05)	6.8 (0.09)	6.7 (0.08)	4.8 (0.09)
6th grade	6.7 (0.02)	6.5 (0.03)	6.5 (0.02)	6.4 (0.05)	6.5 (0.07)	6.5 (0.06)	6.9 (0.09)	6.9 (0.10)	5.3 (0.12)
7th grade	6.4 (0.02)	6.4 (0.04)	6.4 (0.02)	6.4 (0.05)	6.4 (0.06)	6.5 (0.07)	6.9 (0.12)	6.7 (0.11)	5.5 (0.11)
8th grade	6.1 (0.02)	6.4 (0.04)	6.4 (0.02)	6.4 (0.04)	6.3 (0.06)	6.5 (0.07)	7.0 (0.11)	6.6 (0.11)	5.8 (0.10)
Elementary ungraded	1.4 (0.02)	1.2 (0.03)	1.0 (0.01)	1.0 (0.02)	1.2 (0.19)	1.3 (0.21)	0.3 (0.01)	0.6! (0.21)	3.8 (0.77)
Grades 9 through 12	20.4 (0.06)	22.2 (0.22)	24.5 (0.23)	24.3 (0.22)	25.1 (0.27)	25.7 (0.35)	30.8 (0.73)	21.1 (0.31)	24.9 (0.38)
9th grade	5.6 (0.02)	5.9 (0.05)	6.3 (0.06)	6.2 (0.05)	6.4 (0.07)	6.5 (0.09)	7.9 (0.18)	5.5 (0.08)	6.2 (0.11)
10th grade	5.2 (0.01)	5.7 (0.08)	6.2 (0.06)	6.1 (0.06)	6.4 (0.07)	6.4 (0.09)	7.7 (0.18)	5.3 (0.08)	6.1 (0.09)
11th grade	4.9 (0.02)	5.4 (0.06)	6.0 (0.05)	6.0 (0.06)	6.2 (0.07)	6.4 (0.09)	7.7 (0.19)	5.2 (0.08)	6.3 (0.10)
12th grade	4.7 (0.02)	5.2 (0.07)	6.0 (0.06)	5.9 (0.06)	6.1 (0.07)	6.3 (0.09)	7.6 (0.18)	5.0 (0.08)	6.3 (0.10)
Secondary ungraded	0.1 (0.02)	0.1 (#)	0.1 (#)	0.1 (#)	0.1 (#)	0.1 (#)	# (†)	0.1 (#)	0.2 (#)

See notes at end of table.

Table 205.15. Private elementary and secondary school enrollment, percentage distribution of private school enrollment, and private enrollment as a percentage of total enrollment in public and private schools, by school orientation and grade: Selected years, fall 1999 through fall 2017—Continued

[Standard errors appear in parentheses]

Private enrollment as a percent of total enrollment

Grade	1999	2005	2011	2013	2015	2017 Total	2017 Catholic	2017 Other religious	2017 Nonsectarian
1	2	3	4	5	6	7	8	9	10
Total, all grades	11.4 (0.05)	11.0 (0.07)	9.7 (0.04)	9.8 (0.08)	10.3 (0.14)	10.2 (0.12)	3.8 (0.07)	3.9 (0.07)	2.5 (0.05)
Prekindergarten through grade 8	12.6 (0.05)	12.2 (0.07)	10.3 (0.04)	10.4 (0.10)	10.9 (0.16)	10.8 (0.16)	3.7 (0.09)	4.4 (0.09)	2.7 (0.06)
Prekindergarten	55.4 (0.20)	52.3 (0.42)	40.4 (0.08)	41.5 (0.30)	41.6 (0.51)	39.6 (0.52)	8.5 (0.23)	15.9 (0.51)	15.2 (0.37)
Kindergarten	14.9 (0.09)	13.2 (0.10)	10.7 (0.06)	10.8 (0.11)	11.2 (0.18)	11.0 (0.17)	3.5 (0.09)	4.5 (0.09)	3.0 (0.09)
1st grade	11.4 (0.04)	10.2 (0.06)	8.5 (0.08)	8.4 (0.11)	9.0 (0.15)	9.0 (0.14)	3.4 (0.09)	3.9 (0.08)	1.7 (0.04)
2nd grade	10.9 (0.05)	10.1 (0.06)	8.4 (0.05)	8.3 (0.11)	8.8 (0.14)	8.7 (0.13)	3.4 (0.09)	3.8 (0.08)	1.6 (0.04)
3rd grade	10.6 (0.04)	10.0 (0.06)	8.3 (0.05)	8.3 (0.09)	8.6 (0.14)	8.6 (0.14)	3.4 (0.09)	3.6 (0.07)	1.5 (0.03)
4th grade	10.3 (0.04)	9.9 (0.05)	8.2 (0.04)	8.4 (0.10)	8.6 (0.14)	8.4 (0.13)	3.4 (0.09)	3.6 (0.07)	1.5 (0.03)
5th grade	10.2 (0.05)	9.7 (0.05)	8.2 (0.05)	8.4 (0.10)	8.5 (0.13)	8.4 (0.13)	3.4 (0.09)	3.5 (0.07)	1.6 (0.04)
6th grade	10.2 (0.05)	9.7 (0.05)	8.4 (0.04)	8.6 (0.11)	8.7 (0.16)	8.9 (0.15)	3.5 (0.09)	3.6 (0.08)	1.8 (0.05)
7th grade	9.8 (0.05)	9.4 (0.09)	8.4 (0.04)	8.4 (0.10)	9.1 (0.15)	9.0 (0.15)	3.6 (0.10)	3.5 (0.08)	1.9 (0.05)
8th grade	9.5 (0.05)	9.3 (0.09)	8.4 (0.04)	8.4 (0.08)	9.0 (0.16)	9.0 (0.14)	3.6 (0.09)	3.5 (0.08)	1.9 (0.05)
Elementary ungraded	16.8 (0.21)	22.8 (0.46)	40.3 (0.30)	38.6 (0.46)	46.6 (4.19)	48.5 (4.26)	4.2 (†)	8.8! (2.98)	35.5 (5.03)
Grades 9 through 12	8.4 (0.05)	8.3 (0.10)	8.1 (0.09)	8.2 (0.09)	8.8 (0.13)	8.8 (0.10)	4.0 (0.09)	2.8 (0.04)	2.1 (0.02)
9th grade	7.9 (0.05)	7.7 (0.09)	7.7 (0.08)	7.8 (0.08)	8.4 (0.13)	8.6 (0.10)	3.9 (0.08)	2.8 (0.05)	2.0 (0.03)
10th grade	8.4 (0.05)	8.3 (0.13)	8.0 (0.09)	8.1 (0.09)	8.7 (0.13)	8.7 (0.09)	3.9 (0.08)	2.8 (0.04)	2.0 (0.02)
11th grade	8.8 (0.06)	8.6 (0.11)	8.3 (0.09)	8.5 (0.09)	9.0 (0.14)	9.1 (0.10)	4.1 (0.10)	2.8 (0.04)	2.2 (0.03)
12th grade	9.1 (0.06)	9.0 (0.13)	8.4 (0.09)	8.5 (0.09)	9.0 (0.13)	9.0 (0.10)	4.1 (0.09)	2.8 (0.04)	2.2 (0.02)
Secondary ungraded	3.6 (1.03)	3.2 (†)	9.5 (0.19)	6.8 (0.03)	11.7 (†)	8.7 (†)	0.4 (†)	2.8 (†)	5.5 (†)

†Not applicable.
#Rounds to zero.
NOTE: Includes enrollment in prekindergarten through grade 12 in schools that offer kindergarten or higher grade. Ungraded students are prorated into prekindergarten through grade 8 and grades 9 through 12. Detail may not sum to totals because of rounding.

SOURCE: U.S. Department of Education, National Center for Education Statistics, Private School Universe Survey (PSS), 1999–2000 through 2017–18; and Common Core of Data (CCD), "Public Elementary/Secondary School Universe Survey," 1999–2000 through 2017–18. (This table was prepared August 2019.)

Table 205.20. Enrollment and percentage distribution of students enrolled in private elementary and secondary schools, by school orientation and grade level: Selected years, fall 1995 through fall 2017

[Standard errors appear in parentheses]

Grade level and year	Total private enrollment	Catholic Total	Catholic Parochial	Catholic Diocesan	Catholic Private	Other religious Total	Other religious Conservative Christian	Other religious Affiliated[1]	Other religious Unaffiliated[1]	Nonsectarian
1	2	3	4	5	6	7	8	9	10	11
					Enrollment					
Total, all grades										
1995	5,918,040 (31,815)	2,660,450 (6,878)	1,458,990 (2,079)	850,560 (5,674)	350,900 (1,176)	2,094,690 (16,956)	786,660 (8,815)	697,280 (4,886)	610,750 (11,831)	1,162,900 (18,443)
1997	5,944,320 (18,543)	2,665,630 (5,472)	1,438,860 (5,331)	873,780 (761)	352,990 (1,405)	2,097,190 (13,733)	823,610 (7,342)	646,500 (3,104)	627,080 (11,133)	1,181,510 (12,013)
1999	6,018,280 (30,179)	2,660,420 (4,831)	1,397,570 (4,421)	880,650 (†)	382,190 (1,945)	2,193,370 (27,176)	871,060 (4,827)	646,280 (4,894)	676,030 (24,593)	1,164,500 (8,156)
2001	6,319,650 (40,272)	2,672,650 (12,460)	1,309,890 (5,626)	979,050 (6,976)	383,710 (3,152)	2,328,160 (17,281)	937,420 (6,070)	663,190 (8,636)	727,550 (13,303)	1,318,840 (27,300)
2003	6,099,220 (41,219)	2,520,120 (10,580)	1,183,250 (9,937)	963,140 (4,754)	373,740 (3,996)	2,228,230 (19,674)	889,710 (8,852)	650,530 (5,860)	688,000 (14,805)	1,350,870 (29,197)
2005	6,073,240 (42,446)	2,402,800 (9,293)	1,062,950 (6,355)	956,610 (6,325)	383,230 (3,996)	2,303,330 (22,368)	957,360 (9,561)	696,910 (6,677)	649,050 (14,200)	1,367,120 (27,558)
2007	5,910,210 (28,363)	2,308,150 (6,083)	945,860 (5,361)	969,940 (1,788)	392,340 (3,432)	2,283,210 (20,628)	883,180 (6,616)	527,040 (3,512)	872,990 (18,217)	1,318,850 (18,235)
2009	5,488,490 (35,857)	2,160,220 (3,494)	856,440 (3,088)	909,010 (4,393)	394,770 (1,087)	2,076,220 (32,751)	787,020 (1,891)	516,310 (4,366)	822,890 (31,180)	1,252,050 (8,849)
2011	5,268,090 (24,908)	2,087,870 (14,426)	804,410 (3,686)	899,810 (14,320)	383,650 (459)	1,991,950 (21,814)	730,570 (4,721)	565,340 (2,990)	696,040 (20,419)	1,188,270 (5,376)
2013	5,395,740 (50,342)	2,055,140 (37,142)	739,850 (18,829)	936,320 (32,000)	378,970 (980)	2,030,930 (30,090)	707,100 (7,544)	565,490 (5,884)	758,350 (28,152)	1,309,670 (14,800)
2015	5,750,520 (85,729)	2,082,660 (42,791)	716,120 (24,336)	960,590 (22,533)	405,950 (14,453)	2,268,820 (68,162)	760,790 (53,772)	587,490 (23,414)	920,550 (45,692)	1,399,030 (29,132)
2017	5,719,990 (74,133)	2,137,330 (40,520)	648,580 (26,112)	1,052,150 (32,312)	436,590 (7,204)	2,188,240 (40,106)	685,070 (13,085)	633,310 (24,576)	869,850 (30,669)	1,394,420 (26,889)
Prekindergarten through grade 8										
1995	4,755,540 (28,435)	2,041,990 (5,249)	1,368,340 (2,079)	575,190 (3,528)	98,460 (1,176)	1,752,510 (14,834)	651,050 (7,219)	574,820 (4,581)	526,630 (11,121)	961,040 (17,471)
1997	4,759,060 (17,323)	2,046,620 (5,469)	1,352,620 (5,331)	598,380 (761)	95,620 (1,393)	1,744,500 (12,194)	678,660 (5,957)	529,050 (2,504)	536,790 (10,120)	967,940 (11,050)
1999	4,788,990 (23,055)	2,033,900 (4,830)	1,317,300 (4,421)	607,860 (†)	108,740 (1,943)	1,818,260 (19,897)	713,020 (3,748)	529,280 (3,866)	575,970 (17,632)	936,820 (7,302)
2001	5,023,160 (36,096)	2,032,080 (10,751)	1,226,960 (4,494)	687,540 (6,976)	117,580 (2,978)	1,926,870 (15,459)	765,080 (5,110)	535,850 (7,370)	625,940 (12,240)	1,064,210 (24,703)
2003	4,788,070 (30,338)	1,886,530 (11,055)	1,108,320 (9,937)	670,910 (4,754)	107,300 (337)	1,835,930 (16,931)	722,460 (6,517)	519,310 (4,134)	594,160 (13,504)	1,065,620 (15,379)
2005	4,724,310 (33,034)	1,779,830 (9,318)	993,390 (6,355)	673,110 (6,286)	113,330 (2,896)	1,865,430 (19,380)	764,920 (8,028)	561,320 (5,730)	539,190 (12,633)	1,079,050 (15,497)
2007	4,545,910 (21,853)	1,685,220 (5,288)	878,830 (4,562)	688,260 (1,640)	118,130 (3,104)	1,833,540 (18,364)	698,930 (5,885)	417,610 (3,218)	717,000 (16,573)	1,027,150 (11,379)
2009	4,179,060 (33,168)	1,541,830 (3,250)	782,050 (3,085)	642,720 (846)	117,050 (578)	1,665,680 (30,216)	579,190 (1,685)	401,430 (3,952)	685,050 (28,928)	971,550 (8,113)
2011	3,976,960 (18,241)	1,481,620 (3,867)	737,090 (3,675)	630,970 (321)	113,560 (459)	1,583,610 (16,558)	568,150 (3,607)	443,780 (2,604)	571,690 (15,197)	911,730 (3,469)
2013	4,083,860 (42,441)	1,466,550 (27,646)	680,370 (18,826)	666,260 (20,228)	119,930 (843)	1,615,120 (29,311)	544,610 (5,638)	446,050 (5,316)	624,470 (27,948)	1,002,180 (11,849)
2015	4,304,470 (69,171)	1,487,620 (42,646)	662,670 (24,233)	677,540 (22,542)	147,410 (14,387)	1,771,440 (47,422)	576,570 (38,496)	445,620 (15,105)	749,250 (33,313)	1,045,410 (27,611)
2017	4,251,960 (69,049)	1,478,040 (37,641)	593,910 (24,950)	738,980 (27,007)	145,150 (7,204)	1,727,280 (36,077)	518,200 (10,946)	486,720 (19,828)	722,360 (29,984)	1,046,640 (24,548)
Grades 9 through 12										
1995	1,162,500 (4,625)	618,460 (2,786)	90,650 (†)	275,370 (2,786)	252,440 (†)	342,180 (3,174)	135,610 (2,338)	122,460 (645)	84,120 (1,720)	201,860 (1,495)
1997	1,185,260 (2,374)	619,010 (96)	86,240 (†)	275,400 (†)	257,370 (96)	352,690 (2,261)	144,950 (1,660)	117,450 (848)	90,290 (1,221)	213,560 (1,860)
1999	1,229,290 (8,260)	626,520 (70)	80,270 (†)	272,790 (†)	273,460 (70)	375,100 (7,920)	158,040 (1,640)	117,000 (1,237)	100,060 (7,461)	227,670 (2,208)
2001	1,296,480 (6,669)	640,570 (2,317)	82,930 (2,293)	291,520 (†)	266,130 (338)	401,290 (3,527)	172,340 (2,633)	127,340 (1,625)	101,600 (1,852)	254,620 (4,465)
2003	1,311,150 (24,733)	633,590 (3,888)	74,930 (†)	292,230 (†)	266,430 (3,888)	392,310 (4,195)	167,250 (3,144)	131,220 (1,924)	93,840 (2,031)	285,250 (23,952)
2005	1,348,930 (18,073)	622,970 (1,538)	69,560 (†)	283,510 (700)	269,900 (1,341)	437,900 (6,541)	192,440 (3,404)	135,590 (1,493)	109,860 (5,190)	288,070 (16,551)
2007	1,364,300 (11,958)	622,930 (1,377)	67,030 (1,201)	281,680 (566)	274,210 (364)	449,680 (3,796)	184,260 (1,768)	109,430 (374)	156,000 (3,052)	291,700 (11,156)
2009	1,309,430 (6,480)	618,390 (4,409)	74,380 (42)	266,290 (4,311)	277,720 (920)	410,540 (4,285)	157,830 (362)	114,880 (1,074)	137,840 (4,111)	280,500 (1,880)
2011	1,291,130 (15,396)	606,250 (14,313)	67,320 (10)	268,840 (14,313)	270,090 (†)	408,330 (5,747)	162,420 (1,349)	121,560 (513)	124,350 (5,792)	276,550 (3,485)
2013	1,311,880 (14,936)	588,580 (13,452)	59,480 (358)	270,060 (13,416)	259,040 (905)	415,810 (2,774)	162,490 (1,942)	119,440 (1,862)	133,880 (1,762)	307,490 (6,938)
2015	1,446,060 (23,777)	595,050 (2,166)	53,450 (1,662)	283,050 (38)	258,550 (1,388)	497,390 (23,622)	184,220 (15,411)	141,870 (9,045)	171,300 (16,438)	353,620 (5,530)
2017	1,468,020 (17,378)	659,290 (15,189)	54,670 (3,818)	313,180 (14,701)	291,440 (†)	460,960 (6,962)	166,870 (2,664)	146,600 (5,627)	147,490 (2,665)	347,780 (4,172)

See notes at end of table.

Table 205.20. Enrollment and percentage distribution of students enrolled in private elementary and secondary schools, by school orientation and grade level: Selected years, fall 1995 through fall 2017—Continued

[Standard errors appear in parentheses]

Grade level and year	Total private enrollment	Catholic				Other religious				Nonsectarian
		Total	Parochial	Diocesan	Private	Total	Conservative Christian	Affiliated[1]	Unaffiliated[1]	
1	2	3	4	5	6	7	8	9	10	11
					Percentage distribution					
Total, all grades										
1995	100.0 (†)	45.0 (0.19)	24.7 (0.13)	14.4 (0.08)	5.9 (0.03)	35.4 (0.19)	13.3 (0.12)	11.8 (0.08)	10.3 (0.18)	19.7 (0.23)
1997	100.0 (†)	44.8 (0.13)	24.2 (0.09)	14.7 (0.05)	5.9 (0.03)	35.3 (0.18)	13.9 (0.12)	10.9 (0.06)	10.5 (0.17)	19.9 (0.17)
1999	100.0 (†)	44.2 (0.24)	23.2 (0.14)	14.6 (0.07)	6.4 (0.04)	36.4 (0.28)	14.5 (0.09)	10.7 (0.08)	11.2 (0.36)	19.3 (0.11)
2001	100.0 (†)	42.3 (0.25)	20.7 (0.14)	15.5 (0.12)	6.1 (0.04)	36.8 (0.22)	14.8 (0.13)	10.5 (0.13)	11.5 (0.18)	20.9 (0.33)
2003	100.0 (†)	41.3 (0.27)	19.4 (0.17)	15.8 (0.14)	6.1 (0.07)	36.5 (0.25)	14.6 (0.13)	10.7 (0.10)	11.3 (0.22)	22.1 (0.36)
2005	100.0 (†)	39.6 (0.26)	17.5 (0.13)	15.8 (0.14)	6.3 (0.07)	37.9 (0.25)	15.8 (0.14)	11.5 (0.09)	10.7 (0.20)	22.5 (0.34)
2007	100.0 (†)	39.1 (0.20)	16.0 (0.11)	16.4 (0.09)	6.6 (0.06)	38.6 (0.25)	14.9 (0.12)	8.9 (0.06)	14.8 (0.26)	22.3 (0.25)
2009	100.0 (†)	39.4 (0.25)	15.6 (0.11)	16.6 (0.13)	7.2 (0.05)	37.8 (0.37)	13.4 (0.09)	9.4 (0.07)	15.0 (0.48)	22.8 (0.16)
2011	100.0 (†)	39.6 (0.25)	15.3 (0.09)	17.1 (0.25)	7.3 (0.04)	37.8 (0.28)	13.9 (0.09)	10.7 (0.08)	13.2 (0.34)	22.6 (0.15)
2013	100.0 (†)	38.1 (0.50)	13.7 (0.33)	17.4 (0.51)	7.0 (0.07)	37.6 (0.44)	13.1 (0.16)	10.5 (0.13)	14.1 (0.47)	24.3 (0.28)
2015	100.0 (†)	36.2 (0.66)	12.5 (0.38)	16.7 (0.40)	7.1 (0.24)	39.5 (0.80)	13.2 (0.85)	10.2 (0.39)	16.0 (0.73)	24.3 (0.51)
2017	100.0 (†)	37.4 (0.53)	11.3 (0.40)	18.4 (0.51)	7.6 (0.16)	38.3 (0.42)	12.0 (0.24)	11.1 (0.40)	15.2 (0.43)	24.4 (0.40)
Prekindergarten through grade 8										
1995	100.0 (†)	42.9 (0.20)	28.8 (0.17)	12.1 (0.06)	2.1 (0.02)	36.9 (0.22)	13.7 (0.13)	12.1 (0.09)	11.1 (0.21)	20.2 (0.28)
1997	100.0 (†)	43.0 (0.15)	28.4 (0.12)	12.6 (0.05)	2.0 (0.03)	36.7 (0.20)	14.3 (0.09)	11.1 (0.06)	11.3 (0.19)	20.3 (0.19)
1999	100.0 (†)	42.5 (0.23)	27.5 (0.16)	12.7 (0.06)	2.3 (0.04)	38.0 (0.26)	14.9 (0.09)	11.1 (0.07)	12.0 (0.32)	19.6 (0.12)
2001	100.0 (†)	40.5 (0.27)	24.4 (0.17)	13.7 (0.14)	2.3 (0.05)	38.4 (0.25)	15.2 (0.15)	10.7 (0.14)	12.5 (0.20)	21.2 (0.37)
2003	100.0 (†)	39.4 (0.25)	23.1 (0.18)	14.0 (0.13)	2.2 (0.01)	38.3 (0.23)	15.1 (0.12)	10.8 (0.09)	12.4 (0.24)	22.3 (0.22)
2005	100.0 (†)	37.7 (0.25)	21.0 (0.14)	14.2 (0.15)	2.4 (0.06)	39.5 (0.21)	16.2 (0.16)	11.9 (0.09)	11.4 (0.22)	22.8 (0.23)
2007	100.0 (†)	37.1 (0.20)	19.3 (0.13)	15.1 (0.09)	2.6 (0.07)	40.3 (0.27)	15.4 (0.14)	9.2 (0.07)	15.8 (0.30)	22.6 (0.21)
2009	100.0 (†)	36.9 (0.29)	18.7 (0.15)	15.4 (0.12)	2.8 (0.03)	39.9 (0.43)	13.9 (0.11)	9.6 (0.10)	16.4 (0.57)	23.2 (0.20)
2011	100.0 (†)	37.3 (0.18)	18.5 (0.11)	15.9 (0.08)	2.9 (0.02)	39.8 (0.24)	14.3 (0.08)	11.2 (0.08)	14.4 (0.32)	22.9 (0.11)
2013	100.0 (†)	35.9 (0.53)	16.7 (0.42)	16.3 (0.44)	2.9 (0.04)	39.5 (0.52)	13.3 (0.17)	10.9 (0.15)	15.3 (0.59)	24.5 (0.31)
2015	100.0 (†)	34.6 (0.78)	15.4 (0.48)	15.7 (0.50)	3.4 (0.31)	41.2 (0.81)	13.4 (0.82)	10.4 (0.35)	17.4 (0.73)	24.3 (0.61)
2017	100.0 (†)	34.8 (0.64)	14.0 (0.52)	17.4 (0.56)	3.4 (0.17)	40.6 (0.52)	12.2 (0.28)	11.4 (0.45)	17.0 (0.56)	24.6 (0.48)
Grades 9 through 12										
1995	100.0 (†)	53.2 (0.20)	7.8 (0.03)	23.7 (0.20)	21.7 (0.09)	29.4 (0.20)	11.7 (0.18)	10.5 (0.06)	7.2 (0.14)	17.4 (0.12)
1997	100.0 (†)	52.2 (0.10)	7.3 (0.01)	23.2 (0.05)	21.7 (0.04)	29.8 (0.16)	12.2 (0.13)	9.9 (0.08)	7.6 (0.10)	18.0 (0.14)
1999	100.0 (†)	51.0 (0.34)	6.5 (0.04)	22.2 (0.15)	22.2 (0.15)	30.5 (0.45)	12.9 (0.14)	9.5 (0.11)	8.1 (0.56)	18.5 (0.19)
2001	100.0 (†)	49.4 (0.26)	6.4 (0.17)	22.5 (0.12)	20.5 (0.10)	31.0 (0.19)	13.3 (0.17)	9.8 (0.12)	7.8 (0.13)	19.6 (0.28)
2003	100.0 (†)	48.3 (0.91)	5.7 (0.11)	22.3 (0.42)	20.3 (0.44)	29.9 (0.59)	12.8 (0.32)	10.0 (0.23)	7.2 (0.20)	21.8 (1.43)
2005	100.0 (†)	46.2 (0.60)	5.2 (0.07)	21.0 (0.18)	20.0 (0.27)	32.5 (0.52)	14.3 (0.28)	10.1 (0.16)	8.1 (0.37)	21.4 (0.97)
2007	100.0 (†)	45.7 (0.40)	4.9 (0.09)	20.6 (0.18)	20.1 (0.17)	33.0 (0.33)	13.5 (0.16)	8.0 (0.07)	11.4 (0.22)	21.4 (0.65)
2009	100.0 (†)	47.2 (0.25)	5.7 (0.03)	20.3 (0.27)	21.2 (0.12)	31.4 (0.25)	12.1 (0.06)	8.8 (0.08)	10.5 (0.28)	21.4 (0.15)
2011	100.0 (†)	47.0 (0.63)	5.2 (0.06)	20.8 (0.88)	20.9 (0.25)	31.6 (0.49)	12.6 (0.18)	9.4 (0.13)	9.6 (0.43)	21.4 (0.35)
2013	100.0 (†)	44.9 (0.64)	4.5 (0.06)	20.6 (0.83)	19.7 (0.24)	31.7 (0.42)	12.4 (0.19)	9.1 (0.17)	10.2 (0.19)	23.4 (0.47)
2015	100.0 (†)	41.1 (0.67)	3.7 (0.13)	19.6 (0.32)	17.9 (0.30)	34.4 (1.11)	12.7 (0.96)	9.8 (0.59)	11.8 (1.02)	24.5 (0.51)
2017	100.0 (†)	44.9 (0.63)	3.7 (0.25)	21.3 (0.80)	19.9 (0.24)	31.4 (0.46)	11.4 (0.21)	10.0 (0.36)	10.0 (0.19)	23.7 (0.34)

†Not applicable.
[1]Affiliated schools belong to associations of schools with a specific religious orientation other than Catholic or conservative Christian. Unaffiliated schools have a religious orientation or purpose but are not classified as Catholic, conservative Christian, or affiliated.

NOTE: Includes enrollment in prekindergarten through grade 12 in schools that offer kindergarten or higher grade. Ungraded students are prorated into prekindergarten through grade 8 and grades 9 through 12. Detail may not sum to totals because of rounding.
SOURCE: U.S. Department of Education, National Center for Education Statistics, Private School Universe Survey (PSS), 1995–96 through 2017–18. (This table was prepared August 2019.)

Table 205.30. Percentage distribution of students enrolled in private elementary and secondary schools, by school orientation and selected characteristics: Selected years, fall 2005 through fall 2017

[Standard errors appear in parentheses]

Selected characteristic	2005	2007	2009	2011	2013	2015	2017 Total	Catholic Total	Catholic Parochial	Catholic Diocesan	Catholic Private	Other religious Total	Other religious Conservative Christian	Other religious Affiliated[1]	Other religious Unaffiliated[1]	Nonsectarian
1	2	3	4	5	6	7	8	9	10	11	12	13	14	15	16	17
Total	100.0 (†)	100.0 (†)	100.0 (†)	100.0 (†)	100.0 (†)	100.0 (†)	100.0 (†)	100.0 (†)	100.0 (†)	100.0 (†)	100.0 (†)	100.0 (†)	100.0 (†)	100.0 (†)	100.0 (†)	100.0 (†)
School level[2]																
Elementary	56.8 (0.34)	54.6 (0.24)	53.5 (0.24)	52.7 (0.23)	52.8 (0.47)	50.3 (0.80)	49.8 (0.55)	63.0 (0.83)	86.0 (1.39)	66.3 (1.27)	21.0 (1.30)	39.7 (0.95)	21.9 (0.81)	41.0 (1.71)	52.7 (1.59)	45.3 (0.62)
Secondary	14.2 (0.34)	14.0 (0.17)	14.3 (0.11)	14.4 (0.25)	13.7 (0.19)	13.5 (0.20)	14.1 (0.32)	27.1 (0.77)	6.0 (0.25)	29.0 (1.24)	53.7 (0.89)	5.5 (0.13)	2.4 (0.05)	8.4 (0.34)	5.8 (0.29)	7.9 (0.18)
Combined	29.1 (0.29)	31.4 (0.25)	32.2 (0.21)	32.9 (0.21)	33.5 (0.48)	36.2 (0.88)	36.1 (0.46)	9.9 (0.42)	8.0 (1.41)	4.7 (0.21)	25.3 (0.42)	54.9 (0.92)	75.7 (0.82)	50.6 (1.93)	41.5 (1.41)	46.8 (0.62)
Student race/ethnicity[3]																
White	75.3 (0.10)	74.5 (0.17)	72.6 (0.20)	71.4 (0.14)	69.6 (0.31)	68.6 (0.34)	66.7 (0.40)	65.6 (0.48)	66.6 (0.96)	66.6 (0.78)	61.7 (0.12)	70.7 (0.50)	67.3 (0.39)	74.2 (1.24)	70.8 (0.96)	62.0 (0.62)
Black	9.6 (0.08)	9.8 (0.08)	9.2 (0.07)	8.9 (0.06)	9.3 (0.27)	9.3 (0.31)	9.3 (0.23)	7.6 (0.15)	6.3 (0.29)	7.5 (0.21)	9.8 (0.11)	10.4 (0.37)	11.6 (0.28)	8.7 (1.22)	10.8 (0.37)	10.2 (0.45)
Hispanic	9.2 (0.05)	9.6 (0.14)	9.4 (0.09)	9.8 (0.05)	10.2 (0.11)	10.4 (0.15)	11.3 (0.22)	15.7 (0.29)	16.1 (0.58)	15.4 (0.57)	15.6 (0.24)	8.0 (0.33)	9.2 (0.15)	6.6 (0.20)	8.0 (0.84)	9.0 (0.33)
Asian[4]	4.1 (0.05)	5.4 (0.07)	5.1 (0.05)	5.5 (0.03)	5.9 (0.05)	6.2 (0.06)	6.5 (0.15)	5.3 (0.07)	4.9 (0.18)	5.1 (0.12)	6.3 (0.09)	5.4 (0.16)	6.3 (0.22)	5.8 (0.20)	4.0 (0.35)	10.5 (0.45)
Pacific Islander[4]	— (†)	— (†)	0.6 (0.02)	0.6 (#)	0.7 (0.01)	0.7 (0.02)	0.8 (0.03)	0.7 (0.07)	0.8 (0.21)	0.6 (0.02)	0.8 (0.08)	0.9 (0.02)	0.7 (0.01)	0.3 (0.01)	1.6 (0.05)	0.9 (0.02)
American Indian/Alaska Native	1.8 (0.01)	0.6 (0.02)	0.4 (0.01)	0.5 (0.01)	0.5 (0.01)	0.5 (0.01)	0.5 (0.03)	0.5 (0.01)	0.5 (0.02)	0.4 (0.01)	0.9 (0.01)	0.5 (0.09)	0.6 (0.04)	0.3 (0.03)	0.61 (0.23)	0.6 (0.01)
Two or more races[4]	— (†)	— (†)	2.7 (0.02)	3.3 (0.01)	3.9 (0.03)	4.3 (0.08)	4.9 (0.06)	4.6 (0.08)	4.7 (0.18)	4.5 (0.09)	4.9 (0.08)	4.1 (0.13)	4.2 (0.25)	4.1 (0.26)	4.1 (0.18)	6.8 (0.09)
School enrollment																
Less than 50	4.5 (0.10)	4.4 (0.12)	5.4 (0.39)	4.6 (0.14)	5.4 (0.47)	5.5 (0.39)	4.9 (0.15)	0.4 (0.01)	0.3 (0.01)	0.2 (0.01)	0.7 (0.01)	7.1 (0.30)	4.5 (0.51)	3.2 (0.39)	12.0 (0.54)	8.2 (0.42)
50 to 149	16.7 (0.17)	16.6 (0.20)	17.3 (0.18)	16.8 (0.15)	17.1 (0.23)	16.8 (0.40)	16.2 (0.37)	7.4 (0.44)	7.3 (0.49)	8.3 (0.83)	5.3 (0.17)	18.3 (0.65)	16.0 (0.34)	13.5 (0.59)	23.6 (1.52)	26.3 (0.90)
150 to 299	26.6 (0.18)	26.0 (0.19)	25.9 (0.17)	26.2 (0.15)	25.5 (0.29)	25.1 (0.49)	25.2 (0.54)	28.9 (0.96)	40.2 (2.10)	28.8 (1.35)	12.5 (0.21)	24.2 (0.80)	24.5 (0.61)	23.6 (1.88)	24.3 (1.45)	21.1 (0.85)
300 to 499	21.1 (0.20)	21.2 (0.11)	21.0 (0.19)	21.0 (0.11)	20.4 (0.21)	19.5 (0.49)	20.3 (0.52)	25.8 (0.74)	28.2 (1.45)	26.5 (1.05)	20.4 (1.31)	18.6 (0.94)	21.6 (1.24)	20.1 (2.04)	15.3 (1.76)	14.3 (0.65)
500 to 749	15.0 (0.31)	14.6 (0.09)	14.0 (0.12)	15.0 (0.25)	14.5 (0.24)	15.8 (0.97)	14.8 (0.49)	19.4 (0.99)	17.6 (2.03)	19.0 (1.55)	23.1 (0.38)	12.8 (0.39)	15.7 (0.89)	14.7 (0.65)	9.1 (0.33)	10.9 (0.59)
750 or more	16.1 (0.24)	17.2 (0.24)	16.3 (0.12)	16.4 (0.29)	17.0 (0.54)	17.3 (0.29)	18.7 (0.34)	18.1 (0.44)	6.4 (0.26)	17.1 (0.76)	38.0 (0.63)	19.0 (0.54)	17.6 (0.34)	24.8 (1.68)	15.8 (0.56)	19.1 (0.37)
Region																
Northeast	23.5 (0.19)	24.1 (0.18)	23.9 (0.26)	23.8 (0.27)	22.3 (0.25)	22.9 (0.59)	21.5 (0.37)	22.5 (0.76)	19.4 (1.28)	21.4 (1.34)	29.7 (0.49)	18.2 (0.38)	7.1 (0.14)	24.3 (0.99)	22.5 (0.89)	25.1 (0.50)
Midwest	23.6 (0.30)	22.9 (0.15)	23.6 (0.38)	24.0 (0.26)	24.6 (0.64)	24.5 (0.77)	24.1 (0.65)	35.2 (1.01)	41.9 (2.12)	35.4 (1.47)	24.7 (0.41)	20.7 (0.94)	16.5 (0.76)	21.4 (2.04)	23.4 (1.99)	12.5 (0.56)
South	32.5 (0.33)	33.3 (0.26)	33.6 (0.29)	33.2 (0.16)	34.1 (0.33)	34.2 (0.73)	35.5 (0.63)	26.0 (0.84)	24.4 (1.76)	27.2 (1.56)	25.6 (1.22)	43.5 (0.93)	49.6 (0.96)	39.4 (2.05)	41.8 (1.69)	37.4 (0.89)
West	20.3 (0.36)	19.7 (0.19)	19.0 (0.17)	19.1 (0.09)	19.1 (0.32)	18.5 (0.33)	18.9 (0.51)	16.3 (0.31)	14.2 (0.61)	16.0 (0.50)	19.9 (0.35)	17.6 (0.55)	26.7 (0.81)	14.9 (0.67)	12.4 (1.21)	25.0 (1.17)
School locale																
City	41.3 (0.26)	41.1 (0.22)	41.0 (0.31)	41.5 (0.27)	42.5 (0.50)	43.0 (0.77)	43.1 (0.63)	46.1 (1.02)	44.2 (2.00)	44.8 (1.38)	52.1 (0.79)	40.0 (0.97)	33.0 (0.74)	45.4 (2.01)	41.5 (1.63)	43.3 (0.92)
Suburban	40.0 (0.35)	40.3 (0.22)	39.0 (0.34)	38.3 (0.20)	41.0 (0.44)	40.2 (0.82)	39.9 (0.58)	40.8 (1.01)	39.3 (1.82)	42.7 (1.55)	38.7 (0.64)	37.7 (0.79)	43.7 (0.96)	39.2 (1.55)	31.9 (1.22)	42.0 (0.79)
Town	7.2 (0.13)	7.0 (0.09)	7.1 (0.17)	6.8 (0.05)	6.3 (0.33)	6.2 (0.56)	8.7 (0.42)	8.7 (1.01)	12.5 (2.13)	9.3 (1.56)	1.8 (0.03)	5.8 (0.12)	6.9 (0.17)	5.0 (0.20)	5.4 (0.19)	4.2 (0.69)
Rural	11.5 (0.37)	11.6 (0.32)	12.9 (0.42)	13.4 (0.33)	10.1 (0.47)	10.7 (0.57)	10.5 (0.41)	4.3 (0.15)	4.0 (0.44)	3.2 (0.10)	7.4 (0.12)	16.5 (0.96)	16.3 (0.50)	10.3 (2.09)	21.3 (1.79)	10.5 (0.46)

—Not available.
†Not applicable.
#Rounds to zero.
‡Interpret data with caution. The coefficient of variation (CV) for this estimate is between 30 and 50 percent.
[1]Affiliated schools belong to associations of schools with a specific religious orientation other than Catholic or conservative Christian. Unaffiliated schools have a religious orientation or purpose but are not classified as Catholic, conservative Christian, or affiliated.
[2]Elementary schools have grade 6 or lower and no grade higher than 8. Secondary schools have no grade lower than 7. Combined schools include those that have grades lower than 7 and higher than 8, as well as those that do not classify students by grade level.
[3]Race categories exclude persons of Hispanic ethnicity. Race/ethnicity was not collected for prekindergarten students (821,800 out of 5,719,990 students in 2017). Percentage distribution is based on the students for whom race/ethnicity was reported.
[4]Prior to 2009, Pacific Islander data are included with Asian data. Separate data on Pacific Islander students and data on students of Two or more races were not collected prior to 2009.
NOTE: Includes enrollment in prekindergarten through grade 12 in schools that offer kindergarten or higher grade. Detail may not sum to totals because of rounding.
SOURCE: U.S. Department of Education, National Center for Education Statistics, Private School Universe Survey (PSS), 2005–06 through 2017–18. (This table was prepared August 2019.)

Table 205.40.   Number and percentage distribution of private elementary and secondary students, teachers, and schools, by orientation of school and selected characteristics: Fall 1999, fall 2009, and fall 2017

[Standard errors appear in parentheses]

Selected characteristic	Fall 1999 Total Number	Fall 1999 Total Percent	Fall 2009 Total Number	Fall 2009 Total Percent	Fall 2017 Total Number	Fall 2017 Total Percent	Fall 2017 Catholic Number	Fall 2017 Catholic Percent	Fall 2017 Other religious Number	Fall 2017 Other religious Percent	Fall 2017 Nonsectarian Number	Fall 2017 Nonsectarian Percent
1	2	3	4	5	6	7	8	9	10	11	12	13
Students[1]												
Total	6,018,280 (30,179)	100.0 (†)	5,488,490 (35,857)	100.0 (†)	5,719,990 (74,133)	100.0 (†)	2,137,330 (40,520)	100.0 (†)	2,188,240 (40,106)	100.0 (†)	1,394,420 (26,889)	100.0 (†)
School level[2]												
Elementary	3,595,020 (11,516)	59.7 (0.22)	2,937,090 (26,807)	53.5 (0.24)	2,846,020 (56,267)	49.8 (0.55)	1,346,850 (36,078)	63.0 (0.83)	867,760 (29,313)	39.7 (0.95)	631,410 (15,274)	45.3 (0.62)
Secondary	806,640 (2,395)	13.4 (0.08)	785,810 (4,810)	14.3 (0.11)	808,630 (16,013)	14.1 (0.32)	578,300 (15,841)	27.1 (0.77)	119,880 (1,910)	5.5 (0.13)	110,450 (1,338)	7.9 (0.18)
Combined	1,616,620 (23,949)	26.9 (0.28)	1,765,590 (15,909)	32.2 (0.21)	2,065,340 (35,992)	36.1 (0.46)	212,190 (9,771)	9.9 (0.42)	1,200,600 (27,105)	54.9 (0.92)	652,550 (16,618)	46.8 (0.62)
School enrollment												
Less than 50	238,980 (5,691)	4.0 (0.09)	296,000 (22,889)	5.4 (0.39)	277,530 (9,120)	4.9 (0.15)	7,490 (0)	0.4 (0.01)	155,760 (6,968)	7.1 (0.30)	114,280 (6,141)	8.2 (0.42)
50 to 149	939,110 (10,717)	15.6 (0.14)	950,050 (12,053)	17.3 (0.18)	924,490 (25,783)	16.2 (0.37)	157,680 (9,882)	7.4 (0.44)	399,970 (16,510)	18.3 (0.65)	366,830 (14,385)	26.3 (0.90)
150 to 299	1,615,970 (7,315)	26.9 (0.16)	1,423,220 (9,951)	25.9 (0.17)	1,441,670 (38,720)	25.2 (0.54)	618,050 (25,586)	28.9 (0.96)	529,270 (20,288)	24.2 (0.80)	294,350 (13,550)	21.1 (0.85)
300 to 499	1,419,360 (13,203)	23.6 (0.18)	1,154,950 (10,730)	21.0 (0.19)	1,158,950 (31,868)	20.3 (0.52)	551,610 (15,687)	25.8 (0.74)	407,920 (23,904)	18.6 (0.94)	199,410 (8,974)	14.3 (0.65)
500 to 749	917,670 (2,330)	15.2 (0.08)	768,540 (†)	14.0 (0.09)	848,140 (30,584)	14.8 (0.49)	415,130 (24,969)	19.4 (0.99)	280,450 (7,412)	12.8 (0.39)	152,570 (9,627)	10.9 (0.59)
750 or more	887,190 (18,232)	14.7 (0.26)	895,720 (6,538)	16.3 (0.12)	1,069,210 (19,363)	18.7 (0.34)	387,370 (†)	18.1 (0.44)	414,870 (12,135)	19.0 (0.54)	266,970 (6,355)	19.1 (0.37)
Student race/ethnicity[3]												
White	4,061,870 (24,242)	77.3 (0.12)	3,410,360 (31,067)	72.6 (0.20)	3,267,740 (46,018)	66.7 (0.40)	1,285,900 (30,147)	65.6 (0.48)	1,312,690 (26,032)	70.7 (0.50)	669,160 (10,377)	62.0 (0.62)
Black	494,530 (5,079)	9.4 (0.09)	430,970 (2,579)	9.2 (0.07)	453,670 (11,354)	9.3 (0.23)	149,800 (2,761)	7.6 (0.15)	193,510 (7,194)	10.4 (0.37)	110,360 (5,814)	10.2 (0.45)
Hispanic	435,890 (1,592)	8.3 (0.04)	443,290 (4,113)	9.4 (0.09)	552,000 (13,863)	11.3 (0.22)	307,230 (7,087)	15.7 (0.29)	148,190 (6,890)	8.0 (0.33)	96,580 (6,348)	9.0 (0.33)
Asian	239,510 (877)	4.6 (0.02)	239,320 (1,894)	5.1 (0.05)	315,970 (8,834)	6.5 (0.15)	104,030 (1,531)	5.3 (0.07)	98,660 (3,190)	5.3 (0.16)	113,270 (6,348)	10.5 (0.45)
Pacific Islander	[†]	[‡]	28,020 (884)	0.6 (0.02)	40,960 (1,418)	0.8 (0.03)	13,510 (1,387)	0.7 (0.07)	17,590 (188)	0.9 (0.02)	9,860 (94)	0.9 (0.02)
American Indian/ Alaska Native	22,690 (164)	0.4 (#)	21,080 (162)	0.4 (0.02)	26,840 (1,659)	0.5 (0.03)	10,340 (126)	0.5 (0.01)	10,060 (1,650)	0.5 (0.09)	6,440 (117)	0.6 (0.01)
Two or more races	—	—	127,090 (781)	2.7	240,970 (3,881)	4.9 (0.06)	90,870 (1,792)	4.6 (0.08)	77,070 (2,904)	4.1 (0.13)	73,020 (1,049)	6.8 (0.09)
School locale												
City	— (†)	—	2,252,780 (12,708)	41.0 (0.31)	2,463,590 (50,197)	43.1 (0.63)	985,600 (23,753)	46.1 (1.02)	874,720 (26,907)	40.0 (0.97)	603,270 (20,872)	43.3 (0.92)
Suburban	— (†)	—	2,137,800 (20,891)	39.0 (0.34)	2,284,510 (35,510)	39.9 (0.58)	873,070 (26,231)	40.8 (1.01)	825,600 (16,957)	37.7 (0.79)	585,830 (11,623)	42.0 (0.79)
Town	— (†)	—	387,920 (9,565)	7.1 (0.17)	371,150 (25,577)	6.5 (0.42)	186,510 (23,522)	8.7 (1.02)	125,930 (730)	5.8 (0.12)	58,710 (10,017)	4.2 (0.69)
Rural	— (†)	—	709,990 (26,462)	12.9 (0.42)	600,740 (25,531)	10.5 (0.41)	92,150 (2,740)	4.3 (0.15)	361,990 (24,792)	16.5 (0.96)	146,590 (5,414)	10.5 (0.46)
Teachers[5]												
Total	408,400 (2,977)	100.0 (†)	437,410 (3,222)	100.0 (†)	482,320 (5,669)	100.0 (†)	152,900 (2,961)	100.0 (†)	182,860 (3,057)	100.0 (†)	146,560 (2,539)	100.0 (†)
School level[2]												
Elementary	200,910 (735)	49.2 (0.31)	194,480 (1,878)	44.5 (0.25)	200,120 (3,691)	41.5 (0.56)	88,590 (2,249)	57.9 (1.17)	60,840 (1,641)	33.3 (0.79)	50,700 (1,339)	34.6 (0.63)
Secondary	62,740 (229)	15.4 (0.12)	67,530 (553)	15.4 (0.14)	73,690 (2,330)	15.3 (0.48)	45,780 (2,271)	29.9 (1.23)	12,920 (443)	7.1 (0.26)	14,990 (276)	10.2 (0.24)
Combined	144,750 (2,682)	35.4 (0.41)	175,410 (1,853)	40.1 (0.26)	208,520 (3,496)	43.2 (0.47)	18,530 (653)	12.1 (0.41)	109,110 (2,639)	59.7 (0.82)	80,870 (1,787)	55.2 (0.64)
School enrollment												
Less than 50	25,970 (488)	6.4 (0.11)	34,120 (1,642)	7.8 (0.34)	35,760 (1,330)	7.4 (0.25)	1,100 (0)	0.7 (0.01)	19,020 (1,077)	10.4 (0.53)	15,640 (782)	10.7 (0.50)
50 to 149	70,800 (983)	17.3 (0.21)	82,460 (1,102)	18.9 (0.23)	85,130 (2,523)	17.6 (0.42)	15,010 (1,508)	9.8 (0.89)	34,680 (1,158)	19.0 (0.56)	35,440 (1,440)	24.2 (0.81)
150 to 299	102,240 (486)	25.0 (0.20)	107,490 (1,873)	24.6 (0.33)	114,100 (2,944)	23.7 (0.53)	43,360 (1,706)	28.4 (0.93)	41,420 (1,498)	22.6 (0.74)	29,330 (1,504)	20.0 (0.94)
300 to 499	90,010 (1,316)	22.0 (0.28)	86,850 (751)	19.9 (0.19)	91,470 (2,245)	19.0 (0.46)	37,920 (1,185)	24.8 (0.91)	31,580 (1,443)	17.3 (0.70)	21,970 (680)	15.0 (0.47)
500 to 749	57,930 (79)	14.2 (0.10)	56,920 (†)	13.0 (0.10)	68,790 (2,335)	14.3 (0.46)	28,290 (2,018)	18.5 (1.17)	23,260 (610)	12.7 (0.36)	17,240 (506)	11.8 (0.27)
750 or more	61,440 (2,143)	15.0 (0.45)	69,570 (566)	15.9 (0.13)	87,090 (1,768)	18.1 (0.34)	27,230 (†)	17.8 (0.43)	32,910 (1,244)	18.0 (0.61)	26,950 (553)	18.4 (0.31)
School locale												
City	— (†)	—	176,740 (799)	40.4 (0.33)	206,880 (3,770)	42.9 (0.58)	69,920 (1,760)	45.7 (1.23)	73,510 (2,032)	40.2 (0.87)	63,450 (1,782)	43.3 (0.76)
Suburban	— (†)	—	166,170 (2,463)	38.0 (0.41)	185,400 (2,704)	38.4 (0.53)	60,840 (2,145)	39.8 (1.23)	65,780 (1,336)	36.0 (0.74)	58,770 (1,342)	40.1 (0.64)
Town	— (†)	—	30,390 (663)	6.9 (0.15)	31,410 (2,294)	6.5 (0.45)	14,830 (2,040)	9.7 (1.21)	10,910 (125)	6.0 (0.13)	5,660 (1,041)	3.9 (0.70)
Rural	— (†)	—	64,120 (1,960)	14.7 (0.39)	58,640 (2,235)	12.2 (0.43)	7,310 (173)	4.8 (0.14)	32,660 (1,970)	17.9 (0.92)	18,670 (1,036)	12.7 (0.74)

See notes at end of table.

Table 205.40. Number and percentage distribution of private elementary and secondary students, teachers, and schools, by orientation of school and selected characteristics: Fall 1999, fall 2009, and fall 2017—Continued

[Standard errors appear in parentheses]

Selected characteristic	Fall 1999 Total		Fall 2009 Total		Fall 2017 Total		Fall 2017 Catholic		Fall 2017 Other religious		Fall 2017 Nonsectarian	
	Number	Percent	Number	Percent	Number	Percent	Number	Percent	Number	Percent	Number	Percent
1	2	3	4	5	6	7	8	9	10	11	12	13
Schools												
Total	33,000 (301)	100.0 (†)	33,370 (834)	100.0 (†)	32,460 (559)	100.0 (†)	7,050 (147)	100.0 (†)	14,500 (319)	100.0 (†)	10,910 (342)	100.0 (†)
School level[2]												
Elementary	22,300 (242)	67.6 (0.43)	21,420 (745)	64.2 (0.70)	20,090 (460)	61.9 (0.82)	5,410 (134)	76.7 (0.78)	8,010 (329)	55.2 (1.53)	6,670 (241)	61.1 (1.18)
Secondary	2,540 (62)	7.7 (0.19)	2,780 (39)	8.3 (0.23)	2,840 (92)	8.8 (0.30)	1,130 (57)	16.1 (0.74)	810 (63)	5.6 (0.45)	900 (28)	8.2 (0.30)
Combined	8,150 (160)	24.7 (0.40)	9,160 (153)	27.5 (0.54)	9,530 (300)	29.3 (0.76)	510 (16)	7.2 (0.26)	5,680 (206)	39.1 (1.42)	3,340 (176)	30.6 (1.13)
School enrollment												
Less than 50	9,160 (210)	27.8 (0.44)	11,070 (801)	33.2 (1.61)	10,300 (323)	31.7 (0.67)	240 (0)	3.4 (0.07)	5,780 (207)	39.9 (0.93)	4,280 (259)	39.2 (1.46)
50 to 149	10,260 (134)	31.1 (0.29)	10,470 (154)	31.4 (0.81)	9,970 (261)	30.7 (0.57)	1,480 (76)	21.0 (0.92)	4,310 (165)	29.7 (0.78)	4,180 (162)	38.3 (1.28)
150 to 299	7,440 (34)	22.5 (0.21)	6,690 (46)	20.1 (0.49)	6,790 (196)	20.9 (0.54)	2,840 (113)	40.3 (1.11)	2,510 (97)	17.3 (0.70)	1,450 (79)	13.3 (0.68)
300 to 499	3,730 (41)	11.3 (0.13)	3,010 (30)	9.0 (0.24)	3,030 (89)	9.3 (0.27)	1,420 (37)	20.2 (0.62)	1,090 (73)	7.5 (0.50)	520 (22)	4.8 (0.25)
500 to 749	1,530 (3)	4.6 (0.04)	1,280 (†)	3.8 (0.10)	1,410 (51)	4.4 (0.17)	690 (42)	9.8 (0.56)	470 (12)	3.2 (0.11)	250 (16)	2.3 (0.17)
750 or more	870 (20)	2.6 (0.06)	850 (7)	2.5 (0.06)	950 (21)	2.9 (0.08)	370 (†)	5.2 (0.16)	350 (12)	2.4 (0.10)	230 (8)	2.1 (0.10)
Racial/ethnic enrollment concentration												
More than 50 percent White	26,490 (290)	80.3 (0.21)	25,110 (818)	75.2 (0.74)	23,250 (434)	71.6 (0.60)	5,180 (†)	73.6 (0.58)	10,940 (303)	75.4 (0.77)	7,120 (259)	65.3 (1.14)
More than 50 percent Black	2,660 (34)	8.0 (0.11)	2,640 (70)	7.9 (0.28)	2,220 (79)	6.8 (0.26)	290 (†)	4.1 (0.13)	1,240 (55)	8.5 (0.40)	690 (49)	6.3 (0.47)
More than 50 percent Hispanic	1,220 (20)	3.7 (0.07)	1,550 (72)	4.6 (0.23)	1,990 (153)	6.1 (0.42)	680 (†)	9.7 (0.32)	620 (100)	4.3 (0.68)	680 (90)	6.2 (0.74)
No racial/ethnic group more than 50 percent	2,150 (36)	6.5 (0.11)	3,300 (103)	9.9 (0.36)	4,080 (121)	12.6 (0.32)	790 (†)	11.2 (0.30)	1,350 (45)	9.3 (0.34)	1,940 (113)	17.8 (0.87)
School locale												
City	— (†)	— (†)	10,810 (171)	32.4 (0.88)	10,530 (221)	32.4 (0.61)	2,830 (69)	40.2 (0.99)	3,910 (117)	26.9 (0.93)	3,790 (128)	34.8 (0.98)
Suburban	— (†)	— (†)	11,610 (176)	34.8 (0.94)	12,150 (300)	37.4 (0.76)	2,660 (69)	37.7 (0.97)	4,420 (144)	30.5 (1.00)	5,070 (180)	46.5 (1.11)
Town	— (†)	— (†)	3,340 (154)	10.0 (0.50)	2,750 (150)	8.5 (0.43)	1,020 (110)	14.5 (1.35)	1,180 (43)	8.1 (0.36)	550 (92)	5.0 (0.77)
Rural	— (†)	— (†)	7,610 (799)	22.8 (1.86)	7,020 (336)	21.6 (0.86)	530 (35)	7.5 (0.48)	4,990 (301)	34.4 (1.47)	1,500 (148)	13.8 (1.19)

—Not available.
†Not applicable.
#Rounds to zero.
[1]Includes students in prekindergarten through grade 12 in schools that offer kindergarten or higher grade.
[2]Elementary schools have grade 6 or lower and no grade higher than 8. Secondary schools have no grade lower than 7. Combined schools include those that have grades lower than 7 and higher than 8, as well as those that do not classify students by grade level.
[3]Race/ethnicity was not collected for prekindergarten students (821,800 in fall 2017). Percentage distribution is based on the students for whom race/ethnicity was reported.

[4]For 1999, Pacific Islander students are included under Asian. Prior to 2009, data were not collected on Pacific Islander students as a separate category.
[5]Reported in full-time equivalents (FTE). Excludes teachers who teach only prekindergarten students.
NOTE: Tabulation includes schools that offer kindergarten or higher grade. Detail may not sum to totals because of rounding.
SOURCE: U.S. Department of Education, National Center for Education Statistics, Private School Universe Survey (PSS), 1999–2000, 2009–10, and 2017–18. (This table was prepared August 2019.)

Table 205.80. Private elementary and secondary schools, enrollment, teachers, and high school graduates, by state: Selected years, 2007 through 2017

[Standard errors appear in parentheses]

State	Schools, fall 2017		Enrollment in prekindergarten through grade 12												Teachers,[1] fall 2017		High school graduates, 2016–17	
			Fall 2007		Fall 2009		Fall 2011		Fall 2013		Fall 2015		Fall 2017					
1	2		3		4		5		6		7		8		9		10	
United States	32,460	(559)	5,910,210	(28,363)	5,488,490	(35,857)	5,268,090	(24,908)	5,395,740	(50,342)	5,750,520	(85,729)	5,719,990	(74,133)	482,320	(5,669)	348,230	(3,751)
Alabama	370	(35)	83,840	(103)	95,570	(11,745)	81,070	(49)	76,400	(295)	75,070	(†)	70,840	(2,360)	5,890	(212)	4,580	(35)
Alaska	50	(†)	4,990	(†)	7,510!	(2,740)	5,170	(†)	5,080	(†)	5,540	(†)	4,470	(†)	410	(†)	‡	(†)
Arizona	330	(32)	64,910	(†)	55,390	(†)	53,120	(229)	55,070	(†)	56,610	(†)	56,800	(1,153)	4,300	(128)	3,570	(†)
Arkansas	230!	(85)	40,120	(11,961)	28,900	(1,371)	29,930	(1,245)	30,340	(1,496)	37,930	(6,108)	30,530	(1,872)	2,460	(85)	1,680	(†)
California	3,340	(47)	703,810	(6,129)	623,150	(4,185)	608,070	(69)	596,160	(3,500)	627,170	(10,231)	643,010	(22,494)	51,490	(2,007)	41,310	(398)
Colorado	410	(62)	64,740	(†)	63,720	(3,486)	61,140	(148)	60,690	(4,498)	68,140	(9,589)	56,420	(2,338)	5,070	(529)	2,960	(62)
Connecticut	370	(38)	85,150	(9,241)	72,540	(464)	66,320	(142)	72,770	(8,293)	66,710	(2,671)	62,680	(4,763)	7,840	(1,070)	5,950	(†)
Delaware	160!	(59)	32,520	(2,701)	26,640	(†)	25,090	(†)	23,640	(†)	19,660	(†)	28,130!	(9,939)	2,530!	(832)	1,390	(147)
District of Columbia	60	(†)	19,640	(†)	17,810	(†)	16,950	(†)	19,790	(277)	17,110	(1,939)	14,280	(†)	1,700	(†)	1,060	(†)
Florida	2,870	(271)	391,660	(6,123)	343,990	(1,023)	340,960	(230)	372,790	(2,812)	389,310	(207)	471,580	(26,070)	37,960	(2,449)	26,900	(215)
Georgia	840	(111)	157,430	(9,185)	150,300	(6,251)	138,080	(†)	150,360	(2,250)	189,630	(27,662)	166,310	(16,140)	14,990	(209)	10,100	(†)
Hawaii	130	(†)	37,300	(290)	37,130	(†)	37,530	(†)	33,820	(32)	45,600	(7,730)	40,840	(†)	3,570	(†)	3,510	(†)
Idaho	280	(81)	24,700!	(11,608)	18,680	(4,814)	13,670	(193)	18,580	(3,090)	20,230	(3,947)	26,040	(5,656)	1,820	(441)	890	(129)
Illinois	1,350	(70)	312,270	(6,638)	289,720	(9,237)	271,030	(1,289)	281,360	(6,026)	280,440	(19,662)	258,280	(16,148)	19,200	(973)	14,450	(192)
Indiana	910	(118)	119,910	(2,284)	120,770	(5,919)	129,120	(12,177)	121,230	(3,928)	171,570	(4,510)	144,780	(16,314)	10,370	(1,117)	6,610	(291)
Iowa	320	(80)	47,820	(†)	45,160	(†)	63,840	(14,665)	56,150	(9,338)	70,870	(16,178)	51,040	(1,661)	4,030	(289)	2,810	(†)
Kansas	200	(†)	47,780	(2,414)	44,680	(1,668)	43,100	(1,640)	41,520	(3,286)	42,270	(†)	43,660	(†)	3,350	(†)	2,870	(†)
Kentucky	420	(79)	76,140	(2,074)	70,590	(2,132)	69,410	(12)	74,750	(4,226)	70,090	(†)	86,880	(19,678)	7,300	(1,962)	7,260!	(2,868)
Louisiana	530	(71)	137,460	(†)	147,040	(9,890)	125,720	(108)	129,720	(2,606)	166,560	(33,949)	146,100	(16,303)	10,940	(1,060)	8,700	(164)
Maine	140	(†)	21,260	(143)	18,310	(†)	18,350	(†)	18,380	(272)	18,600	(†)	18,340	(†)	1,990	(†)	2,530	(†)
Maryland	750	(53)	165,760	(1,160)	145,690	(160)	137,450	(564)	143,530	(2,030)	142,630	(3,549)	157,180	(14,193)	14,050	(673)	9,830	(†)
Massachusetts	660	(22)	151,640	(2,516)	137,110	(1,169)	130,940	(1,596)	134,560	(943)	123,230	(865)	121,040	(658)	14,540	(61)	10,700	(†)
Michigan	840	(94)	159,100	(2,047)	153,230	(5,828)	135,580	(544)	141,590	(6,240)	172,130	(34,196)	147,650	(10,736)	10,940	(983)	7,930	(124)
Minnesota	810	(220)	101,740	(3,903)	89,530	(†)	87,620	(†)	85,260	(†)	75,630	(†)	128,690	(30,057)	9,640	(2,104)	6,260	(922)
Mississippi	200	(†)	55,270	(†)	54,650	(2,458)	52,060	(†)	50,330	(3,333)	43,580	(†)	47,450	(†)	3,800	(†)	3,030	(†)
Missouri	780	(182)	125,610	(3,685)	117,970	(2,065)	130,130	(8,715)	139,570	(25,980)	125,290	(8,723)	132,030	(16,277)	10,100	(1,442)	8,250	(401)
Montana	120	(†)	15,030!	(5,465)	10,390	(1,221)	10,550	(†)	10,560	(521)	11,690	(†)	10,390	(†)	1,040	(†)	530	(†)
Nebraska	270	(53)	40,320	(†)	39,040	(†)	40,750	(†)	42,300	(†)	48,960	(5,442)	50,940	(7,667)	4,420!	(1,451)	3,900!	(1,348)
Nevada	140	(†)	29,820	(2,009)	25,060	(†)	26,130	(†)	21,980	(†)	23,910	(†)	26,330	(†)	1,830	(†)	1,330	(†)
New Hampshire	350	(97)	30,920	(†)	26,470	(†)	27,350	(†)	26,700	(†)	25,330	(†)	32,490	(7,282)	3,460	(983)	2,840	(343)
New Jersey	1,100	(83)	253,250	(5,016)	232,020	(16,536)	210,220	(1,211)	211,150	(4,607)	213,170	(13,684)	214,840	(12,022)	18,990	(564)	15,070	(†)
New Mexico	‡	(†)	27,290	(1,388)	23,730	(507)	22,680	(10)	21,750	(†)	22,230	(†)	‡	(†)	‡	(†)	1,080	(†)
New York	1,690	(4)	518,850	(7,196)	486,310	(5,211)	487,810	(19,574)	452,380	(901)	520,660	(16,620)	469,720	(2,192)	43,290	(118)	31,020	(†)
North Carolina	640	(9)	121,660	(2,226)	110,740	(1,851)	119,070	(†)	118,090	(492)	124,030	(†)	122,060	(3,653)	11,730	(254)	6,820	(28)
North Dakota	50	(†)	7,430	(†)	7,750	(†)	7,770	(†)	8,290	(†)	7,830	(†)	9,260	(†)	790	(†)	‡	(†)
Ohio	1,430	(186)	239,520	(2,741)	246,250	(24,214)	213,990	(3,419)	238,620	(19,487)	255,690	(40,837)	247,790	(24,684)	18,190	(1,508)	14,640	(730)
Oklahoma	150	(†)	40,320	(5,032)	34,000	(716)	35,750	(847)	32,740	(†)	32,160	(1,061)	31,550	(†)	2,790	(†)	1,770	(†)
Oregon	400	(49)	66,260	(5,188)	56,820	(3,502)	53,200	(†)	58,830	(3,109)	57,310	(†)	52,960	(787)	4,410	(394)	3,260	(197)
Pennsylvania	2,500	(126)	324,020	(6,253)	301,640	(5,036)	276,300	(3,668)	253,800	(756)	315,830	(38,974)	282,330	(13,928)	23,630	(793)	18,060	(244)
Rhode Island	110	(†)	28,260	(1,096)	24,940	(†)	25,420	(†)	22,180	(†)	20,620	(2,711)	18,770	(†)	1,750	(†)	1,780	(†)
South Carolina	390	(33)	71,430	(1,043)	62,320	(311)	60,890	(†)	65,350	(4,447)	62,830	(†)	65,200	(2,438)	5,620	(367)	3,260	(33)
South Dakota	80	(†)	12,280	(†)	11,470	(†)	12,490	(†)	9,950	(†)	10,740	(†)	12,170	(†)	1,000	(†)	690	(†)
Tennessee	490	(9)	117,540	(12,851)	98,310	(4,176)	92,430	(34)	93,990	(3,210)	91,950	(†)	99,110	(7,467)	9,200	(674)	7,790	(583)
Texas	2,090	(180)	296,540	(4,132)	313,360	(11,968)	285,320	(2,046)	312,640	(5,896)	351,270	(26,334)	347,430	(28,896)	31,300	(2,472)	17,390	(1,399)
Utah	150	(†)	20,860	(†)	21,990	(1,558)	18,660	(55)	23,310	(†)	21,140	(†)	22,650	(†)	1,820	(†)	1,690	(†)
Vermont	100	(†)	12,600	(232)	10,350	(†)	9,030	(†)	8,890	(†)	10,040	(†)	9,090	(†)	1,120	(†)	870	(†)
Virginia	820	(40)	143,140	(7,988)	128,140	(2,581)	123,780	(82)	131,330	(1,828)	140,350	(12,832)	131,290	(281)	11,710	(80)	7,440	(160)
Washington	620	(20)	104,070	(3,054)	94,340	(625)	93,630	(234)	119,730	(17,349)	100,140	(479)	99,620	(762)	7,870	(78)	4,330	(†)
West Virginia	120	(†)	14,980	(†)	13,860	(†)	13,430	(1)	14,350	(†)	14,780	(†)	14,310	(†)	1,280	(†)	860	(†)
Wisconsin	910	(67)	138,290	(1,597)	130,510	(†)	127,250	(†)	160,650	(32,980)	144,020	(11,405)	151,990	(15,852)	11,280	(896)	6,160	(†)
Wyoming	40	(†)	2,930	(†)	2,910	(†)	2,740	(†)	2,780	(†)	2,240	(†)	2,320	(†)	220	(†)	‡	(†)

†Not applicable.
!Interpret data with caution. The coefficient of variation (CV) for this estimate is between 30 and 50 percent.
‡Reporting standards not met. Either there are too few cases for a reliable estimate or the coefficient of variation (CV) is 50 percent or greater.
[1]Reported in full-time equivalents (FTE). Excludes teachers who teach only prekindergarten students.
NOTE: Includes special education, vocational/technical education, and alternative schools. Tabulation includes schools that offer kindergarten or higher grade. Includes enrollment of students in prekindergarten through grade 12 in schools that offer kindergarten or higher grade. Some state counts are based on a census of schools in that state rather than a sample; for these counts, standard errors are not applicable. Detail may not sum to totals because of rounding.
SOURCE: U.S. Department of Education, National Center for Education Statistics, Private School Universe Survey (PSS), 2007–08 through 2017–18. (This table was prepared August 2019.)

Table 206.10. Number and percentage of homeschooled students ages 5 through 17 with a grade equivalent of kindergarten through 12th grade, by selected child, parent, and household characteristics: Selected years, 1999 through 2016

[Standard errors appear in parentheses]

Selected child, parent, or household characteristic	1999 Number homeschooled[1] (in thousands)	1999 Percent homeschooled[1]	2003 Number homeschooled[1] (in thousands)	2003 Percent homeschooled[1]	2007 Number homeschooled[1] (in thousands)	2007 Percent homeschooled[1]	2012 Number homeschooled[1,2] (in thousands)	2012 Percent homeschooled[1,2]	2016 Number homeschooled[1] (in thousands)	2016 Percent homeschooled[1]
1	2	3	4	5	6	7	8	9	10	11
Total	850 (71.1)	1.7 (0.14)	1,096 (92.3)	2.2 (0.18)	1,520 (118.0)	3.0 (0.23)	1,773 (115.7)	3.4 (0.23)	1,690 (118.4)	3.3 (0.23)
Sex of child										
Male	417 (43.9)	1.6 (0.17)	569 (61.9)	2.2 (0.24)	639 (75.1)	2.4 (0.28)	875 (73.7)	3.3 (0.28)	807 (79.2)	3.0 (0.30)
Female	434 (46.1)	1.8 (0.19)	527 (58.2)	2.1 (0.23)	881 (97.4)	3.5 (0.39)	898 (80.3)	3.6 (0.32)	882 (74.8)	3.5 (0.29)
Race/ethnicity of child										
White	640 (62.3)	2.0 (0.19)	843 (77.5)	2.7 (0.25)	1,171 (102.2)	3.9 (0.34)	1,205 (95.7)	4.5 (0.35)	998 (92.6)	3.8 (0.35)
Black	84 (24.8)	1.0 (0.31)	103! (33.9)	1.3! (0.42)	61! (21.2)	0.8! (0.28)	140 (37.1)	2.0 (0.52)	132 (27.6)	1.9 (0.39)
Hispanic	77 (17.7)	1.1 (0.25)	59! (21.1)	0.7! (0.26)	147 (27.5)	1.5 (0.29)	265 (41.1)	2.3 (0.35)	444 (62.2)	3.5 (0.50)
Asian/Pacific Islander	‡ (†)	‡ (†)	‡ (†)	‡ (†)	‡ (†)	‡ (†)	—	—	—	—
Asian	—	—	—	—	—	—	73! (21.0)	2.8! (0.90)	44 (12.6)	1.4 (0.40)
Pacific Islander	—	—	—	—	—	—	‡ (†)	‡ (†)	42 (12.0)	‡ (†)
American Indian/Alaska Native	‡ (†)	‡ (†)	‡ (†)	‡ (†)	‡ (†)	‡ (†)	‡ (†)	‡ (†)	‡ (†)	‡ (†)
Other[3]	16! (6.4)	1.6! (0.62)	59! (26.9)	4.9! (2.13)	111 (29.5)	4.8 (1.30)	82 (16.3)	3.2 (0.61)	69 (15.2)	2.7 (0.62)
Grade equivalent[4]										
Kindergarten through grade 5	428 (48.1)	1.8 (0.20)	472 (55.3)	1.9 (0.23)	717 (83.8)	3.0 (0.36)	833 (84.8)	4.0 (0.33)	767 (74.4)	3.0 (0.29)
Kindergarten	92 (19.7)	2.4 (0.52)	98	1.9	114	3.2	212 (47.3)	4.0 (0.90)	181 (40.7)	3.5 (0.80)
Grades 1 through 3	199 (36.7)	1.6 (0.29)	214 (33.1)	1.8 (0.28)	406 (64.5)	3.4 (0.54)	353 (50.9)	2.9 (0.42)	300 (34.1)	2.4 (0.62)
Grades 4 and 5	136 (22.5)	1.7 (0.28)	160 (30.1)	1.9 (0.35)	197 (41.4)	2.5 (0.52)	268 (44.2)	3.5 (0.52)	287 (51.8)	3.3 (0.62)
Grades 6 through 8	186 (28.0)	1.6 (0.24)	302 (44.9)	2.4 (0.36)	371 (65.3)	3.0 (0.53)	424 (49.0)	3.8 (0.41)	398 (49.1)	3.8 (0.41)
Grades 9 through 12	235 (33.3)	1.7 (0.24)	315 (47.0)	2.3 (0.33)	422 (58.2)	2.8 (0.38)	516 (53.6)	3.8 (0.39)	525 (55.9)	3.8 (0.40)
Number of children in the household										
One child	132 (18.0)	1.3 (0.17)	110 (22.3)	1.4 (0.27)	197 (32.5)	1.4 (0.38)	418 (29.6)	3.4 (0.23)	338 (35.5)	2.7 (0.27)
Two children	248 (28.4)	1.3 (0.15)	306 (45.1)	1.5 (0.26)	414 (67.2)	1.5 (0.32)	493 (51.5)	2.5 (0.26)	475 (55.3)	2.3 (0.27)
Three or more children	470 (63.9)	2.3 (0.31)	679 (80.2)	3.1 (0.36)	909 (102.4)	4.1 (0.46)	862 (88.4)	4.5 (0.47)	877 (84.8)	4.7 (0.45)
Number of parents in the household										
Two parents	683 (68.3)	2.1 (0.21)	886 (82.7)	2.5 (0.32)	1,357 (111.5)	3.6 (0.30)	1,354 (104.2)	3.8 (0.29)	1,358 (103.7)	3.7 (0.28)
One parent	142 (25.0)	0.9 (0.16)	196! (42.6)	1.5! (0.32)	118! (28.4)	1.0! (0.24)	342 (51.6)	2.5 (0.37)	293 (38.4)	2.3 (0.37)
Nonparental guardians	25! (14.4)	‡ (†)	‡ (†)	‡ (†)	‡ (†)	‡ (†)	77! (31.9)	4.0! (1.60)	38 (9.9)	2.0 (0.54)
Parent participation in the labor force										
Two parents—both in labor force	237 (39.8)	1.0 (0.17)	274 (44.1)	1.1 (0.18)	518 (76.2)	2.0 (0.29)	588 (63.5)	2.5 (0.27)	427 (56.5)	1.7 (0.23)
Two parents—one in labor force	444 (53.9)	4.6 (0.55)	594 (73.7)	5.6 (0.67)	808 (94.3)	7.5 (0.82)	719 (76.3)	6.2 (0.65)	935 (87.8)	7.2 (0.68)
One parent in labor force	98 (21.8)	0.9 (0.16)	174! (39.8)	1.4 (0.33)	127! (29.5)	1.3! (0.30)	247 (40.9)	2.2 (0.36)	189 (29.6)	1.8 (0.29)
No parent participation in labor force	71 (18.8)	1.9 (0.48)	‡ (†)	‡ (†)	‡ (†)	‡ (†)	130 (31.9)	4.8 (1.15)	139 (23.9)	4.0 (0.72)
Highest education level of parents										
High school diploma or less	160 (26.5)	0.9 (0.15)	269 (51.6)	1.7 (0.32)	208 (35.5)	1.5 (0.24)	560 (81.7)	3.4 (0.50)	510 (66.1)	3.3 (0.43)
Vocational/technical, associate's degree, or some college	287 (37.3)	1.9 (0.24)	338 (57.7)	2.1 (0.36)	559 (77.5)	3.8 (0.52)	525 (45.6)	3.7 (0.29)	418 (49.2)	3.1 (0.36)
Bachelor's degree/some graduate school	213 (36.2)	2.6 (0.42)	309 (48.5)	2.8 (0.45)	444 (64.7)	3.9 (0.57)	434 (51.4)	3.7 (0.43)	501 (64.0)	3.6 (0.45)
Graduate/professional degree	190 (39.8)	2.3 (0.46)	180 (41.6)	2.3 (0.55)	309 (50.0)	2.9 (0.46)	255 (27.3)	3.3 (0.36)	260 (30.7)	3.0 (0.35)
Household income[5]										
$20,000 or less	184 (35.2)	1.5 (0.28)	164 (38.9)	1.8 (0.43)	186 (42.1)	2.2 (0.50)	219 (41.8)	2.9 (0.56)	184 (29.0)	2.9 (0.46)
$20,001 to $50,000	356 (42.9)	1.8 (0.22)	430 (60.3)	2.6 (0.36)	420 (59.8)	3.1 (0.42)	528 (65.5)	3.8 (0.47)	483 (59.4)	3.7 (0.46)
$50,001 to $75,000	162 (25.5)	1.9 (0.30)	264 (51.1)	2.4 (0.46)	414 (58.8)	4.0 (0.57)	370 (48.9)	3.9 (0.53)	435 (58.6)	4.8 (0.65)
$75,001 to $100,000	148 (26.5)	1.5 (0.28)	169! (42.9)	2.6! (0.66)	264 (57.2)	3.8 (0.83)	288 (47.3)	4.2 (0.69)	268 (38.4)	3.8 (0.55)
Over $100,000	—	—	—	—	236 (57.5)	2.0 (0.49)	367 (42.8)	2.7 (0.31)	319 (39.0)	1.9 (0.24)
Locale										
City	—	—	—	—	327 (40.4)	2.0 (0.26)	493 (59.5)	3.1 (0.40)	493 (56.0)	3.0 (0.33)
Suburban	—	—	—	—	503 (78.8)	2.6 (0.41)	601 (66.8)	3.3 (0.34)	651 (76.2)	2.9 (0.33)
Town	—	—	—	—	168 (37.1)	3.0 (0.65)	127 (30.8)	2.6 (0.41)	177 (30.0)	4.3 (0.70)
Rural	—	—	—	—	523 (75.9)	4.9 (0.71)	552 (68.2)	4.5 (0.55)	368 (45.1)	4.4 (0.54)

—Not available.
†Not applicable.
‡Reporting standards not met (too few cases for a reliable estimate).
!Interpret data with caution. The coefficient of variation (CV) for this estimate is between 30 and 50 percent.
[1] Excludes students who were enrolled in school for more than 25 hours a week. Also excludes students who were homeschooled only due to a temporary illness.
[2] The National Center for Education Statistics uses a statistical adjustment for estimates of homeschoolers in 2012. For more information about this adjustment, please see Homeschooling in the United States: 2012 (NCES 2016-096REV).
[3] Includes Two or more races and race/ethnicity not reported.
[4] Students whose grade equivalent was "ungraded" were excluded from the grade analysis. The percentage of students with an "ungraded" grade equivalent was 0.02 percent in 2003 and 2007. There were no students with an "ungraded" grade equivalent in 2012.

[5] For 1999, estimates combine the "$75,001 to $100,000" and "Over $100,000" categories.
NOTE: While National Household Education Surveys Program (NHES) administrations prior to 2012 were administered via telephone with an interviewer, NHES:2012 and NHES:2016 used self-administered paper-and-pencil questionnaires that were mailed to respondents. Measurable differences between estimates for years prior to 2012 and estimates for later years could reflect actual changes in the population, or the changes could be due to the mode change from telephone to mail. Race categories exclude persons of Hispanic ethnicity. Detail may not sum to totals because of rounding. Some data have been revised from previously published figures.
SOURCE: U.S. Department of Education, National Center for Education Statistics, Parent Survey and Parent and Family Involvement in Education Survey of the National Household Education Surveys Program (Parent-NHES:1999 and PFI-NHES:2003, 2007, 2012, and 2016). (This table was prepared February 2018.)

Table 206.30. Percentage distribution of students enrolled in grades 1 through 12, by public school type and charter status, private school orientation, and selected child and household characteristics: 2016

[Standard errors appear in parentheses]

Selected child or household characteristic and public school type	Total, all schools	Public school, total	Public school type[1] Assigned	Chosen	Public school charter status Traditional[2]	Charter	Private school, total	Private school orientation Religious	Nonsectarian
1	2	3	4	5	6	7	8	9	10
Percentage distribution of all enrolled students, by school type and charter status	100.0 (†)	90.5 (0.32)	70.6 (0.61)	19.8 (0.52)	85.9 (0.44)	4.6 (0.31)	9.5 (0.32)	7.6 (0.32)	1.9 (0.18)
Percentage distribution of students in schools of each type or status, by characteristic									
Total, all students	100.0 (†)	100.0 (†)	100.0 (†)	100.0 (†)	100.0 (†)	100.0 (†)	100.0 (†)	100.0 (†)	100.0 (†)
Sex of child									
Male	51.8 (0.67)	52.0 (0.72)	52.2 (0.87)	51.2 (1.69)	52.0 (0.78)	51.4 (3.38)	50.3 (1.92)	50.2 (2.18)	50.9 (5.01)
Female	48.2 (0.67)	48.0 (0.72)	47.8 (0.87)	48.8 (1.69)	48.0 (0.78)	48.6 (3.38)	49.7 (1.92)	49.8 (2.18)	49.1 (5.01)
Race/ethnicity of child									
White	51.8 (0.41)	50.7 (0.44)	54.6 (0.57)	36.9 (1.19)	51.8 (0.47)	30.4 (2.85)	62.1 (1.85)	64.0 (2.15)	54.6 (5.02)
Black	14.3 (0.19)	14.5 (0.26)	12.1 (0.41)	23.2 (1.27)	13.9 (0.31)	26.2 (3.63)	12.2 (1.34)	12.3 (1.57)	11.6 (2.75)
Hispanic	23.8 (0.28)	24.7 (0.35)	23.3 (0.52)	29.9 (1.43)	24.1 (0.37)	36.0 (3.09)	15.0 (1.38)	15.4 (1.51)	13.5 (3.25)
Asian/Pacific Islander	5.7 (0.26)	5.6 (0.29)	5.6 (0.30)	5.7 (0.63)	5.6 (0.30)	4.7 (1.37)	6.3 (1.05)	4.4 (0.90)	13.7 (3.54)
Asian	5.4 (0.25)	5.3 (0.28)	5.3 (0.29)	5.3 (0.60)	5.4 (0.28)	4.0 (1.15)	6.0 (1.02)	4.1 (0.85)	13.7 (3.54)
Pacific Islander	0.3 (0.05)	0.3 (0.06)	0.2 (0.06)	0.4! (0.19)	0.2 (0.05)	‡ (†)	‡ (†)	‡ (†)	‡ (†)
Other[3]	4.5 (0.26)	4.5 (0.29)	4.5 (0.33)	4.3 (0.49)	4.6 (0.30)	2.7 (0.71)	4.4 (0.63)	3.9 (0.64)	6.7 (1.85)
Disability status of child as reported by parent									
Has a disability	16.9 (0.57)	17.3 (0.61)	17.4 (0.68)	17.0 (1.04)	17.3 (0.61)	15.9 (2.00)	13.3 (1.20)	12.7 (1.40)	15.8 (2.86)
Does not have a disability	83.1 (0.57)	82.7 (0.61)	82.6 (0.68)	83.0 (1.04)	82.7 (0.61)	84.1 (2.00)	86.7 (1.20)	87.3 (1.40)	84.2 (2.86)
Grade level									
Grades 1 through 5	43.5 (0.33)	43.6 (0.35)	44.2 (0.51)	41.3 (1.15)	43.2 (0.40)	51.6 (3.23)	42.7 (1.89)	43.2 (2.14)	40.9 (4.79)
Grades 6 through 8	25.2 (0.33)	24.9 (0.34)	25.3 (0.52)	23.8 (1.11)	24.8 (0.37)	27.9 (2.89)	27.4 (1.55)	27.8 (1.74)	25.8 (3.80)
Grades 9 through 12	31.3 (0.27)	31.5 (0.32)	30.5 (0.44)	34.8 (1.09)	32.0 (0.35)	20.5 (2.13)	29.9 (1.60)	29.0 (1.84)	33.4 (3.54)
Number of parents in the household									
Two parents	70.3 (0.51)	69.3 (0.57)	70.5 (0.72)	64.9 (1.34)	69.3 (0.57)	68.2 (3.61)	80.6 (1.52)	80.0 (1.71)	82.7 (2.59)
One parent	25.7 (0.55)	26.6 (0.62)	25.4 (0.73)	30.7 (1.29)	26.4 (0.62)	28.7 (3.43)	17.7 (1.46)	18.2 (1.67)	15.4 (2.46)
Nonparental guardians	3.9 (0.26)	4.2 (0.28)	4.1 (0.37)	4.5 (0.62)	4.2 (0.30)	3.0 (0.59)	1.8 (0.37)	1.8 (0.36)	‡ (†)
Highest education level of parents									
Less than a high school diploma	10.7 (0.30)	11.3 (0.34)	10.9 (0.44)	12.4 (1.13)	11.0 (0.35)	17.1 (3.53)	5.5 (1.27)	5.8 (1.37)	‡ (†)
High school diploma or GED	20.0 (0.27)	21.3 (0.30)	21.3 (0.48)	21.4 (1.28)	21.5 (0.36)	17.7 (3.26)	8.0 (1.43)	8.9 (1.62)	‡ (†)
Vocational/technical, associate's degree, or some college	25.7 (0.44)	26.6 (0.45)	26.7 (0.58)	26.0 (1.07)	26.7 (0.47)	25.0 (2.57)	17.5 (1.57)	19.5 (1.76)	9.7 (2.46)
Bachelor's degree/some graduate school	26.7 (0.46)	25.6 (0.47)	26.0 (0.60)	24.2 (0.99)	25.8 (0.50)	22.8 (1.96)	37.2 (1.60)	38.2 (1.89)	33.1 (3.76)
Graduate/professional degree	16.8 (0.18)	15.2 (0.19)	15.0 (0.27)	16.0 (0.78)	15.1 (0.19)	17.4 (1.87)	31.8 (1.68)	27.5 (1.75)	49.0 (5.11)
Poverty status of household[4]									
Poor	17.3 (0.42)	18.3 (0.47)	18.1 (0.50)	18.8 (1.26)	18.2 (0.46)	19.9 (2.80)	7.6 (1.36)	7.0 (1.38)	9.9! (4.05)
Near-poor	21.4 (0.45)	22.2 (0.51)	21.3 (0.59)	25.6 (1.50)	21.9 (0.52)	28.2 (4.09)	13.1 (1.59)	14.9 (1.90)	6.0 (1.70)
Nonpoor	61.4 (0.46)	59.5 (0.49)	60.6 (0.66)	55.6 (1.33)	59.9 (0.51)	51.8 (3.60)	79.3 (1.79)	78.1 (2.07)	84.1 (3.83)
Locale									
City	31.2 (0.74)	30.5 (0.79)	25.6 (0.80)	48.1 (1.58)	29.1 (0.74)	57.8 (3.20)	37.2 (1.76)	36.8 (2.02)	38.6 (3.24)
Suburban	44.5 (0.73)	44.1 (0.77)	46.0 (0.82)	37.7 (1.47)	44.6 (0.76)	34.8 (2.90)	48.1 (1.90)	47.9 (2.19)	48.6 (3.38)
Town	7.9 (0.37)	8.5 (0.40)	9.3 (0.47)	5.4 (0.56)	8.7 (0.42)	3.4 (0.95)	3.0 (0.42)	3.0 (0.49)	2.6! (0.89)
Rural	16.4 (0.42)	16.9 (0.45)	19.1 (0.51)	8.7 (0.66)	17.5 (0.46)	4.0 (1.14)	11.8 (1.19)	12.2 (1.33)	10.2 (2.42)
Region									
Northeast	19.9 (0.50)	19.3 (0.57)	20.8 (0.65)	13.8 (1.23)	19.4 (0.57)	16.8 (2.93)	26.1 (1.81)	25.0 (2.02)	30.4 (4.34)
South	23.9 (0.53)	24.0 (0.56)	23.2 (0.65)	26.8 (1.57)	24.4 (0.56)	16.7 (2.15)	23.3 (1.51)	21.8 (1.73)	29.2 (3.50)
Midwest	21.9 (0.55)	21.5 (0.60)	22.3 (0.66)	18.2 (1.42)	21.5 (0.58)	20.6 (3.61)	26.5 (1.65)	31.0 (1.83)	8.4 (1.65)
West	34.2 (0.63)	35.3 (0.68)	33.7 (0.79)	41.2 (1.73)	34.7 (0.71)	45.9 (3.25)	24.1 (1.59)	22.2 (1.82)	32.1 (3.71)
Public school type[1]									
Assigned	70.6 (0.61)	78.0 (0.57)	100.0 (†)	† (†)	82.1 (0.53)	100.0 (†)	† (†)	† (†)	† (†)
Chosen	19.8 (0.52)	21.8 (0.58)	† (†)	100.0 (†)	17.6 (0.54)	† (†)	† (†)	† (†)	† (†)

†Not applicable.
!Interpret data with caution. The coefficient of variation (CV) for this estimate is between 30 and 50 percent.
‡Reporting standards not met. The coefficient of variation (CV) for this estimate is 50 percent or greater.
[1]In 31 cases, questions about whether a student's school was assigned were not asked because parents reported the school as a private school, and it was only later identified as a public school based on administrative data. Due to the missing data on whether the school was assigned or chosen, these cases were included neither with assigned public schools nor with chosen public schools. These cases were included in the public school totals, however, and they could still be accurately classified as either traditional or charter schools based on administrative data.
[2]Includes all types of public noncharter schools.
[3]Includes American Indian/Alaska Native, Two or more races, and race/ethnicity not reported.

[4]Poor children are those whose family incomes were below the Census Bureau's poverty threshold in the year prior to data collection; near-poor children are those whose family incomes ranged from the poverty threshold to 199 percent of the poverty threshold; and nonpoor children are those whose family incomes were at or above 200 percent of the poverty threshold. The poverty threshold is a dollar amount that varies depending on a family's size and composition and is updated annually to account for inflation. In 2015, for example, the poverty threshold for a family of four with two children was $24,257. Survey respondents are asked to select the range within which their income falls, rather than giving the exact amount of their income; therefore, the measure of poverty status is an approximation.
NOTE: Data exclude homeschooled children. Race categories exclude persons of Hispanic ethnicity. Detail may not sum to totals because of rounding.
SOURCE: U.S. Department of Education, National Center for Education Statistics, Parent and Family Involvement in Education Survey of the National Household Education Surveys Program (PFI-NHES:2016). (This table was prepared February 2018.)

Table 207.10. Number of 3- to 5-year-olds not yet enrolled in kindergarten and percentage participating in home literacy activities with a family member, by type and frequency of activity and selected child and family characteristics: 2001, 2012, and 2016

[Standard errors appear in parentheses]

Selected child or family characteristic	Number of children (in thousands)			Percent of children participating in literacy activity with family member[1]														
				Read by family member three or more times in past week			Told a story by family member (At least once in past week)			Taught letters, words, or numbers			Did arts and crafts			Visited a library at least once in past month		
	2001	2012	2016	2001	2012	2016	2001	2012	2016	2001	2012	2016	2001	2012	2016	2001	2012	2016
1	2	3	4	5	6	7	8	9	10	11	12	13	14	15	16	17	18	19
Total	8,551 (11.0)	8,244 (85.1)	8,087 (91.1)	84 (0.8)	83 (0.8)	81 (1.1)	84 (0.8)	83 (0.9)	84 (1.2)	94 (0.6)	98 (0.3)	97 (0.6)	79 (0.9)	86 (0.8)	87 (1.1)	36 (1.1)	42 (1.2)	41 (1.4)
Age																		
3 years old	3,795 (91.4)	3,674 (89.8)	3,404 (123.0)	84 (1.1)	82 (1.3)	82 (1.7)	83 (1.2)	82 (1.4)	84 (1.6)	93 (1.0)	97 (0.5)	96 (1.1)	77 (1.3)	85 (1.1)	85 (1.7)	35 (1.9)	38 (1.6)	39 (2.1)
4 years old	3,861 (89.0)	3,508 (90.4)	3,379 (109.8)	85 (1.2)	84 (1.3)	81 (2.1)	84 (1.1)	85 (1.3)	85 (1.9)	95 (0.7)	98 (0.3)	96 (0.8)	82 (1.2)	87 (1.2)	89 (1.3)	37 (1.4)	43 (1.8)	40 (2.1)
5 years old	896 (47.0)	1,062 (59.6)	1,303 (84.9)	81 (2.7)	80 (2.7)	80 (3.3)	82 (2.4)	81 (2.6)	82 (3.3)	93 (1.8)	98 (0.7)	97 (1.0)	80 (2.4)	88 (1.9)	85 (3.9)	37 (3.4)	49 (3.8)	46 (3.6)
Sex																		
Male	4,292 (79.9)	4,251 (103.9)	4,184 (118.8)	82 (1.2)	82 (1.2)	80 (1.5)	82 (1.1)	82 (1.4)	82 (1.5)	94 (0.7)	97 (0.4)	96 (1.0)	76 (1.3)	84 (1.1)	85 (1.4)	35 (1.4)	41 (1.7)	40 (2.1)
Female	4,260 (79.6)	3,993 (104.2)	3,903 (117.5)	86 (1.0)	84 (1.4)	83 (1.9)	85 (1.0)	85 (1.0)	86 (1.9)	94 (0.8)	98 (0.4)	97 (0.6)	83 (1.3)	88 (1.1)	89 (1.7)	37 (1.6)	42 (1.4)	42 (2.0)
Race/ethnicity																		
White	5,313 (68.0)	4,062 (97.4)	4,003 (96.8)	89 (0.8)	90 (1.0)	88 (1.2)	86 (1.0)	87 (1.1)	86 (1.1)	95 (0.7)	98 (0.4)	96 (0.9)	85 (1.0)	90 (0.9)	90 (1.2)	39 (1.3)	44 (1.4)	44 (1.7)
Black	1,251 (55.1)	1,154 (63.4)	1,086 (67.4)	77 (2.6)	77 (3.3)	79 (3.3)	81 (2.1)	80 (2.3)	85 (3.0)	94 (1.8)	99 (0.6)	98 (1.2)	70 (3.1)	83 (2.8)	85 (3.2)	31 (2.6)	41 (3.8)	42 (4.5)
Hispanic	1,506 (43.5)	2,100 (76.1)	2,133 (84.9)	71 (1.9)	71 (2.0)	71 (3.4)	75 (2.0)	78 (2.7)	78 (3.6)	92 (2.2)	97 (0.7)	97 (1.1)	67 (2.2)	80 (1.9)	82 (2.7)	30 (2.0)	34 (2.2)	33 (3.0)
Asian/Pacific Islander[2]	202 (29.0)	420 (32.7)	400 (44.7)	87 (4.1)	77 (3.3)	74 (6.5)	81 (5.8)	85 (3.0)	88 (3.2)	96 (2.2)	98 (1.1)	98 (0.9)	74 (6.9)	84 (2.6)	79 (6.6)	47 (7.5)	55 (4.4)	49 (5.8)
Asian	— (†)	374 (30.3)	386 (43.4)	— (†)	75 (3.5)	74 (6.7)	— (†)	83 (3.0)	88 (3.2)	— (†)	98 (1.2)	98 (0.9)	— (†)	84 (2.9)	78 (6.7)	— (—)	55 (4.4)	49 (5.9)
Pacific Islander	— (†)	‡ (†)	‡ (†)	— (†)	‡ (†)	‡ (†)	— (†)	‡ (†)	‡ (†)	— (†)	‡ (†)	‡ (†)	— (†)	‡ (†)	‡ (†)	— (—)	‡ (†)	‡ (†)
American Indian/Alaska Native	‡ (†)	‡ (†)	‡ (†)	‡ (†)	‡ (†)	‡ (†)	‡ (†)	‡ (†)	‡ (†)	‡ (†)	‡ (†)	‡ (†)	‡ (†)	‡ (†)	‡ (†)	‡ (†)	‡ (†)	‡ (†)
Two or more races	240 (26.9)	463 (41.1)	418 (47.8)	84 (3.9)	87 (3.2)	81 (4.0)	92 (2.7)	83 (3.8)	83 (5.0)	93 (3.1)	99 (0.8)	97 (1.3)	86 (3.7)	88 (3.8)	90 (2.6)	31 (5.8)	44 (4.2)	38 (5.0)
Mother's highest level of education[3]																		
Less than high school	996 (54.5)	1,291 (71.9)	1,093 (90.7)	69 (2.8)	73 (3.1)	61 (5.9)	72 (2.7)	75 (3.5)	77 (6.1)	91 (2.0)	98 (0.8)	94 (2.9)	62 (3.0)	82 (2.6)	77 (5.4)	21 (2.4)	26 (3.1)	27 (4.1)
High school/GED	2,712 (89.0)	1,614 (64.0)	1,482 (87.1)	81 (1.6)	75 (2.5)	79 (2.7)	83 (1.3)	83 (1.8)	78 (2.9)	95 (0.9)	97 (0.9)	96 (1.4)	77 (1.8)	84 (1.8)	86 (2.3)	30 (1.9)	38 (2.8)	35 (4.4)
Vocational/technical or some college	1,833 (73.9)	1,663 (77.3)	1,400 (64.0)	85 (1.8)	85 (1.7)	80 (2.3)	85 (1.7)	83 (1.5)	83 (2.3)	94 (1.2)	97 (0.8)	97 (1.1)	81 (1.9)	86 (1.6)	88 (2.2)	38 (2.2)	40 (2.0)	38 (2.7)
Associate's degree	573 (40.9)	678 (50.0)	700 (53.7)	89 (2.5)	85 (2.3)	85 (2.7)	84 (2.7)	84 (2.2)	87 (2.4)	92 (2.3)	98 (0.7)	98 (1.3)	82 (3.2)	86 (2.3)	89 (2.2)	42 (4.3)	43 (3.9)	42 (3.2)
Bachelor's degree/some graduate school	1,553 (68.4)	1,870 (65.9)	2,078 (75.4)	93 (1.2)	92 (1.2)	90 (1.4)	88 (1.5)	90 (1.2)	89 (1.6)	95 (1.1)	99 (0.3)	98 (0.5)	89 (1.4)	92 (1.0)	89 (1.4)	46 (2.4)	49 (2.2)	47 (2.2)
Graduate/professional degree	685 (45.7)	680 (30.8)	1,036 (45.0)	96 (1.1)	95 (1.0)	91 (1.4)	89 (2.3)	89 (1.5)	89 (1.5)	95 (1.3)	97 (0.8)	97 (0.8)	86 (2.2)	91 (1.5)	91 (1.4)	55 (3.8)	64 (2.5)	56 (2.0)
Mother's employment status[3]																		
Employed	5,148 (84.2)	4,491 (88.6)	4,782 (116.5)	86 (1.0)	84 (1.1)	83 (1.4)	84 (1.0)	84 (1.2)	85 (1.3)	94 (0.7)	98 (0.3)	96 (0.8)	80 (1.2)	86 (0.9)	86 (1.3)	36 (1.2)	42 (1.5)	41 (1.8)
Unemployed	550 (36.9)	396 (52.0)	269 (37.7)	77 (5.0)	80 (4.4)	91 (3.9)	80 (4.7)	84 (3.5)	82 (6.5)	94 (3.3)	98 (1.1)	98 (1.8)	69 (5.5)	89 (4.0)	88 (5.4)	37 (4.8)	33 (4.2)	36 (7.6)
Not in labor force	2,756 (73.3)	2,737 (86.9)	2,737 (104.2)	83 (1.4)	84 (1.7)	79 (2.7)	82 (1.5)	84 (1.6)	84 (2.6)	94 (0.9)	97 (0.7)	97 (0.8)	80 (1.3)	87 (1.4)	87 (2.0)	38 (1.9)	43 (1.9)	41 (2.6)
Family income (in current dollars)																		
$20,000 or less	2,106 (58.4)	1,480 (60.3)	1,162 (63.5)	74 (2.1)	76 (2.3)	70 (3.1)	81 (1.6)	83 (1.9)	82 (2.9)	92 (1.5)	97 (0.9)	95 (2.1)	72 (2.2)	84 (1.6)	85 (2.5)	27 (2.0)	39 (2.5)	40 (3.9)
$20,001 to $50,000	2,934 (86.6)	2,372 (77.4)	2,211 (93.6)	83 (1.4)	78 (2.1)	76 (2.7)	83 (1.4)	82 (1.6)	83 (1.9)	95 (0.7)	98 (0.5)	96 (0.9)	79 (1.4)	83 (1.6)	85 (2.2)	35 (1.8)	35 (2.2)	35 (2.9)
$50,001 to $75,000	1,724 (74.4)	1,510 (67.2)	1,342 (84.5)	88 (1.4)	82 (2.3)	79 (4.0)	87 (1.6)	82 (2.4)	82 (4.4)	95 (1.1)	98 (0.6)	96 (0.9)	82 (1.7)	87 (2.3)	87 (2.4)	38 (2.3)	38 (2.5)	37 (3.4)
$75,001 to $100,000	879 (49.4)	1,082 (46.5)	1,047 (58.6)	91 (1.6)	86 (2.5)	88 (2.3)	85 (2.2)	89 (2.1)	89 (3.5)	93 (1.7)	98 (0.6)	98 (0.6)	87 (2.1)	91 (2.2)	91 (3.6)	47 (3.1)	44 (2.9)	41 (3.5)
Over $100,000	909 (43.2)	1,800 (66.3)	2,325 (70.0)	96 (1.2)	93 (1.0)	90 (1.5)	84 (2.3)	83 (2.0)	84 (1.7)	96 (1.2)	98 (0.7)	98 (0.6)	87 (2.1)	89 (1.4)	89 (1.4)	45 (2.7)	48 (2.4)	48 (2.2)

See notes at end of table.

Table 207.10. Number of 3- to 5-year-olds not yet enrolled in kindergarten and percentage participating in home literacy activities with a family member, by type and frequency of activity and selected child and family characteristics: 2001, 2012, and 2016—Continued

[Standard errors appear in parentheses]

Selected child or family characteristic	Number of children (in thousands)			Percent of children participating in literacy activity with family member[1]														
				Read to by family member three or more times in past week			Told a story by family member			At least once in past week								
										Taught letters, words, or numbers			Did arts and crafts			Visited a library at least once in past month		
	2001	2012	2016	2001	2012	2016	2001	2012	2016	2001	2012	2016	2001	2012	2016	2001	2012	2016
1	2	3	4	5	6	7	8	9	10	11	12	13	14	15	16	17	18	19
Number of parents in the household																		
Two parents	6,429 (75.0)	5,958 (95.6)	5,969 (117.0)	87 (0.8)	85 (0.9)	84 (1.3)	84 (0.9)	85 (1.0)	84 (1.3)	94 (0.6)	98 (0.3)	97 (0.7)	81 (0.9)	87 (0.9)	88 (1.2)	38 (1.2)	42 (1.4)	43 (1.6)
None or one parent	2,123 (75.0)	2,286 (81.1)	2,117 (91.9)	76 (2.0)	77 (1.8)	74 (2.6)	82 (1.6)	79 (1.5)	83 (2.0)	93 (1.3)	97 (0.7)	97 (1.0)	74 (2.3)	84 (1.6)	84 (2.3)	30 (2.1)	40 (2.3)	33 (2.6)
Poverty status[4]																		
Poor	2,008 (60.4)	1,958 (77.8)	1,536 (67.1)	74 (2.1)	74 (2.2)	71 (3.0)	81 (1.7)	82 (1.7)	83 (2.8)	92 (1.6)	96 (0.8)	94 (1.7)	73 (2.3)	83 (1.7)	85 (2.6)	27 (2.1)	39 (2.2)	38 (3.3)
Near-poor	1,782 (70.5)	1,960 (86.5)	1,984 (112.9)	81 (1.8)	81 (2.1)	75 (3.4)	82 (2.0)	81 (2.0)	82 (3.0)	95 (1.0)	98 (0.5)	97 (1.0)	76 (1.9)	82 (2.1)	86 (2.3)	33 (2.8)	38 (2.6)	36 (3.1)
Nonpoor	4,762 (71.9)	4,327 (87.6)	4,567 (108.9)	90 (0.9)	88 (1.0)	87 (1.0)	85 (1.0)	85 (1.2)	85 (1.4)	95 (0.6)	98 (0.4)	97 (0.4)	84 (1.0)	89 (1.0)	88 (1.3)	41 (1.4)	44 (1.5)	44 (1.7)

—Not available.
†Not applicable.
‡Reporting standards not met. Either there are too few cases for a reliable estimate or the coefficient of variation (CV) is 50 percent or greater.
[1]The respondent was the parent most knowledgeable about the child's care and education. Responding parents reported on their own activities and the activities of their spouse/other adults in the household.
[2]The 2001 questionnaire included a single item for "Asian or Pacific Islander," whereas questionnaires for later years included one item for Asian and a separate item for Pacific Islander.
[3]Excludes children living in households with no mother or female guardian present.
[4]Poor children are those whose family incomes were below the Census Bureau's poverty threshold in the year prior to data collection; near-poor children are those whose family incomes ranged from the poverty threshold to 199 percent of the poverty threshold; and nonpoor children are those whose family incomes were at or above 200 percent of the poverty threshold. The poverty threshold is a dollar amount that varies depending on a family's size and composition and is updated annually

to account for inflation. In 2015, for example, the poverty threshold for a family of four with two children was $24,257. Survey respondents are asked to select the range within which their income falls, rather than giving the exact amount of their income; therefore, the measure of poverty status is an approximation.
NOTE: Prior to 2012, National Household Education Surveys Program (NHES) surveys were administered via telephone with an interviewer. NHES:2012 used self-administered paper-and-pencil questionnaires that were mailed to respondents. For NHES:2016, initial contact with all respondents was by mail, and the majority of respondents received paper-and-pencil questionnaires. However, as an experiment with web use, a small sample of NHES:2016 respondents received mailed invitations to complete the survey online. Race categories exclude persons of Hispanic ethnicity. Detail may not sum to totals because of rounding and suppression of estimates that did not meet reporting standards. Some data have been revised from previously published figures.
SOURCE: U.S. Department of Education, National Center for Education Statistics, Early Childhood Program Participation Survey of the National Household Education Surveys Program (ECPP-NHES:2001, 2012, and 2016). (This table was prepared October 2017.)

Table 207.30. Number of kindergartners through fifth-graders and percentage whose parents reported doing education-related activities with their children in the past week, by selected child, parent, and school characteristics: 2003, 2012, and 2016

[Standard errors appear in parentheses]

Selected child, parent, or school characteristic	Number of children (in thousands)			Percent of children whose parents reported doing education-related activities with them in the past week											
				Told child a story			Did arts and crafts			Discussed family history/ethnic heritage			Played board games or did puzzles		
	2003	2012	2016	2003	2012	2016	2003	2012	2016	2003	2012	2016	2003	2012	2016
1	2	3	4	5	6	7	8	9	10	11	12	13	14	15	16
Total	23,887 (55.7)	25,331 (137.9)	25,085 (167.1)	74.9 (0.66)	68.8 (0.91)	72.0 (0.94)	74.9 (0.70)	67.0 (0.84)	68.8 (1.11)	53.1 (0.89)	49.4 (1.00)	50.8 (0.99)	72.9 (0.68)	64.0 (0.94)	67.4 (1.13)
Sex of child															
Male	12,192 (215.7)	13,103 (241.4)	12,925 (281.3)	73.3 (0.86)	68.2 (1.27)	71.3 (1.59)	69.7 (0.98)	60.7 (1.19)	61.8 (1.62)	51.1 (1.16)	47.6 (1.10)	47.9 (1.49)	71.8 (0.92)	63.0 (1.20)	66.5 (1.73)
Female	11,695 (207.6)	12,228 (234.7)	12,160 (221.5)	76.6 (0.96)	69.5 (1.22)	72.8 (1.27)	80.2 (1.01)	73.8 (1.25)	76.3 (1.29)	55.1 (1.28)	51.2 (1.47)	53.9 (1.35)	74.1 (1.05)	65.2 (1.14)	68.2 (1.37)
Race/ethnicity of child															
White	14,419 (155.8)	12,600 (173.4)	12,190 (262.3)	76.0 (0.96)	71.9 (0.98)	72.8 (1.21)	75.4 (0.89)	67.5 (1.08)	68.3 (1.17)	44.7 (1.13)	37.3 (1.21)	36.7 (1.18)	73.8 (0.87)	66.6 (1.03)	68.2 (1.19)
Black	3,765 (111.4)	3,642 (107.8)	3,450 (136.5)	69.6 (2.00)	64.3 (2.40)	73.8 (2.41)	68.1 (2.14)	64.0 (2.76)	66.1 (3.01)	66.6 (2.45)	67.4 (2.44)	69.9 (3.10)	72.9 (1.92)	60.1 (2.94)	64.7 (3.83)
Hispanic	4,220 (98.3)	6,051 (126.3)	6,234 (183.7)	74.2 (1.55)	65.4 (2.15)	69.9 (1.99)	79.6 (1.45)	67.7 (1.69)	71.9 (2.22)	64.5 (1.71)	58.1 (2.09)	64.5 (2.14)	68.5 (1.82)	62.2 (1.88)	69.2 (1.99)
Asian/Pacific Islander[1]	709 (82.9)	1,398 (93.2)	1,735 (171.4)	75.8 (3.73)	69.2 (3.38)	66.8 (6.31)	63.4 (4.34)	63.4 (3.45)	63.0 (7.10)	68.2 (4.83)	69.8 (3.56)	56.2 (5.10)	77.0 (3.82)	61.5 (3.87)	60.4 (6.54)
Asian	— (†)	1,331 (88.9)	1,676 (172.0)	— (†)	68.0 (3.52)	66.6 (6.54)	— (†)	62.7 (3.52)	62.8 (7.33)	— (†)	68.8 (3.78)	55.3 (5.19)	— (†)	60.6 (3.94)	61.1 (6.87)
Pacific Islander	— (†)	‡ (†)	‡ (†)	— (†)	‡	‡	— (†)	‡	‡	— (†)	‡	‡	— (†)	‡	‡
American Indian/Alaska Native	171 (36.3)	228 (54.2)	‡ (†)	84.1 (7.22)	70.3 (11.26)	‡ (†)	76.5 (8.06)	66.9 (9.66)	‡ (†)	82.4 (6.82)	56.0 (12.17)	‡ (†)	72.6 (10.24)	49.7 (11.34)	‡ (†)
Two or more races	603 (62.8)	1,411 (93.6)	1,410 (124.7)	83.5 (5.40)	66.4 (3.35)	77.5 (3.58)	69.7 (3.86)	69.7 (2.91)	73.6 (3.47)	63.3 (5.82)	51.7 (3.79)	58.5 (4.64)	77.8 (4.54)	64.2 (3.93)	67.0 (4.08)
Grade of child															
Kindergarten and grade 1	7,823 (32.5)	9,219 (140.6)	9,130 (174.2)	84.5 (0.93)	78.0 (1.60)	79.1 (1.72)	89.3 (0.84)	81.2 (1.14)	79.2 (2.22)	47.7 (1.38)	44.4 (1.89)	43.9 (2.00)	77.5 (1.17)	69.3 (1.56)	71.9 (2.28)
Grades 2 and 3	7,696 (24.5)	7,965 (155.5)	7,922 (183.1)	74.5 (1.21)	66.9 (1.51)	72.6 (1.68)	74.0 (1.12)	66.7 (1.54)	69.3 (1.57)	54.7 (1.34)	52.1 (1.53)	52.5 (1.88)	72.7 (1.09)	65.5 (1.44)	68.1 (1.99)
Grades 4 and 5	8,368 (30.1)	8,146 (130.5)	8,033 (167.3)	66.4 (1.20)	60.2 (1.55)	63.4 (1.55)	62.2 (1.36)	51.2 (1.45)	56.6 (1.56)	56.5 (1.42)	52.3 (1.44)	56.9 (1.59)	68.9 (1.18)	56.6 (1.50)	61.4 (1.62)
Language spoken most at home by child[2]															
English	21,595 (104.8)	21,763 (198.7)	20,716 (269.5)	75.4 (0.73)	69.4 (1.00)	73.2 (0.92)	74.4 (0.72)	67.2 (0.81)	68.5 (1.11)	51.5 (0.93)	46.8 (1.06)	47.2 (1.06)	73.7 (0.73)	64.0 (1.06)	67.0 (1.08)
Spanish	1,272 (69.2)	1,145 (78.2)	1,438 (151.4)	65.6 (2.85)	56.4 (5.08)	62.3 (5.94)	81.7 (2.16)	70.7 (3.63)	66.5 (5.88)	60.2 (3.11)	64.7 (4.04)	70.9 (5.69)	58.1 (3.10)	60.2 (4.36)	69.7 (5.49)
English and Spanish equally	559 (47.9)	1,310 (104.9)	1,398 (117.1)	76.6 (3.83)	68.7 (4.01)	69.0 (4.54)	78.7 (3.88)	64.5 (4.01)	78.3 (3.78)	77.3 (4.18)	64.0 (3.84)	75.9 (4.22)	75.2 (3.73)	67.0 (3.51)	72.8 (4.14)
English and other language equally	‡ (†)	705 (60.9)	1,038 (176.8)	‡ (†)	74.6 (3.94)	66.0 (8.87)	‡ (†)	66.9 (4.78)	66.9 (9.27)	‡ (†)	72.2 (4.54)	63.3 (8.85)	‡ (†)	68.2 (3.67)	63.8 (8.86)
Other language	375 (60.5)	335 (68.9)	415 (91.7)	81.7 (6.95)	66.1 (9.93)	77.6 (7.42)	76.7 (4.81)	55.2 (10.98)	70.1 (7.17)	75.1 (6.13)	63.1 (11.51)	47.6 (8.04)	74.8 (7.43)	65.5 (11.12)	66.9 (10.08)
Highest education level of parents/guardians in the household[3]															
Less than a high school diploma	1,664 (120.3)	2,933 (115.7)	2,690 (173.3)	67.2 (3.16)	65.0 (3.19)	59.6 (5.53)	74.8 (3.20)	67.2 (3.32)	66.1 (4.93)	60.4 (2.98)	60.7 (3.45)	59.6 (5.02)	66.8 (3.16)	61.7 (3.09)	59.3 (5.46)
High school diploma/equivalent (e.g., GED)	5,604 (163.6)	4,898 (146.9)	4,819 (168.4)	71.3 (1.59)	65.7 (2.45)	72.4 (2.45)	75.5 (1.32)	70.3 (2.50)	71.4 (2.76)	54.9 (1.91)	50.8 (2.04)	56.1 (3.27)	73.2 (1.39)	64.8 (2.32)	68.8 (2.40)
Vocational/technical or some college	5,466 (189.4)	5,044 (129.5)	4,043 (166.7)	75.9 (1.54)	69.1 (1.56)	70.3 (2.32)	76.2 (1.51)	64.4 (1.87)	68.9 (2.33)	50.8 (1.75)	47.0 (1.90)	49.0 (2.44)	71.6 (1.58)	63.9 (1.72)	70.8 (2.05)
Associate's degree	2,320 (139.6)	2,617 (141.8)	2,392 (138.2)	76.0 (2.00)	67.0 (3.80)	71.6 (2.57)	73.6 (2.47)	66.0 (2.45)	72.2 (2.69)	50.9 (3.16)	44.6 (3.22)	51.5 (3.36)	70.1 (2.50)	57.9 (3.69)	67.1 (2.70)
Bachelor's degree/some graduate school	5,214 (179.1)	6,485 (152.8)	6,688 (198.9)	77.3 (1.60)	71.3 (1.37)	76.0 (1.47)	74.0 (1.48)	66.8 (1.47)	68.4 (1.72)	47.3 (1.74)	45.6 (1.49)	46.3 (1.98)	75.8 (1.27)	65.1 (1.67)	67.8 (1.76)
Graduate/professional degree	3,618 (149.8)	3,354 (69.8)	4,452 (110.9)	78.6 (1.64)	72.7 (1.41)	75.0 (1.64)	73.9 (1.72)	67.3 (1.41)	66.4 (1.66)	60.1 (2.16)	51.9 (1.74)	47.8 (1.76)	74.9 (1.82)	67.8 (1.39)	67.0 (1.87)
Family income (in current dollars)															
$20,000 or less	4,418 (150.4)	3,838 (112.7)	3,324 (160.2)	73.9 (1.61)	68.7 (1.81)	65.6 (3.67)	76.0 (1.87)	71.4 (2.08)	67.1 (3.82)	61.6 (2.05)	54.3 (2.17)	57.9 (3.38)	73.3 (1.70)	61.7 (2.22)	64.7 (3.81)
$20,001 to $50,000	7,857 (230.1)	7,166 (155.7)	6,533 (154.9)	74.0 (1.31)	68.6 (1.87)	70.6 (1.94)	75.3 (1.05)	68.1 (1.86)	70.3 (2.41)	53.5 (1.59)	53.6 (2.07)	55.4 (2.38)	72.3 (1.45)	63.6 (1.80)	67.4 (2.16)
$50,001 to $75,000	5,024 (187.5)	4,380 (123.2)	4,159 (140.3)	74.9 (1.53)	68.5 (2.31)	71.9 (2.17)	75.3 (1.55)	67.5 (1.86)	68.8 (2.31)	49.6 (1.99)	47.7 (2.35)	54.7 (3.01)	72.1 (1.51)	63.3 (2.35)	68.1 (2.64)
$75,001 to $100,000	3,044 (127.1)	3,279 (81.0)	3,277 (99.8)	74.7 (2.02)	68.4 (2.03)	75.1 (2.30)	71.2 (1.98)	64.7 (2.13)	68.4 (2.78)	48.8 (2.28)	46.3 (2.46)	46.4 (2.39)	73.3 (2.30)	65.6 (2.29)	65.8 (2.46)
Over $100,000	3,543 (139.6)	6,668 (133.0)	7,790 (166.4)	78.6 (1.52)	69.4 (1.35)	74.7 (1.48)	75.1 (1.87)	64.1 (1.62)	68.6 (1.53)	50.1 (1.93)	44.5 (1.48)	43.8 (1.58)	74.7 (1.81)	65.5 (1.50)	68.7 (1.39)

See notes at end of table.

Table 207.30. Number of kindergartners through fifth-graders and percentage whose parents reported doing education-related activities with their children in the past week, by selected child, parent, and school characteristics: 2003, 2012, and 2016—Continued

[Standard errors appear in parentheses]

Selected child, parent, or school characteristic	Number of children (in thousands)			Percent of children whose parents reported doing education-related activities with them in the past week												
				Told child a story			Did arts and crafts			Discussed family history/ethnic heritage			Played board games or did puzzles		
	2003	2012	2016	2003	2012	2016	2003	2012	2016	2003	2012	2016	2003	2012	2016
1	2	3	4	5	6	7	8	9	10	11	12	13	14	15	16
Poverty status[4]															
Poor	4,396 (162.4)	5,489 (157.3)	4,771 (191.4)	73.2 (1.67)	68.6 (2.15)	67.3 (2.87)	76.9 (1.85)	72.0 (2.01)	68.2 (2.85)	60.9 (2.13)	57.6 (2.64)	55.8 (2.72)	72.4 (1.88)	61.7 (2.29)	66.8 (3.08)
Near-poor	5,332 (218.0)	5,495 (162.0)	5,470 (231.4)	74.3 (1.30)	68.3 (1.88)	70.6 (2.37)	76.7 (1.24)	67.5 (1.63)	70.6 (2.44)	53.3 (1.79)	49.8 (2.18)	57.4 (2.73)	73.6 (1.85)	63.3 (1.71)	66.6 (2.68)
Nonpoor	14,159 (182.1)	14,346 (167.4)	14,843 (209.6)	75.7 (0.85)	69.0 (1.07)	74.1 (1.02)	73.6 (0.92)	64.9 (0.98)	68.4 (1.11)	50.6 (1.11)	46.1 (1.09)	46.8 (1.19)	72.8 (0.87)	65.2 (1.16)	67.8 (1.09)
Control of school															
Public	21,004 (140.8)	22,797 (186.8)	22,626 (195.3)	75.0 (0.68)	68.2 (1.04)	71.3 (1.00)	75.2 (0.72)	67.0 (0.89)	68.2 (1.25)	52.4 (0.98)	49.6 (1.07)	50.7 (1.06)	73.4 (0.74)	63.7 (1.04)	67.4 (1.24)
Private	2,882 (127.8)	2,534 (113.4)	2,389 (134.3)	74.2 (2.09)	73.7 (2.08)	78.7 (2.48)	72.1 (1.94)	67.0 (2.45)	75.3 (2.31)	58.1 (2.17)	47.0 (2.75)	51.3 (3.22)	69.1 (1.99)	67.2 (2.25)	66.8 (2.71)
Locale of household[5]															
City	— (†)	7,473 (195.8)	8,376 (308.6)	— (†)	68.7 (1.64)	73.2 (1.98)	(†)	68.1 (1.55)	69.6 (2.23)	(†)	54.8 (1.69)	57.0 (1.99)	(†)	64.1 (1.72)	66.9 (2.33)
Suburban	— (†)	9,418 (211.3)	10,797 (275.6)	— (†)	72.1 (1.37)	72.6 (1.35)	(†)	67.6 (1.23)	69.7 (1.36)	(†)	49.9 (1.59)	52.5 (1.48)	(†)	65.2 (1.44)	68.1 (1.26)
Town	— (†)	2,483 (167.3)	2,019 (128.8)	— (†)	64.8 (4.83)	71.0 (2.64)	(†)	67.4 (3.35)	64.2 (3.70)	(†)	48.5 (3.24)	42.8 (3.62)	(†)	57.6 (3.38)	65.0 (3.20)
Rural	— (†)	5,956 (191.3)	3,893 (189.6)	— (†)	65.3 (1.45)	68.4 (2.45)	(†)	64.7 (1.54)	67.3 (2.42)	(†)	42.2 (1.75)	36.9 (2.28)	(†)	64.8 (1.45)	67.4 (2.24)

—Not available.
†Not applicable.
‡Reporting standards not met. Either there are too few cases for a reliable estimate or the coefficient of variation (CV) is 50 percent or greater.
[1]The 2003 questionnaire included a single item for "Asian or Pacific Islander," whereas questionnaires for later years included one item for Asian and a separate item for Pacific Islander.
[2]The 2012 and 2016 questionnaires included an item specifying that the child was not able to speak. Children who were not able to speak are excluded from this analysis.
[3]In 2003, education level was not collected for the second parent in a same sex couple.
[4]Poor children are those whose family incomes were below the Census Bureau's poverty threshold in the year prior to data collection; near-poor children are those whose family incomes ranged from the poverty threshold to 199 percent of the poverty threshold; and nonpoor children are those whose family incomes were at or above 200 percent of the poverty threshold. The poverty threshold is a dollar amount that varies depending on a family's size and composition and is updated annually to account for inflation. In 2015, or example, the poverty threshold for a family of four with two children was

$24,257. Survey respondents are asked to select the range within which their income falls, rather than giving the exact amount of their income; therefore, the measure of poverty status is an approximation.
[5]Based on zip code of the household.
NOTE: While National Household Education Surveys Program (NHES) administrations prior to 2012 were administered via telephone with an interviewer, NHES:2012 and NHES:2016 used self-administered paper-and-pencil questionnaires that were mailed to respondents. Measurable differences between estimates for years prior to 2012 and estimates for later years could reflect actual changes in the population, or the changes could be due to the mode change from telephone to mail. The respondent was the parent most knowledgeable about the child's education. Responding parents reported on their own activities and the activities of their spouse/other adults in the household. Unless otherwise noted, all information is based on parent reports. Excludes homeschooled children. Race categories exclude persons of Hispanic ethnicity. Some data have been revised from previously published figures.
SOURCE: U.S. Department of Education, National Center for Education Statistics, Parent and Family Involvement in Education Survey of the National Household Education Surveys Program (PFI-NHES:2003, 2012, and 2016). (This table was prepared April 2019.)

Table 207.40. Percentage of elementary and secondary school children whose parents were involved in school activities, by selected child, parent, and school characteristics: 2003, 2012, and 2016

Percent of children whose parents reported the following types of involvement in school activities
[Standard errors appear in parentheses]

Selected child, parent, or school characteristic	2003				2012				2016			
	Attended a general school or PTO/PTA¹ meeting	Attended a parent-teacher conference	Attended a class event	Volunteered at school	Attended a general school or PTO/PTA¹ meeting	Attended a parent-teacher conference	Attended a class event	Volunteered at school	Attended a general school or PTO/PTA¹ meeting	Attended a parent-teacher conference	Attended a class event	Volunteered at school
1	2	3	4	5	6	7	8	9	10	11	12	13
Total	**87.7 (0.37)**	**77.1 (0.42)**	**69.9 (0.42)**	**41.8 (0.61)**	**87.4 (0.41)**	**75.8 (0.43)**	**74.4 (0.45)**	**41.7 (0.49)**	**88.6 (0.47)**	**77.7 (0.53)**	**79.3 (0.54)**	**43.4 (0.67)**
Sex of child												
Male	87.4 (0.49)	77.7 (0.63)	67.4 (0.75)	41.2 (0.88)	87.1 (0.66)	76.4 (0.61)	72.3 (0.65)	40.0 (0.71)	87.5 (0.80)	78.6 (0.74)	77.2 (0.97)	41.9 (0.82)
Female	87.9 (0.56)	76.5 (0.63)	72.6 (0.62)	42.4 (0.83)	87.7 (0.50)	75.1 (0.61)	76.7 (0.68)	43.5 (0.88)	89.8 (0.56)	76.6 (0.76)	81.6 (0.60)	45.0 (0.87)
Race/ethnicity of child												
White	88.7 (0.50)	76.3 (0.62)	74.1 (0.65)	48.3 (0.82)	89.1 (0.50)	77.2 (0.56)	81.5 (0.54)	49.6 (0.72)	90.6 (0.52)	78.8 (0.67)	85.8 (0.63)	49.1 (0.83)
Black	88.7 (0.85)	78.7 (1.35)	63.3 (1.54)	31.9 (1.64)	85.0 (1.35)	76.1 (1.35)	68.0 (1.66)	30.3 (1.33)	87.2 (1.72)	78.9 (1.60)	72.2 (2.02)	33.9 (1.81)
Hispanic	82.6 (1.05)	78.1 (1.10)	60.9 (1.36)	27.7 (1.23)	85.7 (0.98)	72.8 (1.08)	64.0 (1.34)	31.7 (1.14)	86.7 (0.98)	74.6 (1.38)	71.1 (1.29)	35.9 (1.49)
Asian/Pacific Islander[2]	88.5 (2.14)	77.7 (3.03)	65.1 (3.65)	33.8 (2.69)	83.0 (1.72)	71.5 (2.01)	65.8 (2.21)	35.2 (2.22)	80.0 (3.59)	76.4 (2.25)	71.9 (2.49)	41.7 (2.96)
Asian	— (†)	— (†)	— (†)	— (†)	82.5 (1.80)	71.5 (2.03)	65.0 (2.30)	34.0 (2.33)	79.5 (3.71)	76.4 (2.36)	71.9 (2.57)	41.4 (3.07)
Pacific Islander	— (†)	— (†)	— (†)	— (†)	90.7 (3.96)	71.4 (8.97)	79.0 (6.32)	54.3 (11.37)	92.0 (5.24)	87.5 (10.09)	52.3 (11.66)	48.2 (10.95)
American Indian/Alaska Native	85.1 (5.22)	85.1 (6.68)	69.5 (7.37)	18.9 (5.57)	85.1 (4.91)	79.9 (6.85)	75.6 (6.61)	42.3 (8.61)	93.0 (3.05)	87.5 (4.36)	80.1 (7.45)	59.4 (10.56)
Two or more races	87.2 (2.45)	74.9 (3.63)	72.3 (2.84)	47.7 (3.79)	88.8 (1.30)	78.4 (2.31)	76.0 (2.52)	45.3 (2.57)	91.2 (1.37)	78.1 (2.29)	83.1 (2.07)	48.0 (3.17)
Highest education level of parents/guardians in the household[3]												
Less than a high school diploma	69.8 (2.04)	67.8 (2.50)	42.4 (2.42)	15.6 (2.04)	77.0 (1.79)	63.3 (1.88)	48.0 (2.04)	18.3 (1.72)	76.4 (2.98)	69.8 (2.74)	54.3 (2.75)	25.0 (2.70)
High school diploma or equivalent	83.8 (0.91)	75.4 (0.94)	62.1 (1.28)	30.3 (1.27)	82.1 (1.42)	72.2 (1.23)	62.3 (1.45)	27.6 (1.38)	82.2 (1.34)	73.1 (1.55)	69.5 (1.70)	26.5 (1.99)
Vocational/technical or some college	88.5 (0.67)	78.0 (1.02)	69.1 (0.94)	38.8 (1.25)	87.5 (0.62)	75.4 (1.02)	76.1 (0.99)	39.0 (1.14)	89.2 (0.75)	75.7 (1.08)	78.2 (1.21)	34.7 (1.20)
Associate's degree	88.6 (1.27)	76.6 (1.68)	73.0 (1.76)	39.7 (1.67)	88.9 (0.91)	79.5 (1.13)	80.5 (1.37)	44.9 (1.77)	90.2 (1.08)	77.6 (1.45)	83.4 (1.45)	44.8 (1.70)
Bachelor's degree/some graduate school	92.0 (0.73)	79.8 (0.89)	80.1 (0.94)	53.9 (1.30)	92.1 (0.53)	79.9 (0.62)	85.0 (0.63)	55.0 (1.11)	92.9 (0.57)	81.5 (0.96)	87.3 (0.71)	54.0 (1.18)
Graduate/professional degree	94.6 (0.74)	79.5 (1.00)	80.8 (1.10)	61.7 (1.57)	95.1 (0.47)	83.0 (0.68)	90.1 (0.59)	61.8 (1.30)	95.3 (0.47)	83.8 (0.75)	92.7 (0.60)	64.9 (1.05)
Family income (in current dollars)												
$20,000 or less	79.8 (1.43)	74.6 (1.33)	56.6 (1.42)	26.1 (1.45)	79.9 (1.15)	69.4 (1.36)	57.2 (1.31)	24.1 (1.18)	79.5 (2.18)	73.7 (1.89)	61.4 (1.98)	24.2 (1.78)
$20,001 to $50,000	85.1 (0.67)	77.3 (0.85)	66.2 (0.94)	34.6 (1.14)	84.3 (0.73)	74.5 (1.04)	67.2 (1.28)	31.1 (1.22)	85.0 (1.12)	76.0 (1.18)	70.2 (1.47)	31.9 (1.63)
$50,001 to $75,000	89.9 (0.79)	76.8 (0.96)	74.5 (1.03)	46.0 (1.26)	88.7 (0.97)	77.3 (1.23)	77.3 (1.19)	43.7 (1.40)	88.7 (1.02)	78.3 (1.13)	81.2 (1.35)	39.7 (1.65)
$75,001 to $100,000	94.0 (0.80)	79.4 (1.28)	77.6 (1.34)	51.5 (1.71)	89.9 (0.88)	77.3 (1.15)	81.9 (1.13)	47.8 (1.24)	91.4 (0.87)	75.9 (1.23)	83.5 (1.32)	49.2 (1.53)
Over $100,000	93.9 (0.71)	77.9 (1.21)	80.7 (1.03)	61.1 (1.19)	92.5 (0.92)	79.0 (0.80)	85.5 (0.96)	57.6 (1.05)	93.6 (0.62)	80.8 (0.95)	90.5 (0.70)	59.1 (0.99)
Poverty status[4]												
Poor	79.4 (1.55)	74.5 (1.37)	56.7 (1.57)	26.8 (1.55)	82.5 (1.08)	71.3 (1.29)	60.0 (1.52)	26.8 (1.28)	81.1 (1.68)	74.8 (1.90)	62.3 (1.78)	26.6 (1.77)
Near-poor	85.1 (0.89)	77.9 (1.05)	64.8 (0.98)	32.5 (1.31)	83.7 (0.78)	75.2 (0.97)	66.5 (1.22)	31.2 (1.35)	85.8 (1.14)	76.4 (1.24)	71.4 (1.42)	33.0 (1.86)
Nonpoor	91.0 (0.46)	77.6 (0.58)	75.7 (0.51)	49.5 (0.76)	90.4 (0.51)	77.5 (0.55)	82.2 (0.61)	50.6 (0.71)	91.7 (0.48)	78.9 (0.66)	86.9 (0.57)	51.7 (0.78)
Control of school and enrollment level of child												
Public school	86.7 (0.40)	75.9 (0.45)	68.0 (0.47)	38.5 (0.64)	86.5 (0.43)	74.8 (0.45)	72.9 (0.50)	39.0 (0.52)	88.2 (0.50)	76.7 (0.56)	77.8 (0.60)	40.3 (0.69)
Elementary (kindergarten to grade 8)	90.9 (0.40)	85.1 (0.42)	71.7 (0.57)	42.8 (0.75)	90.0 (0.42)	82.4 (0.47)	76.0 (0.64)	44.1 (0.69)	91.0 (0.59)	84.8 (0.62)	80.5 (0.70)	44.6 (0.89)
Secondary (grades 9 to 12)	76.9 (1.06)	54.8 (1.03)	59.4 (1.06)	28.5 (0.98)	77.8 (0.92)	55.5 (1.04)	65.1 (0.90)	26.2 (0.71)	81.2 (0.88)	56.1 (1.21)	71.0 (1.01)	29.4 (0.95)
Private school	95.8 (0.61)	86.6 (1.02)	85.8 (1.20)	68.6 (1.57)	96.2 (0.58)	86.9 (1.13)	90.1 (1.18)	69.5 (1.63)	92.2 (1.39)	87.3 (1.21)	93.5 (1.14)	72.6 (1.91)
Elementary (kindergarten to grade 8)	96.6 (0.70)	91.6 (0.93)	88.4 (1.23)	73.3 (1.91)	97.4 (0.63)	91.2 (1.47)	91.8 (1.39)	74.4 (1.87)	92.1 (1.76)	90.5 (1.51)	94.2 (1.41)	78.2 (2.27)
Secondary (grades 9 to 12)	93.3 (1.55)	72.3 (2.49)	78.3 (2.77)	54.8 (2.82)	92.5 (1.20)	73.6 (2.19)	84.9 (2.08)	54.6 (2.44)	92.5 (2.36)	78.7 (1.89)	91.5 (1.30)	57.5 (2.80)
Locale of household[5]												
City	— (†)	— (†)	— (†)	— (†)	86.1 (0.76)	74.9 (0.84)	68.4 (0.93)	36.3 (0.98)	86.4 (1.02)	78.7 (1.10)	75.5 (1.25)	42.2 (1.39)
Suburban	— (†)	— (†)	— (†)	— (†)	88.3 (0.63)	74.9 (0.74)	74.5 (0.76)	44.2 (0.83)	90.0 (0.65)	77.5 (0.88)	80.9 (0.79)	45.5 (0.88)
Town	— (†)	— (†)	— (†)	— (†)	87.3 (1.27)	76.9 (1.78)	76.5 (1.92)	37.3 (1.90)	87.4 (1.51)	77.0 (1.72)	76.3 (1.76)	34.9 (1.99)
Rural	— (†)	— (†)	— (†)	— (†)	87.6 (0.87)	78.0 (0.76)	81.0 (0.97)	46.1 (1.15)	89.8 (1.02)	76.3 (1.34)	84.2 (1.15)	44.0 (1.75)

See notes at end of table.

Table 207.40. Percentage of elementary and secondary school children whose parents were involved in school activities, by selected child, parent, and school characteristics: 2003, 2012, and 2016—Continued

[Standard errors appear in parentheses]

Selected child, parent, or school characteristic	Percent of children whose parents reported the following types of involvement in school activities											
	2003				2012				2016			
	Attended a general school or PTO/PTA[1] meeting	Attended a parent-teacher conference	Attended a class event	Volunteered at school	Attended a general school or PTO/PTA[1] meeting	Attended a parent-teacher conference	Attended a class event	Volunteered at school	Attended a general school or PTO/PTA[1] meeting	Attended a parent-teacher conference	Attended a class event	Volunteered at school
1	2	3	4	5	6	7	8	9	10	11	12	13
Enrollment level of child and locale of household												
Elementary												
City	— (†)	— (†)	— (†)	— (†)	88.9 (0.77)	81.1 (0.93)	71.7 (1.15)	40.4 (1.25)	88.8 (1.25)	86.9 (1.13)	78.3 (1.41)	46.4 (1.85)
Suburban	— (†)	— (†)	— (†)	— (†)	91.8 (0.62)	83.6 (0.71)	77.8 (0.97)	50.6 (0.96)	92.4 (0.75)	85.4 (0.95)	83.4 (0.96)	51.1 (1.13)
Town	— (†)	— (†)	— (†)	— (†)	91.2 (1.39)	83.4 (2.30)	77.9 (2.37)	41.2 (2.41)	90.9 (1.74)	84.8 (1.98)	79.5 (2.52)	37.4 (2.58)
Rural	— (†)	— (†)	— (†)	— (†)	91.0 (0.74)	85.0 (0.84)	84.1 (1.00)	51.6 (1.41)	92.4 (1.17)	82.2 (1.67)	86.1 (1.57)	47.5 (2.10)
Secondary												
City	— (†)	— (†)	— (†)	— (†)	78.0 (1.47)	57.2 (1.64)	59.1 (1.81)	24.8 (1.38)	79.6 (1.66)	55.6 (1.92)	67.3 (1.74)	30.4 (1.57)
Suburban	— (†)	— (†)	— (†)	— (†)	79.8 (1.47)	54.0 (1.58)	66.3 (1.55)	28.7 (1.35)	84.1 (1.18)	58.7 (1.61)	74.8 (1.35)	32.2 (1.26)
Town	— (†)	— (†)	— (†)	— (†)	76.6 (2.38)	59.2 (2.81)	72.6 (2.35)	26.6 (2.24)	78.1 (3.12)	55.9 (3.63)	67.8 (3.32)	28.1 (3.18)
Rural	— (†)	— (†)	— (†)	— (†)	79.2 (2.05)	60.6 (1.86)	73.5 (2.20)	32.7 (1.76)	83.6 (1.72)	61.9 (1.87)	79.7 (1.68)	35.5 (2.07)

—Not available.
†Not applicable.
[1]PTO stands for Parent Teacher Organization and PTA stands for Parent Teacher Association.
[2]The 2003 questionnaire included a single item for "Asian or Pacific Islander," whereas questionnaires for later years included one item for Asian and a separate item for Pacific Islander.
[3]In 2003, education level was not collected for the second parent in a same sex couple.
[4]Poor children are those whose family incomes were below the Census Bureau's poverty threshold in the year prior to data collection; near-poor children are those whose family incomes ranged from the poverty threshold to 199 percent of the poverty threshold; and nonpoor children are those whose family incomes were at or above 200 percent of the poverty threshold. The poverty threshold is a dollar amount that varies depending on a family's size and composition and is updated annually to account for inflation. In 2015, for example, the poverty threshold for a family of four with two children was $24,257. Survey respondents are asked to select the range within which their income falls, rather than giving the exact amount of their income; therefore, the measure of poverty status is an approximation.

[5]Based on zip code of the household.
NOTE: While National Household Education Surveys Program (NHES) administrations prior to 2012 were administered via telephone with an interviewer, NHES:2012 and NHES:2016 used self-administered paper-and-pencil questionnaires that were mailed to respondents. Measurable differences between estimates for years prior to 2012 and estimates for later years could reflect actual changes in the population, or the changes could be due to the mode change from telephone to mail. Includes children enrolled in kindergarten through grade 12 and ungraded students. Excludes homeschooled children. The respondent was the parent most knowledgeable about the child's education. Responding parents reported on their own activities and the activities of their spouse/other adults in the household. Race categories exclude persons of Hispanic ethnicity. Some data have been revised from previously published figures.
SOURCE: U.S. Department of Education, National Center for Education Statistics, Parent and Family Involvement in Education Survey of the National Household Education Surveys Program (PFI-NHES:2003, 2012, and 2016). (This table was prepared April 2019.)

Table 208.10. Public elementary and secondary pupil/teacher ratios, by selected school characteristics: Selected years, fall 1990 through fall 2017

Selected school characteristic	1990	1995	1999	2000	2001	2002	2003	2004	2005	2006	2007	2008	2009	2010[1]	2011	2012	2013	2014	2015	2016	2017
1	2	3	4	5	6	7	8	9	10	11	12	13	14	15	16	17	18	19	20	21	22
All schools	**17.4**	**17.8**	**16.6**	**16.4**	**16.3**	**16.2**	**16.4**	**16.2**	**16.0**	**15.8**	**15.7**	**15.7**	**16.0**	**16.4**	**16.3**	**16.4**	**16.3**	**16.2**	**16.2**	**16.2**	**16.1**
Enrollment size of school																					
Under 300	14.0	14.1	13.3	13.1	12.9	12.8	13.0	12.8	12.7	12.7	12.7	12.5	12.6	12.9	12.8	12.8	12.7	12.7	12.8	12.8	12.7
300 to 499	17.0	17.1	15.8	15.5	15.4	15.3	15.5	15.2	15.0	14.9	15.0	14.8	15.2	15.4	15.4	15.5	15.4	15.3	15.3	15.2	15.2
500 to 999	18.0	18.2	16.8	16.7	16.5	16.5	16.6	16.4	16.2	15.9	15.9	15.9	16.3	16.7	16.7	16.7	16.7	16.5	16.5	16.5	16.4
1,000 to 1,499	17.9	18.7	17.6	17.4	17.4	17.4	17.6	17.3	16.9	16.7	16.5	16.5	16.8	17.3	17.1	17.1	17.1	16.9	16.9	17.0	16.8
1,500 or more	19.2	20.0	19.3	19.1	19.0	18.9	19.2	19.1	18.8	18.6	18.1	18.3	18.7	19.5	19.0	19.0	19.1	19.0	19.0	18.9	18.8
Type																					
Regular schools	17.6	17.9	16.7	16.5	16.4	16.3	16.5	16.3	16.1	15.9	15.8	15.8	16.1	16.5	16.4	16.5	16.5	16.3	16.3	16.3	16.2
Alternative	14.2	16.6	15.8	15.2	14.9	14.9	15.0	14.4	14.0	14.7	13.5	14.2	14.3	14.8	14.7	14.8	14.3	14.5	14.4	14.4	13.9
Special education	6.5	7.2	7.2	7.0	6.4	7.0	7.3	7.4	6.2	6.6	7.1	6.8	7.1	6.9	7.1	7.2	6.6	7.0	7.4	7.2	7.3
Vocational	13.0	12.7	13.0	12.7	12.7	9.9	10.3	11.5	12.0	13.3	11.3	10.7	10.2	11.7	11.8	11.6	11.8	11.8	11.9	11.8	11.7
Percent of students eligible for free or reduced-price lunch																					
25 percent or less	—	—	16.9	16.7	16.7	16.6	16.8	16.8	16.5	16.4	16.3	16.1	16.5	16.8	16.9	16.5	16.5	16.4	16.5	16.5	16.2
26 percent to 50 percent	—	—	16.4	16.2	16.1	16.2	16.4	16.2	16.1	15.8	15.7	15.7	16.1	16.5	16.2	16.4	16.3	16.2	16.2	16.1	16.1
51 percent to 75 percent	—	—	16.2	16.1	16.0	16.0	16.0	15.9	15.6	15.3	15.2	15.4	15.8	16.2	15.8	16.2	16.1	16.0	16.0	15.9	15.9
More than 75 percent	—	—	16.3	16.1	16.0	16.0	16.1	15.9	15.5	15.4	15.0	15.1	15.6	16.0	15.5	16.3	16.5	16.4	16.4	16.4	16.2
Level and size																					
Elementary schools	18.1	18.1	16.7	16.5	16.3	16.2	16.3	16.0	15.8	15.6	15.6	15.5	15.9	16.3	16.3	16.4	16.3	16.1	16.1	16.1	16.0
Regular	18.2	18.1	16.7	16.5	16.3	16.2	16.3	16.0	15.8	15.6	15.6	15.5	15.9	16.3	16.3	16.4	16.4	16.2	16.1	16.1	16.0
Under 300	16.0	15.7	14.6	14.4	14.1	13.9	14.0	13.7	13.6	13.5	13.7	13.5	13.7	14.0	14.0	14.0	14.0	13.8	13.8	13.7	13.8
300 to 499	17.6	17.5	16.1	15.8	15.6	15.5	15.6	15.3	15.2	15.1	15.2	15.0	15.4	15.6	15.7	15.7	15.6	15.5	15.4	15.4	15.3
500 to 999	18.8	18.6	17.1	16.9	16.8	16.7	16.8	16.5	16.3	16.0	16.0	16.0	16.5	16.9	16.9	17.0	17.0	16.7	16.7	16.7	16.5
1,000 to 1,499	19.5	19.7	18.3	18.1	18.0	18.0	18.1	17.7	17.2	17.0	16.7	16.8	17.2	17.8	17.7	17.8	17.7	17.5	17.4	17.4	17.3
1,500 or more	19.9	20.9	20.0	20.5	20.2	20.3	20.8	20.5	19.6	19.4	18.0	18.1	18.5	19.3	19.0	18.9	19.1	19.0	18.8	18.6	18.0
Secondary schools	16.6	17.6	16.8	16.6	16.6	16.7	16.9	16.8	16.6	16.4	16.3	16.2	16.4	16.8	16.5	16.6	16.6	16.6	16.6	16.6	16.5
Regular	16.7	17.7	16.9	16.7	16.7	16.8	17.0	16.9	16.8	16.6	16.4	16.3	16.6	16.9	16.7	16.7	16.7	16.7	16.7	16.7	16.6
Under 300	12.3	12.8	12.0	12.0	11.9	12.0	12.3	12.0	12.2	12.0	12.1	11.9	11.9	12.2	12.0	12.1	12.1	11.9	12.1	12.2	12.1
300 to 499	14.9	15.7	14.6	14.5	14.4	14.4	14.7	14.7	14.6	14.4	14.4	14.3	14.3	14.6	14.6	14.5	14.4	14.6	14.6	14.5	14.5
500 to 999	16.1	16.9	16.0	15.8	15.7	15.8	16.0	15.9	15.8	15.6	15.4	15.4	15.6	15.8	15.7	15.7	15.7	15.7	15.7	15.8	15.7
1,000 to 1,499	17.2	18.0	17.1	16.8	16.8	16.9	17.2	17.0	16.8	16.5	16.5	16.3	16.6	16.9	16.6	16.6	16.6	16.5	16.5	16.6	16.5
1,500 or more	19.3	20.0	19.2	18.9	18.8	18.8	19.0	19.0	18.8	18.5	18.2	18.2	18.6	19.3	18.8	18.9	18.9	18.9	18.7	18.7	18.6
Combined schools	14.5	15.0	13.4	13.7	13.4	13.5	13.8	13.9	14.1	14.7	13.4	13.9	14.0	15.4	14.4	14.4	14.7	14.2	15.2	15.0	14.8
Under 300	8.9	9.0	9.1	9.2	9.1	9.1	9.5	9.2	9.5	10.1	9.2	8.9	9.1	9.2	9.4	9.3	9.1	9.2	9.6	9.7	9.4
300 to 499	14.2	14.7	13.8	13.5	13.1	13.1	14.4	13.4	13.9	14.3	13.7	13.9	13.8	13.6	13.3	13.3	13.5	13.6	14.3	14.0	13.6
500 to 999	16.3	16.6	14.9	15.8	15.6	16.0	15.4	15.8	15.9	16.0	15.2	15.6	15.8	16.9	15.6	15.5	15.5	15.1	16.3	15.9	15.7
1,000 to 1,499	17.8	18.2	16.9	17.5	18.1	17.7	17.5	17.4	16.4	17.3	15.9	16.7	17.9	19.2	18.1	17.8	17.9	17.3	17.5	17.3	16.9
1,500 or more	17.7	19.6	19.2	18.6	18.9	19.1	19.2	18.7	20.0	20.3	18.0	21.7	21.7	25.7	23.4	23.3	24.7	20.9	23.6	22.9	22.9
Ungraded	6.4	6.9	5.3	7.0	6.3	6.8	9.6	8.0	7.7	7.2	7.3	5.5	8.5	5.3	6.0	5.9	3.0	8.1	9.0	5.1	5.7
Level, type, and percent of students eligible for free or reduced-price lunch																					
Elementary, regular																					
25 percent or less	—	—	17.1	16.9	16.7	16.5	16.7	16.6	16.4	16.2	16.2	16.0	16.4	16.8	16.6	16.5	16.5	16.3	16.4	16.3	16.1
26 to 50 percent	—	—	16.5	16.3	16.2	16.1	16.2	16.0	15.8	15.5	15.6	15.6	16.0	16.4	16.3	16.4	16.3	16.1	16.1	16.0	15.9
51 to 75 percent	—	—	16.3	16.2	16.1	16.0	16.0	15.7	15.5	15.1	15.2	15.2	15.7	16.0	15.9	16.2	16.1	15.8	15.8	15.8	15.7
More than 75 percent	—	—	16.6	16.4	16.2	16.1	16.3	16.0	15.6	15.4	15.1	15.2	15.8	16.1	15.7	16.5	16.6	16.5	16.4	16.4	16.3
Secondary, regular																					
25 percent or less	—	—	17.0	16.9	16.9	16.9	17.2	17.5	17.0	16.9	16.8	16.6	16.8	17.1	17.4	16.7	16.8	16.7	16.9	16.8	16.4
26 to 50 percent	—	—	16.6	16.4	16.3	16.5	16.9	16.9	16.8	16.4	16.4	16.2	16.5	16.8	16.4	16.6	16.5	16.5	16.6	16.6	16.5
51 to 75 percent	—	—	16.8	16.6	16.6	16.6	17.0	16.9	16.7	16.3	16.1	16.4	16.5	17.1	16.1	16.7	16.8	16.9	16.9	16.8	16.8
More than 75 percent	—	—	16.8	16.5	16.5	16.3	16.6	16.2	16.7	16.2	15.7	15.9	16.0	16.5	15.5	16.6	17.0	17.0	17.1	17.1	17.0

—Not available.

[1]Includes imputations for California and Wyoming.

NOTE: Includes only schools that reported both enrollment and teacher data. Ratios are based on data reported by schools and may differ from data reported in other tables that reflect aggregate totals reported by states.

SOURCE: U.S. Department of Education, National Center for Education Statistics, Common Core of Data (CCD), "Public Elementary/Secondary School Universe Survey," 1990–91 through 2017–18. (This table was prepared February 2020.)

Table 208.20. Public and private elementary and secondary teachers, enrollment, pupil/teacher ratios, and new teacher hires: Selected years, fall 1955 through fall 2029

Year	Teachers (in thousands)			Enrollment (in thousands)			Pupil/teacher ratio			Number of new teacher hires (in thousands)[1]		
	Total	Public	Private	Total	Public	Private	Total	Public	Private	Total	Public	Private
1	2	3	4	5	6	7	8	9	10	11	12	13
1955	1,286	1,141	145[2]	35,280	30,680	4,600[2]	27.4	26.9	31.7[2]	—	—	—
1960	1,600	1,408	192[2]	42,181	36,281	5,900[2]	26.4	25.8	30.7[2]	—	—	—
1965	1,933	1,710	223	48,473	42,173	6,300	25.1	24.7	28.3	—	—	—
1970	2,292	2,059	233	51,257	45,894	5,363	22.4	22.3	23.0	—	—	—
1975	2,453	2,198	255[2]	49,819	44,819	5,000[2]	20.3	20.4	19.6[2]	—	—	—
1976	2,457	2,189	268	49,478	44,311	5,167	20.1	20.2	19.3	—	—	—
1977	2,488	2,209	279	48,717	43,577	5,140	19.6	19.7	18.4	—	—	—
1978	2,479	2,207	272	47,637	42,551	5,086	19.2	19.3	18.7	—	—	—
1979	2,461	2,185	276[2]	46,651	41,651	5,000[2]	19.0	19.1	18.1[2]	—	—	—
1980	2,485	2,184	301	46,208	40,877	5,331	18.6	18.7	17.7	—	—	—
1981	2,440	2,127	313[2]	45,544	40,044	5,500[2]	18.7	18.8	17.6[2]	—	—	—
1982	2,458	2,133	325[2]	45,166	39,566	5,600[2]	18.4	18.6	17.2[2]	—	—	—
1983	2,476	2,139	337	44,967	39,252	5,715	18.2	18.4	17.0	—	—	—
1984	2,508	2,168	340[2]	44,908	39,208	5,700[2]	17.9	18.1	16.8[2]	—	—	—
1985	2,549	2,206	343	44,979	39,422	5,557	17.6	17.9	16.2	—	—	—
1986	2,592	2,244	348[2]	45,205	39,753	5,452[2]	17.4	17.7	15.7[2]	—	—	—
1987	2,631	2,279	352	45,488	40,008	5,479	17.3	17.6	15.6	—	—	—
1988	2,668	2,323	345[2]	45,430	40,189	5,242[2]	17.0	17.3	15.2[2]	—	—	—
1989	2,713	2,357	356	46,141	40,543	5,599	17.0	17.2	15.7	—	—	—
1990	2,759	2,398	361[2]	46,864	41,217	5,648[2]	17.0	17.2	15.6[2]	—	—	—
1991	2,797	2,432	365	47,728	42,047	5,681	17.1	17.3	15.6	—	—	—
1992	2,823	2,459	364[2]	48,694	42,823	5,870[2]	17.2	17.4	16.1[2]	—	—	—
1993	2,868	2,504	364	49,532	43,465	6,067	17.3	17.4	16.7	—	—	—
1994	2,922	2,552	370[2]	50,106	44,111	5,994[2]	17.1	17.3	16.2[2]	—	—	—
1995	2,974	2,598	376	50,759	44,840	5,918	17.1	17.3	15.7	—	—	—
1996	3,051	2,667	384[2]	51,544	45,611	5,933[2]	16.9	17.1	15.5[2]	—	—	—
1997	3,138	2,746	391	52,071	46,127	5,944	16.6	16.8	15.2	—	—	—
1998	3,230	2,830	400[2]	52,526	46,539	5,988[2]	16.3	16.4	15.0[2]	—	—	—
1999	3,319	2,911	408	52,875	46,857	6,018	15.9	16.1	14.7	305	222	83
2000	3,366	2,941	424[2]	53,373	47,204	6,169[2]	15.9	16.0	14.5[2]	—	—	—
2001	3,440	3,000	441	53,992	47,672	6,320	15.7	15.9	14.3	—	—	—
2002	3,476	3,034	442[2]	54,403	48,183	6,220[2]	15.7	15.9	14.1[2]	—	—	—
2003	3,490	3,049	441	54,639	48,540	6,099	15.7	15.9	13.8	311	236	74
2004	3,536	3,091	445[2]	54,882	48,795	6,087[2]	15.5	15.8	13.7[2]	—	—	—
2005	3,593	3,143	450	55,187	49,113	6,073	15.4	15.6	13.5	—	—	—
2006	3,622	3,166	456[2]	55,307	49,316	5,991[2]	15.3	15.6	13.2[2]	—	—	—
2007	3,656	3,200	456	55,201	49,291	5,910	15.1	15.4	13.0	327	246	80
2008	3,670	3,222	448[2]	54,973	49,266	5,707[2]	15.0	15.3	12.8[2]	—	—	—
2009	3,647	3,210	437	54,849	49,361	5,488	15.0	15.4	12.5	—	—	—
2010	3,512	3,099	413[2]	54,867	49,484	5,382[2]	15.6	16.0	13.0[2]	—	—	—
2011	3,508	3,103	405	54,790	49,522	5,268	15.6	16.0	13.0	241	173	68
2012	3,517	3,109	408[2]	55,104	49,771	5,333[2]	15.7	16.0	13.1[2]	—	—	—
2013	3,555	3,114	441	55,440	50,045	5,396	15.6	16.1	12.2	—	—	—
2014	3,594	3,132	461[2]	55,888	50,313	5,575[2]	15.6	16.1	12.1[2]	—	—	—
2015	3,633	3,151	482	56,189	50,438	5,751	15.5	16.0	11.9	325	218	107
2016	3,653	3,169	483[2]	56,369	50,615	5,754[2]	15.4	16.0	11.9[2]	351	257	94
2017	3,652	3,170	482	56,406	50,686	5,720	15.4	16.0	11.9	329	241	89
2018[3]	3,639	3,157	482	56,367	50,650	5,717	15.5	16.0	11.9	317	226	91
2019[3]	3,661	3,176	485	56,350	50,634	5,716	15.4	15.9	11.8	351	258	93
2020[3]	3,670	3,184	486	56,368	50,654	5,714	15.4	15.9	11.8	340	248	92
2021[3]	3,684	3,197	488	56,343	50,643	5,700	15.3	15.8	11.7	346	253	92
2022[3]	3,708	3,217	491	56,434	50,721	5,713	15.2	15.8	11.6	357	263	94
2023[3]	3,731	3,237	494	56,480	50,768	5,712	15.1	15.7	11.6	357	262	95
2024[3]	3,758	3,260	498	56,460	50,758	5,702	15.0	15.6	11.5	363	267	96
2025[3]	3,786	3,284	502	56,404	50,704	5,700	14.9	15.4	11.4	367	269	97
2026[3]	3,813	3,307	506	56,370	50,672	5,699	14.8	15.3	11.3	368	270	98
2027[3]	3,842	3,332	510	56,439	50,734	5,704	14.7	15.2	11.2	373	274	99
2028[3]	3,880	3,364	516	56,605	50,885	5,720	14.6	15.1	11.1	384	283	101
2029[3]	3,909	3,390	520	56,806	51,068	5,738	14.5	15.1	11.0	377	280	97

—Not available.

[1]A teacher is considered to be a new hire for a public or private school if the teacher had not taught in that control of school in the previous year. A teacher who moves from a public to private or a private to public school is considered a new teacher hire, but a teacher who moves from one public school to another public school or one private school to another private school is not considered a new teacher hire.

[2]Estimated.

[3]Projected.

NOTE: Data for teachers are expressed in full-time equivalents (FTE). Counts of private school teachers and enrollment include prekindergarten through grade 12 in schools offering kindergarten or higher grades. Counts of public school teachers and enrollment include prekindergarten through grade 12. The pupil/teacher ratio includes teachers for students with disabilities and other special teachers, while these teachers are generally excluded from class size calculations. Ratios for public schools reflect totals reported by states and differ from totals reported for schools or school districts. Some data have been revised from previously published figures. Detail may not sum to totals because of rounding.

SOURCE: U.S. Department of Education, National Center for Education Statistics, *Statistics of Public Elementary and Secondary Day Schools*, 1955–56 through 1980–81; *Statistics of Nonpublic Elementary and Secondary Schools*, 1955 through 1980; 1983–84, 1985–86, and 1987–88 Private School Survey; Common Core of Data (CCD), "State Nonfiscal Survey of Public Elementary/Secondary Education," 1981–82 through 2017–18; Private School Universe Survey (PSS), 1989–90 through 2017–18; Schools and Staffing Survey (SASS), "Public School Teacher Data File" and "Private School Teacher Data File," 1999–2000 through 2011–12; National Teacher and Principal Survey (NTPS), 2015–16; Elementary and Secondary Teacher Projection Model, 1973 through 2029; and New Teacher Hires Projection Model, 1988 through 2029. (This table was prepared December 2019.)

Table 208.30. Public elementary and secondary teachers, by level and state or jurisdiction: Selected years, fall 2000 through fall 2017

[In full-time equivalents]

State or jurisdiction	Fall 2000	Fall 2005	Fall 2010	Fall 2014	Fall 2015	Fall 2016 Total	Fall 2016 Elementary	Fall 2016 Secondary	Fall 2016 Ungraded	Fall 2017 Total	Fall 2017 Elementary	Fall 2017 Secondary	Fall 2017 Ungraded
1	2	3	4	5	6	7	8	9	10	11	12	13	14
United States	2,941,461[1]	3,143,003[1]	3,099,095[1]	3,132,351[1]	3,151,497[1]	3,169,499[1]	1,759,610[1]	1,232,805[1]	177,083[1]	3,169,750[1]	1,746,538[1]	1,233,360[1]	189,851[1]
Alabama	48,194[2]	57,757	49,363	42,737	40,766	42,533	22,476	20,057	0	41,802	22,301	19,501	0
Alaska	7,880	7,912	8,171	7,759	7,832	7,825	4,070	3,754	0	7,743	4,070	3,673	0
Arizona	44,438	51,376	50,031	48,124	47,944	48,220	33,135	15,085	0	47,868	33,299	14,569	0
Arkansas	31,947	32,997	34,273	35,430	35,804	35,730	18,317	14,768	2,645	35,800	18,177	14,862	2,760
California	298,021[2]	309,222[2]	260,806[2]	267,685[2]	263,475	271,287[2]	182,600[2]	86,140	2,547	271,523[2]	181,402[2]	85,849	4,272
Colorado	41,983	45,841	48,543	51,388	51,798	52,014	29,401	22,613	0	52,373	29,341	23,033	0
Connecticut	41,044	39,687	42,951	42,062	43,772	42,343	26,744	15,373	226	45,081	29,414	15,428	239
Delaware	7,469	7,998	8,933	9,649	8,962	9,208	4,678	4,530	0	9,399	4,788	4,611	0
District of Columbia	4,949	5,481[3]	5,925	6,565	6,789	6,727	3,990	2,713	24	6,659	4,078	2,581	0
Florida	132,030	158,962	175,609	180,442	182,586	186,339	76,301	67,849	42,190	186,128	75,746	67,474	42,908
Georgia	91,043	108,535	112,460	111,470	113,031	114,763	52,918	44,721	17,124	116,022	53,116	45,502	17,403
Hawaii	10,927	11,226	11,396	11,663	11,747	11,782	6,397	5,315	70	12,033	6,518	5,450	66
Idaho	13,714	14,521	15,673	15,609	15,656	16,204	7,648	8,556	0	16,592	7,764	8,828	0
Illinois	127,620	133,857	132,983	132,456[4]	129,948	128,893	90,125	38,506	263	128,204	89,854	38,018	332
Indiana	59,226	60,592	58,121[2]	56,547	57,675	60,162	31,163	28,999	0	61,018	31,621	29,398	0
Iowa	34,636	35,181	34,642	35,684	35,687	35,808	25,205	10,603	0	35,553	25,007	10,546	0
Kansas	32,742	33,608	34,644	37,659	40,035	36,193	18,496	17,697	0	36,387	18,729	17,658	0
Kentucky	39,589	42,413	42,042	41,586	41,902	42,029	24,772	10,058	7,199	42,064	24,701	10,092	7,270
Louisiana	49,915	44,660	48,655	46,340	58,469	48,408	32,806	15,602	0	40,281	27,409	12,872	0
Maine	16,559	16,684	15,384	14,937	14,857	14,750	10,284	4,467	0	14,760	10,329	4,431	0
Maryland	52,433	56,685	58,428	59,194	59,414	59,703	36,442	23,261	0	60,175	36,657	23,518	0
Massachusetts	67,432	73,596	68,754	71,859	71,969	72,413	47,382	25,031	0	73,381	47,733	25,648	0
Michigan	97,031	98,069	88,615	85,038	84,181	83,597	34,756	32,785	16,057	84,473	35,276	32,978	16,219
Minnesota	53,457	51,107	52,672	55,690	55,985	56,715	30,555	24,270	1,889	57,260	30,816	24,497	1,947
Mississippi	31,006	31,433	32,255	32,311	32,175	31,924	14,907	13,196	3,822	31,625	14,795	13,117	3,713
Missouri	64,735	67,076	66,735	67,356	67,635	67,926	35,235	32,691	0	68,496	35,725	32,771	0
Montana	10,411	10,369	10,361	10,234	10,412	10,555	7,391	3,127	36	10,515	7,383	3,097	35
Nebraska	20,983	21,359	22,345	22,998	23,308	23,611	15,221	8,390	0	23,771	15,321	8,450	0
Nevada	18,293	21,744	21,839	21,656	22,702	23,705	11,422	8,486	3,797	23,709	11,348	8,453	3,908
New Hampshire	14,341	15,536	15,365	14,773	14,770	14,760	9,761	4,999	0	14,589	9,859	4,730	0
New Jersey	99,061	112,673	110,202	115,067	114,968	115,729	61,286	37,911	16,532	115,496	61,197	37,635	16,664
New Mexico	21,042	22,021	22,437	22,411	21,722	21,331	9,454	8,123	3,754	21,092	9,387	7,960	3,745
New York	206,961	218,989	211,606	203,781	206,086	209,151	105,341	93,792	10,018	213,159	108,893	95,744	8,522
North Carolina	83,680	95,664	98,357	99,320	99,355	100,220	69,663	29,741	816	100,401	70,004	29,641	756
North Dakota	8,141	8,003	8,417	9,049	9,195	9,265	6,122	3,143	0	9,284	6,163	3,121	0
Ohio	118,361	117,982	109,282	106,526[3]	101,742	102,600	57,122	41,128	4,350	98,912	43,987	41,543	13,382
Oklahoma	41,318	41,833	41,278	42,073	42,452	41,090	23,119	17,970	0	41,597	23,643	17,954	0
Oregon	28,094	28,346	28,109	27,850	29,086	29,756	21,089	8,667	0	29,909	21,158	8,752	0
Pennsylvania	116,963	122,397	129,911	122,030	120,893	122,552	58,732	52,965	10,855	121,918	58,334	52,638	10,946
Rhode Island	10,645	14,180[2]	11,212	9,471	10,631	10,689	5,965	4,724	0	10,687	5,939	4,748	0
South Carolina	45,380	48,212	45,210	49,475	50,237	50,789	35,712	15,078	0	52,467	36,969	15,498	0
South Dakota	9,397	9,129	9,512	9,618	9,638	9,777	6,364	2,499	914	9,833	6,250	2,495	1,087
Tennessee	57,164	59,596	66,558	65,341	66,488	64,270	45,296	18,975	0	64,019	45,462	18,558	0
Texas	274,826	302,425	334,997	342,257	347,329	352,809	175,290	153,142	24,377	356,877	176,132	155,342	25,403
Utah	22,008	22,993	25,677	27,374[3]	28,348[3]	28,841[3]	14,050[3]	11,882[3]	2,909[3]	29,212[3]	14,230[3]	12,035[3]	2,946[3]
Vermont	8,414	8,851	8,382	8,276	8,338	8,187	3,326	2,736	2,124	8,313	3,176	2,745	2,392
Virginia	86,977[2]	103,944	70,947	89,968	90,255	91,628	42,155	49,473	0	85,936	37,097	48,840	0
Washington	51,098	53,508	53,934	59,555	57,942	58,815	32,242	24,507	2,067	60,183	33,057	24,810	2,316
West Virginia	20,930	19,940	20,338	20,029	19,664	19,356	9,168	10,167	21	19,239	9,951	9,083	205
Wisconsin	60,165	60,127	57,625	58,376[3]	58,185	59,011	29,429	29,125	457	58,598	28,986	29,198	414
Wyoming	6,783	6,706	7,127	7,615	7,653	7,506	4,089	3,417	0	7,335	3,948	3,387	0
Jurisdiction													
Bureau of Indian Education	—	—	—	—	—	—	—	—	—	—	—	—	—
DoDEA[5]	7,504	7,759	—	—	—	—	—	—	—	—	—	—	—
Other jurisdictions													
American Samoa	820	989	—	—	—	—	—	—	—	—	—	—	—
Guam	1,975	1,804	1,843	2,286	2,336	2,289	1,154	1,135	0	2,202	1,068	1,134	0
Northern Marianas	526	614	607	—	—	—	—	—	—	—	—	—	—
Puerto Rico	37,620	42,036	36,506	31,186	30,438	28,899	13,097	10,140	5,661	28,039	16,617	6,275	5,147
U.S. Virgin Islands	1,511	1,434	1,457	1,131	1,106	1,154	546	593	15	1,066	500	553	13

—Not available.
[1]Includes imputed values for states.
[2]Includes imputations to correct for underreporting of prekindergarten teachers.
[3]Imputed.
[4]Includes imputations to correct for underreporting of prekindergarten, kindergarten, and ungraded teachers.

[5]DoDEA = Department of Defense Education Activity. Includes both domestic and overseas schools.
NOTE: Distribution of elementary and secondary teachers determined by reporting units.
SOURCE: U.S. Department of Education, National Center for Education Statistics, Common Core of Data (CCD), "State Nonfiscal Survey of Public Elementary/Secondary Education," 2000–01 through 2017–18. (This table was prepared August 2019.)

Table 208.40. Public elementary and secondary teachers, enrollment, and pupil/teacher ratios, by state or jurisdiction: Selected years, fall 2000 through fall 2017

| State or jurisdiction | Pupil/teacher ratio | | | | Fall 2015 | | | Fall 2016 | | | Fall 2017 | | |
	Fall 2000	Fall 2005	Fall 2010	Fall 2014	Teachers	Enrollment	Pupil/teacher ratio	Teachers	Enrollment	Pupil/teacher ratio	Teachers	Enrollment	Pupil/teacher ratio
1	2	3	4	5	6	7	8	9	10	11	12	13	14
United States	16.0[1]	15.6[1]	16.0[1]	16.1[1]	3,151,497[1]	50,438,043[1]	16.0[1]	3,169,499[1]	50,615,189[1]	16.0[1]	3,169,750[1]	50,685,567[1]	16.0[1]
Alabama	15.4[2]	12.8	15.3	17.4	40,766	743,789	18.2	42,533	744,930	17.5	41,802	742,444	17.8
Alaska	16.9	16.8	16.2	16.9	7,832	132,477	16.9	7,825	132,737	17.0	7,743	132,872	17.2
Arizona	19.8	21.3	21.4	23.1	47,944	1,109,040	23.1	48,220	1,123,137	23.3	47,868	1,110,851	23.2
Arkansas	14.1	14.4	14.1	13.9	35,804	492,132	13.7	35,730	493,447	13.8	35,800	496,085	13.9
California	20.6[2]	20.8[2]	24.1[2]	23.6[2]	263,475	6,305,347[2]	23.9[2]	271,287[2]	6,309,138[2]	23.3[2]	271,523[2]	6,304,266[2]	23.2[2]
Colorado	17.3	17.0	17.4	17.3	51,798	899,112	17.4	52,014	905,019	17.4	52,373	910,280	17.4
Connecticut	13.7	14.5	13.1	12.9	43,772	537,933	12.3	42,343	535,118	12.6	45,081	531,288	11.8
Delaware	15.4	15.1	14.5	13.9	8,962	134,847	15.0	9,208	136,264	14.8	9,399	136,293	14.5
District of Columbia	13.9	14.0[3]	12.0	12.3	6,789	84,024	12.4	6,727	85,850	12.8	6,659	87,315	13.1
Florida	18.4	16.8	15.1	15.3	182,586	2,792,234	15.3	186,339	2,816,791	15.1	186,128	2,832,424	15.2
Georgia	15.9	14.7	14.9	15.6	113,031	1,757,237	15.5	114,763	1,764,346	15.4	116,022	1,768,642	15.2
Hawaii	16.9	16.3	15.8	15.6	11,747	181,995	15.5	11,782	181,550	15.4	12,033	180,837	15.0
Idaho	17.9	18.0	17.6	18.6	15,656	292,277	18.7	16,204	297,200	18.3	16,592	301,186	18.2
Illinois	16.1	15.8	15.7	15.5[4]	129,948	2,041,779	15.7	128,893	2,026,718	15.7	128,204	2,005,153	15.6
Indiana	16.7	17.1	18.0[2]	18.5	57,675	1,046,757	18.1	60,162	1,049,547	17.4	61,018	1,054,187	17.3
Iowa	14.3	13.7	14.3	14.2	35,687	508,014	14.2	35,808	509,831	14.2	35,553	511,850	14.4
Kansas	14.4	13.9	14.0	13.2	40,035	495,884	12.4	36,193	494,347	13.7	36,387	497,088	13.7
Kentucky	16.8	16.0	16.0	16.6	41,902	686,598	16.4	42,029	684,017	16.3	42,064	680,978	16.2
Louisiana	14.9	14.7	14.3	15.5	58,469	718,711	12.3	48,408	716,293	14.8	40,281	715,135	17.8
Maine	12.5	11.7	12.3	12.2	14,857	181,613	12.2	14,750	180,512	12.2	14,760	180,473	12.2
Maryland	16.3	15.2	14.6	14.8	59,414	879,601	14.8	59,703	886,221	14.8	60,175	893,684	14.9
Massachusetts	14.5	13.2	13.9	13.3	71,969	964,026	13.4	72,413	964,514	13.3	73,381	964,791	13.1
Michigan	17.7[2]	17.8	17.9	18.1	84,181	1,536,231	18.2	83,597	1,528,666	18.3	84,473	1,516,398	18.0
Minnesota	16.0	16.4	15.9	15.4	55,985	864,384	15.4	56,715	875,021	15.4	57,260	884,944	15.5
Mississippi	16.1	15.7	15.2	15.2	32,175	487,200	15.1	31,924	483,150	15.1	31,625	478,321	15.1
Missouri	14.1	13.7	13.8	13.6	67,635	919,234	13.6	67,926	915,040	13.5	68,496	915,472	13.4
Montana	14.9	14.0	13.7	14.1	10,412	145,319	14.0	10,555	146,375	13.9	10,515	149,474	14.2
Nebraska	13.6	13.4	13.4	13.6	23,308	316,014	13.6	23,611	319,194	13.5	23,771	323,766	13.6
Nevada	18.6	19.0	20.0	21.2	22,702	467,527	20.6	23,705	473,744	20.0	23,709	485,785	20.5
New Hampshire	14.5	13.2	12.7	12.5	14,770	182,425	12.4	14,760	180,888	12.3	14,589	179,433	12.3
New Jersey	13.3	12.4	12.7	12.2	114,968	1,408,845	12.3	115,729	1,410,421	12.2	115,496	1,408,102	12.2
New Mexico	15.2	14.8	15.1	15.2	21,722	335,694	15.5	21,331	336,263	15.8	21,092	334,345	15.9
New York	13.9	12.9	12.9	13.5	206,086	2,711,626	13.2	209,151	2,729,776	13.1	213,159	2,724,663	12.8
North Carolina	15.5	14.8	15.2	15.6	99,355	1,544,934	15.5	100,220	1,550,062	15.5	100,401	1,553,513	15.5
North Dakota	13.4	12.3	11.4	11.8	9,195	108,644	11.8	9,265	109,706	11.8	9,284	111,920	12.1
Ohio	15.5	15.6	16.1	16.2[3]	101,742	1,716,585	16.9	102,600	1,710,143	16.7	98,912	1,704,399	17.2
Oklahoma	15.1	15.2	16.0	16.4	42,452	692,878	16.3	41,090	693,903	16.9	41,597	695,092	16.7
Oregon	19.4	19.5	20.3	21.6	29,086	608,825[2]	20.9[2]	29,756	606,277[2]	20.4[2]	29,909	608,014[2]	20.3[2]
Pennsylvania	15.5	15.0	13.8	14.3	120,893	1,717,414	14.2	122,552	1,727,497	14.1	121,918	1,726,809	14.2
Rhode Island	14.8	10.8	12.8	15.0	10,631	142,014	13.4	10,689	142,150	13.3	10,687	142,949	13.4
South Carolina	14.9	14.6	16.1	15.3	50,237	763,533	15.2	50,789	771,250	15.2	52,467	777,507	14.8
South Dakota	13.7	13.4	13.3	13.8	9,638	134,253	13.9	9,777	136,302	13.9	9,833	137,823	14.0
Tennessee	15.9[2]	16.0	14.8	15.2	66,488	1,001,235	15.1	64,270	1,001,562	15.6	64,019	1,001,967	15.7
Texas	14.8	15.0	14.7	15.3	347,329	5,301,477	15.3	352,809	5,360,849	15.2	356,877	5,401,341	15.1
Utah	21.9	22.1	22.8	23.2[3]	28,348[3]	647,870	22.9[3]	28,841[3]	659,801	22.9	29,212[3]	668,274	22.9
Vermont	12.1	10.9	11.6	10.6	8,338	87,866	10.5	8,187	88,428	10.8	8,313	88,028	10.6
Virginia	13.2[2]	11.7	17.6	14.2	90,255	1,283,590	14.2	91,628	1,287,026	14.0	85,936	1,291,462	15.0
Washington	19.7	19.3	19.4	18.0	57,942	1,087,030	18.8	58,815	1,101,711	18.7	60,183	1,110,367	18.4
West Virginia	13.7	14.1	13.9	14.0	19,664	277,452	14.1	19,356	273,855	14.1	19,239	272,266	14.2
Wisconsin	14.6	14.6	15.1	14.9[3]	58,185	867,800	14.9	59,011	864,432	14.6	58,598	860,753	14.7
Wyoming	13.3	12.6	12.5	12.4	7,653	94,717	12.4	7,506	94,170	12.5	7,335	94,258	12.9
Jurisdiction													
Bureau of Indian Education	—	—	—	—	—	—	—	—	45,399	—	—	46,330	—
DoDEA[5]	14.4	11.7	—	—	—	74,970	—	—	—	—	—	71,134	—
Other jurisdictions													
American Samoa	19.1	16.6	—	—	—	—	—	—	—	—	—	12,620	—
Guam	16.4	—	17.2	13.6	2,336	30,821	13.2	2,289	30,758	13.4	2,202	30,112	13.7
Northern Marianas	19.0	19.1	18.3	—	—	—	—	—	—	—	—	—	—
Puerto Rico	16.3	13.4	13.0	13.2	30,438	379,818	12.5	28,899	365,181	12.6	28,039	346,096	12.3
U.S. Virgin Islands	12.9	11.7	10.6	12.6	1,106	13,805	12.5	1,154	13,194	11.4	1,066	16,139	15.1

—Not available.
[1]Includes imputed values for states.
[2]Includes imputations to correct for underreporting of prekindergarten teachers/enrollment.
[3]Imputed.
[4]Includes imputations to correct for underreporting of prekindergarten, kindergarten, and ungraded teachers.
[5]DoDEA = Department of Defense Education Activity. Includes both domestic and overseas schools.

NOTE: Teachers reported in full-time equivalents (FTE). Ratios reflect totals reported by states and differ from totals reported for schools or school districts.
SOURCE: U.S. Department of Education, National Center for Education Statistics, Common Core of Data (CCD), "State Nonfiscal Survey of Public Elementary/Secondary Education," 2000–01 through 2017–18. (This table was prepared February 2020.)

Table 209.10. Number and percentage distribution of teachers in public and private elementary and secondary schools, by selected teacher characteristics: Selected years, 1987–88 through 2017–18

[Standard errors appear in parentheses]

Selected teacher characteristic	Number of teachers (in thousands)							Percentage distribution of teachers						
	1987–88	1990–91	1999–2000	2003–04	2007–08	2011–12	2017–18	1987–88	1990–91	1999–2000	2003–04	2007–08	2011–12	2017–18
1	2	3	4	5	6	7	8	9	10	11	12	13	14	15
Public schools														
Total	2,323 (13.2)	2,559 (20.7)	3,002 (19.4)	3,251 (29.2)	3,405 (44.0)	3,385 (41.4)	3,545 (23.5)	100.0 (†)	100.0 (†)	100.0 (†)	100.0 (†)	100.0 (†)	100.0 (†)	100.0 (†)
Sex														
Male	685 (6.8)	719 (11.2)	754 (10.7)	813 (13.3)	821 (20.4)	802 (22.2)	834 (11.6)	29.5 (0.22)	28.1 (0.31)	25.1 (0.30)	25.0 (0.32)	24.1 (0.47)	23.7 (0.49)	23.5 (0.28)
Female	1,638 (10.1)	1,840 (14.7)	2,248 (16.0)	2,438 (23.5)	2,584 (34.6)	2,584 (30.5)	2,712 (20.2)	70.5 (0.22)	71.9 (0.31)	74.9 (0.30)	75.0 (0.32)	75.9 (0.47)	76.3 (0.49)	76.5 (0.28)
Race/ethnicity														
White[1]	2,018 (12.6)	2,214 (20.0)	2,532 (17.2)	2,702 (30.1)	2,829 (38.7)	2,773 (30.5)	2,811 (22.7)	86.9 (0.24)	86.5 (0.29)	84.3 (0.30)	83.1 (0.53)	83.1 (0.53)	81.9 (0.53)	79.3 (0.35)
Black[1]	191 (4.6)	212 (6.4)	228 (6.0)	257 (11.0)	239 (15.8)	231 (12.1)	239 (7.4)	8.2 (0.19)	8.3 (0.25)	7.6 (0.19)	7.9 (0.34)	7.0 (0.45)	6.8 (0.31)	6.7 (0.20)
Hispanic[1]	69 (2.6)	87 (4.5)	169 (6.4)	202 (11.3)	240 (16.6)	264 (13.4)	331 (9.2)	3.0 (0.11)	3.4 (0.17)	5.6 (0.20)	6.2 (0.34)	7.1 (0.46)	7.8 (0.37)	9.3 (0.26)
Asian[1,2]	21 (1.1)	27 (1.7)	48 (2.7)	42 (2.5)	42 (7.2)	61 (7.3)	75 (3.5)	0.9 (0.05)	1.0 (0.06)	1.6 (†)	1.3 (0.08)	1.2 (0.21)	1.8 (0.21)	2.1 (0.10)
Pacific Islander[1,2]	— (†)	— (†)	— (†)	6 (0.8)	6 (1.3)	5 (1.4)	8 (1.0)	— (†)	— (†)	— (†)	0.2 (0.03)	0.2 (0.04)	0.1 (0.04)	0.2 (0.03)
American Indian/Alaska Native[1]	24 (1.3)	20 (1.4)	26 (1.9)	17 (1.2)	17 (1.9)	17 (2.9)	18 (1.7)	1.0 (0.06)	0.8 (0.05)	0.9 (0.06)	0.5 (0.04)	0.5 (0.06)	0.5 (0.08)	0.5 (0.05)
Two or more races	— (†)	— (†)	— (†)	24 (2.2)	31 (2.9)	35 (3.7)	63 (3.1)	— (†)	— (†)	— (†)	0.7 (0.07)	0.9 (0.09)	1.0 (0.11)	1.8 (0.09)
Age														
Under 30	313 (5.0)	257 (5.7)	509 (9.2)	540 (27.4)	612 (22.4)	518 (15.9)	531 (9.4)	13.5 (0.19)	10.0 (0.23)	17.0 (0.28)	16.6 (0.84)	18.0 (0.61)	15.3 (0.44)	15.0 (0.24)
30 to 39	823 (7.7)	684 (10.8)	661 (9.8)	798 (14.5)	898 (16.8)	979 (19.3)	991 (12.9)	35.4 (0.30)	26.7 (0.35)	22.0 (0.29)	24.5 (0.38)	26.4 (0.39)	28.9 (0.53)	27.9 (0.29)
40 to 49	762 (7.4)	1,034 (13.3)	953 (10.3)	840 (14.3)	808 (19.2)	849 (19.2)	1,028 (12.3)	32.8 (0.25)	40.4 (0.37)	31.8 (0.32)	25.9 (0.38)	23.7 (0.47)	25.1 (0.51)	29.0 (0.32)
50 to 59	357 (5.7)	477 (8.6)	786 (12.6)	942 (26.0)	879 (21.1)	783 (20.5)	732 (11.6)	15.4 (0.23)	18.7 (0.29)	26.2 (0.35)	29.0 (0.74)	25.8 (0.51)	23.1 (0.49)	20.7 (0.29)
60 and over	68 (2.5)	107 (4.1)	93 (4.0)	131 (4.8)	207 (10.3)	256 (13.2)	263 (6.1)	2.9 (0.11)	4.2 (0.16)	3.1 (0.13)	4.0 (0.14)	6.1 (0.29)	7.6 (0.34)	7.4 (0.17)
Highest degree earned														
Less than bachelor's	15 (1.0)	17 (1.2)	20 (1.3)	35 (2.5)	27 (2.1)	128 (8.6)	97 (3.6)	0.7 (0.04)	0.7 (0.05)	0.7 (0.04)	1.1 (0.08)	0.8 (0.06)	3.8 (0.24)	2.7 (0.10)
Bachelor's	1,214 (9.8)	1,327 (11.7)	1,560 (15.8)	1,651 (22.8)	1,612 (28.8)	1,350 (21.1)	1,393 (15.8)	52.3 (0.28)	51.9 (0.31)	52.0 (0.40)	50.8 (0.56)	47.4 (0.59)	39.9 (0.52)	39.3 (0.36)
Master's	932 (8.5)	1,077 (13.5)	1,257 (13.9)	1,331 (21.7)	1,517 (27.8)	1,614 (29.1)	1,744 (17.5)	40.1 (0.30)	42.1 (0.34)	41.9 (0.38)	40.9 (0.56)	44.5 (0.55)	47.7 (0.57)	49.2 (0.36)
Education specialist[3]	146 (3.4)	118 (5.3)	143 (5.2)	195 (6.8)	218 (8.6)	257 (9.7)	271 (6.8)	6.3 (0.14)	4.6 (0.20)	4.7 (0.17)	6.0 (0.19)	6.4 (0.25)	7.6 (0.27)	7.6 (0.18)
Doctor's	16 (1.2)	20 (1.7)	22 (1.8)	38 (3.5)	30 (2.7)	37 (4.0)	41 (2.5)	0.7 (0.05)	0.8 (0.07)	0.7 (0.06)	1.2 (0.11)	0.9 (0.08)	1.1 (0.11)	1.2 (0.07)
Years of teaching experience														
Less than 3	145 (3.2)	185 (4.8)	325 (7.7)	339 (36.6)	392 (18.1)	244 (8.5)	318 (7.2)	6.2 (0.14)	7.2 (0.19)	10.8 (0.24)	10.4 (1.13)	11.5 (0.48)	7.2 (0.24)	9.0 (0.19)
3 to 9	568 (6.3)	596 (9.4)	854 (12.3)	1,043 (14.1)	1,125 (19.6)	1,104 (20.6)	1,003 (14.1)	24.4 (0.22)	23.3 (0.30)	28.5 (0.37)	32.1 (0.33)	33.0 (0.52)	32.6 (0.52)	28.3 (0.34)
10 to 20	1,072 (8.7)	1,056 (11.8)	865 (10.1)	946 (21.5)	1,017 (24.3)	1,265 (21.0)	1,416 (14.4)	46.1 (0.27)	41.3 (0.35)	28.8 (0.33)	29.1 (0.58)	29.9 (0.57)	37.4 (0.53)	39.9 (0.35)
Over 20	539 (6.1)	721 (10.6)	958 (13.5)	922 (27.9)	871 (23.9)	772 (23.8)	808 (11.8)	23.2 (0.23)	28.2 (0.30)	31.9 (0.36)	28.4 (0.81)	25.6 (0.62)	22.8 (0.54)	22.8 (0.29)
Level of instruction[4]														
Elementary	1,292 (9.5)	1,442 (11.8)	1,602 (13.5)	1,716 (25.8)	1,725 (37.1)	1,726 (20.2)	1,779 (24.5)	55.6 (0.33)	56.3 (0.40)	53.3 (0.42)	52.8 (0.66)	50.7 (0.91)	51.0 (0.65)	50.2 (0.62)
General	788 (7.4)	887 (10.6)	1,042 (12.5)	1,130 (29.8)	1,100 (26.5)	1,078 (22.1)	1,097 (17.3)	33.9 (0.29)	34.6 (0.39)	34.7 (0.41)	34.8 (0.86)	32.3 (0.70)	31.8 (0.71)	30.9 (0.45)
Arts/music	116 (3.0)	110 (4.3)	99 (3.7)	101 (5.3)	103 (6.6)	82 (5.4)	99 (4.2)	5.0 (0.13)	4.3 (0.17)	3.3 (0.13)	3.1 (0.17)	3.0 (0.19)	2.4 (0.16)	2.8 (0.11)
English	60 (2.3)	72 (3.8)	66 (3.8)	70 (5.1)	104 (9.9)	92 (6.9)	117 (4.6)	2.6 (0.10)	2.8 (0.14)	2.2 (0.13)	2.2 (0.16)	3.0 (0.29)	2.7 (0.21)	3.3 (0.13)
ESL/bilingual	18 (1.1)	20 (1.3)	28 (1.8)	25 (3.6)	24 (3.3)	51 (6.8)	48 (3.4)	0.8 (0.05)	0.8 (0.05)	0.9 (0.06)	0.8 (0.11)	0.7 (0.10)	1.5 (0.20)	1.4 (0.10)
Health/physical ed	56 (2.0)	66 (3.2)	57 (3.5)	73 (5.0)	63 (6.0)	79 (8.1)	65 (3.5)	2.4 (0.09)	2.6 (0.12)	1.9 (0.12)	2.2 (0.15)	1.8 (0.18)	2.3 (0.23)	1.8 (0.10)
Mathematics	31 (2.0)	30 (1.9)	23 (2.4)	19 (2.3)	28 (3.8)	32 (6.5)	36 (2.3)	1.3 (0.09)	1.2 (0.08)	0.8 (0.08)	0.6 (0.07)	0.8 (0.11)	0.9 (0.19)	1.0 (0.07)
Science	18 (1.5)	21 (1.9)	11 (1.3)	19 (3.0)	15 (3.4)	18 (3.3)	23 (1.8)	0.8 (0.06)	0.8 (0.07)	0.4 (0.04)	0.6 (0.09)	0.4 (0.10)	0.5 (0.10)	0.6 (0.05)
Special education	168 (3.9)	176 (5.9)	227 (5.6)	240 (20.6)	230 (13.0)	239 (10.3)	235 (6.3)	7.2 (0.16)	6.9 (0.23)	7.6 (0.18)	7.4 (0.63)	6.7 (0.37)	7.1 (0.31)	6.6 (0.17)
Other elementary	37 (2.4)	60 (3.2)	49 (3.5)	40 (3.5)	58 (4.2)	55 (5.2)	60 (3.0)	1.6 (0.10)	2.4 (0.12)	1.6 (0.12)	1.2 (0.11)	1.7 (0.12)	1.6 (0.15)	1.7 (0.08)
Secondary	1,031 (10.5)	1,118 (16.5)	1,401 (17.7)	1,534 (26.0)	1,680 (39.0)	1,659 (37.8)	1,766 (25.2)	44.4 (0.33)	43.7 (0.40)	46.7 (0.42)	47.2 (0.66)	49.3 (0.91)	49.0 (0.65)	49.8 (0.62)
Arts/music	73 (2.0)	74 (2.3)	110 (3.4)	112 (4.1)	121 (6.2)	121 (5.6)	130 (4.5)	3.1 (0.09)	2.9 (0.08)	3.7 (0.11)	3.4 (0.12)	3.6 (0.18)	3.6 (0.14)	3.7 (0.13)
English	171 (3.2)	195 (5.1)	245 (5.1)	269 (9.0)	289 (10.0)	289 (9.9)	294 (6.6)	7.4 (0.12)	7.6 (0.15)	8.2 (0.15)	8.3 (0.25)	9.0 (0.27)	8.5 (0.25)	8.3 (0.18)
ESL/bilingual	6 (0.5)	10 (0.7)	16 (1.2)	18 (2.5)	21 (2.5)	20 (2.4)	24 (1.9)	0.3 (0.02)	0.4 (0.03)	0.5 (0.04)	0.6 (0.08)	0.6 (0.07)	0.6 (0.07)	0.7 (0.05)
Foreign language	43 (1.2)	52 (2.4)	71 (2.4)	73 (3.3)	78 (5.0)	88 (4.5)	85 (3.5)	1.9 (0.05)	2.0 (0.09)	2.4 (0.08)	2.3 (0.10)	2.3 (0.14)	2.6 (0.12)	2.4 (0.10)
Health/physical ed	76 (2.4)	76 (2.2)	99 (3.1)	102 (4.3)	119 (5.7)	101 (3.9)	97 (3.2)	3.3 (0.10)	3.0 (0.10)	3.3 (0.10)	3.1 (0.12)	3.5 (0.17)	3.0 (0.11)	2.7 (0.09)
Mathematics	139 (2.5)	155 (4.3)	207 (4.5)	213 (5.5)	252 (9.1)	250 (7.5)	265 (6.6)	6.0 (0.10)	6.0 (0.15)	6.9 (0.14)	6.5 (0.17)	7.4 (0.25)	7.4 (0.19)	7.5 (0.18)
Science	115 (2.9)	128 (4.0)	169 (4.0)	189 (6.8)	195 (8.3)	209 (6.1)	220 (5.6)	4.9 (0.11)	5.0 (0.15)	5.6 (0.14)	5.8 (0.20)	5.7 (0.24)	6.2 (0.16)	6.2 (0.15)
Social studies	118 (2.4)	124 (3.3)	163 (4.4)	178 (5.7)	209 (9.9)	197 (6.3)	214 (5.2)	5.1 (0.10)	4.8 (0.14)	5.4 (0.14)	5.5 (0.16)	6.1 (0.27)	5.8 (0.16)	6.0 (0.14)
Special education	100 (2.2)	113 (3.5)	113 (2.8)	174 (7.5)	165 (9.7)	191 (12.2)	199 (5.5)	4.3 (0.09)	4.4 (0.13)	3.8 (0.09)	5.4 (0.23)	4.9 (0.28)	5.7 (0.32)	5.6 (0.15)
Vocational/technical	166 (3.0)	160 (3.7)	161 (3.5)	169 (5.7)	164 (6.3)	147 (5.7)	139 (4.4)	7.1 (0.12)	6.3 (0.12)	5.4 (0.10)	5.2 (0.17)	4.8 (0.17)	4.3 (0.16)	3.9 (0.12)
Other secondary	25 (1.3)	30 (1.5)	47 (2.0)	36 (2.1)	47 (3.4)	46 (4.0)	98 (3.9)	1.1 (0.06)	1.2 (0.06)	1.6 (0.07)	1.1 (0.06)	1.4 (0.10)	1.4 (0.12)	2.8 (0.11)

See notes at end of table.

Table 209.10. Number and percentage distribution of teachers in public and private elementary and secondary schools, by selected teacher characteristics: Selected years, 1987–88 through 2017–18—Continued

[Standard errors appear in parentheses]

Selected teacher characteristic	Number of teachers (in thousands)							Percentage distribution of teachers						
	1987–88	1990–91	1999–2000	2003–04	2007–08	2011–12	2017–18	1987–88	1990–91	1999–2000	2003–04	2007–08	2011–12	2017–18
1	2	3	4	5	6	7	8	9	10	11	12	13	14	15
Private schools														
Total	307 (8.5)	356 (7.2)	449 (10.6)	467 (10.3)	490 (9.2)	465 (11.1)	509 (9.1)	100.0 (†)	100.0 (†)	100.0 (†)	100.0 (†)	100.0 (†)	100.0 (†)	100.0 (†)
Sex														
Male	67 (3.3)	82 (3.3)	107 (3.8)	110 (8.4)	127 (4.6)	117 (6.9)	133 (4.1)	21.8 (0.86)	22.9 (0.74)	23.9 (0.48)	23.6 (1.93)	26.0 (0.78)	25.2 (1.33)	26.0 (0.63)
Female	240 (7.2)	275 (5.8)	342 (7.7)	357 (14.3)	362 (7.7)	348 (10.1)	377 (7.3)	78.2 (0.86)	77.1 (0.74)	76.1 (0.48)	76.4 (1.93)	74.0 (0.78)	74.8 (1.33)	74.0 (0.63)
Race/ethnicity														
White[1]	285 (8.3)	329 (7.0)	402 (9.6)	411 (12.0)	423 (8.8)	411 (11.1)	433 (8.3)	92.8 (0.50)	92.2 (0.46)	89.5 (0.42)	88.0 (0.99)	86.4 (0.80)	88.3 (0.69)	85.1 (0.61)
Black[1]	7 (0.8)	9 (1.0)	17 (1.4)	19 (2.9)	20 (2.2)	17 (2.4)	16 (1.5)	2.3 (0.27)	2.7 (0.28)	3.7 (0.29)	4.0 (0.65)	4.0 (0.44)	3.6 (0.54)	3.2 (0.29)
Hispanic[1]	9 (1.1)	12 (1.0)	21 (1.5)	23 (3.1)	29 (2.1)	24 (2.4)	37 (2.2)	2.8 (0.36)	3.3 (0.26)	4.7 (0.30)	4.8 (0.71)	5.9 (0.38)	5.2 (0.51)	7.2 (0.43)
Asian[1,2]	4 (0.8)	5 (0.6)	7 (0.6)	9 (1.0)	11 (1.5)	9 (1.4)	14 (1.4)	1.2 (0.26)	1.5 (0.18)	1.6 (0.14)	1.8 (0.20)	2.2 (0.29)	1.8 (0.31)	2.7 (0.27)
Pacific Islander	—	—	—	‡	‡	‡	‡	— (†)	— (†)	— (†)	0.21 (0.07)	0.3! (0.14)	‡ (†)	0.1! (0.04)
American Indian/Alaska Native[1]	3 (0.4)	1 (0.3)	2 (0.4)	‡ (†)	‡ (†)	‡ (†)	‡ (†)	0.9 (0.12)	0.4 (0.09)	0.6 (0.08)	‡ (†)	‡ (†)	‡ (†)	0.3! (0.10)
Two or more races	—	—	—	3! (1.4)	4 (0.6)	4 (0.9)	7 (0.9)	—	—	—	0.6! (0.28)	0.7 (0.12)	0.8 (0.19)	1.3 (0.17)
Age														
Under 30	67 (2.6)	60 (2.2)	87 (3.1)	88 (3.7)	80 (3.9)	78 (6.8)	83 (3.5)	21.8 (0.77)	16.7 (0.61)	19.3 (0.43)	18.9 (0.78)	16.3 (0.67)	16.7 (1.48)	16.2 (0.65)
30 to 39	106 (3.6)	100 (4.0)	101 (3.2)	103 (5.8)	109 (5.2)	112 (6.2)	124 (4.1)	34.5 (0.81)	28.1 (0.78)	22.4 (0.50)	22.0 (1.36)	22.3 (0.91)	24.0 (1.07)	24.4 (0.66)
40 to 49	84 (3.4)	121 (3.1)	131 (4.2)	119 (7.1)	116 (3.6)	110 (6.3)	115 (4.0)	27.4 (0.78)	33.9 (0.74)	29.2 (0.62)	25.4 (1.41)	23.8 (0.65)	23.8 (1.06)	22.7 (0.68)
50 to 59	34 (2.2)	53 (2.3)	106 (3.2)	121 (11.1)	128 (4.5)	99 (5.0)	108 (3.8)	11.1 (0.57)	14.8 (0.55)	23.5 (0.46)	25.8 (2.07)	26.2 (0.87)	21.3 (1.06)	21.2 (0.64)
60 and over	16 (1.7)	23 (1.6)	25 (1.2)	37 (4.7)	56 (3.1)	66 (5.0)	79 (3.4)	5.3 (0.49)	6.4 (0.41)	5.7 (0.24)	8.0 (0.99)	11.5 (0.62)	14.2 (1.05)	15.5 (0.58)
Highest degree earned														
Less than bachelor's	13 (1.4)	23 (1.6)	33 (2.3)	43! (21.5)	40 (2.9)	39 (5.2)	51 (2.8)	4.4 (0.42)	6.4 (0.45)	7.3 (0.46)	9.2! (4.41)	8.1 (0.58)	8.4 (1.07)	10.0 (0.53)
Bachelor's	189 (5.1)	221 (5.7)	258 (5.8)	259 (11.2)	264 (6.8)	225 (6.7)	216 (5.3)	61.4 (0.75)	61.9 (0.90)	57.5 (0.64)	55.5 (2.90)	53.9 (0.95)	48.5 (1.37)	42.4 (0.83)
Master's	92 (3.8)	96 (3.1)	136 (4.5)	138 (6.1)	161 (5.3)	166 (7.5)	204 (5.9)	29.8 (0.73)	27.0 (0.71)	30.3 (0.58)	29.5 (1.35)	32.8 (0.84)	35.8 (1.16)	40.0 (0.80)
Education specialist[3]	9 (0.9)	11 (0.9)	14 (1.0)	17 (2.4)	14 (1.3)	23 (2.3)	25 (1.8)	3.0 (0.30)	2.9 (0.24)	3.1 (0.19)	3.6 (0.54)	2.8 (0.25)	5.0 (0.48)	4.8 (0.33)
Doctor's	4 (0.7)	6 (0.8)	8 (0.8)	10 (1.2)	12 (1.9)	11 (2.0)	14 (1.2)	1.5 (0.23)	1.8 (0.22)	1.8 (0.16)	2.2 (0.26)	2.4 (0.38)	2.3 (0.41)	2.8 (0.23)
Years of teaching experience														
Less than 3	38 (1.4)	47 (1.8)	73 (3.0)	71 (17.5)	72 (4.8)	52 (7.1)	62 (2.4)	12.4 (0.44)	13.2 (0.47)	16.3 (0.44)	15.2 (3.50)	14.7 (0.92)	11.2 (1.54)	12.1 (0.45)
3 to 9	111 (3.4)	123 (3.6)	144 (4.1)	162 (7.1)	163 (5.9)	150 (6.3)	152 (4.8)	36.1 (0.85)	34.6 (0.67)	32.0 (0.56)	34.6 (1.65)	33.2 (1.05)	32.3 (1.07)	29.8 (0.74)
10 to 20	109 (4.3)	122 (3.9)	137 (4.1)	130 (7.3)	133 (4.8)	147 (7.6)	167 (4.7)	35.6 (0.78)	34.4 (0.77)	30.6 (0.54)	27.9 (1.63)	27.1 (0.83)	31.6 (1.38)	32.9 (0.71)
Over 20	49 (2.8)	63 (2.8)	95 (2.8)	105 (7.0)	122 (4.7)	116 (7.2)	128 (4.2)	15.8 (0.65)	17.8 (0.73)	21.2 (0.47)	22.4 (1.62)	24.9 (0.88)	24.9 (1.44)	25.2 (0.67)
Level of instruction[4]														
Elementary	179 (5.6)	225 (4.7)	261 (5.8)	263 (17.5)	258 (6.5)	245 (9.3)	262 (6.1)	58.3 (0.92)	63.2 (0.72)	58.1 (0.66)	56.4 (3.06)	52.8 (1.03)	52.8 (1.67)	51.4 (0.85)
Secondary	128 (4.7)	131 (4.0)	188 (6.2)	204 (13.4)	231 (7.1)	219 (9.9)	247 (6.5)	41.7 (0.92)	36.8 (0.72)	41.9 (0.66)	43.6 (3.06)	47.2 (1.03)	47.2 (1.67)	48.6 (0.78)

—Not available.
†Not applicable.
‡Reporting standards not met. Either there are too few cases for a reliable estimate or the coefficient of variation (CV) is 50 percent or greater.
!Interpret data with caution. The coefficient of variation (CV) for this estimate is between 30 and 50 percent.
[1]Data for 1987–88 through 1999–2000 are only roughly comparable to data for later years, because the new category of Two or more races was introduced in 2003–04.
[2]Includes Pacific Islander for 1987–88 through 1999–2000.
[3]Education specialist degrees or certificates are generally awarded for 1 year's work beyond the master's level. Includes certificate of advanced graduate studies.
[4]Teachers were classified as elementary or secondary on the basis of the grades they taught, rather than on the level of the school in which they taught. In general, elementary teachers include those teaching prekindergarten through grade 6 and those teaching multiple grades, with a preponderance of grades taught being kindergarten through grade 6. In general, secondary teachers include those teaching any of grades 7 through 12 and those teaching multiple grades, with a preponderance of grades taught being grades 7 through 12 and usually with no grade taught being lower than grade 5.
NOTE: Excludes teachers who teach only prekindergarten. Data are based on a head count of full-time and part-time teachers rather than on the number of full-time-equivalent teachers reported in other tables. Detail may not sum to totals because of rounding and cell suppression. Race categories exclude persons of Hispanic ethnicity.
SOURCE: U.S. Department of Education, National Center for Education Statistics, Schools and Staffing Survey (SASS), "Public School Teacher Data File" and "Private School Teacher Data File," 1987–88 through 2011–12; SASS, "Charter School Teacher Data File," 1999–2000; and National Teacher and Principal Survey (NTPS), "Public School Teacher Data File" and "Private School Teacher Data File," 2017–18. (This table was prepared November 2019.)

Table 209.20. Number, highest degree, and years of teaching experience of teachers in public and private elementary and secondary schools, by selected teacher characteristics: Selected years, 1999–2000 through 2017–18

[Standard errors appear in parentheses]

Selected teacher characteristic	Number of teachers (in thousands)				Percent of teachers, by highest degree earned, 2017–18					Percent of teachers, by years of full-time and part-time teaching experience, 2017–18			
	1999–2000	2007–08	2011–12	2017–18	Less than bachelor's	Bachelor's	Master's	Education specialist[1]	Doctor's	Less than 3	3 to 9	10 to 20	Over 20
1	2	3	4	5	6	7	8	9	10	11	12	13	14
Public schools													
Total	3,002 (19.4)	3,405 (44.0)	3,385 (41.4)	3,545 (23.5)	2.7 (0.10)	39.3 (0.36)	49.2 (0.36)	7.6 (0.18)	1.2 (0.07)	9.0 (0.19)	28.3 (0.34)	39.9 (0.35)	22.8 (0.29)
Sex													
Male	754 (10.7)	821 (20.4)	802 (22.2)	834 (11.6)	4.0 (0.24)	39.0 (0.64)	49.6 (0.65)	5.7 (0.26)	1.7 (0.18)	8.9 (0.38)	27.4 (0.60)	40.6 (0.68)	23.2 (0.52)
Female	2,248 (16.0)	2,584 (34.6)	2,584 (30.5)	2,712 (20.2)	2.3 (0.11)	39.4 (0.39)	49.1 (0.40)	8.2 (0.22)	1.0 (0.07)	9.0 (0.21)	28.6 (0.39)	39.7 (0.40)	22.7 (0.38)
Race/ethnicity													
White[2]	2,532 (17.2)	2,829 (38.7)	2,773 (30.5)	2,811 (22.7)	2.6 (0.12)	38.6 (0.39)	50.4 (0.39)	7.4 (0.19)	1.0 (0.07)	8.3 (0.21)	27.3 (0.37)	40.1 (0.39)	24.3 (0.34)
Black[2]	228 (6.0)	239 (15.8)	231 (12.1)	239 (7.4)	3.0 (0.42)	32.9 (1.23)	50.7 (1.40)	11.3 (0.85)	2.1 (0.37)	10.8 (0.75)	30.3 (1.27)	38.7 (1.25)	20.2 (1.03)
Hispanic[2]	169 (6.4)	240 (16.6)	263 (13.4)	331 (9.2)	3.6 (0.41)	51.1 (1.20)	37.9 (1.06)	6.1 (0.49)	1.3 (0.20)	11.8 (0.71)	34.0 (0.99)	39.6 (1.03)	14.6 (0.75)
Asian[2,3]	48 (2.7)	42 (7.2)	61 (7.3)	75 (3.5)	1.7 (0.45)	29.0 (1.85)	55.1 (2.00)	11.3 (1.24)	2.8 (0.77)	12.0 (1.33)	31.1 (2.01)	42.1 (2.06)	14.8 (1.44)
Pacific Islander	— (†)	6 (1.3)	5 (1.4)	8 (1.0)	‡ (†)	44.2 (6.46)	38.6 (6.15)	8.7! (2.64)	† (†)	6.7! (2.41)	24.0 (5.02)	44.2 (6.58)	25.1 (5.45)
American Indian/Alaska Native[2]	26 (1.9)	17 (1.9)	17 (2.9)	18 (1.7)	5.3! (2.63)	51.6 (3.93)	36.2 (4.05)	6.2 (1.63)	† (†)	9.0 (2.03)	20.9 (2.68)	42.5 (4.31)	27.6 (3.92)
Two or more races	— (†)	31 (2.9)	35 (3.8)	63 (3.1)	3.2 (0.92)	40.8 (2.33)	47.0 (2.50)	7.8 (1.35)	1.2! (0.41)	12.5 (1.40)	35.5 (2.41)	34.6 (2.13)	17.4 (1.86)
Age													
Under 30	509 (9.2)	612 (22.4)	518 (15.9)	531 (9.4)	2.7 (0.29)	64.8 (0.88)	30.3 (0.85)	2.1 (0.24)	‡ (†)	37.1 (0.80)	62.8 (0.79)	‡ (†)	‡ (†)
30 to 39	661 (9.8)	898 (16.8)	979 (19.3)	991 (12.9)	2.2 (0.18)	37.9 (0.62)	52.9 (0.65)	6.5 (0.34)	0.6 (0.08)	6.7 (0.29)	42.9 (0.65)	50.3 (0.65)	‡ (†)
40 to 49	953 (10.3)	808 (19.2)	849 (19.2)	1,028 (12.3)	2.9 (0.19)	33.5 (0.60)	53.3 (0.67)	9.2 (0.34)	1.1 (0.12)	3.4 (0.23)	15.5 (0.45)	58.1 (0.57)	23.0 (0.49)
50 to 59	786 (12.6)	879 (21.1)	783 (20.5)	732 (11.6)	2.9 (0.25)	33.4 (0.69)	52.1 (0.75)	9.5 (0.40)	2.1 (0.22)	2.0 (0.19)	9.2 (0.39)	33.5 (0.68)	55.2 (0.72)
60 and over	93 (4.0)	207 (10.3)	256 (13.2)	263 (6.1)	3.6 (0.38)	32.1 (1.05)	49.2 (1.08)	12.0 (0.75)	3.1 (0.39)	1.7 (0.30)	6.5 (0.54)	28.2 (1.07)	63.6 (1.05)
Level of instruction[4]													
Elementary	1,602 (13.5)	1,725 (37.1)	1,726 (20.2)	1,779 (24.5)	2.1 (0.15)	42.6 (0.53)	47.1 (0.53)	7.6 (0.27)	0.7 (0.08)	9.4 (0.30)	29.2 (0.50)	39.0 (0.51)	22.4 (0.42)
General	1,019 (13.6)	1,100 (26.5)	1,078 (22.1)	1,097 (17.3)	2.1 (0.21)	45.0 (0.68)	45.5 (0.67)	6.9 (0.33)	0.5 (0.10)	9.4 (0.40)	28.8 (0.58)	39.9 (0.66)	21.9 (0.55)
Arts/music	33 (2.8)	103 (6.6)	82 (5.4)	99 (4.2)	1.4 (0.34)	49.1 (2.12)	42.9 (2.10)	5.5 (0.90)	1.1! (0.53)	9.1 (1.12)	29.7 (1.94)	37.0 (2.15)	24.2 (1.77)
English	‡ (†)	104 (9.9)	92 (6.8)	117 (4.6)	1.9 (0.50)	35.4 (1.78)	51.3 (1.84)	10.4 (1.01)	1.0! (0.39)	7.7 (1.02)	25.5 (1.64)	39.0 (1.77)	27.8 (1.54)
ESL/bilingual	‡ (†)	24 (3.3)	51 (6.8)	48 (3.4)	1.8! (0.81)	32.9 (3.15)	51.2 (3.15)	13.3 (2.03)	0.9! (0.35)	8.8 (1.52)	29.8 (3.27)	39.3 (3.26)	22.1 (2.76)
Health/physical ed	26 (2.5)	63 (6.0)	79 (8.1)	65 (3.5)	5.1 (1.27)	50.2 (2.32)	41.5 (2.40)	3.0 (0.76)	† (†)	7.6 (1.25)	24.1 (2.07)	38.9 (2.59)	29.4 (2.24)
Mathematics	‡ (†)	28 (3.8)	32 (6.5)	36 (2.3)	2.7! (0.88)	43.1 (3.17)	48.0 (3.31)	6.2 (1.60)	‡ (†)	7.5 (1.44)	31.2 (3.18)	41.4 (3.31)	19.8 (2.40)
Science	‡ (†)	15 (3.4)	18 (3.3)	23 (1.8)	4.3! (1.48)	45.8 (3.88)	44.9 (3.98)	3.8! (1.23)	‡ (†)	8.6! (2.62)	29.3 (3.61)	42.9 (3.52)	19.2 (3.37)
Special education	210 (5.8)	230 (13.0)	239 (10.3)	235 (6.3)	1.2 (0.23)	33.9 (1.34)	53.2 (1.40)	10.3 (0.82)	1.3 (0.35)	11.8 (0.82)	33.6 (1.29)	34.8 (1.31)	19.8 (1.05)
Other elementary	314 (8.4)	58 (4.2)	55 (5.2)	60 (3.0)	2.3 (0.49)	33.4 (2.47)	54.2 (2.66)	9.5 (1.38)	1.4! (0.65)	8.6 (1.23)	29.9 (2.31)	38.9 (2.46)	24.4 (2.08)
Secondary	1,401 (17.7)	1,680 (39.0)	1,659 (37.8)	1,766 (25.2)	3.4 (0.16)	36.0 (0.49)	51.3 (0.49)	7.7 (0.26)	1.6 (0.11)	8.6 (0.23)	27.4 (0.41)	40.9 (0.45)	23.2 (0.43)
Arts/music	235 (5.0)	121 (6.2)	121 (5.6)	130 (4.5)	3.3 (0.69)	44.8 (1.58)	44.6 (1.59)	5.8 (0.72)	1.4 (0.28)	9.7 (1.03)	28.6 (1.39)	35.9 (1.31)	25.9 (1.38)
English	‡ (†)	306 (10.0)	289 (9.9)	294 (6.6)	1.5 (0.28)	34.1 (0.98)	54.2 (0.95)	8.4 (0.64)	1.8 (0.27)	8.4 (0.55)	27.6 (0.98)	41.2 (1.06)	22.7 (0.87)
ESL/bilingual	‡ (†)	21 (2.5)	20 (2.4)	24 (1.9)	‡ (†)	24.0 (3.58)	58.1 (3.98)	14.7 (2.79)	1.7! (0.85)	6.8 (1.33)	25.8 (3.30)	43.7 (3.66)	23.6 (3.35)
Foreign language	‡ (†)	78 (5.0)	88 (4.5)	85 (3.2)	0.8 (0.22)	31.3 (1.89)	57.5 (1.90)	7.5 (0.99)	2.9 (0.65)	8.7 (1.47)	26.0 (1.62)	43.8 (1.93)	21.5 (1.55)
Health/physical ed	191 (4.3)	119 (5.7)	101 (3.9)	97 (3.2)	2.8 (0.57)	45.0 (1.73)	47.7 (1.66)	4.0 (0.85)	0.4! (0.17)	5.6 (0.69)	22.3 (1.19)	41.7 (1.59)	30.4 (1.46)
Mathematics	159 (3.7)	252 (9.1)	250 (7.5)	265 (6.6)	2.5 (0.35)	37.5 (1.10)	53.1 (1.12)	5.8 (0.48)	1.1 (0.21)	8.9 (0.62)	28.3 (1.12)	40.9 (1.09)	21.8 (0.94)
Science	147 (4.3)	195 (8.3)	197 (6.1)	220 (5.6)	2.9 (0.41)	33.7 (1.27)	54.5 (1.32)	6.4 (0.64)	2.5 (0.32)	9.1 (0.67)	27.1 (1.12)	42.5 (1.19)	21.3 (1.05)
Social studies	99 (2.3)	209 (9.9)	191 (6.3)	214 (5.2)	2.2 (0.29)	35.9 (1.28)	55.3 (1.31)	6.8 (0.59)	1.8 (0.34)	8.0 (0.60)	27.3 (1.13)	42.8 (1.19)	21.9 (0.97)
Special education	125 (3.2)	165 (9.7)	147 (12.2)	199 (5.5)	2.6 (0.43)	30.7 (1.13)	50.9 (1.32)	14.6 (0.97)	1.2 (0.30)	9.3 (0.73)	30.6 (1.14)	37.3 (1.36)	22.8 (1.31)
Vocational/technical	‡ (†)	164 (6.3)	139 (5.7)	139 (4.4)	14.4 (1.14)	37.8 (1.59)	40.1 (1.40)	6.0 (0.68)	1.7 (0.32)	9.3 (0.76)	27.6 (1.34)	40.9 (1.39)	22.2 (1.19)
Other secondary	443 (8.5)	47 (3.4)	46 (4.0)	98 (3.9)	4.3 (0.71)	37.6 (1.66)	49.0 (1.72)	8.4 (1.01)	0.7! (0.23)	7.6 (0.89)	23.5 (1.42)	41.4 (1.82)	27.6 (1.60)

See notes at end of table.

Table 209.20. Number, highest degree, and years of teaching experience of teachers in public and private elementary and secondary schools, by selected teacher characteristics: Selected years, 1999–2000 through 2017–18—Continued

[Standard errors appear in parentheses]

Selected teacher characteristic	Number of teachers (in thousands)				Percent of teachers, by highest degree earned, 2017–18					Percent of teachers, by years of full-time and part-time teaching experience, 2017–18			
	1999–2000	2007–08	2011–12	2017–18	Less than bachelor's	Bachelor's	Master's	Education specialist[1]	Doctor's	Less than 3	3 to 9	10 to 20	Over 20
1	2	3	4	5	6	7	8	9	10	11	12	13	14
Private schools													
Total	449 (10.6)	490 (9.2)	465 (11.1)	509 (9.1)	10.0 (0.53)	42.4 (0.83)	40.0 (0.80)	4.8 (0.33)	2.8 (0.23)	12.1 (0.45)	29.8 (0.74)	32.9 (0.71)	25.2 (0.67)
Sex													
Male	107 (3.8)	127 (4.6)	117 (6.9)	133 (4.1)	8.7 (0.87)	37.6 (1.39)	44.0 (1.42)	3.8 (0.53)	5.9 (0.65)	12.0 (0.90)	30.1 (1.32)	31.6 (1.21)	26.3 (1.25)
Female	342 (7.7)	362 (7.7)	348 (10.1)	377 (7.3)	10.4 (0.60)	44.1 (0.97)	38.5 (0.90)	5.2 (0.41)	1.7 (0.19)	12.2 (0.54)	29.7 (0.86)	33.3 (0.86)	24.8 (0.77)
Race/ethnicity													
White[2]	402 (9.6)	423 (8.8)	411 (11.1)	433 (8.3)	9.3 (0.57)	42.2 (0.89)	40.7 (0.86)	4.8 (0.36)	2.9 (0.25)	11.3 (0.49)	28.8 (0.81)	33.4 (0.78)	26.6 (0.73)
Black[2]	17 (1.4)	20 (2.2)	17 (2.4)	16 (1.5)	10.1 (2.26)	48.1 (4.12)	34.4 (3.77)	5.4! (1.71)	† (†)	16.2 (3.56)	35.6 (4.14)	30.9 (3.99)	17.3 (2.94)
Hispanic[2]	21 (1.5)	29 (2.1)	24 (2.4)	37 (1.5)	15.1 (2.07)	45.2 (2.70)	33.0 (2.78)	5.1 (1.37)	1.7! (0.53)	17.7 (2.31)	34.3 (2.64)	30.2 (2.64)	17.8 (2.44)
Asian[3]	‡ (†)	11 (1.5)	9 (1.4)	14 (1.4)	10.0 (2.25)	37.2 (4.40)	44.1 (4.38)	‡ (†)	3.3! (1.41)	15.3 (2.69)	37.9 (4.12)	32.2 (4.21)	14.5 (3.49)
Pacific Islander	—	‡ (†)	‡ (†)	‡ (†)	‡ (†)	‡ (†)	‡ (†)	‡ (†)	‡ (†)	‡ (†)	‡ (†)	‡ (†)	‡ (†)
American Indian/Alaska Native	‡ (†)	‡ (†)	‡ (†)	‡ (†)	‡ (†)	‡ (†)	‡ (†)	‡ (†)	‡ (†)	‡ (†)	‡ (†)	‡ (†)	‡ (†)
Two or more races	—	4 (0.6)	4 (0.9)	7 (0.9)	12.5! (5.41)	43.4 (6.37)	37.9 (6.04)	‡ (†)	3.9! (1.75)	15.5! (5.38)	41.1 (6.64)	24.3 (5.49)	19.2 (4.34)
Age													
Under 30	87 (3.1)	80 (3.9)	78 (6.8)	83 (3.5)	26.5 (1.64)	46.7 (1.80)	25.3 (1.42)	1.4! (0.41)	‡ (†)	42.2 (1.87)	57.6 (1.87)	‡ (†)	‡ (†)
30 to 39	101 (3.2)	109 (5.2)	112 (6.2)	124 (4.1)	7.3 (0.88)	40.9 (1.44)	44.3 (1.52)	4.2 (0.56)	3.3 (0.49)	11.7 (0.98)	46.9 (1.53)	41.3 (1.60)	‡ (†)
40 to 49	131 (4.2)	116 (3.6)	110 (6.3)	115 (4.0)	5.0 (0.67)	43.1 (1.56)	43.9 (1.56)	5.4 (0.65)	2.6 (0.39)	5.9 (0.60)	23.8 (1.39)	53.8 (1.64)	16.5 (1.19)
50 to 59	106 (3.2)	128 (4.5)	99 (5.0)	108 (3.8)	7.9 (0.85)	42.8 (1.69)	39.6 (1.72)	6.4 (0.82)	3.3 (0.52)	3.6 (0.49)	12.3 (0.99)	36.6 (1.51)	47.5 (1.51)
60 and over	25 (1.2)	56 (3.1)	66 (5.0)	79 (3.4)	6.8 (1.14)	38.7 (1.92)	43.4 (1.95)	6.4 (0.88)	4.6 (0.80)	2.0 (0.53)	6.6 (1.05)	18.3 (1.43)	73.1 (1.75)
Level of instruction[4]													
Elementary	261 (5.8)	258 (6.5)	245 (9.3)	262 (6.1)	11.7 (0.76)	48.3 (1.20)	34.2 (1.12)	5.1 (0.51)	0.8 (0.18)	12.6 (0.69)	29.5 (1.07)	33.3 (1.07)	24.6 (0.96)
General	168 (4.0)	163 (3.9)	151 (7.0)	154 (4.7)	11.5 (0.91)	51.1 (1.51)	32.8 (1.36)	4.1 (0.60)	0.6! (0.20)	12.3 (0.97)	30.4 (1.35)	33.1 (1.39)	24.2 (1.21)
Arts/music	[5]	20 (1.6)	20 (1.8)	23 (1.3)	8.0 (1.97)	47.5 (3.81)	41.9 (3.87)	1.9! (0.85)	‡ (†)	10.0 (2.05)	22.5 (3.03)	37.2 (3.65)	30.4 (3.60)
English	[5]	13 (1.2)	16 (2.8)	12 (1.3)	13.1 (3.61)	38.1 (5.07)	33.3 (5.01)	14.5 (3.29)	‡ (†)	13.1 (3.25)	26.0 (4.37)	27.9 (3.98)	30.4 (4.74)
ESL/bilingual	[5]	[5]	[5]	‡ (†)	‡ (†)	‡ (†)	‡ (†)	‡ (†)	‡ (†)	‡ (†)	‡ (†)	‡ (†)	‡ (†)
Health/physical ed	[5]	14 (1.7)	11 (1.2)	13 (1.1)	10.3! (3.11)	57.9 (4.39)	27.0 (3.86)	4.4! (2.02)	‡ (†)	8.9 (2.26)	33.1 (4.34)	31.7 (4.33)	26.3 (3.96)
Mathematics	[5]	7 (1.0)	6 (1.1)	8 (1.2)	15.0 (4.04)	56.2 (6.27)	24.0 (4.92)	4.0! (1.85)	‡ (†)	18.3 (4.59)	26.2 (5.11)	35.9 (7.62)	19.6 (4.94)
Science	[5]	6 (0.8)	5 (1.0)	8 (1.0)	‡ (†)	55.1 (6.75)	38.3 (6.64)	‡ (†)	‡ (†)	‡ (†)	28.7 (6.12)	42.2 (7.22)	20.6 (4.46)
Special education	16 (1.6)	9 (1.0)	10 (1.9)	16 (1.7)	10.0 (2.84)	33.7 (3.66)	44.5 (3.75)	11.8 (2.52)	‡ (†)	16.1 (2.84)	42.0 (3.73)	19.8 (3.31)	22.1 (3.44)
Other elementary	77 (2.2)	27 (2.3)	25 (2.8)	26 (2.0)	18.8 (3.29)	37.7 (3.74)	34.9 (4.09)	6.3 (1.88)	2.2! (1.00)	15.1 (3.23)	24.2 (2.96)	39.0 (3.83)	21.8 (3.16)
Secondary	188 (6.2)	231 (7.1)	219 (9.9)	247 (6.5)	8.1 (0.55)	36.2 (0.98)	46.1 (1.07)	4.5 (0.40)	5.0 (0.40)	11.7 (0.64)	30.1 (0.99)	32.4 (0.93)	25.8 (0.90)
Arts/music	33 (1.7)	19 (1.8)	21 (2.2)	24 (1.7)	10.3 (1.85)	41.7 (3.04)	39.4 (3.07)	4.7 (1.28)	3.8 (1.10)	10.4 (1.65)	31.3 (3.00)	35.4 (3.14)	22.9 (2.90)
English	[6]	39 (2.8)	39 (4.1)	43 (2.1)	6.1 (1.27)	32.3 (2.19)	52.6 (2.45)	4.7 (0.82)	4.2 (0.89)	10.3 (1.44)	31.8 (2.44)	33.0 (2.16)	24.9 (2.22)
ESL/bilingual	[6]	[6]	[6]	‡ (†)	‡ (†)	‡ (†)	‡ (†)	‡ (†)	‡ (†)	‡ (†)	‡ (†)	‡ (†)	‡ (†)
Foreign language	33 (3.5)	22 (2.6)	22 (3.5)	24 (1.7)	6.9 (1.45)	35.9 (3.15)	47.8 (3.30)	4.7 (1.37)	4.6 (0.89)	11.5 (2.17)	26.1 (3.04)	34.0 (3.04)	28.3 (2.96)
Health/physical ed	12 (1.8)	12 (1.8)	10 (1.8)	10 (0.9)	13.3! (4.32)	47.2 (4.92)	36.2 (4.49)	3.3! (1.13)	‡ (†)	9.4 (1.48)	24.9 (3.94)	33.5 (4.56)	21.6 (3.99)
Mathematics	36 (1.6)	36 (2.6)	38 (5.1)	41 (2.0)	6.4 (1.17)	39.5 (2.44)	45.5 (2.65)	‡ (†)	5.3 (1.13)	11.4 (1.52)	30.5 (2.35)	31.8 (2.26)	28.4 (2.36)
Science	31 (1.9)	31 (1.9)	28 (2.7)	31 (1.7)	7.2 (1.23)	37.9 (2.90)	43.3 (2.98)	2.8 (0.82)	8.8 (1.31)	11.4 (1.52)	29.3 (2.53)	32.7 (2.84)	27.1 (2.63)
Social studies	23 (1.3)	31 (2.6)	28 (2.9)	29 (1.6)	5.3 (1.23)	31.4 (2.73)	51.7 (2.99)	3.7 (0.99)	7.9 (1.59)	10.9 (1.60)	33.2 (2.61)	33.2 (2.84)	27.0 (2.42)
Special education	19 (1.1)	6 (1.0)	9 (1.5)	10 (1.4)	9.5 (2.15)	31.1 (4.01)	50.7 (4.01)	7.8 (2.05)	‡ (†)	12.4 (2.76)	37.8 (5.21)	32.7 (4.38)	17.1 (3.47)
Vocational/technical	4 (0.6)	5 (0.8)	5 (1.2)	5 (0.7)	13.8! (4.54)	44.4 (7.28)	30.9 (7.02)	7.7! (3.27)	‡ (†)	19.9 (5.06)	17.0! (5.80)	36.3 (5.93)	26.7 (5.30)
Other secondary	69 (2.6)	29 (2.3)	20 (2.2)	30 (1.7)	12.5 (2.03)	33.6 (2.69)	43.3 (2.61)	6.9 (1.45)	3.6 (0.86)	14.1 (1.86)	30.7 (2.47)	29.4 (2.17)	25.8 (2.43)

—Not available.
†Not applicable.
‡Reporting standards not met. Either there are too few cases for a reliable estimate or the coefficient of variation (CV) is 50 percent or greater.
!Interpret data with caution. The coefficient of variation (CV) for this estimate is between 30 and 50 percent.
[1]Education specialist degrees or certificates are generally awarded for 1 year's work beyond the master's level. Includes certificate of advanced graduate studies.
[2]Data for 1999–2000 are only roughly comparable to data for later years, because the new category of Two or more races was introduced in 2003–04.
[3]Includes Pacific Islander for 1999–2000.
[4]Teachers were classified as elementary or secondary on the basis of the grades they taught, rather than on the level of the school in which they taught. In general, elementary teachers include those teaching prekindergarten through grade 6 and those teaching multiple grades, with a preponderance of grades taught being kindergarten through grade 6. In general, secondary teachers include those teaching any of grades 7 through 12 and those teaching multiple grades, with a preponderance of grades taught being grades 7 through 12 and usually with no grade taught being lower than grade 5.
[5]Included under Other elementary.
[6]Included under Other secondary.

NOTE: Excludes teachers who teach only prekindergarten. Data are based on a head count of full-time and part-time teachers rather than on the number of full-time-equivalent teachers reported in other tables. Detail may not sum to totals because of rounding and cell suppression. Race categories exclude persons of Hispanic ethnicity.
SOURCE: U.S. Department of Education, National Center for Education Statistics, Schools and Staffing Survey (SASS), "Public School Teacher Data File" and "Private School Teacher Data File," 1999–2000, 2003–04, 2007–08, and 2011–12; and National Teacher and Principal Survey (NTPS), "Public School Teacher Data File" and "Private School Teacher Data File," 2017–18. (This table was prepared November 2019.)

Table 209.30.   Highest degree earned, years of full-time teaching experience, and average class size for teachers in public elementary and secondary schools, by state: 2011–12

[Standard errors appear in parentheses]

State	Total number of teachers (in thousands)	Percent of teachers, by highest degree earned — Less than bachelor's	Bachelor's	Master's	Education specialist[2] or doctor's	Percent of teachers, by years of full-time teaching experience — Less than 3	3 to 9	10 to 20	Over 20	Average class size, by level of instruction[1] — Elementary	Secondary
1	2	3	4	5	6	7	8	9	10	11	12
United States	3,385.2 (41.42)	3.8 (0.24)	39.9 (0.52)	47.7 (0.57)	8.7 (0.28)	9.0 (0.29)	33.3 (0.52)	36.4 (0.51)	21.3 (0.54)	21.2 (0.18)	26.8 (0.22)
Alabama	45.0 (2.61)	3.8! (1.51)	34.5 (2.69)	52.8 (2.81)	8.9 (1.64)	8.0 (1.28)	30.9 (2.75)	39.2 (2.85)	21.9 (2.34)	19.2 (0.42)	27.4 (0.94)
Alaska	7.5 (0.70)	4.4! (1.78)	45.6 (4.44)	41.9 (4.01)	8.2 (2.37)	12.9 (3.30)	30.8 (4.15)	39.6 (4.16)	16.7 (3.76)	18.3 (1.35)	18.7 (1.22)
Arizona	61.7 (2.61)	4.6 (1.16)	44.4 (3.67)	44.1 (3.49)	6.9 (1.71)	16.4 (2.29)	38.0 (2.75)	28.5 (2.60)	17.2 (2.02)	24.1 (0.67)	27.7 (0.96)
Arkansas	37.7 (2.01)	3.7! (1.45)	54.7 (3.36)	35.0 (3.13)	6.6 (1.72)	11.5 (2.03)	28.9 (3.38)	32.3 (3.93)	27.3 (3.37)	20.4 (0.73)	25.4 (1.69)
California	285.5 (7.27)	4.8 (0.91)	43.4 (2.33)	39.2 (2.18)	12.7 (1.56)	9.4 (1.29)	29.1 (2.13)	42.3 (2.25)	19.1 (1.89)	25.0 (0.52)	32.0 (0.53)
Colorado	55.9 (3.14)	2.8! (1.00)	36.1 (3.51)	49.9 (4.26)	11.2 (2.79)	10.8 (2.25)	33.4 (3.50)	42.9 (3.96)	12.9 (2.51)	22.8 (1.29)	29.1 (1.25)
Connecticut	44.9 (2.51)	‡ (†)	15.3 (1.86)	64.4 (3.01)	17.7 (2.37)	10.0 (1.43)	29.1 (2.66)	37.1 (2.43)	23.8 (3.34)	19.6 (0.68)	22.0 (0.71)
Delaware	9.3 (0.70)	4.0! (1.50)	34.5 (4.36)	49.7 (4.55)	11.8 (2.85)	12.6 (3.31)	35.0 (3.59)	33.8 (4.04)	18.6 (2.75)	20.3 (0.82)	25.8 (2.09)
District of Columbia	‡ (†)	‡ (†)	‡ (†)	‡ (†)	‡ (†)	‡ (†)	‡ (†)	‡ (†)	‡ (†)	‡ (†)	‡ (†)
Florida	‡ (†)	‡ (†)	‡ (†)	‡ (†)	‡ (†)	‡ (†)	‡ (†)	‡ (†)	‡ (†)	‡ (†)	‡ (†)
Georgia	123.3 (3.97)	3.4! (1.15)	29.5 (3.48)	43.5 (3.79)	23.6 (3.00)	6.3 (1.70)	34.2 (3.42)	39.8 (3.34)	19.7 (2.58)	21.0 (0.91)	27.5 (1.42)
Hawaii	‡ (†)	‡ (†)	‡ (†)	‡ (†)	‡ (†)	‡ (†)	‡ (†)	‡ (†)	‡ (†)	‡ (†)	‡ (†)
Idaho	16.3 (1.83)	4.6 (1.37)	55.6 (3.30)	35.3 (3.18)	4.4 (1.20)	10.4 (1.93)	30.4 (3.18)	35.2 (3.02)	24.0 (2.89)	24.5 (0.63)	25.4 (2.13)
Illinois	140.9 (9.09)	2.7! (0.81)	32.6 (2.53)	57.8 (2.44)	7.0 (1.34)	9.3 (1.56)	36.4 (2.59)	34.4 (2.85)	20.0 (2.51)	22.9 (1.26)	27.3 (1.00)
Indiana	64.0 (2.98)	2.2 (0.52)	43.6 (3.04)	47.4 (3.29)	6.9 (1.45)	10.0 (1.92)	26.1 (2.42)	35.6 (3.01)	28.3 (3.02)	21.4 (0.45)	27.3 (1.07)
Iowa	36.1 (2.28)	3.5! (1.22)	52.8 (3.89)	39.7 (3.60)	4.1! (1.26)	8.8 (1.85)	29.0 (2.98)	33.0 (2.77)	29.2 (2.55)	20.3 (0.93)	27.4 (1.35)
Kansas	36.5 (2.27)	3.8 (0.83)	43.8 (3.52)	47.0 (3.66)	5.4 (1.38)	12.5 (2.98)	27.4 (3.00)	32.7 (3.15)	27.4 (2.83)	20.4 (0.86)	24.6 (1.21)
Kentucky	46.8 (2.51)	5.1 (1.22)	17.5 (2.24)	57.5 (2.58)	20.0 (2.11)	10.1 (1.83)	32.2 (2.82)	38.5 (2.81)	19.2 (2.02)	23.3 (1.92)	26.6 (1.09)
Louisiana	44.5 (2.39)	3.5! (1.72)	61.9 (3.12)	27.0 (2.68)	7.6 (1.55)	8.6 (1.51)	31.2 (3.13)	33.4 (3.31)	26.8 (3.10)	19.0 (0.80)	23.4 (0.78)
Maine	18.4 (0.90)	4.9! (1.60)	46.3 (3.41)	42.8 (3.30)	6.0 (1.36)	5.8 (1.47)	24.1 (2.57)	39.4 (3.32)	30.6 (2.81)	17.6 (0.64)	19.9 (1.76)
Maryland	‡ (†)	‡ (†)	‡ (†)	‡ (†)	‡ (†)	‡ (†)	‡ (†)	‡ (†)	‡ (†)	‡ (†)	‡ (†)
Massachusetts	79.2 (4.42)	3.9 (1.08)	21.8 (2.33)	67.5 (2.54)	6.8 (1.48)	12.4 (1.96)	33.4 (3.04)	36.8 (3.02)	17.4 (3.09)	19.9 (1.72)	24.5 (1.18)
Michigan	96.7 (3.73)	2.3 (0.55)	29.8 (2.50)	62.9 (2.52)	5.0 (1.40)	7.3 (1.00)	31.4 (2.68)	42.7 (2.44)	18.7 (2.12)	23.8 (0.93)	28.9 (0.81)
Minnesota	62.3 (2.99)	4.4 (0.77)	35.3 (2.06)	50.1 (1.87)	10.2 (1.40)	9.5 (1.20)	27.4 (2.05)	40.3 (2.14)	22.9 (2.00)	22.8 (0.70)	29.9 (0.86)
Mississippi	37.6 (2.11)	5.3 (1.45)	54.4 (3.87)	35.2 (3.57)	5.1 (1.51)	10.3 (1.97)	41.0 (3.45)	30.5 (3.35)	18.2 (3.18)	21.6 (1.01)	22.8 (1.15)
Missouri	68.7 (2.34)	4.4 (0.91)	33.3 (2.90)	57.5 (2.96)	4.8 (0.94)	10.4 (1.90)	35.3 (2.21)	35.2 (2.31)	19.2 (2.31)	20.2 (0.83)	26.8 (1.18)
Montana	12.4 (0.90)	6.4 (1.52)	55.2 (3.34)	34.6 (3.39)	3.8! (1.66)	9.6 (2.33)	31.3 (3.17)	30.5 (3.04)	28.6 (3.65)	18.9 (0.80)	21.7 (1.81)
Nebraska	23.9 (1.73)	5.5 (1.31)	44.9 (3.29)	45.9 (3.15)	3.7 (0.98)	10.6 (1.74)	27.2 (2.52)	34.6 (2.63)	27.6 (2.54)	17.9 (0.72)	23.5 (0.99)
Nevada	25.2 (2.63)	4.5! (1.85)	25.1 (3.92)	49.8 (4.26)	20.6 (3.23)	6.5! (2.17)	39.0 (4.02)	36.2 (4.29)	18.2 (3.55)	25.3 (1.41)	34.5 (1.54)
New Hampshire	15.7 (1.05)	3.0! (1.12)	40.2 (3.49)	48.7 (3.55)	8.1 (1.82)	8.1 (1.54)	32.8 (3.41)	31.5 (3.57)	27.5 (3.54)	20.4 (3.09)	21.7 (1.16)
New Jersey	125.2 (4.16)	3.0 (0.74)	48.5 (2.47)	40.8 (2.30)	7.6 (1.60)	7.3 (1.24)	35.4 (2.45)	37.4 (2.66)	20.0 (2.03)	18.5 (0.81)	23.9 (0.68)
New Mexico	21.7 (2.83)	4.3! (2.01)	43.3 (3.80)	42.1 (3.72)	10.3 (2.82)	8.0! (2.46)	30.9 (3.73)	40.3 (5.11)	20.8 (5.19)	19.8 (0.76)	23.7 (1.58)
New York	241.4 (14.58)	2.8! (1.00)	4.4 (1.09)	84.2 (1.56)	8.6 (1.32)	5.3 (1.38)	30.0 (2.81)	45.5 (2.35)	19.1 (2.41)	20.7 (1.36)	25.1 (0.96)
North Carolina	104.3 (5.71)	4.1! (1.57)	54.2 (3.16)	33.8 (2.80)	7.8 (1.84)	8.4 (1.52)	35.8 (3.13)	34.8 (3.05)	21.1 (2.74)	18.8 (0.65)	25.8 (1.25)
North Dakota	10.3 (0.74)	6.9 (1.63)	59.2 (3.08)	30.1 (2.60)	3.9 (1.13)	12.2 (2.09)	24.6 (3.06)	30.6 (3.28)	32.6 (3.45)	17.8 (0.60)	19.2 (1.41)
Ohio	122.1 (4.29)	5.3 (1.17)	24.0 (1.79)	64.5 (2.16)	6.2 (1.28)	7.1 (1.11)	28.8 (2.48)	40.8 (2.67)	23.3 (2.00)	21.3 (0.99)	26.7 (0.85)
Oklahoma	46.2 (2.49)	4.3 (1.04)	65.6 (2.66)	26.9 (2.56)	3.2! (1.12)	9.8 (1.84)	30.1 (2.58)	36.9 (2.93)	23.3 (2.27)	20.7 (0.56)	23.7 (0.88)
Oregon	31.8 (1.28)	4.2! (1.53)	26.3 (3.18)	59.8 (3.62)	9.7 (1.94)	7.2 (1.54)	37.0 (3.58)	35.6 (3.58)	20.2 (2.45)	26.4 (0.96)	30.0 (1.05)
Pennsylvania	148.8 (7.48)	4.5! (1.94)	32.9 (2.52)	53.9 (3.34)	8.7 (1.77)	6.2 (1.78)	37.0 (2.55)	35.8 (2.17)	21.0 (2.30)	22.4 (0.99)	25.2 (0.96)
Rhode Island	‡ (†)	‡ (†)	‡ (†)	‡ (†)	‡ (†)	‡ (†)	‡ (†)	‡ (†)	‡ (†)	‡ (†)	‡ (†)
South Carolina	51.8 (1.76)	3.0! (1.34)	28.8 (3.14)	57.9 (3.95)	10.3 (2.15)	8.4 (1.58)	30.5 (3.22)	32.3 (3.54)	28.9 (3.38)	19.1 (0.75)	26.0 (1.98)
South Dakota	10.8 (0.92)	2.3! (0.73)	68.8 (3.52)	26.6 (3.13)	2.3! (1.14)	8.8 (1.65)	24.6 (2.76)	32.9 (3.63)	33.7 (3.38)	20.4 (0.66)	22.3 (1.31)
Tennessee	76.5 (2.91)	4.4! (1.52)	35.1 (3.54)	46.3 (3.44)	14.2 (2.83)	10.6 (1.80)	34.0 (3.66)	34.1 (3.48)	21.3 (3.28)	17.7 (0.52)	26.9 (1.60)
Texas	350.8 (22.99)	3.3 (0.65)	66.4 (2.09)	25.8 (2.12)	4.6 (0.77)	8.9 (0.95)	40.4 (2.05)	31.1 (1.88)	19.7 (1.74)	18.2 (0.82)	26.9 (1.07)
Utah	27.9 (1.67)	4.2 (1.10)	56.8 (3.96)	27.3 (3.88)	11.7! (3.94)	15.0 (2.43)	39.9 (4.49)	25.6 (4.52)	19.5 (3.12)	27.4 (2.09)	31.5 (1.29)
Vermont	9.4 (0.34)	6.6 (1.46)	35.4 (2.78)	52.0 (2.87)	6.0 (1.59)	12.9 (1.60)	22.1 (2.38)	37.0 (2.56)	28.0 (2.73)	16.6 (0.40)	19.8 (1.25)
Virginia	88.5 (3.35)	3.3! (1.07)	47.5 (3.08)	41.6 (3.17)	7.6 (1.26)	9.1 (1.68)	31.5 (3.20)	34.2 (2.73)	25.2 (2.43)	20.4 (1.27)	23.8 (0.90)
Washington	55.5 (3.15)	2.9 (0.59)	23.1 (2.61)	62.9 (2.92)	11.1 (1.96)	6.2 (1.45)	32.2 (3.00)	34.8 (2.82)	26.8 (3.03)	23.7 (0.60)	29.7 (0.99)
West Virginia	24.2 (0.79)	3.1 (0.90)	46.6 (4.82)	43.2 (4.71)	7.1 (1.73)	12.0 (2.26)	31.2 (4.12)	30.5 (3.82)	26.3 (3.24)	18.7 (1.00)	24.0 (1.65)
Wisconsin	66.8 (3.42)	2.7 (0.79)	36.7 (2.96)	55.1 (2.98)	5.5 (1.41)	10.5 (1.67)	26.2 (3.12)	42.1 (3.24)	21.3 (2.73)	20.8 (0.55)	27.9 (0.95)
Wyoming	8.5 (0.57)	7.0! (3.08)	44.3 (4.47)	41.2 (4.18)	7.5! (2.74)	7.6! (2.62)	25.2 (4.09)	35.1 (3.73)	32.1 (4.30)	17.0 (1.05)	19.6 (1.22)

†Not applicable.

!Interpret data with caution. The coefficient of variation (CV) for this estimate is between 30 and 50 percent.

‡Reporting standards not met. Data may be suppressed because the response rate is under 50 percent, there are too few cases for a reliable estimate, or the coefficient of variation (CV) is 50 percent or greater.

[1]Elementary teachers are those who taught self-contained classes at the elementary level, and secondary teachers are those who taught departmentalized classes (e.g., science, art, social science, or other course subjects) at the secondary level. Teachers were classified as elementary or secondary on the basis of the grades they taught, rather than on the level of the school in which they taught. In general, elementary teachers include those teaching prekindergarten through grade 5 and those teaching multiple grades, with a preponderance of grades taught being kindergarten through grade 6. In general, secondary teachers include those teaching any of grades 7 through 12 and those teaching multiple grades, with a preponderance of grades taught being grades 7 through 12 and usually with no grade taught being lower than grade 5.

[2]Education specialist degrees or certificates are generally awarded for 1 year's work beyond the master's level. Includes certificate of advanced graduate studies.

NOTE: Data are based on a head count of all teachers rather than on the number of full-time-equivalent teachers appearing in other tables. Excludes prekindergarten teachers. Detail may not sum to totals because of rounding and cell suppression.

SOURCE: U.S. Department of Education, National Center for Education Statistics, Schools and Staffing Survey (SASS), "Public School Teacher Data File," 2011–12. (This table was prepared May 2013.)

Table 211.20. Average base salary for full-time teachers in public elementary and secondary schools, by highest degree earned and years of teaching experience: Selected years, 1990–91 through 2017–18

[Standard errors appear in parentheses]

Years of full- and part-time teaching experience[1]	Number of full-time teachers	Base salary[2] (current dollars)					Base salary[2] (constant 2018–19 dollars)[3]				
		All teachers[4]	Bachelor's degree	Master's degree	Education specialist[5]	Doctor's degree	All teachers[4]	Bachelor's degree	Master's degree	Education specialist[5]	Doctor's degree
1	2	3	4	5	6	7	8	9	10	11	12
1990–91											
Total	2,336,750 (20,958)	$31,330 (97)	$27,740 (103)	$34,960 (125)	$37,230 (391)	$40,070 (817)	$59,250 (184)	$52,460 (194)	$66,110 (237)	$70,410 (739)	$75,770 (1,544)
1 year or less	80,770 (2,952)	21,640 (182)	21,170 (172)	25,330 (772)	‡ (†)	‡ (†)	40,920 (345)	40,040 (324)	47,910 (1,461)	‡ (†)	‡ (†)
2 years	80,330 (2,981)	21,990 (166)	21,590 (157)	24,650 (527)	‡ (†)	‡ (†)	41,590 (314)	40,820 (297)	46,620 (997)	‡ (†)	‡ (†)
3 years	77,380 (2,796)	22,770 (189)	22,170 (179)	25,980 (760)	‡ (†)	‡ (†)	43,060 (357)	41,940 (339)	49,130 (1,438)	‡ (†)	‡ (†)
4 years	75,400 (3,346)	23,690 (228)	23,090 (232)	25,570 (425)	30,280 (1,601)	‡ (†)	44,810 (430)	43,660 (438)	48,350 (804)	57,270 (3,028)	‡ (†)
5 years	77,130 (3,280)	24,710 (182)	23,840 (216)	26,530 (394)	29,280 (1,325)	‡ (†)	46,740 (344)	45,090 (409)	50,170 (746)	55,380 (2,506)	‡ (†)
6 to 9 years	299,950 (6,518)	26,180 (114)	24,650 (135)	28,570 (215)	29,810 (765)	30,060 (1,551)	49,510 (216)	46,620 (255)	54,040 (406)	56,380 (1,448)	56,860 (2,934)
10 to 14 years	406,650 (7,245)	29,120 (120)	26,980 (156)	31,240 (217)	32,940 (601)	35,430 (1,665)	55,070 (226)	51,020 (296)	59,080 (410)	62,300 (1,137)	67,000 (3,149)
15 to 19 years	459,540 (7,922)	33,350 (191)	30,580 (234)	35,110 (251)	37,460 (836)	39,890 (1,495)	63,080 (360)	57,830 (443)	66,410 (474)	70,850 (1,582)	75,440 (2,827)
20 to 24 years	404,020 (8,354)	36,750 (214)	33,750 (280)	38,330 (243)	39,190 (840)	43,070 (1,387)	69,500 (406)	63,830 (529)	72,500 (459)	74,110 (1,588)	81,460 (2,622)
25 to 29 years	233,620 (6,196)	38,070 (279)	34,960 (358)	39,730 (362)	42,320 (1,106)	43,560 (2,031)	72,010 (527)	66,120 (677)	75,140 (684)	80,040 (2,092)	82,280 (3,841)
30 to 34 years	106,160 (4,942)	38,430 (379)	34,840 (461)	40,510 (450)	41,460 (1,591)	‡ (†)	72,680 (717)	65,900 (871)	76,610 (850)	78,410 (3,010)	‡ (†)
35 years or more	35,790 (2,404)	39,180 (744)	34,650 (1,013)	41,430 (983)	48,740 (3,767)	‡ (†)	74,100 (1,408)	65,540 (1,916)	78,360 (1,859)	92,180 (7,125)	‡ (†)
1999–2000											
Total	2,742,210 (20,301)	$39,900 (118)	$35,310 (116)	$44,730 (174)	$48,000 (438)	$48,180 (1,418)	$59,690 (177)	$52,820 (173)	$66,910 (260)	$71,810 (656)	$72,070 (2,122)
1 year or less	143,610 (4,949)	29,090 (179)	28,110 (160)	33,170 (543)	33,680 (1,012)	‡ (†)	43,520 (268)	42,060 (239)	49,620 (812)	50,380 (1,514)	‡ (†)
2 years	150,130 (5,012)	29,420 (186)	28,560 (178)	32,990 (423)	‡ (†)	‡ (†)	44,010 (279)	42,730 (266)	49,360 (633)	‡ (†)	‡ (†)
3 years	144,250 (4,943)	30,270 (150)	29,240 (190)	34,020 (298)	34,050 (1,629)	‡ (†)	45,290 (225)	43,750 (285)	50,900 (446)	50,940 (2,437)	‡ (†)
4 years	127,330 (5,613)	31,810 (249)	30,540 (213)	35,380 (735)	33,960 (1,089)	‡ (†)	47,590 (372)	45,700 (319)	52,930 (1,099)	50,800 (1,629)	‡ (†)
5 years	121,310 (4,583)	32,220 (272)	30,940 (273)	34,750 (412)	37,240 (2,225)	‡ (†)	48,210 (408)	46,280 (408)	51,990 (617)	55,710 (3,329)	‡ (†)
6 to 9 years	387,160 (8,145)	34,640 (154)	32,350 (173)	37,480 (227)	39,980 (753)	39,610 (2,802)	51,830 (231)	48,400 (259)	56,070 (339)	59,810 (1,127)	59,260 (4,192)
10 to 14 years	375,830 (6,514)	38,710 (254)	35,510 (364)	41,430 (330)	44,560 (1,022)	43,370 (2,096)	57,910 (380)	53,130 (545)	61,980 (494)	66,660 (1,529)	64,890 (3,135)
15 to 19 years	325,840 (7,677)	42,940 (222)	39,930 (334)	45,380 (341)	47,150 (1,397)	46,470 (1,481)	64,250 (332)	59,740 (499)	67,890 (511)	70,540 (1,409)	69,510 (2,216)
20 to 24 years	361,420 (7,306)	45,300 (252)	41,160 (290)	48,260 (392)	47,970 (874)	47,150 (1,410)	67,770 (376)	61,580 (434)	72,200 (587)	71,770 (1,308)	70,540 (2,110)
25 to 29 years	349,650 (7,057)	48,550 (267)	44,540 (320)	50,400 (390)	53,330 (743)	60,790 (2,519)	72,630 (400)	66,630 (478)	75,390 (584)	79,790 (1,112)	90,940 (3,768)
30 to 34 years	199,420 (5,990)	51,910 (375)	47,040 (601)	53,940 (435)	56,590 (1,381)	‡ (†)	77,660 (561)	70,380 (900)	80,700 (651)	84,660 (2,066)	‡ (†)
35 years or more	56,270 (3,030)	50,640 (635)	46,440 (1,234)	52,270 (878)	57,160 (2,395)	‡ (†)	75,760 (950)	69,470 (1,847)	78,200 (1,314)	85,520 (3,582)	‡ (†)
2007–08											
Total	3,114,690 (41,111)	$49,630 (203)	$43,650 (220)	$54,810 (281)	$58,420 (722)	$59,150 (1,620)	$59,370 (243)	$52,220 (263)	$65,570 (336)	$69,890 (863)	$70,770 (1,938)
1 year or less	181,340 (10,618)	37,660 (296)	36,210 (301)	42,370 (855)	45,930 (3,571)	‡ (†)	45,060 (354)	43,310 (361)	50,680 (1,022)	54,950 (4,272)	‡ (†)
2 years	176,370 (10,008)	38,420 (365)	36,860 (372)	42,230 (792)	46,720 (4,534)	‡ (†)	45,960 (436)	44,100 (445)	50,520 (947)	55,900 (5,424)	‡ (†)
3 years	174,150 (8,827)	39,720 (344)	37,570 (366)	44,210 (627)	51,270 (4,903)	‡ (†)	47,520 (412)	44,940 (438)	52,890 (750)	61,340 (5,865)	‡ (†)
4 years	172,750 (7,679)	41,000 (413)	38,440 (416)	45,090 (640)	48,460 (2,574)	‡ (†)	49,050 (497)	45,990 (497)	53,950 (766)	57,970 (3,079)	‡ (†)
5 years	147,760 (7,678)	42,370 (515)	39,200 (449)	46,170 (883)	47,630 (3,308)	‡ (†)	50,690 (616)	46,900 (537)	55,230 (1,057)	56,980 (3,958)	‡ (†)
6 to 9 years	546,350 (12,759)	46,020 (265)	41,640 (372)	49,860 (500)	51,030 (1,128)	52,390 (2,491)	55,060 (317)	49,820 (445)	59,650 (598)	61,050 (1,349)	62,670 (2,980)
10 to 14 years	515,020 (17,292)	49,920 (369)	44,880 (443)	52,920 (544)	56,120 (1,259)	60,920 (4,249)	59,720 (441)	53,690 (530)	63,310 (651)	67,140 (1,506)	72,880 (5,083)
15 to 19 years	351,510 (13,286)	54,550 (465)	48,360 (549)	58,590 (684)	59,930 (1,397)	63,190 (3,501)	65,260 (557)	57,840 (657)	70,090 (818)	71,690 (1,671)	75,600 (4,188)
20 to 24 years	297,710 (12,318)	57,570 (591)	52,550 (811)	60,530 (739)	63,620 (1,960)	66,600 (6,196)	68,870 (707)	62,870 (970)	72,420 (885)	76,110 (2,345)	79,670 (7,412)
25 to 29 years	236,280 (9,186)	59,890 (676)	54,090 (822)	63,460 (1,025)	64,410 (2,199)	‡ (†)	71,640 (808)	64,720 (983)	75,920 (1,226)	77,060 (2,631)	‡ (†)
30 to 34 years	208,120 (9,566)	60,940 (656)	55,080 (1,007)	62,900 (848)	66,540 (2,552)	71,350 (4,668)	72,900 (785)	65,820 (1,204)	75,230 (1,015)	79,600 (3,053)	85,360 (5,584)
35 years or more	107,310 (6,873)	62,530 (1,002)	55,230 (1,467)	65,570 (1,488)	67,740 (2,872)	‡ (†)	74,800 (1,198)	66,080 (1,755)	78,450 (1,780)	81,040 (3,436)	‡ (†)
2011–12											
Total	3,139,250 (38,342)	$53,070 (213)	$46,340 (225)	$57,830 (352)	$59,680 (642)	$60,230 (1,775)	$59,060 (237)	$51,580 (250)	$64,360 (392)	$66,420 (714)	$67,030 (1,975)
1 year or less	109,060 (6,116)	38,310 (483)	37,140 (496)	41,650 (1,134)	45,970 (4,231)	‡ (†)	42,640 (538)	41,340 (552)	46,350 (1,263)	51,160 (4,709)	‡ (†)
2 years	113,470 (5,654)	39,490 (348)	38,180 (399)	42,690 (695)	41,470 (2,831)	‡ (†)	43,950 (387)	42,490 (444)	47,510 (773)	46,150 (3,151)	‡ (†)
3 years	127,030 (7,212)	41,170 (451)	38,950 (494)	45,250 (786)	48,160 (2,529)	‡ (†)	45,820 (502)	43,340 (550)	50,360 (875)	53,600 (2,814)	‡ (†)
4 years	148,720 (8,316)	42,530 (422)	39,900 (423)	45,780 (653)	46,530 (2,181)	‡ (†)	47,340 (470)	44,400 (471)	50,950 (727)	51,790 (2,427)	‡ (†)
5 years	169,220 (8,284)	43,420 (805)	40,020 (398)	47,220 (1,647)	46,960 (1,639)	‡ (†)	48,320 (895)	44,540 (443)	52,560 (1,833)	52,270 (1,824)	‡ (†)
6 to 9 years	597,980 (16,175)	47,820 (322)	43,020 (334)	50,960 (464)	50,940 (1,177)	51,330 (2,288)	53,220 (358)	47,880 (371)	56,710 (516)	56,700 (1,309)	57,120 (2,547)
10 to 14 years	655,560 (17,292)	54,370 (390)	48,360 (542)	57,750 (553)	57,280 (1,075)	60,940 (2,880)	60,510 (434)	53,820 (604)	64,270 (616)	63,750 (1,196)	67,830 (3,205)
15 to 19 years	435,300 (15,477)	58,800 (600)	51,410 (759)	62,410 (809)	65,390 (1,611)	63,350 (3,950)	65,440 (668)	57,210 (845)	69,460 (900)	72,780 (1,793)	70,500 (4,397)
20 to 24 years	312,010 (10,430)	60,880 (599)	54,230 (788)	65,160 (845)	64,460 (1,666)	66,930 (4,546)	67,760 (667)	60,350 (877)	72,520 (940)	71,740 (1,855)	74,490 (5,059)
25 to 29 years	230,570 (10,871)	63,300 (778)	56,430 (1,023)	67,330 (1,246)	67,840 (1,906)	‡ (†)	70,450 (866)	62,800 (1,139)	74,930 (1,386)	75,500 (2,121)	‡ (†)
30 to 34 years	153,840 (9,375)	65,770 (796)	58,570 (1,080)	69,180 (1,117)	70,100 (4,586)	‡ (†)	73,190 (1,202)	65,180 (1,202)	76,990 (1,244)	78,020 (5,104)	‡ (†)
35 years or more	86,470 (5,303)	63,570 (953)	59,740 (1,472)	66,250 (1,136)	65,560 (2,379)	‡ (†)	70,750 (1,061)	66,490 (1,639)	73,730 (1,264)	72,960 (2,648)	‡ (†)

See notes at end of table.

Table 211.20. Average base salary for full-time teachers in public elementary and secondary schools, by highest degree earned and years of teaching experience: Selected years, 1990–91 through 2017–18—Continued

[Standard errors appear in parentheses]

Years of full- and part-time teaching experience[1]	Number of full-time teachers	Base salary[2] (current dollars)					Base salary[2] (constant 2018–19 dollars)[3]				
		Highest degree earned					Highest degree earned				
		All teachers[4]	Bachelor's degree	Master's degree	Education specialist[5]	Doctor's degree	All teachers[4]	Bachelor's degree	Master's degree	Education specialist[5]	Doctor's degree
1	2	3	4	5	6	7	8	9	10	11	12
2017–18											
Total	3,323,200 (22,973)	$57,950 (174)	$49,890 (164)	$63,120 (240)	$66,510 (511)	$69,520 (1,220)	$59,150 (177)	$50,920 (167)	$64,430 (245)	$67,890 (521)	$70,960 (1,246)
1 year or less	230,500 (6,131)	44,150 (327)	42,130 (317)	49,310 (692)	49,480 (1,197)	50,100 (2,205)	45,070 (334)	43,010 (323)	50,330 (707)	50,500 (1,221)	51,140 (2,250)
2 years	171,770 (4,940)	46,000 (337)	42,890 (330)	51,180 (669)	52,600 (1,786)	† (†)	46,960 (344)	43,780 (337)	52,240 (683)	53,690 (1,823)	† (†)
3 years	154,040 (4,999)	47,370 (370)	44,350 (398)	51,440 (598)	52,690 (2,710)	† (†)	48,350 (378)	45,260 (406)	52,500 (610)	53,780 (2,766)	† (†)
4 years	159,610 (4,784)	47,320 (337)	44,180 (345)	50,950 (513)	55,590 (2,471)	‡ (‡)	48,300 (344)	45,100 (352)	52,000 (524)	56,740 (2,523)	‡ (‡)
5 years	144,770 (4,745)	48,780 (334)	45,070 (359)	52,180 (588)	51,430 (1,404)	‡ (‡)	49,790 (341)	46,010 (367)	53,270 (600)	52,500 (1,433)	‡ (‡)
6 to 9 years	452,970 (8,407)	51,380 (242)	46,410 (277)	54,950 (358)	57,690 (1,035)	60,220 (3,440)	52,450 (247)	47,380 (282)	56,090 (366)	58,890 (1,057)	61,470 (3,512)
10 to 14 years	647,230 (8,907)	57,860 (277)	50,630 (358)	61,040 (337)	65,040 (1,037)	66,160 (1,856)	59,060 (282)	51,680 (365)	62,300 (344)	66,390 (1,058)	67,530 (1,895)
15 to 19 years	556,500 (9,214)	64,980 (361)	56,600 (509)	68,490 (454)	69,750 (1,013)	79,120 (3,183)	66,320 (369)	57,770 (520)	69,910 (464)	71,200 (1,034)	80,760 (3,249)
20 to 24 years	384,560 (7,078)	68,440 (468)	59,690 (702)	72,500 (637)	72,940 (1,331)	73,100 (2,559)	69,860 (477)	60,930 (716)	74,010 (650)	74,450 (1,359)	74,610 (2,612)
25 to 29 years	237,750 (6,543)	69,170 (616)	59,960 (712)	73,450 (827)	73,240 (1,952)	74,570 (2,633)	70,610 (629)	61,200 (727)	74,970 (844)	74,760 (1,993)	76,120 (2,687)
30 to 34 years	119,120 (4,303)	71,000 (729)	64,010 (1,207)	74,040 (991)	74,680 (2,562)	‡ (‡)	72,470 (744)	65,340 (1,232)	75,580 (1,012)	76,230 (2,615)	‡ (‡)
35 years or more	64,380 (2,845)	69,420 (964)	61,090 (1,256)	73,090 (1,339)	72,240 (2,775)	† (†)	70,860 (984)	62,350 (1,282)	74,600 (1,367)	73,740 (2,832)	† (†)

†Not applicable.
‡Reporting standards not met (too few cases for a reliable estimate).
[1]Teachers were asked how many school years they had worked as a teacher. In 2011–12 and earlier years, teachers were also asked how many of their teaching years were full time and how many were part time. After 2011–12, teachers were no longer asked how many years were full time versus part time. Throughout this table, all school years are counted, regardless of whether teachers taught full time or part time.
[2]Teachers' base salary does not include any supplemental contracts for additional work at a school during the school year (e.g., coaching) or during the summer (e.g., teaching summer sessions). Also does not include any income from nonschool sources.
[3]Constant dollars based on the Consumer Price Index, prepared by the Bureau of Labor Statistics, U.S. Department of Labor, adjusted to a school-year basis.

[4]Includes teachers with levels of education below the bachelor's degree (not shown separately).
[5]Education specialist degrees or certificates are generally awarded for 1 year's work beyond the master's level. Includes certificate of advanced graduate studies.
NOTE: This table includes regular full-time teachers only; it excludes other staff even when they have full-time teaching duties (regular part-time teachers, itinerant teachers, long-term substitutes, administrators, library media specialists, other professional staff, and support staff). Detail may not sum to totals because of rounding.
SOURCE: U.S. Department of Education, National Center for Education Statistics, Schools and Staffing Survey (SASS), "Public School Teacher Data File," 1990–91, 1999–2000, 2007–08, and 2011–12; and "Charter School Teacher Data File," 1999–2000; and National Teacher and Principal Survey (NTPS), "Public School Teacher Data File," 2017–18. (This table was prepared November 2019.)

Table 211.50. Estimated average annual salary of teachers in public elementary and secondary schools: Selected years, 1959–60 through 2018–19

	Current dollars					Average public school teachers' salary in constant 2018–19 dollars[1]		
	Average public school teachers' salary			Wage and salary accruals per full-time-equivalent (FTE) employee[2]	Ratio of average teachers' salary to accruals per FTE employee			
School year	All teachers	Elementary teachers[3]	Secondary teachers[4]			All teachers	Elementary teachers[3]	Secondary teachers[4]
1	2	3	4	5	6	7	8	9
1959–60	$4,995	$4,815	$5,276	$4,749	1.05	$43,055	$41,503	$45,477
1961–62	5,515	5,340	5,775	5,063	1.09	46,469	44,995	48,660
1963–64	5,995	5,805	6,266	5,478	1.09	49,230	47,669	51,455
1965–66	6,485	6,279	6,761	5,934	1.09	51,474	49,839	53,665
1967–68	7,423	7,208	7,692	6,533	1.14	55,281	53,680	57,285
1969–70	8,626	8,412	8,891	7,486	1.15	57,834	56,399	59,611
1970–71	9,268	9,021	9,568	7,998	1.16	59,088	57,514	61,001
1971–72	9,705	9,424	10,031	8,521	1.14	59,732	58,002	61,738
1972–73	10,174	9,893	10,507	9,056	1.12	60,193	58,531	62,163
1973–74	10,770	10,507	11,077	9,667	1.11	58,503	57,074	60,171
1974–75	11,641	11,334	12,000	10,411	1.12	56,926	55,424	58,681
1975–76	12,600	12,280	12,937	11,194	1.13	57,542	56,081	59,081
1976–77	13,354	12,989	13,776	11,971	1.12	57,625	56,050	59,446
1977–78	14,198	13,845	14,602	12,811	1.11	57,412	55,985	59,046
1978–79	15,032	14,681	15,450	13,808	1.09	55,578	54,281	57,124
1979–80	15,970	15,569	16,459	15,051	1.06	52,100	50,792	53,695
1980–81	17,644	17,230	18,142	16,462	1.07	51,586	50,376	53,042
1981–82	19,274	18,853	19,805	17,838	1.08	51,871	50,738	53,300
1982–83	20,695	20,227	21,291	18,962	1.09	53,402	52,194	54,940
1983–84	21,935	21,487	22,554	19,892	1.10	54,581	53,466	56,121
1984–85	23,600	23,200	24,187	20,840	1.13	56,512	55,554	57,918
1985–86	25,199	24,718	25,846	21,767	1.16	58,650	57,530	60,156
1986–87	26,569	26,057	27,244	22,700	1.17	60,495	59,330	62,032
1987–88	28,034	27,519	28,798	23,777	1.18	61,291	60,165	62,962
1988–89	29,564	29,022	30,218	24,752	1.19	61,783	60,650	63,150
1989–90	31,367	30,832	32,049	25,762	1.22	62,566	61,498	63,926
1990–91	33,084	32,490	33,896	26,935	1.23	62,569	61,446	64,105
1991–92	34,063	33,479	34,827	28,207	1.21	62,421	61,351	63,821
1992–93	35,029	34,350	35,880	29,266	1.20	62,247	61,040	63,759
1993–94	35,737	35,233	36,566	29,956	1.19	61,901	61,028	63,337
1994–95	36,675	36,088	37,523	30,726	1.19	61,756	60,768	63,184
1995–96	37,642	37,138	38,397	31,732	1.19	61,706	60,879	62,943
1996–97	38,443	38,039	39,184	33,057	1.16	61,271	60,627	62,452
1997–98	39,350	39,002	39,944	34,651	1.14	61,617	61,072	62,547
1998–99	40,544	40,165	41,203	36,280	1.12	62,407	61,823	63,421
1999–2000	41,807	41,306	42,546	38,144	1.10	62,545	61,796	63,651
2000–01	43,378	42,910	44,053	39,729	1.09	62,746	62,069	63,722
2001–02	44,655	44,177	45,310	40,600	1.10	63,469	62,790	64,400
2002–03	45,686	45,408	46,106	41,659	1.10	63,538	63,151	64,122
2003–04	46,542	46,187	46,976	43,303	1.07	63,343	62,860	63,934
2004–05	47,516	47,122	47,688	44,957	1.06	62,779	62,259	63,007
2005–06	49,086	48,573	49,496	46,690	1.05	62,474	61,822	62,996
2006–07	51,052	50,740	51,529	48,816	1.05	63,339	62,952	63,931
2007–08	52,800	52,385	53,262	50,649	1.04	63,167	62,670	63,720
2008–09	54,368	53,998	54,552	51,594	1.05	64,147	63,710	64,364
2009–10	55,370	54,918	55,595	52,512	1.05	64,703	64,175	64,966
2010–11	55,495	55,217	56,225	53,966	1.03	63,573	63,254	64,409
2011–12	55,871	54,704	56,226	55,391	1.01	62,182	60,883	62,577
2012–13	56,212	55,344	57,077	56,373	1.00	61,537	60,587	62,484
2013–14	56,826	56,395	56,886	57,501	0.99	61,252	60,788	61,317
2014–15	57,626	57,092	57,678	59,147	0.97	61,666	61,094	61,721
2015–16	58,316	58,225	58,385	60,382	0.97	61,986	61,889	62,059
2016–17	59,539	58,773	58,978	61,740	0.96	62,143	61,343	61,557
2017–18	60,477	—	—	63,674	0.95	61,730	—	—
2018–19	61,730	—	—	—	—	61,730	—	—

—Not available.

[1]Constant dollars based on the Consumer Price Index, prepared by the Bureau of Labor Statistics, U.S. Department of Labor, adjusted to a school-year basis.
[2]The average monetary remuneration earned by FTE employees across all industries in a given year, including wages, salaries, commissions, tips, bonuses, voluntary employee contributions to certain deferred compensation plans, and receipts in kind that represent income. Calendar-year data from the U.S. Department of Commerce, Bureau of Economic Analysis, have been converted to a school-year basis by averaging the two appropriate calendar years in each case.
[3]Teachers at schools that are classified as elementary by state and local practice and composed of any span of grades not above grade 8. Preschool or kindergarten schools are included only if they are an integral part of an elementary school or a regularly established school system.

[4]Teachers at schools comprising any span of grades beginning with the next grade following elementary or middle school (usually 7, 8, or 9) and ending with or below grade 12. Includes both junior high schools and senior high schools.
NOTE: Some data have been revised from previously published figures. Standard errors are not available for these estimates, which are based on state reports.
SOURCE: National Education Association, *Estimates of School Statistics*, 1960 through 2019; and unpublished tabulations. U.S. Department of Commerce, Bureau of Economic Analysis, National Income and Product Accounts, table 6.6D, retrieved September 4, 2019, from https://apps.bea.gov/iTable/iTable.cfm?reqid=19&step=2#reqid=19&step=2&isuri=1&1921=survey. (This table was prepared September 2019.)

Table 212.08. Number and percentage distribution of principals in public and private elementary and secondary schools, by selected characteristics: Selected years, 1993–94 through 2017–18

[Standard errors appear in parentheses]

Selected characteristic	Number of principals					Percentage distribution of principals				
	1993–94	1999–2000	2011–12	2015–16	2017–18	1993–94	1999–2000	2011–12	2015–16	2017–18
1	2	3	4	5	6	7	8	9	10	11
Public schools										
Total	79,620 (235)	83,790 (327)	89,810 (406)	90,410 (298)	90,850 (229)	100.0 (†)	100.0 (†)	100.0 (†)	100.0 (†)	100.0 (†)
Sex										
Male	52,110 (613)	47,130 (604)	43,450 (901)	41,380 (690)	42,100 (540)	65.5 (0.70)	56.2 (0.69)	48.4 (0.92)	45.8 (0.74)	46.3 (0.59)
Female	27,500 (542)	36,660 (598)	46,360 (801)	49,030 (672)	48,750 (559)	34.5 (0.70)	43.8 (0.69)	51.6 (0.92)	54.2 (0.74)	53.7 (0.59)
Race/ethnicity										
White[1]	67,080 (540)	68,930 (579)	72,070 (723)	70,340 (541)	70,580 (498)	84.3 (0.54)	82.3 (0.57)	80.3 (0.66)	77.8 (0.52)	77.7 (0.49)
Black[1]	8,020 (351)	9,240 (321)	9,110 (394)	9,550 (354)	9,570 (367)	10.1 (0.45)	11.0 (0.39)	10.1 (0.43)	10.6 (0.39)	10.5 (0.41)
Hispanic[1]	3,270 (258)	4,330 (300)	6,130 (404)	7,430 (361)	8,090 (328)	4.1 (0.33)	5.2 (0.36)	6.8 (0.46)	8.2 (0.40)	8.9 (0.36)
Asian[1,2]	620 (109)	630 (124)	820 (154)	1,290 (192)	860 (111)	0.8 (0.14)	0.8 (0.15)	0.9 (0.17)	1.4 (0.21)	0.9 (0.12)
Pacific Islander	— (†)	— (†)	‡ (†)	‡ (†)	‡ (†)	— (†)	— (†)	# (†)	0.2 (0.06)	0.2 (0.04)
American Indian/Alaska Native[1]	630 (67)	660 (60)	650 (123)	620 (114)	630 (97)	0.8 (0.08)	0.8 (0.07)	0.7 (0.14)	0.7 (0.13)	0.7 (0.11)
Two or more races	— (†)	— (†)	1,010 (183)	980 (131)	930 (118)	— (†)	— (†)	1.1 (0.20)	1.1 (0.15)	1.0 (0.13)
Age										
Under 40	5,940 (273)	8,440 (302)	18,040 (523)	17,360 (507)	15,210 (445)	7.5 (0.34)	10.1 (0.35)	20.1 (0.58)	19.2 (0.56)	16.7 (0.48)
40 to 44	14,570 (496)	10,510 (317)	17,650 (565)	19,150 (515)	18,330 (472)	18.3 (0.61)	12.5 (0.37)	19.7 (0.62)	21.2 (0.56)	20.2 (0.52)
45 to 49	25,430 (429)	19,600 (535)	14,700 (541)	19,460 (599)	21,100 (447)	31.9 (0.55)	23.4 (0.63)	16.4 (0.60)	21.5 (0.65)	23.2 (0.49)
50 to 54	18,870 (539)	27,120 (606)	15,060 (668)	13,910 (438)	15,980 (498)	23.7 (0.68)	32.4 (0.71)	16.8 (0.73)	15.4 (0.49)	17.6 (0.55)
55 or over	14,820 (441)	18,130 (500)	24,350 (655)	20,540 (631)	20,230 (468)	18.6 (0.55)	21.6 (0.60)	27.1 (0.74)	22.7 (0.70)	22.3 (0.51)
School level										
Elementary	53,680[4] (294)	60,110 (253)	61,250 (443)	62,090 (276)	62,030 (273)	71.9 (0.21)	71.7 (0.21)	68.2 (0.38)	68.7 (0.31)	68.3 (0.28)
Secondary	18,260[4] (161)	20,450 (197)	20,470 (537)	20,280 (395)	20,240 (275)	24.4 (0.20)	24.4 (0.20)	22.8 (0.56)	22.4 (0.41)	22.3 (0.29)
Combined	2,750[4] (143)	3,230 (146)	8,090 (658)	8,050 (332)	8,570 (239)	3.7 (0.19)	3.9 (0.17)	9.0 (0.74)	8.9 (0.37)	9.4 (0.26)
Highest degree earned										
Bachelor's or less	1,150 (167)	1,540 (182)	1,960 (272)	2,030 (212)	1,670 (201)	1.4 (0.21)	1.8 (0.22)	2.2 (0.30)	2.2 (0.23)	1.8 (0.22)
Master's	50,470 (536)	45,440 (579)	55,420 (678)	55,390 (682)	56,110 (602)	63.4 (0.65)	54.2 (0.63)	61.7 (0.71)	61.3 (0.73)	61.8 (0.65)
Education specialist[3]	20,570 (459)	28,280 (493)	23,560 (492)	24,020 (570)	23,500 (551)	25.8 (0.57)	33.8 (0.60)	26.2 (0.54)	26.6 (0.62)	25.9 (0.60)
Doctor's or first professional	7,430 (263)	8,530 (386)	8,870 (442)	8,970 (415)	9,580 (372)	9.3 (0.33)	10.2 (0.46)	9.9 (0.49)	9.9 (0.46)	10.5 (0.41)
Number of years as a principal										
3 or fewer	24,450 (451)	25,080 (513)	29,520 (758)	35,420 (644)	33,390 (633)	30.7 (0.56)	29.9 (0.60)	32.9 (0.84)	39.2 (0.71)	36.7 (0.69)
4 to 9	26,600 (548)	25,900 (524)	35,500 (886)	31,370 (618)	32,420 (597)	33.4 (0.68)	30.9 (0.61)	39.5 (0.96)	34.7 (0.67)	35.7 (0.65)
10 to 19	19,730 (412)	23,230 (525)	19,870 (634)	19,960 (533)	21,600 (548)	24.8 (0.52)	27.7 (0.62)	22.1 (0.70)	22.1 (0.58)	23.8 (0.60)
20 or more	8,840 (377)	9,580 (331)	4,920 (273)	3,670 (285)	3,450 (233)	11.1 (0.47)	11.4 (0.39)	5.5 (0.31)	4.1 (0.31)	3.8 (0.26)
Years of full- and part-time teaching experience prior to becoming a principal										
3 or fewer	5,690 (251)	3,210 (186)	4,040 (264)	3,360 (235)	4,190 (233)	7.1 (0.31)	3.8 (0.22)	4.5 (0.30)	3.7 (0.26)	4.6 (0.26)
4 to 9	29,500 (516)	22,510 (491)	34,240 (792)	34,970 (639)	34,600 (575)	37.1 (0.63)	26.9 (0.57)	38.1 (0.84)	38.7 (0.69)	38.1 (0.62)
10 to 19	36,680 (558)	38,110 (597)	39,160 (752)	41,970 (710)	41,910 (547)	46.1 (0.70)	45.5 (0.69)	43.6 (0.82)	46.4 (0.77)	46.1 (0.60)
20 or more	7,740 (275)	19,960 (485)	12,380 (519)	10,110 (418)	10,160 (367)	9.7 (0.34)	23.8 (0.57)	13.8 (0.58)	11.2 (0.46)	11.2 (0.40)
School locale										
City	— (†)	20,100 (328)	23,440 (274)	24,770 (190)	25,360 (091)	27.4 (0.34)	24.0 (0.40)	26.1 (0.28)	27.4 (0.17)	27.9 (0.10)
Suburban	— (†)	30,640 (440)	24,520 (356)	29,120 (180)	29,640 (123)	25.9 (0.45)	36.6 (0.53)	27.3 (0.36)	32.2 (0.17)	32.6 (0.12)
Town	— (†)	10,860 (228)	12,330 (341)	12,360 (372)	12,060 (101)	22.0 (0.43)	13.0 (0.26)	13.7 (0.40)	13.7 (0.41)	13.3 (0.10)
Rural	— (†)	22,200 (404)	29,520 (430)	24,170 (399)	23,800 (145)	24.7 (0.43)	26.5 (0.44)	32.9 (0.43)	26.7 (0.43)	26.2 (0.13)

See notes at end of table.

Table 212.08. Number and percentage distribution of principals in public and private elementary and secondary schools, by selected characteristics: Selected years, 1993–94 through 2017–18—Continued

[Standard errors appear in parentheses]

Selected characteristic	Number of principals					Percentage distribution of principals				
	1993–94	1999–2000	2011–12	2015–16	2017–18	1993–94	1999–2000	2011–12	2015–16	2017–18
1	2	3	4	5	6	7	8	9	10	11
Private schools										
Total	25,020 (198)	26,230 (259)	25,730 (605)	—	26,260 (149)	100.0 (†)	100.0 (†)	100.0 (†)	—	100.0 (†)
Sex										
Male	11,610 (301)	11,900 (308)	11,490 (501)	—	11,030 (327)	46.4 (1.10)	45.4 (1.06)	44.6 (1.48)	—	42.0 (1.23)
Female	13,410 (283)	14,330 (307)	14,240 (462)	—	15,230 (335)	53.6 (1.10)	54.6 (1.06)	55.4 (1.48)	—	58.0 (1.23)
Race/ethnicity										
White[1]	23,130 (270)	23,320 (309)	22,470 (628)	—	22,620 (232)	92.5 (0.70)	88.9 (0.76)	87.3 (1.08)	—	86.2 (0.81)
Black[1]	1,060 (124)	1,570 (164)	1,750 (193)	—	1,410 (168)	4.2 (0.50)	6.0 (0.62)	6.8 (0.75)	—	5.4 (0.64)
Hispanic[1]	520 (91)	830 (135)	860 (141)	—	1,260 (118)	2.1 (0.37)	3.2 (0.52)	3.3 (0.56)	—	4.8 (0.45)
Asian[1,2]	‡ (†)	350 (64)	‡ (†)	—	510 (87)	0.7 (0.17)	1.3 (0.25)	1.8 (0.38)	—	1.9 (0.33)
Pacific Islander[1]	—	—	‡ (†)	—	‡ (†)	—	—	‡ (†)	—	0.3! (0.12)
American Indian/Alaska Native[1]	‡ (†)	‡ (†)	‡ (†)	—	‡ (†)	0.5 (0.15)	0.6 (0.15)	‡ (†)	—	0.3! (0.12)
Two or more races[1]	—	—	90! (45)	—	‡ (†)	—	—	0.4! (0.17)	—	1.2 (0.27)
Age										
Under 40	4,790 (302)	3,750 (223)	4,360 (392)	—	4,470 (298)	19.2 (1.21)	14.3 (0.80)	16.9 (1.44)	—	17.0 (1.14)
40 to 44	4,400 (217)	3,450 (212)	3,130 (300)	—	3,130 (217)	17.6 (0.83)	13.2 (0.83)	12.2 (1.05)	—	11.9 (0.83)
45 to 49	5,140 (216)	5,210 (261)	2,630 (281)	—	3,610 (240)	20.6 (0.87)	19.9 (0.96)	10.2 (1.00)	—	13.8 (0.91)
50 to 54	4,120 (228)	5,840 (291)	3,480 (247)	—	3,610 (237)	16.5 (0.90)	22.3 (1.11)	13.5 (0.93)	—	13.7 (0.89)
55 or over	6,550 (244)	7,980 (276)	12,120 (424)	—	11,430 (372)	26.2 (0.95)	30.4 (1.01)	47.1 (1.66)	—	43.5 (1.38)
School level										
Elementary	13,350[4] (244)	15,810 (245)	14,510 (505)	—	14,380 (223)	59.5 (0.74)	60.3 (0.85)	56.4 (0.90)	—	54.8 (0.80)
Secondary	2,300[4] (115)	2,630 (133)	2,660 (138)	—	3,900 (209)	10.3 (0.52)	10.0 (0.51)	10.3 (0.57)	—	14.9 (0.78)
Combined	6,770[4] (174)	7,800 (265)	8,570 (210)	—	7,980 (209)	30.2 (0.77)	29.7 (0.89)	33.3 (0.71)	—	30.4 (0.78)
Highest degree earned										
Bachelor's or less	8,590 (337)	8,050 (334)	7,990 (570)	—	8,080 (397)	34.3 (1.23)	30.7 (1.16)	31.0 (1.73)	—	30.8 (1.52)
Master's	12,900 (292)	13,370 (288)	12,800 (363)	—	13,280 (399)	51.6 (1.28)	51.0 (1.09)	49.7 (1.49)	—	50.6 (1.47)
Education specialist[3]	2,050 (103)	2,600 (159)	2,610 (200)	—	2,830 (172)	8.2 (0.41)	9.9 (0.60)	10.1 (0.80)	—	10.8 (0.66)
Doctor's or first professional	1,480 (138)	2,220 (167)	2,340 (224)	—	2,060 (179)	5.9 (0.54)	8.5 (0.64)	9.1 (0.87)	—	7.9 (0.68)
Number of years as a principal										
3 or fewer	8,270 (341)	7,540 (327)	7,100 (516)	—	9,380 (422)	33.1 (1.32)	28.7 (1.19)	27.6 (1.74)	—	35.7 (1.63)
4 to 9	7,080 (269)	6,990 (320)	6,750 (415)	—	6,430 (318)	28.3 (1.03)	26.6 (1.16)	26.2 (1.45)	—	24.5 (1.17)
10 to 19	6,950 (310)	7,340 (250)	6,910 (350)	—	6,360 (285)	27.8 (1.23)	28.0 (0.93)	26.8 (1.33)	—	24.2 (1.08)
20 or more	2,710 (189)	4,360 (230)	4,970 (318)	—	4,100 (257)	10.8 (0.77)	16.6 (0.90)	19.3 (1.27)	—	15.6 (0.97)
Years of full- and part-time teaching experience prior to becoming a principal										
3 or fewer	6,290 (335)	3,610 (241)	6,820 (473)	—	5,150 (296)	25.2 (1.27)	13.8 (0.87)	26.5 (1.48)	—	19.6 (1.14)
4 to 9	6,940 (268)	5,560 (244)	6,810 (363)	—	5,220 (255)	27.8 (1.05)	21.2 (0.88)	26.5 (1.36)	—	19.9 (0.97)
10 to 19	9,240 (251)	9,070 (260)	7,790 (403)	—	9,220 (321)	36.9 (1.03)	34.6 (1.04)	30.3 (1.50)	—	35.1 (1.19)
20 or more	2,540 (136)	7,990 (265)	4,310 (249)	—	6,680 (292)	10.1 (0.54)	30.4 (0.98)	16.7 (0.99)	—	25.4 (1.08)
School locale										
City	—	11,250 (226)	8,590 (267)	—	8,870 (107)	—	42.9 (0.78)	33.4 (1.28)	—	33.8 (0.33)
Suburban	—	9,190 (229)	8,110 (298)	—	9,030 (84)	—	35.0 (0.80)	31.5 (1.27)	—	34.4 (0.28)
Town	—	3,250 (190)	2,630 (323)	—	2,440 (60)	—	12.4 (0.73)	10.2 (1.16)	—	9.3 (0.22)
Rural	—	2,540 (211)	6,390 (510)	—	5,890 (93)	—	9.7 (0.78)	24.8 (1.57)	—	22.5 (0.34)

—Not available.
†Not applicable.
#Rounds to zero.
!Interpret data with caution. The coefficient of variation (CV) for this estimate is between 30 and 50 percent.
‡Reporting standards not met. Either there are too few cases for a reliable estimate or the coefficient of variation (CV) is 50 percent or greater.
[1]Data for 1993–94 and 1999–2000 are only roughly comparable to data for later years, because the new category of Two or more races was introduced in 2003–04.
[2]Includes Pacific Islander for 1993–94 and 1999–2000.
[3]Education specialist degrees or certificates are generally awarded for 1 year's work beyond the master's level. Includes certificate of advanced graduate studies.
[4]Excludes data for 4,930 public and 2,690 private school principals whose school level could not be determined.

NOTE: Data are based on a head count of full-time and part-time principals rather than on the number of full-time-equivalent principals reported in other tables. Detail may not sum to totals because of rounding and cell suppression. Some data have been revised from previously published figures. Race categories exclude persons of Hispanic ethnicity.

SOURCE: U.S. Department of Education, National Center for Education Statistics, Schools and Staffing Survey (SASS), "Public School Principal Data File" and "Private School Principal Data File," 1993–94, 1999–2000, and 2011–12; SASS, "Charter School Principal Data File," 1999–2000; National Teacher and Principal Survey (NTPS), "Public School Principal Data File," 2015–16 and 2017–18; and NTPS, "Private School Principal Data File," 2017–18. (This table was prepared November 2019.)

Table 213.10. Staff employed in public elementary and secondary school systems, by type of assignment: Selected years, 1949–50 through fall 2017

[In full-time equivalents]

School year	Total	School district administrative staff			Instructional staff						Support staff[1]
		Total	Officials and administrators	Instruction coordinators	Total	Principals and assistant principals	Teachers	Instructional aides	Librarians	Guidance counselors	
1	2	3	4	5	6	7	8	9	10	11	12
					Number						
1949–50[2]	1,300,031	33,642	23,868	9,774	956,808	43,137	913,671	(3)	(3)	(3)	309,582
1959–60[2]	2,089,283	42,423	28,648	13,775	1,448,931	63,554	1,353,372	(3)	17,363	14,643	597,929
1969–70[2]	3,360,763	65,282	33,745	31,537	2,255,707	90,593	2,016,244	57,418	42,689	48,763	1,039,774
Fall 1980[2]	4,168,286	78,784	58,230	20,554	2,729,023	107,061	2,184,216	325,755	48,018	63,973	1,360,479
Fall 1990	4,494,076	75,868	—	—	3,051,404	127,417	2,398,169	395,959	49,909	79,950	1,366,804
Fall 2000	5,709,753	97,270	57,837	39,433	3,876,628	141,792	2,941,461	641,392	54,246	97,737	1,735,855
Fall 2002	5,954,661	110,777	62,781	47,996	4,016,963	164,171	3,034,123	663,552	54,205	100,912	1,826,921
Fall 2003	5,953,667	107,483	63,418	44,065	4,052,739	165,233	3,048,652	685,118	54,349	99,387	1,793,445
Fall 2004	6,058,174	111,832	64,101	47,731	4,120,063	165,657	3,090,925	707,514	54,145	101,822	1,826,279
Fall 2005	6,130,686	121,164	62,464	58,700	4,151,236	156,454	3,143,003	693,792	54,057	103,930	1,858,286
Fall 2006	6,153,735	118,707	53,722	64,985	4,186,968	153,673	3,166,391	709,715	54,444	102,745	1,848,060
Fall 2007	6,232,911	130,044	59,361	70,683	4,235,238	157,539	3,199,995	717,806	54,386	105,512	1,867,629
Fall 2008	6,326,702	135,706	62,153	73,553	4,277,674	159,897	3,222,154	734,010	53,805	107,808	1,913,322
Fall 2009	6,351,157	138,471	63,969	74,502	4,279,488	168,450	3,209,672	741,337	52,545	107,484	1,933,198
Fall 2010	6,195,207	133,833	64,597	69,236	4,151,225	165,047	3,099,095	731,705	50,300	105,079	1,910,150
Fall 2011	6,138,890	130,595	62,884	67,711	4,133,767	166,416	3,103,263	710,335	48,402	105,351	1,874,528
Fall 2012	6,181,238	136,387	65,420	70,967	4,158,000	169,240	3,109,101	729,756	46,685	103,218	1,886,851
Fall 2013	6,187,901	139,667	66,732	72,935	4,167,118	168,101	3,113,764	738,226	45,106	101,920	1,881,116
Fall 2014	6,258,543	148,229	68,962	79,267	4,205,088	174,664	3,132,351	749,143	44,624	104,306	1,905,226
Fall 2015	6,373,406	155,273	67,778	87,495	4,249,784	182,006	3,151,497	764,537	43,368	108,376	1,968,350
Fall 2016	6,484,723	160,540	70,357	90,183	4,294,185	183,671	3,169,499	786,773	42,964	111,278	2,029,998
Fall 2017	6,544,767	170,158	74,411	95,746	4,340,264	189,155	3,169,750	824,051	42,605	114,703	2,034,346
					Percentage distribution						
1949–50[2]	100.0	2.6	1.8	0.8	73.6	3.3	70.3	(3)	(3)	(3)	23.8
1959–60[2]	100.0	2.0	1.4	0.7	69.4	3.0	64.8	(3)	0.8	0.7	28.6
1969–70[2]	100.0	1.9	1.0	0.9	67.1	2.7	60.0	1.7	1.3	1.5	30.9
Fall 1980[2]	100.0	1.9	1.4	0.5	65.5	2.6	52.4	7.8	1.2	1.5	32.6
Fall 1990	100.0	1.7	—	—	67.9	2.8	53.4	8.8	1.1	1.8	30.4
Fall 2000	100.0	1.7	1.0	0.7	67.9	2.5	51.5	11.2	1.0	1.7	30.4
Fall 2002	100.0	1.9	1.1	0.8	67.5	2.8	51.0	11.1	0.9	1.7	30.7
Fall 2003	100.0	1.8	1.1	0.7	68.1	2.8	51.2	11.5	0.9	1.7	30.1
Fall 2004	100.0	1.8	1.1	0.8	68.0	2.7	51.0	11.7	0.9	1.7	30.1
Fall 2005	100.0	2.0	1.0	1.0	67.7	2.6	51.3	11.3	0.9	1.7	30.3
Fall 2006	100.0	1.9	0.9	1.1	68.0	2.5	51.5	11.5	0.9	1.7	30.0
Fall 2007	100.0	2.1	1.0	1.1	67.9	2.5	51.3	11.5	0.9	1.7	30.0
Fall 2008	100.0	2.1	1.0	1.2	67.6	2.5	50.9	11.6	0.9	1.7	30.2
Fall 2009	100.0	2.2	1.0	1.2	67.4	2.7	50.5	11.7	0.8	1.7	30.4
Fall 2010	100.0	2.2	1.0	1.1	67.0	2.7	50.0	11.8	0.8	1.7	30.8
Fall 2011	100.0	2.1	1.0	1.1	67.3	2.7	50.6	11.6	0.8	1.7	30.5
Fall 2012	100.0	2.2	1.1	1.1	67.3	2.7	50.3	11.8	0.8	1.7	30.5
Fall 2013	100.0	2.3	1.1	1.2	67.3	2.7	50.3	11.9	0.7	1.6	30.4
Fall 2014	100.0	2.4	1.1	1.3	67.2	2.8	50.0	12.0	0.7	1.7	30.4
Fall 2015	100.0	2.4	1.1	1.4	66.7	2.9	49.4	12.0	0.7	1.7	30.9
Fall 2016	100.0	2.5	1.1	1.4	66.2	2.8	48.9	12.1	0.7	1.7	31.3
Fall 2017	100.0	2.6	1.1	1.5	66.3	2.9	48.4	12.6	0.7	1.8	31.1
					Pupils per staff member						
1949–50[2]	19.3	746.4	1,052.1	2,569.2	26.2	582.1	27.5	(3)	(3)	(3)	81.1
1959–60[2]	16.8	829.3	1,228.1	2,554.1	24.3	553.6	26.0	(3)	2,026.3	2,402.7	58.8
1969–70[2]	13.6	697.7	1,349.8	1,444.3	20.2	502.8	22.6	793.3	1,067.0	934.1	43.8
Fall 1980[2]	9.8	518.9	702.0	1,988.8	15.0	381.8	18.7	125.5	851.3	639.0	30.0
Fall 1990	9.2	543.3	—	—	13.5	323.5	17.2	104.1	825.8	515.5	30.2
Fall 2000	8.3	485.3	816.1	1,197.1	12.2	332.9	16.0	73.6	870.2	483.0	27.2
Fall 2002	8.1	435.0	767.5	1,003.9	12.0	293.5	15.9	72.6	888.9	477.5	26.4
Fall 2003	8.2	451.6	765.4	1,101.6	12.0	293.8	15.9	70.8	893.1	488.4	27.1
Fall 2004	8.1	436.3	761.2	1,022.3	11.8	294.6	15.8	69.0	901.2	479.2	26.7
Fall 2005	8.0	405.3	786.3	836.7	11.8	313.9	15.6	70.8	908.5	472.6	26.4
Fall 2006	8.0	415.4	918.0	758.9	11.8	320.9	15.6	69.5	905.8	480.0	26.7
Fall 2007	7.9	379.0	830.4	697.3	11.6	312.9	15.4	68.7	906.3	467.2	26.4
Fall 2008	7.8	363.0	792.6	669.8	11.5	308.1	15.3	67.1	915.6	457.0	25.7
Fall 2009	7.8	356.5	771.6	662.5	11.5	293.0	15.4	66.6	939.4	459.2	25.5
Fall 2010	8.0	369.7	766.0	714.7	11.9	299.8	16.0	67.6	983.8	470.9	25.9
Fall 2011	8.1	379.2	787.5	731.4	12.0	297.6	16.0	69.7	1,023.1	470.1	26.4
Fall 2012	8.1	364.9	760.8	701.3	12.0	294.1	16.0	68.2	1,066.1	482.2	26.4
Fall 2013	8.1	358.3	749.9	686.2	12.0	297.7	16.1	67.8	1,109.5	491.0	26.6
Fall 2014	8.0	339.4	729.6	634.7	12.0	288.1	16.1	67.2	1,127.5	482.4	26.4
Fall 2015	7.9	324.8	744.2	576.5	11.9	277.1	16.0	66.0	1,163.0	465.4	25.6
Fall 2016	7.8	315.3	719.4	561.2	11.8	275.6	16.0	64.3	1,178.1	454.9	24.9
Fall 2017	7.7	297.9	681.2	529.4	11.7	268.0	16.0	61.5	1,189.7	441.9	24.9

—Not available.
[1]Includes school district administrative support staff, school and library support staff, student support staff, and other support services staff.
[2]Because of classification revisions, categories other than teachers, principals, librarians, and guidance counselors are only roughly comparable to figures for years after 1980.
[3]Data included in column 8.

NOTE: Data for 1949–50 through 1969–70 are cumulative for the entire school year, rather than counts as of the fall of the year. Detail may not sum to totals because of rounding.
SOURCE: U.S. Department of Education, National Center for Education Statistics, *Statistics of State School Systems*, various years; *Statistics of Public Elementary and Secondary Schools*, various years; and Common Core of Data (CCD), "State Nonfiscal Survey of Public Elementary/Secondary Education," 1986–87 through 2017–18. (This table was prepared August 2019.)

Table 213.20. Staff employed in public elementary and secondary school systems, by type of assignment and state or jurisdiction: Fall 2017

[In full-time equivalents]

| State or jurisdiction | Total | School district staff | | | School staff | | | | | | | Student support staff | Other support services staff |
		Officials and administrators	Administrative support staff	Instruction coordinators	Principals and assistant principals	School and library support staff	Teachers	Instructional aides	Guidance counselors	Librarians		
1	2	3	4	5	6	7	8	9	10	11	12	13
United States[1]	6,544,767	74,411	194,312	95,746	189,155	284,192	3,169,750	824,051	114,703	42,605	356,959	1,198,883
Alabama	91,778	1,789	1,895	122	3,930	3,289	41,802	7,028	1,796	1,323	8,004	20,801
Alaska	17,154	707	813	0	646	1,165	7,743	2,608	312	136	688	2,337
Arizona	103,508	1,409	4,093	629	2,452	3,851	47,868	15,694	1,201	419	11,812	14,080
Arkansas	73,587	643	2,587	986	1,880	3,088	35,800	9,128	1,288	954	7,461	9,772
California[2]	604,248	3,821	21,873	25,495	17,719	35,181	271,523	81,898	9,794	93	20,544	116,308
Colorado	113,320	1,400	4,707	3,325	3,629	6,078	52,373	17,199	2,598	551	7,429	14,031
Connecticut	97,989	2,052	1,572	5,119	2,311	3,451	45,081	16,039	1,204	768	2,931	17,460
Delaware	18,398	469	340	336	505	402	9,399	2,572	344	114	841	3,076
District of Columbia	14,171	663	930	85	561	739	6,659	1,983	156	118	1,465	811
Florida	352,746	2,318	15,597	759	8,826	16,780	186,128	33,375	5,931	1,972	12,049	69,012
Georgia	231,644	2,711	2,683	3,882	6,590	10,325	116,022	25,882	3,854	2,075	8,841	48,780
Hawaii	23,141	324	735	613	712	1,020	12,033	2,626	653	143	1,748	2,534
Idaho	28,860	143	713	238	728	1,245	16,592	3,164	572	47	550	4,868
Illinois	248,682	3,475	6,379	1,513	6,818	10,130	128,204	28,848	2,963	1,475	31,020	27,856
Indiana	142,014	604	749	4,832	3,504	7,489	61,018	16,541	2,140	643	8,680	35,815
Iowa	75,694	1,898	1,931	2,527	1,744	2,685	35,553	12,868	1,296	407	4,595	10,191
Kansas	69,442	450	1,392	1,056	1,899	2,657	36,387	8,969	1,068	567	4,566	10,432
Kentucky	98,363	961	2,314	1,661	3,522	5,610	42,064	13,134	1,592	1,053	3,255	23,197
Louisiana	81,650	95	427	1,376	3,282	3,589	40,281	11,617	1,567	984	3,887	14,547
Maine	35,983	639	714	515	956	1,737	14,760	6,171	566	195	4,249	5,482
Maryland	118,384	3,740	1,969	1,998	3,612	5,997	60,175	11,434	2,415	1,162	6,550	19,333
Massachusetts	132,727	2,640	2,880	469	5,051	6,761	73,381	26,065	2,377	644	10,648	1,809
Michigan	184,986	4,232	1,149	1,289	6,741	11,786	84,473	20,410	2,092	437	14,653	37,725
Minnesota	121,035	2,451	2,084	2,934	2,572	4,576	57,260	19,975	1,323	537	14,402	12,920
Mississippi	67,521	1,012	2,077	670	2,044	2,568	31,625	8,265	1,072	766	3,225	14,198
Missouri	125,779	898	6,200	1,449	3,379	329	68,496	14,305	2,706	1,383	5,725	20,909
Montana	21,223	483	687	208	527	734	10,515	2,717	478	375	749	3,749
Nebraska	48,012	673	1,302	767	1,094	1,910	23,771	6,544	842	540	1,633	8,936
Nevada[3]	35,848	38	79	36	1,194	1,822	23,709	6,196	1,016	298	369	1,092
New Hampshire[4]	31,618	758	763	271	527	777	14,589	7,143	825	323	687	4,957
New Jersey	238,785	1,455	5,503	3,836	5,215	9,587	115,496	39,356	3,810	1,333	13,452	39,742
New Mexico	36,473	206	32	360	1,125	2,052	21,092	5,818	690	217	1,345	3,536
New York	425,292	4,384	21,058	2,671	13,075	11,450	213,159	67,567	9,347	2,593	15,116	64,872
North Carolina	193,798	1,711	5,688	1,209	5,933	7,252	100,401	22,366	4,300	2,127	11,420	31,390
North Dakota	18,599	516	287	202	498	770	9,284	2,849	369	190	942	2,691
Ohio	323,566	2,610	14,785	2,374	5,458	13,965	98,912	23,002	3,844	803	27,170	130,643
Oklahoma	85,021	833	3,088	334	2,273	4,455	41,597	10,232	1,604	900	4,771	14,933
Oregon	68,520	481	2,575	553	1,741	4,838	29,909	11,516	1,255	159	3,063	12,431
Pennsylvania	244,015	2,447	7,256	1,738	5,319	10,645	121,918	31,419	4,550	1,633	9,633	47,456
Rhode Island	20,376	297	540	212	549	747	10,687	2,662	340	202	2,130	2,011
South Carolina	88,410	864	2,585	1,533	3,336	3,000	52,467	11,835	2,205	1,113	2,926	6,547
South Dakota	19,787	710	353	141	459	611	9,833	2,877	354	96	1,010	3,343
Tennessee	131,312	401	1,494	974	3,860	5,385	64,019	17,396	3,045	1,536	4,152	29,051
Texas	713,764	7,232	22,770	4,245	27,347	28,622	356,877	72,123	12,546	4,626	25,990	151,385
Utah[5]	60,086	925	1,671	2,199	1,545	2,709	29,212	10,061	1,032	229	2,086	8,417
Vermont	18,268	132	488	281	497	860	8,313	4,043	449	204	1,030	1,971
Virginia	183,485	1,876	4,411	2,082	4,333	8,640	85,936	19,676	3,576	1,782	12,436	38,736
Washington	99,520	1,456	3,368	3,734	3,499	4,956	60,183	12,883	2,285	1,067	3,648	2,441
West Virginia	37,603	872	1,355	373	1,119	465	19,239	3,612	726	243	1,154	8,445
Wisconsin	112,001	1,132	2,907	1,289	2,640	4,458	58,598	9,938	2,050	960	9,332	18,697
Wyoming	16,580	376	466	247	381	952	7,335	2,424	282	88	896	3,133
Bureau of Indian Education	—	—	—	—	—	—	—	—	—	—	—	—
DoDEA[6]	—	—	—	—	—	—	—	—	—	—	—	—
Other jurisdictions												
American Samoa	—	—	—	—	—	—	—	—	—	—	—	—
Guam	3,852	44	145	143	87	173	2,202	641	85	38	126	168
Northern Marianas	—	—	—	—	—	—	—	—	—	—	—	—
Puerto Rico	39,301	267	1,111	266	1,153	1,013	28,039	61	607	697	1,607	4,480
U.S. Virgin Islands	2,238	4	51	20	76	197	1,066	271	58	0	63	432

—Not available.
[1]Includes imputations to correct for undercounts in states as designated in footnotes 2 through 5.
[2]Includes imputations for prekindergarten teachers.
[3]Includes imputations for school district administrative support staff, school and library support staff, and instructional aides.
[4]Distributions of school district administrators and instruction coordinators, school support staff, and student support staff were estimated.
[5]Imputed.
[6]DoDEA = Department of Defense Education Activity. Includes both domestic and overseas schools.
SOURCE: U.S. Department of Education, National Center for Education Statistics, Common Core of Data (CCD), "State Nonfiscal Survey of Public Elementary/Secondary Education," 2017–18. (This table was prepared March 2020.)

Table 213.40. Staff, teachers, and teachers as a percentage of staff in public elementary and secondary school systems, by state or jurisdiction: Selected years, fall 2000 through fall 2017

[In full-time equivalents]

State or jurisdiction	Teachers as a percent of staff						Fall 2015			Fall 2016			Fall 2017		
	Fall 2000	Fall 2005	Fall 2010	Fall 2012	Fall 2013	Fall 2014	All staff	Teachers	Teachers as a percent of staff	All staff	Teachers	Teachers as a percent of staff	All staff	Teachers	Teachers as a percent of staff
1	2	3	4	5	6	7	8	9	10	11	12	13	14	15	16
United States[1]	51.5	51.3	50.0	50.3	50.3	50.0	6,373,406	3,151,497	49.4	6,484,723	3,169,499	48.9	6,544,767	3,169,750	48.4
Alabama	53.7[2]	55.7	51.9	53.8[2]	51.4	48.9	71,628[2]	40,766	56.9[2]	87,251[2]	42,533	48.7[2]	91,778	41,802	45.5
Alaska	49.3[2]	44.1[2]	45.1[2]	44.9[2]	46.1[2]	45.4[2]	16,982	7,832	46.1	17,231	7,825	45.4	17,154	7,743	45.1
Arizona	49.3	51.3	51.8	47.3	46.8	47.0	103,175	47,944	46.5	104,170	48,220	46.3	103,508	47,868	46.2
Arkansas	50.6	46.7	47.5	47.9	49.6	47.8	73,658	35,804	48.6	73,599	35,730	48.5	73,587	35,800	48.6
California	54.1[2]	53.4[2]	49.2[2]	48.9[2]	47.9[2]	46.8[2]	577,836	263,475	45.6	599,786	271,287[2]	45.2[2]	604,248	271,523[2]	44.9[2]
Colorado	50.7	49.2	47.9	47.7	48.2	47.3	111,939	51,798	46.3	111,293	52,014	46.7	113,320	52,373	46.2
Connecticut	50.0	46.9	46.1	48.1	46.1	44.7	98,166	43,772	44.6	96,047	42,343	44.1	97,989	45,081	46.0
Delaware	59.2	51.7	54.2	52.7	51.4	52.0	17,097	8,962	52.4	17,142	9,208	53.7	18,398	9,399	51.1
District of Columbia	46.2	44.3[2]	52.1	47.5	52.5	48.2	14,106	6,789	48.1	13,402	6,727	50.2	14,171	6,659	47.0
Florida	47.8	50.6	52.7	52.7	53.1	52.8	345,645	182,586	52.8	351,531	186,339	53.0	352,746	186,128	52.8
Georgia	49.2	49.6	49.5	49.6	50.2	50.2	224,488	113,031	50.4	228,523	114,763	50.2	231,644	116,022	50.1
Hawaii	59.5	53.3	52.5	52.2	52.5	52.0	22,596	11,747	52.0	22,598	11,782[2]	52.1[2]	23,141	12,033	52.0
Idaho	56.2	55.8	56.4	55.3[2]	63.0[2]	56.9	27,186	15,656	57.6	28,079	16,204	57.7	28,860	16,592	57.5
Illinois	51.1[2]	53.2[2]	61.6[2]	51.5[2]	51.1[2]	50.6	260,463	129,948	49.9	259,560	128,893	49.7	248,682	128,204	51.6
Indiana	46.7	45.5	41.9[2]	40.5	41.4	40.5	143,417	57,675	40.2	144,997	60,162	41.5	142,014	61,018	43.0
Iowa	51.1	50.9	49.8	49.3	49.5	49.5	72,887	35,687	49.0	73,495	35,808	48.7	75,694	35,553	47.0
Kansas	50.9	51.3	51.1	56.5	53.0	52.9	73,272	40,035	54.6	68,847	36,193	52.6	69,442	36,387	52.4
Kentucky	44.1	43.3	42.4	43.1	42.8	42.8	97,712	41,902	42.9	97,694	42,029	43.0	98,363	42,064	42.8
Louisiana	49.3	48.2	48.2	48.6	48.5	54.3	107,600	58,469	54.3	97,152	48,408	49.8	81,650	40,281	49.3
Maine	49.7	47.3	47.3	46.3	45.1	46.4	35,241	14,857	42.2	35,607	14,750	41.4	35,983	14,760	41.0
Maryland	54.3	51.0	50.6	51.0	50.9	50.5	115,517	59,414	51.4	117,750	59,703	50.7	118,384	60,175	50.8
Massachusetts	55.1	53.0[2]	56.3	56.4	55.5	55.8	128,291	71,969	56.1	130,732	72,413	55.4	132,727	73,381	55.3
Michigan	46.1	47.9[2]	45.8	46.3	46.6	46.3	181,468	84,181	46.4	181,556	83,597	46.0	184,986	84,473	45.7
Minnesota	51.6[2]	48.9	48.3	48.2	48.3	48.0	117,236	55,985	47.8	118,632	56,715	47.8	121,035	57,260	47.3
Mississippi	47.9	46.5	47.5	47.8	47.3	47.5	67,757	32,175	47.5	67,583	31,924	47.2	67,521	31,625	46.8
Missouri	53.2	52.1	52.0	52.2	54.0	53.0	128,938	67,635	52.5	124,666	67,926	54.5	125,779	68,496	54.5
Montana	53.5[2]	52.9[2]	53.8[2]	54.0[2]	49.4[2]	50.0[2]	21,330	10,412	48.8	21,233	10,555[2]	49.7[2]	21,223	10,515	49.5
Nebraska	52.6	51.9	49.1	48.7	48.8	49.0	47,292	23,308	49.3	47,979	23,611[2]	49.2[2]	48,012	23,771	49.5
Nevada	58.6	67.2[2]	65.4[2]	63.3[2]	64.5[2]	64.2[2]	26,430	22,702	85.9	35,878[2]	23,705	66.1[2]	35,848[2]	23,709	66.1[2]
New Hampshire	51.1	48.5	46.6	47.0	46.6	46.4	31,980	14,770	46.2	31,622[2]	14,760	46.7[2]	31,618	14,589	46.1
New Jersey	53.4	53.2[2]	54.4[2]	49.7[2]	49.6[2]	48.9[2]	236,558	114,968	48.6	237,561	115,729	48.7	238,785	115,496	48.4
New Mexico	46.8	45.9	48.2	48.0	47.9	47.8	37,573	21,722	57.8	36,506	21,331	58.4	36,473	21,092	57.8
New York	49.7	58.6	51.1	55.9	57.5	57.2	372,692	206,086	55.3	386,801	209,151	54.1	425,292	213,159	50.1
North Carolina	51.5	52.5	51.0	51.4	51.6	51.9	190,855	99,355	52.1	193,031	100,220	51.9	193,798	100,401	51.8
North Dakota	53.9	52.9	51.8	51.9	51.7	51.4	17,983	9,195	51.1	18,412	9,265	50.3	18,599	9,284	49.9
Ohio	53.1	49.4	45.3	43.7	42.7	42.6[2]	322,611	101,742	31.5	325,387	102,600	31.5	323,566	98,912	30.6
Oklahoma	55.0	51.1	50.2	49.5	49.3	49.0	85,915	42,452	49.4	84,115	41,090	48.8	85,021	41,597	48.9
Oregon	50.0	47.0	44.2	44.2	44.7	44.2	65,928	29,086	44.1	68,089	29,756	43.7	68,520	29,909	43.7
Pennsylvania	52.2	50.9	48.7	48.8	49.9[2]	50.2	241,548	120,893	50.0	247,299	122,552	49.6	244,015	121,918	50.0
Rhode Island	60.0	58.4[2]	60.2	58.3	56.7	60.3	19,483	10,631	54.6	20,233	10,689	52.8	20,376	10,687	52.4
South Carolina	65.7[2]	70.9[2]	69.0	66.3	66.5	65.3	78,108	50,237	64.3	87,314	50,789	58.2	88,410	52,467	59.3
South Dakota	52.0	48.0	48.7	48.8	49.5	49.8	19,543	9,638	49.3	19,732	9,777	49.5	19,787	9,833	49.7
Tennessee	52.1	52.2	51.9	52.0	52.5	51.4	128,469	66,488	51.8	128,323	64,270	50.1	131,312	64,019	48.8
Texas	50.6	50.5	50.3	50.8	50.8	50.7	690,077	347,329	50.3	707,173	352,809	49.9	713,764	356,877	50.0
Utah	54.1	50.2	49.1	49.5	49.6	49.5[2]	56,146[3]	28,348[3]	50.5[3]	59,325	28,841	48.6	60,086[3]	29,212[3]	48.6[3]
Vermont	47.3	46.5	45.3	45.6	45.8	45.6	18,183	8,338	45.9	18,048	8,187	45.4	18,268	8,313	45.5
Virginia	54.1[2]	44.4	35.3	50.4	50.6	50.6	178,551	90,255	50.5	180,091	91,628	50.9	183,485	85,936	46.8
Washington	52.3	47.0	52.0	52.4	52.1	53.3	94,883[2]	57,942	61.1[2]	94,685	58,815	62.1	99,520	60,183	60.5
West Virginia	54.3	52.3	51.8[2]	51.2[2]	51.1[2]	51.0[2]	38,452	19,664	51.1	36,885	19,356	52.5	37,603	19,239	51.2
Wisconsin	56.3	57.0	55.5	56.6	56.6	56.6[2]	101,250	58,185	57.5	113,145	59,011	52.2	112,001	58,598	52.3
Wyoming	48.6	46.2	43.4	44.3	44.6	44.9	17,269	7,653	44.3	16,933	7,506	44.3	16,580	7,335	44.2
Bureau of Indian Education	—	—	—	42.9[4]	—	—	—	—	—	—	—	—	—	—	—
DoDEA,[5] overseas	66.0	62.9	—	—	—	—	—	—	—	—	—	—	—	—	—
DoDEA,[5] domestic	59.2	55.4	—	—	—	—	—	—	—	—	—	—	—	—	—
Other jurisdictions															
American Samoa	50.0	68.4	—	—	—	—	—	—	—	—	—	—	—	—	—
Guam	51.5	52.2	54.5	58.4	58.4	58.0	4,019	2,336	58.1	3,954	2,289	57.9	3,852	2,202	57.2
Northern Marianas	50.2	49.8	50.0	45.9	47.6	—	—	—	—	—	—	—	—	—	—
Puerto Rico	54.4	56.0	61.6	57.0	61.4	62.2	48,820	30,438	62.3	41,012	28,899[2]	70.5[2]	39,301	28,039	71.3
U.S. Virgin Islands	52.1	53.8	49.9	51.1	49.9	51.1	2,284	1,106	48.4	2,377	1,154	48.5	2,238	1,066	47.6

—Not available.
[1]U.S. totals include imputations for underreporting and nonreporting states.
[2]Includes imputations to correct for underreporting.
[3]Imputed. State did not report staff data.
[4]Total staff count excludes officials and administrators and administrative support staff, so computed percentage of teachers may be overstated.

[5]DoDEA = Department of Defense Education Activity.
SOURCE: U.S. Department of Education, National Center for Education Statistics, Common Core of Data (CCD), "State Nonfiscal Survey of Public Elementary/Secondary Education," 2000–01 through 2017–18. (This table was prepared February 2020.)

Table 213.50. Staff, enrollment, and pupil/staff ratios in public elementary and secondary school systems, by state or jurisdiction: Selected years, fall 2000 through fall 2017

State or jurisdiction	Pupil/staff ratio						Fall 2015			Fall 2016			Fall 2017		
	Fall 2000	Fall 2005	Fall 2010	Fall 2012	Fall 2013	Fall 2014	Staff	Enrollment	Pupil/staff ratio	Staff	Enrollment	Pupil/staff ratio	Staff	Enrollment	Pupil/staff ratio
1	2	3	4	5	6	7	8	9	10	11	12	13	14	15	16
United States[1]	8.3	8.0	8.0	8.1	8.1	8.0	6,373,406	50,438,043	7.9	6,484,723	50,615,189	7.8	6,544,767	50,685,567	7.7
Alabama	8.2[2]	7.1	7.9	7.7[2]	8.1	8.5	71,628[2]	743,789	10.4[2]	87,251[2]	744,930	8.5[2]	91,778	742,444	8.1
Alaska	8.3[2]	7.4[2]	7.3[2]	7.7[2]	7.6[2]	7.7[2]	16,982	132,477	7.8	17,231	132,737	7.7	17,154	132,872	7.7
Arizona	9.7	10.9	11.1	10.6	10.7	10.9	103,175	1,109,040	10.7	104,170	1,123,137	10.8	103,508	1,110,851	10.7
Arkansas	7.1	6.7	6.7	6.8	7.0	6.6	73,658	492,132	6.7	73,599	493,447	6.7	73,587	496,085	6.7
California	11.1[2]	11.1[2]	11.9[2]	11.6[2]	11.7[2]	11.0[2]	577,836	6,305,347	10.9	599,786[2]	6,309,138	10.5[2]	604,248[2]	6,304,266	10.4[2]
Colorado	8.7	8.4	8.3	8.4	8.4	8.2	111,939	899,112	8.0	111,293	905,019	8.1	113,320	910,280	8.0
Connecticut	6.8	6.8	6.0	6.0	5.8	5.8	98,166	537,933	5.5	96,047	535,118	5.6	97,989	531,288	5.4
Delaware	9.1	7.8	7.9	7.4	7.2	7.2	17,097	134,847	7.9	17,142	136,264	7.9	18,398	136,293	7.4
District of Columbia	6.4	6.2[3]	6.3	6.1	6.9	5.9	14,106	84,024	6.0	13,402	85,850	6.4	14,171	87,315	6.2
Florida	8.8	8.5	7.9	8.0	8.1	8.1	345,645	2,792,234	8.1	351,531	2,816,791	8.0	352,746	2,832,424	8.0
Georgia	7.8	7.3	7.4	7.7	7.9	7.9	224,488	1,757,237	7.8	228,523	1,764,346	7.7	231,644	1,768,642	7.6
Hawaii	10.0	8.7	8.3	8.3	8.3	8.1	22,596	181,995	8.1	22,598[2]	181,550	8.0[2]	23,141	180,837	7.8
Idaho	10.1	10.1	9.9	10.8[2]	12.5[2]	10.6	27,186	292,277	10.8	28,079	297,200	10.6	28,860	301,186	10.4
Illinois	8.2[2]	8.4[2]	9.7[2]	7.9[2]	7.8[2]	7.8	260,463	2,041,779	7.8	259,560	2,026,718	7.8	248,682	2,005,153	8.1
Indiana	7.8	7.8	7.5[2]	7.0	7.3	7.5	143,417	1,046,757	7.3	144,997	1,049,547	7.2	142,014	1,054,187	7.4
Iowa	7.3	7.0	7.1	7.0	7.0	7.0	72,887	508,014	7.0	73,495	509,831	6.9	75,694	511,850	6.8
Kansas	7.3	7.1	7.1	6.7	6.9	7.0	73,272	495,884	6.8	68,847	494,347	7.2	69,442	497,088	7.2
Kentucky	7.4	6.9	6.8	6.9	6.9	7.1	97,712	686,598	7.0	97,694	684,017	7.0	98,363	680,978	6.9
Louisiana	7.3	7.1	6.9	7.4	7.4	8.4	107,600	718,711	6.7	97,152	716,293	7.4	81,650	715,135	8.8
Maine	6.2	5.5	5.8	5.7	5.4	5.7	35,241	181,613	5.2	35,607	180,512	5.1	35,983	180,473	5.0
Maryland	8.8	7.7	7.4	7.6	7.5	7.5	115,517	879,601	7.6	117,750	886,221	7.5	118,384	893,684	7.5
Massachusetts	8.0	7.0[2]	7.8	7.6	7.5	7.4	128,291	964,026	7.5	130,732	964,514	7.4	132,727	964,791	7.3
Michigan	8.2[2]	8.5[2]	8.2	8.4	8.4	8.4	181,468	1,536,231	8.5	181,556	1,528,666	8.4	184,986	1,516,398	8.2
Minnesota	8.2[2]	8.0	7.7	7.6	7.5	7.4	117,236	864,384	7.4	118,632	875,021	7.4	121,035	884,944	7.3
Mississippi	7.7	7.3	7.2	7.2	7.2	7.2	67,757	487,200	7.2	67,583	483,150	7.1	67,521	478,321	7.1
Missouri	7.5	7.1	7.2	7.2	7.4	7.2	128,938	919,234	7.1	124,666	915,040	7.3	125,779	915,472	7.3
Montana	8.0[2]	7.4[2]	7.4[2]	7.6[2]	6.9[2]	7.1[2]	21,330	145,319	6.8	21,233[2]	146,375	6.9[2]	21,223	149,474	7.0
Nebraska	7.2	7.0	6.6	6.7	6.7	6.7	47,292	316,014	6.7	47,979[2]	319,194	6.7[2]	48,012	323,766	6.7
Nevada	10.9	12.7[2]	13.1[2]	13.6[2]	13.3[2]	13.6[2]	26,430	467,527	17.7	35,878[2]	473,744	13.2[2]	35,848[2]	485,785	13.6[2]
New Hampshire	7.4	6.4	5.9	6.0	5.9	5.8	31,980	182,425	5.7	31,622[2]	180,888	5.7[2]	31,618	179,433	5.7
New Jersey	7.1	6.6[2]	6.9[2]	6.1[2]	5.9[2]	6.0[2]	236,558	1,408,845	6.0	237,561	1,410,421	5.9	238,785	1,408,102	5.9
New Mexico	7.1	6.8	7.3	7.3	7.3	7.3	37,573	335,694	8.9	36,506	336,263	9.2	36,473	334,345	9.2
New York	6.9	7.5	6.6	7.3	7.6	7.7	372,692	2,711,626	7.3	386,801	2,729,776	7.1	425,292	2,724,663	6.4
North Carolina	8.0	7.8	7.7	7.9	8.0	8.1	190,855	1,544,934	8.1	193,031	1,550,062	8.0	193,798	1,553,513	8.0
North Dakota	7.2	6.5	5.9	6.0	6.1	6.1	17,983	108,644	6.0	18,412	109,706	6.0	18,599	111,920	6.0
Ohio	8.2	7.7	7.3	7.1	6.9	6.9[3]	322,611	1,716,585	5.3	325,387	1,710,143	5.3	323,566	1,704,399	5.3
Oklahoma	8.3	7.8	8.0	8.0	8.0	8.0	85,915	692,878	8.1	84,115	693,903	8.2	85,021	695,092	8.2
Oregon	9.7	9.2	9.0	9.8	9.9	9.6	65,928	608,825	9.2	68,089	606,277	8.9	68,520	608,014	8.9
Pennsylvania	8.1	7.6	6.7	7.0	7.2[2]	7.2	241,548	1,717,414	7.1	247,299	1,727,497	7.0	244,015	1,726,809	7.1
Rhode Island	8.9	6.3[2]	7.7	8.4	8.2	9.0	19,483	142,014	7.3	20,233	142,150	7.0	20,376	142,949	7.0
South Carolina	9.8[2]	10.3[2]	11.1	10.2	10.3	10.0	78,108	763,533	9.8	87,314	771,250	8.8	88,410	777,507	8.8
South Dakota	7.1	6.4	6.5	6.8	6.8	6.9	19,543	134,253	6.9	19,732	136,302	6.9	19,787	137,823	7.0
Tennessee	8.3[2]	8.4	7.7	7.8	7.9	7.8	128,469	1,001,235	7.8	128,323	1,001,562	7.8	131,312	1,001,967	7.6
Texas	7.5	7.6	7.4	7.9	7.8	7.8	690,077	5,301,477	7.7	707,173	5,360,849	7.6	713,764	5,401,341	7.6
Utah	11.8	11.1	11.2	11.4	11.4	11.5[3]	56,146[3]	647,870	11.5[3]	59,325	659,801	11.1	60,086[3]	668,274	11.1[3]
Vermont	5.7	5.1	5.2	4.9	4.8	4.8	18,183	87,866	4.8	18,048	88,428	4.9	18,268	88,028	4.8
Virginia	7.1[2]	5.2	6.2	7.1	7.1	7.2	178,551	1,283,590	7.2	180,091	1,287,026	7.1	183,485	1,291,462	7.0
Washington	10.3	9.1	10.1	10.3	10.1	9.6	94,883[2]	1,087,030	11.5[2]	94,685	1,101,711	11.6	99,520	1,110,367	11.2
West Virginia	7.4	7.4	7.2[2]	7.2[2]	7.2[2]	7.1[2]	38,452	277,452	7.2	36,885	273,855	7.4	37,603	272,266	7.2
Wisconsin	8.2	8.3	8.4	8.6	8.5	8.4[3]	101,250	867,800	8.6	113,145	864,432	7.6	112,001	860,753	7.7
Wyoming	6.4	5.8	5.4	5.5	5.5	5.6	17,269	94,717	5.5	16,933	94,170	5.6	16,580	94,258	5.7
Bureau of Indian Education	—	—	—	—	—	—	—	—	—	—	45,399	—	—	46,330	—
DoDEA,[4] overseas	9.5	6.9	—	—	—	—	—	74,970	—	—	—	—	—	—	—
DoDEA,[4] domestic	8.4	7.7	—	—	—	—	—	—	—	—	—	—	—	—	—
Other jurisdictions															
American Samoa	9.6	11.4	—	—	—	—	—	—	—	—	—	—	—	12,620	—
Guam	8.5	9.0	9.3	7.9	8.5	7.9	4,019	30,821	7.7	3,954	30,758	7.8	3,852	30,112	7.8
Northern Marianas	9.6	9.5	9.1	11.9	12.1	—	—	—	—	—	—	—	—	—	—
Puerto Rico	8.9	7.5	8.0	8.0	7.8	8.2	48,820	379,818	7.8	41,012	365,181	8.9	39,301	346,096	8.8
U.S. Virgin Islands	6.7	6.3	5.3	6.9	6.9	6.4	2,284	13,805	6.0	2,377	13,194	5.6	2,238	10,868	4.9

—Not available.
[1]U.S. totals include imputations for underreporting and nonreporting states.
[2]Includes imputations to correct for underreporting.
[3]Staff data imputed.
[4]DoDEA = Department of Defense Education Activity.

NOTE: Staff reported in full-time equivalents.
SOURCE: U.S. Department of Education, National Center for Education Statistics, Common Core of Data (CCD), "State Nonfiscal Survey of Public Elementary/Secondary Education," 2000–01 through 2017–18. (This table was prepared February 2020.)

Table 214.10. Number of public school districts and public and private elementary and secondary schools: Selected years, 1869–70 through 2017–18

School year	Regular public school districts[1]	Total, all public and private schools	Total, all public schools[4]	Total, schools with reported grade spans[5]	Schools with elementary grades — Total	Schools with elementary grades — One-teacher[6]	Schools with secondary grades	Total, all private schools[4]	Schools with elementary grades	Schools with secondary grades
1	2	3	4	5	6	7	8	9	10	11
1869–70	—	—	116,312	—	—	—	—	—	—	—
1879–80	—	—	178,122	—	—	—	—	—	—	—
1889–90	—	—	224,526	—	—	—	—	—	—	—
1899–1900	—	—	248,279	—	—	—	—	—	—	—
1909–10	—	—	265,474	—	—	212,448	—	—	—	—
1919–20	—	—	271,319	—	—	187,948	—	—	—	—
1929–30	—	—	248,117	—	238,306	148,712	23,930	—	9,275[7]	3,258[7]
1939–40	117,108[8]	—	226,762	—	—	113,600	—	—	11,306[7]	3,568[7]
1949–50	83,718[8]	—	—	—	128,225	59,652	24,542	—	10,375[7]	3,331[7]
1959–60	40,520[8]	—	—	—	91,853	20,213	25,784	—	13,574[7]	4,061[7]
1961–62	35,676[8]	125,634	107,260	—	81,910	13,333	25,350	18,374	14,762[7]	4,129[7]
1963–64	31,705[8]	—	104,015	—	77,584	9,895	26,431	—	—	4,451[7]
1965–66	26,983[8]	117,662	99,813	—	73,216	6,491	26,597	17,849[7]	15,340[7]	4,606[7]
1967–68	22,010[8]	—	—	94,197	70,879	4,146	27,011	—	—	—
1970–71	17,995[8]	—	—	89,372	65,800	1,815	25,352	—	14,372[7]	3,770[7]
1973–74	16,730[8]	—	—	88,655	65,070	1,365	25,906	—	—	—
1975–76	16,376[8]	—	88,597	87,034	63,242	1,166	25,330	—	—	—
1976–77	16,271[8]	—	—	86,501	62,644	1,111	25,378	19,910[7]	16,385[7]	5,904[7]
1978–79	16,014[8]	—	—	84,816	61,982	1,056	24,504	19,489[7]	16,097[7]	5,766[7]
1979–80	15,944[8]	—	87,004	—	—	—	—	—	—	—
1980–81	15,912[8]	106,746	85,982	83,688	61,069	921	24,362	20,764[7]	16,792[7]	5,678[7]
1982–83	15,824[8]	—	84,740	82,039	59,656	798	23,988	—	—	—
1983–84	15,747[8]	111,872	84,178	81,418	59,082	838	23,947	27,694	20,872	7,862
1984–85	—	—	84,007	81,147	58,827	825	23,916	—	—	—
1985–86	—	—	—	—	—	—	—	25,616	20,252	7,387
1986–87	15,713	—	83,421	82,316	60,811	763	23,481	—	—	—
1987–88	15,577	110,055	83,248	81,416	59,754	729	23,841	26,807	22,959	8,418
1988–89	15,376	—	83,165	81,579	60,176	583	23,638	—	—	—
1989–90	15,367	110,137	83,425	81,880	60,699	630	23,461	26,712	24,221	10,197
1990–91	15,358	109,228	84,538	82,475	61,340	617	23,460	24,690	22,223	8,989
1991–92	15,173	110,576	84,578	82,506	61,739	569	23,248	25,998	23,523	9,282
1992–93	15,025	—	84,497	82,896	62,225	430	23,220	—	—	—
1993–94	14,881	111,486	85,393	83,431	62,726	442	23,379	26,093	23,543	10,555
1994–95	14,772	—	86,221	84,476	63,572	458	23,668	—	—	—
1995–96	14,766	121,519	87,125	84,958	63,961	474	23,793	34,394	32,401	10,942
1996–97	14,841	—	88,223	86,092	64,785	487	24,287	—	—	—
1997–98	14,805	123,403	89,508	87,541	65,859	476	24,802	33,895	31,408	10,779
1998–99	14,891	—	90,874	89,259	67,183	463	25,797	—	—	—
1999–2000	14,928	125,007	92,012	90,538	68,173	423	26,407	32,995	30,457	10,693
2000–01	14,859	—	93,273	91,691	69,697	411	27,090	—	—	—
2001–02	14,559	130,007	94,112	92,696	70,516	408	27,468	35,895	33,191	11,846
2002–03	14,465	—	95,615	93,869	71,270	366	28,151	—	—	—
2003–04	14,383	130,407	95,726	93,977	71,195	376	28,219	34,681	31,988	11,188
2004–05	14,205	—	96,513	95,001	71,556	338	29,017	—	—	—
2005–06	14,166	132,436	97,382	95,731	71,733	326	29,705	35,054	32,127	12,184
2006–07	13,856	—	98,793	96,362	72,442	313	29,904	—	—	—
2007–08	13,838	132,656	98,916	97,654	73,011	288	30,542	33,740	30,808	11,870
2008–09	13,809	—	98,706	97,119	72,771	237	29,971	—	—	—
2009–10	13,625	132,183	98,817	97,521	72,870	217	30,381	33,366	30,590	11,941
2010–11	13,588	—	98,817	97,767	73,223	224	30,681	—	—	—
2011–12	13,567	129,189	98,328	97,357	73,000	205	30,668	30,861	28,184	11,165
2012–13	13,515	—	98,454	97,331	73,037	196	30,623	—	—	—
2013–14	13,491	131,890	98,271	97,290	73,223	193	30,256	33,619	30,919	11,110
2014–15	13,601	—	98,176	97,601	73,420	165	30,528	—	—	—
2015–16	13,584	132,853	98,277	97,586	73,546	197	30,828	34,576	31,630	12,669
2016–17	13,598	—	98,158	97,434	73,620	203	30,597	—	—	—
2017–18	13,551	130,930	98,469	97,568	73,686	188	30,160	32,461	29,616	12,371

—Not available.

[1]Regular districts exclude regional education service agencies and supervisory union administrative centers, state-operated agencies, federally operated agencies, and other types of local education agencies, such as independent charter schools.

[2]Schools with both elementary and secondary grades are included under elementary schools and also under secondary schools.

[3]Data for most years prior to 1976–77 are partly estimated. Prior to 1995–96, excludes schools with highest grade of kindergarten.

[4]Includes schools not classified by grade span, which are not shown separately.

[5]Includes elementary, secondary, and combined elementary/secondary schools.

[6]Excludes alternative schools, academies, hospitals, virtual schools, prisons, and juvenile detention facilities.

[7]These data cannot be compared directly with the data for years after 1980–81.

[8]Because of expanded survey coverage, data are not directly comparable with data for years after 1983–84.

SOURCE: U.S. Department of Education, National Center for Education Statistics, *Annual Report of the Commissioner of Education*, 1870 through 1910; *Biennial Survey of Education in the United States*, 1919–20 through 1949–50; *Statistics of State School Systems*, 1951–52 through 1967–68; *Statistics of Public Elementary and Secondary School Systems*, 1970–71 through 1980–81; *Statistics of Public and Nonpublic Elementary and Secondary Day Schools*, 1968–69; *Statistics of Nonpublic Elementary and Secondary Schools*, 1970–71; *Private Schools in American Education*; Schools and Staffing Survey (SASS), "Private School Questionnaire," 1987–88 and 1990–91; Private School Universe Survey (PSS), 1989–90 through 2017–18; and Common Core of Data (CCD), "Local Education Agency Universe Survey" and "Public Elementary/Secondary School Universe Survey," 1982–83 through 2017–18. (This table was prepared February 2020.)

Table 214.20. Number and percentage distribution of regular public school districts and students, by enrollment size of district: Selected years, 1979–80 through 2017–18

Year	Total	25,000 or more	10,000 to 24,999	5,000 to 9,999	2,500 to 4,999	1,000 to 2,499	600 to 999	300 to 599	1 to 299	Size not reported
1	2	3	4	5	6	7	8	9	10	11
Number of districts										
1979–80[1]	15,944	181	478	1,106	2,039	3,475	1,841	2,298	4,223	303
1989–90	15,367	179	479	913	1,937	3,547	1,801	2,283	3,910	318
1999–2000	14,928	238	579	1,036	2,068	3,457	1,814	2,081	3,298	357
2005–06	14,166	269	594	1,066	2,015	3,335	1,768	1,895	2,857	367
2006–07	13,856	275	598	1,066	2,006	3,334	1,730	1,898	2,685	264
2007–08	13,838	281	589	1,062	2,006	3,292	1,753	1,890	2,692	273
2008–09	13,809	280	594	1,049	1,995	3,272	1,766	1,886	2,721	246
2009–10	13,625	284	598	1,044	1,985	3,242	1,750	1,891	2,707	124
2010–11	13,588	282	600	1,052	1,975	3,224	1,738	1,887	2,687	143
2011–12	13,567	286	592	1,044	1,952	3,222	1,755	1,911	2,676	129
2012–13	13,515	290	588	1,048	1,924	3,227	1,751	1,908	2,678	101
2013–14	13,491	286	596	1,046	1,920	3,186	1,791	1,894	2,668	104
2014–15	13,601	288	609	1,046	1,898	3,221	1,766	1,880	2,687	206
2015–16	13,584	287	613	1,040	1,888	3,214	1,782	1,909	2,643	208
2016–17	13,598	287	613	1,044	1,908	3,236	1,776	1,926	2,647	161
2017–18	13,551	288	618	1,034	1,918	3,218	1,773	1,936	2,561	205
Percentage distribution of districts										
1979–80[1]	100.0	1.1	3.0	6.9	12.8	21.8	11.5	14.4	26.5	1.9
1989–90	100.0	1.2	3.1	5.9	12.6	23.1	11.7	14.9	25.4	2.1
1999–2000	100.0	1.6	3.9	6.9	13.9	23.2	12.2	13.9	22.1	2.4
2005–06	100.0	1.9	4.2	7.5	14.2	23.5	12.5	13.4	20.2	2.6
2006–07	100.0	2.0	4.3	7.7	14.5	24.1	12.5	13.7	19.4	1.9
2007–08	100.0	2.0	4.3	7.7	14.5	23.8	12.7	13.7	19.5	2.0
2008–09	100.0	2.0	4.3	7.6	14.4	23.7	12.8	13.7	19.7	1.8
2009–10	100.0	2.1	4.4	7.7	14.6	23.8	12.8	13.9	19.9	0.9
2010–11	100.0	2.1	4.4	7.7	14.5	23.7	12.8	13.9	19.8	1.1
2011–12	100.0	2.1	4.4	7.7	14.4	23.7	12.9	14.1	19.7	1.0
2012–13	100.0	2.1	4.4	7.8	14.2	23.9	13.0	14.1	19.8	0.7
2013–14	100.0	2.1	4.4	7.8	14.2	23.6	13.3	14.0	19.8	0.8
2014–15	100.0	2.1	4.5	7.7	14.0	23.7	13.0	13.8	19.8	1.5
2015–16	100.0	2.1	4.5	7.7	13.9	23.7	13.1	14.1	19.5	1.5
2016–17	100.0	2.1	4.5	7.7	14.0	23.8	13.1	14.2	19.5	1.2
2017–18	100.0	2.1	4.6	7.6	14.2	23.7	13.1	14.3	18.9	1.5
Number of students										
1979–80[1]	41,882,000	11,415,000	7,004,000	7,713,000	7,076,000	5,698,000	1,450,000	1,005,000	521,000	†
1989–90	40,069,756	11,209,889	7,107,362	6,347,103	6,731,334	5,763,282	1,402,623	997,434	510,729	†
1999–2000	46,318,635	14,886,636	8,656,672	7,120,704	7,244,407	5,620,962	1,426,280	911,127	451,847	†
2005–06	48,013,931	16,376,213	9,055,547	7,394,010	7,114,942	5,442,588	1,391,314	835,430	403,887	†
2006–07	48,105,666	16,496,573	9,083,944	7,395,889	7,092,532	5,433,770	1,363,287	840,032	399,639	†
2007–08	48,096,140	16,669,611	8,946,432	7,408,553	7,103,274	5,358,492	1,381,342	834,295	394,141	†
2008–09	48,033,126	16,634,807	9,043,665	7,324,565	7,079,061	5,329,406	1,392,110	832,262	397,250	†
2009–10	48,021,335	16,788,789	9,053,144	7,265,111	7,034,640	5,266,945	1,381,415	835,035	396,256	†
2010–11	48,059,830	16,803,247	9,150,912	7,318,413	6,973,720	5,215,389	1,372,759	833,764	391,626	†
2011–12	47,973,834	16,934,369	9,031,528	7,266,770	6,907,658	5,218,533	1,381,289	842,134	391,553	†
2012–13	48,033,002	17,101,040	8,967,874	7,300,285	6,817,724	5,232,487	1,377,490	841,150	394,952	†
2013–14	48,124,386	17,125,416	9,128,194	7,270,070	6,792,172	5,169,748	1,412,987	832,091	393,708	†
2014–15	48,390,432	17,267,232	9,275,438	7,270,961	6,740,298	5,214,007	1,393,249	831,703	397,544	†
2015–16	48,413,211	17,301,641	9,347,240	7,223,779	6,693,454	5,202,470	1,405,851	844,470	394,306	†
2016–17	48,599,865	17,353,942	9,363,219	7,274,211	6,748,580	5,214,673	1,397,636	851,548	396,056	†
2017–18	48,560,014	17,366,407	9,397,505	7,196,218	6,780,881	5,187,521	1,396,908	852,353	382,221	†
Percentage distribution of students										
1979–80[1]	100.0	27.3	16.7	18.4	16.9	13.6	3.5	2.4	1.2	†
1989–90	100.0	28.0	17.7	15.8	16.8	14.4	3.5	2.5	1.3	†
1999–2000	100.0	32.1	18.7	15.4	15.6	12.1	3.1	2.0	1.0	†
2005–06	100.0	34.1	18.9	15.4	14.8	11.3	2.9	1.7	0.8	†
2006–07	100.0	34.3	18.9	15.4	14.7	11.3	2.8	1.7	0.8	†
2007–08	100.0	34.7	18.6	15.4	14.8	11.1	2.9	1.7	0.8	†
2008–09	100.0	34.6	18.8	15.2	14.7	11.1	2.9	1.7	0.8	†
2009–10	100.0	35.0	18.9	15.1	14.6	11.0	2.9	1.7	0.8	†
2010–11	100.0	35.0	19.0	15.2	14.5	10.9	2.9	1.7	0.8	†
2011–12	100.0	35.3	18.8	15.1	14.4	10.9	2.9	1.8	0.8	†
2012–13	100.0	35.6	18.7	15.2	14.2	10.9	2.9	1.8	0.8	†
2013–14	100.0	35.6	19.0	15.1	14.1	10.7	2.9	1.7	0.8	†
2014–15	100.0	35.7	19.2	15.0	13.9	10.8	2.9	1.7	0.8	†
2015–16	100.0	35.7	19.3	14.9	13.8	10.7	2.9	1.7	0.8	†
2016–17	100.0	35.7	19.3	15.0	13.9	10.7	2.9	1.8	0.8	†
2017–18	100.0	35.8	19.4	14.8	14.0	10.7	2.9	1.8	0.8	†

†Not applicable.
[1]Because of expanded survey coverage, data for 1979-89 are not directly comparable with figures for later years.
NOTE: Size not reported (column 11) includes school districts reporting enrollment of zero and school districts whose enrollment counts were suppressed because they failed data quality edits. Regular districts exclude regional education service agencies and supervisory union administrative centers, state-operated agencies, federally operated agencies, and other types of local education agencies, such as independent charter schools. Enrollment totals differ from other tables because this table represents data reported by regular school districts rather than states or schools. Detail may not sum to totals because of rounding. SOURCE: U.S. Department of Education, National Center for Education Statistics, Common Core of Data (CCD), "Local Education Agency Universe Survey," 1979–80 through 2017–18. (This table was prepared March 2020.)

Table 214.30. Number of public elementary and secondary education agencies, by type of agency and state or jurisdiction: 2016–17 and 2017–18

State or jurisdiction	Total agencies		Regular school districts[1]		Regional education service agencies and supervisory union administrative centers		State-operated agencies		Federally operated agencies		Independent charter schools		Other agencies[2]	
	2016–17	2017–18	2016–17	2017–18	2016–17	2017–18	2016–17	2017–18	2016–17	2017–18	2016–17	2017–18	2016–17	2017–18
1	2	3	4	5	6	7	8	9	10	11	12	13	14	15
United States	**18,343**	**18,297**	**13,598**	**13,551**	**1,350**	**1,338**	**254**	**244**	**4**	**4**	**2,998**	**3,021**	**139**	**139**
Alabama	178	176	134	137	0	2	43	34	0	0	1	1	0	2
Alaska	54	54	53	53	0	0	1	1	0	0	0	0	0	0
Arizona	699	700	226	225	16	19	9	9	0	0	434	433	14	14
Arkansas	292	293	234	234	15	15	5	5	0	0	25	26	13	13
California	1,159	1,156	1,057	1,051	73	71	4	4	0	0	25	30	0	0
Colorado	267	270	178	178	83	86	4	4	0	0	2	2	0	0
Connecticut	205	205	169	169	6	6	6	6	0	0	24	24	0	0
Delaware	49	46	19	19	1	1	2	2	0	0	27	24	0	0
District of Columbia	61	63	1	1	0	0	1	1	0	0	59	61	0	0
Florida	76	77	67	67	0	0	2	2	0	0	2	3	5	5
Georgia	226	232	180	180	16	16	7	7	0	0	23	29	0	0
Hawaii	1	1	1	1	0	0	0	0	0	0	0	0	0	0
Idaho	160	162	115	115	2	2	3	3	0	0	40	42	0	0
Illinois	1,057	1,056	854	854	187	186	6	6	0	0	8	8	2	2
Indiana	423	427	294	294	30	29	4	3	0	0	93	99	2	2
Iowa	342	342	333	333	9	9	0	0	0	0	0	0	0	0
Kansas	317	317	307	307	0	0	10	10	0	0	0	0	0	0
Kentucky	186	186	173	173	9	9	3	3	0	0	0	0	1	1
Louisiana	185	201	69	69	0	0	6	7	0	0	105	121	5	4
Maine	268	271	249	252	8	8	2	2	0	0	9	9	0	0
Maryland	25	25	24	24	0	0	1	1	0	0	0	0	0	0
Massachusetts	431	432	326	326	26	25	1	1	0	0	78	80	0	0
Michigan	901	892	540	537	56	56	4	4	0	0	301	295	0	0
Minnesota	567	564	332	331	65	66	4	3	0	0	166	164	0	0
Mississippi	158	157	144	144	0	0	11	10	0	0	3	3	0	0
Missouri	566	566	518	518	0	0	6	6	0	0	38	38	4	4
Montana	487	485	401	399	77	77	4	4	0	0	0	0	5	5
Nebraska	284	279	245	244	34	30	5	5	0	0	0	0	0	0
Nevada	19	21	18	19	0	0	0	0	0	0	1	1	0	1
New Hampshire	301	305	180	180	97	101	0	0	0	0	24	24	0	0
New Jersey	678	681	565	567	20	21	4	4	0	0	88	89	1	0
New Mexico	157	151	89	89	0	0	6	6	0	0	62	56	0	0
New York[3]	999	1,011	689	689	37	37	6	6	0	0	267	279	0	0
North Carolina	306	314	115	117	1	1	4	4	3	3	167	173	16	16
North Dakota	226	225	178	178	45	44	3	3	0	0	0	0	0	0
Ohio	1,088	1,064	620	619	102	101	4	4	0	0	362	340	0	0
Oklahoma	600	595	513	512	0	0	3	3	0	0	31	28	53	52
Oregon	221	222	179	178	19	19	5	6	0	0	18	19	0	0
Pennsylvania	789	788	500	500	102	102	7	6	0	0	179	179	1	1
Rhode Island	63	63	32	32	4	4	8	8	0	0	19	19	0	0
South Carolina	101	101	84	84	11	11	3	3	0	0	1	1	2	2
South Dakota	167	166	150	149	14	14	3	3	0	0	0	0	0	0
Tennessee	146	147	146	147	0	0	0	0	0	0	0	0	0	0
Texas	1,228	1,225	1,025	1,025	20	20	3	3	0	0	180	177	0	0
Utah	156	160	41	41	4	4	3	2	0	0	108	113	0	0
Vermont	342	298	278	235	63	62	1	1	0	0	0	0	0	0
Virginia	222	210	130	132	71	57	20	20	1	1	0	0	0	0
Washington	332	334	299	299	10	10	0	0	0	0	8	10	15	15
West Virginia	57	57	55	55	0	0	2	2	0	0	0	0	0	0
Wisconsin	461	462	421	421	17	17	3	3	0	0	20	21	0	0
Wyoming	60	62	48	48	0	0	12	14	0	0	0	0	0	0
Jurisdiction														
Bureau of Indian Education	174	174	0	0	174	174	0	0	0	0	0	0	0	0
DoDEA[4]	8	—	0	0	0	0	0	0	8	—	0	0	0	0
Other jurisdictions														
American Samoa	1	1	1	1	0	0	0	0	0	0	0	0	0	0
Guam	1	1	1	1	0	0	0	0	0	0	0	0	0	0
Northern Marianas	—	—	—	—	—	—	—	—	—	—	—	—	—	—
Puerto Rico	1	1	1	1	0	0	0	0	0	0	0	0	0	0
U.S. Virgin Islands	2	2	2	2	0	0	0	0	0	0	0	0	0	0

—Not available.
[1]Includes both independent districts and those that are a dependent segment of a local government. Also includes components of supervisory unions that operate schools but share superintendent services with other districts.
[2]Includes public agencies that provide education but are not school districts, such as juvenile correctional institutions, sheriff's offices, hospitals, residential treatment centers, and university lab schools.

[3]New York City is counted as one school district.
[4]DoDEA = Department of Defense Education Activity. Includes both domestic and overseas schools.
SOURCE: U.S. Department of Education, National Center for Education Statistics, Common Core of Data (CCD), "Local Education Agency Universe Survey," 2016–17 and 2017–18. (This table was prepared February 2020.)

Table 214.40. Public elementary and secondary school enrollment, number of schools, and other selected characteristics, by locale: Fall 2014 through fall 2017

Enrollment, number of schools, and other characteristics	Total	City				Suburban				Town				Rural				Locale unknown
		Total	Large[1]	Mid-size[2]	Small[3]	Total	Large[4]	Mid-size[5]	Small[6]	Total	Fringe[7]	Distant[8]	Remote[9]	Total	Fringe[10]	Distant[11]	Remote[12]	
1	2	3	4	5	6	7	8	9	10	11	12	13	14	15	16	17	18	19
Fall 2014																		
Enrollment (in thousands)	50,010	15,235	8,042	3,319	3,874	19,882	17,072	1,821	989	5,680	1,436	2,694	1,549	9,213	5,310	2,881	1,022	†
Percentage distribution of enrollment, by race/ethnicity	100.0	100.0	100.0	100.0	100.0	100.0	100.0	100.0	100.0	100.0	100.0	100.0	100.0	100.0	100.0	100.0	100.0	†
White	49.6	29.5	20.4	32.5	45.8	50.6	48.7	60.7	64.4	64.2	67.8	65.4	58.9	71.6	66.9	79.6	73.3	
Black	15.5	23.7	26.1	25.0	17.5	13.7	14.4	10.1	8.4	10.0	7.0	11.6	10.1	9.4	10.9	7.5	6.8	
Hispanic	25.4	35.6	42.0	32.1	25.4	25.4	26.2	21.0	19.8	18.9	19.0	17.3	21.6	12.7	15.9	8.1	9.5	
Asian	4.9	6.8	7.6	5.5	6.2	6.1	6.6	3.0	3.2	1.3	1.5	1.0	1.6	1.4	2.1	0.5	0.3	
Pacific Islander	0.3	0.4	0.4	0.4	0.8	0.4	0.4	0.5	0.2	0.4	0.4	0.1	0.9	0.2	0.2	0.1	0.3	
American Indian/Alaska Native	1.0	0.7	0.7	0.6	0.8	0.5	0.4	0.7	0.7	2.2	1.2	1.6	4.1	2.1	1.1	2.0	7.5	
Two or more races	3.2	3.4	2.9	3.9	4.0	3.4	3.3	4.1	3.4	3.0	3.1	3.0	2.8	2.6	2.9	2.2	2.1	
Students participating in English language learner (ELL) programs (in thousands)[13]	4,670	2,186	1,358	441	387	1,879	1,696	116	67	352	79	160	113	255	159	61	35	†
ELL program participants as a percent of enrollment[13]	9.3	13.8	16.2	12.2	10.2	8.8	9.1	6.2	6.7	6.2	5.9	5.9	6.8	3.5	4.5	2.2	3.6	†
Schools	98,176	26,560	13,870	5,745	6,945	31,099	25,966	3,217	1,916	13,391	2,949	6,299	4,143	27,126	10,422	10,315	6,389	†
Average school size[14]	525	591	593	599	579	655	673	579	537	445	500	448	398	350	528	286	165	†
Pupil/teacher ratio[15]	16.2	16.9	17.1	17.0	16.3	16.5	16.5	16.2	16.9	15.8	16.4	15.6	15.5	14.9	15.9	14.2	12.5	†
Enrollment (percentage distribution)	100.0	30.5	16.1	6.6	7.7	39.8	34.1	3.6	2.0	11.4	2.9	5.4	3.1	18.4	10.6	5.8	2.0	†
Schools (percentage distribution)	100.0	27.1	14.1	5.9	7.1	31.7	26.4	3.3	2.0	13.6	3.0	6.4	4.2	27.6	10.6	10.5	6.5	†
Fall 2015																		
Enrollment (in thousands)	50,112	15,276	8,276	3,368	3,632	19,903	17,095	1,819	989	5,630	1,422	2,670	1,538	9,303	5,434	2,855	1,014	3
Percentage distribution of enrollment, by race/ethnicity	100.0	100.0	100.0	100.0	100.0	100.0	100.0	100.0	100.0	100.0	100.0	100.0	100.0	100.0	100.0	100.0	100.0	100.0
White	48.9	29.1	20.2	32.6	46.0	49.7	47.8	59.9	63.6	63.6	67.1	64.8	58.3	70.8	65.9	79.3	73.1	48.7
Black	15.4	23.4	25.7	24.2	17.4	13.7	14.4	10.2	8.4	10.0	7.0	11.5	10.1	9.4	11.0	7.3	6.6	11.5
Hispanic	25.9	36.0	42.4	32.4	24.8	25.9	26.7	21.5	20.3	19.4	19.5	17.8	22.1	13.2	16.4	8.4	9.7	30.1
Asian	5.0	6.8	7.6	5.6	6.4	6.3	6.8	3.0	3.2	1.3	1.5	1.0	1.6	1.5	2.3	0.5	0.5	5.5
Pacific Islander	0.4	0.4	0.4	0.4	0.4	0.4	0.4	0.5	0.2	0.4	0.4	0.1	0.9	0.2	0.2	0.1	0.3	0.2
American Indian/Alaska Native	1.0	0.7	0.7	0.6	0.8	0.4	0.4	0.6	0.7	2.1	1.1	1.5	4.0	2.1	1.1	2.0	7.5	0.3
Two or more races	3.4	3.6	3.0	4.2	4.3	3.6	3.5	4.4	3.6	3.2	3.3	3.2	3.0	2.8	3.1	2.4	2.3	3.6
Number of English language learner (ELL) students (in thousands)[13]	4,795	2,217	1,402	452	363	1,941	1,754	119	68	365	81	164	120	272	173	64	36	#
ELL students as a percent of enrollment[13]	9.5	14.0	16.3	12.4	10.0	9.1	9.5	6.5	6.7	6.5	6.2	6.1	7.4	3.6	4.5	2.4	3.7	0.9
Schools	98,277	26,636	14,214	5,828	6,594	31,081	25,963	3,209	1,909	13,307	2,922	6,279	4,106	27,146	10,546	10,262	6,338	107
Average school size[14]	526	591	595	598	575	657	675	582	538	445	500	447	401	354	535	285	165	26
Pupil/teacher ratio[15]	16.2	16.8	17.1	16.8	16.3	16.5	16.5	16.4	16.8	15.8	16.3	15.7	15.4	14.9	15.9	14.3	12.5	11.8
Enrollment (percentage distribution)	100.0	30.5	16.5	6.7	7.2	39.7	34.1	3.6	2.0	11.2	2.8	5.3	3.1	18.6	10.8	5.7	2.0	#
Schools (percentage distribution)	100.0	27.1	14.5	5.9	6.7	31.6	26.4	3.3	1.9	13.5	3.0	6.4	4.2	27.6	10.7	10.4	6.4	0.1
Fall 2016																		
Enrollment (in thousands)	50,283	15,316	8,356	3,386	3,573	19,918	17,107	1,822	989	5,560	1,415	2,631	1,513	9,489	5,635	2,845	1,010	†
Percentage distribution of enrollment, by race/ethnicity	100.0	100.0	100.0	100.0	100.0	100.0	100.0	100.0	100.0	100.0	100.0	100.0	100.0	100.0	100.0	100.0	100.0	†
White	48.2	28.7	20.1	32.2	45.3	48.7	46.9	58.9	62.8	63.1	66.4	64.2	58.0	69.9	64.9	78.9	72.8	
Black	15.3	23.2	25.3	23.9	17.4	13.6	14.3	10.3	8.3	9.9	7.0	11.3	10.0	9.4	11.0	7.2	6.4	
Hispanic	26.4	36.4	42.5	33.3	25.0	26.5	27.3	22.1	20.8	19.8	19.9	18.3	22.2	13.8	17.2	8.7	9.8	
Asian	5.1	6.9	7.8	5.2	6.4	6.4	7.0	3.1	3.3	1.3	1.5	1.0	1.6	1.6	2.4	0.5	0.5	
Pacific Islander	0.4	0.4	0.4	0.4	0.4	0.4	0.4	0.4	0.2	0.4	0.4	0.1	0.9	0.2	0.3	0.1	0.3	
American Indian/Alaska Native	1.0	0.7	0.7	0.6	0.8	0.4	0.4	0.6	0.6	2.1	1.1	1.6	4.1	2.0	1.0	2.0	7.7	
Two or more races	3.6	3.8	3.2	4.4	4.6	3.9	3.8	4.7	3.9	3.4	3.6	3.4	3.2	3.0	3.3	2.6	2.5	
Number of English language learner (ELL) students (in thousands)[13]	4,857	2,238	1,420	459	360	1,974	1,795	111	68	358	80	160	118	286	187	64	35	†
ELL students as a percent of enrollment[13]	9.6	14.0	16.2	12.4	10.1	9.3	9.7	6.3	6.9	6.5	6.4	6.0	7.4	3.8	4.7	2.4	3.6	†
Number of students with disabilities (in thousands)[13]	6,756	2,127	1,183	465	479	2,793	2,417	242	135	773	171	380	222	1,063	549	374	141	†
Students with disabilities as a percent of enrollment[13]	13.4	13.3	13.5	12.6	13.4	13.1	13.0	13.6	13.6	14.0	13.6	14.3	13.9	13.9	13.8	13.9	14.6	†

See notes at end of table.

Table 214.40. Public elementary and secondary school enrollment, number of schools, and other selected characteristics, by locale: Fall 2014 through fall 2017—Continued

Enrollment, number of schools, and other characteristics	Total	City				Suburban				Town				Rural				Locale unknown
		Total	Large[1]	Mid-size[2]	Small[3]	Total	Large[4]	Mid-size[5]	Small[6]	Total	Fringe[7]	Distant[8]	Remote[9]	Total	Fringe[10]	Distant[11]	Remote[12]	
1	2	3	4	5	6	7	8	9	10	11	12	13	14	15	16	17	18	19
Schools	98,169	26,658	14,315	5,865	6,478	31,068	25,950	3,218	1,900	13,148	2,912	6,205	4,031	27,295	10,791	10,193	6,311	†
Average school size[14]	528	591	596	597	574	656	674	580	538	444	500	446	399	358	541	285	165	†
Pupil/teacher ratio[15]	16.2	16.8	16.9	16.8	16.3	16.5	16.5	16.3	17.0	15.8	16.3	15.7	15.5	15.0	15.9	14.3	12.6	†
Enrollment (percentage distribution)	100.0	30.5	16.6	6.7	7.1	39.6	34.0	3.6	2.0	11.1	2.8	5.2	3.0	18.9	11.2	5.7	2.0	†
Schools (percentage distribution)	100.0	27.2	14.6	6.0	6.6	31.6	26.4	3.3	1.9	13.4	3.0	6.3	4.1	27.8	11.0	10.4	6.4	†
Fall 2017																		
Enrollment (in thousands)	50,345	15,283	8,386	3,313	3,584	19,939	17,123	1,826	990	5,522	1,409	2,614	1,500	9,601	5,755	2,841	1,005	†
Percentage distribution of enrollment, by race/ethnicity	100.0	100.0	100.0	100.0	100.0	100.0	100.0	100.0	100.0	100.0	100.0	100.0	100.0	100.0	100.0	100.0	100.0	†
White	47.6	28.4	20.1	31.7	44.6	47.9	46.0	58.0	62.0	62.6	65.8	63.7	57.6	69.2	64.0	78.5	72.6	†
Black	15.2	22.9	24.9	24.0	17.3	13.7	14.3	10.4	8.4	9.7	6.9	11.2	9.9	9.3	11.0	7.1	6.3	†
Hispanic	26.7	36.6	42.6	33.4	25.4	27.0	27.8	22.5	21.2	20.2	20.4	18.8	22.6	14.3	17.7	9.0	10.0	†
Asian	5.2	7.0	7.8	5.3	6.5	6.6	7.2	3.1	3.4	1.3	1.5	1.0	1.5	1.7	2.5	0.5	0.5	†
Pacific Islander	0.4	0.4	0.4	0.5	0.4	0.4	0.4	0.4	0.2	0.4	0.4	0.2	0.9	0.2	0.3	0.1	0.3	†
American Indian/Alaska Native	1.0	0.7	0.7	0.6	0.8	0.4	0.4	0.6	0.6	2.1	1.0	1.5	4.0	2.0	1.0	2.0	7.7	†
Two or more races	3.9	4.0	3.4	4.6	4.9	4.1	4.0	4.9	4.1	3.6	3.8	3.6	3.5	3.2	3.6	2.8	2.6	†
Number of English language learner (ELL) students (in thousands)[13]	4,953	2,275	1,451	456	367	2,015	1,831	116	68	360	80	163	117	303	196	68	39	†
ELL students as a percent of enrollment[13]	10.1	14.7	17.1	13.1	10.5	9.6	10.0	6.6	7.1	6.8	6.6	6.4	7.6	4.1	5.1	2.6	4.2	†
Number of students with disabilities (in thousands)[13]	6,953	2,195	1,227	468	499	2,870	2,481	252	137	789	173	390	226	1,100	564	389	147	†
Students with disabilities as a percent of enrollment[13]	13.8	13.8	14.0	13.1	13.9	13.4	13.3	13.9	14.0	14.4	13.9	14.7	14.2	14.4	14.2	14.4	15.0	†
Schools	98,480	26,781	14,564	5,731	6,486	31,217	26,112	3,208	1,897	13,098	2,890	6,198	4,010	27,384	10,943	10,175	6,266	†
Average school size[14]	528	589	588	599	580	657	674	586	543	445	502	445	400	362	546	286	165	†
Pupil/teacher ratio[15]	16.1	16.7	16.8	16.9	16.2	16.3	16.3	16.3	16.9	15.7	16.2	15.7	15.4	15.0	15.9	14.3	12.7	†
Enrollment (percentage distribution)	100.0	30.4	16.7	6.6	7.1	39.6	34.0	3.6	2.0	11.0	2.8	5.2	3.0	19.1	11.4	5.6	2.0	†
Schools (percentage distribution)	100.0	27.2	14.8	5.8	6.6	31.7	26.5	3.3	1.9	13.3	2.9	6.3	4.1	27.8	11.1	10.3	6.4	†

†Not applicable.
#Rounds to zero.
[1]Located inside an urbanized area and inside a principal city with a population of 250,000 or more.
[2]Located inside an urbanized area and inside a principal city with a population of at least 100,000, but less than 250,000.
[3]Located inside an urbanized area and inside a principal city with a population less than 100,000.
[4]Located inside an urbanized area and outside a principal city with a population of 250,000 or more.
[5]Located inside an urbanized area and outside a principal city with a population of at least 100,000, but less than 250,000.
[6]Located inside an urbanized area and outside a principal city with a population less than 100,000.
[7]Located inside an urban cluster that is 10 miles or less from an urbanized area.
[8]Located inside an urban cluster that is more than 10 but less than or equal to 35 miles from an urbanized area.
[9]Located inside an urban cluster that is more than 35 miles from an urbanized area.
[10]Located outside any urbanized area or urban cluster, but 5 miles or less from an urbanized area or 2.5 miles or less from an urban cluster.
[11]Located outside any urbanized area or urban cluster and more than 5 miles but less than or equal to 25 miles from an urbanized area, or more than 2.5 miles but less than or equal to 10 miles from an urban cluster.
[12]Located outside any urbanized area or urban cluster, more than 25 miles from an urbanized area, and more than 10 miles from an urban cluster.

[13]Data are based on locales of school districts rather than locales of schools as in the rest of the table. Data for 2014 and earlier years include only those ELL students who participated in ELL programs. Starting with 2015, data include all ELL students, regardless of program participation. Data exclude ELL students who are enrolled in prekindergarten.
[14]Average for schools reporting enrollment. Enrollment data were available for 95,230 out of 98,176 schools in 2014–15, 95,240 out of 98,277 schools in 2015–16, 95,306 out of 98,169 schools in 2016–17, and 95,265 out of 98,480 schools in 2017–18.
[15]Ratio for schools reporting both full-time-equivalent teachers and fall enrollment data.
NOTE: Detail may not sum to totals because of rounding. Race categories exclude persons of Hispanic ethnicity. Enrollment and ratios are based on data reported by schools and may differ from data reported in other tables that reflect aggregate totals reported by states.
SOURCE: U.S. Department of Education, National Center for Education Statistics, Common Core of Data (CCD), "Public Elementary/Secondary School Universe Survey," 2014–15, 2015–16, 2016–17, and 2017–18; CCD, "Local Education Agency Universe Survey," 2014–15, 2015–16, 2016–17, and 2017–18; and Education Demographic and Geographic Estimates (EDGE), "Public School File," 2015–16, 2016–17, and 2017–18. (This table was prepared November 2019.)

Table 216.10. Public elementary and secondary schools, by level of school: Selected years, 1967–68 through 2017–18

		Schools with reported grade spans											
			Elementary schools				Secondary schools					Combined elementary/ secondary schools[2]	Other schools[1]
Year	Total, all public schools	Total	Total[3]	Middle schools[4]	One-teacher schools	Other elementary schools	Total[5]	Junior high[6]	3-year or 4-year high schools	5-year or 6-year high schools	Other secondary schools		
1	2	3	4	5	6	7	8	9	10	11	12	13	14
1967–68	—	94,197	67,186	—	4,146	63,040	23,318	7,437	10,751	4,650	480	3,693	—
1970–71	—	89,372	64,020	2,080	1,815	60,125	23,572	7,750	11,265	3,887	670	1,780	—
1972–73	—	88,864	62,942	2,308	1,475	59,159	23,919	7,878	11,550	3,962	529	2,003	—
1974–75	—	87,456	61,759	3,224	1,247	57,288	23,837	7,690	11,480	4,122	545	1,860	—
1975–76	88,597	87,034	61,704	3,916	1,166	56,622	23,792	7,521	11,572	4,113	586	1,538	1,563
1976–77	—	86,501	61,123	4,180	1,111	55,832	23,857	7,434	11,658	4,130	635	1,521	—
1978–79	—	84,816	60,312	5,879	1,056	53,377	22,834	6,282	11,410	4,429	713	1,670	—
1980–81	85,982	83,688	59,326	6,003	921	52,402	22,619	5,890	10,758	4,193	1,778	1,743	2,294
1982–83	84,740	82,039	58,051	6,875	798	50,378	22,383	5,948	11,678	4,067	690	1,605	2,701
1983–84	84,178	81,418	57,471	6,885	838	49,748	22,336	5,936	11,670	4,046	684	1,611	2,760
1984–85	84,007	81,147	57,231	6,893	825	49,513	22,320	5,916	11,671	4,021	712	1,596	2,860
1986–87	83,421	82,316	58,835	7,483	763	50,589	21,505	5,109	11,430	4,196	770	1,976	1,105[7]
1987–88	83,248	81,416	57,575	7,641	729	49,205	21,662	4,900	11,279	4,048	1,435	2,179	1,832[7]
1988–89	83,165	81,579	57,941	7,957	583	49,401	21,403	4,687	11,350	3,994	1,372	2,235	1,586[7]
1989–90	83,425	81,880	58,419	8,272	630	49,517	21,181	4,512	11,492	3,812	1,365	2,280	1,545[7]
1990–91	84,538	82,475	59,015	8,545	617	49,853	21,135	4,561	11,537	3,723	1,314	2,325	2,063
1991–92	84,578	82,506	59,258	8,829	569	49,860	20,767	4,298	11,528	3,699	1,242	2,481	2,072
1992–93	84,497	82,896	59,676	9,152	430	50,094	20,671	4,115	11,651	3,613	1,292	2,549	1,601
1993–94	85,393	83,431	60,052	9,573	442	50,037	20,705	3,970	11,858	3,595	1,282	2,674	1,962
1994–95	86,221	84,476	60,808	9,954	458	50,396	20,904	3,859	12,058	3,628	1,359	2,764	1,745
1995–96	87,125	84,958	61,165	10,205	474	50,486	20,997	3,743	12,168	3,621	1,465	2,796	2,167
1996–97	88,223	86,092	61,805	10,499	487	50,819	21,307	3,707	12,424	3,614	1,562	2,980	2,131
1997–98	89,508	87,541	62,739	10,944	476	51,319	21,682	3,599	12,734	3,611	1,738	3,120	1,967
1998–99	90,874	89,259	63,462	11,202	463	51,797	22,076	3,607	13,457	3,707	1,305	3,721	1,615
1999–2000	92,012	90,538	64,131	11,521	423	52,187	22,365	3,566	13,914	3,686	1,199	4,042	1,474
2000–01	93,273	91,691	64,601	11,696	411	52,494	21,994	3,318	13,793	3,974	909	5,096	1,582
2001–02	94,112	92,696	65,228	11,983	408	52,837	22,180	3,285	14,070	3,917	908	5,288	1,416
2002–03	95,615	93,869	65,718	12,174	366	53,178	22,599	3,263	14,330	4,017	989	5,552	1,746
2003–04	95,726	93,977	65,758	12,341	376	53,041	22,782	3,251	14,595	3,840	1,096	5,437	1,749
2004–05	96,513	95,001	65,984	12,530	338	53,116	23,445	3,250	14,854	3,945	1,396	5,572	1,512
2005–06	97,382	95,731	66,026	12,545	326	53,155	23,998	3,249	15,103	3,910	1,736	5,707	1,651
2006–07	98,793	96,362	66,458	12,773	313	53,372	23,920	3,112	15,043	4,048	1,717	5,984	2,431
2007–08	98,916	97,654	67,112	13,014	288	53,810	24,643	3,117	16,146	3,981	1,399	5,899	1,262
2008–09	98,706	97,119	67,148	13,060	237	53,851	24,348	3,037	16,246	3,761	1,304	5,623	1,587
2009–10	98,817	97,521	67,140	13,163	217	53,760	24,651	2,953	16,706	3,778	1,214	5,730	1,296
2010–11	98,817	97,767	67,086	13,045	224	53,817	24,544	2,855	16,321	4,047	1,321	6,137	1,050
2011–12	98,328	97,357	66,689	12,963	205	53,521	24,357	2,865	16,586	3,899	1,007	6,311	971
2012–13	98,454	97,331	66,708	13,064	196	53,448	24,294	2,816	16,393	3,875	1,210	6,329	1,123
2013–14	98,271	97,290	67,034	13,234	193	53,517	24,067	2,721	16,704	3,467	1,175	6,189	981
2014–15	98,176	97,601	67,073	13,250	165	53,658	24,181	2,706	16,603	3,585	1,287	6,347	575
2015–16	98,277	97,586	66,758	13,022	197	53,539	24,040	2,594	16,243	3,995	1,208	6,788	691
2016–17	98,158	97,434	66,837	13,253	203	53,381	23,814	2,527	16,514	3,523	1,250	6,783	724
2017–18	98,469	97,568	67,408	13,437	188	53,783	23,882	2,479	16,677	3,390	1,336	6,278	901

—Not available.
[1]Includes special education, alternative, and other schools not reported by grade span.
[2]Includes schools beginning with grade 6 or below and ending with grade 9 or above.
[3]Includes schools beginning with grade 6 or below and with no grade higher than 8.
[4]Includes schools with grade spans beginning with 4, 5, or 6 and ending with 6, 7, or 8.
[5]Includes schools with no grade lower than 7.
[6]Includes schools with grades 7 and 8 or grades 7 through 9.

[7]Because of revision in data collection procedures, figures not comparable to data for other years.
SOURCE: U.S. Department of Education, National Center for Education Statistics, *Statistics of State School Systems*, 1967–68 and 1975–76; *Statistics of Public Elementary and Secondary Day Schools*, 1970–71, 1972–73, 1974–75, and 1976–77 through 1980–81; and Common Core of Data (CCD), "Public Elementary/Secondary School Universe Survey," 1982–83 through 2017–18. (This table was prepared December 2019.)

Table 216.20. Number and enrollment of public elementary and secondary schools, by school level, type, and charter, magnet, and virtual status: Selected years, 1990–91 through 2017–18

School level, type, and charter, magnet, or virtual status	Number of schools										Fall enrollment									
	1990–91	2000–01	2005–06	2010–11	2012–13	2013–14	2014–15	2015–16	2016–17	2017–18	1990–91	2000–01	2005–06	2010–11	2012–13	2013–14	2014–15	2015–16	2016–17	2017–18
1	2	3	4	5	6	7	8	9	10	11	12	13	14	15	16	17	18	19	20	21
Total, all schools	84,538	93,273	97,382	98,817	98,454	98,271	98,176	98,277	98,158	98,469	41,141,366	47,060,714	48,912,085	49,177,617	49,519,559	49,777,410	50,009,771	50,115,178	50,274,747	50,330,241
School type																				
Regular	80,395	85,422	87,585	88,929	89,031	89,183	89,386	89,501	89,527	89,914	40,599,943	46,194,730	47,957,375	48,259,245	48,583,049	48,863,752	49,178,890	49,313,134	49,468,870	49,531,526
Special education	1,932	2,008	2,128	2,206	2,034	2,010	1,954	2,005	1,991	1,903	209,145	174,577	222,497	190,910	198,626	214,611	186,269	180,155	184,261	185,073
Vocational	1,060	1,025	1,221	1,485	1,403	1,380	1,387	1,396	1,391	1,467	198,117	199,669	217,621	164,013	160,207	148,447	147,550	146,321	146,601	147,516
Alternative[1]	1,151	4,818	6,448	6,197	5,986	5,698	5,449	5,375	5,249	5,185	134,161	491,738	514,592	563,449	577,677	550,600	497,062	475,568	475,015	466,126
School level and type																				
Elementary[2]	59,015	64,601	66,026	67,086	66,708	67,034	67,073	66,758	66,837	67,408	26,503,677	30,673,453	31,104,018	31,581,751	31,918,613	32,226,881	32,225,908	32,035,708	32,132,682	32,346,383
Regular	58,440	63,674	64,996	65,874	65,572	65,948	66,036	65,734	65,853	66,436	26,400,740	30,582,610	31,003,942	31,441,027	31,772,432	32,083,759	32,116,995	31,930,363	32,034,365	32,241,347
Special education	419	496	508	587	541	543	578	568	551	555	58,204	42,127	49,652	58,987	59,826	62,596	54,161	50,508	43,555	52,522
Vocational	31	8	8	16	15	7	6	5	5	4	17,686	2,409	1,713	3,495	3,734	1,791	1,749	1,729	1,960	1,831
Alternative[1]	125	423	514	609	580	536	453	451	428	413	27,047	46,307	48,711	78,242	82,621	78,735	53,003	53,108	52,802	50,683
Secondary[3]	21,135	21,994	23,998	24,544	24,294	24,067	24,181	24,040	23,814	23,816	13,569,787	15,038,171	16,219,309	15,692,610	15,670,275	15,640,128	15,731,561	15,748,184	15,798,446	15,759,707
Regular	19,459	18,456	19,252	19,449	19,479	19,411	19,441	19,325	19,264	19,171	13,313,097	14,567,969	15,685,032	15,197,786	15,161,226	15,167,671	15,270,834	15,296,173	15,355,391	15,324,419
Special education	165	219	368	359	333	331	339	313	316	296	11,913	12,607	42,696	27,990	28,235	28,312	24,729	21,929	21,700	21,710
Vocational	1,010	997	1,185	1,387	1,324	1,311	1,318	1,329	1,332	1,427	174,105	193,981	209,762	154,088	154,610	144,066	144,042	142,611	142,332	142,915
Alternative[1]	501	2,322	3,193	3,349	3,158	3,014	3,083	3,073	2,902	2,922	70,672	263,614	281,819	312,746	326,204	300,079	291,956	287,471	279,023	270,663
Combined elementary/secondary[4]	2,325	5,096	5,707	6,137	6,329	6,189	6,347	6,788	6,783	6,344	925,887	1,266,778	1,526,186	1,897,712	1,926,786	1,898,252	2,049,039	2,329,346	2,335,618	2,216,403
Regular	1,784	2,780	3,121	3,363	3,558	3,446	3,713	4,236	4,236	3,936	855,814	1,007,368	1,263,952	1,620,031	1,649,010	1,611,918	1,790,208	2,085,918	2,078,659	1,965,052
Special education	376	715	735	964	935	940	935	923	907	877	43,992	86,253	91,966	99,120	107,295	111,958	106,500	107,658	112,826	105,334
Vocational	19	20	28	82	64	62	63	62	54	36	6,326	3,279	6,146	6,430	1,863	2,590	1,759	1,981	2,309	2,770
Alternative[1]	146	1,581	1,823	1,728	1,772	1,741	1,636	1,567	1,586	1,495	19,755	169,878	164,122	172,131	168,618	171,786	150,572	133,789	141,824	143,247
Other (not classified by grade span)	2,063	1,582	1,651	1,050	1,123	981	575	691	724	901	142,015	82,312	62,572	5,544	3,885	12,149	3,263	1,940	8,001	7,748
Regular	712	512	216	243	422	378	196	206	174	371	30,292	36,783	4,449	401	381	404	853	680	455	708
Special education	972	578	517	296	225	196	102	201	217	175	95,036	33,590	38,183	4,813	3,270	11,745	879	60	6,180	5,507
Vocational	0	0	0	0	0	0	0	0	0	0	0	0	0	0	0	0	0	0	0	0
Alternative[1]	379	492	918	511	476	407	277	284	333	355	16,687	11,939	19,940	330	234	0	1,531	1,200	1,366	1,533
Charter status and level																				
All charter schools[5]	—	1,993	3,780	5,274	6,079	6,465	6,747	6,855	7,011	7,193	—	448,343	1,012,906	1,787,091	2,269,435	2,522,022	2,721,786	2,845,322	3,010,287	3,143,269
Elementary[2]	—	1,011	1,969	2,866	3,388	3,634	3,851	3,854	3,934	4,064	—	249,101	532,217	905,575	1,156,075	1,288,568	1,405,015	1,448,523	1,511,812	1,601,350
Secondary[3]	—	467	1,057	1,368	1,465	1,522	1,563	1,576	1,618	1,667	—	79,588	219,627	341,534	399,921	443,423	467,231	482,296	504,301	539,890
Combined elementary/secondary[4]	—	448	704	1,027	1,204	1,268	1,330	1,406	1,454	1,458	—	117,377	259,837	539,653	713,073	789,883	848,875	914,110	994,021	1,001,788
Other (not classified by grade span)	—	67	50	13	22	41	3	19	5	4	—	2,277	1,225	329	366	148	665	393	153	241
Magnet status and level																				
All magnet schools[5]	—	1,469	2,736	2,722	3,151	3,254	3,285	3,237	3,164	3,421	—	1,213,976	2,103,013	2,055,133	2,478,531	2,556,644	2,609,104	2,604,145	2,537,011	2,665,820
Elementary[2]	—	1,111	1,994	1,849	2,150	2,164	2,216	2,135	2,087	2,307	—	704,763	1,186,160	1,035,288	1,287,771	1,300,317	1,312,571	1,281,873	1,266,076	1,370,347
Secondary[3]	—	328	643	746	862	939	911	884	853	931	—	484,684	869,010	944,434	1,118,574	1,178,272	1,207,248	1,188,316	1,141,181	1,184,412
Combined elementary/secondary[4]	—	29	80	103	121	133	142	203	205	165	—	24,529	47,509	75,411	72,148	78,055	89,277	133,956	129,752	111,056
Other (not classified by grade span)	—	1	19	24	18	18	16	15	19	18	—	0	334	0	38	0	8	0	2	5
Virtual status and level																				
All virtual schools[5,6]	—	—	—	—	—	477	576	592	562	656	—	—	—	—	—	200,343	229,608	234,148	212,311	278,783
Elementary[2]	—	—	—	—	—	65	77	74	68	77	—	—	—	—	—	14,277	19,341	19,064	14,669	20,941
Secondary[3]	—	—	—	—	—	100	132	144	132	159	—	—	—	—	—	18,625	29,303	32,535	23,355	36,505
Combined elementary/secondary[4]	—	—	—	—	—	310	366	373	361	415	—	—	—	—	—	167,441	180,964	182,549	174,287	221,337
Other (not classified by grade span)	—	—	—	—	—	2	1	1	1	5	—	—	—	—	—	0	0	0	0	0

—Not available.
[1]Includes schools that provide nontraditional education, address needs of students that typically cannot be met in regular schools, serve as adjuncts to regular schools, or fall outside the categories of regular, special education, or vocational education.
[2]Includes schools beginning with grade 6 or below and with no grade higher than 8.
[3]Includes schools with no grade lower than 7.
[4]Includes schools beginning with grade 6 or below and ending with grade 9 or above.
[5]Magnet, charter, and virtual schools are also included under regular, special education, vocational, or alternative schools as appropriate.
[6]Virtual schools are defined as having instruction during which students and teachers are separated by time and/or location and interact via internet-connected computers or other electronic devices.
SOURCE: U.S. Department of Education, National Center for Education Statistics, Common Core of Data (CCD), "Public Elementary/Secondary School Universe Survey," 1990–91 through 2017–18. (This table was prepared November 2019.)

Table 216.30. Number and percentage distribution of public elementary and secondary students and schools, by traditional or charter school status and selected characteristics: Selected years, 1999–2000 through 2017–18

| Selected characteristic | 1999–2000 | | | 2000–01 | | | 2010–11 | | | 2017–18 | | |
	Total, all public schools	Traditional (non-charter) schools	Charter schools	Total, all public schools	Traditional (non-charter) schools	Charter schools	Total, all public schools	Traditional (non-charter) schools	Charter schools	Total, all public schools	Traditional (non-charter) schools	Charter schools
1	2	3	4	5	6	7	8	9	10	11	12	13
Fall enrollment (in thousands)	46,689	46,350	340	47,061	46,612	448	49,178	47,391	1,787	50,330	47,187	3,143
Percentage distribution of students												
Sex	100.0	100.0	100.0	100.0	100.0	100.0	100.0	100.0	100.0	100.0	100.0	100.0
Male	51.4	51.4	51.1	51.4	51.4	51.2	51.4	51.4	49.5	51.4	51.5	49.6
Female	48.6	48.6	48.9	48.6	48.6	48.8	48.6	48.6	50.5	48.6	48.5	50.4
Race/ethnicity	100.0	100.0	100.0	100.0	100.0	100.0	100.0	100.0	100.0	100.0	100.0	100.0
White	61.8	61.9	42.5	61.0	61.2	42.7	52.5	53.1	36.2	47.6	48.7	32.1
Black	17.1	16.9	33.5	17.0	16.9	33.2	16.0	15.5	28.9	15.2	14.5	25.8
Hispanic	15.9	15.9	19.6	16.6	16.6	19.4	23.1	22.9	27.3	26.7	26.3	33.1
Asian/Pacific Islander	4.1	4.1	2.8	4.2	4.2	2.9	5.0	5.0	3.7	5.6	5.6	4.4
Asian	—	—	—	—	—	—	4.6	4.7	3.3	5.2	5.3	4.0
Pacific Islander	—	—	—	—	—	—	0.3	0.3	0.5	0.4	0.4	0.4
American Indian/Alaska Native	1.2	1.2	1.5	1.2	1.2	1.8	1.1	1.1	0.9	1.0	1.0	0.7
Two or more races	—	—	—	—	—	—	2.4	2.3	2.9	3.9	3.9	3.9
Percent of students eligible for free or reduced-price lunch program[1]	100.0	100.0	100.0	100.0	100.0	100.0	100.0	100.0	100.0	100.0	100.0	100.0
0 to 25.0	44.9	45.0	36.9	34.3	34.3	39.3	23.9	23.8	26.7	21.0	21.2	18.2
25.1 to 50.0	25.4	25.5	12.7	24.7	24.8	12.7	28.9	29.2	18.9	28.3	28.9	19.5
50.1 to 75.0	16.0	16.1	13.0	16.0	16.1	14.9	26.6	26.8	20.4	25.3	25.6	21.6
More than 75.0	12.2	12.2	14.3	12.4	12.4	14.7	20.1	19.7	30.7	24.8	24.2	34.5
Missing/school does not participate	1.4	1.2	23.2	12.5	12.4	18.4	0.5	0.4	3.2	0.6	0.2	6.2
Number of teachers	2,636,277	2,622,678	13,599	2,747,649	2,729,033	18,616	3,001,994	2,910,869	91,126	3,079,590	2,922,634	156,956
Pupil/teacher ratio[2]	16.6	16.6	18.8	16.4	16.4	18.2	16.4	16.4	18.0	16.1	16.0	17.7
Total number of schools	92,012	90,488	1,524	93,273	91,280	1,993	98,817	93,543	5,274	98,469	91,276	7,193
Percentage distribution of schools												
School level	100.0	100.0	100.0	100.0	100.0	100.0	100.0	100.0	100.0	100.0	100.0	100.0
Elementary[3]	69.7	70.0	54.6	69.3	69.7	50.7	67.9	68.7	54.3	68.5	69.4	56.5
Secondary[4]	24.3	24.3	25.9	23.6	23.6	23.4	24.8	24.8	25.9	24.3	24.3	23.2
Combined[5]	4.4	4.2	18.6	5.5	5.1	22.5	6.2	5.5	19.5	6.4	5.3	20.3
Ungraded	1.6	1.6	0.9	1.7	1.7	3.4	1.1	1.1	0.2	0.9	1.0	0.1
Size of enrollment	100.0	100.0	100.0	100.0	100.0	100.0	100.0	100.0	100.0	100.0	100.0	100.0
Less than 300	31.3	30.5	77.0	31.9	31.0	75.2	30.9	29.3	59.0	29.8	28.6	44.8
300 to 499	26.5	26.7	12.0	26.5	26.8	12.7	27.8	28.1	22.3	28.1	28.3	25.5
500 to 999	32.8	33.2	8.7	32.0	32.5	9.7	32.3	33.4	14.8	32.7	33.5	23.3
1,000 or more	9.5	9.7	2.4	9.6	9.8	2.4	9.0	9.3	3.9	9.4	9.6	6.3
Racial/ethnic concentration												
More than 50 percent White	70.9	71.2	51.1	70.2	70.6	51.6	60.4	61.7	38.4	54.8	56.6	32.3
More than 50 percent Black	11.1	10.8	26.5	11.1	10.8	25.1	10.7	9.8	25.4	9.8	8.7	22.8
More than 50 percent Hispanic	8.8	8.7	11.4	9.2	9.1	11.5	14.5	14.1	20.8	17.3	16.6	26.6
No majority racial/ethnic group	7.8	7.8	9.1	8.0	8.0	9.7	13.1	13.0	14.1	16.5	16.4	16.8
Percent of students eligible for free or reduced-price lunch program[1]	100.0	100.0	100.0	100.0	100.0	100.0	100.0	100.0	100.0	100.0	100.0	100.0
0 to 25.0	42.3	42.3	44.5	29.9	29.8	33.1	23.2	22.9	27.7	17.9	18.0	16.6
25.1 to 50.0	25.6	25.9	11.1	25.0	25.3	11.5	26.9	27.4	17.4	26.6	27.3	18.2
50.1 to 75.0	16.8	16.9	10.2	16.8	16.9	11.1	26.4	26.8	20.1	25.1	25.4	21.5
More than 75.0	11.9	11.9	12.4	12.2	12.2	13.1	21.3	20.7	33.1	25.8	24.9	37.0
Missing/school does not participate	3.3	3.0	21.9	16.2	15.8	31.1	2.2	2.3	1.7	4.6	4.4	6.6
Locale	—	—	—	—	—	—	100.0	100.0	100.0	100.0	100.0	100.0
City	—	—	—	—	—	—	26.2	24.5	55.5	27.2	24.9	56.1
Suburban	—	—	—	—	—	—	27.4	27.8	21.3	31.7	32.1	26.3
Town	—	—	—	—	—	—	14.0	14.4	7.6	13.3	13.9	6.1
Rural	—	—	—	—	—	—	32.3	33.3	15.6	27.8	29.1	11.5
Region	100.0	100.0	100.0	100.0	100.0	100.0	100.0	100.0	100.0	100.0	100.0	100.0
Northeast	16.1	16.3	7.2	16.2	16.3	10.9	15.5	15.9	9.5	15.2	15.6	10.1
Midwest	28.9	29.0	24.9	28.7	28.8	23.3	26.4	26.6	23.1	26.0	26.5	20.6
South	33.1	33.2	28.9	33.1	33.2	27.5	34.7	35.0	29.5	34.8	35.0	32.6
West	21.8	21.6	38.9	22.0	21.6	38.3	23.4	22.5	37.9	23.9	22.9	36.7

—Not available.
[1]The National School Lunch Program (NSLP) is a federally assisted meal program. To be eligible for free lunch under the program, a student must be from a household with an income at or below 130 percent of the poverty threshold; to be eligible for reduced-price lunch, a student must be from a household with an income between 130 percent and 185 percent of the poverty threshold. Data for 2017–18 include students whose NSLP eligibility has been determined through direct certification.
[2]Pupil/teacher ratio based on schools that reported both enrollment and teacher data.
[3]Includes schools beginning with grade 6 or below and with no grade higher than 8.

[4]Includes schools with no grade lower than 7.
[5]Includes schools beginning with grade 6 or below and ending with grade 9 or above.
NOTE: Detail may not sum to totals because of rounding. Race categories exclude persons of Hispanic ethnicity.
SOURCE: U.S. Department of Education, National Center for Education Statistics, Common Core of Data (CCD), "Public Elementary/Secondary School Universe Survey," 1999–2000 through 2017–18; and Education Demographic and Geographic Estimates (EDGE), "Public School File," 2017–18. (This table was prepared January 2020.)

Table 216.40. Number and percentage distribution of public elementary and secondary schools and enrollment, by level, type, and enrollment size of school: 2015–16, 2016–17, and 2017–18

Enrollment size of school	Number and percentage distribution of schools, by level and type						Enrollment totals and percentage distribution, by level and type of school[1]					
			Secondary[4]		Combined elementary/ secondary[5]	Other[6]			Secondary[4]		Combined elementary/ secondary[5]	Other[6]
	Total[2]	Elementary[3]	All schools	Regular schools[7]			Total[2]	Elementary[3]	All schools	Regular schools[7]		
1	2	3	4	5	6	7	8	9	10	11	12	13
2015–16												
Total	98,277	66,758	24,040	19,325	6,788	691	50,115,178	32,035,708	15,748,184	15,296,173	2,329,346	1,940
Percent[8]	100.00	100.00	100.00	100.00	100.00	100.00	100.00	100.00	100.00	100.00	100.00	100.00
Under 100	10.14	5.32	17.94	9.39	33.11	88.89	0.86	0.55	1.07	0.64	3.57	18.87
100 to 199	8.91	7.62	11.04	10.15	15.03	0.00	2.53	2.40	2.32	1.88	5.76	0.00
200 to 299	10.94	11.59	9.28	9.75	10.06	0.00	5.25	6.10	3.31	3.05	6.64	0.00
300 to 399	13.48	15.88	7.84	8.61	8.24	5.56	8.97	11.56	3.92	3.77	7.64	20.26
400 to 499	14.11	17.13	7.15	8.13	7.03	0.00	12.02	15.95	4.58	4.56	8.40	0.00
500 to 599	11.63	14.21	5.71	6.46	5.65	0.00	12.10	16.12	4.48	4.44	8.23	0.00
600 to 699	8.67	10.32	4.85	5.51	4.98	0.00	10.66	13.84	4.51	4.48	8.62	0.00
700 to 799	6.10	7.02	3.96	4.56	4.02	0.00	8.65	10.87	4.24	4.28	7.99	0.00
800 to 999	6.73	6.91	6.69	7.75	4.97	0.00	11.31	12.63	8.55	8.68	11.77	0.00
1,000 to 1,499	5.53	3.67	11.28	13.03	4.53	5.56	12.54	8.79	19.86	20.09	14.44	60.88
1,500 to 1,999	2.05	0.28	7.46	8.71	1.34	0.00	6.72	0.95	18.52	18.93	6.17	0.00
2,000 to 2,999	1.42	0.04	5.72	6.70	0.58	0.00	6.36	0.19	19.30	19.79	3.62	0.00
3,000 or more	0.29	#	1.07	1.25	0.45	0.00	2.03	0.04	5.34	5.41	7.16	0.00
Average enrollment[8]	526	482	698	797	376	108	526	482	698	797	376	108
2016–17												
Total	98,158	66,837	23,814	19,264	6,783	724	50,274,747	32,132,682	15,798,446	15,355,391	2,335,618	8,001
Percent[8]	100.00	100.00	100.00	100.00	100.00	100.00	100.00	100.00	100.00	100.00	100.00	100.00
Under 100	10.02	5.25	17.22	9.38	33.67	81.74	0.85	0.54	1.05	0.64	3.61	48.09
100 to 199	8.93	7.60	11.11	10.06	15.24	14.78	2.54	2.40	2.32	1.87	5.92	28.52
200 to 299	10.95	11.59	9.23	9.60	10.42	1.74	5.24	6.10	3.25	2.98	7.03	5.36
300 to 399	13.68	16.05	8.04	8.80	8.79	0.87	9.09	11.66	3.97	3.84	8.27	3.97
400 to 499	14.12	17.10	7.14	8.02	7.55	0.00	12.00	15.89	4.51	4.47	9.08	0.00
500 to 599	11.57	14.08	5.94	6.70	5.32	0.00	12.01	15.96	4.60	4.58	7.88	0.00
600 to 699	8.62	10.36	4.71	5.32	4.24	0.00	10.58	13.88	4.32	4.31	7.44	0.00
700 to 799	6.03	6.99	3.95	4.50	3.38	0.00	8.54	10.81	4.18	4.20	6.85	0.00
800 to 999	6.72	6.96	6.82	7.86	4.04	0.00	11.28	12.71	8.61	8.76	9.70	0.00
1,000 to 1,499	5.54	3.69	11.33	12.97	4.67	0.87	12.54	8.85	19.69	19.89	15.02	14.05
1,500 to 1,999	2.02	0.28	7.38	8.54	1.40	0.00	6.59	0.98	18.04	18.42	6.40	0.00
2,000 to 2,999	1.49	0.04	6.04	7.01	0.78	0.00	6.66	0.18	20.11	20.62	4.87	0.00
3,000 or more	0.29	0.01	1.08	1.24	0.51	0.00	2.08	0.04	5.35	5.42	7.93	0.00
Average enrollment[8]	528	483	708	802	371	70	528	483	708	802	371	70
2017–18												
Total	98,469	67,408	23,882	19,231	6,278	901	50,330,241	32,346,383	15,811,242	15,374,566	2,164,868	7,748
Percent[8]	100.00	100.00	100.00	100.00	100.00	100.00	100.00	100.00	100.00	100.00	100.00	100.00
Under 100	9.86	5.04	17.40	9.46	34.98	85.25	0.85	0.53	1.07	0.65	3.84	53.41
100 to 199	8.82	7.53	10.96	9.88	15.44	10.66	2.50	2.37	2.28	1.83	6.01	22.73
200 to 299	11.01	11.71	9.17	9.68	10.15	3.28	5.26	6.16	3.21	3.00	6.70	10.74
300 to 399	13.86	16.31	8.13	8.94	7.77	0.00	9.19	11.85	4.01	3.89	7.25	0.00
400 to 499	14.26	17.28	7.29	8.10	6.41	0.00	12.10	16.07	4.60	4.50	7.76	0.00
500 to 599	11.53	14.04	5.66	6.40	5.37	0.00	11.95	15.92	4.37	4.36	7.86	0.00
600 to 699	8.56	10.20	4.73	5.35	4.45	0.00	10.48	13.67	4.32	4.31	7.76	0.00
700 to 799	6.10	7.02	4.13	4.68	3.18	0.00	8.62	10.86	4.36	4.36	6.39	0.00
800 to 999	6.64	6.89	6.53	7.53	4.40	0.00	11.14	12.62	8.22	8.38	10.54	0.00
1,000 to 1,499	5.49	3.61	11.42	13.10	4.59	0.82	12.41	8.67	19.75	19.99	14.79	13.13
1,500 to 1,999	2.07	0.32	7.42	8.57	1.82	0.00	6.76	1.10	18.13	18.48	8.28	0.00
2,000 to 2,999	1.50	0.04	6.04	7.02	0.93	0.00	6.66	0.16	20.10	20.62	5.66	0.00
3,000 or more	0.30	#	1.13	1.30	0.50	0.00	2.08	0.02	5.58	5.63	7.16	0.00
Average enrollment[8]	528	483	709	804	372	64	528	483	709	804	372	64

#Rounds to zero.
[1]Because the data reflect reports by schools, totals differ from those in tables based on reports by states or school districts. Percentage distribution and average enrollment calculations exclude data for schools not reporting enrollment.
[2]Includes elementary, secondary, combined elementary/secondary, and other schools.
[3]Includes schools beginning with grade 6 or below and with no grade higher than 8.
[4]Includes schools with no grade lower than 7.
[5]Includes schools beginning with grade 6 or below and ending with grade 9 or above.
[6]Includes special education, alternative, and other schools not reported by grade span.

[7]Excludes special education schools, vocational schools, and alternative schools.
[8]Data are for schools reporting enrollments greater than zero. Enrollments greater than zero were reported for 95,240 out of 98,277 schools in 2015–16, 95,283 out of 98,158 in 2016–17, and 95,240 out of 98,469 in 2017–18.
NOTE: Detail may not sum to totals because of rounding.
SOURCE: U.S. Department of Education, National Center for Education Statistics, Common Core of Data (CCD), "Public Elementary/Secondary School Universe Survey," 2015–16, 2016–17, and 2017–18. (This table was prepared December 2019.)

Table 216.45. Average enrollment and percentage distribution of public elementary and secondary schools, by level, type, and enrollment size: Selected years, 1982–83 through 2017–18

| | Average enrollment in schools, by level and type | | | | | | Percentage distribution of schools, by enrollment size | | | | | | | |
| | | | Secondary[3] | | Combined elementary/secondary[4] | | | | | | | | | |
Year	Total[1]	Elementary[2]	All schools	Regular schools[6]		Other[5]	Under 200	200 to 299	300 to 399	400 to 499	500 to 599	600 to 699	700 to 999	1,000 or more
1	2	3	4	5	6	7	8	9	10	11	12	13	14	15
1982–83	478	399	719	—	478	142	21.9	13.8	15.5	13.1	10.2	7.1	10.2	8.3
1983–84	480	401	720	—	475	145	21.7	13.7	15.5	13.2	10.2	7.1	10.3	8.3
1984–85	482	403	721	—	476	146	21.5	13.6	15.5	13.2	10.3	7.1	10.4	8.4
1986–87	489	416	707	714	426	118	21.1	13.1	15.0	13.5	10.8	7.5	10.7	8.1
1987–88	490	424	695	711	420	122	20.3	12.9	14.9	13.8	11.1	7.8	11.2	8.0
1988–89	494	433	689	697	412	142	20.0	12.5	14.7	13.8	11.4	8.0	11.6	8.0
1989–90	493	441	669	689	402	142	19.8	12.2	14.5	13.7	11.5	8.3	12.0	7.9
1990–91	497	449	663	684	398	150	19.7	11.9	14.2	13.6	11.7	8.5	12.3	8.1
1991–92	507	458	677	717	407	152	19.1	11.7	14.1	13.5	11.8	8.6	12.8	8.5
1992–93	513	464	688	733	423	135	18.6	11.6	13.9	13.5	11.9	8.7	13.1	8.7
1993–94	518	468	693	748	418	136	18.6	11.5	13.6	13.5	11.7	8.8	13.3	9.0
1994–95	520	471	696	759	412	131	18.6	11.4	13.6	13.4	11.8	8.7	13.3	9.2
1995–96	525	476	703	771	401	136	18.5	11.2	13.5	13.4	11.8	8.8	13.4	9.4
1996–97	527	478	703	777	387	135	18.7	11.3	13.2	13.2	11.8	8.8	13.6	9.5
1997–98	525	478	699	779	374	121	19.3	11.2	13.1	13.3	11.6	8.6	13.4	9.6
1998–99	524	478	707	786	290	135	19.6	11.2	13.1	13.2	11.5	8.5	13.3	9.6
1999–2000	521	477	706	785	282	123	20.0	11.3	13.3	13.2	11.2	8.4	13.1	9.5
2000–01	519	477	714	795	274	136	20.4	11.4	13.2	13.3	11.0	8.2	12.9	9.6
2001–02	520	477	718	807	270	138	20.5	11.5	13.3	13.1	10.9	8.1	12.7	9.7
2002–03	519	476	720	813	265	136	20.7	11.6	13.4	13.0	10.9	8.1	12.4	9.8
2003–04	521	476	722	816	269	142	20.7	11.6	13.5	13.2	10.8	8.0	12.3	9.9
2004–05	521	474	713	815	298	143	20.7	11.6	13.5	13.2	10.8	8.1	12.2	9.9
2005–06	521	473	709	819	318	128	20.7	11.5	13.6	13.2	11.0	8.1	12.2	9.8
2006–07	521	473	711	818	325	138	20.3	11.5	13.8	13.4	11.0	8.2	12.2	9.6
2007–08	516	469	704	816	292	136	20.4	11.5	13.9	13.6	11.1	8.1	12.0	9.3
2008–09	517	470	704	807	308	177	20.0	11.4	13.8	13.9	11.3	8.3	12.2	9.1
2009–10	516	473	692	796	300	191	20.0	11.3	13.7	13.9	11.4	8.5	12.3	9.0
2010–11	517	475	684	790	343	57	19.8	11.0	13.9	13.9	11.5	8.5	12.5	9.0
2011–12	520	479	690	788	322	84	19.4	11.0	13.8	13.9	11.7	8.6	12.7	9.0
2012–13	522	481	689	785	337	84	19.3	10.9	13.6	13.9	11.7	8.6	12.8	9.1
2013–14	525	483	693	788	340	238	19.2	10.9	13.4	13.9	11.8	8.7	13.0	9.1
2014–15	525	483	694	791	354	131	19.2	10.9	13.4	13.9	11.8	8.6	12.9	9.2
2015–16	526	482	698	797	376	108	19.0	10.9	13.5	14.1	11.6	8.7	12.8	9.3
2016–17	528	483	708	802	371	70	19.0	11.0	13.7	14.1	11.6	8.6	12.8	9.3
2017–18	528	483	709	804	372	64	18.7	11.0	13.9	14.3	11.5	8.6	12.7	9.4

—Not available.

[1]Includes elementary, secondary, combined elementary/secondary, and other schools.
[2]Includes schools beginning with grade 6 or below and with no grade higher than 8.
[3]Includes schools with no grade lower than 7.
[4]Includes schools beginning with grade 6 or below and ending with grade 9 or above.
[5]Includes special education, alternative, and other schools not reported by grade span.
[6]Excludes special education schools, vocational schools, and alternative schools.

NOTE: Data reflect reports by schools rather than by states or school districts. Percentage distribution and average enrollment calculations include data only for schools reporting enrollments greater than zero. Enrollments greater than zero were reported for 95,240 out of 98,469 schools in 2017–18. Detail may not sum to totals because of rounding.
SOURCE: U.S. Department of Education, National Center for Education Statistics, Common Core of Data (CCD), "Public Elementary/Secondary School Universe Survey," 1982–83 through 2017–18. (This table was prepared December 2019.)

Table 216.50. Number and percentage distribution of public elementary and secondary school students, by percentage of minority enrollment in the school and student's racial/ethnic group: Selected years, fall 1995 through fall 2017

Year and racial/ethnic group	Number of students in racial/ethnic group, by percent minority enrollment in the school							Percentage distribution of students in racial/ethnic group, by percent minority enrollment in the school						
	Total	Less than 10 percent	10 to 24 percent	25 to 49 percent	50 to 74 percent	75 to 89 percent	90 percent or more	Total	Less than 10 percent	10 to 24 percent	25 to 49 percent	50 to 74 percent	75 to 89 percent	90 percent or more
1	2	3	4	5	6	7	8	9	10	11	12	13	14	15
Total, 1995	44,424,467	14,508,573	8,182,484	8,261,110	5,467,784	2,876,302	5,128,214	100.0	32.7	18.4	18.6	12.3	6.5	11.5
White	28,736,961	13,939,633	6,812,196	5,246,785	2,094,440	499,884	144,023	100.0	48.5	23.7	18.3	7.3	1.7	0.5
Minority	15,687,506	568,940	1,370,288	3,014,325	3,373,344	2,376,418	4,984,191	100.0	3.6	8.7	19.2	21.5	15.1	31.8
Black	7,510,678	198,386	598,716	1,588,850	1,622,448	941,335	2,560,943	100.0	2.6	8.0	21.2	21.6	12.5	34.1
Hispanic	6,016,293	174,140	415,761	932,949	1,289,184	1,099,109	2,105,150	100.0	2.9	6.9	15.5	21.4	18.3	35.0
Asian/Pacific Islander	1,656,787	142,886	259,335	367,888	379,110	297,680	209,888	100.0	8.6	15.7	22.2	22.9	18.0	12.7
American Indian/Alaska Native	503,748	53,528	96,476	124,638	82,602	38,294	108,210	100.0	10.6	19.2	24.7	16.4	7.6	21.5
Total, 2000	46,120,425	12,761,478	8,736,252	8,760,300	6,013,131	3,472,083	6,377,181	100.0	27.7	18.9	19.0	13.0	7.5	13.8
White	28,146,613	12,218,862	7,271,285	5,566,681	2,303,106	596,478	190,201	100.0	43.4	25.8	19.8	8.2	2.1	0.7
Minority	17,973,812	542,616	1,464,967	3,193,619	3,710,025	2,875,605	6,186,980	100.0	3.0	8.2	17.8	20.6	16.0	34.4
Black	7,854,032	178,185	561,488	1,485,130	1,652,393	1,043,907	2,932,929	100.0	2.3	7.1	18.9	21.0	13.3	37.3
Hispanic	7,649,728	181,685	505,612	1,121,809	1,542,982	1,432,639	2,865,001	100.0	2.4	6.6	14.7	20.2	18.7	37.5
Asian/Pacific Islander	1,924,875	132,813	295,437	441,769	423,175	353,395	278,286	100.0	6.9	15.3	23.0	22.0	18.4	14.5
American Indian/Alaska Native	545,177	49,933	102,430	144,911	91,475	45,664	110,764	100.0	9.2	18.8	26.6	16.8	8.4	20.3
Total, 2005	48,584,980	10,711,307	9,283,783	9,865,121	6,839,850	4,149,802	7,735,117	100.0	22.0	19.1	20.3	14.1	8.5	15.9
White	27,742,612	10,208,608	7,720,632	6,259,485	2,604,846	707,603	241,438	100.0	36.8	27.8	22.6	9.4	2.6	0.9
Minority	20,842,368	502,699	1,563,151	3,605,636	4,235,004	3,442,199	7,493,679	100.0	2.4	7.5	17.3	20.3	16.5	36.0
Black	8,366,722	162,455	560,928	1,513,020	1,752,207	1,176,649	3,201,463	100.0	1.9	6.7	18.1	20.9	14.1	38.3
Hispanic	9,638,712	182,039	581,533	1,388,496	1,873,877	1,803,567	3,809,200	100.0	1.9	6.0	14.4	19.4	18.7	39.5
Asian/Pacific Islander	2,242,628	115,084	319,524	543,952	496,515	406,788	360,765	100.0	5.1	14.2	24.3	22.1	18.1	16.1
American Indian/Alaska Native	594,306	43,121	101,166	160,168	112,405	55,195	122,251	100.0	7.3	17.0	27.0	18.9	9.3	20.6
Total, 2010	49,212,031	7,395,549	9,177,649	11,236,328	7,904,340	4,718,126	8,780,039	100.0	15.0	18.6	22.8	16.1	9.6	17.8
White	25,801,021	6,987,898	7,614,557	7,097,284	3,003,599	808,637	289,046	100.0	27.1	29.5	27.5	11.6	3.1	1.1
Minority	23,411,010	407,651	1,563,092	4,139,044	4,900,741	3,909,489	8,490,993	100.0	1.7	6.7	17.7	20.9	16.7	36.3
Black	7,873,809	95,108	415,807	1,335,674	1,697,727	1,236,333	3,093,160	100.0	1.2	5.3	17.0	21.6	15.7	39.3
Hispanic	11,367,157	142,927	583,019	1,654,084	2,238,071	2,063,492	4,685,564	100.0	1.3	5.1	14.6	19.7	18.2	41.2
Asian	2,281,908	63,974	259,910	585,447	552,633	390,731	429,213	100.0	2.8	11.4	25.7	24.2	17.1	18.8
Pacific Islander	169,678	4,958	13,772	27,478	32,241	41,652	49,577	100.0	2.9	8.1	16.2	19.0	24.5	29.2
American Indian/Alaska Native	561,126	26,066	77,990	157,300	116,787	58,476	124,507	100.0	4.6	13.9	28.0	20.8	10.4	22.2
Two or more races	1,157,332	74,618	212,594	379,061	263,282	118,805	108,972	100.0	6.4	18.4	32.8	22.7	10.3	9.4
Total, 2015	50,115,178	5,396,946	8,879,198	11,705,331	9,039,153	5,397,826	9,696,724	100.0	10.8	17.7	23.4	18.0	10.8	19.3
White	24,505,632	5,072,523	7,350,271	7,372,017	3,444,117	927,072	339,632	100.0	20.7	30.0	30.1	14.1	3.8	1.4
Minority	25,609,546	324,423	1,528,927	4,333,314	5,595,036	4,470,754	9,357,092	100.0	1.3	6.0	16.9	21.8	17.5	36.5
Black	7,731,426	57,618	326,861	1,195,388	1,705,877	1,334,427	3,111,255	100.0	0.7	4.2	15.5	22.1	17.3	40.2
Hispanic	12,982,345	121,565	612,478	1,800,949	2,628,585	2,392,367	5,426,401	100.0	0.9	4.7	13.9	20.2	18.4	41.8
Asian	2,504,848	38,098	222,680	606,969	685,774	458,658	492,669	100.0	1.5	8.9	24.2	27.4	18.3	19.7
Pacific Islander	175,646	3,654	13,358	28,769	37,209	36,554	56,102	100.0	2.1	7.6	16.4	21.2	20.8	31.9
American Indian/Alaska Native	504,365	15,229	54,626	136,002	109,499	58,998	130,011	100.0	3.0	10.8	27.0	21.7	11.7	25.8
Two or more races	1,710,916	88,259	298,924	565,237	428,092	189,750	140,654	100.0	5.2	17.5	33.0	25.0	11.1	8.2
Total, 2016	50,274,747	5,022,678	8,774,358	11,786,119	9,298,054	5,573,066	9,820,472	100.0	10.0	17.5	23.4	18.5	11.1	19.5
White	24,237,835	4,718,110	7,259,945	7,417,761	3,541,807	953,713	346,499	100.0	19.5	30.0	30.6	14.6	3.9	1.4
Minority	26,036,912	304,568	1,514,413	4,368,358	5,756,247	4,619,353	9,473,973	100.0	1.2	5.8	16.8	22.1	17.7	36.4
Black	7,698,283	51,649	309,819	1,168,994	1,714,844	1,360,977	3,092,000	100.0	0.7	4.0	15.2	22.3	17.7	40.2
Hispanic	13,262,558	114,844	615,713	1,823,154	2,708,043	2,475,126	5,525,678	100.0	0.9	4.6	13.7	20.4	18.7	41.7
Asian	2,560,906	32,890	213,564	612,963	720,640	472,524	508,325	100.0	1.3	8.3	23.9	28.1	18.5	19.8
Pacific Islander	183,415	3,708	13,567	29,378	38,580	38,780	59,402	100.0	2.0	7.4	16.0	21.0	21.1	32.4
American Indian/Alaska Native	502,152	13,441	51,288	133,381	108,048	62,795	133,199	100.0	2.7	10.2	26.6	21.5	12.5	26.5
Two or more races	1,829,598	88,036	310,462	600,488	466,092	209,151	155,369	100.0	4.8	17.0	32.8	25.5	11.4	8.5
Total, 2017	50,330,241	4,721,887	8,591,274	11,880,887	9,541,134	5,696,069	9,898,990	100.0	9.4	17.1	23.6	19.0	11.3	19.7
White	23,976,394	4,432,804	7,106,209	7,478,286	3,630,789	975,815	352,491	100.0	18.5	29.6	31.2	15.1	4.1	1.5
Minority	26,353,847	289,083	1,485,065	4,402,601	5,910,345	4,720,254	9,546,499	100.0	1.1	5.6	16.7	22.4	17.9	36.2
Black	7,657,704	46,803	293,409	1,147,199	1,724,050	1,371,883	3,074,360	100.0	0.6	3.8	15.0	22.5	17.9	40.1
Hispanic	13,461,088	110,151	609,252	1,850,857	2,772,521	2,519,689	5,598,618	100.0	0.8	4.5	13.7	20.6	18.7	41.6
Asian	2,619,963	29,465	200,698	615,105	756,748	499,451	518,496	100.0	1.1	7.7	23.5	28.9	19.1	19.8
Pacific Islander	183,919	3,479	13,333	29,568	39,929	39,258	58,352	100.0	1.9	7.2	16.1	21.7	21.3	31.7
American Indian/Alaska Native	490,714	11,993	47,979	129,037	108,045	63,294	130,366	100.0	2.4	9.8	26.3	22.0	12.9	26.6
Two or more races	1,940,459	87,192	320,394	630,835	509,052	226,679	166,307	100.0	4.5	16.5	32.5	26.2	11.7	8.6

NOTE: Data reflect racial/ethnic data reported by schools. Because some schools do not report complete racial/ethnic data, totals may differ from figures in other tables. Excludes 1995 data for Idaho and 2000 data for Tennessee because racial/ethnic data were not reported. Race categories exclude persons of Hispanic ethnicity. Detail may not sum to totals because of rounding.

SOURCE: U.S. Department of Education, National Center for Education Statistics, Common Core of Data (CCD), "Public Elementary/Secondary School Universe Survey," 1995–96 through 2017–18. (This table was prepared December 2019.)

Table 216.55. Number and percentage distribution of public elementary and secondary school students, by percentage of student's racial/ethnic group enrolled in the school and student's racial/ethnic group: Selected years, fall 1995 through fall 2017

Year and racial/ethnic group	Number of students in each racial/ethnic group, by percent of that racial/ethnic group in the school							Percentage distribution of students in each racial/ethnic group, by percent of that racial/ethnic group in the school						
	Total	Less than 10 percent	10 to 24 percent	25 to 49 percent	50 to 74 percent	75 to 89 percent	90 percent or more	Total	Less than 10 percent	10 to 24 percent	25 to 49 percent	50 to 74 percent	75 to 89 percent	90 percent or more
1	2	3	4	5	6	7	8	9	10	11	12	13	14	15
1995														
White	28,736,961	143,787	498,649	2,084,689	5,244,015	6,813,804	13,952,017	100.0	0.5	1.7	7.3	18.2	23.7	48.6
Black	7,510,678	657,403	1,119,556	1,873,303	1,386,802	811,898	1,661,716	100.0	8.8	14.9	24.9	18.5	10.8	22.1
Hispanic	6,016,293	646,364	847,792	1,359,649	1,360,020	874,878	927,590	100.0	10.7	14.1	22.6	22.6	14.5	15.4
Asian/Pacific Islander	1,656,787	703,101	435,495	301,984	135,001	67,558	13,648	100.0	42.4	26.3	18.2	8.1	4.1	0.8
American Indian/Alaska Native	503,748	223,244	75,019	63,070	39,200	15,084	88,131	100.0	44.3	14.9	12.5	7.8	3.0	17.5
2000														
White	28,146,613	189,779	595,137	2,294,232	5,556,108	7,279,301	12,232,056	100.0	0.7	2.1	8.2	19.7	25.9	43.5
Black	7,854,032	735,459	1,199,865	1,899,982	1,366,363	871,399	1,780,964	100.0	9.4	15.3	24.2	17.4	11.1	22.7
Hispanic	7,649,728	738,509	1,054,396	1,696,944	1,739,038	1,134,466	1,286,375	100.0	9.7	13.8	22.2	22.7	14.8	16.8
Asian/Pacific Islander	1,924,875	799,220	524,279	331,576	171,739	81,461	16,600	100.0	41.5	27.2	17.2	8.9	4.2	0.9
American Indian/Alaska Native	545,177	251,983	81,119	75,831	39,944	15,363	80,937	100.0	46.2	14.9	13.9	7.3	2.8	14.8
2005														
White	27,742,612	240,614	705,300	2,596,310	6,256,109	7,718,175	10,226,104	100.0	0.9	2.5	9.4	22.6	27.8	36.9
Black	8,366,722	849,399	1,396,670	2,004,856	1,453,759	884,663	1,777,375	100.0	10.2	16.7	24.0	17.4	10.6	21.2
Hispanic	9,638,712	848,160	1,316,558	2,071,303	2,218,616	1,545,322	1,638,753	100.0	8.8	13.7	21.5	23.0	16.0	17.0
Asian/Pacific Islander	2,242,628	925,411	616,762	363,562	214,304	100,845	21,744	100.0	41.3	27.5	16.2	9.6	4.5	1.0
American Indian/Alaska Native	594,306	276,846	86,978	84,665	43,272	21,275	81,270	100.0	46.6	14.6	14.2	7.3	3.6	13.7
2010														
White	25,801,021	288,136	807,107	2,991,928	7,090,581	7,620,071	7,003,198	100.0	1.1	3.1	11.6	27.5	29.5	27.1
Black	7,873,809	904,777	1,453,068	1,907,158	1,328,164	859,843	1,420,799	100.0	11.5	18.5	24.2	16.9	10.9	18.0
Hispanic	11,367,157	896,796	1,603,546	2,473,080	2,657,108	1,791,161	1,945,466	100.0	7.9	14.1	21.8	23.4	15.8	17.1
Asian	2,281,908	944,657	633,149	431,446	219,381	43,509	9,766	100.0	41.4	27.7	18.9	9.6	1.9	0.4
Pacific Islander	169,678	104,646	15,170	27,558	14,860	5,146	2,298	100.0	61.7	8.9	16.2	8.8	3.0	1.4
American Indian/Alaska Native	561,126	276,859	76,874	78,978	38,349	21,156	68,910	100.0	49.3	13.7	14.1	6.8	3.8	12.3
Two or more races	1,157,332	996,181	128,813	15,347	6,709	3,286	6,996	100.0	86.1	11.1	1.3	0.6	0.3	0.6
2015														
White	24,505,632	338,854	925,174	3,433,953	7,370,748	7,349,746	5,087,157	100.0	1.4	3.8	14.0	30.1	30.0	20.8
Black	7,731,426	926,749	1,501,089	1,921,738	1,359,513	867,967	1,154,370	100.0	12.0	19.4	24.9	17.6	11.2	14.9
Hispanic	12,982,345	917,357	1,853,764	2,853,336	3,113,283	2,063,469	2,181,136	100.0	7.1	14.3	22.0	24.0	15.9	16.8
Asian	2,504,848	958,423	688,104	525,789	264,939	51,494	16,099	100.0	38.3	27.5	21.0	10.6	2.1	0.6
Pacific Islander	175,646	115,753	16,543	26,626	12,225	4,398	101	100.0	65.9	9.4	15.2	7.0	2.5	0.1
American Indian/Alaska Native	504,365	244,771	70,672	70,002	31,830	20,554	66,536	100.0	48.5	14.0	13.9	6.3	4.1	13.2
Two or more races	1,710,916	1,441,131	257,234	9,985	1,644	915	7	100.0	84.2	15.0	0.6	0.1	0.1	#
2016														
White	24,237,835	345,391	951,004	3,526,424	7,414,830	7,269,692	4,730,494	100.0	1.4	3.9	14.5	30.6	30.0	19.5
Black	7,698,283	934,011	1,525,821	1,918,536	1,370,443	847,520	1,101,952	100.0	12.1	19.8	24.9	17.8	11.0	14.3
Hispanic	13,262,558	915,163	1,908,509	2,959,009	3,184,219	2,112,281	2,183,377	100.0	6.9	14.4	22.3	24.0	15.9	16.5
Asian	2,560,906	957,860	699,521	554,255	277,419	56,823	15,028	100.0	37.4	27.3	21.6	10.8	2.2	0.6
Pacific Islander	183,415	124,482	18,105	25,524	12,050	3,142	112	100.0	67.9	9.9	13.9	6.6	1.7	0.1
American Indian/Alaska Native	502,152	243,356	69,973	70,719	32,069	21,969	64,066	100.0	48.5	13.9	14.1	6.4	4.4	12.8
Two or more races	1,829,598	1,510,009	301,306	15,955	808	1,074	446	100.0	82.5	16.5	0.9	0.0	0.1	#
2017														
White	23,976,394	351,591	972,907	3,617,008	7,478,175	7,104,442	4,452,271	100.0	1.5	4.1	15.1	31.2	29.6	18.6
Black	7,657,704	937,456	1,540,064	1,930,181	1,347,953	841,625	1,060,425	100.0	12.2	20.1	25.2	17.6	11.0	13.8
Hispanic	13,461,088	909,319	1,958,390	3,020,258	3,251,806	2,108,336	2,212,979	100.0	6.8	14.5	22.4	24.2	15.7	16.4
Asian	2,619,963	960,701	714,338	574,139	292,198	64,730	13,857	100.0	36.7	27.3	21.9	11.2	2.5	0.5
Pacific Islander	183,919	127,122	18,381	23,397	11,678	3,237	104	100.0	69.1	10.0	12.7	6.3	1.8	0.1
American Indian/Alaska Native	490,714	239,389	68,775	65,205	32,948	20,172	64,225	100.0	48.8	14.0	13.3	6.7	4.1	13.1
Two or more races	1,940,459	1,573,163	343,041	21,498	2,752	0	5	100.0	81.1	17.7	1.1	0.1	0.0	#

#Rounds to zero.
NOTE: Data reflect racial/ethnic data reported by schools. Because some schools do not report complete racial/ethnic data, totals may differ from figures in other tables. Excludes 1995 data for Idaho and 2000 data for Tennessee because racial/ethnic data were not reported. Race categories exclude persons of Hispanic ethnicity. Detail may not sum to totals because of rounding.

SOURCE: U.S. Department of Education, National Center for Education Statistics, Common Core of Data (CCD), "Public Elementary/Secondary School Universe Survey," 1995–96 through 2017–18. (This table was prepared December 2019.)

Table 216.60. Number and percentage distribution of public school students, by percentage of students in school who are eligible for free or reduced-price lunch, school level, locale, and student race/ethnicity: Fall 2017

School level, locale, and student race/ethnicity	Number of students, by percent of students in school eligible for free or reduced-price lunch						Percentage distribution of students, by percent of students in school eligible for free or reduced-price lunch					
	Total	0 to 25.0 percent	25.1 to 50.0 percent	50.1 to 75.0 percent	More than 75.0 percent	Missing/ school does not participate	Total	0 to 25.0 percent	25.1 to 50.0 percent	50.1 to 75.0 percent	More than 75.0 percent	Missing/ school does not participate
1	2	3	4	5	6	7	8	9	10	11	12	13
Total	50,330,241	10,575,788	14,236,362	12,740,656	12,491,910	285,525	100.0	21.0	28.3	25.3	24.8	0.6
White	23,976,394	7,378,741	8,876,623	5,520,817	2,033,096	167,117	100.0	30.8	37.0	23.0	8.5	0.7
Black	7,657,704	567,654	1,438,606	2,159,919	3,457,276	34,249	100.0	7.4	18.8	28.2	45.1	0.4
Hispanic	13,461,088	1,097,002	2,476,376	3,839,382	5,996,254	52,074	100.0	8.1	18.4	28.5	44.5	0.4
Asian	2,619,963	1,013,918	673,157	513,707	403,943	15,238	100.0	38.7	25.7	19.6	15.4	0.6
Pacific Islander	183,919	22,183	51,720	64,784	44,348	884	100.0	12.1	28.1	35.2	24.1	0.5
American Indian/Alaska Native	490,714	40,556	109,998	133,764	202,716	·3,680	100.0	8.3	22.4	27.3	41.3	0.7
Two or more races	1,940,459	455,734	609,882	508,283	354,277	12,283	100.0	23.5	31.4	26.2	18.3	0.6
School level[1]												
Elementary[2]	32,346,383	6,398,292	8,262,515	8,264,994	9,310,792	109,790	100.0	19.8	25.5	25.6	28.8	0.3
White	15,070,919	4,407,423	5,213,146	3,813,266	1,577,427	59,657	100.0	29.2	34.6	25.3	10.5	0.4
Black	4,976,996	310,931	786,604	1,308,539	2,554,563	16,359	100.0	6.2	15.8	26.3	51.3	0.3
Hispanic	8,847,659	663,432	1,401,848	2,335,243	4,426,259	20,877	100.0	7.5	15.8	26.4	50.0	0.2
Asian	1,672,851	674,378	384,908	315,435	291,864	6,266	100.0	40.3	23.0	18.9	17.4	0.4
Pacific Islander	113,715	12,792	26,892	40,366	33,319	346	100.0	11.2	23.6	35.5	29.3	0.3
American Indian/Alaska Native	304,152	21,452	56,800	84,578	140,243	1,079	100.0	7.1	18.7	27.8	46.1	0.4
Two or more races	1,360,091	307,884	392,317	367,567	287,117	5,206	100.0	22.6	28.8	27.0	21.1	0.4
Secondary[3]	15,811,242	3,802,293	5,429,067	3,891,915	2,618,320	69,647	100.0	24.0	34.3	24.6	16.6	0.4
White	7,867,081	2,715,719	3,325,684	1,418,598	363,107	43,973	100.0	34.5	42.3	18.0	4.6	0.6
Black	2,290,686	224,518	596,962	746,768	716,801	5,637	100.0	9.8	26.1	32.6	31.3	0.2
Hispanic	4,066,826	389,982	972,105	1,357,831	1,333,044	13,864	100.0	9.6	23.9	33.4	32.8	0.3
Asian	872,396	318,616	268,325	184,948	97,431	3,076	100.0	36.5	30.8	21.2	11.2	0.4
Pacific Islander	61,639	8,218	23,022	21,584	8,667	148	100.0	13.3	37.3	35.0	14.1	0.2
American Indian/Alaska Native	152,289	15,752	49,246	40,594	45,267	1,115	100.0	10.3	32.3	26.9	29.7	0.7
Two or more races	500,325	129,488	193,723	121,277	54,003	1,834	100.0	25.9	38.7	24.2	10.8	0.4
School locale												
City	15,282,104	1,877,136	3,169,673	3,735,112	6,408,206	91,977	100.0	12.3	20.7	24.4	41.9	0.6
White	4,335,254	1,081,252	1,492,990	1,049,836	671,185	39,991	100.0	24.9	34.4	24.2	15.5	0.9
Black	3,504,501	143,097	479,468	861,979	2,003,035	16,922	100.0	4.1	13.7	24.6	57.2	0.5
Hispanic	5,591,844	250,427	748,011	1,362,064	3,206,857	24,485	100.0	4.5	13.4	24.4	57.3	0.4
Asian	1,066,561	278,047	248,414	252,068	283,292	4,740	100.0	26.1	23.3	23.6	26.6	0.4
Pacific Islander	66,516	5,666	15,017	21,965	23,587	281	100.0	8.5	22.6	33.0	35.5	0.4
American Indian/Alaska Native	104,866	8,458	23,341	27,386	44,305	1,376	100.0	8.1	22.3	26.1	42.2	1.3
Two or more races	612,562	110,189	162,432	159,814	175,945	4,182	100.0	18.0	26.5	26.1	28.7	0.7
Suburban	19,928,348	6,364,619	5,651,985	4,301,976	3,491,758	118,010	100.0	31.9	28.4	21.6	17.5	0.6
White	9,541,064	4,421,808	3,174,211	1,411,315	460,394	73,336	100.0	46.3	33.3	14.8	4.8	0.8
Black	2,721,131	330,255	655,582	860,948	860,778	13,568	100.0	12.1	24.1	31.6	31.6	0.5
Hispanic	5,376,104	662,692	1,152,655	1,593,642	1,950,577	16,538	100.0	12.3	21.4	29.6	36.3	0.3
Asian	1,316,933	648,967	350,005	211,562	97,703	8,696	100.0	49.3	26.6	16.1	7.4	0.7
Pacific Islander	73,645	13,177	23,422	23,780	12,898	368	100.0	17.9	31.8	32.3	17.5	0.5
American Indian/Alaska Native	83,531	17,259	28,067	22,436	15,059	710	100.0	20.7	33.6	26.9	18.0	0.8
Two or more races	815,940	270,461	268,043	178,293	94,349	4,794	100.0	33.1	32.9	21.9	11.6	0.6
Town	5,522,279	509,799	1,903,810	1,941,965	1,135,097	31,608	100.0	9.2	34.5	35.2	20.6	0.6
White	3,456,185	422,645	1,473,381	1,189,836	347,423	22,900	100.0	12.2	42.6	34.4	10.1	0.7
Black	536,796	15,348	87,609	171,478	260,459	1,902	100.0	2.9	16.3	31.9	48.5	0.4
Hispanic	1,117,990	40,363	216,053	434,378	423,008	4,188	100.0	3.6	19.3	38.9	37.8	0.4
Asian	71,937	9,416	26,307	23,453	12,359	402	100.0	13.1	36.6	32.6	17.2	0.6
Pacific Islander	23,123	834	7,401	10,652	4,163	73	100.0	3.6	32.0	46.1	18.0	0.3
American Indian/Alaska Native	114,712	5,004	26,386	34,621	48,021	680	100.0	4.4	23.0	30.2	41.9	0.6
Two or more races	201,536	16,189	66,673	77,547	39,664	1,463	100.0	8.0	33.1	38.5	19.7	0.7
Rural	9,597,510	1,824,234	3,510,894	2,761,603	1,456,849	43,930	100.0	19.0	36.6	28.8	15.2	0.5
White	6,643,891	1,453,036	2,736,041	1,869,830	554,094	30,890	100.0	21.9	41.2	28.1	8.3	0.5
Black	895,276	78,954	215,947	265,514	333,004	1,857	100.0	8.8	24.1	29.7	37.2	0.2
Hispanic	1,375,150	143,520	359,657	449,298	415,812	6,863	100.0	10.4	26.2	32.7	30.2	0.5
Asian	164,532	77,488	48,431	26,624	10,589	1,400	100.0	47.1	29.4	16.2	6.4	0.9
Pacific Islander	20,635	2,506	5,880	8,387	3,700	162	100.0	12.1	28.5	40.6	17.9	0.8
American Indian/Alaska Native	187,605	9,835	32,204	49,321	95,331	914	100.0	5.2	17.2	26.3	50.8	0.5
Two or more races	310,421	58,895	112,734	92,629	44,319	1,844	100.0	19.0	36.3	29.8	14.3	0.6

[1]Combined elementary/secondary schools and schools not reported by grade span are not shown separately.
[2]Includes schools beginning with grade 6 or below and with no grade higher than 8.
[3]Includes schools with no grade lower than 7.
NOTE: Students with household incomes under 185 percent of the poverty threshold are eligible for free or reduced-price lunch under the National School Lunch Program (NSLP). In addition, some groups of children—such as foster children, children participating in the Head Start and Migrant Education programs, and children receiving services under the Runaway and Homeless Youth Act—are assumed to be categorically eligible to participate in the NSLP. Data include students whose NSLP eligibility has been determined through direct certification. Also, under the Community Eligibility option, some nonpoor children who attend school in a low-income area may participate if the district decides that it would be more efficient to provide free lunch to all children in the school. For more information, see https://www.fns.usda.gov/nslp. Race categories exclude persons of Hispanic ethnicity. Detail may not sum to totals because of rounding.
SOURCE: U.S. Department of Education, National Center for Education Statistics, Common Core of Data (CCD), "Public Elementary/Secondary School Universe Survey," 2017–18; and Education Demographic and Geographic Estimates (EDGE), "Public School File," 2017–18. (This table was prepared November 2019.)

Table 216.70. Public elementary and secondary schools, by level, type, and state or jurisdiction: 1990–91, 2000–01, 2010–11, and 2017–18

State or jurisdiction	Total, all schools, 1990–91	Total, all schools, 2000–01	Total, all schools, 2010–11	Schools by level, 2017–18								Selected types of schools, 2017–18		
				Total, all schools	Elementary[1]	Secondary[2]	Combined elementary/secondary[3]				Other[4]	Alternative[5]	Special education[5]	One-teacher schools[5]
							Total	Prekindergarten, kindergarten, or grade 1 to grade 12	Other schools ending with grade 12	Other combined schools				
1	2	3	4	5	6	7	8	9	10	11	12	13	14	15
United States	84,538	93,273	98,817	98,469	67,408	23,882	6,278	3,267	2,509	502	901	5,185	1,903	188
Alabama	1,297	1,517	1,600	1,474	922	399	149	96	49	4	4	63	23	0
Alaska	498	515	509	509	198	79	232	216	15	1	0	22	3	4
Arizona	1,049	1,724	2,265	2,330	1,391	762	162	89	58	15	15	59	20	4
Arkansas	1,098	1,138	1,110	1,086	689	373	23	8	10	5	1	5	4	0
California	7,913	8,773	10,124	10,319	7,028	2,488	651	503	139	9	152	1,075	155	34
Colorado	1,344	1,632	1,796	1,900	1,337	396	167	78	82	7	0	97	6	0
Connecticut	985	1,248	1,157	1,031	784	222	23	10	12	1	2	5	6	0
Delaware	173	191	214	227	165	38	19	11	5	3	5	6	19	0
District of Columbia	181	198	228	224	177	37	10	1	7	2	0	4	2	0
Florida	2,516	3,316	4,131	4,322	2,843	679	662	288	356	18	138	388	163	0
Georgia	1,734	1,946	2,449	2,307	1,775	457	68	17	38	13	7	39	19	0
Hawaii	235	261	289	292	212	53	27	22	3	2	0	1	1	0
Idaho	582	673	748	741	466	189	86	44	41	1	0	72	11	11
Illinois	4,239	4,342	4,361	4,241	3,086	989	73	19	49	5	93	144	113	1
Indiana	1,915	1,976	1,936	1,920	1,370	458	92	49	37	6	0	8	22	0
Iowa	1,588	1,534	1,436	1,322	935	348	39	4	35	0	0	17	3	1
Kansas	1,477	1,430	1,378	1,319	917	342	57	21	36	0	3	1	4	0
Kentucky	1,400	1,526	1,554	1,533	966	423	142	44	93	5	2	184	8	0
Louisiana	1,533	1,530	1,471	1,390	959	281	150	99	44	7	0	5	30	0
Maine	747	714	631	599	439	145	15	9	6	0	0	0	1	2
Maryland	1,220	1,383	1,449	1,420	1,120	240	48	19	23	6	12	44	37	0
Massachusetts	1,842	1,905	1,829	1,854	1,413	372	61	20	34	7	8	22	11	0
Michigan	3,313	3,998	3,877	3,730	2,272	959	453	257	188	8	46	378	269	5
Minnesota	1,590	2,362	2,392	2,525	1,379	851	292	140	140	12	3	493	314	0
Mississippi	972	1,030	1,083	1,060	614	329	44	36	7	1	73	67	0	0
Missouri	2,199	2,368	2,410	2,414	1,611	628	155	74	81	0	20	59	52	0
Montana	900	879	827	820	496	324	0	0	0	0	0	4	2	60
Nebraska	1,506	1,326	1,096	1,095	731	305	12	11	0	1	47	47	27	4
Nevada	354	511	645	691	513	127	50	17	28	5	1	32	14	14
New Hampshire	439	526	480	490	382	108	0	0	0	0	0	0	0	0
New Jersey	2,272	2,410	2,607	2,594	1,952	539	82	45	26	11	21	89	65	0
New Mexico	681	765	862	881	600	229	33	13	17	3	19	41	5	0
New York	4,010	4,336	4,757	4,795	3,286	1,121	385	175	154	56	3	53	133	0
North Carolina	1,955	2,207	2,567	2,647	1,939	553	155	73	63	19	0	73	25	0
North Dakota	663	579	516	516	305	178	0	0	0	0	33	0	32	7
Ohio	3,731	3,916	3,758	3,604	2,430	989	148	42	69	37	37	0	47	0
Oklahoma	1,880	1,821	1,785	1,800	1,234	564	2	1	1	0	0	5	4	0
Oregon	1,199	1,273	1,296	1,249	890	274	85	57	24	4	0	35	1	13
Pennsylvania	3,260	3,252	3,233	2,982	2,102	783	97	47	40	10	0	6	4	0
Rhode Island	309	328	317	317	241	70	6	5	1	0	0	2	1	0
South Carolina	1,097	1,127	1,214	1,255	933	282	40	13	22	5	0	12	7	0
South Dakota	802	769	710	697	442	240	15	8	7	0	0	30	12	12
Tennessee	1,543	1,624	1,784	1,782	1,351	351	80	30	40	10	0	19	16	0
Texas	5,991	7,519	8,732	8,905	6,156	2,076	673	274	242	157	0	874	12	0
Utah	714	793	1,016	1,051	688	282	81	42	10	29	0	29	59	0
Vermont	397	393	320	311	228	65	18	11	7	0	0	1	0	1
Virginia	1,811	1,969	2,175	2,113	1,490	436	35	25	10	0	152	125	33	0
Washington	1,936	2,305	2,338	2,425	1,583	625	217	135	71	11	0	312	89	3
West Virginia	1,015	840	757	730	544	155	31	11	19	1	0	33	3	0
Wisconsin	2,018	2,182	2,238	2,261	1,577	568	112	45	64	3	4	95	13	2
Wyoming	415	393	360	369	247	101	21	13	6	2	0	10	3	10
Jurisdiction														
Bureau of Indian Education	—	189	173	174	111	19	44	37	5	2	0	0	0	0
DoDEA[6]	—	227	191	—	—	—	—	—	—	—	—	—	—	—
Other jurisdictions														
American Samoa	30	31	28	28	22	6	0	0	0	0	0	0	0	0
Guam	35	38	40	—	—	—	—	—	—	—	—	—	—	—
Northern Marianas	26	29	30	41	34	7	0	0	0	0	0	1	0	—
Puerto Rico	1,619	1,543	1,473	1,121	855	182	60	7	26	27	24	0	17	0
U.S. Virgin Islands	33	36	32	28	19	9	0	0	0	0	0	0	0	0

—Not available.
[1]Includes schools beginning with grade 6 or below and with no grade higher than 8.
[2]Includes schools with no grade lower than 7.
[3]Includes schools beginning with grade 6 or below and ending with grade 9 or above.
[4]Includes schools not reported by grade span.
[5]Schools are also included under elementary, secondary, combined, or other as appropriate.

[6]DoDEA = Department of Defense Education Activity. Includes both domestic and overseas schools.
SOURCE: U.S. Department of Education, National Center for Education Statistics, Common Core of Data (CCD), "Public Elementary/Secondary School Universe Survey," 1990–91, 2000–01, 2010–11, and 2017–18. (This table was prepared December 2019.)

Table 216.75. Public elementary schools, by grade span, average school enrollment, and state or jurisdiction: 2017–18

State or jurisdiction	Total, all elementary schools	Total, all regular elementary schools[1]	Schools, by grade span						Average school enrollment[2]	
			Prekindergarten, kindergarten, or grade 1 to grade 3 or 4	Prekindergarten, kindergarten, or grade 1 to grade 5	Prekindergarten, kindergarten, or grade 1 to grade 6	Prekindergarten, kindergarten, or grade 1 to grade 8	Grade 4, 5, or 6 to grade 6, 7, or 8	Other grade spans	All elementary schools	Regular elementary schools[1]
1	2	3	4	5	6	7	8	9	10	11
United States	67,408	66,436	4,985	25,906	9,470	6,826	13,437	6,784	483	487
Alabama	922	913	95	288	140	62	215	122	498	500
Alaska	198	198	0	42	96	22	25	13	335	335
Arizona	1,391	1,374	48	236	376	484	174	73	505	507
Arkansas	689	687	129	142	154	7	153	104	450	452
California	7,028	6,882	118	2,569	2,043	1,068	1,057	173	545	553
Colorado	1,337	1,332	26	641	188	137	246	99	434	435
Connecticut	784	779	87	270	67	104	155	101	425	427
Delaware	165	156	14	83	4	7	38	19	538	553
District of Columbia	177	177	21	73	1	33	33	16	369	369
Florida	2,843	2,786	31	1,656	123	338	568	127	670	682
Georgia	1,775	1,774	36	1,060	22	42	464	151	684	684
Hawaii	212	212	0	87	85	10	28	2	534	534
Idaho	466	454	34	163	126	33	86	24	393	402
Illinois	3,086	3,058	283	774	285	660	580	504	426	429
Indiana	1,370	1,367	167	469	294	44	267	129	476	477
Iowa	935	934	112	322	137	10	226	128	355	355
Kansas	917	915	67	371	180	51	190	58	350	350
Kentucky	966	954	31	466	104	76	194	95	476	481
Louisiana	959	958	79	307	108	133	201	131	474	474
Maine	439	439	46	96	55	90	77	75	269	269
Maryland	1,120	1,107	11	685	51	102	222	49	558	563
Massachusetts	1,413	1,408	178	486	115	103	285	246	435	435
Michigan	2,272	2,175	218	760	185	246	453	410	421	424
Minnesota	1,379	1,201	115	433	238	80	274	239	427	468
Mississippi	614	614	69	140	87	40	153	125	495	495
Missouri	1,611	1,603	143	517	294	115	322	220	372	373
Montana	496	493	17	76	185	110	74	34	193	194
Nebraska	731	727	46	198	239	19	110	119	298	298
Nevada	513	504	11	283	72	32	98	17	633	643
New Hampshire	382	382	51	113	37	54	83	44	313	313
New Jersey	1,952	1,932	263	555	133	287	369	345	456	460
New Mexico	600	596	20	250	109	33	130	58	361	363
New York	3,286	3,262	287	1,293	343	292	716	355	514	516
North Carolina	1,939	1,927	77	1,100	53	141	468	100	527	530
North Dakota	305	305	13	88	95	67	33	9	247	247
Ohio	2,430	2,408	351	608	328	229	529	385	437	440
Oklahoma	1,234	1,230	82	308	157	275	257	155	387	387
Oregon	890	887	27	411	113	127	178	34	416	416
Pennsylvania	2,102	2,102	298	671	312	191	424	206	494	494
Rhode Island	241	240	35	103	17	3	50	33	391	392
South Carolina	933	931	45	479	33	49	230	97	567	568
South Dakota	442	432	29	128	57	95	107	26	218	220
Tennessee	1,351	1,342	179	528	48	180	327	89	504	506
Texas	6,156	6,047	607	2,933	430	149	1,381	656	570	577
Utah	688	651	5	124	433	33	45	48	541	562
Vermont	228	228	15	24	97	63	17	12	243	243
Virginia	1,490	1,490	40	845	148	11	311	135	578	578
Washington	1,583	1,504	62	736	248	84	315	138	457	473
West Virginia	544	543	70	251	28	39	113	43	349	350
Wisconsin	1,577	1,570	171	601	125	148	340	192	359	360
Wyoming	247	246	26	64	72	18	46	21	242	242
Jurisdiction										
Bureau of Indian Education	111	111	7	6	28	62	4	4	212	212
DoDEA[3]	—	—	—	—	—	—	—	—	—	—
Other jurisdictions										
American Samoa	22	22	0	0	0	22	0	0	349	349
Guam	34	34	0	24	0	0	8	2	595	595
Northern Marianas	—	—	—	—	—	—	—	—	—	—
Puerto Rico	855	854	10	449	79	183	125	9	263	263
U.S. Virgin Islands	19	19	1	1	14	1	2	0	326	326

—Not available.
[1]Excludes special education and alternative schools.
[2]Average for schools reporting enrollment data. Enrollment data were available for 67,010 out of 67,408 public elementary schools in 2017–18.
[3]DoDEA = Department of Defense Education Activity. Includes both domestic and overseas schools.

NOTE: Includes schools beginning with grade 6 or below and with no grade higher than 8. Excludes schools not reported by grade level, such as some special education schools for students with disabilities.
SOURCE: U.S. Department of Education, National Center for Education Statistics, Common Core of Data (CCD), "Public Elementary/Secondary School Universe Survey," 2017–18. (This table was prepared December 2019.)

Table 216.80. Public secondary schools, by grade span, average school enrollment, and state or jurisdiction: 2017–18

State or jurisdiction	Total, all secondary schools	Total, all regular secondary schools[1]	Schools, by grade span							Vocational schools[2]	Average school enrollment[3]	
			Grades 7 and 8 or grades 7 to 9	Grades 7 to 12	Grades 8 to 12	Grades 9 to 12	Grades 10 to 12	Other spans ending with grade 12	Other grade spans		All secondary schools	Regular secondary schools[1]
1	2	3	4	5	6	7	8	9	10	11	12	13
United States	23,882	19,231	2,479	2,864	526	16,119	558	401	935	1,467	709	804
Alabama	399	317	40	68	10	245	28	1	7	65	702	712
Alaska	79	62	12	19	2	41	2	2	1	3	448	525
Arizona	762	473	54	78	25	575	12	3	15	260	654	732
Arkansas	373	344	50	117	10	136	36	1	23	24	514	520
California	2,488	1,657	354	269	13	1,752	67	23	10	66	878	1,215
Colorado	396	336	35	42	2	299	4	2	12	7	669	748
Connecticut	222	201	29	4	3	182	2	2	0	17	772	798
Delaware	38	32	1	1	9	25	0	0	2	6	996	961
District of Columbia	37	33	0	0	2	33	0	0	2	0	429	462
Florida	679	508	18	32	28	558	6	20	17	50	1,293	1,585
Georgia	457	427	15	7	11	388	5	0	31	0	1,131	1,206
Hawaii	53	52	12	7	0	33	0	0	1	0	1,105	1,125
Idaho	189	142	26	33	1	124	5	0	0	6	526	653
Illinois	989	855	125	55	8	647	34	70	50	0	671	767
Indiana	458	436	72	74	8	275	11	8	10	28	818	827
Iowa	348	332	33	68	1	229	10	0	7	0	466	484
Kansas	342	339	34	96	3	207	1	1	0	0	456	459
Kentucky	423	236	26	35	6	227	5	5	119	122	684	858
Louisiana	281	260	28	39	54	141	12	0	7	11	730	759
Maine	145	117	8	17	1	92	0	0	27	27	459	463
Maryland	240	184	4	5	3	201	2	7	18	25	1,120	1,309
Massachusetts	372	318	28	36	13	283	5	6	1	37	810	830
Michigan	959	629	54	99	44	702	24	31	5	57	540	696
Minnesota	851	435	28	274	34	432	32	48	3	8	394	622
Mississippi	329	236	31	43	1	149	4	2	99	93	630	630
Missouri	628	551	57	174	2	367	13	8	7	63	542	544
Montana	324	321	153	0	0	171	0	0	0	0	158	159
Nebraska	305	294	25	157	1	115	1	6	0	0	380	380
Nevada	127	112	12	7	6	95	1	6	0	0	1,107	1,221
New Hampshire	108	108	13	0	0	93	1	0	1	0	549	549
New Jersey	539	406	54	38	12	409	6	6	14	69	832	1,027
New Mexico	229	207	32	26	2	149	8	0	12	0	465	498
New York	1,121	1,030	57	146	29	840	23	5	21	20	716	745
North Carolina	553	522	19	9	4	488	1	10	22	9	839	874
North Dakota	178	166	4	85	0	75	0	1	13	12	208	208
Ohio	989	915	128	142	41	624	16	20	18	73	597	606
Oklahoma	564	559	88	2	3	439	24	0	8	0	387	390
Oregon	274	250	25	40	4	203	1	1	0	0	645	695
Pennsylvania	783	694	96	153	11	502	13	2	6	84	807	815
Rhode Island	70	59	5	2	0	54	0	0	9	10	714	722
South Carolina	282	229	19	2	1	235	7	4	14	42	927	969
South Dakota	240	220	59	0	1	176	1	3	0	2	174	184
Tennessee	351	337	11	21	8	271	11	12	17	4	810	842
Texas	2,076	1,526	248	130	47	1,376	37	45	193	0	813	1,067
Utah	282	252	90	48	7	74	51	1	11	6	945	1,008
Vermont	65	49	7	17	0	41	0	0	0	15	469	479
Virginia	436	344	34	6	24	282	1	0	89	89	1,202	1,212
Washington	625	417	54	48	25	446	22	20	10	18	628	860
West Virginia	155	106	1	21	3	129	0	1	0	33	690	716
Wisconsin	568	498	54	57	3	420	13	18	3	6	487	536
Wyoming	101	98	17	15	0	69	0	0	0	0	325	334
Jurisdiction												
Bureau of Indian Education	19	19	1	4	2	12	0	0	0	0	337	337
DoDEA[4]	—	—	—	—	0	—	—	—	—	—	—	—
Other jurisdictions												
American Samoa	6	5	0	0	0	6	0	0	0	1	623	679
Guam	7	6	0	0	0	7	0	0	0	0	1,412	1,619
Northern Marianas	—	—	—	—	0	—	—	—	—	—	—	—
Puerto Rico	182	151	7	5	0	159	6	0	5	31	545	517
U.S. Virgin Islands	9	8	4	0	0	5	0	0	0	1	585	585

—Not available.
[1]Excludes vocational, special education, and alternative schools.
[2]Vocational schools are also included under appropriate grade span.
[3]Average for schools reporting enrollment data. Enrollment data were available for 22,293 out of 23,882 public secondary schools in 2017–18.
[4]DoDEA = Department of Defense Education Activity. Includes both domestic and overseas schools.

NOTE: Includes schools with no grade lower than 7. Excludes schools not reported by grade level, such as some special education schools for students with disabilities.
SOURCE: U.S. Department of Education, National Center for Education Statistics, Common Core of Data (CCD), "Public Elementary/Secondary School Universe Survey," 2017–18. (This table was prepared December 2019.)

Table 216.90. Public elementary and secondary charter schools and enrollment, and charter schools and enrollment as a percentage of total public schools and total enrollment in public schools, by state: Selected years, 2000–01 through 2017–18

State	Number of charter schools — 2000–01	2010–11	2015–16	2016–17	2017–18	Fall enrollment in charter schools — 2000–01	2010–11	2015–16	2016–17	2017–18	Charter schools as a percent of total public schools — 2000–01	2010–11	2016–17	2017–18	Charter school enrollment as a percent of total fall enrollment in public schools — 2000–01	2010–11	2016–17	2017–18
1	2	3	4	5	6	7	8	9	10	11	12	13	14	15	16	17	18	19
United States	**1,993**	**5,274**	**6,855**	**7,011**	**7,193**	**448,343**	**1,787,091**	**2,845,322**	**3,010,287**	**3,143,269**	**2.1**	**5.3**	**7.1**	**7.3**	**1.0**	**3.6**	**6.0**	**6.2**
Alabama	0	0	0	1	1	0	0	0	—	245	0.0	0.0	0.1	0.1	0.0	0.0	—	#
Alaska	19	27	28	28	29	2,594	5,751	6,343	6,677	7,007	3.7	5.3	5.5	5.7	1.9	4.4	5.0	5.3
Arizona	313	519	552	550	557	45,596	124,467	176,894	185,588	189,686	18.2	22.9	23.8	23.9	5.4	11.6	16.6	17.2
Arkansas	3	40	65	75	82	708	10,209	24,182	27,896	31,545	0.3	3.6	6.9	7.6	0.2	2.1	5.7	6.4
California	302	908	1,224	1,248	1,268	115,582	363,916	568,774	602,837	626,982	3.4	9.0	12.1	12.3	1.9	5.9	9.7	10.1
Colorado	77	168	226	238	250	20,155	74,685	108,793	114,694	120,739	4.7	9.4	12.6	13.2	2.8	8.9	12.7	13.3
Connecticut	16	18	24	24	24	2,429	5,139	9,132	9,573	10,187	1.3	1.6	1.9	2.3	0.4	0.9	1.8	2.0
Delaware	7	19	28	27	24	2,716	9,525	13,622	14,722	15,337	3.7	8.9	11.8	10.6	2.4	7.4	10.8	11.3
District of Columbia	33	97	109	110	111	—	26,910	35,798	37,151	38,696	16.7	42.5	49.3	49.6	—	37.8	43.7	44.8
Florida	148	458	653	655	654	26,893	154,703	270,953	283,560	295,814	4.5	11.1	15.7	15.1	1.1	5.9	10.1	10.4
Georgia	30	67	82	84	93	20,066	41,981	72,170	66,905	72,716	1.5	2.7	3.7	4.0	1.4	2.5	3.8	4.1
Hawaii	6	31	34	34	36	1,343	8,289	10,444	10,669	11,168	2.3	10.7	11.7	12.3	0.7	4.6	5.9	6.2
Idaho	9	40	54	57	59	1,083	15,330	19,381	20,579	21,070	1.3	5.3	7.7	8.0	0.4	5.6	6.9	7.0
Illinois	20	50	64	63	142	7,552	43,049	64,108	65,169	64,925	0.5	1.1	1.5	3.3	0.4	2.1	3.2	3.3
Indiana	0	60	88	93	99	0	22,472	39,671	43,079	47,089	0.0	3.1	4.8	5.2	0.0	2.2	4.1	4.5
Iowa	0	7	3	3	3	0	298	430	398	428	0.0	0.5	0.2	0.2	0.0	0.1	0.1	0.1
Kansas	1	25	10	10	10	67	4,618	3,186	3,159	3,191	0.1	1.8	0.8	0.8	#	1.0	0.6	0.7
Kentucky	0	0	0	0	0	0	0	0	0	0	0.0	0.0	0.0	0.0	0.0	0.0	0.0	0.0
Louisiana	19	78	138	151	150	3,212	29,199	74,030	79,022	80,726	1.2	5.3	10.8	10.8	0.4	4.2	11.0	11.3
Maine	1	0	7	9	11	154	0	1,518	1,955	2,240	0.1	0.0	1.5	1.8	0.1	0.0	1.1	1.3
Maryland	0	44	50	49	50	0	14,492	20,988	22,366	23,819	0.0	3.0	3.4	3.5	0.0	1.7	2.5	2.7
Massachusetts	41	63	81	78	80	13,712	28,422	40,199	42,596	45,238	2.2	3.4	4.2	4.3	1.4	3.0	4.5	4.7
Michigan	205	300	370	376	366	54,751	111,344	145,483	147,061	145,948	5.1	7.7	10.9	9.8	3.3	7.2	10.0	9.9
Minnesota	73	176	216	220	221	9,395	37,253	50,812	54,211	56,769	3.1	7.4	8.8	8.8	1.1	4.4	6.2	6.4
Mississippi	1	0	2	3	3	367	0	226	523	944	0.1	0.0	0.3	0.3	0.1	0.0	0.1	0.2
Missouri	21	53	70	72	68	7,061	20,076	21,619	22,803	23,624	0.9	2.2	3.0	2.8	0.8	2.2	2.5	2.6
Montana	0	0	0	0	0	0	0	0	0	0	0.0	0.0	0.0	0.0	0.0	0.0	0.0	0.0
Nebraska	0	0	0	0	0	0	0	0	0	0	0.0	0.0	0.0	0.0	0.0	0.0	0.0	0.0
Nevada	8	34	47	49	72	1,255	14,127	35,130	40,074	45,270	1.6	5.3	7.5	10.4	0.4	3.2	8.5	9.3
New Hampshire	0	14	31	31	31	0	983	3,011	3,422	3,543	0.0	2.9	6.3	6.3	0.0	0.5	1.9	2.0
New Jersey	53	76	89	88	89	10,179	24,591	41,026	46,274	49,447	2.2	2.9	3.4	3.4	0.8	1.8	3.4	3.6
New Mexico	10	81	99	99	97	1,335	15,290	22,079	25,139	26,116	1.3	9.4	11.4	11.0	0.4	4.6	7.6	7.8
New York	38	170	256	267	279	15,523	54,443	117,710	128,784	139,385	0.9	3.6	5.6	5.8	0.5	2.0	4.8	5.2
North Carolina	90	99	158	167	173	—	42,141	82,521	92,281	100,986	4.1	3.9	6.4	6.5	1.2	2.8	6.0	6.5
North Dakota	0	0	0	0	0	0	0	0	0	0	0.0	0.0	0.0	0.0	0.0	0.0	0.0	0.0
Ohio	66	339	373	362	340	14,745	96,669	118,603	116,279	113,162	1.7	9.0	10.1	9.4	0.8	5.5	6.8	6.6
Oklahoma	6	18	45	48	58	1,208	6,585	19,893	24,248	29,033	0.3	1.0	2.7	3.2	0.2	1.0	3.5	4.2
Oregon	12	108	126	124	127	559	20,372	30,728	32,323	33,677	0.9	8.3	10.0	10.2	0.1	3.7	5.7	5.9
Pennsylvania	65	145	175	179	179	18,981	90,613	130,940	132,979	137,712	2.0	4.5	6.0	6.0	1.0	5.1	7.8	8.1
Rhode Island	3	16	29	30	31	557	3,971	7,310	8,137	8,859	0.9	5.0	9.5	9.8	0.4	2.8	5.8	6.3
South Carolina	8	44	68	70	70	484	16,390	29,470	32,343	34,857	0.7	3.6	5.6	5.6	0.1	2.3	4.2	4.5
South Dakota	0	0	0	0	0	0	0	0	0	0	0.0	0.0	0.0	0.0	0.0	0.0	0.0	0.0
Tennessee	0	29	100	104	110	0	6,517	29,274	34,984	37,713	0.0	1.6	5.9	6.2	0.0	0.7	3.5	3.8
Texas	201	561	702	753	759	37,978	164,940	284,617	310,846	325,165	2.7	6.4	8.5	8.5	1.0	3.3	5.8	6.0
Utah	8	78	117	124	131	537	39,862	67,398	71,417	75,467	1.0	7.7	12.0	12.5	0.1	6.8	10.8	11.3
Vermont	0	0	0	0	0	0	0	0	0	0	0.0	0.0	0.0	0.0	0.0	0.0	0.0	0.0
Virginia	2	4	7	8	8	55	348	1,001	1,176	1,178	0.1	0.2	0.4	0.4	#	#	0.1	0.1
Washington	0	0	9	8	10	0	0	1,225	1,676	2,498	0.0	0.0	0.3	0.4	0.0	0.0	0.2	0.2
West Virginia	0	0	0	0	0	0	0	0	0	0	0.0	0.0	0.0	0.0	0.0	0.0	0.0	0.0
Wisconsin	78	207	242	237	233	9,511	36,863	44,162	44,209	42,499	3.6	9.2	10.5	10.3	1.1	4.2	5.1	4.9
Wyoming	0	3	4	5	5	0	258	468	503	569	0.0	0.8	0.8	1.4	0.0	0.3	0.5	0.6

—Not available.
#Rounds to zero.

SOURCE: U.S. Department of Education, National Center for Education Statistics, Common Core of Data (CCD), "Public Elementary/Secondary School Universe Survey," 2000–01 through 2017–18. (This table was prepared November 2019.)

Table 218.16. Percentage of students ages 5 through 17 enrolled in kindergarten through grade 12 who took any school-related courses online and, among those taking courses online, percentage who took courses from various providers, by selected child, parent, and household characteristics: 2016

[Standard errors appear in parentheses]

Selected child, parent, or household characteristic	Percent who took any school-related courses online		Among those taking school-related courses online, percent taking courses from various providers[1]								
			Local public school		State		Charter school, another public school, or private school		College, community college, or university		Someplace else	
1	2		3		4		5		6		7	
Total	3.1	(0.20)	55.3	(2.96)	11.6	(1.62)	16.0	(2.80)	13.9	(1.64)	13.6	(2.33)
Sex of child												
Male	3.0	(0.26)	55.9	(4.74)	10.0	(2.25)	19.4	(4.16)	10.5	(2.11)	15.3	(3.27)
Female	3.3	(0.29)	54.7	(3.96)	13.2	(2.64)	12.7	(3.51)	17.3	(2.91)	11.9	(2.89)
Race/ethnicity of child												
White	2.5	(0.21)	50.6	(3.90)	10.1	(1.80)	12.8	(2.40)	23.7	(3.25)	11.1	(2.48)
Black	4.5	(0.74)	61.2	(8.91)	7.1!	(3.12)	27.6!	(9.89)	‡	(†)	12.1!	(4.98)
Hispanic	2.8	(0.47)	51.4	(5.96)	17.4	(5.02)	18.5	(5.53)	‡	(†)	18.0!	(5.83)
Asian/Pacific Islander	5.9	(1.04)	52.7	(8.08)	18.7!	(6.92)	9.5!	(3.53)	13.7!	(4.92)	18.8!	(5.70)
Asian	5.6	(0.99)	55.6	(8.52)	12.6!	(5.41)	8.8!	(3.46)	15.2!	(5.40)	20.9	(6.19)
Pacific Islander	‡	(†)	‡	(†)	‡	(†)	‡	(†)	‡	(†)	‡	(†)
American Indian/Alaska Native	‡	(†)	‡	(†)	‡	(†)	‡	(†)	‡	(†)	‡	(†)
Two or more races	3.2!	(1.10)	‡	(†)	‡	(†)	‡	(†)	‡	(†)	‡	(†)
Grade equivalent												
Kindergarten through grade 5	2.1	(0.27)	66.5	(6.17)	‡	(†)	21.1!	(6.59)	‡	(†)	17.5	(4.93)
Kindergarten and grade 1	1.7	(0.47)	‡	(†)	‡	(†)	‡	(†)	‡	(†)	‡	(†)
Grades 2 and 3	2.3	(0.48)	76.7	(8.55)	‡	(†)	‡	(†)	‡	(†)	18.1!	(7.57)
Grades 4 and 5	2.3	(0.55)	66.1	(12.02)	‡	(†)	31.2!	(13.53)	‡	(†)	‡	(†)
Grades 6 through 8	1.6	(0.30)	55.0	(9.85)	‡	(†)	16.0!	(5.85)	‡	(†)	25.9	(7.66)
Grades 9 through 12	6.6	(0.43)	48.8	(3.48)	16.0	(2.29)	13.0	(2.44)	23.2	(2.56)	8.7	(2.02)
Number of children in the household												
One child	4.0	(0.29)	46.5	(4.00)	15.4	(2.46)	16.3	(2.73)	17.7	(2.55)	14.1	(2.98)
Two children	3.3	(0.29)	58.8	(4.70)	14.3	(3.45)	10.6	(2.11)	12.1	(2.58)	14.2	(3.52)
Three or more children	2.4	(0.42)	60.1	(8.50)	‡	(†)	23.8!	(9.37)	12.4!	(4.23)	12.1!	(4.53)
Number of parents in the household												
Two parents	3.4	(0.24)	53.9	(3.53)	11.2	(1.84)	17.4	(3.71)	15.3	(1.98)	13.2	(2.63)
One parent	2.7	(0.36)	58.9	(5.75)	12.6	(2.91)	12.1!	(3.75)	8.2!	(2.64)	15.5	(4.10)
Nonparental guardians	2.3	(0.66)	‡	(†)	‡	(†)	‡	(†)	‡	(†)	‡	(†)
Highest education level of parents/guardians in the household												
Less than a high school diploma	2.9	(0.72)	67.6	(12.15)	‡	(†)	‡	(†)	‡	(†)	‡	(†)
High school diploma/equivalent (e.g., GED)	2.2	(0.48)	54.4	(9.62)	14.6!	(7.13)	15.1!	(7.33)	11.7!	(4.48)	17.1!	(7.31)
Vocational/technical, associate's degree, or some college	2.9	(0.38)	63.9	(6.24)	10.1	(2.91)	18.9!	(6.22)	7.3	(2.05)	8.1!	(2.84)
Bachelor's degree/some graduate school	3.8	(0.41)	46.4	(4.88)	13.0	(2.99)	12.7	(3.18)	19.0	(3.36)	15.7	(3.45)
Graduate/professional degree	3.7	(0.43)	54.1	(6.42)	9.9	(2.89)	13.1	(3.83)	17.1	(3.55)	17.7	(4.12)
Household income												
$20,000 or less	3.0	(0.59)	72.8	(7.06)	‡	(†)	13.8!	(5.42)	8.0!	(2.68)	‡	(†)
$20,001 to $50,000	2.9	(0.46)	59.7	(8.71)	10.2!	(3.23)	16.1!	(6.62)	‡	(†)	18.7!	(6.38)
$50,001 to $75,000	2.9	(0.47)	49.6	(7.06)	15.0!	(5.30)	18.2!	(7.04)	10.3!	(4.10)	14.2!	(5.65)
$75,001 to $100,000	3.5	(0.68)	44.3	(9.74)	9.8!	(3.48)	33.6!	(11.93)	16.3!	(5.44)	8.4!	(3.78)
Over $100,000	3.4	(0.33)	53.8	(4.30)	11.2	(2.08)	8.2	(2.07)	20.4	(3.33)	14.9	(3.25)
Locale												
City	2.9	(0.35)	47.1	(5.73)	11.0	(2.58)	26.4	(6.33)	7.1	(1.89)	19.2	(4.44)
Suburban	3.5	(0.30)	56.5	(3.74)	12.6	(2.48)	10.5	(2.35)	15.1	(2.73)	14.5	(3.26)
Town	2.6	(0.58)	43.8	(13.06)	‡	(†)	‡	(†)	33.1!	(13.40)	‡	(†)
Rural	3.0	(0.50)	71.6	(6.45)	8.7!	(3.26)	‡	(†)	14.7	(4.03)	‡	(†)

†Not applicable.
!Interpret data with caution. The coefficient of variation (CV) for this estimate is between 30 and 50 percent.
‡Reporting standards not met. Either there are too few cases for a reliable estimate or the coefficient of variation (CV) is 50 percent or greater.
[1]One student could take courses from more than one provider. Therefore, the percentages sum to more than 100.

NOTE: Excludes homeschooled students and any enrolled students whose parents filled out the questionnaire that was intended for homeschooled students. Race categories exclude persons of Hispanic ethnicity. Detail may not sum to totals because of rounding. SOURCE: U.S. Department of Education, National Center for Education Statistics, Parent and Family Involvement in Education Survey of the National Household Education Surveys Program (PFI-NHES:2016). (This table was prepared April 2019.)

Table 219.10. High school graduates, by sex and control of school; public high school averaged freshman graduation rate (AFGR); and total graduates as a ratio of 17-year-old population: Selected years, 1869–70 through 2029–30

School year	High school graduates							Public school AFGR[3]	Population 17 years old[4]	Graduates as a ratio of 17-year-old population[5]
	Sex			Control						
				Public[2]			Private, total			
	Total[1]	Males	Females	Total	Males	Females				
1	2	3	4	5	6	7	8	9	10	11
1869–70	16,000	7,064	8,936	—	—	—	—	—	815,000	2.0
1879–80	23,634	10,605	13,029	—	—	—	—	—	946,026	2.5
1889–90	43,731	18,549	25,182	21,882	—	—	21,849[6]	—	1,259,177	3.5
1899–1900	94,883	38,075	56,808	61,737	—	—	33,146[6]	—	1,489,146	6.4
1909–10	156,429	63,676	92,753	111,363	—	—	45,066[6]	—	1,786,240	8.8
1919–20	311,266	123,684	187,582	230,902	—	—	80,364[6]	—	1,855,173	16.8
1929–30	666,904	300,376	366,528	591,719	—	—	75,185[6]	—	2,295,822	29.0
1939–40	1,221,475	578,718	642,757	1,143,246	538,273	604,973	78,229[6]	—	2,403,074	50.8
1949–50	1,199,700	570,700	629,000	1,063,444	505,394	558,050	136,256[6]	—	2,034,450	59.0
1959–60	1,858,023	895,000	963,000	1,627,050	791,426	835,624	230,973	—	2,672,000	69.5
1969–70	2,888,639	1,430,000	1,459,000	2,588,639	1,285,895	1,302,744	300,000[6]	78.7	3,757,000	76.9
1975–76	3,142,120	1,552,000	1,590,000	2,837,129	1,401,064	1,436,065	304,991	74.9	4,272,000	73.6
1979–80	3,042,214	1,503,000	1,539,000	2,747,678	—	—	294,536	71.5	4,262,000	71.4
1985–86	2,642,616	—	—	2,382,616	—	—	260,000[6]	74.3	3,670,000	72.0
1986–87	2,693,803	—	—	2,428,803	—	—	265,000[6]	74.3	3,754,000	71.8
1987–88	2,773,020	—	—	2,500,020	—	—	273,000[6]	74.2	3,849,000	72.0
1988–89	2,743,743	—	—	2,458,800	—	—	284,943	73.4	3,842,000	71.4
1989–90[7]	2,574,162	—	—	2,320,337	—	—	253,825[8]	73.6	3,505,000	73.4
1990–91	2,492,988	—	—	2,234,893	—	—	258,095	73.7	3,417,913	72.9
1991–92	2,480,399	—	—	2,226,016	—	—	254,383[8]	74.2	3,398,884	73.0
1992–93	2,480,519	—	—	2,233,241	—	—	247,278	73.8	3,449,143	71.9
1993–94	2,463,849	—	—	2,220,849	—	—	243,000[6]	73.1	3,442,521	71.6
1994–95	2,519,084	—	—	2,273,541	—	—	245,543	71.8	3,635,803	69.3
1995–96	2,518,109	—	—	2,273,109	—	—	245,000[6]	71.0	3,640,132	69.2
1996–97	2,611,988	—	—	2,358,403	—	—	253,585	71.3	3,792,207	68.9
1997–98	2,704,050	—	—	2,439,050	1,187,647	1,251,403	265,000[6]	71.3	4,008,416	67.5
1998–99	2,758,655	—	—	2,485,630	1,212,924	1,272,706	273,025	71.1	3,917,885	70.4
1999–2000	2,832,844	—	—	2,553,844	1,241,631	1,312,213	279,000[6]	71.7	4,056,639	69.8
2000–01	2,847,973	—	—	2,569,200	1,251,931	1,317,269	278,773	71.7	4,023,686	70.8
2001–02	2,906,534	—	—	2,621,534	1,275,813	1,345,721	285,000[6]	72.6	4,023,968	72.2
2002–03	3,015,735	—	—	2,719,947	1,330,973	1,388,974	295,788	73.9	4,125,087	73.1
2003–04[7,9]	3,054,438	—	—	2,753,438	1,347,800	1,405,638	301,000[6]	74.3	4,113,074	74.3
2004–05	3,106,499	—	—	2,799,250	1,369,749	1,429,501	307,249	74.7	4,120,073	75.4
2005–06[7]	3,122,544	—	—	2,815,544	1,376,458	1,439,086	307,000[6]	73.4	4,200,554	74.3
2006–07	3,199,650	—	—	2,893,045	1,414,069	1,478,976	306,605	73.9	4,297,239	74.5
2007–08	3,312,337	—	—	3,001,337	1,467,180	1,534,157	311,000[6]	74.7	4,436,955	74.7
2008–09[7]	3,347,828	—	—	3,039,015	1,490,317	1,548,698	308,813	75.5	4,336,950	77.2
2009–10	3,435,022	—	—	3,128,022	1,542,684[10]	1,585,338[10]	307,000[6]	78.2	4,311,831	79.7
2010–11	3,449,940	—	—	3,144,100	1,552,981	1,591,110	305,840	79.6	4,367,816	79.0
2011–12	3,454,095	—	—	3,149,185	1,558,489	1,590,694	304,910[6]	80.8	4,294,110	80.4
2012–13	3,478,027	—	—	3,169,257	1,569,675	1,599,579	308,770	81.9	4,255,798	81.7
2013–14[11]	3,488,310	—	—	3,168,450	—	—	319,860	83.1	4,184,556	83.4
2014–15[12]	3,530,250	—	—	3,187,000	—	—	343,250	—	4,170,348	84.7
2015–16[11]	3,574,730	—	—	3,224,140	—	—	350,590	—	4,203,329	85.0
2016–17[12]	3,603,550	—	—	3,255,320	—	—	348,230	—	4,217,905	85.4
2017–18[11]	3,663,530	—	—	3,310,020	—	—	353,510	—	4,291,210	85.4
2018–19[11]	3,674,130	—	—	3,316,970	—	—	357,160	—	4,223,346	87.0
2019–20[11]	3,652,130	—	—	3,294,660	—	—	357,460	—	4,179,612	87.4
2020–21[11]	3,662,860	—	—	3,302,430	—	—	360,430	—	—	—
2021–22[11]	3,688,550	—	—	3,323,040	—	—	365,510	—	—	—
2022–23[11]	3,703,000	—	—	3,337,740	—	—	365,260	—	—	—
2023–24[11]	3,779,770	—	—	3,404,190	—	—	375,580	—	—	—
2024–25[11]	3,831,290	—	—	3,463,190	—	—	368,100	—	—	—
2025–26[11]	3,827,340	—	—	3,458,860	—	—	368,480	—	—	—
2026–27[11]	3,746,800	—	—	3,384,860	—	—	361,940	—	—	—
2027–28[11]	3,667,760	—	—	3,314,690	—	—	353,070	—	—	—
2028–29[11]	3,640,620	—	—	3,290,850	—	—	349,770	—	—	—
2029–30[11]	3,612,400	—	—	3,265,340	—	—	347,060	—	—	—

—Not available.
[1]Includes graduates of public and private schools.
[2]Includes estimates for states not reporting counts of graduates by sex. Data for 1929–30 and preceding years are from Statistics of Public High Schools and exclude graduates from high schools that failed to report to the Office of Education.
[3]The averaged freshman graduation rate provides an estimate of the percentage of students who receive a regular diploma within 4 years of entering ninth grade. The rate uses aggregate student enrollment data to estimate the size of an incoming freshman class and aggregate counts of the number of diplomas awarded 4 years later. Averaged freshman graduation rates in this table are based on reported totals of enrollment by grade and high school graduates, rather than on details reported by race/ethnicity.
[4]Derived from Current Population Reports, Series P-25. For years 1869–70 through 1989–90, 17-year-old population is an estimate of the October 17-year-old population based on July data. Data for 1990–91 and later years are October resident population estimates prepared by the Census Bureau.
[5]Based on persons of all ages graduating from high school in a given year divided by the 17-year-old population in the same year. This ratio allows for comparisons over time but does not provide a measure of graduation rates for incoming freshmen who form a cohort (or class) that is scheduled to graduate 4 years later. The ratio of high school graduates to the 17-year-old population differs from measures such as the AFGR (shown in column 9), which are designed to estimate high school cohort graduation rates.
[6]Estimated.
[7]Includes imputations for nonreporting states.
[8]Projected by private schools responding to the Private School Universe Survey.
[9]Includes estimates for public schools in New York and Wisconsin. Without estimates for these two states, the averaged freshman graduation rate for the remaining 48 states and the District of Columbia is 75.0 percent.

[10]Includes estimate for Connecticut, which did not report graduates by sex.
[11]Projected by the National Center for Education Statistics (NCES).
[12]Public school data are projected by NCES; private school data are actual.
NOTE: Includes graduates of regular day school programs. Excludes graduates of other programs, when separately reported, and recipients of high school equivalency certificates. Some data have been revised from previously published figures. Detail may not sum to totals because of rounding and adjustments to protect student privacy.
SOURCE: U.S. Department of Education, National Center for Education Statistics, Annual Report of the Commissioner of Education, 1870 through 1910; Biennial Survey of Education in the United States, 1919–20 through 1949–50; Statistics of Public Elementary and Secondary School Systems, 1958–59 through 1979–80; Statistics of Nonpublic Elementary and Secondary Schools, 1959 through 1980; Common Core of Data (CCD), "State Nonfiscal Survey of Public Elementary/Secondary Education," 1985–86 through 2009–10; "State Dropout and Completion Data File," 2005–06 through 2012–13; Public School Graduates and Dropouts from the Common Core of Data, 2007–08 and 2008–09; Private School Universe Survey (PSS), 1989 through 2017; and National High School Graduates Projection Model, 1972–73 through 2029–30. U.S. Department of Commerce, Census Bureau, Current Population Reports, Series P-25, Nos. 1000, 1022, 1045, 1057, 1059, 1092, and 1095; 2000 through 2009 Population Estimates, retrieved August 14, 2012, from https://www.census.gov/popest/data/national/asrh/2011/index.html; and 2010 through 2019 Population Estimates, retrieved November 29, 2019, from https://www.census.gov/data/datasets/time-series/demo/popest/2010s-national-detail.html#par_textimage_57373479. (This table was prepared December 2019.)

Table 219.20. Public high school graduates, by region, state, and jurisdiction: Selected years, 1980–81 through 2029–30

Region, state, and jurisdiction	Actual data						Projected data					
	1980–81	1989–90	1999–2000	2009–10	2011–12	2012–13	2013–14	2014–15	2015–16	2016–17	2017–18	2018–19
1	2	3	4	5	6	7	8	9	10	11	12	13
United States	2,725,285	2,320,337[1]	2,553,844	3,128,022	3,149,185	3,169,257	3,168,450	3,187,000	3,224,140	3,255,320	3,310,020	3,316,970
Region												
Northeast	593,727	446,045	453,814	556,400	554,705	555,202	546,910	543,080	545,820	551,480	553,700	550,610
Midwest	784,071	616,700	648,020	726,844	716,072	713,662	705,550	708,240	714,040	719,240	728,420	728,250
South	868,068	796,385	861,498	1,104,770	1,121,400	1,138,965	1,145,570	1,162,950	1,189,220	1,211,650	1,247,860	1,260,960
West	479,419	461,207	590,512	740,008	757,008	761,428	770,420	772,720	775,060	772,950	780,030	777,150
State												
Alabama	44,894	40,485	37,819	43,166	45,394	44,233	44,540	45,420	46,070	47,560	48,030	47,610
Alaska	5,343	5,386	6,615	8,245	7,989	7,860	7,720	7,860	7,840	7,910	8,030	7,910
Arizona	28,416	32,103	38,304	61,145	63,208	62,208	66,700	67,200	67,120	68,770	66,670	66,370
Arkansas	29,577	26,475	27,335	28,276	28,419	28,928	29,610	30,350	30,290	30,750	30,940	31,260
California	242,172	236,291	309,866	404,987	418,664	422,125	424,080	422,830	419,190	411,710	415,890	411,260
Colorado	35,897	32,967	38,924	49,321	50,087	50,968	51,310	51,450	53,310	54,060	55,560	56,330
Connecticut	38,369	27,878	31,562	34,495	38,681	38,722	37,860	37,160	37,420	37,890	37,850	37,310
Delaware	7,349	5,550	6,108	8,133	8,247	8,070	8,240	8,390	8,480	8,690	8,780	8,940
District of Columbia[2]	4,848	3,626	2,695	3,602	3,860	3,961	3,880	3,990	4,510	4,430	4,780	4,660
Florida	88,755	88,934	106,708	156,130	151,964	158,029	158,440	163,740	166,540	170,820	175,140	177,240
Georgia	62,963	56,605	62,563	91,561	90,582	92,416	94,380	97,420	100,070	102,050	105,810	107,740
Hawaii	11,472	10,325	10,437	10,998	11,360	10,790	11,050	10,760	10,860	10,690	11,180	10,550
Idaho	12,679	11,971	16,170	17,793	17,568	17,198	19,120	18,050	18,230	19,130	19,510	19,780
Illinois	136,795	108,119	111,835	139,035	139,575	139,228	137,640	140,520	140,850	141,250	142,720	142,810
Indiana	73,381	60,012	57,012	64,551	65,667	66,595	67,560	66,750	66,720	68,970	71,590	74,270
Iowa	42,635	31,796	33,926	34,462	33,230	32,548	32,590	32,450	32,700	32,850	33,280	33,050
Kansas	29,397	25,367	29,102	31,642	31,898	31,922	32,150	31,900	32,790	32,900	33,530	33,270
Kentucky	41,714	38,005	36,830	42,664	42,642	42,888	42,400	42,530	43,280	43,280	44,160	44,240
Louisiana	46,199	36,053	38,430	36,573	36,675	37,508	38,180	37,720	38,790	39,380	41,860	41,730
Maine	15,554	13,839	12,211	14,069	13,473	13,170	12,730	12,560	12,790	12,640	12,690	12,600
Maryland	54,050	41,566	47,849	59,078	58,811	58,896	58,120	57,650	57,490	57,290	59,120	58,430
Massachusetts	74,831	55,941[3]	52,950	64,462	65,157	66,360	65,200	65,790	68,630	68,610	69,250	69,610
Michigan	124,372	93,807	97,679	110,682	105,446	104,210	102,520	102,020	100,800	101,570	102,940	101,830
Minnesota	64,166	49,087	57,372	59,667	57,501	58,255	56,370	56,800	56,640	57,250	57,740	58,850
Mississippi	28,083	25,182	24,232	25,478	26,158	26,502	26,650	26,260	26,770	26,900	28,000	27,360
Missouri	60,359	48,957	52,848	63,994	61,313	61,407	60,900	60,590	61,600	60,890	61,380	60,990
Montana	11,634	9,370	10,903	10,075	9,750	9,369	9,470	9,390	9,320	9,380	9,480	9,850
Nebraska	21,411	17,664	20,149	19,370	20,464	20,442	20,580	20,650	21,090	21,130	21,800	21,900
Nevada	9,069	9,477	14,551	20,956	21,891	23,038	22,720	23,040	23,190	23,780	24,140	24,610
New Hampshire	11,552	10,766	11,829	15,034	14,426	14,262	13,790	13,520	13,600	13,160	13,100	12,910
New Jersey	93,168	69,824	74,420	96,225	93,819	96,490	95,220	95,250	97,130	97,990	98,320	97,940
New Mexico	17,915	14,884	18,031	18,595	20,315	19,232	18,590	19,530	19,480	19,770	19,900	19,730
New York	198,465	143,318	141,731	183,826	180,806	180,351	178,810	179,110	178,260	181,790	182,400	181,210
North Carolina	69,395	64,782	62,140	88,704	93,977	94,339	96,210	97,020	98,970	101,710	104,850	106,870
North Dakota	9,924	7,690	8,606	7,155	6,942	6,900	6,960	7,040	7,020	6,940	6,940	7,120
Ohio	143,503	114,513	111,668	123,437	123,135	122,491	119,520	120,940	125,050	126,590	126,900	125,270
Oklahoma	38,875	35,606	37,646	38,503	37,305	37,033	37,260	38,420	39,690	40,230	41,030	41,350
Oregon	28,729	25,473	30,151	34,671	34,261	33,899	34,440	34,800	35,650	34,700	34,540	34,920
Pennsylvania	144,645	110,527	113,959	131,182	131,733	129,777	127,200	123,560	121,840	123,990	124,750	123,070
Rhode Island	10,719	7,825	8,477	9,908	9,751	9,579	9,730	9,900	10,050	9,390	9,620	10,250
South Carolina	38,347	32,483	31,617	40,438	41,442	42,246	41,720	42,650	43,840	45,090	46,790	47,060
South Dakota	10,385	7,650	9,278	8,162	8,196	8,239	7,960	8,140	8,080	8,160	8,230	8,200
Tennessee	50,648	46,094	41,568	62,408	62,454	61,323	60,970	62,010	63,480	63,710	64,290	65,110
Texas	171,665	172,480	212,925	280,894	292,531	301,390	304,360	309,280	318,660	327,690	339,670	346,980
Utah	19,886	21,196	32,501	31,481	31,157	33,186	33,400	34,070	35,400	36,560	37,550	38,160
Vermont	6,424	6,127	6,675	7,199	6,859	6,491	6,360	6,240	6,090	6,010	5,740	5,700
Virginia	67,126	60,605	65,596	81,511	83,336	83,279	83,100	82,680	84,640	84,720	87,150	87,260
Washington	50,046	45,941	57,597	66,046	65,205	66,066	66,240	68,200	69,770	70,840	71,790	71,850
West Virginia	23,580	21,854	19,437	17,651	17,603	17,924	17,510	17,460	17,640	17,370	17,480	17,140
Wisconsin	67,743	52,038	58,545	64,687	62,705	61,425	60,810	60,460	60,710	60,740	61,380	60,700
Wyoming	6,161	5,823	6,462	5,695	5,553	5,489	5,590	5,550	5,700	5,660	5,790	5,840
Jurisdiction												
Bureau of Indian Education	—	—	—	—	—	—	—	—	—	—	—	—
DoDEA[4]	—	—	3,202	—	—	—	—	—	—	—	—	—
Other jurisdictions												
American Samoa	—	703	698	—	—	—	—	—	—	—	—	—
Guam	—	1,033	1,406	—	—	—	—	—	—	—	—	—
Northern Marianas	—	227	360	—	—	—	—	—	—	—	—	—
Puerto Rico	—	29,049	30,856	25,514	25,720	—	—	—	—	—	—	—
U.S. Virgin Islands	—	1,260	1,060	958	1,046	897	—	—	—	—	—	—

See notes at end of table.

Table 219.20. Public high school graduates, by region, state, and jurisdiction: Selected years, 1980–81 through 2029–30—Continued

Region, state, and jurisdiction	2019–20	2020–21	2021–22	2022–23	2023–24	2024–25	2025–26	2026–27	2027–28	2028–29	2029–30	Percent change, 2012–13 to 2029–30
1	14	15	16	17	18	19	20	21	22	23	24	25
United States	3,294,660	3,302,430	3,323,040	3,337,740	3,404,190	3,463,190	3,458,860	3,384,860	3,314,690	3,290,850	3,265,340	3.0
Region												
Northeast	545,780	546,720	547,000	543,310	549,940	559,110	554,400	544,550	532,560	530,600	525,610	-5.3
Midwest	715,220	715,460	727,280	721,220	731,350	746,070	741,560	726,570	709,840	698,670	694,010	-2.8
South	1,255,600	1,250,440	1,255,270	1,272,010	1,302,070	1,339,300	1,346,460	1,323,500	1,280,680	1,270,240	1,262,520	10.8
West	778,050	789,810	793,490	801,200	820,840	818,720	816,440	790,240	791,620	791,350	783,210	2.9
State												
Alabama	45,440	44,150	44,470	44,640	44,970	46,610	46,950	46,080	44,370	44,160	43,750	-1.1
Alaska	7,710	7,700	7,740	7,860	8,060	8,230	8,450	8,460	8,400	8,270	8,210	4.4
Arizona	67,510	67,700	67,890	67,580	69,090	71,250	71,800	70,290	68,130	67,090	66,470	6.9
Arkansas	31,640	31,140	31,290	31,160	31,380	33,640	33,580	32,800	31,940	31,580	31,160	7.7
California	410,090	416,980	418,020	421,720	431,060	417,610	412,760	396,860	405,510	406,210	400,550	-5.1
Colorado	57,010	58,350	58,360	58,680	60,270	61,040	61,290	60,170	58,470	58,190	57,450	12.7
Connecticut	36,670	36,510	35,750	35,710	35,400	35,790	34,580	33,770	32,820	32,760	32,100	-17.1
Delaware	8,930	9,130	9,050	9,130	9,260	9,690	9,910	9,770	9,530	9,380	9,320	15.4
District of Columbia[2]	4,750	4,390	4,590	4,890	5,140	5,760	5,830	5,840	5,830	5,970	6,220	57.0
Florida	174,180	174,830	176,640	179,000	188,030	186,200	192,520	187,610	182,600	184,380	184,370	16.7
Georgia	107,290	105,750	106,870	107,910	110,690	113,680	113,570	111,590	107,580	106,390	104,890	13.5
Hawaii	10,820	10,840	10,930	11,070	11,150	11,410	11,400	8,750	10,850	10,600	10,580	-2.0
Idaho	19,960	19,940	20,410	21,160	21,290	22,100	22,250	21,790	21,410	21,440	21,390	24.3
Illinois	140,130	139,520	145,620	144,750	144,650	150,190	149,490	144,900	141,730	136,270	135,930	-2.4
Indiana	72,010	70,760	72,520	71,730	73,170	74,570	76,020	72,880	71,890	71,250	70,600	6.0
Iowa	33,300	33,780	33,660	34,460	35,300	35,980	36,020	34,960	34,490	33,520	33,090	1.7
Kansas	33,250	33,560	33,760	33,740	34,380	35,030	34,930	34,220	33,810	32,790	32,270	1.1
Kentucky	43,510	43,670	43,730	43,700	44,490	45,800	45,400	44,570	42,730	42,320	42,020	-2.0
Louisiana	41,500	39,860	40,290	40,330	40,760	42,750	42,100	41,430	39,400	39,020	38,690	3.2
Maine	12,310	12,190	12,420	12,490	12,350	12,590	12,340	12,280	11,830	11,760	11,590	-12.0
Maryland	60,940	61,140	61,920	62,350	64,270	66,460	67,230	65,980	64,730	64,490	63,770	8.3
Massachusetts	69,390	69,720	69,840	69,170	69,930	71,090	70,870	69,120	67,430	67,330	67,270	1.4
Michigan	97,340	97,200	97,780	94,520	95,430	96,050	92,160	89,790	88,410	89,440	88,440	-15.1
Minnesota	58,170	59,290	61,150	61,270	62,660	64,450	64,510	63,740	63,050	62,390	62,410	7.1
Mississippi	26,620	25,880	26,230	25,950	25,830	27,810	27,500	26,080	24,590	23,900	23,470	-11.4
Missouri	60,180	60,340	60,580	60,920	61,860	63,380	63,220	61,880	60,610	59,880	59,120	-3.7
Montana	10,110	10,310	10,420	10,460	11,030	10,980	11,240	10,860	10,480	10,740	10,630	13.5
Nebraska	22,390	22,880	23,350	23,120	23,640	22,600	24,330	24,460	23,980	23,490	23,690	15.9
Nevada	25,080	25,340	25,590	26,510	27,540	29,000	29,020	28,190	28,200	28,630	28,620	24.2
New Hampshire	13,010	12,740	12,780	12,490	12,520	12,450	12,260	11,930	11,490	11,770	11,650	-18.3
New Jersey	96,730	97,140	98,150	96,730	98,320	99,260	98,050	96,830	94,110	93,630	92,680	-3.9
New Mexico	19,540	19,430	19,380	19,710	19,730	20,150	20,240	19,840	18,430	18,050	17,630	-8.3
New York	182,650	182,770	181,350	181,310	183,920	187,960	186,630	184,630	181,070	178,810	177,180	-1.8
North Carolina	104,980	104,950	97,800	104,330	107,290	110,360	110,710	109,090	105,350	103,470	102,970	9.2
North Dakota	7,070	7,260	7,540	7,640	8,090	8,380	8,450	8,560	8,400	8,390	8,570	24.2
Ohio	123,090	122,280	121,570	119,450	122,070	123,670	121,360	121,300	115,910	114,420	113,900	-7.0
Oklahoma	41,390	42,270	42,160	40,930	43,180	44,880	44,840	44,530	43,390	42,170	42,060	13.6
Oregon	34,500	35,000	35,340	35,370	36,760	37,880	38,160	37,020	36,230	36,320	35,980	6.1
Pennsylvania	118,860	119,840	120,690	119,480	121,600	123,690	123,520	120,490	118,390	119,080	117,900	-9.2
Rhode Island	10,500	10,280	10,490	10,300	10,410	10,580	10,490	10,170	10,040	10,110	9,940	3.7
South Carolina	47,100	46,220	46,980	47,850	49,410	52,020	51,900	51,650	49,050	49,110	48,770	15.4
South Dakota	8,230	8,520	8,800	9,140	9,310	9,610	9,650	9,440	9,300	9,240	9,250	12.3
Tennessee	63,860	62,930	63,270	63,910	65,630	66,960	66,380	63,660	63,020	63,090	62,560	2.0
Texas	349,340	350,570	355,170	361,120	365,740	378,180	379,960	377,200	363,850	357,810	356,220	18.2
Utah	39,000	40,170	40,920	41,400	42,780	44,110	43,880	43,050	42,330	42,080	42,190	27.1
Vermont	5,670	5,530	5,540	5,640	5,490	5,700	5,670	5,330	5,380	5,360	5,290	-18.5
Virginia	87,080	87,070	88,330	88,640	90,150	92,180	91,980	89,990	87,630	88,000	87,480	5.0
Washington	70,920	72,030	72,530	73,490	75,810	78,550	79,670	78,850	77,280	77,980	77,960	18.0
West Virginia	17,070	16,500	16,500	16,180	15,860	16,320	16,070	15,660	15,090	14,980	14,820	-17.3
Wisconsin	60,060	60,090	60,970	60,490	60,800	62,160	61,430	60,440	58,260	57,590	56,710	-7.7
Wyoming	5,810	6,020	5,960	6,210	6,280	6,400	6,290	6,110	5,900	5,740	5,560	1.4
Jurisdiction												
Bureau of Indian Education	—	—	—	—	—	—	—	—	—	—	—	—
DoDEA[4]	—	—	—	—	—	—	—	—	—	—	—	—
Other jurisdictions												
American Samoa	—	—	—	—	—	—	—	—	—	—	—	—
Guam	—	—	—	—	—	—	—	—	—	—	—	—
Northern Marianas	—	—	—	—	—	—	—	—	—	—	—	—
Puerto Rico	—	—	—	—	—	—	—	—	—	—	—	—
U.S. Virgin Islands	—	—	—	—	—	—	—	—	—	—	—	—

—Not available.
[1]U.S. total includes estimates for nonreporting states.
[2]Beginning in 1989–90, graduates from adult programs are excluded.
[3]Projected data from NCES 91-490, *Projections of Education Statistics to 2002.*
[4]DoDEA = Department of Defense Education Activity. Includes both domestic and overseas schools.
NOTE: Data include regular diploma recipients, but exclude students receiving a certificate of attendance and persons receiving high school equivalency certificates. Some data have been revised from previously published figures. Detail may not sum to totals because of rounding.
SOURCE: U.S. Department of Education, National Center for Education Statistics, Common Core of Data (CCD), "State Nonfiscal Survey of Public Elementary/Secondary Education," 1981–82 through 2005–06; "State Dropout and Completion Data File," 2005–06 through 2012–13; and State High School Graduates Projection Model, 1980–81 through 2029–30. (This table was prepared December 2019.)

Table 219.30. Public high school graduates, by race/ethnicity: 1998–99 through 2029–30

Year	Number of high school graduates							Percentage distribution of graduates						
	Total	White	Black	Hispanic	Asian/ Pacific Islander	American Indian/ Alaska Native	Two or more races	Total	White	Black	Hispanic	Asian/ Pacific Islander	American Indian/ Alaska Native	Two or more races
1	2	3	4	5	6	7	8	9	10	11	12	13	14	15
1998–99	2,485,630	1,749,561	325,708	270,836	115,216	24,309	—	100.0	70.4	13.1	10.9	4.6	1.0	†
1999–2000	2,553,844	1,778,370	338,116	289,139	122,344	25,875	—	100.0	69.6	13.2	11.3	4.8	1.0	†
2000–01	2,569,200	1,775,036	339,578	301,740	126,465	26,381	—	100.0	69.1	13.2	11.7	4.9	1.0	†
2001–02	2,621,534	1,796,110	348,969	317,197	132,182	27,076	—	100.0	68.5	13.3	12.1	5.0	1.0	†
2002–03	2,719,947	1,856,454	359,920	340,182	135,588	27,803	—	100.0	68.3	13.2	12.5	5.0	1.0	†
2003–04	2,753,438	1,829,177	383,443	374,492	137,496	28,830	—	100.0	66.4	13.9	13.6	5.0	1.0	†
2004–05	2,799,250	1,855,198	385,987	383,714	143,729	30,622	—	100.0	66.3	13.8	13.7	5.1	1.1	†
2005–06	2,815,544	1,838,765	399,406	396,820	150,925	29,628	—	100.0	65.3	14.2	14.1	5.4	1.1	†
2006–07	2,893,045	1,868,056	418,113	421,036	154,837	31,003	—	100.0	64.6	14.5	14.6	5.4	1.1	†
2007–08	3,001,337	1,898,367	429,840	448,887	159,410	32,036	32,797[1]	100.0	63.3	14.3	15.0	5.3	1.1	1.1[1]
2008–09	3,039,015	1,883,382	451,384	481,698	163,575	32,213	26,763[1]	100.0	62.0	14.9	15.9	5.4	1.1	0.9[1]
2009–10	3,128,022	1,871,980	472,261	545,518	167,840	34,131	36,292[1]	100.0	59.8	15.1	17.4	5.4	1.1	1.2[1]
2010–11	3,144,100	1,835,332	471,461	583,907	168,875	32,768	51,748	100.0	58.4	15.0	18.6	5.4	1.0	1.6
2011–12	3,149,185	1,807,528	467,932	608,726	173,835	32,450	58,703	100.0	57.4	14.9	19.3	5.5	1.0	1.9
2012–13	3,169,257	1,791,147	461,919	640,413	179,101	31,100	65,569	100.0	56.5	14.6	20.2	5.7	1.0	2.1
2013–14[2]	3,168,450	1,765,670	441,190	678,020	181,550	30,120	71,890	100.0	55.7	13.9	21.4	5.7	1.0	2.3
2014–15[2]	3,187,000	1,746,730	446,000	703,430	184,780	29,990	76,060	100.0	54.8	14.0	22.1	5.8	0.9	2.4
2015–16[2]	3,224,140	1,742,530	451,780	731,860	184,660	30,160	83,160	100.0	54.0	14.0	22.7	5.7	0.9	2.6
2016–17[2]	3,255,320	1,737,890	455,260	755,350	186,390	30,120	90,310	100.0	53.4	14.0	23.2	5.7	0.9	2.8
2017–18[2]	3,310,020	1,733,070	461,460	787,440	200,160	29,920	97,970	100.0	52.4	13.9	23.8	6.0	0.9	3.0
2018–19[2]	3,316,970	1,708,880	457,520	816,590	201,210	29,420	103,350	100.0	51.5	13.8	24.6	6.1	0.9	3.1
2019–20[2]	3,294,660	1,669,470	450,140	833,680	203,790	28,640	108,950	100.0	50.7	13.7	25.3	6.2	0.9	3.3
2020–21[2]	3,302,430	1,659,350	438,840	847,220	210,500	28,010	118,520	100.0	50.2	13.3	25.7	6.4	0.8	3.6
2021–22[2]	3,323,040	1,644,960	437,670	867,260	215,970	28,630	128,550	100.0	49.5	13.2	26.1	6.5	0.9	3.9
2022–23[2]	3,337,740	1,619,670	437,020	897,540	216,500	28,350	138,660	100.0	48.5	13.1	26.9	6.5	0.8	4.2
2023–24[2]	3,404,190	1,617,130	448,210	938,810	217,600	28,450	154,000	100.0	47.5	13.2	27.6	6.4	0.8	4.5
2024–25[2]	3,463,190	1,621,480	460,190	964,330	220,810	28,420	167,960	100.0	46.8	13.3	27.8	6.4	0.8	4.8
2025–26[2]	3,458,860	1,593,110	461,810	974,170	224,280	27,780	177,720	100.0	46.1	13.4	28.2	6.5	0.8	5.1
2026–27[2]	3,384,860	1,545,340	453,610	957,640	220,380	27,160	180,730	100.0	45.7	13.4	28.3	6.5	0.8	5.3
2027–28[2]	3,314,690	1,503,860	435,320	937,280	225,420	25,930	186,900	100.0	45.4	13.1	28.3	6.8	0.8	5.6
2028–29[2]	3,290,850	1,486,770	428,000	927,090	229,260	24,670	195,070	100.0	45.2	13.0	28.2	7.0	0.7	5.9
2029–30[2]	3,265,340	1,475,140	425,170	908,160	237,300	24,420	195,160	100.0	45.2	13.0	27.8	7.3	0.7	6.0

—Not available.
†Not applicable.
[1]Data on students of Two or more races were not reported by all states; therefore, the data are not comparable to figures for 2010–11 and later years.
[2]Projected.
NOTE: Race categories exclude persons of Hispanic ethnicity. Prior to 2007–08, data on students of Two or more races were not collected separately. Some data have been revised from previously published figures. Detail may not sum to totals because of rounding and statistical methods used to prevent the identification of individual students.
SOURCE: U.S. Department of Education, National Center for Education Statistics, Common Core of Data (CCD), "State Nonfiscal Survey of Public Elementary/Secondary Education," 1981–82 through 2005–06; "State Dropout and Completion Data File," 2005–06 through 2012–13; and National Public High School Graduates by Race/Ethnicity Projections Model, 1995–96 through 2029–30. (This table was prepared December 2019.)

Table 219.46. Public high school 4-year adjusted cohort graduation rate (ACGR), by selected student characteristics and state: 2010–11 through 2017–18

State	Total, ACGR for all students								ACGR for students with selected characteristics,[1] 2017–18													
									Race/ethnicity													
												Asian/Pacific Islander[5]										
	2010–11	2011–12	2012–13	2013–14	2014–15	2015–16	2016–17	2017–18	White	Black	Hispanic	Total	Asian	Pacific Islander	American Indian/ Alaska Native	Two or more races	Students with disabili- ties[2]	Limited English proficient[3]	Econom- ically disad- vantaged[4]	Homeless enrolled	Foster care
1	2	3	4	5	6	7	8	9	10	11	12	13	14	15	16	17	18	19	20	21	22
United States	79[6]	80[6]	81[7]	82	83	84	85	85	89	79	81	92	—	—	74[8]	—	67	68	80	—	—
Alabama[9]	72	75	80	86	89	87	89	90	92	88	88	94	94	85	90	91	68	64	84	78	77
Alaska	68	70	72	71	76	76	78	79	84	73	76	84	88	74	69	74	57	61	72	57	55
Arizona	78	76	75	76	77	80	78	79	83	74	76	89	90	76	68	75	68	47	73	52	45
Arkansas	81	84	85	87	85	87	88	89	91	86	86	88	95	73	84	90	85	83	87	81	74
California	76	79	80	81	82	83	83	83	87	73	81	93	94	81	71	73	66	68	80	69	53
Colorado	74	75	77	77	79	79	79	81	85	74	73	89	90	74	68	83	59	67	71	55	25
Connecticut	83	85	86	87	87	87	88	88	93	81	79	96	‡	>=90	85	88	65	67	80	70	48
Delaware	78	80	80	87	86	87	87	87	90	83	82	95	‡	>=50	76	91	68	69	78	83	62
District of Columbia	59	59	62	61	69	69	73	69	89	67	65	88	‡	‡	‡	>=90	47	56	59	44	46
Florida	71	75	76	76	78	81	82	86	89	81	85	96	96	89	80	87	77	75	82	74	50
Georgia	67	70	72	73	79	79	81	82	85	79	75	90	—	77	77	82	61	58	77	61	37
Hawaii	80	81	82	82	83	83	85	85	86	82	80	85	92	77	—	—	64	68	80	66	57
Idaho	—	—	—	77	79	80	80	81	82	71	76	83	86	72	61	74	59	76	72	58	47
Illinois	84	82	83	86	86	87	87	85	91	78	82	94	94	84	80	86	72	72	79	68	56
Indiana	86	86	87	88	87	84	84	88	90	79	84	95	96	83	84	85	73	69	78	82	68
Iowa	88	89	90	91	91	91	91	91	93	81	84	91	93	75	76	88	77	79	84	73	76
Kansas	83	85	86	86	86	86	87	87	90	79	81	93	93	81	79	86	80	81	80	68	61
Kentucky	—	—	86	88	88	89	90	90	92	82	83	95	95	85	89	88	75	71	88	84	—
Louisiana	71	72	74	75	78	79	78	81	86	78	68	92	92	76	89	81	59	36	70	60	35
Maine	84	85	87	88	88	87	87	87	87	78	83	92	‡	>=80	71	79	74	76	78	57	56
Maryland	83	84	86	87	88	88	88	87	93	85	72	96	97	84	90	90	67	51	79	67	59
Massachusetts	83	85	85	86	87	88	88	88	92	80	74	94	94	90	83	87	72	64	77	71	61
Michigan	74	76	77	79	80	80	80	81	84	70	74	91	91	87	70	85	58	71	70	57	40
Minnesota	77	78	80	81	82	82	83	83	88	67	67	87	87	76	51	72	62	66	70	47	—
Mississippi	75	75	78	78	81	82	83	84	88	78	79	93	‡	>=80	86	82	38	55	81	71	80
Missouri	81	84	86	87	89	88	88	89	92	80	85	92	97	76	87	90	76	71	82	76	69
Montana	82	84	85	85	86	86	86	86	89	80	79	90	94	‡	68	82	77	63	78	66	75
Nebraska	86	88	89	90	89	89	89	89	93	78	81	82	91	>=80	71	85	69	49	81	59	46
Nevada	62	63	71	70	71	74	81	83	86	72	82	92	94	84	80	83	66	76	81	76	44
New Hampshire	86	86	87	88	88	88	89	89	89	81	76	93	94	75	85	92	74	65	78	65	44
New Jersey	83	86	88	89	90	90	91	91	95	84	85	97	97	93	87	92	80	76	85	73	63
New Mexico	63	70	70	69	69	71	71	74	79	69	73	86	86	‡	66	—	66	71	69	53	46
New York	77	77	77	78	79	80	82	82	90	73	72	89	89	77	69	84	57	31	76	56	61
North Carolina	78	80	83	84	86	86	87	86	90	83	80	93	93	90	84	84	70	68	80	67	73
North Dakota	86	87	88	87	87	88	87	88	91	76	79	89	89	—	72	—	69	68	75	52	71
Ohio	80	81	82	81	80	84	84	82	86	69	73	90	90	—	70	77	51	65	71	51	52
Oklahoma	—	—	85	83	84	83	83	82	83	77	79	86	87	74	81	84	58	61	75	67	61
Oregon	68	68	69	72	74	75	77	79	80	68	75	88	91	75	65	78	61	56	72	54	—
Pennsylvania	83	84	86	85	86	87	87	86	91	72	74	92	93	90	79	79	70	66	78	70	—
Rhode Island	77	77	80	83	81	83	84	84	87	83	77	91	‡	>=50	69	78	62	72	77	57	>=50
South Carolina	74	75	78	80	83	84	84	81	84	77	81	93	‡	>=80	73	80	52	80	83	64	48
South Dakota	83	83	83	84	84	84	83	84	90	75	71	87	87	‡	50	—	63	77	69	60	—
Tennessee	86	87	86	88	89	89	90	90	93	84	83	95	95	91	90	80	73	77	84	75	67
Texas	86	88	88	89	89	90	90	90	94	87	88	96	96	86	85	91	78	77	87	80	63
Utah	76	80	83	84	85	85	86	87	89	76	78	89	92	85	77	78	70	72	77	—	—
Vermont	87	88	87	88	88	88	89	85	86	70	79	72	‡	‡	—	80	68	58	76	60	—
Virginia	82	83	85	85	86	87	87	88	92	84	74	95	95	93	84	91	61	57	80	60	63
Washington	76	77	76	78	79	79	79	81	88	80	83	92	93	81	71	87	70	76	80	65	70
West Virginia	78	79	81	85	88	90	89	90	90	86	92	>=95	>=95	>=50	87	86	70	93	88	87	72
Wisconsin	87	88	88	89	88	88	89	90	94	70	82	91	91	>=90	78	85	69	70	80	70	51
Wyoming	80	79	77	79	79	80	86	82	84	77	75	86	86	>=50	59	78	63	61	70	62	—

See notes at end of table.

Table 219.46. Public high school 4-year adjusted cohort graduation rate (ACGR), by selected student characteristics and state: 2010–11 through 2017–18—Continued

—Not available.

‡Reporting standards not met (too few cases).

[1]The time when students are identified as having certain characteristics varies by state. Depending on the state, a student may be included in a category if the relevant characteristic is reported in 9th-grade data, if the characteristic is reported in 12th-grade data, or if it is reported at any point during the student's high school years.

[2]Students identified as children with disabilities under the Individuals with Disabilities Education Act (IDEA).

[3]Students who met the definition of limited English proficient students as outlined in the EDFacts workbook. For more information, see https://www2.ed.gov/about/inits/ed/edfacts/eden-workbook.html.

[4]Students who met the state criteria for classification as economically disadvantaged.

[5]States either report data for a combined "Asian/Pacific Islander" group or report the "Asian" and "Pacific Islander" groups separately. Total represents either a single value reported by the state for "Asian/Pacific Islander" or an aggregation of separate values reported for "Asian" and "Pacific Islander." "Asian/Pacific Islander" includes the "Filipino" group, which only California and Hawaii report separately.

[6]Includes imputed data for Idaho, Kentucky, and Oklahoma. Data were not available for these states because they had not yet started reporting ACGR data in 2010–11 and 2011–12.

[7]Includes imputed data for Idaho. Data were not available for Idaho because this state had not yet started reporting ACGR data in 2012–13.

[8]Estimated assuming a count of zero American Indian/Alaska Native students for Hawaii.

[9]Use data with caution. The Alabama State Department of Education has indicated that their ACGR data for some years was misstated. For more information, please see the following press release issued by the state: https://www.alsde.edu/sec/comm/News%20Releases/12-08-2016%20Graduation%20Rate%20Review.pdf.

NOTE: The adjusted cohort graduation rate (ACGR) is the percentage of public high school freshmen who graduate with a regular diploma within 4 years of starting 9th grade. Students who are entering 9th grade for the first time form a cohort for the graduating class. This cohort is "adjusted" by adding any students who subsequently transfer into the cohort and subtracting any students who subsequently transfer out, emigrate to another country, or die. Values preceded by the ">=" symbol have been "blurred" (rounded) to protect student privacy. Race categories exclude persons of Hispanic ethnicity.

SOURCE: U.S. Department of Education, Office of Elementary and Secondary Education, Consolidated State Performance Report, 2010–11 through 2017–18. (This table was prepared February 2020.)

Table 219.55. Among 15- to 24-year-olds enrolled in grades 10 through 12, percentage who dropped out (event dropout rate), by sex and race/ethnicity: 1972 through 2018

[Standard errors appear in parentheses]

Year	Total[2]		Sex				Race/ethnicity					
			Male		Female		White		Black		Hispanic	
1	2		3		4		5		6		7	
1972	6.1	(0.34)	5.9	(0.47)	6.3	(0.49)	5.3	(0.35)	9.6	(1.36)	11.2!	(3.70)
1973	6.3	(0.34)	6.8	(0.50)	5.7	(0.46)	5.5	(0.35)	10.0	(1.39)	10.0!	(3.50)
1974	6.7	(0.35)	7.4	(0.52)	6.0	(0.47)	5.8	(0.36)	11.6	(1.44)	9.9!	(3.34)
1975	5.8	(0.32)	5.4	(0.45)	6.1	(0.47)	5.1	(0.34)	8.7	(1.28)	10.9!	(3.30)
1976	5.9	(0.33)	6.6	(0.49)	5.2	(0.44)	5.6	(0.36)	7.4	(1.18)	7.3!	(2.71)
1977	6.5	(0.34)	6.9	(0.49)	6.1	(0.47)	6.1	(0.37)	8.6	(1.21)	7.8!	(2.79)
1978	6.7	(0.35)	7.5	(0.52)	5.9	(0.46)	5.8	(0.36)	10.2	(1.32)	12.3	(3.60)
1979	6.7	(0.35)	6.8	(0.50)	6.7	(0.49)	6.1	(0.37)	10.0	(1.34)	9.8!	(3.20)
1980	6.1	(0.33)	6.7	(0.49)	5.5	(0.45)	5.3	(0.35)	8.3	(1.22)	11.7	(3.36)
1981	5.9	(0.33)	6.0	(0.47)	5.8	(0.46)	4.9	(0.34)	9.7	(1.30)	10.7	(3.00)
1982	5.5	(0.34)	5.8	(0.50)	5.2	(0.47)	4.8	(0.37)	7.8	(1.23)	9.2!	(3.04)
1983	5.2	(0.34)	5.8	(0.50)	4.7	(0.46)	4.4	(0.36)	7.0	(1.20)	10.1!	(3.18)
1984	5.1	(0.34)	5.5	(0.50)	4.8	(0.47)	4.5	(0.37)	5.8	(1.08)	11.1	(3.28)
1985	5.3	(0.35)	5.4	(0.51)	5.1	(0.49)	4.4	(0.37)	7.8	(1.29)	9.8	(2.58)
1986	4.7	(0.33)	4.7	(0.46)	4.7	(0.46)	3.8	(0.34)	5.5	(1.08)	11.9	(2.70)
1987	4.1	(0.31)	4.4	(0.45)	3.8	(0.42)	3.6	(0.33)	6.4	(1.16)	5.6!	(1.94)
1988	4.8	(0.37)	5.4	(0.55)	4.6	(0.53)	4.4	(0.42)	6.3	(1.28)	11.0	(3.08)
1989	4.5	(0.35)	4.6	(0.50)	4.6	(0.50)	3.6	(0.37)	8.2	(1.40)	8.1	(2.43)
1990	4.0	(0.33)	4.2	(0.49)	4.1	(0.49)	3.5	(0.37)	5.2	(1.17)	8.4	(2.41)
1991	4.0	(0.33)	3.9	(0.47)	4.4	(0.51)	3.3	(0.37)	6.4	(1.27)	7.8	(2.33)
1992	4.4	(0.35)	3.9	(0.46)	4.9	(0.53)	3.7	(0.38)	5.0	(1.09)	8.2	(2.23)
1993	4.5	(0.36)	4.6	(0.51)	4.3	(0.50)	3.9	(0.40)	5.8	(1.20)	6.7!	(2.02)
1994	5.3	(0.37)	5.2	(0.51)	5.4	(0.53)	4.2	(0.40)	6.6	(1.21)	10.0	(2.18)
1995	5.7	(0.35)	6.2	(0.51)	5.3	(0.48)	4.5	(0.38)	6.4	(1.01)	12.4	(1.62)
1996	5.0	(0.34)	5.0	(0.48)	5.1	(0.49)	4.1	(0.38)	6.7	(1.05)	9.0	(1.49)
1997	4.6	(0.32)	5.0	(0.47)	4.1	(0.43)	3.6	(0.35)	5.0	(0.91)	9.5	(1.45)
1998	4.8	(0.33)	4.6	(0.45)	4.9	(0.47)	3.9	(0.36)	5.2	(0.91)	9.4	(1.46)
1999	5.0	(0.33)	4.6	(0.44)	5.4	(0.49)	4.0	(0.36)	6.5	(0.99)	7.8	(1.27)
2000	4.8	(0.33)	5.5	(0.49)	4.1	(0.43)	4.1	(0.37)	6.1	(1.00)	7.4	(1.24)
2001	5.0	(0.32)	5.6	(0.46)	4.3	(0.42)	4.1	(0.35)	6.3	(0.96)	8.8	(1.31)
2002	3.5	(0.27)	3.7	(0.39)	3.4	(0.37)	2.6	(0.28)	4.9	(0.87)	5.8	(1.01)
2003	4.0	(0.28)	4.2	(0.40)	3.8	(0.38)	3.2	(0.31)	4.8	(0.85)	7.1	(1.06)
2004	4.7	(0.30)	5.1	(0.44)	4.3	(0.41)	3.7	(0.34)	5.7	(0.94)	8.9	(1.20)
2005	3.8	(0.27)	4.2	(0.40)	3.4	(0.36)	2.8	(0.29)	7.3	(1.03)	5.0	(0.87)
2006	3.8	(0.27)	4.1	(0.39)	3.4	(0.36)	2.9	(0.30)	3.8	(0.77)	7.0	(1.01)
2007	3.5	(0.26)	3.7	(0.37)	3.3	(0.35)	2.2	(0.26)	4.5	(0.80)	6.0	(0.98)
2008	3.5	(0.26)	3.1	(0.34)	4.0	(0.39)	2.3	(0.27)	6.4	(0.94)	5.3	(0.85)
2009	3.4	(0.25)	3.5	(0.36)	3.4	(0.35)	2.4	(0.28)	4.8	(0.83)	5.8	(0.87)
2010	3.0	(0.26)	3.0	(0.36)	2.9	(0.35)	2.3	(0.29)	3.6	(0.88)	4.1	(0.73)
2011	3.4	(0.30)	3.6	(0.43)	3.1	(0.37)	2.7	(0.38)	4.4	(0.87)	4.6	(0.81)
2012	3.4	(0.32)	3.6	(0.48)	3.3	(0.49)	1.6	(0.24)	6.8	(1.35)	5.4	(0.93)
2013	4.7	(0.40)	4.8	(0.53)	4.5	(0.55)	4.3	(0.51)	5.8	(1.17)	5.7	(0.95)
2014	5.2	(0.38)	5.4	(0.58)	5.0	(0.53)	4.7	(0.43)	5.7	(1.21)	7.9	(1.05)
2015	4.9	(0.43)	5.1	(0.60)	4.6	(0.57)	3.8	(0.47)	6.8	(1.37)	6.2	(1.12)
2016	4.8	(0.36)	5.4	(0.57)	4.1	(0.52)	4.5	(0.45)	5.9	(1.19)	4.7	(0.76)
2017	4.7	(0.37)	5.4	(0.52)	3.9	(0.49)	3.9	(0.43)	5.5	(1.16)	6.5	(0.98)
2018	4.7	(0.43)	4.2	(0.48)	5.2	(0.66)	3.6	(0.50)	6.8	(1.35)	6.1	(1.03)

!Interpret data with caution. The coefficient of variation (CV) for this estimate is between 30 and 50 percent.
[1]The event dropout rate is the percentage of 15- to 24-year-olds in grades 10 through 12 who dropped out between one October and the next (e.g., the 2018 data refer to 10th- through 12th-graders who were enrolled in October 2017 but had dropped out by October 2018). Dropping out is defined as leaving school without a high school diploma or alternative credential such as a GED certificate.
[2]Includes other racial/ethnic groups not separately shown.

NOTE: Data are based on sample surveys of the civilian noninstitutionalized population, which excludes persons in the military and persons living in institutions (e.g., prisons or nursing facilities). Because of changes in data collection procedures, data for 1992 and later years may not be comparable with figures for prior years. Prior to 2010, standard errors were computed using generalized variance function methodology rather than the more precise replicate weight methodology used in later years. Race categories exclude persons of Hispanic ethnicity. Detail may not sum to totals because of rounding.
SOURCE: U.S. Department of Commerce, Census Bureau, Current Population Survey (CPS), October, 1972 through 2018. (This table was prepared October 2019.)

Table 219.57. Among 15- to 24-year-olds enrolled in grades 10 through 12, percentage who dropped out (event dropout rate), and number and percentage distribution of 15- to 24-year-olds in grades 10 through 12, by selected characteristics: Selected years, 2008 through 2018

[Standard errors appear in parentheses]

Selected characteristic	Event dropout rate[1] 2008		2013		2017		2018		2018 — Number of 15- to 24-year-olds enrolled in grades 10 through 12 (in thousands) Total population[2]		Event dropouts only[3]		2018 — Percentage distribution of 15- to 24-year-olds enrolled in grades 10 through 12 Total population[2]		Event dropouts only[3]	
1	2		3		4		5		6		7		8		9	
Total	**3.5**	**(0.26)**	**4.7**	**(0.40)**	**4.7**	**(0.37)**	**4.7**	**(0.43)**	**11,033**	**(155.2)**	**518**	**(46.0)**	**100.0**	**(†)**	**100.0**	**(†)**
Sex																
Male	3.1	(0.34)	4.8	(0.53)	5.4	(0.52)	4.2	(0.48)	5,646	(92.2)	236	(27.1)	51.2	(0.54)	45.6	(4.09)
Female	4.0	(0.39)	4.5	(0.55)	3.9	(0.49)	5.2	(0.66)	5,387	(103.5)	282	(34.9)	48.8	(0.54)	54.4	(4.09)
Race/ethnicity																
White	2.3	(0.27)	4.3	(0.51)	3.9	(0.43)	3.6	(0.50)	5,878	(110.2)	213	(29.4)	53.3	(0.61)	41.1	(4.52)
Black	6.4	(0.94)	5.8	(1.17)	5.5	(1.16)	6.8	(1.35)	1,508	(58.8)	‡	(†)	13.7	(0.51)	19.9	(3.73)
Hispanic	5.3	(0.85)	5.7	(0.95)	6.5	(0.98)	6.1	(1.03)	2,513	(65.3)	153	(26.4)	22.8	(0.64)	29.5	(4.32)
Asian	4.2!	(1.57)	1.8!	(0.78)	4.7!	(1.53)	4.7!	(1.79)	588	(47.8)	‡	(†)	5.3	(0.40)	5.4!	(2.03)
Pacific Islander	‡	(†)	‡	(†)	‡	(†)	‡	(†)	‡	(†)	‡	(†)	0.4	(0.10)	‡	(†)
American Indian/Alaska Native	‡	(†)	‡	(†)	4.4!	(1.86)	‡	(†)	100	(18.8)	‡	(†)	0.9	(0.17)	‡	(†)
Two or more races	‡	(†)	5.0!	(2.34)	‡	(†)	‡	(†)	399	(39.9)	‡	(†)	3.6	(0.34)	‡	(†)
Age[4]																
15 and 16	2.4	(0.40)	5.2	(0.73)	4.5	(0.64)	5.6	(0.94)	3,047	(96.6)	169	(27.2)	27.6	(0.69)	32.7	(4.11)
17	3.1	(0.41)	4.0	(0.62)	4.1	(0.55)	4.2	(0.59)	3,657	(70.3)	153	(21.9)	33.1	(0.55)	29.6	(3.53)
18	3.6	(0.50)	2.9	(0.58)	5.2	(0.79)	3.5	(0.64)	3,046	(72.6)	108	(19.4)	27.6	(0.54)	20.8	(3.22)
19	4.9	(1.11)	7.2	(1.61)	6.1!	(1.89)	6.5	(1.62)	877	(55.9)	‡	(†)	8.0	(0.49)	11.1	(2.87)
20 to 24	14.9	(2.79)	14.4	(3.41)	5.8!	(2.31)	7.5!	(2.71)	406	(47.3)	‡	(†)	3.7	(0.43)	5.9!	(2.04)
Recency of immigration[5]																
Born outside the United States	6.3	(1.49)	4.8	(1.24)	8.0	(1.72)	10.4	(2.48)	721	(50.1)	‡	(†)	6.5	(0.44)	14.5	(3.32)
Hispanic	7.2!	(2.18)	5.5!	(2.19)	5.9!	(2.27)	15.6	(4.53)	345	(35.7)	‡	(†)	3.1	(0.33)	10.4	(3.09)
Non-Hispanic	5.3!	(1.98)	4.1!	(1.52)	9.6	(2.53)	5.7!	(2.30)	376	(35.2)	‡	(†)	3.4	(0.31)	4.1!	(1.68)
First generation	2.5	(0.58)	4.4	(0.86)	4.2	(0.85)	6.4	(1.30)	2,208	(86.0)	142	(29.0)	20.0	(0.75)	27.4	(4.74)
Hispanic	3.6!	(1.11)	6.5	(1.48)	4.7	(1.17)	5.2	(1.21)	1,239	(62.4)	‡	(†)	11.2	(0.59)	12.5	(2.69)
Non-Hispanic	1.4!	(0.60)	1.9!	(0.74)	3.5	(1.04)	8.0	(2.20)	969	(62.5)	‡	(†)	8.8	(0.53)	14.9	(3.90)
Second or later generation	3.5	(0.29)	4.8	(0.46)	4.5	(0.45)	3.7	(0.40)	8,103	(150.5)	301	(32.0)	73.4	(0.78)	58.1	(4.98)
Hispanic	6.1	(1.47)	5.0	(1.16)	8.8	(1.93)	3.7!	(1.29)	929	(57.1)	‡	(†)	8.4	(0.51)	6.7!	(2.37)
Non-Hispanic	3.2	(0.29)	4.7	(0.47)	4.0	(0.40)	3.7	(0.43)	7,175	(144.9)	266	(30.4)	65.0	(0.80)	51.4	(4.81)
Disability status[6]																
With a disability	—	(†)	7.8!	(2.84)	6.2!	(2.10)	7.3	(1.83)	426	(39.8)	‡	(†)	3.9	(0.36)	6.0	(1.67)
Without a disability	—	(†)	4.6	(0.39)	4.6	(0.39)	4.6	(0.44)	10,607	(154.3)	487	(45.2)	96.1	(0.36)	94.0	(1.67)
Region																
Northeast	2.3	(0.50)	2.2	(0.57)	4.9	(1.01)	3.8	(0.99)	1,878	(86.6)	‡	(†)	17.0	(0.71)	13.7	(3.44)
Midwest	2.7	(0.47)	4.5	(0.85)	3.2	(0.63)	2.7	(0.57)	2,512	(85.0)	‡	(†)	22.8	(0.69)	13.2	(2.69)
South	4.3	(0.50)	5.8	(0.79)	5.2	(0.62)	5.6	(0.76)	4,016	(105.7)	225	(31.5)	36.4	(0.88)	43.4	(4.61)
West	4.1	(0.58)	4.9	(0.68)	5.1	(0.73)	5.8	(0.93)	2,627	(84.3)	154	(24.5)	23.8	(0.70)	29.6	(4.06)

—Not available.

†Not applicable.

!Interpret data with caution. The coefficient of variation (CV) for this estimate is between 30 and 50 percent.

‡Reporting standards not met. Either there are too few cases for a reliable estimate or the coefficient of variation (CV) is 50 percent or greater.

[1]The event dropout rate is the percentage of 15- to 24-year-olds in grades 10 through 12 who dropped out between one October and the next (e.g., the 2018 data refer to 10th- through 12th-graders who were enrolled in October 2017 but had dropped out by October 2018). Dropping out is defined as leaving school without a high school diploma or alternative credential such as a GED certificate.

[2]Includes all 15- to 24-year-olds who were enrolled in grades 10 through 12 in October 2017.

[3]Includes only those 15- to 24-year-olds who dropped out of grades 10 through 12 between October 2017 and October 2018. Dropping out is defined as leaving school without a high school diploma or alternative credential such as a GED certificate.

[4]Age at the time of data collection. A person's age at the time of dropping out may be 1 year younger, because the dropout event could occur at any time over the previous 12-month period.

[5]United States refers to the 50 states, the District of Columbia, Puerto Rico, American Samoa, Guam, the U.S. Virgin Islands, and the Northern Marianas. Children born abroad to U.S.-citizen parents are counted as born in the United States. Individuals defined as "first generation" were born in the United States, but one or both of their parents were born outside the United States. Individuals defined as "second generation or higher" were born in the United States, as were both of their parents.

[6]Individuals identified as having a disability reported difficulty with at least one of the following: hearing, seeing even when wearing glasses, walking or climbing stairs, dressing or bathing, doing errands alone, concentrating, remembering, or making decisions.

NOTE: Data are based on sample surveys of the civilian noninstitutionalized population, which excludes persons in the military and persons living in institutions (e.g., prisons or nursing facilities). Race categories exclude persons of Hispanic ethnicity. Detail may not sum to totals because of rounding. Prior to 2010, standard errors were computed using generalized variance function methodology rather than the more precise replicate weight methodology used in later years.

SOURCE: U.S. Department of Commerce, Census Bureau, Current Population Survey (CPS), October, 2008 through 2018. (This table was prepared October 2019.)

Table 219.65. High school completion rate of 18- to 24-year-olds not enrolled in high school (status completion rate), by sex and race/ethnicity: 1972 through 2018

[Standard errors appear in parentheses]

Year	Total		Sex				Race/ethnicity							
			Male		Female		White		Black		Hispanic		Asian[2]	
1	2		3		4		5		6		7		8	
1972	82.8	(0.36)	83.0	(0.52)	82.7	(0.49)	86.0	(0.36)	72.1	(1.45)	56.2	(3.67)	—	(†)
1973	83.7	(0.34)	84.0	(0.50)	83.4	(0.48)	87.0	(0.35)	71.6	(1.42)	58.7	(3.68)	—	(†)
1974	83.6	(0.34)	83.4	(0.50)	83.8	(0.47)	86.7	(0.35)	72.9	(1.41)	60.1	(3.40)	—	(†)
1975	83.8	(0.34)	84.1	(0.48)	83.6	(0.47)	87.2	(0.34)	70.2	(1.43)	62.2	(3.45)	—	(†)
1976	83.5	(0.33)	83.0	(0.49)	84.0	(0.46)	86.4	(0.34)	73.5	(1.36)	60.3	(3.36)	—	(†)
1977	83.6	(0.33)	82.8	(0.49)	84.4	(0.45)	86.7	(0.34)	73.9	(1.34)	58.6	(3.50)	—	(†)
1978	83.6	(0.33)	82.8	(0.48)	84.2	(0.45)	86.9	(0.34)	73.4	(1.33)	58.8	(3.21)	—	(†)
1979	83.1	(0.33)	82.1	(0.49)	84.0	(0.45)	86.5	(0.34)	72.6	(1.33)	58.5	(3.15)	—	(†)
1980	83.9	(0.32)	82.3	(0.48)	85.3	(0.43)	87.5	(0.33)	75.2	(1.28)	57.1	(2.99)	—	(†)
1981	83.8	(0.32)	82.0	(0.48)	85.4	(0.43)	87.1	(0.33)	76.7	(1.22)	59.1	(2.90)	—	(†)
1982	83.8	(0.34)	82.7	(0.50)	84.9	(0.46)	87.0	(0.35)	76.4	(1.28)	60.9	(2.61)	—	(†)
1983	83.9	(0.34)	82.1	(0.51)	85.6	(0.45)	87.4	(0.35)	76.8	(1.27)	59.4	(3.13)	—	(†)
1984	84.7	(0.34)	83.3	(0.50)	85.9	(0.45)	87.5	(0.35)	80.3	(1.19)	63.7	(3.03)	—	(†)
1985	85.4	(0.34)	84.0	(0.50)	86.7	(0.45)	88.2	(0.35)	81.0	(1.20)	66.6	(2.40)	—	(†)
1986	85.5	(0.34)	84.2	(0.51)	86.7	(0.45)	88.8	(0.35)	81.8	(1.19)	63.5	(2.30)	—	(†)
1987	84.7	(0.35)	83.6	(0.52)	85.8	(0.47)	87.7	(0.37)	81.9	(1.20)	65.1	(2.24)	—	(†)
1988	84.5	(0.39)	83.2	(0.58)	85.8	(0.52)	88.6	(0.40)	80.9	(1.35)	58.2	(2.56)	—	(†)
1989	84.7	(0.37)	83.2	(0.55)	86.2	(0.49)	89.0	(0.38)	81.9	(1.25)	59.4	(2.29)	89.3	(2.46)
1990	85.6	(0.36)	85.1	(0.53)	86.0	(0.50)	89.6	(0.37)	83.2	(1.22)	59.1	(2.35)	94.2	(1.72)
1991	84.9	(0.37)	83.8	(0.55)	85.9	(0.51)	89.4	(0.38)	82.5	(1.26)	56.5	(2.32)	95.2	(1.42)
1992	86.4	(0.36)	85.3	(0.53)	87.4	(0.49)	90.7	(0.36)	82.0	(1.26)	62.1	(2.32)	93.1	(1.73)
1993	86.2	(0.36)	85.4	(0.53)	86.9	(0.50)	90.1	(0.37)	81.9	(1.27)	64.4	(2.26)	93.9	(1.66)
1994	85.8	(0.36)	84.5	(0.53)	87.0	(0.49)	90.7	(0.36)	83.3	(1.19)	61.8	(2.06)	92.4	(1.83)
1995	85.0	(0.34)	84.3	(0.50)	85.7	(0.47)	89.5	(0.36)	84.1	(1.01)	62.6	(1.40)	94.8	(1.43)
1996	86.2	(0.35)	85.7	(0.50)	86.8	(0.48)	91.5	(0.34)	83.0	(1.08)	61.9	(1.49)	93.5	(1.24)
1997	85.9	(0.35)	84.6	(0.51)	87.2	(0.47)	90.5	(0.36)	82.0	(1.10)	66.7	(1.42)	90.6	(1.58)
1998	84.8	(0.36)	82.6	(0.53)	87.0	(0.47)	90.2	(0.36)	81.4	(1.11)	62.8	(1.37)	94.2	(1.22)
1999	85.9	(0.34)	84.8	(0.50)	87.0	(0.46)	91.2	(0.34)	83.5	(1.04)	63.4	(1.39)	94.0	(1.19)
2000	86.5	(0.33)	84.9	(0.49)	88.1	(0.44)	91.8	(0.33)	83.7	(1.01)	64.1	(1.36)	94.6	(1.13)
2001	86.5	(0.31)	84.6	(0.47)	88.3	(0.41)	91.1	(0.32)	85.7	(0.92)	65.7	(1.24)	96.1	(0.91)
2002	86.6	(0.31)	84.8	(0.46)	88.4	(0.41)	91.8	(0.31)	84.7	(0.95)	67.3	(1.15)	95.7	(0.89)
2003	87.1	(0.30)	85.1	(0.46)	89.2	(0.40)	91.9	(0.31)	85.0	(0.96)	69.2	(1.15)	94.8	(1.06)
2004	86.9	(0.30)	84.9	(0.46)	88.8	(0.40)	91.7	(0.31)	83.5	(0.98)	69.9	(1.12)	95.2	(1.00)
2005	87.6	(0.30)	85.4	(0.45)	89.8	(0.38)	92.3	(0.30)	86.0	(0.91)	70.3	(1.12)	96.0	(0.93)
2006	87.8	(0.29)	86.5	(0.43)	89.2	(0.39)	92.6	(0.30)	84.9	(0.93)	70.9	(1.11)	95.8	(0.95)
2007	89.0	(0.28)	87.4	(0.42)	90.6	(0.37)	93.5	(0.28)	88.8	(0.80)	72.7	(1.07)	92.8	(1.23)
2008	89.9	(0.27)	89.3	(0.39)	90.5	(0.37)	94.2	(0.26)	86.9	(0.86)	75.5	(1.03)	95.5	(1.01)
2009	89.8	(0.27)	88.3	(0.40)	91.2	(0.35)	93.8	(0.27)	87.1	(0.84)	76.8	(1.00)	97.6	(0.72)
2010	90.4	(0.35)	89.2	(0.53)	91.6	(0.38)	93.7	(0.38)	89.2	(1.08)	79.4	(1.21)	95.3	(1.26)
2011	90.8	(0.35)	89.9	(0.50)	91.8	(0.46)	93.8	(0.39)	90.1	(0.98)	82.2	(1.04)	94.1	(1.48)
2012	91.3	(0.33)	90.3	(0.47)	92.3	(0.45)	94.6	(0.38)	90.0	(1.01)	82.8	(1.02)	95.3	(1.24)
2013	92.0	(0.35)	91.4	(0.47)	92.6	(0.45)	94.3	(0.38)	91.5	(1.13)	85.0	(0.98)	96.3	(1.27)
2014	92.4	(0.32)	91.8	(0.46)	93.1	(0.38)	94.2	(0.40)	91.7	(0.91)	87.1	(0.88)	98.8	(0.47)
2015	93.0	(0.33)	92.5	(0.44)	93.4	(0.45)	94.7	(0.36)	91.9	(0.91)	88.4	(0.93)	97.3	(0.75)
2016	92.9	(0.32)	91.6	(0.46)	94.3	(0.37)	94.5	(0.36)	92.2	(1.02)	89.1	(0.81)	96.8	(0.75)
2017	93.3	(0.33)	92.3	(0.44)	94.3	(0.41)	94.8	(0.38)	93.8	(0.84)	88.3	(0.90)	98.6	(0.51)
2018	93.6	(0.32)	92.3	(0.46)	94.9	(0.39)	94.9	(0.37)	94.4	(0.85)	89.2	(0.85)	96.9	(0.92)

—Not available.
†Not applicable.
[1]The status completion rate is the number of 18- to 24-year-olds who are high school completers as a percentage of the total number of 18- to 24-year-olds who are not enrolled in high school or a lower level of education. High school completers include those with a high school diploma, as well as those with an alternative credential, such as a GED.
[2]Prior to 2003, Asian data include Pacific Islanders.
NOTE: Data are based on sample surveys of the civilian noninstitutionalized population, which excludes persons in the military and persons living in institutions (e.g., prisons or nursing facilities). Because of changes in data collection procedures, data for 1992 and later years may not be comparable with figures for prior years. Prior to 2010, standard errors were computed using generalized variance function methodology rather than the more precise replicate weight methodology used in later years. Race categories exclude persons of Hispanic ethnicity. Totals include other racial/ethnic groups not separately shown.
SOURCE: U.S. Department of Commerce, Census Bureau, Current Population Survey (CPS), October, 1972 through 2018. (This table was prepared November 2019.)

Table 219.67. High school completion rate of 18- to 24-year-olds not enrolled in high school (status completion rate), number of 18- to 24-year-olds not in high school, and number who are high school completers (status completers), by selected characteristics: Selected years, 2008 through 2018

[Standard errors appear in parentheses]

Selected characteristic	Status completion rate[1] 2008		2013		2017		2018		2018 Number of 18- to 24-year-olds not enrolled in high school (in thousands) Total population[2]		Status completers only[3]		2018 Percentage distribution of 18- to 24-year-olds not enrolled in high school Total population[2]		Status completers only[3]	
1	2		3		4		5		6		7		8		9	
Total	**89.9**	**(0.27)**	**92.0**	**(0.35)**	**93.3**	**(0.33)**	**93.6**	**(0.32)**	**27,713**	**(198.9)**	**25,950**	**(209.8)**	**100.0**	**(†)**	**100.0**	**(†)**
Sex																
Male	89.3	(0.39)	91.4	(0.47)	92.3	(0.44)	92.3	(0.46)	13,811	(111.7)	12,754	(125.5)	49.8	(0.16)	49.1	(0.23)
Female	90.5	(0.37)	92.6	(0.45)	94.3	(0.41)	94.9	(0.39)	13,902	(106.5)	13,196	(115.4)	50.2	(0.16)	50.9	(0.23)
Race/ethnicity																
White	94.2	(0.26)	94.3	(0.38)	94.8	(0.38)	94.9	(0.37)	14,887	(96.7)	14,134	(107.8)	53.7	(0.39)	54.5	(0.40)
Black	86.9	(0.86)	91.5	(1.13)	93.8	(0.84)	94.4	(0.85)	3,801	(89.9)	3,588	(91.5)	13.7	(0.26)	13.8	(0.29)
Hispanic	75.5	(1.03)	85.0	(0.98)	88.3	(0.90)	89.2	(0.85)	6,316	(80.9)	5,636	(87.8)	22.8	(0.22)	21.7	(0.27)
Asian	95.5	(1.01)	96.3	(1.27)	98.6	(0.51)	96.9	(0.92)	1,694	(55.5)	1,642	(55.7)	6.1	(0.18)	6.3	(0.19)
Pacific Islander	95.9	(3.99)	99.3	(0.79)	89.2	(7.65)	93.1	(4.39)	99	(18.3)	92	(17.3)	0.4	(0.07)	0.4	(0.07)
American Indian/Alaska Native	82.5	(4.03)	91.7	(2.97)	86.3	(3.21)	91.1	(2.21)	233	(31.7)	212	(30.4)	0.8	(0.11)	0.8	(0.12)
Two or more races	94.2	(1.72)	93.6	(1.83)	96.4	(1.28)	94.5	(1.85)	683	(40.3)	646	(41.3)	2.5	(0.15)	2.5	(0.16)
Race/ethnicity by sex																
Male																
White	93.6	(0.39)	93.8	(0.48)	94.3	(0.51)	93.9	(0.57)	7,461	(88.3)	7,008	(95.9)	54.0	(0.47)	54.9	(0.53)
Black	89.1	(1.15)	90.3	(1.41)	92.1	(1.48)	93.0	(1.19)	1,814	(48.7)	1,688	(51.6)	13.1	(0.31)	13.2	(0.36)
Hispanic	73.2	(1.48)	83.8	(1.35)	85.9	(1.22)	86.9	(1.19)	3,192	(48.7)	2,774	(56.1)	23.1	(0.33)	21.8	(0.40)
Asian	95.3	(1.49)	97.6	(1.17)	99.3	(0.41)	97.0	(1.17)	876	(34.8)	849	(37.2)	6.3	(0.24)	6.7	(0.27)
Pacific Islander	‡	(†)	‡	(†)	‡	(†)	‡	(†)	‡	(†)	‡	(†)	0.3!	(0.09)	0.3!	(0.09)
American Indian/Alaska Native	74.7	(7.04)	90.5	(6.44)	85.8	(5.00)	91.9	(3.13)	108	(20.3)	99	(19.5)	0.8	(0.15)	0.8	(0.15)
Two or more races	95.2	(2.18)	94.7	(2.65)	95.1	(2.14)	94.1	(2.99)	319	(37.0)	300	(37.3)	2.3	(0.27)	2.4	(0.30)
Female																
White	94.9	(0.35)	94.7	(0.45)	95.2	(0.49)	96.0	(0.46)	7,426	(67.6)	7,126	(71.5)	53.4	(0.69)	54.0	(0.70)
Black	85.0	(1.25)	92.6	(1.39)	95.3	(0.96)	95.7	(1.06)	1,987	(57.6)	1,901	(57.6)	14.3	(0.34)	14.4	(0.37)
Hispanic	77.9	(1.42)	86.2	(1.30)	90.7	(1.16)	91.6	(1.03)	3,124	(60.7)	2,862	(63.8)	22.5	(0.34)	21.7	(0.38)
Asian	95.6	(1.36)	94.9	(1.94)	97.9	(0.90)	96.8	(1.45)	818	(37.6)	793	(37.3)	5.9	(0.26)	6.0	(0.27)
Pacific Islander	‡	(†)	‡	(†)	‡	(†)	‡	(†)	‡	(†)	‡	(†)	0.4	(0.11)	0.4	(0.11)
American Indian/Alaska Native	88.2	(4.51)	92.5	(4.02)	87.0	(5.29)	90.4	(3.31)	125	(19.7)	113	(18.5)	0.9	(0.14)	0.9	(0.14)
Two or more races	93.1	(2.69)	92.5	(2.88)	97.4	(1.41)	94.9	(1.70)	364	(28.1)	346	(28.2)	2.6	(0.20)	2.6	(0.21)
Age																
18 and 19	89.0	(0.55)	91.4	(0.69)	90.6	(0.70)	91.4	(0.62)	6,802	(86.5)	6,218	(92.8)	24.5	(0.37)	24.0	(0.41)
20 and 21	91.0	(0.47)	92.4	(0.63)	94.2	(0.54)	94.3	(0.51)	8,185	(194.5)	7,720	(189.3)	29.5	(0.59)	29.8	(0.61)
22 to 24	89.7	(0.40)	92.1	(0.51)	94.2	(0.41)	94.4	(0.44)	12,725	(163.6)	12,011	(167.5)	45.9	(0.51)	46.3	(0.54)
Recency of immigration[4]																
Born outside the United States	73.9	(1.33)	82.2	(1.52)	86.6	(1.34)	87.2	(1.43)	2,780	(110.5)	2,425	(105.4)	10.0	(0.38)	9.3	(0.39)
Hispanic	59.0	(1.97)	71.8	(2.53)	78.1	(2.25)	79.1	(2.46)	1,296	(75.0)	1,025	(64.4)	4.7	(0.27)	3.9	(0.25)
Non-Hispanic	93.4	(1.15)	92.7	(1.50)	94.7	(1.23)	94.3	(1.39)	1,485	(82.0)	1,401	(83.3)	5.4	(0.29)	5.4	(0.31)
First generation	91.3	(0.73)	92.3	(0.86)	94.3	(0.75)	94.1	(0.79)	5,073	(135.8)	4,771	(134.2)	18.3	(0.47)	18.4	(0.49)
Hispanic	85.4	(1.51)	89.9	(1.29)	91.7	(1.18)	91.4	(1.22)	2,801	(94.5)	2,561	(91.4)	10.1	(0.33)	9.9	(0.34)
Non-Hispanic	96.4	(0.66)	95.5	(1.15)	97.9	(0.64)	97.3	(0.73)	2,272	(90.3)	2,210	(91.1)	8.2	(0.32)	8.5	(0.34)
Second generation or higher	92.0	(0.27)	93.3	(0.38)	94.1	(0.37)	94.4	(0.34)	19,860	(196.8)	18,754	(200.7)	71.7	(0.57)	72.3	(0.60)
Hispanic	84.0	(1.53)	88.7	(1.47)	90.8	(1.37)	92.4	(1.25)	2,219	(108.4)	2,051	(104.5)	8.0	(0.39)	7.9	(0.40)
Non-Hispanic	92.6	(0.27)	93.8	(0.38)	94.5	(0.37)	94.7	(0.36)	17,640	(163.2)	16,703	(171.6)	63.7	(0.47)	64.4	(0.52)
Disability[5]																
With a disability	—	(†)	81.3	(2.27)	84.8	(2.28)	84.7	(2.00)	1,104	(71.7)	935	(62.3)	4.0	(0.26)	3.6	(0.24)
Without a disability	—	(†)	92.4	(0.33)	93.6	(0.34)	94.0	(0.32)	26,609	(207.0)	25,014	(215.0)	96.0	(0.26)	96.4	(0.24)
Region																
Northeast	92.7	(0.56)	93.4	(0.79)	94.9	(0.64)	94.7	(0.82)	4,753	(149.8)	4,500	(150.4)	17.1	(0.52)	17.3	(0.56)
Midwest	90.3	(0.58)	93.2	(0.71)	93.3	(0.73)	93.0	(0.75)	5,649	(126.0)	5,256	(120.7)	20.4	(0.46)	20.3	(0.46)
South	89.1	(0.47)	91.2	(0.60)	92.8	(0.56)	93.5	(0.55)	10,770	(190.9)	10,071	(189.5)	38.9	(0.61)	38.8	(0.65)
West	88.7	(0.57)	91.2	(0.70)	93.1	(0.71)	93.6	(0.52)	6,542	(155.3)	6,123	(149.4)	23.6	(0.53)	23.6	(0.53)

—Not available.
†Not applicable.
‡Reporting standards not met (too few cases for a reliable estimate).
[1]The status completion rate is the number of 18- to 24-year-olds who are high school completers as a percentage of the total number of 18- to 24-year-olds who are not enrolled in high school or a lower level of education. High school completers include those with a high school diploma, as well as those with an alternative credential, such as a GED.
[2]Includes all 18- to 24-year-olds who are not enrolled in high school or a lower level of education.
[3]Status completers are 18- to 24-year-olds who are not enrolled in high school or a lower level of education and who also are high school completers—that is, have either a high school diploma or an alternative credential, such as a GED.
[4]United States refers to the 50 states, the District of Columbia, Puerto Rico, American Samoa, Guam, the U.S. Virgin Islands, and the Northern Marianas. Children born abroad

to U.S.-citizen parents are counted as born in the United States. Individuals defined as "first generation" were born in the United States, but one or both of their parents were born outside the United States. Individuals defined as "second generation or higher" were born in the United States, as were both of their parents.
[5]Individuals identified as having a disability reported difficulty in at least one of the following: hearing, seeing even when wearing glasses, walking or climbing stairs, dressing or bathing, doing errands alone, concentrating, remembering, or making decisions.
NOTE: Data are based on sample surveys of the civilian noninstitutionalized population, which excludes persons in the military and persons living in institutions (e.g., prisons or nursing facilities). Race categories exclude persons of Hispanic ethnicity. Detail may not sum to totals because of rounding and the suppression of cells that do not meet National Center for Education Statistics reporting standards.
SOURCE: U.S. Department of Commerce, Census Bureau, Current Population Survey (CPS), October, 2008 through 2018. (This table was prepared October 2019.)

Table 219.70. Percentage of high school dropouts among persons 16 to 24 years old (status dropout rate), by sex and race/ethnicity: Selected years, 1960 through 2018

[Standard errors appear in parentheses]

Year	Total All races/ ethnicities[1]	Total White	Total Black	Total Hispanic	Male All races/ ethnicities[1]	Male White	Male Black	Male Hispanic	Female All races/ ethnicities[1]	Female White	Female Black	Female Hispanic
1	2	3	4	5	6	7	8	9	10	11	12	13
1960[2]	27.2 (—)	— (†)	— (†)	— (†)	27.8 (—)	— (†)	— (†)	— (†)	26.7 (—)	— (†)	— (†)	— (†)
1967[3]	17.0 (—)	15.4 (—)	28.6 (—)	— (†)	16.5 (—)	14.7 (—)	30.6 (—)	— (†)	17.3 (—)	16.1 (—)	26.9 (—)	— (†)
1968[3]	16.2 (—)	14.7 (—)	27.4 (—)	— (†)	15.8 (—)	14.4 (—)	27.1 (—)	— (†)	16.5 (—)	15.0 (—)	27.6 (—)	— (†)
1969[3]	15.2 (—)	13.6 (—)	26.7 (—)	— (†)	14.3 (—)	12.6 (—)	26.9 (—)	— (†)	16.0 (—)	14.6 (—)	26.7 (—)	— (†)
1970[3]	15.0 (0.30)	13.2 (0.30)	27.9 (1.25)	— (†)	14.2 (0.42)	12.2 (0.43)	29.4 (1.87)	— (†)	15.7 (0.42)	14.1 (0.43)	26.6 (1.69)	— (†)
1971[3]	14.7 (0.29)	13.4 (0.30)	24.0 (1.17)	— (†)	14.2 (0.41)	12.6 (0.42)	25.5 (1.74)	— (†)	15.2 (0.41)	14.2 (0.42)	22.6 (1.58)	— (†)
1972	14.6 (0.28)	12.3 (0.29)	21.3 (1.09)	34.3 (2.93)	14.1 (0.40)	11.6 (0.41)	22.3 (1.63)	33.7 (4.26)	15.1 (0.40)	12.8 (0.42)	20.5 (1.48)	34.8 (4.03)
1973	14.1 (0.28)	11.6 (0.28)	22.2 (1.09)	33.5 (2.96)	13.7 (0.40)	11.5 (0.40)	21.5 (1.57)	30.4 (4.17)	14.5 (0.39)	11.8 (0.40)	22.8 (1.51)	36.4 (4.18)
1974	14.3 (0.28)	11.9 (0.28)	21.2 (1.07)	33.0 (2.74)	14.2 (0.39)	12.0 (0.41)	20.1 (1.55)	33.8 (3.94)	14.3 (0.39)	11.8 (0.40)	22.1 (1.49)	32.2 (3.82)
1975	13.9 (0.27)	11.4 (0.28)	22.9 (1.08)	29.2 (2.67)	13.3 (0.38)	11.0 (0.39)	23.0 (1.60)	26.7 (3.75)	14.5 (0.38)	11.8 (0.39)	22.9 (1.48)	31.6 (3.78)
1976	14.1 (0.27)	12.0 (0.28)	20.5 (1.03)	31.4 (2.66)	14.1 (0.39)	12.1 (0.40)	21.2 (1.53)	30.3 (3.88)	14.2 (0.38)	11.8 (0.39)	19.9 (1.39)	32.3 (3.64)
1977	14.1 (0.27)	11.9 (0.28)	19.8 (1.00)	33.0 (2.65)	14.5 (0.39)	12.6 (0.41)	19.5 (1.47)	31.6 (3.79)	13.8 (0.37)	11.2 (0.38)	20.0 (1.38)	34.3 (3.71)
1978	14.2 (0.27)	11.9 (0.28)	20.2 (1.01)	33.3 (2.62)	14.6 (0.39)	12.2 (0.40)	22.5 (1.54)	33.6 (3.77)	13.9 (0.37)	11.6 (0.39)	18.3 (1.32)	33.1 (3.65)
1979	14.6 (0.27)	12.0 (0.28)	21.1 (1.02)	33.8 (2.60)	15.0 (0.39)	12.6 (0.40)	22.4 (1.53)	33.0 (3.71)	14.2 (0.37)	11.5 (0.39)	20.0 (1.36)	34.5 (3.63)
1980	14.1 (0.27)	11.4 (0.27)	19.1 (0.98)	35.2 (2.47)	15.1 (0.39)	12.3 (0.40)	20.8 (1.48)	37.2 (3.57)	13.1 (0.36)	10.5 (0.37)	17.7 (1.29)	33.2 (3.42)
1981	13.9 (0.26)	11.3 (0.27)	18.4 (0.94)	33.2 (2.36)	15.1 (0.39)	12.5 (0.40)	19.9 (1.41)	36.0 (3.42)	12.8 (0.35)	10.2 (0.37)	17.1 (1.25)	30.4 (3.25)
1982	13.9 (0.28)	11.4 (0.29)	18.4 (0.99)	31.7 (2.51)	14.5 (0.40)	12.0 (0.43)	21.2 (1.52)	30.5 (3.57)	13.3 (0.38)	10.8 (0.40)	15.9 (1.28)	32.8 (3.53)
1983	13.7 (0.28)	11.1 (0.29)	18.0 (0.98)	31.6 (2.51)	14.9 (0.41)	12.2 (0.43)	19.9 (1.48)	34.3 (3.71)	12.5 (0.38)	10.1 (0.40)	16.2 (1.30)	29.1 (3.41)
1984	13.1 (0.28)	11.0 (0.28)	15.5 (0.93)	29.8 (2.49)	14.0 (0.41)	11.9 (0.43)	16.8 (1.39)	30.6 (3.62)	12.3 (0.38)	10.1 (0.40)	14.3 (1.24)	29.0 (3.42)
1985	12.6 (0.28)	10.4 (0.29)	15.2 (0.93)	27.6 (1.93)	13.4 (0.40)	11.1 (0.43)	16.1 (1.39)	29.9 (2.77)	11.8 (0.37)	9.8 (0.40)	14.3 (1.25)	25.2 (2.68)
1986	12.2 (0.27)	9.7 (0.29)	14.2 (0.91)	30.1 (1.88)	13.1 (0.40)	10.3 (0.42)	15.0 (1.36)	32.8 (2.67)	11.4 (0.37)	9.1 (0.39)	13.5 (1.23)	27.2 (2.64)
1987	12.6 (0.28)	10.4 (0.30)	14.1 (0.92)	28.6 (1.85)	13.2 (0.41)	10.8 (0.43)	15.0 (1.37)	29.1 (2.58)	12.1 (0.39)	10.0 (0.41)	13.3 (1.23)	28.1 (2.65)
1988	12.9 (0.31)	9.6 (0.32)	14.5 (1.01)	35.8 (2.17)	13.5 (0.45)	10.3 (0.47)	15.0 (1.50)	36.0 (3.02)	12.2 (0.42)	8.9 (0.43)	14.0 (1.38)	35.4 (3.13)
1989	12.6 (0.30)	9.4 (0.31)	13.9 (0.94)	33.0 (1.92)	13.6 (0.43)	10.3 (0.45)	14.9 (1.41)	34.4 (2.70)	11.7 (0.40)	8.5 (0.41)	13.0 (1.27)	31.6 (2.73)
1990	12.1 (0.29)	9.0 (0.30)	13.2 (0.94)	32.4 (1.91)	12.3 (0.42)	9.3 (0.44)	11.9 (1.30)	34.3 (2.71)	11.8 (0.41)	8.7 (0.42)	14.4 (1.34)	30.3 (2.70)
1991	12.5 (0.30)	8.9 (0.31)	13.6 (0.95)	35.3 (1.93)	13.0 (0.43)	8.9 (0.44)	13.5 (1.37)	39.2 (2.74)	11.9 (0.41)	8.9 (0.43)	13.7 (1.31)	30.1 (2.70)
1992[4]	11.0 (0.28)	7.7 (0.29)	13.7 (0.95)	29.4 (1.86)	11.3 (0.41)	8.0 (0.42)	12.5 (1.31)	32.1 (2.67)	10.7 (0.39)	7.4 (0.40)	14.8 (1.35)	26.6 (2.56)
1993[4]	11.0 (0.28)	7.9 (0.29)	13.6 (0.94)	27.5 (1.79)	11.2 (0.40)	8.2 (0.42)	12.6 (1.32)	28.1 (2.54)	10.9 (0.40)	7.6 (0.41)	14.4 (1.34)	26.9 (2.51)
1994[4]	11.4 (0.28)	7.7 (0.29)	12.6 (0.89)	30.0 (1.66)	12.3 (0.41)	8.0 (0.41)	14.1 (1.34)	31.6 (2.30)	10.6 (0.38)	7.5 (0.40)	11.3 (1.17)	28.1 (2.38)
1995[4]	12.0 (0.27)	8.6 (0.28)	12.1 (0.75)	30.0 (1.15)	12.2 (0.38)	9.0 (0.40)	11.1 (1.05)	30.0 (1.59)	11.7 (0.37)	8.2 (0.39)	12.9 (1.06)	30.0 (1.66)
1996[4]	11.1 (0.27)	7.3 (0.27)	13.0 (0.80)	29.4 (1.19)	11.4 (0.38)	7.3 (0.38)	13.5 (1.18)	30.3 (1.67)	10.9 (0.38)	7.3 (0.39)	12.5 (1.08)	28.3 (1.69)
1997[4]	11.0 (0.27)	7.6 (0.28)	13.4 (0.80)	25.3 (1.11)	11.9 (0.39)	8.5 (0.41)	13.3 (1.16)	27.0 (1.55)	10.1 (0.36)	6.7 (0.37)	13.5 (1.11)	24.1 (1.59)
1998[4]	11.8 (0.27)	7.7 (0.28)	13.8 (0.81)	29.5 (1.12)	13.3 (0.40)	8.6 (0.41)	15.5 (1.23)	33.5 (1.59)	10.3 (0.36)	6.9 (0.37)	12.2 (1.05)	25.0 (1.56)
1999[4]	11.2 (0.26)	7.3 (0.27)	12.6 (0.77)	28.6 (1.11)	11.9 (0.38)	7.7 (0.39)	12.1 (1.10)	31.0 (1.58)	10.5 (0.36)	6.9 (0.37)	13.0 (1.08)	26.0 (1.54)
2000[4]	10.9 (0.26)	6.9 (0.26)	13.1 (0.78)	27.8 (1.08)	12.0 (0.38)	7.0 (0.37)	15.3 (1.20)	31.8 (1.56)	9.9 (0.35)	6.9 (0.37)	11.1 (1.00)	23.5 (1.48)
2001[4]	10.7 (0.24)	7.3 (0.25)	10.9 (0.68)	27.0 (1.01)	12.2 (0.36)	7.9 (0.37)	13.0 (1.06)	31.6 (1.47)	9.3 (0.32)	6.7 (0.34)	9.0 (0.86)	22.1 (1.35)
2002[4]	10.5 (0.24)	6.5 (0.24)	11.3 (0.70)	25.7 (0.93)	11.8 (0.35)	6.7 (0.35)	12.8 (1.07)	29.6 (1.32)	9.2 (0.32)	6.3 (0.34)	9.9 (0.91)	21.2 (1.27)
2003[4,5]	9.9 (0.23)	6.3 (0.24)	10.9 (0.69)	23.5 (0.90)	11.3 (0.34)	7.1 (0.35)	12.5 (1.05)	26.7 (1.29)	8.4 (0.30)	5.6 (0.32)	9.5 (0.89)	20.1 (1.23)
2004[4,5]	10.3 (0.23)	6.8 (0.24)	11.8 (0.70)	23.8 (0.89)	11.6 (0.34)	7.1 (0.35)	13.5 (1.08)	28.5 (1.30)	9.0 (0.31)	6.4 (0.34)	10.2 (0.92)	18.5 (1.18)
2005[4,5]	9.4 (0.22)	6.0 (0.23)	10.4 (0.66)	22.4 (0.87)	10.8 (0.33)	6.6 (0.34)	12.0 (1.02)	26.4 (1.26)	8.0 (0.29)	5.3 (0.31)	9.0 (0.86)	18.1 (1.16)
2006[4,5]	9.3 (0.22)	5.8 (0.23)	10.7 (0.66)	22.1 (0.86)	10.3 (0.33)	6.4 (0.33)	9.7 (0.91)	25.7 (1.25)	8.3 (0.30)	5.3 (0.31)	11.7 (0.96)	18.1 (1.15)
2007[4,5]	8.7 (0.21)	5.3 (0.22)	8.4 (0.59)	21.4 (0.83)	9.8 (0.32)	6.0 (0.32)	8.0 (0.82)	24.7 (1.22)	7.7 (0.29)	4.5 (0.28)	8.8 (0.84)	18.0 (1.13)
2008[4,5]	8.0 (0.20)	4.8 (0.21)	9.9 (0.63)	18.3 (0.78)	8.5 (0.30)	5.4 (0.30)	8.7 (0.85)	19.9 (1.12)	7.5 (0.28)	4.2 (0.28)	11.1 (0.93)	16.7 (1.08)
2009[4,5]	8.1 (0.20)	5.2 (0.21)	9.3 (0.61)	17.6 (0.76)	9.1 (0.31)	6.3 (0.33)	10.6 (0.93)	19.0 (1.10)	7.0 (0.27)	4.1 (0.27)	8.1 (0.80)	16.1 (1.06)
2010[4,5]	7.4 (0.27)	5.1 (0.30)	8.0 (0.76)	15.1 (0.87)	8.5 (0.40)	5.9 (0.42)	9.5 (1.11)	17.3 (1.24)	6.3 (0.28)	4.2 (0.35)	6.7 (0.85)	12.8 (0.97)
2011[4,5]	7.1 (0.26)	5.0 (0.31)	7.3 (0.67)	13.6 (0.78)	7.7 (0.36)	5.4 (0.41)	8.3 (0.98)	14.6 (1.09)	6.5 (0.34)	4.6 (0.38)	6.4 (0.94)	12.4 (0.97)
2012[4,5]	6.6 (0.25)	4.3 (0.31)	7.5 (0.76)	12.7 (0.72)	7.3 (0.36)	4.8 (0.40)	8.1 (1.15)	13.9 (1.04)	5.9 (0.33)	3.8 (0.37)	7.0 (1.01)	11.3 (1.00)
2013[4,5]	6.8 (0.28)	5.1 (0.31)	7.3 (0.87)	11.7 (0.74)	7.2 (0.37)	5.5 (0.39)	8.2 (1.11)	12.6 (1.01)	6.3 (0.34)	4.7 (0.36)	6.6 (1.07)	10.8 (0.98)
2014[4,5]	6.5 (0.25)	5.2 (0.32)	7.4 (0.74)	10.6 (0.68)	7.1 (0.37)	5.7 (0.42)	7.1 (1.02)	11.8 (1.04)	5.9 (0.34)	4.8 (0.41)	7.7 (1.02)	9.3 (0.84)
2015[4,5]	5.9 (0.26)	4.6 (0.29)	6.5 (0.70)	9.2 (0.71)	6.3 (0.37)	5.0 (0.40)	6.4 (1.04)	9.9 (0.93)	5.4 (0.33)	4.1 (0.37)	6.5 (0.98)	8.4 (0.97)
2016[4,5]	6.1 (0.27)	5.2 (0.31)	6.2 (0.80)	8.6 (0.64)	7.1 (0.38)	5.8 (0.42)	8.2 (1.22)	10.1 (1.06)	5.1 (0.31)	4.6 (0.39)	4.3 (0.84)	7.0 (0.76)
2017[4,5]	5.8 (0.26)	4.6 (0.30)	5.7 (0.66)	9.5 (0.67)	6.6 (0.36)	5.0 (0.43)	7.0 (1.08)	11.5 (0.95)	5.0 (0.31)	4.3 (0.36)	4.4 (0.78)	7.4 (0.83)
2018[4,5]	5.7 (0.27)	4.5 (0.29)	5.8 (0.74)	9.0 (0.69)	6.3 (0.35)	5.1 (0.42)	6.0 (0.92)	10.4 (0.93)	5.1 (0.34)	3.8 (0.38)	5.6 (1.04)	7.5 (0.83)

—Not available.
†Not applicable.
[1]Includes other racial/ethnic groups not separately shown.
[2]Based on the April 1960 decennial census.
[3]For 1967 through 1971, White and Black include persons of Hispanic ethnicity.
[4]Because of changes in data collection procedures, data may not be comparable with figures for years prior to 1992.
[5]After 2002, White and Black exclude persons of Two or more races.
NOTE: Status dropouts are 16- to 24-year-olds who are not enrolled in school and who have not completed a high school program, regardless of when they left school. People who have received equivalency credentials, such as the GED, are counted as high school completers. All data except for 1960 are based on October counts. Data are based on sample surveys of the civilian noninstitutionalized population, which excludes persons in the military and persons living in institutions (e.g., prisons or nursing facilities). Prior to 2010, standard errors were computed using generalized variance function methodology rather than the more precise replicate weight methodology used in later years. Race categories exclude persons of Hispanic ethnicity except where otherwise noted.
SOURCE: U.S. Department of Commerce, Census Bureau, Current Population Survey (CPS), October, 1967 through 2018. (This table was prepared November 2019.)

Table 219.75. Percentage of high school dropouts among persons 16 to 24 years old (status dropout rate) and percentage distribution of status dropouts, by labor force status and years of school completed: Selected years, 1970 through 2018

[Standard errors appear in parentheses]

Year	Status dropout rate	Percentage distribution of status dropouts, by labor force status[1]				Percentage distribution of status dropouts, by years of school completed					
		Total	In labor force		Not in labor force	Total	Less than 9 years	9 years	10 years	11 or 12 years
			Employed[2]	Unemployed						
1	2	3	4	5	6	7	8	9	10	11
1970	15.0 (0.30)	100.0 (†)	49.8 (1.08)	10.3 (0.66)	39.9 (1.06)	100.0 (†)	28.5 (0.98)	20.6 (0.87)	26.8 (0.96)	24.0 (0.92)
1975	13.9 (0.27)	100.0 (†)	46.0 (1.04)	15.6 (0.76)	38.4 (1.02)	100.0 (†)	23.5 (0.89)	21.1 (0.85)	27.5 (0.93)	27.9 (0.94)
1976	14.1 (0.27)	100.0 (†)	48.8 (1.03)	16.0 (0.75)	35.2 (0.98)	100.0 (†)	24.3 (0.88)	20.1 (0.82)	27.8 (0.92)	27.8 (0.92)
1977	14.1 (0.27)	100.0 (†)	52.9 (1.02)	13.6 (0.70)	33.6 (0.97)	100.0 (†)	24.3 (0.88)	21.7 (0.84)	27.3 (0.91)	26.6 (0.91)
1978	14.2 (0.27)	100.0 (†)	54.3 (1.01)	12.4 (0.67)	33.3 (0.96)	100.0 (†)	22.9 (0.85)	20.2 (0.81)	28.2 (0.91)	28.8 (0.92)
1979	14.6 (0.27)	100.0 (†)	54.0 (1.00)	12.7 (0.67)	33.3 (0.94)	100.0 (†)	22.6 (0.84)	21.0 (0.82)	28.6 (0.90)	27.8 (0.90)
1980	14.1 (0.27)	100.0 (†)	50.4 (1.02)	17.0 (0.77)	32.6 (0.95)	100.0 (†)	23.6 (0.86)	19.7 (0.81)	29.8 (0.93)	27.0 (0.90)
1981	13.9 (0.26)	100.0 (†)	49.8 (1.01)	18.3 (0.78)	31.9 (0.94)	100.0 (†)	24.3 (0.87)	18.6 (0.79)	30.2 (0.93)	26.9 (0.90)
1982	13.9 (0.28)	100.0 (†)	45.2 (1.08)	21.1 (0.88)	33.7 (1.02)	100.0 (†)	22.9 (0.91)	20.8 (0.88)	28.8 (0.98)	27.6 (0.97)
1983	13.7 (0.28)	100.0 (†)	48.4 (1.10)	18.2 (0.85)	33.4 (1.04)	100.0 (†)	23.0 (0.92)	19.3 (0.87)	28.8 (0.99)	28.8 (0.99)
1984	13.1 (0.28)	100.0 (†)	49.7 (1.13)	17.3 (0.86)	32.9 (1.06)	100.0 (†)	23.6 (0.96)	21.4 (0.93)	27.5 (1.01)	27.5 (1.01)
1985	12.6 (0.28)	100.0 (†)	50.1 (1.17)	17.5 (0.89)	32.4 (1.09)	100.0 (†)	23.9 (1.00)	21.0 (0.95)	27.9 (1.05)	27.2 (1.04)
1986	12.2 (0.27)	100.0 (†)	51.1 (1.19)	16.4 (0.88)	32.5 (1.12)	100.0 (†)	25.4 (1.04)	21.5 (0.98)	25.7 (1.04)	27.4 (1.07)
1987	12.6 (0.28)	100.0 (†)	52.4 (1.18)	13.6 (0.81)	34.0 (1.12)	100.0 (†)	25.9 (1.04)	20.7 (0.96)	26.0 (1.04)	27.5 (1.06)
1988	12.9 (0.31)	100.0 (†)	52.9 (1.29)	— (†)	— (†)	100.0 (†)	28.9 (1.17)	19.3 (1.02)	25.1 (1.12)	26.8 (1.14)
1989	12.6 (0.30)	100.0 (†)	53.2 (1.25)	13.8 (0.86)	33.0 (1.18)	100.0 (†)	29.4 (1.14)	20.8 (1.02)	24.9 (1.08)	25.0 (1.09)
1990	12.1 (0.29)	100.0 (†)	52.5 (1.29)	13.3 (0.88)	34.2 (1.23)	100.0 (†)	28.6 (1.17)	20.9 (1.05)	24.4 (1.11)	26.1 (1.14)
1991	12.5 (0.30)	100.0 (†)	47.5 (1.28)	15.8 (0.93)	36.7 (1.23)	100.0 (†)	28.6 (1.15)	20.5 (1.03)	26.1 (1.12)	24.9 (1.10)
1992[3]	11.0 (0.28)	100.0 (†)	47.6 (1.36)	15.0 (0.97)	37.4 (1.32)	100.0 (†)	21.6 (1.12)	17.5 (1.04)	24.4 (1.17)	36.5 (1.31)
1993[3]	11.0 (0.28)	100.0 (†)	48.7 (1.37)	12.8 (0.91)	38.5 (1.33)	100.0 (†)	20.5 (1.10)	16.6 (1.02)	24.1 (1.17)	38.8 (1.33)
1994[3]	11.4 (0.28)	100.0 (†)	49.5 (1.30)	13.0 (0.88)	37.5 (1.26)	100.0 (†)	23.9 (1.11)	16.2 (0.96)	20.3 (1.05)	39.6 (1.28)
1995[3]	12.0 (0.27)	100.0 (†)	48.9 (1.19)	14.2 (0.83)	37.0 (1.15)	100.0 (†)	22.2 (0.99)	17.0 (0.89)	22.5 (0.99)	38.3 (1.16)
1996[3]	11.1 (0.27)	100.0 (†)	47.3 (1.28)	15.0 (0.91)	37.7 (1.24)	100.0 (†)	20.3 (1.03)	17.7 (0.98)	22.6 (1.07)	39.4 (1.25)
1997[3]	11.0 (0.27)	100.0 (†)	53.3 (1.27)	13.2 (0.86)	33.5 (1.21)	100.0 (†)	19.9 (1.02)	15.7 (0.93)	22.3 (1.06)	42.1 (1.26)
1998[3]	11.8 (0.27)	100.0 (†)	55.1 (1.22)	10.3 (0.74)	34.6 (1.17)	100.0 (†)	21.0 (1.00)	14.9 (0.87)	21.4 (1.00)	42.6 (1.21)
1999[3]	11.2 (0.26)	100.0 (†)	55.6 (1.23)	10.0 (0.74)	34.4 (1.18)	100.0 (†)	22.2 (1.03)	16.3 (0.92)	22.5 (1.04)	39.0 (1.21)
2000[3]	10.9 (0.26)	100.0 (†)	56.9 (1.24)	12.3 (0.82)	30.8 (1.16)	100.0 (†)	21.5 (1.03)	15.3 (0.90)	23.1 (1.06)	40.0 (1.23)
2001[3]	10.7 (0.24)	100.0 (†)	58.3 (1.17)	14.8 (0.85)	26.9 (1.05)	100.0 (†)	18.4 (0.92)	16.8 (0.89)	23.8 (1.01)	40.9 (1.17)
2002[3]	10.5 (0.24)	100.0 (†)	57.4 (1.18)	13.3 (0.81)	29.2 (1.09)	100.0 (†)	22.8 (1.00)	17.1 (0.90)	21.3 (0.98)	38.9 (1.17)
2003[3]	9.9 (0.23)	100.0 (†)	53.5 (1.22)	13.7 (0.84)	32.9 (1.15)	100.0 (†)	21.2 (1.00)	18.2 (0.94)	20.7 (0.99)	40.0 (1.20)
2004[3]	10.3 (0.23)	100.0 (†)	53.0 (1.19)	14.3 (0.83)	32.7 (1.12)	100.0 (†)	21.4 (0.97)	15.9 (0.87)	22.5 (0.99)	40.3 (1.17)
2005[3]	9.4 (0.22)	100.0 (†)	56.9 (1.23)	11.9 (0.80)	31.2 (1.15)	100.0 (†)	18.9 (0.97)	16.8 (0.93)	21.4 (1.02)	42.9 (1.23)
2006[3]	9.3 (0.22)	100.0 (†)	56.4 (1.23)	11.7 (0.80)	32.0 (1.16)	100.0 (†)	22.1 (1.03)	13.4 (0.85)	20.7 (1.01)	43.9 (1.23)
2007[3]	8.7 (0.21)	100.0 (†)	55.5 (1.27)	11.2 (0.80)	33.3 (1.20)	100.0 (†)	21.2 (1.04)	16.9 (0.96)	22.9 (1.07)	39.0 (1.24)
2008[3]	8.0 (0.20)	100.0 (†)	46.8 (1.33)	16.3 (0.98)	36.9 (1.28)	100.0 (†)	18.4 (1.03)	15.2 (0.96)	23.8 (1.13)	42.6 (1.32)
2009[3]	8.1 (0.20)	100.0 (†)	43.2 (1.31)	19.9 (1.06)	36.9 (1.28)	100.0 (†)	17.7 (1.01)	13.6 (0.91)	24.4 (1.14)	44.3 (1.32)
2010[3]	7.4 (0.27)	100.0 (†)	45.8 (1.64)	18.7 (1.38)	35.5 (1.70)	100.0 (†)	19.2 (1.48)	13.1 (1.07)	22.5 (1.59)	45.2 (1.89)
2011[3]	7.1 (0.26)	100.0 (†)	49.8 (1.77)	16.0 (1.33)	34.2 (1.69)	100.0 (†)	18.1 (1.72)	12.9 (1.15)	21.2 (1.39)	47.7 (1.87)
2012[3]	6.6 (0.25)	100.0 (†)	44.8 (2.07)	18.1 (1.49)	37.1 (1.83)	100.0 (†)	18.3 (1.76)	10.2 (1.21)	21.9 (1.57)	49.6 (2.20)
2013[3]	6.8 (0.28)	100.0 (†)	41.1 (2.01)	16.8 (1.58)	42.1 (1.84)	100.0 (†)	18.3 (1.70)	13.3 (1.34)	21.1 (1.63)	47.4 (2.31)
2014[3]	6.5 (0.25)	100.0 (†)	44.7 (1.84)	17.0 (1.41)	38.3 (1.61)	100.0 (†)	15.0 (1.58)	13.7 (1.28)	21.3 (1.56)	50.0 (1.94)
2015[3]	5.9 (0.26)	100.0 (†)	41.7 (2.10)	14.2 (1.48)	44.1 (2.10)	100.0 (†)	14.5 (1.67)	13.9 (1.40)	21.3 (1.65)	50.2 (2.00)
2016[3]	6.1 (0.27)	100.0 (†)	46.6 (1.99)	13.9 (1.31)	39.6 (1.90)	100.0 (†)	17.6 (1.91)	10.8 (1.14)	21.9 (1.64)	49.7 (2.22)
2017[3]	5.8 (0.26)	100.0 (†)	46.7 (1.91)	8.3 (1.09)	44.9 (1.98)	100.0 (†)	21.0 (2.14)	9.8 (1.22)	20.3 (1.76)	49.0 (2.41)
2018[3]	5.7 (0.27)	100.0 (†)	50.7 (2.02)	8.5 (1.24)	40.8 (2.10)	100.0 (†)	17.0 (2.03)	10.3 (1.26)	20.6 (1.74)	52.0 (2.29)

—Not available.
†Not applicable.
[1]Data are not comparable to employment and unemployment rate data produced by the Bureau of Labor Statistics because the percentage distributions presented here include persons who are not in the labor force. The labor force consists of those who are employed and those who are unemployed (i.e., seeking employment); persons who are neither employed nor seeking employment are not in the labor force.
[2]Includes persons who were employed but not at work during the survey week.
[3]Because of changes in data collection procedures, data may not be comparable with figures for years prior to 1992.

NOTE: Status dropouts are 16- to 24-year-olds who are not enrolled in school and who have not completed a high school program, regardless of when they left school. People who have received equivalency credentials, such as the GED, are counted as high school completers. Data are based on sample surveys of the civilian noninstitutionalized population, which excludes persons in the military and persons living in institutions (e.g., prisons or nursing facilities). Prior to 2010, standard errors were computed using generalized variance function methodology rather than the more precise replicate weight methodology used in later years. Detail may not sum to totals because of rounding.
SOURCE: U.S. Department of Commerce, Census Bureau, Current Population Survey (CPS), October, 1970 through 2018. (This table was prepared November 2019.)

Table 219.90. Number and percentage distribution of 14- through 21-year-old students served under Individuals with Disabilities Education Act (IDEA), Part B, who exited school, by exit reason, sex, race/ethnicity, age, and type of disability: 2016–17 and 2017–18

Year, sex, race/ethnicity, age, and type of disability		Exited school					Transferred to regular education[4]	Moved, known to be continuing[5]
	Total	Graduated with regular diploma	Received alternative certificate[1]	Reached maximum age[2]	Dropped out[3]	Died		
1	2	3	4	5	6	7	8	9
2016–17								
Total number	413,353	293,096	42,857	5,219	70,636	1,545	64,962	157,645
Percentage distribution of total	100.0	70.9	10.4	1.3	17.1	0.4	†	†
Number by sex								
Male	268,210	187,865	27,314	3,433	48,518	1,080	42,570	103,784
Female	145,140	105,229	15,543	1,786	22,117	465	22,392	53,860
Number by race/ethnicity								
White	203,362	151,159	19,663	2,357	29,433	750	36,414	72,481
Black	86,180	54,857	11,714	984	18,258	367	9,584	40,169
Hispanic	96,796	68,017	9,114	1,448	17,907	310	12,932	34,662
Asian	7,365	5,634	885	252	559	35	1,629	1,724
Pacific Islander	1,736	1,205	110	37	372	12	353	513
American Indian/Alaska Native	6,511	4,449	271	35	1,726	30	1,817	2,381
Two or more races	11,403	7,775	1,100	106	2,381	41	2,233	5,715
Number by age[6]								
14	3,468	18	2	†	3,236	211	16,805	36,133
15	5,989	64	40	†	5,647	238	15,302	36,814
16	18,179	4,876	455	†	12,536	312	15,179	36,156
17	172,682	141,114	11,815	1	19,428	324	11,406	27,703
18	149,070	115,314	15,630	1	17,919	206	4,601	14,061
19	34,341	20,738	5,735	10	7,730	128	1,006	4,414
20	16,986	7,563	5,037	1,242	3,062	82	457	1,686
21	12,638	3,409	4,143	3,964	1,078	44	206	678
Number by type of disability								
Autism	29,295	20,568	5,596	1,083	1,985	63	2,966	7,972
Deaf-blindness	77	42	19	9	4	3	3	34
Emotional disturbance	37,891	22,017	2,355	250	13,128	141	5,844	23,402
Hearing impairment	4,667	3,734	468	52	404	9	733	1,293
Intellectual disability	35,338	15,180	12,446	2,069	5,407	236	1,773	12,313
Multiple disabilities	8,506	3,878	2,684	649	969	326	404	2,671
Orthopedic impairment	2,697	1,730	562	149	198	58	246	528
Other health impairment[7]	71,481	53,396	4,940	279	12,558	308	11,463	30,029
Specific learning disability	207,649	159,563	12,910	540	34,282	354	31,558	73,438
Speech or language impairment	11,314	9,600	388	30	1,283	13	9,473	4,898
Traumatic brain injury	2,641	1,933	317	74	295	22	282	645
Visual impairment	1,797	1,455	172	35	123	12	217	422
2017–18								
Total number	414,051	301,035	40,313	4,948	66,301	1,454	60,474	159,665
Percentage distribution of total	100.0	72.7	9.7	1.2	16.0	0.4	†	†
Number by sex								
Male	268,660	192,705	26,156	3,251	45,541	1,007	39,673	104,974
Female	145,385	108,329	14,157	1,697	20,755	447	20,801	54,690
Number by race/ethnicity								
White	199,998	153,184	17,265	2,265	26,612	672	34,598	71,788
Black	86,203	56,745	10,651	832	17,602	373	8,209	39,870
Hispanic	99,834	70,593	10,245	1,399	17,311	286	12,445	36,992
Asian	7,623	6,017	816	248	508	34	1,565	1,859
Pacific Islander	1,779	1,209	102	43	415	10	432	512
American Indian/Alaska Native	6,229	4,429	225	48	1,493	34	1,088	2,508
Two or more races	12,385	8,858	1,009	113	2,360	45	2,137	6,136
Number by age[6]								
14	3,675	3	1	0	3,464	207	15,650	38,731
15	5,749	60	13	0	5,429	247	13,237	36,702
16	16,954	4,862	400	0	11,415	277	13,300	35,511
17	172,234	142,437	11,067	1	18,451	279	11,001	27,120
18	146,347	115,063	14,680	11	16,373	220	5,152	14,039
19	38,517	25,938	5,208	29	7,227	115	1,203	4,895
20	17,980	8,657	5,050	1,301	2,900	72	634	1,909
21	12,595	4,016	3,894	3,606	1,042	37	297	758

See notes at end of table.

Table 219.90. Number and percentage distribution of 14- through 21-year-old students served under Individuals with Disabilities Education Act (IDEA), Part B, who exited school, by exit reason, sex, race/ethnicity, age, and type of disability: 2016–17 and 2017–18—Continued

| Year, sex, race/ethnicity, age, and type of disability | Exited school | | | | | | Transferred to regular education[4] | Moved, known to be continuing[5] |
	Total	Graduated with regular diploma	Received alternative certificate[1]	Reached maximum age[2]	Dropped out[3]	Died		
1	2	3	4	5	6	7	8	9
Number by type of disability								
Autism	32,617	23,494	5,837	1,113	2,090	83	3,196	9,385
Deaf-blindness	82	56	14	6	4	2	5	31
Emotional disturbance	36,754	22,204	2,238	246	11,934	132	5,159	22,299
Hearing impairment	4,502	3,753	353	45	340	11	691	1,230
Intellectual disability	35,194	16,760	11,136	1,967	5,141	190	1,600	12,583
Multiple disabilities	8,672	4,041	2,734	562	1,042	293	397	2,816
Orthopedic impairment	2,444	1,637	484	114	159	50	221	528
Other health impairment[7]	74,103	56,183	4,832	289	12,496	303	11,161	31,832
Specific learning disability	203,805	159,620	11,918	483	31,440	345	28,942	72,981
Speech or language impairment	11,429	9,820	303	30	1,256	20	8,647	4,897
Traumatic brain injury	2,667	1,990	321	66	274	16	256	663
Visual impairment	1,782	1,478	143	27	125	9	199	420

†Not applicable.
[1]Received a certificate of completion, modified diploma, or some similar document, but did not meet the same standards for graduation as those for students without disabilities.
[2]Each state determines its maximum age to receive special education services. At the time these data were collected, the maximum age across states generally ranged from 20 to 22 years old.
[3]"Dropped out" is defined as the total who were enrolled at some point in the reporting year, were not enrolled at the end of the reporting year, and did not exit for any of the other reasons described. Includes students previously categorized as "moved, not known to continue."
[4]"Transferred to regular education" was previously labeled "no longer receives special education."
[5]"Moved, known to be continuing" is the total number of students who moved out of the administrative area or transferred to another district and are known to be continuing in an educational program.

[6]Age data are as of fall of the school year, so some students may have been 1 year older at the time they exited school.
[7]Other health impairments include having limited strength, vitality, or alertness due to chronic or acute health problems such as a heart condition, tuberculosis, rheumatic fever, nephritis, asthma, sickle cell anemia, hemophilia, epilepsy, lead poisoning, leukemia, or diabetes.
NOTE: Data are for the 50 states, the District of Columbia, the Bureau of Indian Education, American Samoa, the Federated States of Micronesia, Guam, the Northern Marianas, Puerto Rico, the Republic of Palau, the Republic of the Marshall Islands, and the U.S. Virgin Islands. Includes imputations for missing or unavailable data from Illinois in 2016–17 and Vermont in 2017–18. Race categories exclude persons of Hispanic ethnicity. Detail may not sum to totals because of reporting anomalies and rounding.
SOURCE: U.S. Department of Education, Office of Special Education Programs, Individuals with Disabilities Education Act (IDEA) Section 618 Data Products: State Level Data Files. Retrieved February 20, 2020, from https://www2.ed.gov/programs/osepidea/618-data/state-level-data-files/index.html. (This table was prepared February 2020.)

Table 220.40. Fall 2010 first-time kindergartners' reading scale scores and standard deviations through spring of fifth grade, by selected child, family, and school characteristics during the kindergarten year: Fall 2010 and spring 2011 through spring 2016

[Standard errors appear in parentheses]

Selected child, family, or school characteristic during the kindergarten year	Kindergarten Fall 2010		Spring 2011		First grade, spring 2012		Second grade, spring 2013		Third grade, spring 2014		Fourth grade, spring 2015		Fifth grade, spring 2016	
1	2		3		4		5		6		7		8	
	Mean reading score[1]													
Total	**54.5**	**(0.24)**	**69.3**	**(0.34)**	**95.3**	**(0.40)**	**112.8**	**(0.37)**	**121.4**	**(0.32)**	**129.7**	**(0.28)**	**136.8**	**(0.30)**
Sex of child														
Male	54.0	(0.30)	68.6	(0.41)	93.7	(0.45)	111.1	(0.44)	119.8	(0.40)	128.8	(0.34)	136.1	(0.36)
Female	55.0	(0.26)	70.1	(0.39)	97.0	(0.48)	114.5	(0.42)	123.0	(0.37)	130.7	(0.32)	137.5	(0.36)
Age of child at kindergarten entry, fall 2010														
Less than 5 years old	50.7	(0.62)	63.8	(0.96)	87.9	(1.40)	107.1	(1.22)	117.3	(1.02)	126.2	(0.98)	134.0	(1.07)
5 years old to 5 1/2 years old	53.0	(0.32)	67.7	(0.41)	93.5	(0.48)	111.3	(0.40)	119.8	(0.38)	128.7	(0.35)	135.6	(0.37)
More than 5 1/2 years old to 6 years old	55.5	(0.30)	70.6	(0.37)	96.9	(0.52)	114.1	(0.49)	122.6	(0.41)	130.6	(0.36)	137.8	(0.38)
More than 6 years old	57.9	(0.45)	73.1	(0.63)	99.6	(0.74)	115.9	(0.74)	124.0	(0.61)	131.9	(0.68)	138.4	(0.74)
Race/ethnicity of child														
White	56.1	(0.33)	71.4	(0.45)	98.6	(0.50)	116.1	(0.43)	124.8	(0.38)	132.8	(0.32)	140.0	(0.35)
Black	53.0	(0.44)	66.5	(0.58)	91.0	(0.90)	107.7	(0.80)	115.3	(0.62)	123.8	(0.68)	130.5	(0.57)
Hispanic	50.8	(0.32)	65.3	(0.33)	89.2	(0.52)	107.1	(0.61)	116.0	(0.56)	125.0	(0.56)	132.0	(0.53)
Asian	59.2	(0.66)	74.4	(0.82)	100.4	(1.00)	117.1	(0.88)	125.2	(0.70)	134.3	(0.81)	141.3	(0.76)
Pacific Islander	52.7	(2.00)	69.9	(2.96)	97.7	(2.87)	115.4	(2.82)	123.2	(2.61)	131.3	(1.87)	138.8	(2.09)
American Indian/Alaska Native	50.3	(0.61)	64.2	(1.08)	91.3	(1.39)	107.5	(1.33)	117.6	(1.21)	126.7	(1.33)	134.0	(1.59)
Two or more races	56.2	(0.74)	70.8	(1.01)	97.0	(1.12)	114.6	(1.08)	123.6	(0.82)	132.0	(0.84)	139.2	(0.82)
How often child exhibited positive learning behaviors, fall 2010[2]														
Never	45.6	(0.81)	55.3	(1.41)	71.8	(1.86)	91.5	(2.15)	103.4	(1.89)	113.9	(1.75)	119.8	(1.97)
Sometimes	49.9	(0.35)	63.5	(0.38)	87.0	(0.59)	105.1	(0.54)	114.4	(0.46)	123.8	(0.48)	130.7	(0.47)
Often	54.3	(0.26)	69.5	(0.43)	96.4	(0.48)	114.0	(0.41)	122.5	(0.38)	130.7	(0.35)	137.9	(0.39)
Very often	59.2	(0.45)	75.4	(0.62)	103.0	(0.62)	119.4	(0.60)	127.3	(0.49)	134.8	(0.46)	141.8	(0.44)
Primary type of nonparental care arrangement prior to kindergarten entry[3]														
No regular nonparental arrangement	52.1	(0.34)	67.1	(0.43)	92.0	(0.61)	109.6	(0.59)	118.9	(0.54)	127.3	(0.46)	135.0	(0.45)
Home-based care														
Relative care	52.4	(0.37)	68.0	(0.40)	93.8	(0.54)	111.4	(0.57)	119.9	(0.49)	128.8	(0.42)	135.2	(0.46)
Nonrelative care	54.7	(0.62)	70.3	(0.82)	98.4	(0.78)	115.3	(0.74)	123.6	(0.71)	132.2	(0.58)	139.5	(0.64)
Center-based care	56.0	(0.28)	70.5	(0.42)	96.7	(0.50)	114.1	(0.41)	122.5	(0.37)	130.6	(0.35)	137.7	(0.38)
Multiple arrangements	55.1	(0.61)	70.8	(0.82)	96.5	(1.05)	114.2	(1.08)	121.2	(1.00)	130.8	(0.92)	137.4	(0.94)
Household type, fall 2010[4]														
Two-parent household	55.6	(0.27)	70.8	(0.38)	97.3	(0.45)	114.8	(0.40)	123.3	(0.35)	131.6	(0.31)	138.7	(0.34)
Mother-only household	51.7	(0.32)	65.6	(0.44)	90.4	(0.60)	108.0	(0.53)	116.9	(0.51)	125.3	(0.49)	132.1	(0.50)
Father-only household	51.6	(0.69)	65.6	(1.01)	89.0	(1.30)	107.0	(1.22)	115.4	(1.06)	123.8	(1.20)	132.2	(1.24)
Other household type	49.4	(0.83)	63.5	(0.86)	87.0	(1.79)	103.5	(1.51)	112.6	(1.57)	120.8	(1.86)	127.0	(1.53)
Primary home language														
English	55.3	(0.25)	70.3	(0.39)	96.8	(0.42)	114.1	(0.37)	122.6	(0.33)	130.8	(0.26)	137.8	(0.29)
Non-English	49.9	(0.44)	63.9	(0.55)	87.4	(0.81)	105.5	(0.72)	115.0	(0.63)	124.1	(0.63)	131.2	(0.68)
Primary language not identified[5]	51.6	(1.24)	66.8	(1.52)	91.0	(1.96)	107.5	(2.22)	115.6	(1.68)	126.2	(1.95)	131.3	(1.81)
Parents' highest level of education[6]														
Less than high school	47.5	(0.43)	61.4	(0.48)	83.5	(0.80)	101.0	(0.81)	110.6	(0.67)	119.2	(0.70)	126.0	(0.67)
High school completion	50.3	(0.31)	64.5	(0.33)	88.7	(0.53)	106.1	(0.51)	115.6	(0.44)	124.3	(0.41)	131.2	(0.44)
Some college/vocational	53.4	(0.27)	68.1	(0.39)	94.3	(0.42)	111.7	(0.41)	120.1	(0.42)	128.7	(0.36)	135.9	(0.36)
Bachelor's degree	57.6	(0.34)	73.1	(0.48)	100.3	(0.58)	118.1	(0.40)	126.2	(0.35)	134.3	(0.35)	141.5	(0.35)
Any graduate education	61.1	(0.51)	76.8	(0.60)	104.7	(0.52)	122.2	(0.41)	130.0	(0.41)	137.8	(0.39)	144.7	(0.36)
Poverty status, spring 2011[7]														
Below poverty threshold	50.0	(0.30)	63.7	(0.37)	86.6	(0.58)	104.4	(0.58)	113.6	(0.56)	122.3	(0.49)	129.4	(0.51)
100 to 199 percent of poverty threshold	53.0	(0.31)	67.9	(0.53)	93.8	(0.64)	111.0	(0.58)	119.9	(0.55)	128.3	(0.55)	135.5	(0.55)
200 percent or more of poverty threshold	57.7	(0.31)	73.0	(0.41)	100.7	(0.44)	118.2	(0.36)	126.3	(0.35)	134.4	(0.27)	141.5	(0.30)
Two risk factors[8]														
Both risk factors: No parent completed high school[9] and family below poverty threshold[7]	47.4	(0.50)	61.2	(0.63)	83.2	(0.99)	101.0	(0.98)	110.2	(0.82)	118.8	(0.87)	125.7	(0.90)
One risk factor: No parent completed high school	49.0	(0.81)	62.4	(0.77)	85.6	(1.09)	103.8	(1.20)	113.3	(1.09)	122.9	(1.05)	130.2	(1.21)
One risk factor: Family below poverty threshold	50.7	(0.33)	64.5	(0.41)	87.6	(0.58)	105.4	(0.65)	114.6	(0.62)	123.4	(0.55)	130.5	(0.57)
Neither risk factor	56.4	(0.27)	71.7	(0.40)	99.0	(0.41)	116.4	(0.36)	124.6	(0.33)	132.8	(0.27)	140.0	(0.30)
Socioeconomic status[10]														
Lowest 20 percent	48.8	(0.35)	62.4	(0.38)	85.0	(0.60)	102.8	(0.58)	112.2	(0.54)	120.9	(0.52)	127.8	(0.51)
Middle 60 percent	54.0	(0.22)	69.0	(0.34)	95.4	(0.37)	112.7	(0.34)	121.2	(0.29)	129.7	(0.27)	136.9	(0.28)
Highest 20 percent	61.0	(0.46)	76.7	(0.58)	104.6	(0.54)	122.0	(0.45)	130.1	(0.40)	137.9	(0.33)	144.8	(0.32)
School control, fall 2010														
Public	54.1	(0.27)	68.9	(0.38)	94.8	(0.44)	112.1	(0.41)	120.7	(0.37)	129.1	(0.32)	136.1	(0.34)
Private	57.4	(0.66)	72.4	(1.06)	99.6	(1.25)	118.5	(0.90)	126.5	(0.86)	134.8	(0.76)	141.9	(0.68)
	Standard deviation of the reading score													
Total	10.5	(0.22)	13.2	(0.26)	16.5	(0.25)	15.6	(0.26)	14.0	(0.24)	13.3	(0.25)	14.0	(0.24)

See notes at end of table.

Table 220.40. Fall 2010 first-time kindergartners' reading scale scores and standard deviations through spring of fifth grade, by selected child, family, and school characteristics during the kindergarten year: Fall 2010 and spring 2011 through spring 2016—Continued

[1]Reflects performance on questions measuring basic skills (e.g., word recognition); vocabulary knowledge; and reading comprehension, including identifying information specifically stated in text (e.g., definitions, facts, and supporting details), making complex inferences from texts, and considering the text objectively and judging its appropriateness and quality. Possible scores for the reading assessment range from 0 to 167.

[2]Derived from child's approaches to learning scale score in fall of the kindergarten year. This score is based on teachers' reports on how often students exhibit positive learning behaviors in seven areas: attentiveness, task persistence, eagerness to learn, learning independence, ability to adapt easily to changes in routine, organization, and ability to follow classroom rules. Possible scores range from 1 to 4, with higher scores indicating that a child exhibits positive learning behaviors more often. Fall 2010 scores were categorized into the four anchor points on the original scale—1 (never), 2 (sometimes), 3 (often), and 4 (very often)—by rounding the mean score to the nearest whole number.

[3]The type of nonparental care in which the child spent the most hours. "Multiple arrangements" refers to children who spent an equal amount of time in each of two or more arrangements.

[4]A two-parent household may have two biological parents, two adoptive parents, or one biological/adoptive parent and one other parent/partner. A mother-only or father-only household has one biological or adoptive parent only, without another parent/partner. In other household types, which do not include biological or adoptive parents, the guardian or guardians may be related or unrelated to the child.

[5]Two or more languages (which could include English) were spoken in the child's home, and the parent respondent was unable to specify which language was the primary one (the one spoken most of the time).

[6]Parents' highest level of education is the highest level of education achieved by either of the parents or guardians in a two-parent household, by the only parent in a single-parent household, or by any guardian in a household with no parents.

[7]Poverty status is based on preliminary U.S. Census income thresholds for 2010, which identify incomes determined to meet household needs, given family size and composition. For example, a family of three with one child was below the poverty threshold if its income was less than $17,552 in 2010.

[8]Includes only children for whom information about both risk factors is available. Excludes children with missing information about parental education or poverty status.

[9]High school not completed by any parent or guardian living with the child.

[10]Socioeconomic status (SES) was measured by a composite score based on parental education and occupations and household income during the child's kindergarten year.

NOTE: Estimates weighted by W9C9P_20. Estimates pertain to a sample of children who were enrolled in kindergarten for the first time in the 2010–11 school year. The same children were assessed in spring 2012 (when the majority were in first grade), spring 2013 (when the majority were in second grade), spring 2014 (when the majority were in third grade), spring 2015 (when the majority were in fourth grade), and spring 2016 (when the majority were in fifth grade). Estimates differ from previously published figures because reading scale scores were recalculated to represent the kindergarten through fifth-grade assessment item pools and because weights were adjusted to account for survey nonresponse at each data collection wave, including the latest round of data collection (spring 2016). Race categories exclude persons of Hispanic ethnicity.

SOURCE: U.S. Department of Education, National Center for Education Statistics, Early Childhood Longitudinal Study, Kindergarten Class of 2010–11 (ECLS-K:2011), Kindergarten–Fifth Grade Restricted-Use Data File. (This table was prepared March 2019.)

Table 221.10. Average National Assessment of Educational Progress (NAEP) reading scale score, by sex, race/ethnicity, and grade: Selected years, 1992 through 2019

[Standard errors appear in parentheses]

Grade and year	All students	Sex — Average reading scale score — Male	Female	Gap between female and male score	Race/ethnicity — Average reading scale score — White	Black	Hispanic	Asian/Pacific Islander Total	Asian[1]	Pacific Islander[1]	American Indian/Alaska Native	Two or more races[1]	Gap between White and Black score	Gap between White and Hispanic score
1	2	3	4	5	6	7	8	9	10	11	12	13	14	15
Grade 4														
1992[2]	217 (0.9)	213 (1.2)	221 (1.0)	8 (1.6)	224 (1.2)	192 (1.7)	197 (2.6)	216 (2.9)	— (†)	— (†)	‡ (†)	— (†)	32 (2.1)	27 (2.9)
1994[2]	214 (1.0)	209 (1.3)	220 (1.1)	10 (1.7)	224 (1.3)	185 (1.8)	188 (3.4)	220 (3.8)	— (†)	— (†)	211 (6.6)	— (†)	38 (2.2)	35 (3.6)
1998	215 (1.1)	212 (1.3)	217 (1.3)	5 (1.8)	225 (1.0)	193 (1.9)	193 (3.2)	215 (5.6)	— (†)	— (†)	‡ (†)	— (†)	32 (2.2)	32 (3.3)
2000	213 (1.3)	208 (1.3)	219 (1.4)	11 (1.9)	224 (1.1)	190 (2.9)	190 (2.9)	225 (5.2)	— (†)	— (†)	214 (6.0)	— (†)	34 (2.1)	35 (3.1)
2002	219 (0.4)	215 (0.4)	222 (0.5)	6 (0.7)	229 (0.3)	199 (0.5)	201 (1.3)	224 (1.6)	— (†)	— (†)	207 (2.0)	— (†)	30 (0.6)	28 (1.4)
2003	218 (0.3)	215 (0.3)	222 (0.3)	7 (0.5)	229 (0.2)	198 (0.4)	200 (0.6)	226 (1.2)	— (†)	— (†)	202 (1.4)	— (†)	31 (0.5)	28 (0.6)
2005	219 (0.2)	216 (0.2)	222 (0.3)	6 (0.4)	229 (0.2)	200 (0.3)	203 (0.5)	229 (0.7)	— (†)	— (†)	204 (1.3)	— (†)	29 (0.4)	26 (0.5)
2007	221 (0.3)	218 (0.3)	224 (0.3)	7 (0.4)	231 (0.2)	203 (0.4)	205 (0.5)	232 (1.0)	— (†)	— (†)	203 (1.2)	— (†)	27 (0.5)	26 (0.6)
2009	221 (0.3)	218 (0.3)	224 (0.3)	7 (0.4)	230 (0.3)	205 (0.5)	205 (0.5)	235 (1.0)	— (†)	— (†)	204 (1.3)	— (†)	26 (0.6)	25 (0.6)
2011	221 (0.3)	218 (0.3)	225 (0.3)	7 (0.5)	231 (0.2)	205 (0.5)	206 (0.5)	235 (1.2)	236 (1.3)	216 (1.9)	202 (1.3)	227 (1.2)	25 (0.5)	24 (0.6)
2013	222 (0.3)	219 (0.3)	225 (0.3)	7 (0.5)	232 (0.3)	206 (0.5)	207 (0.5)	235 (1.1)	237 (1.3)	212 (2.5)	205 (1.3)	227 (1.0)	26 (0.6)	25 (0.6)
2015	223 (0.4)	219 (0.4)	226 (0.4)	7 (0.6)	232 (0.3)	206 (0.5)	208 (0.8)	239 (1.4)	241 (1.6)	215 (2.9)	205 (1.5)	227 (1.2)	26 (0.6)	24 (0.9)
2017	222 (0.3)	219 (0.3)	225 (0.3)	6 (0.4)	232 (0.3)	206 (0.5)	209 (0.5)	239 (0.9)	241 (1.0)	212 (2.7)	202 (1.8)	227 (0.9)	26 (0.6)	23 (0.5)
2019	220 (0.2)	217 (0.3)	224 (0.2)	7 (0.4)	230 (0.2)	204 (0.5)	209 (0.5)	237 (0.9)	239 (1.0)	212 (2.0)	204 (1.7)	226 (0.8)	27 (0.6)	21 (0.5)
Grade 8														
1992[2]	260 (0.9)	254 (1.1)	267 (1.0)	13 (1.5)	267 (1.1)	237 (1.7)	241 (1.6)	268 (3.9)	— (†)	— (†)	‡ (†)	— (†)	30 (2.0)	26 (2.0)
1994[2]	260 (0.8)	252 (1.0)	267 (1.0)	15 (1.4)	267 (1.0)	236 (1.8)	243 (1.2)	265 (3.0)	— (†)	— (†)	248 (4.7)	— (†)	30 (2.1)	24 (1.5)
1998	263 (0.8)	256 (1.0)	270 (0.8)	14 (1.3)	270 (0.9)	244 (1.2)	243 (1.7)	264 (7.1)	— (†)	— (†)	‡ (†)	— (†)	26 (1.5)	27 (1.9)
2000	— (†)	— (†)	— (†)	— (†)	— (†)	— (†)	— (†)	— (†)	— (†)	— (†)	— (†)	— (†)	— (†)	— (†)
2002	264 (0.4)	260 (0.5)	269 (0.5)	9 (0.7)	272 (0.4)	245 (0.7)	247 (0.8)	267 (1.7)	— (†)	— (†)	250 (3.5)	— (†)	27 (0.9)	26 (0.9)
2003	263 (0.3)	258 (0.3)	269 (0.3)	11 (0.4)	272 (0.2)	244 (0.5)	245 (0.7)	270 (1.1)	— (†)	— (†)	246 (3.0)	— (†)	28 (0.5)	27 (0.7)
2005	262 (0.2)	257 (0.2)	267 (0.2)	10 (0.3)	271 (0.2)	243 (0.4)	246 (0.4)	271 (0.8)	— (†)	— (†)	249 (1.4)	— (†)	28 (0.5)	25 (0.5)
2007	263 (0.2)	258 (0.3)	268 (0.3)	10 (0.4)	272 (0.2)	245 (0.4)	247 (0.4)	271 (1.1)	— (†)	— (†)	247 (1.2)	— (†)	27 (0.4)	25 (0.5)
2009	264 (0.3)	259 (0.3)	269 (0.3)	9 (0.5)	273 (0.2)	246 (0.4)	249 (0.6)	274 (1.1)	— (†)	— (†)	251 (1.2)	— (†)	26 (0.5)	24 (0.7)
2011	265 (0.2)	261 (0.3)	270 (0.2)	9 (0.4)	274 (0.2)	249 (0.5)	252 (0.5)	275 (1.0)	277 (1.0)	254 (2.2)	252 (1.2)	269 (1.2)	25 (0.5)	22 (0.5)
2013	268 (0.3)	263 (0.3)	273 (0.3)	10 (0.4)	276 (0.3)	250 (0.4)	256 (0.5)	280 (0.9)	282 (0.9)	259 (2.6)	251 (1.0)	271 (0.9)	26 (0.5)	21 (0.5)
2015	265 (0.2)	261 (0.2)	270 (0.3)	10 (0.4)	274 (0.2)	248 (0.5)	253 (0.4)	280 (1.3)	281 (1.3)	255 (2.4)	252 (1.7)	269 (1.1)	26 (0.5)	21 (0.5)
2017	267 (0.3)	262 (0.3)	272 (0.4)	10 (0.5)	275 (0.3)	249 (0.5)	255 (0.5)	282 (1.0)	284 (1.0)	255 (2.5)	253 (1.3)	272 (1.1)	25 (0.6)	19 (0.6)
2019	263 (0.3)	258 (0.3)	269 (0.3)	11 (0.5)	272 (0.3)	244 (0.5)	252 (0.6)	281 (0.9)	284 (0.9)	252 (2.3)	248 (1.6)	267 (0.9)	28 (0.5)	20 (0.6)
Grade 12														
1992[2]	292 (0.6)	287 (0.7)	297 (0.7)	10 (1.0)	297 (0.6)	273 (1.4)	279 (2.7)	290 (3.2)	— (†)	— (†)	‡ (†)	— (†)	24 (1.5)	19 (2.7)
1994[2]	287 (0.7)	280 (0.8)	294 (0.8)	14 (1.2)	293 (0.7)	265 (1.6)	270 (1.7)	278 (2.4)	— (†)	— (†)	274 (5.8)	— (†)	29 (1.8)	23 (1.9)
1998	290 (0.6)	282 (0.8)	298 (0.8)	16 (1.1)	297 (0.7)	269 (1.4)	275 (1.5)	287 (2.7)	— (†)	— (†)	‡ (†)	— (†)	27 (1.6)	22 (1.6)
2000	— (†)	— (†)	— (†)	— (†)	— (†)	— (†)	— (†)	— (†)	— (†)	— (†)	— (†)	— (†)	— (†)	— (†)
2002	287 (0.7)	279 (0.9)	295 (0.7)	16 (1.1)	292 (0.7)	267 (1.3)	273 (1.5)	286 (2.0)	— (†)	— (†)	‡ (†)	— (†)	25 (1.5)	20 (1.6)
2003	— (†)	— (†)	— (†)	— (†)	— (†)	— (†)	— (†)	— (†)	— (†)	— (†)	— (†)	— (†)	— (†)	— (†)
2005	286 (0.6)	279 (0.8)	292 (0.7)	13 (1.1)	293 (0.7)	267 (1.2)	272 (1.2)	287 (1.9)	— (†)	— (†)	279 (6.3)	— (†)	26 (1.4)	21 (1.4)
2007	— (†)	— (†)	— (†)	— (†)	— (†)	— (†)	— (†)	— (†)	— (†)	— (†)	— (†)	— (†)	— (†)	— (†)
2009	288 (0.7)	282 (0.7)	294 (0.8)	12 (1.1)	296 (0.6)	269 (1.1)	274 (1.0)	298 (2.4)	— (†)	— (†)	283 (3.7)	— (†)	27 (1.3)	22 (1.2)
2011	— (†)	— (†)	— (†)	— (†)	— (†)	— (†)	— (†)	— (†)	— (†)	— (†)	— (†)	— (†)	— (†)	— (†)
2013	288 (0.6)	284 (0.6)	293 (0.7)	10 (0.9)	297 (0.6)	268 (0.9)	276 (0.9)	296 (1.9)	296 (2.0)	289 (6.0)	277 (3.5)	291 (2.5)	30 (1.0)	22 (1.0)
2015	287 (0.5)	282 (0.6)	292 (0.7)	10 (1.0)	295 (0.7)	266 (1.1)	276 (0.9)	297 (2.1)	297 (2.1)	‡ (†)	279 (6.2)	295 (2.9)	30 (1.3)	20 (1.1)
2017	— (†)	— (†)	— (†)	— (†)	— (†)	— (†)	— (†)	— (†)	— (†)	— (†)	— (†)	— (†)	— (†)	— (†)
2019	— (†)	— (†)	— (†)	— (†)	— (†)	— (†)	— (†)	— (†)	— (†)	— (†)	— (†)	— (†)	— (†)	— (†)

—Not available.
†Not applicable.
‡Reporting standards not met. Either there are too few cases for a reliable estimate or the coefficient of variation (CV) is 50 percent or greater.
[1]Prior to 2011, separate data for Asian students, Pacific Islander students, and students of Two or more races were not collected.
[2]Accommodations were not permitted for this assessment.
NOTE: Scale ranges from 0 to 500. Includes public, private, Bureau of Indian Education, and Department of Defense Education Activity schools. For 1998 and later years, includes students tested with accommodations (2 to 14 percent of all students, depending on grade level and year); excludes only those students with disabilities and English language learners who were unable to be tested even with accommodations (2 to 6 percent of all students). Data on race/ethnicity are based on school reports. Race categories exclude persons of Hispanic ethnicity.
SOURCE: U.S. Department of Education, National Center for Education Statistics, National Assessment of Educational Progress (NAEP), 1992, 1994, 1998, 2000, 2002, 2003, 2005, 2007, 2009, 2011, 2013, 2015, 2017, and 2019 Reading Assessments, retrieved October 30, 2019, from the Main NAEP Data Explorer (https://nces.ed.gov/nationsreportcard/naepdata/). (This table was prepared October 2019.)

Table 221.20. Percentage of students at or above selected National Assessment of Educational Progress (NAEP) reading achievement levels, by grade and selected student characteristics: Selected years, 2005 through 2019

[Standard errors appear in parentheses]

Column headers: each year has "At or above NAEP Basic[1]" and "At or above NAEP Proficient[2]". Column numbers 1–17.

Grade and selected student characteristic (1)	2005 Basic[1] (2)	2005 Prof.[2] (3)	2007 Basic[1] (4)	2007 Prof.[2] (5)	2009 Basic[1] (6)	2009 Prof.[2] (7)	2011 Basic[1] (8)	2011 Prof.[2] (9)	2013 Basic[1] (10)	2013 Prof.[2] (11)	2015 Basic[1] (12)	2015 Prof.[2] (13)	2017 Basic[1] (14)	2017 Prof.[2] (15)	2019 Basic[1] (16)	2019 Prof.[2] (17)
4th grade, all students	64 (0.3)	31 (0.2)	67 (0.3)	33 (0.3)	67 (0.3)	33 (0.4)	67 (0.3)	34 (0.4)	68 (0.3)	35 (0.3)	69 (0.4)	36 (0.4)	68 (0.3)	37 (0.3)	66 (0.3)	35 (0.3)
Sex																
Male	61 (0.4)	29 (0.3)	64 (0.4)	30 (0.4)	64 (0.3)	30 (0.4)	64 (0.4)	31 (0.4)	65 (0.3)	32 (0.3)	66 (0.5)	33 (0.5)	65 (0.4)	34 (0.4)	63 (0.4)	32 (0.4)
Female	67 (0.3)	34 (0.3)	70 (0.3)	36 (0.3)	70 (0.4)	36 (0.4)	71 (0.4)	37 (0.4)	72 (0.4)	38 (0.4)	72 (0.4)	39 (0.5)	71 (0.4)	39 (0.4)	70 (0.3)	38 (0.3)
Race/ethnicity																
White	76 (0.3)	41 (0.3)	78 (0.3)	43 (0.3)	78 (0.3)	42 (0.3)	78 (0.3)	44 (0.3)	79 (0.3)	46 (0.3)	79 (0.3)	46 (0.5)	78 (0.3)	47 (0.4)	77 (0.3)	45 (0.4)
Black	42 (0.5)	13 (0.3)	46 (0.6)	14 (0.4)	48 (0.8)	16 (0.5)	49 (0.6)	17 (0.5)	50 (0.6)	18 (0.5)	52 (0.6)	18 (0.6)	51 (0.8)	20 (0.5)	48 (0.7)	18 (0.5)
Hispanic	46 (0.7)	16 (0.5)	50 (0.6)	17 (0.5)	49 (0.7)	17 (0.5)	51 (0.8)	18 (0.6)	53 (0.6)	20 (0.6)	55 (1.0)	21 (0.7)	54 (0.6)	23 (0.5)	55 (0.8)	23 (0.6)
Asian/Pacific Islander	73 (0.9)	42 (0.9)	77 (1.0)	46 (1.4)	80 (1.0)	49 (1.3)	80 (1.2)	49 (1.2)	82 (1.0)	51 (1.2)	82 (1.3)	55 (1.3)	82 (0.9)	56 (1.3)	81 (0.8)	55 (1.3)
Asian	— (†)	— (†)	— (†)	— (†)	— (†)	— (†)	81 (1.2)	50 (1.7)	82 (1.0)	53 (1.7)	84 (1.4)	57 (1.4)	84 (0.9)	59 (1.4)	82 (0.8)	57 (1.4)
Pacific Islander	— (†)	— (†)	— (†)	— (†)	— (†)	— (†)	61 (2.4)	28 (3.0)	57 (3.2)	27 (3.0)	60 (3.7)	28 (3.7)	58 (3.7)	27 (3.3)	58 (3.3)	25 (3.3)
American Indian/Alaska Native	48 (1.5)	18 (1.0)	49 (1.4)	18 (1.1)	50 (1.7)	20 (1.4)	47 (1.7)	18 (1.7)	51 (1.6)	21 (1.4)	52 (2.1)	21 (1.9)	48 (2.3)	22 (1.9)	50 (2.3)	19 (1.7)
Two or more races	— (†)	— (†)	— (†)	— (†)	— (†)	— (†)	73 (1.1)	39 (1.6)	73 (1.2)	40 (1.4)	73 (1.4)	40 (1.6)	73 (1.3)	42 (1.3)	72 (1.0)	40 (1.3)
Eligibility for free or reduced-price lunch																
Eligible	46 (0.4)	16 (0.3)	50 (0.4)	17 (0.3)	51 (0.4)	17 (0.3)	52 (0.4)	18 (0.3)	53 (0.3)	20 (0.3)	56 (0.5)	21 (0.3)	54 (0.4)	22 (0.3)	53 (0.4)	21 (0.4)
Not eligible	77 (0.2)	42 (0.2)	79 (0.3)	44 (0.4)	80 (0.3)	45 (0.4)	82 (0.4)	48 (0.5)	83 (0.3)	51 (0.5)	83 (0.3)	52 (0.6)	82 (0.3)	52 (0.4)	81 (0.3)	51 (0.4)
Unknown	77 (1.1)	45 (1.4)	80 (1.3)	46 (1.8)	81 (1.9)	50 (1.9)	82 (1.0)	48 (1.0)	83 (1.6)	51 (1.2)	81 (1.3)	52 (1.8)	80 (1.5)	51 (1.7)	78 (1.2)	47 (1.8)
8th grade, all students	73 (0.2)	31 (0.2)	74 (0.2)	31 (0.2)	75 (0.3)	32 (0.3)	76 (0.3)	34 (0.3)	78 (0.3)	36 (0.3)	76 (0.3)	34 (0.3)	76 (0.3)	36 (0.3)	73 (0.3)	34 (0.3)
Sex																
Male	68 (0.3)	26 (0.3)	69 (0.3)	26 (0.3)	71 (0.4)	28 (0.4)	72 (0.3)	29 (0.3)	74 (0.4)	31 (0.4)	72 (0.3)	29 (0.3)	72 (0.4)	31 (0.4)	68 (0.4)	28 (0.4)
Female	78 (0.2)	36 (0.3)	79 (0.3)	36 (0.3)	79 (0.4)	37 (0.5)	80 (0.3)	38 (0.4)	82 (0.3)	42 (0.3)	80 (0.3)	39 (0.3)	81 (0.4)	41 (0.5)	78 (0.4)	39 (0.4)
Race/ethnicity																
White	82 (0.2)	39 (0.3)	84 (0.3)	40 (0.3)	84 (0.2)	41 (0.4)	85 (0.2)	43 (0.4)	86 (0.2)	46 (0.5)	85 (0.2)	44 (0.5)	84 (0.3)	45 (0.4)	82 (0.3)	42 (0.4)
Black	52 (0.6)	12 (0.4)	55 (0.6)	13 (0.4)	57 (0.6)	14 (0.6)	59 (0.7)	15 (0.7)	61 (0.6)	17 (0.6)	58 (0.7)	16 (0.7)	60 (0.6)	18 (0.5)	54 (0.7)	15 (0.6)
Hispanic	56 (0.6)	15 (0.6)	58 (0.5)	15 (0.4)	61 (0.8)	17 (0.6)	64 (0.8)	19 (0.5)	68 (0.7)	22 (0.5)	66 (0.6)	21 (0.6)	67 (0.6)	23 (0.6)	63 (0.7)	22 (0.7)
Asian/Pacific Islander	80 (0.8)	40 (1.2)	80 (1.0)	41 (1.1)	83 (1.1)	45 (1.1)	83 (1.0)	47 (1.4)	87 (0.7)	54 (1.8)	86 (1.0)	52 (1.8)	86 (0.9)	57 (1.5)	85 (0.8)	54 (1.4)
Asian	— (†)	— (†)	— (†)	— (†)	— (†)	— (†)	84 (1.0)	49 (1.5)	87 (0.9)	54 (1.9)	86 (1.0)	54 (1.9)	87 (0.9)	57 (1.5)	87 (0.8)	57 (1.4)
Pacific Islander	— (†)	— (†)	— (†)	— (†)	— (†)	— (†)	63 (2.7)	24 (3.2)	70 (3.5)	27 (3.5)	66 (3.3)	24 (3.0)	65 (3.9)	23 (3.3)	63 (3.6)	25 (3.6)
American Indian/Alaska Native	59 (2.1)	17 (1.7)	56 (1.9)	18 (1.3)	62 (2.0)	21 (1.2)	63 (1.4)	22 (1.4)	62 (1.8)	19 (1.1)	63 (2.2)	22 (1.8)	63 (1.8)	22 (2.1)	59 (2.3)	19 (2.1)
Two or more races	— (†)	— (†)	— (†)	— (†)	— (†)	— (†)	79 (1.7)	39 (1.7)	81 (1.1)	40 (1.4)	79 (1.2)	38 (1.2)	82 (1.2)	42 (1.4)	76 (1.1)	37 (1.3)
Eligibility for free or reduced-price lunch																
Eligible	57 (0.4)	15 (0.3)	58 (0.4)	15 (0.4)	60 (0.5)	16 (0.3)	63 (0.5)	18 (0.3)	66 (0.4)	20 (0.4)	64 (0.4)	20 (0.4)	65 (0.4)	21 (0.3)	60 (0.5)	20 (0.4)
Not eligible	81 (0.3)	39 (0.3)	83 (0.3)	40 (0.3)	85 (0.3)	42 (0.3)	86 (0.3)	45 (0.4)	87 (0.4)	48 (0.4)	87 (0.3)	47 (0.3)	86 (0.3)	48 (0.3)	83 (0.5)	46 (0.4)
Unknown	84 (1.0)	45 (1.3)	86 (1.0)	48 (1.1)	89 (1.3)	51 (1.3)	90 (0.8)	54 (1.8)	92 (0.9)	59 (1.6)	89 (0.9)	53 (1.5)	87 (1.1)	52 (1.8)	84 (1.1)	47 (1.7)
12th grade, all students	73 (0.8)	35 (0.7)	—	—	74 (0.6)	38 (0.8)	—	—	75 (0.6)	38 (0.6)	72 (0.5)	37 (0.6)	—	—	— (†)	— (†)
Sex																
Male	67 (0.9)	29 (0.9)	—	—	69 (0.8)	32 (0.9)	—	—	70 (0.7)	33 (0.7)	68 (0.6)	33 (0.7)	—	—	— (†)	— (†)
Female	78 (0.9)	41 (0.9)	—	—	80 (0.6)	43 (1.0)	—	—	79 (0.7)	42 (0.9)	76 (0.8)	42 (0.8)	—	—	— (†)	— (†)
Race/ethnicity																
White	79 (0.8)	43 (0.9)	—	—	81 (0.5)	46 (0.8)	—	—	83 (0.6)	47 (1.2)	79 (0.7)	46 (0.9)	—	—	— (†)	— (†)
Black	54 (1.5)	16 (1.2)	—	—	57 (1.3)	17 (1.2)	—	—	56 (1.2)	16 (1.0)	52 (1.5)	17 (1.0)	—	—	— (†)	— (†)
Hispanic	60 (1.9)	20 (1.3)	—	—	61 (1.1)	22 (1.3)	—	—	64 (1.8)	23 (2.3)	63 (1.1)	25 (1.0)	—	—	— (†)	— (†)
Asian/Pacific Islander	74 (2.3)	36 (2.3)	—	—	81 (1.5)	49 (2.9)	—	—	80 (1.9)	47 (2.5)	79 (1.7)	48 (3.0)	—	—	— (†)	— (†)
Asian	— (†)	— (†)	—	—	— (†)	— (†)	—	—	80 (1.8)	48 (2.6)	79 (1.8)	49 (3.0)	—	—	— (†)	— (†)
Pacific Islander	— (†)	— (†)	—	—	— (†)	— (†)	—	—	75 (8.2)	39 (8.4)	‡ (†)	‡ (6.0)	—	—	— (†)	— (†)
American Indian/Alaska Native	67 (10.1)	26 (8.6)	—	—	70 (6.4)	29 (5.5)	—	—	65 (5.0)	26 (4.8)	65 (8.6)	28 (3.4)	—	—	— (†)	— (†)
Two or more races	— (†)	— (†)	—	—	— (†)	— (†)	—	—	77 (2.9)	38 (3.4)	45 (3.4)	—	—	—	— (†)	— (†)

—Not available.
†Not applicable.
‡Reporting standards not met (too few cases for a reliable estimate).
[1]NAEP Basic denotes partial mastery of the knowledge and skills that are fundamental for proficient work at a given grade.
[2]NAEP Proficient represents solid academic performance. Students reaching this level have demonstrated competency over challenging subject matter.
NOTE: Includes public, private, Bureau of Indian Education, and Department of Defense Education Activity schools. Includes students tested with accommodations (2 to 14 percent of all students, depending on grade level and year); excludes only those students with disabilities and English language learners who were unable to be tested even with accommodations (2 to 6 percent of all students). Race categories exclude persons of Hispanic ethnicity. Prior to 2011, separate data for Asian students, Pacific Islander students, and students of Two or more races were not collected.
SOURCE: U.S. Department of Education, National Center for Education Statistics, National Assessment of Educational Progress (NAEP), 2005, 2007, 2009, 2011, 2013, 2015, 2017, and 2019 Reading Assessments, retrieved November 6, 2019, from the Main NAEP Data Explorer (https://nces.ed.gov/nationsreportcard/naepdata). (This table was prepared November 2019.)

Table 221.40. Average National Assessment of Educational Progress (NAEP) reading scale score of 4th-grade public school students, by state: Selected years, 1992 through 2019

[Standard errors appear in parentheses]

State	1992[1]	1994[1]	1998	2002	2003	2005	2007	2009	2011	2013	2015	2017	2019
1	2	3	4	5	6	7	8	9	10	11	12	13	14
United States	215 (1.0)	212 (1.1)	213 (1.2)	217 (0.5)	216 (0.3)	217 (0.2)	220 (0.3)	220 (0.3)	220 (0.3)	221 (0.3)	221 (0.4)	221 (0.2)	219 (0.2)
Alabama	207 (1.7)	208 (1.5)	211 (1.9)	207 (1.4)	207 (1.7)	208 (1.2)	216 (1.3)	216 (1.2)	220 (1.3)	219 (1.2)	217 (1.4)	216 (1.2)	212 (1.2)
Alaska	— (†)	— (†)	— (†)	— (†)	212 (1.6)	211 (1.4)	214 (1.0)	211 (1.2)	208 (1.1)	209 (1.0)	213 (1.3)	207 (1.2)	204 (1.2)
Arizona	209 (1.2)	206 (1.9)	206 (1.4)	205 (1.5)	209 (1.2)	207 (1.6)	210 (1.6)	210 (1.2)	212 (1.2)	213 (1.4)	215 (1.3)	215 (1.5)	216 (1.3)
Arkansas	211 (1.2)	209 (1.7)	209 (1.6)	213 (1.4)	214 (1.4)	217 (1.2)	217 (1.2)	216 (1.1)	217 (1.0)	219 (0.9)	218 (1.1)	216 (1.2)	215 (1.2)
California[2,3]	202 (2.0)	197 (1.8)	202 (2.5)	206 (2.5)	206 (1.2)	207 (0.7)	209 (1.0)	210 (1.5)	211 (1.8)	213 (1.2)	213 (1.7)	215 (1.3)	216 (1.0)
Colorado	217 (1.1)	213 (1.3)	220 (1.4)	— (†)	224 (1.2)	224 (1.1)	224 (1.1)	226 (1.2)	223 (1.3)	227 (1.0)	224 (1.6)	225 (1.5)	225 (1.1)
Connecticut	222 (1.3)	222 (1.6)	230 (1.6)	229 (1.1)	228 (1.1)	226 (1.0)	227 (1.3)	229 (1.1)	227 (1.3)	230 (0.9)	229 (1.1)	228 (1.2)	224 (1.3)
Delaware[4]	213 (0.6)	206 (1.1)	207 (1.7)	224 (0.6)	224 (0.7)	226 (0.8)	225 (0.7)	226 (0.5)	225 (0.7)	226 (0.8)	224 (0.8)	221 (0.8)	218 (0.9)
District of Columbia	188 (0.8)	179 (0.7)	179 (1.2)	191 (0.9)	188 (0.7)	191 (1.0)	197 (0.9)	202 (1.0)	201 (0.8)	206 (0.9)	212 (0.9)	213 (0.8)	214 (0.8)
Florida	208 (1.2)	205 (1.7)	206 (1.4)	214 (1.4)	218 (1.1)	219 (0.9)	224 (0.8)	226 (1.0)	225 (1.1)	227 (1.1)	227 (1.0)	228 (1.1)	225 (1.1)
Georgia	212 (1.5)	207 (2.4)	209 (1.4)	215 (1.4)	214 (1.3)	214 (1.2)	219 (0.9)	218 (1.1)	221 (1.1)	222 (1.1)	222 (1.2)	220 (1.2)	218 (1.2)
Hawaii	203 (1.7)	201 (1.7)	200 (1.5)	208 (0.9)	208 (1.4)	210 (1.0)	213 (1.1)	211 (1.0)	214 (1.0)	215 (1.0)	215 (1.0)	216 (1.0)	218 (1.1)
Idaho	219 (0.9)	‡ (†)	— (†)	220 (1.1)	218 (1.0)	222 (0.9)	223 (0.8)	221 (0.9)	221 (0.8)	219 (0.9)	222 (1.0)	223 (1.0)	223 (1.2)
Illinois	— (†)	— (†)	‡ (†)	‡ (†)	216 (1.6)	216 (1.2)	219 (1.2)	219 (1.4)	219 (1.1)	219 (1.4)	222 (1.2)	220 (1.2)	218 (1.3)
Indiana	221 (1.3)	220 (1.3)	— (†)	222 (1.4)	220 (1.0)	218 (1.1)	222 (0.9)	223 (1.1)	221 (0.9)	225 (1.0)	227 (1.1)	226 (1.1)	222 (1.2)
Iowa[2,3]	225 (1.1)	223 (1.3)	220 (1.0)	223 (1.1)	223 (1.1)	221 (0.9)	225 (1.1)	221 (1.2)	221 (0.8)	224 (1.1)	224 (1.1)	222 (1.2)	221 (1.1)
Kansas[2,3]	— (†)	— (†)	221 (1.4)	222 (1.4)	220 (1.2)	220 (1.3)	225 (1.1)	224 (1.3)	224 (1.0)	223 (1.3)	221 (1.5)	223 (1.2)	219 (1.2)
Kentucky	213 (1.3)	212 (1.6)	218 (1.5)	219 (1.1)	219 (1.3)	220 (1.1)	222 (1.1)	226 (1.1)	225 (1.0)	224 (1.2)	228 (1.2)	224 (1.1)	221 (1.2)
Louisiana	204 (1.2)	197 (1.3)	200 (1.6)	207 (1.7)	205 (1.4)	209 (1.3)	207 (1.6)	207 (1.1)	210 (1.4)	210 (1.3)	216 (1.5)	212 (1.4)	210 (1.4)
Maine[4]	227 (1.1)	228 (1.3)	225 (1.4)	225 (1.1)	224 (0.9)	225 (0.9)	226 (0.9)	224 (0.9)	222 (0.7)	225 (0.9)	224 (0.9)	221 (1.1)	221 (0.9)
Maryland	211 (1.6)	210 (1.5)	212 (1.6)	217 (1.5)	219 (1.4)	220 (1.3)	225 (1.1)	226 (1.4)	231 (0.9)	232 (1.3)	223 (1.3)	225 (1.3)	220 (1.3)
Massachusetts[2]	226 (0.9)	223 (1.3)	223 (1.4)	234 (1.1)	228 (1.2)	231 (0.9)	236 (1.1)	234 (1.1)	237 (1.0)	232 (1.1)	235 (1.0)	236 (1.1)	231 (1.1)
Michigan	216 (1.5)	‡ (†)	216 (1.5)	219 (1.1)	219 (1.2)	218 (1.5)	220 (1.4)	218 (1.0)	219 (1.2)	217 (1.4)	216 (1.3)	218 (1.5)	218 (1.2)
Minnesota[2,3]	221 (1.2)	218 (1.4)	219 (1.7)	225 (1.1)	223 (1.1)	225 (1.3)	225 (1.1)	223 (1.3)	222 (1.2)	227 (1.2)	223 (1.3)	225 (1.3)	222 (1.1)
Mississippi	199 (1.3)	202 (1.6)	203 (1.3)	203 (1.3)	205 (1.3)	204 (1.3)	208 (1.0)	211 (1.1)	209 (1.2)	209 (0.9)	214 (1.0)	215 (1.2)	219 (1.1)
Missouri	220 (1.2)	217 (1.5)	216 (1.3)	220 (1.3)	222 (1.2)	221 (0.9)	221 (1.1)	224 (1.1)	220 (0.9)	222 (1.0)	223 (1.1)	223 (1.1)	218 (1.2)
Montana[2,3,5]	— (†)	222 (1.4)	225 (1.5)	224 (1.8)	223 (1.2)	225 (1.1)	227 (1.0)	225 (0.8)	225 (0.6)	223 (0.8)	225 (0.8)	222 (0.9)	222 (1.0)
Nebraska[4,5]	221 (1.1)	220 (1.5)	— (†)	222 (1.5)	221 (1.0)	221 (1.2)	223 (1.3)	223 (1.0)	223 (1.0)	223 (1.0)	227 (1.1)	224 (1.2)	222 (1.0)
Nevada	— (†)	— (†)	206 (1.8)	209 (1.2)	207 (1.2)	207 (1.2)	211 (1.2)	211 (1.1)	213 (1.0)	214 (1.1)	214 (1.2)	215 (1.6)	218 (1.1)
New Hampshire[2,4,5]	228 (1.2)	223 (1.5)	226 (1.7)	— (†)	228 (1.0)	227 (0.9)	229 (0.9)	229 (1.0)	230 (0.8)	232 (0.9)	232 (1.0)	229 (1.0)	224 (1.1)
New Jersey[4]	223 (1.4)	219 (1.2)	— (†)	— (†)	225 (1.2)	223 (1.3)	231 (1.2)	229 (0.9)	231 (1.2)	229 (1.3)	229 (1.4)	233 (1.2)	227 (1.3)
New Mexico	211 (1.5)	205 (1.7)	205 (1.4)	208 (1.6)	203 (1.5)	207 (1.3)	212 (1.3)	208 (1.4)	208 (1.0)	206 (1.1)	207 (1.0)	208 (1.1)	208 (1.2)
New York[2,3,4]	215 (1.4)	212 (1.4)	215 (1.6)	222 (1.5)	222 (1.1)	223 (1.0)	224 (1.0)	224 (1.0)	222 (1.1)	224 (1.2)	223 (1.1)	222 (1.3)	220 (1.3)
North Carolina	212 (1.1)	214 (1.5)	213 (1.6)	222 (1.0)	221 (1.0)	217 (1.0)	218 (0.9)	219 (1.1)	221 (1.2)	222 (1.1)	226 (1.1)	224 (1.0)	221 (1.0)
North Dakota[3]	226 (1.1)	225 (1.2)	— (†)	224 (1.0)	222 (0.9)	225 (0.7)	226 (0.9)	226 (0.8)	226 (0.5)	224 (0.5)	225 (0.7)	222 (0.8)	221 (0.8)
Ohio	217 (1.3)	— (†)	— (†)	222 (1.3)	222 (1.2)	223 (1.4)	226 (1.1)	225 (1.1)	224 (1.0)	224 (1.2)	225 (1.2)	225 (1.0)	222 (1.1)
Oklahoma	220 (0.9)	— (†)	219 (1.2)	213 (1.2)	214 (1.2)	214 (1.1)	217 (1.1)	217 (1.1)	215 (1.1)	217 (1.1)	222 (1.1)	217 (1.1)	216 (1.1)
Oregon	— (†)	— (†)	212 (1.8)	220 (1.4)	218 (1.3)	217 (1.4)	215 (1.4)	218 (1.2)	216 (1.1)	219 (1.3)	220 (1.4)	218 (1.4)	218 (1.1)
Pennsylvania[5]	221 (1.3)	215 (1.6)	— (†)	221 (1.2)	219 (1.3)	223 (1.3)	226 (1.0)	224 (1.4)	227 (1.2)	226 (1.3)	227 (1.8)	225 (1.1)	223 (1.2)
Rhode Island[5]	217 (1.8)	220 (1.3)	218 (1.4)	220 (1.2)	216 (1.3)	216 (1.2)	219 (1.0)	223 (1.1)	222 (0.8)	223 (0.9)	225 (0.9)	223 (1.0)	220 (0.9)
South Carolina	210 (1.3)	203 (1.4)	209 (1.4)	214 (1.3)	215 (1.3)	213 (1.3)	214 (1.2)	216 (1.1)	215 (1.2)	214 (1.2)	218 (1.4)	213 (1.2)	216 (1.3)
South Dakota	— (†)	— (†)	— (†)	— (†)	222 (1.2)	222 (0.5)	223 (1.0)	222 (0.6)	220 (0.9)	218 (1.0)	220 (0.9)	222 (1.0)	222 (1.0)
Tennessee[3,5]	212 (1.4)	213 (1.7)	212 (1.4)	214 (1.2)	212 (1.6)	214 (1.4)	216 (1.2)	217 (1.2)	215 (1.1)	220 (1.4)	219 (1.4)	219 (1.1)	219 (1.0)
Texas	213 (1.6)	212 (1.9)	214 (1.9)	217 (1.7)	215 (1.2)	219 (0.8)	220 (0.9)	219 (1.2)	218 (1.5)	217 (1.1)	218 (1.7)	215 (1.1)	216 (1.1)
Utah	220 (1.1)	217 (1.3)	216 (1.2)	222 (1.0)	219 (1.0)	221 (1.0)	221 (1.2)	219 (1.0)	220 (1.0)	223 (1.1)	226 (1.1)	225 (1.1)	225 (1.1)
Vermont	— (†)	— (†)	— (†)	227 (1.1)	226 (0.9)	227 (0.9)	228 (0.8)	229 (0.8)	227 (0.6)	228 (0.6)	230 (0.8)	226 (0.8)	222 (0.8)
Virginia	221 (1.4)	213 (1.5)	217 (1.2)	225 (1.3)	223 (1.5)	226 (0.8)	227 (1.1)	227 (1.2)	226 (1.1)	229 (1.3)	229 (1.7)	228 (1.5)	224 (1.2)
Washington[3]	— (†)	213 (1.5)	218 (1.4)	224 (1.2)	221 (1.1)	223 (1.1)	224 (1.4)	221 (1.2)	221 (1.1)	225 (1.4)	226 (1.5)	223 (1.4)	220 (1.3)
West Virginia	216 (1.3)	213 (1.1)	216 (1.7)	219 (1.2)	219 (1.0)	215 (0.8)	215 (1.0)	215 (1.0)	214 (0.8)	215 (0.8)	216 (1.2)	217 (1.2)	213 (1.1)
Wisconsin[2,5]	224 (1.0)	224 (1.1)	222 (1.1)	‡ (†)	221 (0.8)	221 (1.0)	223 (1.2)	220 (1.1)	221 (0.8)	221 (1.6)	223 (1.1)	220 (0.9)	220 (1.1)
Wyoming	223 (1.1)	221 (1.2)	218 (1.5)	221 (1.0)	222 (0.8)	223 (0.7)	225 (0.5)	223 (0.7)	224 (0.8)	226 (0.6)	228 (0.7)	227 (0.9)	227 (0.9)
Department of Defense Education Activity (DoDEA)[6]	— (†)	— (†)	220 (0.7)	224 (0.4)	224 (0.5)	226 (0.6)	229 (0.5)	228 (0.5)	229 (0.5)	232 (0.6)	234 (0.7)	234 (0.6)	235 (0.7)

—Not available.
†Not applicable.
‡Reporting standards not met (too few cases for a reliable estimate).
[1]Accommodations were not permitted for this assessment.
[2]Did not meet one or more of the guidelines for school participation in 1998. Data are subject to appreciable nonresponse bias.
[3]Did not meet one or more of the guidelines for school participation in 2002. Data are subject to appreciable nonresponse bias.
[4]Did not meet one or more of the guidelines for school participation in 1992. Data are subject to appreciable nonresponse bias.
[5]Did not meet one or more of the guidelines for school participation in 1994. Data are subject to appreciable nonresponse bias.
[6]Prior to 2005, NAEP divided the DoDEA schools into two jurisdictions, domestic and overseas. In 2005, NAEP began combining the domestic and overseas schools into a single jurisdiction. Data shown in this table for years prior to 2005 were recalculated for comparability.

NOTE: Scale ranges from 0 to 500. State-level data for 2000 are not available. Table does not include private schools, Bureau of Indian Education schools, or (except in the final row) DoDEA schools. For 1998 and later years, includes public school students who were tested with accommodations; excludes only those students with disabilities (SD) and English language learners (ELL) who were unable to be tested even with accommodations. SD and ELL populations, accommodation rates, and exclusion rates vary from state to state.
SOURCE: U.S. Department of Education, National Center for Education Statistics, National Assessment of Educational Progress (NAEP), 1992, 1994, 1998, 2002, 2003, 2005, 2007, 2009, 2011, 2013, 2015, 2017, and 2019 Reading Assessments, retrieved October 30, 2019, from the Main NAEP Data Explorer (https://nces.ed.gov/nationsreportcard/naepdata/). (This table was prepared October 2019.)

Table 221.60. Average National Assessment of Educational Progress (NAEP) reading scale score of 8th-grade public school students, by state: Selected years, 1998 through 2019

[Standard errors appear in parentheses]

State	1998		2002		2003		2005		2007		2009		2011		2013		2015		2017		2019	
1	2		3		4		5		6		7		8		9		10		11		12	
United States	261	(0.8)	263	(0.5)	261	(0.2)	260	(0.2)	261	(0.2)	262	(0.3)	264	(0.2)	266	(0.2)	264	(0.2)	265	(0.3)	262	(0.3)
Alabama	255	(1.4)	253	(1.3)	253	(1.5)	252	(1.4)	252	(1.0)	255	(1.1)	258	(1.5)	257	(1.2)	259	(1.1)	258	(1.0)	253	(1.4)
Alaska	—	(†)	—	(†)	256	(1.1)	259	(0.9)	259	(1.0)	259	(0.9)	261	(0.9)	261	(0.8)	260	(1.1)	258	(0.8)	252	(1.1)
Arizona	260	(1.1)	257	(1.3)	255	(1.4)	255	(1.0)	255	(1.2)	258	(1.2)	260	(1.2)	260	(1.1)	263	(1.2)	263	(0.9)	259	(1.2)
Arkansas	256	(1.3)	260	(1.1)	258	(1.3)	258	(1.1)	258	(1.0)	258	(1.2)	259	(0.9)	262	(1.1)	259	(1.2)	260	(0.8)	259	(1.1)
California[1,2]	252	(1.6)	250	(1.8)	251	(1.3)	250	(0.6)	251	(0.8)	253	(1.2)	255	(1.0)	262	(1.2)	259	(1.2)	263	(1.2)	259	(1.4)
Colorado	264	(1.0)	—	(†)	268	(1.2)	265	(1.1)	266	(1.0)	266	(0.8)	271	(1.4)	271	(1.1)	268	(1.4)	270	(1.3)	267	(0.9)
Connecticut	270	(1.0)	267	(1.2)	267	(1.1)	264	(1.3)	267	(1.6)	272	(0.9)	275	(0.9)	274	(1.0)	273	(1.1)	273	(0.9)	270	(1.2)
Delaware	254	(1.3)	267	(0.5)	265	(0.7)	266	(0.6)	265	(0.6)	265	(0.7)	266	(0.6)	266	(0.7)	263	(0.8)	263	(0.8)	260	(0.8)
District of Columbia	236	(2.1)	240	(0.9)	239	(0.8)	238	(0.9)	241	(0.7)	242	(0.9)	242	(0.9)	248	(0.9)	248	(1.0)	247	(1.0)	250	(0.9)
Florida	255	(1.4)	261	(1.6)	257	(1.3)	256	(1.2)	260	(1.2)	264	(1.2)	262	(1.0)	266	(1.1)	263	(1.0)	267	(1.1)	263	(1.1)
Georgia	257	(1.4)	258	(1.0)	258	(1.1)	257	(1.3)	259	(1.0)	260	(1.0)	262	(1.1)	265	(1.2)	262	(1.3)	266	(1.1)	262	(1.0)
Hawaii	249	(1.0)	252	(0.9)	251	(0.9)	249	(0.9)	251	(0.8)	255	(0.6)	257	(0.7)	260	(0.8)	257	(0.9)	261	(0.8)	258	(1.0)
Idaho	—	(†)	266	(1.1)	264	(0.9)	264	(1.1)	265	(0.9)	265	(0.9)	268	(0.7)	270	(0.8)	269	(0.9)	270	(0.9)	266	(0.9)
Illinois	‡	(†)	‡	(†)	266	(1.0)	264	(1.0)	263	(1.0)	265	(1.2)	266	(0.8)	267	(1.0)	267	(1.0)	267	(1.1)	265	(1.0)
Indiana	—	(†)	265	(1.3)	265	(1.0)	261	(1.1)	264	(1.1)	266	(1.0)	265	(1.0)	267	(1.2)	268	(1.1)	272	(1.0)	266	(1.3)
Iowa	—	(†)	—	(†)	268	(0.8)	267	(0.9)	267	(0.9)	265	(0.9)	265	(1.0)	269	(0.8)	268	(1.0)	268	(1.1)	262	(1.1)
Kansas[1,2]	268	(1.4)	269	(1.3)	266	(1.5)	267	(1.0)	267	(0.8)	267	(1.1)	267	(1.0)	267	(1.0)	267	(1.2)	267	(1.0)	263	(0.9)
Kentucky	262	(1.4)	265	(1.0)	266	(1.3)	264	(1.1)	262	(1.0)	267	(0.9)	269	(0.8)	270	(0.8)	268	(1.0)	265	(0.8)	263	(1.0)
Louisiana	252	(1.4)	256	(1.5)	253	(1.6)	253	(1.6)	253	(1.1)	253	(1.6)	255	(1.5)	257	(1.0)	255	(1.2)	257	(1.5)	257	(1.4)
Maine	271	(1.2)	270	(0.9)	268	(1.0)	270	(1.0)	270	(0.8)	268	(0.7)	270	(0.8)	269	(0.8)	268	(0.9)	269	(0.9)	265	(0.9)
Maryland[1]	261	(1.8)	263	(1.7)	262	(1.4)	261	(1.2)	265	(1.2)	267	(1.1)	271	(1.2)	274	(1.1)	268	(1.1)	267	(1.0)	264	(1.0)
Massachusetts	269	(1.4)	271	(1.3)	273	(1.0)	274	(1.0)	273	(1.0)	274	(1.2)	275	(1.0)	277	(1.0)	274	(1.1)	278	(1.1)	273	(1.0)
Michigan	—	(†)	265	(1.6)	264	(1.8)	261	(1.2)	260	(1.2)	262	(1.4)	265	(0.9)	266	(1.0)	264	(1.2)	265	(1.1)	263	(1.2)
Minnesota[1]	265	(1.4)	‡	(†)	268	(1.1)	268	(1.2)	268	(0.9)	270	(1.0)	270	(1.0)	271	(1.0)	270	(1.1)	269	(1.0)	264	(1.1)
Mississippi	251	(1.2)	255	(0.9)	255	(1.4)	251	(1.3)	250	(1.1)	251	(1.0)	254	(1.2)	253	(1.0)	252	(1.0)	256	(0.7)	256	(1.0)
Missouri	262	(1.3)	268	(1.0)	267	(1.0)	265	(1.0)	263	(1.0)	267	(1.0)	267	(1.1)	267	(1.1)	267	(1.1)	266	(1.2)	263	(1.2)
Montana[1,2]	271	(1.3)	270	(1.0)	270	(1.0)	269	(0.7)	271	(0.8)	270	(0.6)	273	(0.6)	272	(0.8)	270	(0.8)	267	(0.8)	265	(0.8)
Nebraska	—	(†)	270	(0.9)	266	(0.9)	267	(0.9)	267	(0.9)	267	(0.9)	268	(0.7)	269	(0.8)	269	(0.9)	269	(0.7)	264	(0.9)
Nevada	258	(1.0)	251	(0.8)	252	(0.8)	253	(0.9)	252	(0.8)	254	(0.9)	258	(0.9)	262	(0.7)	259	(0.9)	260	(0.8)	258	(0.9)
New Hampshire	—	(†)	—	(†)	271	(0.9)	270	(1.2)	270	(0.9)	271	(1.0)	272	(0.7)	274	(0.8)	275	(0.9)	275	(0.9)	268	(1.0)
New Jersey	—	(†)	—	(†)	268	(1.2)	269	(1.2)	270	(1.1)	273	(1.3)	275	(1.2)	276	(1.1)	271	(1.0)	275	(1.1)	270	(1.2)
New Mexico	258	(1.2)	254	(1.0)	252	(0.9)	251	(1.0)	251	(0.8)	254	(1.2)	256	(0.9)	256	(0.8)	253	(0.9)	256	(0.9)	252	(1.0)
New York[1,2]	265	(1.5)	264	(1.5)	265	(1.3)	265	(1.0)	264	(1.1)	264	(1.2)	266	(1.1)	266	(1.1)	263	(1.4)	264	(1.0)	262	(1.2)
North Carolina	262	(1.1)	265	(1.1)	262	(1.0)	258	(0.9)	259	(1.1)	260	(1.2)	263	(0.9)	265	(1.1)	261	(1.3)	263	(1.2)	263	(1.1)
North Dakota[2]	—	(†)	268	(0.8)	270	(0.8)	270	(0.6)	268	(0.7)	269	(0.6)	269	(0.7)	268	(0.6)	267	(0.6)	265	(0.8)	263	(0.9)
Ohio	—	(†)	268	(1.6)	267	(1.3)	267	(1.3)	268	(1.2)	269	(1.3)	268	(1.1)	269	(1.0)	266	(1.5)	268	(1.9)	267	(1.2)
Oklahoma	265	(1.2)	262	(0.8)	262	(0.9)	260	(1.1)	260	(0.8)	259	(0.9)	260	(1.1)	262	(0.9)	263	(1.3)	261	(1.0)	258	(0.9)
Oregon[2]	266	(1.5)	268	(1.3)	264	(1.2)	263	(1.1)	266	(0.9)	265	(1.0)	264	(0.9)	268	(0.9)	268	(1.3)	266	(1.2)	264	(1.1)
Pennsylvania	—	(†)	265	(1.0)	264	(1.2)	267	(1.3)	268	(1.2)	271	(0.8)	268	(1.3)	272	(1.0)	269	(1.5)	270	(1.1)	264	(1.1)
Rhode Island	264	(0.9)	262	(0.8)	261	(0.7)	261	(0.7)	258	(0.9)	260	(0.6)	265	(0.7)	267	(0.6)	265	(1.0)	266	(0.8)	262	(0.9)
South Carolina	255	(1.1)	258	(1.1)	258	(1.3)	257	(1.1)	257	(0.9)	257	(1.2)	260	(0.9)	261	(1.0)	260	(1.2)	260	(1.0)	259	(0.9)
South Dakota	—	(†)	—	(†)	270	(0.8)	269	(0.6)	270	(0.7)	270	(0.5)	269	(0.8)	268	(0.8)	267	(1.0)	267	(0.7)	263	(0.9)
Tennessee[2]	258	(1.2)	260	(1.4)	258	(1.2)	259	(0.9)	259	(1.0)	261	(1.1)	259	(1.0)	265	(1.1)	265	(1.4)	262	(1.1)	262	(1.1)
Texas	261	(1.4)	262	(1.4)	259	(1.1)	258	(0.6)	261	(0.9)	260	(1.1)	261	(1.0)	264	(1.1)	261	(1.0)	260	(1.2)	256	(1.2)
Utah	263	(1.0)	263	(1.1)	264	(0.8)	262	(0.8)	262	(1.0)	266	(0.8)	267	(0.8)	270	(0.9)	269	(1.0)	269	(0.9)	267	(1.2)
Vermont	—	(†)	272	(0.9)	271	(0.8)	269	(0.7)	273	(0.8)	272	(0.6)	274	(0.9)	274	(0.7)	274	(0.8)	273	(0.8)	268	(0.8)
Virginia	266	(1.1)	269	(1.0)	268	(1.1)	268	(1.0)	267	(1.1)	266	(1.1)	267	(1.2)	268	(1.3)	267	(1.2)	268	(1.3)	262	(1.3)
Washington[2]	264	(1.2)	268	(1.2)	264	(0.9)	265	(1.3)	265	(0.9)	267	(1.1)	268	(1.0)	272	(1.0)	267	(1.2)	272	(1.4)	266	(1.3)
West Virginia	262	(1.0)	264	(1.0)	260	(1.0)	255	(1.2)	255	(1.0)	255	(0.9)	256	(0.9)	257	(0.9)	260	(0.9)	259	(0.9)	256	(1.0)
Wisconsin[1]	265	(1.8)	‡	(†)	266	(1.3)	266	(1.1)	264	(1.0)	266	(1.0)	267	(0.9)	268	(0.9)	270	(1.1)	269	(1.0)	267	(0.9)
Wyoming	263	(1.3)	265	(0.7)	267	(0.5)	268	(0.7)	266	(0.7)	268	(1.0)	270	(1.0)	271	(0.6)	269	(0.7)	269	(0.7)	265	(0.8)
Department of Defense Education Activity (DoDEA)[3]	269	(1.3)	273	(0.5)	272	(0.6)	271	(0.7)	273	(1.0)	272	(0.7)	272	(0.7)	277	(0.7)	277	(0.7)	280	(0.8)	280	(0.7)

—Not available.
†Not applicable.
‡Reporting standards not met. Participation rates fell below the required standards for reporting.
[1]Did not meet one or more of the guidelines for school participation in 1998. Data are subject to appreciable nonresponse bias.
[2]Did not meet one or more of the guidelines for school participation in 2002. Data are subject to appreciable nonresponse bias.
[3]Prior to 2005, NAEP divided the DoDEA schools into two jurisdictions, domestic and overseas. In 2005, NAEP began combining the domestic and overseas schools into a single jurisdiction. Data shown in this table for years prior to 2005 were recalculated for comparability.

NOTE: Scale ranges from 0 to 500. State-level data for 1992 and 1994 are not available. Table does not include private schools, Bureau of Indian Education schools, or (except in the final row) DoDEA schools. Includes public school students who were tested with accommodations; excludes only those students with disabilities (SD) and English language learners (ELL) who were unable to be tested even with accommodations. SD and ELL populations, accommodation rates, and exclusion rates vary from state to state.
SOURCE: U.S. Department of Education, National Center for Education Statistics, National Assessment of Educational Progress (NAEP), 1998, 2002, 2003, 2005, 2007, 2009, 2011, 2013, 2015, 2017, and 2019 Reading Assessments, retrieved November 3, 2019, from the Main NAEP Data Explorer (https://nces.ed.gov/nationsreportcard/naepdata/). (This table was prepared November 2019.)

Table 222.10.   Average National Assessment of Educational Progress (NAEP) mathematics scale score, by sex, race/ethnicity, and grade: Selected years, 1990 through 2019

[Standard errors appear in parentheses]

Grade and year	All students	Sex — Average mathematics scale score: Male	Female	Gap between female and male score	Race/ethnicity — Average mathematics scale score: White	Black	Hispanic	Asian/Pacific Islander Total	Asian[1]	Pacific Islander[1]	American Indian/Alaska Native	Two or more races[1]	Gap between White and Black score	Gap between White and Hispanic score
1	2	3	4	5	6	7	8	9	10	11	12	13	14	15
Grade 4														
1990[2]	213 (0.9)	214 (1.2)	213 (1.1)	-1 (1.7)	220 (1.0)	188 (1.8)	200 (2.2)	225 (4.1)	— (†)	— (†)	‡ (†)	— (†)	32 (2.0)	20 (2.4)
1992[2]	220 (0.7)	221 (0.8)	219 (1.0)	-2 (1.2)	227 (0.8)	193 (1.4)	202 (1.5)	231 (2.1)	— (†)	— (†)	‡ (†)	— (†)	35 (1.6)	25 (1.7)
1996	224 (1.0)	224 (1.1)	223 (1.1)	# (†)	232 (1.0)	198 (1.6)	207 (1.9)	229 (4.2)	— (†)	— (†)	217 (5.6)	— (†)	34 (1.8)	25 (2.1)
2000	226 (0.9)	227 (1.0)	224 (0.9)	-3 (1.4)	234 (0.8)	203 (1.2)	208 (1.5)	‡ (†)	— (†)	— (†)	208 (3.5)	— (†)	31 (1.5)	27 (1.7)
2003	235 (0.2)	236 (0.3)	233 (0.2)	-3 (0.3)	243 (0.2)	216 (0.4)	222 (0.4)	246 (1.1)	— (†)	— (†)	223 (1.0)	— (†)	27 (0.4)	22 (0.5)
2005	238 (0.1)	239 (0.2)	237 (0.2)	-3 (0.2)	246 (0.1)	220 (0.3)	226 (0.3)	251 (0.7)	— (†)	— (†)	226 (0.9)	— (†)	26 (0.3)	20 (0.3)
2007	240 (0.2)	241 (0.2)	239 (0.2)	-2 (0.3)	248 (0.2)	222 (0.3)	227 (0.3)	253 (0.8)	— (†)	— (†)	228 (0.7)	— (†)	26 (0.4)	21 (0.4)
2009	240 (0.2)	241 (0.3)	239 (0.3)	-2 (0.4)	248 (0.2)	222 (0.3)	227 (0.4)	255 (1.0)	— (†)	— (†)	225 (0.9)	— (†)	26 (0.4)	21 (0.5)
2011	241 (0.2)	241 (0.2)	240 (0.2)	-1 (0.3)	249 (0.2)	224 (0.4)	229 (0.3)	256 (1.0)	257 (1.0)	236 (2.1)	225 (0.9)	245 (0.6)	25 (0.4)	20 (0.4)
2013	242 (0.2)	242 (0.3)	241 (0.2)	-1 (0.4)	250 (0.2)	224 (0.3)	231 (0.4)	258 (0.8)	259 (0.8)	236 (2.0)	227 (1.1)	245 (0.7)	26 (0.4)	19 (0.5)
2015	240 (0.3)	241 (0.3)	239 (0.3)	-2 (0.4)	248 (0.3)	224 (0.4)	230 (0.5)	257 (1.2)	259 (1.2)	231 (2.3)	227 (1.0)	245 (0.8)	24 (0.5)	18 (0.5)
2017	240 (0.2)	241 (0.3)	239 (0.2)	-2 (0.4)	248 (0.2)	223 (0.5)	229 (0.4)	258 (1.1)	260 (1.0)	229 (2.7)	227 (1.3)	245 (0.8)	25 (0.5)	19 (0.5)
2019	241 (0.2)	242 (0.3)	239 (0.2)	-3 (0.4)	249 (0.3)	224 (0.4)	231 (0.3)	260 (1.4)	263 (1.0)	226 (7.9)	227 (1.2)	244 (0.6)	25 (0.5)	18 (0.4)
Grade 8														
1990[2]	263 (1.3)	263 (1.6)	262 (1.3)	-1 (2.1)	270 (1.3)	237 (2.7)	246 (4.3)	275 (5.0)	— (†)	— (†)	‡ (†)	— (†)	33 (3.0)	24 (4.5)
1992[2]	268 (0.9)	268 (1.1)	269 (1.0)	1 (1.5)	277 (1.0)	237 (1.3)	249 (1.2)	290 (5.9)	— (†)	— (†)	‡ (†)	— (†)	40 (1.7)	28 (1.5)
1996	270 (0.9)	271 (1.1)	269 (1.1)	-2 (1.5)	281 (1.1)	240 (1.9)	251 (1.7)	‡ (†)	— (†)	— (†)	‡ (†)	— (†)	41 (2.2)	30 (2.0)
2000	273 (0.8)	274 (0.9)	272 (0.9)	-2 (1.3)	284 (0.8)	244 (1.2)	253 (1.3)	288 (3.5)	— (†)	— (†)	259 (7.5)	— (†)	40 (1.5)	31 (1.6)
2003	278 (0.3)	278 (0.3)	277 (0.3)	-2 (0.4)	288 (0.3)	252 (0.5)	259 (0.6)	291 (1.1)	— (†)	— (†)	263 (1.8)	— (†)	35 (0.6)	29 (0.7)
2005	279 (0.2)	280 (0.2)	278 (0.2)	-2 (0.3)	289 (0.2)	255 (0.4)	262 (0.4)	295 (0.9)	— (†)	— (†)	264 (0.9)	— (†)	34 (0.4)	27 (0.5)
2007	281 (0.3)	282 (0.3)	280 (0.3)	-2 (0.4)	291 (0.3)	260 (0.4)	265 (0.4)	297 (0.9)	— (†)	— (†)	264 (1.2)	— (†)	32 (0.5)	26 (0.5)
2009	283 (0.3)	284 (0.3)	282 (0.4)	-2 (0.5)	293 (0.3)	261 (0.5)	266 (0.6)	301 (1.2)	— (†)	— (†)	266 (1.1)	— (†)	32 (0.5)	26 (0.6)
2011	284 (0.2)	284 (0.3)	283 (0.2)	-1 (0.4)	293 (0.2)	262 (0.5)	270 (0.5)	303 (1.0)	305 (1.1)	269 (2.4)	265 (0.9)	288 (1.3)	31 (0.5)	23 (0.5)
2013	285 (0.3)	285 (0.3)	284 (0.4)	-1 (0.4)	294 (0.3)	263 (0.4)	272 (0.5)	306 (1.1)	309 (1.1)	275 (2.3)	269 (1.2)	288 (1.2)	31 (0.5)	22 (0.5)
2015	282 (0.3)	282 (0.3)	282 (0.4)	# (†)	292 (0.3)	260 (0.5)	270 (0.5)	306 (1.5)	307 (1.5)	276 (2.9)	267 (1.3)	285 (1.1)	32 (0.6)	22 (0.6)
2017	283 (0.3)	283 (0.3)	282 (0.3)	-1 (0.4)	293 (0.3)	260 (0.5)	269 (0.5)	310 (1.5)	312 (1.5)	274 (2.2)	267 (1.4)	287 (1.1)	32 (0.6)	24 (0.6)
2019	282 (0.3)	282 (0.3)	282 (0.3)	# (†)	292 (0.3)	260 (0.4)	268 (0.4)	310 (1.1)	313 (1.0)	266 (2.3)	262 (1.3)	286 (1.0)	32 (0.5)	24 (0.5)
Grade 12														
1990[2]	[3] (†)	[3] (†)	[3] (†)	[3] (†)	[3] (†)	[3] (†)	[3] (†)	[3] (†)	[3] (†)	[3] (†)	[3] (†)	[3] (†)	[3] (†)	[3] (†)
1992[2]	[3] (†)	[3] (†)	[3] (†)	[3] (†)	[3] (†)	[3] (†)	[3] (†)	[3] (†)	[3] (†)	[3] (†)	[3] (†)	[3] (†)	[3] (†)	[3] (†)
1996	[3] (†)	[3] (†)	[3] (†)	[3] (†)	[3] (†)	[3] (†)	[3] (†)	[3] (†)	[3] (†)	[3] (†)	[3] (†)	[3] (†)	[3] (†)	[3] (†)
2000	[3] (†)	[3] (†)	[3] (†)	[3] (†)	[3] (†)	[3] (†)	[3] (†)	[3] (†)	[3] (†)	[3] (†)	[3] (†)	[3] (†)	[3] (†)	[3] (†)
2003	— (†)	— (†)	— (†)	— (†)	— (†)	— (†)	— (†)	— (†)	— (†)	— (†)	— (†)	— (†)	— (†)	— (†)
2005	150 (0.6)	151 (0.7)	149 (0.7)	-3 (1.0)	157 (0.6)	127 (1.1)	133 (1.3)	163 (2.0)	— (†)	— (†)	134 (4.1)	— (†)	31 (1.2)	24 (1.4)
2007	— (†)	— (†)	— (†)	— (†)	— (†)	— (†)	— (†)	— (†)	— (†)	— (†)	— (†)	— (†)	— (†)	— (†)
2009	153 (0.7)	155 (0.9)	152 (0.7)	-3 (1.1)	161 (0.6)	131 (0.8)	138 (0.8)	175 (2.7)	— (†)	— (†)	144 (2.8)	— (†)	30 (1.0)	23 (1.0)
2011	— (†)	— (†)	— (†)	— (†)	— (†)	— (†)	— (†)	— (†)	— (†)	— (†)	— (†)	— (†)	— (†)	— (†)
2013	153 (0.5)	155 (0.6)	152 (0.6)	-3 (0.9)	162 (0.6)	132 (0.8)	141 (0.8)	172 (1.3)	174 (1.3)	151 (2.8)	142 (3.2)	155 (1.7)	30 (1.0)	21 (1.0)
2015	152 (0.5)	153 (0.7)	150 (0.6)	-3 (0.9)	160 (0.6)	130 (1.0)	139 (0.8)	170 (2.0)	171 (1.9)	‡ (†)	138 (2.8)	157 (2.2)	30 (1.2)	22 (1.0)
2017	— (†)	— (†)	— (†)	— (†)	— (†)	— (†)	— (†)	— (†)	— (†)	— (†)	— (†)	— (†)	— (†)	— (†)
2019	— (†)	— (†)	— (†)	— (†)	— (†)	— (†)	— (†)	— (†)	— (†)	— (†)	— (†)	— (†)	— (†)	— (†)

—Not available.
†Not applicable.
#Rounds to zero.
‡Reporting standards not met. Either there are too few cases for a reliable estimate or the coefficient of variation (CV) is 50 percent or greater.
[1]Prior to 2011, separate data for Asian students, Pacific Islander students, and students of Two or more races were not collected.
[2]Accommodations were not permitted for this assessment.
[3]Because of major changes to the framework and content of the grade 12 assessment, scores from 2005 and later assessment years cannot be compared with scores from earlier assessment years. Therefore, this table does not include scores from the earlier grade 12 assessment years (1990, 1992, 1996, and 2000). For data pertaining to scale score comparisons between earlier years, see the *Digest of Education Statistics 2009*, table 138 (https://nces.ed.gov/programs/digest/d09/tables/dt09_138.asp).

NOTE: For the grade 4 and grade 8 assessments, the scale ranges from 0 to 500. For the grade 12 assessment, the scale ranges from 0 to 300. Includes public, private, Bureau of Indian Education, and Department of Defense Education Activity schools. For 1996 and later years, includes students tested with accommodations (3 to 14 percent of all students, depending on grade level and year); excludes only those students with disabilities and English language learners who were unable to be tested even with accommodations (1 to 4 percent of all students). Race categories exclude persons of Hispanic ethnicity.
SOURCE: U.S. Department of Education, National Center for Education Statistics, National Assessment of Educational Progress (NAEP), 1990, 1992, 1996, 2000, 2003, 2005, 2007, 2009, 2011, 2013, 2015, 2017, and 2019 Mathematics Assessments, retrieved November 6, 2019, from the Main NAEP Data Explorer (https://nces.ed.gov/nationsreportcard/naepdata/). (This table was prepared November 2019.)

Table 222.20. Percentage of students at or above selected National Assessment of Educational Progress (NAEP) mathematics achievement levels, by grade and selected student characteristics: Selected years, 2005 through 2019

[Standard errors appear in parentheses]

In the table below, "Basic[1]" = "At or above NAEP Basic"; "Prof[2]" = "At or above NAEP Proficient".

Grade and selected student characteristic	2005 Basic[1]	2005 Prof[2]	2007 Basic[1]	2007 Prof[2]	2009 Basic[1]	2009 Prof[2]	2011 Basic[1]	2011 Prof[2]	2013 Basic[1]	2013 Prof[2]	2015 Basic[1]	2015 Prof[2]	2017 Basic[1]	2017 Prof[2]	2019 Basic[1]	2019 Prof[2]
(col) 1	2	3	4	5	6	7	8	9	10	11	12	13	14	15	16	17
4th grade, all students	80 (0.2)	36 (0.2)	82 (0.2)	39 (0.2)	82 (0.3)	39 (0.3)	82 (0.2)	40 (0.3)	83 (0.2)	42 (0.3)	82 (0.3)	40 (0.4)	80 (0.3)	40 (0.4)	81 (0.2)	41 (0.3)
Sex																
Male	81 (0.2)	38 (0.3)	82 (0.2)	41 (0.2)	82 (0.3)	41 (0.4)	83 (0.3)	42 (0.4)	82 (0.3)	43 (0.3)	82 (0.4)	42 (0.5)	80 (0.4)	42 (0.4)	81 (0.3)	44 (0.4)
Female	80 (0.2)	34 (0.3)	82 (0.2)	37 (0.2)	82 (0.3)	37 (0.4)	82 (0.3)	39 (0.4)	83 (0.2)	41 (0.4)	82 (0.3)	38 (0.5)	80 (0.3)	38 (0.4)	80 (0.3)	38 (0.4)
Race/ethnicity																
White	90 (0.2)	47 (0.2)	91 (0.2)	51 (0.2)	91 (0.2)	51 (0.2)	91 (0.2)	52 (0.2)	91 (0.2)	54 (0.2)	90 (0.3)	51 (0.5)	88 (0.3)	51 (0.4)	89 (0.3)	52 (0.4)
Black	60 (0.5)	13 (0.3)	64 (0.6)	15 (0.6)	64 (0.6)	16 (0.6)	66 (0.6)	17 (0.5)	66 (0.6)	18 (0.6)	65 (0.7)	19 (0.6)	63 (0.8)	19 (0.6)	65 (0.7)	20 (0.5)
Hispanic	68 (0.5)	19 (0.3)	70 (0.5)	22 (0.5)	71 (0.7)	22 (0.4)	72 (0.6)	24 (0.5)	73 (0.6)	26 (0.6)	73 (0.6)	26 (0.7)	70 (0.5)	26 (0.5)	73 (0.7)	28 (0.6)
Asian/Pacific Islander	90 (0.5)	55 (1.1)	91 (0.7)	58 (1.3)	92 (0.6)	60 (1.0)	91 (1.0)	62 (1.2)	91 (0.8)	64 (1.3)	93 (0.8)	62 (1.7)	92 (0.8)	64 (1.5)	91 (0.9)	66 (1.4)
Asian	— (†)	— (†)	— (†)	— (†)	— (†)	— (†)	93 (1.0)	64 (1.4)	92 (3.1)	66 (3.2)	93 (0.7)	65 (1.7)	92 (2.8)	67 (3.5)	93 (0.8)	69 (4.7)
Pacific Islander	— (†)	— (†)	— (†)	— (†)	— (†)	— (†)	77 (2.7)	34 (3.2)	77 (3.1)	33 (3.1)	68 (4.0)	30 (4.2)	71 (3.7)	29 (3.3)	64 (5.5)	28 (1.9)
American Indian/Alaska Native	68 (1.5)	21 (1.2)	70 (1.2)	25 (1.1)	66 (1.6)	21 (1.5)	66 (1.2)	22 (1.4)	68 (1.7)	23 (1.4)	69 (1.8)	23 (1.7)	69 (2.0)	24 (1.9)	67 (1.9)	24 (1.8)
Two or more races	— (†)	— (†)	— (†)	— (†)	— (†)	— (†)	87 (0.7)	45 (1.7)	85 (1.0)	46 (1.3)	86 (0.9)	45 (1.7)	85 (0.9)	45 (1.3)	84 (0.9)	44 (1.2)
Eligibility for free or reduced-price lunch																
Eligible	67 (0.3)	19 (0.2)	70 (0.4)	22 (0.3)	70 (0.4)	22 (0.3)	72 (0.2)	24 (0.3)	73 (0.4)	25 (0.4)	72 (0.4)	24 (0.4)	69 (0.4)	25 (0.3)	71 (0.3)	26 (0.4)
Not eligible	90 (0.2)	49 (0.3)	91 (0.2)	53 (0.3)	91 (0.3)	54 (0.4)	92 (0.2)	57 (0.4)	93 (0.2)	59 (0.4)	92 (0.3)	58 (0.6)	91 (0.3)	57 (0.5)	91 (0.2)	58 (0.5)
Unknown	87 (0.7)	45 (1.2)	90 (0.9)	48 (1.5)	88 (1.3)	47 (1.7)	90 (0.8)	52 (2.2)	90 (1.0)	52 (1.7)	89 (1.2)	50 (1.7)	87 (1.1)	49 (1.7)	88 (1.2)	48 (1.7)
8th grade, all students	69 (0.2)	30 (0.2)	71 (0.3)	32 (0.3)	73 (0.3)	34 (0.3)	73 (0.2)	35 (0.3)	74 (0.3)	35 (0.3)	71 (0.3)	33 (0.3)	70 (0.3)	34 (0.3)	69 (0.3)	34 (0.3)
Sex																
Male	70 (0.3)	31 (0.3)	72 (0.3)	34 (0.3)	73 (0.3)	36 (0.3)	73 (0.4)	36 (0.4)	74 (0.3)	36 (0.3)	71 (0.4)	34 (0.4)	70 (0.3)	35 (0.4)	68 (0.3)	34 (0.4)
Female	69 (0.3)	28 (0.3)	71 (0.3)	30 (0.3)	72 (0.4)	32 (0.3)	73 (0.2)	34 (0.3)	74 (0.4)	35 (0.3)	72 (0.4)	33 (0.4)	70 (0.3)	33 (0.5)	70 (0.4)	33 (0.4)
Race/ethnicity																
White	80 (0.2)	39 (0.3)	82 (0.3)	42 (0.3)	83 (0.3)	44 (0.3)	84 (0.3)	44 (0.2)	84 (0.2)	45 (0.4)	82 (0.3)	43 (0.4)	80 (0.3)	44 (0.4)	80 (0.3)	44 (0.4)
Black	42 (0.6)	9 (0.6)	47 (0.7)	11 (0.7)	50 (0.6)	12 (0.6)	51 (0.7)	13 (0.6)	52 (0.6)	14 (0.6)	48 (0.9)	13 (0.7)	47 (0.7)	13 (0.6)	47 (0.8)	14 (0.6)
Hispanic	52 (0.6)	13 (0.4)	55 (0.7)	15 (0.4)	57 (0.8)	17 (0.5)	61 (0.7)	20 (0.5)	62 (0.6)	21 (0.7)	59 (0.9)	19 (0.7)	57 (0.7)	20 (0.9)	57 (0.9)	20 (0.9)
Asian/Pacific Islander	81 (0.8)	47 (1.2)	83 (0.8)	50 (1.1)	85 (1.0)	54 (1.8)	86 (1.0)	55 (1.3)	87 (0.8)	60 (1.3)	87 (0.9)	59 (1.7)	88 (0.9)	64 (1.5)	88 (0.8)	64 (1.4)
Asian	— (†)	— (†)	— (†)	— (†)	— (†)	— (†)	88 (1.0)	58 (1.3)	89 (0.8)	63 (1.2)	88 (0.9)	61 (1.7)	88 (0.9)	64 (2.8)	88 (0.8)	64 (3.6)
Pacific Islander	— (†)	— (†)	— (†)	— (†)	— (†)	— (†)	59 (4.7)	22 (3.5)	67 (3.5)	24 (2.9)	63 (4.2)	29 (3.9)	64 (2.8)	25 (3.1)	51 (3.1)	18 (1.6)
American Indian/Alaska Native	53 (1.3)	14 (1.2)	53 (1.8)	16 (1.8)	56 (1.5)	18 (1.3)	55 (1.5)	17 (1.5)	59 (1.7)	21 (1.5)	57 (1.8)	20 (1.7)	56 (1.6)	18 (1.6)	51 (1.6)	15 (1.6)
Two or more races	— (†)	— (†)	— (†)	— (†)	— (†)	— (†)	78 (1.1)	39 (1.7)	76 (1.2)	38 (1.4)	74 (1.5)	36 (1.3)	73 (1.3)	37 (1.4)	73 (1.2)	38 (1.4)
Eligibility for free or reduced-price lunch																
Eligible	51 (0.4)	13 (0.4)	55 (0.5)	15 (0.3)	57 (0.5)	17 (0.4)	59 (0.4)	19 (0.4)	60 (0.3)	20 (0.4)	58 (0.4)	18 (0.5)	55 (0.4)	18 (0.4)	54 (0.4)	18 (0.3)
Not eligible	79 (0.4)	39 (0.3)	81 (0.3)	42 (0.3)	83 (0.3)	45 (0.3)	84 (0.2)	47 (0.4)	86 (0.3)	49 (0.3)	84 (0.3)	48 (0.5)	82 (0.3)	48 (0.4)	82 (0.3)	48 (0.5)
Unknown	79 (1.1)	40 (1.4)	81 (1.7)	43 (1.7)	83 (1.3)	48 (1.9)	85 (0.9)	48 (1.5)	84 (1.3)	50 (2.6)	81 (1.5)	46 (1.9)	83 (1.1)	47 (1.8)	80 (1.2)	45 (1.8)
12th grade, all students	61 (0.8)	23 (0.7)	— (†)	— (†)	64 (0.8)	26 (0.8)	— (†)	— (†)	65 (0.7)	26 (0.6)	62 (0.8)	25 (0.7)	— (†)	— (†)	— (†)	— (†)
Sex																
Male	62 (0.9)	25 (1.0)	— (†)	— (†)	65 (0.9)	28 (1.0)	— (†)	— (†)	66 (0.8)	28 (0.8)	63 (1.0)	26 (0.7)	— (†)	— (†)	— (†)	— (†)
Female	60 (1.0)	21 (0.8)	— (†)	— (†)	63 (0.8)	24 (0.8)	— (†)	— (†)	64 (0.9)	24 (0.7)	61 (0.9)	23 (0.7)	— (†)	— (†)	— (†)	— (†)
Race/ethnicity																
White	70 (0.8)	29 (0.8)	— (†)	— (†)	75 (0.7)	33 (0.8)	— (†)	— (†)	75 (0.8)	33 (0.8)	73 (0.9)	32 (0.9)	— (†)	— (†)	— (†)	— (†)
Black	30 (1.7)	6 (0.8)	— (†)	— (†)	37 (1.2)	6 (0.6)	— (†)	— (†)	38 (1.5)	7 (0.6)	36 (1.6)	7 (0.7)	— (†)	— (†)	— (†)	— (†)
Hispanic	40 (2.1)	8 (1.0)	— (†)	— (†)	45 (1.1)	11 (0.7)	— (†)	— (†)	51 (1.4)	12 (0.7)	47 (1.3)	12 (1.0)	— (†)	— (†)	— (†)	— (†)
Asian/Pacific Islander	73 (2.6)	36 (3.0)	— (†)	— (†)	84 (1.9)	52 (3.4)	— (†)	— (†)	81 (1.4)	47 (2.0)	78 (2.1)	46 (2.6)	— (†)	— (†)	— (†)	— (†)
Asian	— (†)	— (†)	— (†)	— (†)	— (†)	— (†)	— (†)	— (†)	83 (1.4)	49 (2.0)	79 (2.0)	47 (2.5)	— (†)	— (†)	— (†)	— (†)
Pacific Islander	— (†)	— (†)	— (†)	— (†)	— (†)	— (†)	— (†)	— (†)	65 (7.3)	16 (6.0)	46 (4.6)	10 (3.3)	— (†)	— (†)	— (†)	— (†)
American Indian/Alaska Native	42 (8.6)	6 (2.9)	— (†)	— (†)	56 (5.4)	12 (3.3)	— (†)	— (†)	54 (5.8)	12 (4.0)	46 (3.2)	31 (3.3)	— (†)	— (†)	— (†)	— (†)
Two or more races	— (†)	— (†)	— (†)	— (†)	— (†)	— (†)	— (†)	— (†)	67 (3.0)	26 (2.7)	31 (3.2)	— (†)	— (†)	— (†)	— (†)	— (†)

—Not available.
†Not applicable.
‡Reporting standards not met (too few cases for a reliable estimate).
[1]NAEP Basic denotes partial mastery of the knowledge and skills that are fundamental for proficient work at a given grade.
[2]NAEP Proficient represents solid academic performance. Students reaching this level have demonstrated competency over challenging subject matter.
NOTE: Includes public, private, Bureau of Indian Education, and Department of Defense Education Activity schools. Includes students tested with accommodations (3 to 14 percent of all students, depending on grade level and year); excludes only those students with disabilities and English language learners who were unable to be tested even with accommodations (1 to 4 percent of all students). Race categories exclude persons of Hispanic ethnicity. Prior to 2011, separate data for Asian students, Pacific Islander students, and students of Two or more races were not collected.
SOURCE: U.S. Department of Education, National Center for Education Statistics, National Assessment of Educational Progress (NAEP), 2005, 2007, 2009, 2011, 2013, 2015, 2017, and 2019 Mathematics Assessments, retrieved November 8, 2019, from the Main NAEP Data Explorer (https://nces.ed.gov/nationsreportcard/naepdata/). (This table was prepared November 2019.)

Table 222.50. Average National Assessment of Educational Progress (NAEP) mathematics scale score of 4th-grade public school students, by state: Selected years, 1992 through 2019

[Standard errors appear in parentheses]

State	1992[1]	1996[2]	2000	2003	2005	2007	2009	2011	2013	2015	2017	2019
1	2	3	4	5	6	7	8	9	10	11	12	13
United States	219 (0.8)	222 (1.0)	224 (1.0)	234 (0.2)	237 (0.2)	239 (0.2)	239 (0.2)	240 (0.2)	241 (0.2)	240 (0.3)	239 (0.2)	240 (0.2)
Alabama	208 (1.6)	212 (1.2)	217 (1.2)	223 (1.2)	225 (0.9)	229 (1.3)	228 (1.1)	231 (1.0)	233 (1.0)	231 (0.9)	232 (1.0)	230 (1.0)
Alaska[3]	— (†)	224 (1.3)	— (†)	233 (0.8)	236 (1.0)	237 (1.0)	237 (0.9)	236 (0.9)	236 (0.8)	236 (1.1)	230 (0.9)	232 (0.7)
Arizona	215 (1.1)	218 (1.7)	219 (1.3)	229 (1.1)	230 (1.1)	232 (1.0)	230 (1.1)	235 (1.1)	240 (1.2)	238 (1.0)	234 (1.1)	238 (0.8)
Arkansas[3]	210 (0.9)	216 (1.5)	216 (1.1)	229 (0.9)	236 (0.9)	238 (1.1)	238 (0.9)	238 (0.8)	240 (0.9)	235 (0.8)	234 (0.9)	233 (1.0)
California[4]	208 (1.6)	209 (1.8)	213 (1.6)	227 (0.9)	230 (0.6)	230 (0.7)	232 (1.2)	234 (1.4)	234 (1.2)	232 (1.4)	232 (1.2)	235 (0.8)
Colorado	221 (1.0)	226 (1.0)	— (†)	235 (1.0)	239 (1.1)	240 (1.0)	243 (1.0)	244 (0.9)	247 (0.8)	242 (1.0)	241 (1.1)	242 (0.9)
Connecticut	227 (1.1)	232 (1.1)	234 (1.1)	241 (0.8)	242 (0.8)	243 (1.1)	245 (1.0)	242 (1.3)	243 (0.9)	240 (0.9)	239 (1.1)	243 (0.8)
Delaware	218 (0.8)	215 (0.6)	— (†)	236 (0.5)	240 (0.5)	242 (0.4)	239 (0.5)	240 (0.6)	243 (0.7)	239 (0.6)	236 (0.8)	239 (0.7)
District of Columbia	193 (0.5)	187 (1.1)	192 (1.1)	205 (0.7)	211 (0.8)	214 (0.8)	219 (0.7)	222 (0.7)	229 (0.7)	231 (0.6)	231 (0.7)	235 (0.7)
Florida	214 (1.5)	216 (1.2)	— (†)	234 (1.1)	239 (0.7)	242 (0.8)	242 (1.0)	240 (0.8)	242 (0.8)	243 (1.0)	246 (0.7)	246 (0.8)
Georgia	216 (1.2)	215 (1.5)	219 (1.1)	230 (1.0)	234 (1.0)	235 (0.8)	236 (0.9)	238 (0.7)	240 (1.0)	236 (1.2)	236 (1.1)	238 (1.0)
Hawaii	214 (1.3)	215 (1.5)	216 (1.0)	227 (1.0)	230 (0.8)	234 (0.8)	236 (1.1)	239 (0.7)	243 (0.8)	238 (0.9)	238 (0.8)	239 (0.7)
Idaho[4]	222 (1.0)	— (†)	224 (1.4)	235 (0.7)	242 (0.7)	241 (0.7)	241 (0.8)	240 (0.6)	241 (0.9)	239 (0.9)	240 (0.9)	242 (0.9)
Illinois[4]	— (†)	— (†)	223 (1.9)	233 (1.1)	233 (1.0)	237 (1.1)	238 (1.0)	239 (1.1)	239 (1.2)	237 (1.2)	238 (1.0)	237 (1.2)
Indiana[4]	221 (1.0)	229 (1.0)	233 (1.1)	238 (0.9)	240 (0.8)	245 (0.8)	243 (0.9)	244 (1.0)	249 (0.9)	248 (1.1)	247 (1.1)	245 (1.1)
Iowa[3,4]	230 (1.0)	229 (1.1)	231 (1.2)	238 (0.7)	240 (0.7)	243 (0.8)	243 (0.8)	243 (0.8)	246 (0.9)	243 (0.9)	243 (1.1)	241 (1.1)
Kansas[4]	— (†)	— (†)	232 (1.6)	242 (1.0)	246 (1.0)	248 (0.9)	245 (1.0)	246 (0.9)	246 (0.8)	241 (1.0)	241 (0.9)	239 (0.8)
Kentucky	215 (1.0)	220 (1.1)	219 (1.4)	229 (1.1)	231 (0.9)	235 (0.9)	239 (1.1)	241 (0.8)	241 (0.9)	242 (1.1)	239 (0.9)	239 (1.1)
Louisiana	204 (1.5)	209 (1.1)	218 (1.4)	226 (1.0)	230 (0.9)	230 (1.0)	229 (1.0)	231 (1.0)	231 (1.2)	234 (1.1)	229 (1.2)	231 (1.1)
Maine[4]	232 (1.0)	232 (1.0)	230 (1.0)	238 (0.7)	241 (0.8)	242 (0.8)	244 (0.8)	244 (0.7)	246 (0.7)	242 (0.8)	240 (0.9)	241 (1.0)
Maryland	217 (1.3)	221 (1.6)	222 (1.2)	233 (1.3)	238 (1.0)	240 (0.9)	244 (0.9)	247 (0.9)	245 (1.3)	239 (1.0)	241 (1.1)	239 (1.2)
Massachusetts	227 (1.2)	229 (1.3)	233 (1.2)	242 (0.8)	247 (0.8)	252 (0.8)	252 (0.9)	253 (0.8)	253 (1.0)	251 (1.2)	249 (1.0)	247 (1.1)
Michigan[3,4]	220 (1.7)	226 (1.3)	229 (1.6)	236 (0.9)	238 (1.2)	238 (1.3)	236 (1.0)	236 (1.1)	237 (1.1)	236 (1.2)	236 (1.3)	236 (1.2)
Minnesota[4]	228 (0.9)	232 (1.1)	234 (1.3)	242 (0.9)	246 (1.0)	247 (1.0)	249 (1.1)	249 (0.9)	253 (1.1)	250 (1.2)	249 (1.2)	248 (1.0)
Mississippi	202 (1.1)	208 (1.2)	211 (1.1)	223 (1.0)	227 (0.9)	228 (1.0)	227 (1.0)	230 (0.9)	231 (0.7)	234 (0.9)	235 (0.8)	241 (0.8)
Missouri	222 (1.2)	225 (1.1)	228 (1.2)	235 (0.9)	235 (0.9)	239 (0.9)	241 (1.2)	240 (0.9)	240 (0.8)	239 (0.9)	240 (1.1)	238 (1.0)
Montana[3,4]	— (†)	228 (1.2)	228 (1.2)	236 (0.8)	241 (0.8)	244 (0.8)	244 (0.7)	244 (0.6)	244 (0.6)	241 (0.7)	241 (0.8)	241 (0.8)
Nebraska	225 (1.1)	228 (1.2)	225 (1.8)	236 (0.8)	238 (0.9)	238 (1.1)	239 (1.0)	240 (1.0)	243 (1.0)	244 (0.9)	246 (0.9)	244 (0.7)
Nevada[3]	— (†)	218 (1.3)	220 (1.0)	228 (0.8)	230 (0.8)	232 (0.9)	235 (0.9)	237 (0.8)	236 (0.8)	234 (1.1)	232 (1.2)	236 (0.8)
New Hampshire	230 (1.2)	— (†)	— (†)	243 (0.9)	246 (0.8)	249 (0.8)	251 (0.8)	252 (0.6)	253 (0.8)	249 (0.8)	245 (0.9)	245 (0.8)
New Jersey[3]	227 (1.5)	227 (1.5)	— (†)	239 (1.1)	244 (1.1)	249 (1.1)	247 (1.0)	248 (0.9)	247 (1.1)	245 (1.2)	248 (1.3)	246 (1.1)
New Mexico	213 (1.4)	214 (1.8)	213 (1.5)	223 (1.1)	224 (0.8)	228 (0.9)	230 (1.0)	233 (0.8)	233 (0.7)	231 (0.8)	230 (0.8)	231 (0.8)
New York[3,4]	218 (1.2)	223 (1.2)	225 (1.4)	236 (0.9)	238 (0.9)	243 (0.8)	241 (0.7)	238 (0.8)	240 (1.0)	237 (0.9)	236 (1.0)	237 (1.1)
North Carolina	213 (1.1)	224 (1.2)	230 (1.1)	242 (0.8)	241 (0.9)	242 (0.8)	244 (0.8)	245 (0.7)	245 (0.9)	244 (1.0)	241 (1.0)	241 (1.0)
North Dakota	229 (0.8)	231 (1.2)	230 (1.2)	238 (0.7)	243 (0.5)	245 (0.5)	245 (0.6)	245 (0.4)	246 (0.5)	245 (0.5)	244 (0.7)	243 (0.7)
Ohio[4]	219 (1.2)	— (†)	230 (1.5)	238 (1.0)	242 (1.0)	245 (1.0)	244 (1.1)	244 (0.8)	246 (1.1)	244 (1.2)	241 (1.0)	241 (1.0)
Oklahoma	220 (1.0)	— (†)	224 (1.0)	229 (1.0)	234 (1.0)	237 (0.8)	237 (0.9)	237 (0.8)	239 (0.7)	240 (1.0)	237 (0.9)	237 (0.8)
Oregon[4]	— (†)	223 (1.4)	224 (1.8)	236 (0.9)	238 (0.8)	236 (1.0)	238 (0.9)	237 (0.9)	240 (1.3)	238 (1.1)	233 (1.1)	236 (1.0)
Pennsylvania[3]	224 (1.3)	226 (1.2)	— (†)	236 (1.1)	241 (1.2)	244 (0.8)	244 (1.1)	246 (1.1)	244 (1.0)	243 (1.4)	242 (1.0)	244 (1.1)
Rhode Island	215 (1.5)	220 (1.4)	224 (1.1)	230 (1.0)	233 (0.9)	236 (0.9)	239 (0.8)	242 (0.7)	241 (0.8)	238 (0.7)	238 (0.7)	239 (0.8)
South Carolina[3]	212 (1.1)	213 (1.3)	220 (1.4)	236 (0.9)	238 (0.9)	237 (0.8)	236 (0.9)	237 (1.0)	237 (1.0)	237 (1.1)	234 (1.0)	237 (1.1)
South Dakota	— (†)	— (†)	— (†)	237 (0.7)	242 (0.5)	241 (0.7)	242 (0.5)	241 (0.6)	241 (0.5)	240 (0.7)	242 (0.8)	241 (0.7)
Tennessee	211 (1.4)	219 (1.4)	220 (1.4)	228 (1.0)	232 (1.2)	233 (0.9)	232 (1.1)	233 (0.9)	240 (0.9)	241 (1.1)	237 (1.0)	240 (1.0)
Texas	218 (1.2)	229 (1.4)	231 (1.1)	237 (0.9)	242 (0.6)	242 (0.7)	240 (0.7)	241 (1.1)	242 (0.9)	244 (1.3)	241 (1.2)	244 (1.0)
Utah	224 (1.0)	227 (1.2)	227 (1.3)	235 (0.8)	239 (0.8)	239 (0.9)	240 (1.0)	243 (0.8)	243 (0.9)	243 (1.3)	242 (1.0)	244 (1.0)
Vermont[3,4]	— (†)	225 (1.2)	232 (1.6)	242 (0.8)	244 (0.5)	246 (0.5)	248 (0.4)	247 (0.5)	248 (0.6)	243 (0.7)	241 (0.7)	239 (0.7)
Virginia	221 (1.3)	223 (1.4)	230 (1.0)	239 (1.1)	240 (0.9)	244 (0.9)	243 (1.0)	245 (0.8)	246 (1.1)	247 (1.3)	248 (1.0)	247 (1.2)
Washington	— (†)	225 (1.2)	— (†)	238 (1.0)	242 (0.9)	243 (1.0)	242 (0.8)	243 (0.9)	246 (1.1)	245 (1.3)	242 (1.3)	240 (1.2)
West Virginia	215 (1.1)	223 (1.0)	223 (1.3)	231 (0.8)	231 (0.7)	236 (0.9)	233 (0.8)	235 (0.7)	237 (0.8)	235 (0.8)	236 (1.0)	231 (0.9)
Wisconsin	229 (1.1)	231 (1.0)	‡ (†)	237 (0.9)	241 (0.9)	244 (0.9)	244 (0.9)	245 (0.8)	245 (1.0)	243 (1.1)	240 (0.9)	242 (1.1)
Wyoming	225 (0.9)	223 (1.4)	229 (1.1)	241 (0.6)	243 (0.6)	244 (0.5)	242 (0.6)	244 (0.4)	247 (0.4)	247 (0.6)	248 (0.6)	246 (0.7)
Department of Defense Education Activity (DoDEA)[5]	— (†)	224 (0.6)	227 (0.6)	237 (0.4)	239 (0.5)	240 (0.4)	240 (0.5)	241 (0.4)	245 (0.4)	248 (0.5)	249 (0.5)	250 (0.5)

—Not available.
†Not applicable.
‡Reporting standards not met. Participation rates fell below the required standards for reporting.
[1]Accommodations were not permitted for this assessment.
[2]The 1996 data in this table do not include students who were tested with accommodations. Data for students tested with accommodations are not available at the state level for 1996.
[3]Did not meet one or more of the guidelines for school participation in 1996. Data are subject to appreciable nonresponse bias.
[4]Did not meet one or more of the guidelines for school participation in 2000. Data are subject to appreciable nonresponse bias.
[5]Prior to 2005, NAEP divided the DoDEA schools into two jurisdictions, domestic and overseas. In 2005, NAEP began combining the domestic and overseas schools into a single jurisdiction. Data shown in this table for years prior to 2005 were recalculated for comparability.

NOTE: Scale ranges from 0 to 500. State-level data for 1990 are not available. Table does not include private schools, Bureau of Indian Education schools, or (except in the final row) DoDEA schools. For 2000 and later years, includes public school students who were tested with accommodations; excludes only those students with disabilities (SD) and English language learners (ELL) who were unable to be tested even with accommodations. SD and ELL populations, accommodation rates, and exclusion rates vary from state to state.
SOURCE: U.S. Department of Education, National Center for Education Statistics, National Assessment of Educational Progress (NAEP), 1992, 1996, 2000, 2003, 2005, 2007, 2009, 2011, 2013, 2015, 2017, and 2019 Mathematics Assessments, retrieved October 30, 2019, from the Main NAEP Data Explorer (https://nces.ed.gov/nationsreportcard/naepdata/). (This table was prepared November 2019.)

Table 222.60. Average National Assessment of Educational Progress (NAEP) mathematics scale score of 8th-grade public school students, by state: Selected years, 1990 through 2019

[Standard errors appear in parentheses]

State	1990[1]	1992[1]	1996[2]	2000	2003	2005	2007	2009	2011	2013	2015	2017	2019
1	2	3	4	5	6	7	8	9	10	11	12	13	14
United States	262 (1.4)	267 (1.0)	271 (1.2)	272 (0.9)	276 (0.3)	278 (0.2)	280 (0.3)	282 (0.3)	283 (0.2)	284 (0.2)	281 (0.3)	282 (0.3)	281 (0.3)
Alabama	253 (1.1)	252 (1.7)	257 (2.1)	264 (1.8)	262 (1.5)	262 (1.5)	266 (1.5)	269 (1.2)	269 (1.4)	269 (1.3)	267 (1.2)	268 (1.3)	269 (1.4)
Alaska[3]	— (†)	— (†)	278 (1.8)	— (†)	279 (0.9)	279 (0.8)	283 (1.1)	283 (1.0)	283 (0.8)	282 (0.9)	280 (1.0)	277 (0.9)	274 (1.1)
Arizona[4]	260 (1.3)	265 (1.3)	268 (1.6)	269 (1.8)	271 (1.2)	274 (1.1)	276 (1.2)	277 (1.4)	279 (1.2)	280 (1.2)	283 (1.4)	282 (1.1)	280 (1.1)
Arkansas[3]	256 (0.9)	256 (1.2)	262 (1.5)	257 (1.5)	266 (1.2)	272 (1.2)	274 (1.1)	276 (1.1)	279 (1.0)	278 (1.1)	275 (1.4)	274 (1.0)	274 (1.2)
California[4]	256 (1.3)	261 (1.7)	263 (1.9)	260 (2.1)	267 (1.2)	269 (0.6)	270 (0.8)	270 (1.3)	273 (1.2)	276 (1.2)	275 (1.3)	277 (1.2)	276 (1.3)
Colorado	267 (0.9)	272 (1.0)	276 (1.1)	— (†)	283 (1.1)	281 (1.1)	286 (0.9)	287 (1.4)	292 (1.1)	290 (1.1)	286 (1.5)	286 (1.4)	285 (1.2)
Connecticut	270 (1.0)	274 (1.1)	280 (1.1)	281 (1.3)	284 (1.2)	281 (1.4)	282 (1.5)	289 (1.0)	287 (1.1)	285 (1.1)	284 (1.2)	284 (0.9)	286 (1.3)
Delaware	261 (0.9)	263 (1.0)	267 (0.9)	— (†)	277 (0.7)	281 (0.6)	283 (0.6)	284 (0.5)	283 (0.7)	282 (0.7)	280 (0.7)	278 (0.7)	277 (0.9)
District of Columbia	231 (0.9)	235 (0.9)	233 (1.3)	235 (1.1)	243 (0.8)	245 (0.9)	248 (0.9)	254 (0.9)	260 (0.7)	265 (0.9)	263 (0.9)	266 (0.9)	269 (0.8)
Florida	255 (1.2)	260 (1.5)	264 (1.8)	— (†)	271 (1.5)	274 (1.1)	277 (1.3)	279 (1.1)	278 (0.8)	281 (0.8)	275 (1.4)	279 (1.1)	279 (1.3)
Georgia	259 (1.3)	259 (1.2)	262 (1.6)	265 (1.2)	270 (1.2)	272 (1.1)	275 (1.0)	278 (0.9)	278 (1.0)	279 (1.2)	279 (1.2)	281 (1.4)	279 (1.0)
Hawaii	251 (0.8)	257 (0.9)	262 (1.0)	262 (1.4)	266 (0.8)	266 (0.7)	269 (0.8)	274 (0.7)	278 (0.7)	281 (0.8)	279 (0.8)	277 (0.8)	275 (1.1)
Idaho[4]	271 (0.8)	275 (0.7)	— (†)	277 (1.0)	280 (0.9)	281 (0.9)	284 (0.9)	287 (0.8)	287 (0.8)	286 (0.9)	284 (0.9)	284 (1.2)	286 (1.0)
Illinois[4]	261 (1.7)	— (†)	— (†)	275 (1.7)	277 (1.2)	278 (1.1)	280 (1.1)	282 (1.2)	283 (1.1)	285 (1.0)	282 (1.3)	282 (1.2)	283 (1.2)
Indiana[4]	267 (1.2)	270 (1.1)	276 (1.4)	281 (1.4)	281 (1.1)	282 (1.0)	285 (1.1)	287 (0.9)	285 (1.0)	288 (1.1)	287 (1.2)	288 (1.3)	286 (1.3)
Iowa[3]	278 (1.1)	283 (1.0)	284 (1.3)	— (†)	284 (0.8)	284 (0.9)	285 (0.9)	284 (1.0)	285 (0.9)	285 (0.9)	286 (1.2)	286 (0.9)	282 (1.0)
Kansas[4]	— (†)	— (†)	— (†)	283 (1.3)	284 (1.3)	284 (1.0)	290 (1.1)	289 (1.0)	290 (0.9)	290 (1.0)	284 (1.3)	285 (1.0)	282 (0.9)
Kentucky	257 (1.2)	262 (1.1)	267 (1.1)	270 (1.3)	274 (1.2)	274 (1.2)	279 (1.1)	279 (1.1)	282 (0.9)	281 (0.9)	278 (0.9)	278 (1.0)	278 (1.1)
Louisiana	246 (1.2)	250 (1.7)	252 (1.6)	259 (1.5)	266 (1.5)	268 (1.4)	272 (1.1)	272 (1.6)	273 (1.2)	273 (0.9)	268 (1.4)	267 (1.3)	272 (1.4)
Maine[4]	— (†)	279 (1.0)	284 (1.3)	281 (1.1)	282 (0.9)	281 (0.8)	286 (0.8)	286 (0.7)	289 (0.8)	289 (0.7)	285 (0.7)	284 (0.9)	282 (0.9)
Maryland[3]	261 (1.4)	265 (1.3)	270 (2.1)	272 (1.7)	278 (1.0)	278 (1.1)	286 (1.2)	288 (1.1)	288 (1.2)	287 (1.1)	283 (1.2)	281 (1.1)	280 (1.1)
Massachusetts	— (†)	273 (1.4)	278 (1.7)	279 (1.5)	287 (0.9)	292 (0.9)	298 (1.3)	299 (1.3)	299 (0.8)	301 (0.9)	297 (1.4)	297 (1.1)	294 (1.2)
Michigan[3,4]	264 (1.2)	267 (1.4)	277 (1.8)	277 (1.9)	276 (2.0)	277 (1.5)	277 (1.4)	278 (1.6)	280 (1.4)	280 (1.3)	278 (1.3)	280 (1.2)	280 (1.3)
Minnesota[4]	275 (0.9)	282 (1.0)	284 (1.3)	287 (1.4)	291 (1.1)	290 (1.2)	292 (1.0)	294 (1.0)	295 (1.0)	295 (1.0)	294 (1.0)	294 (1.5)	291 (1.2)
Mississippi	— (†)	246 (1.2)	250 (1.2)	254 (1.1)	261 (1.1)	262 (1.2)	265 (0.8)	265 (1.2)	269 (1.4)	271 (0.9)	271 (1.1)	271 (0.9)	274 (0.9)
Missouri	— (†)	271 (1.2)	273 (1.4)	271 (1.5)	279 (1.1)	276 (1.3)	281 (1.0)	286 (1.0)	282 (1.1)	283 (1.0)	281 (1.2)	281 (1.1)	281 (1.0)
Montana[3,4]	280 (0.9)	— (†)	283 (1.3)	285 (1.4)	286 (0.8)	286 (0.7)	287 (0.7)	292 (0.9)	293 (0.6)	289 (0.9)	287 (0.8)	286 (0.8)	284 (0.8)
Nebraska	276 (1.0)	278 (1.1)	283 (1.0)	280 (1.2)	282 (0.9)	284 (1.0)	284 (1.0)	284 (1.1)	283 (0.8)	285 (0.9)	286 (0.8)	288 (1.0)	285 (0.9)
Nevada	— (†)	— (†)	‡ (†)	265 (0.8)	268 (0.8)	270 (0.8)	271 (0.8)	274 (0.7)	278 (0.8)	278 (0.7)	275 (0.7)	275 (0.7)	274 (0.8)
New Hampshire	273 (0.9)	278 (1.0)	‡ (†)	— (†)	286 (0.8)	285 (0.8)	288 (0.7)	292 (0.9)	292 (0.7)	296 (0.8)	294 (0.9)	293 (0.8)	287 (0.9)
New Jersey	270 (1.1)	272 (1.6)	‡ (†)	— (†)	281 (1.1)	284 (1.4)	289 (1.2)	293 (1.4)	294 (1.2)	296 (1.1)	293 (1.2)	292 (1.0)	292 (1.5)
New Mexico	256 (0.7)	260 (0.9)	262 (1.2)	259 (1.3)	263 (1.0)	263 (0.9)	268 (0.9)	270 (1.1)	274 (0.8)	273 (0.7)	271 (1.0)	269 (1.0)	269 (0.9)
New York[3,4]	261 (1.4)	266 (2.1)	270 (1.7)	271 (2.2)	280 (1.1)	280 (0.9)	280 (1.2)	283 (1.2)	280 (0.9)	282 (0.9)	280 (1.4)	282 (1.2)	280 (1.3)
North Carolina	250 (1.1)	258 (1.2)	268 (1.4)	276 (1.3)	281 (1.0)	282 (0.9)	284 (1.1)	284 (1.3)	286 (1.0)	286 (1.1)	281 (1.6)	282 (1.2)	284 (1.1)
North Dakota	281 (1.2)	283 (1.1)	284 (0.9)	282 (1.1)	287 (0.8)	287 (0.6)	292 (0.7)	293 (0.7)	292 (0.6)	291 (0.5)	288 (0.7)	288 (0.8)	286 (0.8)
Ohio	264 (1.0)	268 (1.5)	— (†)	281 (1.6)	282 (1.3)	283 (1.1)	285 (1.2)	286 (1.0)	289 (1.0)	290 (1.1)	285 (1.6)	288 (2.0)	286 (1.1)
Oklahoma	263 (1.3)	268 (1.1)	— (†)	270 (1.3)	272 (1.1)	271 (1.0)	275 (0.9)	276 (1.0)	279 (1.0)	276 (1.0)	275 (1.3)	275 (1.1)	276 (1.0)
Oregon[4]	271 (1.0)	— (†)	276 (1.5)	280 (1.5)	281 (1.3)	282 (1.0)	284 (1.1)	285 (1.0)	283 (1.0)	284 (1.1)	283 (1.2)	282 (1.2)	280 (1.2)
Pennsylvania	266 (1.6)	271 (1.5)	— (†)	— (†)	279 (1.1)	281 (1.5)	286 (1.1)	288 (1.3)	286 (1.2)	290 (1.0)	284 (1.5)	286 (1.2)	285 (1.2)
Rhode Island	260 (0.6)	266 (0.7)	269 (0.9)	269 (1.3)	272 (0.7)	272 (0.8)	275 (0.7)	278 (0.8)	283 (0.5)	284 (0.6)	281 (0.7)	277 (0.8)	276 (0.7)
South Carolina[3]	— (†)	261 (1.0)	261 (1.5)	265 (1.5)	277 (1.3)	281 (0.9)	282 (1.0)	280 (1.3)	281 (1.1)	280 (1.1)	276 (1.3)	275 (1.0)	276 (1.0)
South Dakota	— (†)	— (†)	— (†)	— (†)	285 (0.8)	287 (0.6)	288 (0.8)	291 (0.5)	291 (0.5)	287 (0.7)	285 (0.9)	286 (0.7)	287 (1.2)
Tennessee	— (†)	259 (1.4)	263 (1.4)	262 (1.5)	268 (1.8)	271 (1.1)	274 (1.1)	275 (1.4)	274 (1.2)	278 (1.3)	278 (1.8)	279 (1.2)	280 (1.3)
Texas	258 (1.4)	265 (1.3)	270 (1.4)	273 (1.6)	277 (1.1)	281 (0.6)	286 (1.0)	287 (1.3)	290 (0.9)	288 (1.0)	284 (1.2)	282 (1.4)	280 (1.0)
Utah	— (†)	274 (0.7)	277 (1.0)	274 (1.2)	281 (1.0)	279 (0.7)	281 (0.9)	284 (0.9)	283 (0.8)	284 (0.9)	286 (1.1)	287 (0.9)	285 (1.0)
Vermont[3,4]	— (†)	— (†)	279 (1.0)	281 (1.5)	286 (0.8)	287 (0.7)	291 (0.7)	293 (0.6)	294 (0.7)	295 (0.7)	290 (0.7)	288 (0.7)	287 (0.7)
Virginia	264 (1.5)	268 (1.2)	270 (1.6)	275 (1.3)	282 (1.3)	284 (1.1)	288 (1.1)	286 (1.1)	289 (1.1)	288 (1.2)	288 (1.2)	290 (1.5)	287 (1.3)
Washington	— (†)	— (†)	276 (1.3)	— (†)	281 (0.9)	285 (1.0)	285 (1.0)	289 (1.0)	288 (1.0)	290 (1.0)	287 (1.3)	289 (1.4)	286 (1.4)
West Virginia	256 (1.0)	259 (1.6)	265 (1.0)	266 (1.2)	271 (1.2)	269 (1.0)	270 (1.0)	270 (1.0)	273 (0.7)	274 (0.9)	271 (0.9)	273 (0.9)	272 (0.9)
Wisconsin[3]	274 (1.3)	278 (1.5)	283 (1.5)	‡ (†)	284 (1.3)	285 (1.1)	286 (1.1)	288 (0.9)	289 (1.0)	289 (0.9)	289 (1.3)	288 (1.0)	289 (1.1)
Wyoming	272 (0.7)	275 (0.9)	275 (0.9)	276 (1.0)	284 (0.7)	282 (0.7)	287 (0.7)	286 (0.6)	288 (0.6)	288 (0.9)	287 (0.6)	289 (0.7)	286 (0.9)
Department of Defense Education Activity (DoDEA)[5]	— (†)	— (†)	274 (0.9)	277 (1.1)	285 (0.7)	284 (0.7)	285 (0.8)	287 (0.9)	288 (0.8)	290 (0.8)	291 (0.7)	293 (0.7)	292 (0.8)

—Not available.
†Not applicable.
‡Reporting standards not met. Participation rates fell below the required standards for reporting.
[1]Accommodations were not permitted for this assessment.
[2]The 1996 data in this table do not include students who were tested with accommodations. Data for students tested with accommodations are not available at the state level for 1996.
[3]Did not meet one or more of the guidelines for school participation in 1996. Data are subject to appreciable nonresponse bias.
[4]Did not meet one or more of the guidelines for school participation in 2000. Data are subject to appreciable nonresponse bias.
[5]Prior to 2005, NAEP divided the DoDEA schools into two jurisdictions, domestic and overseas. In 2005, NAEP began combining the domestic and overseas schools into a single jurisdiction. Data shown in this table for years prior to 2005 were recalculated for comparability.

NOTE: Scale ranges from 0 to 500. Table does not include private schools, Bureau of Indian Education schools, or (except in the final row) DoDEA schools. For 2000 and later years, includes public school students who were tested with accommodations; excludes only those students with disabilities (SD) and English language learners (ELL) who were unable to be tested even with accommodations. SD and ELL populations, accommodation rates, and exclusion rates vary from state to state.
SOURCE: U.S. Department of Education, National Center for Education Statistics, National Assessment of Educational Progress (NAEP), 1990, 1992, 1996, 2000, 2003, 2005, 2007, 2009, 2011, 2013, 2015, 2017, and 2019 Mathematics Assessments, retrieved October 30, 2019, from the Main NAEP Data Explorer (https://nces.ed.gov/nationsreportcard/naepdata/). (This table was prepared November 2019.)

Table 223.10. Average National Assessment of Educational Progress (NAEP) science scale score, standard deviation, and percentage of students attaining science achievement levels, by grade level, selected student and school characteristics, and percentile: 2009, 2011, and 2015

[Standard errors appear in parentheses]

Selected characteristic, percentile, and achievement level	Grade 4			Grade 8			Grade 12		
	2009	2011	2015	2009	2011	2015	2009	2011	2015
1	2	3	4	5	6	7	8	9	10
Average science scale score[1]									
All students	150 (0.3)	— (†)	154 (0.3)	150 (0.3)	152 (0.3)	154 (0.3)	150 (0.8)	— (†)	150 (0.6)
Sex									
Male	151 (0.3)	— (†)	154 (0.4)	152 (0.4)	154 (0.3)	155 (0.3)	153 (0.9)	— (†)	153 (0.8)
Female	149 (0.3)	— (†)	154 (0.3)	148 (0.3)	149 (0.3)	152 (0.4)	147 (0.9)	— (†)	148 (0.7)
Gap between male and female score	1 (0.4)	— (†)	1 (0.5)	4 (0.5)	5 (0.5)	3 (0.5)	6 (1.3)	— (†)	5 (1.0)
Race/ethnicity									
White	163 (0.2)	— (†)	166 (0.3)	162 (0.2)	163 (0.2)	166 (0.3)	159 (0.7)	— (†)	160 (0.7)
Black	127 (0.4)	— (†)	133 (0.4)	126 (0.4)	129 (0.5)	132 (0.5)	125 (1.2)	— (†)	125 (1.5)
Hispanic	131 (0.5)	— (†)	139 (0.7)	132 (0.6)	137 (0.5)	140 (0.5)	134 (1.3)	— (†)	136 (1.0)
Asian/Pacific Islander	160 (1.2)	— (†)	167 (1.4)	160 (1.0)	159 (1.3)	164 (0.9)	164 (3.0)	— (†)	166 (2.3)
Asian	— (†)	— (†)	169 (1.4)	— (†)	161 (1.3)	166 (0.9)	— (†)	— (†)	167 (2.3)
Pacific Islander	— (†)	— (†)	143 (2.2)	— (†)	139 (1.9)	138 (2.5)	— (†)	— (†)	‡ (†)
American Indian/Alaska Native	135 (1.3)	— (†)	139 (1.5)	137 (1.4)	141 (1.4)	139 (1.6)	144 (3.7)	— (†)	135 (5.3)
Two or more races[2]	154 (1.1)	— (†)	158 (1.0)	151 (1.2)	156 (1.3)	159 (1.3)	151 (3.7)	— (†)	156 (2.5)
Gap between White and Black score	36 (0.4)	— (†)	33 (0.5)	36 (0.5)	35 (0.6)	34 (0.5)	34 (1.4)	— (†)	36 (1.6)
Gap between White and Hispanic score	32 (0.6)	— (†)	27 (0.7)	30 (0.6)	27 (0.6)	26 (0.6)	25 (1.5)	— (†)	24 (1.2)
English language learner (ELL) status									
ELL	114 (0.8)	— (†)	121 (1.0)	103 (1.0)	106 (1.2)	110 (1.1)	104 (2.4)	— (†)	105 (2.7)
Non-ELL	154 (0.2)	— (†)	158 (0.3)	153 (0.3)	154 (0.2)	157 (0.3)	151 (0.8)	— (†)	152 (0.5)
Gap between ELL and non-ELL score	39 (0.8)	— (†)	36 (1.0)	49 (1.0)	48 (1.3)	46 (1.2)	47 (2.6)	— (†)	47 (2.7)
Disability status[3]									
Identified as student with disability (SD)	129 (0.6)	— (†)	131 (0.6)	123 (0.5)	124 (0.6)	124 (0.6)	121 (1.8)	— (†)	124 (1.8)
Not identified as SD	153 (0.3)	— (†)	157 (0.3)	153 (0.3)	155 (0.3)	158 (0.3)	153 (0.8)	— (†)	153 (0.6)
Gap between SD and non-SD score	23 (0.7)	— (†)	26 (0.7)	31 (0.6)	31 (0.7)	34 (0.7)	31 (2.0)	— (†)	29 (1.9)
Highest education level of either parent									
Did not finish high school	— (†)	— (†)	— (†)	131 (0.6)	132 (0.7)	137 (0.7)	131 (1.4)	— (†)	131 (1.4)
Graduated high school	— (†)	— (†)	— (†)	139 (0.4)	140 (0.4)	142 (0.5)	138 (1.2)	— (†)	136 (1.2)
Some education after high school	— (†)	— (†)	— (†)	152 (0.4)	153 (0.4)	155 (0.5)	147 (0.9)	— (†)	148 (0.9)
Graduated college	— (†)	— (†)	— (†)	161 (0.4)	162 (0.3)	165 (0.3)	161 (0.7)	— (†)	162 (0.7)
Percent of students in school eligible for free or reduced-price lunch									
0–25 percent eligible (low poverty)	167 (0.4)	— (†)	172 (0.6)	165 (0.5)	167 (0.4)	170 (0.6)	163 (1.2)	— (†)	165 (1.1)
26–50 percent eligible	155 (0.5)	— (†)	161 (0.7)	154 (0.5)	157 (0.5)	161 (0.5)	148 (1.1)	— (†)	154 (1.0)
51–75 percent eligible	144 (0.5)	— (†)	151 (0.7)	141 (0.6)	146 (0.5)	150 (0.6)	136 (1.7)	— (†)	143 (1.1)
76–100 percent eligible (high poverty)	126 (0.6)	— (†)	134 (0.6)	124 (0.7)	129 (0.7)	134 (0.8)	124 (2.1)	— (†)	126 (1.7)
Gap between low- and high-poverty score	41 (0.8)	— (†)	38 (0.8)	41 (0.9)	38 (0.8)	36 (1.0)	38 (2.5)	— (†)	39 (2.0)
School locale									
City	142 (0.6)	— (†)	148 (0.6)	142 (0.6)	144 (0.6)	148 (0.6)	146 (1.8)	— (†)	145 (1.2)
Suburban	154 (0.4)	— (†)	157 (0.6)	154 (0.5)	155 (0.5)	158 (0.4)	154 (1.4)	— (†)	153 (1.0)
Town	150 (0.6)	— (†)	153 (0.8)	149 (1.0)	153 (0.7)	154 (0.7)	150 (1.2)	— (†)	150 (2.1)
Rural	155 (0.5)	— (†)	157 (0.7)	154 (0.4)	156 (0.5)	156 (0.6)	150 (1.2)	— (†)	152 (1.3)
Percentile[4]									
10th	104 (0.6)	— (†)	108 (0.6)	103 (0.6)	106 (0.5)	109 (0.6)	104 (1.2)	— (†)	103 (1.0)
25th	128 (0.4)	— (†)	132 (0.4)	128 (0.4)	131 (0.4)	133 (0.5)	126 (0.8)	— (†)	126 (0.9)
50th	153 (0.3)	— (†)	157 (0.4)	153 (0.3)	155 (0.3)	157 (0.4)	151 (1.1)	— (†)	151 (0.6)
75th	175 (0.3)	— (†)	178 (0.3)	175 (0.2)	176 (0.4)	178 (0.4)	174 (1.0)	— (†)	176 (0.6)
90th	192 (0.3)	— (†)	196 (0.4)	192 (0.3)	193 (0.4)	195 (0.3)	194 (1.0)	— (†)	196 (0.6)
Standard deviation of the science scale score[5]									
All students	35 (0.2)	— (†)	35 (0.2)	35 (0.2)	34 (0.2)	34 (0.2)	35 (0.4)	— (†)	36 (0.4)
Percent of students attaining science achievement levels									
Achievement level									
Below *Basic*	28 (0.3)	— (†)	24 (0.3)	37 (0.4)	35 (0.3)	32 (0.4)	40 (1.0)	— (†)	40 (0.7)
At or above *Basic*[6]	72 (0.3)	— (†)	76 (0.3)	63 (0.4)	65 (0.3)	68 (0.4)	60 (1.0)	— (†)	60 (0.7)
At or above *Proficient*[7]	34 (0.3)	— (†)	38 (0.4)	30 (0.3)	32 (0.4)	34 (0.4)	21 (0.8)	— (†)	22 (0.6)
At *Advanced*[8]	1 (0.1)	— (†)	1 (0.1)	2 (0.1)	2 (0.1)	2 (0.1)	1 (0.2)	— (†)	2 (0.2)

—Not available.
†Not applicable.
‡Reporting standards not met (too few cases for a reliable estimate).
[1]Scale ranges from 0 to 300 for all three grades, but scores cannot be compared across grades. For example, the average score of 166 for White 4th-graders in 2015 does not denote higher performance than the score of 160 for White 12th-graders.
[2]Prior to 2011, students in the "Two or more races" category were categorized as "Unclassified."
[3]The student with disability (SD) variable used in this table includes students who have a 504 plan, even if they do not have an Individualized Education Plan (IEP).
[4]The percentile represents a specific point on the percentage distribution of all students ranked by their science score from low to high. For example, 10 percent of students scored at or below the 10th percentile score, while 90 percent of students scored above it.
[5]The standard deviation provides an indication of how much the test scores varied. The lower the standard deviation, the closer the scores were clustered around the average score. About two-thirds of the student scores can be expected to fall within the range of one standard deviation above and one standard deviation below the average score. In 2015, for example, the average score for all 4th-graders was 154, and the standard

deviation was 35. This means that one would expect about two-thirds of the students to have scores between 189 (one standard deviation above the average) and 119 (one standard deviation below). Standard errors also must be taken into account when making comparisons of these ranges.
[6]*Basic* denotes partial mastery of the knowledge and skills that are fundamental for proficient work.
[7]*Proficient* represents solid academic performance. Students reaching this level have demonstrated competency over challenging subject matter.
[8]*Advanced* signifies superior performance.
NOTE: In 2011, only 8th-grade students were assessed in science. Includes students tested with accommodations (7 to 14 percent of all students, depending on grade level and year); excludes only those students with disabilities and English language learners who were unable to be tested even with accommodations (1 to 3 percent of all students). Race categories exclude persons of Hispanic ethnicity.
SOURCE: U.S. Department of Education, National Center for Education Statistics, National Assessment of Educational Progress (NAEP), 2009, 2011, and 2015 Science Assessments, retrieved January 10, 2017, from the Main NAEP Data Explorer (http://nces.ed.gov/nationsreportcard/naepdata/). (This table was prepared January 2017.)

Table 224.10. Average National Assessment of Educational Progress (NAEP) music and visual arts scale scores of 8th-graders, percentage distribution by frequency of instruction at their school, and percentage participating in selected musical activities in school, by selected characteristics: 2016

[Standard errors appear in parentheses]

Selected characteristic	Average scale score[1] — Music[3]	Average scale score[1] — Visual arts[4]	Music[2] — Subject not offered	Music — Less than once a week	Music — Once or twice a week	Music — 3 or 4 times a week	Music — Every day	Visual arts[2] — Subject not offered	Visual arts — Less than once a week	Visual arts — Once or twice a week	Visual arts — 3 or 4 times a week	Visual arts — Every day	Play in band	Play in orchestra	Sing in chorus or choir
1	2	3	4	5	6	7	8	9	10	11	12	13	14	15	16
All students	147 (1.0)	149 (0.9)	8 (1.7)	5 (1.4)	23 (3.0)	19 (3.0)	45 (3.4)	14 (3.0)	7 (1.8)	24 (3.1)	18 (2.9)	37 (3.5)	17 (0.8)	5 (0.6)	16 (1.0)
Sex															
Male	140 (1.1)	142 (1.1)	7 (1.6)	5 (1.4)	24 (3.2)	19 (3.0)	45 (3.3)	14 (3.0)	7 (1.8)	24 (3.2)	18 (2.8)	37 (3.4)	18 (1.0)	5 (0.7)	8 (0.9)
Female	155 (1.1)	156 (1.0)	9 (1.9)	5 (1.3)	22 (2.8)	19 (3.1)	45 (3.5)	14 (3.0)	7 (1.8)	23 (3.1)	19 (2.9)	37 (3.7)	16 (1.2)	6 (0.7)	24 (1.3)
Race/ethnicity															
White	158 (1.2)	158 (1.1)	8 (2.2)	4 (1.6)	27 (4.2)	19 (4.2)	42 (4.2)	13 (3.9)	8 (2.6)	28 (4.2)	17 (3.5)	34 (4.4)	19 (1.3)	5 (0.9)	19 (1.5)
Black	129 (2.0)	128 (2.0)	9 (3.8)	10 (3.7)	21 (4.2)	16 (4.2)	43 (5.0)	20 (5.5)	7 (2.9)	17 (3.7)	19 (4.5)	37 (4.9)	12 (1.6)	4 (1.0)	16 (1.5)
Hispanic	135 (1.2)	139 (1.3)	2 (2.5)	4 (1.6)	17 (3.0)	17 (3.3)	53 (3.8)	15 (3.5)	5 (1.7)	18 (3.1)	17 (3.3)	44 (3.9)	15 (1.2)	5 (0.8)	10 (1.1)
Asian	163 (2.5)	167 (2.6)	‡ (†)	4 (2.4)	22 (5.4)	34 (6.2)	38 (6.2)	4 (1.7)	6 (2.5)	26 (5.6)	32 (5.8)	32 (5.5)	17 (2.5)	15 (2.5)	13 (2.3)
Pacific Islander	‡ (†)	‡ (†)	‡ (†)	‡ (†)	‡ (†)	‡ (†)	‡ (†)	‡ (†)	‡ (†)	‡ (†)	‡ (†)	‡ (†)	‡ (†)	‡ (†)	‡ (†)
American Indian/Alaska Native	‡ (†)	‡ (†)	‡ (†)	‡ (†)	‡ (†)	‡ (†)	‡ (†)	‡ (†)	‡ (†)	‡ (†)	‡ (†)	‡ (†)	‡ (†)	‡ (†)	‡ (†)
Two or more races	149 (3.3)	155 (4.5)	4 (2.1)	6 (2.2)	14 (3.0)	20 (4.4)	56 (5.9)	9 (3.2)	3 (1.9)	26 (4.8)	25 (7.0)	37 (6.6)	21 (4.1)	3 (1.9)	24 (3.6)
Free or reduced-price lunch eligibility															
Eligible	134 (1.1)	137 (1.2)	9 (2.1)	5 (1.7)	20 (3.3)	17 (3.2)	48 (4.0)	18 (3.8)	5 (1.6)	18 (3.4)	17 (3.1)	42 (4.5)	15 (1.0)	4 (0.7)	14 (1.2)
Not eligible	160 (1.1)	159 (1.2)	6 (1.8)	4 (1.7)	22 (3.5)	22 (4.3)	47 (4.2)	12 (3.9)	9 (2.8)	24 (4.0)	20 (3.9)	36 (3.8)	19 (1.4)	7 (1.1)	18 (1.5)
Unknown	157 (3.1)	161 (3.7)	13 (8.0)	8 (†)	49 (11.1)	12 (6.3)	17 (7.9)	2 (†)	12 (7.0)	57 (10.0)	16 (7.3)	12 (7.8)	16 (2.7)	4 (0.9)	18 (3.4)
Control of school															
Public	146 (1.0)	148 (0.9)	8 (1.7)	5 (1.4)	20 (3.1)	20 (3.2)	48 (3.6)	15 (3.2)	6 (1.9)	21 (3.4)	19 (3.0)	39 (3.7)	17 (0.9)	6 (0.7)	15 (1.0)
Private	160 (2.6)	164 (3.2)	14 (8.5)	8 (†)	59 (10.8)	8 (4.5)	10 (†)	5 (†)	17 (8.2)	61 (10.2)	11 (5.8)	6 (1.3)	16 (2.9)	3 (0.8)	23 (4.3)
School location															
City	140 (1.9)	145 (1.8)	7 (2.8)	6 (2.8)	25 (4.4)	18 (4.7)	43 (5.1)	13 (3.6)	2 (1.7)	29 (4.1)	19 (4.6)	36 (4.6)	13 (1.1)	6 (0.9)	14 (1.4)
Suburban	153 (1.5)	152 (1.6)	4 (1.7)	3 (1.7)	26 (4.2)	18 (4.2)	49 (5.1)	11 (2.0)	9 (2.9)	21 (3.9)	21 (4.8)	38 (5.3)	16 (1.3)	7 (1.1)	16 (1.3)
Town	143 (4.4)	147 (3.6)	25 (11.3)	4 (0.7)	8 (1.8)	31 (12.1)	32 (9.2)	26 (12.9)	8 (5.2)	19 (9.4)	12 (7.8)	34 (9.0)	22 (5.2)	1 (0.4)	19 (4.2)
Rural	149 (2.1)	148 (2.0)	14 (5.7)	7 (3.6)	18 (4.8)	18 (6.7)	43 (7.6)	17 (8.5)	9 (5.6)	24 (7.8)	13 (5.7)	37 (8.3)	21 (2.0)	2 (0.8)	19 (2.8)
Region															
Northeast	152 (2.3)	160 (1.4)	3 (0.4)	9 (5.4)	61 (11.2)	25 (8.3)	2 (1.1)	8 (1.0)	11 (5.9)	54 (8.8)	22 (6.1)	4 (†)	17 (1.8)	8 (2.8)	24 (2.7)
Midwest	152 (2.2)	148 (2.2)	4 (4.3)	4 (†)	23 (5.1)	27 (8.9)	37 (9.4)	11 (3.6)	11 (5.2)	31 (7.9)	19 (6.3)	29 (8.8)	20 (2.5)	6 (1.3)	20 (3.7)
South	146 (1.6)	146 (1.7)	10 (3.6)	6 (1.9)	15 (4.4)	11 (3.5)	58 (5.8)	16 (6.6)	6 (2.7)	14 (5.2)	12 (6.0)	52 (6.1)	17 (1.3)	5 (0.5)	14 (0.9)
West	143 (1.6)	148 (1.4)	7 (2.3)	2 (0.1)	11 (3.4)	23 (5.2)	57 (5.1)	17 (5.1)	3 (†)	12 (3.0)	27 (6.3)	42 (5.5)	14 (1.2)	5 (0.8)	11 (1.4)
Frequency of instruction[2,5]															
Subject not offered	133 (3.3)	139 (2.6)	†	†	†	†	†	†	†	†	†	†	13 (2.9)	# (†)	13 (3.4)
Less than once a week	145 (5.9)	153 (5.5)	†	†	†	†	†	†	†	†	†	†	14 (2.7)	3 (1.2)	19 (5.0)
Once or twice a week	151 (2.1)	155 (2.5)	†	†	†	†	†	†	†	†	†	†	18 (1.7)	6 (1.7)	20 (2.2)
3 or 4 times a week	152 (3.4)	150 (2.5)	†	†	†	†	†	†	†	†	†	†	18 (3.0)	8 (1.3)	16 (2.0)
Every day	147 (1.7)	149 (1.7)	†	†	†	†	†	†	†	†	†	†	17 (1.2)	5 (0.6)	14 (1.1)

†Not applicable.
#Rounds to zero.
‡Reporting standards not met (too few cases for a reliable estimate).
[1]Scale ranges from 0 to 300 for both music and visual arts.
[2]Based on principals' responses to the following question: "How often does a typical eighth-grade student in your school receive instruction in each of the following subjects?"
[3]Students were asked to analyze, interpret, or critique a piece of music that they listened to or to describe the social, historical, or cultural context of a piece of music.
[4]Students were asked to analyze, describe, or judge works of art and design to show understanding of form, aesthetics, and cultural or historical context.

[5]For columns 2, 14, 15, and 16, refers to music instruction. For column 3, refers to visual arts instruction.
NOTE: Includes students tested with accommodations (10 percent of all 8th-graders for visual arts and 11 percent for music); excludes only those students with disabilities and English language learners who were unable to be tested even with accommodations (2 percent of all 8th-graders both for visual arts and for music). Detail may not sum to totals because of rounding. Race categories exclude persons of Hispanic ethnicity.
SOURCE: U.S. Department of Education, National Center for Education Statistics, National Assessment of Educational Progress (NAEP), 2016 Arts Assessment, retrieved May 11, 2017, from the Main NAEP Data Explorer (http://nces.ed.gov/nationsreportcard/naepdata/). (This table was prepared May 2017.)

Table 224.70. Average National Assessment of Educational Progress (NAEP) technology and engineering literacy (TEL) overall and content area scale scores of 8th-graders and percentage of 8th-graders attaining TEL achievement levels, by selected student and school characteristics: 2018

[Standard errors appear in parentheses]

Selected student or school characteristic	Average scale score[1]				Percent attaining TEL achievement levels[2]						
		Content area				At or above Basic[3]					
									At or above Proficient[4]		
	Overall TEL score	Technology and society	Design and systems	Information and communication technology	Below Basic[3]	Total at or above Basic[3]	At Basic[3]	Total at or above Proficient[4]	At Proficient[4]	At Advanced[5]
1	2	3	4	5	6	7	8	9	10	11
All students	152 (0.6)	152 (0.7)	153 (0.8)	153 (0.7)	16 (0.6)	84 (0.6)	38 (0.7)	46 (0.8)	42 (0.7)	5 (0.3)
Sex										
Male	150 (0.7)	151 (0.7)	152 (0.9)	149 (0.7)	18 (0.7)	82 (0.7)	38 (0.8)	44 (0.9)	40 (0.9)	4 (0.4)
Female	155 (0.8)	154 (0.8)	154 (0.9)	156 (0.9)	14 (0.6)	86 (0.6)	37 (0.8)	49 (1.0)	44 (1.0)	5 (0.4)
Race/ethnicity										
White	163 (0.7)	163 (0.7)	164 (1.0)	162 (0.8)	8 (0.6)	92 (0.6)	33 (0.9)	59 (1.0)	52 (1.0)	7 (0.5)
Black	132 (1.1)	132 (1.1)	131 (1.3)	133 (1.3)	32 (1.4)	68 (1.4)	44 (1.4)	23 (1.3)	23 (1.2)	1 (0.3)
Hispanic	139 (0.8)	139 (0.9)	141 (1.0)	140 (0.9)	24 (0.9)	76 (0.9)	45 (1.0)	31 (1.0)	29 (1.0)	2 (0.3)
Asian	169 (2.0)	167 (2.4)	168 (2.4)	172 (2.7)	8 (1.0)	92 (1.0)	25 (2.7)	66 (2.8)	53 (2.4)	13 (1.4)
Pacific Islander	‡ (†)	‡ (†)	‡ (†)	‡ (†)	‡ (†)	‡ (†)	‡ (†)	‡ (†)	‡ (†)	‡ (†)
American Indian/Alaska Native	133 (6.2)	135 (6.4)	135 (5.7)	131 (5.0)	33 (6.6)	67 (6.6)	38 (4.2)	29 (5.8)	27 (5.6)	2 (†)
Two or more races	157 (1.9)	157 (2.2)	156 (2.7)	157 (2.0)	13 (1.9)	87 (1.9)	34 (2.9)	53 (3.2)	48 (3.3)	5 (1.2)
English language learner (ELL) status										
ELL	106 (1.3)	109 (1.4)	106 (1.8)	106 (1.5)	61 (2.1)	39 (2.1)	34 (2.1)	5 (0.9)	5 (0.9)	# (†)
Non-ELL	155 (0.6)	155 (0.7)	156 (0.8)	156 (0.7)	13 (0.6)	87 (0.6)	38 (0.7)	49 (0.8)	44 (0.7)	5 (0.3)
Disability status[6]										
Identified as student with a disability (SD)	118 (1.1)	120 (1.1)	120 (1.4)	117 (1.3)	48 (1.4)	52 (1.4)	39 (1.5)	13 (1.2)	13 (1.1)	1 (0.2)
Not identified as SD	157 (0.6)	157 (0.6)	158 (0.8)	158 (0.7)	11 (0.5)	89 (0.5)	37 (0.7)	51 (0.8)	46 (0.7)	5 (0.3)
Access to desktop or laptop computer at home										
Yes	156 (0.6)	155 (0.6)	156 (0.8)	156 (0.7)	13 (0.5)	87 (0.5)	37 (0.7)	50 (0.8)	44 (0.7)	5 (0.3)
No	134 (1.1)	134 (1.1)	134 (1.4)	134 (1.0)	31 (1.5)	69 (1.5)	43 (1.5)	26 (1.4)	25 (1.4)	1 (0.4)
Access to Internet at home										
Yes	153 (0.7)	153 (0.6)	154 (0.8)	154 (0.7)	15 (0.6)	85 (0.6)	37 (0.7)	47 (0.8)	42 (0.7)	5 (0.3)
No	127 (2.0)	128 (2.2)	129 (2.9)	126 (2.2)	38 (3.0)	62 (3.0)	41 (3.4)	21 (2.8)	21 (2.9)	1 (†)
Highest education level of either parent[7]										
Did not finish high school	138 (1.3)	138 (1.3)	138 (1.5)	140 (1.5)	24 (1.9)	76 (1.9)	47 (2.3)	29 (1.9)	28 (1.9)	1 (0.4)
Graduated high school	138 (1.0)	138 (1.0)	139 (1.3)	138 (1.0)	26 (1.4)	74 (1.4)	45 (1.6)	29 (1.2)	28 (1.2)	1 (0.4)
Some education after high school	151 (1.1)	151 (1.2)	152 (1.5)	152 (1.2)	14 (0.9)	86 (0.9)	42 (1.4)	44 (1.7)	41 (1.6)	3 (0.7)
Graduated college	163 (0.7)	163 (0.7)	163 (1.0)	163 (0.8)	9 (0.5)	91 (0.5)	32 (0.8)	59 (0.9)	51 (0.9)	7 (0.5)
Percent of students in school eligible for free or reduced-price lunch[8]										
0 to 25 percent eligible	170 (1.4)	169 (1.8)	169 (1.8)	170 (1.7)	6 (0.8)	94 (0.8)	27 (1.7)	67 (2.0)	57 (1.8)	10 (1.2)
26 to 50 percent eligible	157 (1.3)	157 (1.5)	159 (1.7)	157 (1.4)	12 (0.9)	88 (0.9)	37 (1.4)	51 (1.9)	46 (1.5)	5 (0.7)
51 to 75 percent eligible	148 (1.0)	148 (0.9)	148 (1.2)	148 (1.1)	17 (1.1)	83 (1.1)	42 (1.3)	41 (1.5)	39 (1.4)	2 (0.4)
76 to 100 percent eligible	134 (1.2)	135 (1.3)	134 (1.5)	135 (1.4)	30 (1.4)	70 (1.4)	45 (1.2)	26 (1.2)	25 (1.1)	1 (0.3)
School control[9]										
Public	151 (0.7)	151 (0.7)	151 (0.8)	151 (0.7)	17 (0.6)	83 (0.6)	38 (0.7)	45 (0.9)	40 (0.8)	4 (0.3)
Private	‡ (†)	‡ (†)	‡ (†)	‡ (†)	‡ (†)	‡ (†)	‡ (†)	‡ (†)	‡ (†)	‡ (†)
School locale										
City	147 (1.4)	148 (1.3)	148 (1.6)	148 (1.5)	21 (1.2)	79 (1.2)	38 (1.2)	42 (1.8)	37 (1.5)	4 (0.5)
Suburb	156 (0.8)	156 (1.0)	156 (0.9)	157 (0.9)	13 (0.7)	87 (0.7)	36 (1.0)	51 (1.2)	45 (1.1)	6 (0.5)
Town	153 (2.6)	153 (2.3)	156 (2.8)	153 (2.6)	14 (2.4)	86 (2.4)	41 (1.8)	46 (3.1)	42 (2.4)	4 (1.1)
Rural	152 (1.7)	153 (2.0)	153 (2.5)	152 (1.8)	15 (1.2)	85 (1.2)	40 (1.5)	45 (2.1)	41 (1.7)	4 (0.8)

†Not applicable.
#Rounds to zero.
‡Reporting standards not met (too few cases for a reliable estimate) or the standard error could not be accurately determined.
[1]Scale ranges from 0 to 300.
[2]TEL achievement levels are for performance on the TEL assessment overall, rather than performance on any specific content area.
[3]Basic denotes partial mastery of the knowledge and skills that are fundamental for proficient work at a given grade.
[4]Proficient represents solid academic performance. Students reaching this level have demonstrated competency over challenging subject matter.
[5]Advanced signifies superior performance.
[6]In addition to students with an Individualized Education Program (IEP), also includes students with a 504 plan.
[7]These data are based on students' responses to questions about their parents' education level. Data for students whose parents have an unknown level of education are included in table totals, but not shown separately.

[8]Nonresponse rate for this item was greater than 15 percent but not greater than 50 percent.
[9]Bureau of Indian Education and Department of Defense schools are excluded from the Public category but included elsewhere in this table. The Private category includes Catholic and Other private schools.
NOTE: Includes students tested with accommodations (11 percent of all 8th-graders); excludes only those students with disabilities and English language learners who were unable to be tested even with accommodations (2 percent of all 8th-graders). Race categories exclude persons of Hispanic ethnicity. Detail may not sum to totals because of rounding.
SOURCE: U.S. Department of Education, National Center for Education Statistics, National Assessment of Educational Progress (NAEP), 2018 Technology and Engineering Literacy (TEL) Assessment, retrieved February 12, 2019, from the Main NAEP Data Explorer (http://nces.ed.gov/nationsreportcard/naepdata/). (This table was prepared February 2019.)

Table 225.10. Average number of Carnegie units earned by public high school graduates in various subject fields, by sex and race/ethnicity: Selected years, 1982 through 2009

[Standard errors appear in parentheses]

Graduation year, sex, and race/ethnicity	Total	English	History/ social studies	Mathematics	Science — Total	Biology	Chemistry	Physics	Other science[4]	Foreign languages	Arts	Career/ technical (occupational) education[1]	Labor market, family, and consumer education[2]	Personal use[3]
1	2	3	4	5	6	7	8	9	10	11	12	13	14	15
1982 graduates	**21.58 (0.090)**	**3.93 (0.022)**	**3.16 (0.028)**	**2.63 (0.022)**	**2.20 (0.025)**	**0.94 (0.014)**	**0.34 (0.010)**	**0.17 (0.008)**	**0.73 (0.016)**	**0.99 (0.029)**	**1.47 (0.035)**	**— (†)**	**— (†)**	**2.58 (0.048)**
Sex														
Male	21.40 (0.108)	3.88 (0.026)	3.16 (0.034)	2.71 (0.030)	2.27 (0.031)	0.91 (0.016)	0.36 (0.014)	0.23 (0.012)	0.76 (0.018)	0.80 (0.030)	1.29 (0.044)	— (†)	— (†)	2.69 (0.056)
Female	21.75 (0.101)	3.98 (0.026)	3.15 (0.029)	2.57 (0.024)	2.13 (0.029)	0.97 (0.017)	0.33 (0.013)	0.12 (0.008)	0.71 (0.017)	1.17 (0.036)	1.63 (0.044)	— (†)	— (†)	2.48 (0.049)
Race/ethnicity														
White	21.69 (0.107)	3.90 (0.025)	3.19 (0.032)	2.68 (0.026)	2.27 (0.029)	0.97 (0.015)	0.38 (0.013)	0.20 (0.010)	0.73 (0.017)	1.06 (0.033)	1.53 (0.042)	—	—	2.52 (0.052)
Black	21.15 (0.169)	4.08 (0.050)	3.08 (0.054)	2.61 (0.043)	2.06 (0.049)	0.90 (0.033)	0.26 (0.023)	0.09 (0.011)	0.81 (0.033)	0.72 (0.042)	1.26 (0.063)	—	—	2.60 (0.094)
Hispanic	21.23 (0.122)	3.94 (0.037)	3.00 (0.037)	2.33 (0.040)	1.80 (0.038)	0.81 (0.025)	0.16 (0.012)	0.07 (0.007)	0.75 (0.026)	0.77 (0.042)	1.29 (0.054)	—	—	2.87 (0.081)
Asian/Pacific Islander	22.46 (0.216)	4.01 (0.091)	3.16 (0.094)	3.15 (0.095)	2.64 (0.125)	1.11 (0.048)	0.61 (0.046)	0.42 (0.048)	0.51 (0.061)	1.79 (0.105)	1.31 (0.124)	—	—	3.05 (0.146)
American Indian/ Alaska Native	21.45 (0.330)	3.98 (0.114)	3.25 (0.207)	2.35 (0.129)	2.04 (0.090)	0.84 (0.124)	0.42 (0.087)	0.12 (0.039)	0.67 (0.087)	0.48 (0.117)	1.72 (0.338)	—	—	2.84 (0.128)
1987 graduates	**23.00 (0.157)**	**4.12 (0.022)**	**3.32 (0.037)**	**3.01 (0.029)**	**2.55 (0.046)**	**1.10 (0.020)**	**0.47 (0.015)**	**0.21 (0.011)**	**0.76 (0.033)**	**1.35 (0.049)**	**1.44 (0.044)**	**— (†)**	**— (†)**	**2.67 (0.073)**
Sex														
Male	22.88 (0.162)	4.08 (0.021)	3.29 (0.037)	3.05 (0.029)	2.59 (0.049)	1.05 (0.021)	0.47 (0.016)	0.26 (0.013)	0.79 (0.032)	1.16 (0.051)	1.24 (0.046)	— (†)	— (†)	2.83 (0.081)
Female	23.12 (0.156)	4.15 (0.026)	3.35 (0.041)	2.96 (0.030)	2.52 (0.048)	1.14 (0.022)	0.47 (0.017)	0.17 (0.012)	0.74 (0.035)	1.53 (0.051)	1.63 (0.050)	— (†)	— (†)	2.51 (0.069)
Race/ethnicity														
White	23.11 (0.189)	4.08 (0.028)	3.29 (0.045)	3.01 (0.034)	2.61 (0.058)	1.12 (0.025)	0.51 (0.020)	0.23 (0.012)	0.75 (0.040)	1.38 (0.055)	1.50 (0.055)	—	—	2.60 (0.082)
Black	22.40 (0.251)	4.22 (0.038)	3.34 (0.073)	2.99 (0.060)	2.33 (0.060)	1.01 (0.036)	0.42 (0.021)	0.16 (0.012)	0.90 (0.051)	1.08 (0.094)	1.20 (0.064)	—	—	2.73 (0.120)
Hispanic	22.84 (0.162)	4.30 (0.055)	3.22 (0.061)	2.81 (0.056)	2.24 (0.045)	1.07 (0.028)	0.29 (0.015)	0.10 (0.013)	0.78 (0.028)	1.25 (0.071)	1.34 (0.056)	—	—	3.19 (0.096)
Asian/Pacific Islander	24.47 (0.332)	4.37 (0.076)	3.65 (0.163)	3.71 (0.094)	3.14 (0.116)	1.17 (0.027)	0.87 (0.069)	0.50 (0.045)	0.59 (0.048)	2.07 (0.105)	1.18 (0.077)	—	—	3.23 (0.185)
American Indian/ Alaska Native	23.23 (0.153)	4.22 (0.033)	3.18 (0.044)	2.98 (0.113)	2.44 (0.104)	1.22 (0.073)	0.32 (0.035)	0.09! (0.027)	0.81 (0.041)	0.75 (0.138)	1.68 (0.112)	—	—	3.06 (0.050)
1990 graduates	**23.53 (0.127)**	**4.19 (0.034)**	**3.47 (0.040)**	**3.15 (0.028)**	**2.75 (0.028)**	**1.14 (0.019)**	**0.53 (0.014)**	**0.23 (0.010)**	**0.85 (0.026)**	**1.54 (0.041)**	**1.55 (0.045)**	**— (†)**	**— (†)**	**2.68 (0.073)**
Sex														
Male	23.35 (0.130)	4.13 (0.035)	3.45 (0.041)	3.16 (0.028)	2.78 (0.033)	1.11 (0.021)	0.52 (0.017)	0.28 (0.012)	0.88 (0.027)	1.33 (0.040)	1.31 (0.047)	— (†)	— (†)	2.87 (0.077)
Female	23.69 (0.132)	4.25 (0.036)	3.50 (0.041)	3.14 (0.033)	2.73 (0.027)	1.17 (0.019)	0.53 (0.014)	0.19 (0.010)	0.83 (0.027)	1.72 (0.045)	1.76 (0.050)	— (†)	— (†)	2.51 (0.072)
Race/ethnicity														
White	23.54 (0.133)	4.12 (0.036)	3.46 (0.045)	3.13 (0.032)	2.80 (0.033)	1.15 (0.020)	0.55 (0.016)	0.25 (0.011)	0.84 (0.022)	1.58 (0.049)	1.61 (0.056)	—	—	2.61 (0.076)
Black	23.40 (0.255)	4.34 (0.044)	3.49 (0.058)	3.20 (0.064)	2.68 (0.061)	1.11 (0.042)	0.42 (0.024)	0.16 (0.020)	0.98 (0.068)	1.20 (0.075)	1.34 (0.052)	—	—	2.74 (0.124)
Hispanic	23.83 (0.210)	4.51 (0.139)	3.42 (0.071)	3.13 (0.058)	2.50 (0.046)	1.10 (0.034)	0.42 (0.034)	0.14 (0.016)	0.83 (0.041)	1.57 (0.060)	1.48 (0.072)	—	—	3.10 (0.103)
Asian/Pacific Islander	24.07 (0.236)	4.50 (0.117)	3.70 (0.126)	3.52 (0.060)	2.97 (0.114)	1.12 (0.085)	0.74 (0.057)	0.42 (0.047)	0.68 (0.080)	2.06 (0.150)	1.29 (0.084)	—	—	2.96 (0.221)
American Indian/ Alaska Native	22.64 (0.267)	4.08 (0.092)	3.34 (0.083)	3.04 (0.152)	2.48 (0.175)	1.09 (0.090)	0.42 (0.072)	0.15 (0.039)	0.83 (0.090)	1.15 (0.188)	1.11 (0.126)	—	—	2.81 (0.148)
1994 graduates	**24.17 (0.144)**	**4.29 (0.028)**	**3.55 (0.041)**	**3.33 (0.021)**	**3.04 (0.028)**	**1.26 (0.018)**	**0.62 (0.013)**	**0.28 (0.011)**	**0.88 (0.024)**	**1.71 (0.033)**	**1.66 (0.041)**	**— (†)**	**— (†)**	**2.63 (0.077)**
Sex														
Male	23.79 (0.146)	4.26 (0.028)	3.51 (0.041)	3.32 (0.022)	3.03 (0.030)	1.20 (0.020)	0.59 (0.015)	0.32 (0.014)	0.91 (0.026)	1.49 (0.034)	1.43 (0.038)	— (†)	— (†)	2.83 (0.081)
Female	24.11 (0.147)	4.32 (0.030)	3.59 (0.041)	3.34 (0.023)	3.06 (0.028)	1.31 (0.018)	0.64 (0.014)	0.24 (0.010)	0.86 (0.024)	1.93 (0.034)	1.87 (0.051)	— (†)	— (†)	2.44 (0.078)
Race/ethnicity														
White	24.08 (0.183)	4.23 (0.035)	3.56 (0.049)	3.36 (0.023)	3.13 (0.032)	1.29 (0.022)	0.65 (0.014)	0.30 (0.014)	0.89 (0.030)	1.76 (0.039)	1.74 (0.049)	—	—	2.61 (0.096)
Black	23.28 (0.132)	4.36 (0.034)	3.51 (0.039)	3.23 (0.030)	2.80 (0.042)	1.21 (0.036)	0.49 (0.028)	0.17 (0.013)	0.92 (0.051)	1.35 (0.052)	1.36 (0.066)	—	—	2.69 (0.101)
Hispanic	23.71 (0.131)	4.61 (0.075)	3.45 (0.046)	3.28 (0.041)	2.69 (0.046)	1.19 (0.027)	0.49 (0.047)	0.17 (0.021)	0.83 (0.058)	1.73 (0.062)	1.51 (0.046)	—	—	2.93 (0.086)
Asian/Pacific Islander	23.84 (0.256)	4.60 (0.091)	3.66 (0.097)	3.66 (0.082)	3.35 (0.131)	1.22 (0.042)	0.81 (0.062)	0.48 (0.058)	0.80 (0.034)	2.09 (0.085)	1.32 (0.121)	—	—	2.78 (0.123)
American Indian/ Alaska Native	23.40 (0.541)	4.27 (0.113)	3.57 (0.201)	3.11 (0.038)	2.82 (0.073)	1.28 (0.069)	0.50 (0.065)	0.13 (0.039)	0.91 (0.057)	1.30 (0.150)	2.01 (0.351)	—	—	3.12 (0.355)
1998 graduates	**25.14 (0.162)**	**4.25 (0.037)**	**3.74 (0.038)**	**3.40 (0.024)**	**3.12 (0.026)**	**1.26 (0.021)**	**0.66 (0.015)**	**0.31 (0.015)**	**0.89 (0.024)**	**1.85 (0.039)**	**1.90 (0.079)**	**— (†)**	**— (†)**	**2.89 (0.076)**
Sex														
Male	24.64 (0.162)	4.19 (0.038)	3.68 (0.040)	3.37 (0.024)	3.09 (0.028)	1.20 (0.021)	0.62 (0.014)	0.33 (0.018)	0.93 (0.026)	1.62 (0.040)	1.61 (0.072)	— (†)	— (†)	3.12 (0.079)
Female	25.04 (0.166)	4.31 (0.039)	3.80 (0.036)	3.42 (0.025)	3.17 (0.029)	1.32 (0.023)	0.70 (0.018)	0.28 (0.015)	0.87 (0.023)	2.06 (0.041)	2.15 (0.094)	— (†)	— (†)	2.67 (0.080)
Race/ethnicity														
White	24.87 (0.178)	4.19 (0.049)	3.77 (0.046)	3.40 (0.028)	3.18 (0.028)	1.28 (0.025)	0.69 (0.017)	0.33 (0.019)	0.87 (0.027)	1.90 (0.049)	2.00 (0.078)	—	—	2.80 (0.088)
Black	24.37 (0.250)	4.28 (0.045)	3.69 (0.050)	3.42 (0.042)	3.03 (0.064)	1.24 (0.038)	0.58 (0.025)	0.22 (0.022)	0.97 (0.045)	1.58 (0.062)	1.57 (0.152)	—	—	2.94 (0.080)
Hispanic	24.69 (0.218)	4.51 (0.055)	3.60 (0.051)	3.28 (0.041)	2.81 (0.054)	1.13 (0.026)	0.50 (0.036)	0.20 (0.020)	0.97 (0.042)	1.78 (0.055)	1.78 (0.113)	—	—	3.36 (0.121)
Asian/Pacific Islander	24.67 (0.195)	4.37 (0.068)	3.92 (0.086)	3.62 (0.029)	3.43 (0.079)	1.26 (0.027)	0.83 (0.037)	0.51 (0.036)	0.81 (0.041)	2.29 (0.129)	1.52 (0.056)	—	—	2.95 (0.208)
American Indian/ Alaska Native	23.81 (0.350)	4.18 (0.082)	3.67 (0.093)	3.10 (0.081)	2.68 (0.081)	1.07 (0.056)	0.49 (0.038)	0.15 (0.024)	0.98 (0.070)	1.45 (0.132)	1.94 (0.146)	—	—	3.40 (0.212)

See notes at end of table.

Table 225.10. Average number of Carnegie units earned by public high school graduates in various subject fields, by sex and race/ethnicity: Selected years, 1982 through 2009—Continued

[Standard errors appear in parentheses]

Graduation year, sex, and race/ethnicity	Total	English	History/ social studies	Mathematics	Science					Foreign languages	Arts	Career/ technical (occupational) education[1]	Labor market, family, and consumer education[2]	Personal use[3]
					Total	Biology	Chemistry	Physics	Other science[4]					
1	2	3	4	5	6	7	8	9	10	11	12	13	14	15
2000 graduates	26.15 (0.204)	4.26 (0.037)	3.89 (0.036)	3.62 (0.029)	3.20 (0.038)	1.28 (0.028)	0.71 (0.020)	0.37 (0.018)	0.84 (0.030)	2.01 (0.045)	2.03 (0.054)	2.86 (0.105)	1.35 (0.044)	3.49 (0.071)
Sex														
Male	26.01 (0.210)	4.18 (0.036)	3.83 (0.036)	3.60 (0.032)	3.15 (0.039)	1.20 (0.030)	0.67 (0.020)	0.42 (0.020)	0.87 (0.029)	1.77 (0.045)	1.75 (0.051)	3.24 (0.133)	1.35 (0.049)	3.76 (0.079)
Female	26.26 (0.204)	4.34 (0.040)	3.95 (0.038)	3.64 (0.028)	3.24 (0.041)	1.36 (0.030)	0.74 (0.022)	0.33 (0.018)	0.81 (0.031)	2.25 (0.050)	2.29 (0.065)	2.48 (0.086)	1.34 (0.047)	3.22 (0.068)
Race/ethnicity														
White	26.31 (0.256)	4.26 (0.037)	3.93 (0.042)	3.63 (0.032)	3.24 (0.038)	1.30 (0.034)	0.72 (0.024)	0.39 (0.021)	0.83 (0.033)	1.98 (0.054)	2.11 (0.068)	2.97 (0.136)	1.37 (0.055)	3.37 (0.080)
Black	25.85 (0.233)	4.36 (0.078)	3.81 (0.068)	3.57 (0.046)	3.12 (0.059)	1.25 (0.041)	0.66 (0.030)	0.30 (0.027)	0.91 (0.043)	1.71 (0.070)	1.94 (0.134)	2.74 (0.143)	1.54 (0.075)	3.60 (0.134)
Hispanic	25.59 (0.358)	4.29 (0.125)	3.84 (0.076)	3.48 (0.069)	2.86 (0.112)	1.18 (0.068)	0.58 (0.055)	0.25 (0.026)	0.84 (0.044)	2.22 (0.063)	1.76 (0.062)	2.64 (0.152)	1.20 (0.082)	3.95 (0.173)
Asian/Pacific Islander	26.23 (0.332)	4.12 (0.060)	3.80 (0.055)	4.01 (0.108)	3.70 (0.162)	1.35 (0.066)	0.97 (0.050)	0.67 (0.042)	0.71 (0.086)	2.90 (0.089)	1.78 (0.085)	1.99 (0.149)	0.81 (0.050)	3.52 (0.221)
American Indian/ Alaska Native	25.24 (0.342)	4.08 (0.069)	3.82 (0.102)	3.35 (0.117)	2.88 (0.086)	1.25 (0.080)	0.45 (0.045)	0.19 (0.042)	0.98 (0.038)	1.41 (0.105)	1.99 (0.220)	3.23 (0.380)	1.60 (0.151)	3.60 (0.365)
2005 graduates	26.88 (0.102)	4.33 (0.022)	4.08 (0.027)	3.80 (0.018)	3.35 (0.019)	1.28 (0.016)	0.75 (0.011)	0.37 (0.012)	0.95 (0.019)	2.07 (0.022)	2.06 (0.035)	2.64 (0.045)	1.38 (0.030)	3.83 (0.047)
Sex														
Male	26.70 (0.107)	4.26 (0.024)	4.01 (0.030)	3.78 (0.021)	3.29 (0.023)	1.19 (0.016)	0.71 (0.012)	0.41 (0.014)	0.98 (0.019)	1.87 (0.025)	1.71 (0.035)	3.01 (0.050)	1.36 (0.032)	4.17 (0.055)
Female	27.05 (0.104)	4.39 (0.022)	4.16 (0.028)	3.83 (0.018)	3.41 (0.019)	1.37 (0.017)	0.79 (0.012)	0.33 (0.012)	0.92 (0.020)	2.25 (0.023)	2.38 (0.045)	2.29 (0.049)	1.41 (0.033)	3.52 (0.050)
Race/ethnicity														
White	27.06 (0.127)	4.30 (0.030)	4.12 (0.030)	3.80 (0.022)	3.44 (0.021)	1.31 (0.018)	0.77 (0.014)	0.39 (0.012)	0.96 (0.021)	2.03 (0.025)	2.17 (0.043)	2.75 (0.059)	1.39 (0.036)	3.64 (0.059)
Black	26.76 (0.151)	4.50 (0.028)	4.10 (0.054)	3.86 (0.036)	3.22 (0.035)	1.27 (0.025)	0.69 (0.017)	0.28 (0.025)	0.99 (0.037)	1.77 (0.041)	1.77 (0.056)	2.58 (0.074)	1.56 (0.065)	4.32 (0.096)
Hispanic	26.18 (0.147)	4.33 (0.026)	3.88 (0.052)	3.64 (0.034)	2.93 (0.036)	1.11 (0.021)	0.64 (0.022)	0.25 (0.017)	0.94 (0.031)	2.39 (0.047)	1.78 (0.055)	2.41 (0.086)	1.30 (0.046)	4.44 (0.100)
Asian/Pacific Islander	26.58 (0.183)	4.28 (0.043)	4.02 (0.048)	4.08 (0.051)	3.65 (0.057)	1.31 (0.035)	0.98 (0.028)	0.59 (0.036)	0.77 (0.061)	2.70 (0.066)	1.80 (0.076)	1.94 (0.116)	0.98 (0.052)	3.53 (0.122)
American Indian/ Alaska Native	26.66 (0.454)	4.42 (0.136)	4.15 (0.151)	3.60 (0.175)	3.00 (0.075)	1.27 (0.061)	0.52 (0.053)	0.17 (0.036)	1.04 (0.063)	1.55 (0.125)	2.45 (0.179)	2.45 (0.208)	1.70 (0.184)	4.24 (0.294)
2009 graduates	27.15 (0.100)	4.37 (0.013)	4.19 (0.027)	3.91 (0.017)	3.47 (0.022)	1.35 (0.014)	0.78 (0.011)	0.42 (0.013)	0.92 (0.017)	2.21 (0.027)	2.12 (0.036)	2.47 (0.059)	1.11 (0.030)	3.86 (0.059)
Sex														
Male	26.98 (0.111)	4.30 (0.015)	4.13 (0.028)	3.88 (0.018)	3.46 (0.027)	1.27 (0.014)	0.74 (0.012)	0.48 (0.017)	0.96 (0.017)	2.01 (0.028)	1.76 (0.034)	2.77 (0.068)	1.13 (0.036)	4.18 (0.070)
Female	27.31 (0.095)	4.42 (0.014)	4.25 (0.027)	3.93 (0.018)	3.49 (0.020)	1.43 (0.015)	0.82 (0.011)	0.37 (0.012)	0.88 (0.019)	2.40 (0.028)	2.46 (0.046)	2.19 (0.055)	1.10 (0.028)	3.57 (0.060)
Race/ethnicity														
White	27.30 (0.151)	4.32 (0.016)	4.23 (0.037)	3.91 (0.021)	3.55 (0.026)	1.37 (0.015)	0.80 (0.013)	0.44 (0.016)	0.94 (0.022)	2.19 (0.032)	2.26 (0.042)	2.55 (0.071)	1.16 (0.040)	3.70 (0.075)
Black	27.42 (0.141)	4.56 (0.039)	4.26 (0.036)	4.02 (0.035)	3.31 (0.027)	1.33 (0.025)	0.68 (0.022)	0.30 (0.019)	1.00 (0.028)	1.87 (0.044)	1.87 (0.067)	2.72 (0.127)	1.21 (0.052)	4.29 (0.102)
Hispanic	26.47 (0.194)	4.43 (0.024)	4.04 (0.040)	3.70 (0.029)	3.13 (0.028)	1.24 (0.019)	0.70 (0.015)	0.32 (0.015)	0.87 (0.024)	2.34 (0.034)	1.85 (0.046)	2.31 (0.101)	1.04 (0.040)	4.26 (0.095)
Asian/Pacific Islander	26.94 (0.190)	4.19 (0.039)	4.13 (0.083)	4.16 (0.052)	4.06 (0.091)	1.56 (0.077)	1.08 (0.035)	0.75 (0.033)	0.68 (0.063)	2.98 (0.090)	1.99 (0.065)	1.63 (0.074)	0.62 (0.054)	3.47 (0.100)
American Indian/ Alaska Native	26.17 (0.409)	4.39 (0.085)	4.11 (0.083)	3.76 (0.125)	3.20 (0.070)	1.38 (0.062)	0.50 (0.051)	0.24 (0.046)	1.09 (0.066)	1.56 (0.097)	2.19 (0.157)	2.35 (0.188)	1.20 (0.117)	4.54 (0.370)

—Not available.
†Not applicable.
Interpret data with caution. The coefficient of variation (CV) for this estimate is between 30 and 50 percent.
[1]Includes occupational education in agriculture; business and marketing; communications and design; computer and information sciences; construction and architecture; engineering technologies; health sciences; manufacturing; repair and transportation; and personal, public, and legal services. Does not include general labor market preparation courses and family and consumer sciences education courses.
[2]Includes general labor market preparation courses and family and consumer sciences education courses.
[3]Includes general skills, personal health and physical education, religion, military sciences, special education, and other courses not included in other academic subject fields. Some personal-use courses are also included in the Career/technical (occupational) education column and the Labor market, family, and consumer education column.
[4]Includes all science credits earned outside of biology, chemistry, and physics.
NOTE: The Carnegie unit is a standard of measurement that represents one credit for the completion of a 1-year course. Data differ slightly from figures appearing in other NCES reports because of differences in taxonomies and case exclusion criteria. Race categories exclude persons of Hispanic ethnicity. Totals include other racial/ethnic groups not separately shown. Detail may not sum to totals because of rounding.
SOURCE: U.S. Department of Education, National Center for Education Statistics, High School and Beyond Longitudinal Study of 1980 Sophomores (HS&B-So:80/82), "High School Transcript Study," and 1987, 1990, 1994, 1998, 2000, 2005, and 2009 High School Transcript Study (HSTS). (This table was prepared September 2011.)

Table 225.30. Percentage of public and private high school graduates taking selected mathematics and science courses in high school, by sex and race/ethnicity: Selected years, 1982 through 2009

[Standard errors appear in parentheses]

Course (Carnegie units)	1982	1990	1994	1998	2000	2005	2009 Total	Sex Male	Sex Female	Race/ethnicity White	Race/ethnicity Black	Race/ethnicity Hispanic	Race/ethnicity Asian/Pacific Islander	Race/ethnicity American Indian/Alaska Native
1	2	3	4	5	6	7	8	9	10	11	12	13	14	15
Mathematics[1]														
Any mathematics (≥10)	98.5 (0.21)	99.6 (0.07)	99.5 (0.07)	99.9 (0.05)	99.8 (0.05)	99.9 (0.02)	100.0 (†)	100.0 (†)	100.0 (†)	100.0 (†)	100.0 (†)	100.0 (†)	100.0 (†)	100.0 (†)
Algebra I (≥10)[2]	55.2 (1.01)	64.5 (1.55)	66.9 (1.33)	63.4 (1.44)	66.5 (1.75)	68.4 (0.99)	68.9 (0.94)	68.5 (0.98)	69.3 (1.01)	67.0 (1.09)	77.2 (1.26)	75.4 (1.60)	53.3 (3.52)	74.8 (5.85)
Geometry (≥10)	47.1 (0.99)	64.1 (1.33)	70.6 (1.25)	75.3 (1.06)	78.3 (1.08)	83.8 (0.63)	88.3 (0.53)	86.6 (0.75)	89.9 (0.54)	88.8 (0.73)	88.4 (1.07)	87.0 (0.96)	86.1 (1.47)	81.6 (4.09)
Algebra II (≥05)[3]	39.9 (0.93)	48.8 (1.39)	61.5 (1.38)	61.7 (1.77)	67.6 (1.43)	70.3 (1.01)	75.5 (0.92)	73.5 (1.09)	77.6 (0.91)	77.1 (1.09)	70.5 (1.68)	71.1 (1.83)	82.8 (2.57)	66.3 (4.12)
Trigonometry (≥05)	8.1 (0.54)	18.2 (1.28)	11.8 (1.16)	8.9 (1.06)	7.9 (1.33)	8.4 (0.88)	6.1 (0.77)	5.8 (0.78)	6.4 (0.81)	7.1 (1.01)	3.2 (0.55)	3.6 (0.69)	8.5 (1.96)	6.5 (1.84)
Analysis/precalculus (≥05)	6.2 (0.46)	13.4 (0.95)	17.4 (0.87)	23.2 (1.44)	26.6 (1.40)	29.4 (0.98)	35.3 (0.84)	33.8 (1.02)	36.6 (0.89)	37.9 (0.98)	22.7 (1.29)	26.5 (1.36)	60.5 (2.88)	18.5 (2.98)
Statistics/probability (≥05)	1.0 (0.16)	1.0 (0.21)	2.0 (0.33)	3.7 (0.54)	5.7 (0.85)	7.7 (0.53)	10.8 (0.49)	10.7 (0.51)	10.9 (0.58)	11.6 (0.64)	7.9 (1.04)	7.5 (0.77)	17.6 (1.69)	5.9! (2.07)
Calculus (≥10)	5.0 (0.43)	6.5 (0.46)	9.4 (0.56)	11.0 (0.85)	11.6 (0.72)	13.6 (0.53)	15.9 (0.66)	16.1 (0.75)	15.7 (0.69)	17.5 (0.69)	6.1 (0.59)	8.6 (0.64)	42.2 (3.11)	6.3 (1.60)
AP/honors calculus (≥10)[4]	1.6 (0.26)	4.2 (0.44)	7.0 (0.54)	6.8 (0.49)	7.8 (0.58)	9.2 (0.44)	11.0 (0.55)	11.3 (0.65)	10.7 (0.54)	11.5 (0.52)	4.0 (0.37)	6.3 (0.46)	34.8 (2.77)	4.9 (1.44)
Science[1]														
Any science (≥10)	96.4 (0.39)	99.4 (0.13)	99.5 (0.09)	99.5 (0.10)	99.8 (0.12)	99.7 (0.05)	99.9 (0.02)	99.8 (0.04)	99.9 (0.02)	99.9 (0.03)	99.9 (0.04)	99.8 (0.06)	100.0 (†)	100.0 (†)
Biology (≥10)	77.4 (0.87)	91.3 (0.98)	93.7 (0.98)	92.9 (0.68)	91.1 (1.01)	92.5 (0.60)	95.6 (0.40)	94.9 (0.45)	96.2 (0.43)	95.6 (0.51)	96.3 (0.56)	94.8 (0.67)	95.8 (0.95)	94.5 (1.64)
AP/honors biology (≥10)[4]	10.0 (0.64)	5.0 (0.76)	12.0 (0.93)	16.3 (1.32)	16.3 (1.45)	16.0 (0.83)	22.4 (0.78)	19.7 (0.76)	25.0 (0.89)	24.2 (0.88)	14.1 (0.80)	16.1 (0.88)	39.7 (3.58)	15.4 (3.38)
Chemistry (≥10)	32.1 (0.84)	49.2 (1.22)	56.1 (1.01)	60.5 (1.29)	61.8 (1.48)	66.4 (0.94)	70.4 (0.75)	67.4 (0.95)	73.4 (0.76)	71.5 (0.87)	65.3 (1.80)	65.7 (1.41)	84.8 (1.72)	44.5 (4.78)
AP/honors chemistry (≥10)[4]	3.0 (0.33)	3.5 (0.47)	3.9 (0.53)	4.8 (0.50)	5.7 (0.84)	7.6 (0.53)	5.9 (0.43)	6.1 (0.52)	5.8 (0.39)	6.5 (0.47)	2.5 (0.46)	2.6 (0.35)	17.0 (2.36)	3.4! (1.39)
Physics (≥10)	15.0 (0.62)	21.3 (0.84)	24.8 (0.86)	28.8 (1.49)	31.3 (1.16)	32.9 (0.91)	36.1 (1.01)	39.2 (1.29)	33.0 (0.92)	37.6 (1.24)	26.9 (1.72)	28.6 (1.33)	61.1 (2.35)	19.8 (3.89)
AP/honors physics (≥10)[4]	1.2 (0.17)	2.0 (0.38)	2.7 (0.34)	3.0 (0.37)	3.9 (0.60)	5.3 (0.33)	5.7 (0.46)	7.7 (0.63)	3.7 (0.38)	6.1 (0.54)	2.5 (0.39)	3.4 (0.39)	15.1 (2.51)	‡ (†)
Engineering (≥10)	1.2 (0.21)	0.1 (0.04)	4.5 (0.80)	6.7 (1.76)	4.1 (0.98)	4.8 (0.56)	8.2 (0.93)	9.0 (1.02)	7.4 (0.93)	8.2 (1.18)	10.1 (1.75)	7.1 (1.06)	6.4 (1.17)	9.0! (3.15)
Astronomy (≥05)	1.2 (0.24)	1.2 (0.31)	1.7 (0.50)	1.9 (0.46)	2.8 (0.59)	2.8 (0.37)	3.3 (0.40)	3.9 (0.51)	2.7 (0.33)	4.0 (0.57)	1.8 (0.38)	2.0 (0.36)	1.9 (0.43)	5.3! (2.51)
Geology/earth science (≥05)	13.6 (1.04)	25.3 (2.47)	23.1 (2.44)	20.9 (2.35)	18.5 (1.92)	24.7 (1.43)	27.7 (1.70)	28.9 (1.88)	26.5 (1.66)	28.2 (2.04)	30.1 (2.57)	27.1 (2.15)	19.1 (2.38)	26.0 (5.25)
Biology and chemistry (≥20)[5]	29.3 (0.83)	47.8 (1.23)	53.8 (1.18)	59.1 (1.22)	59.2 (1.50)	64.3 (0.97)	68.3 (0.77)	65.0 (0.91)	71.4 (0.84)	68.9 (0.93)	64.3 (1.74)	64.2 (1.45)	82.7 (1.93)	43.9 (4.77)
Biology, chemistry, and physics (≥30)[5]	11.2 (0.51)	18.7 (0.71)	21.4 (0.83)	25.6 (1.34)	25.0 (1.10)	27.4 (0.89)	30.1 (0.87)	31.9 (1.08)	28.3 (0.85)	31.4 (1.04)	21.9 (1.48)	22.7 (1.19)	54.4 (2.77)	13.6 (2.87)

†Not applicable.
!Interpret data with caution. The coefficient of variation (CV) for this estimate is between 30 and 50 percent.
‡Reporting standards not met. The coefficient of variation (CV) for this estimate is 50 percent or greater.
[1]For each course category, percentages include only students who earned at least the number of credits shown in parentheses.
[2]Excludes prealgebra.
[3]Includes courses where trigonometry or geometry has been combined with algebra II.
[4]For 2000 and later years, includes International Baccalaureate (IB) courses in addition to Advanced Placement (AP) and honors courses.
[5]Percentages include only students who earned at least one credit in each of the indicated courses.

NOTE: For a transcript to be included in the analyses, it had to meet three requirements: (1) the student graduated with either a standard or honors diploma, (2) the student's transcript contained 16 or more Carnegie units, and (3) the student's transcript contained more than 0 Carnegie units in English courses. The Carnegie unit is a standard of measurement that represents one credit for the completion of a 1-year course (0.5 = one semester; 1.0 = one academic year). Data differ slightly from figures appearing in other National Center for Education Statistics reports because of differences in taxonomies and case exclusion criteria. Race categories exclude persons of Hispanic ethnicity. Totals include other racial/ethnic groups not separately shown. Some data have been revised from previously published figures.
SOURCE: U.S. Department of Education, National Center for Education Statistics, High School and Beyond Longitudinal Study of 1980 Sophomores (HS&B-So:80/82), "High School Transcript Study", and 1990, 1994, 1998, 2000, 2005, and 2009 High School Transcript Study (HSTS). (This table was prepared October 2012.)

Table 225.70. Number and percentage of high school graduates who took foreign language courses in high school and average number of credits earned, by language and number of credits: 2000, 2005, and 2009

[Standard errors appear in parentheses]

Language and number of credits	2000			2005			2009		
	Number of graduates (in thousands)	Percent of graduates	Average credits[1]	Number of graduates (in thousands)	Percent of graduates	Average credits[1]	Number of graduates (in thousands)	Percent of graduates	Average credits[1]
1	2	3	4	5	6	7	8	9	10
All foreign languages **Any credit**	**2,487** (33.8)	**84.0** (0.92)	**2.5** (0.03)	**2,295** (51.1)	**85.7** (0.49)	**2.5** (0.02)	**2,599** (52.7)	**88.5** (0.45)	**2.6** (0.02)
Spanish									
Any credit	1,780 (31.9)	60.1 (0.90)	2.2 (0.03)	1,705 (42.2)	63.7 (0.66)	2.2 (0.02)	2,032 (45.0)	69.2 (0.70)	2.3 (0.02)
2 or more credits	1,369 (32.2)	46.2 (1.04)	2.6 (0.03)	1,344 (35.9)	50.2 (0.67)	2.6 (0.01)	1,638 (39.2)	55.8 (0.73)	2.6 (0.02)
3 or more credits	554 (26.3)	18.7 (0.90)	3.4 (0.03)	531 (20.1)	19.8 (0.57)	3.4 (0.01)	721 (30.2)	24.5 (0.78)	3.4 (0.02)
French									
Any credit	528 (21.5)	17.8 (0.73)	2.3 (0.05)	414 (14.1)	15.5 (0.49)	2.3 (0.03)	411 (16.1)	14.0 (0.47)	2.4 (0.04)
2 or more credits	398 (17.8)	13.4 (0.61)	2.7 (0.04)	309 (11.1)	11.5 (0.38)	2.7 (0.03)	314 (14.1)	10.7 (0.42)	2.8 (0.03)
3 or more credits	190 (12.1)	6.4 (0.42)	3.5 (0.04)	143 (7.2)	5.4 (0.25)	3.5 (0.03)	167 (10.6)	5.7 (0.32)	3.5 (0.03)
German									
Any credit	142 (17.2)	4.8 (0.57)	2.3 (0.08)	139 (10.0)	5.2 (0.36)	2.3 (0.04)	122 (8.6)	4.2 (0.29)	2.3 (0.06)
2 or more credits	104 (14.6)	3.5 (0.49)	2.8 (0.07)	102 (8.2)	3.8 (0.29)	2.8 (0.04)	91 (7.8)	3.1 (0.27)	2.8 (0.05)
3 or more credits	55 (8.6)	1.8 (0.29)	3.5 (0.06)	53 (4.7)	2.0 (0.17)	3.5 (0.04)	46 (5.3)	1.6 (0.18)	3.5 (0.03)
Latin									
Any credit	120 (15.3)	4.0 (0.52)	2.1 (0.08)	106 (10.4)	4.0 (0.36)	2.1 (0.05)	108 (10.6)	3.7 (0.35)	2.2 (0.07)
Italian									
Any credit	29 (5.5)	1.0 (0.19)	2.2 (0.20)	29 (5.3)	1.1 (0.20)	2.4 (0.16)	36 (7.0)	1.2 (0.23)	2.3 (0.18)
Japanese									
Any credit	36 (7.3)	1.2 (0.25)	2.3 (0.15)	30 (4.4)	1.1 (0.16)	2.1 (0.12)	28 (4.3)	1.0 (0.15)	2.5 (0.12)
Chinese									
Any credit	12 (3.1)	0.4 (0.10)	2.4 (0.20)	8 (2.1)	0.3 (0.08)	2.1 (0.23)	20 (4.1)	0.7 (0.14)	1.9 (0.13)
Arabic									
Any credit	‡ (†)	‡ (†)	‡ (†)	‡ (†)	‡ (†)	‡ (†)	‡ (†)	‡ (†)	2.8 (0.36)
Russian									
Any credit	10 (2.7)	0.3 (0.09)	1.9 (0.24)	5 (1.3)	0.2 (0.05)	1.5 (0.17)	3! (1.3)	0.1! (0.04)	2.4 (0.14)
Other foreign languages									
Any credit	106 (12.0)	3.6 (0.40)	2.5 (0.17)	89 (5.9)	3.3 (0.23)	2.8 (0.10)	105 (10.6)	3.6 (0.37)	2.5 (0.18)
AP/IB/honors foreign languages									
Any credit	183 (23.9)	6.2 (0.81)	1.2 (0.04)	157 (10.3)	5.9 (0.38)	1.2 (0.02)	233 (15.9)	7.9 (0.52)	1.2 (0.02)

†Not applicable.
!Interpret data with caution. The coefficient of variation (CV) for this estimate is between 30 and 50 percent.
‡Reporting standards not met. Either there are too few cases for a reliable estimate or the coefficient of variation (CV) is 50 percent or greater.
[1]Average credits earned are shown only for those graduates who earned any credit in the specified language while in high school. For these students, however, credits earned include both courses taken in high school and courses taken prior to entering high school.

Credits are shown in Carnegie units. The Carnegie unit is a standard unit of measurement that represents one credit for the completion of a 1-year course.
NOTE: For a transcript to be included in the analyses, it had to meet three requirements: (1) the graduate received either a standard or honors diploma, (2) the graduate's transcript contained 16 or more Carnegie credits, and (3) the graduate's transcript contained more than 0 Carnegie credits in English courses.
SOURCE: U.S. Department of Education, National Center for Education Statistics, 2000, 2005, and 2009 High School Transcript Study (HSTS). (This table was prepared April 2014.)

Table 225.80. Percentage distribution of elementary and secondary school children, by average grades and selected child and school characteristics: 2003, 2012, and 2016

[Standard errors appear in parentheses]

Percentage distribution of children, by parental reports of average grades in all subjects

Selected child or school characteristic	2003				2012				2016			
	Mostly A's	Mostly B's	Mostly C's	Mostly D's or F's	Mostly A's	Mostly B's	Mostly C's	Mostly D's or F's	Mostly A's	Mostly B's	Mostly C's	Mostly D's or F's
1	2	3	4	5	6	7	8	9	10	11	12	13
All students	43.6 (0.62)	37.0 (0.58)	15.9 (0.52)	3.6 (0.24)	49.2 (0.53)	35.6 (0.57)	12.8 (0.37)	2.5 (0.21)	49.2 (0.60)	34.6 (0.69)	13.0 (0.56)	3.2 (0.30)
Sex of child												
Male	36.4 (0.72)	38.6 (0.86)	19.8 (0.74)	5.2 (0.40)	42.9 (0.74)	37.7 (0.78)	16.1 (0.58)	3.3 (0.34)	42.8 (0.97)	36.8 (1.08)	16.0 (0.86)	4.3 (0.50)
Female	51.0 (0.84)	35.3 (0.76)	11.9 (0.61)	1.9 (0.24)	55.9 (0.82)	33.3 (0.80)	9.3 (0.51)	1.5 (0.22)	56.1 (0.95)	32.1 (0.95)	9.7 (0.70)	2.1 (0.23)
Race/ethnicity of child												
White	47.8 (0.86)	35.2 (0.75)	14.0 (0.63)	3.1 (0.25)	53.6 (0.74)	33.5 (0.77)	10.8 (0.48)	2.1 (0.22)	55.3 (0.82)	32.0 (0.87)	10.3 (0.59)	2.4 (0.29)
Black	34.5 (1.75)	39.5 (1.65)	20.9 (1.33)	5.0 (0.82)	37.0 (1.88)	39.7 (1.97)	19.9 (1.19)	3.4 (0.75)	36.7 (2.18)	37.6 (1.99)	20.4 (1.51)	5.3 (1.40)
Hispanic	34.9 (1.14)	42.3 (1.24)	18.6 (1.03)	4.2 (0.48)	43.2 (1.09)	39.9 (1.05)	14.3 (0.83)	2.6 (0.41)	40.2 (1.37)	40.5 (1.58)	15.2 (1.40)	4.1 (0.60)
Asian/Pacific Islander[1]	62.0 (3.47)	25.5 (2.76)	11.3 (3.06)	‡ (†)	60.9 (2.74)	32.5 (2.83)	5.9 (0.98)	0.7! (0.28)	64.6 (4.52)	23.7 (2.54)	10.9! (4.81)	‡ (†)
Asian	— (†)	— (†)	— (†)	— (†)	63.2 (2.82)	31.8 (2.86)	4.6 (0.98)	0.4! (0.20)	64.9 (4.64)	23.3 (2.42)	11.2! (5.02)	‡ (†)
Pacific Islander	— (†)	— (†)	— (†)	— (†)	27.5! (7.70)	43.4 (10.65)	27.5! (8.38)	‡ (†)	59.2 (12.85)	32.3! (13.31)	‡ (†)	‡ (†)
American Indian/Alaska Native	29.5 (6.53)	53.3 (6.42)	12.1! (4.90)	5.1! (2.54)	54.6 (8.07)	28.2 (6.56)	16.3! (5.26)	‡ (†)	36.5 (9.40)	45.8 (10.14)	‡ (†)	‡ (†)
Two or more races[2]	41.4 (4.34)	36.2 (3.91)	18.8 (2.81)	3.5! (1.38)	55.7 (2.79)	28.2 (2.68)	11.1 (1.68)	5.0! (2.28)	53.7 (3.55)	33.9 (4.00)	8.6 (1.53)	3.8 (1.07)
Highest education level of parents/ guardians in the household[3]												
Less than high school	27.8 (2.17)	41.6 (2.05)	22.7 (2.27)	7.8 (1.46)	39.5 (2.25)	39.7 (2.02)	16.8 (1.73)	4.0 (0.93)	30.2 (2.46)	36.3 (2.75)	26.0 (3.28)	7.5 (1.88)
High school/GED	32.1 (1.20)	41.4 (1.23)	21.7 (1.12)	4.8 (0.57)	37.7 (1.51)	40.8 (1.62)	17.6 (1.31)	4.0 (0.71)	35.3 (1.91)	43.0 (1.96)	17.1 (1.63)	4.6 (0.64)
Vocational/technical or some college	39.8 (1.34)	38.3 (1.36)	17.2 (0.95)	4.7 (0.58)	43.5 (1.07)	38.1 (1.05)	15.6 (0.87)	2.8 (0.32)	41.5 (1.59)	38.0 (1.62)	16.2 (1.25)	4.3 (0.68)
Associate's degree	46.7 (2.13)	34.5 (1.94)	16.4 (1.51)	2.4 (0.57)	47.0 (1.82)	34.9 (1.78)	15.4 (1.29)	2.7 (0.52)	49.4 (1.89)	35.0 (1.98)	12.6 (1.32)	3.0 (0.62)
Bachelor's degree/some graduate school	53.0 (1.26)	34.2 (1.29)	11.1 (0.85)	1.7 (0.28)	60.1 (1.05)	31.4 (1.02)	7.5 (0.53)	1.0 (0.19)	60.2 (1.04)	31.1 (0.94)	7.6 (0.69)	1.2 (0.21)
Graduate/professional degree	61.9 (1.71)	30.5 (1.75)	6.7 (0.67)	0.9 (0.24)	68.1 (1.04)	27.3 (1.04)	4.2 (0.36)	0.5 (0.10)	69.4 (1.07)	25.0 (0.98)	4.7 (0.39)	0.9 (0.24)
Family income (in current dollars)												
$20,000 or less	33.1 (1.53)	38.9 (1.56)	22.0 (1.30)	6.0 (0.85)	37.2 (1.35)	40.2 (1.19)	18.3 (1.04)	4.4 (0.59)	31.4 (2.04)	36.4 (2.32)	25.8 (2.49)	6.5 (1.03)
$20,001 to $50,000	37.8 (1.20)	40.0 (1.19)	17.7 (0.85)	4.5 (0.42)	41.3 (1.22)	38.9 (1.19)	16.7 (0.90)	3.1 (0.44)	37.6 (1.41)	40.9 (1.61)	16.6 (1.15)	4.9 (0.90)
$50,001 to $75,000	48.0 (1.29)	35.0 (1.22)	14.0 (0.81)	3.0 (0.45)	49.3 (1.45)	35.8 (1.37)	12.6 (1.07)	1.9 (0.32)	48.6 (1.84)	34.7 (1.85)	13.5 (1.25)	3.2 (0.59)
$75,001 to $100,000	51.8 (1.66)	33.7 (1.45)	13.3 (1.23)	1.3 (0.32)	53.7 (1.64)	33.5 (1.42)	10.6 (1.03)	2.3 (0.50)	54.3 (1.70)	33.4 (1.73)	9.8 (0.98)	2.5 (0.55)
Over $100,000	55.8 (1.74)	33.9 (1.72)	9.1 (1.09)	1.2 (0.24)	61.8 (1.15)	30.4 (1.19)	6.6 (0.61)	1.1! (0.41)	63.9 (1.09)	29.2 (1.12)	6.0 (0.63)	0.9 (0.23)
Poverty status[4]												
Poor	33.1 (1.61)	39.4 (1.65)	21.9 (1.39)	5.6 (0.91)	39.1 (1.39)	38.9 (1.33)	17.8 (1.06)	4.2 (0.54)	32.7 (1.78)	37.0 (1.83)	24.5 (2.07)	5.8 (0.78)
Near-poor	34.8 (1.39)	42.0 (1.26)	18.2 (1.08)	5.0 (0.59)	40.1 (1.19)	40.3 (1.07)	17.0 (0.93)	2.7 (0.45)	38.5 (1.57)	40.8 (1.44)	15.2 (1.08)	5.5 (1.00)
Nonpoor	49.9 (0.83)	34.5 (0.76)	13.2 (0.54)	2.4 (0.23)	56.0 (0.75)	32.7 (0.75)	9.5 (0.45)	1.8 (0.25)	57.9 (0.75)	31.6 (0.79)	8.8 (0.42)	1.7 (0.20)
Control of school and enrollment level of child												
Public school	41.8 (0.64)	37.5 (0.62)	16.8 (0.57)	3.8 (0.26)	47.9 (0.55)	36.0 (0.60)	13.5 (0.39)	2.6 (0.23)	47.4 (0.64)	35.4 (0.77)	13.6 (0.61)	3.5 (0.33)
Elementary (kindergarten to grade 8)	46.1 (0.80)	35.9 (0.84)	14.6 (0.74)	3.4 (0.32)	52.9 (0.69)	34.2 (0.73)	11.0 (0.49)	1.8 (0.22)	50.5 (0.83)	34.6 (1.00)	11.9 (0.76)	3.0 (0.41)
Secondary (grades 9 to 12)	34.6 (0.96)	40.2 (0.97)	20.6 (0.94)	4.6 (0.46)	37.5 (0.83)	39.7 (1.03)	18.4 (0.84)	4.4 (0.54)	41.1 (0.99)	37.2 (1.20)	17.1 (1.01)	4.5 (0.50)
Private school	57.6 (1.72)	33.0 (1.68)	8.1 (0.91)	1.3! (0.45)	63.9 (1.63)	30.8 (1.51)	5.4 (0.68)	0.4! (0.20)	66.4 (1.81)	26.2 (1.49)	7.0 (1.17)	0.4! (0.14)
Elementary (kindergarten to grade 8)	61.6 (2.39)	30.3 (2.28)	7.3 (1.03)	0.8! (0.28)	67.8 (1.91)	28.2 (1.91)	3.5 (0.61)	‡ (†)	71.2 (2.45)	22.4 (2.11)	6.1 (1.52)	‡ (†)
Secondary (grades 9 to 12)	48.8 (3.22)	38.9 (2.94)	10.0 (1.77)	‡ (†)	52.8 (2.70)	37.2 (2.58)	9.9 (1.60)	‡ (†)	55.6 (2.76)	34.6 (2.42)	9.0 (1.95)	0.7! (0.32)

—Not available.
†Not applicable.
‡Reporting standards not met. Either there are too few cases for a reliable estimate or the coefficient of variation (CV) is 50 percent or greater.
!Interpret data with caution. The coefficient of variation (CV) for this estimate is between 30 and 50 percent.
[1]The 2003 questionnaire included a single item for "Asian or Pacific Islander," whereas questionnaires for later years included one item for Asian and a separate item for Pacific Islander.
[2]For 2003, the "Two or more races" row also includes children whose race was reported as "Other." The "Other" race category was not included on the 2012 and 2016 questionnaires.
[3]In 2003, education level was not collected for the second parent in a same sex couple.
[4]Poor children are those whose family incomes were below the Census Bureau's poverty threshold in the year prior to data collection; near-poor children are those whose family incomes ranged from the poverty threshold to 199 percent of the poverty threshold; and nonpoor children are those whose family incomes were at or above 200 percent of the poverty threshold.

The poverty threshold is a dollar amount that varies depending on a family's size and composition and is updated annually to account for inflation. In 2015, for example, the poverty threshold for a family of four with two children was $24,257. Survey respondents are asked to select the range within which their income falls, rather than giving the exact amount of their income; therefore, the measure of poverty status is an approximation.
NOTE: While National Household Education Surveys Program (NHES) administrations prior to 2012 were administered via telephone with an interviewer, NHES:2012 and NHES:2016 used self-administered paper-and-pencil questionnaires that were mailed to respondents. Measurable differences between estimates for years prior to 2012 and estimates for later years could reflect actual changes in the population, or the changes could be due to the mode change from telephone to mail. Excludes children whose programs have no classes with lettered grades. Race categories exclude persons of Hispanic ethnicity. Detail may not sum to totals because of rounding. Some data have been revised from previously published figures.
SOURCE: U.S. Department of Education, National Center for Education Statistics, Parent and Family Involvement in Education Survey of the National Household Education Surveys Program (PFI-NHES:2003, 2012, and 2016). (This table was prepared June 2018.)

Table 228.30. Percentage of students ages 12–18 who reported criminal victimization at school during the previous 6 months, by type of victimization and selected student and school characteristics: Selected years, 1995 through 2017

[Standard errors appear in parentheses]

Type of victimization and student or school characteristic	1995	2001	2003	2005	2007	2009	2011	2013	2015	2017
1	2	3	4	5	6	7	8	9	10	11
Total	9.1 (0.33)	5.5 (0.31)	5.1 (0.24)	4.3 (0.31)	4.3 (0.29)	3.9 (0.28)	3.5 (0.28)	3.0 (0.25)	2.7 (0.25)	2.2 (0.22)
Sex										
Male	9.6 (0.44)	6.1 (0.41)	5.3 (0.33)	4.6 (0.43)	4.5 (0.43)	4.6 (0.40)	3.7 (0.35)	3.2 (0.40)	2.6 (0.35)	2.6 (0.34)
Female	8.5 (0.45)	4.9 (0.39)	4.8 (0.36)	3.9 (0.38)	3.9 (0.38)	3.2 (0.35)	3.4 (0.38)	2.8 (0.34)	2.8 (0.38)	1.8 (0.28)
Race/ethnicity[1]										
White	9.4 (0.36)	5.7 (0.40)	5.4 (0.32)	4.6 (0.36)	4.2 (0.38)	3.9 (0.37)	3.6 (0.35)	3.0 (0.32)	2.9 (0.36)	2.2 (0.27)
Black	9.6 (1.02)	6.1 (0.78)	5.1 (0.78)	3.9 (0.80)	4.3 (0.83)	4.4 (0.74)	4.6 (0.89)	3.2 (0.71)	2.2! (0.77)	2.6 (0.52)
Hispanic	7.1 (0.96)	4.6 (0.64)	3.9 (0.50)	3.9 (0.70)	3.6 (0.54)	3.9 (0.75)	2.9 (0.47)	3.2 (0.46)	2.3 (0.47)	2.0 (0.45)
Asian/Pacific Islander	8.3 (1.63)	3.7 (1.08)	3.2 (0.93)	1.4! (0.64)	3.4! (1.33)	‡ (†)	2.3! (1.13)	2.4! (0.99)	‡ (†)	2.1! (1.02)
Asian	— (†)	— (†)	3.3! (1.00)	1.5! (0.69)	3.6! (1.38)	‡ (†)	2.5! (1.23)	2.6! (1.08)	‡ (†)	2.1! (1.05)
Pacific Islander	— (†)	— (†)	‡ (†)	‡ (†)	‡ (†)	‡ (†)	‡ (†)	‡ (†)	‡ (†)	‡ (†)
American Indian/Alaska Native	9.6! (3.27)	‡ (†)	‡ (†)	‡ (†)	‡ (†)	‡ (†)	‡ (†)	‡ (†)	‡ (†)	11.1! (4.80)
Two or more races	— (†)	— (†)	9.8 (2.85)	‡ (†)	10.1 (2.59)	‡ (†)	4.9! (1.77)	3.0! (1.46)	6.5! (2.24)	‡ (†)
Grade										
6th	8.8 (0.92)	5.9 (0.90)	3.8 (0.77)	4.6 (0.83)	3.9 (0.86)	3.7 (0.91)	3.8 (0.85)	4.1 (0.92)	3.1 (0.79)	3.1 (0.75)
7th	10.6 (0.79)	5.8 (0.67)	6.3 (0.74)	5.4 (0.71)	4.7 (0.69)	3.4 (0.70)	3.1 (0.61)	2.5 (0.51)	3.4 (0.70)	2.6 (0.60)
8th	10.1 (0.76)	4.3 (0.61)	5.2 (0.65)	3.6 (0.63)	4.4 (0.63)	3.8 (0.78)	3.8 (0.67)	2.3 (0.52)	2.3 (0.57)	1.8 (0.51)
9th	11.4 (0.86)	7.9 (0.81)	6.3 (0.70)	4.7 (0.69)	5.3 (0.75)	5.3 (0.85)	5.1 (0.83)	4.1 (0.76)	3.0 (0.62)	2.7 (0.67)
10th	8.7 (0.73)	6.5 (0.77)	4.7 (0.63)	4.3 (0.71)	4.4 (0.67)	4.2 (0.79)	3.0 (0.58)	3.3 (0.57)	1.6 (0.47)	2.7 (0.49)
11th	7.0 (0.72)	4.8 (0.62)	5.0 (0.69)	3.6 (0.51)	4.0 (0.75)	4.7 (0.88)	3.1 (0.65)	3.3 (0.65)	4.4 (1.04)	1.4 (0.40)
12th	5.8 (0.73)	2.9 (0.52)	3.6 (0.71)	3.7 (0.85)	2.7 (0.70)	2.0 (0.52)	2.9 (0.68)	2.0! (0.67)	1.3! (0.45)	1.4 (0.41)
Urbanicity[2]										
Urban	8.6 (0.59)	5.9 (0.58)	6.0 (0.58)	5.3 (0.66)	4.5 (0.58)	4.2 (0.56)	4.3 (0.56)	3.3 (0.47)	3.3 (0.51)	2.7 (0.45)
Suburban	9.9 (0.48)	5.6 (0.41)	4.7 (0.32)	4.2 (0.34)	4.1 (0.38)	4.0 (0.36)	3.3 (0.34)	3.2 (0.35)	2.8 (0.35)	2.1 (0.25)
Rural	8.1 (0.78)	4.7 (0.93)	4.7 (0.75)	2.8 (0.69)	4.4 (0.55)	3.1 (0.66)	2.8 (0.57)	2.0 (0.58)	1.5 (0.37)	1.6! (0.49)
Control of school										
Public	9.3 (0.37)	5.7 (0.34)	5.1 (0.26)	4.4 (0.32)	4.5 (0.32)	4.1 (0.30)	3.7 (0.29)	3.1 (0.27)	2.8 (0.26)	2.3 (0.23)
Private	6.2 (0.89)	3.4 (0.72)	4.9 (0.79)	2.7 (0.77)	1.1! (0.50)	1.8! (0.76)	1.9! (0.68)	2.8! (0.89)	‡ (†)	‡ (†)
Theft	7.0 (0.28)	4.2 (0.24)	4.0 (0.20)	3.1 (0.27)	3.0 (0.23)	2.8 (0.23)	2.6 (0.23)	1.9 (0.20)	1.9 (0.22)	1.5 (0.17)
Sex										
Male	7.0 (0.37)	4.5 (0.34)	3.9 (0.27)	3.1 (0.34)	3.0 (0.34)	3.4 (0.36)	2.6 (0.29)	2.0 (0.30)	1.7 (0.26)	1.6 (0.27)
Female	7.0 (0.41)	3.8 (0.33)	4.1 (0.31)	3.2 (0.36)	3.0 (0.32)	2.1 (0.28)	2.6 (0.33)	1.8 (0.28)	2.0 (0.34)	1.3 (0.24)
Race/ethnicity[1]										
White	7.3 (0.32)	4.1 (0.31)	4.3 (0.28)	3.4 (0.32)	3.1 (0.29)	2.9 (0.31)	2.5 (0.28)	1.6 (0.22)	2.0 (0.28)	1.3 (0.20)
Black	6.9 (0.87)	5.0 (0.68)	3.8 (0.64)	2.7 (0.66)	3.1 (0.70)	2.5 (0.61)	3.7 (0.78)	2.7 (0.67)	1.3! (0.63)	1.8 (0.51)
Hispanic	5.7 (0.79)	3.7 (0.69)	3.0 (0.41)	3.1 (0.64)	2.2 (0.47)	3.0 (0.63)	2.0 (0.41)	1.8 (0.39)	1.6 (0.39)	1.4 (0.36)
Asian/Pacific Islander	6.4 (1.47)	3.5 (1.03)	3.2 (0.93)	‡ (†)	3.0! (1.27)	‡ (†)	2.3! (1.13)	2.4! (0.99)	‡ (†)	2.1! (1.02)
Asian	— (†)	— (†)	3.3! (1.00)	‡ (†)	3.2! (1.32)	‡ (†)	2.5! (1.23)	2.6! (1.08)	‡ (†)	2.1! (1.05)
Pacific Islander	— (†)	— (†)	‡ (†)	‡ (†)	‡ (†)	‡ (†)	‡ (†)	‡ (†)	‡ (†)	‡ (†)
American Indian/Alaska Native	7.2! (3.04)	‡ (†)	‡ (†)	‡ (†)	‡ (†)	‡ (†)	‡ (†)	‡ (†)	‡ (†)	7.2! (3.37)
Two or more races	— (†)	— (†)	8.3! (2.72)	‡ (†)	5.3! (2.01)	‡ (†)	3.7! (1.56)	‡ (†)	4.3! (1.80)	‡ (†)
Grade										
6th	5.4 (0.66)	4.0 (0.70)	2.2 (0.63)	2.8 (0.75)	2.6 (0.75)	1.3! (0.52)	2.7 (0.70)	1.4! (0.57)	1.6! (0.65)	1.0! (0.42)
7th	8.1 (0.72)	3.4 (0.51)	4.8 (0.67)	2.9 (0.50)	2.7 (0.54)	2.1 (0.57)	1.9 (0.44)	1.4 (0.38)	1.6! (0.54)	1.3! (0.39)
8th	7.8 (0.72)	3.3 (0.50)	4.1 (0.57)	2.4 (0.53)	2.5 (0.54)	2.0 (0.55)	2.0 (0.48)	1.0! (0.33)	1.8 (0.50)	1.1! (0.41)
9th	8.8 (0.76)	6.2 (0.76)	5.2 (0.63)	3.7 (0.61)	4.6 (0.70)	4.9 (0.80)	4.4 (0.78)	2.7 (0.58)	2.1 (0.52)	2.4 (0.60)
10th	7.6 (0.70)	5.7 (0.72)	3.7 (0.59)	3.8 (0.66)	3.6 (0.63)	3.5 (0.72)	2.1 (0.50)	2.6 (0.48)	1.4! (0.43)	2.1 (0.39)
11th	5.4 (0.66)	3.8 (0.57)	4.1 (0.64)	2.8 (0.45)	2.6 (0.61)	3.3 (0.74)	2.7 (0.58)	2.3 (0.50)	3.4 (0.85)	1.1! (0.36)
12th	4.5 (0.67)	2.3 (0.45)	3.1 (0.68)	3.4 (0.84)	1.9 (0.55)	1.5 (0.44)	2.4 (0.62)	1.6! (0.62)	1.0! (0.40)	1.2! (0.42)
Urbanicity[2]										
Urban	6.4 (0.51)	4.5 (0.52)	4.5 (0.46)	3.6 (0.52)	2.8 (0.48)	2.9 (0.45)	3.0 (0.45)	2.4 (0.44)	2.3 (0.45)	1.8 (0.39)
Suburban	7.5 (0.40)	4.3 (0.32)	3.8 (0.26)	3.2 (0.31)	3.0 (0.31)	2.8 (0.32)	2.5 (0.30)	1.9 (0.27)	1.8 (0.30)	1.4 (0.18)
Rural	6.8 (0.66)	3.4 (0.65)	3.9 (0.66)	2.2! (0.68)	3.2 (0.46)	2.3 (0.59)	2.0 (0.47)	0.8 (0.24)	1.2 (0.32)	0.9! (0.35)
Control of school										
Public	7.2 (0.31)	4.4 (0.26)	4.0 (0.22)	3.3 (0.28)	3.2 (0.25)	2.9 (0.25)	2.7 (0.24)	1.9 (0.21)	1.9 (0.22)	1.6 (0.19)
Private	4.9 (0.73)	2.4 (0.67)	4.0 (0.77)	1.3! (0.48)	1.1! (0.50)	‡ (†)	1.2! (0.52)	2.0! (0.76)	‡ (†)	‡ (†)
Violent	2.5 (0.19)	1.8 (0.19)	1.3 (0.15)	1.2 (0.15)	1.6 (0.18)	1.4 (0.17)	1.1 (0.15)	1.2 (0.15)	0.9 (0.15)	0.7 (0.12)
Sex										
Male	3.0 (0.26)	2.1 (0.26)	1.7 (0.23)	1.6 (0.25)	1.7 (0.26)	1.6 (0.25)	1.2 (0.21)	1.3 (0.23)	1.0 (0.21)	1.0 (0.20)
Female	2.0 (0.22)	1.4 (0.24)	0.9 (0.16)	0.8 (0.15)	1.4 (0.23)	1.1 (0.21)	0.9 (0.17)	1.1 (0.23)	0.9 (0.19)	0.5 (0.14)
Race/ethnicity[1]										
White	2.5 (0.21)	2.0 (0.24)	1.4 (0.17)	1.3 (0.21)	1.5 (0.22)	1.2 (0.21)	1.2 (0.17)	1.5 (0.24)	1.0 (0.22)	0.9 (0.19)
Black	3.0 (0.57)	1.3! (0.40)	1.5 (0.41)	1.3! (0.47)	1.6! (0.50)	2.3 (0.62)	1.1! (0.42)	‡ (†)	0.9! (0.44)	0.8! (0.31)
Hispanic	2.0 (0.47)	1.5 (0.41)	1.1 (0.28)	0.9 (0.24)	1.4 (0.42)	1.3! (0.40)	1.0 (0.28)	1.5 (0.26)	0.6! (0.23)	0.5! (0.23)
Asian/Pacific Islander	2.2! (0.98)	‡ (†)	‡ (†)	‡ (†)	‡ (†)	‡ (†)	‡ (†)	‡ (†)	‡ (†)	‡ (†)
Asian	— (†)	— (†)	‡ (†)	‡ (†)	‡ (†)	‡ (†)	‡ (†)	‡ (†)	‡ (†)	‡ (†)
Pacific Islander	— (†)	— (†)	‡ (†)	‡ (†)	‡ (†)	‡ (†)	‡ (†)	‡ (†)	‡ (†)	‡ (†)
American Indian/Alaska Native	‡ (†)	‡ (†)	‡ (†)	‡ (†)	‡ (†)	‡ (†)	‡ (†)	‡ (†)	‡ (†)	‡ (†)
Two or more races	— (†)	— (†)	‡ (†)	‡ (†)	5.3! (1.90)	‡ (†)	‡ (†)	‡ (†)	3.6! (1.64)	‡ (†)

See notes at end of table.

Table 228.30. Percentage of students ages 12–18 who reported criminal victimization at school during the previous 6 months, by type of victimization and selected student and school characteristics: Selected years, 1995 through 2017—Continued

[Standard errors appear in parentheses]

Type of victimization and student or school characteristic	1995	2001	2003	2005	2007	2009	2011	2013	2015	2017
1	2	3	4	5	6	7	8	9	10	11
Grade										
6th	4.3 (0.68)	2.6 (0.66)	1.9 (0.53)	1.9 (0.55)	1.5! (0.54)	2.6! (0.83)	1.3! (0.49)	2.7 (0.73)	1.6! (0.65)	2.1 (0.60)
7th	3.1 (0.50)	2.6 (0.46)	1.7 (0.43)	2.6 (0.53)	2.4 (0.50)	1.2! (0.42)	1.2! (0.41)	1.2! (0.38)	1.9 (0.47)	1.4! (0.45)
8th	2.7 (0.39)	1.3 (0.34)	1.4 (0.34)	1.4 (0.39)	2.1 (0.47)	2.0 (0.60)	2.1 (0.50)	1.4 (0.42)	0.6! (0.30)	0.7! (0.29)
9th	2.9 (0.47)	2.4 (0.46)	1.5 (0.31)	1.0 (0.29)	1.2! (0.37)	0.9! (0.37)	1.1! (0.35)	1.4! (0.44)	0.8! (0.34)	‡ (†)
10th	1.8 (0.35)	1.2 (0.31)	1.3 (0.36)	0.5! (0.24)	1.2! (0.39)	1.0! (0.37)	0.9! (0.34)	1.0! (0.35)	‡ (†)	0.7! (0.32)
11th	1.6 (0.35)	1.6 (0.39)	0.9! (0.32)	0.7! (0.31)	1.5 (0.46)	1.5! (0.51)	‡ (†)	1.0! (0.43)	1.3! (0.49)	‡ (†)
12th	1.6 (0.36)	0.9! (0.31)	0.5! (0.26)	‡ (†)	0.8! (0.35)	‡ (†)	‡ (†)	‡ (†)	‡ (†)	‡ (†)
Urbanicity[2]										
Urban	2.6 (0.34)	1.7 (0.29)	1.8 (0.31)	1.8 (0.34)	2.0 (0.35)	1.8 (0.41)	1.4 (0.31)	0.9 (0.21)	1.0 (0.27)	0.9 (0.21)
Suburban	3.0 (0.29)	1.7 (0.20)	1.2 (0.19)	1.1 (0.18)	1.3 (0.23)	1.3 (0.23)	0.9 (0.16)	1.4 (0.21)	1.0 (0.20)	0.6 (0.17)
Rural	1.5 (0.27)	2.0! (0.64)	0.9! (0.31)	0.6! (0.26)	1.7 (0.36)	0.8! (0.32)	1.0! (0.31)	1.1! (0.46)	0.5! (0.22)	0.7! (0.33)
Control of school										
Public	2.6 (0.19)	1.8 (0.20)	1.4 (0.15)	1.2 (0.15)	1.7 (0.20)	1.4 (0.19)	1.1 (0.15)	1.2 (0.16)	1.0 (0.15)	0.8 (0.12)
Private	1.6 (0.44)	1.0! (0.32)	0.9! (0.39)	1.4! (0.60)	‡ (†)	‡ (†)	‡ (†)	‡ (†)	‡ (†)	‡ (†)
Serious violent[3]	**0.5 (0.08)**	**0.4 (0.08)**	**0.2 (0.05)**	**0.3 (0.07)**	**0.4 (0.08)**	**0.3 (0.09)**	**0.1! (0.05)**	**0.2! (0.07)**	**0.2! (0.07)**	**0.2! (0.06)**
Sex										
Male	0.7 (0.12)	0.5 (0.11)	0.3! (0.09)	0.3! (0.10)	0.5! (0.14)	0.6 (0.16)	0.2! (0.08)	0.2! (0.10)	0.2! (0.12)	0.2! (0.10)
Female	0.3 (0.08)	0.4! (0.12)	‡ (†)	0.3 (0.07)	0.2! (0.08)	‡ (†)	‡ (†)	0.2! (0.10)	‡ (†)	0.2! (0.08)
Race/ethnicity[1]										
White	0.5 (0.08)	0.4 (0.08)	0.2! (0.07)	0.3! (0.09)	0.2! (0.08)	0.3! (0.10)	0.2! (0.07)	0.2! (0.09)	0.3! (0.10)	0.3! (0.11)
Black	0.8! (0.28)	0.5! (0.25)	‡ (†)	‡ (†)	‡ (†)	‡ (†)	‡ (†)	‡ (†)	‡ (†)	‡ (†)
Hispanic	0.4! (0.18)	0.8! (0.33)	0.4! (0.18)	0.4! (0.16)	0.8! (0.32)	‡ (†)	‡ (†)	0.4! (0.17)	‡ (†)	‡ (†)
Asian/Pacific Islander	‡ (†)	‡ (†)	‡ (†)	‡ (†)	‡ (†)	‡ (†)	‡ (†)	‡ (†)	‡ (†)	‡ (†)
Asian	— (†)	— (†)	‡ (†)	‡ (†)	‡ (†)	‡ (†)	‡ (†)	‡ (†)	‡ (†)	‡ (†)
Pacific Islander	— (†)	— (†)	‡ (†)	‡ (†)	‡ (†)	‡ (†)	‡ (†)	‡ (†)	‡ (†)	‡ (†)
American Indian/Alaska Native	‡ (†)	‡ (†)	‡ (†)	‡ (†)	‡ (†)	‡ (†)	‡ (†)	‡ (†)	‡ (†)	‡ (†)
Two or more races	— (†)	— (†)	‡ (†)	‡ (†)	‡ (†)	‡ (†)	‡ (†)	‡ (†)	‡ (†)	‡ (†)
Grade										
6th	1.2! (0.38)	‡ (†)	‡ (†)	‡ (†)	‡ (†)	‡ (†)	‡ (†)	0.8! (0.42)	‡ (†)	‡ (†)
7th	0.5! (0.19)	0.6! (0.24)	‡ (†)	‡ (†)	0.4! (0.20)	‡ (†)	0.5! (0.23)	‡ (†)	‡ (†)	‡ (†)
8th	0.6! (0.19)	0.3! (0.14)	‡ (†)	‡ (†)	‡ (†)	‡ (†)	# (†)	‡ (†)	‡ (†)	‡ (†)
9th	0.5! (0.19)	0.8! (0.31)	0.6! (0.21)	‡ (†)	‡ (†)	‡ (†)	‡ (†)	‡ (†)	‡ (†)	‡ (†)
10th	0.2! (0.11)	0.4! (0.18)	‡ (†)	‡ (†)	‡ (†)	‡ (†)	# (†)	‡ (†)	‡ (†)	‡ (†)
11th	0.3! (0.16)	‡ (†)	‡ (†)	‡ (†)	0.6! (0.27)	‡ (†)	# (†)	‡ (†)	‡ (†)	‡ (†)
12th	‡ (†)	‡ (†)	‡ (†)	‡ (†)	‡ (†)	‡ (†)	# (†)	‡ (†)	‡ (†)	‡ (†)
Urbanicity[2]										
Urban	0.9 (0.20)	0.5 (0.15)	0.3! (0.14)	0.4! (0.17)	0.7! (0.23)	0.6! (0.22)	‡ (†)	0.3! (0.16)	‡ (†)	‡ (†)
Suburban	0.4 (0.10)	0.4 (0.09)	0.1! (0.05)	0.3! (0.08)	0.2! (0.09)	0.3! (0.11)	‡ (†)	0.2! (0.08)	0.3! (0.12)	0.2! (0.09)
Rural	0.2! (0.09)	0.5! (0.24)	‡ (†)	‡ (†)	‡ (†)	‡ (†)	‡ (†)	‡ (†)	‡ (†)	‡ (†)
Control of school										
Public	0.5 (0.08)	0.5 (0.09)	0.2 (0.06)	0.3 (0.06)	0.4 (0.09)	0.4 (0.10)	0.1! (0.06)	0.2! (0.08)	0.2! (0.08)	0.2! (0.07)
Private	‡ (†)	‡ (†)	‡ (†)	‡ (†)	‡ (†)	‡ (†)	# (†)	‡ (†)	‡ (†)	‡ (†)

—Not available.
†Not applicable.
#Rounds to zero.
!Interpret data with caution. The coefficient of variation (CV) for this estimate is between 30 and 50 percent.
‡Reporting standards not met. Either there are too few cases for a reliable estimate or the coefficient of variation (CV) is 50 percent or greater.
[1]Race categories exclude persons of Hispanic ethnicity. Prior to 2003, separate data for Asian students, Pacific Islander students, and students of Two or more races were not collected.
[2]Refers to the Standard Metropolitan Statistical Area (MSA) status of the respondent's household as defined by the U.S. Census Bureau. Categories include "central city of an MSA (Urban)," "in MSA but not in central city (Suburban)," and "not MSA (Rural)."
[3]Serious violent victimization is also included in violent victimization.

NOTE: "Total victimization" includes theft and violent victimization. A single student could report more than one type of victimization. In the total victimization section, students who reported both theft and violent victimization are counted only once. "Theft" includes attempted and completed purse-snatching, completed pickpocketing, and all attempted and completed thefts, with the exception of motor vehicle thefts. Theft does not include robbery, which involves the threat or use of force and is classified as a violent crime. "Serious violent victimization" includes the crimes of rape, sexual assault, robbery, and aggravated assault. "Violent victimization" includes the serious violent crimes as well as simple assault. "At school" includes in the school building, on school property, on a school bus, and, from 2001 onward, going to and from school. Some data have been revised from previously published figures.
SOURCE: U.S. Department of Justice, Bureau of Justice Statistics, School Crime Supplement (SCS) to the National Crime Victimization Survey, 1995 through 2017. (This table was prepared September 2018.)

Table 229.10. Percentage of public schools recording incidents of crime at school, percentage reporting incidents of crime at school to police, and number of incidents recorded or reported, by type of crime: Selected years, 1999–2000 through 2017–18

[Standard errors appear in parentheses]

Type of crime recorded or reported to police	1999–2000	2003–04	2005–06	2007–08	2009–10	2013–14[1]	2015–16 Percent of schools	2015–16 Number of incidents	2017–18 Percent of schools	2017–18 Number of incidents
1	2	3	4	5	6	7	8	9	10	11
Recorded incidents										
Total	86.4 (1.23)	88.5 (0.85)	85.7 (1.07)	85.5 (0.87)	85.0 (1.07)	— (†)	78.9 (1.28)	1,381,200 (42,660)	79.8 (1.23)	1,438,500 (54,530)
Violent incidents	71.4 (1.37)	81.4 (1.05)	77.7 (1.11)	75.5 (1.09)	73.8 (1.07)	65.0 (1.46)	68.9 (1.30)	864,900 (42,950)	70.7 (1.38)	962,300 (45,850)
Serious violent incidents	19.7 (0.98)	18.3 (0.99)	17.1 (0.91)	17.2 (1.06)	16.4 (0.94)	13.1 (1.00)	15.5 (0.93)	40,800 (3,460)	21.3 (0.98)	54,400 (7,770)
Rape or attempted rape	0.7 (0.10)	0.8 (0.17)	0.3 (0.07)	0.8 (0.17)	0.5 (0.10)	0.2! (0.10)	0.9 (0.19)	1,100 (190)	0.9 (0.16)	1,100 (200)
Sexual assault other than rape[2]	2.5 (0.33)	3.0 (0.32)	2.8 (0.24)	2.5 (0.33)	2.3 (0.34)	1.7 (0.37)	3.4 (0.38)	6,100 (1,360)	5.2 (0.46)	7,100 (690)
Physical attack or fight with a weapon	5.2 (0.60)	4.0 (0.46)	3.0 (0.38)	3.0 (0.33)	3.9 (0.48)	1.8 (0.34)	2.6 (0.38)	5,300 (1,280)	3.0 (0.42)	10,500 (2,850)
Threat of physical attack with a weapon	11.1 (0.70)	8.6 (0.71)	8.8 (0.66)	9.3 (0.77)	7.7 (0.72)	8.7 (0.78)	8.5 (0.79)	18,300 (2,420)	13.2 (0.86)	26,700 (4,460)
Robbery with a weapon	0.5! (0.15)	0.6 (0.15)	0.4 (0.12)	0.4! (0.14)	0.2 (0.05)	‡ (†)	0.5! (0.16)	600 (160)	0.4 (0.10)	500 (140)
Robbery without a weapon	5.3 (0.56)	6.3 (0.60)	6.4 (0.59)	5.2 (0.56)	4.4 (0.49)	2.5 (0.42)	2.7 (0.36)	9,500 (1,440)	3.5 (0.39)	8,500 (1,050)
Physical attack or fight without a weapon	63.7 (1.52)	76.7 (1.21)	74.3 (1.20)	72.7 (1.07)	70.5 (1.11)	57.5 (1.43)	64.9 (1.28)	567,000 (36,780)	65.7 (1.39)	597,300 (34,030)
Threat of physical attack without a weapon	52.2 (1.47)	53.0 (1.34)	52.2 (1.27)	47.8 (1.19)	46.4 (1.33)	47.1 (1.50)	39.4 (1.48)	257,000 (15,630)	41.4 (1.38)	310,700 (18,050)
Theft/larceny[3]	45.6 (1.37)	46.0 (1.29)	46.0 (1.07)	47.3 (1.29)	44.1 (1.31)	— (†)	38.7 (1.29)	166,000 (5,190)	33.4 (1.31)	132,500 (6,130)
Other incidents[4]	72.7 (1.30)	64.0 (1.27)	68.2 (1.07)	67.4 (1.13)	68.1 (1.12)	— (†)	58.5 (1.68)	350,400 (10,710)	59.8 (1.18)	343,700 (9,270)
Possession of a firearm/explosive device	5.5 (0.44)	6.1 (0.49)	7.2 (0.60)	4.7 (0.38)	4.7 (0.52)	— (†)	4.0 (0.50)	10,500! (3,220)	3.3 (0.37)	3,600 (390)
Possession of a knife or sharp object	42.6 (1.28)	— (—)	42.8 (1.23)	40.6 (1.10)	39.7 (1.06)	— (†)	38.4 (1.26)	70,600 (3,210)	38.2 (1.12)	69,100 (2,220)
Distribution of illegal drugs[5]	12.3 (0.50)	12.9 (0.55)	— (†)	— (†)	— (†)	— (†)	— (†)	— (†)	— (†)	— (†)
Possession or use of alcohol or illegal drugs[5]	26.6 (0.72)	29.3 (0.87)	— (†)	— (†)	— (†)	— (†)	— (†)	— (†)	— (†)	— (†)
Distribution, possession, or use of illegal drugs[6]	— (†)	— (†)	25.9 (0.68)	23.2 (0.68)	24.6 (0.57)	— (†)	24.9 (0.85)	112,100 (4,250)	24.9 (0.69)	120,300 (4,480)
Inappropriate distribution, possession, or use of prescription drugs[7]	— (†)	— (†)	— (†)	— (†)	— (†)	— (†)	9.5 (0.55)	20,100 (1,580)	9.7 (0.46)	21,100 (1,350)
Distribution, possession, or use of alcohol[6]	— (†)	— (†)	16.2 (0.68)	14.9 (0.57)	14.1 (0.50)	— (†)	13.3 (0.50)	29,900 (1,620)	13.4 (0.45)	29,000 (1,420)
Sexual harassment	36.3 (1.26)	— (†)	— (†)	— (†)	— (†)	— (†)	— (†)	— (†)	— (†)	— (†)
Vandalism	51.4 (1.61)	51.4 (1.17)	50.5 (1.17)	49.3 (1.16)	45.8 (1.12)	— (†)	33.4 (1.25)	107,200 (7,040)	33.1 (1.10)	100,600 (5,720)
Reported incidents to police										
Total	62.5 (1.37)	65.2 (1.35)	60.9 (1.15)	62.0 (1.24)	60.0 (1.58)	— (†)	47.4 (1.54)	448,900 (13,330)	46.9 (1.04)	422,800 (12,650)
Violent incidents	36.0 (0.82)	43.6 (1.15)	37.7 (1.09)	37.8 (1.16)	39.9 (1.13)	— (†)	32.7 (1.13)	195,600 (9,620)	32.5 (1.08)	192,100 (8,050)
Serious violent incidents	14.8 (0.84)	13.3 (0.88)	12.6 (0.70)	12.6 (0.86)	10.4 (0.62)	— (†)	10.0 (0.68)	20,000 (1,700)	14.9 (0.86)	26,100 (1,680)
Rape or attempted rape	0.6 (0.34)	0.8 (0.17)	0.3 (0.07)	0.8 (0.17)	0.5 (0.10)	— (†)	0.7 (0.14)	900 (160)	0.8 (0.16)	1,000 (190)
Sexual assault other than rape[2]	2.3 (0.50)	2.6 (0.28)	2.6 (0.26)	2.1 (0.29)	1.4 (0.20)	— (†)	2.7 (0.28)	3,600 (490)	4.3 (0.42)	5,600 (440)
Physical attack or fight with a weapon	3.9 (0.59)	2.8 (0.38)	2.2 (0.27)	2.1 (0.27)	2.2 (0.32)	— (†)	1.3 (0.24)	2,500! (830)	1.5 (0.23)	2,400 (390)
Threat of physical attack with a weapon	8.5 (0.69)	6.0 (0.55)	5.9 (0.49)	5.7 (0.59)	4.5 (0.43)	— (†)	5.3 (0.53)	7,500 (770)	9.0 (0.67)	12,400 (1,290)
Robbery with a weapon	0.3! (0.41)	0.6 (0.15)	0.4 (0.12)	0.4 (0.14)	0.2 (0.05)	— (†)	0.3! (0.13)	400! (140)	0.3 (0.08)	400 (90)
Robbery without a weapon	3.4 (0.91)	4.2 (0.51)	4.9 (0.48)	4.1 (0.42)	3.5 (0.40)	— (†)	1.9 (0.28)	5,000 (690)	2.4 (0.33)	4,300 (560)
Physical attack or fight without a weapon	25.8 (0.94)	35.6 (0.98)	29.2 (1.00)	28.2 (0.90)	34.3 (0.90)	— (†)	25.1 (1.03)	121,500 (8,560)	21.7 (0.70)	107,600 (5,570)
Threat of physical attack without a weapon	18.9 (0.94)	21.0 (0.82)	19.7 (0.69)	19.5 (0.76)	15.2 (0.79)	— (†)	12.9 (0.65)	54,200 (3,680)	14.3 (0.63)	58,400 (4,090)
Theft/larceny[3]	28.5 (1.04)	30.5 (1.17)	27.9 (0.97)	31.0 (1.12)	25.4 (1.01)	— (†)	18.1 (0.80)	71,600 (3,280)	14.9 (0.75)	53,900 (2,780)
Other incidents[4]	52.0 (1.14)	50.0 (1.18)	50.6 (1.00)	48.7 (1.17)	46.3 (1.23)	— (†)	33.5 (1.15)	181,700 (5,500)	35.1 (0.86)	176,900 (5,210)
Possession of a firearm/explosive device	4.5 (0.41)	4.9 (0.44)	5.5 (0.51)	3.6 (0.32)	3.1 (0.39)	— (†)	1.9 (0.29)	7,500! (2,760)	2.1 (0.30)	2,300 (320)
Possession of a knife or sharp object	23.0 (0.84)	— (—)	25.0 (1.00)	23.3 (0.69)	20.0 (0.88)	— (†)	15.8 (0.66)	27,700 (1,330)	18.0 (0.68)	30,500 (1,260)
Distribution of illegal drugs[5]	11.4 (0.48)	12.4 (0.57)	— (†)	— (†)	— (†)	— (†)	— (†)	— (†)	— (†)	— (†)
Possession or use of alcohol or illegal drugs[5]	22.2 (0.67)	26.0 (0.76)	— (†)	— (†)	— (†)	— (†)	— (†)	— (†)	— (†)	— (†)
Distribution, possession, or use of illegal drugs[6]	— (†)	— (†)	22.8 (0.62)	20.7 (0.60)	21.4 (0.57)	— (†)	19.9 (0.71)	82,200 (3,300)	19.9 (0.52)	84,800 (3,380)
Inappropriate distribution, possession, or use of prescription drugs[7]	— (†)	— (†)	— (†)	— (†)	— (†)	— (†)	7.4 (0.56)	15,100 (1,270)	7.1 (0.36)	15,100 (960)
Distribution, possession, or use of alcohol[6]	— (†)	— (†)	11.6 (0.61)	10.6 (0.55)	10.0 (0.41)	— (†)	8.6 (0.41)	17,800 (1,330)	8.0 (0.39)	16,900 (950)
Sexual harassment	14.7 (0.78)	— (†)	— (†)	— (†)	— (†)	— (†)	— (†)	— (†)	— (†)	— (†)
Vandalism	32.7 (1.10)	34.3 (1.06)	31.9 (1.02)	30.8 (1.18)	26.8 (1.09)	— (†)	12.9 (0.86)	31,600 (2,370)	12.0 (0.66)	27,300 (2,220)

See notes at end of table.

Table 229.10. Percentage of public schools recording incidents of crime at school, percentage reporting incidents of crime at school to police, and number of incidents recorded or reported, by type of crime: Selected years, 1999–2000 through 2017–18—Continued

—Not available.

†Not applicable.

‡Reporting standards not met. The coefficient of variation (CV) for this estimate is between 30 and 50 percent.

‡Interpret data with caution. Either there are too few cases for a reliable estimate or the coefficient of variation (CV) is 50 percent or greater.

[1]Data for 2013–14 were collected using the Fast Response Survey System (FRSS), while data for all other years were collected using the School Survey on Crime and Safety (SSOCS). The 2013–14 FRSS survey was designed to allow comparisons with SSOCS data. However, all respondents to the 2013–14 survey could choose either to complete the survey on paper (and mail it back) or to complete the survey online, whereas all respondents to SSOCS had only the option of completing a paper survey prior to 2017–18, when SSOCS experimented with offering an online option to some respondents. The 2013–14 FRSS survey also relied on a smaller sample than SSOCS. The FRSS survey's smaller sample size and difference in survey administration may have impacted the 2013–14 results.

[2]Prior to 2015–16, the wording of the survey item was "sexual battery other than rape."

[3]Theft/larceny is taking things worth over $10 without personal confrontation.

[4]Caution should be used when making direct comparisons of "Other incidents" between years because the survey questions about alcohol and drugs changed, as outlined in footnotes 5, 6, and 7, and because sexual harrassment was only included in 1999–2000.

[5]The survey items "Distribution of illegal drugs" and "Possession or use of alcohol or illegal drugs" appear only on the 1999–2000 and 2003–04 questionnaires. Different alcohol- and drug-related survey items were used on the SSOCS questionnaires for later years.

[6]The survey items "Distribution, possession, or use of illegal drugs" and "Distribution, possession, or use of alcohol" appear only on the SSOCS questionnaires for 2005–06 and later years.

[7]The survey item "Inappropriate distribution, possession, or use of prescription drugs" appears only on the SSOCS questionnaires for 2009–10 and later years.

NOTE: Responses were provided by the principal or the person most knowledgeable about crime and safety issues at the school. "At school" was defined to include activities that happen in school buildings, on school grounds, on school buses, and at places that hold school-sponsored events or activities. Respondents were instructed to include incidents that occurred before, during, and after normal school hours or when school activities or events were in session. Detail may not sum to totals because of rounding and because schools that recorded or reported more than one type of crime incident were counted only once in the total percentage of schools recording or reporting incidents.

SOURCE: U.S. Department of Education, National Center for Education Statistics, 1999–2000, 2003–04, 2005–06, 2007–08, 2009–10, 2015–16, and 2017–18 School Survey on Crime and Safety (SSOCS), 2000, 2004, 2006, 2008, 2010, 2016, and 2018; and Fast Response Survey System (FRSS), "School Safety and Discipline: 2013–14," FRSS 106, 2014. (This table was prepared July 2019.)

Table 230.10. Percentage of public schools reporting selected discipline problems that occurred at school, by frequency and selected school characteristics: Selected years, 1999–2000 through 2017–18

[Standard errors appear in parentheses]

Year and school characteristic	Happens at least once a week[1]							Happens at all[2]	
	Student racial/ ethnic tensions[3]	Student bullying[4]	Student sexual harassment of other students	Student harassment of other students based on sexual orientation or gender identity[5]	Student verbal abuse of teachers	Widespread disorder in classrooms	Student acts of disrespect for teachers other than verbal abuse	Gang activities	Cult or extremist group activities
1	2	3	4	5	6	7	8	9	10
All schools									
1999–2000	3.4 (0.41)	29.3 (1.21)	— (†)	— (†)	12.5 (0.69)	3.1 (0.44)	— (†)	18.7 (0.85)	6.7 (0.46)
2003–04	2.1 (0.28)	26.8 (1.09)	4.0 (0.40)	— (†)	10.7 (0.80)	2.8 (0.39)	— (†)	16.7 (0.78)	3.4 (0.35)
2005–06	2.8 (0.31)	24.5 (1.14)	3.5 (0.40)	— (†)	9.5 (0.61)	2.3 (0.24)	— (†)	16.9 (0.76)	3.7 (0.41)
2007–08	3.7 (0.49)	25.3 (1.11)	3.0 (0.39)	— (†)	6.0 (0.48)	4.0 (0.45)	10.5 (0.71)	19.8 (0.88)	2.6 (0.36)
2009–10	2.8 (0.39)	23.1 (1.12)	3.2 (0.55)	2.5 (0.41)	4.8 (0.49)	2.5 (0.37)	8.6 (0.67)	16.4 (0.84)	1.7 (0.31)
2013–14[6]	1.4 (0.31)	15.7 (1.12)	1.4 (0.26)	0.8 (0.19)	5.1 (0.54)	2.3 (0.45)	8.6 (0.74)	— (†)	— (†)
2015–16	1.7 (0.33)	11.9 (0.79)	1.0 (0.19)	0.6 (0.13)	4.8 (0.51)	2.3 (0.38)	10.3 (0.80)	10.4 (0.62)	— (†)
2017–18									
All schools	**2.8 (0.42)**	**13.6 (0.72)**	**1.4 (0.27)**	**1.0 (0.19)**	**6.0 (0.53)**	**3.1 (0.41)**	**11.8 (0.72)**	**11.0 (0.66)**	**— (†)**
School level[7]									
Primary	1.9 (0.51)	8.7 (0.94)	‡ (†)	‡ (†)	4.6 (0.83)	2.6 (0.62)	10.1 (1.02)	4.9 (0.85)	— (†)
Middle	4.9 (0.68)	27.9 (1.51)	3.3 (0.58)	2.6 (0.47)	10.3 (0.89)	5.5 (0.79)	17.3 (1.18)	19.0 (1.19)	— (†)
High school	4.5 (0.69)	15.8 (1.25)	2.8 (0.49)	2.3 (0.49)	7.1 (0.81)	2.6 (0.60)	13.1 (1.25)	27.9 (1.20)	— (†)
Combined	‡ (†)	12.3 (3.17)	‡ (†)	‡ (†)	4.3! (1.98)	‡ (†)	8.2! (2.67)	4.5! (1.46)	— (†)
Enrollment size									
Less than 300	‡ (†)	9.6 (1.89)	‡ (†)	‡ (†)	3.0! (1.04)	1.5! (0.64)	4.9 (1.29)	3.3 (0.56)	— (†)
300 to 499	3.4 (0.76)	11.3 (1.26)	1.2! (0.41)	0.6! (0.23)	5.9 (1.18)	4.3 (0.97)	14.4 (1.60)	6.6 (1.19)	— (†)
500 to 999	2.3 (0.45)	15.6 (1.20)	0.9 (0.25)	0.8 (0.18)	6.8 (0.87)	2.7 (0.51)	12.1 (1.09)	12.3 (1.15)	— (†)
1,000 or more	5.9 (0.89)	20.7 (1.67)	3.3 (0.56)	2.2 (0.45)	9.5 (1.29)	3.9 (0.71)	16.2 (1.48)	33.4 (1.61)	— (†)
Locale									
City	3.1 (0.69)	13.4 (1.11)	0.9 (0.24)	0.6! (0.18)	8.9 (1.32)	3.9 (0.74)	14.9 (1.64)	17.8 (1.37)	— (†)
Suburban	3.7 (0.79)	13.0 (1.51)	1.4 (0.36)	0.7 (0.18)	5.3 (0.74)	2.7 (0.64)	10.5 (1.23)	10.1 (0.89)	— (†)
Town	2.6! (0.85)	17.9 (2.35)	2.4! (0.73)	1.8! (0.57)	6.6 (1.80)	4.8! (1.63)	14.8 (2.16)	10.0 (1.20)	— (†)
Rural	1.4! (0.60)	12.5 (1.53)	1.5! (0.62)	1.3! (0.60)	3.7 (0.90)	1.8! (0.66)	8.7 (1.44)	5.7 (0.84)	— (†)
Percent minority enrollment[8]									
0 to 25 percent	1.7 (0.40)	13.0 (1.10)	1.5! (0.49)	1.5! (0.45)	2.3 (0.44)	1.5! (0.46)	7.8 (1.10)	2.7 (0.48)	— (†)
26 to 50 percent	2.4 (0.57)	11.7 (1.48)	1.3 (0.29)	0.7! (0.24)	5.2 (1.17)	3.6 (0.98)	10.1 (1.50)	9.8 (1.13)	— (†)
51 to 75 percent	5.1 (1.52)	16.5 (2.45)	2.3! (0.82)	0.9! (0.37)	10.1 (1.91)	4.2! (1.38)	18.9 (2.45)	17.8 (1.62)	— (†)
76 to 100 percent	3.3 (0.85)	14.3 (1.50)	0.8 (0.25)	0.6! (0.23)	9.5 (1.23)	4.1 (0.77)	14.5 (1.47)	19.3 (1.52)	— (†)
Percent of students eligible for free or reduced-price lunch									
0 to 25 percent	1.5 (0.36)	8.5 (0.97)	1.5! (0.49)	1.2 (0.32)	1.4 (0.36)	1.1! (0.44)	5.8 (1.43)	3.2 (0.54)	— (†)
26 to 50 percent	3.5 (0.76)	13.8 (1.45)	1.9 (0.55)	1.1 (0.28)	3.0 (0.71)	2.5! (0.77)	8.1 (1.07)	7.5 (0.79)	— (†)
51 to 75 percent	2.2 (0.61)	14.5 (1.63)	0.4! (0.15)	‡ (†)	7.1 (0.98)	3.3 (0.83)	13.8 (1.35)	12.2 (1.39)	— (†)
76 to 100 percent	3.5 (0.93)	15.6 (1.52)	1.7! (0.63)	0.7! (0.24)	10.0 (1.25)	4.4 (0.82)	16.2 (1.73)	16.9 (1.43)	— (†)
Prevalence of violent incidents[9] at school during school year									
No violent incidents	‡ (†)	4.2 (1.06)	‡ (†)	‡ (†)	‡ (†)	‡ (†)	3.0! (0.95)	2.6 (0.65)	— (†)
Any violent incidents	3.9 (0.61)	17.5 (0.93)	1.7 (0.29)	1.4 (0.26)	8.2 (0.74)	3.9 (0.50)	15.4 (0.98)	14.5 (0.86)	— (†)

See notes at end of table.

Table 230.10. Percentage of public schools reporting selected discipline problems that occurred at school, by frequency and selected school characteristics: Selected years, 1999–2000 through 2017–18—Continued

—Not available.

†Not applicable.

!Interpret data with caution. The coefficient of variation (CV) for this estimate is between 30 and 50 percent.

‡Reporting standards not met. Either there are too few cases for a reliable estimate or the coefficient of variation (CV) is 50 percent or greater.

[1]Includes schools that reported the problem happens either at least once a week or daily.

[2]Includes schools that reported the problem happens at all at their school during the school year. In the 1999–2000 survey administration, the questionnaire specified "undesirable" gang activities and "undesirable" cult or extremist group activities. As of 2013–14, the questionnaires have no longer asked about cult or extremist group activities.

[3]Prior to the 2007–08 survey administration, the questionnaire wording was "student racial tensions."

[4]The 2015–16 and 2017–18 questionnaires defined bullying as "any unwanted aggressive behavior(s) by another youth or group of youths who are not siblings or current dating partners that involves an observed or perceived power imbalance and is repeated multiple times or is highly likely to be repeated." The term was not defined for respondents in previous survey administrations.

[5]Prior to 2015–16, the questionnaire asked about "student harassment of other students based on sexual orientation or gender identity (i.e., lesbian, gay, bisexual, transgender, questioning)" in one single item. The 2015–16 and 2017–18 questionnaires had one item asking about "student harassment of other students based on sexual orientation," followed by a separate item asking about "student harassment of other students based on gender identity." For 2015–16 and 2017–18, schools are included in this column if they responded "daily" or "at least once a week" to either or both of these items; each school is counted only once, even if it indicated daily/weekly frequency for both items. The 2015–16 and 2017–18 questionnaires provided definitions for sexual orientation—"one's emotional or physical attraction to the same and/or opposite sex"—and gender identity—"one's inner sense of one's own gender, which may or may not match the sex assigned at birth." These terms were not defined for respondents in previous survey administrations.

[6]Data for 2013–14 were collected using the Fast Response Survey System (FRSS), while data for all other years were collected using the School Survey on Crime and Safety (SSOCS). The 2013–14 FRSS survey was designed to allow comparisons with SSOCS data. However, all respondents to the 2013–14 survey could choose either to complete the survey on paper (and mail it back) or to complete the survey online, whereas all respondents to SSOCS had only the option of completing a paper survey prior to 2017–18, when SSOCS experimented with offering an online option to some respondents. The 2013–14 FRSS survey also relied on a smaller sample than SSOCS. The FRSS survey's smaller sample size and difference in survey administration may have impacted the 2013–14 results.

[7]Primary schools are defined as schools in which the lowest grade is not higher than grade 3 and the highest grade is not higher than grade 8. Middle schools are defined as schools in which the lowest grade is not lower than grade 4 and the highest grade is not higher than grade 9. High schools are defined as schools in which the lowest grade is not lower than grade 9. Combined schools include all other combinations of grades, including K–12 schools.

[8]Percent combined enrollment of Black, Hispanic, Asian, Pacific Islander, and American Indian/Alaska Native students, and students of Two or more races.

[9]"Violent incidents" include rape or attempted rape, sexual assault other than rape, physical attack or fight with or without a weapon, threat of physical attack or fight with or without a weapon, and robbery with or without a weapon. Respondents were instructed to include violent incidents that occurred before, during, or after normal school hours or when school activities or events were in session.

NOTE: Responses were provided by the principal or the person most knowledgeable about crime and safety issues at the school. "At school" was defined for respondents to include activities that happen in school buildings, on school grounds, on school buses, and at places that hold school-sponsored events or activities. Respondents were instructed to respond only for those times that were during normal school hours or when school activities or events were in session, unless the survey specified otherwise.

SOURCE: U.S. Department of Education, National Center for Education Statistics, 1999–2000, 2003–04, 2005–06, 2007–08, 2009–10, 2015–16, and 2017–18 School Survey on Crime and Safety (SSOCS), 2000, 2004, 2006, 2008, 2010, 2016, and 2018; and Fast Response Survey System (FRSS), "School Safety and Discipline: 2013–14," FRSS 106, 2014. (This table was prepared July 2019.)

Table 230.40. Percentage of students ages 12–18 who reported being bullied at school during the school year, by selected student and school characteristics: Selected years, 2005 through 2017

[Standard errors appear in parentheses]

Student or school characteristic	2005[1]		2007		2009		2011		2013		2015		2017	
1	2		3		4		5		6		7		8	
Total	**28.5**	**(0.70)**	**31.7**	**(0.74)**	**28.0**	**(0.83)**	**27.8**	**(0.76)**	**21.5**	**(0.66)**	**20.8**	**(0.99)**	**20.2**	**(0.71)**
Sex														
Male	27.5	(0.90)	30.3	(0.96)	26.6	(1.04)	24.5	(0.91)	19.5	(0.81)	18.8	(1.31)	16.7	(0.87)
Female	29.7	(0.85)	33.2	(0.99)	29.5	(1.08)	31.4	(0.99)	23.7	(0.98)	22.8	(1.39)	23.8	(1.01)
Race/ethnicity														
White	30.3	(0.85)	34.1	(0.97)	29.3	(1.03)	31.5	(1.07)	23.7	(0.93)	21.6	(1.43)	22.8	(1.02)
Black	29.2	(2.23)	30.4	(2.18)	29.1	(2.29)	27.2	(1.97)	20.3	(1.81)	24.7	(3.29)	22.9	(1.98)
Hispanic	22.3	(1.29)	27.3	(1.53)	25.5	(1.71)	21.9	(1.07)	19.2	(1.30)	17.2	(1.58)	15.7	(1.12)
Asian/Pacific Islander	20.8	(2.61)	17.2	(2.47)	17.8	(2.79)	13.8	(2.48)	9.3	(1.67)	19.4	(4.45)	7.3	(1.54)
Asian	20.9	2.7	18.1	(2.60)	17.3	(3.01)	14.9	(2.70)	9.2	(1.67)	15.6	(4.02)	7.3	(1.56)
Pacific Islander	‡	(†)	‡	(†)	‡	(†)	‡	(†)	‡	(†)	‡	(†)	‡	(†)
American Indian/Alaska Native	‡	(†)	29.8	(7.40)	‡	(†)	21.1!	(6.72)	24.3!	(9.87)	‡	(†)	27.2	(5.93)
Two or more races	34.6	(4.44)	38.2	(3.95)	27.3	(5.56)	26.9	(4.30)	27.6	(4.50)	17.7	(3.96)	23.2	(3.03)
Grade														
6th	37.0	(2.06)	42.7	(2.23)	39.4	(2.60)	37.0	(2.17)	27.8	(2.31)	31.0	(3.53)	29.5	(2.79)
7th	35.1	(1.70)	35.6	(1.78)	33.1	(1.87)	30.3	(1.64)	26.4	(1.65)	25.1	(2.48)	24.4	(1.60)
8th	31.3	(1.60)	36.9	(1.84)	31.7	(1.85)	30.7	(1.68)	21.7	(1.42)	22.2	(2.41)	25.3	(1.69)
9th	28.3	(1.59)	30.6	(1.72)	28.0	(1.90)	26.5	(1.66)	23.0	(1.42)	19.0	(2.11)	19.3	(1.52)
10th	25.1	(1.42)	27.7	(1.44)	26.6	(1.71)	28.0	(1.56)	19.5	(1.48)	21.2	(2.13)	18.9	(1.67)
11th	23.5	(1.62)	28.5	(1.48)	21.1	(1.69)	23.8	(1.72)	20.0	(1.50)	15.8	(2.24)	14.7	(1.45)
12th	20.8	(1.83)	23.0	(1.60)	20.4	(1.63)	22.0	(1.34)	14.1	(1.51)	14.9	(2.18)	12.2	(1.34)
Urbanicity[2]														
Urban	26.2	(1.32)	30.7	(1.36)	27.4	(1.25)	24.8	(1.28)	20.7	(1.10)	21.5	(1.84)	18.3	(1.32)
Suburban	29.4	(0.80)	31.2	(1.07)	27.5	(1.06)	29.0	(1.07)	22.0	(0.90)	21.1	(1.22)	19.7	(0.80)
Rural	29.5	(1.97)	35.2	(1.73)	30.7	(1.99)	29.7	(1.82)	21.4	(1.86)	18.2	(2.86)	26.7	(2.13)
Control of school[3]														
Public	29.0	(0.74)	32.0	(0.76)	28.8	(0.88)	28.4	(0.82)	21.5	(0.67)	21.1	(1.06)	20.6	(0.73)
Private	23.3	(2.16)	29.1	(2.10)	18.9	(2.16)	21.5	(1.91)	22.4	(2.71)	16.1	(3.40)	16.0	(2.39)

†Not applicable.
!Interpret data with caution. The coefficient of variation (CV) for this estimate is between 30 and 50 percent.
‡Reporting standards not met. Either there are too few cases for a reliable estimate or the coefficient of variation (CV) is 50 percent or greater.
[1]In 2005, the period covered by the survey question was "during the last 6 months," whereas the period was "during this school year" beginning in 2007. Cognitive testing showed that estimates for 2005 are comparable to those for 2007 and later years.
[2]Refers to the Standard Metropolitan Statistical Area (MSA) status of the respondent's household as defined by the U.S. Census Bureau. Categories include "central city of an MSA (Urban)," "in MSA but not in central city (Suburban)," and "not MSA (Rural)." These data by metropolitan status were based on the location of households and differ from those published in *Student Reports of Bullying: Results From the 2015 School Crime*

Supplement to the National Crime Victimization Survey, which were based on the urban-centric measure of the location of the school that the child attended.
[3]Control of school as reported by the respondent. These data differ from those based on a matching of the respondent-reported school name to the Common Core of Data's Public Elementary/Secondary School Universe Survey or the Private School Survey, as reported in *Student Reports of Bullying: Results From the 2015 School Crime Supplement to the National Crime Victimization Survey*.
NOTE: "At school" includes in the school building, on school property, on a school bus, and going to and from school. Race categories exclude persons of Hispanic ethnicity. Some data have been revised from previously published figures.
SOURCE: U.S. Department of Justice, Bureau of Justice Statistics, School Crime Supplement (SCS) to the National Crime Victimization Survey, selected years, 2005 through 2017. (This table was prepared September 2018.)

Table 231.10. Percentage of students in grades 9–12 who reported having been in a physical fight at least one time during the previous 12 months, by location and selected student characteristics: Selected years, 1993 through 2017

[Standard errors appear in parentheses]

Location and student characteristic	1993	1997	1999	2001	2003	2005	2007	2009	2011	2013	2015	2017
1	2	3	4	5	6	7	8	9	10	11	12	13
Anywhere (including on school property)[1]												
Total	41.8 (0.99)	36.6 (1.01)	35.7 (1.17)	33.2 (0.71)	33.0 (0.99)	35.9 (0.77)	35.5 (0.77)	31.5 (0.70)	32.8 (0.65)	24.7 (0.74)	22.6 (0.87)	23.6 (0.97)
Sex												
Male	51.2 (1.05)	45.5 (1.07)	44.0 (1.27)	43.1 (0.84)	40.5 (1.32)	43.4 (1.01)	44.4 (0.89)	39.3 (1.20)	40.7 (0.74)	30.2 (1.10)	28.4 (1.04)	30.0 (1.14)
Female	31.7 (1.19)	26.0 (1.26)	27.3 (1.70)	23.9 (0.95)	25.1 (0.85)	28.1 (0.94)	26.5 (0.99)	22.9 (0.74)	24.4 (0.92)	19.2 (0.72)	16.5 (1.04)	17.2 (1.01)
Race/ethnicity												
White	40.3 (1.13)	33.7 (1.29)	33.1 (1.45)	32.2 (0.95)	30.5 (1.11)	33.1 (0.88)	31.7 (0.96)	27.8 (0.88)	29.4 (0.74)	20.9 (0.70)	20.1 (1.13)	20.8 (0.82)
Black	49.5 (1.82)	43.0 (1.92)	41.4 (3.12)	36.5 (1.60)	39.7 (1.23)	43.1 (1.74)	44.7 (1.33)	41.1 (1.71)	39.1 (1.52)	34.7 (1.67)	32.4 (2.11)	33.2 (2.49)
Hispanic	43.2 (1.58)	40.7 (1.68)	39.9 (1.65)	35.8 (0.91)	36.1 (0.98)	41.0 (1.64)	40.4 (1.25)	36.2 (0.95)	36.8 (1.44)	28.4 (1.15)	23.0 (1.10)	25.7 (1.85)
Asian[2]	(†)	(†)	22.7 (2.71)	22.3 (2.73)	25.9 (2.99)	21.6 (2.43)	24.3 (3.50)	18.9 (1.72)	18.4 (1.87)	16.1 (1.87)	14.7 (1.12)	11.0 (1.61)
Pacific Islander[2]	(†)	(†)	50.7 (3.42)	51.7 (6.25)	30.0 (5.21)	34.4 (5.58)	42.6 (7.74)	32.6 (3.50)	43.0 (5.14)	22.0 (4.95)	29.2 (7.98)	22.6 (2.47)
American Indian/Alaska Native	49.8 (4.79)	54.7 (5.75)	48.7 (6.78)	49.2 (6.58)	46.6 (6.53)	44.2 (3.40)	36.0 (1.49)	42.4 (5.23)	42.4 (2.12)	32.1 (7.39)	29.9 (5.07)	34.7 (6.36)
Two or more races[2]	(†)	(†)	40.2 (2.76)	39.6 (2.85)	38.2 (3.64)	46.9 (4.16)	47.8 (3.30)	34.2 (3.51)	45.0 (2.60)	28.5 (2.31)	27.6 (2.58)	25.5 (2.30)
Sexual orientation[3]												
Heterosexual	—	—	—	—	—	—	—	—	—	—	21.7 (0.78)	23.2 (0.95)
Gay, lesbian, or bisexual	—	—	—	—	—	—	—	—	—	—	28.4 (2.34)	27.9 (1.66)
Not sure	—	—	—	—	—	—	—	—	—	—	34.5 (4.44)	19.8 (2.83)
Grade												
9th	50.4 (1.54)	44.8 (1.98)	41.1 (1.96)	39.5 (1.27)	38.6 (1.38)	43.5 (1.15)	40.9 (1.16)	37.0 (1.21)	37.7 (1.11)	28.3 (1.17)	27.9 (1.51)	28.3 (1.53)
10th	42.2 (1.45)	40.2 (1.91)	37.7 (2.11)	34.7 (1.37)	33.5 (1.20)	36.6 (1.09)	36.2 (1.34)	33.5 (1.19)	35.3 (1.35)	26.4 (1.42)	23.4 (1.46)	26.2 (1.14)
11th	40.5 (1.52)	34.2 (1.72)	31.3 (1.55)	29.1 (1.10)	30.9 (1.38)	31.6 (1.44)	34.8 (1.36)	28.6 (0.93)	29.7 (1.14)	24.0 (1.04)	20.5 (1.23)	20.4 (0.91)
12th	34.8 (1.56)	28.8 (1.36)	30.4 (1.91)	26.5 (1.01)	26.5 (1.08)	29.1 (1.26)	28.0 (1.42)	24.9 (0.99)	26.9 (0.95)	18.8 (1.19)	17.4 (1.23)	17.8 (1.52)
Urbanicity[4]												
Urban	—	38.2 (2.00)	37.0 (2.66)	36.8 (1.53)	35.5 (2.17)	(†)	(†)	(†)	(†)	(†)	(†)	(†)
Suburban	—	36.7 (1.59)	35.0 (1.56)	31.3 (0.80)	33.1 (1.23)	(†)	(†)	(†)	(†)	(†)	(†)	(†)
Rural	—	32.9 (2.91)	36.6 (2.14)	33.8 (2.58)	29.7 (1.61)	(†)	(†)	(†)	(†)	(†)	(†)	(†)
On school property[5]												
Total	16.2 (0.59)	14.8 (0.64)	14.2 (0.62)	12.5 (0.49)	12.8 (0.76)	13.6 (0.56)	12.4 (0.48)	11.1 (0.54)	12.0 (0.39)	8.1 (0.35)	7.8 (0.54)	8.5 (0.53)
Sex												
Male	23.5 (0.71)	20.0 (1.04)	18.5 (0.66)	18.0 (0.74)	17.1 (0.92)	18.2 (0.93)	16.3 (0.60)	15.1 (1.05)	16.0 (0.58)	10.7 (0.55)	10.3 (0.79)	11.6 (0.62)
Female	8.6 (0.73)	8.6 (0.78)	9.8 (0.95)	7.2 (0.47)	8.0 (0.70)	8.8 (0.52)	8.5 (0.62)	6.7 (0.42)	7.8 (0.43)	5.6 (0.38)	5.0 (0.45)	5.6 (0.54)
Race/ethnicity												
White	15.0 (0.68)	13.3 (0.84)	12.3 (0.86)	11.2 (0.60)	10.0 (0.73)	11.6 (0.66)	10.2 (0.56)	8.6 (0.58)	9.9 (0.51)	6.4 (0.45)	5.6 (0.35)	6.5 (0.64)
Black	22.0 (1.39)	20.7 (1.20)	18.7 (1.51)	16.8 (1.26)	17.1 (1.30)	16.9 (1.39)	17.6 (1.10)	17.4 (0.99)	16.4 (0.89)	12.8 (0.84)	12.6 (1.96)	15.3 (1.45)
Hispanic	17.9 (1.75)	19.0 (1.50)	15.7 (0.91)	14.1 (0.89)	16.7 (1.14)	18.3 (1.62)	15.5 (0.81)	13.5 (0.82)	14.4 (0.79)	9.4 (0.44)	8.9 (0.87)	9.4 (0.90)
Asian[2]	(†)	(†)	10.4 (0.95)	10.8 (1.92)	13.1 (2.26)	5.9 (1.53)	8.5 (1.99)	7.7 (1.09)	6.2 (1.06)	5.5 (1.39)	6.3 (1.63)	3.7 (1.00)
Pacific Islander[2]	(†)	(†)	25.3 (4.60)	29.1 (7.63)	22.2 (4.82)	24.5 (5.60)	9.6! (3.47)	14.8 (2.37)	20.9 (4.41)	7.1! (2.58)	20.9! (7.11)	14.2 (3.58)
American Indian/Alaska Native	18.6 (2.74)	18.9 (5.55)	16.2! (5.23)	18.2 (4.41)	24.2 (5.03)	22.0 (3.16)	15.0 (1.12)	20.7 (3.73)	12.0 (1.77)	10.7 (3.13)	13.2 (3.54)	8.6! (3.74)
Two or more races[2]	(†)	(†)	16.9 (2.40)	14.7 (1.97)	20.2 (3.83)	15.8 (2.61)	19.6 (2.39)	12.4 (2.19)	16.6 (1.41)	10.0 (1.04)	9.3 (1.49)	9.2 (1.36)
Sexual orientation[3]												
Heterosexual	—	—	—	—	—	—	—	—	—	—	7.1 (0.51)	8.3 (0.56)
Gay, lesbian, or bisexual	—	—	—	—	—	—	—	—	—	—	11.2 (1.22)	9.6 (1.16)
Not sure	—	—	—	—	—	—	—	—	—	—	14.6 (2.38)	11.8 (2.25)
Grade												
9th	23.1 (1.55)	21.3 (1.29)	18.6 (1.02)	17.3 (0.77)	18.0 (1.24)	18.9 (0.93)	17.0 (0.67)	14.9 (0.98)	16.2 (0.77)	10.9 (0.78)	11.6 (0.82)	12.3 (1.05)
10th	17.2 (1.07)	17.0 (1.67)	17.2 (1.23)	13.5 (0.88)	12.8 (0.89)	14.4 (1.08)	11.7 (0.86)	12.1 (0.83)	12.8 (0.86)	8.3 (0.61)	7.3 (0.76)	9.6 (0.74)
11th	13.8 (1.27)	12.5 (0.87)	10.8 (1.01)	9.4 (0.71)	10.4 (0.89)	10.4 (0.75)	11.0 (0.73)	9.5 (0.63)	9.2 (0.55)	7.5 (0.53)	6.5 (0.83)	6.0 (0.66)
12th	11.4 (0.66)	9.5 (0.73)	8.1 (1.00)	7.5 (0.56)	7.3 (0.70)	8.5 (0.70)	8.6 (0.62)	6.6 (0.59)	8.8 (0.69)	4.9 (0.63)	4.5 (0.51)	5.0 (0.61)
Urbanicity[4]												
Urban	—	15.8 (1.50)	14.4 (1.08)	14.8 (0.90)	14.8 (1.31)	(†)	(†)	(†)	(†)	(†)	(†)	(†)
Suburban	—	14.2 (0.95)	13.7 (0.86)	11.0 (0.75)	12.8 (1.23)	(†)	(†)	(†)	(†)	(†)	(†)	(†)
Rural	—	14.7 (2.09)	16.3 (2.33)	13.8 (1.10)	10.0 (1.36)	(†)	(†)	(†)	(†)	(†)	(†)	(†)

—Not available.
†Not applicable.
!Interpret data with caution. The coefficient of variation (CV) for this estimate is between 30 and 50 percent.
[1]The term "anywhere" is not used in the Youth Risk Behavior Survey (YRBS) questionnaire; students were simply asked how many times in the past 12 months they had been in a physical fight.
[2]Before 1999, Asian students and Pacific Islander students were not categorized separately, and students could not be classified as Two or more races. Because the response categories changed in 1999, caution should be used in comparing data on race from 1993 and 1997 with data from later years.

[3]Students were asked which sexual orientation—"heterosexual (straight)," "gay or lesbian," "bisexual," or "not sure"—best described them.
[4]Refers to the Standard Metropolitan Statistical Area (MSA) status of the respondent's household as defined by the U.S. Census Bureau. Categories include "central city of an MSA (Urban)," "in MSA but not in central city (Suburban)," and "not MSA (Rural)."
[5]In the question asking students about physical fights at school, "on school property" was not defined for survey respondents.
NOTE: Race categories exclude persons of Hispanic ethnicity.
SOURCE: Centers for Disease Control and Prevention, Division of Adolescent and School Health, Youth Risk Behavior Surveillance System (YRBSS), 1993 through 2017. (This table was prepared July 2018.)

Table 232.10. Percentage of students in grades 9–12 who reported using alcohol at least 1 day during the previous 30 days, by location and selected student characteristics: Selected years, 1993 through 2017

[Standard errors appear in parentheses]

Location and student characteristic	1993	1997	1999	2001	2003	2005	2007	2009	2011	2013	2015	2017
1	2	3	4	5	6	7	8	9	10	11	12	13
Anywhere (including on school property)[1]												
Total	48.0 (1.06)	50.8 (1.43)	50.0 (1.30)	47.1 (1.11)	44.9 (1.21)	43.3 (1.38)	44.7 (1.15)	41.8 (0.80)	38.7 (0.75)	34.9 (1.08)	32.8 (1.18)	29.8 (1.27)
Sex												
Male	50.1 (1.23)	53.3 (1.22)	52.3 (1.47)	49.2 (1.42)	43.8 (1.31)	43.8 (1.40)	44.7 (1.39)	40.8 (1.11)	39.5 (0.93)	34.4 (1.30)	32.2 (0.89)	27.6 (1.24)
Female	45.9 (1.32)	47.8 (1.99)	47.7 (1.45)	45.0 (1.11)	45.8 (1.29)	42.8 (1.56)	44.6 (1.42)	42.9 (0.85)	37.9 (0.91)	35.5 (1.39)	33.5 (1.89)	31.8 (1.57)
Race/ethnicity												
White	49.9 (1.26)	54.0 (1.51)	52.5 (1.62)	50.4 (1.12)	47.1 (1.51)	46.4 (1.84)	47.3 (1.67)	44.7 (1.16)	40.3 (0.97)	36.3 (1.63)	35.2 (2.00)	32.4 (1.73)
Black	42.5 (1.82)	36.9 (1.46)	39.9 (4.07)	32.7 (2.33)	37.4 (1.67)	31.2 (1.05)	34.5 (1.65)	33.4 (1.45)	30.5 (1.40)	29.6 (1.65)	23.8 (2.82)	20.8 (2.27)
Hispanic	50.8 (2.82)	53.9 (1.96)	52.8 (2.41)	49.2 (1.52)	45.6 (1.39)	46.8 (1.39)	47.6 (1.80)	42.9 (1.43)	42.3 (1.38)	37.5 (2.11)	34.4 (1.28)	31.3 (1.53)
Asian[2]	— (†)	— (†)	25.7 (2.24)	28.4 (3.22)	27.5 (3.47)	25.6 (1.98)	25.4 (2.17)	18.3 (1.60)	25.6 (2.90)	21.7 (1.80)	13.1 (1.83)	12.2 (1.74)
Pacific Islander[2]	— (†)	— (†)	60.8 (6.11)	52.3 (8.54)	40.0 (7.04)	38.7 (8.43)	48.8 (6.58)	34.8 (4.36)	38.4 (6.40)	26.8 (5.84)	36.9 (10.62)	18.7 (3.17)
American Indian/Alaska Native	45.3 (7.18)	57.6 (3.79)	49.4 (6.43)	51.4 (3.97)	51.9 (5.29)	57.4 (4.13)	34.5 (1.77)	42.8 (5.43)	44.9 (2.26)	33.4 (5.13)	46.0 (8.12)	31.8 (8.15)
Two or more races[2]	— (†)	— (†)	51.1 (3.98)	45.4 (4.11)	47.1 (3.59)	39.0 (3.59)	46.2 (2.89)	44.3 (2.42)	36.9 (3.08)	36.1 (2.87)	39.6 (2.68)	32.7 (2.50)
Sexual orientation[3]												
Heterosexual	— (†)	— (†)	— (†)	— (†)	— (†)	— (†)	— (†)	— (†)	— (†)	—	32.1 (1.30)	29.7 (1.02)
Gay, lesbian, or bisexual	— (†)	— (†)	— (†)	— (†)	— (†)	— (†)	— (†)	— (†)	— (†)	—	40.5 (2.07)	37.4 (2.39)
Not sure	— (†)	— (†)	— (†)	— (†)	— (†)	— (†)	— (†)	— (†)	— (†)	—	34.6 (2.81)	21.5 (2.77)
Grade												
9th	40.5 (1.79)	44.2 (3.12)	40.6 (2.17)	41.1 (1.82)	36.2 (1.43)	36.2 (1.23)	35.7 (1.15)	31.5 (1.28)	29.8 (1.35)	24.4 (1.13)	23.4 (1.28)	18.8 (1.23)
10th	44.0 (2.00)	47.2 (2.19)	49.7 (1.89)	45.2 (1.29)	43.5 (1.66)	42.0 (1.95)	41.8 (1.68)	40.6 (1.42)	35.7 (1.37)	30.9 (1.84)	29.0 (2.49)	27.0 (1.60)
11th	49.7 (1.73)	53.2 (1.49)	50.9 (1.98)	49.3 (1.70)	47.0 (2.08)	46.0 (1.98)	49.0 (1.83)	45.7 (2.05)	42.7 (1.28)	39.2 (1.52)	38.0 (1.68)	34.4 (1.68)
12th	56.4 (1.35)	57.3 (2.50)	61.7 (2.25)	55.2 (1.53)	55.9 (1.65)	50.8 (2.12)	54.9 (2.09)	51.7 (1.37)	48.4 (1.29)	46.8 (1.85)	42.4 (2.00)	40.8 (1.92)
Urbanicity[4]												
Urban	—	48.9 (2.07)	46.5 (2.75)	45.2 (1.97)	41.5 (1.48)	—	† (†)	† (†)	† (†)	† (†)	† (†)	† (†)
Suburban	—	50.5 (2.11)	51.4 (1.32)	47.6 (1.26)	46.5 (2.10)	—	† (†)	† (†)	† (†)	† (†)	† (†)	† (†)
Rural	—	55.4 (5.36)	52.2 (4.51)	50.2 (1.91)	45.3 (2.35)	—	† (†)	† (†)	† (†)	† (†)	† (†)	† (†)
On school property[5]												
Total	5.2 (0.39)	5.6 (0.34)	4.9 (0.39)	4.9 (0.28)	5.2 (0.46)	4.3 (0.30)	4.1 (0.32)	4.5 (0.29)	5.1 (0.33)	† (†)	† (†)	† (†)
Sex												
Male	6.2 (0.39)	7.2 (0.66)	6.1 (.54)	6.1 (0.43)	6.0 (0.61)	5.3 (0.39)	4.6 (0.35)	5.3 (0.41)	5.4 (0.43)	† (†)	† (†)	† (†)
Female	4.2 (0.54)	3.6 (0.37)	3.6 (.39)	3.8 (0.39)	4.2 (0.41)	3.3 (0.32)	3.6 (0.37)	3.6 (0.34)	4.7 (0.35)	† (†)	† (†)	† (†)
Race/ethnicity												
White	4.6 (0.44)	4.8 (0.42)	4.8 (.55)	4.2 (0.26)	3.9 (0.45)	3.8 (0.38)	3.2 (0.35)	3.3 (0.27)	4.0 (0.38)	† (†)	† (†)	† (†)
Black	6.9 (0.98)	5.6 (0.72)	4.3 (.52)	5.3 (0.65)	5.8 (0.80)	3.2 (0.45)	3.4 (0.63)	5.4 (0.59)	5.1 (0.50)	† (†)	† (†)	† (†)
Hispanic	6.8 (0.84)	8.2 (0.96)	7.0 (.88)	7.0 (0.71)	7.6 (1.08)	7.7 (1.04)	7.5 (0.86)	6.9 (0.70)	7.3 (0.68)	† (†)	† (†)	† (†)
Asian[2]	— (†)	— (†)	2.0 (.42)	6.8 (1.42)	5.6 (1.55)	1.3! (0.62)	4.4 (1.17)	2.9 (0.65)	3.5! (1.21)	† (†)	† (†)	† (†)
Pacific Islander[2]	— (†)	— (†)	6.7 (1.59)	12.4 (3.50)	8.5! (3.29)	‡ (†)	‡ (†)	10.0 (2.34)	8.3! (3.61)	† (†)	† (†)	† (†)
American Indian/Alaska Native	6.7! (3.06)	8.6! (4.15)	‡ (†)	8.2 (1.69)	7.1! (2.61)	6.2! (2.05)	5.0 (0.89)	4.3! (1.58)	20.9 (4.15)	† (†)	† (†)	† (†)
Two or more races[2]	—	—	5.2 (1.09)	7.0! (2.36)	13.3 (2.93)	3.5 (1.02)	5.4 (1.25)	6.7 (1.37)	5.8 (1.32)	† (†)	† (†)	† (†)
Grade												
9th	5.2 (0.38)	5.9 (0.83)	4.4 (.60)	5.3 (0.47)	5.1 (0.69)	3.7 (0.48)	3.4 (0.43)	4.4 (0.37)	5.4 (0.56)	† (†)	† (†)	† (†)
10th	4.7 (0.43)	4.6 (0.71)	5.0 (.67)	5.1 (0.45)	5.6 (0.60)	4.5 (0.45)	4.1 (0.50)	4.8 (0.46)	4.4 (0.51)	† (†)	† (†)	† (†)
11th	5.2 (0.80)	6.0 (0.86)	4.7 (.57)	4.7 (0.45)	5.0 (0.57)	4.0 (0.47)	4.2 (0.54)	4.6 (0.44)	5.2 (0.56)	† (†)	† (†)	† (†)
12th	5.5 (0.64)	5.9 (0.66)	5.0 (.89)	4.3 (0.44)	4.5 (0.68)	4.8 (0.57)	4.8 (0.55)	4.1 (0.44)	5.1 (0.48)	† (†)	† (†)	† (†)
Urbanicity[4]												
Urban	—	6.4 (0.85)	5.0 (.60)	5.4 (0.61)	6.1 (0.94)	—	† (†)	† (†)	† (†)	† (†)	† (†)	† (†)
Suburban	—	5.2 (0.43)	4.6 (.61)	4.9 (0.37)	4.8 (0.54)	—	† (†)	† (†)	† (†)	† (†)	† (†)	† (†)
Rural	—	5.3 (0.55)	5.6 (.67)	4.0 (0.83)	4.7 (0.49)	—	† (†)	† (†)	† (†)	† (†)	† (†)	† (†)

—Not available.
†Not applicable.
!Interpret data with caution. The coefficient of variation (CV) for this estimate is between 30 and 50 percent.
‡Reporting standards not met. The coefficient of variation (CV) for this estimate is 50 percent or greater.
[1]The term "anywhere" is not used in the Youth Risk Behavior Survey (YRBS) questionnaire; students were simply asked how many days during the previous 30 days they had at least one drink of alcohol.
[2]Before 1999, Asian students and Pacific Islander students were not categorized separately, and students could not be classified as Two or more races. Because the response categories changed in 1999, caution should be used in comparing data on race from 1993 and 1997 with data from later years.
[3]Students were asked which sexual orientation—"heterosexual (straight)," "gay or lesbian," "bisexual," or "not sure"—best described them.
[4]Refers to the Standard Metropolitan Statistical Area (MSA) status of the respondent's household as defined by the U.S. Census Bureau. Categories include "central city of an MSA (Urban)," "In MSA but not in central city (Suburban)," and "not MSA (Rural)."
[5]In the question about drinking alcohol at school, "on school property" was not defined for survey respondents. Data on alcohol use at school were not collected from 2013 onward.
NOTE: Race categories exclude persons of Hispanic ethnicity.
SOURCE: Centers for Disease Control and Prevention, Division of Adolescent and School Health, Youth Risk Behavior Surveillance System (YRBSS), 1993 through 2017. (This table was prepared July 2018.)

Table 232.40. Percentage of students in grades 9–12 who reported using marijuana at least one time during the previous 30 days, by location and selected student characteristics: Selected years, 1993 through 2017

[Standard errors appear in parentheses]

Location and student characteristic	1993	1997	1999	2001	2003	2005	2007	2009	2011	2013	2015	2017
	2	3	4	5	6	7	8	9	10	11	12	13
Anywhere (including on school property)[1]												
Total	17.7 (1.22)	26.2 (1.11)	26.7 (1.30)	23.9 (0.77)	22.4 (1.09)	20.2 (0.84)	19.7 (0.97)	20.8 (0.70)	23.1 (0.80)	23.4 (1.08)	21.7 (1.22)	19.8 (0.84)
Sex												
Male	20.6 (1.61)	30.2 (1.46)	30.8 (1.92)	27.9 (0.81)	25.1 (1.25)	22.1 (0.98)	22.4 (1.02)	23.4 (0.80)	25.9 (1.01)	25.0 (1.14)	23.2 (1.46)	20.0 (0.89)
Female	14.6 (1.02)	21.4 (1.04)	22.6 (0.96)	20.0 (0.87)	19.3 (0.96)	18.2 (0.99)	17.0 (1.13)	17.9 (0.87)	20.1 (0.95)	21.9 (1.28)	20.1 (1.33)	19.6 (1.14)
Race/ethnicity												
White	17.3 (1.41)	25.0 (1.56)	26.4 (1.59)	24.4 (1.04)	21.7 (1.20)	20.3 (1.11)	19.9 (1.28)	20.7 (0.93)	21.7 (1.09)	20.4 (1.36)	19.9 (1.67)	17.7 (1.12)
Black	18.6 (1.84)	28.2 (1.67)	26.4 (3.49)	21.8 (2.12)	23.9 (1.58)	20.4 (1.11)	21.5 (1.64)	22.2 (1.44)	25.1 (1.35)	28.9 (1.30)	27.1 (1.57)	25.3 (1.24)
Hispanic	19.4 (1.33)	28.6 (2.06)	28.2 (2.29)	24.6 (0.81)	23.8 (1.16)	23.0 (1.22)	18.5 (1.41)	21.6 (1.04)	24.4 (1.27)	27.6 (1.50)	24.5 (1.49)	23.4 (1.85)
Asian[2]	—	—	13.5 (2.04)	10.9 (2.12)	9.5 (2.21)	6.7 (1.64)	9.4 (1.63)	7.5 (1.40)	13.6 (3.75)	16.4 (2.99)	8.2 (1.58)	7.3 (1.79)
Pacific Islander[2]	—	—	33.8 (4.11)	21.9 (4.07)	28.1 (6.47)	12.4! (3.87)	28.7 (6.14)	24.8 (5.50)	31.1 (7.08)	23.4! (7.35)	17.4 (4.88)	16.1 (4.08)
American Indian/Alaska Native	17.4 (4.77)	44.2 (4.31)	36.2 (6.55)	36.4 (5.48)	32.8 (5.29)	30.3 (4.36)	27.4 (5.26)	31.6 (5.26)	47.4 (4.05)	35.5 (6.37)	26.9 (5.20)	29.7 (6.30)
Two or more races[2]	—	—	29.1 (4.00)	31.8 (3.22)	28.3 (5.57)	16.9 (2.43)	20.5 (2.73)	21.7 (2.33)	26.8 (2.10)	28.8 (2.55)	23.5 (2.18)	20.3 (2.27)
Sexual orientation[3]												
Heterosexual	—	(†)	(†)	(†)	(†)	(†)	(†)	(†)	(†)	(†)	20.7 (1.29)	19.1 (0.83)
Gay, lesbian, or bisexual	—	(†)	(†)	(†)	(†)	(†)	(†)	(†)	(†)	(†)	32.0 (1.64)	30.6 (1.68)
Not sure	—	(†)	(†)	(†)	(†)	(†)	(†)	(†)	(†)	(†)	26.0 (2.28)	18.9 (2.76)
Grade												
9th	13.2 (1.10)	23.6 (1.95)	21.7 (1.84)	19.4 (1.25)	18.5 (1.52)	17.4 (1.16)	14.7 (1.02)	15.5 (0.97)	18.0 (1.11)	17.7 (1.13)	15.2 (0.98)	13.1 (1.07)
10th	16.5 (1.79)	25.0 (1.29)	27.8 (2.21)	24.8 (1.12)	22.0 (1.47)	20.2 (1.27)	19.3 (1.12)	21.1 (1.11)	21.6 (1.15)	23.5 (1.89)	20.0 (1.87)	18.7 (0.93)
11th	18.4 (1.77)	29.3 (1.81)	26.7 (2.47)	25.8 (1.33)	24.1 (1.56)	21.0 (1.24)	21.4 (1.49)	23.2 (1.52)	25.5 (1.44)	25.5 (1.37)	24.8 (1.27)	22.6 (1.23)
12th	22.0 (1.40)	26.6 (2.09)	31.5 (2.81)	26.9 (1.77)	25.8 (1.19)	22.8 (1.23)	25.1 (1.96)	24.6 (1.49)	28.0 (1.08)	27.7 (1.58)	27.6 (1.93)	25.7 (1.43)
Urbanicity[4]												
Urban	—	26.8 (1.50)	27.5 (2.32)	25.6 (1.23)	23.4 (1.65)	—	—	—	—	—	—	—
Suburban	—	27.0 (1.05)	26.1 (1.60)	22.5 (0.96)	22.8 (1.90)	—	—	—	—	—	—	—
Rural	—	21.9 (3.23)	28.0 (4.36)	26.2 (2.49)	19.9 (2.80)	—	—	—	—	—	—	—
On school property[5]												
Total	5.6 (0.65)	7.0 (0.52)	7.2 (0.73)	5.4 (0.37)	5.8 (0.68)	4.5 (0.32)	4.5 (0.46)	4.6 (0.35)	5.9 (0.39)	(†)	(†)	(†)
Sex												
Male	7.8 (0.83)	9.0 (0.68)	10.1 (1.30)	8.0 (0.54)	7.6 (0.88)	6.0 (0.44)	5.9 (0.61)	6.3 (0.54)	7.5 (0.56)	(†)	(†)	(†)
Female	3.3 (0.48)	4.6 (0.56)	4.4 (0.40)	2.9 (0.28)	3.7 (0.48)	3.0 (0.31)	3.0 (0.39)	2.8 (0.32)	4.1 (0.32)	(†)	(†)	(†)
Race/ethnicity												
White	5.0 (0.72)	5.8 (0.69)	6.5 (0.84)	4.8 (0.45)	4.5 (0.66)	3.8 (0.41)	4.0 (0.63)	3.8 (0.38)	4.5 (0.42)	(†)	(†)	(†)
Black	7.3 (1.23)	9.1 (1.07)	7.2 (1.10)	6.1 (0.60)	6.6 (0.89)	4.9 (0.65)	5.0 (0.73)	5.6 (0.76)	6.7 (0.77)	(†)	(†)	(†)
Hispanic	7.5 (1.10)	10.4 (1.03)	10.7 (1.21)	7.4 (0.58)	8.2 (0.72)	7.7 (0.76)	5.4 (0.80)	6.5 (0.76)	7.7 (0.54)	(†)	(†)	(†)
Asian[2]	—	—	4.3 (0.71)	4.7! (1.56)	4.3! (1.38)	‡	2.7! (1.06)	2.0 (0.54)	4.5 (1.34)	(†)	(†)	(†)
Pacific Islander[2]	—	—	11.0 (3.21)	6.4! (2.46)	9.1! (3.17)	‡	13.4! (5.38)	9.0 (2.40)	12.5! (4.94)	(†)	(†)	(†)
American Indian/Alaska Native	‡	16.2! (5.56)	‡	21.5! (6.55)	11.4! (4.42)	9.2 (1.85)	8.2 (2.30)	2.9! (1.25)	20.9 (4.05)	(†)	(†)	(†)
Two or more races[2]	—	—	7.8 (1.81)	5.2 (1.24)	11.4! (5.49)	3.6 (0.91)	3.6! (1.08)	5.4 (1.34)	8.1 (1.79)	(†)	(†)	(†)
Grade												
9th	4.4 (0.40)	8.1 (0.90)	6.6 (0.97)	5.5 (0.62)	6.6 (1.03)	5.0 (0.59)	4.0 (0.52)	4.3 (0.38)	5.4 (0.65)	(†)	(†)	(†)
10th	6.5 (0.94)	6.4 (0.73)	7.6 (1.14)	5.8 (0.51)	5.2 (0.70)	4.6 (0.54)	4.8 (0.60)	4.6 (0.50)	6.2 (0.63)	(†)	(†)	(†)
11th	6.5 (1.07)	7.9 (1.17)	7.0 (0.72)	5.1 (0.48)	5.6 (0.71)	4.1 (0.49)	4.1 (0.73)	5.0 (0.55)	6.2 (0.70)	(†)	(†)	(†)
12th	5.1 (0.78)	5.7 (0.61)	7.3 (1.14)	4.9 (0.71)	5.0 (0.75)	4.1 (0.45)	5.1 (0.73)	4.6 (0.49)	5.4 (0.39)	(†)	(†)	(†)
Urbanicity[4]												
Urban	—	8.0 (1.11)	8.5 (1.03)	6.8 (0.56)	6.8 (1.05)	(†)	(†)	(†)	(†)	(†)	(†)	(†)
Suburban	—	7.0 (0.67)	6.4 (1.03)	4.7 (0.46)	6.0 (1.03)	(†)	(†)	(†)	(†)	(†)	(†)	(†)
Rural	—	4.9! (2.02)	8.1 (1.57)	5.3 (0.93)	3.9 (0.64)	(†)	(†)	(†)	(†)	(†)	(†)	(†)

—Not available.
†Not applicable.
!Interpret data with caution. The coefficient of variation (CV) for this estimate is between 30 and 50 percent.
‡Reporting standards not met. The coefficient of variation (CV) for this estimate is 50 percent or greater.
[1]The term "anywhere" is not used in the Youth Risk Behavior Survey (YRBS) questionnaire; students were simply asked how many times during the previous 30 days they had used marijuana.
[2]Before 1999, Asian students and Pacific Islander students were not categorized separately, and students could not be classified as Two or more races. Because the response categories changed in 1999, caution should be used in comparing data on race from 1993, 1995, and 1997 with data from later years.

[3]Students were asked which sexual orientation—"heterosexual (straight)," "gay or lesbian," "bisexual," or "not sure"—best described them.
[4]Refers to the Standard Metropolitan Statistical Area (MSA) status of the respondent's household as defined by the U.S. Census Bureau. Categories include "central city of an MSA (Urban)," "in MSA but not in central city (Suburban)," and "not MSA (Rural)."
[5]In the question about using marijuana at school, "on school property" was not defined for survey respondents. Data on marijuana use at school were not collected from 2013 onward.
NOTE: Race categories exclude persons of Hispanic ethnicity.
SOURCE: Centers for Disease Control and Prevention, Division of Adolescent and School Health, Youth Risk Behavior Surveillance System (YRBSS), 1993 through 2017. (This table was prepared August 2018.)

Table 233.40. Percentage of students suspended and expelled from public elementary and secondary schools, by sex, race/ethnicity, and state: 2013–14

	Percent receiving out-of-school suspensions[1]										Percent expelled[2]									
		Sex		Race/ethnicity[3]								Sex		Race/ethnicity[3]						
State	Total	Male	Female	White	Black	Hispanic	Asian	Pacific Islander[1]	American Indian/Alaska Native	Two or more races	Total	Male	Female	White	Black	Hispanic	Asian	Pacific Islander	American Indian/Alaska Native	Two or more races
1	2	3	4	5	6	7	8	9	10	11	12	13	14	15	16	17	18	19	20	21
United States	**5.28**	**7.25**	**3.20**	**3.43**	**13.68**	**4.54**	**1.11**	**4.53**	**6.74**	**5.26**	**0.22**	**0.32**	**0.12**	**0.20**	**0.44**	**0.15**	**0.03**	**0.12**	**0.37**	**0.31**
Alabama	7.98	10.50	5.30	4.51	15.25	2.97	1.58	4.03	3.87	5.90	0.19	0.28	0.09	0.09	0.36	0.06	0.00	0.14–0.43	0.02–0.05	0.49
Alaska	5.06	7.24	2.72	3.47	8.81	4.80	2.03	6.49	8.48	4.82	0.08	0.13	0.03	0.05	0.21	0.16	0.00	0.03–0.09	0.03–0.09	0.11
Arizona	5.18	7.45	2.78	3.90	11.54	5.50	1.54	4.81	8.90	5.02	0.04	0.06	0.02	0.04	0.07	0.04	0.00–0.01	0.10	0.04	0.05
Arkansas	7.00	9.63	4.25	4.47	17.87	3.82	1.45	3.11	4.83	4.34	0.18	0.25	0.09	0.17	0.23	0.10	0.07	0.04–0.11	0.46	0.10
California	3.99	5.74	2.14	3.25	11.24	4.03	1.18	4.80	7.11	3.43	0.14	0.22	0.06	0.13	0.35	0.14	0.04	0.13	0.26	0.12
Colorado	4.41	6.27	2.45	3.13	11.04	5.84	1.35	3.64	6.80	4.87	0.15	0.24	0.06	0.11	0.41	0.18	0.06	0.35	0.38	0.15
Connecticut	3.94	5.23	2.57	1.99	9.02	6.61	0.82	(†)	6.23	3.31	0.22	0.36	0.08	0.16	0.49	0.27	0.04	0.00	0.26	0.16
Delaware	8.48	10.72	6.05	4.43	15.64	5.83	1.68	6.08	9.18	6.25	0.09	0.12	0.05	0.06	0.15	0.06	0.00	0.00	0.00	0.03–0.09
District of Columbia	12.44	15.52	9.37	0.90	15.98	4.26	1.52	10.00	9.86	3.83	0.15	0.18	0.12	0.01–0.04	0.19	0.04	0.00	0.00	1.41–4.23	—0.09
Florida	5.04	7.06	2.90	3.67	9.89	3.86	1.00	2.92	4.65	4.91	0.01	0.01	#	#	0.01	#	0.00	0.00	0.01–0.03	0.01
Georgia	7.29	9.86	4.59	3.52	13.38	4.46	1.28	6.53	4.57	6.71	0.16	0.23	0.08	0.11	0.26	0.06	0.02	0.86	0.19	0.19
Hawaii	3.47	4.76	2.06	2.54	4.53	2.96	2.05	5.58	6.16	2.22	#	0.01	#	0.00	0.00	0.01–0.02	0.00–0.01	0.00–0.01	0.00	0.00
Idaho	2.57	3.82	1.25	2.37	3.61	3.43	1.27	2.38	4.66	2.33	0.06	0.09	0.02	0.05	0.13	0.10	0.03–0.08	0.00	0.22	0.02–0.05
Illinois	6.83	9.02	4.51	2.88	21.91	5.45	0.87	3.56	4.57	5.78	0.13	0.18	0.08	0.11	0.35	0.05	0.02	0.00	0.18	0.19
Indiana	6.79	9.35	4.09	4.50	20.58	6.21	1.44	2.78	5.93	10.00	0.51	0.69	0.31	0.38	1.26	0.53	0.10	0.70	0.63	0.53
Iowa	2.60	3.68	1.45	1.96	11.03	2.99	1.08	2.57	4.27	4.66	0.04	0.06	0.01	0.03	0.09	0.04	0.01–0.03	0.00	0.00	0.03
Kansas	4.04	5.73	2.24	2.82	14.03	4.40	1.22	3.41	6.21	5.51	0.16	0.24	0.08	0.13	0.34	0.16	0.05	0.12–0.35	0.32	0.29
Kentucky	4.87	6.91	2.71	4.08	12.21	3.08	0.90	3.12	5.67	5.82	0.05	0.08	0.02	0.05	0.06	0.04	0.00	0.00	0.12–0.35	0.06
Louisiana	8.38	11.08	5.54	4.70	12.61	4.22	1.83	5.68	6.44	5.90	0.62	0.89	0.34	0.31	1.00	0.17	0.07	0.22–0.66	0.49	0.36
Maine	3.45	4.96	1.84	3.36	6.62	4.56	1.26	2.08	3.51	2.75	0.11	0.16	0.05	0.11	0.14	0.14	0.00	0.00	0.00	0.25
Maryland	5.19	6.95	3.34	2.89	9.26	3.34	0.76	2.69	5.86	4.56	0.09	0.13	0.05	0.02	0.20	0.03	0.00–0.01	0.08–0.24	0.16	0.04
Massachusetts	4.28	5.92	2.55	2.61	10.46	8.60	1.26	2.13	5.94	5.34	0.03	0.05	0.02	0.03	0.06	0.04	0.00–0.01	0.00	0.04–0.13	0.09
Michigan	7.34	9.91	4.62	4.51	19.23	6.60	1.69	3.22	7.96	7.48	0.14	0.21	0.07	0.12	0.27	0.14	0.04	0.00	0.12	0.12
Minnesota	3.30	4.57	1.95	2.00	12.29	4.04	1.11	2.69	9.50	4.00	0.10	0.15	0.05	0.08	0.21	0.10	0.03	0.00	0.20	0.17
Mississippi	9.67	12.83	6.35	4.77	14.80	4.08	1.76	3.85	6.03	3.77	0.29	0.42	0.14	0.15	0.43	0.06	0.12	0.00	0.09–0.27	0.45
Missouri	5.74	7.86	3.48	3.87	17.02	4.38	1.62	2.90	5.96	5.33	0.35	0.45	0.23	0.34	0.37	0.51	0.01–0.02	0.41	0.47	0.45
Montana	3.66	5.12	2.10	2.54	4.44	2.85	1.14	1.99	11.84	2.26	0.14	0.19	0.09	0.07	0.07–0.21	0.11	0.00	0.00	0.52	0.61
Nebraska	4.27	5.95	2.48	2.88	16.20	4.68	1.83	3.26	9.23	6.82	0.30	0.43	0.17	0.17	1.37	0.35	0.17	0.00	0.64	0.54
Nevada	4.60	6.38	2.70	3.52	10.87	4.42	1.55	3.33	6.47	4.41	0.42	0.61	0.21	0.22	1.23	0.43	0.14	0.24	0.31	0.38
New Hampshire	4.88	6.95	2.67	4.29	19.21	14.21	2.22	7.51	7.30	3.71	0.02	0.03	0.01	0.02	0.00	0.00	0.00	0.00	0.00	0.00
New Jersey	4.44	5.95	2.84	2.21	12.79	5.59	0.80	1.26	3.70	3.10	0.01	0.02	0.01	0.01	0.04	0.01	#	0.00	0.00	0.03
New Mexico	6.25	8.20	4.19	4.82	10.22	6.78	2.83	2.52	6.03	8.55	0.58	0.80	0.35	0.36	1.24	0.69	0.33	0.00	0.29	1.13
New York	3.22	4.36	2.01	2.68	7.05	2.29	0.49	1.20	4.00	4.23	0.09	0.13	0.05	0.11	0.13	0.05	0.01	0.00	0.13	0.14
North Carolina	6.67	9.19	4.00	3.77	13.42	4.92	1.17	4.68	11.57	7.01	0.06	0.08	0.03	0.03	0.11	0.04	0.01	0.06–0.17	0.09	0.08
North Dakota	2.21	3.09	1.27	1.49	5.21	2.50	0.74	0.31–0.93	8.13	0.50	0.09	0.13	0.04	0.03	0.61	0.17	0.00	0.00	0.41	0.00
Ohio	7.14	9.71	4.42	4.68	18.70	6.79	1.47	3.47	7.73	9.24	1.76	2.49	0.99	1.53	2.83	1.31	0.28	1.84	2.58	2.23
Oklahoma	5.64	7.86	3.29	4.33	16.99	5.75	1.22	4.22	4.42	4.29	1.07	1.46	0.65	0.72	3.68	0.98	0.12	0.63	0.84	1.29
Oregon	4.12	6.03	2.11	3.86	9.24	4.46	1.22	4.18	6.45	4.52	0.20	0.31	0.09	0.20	0.26	0.22	0.04	0.23	0.45	0.21
Pennsylvania	5.62	7.52	3.61	3.01	17.13	7.53	1.28	4.23	4.43	7.30	0.11	0.16	0.06	0.08	0.19	0.18	0.01	0.08–0.23	0.21	0.17
Rhode Island	6.24	8.57	3.75	4.28	12.41	9.29	2.93	4.69	9.33	6.95	0.04	0.06	0.03	0.04	0.04	0.05	0.00	0.00	0.08–0.23	0.11

See notes at end of table.

Table 233.40. Percentage of students suspended and expelled from public elementary and secondary schools, by sex, race/ethnicity, and state: 2013–14—Continued

	Percent receiving out-of-school suspensions[1]										Percent expelled[2]										
		Sex		Race/ethnicity[3]								Sex		Race/ethnicity[3]						
State	Total	Male	Female	White	Black	Hispanic	Asian	Pacific Islander[4]	American Indian/ Alaska Native	Two or more races	Total	Male	Female	White	Black	Hispanic	Asian	Pacific Islander	American Indian/ Alaska Native	Two or more races
1	2	3	4	5	6	7	8	9	10	11	12	13	14	15	16	17	18	19	20	21
South Carolina	10.29	13.68	6.72	6.17	17.88	5.88	1.94	5.43	9.22	8.56	0.38	0.57	0.19	0.23	0.68	0.15	0.09	0.00	0.65	0.28
South Dakota	2.70	3.77	1.55	1.93	7.03	3.95	1.43	0.76–2.27	6.20	2.88	0.03	0.04	0.01	0.01	0.11	0.02–0.05	0.00	0.76–2.27	0.09	0.00
Tennessee	6.70	8.97	4.30	3.55	17.10	4.22	1.69	2.87	5.19	4.52	0.43	0.63	0.22	0.25	1.01	0.29	0.08	0.40	0.22	0.34
Texas	4.77	6.53	2.91	2.49	12.14	4.57	0.91	3.60	4.38	3.51	0.15	0.23	0.07	0.12	0.30	0.14	0.03	0.11	0.36	0.12
Utah	1.70	2.53	0.82	1.32	4.29	3.00	1.19	2.52	5.17	1.72	0.02	0.04	0.01	0.02	0.05	0.04	0.07	0.01–0.03	0.07	0.01–0.02
Vermont	3.88	5.48	2.17	3.79	6.59	3.49	0.68	0.90–2.70	12.60	2.83	0.05	0.08	0.03	0.05	0.27	0.00	0.00	0.00	0.00	0.00
Virginia	5.68	7.80	3.43	3.74	12.72	3.40	0.82	3.81	4.65	4.95	0.06	0.10	0.03	0.05	0.11	0.07	0.01	0.05–0.16	0.15	0.08
Washington	4.58	6.68	2.34	3.89	10.52	5.35	1.44	6.42	9.31	5.34	0.33	0.49	0.15	0.26	0.55	0.45	0.11	0.48	0.84	0.39
West Virginia	7.30	10.27	4.12	7.11	13.60	4.35	1.04	3.60	4.53	5.72	0.17	0.27	0.06	0.17	0.33	0.15	0.05–0.16	0.00	0.32–0.97	0.07
Wisconsin	3.96	5.46	2.36	2.27	17.03	4.22	0.76	3.01	6.53	4.82	0.12	0.18	0.06	0.08	0.53	0.11	0.02	0.00	0.21	0.07
Wyoming	3.12	4.61	1.51	2.92	6.05	3.79	1.69	3.17	5.18	3.03	0.11	0.19	0.03	0.10	0.09–0.28	0.15	0.00	0.00	0.24	0.06–0.17

#Rounds to zero.
[1]An out-of-school suspension is an instance in which a student is temporarily removed from his or her regular school for disciplinary purposes for at least half a day (but less than the remainder of the school year) to another setting (e.g., home or behavior center).
[2]Expulsions are actions taken by a local education agency that result in the removal of a student from his or her regular school for disciplinary purposes, with or without the continuation of educational services, for the remainder of the school year or longer in accordance with local education agency policy. Expulsions also include removals resulting from violations of the Gun Free Schools Act that are modified to less than 365 days.
[3]Data by race/ethnicity exclude students with disabilities served only under Section 504 (not receiving services under IDEA).

[4]Connecticut Pacific Islander data are suppressed and excluded from the Pacific Islander U.S. total pending further data quality review.
NOTE: The percentage of students receiving a disciplinary action is calculated by dividing the cumulative number of students receiving that type of disciplinary action for the entire 2013–14 school year by the student enrollment based on a count of students taken on a single day between September 27 and December 31. Percentages based on suspension or expulsion counts of between 1 and 3 students are displayed as ranges to protect student privacy. Race categories exclude persons of Hispanic ethnicity.
SOURCE: U.S. Department of Education, Office for Civil Rights, Civil Rights Data Collection, "2013–14 Discipline Estimations by Discipline Type" and "2013–14 Estimations for Enrollment." (This table was prepared January 2018.)

Table 233.50. Percentage of public schools with various safety and security measures: Selected years, 1999–2000 through 2017–18

[Standard errors appear in parentheses]

School safety and security measures	1999–2000		2003–04		2005–06		2007–08		2009–10		2013–14[1]		2015–16		2017–18	
1	2		3		4		5		6		7		8		9	
Controlled access during school hours																
Buildings (e.g., locked or monitored doors, loading docks)[2]	74.6	(1.35)	83.0	(1.04)	84.9	(0.89)	89.5	(0.80)	91.7	(0.80)	93.3	(0.95)	94.1	(0.64)	95.4	(0.52)
Grounds (e.g., locked or monitored gates)	33.7	(1.26)	36.2	(1.08)	41.1	(1.25)	42.6	(1.41)	46.0	(1.26)	42.7	(1.53)	49.9	(1.53)	50.8	(1.38)
Visitors required to sign or check in and wear badges[3]	96.6	(0.54)	98.3	(0.40)	97.6	(0.42)	98.7	(0.37)	99.3	(0.27)	98.6	(0.49)	93.5	(0.69)	94.6	(0.65)
Classrooms equipped with locks so that doors can be locked from inside	—	(†)	—	(†)	—	(†)	—	(†)	—	(†)	—	(†)	66.7	(1.34)	64.8	(1.01)
Student dress, IDs, and school supplies																
Required students to wear uniforms	11.8	(0.82)	13.8	(0.85)	13.8	(0.78)	17.5	(0.70)	18.9	(1.02)	20.4	(1.27)	21.5	(1.36)	19.8	(0.87)
Enforced a strict dress code	47.4	(1.50)	55.1	(1.24)	55.3	(1.18)	54.8	(1.20)	56.9	(1.56)	58.5	(1.60)	53.1	(1.22)	48.8	(1.32)
Required students to wear badges or picture IDs	3.9	(0.32)	6.4	(0.64)	6.2	(0.47)	7.6	(0.60)	6.9	(0.57)	8.9	(0.81)	7.0	(0.53)	9.2	(0.60)
Required faculty and staff to wear badges or picture IDs	25.4	(1.39)	48.0	(1.21)	47.9	(1.12)	58.3	(1.37)	62.9	(1.14)	68.0	(1.65)	67.9	(1.36)	69.9	(1.18)
Required clear book bags or banned book bags on school grounds	5.9	(0.50)	6.2	(0.63)	6.4	(0.43)	6.0	(0.48)	5.5	(0.53)	6.3	(0.81)	3.9	(0.44)	3.5	(0.42)
Provided school lockers to students	46.5	(1.07)	49.5	(1.24)	50.5	(1.08)	48.9	(1.17)	52.1	(1.10)	49.9	(1.35)	50.4	(1.24)	49.0	(1.25)
Drug testing																
Students participating in athletics or other extracurricular activities[4]	—	(†)	4.3	(0.44)	5.0	(0.46)	6.6	(0.53)	6.2	(0.51)	6.7	(0.61)	7.7	(0.57)	8.9	(0.57)
Athletes	—	(†)	4.2	(0.44)	5.0	(0.46)	6.4	(0.48)	6.0	(0.52)	6.6	(0.59)	7.2	(0.55)	—	(†)
Students in extracurricular activities (other than athletes)	—	(†)	2.6	(0.37)	3.4	(0.32)	4.5	(0.51)	4.6	(0.47)	4.3	(0.47)	6.0	(0.53)	—	(†)
Any other students	—	(†)	—	(†)	3.0	(0.34)	3.0	(0.42)	3.0	(0.26)	3.5	(0.44)	—	(†)	—	(†)
Metal detectors, dogs, and sweeps																
Random metal detector checks on students	7.2	(0.54)	5.6	(0.55)	4.9	(0.40)	5.3	(0.37)	5.2	(0.42)	4.2	(0.48)	4.5	(0.48)	4.9	(0.49)
Metal detector checks on students every day[5]	0.9	(0.16)	1.1	(0.16)	1.1	(0.18)	1.3	(0.20)	1.4	(0.24)	2.0	(0.40)	1.8	(0.32)	2.2	(0.35)
Random sweeps (e.g., locker checks, dog sniffs) for contraband (e.g., drugs or weapons)[6]	25.3	(0.77)	26.6	(0.73)	28.0	(0.89)	26.3	(0.77)	27.7	(0.86)	28.2	(1.02)	28.2	(0.89)	27.4	(0.88)
Random dog sniffs to check for drugs	20.6	(0.75)	21.3	(0.77)	23.0	(0.79)	21.5	(0.59)	22.9	(0.71)	24.1	(0.97)	24.6	(0.85)	—	(†)
Random sweeps (not including dog sniffs) for contraband	11.8	(0.54)	12.8	(0.58)	13.1	(0.76)	11.4	(0.71)	12.1	(0.68)	11.4	(0.86)	11.9	(0.78)	—	(†)
Communication systems and technology																
Provided telephones in most classrooms	44.6	(1.80)	60.8	(1.48)	66.9	(1.30)	71.6	(1.16)	74.0	(1.13)	78.7	(1.34)	79.3	(1.14)	—	(†)
Provided electronic notification system for schoolwide emergency	—	(†)	—	(†)	—	(†)	43.2	(1.26)	63.1	(1.40)	81.6	(1.12)	73.0	(1.35)	71.6	(1.17)
Provided structured anonymous threat reporting system[7]	—	(†)	—	(†)	—	(†)	31.2	(1.22)	35.9	(1.19)	46.5	(1.63)	43.9	(1.58)	49.3	(1.32)
Had silent alarms directly connected to law enforcement	—	(†)	—	(†)	—	(†)	—	(†)	—	(†)	—	(†)	27.1	(1.23)	29.1	(1.15)
Used security cameras to monitor the school	19.4	(0.88)	36.0	(1.28)	42.8	(1.29)	55.0	(1.37)	61.1	(1.16)	75.1	(1.31)	80.6	(0.96)	83.5	(1.09)
Provided two-way radios to any staff	—	(†)	71.2	(1.18)	70.9	(1.22)	73.1	(1.15)	73.3	(1.33)	74.2	(1.42)	73.3	(1.22)	77.8	(1.06)
Limited access to social networking sites from school computers	—	(†)	—	(†)	—	(†)	—	(†)	93.4	(0.59)	91.9	(0.80)	89.1	(0.88)	—	(†)
Prohibited non-academic use of cell phones or smartphones during school hours[8]	—	(†)	—	(†)	—	(†)	—	(†)	90.9	(0.67)	75.9	(1.07)	65.8	(1.36)	70.3	(1.30)

—Not available.
†Not applicable.
[1]Data for 2013–14 were collected using the Fast Response Survey System (FRSS), while data for all other years were collected using the School Survey on Crime and Safety (SSOCS). The 2013–14 FRSS survey was designed to allow comparisons with SSOCS data. However, all respondents to the 2013–14 survey could choose either to complete the survey on paper (and mail it back) or to complete the survey online, whereas all respondents to SSOCS had only the option of completing a paper survey prior to 2017–18, when SSOCS experimented with offering an online option to some respondents. The 2013–14 FRSS survey also relied on a smaller sample than SSOCS. The FRSS survey's smaller sample size and difference in survey administration may have impacted the 2013–14 results.
[2]Prior to 2017–18, the examples of controlled access to buildings included only "locked or monitored doors" and did not include loading docks.
[3]Prior to 2015–16, the questionnaire asked if visitors were required "to sign or check in" and did not include the requirement to wear badges.
[4]In the 2017–18 questionnaire, a single item asked about drug testing "for students participating in athletics or other extracurricular activities." Prior to 2017–18, the questionnaire included one item about testing for athletes, followed by a separate item about testing for students in other extracurricular activities. For years prior to 2017–18, schools are included in this row if they answered "yes" to either or both of these items; each school is counted only once in this row, even if it answered "yes" to both items.

[5]The wording of this item was revised in 2015–16. Prior to 2015–16, the item asked whether students were required "to pass through metal detectors each day."
[6]The 2017–18 questionnaire included only a single item about random sweeps for contraband, and it provided locker checks and dog sniffs as examples of types of sweeps. Prior to 2017–18, the questionnaire included one item about dog sniffs for drugs, followed by a separate item about sweeps not including dog sniffs. For years prior to 2017–18, schools are included in this row if they answered "yes" to either or both of these items; each school is counted only once in this row, even if it answered "yes" to both items.
[7]For example, a system for reporting threats through online submission, telephone hotline, or written submission via drop box.
[8]Prior to 2017–18, the questionnaire asked about prohibiting the "use of cell phones and text messaging devices during school hours." It did not refer to "nonacademic" use or "smartphones."
NOTE: Responses were provided by the principal or the person most knowledgeable about crime and safety issues at the school.
SOURCE: U.S. Department of Education, National Center for Education Statistics, 1999–2000, 2003–04, 2005–06, 2007–08, 2009–10, 2015–16, and 2017–18 School Survey on Crime and Safety (SSOCS), 2000, 2004, 2006, 2008, 2010, 2016, and 2018; and Fast Response Survey System (FRSS), "School Safety and Discipline: 2013–14," FRSS 106, 2014. (This table was prepared August 2019.)

Table 234.10. Age range for compulsory school attendance and special education services, and policies on year-round schools and kindergarten programs, by state: Selected years, 2000 through 2018

State	Compulsory attendance							Compulsory special education services, 2004[1]	Year-round schools, 2008		Kindergarten programs, 2018		
	2000	2002	2004	2006	2010	2015	2017		Has policy on year-round schools	Has districts with year-round schools	School districts required to offer		Attendance required
											Program	Full-day program	
1	2	3	4	5	6	7	8	9	10	11	12	13	14
Alabama	7 to 16	7 to 16	7 to 16[2]	7 to 16	7 to 17	6 to 17[3]	6 to 17[3]	6 to 21		Yes	X	X	
Alaska	7 to 16	7 to 16	7 to 16[2]	7 to 16	7 to 16	7 to 16[2]	7 to 16[2]	3 to 22		Yes			
Arizona	6 to 16[2]	6 to 16[2]	6 to 16[2]	6 to 16[2]	6 to 16[2]	6 to 16[2]	6 to 16[2]	3 to 21	—	—	X		
Arkansas	5 to 17[2,3]	5 to 17[2,3]	5 to 17[2,3]	5 to 17[2,3]	5 to 17[2,3]	5 to 18	5 to 18	5 to 21	X	Yes	X	X	X
California	6 to 18[2]	6 to 18	6 to 18	6 to 18	6 to 18	6 to 18	6 to 18	Birth to 21[4]	X	Yes	X		
Colorado	—	—	7 to 16	7 to 16	6 to 17	6 to 17	6 to 17	3 to 21		Yes	X		
Connecticut	7 to 16	7 to 18[2]	7 to 18[2]	5 to 18[3]	5 to 18[3]	5 to 18[3]	5 to 18[3]	3 to 21		—	X		X
Delaware	5 to 16	5 to 16	5 to 16[2]	5 to 16	5 to 16	5 to 16	5 to 16	Birth to 20		Yes	X	X	X
District of Columbia	—	5 to 18	5 to 18	5 to 18	5 to 18	5 to 18	5 to 18	—	—	X	X	X	
Florida	6 to 16[5]	6 to 16[5]	6 to 16[5]	6 to 16[5]	6 to 16[5]	6 to 16	6 to 16	3 to 21	X	Yes	X		
Georgia	6 to 16	6 to 16	6 to 16	6 to 16	6 to 16	6 to 16	6 to 16	Birth to 21[6]		Yes	X		
Hawaii	6 to 18	6 to 18	6 to 18	6 to 18	6 to 18	5 to 18	5 to 18	Birth to 19		([7])	X	X	X
Idaho	7 to 16	7 to 16	7 to 16	7 to 16	7 to 16	7 to 16	7 to 16	3 to 21		Yes	X		
Illinois	7 to 16	7 to 16	7 to 17	7 to 17	7 to 17	6 to 17	6 to 17	3 to 21	X	Yes	X	([8])	
Indiana	7 to 16	7 to 16	7 to 16	7 to 18[2]	7 to 18[2]	7 to 18	7 to 18	3 to 22		Yes	X		
Iowa	6 to 16[2]	6 to 16[2]	6 to 16	6 to 16	6 to 16	6 to 16[9]	6 to 16[9]	Birth to 21	X	Yes	X		([10])
Kansas	7 to 18[2]	7 to 18[2]	7 to 18[2]	7 to 18[2]	7 to 18[2]	7 to 18	7 to 18	3 to 21[11]		—	X		
Kentucky	6 to 16	6 to 16	6 to 16[2]	6 to 16	6 to 16	6 to 18[12]	6 to 18	Birth to 21		Yes	X		
Louisiana	7 to 17	7 to 17	7 to 17[2]	7 to 18[2]	7 to 18[2]	7 to 18	7 to 18	3 to 21[13]		Yes	X	X	X[14]
Maine	7 to 17	7 to 17	7 to 17[2]	7 to 17[2]	7 to 17[2]	7 to 17	7 to 17	5 to 19[13,15]		—	X		([10])
Maryland	5 to 16	5 to 16	5 to 16	5 to 16	5 to 16[3]	5 to 17	5 to 18	Birth to 21	X	—	X	X	X
Massachusetts	6 to 16	6 to 16	6 to 16	6 to 16[2]	6 to 16[2]	6 to 16	6 to 16[16]	3 to 21[6]	([17])	—	X		([10])
Michigan	6 to 16	6 to 16	6 to 16	6 to 16	6 to 18	6 to 18	6 to 18	Birth to 25	X	Yes			
Minnesota	7 to 18[2]	7 to 16	7 to 16	7 to 16[2]	7 to 16[2]	7 to 17	7 to 17	Birth to 21	X	Yes			
Mississippi	6 to 17	6 to 17	6 to 16	6 to 16	6 to 17	6 to 17	6 to 17	Birth to 20		—	X	X	([10])
Missouri	7 to 16	7 to 16	7 to 16	7 to 16	7 to 17	7 to 17[2,3]	7 to 17[2,3]	Birth to 20		Yes[18]	X		
Montana	7 to 16[2]	7 to 16[2]	7 to 16[2]	7 to 16[2]	7 to 16[2]	7 to 16[2]	7 to 16	3 to 18[13]		—	X	([8])	
Nebraska	7 to 16	7 to 16	6 to 18	6 to 18	6 to 18	6 to 18	6 to 18	Birth to 20		Yes	X		
Nevada	7 to 17	7 to 17	7 to 17	7 to 17	7 to 18[2]	7 to 18	7 to 18	Birth to 21[4]		Yes	X		X[14]
New Hampshire	6 to 16	6 to 16	6 to 16	6 to 16	6 to 18	6 to 18	6 to 18	3 to 21		—			
New Jersey	6 to 16	6 to 16	6 to 16	6 to 16	6 to 16	6 to 16	6 to 16	5 to 21		—		([19])	([19])
New Mexico	5 to 18	5 to 18	5 to 18[2]	5 to 18[2]	5 to 18[2]	5 to 18	5 to 18	3 to 21	X	Yes	X		X
New York	6 to 16[2]	6 to 16	6 to 16	6 to 16[20]	6 to 16[20]	6 to 16[20]	6 to 16[20]	Birth to 20		—		([20])	([20])
North Carolina	7 to 16	7 to 16	7 to 16	7 to 16	7 to 16	7 to 16	7 to 16	5 to 20	X	Yes	X	X	
North Dakota	7 to 16	7 to 16	7 to 16	7 to 16	7 to 16	7 to 16	7 to 16	3 to 21		No	X		
Ohio	6 to 18	6 to 18	6 to 18	6 to 18	6 to 18	6 to 18	6 to 18	3 to 21	X	—	X		X
Oklahoma	5 to 18	5 to 18	5 to 18	5 to 18	5 to 18	5 to 18	5 to 18	Birth to 21[13]		Yes	X	X	X
Oregon	7 to 18	7 to 18	7 to 18[2]	7 to 18	7 to 18	7 to 18	6 to 18	3 to 20		Yes	X		
Pennsylvania	8 to 17	8 to 17	8 to 17[2]	8 to 17[2]	8 to 17[2]	8 to 17	8 to 17	6 to 21	X[18]	—[18]			
Rhode Island	6 to 16	6 to 16	6 to 16	6 to 16	6 to 16	6 to 18[2]	5 to 18[2]	3 to 21		—	X	X	X
South Carolina	5 to 16	5 to 16	5 to 16	5 to 17[3]	5 to 17[3]	5 to 17	5 to 17	3 to 21[21]		—	X		X
South Dakota	6 to 16	6 to 16	6 to 16	6 to 16	6 to 18[2]	6 to 18[2]	6 to 18[2]	Birth to 21	X	—	X		X[22]
Tennessee	6 to 17	6 to 17	6 to 17	6 to 17[3]	6 to 17[3]	6 to 18	6 to 18	3 to 21[4]	X	Yes	X	X	X
Texas	6 to 18	6 to 18	6 to 18	6 to 18	6 to 18	6 to 18	6 to 19	3 to 21	X	Yes	X		
Utah	6 to 18	6 to 18	6 to 18	6 to 18	6 to 18	6 to 18	6 to 18	3 to 22		Yes	X		
Vermont	7 to 16	6 to 16	6 to 16	6 to 16[2]	6 to 16[2]	6 to 16[2]	6 to 16[2]	3 to 21		—[18]	X		
Virginia	5 to 18	5 to 18	5 to 18	5 to 18[2]	5 to 18[2,3]	5 to 18	5 to 18	2 to 21	X	Yes	X		X
Washington	8 to 17[2]	8 to 17[2]	8 to 16[2]	8 to 18	8 to 18	8 to 18	8 to 18	3 to 21[21]		Yes	X	X	X
West Virginia	6 to 16	6 to 16	6 to 16	6 to 16	6 to 17	6 to 17	6 to 17	5 to 21[23]	X	Yes	X	X	X[24]
Wisconsin	6 to 18	6 to 18	6 to 18	6 to 18	6 to 18	6 to 18	6 to 18	3 to 21		Yes	X		
Wyoming	6 to 16[2]	6 to 16[2]	7 to 16[2]	7 to 16[2]	7 to 16[2]	7 to 16[2]	7 to 16[2]	3 to 21			X	([25])	([10])

—Not available.
X Denotes that the state has a policy. A blank denotes that the state does not have a policy.
[1] Most states have a provision whereby education is provided up to a certain age or completion of secondary school, whichever comes first.
[2] Child may be exempted from compulsory attendance if he/she meets state requirements for early withdrawal with or without meeting conditions for a diploma or equivalency.
[3] Parent/guardian may delay child's entry until a later age per state law/regulation.
[4] Student may continue in the program if 22nd birthday falls before the end of the school year.
[5] Attendance is compulsory until age 18 for Manatee County students, unless they earn a high school diploma prior to reaching their 18th birthday.
[6] Through age 21 or until child graduates with a high school or special education diploma or equivalent.
[7] Some schools operate on a multitrack system; the schools are open year round, but different cohorts start and end at different times.
[8] District must offer either a half-day or full-day program.
[9] Children enrolled in preschool programs (who must be 4 years old on or before September 15) are considered to be of compulsory school attendance age.
[10] Not specified in statute, rules, or regulations.
[11] To be determined by rules and regulations adopted by the state board.
[12] All districts adopted a policy to raise the upper compulsory school age from 16 to 18. The policy took effect for most districts in the 2015-16 school year.
[13] Children from birth through age 2 are eligible for additional services.
[14] Attendance is required unless the student otherwise satisfactorily passes an academic readiness screening upon enrollment in grade 1.
[15] Must be age 5 before October 15 and not age 20 before start of school year.
[16] Each school committee is permitted to establish its own minimum age for school attendance, provided that it is not older than the mandatory minimum age established by the state.
[17] Policies about year-round schools are decided locally.
[18] State did not participate in 2008 online survey. Data are from 2006.

[19] Abbott Districts are required to offer full-day kindergarten and students are required to attend.
[20] Local boards of education can require school attendance until age 17 unless employed. In Syracuse, New York City, Rochester, Utica, Buffalo, Cohoes, Watervliet, and Yonkers, districts are required to offer full-day kindergarten and children are required to attend full-day kindergarten.
[21] Student may complete school year if 21st birthday occurs while attending school.
[22] All children must attend kindergarten before age 7.
[23] Children with severe disabilities may begin receiving services at age 3.
[24] Children must attend in districts that offer kindergarten.
[25] School districts must establish and maintain relationships with a district that offers full-day kindergarten.
NOTE: The Education of the Handicapped Act (EHA) Amendments of 1986 make it mandatory for all states receiving EHA funds to serve all 3- to 18-year-old disabled children.
SOURCE: Council of Chief State School Officers, *Key State Education Policies on PK–12 Education*, 2000, 2002, 2004, 2006, and 2008; Education Commission of the States (ECS), ECS StateNotes, *Compulsory School Age Requirements*, retrieved August 9, 2010, from http://www.ecs.org/clearinghouse/86/62/8662.pdf; ECS StateNotes, *Special Education: State Special Education Definitions, Ages Served*, retrieved August 9, 2010, from http://www.ecs.org/clearinghouse/52/29/5229.pdf; ECS StateNotes, *Compulsory School Age Requirements*, retrieved May 19, 2015, from http://www.ecs.org/clearinghouse/01/18/68/11868.pdf; ECS StateNotes, *Age Requirements for Free and Compulsory Education*, retrieved July 2, 2018, from https://www.ecs.org/age-requirements-for-free-and-compulsory-education/; ECS StateNotes, *Does the state require the district to offer kindergarten and if so, full day or half day? What exemptions exist for districts?*, retrieved July 2, 2018, from http://ecs.force.com/mbdata/MBQuest2RTanw?rep=KK3Q1805; ECS StateNotes, *Does the state require children to attend kindergarten?*, retrieved July 2, 2018, from http://ecs.force.com/mbdata/MBQuest2RTanw?rep=KK3Q1804; and supplemental information retrieved from various state websites. (This table was prepared July 2018.)

Table 234.20. Minimum amount of instructional time per year and policies on textbooks, by state: Selected years, 2000 through 2020

State	Minimum amount of instructional time per year — In days					In hours	Policies on textbooks, 2014 — Textbook selection level		Free textbooks provided to students
	2000	2006	2011	2014	2020	2020	State	Local education agency	
1	2	3	4	5	6	7	8	9	10
Alabama	175	175	180	180[1]	180[1]	1,080	X		X
Alaska	180	180	170[2]	180[3]	180[1]	740 (K-3); 900 (4-12)		X	X
Arizona	—	180	180[1]	180[1]	180[1]	712 (1-3); 890 (4-8); 720 (9-12)		X	X[4]
Arkansas	178	178	178[2]	178[3]	178	†		X[5]	X
California	175	180	180/175[6]	180/175[6]	180[7]	600 (K); 840 (1-3); 900 (4-8); 1,080 (9-12)	X[8]		X
Colorado	[9]	160	160	160	160	450/900 (K); 990 (1-5); 1,080 (6-12)		X	
Connecticut	180	180	180	180	180	450/900 (K); 900 (1-12)		X	X
Delaware	[9]	†	†	†	†	1,060 (K-11); 1,032 (12)		X	X
District of Columbia	180[10]	180	178	180	180	†			X
Florida	180	180	180	180	180[1]	720 (K-3); 900 (4-12)	X		X
Georgia	180[10]	180	180	180	180[1]	†	X		X
Hawaii	184	179	180[11]	180[11]	180[2,11]	1,080[11]	X		X[12]
Idaho	180	†	†	†	†	450[3] (K); 810[3] (1-3); 900[3] (4-8); 990[3] (9-12)	X		X
Illinois	180[13]	176	176	180[3]	185	†		X	[14]
Indiana	180	180	180	180	180	†		X	
Iowa	180	180	180	180	180	1,080		X	
Kansas	186	186 (K-11); 181 (12)	186 (K-11); 181 (12)	186 (K-11); 181 (12)	186 (1-11); 181 (12)	465 (K); 1,116 (1-11); 1,086 (12)	X	X	
Kentucky	175	175	175[2]	170[2]	170[3]	1,062	X		X[15]
Louisiana	175	177	177[2]	177[2,16]	177[1]	1,062			X
Maine	175	175	175[2]	175[2]	180[16]	†		X	X
Maryland	180	180	180	180	180	1,080; 1,170 (High)		X	
Massachusetts	180	180	180	180	180[16]	425 (K); 900 (1-5); 990 (6-12)		X	X
Michigan	180	†	165	175	180	1,098		X	X[17]
Minnesota	[9]	[9]	†	†	165 (1-11)	425/850 (K); 935 (1-6); 1,020 (7-12)		X	X
Mississippi	180	180	180	180	180	†	X		X
Missouri	174	174	174/142[18]	174/142[18]	†	522 (K); 1,044 (1-12)		X	X
Montana	180	90 (K); 180 (K-12)	†	†	†	360/720 (K); 720 (1-3); 1,080[16] (4-12)		X	
Nebraska	[9]	†	†	†	†	400 (K); 1,032 (1-8); 1,080 (9-12)			X
Nevada	180	180	180	180	180	†	X		X[12]
New Hampshire	180	180	180	180	180[1,16]	450 (K); 945 (Elementary); 990 (Middle); 990 (High)		X	X
New Jersey	180	180	180	180	180	†		X	
New Mexico	180	180	180	180	180	450/990 (K); 990 (1-6); 1,080 (7-12)	X		X
New York	180[10]	180	180	180	180	450/900 (K); 900 (1-6); 990 (7-12)		X	X
North Carolina	180	180	180	185	185[1]	1,025	X		X
North Dakota	173	173	175[2]	175[2]	†	481.25/962.5[3] (K); 962.5[3] (1-5); 1,050[3] (6-12)		X	X[17]
Ohio	182	182	182[3]	†	†	450/910 (K); 910 (1-6); 1,001 (7-12)		X	
Oklahoma	180	180	180[3]	180	180[1]	1,080[3]	X		X
Oregon	[9]	†	†	†	†	450/900 (K); 900 (1-8); 990 (9-11); 966 (12)	X		X
Pennsylvania	180	180	180	180	180[1]	450 (K); 900 (1-6); 990 (7-12)		X	X
Rhode Island	180	180	180	180	180[1]	1,080		X	X[17]
South Carolina	180	180	180[2]	180[2]	180[3]	†	X		
South Dakota	—	†	†	180[2]	180[3]	437.5 (K); 875 (1-5); 962.5[16] (6-12)		X	
Tennessee	180	180	180	180	†	†	X		X
Texas	187	180	180	180	180	1,260	X	X	X
Utah	180	180	180	180	180	990	X	[19]	X

See notes at end of table.

Table 234.20. Minimum amount of instructional time per year and policies on textbooks, by state: Selected years, 2000 through 2020—Continued

State	Minimum amount of instructional time per year						Policies on textbooks, 2014		
	In days					In hours	Textbook selection level		Free textbooks provided to students
	2000	2006	2011	2014	2020	2020	State	Local education agency	
1	2	3	4	5	6	7	8	9	10
Vermont	175	175	175	175	175[3]	†		X	X
Virginia	180	180	180	180	180[1]	540 (K); 990 (1-12)	X	X	X
Washington	180[13]	180	180	180	180[20]	450 (K); 1,000 (1-8); 1,080 (9-12)	X		[21]
West Virginia	180	180	180	180	180	†			X
Wisconsin	180	180	180	†	†	437 (K); 1,050 (1-6); 1,137 (7-12)		X	
Wyoming	175	175	180	175	175	450 (K); 900 (1-5); 1,050 (6-8); 1,100 (9-12)		X	X

—Not available.
†Not applicable.
X Denotes that the state has a policy. A blank denotes that the state does not have a policy.
[1]Or an equivalent number of hours or minutes of instruction per year.
[2]Does not include time for in-service or staff development or parent-teacher conferences.
[3]Includes time for in-service or staff development or parent-teacher conferences. No more than 22 hours of staff development can be counted toward Idaho's instructional time requirement, and no more than 30 hours of staff development can be counted toward Oklahoma's requirement.
[4]Fees permitted at the high school level for nonrequired or supplementary textbooks.
[5]State Department of Education prepares a list of suggestions, but the districts choose.
[6]Through 2014–15, districts were allowed to shorten the 180-day instructional year to 175 days without fiscal penalty.
[7]Select districts are required to have 175 days.
[8]Statewide textbook adoption is only at the elementary level. Adoption practices have been suspended until the 2015–16 school year.
[9]No statewide policy; varies by district.
[10]1996 data.
[11]Does not apply to charter and multitrack schools.
[12]Fees for lost or damaged books permitted.
[13]1998 data.
[14]Fees permitted, but if 5 percent or more of the voters in a district petition the school board, a majority of the district's voters may decide to furnish free textbooks to students.

[15]Fees permitted for students in grades 9–12, but students who qualify for free or reduced-price lunch are exempted.
[16]Instructional time for graduating seniors may be reduced.
[17]Refundable or security deposits permitted.
[18]174 days required for a 5-day week; 142 days required for a 4-day week.
[19]Local districts may select textbooks not on the state recommended list provided the textbooks meet specific criteria and the selection is based on recommendations by the district's curriculum materials review committee.
[20]180 half-days for kindergarten.
[21]A district may provide free textbooks to students when, in its judgment, the best interests of the district will be served.

NOTE: Minimum number of instructional days refers to the actual number of days that pupils have contact with a teacher. Some states allow for different types of school calendars by setting instructional time in both days and hours, while others use only days or only hours. For states in which the number of days or hours varies by grade, the relevant grade(s) appear in parentheses. For states that specify minimum hours both for part-day kindergarten and for full-day kindergarten, a slash separates the part-day hours from the full-day hours.
SOURCE: Council of Chief State School Officers, Key State Education Policies on PK–12 Education, 2000 and 2006; Education Commission of the States, StateNotes, Number of Instructional Days/Hours in the School Year (August 2011 and October 2014 revisions), retrieved September 22, 2011, from http://www.ecs.org/clearinghouse/95/9505.pdf and May 9, 2015, from http://www.ecs.org/clearinghouse/01/15/05/11505.pdf; State Textbook Adoption (September 2013 edition), retrieved May 19, 2015, from http://www.ecs.org/clearinghouse/01/09/23/10923.pdf; Instructional Time: What's the State's Requirement of Minimum Number of Days or Hours/Minutes in a School Year?, retrieved May 20, 2020, from https://www.ecs.org/50-state-comparison-instructional-time-policies/; and supplemental information retrieved from various state websites. (This table was prepared May 2020.)

Table 235.10. Revenues for public elementary and secondary schools, by source of funds: Selected years, 1919–20 through 2016–17

School year	Revenues (in thousands)							Revenues per pupil						
				Local (including intermediate sources below the state level)							Local (including intermediate sources below the state level)			
	Total	Federal	State	Total	Property taxes	Other public revenue	Private[1]	Total	Federal	State	Total	Property taxes	Other public revenue	Private[1]
1	2	3	4	5	6	7	8	9	10	11	12	13	14	15
							Current dollars							
1919–20	$970,121	$2,475	$160,085	$807,561	—	—	—	$45	#	$7	$37	—	—	—
1929–30	2,088,557	7,334	353,670	1,727,553	—	—	—	81	#	14	67	—	—	—
1939–40	2,260,527	39,810	684,354	1,536,363	—	—	—	89	$2	27	60	—	—	—
1949–50	5,437,044	155,848	2,165,689	3,115,507	—	—	—	217	6	86	124	—	—	—
1959–60	14,746,618	651,639	5,768,047	8,326,932	—	—	—	419	19	164	237	—	—	—
1969–70	40,266,922	3,219,557	16,062,776	20,984,589	—	—	—	884	71	353	461	—	—	—
1979–80	96,881,164	9,503,537	45,348,814	42,028,813	—	—	—	2,326	228	1,089	1,009	—	—	—
1989–90	208,547,573	12,700,784	98,238,633	97,608,157	$74,867,627	$17,084,494	$5,656,036	5,144	313	2,423	2,408	$1,847	$421	$140
1994–95	273,149,449	18,582,157	127,729,576	126,837,717	97,978,129	21,560,162	7,299,425	6,192	421	2,896	2,875	2,221	489	165
1996–97	305,065,192	20,081,287	146,435,584	138,548,321	106,545,881	24,288,693	7,713,747	6,688	440	3,211	3,038	2,336	533	169
1997–98	325,925,708	22,201,965	157,645,372	146,078,370	111,184,150	26,676,244	8,217,977	7,066	481	3,418	3,167	2,410	578	178
1998–99	347,377,993	24,521,817	169,298,232	153,557,944	119,483,487	25,348,879	8,725,578	7,464	527	3,638	3,300	2,567	545	187
1999–2000	372,943,802	27,097,866	184,613,352	161,232,584	124,735,516	27,628,923	8,868,145	7,959	578	3,940	3,441	2,662	590	189
2000–01	401,356,120	29,100,183	199,583,097	172,672,840	132,575,925	30,889,273	9,207,643	8,503	616	4,228	3,658	2,809	654	195
2001–02	419,501,976	33,144,633	206,541,793	179,815,551	141,095,685	28,924,825	9,795,041	8,800	695	4,333	3,772	2,960	607	205
2002–03	440,111,653	37,515,909	214,277,407	188,318,337	148,511,786	29,579,240	10,227,310	9,134	779	4,447	3,908	3,082	614	212
2003–04	462,026,099	41,923,435	217,384,191	202,718,474	160,602,055	31,651,489	10,464,930	9,518	864	4,478	4,176	3,309	652	216
2004–05	487,753,525	44,809,532	228,553,579	214,390,414	167,909,883	35,433,486	11,047,044	9,996	918	4,684	4,394	3,441	726	226
2005–06	520,621,788	47,553,778	242,151,076	230,916,934	178,279,408	41,111,066	11,526,460	10,600	968	4,930	4,702	3,630	837	235
2006–07	555,710,762	47,150,608	263,608,741	244,951,413	188,287,298	44,806,422	11,857,694	11,281	957	5,351	4,972	3,822	910	241
2007–08	584,683,686	47,788,467	282,622,523	254,272,697	196,521,569	45,314,965	12,436,163	11,879	971	5,742	5,166	3,993	921	253
2008–09	592,422,033	56,670,261	276,525,603	259,226,169	205,821,844	41,195,313	12,209,012	12,032	1,151	5,616	5,265	4,180	837	248
2009–10	596,390,664	75,997,858	258,863,973	261,528,833	210,837,095	38,771,186	11,920,551	12,089	1,540	5,247	5,301	4,274	786	242
2010–11	604,228,585	75,549,471	266,786,402	261,892,711	211,649,523	38,558,755	11,684,433	12,218	1,528	5,395	5,296	4,280	780	236
2011–12	597,885,111	60,921,462	269,043,077	267,920,572	215,830,316	40,290,007	11,800,249	12,075	1,230	5,434	5,411	4,359	814	238
2012–13	603,769,917	55,860,888	273,215,485	274,693,545	221,970,384	41,129,568	11,593,592	12,137	1,123	5,492	5,522	4,462	827	233
2013–14	623,649,738	54,505,981	288,637,122	280,506,635	227,019,185	41,943,022	11,544,428	12,469	1,090	5,771	5,608	4,539	839	231
2014–15	647,679,130	55,002,853	301,529,692	291,146,585	235,870,943	43,978,246	11,297,396	12,884	1,094	5,998	5,792	4,692	875	225
2015–16	677,218,527	55,975,104	317,660,406	303,583,016	246,997,299	45,057,328	11,528,389	13,451	1,112	6,310	6,030	4,906	895	229
2016–17	705,267,398	57,310,693	331,322,010	316,634,696	258,159,622	46,809,893	11,665,181	13,962	1,135	6,559	6,268	5,111	927	231
							Constant 2018–19 dollars[2]							
1919–20	$12,892,256	$32,891	$2,127,422	$10,731,942	—	—	—	$597	$2	$99	$497	—	—	—
1929–30	30,902,883	108,516	5,233,002	25,561,365	—	—	—	1,203	4	204	995	—	—	—
1939–40	40,967,381	721,474	12,402,502	27,843,405	—	—	—	1,611	28	488	1,095	—	—	—
1949–50	58,144,207	1,666,652	23,160,061	33,317,495	—	—	—	2,315	66	922	1,327	—	—	—
1959–60	127,109,092	5,616,830	49,717,923	71,774,339	—	—	—	3,613	160	1,413	2,040	—	—	—
1969–70	269,975,455	21,585,990	107,695,226	140,694,239	—	—	—	5,927	474	2,364	3,089	—	—	—
1979–80	316,062,739	31,004,107	147,944,861	137,113,771	—	—	—	7,588	744	3,552	3,292	—	—	—
1989–90	415,975,009	25,333,350	195,949,612	194,692,047	$149,333,130	$34,077,226	$11,281,692	10,260	625	4,833	4,802	$3,683	$841	$278
1994–95	459,949,037	31,289,996	215,080,409	213,578,631	164,982,745	36,304,580	12,291,306	10,427	709	4,876	4,842	3,740	823	279
1996–97	486,213,727	32,005,609	233,389,457	220,818,689	169,813,113	38,711,385	12,294,191	10,660	702	5,117	4,841	3,723	849	270
1997–98	510,359,413	34,765,536	246,853,187	228,740,690	174,100,649	41,771,703	12,868,337	11,064	754	5,352	4,959	3,774	906	279
1998–99	534,694,665	37,744,720	260,588,935	236,361,011	183,912,580	39,017,758	13,430,672	11,489	811	5,599	5,079	3,952	838	289
1999–2000	557,939,718	40,539,555	276,189,391	241,210,772	186,609,613	41,334,038	13,267,121	11,907	865	5,894	5,148	3,983	882	283
2000–01	580,555,718	42,092,986	288,694,012	249,768,721	191,769,123	44,680,878	13,318,719	12,299	892	6,116	5,291	4,063	947	282
2001–02	596,246,894	47,109,157	293,562,151	255,575,586	200,542,235	41,111,456	13,921,895	12,507	988	6,158	5,361	4,207	862	292
2002–03	612,088,421	52,175,518	298,007,832	261,905,070	206,543,826	41,137,540	14,223,704	12,703	1,083	6,185	5,436	4,287	854	295
2003–04	628,809,546	57,057,071	295,856,131	275,896,344	218,576,624	43,077,131	14,242,589	12,954	1,175	6,095	5,684	4,503	887	293
2004–05	644,431,482	59,203,412	301,970,389	283,257,681	221,846,505	46,815,559	14,595,616	13,207	1,213	6,188	5,805	4,546	959	299

See notes at end of table.

Table 235.10. Revenues for public elementary and secondary schools, by source of funds: Selected years, 1919–20 through 2016–17—Continued

School year	Revenues (in thousands)							Revenues per pupil						
	Total	Federal	State	Local (including intermediate sources below the state level)				Total	Federal	State	Local (including intermediate sources below the state level)			
				Total	Property taxes	Other public revenue	Private[1]				Total	Property taxes	Other public revenue	Private[1]
1	2	3	4	5	6	7	8	9	10	11	12	13	14	15
2005–06	662,623,819	60,524,294	308,198,916	293,900,609	226,905,951	52,324,301	14,670,356	13,492	1,232	6,275	5,984	4,620	1,065	299
2006–07	689,453,964	58,498,370	327,051,595	303,903,999	233,602,501	55,590,007	14,711,491	13,996	1,187	6,639	6,169	4,742	1,128	299
2007–08	699,481,666	57,171,351	338,113,202	304,197,114	235,107,012	54,212,197	14,877,905	14,211	1,162	6,869	6,180	4,777	1,101	302
2008–09	698,979,509	66,863,400	326,263,575	305,852,534	242,842,507	48,605,011	14,405,016	14,197	1,358	6,627	6,212	4,932	987	293
2009–10	696,918,683	88,808,109	302,498,262	305,612,312	246,375,941	45,306,484	13,929,887	14,127	1,800	6,132	6,195	4,994	918	282
2010–11	692,178,940	86,546,307	305,619,320	300,013,313	242,456,821	44,171,294	13,385,197	13,997	1,750	6,180	6,067	4,903	893	271
2011–12	665,415,008	67,802,416	299,430,941	298,181,651	240,207,908	44,840,680	13,133,063	13,439	1,369	6,047	6,022	4,851	906	265
2012–13	660,965,107	61,152,596	299,097,217	300,715,294	242,997,662	45,025,777	12,691,855	13,287	1,229	6,012	6,045	4,885	905	255
2013–14	672,227,138	58,751,568	311,119,679	302,355,891	244,702,191	45,210,053	12,443,648	13,440	1,175	6,220	6,045	4,892	904	249
2014–15	693,081,279	58,858,539	322,666,850	311,555,890	252,405,439	47,061,110	12,089,340	13,787	1,171	6,419	6,198	5,021	936	240
2015–16	719,837,253	59,497,730	337,651,416	322,688,107	262,541,337	47,892,877	12,253,894	14,298	1,182	6,707	6,409	5,215	951	243
2016–17	736,110,640	59,817,043	345,811,613	330,481,984	269,449,637	48,857,016	12,175,331	14,573	1,184	6,846	6,543	5,334	967	241
	Percentage distribution													
1919–20	100.0	0.3	16.5	83.2	—	—	—	100.0	0.3	16.5	83.2	—	—	—
1929–30	100.0	0.4	16.9	82.7	—	—	—	100.0	0.4	16.9	82.7	—	—	—
1939–40	100.0	1.8	30.3	68.0	—	—	—	100.0	1.8	30.3	68.0	—	—	—
1949–50	100.0	2.9	39.8	57.3	—	—	—	100.0	2.9	39.8	57.3	—	—	—
1959–60	100.0	4.4	39.1	56.5	—	—	—	100.0	4.4	39.1	56.5	—	—	—
1969–70	100.0	8.0	39.9	52.1	—	—	—	100.0	8.0	39.9	52.1	—	—	—
1979–80	100.0	9.8	46.8	43.4	—	—	—	100.0	9.8	46.8	43.4	—	—	—
1989–90	100.0	6.1	47.1	46.8	35.9	8.2	2.7	100.0	6.1	47.1	46.8	35.9	8.2	2.7
1994–95	100.0	6.8	46.8	46.4	35.9	7.9	2.7	100.0	6.8	46.4	46.4	35.9	7.9	2.7
1996–97	100.0	6.6	48.0	45.4	34.9	8.0	2.5	100.0	6.6	48.0	45.4	34.9	8.0	2.5
1997–98	100.0	6.8	48.4	44.8	34.1	8.2	2.5	100.0	6.8	48.4	44.8	34.1	8.2	2.5
1998–99	100.0	7.1	48.7	44.2	34.4	7.3	2.5	100.0	7.1	48.7	44.2	34.4	7.3	2.5
1999–2000	100.0	7.3	49.5	43.2	33.4	7.4	2.4	100.0	7.3	49.5	43.2	33.4	7.4	2.4
2000–01	100.0	7.3	49.7	43.0	33.0	7.7	2.3	100.0	7.3	49.7	43.0	33.0	7.7	2.3
2001–02	100.0	7.9	49.2	42.9	33.6	6.9	2.3	100.0	7.9	49.2	42.9	33.6	6.9	2.3
2002–03	100.0	8.5	48.7	42.8	33.7	6.7	2.3	100.0	8.5	48.8	42.8	33.7	6.7	2.3
2003–04	100.0	9.1	47.1	43.9	34.8	6.9	2.3	100.0	9.1	47.1	43.9	34.8	6.9	2.3
2004–05	100.0	9.2	46.9	44.0	34.4	7.3	2.3	100.0	9.2	46.9	44.0	34.4	7.3	2.3
2005–06	100.0	9.1	46.5	44.4	34.2	7.9	2.2	100.0	9.1	46.5	44.4	34.2	7.9	2.2
2006–07	100.0	8.5	47.4	44.1	33.9	8.1	2.1	100.0	8.5	47.4	44.1	33.9	8.1	2.1
2007–08	100.0	8.2	48.3	43.5	33.6	7.8	2.1	100.0	8.2	48.3	43.5	33.6	7.8	2.1
2008–09	100.0	9.6	46.7	43.8	34.7	7.0	2.1	100.0	9.6	46.7	43.9	34.7	7.0	2.0
2009–10	100.0	12.7	43.4	43.9	35.4	6.5	2.0	100.0	12.7	43.4	43.9	35.4	6.5	2.0
2010–11	100.0	12.5	44.2	43.3	35.0	6.4	1.9	100.0	12.5	44.2	43.3	35.0	6.4	1.9
2011–12	100.0	10.2	45.0	44.8	36.1	6.7	2.0	100.0	10.2	45.0	44.8	36.1	6.7	2.0
2012–13	100.0	9.3	45.3	45.5	36.8	6.8	1.9	100.0	9.3	45.5	45.5	36.8	6.8	1.9
2013–14	100.0	8.7	46.3	45.0	36.4	6.7	1.9	100.0	8.7	46.3	45.0	36.4	6.7	1.9
2014–15	100.0	8.5	46.6	45.0	36.4	6.8	1.7	100.0	8.5	46.6	45.0	36.4	6.8	1.7
2015–16	100.0	8.3	46.9	44.8	36.5	6.7	1.7	100.0	8.3	46.9	44.8	36.5	6.7	1.7
2016–17	100.0	8.1	47.0	44.9	36.6	6.6	1.7	100.0	8.1	47.0	44.9	36.6	6.6	1.7

—Not available.
#Rounds to zero.
[1]Includes revenues from gifts, and tuition and fees from patrons.
[2]Constant dollars based on the Consumer Price Index, prepared by the Bureau of Labor Statistics, U.S. Department of Labor, adjusted to a school-year basis.

NOTE: Beginning in 1989–90, revenues for state education agencies were excluded and new survey collection procedures were initiated; data may not be entirely comparable with figures for earlier years. Detail may not sum to totals because of rounding.
SOURCE: U.S. Department of Education, National Center for Education Statistics, *Biennial Survey of Education in the United States*, 1919–20 through 1949–50; *Statistics of State School Systems*, 1959–60 and 1969–70; *Revenues and Expenditures for Public Elementary and Secondary Education*, 1979–80; and Common Core of Data (CCD), "National Public Education Financial Survey," 1989–90 through 2016–17. (This table was prepared August 2019.)

Table 235.20. Revenues for public elementary and secondary schools, by source of funds and state or jurisdiction: 2016–17

[In current dollars]

State or jurisdiction	Total (in thousands)	Federal Amount (in thousands)	Federal Per pupil	Federal Percent of total	State Amount (in thousands)	State Percent of total	Local Amount (in thousands)[1]	Local Percent of total	Property taxes Amount (in thousands)	Property taxes Percent of total	Private[2] Amount (in thousands)	Private[2] Percent of total
1	2	3	4	5	6	7	8	9	10	11	12	13
United States	**$705,267,398**	**$57,310,693**	**$1,135**	**8.1**	**$331,322,010**	**47.0**	**$316,634,696**	**44.9**	**$258,159,622**	**36.6**	**$11,665,181**	**1.7**
Alabama	7,889,120	863,637	1,159	10.9	4,350,890	55.2	2,674,593	33.9	1,223,602	15.5	325,777	4.1
Alaska	2,508,281	354,045	2,667	14.1	1,600,510	63.8	553,726	22.1	319,889	12.8	18,951	0.8
Arizona	10,259,496	1,326,469	1,191	12.9	4,778,454	46.6	4,154,572	40.5	3,182,393	31.0	248,513	2.4
Arkansas	5,619,332	625,993	1,269	11.1	2,950,895	52.5	2,042,443	36.3	1,782,061	31.7	158,048	2.8
California	88,108,864	7,455,046	1,182	8.5	50,841,072	57.7	29,812,746	33.8	24,101,208	27.4	394,460	0.4
Colorado	10,600,561	706,162	780	6.7	4,602,299	43.4	5,292,101	49.9	4,287,369	40.4	393,355	3.7
Connecticut	11,583,918	503,812	941	4.3	4,494,453	38.8	6,585,653	56.9	6,431,528	55.5	92,242	0.8
Delaware	2,729,986	188,717	1,385	6.9	1,323,678	48.5	1,217,591	44.6	646,622	23.7	17,771	0.7
District of Columbia	2,526,099	237,820	2,770	9.4	†	†	2,288,279	90.6	767,117	30.4	11,358	0.4
Florida	28,808,723	3,288,570	1,167	11.4	11,346,675	39.4	14,173,479	49.2	11,738,747	40.7	935,775	3.2
Georgia	20,443,717	1,925,205	1,091	9.4	9,439,804	46.2	9,078,707	44.4	6,020,224	29.4	474,428	2.3
Hawaii	2,844,167	252,145	1,389	8.9	2,534,177	89.1	57,844	2.0	0	0.0	28,852	1.0
Idaho	2,575,178	252,533	850	9.8	1,706,894	66.3	615,751	23.9	517,769	20.1	35,395	1.4
Illinois	35,480,443	2,312,325	1,141	6.5	13,710,764	38.6	19,457,354	54.8	17,082,907	48.1	480,875	1.4
Indiana	11,952,546	974,150	928	8.2	7,087,311	59.3	3,891,085	32.6	3,005,433	25.1	342,023	2.9
Iowa	6,904,458	497,385	976	7.2	3,732,324	54.1	2,674,750	38.7	2,187,985	31.7	145,240	2.1
Kansas	6,344,151	537,797	1,088	8.5	4,031,070	63.5	1,775,284	28.0	1,103,725	17.4	152,835	2.4
Kentucky	7,782,860	912,224	1,334	11.7	4,229,780	54.3	2,640,856	33.9	1,975,137	25.4	85,541	1.1
Louisiana	8,949,726	1,168,690	1,632	13.1	3,903,101	43.6	3,877,936	43.3	1,689,558	18.9	50,474	0.6
Maine	2,820,246	195,168	1,081	6.9	1,093,382	38.8	1,531,696	54.3	1,457,658	51.7	36,636	1.3
Maryland	15,045,717	851,860	961	5.7	6,625,703	44.0	7,568,154	50.3	3,703,439	24.6	115,109	0.8
Massachusetts	18,423,533	929,798	964	5.0	6,999,777	38.0	10,493,958	57.0	9,766,156	53.0	273,640	1.5
Michigan	20,163,387	1,734,557	1,135	8.6	12,224,090	60.6	6,204,741	30.8	5,289,166	26.2	273,047	1.4
Minnesota	13,242,082	743,953	850	5.6	8,762,296	66.2	3,735,833	28.2	2,449,514	18.5	350,318	2.6
Mississippi	4,753,225	672,881	1,393	14.2	2,415,769	50.8	1,664,576	35.0	1,393,467	29.3	110,153	2.3
Missouri	11,485,402	1,003,289	1,096	8.7	3,749,129	32.6	6,732,984	58.6	5,286,304	46.0	349,579	3.0
Montana	1,841,286	225,892	1,543	12.3	867,286	47.1	748,107	40.6	476,318	25.9	62,801	3.4
Nebraska	4,470,153	349,144	1,094	7.8	1,450,774	32.5	2,670,235	59.7	2,369,879	53.0	161,587	3.6
Nevada	4,919,401	444,730	939	9.0	1,780,380	36.2	2,694,292	54.8	1,201,302	24.4	28,596	0.6
New Hampshire	3,132,306	173,816	961	5.5	1,007,310	32.2	1,951,180	62.3	1,859,886	59.4	46,040	1.5
New Jersey	30,368,383	1,269,661	900	4.2	12,920,845	42.5	16,177,878	53.3	15,304,628	50.4	581,364	1.9
New Mexico	4,023,795	589,017	1,752	14.6	2,726,305	67.8	708,473	17.6	572,792	14.2	54,087	1.3
New York	69,228,226	3,657,578	1,373	5.3	28,253,045	40.8	37,317,603	53.9	34,657,273	50.1	305,467	0.4
North Carolina	14,481,275	1,641,260	1,059	11.3	9,057,842	62.5	3,782,173	26.1	3,290,986	22.7	166,817	1.2
North Dakota	1,757,100	163,446	1,490	9.3	1,014,779	57.8	578,875	32.9	423,505	24.1	69,564	4.0
Ohio	24,762,785	1,949,822	1,140	7.9	10,538,278	42.6	12,274,685	49.6	10,070,121	40.7	642,876	2.6
Oklahoma	6,361,194	726,159	1,046	11.4	3,007,742	47.3	2,627,292	41.3	2,007,824	31.6	281,400	4.4
Oregon	7,689,411	550,627	951	7.2	4,018,900	52.3	3,119,884	40.6	2,524,905	32.8	137,680	1.8
Pennsylvania	31,353,132	2,152,130	1,246	6.9	12,104,094	38.6	17,096,908	54.5	13,601,256	43.4	385,862	1.2
Rhode Island	2,561,477	192,929	1,357	7.5	1,087,361	42.5	1,281,187	50.0	1,242,366	48.5	25,406	1.0
South Carolina	9,992,973	913,225	1,184	9.1	4,867,687	48.7	4,212,060	42.2	3,195,782	32.0	245,374	2.5
South Dakota	1,580,004	205,299	1,506	13.0	540,408	34.2	834,297	52.8	716,885	45.4	44,816	2.8
Tennessee	10,077,253	1,161,636	1,160	11.5	4,629,304	45.9	4,286,312	42.5	2,008,470	19.9	438,170	4.3
Texas	60,006,975	6,298,581	1,175	10.5	23,339,969	38.9	30,368,425	50.6	27,675,817	46.1	1,022,545	1.7
Utah	5,757,609	459,308	696	8.0	3,183,265	55.3	2,115,036	36.7	1,598,326	27.8	241,408	4.2
Vermont	1,742,206	113,778	1,287	6.5	1,560,743	89.6	67,685	3.9	2,385	0.1	21,859	1.3
Virginia	16,611,639	1,131,683	879	6.8	6,565,661	39.5	8,914,296	53.7	5,399,824	32.5	241,647	1.5
Washington	15,654,623	1,071,035	972	6.8	9,846,364	62.9	4,737,224	30.3	4,056,493	25.9	299,337	1.9
West Virginia	3,526,416	404,295	1,476	11.5	1,917,056	54.4	1,205,066	34.2	1,115,409	31.6	19,618	0.6
Wisconsin	11,591,278	832,985	964	7.2	5,360,746	46.2	5,397,548	46.6	4,891,353	42.2	224,031	1.9
Wyoming	1,931,277	118,429	1,258	6.1	1,141,567	59.1	671,281	34.8	486,856	25.2	16,436	0.9
Other jurisdictions												
American Samoa	73,876	62,906	—	85.2	10,738	14.5	232	0.3	0	0.0	14	#
Guam	332,552	60,166	1,956	18.1	0	0.0	272,386	81.9	0	0.0	147	#
Northern Marianas	87,683	39,503	—	45.1	47,227	53.9	953	1.1	0	0.0	711	0.8
Puerto Rico	2,819,791	935,887	2,563	33.2	1,883,850	66.8	55	#	0	0.0	55	#
U.S. Virgin Islands	193,314	26,259	1,990	13.6	0	0.0	167,056	86.4	0	0.0	5	#

—Not available.
†Not applicable.
#Rounds to zero.
[1]Includes other categories of revenue not separately shown.
[2]Includes revenues from gifts, and tuition and fees from patrons.

NOTE: Excludes revenues for state education agencies. Detail may not sum to totals because of rounding.
SOURCE: U.S. Department of Education, National Center for Education Statistics, Common Core of Data (CCD), "National Public Education Financial Survey," 2016–17. (This table was prepared August 2019.)

Table 235.40. Public elementary and secondary revenues and expenditures, by locale, source of revenue, and purpose of expenditure: 2016–17

Source of revenue and purpose of expenditure	Total	City, large	City, midsize	City, small	Suburban, large	Suburban, midsize	Suburban, small	Town, fringe	Town, distant	Town, remote	Rural, fringe	Rural, distant	Rural, remote
1	2	3	4	5	6	7	8	9	10	11	12	13	14
Revenue amounts (in millions of current dollars)													
Total revenue[1]	$708,834	$135,044	$50,112	$48,905	$266,735	$23,599	$13,138	$16,533	$33,777	$19,814	$51,673	$35,081	$14,423
Federal	56,838	13,752	5,051	4,236	16,072	1,650	945	1,225	3,155	2,278	4,020	2,854	1,600
Title I	14,602	4,392	1,289	1,098	3,597	401	214	272	812	531	916	715	366
Child Nutrition Act	16,553	3,849	1,396	1,235	4,850	520	272	366	992	556	1,231	914	371
Children with disabilities (IDEA)	11,473	1,983	991	880	4,192	369	230	249	615	362	883	525	194
Impact aid	1,363	122	78	64	165	27	8	67	45	232	139	89	329
Bilingual education	338	93	37	30	122	8	6	6	11	7	13	4	2
Indian education	98	11	3	4	7	2	3	2	9	17	5	9	27
Math, science, and professional development	1,470	338	134	114	369	44	30	32	97	67	105	91	49
Safe and drug-free schools	70	16	4	6	16	2	#	2	5	5	9	3	2
Vocational and technical education	556	119	46	42	169	17	12	12	36	24	47	23	10
Other and unclassified	10,313	2,828	1,074	762	2,588	260	171	219	533	477	671	481	249
State	331,912	59,083	25,082	24,371	115,524	11,817	6,493	8,828	18,350	10,340	25,694	19,058	7,271
Special education programs	20,889	4,365	1,619	1,421	8,132	650	304	445	921	505	1,418	815	293
Compensatory and basic skills	5,282	824	407	476	1,910	263	79	99	281	130	418	286	110
Bilingual education	1,185	108	67	68	784	36	10	6	32	12	47	10	4
Gifted and talented	1,193	42	100	53	749	19	10	11	34	9	131	28	7
Vocational education	1,241	47	82	85	497	49	27	22	93	56	159	91	33
Other[2]	302,122	53,698	22,808	22,267	103,451	10,800	6,063	8,245	16,989	9,628	23,521	17,829	6,823
Local[1]	320,084	62,209	19,978	20,299	135,139	10,132	5,700	6,480	12,272	7,196	21,960	13,168	5,553
Property tax[3]	203,125	29,852	12,357	13,070	92,794	5,741	3,998	4,635	8,490	5,242	13,839	9,126	3,983
Parent government contribution[3]	57,983	21,085	3,298	2,732	21,882	2,565	557	389	871	190	3,126	986	301
Private[4]	13,905	1,519	862	809	5,897	486	263	361	727	443	1,276	892	369
Other[5]	45,071	9,753	3,461	3,688	14,565	1,340	883	1,095	2,184	1,320	3,718	2,163	900
Percentage distribution of revenue													
Total revenue	100.0	100.0	100.0	100.0	100.0	100.0	100.0	100.0	100.0	100.0	100.0	100.0	100.0
Federal	8.0	10.2	10.1	8.7	6.0	7.0	7.2	7.4	9.3	11.5	7.8	8.1	11.1
State	46.8	43.8	50.1	49.8	43.3	50.1	49.4	53.4	54.3	52.2	49.7	54.3	50.4
Local	45.2	46.1	39.9	41.5	50.7	42.9	43.4	39.2	36.3	36.3	42.5	37.5	38.5
Expenditure amounts (in millions of current dollars)													
Total expenditures	$725,239	$138,911	$51,060	$50,310	$272,398	$23,958	$13,265	$17,379	$34,861	$20,411	$52,621	$35,254	$14,811
Current expenditures for schools	609,072	113,540	42,997	42,147	229,779	20,522	11,486	14,338	29,453	17,223	44,769	30,367	12,451
Instruction	368,949	70,341	25,043	25,301	140,942	12,287	6,878	8,656	17,563	10,110	26,782	17,917	7,128
Student support[6]	35,605	5,372	2,848	2,705	14,707	1,255	734	798	1,623	1,008	2,550	1,462	542
Instructional staff support services[7]	28,706	5,189	2,605	2,239	10,614	1,032	530	614	1,372	802	1,953	1,225	531
General and school administration	46,120	7,784	3,252	3,110	16,823	1,497	880	1,165	2,471	1,483	3,581	2,814	1,260
Operation and maintenance	56,489	11,066	3,861	3,858	20,662	1,936	1,059	1,343	2,728	1,702	4,126	2,866	1,283
Student transportation	25,523	4,363	1,627	1,509	9,529	849	498	642	1,262	667	2,275	1,672	630
Food services	23,723	4,481	1,761	1,691	7,762	811	439	580	1,393	821	1,920	1,450	612
Other	23,957	4,943	1,999	1,734	8,739	855	469	539	1,041	629	1,583	961	464
Other current expenditures	33,921	9,361	2,568	2,215	11,967	858	424	617	1,231	671	2,064	1,328	615
Interest on school debt	18,271	4,076	1,270	1,209	7,021	508	324	500	755	388	1,328	690	202
Capital outlay	63,975	11,935	4,225	4,738	23,632	2,070	1,030	1,924	3,421	2,128	4,459	2,869	1,543
Percentage distribution of current expenditures for schools													
All current expenditures for schools	100.0	100.0	100.0	100.0	100.0	100.0	100.0	100.0	100.0	100.0	100.0	100.0	100.0
Instruction	60.6	62.0	58.2	60.0	61.3	59.9	59.9	60.4	59.6	58.7	59.8	59.0	57.3
Support services	10.6	9.3	12.7	11.7	11.0	11.1	11.0	9.8	10.2	10.5	10.1	8.8	8.6
General and school administration	7.6	6.9	7.6	7.4	7.3	7.3	7.7	8.1	8.4	8.6	8.0	9.3	10.1
Operation and maintenance	9.3	9.7	9.0	9.2	9.0	9.4	9.2	9.4	9.3	9.9	9.2	9.4	10.3
Student transportation	4.2	3.8	3.8	3.6	4.1	4.1	4.3	4.5	4.3	3.9	5.1	5.5	5.1
Food service and other	7.8	8.3	8.7	8.1	7.2	8.1	7.9	7.8	8.3	8.4	7.8	7.9	8.6
Per student amounts (in current dollars)													
Current expenditure per student	$12,089	$12,980	$11,648	$11,869	$12,397	$11,550	$11,698	$11,523	$11,083	$10,801	$11,301	$11,336	$12,954
Instruction expenditure per student	7,323	8,041	6,784	7,125	7,604	6,915	7,005	6,957	6,609	6,340	6,760	6,689	7,416

#Rounds to zero.
[1] Excludes revenues from other in-state school systems.
[2] Includes general formula assistance, staff improvement programs, school lunch programs, capital outlay and debt service programs, transportation programs, all other revenues from state sources, state payments on behalf of the local education agency, Census state NCES local revenue, and unspecified state revenue.
[3] Property tax and parent government contributions are determined on the basis of independence or dependence of the local school system and are mutually exclusive.
[4] Includes tuition fees, transportation fees, textbook sales and rentals, school lunch revenues, district activity receipts, other student fees, and private contributions.
[5] Includes revenues from other taxes, rents and royalties, sales and services, interest earnings, and other local revenues.

[6] Includes expenditures for guidance, health, attendance, social work, student accounting, counseling, student appraisal, information, record maintenance, placement services, and medical, dental, nursing, psychological, and speech pathology services.
[7] Includes expenditures for curriculum development, staff training, supervision of instruction service improvements, academic assessment, and media, library, and instruction-related technology services.
NOTE: Detail may not sum to totals because of rounding.
SOURCE: U.S. Department of Education, National Center for Education Statistics, Common Core of Data (CCD), "School District Finance Survey (F33), Fiscal year 2017"; and Education Demographic and Geographic Estimates (EDGE) program, "Public Local Education Agency Geocode File," 2016–17. (This table was prepared April 2020.)

Table 236.10. Summary of expenditures for public elementary and secondary education and other related programs, by purpose: Selected years, 1919–20 through 2016–17

School year	Total expenditures	Current expenditures for public elementary and secondary education							Current expenditures for other programs[1]	Capital outlay[2]	Interest on school debt
		Total	Admin- istration	Instruction	Plant operation	Plant main- tenance	Fixed charges	Other school services[3]			
1	2	3	4	5	6	7	8	9	10	11	12
					Amounts in thousands of current dollars						
1919–20	$1,036,151	$861,120	$36,752	$632,556	$115,707	$30,432	$9,286	$36,387	$3,277	$153,543	$18,212
1929–30	2,316,790	1,843,552	78,680	1,317,727	216,072	78,810	50,270	101,993	9,825	370,878	92,536
1939–40	2,344,049	1,941,799	91,571	1,403,285	194,365	73,321	50,116	129,141	13,367	257,974	130,909
1949–50	5,837,643	4,687,274	220,050	3,112,340	427,587	214,164	261,469	451,663	35,614	1,014,176	100,578
1959–60	15,613,254	12,329,388	528,408	8,350,738	1,085,036	422,586	909,323	1,033,297	132,566	2,661,786	489,514
1969–70	40,683,429	34,217,773	1,606,646	23,270,158	2,537,257	974,941	3,266,920	2,561,856	635,803	4,659,072	1,170,782
1979–80	95,961,561	86,984,142	4,263,757	53,257,937	9,744,785	(4)	11,793,934	7,923,729	597,585	6,506,167	1,873,666
1989–90	212,769,564	188,229,359	16,346,991[5]	113,550,405[5]	20,261,415[5]	(4)	—	38,070,548[5]	2,982,543	17,781,342	3,776,321
1999–2000	381,838,155	323,888,508	25,079,298[5]	199,968,138[5]	31,190,295[5]	(4)	—	67,650,776[5]	5,457,015	43,357,186	9,135,445
2000–01	410,811,185	348,360,841	26,689,182[5]	214,333,003[5]	34,034,158[5]	(4)	—	73,304,498[5]	6,063,700	46,220,704	10,165,940
2006–07	562,194,807	476,814,206	36,213,814[5]	290,678,482[5]	46,828,916[5]	(4)	—	103,092,995[5]	7,804,253	62,863,465	14,712,882
2007–08	597,313,726	506,884,219	38,203,341[5]	308,238,664[5]	49,362,661[5]	(4)	—	111,079,554[5]	8,307,720	66,426,299	15,695,488
2008–09	610,326,007	518,922,842	38,811,325[5]	316,075,710[5]	50,559,027[5]	(4)	—	113,476,779[5]	8,463,793	65,890,367	17,049,004
2009–10	607,018,292	524,715,242	38,972,700[5]	321,213,401[5]	50,023,919[5]	(4)	—	114,505,223[5]	8,355,761	56,714,992	17,232,297
2010–11	604,355,852	527,291,339	39,154,833[5]	322,536,983[5]	50,214,709[5]	(4)	—	115,384,813[5]	8,161,474	50,968,815	17,934,224
2011–12	601,993,584	527,207,246	39,491,926[5]	320,994,474[5]	49,834,165[5]	(4)	—	116,886,681[5]	8,188,640	48,793,436	17,804,262
2012–13	606,813,352	535,795,823	40,349,598[5]	325,682,380[5]	50,674,499[5]	(4)	—	119,089,346[5]	8,031,416	45,720,570	17,265,542
2013–14	625,018,277	553,501,209	41,538,042[5]	336,426,927[5]	53,051,141[5]	(4)	—	122,485,100[5]	7,926,285	46,438,323	17,152,459
2014–15	651,135,383	575,331,825	43,328,198[5]	349,453,258[5]	54,200,172[5]	(4)	—	128,350,197[5]	7,713,966	50,610,125	17,479,466
2015–16	677,605,095	596,201,554	45,252,877[5]	363,106,915[5]	55,045,039[5]	(4)	—	132,796,722[5]	7,913,839	55,989,128	17,500,574
2016–17	707,601,350	619,164,572	46,874,132[5]	376,069,486[5]	57,433,468[5]	(4)	—	138,787,485[5]	8,660,874	61,441,963	18,333,942
					Amounts in thousands of constant 2018–19 dollars[6]						
1919–20	$13,769,750	$11,443,706	$488,409	$8,406,244	$1,537,668	$404,421	$123,405	$483,559	$43,549	$2,040,483	$242,025
1929–30	34,279,884	27,277,720	1,164,172	19,497,463	3,197,063	1,166,095	743,809	1,509,117	145,373	5,487,616	1,369,189
1939–40	42,481,045	35,191,095	1,659,535	25,431,641	3,522,464	1,328,792	908,249	2,340,414	242,249	4,675,246	2,372,455
1949–50	62,428,247	50,126,093	2,353,233	33,283,627	4,572,651	2,290,288	2,796,172	4,830,122	380,859	10,845,684	1,075,590
1959–60	134,579,097	106,273,677	4,554,635	71,979,536	9,352,513	3,642,498	7,837,948	8,906,547	1,142,658	22,943,376	4,219,386
1969–70	272,767,987	229,418,086	10,771,993	156,018,170	17,011,410	6,536,634	21,903,542	17,176,337	4,262,834	31,237,428	7,849,679
1979–80	313,062,649	283,774,937	13,909,977	173,747,391	31,791,148	(4)	38,476,242	25,850,180	1,949,547	21,225,560	6,112,602
1989–90	424,396,314	375,447,713	32,606,180[5]	226,490,915[5]	40,414,003[5]	(4)	—	75,936,614[5]	5,949,066	35,467,178	7,532,359
1999–2000	571,246,047	484,550,921	37,519,692[5]	299,160,801[5]	46,662,001[5]	(4)	—	101,208,425[5]	8,163,926	64,864,187	13,667,013
2000–01	594,232,331	503,898,830	38,605,508[5]	310,029,533[5]	49,229,909[5]	(4)	—	106,033,877[5]	8,771,053	66,857,568	14,704,882
2006–07	697,498,527	591,569,332	44,929,412[5]	360,636,225[5]	58,099,255[5]	(4)	—	127,904,440[5]	9,682,507	77,992,848	18,253,840
2007–08	714,591,514	606,406,895	45,704,263[5]	368,758,868[5]	59,054,626[5]	(4)	—	132,889,139[5]	9,938,874	79,468,573	18,777,172
2008–09	720,103,826	612,260,201	45,792,222[5]	372,927,461[5]	59,652,954[5]	(4)	—	133,887,565[5]	9,986,155	77,741,904	20,115,566
2009–10	709,337,711	613,161,603	45,541,965[5]	375,357,351[5]	58,455,985[5]	(4)	—	133,806,302[5]	9,764,214	66,274,909	20,136,985
2010–11	692,324,731	604,042,855	44,854,135[5]	369,484,848[5]	57,523,866[5]	(4)	—	132,180,006[5]	9,349,442	58,387,738	20,544,696
2011–12	669,987,525	586,754,223	43,952,458[5]	357,250,142[5]	55,462,831[5]	(4)	—	130,088,792[5]	9,113,530	54,304,555	19,815,217
2012–13	664,296,846	586,551,819	44,171,920[5]	356,534,307[5]	55,474,900[5]	(4)	—	130,370,693[5]	8,792,233	50,051,685	18,901,109
2013–14	673,702,276	596,614,592	44,773,528[5]	362,631,933[5]	57,183,406[5]	(4)	—	132,025,724[5]	8,543,681	50,055,503	18,488,500
2014–15	696,779,814	615,662,446	46,365,494[5]	373,949,847[5]	57,999,590[5]	(4)	—	137,347,514[5]	8,254,713	54,157,883	18,704,773
2015–16	720,248,149	633,721,719	48,100,732[5]	385,957,965[5]	58,509,134[5]	(4)	—	141,153,887[5]	8,411,873	59,512,637	18,601,920
2016–17	738,546,661	646,242,305	48,924,064[5]	392,516,017[5]	59,945,188[5]	(4)	—	144,857,035[5]	9,039,637	64,128,985	19,135,734
					Percentage distribution						
1919–20	100.0	83.1	3.5	61.0	11.2	2.9	0.9	3.5	0.3	14.8	1.8
1929–30	100.0	79.6	3.4	56.9	9.3	3.4	2.2	4.4	0.4	16.0	4.0
1939–40	100.0	82.8	3.9	59.9	8.3	3.1	2.1	5.5	0.6	11.0	5.6
1949–50	100.0	80.3	3.8	53.3	7.3	3.7	4.5	7.7	0.6	17.4	1.7
1959–60	100.0	79.0	3.4	53.5	6.9	2.7	5.8	6.6	0.8	17.0	3.1
1969–70	100.0	84.1	3.9	57.2	6.2	2.4	8.0	6.3	1.6	11.5	2.9
1979–80	100.0	90.6	4.4	55.5	10.2	(4)	12.3	8.3	0.6	6.8	2.0
1989–90	100.0	88.5	7.7[5]	53.4[5]	9.5[5]	(4)	—	17.9[5]	1.4	8.4	1.8
1999–2000	100.0	84.8	6.6[5]	52.4[5]	8.2[5]	(4)	—	17.7[5]	1.4	11.4	2.4
2000–01	100.0	84.8	6.5[5]	52.2[5]	8.3[5]	(4)	—	17.8[5]	1.5	11.3	2.5
2006–07	100.0	84.8	6.4[5]	51.7[5]	8.3[5]	(4)	—	18.3[5]	1.4	11.2	2.6
2007–08	100.0	84.9	6.4[5]	51.6[5]	8.3[5]	(4)	—	18.6[5]	1.4	11.1	2.6
2008–09	100.0	85.0	6.4[5]	51.8[5]	8.3[5]	(4)	—	18.6[5]	1.4	10.8	2.8
2009–10	100.0	86.4	6.4[5]	52.9[5]	8.2[5]	(4)	—	18.9[5]	1.4	9.3	2.8
2010–11	100.0	87.2	6.5[5]	53.4[5]	8.3[5]	(4)	—	19.1[5]	1.4	8.4	3.0
2011–12	100.0	87.6	6.6[5]	53.3[5]	8.3[5]	(4)	—	19.4[5]	1.4	8.1	3.0
2012–13	100.0	88.3	6.6[5]	53.7[5]	8.4[5]	(4)	—	19.6[5]	1.3	7.5	2.8
2013–14	100.0	88.6	6.6[5]	53.8[5]	8.5[5]	(4)	—	19.6[5]	1.3	7.4	2.7
2014–15	100.0	88.4	6.7[5]	53.7[5]	8.3[5]	(4)	—	19.7[5]	1.2	7.8	2.7
2015–16	100.0	88.0	6.7[5]	53.6[5]	8.1[5]	(4)	—	19.6[5]	1.2	8.3	2.6
2016–17	100.0	87.5	6.6[5]	53.1[5]	8.1[5]	(4)	—	19.6[5]	1.2	8.7	2.6

—Not available.
[1]Includes expenditures for summer schools, adult education, community colleges, and community services.
[2]Prior to 1969–70, excludes capital outlay by state and local school housing authorities.
[3]Prior to 1959–60, items included under "other school services" were listed under "auxiliary services," a more comprehensive classification that also included community services.
[4]Plant operation also includes plant maintenance.
[5]Data not comparable to figures prior to 1989–90.
[6]Constant dollars based on the Consumer Price Index, prepared by the Bureau of Labor Statistics, U.S. Department of Labor, adjusted to a school-year basis.

NOTE: Beginning in 1959–60, includes Alaska and Hawaii. Beginning in 1989–90, state administration expenditures were excluded from both "total" and "current" expenditures. Beginning in 1989–90, extensive changes were made in the data collection procedures. Detail may not sum to totals because of rounding. Some data have been revised from previously published figures.
SOURCE: U.S. Department of Education, National Center for Education Statistics, *Biennial Survey of Education in the United States*, 1919–20 through 1949–50; *Statistics of State School Systems*, 1959–60 and 1969–70; *Revenues and Expenditures for Public Elementary and Secondary Education*, 1979–80; and Common Core of Data (CCD), "National Public Education Financial Survey," 1989–90 through 2016–17. (This table was prepared August 2019.)

Table 236.15. Current expenditures and current expenditures per pupil in public elementary and secondary schools: 1989–90 through 2029–30

School year	Current expenditures in unadjusted dollars[1]			Current expenditures in constant 2018–19 dollars[2]					
				Total current expenditures		Per pupil in fall enrollment		Per pupil in average daily attendance (ADA)	
	Total, in billions	Per pupil in fall enrollment	Per pupil in average daily attendance (ADA)	In billions	Annual percentage change	Per pupil enrolled	Annual percentage change	Per pupil in ADA	Annual percentage change
1	2	3	4	5	6	7	8	9	10
1989–90	$188.2	$4,643	$4,980	$375.4	3.8	$9,261	2.9	$9,933	2.3
1990–91	202.0	4,902	5,258	382.1	1.8	9,271	0.1	9,944	0.1
1991–92	211.2	5,023	5,421	387.0	1.3	9,205	-0.7	9,934	-0.1
1992–93	220.9	5,160	5,584	392.6	1.4	9,169	-0.4	9,922	-0.1
1993–94	231.5	5,327	5,767	401.1	2.1	9,227	0.6	9,990	0.7
1994–95	243.9	5,529	5,989	410.7	2.4	9,310	0.9	10,085	0.9
1995–96	255.1	5,689	6,147	418.2	1.8	9,326	0.2	10,076	-0.1
1996–97	270.2	5,923	6,393	430.6	3.0	9,441	1.2	10,189	1.1
1997–98	285.5	6,189	6,676	447.0	3.8	9,691	2.7	10,453	2.6
1998–99	302.9	6,508	7,013	466.2	4.3	10,017	3.4	10,795	3.3
1999–2000	323.9	6,912	7,394	484.6	3.9	10,341	3.2	11,061	2.5
2000–01	348.4	7,380	7,904	503.9	4.0	10,675	3.2	11,433	3.4
2001–02	368.4	7,727	8,259	523.6	3.9	10,983	2.9	11,738	2.7
2002–03	387.6	8,044	8,610	539.0	3.0	11,188	1.9	11,974	2.0
2003–04	403.4	8,310	8,900	549.0	1.8	11,310	1.1	12,112	1.2
2004–05	425.0	8,711	9,316	561.6	2.3	11,509	1.8	12,309	1.6
2005–06	449.1	9,145	9,778	571.6	1.8	11,639	1.1	12,445	1.1
2006–07	476.8	9,679	10,336	591.6	3.5	12,009	3.2	12,823	3.0
2007–08	506.9	10,298	10,982	606.4	2.5	12,320	2.6	13,138	2.5
2008–09	518.9	10,540	11,239	612.3	1.0	12,435	0.9	13,260	0.9
2009–10	524.7	10,636	11,427	613.2	0.1	12,429	-0.1	13,353	0.7
2010–11	527.3	10,663	11,433	604.0	-1.5	12,215	-1.7	13,098	-1.9
2011–12	527.2	10,648	11,362	586.8	-2.9	11,850	-3.0	12,645	-3.5
2012–13	535.8	10,771	11,509	586.6	#	11,791	-0.5	12,599	-0.4
2013–14	553.5	11,066	11,819	596.6	1.7	11,928	1.2	12,740	1.1
2014–15	575.3	11,445	12,224	615.7	3.2	12,247	2.7	13,081	2.7
2015–16	596.2	11,842	12,619	633.7	2.9	12,587	2.8	13,413	2.5
2016–17	619.2	12,258	13,094	646.2	2.0	12,794	1.6	13,667	1.9
2017–18[3]	643.8	12,700	13,590	657.1	1.7	12,970	1.4	13,870	1.5
2018–19[3]	669.6	13,220	14,140	669.6	1.9	13,220	1.9	14,140	1.9
2019–20[3]	691.8	13,660	14,610	678.4	1.3	13,400	1.3	14,330	1.3
2020–21[3]	709.2	14,000	14,980	684.1	0.8	13,500	0.8	14,450	0.8
2021–22[3]	731.5	14,440	15,450	690.1	0.9	13,630	0.9	14,570	0.9
2022–23[3]	757.1	14,930	15,970	696.9	1.0	13,740	0.8	14,700	0.8
2023–24[3]	783.4	15,430	16,500	703.6	1.0	13,860	0.9	14,820	0.9
2024–25[3]	810.9	15,980	17,090	711.2	1.1	14,010	1.1	14,990	1.1
2025–26[3]	838.8	16,540	17,690	718.5	1.0	14,170	1.1	15,160	1.1
2026–27[3]	867.2	17,110	18,310	725.7	1.0	14,320	1.1	15,320	1.1
2027–28[3]	898.4	17,710	18,940	734.8	1.3	14,480	1.1	15,490	1.1
2028–29[3]	932.7	18,330	19,610	746.0	1.5	14,660	1.2	15,680	1.2
2029–30[3]	959.0	18,780	20,090	754.6	1.2	14,780	0.8	15,810	0.8

#Rounds to zero.
[1]Unadjusted (or "current") dollars have not been adjusted to compensate for inflation.
[2]Constant dollars based on the Consumer Price Index, prepared by the Bureau of Labor Statistics, U.S. Department of Labor, adjusted to a school-year basis.
[3]Projected.
NOTE: Current expenditures include instruction, support services, food services, and enterprise operations. Some data have been revised from previously published figures.

SOURCE: U.S. Department of Education, National Center for Education Statistics, Common Core of Data (CCD), "National Public Education Financial Survey," 1989–90 through 2016–17; National Elementary and Secondary Enrollment Projection Model, 1972 through 2029; and Public Elementary and Secondary Education Current Expenditure Projection Model, 1973–74 through 2029–30. (This table was prepared December 2019.)

Table 236.20. Total expenditures for public elementary and secondary education and other related programs, by function and subfunction: Selected years, 1990–91 through 2016–17

Function and subfunction	Expenditures (in thousands of current dollars)								Percentage distribution of current expenditures for public schools							
	1990–91	2000–01	2006–07	2010–11	2013–14	2014–15	2015–16	2016–17	1990–91	2000–01	2006–07	2010–11	2013–14	2014–15	2015–16	2016–17
1	2	3	4	5	6	7	8	9	10	11	12	13	14	15	16	17
Total expenditures	$229,429,715	$410,811,185	$562,194,807	$604,355,852	$625,018,277	$651,135,383	$677,605,095	$707,601,350	†	†	†	†	†	†	†	†
Current expenditures for public schools	202,037,752	348,360,841	476,814,206	527,291,339	553,501,209	575,331,825	596,201,554	619,164,572	100.00	100.00	100.00	100.00	100.00	100.00	100.00	100.00
Salaries	132,730,931[1]	224,305,806	288,146,674	311,541,792	318,705,822	328,252,700	339,731,757	349,913,306	65.70	64.39	60.43	59.08	57.58	57.05	56.98	56.51
Employee benefits	33,954,456[1]	57,976,490	95,308,994	111,750,200	123,655,529	130,868,877	136,788,690	145,381,103	16.81	16.64	19.99	21.19	22.34	22.75	22.94	23.48
Purchased services	16,380,643[1]	31,778,754	46,266,516	53,498,786	58,171,703	61,118,818	64,572,861	66,905,790	8.11	9.12	9.70	10.15	10.51	10.62	10.83	10.81
Tuition	1,192,505[1]	2,458,366	3,951,411	4,988,203	5,296,241	5,572,087	5,743,719	6,135,308	0.59	0.71	0.83	0.95	0.96	0.97	0.96	0.99
Supplies	14,805,956[1]	28,262,078	38,378,936	40,417,163	42,895,737	43,793,547	43,774,032	44,771,753	7.33	8.11	8.05	7.67	7.75	7.61	7.34	7.23
Other	2,973,261[1]	3,579,347	4,761,675	5,095,195	4,776,178	5,725,796	5,590,495	6,057,312	1.47	1.03	1.00	0.97	0.86	1.00	0.94	0.98
Instruction	122,223,362	214,333,003	290,678,482	322,536,983	336,426,927	349,453,258	363,069,486	376,069,486	60.50	61.53	60.96	61.17	60.78	60.74	60.90	60.74
Salaries	90,742,284	154,512,089	196,900,968	212,998,609	217,274,753	223,044,251	230,477,780	236,792,085	44.91	44.35	41.30	40.39	39.25	38.77	38.66	38.24
Employee benefits	22,347,524	39,522,678	64,153,369	75,248,811	83,946,609	88,840,559	92,808,865	98,321,490	11.06	11.35	13.45	14.27	15.17	15.44	15.57	15.88
Purchased services	2,722,639	6,430,708	10,997,609	14,694,620	15,177,204	16,559,278	18,048,424	18,476,414	1.35	1.85	2.31	2.79	2.74	2.88	3.03	2.98
Tuition	1,192,505	2,458,366	3,951,411	4,988,203	5,296,241	5,572,087	5,743,719	6,135,308	0.59	0.71	0.83	0.95	0.96	0.97	0.96	0.99
Supplies	4,584,754	10,377,554	13,359,899	13,135,284	13,344,523	14,060,733	14,602,677	14,900,908	2.27	2.98	2.80	2.49	2.41	2.44	2.45	2.41
Textbooks	—	—	2,779,800	2,324,846	2,321,424	2,438,331	2,540,299	2,636,445	—	—	0.58	0.44	0.42	0.42	0.43	0.43
Other	633,656	1,031,608	1,315,226	1,471,457	1,387,596	1,376,350	1,425,450	1,443,281	0.31	0.30	0.28	0.28	0.25	0.24	0.24	0.23
Student support[2]	8,926,010	17,292,756	25,207,881	29,368,646	30,754,056	32,363,375	34,013,896	35,946,038	4.42	4.96	5.29	5.57	5.56	5.63	5.71	5.81
Salaries	6,565,965	12,354,464	16,868,875	19,367,865	19,823,136	20,658,101	21,598,398	22,550,036	3.25	3.55	3.54	3.67	3.58	3.59	3.62	3.64
Employee benefits	1,660,082	3,036,037	5,352,820	6,533,691	7,315,689	7,872,711	8,360,099	9,135,154	0.82	0.87	1.12	1.24	1.32	1.37	1.40	1.48
Purchased services	455,996	1,328,600	2,141,301	2,583,714	2,850,087	3,024,871	3,202,463	3,390,784	0.23	0.38	0.45	0.49	0.51	0.53	0.54	0.55
Supplies	191,482	421,838	521,050	521,729	564,419	599,269	628,105	645,129	0.09	0.12	0.11	0.10	0.10	0.10	0.11	0.10
Other	52,485	151,817	323,835	361,647	200,727	208,422	224,831	224,936	0.03	0.04	0.07	0.07	0.04	0.04	0.04	0.04
Instructional staff services[3]	8,467,142	15,926,856	23,156,534	24,893,140	25,354,104	26,953,637	28,015,976	29,169,348	4.19	4.57	4.86	4.72	4.58	4.68	4.70	4.71
Salaries	5,560,129	9,790,767	13,753,355	14,490,521	14,685,427	15,490,102	16,082,881	16,712,372	2.75	2.81	2.88	2.75	2.65	2.69	2.70	2.70
Employee benefits	1,408,217	2,356,440	4,225,114	4,933,118	5,234,451	5,640,401	5,899,056	6,354,157	0.70	0.68	0.89	0.94	0.95	0.98	0.99	1.03
Purchased services	622,487	2,003,598	3,071,613	3,438,979	3,444,243	3,659,324	3,942,599	3,966,323	0.31	0.58	0.64	0.65	0.62	0.64	0.66	0.64
Supplies	776,863	1,566,954	1,894,927	1,810,950	1,786,877	1,950,698	1,875,189	1,920,987	0.38	0.45	0.40	0.34	0.32	0.34	0.31	0.31
Other	99,445	209,097	211,525	219,573	203,106	213,112	216,251	215,509	0.05	0.06	0.04	0.04	0.04	0.04	0.04	0.03
General administration	5,791,253	7,108,291	9,338,308	10,494,526	11,117,393	11,535,748	12,052,726	12,305,191	2.87	2.04	1.96	1.99	2.01	2.01	2.02	1.99
Salaries	2,603,562	3,351,554	4,024,030	4,401,697	4,622,952	4,746,838	4,883,367	5,074,357	1.29	0.96	0.84	0.83	0.84	0.83	0.82	0.82
Employee benefits	777,381	1,000,698	1,560,360	1,856,221	1,915,512	2,036,756	2,089,102	2,243,394	0.38	0.29	0.33	0.35	0.35	0.35	0.35	0.36
Purchased services	1,482,427	2,099,032	2,902,431	3,236,857	3,585,418	3,735,708	4,037,348	3,903,190	0.73	0.60	0.61	0.61	0.65	0.65	0.68	0.63
Supplies	172,898	206,137	227,885	228,417	237,184	249,401	265,647	276,833	0.09	0.06	0.05	0.04	0.04	0.04	0.04	0.04
Other	754,985	450,870	623,601	771,334	756,327	767,045	777,262	807,418	0.37	0.13	0.13	0.15	0.14	0.13	0.13	0.13
School administration	11,695,344	19,580,890	26,875,507	28,660,307	30,420,650	31,792,450	33,200,151	34,568,941	5.79	5.62	5.64	5.44	5.50	5.53	5.57	5.58
Salaries	8,935,903	14,817,213	19,209,872	20,191,545	21,132,933	21,921,938	22,759,806	23,536,654	4.42	4.25	4.03	3.83	3.82	3.81	3.82	3.80
Employee benefits	2,257,783	3,689,689	6,092,292	6,972,708	7,718,180	8,194,129	8,633,567	9,222,994	1.12	1.06	1.28	1.32	1.39	1.42	1.45	1.49
Purchased services	247,750	611,638	947,665	931,765	973,307	1,067,751	1,159,015	1,145,693	0.12	0.18	0.20	0.18	0.18	0.19	0.19	0.19
Supplies	189,711	369,257	481,794	426,864	435,786	443,385	475,970	485,616	0.09	0.11	0.10	0.08	0.08	0.08	0.08	0.08
Other	64,197	93,093	143,884	137,426	160,463	165,248	171,794	177,984	0.03	0.03	0.03	0.03	0.03	0.03	0.03	0.03
Operation and maintenance	21,290,655	34,034,158	46,828,916	50,214,709	53,051,141	54,200,172	55,045,039	57,433,468	10.54	9.77	9.82	9.52	9.58	9.42	9.23	9.28
Salaries	8,849,559	13,461,242	16,837,148	17,604,634	17,846,272	18,205,576	18,735,694	19,288,241	4.38	3.86	3.53	3.34	3.22	3.16	3.14	3.12
Employee benefits	2,633,075	3,778,520	6,276,703	7,195,927	7,694,270	8,024,419	8,293,750	8,794,259	1.30	1.08	1.32	1.36	1.39	1.39	1.39	1.42
Purchased services	5,721,125	9,642,217	12,650,704	13,351,922	15,022,138	15,514,037	15,895,748	16,881,488	2.83	2.77	2.65	2.53	2.71	2.70	2.67	2.73
Supplies	3,761,738	6,871,845	10,648,015	11,638,187	12,078,609	12,047,041	11,728,040	12,075,145	1.86	1.97	2.23	2.21	2.18	2.09	1.97	1.95
Other	325,157	280,334	416,345	424,039	409,852	409,098	391,807	394,335	0.16	0.08	0.09	0.08	0.07	0.07	0.07	0.06
Student transportation	8,678,954	14,052,654	19,979,068	22,370,807	23,845,036	23,961,692	24,325,727	25,350,286	4.30	4.03	4.19	4.24	4.31	4.16	4.08	4.09
Salaries	3,285,127	5,406,092	7,080,752	7,527,611	7,683,616	7,897,110	8,198,056	8,513,080	1.63	1.55	1.49	1.43	1.39	1.37	1.38	1.37
Employee benefits	892,985	1,592,127	2,719,742	3,124,937	3,296,150	3,412,883	3,599,805	3,808,782	0.44	0.46	0.57	0.59	0.60	0.59	0.60	0.62
Purchased services	3,345,232	5,767,462	8,085,392	9,153,621	9,926,270	10,063,360	10,392,864	10,819,968	1.66	1.66	1.70	1.74	1.79	1.75	1.74	1.75
Supplies	961,447	1,159,350	1,937,360	2,370,182	2,695,508	2,356,982	1,886,842	1,955,427	0.48	0.33	0.41	0.45	0.49	0.41	0.32	0.32
Other	194,163	127,623	155,822	194,456	243,492	231,357	248,160	253,029	0.10	0.04	0.03	0.04	0.04	0.04	0.04	0.04

See notes at end of table.

Table 236.20. Total expenditures for public elementary and secondary education and other related programs, by function and subfunction: Selected years, 1990–91 through 2016–17—Continued

Function and subfunction	Expenditures (in thousands of current dollars)								Percentage distribution of current expenditures for public schools							
	1990–91	2000–01	2006–07	2010–11	2013–14	2014–15	2015–16	2016–17	1990–91	2000–01	2006–07	2010–11	2013–14	2014–15	2015–16	2016–17
1	2	3	4	5	6	7	8	9	10	11	12	13	14	15	16	17
Other support services[4]	5,587,837	11,439,134	15,514,445	17,246,807	19,034,045	20,885,114	21,595,016	22,981,403	2.77	3.28	3.25	3.27	3.44	3.63	3.62	3.71
Salaries	2,900,394	5,521,381	7,140,671	8,139,084	8,618,767	9,104,041	9,565,073	9,879,480	1.44	1.58	1.50	1.54	1.56	1.58	1.60	1.60
Employee benefits	980,859	1,594,540	2,658,808	3,295,052	3,694,720	3,912,721	4,061,850	4,313,953	0.49	0.46	0.56	0.62	0.67	0.68	0.68	0.70
Purchased services	798,922	2,783,176	3,664,598	3,876,650	4,671,337	4,853,416	5,120,351	5,442,999	0.40	0.80	0.77	0.74	0.84	0.84	0.86	0.88
Supplies	294,527	626,889	874,764	876,293	1,097,951	1,163,493	1,241,221	1,337,399	0.15	0.18	0.18	0.17	0.20	0.20	0.21	0.22
Other	613,135	913,148	1,175,605	1,059,728	951,270	1,851,443	1,606,520	2,007,572	0.30	0.26	0.25	0.20	0.17	0.32	0.27	0.32
Food services	8,430,490	13,816,635	18,150,488	20,394,768	22,342,085	23,064,706	23,643,250	24,095,216	4.17	3.97	3.81	3.87	4.04	4.01	3.97	3.89
Salaries	—	4,966,092	6,092,744	6,482,085	6,699,499	6,873,015	7,098,376	7,215,563	—	1.43	1.28	1.23	1.21	1.19	1.19	1.17
Employee benefits	—	1,381,923	2,186,495	2,492,673	2,731,484	2,818,033	2,923,479	3,055,407	—	0.40	0.46	0.47	0.49	0.49	0.49	0.49
Purchased services	—	923,091	1,558,949	2,058,018	2,335,017	2,460,967	2,566,875	2,671,160	—	0.26	0.33	0.39	0.42	0.43	0.43	0.43
Supplies	—	6,420,201	8,123,362	9,118,886	10,333,931	10,628,481	10,753,015	10,843,608	—	1.84	1.70	1.73	1.87	1.85	1.80	1.75
Other	—	125,327	188,937	243,105	242,155	284,209	301,505	309,478	—	0.04	0.04	0.05	0.04	0.05	0.05	0.05
Enterprise operations[5]	946,705	776,463	1,084,578	1,110,646	1,155,773	1,121,673	1,202,858	1,245,194	0.47	0.22	0.23	0.21	0.21	0.19	0.20	0.20
Salaries	—	124,913	238,259	338,141	318,467	311,727	332,327	351,440	—	0.04	0.05	0.06	0.06	0.05	0.06	0.06
Employee benefits	—	23,837	83,290	97,063	108,464	116,266	119,116	131,513	—	0.01	0.02	0.02	0.02	0.02	0.02	0.02
Purchased services	—	189,230	246,253	172,641	186,682	180,106	207,176	207,769	—	0.05	0.05	0.03	0.03	0.03	0.03	0.03
Supplies	—	242,052	309,881	290,372	320,969	294,064	317,326	330,702	—	0.07	0.06	0.06	0.06	0.05	0.05	0.05
Other	—	196,430	206,895	212,430	221,191	219,510	226,914	223,771	—	0.06	0.04	0.04	0.04	0.04	0.04	0.04
Current expenditures for other programs	3,295,717	6,063,700	7,804,253	8,161,474	7,926,285	7,713,966	7,913,839	8,660,874	†	†	†	†	†	†	†	†
Community services	964,370	2,426,189	3,105,955	3,269,802	3,187,692	3,279,485	3,426,859	3,576,730	†	†	†	†	†	†	†	†
Private school programs	527,609	1,026,695	1,445,984	1,427,539	1,431,807	1,590,684	1,662,359	1,674,995	†	†	†	†	†	†	†	†
Adult education	1,365,523	1,838,265	2,047,409	2,013,156	1,804,646	1,815,963	1,946,215	2,039,281	†	†	†	†	†	†	†	†
Community colleges	5,356	351	31,352	34,045	30,906	28,238	29,113	10,659	†	†	†	†	†	†	†	†
Other	432,858	772,200	1,173,552	1,416,931	1,471,234	999,597	849,293	1,359,209	†	†	†	†	†	†	†	†
Capital outlay[6]	19,771,478	46,220,704	62,863,465	50,968,815	46,438,323	50,610,125	55,989,128	61,441,963	†	†	†	†	†	†	†	†
Public schools	19,655,496	46,078,494	62,763,411	50,888,951	46,297,257	50,448,404	55,841,211	61,280,584	†	†	†	†	†	†	†	†
Other current expenditures	115,982	142,210	100,054	79,864	141,066	161,722	147,917	161,379	†	†	†	†	†	†	†	†
Interest on school debt	4,324,768	10,165,940	14,712,882	17,934,224	17,152,459	17,479,466	17,500,574	18,333,942	†	†	†	†	†	†	†	†

—Not available.
†Not applicable.
[1]Includes estimated data for subfunctions of food services and enterprise operations.
[2]Includes expenditures for guidance, health, attendance, and speech pathology services.
[3]Includes expenditures for curriculum development, staff training, libraries, and media and computer centers.
[4]Includes business support services concerned with paying, transporting, exchanging, and maintaining goods and services for local education agencies; central support services, including planning, research, evaluation, information, staff, and data processing services; and other support services.

[5]Includes expenditures for operations funded by sales of products or services (e.g., school bookstore or computer time).
Includes very small amounts for direct program support made by state education agencies for local school districts.
[6]Includes expenditures for property and for buildings and alterations completed by school district staff or contractors.
NOTE: Excludes expenditures for state education agencies. Detail may not sum to totals because of rounding. Some data have been revised from previously published figures.
SOURCE: U.S. Department of Education, National Center for Education Statistics, Common Core of Data (CCD), "National Public Education Financial Survey," 1990–91 through 2016–17. (This table was prepared August 2019.)

Table 236.25. Current expenditures for public elementary and secondary education, by state or jurisdiction: Selected years, 1969–70 through 2016–17

[In thousands of current dollars]

State or jurisdiction	1969–70	1979–80	1989–90	1999–2000	2004–05	2006–07	2007–08	2008–09	2009–10	2010–11	2011–12	2012–13	2013–14	2014–15	2015–16	2016–17
1	2	3	4	5	6	7	8	9	10	11	12	13	14	15	16	17
United States	**$34,217,773**	**$86,984,142**	**$188,229,359**	**$323,888,508**	**$425,047,565**	**$476,814,206**	**$506,884,219**	**$518,922,842**	**$524,715,242**	**$527,291,339**	**$527,207,246**	**$535,795,823**	**$553,501,209**	**$575,331,825**	**$596,201,554**	**$619,164,572**
Alabama	422,730	1,146,713	2,275,233	4,176,082	5,164,406	6,245,031	6,832,439	6,683,843	6,670,517	6,592,925	6,386,517	6,532,358	6,742,829	6,806,467	6,885,677	7,097,472
Alaska	81,374	377,947	828,051	1,183,499	1,442,269	1,634,316	1,918,375	2,007,319	2,084,019	2,201,270	2,292,205	2,395,354	2,418,000	2,648,552	2,319,662	2,367,707
Arizona	281,941	949,753	2,258,660	4,288,739	6,579,957	7,815,720	8,403,221	8,726,755	8,482,552	8,340,211	7,976,089	8,164,529	8,187,607	8,370,884	8,551,673	8,966,684
Arkansas	235,083	666,949	1,404,545	2,380,331	3,546,999	3,997,701	4,156,368	4,240,839	4,459,910	4,578,136	4,606,995	4,637,169	4,778,074	4,813,321	4,872,214	4,936,465
California	3,831,595	9,172,158	21,485,782	38,129,479	50,918,654	57,352,599	61,570,555	60,080,929	58,248,662	57,526,835	57,975,189	58,323,458	61,050,894	65,953,946	72,003,129	76,663,731
Colorado	369,218	1,243,049	2,451,833	4,401,010	5,994,440	6,579,053	7,338,766	7,187,267	7,429,302	7,409,462	7,341,585	7,506,978	7,924,319	8,260,461	8,648,369	8,913,931
Connecticut	588,710	1,227,892	3,444,520	5,402,836	7,080,396	7,855,459	8,336,789	8,708,294	8,853,337	9,094,036	9,344,999	9,543,010	10,050,439	10,321,511	10,551,327	10,664,567
Delaware	108,747	269,108	520,953	937,630	1,299,349	1,437,707	1,489,594	1,518,786	1,549,812	1,613,304	1,751,143	1,761,559	1,816,383	1,860,732	1,941,408	2,029,229
District of Columbia	141,138	298,448	639,983	780,192	1,067,500	1,130,006	1,282,437	1,352,905	1,451,870	1,482,202	1,466,888	1,557,117	1,605,030	1,668,528	1,778,057	1,936,852
Florida	961,273	2,766,468	8,228,531	13,885,988	19,042,877	22,887,024	24,224,114	23,328,028	23,349,314	23,870,090	22,732,752	23,214,634	24,363,817	25,123,548	25,621,239	26,404,135
Georgia	599,371	1,608,028	4,505,962	9,158,624	12,528,856	14,828,715	16,030,039	15,976,945	15,730,409	15,527,907	15,623,633	15,536,733	15,921,673	16,530,506	17,283,295	18,126,272
Hawaii	141,324	351,889	700,012	1,213,695	1,648,086	2,045,198	2,122,779	2,225,438	2,136,144	2,141,561	2,187,480	2,178,284	2,316,586	2,344,496	2,502,117	2,600,074
Idaho	103,107	313,927	627,794	1,302,817	1,618,215	1,777,491	1,891,505	1,957,740	1,961,857	1,881,746	1,854,556	1,925,676	1,949,963	2,015,654	2,107,693	2,245,167
Illinois	1,896,067	4,579,355	8,125,493	14,462,773	18,658,428	20,326,591	21,874,484	23,495,271	24,695,773	24,554,467	25,012,915	25,783,911	27,289,963	28,545,089	29,253,457	31,449,028
Indiana	809,105	1,851,292	4,074,578	7,110,930	9,108,931	9,497,077	9,281,709	9,680,895	9,921,243	9,687,949	9,978,491	9,811,166	9,841,337	9,970,350	10,140,639	10,309,827
Iowa	527,086	1,186,659	2,004,742	3,264,336	3,808,200	4,231,932	4,499,236	4,731,463	4,794,308	4,855,871	4,971,944	5,143,771	5,354,843	5,526,877	5,663,444	5,840,808
Kansas	362,593	830,133	1,848,302	2,971,814	3,718,153	4,339,477	4,633,517	4,806,603	4,731,676	4,741,372	4,871,381	4,895,863	5,083,374	5,136,532	5,065,968	5,154,894
Kentucky	353,265	1,054,459	2,134,011	3,837,794	4,812,591	5,424,621	5,822,550	5,886,890	6,091,814	6,211,453	6,360,799	6,354,306	6,375,119	6,583,287	6,750,052	6,897,155
Louisiana	503,217	1,303,902	2,838,283	4,391,189	5,554,766	6,040,368	6,814,455	7,276,651	7,393,452	7,522,098	7,544,782	7,492,539	7,721,469	7,960,448	8,027,058	8,150,463
Maine	155,907	385,492	1,048,195	1,604,438	2,056,266	2,258,764	2,308,071	2,350,447	2,370,085	2,377,878	2,330,842	2,357,739	2,441,064	2,538,313	2,579,299	2,641,420
Maryland	721,794	1,783,056	3,894,644	6,545,135	8,682,586	10,210,303	11,211,176	11,591,965	11,883,677	11,885,333	11,850,634	12,108,546	12,314,446	12,620,036	12,774,063	13,233,589
Massachusetts	907,341	2,638,734	4,760,390	8,564,039	11,357,857	12,383,447	13,182,987	13,937,097	13,356,373	13,962,366	14,151,659	14,627,898	15,183,018	15,723,617	16,374,676	17,089,142
Michigan	1,799,945	4,642,847	8,025,621	13,994,294	16,353,921	17,013,259	17,053,521	17,217,584	17,227,515	16,786,444	16,485,178	16,354,807	16,493,575	16,849,135	16,977,163	17,206,122
Minnesota	781,243	1,786,768	3,474,398	6,140,442	7,310,284	8,060,410	8,426,264	9,182,281	8,927,288	8,944,867	9,053,021	9,354,376	9,723,759	10,222,017	10,687,048	11,056,128
Mississippi	262,760	756,018	1,472,710	2,510,376	3,243,888	3,692,358	3,898,401	3,967,232	3,990,876	3,887,981	3,972,787	4,006,798	4,071,006	4,145,632	4,234,977	4,229,767
Missouri	642,030	1,504,988	3,288,738	5,655,531	7,115,207	7,957,705	8,526,641	8,827,224	8,923,448	8,691,887	8,719,925	8,905,756	9,125,949	9,390,061	9,545,816	9,776,478
Montana	127,176	358,118	641,345	994,770	1,193,182	1,320,112	1,392,449	1,436,062	1,498,252	1,518,818	1,504,531	1,523,696	1,576,937	1,601,097	1,652,848	1,688,944
Nebraska	231,612	581,615	1,233,431	1,926,500	2,512,914	2,825,608	2,970,323	3,053,575	3,213,646	3,345,530	3,462,575	3,563,939	3,654,376	3,805,871	3,911,805	4,041,479
Nevada	87,273	281,901	712,898	1,875,467	2,722,264	3,311,471	3,515,004	3,606,035	3,592,994	3,676,997	3,574,233	3,577,346	3,738,777	3,880,472	4,092,457	4,320,504
New Hampshire	101,370	295,400	821,671	1,418,503	2,021,144	2,246,692	2,399,330	2,490,623	2,576,956	2,637,911	2,643,256	2,655,077	2,720,225	2,764,233	2,833,893	2,886,649
New Jersey	1,343,564	3,638,533	8,119,336	13,327,645	19,669,576	22,448,262	24,357,079	23,446,911	24,261,392	23,639,281	24,391,278	25,417,320	25,733,921	25,993,208	26,825,114	27,622,861
New Mexico	183,736	515,451	1,020,148	1,890,274	2,554,638	2,904,474	3,057,061	3,186,252	3,217,328	3,127,463	3,039,461	3,099,308	3,189,842	3,309,622	3,343,152	3,345,338
New York	4,111,839	8,760,500	18,090,978	28,433,240	38,866,853	43,679,908	46,443,426	48,635,363	50,251,461	51,574,134	52,460,494	52,938,586	55,080,662	56,862,010	59,161,439	60,905,055
North Carolina	676,193	1,880,862	4,342,826	7,713,293	9,835,550	11,248,336	11,482,912	12,598,382	12,200,362	12,322,555	12,303,426	12,666,607	12,685,461	13,210,839	13,466,942	13,943,070
North Dakota	97,895	228,483	459,391	638,946	832,157	838,221	886,317	928,528	1,000,095	1,049,772	1,098,090	1,174,364	1,287,133	1,373,266	1,451,309	1,510,292
Ohio	1,639,805	3,836,576	7,994,379	12,974,575	17,167,866	18,251,361	18,892,374	19,387,318	19,801,670	19,988,921	19,701,810	19,506,123	19,714,149	20,231,423	20,484,182	21,494,254
Oklahoma	339,105	1,055,844	1,905,332	3,382,581	4,161,024	4,750,536	4,932,913	5,082,062	5,192,124	5,036,031	5,170,978	5,329,897	5,451,048	5,560,047	5,606,044	5,496,402
Oregon	403,844	1,126,812	2,297,944	3,896,287	4,458,028	5,039,632	5,409,630	5,529,831	5,401,667	5,430,888	5,389,273	5,395,742	5,647,470	5,969,321	6,238,574	6,514,334
Pennsylvania	1,912,644	4,584,320	9,496,788	14,120,112	18,711,100	20,404,304	21,157,430	21,831,816	22,733,518	23,485,203	23,190,198	23,712,931	24,264,551	25,109,991	26,045,127	27,263,106
Rhode Island	145,443	362,046	801,908	1,393,143	1,825,900	2,039,633	2,134,609	2,139,317	2,136,582	2,149,366	2,167,450	2,121,403	2,182,976	2,242,486	2,283,927	2,362,463
South Carolina	367,689	997,984	2,322,618	4,087,355	5,312,739	6,023,043	6,453,817	6,626,763	6,566,165	6,465,486	6,619,072	6,950,410	7,163,995	7,437,182	7,727,135	8,035,426
South Dakota	109,375	238,332	447,074	737,998	916,563	977,006	1,037,875	1,080,054	1,115,861	1,126,503	1,100,100	1,125,929	1,182,721	1,211,080	1,253,268	1,379,026
Tennessee	473,226	1,319,303	2,790,808	4,931,734	6,446,691	6,975,099	7,540,306	7,768,063	7,894,661	8,225,374	8,345,584	8,531,675	8,606,624	8,736,367	8,886,994	9,260,615
Texas	1,518,181	4,997,689	12,763,954	25,098,703	31,919,107	36,105,784	39,033,235	40,688,181	42,621,886	42,864,291	41,067,619	42,066,035	44,330,579	47,527,971	49,577,688	51,033,537
Utah	179,981	518,251	1,130,135	2,102,655	2,627,022	2,987,810	3,444,936	3,638,775	3,635,085	3,704,133	3,779,760	3,944,736	4,094,074	4,290,876	4,539,291	4,754,714
Vermont	78,921	189,811	546,901	870,198	1,177,478	1,300,149	1,356,165	1,413,329	1,432,683	1,424,507	1,497,093	1,549,228	1,602,256	1,638,720	1,671,433	1,722,621
Virginia	704,677	1,881,519	4,621,071	7,757,598	10,705,162	12,465,858	13,125,666	13,505,290	13,193,633	12,968,457	13,403,576	13,868,587	13,955,249	14,384,705	14,677,698	15,296,646
Washington	699,984	1,825,782	3,550,819	6,399,885	7,870,979	8,752,007	9,331,539	9,940,325	9,832,913	10,040,312	10,040,607	10,216,676	10,911,929	11,470,245	12,483,668	13,188,097
West Virginia	249,404	678,386	1,316,637	2,086,937	2,527,767	2,742,344	2,841,962	2,998,657	3,328,177	3,388,294	3,275,246	3,188,181	3,194,770	3,226,918	3,169,684	3,216,323
Wisconsin	777,288	1,908,523	3,929,920	6,852,178	8,435,359	9,029,660	9,366,134	9,696,228	9,966,244	10,333,016	9,704,932	9,758,650	9,920,370	10,054,346	10,122,041	10,340,697
Wyoming	69,584	226,067	509,084	683,918	863,423	1,124,564	1,191,736	1,268,407	1,334,655	1,398,444	1,432,216	1,439,041	1,466,579	1,509,532	1,556,321	1,555,016
Other jurisdictions																
American Samoa	—	—	21,838	42,395	58,163	57,093	63,105	65,436	70,305	75,355	80,105	65,039	71,709	63,693	58,675	65,490
Guam	16,652	—	101,130	—	—	219,881	229,243	235,711	235,639	266,952	290,575	279,077	286,844	293,713	298,708	298,340
Northern Marianas	—	—	20,476	49,832	58,400	55,048	51,241	62,787	62,210	84,657	68,775	61,029	62,502	65,304	75,562	87,920
Puerto Rico	—	—	1,045,407	2,086,414	2,865,945	3,268,200	3,433,229	3,502,757	3,464,044	3,519,547	3,351,423	3,676,880	3,510,706	3,247,136	2,970,386	2,789,459
U.S. Virgin Islands	—	—	128,065	135,174	137,793	157,446	196,533	201,326	220,234	204,932	183,333	161,955	175,022	158,652	160,559	171,521

—Not available.
NOTE: Current expenditures include instruction, support services, food services, and enterprise operations. Beginning in 1989–90, expenditures for state administration are excluded. Data are not adjusted for changes in the purchasing power of the dollar due to inflation. Detail may not sum to totals because of rounding. Some data have been revised from previously published figures.

SOURCE: U.S. Department of Education, National Center for Education Statistics, *Statistics of State School Systems, 1969–70*; *Revenues and Expenditures for Public Elementary and Secondary Education, 1979–80*; and Common Core of Data (CCD), "National Public Education Financial Survey," 1989–90 through 2016–17. (This table was prepared August 2019.)

Table 236.30. Total expenditures for public elementary and secondary education and other related programs, by function and state or jurisdiction: 2016–17

[In thousands of current dollars]

State or jurisdiction	Total	Elementary/ secondary current expenditures, total	Instruction	Support services, total	Student support[6]	Instructional staff[5]	General administration	School administration	Operation and maintenance	Student transportation	Other support services	Food services	Enterprise operations[3]	Current expenditures for other programs[1]	Capital outlay[2]	Interest on school debt
1	2	3	4	5	6	7	8	9	10	11	12	13	14	15	16	17
United States	$707,601,350	$619,164,572	$376,069,486	$217,754,675	$35,946,038	$29,169,348	$12,305,191	$34,568,941	$57,433,468	$25,350,286	$22,981,403	$24,095,216	$1,245,194	$8,660,874	$61,441,963	$18,333,942
Alabama	8,030,225	7,097,472	4,049,192	2,563,159	446,175	298,519	182,443	442,733	660,054	366,671	166,563	485,121		122,765	637,471	172,517
Alaska	2,582,582	2,367,707	1,266,042	1,013,894	183,607	196,525	33,856	144,766	283,842	80,673	90,624	76,820	10,952	7,959	169,582	37,334
Arizona	10,530,826	8,966,684	4,828,965	3,669,286	687,666	434,553	173,941	502,905	1,098,094	371,832	400,295	467,132	1,301	92,293	1,220,401	251,447
Arkansas	5,622,673	4,936,465	2,769,224	1,898,530	266,940	415,124	124,843	258,857	500,434	181,436	150,896	263,084	5,627	30,111	529,540	126,558
California	87,968,218	76,663,731	45,442,062	28,155,354	4,598,429	4,880,860	753,775	5,082,339	7,573,197	1,679,133	3,587,603	2,878,381	187,935	924,523	7,470,798	2,909,165
Colorado	10,632,736	8,913,931	4,989,814	3,570,698	502,458	513,143	144,538	679,279	814,583	265,301	651,397	305,496	47,923	77,653	1,183,120	458,032
Connecticut	11,573,665	10,664,567	6,722,928	3,614,923	684,769	335,452	239,206	624,118	915,695	537,460	278,224	234,506	92,211	146,121	641,349	121,628
Delaware	2,247,039	2,029,229	1,269,553	691,907	90,650	37,248	31,895	128,691	216,676	100,560	86,188	67,769		53,793	141,956	22,062
District of Columbia	2,625,829	1,936,852	1,039,933	826,686	86,016	97,241	141,543	134,950	190,735	117,259	58,942	69,429	804	39,350	510,487	139,140
Florida	29,875,971	26,404,135	16,305,281	8,782,010	1,161,081	1,660,734	242,525	1,470,634	2,548,825	1,017,779	680,431	1,316,843		566,061	2,292,633	613,143
Georgia	20,344,480	18,126,272	11,061,068	6,035,059	943,009	941,356	231,190	1,144,159	1,361,543	847,547	566,256	977,222	52,922	33,899	1,959,953	224,356
Hawaii	2,778,688	2,600,074	1,520,054	949,131	244,802	87,772	13,048	186,738	289,131	63,216	64,424	130,889		16,960	161,655	0
Idaho	2,560,406	2,245,167	1,323,118	811,616	125,438	130,399	56,390	129,058	212,304	97,989	60,038	109,263	1,170	4,852	251,888	58,499
Illinois	34,588,140	31,449,028	19,603,947	11,068,443	2,214,977	1,134,511	1,182,158	1,638,178	2,440,415	1,334,997	1,123,207	776,639		162,530	2,018,535	958,047
Indiana	11,866,554	10,309,827	5,939,926	3,872,427	537,800	414,873	212,946	671,823	1,161,592	623,109	250,283	497,474		167,568	1,095,237	293,922
Iowa	6,809,987	5,840,808	3,524,206	2,050,887	341,231	364,865	148,834	330,146	484,172	205,084	176,556	258,951	6,764	38,180	813,457	117,542
Kansas	6,279,467	5,154,894	3,074,527	1,836,380	328,022	212,934	138,347	299,424	503,876	209,520	144,257	243,986		4,285	877,514	242,774
Kentucky	7,878,382	6,897,155	3,954,611	2,472,297	336,798	384,692	155,583	401,723	614,507	393,211	185,782	451,699	18,548	77,289	721,214	182,724
Louisiana	8,983,530	8,150,463	4,551,129	3,169,566	495,861	406,228	211,453	523,649	822,880	465,492	244,002	429,670	99	28,511	690,293	114,263
Maine	2,838,337	2,641,420	1,545,474	989,537	180,995	149,247	89,805	139,360	265,690	129,800	34,641	106,085	324	27,954	123,321	45,642
Maryland	14,669,628	13,233,589	8,432,187	4,424,391	595,713	610,473	128,514	893,341	1,116,465	691,807	388,078	377,011		39,956	1,237,379	158,705
Massachusetts	17,909,571	17,089,142	10,912,548	5,698,222	1,270,086	788,946	275,981	731,675	1,437,462	776,589	417,483	478,372		76,127	507,504	236,798
Michigan	19,612,463	17,206,122	9,875,810	6,695,573	1,360,804	871,777	386,016	960,612	1,510,634	720,147	885,583	634,739		290,037	1,393,502	722,803
Minnesota	14,127,456	11,056,128	7,153,109	3,388,197	323,867	565,322	415,002	444,288	746,716	625,079	267,924	467,516	47,304	513,373	2,160,797	397,158
Mississippi	4,673,532	4,229,767	2,400,216	1,570,271	224,419	196,756	142,223	257,398	433,815	202,096	113,565	259,057	223	29,715	360,550	53,501
Missouri	11,189,561	9,776,478	5,767,922	3,552,049	441,238	447,079	362,602	573,398	977,605	505,638	244,489	456,507		259,729	841,235	312,118
Montana	1,908,339	1,688,944	991,332	619,787	115,746	59,838	53,622	94,081	169,682	79,292	47,525	75,187	2,638	10,712	185,247	23,436
Nebraska	4,844,039	4,041,479	2,616,805	1,150,951	154,575	129,927	118,339	191,203	345,168	119,441	92,298	168,307	105,416	2,062	704,266	96,233
Nevada	4,987,380	4,320,504	2,554,828	1,597,247	237,070	238,700	69,977	317,085	400,038	169,077	165,299	168,244	185	25,125	477,784	163,967
New Hampshire	3,082,887	2,886,649	1,839,343	977,914	222,126	94,964	103,951	160,992	231,303	127,292	37,285	69,392		6,427	144,183	45,629
New Jersey	29,839,108	27,622,861	16,589,382	10,140,298	2,858,018	864,829	563,247	1,369,401	2,686,395	1,139,284	659,124	617,300	275,881	248,666	1,301,715	665,866
New Mexico	3,901,217	3,345,338	1,914,568	1,268,925	337,928	91,409	79,625	198,495	349,245	103,752	108,472	159,640	2,205	1,959	553,767	152
New York	67,194,754	60,905,055	42,389,679	17,303,620	1,950,611	1,567,910	984,799	2,332,684	5,600,964	3,073,409	1,793,244	1,211,757		2,236,181	2,588,199	1,465,319
North Carolina	15,389,536	13,943,070	8,718,633	4,488,163	758,525	479,501	241,840	826,515	1,146,436	568,542	466,805	736,274		65,366	1,359,657	21,444
North Dakota	1,824,684	1,510,292	906,313	491,975	60,781	51,919	65,204	78,090	129,557	60,165	46,259	70,245	41,759	11,520	270,221	32,651
Ohio	24,503,675	21,494,254	12,702,608	8,083,921	1,454,986	856,705	674,296	1,188,192	1,840,936	1,020,880	1,047,926	705,533	1,192	468,613	1,921,438	619,370
Oklahoma	6,228,822	5,496,402	3,072,797	2,004,138	374,211	221,748	164,623	306,275	576,296	173,226	187,759	363,634	55,833	28,946	637,138	66,337
Oregon	7,731,996	6,514,334	3,807,508	2,478,957	494,587	262,616	91,127	415,589	516,505	286,763	411,770	224,745	3,123	32,995	827,259	357,408
Pennsylvania	30,765,985	27,263,106	16,871,795	9,385,807	1,538,734	976,882	823,115	1,214,207	2,495,880	1,297,216	1,039,772	889,644	115,861	568,044	1,992,715	942,120
Rhode Island	2,591,928	2,362,463	1,428,107	869,618	248,744	90,506	35,431	112,808	183,344	102,335	96,450	64,216	522	57,258	132,829	39,378
South Carolina	9,721,717	8,035,426	4,455,636	3,147,018	619,625	497,997	78,239	520,441	788,674	303,877	338,165	412,078	20,694	61,891	1,286,658	337,743
South Dakota	1,571,670	1,379,026	816,490	484,102	76,803	48,890	46,268	66,995	143,576	49,059	52,510	71,486	6,948	7,171	152,374	33,099
Tennessee	10,418,228	9,260,615	5,652,110	3,091,904	416,268	546,464	192,701	560,592	767,734	347,912	260,232	516,601		82,703	849,531	225,379
Texas	64,601,315	51,033,537	29,431,662	18,755,366	2,515,067	2,622,675	750,018	2,926,014	5,379,370	1,485,564	3,076,659	2,846,509		349,734	9,830,252	3,387,792
Utah	5,813,157	4,754,714	3,019,473	1,485,927	185,373	190,712	53,508	312,558	432,719	140,222	170,835	238,818	10,496	10,557	929,100	118,786

See notes at end of table.

Table 236.30. Total expenditures for public elementary and secondary education and other related programs, by function and state or jurisdiction: 2016–17—Continued

[In thousands of current dollars]

State or jurisdiction	Total	Total expenditures												Current expenditures for other programs[1]	Capital outlay[2]	Interest on school debt
		Current expenditures for elementary and secondary programs														
		Elementary/ secondary current expenditures, total	Instruction	Support services												
				Support services, total	Student support[4]	Instructional staff[5]	General adminis-tration	School adminis-tration	Operation and maintenance	Student transpor-tation	Other support services	Food services	Enterprise operations[3]			
1	2	3	4	5	6	7	8	9	10	11	12	13	14	15	16	17
Vermont	1,797,465	1,722,621	1,107,391	570,073	133,216	71,370	36,224	108,604	128,666	56,760	35,234	43,217	1,940	10,448	55,204	9,193
Virginia	16,798,809	15,296,646	9,313,749	5,390,585	774,800	1,013,488	247,977	897,282	1,365,285	787,814	303,939	588,958	3,354	77,176	1,328,791	96,197
Washington	16,007,632	13,188,097	7,646,339	5,018,087	967,929	854,897	225,675	800,156	1,118,968	493,731	556,730	401,398	122,273	50,814	2,329,122	439,599
West Virginia	3,487,741	3,216,323	1,842,144	1,167,027	166,921	127,203	55,147	172,428	346,891	238,828	59,608	207,152	0	46,028	210,863	14,527
Wisconsin	11,876,059	10,340,697	6,136,689	3,824,345	516,870	545,466	298,849	521,086	958,276	438,470	545,329	379,585	78	363,949	1,011,285	160,128
Wyoming	1,913,258	1,555,016	920,260	588,428	93,676	86,084	32,731	82,920	150,621	77,950	64,448	45,637	691	4,935	350,996	2,312
Other jurisdictions																
American Samoa	76,797	65,490	31,446	14,110	35	7,235	891	4,188	0	531	1,231	19,934	0	1,800	9,507	0
Guam	361,502	298,340	142,210	136,084	28,008	16,535	4,802	18,225	38,523	7,948	22,043	20,046	0	0	50,806	12,356
Northern Marianas	92,633	87,920	41,483	33,459	6,742	8,246	1,727	4,276	7,083	1,443	3,942	12,977	0	2,993	1,720	0
Puerto Rico	2,891,749	2,789,459	1,128,669	1,262,150	317,681	166,391	79,112	121,196	407,424	93,059	77,287	398,641		67,690	34,600	0
U.S. Virgin Islands	172,940	171,521	100,419	59,708	14,841	4,219	8,199	9,465	6,854	7,536	8,592	11,236	158	1,303	116	0

[1]Includes expenditures for adult education, community colleges, private school programs funded by local and state education agencies, and community services.
[2]Includes expenditures for property and for buildings and alterations completed by school district staff or contractors.
[3]Includes expenditures for operations funded by sales of products or services (e.g., school bookstore or computer time). Also includes small amounts for direct program support made by state education agencies for local school districts.
[4]Includes expenditures for guidance, health, attendance, and speech pathology services.
[5]Includes expenditures for curriculum development, staff training, libraries, and media and computer centers.
NOTE: Excludes expenditures for state education agencies. Detail may not sum to totals because of rounding.
SOURCE: U.S. Department of Education, National Center for Education Statistics, Common Core of Data (CCD), "National Public Education Financial Survey," 2016–17. (This table was prepared August 2019.)

Table 236.50. Expenditures for instruction in public elementary and secondary schools, by subfunction and state or jurisdiction: 2015–16 and 2016–17

In thousands of current dollars

State or jurisdiction	2015–16 Total	Salaries	Employee benefits	Purchased services[2]	Supplies	Tuition and other	2016–17 Total	Salaries	Employee benefits	Purchased services[2]	Supplies	Tuition and other
	2	3	4	5	6	7	8	9	10	11	12	13
United States	$363,106,915	$230,477,780	$92,808,865	$18,048,424	$14,602,677	$7,169,169	$376,069,486	$236,792,085	$98,321,490	$18,476,414	$14,900,908	$7,578,589
Alabama	3,919,656	2,477,404	965,949	169,353	285,000	21,950	4,049,192	2,582,189	996,372	177,983	270,097	22,552
Alaska	1,251,726	711,182	414,485	58,577	56,348	11,134	1,266,042	721,744	414,054	61,383	57,179	11,682
Arizona	4,596,134	3,126,187	934,003	309,608	194,855	31,482	4,828,965	3,260,105	972,152	338,868	221,550	36,290
Arkansas	2,734,078	1,846,357	524,988	126,960	197,711	38,062	2,769,224	1,876,614	530,842	124,196	201,653	35,919
California	42,606,846	27,148,052	10,154,297	2,228,377	2,185,023	891,098	45,442,062	28,385,595	11,385,176	2,364,304	2,359,697	947,290
Colorado	4,872,737	3,348,613	953,906	133,253	304,275	132,690	4,989,814	3,421,045	1,004,243	135,159	298,385	130,982
Connecticut	6,664,475	3,909,375	1,885,230	220,157	112,589	527,124	6,722,928	3,963,987	1,899,984	217,458	103,922	537,577
Delaware	1,217,984	732,116	382,812	13,611	55,002	34,444	1,269,553	758,279	419,882	17,908	51,864	21,620
District of Columbia	985,046	687,092	139,236	42,456	24,852	91,410	1,039,933	709,164	167,435	48,003	22,171	93,159
Florida	15,763,102	9,227,638	2,794,944	3,131,946	487,810	120,763	16,305,281	9,375,840	2,907,840	3,366,298	529,449	125,854
Georgia	10,690,729	6,932,398	2,674,848	399,785	625,381	58,319	11,061,068	7,297,731	2,824,024	258,060	620,321	60,934
Hawaii	1,466,292	948,100	381,962	55,103	71,682	9,444	1,520,054	955,344	420,171	53,923	80,064	10,552
Idaho	1,249,823	854,488	300,346	45,711	47,744	1,533	1,323,118	902,280	316,921	50,903	51,567	1,448
Illinois	18,155,294	10,057,461	6,270,188	1,024,980	444,020	358,645	19,603,947	10,142,329	7,673,293	1,007,196	423,696	357,434
Indiana	5,829,338	3,622,089	1,891,038	104,080	202,779	9,352	5,939,926	3,687,499	1,911,384	113,159	218,550	9,334
Iowa	3,431,757	2,414,681	786,969	90,387	104,827	34,894	3,524,206	2,487,050	812,850	81,752	106,932	35,622
Kansas	3,027,649	2,153,182	624,906	89,900	135,838	23,823	3,074,527	2,173,096	633,067	94,200	147,246	26,919
Kentucky	3,909,722	2,653,544	1,049,594	61,715	130,899	13,970	3,954,611	2,678,619	1,061,769	63,738	136,607	13,878
Louisiana	4,518,231	2,781,019	1,326,846	144,110	206,561	59,697	4,551,129	2,786,077	1,331,231	152,312	215,036	66,472
Maine	1,516,283	964,407	394,300	39,953	36,233	81,389	1,545,474	993,471	386,470	42,733	35,655	87,145
Maryland	8,028,897	5,029,476	2,283,910	250,071	187,431	278,008	8,432,187	5,256,375	2,387,876	299,548	198,799	289,589
Massachusetts	10,492,714	6,656,111	2,641,926	95,886	277,803	820,988	10,912,548	6,823,131	2,863,534	99,994	273,503	852,386
Michigan	9,766,683	5,176,562	3,368,889	947,726	254,201	19,306	9,875,810	5,203,188	3,414,023	976,162	261,915	20,522
Minnesota	6,949,478	4,641,312	1,642,237	367,612	207,138	91,179	7,153,109	4,835,058	1,613,811	378,176	224,881	101,184
Mississippi	2,414,582	1,667,459	552,238	72,636	102,866	19,384	2,400,216	1,658,005	549,816	70,947	100,228	21,220
Missouri	5,651,864	3,890,461	1,178,624	191,790	358,768	32,221	5,767,922	3,973,411	1,213,296	185,357	365,050	30,808
Montana	970,897	643,783	195,581	58,266	68,008	5,259	991,332	660,424	201,945	59,733	63,835	5,395
Nebraska	2,486,681	1,637,339	583,658	131,445	112,253	21,987	2,616,805	1,679,453	660,061	134,212	119,991	23,089
Nevada	2,398,324	1,565,794	640,137	47,619	140,144	4,631	2,554,828	1,648,455	669,525	48,597	182,143	6,108
New Hampshire	1,804,284	1,070,727	499,636	48,479	35,651	149,791	1,839,343	1,085,209	510,293	50,275	35,204	158,362
New Jersey	16,132,662	9,674,517	4,594,280	636,802	455,518	771,545	16,589,382	9,803,635	4,888,507	660,988	443,100	793,153
New Mexico	1,902,034	1,284,541	443,881	67,436	105,846	331	1,914,568	1,282,898	450,510	74,019	106,860	280
New York	41,924,498	24,955,914	13,224,238	2,330,671	729,050	684,624	42,389,679	25,538,666	13,445,451	1,947,701	752,814	705,047
North Carolina	8,395,193	5,810,078	1,895,980	284,479	404,208	449	8,718,633	5,972,552	2,014,735	295,971	435,369	6
North Dakota	869,633	590,288	221,357	23,072	28,732	6,183	906,313	616,846	231,438	22,323	29,926	5,780
Ohio	11,954,341	7,526,394	2,775,349	725,767	459,953	466,877	12,703,608	7,852,213	2,868,220	934,872	475,638	572,665
Oklahoma	3,125,438	2,163,799	696,168	59,181	193,959	12,330	3,072,797	2,124,218	695,511	58,739	182,005	12,324
Oregon	3,650,480	2,144,702	1,138,171	130,150	197,142	40,315	3,807,508	2,239,094	1,186,291	139,382	202,781	39,959
Pennsylvania	16,083,136	9,192,617	5,305,250	783,388	474,936	326,944	16,871,795	9,396,615	5,724,229	833,924	541,482	375,546
Rhode Island	1,393,738	870,708	420,972	11,913	23,693	66,453	1,428,107	892,529	433,087	14,093	23,157	65,241
South Carolina	4,294,386	2,842,958	1,027,856	174,223	225,632	23,717	4,455,636	2,922,021	1,075,491	192,972	240,425	24,728
South Dakota	730,833	492,308	148,723	28,656	48,482	12,665	816,490	552,513	162,846	32,537	54,046	14,549
Tennessee	5,465,563	3,665,541	1,205,593	127,147	454,033	13,249	5,652,110	3,791,470	1,258,410	126,009	461,240	14,980
Texas	28,970,556	22,035,575	3,664,960	1,003,668	1,928,691	337,661	29,431,662	22,537,224	3,794,495	1,058,061	1,687,197	354,685
Utah	2,868,057	1,748,837	810,108	101,254	192,319	15,539	3,019,473	1,831,170	846,311	105,540	217,834	18,617
Vermont	1,061,379	599,678	291,342	61,557	21,518	87,283	1,107,391	613,350	317,302	58,196	20,116	98,428
Virginia	8,944,628	6,054,755	2,366,965	188,634	321,229	13,045	9,313,749	6,256,908	2,499,818	206,591	342,165	8,266
Washington	7,211,513	4,685,619	1,732,671	445,329	284,788	63,107	7,646,339	5,000,463	1,826,380	471,563	283,814	64,118
West Virginia	1,824,705	1,122,269	526,003	39,033	131,236	6,164	1,842,144	1,104,748	558,286	38,753	132,865	7,492
Wisconsin	6,018,974	3,856,289	1,623,439	90,922	225,236	223,087	6,136,689	3,898,231	1,631,245	100,318	248,504	258,391
Wyoming	923,865	585,983	257,877	33,597	42,785	3,623	920,260	583,957	259,585	31,325	42,383	3,010
Other jurisdictions												
American Samoa	29,612	21,780	4,591	450	985	1,806	31,446	22,500	4,691	1,230	1,193	1,831
Guam	143,897	105,474	36,814	166	1,441	2	142,210	104,755	36,469	479	507	0
Northern Marianas	36,419	25,031	4,666	3,424	2,054	1,244	41,483	24,861	6,288	3,828	4,502	2,004
Puerto Rico	1,194,926	886,323	240,157	51,266	16,900	280	1,128,669	836,793	225,101	53,047	13,402	326
U.S. Virgin Islands	94,624	63,079	26,493	2,136	2,915	0	100,419	66,997	28,139	2,249	3,034	0

See notes at end of table.

Table 236.50. Expenditures for instruction in public elementary and secondary schools, by subfunction and state or jurisdiction: 2015–16 and 2016–17—Continued

In thousands of constant 2018–19 dollars[1]

State or jurisdiction	2015–16						2016–17					
	Total	Salaries	Employee benefits	Purchased services[2]	Supplies	Tuition and other	Total	Salaries	Employee benefits	Purchased services[2]	Supplies	Tuition and other
1	14	15	16	17	18	19	20	21	22	23	24	25
United States	**$385,957,965**	**$244,982,211**	**$98,649,514**	**$19,184,248**	**$15,521,653**	**$7,620,340**	**$392,516,017**	**$247,147,640**	**$102,621,354**	**$19,284,438**	**$15,552,565**	**$7,910,021**
Alabama	4,166,328	2,633,312	1,026,738	180,011	302,936	23,332	4,226,274	2,695,115	1,039,946	185,766	281,909	23,538
Alaska	1,330,499	755,938	440,569	62,263	59,894	11,835	1,321,409	753,308	432,161	64,068	59,679	12,192
Arizona	4,885,378	3,322,924	992,781	329,092	207,118	33,463	5,040,149	3,402,678	1,014,667	353,687	231,239	37,877
Arkansas	2,906,139	1,962,552	558,027	134,950	210,153	40,457	2,890,329	1,958,683	554,057	129,627	210,472	37,490
California	45,288,181	28,856,553	10,793,328	2,368,613	2,322,530	947,176	47,429,366	29,626,973	11,883,080	2,467,702	2,462,893	988,718
Colorado	5,179,389	3,559,348	1,013,937	141,639	323,424	141,040	5,208,032	3,570,657	1,048,161	141,070	311,434	136,710
Connecticut	7,073,254	4,155,400	2,003,871	234,012	119,675	560,297	7,016,939	4,137,343	1,983,075	226,968	108,466	561,087
Delaware	1,294,634	778,189	406,903	14,467	58,463	36,611	1,325,074	791,440	438,244	18,691	54,132	22,565
District of Columbia	1,047,037	730,332	147,999	45,128	26,416	97,163	1,085,411	740,177	174,758	50,103	23,141	97,233
Florida	16,755,105	9,808,352	2,970,836	3,329,046	518,508	128,363	17,018,355	9,785,871	3,035,008	3,513,516	552,603	131,358
Georgia	11,363,519	7,368,667	2,843,181	424,944	664,737	61,989	11,544,799	7,616,880	2,947,526	269,346	647,449	63,598
Hawaii	1,558,568	1,007,766	405,999	58,571	76,194	10,039	1,586,530	997,124	438,546	55,281	83,565	11,014
Idaho	1,328,476	908,263	319,248	48,588	50,748	1,630	1,380,982	941,739	330,781	53,129	53,822	1,511
Illinois	19,297,843	10,690,398	6,664,784	1,089,484	471,963	381,215	20,461,280	10,585,880	8,008,866	1,051,243	442,225	373,065
Indiana	6,196,190	3,850,034	2,010,045	1,110,630	215,540	9,941	6,199,695	3,848,764	1,994,974	118,108	228,107	9,742
Iowa	3,647,724	2,566,641	836,495	96,075	111,424	37,090	3,678,329	2,595,816	848,398	85,327	111,608	37,180
Kansas	3,218,185	2,288,686	664,233	95,557	144,386	25,322	3,208,984	2,268,131	660,753	98,319	153,685	28,096
Kentucky	4,155,769	2,820,536	1,115,648	65,599	139,137	14,849	4,127,557	2,795,762	1,108,203	66,526	142,581	14,485
Louisiana	4,802,572	2,956,034	1,410,347	153,177	219,560	63,454	4,750,162	2,907,920	1,389,450	158,973	224,440	69,378
Maine	1,611,705	1,025,099	419,114	42,467	38,514	86,511	1,613,062	1,036,918	403,372	44,602	37,214	90,956
Maryland	8,534,171	5,345,991	2,427,641	265,808	199,227	295,504	8,800,944	5,486,250	2,492,304	312,649	207,493	302,253
Massachusetts	11,153,042	7,074,993	2,808,188	101,920	295,286	872,654	11,389,783	7,121,525	2,988,764	104,367	285,464	889,663
Michigan	10,381,320	5,502,333	3,580,900	1,007,369	270,198	20,521	10,307,706	5,430,738	3,563,327	1,018,852	273,369	21,419
Minnesota	7,386,822	4,933,399	1,745,586	390,747	220,174	96,917	7,465,934	5,046,508	1,684,387	394,714	234,715	105,609
Mississippi	2,566,537	1,772,396	586,991	77,207	109,339	20,604	2,505,184	1,730,514	573,861	74,050	104,611	22,148
Missouri	6,007,548	4,135,296	1,252,797	203,860	381,346	34,249	6,020,168	4,147,178	1,266,357	193,463	381,015	32,155
Montana	1,031,997	684,298	207,889	61,930	72,288	5,590	1,034,685	689,306	210,777	62,345	66,626	5,631
Nebraska	2,643,173	1,740,380	620,388	139,717	119,317	23,370	2,731,245	1,752,900	688,928	140,081	125,238	24,099
Nevada	2,549,256	1,664,333	680,422	50,615	148,963	4,922	2,666,558	1,720,546	698,805	50,723	190,109	6,375
New Hampshire	1,917,832	1,138,110	531,079	51,530	37,894	159,218	1,919,782	1,132,668	532,609	52,474	36,743	165,287
New Jersey	17,147,923	10,283,354	4,883,407	676,877	484,185	820,100	17,314,880	10,232,374	5,102,294	689,894	462,478	827,840
New Mexico	2,021,733	1,365,379	471,815	71,680	112,507	352	1,998,297	1,339,003	470,212	77,256	111,533	293
New York	44,562,891	26,526,440	14,056,466	2,477,345	774,931	727,709	44,243,493	26,655,540	14,033,456	2,032,879	785,737	735,881
North Carolina	8,923,519	6,175,718	2,015,298	302,382	429,645	477	9,099,922	6,233,748	2,102,845	308,915	454,408	6
North Dakota	924,360	627,436	235,288	24,524	30,541	6,572	945,948	643,823	241,559	23,299	31,235	6,033
Ohio	12,706,652	8,000,045	2,950,007	771,441	488,899	496,259	13,259,171	8,195,612	2,993,655	975,756	496,439	597,710
Oklahoma	3,322,128	2,299,971	739,980	62,906	206,165	13,106	3,207,179	2,217,116	725,927	61,307	189,965	12,863
Oregon	3,880,212	2,279,673	1,209,798	138,340	209,548	42,852	3,974,021	2,337,015	1,238,171	145,478	211,650	41,707
Pennsylvania	17,095,280	9,771,127	5,639,120	832,689	504,825	347,520	17,609,644	9,807,554	5,974,565	870,393	565,162	391,970
Rhode Island	1,481,449	925,503	447,465	12,662	25,184	70,635	1,490,562	931,562	452,027	14,710	24,170	68,094
South Carolina	4,564,641	3,021,871	1,092,541	185,188	239,832	25,209	4,650,493	3,049,809	1,122,525	201,411	250,939	25,809
South Dakota	776,826	523,289	158,082	30,459	51,533	13,462	852,197	576,676	169,968	33,960	56,410	15,185
Tennessee	5,809,522	3,896,221	1,281,463	135,149	482,606	14,083	5,899,292	3,957,281	1,313,444	131,520	481,412	15,635
Texas	30,793,731	23,422,318	3,895,603	1,066,831	2,050,068	358,911	30,718,788	23,522,838	3,960,438	1,104,332	1,760,983	370,196
Utah	3,048,549	1,858,895	861,090	107,626	204,422	16,517	3,151,523	1,911,252	883,323	110,156	227,361	19,431
Vermont	1,128,174	637,417	309,677	65,431	22,873	92,776	1,155,820	640,173	331,178	60,741	20,996	102,732
Virginia	9,507,532	6,435,793	2,515,923	200,505	341,445	13,866	9,721,064	6,530,540	2,609,142	215,626	357,129	8,627
Washington	7,665,348	4,980,495	1,841,711	473,354	302,710	67,078	7,980,734	5,219,147	1,906,253	492,186	296,226	66,922
West Virginia	1,939,537	1,192,896	559,105	41,489	139,495	6,552	1,922,706	1,153,062	582,702	40,447	138,676	7,820
Wisconsin	6,397,760	4,098,973	1,725,605	96,644	239,411	237,126	6,405,063	4,068,711	1,702,584	104,705	259,372	269,691
Wyoming	982,005	622,861	274,106	35,711	45,477	3,851	960,506	609,495	270,937	32,695	44,236	3,142
Other jurisdictions												
American Samoa	31,476	23,151	4,880	479	1,047	1,919	32,821	23,484	4,896	1,284	1,245	1,912
Guam	152,952	112,112	39,131	176	1,532	2	148,429	109,336	38,063	500	529	0
Northern Marianas	38,711	26,607	4,959	3,639	2,183	1,322	43,297	25,948	6,563	3,995	4,699	2,091
Puerto Rico	1,270,125	942,101	255,271	54,492	17,963	297	1,178,028	873,388	234,945	55,367	13,988	340
U.S. Virgin Islands	100,578	67,049	28,161	2,270	3,098	0	104,811	69,927	29,369	2,348	3,167	0

[1]Constant dollars based on the Consumer Price Index (CPI), prepared by the Bureau of Labor Statistics, U.S. Department of Labor, adjusted to a school-year basis. The CPI does not account for differences in inflation rates from state to state. For more information about adjusting for differences in the cost of living from state to state, see the American Community Survey Comparable Wage Index for Teachers (ACS-CWIFT) at https://nces.ed.gov/programs/edge/Docs/EDGE_ACS_CWIFT2015_FILEDOC.pdf.

[2]Includes purchased professional services of teachers or others who provide instruction for students.

NOTE: Excludes expenditures for state education agencies. Detail may not sum to totals because of rounding. Some data have been revised from previously published figures.

SOURCE: U.S. Department of Education, National Center for Education Statistics, Common Core of Data (CCD), "National Public Education Financial Survey," 2015–16 and 2016–17. (This table was prepared November 2019.)

Table 236.55. Total and current expenditures per pupil in public elementary and secondary schools: Selected years, 1919–20 through 2016–17

| | Expenditure per pupil in average daily attendance | | | | Expenditure per pupil in fall enrollment[1] | | | | |
| | Unadjusted dollars[2] | | Constant 2018–19 dollars[3] | | Unadjusted dollars[2] | | Constant 2018–19 dollars[3] | | |
School year	Total expenditure[4]	Current expenditure	Total expenditure[4]	Current expenditure	Total expenditure[4]	Current expenditure	Total expenditure[4]	Current expenditure	Annual percent change in current expenditure
1	2	3	4	5	6	7	8	9	10
1919–20	$64	$53	$850	$709	$48	$40	$636	$530	—
1929–30	108	87	1,605	1,283	90	72	1,329	1,062	—
1931–32	97	81	1,702	1,424	82	69	1,441	1,206	—
1933–34	76	67	1,458	1,291	65	57	1,239	1,097	—
1935–36	88	74	1,621	1,369	74	63	1,371	1,158	—
1937–38	100	84	1,763	1,483	86	72	1,513	1,273	—
1939–40	106	88	1,916	1,597	92	76	1,661	1,384	—
1941–42	110	98	1,787	1,597	94	84	1,530	1,367	—
1943–44	125	117	1,812	1,700	105	99	1,527	1,433	—
1945–46	146	136	2,025	1,894	124	116	1,725	1,613	—
1947–48	205	181	2,227	1,973	179	158	1,945	1,723	—
1949–50	260	210	2,784	2,249	231	187	2,471	1,996	—
1951–52	314	246	3,030	2,371	275	215	2,653	2,076	—
1953–54	351	265	3,305	2,494	312	236	2,939	2,218	—
1955–56	387	294	3,646	2,772	354	269	3,333	2,534	—
1957–58	447	341	3,968	3,025	408	311	3,619	2,759	—
1959–60	471	375	4,060	3,234	440	350	3,793	3,021	—
1961–62	517	419	4,357	3,530	485	393	4,089	3,313	—
1963–64	559	460	4,588	3,780	520	428	4,270	3,518	—
1965–66	654	538	5,190	4,268	607	499	4,818	3,962	—
1967–68	786	658	5,857	4,903	732	612	5,448	4,560	—
1969–70	955	816	6,403	5,471	879	751	5,895	5,037	—
1970–71	1,049	911	6,691	5,809	970	842	6,186	5,370	6.6
1971–72	1,128	990	6,941	6,091	1,034	908	6,366	5,587	4.0
1972–73	1,211	1,077	7,162	6,371	1,117	993	6,607	5,877	5.2
1973–74	1,364	1,207	7,409	6,558	1,244	1,101	6,756	5,979	1.7
1974–75	1,545	1,365	7,554	6,673	1,423	1,257	6,959	6,147	2.8
1975–76	1,697	1,504	7,751	6,867	1,563	1,385	7,137	6,323	2.9
1976–77	1,816	1,638	7,838	7,066	1,674	1,509	7,222	6,512	3.0
1977–78	2,002	1,823	8,097	7,371	1,842	1,677	7,447	6,779	4.1
1978–79	2,210	2,020	8,171	7,470	2,029	1,855	7,504	6,860	1.2
1979–80	2,491	2,272	8,125	7,411	2,290	2,088	7,470	6,813	-0.7
1980–81	2,742[5]	2,502	8,018[5]	7,314	2,529[5]	2,307	7,395[5]	6,746	-1.0
1981–82	2,973[5]	2,726	8,002[5]	7,336	2,754[5]	2,525	7,413[5]	6,795	0.7
1982–83	3,203[5]	2,955	8,266[5]	7,626	2,966[5]	2,736	7,654[5]	7,061	3.9
1983–84	3,471[5]	3,173	8,638[5]	7,896	3,216[5]	2,940	8,002[5]	7,315	3.6
1984–85	3,722[5]	3,470	8,912[5]	8,310	3,456[5]	3,222	8,275[5]	7,716	5.5
1985–86	4,020[5]	3,756	9,356[5]	8,741	3,724[5]	3,479	8,668[5]	8,098	5.0
1986–87	4,308[5]	3,970	9,809[5]	9,040	3,995[5]	3,682	9,096[5]	8,383	3.5
1987–88	4,654[5]	4,240	10,175[5]	9,270	4,310[5]	3,927	9,423[5]	8,585	2.4
1988–89	5,108	4,645	10,674	9,707	4,737	4,307	9,899	9,001	4.8
1989–90	5,547	4,980	11,064	9,933	5,172	4,643	10,316	9,261	2.9
1990–91	5,882	5,258	11,124	9,944	5,484	4,902	10,371	9,271	0.1
1991–92	6,072	5,421	11,127	9,934	5,626	5,023	10,310	9,205	-0.7
1992–93	6,279	5,584	11,158	9,922	5,802	5,160	10,311	9,169	-0.4
1993–94	6,489	5,767	11,240	9,990	5,994	5,327	10,382	9,227	0.6
1994–95	6,723	5,989	11,320	10,085	6,206	5,529	10,450	9,310	0.9
1995–96	6,959	6,147	11,408	10,076	6,441	5,689	10,559	9,326	0.2
1996–97	7,297	6,393	11,630	10,189	6,761	5,923	10,776	9,441	1.2
1997–98	7,701	6,676	12,058	10,453	7,139	6,189	11,179	9,691	2.7
1998–99	8,115	7,013	12,492	10,795	7,531	6,508	11,592	10,017	3.4
1999–2000	8,589	7,394	12,849	11,061	8,030	6,912	12,013	10,341	3.2
2000–01	9,180	7,904	13,278	11,433	8,572	7,380	12,399	10,675	3.2
2001–02	9,611	8,259	13,661	11,738	8,993	7,727	12,782	10,983	2.9
2002–03	9,950	8,610	13,838	11,974	9,296	8,044	12,929	11,188	1.9
2003–04	10,308	8,900	14,029	12,112	9,625	8,310	13,100	11,310	1.1
2004–05	10,779	9,316	14,241	12,309	10,078	8,711	13,316	11,509	1.8
2005–06	11,338	9,778	14,430	12,445	10,603	9,145	13,495	11,639	1.1
2006–07	12,015	10,336	14,907	12,823	11,252	9,679	13,960	12,009	3.2
2007–08	12,759	10,982	15,264	13,138	11,965	10,298	14,314	12,320	2.6
2008–09	13,033	11,239	15,377	13,260	12,222	10,540	14,421	12,435	0.9
2009–10	13,035	11,427	15,232	13,353	12,133	10,636	14,178	12,429	-0.1
2010–11	12,926	11,433	14,807	13,098	12,054	10,663	13,809	12,215	-1.7
2011–12	12,796	11,362	14,241	12,645	11,991	10,648	13,346	11,850	-3.0
2012–13	12,859	11,509	14,077	12,599	12,033	10,771	13,173	11,791	-0.5
2013–14	13,174	11,819	14,201	12,740	12,335	11,066	13,296	11,928	1.2
2014–15	13,668	12,224	14,626	13,081	12,796	11,445	13,693	12,247	2.7
2015–16	14,171	12,619	15,063	13,413	13,299	11,842	14,136	12,587	2.8
2016–17	14,778	13,094	15,424	13,667	13,834	12,258	14,439	12,794	1.6

—Not available.
[1]Data for 1919–20 to 1953–54 are based on school-year enrollment.
[2]Unadjusted (or "current") dollars have not been adjusted to compensate for inflation.
[3]Constant dollars based on the Consumer Price Index, prepared by the Bureau of Labor Statistics, U.S. Department of Labor, adjusted to a school-year basis.
[4]Excludes "Other current expenditures," such as community services, private school programs, adult education, and other programs not allocable to expenditures per student at public schools.
[5]Estimated.
NOTE: Beginning in 1980–81, state administration expenditures are excluded from both "total" and "current" expenditures. Current expenditures include instruction, support services, food services, and enterprise operations. Total expenditures include current expenditures, capital outlay, and interest on debt. Beginning in 1988–89, extensive changes were made in the data collection procedures. Some data have been revised from previously published figures.
SOURCE: U.S. Department of Education, National Center for Education Statistics, *Biennial Survey of Education in the United States*, 1919–20 through 1955–56; *Statistics of State School Systems*, 1957–58 through 1969–70; *Revenues and Expenditures for Public Elementary and Secondary Education*, 1970–71 through 1986–87; and Common Core of Data (CCD), "National Public Education Financial Survey," 1987–88 through 2016–17. (This table was prepared August 2019.)

Table 236.60. Total and current expenditures per pupil in fall enrollment in public elementary and secondary schools, by function and subfunction: Selected years, 1990–91 through 2016–17

Function and subfunction	Expenditures per pupil in current dollars									Expenditures per pupil in constant 2018–19 dollars[1]								
	1990–91	2000–01	2006–07	2010–11	2012–13	2013–14	2014–15	2015–16	2016–17	1990–91	2000–01	2006–07	2010–11	2012–13	2013–14	2014–15	2015–16	2016–17
1	2	3	4	5	6	7	8	9	10	11	12	13	14	15	16	17	18	19
Total expenditures	**$5,484**	**$8,572**	**$11,252**	**$12,054**	**$12,033**	**$12,335**	**$12,796**	**$13,299**	**$13,834**	**$10,371**	**$12,399**	**$13,960**	**$13,809**	**$13,173**	**$13,296**	**$13,693**	**$14,136**	**$14,439**
Current expenditures for public schools	4,902	7,380	9,679	10,663	10,771	11,066	11,445	11,842	12,258	9,271	10,675	12,009	12,215	11,791	11,928	12,247	12,587	12,794
Salaries	3,220[2]	4,752	5,849	6,300	6,265	6,372	6,530	6,748	6,927	6,090[2]	6,874	7,257	7,217	6,858	6,868	6,987	7,173	7,230
Employee benefits	824[2]	1,228	1,935	2,260	2,372	2,472	2,603	2,717	2,878	1,558[2]	1,777	2,400	2,589	2,596	2,665	2,786	2,888	3,004
Purchased services	397[2]	673	939	1,082	1,121	1,163	1,216	1,283	1,325	752[2]	974	1,165	1,239	1,228	1,254	1,301	1,363	1,382
Tuition	29[2]	52	80	101	102	106	111	114	121	55[2]	75	100	116	112	114	119	121	127
Supplies	359[2]	599	779	817	817	858	871	869	886	679[2]	866	967	936	895	924	932	924	925
Other	72[2]	76	97	103	93	95	114	111	120	136[2]	110	120	118	102	103	122	118	125
Instruction	2,965	4,541	5,901	6,522	6,547	6,726	6,951	7,212	7,445	5,608	6,568	7,321	7,471	7,167	7,250	7,439	7,666	7,771
Salaries	2,202	3,273	3,997	4,307	4,273	4,344	4,437	4,578	4,688	4,164	4,735	4,959	4,934	4,678	4,682	4,748	4,866	4,893
Employee benefits	542	837	1,302	1,522	1,598	1,678	1,767	1,843	1,946	1,025	1,211	1,616	1,743	1,750	1,809	1,891	1,959	2,032
Purchased services	66	136	223	297	297	303	329	358	366	125	197	277	340	325	327	352	381	382
Tuition	29	52	80	101	102	106	111	114	121	55	75	100	116	112	114	119	121	127
Supplies	111	220	271	266	250	267	280	290	295	210	318	336	304	273	288	299	308	308
Textbooks	—	—	—	47	43	46	49	50	52	—	—	—	54	47	50	52	54	54
Other	15	22	27	30	27	28	27	28	29	29	32	33	34	30	30	29	30	30
Student support[3]	217	366	512	594	601	615	644	676	712	410	530	635	680	658	663	689	718	743
Salaries	159	262	342	392	389	396	411	429	446	301	379	425	449	425	427	440	456	466
Employee benefits	40	64	109	132	142	146	157	166	181	76	93	135	151	155	158	168	177	189
Purchased services	11	28	43	52	56	57	60	64	67	21	41	54	60	61	61	64	68	70
Supplies	5	9	11	11	11	11	12	12	13	9	13	13	12	12	12	13	13	13
Other	1	3	7	7	4	4	4	4	4	2	5	8	8	4	4	4	5	5
Instructional staff services[4]	205	337	470	503	501	507	536	556	577	389	488	583	577	549	546	574	591	603
Salaries	135	207	279	293	291	294	308	319	331	255	300	346	336	319	316	330	340	345
Employee benefits	34	50	86	100	102	105	112	117	126	65	72	106	114	112	113	120	125	131
Purchased services	15	42	62	70	70	69	73	78	79	29	61	77	80	77	74	78	83	82
Supplies	19	33	38	37	33	36	39	37	38	36	48	48	42	37	39	42	40	40
Other	2	4	4	4	4	4	4	4	4	5	6	5	5	5	4	5	5	4
General administration	141	151	190	212	218	222	229	239	244	266	218	235	243	238	240	246	254	254
Salaries	63	71	82	89	90	92	94	97	100	119	103	101	102	98	100	101	103	105
Employee benefits	19	21	32	38	39	38	41	41	44	36	31	39	43	43	41	43	44	46
Purchased services	36	44	59	65	69	72	74	80	77	68	64	73	75	76	77	80	85	81
Supplies	4	4	5	5	5	5	5	6	5	8	6	6	5	5	5	5	6	6
Other	18	10	13	16	14	15	15	15	16	35	14	16	18	16	16	16	16	17
School administration	284	415	546	580	593	608	632	659	684	537	600	677	664	650	656	677	701	714
Salaries	217	314	390	408	414	423	436	452	466	410	454	484	468	453	455	467	481	486
Employee benefits	55	78	124	141	149	154	163	171	183	104	113	153	162	163	166	174	182	191
Purchased services	6	13	19	19	19	19	21	23	23	11	19	24	22	21	21	23	24	24
Supplies	5	8	10	9	9	9	9	9	10	9	11	12	10	10	9	9	10	10
Other	2	2	3	3	3	3	3	3	4	3	3	4	3	3	3	4	4	4
Operation and maintenance	517	721	951	1,015	1,019	1,061	1,078	1,093	1,137	977	1,043	1,179	1,163	1,115	1,143	1,154	1,162	1,187
Salaries	215	285	342	356	351	357	362	372	382	406	413	424	408	384	385	388	396	399
Employee benefits	64	80	127	146	150	154	160	165	174	121	116	158	167	164	166	171	175	182
Purchased services	139	204	257	270	282	300	309	316	334	263	295	319	309	308	324	330	336	349
Supplies	91	146	216	235	228	241	240	233	239	173	211	268	270	250	260	256	248	250
Other	8	6	8	9	7	8	8	8	8	15	9	10	10	8	9	9	8	8

See notes at end of table.

Table 236.60. Total and current expenditures per pupil in fall enrollment in public elementary and secondary schools, by function and subfunction: Selected years, 1990–91 through 2016–17—Continued

Function and subfunction	Expenditures per pupil in current dollars									Expenditures per pupil in constant 2018–19 dollars[1]								
	1990–91	2000–01	2006–07	2010–11	2012–13	2013–14	2014–15	2015–16	2016–17	1990–91	2000–01	2006–07	2010–11	2012–13	2013–14	2014–15	2015–16	2016–17
1	2	3	4	5	6	7	8	9	10	11	12	13	14	15	16	17	18	19
Student transportation	211	298	406	452	467	477	477	483	502	398	431	503	518	511	514	510	514	524
Salaries	80	115	144	152	151	154	157	163	169	151	166	178	174	166	166	168	173	176
Employee benefits	22	34	55	63	65	66	68	72	75	41	49	49	72	72	71	73	76	79
Purchased services	81	122	164	185	193	198	200	206	214	153	177	204	212	211	214	214	219	224
Supplies	23	25	39	48	53	54	47	37	39	44	36	49	55	58	58	50	40	40
Other	5	3	3	4	5	5	5	5	5	9	4	4	5	5	5	5	5	5
Other support services[5]	136	242	315	349	363	381	415	429	455	256	351	391	400	397	410	445	456	475
Salaries	70	117	145	165	167	172	181	190	196	133	169	180	189	183	186	194	202	204
Employee benefits	24	34	54	67	70	74	78	81	85	45	49	67	76	77	80	83	86	89
Purchased services	19	59	74	78	87	93	97	102	108	37	85	92	90	95	101	103	108	112
Supplies	7	13	18	18	19	22	23	25	26	14	19	22	20	21	24	25	26	28
Other	15	19	24	21	19	19	37	32	40	28	28	30	25	21	21	39	34	41
Food services	205	293	368	412	439	447	459	470	477	387	423	457	472	481	481	491	499	498
Salaries	—	105	124	131	133	134	137	141	143	—	152	153	150	145	144	146	150	149
Employee benefits	—	29	44	50	52	55	56	58	60	—	42	55	58	57	59	60	54	63
Purchased services	—	20	32	42	46	47	49	51	53	—	28	39	48	50	50	52	54	55
Supplies	—	136	165	184	203	207	211	214	215	—	197	205	211	223	223	226	227	224
Other	—	3	4	5	5	5	6	6	6	—	4	5	6	5	5	6	6	6
Enterprise operations[6]	23	16	22	22	22	23	22	24	25	43	24	27	26	24	25	24	25	26
Salaries	—	3	5	7	6	6	6	7	7	—	4	6	8	7	7	7	7	7
Employee benefits	—	1	2	2	2	2	2	2	3	—	1	2	2	2	2	2	3	3
Purchased services	—	4	5	3	4	4	4	4	4	—	6	6	4	4	4	4	4	4
Supplies	—	5	6	6	6	6	6	6	7	—	7	8	7	7	7	6	7	7
Other	—	4	4	4	4	4	4	5	4	—	6	5	5	5	5	5	5	5
Capital outlay[7]	477	976	1,274	1,029	916	926	1,004	1,109	1,213	902	1,412	1,581	1,179	1,003	998	1,074	1,179	1,266
Interest on school debt	105	215	299	363	347	343	348	348	363	198	312	371	415	380	370	372	369	379

—Not available.
[1]Constant dollars based on the Consumer Price Index, prepared by the Bureau of Labor Statistics, U.S. Department of Labor, adjusted to a school-year basis.
[2]Includes estimated data for subfunctions of food services and enterprise operations.
[3]Includes expenditures for guidance, health, attendance, and speech pathology services.
[4]Includes expenditures for curriculum development, staff training, libraries, and media and computer centers.
[5]Includes business support services concerned with paying, transporting, exchanging, and maintaining goods and services for local education agencies; central support services, including planning, research, evaluation, information, staff, and data processing services; and other support services.
[6]Includes expenditures for operations funded by sales of products or services (e.g., school bookstore or computer time).
[7]Includes expenditures for property and for buildings and alterations completed by school district staff or contractors.
NOTE: Excludes expenditures for state education agencies. Detail may not sum to totals because of rounding. Some data have been revised from previously published figures.
SOURCE: U.S. Department of Education, National Center for Education Statistics, Common Core of Data (CCD), "National Public Education Financial Survey," 1990–91 through 2016–17. (This table was prepared August 2019.)

Table 236.65. Current expenditure per pupil in fall enrollment in public elementary and secondary schools, by state or jurisdiction: Selected years, 1969–70 through 2016–17

State or jurisdiction	1969–70	1979–80	1989–90	1999–2000	2006–07	2007–08	2008–09	2009–10	2010–11	2011–12	2012–13	2013–14	2014–15	2015–16	2016–17
1	2	3	4	5	6	7	8	9	10	11	12	13	14	15	16
					Unadjusted dollars[1]										
United States	**$751**	**$2,088**	**$4,643**	**$6,912**	**$9,679**	**$10,298**	**$10,540**	**$10,636**	**$10,663**	**$10,648**	**$10,771**	**$11,066**	**$11,445**	**$11,842**	**$12,258**
Alabama	512	1,520	3,144	5,638	8,398	9,197	8,964	8,907	8,726	8,577	8,773	9,036	9,146	9,258	9,528
Alaska	1,059	4,267	7,577	8,806	12,324	14,641	15,363	15,829	16,663	17,475	18,217	18,466	20,191	17,510	17,838
Arizona	674	1,865	3,717	5,030	7,316	7,727	8,022	7,870	7,782	7,383	7,495	7,427	7,590	7,772	8,053
Arkansas	511	1,472	3,229	5,277	8,391	8,677	8,854	9,281	9,496	9,536	9,538	9,752	9,805	9,900	10,004
California	833	2,227	4,502	6,314	8,952	9,706	9,503	9,300	9,146	9,220	9,258	9,671	10,449	11,420	12,151
Colorado	686	2,258	4,357	6,215	8,286	9,152	8,782	8,926	8,786	8,594	8,693	9,036	9,292	9,619	9,849
Connecticut	911	2,167	7,463	9,753	13,659	14,610	15,353	15,698	16,224	16,855	17,321	18,401	19,020	19,615	19,929
Delaware	833	2,587	5,326	8,310	11,760	12,153	12,109	12,222	12,467	13,580	13,653	13,793	13,882	14,397	14,892
District of Columbia	947	2,811	7,872	10,107	15,511	16,353	19,698	20,910	20,793	19,847	20,451	20,537	20,610	21,161	22,561
Florida	683	1,834	4,597	5,831	8,567	9,084	8,867	8,863	9,030	8,520	8,623	8,955	9,113	9,176	9,374
Georgia	539	1,491	4,000	6,437	9,102	9,718	9,649	9,432	9,259	9,272	9,121	9,236	9,476	9,835	10,274
Hawaii	792	2,086	4,130	6,530	11,316	11,800	12,400	11,855	11,924	11,973	11,790	12,400	12,855	13,748	14,322
Idaho	573	1,548	2,921	5,315	6,648	6,951	7,118	7,100	6,821	6,626	6,761	6,577	6,929	7,211	7,554
Illinois	816	2,241	4,521	7,133	9,596	10,353	11,097	11,739	11,742	12,011	12,443	13,213	13,935	14,327	15,517
Indiana	661	1,708	4,270	7,192	9,080	8,867	9,254	9,479	9,251	9,588	9,421	9,396	9,529	9,688	9,823
Iowa	798	2,164	4,190	6,564	8,791	9,520	9,704	9,748	9,795	10,027	10,291	10,647	10,938	11,148	11,456
Kansas	699	1,963	4,290	6,294	9,243	9,894	10,204	9,972	9,802	10,021	10,011	10,240	10,329	10,216	10,428
Kentucky	502	1,557	3,384	5,921	7,941	8,740	8,786	8,957	9,228	9,327	9,274	9,411	9,560	9,831	10,083
Louisiana	589	1,629	3,625	5,804	8,937	10,006	10,625	10,701	10,799	10,726	10,539	10,853	11,106	11,169	11,379
Maine	649	1,692	4,903	7,667	11,644	11,761	12,183	12,525	12,576	12,335	12,694	13,267	13,976	14,202	14,633
Maryland	809	2,293	5,573	7,731	11,989	13,257	13,737	14,007	13,946	13,875	14,086	14,217	14,431	14,523	14,933
Massachusetts	791	2,548	5,766	8,816	12,784	13,690	14,534	13,956	14,612	14,844	15,321	15,886	16,450	16,986	17,718
Michigan	841	2,495	5,090	8,110	9,876	10,075	10,373	10,447	10,577	10,477	10,515	10,649	10,956	11,051	11,256
Minnesota	855	2,296	4,698	7,190	9,589	10,060	10,983	10,665	10,674	10,781	11,065	11,427	11,924	12,364	12,635
Mississippi	457	1,568	2,934	5,014	7,459	7,890	8,064	8,104	7,926	8,097	8,117	8,265	8,445	8,692	8,755
Missouri	596	1,724	4,071	6,187	8,848	9,532	9,617	9,702	9,461	9,514	9,702	9,938	10,231	10,385	10,684
Montana	728	2,264	4,240	6,314	9,191	9,786	10,120	10,565	10,719	10,569	10,662	10,941	11,078	11,374	11,538
Nebraska	700	2,025	4,553	6,683	10,068	10,565	10,846	11,339	11,704	11,492	11,743	11,877	12,174	12,379	12,662
Nevada	706	1,908	3,816	5,760	7,796	8,187	8,321	8,376	8,411	8,160	8,026	8,275	8,451	8,753	9,120
New Hampshire	666	1,732	4,786	6,860	11,036	11,951	12,583	13,072	13,548	13,774	14,050	14,601	14,969	15,535	15,958
New Jersey	924	2,825	7,546	10,337	16,163	17,620	16,973	17,379	16,855	17,982	18,523	18,780	18,559	19,041	19,585
New Mexico	665	1,870	3,446	5,825	8,849	9,291	9,648	9,621	9,250	9,763	9,164	9,403	9,724	9,959	9,949
New York	1,194	2,950	7,051	9,846	15,546	16,794	17,746	18,167	18,857	19,396	19,529	20,156	20,744	22,231	22,861
North Carolina	570	1,635	4,018	6,045	7,878	7,798	8,463	8,225	8,267	8,160	8,342	8,287	8,529	8,717	8,995
North Dakota	662	1,941	3,899	5,667	8,671	9,324	9,802	10,519	10,898	11,246	11,615	12,383	12,884	13,358	13,767
Ohio	677	1,894	4,531	7,065	9,937	10,340	10,669	11,224	11,395	11,323	11,276	11,434	11,730	11,933	12,569
Oklahoma	554	1,810	3,293	5,395	7,430	7,683	7,878	7,929	7,631	7,763	7,914	7,995	8,075	8,091	7,921
Oregon	843	2,412	4,864	7,149	8,958	9,565	9,611	9,268	9,516	9,485	9,572	9,959	10,457	10,823	11,252
Pennsylvania	815	2,328	5,737	7,772	10,905	11,741	12,299	12,729	13,096	13,091	13,445	13,824	14,405	15,165	15,782
Rhode Island	807	2,340	5,908	8,904	13,453	14,459	14,719	14,723	14,948	15,172	14,889	15,372	15,797	16,082	16,620
South Carolina	567	1,597	3,769	6,130	8,507	9,060	9,228	9,080	8,908	9,102	9,444	9,608	9,831	10,120	10,419
South Dakota	656	1,781	3,511	5,632	8,064	8,535	8,543	9,020	8,931	8,593	8,630	9,036	9,103	9,335	10,117
Tennessee	531	1,523	3,405	5,383	7,129	7,820	7,992	8,177	8,330	8,348	8,588	8,662	8,776	8,876	9,246
Texas	551	1,740	3,835	6,288	7,850	8,350	8,562	8,788	8,685	8,213	8,285	8,602	9,001	9,352	9,520
Utah	595	1,556	2,577	4,378	5,709	5,978	6,612	6,452	6,440	6,312	6,432	6,546	6,751	7,006	7,206
Vermont	790	1,930	5,770	8,323	13,629	14,421	15,096	15,666	14,707	16,651	17,286	18,066	18,769	19,023	19,480
Virginia	654	1,824	4,690	6,841	10,214	10,664	10,928	10,594	10,363	10,656	10,960	10,955	11,235	11,435	11,885
Washington	853	2,387	4,382	6,376	8,524	9,058	9,585	9,497	9,619	9,604	9,714	10,305	10,684	11,484	11,971
West Virginia	621	1,749	4,020	7,152	9,727	10,059	10,606	11,774	11,978	11,579	11,264	11,371	11,512	11,424	11,745
Wisconsin	793	2,225	5,020	7,806	10,372	10,791	11,183	11,507	11,947	11,233	11,186	11,345	11,538	11,664	11,962
Wyoming	805	2,369	5,239	7,425	13,266	13,856	14,628	15,232	15,815	15,988	15,815	15,903	16,047	16,431	16,513
Other jurisdictions															
American Samoa	—	—	1,781	2,739	3,481	—	—	—	—	—	—	—	—	—	—
Guam	766	—	3,817	—	—	—	—	—	8,443	9,300	8,949	8,585	9,431	9,692	9,700
Northern Marianas	—	—	3,356	5,120	4,707	4,535	5,753	5,676	7,623	6,246	5,733	5,875	—	—	—
Puerto Rico	—	—	1,605	3,404	6,006	6,520	6,955	7,021	7,429	7,403	8,460	8,281	7,902	7,821	7,639
U.S. Virgin Islands	—	—	6,043	6,478	9,669	12,358	12,768	14,215	13,226	11,669	10,661	11,705	11,141	11,631	13,000

See notes at end of table.

Table 236.65. Current expenditure per pupil in fall enrollment in public elementary and secondary schools, by state or jurisdiction: Selected years, 1969–70 through 2016–17—Continued

State or jurisdiction	Constant 2018–19 dollars[2]														
	1969–70	1979–80	1989–90	1999–2000	2006–07	2007–08	2008–09	2009–10	2010–11	2011–12	2012–13	2013–14	2014–15	2015–16	2016–17
1	17	18	19	20	21	22	23	24	25	26	27	28	29	30	31
United States	**$5,037**	**$6,813**	**$9,261**	**$10,341**	**$12,009**	**$12,320**	**$12,435**	**$12,429**	**$12,215**	**$11,850**	**$11,791**	**$11,928**	**$12,247**	**$12,587**	**$12,794**
Alabama	3,430	4,960	6,271	8,434	10,419	11,002	10,576	10,409	9,996	9,546	9,604	9,740	9,788	9,840	9,944
Alaska	7,101	13,921	15,114	13,175	15,291	17,515	18,126	18,497	19,089	19,449	19,943	19,904	21,606	18,612	18,618
Arizona	4,522	6,084	7,415	7,525	9,077	9,245	9,465	9,197	8,915	8,217	8,205	8,005	8,122	8,261	8,405
Arkansas	3,426	4,802	6,441	7,895	10,411	10,381	10,447	10,845	10,878	10,613	10,442	10,511	10,492	10,523	10,442
California	5,587	7,264	8,981	9,446	11,106	11,612	11,212	10,867	10,478	10,262	10,136	10,425	11,181	12,139	12,683
Colorado	4,600	7,366	8,690	9,298	10,280	10,949	10,361	10,430	10,065	9,565	9,517	9,740	9,943	10,224	10,280
Connecticut	6,106	7,070	14,885	14,590	16,947	17,478	18,115	18,344	18,585	18,759	18,962	19,834	20,353	20,849	20,801
Delaware	5,588	8,439	10,624	12,432	14,550	14,539	14,287	14,283	15,114	15,114	14,946	14,868	14,855	15,303	15,543
District of Columbia	6,349	9,172	15,701	15,120	19,245	19,564	23,241	24,435	23,819	22,088	22,388	22,137	22,055	22,493	23,548
Florida	4,577	5,984	9,170	8,723	10,629	10,867	10,461	10,357	10,345	9,482	9,440	9,652	9,752	9,753	9,784
Georgia	3,612	4,864	7,978	9,603	11,293	11,626	11,385	11,022	10,607	10,319	9,985	9,955	10,140	10,454	10,723
Hawaii	5,310	6,807	8,238	9,769	14,040	14,117	14,630	13,853	13,660	13,325	12,907	13,366	13,756	14,613	14,948
Idaho	3,843	5,051	5,826	7,951	8,248	8,316	8,398	8,297	7,814	7,375	7,401	7,089	7,415	7,665	7,885
Illinois	5,469	7,312	9,017	10,671	11,905	12,386	13,093	13,717	13,451	13,368	13,622	14,242	14,912	15,229	16,196
Indiana	4,433	5,572	8,518	10,760	11,265	10,608	10,918	11,077	10,598	10,671	10,314	10,128	10,197	10,297	10,253
Iowa	5,351	7,060	8,357	9,820	10,907	11,389	11,450	11,391	11,220	11,159	11,266	11,476	11,704	11,850	11,957
Kansas	4,685	6,404	8,556	9,416	11,467	11,837	12,039	11,653	11,229	11,153	10,959	11,037	11,053	10,859	10,884
Kentucky	3,366	5,080	6,749	8,858	9,852	10,456	10,366	10,467	10,571	10,380	10,153	10,144	10,230	10,450	10,524
Louisiana	3,952	5,314	7,230	8,683	11,088	11,971	12,536	12,550	12,371	11,938	11,538	11,698	11,884	11,872	11,876
Maine	4,352	5,520	9,780	11,471	14,446	14,070	14,374	14,636	14,407	13,728	13,896	14,300	14,956	15,096	15,273
Maryland	5,425	7,480	11,117	11,566	14,874	15,860	16,208	16,368	15,976	15,442	15,420	15,325	15,443	15,436	15,586
Massachusetts	5,301	8,312	11,501	13,189	15,861	16,378	17,149	16,308	16,739	16,520	16,772	17,124	17,603	18,055	18,493
Michigan	5,642	8,141	10,624	12,132	12,253	12,053	12,238	12,208	12,117	11,660	11,511	11,478	11,724	11,747	11,748
Minnesota	5,731	7,492	9,371	10,756	11,897	12,036	12,958	12,463	12,227	11,998	12,113	12,317	12,760	13,142	13,188
Mississippi	3,062	5,117	5,851	7,501	9,254	9,439	9,515	9,470	9,080	9,012	8,886	8,908	9,037	9,240	9,137
Missouri	3,996	5,625	8,119	9,256	10,977	11,404	11,347	11,359	10,838	10,588	10,621	10,712	10,948	11,038	11,151
Montana	4,878	7,385	8,457	9,446	11,404	11,708	11,941	12,346	12,279	11,763	11,672	11,793	11,854	12,090	12,043
Nebraska	4,692	6,605	9,081	9,998	12,491	12,639	12,797	13,250	13,408	12,790	12,802	12,880	13,027	13,158	13,215
Nevada	4,732	6,225	7,611	8,617	9,672	9,794	9,818	9,788	9,636	9,048	8,787	8,919	9,043	9,304	9,519
New Hampshire	4,466	5,651	9,546	10,263	13,692	14,297	14,846	15,275	15,520	15,330	15,381	15,738	16,018	16,512	16,656
New Jersey	6,194	9,217	15,051	15,465	20,053	21,080	20,026	20,308	19,308	20,013	20,278	20,243	19,860	20,239	20,441
New Mexico	4,459	6,102	6,873	8,715	10,979	11,115	11,384	11,242	10,596	10,031	10,032	10,135	10,405	10,586	10,384
New York	8,008	9,625	14,064	14,730	19,288	20,092	20,938	21,229	21,602	21,587	21,379	21,726	22,198	23,630	23,861
North Carolina	3,824	5,335	8,015	9,044	9,774	9,329	9,985	9,611	9,470	9,081	9,132	8,932	9,127	9,265	9,389
North Dakota	4,441	5,651	7,777	8,478	10,758	11,155	11,565	12,292	12,485	12,516	12,715	13,347	13,787	14,199	14,369
Ohio	4,536	6,180	9,037	10,569	12,328	12,370	12,588	13,115	13,054	12,602	12,344	12,325	12,552	12,684	13,118
Oklahoma	3,713	5,904	6,569	8,071	9,218	9,191	9,295	9,266	8,742	8,640	8,664	8,617	8,642	8,600	8,267
Oregon	5,654	7,870	9,703	10,695	11,114	11,443	11,339	10,830	10,901	10,556	10,479	10,734	11,190	11,504	11,744
Pennsylvania	5,466	7,596	11,444	11,628	13,530	14,047	14,512	14,874	15,002	14,570	14,719	14,901	15,415	16,120	16,472
Rhode Island	5,409	7,635	11,785	13,321	16,691	17,298	17,367	17,205	17,123	16,886	16,299	16,570	16,904	17,095	17,346
South Carolina	3,803	5,211	7,519	9,171	10,554	10,839	10,888	10,611	10,204	10,130	10,338	10,356	10,520	10,757	10,874
South Dakota	4,399	5,809	7,003	8,426	10,005	10,210	10,079	10,540	10,231	9,564	9,447	9,740	9,741	9,435	10,560
Tennessee	3,559	4,969	6,791	8,053	8,845	9,355	9,430	9,486	9,543	9,291	9,401	9,337	9,391	9,940	9,651
Texas	3,695	5,676	7,649	9,407	9,739	9,989	10,102	10,269	9,949	9,140	9,069	9,272	9,718	9,940	9,936
Utah	3,991	5,077	5,140	6,550	7,083	7,152	7,802	7,540	7,377	7,025	7,042	7,056	7,224	7,447	7,521
Vermont	5,294	6,297	11,510	12,451	16,909	17,253	17,811	18,307	16,848	18,532	18,923	19,473	20,084	20,220	20,332
Virginia	4,388	5,951	9,354	10,234	12,672	12,758	12,894	12,380	11,871	11,859	11,998	11,809	12,022	12,155	12,405
Washington	5,720	7,787	8,741	9,539	10,575	10,836	11,310	11,098	11,019	10,689	10,635	11,107	11,432	12,207	12,494
West Virginia	4,166	5,704	8,018	10,699	12,068	12,034	12,514	13,759	13,721	12,886	12,331	12,257	12,319	12,143	12,258
Wisconsin	5,317	7,258	10,012	11,679	12,868	12,910	13,195	13,447	13,686	12,502	12,245	12,229	12,347	12,398	12,486
Wyoming	5,397	7,729	10,450	11,109	16,459	16,576	17,259	17,800	18,117	17,794	17,313	17,142	17,172	17,465	17,235
Other jurisdictions															
American Samoa	5,139	—	3,553	4,098	4,319	—	—	—	—	—	—	—	—	—	—
Guam	—	—	7,614	—	—	—	—	—	9,672	10,351	9,796	9,253	10,092	10,302	10,124
Northern Marianas	—	—	6,694	7,660	5,840	5,425	6,788	6,632	8,733	6,952	6,276	6,333	—	—	—
Puerto Rico	—	—	3,202	5,092	7,452	7,800	8,206	8,204	8,511	8,239	9,262	8,926	8,455	8,313	7,973
U.S. Virgin Islands	—	—	12,053	9,692	11,996	14,785	15,065	16,611	15,151	12,987	11,670	12,617	11,921	12,362	13,568

—Not available.
[1] Unadjusted (or "current") dollars have not been adjusted to compensate for inflation.
[2] Constant dollars based on the Consumer Price Index (CPI), prepared by the Bureau of Labor Statistics, U.S. Department of Labor, adjusted to a school-year basis. The CPI does not account for differences in inflation rates from state to state.

NOTE: Current expenditures include instruction, support services, food services, and enterprise operations. Expenditures for state administration are excluded in all years except 1969–70 and 1979–80. Beginning in 1989–90, extensive changes were made in the data collection procedures. Some data have been revised from previously published figures.
SOURCE: U.S. Department of Education, National Center for Education Statistics, *Statistics of State School Systems*, 1969–70; *Revenues and Expenditures for Public Elementary and Secondary Schools*, 1979–80; and Common Core of Data (CCD), "National Public Education Financial Survey," 1989–90 through 2016–17. (This table was prepared August 2019.)

Table 236.70. Current expenditure per pupil in average daily attendance in public elementary and secondary schools, by state or jurisdiction: Selected years, 1969–70 through 2016–17

State or jurisdiction	Unadjusted dollars[1]														
	1969–70	1979–80	1989–90	1999–2000	2006–07	2007–08	2008–09	2009–10	2010–11	2011–12	2012–13	2013–14	2014–15	2015–16	2016–17
1	2	3	4	5	6	7	8	9	10	11	12	13	14	15	16
United States	**$816**	**$2,272**	**$4,980**	**$7,394**	**$10,336**	**$10,982**	**$11,239**	**$11,427**	**$11,433**	**$11,362**	**$11,509**	**$11,819**	**$12,224**	**$12,619**	**$13,094**
Alabama	544	1,612	3,327	5,758	8,743	9,345	9,385	9,554	9,296	8,927	9,486	9,543	9,690	9,870	10,161
Alaska	1,123	4,728	8,431	9,668	13,508	16,002	16,822	17,350	18,352	19,134	19,982	20,254	22,161	19,242	19,550
Arizona	720	1,971	4,053	5,478	8,038	8,630	8,732	8,756	8,646	8,224	8,388	8,278	8,426	8,572	8,867
Arkansas	568	1,574	3,485	5,628	9,152	9,460	9,651	10,237	10,332	10,397	9,853	10,622	10,756	10,837	10,968
California	867	2,268	4,391	6,401	9,029	9,673	9,439	9,680	9,540	9,608	9,686	10,094	10,924	11,937	12,730
Colorado	738	2,421	4,720	6,702	9,110	9,977	9,611	9,747	9,709	9,415	9,572	9,924	10,349	10,619	10,946
Connecticut	951	2,420	7,837	10,122	14,143	15,063	15,840	16,133	16,932	17,472	17,859	19,029	19,731	20,380	20,731
Delaware	900	2,861	5,799	8,809	12,612	12,789	12,753	12,928	13,228	14,253	14,129	14,203	14,556	15,150	15,824
District of Columbia	1,018	3,259	8,955	11,935	18,285	20,807	19,766	21,283	21,304	20,399	20,333	21,629	21,362	22,340	23,632
Florida	732	1,889	4,997	6,383	9,055	9,711	9,452	9,363	9,394	8,825	8,925	9,189	9,295	9,337	9,571
Georgia	588	1,625	4,275	6,903	9,615	10,263	10,178	9,855	9,577	9,492	9,437	9,529	9,809	10,185	10,722
Hawaii	841	2,322	4,448	7,090	12,364	12,774	13,397	12,887	12,603	12,735	12,585	13,219	13,849	14,728	15,325
Idaho	603	1,659	3,078	5,644	7,074	7,402	7,567	7,481	7,115	7,041	7,273	7,215	7,409	7,642	8,024
Illinois	909	2,587	5,118	8,084	10,816	11,624	12,489	13,083	13,180	13,459	13,808	14,682	15,473	15,909	17,332
Indiana	728	1,882	4,606	7,652	9,727	9,569	9,946	10,160	9,924	10,220	10,037	10,078	10,202	10,368	10,472
Iowa	844	2,326	4,453	6,925	8,789	9,128	10,482	10,524	10,565	10,748	10,915	11,359	11,698	11,846	12,167
Kansas	771	2,173	4,752	6,962	10,280	11,085	11,485	10,859	10,700	10,712	10,789	11,180	11,106	10,815	11,159
Kentucky	545	1,701	3,745	6,784	9,300	9,940	10,054	10,376	10,469	10,700	10,269	10,248	10,659	10,912	11,193
Louisiana	648	1,792	3,903	6,256	9,650	10,797	11,410	11,492	11,500	11,352	11,118	11,415	11,697	11,775	12,051
Maine	692	1,824	5,373	8,247	12,628	13,177	13,558	14,090	14,406	14,000	14,347	14,926	15,839	16,060	16,103
Maryland	918	2,598	6,275	8,273	12,836	14,122	14,612	14,937	14,876	14,746	15,010	15,109	15,403	15,478	15,982
Massachusetts	859	2,819	6,237	9,375	13,263	14,373	15,249	14,632	15,334	15,607	16,111	16,646	17,311	18,026	18,853
Michigan	904	2,640	5,546	8,886	10,932	11,155	11,493	11,661	11,560	11,462	11,495	11,678	12,048	12,243	12,448
Minnesota	904	2,387	4,971	7,499	10,185	10,663	11,602	11,366	11,368	11,424	11,754	12,140	12,707	13,169	13,496
Mississippi	501	1,664	3,094	5,356	7,988	8,448	8,610	8,670	8,436	8,623	8,685	8,926	9,129	9,380	9,467
Missouri	709	1,936	4,507	6,764	9,266	10,007	10,341	10,468	10,348	10,370	10,555	10,764	11,079	11,233	11,527
Montana	782	2,476	4,736	6,990	10,244	10,541	10,881	11,463	11,599	11,290	11,493	11,840	11,990	12,379	12,489
Nebraska	736	2,150	4,842	7,360	10,711	11,217	11,457	11,920	12,324	12,114	12,374	12,502	12,825	13,700	14,062
Nevada	769	2,088	4,117	6,148	8,372	8,891	8,865	8,869	9,035	8,677	8,525	8,734	8,939	9,233	9,620
New Hampshire	723	1,916	5,304	7,082	11,347	12,280	12,912	13,424	13,964	14,215	14,463	15,013	15,380	15,934	16,360
New Jersey	1,016	3,191	8,139	10,903	16,650	18,174	17,466	18,060	17,654	18,197	19,020	19,282	19,296	20,055	20,735
New Mexico	707	2,034	3,515	5,835	8,876	9,377	9,727	9,716	9,356	9,069	9,230	9,546	9,891	9,954	9,978
New York	1,327	3,462	8,062	10,957	17,182	18,423	19,373	19,965	20,517	20,881	21,172	22,048	22,771	23,678	24,480
North Carolina	612	1,754	4,290	6,505	8,373	8,415	9,167	8,930	8,943	8,828	9,041	8,948	9,245	9,347	9,708
North Dakota	690	1,920	4,189	6,078	9,203	9,637	10,113	10,976	11,356	11,643	12,090	12,952	13,552	14,002	14,443
Ohio	730	2,075	5,045	7,816	10,792	11,374	11,905	12,307	12,484	12,271	12,284	12,447	12,285	12,488	13,019
Oklahoma	604	1,926	3,508	5,770	7,968	8,270	8,423	8,511	8,165	8,281	8,450	8,526	8,633	8,624	8,469
Oregon	925	2,692	5,474	8,129	9,762	9,846	10,673	10,476	10,497	10,386	10,370	10,739	11,356	11,856	12,320
Pennsylvania	882	2,535	6,228	8,380	11,995	12,493	12,989	13,678	14,072	13,973	14,378	14,789	15,405	15,997	16,828
Rhode Island	891	2,601	6,368	9,646	14,674	15,843	16,211	16,243	16,346	16,498	16,187	16,702	17,151	17,332	17,929
South Carolina	613	1,752	4,082	6,545	9,226	9,823	10,007	9,887	9,735	9,823	10,200	10,408	10,670	10,910	11,306
South Dakota	690	1,908	3,731	6,037	8,506	9,047	9,457	9,683	9,431	9,095	9,138	9,539	9,637	9,897	10,905
Tennessee	566	1,635	3,664	5,837	7,843	8,459	8,676	8,810	9,146	9,235	9,370	9,431	9,549	9,719	10,106
Texas	624	1,916	4,150	6,771	8,484	9,029	9,260	9,528	9,418	8,862	8,951	9,273	9,789	10,067	10,264
Utah	626	1,657	2,764	4,692	6,116	6,841	7,081	6,877	6,851	6,787	7,023	7,156	7,375	7,659	7,892
Vermont	807	1,997	6,227	8,799	14,219	15,089	16,073	16,586	16,661	17,575	18,372	19,032	19,793	20,196	20,929
Virginia	708	1,970	4,672	6,491	10,913	11,410	11,696	11,383	11,123	11,385	11,748	11,716	11,810	12,022	12,535
Washington	915	2,568	4,702	6,914	9,233	9,846	10,422	10,242	10,402	10,413	10,553	11,199	11,648	12,533	13,099
West Virginia	670	1,920	4,360	7,637	10,080	10,605	11,122	12,378	12,505	11,982	11,665	11,800	12,414	12,299	12,649
Wisconsin	883	2,477	5,524	8,299	10,813	11,370	11,773	12,194	12,515	11,750	11,768	11,963	12,227	12,312	12,716
Wyoming	856	2,527	5,577	7,944	14,219	14,936	15,658	16,535	17,126	17,228	17,135	17,165	17,445	17,796	17,950
Other jurisdictions															
American Samoa	820	—	1,908	2,807	3,909	4,309	4,468	4,881	4,877	5,154	4,870	5,504	5,120	5,235	5,817
Guam	—	—	4,234	—	7,450	8,084	8,264	8,393	9,280	10,112	9,431	9,914	10,120	9,983	9,939
Northern Marianas	—	—	3,007	5,720	5,356	5,162	6,397	6,284	8,495	7,068	6,381	6,548	6,921	8,127	9,529
Puerto Rico	—	—	1,750	3,859	6,152	6,937	7,329	7,426	8,560	7,798	8,701	8,822	8,025	8,124	7,697
U.S. Virgin Islands	—	—	6,767	7,238	10,548	12,358	12,768	14,215	13,014	11,669	10,661	14,372	14,849	15,805	16,117

See notes at end of table.

Table 236.70. Current expenditure per pupil in average daily attendance in public elementary and secondary schools, by state or jurisdiction: Selected years, 1969–70 through 2016–17—Continued

Constant 2018–19 dollars[2]

State or jurisdiction	1969–70	1979–80	1989–90	1999–2000	2006–07	2007–08	2008–09	2009–10	2010–11	2011–12	2012–13	2013–14	2014–15	2015–16	2016–17
1	17	18	19	20	21	22	23	24	25	26	27	28	29	30	31
United States	$5,471	$7,411	$9,933	$11,061	$12,823	$13,138	$13,260	$13,353	$13,098	$12,645	$12,599	$12,740	$13,081	$13,413	$13,667
Alabama	3,647	5,258	6,636	8,615	10,847	11,179	11,073	11,164	10,649	9,935	10,385	10,286	10,369	10,491	10,605
Alaska	7,526	15,423	16,817	14,464	16,759	19,144	20,274	20,232	21,023	21,295	21,875	21,832	23,714	20,453	20,405
Arizona	4,828	6,430	8,085	8,196	9,972	10,325	10,303	10,232	9,904	9,153	9,182	8,923	9,017	9,111	9,255
Arkansas	3,806	5,136	6,951	8,419	11,355	11,318	11,387	11,962	11,835	11,450	10,786	11,450	11,690	11,519	11,448
California	5,814	7,398	8,758	9,575	11,202	11,572	11,137	11,312	10,929	10,693	10,603	10,880	11,690	12,688	13,287
Colorado	4,947	7,898	9,415	10,026	11,303	11,936	11,339	11,390	11,122	10,479	10,479	10,697	11,075	11,287	11,424
Connecticut	6,378	7,895	15,632	15,143	17,547	18,021	18,689	19,446	19,396	19,446	19,551	20,511	21,115	21,662	21,637
Delaware	6,035	9,334	11,566	15,178	15,648	15,300	15,047	15,107	15,154	15,863	15,468	15,309	15,576	16,104	16,516
District of Columbia	6,827	10,632	17,862	17,855	22,686	24,892	23,321	24,871	24,405	22,703	22,260	23,314	22,859	23,746	24,665
Florida	4,910	6,163	9,968	9,549	11,235	11,618	11,152	10,942	10,761	9,822	9,771	9,905	9,947	9,925	9,989
Georgia	3,942	5,302	8,526	10,328	11,929	12,278	12,009	11,516	10,971	10,564	10,331	10,271	10,496	10,826	11,191
Hawaii	5,635	7,574	8,873	10,607	15,340	15,282	15,806	15,059	14,437	14,174	13,777	14,249	14,819	15,654	15,995
Idaho	4,045	5,413	6,139	8,444	8,776	8,856	8,928	8,742	8,196	7,837	7,962	7,777	7,928	8,123	8,374
Illinois	6,098	8,438	10,208	12,094	13,419	13,906	14,735	15,289	15,098	14,980	15,116	15,825	16,557	16,910	18,090
Indiana	4,881	6,141	9,188	11,448	12,068	11,448	11,735	11,873	11,368	11,375	10,988	10,863	10,917	11,021	10,930
Iowa	5,660	7,590	8,882	10,360	10,904	10,920	12,367	12,289	12,103	11,962	11,949	12,243	12,518	12,592	12,699
Kansas	5,169	7,089	9,478	10,416	12,754	13,238	13,551	12,689	12,257	11,922	11,811	12,051	11,884	11,496	11,647
Kentucky	3,655	5,550	7,470	10,150	11,542	11,892	11,862	12,125	11,993	11,909	11,242	11,046	11,406	11,598	11,683
Louisiana	4,345	5,846	7,786	9,359	11,973	12,917	13,462	13,429	13,174	12,634	12,171	12,304	12,517	12,516	12,578
Maine	4,643	5,949	10,717	12,337	15,667	15,764	15,997	16,465	16,502	15,582	15,706	16,089	16,949	17,071	16,807
Maryland	6,157	8,475	12,517	12,377	15,925	16,895	17,240	17,455	17,041	16,411	16,432	16,286	16,483	16,452	16,681
Massachusetts	5,760	9,198	12,441	14,025	16,455	17,195	17,992	17,099	17,566	17,370	17,637	17,943	18,524	19,161	19,678
Michigan	6,061	8,614	11,063	13,294	13,563	13,345	13,560	13,627	13,243	12,756	12,584	12,588	12,893	13,014	12,993
Minnesota	6,058	7,787	11,914	13,219	12,636	12,757	13,689	13,462	13,023	12,715	12,868	13,086	13,597	13,997	14,087
Mississippi	3,358	5,428	6,171	8,012	9,910	10,107	10,158	10,131	9,664	9,597	9,508	9,621	9,769	9,970	9,881
Missouri	4,751	6,317	8,990	10,119	11,496	11,971	12,201	12,232	11,854	11,541	11,555	11,602	11,856	11,940	12,031
Montana	5,242	8,079	9,447	10,457	12,709	12,610	12,838	12,395	13,287	12,565	12,581	12,762	12,840	13,158	13,035
Nebraska	4,937	7,014	9,657	11,010	13,289	13,419	13,517	13,930	14,118	13,482	13,546	13,476	13,724	14,562	14,677
Nevada	5,159	6,813	8,212	9,197	10,387	10,636	10,459	10,365	10,350	9,657	9,332	9,414	9,566	9,814	10,041
New Hampshire	4,848	6,250	10,580	10,596	14,078	14,691	15,235	15,687	15,996	15,821	15,834	16,182	16,458	16,937	17,076
New Jersey	6,813	10,411	16,235	16,311	20,657	21,742	20,608	21,104	20,224	20,253	20,822	20,784	20,649	21,317	21,642
New Mexico	4,740	7,635	7,011	8,729	11,012	11,218	11,477	11,353	10,718	10,093	10,105	10,290	10,384	10,581	10,414
New York	8,895	11,295	16,080	16,392	21,317	22,040	22,857	23,331	23,503	23,240	23,178	23,766	24,368	25,168	25,551
North Carolina	4,105	5,723	8,557	9,732	10,389	10,067	10,816	10,436	10,245	9,826	9,898	9,645	9,894	9,936	10,133
North Dakota	4,623	6,265	8,356	9,093	11,418	11,529	11,932	12,826	13,009	12,959	13,235	13,960	14,502	14,883	15,075
Ohio	4,894	6,768	10,062	11,694	13,389	13,607	14,046	14,381	14,301	13,657	13,448	13,416	13,146	13,273	13,588
Oklahoma	4,053	6,285	6,997	8,632	9,886	9,894	9,938	9,946	9,354	9,217	9,250	9,190	9,238	9,167	8,839
Oregon	6,200	8,782	10,919	12,161	12,111	12,546	12,593	12,241	12,025	11,559	11,552	11,576	12,152	12,602	12,859
Pennsylvania	5,912	8,266	12,423	12,537	14,882	14,946	15,325	15,984	16,120	15,551	15,740	15,941	16,485	17,004	17,564
Rhode Island	5,975	8,485	12,701	14,431	18,206	18,953	19,127	18,981	18,725	18,361	17,720	18,002	18,354	18,422	18,713
South Carolina	4,107	5,716	8,142	9,792	11,447	11,752	11,807	11,553	11,152	10,932	11,166	11,219	11,418	11,596	11,800
South Dakota	4,625	6,224	7,442	9,031	10,553	10,823	11,158	11,315	10,804	10,123	10,258	10,166	10,312	10,520	11,382
Tennessee	3,795	5,335	7,308	8,733	9,731	10,119	10,237	11,134	10,477	10,278	9,799	9,995	10,475	10,700	10,713
Utah	4,199	5,405	5,513	7,020	7,588	8,184	8,355	8,036	7,848	7,554	7,688	7,714	7,892	8,141	8,237
Vermont	5,412	6,515	12,420	13,164	17,641	18,051	18,964	19,382	19,086	19,560	20,112	20,515	21,181	21,467	21,845
Virginia	4,746	6,427	9,318	9,711	13,539	13,651	13,800	13,301	12,742	12,671	12,629	12,638	12,658	12,778	13,083
Washington	6,137	8,378	9,379	10,343	11,456	11,779	12,297	11,968	11,917	11,589	11,552	12,071	12,464	13,321	13,672
West Virginia	4,492	8,265	8,698	11,425	12,507	12,687	13,122	14,465	14,325	13,335	12,770	12,719	13,284	13,073	13,202
Wisconsin	5,918	8,080	11,018	12,415	13,415	13,602	13,891	14,250	14,337	13,077	12,883	12,895	13,084	13,087	13,272
Wyoming	5,739	8,243	11,125	11,885	17,641	17,869	18,475	19,322	19,619	19,174	18,758	18,502	18,668	18,916	18,735
Other jurisdictions															
American Samoa	5,496	—	3,805	4,200	4,850	5,155	5,271	5,704	5,587	5,737	5,331	5,933	5,479	5,565	6,071
Guam	—	—	8,446	—	9,243	9,671	9,751	9,808	10,631	11,254	10,325	10,687	10,830	10,611	10,374
Northern Marianas	—	—	5,998	8,557	6,646	6,175	7,548	7,343	9,732	7,866	6,986	7,058	7,406	8,638	9,945
Puerto Rico	—	—	3,490	5,773	7,632	8,300	8,647	8,678	9,806	8,678	9,526	9,509	8,588	8,635	8,033
U.S. Virgin Islands	—	—	13,498	10,828	13,086	14,785	15,065	16,611	14,908	12,987	11,670	15,491	15,890	16,799	16,822

—Not available.
[1]Unadjusted (or "current") dollars have not been adjusted to compensate for inflation.
[2]Constant dollars based on the Consumer Price Index (CPI), prepared by the Bureau of Labor Statistics, U.S. Department of Labor, adjusted to a school-year basis. The CPI does not account for differences in inflation rates from state to state. Expenditures include instruction, support services, food services, and enterprise operations. Expenditures for state administration are excluded in all years except 1969–70 and 1979–80. Beginning in 1989–90, extensive changes were made in the data collection procedures. There are discrepancies in average daily attendance reporting practices from state to state. Some data have been revised from previously published figures.
SOURCE: U.S. Department of Education, National Center for Education Statistics, Statistics of State School Systems, 1969–70; Revenues and Expenditures for Public Elementary and Secondary Education, 1979–80; and Common Core of Data (CCD), "National Public Education Financial Survey," 1989–90 through 2016–17. (This table was prepared August 2019.)

Table 236.75. Total and current expenditures per pupil in fall enrollment in public elementary and secondary schools, by function and state or jurisdiction: 2016–17

Current expenditures, capital expenditures, and interest on school debt per pupil

State or jurisdiction	Total[1]	Current expenditures — Total	Current expenditures — Instruction	Support services — Total	Support services — Student support[4]	Support services — Instructional staff[5]	Support services — General administration	Support services — School administration	Support services — Operation and maintenance	Support services — Student transportation	Support services — Other support services	Food services	Enterprise operations[3]	Capital outlay[2]	Interest on school debt
1	2	3	4	5	6	7	8	9	10	11	12	13	14	15	16
United States	**$13,834**	**$12,258**	**$7,445**	**$4,311**	**$712**	**$577**	**$244**	**$684**	**$1,137**	**$502**	**$455**	**$477**	**$25**	**$1,213**	**$363**
Alabama	10,615	9,528	5,436	3,441	599	401	245	594	886	492	224	651	0	856	232
Alaska	19,396	17,838	9,538	7,638	1,383	1,481	255	1,091	2,138	608	683	579	83	1,277	281
Arizona	9,374	8,053	4,337	3,295	618	390	156	452	986	334	360	420	0	1,095	226
Arkansas	11,332	10,004	5,612	3,847	541	841	253	525	1,014	368	306	533	11	1,072	256
California	13,796	12,151	7,203	4,463	729	774	119	806	1,200	266	569	456	30	1,184	461
Colorado	11,662	9,849	5,513	3,945	555	567	160	751	900	293	720	338	53	1,306	506
Connecticut	21,354	19,929	12,563	6,755	1,280	627	447	1,166	1,711	1,004	520	438	172	1,197	227
Delaware	16,096	14,892	9,317	5,078	665	273	234	944	1,590	738	633	497	0	1,042	162
District of Columbia	30,115	22,561	12,113	9,625	1,002	1,133	1,649	1,572	2,222	1,366	687	809	9	5,934	1,621
Florida	10,405	9,374	5,789	3,118	412	590	86	522	905	361	242	467	0	813	218
Georgia	11,512	10,274	6,269	3,421	534	534	131	648	772	480	321	554	30	1,111	127
Hawaii	15,210	14,322	8,373	5,228	1,348	483	72	1,029	1,593	348	355	721	0	889	0
Idaho	8,599	7,554	4,452	2,731	422	439	190	434	714	330	202	368	4	847	197
Illinois	16,985	15,517	9,673	5,461	1,093	560	583	808	1,204	659	554	383	0	995	473
Indiana	11,145	9,823	5,660	3,690	512	395	203	640	1,107	594	238	474	0	1,042	280
Iowa	13,282	11,456	6,912	4,023	669	716	292	648	950	402	346	508	13	1,595	231
Kansas	12,694	10,428	6,219	3,715	664	431	280	606	1,019	424	292	494	0	1,775	491
Kentucky	11,404	10,083	5,781	3,612	492	562	227	587	898	575	272	660	27	1,054	267
Louisiana	12,502	11,379	6,354	4,425	692	567	295	731	1,149	650	341	600	0	964	160
Maine	15,568	14,633	8,562	5,482	1,003	827	498	772	1,472	719	192	588	2	682	253
Maryland	16,508	14,933	9,515	4,992	672	689	145	1,008	1,260	781	438	425	0	1,396	179
Massachusetts	18,490	17,718	11,314	5,906	1,317	818	286	759	1,490	805	433	496	18	526	246
Michigan	12,639	11,256	6,460	4,380	890	570	253	628	988	471	579	415	0	910	473
Minnesota	15,554	12,635	8,175	3,872	370	646	474	508	853	714	306	534	54	2,465	454
Mississippi	9,611	8,755	4,968	3,250	464	407	294	533	898	357	235	536	2	746	111
Missouri	11,943	10,684	6,303	3,882	482	489	396	627	1,068	553	267	499	0	917	341
Montana	12,964	11,538	6,773	4,234	791	409	366	643	1,159	542	325	514	18	1,265	160
Nebraska	15,169	12,662	8,198	3,606	484	407	371	599	1,081	374	289	527	330	2,206	301
Nevada	10,475	9,120	5,393	3,372	370	504	148	669	844	357	349	355	0	1,009	346
New Hampshire	17,006	15,958	10,168	5,406	1,228	525	575	890	1,279	704	206	384	0	796	252
New Jersey	20,980	19,585	11,762	7,190	2,026	613	399	971	1,905	808	467	438	196	923	472
New Mexico	11,596	9,949	5,694	3,774	1,005	272	237	590	1,039	309	323	475	7	1,647	0
New York	24,377	22,861	15,911	6,495	732	589	370	876	2,102	1,154	673	455	0	967	550
North Carolina	9,886	8,995	5,625	2,895	489	309	156	533	740	367	301	475	0	877	14
North Dakota	16,526	13,767	8,261	4,484	554	473	594	712	1,181	548	422	640	381	2,462	298
Ohio	12,525	11,066	5,945	4,707	851	501	394	675	1,076	597	613	413	1	1,097	362
Oklahoma	8,935	7,921	4,428	2,888	539	320	237	441	831	250	271	524	80	918	96
Oregon	13,298	11,252	6,577	4,282	854	454	157	718	892	495	711	388	5	1,429	617
Pennsylvania	17,479	15,782	9,767	5,433	891	565	476	703	1,445	751	602	515	67	1,152	545
Rhode Island	17,345	16,620	10,046	6,118	1,750	637	249	794	1,290	720	679	452	4	449	277
South Carolina	12,525	10,419	5,777	4,080	803	646	101	675	1,023	394	438	534	27	1,668	438
South Dakota	11,478	10,117	5,990	3,552	563	359	339	492	1,053	360	385	524	51	1,118	243
Tennessee	10,318	9,246	5,643	3,087	416	546	192	560	767	347	260	516	0	847	225
Texas	11,985	9,520	5,490	3,499	469	489	140	546	1,003	277	574	531	0	1,833	632
Utah	8,794	7,206	4,576	2,252	281	289	81	474	656	213	259	362	16	1,408	180
Vermont	20,207	19,480	12,523	6,447	1,506	807	410	1,228	1,455	642	398	489	22	623	104
Virginia	12,992	11,885	7,237	4,188	602	787	193	697	1,061	612	236	458	3	1,032	75
Washington	14,483	11,971	6,940	4,555	879	776	205	726	1,016	448	505	364	111	2,114	399
West Virginia	12,566	11,745	6,727	4,261	610	464	201	630	1,267	872	218	756	0	768	53
Wisconsin	13,315	11,962	7,099	4,424	598	631	346	603	1,109	507	631	439	0	1,167	185
Wyoming	20,264	16,513	9,772	6,249	995	914	348	881	1,599	828	684	485	7	3,727	25
Other jurisdictions															
American Samoa	—	—	—	—	—	—	—	—	—	—	—	—	—	—	—
Guam	11,753	9,700	4,624	4,424	911	538	156	593	1,252	258	717	652	0	1,652	402
Northern Marianas	—	—	—	—	—	—	—	—	—	—	—	—	—	—	—
Puerto Rico	7,731	7,639	3,091	3,456	870	456	217	332	1,116	255	212	1,092	0	93	0
U.S. Virgin Islands	13,009	13,000	7,611	4,525	1,125	320	621	717	519	571	651	852	12	9	0

—Not available.
[1]Excludes "Other current expenditures," such as community services, private school programs, adult education, and other programs not allocable to expenditures per pupil in public schools.
[2]Includes expenditures for property and for buildings and alterations completed by school district staff or contractors.
[3]Includes expenditures for operations funded by sales of products or services (e.g., school bookstore or computer time).
[4]Includes expenditures for guidance, health, attendance, and speech pathology services.
[5]Includes expenditures for curriculum development, staff training, libraries, and media and computer centers.
NOTE: Excludes expenditures for state education agencies. "0" indicates none or less than $0.50. Detail may not sum to totals because of rounding.
SOURCE: U.S. Department of Education, National Center for Education Statistics, Common Core of Data (CCD), "National Public Education Financial Survey," 2016–17. (This table was prepared August 2019.)

CHAPTER 3
Postsecondary Education

Postsecondary education includes academic, career and technical, and continuing professional education programs after high school. American colleges and universities and career/technical institutions offer a diverse array of postsecondary educational experiences. For example, a community college normally offers the first 2 years of a standard college curriculum as well as a selection of terminal career and technical education programs. A university typically offers a full undergraduate course of study leading to a bachelor's degree, as well as programs leading to advanced degrees. A specialized career/technical institution offers training programs of varying lengths that are designed to prepare students for specific careers

This chapter provides an overview of the latest statistics on postsecondary education, including data on various types of postsecondary institutions and programs. However, to maintain comparability over time, most of the data in the *Digest* are for degree-granting institutions, which are define as postsecondary institutions that grant an associate's or higher degree and whose students are eligible to participate in Title I federal financial aid programs.[1] These include almost all 2- and 4-year colleges and universities. Non-degree-granting institutions are those that offer only career and technical programs of less than 2 years' duration and continuing education programs, and therefore do not award associate's or bachelor's degrees. The degree-granting institution classification currently used by the National Center for Education tatistics (NCE) includes approximately the same set of institutions as the higher education institution classification that was used by NCE prior to 1996–97.[2] This chapter highlights historical data that enable the reader to observe long-range trends in postsecondary education in America.

Other chapters provide related information on postsecondary education. Data on price indexes and on the number of degrees held by the general population are shown in chapter 1. Chapter 4 contains tabulations on federal funding for postsecondary education. Information on employment outcomes for college graduates is shown in chapter 5. Chapter 7 contains data on college libraries. Further information on survey methodologies is presented in Appendix A: Guide to Sources and in the publications cited in the table source notes. See chapter 5 for information on adults' participation in nonpostsecondary education, such as adult secondary education classes (e.g., to prepare for the GED test) or English as a Second Language (ESL) classes.

Enrollment

In 2018, 19.6 million students were enrolled in degree-granting postsecondary institutions. In addition to the students enrolled in degree-granting institutions, about 363,000 students attended non-degree-granting Title IV-eligible postsecondary institutions in fall 2018 (table 303.20). The remainder of this chapter focuses primarily on degree-granting institutions.

Who Enrolls?—Enrollment and Enrollment Rates

Fall enrollment in degree-granting postsecondary institutions increased 32 percent between 1998 and 2008 (table 303.10 and figure 12). In 2018, fall enrollment in degree-granting postsecondary institutions (19.6 million) was 3 percent higher than in 2008 (19.1 million). However, during this period, enrollment reached a peak in 2010 (21.0 million or 10 percent higher than in 2008), followed by a decrease of 7 percent between 2010 and 2018. imilar patterns held for different groups of students, including by sex and enrollment status. For example, postsecondary enrollment was 3 percent higher in 2018 than in 2008 for both male and female students. For each, this overall increase reflects annual increases during the early part of the period followed by decreases during the most recent part of the period (a decrease of 7 percent for males and 6 percent for females from 2010 to 2018).

Such trends in overall enrollment are shaped both by the size of the college-age population and by rates of enrollment. While the traditional college-age population (18- to 24-year-olds) was about 1 percent higher in 2018 (30.5 million) than in 2008 (30.2 million), the percentage of this age group who enrolled in degree-granting postsecondary institutions (41 percent) was not measurably different from the percentage in 2008 (tables 101.10 and 302.60). However, whereas percentage increases in total enrollment were similar for male and female students, trends in enrollment

---

[1] Title IV programs, which are administered by the U.S. Department of Education, provide financial aid to postsecondary students
[2] Included in the current degree-granting classification are some institutions (primarily 2-year colleges) that were not previously designated as higher education institutions. Excluded from the current degree-granting classification are a few institutions that were previously designated as higher education institutions even though they did not award an associate's or higher degree. The former higher education classification was defined as including institutions that were accredited by an agency or association that was recognized by the U.S. Department of Education or recognized directly by the Secretary of Education. The former higher education institutions offered courses that led to an associate's or higher degree or were accepted for credit toward a degree.

rates differed. Like the general population, the enrollment rate for male 18- to 24-year-olds in 2018 (38 percent) was not measurably different from the rate in 2008. For females, in contrast, the enrollment rate in 2018 (44 percent) was 2 percentage points higher than the rate in 2008 (42 percent). Additional differences in enrollment rates were observed by race. The enrollment rate for Hispanic 18- to 24-year-olds rose from 26 percent in 2008 to 36 percent in 2018. The enrollment rate for Black 18- to 24-year-olds in 2018 (37 percent) was 5 percentage points higher than in 2008 (32 percent). eanwhile,` the rate for White 18- to 24-year-olds in 2018 (42 percent) was 2 percentage points lower than in 2008 (44 percent).

Although 18- to 24-year-olds are our best approximation of the college-age population, not all college students are part of this age group and trends in enrollment differ by age. The number of students under age 25 enrolled in degree-granting institutions was 6 percent higher in 2018 than in 2008, while the number of students age 25 and over decreased 2 percent (table 303.40 and figure 14). A similar pattern is expected to continue in the coming years. NCE` projects that enrollment for students under age 25 will increase 5 percent between 2018 and 2029, while the enrollment of students age 25 and over will be 1 percent lower in 2029 than in 2018.

Postsecondary enrollment also differs across states. Overall, fall enrollment in degree-granting institutions declined 4 percent between 2013 and 2018, driven by declines across 40 states (table 304.10 and figure 13). The largest declines were in Alaska (-26 percent) and Iowa (-25 percent). In contrast, enrollment was higher in 2018 than in 2013 in 10 states and the District of Columbia. The largest increases were in New Hampshire (74 percent),[3] followed by tah` (37 percent), Idaho (13 percent), the District of Columbia (10 percent), and Texas (7 percent). The overall enrollment decline in Iowa between 2013 and 2018 resulted primarily from declines among private for-profit institutions, while the enrollment increases in New Hampshire, Utah, and Idaho during the same period resulted primarily from increases among private nonprofit institutions (tables 304.15, 304.21, and 304.22).

Characteristics of Enrolled Students

As enrollment has changed at different rates for different groups of students, the composition of colleges and universities has shifted. The percentage of U.S. resident postsecondary students who are Hispanic, Asian/Pacific Islander, and Black has been increasing (table 306.30). From fall 1976 to fall 2018, the percentage of Hispanic students rose from 4 to 20 percent of all U.S. residents enrolled in degree-granting postsecondary institutions, and the percentage of Asian/Pacific Islander students rose from 2 to 7 percent. The percentage of Black students increased

overall from 10 percent in 1976 to 13 percent in 2018, but the 2018 percentage reflects a decrease since 2011, when Black students made up 15 percent of all enrolled U.S. residents. The percentage of American Indian/Alaska Native students in 2018 (0.7 percent) was about the same as in 1976 (0.7 percent). During the same period, the percentage of White students fell from 84 to 55 percent. Four percent of students in 2018 were of Two or more races. Race/ethnicity is not reported for nonresident aliens, who made up 5 percent of total enrollment in 2018 (table 306.10).

Nineteen percent of undergraduates in 2015–16 reported having a disability (table 311.10). In 2015–16, the percentage of undergraduates who reported having a disability was 19 percent for male students and 20 percent for female students. There were some differences in the percentages of undergraduates with disabilities by characteristics such as veteran status, age, dependency status, and race/ethnicity. For example, 26 percent of undergraduates who were veterans reported having a disability, compared with 19 percent of undergraduates who were not veterans. The percentage of undergraduates having a disability was higher among those age 30 and over (23 percent) than among 15- to 23-year-olds (18 percent). Among dependent undergraduates, 17 percent reported having a disability, which was lower than the percentages for independent undergraduates who were married (21 percent) or unmarried (24 percent). A lower percentage of Asian undergraduates (15 percent) had a disability than White, Hispanic, and Black undergraduates (21, 18, and 17 percent, respectively).

Of the 19.6 million students enrolled in degree-granting postsecondary institutions in fall 2018, some 35 percent took at least one distance education course, including 17 percent who took their courses exclusively through distance education programs (table 311.15). Distance learning varied across the level and control of institutions. Twelve percent of students at public institutions took their coursework exclusively through distance education courses, compared with 20 percent of students at private nonprofit institutions and 63 percent of students at private for-profit institutions. Fourteen percent of undergraduates took their coursework exclusively through distance education courses, compared with 31 percent of postbaccalaureate students.

In fall 2018, the five institutions with the highest enrollment (including distance education as well as in-person enrollment) were Western overnors` niversity` (121,400 students); outhern` New Hampshire niversity` (104,100 students); niversity` of Phoenix, Ariona` (95,800 students); rand` Canyon niversity` (90,300 students); and Liberty niversity` (79,200 students; table 312.10). Enrollments in these institutions were predominantly students enrolled in distance learning only. Overall, despite the sizable numbers of small degree-granting postsecondary institutions, most students attend larger colleges and universities. Although only 14 percent of campuses enrolled 10,000 or more students, these institutions accounted for 61 percent of total

---

[3] Enrollment growth in New Hampshire was primarily driven by increases in online enrollment at Southern New Hampshire University.

postsecondary enrollment in fall 2018. In contrast, some 39 percent of institutions had fewer than 1,000 students; however, these campuses enrolled 3 percent of all postsecondary students (table 317.40).

Changes in Undergraduate and Postbaccalaureate Enrollment

Enrollment trends have differed at the undergraduate and postbaccalaureate levels. Undergraduate enrollment increased 47 percent between fall 1970 and fall 1983, when it reached 10.8 million (table 303.70 and *Digest of Education Statistics 2016*, table 303.70). Undergraduate enrollment dipped to 10.6 million in 1984 and 1985 but then increased each year from 1985 to 1992, rising 18 percent before stabiliing between 1992 and 1998. Undergraduate enrollment increased every year between 1998 and 2008. ndergraduate enrollment was 2 percent higher in 2018 (16.6 million) than in 2008 (16.3 million). This overall change reflects increases in undergraduate enrollment in 2008, 2009, and 2010 (when undergraduate enrollment reached 18.1 million), followed by an 8 percent decrease between 2010 and 2018.

Postbaccalaureate enrollment increased 34 percent between 1970 and 1984, with most of this increase occurring in the early and mid-1970s (table 303.80). Postbaccalaureate enrollment increased between 1985 and 2018, rising a total of 84 percent. During the last decade of this period, between 2008 and 2018, postbaccalaureate enrollment rose 11 percent, from 2.7 million to 3.0 million. nlike undergraduate enrollment, which was lower in 2018 than in 2010, postbaccalaureate enrollment was higher in 2018 than in 2010.

ince fall 1988, the number of female students in post-baccalaureate programs has exceeded the number of male students (table 303.80). Between 2008 and 2018, the number of full-time male postbaccalaureate students increased 12 percent, compared with an 18 percent increase in the number of full-time female postbaccalaureate students. Among part-time postbaccalaureate students, the number of males enrolled in 2018 was 3 percent higher than in 2008, while the number of females was 6 percent higher.

The percentage of postbaccalaureate students who reported having a disability (12 percent) was lower than the percentage for undergraduates (19 percent).

Faculty, Staff, and Salaries

Characteristics of Faculty and Staff

Approximately 3.9 million people were employed in degree-granting postsecondary institutions in fall 2018, including 1.5 million faculty, 0.4 million graduate assistants, and 2.0 million other staff (table 314.20). Out of the 1.5 million faculty in 2018, about 0.8 million were full-time and 0.7 million were part-time. In 2019, the proportion of

staff who were faculty was 39 percent, about the same as in 2009. During the same period, the proportion of staff who were graduate assistants increased from 9 to 10 percent. The proportion of staff who were not engaged in teaching—that is, staff in any occupational category except the faculty and graduate assistant categoriesdecreased from 52 percent in 2009 to 51 percent in 2018. The full-time-equivalent (FTE) student/FTE staff ratio at degree-granting institutions in 2018 (4.9) was lower than in 2009 (5.4; table 314.10 and figure 15). Also, the FTE student/FTE faculty ratio was lower in 2018 (13.8) than in 2009 (15.9).

Degree-granting postsecondary institutions differ in their practices of employing part-time and full-time staff. In fall 2018, some 45 percent of the employees at private for-profit 4-year institutions and 49 percent at public 2-year institutions were employed full time, compared with 61 percent at private for-profit 2-year institutions, 68 percent at public 4-year institutions, 69 percent at private non-profit 4-year institutions, and 70 percent at private nonprofit 2-year institutions (table 314.30). Between 2009 and 2018, the number of full-time staff increased 7 percent, while the number of part-time staff was 2 percent higher in 2018 than in 2009 (table 314.20). For faculty specifically, the percentage employed full time was higher at public 4-year institutions (66 percent) than at private nonprofit 4-year institutions (56 percent), private nonprofit 2-year institutions (46 percent), private for-profit 2-year institutions (41 percent), public 2-year institutions (33 percent), and private for-profit 4-year institutions (18 percent; table 314.30). The number of full-time faculty increased 14 percent between 2009 and 2018, while the number of part-time faculty was less than 1 percent higher in 2018 than in 2009 (table 314.20). The number of part-time graduate assistants increased 12 percent during this period.

In fall 2018, some 9 percent of faculty at degree-granting institutions were Asian (based on a faculty count that excludes nonresident aliens and other persons whose race/ethnicity was unknown), 8 percent were Black, 6 percent were Hispanic, 1 percent were of Two or more races, 0.5 percent were American Indian/Alaska Native, and 0.2 percent were Pacific Islander (table 314.40). About 76 percent of all faculty were White 38 percent were White males and 38 percent were White females. taff who were Black, Hispanic, Asian, Pacific Islander, American Indian/Alaska Native, or of Two or more races made up 30 percent of graduate assistants and 32 percent of other staff in non-faculty positions in 2018, compared with 24 percent of faculty. The proportion of total staff who were Black, Hispanic, Asian, Pacific Islander, American Indian/Alaska Native, and of Two or more races was similar at public 4-year institutions (29 percent), public 2-year institutions (28 percent), and private nonprofit 4-year institutions (27 percent), but the proportion was higher at private for-profit 2-year institutions (43 percent), private nonprofit 2-year institutions (36 percent), and private for-profit 4-year institutions (35 percent).

Salary and Tenure

Faculty salaries generally lost purchasing power during the 1970s. In constant 2018–19 dollars, average salaries for faculty on 9-month contracts declined 16 percent during the period from 1970–71 ($81,000 in constant 2018–19 dollars) to 1980–81 ($68,100; table 316.10). During the 1980s, average salaries rose and recouped most of the losses. Between 1990–91 and 2018–19, there was a further increase in average faculty salaries, resulting in an average salary in 2018–19 ($88,700) that was 9 percent higher than the average salary in 1970–71. The average salary for male faculty in 2018–19 ($96,400) was 2 percent higher than in 2008–09 ($94,100). The average salary for female faculty in 2018–19 ($80,000) was 3 percent higher than in 2008–09 ($77,500). The average salary for male faculty was higher than the average salary for female faculty in all years for which data are available. In 2018–19, average salaries for male faculty were 20 percent higher than for female faculty, nearly the same percentage difference as in 2008–09 (21 percent).

The percentage of faculty with tenure has declined since 1993–94, both because of declines in the percentage of institutions with tenure systems and declines in the percentage of faculty receiving tenure at these institutions. The percentage of institutions with tenure systems in 2018–19 (57 percent) was lower than in 1993–94 (63 percent; table 316.80). Part of this change was due to the expansion in the number of for-profit institutions, relatively few of which have tenure systems (1.3 percent in 2018–19; tables 316.80 and 317.10). Between 1993–94 and 2011–12, the percentage of institutions with tenure systems decreased from 63 to 45 percent, while the number of for-profit institutions increased from 320 to 1,404. In more recent years, the growth of for-profit institutions has reversed, declining to 742 in 2018–19. During the same period as this decline, the percent of institutions with tenure systems increased from 45 percent in 2011–12 to 57 percent in 2018–19. In addition to the compositional change in postsecondary institutions, there was also an increase in the percentage of public institutions with a tenure system, from 71 percent in 2009–10 to 74 percent in 2018–19.

At institutions with tenure systems, the percentage of full-time faculty with tenure decreased from 56 percent in 1993–94 to 45 percent in 2018–19 (table 316.80). Among these institutions, there were differences between males and females in the percentage of full-time instructional faculty having tenure: 54 percent of males had tenure in 2018–19, compared with 40 percent of females. In 2018–19, about 49 percent of full-time instructional faculty had tenure at public institutions with tenure systems, compared with 44 percent at private nonprofit institutions with tenure systems and 13 percent at private for-profit institutions with tenure systems.

Degrees

During the 2018–19 academic year, 4,042 accredited institutions offered degrees at the associate's level or above (table 317.10). These included 1,636 public institutions, 1,664 private nonprofit institutions, and 742 private for-profit institutions. Of the 4,042 degree-granting institutions, 2,703 were 4-year institutions that awarded degrees at the bachelor's or higher level, and 1,339 were 2-year institutions that offered associate's degrees as their highest award. In 2017–18, associate's degrees were awarded by 2,457 institutions, bachelor's degrees by 2,335 institutions, master's degrees by 1,884 institutions, and doctor's degrees by 1,011 institutions (table 318.60). In addition to degree-granting institutions, 2,096 institutions offered postsecondary education in 2018–19 but did not grant degrees at the associate's level or higher (web-only table 317.30).

A growing number of people are completing postsecondary degrees. Between 2007–08 and 2017–18, the number of associate's, bachelor's, master's, and doctor's degrees that were conferred increased (table 318.10). During this period, the number of associate's degrees increased 35 percent (from 750,000 to 1,011,000), the number of bachelor's degrees increased 27 percent (from 1,564,000 to 1,981,000), the number of master's degrees increased 30 percent (from 631,000 to 820,000), and the number of doctor's degrees increased 23 percent (from 149,000 to 184,000). The doctor's degree total includes most degrees formerly classified as first-professional, such as .D.` (medical), D.D..` (dental), and .D.` (law) degrees. In addition to degrees awarded at the associate's level or higher, 955,000 certificates were awarded by postsecondary institutions participating in federal Title I` financial aid programs in 2017–18 (table 320.20).

ince` the mid-1980s, more females than males have earned associate's, bachelor's, and master's degrees (table 318.10). Beginning in 2005–06, the number of females earning doctor's degrees has also exceeded the number of males. Between 2007–08 and 2017–18, the numbers of associate's and master's degrees awarded to males increased at higher rates than the numbers awarded to females, while the numbers of bachelor's and doctor's degrees have increased by higher percentages for females. The number of associate's degrees awarded to males increased 41 percent during this period, while the number awarded to females increased 31 percent. The number of master's degrees awarded to males increased 31 percent, while the number awarded to females increased 30 percent. In contrast, the number of bachelor's degrees awarded to males increased 26 percent, while the number awarded to females increased 27 percent. Also, the number of doctor's degrees awarded to females increased 30 percent between 2007–08 and 2017–18, while the number awarded to males increased 17 percent.

Of the 1,981,000 bachelor's degrees conferred in 2017–18, the greatest numbers of degrees were conferred in the fields of business (386,000), health professions and related programs (245,000), social sciences and history (160,000), engineering (122,000), biological and biomedical sciences (119,000), psychology (116,000), communication, journalism, and related programs (92,000), and visual and performing arts (89,000; table 322.10). At the master's degree level, the greatest numbers of degrees were conferred in the fields of business (192,000), education (146,000), and health professions and related programs (125,000; table 323.10). At the doctor's degree level, the greatest numbers of degrees were conferred in the fields of health professions and related programs (80,300), legal professions and studies (34,500), education (12,800), engineering (10,800), biological and biomedical sciences (8,200), psychology (6,300), and physical sciences and science technologies (6,200; table 324.10).

In recent years, the numbers of bachelor's degrees conferred have followed patterns that differed significantly by field of study. While the number of bachelor's degrees conferred increased 27 percent overall between 2007–08 and 2017–18, there was substantial variation among the different fields of study, as well as shifts in the patterns of change during this time period (table 322.10 and figure 16). For example, the number of degrees conferred in foreign languages, literatures, and linguistics increased 3 percent between 2007–08 and 2012–13 but then decreased 22 percent between 2012–13 and 2017–18. Also, the number of degrees in social sciences and history increased 6 percent between 2007–08 and 2012–13 but then decreased 10 percent between 2012–13 and 2017–18. In a number of other major fields, the number of bachelor's degrees increased by higher percentages in the second half of the 10-year period than in the first half. The number of bachelor's degrees conferred in the combined fields of engineering and engineering technologies increased 23 percent between 2007–08 and 2012–13 and then increased a further 37 percent between 2012–13 and 2017–18. Also, computer and information sciences increased 32 percent between 2007–08 and 2012–13 and then increased 56 percent between 2012–13 and 2017–18. ome` other major fields had smaller increases between 2012–13 and 2017–18 than between 2007–08 and 2012–13. For example, the number of degrees conferred in agriculture and natural resources increased 39 percent between 2007–08 and 2012–13 and then 17 percent between 2012–13 and 2017–18. The number of degrees conferred in health professions and related programs increased 62 percent between 2007–08 and 2012–13 and then 35 percent between 2012–13 and 2017–18. Also, the number of degrees conferred in public administration and social services increased 36 percent between 2007–08 and 2012–13 and then 12 percent between 2012–13 and 2017–18. The other field with a large number of degrees (over 10,000 in 2017–18) that showed increases of 25 percent or more between 2012–13 and 2017–18 was parks, recreation, leisure, and fitness studies

(26 percent). ome` other fields with si. able numbers of degrees saw decreases during the 2012–13 to 2017–18 period. For example, the number of degrees in philosophy and religious studies decreased 25 percent between 2012–13 and 2017–18. Also, the number of degrees in English language and literature/letters decreased 24 percent; the number of degrees in education decreased 21 percent; and the number of degrees in visual and performing arts decreased 9 percent. Additionally, the number of degrees in liberal arts and sciences, general studies, and humanities was 5 percent lower in 2017–18 than in 2012–13, and the number of degrees in homeland security, law enforcement, and firefighting was 4 percent lower in 2017–18 than in 2012–13.

Among first-time students who were seeking a bachelor's degree or its equivalent and attending a 4-year institution full time in 2012, about 44 percent completed a bachelor's degree or its equivalent at that institution within 4 years, while 59 percent did so within 5 years, and 62 percent did so within 6 years (web-only table 326.10). These graduation rates were calculated as the total number of completers within the specified time to degree attainment divided by the cohort of students who first enrolled at that institution in 2012. Graduation rates were higher at private nonprofit institutions than at public or private for-profit institutions. For example, the 6-year graduation rate for the 2012 cohort at private nonprofit institutions was 67 percent, compared with 61 percent at public institutions and 25 percent at private for-profit institutions. Graduation rates also varied by race/ethnicity. At 4-year institutions overall, the 6-year graduation rate for Asian students in the 2012 cohort was 75 percent, compared with 66 percent for White students, 58 percent for students of Two or more races, 57 percent for Hispanic students, 49 percent for Pacific Islander students, 42 percent for Black students, and 41 percent for American Indian/Alaska Native students.

Finances and Financial Aid

For the 2018–19 academic year, annual current dollar prices for undergraduate tuition, fees, room, and board were estimated to be $18,383 at public institutions, $47,419 at private nonprofit institutions, and $27,040 at private for-profit institutions (table 330.10). Between 2008–09 and 2018–19, prices for undergraduate tuition, fees, room, and board at public institutions rose 28 percent, and prices at private nonprofit institutions rose 19 percent, after adjustment for inflation. In contrast, the price for undergraduate tuition, fees, room, and board at private for-profit institutions were 6 percent lower in 2018–19 than in 2008–09, after adjustment for inflation.

In 2015–16, about 86 percent of full-time undergraduate students received financial aid (grants, loans, work-study, or aid of multiple types; table 331.10). About 70 percent of full-time undergraduates received financial aid in 2015–16 from federal sources, and 67 percent received aid from nonfederal sources. (Many students receive aid from both federal and nonfederal sources.) Section 484(r) of the Higher Education Act of 1965, as amended, suspends a student's eligibility for Title IV federal financial aid if the student is convicted of certain drug-related offenses that were committed while the student was receiving Title IV aid. For 2016–17, less than 0.01 percent of postsecondary students had their eligibility to receive aid suspended due to a conviction (table C).

Table C. Suspension of eligibility for Title IV federal student financial aid due to a drug-related conviction or failure to report conviction status on aid application form: 2007–08 through 2016–17

| | | Suspension of eligibility | | |
| | | | For full award year | |
Award year	No suspension of eligibility	For part of award year	Due to conviction	Due to failure to report
2007–08				
Number	14,610,371	361	2,832	2,433
Percent	99.96	#	0.02	0.02
2008–09				
Number	16,410,285	398	1,064	724
Percent	99.99	#	0.01	#
2009–10				
Number	19,487,370	666	1,751	879
Percent	99.98	#	0.01	#
2010–11				
Number	21,114,404	606	1,284	406
Percent	99.99	#	0.01	#
2011–12				
Number	21,947,204	404	968	732
Percent	99.99	#	#	#
2012–13				
Number	21,803,176	322	778	432
Percent	99.99	#	#	#
2013–14				
Number	21,192,389	257	572	535
Percent	99.99	#	#	#
2014–15				
Number	20,560,709	242	474	504
Percent	99.99	#	#	#
2015–16				
Number	19,756,619	273	564	308
Percent	99.99	#	#	#
2016–17				
Number	18,739,769	254	657	375
Percent	99.99	#	#	#

Rounds to zero.
NOTE: It is not possible to determine whether a student who lost eligibility due to a drug conviction otherwise would have received Title IV aid, since there are other reasons why an applicant may not receive aid. Detail may not sum to totals because of rounding.
SOURCE: U.S. Department of Education, Federal Student Aid, Free Application for Federal Student Aid (FAFSA), unpublished data.

In 2017–18, total revenue was $409 billion at public institutions, $248 billion at private nonprofit institutions, and $13 billion at private for-profit institutions (tables 333.10, 333.40, and 333.55 and figures 17, 18, and 19). The category of student tuition and fees typically accounts for a significant percentage of total revenue and was the largest single revenue source at both private nonprofit and for-profit institutions in 2017–18 (31 and 94 percent, respectively). Tuition and fees accounted for 20 percent of revenue at public institutions in 2017–18. Public institutions typically report Pell grants as revenue from federal grants, while private institutions report Pell grants as revenue

from tuition and fees; this difference in reporting contributes to the smaller percentage of revenue reported as tuition and fees at public institutions compared with private institutions. At public institutions, the share of revenue from tuition and fees in 2017–18 (20 percent) was higher than the share from state appropriations (18 percent), while in 2007–08 the share from tuition and fees (18 percent) was lower than the share from state appropriations (25 percent; table 333.10). In 2017–18, tuition and fees constituted the largest single revenue category at private nonprofit 2-year and 4-year institutions, private for-profit 2-year and 4-year institutions, and public 4-year institutions (tables 333.10, 333.40, and 333.55). At public 2-year institutions, tuition and fees (16 percent) constituted the third-largest revenue category, below state (26 percent) and local (21 percent) appropriations.

Average total expenditures per full-time-equivalent (FTE) student in 2017–18—shown in constant 2018–19 dollars throughout this paragraph—varied by institution control and level, as did changes in average total expenditures per FTE student between 2009–10 and 2017–18 (after adjustment for inflation). In 2017–18, average total expenditures per FTE student at public degree-granting institutions were $37,200, reflecting an increase of 22 percent from $30,600 in 2009–10 (table 334.10). At public 4-year institutions, the average total expenditures per FTE student were $46,200 in 2017–18, compared with $16,900 at public 2-year institutions. At private nonprofit institutions, the average total expenditures per FTE student increased 14 percent between 2009–10 and 2017–18, from $53,600 to $60,900 (table 334.30). In 2017–18, average total expenditures per FTE student at private nonprofit institutions were $61,400 at 4-year institutions and $19,500 at 2-year institutions. The average total expenditures per FTE student at private for-profit institutions in 2017–18 ($16,500) were 6 percent higher than in 2009–10 ($15,700; table 334.50). In 2017–18, average total expenditures per FTE student at private for-profit institutions were $16,400 at 4-year institutions and $17,000 at 2-year institutions. This difference in expenditures per FTE student between 4-year and 2-year private for-profit institutions was relatively small compared with the differences between 4-year and 2-year institutions in the public and private nonprofit sectors, due to relatively low spending at 4-year private for-profit institutions.

At the end of fiscal year 2018, the market value of the endowment funds of colleges and universities was $648 billion, reflecting an increase of 9 percent since the beginning of the fiscal year, when the total was $597 billion (*web-only table 333.90*). At the end of fiscal year 2018, the 120 institutions with the largest endowments accounted for $482 billion, or about three-fourths of the national total. The five institutions with the largest endowments at the end of fiscal year 2018 were Harvard University ($39 billion), the University of Texas System ($31 billion), Yale University ($29 billion), Stanford University ($26 billion), and Princeton University ($25 billion).

Figure 12. Fall enrollment, degrees conferred, and total expenditures in degree-granting postsecondary institutions: 1960–61 through 2018–19

Fall enrollment, in millions

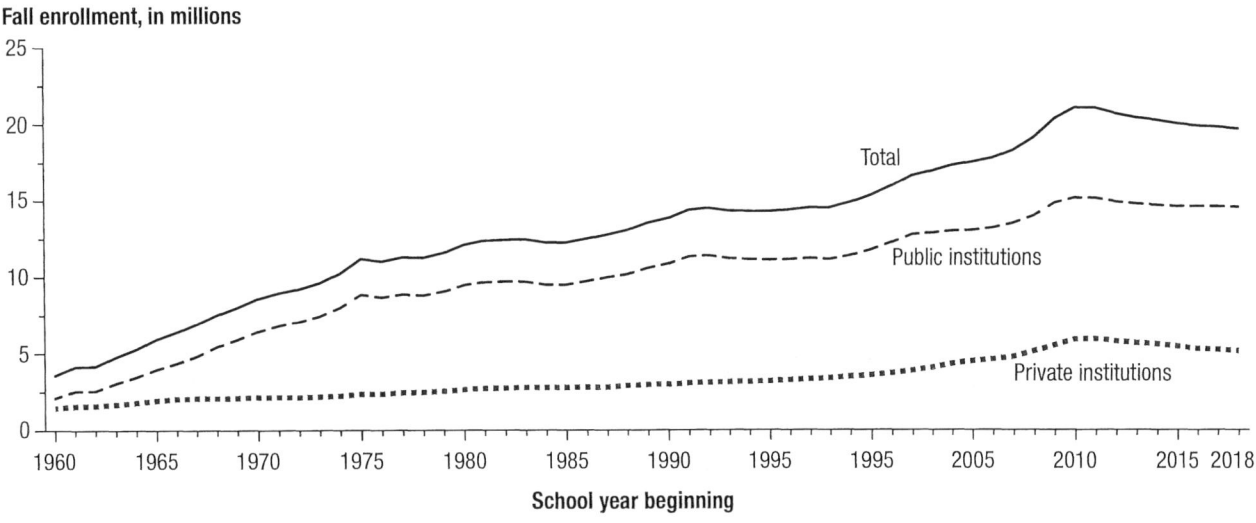

School year beginning

Degrees conferred, in millions

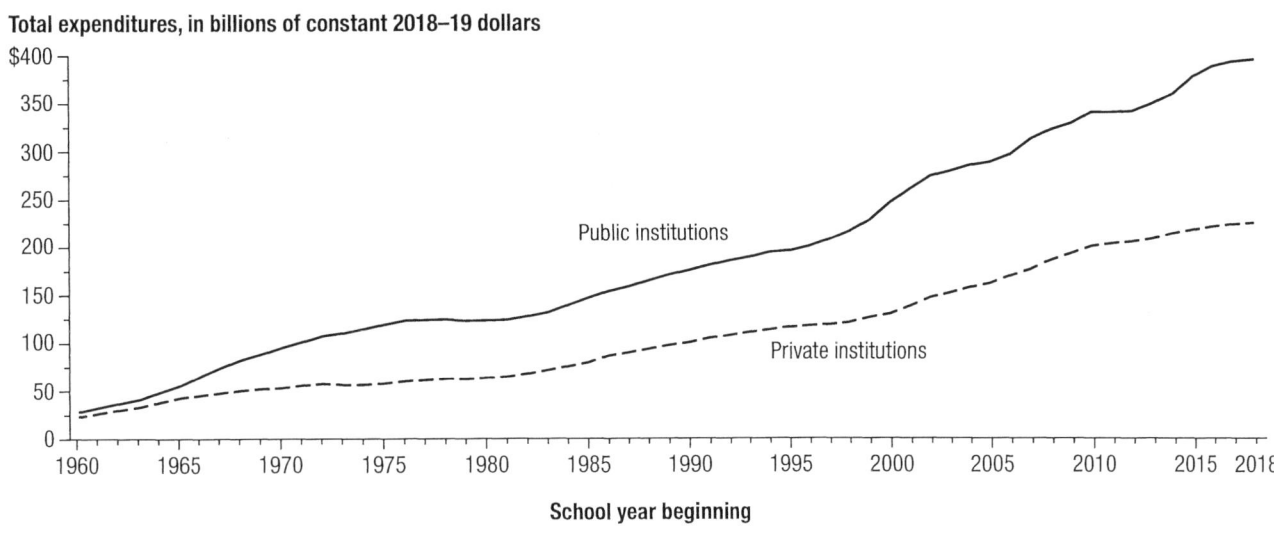

School year beginning

Total expenditures, in billions of constant 2018–19 dollars

School year beginning

NOTE: Expenditure data for the school year beginning in 2018 (2018–19) are estimated. Degree data for the school year beginning in 2018 are projected. Doctor's degrees include Ph.D., Ed.D., and comparable degrees at the doctoral level, as well as such degrees as M.D., D.D.S., and law degrees that were classified as first-professional degrees prior to 2010–11. Constant dollars based on the Consumer Price Index, prepared by the Bureau of Labor Statistics, U.S. Department of Labor, adjusted to a school-year basis.
SOURCE: U.S. Department of Education, National Center for Education Statistics, *Opening Fall Enrollment in Higher Education*, 1960 through 1965; *Financial Statistics of Higher Education*, 1959–60 through 1964–65; *Earned Degrees Conferred*, 1959–60 through 1964–65; Degrees Conferred Projection Model, 1980–81 through 2029–30; Higher Education General Information Survey (HEGIS), "Fall Enrollment in Institutions of Higher Education," "Degrees and Other Formal Awards Conferred," and "Financial Statistics of Institutions of Higher Education" surveys, 1965–66 through 1985–86; Integrated Postsecondary Education Data System (IPEDS), "Fall Enrollment Survey" (IPEDS-EF:86–99), "Completions Survey" (IPEDS-C:87–99), and "Finance Survey" (IPEDS-F:FY87–99); IPEDS Fall 2000 through Fall 2018, Completions component; and IPEDS Spring 2001 through Spring 2019, Fall Enrollment and Finance components.

Figure 13. Percentage change in total enrollment in degree-granting postsecondary institutions, by state: Fall 2013 to fall 2018

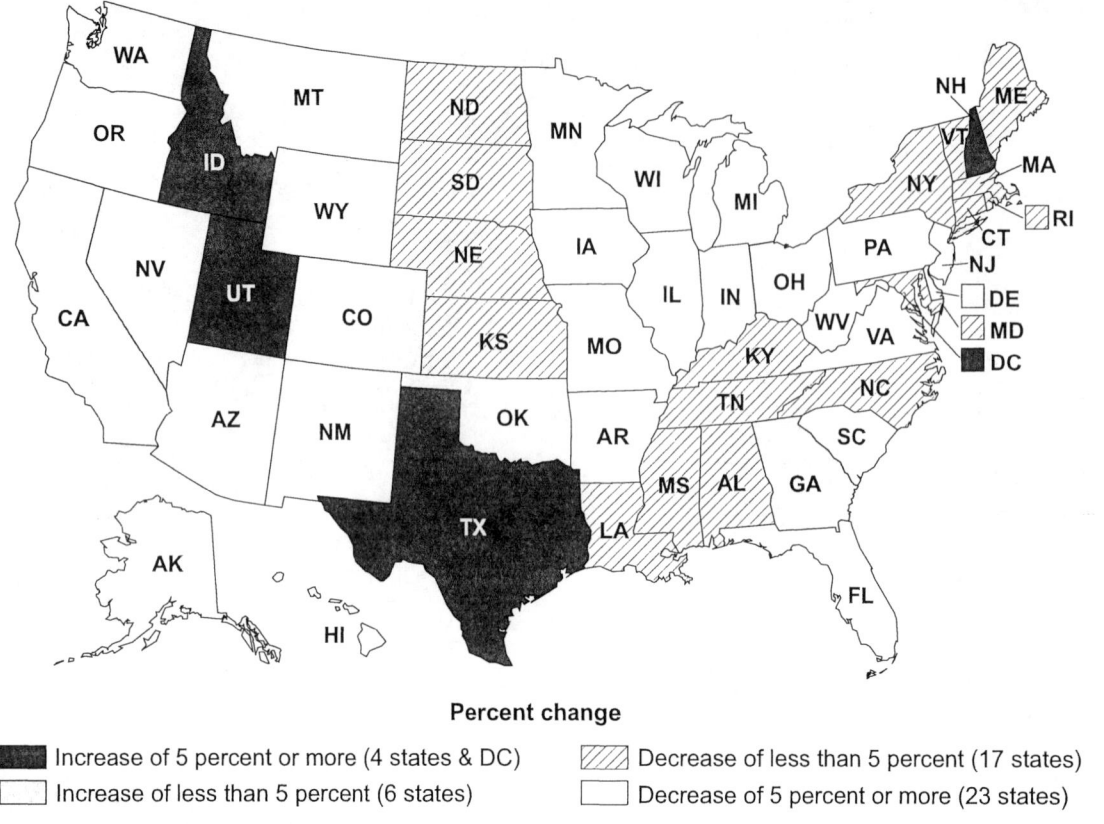

Percent change

■ Increase of 5 percent or more (4 states & DC)   ▨ Decrease of less than 5 percent (17 states)

☐ Increase of less than 5 percent (6 states)   ☐ Decrease of 5 percent or more (23 states)

NOTE: Graphic display was generated using unrounded data.
SOURCE: U.S. Department of Education, National Center for Education Statistics, Integrated Postsecondary Education Data System (IPEDS), Spring 2014 and Spring 2019, Fall Enrollment component.

Figure 14. Fall enrollment in degree-granting postsecondary institutions, by age of student: 1970 through 2029

Fall enrollment, in millions

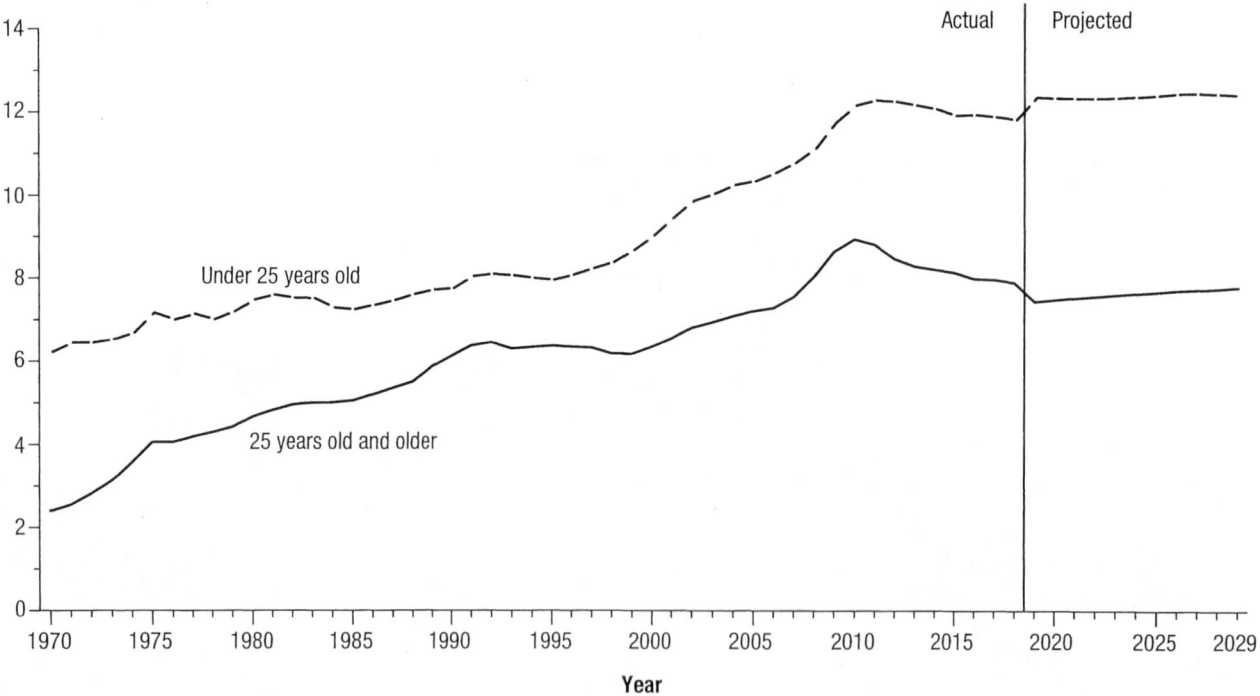

Year

SOURCE: U.S. Department of Education, National Center for Education Statistics, Higher Education General Information Survey (HEGIS), "Fall Enrollment in Colleges and Universities" surveys, 1970 through 1985; Integrated Postsecondary Education Data System (IPEDS), "Fall Enrollment Survey" (IPEDS-EF:86–99); IPEDS Spring 2001 through Spring 2019, Fall Enrollment component; and Enrollment in Degree-Granting Institutions Projection Model, 2000 through 2029. U.S. Department of Commerce, Census Bureau, Current Population Survey (CPS), October, selected years, 1970 through 2018.

Figure 15. Ratio of full-time-equivalent (FTE) students to total FTE staff and to FTE faculty in degree-granting postsecondary institutions, by control of institution: 1999, 2009, and 2018

FTE students per FTE staff member

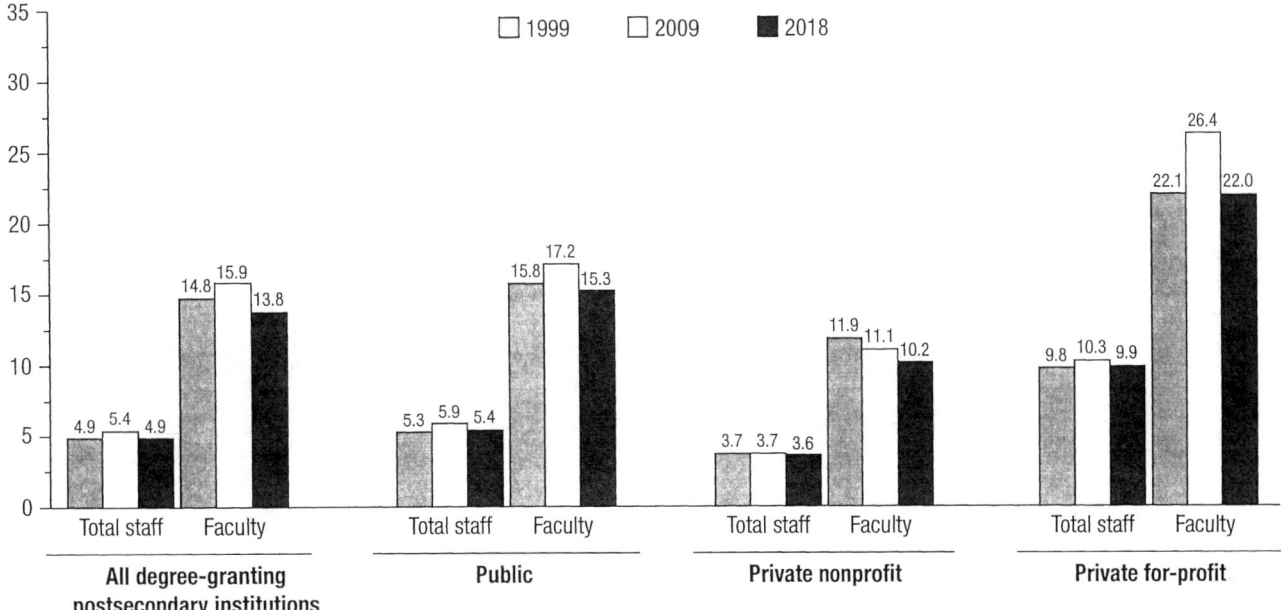

Control of institution and type of staff

NOTE: Graphic display was generated using unrounded data.
SOURCE: U.S. Department of Education, National Center for Education Statistics, Integrated Postsecondary Education Data System (IPEDS), "Fall Enrollment Survey" (IPEDS-EF:99) and "Fall Staff Survey" (IPEDS-S:99); IPEDS Spring 2010 and Spring 2019, Fall Enrollment component; IPEDS Winter 2009–10, Human Resources component, Fall Staff section; and IPEDS Spring 2019, Human Resources component, Fall Staff section.

Figure 16. Number of bachelor's degrees conferred by postsecondary institutions in selected fields of study: 2007–08, 2012–13, and 2017–18

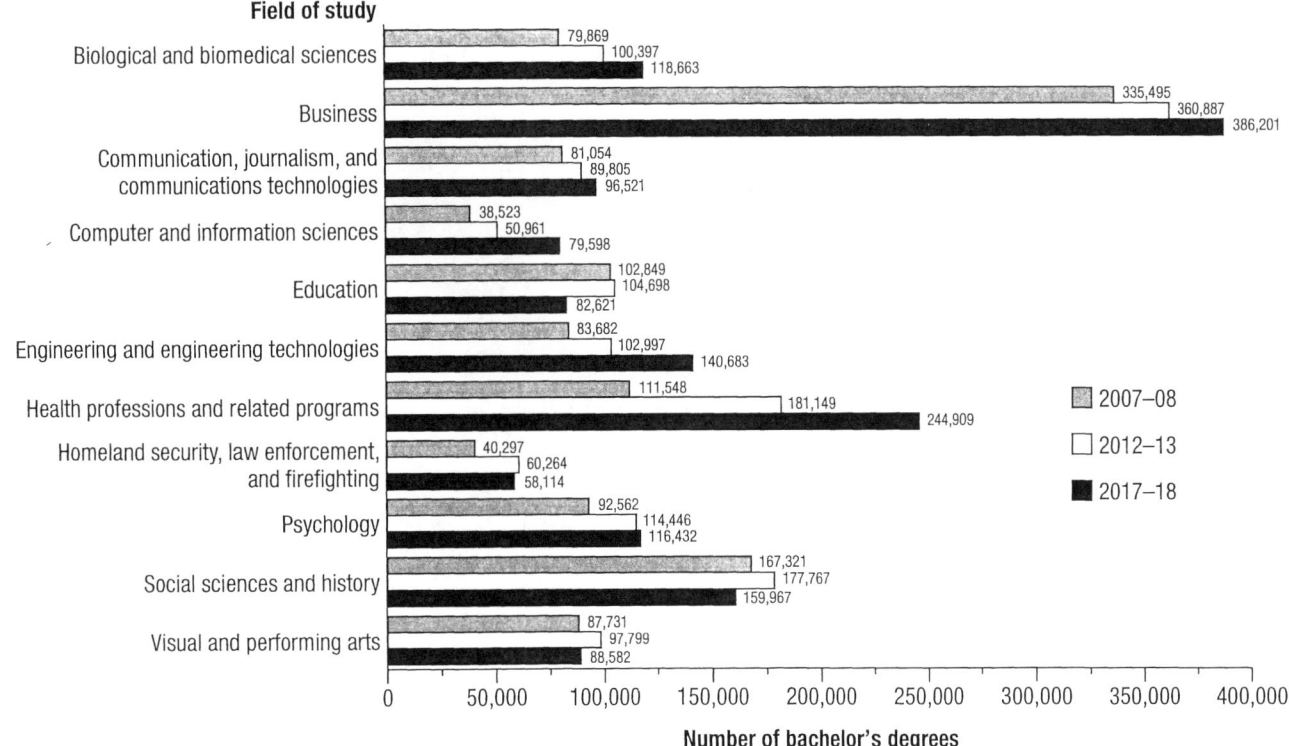

SOURCE: U.S. Department of Education, National Center for Education Statistics, Integrated Postsecondary Education Data System (IPEDS), Fall 2008, Fall 2013, and Fall 2018, Completions component.

Figure 17. Percentage distribution of total revenues of public degree-granting postsecondary institutions, by source of funds: 2017–18

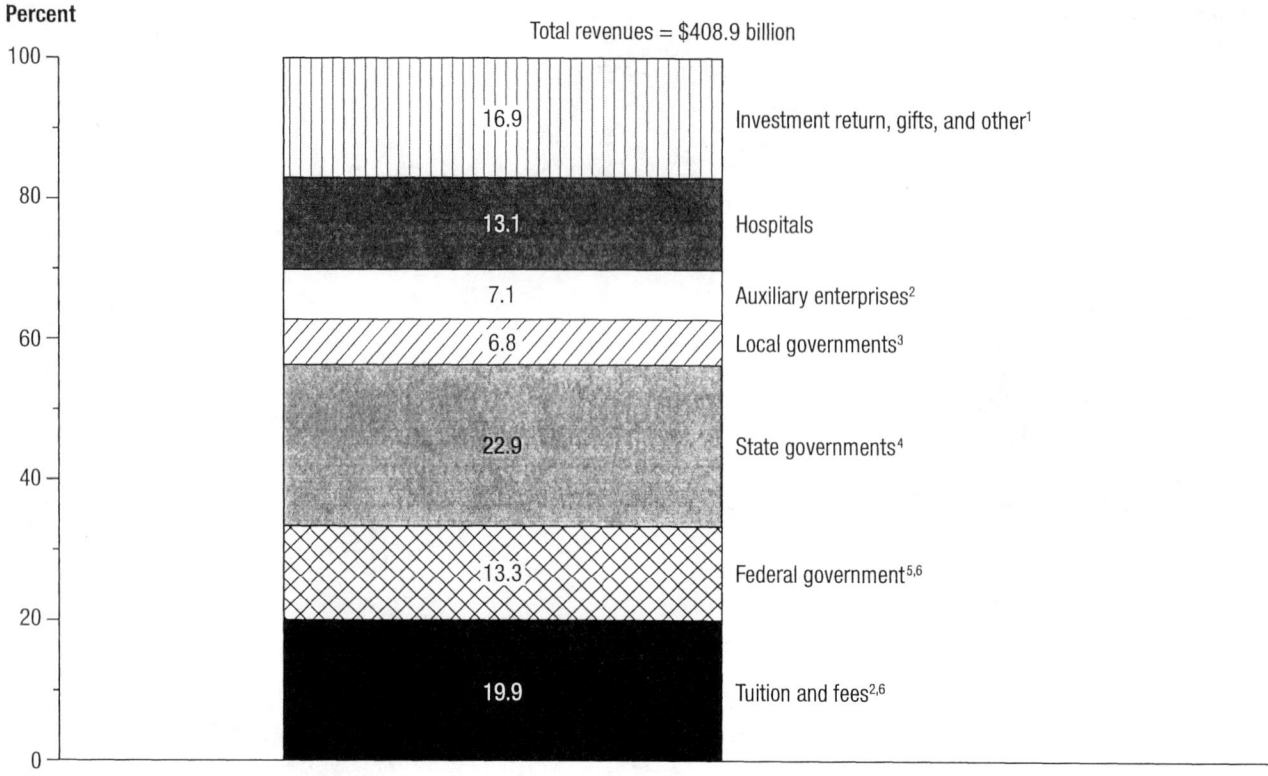

Percent

Total revenues = $408.9 billion

- 16.9 — Investment return, gifts, and other[1]
- 13.1 — Hospitals
- 7.1 — Auxiliary enterprises[2]
- 6.8 — Local governments[3]
- 22.9 — State governments[4]
- 13.3 — Federal government[5,6]
- 19.9 — Tuition and fees[2,6]

Source of funds

[1]In addition to the categories listed, includes capital grants and gifts, additions to permanent endowments, and operating and nonoperating revenues not included elsewhere.
[2]After deducting discounts and allowances.
[3]Revenues from local governments include operating grants and contracts (including private grants and contracts), nonoperating appropriations, and nonoperating grants.
[4]Revenues from state governments include operating grants and contracts, nonoperating appropriations, nonoperating grants, and capital appropriations.
[5]Revenues from the federal government include operating grants and contracts, funds for independent operations, nonoperating appropriations, and nonoperating grants.
[6]Public institutions typically report Pell grants as revenues from federal grants and as allowances that reduce tuition revenues.
NOTE: Graphic display was generated using unrounded data. Detail may not sum to totals because of rounding.
SOURCE: U.S. Department of Education, National Center for Education Statistics, Integrated Postsecondary Education Data System (IPEDS), Spring 2019, Finance component.

Figure 18. Percentage distribution of total revenues of private nonprofit degree-granting postsecondary institutions, by source of funds: 2017–18

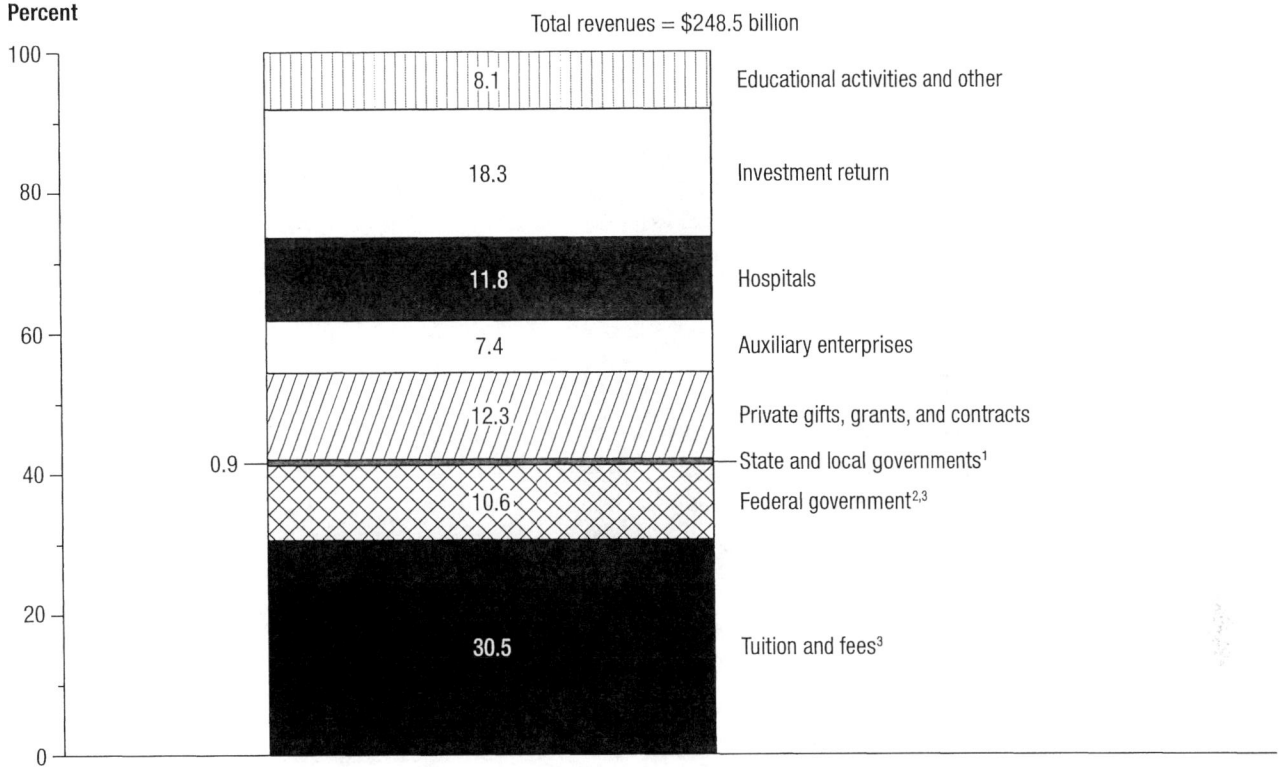

Percent

Total revenues = $248.5 billion

- 8.1 — Educational activities and other
- 18.3 — Investment return
- 11.8 — Hospitals
- 7.4 — Auxiliary enterprises
- 12.3 — Private gifts, grants, and contracts
- 0.9 — State and local governments[1]
- 10.6 — Federal government[2,3]
- 30.5 — Tuition and fees[3]

Source of funds

[1]Includes appropriations, grants, and contracts.
[2]Includes appropriations, grants, contracts, and independent operations.
[3]Private institutions typically report Pell grants as tuition revenues rather than as revenues from federal grants.
NOTE: Graphic display was generated using unrounded data. Detail may not sum to totals because of rounding.
SOURCE: U.S. Department of Education, National Center for Education Statistics, Integrated Postsecondary Education Data System (IPEDS), Spring 2019, Finance component.

Figure 19. Percentage distribution of total revenues of private for-profit degree-granting postsecondary institutions, by source of funds: 2017–18

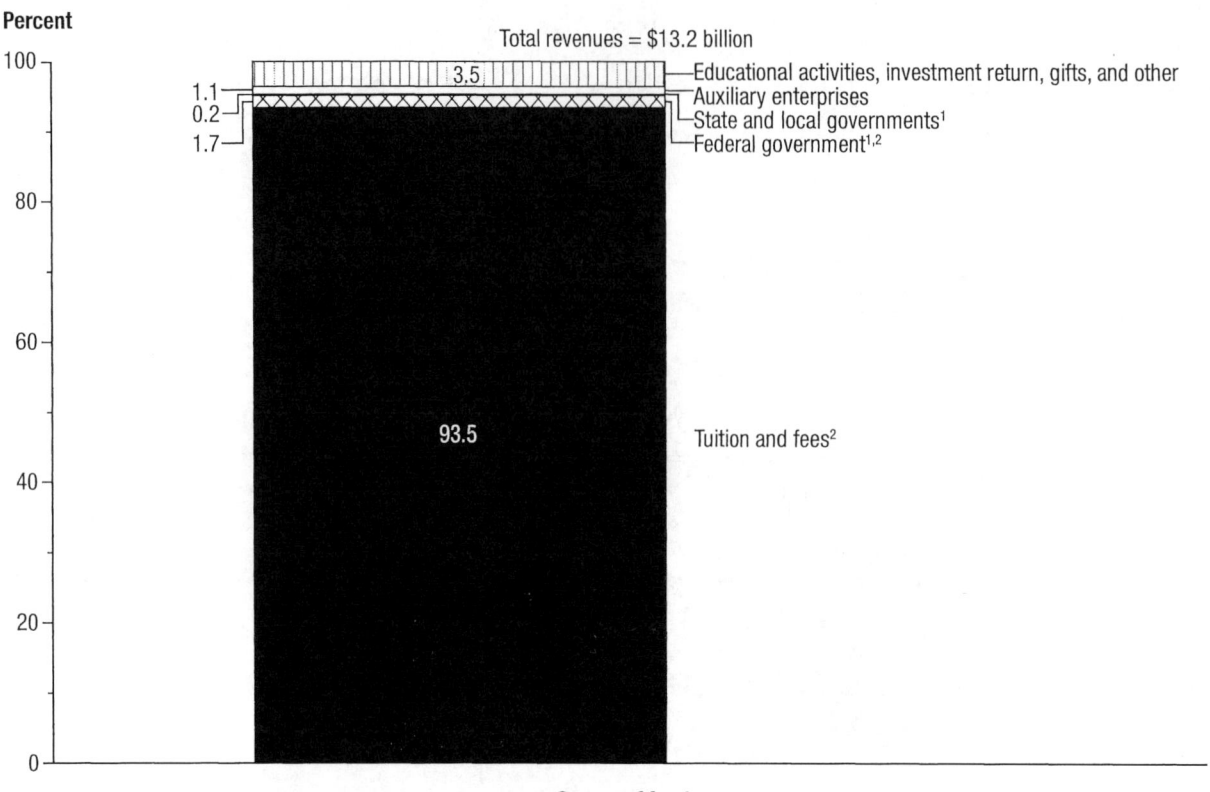

Percent

Total revenues = $13.2 billion

Educational activities, investment return, gifts, and other
Auxiliary enterprises
State and local governments[1]
Federal government[1,2]

1.1
0.2
1.7

3.5

93.5

Tuition and fees[2]

Source of funds

[1]Includes appropriations, grants, and contracts.
[2]Private institutions typically report Pell grants as tuition revenues rather than as revenues from federal grants.
NOTE: Graphic display was generated using unrounded data. Detail may not sum to totals because of rounding.
SOURCE: U.S. Department of Education, National Center for Education Statistics, Integrated Postsecondary Education Data System (IPEDS), Spring 2019, Finance component.

Table 301.10. Enrollment, staff, and degrees/certificates conferred in degree-granting and non-degree-granting postsecondary institutions, by control and level of institution, sex of student, type of staff, and level of degree: Fall 2018 and 2017–18

Level of institution, sex of student, type of staff, and level of degree	Total[1]	Degree-granting institutions					Non-degree-granting institutions				
		Total	Public	Private			Total	Public	Private		
				Total	Nonprofit	For-profit			Total	Nonprofit	For-profit
1	2	3	4	5	6	7	8	9	10	11	12
Enrollment, fall 2018											
Total	20,008,434	19,645,918	14,529,264	5,116,654	4,134,244	982,410	362,516	110,417	252,099	13,360	238,739
4-year institutions	13,901,011	13,900,710	8,982,560	4,918,150	4,089,090	829,060	301	5	296	296	0
Males	5,991,066	5,990,993	4,005,748	1,985,245	1,711,257	273,988	73	2	71	71	0
Females	7,909,945	7,909,717	4,976,812	2,932,905	2,377,833	555,072	228	3	225	225	0
2-year institutions	5,849,184	5,745,208	5,546,704	198,504	45,154	153,350	103,976	57,824	46,152	5,468	40,684
Males	2,506,453	2,451,669	2,385,723	65,946	11,260	54,686	54,784	34,485	20,299	1,289	19,010
Females	3,342,731	3,293,539	3,160,981	132,558	33,894	98,664	49,192	23,339	25,853	4,179	21,674
Less-than-2-year institutions	258,239	†	†	†	†	†	258,239	52,588	205,651	7,596	198,055
Males	83,005	†	†	†	†	†	83,005	26,283	56,722	2,949	53,773
Females	175,234	†	†	†	†	†	175,234	26,305	148,929	4,647	144,282
Staff, fall 2018											
Total	3,983,860	3,923,374	2,586,155	1,337,219	1,221,378	115,841	60,486	22,262	38,224	3,052	35,172
Faculty (instruction/research/public service)	1,573,995	1,542,613	980,835	561,778	491,014	70,764	31,382	11,815	19,567	1,473	18,094
Instruction	1,454,136	1,422,754	905,307	517,447	446,789	70,658	31,382	11,815	19,567	1,473	18,094
Research	90,489	90,489	55,909	34,580	34,526	54	†	†	†	†	†
Public service	29,370	29,370	19,619	9,751	9,699	52	†	†	†	†	†
Graduate assistants	382,715	382,715	299,271	83,444	83,077	367	†	†	†	†	†
Librarians, curators, and archivists	41,637	41,495	24,166	17,329	16,470	859	142	41	101	43	58
Student and academic affairs and other education services	188,440	182,831	122,638	60,193	50,369	9,824	5,609	2,573	3,036	338	2,698
Management	268,530	262,919	152,673	110,246	101,042	9,204	5,611	1,299	4,312	339	3,973
Business and financial operations	222,388	219,793	147,797	71,996	67,858	4,138	2,595	567	2,028	132	1,896
Computer, engineering, and science	238,588	238,073	162,518	75,555	73,695	1,860	515	321	194	34	160
Community, social service, legal, arts, design, entertainment, sports, and media	186,297	185,765	113,130	72,635	69,534	3,101	532	310	222	54	168
Healthcare practitioners and technicians	111,519	111,076	75,116	35,960	35,692	268	443	332	111	23	88
Service occupations	244,842	242,151	161,701	80,450	78,364	2,086	2,691	1,534	1,157	150	1,007
Sales and related occupations	14,533	12,534	4,748	7,786	3,970	3,816	1,999	110	1,889	81	1,808
Office and administrative support	417,271	409,591	273,892	135,699	126,783	8,916	7,680	2,582	5,098	334	4,764
Natural resources, construction, and maintenance	74,097	73,098	53,940	19,158	18,686	472	999	542	457	43	414
Production, transportation, and material moving	19,008	18,720	13,730	4,990	4,824	166	288	236	52	8	44
Degrees/certificates conferred, 2017–18											
Total	4,951,142	4,714,760	3,285,726	1,429,034	1,100,383	328,651	236,382	59,796	176,586	8,722	167,864
Less-than-1-year and 1- to less-than-4-year certificates	954,738	718,453	612,084	106,369	17,067	89,302	236,285	59,796	176,489	8,722	167,767
4-year institutions	166,318	166,278	125,608	40,670	11,264	29,406	40	3	37	37	0
Males	75,999	75,996	62,780	13,216	4,406	8,810	3	2	1	1	0
Females	90,319	90,282	62,828	27,454	6,858	20,596	37	1	36	36	0
2-year institutions	608,547	552,175	486,476	65,699	5,803	59,896	56,372	30,446	25,926	2,236	23,690
Males	289,774	263,875	241,157	22,718	2,073	20,645	25,899	15,436	10,463	639	9,824
Females	318,773	288,300	245,319	42,981	3,730	39,251	30,473	15,010	15,463	1,597	13,866
Less-than-2-year institutions	179,873	†	†	†	†	†	179,873	29,347	150,526	6,449	144,077
Males	54,411	†	†	†	†	†	54,411	11,891	42,520	2,762	39,758
Females	125,462	†	†	†	†	†	125,462	17,456	108,006	3,687	104,319
Associate's degrees	1,011,582	1,011,487	885,870	125,617	56,187	69,430	95	0	95	0	95
4-year institutions	297,139	297,139	209,841	87,298	43,666	43,632	0	0	0	0	0
Males	115,054	115,054	83,613	31,441	16,742	14,699	0	0	0	0	0
Females	182,085	182,085	126,228	55,857	26,924	28,933	0	0	0	0	0
2-year institutions	714,348	714,348	676,029	38,319	12,521	25,798	0	0	0	0	0
Males	283,546	283,546	270,799	12,747	2,593	10,154	0	0	0	0	0
Females	430,802	430,802	405,230	25,572	9,928	15,644	0	0	0	0	0
Less-than-2-year institutions	95	†	†	†	†	†	95	0	95	0	95
Males	34	†	†	†	†	†	34	0	34	0	34
Females	61	†	†	†	†	†	61	0	61	0	61
Bachelor's degrees	1,980,646	1,980,644	1,310,988	669,656	571,155	98,501	2	0	2	0	2
Males	844,961	844,960	574,520	270,440	233,670	36,770	1	0	1	0	1
Females	1,135,685	1,135,684	736,468	399,216	337,485	61,731	1	0	1	0	1
Master's degrees	820,102	820,102	383,929	436,173	372,086	64,087	0	0	0	0	0
Males	326,870	326,870	159,310	167,560	147,892	19,668	0	0	0	0	0
Females	493,232	493,232	224,619	268,613	224,194	44,419	0	0	0	0	0
Doctor's degrees	184,074	184,074	92,855	91,219	83,888	7,331	0	0	0	0	0
Males	85,568	85,568	44,521	41,047	38,497	2,550	0	0	0	0	0
Females	98,506	98,506	48,334	50,172	45,391	4,781	0	0	0	0	0

†Not applicable.
[1]Includes both degree-granting and non-degree-granting institutions.
NOTE: Data are for postsecondary institutions participating in Title IV federal financial aid programs. Degree-granting institutions grant degrees at the associate's or higher level, while non-degree-granting institutions grant only awards below that level. The non-degree-granting classification includes some institutions transitioning to higher level program offerings, though still classified at a lower level; therefore, a small number of associate's degrees are shown as awarded by non-degree-granting institutions.
SOURCE: U.S. Department of Education, National Center for Education Statistics, Integrated Postsecondary Education Data System (IPEDS), Spring 2019, Fall Enrollment component; Spring 2019, Human Resources component; and Fall 2018, Completions component. (This table was prepared February 2020.)

Table 301.20. Historical summary of faculty, enrollment, degrees conferred, and finances in degree-granting postsecondary institutions: Selected years, 1869–70 through 2017–18

Selected characteristic	1869–70	1879–80	1889–90	1899–1900	1909–10	1919–20	1929–30	1939–40	1949–50	1959–60	1969–70	1979–80	1989–90	1999–2000	2009–10	2017–18
	1	2	3	4	5	6	7	8	9	10	11	12	13	14	15	16	17
Total institutions[1]	563	811	998	977	951	1,041	1,409	1,708	1,851	2,004	2,525	3,152	3,535	4,084	4,495	4,313
Total faculty[2]																
Males	5,553[3]	11,522[3]	15,809	23,868	36,480	48,615	82,386	146,929	246,722	380,554	450,000[4]	675,000[4]	824,220[5]	1,027,830[5]	1,439,074[5]	1,545,653[5]
Females	4,887[3]	7,328[3]	12,704[3]	19,151	29,132	35,807	60,017	106,328	186,189	296,773	346,000[4]	479,000[4]	534,254[5]	602,469[5]	761,002[5]	778,873[5]
Total	_663[3]_	_4,194[3]_	_3,105[3]_	_4,717_	_7,348_	_12,808_	_22,369_	_40,601_	_60,533_	_83,781_	_104,000[4]_	_196,000[4]_	_289,966[5]_	_425,361[5]_	_678,072[5]_	_766,780[5]_
Total fall enrollment[6]	52,286	115,817	156,756	237,592	355,213	597,880	1,100,737	1,494,203	2,444,900	3,639,847	8,004,660	11,569,899	13,538,560	14,791,224	20,313,594	19,778,151
Males	41,160[3]	77,972[3]	100,453[3]	152,254	214,648[3]	314,938	619,935	893,250	1,721,572	2,332,617	4,746,201	5,682,877	6,190,015	6,490,646	8,732,963	8,571,314
Females	11,126[3]	37,845[3]	56,303[3]	85,338	140,565[3]	282,942	480,802	600,953	723,328	1,307,230	3,258,459	5,887,022	7,348,545	8,300,578	11,580,641	11,206,837
Degrees conferred																
Associate's, total	—	—	—	—	—	—	—	—	—	—	—	400,910	455,102	564,933	848,856	1,011,487
Bachelor's, total[7]	9,371	12,896	15,539	27,410	37,199	48,622	122,484	186,500	432,058	392,440	792,316	929,417	1,051,344	1,237,875	1,649,919	1,980,644
Males	7,993	10,411	12,857	22,173	28,762	31,980	73,615	109,546	328,841	254,063	451,097	473,611	491,696	530,367	706,660	844,960
Females	1,378	2,485	2,682	5,237	8,437	16,642	48,869	76,954	103,217	138,377	341,219	455,806	559,648	707,508	943,259	1,135,684
Master's, total[8]	0	879	1,015	1,583	2,113	4,279	14,969	26,731	58,183	74,435	213,589	305,196	330,152	463,185	693,313	820,102
Males	—	868	821	1,280	1,555	2,985	8,925	16,508	41,220	50,898	130,799	156,882	158,052	196,129	275,317	326,870
Females	—	11	194	303	558	1,294	6,044	10,223	16,963	23,537	82,790	148,314	172,100	267,056	417,996	493,232
Doctor's, total[9]	1	54	149	382	443	615	2,299	3,290	6,420	9,829	59,486	95,631	103,508	118,736	158,590	184,074
Males	1	51	147	359	399	522	1,946	2,861	5,804	8,801	53,792	69,526	63,963	64,930	76,610	85,568
Females	0	3	2	23	44	93	353	429	616	1,028	5,694	26,105	39,545	53,806	81,980	98,506
Finances																
In thousands of current dollars																
Revenue[10]	—	—	$21,464	$35,084	$76,883	$199,922	$554,511	$715,211	$2,374,645	$5,785,537	$21,515,242	$58,519,982	$139,635,477	$282,261,000	$496,720,000	$670,555,000
Educational and general income[11]	—	—	—	—	$67,917	$172,929	$483,065	$571,288	$1,833,845	$4,688,352	$16,486,177	$56,913,588	$134,655,571	$236,784,000	$446,479,000	$603,915,000
Expenditures[12]	—	—	—	—	—	—	$507,142	$674,688	$2,245,661	$5,601,376	$21,043,113	—	—	—	—	—
Value of physical property	—	—	$95,426	$253,599	$457,594	$747,333	$2,065,049	$2,753,780[13]	$4,799,964	$13,548,548	$42,093,580	$83,733,387	$164,635,000	—	—	—
Market value of endowment funds	—	—	$78,788[14]	$194,998[14]	$323,661[14]	$569,071[14]	$1,372,068[14]	$1,686,283[14]	$2,601,223[14]	$5,322,080[14]	$11,206,632	$20,743,045	$67,978,726	—	$355,910,203	$648,043,000
In thousands of constant 2018–19 dollars[15]																
Revenue[10]							$8,204,702	$12,961,722	$25,394,654	$49,868,679	$144,252,080	$190,914,158	$278,520,953	$422,275,000	$580,447,000	$684,451,000
Educational and general income[11]							$7,147,567	$10,353,415	$19,611,293	$40,411,447	$110,533,980	$185,673,497	$268,587,889	$354,239,000	$521,737,000	$616,430,000
Expenditures[12]							$7,503,817	$12,227,326	$24,015,288	$48,281,295	$141,086,622	—	—	—	—	—
Value of physical property							$30,555,052	$49,906,573[13]	$51,331,220	$116,782,277	$282,222,550	$273,169,753	$328,385,723	—	—	—
Market value of endowment funds							$20,301,508[14]	$27,817,698[14]	$45,873,892[14]	$75,136,500	$67,671,603	$135,592,329	$135,910,203	—	$415,902,671	$661,473,000

—Not available.

[1]Prior to 1979–80, excludes branch campuses.
[2]Total number of different individuals (not reduced to full-time equivalent). Beginning in 1959–60, data are for the first term of the academic year.
[3]Estimated.
[4]Estimated number of senior instructional staff based on actual enrollment data for the prior staff survey. Excludes graduate assistants.
[5]Because of revised survey procedures, data may not be directly comparable with figures prior to 1989–90.
[6]Data for 1869–70 to 1939–40 are for resident degree-credit students who enrolled at any time during the academic year. Excludes graduate assistants.
[7]From 1869–70 to 1959–60, bachelor's degrees include degrees that were classified as first-professional prior to 2010–11, such as M.D., D.D.S., and law degrees.
[8]Data for 1869–70 to 1939–40 are not precisely comparable with later data.
[9]Includes Ph.D., Ed.D., and comparable degrees at the doctoral level. Includes most degrees that were classified as first-professional prior to 2010–11, such as M.D., D.D.S., and law degrees.
[10]Figures for years prior to 1969–70 are not precisely comparable with later data.
[11]Data for 1929–30 through 1989–90 are current-fund revenues for public institutions and current-fund expenditures for private institutions. Data for later years are for total revenues only.
[12]Data for 1929–30 through 1989–90 are current-fund expenditures for public institutions and current-fund expenditures for private institutions. Data for later years are for total expenditures.
[13]Includes revenues from student tuition payments, government appropriations, endowment income, private gifts, sponsored research funds, and other separately budgeted research and sponsored programs.
[14]Book value. Includes other nonexpendable funds.
[15]Constant dollars based on the Consumer Price Index, prepared by the Bureau of Labor Statistics, U.S. Department of Labor, adjusted to a school-year basis.

NOTE: Data through 1989–90 are for institutions of higher education, while later data are for degree-granting institutions. Degree-granting institutions grant associate's or higher degrees and participate in Title IV federal financial aid programs. The degree-granting classification is very similar to the earlier higher education classification, but it includes more 2-year colleges and excludes a few higher education institutions that did not grant degrees. Detail may not sum to totals because of rounding.

SOURCE: U.S. Department of Education, National Center for Education Statistics, Biennial Survey of Education in the United States; Education Directory, Colleges and Universities; Faculty and Other Professional Staff in Institutions of Higher Education; Fall Enrollment in Colleges and Universities; Earned Degrees Conferred; Financial Statistics of Institutions of Higher Education; Higher Education General Information Survey (HEGIS), "Fall Enrollment in Institutions of Higher Education," "Degrees and Other Formal Awards Conferred," and "Financial Statistics of Institutions of Higher Education" surveys; Integrated Postsecondary Education Data System (IPEDS), "Fall Enrollment Survey" (IPEDS-EF:90–99), "Completions Survey" (IPEDS-C:90–00), and "Institutional Characteristics Survey" (IPEDS-IC:89–99), "Fall Staff Survey" (IPEDS-S:89–99), "Finance Survey" (IPEDS-F:FY90–00); IPEDS Winter 2009–10 and Spring 2018, Human Resources component, Fall Staff section; IPEDS Fall 2010 and Fall 2018, Completions component; and IPEDS Spring 2010 and Spring 2018, Fall Enrollment component; IPEDS Spring 2010 and Spring 2019, Finance component. IPEDS Fall 2010 and Fall 2018, Completions component; and IPEDS Spring 2011 and Spring 2019, Finance component. (This table was prepared February 2020.)

Table 302.10. Recent high school completers and their enrollment in college, by sex and level of institution: 1960 through 2018

[Standard errors appear in parentheses]

	Number of high school completers[1] (in thousands)			Percent of recent high school completers[1] enrolled in college[2]								
	Total	Males	Females	Total			Males			Females		
Year	Total	Males	Females	Total	2-year college	4-year college or university	Total	2-year college	4-year college or university	Total	2-year college	4-year college or university
1	2	3	4	5	6	7	8	9	10	11	12	13
1960	1,679 (44.5)	756 (32.3)	923 (30.1)	45.1 (2.16)	— (†)	— (†)	54.0 (3.23)	— (†)	— (†)	37.9 (2.85)	— (†)	— (†)
1961	1,763 (46.7)	790 (33.7)	973 (31.8)	48.0 (2.12)	— (†)	— (†)	56.3 (3.14)	— (†)	— (†)	41.3 (2.81)	— (†)	— (†)
1962	1,838 (44.3)	872 (32.0)	966 (30.4)	49.0 (2.08)	— (†)	— (†)	55.0 (3.00)	— (†)	— (†)	43.5 (2.84)	— (†)	— (†)
1963	1,741 (44.9)	794 (32.6)	947 (30.5)	45.0 (2.12)	— (†)	— (†)	52.3 (3.16)	— (†)	— (†)	39.0 (2.82)	— (†)	— (†)
1964	2,145 (43.6)	997 (32.3)	1,148 (28.9)	48.3 (1.92)	— (†)	— (†)	57.2 (2.79)	— (†)	— (†)	40.7 (2.58)	— (†)	— (†)
1965	2,659 (48.5)	1,254 (35.7)	1,405 (32.5)	50.9 (1.73)	— (†)	— (†)	57.3 (2.49)	— (†)	— (†)	45.3 (2.37)	— (†)	— (†)
1966	2,612 (45.7)	1,207 (34.4)	1,405 (29.5)	50.1 (1.74)	— (†)	— (†)	58.7 (2.53)	— (†)	— (†)	42.7 (2.35)	— (†)	— (†)
1967	2,525 (38.5)	1,142 (28.9)	1,383 (24.7)	51.9 (1.48)	— (†)	— (†)	57.6 (2.12)	— (†)	— (†)	47.2 (1.95)	— (†)	— (†)
1968	2,606 (38.0)	1,184 (28.7)	1,422 (24.2)	55.4 (1.41)	— (†)	— (†)	63.2 (2.04)	— (†)	— (†)	48.9 (1.93)	— (†)	— (†)
1969	2,842 (36.6)	1,352 (27.3)	1,490 (24.2)	53.3 (1.36)	— (†)	— (†)	60.1 (1.93)	— (†)	— (†)	47.2 (1.88)	— (†)	— (†)
1970	2,758 (38.1)	1,343 (26.6)	1,415 (27.3)	51.7 (1.38)	— (†)	— (†)	55.2 (1.97)	— (†)	— (†)	48.5 (1.93)	— (†)	— (†)
1971	2,875 (38.7)	1,371 (27.1)	1,504 (27.6)	53.5 (1.35)	— (†)	— (†)	57.6 (1.94)	— (†)	— (†)	49.8 (1.87)	— (†)	— (†)
1972	2,964 (38.5)	1,423 (27.5)	1,542 (26.9)	49.2 (1.33)	— (†)	— (†)	52.7 (1.92)	— (†)	— (†)	46.0 (1.84)	— (†)	— (†)
1973	3,058 (37.7)	1,460 (28.0)	1,599 (25.0)	46.6 (1.31)	14.9 (0.94)	31.6 (1.22)	50.0 (1.90)	14.6 (1.34)	35.4 (1.82)	43.4 (1.80)	15.2 (1.30)	28.2 (1.63)
1974	3,101 (39.3)	1,491 (28.2)	1,611 (27.3)	47.6 (1.30)	15.2 (0.94)	32.4 (1.22)	49.4 (1.88)	16.6 (1.40)	32.8 (1.77)	45.9 (1.80)	13.9 (1.25)	32.0 (1.69)
1975	3,185 (39.3)	1,513 (27.8)	1,672 (27.7)	50.7 (1.29)	18.2 (0.99)	32.6 (1.21)	52.6 (1.86)	19.0 (1.47)	33.6 (1.76)	49.0 (1.78)	17.4 (1.35)	31.6 (1.65)
1976	2,986 (40.5)	1,451 (29.4)	1,535 (27.8)	48.8 (1.33)	15.6 (0.96)	33.3 (1.25)	47.2 (1.90)	14.5 (1.34)	32.7 (1.79)	50.3 (1.85)	16.6 (1.38)	33.8 (1.75)
1977	3,141 (41.0)	1,483 (29.8)	1,659 (27.9)	50.6 (1.30)	17.5 (0.98)	33.1 (1.22)	52.1 (1.88)	17.2 (1.42)	35.0 (1.80)	49.3 (1.78)	17.8 (1.36)	31.5 (1.66)
1978	3,163 (40.0)	1,485 (29.4)	1,677 (26.8)	50.1 (1.29)	17.0 (0.97)	33.1 (1.22)	51.1 (1.88)	15.6 (1.37)	35.5 (1.80)	49.3 (1.77)	18.3 (1.37)	31.0 (1.64)
1979	3,160 (40.3)	1,475 (29.4)	1,685 (27.4)	49.3 (1.29)	17.5 (0.98)	31.8 (1.20)	50.4 (1.89)	16.9 (1.42)	33.5 (1.79)	48.4 (1.77)	18.1 (1.36)	30.3 (1.63)
1980	3,088 (39.6)	1,498 (28.5)	1,589 (27.5)	49.3 (1.31)	19.4 (1.03)	29.9 (1.20)	46.7 (1.87)	17.1 (1.41)	29.7 (1.71)	51.8 (1.82)	21.6 (1.50)	30.2 (1.67)
1981	3,056 (42.4)	1,491 (30.6)	1,565 (29.3)	53.9 (1.31)	20.5 (1.06)	33.5 (1.24)	54.8 (1.87)	20.9 (1.53)	33.9 (1.78)	53.1 (1.83)	20.1 (1.47)	33.0 (1.73)
1982	3,100 (41.0)	1,509 (29.4)	1,592 (28.6)	50.6 (1.38)	19.1 (1.09)	31.5 (1.28)	49.1 (1.98)	17.5 (1.50)	31.6 (1.84)	52.0 (1.93)	20.6 (1.56)	31.4 (1.79)
1983	2,963 (42.2)	1,389 (30.8)	1,573 (28.6)	52.7 (1.41)	19.2 (1.11)	33.5 (1.33)	51.9 (2.06)	20.2 (1.66)	31.7 (1.92)	53.4 (1.93)	18.4 (1.50)	35.1 (1.85)
1984	3,012 (37.0)	1,429 (29.1)	1,584 (22.2)	55.2 (1.39)	19.4 (1.11)	35.8 (1.34)	56.0 (2.02)	17.7 (1.55)	38.4 (1.98)	54.5 (1.92)	21.0 (1.57)	33.5 (1.82)
1985	2,668 (40.7)	1,287 (29.1)	1,381 (28.3)	57.7 (1.47)	19.6 (1.18)	38.1 (1.45)	58.6 (2.11)	19.9 (1.71)	38.8 (2.09)	56.8 (2.05)	19.3 (1.63)	37.5 (2.00)
1986	2,786 (39.2)	1,332 (28.9)	1,454 (26.4)	53.8 (1.45)	19.2 (1.15)	34.5 (1.39)	55.8 (2.09)	21.3 (1.73)	34.5 (2.00)	51.9 (2.02)	17.3 (1.53)	34.6 (1.92)
1987	2,647 (41.5)	1,278 (30.2)	1,369 (28.4)	56.8 (1.48)	18.9 (1.17)	37.9 (1.45)	58.3 (2.12)	17.3 (1.63)	41.0 (2.12)	55.3 (2.07)	20.3 (1.67)	35.0 (1.98)
1988	2,673 (47.7)	1,334 (34.6)	1,339 (32.8)	58.9 (1.60)	21.9 (1.34)	37.1 (1.57)	57.1 (2.27)	21.3 (1.88)	35.8 (2.20)	60.7 (2.24)	22.4 (1.91)	38.3 (2.23)
1989	2,450 (44.8)	1,204 (31.7)	1,246 (31.7)	59.6 (1.58)	20.7 (1.30)	38.9 (1.57)	57.6 (2.27)	18.3 (1.77)	39.3 (2.24)	61.6 (2.19)	23.1 (1.90)	38.5 (2.20)
1990	2,362 (43.0)	1,173 (30.6)	1,189 (30.2)	60.1 (1.60)	20.1 (1.31)	40.0 (1.61)	58.0 (2.29)	19.6 (1.85)	38.4 (2.26)	62.2 (2.24)	20.6 (1.87)	41.6 (2.28)*
1991	2,276 (41.1)	1,140 (29.0)	1,136 (29.0)	62.5 (1.62)	24.9 (1.44)	37.7 (1.62)	57.9 (2.33)	22.9 (1.98)	35.0 (2.25)	67.1 (2.22)	26.8 (2.09)	40.3 (2.32)
1992	2,397 (40.5)	1,216 (29.1)	1,180 (28.1)	61.9 (1.58)	23.0 (1.37)	38.9 (1.59)	60.0 (2.24)	22.1 (1.89)	37.8 (2.21)	63.8 (2.23)	23.9 (1.98)	40.0 (2.27)
1993	2,342 (41.4)	1,120 (30.6)	1,223 (27.7)	62.6 (1.59)	22.8 (1.38)	39.8 (1.61)	59.9 (2.33)	22.9 (2.00)	37.0 (2.30)	65.2 (2.17)	22.8 (1.91)	42.4 (2.25)
1994	2,517 (41.1)	1,244 (30.1)	1,273 (27.9)	61.9 (1.54)	21.0 (1.29)	40.9 (1.56)	60.6 (2.21)	23.0 (1.90)	37.5 (2.19)	63.2 (2.15)	19.1 (1.75)	44.1 (2.22)
1995	2,599 (41.0)	1,238 (30.0)	1,361 (27.7)	61.9 (1.41)	21.5 (1.19)	40.4 (1.43)	62.6 (2.04)	25.3 (1.83)	37.4 (2.04)	61.3 (1.96)	18.1 (1.55)	43.2 (1.99)
1996	2,660 (40.5)	1,297 (29.5)	1,363 (27.7)	65.0 (1.42)	23.1 (1.26)	41.9 (1.47)	60.1 (2.09)	21.5 (1.76)	38.5 (2.08)	69.7 (1.91)	24.6 (1.79)	45.1 (2.07)
1997	2,769 (41.8)	1,354 (31.0)	1,415 (27.9)	67.0 (1.37)	22.8 (1.23)	44.3 (1.45)	63.6 (2.01)	21.4 (1.71)	42.2 (2.06)	70.3 (1.87)	24.1 (1.75)	46.2 (2.04)
1998	2,810 (43.9)	1,452 (31.0)	1,358 (31.0)	65.6 (1.38)	24.4 (1.25)	41.3 (1.43)	62.4 (1.96)	24.4 (1.73)	38.0 (1.96)	69.1 (1.93)	24.3 (1.79)	44.8 (2.08)
1999	2,897 (41.5)	1,474 (29.9)	1,423 (28.8)	62.9 (1.38)	21.0 (1.16)	41.9 (1.41)	61.4 (1.95)	21.0 (1.63)	40.5 (1.97)	64.4 (1.95)	21.1 (1.66)	43.3 (2.02)
2000	2,756 (45.3)	1,251 (33.6)	1,505 (29.7)	63.3 (1.41)	21.4 (1.20)	41.9 (1.45)	59.9 (2.13)	23.1 (1.83)	36.8 (2.10)	66.2 (1.88)	20.0 (1.59)	46.2 (1.98)
2001	2,549 (44.1)	1,277 (32.0)	1,273 (30.3)	61.8 (1.41)	19.6 (1.15)	42.1 (1.43)	60.1 (2.00)	18.6 (1.59)	41.4 (2.01)	63.5 (1.97)	20.6 (1.66)	42.8 (2.02)
2002	2,796 (42.7)	1,412 (31.3)	1,384 (29.0)	65.2 (1.31)	21.6 (1.14)	43.6 (1.37)	62.1 (1.88)	20.4 (1.57)	41.7 (1.92)	68.4 (1.82)	22.8 (1.65)	45.6 (1.95)
2003	2,677 (42.2)	1,306 (29.9)	1,372 (29.6)	63.9 (1.35)	21.5 (1.16)	42.5 (1.39)	61.2 (1.97)	21.9 (1.67)	39.3 (1.97)	66.5 (1.86)	21.0 (1.61)	45.5 (1.96)
2004	2,752 (40.0)	1,327 (29.1)	1,425 (27.3)	66.7 (1.31)	22.4 (1.16)	44.2 (1.38)	61.4 (1.95)	21.8 (1.65)	39.6 (1.96)	71.5 (1.74)	23.1 (1.63)	48.5 (1.93)
2005	2,675 (40.8)	1,262 (31.5)	1,414 (24.9)	68.6 (1.31)	24.0 (1.21)	44.6 (1.40)	66.5 (1.94)	24.7 (1.77)	41.8 (2.03)	70.4 (1.77)	23.4 (1.64)	47.0 (1.94)
2006	2,692 (44.6)	1,328 (32.7)	1,363 (30.1)	66.0 (1.33)	24.7 (1.21)	41.3 (1.39)	65.8 (1.90)	24.9 (1.73)	40.9 (1.97)	66.1 (1.87)	24.5 (1.70)	41.7 (1.95)
2007	2,955 (42.6)	1,511 (30.0)	1,444 (30.3)	67.2 (1.26)	24.1 (1.15)	43.1 (1.33)	66.1 (1.78)	22.7 (1.57)	43.4 (1.86)	68.3 (1.79)	25.5 (1.67)	42.8 (1.90)
2008	3,151 (42.8)	1,640 (29.6)	1,511 (30.9)	68.6 (1.21)	27.7 (1.16)	40.9 (1.28)	65.9 (1.71)	24.9 (1.56)	41.0 (1.77)	71.6 (1.69)	30.6 (1.73)	40.9 (1.85)
2009	2,937 (45.0)	1,407 (32.8)	1,531 (30.6)	70.1 (1.23)	27.7 (1.21)	42.4 (1.33)	66.0 (1.84)	25.1 (1.69)	40.9 (1.91)	73.8 (1.64)	30.1 (1.71)	43.8 (1.85)
2010	3,160 (91.8)	1,679 (64.6)	1,482 (58.4)	68.1 (1.49)	26.7 (1.52)	41.4 (1.61)	62.8 (1.88)	28.5 (2.03)	34.3 (1.97)	74.0 (2.31)	24.6 (2.32)	49.5 (2.59)
2011	3,079 (88.3)	1,611 (60.6)	1,468 (58.4)	68.2 (1.45)	25.9 (1.49)	42.3 (1.44)	64.7 (2.16)	24.7 (1.79)	40.0 (2.10)	72.2 (1.98)	27.3 (2.17)	44.9 (2.37)
2012	3,203 (96.2)	1,622 (70.1)	1,581 (54.0)	66.2 (1.59)	28.8 (1.57)	37.5 (1.60)	61.3 (2.17)	26.9 (2.20)	34.4 (2.15)	71.3 (2.11)	30.7 (2.09)	40.6 (2.21)
2013	2,977 (84.4)	1,524 (62.9)	1,453 (57.0)	65.9 (1.58)	23.8 (1.44)	42.1 (1.76)	63.5 (2.20)	24.5 (2.14)	39.0 (2.48)	68.4 (2.17)	23.0 (2.15)	45.3 (2.21)
2014	2,868 (78.5)	1,423 (58.1)	1,445 (57.5)	68.4 (1.67)	24.6 (1.56)	43.7 (1.81)	64.0 (2.32)	21.2 (2.07)	42.8 (2.69)	72.6 (2.50)	28.0 (2.35)	44.6 (2.57)
2015	2,965 (87.5)	1,448 (64.6)	1,516 (56.6)	69.2 (1.54)	25.2 (1.48)	44.0 (1.61)	65.8 (2.27)	24.3 (2.00)	41.5 (2.27)	72.5 (2.18)	26.2 (2.08)	46.4 (2.42)
2016	3,137 (102.3)	1,517 (70.6)	1,620 (66.7)	69.8 (1.64)	23.7 (1.56)	46.0 (1.85)	67.5 (2.12)	25.3 (2.26)	42.2 (2.47)	71.9 (2.40)	22.3 (1.99)	49.6 (2.46)
2017	2,870 (95.9)	1,345 (60.2)	1,525 (71.3)	66.7 (1.68)	22.6 (1.50)	44.2 (1.83)	61.1 (2.57)	23.9 (2.36)	37.2 (2.32)	71.7 (2.29)	21.4 (2.09)	50.3 (2.70)
2018	3,212 (94.6)	1,614 (61.2)	1,598 (69.9)	69.1 (1.62)	25.5 (1.54)	43.6 (1.76)	66.9 (2.22)	24.9 (1.92)	42.0 (2.23)	71.4 (2.32)	26.1 (2.19)	45.2 (2.75)

—Not available.
†Not applicable.
[1]Individuals ages 16 to 24 who graduated from high school or completed a GED or other high school equivalency credential.
[2]Enrollment in college as of October of each year for individuals ages 16 to 24 who had completed high school earlier in the calendar year.
NOTE: Data are based on sample surveys of the civilian noninstitutionalized population. High school completion data in this table differ from figures appearing in other tables because of varying survey procedures and coverage. Prior to 2010, standard errors were computed using generalized variance function methodology rather than the more precise replicate weight methodology used in later years. Detail may not sum to totals because of rounding.
SOURCE: American College Testing Program, unpublished tabulations, derived from statistics collected by the Census Bureau, 1960 through 1969. U.S. Department of Commerce, Census Bureau, Current Population Survey (CPS), October, 1970 through 2018. (This table was prepared August 2019.)

Table 302.20. Percentage of recent high school completers enrolled in college, by race/ethnicity: 1960 through 2018

[Standard errors appear in parentheses]

	Percent of recent high school completers[1] enrolled in college[2] (annual data)					3-year moving averages[3]							
						Percent of recent high school completers[1] enrolled in college[2]					Difference between percent enrolled		
Year	Total	White	Black	Hispanic	Asian[4]	Total	White	Black	Hispanic	Asian[4]	White-Black	White-Hispanic	White-Asian[4]
1	2	3	4	5	6	7	8	9	10	11	12	13	14
1960[5]	45.1 (2.16)	45.8 (2.24)	— (†)	— (†)	— (†)	46.6 (1.52)	47.7 (1.58)	— (†)	— (†)	— (†)	— (†)	— (†)	— (†)
1961[5]	48.0 (2.12)	49.5 (2.22)	— (†)	— (†)	— (†)	47.4 (1.22)	48.7 (1.28)	— (†)	— (†)	— (†)	— (†)	— (†)	— (†)
1962[5]	49.0 (2.08)	50.6 (2.19)	— (†)	— (†)	— (†)	47.4 (1.22)	48.6 (1.27)	— (†)	— (†)	— (†)	— (†)	— (†)	— (†)
1963[5]	45.0 (2.12)	45.6 (2.21)	— (†)	— (†)	— (†)	47.5 (1.18)	48.5 (1.23)	— (†)	— (†)	— (†)	— (†)	— (†)	— (†)
1964[5]	48.3 (1.92)	49.2 (2.01)	— (†)	— (†)	— (†)	48.5 (1.10)	49.2 (1.15)	— (†)	— (†)	— (†)	— (†)	— (†)	— (†)
1965[5]	50.9 (1.73)	51.7 (1.81)	— (†)	— (†)	— (†)	49.9 (1.03)	51.0 (1.08)	— (†)	— (†)	— (†)	— (†)	— (†)	— (†)
1966[5]	50.1 (1.74)	51.7 (1.82)	— (†)	— (†)	— (†)	51.0 (1.01)	52.1 (1.06)	— (†)	— (†)	— (†)	— (†)	— (†)	— (†)
1967[5]	51.9 (1.44)	53.0 (1.52)	— (†)	— (†)	— (†)	52.5 (0.82)	53.8 (0.87)	— (†)	— (†)	— (†)	— (†)	— (†)	— (†)
1968[5]	55.4 (1.41)	56.6 (1.50)	— (†)	— (†)	— (†)	53.6 (0.81)	55.0 (0.86)	— (†)	— (†)	— (†)	— (†)	— (†)	— (†)
1969[5]	53.3 (1.36)	55.2 (1.43)	— (†)	— (†)	— (†)	53.5 (0.80)	54.6 (0.85)	— (†)	— (†)	— (†)	— (†)	— (†)	— (†)
1970[5]	51.7 (1.38)	52.0 (1.46)	— (†)	— (†)	— (†)	52.9 (0.79)	53.8 (0.83)	— (†)	— (†)	— (†)	— (†)	— (†)	— (†)
1971[5]	53.5 (1.35)	54.0 (1.42)	— (†)	— (†)	— (†)	51.5 (0.78)	51.9 (0.83)	— (†)	— (†)	— (†)	— (†)	— (†)	— (†)
1972	49.2 (1.33)	49.7 (1.45)	44.6 (4.74)	45.0 (12.85)	— (†)	49.7 (0.77)	50.5 (0.83)	38.4 (3.26)	49.9 (8.76)	— (†)	12.1 (3.36)	‡ (†)	— (†)
1973	46.6 (1.31)	47.8 (1.43)	32.5 (4.40)	54.1 (11.89)	— (†)	47.8 (0.76)	48.2 (0.83)	41.4 (2.68)	48.8 (7.04)	— (†)	6.8! (2.81)	‡ (†)	— (†)
1974	47.6 (1.30)	47.2 (1.42)	47.2 (4.69)	46.9 (11.79)	— (†)	48.3 (0.75)	48.7 (0.82)	40.5 (2.69)	53.1 (6.72)	— (†)	8.3! (2.82)	‡ (†)	— (†)
1975	50.7 (1.29)	51.1 (1.40)	41.7 (4.81)	58.0 (11.14)	— (†)	49.1 (0.75)	49.1 (0.82)	44.5 (2.78)	52.7 (6.44)	— (†)	‡ (†)	‡ (†)	— (†)
1976	48.8 (1.33)	48.8 (1.45)	44.4 (4.94)	52.7 (10.52)	— (†)	50.1 (0.75)	50.3 (0.82)	45.3 (2.78)	53.6 (6.18)	— (†)	‡ (†)	‡ (†)	— (†)
1977	50.6 (1.30)	50.8 (1.42)	49.5 (4.70)	50.8 (10.43)	— (†)	49.9 (0.75)	50.1 (0.83)	46.8 (2.73)	48.8 (6.18)	— (†)	‡ (†)	‡ (†)	— (†)
1978	50.1 (1.29)	50.5 (1.42)	46.4 (4.55)	42.0 (11.06)	— (†)	50.0 (0.75)	50.4 (0.82)	47.5 (2.69)	46.1 (6.14)	— (†)	‡ (†)	‡ (†)	— (†)
1979	49.3 (1.29)	49.9 (1.42)	46.7 (4.73)	45.0 (10.37)	— (†)	49.6 (0.75)	50.1 (0.82)	45.2 (2.65)	46.3 (6.32)	— (†)	‡ (†)	‡ (†)	— (†)
1980	49.3 (1.31)	49.8 (1.44)	42.7 (4.48)	52.3 (11.39)	— (†)	50.8 (0.75)	51.5 (0.83)	44.0 (2.64)	49.6 (6.25)	— (†)	7.5! (2.76)	‡ (†)	— (†)
1981	53.9 (1.31)	54.9 (1.45)	42.7 (4.48)	52.1 (10.73)	— (†)	51.3 (0.76)	52.4 (0.84)	40.3 (2.53)	48.7 (6.13)	— (†)	12.2 (2.66)	‡ (†)	— (†)
1982	50.6 (1.38)	52.7 (1.54)	35.8 (4.39)	43.2 (10.37)	— (†)	52.4 (0.80)	54.2 (0.90)	38.8 (2.61)	49.4 (6.44)	— (†)	15.4 (2.76)	‡ (†)	— (†)
1983	52.7 (1.41)	55.0 (1.57)	38.2 (4.41)	54.2 (11.69)	— (†)	52.8 (0.81)	55.5 (0.90)	38.0 (2.50)	46.7 (6.16)	— (†)	17.5 (2.66)	‡ (†)	— (†)
1984	55.2 (1.39)	59.0 (1.57)	39.8 (4.21)	44.3 (10.00)	— (†)	55.1 (0.82)	57.9 (0.92)	39.9 (2.58)	49.3 (6.38)	— (†)	18.0 (2.74)	‡ (†)	— (†)
1985	57.7 (1.47)	60.1 (1.64)	42.2 (4.86)	51.0 (9.79)	— (†)	55.5 (0.83)	58.6 (0.93)	39.5 (2.59)	46.1 (5.20)	— (†)	19.1 (2.75)	12.5! (5.28)	— (†)
1986	53.8 (1.45)	56.8 (1.64)	36.9 (4.44)	44.0 (8.88)	— (†)	56.1 (0.85)	58.5 (0.96)	43.5 (2.75)	42.3 (5.21)	— (†)	15.0 (2.91)	16.2! (5.30)	— (†)
1987	56.8 (1.48)	58.6 (1.68)	52.2 (4.90)	33.5 (8.28)	— (†)	56.5 (0.85)	58.8 (0.96)	44.2 (2.69)	45.0 (5.06)	— (†)	14.6 (2.86)	13.8! (5.15)	— (†)
1988	58.9 (1.60)	61.1 (1.82)	44.4 (4.98)	57.1 (9.60)	— (†)	58.4 (0.94)	60.1 (1.07)	49.7 (3.02)	48.5 (5.67)	— (†)	10.4! (3.20)	11.6! (5.77)	— (†)
1989	59.6 (1.58)	60.7 (1.79)	53.4 (5.07)	55.1 (9.21)	81.1 (10.23)	59.5 (0.90)	61.6 (1.02)	48.0 (2.87)	52.7 (5.54)	81.4 (6.36)	13.6 (3.04)	‡ (†)	-19.8! (6.44)
1990	60.1 (1.60)	63.0 (1.80)	46.8 (5.08)	42.7 (10.82)	81.7 (8.12)	60.7 (0.92)	63.0 (1.04)	48.9 (2.97)	52.5 (5.70)	81.4 (6.36)	14.0 (3.14)	‡ (†)	-18.5! (6.44)
1991	62.5 (1.62)	65.4 (1.82)	46.4 (5.24)	57.2 (9.57)	78.9 (9.04)	61.5 (0.92)	64.2 (1.05)	47.2 (2.93)	52.6 (5.52)	80.6 (5.21)	17.0 (3.11)	11.7! (5.62)	-16.3! (5.31)
1992	61.9 (1.58)	64.3 (1.84)	48.2 (4.91)	55.0 (8.50)	81.7 (7.00)	62.3 (0.92)	64.2 (1.06)	50.0 (2.97)	58.2 (5.04)	80.9 (4.58)	14.2 (3.16)	‡ (†)	-16.7 (4.70)
1993	62.6 (1.59)	62.9 (1.86)	55.6 (5.27)	62.2 (8.21)	86.2 (6.63)	62.1 (0.91)	63.9 (1.04)	51.3 (2.96)	55.7 (4.97)	82.5 (4.30)	12.6 (3.14)	‡ (†)	-18.6 (4.42)
1994	61.9 (1.54)	64.5 (1.74)	50.8 (5.20)	49.1 (9.00)	78.3 (8.55)	62.1 (0.89)	64.0 (1.03)	52.4 (2.97)	55.0 (4.63)	82.2 (4.25)	11.5 (3.14)	‡ (†)	-18.2 (4.37)
1995	61.9 (1.41)	64.3 (1.65)	51.2 (4.22)	53.7 (4.94)	83.0 (6.94)	63.0 (0.81)	65.4 (0.94)	52.9 (2.40)	51.6 (3.19)	82.7 (4.47)	12.5 (2.58)	13.8 (3.33)	-17.3 (4.57)
1996	65.0 (1.42)	67.4 (1.66)	56.0 (4.03)	50.8 (5.79)	85.3 (5.21)	64.7 (0.82)	66.6 (0.97)	55.4 (2.41)	57.6 (2.96)	82.7 (3.59)	11.3 (2.60)	9.0! (3.11)	-16.0 (3.72)
1997	67.0 (1.37)	68.2 (1.64)	58.5 (4.11)	65.6 (4.52)	80.5 (6.09)	65.9 (0.80)	68.1 (0.94)	58.8 (2.35)	55.3 (2.93)	83.0 (3.49)	9.3 (2.53)	12.8 (3.08)	-15.0 (3.62)
1998	65.6 (1.38)	68.5 (1.61)	61.9 (4.04)	47.4 (4.92)	85.5 (5.71)	65.2 (0.80)	67.7 (0.94)	59.8 (2.31)	51.9 (2.79)	83.8 (3.28)	7.9! (2.49)	15.7 (2.94)	-16.1 (3.41)
1999	62.9 (1.38)	66.3 (1.63)	58.9 (3.85)	42.3 (4.76)	78.3 (5.73)	64.0 (0.80)	66.8 (0.94)	58.6 (2.31)	47.4 (2.84)	81.1 (3.40)	8.3! (2.50)	19.5 (2.99)	-14.3 (3.53)
2000	63.3 (1.41)	65.7 (1.66)	54.9 (4.10)	52.9 (5.03)	81.0 (6.29)	62.7 (0.82)	65.4 (0.96)	56.4 (2.33)	48.6 (2.96)	81.3 (3.44)	9.1 (2.52)	16.9 (3.11)	-15.8 (3.57)
2001	61.8 (1.41)	64.3 (1.63)	55.0 (3.96)	51.7 (5.33)	73.8 (8.71)	63.5 (0.78)	66.3 (0.92)	56.4 (2.26)	52.8 (2.78)	78.4 (3.87)	10.0 (2.44)	13.5 (2.93)	-12.0! (3.97)
2002	65.2 (1.31)	69.1 (1.55)	59.4 (3.90)	53.6 (4.46)	63.7 (6.51)	63.7 (0.78)	66.5 (0.92)	57.3 (2.33)	54.8 (2.75)	71.9 (4.05)	9.3 (2.50)	11.7 (2.90)	‡ (†)
2003[6]	63.9 (1.35)	66.2 (1.61)	57.5 (4.25)	58.6 (4.61)	84.1 (5.10)	65.3 (0.77)	68.0 (0.91)	59.9 (2.29)	57.7 (2.66)	74.2 (3.51)	8.1! (2.46)	10.3 (2.81)	‡ (†)
2004[6]	66.7 (1.31)	68.8 (1.57)	62.5 (3.77)	61.8 (4.76)	75.6 (6.13)	66.4 (0.77)	69.4 (0.91)	58.8 (2.34)	57.7 (2.60)	81.6 (3.37)	10.6 (2.51)	11.7 (2.75)	-12.2 (3.49)
2005[6]	68.6 (1.31)	73.2 (1.52)	55.7 (4.15)	54.0 (4.18)	86.7 (5.99)	67.1 (0.76)	70.2 (0.90)	58.2 (2.35)	57.5 (2.52)	80.9 (3.64)	12.0 (2.52)	12.6 (2.67)	-10.7! (3.75)
2006[6]	66.0 (1.33)	68.5 (1.60)	55.5 (4.33)	57.9 (4.18)	82.3 (5.32)	67.2 (0.75)	70.4 (0.89)	55.6 (2.35)	58.5 (2.43)	85.1 (3.64)	14.7 (2.51)	11.9 (2.59)	-14.7 (3.74)
2007[6]	67.2 (1.26)	69.5 (1.49)	55.7 (3.78)	64.0 (4.22)	88.8 (6.26)	67.3 (0.73)	70.0 (0.87)	55.7 (2.27)	62.0 (2.33)	85.8 (3.45)	14.3 (2.43)	8.0! (2.48)	-15.8 (3.56)
2008[6]	68.6 (1.21)	71.7 (1.44)	55.7 (3.78)	63.9 (3.72)	88.4 (5.08)	68.6 (0.71)	70.8 (0.86)	60.3 (2.15)	62.3 (2.25)	90.1 (3.01)	10.5 (2.31)	8.6 (2.41)	-19.2 (3.13)
2009[6]	70.1 (1.23)	71.3 (1.53)	69.5 (3.51)	59.3 (3.80)	92.1 (3.90)	68.9 (0.70)	71.2 (0.86)	62.4 (2.09)	60.9 (2.14)	88.1 (2.85)	8.8 (2.26)	10.3 (2.31)	-16.9 (2.98)
2010[6]	68.1 (1.49)	70.5 (1.68)	62.0 (4.81)	59.7 (4.18)	84.7 (5.27)	68.8 (0.71)	70.1 (0.90)	66.1 (2.01)	62.3 (2.01)	87.4 (2.78)	‡ (†)	7.8 (2.21)	-17.3 (2.92)
2011[6]	68.2 (1.45)	68.3 (1.86)	67.1 (4.01)	66.6 (3.50)	86.1 (4.25)	67.5 (0.89)	68.2 (1.03)	62.1 (2.86)	66.1 (2.17)	83.9 (2.79)	6.1! (3.04)	‡ (†)	-15.7 (2.97)
2012[6]	66.2 (1.59)	65.7 (1.94)	56.4 (4.84)	70.3 (3.22)	81.5 (5.15)	66.8 (0.94)	67.6 (1.12)	60.5 (2.64)	65.9 (1.99)	82.3 (3.59)	7.1! (2.87)	‡ (†)	-14.7 (3.76)
2013[6]	65.9 (1.58)	68.8 (1.90)	56.7 (5.59)	59.8 (3.62)	80.1 (6.52)	66.8 (0.98)	67.4 (1.26)	60.7 (3.09)	65.5 (2.06)	83.6 (3.20)	6.7! (3.34)	‡ (†)	-16.2 (3.44)
2014[6]	68.4 (1.67)	67.7 (2.25)	70.2 (4.56)	65.2 (4.08)	90.9 (3.91)	67.8 (1.00)	69.3 (1.17)	60.6 (3.40)	64.7 (2.16)	84.2 (3.16)	8.8! (3.59)	‡ (†)	-14.9 (3.37)
2015[6]	69.2 (1.54)	71.3 (1.74)	55.6 (5.69)	68.9 (3.64)	83.2 (4.65)	69.1 (1.07)	69.6 (1.32)	60.8 (3.41)	69.0 (2.05)	88.5 (2.48)	8.8! (3.66)	‡ (†)	-18.9 (2.81)
2016[6]	69.8 (1.64)	69.7 (2.34)	57.3 (6.11)	72.0 (3.24)	91.9 (3.65)	68.6 (1.02)	70.1 (1.28)	57.5 (3.44)	67.6 (2.20)	85.7 (2.60)	12.6 (3.67)	‡ (†)	-15.7 (2.90)
2017[6]	66.7 (1.68)	69.1 (2.09)	59.4 (4.79)	61.0 (3.98)	82.7 (5.20)	68.6 (1.00)	69.9 (1.23)	60.7 (2.86)	66.5 (2.19)	82.0 (2.96)	9.2! (3.11)	‡ (†)	-12.1 (3.20)
2018[6]	69.1 (1.62)	70.9 (1.93)	64.5 (4.37)	65.4 (3.59)	73.6 (5.64)	68.0 (1.19)	70.0 (1.42)	62.1 (3.22)	63.4 (2.58)	77.9 (3.74)	7.9! (3.52)	6.6! (2.95)	‡ (†)

—Not available.
†Not applicable.
!Interpret data with caution. The coefficient of variation (CV) for this estimate is between 30 and 50 percent.
‡Reporting standards not met. The coefficient of variation (CV) for this estimate is 50 percent or greater.
[1]Individuals ages 16 to 24 who graduated from high school or completed a GED or other high school equivalency credential.
[2]Enrollment in college as of October of each year for individuals ages 16 to 24 who had completed high school earlier in the calendar year.
[3]A 3-year moving average is a weighted average of the year indicated, the year immediately preceding, and the year immediately following. For the first and final years of available data, a 2-year moving average is used: The moving average for 1960 reflects an average of 1960 and 1961; for Black and Hispanic data, the moving average for 1972 reflects an average of 1972 and 1973; for Asian data, the moving average for 2003 reflects an average of 2003 and 2004; and the moving average for 2018 reflects an average of 2017 and 2018. Moving averages are used to produce more stable estimates.
[4]Prior to 2003, Asian data include Pacific Islanders.
[5]Prior to 1972, White data include persons of Hispanic ethnicity.
[6]After 2002, White, Black, and Asian data exclude persons of Two or more races.
NOTE: Data are based on sample surveys of the civilian noninstitutionalized population. Includes enrollment in 2-year colleges and in 4-year colleges and universities. Race categories exclude persons of Hispanic ethnicity except where otherwise noted. Total includes persons of other racial/ethnic groups not separately shown. Prior to 2010, standard errors were computed using generalized variance function methodology rather than the more precise replicate weight methodology used in later years. Some data have been revised from previously published figures.
SOURCE: American College Testing Program, unpublished tabulations, derived from statistics collected by the Census Bureau, 1960 through 1969. U.S. Department of Commerce, Census Bureau, Current Population Survey (CPS), October, 1970 through 2018. (This table was prepared August 2019.)

Table 302.40. Number of high schools with 12th-graders and percentage of high school graduates attending 4-year colleges, by selected high school characteristics: Selected years, 1998–99 through 2011–12

[Standard errors appear in parentheses]

Selected high school characteristic	Number of high schools with 12th-graders					Percent of graduates attending 4-year colleges			
	1998–99	2002–03	2006–07	2010–11	Graduation rate of 12th-graders in 2010–11[1]	1998–99 graduates attending in 1999–2000	2002–03 graduates attending in 2003–04	2006–07 graduates attending in 2007–08	2010–11 graduates attending in 2011–12
1	2	3	4	5	6	7	8	9	10
Public high schools	20,000 (230)	22,500 (400)	24,100 (540)	23,300 (330)	88.7 (0.90)	35.4 (0.43)	35.0 (0.61)	39.5 (0.91)	39.4 (0.59)
Percent of students who are Black, Hispanic, Asian, Pacific Islander, American Indian/Alaska Native, or of Two or more races									
Less than 5 percent	6,400 (170)	6,100 (220)	5,200 (270)	3,600 (140)	94.7 (1.19)	41.3 (0.67)	42.6 (0.96)	46.8 (1.54)	43.9 (1.40)
5 to 19 percent	4,800 (180)	5,200 (270)	5,400 (320)	5,700 (310)	92.4 (2.55)	36.6 (0.88)	38.0 (1.77)	48.4 (2.06)	44.9 (1.02)
20 to 49 percent	4,000 (170)	4,700 (180)	6,200 (440)	5,900 (270)	91.2 (1.14)	32.5 (0.92)	34.1 (1.27)	35.0 (1.89)	39.6 (1.31)
50 percent or more	4,800 (150)	6,500 (280)	7,300 (430)	8,100 (320)	81.7 (1.58)	28.7 (0.89)	25.8 (1.43)	30.8 (2.00)	33.0 (1.17)
Percent of students approved for free or reduced-price lunch									
School does not participate	2,400 (130)	2,400 (230)	2,800 (320)	1,900 (250)	72.8 (7.11)	30.0 (1.75)	23.2 (2.26)	25.4 (4.12)	27.6 (5.24)
0 to 25 percent	8,600 (180)	6,800 (230)	6,700 (360)	5,100 (220)	93.3 (1.02)	42.6 (0.67)	46.9 (0.78)	52.1 (1.63)	50.7 (1.42)
26 to 50 percent	4,800 (160)	7,300 (220)	6,800 (350)	6,800 (230)	92.8 (0.91)	33.4 (0.81)	36.7 (1.08)	41.5 (1.44)	42.5 (1.00)
51 to 75 percent	2,300 (140)	4,000 (260)	4,100 (290)	5,100 (260)	90.3 (1.06)	29.1 (1.57)	27.3 (1.58)	33.2 (1.91)	35.8 (1.35)
76 to 100 percent	2,000 (100)	2,600 (270)	3,300 (360)	4,300 (230)	82.3 (1.93)	22.2 (1.35)	20.7 (2.79)	26.0 (2.93)	29.1 (1.66)
School locale									
City	—	4,500 (240)	4,800 (300)	5,100 (220)	81.3 (3.11)	—	32.5 (1.61)	36.1 (2.73)	38.6 (1.53)
Suburb	—	4,800 (200)	4,800 (360)	4,800 (160)	86.1 (1.50)	—	40.3 (1.11)	41.2 (2.35)	42.2 (1.42)
Town	—	3,700 (200)	3,900 (350)	3,300 (260)	89.9 (2.21)	—	31.1 (1.65)	35.2 (2.28)	35.3 (1.76)
Rural	—	9,500 (390)	10,000 (390)	10,100 (260)	93.4 (0.67)	—	35.2 (1.28)	41.9 (1.47)	39.8 (0.88)
Private high schools	7,600 (240)	8,200 (260)	8,900 (280)	8,900 (310)	92.4 (1.34)	55.6 (1.74)	56.2 (1.77)	66.5 (1.57)	64.3 (2.10)
Percent of students who are Black, Hispanic, Asian, Pacific Islander, American Indian/Alaska Native, or of Two or more races									
Less than 5 percent	2,700 (150)	2,500 (180)	2,100 (160)	1,600 (190)	96.1 (1.72)	53.3 (2.85)	54.4 (3.31)	68.2 (3.81)	58.0 (6.31)
5 to 19 percent	2,500 (130)	2,900 (170)	3,500 (200)	3,100 (230)	95.1 (1.90)	63.6 (2.37)	64.2 (2.71)	70.3 (2.24)	67.9 (3.40)
20 to 49 percent	1,400 (100)	1,700 (140)	2,000 (190)	2,200 (200)	90.4 (2.33)	55.3 (3.29)	56.7 (3.70)	58.7 (3.39)	69.4 (3.89)
50 percent or more	1,000 (110)	1,100 (140)	1,400 (130)	1,900 (190)	87.1 (3.49)	41.6 (5.34)	38.3 (4.52)	65.3 (3.37)	57.6 (5.18)
Percent of students approved for free or reduced-price lunch									
School does not participate	6,700 (230)	7,100 (250)	7,300 (280)	7,400 (280)	93.3 (1.27)	57.0 (1.74)	56.2 (2.00)	68.3 (1.77)	66.5 (2.29)
0 to 25 percent	700 (70)	600 (80)	700 (100)	600 (80)	96.8 (2.45)	53.8 (5.69)	66.2 (4.35)	73.2 (4.64)	74.6 (5.23)
26 to 100 percent	‡ (†)	400 (80)	1,000 (130)	900 (140)	83.0 (5.65)	‡ (†)	38.9 (6.70)	46.7 (6.86)	37.8 (8.06)
School locale									
City	—	—	3,100 (170)	‡ (†)	‡ (†)	—	—	71.8 (2.62)	‡ (†)
Suburb	—	—	2,800 (180)	‡ (†)	‡ (†)	—	—	67.0 (2.99)	‡ (†)
Town	—	—	1,000 (150)	‡ (†)	‡ (†)	—	—	63.8 (5.02)	‡ (†)
Rural	—	—	2,000 (190)	‡ (†)	‡ (†)	—	—	58.9 (3.54)	‡ (†)

—Not available.
†Not applicable.
‡Reporting standards not met. Data may be suppressed because the response rate is under 50 percent, there are too few cases for a reliable estimate, or the coefficient of variation (CV) is 50 percent or greater.
[1]The 12th-grade graduation rate is the number of students who graduated from grade 12 with a diploma during the 2010–11 school year divided by 12th-grade enrollment in October 2010.

NOTE: Data are based on a sample survey and may not be strictly comparable with data reported elsewhere. Includes all schools, including combined schools, with students enrolled in the 12th grade. Some data have been revised from previously published figures. Detail may not sum to totals because of rounding.
SOURCE: U.S. Department of Education, National Center for Education Statistics, Schools and Staffing Survey (SASS), "Public School Teacher Data File" and "Private School Teacher Data File," 1999–2000, 2003–04, 2007–08, and 2011–12; and "Charter School Teacher Data File," 1999–2000. (This table was prepared April 2014.)

Table 302.50. Estimated rate of 2011–12 high school graduates attending degree-granting postsecondary institutions, by state: 2012

State	Number of graduates from high schools located in the state			Number of fall 2012 first-time freshmen graduating from high school in the previous 12 months		Estimated rate of high school graduates going to college	
	Total[1]	Public, 2011–12	Private, 2012–13	State residents enrolled in institutions in any state[2]	State residents enrolled in institutions in their home state[3]	In any state	In their home state
1	2	3	4	5	6	7	8
United States	3,457,955	3,149,185	308,770	2,132,264[4]	1,729,792	61.7	50.0
Alabama	50,164	45,394	4,770	29,728	26,567	59.3	53.0
Alaska	8,189	7,989	200	3,732	2,413	45.6	29.5
Arizona	66,218	63,208	3,010	35,181	31,132	53.1	47.0
Arkansas	30,019	28,419	1,600	20,185	18,244	67.2	60.8
California	451,364	418,664	32,700	263,843	231,215	58.5	51.2
Colorado	52,607	50,087	2,520	31,139	23,268	59.2	44.2
Connecticut	44,751	38,681	6,070	31,662	17,396	70.8	38.9
Delaware	10,037	8,247	1,790	6,500	4,632	64.8	46.1
District of Columbia[5]	5,680	3,860	1,820	2,463	450	43.4	7.9
Florida	171,404	151,964	19,440	107,716	94,985	62.8	55.4
Georgia	99,952	90,582	9,370	66,494	55,399	66.5	55.4
Hawaii	13,970	11,360	2,610	9,040	6,091	64.7	43.6
Idaho	18,238	17,568	670	8,782	6,179	48.2	33.9
Illinois	153,605	139,575	14,030	92,394	63,610	60.2	41.4
Indiana	70,767	65,667	5,100	44,612	38,812	63.0	54.8
Iowa	41,550	33,230	2,400	23,488	20,340	56.5	49.0
Kansas	34,078	31,898	2,180	22,239	19,058	65.3	55.9
Kentucky	47,442	42,642	4,800	29,830	26,624	62.9	56.1
Louisiana	44,575	36,675	7,900	28,831	26,024	64.7	58.4
Maine	16,103	13,473	2,630	8,681	5,829	53.9	36.2
Maryland	67,781	58,811	8,970	41,033	25,773	60.5	38.0
Massachusetts	76,177	65,157	11,020	53,836	36,132	70.7	47.4
Michigan	115,256	105,446	9,810	70,843	63,296	61.5	54.9
Minnesota	61,891	57,501	4,390	43,264	30,237	69.9	48.9
Mississippi	29,748	26,158	3,590	23,436	21,752	78.8	73.1
Missouri	69,053	61,313	7,740	42,762	35,648	61.9	51.6
Montana	10,140	9,750	390	5,907	4,598	58.3	45.3
Nebraska	22,844	20,464	2,380	14,750	11,969	64.6	52.4
Nevada	22,731	21,891	840	12,288	9,310	54.1	41.0
New Hampshire	16,886	14,426	2,460	10,418	5,618	61.7	33.3
New Jersey	106,919	93,819	13,100	72,631	41,204	67.9	38.5
New Mexico	21,375	20,315	1,060	14,831	12,903	69.4	60.4
New York	209,216	180,806	28,410	146,458	117,960	70.0	56.4
North Carolina	101,097	93,977	7,120	62,531	55,578	61.9	55.0
North Dakota	7,322	6,942	380	4,751	3,527	64.9	48.2
Ohio	135,885	123,135	12,750	81,428	69,039	59.9	50.8
Oklahoma	39,295	37,305	1,990	22,667	20,207	57.7	51.4
Oregon	37,301	34,261	3,040	17,509	13,343	46.9	35.8
Pennsylvania	146,493	131,733	14,760	87,075	70,625	59.4	48.2
Rhode Island	11,501	9,751	1,750	7,715	5,056	67.1	44.0
South Carolina	44,452	41,442	3,010	29,023	26,154	65.3	58.8
South Dakota	8,456	8,196	260	5,825	4,443	68.9	52.5
Tennessee	67,964	62,454	5,510	41,027	34,318	60.4	50.5
Texas	306,591	292,531	14,060	176,871	156,566	57.7	51.1
Utah	32,757	31,157	1,600	16,650	15,101	50.8	46.1
Vermont	7,789	6,859	930	4,142	2,040	53.2	26.2
Virginia	89,866	83,336	6,530	58,035	47,582	64.6	52.9
Washington	71,165	65,205	5,960	34,168	25,854	48.0	36.3
West Virginia	18,383	17,603	780	10,241	9,110	55.7	49.6
Wisconsin	71,225	62,705	8,520	41,715	33,972	58.6	47.7
Wyoming	5,603	5,553	50	3,170	2,426	56.6	43.3

[1]Total includes public high school graduates for 2011–12 and private high school graduates for 2012–13. Data on private high school graduates are not available for 2011–12.
[2]All U.S. resident students living in a particular state when admitted to an institution in any state. Students may be enrolled in any state.
[3]Students who attend institutions in their home state. Total includes 183 students attending U.S. Service Academies in their home state, not shown separately.
[4]U.S. total includes some U.S. residents whose home state is unknown.
[5]A percentage of the private high school graduates are not residents of the District of Columbia.

NOTE: Degree-granting institutions grant associate's or higher degrees and participate in Title IV federal financial aid programs. Detail may not sum to totals because of rounding.
SOURCE: U.S. Department of Education, National Center for Education Statistics, Common Core of Data (CCD), "NCES Common Core of Data State Dropout and Completion Data File," 2011–12; Private School Universe Survey (PSS), 2013–14; and Integrated Postsecondary Education Data System (IPEDS), Spring 2013, Fall Enrollment component. (This table was prepared January 2016.)

Table 302.60. Percentage of 18- to 24-year-olds enrolled in college, by level of institution and sex and race/ethnicity of student: 1970 through 2018

[Standard errors appear in parentheses]

Year	Total, all students	Level of institution: 2-year college	Level of institution: 4-year college or university	Sex: Male	Sex: Female	Race/ethnicity: White	Black	Hispanic	Asian[1]	Pacific Islander	American Indian/Alaska Native	Two or more races	Race/ethnicity, by sex: White Male	White Female	Black Male	Black Female	Hispanic Male	Hispanic Female
1	2	3	4	5	6	7	8	9	10	11	12	13	14	15	16	17	18	19
1970[2]	25.7 (0.42)	— (†)	— (†)	32.1 (0.67)	20.3 (0.53)	27.1 (0.46)	15.5 (1.18)	— (†)	— (†)	— (†)	— (†)	— (†)	— (†)	— (†)	— (†)	— (†)	— (†)	— (†)
1971[2]	26.2 (0.42)	— (†)	— (†)	32.5 (0.65)	20.8 (0.53)	27.2 (0.45)	18.2 (1.22)	— (†)	— (†)	— (†)	— (†)	— (†)	— (†)	— (†)	— (†)	— (†)	— (†)	— (†)
1972	25.5 (0.40)	— (†)	— (†)	30.2 (0.62)	21.2 (0.52)	27.2 (0.46)	18.3 (1.20)	13.4 (2.42)	— (†)	— (†)	— (†)	— (†)	32.3 (0.69)	22.5 (0.60)	21.1 (1.87)	15.9 (1.55)	15.1 (3.77)	12.0 (3.13)
1973	24.0 (0.39)	6.9 (0.23)	17.1 (0.34)	27.7 (0.59)	20.5 (0.51)	25.5 (0.44)	15.9 (1.11)	16.1 (2.66)	— (†)	— (†)	— (†)	— (†)	29.6 (0.67)	21.8 (0.58)	18.7 (1.75)	13.5 (1.42)	16.7 (3.88)	15.5 (3.66)
1974	24.6 (0.39)	7.6 (0.24)	17.0 (0.34)	27.7 (0.59)	21.7 (0.52)	25.8 (0.44)	17.6 (1.17)	18.0 (2.57)	— (†)	— (†)	— (†)	— (†)	28.9 (0.66)	22.9 (0.59)	19.8 (1.82)	15.9 (1.51)	19.7 (3.85)	16.5 (3.44)
1975	26.3 (0.39)	9.0 (0.26)	17.3 (0.34)	29.0 (0.58)	23.7 (0.53)	27.4 (0.44)	20.4 (1.21)	20.4 (2.75)	— (†)	— (†)	— (†)	— (†)	30.7 (0.66)	24.3 (0.60)	19.9 (1.78)	20.8 (1.65)	21.4 (4.10)	19.5 (3.71)
1976	26.7 (0.39)	6.4 (0.22)	20.2 (0.36)	28.2 (0.57)	25.2 (0.53)	27.6 (0.44)	22.5 (1.23)	20.0 (2.64)	— (†)	— (†)	— (†)	— (†)	29.3 (0.64)	26.1 (0.61)	22.0 (1.82)	22.9 (1.68)	21.3 (4.02)	18.8 (3.48)
1977	26.1 (0.39)	6.8 (0.22)	19.4 (0.35)	28.1 (0.57)	24.3 (0.52)	27.2 (0.44)	21.1 (1.19)	17.2 (2.45)	— (†)	— (†)	— (†)	— (†)	29.4 (0.64)	25.1 (0.60)	20.3 (1.74)	21.9 (1.63)	18.3 (3.66)	16.3 (3.28)
1978	25.3 (0.38)	6.6 (0.22)	18.7 (0.34)	27.1 (0.56)	23.6 (0.52)	26.5 (0.43)	20.1 (1.16)	15.2 (2.28)	— (†)	— (†)	— (†)	— (†)	28.4 (0.63)	24.6 (0.59)	19.7 (1.72)	20.4 (1.57)	16.1 (3.42)	14.3 (3.05)
1979	25.0 (0.38)	6.3 (0.21)	18.7 (0.34)	25.9 (0.55)	24.2 (0.52)	26.3 (0.43)	19.8 (1.14)	16.7 (2.31)	— (†)	— (†)	— (†)	— (†)	27.1 (0.62)	25.5 (0.60)	19.1 (1.69)	20.3 (1.55)	18.3 (3.47)	15.2 (3.08)
1980	25.7 (0.38)	7.1 (0.22)	18.6 (0.34)	26.4 (0.55)	25.0 (0.52)	27.3 (0.44)	19.4 (1.13)	16.1 (2.15)	— (†)	— (†)	— (†)	— (†)	28.4 (0.63)	26.3 (0.60)	17.5 (1.62)	20.9 (1.57)	15.9 (3.05)	16.2 (3.04)
1981	26.1 (0.38)	7.5 (0.22)	18.6 (0.33)	27.1 (0.54)	25.2 (0.52)	27.7 (0.43)	19.9 (1.10)	16.6 (2.14)	— (†)	— (†)	— (†)	— (†)	28.7 (0.62)	26.6 (0.60)	18.9 (1.60)	20.7 (1.52)	16.6 (3.08)	16.7 (2.97)
1982	26.6 (0.40)	7.7 (0.24)	18.9 (0.35)	27.2 (0.58)	26.0 (0.56)	28.1 (0.46)	19.9 (1.16)	16.8 (2.30)	— (†)	— (†)	— (†)	— (†)	28.9 (0.67)	27.4 (0.64)	18.7 (1.66)	21.0 (1.61)	14.9 (3.19)	18.6 (3.29)
1983	26.2 (0.40)	7.4 (0.24)	18.8 (0.36)	27.3 (0.58)	25.1 (0.55)	27.9 (0.47)	19.2 (1.14)	17.3 (2.31)	— (†)	— (†)	— (†)	— (†)	29.4 (0.67)	26.5 (0.64)	18.1 (1.63)	20.1 (1.59)	15.6 (3.21)	18.8 (3.31)
1984	27.1 (0.41)	7.3 (0.24)	19.8 (0.37)	28.6 (0.59)	25.6 (0.56)	28.9 (0.48)	20.3 (1.16)	17.9 (2.35)	— (†)	— (†)	— (†)	— (†)	30.8 (0.69)	27.1 (0.66)	20.3 (1.70)	20.3 (1.60)	16.1 (3.27)	19.6 (3.35)
1985	27.8 (0.42)	7.4 (0.24)	20.4 (0.38)	28.4 (0.60)	27.2 (0.58)	30.0 (0.49)	19.6 (1.17)	16.9 (1.85)	— (†)	— (†)	— (†)	— (†)	30.9 (0.71)	29.2 (0.68)	20.2 (1.74)	19.1 (1.58)	14.9 (2.46)	18.9 (2.75)
1986	27.9 (0.42)	7.6 (0.25)	20.3 (0.38)	28.2 (0.61)	27.6 (0.59)	29.7 (0.50)	21.9 (1.23)	17.6 (1.77)	— (†)	— (†)	— (†)	— (†)	30.6 (0.73)	28.8 (0.69)	20.0 (1.75)	23.4 (1.72)	16.7 (2.37)	18.7 (2.65)
1987	29.6 (0.44)	8.1 (0.26)	21.5 (0.39)	30.6 (0.63)	28.7 (0.60)	31.9 (0.52)	22.8 (1.26)	17.5 (1.74)	— (†)	— (†)	— (†)	— (†)	33.0 (0.75)	30.8 (0.72)	22.6 (1.86)	22.9 (1.72)	18.5 (2.47)	16.5 (2.44)
1988	30.3 (0.48)	8.8 (0.30)	21.5 (0.43)	30.2 (0.69)	30.4 (0.67)	33.2 (0.58)	21.2 (1.35)	17.0 (1.90)	— (†)	— (†)	— (†)	— (†)	33.4 (0.83)	33.0 (0.80)	18.5 (1.90)	23.5 (1.91)	16.5 (2.60)	17.6 (2.77)
1989	30.9 (0.46)	8.0 (0.27)	22.9 (0.42)	30.2 (0.66)	31.6 (0.65)	34.2 (0.56)	23.4 (1.32)	16.1 (1.66)	46.1 (3.77)	— (†)	15.7! (5.13)	— (†)	34.1 (0.80)	34.4 (0.79)	19.7 (1.82)	26.7 (1.89)	14.6 (2.23)	17.6 (2.47)
1990	32.0 (0.47)	8.7 (0.28)	23.3 (0.43)	32.3 (0.68)	31.8 (0.66)	35.1 (0.57)	25.4 (1.37)	15.8 (1.67)	56.9 (3.56)	— (†)	15.8! (5.07)	— (†)	35.5 (0.82)	34.7 (0.80)	26.0 (2.03)	24.8 (1.85)	15.3 (2.31)	16.4 (2.42)
1991	33.3 (0.48)	9.7 (0.30)	23.6 (0.43)	32.8 (0.68)	33.6 (0.67)	36.8 (0.58)	23.5 (1.34)	17.9 (1.72)	57.1 (3.19)	— (†)	15.9! (5.45)	— (†)	36.5 (0.83)	37.0 (0.82)	23.2 (1.95)	23.8 (1.84)	14.0 (2.15)	22.2 (2.70)
1992	34.4 (0.49)	9.9 (0.31)	24.4 (0.44)	32.7 (0.68)	36.0 (0.69)	37.3 (0.59)	25.2 (1.36)	21.3 (1.87)	58.4 (3.27)	— (†)	18.5! (6.17)	— (†)	36.2 (0.83)	38.3 (0.83)	21.3 (1.87)	28.8 (1.96)	17.8 (2.47)	24.7 (2.80)
1993	34.0 (0.49)	9.8 (0.30)	24.2 (0.44)	33.6 (0.69)	34.4 (0.68)	36.8 (0.59)	24.5 (1.35)	21.7 (1.88)	61.2 (3.26)	— (†)	18.9 (5.65)	— (†)	36.5 (0.84)	37.1 (0.83)	22.9 (1.92)	26.0 (1.90)	19.7 (2.59)	23.7 (2.71)
1994	34.6 (0.48)	9.1 (0.29)	25.5 (0.44)	33.1 (0.67)	36.0 (0.68)	38.1 (0.59)	27.7 (1.38)	18.8 (1.58)	62.7 (3.31)	— (†)	29.4 (6.65)	— (†)	37.0 (0.84)	39.2 (0.84)	25.6 (1.95)	29.5 (1.94)	16.5 (2.04)	21.5 (2.44)
1995	34.3 (0.45)	8.9 (0.27)	25.4 (0.41)	33.1 (0.63)	35.5 (0.63)	37.9 (0.55)	27.5 (1.18)	20.7 (1.13)	54.6 (3.11)	— (†)	27.6 (6.16)	— (†)	37.0 (0.78)	38.8 (0.78)	26.0 (1.72)	28.7 (1.63)	18.7 (1.50)	23.0 (1.72)
1996	35.5 (0.47)	9.5 (0.29)	26.1 (0.43)	34.1 (0.66)	37.0 (0.67)	39.5 (0.59)	27.4 (1.23)	20.1 (1.18)	53.9 (2.47)	— (†)	30.3 (5.24)	— (†)	38.3 (0.83)	40.6 (0.84)	25.7 (1.77)	28.8 (1.70)	16.5 (1.52)	24.0 (1.81)
1997	36.8 (0.47)	9.9 (0.29)	27.0 (0.43)	35.0 (0.66)	38.7 (0.67)	40.6 (0.59)	29.8 (1.25)	22.4 (1.21)	55.1 (2.60)	— (†)	27.1 (4.62)	— (†)	39.3 (0.82)	41.8 (0.84)	25.4 (1.75)	33.7 (1.77)	19.2 (1.56)	26.1 (1.88)
1998	36.5 (0.46)	10.2 (0.29)	26.3 (0.42)	34.5 (0.65)	38.6 (0.66)	40.6 (0.59)	29.8 (1.24)	20.4 (1.11)	60.4 (2.49)	— (†)	20.3 (4.90)	— (†)	39.4 (0.82)	41.9 (0.84)	26.1 (1.76)	32.9 (1.73)	16.4 (1.41)	24.9 (1.73)
1999	35.6 (0.46)	9.1 (0.27)	26.5 (0.42)	34.1 (0.64)	37.0 (0.65)	39.4 (0.58)	30.4 (1.24)	18.7 (1.08)	55.7 (2.42)	— (†)	19.5 (4.70)	— (†)	38.3 (0.81)	40.6 (0.82)	28.9 (1.81)	31.6 (1.69)	15.8 (1.41)	21.9 (1.65)
2000	35.5 (0.45)	9.4 (0.27)	26.0 (0.41)	32.6 (0.62)	38.4 (0.65)	38.7 (0.57)	30.5 (1.21)	21.7 (1.12)	55.9 (2.42)	— (†)	15.9 (4.30)	— (†)	36.2 (0.79)	41.3 (0.81)	25.1 (1.67)	35.2 (1.72)	18.5 (1.45)	25.4 (1.71)
2001	36.3 (0.43)	9.8 (0.26)	26.6 (0.39)	33.6 (0.59)	39.0 (0.61)	39.5 (0.54)	31.4 (1.15)	21.7 (1.04)	61.3 (2.23)	— (†)	23.3 (4.07)	— (†)	37.2 (0.75)	41.9 (0.77)	26.7 (1.62)	35.5 (1.62)	17.4 (1.35)	26.1 (1.58)
2002	36.7 (0.43)	9.7 (0.26)	27.0 (0.39)	33.7 (0.59)	39.7 (0.61)	40.9 (0.55)	31.9 (1.18)	19.9 (0.94)	60.9 (2.10)	— (†)	23.6 (3.96)	— (†)	38.9 (0.77)	42.8 (0.78)	26.3 (1.63)	36.9 (1.68)	16.2 (1.17)	24.4 (1.51)
2003[3]	37.8 (0.43)	10.2 (0.27)	27.7 (0.39)	34.3 (0.59)	41.3 (0.61)	41.6 (0.55)	32.3 (1.20)	23.5 (1.02)	61.2 (2.27)	43.3 (9.97)	17.7 (4.45)	41.6 (3.58)	38.5 (0.77)	44.5 (0.78)	28.2 (1.68)	36.0 (1.69)	18.3 (1.27)	29.4 (1.60)
2004[3]	38.0 (0.42)	9.4 (0.25)	28.6 (0.39)	34.7 (0.59)	41.2 (0.61)	41.7 (0.55)	31.8 (1.18)	24.7 (1.02)	60.6 (2.24)	55.8 (8.99)	24.4 (4.52)	36.8 (3.44)	38.4 (0.76)	45.0 (0.78)	26.5 (1.63)	36.6 (1.67)	21.7 (1.33)	28.2 (1.56)
2005[3]	38.9 (0.43)	9.6 (0.26)	29.2 (0.40)	35.3 (0.59)	42.5 (0.61)	42.8 (0.55)	33.1 (1.18)	24.8 (1.02)	61.0 (2.26)	50.6 (10.95)	27.8 (4.88)	41.8 (3.48)	39.4 (0.76)	46.1 (0.79)	28.2 (1.64)	37.6 (1.69)	20.7 (1.31)	29.5 (1.58)
2006[3]	37.3 (0.42)	9.6 (0.25)	27.8 (0.39)	34.1 (0.58)	40.6 (0.60)	41.0 (0.54)	32.6 (1.16)	23.6 (0.99)	58.3 (2.28)	39.1 (8.36)	26.2 (5.18)	38.5 (3.51)	37.9 (0.75)	44.1 (0.78)	28.1 (1.60)	36.9 (1.65)	20.0 (1.29)	27.6 (1.52)
2007[3]	38.8 (0.42)	10.9 (0.27)	27.9 (0.39)	35.5 (0.58)	42.1 (0.60)	42.6 (0.54)	33.1 (1.15)	26.6 (1.02)	57.2 (2.28)	37.1 (9.07)	24.7 (4.63)	39.2 (3.48)	39.6 (0.76)	45.7 (0.78)	32.2 (1.63)	34.0 (1.61)	20.7 (1.29)	33.0 (1.57)
2008[3]	39.6 (0.42)	11.8 (0.28)	27.8 (0.38)	37.0 (0.58)	42.3 (0.60)	44.2 (0.54)	32.1 (1.13)	25.8 (1.01)	59.3 (2.32)	27.3! (8.92)	21.9 (4.22)	45.7 (3.55)	41.7 (0.76)	46.9 (0.78)	29.7 (1.61)	34.2 (1.59)	23.0 (1.35)	28.9 (1.50)
2009[3]	41.3 (0.42)	11.7 (0.27)	29.6 (0.39)	38.4 (0.59)	44.2 (0.60)	45.0 (0.55)	37.7 (1.17)	27.5 (1.01)	65.2 (2.17)	33.4 (7.45)	29.8 (5.10)	39.3 (3.32)	42.3 (0.76)	47.7 (0.78)	33.2 (1.64)	41.9 (1.64)	24.2 (1.35)	31.0 (1.50)
2010[3]	41.2 (0.57)	12.9 (0.36)	28.2 (0.53)	38.3 (0.78)	44.1 (0.84)	43.3 (0.81)	38.4 (1.66)	31.9 (1.15)	63.6 (2.70)	36.0 (8.36)	41.4 (6.60)	38.3 (4.38)	40.6 (1.00)	46.1 (1.17)	35.2 (2.13)	41.4 (2.16)	27.9 (1.57)	36.1 (1.60)
2011[3]	42.0 (0.59)	12.0 (0.35)	30.0 (0.58)	39.1 (0.80)	44.9 (0.80)	44.7 (0.77)	37.1 (1.53)	34.8 (1.20)	60.1 (2.45)	37.8 (7.93)	23.5 (5.30)	38.8 (3.60)	42.4 (0.96)	47.1 (1.08)	34.0 (2.29)	39.9 (1.90)	31.0 (1.63)	39.4 (1.58)
2012[3]	41.0 (0.62)	12.7 (0.38)	28.3 (0.58)	37.6 (0.79)	44.5 (0.86)	42.1 (0.83)	36.4 (1.62)	37.5 (1.18)	59.8 (2.61)	50.3 (9.60)	27.8 (4.43)	39.4 (3.64)	38.3 (1.06)	46.0 (1.08)	33.9 (2.04)	38.7 (2.33)	33.5 (1.58)	41.7 (1.73)
2013[3]	39.9 (0.63)	11.6 (0.36)	28.3 (0.57)	36.6 (0.85)	43.3 (0.80)	41.6 (0.90)	34.2 (1.58)	33.8 (1.24)	62.3 (2.62)	32.9 (8.26)	31.8 (5.58)	44.7 (3.99)	38.1 (1.11)	45.3 (1.11)	30.6 (2.13)	37.6 (2.18)	29.1 (1.72)	38.8 (1.58)
2014[3]	40.0 (0.65)	10.6 (0.40)	29.4 (0.61)	37.3 (0.89)	42.8 (0.79)	42.2 (0.87)	32.6 (1.48)	34.7 (1.21)	65.2 (2.27)	41.0 (11.29)	35.4 (4.63)	31.6 (3.20)	40.2 (1.28)	44.2 (0.99)	28.5 (1.95)	36.6 (2.04)	30.3 (1.65)	39.4 (1.70)
2015[3]	40.5 (0.70)	10.6 (0.35)	29.9 (0.69)	37.8 (0.91)	43.2 (0.93)	41.8 (0.88)	34.9 (1.54)	36.6 (1.31)	62.6 (2.65)	24.1! (7.29)	23.0 (4.45)	38.3 (3.86)	39.1 (1.16)	44.5 (1.10)	34.1 (2.21)	35.7 (2.17)	32.8 (1.76)	40.5 (1.91)
2016[3]	41.2 (0.71)	10.1 (0.36)	31.1 (0.64)	38.6 (0.83)	43.9 (0.91)	42.1 (0.88)	36.2 (1.69)	39.2 (1.28)	57.6 (2.17)	20.7! (8.02)	18.6 (3.72)	42.3 (3.64)	39.8 (1.09)	44.5 (1.12)	33.0 (2.18)	39.4 (2.51)	34.9 (1.67)	43.6 (1.76)
2017[3]	40.4 (0.66)	10.0 (0.37)	30.4 (0.64)	36.8 (0.84)	44.0 (0.91)	41.0 (0.76)	36.5 (1.71)	36.2 (1.50)	64.7 (2.49)	32.6! (10.94)	20.1 (4.47)	41.5 (3.66)	37.8 (1.05)	44.4 (1.12)	33.1 (2.45)	39.6 (2.18)	31.1 (1.82)	41.4 (2.02)
2018[3]	40.9 (0.68)	9.9 (0.37)	31.0 (0.64)	37.6 (0.90)	44.3 (0.80)	42.3 (0.86)	37.2 (1.58)	35.9 (1.25)	59.0 (3.20)	23.8! (8.62)	24.2 (5.60)	44.3 (3.86)	39.1 (1.08)	45.4 (1.08)	33.3 (1.86)	40.9 (2.43)	31.6 (1.59)	40.4 (1.80)

—Not available.
†Not applicable.
!Interpret data with caution. The coefficient of variation (CV) for this estimate is between 30 and 50 percent.
[1]Prior to 2003, Asian data include Pacific Islanders.
[2]Prior to 1972, White and Black data include persons of Hispanic ethnicity.
[3]After 2002, data for individual race categories exclude persons of Two or more races. In 2002 and earlier years, the questionnaire did not include the "Two or more races" category, and each respondent could select only one race category.

NOTE: Data are based on sample surveys of the civilian noninstitutionalized population. Totals include other racial/ethnic groups not separately shown. Race categories exclude persons of Hispanic ethnicity except where otherwise noted. Prior to 2010, standard errors were computed using generalized variance function methodology rather than the more precise replicate weight methodology used in later years.
SOURCE: U.S. Department of Commerce, Census Bureau, Current Population Survey (CPS), October, 1970 through 2018. (This table was prepared August 2019.)

Table 303.10. Total fall enrollment in degree-granting postsecondary institutions, by attendance status, sex of student, and control of institution: Selected years, 1947 through 2029

Year	Total enrollment	Attendance status			Sex of student			Control of institution			
		Full-time	Part-time	Percent part-time	Male	Female	Percent female	Public	Private		
									Total	Nonprofit	For-profit
1	2	3	4	5	6	7	8	9	10	11	12
1947[1]	2,338,226	—	—	—	1,659,249	678,977	29.0	1,152,377	1,185,849	—	—
1948[1]	2,403,396	—	—	—	1,709,367	694,029	28.9	1,185,588	1,217,808	—	—
1949[1]	2,444,900	—	—	—	1,721,572	723,328	29.6	1,207,151	1,237,749	—	—
1950[1]	2,281,298	—	—	—	1,560,392	720,906	31.6	1,139,699	1,141,599	—	—
1951[1]	2,101,962	—	—	—	1,390,740	711,222	33.8	1,037,938	1,064,024	—	—
1952[1]	2,134,242	—	—	—	1,380,357	753,885	35.3	1,101,240	1,033,002	—	—
1953[1]	2,231,054	—	—	—	1,422,598	808,456	36.2	1,185,876	1,045,178	—	—
1954[1]	2,446,693	—	—	—	1,563,382	883,311	36.1	1,353,531	1,093,162	—	—
1955[1]	2,653,034	—	—	—	1,733,184	919,850	34.7	1,476,282	1,176,752	—	—
1956[1]	2,918,212	—	—	—	1,911,458	1,006,754	34.5	1,656,402	1,261,810	—	—
1957	3,323,783	—	—	—	2,170,765	1,153,018	34.7	1,972,673	1,351,110	—	—
1959	3,639,847	2,421,016	1,218,831[2]	33.5	2,332,617	1,307,230	35.9	2,180,982	1,458,865	—	—
1961	4,145,065	2,785,133	1,359,932[2]	32.8	2,585,821	1,559,244	37.6	2,561,447	1,583,618	—	—
1963	4,779,609	3,183,833	1,595,776[2]	33.4	2,961,540	1,818,069	38.0	3,081,279	1,698,330	—	—
1964	5,280,020	3,573,238	1,706,782[2]	32.3	3,248,713	2,031,307	38.5	3,467,708	1,812,312	—	—
1965	5,920,864	4,095,728	1,825,136[2]	30.8	3,630,020	2,290,844	38.7	3,969,596	1,951,268	—	—
1966	6,389,872	4,438,606	1,951,266[2]	30.5	3,856,216	2,533,656	39.7	4,348,917	2,040,955	—	—
1967	6,911,748	4,793,128	2,118,620[2]	30.7	4,132,800	2,778,948	40.2	4,816,028	2,095,720	2,074,041	21,679
1968	7,513,091	5,210,155	2,302,936	30.7	4,477,649	3,035,442	40.4	5,430,652	2,082,439	2,061,211	21,228
1969	8,004,660	5,498,883	2,505,777	31.3	4,746,201	3,258,459	40.7	5,896,868	2,107,792	2,087,653	20,139
1970	8,580,887	5,816,290	2,764,597	32.2	5,043,642	3,537,245	41.2	6,428,134	2,152,753	2,134,420	18,333
1971	8,948,644	6,077,232	2,871,412	32.1	5,207,004	3,741,640	41.8	6,804,309	2,144,335	2,121,913	22,422
1972	9,214,860	6,072,389	3,142,471	34.1	5,238,757	3,976,103	43.1	7,070,635	2,144,225	2,123,245	20,980
1973	9,602,123	6,189,493	3,412,630	35.5	5,371,052	4,231,071	44.1	7,419,516	2,182,607	2,148,784	33,823
1974	10,223,729	6,370,273	3,853,456	37.7	5,622,429	4,601,300	45.0	7,988,500	2,235,229	2,200,963	34,266
1975	11,184,859	6,841,334	4,343,525	38.8	6,148,997	5,035,862	45.0	8,834,508	2,350,351	2,311,448	38,903
1976	11,012,137	6,717,058	4,295,079	39.0	5,810,828	5,201,309	47.2	8,653,477	2,358,660	2,314,298	44,362
1977	11,285,787	6,792,925	4,492,862	39.8	5,789,016	5,496,771	48.7	8,846,993	2,438,794	2,386,652	52,142
1978	11,260,092	6,667,657	4,592,435	40.8	5,640,998	5,619,094	49.9	8,785,893	2,474,199	2,408,331	65,868
1979	11,569,899	6,794,039	4,775,860	41.3	5,682,877	5,887,022	50.9	9,036,822	2,533,077	2,461,773	71,304
1980	12,096,895	7,097,958	4,998,937	41.3	5,874,374	6,222,521	51.4	9,457,394	2,639,501	2,527,787	111,714[3]
1981	12,371,672	7,181,250	5,190,422	42.0	5,975,056	6,396,616	51.7	9,647,032	2,724,640	2,572,405	152,235[3]
1982	12,425,780	7,220,618	5,205,162	41.9	6,031,384	6,394,396	51.5	9,696,087	2,729,693	2,552,739	176,954[3]
1983	12,464,661	7,261,050	5,203,611	41.7	6,023,725	6,440,936	51.7	9,682,734	2,781,927	2,589,187	192,740
1984	12,241,940	7,098,388	5,143,552	42.0	5,863,574	6,378,366	52.1	9,477,370	2,764,570	2,574,419	190,151
1985	12,247,055	7,075,221	5,171,834	42.2	5,818,450	6,428,605	52.5	9,479,273	2,767,782	2,571,791	195,991
1986	12,503,511	7,119,550	5,383,961	43.1	5,884,515	6,618,996	52.9	9,713,893	2,789,618	2,572,479	217,139[4]
1987	12,766,642	7,231,085	5,535,557	43.4	5,932,056	6,834,586	53.5	9,973,254	2,793,388	2,602,350	191,038[4]
1988	13,055,337	7,436,768	5,618,569	43.0	6,001,896	7,053,441	54.0	10,161,388	2,893,949	2,673,567	220,382
1989	13,538,560	7,660,950	5,877,610	43.4	6,190,015	7,348,545	54.3	10,577,963	2,960,597	2,731,174	229,423
1990	13,818,637	7,820,985	5,997,652	43.4	6,283,909	7,534,728	54.5	10,844,717	2,973,920	2,760,227	213,693
1991	14,358,953	8,115,329	6,243,624	43.5	6,501,844	7,857,109	54.7	11,309,563	3,049,390	2,819,041	230,349
1992	14,487,359	8,162,118	6,325,241	43.7	6,523,989	7,963,370	55.0	11,384,567	3,102,792	2,872,523	230,269
1993	14,304,803	8,127,618	6,177,185	43.2	6,427,450	7,877,353	55.1	11,189,088	3,115,715	2,888,897	226,818
1994	14,278,790	8,137,776	6,141,014	43.0	6,371,898	7,906,892	55.4	11,133,680	3,145,110	2,910,107	235,003
1995	14,261,781	8,128,802	6,132,979	43.0	6,342,539	7,919,242	55.5	11,092,374	3,169,407	2,929,044	240,363
1996	14,367,520	8,302,953	6,064,567	42.2	6,352,825	8,014,695	55.8	11,120,499	3,247,021	2,942,556	304,465
1997	14,502,334	8,438,062	6,064,272	41.8	6,396,028	8,106,306	55.9	11,196,119	3,306,215	2,977,614	328,601
1998	14,506,967	8,563,338	5,943,629	41.0	6,369,265	8,137,702	56.1	11,137,769	3,369,198	3,004,925	364,273
1999	14,849,691	8,803,139	6,046,552	40.7	6,515,164	8,334,527	56.1	11,375,739	3,473,952	3,055,029	418,923
2000	15,312,289	9,009,600	6,302,689	41.2	6,721,769	8,590,520	56.1	11,752,786	3,559,503	3,109,419	450,084
2001	15,927,987	9,447,502	6,480,485	40.7	6,960,815	8,967,172	56.3	12,233,156	3,694,831	3,167,330	527,501
2002	16,611,711	9,946,359	6,665,352	40.1	7,202,116	9,409,595	56.6	12,751,993	3,859,718	3,265,476	594,242
2003	16,911,481	10,326,133	6,585,348	38.9	7,260,264	9,651,217	57.1	12,858,698	4,052,783	3,341,048	711,735
2004	17,272,044	10,610,177	6,661,867	38.6	7,387,262	9,884,782	57.2	12,980,112	4,291,932	3,411,685	880,247
2005	17,487,475	10,797,011	6,690,464	38.3	7,455,925	10,031,550	57.4	13,021,834	4,465,641	3,454,692	1,010,949
2006	17,754,230	10,957,538	6,796,692	38.3	7,572,265	10,181,965	57.3	13,175,350	4,578,880	3,512,929	1,065,951
2007	18,258,138	11,270,929	6,987,209	38.3	7,819,938	10,438,200	57.2	13,500,894	4,757,244	3,571,395	1,185,849
2008	19,081,686	11,734,636	7,347,050	38.5	8,177,714	10,903,972	57.1	13,970,862	5,110,824	3,660,827	1,449,997
2009	20,313,594	12,605,355	7,708,239	37.9	8,732,953	11,580,641	57.0	14,810,768	5,502,826	3,767,672	1,735,154
2010	21,019,438	13,087,182	7,932,256	37.7	9,045,759	11,973,679	57.0	15,142,171	5,877,267	3,854,482	2,022,785
2011	21,010,590	13,002,531	8,008,059	38.1	9,034,256	11,976,334	57.0	15,116,303	5,894,287	3,926,819	1,967,468
2012	20,644,478	12,734,404	7,910,074	38.3	8,919,006	11,725,472	56.8	14,884,667	5,759,811	3,951,388	1,808,423
2013	20,376,677	12,596,610	7,780,067	38.2	8,861,197	11,515,480	56.5	14,746,848	5,629,829	3,971,390	1,658,439
2014	20,209,092	12,454,464	7,754,628	38.4	8,797,530	11,411,562	56.5	14,654,660	5,554,432	3,997,249	1,557,183

See notes at end of table.

Table 303.10. Total fall enrollment in degree-granting postsecondary institutions, by attendance status, sex of student, and control of institution: Selected years, 1947 through 2029—Continued

Year	Total enrollment	Attendance status			Sex of student			Control of institution			
		Full-time	Part-time	Percent part-time	Male	Female	Percent female	Public	Private		
									Total	Nonprofit	For-profit
1	2	3	4	5	6	7	8	9	10	11	12
2015	19,988,204	12,287,512	7,700,692	38.5	8,723,819	11,264,385	56.4	14,572,843	5,415,361	4,065,891	1,349,470
2016	19,846,904	12,125,314	7,721,590	38.9	8,638,422	11,208,482	56.5	14,585,840	5,261,064	4,078,956	1,182,108
2017	19,778,151	12,076,141	7,702,010	38.9	8,571,314	11,206,837	56.7	14,571,739	5,206,412	4,108,489	1,097,923
2018	19,645,918	11,991,721	7,654,197	39.0	8,442,662	11,203,256	57.0	14,529,264	5,116,654	4,134,244	982,410
2019[5]	19,720,000	12,025,000	7,695,000	39.0	8,470,000	11,250,000	57.0	14,586,000	5,135,000	—	—
2020[5]	19,744,000	12,022,000	7,722,000	39.1	8,476,000	11,268,000	57.1	14,605,000	5,139,000	—	—
2021[5]	19,778,000	12,021,000	7,757,000	39.2	8,487,000	11,292,000	57.1	14,633,000	5,145,000	—	—
2022[5]	19,813,000	12,027,000	7,786,000	39.3	8,498,000	11,315,000	57.1	14,661,000	5,152,000	—	—
2023[5]	19,862,000	12,045,000	7,817,000	39.4	8,515,000	11,346,000	57.1	14,698,000	5,163,000	—	—
2024[5]	19,926,000	12,078,000	7,848,000	39.4	8,544,000	11,382,000	57.1	14,747,000	5,179,000	—	—
2025[5]	19,993,000	12,120,000	7,873,000	39.4	8,574,000	11,419,000	57.1	14,796,000	5,197,000	—	—
2026[5]	20,070,000	12,165,000	7,905,000	39.4	8,608,000	11,463,000	57.1	14,854,000	5,217,000	—	—
2027[5]	20,099,000	12,169,000	7,930,000	39.5	8,621,000	11,478,000	57.1	14,877,000	5,222,000	—	—
2028[5]	20,110,000	12,159,000	7,951,000	39.5	8,627,000	11,483,000	57.1	14,887,000	5,223,000	—	—
2029[5]	20,115,000	12,144,000	7,971,000	39.6	8,630,000	11,485,000	57.1	14,893,000	5,222,000	—	—

—Not available.

[1]Degree-credit enrollment only.

[2]Includes part-time resident students and all extension students (students attending courses at sites separate from the primary reporting campus). In later years, part-time student enrollment was collected as a distinct category.

[3]Large increases are due to the addition of schools accredited by the Accrediting Commission of Career Schools and Colleges of Technology.

[4]Because of imputation techniques, data are not consistent with figures for other years.

[5]Projected.

NOTE: Data through 1995 are for institutions of higher education, while later data are for degree-granting institutions. Degree-granting institutions grant associate's or higher degrees and participate in Title IV federal financial aid programs. The degree-granting classification is very similar to the earlier higher education classification, but it includes more 2-year colleges and excludes a few higher education institutions that did not grant degrees. Some data have been revised from previously published figures.

SOURCE: U.S. Department of Education, National Center for Education Statistics, *Biennial Survey of Education in the United States; Opening Fall Enrollment in Higher Education*, 1963 through 1965; Higher Education General Information Survey (HEGIS), "Fall Enrollment in Colleges and Universities" surveys, 1966 through 1985; Integrated Postsecondary Education Data System (IPEDS), "Fall Enrollment Survey" (IPEDS-EF:86-99); IPEDS Spring 2001 through Spring 2019, Fall Enrollment component; and Enrollment in Degree-Granting Institutions Projection Model, 2000 through 2029. (This table was prepared December 2019.)

Table 303.20. Total fall enrollment in all postsecondary institutions participating in Title IV aid programs and annual percentage change in enrollment, by degree-granting status and control of institution: 1995 through 2018

Year	All Title IV institutions[1]		Private		Degree-granting institutions[2]		Private			Non-degree-granting institutions[3]		Private	
	Total	Public	Nonprofit	For-profit	Total	Public	Total	Nonprofit	For-profit	Total	Public	Nonprofit	For-profit
1	2	3	4	5	6	7	8	9	10	11	12	13	14
						Enrollment							
1995	14,836,338	11,312,491	2,977,794	546,053	14,261,781	11,092,374	3,169,407	2,929,044	240,363	574,557	220,117	48,750	305,690
1996	14,809,897	11,312,775	2,976,850	520,272	14,367,520	11,120,499	3,247,021	2,942,556	304,465	442,377	192,276	34,294	215,807
1997	14,900,416	11,370,755	3,012,106	517,555	14,502,334	11,196,119	3,306,215	2,977,614	328,601	398,082	174,636	34,492	188,954
1998	14,923,839	11,330,811	3,040,251	552,777	14,506,967	11,137,769	3,369,198	3,004,925	364,273	416,872	193,042	35,326	188,504
1999	15,262,888	11,556,731	3,088,233	617,924	14,849,691	11,375,739	3,473,952	3,055,029	418,923	413,197	180,992	33,204	199,001
2000	15,701,409	11,891,450	3,137,108	672,851	15,312,289	11,752,786	3,559,503	3,109,419	450,084	389,120	138,664	27,689	222,767
2001	16,334,134	12,370,079	3,198,354	765,701	15,927,987	12,233,156	3,694,831	3,167,330	527,501	406,147	136,923	31,024	238,200
2002	17,035,027	12,883,071	3,299,094	852,862	16,611,711	12,751,993	3,859,718	3,265,476	594,242	423,316	131,078	33,618	258,620
2003	17,330,775	12,965,502	3,372,647	992,626	16,911,481	12,858,698	4,052,783	3,341,048	711,735	419,294	106,804	31,599	280,891
2004	17,710,798	13,081,358	3,440,559	1,188,881	17,272,044	12,980,112	4,291,932	3,411,685	880,247	438,754	101,246	28,874	308,634
2005	17,921,804	13,115,177	3,484,013	1,322,614	17,487,475	13,021,834	4,465,641	3,454,692	1,010,949	434,329	93,343	29,321	311,665
2006	18,198,370	13,276,881	3,543,064	1,378,425	17,754,230	13,175,350	4,578,880	3,512,929	1,065,951	444,140	101,531	30,135	312,474
2007	18,677,469	13,603,772	3,595,466	1,478,231	18,258,138	13,500,894	4,757,244	3,571,395	1,185,849	419,331	102,878	24,071	292,382
2008	19,553,784	14,090,863	3,684,190	1,778,731	19,081,686	13,970,862	5,110,824	3,660,827	1,449,997	472,098	120,001	23,363	328,734
2009	20,853,423	14,936,402	3,793,751	2,123,270	20,313,594	14,810,768	5,502,826	3,767,672	1,735,154	539,829	125,634	26,079	388,116
2010	21,591,742	15,279,455	3,881,630	2,430,657	21,019,438	15,142,171	5,877,267	3,854,482	2,022,785	572,304	137,284	27,148	407,872
2011	21,573,798	15,251,185	3,954,173	2,368,440	21,010,590	15,116,303	5,894,287	3,926,819	1,967,468	563,208	134,882	27,354	400,972
2012	21,148,181	15,000,302	3,973,422	2,174,457	20,644,478	14,884,667	5,759,811	3,951,388	1,808,423	503,703	115,635	22,034	366,034
2013	20,848,050	14,856,309	3,990,858	2,000,883	20,376,677	14,746,848	5,629,829	3,971,390	1,658,439	471,373	109,461	19,468	342,444
2014	20,664,180	14,764,741	4,016,240	1,883,199	20,209,092	14,654,660	5,554,432	3,997,249	1,557,183	455,088	110,081	18,991	326,016
2015	20,400,164	14,682,321	4,088,450	1,629,393	19,988,204	14,572,843	5,415,361	4,065,891	1,349,470	411,960	109,478	22,559	279,923
2016	20,230,012	14,695,538	4,097,022	1,437,452	19,846,904	14,585,840	5,261,064	4,078,956	1,182,108	383,108	109,698	18,066	255,344
2017	20,151,151	14,681,145	4,125,316	1,344,690	19,778,151	14,571,739	5,206,412	4,108,489	1,097,923	373,000	109,406	16,827	246,767
2018	20,008,434	14,639,681	4,147,604	1,221,149	19,645,918	14,529,264	5,116,654	4,134,244	982,410	362,516	110,417	13,360	238,739
						Annual percentage change							
1995 to 1996	-0.2	#	#	-4.7	0.7	0.3	2.4	0.5	26.7	-23.0	-12.6	-29.7	-29.4
1996 to 1997	0.6	0.5	1.2	-0.5	0.9	0.7	1.8	1.2	7.9	-10.0	-9.2	0.6	-12.4
1997 to 1998	0.2	-0.4	0.9	6.8	#	-0.5	1.9	0.9	10.9	4.7	10.5	2.4	-0.2
1998 to 1999	2.3	2.0	1.6	11.8	2.4	2.1	3.1	1.7	15.0	-0.9	-6.2	-6.0	5.6
1999 to 2000	2.9	2.9	1.6	8.9	3.1	3.3	2.5	1.8	7.4	-5.8	-23.4	-16.6	11.9
2000 to 2001	4.0	4.0	2.0	13.8	4.0	4.1	3.8	1.9	17.2	4.4	-1.3	12.0	6.9
2001 to 2002	4.3	4.1	3.1	11.4	4.3	4.2	4.5	3.1	12.7	4.2	-4.3	8.4	8.6
2002 to 2003	1.7	0.6	2.2	16.4	1.8	0.8	5.0	2.3	19.8	-1.0	-18.5	-6.0	8.6
2003 to 2004	2.2	0.9	2.0	19.8	2.1	0.9	5.9	2.1	23.7	4.6	-5.2	-8.6	9.9
2004 to 2005	1.2	0.3	1.3	11.2	1.2	0.3	4.0	1.3	14.8	-1.0	-7.8	1.5	1.0
2005 to 2006	1.5	1.2	1.7	4.2	1.5	1.2	2.5	1.7	5.4	2.3	8.8	2.8	0.3
2006 to 2007	2.6	2.5	1.5	7.2	2.8	2.5	3.9	1.7	11.2	-5.6	1.3	-20.1	-6.4
2007 to 2008	4.7	3.6	2.5	20.3	4.5	3.5	7.4	2.5	22.3	12.6	16.6	-2.9	12.4
2008 to 2009	6.6	6.0	3.0	19.4	6.5	6.0	7.7	2.9	19.7	14.3	4.7	11.6	18.1
2009 to 2010	3.5	2.3	2.3	14.5	3.5	2.2	6.8	2.3	16.6	6.0	9.3	4.1	5.1
2010 to 2011	-0.1	-0.2	1.9	-2.6	#	-0.2	0.3	1.9	-2.7	-1.6	-1.7	0.8	-1.7
2011 to 2012	-2.0	-1.6	0.5	-8.2	-1.7	-1.5	-2.3	0.6	-8.1	-10.6	-14.3	-19.4	-8.7
2012 to 2013	-1.4	-1.0	0.4	-8.0	-1.3	-0.9	-2.3	0.5	-8.3	-6.4	-5.3	-11.6	-6.4
2013 to 2014	-0.9	-0.6	0.6	-5.9	-0.8	-0.6	-1.3	0.7	-6.1	-3.5	0.6	-2.5	-4.8
2014 to 2015	-1.3	-0.6	1.8	-13.5	-1.1	-0.6	-2.5	1.7	-13.3	-9.5	-0.5	18.8	-14.1
2015 to 2016	-0.8	0.1	0.2	-11.8	-0.7	0.1	-2.8	0.3	-12.4	-7.0	0.2	-19.9	-8.8
2016 to 2017	-0.4	-0.1	0.7	-6.5	-0.3	-0.1	-1.0	0.7	-7.1	-2.6	-0.3	-6.9	-3.4
2017 to 2018	-0.7	-0.3	0.5	-9.2	-0.7	-0.3	-1.7	0.6	-10.5	-2.8	0.9	-20.6	-3.3

#Rounds to zero.
[1]Includes degree-granting and non-degree-granting institutions.
[2]Data for 1995 are for institutions of higher education, while later data are for degree-granting institutions. Degree-granting institutions grant associate's or higher degrees and participate in Title IV federal financial aid programs. The degree-granting classification is very similar to the earlier higher education classification, but it includes more 2-year colleges and excludes a few higher education institutions that did not grant degrees.

[3]Data are for institutions that did not offer accredited 4-year or 2-year programs, but were participating in Title IV federal financial aid programs. Includes some institutions transitioning to higher level program offerings, though still classified at a lower level.
NOTE: Some data have been revised from previously published figures.
SOURCE: U.S. Department of Education, National Center for Education Statistics, Integrated Postsecondary Education Data System (IPEDS), "Fall Enrollment Survey" (IPEDS-EF:95–99); and IPEDS Spring 2001 through Spring 2019, Fall Enrollment component. (This table was prepared November 2019.)

Table 303.25. Total fall enrollment in degree-granting postsecondary institutions, by control and level of institution: 1970 through 2018

	All institutions			Public institutions			All private institutions			Private institutions					
										Nonprofit			For-profit		
Year	Total	4-year	2-year	Total	4-year	2-year	Total	4-year	2-year	Total	4-year	2-year	Total	4-year	2-year
1	2	3	4	5	6	7	8	9	10	11	12	13	14	15	16
1970	8,580,887	6,261,502	2,319,385	6,428,134	4,232,722	2,195,412	2,152,753	2,028,780	123,973	2,134,420	2,021,121	113,299	18,333	7,659	10,674
1971	8,948,644	6,369,355	2,579,289	6,804,309	4,346,590	2,457,319	2,144,335	2,022,765	121,970	2,121,913	2,011,682	110,231	22,422	10,683	11,739
1972	9,214,860	6,458,674	2,756,186	7,070,635	4,429,696	2,640,939	2,144,225	2,028,978	115,247	2,123,245	2,019,380	103,865	20,980	9,598	11,382
1973	9,602,123	6,590,023	3,012,100	7,419,516	4,529,895	2,889,621	2,182,607	2,060,128	122,479	2,148,784	2,045,804	102,980	33,823	14,324	19,499
1974	10,223,729	6,819,735	3,403,994	7,988,500	4,703,018	3,285,482	2,235,229	2,116,717	118,512	2,200,963	2,098,599	102,364	34,266	18,118	16,148
1975	11,184,859	7,214,740	3,970,119	8,834,508	4,998,142	3,836,366	2,350,351	2,216,598	133,753	2,311,448	2,198,451	112,997	38,903	18,147	20,756
1976	11,012,137	7,128,816	3,883,321	8,653,477	4,901,691	3,751,786	2,358,660	2,227,125	131,535	2,314,298	2,206,457	107,841	44,362	20,668	23,694
1977	11,285,787	7,242,845	4,042,942	8,846,993	4,945,224	3,901,769	2,438,794	2,297,621	141,173	2,386,652	2,277,072	109,580	52,142	20,549	31,593
1978	11,260,092	7,231,625	4,028,467	8,785,893	4,912,203	3,873,690	2,474,199	2,319,422	154,777	2,408,331	2,299,132	109,199	65,868	20,290	45,578
1979	11,569,899	7,353,233	4,216,666	9,036,822	4,980,012	4,056,810	2,533,077	2,373,221	159,856	2,461,773	2,351,364	110,409	71,304	21,857	49,447
1980	12,096,895	7,570,608	4,526,287	9,457,394	5,128,612	4,328,782	2,639,501	2,441,996	197,505[1]	2,527,787	2,413,693	114,094	111,714	28,303	83,411[1]
1981	12,371,672	7,655,461	4,716,211	9,647,032	5,166,324	4,480,708	2,724,640	2,489,137	235,503[1]	2,572,465	2,453,239	119,166	152,235	35,898	116,337[1]
1982	12,425,780	7,654,074	4,771,706	9,696,087	5,176,434	4,519,653	2,729,693	2,477,640	252,053[1]	2,552,739	2,437,763	114,976	176,954	39,877	137,077[1]
1983	12,464,661	7,741,195	4,723,466	9,682,734	5,223,404	4,459,330	2,781,927	2,517,791	264,136	2,589,187	2,472,894	116,293	192,740	44,897	147,843
1984	12,241,940	7,711,167	4,530,773	9,477,370	5,198,273	4,279,097	2,764,570	2,512,894	251,676	2,574,419	2,466,172	108,247	190,151	46,722	143,429
1985	12,247,055	7,715,978	4,531,077	9,479,273	5,209,540	4,269,733	2,767,782	2,506,438	261,344	2,571,791	2,463,000	108,791	195,991	43,438	152,553
1986	12,503,511	7,823,963	4,679,548	9,713,893	5,300,202	4,413,691	2,789,618	2,523,761	265,857[2]	2,572,479	2,470,981	101,498	217,139	52,780	164,359[2]
1987	12,766,642	7,990,420	4,776,222	9,973,254	5,432,200	4,541,054	2,793,388	2,558,220	235,168[2]	2,602,350	2,512,248	90,102	191,038	45,972	145,066[2]
1988	13,055,337	8,180,182	4,875,155	10,161,388	5,545,901	4,615,487	2,893,949	2,634,281	259,668	—	—	—	—	—	—
1989	13,538,560	8,387,671	5,150,889	10,577,963	5,694,303	4,883,660	2,960,597	2,693,368	267,229	—	—	—	—	—	—
1990	13,818,637	8,578,554	5,240,083	10,844,717	5,848,242	4,996,475	2,973,920	2,730,312	243,608	2,760,227	2,671,069	89,158	213,693	59,243	154,450
1991	14,358,953	8,707,053	5,651,900	11,309,563	5,904,748	5,404,815	3,049,390	2,802,305	247,085	2,819,041	2,729,752	89,289	230,349	72,553	157,796
1992	14,487,359	8,764,969	5,722,390	11,384,567	5,900,012	5,484,555	3,102,792	2,864,957	237,835	2,872,523	2,789,235	83,288	230,269	75,722	154,547
1993	14,304,803	8,738,936	5,565,867	11,189,088	5,851,760	5,337,328	3,115,715	2,887,176	228,539	2,888,897	2,802,540	86,357	226,818	84,636	142,182
1994	14,278,790	8,749,080	5,529,710	11,133,680	5,825,213	5,308,467	3,145,110	2,923,867	221,243	2,910,107	2,824,500	85,607	235,003	99,367	135,636
1995	14,261,781	8,769,252	5,492,529	11,092,374	5,814,545	5,277,829	3,169,407	2,954,707	214,700	2,929,044	2,853,890	75,154	240,363	100,817	139,546
1996	14,367,520	8,804,193	5,563,327	11,120,499	5,806,036	5,314,463	3,247,021	2,998,157	248,864	2,942,556	2,867,181	75,375	304,465	130,976	173,489
1997	14,502,334	8,896,765	5,605,569	11,196,119	5,835,433	5,360,686	3,306,215	3,061,332	244,883	2,977,614	2,905,820	71,794	328,601	155,512	173,089
1998	14,506,967	9,017,653	5,489,314	11,137,769	5,891,806	5,245,963	3,369,198	3,125,847	243,351	3,004,925	2,939,055	65,870	364,273	186,792	177,481
1999	14,849,691	9,196,160	5,653,531	11,375,739	5,977,678	5,398,061	3,473,952	3,218,482	255,470	3,055,029	2,991,728	63,301	418,923	226,754	192,169
2000	15,312,289	9,363,858	5,948,431	11,752,786	6,055,398	5,697,388	3,559,503	3,308,460	251,043	3,109,419	3,050,575	58,844	450,084	257,885	192,199
2001	15,927,987	9,677,408	6,250,579	12,233,156	6,236,455	5,996,701	3,694,831	3,440,953	253,878	3,167,330	3,119,781	47,549	527,501	321,172	206,329
2002	16,611,711	10,082,332	6,529,379	12,751,993	6,481,613	6,270,380	3,859,718	3,600,719	258,999	3,265,476	3,218,389	47,087	594,242	382,330	211,912
2003	16,911,481	10,417,247	6,494,234	12,858,698	6,649,441	6,209,257	4,052,783	3,767,806	284,977	3,341,048	3,297,180	43,868	711,735	470,626	241,109
2004	17,272,044	10,726,181	6,545,863	12,980,112	6,736,536	6,243,576	4,291,932	3,989,645	302,287	3,411,685	3,369,435	42,250	880,247	620,210	260,037
2005	17,487,475	10,999,420	6,488,055	13,021,834	6,837,605	6,184,229	4,465,641	4,161,815	303,826	3,454,692	3,411,170	43,522	1,010,949	750,645	260,304
2006	17,754,230	11,240,678	6,513,552	13,175,350	6,955,221	6,220,129	4,578,880	4,285,457	293,423	3,512,929	3,473,773	39,156	1,065,951	811,684	254,267
2007	18,258,138	11,628,893	6,629,245	13,500,894	7,164,759	6,336,135	4,757,244	4,464,134	293,110	3,571,395	3,537,903	33,492	1,185,849	926,231	259,618
2008	19,081,686	12,110,487	6,971,199	13,970,862	7,330,682	6,640,180	5,110,824	4,779,805	331,019	3,660,827	3,625,469	35,358	1,449,997	1,154,336	295,661
2009	20,313,594	12,791,012	7,522,582	14,810,768	7,709,198	7,101,570	5,502,826	5,081,814	421,012	3,787,672	3,732,900	34,772	1,735,154	1,348,914	386,240
2010	21,019,438	13,335,841	7,683,597	15,142,171	7,924,108	7,218,063	5,877,267	5,411,733	465,534	3,854,482	3,821,799	32,683	2,022,785	1,589,934	432,851
2011	21,010,590	13,499,440	7,511,150	15,116,303	8,048,145	7,068,158	5,894,287	5,451,295	442,992	3,926,819	3,886,964	39,855	1,967,468	1,564,331	403,137
2012	20,644,478	13,476,638	7,167,840	14,884,667	8,092,602	6,792,065	5,759,811	5,384,036	375,775	3,951,388	3,913,690	37,698	1,808,423	1,470,346	338,077
2013	20,376,677	13,406,033	6,970,644	14,746,848	8,120,437	6,626,411	5,629,829	5,285,596	344,233	3,971,390	3,939,199	32,191	1,658,439	1,346,397	312,042
2014	20,209,092	13,494,414	6,714,678	14,654,660	8,257,108	6,397,552	5,554,432	5,237,306	317,126	3,997,249	3,966,873	30,376	1,557,183	1,270,433	286,750
2015	19,988,204	13,488,743	6,499,461	14,572,843	8,348,539	6,224,304	5,415,361	5,140,204	275,157	4,065,891	4,015,882	50,009	1,349,470	1,124,322	225,148
2016	19,846,904	13,754,486	6,092,418	14,585,840	8,742,931	5,842,909	5,261,064	5,011,555	249,509	4,078,956	4,028,401	50,555	1,182,108	983,154	198,954
2017	19,778,151	13,825,380	5,952,771	14,571,739	8,854,279	5,717,460	5,206,412	4,971,101	235,311	4,108,489	4,060,094	48,395	1,097,923	911,007	186,916
2018	19,645,918	13,900,710	5,745,208	14,529,264	8,982,560	5,546,704	5,116,654	4,918,150	198,504	4,134,244	4,089,090	45,154	982,410	829,060	153,350

—Not available.

[1] Large increases are due to the addition of schools accredited by the Accrediting Commission of Career Schools and Colleges of Technology.

[2] Because of imputation techniques, data are not consistent with figures for other years.

NOTE: Data through 1995 are for institutions of higher education, while later data are for degree-granting institutions. Degree-granting institutions grant associate's or higher degrees and participate in Title IV federal financial aid programs.

The degree-granting classification is very similar to the earlier higher education classification, but it includes more 2-year colleges and excludes a few higher education institutions that did not grant degrees. Some data have been revised from previously published figures.

SOURCE: U.S. Department of Education, National Center for Education Statistics, Higher Education General Information Survey (HEGIS), "Fall Enrollment in Institutions of Higher Education" surveys, 1970 through 1985; Integrated Postsecondary Education Data System (IPEDS), "Fall Enrollment Survey" (IPEDS-EF:86–99); and IPEDS Spring 2001 through Spring 2019, Fall Enrollment component. (This table was prepared November 2019.)

Table 303.30. Total fall enrollment in degree-granting postsecondary institutions, by level and control of institution, attendance status, and sex of student: Selected years, 1970 through 2029

Level and control of institution, attendance status, and sex of student	Actual													
	1970	1975	1980[1]	1985	1990	1995	2000	2005	2010	2014	2015	2016	2017	2018
1	2	3	4	5	6	7	8	9	10	11	12	13	14	15
Total	8,580,887	11,184,859	12,096,895	12,247,055	13,818,637	14,261,781	15,312,289	17,487,475	21,019,438	20,209,092	19,988,204	19,846,904	19,778,151	19,645,918
Full-time	5,816,290	6,841,334	7,097,958	7,075,221	7,820,985	8,128,802	9,009,600	10,797,011	13,087,182	12,454,464	12,287,512	12,125,314	12,076,141	11,991,721
Males	3,504,095	3,926,753	3,689,244	3,607,720	3,807,752	3,807,392	4,111,093	4,803,388	5,838,383	5,619,778	5,558,447	5,472,798	5,423,955	5,338,934
Females	2,312,195	2,914,581	3,408,714	3,467,501	4,013,233	4,321,410	4,898,507	5,993,623	7,248,799	6,834,686	6,729,065	6,652,516	6,652,186	6,652,787
Part-time	2,764,597	4,343,525	4,998,937	5,171,834	5,997,652	6,132,979	6,302,689	6,690,464	7,932,256	7,754,628	7,700,692	7,721,590	7,702,010	7,654,197
Males	1,539,547	2,222,244	2,185,130	2,210,730	2,476,157	2,535,147	2,610,676	2,652,537	3,207,376	3,177,752	3,165,372	3,165,624	3,147,359	3,103,728
Females	1,225,050	2,121,281	2,813,807	2,961,104	3,521,495	3,597,832	3,692,013	4,037,927	4,724,880	4,576,876	4,535,320	4,555,966	4,554,651	4,550,469
4-year	6,261,502	7,214,740	7,570,608	7,715,978	8,578,554	8,769,252	9,363,858	10,999,420	13,335,841	13,494,414	13,488,743	13,754,486	13,825,380	13,900,710
Full-time	4,587,379	5,080,256	5,344,163	5,384,614	5,937,023	6,151,755	6,792,551	8,150,209	9,721,803	9,793,357	9,776,828	9,815,967	9,848,817	9,880,953
Males	2,732,796	2,891,192	2,809,528	2,781,412	2,926,360	2,929,177	3,115,252	3,649,622	4,355,153	4,419,130	4,414,743	4,414,959	4,410,360	4,385,208
Females	1,854,583	2,189,064	2,534,635	2,603,202	3,010,663	3,222,578	3,677,299	4,500,587	5,366,650	5,374,227	5,362,085	5,401,008	5,438,457	5,495,745
Part-time	1,674,123	2,134,484	2,226,445	2,331,364	2,641,531	2,617,497	2,571,307	2,849,211	3,614,038	3,701,057	3,711,915	3,938,519	3,976,563	4,019,757
Males	936,189	1,092,461	1,017,813	1,034,804	1,124,780	1,084,753	1,047,917	1,125,935	1,424,721	1,484,380	1,491,001	1,586,069	1,594,427	1,605,785
Females	737,934	1,042,023	1,208,632	1,296,560	1,516,751	1,532,744	1,523,390	1,723,276	2,189,317	2,216,677	2,220,914	2,352,450	2,382,136	2,413,972
Public 4-year	4,232,722	4,998,142	5,128,612	5,209,540	5,848,242	5,814,545	6,055,398	6,837,605	7,924,108	8,257,108	8,348,539	8,742,931	8,854,279	8,982,560
Full-time	3,086,491	3,469,821	3,592,193	3,623,341	4,033,654	4,084,711	4,371,218	5,021,745	5,811,214	6,011,908	6,081,177	6,236,018	6,309,569	6,336,978
Males	1,813,584	1,947,823	1,873,397	1,863,689	1,982,369	1,951,140	2,008,618	2,295,456	2,707,307	2,806,792	2,833,998	2,894,232	2,911,441	2,895,088
Females	1,272,907	1,521,998	1,718,796	1,759,652	2,051,285	2,133,571	2,362,600	2,726,289	3,103,907	3,205,116	3,247,179	3,341,786	3,398,128	3,441,890
Part-time	1,146,231	1,528,321	1,536,419	1,586,199	1,814,588	1,729,834	1,684,180	1,815,860	2,112,894	2,245,200	2,267,362	2,506,913	2,544,710	2,645,582
Males	609,422	760,469	685,051	693,115	764,248	720,402	683,100	724,375	860,968	941,104	955,658	1,065,112	1,077,611	1,110,660
Females	536,809	767,852	851,368	893,084	1,050,340	1,009,432	1,001,080	1,091,485	1,251,926	1,304,096	1,311,704	1,441,801	1,467,099	1,534,922
Private 4-year	2,028,780	2,216,598	2,441,996	2,506,438	2,730,312	2,954,707	3,308,460	4,161,815	5,411,733	5,237,306	5,140,204	5,011,555	4,971,101	4,918,150
Full-time	1,500,888	1,610,435	1,751,970	1,761,273	1,903,369	2,067,044	2,421,333	3,128,464	3,910,589	3,781,449	3,695,651	3,579,949	3,539,248	3,543,975
Males	919,212	943,369	936,131	917,723	943,991	978,037	1,106,634	1,354,166	1,647,846	1,612,338	1,580,745	1,520,727	1,498,919	1,490,120
Females	581,676	667,066	815,839	843,550	959,378	1,089,007	1,314,699	1,774,298	2,262,743	2,169,111	2,114,906	2,059,222	2,040,329	2,053,855
Part-time	527,892	606,163	690,026	745,165	826,943	887,663	887,127	1,033,351	1,501,144	1,455,857	1,444,553	1,431,606	1,431,853	1,374,175
Males	326,767	331,992	332,762	341,689	360,532	364,351	364,817	401,560	563,753	543,276	535,343	520,957	516,816	495,125
Females	201,125	274,171	357,264	403,476	466,411	523,312	522,310	631,791	937,391	912,581	909,210	910,649	915,037	879,050
Nonprofit 4-year	2,021,121	2,198,451	2,413,693	2,463,000	2,671,069	2,853,890	3,050,575	3,411,170	3,821,799	3,966,873	4,015,882	4,028,401	4,060,094	4,089,090
Full-time	1,494,625	1,596,074	1,733,014	1,727,707	1,859,124	1,989,457	2,226,028	2,534,793	2,864,640	2,981,188	3,009,240	3,019,342	3,040,980	3,088,150
Males	914,020	930,842	921,253	894,080	915,100	931,956	996,113	1,109,075	1,259,638	1,313,286	1,320,947	1,318,323	1,318,131	1,328,444
Females	580,605	665,232	811,761	833,627	944,024	1,057,501	1,229,915	1,425,718	1,605,002	1,667,902	1,688,293	1,701,019	1,722,849	1,759,706
Part-time	526,496	602,377	680,679	735,293	811,945	864,433	824,547	876,377	957,159	985,685	1,006,642	1,009,059	1,019,114	1,000,940
Males	325,693	329,662	327,986	336,168	352,106	351,874	332,814	339,572	366,735	379,513	385,942	385,008	389,975	382,813
Females	200,803	272,715	352,693	399,125	459,839	512,559	491,733	536,805	590,424	606,172	620,700	624,051	629,139	618,127
For-profit 4-year	7,659	18,147	28,303	43,438	59,243	100,817	257,885	750,645	1,589,934	1,270,433	1,124,322	983,154	911,007	829,060
2-year	2,319,385	3,970,119	4,526,287	4,531,077	5,240,083	5,492,529	5,948,431	6,488,055	7,683,597	6,714,678	6,499,461	6,092,418	5,952,771	5,745,208
Full-time	1,228,911	1,761,078	1,753,795	1,690,607	1,883,962	1,977,047	2,217,049	2,646,802	3,365,379	2,661,107	2,510,684	2,309,347	2,227,324	2,110,768
Males	771,299	1,035,561	879,716	826,308	881,392	878,215	995,841	1,153,766	1,483,230	1,200,648	1,143,704	1,057,839	1,013,595	953,726
Females	457,612	725,517	874,079	864,299	1,002,570	1,098,832	1,221,208	1,493,036	1,882,149	1,460,459	1,366,980	1,251,508	1,213,729	1,157,042
Part-time	1,090,474	2,209,041	2,772,492	2,840,470	3,356,121	3,515,482	3,731,382	3,841,253	4,318,218	4,053,571	3,988,777	3,783,071	3,725,447	3,634,440
Males	603,358	1,129,783	1,167,317	1,175,926	1,351,377	1,450,394	1,562,759	1,526,602	1,782,655	1,693,372	1,674,371	1,579,555	1,552,932	1,497,943
Females	487,116	1,079,258	1,605,175	1,664,544	2,004,744	2,065,088	2,168,623	2,314,651	2,535,563	2,360,199	2,314,406	2,203,516	2,172,515	2,136,497
Public 2-year	2,195,412	3,836,366	4,328,782	4,269,733	4,996,475	5,277,829	5,697,388	6,184,229	7,218,063	6,397,552	6,224,304	5,842,909	5,717,460	5,546,704
Full-time	1,129,165	1,662,621	1,595,493	1,496,905	1,716,843	1,840,590	2,000,008	2,387,016	2,950,024	2,385,023	2,272,769	2,091,361	2,016,905	1,931,842
Males	720,440	988,701	811,871	742,673	810,664	818,605	891,282	1,055,029	1,340,820	1,107,410	1,062,633	983,567	945,990	892,853
Females	408,725	673,920	783,622	754,232	906,179	1,021,985	1,108,726	1,331,987	1,609,204	1,277,613	1,210,136	1,107,794	1,070,915	1,038,989
Part-time	1,066,247	2,173,745	2,733,289	2,772,828	3,279,632	3,437,239	3,697,380	3,797,213	4,268,039	4,012,529	3,951,535	3,751,548	3,700,555	3,614,862
Males	589,439	1,107,680	1,152,268	1,138,011	1,317,730	1,417,488	1,549,407	1,514,363	1,769,737	1,683,249	1,665,373	1,571,824	1,546,504	1,492,870
Females	476,808	1,066,065	1,581,021	1,634,817	1,961,902	2,019,751	2,147,973	2,282,850	2,498,302	2,329,280	2,286,162	2,179,724	2,154,051	2,121,992
Private 2-year	123,973	133,753	197,505	261,344	243,608	214,700	251,043	303,826	465,534	317,126	275,157	249,509	235,311	198,504
Full-time	99,746	98,457	158,302	193,702	167,119	136,457	217,041	259,786	415,355	276,084	237,915	217,986	210,419	178,926
Males	50,859	46,860	67,845	83,635	70,728	59,610	104,559	98,737	142,410	93,238	81,071	74,272	67,605	60,873
Females	48,887	51,597	90,457	110,067	96,391	76,847	112,482	161,049	272,945	182,846	156,844	143,714	142,814	118,053
Part-time	24,227	35,296	39,203	67,642	76,489	78,243	34,002	44,040	50,179	41,042	37,242	31,523	24,892	19,578
Males	13,919	22,103	15,049	37,915	33,647	32,906	13,352	12,239	12,918	10,123	8,998	7,731	6,428	5,073
Females	10,308	13,193	24,154	29,727	42,842	45,337	20,650	31,801	37,261	30,919	28,244	23,792	18,464	14,505
Nonprofit 2-year	113,299	112,997	114,094	108,791	89,158	75,154	58,844	43,522	32,683	30,376	50,009	50,555	48,395	45,154
Full-time	91,514	82,158	83,000	76,547	62,003	54,033	46,670	28,939	23,127	22,789	36,027	39,513	41,091	37,980
Males	46,030	40,548	34,968	30,878	25,946	23,265	21,950	12,086	9,944	9,074	11,972	11,950	10,794	9,397
Females	45,484	41,610	48,041	45,669	36,057	30,768	24,720	16,853	13,183	13,715	24,055	27,563	30,297	28,583
Part-time	21,785	30,839	31,085	32,244	27,155	21,121	12,174	14,583	9,556	7,587	13,982	11,042	7,304	7,174
Males	12,097	18,929	11,445	10,786	7,970	6,080	4,499	3,566	2,585	2,198	2,707	2,547	1,925	1,863
Females	9,688	11,910	19,640	21,458	19,185	15,041	7,675	11,017	6,971	5,389	11,275	8,495	5,379	5,311
For-profit 2-year	10,674	20,756	83,411	152,553	154,450	139,546	192,199	260,304	432,851	286,750	225,148	198,954	186,916	153,350

See notes at end of table.

Table 303.30. Total fall enrollment in degree-granting postsecondary institutions, by level and control of institution, attendance status, and sex of student: Selected years, 1970 through 2029—Continued

Level and control of institution, attendance status, and sex of student	Projected										
	2019	2020	2021	2022	2023	2024	2025	2026	2027	2028	2029
1	16	17	18	19	20	21	22	23	24	25	26
Total	**19,720,000**	**19,744,000**	**19,778,000**	**19,813,000**	**19,862,000**	**19,926,000**	**19,993,000**	**20,070,000**	**20,099,000**	**20,110,000**	**20,115,000**
Full-time	12,025,000	12,022,000	12,021,000	12,027,000	12,045,000	12,078,000	12,120,000	12,165,000	12,169,000	12,159,000	12,144,000
Males	5,350,000	5,345,000	5,343,000	5,343,000	5,347,000	5,361,000	5,381,000	5,400,000	5,403,000	5,400,000	5,395,000
Females	6,676,000	6,677,000	6,678,000	6,685,000	6,698,000	6,716,000	6,740,000	6,765,000	6,767,000	6,759,000	6,748,000
Part-time	7,695,000	7,722,000	7,757,000	7,786,000	7,817,000	7,848,000	7,873,000	7,905,000	7,930,000	7,951,000	7,971,000
Males	3,121,000	3,131,000	3,143,000	3,155,000	3,169,000	3,182,000	3,193,000	3,207,000	3,219,000	3,226,000	3,235,000
Females	4,574,000	4,591,000	4,614,000	4,631,000	4,648,000	4,666,000	4,680,000	4,698,000	4,711,000	4,724,000	4,736,000
4-year	**13,950,000**	**13,961,000**	**13,979,000**	**13,999,000**	**14,030,000**	**14,074,000**	**14,122,000**	**14,175,000**	**14,192,000**	**14,194,000**	**14,192,000**
Full-time	9,909,000	9,906,000	9,905,000	9,910,000	9,925,000	9,952,000	9,987,000	10,024,000	10,027,000	10,019,000	10,006,000
Males	4,394,000	4,390,000	4,389,000	4,388,000	4,392,000	4,404,000	4,420,000	4,436,000	4,438,000	4,436,000	4,431,000
Females	5,515,000	5,516,000	5,517,000	5,522,000	5,533,000	5,548,000	5,567,000	5,588,000	5,590,000	5,583,000	5,575,000
Part-time	4,041,000	4,055,000	4,074,000	4,089,000	4,105,000	4,122,000	4,134,000	4,152,000	4,165,000	4,175,000	4,186,000
Males	1,615,000	1,620,000	1,626,000	1,632,000	1,639,000	1,646,000	1,652,000	1,659,000	1,665,000	1,669,000	1,674,000
Females	2,427,000	2,436,000	2,447,000	2,457,000	2,466,000	2,475,000	2,483,000	2,492,000	2,499,000	2,506,000	2,513,000
Public 4-year	9,014,000	9,022,000	9,033,000	9,046,000	9,066,000	9,095,000	9,126,000	9,161,000	9,171,000	9,173,000	9,172,000
Full-time	6,355,000	6,353,000	6,352,000	6,355,000	6,365,000	6,382,000	6,405,000	6,428,000	6,430,000	6,425,000	6,417,000
Males	2,901,000	2,898,000	2,897,000	2,897,000	2,899,000	2,907,000	2,918,000	2,928,000	2,930,000	2,928,000	2,926,000
Females	3,454,000	3,454,000	3,455,000	3,458,000	3,465,000	3,475,000	3,487,000	3,500,000	3,501,000	3,497,000	3,491,000
Part-time	2,660,000	2,669,000	2,681,000	2,691,000	2,702,000	2,713,000	2,721,000	2,732,000	2,741,000	2,748,000	2,755,000
Males	1,117,000	1,120,000	1,125,000	1,129,000	1,134,000	1,139,000	1,143,000	1,148,000	1,152,000	1,155,000	1,158,000
Females	1,543,000	1,549,000	1,556,000	1,562,000	1,568,000	1,574,000	1,579,000	1,585,000	1,589,000	1,594,000	1,598,000
Private 4-year	4,935,000	4,940,000	4,946,000	4,953,000	4,964,000	4,979,000	4,996,000	5,015,000	5,021,000	5,021,000	5,020,000
Full-time	3,554,000	3,553,000	3,553,000	3,555,000	3,560,000	3,570,000	3,582,000	3,596,000	3,597,000	3,594,000	3,589,000
Males	1,493,000	1,492,000	1,491,000	1,491,000	1,492,000	1,496,000	1,502,000	1,507,000	1,508,000	1,507,000	1,506,000
Females	2,061,000	2,061,000	2,062,000	2,064,000	2,068,000	2,073,000	2,081,000	2,088,000	2,089,000	2,087,000	2,083,000
Part-time	1,381,000	1,386,000	1,393,000	1,398,000	1,403,000	1,409,000	1,413,000	1,419,000	1,424,000	1,427,000	1,431,000
Males	498,000	499,000	501,000	503,000	505,000	508,000	509,000	512,000	513,000	515,000	516,000
Females	884,000	887,000	891,000	895,000	898,000	901,000	904,000	908,000	910,000	913,000	915,000
Nonprofit 4-year	—	—	—	—	—	—	—	—	—	—	—
Full-time	—	—	—	—	—	—	—	—	—	—	—
Males	—	—	—	—	—	—	—	—	—	—	—
Females	—	—	—	—	—	—	—	—	—	—	—
Part-time	—	—	—	—	—	—	—	—	—	—	—
Males	—	—	—	—	—	—	—	—	—	—	—
Females	—	—	—	—	—	—	—	—	—	—	—
For-profit 4-year	—	—	—	—	—	—	—	—	—	—	—
2-year	**5,770,000**	**5,783,000**	**5,799,000**	**5,814,000**	**5,832,000**	**5,853,000**	**5,872,000**	**5,895,000**	**5,907,000**	**5,915,000**	**5,922,000**
Full-time	2,117,000	2,116,000	2,116,000	2,117,000	2,120,000	2,126,000	2,133,000	2,141,000	2,142,000	2,140,000	2,137,000
Males	956,000	955,000	955,000	954,000	955,000	958,000	961,000	965,000	965,000	965,000	964,000
Females	1,161,000	1,161,000	1,161,000	1,163,000	1,165,000	1,168,000	1,172,000	1,176,000	1,177,000	1,175,000	1,174,000
Part-time	3,654,000	3,667,000	3,683,000	3,697,000	3,712,000	3,727,000	3,738,000	3,754,000	3,765,000	3,775,000	3,785,000
Males	1,506,000	1,511,000	1,517,000	1,523,000	1,529,000	1,536,000	1,541,000	1,548,000	1,553,000	1,557,000	1,561,000
Females	2,148,000	2,156,000	2,166,000	2,174,000	2,183,000	2,191,000	2,197,000	2,206,000	2,212,000	2,218,000	2,224,000
Public 2-year	5,571,000	5,584,000	5,600,000	5,614,000	5,632,000	5,652,000	5,670,000	5,693,000	5,705,000	5,714,000	5,721,000
Full-time	1,937,000	1,937,000	1,937,000	1,937,000	1,940,000	1,946,000	1,952,000	1,960,000	1,960,000	1,959,000	1,956,000
Males	895,000	894,000	894,000	893,000	894,000	897,000	900,000	903,000	904,000	903,000	902,000
Females	1,043,000	1,043,000	1,043,000	1,044,000	1,046,000	1,049,000	1,053,000	1,056,000	1,057,000	1,056,000	1,054,000
Part-time	3,634,000	3,647,000	3,663,000	3,677,000	3,692,000	3,707,000	3,718,000	3,734,000	3,745,000	3,755,000	3,765,000
Males	1,501,000	1,506,000	1,512,000	1,518,000	1,524,000	1,531,000	1,536,000	1,543,000	1,548,000	1,552,000	1,556,000
Females	2,133,000	2,141,000	2,151,000	2,159,000	2,168,000	2,176,000	2,182,000	2,191,000	2,197,000	2,203,000	2,209,000
Private 2-year	199,000	199,000	199,000	199,000	200,000	200,000	201,000	202,000	202,000	202,000	202,000
Full-time	179,000	179,000	179,000	180,000	180,000	180,000	181,000	182,000	182,000	182,000	181,000
Males	61,000	61,000	61,000	61,000	61,000	61,000	61,000	62,000	62,000	62,000	62,000
Females	118,000	118,000	119,000	119,000	119,000	119,000	120,000	120,000	120,000	120,000	120,000
Part-time	20,000	20,000	20,000	20,000	20,000	20,000	20,000	20,000	20,000	20,000	20,000
Males	5,000	5,000	5,000	5,000	5,000	5,000	5,000	5,000	5,000	5,000	5,000
Females	15,000	15,000	15,000	15,000	15,000	15,000	15,000	15,000	15,000	15,000	15,000
Nonprofit 2-year	—	—	—	—	—	—	—	—	—	—	—
Full-time	—	—	—	—	—	—	—	—	—	—	—
Males	—	—	—	—	—	—	—	—	—	—	—
Females	—	—	—	—	—	—	—	—	—	—	—
Part-time	—	—	—	—	—	—	—	—	—	—	—
Males	—	—	—	—	—	—	—	—	—	—	—
Females	—	—	—	—	—	—	—	—	—	—	—
For-profit 2-year	—	—	—	—	—	—	—	—	—	—	—

—Not available.
[1]Large increase in private 2-year institutions in 1980 is due to the addition of schools accredited by the Accrediting Commission of Career Schools and Colleges of Technology. NOTE: Data through 1995 are for institutions of higher education, while later data are for degree-granting institutions. Degree-granting institutions grant associate's or higher degrees and participate in Title IV federal financial aid programs. The degree-granting classification is very similar to the earlier higher education classification, but it includes more 2-year colleges and excludes a few higher education institutions that did not grant degrees. Some data have been revised from previously published figures.

SOURCE: U.S. Department of Education, National Center for Education Statistics, Higher Education General Information Survey (HEGIS), "Fall Enrollment in Colleges and Universities" surveys, 1970 through 1985; Integrated Postsecondary Education Data System (IPEDS), "Fall Enrollment Survey" (IPEDS-EF:90–99); IPEDS Spring 2001 through Spring 2019, Fall Enrollment component; and Enrollment in Degree-Granting Institutions Projection Model, 2000 through 2029. (This table was prepared December 2019.)

Table 303.40. Total fall enrollment in degree-granting postsecondary institutions, by attendance status, sex, and age of student: Selected years, 1970 through 2029

[In thousands]

Attendance status, sex, and age	1970	1980	1990	2000	2005	2009	2010	2011	2012	2013	2014	2015	2016	2017	2018	Projected 2019	Projected 2020	Projected 2021	Projected 2029
1	2	3	4	5	6	7	8	9	10	11	12	13	14	15	16	17	18	19	20
All students	**8,581**	**12,097**	**13,819**	**15,312**	**17,487**	**20,314**	**21,019**	**21,011**	**20,644**	**20,377**	**20,209**	**19,988**	**19,847**	**19,778**	**19,646**	**19,720**	**19,744**	**19,778**	**20,115**
14 to 17 years old	263	257	153	131	187	215	202	221	242	256	239	214	214	210	206	204	205	207	204
18 and 19 years old	2,579	2,852	2,777	3,258	3,444	4,009	4,057	3,956	3,782	3,720	3,720	3,732	3,738	3,782	3,768	4,091	4,029	3,996	4,025
20 and 21 years old	1,885	2,395	2,593	3,005	3,563	3,916	4,103	4,269	4,235	4,183	4,163	4,148	4,204	4,160	4,142	4,467	4,519	4,537	4,517
22 to 24 years old	1,469	1,947	2,202	2,600	3,114	3,571	3,759	3,793	3,951	3,964	3,910	3,785	3,736	3,691	3,666	3,551	3,540	3,547	3,619
25 to 29 years old	1,091	1,843	2,083	2,044	2,469	3,082	3,254	3,272	3,155	3,050	3,084	3,165	3,192	3,226	3,194	3,058	3,033	2,996	2,957
30 to 34 years old	527	1,227	1,384	1,333	1,438	1,735	1,805	1,788	1,684	1,606	1,586	1,600	1,589	1,587	1,562	1,565	1,597	1,632	1,625
35 years old and over	767	1,577	2,627	2,942	3,272	3,785	3,840	3,712	3,597	3,597	3,507	3,344	3,174	3,123	3,107	2,785	2,821	2,864	3,166
Males	**5,044**	**5,874**	**6,284**	**6,722**	**7,456**	**8,733**	**9,046**	**9,034**	**8,919**	**8,861**	**8,798**	**8,724**	**8,638**	**8,571**	**8,443**	**8,470**	**8,476**	**8,487**	**8,630**
14 to 17 years old	125	106	66	58	68	103	94	104	119	125	117	94	83	75	77	81	81	82	81
18 and 19 years old	1,355	1,368	1,298	1,464	1,523	1,795	1,820	1,782	1,707	1,661	1,673	1,684	1,688	1,686	1,654	1,815	1,784	1,769	1,786
20 and 21 years old	1,064	1,219	1,259	1,411	1,658	1,866	1,948	1,985	1,960	1,955	1,960	1,954	1,945	1,915	1,889	2,025	2,048	2,055	2,044
22 to 24 years old	1,004	1,075	1,129	1,222	1,410	1,599	1,723	1,769	1,864	1,846	1,789	1,746	1,739	1,690	1,653	1,613	1,606	1,608	1,639
25 to 29 years old	796	983	1,024	908	1,057	1,378	1,410	1,404	1,353	1,356	1,379	1,382	1,366	1,385	1,378	1,299	1,291	1,276	1,251
30 to 34 years old	333	564	605	581	591	707	731	700	661	634	643	655	670	667	662	623	636	651	652
35 years old and over	366	559	902	1,077	1,149	1,285	1,320	1,290	1,255	1,283	1,237	1,208	1,148	1,154	1,131	1,015	1,030	1,047	1,177
Females	**3,537**	**6,223**	**7,535**	**8,591**	**10,032**	**11,581**	**11,974**	**11,976**	**11,725**	**11,515**	**11,412**	**11,264**	**11,208**	**11,207**	**11,203**	**11,250**	**11,268**	**11,292**	**11,485**
14 to 17 years old	137	151	87	73	119	113	108	116	123	131	121	120	131	135	130	123	124	125	123
18 and 19 years old	1,224	1,484	1,479	1,794	1,920	2,214	2,237	2,173	2,074	2,059	2,047	2,049	2,050	2,096	2,115	2,276	2,244	2,227	2,239
20 and 21 years old	821	1,177	1,334	1,593	1,905	2,050	2,155	2,284	2,276	2,228	2,203	2,194	2,259	2,245	2,253	2,442	2,470	2,482	2,473
22 to 24 years old	464	871	1,073	1,378	1,704	1,972	2,036	2,024	2,087	2,118	2,122	2,038	1,997	2,001	2,014	1,937	1,934	1,939	1,980
25 to 29 years old	296	859	1,059	1,136	1,413	1,704	1,844	1,868	1,802	1,694	1,706	1,783	1,826	1,841	1,816	1,759	1,743	1,720	1,706
30 to 34 years old	194	663	779	752	847	1,028	1,074	1,088	1,022	972	943	945	919	920	899	943	961	981	973
35 years old and over	401	1,018	1,725	1,865	2,123	2,500	2,520	2,422	2,341	2,314	2,270	2,136	2,026	1,969	1,976	1,770	1,791	1,816	1,990
Full-time	**5,816**	**7,098**	**7,821**	**9,010**	**10,797**	**12,605**	**13,087**	**13,003**	**12,734**	**12,597**	**12,454**	**12,288**	**12,125**	**12,076**	**11,992**	**12,025**	**12,022**	**12,021**	**12,144**
14 to 17 years old	246	231	134	121	152	179	170	185	207	210	200	182	186	183	179	178	179	181	178
18 and 19 years old	2,374	2,544	2,471	2,823	3,026	3,481	3,496	3,351	3,226	3,199	3,174	3,188	3,161	3,242	3,238	3,390	3,339	3,313	3,337
20 and 21 years old	1,649	2,007	2,137	2,452	2,976	3,241	3,364	3,427	3,386	3,327	3,326	3,290	3,365	3,332	3,361	3,419	3,460	3,471	3,455
22 to 24 years old	904	1,181	1,405	1,714	2,122	2,511	2,585	2,580	2,603	2,650	2,597	2,568	2,502	2,433	2,374	2,244	2,238	2,243	2,290
25 to 29 years old	426	641	791	886	1,174	1,506	1,605	1,600	1,555	1,528	1,525	1,519	1,478	1,480	1,453	1,385	1,375	1,358	1,339
30 to 34 years old	113	272	383	418	547	657	745	763	711	664	626	601	583	570	563	564	575	588	586
35 years old and over	104	221	500	596	800	1,030	1,122	1,096	1,047	1,018	1,005	941	852	835	824	844	855	868	959
Males	**3,504**	**3,689**	**3,808**	**4,111**	**4,803**	**5,632**	**5,838**	**5,793**	**5,708**	**5,682**	**5,620**	**5,558**	**5,473**	**5,424**	**5,339**	**5,350**	**5,345**	**5,343**	**5,395**
14 to 17 years old	121	95	55	51	53	77	71	85	102	106	100	81	71	65	66	68	69	69	69
18 and 19 years old	1,261	1,219	1,171	1,252	1,339	1,570	1,574	1,510	1,461	1,423	1,402	1,414	1,416	1,435	1,407	1,458	1,433	1,422	1,436
20 and 21 years old	955	1,046	1,035	1,156	1,398	1,536	1,586	1,586	1,537	1,542	1,549	1,546	1,552	1,536	1,546	1,564	1,582	1,587	1,579
22 to 24 years old	686	717	768	834	982	1,169	1,215	1,217	1,254	1,270	1,236	1,208	1,173	1,129	1,099	1,032	1,028	1,030	1,050
25 to 29 years old	346	391	433	410	506	661	715	727	728	734	732	709	689	693	683	672	667	660	647
30 to 34 years old	77	142	171	186	225	279	301	299	278	257	242	251	253	256	244	249	255	261	261
35 years old and over	58	80	174	222	300	341	376	369	349	351	360	349	320	310	293	306	310	315	354
Females	**2,312**	**3,409**	**4,013**	**4,899**	**5,994**	**6,973**	**7,249**	**7,210**	**7,026**	**6,914**	**6,835**	**6,729**	**6,653**	**6,652**	**6,653**	**6,676**	**6,677**	**6,678**	**6,748**
14 to 17 years old	125	136	78	70	98	102	99	100	105	104	101	101	115	118	113	110	111	111	110
18 and 19 years old	1,113	1,325	1,300	1,571	1,687	1,911	1,922	1,842	1,765	1,776	1,773	1,774	1,745	1,807	1,831	1,932	1,906	1,891	1,901
20 and 21 years old	693	961	1,101	1,296	1,578	1,705	1,778	1,840	1,849	1,785	1,777	1,744	1,813	1,795	1,815	1,855	1,878	1,885	1,876
22 to 24 years old	218	464	638	880	1,140	1,343	1,370	1,364	1,349	1,380	1,362	1,359	1,329	1,305	1,275	1,212	1,210	1,213	1,240
25 to 29 years old	80	250	358	476	668	845	891	873	827	794	793	810	789	788	769	714	707	698	692
30 to 34 years old	37	130	212	232	322	378	444	464	433	408	384	350	330	314	318	314	320	327	325
35 years old and over	46	141	326	374	500	690	746	727	698	667	645	592	532	526	531	538	545	552	605
Part-time	**2,765**	**4,999**	**5,998**	**6,303**	**6,690**	**7,708**	**7,932**	**8,008**	**7,910**	**7,780**	**7,755**	**7,701**	**7,722**	**7,702**	**7,654**	**7,695**	**7,722**	**7,757**	**7,971**
14 to 17 years old	16	26	19	10	36	36	32	36	35	47	38	32	28	27	27	26	26	26	26
18 and 19 years old	205	308	306	435	417	528	561	604	556	521	546	545	577	540	531	700	690	683	688
20 and 21 years old	236	388	456	553	586	675	738	842	850	855	836	858	839	828	781	1,048	1,058	1,065	1,062
22 to 24 years old	564	765	796	886	992	1,059	1,174	1,212	1,348	1,314	1,313	1,217	1,235	1,257	1,292	1,306	1,302	1,304	1,330
25 to 29 years old	665	1,202	1,291	1,158	1,296	1,576	1,648	1,672	1,600	1,522	1,560	1,646	1,715	1,745	1,741	1,672	1,659	1,638	1,618
30 to 34 years old	414	954	1,001	915	891	1,079	1,060	1,025	973	942	960	1,000	1,006	1,016	999	1,002	1,022	1,044	1,040
35 years old and over	663	1,356	2,127	2,345	2,472	2,754	2,718	2,616	2,550	2,579	2,502	2,404	2,322	2,288	2,283	1,941	1,966	1,996	2,207
Males	**1,540**	**2,185**	**2,476**	**2,611**	**2,653**	**3,101**	**3,207**	**3,241**	**3,211**	**3,179**	**3,178**	**3,165**	**3,166**	**3,147**	**3,104**	**3,121**	**3,131**	**3,143**	**3,235**
14 to 17 years old	4	12	11	7	15	25	23	20	17	20	18	13	12	10	10	12	12	12	12
18 and 19 years old	94	149	127	212	184	226	245	273	246	239	271	270	272	251	247	357	351	347	351
20 and 21 years old	108	172	224	255	260	330	362	398	423	413	411	408	393	378	342	461	466	468	465
22 to 24 years old	318	359	361	388	428	430	508	552	610	576	553	538	566	561	554	581	578	578	589
25 to 29 years old	450	592	591	498	551	718	695	677	625	622	646	673	677	692	695	627	623	616	604
30 to 34 years old	257	422	435	395	365	428	430	401	383	377	401	405	417	410	418	373	381	390	391
35 years old and over	309	479	728	855	850	944	944	921	906	932	877	859	829	845	838	710	720	732	822
Females	**1,225**	**2,814**	**3,521**	**3,692**	**4,038**	**4,607**	**4,725**	**4,767**	**4,699**	**4,601**	**4,577**	**4,535**	**4,556**	**4,555**	**4,550**	**4,574**	**4,591**	**4,614**	**4,736**
14 to 17 years old	12	14	9	3	21	11	9	16	18	27	20	19	16	17	16	14	14	14	14
18 and 19 years old	112	159	179	223	233	303	316	332	310	283	274	275	305	289	284	343	339	336	338
20 and 21 years old	128	216	233	298	327	345	377	444	427	443	425	450	446	450	439	587	592	598	597
22 to 24 years old	246	407	435	497	564	629	666	660	738	738	760	679	668	696	738	725	724	725	741
25 to 29 years old	216	609	700	660	745	859	953	995	975	900	913	973	1,037	1,053	1,047	1,045	1,036	1,022	1,014
30 to 34 years old	158	532	567	520	526	651	630	624	589	565	559	595	589	606	581	629	641	654	649
35 years old and over	354	876	1,399	1,491	1,623	1,810	1,774	1,695	1,643	1,647	1,625	1,544	1,493	1,443	1,445	1,232	1,247	1,264	1,385

NOTE: Distributions by age are estimates based on samples of the civilian noninstitutionalized population from the U.S. Census Bureau's Current Population Survey. Data through 1995 are for institutions of higher education, while later data are for degree-granting institutions. Degree-granting institutions grant associate's or higher degrees and participate in Title IV federal financial aid programs. The degree-granting classification is very similar to the earlier higher education classification, but it includes more 2-year colleges and excludes a few higher education institutions that did not grant degrees. Some data have been revised from previously published figures. Detail may not sum to totals because of rounding.

SOURCE: U.S. Department of Education, National Center for Education Statistics, Higher Education General Information Survey (HEGIS), "Fall Enrollment in Colleges and Universities" surveys, 1970 and 1980; Integrated Postsecondary Education Data System (IPEDS), "Fall Enrollment Survey" (IPEDS-EF:90–99); IPEDS Spring 2001 through Spring 2019, Fall Enrollment component; and Enrollment in Degree-Granting Institutions Projection Model, 2000 through 2029. U.S. Department of Commerce, Census Bureau, Current Population Survey (CPS), October, selected years, 1970 through 2018. (This table was prepared April 2020.)

Table 303.45. Total fall enrollment in degree-granting postsecondary institutions, by level of enrollment, sex, attendance status, and age of student: 2013, 2015, and 2017

Attendance status and age of student	Fall 2013 All levels Total	Fall 2015 All levels Total	Males	Females	Fall 2017 All levels Total	Males	Females	Undergraduate Total	Males	Females	Postbaccalaureate Total	Males	Females
1	2	3	4	5	6	7	8	9	10	11	12	13	14
All students	20,376,677	19,988,204	8,723,819	11,264,385	19,778,151	8,571,314	11,206,837	16,773,036	7,351,259	9,421,777	3,005,115	1,220,055	1,785,060
Under 18	878,766	1,053,854	435,452	618,402	1,233,155	506,387	726,768	1,233,021	506,327	726,694	134	60	74
18 and 19	4,265,916	4,341,382	1,954,795	2,386,587	4,446,105	1,994,211	2,451,894	4,445,215	1,993,914	2,451,301	890	297	593
20 and 21	4,086,686	4,078,990	1,849,082	2,229,908	4,096,336	1,844,738	2,251,598	4,059,944	1,831,887	2,228,057	36,392	12,851	23,541
22 to 24	3,431,880	3,324,891	1,540,990	1,783,901	3,204,527	1,471,011	1,733,516	2,541,944	1,208,478	1,333,466	662,583	262,533	400,050
25 to 29	2,856,287	2,778,912	1,227,002	1,551,910	2,694,183	1,167,840	1,526,343	1,732,765	752,678	980,087	961,418	415,162	546,256
30 to 34	1,641,631	1,511,847	644,424	867,423	1,421,657	597,664	823,993	946,325	389,598	556,727	475,332	208,066	267,266
35 to 39	1,033,809	973,402	384,395	589,007	933,343	366,653	566,690	634,889	246,082	388,807	298,454	120,571	177,883
40 to 49	1,346,668	1,190,153	428,681	761,472	1,090,103	389,284	700,819	727,226	260,318	466,908	362,877	128,966	233,911
50 to 64	717,355	627,528	214,632	412,896	560,173	192,051	368,122	372,091	128,351	243,740	188,082	63,700	124,382
65 and over	66,202	66,683	28,234	38,449	67,094	28,537	38,557	53,541	22,728	30,813	13,553	5,809	7,744
Age unknown	51,477	40,562	16,132	24,430	31,475	12,938	18,537	26,075	10,898	15,177	5,400	2,040	3,360
Full-time	12,596,610	12,287,512	5,558,447	6,729,065	12,076,141	5,423,955	6,652,186	10,371,863	4,683,715	5,688,148	1,704,278	740,240	964,038
Under 18	185,285	206,770	83,135	123,635	220,590	86,108	134,482	220,547	86,084	134,463	43	24	19
18 and 19	3,549,171	3,612,294	1,612,557	1,999,737	3,695,990	1,644,606	2,051,384	3,695,241	1,644,373	2,050,868	749	233	516
20 and 21	3,245,703	3,241,515	1,470,848	1,770,667	3,267,198	1,475,104	1,792,094	3,234,340	1,463,343	1,770,997	32,858	11,761	21,097
22 to 24	2,240,365	2,156,073	1,033,642	1,122,431	2,068,425	983,041	1,085,384	1,538,218	768,645	769,573	530,207	214,396	315,811
25 to 29	1,497,997	1,442,151	681,881	760,270	1,372,010	636,740	735,270	761,468	353,742	407,726	610,542	282,998	327,544
30 to 34	724,235	649,695	296,410	353,285	591,317	266,301	325,016	361,865	156,078	205,787	229,452	110,223	119,229
35 to 39	408,932	368,319	151,776	216,543	338,499	138,827	199,672	221,791	87,570	134,221	116,708	51,257	65,451
40 to 49	483,716	403,959	151,610	252,349	350,409	129,668	220,741	229,041	83,394	145,647	121,368	46,274	75,094
50 to 64	226,402	177,157	64,530	112,627	148,671	53,859	94,812	91,788	33,175	58,613	56,883	20,684	36,199
65 and over	9,105	10,556	4,747	5,809	8,951	3,941	5,010	5,161	2,318	2,843	3,790	1,623	2,167
Age unknown	25,699	19,023	7,311	11,712	14,081	5,760	8,321	12,403	4,993	7,410	1,678	767	911
Part-time	7,780,067	7,700,692	3,165,372	4,535,320	7,702,010	3,147,359	4,554,651	6,401,173	2,667,544	3,733,629	1,300,837	479,815	821,022
Under 18	693,481	847,084	352,317	494,767	1,012,565	420,279	592,286	1,012,474	420,243	592,231	91	36	55
18 and 19	716,745	729,088	342,238	386,850	750,115	349,605	400,510	749,974	349,541	400,433	141	64	77
20 and 21	840,983	837,475	378,234	459,241	829,138	369,634	459,504	825,604	368,544	457,060	3,534	1,090	2,444
22 to 24	1,191,515	1,168,818	507,348	661,470	1,136,102	487,970	648,132	1,003,726	439,833	563,893	132,376	48,137	84,239
25 to 29	1,358,290	1,336,761	545,121	791,640	1,322,173	531,100	791,073	971,297	398,936	572,361	350,876	132,164	218,712
30 to 34	917,396	862,152	348,014	514,138	830,340	331,363	498,977	584,460	233,520	350,940	245,880	97,843	148,037
35 to 39	624,877	605,083	232,619	372,464	594,844	227,826	367,018	413,098	158,512	254,586	181,746	69,314	112,432
40 to 49	862,952	786,194	277,071	509,123	739,694	259,616	480,078	498,185	176,924	321,261	241,509	82,692	158,817
50 to 64	490,953	450,371	150,102	300,269	411,502	138,192	273,310	280,303	95,176	185,127	131,199	43,016	88,183
65 and over	57,097	56,127	23,487	32,640	58,143	24,596	33,547	48,380	20,410	27,970	9,763	4,186	5,577
Age unknown	25,778	21,539	8,821	12,718	17,394	7,178	10,216	13,672	5,905	7,767	3,722	1,273	2,449

Percentage distribution of students with known age[1]

All students	100.0	100.0	100.0	100.0	100.0	100.0	100.0	100.0	100.0	100.0	100.0	100.0	100.0
Under 18	4.3	5.3	5.0	5.5	6.2	5.9	6.5	7.4	6.9	7.7	#	#	#
18 and 19	21.0	21.8	22.4	21.2	22.5	23.3	21.9	26.5	27.2	26.1	#	#	#
20 and 21	20.1	20.4	21.2	19.8	20.7	21.6	20.1	24.2	25.0	23.7	1.2	1.1	1.3
22 to 24	16.9	16.7	17.7	15.9	16.2	17.2	15.5	15.2	16.5	14.2	22.1	21.6	22.5
25 to 29	14.1	13.9	14.1	13.8	13.6	13.6	13.6	10.3	10.3	10.4	32.1	34.1	30.7
30 to 34	8.1	7.6	7.4	7.7	7.2	7.0	7.4	5.7	5.3	5.9	15.8	17.1	15.0
35 to 39	5.1	4.9	4.4	5.2	4.7	4.3	5.1	3.8	3.4	4.1	9.9	9.9	10.0
40 to 49	6.6	6.0	4.9	6.8	5.5	4.5	6.3	4.3	3.5	5.0	12.1	10.6	13.1
50 to 64	3.5	3.1	2.5	3.7	2.8	2.2	3.3	2.2	1.7	2.6	6.3	5.2	7.0
65 and over	0.3	0.3	0.3	0.3	0.3	0.3	0.3	0.3	0.3	0.3	0.5	0.5	0.4
Full-time	100.0	100.0	100.0	100.0	100.0	100.0	100.0	100.0	100.0	100.0	100.0	100.0	100.0
Under 18	1.5	1.7	1.5	1.8	1.8	1.6	2.0	2.1	1.8	2.4	#	#	#
18 and 19	28.2	29.4	29.0	29.8	30.6	30.4	30.9	35.7	35.1	36.1	#	#	0.1
20 and 21	25.8	26.4	26.5	26.4	27.1	27.2	27.0	31.2	31.3	31.2	1.9	1.6	2.2
22 to 24	17.8	17.6	18.6	16.7	17.1	18.1	16.3	14.8	16.4	13.5	31.1	29.0	32.8
25 to 29	11.9	11.8	12.3	11.3	11.4	11.8	11.1	7.4	7.6	7.2	35.9	38.3	34.0
30 to 34	5.8	5.3	5.3	5.3	4.9	4.9	4.9	3.5	3.3	3.6	13.5	14.9	12.4
35 to 39	3.3	3.0	2.7	3.2	2.8	2.6	3.0	2.1	1.9	2.4	6.9	6.9	6.8
40 to 49	3.8	3.3	2.7	3.8	2.9	2.4	3.3	2.2	1.8	2.6	7.1	6.3	7.8
50 to 64	1.8	1.4	1.2	1.7	1.2	1.0	1.4	0.9	0.7	1.0	3.3	2.8	3.8
65 and over	0.1	0.1	0.1	0.1	0.1	0.1	0.1	#	#	0.1	0.2	0.2	0.2
Part-time	100.0	100.0	100.0	100.0	100.0	100.0	100.0	100.0	100.0	100.0	100.0	100.0	100.0
Under 18	8.9	11.0	11.2	10.9	13.2	13.4	13.0	15.9	15.8	15.9	#	#	#
18 and 19	9.2	9.5	10.8	8.6	9.8	11.1	8.8	11.7	13.1	10.7	#	#	#
20 and 21	10.8	10.9	12.0	10.2	10.8	11.8	10.1	12.9	13.8	12.3	0.3	0.2	0.3
22 to 24	15.4	15.2	16.1	14.6	14.8	15.5	14.3	15.7	16.5	15.1	10.2	10.1	10.3
25 to 29	17.5	17.4	17.3	17.5	17.2	16.9	17.4	15.2	15.0	15.4	27.1	27.6	26.7
30 to 34	11.8	11.2	11.0	11.4	10.8	10.6	11.0	9.2	8.8	9.4	19.0	20.4	18.1
35 to 39	8.1	7.9	7.4	8.2	7.7	7.3	8.1	6.5	6.0	6.8	14.0	14.5	13.7
40 to 49	11.1	10.2	8.8	11.3	9.6	8.3	10.6	7.8	6.6	8.6	18.6	17.3	19.4
50 to 64	6.3	5.9	4.8	6.6	5.4	4.4	6.0	4.4	3.6	5.0	10.1	9.0	10.8
65 and over	0.7	0.7	0.7	0.7	0.8	0.8	0.7	0.8	0.8	0.8	0.8	0.9	0.7

#Rounds to zero.
[1]Percentage distributions exclude students whose age is unknown.
NOTE: Degree-granting institutions grant associate's or higher degrees and participate in Title IV federal financial aid programs. Detail may not sum to totals because of rounding.

Some data have been revised from previously published figures.
SOURCE: U.S. Department of Education, National Center for Education Statistics, Integrated Postsecondary Education Data System (IPEDS), Spring 2014, 2016, and 2018, Fall Enrollment component. (This table was prepared September 2019.)

Table 303.50. Total fall enrollment in degree-granting postsecondary institutions, by level of enrollment, control and level of institution, attendance status, and age of student: 2017

Attendance status and age of student	Undergraduate											Postbaccalaureate			
	Total	Public			Private nonprofit			Private for-profit				Total	Public	Private nonprofit	Private for-profit
		Total	4-year	2-year	Total	4-year	2-year	Total	4-year	2-year					
1	2	3	4	5	6	7	8	9	10	11		12	13	14	15
All students	16,773,036	13,112,594	7,395,134	5,717,460	2,819,080	2,770,685	48,395	841,362	654,446	186,916		3,005,115	1,459,145	1,289,409	256,561
Under 18	1,233,021	1,132,042	379,252	752,790	96,410	95,753	657	4,569	3,457	1,112		134	40	92	2
18 and 19	4,445,215	3,526,795	2,172,927	1,353,868	859,865	852,685	7,180	58,555	36,666	21,889		890	449	413	28
20 and 21	4,059,944	3,132,168	2,171,402	960,766	847,338	841,906	5,432	80,438	54,061	26,377		36,392	19,785	16,146	461
22 to 24	2,541,944	2,063,145	1,293,776	769,369	362,913	355,868	7,045	115,886	82,912	32,974		662,583	358,913	290,793	12,877
25 to 29	1,732,765	1,339,447	630,619	708,828	209,967	200,300	9,667	183,351	143,343	40,008		961,418	492,261	422,550	46,607
30 to 34	946,325	674,873	283,074	391,799	134,710	128,665	6,045	136,742	113,202	23,540		475,332	234,815	195,546	44,971
35 to 39	634,889	432,454	172,682	259,772	103,114	98,923	4,191	99,321	83,715	15,606		298,454	134,762	121,331	42,361
40 to 49	727,226	487,302	185,390	301,912	128,754	123,608	5,146	111,170	94,363	16,807		362,877	146,499	150,493	65,885
50 to 64	372,091	262,585	88,723	173,862	62,440	59,712	2,728	47,066	39,662	7,404		188,082	66,177	81,872	40,033
65 and over	53,541	47,310	13,167	34,143	4,421	4,206	215	1,810	1,464	346		13,553	5,014	5,734	2,805
Age unknown	26,075	14,473	4,122	10,351	9,148	9,059	89	2,454	1,601	853		5,400	430	4,439	531
Full-time	10,371,863	7,515,398	5,498,493	2,016,905	2,300,518	2,259,427	41,091	555,947	386,619	169,328		1,704,278	811,076	781,553	111,649
Under 18	220,547	185,310	103,906	81,404	33,098	32,834	264	2,139	1,052	1,087		43	18	24	1
18 and 19	3,695,241	2,812,605	1,983,407	829,198	830,043	823,231	6,812	52,593	31,590	21,003		749	404	327	18
20 and 21	3,234,340	2,354,762	1,921,413	433,349	813,857	809,134	4,723	65,721	41,211	24,510		32,858	18,007	14,515	336
22 to 24	1,538,218	1,161,147	924,814	236,333	293,846	288,032	5,814	83,225	53,388	29,837		530,207	285,663	236,769	7,775
25 to 29	761,468	515,303	320,680	194,623	124,840	116,701	8,139	121,325	85,420	35,905		610,542	302,408	285,291	22,843
30 to 34	361,865	208,220	112,487	95,733	69,373	64,304	5,069	84,272	63,342	20,930		229,452	106,932	103,218	19,302
35 to 39	221,791	114,346	57,303	57,043	49,018	45,528	3,490	58,427	44,532	13,895		116,708	46,004	52,918	17,786
40 to 49	229,041	109,944	51,973	57,971	57,059	52,763	4,296	62,038	47,218	14,820		121,368	37,424	57,399	26,545
50 to 64	91,788	44,149	18,726	25,423	23,781	21,524	2,257	23,858	17,620	6,238		56,883	13,387	27,886	15,610
65 and over	5,161	3,273	1,022	2,251	953	775	178	935	632	303		3,790	745	1,903	1,142
Age unknown	12,403	6,339	2,762	3,577	4,650	4,601	49	1,414	614	800		1,678	84	1,303	291
Part-time	6,401,173	5,597,196	1,896,641	3,700,555	518,562	511,258	7,304	285,415	267,827	17,588		1,300,837	648,069	507,856	144,912
Under 18	1,012,474	946,732	275,346	671,386	63,312	62,919	393	2,430	2,405	25		91	22	68	1
18 and 19	749,974	714,190	189,520	524,670	29,822	29,454	368	5,962	5,076	886		141	45	86	10
20 and 21	825,604	777,406	249,989	527,417	33,481	32,772	709	14,717	12,850	1,867		3,534	1,778	1,631	125
22 to 24	1,003,726	901,998	368,962	533,036	69,067	67,836	1,231	32,661	29,524	3,137		132,376	73,250	54,024	5,102
25 to 29	971,297	824,144	309,939	514,205	85,127	83,599	1,528	62,026	57,923	4,103		350,876	189,853	137,259	23,764
30 to 34	584,460	466,653	170,587	296,066	65,337	64,361	976	52,470	49,860	2,610		245,880	127,883	92,328	25,669
35 to 39	413,098	318,108	115,379	202,729	54,096	53,395	701	40,894	39,183	1,711		181,746	88,758	68,413	24,575
40 to 49	498,185	377,358	133,417	243,941	71,695	70,845	850	49,132	47,145	1,987		241,509	109,075	93,094	39,340
50 to 64	280,303	218,436	69,997	148,439	38,659	38,188	471	23,208	22,042	1,166		131,199	52,790	53,986	24,423
65 and over	48,380	44,037	12,145	31,892	3,468	3,431	37	875	832	43		9,763	4,269	3,831	1,663
Age unknown	13,672	8,134	1,360	6,774	4,498	4,458	40	1,040	987	53		3,722	346	3,136	240
Percentage distribution of students with known age[1]															
All students	100.0	100.0	100.0	100.0	100.0	100.0	100.0	100.0	100.0	100.0		100.0	100.0	100.0	100.0
Under 18	7.4	8.6	5.1	13.2	3.4	3.5	1.4	0.5	0.5	0.6		#	#	#	#
18 and 19	26.5	26.9	29.4	23.7	30.6	30.9	14.9	7.0	5.6	11.8		#	#	#	#
20 and 21	24.2	23.9	29.4	16.8	30.2	30.5	11.2	9.6	8.3	14.2		1.2	1.4	1.3	0.2
22 to 24	15.2	15.8	17.5	13.5	12.9	12.9	14.6	13.8	12.7	17.7		22.1	24.6	22.6	5.0
25 to 29	10.3	10.2	8.5	12.4	7.5	7.3	20.0	21.9	22.0	21.5		32.1	33.7	32.9	18.2
30 to 34	5.7	5.2	3.8	6.9	4.8	4.7	12.5	16.3	17.3	12.7		15.8	16.1	15.2	17.6
35 to 39	3.8	3.3	2.3	4.6	3.7	3.6	8.7	11.8	12.8	8.4		9.9	9.2	9.4	16.5
40 to 49	4.3	3.7	2.5	5.3	4.6	4.5	10.7	13.3	14.5	9.0		12.1	10.0	11.7	25.7
50 to 64	2.2	2.0	1.2	3.0	2.2	2.2	5.6	5.6	6.1	4.0		6.3	4.5	6.4	15.6
65 and over	0.3	0.4	0.2	0.6	0.2	0.2	0.4	0.2	0.2	0.2		0.5	0.3	0.4	1.1
Full-time	100.0	100.0	100.0	100.0	100.0	100.0	100.0	100.0	100.0	100.0		100.0	100.0	100.0	100.0
Under 18	2.1	2.5	1.9	4.0	1.4	1.5	0.6	0.4	0.3	0.6		#	#	#	#
18 and 19	35.7	37.5	36.1	41.2	36.2	36.5	16.6	9.5	8.2	12.5		#	#	#	#
20 and 21	31.2	31.4	35.0	21.5	35.4	35.9	11.5	11.9	10.7	14.5		1.9	2.2	1.9	0.3
22 to 24	14.8	15.5	16.8	11.7	12.8	12.8	14.2	15.0	13.8	17.7		31.1	35.2	30.3	7.0
25 to 29	7.4	6.9	5.8	9.7	5.4	5.2	19.8	21.9	22.1	21.3		35.9	37.3	36.6	20.5
30 to 34	3.5	2.8	2.0	4.8	3.0	2.9	12.4	15.2	16.4	12.4		13.5	13.2	13.2	17.3
35 to 39	2.1	1.5	1.0	2.8	2.1	2.0	8.5	10.5	11.5	8.2		6.9	5.7	6.8	16.0
40 to 49	2.2	1.5	0.9	2.9	2.5	2.3	10.5	11.2	12.2	8.8		7.1	4.6	7.4	23.8
50 to 64	0.9	0.6	0.3	1.3	1.0	1.0	5.5	4.3	4.6	3.7		3.3	1.7	3.6	14.0
65 and over	#	#	#	0.1	#	#	0.4	0.2	0.2	0.2		0.2	0.1	0.2	1.0
Part-time	100.0	100.0	100.0	100.0	100.0	100.0	100.0	100.0	100.0	100.0		100.0	100.0	100.0	100.0
Under 18	15.9	16.9	14.5	18.2	12.3	12.4	5.4	0.9	0.9	0.1		#	#	#	#
18 and 19	11.7	12.8	10.0	14.2	5.8	5.8	5.1	2.1	1.9	5.1		#	#	#	#
20 and 21	12.9	13.9	13.2	14.3	6.5	6.5	9.8	5.2	4.8	10.6		0.3	0.3	0.3	0.1
22 to 24	15.7	16.1	19.5	14.4	13.4	13.4	16.9	11.5	11.1	17.9		10.2	11.3	10.7	3.5
25 to 29	15.2	14.7	16.4	13.9	16.6	16.5	21.0	21.8	21.7	23.4		27.1	29.3	27.2	16.4
30 to 34	9.2	8.3	9.0	8.0	12.7	12.7	13.4	18.5	18.7	14.9		19.0	19.7	18.3	17.7
35 to 39	6.5	5.7	6.1	5.5	10.5	10.5	9.7	14.4	14.7	9.8		14.0	13.7	13.6	17.0
40 to 49	7.8	6.8	7.0	6.6	13.9	14.0	11.7	17.3	17.7	11.3		18.6	16.8	18.4	27.2
50 to 64	4.4	3.9	3.7	4.0	7.5	7.5	6.5	8.2	8.3	6.6		10.1	8.2	10.7	16.9
65 and over	0.8	0.8	0.6	0.9	0.7	0.7	0.5	0.3	0.3	0.2		0.8	0.7	0.8	1.1

#Rounds to zero.
[1]Percentage distributions exclude students whose age is unknown.
NOTE: Degree-granting institutions grant associate's or higher degrees and participate in Title IV federal financial aid programs. Detail may not sum to totals because of rounding. Some data have been revised from previously published figures.

SOURCE: U.S. Department of Education, National Center for Education Statistics, Integrated Postsecondary Education Data System (IPEDS), Spring 2018, Fall Enrollment component. (This table was prepared September 2019.)

Table 303.55. Total fall enrollment in degree-granting postsecondary institutions, by control and level of institution, attendance status, and age of student: 2017

Attendance status and age of student	All institutions			Public institutions			Private (nonprofit and for-profit) institutions						
								Nonprofit institutions			For-profit institutions		
	Total	4-year	2-year	Total	4-year	2-year	Total	Total	4-year	2-year	Total	4-year	2-year
1	2	3	4	5	6	7	8	9	10	11	12	13	14
All students	19,778,151	13,825,380	5,952,771	14,571,739	8,854,279	5,717,460	5,206,412	4,108,489	4,060,094	48,395	1,097,923	911,007	186,916
Under 18	1,233,155	478,596	754,559	1,132,082	379,292	752,790	101,073	96,502	95,845	657	4,571	3,459	1,112
18 and 19	4,446,105	3,063,168	1,382,937	3,527,244	2,173,376	1,353,868	918,861	860,278	853,098	7,180	58,583	36,694	21,889
20 and 21	4,096,336	3,103,761	992,575	3,151,953	2,191,187	960,766	944,383	863,484	858,052	5,432	80,899	54,522	26,377
22 to 24	3,204,527	2,395,139	809,388	2,422,058	1,652,689	769,369	782,469	653,706	646,661	7,045	128,763	95,789	32,974
25 to 29	2,694,183	1,935,680	758,503	1,831,708	1,122,880	708,828	862,475	632,517	622,850	9,667	229,958	189,950	40,008
30 to 34	1,421,657	1,000,273	421,384	909,688	517,889	391,799	511,969	330,256	324,211	6,045	181,713	158,173	23,540
35 to 39	933,343	653,774	279,569	567,216	307,444	259,772	366,127	224,445	220,254	4,191	141,682	126,076	15,606
40 to 49	1,090,103	766,238	323,865	633,801	331,889	301,912	456,302	279,247	274,101	5,146	177,055	160,248	16,807
50 to 64	560,173	376,179	183,994	328,762	154,900	173,862	231,411	144,312	141,584	2,728	87,099	79,695	7,404
65 and over	67,094	32,390	34,704	52,324	18,181	34,143	14,770	10,155	9,940	215	4,615	4,269	346
Age unknown	31,475	20,182	11,293	14,903	4,552	10,351	16,572	13,587	13,498	89	2,985	2,132	853
Full-time	12,076,141	9,848,817	2,227,324	8,326,474	6,309,569	2,016,905	3,749,667	3,082,071	3,040,980	41,091	667,596	498,268	169,328
Under 18	220,590	137,835	82,755	185,328	103,924	81,404	35,262	33,122	32,858	264	2,140	1,053	1,087
18 and 19	3,695,990	2,838,977	857,013	2,813,009	1,983,811	829,198	882,981	830,370	823,558	6,812	52,611	31,608	21,003
20 and 21	3,267,198	2,804,616	462,582	2,372,769	1,939,420	433,349	894,429	828,372	823,649	4,723	66,057	41,547	24,510
22 to 24	2,068,425	1,796,441	271,984	1,446,810	1,210,477	236,333	621,615	530,615	524,801	5,814	91,000	61,163	29,837
25 to 29	1,372,010	1,133,343	238,667	817,711	623,088	194,623	554,299	410,131	401,992	8,139	144,168	108,263	35,905
30 to 34	591,317	469,585	121,732	315,152	219,419	95,733	276,165	172,591	167,522	5,069	103,574	82,644	20,930
35 to 39	338,499	264,071	74,428	160,350	103,307	57,043	178,149	101,936	98,446	3,490	76,213	62,318	13,895
40 to 49	350,409	273,322	77,087	147,368	89,397	57,971	203,041	114,458	110,162	4,296	88,583	73,763	14,820
50 to 64	148,671	114,753	33,918	57,536	32,113	25,423	91,135	51,667	49,410	2,257	39,468	33,230	6,238
65 and over	8,951	6,219	2,732	4,018	1,767	2,251	4,933	2,856	2,678	178	2,077	1,774	303
Age unknown	14,081	9,655	4,426	6,423	2,846	3,577	7,658	5,953	5,904	49	1,705	905	800
Part-time	7,702,010	3,976,563	3,725,447	6,245,265	2,544,710	3,700,555	1,456,745	1,026,418	1,019,114	7,304	430,327	412,739	17,588
Under 18	1,012,565	340,761	671,804	946,754	275,368	671,386	65,811	63,380	62,987	393	2,431	2,406	25
18 and 19	750,115	224,191	525,924	714,235	189,565	524,670	35,880	29,908	29,540	368	5,972	5,086	886
20 and 21	829,138	299,145	529,993	779,184	251,767	527,417	49,954	35,112	34,403	709	14,842	12,975	1,867
22 to 24	1,136,102	598,698	537,404	975,248	442,212	533,036	160,854	123,091	121,860	1,231	37,763	34,626	3,137
25 to 29	1,322,173	802,337	519,836	1,013,997	499,792	514,205	308,176	222,386	220,858	1,528	85,790	81,687	4,103
30 to 34	830,340	530,688	299,652	594,536	298,470	296,066	235,804	157,665	156,689	976	78,139	75,529	2,610
35 to 39	594,844	389,703	205,141	406,866	204,137	202,729	187,978	122,509	121,808	701	65,469	63,758	1,711
40 to 49	739,694	492,916	246,778	486,433	242,492	243,941	253,261	164,789	163,939	850	88,472	86,485	1,987
50 to 64	411,502	261,426	150,076	271,226	122,787	148,439	140,276	92,645	92,174	471	47,631	46,465	1,166
65 and over	58,143	26,171	31,972	48,306	16,414	31,892	9,837	7,299	7,262	37	2,538	2,495	43
Age unknown	17,394	10,527	6,867	8,480	1,706	6,774	8,914	7,634	7,594	40	1,280	1,227	53
	Percentage distribution of students with known age[1]												
All students	100.0	100.0	100.0	100.0	100.0	100.0	100.0	100.0	100.0	100.0	100.0	100.0	100.0
Under 18	6.2	3.5	12.7	7.8	4.3	13.2	1.9	2.4	2.4	1.4	0.4	0.4	0.6
18 and 19	22.5	22.2	23.3	24.2	24.6	23.7	17.7	21.0	21.1	14.9	5.4	4.0	11.8
20 and 21	20.7	22.5	16.7	21.7	24.8	16.8	18.2	21.1	21.2	11.2	7.4	6.0	14.2
22 to 24	16.2	17.3	13.6	16.6	18.7	13.5	15.1	16.0	16.0	14.6	11.8	10.5	17.7
25 to 29	13.6	14.0	12.8	12.6	12.7	12.4	16.6	15.4	15.4	20.0	21.0	20.9	21.5
30 to 34	7.2	7.2	7.1	6.2	5.9	6.9	9.9	8.1	8.0	12.5	16.6	17.4	12.7
35 to 39	4.7	4.7	4.7	3.9	3.5	4.6	7.1	5.5	5.4	8.7	12.9	13.9	8.4
40 to 49	5.5	5.6	5.5	4.4	3.8	5.3	8.8	6.8	6.8	10.7	16.2	17.6	9.0
50 to 64	2.8	2.7	3.1	2.3	1.8	3.0	4.5	3.5	3.5	5.6	8.0	8.8	4.0
65 and over	0.3	0.2	0.6	0.4	0.2	0.6	0.3	0.2	0.2	0.4	0.4	0.5	0.2
Full-time	100.0	100.0	100.0	100.0	100.0	100.0	100.0	100.0	100.0	100.0	100.0	100.0	100.0
Under 18	1.8	1.4	3.7	2.2	1.6	4.0	0.9	1.1	1.1	0.6	0.3	0.2	0.6
18 and 19	30.6	28.9	38.6	33.8	31.5	41.2	23.6	27.0	27.1	16.6	7.9	6.4	12.5
20 and 21	27.1	28.5	20.8	28.5	30.8	21.5	23.9	26.9	27.1	11.5	9.9	8.4	14.5
22 to 24	17.1	18.3	12.2	17.4	19.2	11.7	16.6	17.2	17.3	14.2	13.7	12.3	17.7
25 to 29	11.4	11.5	10.7	9.8	9.9	9.7	14.8	13.3	13.2	19.8	21.7	21.8	21.3
30 to 34	4.9	4.8	5.5	3.8	3.5	4.8	7.4	5.6	5.5	12.4	15.6	16.6	12.4
35 to 39	2.8	2.7	3.3	1.9	1.6	2.8	4.8	3.3	3.2	8.5	11.4	12.5	8.2
40 to 49	2.9	2.8	3.5	1.8	1.4	2.9	5.4	3.7	3.6	10.5	13.3	14.8	8.8
50 to 64	1.2	1.2	1.5	0.7	0.5	1.3	2.4	1.7	1.6	5.5	5.9	6.7	3.7
65 and over	0.1	0.1	0.1	#	#	0.1	0.1	0.1	0.1	0.4	0.3	0.4	0.2
Part-time	100.0	100.0	100.0	100.0	100.0	100.0	100.0	100.0	100.0	100.0	100.0	100.0	100.0
Under 18	13.2	8.6	18.1	15.2	10.8	18.2	4.5	6.2	6.2	5.4	0.6	0.6	0.1
18 and 19	9.8	5.7	14.1	11.5	7.5	14.2	2.5	2.9	2.9	5.1	1.4	1.2	5.1
20 and 21	10.8	7.5	14.3	12.5	9.9	14.3	3.5	3.4	3.4	9.8	3.5	3.2	10.6
22 to 24	14.8	15.1	14.5	15.6	17.4	14.4	11.1	12.1	12.0	16.9	8.8	8.4	17.9
25 to 29	17.2	20.2	14.0	16.3	19.7	13.9	21.3	21.8	21.8	21.0	20.0	19.9	23.4
30 to 34	10.8	13.4	8.1	9.5	11.7	8.0	16.3	15.5	15.5	13.4	18.2	18.4	14.9
35 to 39	7.7	9.8	5.5	6.5	8.0	5.5	13.0	12.0	12.0	9.7	15.3	15.5	9.8
40 to 49	9.6	12.4	6.6	7.8	9.5	6.6	17.5	16.2	16.2	11.7	20.6	21.0	11.3
50 to 64	5.4	6.6	4.0	4.3	4.8	4.0	9.7	9.1	9.1	6.5	11.1	11.3	6.6
65 and over	0.8	0.7	0.9	0.8	0.6	0.9	0.7	0.7	0.7	0.5	0.6	0.6	0.2

#Rounds to zero.
[1]Percentage distributions exclude students whose age is unknown.
NOTE: Degree-granting institutions grant associate's or higher degrees and participate in Title IV federal financial aid programs. Detail may not sum to totals because of rounding. Some data have been revised from previously published figures.

SOURCE: U.S. Department of Education, National Center for Education Statistics, Integrated Postsecondary Education Data System (IPEDS), Spring 2018, Fall Enrollment component. (This table was prepared September 2019.)

Table 303.60. Total fall enrollment in degree-granting postsecondary institutions, by level of enrollment, sex of student, level and control of institution, and attendance status of student: 2018

Level and control of institution and attendance status of student	Total			Undergraduate			Postbaccalaureate		
	Total	Males	Females	Total	Males	Females	Total	Males	Females
1	2	3	4	5	6	7	8	9	10
Total	**19,645,918**	**8,442,662**	**11,203,256**	**16,610,235**	**7,225,999**	**9,384,236**	**3,035,683**	**1,216,663**	**1,819,020**
Full-time	11,991,721	5,338,934	6,652,787	10,267,135	4,602,752	5,664,383	1,724,586	736,182	988,404
Part-time	7,654,197	3,103,728	4,550,469	6,343,100	2,623,247	3,719,853	1,311,097	480,481	830,616
4-year	**13,900,710**	**5,990,993**	**7,909,717**	**10,865,027**	**4,774,330**	**6,090,697**	**3,035,683**	**1,216,663**	**1,819,020**
Full-time	9,880,953	4,385,208	5,495,745	8,156,367	3,649,026	4,507,341	1,724,586	736,182	988,404
Part-time	4,019,757	1,605,785	2,413,972	2,708,660	1,125,304	1,583,356	1,311,097	480,481	830,616
2-year	**5,745,208**	**2,451,669**	**3,293,539**	**5,745,208**	**2,451,669**	**3,293,539**	†	†	†
Full-time	2,110,768	953,726	1,157,042	2,110,768	953,726	1,157,042	†	†	†
Part-time	3,634,440	1,497,943	2,136,497	3,634,440	1,497,943	2,136,497	†	†	†
Public	**14,529,264**	**6,391,471**	**8,137,793**	**13,049,326**	**5,774,848**	**7,274,478**	**1,479,938**	**616,623**	**863,315**
Full-time	8,268,820	3,787,941	4,480,879	7,451,638	3,427,581	4,024,057	817,182	360,360	456,822
Part-time	6,260,444	2,603,530	3,656,914	5,597,688	2,347,267	3,250,421	662,756	256,263	406,493
Public 4-year	8,982,560	4,005,748	4,976,812	7,502,622	3,389,125	4,113,497	1,479,938	616,623	863,315
Full-time	6,336,978	2,895,088	3,441,890	5,519,796	2,534,728	2,985,068	817,182	360,360	456,822
Part-time	2,645,582	1,110,660	1,534,922	1,982,826	854,397	1,128,429	662,756	256,263	406,493
Public 2-year	5,546,704	2,385,723	3,160,981	5,546,704	2,385,723	3,160,981	†	†	†
Full-time	1,931,842	892,853	1,038,989	1,931,842	892,853	1,038,989	†	†	†
Part-time	3,614,862	1,492,870	2,121,992	3,614,862	1,492,870	2,121,992	†	†	†
Private	**5,116,654**	**2,051,191**	**3,065,463**	**3,560,909**	**1,451,151**	**2,109,758**	**1,555,745**	**600,040**	**955,705**
Full-time	3,722,901	1,550,993	2,171,908	2,815,497	1,175,171	1,640,326	907,404	375,822	531,582
Part-time	1,393,753	500,198	893,555	745,412	275,980	469,432	648,341	224,218	424,123
Private 4-year	4,918,150	1,985,245	2,932,905	3,362,405	1,385,205	1,977,200	1,555,745	600,040	955,705
Full-time	3,543,975	1,490,120	2,053,855	2,636,571	1,114,298	1,522,273	907,404	375,822	531,582
Part-time	1,374,175	495,125	879,050	725,834	270,907	454,927	648,341	224,218	424,123
Private 2-year	198,504	65,946	132,558	198,504	65,946	132,558	†	†	†
Full-time	178,926	60,873	118,053	178,926	60,873	118,053	†	†	†
Part-time	19,578	5,073	14,505	19,578	5,073	14,505	†	†	†
Nonprofit	4,134,244	1,722,517	2,411,727	2,821,653	1,191,128	1,630,525	1,312,591	531,389	781,202
Full-time	3,126,130	1,337,841	1,788,289	2,321,433	995,083	1,326,350	804,697	342,758	461,939
Part-time	1,008,114	384,676	623,438	500,220	196,045	304,175	507,894	188,631	319,263
Nonprofit 4-year	4,089,090	1,711,257	2,377,833	2,776,499	1,179,868	1,596,631	1,312,591	531,389	781,202
Full-time	3,088,150	1,328,444	1,759,706	2,283,453	985,686	1,297,767	804,697	342,758	461,939
Part-time	1,000,940	382,813	618,127	493,046	194,182	298,864	507,894	188,631	319,263
Nonprofit 2-year	45,154	11,260	33,894	45,154	11,260	33,894	†	†	†
Full-time	37,980	9,397	28,583	37,980	9,397	28,583	†	†	†
Part-time	7,174	1,863	5,311	7,174	1,863	5,311	†	†	†
For-profit	982,410	328,674	653,736	739,256	260,023	479,233	243,154	68,651	174,503
Full-time	596,771	213,152	383,619	494,064	180,088	313,976	102,707	33,064	69,643
Part-time	385,639	115,522	270,117	245,192	79,935	165,257	140,447	35,587	104,860
For-profit 4-year	829,060	273,988	555,072	585,906	205,337	380,569	243,154	68,651	174,503
Full-time	455,825	161,676	294,149	353,118	128,612	224,506	102,707	33,064	69,643
Part-time	373,235	112,312	260,923	232,788	76,725	156,063	140,447	35,587	104,860
For-profit 2-year	153,350	54,686	98,664	153,350	54,686	98,664	†	†	†
Full-time	140,946	51,476	89,470	140,946	51,476	89,470	†	†	†
Part-time	12,404	3,210	9,194	12,404	3,210	9,194	†	†	†

†Not applicable.
NOTE: Degree-granting institutions grant associate's or higher degrees and participate in Title IV federal financial aid programs.

SOURCE: U.S. Department of Education, National Center for Education Statistics, Integrated Postsecondary Education Data System (IPEDS), Spring 2019, Fall Enrollment component. (This table was prepared September 2019.)

Table 303.70. Total undergraduate fall enrollment in degree-granting postsecondary institutions, by attendance status, sex of student, and control and level of institution: Selected years, 1970 through 2029

Level and year	Total	Full-time	Part-time	Males	Females	Males		Females		Public	Private		
						Full-time	Part-time	Full-time	Part-time		Total	Nonprofit	For-profit
1	2	3	4	5	6	7	8	9	10	11	12	13	14
Total, all levels													
1970	7,368,644	5,280,064	2,088,580	4,249,702	3,118,942	3,096,371	1,153,331	2,183,693	935,249	5,620,255	1,748,389	1,730,133	18,256
1975	9,679,455	6,168,396	3,511,059	5,257,005	4,422,450	3,459,328	1,797,677	2,709,068	1,713,382	7,826,032	1,853,423	1,814,844	38,579
1980	10,475,055	6,361,744	4,113,311	5,000,177	5,474,878	3,226,857	1,773,320	3,134,887	2,339,991	8,441,955	2,033,100	1,926,703	106,397
1985	10,596,674	6,319,592	4,277,082	4,962,080	5,634,594	3,156,446	1,805,634	3,163,146	2,471,448	8,477,125	2,119,549	1,928,996	190,553
1986	10,797,975	6,352,073	4,445,902	5,017,505	5,780,470	3,146,330	1,871,175	3,205,743	2,574,727	8,660,716	2,137,259	1,928,294	208,965
1987	11,046,235	6,462,549	4,583,686	5,068,457	5,977,778	3,163,676	1,904,781	3,298,873	2,678,905	8,918,589	2,127,646	1,939,942	187,704
1988	11,316,548	6,642,428	4,674,120	5,137,644	6,178,904	3,206,442	1,931,202	3,435,986	2,742,918	9,103,146	2,213,402	—	—
1989	11,742,531	6,840,696	4,901,835	5,310,990	6,431,541	3,278,647	2,032,343	3,562,049	2,869,492	9,487,742	2,254,789	—	—
1990	11,959,106	6,976,030	4,983,076	5,379,759	6,579,347	3,336,535	2,043,224	3,639,495	2,939,852	9,709,596	2,249,510	2,043,407	206,103
1991	12,439,287	7,221,412	5,217,875	5,571,003	6,868,284	3,435,526	2,135,477	3,785,886	3,082,398	10,147,957	2,291,330	2,072,354	218,976
1992	12,537,700	7,244,442	5,293,258	5,582,936	6,954,764	3,424,739	2,158,197	3,819,703	3,135,061	10,216,297	2,321,403	2,101,721	219,682
1993	12,323,959	7,179,482	5,144,477	5,483,682	6,840,277	3,381,997	2,101,685	3,797,485	3,042,792	10,011,787	2,312,172	2,099,197	212,975
1994	12,262,608	7,168,706	5,093,902	5,422,113	6,840,495	3,341,591	2,080,522	3,827,115	3,013,380	9,945,128	2,317,480	2,100,465	217,015
1995	12,231,719	7,145,268	5,086,451	5,401,130	6,830,589	3,296,610	2,104,520	3,848,658	2,981,931	9,903,626	2,328,093	2,104,693	223,400
1996	12,326,948	7,298,839	5,028,109	5,420,672	6,906,276	3,339,108	2,081,564	3,959,731	2,946,545	9,935,283	2,391,665	2,112,318	279,347
1997	12,450,587	7,418,598	5,031,989	5,468,532	6,982,055	3,379,597	2,088,935	4,039,001	2,943,054	10,007,479	2,443,108	2,139,824	303,284
1998	12,436,937	7,538,711	4,898,226	5,446,133	6,990,804	3,428,161	2,017,972	4,110,550	2,880,254	9,950,212	2,486,725	2,152,655	334,070
1999	12,739,445	7,753,548	4,985,897	5,584,234	7,155,211	3,524,586	2,059,648	4,228,962	2,926,249	10,174,228	2,565,217	2,185,290	379,927
2000	13,155,393	7,922,926	5,232,467	5,778,268	7,377,125	3,588,246	2,190,022	4,334,680	3,042,445	10,539,322	2,616,071	2,213,180	402,891
2001	13,715,610	8,327,640	5,387,970	6,004,431	7,711,179	3,768,630	2,235,801	4,559,010	3,152,169	10,985,871	2,729,739	2,257,718	472,021
2002	14,257,077	8,734,252	5,522,825	6,192,390	8,064,687	3,934,168	2,258,222	4,800,084	3,264,603	11,432,855	2,824,222	2,306,091	518,131
2003	14,480,364	9,045,253	5,435,111	6,227,372	8,252,992	4,048,682	2,178,690	4,996,571	3,256,421	11,523,103	2,957,261	2,346,673	610,588
2004	14,780,630	9,284,336	5,496,294	6,340,048	8,440,582	4,140,628	2,199,420	5,143,708	3,296,874	11,650,580	3,130,050	2,389,366	740,684
2005	14,963,964	9,446,430	5,517,534	6,408,871	8,555,093	4,200,863	2,208,008	5,245,567	3,309,526	11,697,730	3,266,234	2,418,368	847,866
2006	15,179,591	9,571,349	5,608,242	6,511,198	8,668,393	4,264,722	2,246,476	5,306,627	3,361,766	11,842,625	3,336,966	2,448,250	888,716
2007	15,613,540	9,841,973	5,771,567	6,731,561	8,881,979	4,397,402	2,334,159	5,444,571	3,437,408	12,147,744	3,465,796	2,470,463	995,333
2008	16,344,592	10,244,174	6,100,418	7,055,640	9,288,952	4,570,913	2,484,727	5,673,261	3,615,691	12,589,947	3,754,645	2,535,789	1,218,856
2009	17,464,179	11,038,275	6,425,904	7,563,176	9,901,003	4,942,120	2,621,056	6,096,155	3,804,848	13,386,375	4,077,804	2,595,171	1,482,633
2010	18,082,427	11,457,040	6,625,387	7,836,282	10,246,145	5,118,975	2,717,307	6,338,065	3,908,080	13,703,000	4,379,427	2,652,993	1,726,434
2011	18,077,303	11,365,175	6,712,128	7,822,992	10,254,311	5,070,553	2,752,439	6,294,622	3,959,689	13,694,899	4,382,404	2,718,923	1,663,481
2012	17,735,638	11,097,092	6,638,546	7,714,938	10,020,700	4,984,389	2,730,549	6,112,703	3,907,997	13,478,100	4,257,538	2,744,400	1,513,138
2013	17,476,304	10,939,276	6,537,028	7,660,140	9,816,164	4,950,210	2,709,930	5,989,066	3,827,098	13,348,292	4,128,012	2,755,463	1,372,549
2014	17,294,136	10,784,392	6,509,744	7,586,299	9,707,837	4,877,531	2,708,768	5,906,861	3,800,976	13,244,533	4,049,603	2,772,065	1,277,538
2015	17,046,673	10,603,030	6,443,643	7,502,254	9,544,419	4,809,098	2,693,156	5,793,932	3,750,487	13,150,823	3,895,850	2,822,122	1,073,728
2016	16,874,649	10,430,068	6,444,581	7,416,859	9,457,790	4,725,510	2,691,349	5,704,558	3,753,232	13,143,979	3,730,670	2,813,742	916,928
2017	16,773,036	10,371,863	6,401,173	7,351,259	9,421,777	4,683,715	2,667,544	5,688,148	3,733,629	13,112,594	3,660,442	2,819,080	841,362
2018	16,610,235	10,267,135	6,343,100	7,225,999	9,384,236	4,602,752	2,623,247	5,664,383	3,719,853	13,049,326	3,560,909	2,821,653	739,256
2019[1]	16,673,000	10,296,000	6,377,000	7,250,000	9,423,000	4,612,000	2,638,000	5,684,000	3,739,000	13,100,000	3,573,000	—	—
2020[1]	16,692,000	10,293,000	6,399,000	7,254,000	9,438,000	4,608,000	2,646,000	5,685,000	3,753,000	13,118,000	3,575,000	—	—
2021[1]	16,721,000	10,292,000	6,428,000	7,263,000	9,457,000	4,606,000	2,657,000	5,686,000	3,771,000	13,142,000	3,578,000	—	—
2022[1]	16,750,000	10,297,000	6,452,000	7,273,000	9,477,000	4,606,000	2,667,000	5,692,000	3,785,000	13,167,000	3,582,000	—	—
2023[1]	16,790,000	10,312,000	6,478,000	7,288,000	9,503,000	4,610,000	2,678,000	5,703,000	3,800,000	13,201,000	3,590,000	—	—
2024[1]	16,845,000	10,341,000	6,504,000	7,312,000	9,533,000	4,622,000	2,690,000	5,718,000	3,814,000	13,244,000	3,600,000	—	—
2025[1]	16,901,000	10,377,000	6,524,000	7,338,000	9,564,000	4,639,000	2,699,000	5,738,000	3,826,000	13,289,000	3,613,000	—	—
2026[1]	16,967,000	10,415,000	6,551,000	7,367,000	9,600,000	4,656,000	2,711,000	5,760,000	3,841,000	13,340,000	3,626,000	—	—
2027[1]	16,991,000	10,419,000	6,572,000	7,378,000	9,613,000	4,658,000	2,720,000	5,761,000	3,851,000	13,361,000	3,630,000	—	—
2028[1]	16,999,000	10,410,000	6,589,000	7,383,000	9,616,000	4,656,000	2,727,000	5,755,000	3,862,000	13,370,000	3,629,000	—	—
2029[1]	17,003,000	10,397,000	6,606,000	7,385,000	9,618,000	4,651,000	2,734,000	5,746,000	3,872,000	13,375,000	3,628,000	—	—
2-year institutions[2]													
1970	2,318,956	1,228,909	1,090,047	1,374,426	944,530	771,298	603,128	457,611	486,919	2,194,983	123,973	113,299	10,674
1975	3,965,726	1,761,009	2,204,717	2,163,604	1,802,122	1,035,531	1,128,073	725,478	1,076,644	3,831,973	133,753	112,997	20,756
1980	4,525,097	1,753,637	2,771,460	2,046,642	2,478,455	879,619	1,167,023	874,018	1,604,437	4,327,592	197,505	114,094	83,411
1985	4,531,077	1,690,607	2,840,470	2,002,234	2,528,843	826,308	1,175,926	864,299	1,664,544	4,269,733	261,344	108,791	152,553
1986	4,679,548	1,696,261	2,983,287	2,060,932	2,618,616	824,551	1,236,381	871,710	1,746,906	4,413,691	265,857	101,498	164,359
1987	4,776,222	1,708,669	3,067,553	2,072,823	2,703,399	820,167	1,252,656	888,502	1,814,897	4,541,054	235,168	90,102	145,066
1988	4,875,155	1,743,592	3,131,563	2,089,689	2,785,466	818,593	1,271,096	924,999	1,860,467	4,615,487	259,668	—	—
1989	5,150,889	1,855,701	3,295,188	2,216,800	2,934,089	869,688	1,347,112	986,013	1,948,076	4,883,660	267,229	—	—
1990	5,240,083	1,883,962	3,356,121	2,232,769	3,007,314	881,392	1,351,377	1,002,570	2,004,744	4,996,475	243,608	89,158	154,450
1991	5,651,900	2,074,530	3,577,370	2,401,910	3,249,990	961,397	1,440,513	1,113,133	2,136,857	5,404,815	247,085	89,289	157,796
1992	5,722,349	2,080,005	3,642,344	2,413,266	3,309,083	951,816	1,461,450	1,128,189	2,180,894	5,484,514	237,835	83,288	154,547
1993	5,565,561	2,043,319	3,522,242	2,345,396	3,220,165	928,216	1,417,180	1,115,103	2,105,062	5,337,022	228,539	86,357	142,182
1994	5,529,609	2,031,713	3,497,896	2,323,161	3,206,448	911,589	1,411,572	1,120,124	2,086,324	5,308,366	221,243	85,607	135,636
1995	5,492,098	1,977,046	3,515,052	2,328,500	3,163,598	878,215	1,450,285	1,098,831	2,064,767	5,277,398	214,700	75,154	139,546
1996	5,562,780	2,072,215	3,490,565	2,358,792	3,203,988	916,452	1,442,340	1,155,763	2,048,225	5,314,038	248,742	75,253	173,489
1997	5,605,569	2,095,171	3,510,398	2,389,711	3,215,858	931,394	1,458,317	1,163,777	2,052,081	5,360,686	244,883	71,794	173,089
1998	5,489,314	2,085,906	3,403,408	2,333,334	3,155,980	936,421	1,396,913	1,149,485	2,006,495	5,245,963	243,351	65,870	177,481
1999	5,653,256	2,167,242	3,486,014	2,413,322	3,239,934	979,203	1,434,119	1,188,039	2,051,895	5,397,786	255,470	63,301	192,169
2000	5,948,104	2,217,044	3,731,060	2,558,520	3,389,584	995,839	1,562,681	1,221,205	2,168,379	5,697,061	251,043	58,844	192,199
2001	6,250,529	2,374,490	3,876,039	2,675,193	3,575,336	1,066,281	1,608,912	1,308,209	2,267,127	5,996,651	253,878	47,549	206,329
2002	6,529,198	2,556,032	3,973,166	2,753,405	3,775,793	1,135,669	1,617,736	1,420,363	2,355,430	6,270,199	258,999	47,087	211,912
2003	6,493,862	2,650,337	3,843,525	2,689,928	3,803,934	1,162,555	1,527,373	1,487,782	2,316,152	6,208,885	284,977	43,868	241,109
2004	6,545,570	2,683,489	3,862,081	2,697,507	3,848,063	1,166,554	1,530,953	1,516,935	2,331,128	6,243,344	302,226	42,250	259,976
2005	6,487,826	2,646,763	3,841,063	2,680,299	3,807,527	1,153,759	1,526,540	1,493,004	2,314,523	6,184,000	303,826	43,522	260,304
2006	6,513,303	2,643,162	3,870,141	2,701,970	3,811,333	1,159,733	1,542,237	1,483,429	2,327,904	6,219,880	293,423	39,156	254,267
2007	6,628,936	2,694,608	3,934,328	2,775,166	3,853,770	1,191,058	1,584,108	1,503,550	2,350,220	6,335,826	293,110	33,492	259,618
2008	6,970,947	2,832,412	4,138,535	2,935,799	4,035,148	1,250,063	1,685,736	1,582,349	2,452,799	6,639,928	331,019	35,358	295,661
2009	7,522,581	3,243,952	4,278,629	3,197,338	4,325,243	1,446,372	1,750,966	1,797,580	2,527,663	7,101,569	421,012	34,772	386,240

See notes at end of table.

Table 303.70. Total undergraduate fall enrollment in degree-granting postsecondary institutions, by attendance status, sex of student, and control and level of institution: Selected years, 1970 through 2029—Continued

Level and year	Total	Full-time	Part-time	Males	Females	Males		Females		Public	Private		
						Full-time	Part-time	Full-time	Part-time		Total	Nonprofit	For-profit
1	2	3	4	5	6	7	8	9	10	11	12	13	14
2010	7,683,597	3,365,379	4,318,218	3,265,885	4,417,712	1,483,230	1,782,655	1,882,149	2,535,563	7,218,063	465,534	32,683	432,851
2011	7,511,150	3,170,207	4,340,943	3,175,803	4,335,347	1,391,183	1,784,620	1,779,024	2,556,323	7,068,158	442,992	39,855	403,137
2012	7,167,840	2,941,797	4,226,043	3,046,093	4,121,747	1,305,657	1,740,436	1,636,140	2,485,607	6,792,065	375,775	37,698	338,077
2013	6,970,644	2,836,274	4,134,370	2,998,440	3,972,204	1,279,794	1,718,646	1,556,480	2,415,724	6,626,411	344,233	32,191	312,042
2014	6,714,678	2,661,107	4,053,571	2,894,020	3,820,658	1,200,648	1,693,372	1,460,459	2,360,199	6,397,552	317,126	30,376	286,750
2015	6,499,461	2,510,684	3,988,777	2,818,075	3,681,386	1,143,704	1,674,371	1,366,980	2,314,406	6,224,304	275,157	50,009	225,148
2016	6,092,418	2,309,347	3,783,071	2,637,394	3,455,024	1,057,839	1,579,555	1,251,508	2,203,516	5,842,909	249,509	50,555	198,954
2017	5,952,771	2,227,324	3,725,447	2,566,527	3,386,244	1,013,595	1,552,932	1,213,729	2,172,515	5,717,460	235,311	48,395	186,916
2018	5,745,208	2,110,768	3,634,440	2,451,669	3,293,539	953,726	1,497,943	1,157,042	2,136,497	5,546,704	198,504	45,154	153,350
2019[1]	5,770,000	2,117,000	3,654,000	2,462,000	3,309,000	956,000	1,506,000	1,161,000	2,148,000	5,571,000	199,000	—	—
2020[1]	5,783,000	2,116,000	3,667,000	2,466,000	3,317,000	955,000	1,511,000	1,161,000	2,156,000	5,584,000	199,000	—	—
2021[1]	5,799,000	2,116,000	3,683,000	2,472,000	3,328,000	955,000	1,517,000	1,161,000	2,166,000	5,600,000	199,000	—	—
2022[1]	5,814,000	2,117,000	3,697,000	2,477,000	3,337,000	954,000	1,523,000	1,163,000	2,174,000	5,614,000	199,000	—	—
2023[1]	5,832,000	2,120,000	3,712,000	2,484,000	3,347,000	955,000	1,529,000	1,165,000	2,183,000	5,632,000	200,000	—	—
2024[1]	5,853,000	2,126,000	3,727,000	2,494,000	3,359,000	958,000	1,536,000	1,168,000	2,191,000	5,652,000	200,000	—	—
2025[1]	5,872,000	2,133,000	3,738,000	2,502,000	3,369,000	961,000	1,541,000	1,172,000	2,197,000	5,670,000	201,000	—	—
2026[1]	5,895,000	2,141,000	3,754,000	2,513,000	3,382,000	965,000	1,548,000	1,176,000	2,206,000	5,693,000	202,000	—	—
2027[1]	5,907,000	2,142,000	3,765,000	2,519,000	3,389,000	965,000	1,553,000	1,177,000	2,212,000	5,705,000	202,000	—	—
2028[1]	5,915,000	2,140,000	3,775,000	2,522,000	3,394,000	965,000	1,557,000	1,175,000	2,218,000	5,714,000	202,000	—	—
2029[1]	5,922,000	2,137,000	3,785,000	2,525,000	3,397,000	964,000	1,561,000	1,174,000	2,224,000	5,721,000	202,000	—	—
4-year institutions													
1970	5,049,688	4,051,155	998,533	2,875,276	2,174,412	2,325,073	550,203	1,726,082	448,330	3,425,272	1,624,416	1,616,834	7,582
1975	5,713,729	4,407,387	1,306,342	3,093,401	2,620,328	2,423,797	669,604	1,983,590	636,738	3,994,059	1,719,670	1,701,847	17,823
1980	5,949,958	4,608,107	1,341,851	2,953,535	2,996,423	2,347,238	606,297	2,260,869	735,554	4,114,363	1,835,595	1,812,609	22,986
1985	6,065,597	4,628,985	1,436,612	2,959,846	3,105,751	2,330,138	629,708	2,298,847	806,904	4,207,392	1,858,205	1,820,205	38,000
1986	6,118,427	4,655,812	1,462,615	2,956,573	3,161,854	2,321,779	634,794	2,334,033	827,821	4,247,025	1,871,402	1,826,796	44,606
1987	6,270,013	4,753,880	1,516,133	2,995,634	3,274,379	2,343,509	652,125	2,410,371	864,008	4,377,535	1,892,478	1,849,840	42,638
1988	6,441,393	4,898,836	1,542,557	3,047,955	3,393,438	2,387,849	660,106	2,510,987	882,451	4,487,659	1,953,734	—	—
1989	6,591,642	4,984,995	1,606,647	3,094,190	3,497,452	2,408,959	685,231	2,576,036	921,416	4,604,082	1,987,560	—	—
1990	6,719,023	5,092,068	1,626,955	3,146,990	3,572,033	2,455,143	691,847	2,636,925	935,108	4,713,121	2,005,902	1,954,249	51,653
1991	6,787,387	5,146,882	1,640,505	3,169,093	3,618,294	2,474,129	694,964	2,672,753	945,541	4,743,142	2,044,245	1,983,065	61,180
1992	6,815,351	5,164,437	1,650,914	3,169,670	3,645,681	2,472,923	696,747	2,691,514	954,167	4,731,783	2,083,568	2,018,433	65,135
1993	6,758,398	5,136,163	1,622,235	3,138,286	3,620,112	2,453,781	684,505	2,682,382	937,730	4,674,765	2,083,633	2,012,840	70,793
1994	6,732,999	5,136,993	1,596,006	3,098,952	3,634,047	2,430,002	668,950	2,706,991	927,056	4,636,762	2,096,237	2,014,858	81,379
1995	6,739,621	5,168,222	1,571,399	3,072,630	3,666,991	2,418,395	654,235	2,749,827	917,164	4,626,228	2,113,393	2,029,539	83,854
1996	6,764,168	5,226,624	1,537,544	3,061,880	3,702,288	2,422,656	639,224	2,803,968	898,320	4,621,245	2,142,923	2,037,065	105,858
1997	6,845,018	5,323,427	1,521,591	3,078,821	3,766,197	2,448,203	630,618	2,875,224	890,973	4,646,793	2,198,225	2,068,030	130,195
1998	6,947,623	5,452,805	1,494,818	3,112,799	3,834,824	2,491,740	621,059	2,961,065	873,759	4,704,249	2,243,374	2,086,785	156,589
1999	7,086,189	5,586,306	1,499,883	3,170,912	3,915,277	2,545,383	625,529	3,040,923	874,354	4,776,442	2,309,747	2,121,989	187,758
2000	7,207,289	5,705,882	1,501,407	3,219,748	3,987,541	2,592,407	627,341	3,113,475	874,066	4,842,261	2,365,028	2,154,336	210,692
2001	7,465,081	5,953,150	1,511,931	3,329,238	4,135,843	2,702,349	626,889	3,250,801	885,042	4,989,220	2,475,861	2,210,169	265,692
2002	7,727,879	6,178,220	1,549,659	3,438,985	4,288,894	2,798,499	640,486	3,379,721	909,173	5,162,656	2,565,223	2,259,004	306,219
2003	7,986,502	6,394,916	1,591,586	3,537,444	4,449,058	2,886,127	651,317	3,508,789	940,269	5,314,218	2,672,284	2,302,805	369,479
2004	8,235,060	6,600,847	1,634,213	3,642,541	4,592,519	2,974,074	668,467	3,626,773	965,746	5,407,236	2,827,824	2,347,116	480,708
2005	8,476,138	6,799,667	1,676,471	3,728,572	4,747,566	3,047,104	681,468	3,752,563	995,003	5,513,730	2,962,408	2,374,846	587,562
2006	8,666,288	6,928,187	1,738,101	3,809,228	4,857,060	3,104,989	704,239	3,823,198	1,033,862	5,622,745	3,043,543	2,409,094	634,449
2007	8,984,604	7,147,365	1,837,239	3,956,395	5,028,209	3,206,344	750,051	3,941,021	1,087,188	5,811,918	3,172,686	2,436,971	735,715
2008	9,373,645	7,411,762	1,961,883	4,119,841	5,253,804	3,320,850	798,991	4,090,912	1,162,892	5,950,019	3,423,626	2,500,431	923,195
2009	9,941,598	7,794,323	2,147,275	4,365,838	5,575,760	3,495,748	870,090	4,298,575	1,277,185	6,284,806	3,656,792	2,560,399	1,096,393
2010	10,398,830	8,091,661	2,307,169	4,570,397	5,828,433	3,635,745	934,652	4,455,916	1,372,517	6,484,937	3,913,893	2,620,310	1,293,583
2011	10,566,153	8,194,968	2,371,185	4,647,189	5,918,964	3,679,370	967,819	4,515,598	1,403,366	6,626,741	3,939,412	2,679,068	1,260,344
2012	10,567,798	8,155,295	2,412,503	4,668,845	5,898,953	3,678,732	990,113	4,476,563	1,422,390	6,686,035	3,881,763	2,706,702	1,175,061
2013	10,505,660	8,103,002	2,402,658	4,661,700	5,843,960	3,670,416	991,284	4,432,586	1,411,374	6,721,881	3,783,779	2,723,272	1,060,507
2014	10,579,458	8,123,285	2,456,173	4,692,279	5,887,179	3,676,883	1,015,396	4,446,402	1,440,777	6,846,981	3,732,477	2,741,689	990,788
2015	10,547,212	8,092,346	2,454,866	4,684,179	5,863,033	3,665,394	1,018,785	4,426,952	1,436,081	6,926,519	3,620,693	2,772,113	848,580
2016	10,782,231	8,120,721	2,661,510	4,779,465	6,002,766	3,667,671	1,111,794	4,453,050	1,549,716	7,301,070	3,481,161	2,763,187	717,974
2017	10,820,265	8,144,539	2,675,726	4,784,732	6,035,533	3,670,120	1,114,612	4,474,419	1,561,114	7,395,134	3,425,131	2,770,685	654,446
2018	10,865,027	8,156,367	2,708,660	4,774,330	6,090,697	3,649,026	1,125,304	4,507,341	1,583,356	7,502,622	3,362,405	2,776,499	585,906
2019[1]	10,902,000	8,179,000	2,723,000	4,788,000	6,114,000	3,656,000	1,131,000	4,523,000	1,592,000	7,528,000	3,374,000	—	—
2020[1]	10,910,000	8,177,000	2,733,000	4,788,000	6,121,000	3,653,000	1,135,000	4,524,000	1,598,000	7,534,000	3,376,000	—	—
2021[1]	10,921,000	8,177,000	2,745,000	4,792,000	6,130,000	3,652,000	1,140,000	4,525,000	1,605,000	7,543,000	3,379,000	—	—
2022[1]	10,936,000	8,180,000	2,755,000	4,795,000	6,140,000	3,652,000	1,144,000	4,529,000	1,611,000	7,553,000	3,383,000	—	—
2023[1]	10,958,000	8,192,000	2,766,000	4,803,000	6,155,000	3,654,000	1,149,000	4,538,000	1,617,000	7,569,000	3,390,000	—	—
2024[1]	10,992,000	8,215,000	2,777,000	4,818,000	6,174,000	3,664,000	1,154,000	4,550,000	1,624,000	7,592,000	3,400,000	—	—
2025[1]	11,030,000	8,244,000	2,786,000	4,835,000	6,194,000	3,678,000	1,158,000	4,566,000	1,628,000	7,618,000	3,412,000	—	—
2026[1]	11,072,000	8,274,000	2,798,000	4,854,000	6,218,000	3,691,000	1,163,000	4,583,000	1,635,000	7,647,000	3,425,000	—	—
2027[1]	11,083,000	8,277,000	2,806,000	4,860,000	6,224,000	3,693,000	1,167,000	4,584,000	1,639,000	7,656,000	3,428,000	—	—
2028[1]	11,084,000	8,270,000	2,814,000	4,861,000	6,223,000	3,691,000	1,170,000	4,579,000	1,644,000	7,656,000	3,428,000	—	—
2029[1]	11,080,000	8,260,000	2,821,000	4,860,000	6,220,000	3,687,000	1,173,000	4,572,000	1,648,000	7,654,000	3,426,000	—	—

—Not available.
[1]Projected.
[2]Beginning in 1980, 2-year institutions include schools accredited by the Accrediting Commission of Career Schools and Colleges of Technology.
NOTE: Data through 1995 are for institutions of higher education, while later data are for degree-granting institutions. Degree-granting institutions grant associate's or higher degrees and participate in Title IV federal financial aid programs. The degree-granting classification is very similar to the earlier higher education classification, but it includes more 2-year colleges and excludes a few higher education institutions that did not grant degrees. Some data have been revised from previously published figures.
SOURCE: U.S. Department of Education, National Center for Education Statistics, Higher Education General Information Survey (HEGIS), "Fall Enrollment in Colleges and Universities" surveys, 1970 through 1985; Integrated Postsecondary Education Data System (IPEDS), "Fall Enrollment Survey" (IPEDS-EF:86–99); IPEDS Spring 2001 through Spring 2019, Fall Enrollment component; and Enrollment in Degree-Granting Institutions Projection Model, 2000 through 2029. (This table was prepared December 2019.)

Table 303.80. Total postbaccalaureate fall enrollment in degree-granting postsecondary institutions, by attendance status, sex of student, and control of institution: 1970 through 2029

Year	Total	Full-time	Part-time	Males	Females	Males Full-time	Males Part-time	Females Full-time	Females Part-time	Public	Private Total	Private Nonprofit	Private For-profit
1	2	3	4	5	6	7	8	9	10	11	12	13	14
1970	1,212,243	536,226	676,017	793,940	418,303	407,724	386,216	128,502	289,801	807,879	404,364	404,287	77
1971	1,204,390	564,236	640,154	789,131	415,259	428,167	360,964	136,069	279,190	796,516	407,874	407,804	70
1972	1,272,421	583,299	689,122	810,164	462,257	436,533	373,631	146,766	315,491	848,031	424,390	424,278	112
1973	1,342,452	610,935	731,517	833,453	508,999	444,219	389,234	166,716	342,283	897,104	445,348	445,205	143
1974	1,425,001	643,927	781,074	856,847	568,154	454,706	402,141	189,221	378,933	956,770	468,231	467,950	281
1975	1,505,404	672,938	832,466	891,992	613,412	467,425	424,567	205,513	407,899	1,008,476	496,928	496,604	324
1976	1,577,546	683,825	893,721	904,551	672,995	459,286	445,265	224,539	448,456	1,033,115	544,431	541,064	3,367
1977	1,569,084	698,902	870,182	891,819	677,265	462,038	429,781	236,864	440,401	1,004,013	565,071	561,384	3,687
1978	1,575,693	704,831	870,862	879,931	695,762	458,865	421,066	245,966	449,796	998,608	577,085	573,563	3,522
1979	1,571,922	714,624	857,298	862,754	709,168	456,197	406,557	258,427	450,741	989,991	581,931	578,425	3,506
1980	1,621,840	736,214	885,626	874,197	747,643	462,387	411,810	273,827	473,816	1,015,439	606,401	601,084	5,317
1981	1,617,150	732,182	884,968	866,785	750,365	452,364	414,421	279,818	470,547	998,669	618,481	613,557	4,924
1982	1,600,718	736,813	863,905	860,890	739,828	453,519	407,371	283,294	456,534	983,014	617,704	613,350	4,354
1983	1,618,666	747,016	871,650	865,425	753,241	455,540	409,885	291,476	461,765	985,616	633,050	628,111	4,939
1984	1,623,869	750,735	873,134	856,761	767,108	452,579	404,182	298,156	468,952	983,879	639,990	634,109	5,881
1985	1,650,381	755,629	894,752	856,370	794,011	451,274	405,096	304,355	489,656	1,002,148	648,233	642,795	5,438
1986	1,705,536	767,477	938,059	867,010	838,526	452,717	414,293	314,760	523,766	1,053,177	652,359	644,185	8,174
1987	1,720,407	768,536	951,871	863,599	856,808	447,212	416,387	321,324	535,484	1,054,665	665,742	662,408	3,334
1988	1,738,789	794,340	944,449	864,252	874,537	455,337	408,915	339,003	535,534	1,058,242	680,547	—	—
1989	1,796,029	820,254	975,775	879,025	917,004	461,596	417,429	358,658	558,346	1,090,221	705,808	—	—
1990	1,859,531	844,955	1,014,576	904,150	955,381	471,217	432,933	373,738	581,643	1,135,121	724,410	716,820	7,590
1991	1,919,666	893,917	1,025,749	930,841	988,825	493,849	436,992	400,068	588,757	1,161,606	758,060	746,687	11,373
1992	1,949,659	917,676	1,031,983	941,053	1,008,606	502,166	438,887	415,510	593,096	1,168,270	781,389	770,802	10,587
1993	1,980,844	948,136	1,032,708	943,768	1,037,076	508,574	435,194	439,562	597,514	1,177,301	803,543	789,700	13,843
1994	2,016,182	969,070	1,047,112	949,785	1,066,397	513,592	436,193	455,478	610,919	1,188,552	827,630	809,642	17,988
1995	2,030,062	983,534	1,046,528	941,409	1,088,653	510,782	430,627	472,752	615,901	1,188,748	841,314	824,351	16,963
1996	2,040,572	1,004,114	1,036,458	932,153	1,108,419	512,100	420,053	492,014	616,405	1,185,216	855,356	830,238	25,118
1997	2,051,747	1,019,464	1,032,283	927,496	1,124,251	510,845	416,651	508,619	615,632	1,188,640	863,107	837,790	25,317
1998	2,070,030	1,024,627	1,045,403	923,132	1,146,898	505,492	417,640	519,135	627,763	1,187,557	882,473	852,270	30,203
1999	2,110,246	1,049,591	1,060,655	930,930	1,179,316	508,930	422,000	540,661	638,655	1,201,511	908,735	869,739	38,996
2000	2,156,896	1,086,674	1,070,222	943,501	1,213,395	522,847	420,654	563,827	649,568	1,213,464	943,432	896,239	47,193
2001	2,212,377	1,119,862	1,092,515	956,384	1,255,993	531,260	425,124	588,602	667,391	1,247,285	965,092	909,612	55,480
2002	2,354,634	1,212,107	1,142,527	1,009,726	1,344,908	566,930	442,796	645,177	699,731	1,319,138	1,035,496	959,385	76,111
2003	2,431,117	1,280,880	1,150,237	1,032,892	1,398,225	589,190	443,702	691,690	706,535	1,335,595	1,095,522	994,375	101,147
2004	2,491,414	1,325,841	1,165,573	1,047,214	1,444,200	598,727	448,487	727,114	717,086	1,329,532	1,161,882	1,022,319	139,563
2005	2,523,511	1,350,581	1,172,930	1,047,054	1,476,457	602,525	444,529	748,056	728,401	1,324,104	1,199,407	1,036,324	163,083
2006	2,574,639	1,386,189	1,188,450	1,061,067	1,513,572	614,706	446,361	771,483	742,089	1,332,725	1,241,914	1,064,679	177,235
2007	2,644,598	1,428,956	1,215,642	1,088,377	1,556,221	632,619	455,758	796,337	759,884	1,353,150	1,291,448	1,100,932	190,516
2008	2,737,094	1,490,462	1,246,632	1,122,074	1,615,020	656,213	465,861	834,249	780,771	1,380,915	1,356,179	1,125,038	231,141
2009	2,849,415	1,567,080	1,282,335	1,169,777	1,679,638	689,977	479,800	877,103	802,535	1,424,393	1,425,022	1,172,501	252,521
2010	2,937,011	1,630,142	1,306,869	1,209,477	1,727,534	719,408	490,069	910,734	816,800	1,439,171	1,497,840	1,201,489	296,351
2011	2,933,287	1,637,356	1,295,931	1,211,264	1,722,023	722,265	488,999	915,091	806,932	1,421,404	1,511,883	1,207,896	303,987
2012	2,908,840	1,637,312	1,271,528	1,204,068	1,704,772	724,017	480,051	913,295	791,477	1,406,567	1,502,273	1,206,988	295,285
2013	2,900,373	1,657,334	1,243,039	1,201,057	1,699,316	732,112	468,945	925,222	774,094	1,398,556	1,501,817	1,215,927	285,890
2014	2,914,956	1,670,072	1,244,884	1,211,231	1,703,725	742,247	468,984	927,825	775,900	1,410,127	1,504,829	1,225,184	279,645
2015	2,941,531	1,684,482	1,257,049	1,221,565	1,719,966	749,349	472,216	935,133	784,833	1,422,020	1,519,511	1,243,769	275,742
2016	2,972,255	1,695,246	1,277,009	1,221,563	1,750,692	747,288	474,275	947,958	802,734	1,441,861	1,530,394	1,265,214	265,180
2017	3,005,115	1,704,278	1,300,837	1,220,055	1,785,060	740,240	479,815	964,038	821,022	1,459,145	1,545,970	1,289,409	256,561
2018	3,035,683	1,724,586	1,311,097	1,216,663	1,819,020	736,182	480,481	988,404	830,616	1,479,938	1,555,745	1,312,591	243,154
2019[1]	3,048,000	1,729,000	1,318,000	1,221,000	1,827,000	738,000	483,000	992,000	835,000	1,486,000	1,562,000	—	—
2020[1]	3,052,000	1,729,000	1,323,000	1,222,000	1,830,000	737,000	485,000	992,000	838,000	1,488,000	1,564,000	—	—
2021[1]	3,058,000	1,729,000	1,329,000	1,223,000	1,834,000	737,000	487,000	992,000	842,000	1,491,000	1,567,000	—	—
2022[1]	3,064,000	1,730,000	1,334,000	1,225,000	1,838,000	737,000	488,000	993,000	845,000	1,494,000	1,570,000	—	—
2023[1]	3,071,000	1,732,000	1,339,000	1,228,000	1,844,000	737,000	491,000	995,000	849,000	1,498,000	1,574,000	—	—
2024[1]	3,081,000	1,737,000	1,344,000	1,232,000	1,850,000	739,000	493,000	998,000	852,000	1,503,000	1,579,000	—	—
2025[1]	3,092,000	1,743,000	1,349,000	1,236,000	1,856,000	742,000	494,000	1,001,000	854,000	1,508,000	1,584,000	—	—
2026[1]	3,104,000	1,750,000	1,354,000	1,241,000	1,863,000	745,000	497,000	1,005,000	858,000	1,514,000	1,590,000	—	—
2027[1]	3,109,000	1,750,000	1,358,000	1,243,000	1,865,000	745,000	498,000	1,005,000	860,000	1,516,000	1,593,000	—	—
2028[1]	3,111,000	1,749,000	1,362,000	1,244,000	1,866,000	745,000	499,000	1,004,000	862,000	1,517,000	1,594,000	—	—
2029[1]	3,112,000	1,747,000	1,365,000	1,245,000	1,867,000	744,000	501,000	1,003,000	865,000	1,518,000	1,594,000	—	—

—Not available.
[1]Projected.
NOTE: Data include unclassified graduate students. Data through 1995 are for institutions of higher education, while later data are for degree-granting institutions. Degree-granting institutions grant associate's or higher degrees and participate in Title IV federal financial aid programs. The degree-granting classification is very similar to the earlier higher education classification, but it includes more 2-year colleges and excludes a few higher education institutions that did not grant degrees. Some data have been revised from previously published figures.

SOURCE: U.S. Department of Education, National Center for Education Statistics, Higher Education General Information Survey (HEGIS), "Fall Enrollment in Colleges and Universities" surveys, 1970 through 1985; Integrated Postsecondary Education Data System (IPEDS), "Fall Enrollment Survey" (IPEDS-EF:86–99); IPEDS Spring 2001 through Spring 2019, Fall Enrollment component; and Enrollment in Degree-Granting Institutions Projection Model, 2000 through 2029. (This table was prepared December 2019.)

Table 303.90. Fall enrollment and number of degree-granting postsecondary institutions, by control and religious affiliation of institution: Selected years, 1980 through 2018

Control and religious affiliation of institution	Total enrollment							Enrollment, fall 2018				Number of institutions				
									Full-time		Part-time						
	Fall 1980	Fall 1990	Fall 2000	Fall 2010	Fall 2016	Fall 2017	Total	Males	Females	Males	Females	Fall 1980	Fall 1990	Fall 2000	Fall 2010	Fall 2018
	2	3	4	5	6	7	8	9	10	11	12	13	14	15	16	17
All institutions	**12,096,895**	**13,818,637**	**15,312,289**	**21,019,438**	**19,846,904**	**19,778,151**	**19,645,918**	**5,338,934**	**6,652,787**	**3,103,728**	**4,550,469**	**3,226**	**3,501**	**4,056**	**4,589**	**4,034**
Public institutions	9,457,394	10,844,717	11,752,786	15,142,171	14,585,840	14,571,739	14,529,264	3,787,941	4,480,879	2,603,530	3,656,914	1,493	1,548	1,676	1,652	1,634
Federal	50,989	50,669	16,917	21,610	19,804	20,265	20,379	12,657	5,978	1,152	592	12	17	12	14	14
State	(†)	7,181,380	9,548,090	12,364,881	12,089,310	12,103,707	12,104,962	3,361,325	4,002,394	1,964,287	2,776,956	(†)	978	1,355	1,331	1,320
Local	(†)	3,508,941	2,078,090	2,542,044	2,276,473	2,246,845	2,206,015	364,309	412,242	604,092	825,372	(†)	523	277	261	258
Other public	9,406,405	103,727	109,669	213,636	200,263	200,922	197,908	49,650	60,265	34,559	53,434	1,481	30	32	46	42
Private institutions	2,639,501	2,973,920	3,559,503	5,877,267	5,261,064	5,206,412	5,116,654	1,550,993	2,171,908	500,198	893,555	1,733	1,953	2,380	2,937	2,400
Independent nonprofit	1,521,614	1,474,818	1,577,242	1,994,900	2,190,233	2,222,677	2,246,622	743,384	968,932	205,119	329,187	795	709	729	736	785
For-profit	111,714	213,693	450,084	2,022,785	1,182,108	1,097,923	982,410	213,152	383,619	115,522	270,117	164	322	724	1,310	736
Religiously affiliated[b]	1,006,173	1,285,409	1,532,177	1,859,582	1,888,723	1,885,812	1,887,622	594,457	819,357	179,557	294,251	774	922	927	891	879
Advent Christian Church	143	88	34	1,536	1,547	1,462	1,484	740	685	33	26	1	1	1	1	1
African Methodist Episcopal Zion Church	1,091	—	—	—	—	—	5,633	1,594	1,586	1,180	1,273	3	3	3	3	4
African Methodist Episcopal	4,541	3,220	5,980	2,674	5,379	5,887	12,622	3,784	5,099	1,274	2,465	6	6	6	5	4
American Baptist	6,131	10,800	15,410	15,120	12,801	12,500	1,443	684	678	33	48	11	8	17	18	18
American Evangelical Lutheran Church	—	—	743	1,340	1,295	1,394	—	—	—	—	—	1	4	1	1	1
American Lutheran and Lutheran Church in America	3,092	—	1,460	—	—	—	—	—	—	—	—	3	—	—	—	—
American Lutheran	21,608	—	—	15,806	17,780	19,240	20,792	6,032	8,198	2,878	3,684	13	11	14	16	13
Assemblies of God Church	7,814	8,307	14,272	15,806	17,780	19,240	20,792	6,032	8,198	2,878	3,684	10	11	14	16	13
Baptist	38,231	99,510	107,610	174,538	111,744	111,124	113,415	34,111	47,269	14,590	17,445	69	69	68	69	63
Brethren Church	3,925	958	2,088	8,506	9,135	8,627	8,656	2,694	3,320	1,455	1,187	3	3	3	3	2
Brethren in Christ Church	1,301	2,239	2,797	6,455	6,094	6,122	6,351	1,791	2,313	969	1,278	1	1	1	1	1
Christian and Missionary Alliance Church	1,705	2,519	5,278	52,839	47,970	46,260	49,521	14,599	21,603	5,615	7,704	3	4	6	4	4
Christian Church (Disciples of Christ)	14,913	30,397	35,984	10,074	10,061	9,970	10,050	3,641	3,432	1,433	1,544	12	18	16	18	19
Christian Churches and Churches of Christ	1,342	2,263	7,277	10,074	10,061	9,970	10,050	3,641	3,432	1,433	1,544	7	8	18	18	17
Christian Methodist Episcopal	2,486	2,174	1,502	4,817	4,207	4,053	3,824	1,890	1,789	57	88	4	4	1	1	3
Christian Reformed Church	5,408	4,488	5,999	5,625	5,710	5,714	5,630	2,465	2,560	325	280	3	2	3	3	3
Church of Christ (Scientist)	2,773	2,557	—	—	—	—	—	—	—	—	—	6	2	—	—	—
Church of God	—	249	—	—	—	—	—	—	—	—	—	1	1	—	—	—
Church of God of Prophecy	6,082	5,627	12,540	16,731	17,768	16,962	16,422	4,653	7,543	1,932	2,294	9	9	7	7	9
Church of New Jerusalem	170	—	—	—	—	—	—	—	—	—	—	3	1	1	1	1
Church of the Brethren	8,482	4,463	4,187	6,154	6,484	6,401	6,255	2,594	3,076	226	359	6	5	4	5	6
Church of the Nazarene	11,716	10,779	16,661	21,144	22,572	23,267	23,353	6,528	10,358	2,136	4,331	10	9	12	10	10
Churches of Christ	9,343	14,611	30,140	35,538	36,299	36,131	35,453	11,200	15,690	3,126	5,437	19	19	19	17	18
Cumberland Presbyterian	594	746	1,112	4,652	6,142	6,007	5,615	1,694	2,010	738	1,173	2	2	3	2	2
Episcopal Church, Reformed	67	—	—	—	1,242	1,286	1,179	66	318	113	682	1	1	1	1	2
Evangelical Christian	—	—	—	—	77,375	76,654	83,835	18,652	27,140	15,932	22,111	—	—	—	—	—
Evangelical Congregational Church	80	88	148	153	120	111	151	28	11	82	30	1	1	1	1	1
Evangelical Covenant Church of America	1,401	1,035	2,387	3,233	3,122	3,011	2,981	755	1,211	362	653	2	2	2	2	2
Evangelical Free Church of America	833	2,355	4,022	2,926	2,391	2,409	1,998	629	368	630	371	2	2	2	2	2
Evangelical Lutheran Church of America	743	49,210	49,085	56,162	49,863	49,960	52,138	20,241	26,905	1,785	3,207	33	33	34	33	27
Free Methodist	5,543	5,902	7,323	12,270	11,324	10,965	10,721	2,880	5,913	545	1,383	5	5	5	5	5
Free Will Baptist Church	1,132	1,177	2,378	528	713	704	733	286	255	103	89	4	3	4	3	3
Friends United Meeting	1,109	—	—	—	—	—	—	—	—	—	—	1	1	3	2	2
Friends	5,157	5,844	10,898	13,876	11,636	11,368	11,070	4,140	4,886	821	1,223	5	3	4	2	7
General Baptist	—	—	—	—	1,469	1,303	1,419	332	353	338	396	1	1	1	1	1

See notes at end of table.

Table 303.90. Fall enrollment and number of degree-granting postsecondary institutions, by control and religious affiliation of institution: Selected years, 1980 through 2018—Continued

Control and religious affiliation of institution	Total enrollment						Enrollment, fall 2018					Number of institutions[1]				
							Total	Full-time		Part-time						
	Fall 1980	Fall 1990	Fall 2000	Fall 2010	Fall 2016	Fall 2017		Males	Females	Males	Females	Fall 1980	Fall 1990	Fall 2000	Fall 2010	Fall 2018
1	2	3	4	5	6	7	8	9	10	11	12	13	14	15	16	17
General Conference Mennonite Church	820	1,243	1,059	—	—	—	—	—	—	—	—	2	2	1	—	—
Greek Orthodox	204	148	132	—	195	170	341	202	110	19	10	2	2	1	1	1
Interdenominational	1,254	11,103	9,788	33,778	41,113	41,175	40,777	12,111	17,164	5,587	5,915	4	17	14	31	34
Jewish	5,738	12,217	14,182	12,755	13,846	14,066	14,221	2,561	10,290	416	954	24	63	62	36	34
Latter-Day Saints	39,172	42,274	44,680	53,514	84,046	91,403	82,012	25,584	27,048	12,322	17,058	4	4	4	4	4
Lutheran Church—Missouri Synod	11,727	13,827	18,866	28,255	36,542	36,243	35,715	7,970	14,710	4,403	8,632	15	14	13	12	11
Lutheran Church in America	23,877	5,796	8,240	8,708	8,181	6,004	6,004	2,218	3,175	182	429	20	18	18	12	13
Mennonite Brethren Church	1,344	1,864	2,390	4,136	4,291	4,875	5,005	1,124	2,400	446	1,035	3	3	3	2	2
Mennonite Church	4,008	2,859	3,553	4,263	4,131	3,886	3,704	1,271	1,639	209	585	6	5	5	5	5
Missionary Church Inc	487	699	1,647	2,152	1,639	1,513	1,513	435	667	109	302	5	5	5	1	1
Moravian Church	2,434	2,511	2,939	3,095	3,513	3,430	3,356	808	1,754	147	647	2	2	2	2	2
Multiple Protestant denominations	5,526	211	4,690	5,350	4,758	4,766	4,663	967	1,555	928	1,213	8	7	7	6	6
Nondenominational	—	—	—	—	—	—	1,364	547	800	7	10	—	—	—	—	2
North American Baptist	—	—	124	120	207	229	306	48	20	167	71	—	—	1	1	1
Original Free Will Baptist	155	—	—	3,855	3,430	3,451	3,208	591	819	541	1,257	1	—	—	1	1
Pentecostal Holiness Church	767	566	976	1,272	1,684	1,623	1,518	712	598	91	117	3	3	2	3	2
Presbyterian	47,144	77,700	78,950	85,719	2,965	3,079	3,295	1,076	1,622	176	421	57	70	64	58	4
Presbyterian USA	—	—	1,877	—	82,215	80,862	80,706	29,177	38,490	4,029	9,010	—	—	1	—	56
Presbyterian Church in America	—	1,877	4,499	2,071	1,611	1,585	1,567	665	588	163	151	—	1	5	2	8
Protestant Episcopal	5,396	4,559	5,479	5,006	3,687	3,719	3,535	1,577	1,645	152	161	12	9	12	11	8
Protestant, other	4,072	38,136	30,116	13,450	19,342	19,238	18,950	5,467	7,378	2,651	3,454	15	44	34	23	25
Reformed Church in America	2,713	5,525	6,002	6,555	6,205	6,125	5,992	2,222	3,006	269	495	4	4	5	5	5
Reformed Presbyterian Church	2,014	1,556	2,355	2,982	2,585	2,393	2,325	1,019	825	257	224	2	2	2	3	3
Reorganized Latter-Day Saints Church	4,274	4,793	3,390	—	—	—	—	—	—	—	—	2	1	2	—	—
Roman Catholic	422,842	530,585	636,336	751,091	720,808	711,801	707,105	217,382	323,277	56,043	110,403	229	239	239	237	227
Russian Orthodox	47	38	106	60	75	89	90	68	6	15	1	1	1	1	1	1
Seventh-Day Adventists	19,168	15,771	19,223	25,430	23,914	23,602	23,315	7,320	10,979	1,831	3,185	11	11	13	14	13
Southern Baptist	85,281	49,493	54,275	49,936	55,308	60,043	65,762	21,888	22,887	8,800	12,187	54	29	32	22	22
Undenominational	—	6,758	23,573	27,748	35,365	36,006	35,983	8,006	12,426	6,009	9,542	—	14	16	16	20
Unitarian Universalist	87	82	132	166	181	178	164	24	76	17	47	2	2	2	2	2
United Brethren Church	545	601	938	1,260	1,295	1,321	1,302	426	698	75	103	1	1	1	1	1
United Church of Christ	14,169	20,175	23,709	20,537	15,641	15,324	15,336	5,042	6,529	1,229	2,536	16	18	18	17	14
United Methodist	127,099	148,851	171,109	206,744	200,792	200,217	199,759	72,248	95,922	11,556	20,033	91	96	100	96	94
Wesleyan Church	3,583	5,311	11,128	20,670	19,240	18,608	18,339	4,765	10,225	1,040	2,309	5	4	4	6	8
Wisconsin Evangelical Lutheran Synod	808	931	1,660	1,677	2,051	2,095	2,220	823	887	215	295	1	3	4	6	8
Other religiously affiliated	462	5,743	2,534	4,778	5,097	5,624	5,426	1,681	2,302	460	983	9	9	4	11	12

—Not available.

[1]Counts of institutions in this table may be lower than reported in other tables because counts in this table include only institutions reporting separate enrollment data.

[2]Included under "Other public."

[3]Religious affiliation as reported by institution.

NOTE: Data for 1980 and 1990 are for institutions of higher education, while later data are for degree-granting institutions. Degree-granting institutions grant associate's or higher degrees and participate in Title IV federal financial aid programs. The degree-granting classification is very similar to the earlier higher education classification, but it includes more 2-year colleges and excludes a few higher education institutions that did not grant degrees. Some data have been revised from previously published figures.

SOURCE: U.S. Department of Education, National Center for Education Statistics, Higher Education General Information Survey (HEGIS), "Fall Enrollment in Institutions of Higher Education" and "Institutional Characteristics" surveys, 1980; Integrated Postsecondary Education Data System (IPEDS), "Fall Enrollment Survey" (IPEDS-EF:90) and "Institutional Characteristics Survey" (IPEDS-IC:90); and IPEDS Spring 2001 through Spring 2019, Fall Enrollment component. (This table was prepared February 2020.)

Table 304.10. Total fall enrollment in degree-granting postsecondary institutions, by state or jurisdiction: Selected years, 1970 through 2018

State or jurisdiction	1970	1980	1990	2000	2010	2013	2015	2016	2017	2018	Percent change, 2013 to 2018
1	2	3	4	5	6	7	8	9	10	11	12
United States	**8,580,887**	**12,096,895**	**13,818,637**	**15,312,289**	**21,019,438**	**20,376,677**	**19,988,204**	**19,846,904**	**19,778,151**	**19,645,918**	**-3.6**
Alabama	103,936	164,306	218,589	233,962	327,606	305,817	302,959	304,052	306,817	304,182	-0.5
Alaska	9,471	21,296	29,833	27,953	34,799	34,890	31,373	28,436	26,905	25,692	-26.4
Arizona	109,619	202,716	264,148	342,490	793,871	693,714	650,422	608,086	591,122	581,982	-16.1
Arkansas	52,039	77,347	90,425	115,172	175,848	172,432	168,402	167,235	163,963	159,738	-7.4
California	1,257,245	1,791,088	1,808,740	2,256,708	2,714,699	2,641,331	2,687,410	2,700,445	2,724,446	2,712,420	2.7
Colorado	123,395	162,916	227,131	263,872	369,450	358,330	348,159	352,255	360,236	360,537	0.6
Connecticut	124,700	159,632	168,604	161,243	199,384	201,028	199,666	198,010	197,534	197,480	-1.8
Delaware	25,260	32,939	42,004	43,897	55,258	59,615	60,392	61,139	60,338	60,700	1.8
District of Columbia	77,158	86,675	79,551	72,689	91,992	89,257	93,972	93,040	95,999	97,776	9.5
Florida	235,525	411,891	588,086	707,684	1,124,778	1,125,872	1,083,570	1,075,527	1,073,338	1,068,063	-5.1
Georgia	126,511	184,159	251,786	346,204	568,916	533,425	530,711	533,073	538,124	543,443	1.9
Hawaii	36,562	49,009	56,436	60,182	78,073	76,434	69,332	65,843	64,125	61,855	-19.1
Idaho	34,567	43,018	51,881	65,594	85,201	109,044	121,109	123,796	131,803	123,487	13.2
Illinois	452,146	645,288	729,246	743,918	906,845	842,888	802,211	777,720	757,001	738,448	-12.4
Indiana	192,668	247,253	284,832	314,334	459,493	444,409	426,364	419,284	398,802	388,348	-12.6
Iowa	108,902	140,449	170,515	188,974	381,867	339,738	275,106	266,513	260,801	254,058	-25.2
Kansas	102,485	136,605	163,733	179,968	214,849	215,855	219,994	215,832	213,997	212,737	-1.4
Kentucky	98,591	143,066	177,852	188,341	291,104	273,073	255,722	255,062	258,498	262,961	-3.7
Louisiana	120,728	160,058	186,840	223,800	263,676	251,935	245,305	239,278	241,567	241,401	-4.2
Maine	34,134	43,264	57,186	58,473	72,406	72,412	71,719	72,116	71,811	71,773	-0.9
Maryland	149,607	225,180	259,700	273,745	377,967	363,699	364,225	366,809	364,178	361,442	-0.6
Massachusetts	303,809	418,415	417,833	421,142	507,753	513,964	510,512	505,722	503,539	499,769	-2.8
Michigan	392,726	520,131	569,803	567,631	697,765	643,575	601,462	583,034	558,072	541,096	-15.9
Minnesota	160,788	206,691	253,789	293,445	465,449	441,637	430,466	422,793	412,966	408,783	-7.4
Mississippi	73,967	102,364	122,883	137,389	179,995	173,084	174,183	172,588	171,824	169,360	-2.2
Missouri	183,930	233,378	289,899	321,348	444,750	438,446	409,999	401,098	385,483	374,424	-14.6
Montana	30,062	35,177	35,876	42,240	53,282	52,777	50,799	50,918	50,642	49,363	-6.5
Nebraska	66,915	89,488	112,831	112,117	144,692	137,943	136,091	136,098	135,710	134,938	-2.2
Nevada	13,669	40,455	61,728	87,893	129,360	116,738	116,101	116,030	117,574	117,798	0.9
New Hampshire	29,400	46,794	59,510	61,718	75,539	92,440	123,508	133,159	149,184	160,743	73.9
New Jersey	216,121	321,610	324,286	335,945	444,092	436,939	423,759	421,386	419,037	414,416	-5.2
New Mexico	44,461	58,629	85,500	110,739	162,552	153,455	138,248	134,607	129,595	123,297	-19.7
New York	806,479	992,349	1,048,286	1,043,395	1,305,151	1,305,121	1,285,406	1,273,634	1,260,557	1,250,287	-4.2
North Carolina	171,925	287,537	352,138	404,652	585,792	575,020	562,442	561,415	564,111	563,710	-2.0
North Dakota	31,495	34,069	37,878	40,248	56,903	55,030	53,834	54,203	53,749	53,286	-3.2
Ohio	376,267	488,938	557,690	549,553	745,115	696,912	664,623	658,043	649,586	644,962	-7.5
Oklahoma	110,155	160,295	173,221	178,016	230,560	220,897	211,117	208,333	202,150	195,943	-11.3
Oregon	122,177	157,458	165,741	183,065	251,708	251,087	240,649	236,851	229,988	228,140	-9.1
Pennsylvania	411,044	507,716	604,060	609,521	804,640	765,581	736,163	725,682	717,025	700,329	-8.5
Rhode Island	45,898	66,869	78,273	75,450	85,110	83,460	82,292	83,348	82,765	80,868	-3.1
South Carolina	69,518	132,476	159,302	185,931	257,064	257,844	249,655	246,563	246,416	240,533	-6.7
South Dakota	30,639	32,761	34,208	43,221	58,360	55,129	53,664	53,683	53,620	53,365	-3.2
Tennessee	135,103	204,841	226,238	263,910	351,762	338,197	323,869	321,752	323,157	322,115	-4.8
Texas	442,225	701,391	901,437	1,033,973	1,535,864	1,541,279	1,579,614	1,605,498	1,630,520	1,643,542	6.6
Utah	81,687	92,159	121,303	163,776	255,653	261,897	292,995	311,450	331,996	359,772	37.4
Vermont	22,209	30,628	36,398	35,489	45,572	43,536	43,865	44,719	43,855	42,914	-1.4
Virginia	151,915	280,504	353,442	381,893	577,922	583,755	569,752	557,444	554,120	552,041	-5.4
Washington	183,544	303,603	263,384	320,840	388,116	363,377	364,844	366,547	367,943	367,056	1.0
West Virginia	63,153	81,973	84,790	87,888	152,431	157,952	150,897	146,608	142,966	140,103	-11.3
Wisconsin	202,058	269,086	299,774	307,179	384,181	362,379	350,255	341,717	340,301	336,409	-7.2
Wyoming	15,220	21,147	31,326	30,004	38,298	37,031	34,205	33,365	33,014	32,510	-12.2
U.S. Service Academies[1]	17,079	49,808	48,692	13,475	15,925	14,997	14,812	15,065	15,281	15,523	3.5
Other jurisdictions	**67,237**	**137,749**	**164,618**	**194,633**	**264,240**	**254,543**	**247,886**	**241,896**	**192,717**	**212,565**	**-16.5**
American Samoa	0	976	1,219	297	2,193	1,488	1,285	1,253	1,095	1,037	-30.3
Federated States of Micronesia	0	224	975	1,576	2,699	2,446	2,215	2,090	2,022	1,931	-21.1
Guam	2,719	3,217	4,741	5,215	6,188	6,518	6,395	6,084	6,027	5,888	-9.7
Marshall Islands	0	0	0	328	869	1,000	995	978	1,032	1,119	11.9
Northern Marianas	0	0	661	1,078	1,137	1,109	1,157	1,038	1,216	1,194	7.7
Palau	0	0	491	581	694	646	627	587	532	497	-23.1
Puerto Rico	63,073	131,184	154,065	183,290	247,727	239,015	232,891	227,496	178,623	198,915	-16.8
U.S. Virgin Islands	1,445	2,148	2,466	2,268	2,733	2,321	2,321	2,370	2,170	1,984	-14.5

[1]Data for 2000 and later years reflect a substantial reduction in the number of Department of Defense institutions included in the IPEDS survey.

NOTE: Data through 1990 are for institutions of higher education, while later data are for degree-granting institutions. Degree-granting institutions grant associate's or higher degrees and participate in Title IV federal financial aid programs. The degree-granting classification is very similar to the earlier higher education classification, but it includes more 2-year colleges and excludes a few higher education institutions that did not grant degrees. Some data have been revised from previously published figures.

SOURCE: U.S. Department of Education, National Center for Education Statistics, Higher Education General Information Survey (HEGIS), "Fall Enrollment in Colleges and Universities" surveys, 1970 and 1980; Integrated Postsecondary Education Data System (IPEDS), "Fall Enrollment Survey" (IPEDS-EF:90); and IPEDS Spring 2001 through Spring 2019, Fall Enrollment component. (This table was prepared January 2020.)

Table 304.15. Total fall enrollment in public degree-granting postsecondary institutions, by state or jurisdiction: Selected years, 1970 through 2018

State or jurisdiction	1970	1980	1990	2000	2010	2013	2015	2016	2017	2018	Percent change, 2013 to 2018
1	2	3	4	5	6	7	8	9	10	11	12
United States	**6,428,134**	**9,457,394**	**10,844,717**	**11,752,786**	**15,142,171**	**14,746,848**	**14,572,843**	**14,585,840**	**14,571,739**	**14,529,264**	**-1.5**
Alabama	87,884	143,674	195,939	207,435	267,083	248,296	247,450	251,038	254,071	255,087	2.7
Alaska	8,563	20,561	27,792	26,559	32,303	31,600	28,429	27,352	25,850	24,649	-22.0
Arizona	107,315	194,034	248,213	284,522	366,976	354,485	360,976	361,400	366,787	367,198	3.6
Arkansas	43,599	66,068	78,645	101,775	155,780	153,898	150,165	149,298	146,578	142,382	-7.5
California	1,123,529	1,599,838	1,594,710	1,927,771	2,223,163	2,151,521	2,202,258	2,228,592	2,257,256	2,250,219	4.6
Colorado	108,562	145,598	200,653	217,897	269,433	271,223	265,828	272,668	278,909	279,495	3.0
Connecticut	73,391	97,788	109,556	101,027	127,194	123,093	119,766	117,345	116,090	114,529	-7.0
Delaware	21,151	28,325	34,252	34,194	39,935	40,992	40,611	41,816	42,321	42,601	3.9
District of Columbia	12,194	13,900	11,990	5,499	5,840	5,347	5,118	4,587	4,529	4,500	-15.8
Florida	189,450	334,349	489,081	556,912	790,027	795,860	794,390	797,048	798,045	800,451	0.6
Georgia	101,900	140,158	196,413	271,755	436,047	413,706	417,860	422,159	428,586	435,744	5.3
Hawaii	32,963	43,269	45,728	44,579	60,090	58,941	55,756	53,418	51,674	51,063	-13.4
Idaho	27,072	34,491	41,315	53,751	64,204	75,910	72,339	74,667	75,792	77,133	1.6
Illinois	315,634	491,274	551,333	534,155	585,515	546,483	509,104	492,578	478,042	465,229	-14.9
Indiana	136,739	189,224	223,953	240,023	337,705	335,923	321,501	319,581	301,562	296,229	-11.8
Iowa	68,390	97,454	117,834	135,008	177,781	168,644	171,005	171,075	170,262	199,231	18.1
Kansas	88,215	121,987	149,117	159,976	185,623	184,075	179,532	180,170	179,624	179,600	-2.4
Kentucky	77,240	114,884	147,095	151,973	229,725	218,472	205,908	205,431	202,266	199,748	-8.6
Louisiana	101,127	136,703	158,290	189,213	224,811	215,701	212,098	208,254	210,166	210,696	-2.3
Maine	25,405	31,878	41,500	40,662	50,903	49,602	47,408	47,763	46,999	48,332	-2.6
Maryland	118,988	195,051	220,783	223,797	309,779	301,565	303,849	306,892	303,614	301,959	0.1
Massachusetts	116,127	183,765	186,035	183,248	224,542	228,253	222,243	218,465	213,388	207,767	-9.0
Michigan	339,625	454,147	487,359	467,861	562,448	527,745	501,411	492,771	478,735	466,806	-11.5
Minnesota	130,567	162,379	199,211	218,617	276,176	266,440	256,187	253,239	249,385	245,164	-8.0
Mississippi	64,968	90,661	109,038	125,355	161,493	154,366	155,334	153,082	152,392	150,583	-2.5
Missouri	132,540	165,179	200,093	201,509	256,030	254,650	248,516	244,921	237,454	232,040	-8.9
Montana	27,287	31,178	31,865	37,387	48,231	47,851	45,935	46,262	46,002	44,925	-6.1
Nebraska	51,454	73,509	94,614	88,531	107,979	101,893	100,030	101,032	101,038	100,594	-1.3
Nevada	13,576	40,280	61,242	83,120	113,103	102,538	104,418	106,196	107,864	108,658	6.0
New Hampshire	15,979	24,119	32,163	35,870	44,077	42,711	42,628	41,170	39,761	38,735	-9.3
New Jersey	145,373	247,028	261,601	266,921	358,256	352,822	339,722	337,099	334,597	329,037	-6.7
New Mexico	40,795	55,077	83,403	101,450	150,844	144,381	131,343	129,038	125,381	120,293	-16.7
New York	449,437	563,251	616,884	583,417	723,500	720,948	709,243	700,875	697,458	690,097	-4.3
North Carolina	123,761	228,154	285,405	329,422	475,064	460,125	448,055	450,080	454,998	456,128	-0.9
North Dakota	30,192	31,709	34,690	36,014	48,904	48,718	48,191	47,964	47,574	46,531	-4.5
Ohio	281,099	381,765	427,613	411,161	547,551	520,039	501,677	501,146	497,409	495,612	-4.7
Oklahoma	91,438	137,188	151,073	153,699	197,641	187,078	179,008	177,629	174,239	170,979	-8.6
Oregon	108,483	140,102	144,427	154,756	208,001	208,317	197,948	197,819	192,402	191,943	-7.9
Pennsylvania	232,982	292,499	343,478	339,229	432,923	419,856	408,522	406,346	401,045	392,771	-6.5
Rhode Island	25,527	35,052	42,350	38,458	43,224	42,786	41,320	41,369	41,018	40,082	-6.3
South Carolina	47,101	107,683	131,134	155,519	205,080	207,717	202,487	200,295	200,622	196,525	-5.4
South Dakota	23,936	24,328	26,596	34,857	44,569	44,272	44,254	44,305	44,630	43,871	-0.9
Tennessee	98,897	156,835	175,049	202,530	242,486	229,302	223,411	221,288	223,179	225,281	-1.8
Texas	365,522	613,552	802,314	896,534	1,334,110	1,349,490	1,388,266	1,423,205	1,448,398	1,468,587	8.8
Utah	49,588	59,598	86,108	123,046	179,061	168,311	170,689	175,308	180,034	183,949	9.3
Vermont	12,536	17,984	20,910	20,021	27,524	25,852	25,383	25,736	25,300	25,197	-2.5
Virginia	123,279	246,500	291,286	313,780	409,004	405,915	394,210	389,446	389,251	384,879	-5.2
Washington	162,718	276,028	227,632	273,928	330,853	310,192	313,964	315,356	318,336	319,377	3.0
West Virginia	51,363	71,228	74,108	76,136	96,104	90,780	86,342	85,099	83,898	81,605	-10.1
Wisconsin	170,374	235,179	253,529	249,737	301,259	287,619	282,250	278,300	279,097	277,178	-3.6
Wyoming	15,220	21,121	30,623	28,715	36,292	35,547	33,693	32,802	32,550	32,472	-8.7
U.S. Service Academies[1]	17,079	49,808	48,692	13,475	15,925	14,997	14,812	15,065	15,281	15,523	3.5
Other jurisdictions	**46,680**	**60,692**	**66,244**	**84,464**	**83,719**	**78,136**	**80,129**	**81,479**	**37,419**	**72,399**	**-7.3**
American Samoa	0	976	1,219	297	2,193	1,488	1,285	1,253	1,095	1,037	-30.3
Federated States of Micronesia	0	224	975	1,576	2,699	2,446	2,215	2,090	2,022	1,931	-21.1
Guam	2,719	3,217	4,741	5,215	6,103	6,439	6,325	6,017	5,972	5,826	-9.5
Marshall Islands	0	0	0	328	869	1,000	995	978	1,032	1,119	11.9
Northern Marianas	0	0	661	1,078	1,137	1,109	1,157	1,038	1,216	1,194	7.7
Palau	0	0	491	581	694	646	627	587	532	497	-23.1
Puerto Rico	42,516	54,127	55,691	73,121	67,291	62,687	65,204	67,146	23,380	58,811	-6.2
U.S. Virgin Islands	1,445	2,148	2,466	2,268	2,733	2,321	2,321	2,370	2,170	1,984	-14.5

[1]Data for 2000 and later years reflect a substantial reduction in the number of Department of Defense institutions included in the IPEDS survey.
NOTE: Data through 1990 are for institutions of higher education, while later data are for degree-granting institutions. Degree-granting institutions grant associate's or higher degrees and participate in Title IV federal financial aid programs. The degree-granting classification is very similar to the earlier higher education classification, but it includes more 2-year colleges and excludes a few higher education institutions that did not grant degrees. Some data have been revised from previously published figures.

SOURCE: U.S. Department of Education, National Center for Education Statistics, Higher Education General Information Survey (HEGIS), "Fall Enrollment in Colleges and Universities" surveys, 1970 and 1980; Integrated Postsecondary Education Data System (IPEDS), "Fall Enrollment Survey" (IPEDS-EF:90); and IPEDS Spring 2001 through Spring 2019, Fall Enrollment component. (This table was prepared January 2020.)

Table 304.21. Total fall enrollment in private nonprofit degree-granting postsecondary institutions, by state or jurisdiction: Selected years, 1980 through 2018

State or jurisdiction	1980	1990	2000	2010	2012	2013	2015	2016	2017	2018	Percent change, 2013 to 2018
1	2	3	4	5	6	7	8	9	10	11	12
United States	**2,527,787**	**2,760,227**	**3,109,419**	**3,854,482**	**3,951,388**	**3,971,390**	**4,065,891**	**4,078,956**	**4,108,489**	**4,134,244**	**4.1**
Alabama	19,233	20,421	22,649	25,136	26,109	25,239	25,967	24,956	26,144	26,261	4.0
Alaska	735	1,647	908	732	715	764	621	660	625	628	-17.8
Arizona	2,949	7,184	11,092	8,817	9,187	9,150	9,606	9,802	9,935	10,923	19.4
Arkansas	9,557	10,078	12,640	16,654	17,152	16,919	17,554	17,446	17,009	16,932	0.1
California	183,700	201,222	252,449	285,898	297,250	306,964	304,296	304,789	309,239	311,573	1.5
Colorado	16,156	19,254	27,548	32,938	33,765	34,530	35,400	34,269	34,081	33,880	-1.9
Connecticut	61,457	58,346	58,444	66,750	67,765	68,779	71,715	72,344	72,360	73,023	6.2
Delaware	4,614	7,752	9,703	14,833	16,627	18,245	19,455	19,022	17,697	17,748	-2.7
District of Columbia	70,894	64,645	64,212	78,215	79,000	78,908	79,276	78,938	81,099	81,391	3.1
Florida	73,767	87,476	113,580	162,311	179,935	180,611	207,518	205,323	205,106	200,329	10.9
Georgia	39,122	46,297	64,123	71,134	73,235	73,395	74,106	76,263	78,855	81,101	10.5
Hawaii	5,740	10,708	13,727	14,273	14,292	13,087	10,586	9,799	10,159	9,695	-25.9
Idaho	8,527	10,133	11,167	18,185	26,749	31,489	47,651	48,492	55,503	45,926	45.8
Illinois	147,269	165,669	184,856	227,482	227,880	224,127	221,310	218,283	215,250	213,452	-4.8
Indiana	54,641	56,929	67,307	88,928	88,916	88,834	90,752	91,604	89,983	88,799	#
Iowa	42,693	51,851	51,625	57,430	56,221	56,283	54,078	53,475	52,882	51,467	-8.6
Kansas	14,618	14,518	19,522	25,212	26,004	26,693	25,249	23,058	23,177	23,312	-12.7
Kentucky	22,326	26,084	28,015	37,554	40,223	39,830	39,483	41,332	47,958	55,504	39.4
Louisiana	22,980	26,183	29,963	27,667	28,881	28,065	26,345	25,676	26,436	27,318	-2.7
Maine	10,258	14,348	16,837	19,578	21,121	21,329	22,424	22,737	23,468	23,234	8.9
Maryland	30,035	38,557	46,529	54,894	54,917	53,856	53,063	53,881	54,644	55,012	2.1
Massachusetts	234,007	231,232	236,050	275,565	278,907	280,088	284,065	284,513	288,019	289,932	3.5
Michigan	65,984	82,444	96,669	124,307	114,676	108,166	95,107	87,297	76,782	72,631	-32.9
Minnesota	42,292	51,502	62,870	73,504	71,446	71,366	70,666	70,356	70,653	71,190	-0.2
Mississippi	10,556	12,034	11,625	15,398	16,058	16,046	16,873	17,856	17,576	17,576	9.5
Missouri	66,440	86,202	109,784	153,918	154,169	152,442	147,328	146,452	139,978	138,418	-9.2
Montana	3,482	4,011	4,853	5,051	4,921	4,926	4,864	4,621	4,603	4,395	-10.8
Nebraska	15,979	17,885	21,608	32,940	32,783	33,400	34,233	33,747	33,700	34,191	2.4
Nevada	175	339	586	3,370	3,421	3,546	4,214	4,057	4,266	4,233	19.4
New Hampshire	20,783	24,900	21,939	26,566	35,681	46,681	79,388	91,989	109,423	122,008	161.4
New Jersey	73,757	59,011	62,049	75,980	74,391	73,483	73,636	73,822	73,693	74,413	1.3
New Mexico	3,552	1,796	4,258	1,120	1,334	1,503	1,617	1,658	1,590	1,498	-0.3
New York	407,101	406,510	424,379	526,357	535,236	533,749	530,798	530,938	524,627	522,350	-2.1
North Carolina	55,729	64,859	74,640	92,031	94,023	96,072	97,684	97,322	97,121	97,122	1.1
North Dakota	2,360	3,188	4,123	6,234	5,313	5,348	5,040	5,690	5,648	6,140	14.8
Ohio	95,918	109,749	124,718	146,389	146,179	142,502	138,542	138,327	136,776	135,303	-5.1
Oklahoma	21,149	18,492	21,094	22,657	24,032	25,117	25,996	26,227	23,919	22,549	-10.2
Oregon	17,192	20,353	25,289	32,811	33,370	35,289	37,533	35,429	34,607	33,809	-4.2
Pennsylvania	207,975	223,478	239,128	298,997	296,704	294,767	292,166	291,914	294,437	294,037	-0.2
Rhode Island	31,817	35,923	36,768	41,886	40,748	40,674	40,972	41,979	41,747	40,786	0.3
South Carolina	21,868	26,734	29,655	35,089	34,601	34,195	34,606	35,106	34,165	36,950	8.1
South Dakota	8,433	6,188	5,660	9,044	7,273	7,153	7,221	7,223	7,060	7,405	3.5
Tennessee	44,711	47,344	55,809	77,764	82,816	83,912	83,352	84,426	84,459	83,974	0.1
Texas	86,001	92,672	120,123	131,485	136,187	136,077	140,057	142,266	142,727	141,753	4.2
Utah	32,561	34,387	35,986	61,310	81,270	85,599	117,009	131,527	147,610	171,644	100.5
Vermont	12,644	15,488	15,131	17,433	17,679	17,222	18,103	18,683	18,411	17,644	2.5
Virginia	33,269	57,142	50,979	110,720	128,323	130,794	135,037	132,850	132,956	137,115	4.8
Washington	27,087	32,145	41,415	43,702	43,177	43,222	44,568	43,992	42,860	42,267	-2.2
West Virginia	10,440	9,822	9,800	12,952	7,683	8,505	8,665	8,809	8,583	8,368	-1.6
Wisconsin	33,254	45,095	55,535	65,281	63,043	62,427	59,584	57,168	58,419	57,035	-8.6
Wyoming	0	0	0	0	0	0	22	512	563	464	-100.0
Other jurisdictions	**70,702**	**164,618**	**194,633**	**137,375**	**138,661**	**134,587**	**127,194**	**122,016**	**118,597**	**108,934**	**-19.1**
American Samoa	0	1,219	297	0	0	0	0	0	0	0	†
Federated States of Micronesia	0	975	1,576	0	0	0	0	0	0	0	†
Guam	0	4,741	5,215	85	77	79	70	67	55	62	-21.5
Marshall Islands	0	0	328	0	0	0	0	0	0	0	†
Northern Marianas	0	661	1,078	0	0	0	0	0	0	0	†
Palau	0	491	581	0	0	0	0	0	0	0	†
Puerto Rico	70,702	154,065	183,290	137,290	138,584	134,508	127,124	121,949	118,542	108,872	-19.1
U.S. Virgin Islands	0	2,466	2,268	0	0	0	0	0	0	0	†

†Not applicable.
#Rounds to zero.
NOTE: Data through 1990 are for institutions of higher education, while later data are for degree-granting institutions. Degree-granting institutions grant associate's or higher degrees and participate in Title IV federal financial aid programs. The degree-granting classification is very similar to the earlier higher education classification, but it includes more 2-year colleges and excludes a few higher education institutions that did not grant degrees. Some data have been revised from previously published figures.

SOURCE: U.S. Department of Education, National Center for Education Statistics, Higher Education General Information Survey (HEGIS), "Fall Enrollment in Colleges and Universities" survey, 1980; Integrated Postsecondary Education Data System (IPEDS), "Fall Enrollment Survey" (IPEDS-EF:90); and IPEDS Spring 2001 through Spring 2019, Fall Enrollment component. (This table was prepared January 2020.)

Table 304.22. Total fall enrollment in private for-profit degree-granting postsecondary institutions, by state or jurisdiction: Selected years, 1980 through 2018

State or jurisdiction	1980	1990	2000	2010	2012	2013	2015	2016	2017	2018	Percent change, 2013 to 2018
1	2	3	4	5	6	7	8	9	10	11	12
United States	111,714	213,693	450,084	2,022,785	1,808,423	1,658,439	1,349,470	1,182,108	1,097,923	982,410	-40.8
Alabama	1,399	2,229	3,878	35,387	33,157	32,282	29,542	28,058	26,602	22,834	-29.3
Alaska	0	394	486	1,764	1,487	2,526	2,323	424	430	415	-83.6
Arizona	5,733	8,751	46,876	418,078	368,049	330,079	279,840	236,884	214,400	203,861	-38.2
Arkansas	1,722	1,702	757	3,414	2,082	1,615	683	491	376	424	-73.7
California	7,550	12,808	76,488	205,638	195,204	182,846	180,856	167,064	157,951	150,628	-17.6
Colorado	1,162	7,224	18,427	67,079	56,961	52,577	46,931	45,318	47,246	47,162	-10.3
Connecticut	387	702	1,772	5,440	8,941	9,156	8,185	8,321	9,084	9,928	8.4
Delaware	0	0	0	490	387	378	326	301	320	351	-7.1
District of Columbia	1,881	2,916	2,978	7,937	5,674	5,002	9,578	9,515	10,371	11,885	137.6
Florida	3,775	11,529	37,192	172,440	169,878	149,401	81,662	73,156	70,187	67,283	-55.0
Georgia	4,879	9,076	10,326	61,735	49,936	46,324	38,745	34,651	30,683	26,598	-42.6
Hawaii	0	0	1,876	3,710	3,869	4,406	2,990	2,626	2,292	1,097	-75.1
Idaho	0	433	676	2,812	2,478	1,645	1,119	637	508	428	-74.0
Illinois	6,745	12,244	24,907	93,848	82,123	72,278	71,797	66,859	63,709	59,767	-17.3
Indiana	3,388	3,950	7,004	32,860	24,578	19,652	14,111	8,099	7,257	3,320	-83.1
Iowa	302	830	2,341	146,656	131,410	114,811	50,023	41,963	37,657	3,360	-97.1
Kansas	0	98	470	4,014	3,937	5,087	15,213	12,604	11,196	9,825	93.1
Kentucky	5,856	4,673	8,353	23,825	17,810	14,771	10,331	8,299	8,274	7,709	-47.8
Louisiana	375	2,367	4,624	11,198	8,994	8,169	6,862	5,348	4,965	3,387	-58.5
Maine	1,128	1,338	974	1,925	1,419	1,481	1,887	1,616	1,344	207	-86.0
Maryland	94	360	3,419	13,294	9,076	8,278	7,313	6,036	5,920	4,471	-46.0
Massachusetts	643	566	1,844	7,646	7,034	5,623	4,204	2,744	2,132	2,070	-63.2
Michigan	0	0	3,101	11,010	8,785	7,664	4,944	2,966	2,555	1,659	-78.4
Minnesota	2,020	3,076	11,958	115,769	107,925	103,831	103,613	99,198	92,928	92,429	-11.0
Mississippi	1,147	1,811	409	3,104	2,565	2,672	1,976	1,650	1,856	1,201	-55.1
Missouri	1,759	3,604	10,055	34,802	29,587	31,354	14,155	9,725	8,051	3,966	-87.4
Montana	517	0	0	0	0	0	0	35	37	43	†
Nebraska	0	332	1,978	3,773	2,609	2,650	1,828	1,319	972	153	-94.2
Nevada	0	147	4,187	12,887	11,260	10,654	7,469	5,777	5,444	4,907	-53.9
New Hampshire	1,892	2,447	3,909	4,896	3,708	3,048	1,492	0	0	0	-100.0
New Jersey	825	3,674	6,975	9,856	9,118	10,634	10,401	10,465	10,747	10,966	3.1
New Mexico	0	301	5,031	10,588	8,298	7,571	5,288	3,911	2,624	1,506	-80.1
New York	21,997	24,892	35,599	55,294	52,174	50,424	45,365	41,821	38,472	37,840	-25.0
North Carolina	3,654	1,874	590	18,697	18,292	18,823	16,703	14,013	11,992	10,460	-44.4
North Dakota	0	0	111	1,765	1,000	964	603	549	527	615	-36.2
Ohio	11,255	20,328	13,674	51,175	39,227	34,371	24,404	18,570	15,401	14,047	-59.1
Oklahoma	1,958	3,656	3,223	10,262	9,342	8,702	6,113	4,477	3,992	2,415	-72.2
Oregon	164	961	3,020	10,896	9,015	7,481	5,168	3,603	2,979	2,388	-68.1
Pennsylvania	7,242	37,104	31,164	72,720	54,756	50,958	35,475	27,422	21,543	13,521	-73.5
Rhode Island	0	0	224	0	0	0	0	0	0	0	†
South Carolina	2,925	1,434	757	16,895	15,993	15,932	12,562	11,162	11,629	7,058	-55.7
South Dakota	0	1,424	2,704	4,747	4,600	3,704	2,189	2,155	1,930	2,089	-43.6
Tennessee	3,295	3,845	5,571	31,512	25,652	24,983	17,106	16,038	15,519	12,860	-48.5
Texas	1,838	6,451	17,316	70,269	56,277	55,712	51,291	40,027	39,395	33,202	-40.4
Utah	0	808	4,744	15,282	15,038	7,987	5,297	4,615	4,352	4,179	-47.7
Vermont	0	0	337	615	517	462	379	300	144	73	-84.2
Virginia	735	5,014	17,134	58,198	50,632	47,046	40,505	35,148	31,913	30,047	-36.1
Washington	488	3,607	5,497	13,561	10,855	9,963	6,312	7,199	6,747	5,412	-45.7
West Virginia	305	860	1,952	43,375	61,482	58,667	55,890	52,700	50,485	50,130	-14.6
Wisconsin	653	1,150	1,907	17,641	13,279	12,333	8,421	6,249	2,785	2,196	-82.2
Wyoming	26	703	1,289	2,006	1,953	1,462	0	0	0	38	-97.4
Other jurisdictions	6,355	164,618	194,633	43,146	42,914	41,820	40,563	38,401	36,701	31,232	-25.3
American Samoa	0	1,219	297	0	0	0	0	0	0	0	†
Federated States of Micronesia	0	975	1,576	0	0	0	0	0	0	0	†
Guam	0	4,741	5,215	0	0	0	0	0	0	0	†
Marshall Islands	0	0	328	0	0	0	0	0	0	0	†
Northern Marianas	0	661	1,078	0	0	0	0	0	0	0	†
Palau	0	491	581	0	0	0	0	0	0	0	†
Puerto Rico	6,355	154,065	183,290	43,146	42,914	41,820	40,563	38,401	36,701	31,232	-25.3
U.S. Virgin Islands	0	2,466	2,268	0	0	0	0	0	0	0	†

†Not applicable.
NOTE: Data through 1990 are for institutions of higher education, while later data are for degree-granting institutions. Degree-granting institutions grant associate's or higher degrees and participate in Title IV federal financial aid programs. The degree-granting classification is very similar to the earlier higher education classification, but it includes more 2-year colleges and excludes a few higher education institutions that did not grant degrees. Some data have been revised from previously published figures.

SOURCE: U.S. Department of Education, National Center for Education Statistics, Higher Education General Information Survey (HEGIS), "Fall Enrollment in Colleges and Universities" survey, 1980; Integrated Postsecondary Education Data System (IPEDS), "Fall Enrollment Survey" (IPEDS-EF:90); and IPEDS Spring 2001 through Spring 2019, Fall Enrollment component. (This table was prepared January 2020.)

Table 304.30. Total fall enrollment in degree-granting postsecondary institutions, by attendance status, sex, and state or jurisdiction: 2017 and 2018

State or jurisdiction	2017 Total	2017 Full-time Males	2017 Full-time Females	2017 Part-time Males	2017 Part-time Females	2018 Total	2018 Full-time Males	2018 Full-time Females	2018 Part-time Males	2018 Part-time Females	Percent change, 2017 to 2018
1	2	3	4	5	6	7	8	9	10	11	12
United States	19,778,151	5,423,955	6,652,186	3,147,359	4,554,651	19,645,918	5,338,934	6,652,787	3,103,728	4,550,469	-0.7
Alabama	306,817	91,970	118,873	39,522	56,452	304,182	89,797	116,948	39,958	57,479	-0.9
Alaska	26,905	5,485	6,705	5,409	9,306	25,692	5,126	6,323	5,057	9,186	-4.5
Arizona	591,122	141,786	196,426	94,483	158,427	581,982	135,977	188,169	94,537	163,299	-1.5
Arkansas	163,963	44,881	58,757	23,301	37,024	159,738	43,198	57,698	22,762	36,080	-2.6
California	2,724,446	665,176	827,351	558,940	672,979	2,712,420	660,564	832,468	550,771	668,617	-0.4
Colorado	360,236	95,560	109,193	64,269	91,214	360,537	94,850	111,629	63,371	90,687	0.1
Connecticut	197,534	58,447	70,992	25,363	42,732	197,480	57,954	71,751	24,775	43,000	#
Delaware	60,338	15,918	21,376	7,965	15,079	60,700	15,831	21,559	7,881	15,429	0.6
District of Columbia	95,999	25,965	38,178	12,279	19,577	97,776	26,073	38,737	12,474	20,492	1.9
Florida	1,073,338	265,282	350,453	182,876	274,727	1,068,063	262,973	353,235	179,316	272,539	-0.5
Georgia	538,124	144,116	194,896	75,723	123,389	543,443	142,719	196,570	79,369	124,785	1.0
Hawaii	64,125	15,659	21,771	10,376	16,319	61,855	14,533	20,926	10,065	16,331	-3.5
Idaho	131,803	27,695	32,239	29,016	42,853	123,487	27,904	33,060	24,625	37,898	-6.3
Illinois	757,001	201,572	236,661	123,667	195,101	738,448	195,385	234,805	118,461	189,797	-2.5
Indiana	398,802	121,301	142,262	57,892	77,347	388,348	118,999	140,588	54,526	74,235	-2.6
Iowa	260,801	73,441	79,614	41,604	66,142	254,058	71,910	78,623	40,862	62,663	-2.6
Kansas	213,997	59,690	64,184	37,923	52,200	212,737	58,189	63,617	37,830	53,101	-0.6
Kentucky	258,498	66,423	89,574	43,704	58,797	262,961	69,016	90,575	44,286	59,084	1.7
Louisiana	241,567	66,556	94,299	29,315	51,397	241,401	66,364	96,614	28,291	50,132	-0.1
Maine	71,811	19,554	24,020	9,644	18,593	71,773	19,187	23,873	10,053	18,660	-0.1
Maryland	364,178	87,111	101,730	74,525	100,812	361,442	85,352	100,876	73,751	101,463	-0.8
Massachusetts	503,539	161,201	192,140	57,461	92,737	499,769	159,187	191,879	57,138	91,565	-0.7
Michigan	558,072	157,306	176,811	95,601	128,354	541,096	153,053	175,363	90,558	122,122	-3.0
Minnesota	412,966	94,227	125,640	66,074	127,025	408,783	92,241	126,186	64,338	126,018	-1.0
Mississippi	171,824	53,131	75,552	15,386	27,755	169,360	50,286	72,829	16,464	29,781	-1.4
Missouri	385,483	105,974	129,656	59,274	90,579	374,424	100,863	125,363	58,730	89,468	-2.9
Montana	50,642	17,412	17,980	5,869	9,381	49,363	16,635	17,498	5,953	9,277	-2.5
Nebraska	135,710	40,242	47,157	19,992	28,319	134,938	38,980	46,347	20,289	29,322	-0.6
Nevada	117,574	26,886	36,078	22,872	31,738	117,798	26,965	36,032	22,807	31,994	0.2
New Hampshire	149,184	29,337	38,914	28,460	52,473	160,743	30,576	42,121	30,624	57,422	7.7
New Jersey	419,037	131,377	143,515	59,872	84,273	414,416	130,541	143,158	58,234	82,483	-1.1
New Mexico	129,595	28,211	35,831	25,972	39,581	123,297	26,026	33,859	24,685	38,727	-4.9
New York	1,260,557	404,510	491,234	146,069	218,744	1,250,287	400,139	491,531	143,092	215,525	-0.8
North Carolina	564,111	156,448	203,139	77,753	126,771	563,710	154,504	201,933	78,070	129,203	-0.1
North Dakota	53,749	18,770	18,292	7,514	9,173	53,286	18,235	18,126	7,489	9,436	-0.9
Ohio	649,586	192,545	219,991	94,259	142,791	644,962	188,767	218,435	92,003	145,757	-0.7
Oklahoma	202,150	60,390	70,764	27,760	43,236	195,943	56,725	69,359	27,009	42,850	-3.1
Oregon	229,988	64,634	78,304	38,827	48,223	228,140	62,439	77,280	39,104	49,317	-0.8
Pennsylvania	717,025	242,852	279,962	72,050	122,161	700,329	234,273	275,567	70,105	120,384	-2.3
Rhode Island	82,765	27,742	34,659	7,682	12,682	80,868	27,453	34,120	7,272	12,023	-2.3
South Carolina	246,416	74,108	97,010	26,901	48,397	240,533	72,906	95,054	25,475	47,098	-2.4
South Dakota	53,620	16,230	16,728	7,984	12,678	53,365	15,905	16,707	8,070	12,683	-0.5
Tennessee	323,157	100,053	130,691	35,515	56,898	322,115	97,314	130,278	35,830	58,693	-0.3
Texas	1,630,520	387,457	465,124	318,908	459,031	1,643,542	384,004	467,710	319,572	472,256	0.8
Utah	331,996	103,814	138,924	43,149	46,309	359,772	111,363	156,848	42,809	48,752	8.4
Vermont	43,855	15,396	16,407	4,724	7,328	42,914	14,973	16,316	4,534	7,091	-2.1
Virginia	554,120	153,150	188,204	86,804	125,962	552,041	152,793	191,686	84,284	123,278	-0.4
Washington	367,943	115,274	138,436	49,054	65,179	367,056	113,364	138,830	49,513	65,349	-0.2
West Virginia	142,966	34,777	39,523	36,928	31,738	140,103	32,257	37,948	37,348	32,550	-2.0
Wisconsin	340,301	96,750	112,774	54,071	76,706	336,409	94,452	112,491	52,641	76,825	-1.1
Wyoming	33,014	8,931	9,364	6,760	7,959	32,510	8,332	9,267	6,650	8,261	-1.5
U.S. Service Academies	15,281	11,432	3,828	18	3	15,523	11,482	4,022	17	2	1.6
Other jurisdictions	192,717	62,759	86,060	17,998	25,900	212,565	69,481	98,503	18,092	26,489	10.3
American Samoa	1,095	205	410	164	316	1,037	195	418	124	300	-5.3
Federated States of Micronesia	2,022	639	815	257	311	1,931	634	781	234	282	-4.5
Guam	6,027	1,695	2,237	886	1,209	5,888	1,651	2,174	896	1,167	-2.3
Marshall Islands	1,032	331	336	196	169	1,119	380	360	191	188	8.4
Northern Marianas	1,216	354	559	124	179	1,194	349	578	104	163	-1.8
Palau	532	164	188	74	106	497	117	150	72	158	-6.6
Puerto Rico	178,623	58,889	80,635	16,067	23,032	198,915	65,722	93,171	16,272	23,750	11.4
U.S. Virgin Islands	2,170	482	880	230	578	1,984	433	871	199	481	-8.6

#Rounds to zero.
NOTE: Degree-granting institutions grant associate's or higher degrees and participate in Title IV federal financial aid programs. Some data have been revised from previously published figures.

SOURCE: U.S. Department of Education, National Center for Education Statistics, Integrated Postsecondary Education Data System (IPEDS), Spring 2018 and Spring 2019, Fall Enrollment component. (This table was prepared January 2020.)

Table 304.35. Total fall enrollment in public degree-granting postsecondary institutions, by attendance status, sex, and state or jurisdiction: 2017 and 2018

State or jurisdiction	2017					2018					Percent change, 2017 to 2018
	Total	Full-time		Part-time		Total	Full-time		Part-time		
		Males	Females	Males	Females		Males	Females	Males	Females	
1	2	3	4	5	6	7	8	9	10	11	12
United States	**14,571,739**	**3,857,431**	**4,469,043**	**2,624,115**	**3,621,150**	**14,529,264**	**3,787,941**	**4,480,879**	**2,603,530**	**3,656,914**	**-0.3**
Alabama	254,071	74,203	96,246	32,969	50,653	255,087	72,952	97,147	33,201	51,787	0.4
Alaska	25,850	5,289	6,133	5,306	9,122	24,649	4,936	5,735	4,953	9,025	-4.6
Arizona	366,787	90,375	98,218	75,047	103,147	367,198	87,940	98,735	74,940	105,583	0.1
Arkansas	146,578	38,360	50,741	22,134	35,343	142,382	36,664	49,735	21,565	34,418	-2.9
California	2,257,256	515,912	604,857	521,696	614,791	2,250,219	514,188	611,606	514,775	609,650	-0.3
Colorado	278,909	74,706	78,038	54,672	71,493	279,495	74,548	78,844	54,141	71,962	0.2
Connecticut	116,090	32,653	36,476	18,798	28,163	114,529	32,028	36,521	18,281	27,699	-1.3
Delaware	42,321	12,727	17,222	4,488	7,884	42,601	12,787	17,560	4,363	7,891	0.7
District of Columbia	4,529	1,050	1,206	830	1,443	4,500	1,036	1,197	848	1,419	-0.6
Florida	798,045	181,640	227,474	155,578	233,353	800,451	180,635	231,016	154,014	234,786	0.3
Georgia	428,586	115,084	146,935	66,216	100,351	435,744	113,576	149,155	70,018	102,995	1.7
Hawaii	51,674	12,080	15,581	9,201	14,812	51,063	11,482	15,453	9,089	15,039	-1.2
Idaho	75,792	18,453	20,740	14,690	21,909	77,133	18,142	21,085	14,870	23,036	1.8
Illinois	478,042	122,250	129,588	96,430	129,774	465,229	117,478	127,488	93,360	126,903	-2.7
Indiana	301,562	87,402	96,787	51,562	65,811	296,229	86,116	97,242	48,548	64,323	-1.8
Iowa	170,262	51,117	50,326	30,347	38,472	199,231	51,927	55,569	36,783	54,952	17.0
Kansas	179,624	49,741	53,637	31,783	44,463	179,600	48,500	53,240	32,132	45,728	#
Kentucky	202,266	53,145	68,233	34,491	46,397	199,748	50,979	67,572	34,719	46,478	-1.2
Louisiana	210,166	57,512	77,279	27,768	47,607	210,696	57,368	80,314	26,701	46,313	0.3
Maine	46,999	12,283	13,326	7,845	13,545	48,332	12,010	13,446	8,281	14,595	2.8
Maryland	303,614	70,748	79,761	66,368	86,737	301,959	69,549	79,629	65,438	87,343	-0.5
Massachusetts	213,388	59,644	64,619	34,182	54,943	207,767	57,016	62,954	33,684	54,113	-2.6
Michigan	478,735	133,968	150,110	83,964	110,693	466,806	130,309	149,192	80,258	107,047	-2.5
Minnesota	249,385	66,561	73,545	45,331	63,948	245,164	64,864	73,047	44,292	62,961	-1.7
Mississippi	152,392	48,624	67,625	13,279	22,864	150,583	45,900	65,448	14,356	24,879	-1.2
Missouri	237,454	66,014	78,906	36,840	55,694	232,040	62,660	76,836	36,225	56,319	-2.3
Montana	46,002	15,834	15,819	5,648	8,701	44,925	15,115	15,466	5,725	8,619	-2.3
Nebraska	101,038	29,570	31,906	17,199	22,363	100,594	29,278	32,112	16,645	22,559	-0.4
Nevada	107,864	23,908	30,673	22,445	30,838	108,658	24,258	30,972	22,387	31,041	0.7
New Hampshire	39,761	12,907	15,160	4,447	7,247	38,735	12,685	14,851	4,375	6,824	-2.6
New Jersey	334,597	99,889	110,370	52,439	71,899	329,037	98,373	109,706	51,043	69,915	-1.7
New Mexico	125,381	27,136	33,469	25,757	39,019	120,293	25,212	32,061	24,566	38,454	-4.1
New York	697,458	215,895	248,886	95,192	137,485	690,097	211,638	247,145	94,227	137,087	-1.1
North Carolina	454,998	118,312	152,809	71,274	112,603	456,128	116,740	152,933	71,619	114,836	0.2
North Dakota	47,574	16,888	15,366	7,034	8,286	46,531	16,257	15,063	6,870	8,341	-2.2
Ohio	497,409	140,321	154,805	82,121	120,162	495,612	136,593	153,336	80,742	124,941	-0.4
Oklahoma	174,239	48,788	58,315	26,081	41,055	170,979	46,536	58,025	25,510	40,908	-1.9
Oregon	192,402	53,364	58,990	36,471	43,577	191,943	51,780	58,291	36,950	44,922	-0.2
Pennsylvania	401,045	132,642	142,412	49,588	76,403	392,771	127,742	139,774	48,664	76,591	-2.1
Rhode Island	41,018	10,563	14,628	5,775	10,052	40,082	10,631	14,810	5,397	9,244	-2.3
South Carolina	200,622	59,898	74,953	24,044	41,727	196,525	59,162	74,160	22,698	40,505	-2.0
South Dakota	44,630	14,203	13,525	6,747	10,155	43,871	13,736	13,441	6,576	10,078	-1.7
Tennessee	223,179	67,470	83,070	28,797	43,842	225,281	65,732	83,417	29,616	46,516	0.9
Texas	1,448,398	326,263	380,891	303,811	437,433	1,468,587	324,380	388,301	305,072	450,834	1.4
Utah	180,034	48,153	48,276	40,039	43,566	183,949	48,712	49,749	39,868	45,620	2.2
Vermont	25,300	7,565	9,503	2,667	5,565	25,197	7,475	9,642	2,629	5,451	-0.4
Virginia	389,251	109,603	127,095	64,099	88,454	384,879	108,617	127,274	62,198	86,790	-1.1
Washington	318,336	99,257	113,978	45,683	59,418	319,377	97,946	115,019	46,438	59,974	0.3
West Virginia	83,898	28,669	32,107	8,648	14,474	81,605	26,750	31,242	8,776	14,837	-2.7
Wisconsin	279,097	78,858	85,271	49,516	65,452	277,178	77,222	84,999	48,437	66,520	-0.7
Wyoming	32,550	8,502	9,329	6,760	7,959	32,472	8,299	9,262	6,650	8,261	-0.2
U.S. Service Academies	15,281	11,432	3,828	18	3	15,523	11,482	4,022	17	2	1.6
Other jurisdictions	**37,419**	**14,488**	**15,921**	**3,145**	**3,865**	**72,399**	**26,338**	**34,587**	**5,004**	**6,470**	**93.5**
American Samoa	1,095	205	410	164	316	1,037	195	418	124	300	-5.3
Federated States of Micronesia	2,022	639	815	257	311	1,931	634	781	234	282	-4.5
Guam	5,972	1,673	2,217	880	1,202	5,826	1,628	2,150	888	1,160	-2.4
Marshall Islands	1,032	331	336	196	169	1,119	380	360	191	188	8.4
Northern Marianas	1,216	354	559	124	179	1,194	349	578	104	163	-1.8
Palau	532	164	188	74	106	497	117	150	72	158	-6.6
Puerto Rico	23,380	10,640	10,516	1,220	1,004	58,811	22,602	29,279	3,192	3,738	151.5
U.S. Virgin Islands	2,170	482	880	230	578	1,984	433	871	199	481	-8.6

#Rounds to zero.
NOTE: Degree-granting institutions grant associate's or higher degrees and participate in Title IV federal financial aid programs. Some data have been revised from previously published figures.

SOURCE: U.S. Department of Education, National Center for Education Statistics, Integrated Postsecondary Education Data System (IPEDS), Spring 2018 and Spring 2019, Fall Enrollment component. (This table was prepared January 2020.)

Table 304.60. Total fall enrollment in degree-granting postsecondary institutions, by control and level of institution and state or jurisdiction: 2017 and 2018

State or jurisdiction	2017						2018					
	Public 4-year	Public 2-year	Private 4-year Nonprofit	Private 4-year For-profit	Private 2-year Nonprofit	Private 2-year For-profit	Public 4-year	Public 2-year	Private 4-year Nonprofit	Private 4-year For-profit	Private 2-year Nonprofit	Private 2-year For-profit
1	2	3	4	5	6	7	8	9	10	11	12	13
United States	**8,854,279**	**5,717,460**	**4,060,094**	**911,007**	**48,395**	**186,916**	**8,982,560**	**5,546,704**	**4,089,090**	**829,060**	**45,154**	**153,350**
Alabama	173,335	80,736	26,144	24,841	†	1,761	174,857	80,230	26,261	22,728	†	106
Alaska	25,850	†	551	†	74	430	24,649	†	547	†	81	415
Arizona	180,262	186,525	9,935	203,877	†	10,523	188,360	178,838	10,923	194,257	†	9,604
Arkansas	100,055	46,523	15,713	323	1,296	53	98,718	43,664	15,606	368	1,326	56
California	1,014,651	1,242,605	307,742	131,822	1,497	26,129	1,016,497	1,233,722	310,313	127,229	1,260	23,399
Colorado	212,011	66,898	33,730	39,861	351	7,385	238,952	40,543	33,750	38,775	130	8,387
Connecticut	66,710	49,380	72,360	9,084	†	†	66,620	47,909	73,023	9,928	†	†
Delaware	42,321	†	17,554	320	143	†	42,601	†	17,630	351	118	†
District of Columbia	4,529	†	81,099	9,984	†	387	4,500	†	81,391	11,537	†	348
Florida	770,419	27,626	184,960	50,603	20,146	19,584	777,268	23,183	179,885	50,822	20,444	16,461
Georgia	314,455	114,131	77,092	24,084	1,763	6,599	318,412	117,332	79,170	21,258	1,931	5,340
Hawaii	27,535	24,139	10,159	1,670	†	622	27,336	23,727	9,695	406	†	691
Idaho	52,432	23,360	55,503	79	†	429	53,392	23,741	45,926	†	†	428
Illinois	184,631	293,411	214,829	59,655	421	4,054	181,814	283,415	213,041	56,854	411	2,913
Indiana	226,076	75,486	89,435	4,403	548	2,854	224,223	72,006	88,384	668	415	2,652
Iowa	80,020	90,242	52,882	37,550	†	107	109,809	89,422	51,467	3,284	†	76
Kansas	100,731	78,893	23,177	10,154	†	1,042	100,937	78,663	23,312	9,015	†	810
Kentucky	124,710	77,556	47,958	7,272	†	1,002	122,074	77,674	55,504	6,726	†	983
Louisiana	143,905	66,261	25,955	56	481	4,909	145,708	64,988	26,826	75	492	3,312
Maine	30,040	16,959	23,226	1,096	242	248	31,720	16,612	23,173	†	61	207
Maryland	184,495	119,119	54,644	3,511	†	2,409	186,212	115,747	55,012	3,181	†	1,290
Massachusetts	125,770	87,618	286,926	1,914	1,093	218	124,447	83,320	288,720	1,937	1,212	133
Michigan	327,750	150,985	76,782	1,411	†	1,144	322,932	143,874	72,631	411	†	1,248
Minnesota	132,119	117,266	70,563	92,658	90	270	128,746	116,418	71,084	92,204	106	225
Mississippi	80,730	71,662	17,576	359	†	1,497	78,558	72,025	17,576	508	†	693
Missouri	148,708	88,746	139,805	4,929	173	3,122	146,372	85,668	138,235	2,885	183	1,081
Montana	38,116	7,886	4,228	†	375	37	36,977	7,948	4,090	†	305	43
Nebraska	60,740	40,298	33,668	903	32	69	60,365	40,229	34,176	107	15	46
Nevada	97,144	10,720	3,994	1,862	272	3,582	108,658	†	4,136	1,836	97	3,071
New Hampshire	27,308	12,453	109,300	†	123	†	26,950	11,785	121,896	†	112	†
New Jersey	187,735	146,862	73,693	6,894	†	3,853	189,539	139,498	74,254	6,891	159	4,075
New Mexico	58,353	67,028	1,590	1,283	†	1,341	55,908	64,385	1,498	519	†	987
New York	400,971	296,487	521,937	27,702	2,696	10,770	403,935	286,162	519,645	27,680	2,705	10,160
North Carolina	232,872	222,126	96,497	8,875	624	3,117	237,460	218,668	96,528	8,335	594	2,125
North Dakota	40,368	7,206	5,648	527	†	†	39,204	7,327	6,140	615	†	†
Ohio	326,478	170,931	135,357	6,092	1,419	9,309	334,004	161,608	134,139	4,904	1,164	9,143
Oklahoma	117,916	56,323	23,338	1,464	581	2,528	116,267	54,712	21,971	1,088	578	1,327
Oregon	104,604	87,798	34,573	2,209	34	770	103,375	88,568	33,764	1,621	45	767
Pennsylvania	277,538	123,507	288,384	8,544	6,053	12,999	271,256	121,515	289,345	4,083	4,692	9,438
Rhode Island	26,260	14,758	41,747	†	†	†	25,543	14,539	40,786	†	†	†
South Carolina	114,569	86,053	33,375	7,883	790	3,746	115,686	80,839	36,081	4,308	869	2,750
South Dakota	37,897	6,733	7,060	1,930	†	†	37,034	6,837	7,405	2,089	†	†
Tennessee	136,810	86,369	83,777	7,698	682	7,821	137,180	88,101	83,265	7,510	709	5,350
Texas	737,555	710,843	140,806	18,175	1,921	21,220	785,517	683,070	140,143	17,501	1,610	15,701
Utah	150,414	29,620	145,565	3,862	2,045	490	154,793	29,156	169,648	3,699	1,996	480
Vermont	19,796	5,504	18,411	144	†	†	19,819	5,378	17,644	73	†	†
Virginia	219,882	169,369	132,378	28,278	578	3,635	220,817	164,062	136,722	26,840	393	3,207
Washington	282,316	36,020	41,472	5,044	1,388	1,703	286,838	32,539	41,326	4,110	941	1,302
West Virginia	67,191	16,707	8,583	47,715	†	2,770	65,121	16,484	8,368	47,815	†	2,315
Wisconsin	189,518	89,579	58,419	2,407	†	378	186,627	90,551	57,035	2,029	†	167
Wyoming	12,397	20,153	†	†	464	†	12,450	20,022	†	†	†	38
U.S. Service Academies	15,281	†	†	†	†	†	15,523	†	†	†	†	†
Other jurisdictions	**29,524**	**7,895**	**118,239**	**18,879**	**358**	**17,822**	**65,951**	**6,448**	**108,807**	**17,989**	**127**	**13,243**
American Samoa	1,095	†	†	†	†	†	1,037	†	†	†	†	†
Federated States of Micronesia	†	2,022	†	†	†	†	†	1,931	†	†	†	†
Guam	3,917	2,055	55	†	†	†	3,744	2,082	62	†	†	†
Marshall Islands	†	1,032	†	†	†	†	1,119	†	†	†	†	†
Northern Marianas	1,216	†	†	†	†	†	1,194	†	†	†	†	†
Palau	†	532	†	†	†	†	†	497	†	†	†	†
Puerto Rico	21,126	2,254	118,184	18,879	358	17,822	56,873	1,938	108,745	17,989	127	13,243
U.S. Virgin Islands	2,170	†	†	†	†	†	1,984	†	†	†	†	†

†Not applicable.
NOTE: Degree-granting institutions grant associate's or higher degrees and participate in Title IV federal financial aid programs. Some data have been revised from previously published figures.

SOURCE: U.S. Department of Education, National Center for Education Statistics, Integrated Postsecondary Education Data System (IPEDS), Spring 2018 and Spring 2019, Fall Enrollment component. (This table was prepared January 2020.)

Table 305.10. Total fall enrollment of first-time degree/certificate-seeking students in degree-granting postsecondary institutions, by attendance status, sex of student, and level and control of institution: 1960 through 2029

Year	Total	Full-time	Part-time	Males Total	Males Full-time	Males Part-time	Females Total	Females Full-time	Females Part-time	4-year Public	4-year Private	2-year Public	2-year Private
1	2	3	4	5	6	7	8	9	10	11	12	13	14
1960[1]	923,069	—	—	539,512	—	—	383,557	—	—	395,884[2]	313,209[2]	181,860[2]	32,116[2]
1961[1]	1,018,361	—	—	591,913	—	—	426,448	—	—	438,135[2]	336,449[2]	210,101[2]	33,676[2]
1962[1]	1,030,554	—	—	598,099	—	—	432,455	—	—	445,191[2]	324,923[2]	224,537[2]	35,903[2]
1963[1]	1,046,424	—	—	604,282	—	—	442,142	—	—	—	—	—	—
1964[1]	1,224,840	—	—	701,524	—	—	523,316	—	—	539,251[2]	363,348[2]	275,413[2]	46,828[2]
1965[1]	1,441,822	—	—	829,215	—	—	612,607	—	—	642,233[2]	398,792[2]	347,788[2]	53,009[2]
1966	1,554,337	—	—	889,516	—	—	664,821	—	—	626,472[2]	382,889[2]	478,459[2]	66,517[2]
1967	1,640,936	1,335,512	305,424	931,127	761,299	169,828	709,809	574,213	135,596	644,525	368,300	561,488	66,623
1968	1,892,849	1,470,653	422,196	1,082,367	847,005	235,362	810,482	623,648	186,834	724,377	378,052	718,562	71,858
1969	1,967,104	1,525,290	441,814	1,118,269	876,280	241,989	848,835	649,010	199,825	699,167	391,508	814,132	62,297
1970	2,063,397	1,587,072	476,325	1,151,960	896,281	255,679	911,437	690,791	220,646	717,449	395,886	890,703	59,359
1971	2,119,018	1,606,036	512,982	1,170,518	895,715	274,803	948,500	710,321	238,179	704,052	384,695	971,295	58,976
1972	2,152,778	1,574,197	578,581	1,157,501	858,254	299,247	995,277	715,943	279,334	680,337	380,982	1,036,616	54,843
1973	2,226,041	1,607,269	618,772	1,182,173	867,314	314,859	1,043,868	739,955	303,913	698,777	378,994	1,089,182	59,088
1974	2,365,761	1,673,333	692,428	1,243,790	896,077	347,713	1,121,971	777,256	344,715	745,637	386,391	1,175,759	57,974
1975	2,515,155	1,763,296	751,859	1,327,935	942,198	385,737	1,187,220	821,098	366,122	771,725	395,440	1,283,523	64,467
1976	2,347,014	1,662,333	684,681	1,170,326	854,597	315,729	1,176,688	807,736	368,952	717,373	413,961	1,152,944	62,736
1977	2,394,426	1,680,916	713,510	1,155,856	839,848	316,008	1,238,570	841,068	397,502	737,497	404,631	1,185,648	66,650
1978	2,389,627	1,650,848	738,779	1,141,777	817,294	324,483	1,247,850	833,554	414,296	736,703	406,669	1,173,544	72,711
1979	2,502,896	1,706,732	796,164	1,179,846	840,315	339,531	1,323,050	866,417	456,633	760,119	415,126	1,253,854	73,797
1980	2,587,644	1,749,928	837,716	1,218,961	862,458	356,503	1,368,683	887,470	481,213	765,395	417,937	1,313,591	90,721[3]
1981	2,595,421	1,737,714	857,707	1,217,680	851,833	365,847	1,377,741	885,881	491,860	754,007	419,257	1,318,436	103,721[3]
1982	2,505,466	1,688,620	816,846	1,199,237	837,223	362,014	1,306,229	851,397	454,832	730,775	404,252	1,254,193	116,246[3]
1983	2,443,703	1,678,071	765,632	1,159,049	824,609	334,440	1,284,654	853,462	431,192	728,244	403,882	1,189,869	121,708
1984	2,356,898	1,613,185	743,713	1,112,303	786,099	326,204	1,244,595	827,086	417,509	713,790	402,959	1,130,311	109,838
1985	2,292,222	1,602,038	690,184	1,075,736	774,858	300,878	1,216,486	827,180	389,306	717,199	398,556	1,060,275	116,192
1986	2,219,208	1,589,451	629,757	1,046,527	768,856	277,671	1,172,681	820,595	352,086	719,974	391,673	990,973	116,588
1987	2,246,359	1,626,719	619,640	1,046,615	779,226	267,389	1,199,744	847,493	352,251	757,833	405,113	979,820	103,593
1988	2,378,803	1,698,927	679,876	1,100,026	807,319	292,707	1,278,777	891,608	387,169	783,358	425,907	1,048,914	120,624
1989	2,341,035	1,656,594	684,441	1,094,750	791,295	303,455	1,246,285	865,299	380,986	762,217	413,836	1,048,529	116,453
1990	2,256,624	1,617,118	639,506	1,045,191	771,372	273,819	1,211,433	845,746	365,687	727,264	400,120	1,041,097	88,143
1991	2,277,920	1,652,983	624,937	1,068,433	798,043	270,390	1,209,487	854,940	354,547	717,697	392,904	1,070,048	97,271
1992	2,184,113	1,603,737	580,376	1,013,058	760,290	252,768	1,171,055	843,447	327,608	697,393	408,306	993,074	85,340
1993	2,160,710	1,608,274	552,436	1,007,647	762,240	245,407	1,153,063	846,034	307,029	702,273	410,688	973,545	74,204
1994	2,133,205	1,603,106	530,099	984,558	751,081	233,477	1,148,647	852,025	296,622	709,042	405,917	952,468	65,778
1995	2,168,831	1,646,812	522,019	1,001,052	767,185	233,867	1,167,779	879,627	288,152	731,836	419,025	954,595	63,375
1996	2,274,319	1,739,852	534,467	1,046,662	805,982	240,680	1,227,657	933,870	293,787	741,164	427,442	989,536	116,177
1997	2,219,255	1,733,512	485,743	1,026,058	806,054	220,004	1,193,197	927,458	265,739	755,362	442,397	923,954	97,542
1998	2,212,593	1,775,412	437,181	1,022,656	825,577	197,079	1,189,937	949,835	240,102	792,772	460,948	858,411	100,456
1999	2,357,590	1,849,741	507,849	1,094,539	865,545	228,994	1,263,051	984,196	278,855	819,503	474,223	955,499	108,365
2000	2,427,551	1,918,093	509,458	1,123,948	894,432	229,516	1,303,603	1,023,661	279,942	842,228	498,532	952,175	134,616
2001	2,497,078	1,989,179	507,899	1,152,837	926,393	226,444	1,344,241	1,062,786	281,455	866,619	508,030	988,726	133,703
2002	2,570,611	2,053,065	517,546	1,170,609	945,938	224,671	1,400,002	1,107,127	292,875	886,297	517,621	1,037,267	129,426
2003	2,591,754	2,102,394	489,360	1,175,856	965,075	210,781	1,415,898	1,137,319	278,579	918,602	537,726	1,004,428	130,998
2004	2,630,243	2,147,546	482,697	1,190,268	981,591	208,677	1,439,975	1,165,955	274,020	925,249	562,485	1,009,082	133,427
2005	2,657,338	2,189,884	467,454	1,200,055	995,610	204,445	1,457,283	1,194,274	263,009	953,903	606,712	977,224	119,499
2006	2,707,205	2,220,184	487,021	1,228,703	1,015,786	212,917	1,478,502	1,204,398	274,104	990,077	598,266	1,013,419	105,443
2007	2,777,168	2,295,518	481,650	1,268,137	1,053,375	214,762	1,509,031	1,242,143	266,888	1,023,789	633,772	1,016,636	102,971
2008	3,022,736	2,425,987	596,749	1,388,441	1,114,724	273,717	1,634,295	1,311,263	323,032	1,053,829	672,372	1,186,640	109,895
2009	3,156,882	2,534,440	622,442	1,464,424	1,177,119	287,305	1,692,458	1,357,321	335,137	1,090,980	658,808	1,275,974	131,120
2010	3,156,727	2,533,636	623,091	1,461,016	1,171,090	289,926	1,695,711	1,362,546	333,165	1,110,601	674,573	1,238,491	133,062
2011	3,091,496	2,479,155	612,341	1,424,140	1,140,843	283,297	1,667,356	1,338,312	329,044	1,131,091	656,864	1,195,083	108,458
2012	2,994,187	2,408,063	586,124	1,387,316	1,115,266	272,050	1,606,871	1,292,797	314,074	1,128,344	642,716	1,137,927	85,200
2013	2,985,366	2,415,969	569,397	1,383,852	1,117,525	266,327	1,601,514	1,298,444	303,070	1,144,102	633,184	1,126,978	81,102
2014	2,925,998	2,383,328	542,670	1,355,164	1,100,005	255,159	1,570,834	1,283,323	287,511	1,170,639	612,162	1,070,625	72,572
2015	2,882,949	2,368,283	514,666	1,338,853	1,096,976	241,877	1,544,096	1,271,307	272,789	1,190,206	599,242	1,031,117	62,384
2016	2,882,991	2,369,021	513,970	1,333,598	1,093,968	239,630	1,549,393	1,275,053	274,340	1,259,214	581,098	981,029	61,650
2017	2,883,001	2,377,999	505,002	1,326,237	1,091,909	234,328	1,556,764	1,286,090	270,674	1,285,500	588,395	954,930	54,176
2018	2,885,818	2,392,319	493,499	1,317,522	1,093,233	224,289	1,568,296	1,299,086	269,210	1,309,453	595,543	934,085	46,737
2019[4]	2,895,000	—	—	1,320,000	—	—	1,575,000	—	—	—	—	—	—
2020[4]	2,898,000	—	—	1,321,000	—	—	1,577,000	—	—	—	—	—	—
2021[4]	2,903,000	—	—	1,323,000	—	—	1,581,000	—	—	—	—	—	—
2022[4]	2,908,000	—	—	1,325,000	—	—	1,584,000	—	—	—	—	—	—
2023[4]	2,915,000	—	—	1,327,000	—	—	1,588,000	—	—	—	—	—	—
2024[4]	2,925,000	—	—	1,332,000	—	—	1,593,000	—	—	—	—	—	—
2025[4]	2,935,000	—	—	1,336,000	—	—	1,598,000	—	—	—	—	—	—
2026[4]	2,946,000	—	—	1,342,000	—	—	1,604,000	—	—	—	—	—	—
2027[4]	2,950,000	—	—	1,344,000	—	—	1,606,000	—	—	—	—	—	—
2028[4]	2,952,000	—	—	1,345,000	—	—	1,607,000	—	—	—	—	—	—
2029[4]	2,952,000	—	—	1,345,000	—	—	1,607,000	—	—	—	—	—	—

—Not available.

[1]Excludes first-time degree/certificate-seeking students in occupational programs not creditable towards a bachelor's degree.

[2]Data for 2-year branches of 4-year college systems are aggregated with the 4-year institutions.

[3]Large increases are due to the addition of schools accredited by the Accrediting Commission of Career Schools and Colleges of Technology.

[4]Projected.

NOTE: Data through 1995 are for institutions of higher education, while later data are for degree-granting institutions. Degree-granting institutions grant associate's or higher degrees and participate in Title IV federal financial aid programs. The degree-granting classification is very similar to the earlier higher education classification, but it includes more 2-year colleges and excludes a few higher education institutions that did not grant degrees. Alaska and Hawaii are included in all years. Some data have been revised from previously published figures.

SOURCE: U.S. Department of Education, National Center for Education Statistics, *Biennial Survey of Education in the United States*; *Opening Fall Enrollment in Higher Education*, 1963 through 1965; Higher Education General Information Survey (HEGIS), "Fall Enrollment in Colleges and Universities" surveys, 1966 through 1985; Integrated Postsecondary Education Data System (IPEDS), "Fall Enrollment Survey" (IPEDS-EF:86–99); IPEDS Spring 2001 through Spring 2019, Fall Enrollment component; and First-Time Freshmen Projection Model, 1980 through 2029. (This table was prepared December 2019.)

Table 305.20. Total fall enrollment of first-time degree/certificate-seeking students in degree-granting postsecondary institutions, by attendance status, sex of student, control of institution, and state or jurisdiction: Selected years, 2000 through 2018

State or jurisdiction	Total, fall 2000	Total, fall 2010	Total, fall 2015	Total, fall 2016	Total, fall 2017	Fall 2018 Total	Full-time Total	Full-time Males	Full-time Females	Part-time Total	Part-time Males	Part-time Females	Public	Private
1	2	3	4	5	6	7	8	9	10	11	12	13	14	15
United States	2,427,551	3,156,727	2,882,949	2,882,991	2,883,001	2,885,818	2,392,319	1,093,233	1,299,086	493,499	224,289	269,210	2,243,538	642,280
Alabama	43,411	52,990	50,151	50,108	50,263	48,346	43,016	18,863	24,153	5,330	2,441	2,889	43,501	4,845
Alaska	2,432	5,400	3,849	3,049	3,234	2,931	2,227	969	1,258	704	279	425	2,623	308
Arizona	46,646	76,832	67,751	65,784	62,440	61,748	44,007	20,329	23,678	17,741	7,594	10,147	51,814	9,934
Arkansas	22,695	29,321	27,388	27,276	26,779	26,567	24,053	10,782	13,271	2,514	1,104	1,410	22,902	3,665
California	246,128	402,832	383,920	394,845	390,289	387,767	277,907	127,275	150,632	109,860	57,322	52,538	344,117	43,650
Colorado	43,201	54,594	43,349	43,832	45,436	45,827	37,808	17,957	19,851	8,019	3,468	4,551	38,288	7,539
Connecticut	24,212	32,719	31,398	31,741	31,804	31,656	27,105	12,308	14,797	4,551	1,953	2,598	19,037	12,619
Delaware	7,636	8,947	9,352	9,727	10,051	9,879	8,469	3,572	4,897	1,410	535	875	8,731	1,148
District of Columbia	9,150	10,747	11,075	9,012	10,617	10,506	9,453	3,501	5,952	1,053	362	691	617	9,889
Florida	109,931	176,040	157,687	158,956	160,114	161,033	123,638	52,844	70,794	37,395	15,818	21,577	119,415	41,618
Georgia	67,616	100,140	86,071	84,932	85,737	87,518	72,456	31,274	41,182	15,062	6,526	8,536	71,495	16,023
Hawaii	8,931	10,740	8,851	8,398	8,691	8,645	7,104	2,720	4,384	1,541	653	888	6,952	1,693
Idaho	10,669	12,668	14,179	14,520	15,450	14,874	12,754	5,481	7,273	2,120	934	1,186	9,781	5,093
Illinois	107,592	114,467	95,852	93,994	92,736	92,486	78,563	37,344	41,219	13,923	6,343	7,580	63,451	29,035
Indiana	59,320	82,406	66,876	64,028	62,696	64,865	57,172	26,689	30,483	7,693	3,603	4,090	48,430	16,435
Iowa	39,564	47,257	37,851	38,130	38,056	35,591	31,645	16,084	15,561	3,946	1,551	2,395	27,103	8,488
Kansas	31,424	33,544	32,268	32,597	32,379	30,960	26,786	13,364	13,422	4,174	1,889	2,285	26,804	4,156
Kentucky	34,140	43,735	37,623	36,378	37,257	38,634	33,950	14,585	19,365	4,684	2,067	2,617	31,356	7,278
Louisiana	45,383	43,144	40,740	40,261	39,782	40,876	36,527	15,419	21,108	4,349	1,804	2,545	35,184	5,692
Maine	9,231	12,203	11,357	11,727	11,597	11,665	10,586	5,044	5,542	1,079	431	648	7,742	3,923
Maryland	35,552	51,104	44,767	47,084	44,436	44,708	35,180	16,491	18,689	9,528	4,104	5,424	37,992	6,716
Massachusetts	66,044	76,857	73,189	72,432	73,366	71,899	64,620	29,717	34,903	7,279	3,058	4,221	33,584	38,315
Michigan	84,998	101,063	89,224	86,314	83,041	81,937	66,626	31,214	35,412	15,311	7,110	8,201	72,113	9,824
Minnesota	63,893	55,723	45,323	45,102	44,752	44,218	38,424	18,361	20,063	5,794	2,553	3,241	33,153	11,065
Mississippi	30,356	37,034	31,185	32,088	31,145	31,041	29,399	12,860	16,539	1,642	744	898	29,084	1,957
Missouri	48,639	64,381	54,660	53,824	52,028	50,900	45,079	20,360	24,719	5,821	2,662	3,159	37,792	13,108
Montana	7,771	9,959	8,749	8,959	8,770	8,511	7,333	3,764	3,569	1,178	535	643	7,657	854
Nebraska	19,027	19,284	18,092	18,423	17,883	18,258	16,612	8,016	8,596	1,646	751	895	14,797	3,461
Nevada	10,490	18,572	15,917	16,112	17,169	18,143	13,744	5,917	7,827	4,399	2,124	2,275	17,118	1,025
New Hampshire	13,143	13,613	17,097	15,728	18,388	20,398	12,826	5,796	7,030	7,572	2,581	4,991	7,802	12,596
New Jersey	52,233	71,296	65,232	65,178	65,109	65,246	57,771	28,056	29,715	7,475	3,385	4,090	53,495	11,751
New Mexico	15,261	22,353	18,045	19,085	18,282	16,654	13,345	5,959	7,386	3,309	1,352	1,957	16,275	379
New York	168,181	197,849	187,059	185,714	187,805	188,267	179,943	84,480	95,463	8,324	3,807	4,517	112,664	75,603
North Carolina	69,343	92,627	88,995	88,547	88,204	88,920	72,867	32,378	40,489	16,053	6,825	9,228	69,228	19,692
North Dakota	8,929	9,073	8,606	8,709	8,874	8,368	8,065	4,281	3,784	303	142	161	7,294	1,074
Ohio	98,823	123,063	100,029	101,393	99,542	107,591	89,106	42,131	46,975	18,485	7,233	11,252	81,991	25,600
Oklahoma	35,094	39,107	36,371	36,266	35,306	33,781	27,445	12,534	14,911	6,336	2,550	3,786	29,494	4,287
Oregon	26,946	35,442	30,765	31,324	32,002	32,046	25,631	11,540	14,091	6,415	3,043	3,372	27,330	4,716
Pennsylvania	125,578	144,184	126,933	125,063	122,264	118,558	106,220	49,337	56,883	12,338	5,088	7,250	69,744	48,814
Rhode Island	13,789	15,698	15,004	14,942	14,602	14,959	14,048	6,582	7,466	911	410	501	7,312	7,647
South Carolina	32,353	47,535	46,080	45,173	46,455	46,053	40,907	18,085	22,822	5,146	2,114	3,032	37,044	9,009
South Dakota	8,597	10,074	8,473	8,316	8,673	8,646	7,993	4,120	3,873	653	247	406	7,200	1,446
Tennessee	43,327	59,279	56,498	56,605	58,398	57,576	53,566	23,075	30,491	4,010	1,479	2,531	42,336	15,240
Texas	181,813	228,503	234,131	235,197	242,984	244,190	181,812	82,378	99,434	62,378	28,385	33,993	214,139	30,051
Utah	24,953	35,126	31,884	32,141	34,851	40,979	35,656	14,149	21,507	5,323	2,566	2,757	26,457	14,522
Vermont	6,810	8,242	7,202	7,474	7,393	7,249	6,626	3,215	3,411	623	209	414	4,343	2,906
Virginia	52,661	83,166	80,362	79,020	79,374	79,615	67,268	30,815	36,453	12,347	5,537	6,810	63,076	16,539
Washington	36,287	41,124	46,370	47,853	48,447	48,363	42,488	19,083	23,405	5,875	2,506	3,369	40,371	7,992
West Virginia	15,659	23,020	18,866	18,874	18,077	17,106	15,050	6,875	8,175	2,056	1,179	877	13,428	3,678
Wisconsin	53,662	61,249	50,978	51,423	50,654	50,357	42,953	20,180	22,773	7,404	3,139	4,265	41,000	9,357
Wyoming	4,209	6,042	5,210	5,227	5,173	4,828	4,411	2,084	2,327	417	194	223	4,803	25
U.S. Service Academies	3,818	4,359	4,065	4,106	4,146	4,079	4,079	2,996	1,083	0	0	0	4,079	†
Other jurisdictions	39,609	52,222	43,746	48,706	31,606	37,759	35,795	15,956	19,839	1,964	867	1,097	13,813	23,946
American Samoa	297	657	382	392	381	309	253	92	161	56	20	36	309	0
Federated States of Micronesia	786	653	708	760	647	698	607	289	318	91	39	52	698	0
Guam	770	1,043	1,101	985	1,275	1,093	792	318	474	301	132	169	1,077	16
Marshall Islands	199	240	327	303	279	336	292	144	148	44	23	21	336	0
Northern Marianas	333	360	290	305	336	343	297	121	176	46	25	21	343	0
Palau	147	114	200	148	165	121	111	53	58	10	4	6	121	0
Puerto Rico	36,773	48,672	40,347	45,468	28,215	34,539	33,149	14,841	18,308	1,390	612	778	10,609	23,930
U.S. Virgin Islands	304	483	391	345	308	320	294	98	196	26	12	14	320	0

†Not applicable.

NOTE: Degree-granting institutions grant associate's or higher degrees and participate in Title IV federal financial aid programs. Some data have been revised from previously published figures.

SOURCE: U.S. Department of Education, National Center for Education Statistics, Integrated Postsecondary Education Data System (IPEDS), Spring 2001 through Spring 2019, Fall Enrollment component. (This table was prepared December 2019.)

Table 305.40. Acceptance rates; number of applications, admissions, and enrollees; and enrollees' SAT and ACT scores for degree-granting postsecondary institutions with first-year undergraduates, by control and level of institution: 2018–19

Acceptance rates, applications, admissions, enrollees, and SAT and ACT scores	All institutions			Public institutions			Private institutions								
							Total			Nonprofit			For-profit		
	Total	4-year	2-year	Total	4-year	2-year	Total	4-year	2-year	Total	4-year	2-year	Total	4-year	2-year
1	2	3	4	5	6	7	8	9	10	11	12	13	14	15	16
Number of institutions reporting application data[1]	3,608	2,296	1,312	1,589	724	865	2,019	1,572	447	1,359	1,280	79	660	292	368
Percentage distribution of institutions by their acceptance of applications	100.0	100.0	100.0	100.0	100.0	100.0	100.0	100.0	100.0	100.0	100.0	100.0	100.0	100.0	100.0
No application criteria	49.3	25.0	92.0	65.3	25.6	98.6	36.8	24.7	79.2	17.4	14.5	64.6	76.5	69.2	82.3
90.0 percent or more accepted	8.0	11.1	2.6	4.5	9.9	0.0	10.7	11.6	7.6	11.8	12.0	7.6	8.6	9.9	7.6
75.0 to 89.9 percent accepted	12.9	19.2	2.0	12.1	26.4	0.1	13.6	15.9	5.6	17.7	18.2	10.1	5.2	5.8	4.6
50.0 to 74.9 percent accepted	20.2	30.3	2.6	13.2	27.6	1.0	25.8	31.6	5.6	35.4	36.8	12.7	6.1	8.6	4.1
25.0 to 49.9 percent accepted	7.0	10.7	0.7	4.2	8.8	0.2	9.3	11.5	1.6	12.6	13.1	3.8	2.6	4.5	1.1
10.0 to 24.9 percent accepted	1.9	2.8	0.2	0.7	1.5	0.0	2.8	3.4	0.4	3.6	3.8	1.3	1.1	2.1	0.3
Less than 10.0 percent accepted	0.6	0.9	0.0	0.1	0.1	0.0	1.0	1.3	0.0	1.5	1.6	0.0	0.0	0.0	0.0
Number of applications (in thousands)	11,273	11,210	63	6,350	6,326	24	4,922	4,884	39	4,834	4,810	24	89	74	15
Percentage distribution of admissions by institutions' acceptance of applications	100.0	100.0	100.0	100.0	100.0	100.0	100.0	100.0	100.0	100.0	100.0	100.0	100.0	100.0	100.0
No application criteria	†	†	†	†	†	†	†	†	†	†	†	†	†	†	†
90.0 percent or more accepted	4.4	4.4	10.6	5.4	5.4	0.0	3.2	3.1	17.3	3.0	3.0	1.2	12.4	6.2	42.4
75.0 to 89.9 percent accepted	20.5	20.6	13.1	24.6	24.7	4.9	15.3	15.3	18.3	15.4	15.4	13.1	10.2	6.8	26.5
50.0 to 74.9 percent accepted	37.4	37.3	46.8	37.8	37.5	91.6	36.9	37.0	18.5	36.3	36.5	14.4	65.0	73.2	24.8
25.0 to 49.9 percent accepted	22.7	22.8	2.7	25.9	26.0	3.5	18.6	18.7	2.2	18.7	18.8	0.8	12.0	13.6	4.4
10.0 to 24.9 percent accepted	10.3	10.2	26.8	6.1	6.1	0.0	15.7	15.5	43.8	16.0	15.8	70.4	0.4	0.1	1.8
Less than 10.0 percent accepted	4.6	4.7	0.0	0.3	0.3	0.0	10.3	10.4	0.0	10.5	10.6	0.0	0.0	0.0	0.0
Number of admissions (in thousands)	6,262	6,225	37	3,806	3,790	16	2,457	2,435	21	2,395	2,385	9	62	50	12
Percentage distribution of admissions by institutions' acceptance of applications	100.0	100.0	100.0	100.0	100.0	100.0	100.0	100.0	100.0	100.0	100.0	100.0	100.0	100.0	100.0
No application criteria	†	†	†	†	†	†	†	†	†	†	†	†	†	†	†
90.0 percent or more accepted	7.5	7.4	17.1	8.4	8.5	0.0	6.0	5.8	29.6	5.7	5.8	3.1	16.9	8.8	49.6
75.0 to 89.9 percent accepted	30.1	30.2	18.2	33.5	33.7	5.9	24.8	24.8	27.2	25.1	25.1	27.9	11.8	8.2	26.6
50.0 to 74.9 percent accepted	42.6	42.6	51.7	39.4	39.2	92.1	47.7	47.9	22.0	47.3	47.4	23.1	64.0	74.5	21.2
25.0 to 49.9 percent accepted	15.9	16.0	1.8	16.8	16.9	2.0	14.6	14.7	1.6	14.8	14.9	0.8	7.1	8.4	2.1
10.0 to 24.9 percent accepted	3.2	3.2	11.3	1.8	1.8	0.0	5.4	5.3	19.7	5.6	5.4	45.1	0.1	#	0.5
Less than 10.0 percent accepted	0.6	0.6	0.0	#	#	0.0	1.5	1.5	0.0	1.5	1.5	0.0	0.0	0.0	0.0
Number of enrollees (in thousands)	1,625	1,610	15	1,090	1,084	7	535	526	9	514	512	3	21	15	6
Percentage distribution of admissions by institutions' acceptance of applications	100.0	100.0	100.0	100.0	100.0	100.0	100.0	100.0	100.0	100.0	100.0	100.0	100.0	100.0	100.0
No application criteria	†	†	†	†	†	†	†	†	†	†	†	†	†	†	†
90.0 percent or more accepted	8.4	8.3	20.0	9.1	9.1	0.0	7.0	6.5	35.3	6.2	6.2	6.1	26.7	17.8	49.4
75.0 to 89.9 percent accepted	29.5	29.6	21.4	33.9	34.0	8.0	20.7	20.5	31.6	21.0	20.8	45.0	13.2	8.5	25.1
50.0 to 74.9 percent accepted	40.1	40.0	52.1	38.5	38.1	88.3	43.5	43.8	24.5	43.2	43.3	28.1	50.2	61.0	22.7
25.0 to 49.9 percent accepted	15.6	15.7	2.6	15.6	15.7	3.7	15.5	15.7	1.8	15.7	15.8	1.8	9.6	12.6	1.8
10.0 to 24.9 percent accepted	4.9	4.9	3.9	2.9	2.9	0.0	9.1	9.1	6.9	9.5	9.4	19.0	0.4	0.1	1.0
Less than 10.0 percent accepted	1.5	1.5	0.0	0.1	0.1	0.0	4.3	4.3	0.0	4.4	4.5	0.0	0.0	0.0	0.0
SAT scores of enrollees															
Evidence-based reading and writing (ERW), 25th percentile[2]	517	517	461	511	512	454	520	520	473	520	521	473	474	474	—
ERW, 75th percentile[2]	613	614	564	607	607	563	618	618	565	618	618	565	583	583	—
Mathematics, 25th percentile[2]	511	511	451	505	506	439	514	514	471	514	515	471	478	478	—
Mathematics, 75th percentile[2]	610	610	563	604	605	551	613	613	583	613	613	583	591	591	—
ACT scores of enrollees															
Composite, 25th percentile[2]	20.6	20.7	15.8	20.1	20.2	15.3	20.9	20.9	16.3	20.9	20.9	16.3	18.8	18.8	—
Composite, 75th percentile[2]	26.0	26.0	20.6	25.6	25.6	21.1	26.2	26.2	20.0	26.2	26.3	20.0	25.2	25.2	—
English, 25th percentile[2]	19.7	19.8	13.0	19.1	19.2	13.6	20.1	20.1	12.2	20.1	20.1	12.2	18.0	18.0	—
English, 75th percentile[2]	26.3	26.4	19.3	25.8	25.8	20.4	26.6	26.7	17.8	26.7	26.7	17.8	24.0	24.0	—
Mathematics, 25th percentile[2]	19.4	19.4	14.6	19.1	19.1	15.4	19.5	19.6	13.4	19.5	19.6	13.4	19.5	19.5	—
Mathematics, 75th percentile[2]	25.4	25.4	19.4	25.2	25.2	20.9	25.5	25.6	17.4	25.5	25.6	17.4	23.5	23.5	—

—Not available.
†Not applicable.
#Rounds to zero.
[1]The total on this table differs slightly from other counts of institutions with first-year undergraduates because approximately 1.0 percent of these institutions did not report application information.
[2]Data are only for institutions that require test scores for admission. Relatively few 2-year institutions require test scores for admission. The SAT evidence-based reading and writing (ERW) and mathematics scales range from 200 to 800. The ACT composite, English, and mathematics scales range from 1 to 36.

NOTE: Degree-granting institutions grant associate's or higher degrees and participate in Title IV federal financial aid programs. Excludes institutions not enrolling any first-time degree/certificate-seeking undergraduates. Detail may not sum to totals because of rounding.
SOURCE: U.S. Department of Education, National Center for Education Statistics, Integrated Postsecondary Education Data System (IPEDS), Winter 2018–19, Admissions component. (This table was prepared November 2019.)

Table 306.10. Total fall enrollment in degree-granting postsecondary institutions, by level of enrollment, sex, attendance status, and race/ethnicity or nonresident alien status of student: Selected years, 1976 through 2018

Columns 2–12 = Fall enrollment (in thousands). Columns 13–23 = Percentage distribution of U.S. resident students (excludes nonresident aliens).

Level of enrollment, sex, attendance status, and race/ethnicity or nonresident alien status of student	1976	1980	1990	2000	2010	2013	2014	2015	2016	2017	2018	1976	1980	1990	2000	2010	2013	2014	2015	2016	2017	2018
1	2	3	4	5	6	7	8	9	10	11	12	13	14	15	16	17	18	19	20	21	22	23
All students, total	10,985.6	12,086.8	13,818.6	15,312.3	21,019.4	20,376.7	20,209.1	19,988.2	19,846.9	19,778.2	19,645.9	100.0	100.0	100.0	100.0	100.0	100.0	100.0	100.0	100.0	100.0	100.0
White	9,076.1	9,833.0	10,722.5	10,462.1	12,720.8	11,589.4	11,239.3	10,939.2	10,716.6	10,517.4	10,301.3	84.3	83.5	79.9	70.8	62.6	59.3	58.3	57.6	56.9	56.0	55.2
Total, selected races/ethnicities	1,690.8	1,948.8	2,704.7	4,321.5	7,591.0	7,947.1	8,052.0	8,066.7	8,132.2	8,260.8	8,352.6	15.7	16.5	20.1	29.2	37.4	40.7	41.7	42.4	43.1	44.0	44.8
Black	1,033.0	1,106.8	1,247.0	1,730.3	3,039.0	2,872.0	2,792.8	2,681.0	2,589.4	2,549.5	2,493.3	9.6	9.4	9.3	11.7	15.0	14.7	14.5	14.1	13.7	13.6	13.4
Hispanic	383.8	471.7	782.4	1,461.8	2,748.8	3,093.2	3,191.9	3,297.7	3,428.0	3,546.0	3,645.0	3.6	4.0	5.8	9.9	13.5	15.8	16.5	17.4	18.2	18.9	19.5
Asian/Pacific Islander	197.9	286.4	572.4	978.2	1,281.6	1,259.7	1,272.2	1,284.3	1,306.7	1,327.8	1,352.6	1.8	2.4	4.3	6.6	6.3	6.4	6.6	6.8	6.9	7.1	7.3
Asian	—	—	—	—	1,217.6	1,198.7	1,213.8	1,229.0	1,253.5	1,275.7	1,302.1	—	—	—	—	6.0	6.1	6.3	6.5	6.7	6.8	7.0
Pacific Islander	—	—	—	—	64.0	61.0	58.5	55.3	53.2	52.0	50.5	—	—	—	—	0.3	0.3	0.3	0.3	0.3	0.3	0.3
American Indian/Alaska Native	76.1	83.9	102.8	151.2	196.2	162.2	152.9	146.1	142.3	137.5	133.8	0.7	0.7	0.8	1.0	1.0	0.8	0.8	0.8	0.8	0.7	0.7
Two or more races	—	—	—	—	325.4	560.0	642.2	657.6	665.3	700.1	727.9	—	—	—	—	1.6	2.9	3.3	3.5	3.5	3.7	3.9
Nonresident alien[1]	218.7	305.0	391.5	528.7	707.7	840.2	917.8	982.3	998.1	1,000.0	992.1	†	†	†	†	†	†	†	†	†	†	†
Male	5,794.4	5,868.1	6,283.9	6,721.8	9,045.8	8,861.2	8,797.5	8,723.8	8,638.4	8,571.3	8,442.7	100.0	100.0	100.0	100.0	100.0	100.0	100.0	100.0	100.0	100.0	100.0
White	4,813.7	4,772.9	4,861.0	4,634.6	5,605.8	5,132.4	4,974.3	4,848.5	4,736.1	4,632.2	4,500.5	85.3	84.4	80.5	72.1	64.7	61.1	60.0	59.3	58.6	57.8	57.0
Total, selected races/ethnicities	826.6	884.4	1,176.6	1,789.8	3,060.3	3,268.7	3,313.4	3,326.8	3,346.7	3,387.5	3,399.3	14.7	15.6	19.5	27.9	35.3	38.9	40.0	40.7	41.4	42.2	43.0
Black	469.9	463.7	484.7	635.3	1,089.0	1,064.9	1,035.1	998.9	959.5	942.0	909.7	8.3	8.2	8.0	9.9	12.6	12.7	12.5	12.2	11.9	11.7	11.5
Hispanic	209.7	231.6	353.9	627.1	1,157.6	1,307.7	1,348.2	1,389.2	1,439.3	1,479.0	1,507.6	3.7	4.1	5.9	9.8	13.4	15.6	16.3	17.0	17.8	18.4	19.1
Asian/Pacific Islander	108.4	151.3	294.9	465.9	600.6	594.3	599.1	602.9	610.1	617.3	625.6	1.9	2.7	4.9	7.3	6.9	7.1	7.2	7.4	7.5	7.7	7.9
Asian	—	—	—	—	572.1	567.1	573.0	577.8	586.4	594.0	603.3	—	—	—	—	6.6	6.8	6.9	7.1	7.3	7.4	7.6
Pacific Islander	—	—	—	—	28.5	27.2	26.1	25.1	23.7	23.3	22.2	—	—	—	—	0.3	0.3	0.3	0.3	0.3	0.3	0.3
American Indian/Alaska Native	38.5	37.8	43.1	61.4	78.7	64.7	61.3	58.2	56.3	53.7	51.6	0.7	0.7	0.7	1.0	0.9	0.8	0.7	0.7	0.7	0.7	0.7
Two or more races	—	—	—	—	134.4	237.1	269.7	277.6	281.7	295.5	304.8	—	—	—	—	1.6	2.8	3.3	3.4	3.5	3.7	3.9
Nonresident alien[1]	154.1	210.8	246.3	297.3	379.6	460.1	509.7	548.6	555.6	551.6	543.0	†	†	†	†	†	†	†	†	†	†	†
Female	5,191.2	6,218.7	7,534.7	8,590.5	11,973.7	11,515.5	11,411.6	11,264.4	11,208.5	11,206.8	11,203.3	100.0	100.0	100.0	100.0	100.0	100.0	100.0	100.0	100.0	100.0	100.0
White	4,262.4	5,060.1	5,861.5	5,827.5	7,115.0	6,457.0	6,265.0	6,090.7	5,980.5	5,885.2	5,800.8	83.1	82.6	79.3	69.7	61.1	58.0	56.9	56.2	55.6	54.7	53.9
Total, selected races/ethnicities	864.2	1,064.4	1,528.1	2,531.7	4,530.7	4,678.4	4,738.6	4,739.9	4,785.4	4,873.2	4,953.3	16.9	17.4	20.7	30.3	38.9	42.0	43.1	43.8	44.4	45.3	46.1
Black	563.1	643.0	762.3	1,095.0	1,950.3	1,807.1	1,757.7	1,682.1	1,630.0	1,607.5	1,583.6	11.0	10.5	10.3	13.1	16.7	16.2	16.0	15.7	15.1	14.9	14.7
Hispanic	174.1	240.1	428.5	834.7	1,591.2	1,785.5	1,843.7	1,908.5	1,988.7	2,067.0	2,137.4	3.4	3.9	5.8	10.0	13.7	16.0	16.8	17.6	18.5	19.2	19.9
Asian/Pacific Islander	89.4	135.2	277.5	512.3	681.0	665.4	673.1	681.5	696.6	710.5	727.0	1.7	2.2	3.8	6.1	5.8	6.0	6.1	6.3	6.5	6.6	6.8
Asian	—	—	—	—	645.5	631.6	640.7	651.3	667.1	681.7	698.8	—	—	—	—	5.5	5.7	5.8	6.0	6.2	6.3	6.5
Pacific Islander	—	—	—	—	35.5	33.7	32.4	30.2	29.5	28.7	28.3	—	—	—	—	0.3	0.3	0.3	0.3	0.3	0.3	0.3
American Indian/Alaska Native	37.6	46.1	59.7	89.7	117.5	97.5	91.6	88.0	86.0	83.7	82.2	0.7	0.8	0.8	1.1	1.0	0.9	0.8	0.8	0.8	0.8	0.8
Two or more races	—	—	—	—	191.0	322.9	372.5	379.9	384.1	404.6	423.1	—	—	—	—	1.6	2.9	3.4	3.5	3.6	3.8	3.9
Nonresident alien[1]	64.6	94.2	145.2	231.4	328.0	380.1	407.9	433.7	442.5	448.4	449.1	†	†	†	†	†	†	†	†	†	†	†
Full-time	6,703.6	7,088.9	7,821.0	9,009.6	13,087.2	12,596.6	12,454.5	12,287.5	12,125.3	12,076.1	11,991.7	100.0	100.0	100.0	100.0	100.0	100.0	100.0	100.0	100.0	100.0	100.0
White	5,512.6	5,717.0	6,016.5	6,231.1	8,053.5	7,237.7	6,983.3	6,784.0	6,611.4	6,482.2	6,359.5	84.2	83.4	79.9	72.5	64.3	60.8	59.7	59.1	58.5	57.6	56.9
Total, selected races/ethnicities	1,030.9	1,137.5	1,514.9	2,368.5	4,468.5	4,663.7	4,708.6	4,690.3	4,686.0	4,768.6	4,814.0	15.8	16.6	20.1	27.5	35.7	39.2	40.3	40.9	41.5	42.4	43.1
Black	659.2	685.6	718.3	982.6	1,811.3	1,669.0	1,600.4	1,537.3	1,469.5	1,453.7	1,416.3	10.1	10.0	9.5	11.4	14.5	14.0	13.7	13.4	13.0	12.9	12.7
Hispanic	211.1	247.0	394.7	710.3	1,501.0	1,701.8	1,747.9	1,786.2	1,843.3	1,913.7	1,964.6	3.2	3.6	5.2	8.3	12.0	14.3	14.9	15.6	16.3	17.0	17.6
Asian/Pacific Islander	117.7	162.0	347.4	591.2	820.8	821.2	832.1	843.8	857.4	870.0	888.0	1.8	2.4	4.6	6.9	6.6	6.9	7.1	7.4	7.6	7.7	7.9
Asian	—	—	—	—	733.0	785.5	798.1	812.2	826.9	840.6	859.6	—	—	—	—	5.9	6.6	6.8	7.1	7.3	7.5	7.7
Pacific Islander	—	—	—	—	37.8	35.7	34.0	31.6	30.4	29.4	28.4	—	—	—	—	0.3	0.3	0.3	0.3	0.3	0.3	0.3
American Indian/Alaska Native	43.0	43.0	54.4	84.4	118.3	94.2	88.0	82.8	80.5	76.3	73.6	0.7	0.6	0.7	1.0	0.9	0.8	0.8	0.7	0.7	0.7	0.7
Two or more races	—	—	—	—	217.2	377.5	440.3	440.2	435.4	454.6	471.5	—	—	—	—	1.7	3.2	3.8	3.8	3.9	4.0	4.2
Nonresident alien[1]	160.0	234.4	289.6	410.0	565.2	695.2	762.6	813.2	827.9	825.3	818.2	†	†	†	†	†	†	†	†	†	†	†
Part-time	4,282.1	4,997.9	5,997.7	6,302.7	7,932.3	7,780.1	7,754.6	7,700.7	7,721.6	7,702.0	7,654.2	100.0	100.0	100.0	100.0	100.0	100.0	100.0	100.0	100.0	100.0	100.0
White	3,563.5	4,116.0	4,706.0	4,231.0	4,667.3	4,351.7	4,256.0	4,155.1	4,105.2	4,035.2	3,941.8	84.4	83.5	79.8	68.4	59.9	57.0	56.0	55.2	54.4	53.6	52.7
Total, selected races/ethnicities	659.9	811.3	1,189.8	1,953.0	3,122.5	3,283.4	3,343.4	3,376.4	3,446.2	3,492.2	3,538.6	15.6	16.5	20.2	31.6	40.1	43.0	44.0	44.8	45.6	46.4	47.3
Black	373.8	421.2	528.7	747.7	1,227.9	1,203.0	1,192.5	1,143.7	1,119.9	1,095.8	1,077.0	8.9	8.5	9.0	12.1	15.8	15.8	15.7	15.2	15.0	14.6	14.4
Hispanic	172.7	224.8	387.7	751.5	1,247.9	1,391.4	1,444.0	1,511.5	1,584.7	1,632.2	1,680.5	4.1	4.6	6.6	12.2	16.0	18.2	19.0	20.1	21.0	21.7	22.5
Asian/Pacific Islander	80.2	124.4	225.1	387.1	460.8	438.5	440.2	440.5	449.3	457.7	464.6	1.9	2.5	3.8	6.3	5.9	5.7	5.8	5.8	5.9	6.1	6.2
Asian	—	—	—	—	434.6	413.2	415.7	416.9	426.5	435.1	442.5	—	—	—	—	5.6	5.4	5.5	5.5	5.6	5.8	5.9
Pacific Islander	—	—	—	—	26.2	25.3	24.4	23.6	22.8	22.6	22.1	—	—	—	—	0.3	0.3	0.3	0.3	0.3	0.3	0.3
American Indian/Alaska Native	33.1	40.9	48.4	66.8	78.0	68.0	64.9	63.3	61.9	61.1	60.2	0.8	0.8	0.8	1.1	1.0	0.9	0.9	0.8	0.8	0.8	0.8
Two or more races	—	—	—	—	108.2	182.5	201.9	217.4	230.4	245.3	256.4	—	—	—	—	1.4	2.4	2.7	2.9	3.1	3.3	3.4
Nonresident alien[1]	58.7	70.6	101.8	118.7	142.5	145.0	155.2	169.1	170.2	174.6	173.8	†	†	†	†	†	†	†	†	†	†	†

See notes at end of table.

Table 306.10. Total fall enrollment in degree-granting postsecondary institutions, by level of enrollment, sex, attendance status, and race/ethnicity or nonresident alien status of student: Selected years, 1976 through 2018—Continued

Level of enrollment, sex, attendance status, and race/ethnicity or nonresident alien status of student	Fall enrollment (in thousands)											Percentage distribution of U.S. resident students (excludes nonresident aliens)										
	1976	1980	1990	2000	2010	2013	2014	2015	2016	2017	2018	1976	1980	1990	2000	2010	2013	2014	2015	2016	2017	2018
1	2	3	4	5	6	7	8	9	10	11	12	13	14	15	16	17	18	19	20	21	22	23
Undergraduate, total	9,419.0	10,469.1	11,959.1	13,155.4	18,082.4	17,476.3	17,294.1	17,046.7	16,874.6	16,773.0	16,610.2	100.0	100.0	100.0	100.0	100.0	100.0	100.0	100.0	100.0	100.0	100.0
White	7,740.5	8,480.7	9,272.6	8,983.5	10,895.9	9,898.1	9,582.5	9,303.8	9,085.6	8,882.8	8,664.5	83.4	82.7	79.0	69.8	61.6	58.2	57.2	56.4	55.7	54.8	54.0
Total, selected races/ethnicities	1,535.3	1,778.5	2,467.7	3,884.0	6,788.1	7,094.6	7,182.3	7,177.8	7,218.9	7,316.2	7,379.1	16.6	17.3	21.0	30.2	38.4	41.8	42.8	43.6	44.3	45.2	46.0
Black	943.4	1,018.8	1,147.2	1,548.9	2,677.1	2,504.7	2,426.7	2,316.5	2,226.4	2,184.0	2,127.9	10.2	9.9	9.8	12.0	15.1	14.7	14.5	14.1	13.7	13.5	13.3
Hispanic	352.9	433.1	724.6	1,351.0	2,551.0	2,872.2	2,962.4	3,055.0	3,168.3	3,270.6	3,352.7	3.8	4.2	6.2	10.5	14.4	16.9	17.7	18.5	19.4	20.2	20.9
Asian/Pacific Islander	169.3	248.7	500.5	845.5	1,087.3	1,064.5	1,074.9	1,084.0	1,100.3	1,113.6	1,131.8	1.8	2.4	4.3	6.6	6.1	6.3	6.4	6.6	6.7	6.9	7.1
Asian	—	—	—	—	1,029.8	1,010.3	1,022.9	1,034.8	1,053.2	1,067.5	1,087.1	—	—	—	—	5.8	5.9	6.1	6.3	6.5	6.6	6.8
Pacific Islander	—	—	—	—	57.5	54.1	52.1	49.2	47.1	46.1	44.7	—	—	—	—	0.3	0.3	0.3	0.3	0.3	0.3	0.3
American Indian/Alaska Native	69.7	77.9	95.5	138.5	179.1	147.4	138.6	132.2	128.6	123.9	120.2	0.8	0.8	0.8	1.1	1.0	0.9	0.8	0.8	0.8	0.8	0.7
Two or more races	—	—	—	—	293.7	505.8	579.6	590.1	595.2	624.0	646.5	—	—	—	—	1.7	3.0	3.5	3.6	3.7	3.9	4.0
Nonresident alien[1]	143.2	209.9	218.7	288.0	398.4	483.6	529.3	565.1	570.2	574.1	566.6	†	†	†	†	†	†	†	†	†	†	†
Male	4,896.8	4,997.4	5,379.8	5,778.3	7,836.3	7,660.1	7,586.3	7,502.3	7,416.9	7,351.3	7,226.0	100.0	100.0	100.0	100.0	100.0	100.0	100.0	100.0	100.0	100.0	100.0
White	4,052.2	4,054.9	4,184.4	4,010.1	4,861.0	4,438.9	4,299.0	4,188.1	4,087.0	3,990.0	3,867.3	84.4	83.5	79.6	71.3	63.7	60.0	58.9	58.2	57.5	56.7	55.9
Total, selected races/ethnicities	748.2	802.7	1,069.3	1,618.0	2,773.8	2,962.7	3,000.4	3,007.0	3,020.2	3,051.8	3,056.3	15.6	16.5	20.4	28.7	36.3	40.0	41.1	41.8	42.5	43.3	44.1
Black	430.7	428.2	448.0	577.0	982.9	955.3	924.9	888.4	849.4	831.7	800.5	9.0	8.8	8.5	10.3	12.9	12.9	12.7	12.3	12.0	11.8	11.6
Hispanic	191.7	211.2	326.9	582.6	1,082.9	1,224.1	1,261.8	1,298.3	1,343.5	1,378.5	1,402.7	4.0	4.3	6.2	10.4	14.2	16.5	17.3	18.0	18.9	19.6	20.3
Asian/Pacific Islander	91.1	128.5	254.5	401.9	513.4	507.5	511.7	515.0	520.6	525.3	531.5	1.9	2.6	4.8	7.1	6.7	6.9	7.0	7.2	7.3	7.5	7.7
Asian	—	—	—	—	487.4	482.9	488.1	492.3	499.2	504.2	511.5	—	—	—	—	6.4	6.5	6.7	6.8	7.0	7.2	7.4
Pacific Islander	—	—	—	—	26.0	24.5	23.5	22.7	21.4	21.1	20.0	—	—	—	—	0.3	0.3	0.3	0.3	0.3	0.3	0.3
American Indian/Alaska Native	34.8	34.8	39.9	56.4	72.3	59.4	56.1	53.2	51.5	49.1	47.1	0.7	0.7	0.8	1.0	0.9	0.8	0.8	0.7	0.7	0.7	0.7
Two or more races	—	—	—	—	122.3	216.6	245.9	252.1	255.2	267.2	274.6	—	—	—	—	1.6	2.9	3.4	3.5	3.6	3.8	4.0
Nonresident alien[1]	96.4	139.8	126.1	150.2	201.5	258.5	286.8	307.2	309.6	309.4	302.5	†	†	†	†	†	†	†	†	†	†	†
Female	4,522.1	5,471.7	6,579.3	7,377.1	10,246.1	9,816.2	9,707.8	9,544.4	9,457.8	9,421.8	9,384.2	100.0	100.0	100.0	100.0	100.0	100.0	100.0	100.0	100.0	100.0	100.0
White	3,688.3	4,425.8	5,088.2	4,973.3	6,035.0	5,459.2	5,283.5	5,115.7	4,998.6	4,892.7	4,797.2	82.4	81.9	78.4	68.7	60.1	56.9	55.8	55.1	54.3	53.4	52.6
Total, selected races/ethnicities	787.0	975.8	1,398.5	2,266.0	4,014.3	4,131.8	4,181.9	4,170.8	4,198.7	4,264.3	4,322.8	17.6	18.1	21.6	31.3	39.9	43.1	44.2	44.9	45.7	46.6	47.4
Black	512.7	590.6	699.2	971.9	1,694.2	1,549.4	1,501.7	1,428.2	1,376.9	1,352.3	1,327.5	11.5	10.9	10.8	13.4	16.9	16.2	15.9	15.4	15.0	14.8	14.6
Hispanic	161.2	221.8	397.6	768.4	1,468.1	1,648.1	1,700.6	1,756.7	1,824.9	1,892.0	1,950.0	3.6	4.1	6.1	10.6	14.6	17.2	18.0	18.9	19.8	20.7	21.4
Asian/Pacific Islander	78.2	120.2	246.0	443.6	573.9	557.0	563.2	569.0	579.7	588.3	600.3	1.7	2.2	3.8	6.1	5.7	5.8	6.0	6.1	6.3	6.4	6.6
Asian	—	—	—	—	542.4	527.4	534.7	542.5	554.0	563.3	575.7	—	—	—	—	5.4	5.5	5.6	5.8	6.0	6.2	6.3
Pacific Islander	—	—	—	—	31.5	29.6	28.5	26.5	25.7	25.0	24.7	—	—	—	—	0.3	0.3	0.3	0.3	0.3	0.3	0.3
American Indian/Alaska Native	34.9	43.1	55.5	82.1	106.8	88.0	82.6	79.1	77.1	74.8	73.1	0.8	0.8	0.9	1.1	1.1	0.9	0.9	0.9	0.8	0.8	0.8
Two or more races	—	—	—	—	171.3	289.2	333.7	337.9	340.0	356.9	372.0	—	—	—	—	1.7	3.0	3.5	3.6	3.7	3.9	4.1
Nonresident alien[1]	46.8	70.1	92.6	137.8	196.9	225.1	242.5	257.9	260.5	264.7	264.2	†	†	†	†	†	†	†	†	†	†	†
Postbaccalaureate, total	1,566.6	1,617.7	1,859.5	2,156.9	2,937.0	2,900.4	2,915.0	2,941.5	2,972.3	3,005.1	3,035.7	100.0	100.0	100.0	100.0	100.0	100.0	100.0	100.0	100.0	100.0	100.0
White	1,335.6	1,352.4	1,449.8	1,478.6	1,824.9	1,691.3	1,656.7	1,635.4	1,631.0	1,634.6	1,636.8	89.6	88.8	86.0	77.2	69.4	66.5	65.6	64.8	64.1	63.4	62.7
Total, selected races/ethnicities	155.5	170.3	237.0	437.5	802.8	852.5	869.7	888.9	913.3	944.6	973.5	10.4	11.2	14.0	22.8	30.6	33.5	34.4	35.2	35.9	36.6	37.3
Black	89.7	87.9	99.8	181.4	361.9	367.3	366.2	364.5	363.0	365.5	365.4	6.0	5.8	5.9	9.5	13.8	14.4	14.5	14.4	14.3	14.2	14.0
Hispanic	30.9	38.6	57.9	110.8	197.8	221.0	229.4	242.7	259.6	275.4	292.4	2.1	2.5	3.4	5.8	7.5	8.7	9.1	9.6	10.2	10.7	11.2
Asian/Pacific Islander	28.6	37.7	72.0	132.7	194.3	195.2	197.3	200.3	206.3	214.2	220.8	1.9	2.5	4.3	6.9	7.4	7.7	7.8	7.9	8.1	8.3	8.5
Asian	—	—	—	—	187.8	188.4	190.9	194.3	200.3	208.2	215.0	—	—	—	—	7.1	7.4	7.6	7.7	7.9	8.1	8.2
Pacific Islander	—	—	—	—	6.5	6.8	6.4	6.1	6.1	5.9	5.8	—	—	—	—	0.2	0.3	0.3	0.2	0.2	0.2	0.2
American Indian/Alaska Native	6.4	6.0	7.3	12.6	17.1	14.8	14.3	13.9	13.7	13.6	13.6	0.4	0.4	0.4	0.7	0.7	0.6	0.6	0.6	0.5	0.5	0.5
Two or more races	—	—	—	—	31.7	54.2	62.6	67.5	70.6	76.1	81.3	—	—	—	—	1.2	2.1	2.5	2.7	2.8	2.9	3.1
Nonresident alien[1]	75.5	95.1	172.7	240.7	309.3	356.5	388.5	417.2	428.0	425.9	425.4	†	†	†	†	†	†	†	†	†	†	†
Male	897.6	870.7	904.2	943.5	1,209.5	1,201.1	1,211.2	1,221.6	1,221.6	1,220.1	1,216.7	100.0	100.0	100.0	100.0	100.0	100.0	100.0	100.0	100.0	100.0	100.0
White	761.6	718.1	676.6	624.5	744.9	693.5	675.2	660.3	649.0	642.1	633.2	90.7	89.8	86.3	78.4	72.2	69.4	68.3	67.4	66.5	65.7	64.9
Total, selected races/ethnicities	78.4	81.7	107.4	171.9	286.5	306.0	313.0	319.8	326.5	335.7	343.0	9.3	10.2	13.7	21.6	27.8	30.6	31.7	32.6	33.5	34.3	35.1
Black	39.2	35.5	36.7	58.3	106.1	109.6	110.2	110.5	110.0	110.3	109.2	4.7	4.4	4.7	7.3	10.3	11.0	11.1	11.3	11.3	11.3	11.2
Hispanic	18.1	20.4	27.0	44.5	74.7	83.6	86.4	90.9	95.8	100.5	104.9	2.2	2.5	3.4	5.6	7.2	8.4	8.7	9.3	9.8	10.3	10.7
Asian/Pacific Islander	17.4	22.8	40.4	64.0	87.2	86.9	87.4	87.8	89.5	92.0	94.1	2.1	2.8	5.2	8.0	8.5	8.7	8.8	9.0	9.2	9.4	9.6
Asian	—	—	—	—	84.7	84.2	84.9	85.5	87.2	89.8	91.9	—	—	—	—	8.2	8.4	8.6	8.7	8.9	9.2	9.4
Pacific Islander	—	—	—	—	2.5	2.7	2.5	2.3	2.3	2.2	2.2	—	—	—	—	0.2	0.3	0.3	0.2	0.2	0.2	0.2
American Indian/Alaska Native	3.7	3.0	3.2	5.0	6.4	5.3	5.3	5.0	4.8	4.6	4.5	0.4	0.4	0.4	0.6	0.6	0.5	0.5	0.5	0.5	0.5	0.5
Two or more races	—	—	—	—	12.0	20.6	23.7	25.5	26.5	28.3	30.2	—	—	—	—	1.2	2.1	2.4	2.6	2.7	2.9	3.1
Nonresident alien[1]	57.7	71.0	120.2	147.1	178.2	201.6	223.0	241.4	246.0	242.2	240.5	†	†	†	†	†	†	†	†	†	†	†

See notes at end of table.

Table 306.10. Total fall enrollment in degree-granting postsecondary institutions, by level of enrollment, sex, attendance status, and race/ethnicity or nonresident alien status of student: Selected years, 1976 through 2018—Continued

Level of enrollment, sex, attendance status, and race/ethnicity or nonresident alien status of student	Fall enrollment (in thousands)											Percentage distribution of U.S. resident students (excludes nonresident aliens)										
	1976	1980	1990	2000	2010	2013	2014	2015	2016	2017	2018	1976	1980	1990	2000	2010	2013	2014	2015	2016	2017	2018
1	2	3	4	5	6	7	8	9	10	11	12	13	14	15	16	17	18	19	20	21	22	23
Female	669.1	747.0	955.4	1,213.4	1,727.5	1,699.3	1,703.7	1,720.0	1,750.7	1,785.1	1,819.0	100.0	100.0	100.0	100.0	100.0	100.0	100.0	100.0	100.0	100.0	100.0
White	574.1	634.3	773.2	854.1	1,080.0	997.8	981.5	975.0	982.0	992.5	1,003.6	88.1	87.7	85.6	76.3	67.7	64.6	63.8	63.1	62.6	62.0	61.4
Total, selected races/ethnicities	77.2	88.6	129.6	265.7	516.4	546.5	556.8	569.2	586.8	608.9	630.5	11.9	12.3	14.4	23.7	32.3	35.4	36.2	36.9	37.4	38.0	38.6
Black	50.5	52.4	63.1	123.1	255.8	257.7	256.0	254.0	253.0	255.1	256.2	7.7	7.2	7.0	11.0	16.0	16.7	16.6	16.4	16.1	15.9	15.7
Hispanic	12.8	18.3	30.9	66.3	123.1	137.4	143.1	151.8	163.8	174.9	187.4	2.0	2.5	3.4	5.9	7.7	8.9	9.3	9.8	10.4	10.9	11.5
Asian/Pacific Islander	11.2	15.0	31.5	68.7	107.0	108.3	109.9	112.5	116.9	122.1	126.7	1.7	2.1	3.5	6.1	7.7	7.0	7.1	7.3	7.5	7.6	7.8
Asian	—	—	—	—	103.1	104.2	106.0	108.8	113.1	118.4	123.1	—	—	—	—	6.5	6.7	6.9	7.0	7.2	7.4	7.5
Pacific Islander	—	—	—	—	3.9	4.1	3.9	3.7	3.8	3.7	3.6	—	—	—	—	0.2	0.3	0.3	0.2	0.2	0.2	0.2
American Indian/Alaska Native	2.7	3.0	4.1	7.6	10.7	9.5	9.0	8.9	8.9	9.0	9.0	0.4	0.4	0.5	0.7	0.7	0.6	0.6	0.6	0.6	0.6	0.6
Two or more races	—	—	—	—	19.7	33.6	38.8	42.0	44.1	47.8	51.1	—	—	—	—	1.2	2.2	2.5	2.7	2.8	3.0	3.1
Nonresident alien[1]	17.8	24.1	52.5	93.6	131.1	155.0	165.5	175.8	182.0	183.6	184.9	†	†	†	†	†	†	†	†	†	†	†

—Not available.
†Not applicable.
[1]Race/ethnicity not collected.
NOTE: Race categories exclude persons of Hispanic ethnicity. Because of underreporting and nonreporting of racial/ethnic data, some figures are slightly lower than corresponding data in other tables. Data through 1990 are for institutions of higher education, while later data are for degree-granting institutions. Degree-granting institutions grant associate's or higher degrees and participate in Title IV federal financial aid programs. The degree-granting classification is very similar to the earlier higher education classification, but it includes more 2-year colleges and excludes a few higher education institutions that did not grant degrees. Some data have been revised from previously published figures. Detail may not sum to totals because of rounding.
SOURCE: U.S. Department of Education, National Center for Education Statistics, Higher Education General Information Survey (HEGIS), "Fall Enrollment in Colleges and Universities" surveys, 1976 and 1980; Integrated Postsecondary Education Data System (IPEDS), "Fall Enrollment Survey" (IPEDS-EF:90); and IPEDS Spring 2001 through Spring 2019, Fall Enrollment component. (This table was prepared September 2019.)

Table 306.20. Total fall enrollment in degree-granting postsecondary institutions, by level and control of institution and race/ethnicity or nonresident alien status of student: Selected years, 1976 through 2018

Level and control of institution and race/ethnicity or nonresident alien status of student	Fall enrollment (in thousands)										
	1976	1980	1990	2000	2010	2013	2014	2015	2016	2017	2018
1	2	3	4	5	6	7	8	9	10	11	12
All students, total	**10,985.6**	**12,086.8**	**13,818.6**	**15,312.3**	**21,019.4**	**20,376.7**	**20,209.1**	**19,988.2**	**19,846.9**	**19,778.2**	**19,645.9**
White	9,076.1	9,833.0	10,722.5	10,462.1	12,720.8	11,589.4	11,239.3	10,939.2	10,716.6	10,517.4	10,301.3
Total, selected races/ethnicities	1,690.8	1,948.8	2,704.7	4,321.5	7,591.0	7,947.1	8,052.0	8,066.7	8,132.2	8,260.8	8,352.6
Black	1,033.0	1,106.8	1,247.0	1,730.3	3,039.0	2,872.0	2,792.8	2,681.0	2,589.4	2,549.5	2,493.3
Hispanic	383.8	471.7	782.4	1,461.8	2,748.8	3,093.2	3,191.9	3,297.7	3,428.0	3,546.0	3,645.0
Asian/Pacific Islander	197.9	286.4	572.4	978.2	1,281.6	1,259.7	1,272.2	1,284.3	1,306.7	1,327.8	1,352.6
Asian	—	—	—	—	1,217.6	1,198.7	1,213.8	1,229.0	1,253.5	1,275.7	1,302.1
Pacific Islander	—	—	—	—	64.0	61.0	58.5	55.3	53.2	52.0	50.5
American Indian/Alaska Native	76.1	83.9	102.8	151.2	196.2	162.2	152.9	146.1	142.3	137.5	133.8
Two or more races	—	—	—	—	325.4	560.0	642.2	657.6	665.8	700.1	727.9
Nonresident alien[1]	218.7	305.0	391.5	528.7	707.7	840.2	917.8	982.3	998.1	1,000.0	992.1
Public	8,641.0	9,456.4	10,844.7	11,752.8	15,142.2	14,746.8	14,654.7	14,572.8	14,585.8	14,571.7	14,529.3
White	7,094.5	7,656.1	8,385.4	7,963.4	9,182.1	8,363.3	8,119.6	7,910.7	7,787.3	7,646.3	7,505.9
Total, selected races/ethnicities	1,401.2	1,596.2	2,199.2	3,446.3	5,507.1	5,849.1	5,947.5	6,035.3	6,165.0	6,301.9	6,412.3
Black	831.2	876.1	976.4	1,319.2	1,988.8	1,886.5	1,840.2	1,775.1	1,739.6	1,725.3	1,711.8
Hispanic	336.8	406.2	671.4	1,229.3	2,163.8	2,479.4	2,580.4	2,694.5	2,819.5	2,929.7	3,016.4
Asian/Pacific Islander	165.7	239.7	461.0	770.5	968.7	944.9	955.9	970.1	990.5	1,007.4	1,027.8
Asian	—	—	—	—	924.8	905.7	918.5	934.3	955.9	973.7	994.5
Pacific Islander	—	—	—	—	43.9	39.2	37.4	35.8	34.6	33.6	33.3
American Indian/Alaska Native	67.5	74.2	90.4	127.3	150.8	124.4	117.8	113.7	110.7	107.7	105.1
Two or more races	—	—	—	—	235.0	414.0	453.2	482.0	504.8	531.8	551.2
Nonresident alien[1]	145.3	204.2	260.0	343.1	453.0	534.5	587.6	626.8	633.5	623.6	611.1
Private	2,344.6	2,630.4	2,973.9	3,559.5	5,877.3	5,629.8	5,554.4	5,415.4	5,261.1	5,206.4	5,116.7
White	1,981.6	2,176.9	2,337.0	2,498.7	3,538.7	3,226.1	3,119.7	3,028.5	2,929.3	2,871.1	2,795.4
Total, selected races/ethnicities	289.6	352.7	505.5	875.2	2,083.9	2,098.0	2,104.5	2,031.4	1,967.2	1,958.9	1,940.3
Black	201.8	230.7	270.6	411.1	1,050.2	985.6	952.7	906.0	849.8	824.2	781.6
Hispanic	47.0	65.6	111.0	232.5	585.0	613.8	611.4	603.2	608.5	616.3	628.7
Asian/Pacific Islander	32.2	46.7	111.5	207.7	312.8	314.8	316.4	314.2	316.2	320.4	324.8
Asian	—	—	—	—	292.7	293.0	295.3	294.7	297.6	302.0	307.6
Pacific Islander	—	—	—	—	20.1	21.8	21.1	19.5	18.6	18.4	17.2
American Indian/Alaska Native	8.6	9.7	12.4	23.9	45.5	37.8	35.1	32.5	31.7	29.7	28.6
Two or more races	—	—	—	—	90.4	146.0	189.0	175.6	161.0	168.3	176.6
Nonresident alien[1]	73.4	100.8	131.4	185.6	254.7	305.7	330.2	355.5	364.6	376.4	380.9
4-year, total	**7,106.5**	**7,565.4**	**8,578.6**	**9,363.9**	**13,335.8**	**13,406.0**	**13,494.4**	**13,488.7**	**13,754.5**	**13,825.4**	**13,900.7**
White	5,999.0	6,274.5	6,768.1	6,658.0	8,399.5	7,954.2	7,829.1	7,713.4	7,715.0	7,637.9	7,574.8
Total, selected races/ethnicities	931.0	1,049.9	1,486.1	2,266.1	4,328.0	4,703.8	4,843.0	4,897.2	5,135.5	5,275.6	5,421.1
Black	603.7	634.3	722.8	995.4	1,840.0	1,799.2	1,778.7	1,740.5	1,724.0	1,704.7	1,689.3
Hispanic	173.6	216.6	358.2	617.9	1,355.9	1,599.6	1,670.8	1,742.1	1,932.5	2,035.7	2,145.1
Asian/Pacific Islander	118.7	162.1	357.2	576.3	818.5	843.7	864.8	882.5	929.6	958.8	986.5
Asian	—	—	—	—	782.5	806.1	827.5	847.1	893.9	923.5	952.1
Pacific Islander	—	—	—	—	36.0	37.6	37.3	35.4	35.7	35.3	34.4
American Indian/Alaska Native	35.0	36.9	47.9	76.5	109.0	91.4	87.0	83.4	83.6	81.7	80.7
Two or more races	—	—	—	—	204.6	369.8	441.7	448.8	465.7	494.7	519.5
Nonresident alien[1]	176.5	240.9	324.3	439.7	608.3	748.0	822.4	878.1	904.0	911.8	904.8
Public	4,892.9	5,127.6	5,848.2	6,055.4	7,924.1	8,120.4	8,257.1	8,348.5	8,742.9	8,854.3	8,982.6
White	4,120.2	4,243.0	4,605.6	4,311.2	5,069.6	4,867.1	4,833.9	4,790.3	4,879.3	4,850.4	4,849.5
Total, selected races/ethnicities	666.7	740.8	1,046.2	1,486.4	2,496.8	2,808.6	2,928.6	3,032.7	3,321.1	3,465.8	3,606.6
Black	421.8	438.2	495.1	627.8	912.6	909.0	914.8	916.0	950.9	956.5	969.1
Hispanic	129.3	156.4	262.5	420.0	869.5	1,063.4	1,133.0	1,199.5	1,379.5	1,472.8	1,561.4
Asian/Pacific Islander	87.5	117.2	250.6	381.3	522.8	544.7	563.1	579.4	623.7	648.2	670.8
Asian	—	—	—	—	504.7	526.1	544.3	562.0	605.2	629.9	652.4
Pacific Islander	—	—	—	—	18.1	18.6	18.7	17.4	18.5	18.2	18.4
American Indian/Alaska Native	28.2	29.0	38.0	57.2	69.5	58.1	56.0	54.6	55.3	55.0	54.9
Two or more races	—	—	—	—	122.4	233.4	261.9	283.2	311.6	333.4	350.4
Nonresident alien[1]	106.0	143.8	196.4	257.8	357.8	444.8	494.6	525.6	542.6	538.1	526.5
Private	2,213.6	2,437.8	2,730.3	3,308.5	5,411.7	5,285.6	5,237.3	5,140.2	5,011.6	4,971.1	4,918.2
White	1,878.8	2,031.5	2,162.5	2,346.9	3,330.0	3,087.1	2,995.2	2,923.1	2,835.7	2,787.6	2,725.3
Total, selected races/ethnicities	264.3	309.2	439.8	779.7	1,831.2	1,895.2	1,914.3	1,864.5	1,814.4	1,809.8	1,814.5
Black	182.0	196.1	227.7	367.6	927.4	890.3	864.0	824.5	773.1	748.2	720.2
Hispanic	44.3	60.2	95.7	197.9	486.3	536.2	537.8	542.7	553.0	563.0	583.7
Asian/Pacific Islander	31.2	44.9	106.6	195.0	295.7	299.0	301.7	303.0	305.9	310.6	315.7
Asian	—	—	—	—	277.8	280.0	283.1	285.1	288.7	293.6	299.8
Pacific Islander	—	—	—	—	17.9	19.0	18.6	18.0	17.2	17.0	16.0
American Indian/Alaska Native	6.8	7.9	9.9	19.3	39.6	33.3	31.0	28.8	28.3	26.7	25.8
Two or more races	—	—	—	—	82.2	136.4	179.8	165.6	154.1	161.3	169.0
Nonresident alien[1]	70.5	97.1	127.9	181.9	250.6	303.2	327.8	352.5	361.5	373.8	378.3

Level and control of institution and race/ethnicity or nonresident alien status of student	Percentage distribution of U.S. resident students (excludes nonresident aliens)										
	1976	1980	1990	2000	2010	2013	2014	2015	2016	2017	2018
1	13	14	15	16	17	18	19	20	21	22	23
All students, total	**100.0**	**100.0**	**100.0**	**100.0**	**100.0**	**100.0**	**100.0**	**100.0**	**100.0**	**100.0**	**100.0**
White	84.3	83.5	79.9	70.8	62.6	59.3	58.3	57.6	56.9	56.0	55.2
Total, selected races/ethnicities	15.7	16.5	20.1	29.2	37.4	40.7	41.7	42.4	43.1	44.0	44.8
Black	9.6	9.4	9.3	11.7	15.0	14.7	14.5	14.1	13.7	13.6	13.4
Hispanic	3.6	4.0	5.8	9.9	13.5	15.8	16.5	17.4	18.2	18.9	19.5
Asian/Pacific Islander	1.8	2.4	4.3	6.6	6.3	6.4	6.6	6.8	6.9	7.1	7.3
Asian	—	—	—	—	6.0	6.1	6.3	6.5	6.7	6.8	7.0
Pacific Islander	—	—	—	—	0.3	0.3	0.3	0.3	0.3	0.3	0.3
American Indian/Alaska Native	0.7	0.7	0.8	1.0	1.0	0.8	0.8	0.8	0.8	0.7	0.7
Two or more races	—	—	—	—	1.6	2.9	3.3	3.5	3.5	3.7	3.9
Nonresident alien[1]	†	†	†	†	†	†	†	†	†	†	†
Public	100.0	100.0	100.0	100.0	100.0	100.0	100.0	100.0	100.0	100.0	100.0
White	83.5	82.7	79.2	69.8	62.5	58.8	57.7	56.7	55.8	54.8	53.9
Total, selected races/ethnicities	16.5	17.3	20.8	30.2	37.5	41.2	42.3	43.3	44.2	45.2	46.1
Black	9.8	9.5	9.2	11.6	13.5	13.3	13.1	12.7	12.5	12.4	12.3
Hispanic	4.0	4.4	6.3	10.8	14.7	17.4	18.3	19.3	20.2	21.0	21.7
Asian/Pacific Islander	2.0	2.6	4.4	6.8	6.6	6.6	6.8	7.0	7.1	7.2	7.4
Asian	—	—	—	—	6.3	6.4	6.5	6.7	6.9	7.0	7.1
Pacific Islander	—	—	—	—	0.3	0.3	0.3	0.3	0.2	0.2	0.2
American Indian/Alaska Native	0.8	0.8	0.9	1.1	1.0	0.9	0.8	0.8	0.8	0.8	0.8
Two or more races	—	—	—	—	1.6	2.9	3.2	3.5	3.6	3.8	4.0
Nonresident alien[1]	†	†	†	†	†	†	†	†	†	†	†
Private	100.0	100.0	100.0	100.0	100.0	100.0	100.0	100.0	100.0	100.0	100.0
White	87.3	86.1	82.2	74.1	62.9	60.6	59.7	59.9	59.8	59.4	59.0
Total, selected races/ethnicities	12.7	13.9	17.8	25.9	37.1	39.4	40.3	40.1	40.2	40.6	41.0
Black	8.9	9.1	9.5	12.2	18.7	18.5	18.2	17.9	17.4	17.1	16.5
Hispanic	2.1	2.6	3.9	6.9	10.4	11.5	11.7	11.9	12.4	12.8	13.3
Asian/Pacific Islander	1.4	1.8	3.9	6.2	5.6	5.9	6.1	6.2	6.5	6.6	6.9
Asian	—	—	—	—	5.2	5.5	5.7	5.8	6.1	6.3	6.5
Pacific Islander	—	—	—	—	0.4	0.4	0.4	0.4	0.4	0.4	0.4
American Indian/Alaska Native	0.4	0.4	0.4	0.7	0.8	0.7	0.7	0.6	0.6	0.6	0.6
Two or more races	—	—	—	—	1.6	2.7	3.6	3.5	3.3	3.5	3.7
Nonresident alien[1]	†	†	†	†	†	†	†	†	†	†	†
4-year, total	**100.0**	**100.0**	**100.0**	**100.0**	**100.0**	**100.0**	**100.0**	**100.0**	**100.0**	**100.0**	**100.0**
White	86.6	85.7	82.0	74.6	66.0	62.8	61.8	61.2	60.0	59.1	58.3
Total, selected races/ethnicities	13.4	14.3	18.0	25.4	34.0	37.2	38.2	38.8	40.0	40.9	41.7
Black	8.7	8.7	8.8	11.2	14.5	14.2	14.0	13.8	13.4	13.2	13.0
Hispanic	2.5	3.0	4.3	6.9	10.7	12.6	13.2	13.8	15.0	15.8	16.5
Asian/Pacific Islander	1.7	2.2	4.3	6.5	6.4	6.7	6.8	7.0	7.2	7.4	7.6
Asian	—	—	—	—	6.1	6.4	6.5	6.7	7.0	7.2	7.3
Pacific Islander	—	—	—	—	0.3	0.3	0.3	0.3	0.3	0.3	0.3
American Indian/Alaska Native	0.5	0.5	0.6	0.9	0.9	0.7	0.7	0.7	0.7	0.6	0.6
Two or more races	—	—	—	—	1.6	2.9	3.5	3.6	3.6	3.8	4.0
Nonresident alien[1]	†	†	†	†	†	†	†	†	†	†	†
Public	100.0	100.0	100.0	100.0	100.0	100.0	100.0	100.0	100.0	100.0	100.0
White	86.1	85.1	81.5	74.4	67.0	63.4	62.3	61.2	59.5	58.3	57.3
Total, selected races/ethnicities	13.9	14.9	18.5	25.6	33.0	36.6	37.7	38.8	40.5	41.7	42.7
Black	8.8	8.8	8.8	10.8	12.1	11.8	11.8	11.7	11.6	11.5	11.5
Hispanic	2.7	3.1	4.6	7.2	11.5	13.9	14.6	15.3	16.8	17.7	18.5
Asian/Pacific Islander	1.8	2.4	4.4	6.6	6.9	7.1	7.3	7.4	7.6	7.8	7.9
Asian	—	—	—	—	6.7	6.9	7.0	7.2	7.4	7.6	7.7
Pacific Islander	—	—	—	—	0.2	0.2	0.2	0.2	0.2	0.2	0.2
American Indian/Alaska Native	0.6	0.6	0.7	1.0	0.9	0.8	0.7	0.7	0.7	0.7	0.6
Two or more races	—	—	—	—	1.6	3.0	3.4	3.6	3.8	4.0	4.1
Nonresident alien[1]	†	†	†	†	†	†	†	†	†	†	†
Private	100.0	100.0	100.0	100.0	100.0	100.0	100.0	100.0	100.0	100.0	100.0
White	87.7	86.8	83.1	75.1	64.5	62.0	61.0	61.1	61.0	60.6	60.0
Total, selected races/ethnicities	12.3	13.2	16.9	24.9	35.5	38.0	39.0	38.9	39.0	39.4	40.0
Black	8.5	8.4	8.7	11.8	18.0	17.9	17.6	17.2	16.6	16.3	15.9
Hispanic	2.1	2.6	3.7	6.3	9.4	10.8	11.0	11.3	11.9	12.2	12.9
Asian/Pacific Islander	1.5	1.9	4.1	6.2	5.7	6.0	6.1	6.3	6.6	6.8	7.0
Asian	—	—	—	—	5.4	5.6	5.8	6.0	6.2	6.4	6.6
Pacific Islander	—	—	—	—	0.3	0.4	0.4	0.4	0.4	0.4	0.4
American Indian/Alaska Native	0.3	0.3	0.4	0.6	0.8	0.7	0.6	0.6	0.6	0.6	0.6
Two or more races	—	—	—	—	1.6	2.7	3.7	3.5	3.3	3.5	3.7
Nonresident alien[1]	†	†	†	†	†	†	†	†	†	†	†

See notes at end of table.

Table 306.20. Total fall enrollment in degree-granting postsecondary institutions, by level and control of institution and race/ethnicity or nonresident alien status of student: Selected years, 1976 through 2018—Continued

Level and control of institution and race/ethnicity or nonresident alien status of student	Fall enrollment (in thousands)											Percentage distribution of U.S. resident students (excludes nonresident aliens)										
	1976	1980	1990	2000	2010	2013	2014	2015	2016	2017	2018	1976	1980	1990	2000	2010	2013	2014	2015	2016	2017	2018
1	2	3	4	5	6	7	8	9	10	11	12	13	14	15	16	17	18	19	20	21	22	23
2-year, total	3,879.1	4,521.4	5,240.1	5,948.4	7,683.6	6,970.6	6,714.7	6,499.5	6,092.4	5,952.8	5,745.2	100.0	100.0	100.0	100.0	100.0	100.0	100.0	100.0	100.0	100.0	100.0
White	3,077.1	3,558.5	3,954.3	3,804.1	4,321.3	3,635.2	3,410.2	3,225.8	3,001.6	2,879.5	2,726.5	80.2	79.8	76.4	64.9	57.0	52.8	51.5	50.4	50.0	49.1	48.2
Total, selected races/ethnicities	759.8	898.9	1,218.6	2,055.4	3,263.0	3,243.3	3,209.1	3,169.5	2,996.7	2,985.2	2,931.5	19.8	20.2	23.6	35.1	43.0	47.2	48.5	49.6	50.0	50.9	51.8
Black	429.3	472.5	524.3	734.9	1,198.9	1,072.8	1,014.1	940.5	865.5	844.8	804.1	11.2	10.6	10.1	12.5	15.8	15.6	15.3	14.7	14.4	14.4	14.2
Hispanic	210.2	255.1	424.2	843.9	1,393.0	1,493.5	1,521.1	1,555.6	1,495.4	1,510.2	1,499.9	5.5	5.7	8.2	14.4	18.4	21.7	23.0	24.3	24.9	25.8	26.5
Asian/Pacific Islander	79.2	124.3	215.2	401.9	463.1	416.0	407.5	401.9	377.1	369.0	366.1	2.1	2.8	4.2	6.9	6.1	6.0	6.2	6.3	6.3	6.3	6.5
Asian	—	—	—	—	435.1	392.6	386.3	381.9	359.6	352.2	350.0	—	—	—	—	5.7	5.7	5.8	6.0	6.0	6.0	6.2
Pacific Islander	—	—	—	—	27.9	23.4	21.2	19.9	17.5	16.7	16.1	—	—	—	—	0.4	0.3	0.3	0.3	0.3	0.3	0.3
American Indian/Alaska Native	41.2	47.0	54.9	74.7	87.2	70.8	66.0	62.8	58.7	55.7	53.0	1.1	1.1	1.1	1.3	1.1	1.0	1.0	1.0	1.0	1.0	0.9
Two or more races	—	—	—	—	120.8	190.2	200.5	208.7	200.0	205.4	208.4	—	—	—	—	1.6	2.8	3.0	3.3	3.3	3.5	3.7
Nonresident alien[1]	42.2	64.1	67.1	89.0	99.3	92.1	95.4	104.2	94.1	88.1	87.2	†	†	†	†	†	†	†	†	†	†	†
Public	3,748.1	4,328.8	4,996.5	5,697.4	7,218.1	6,626.4	6,397.6	6,224.3	5,842.9	5,717.5	5,546.7	100.0	100.0	100.0	100.0	100.0	100.0	100.0	100.0	100.0	100.0	100.0
White	2,974.3	3,413.1	3,779.8	3,652.2	4,112.5	3,496.2	3,285.7	3,120.4	2,908.0	2,795.9	2,656.4	80.2	80.0	76.6	65.1	57.7	53.5	52.1	51.0	50.6	49.6	48.6
Total, selected races/ethnicities	734.3	855.4	1,153.0	1,959.9	3,010.3	3,040.5	3,018.9	3,002.6	2,844.0	2,836.0	2,805.7	19.8	20.0	23.4	34.9	42.3	46.5	47.9	49.0	49.4	50.4	51.4
Black	409.5	437.9	481.4	691.4	1,076.1	977.5	925.4	859.0	788.7	768.8	742.7	11.0	10.3	9.8	12.3	15.1	15.0	14.7	14.0	13.7	13.7	13.6
Hispanic	207.5	249.8	408.9	809.2	1,294.3	1,415.9	1,447.5	1,495.1	1,439.9	1,456.9	1,455.0	5.6	5.9	8.3	14.4	18.2	21.7	23.0	24.4	25.0	25.9	26.6
Asian/Pacific Islander	78.2	122.5	210.3	389.2	445.9	400.2	392.9	390.7	366.8	359.2	357.0	2.1	2.9	4.3	6.9	6.3	6.1	6.2	6.4	6.4	6.4	6.5
Asian	—	—	—	—	420.2	379.6	374.2	372.3	350.7	343.8	342.2	—	—	—	—	5.9	5.8	5.9	6.1	6.1	6.1	6.3
Pacific Islander	—	—	—	—	25.7	20.6	18.7	18.4	16.1	15.4	14.9	—	—	—	—	0.4	0.3	0.3	0.3	0.3	0.3	0.3
American Indian/Alaska Native	39.3	45.2	52.4	70.1	81.3	66.3	61.9	59.1	55.3	52.7	50.2	1.1	1.1	1.1	1.2	1.1	1.0	1.0	1.0	1.0	0.9	0.9
Two or more races	—	—	—	—	112.7	180.6	191.3	198.8	193.2	198.4	200.8	—	—	—	—	1.6	2.8	3.0	3.2	3.4	3.5	3.7
Nonresident alien[1]	39.2	60.3	63.6	85.2	95.2	89.7	93.0	101.3	91.0	85.5	84.6	†	†	†	†	†	†	†	†	†	†	†
Private	131.0	192.6	243.6	251.0	465.5	344.2	317.1	275.2	249.5	235.3	198.5	100.0	100.0	100.0	100.0	100.0	100.0	100.0	100.0	100.0	100.0	100.0
White	102.8	145.4	174.5	151.8	208.8	139.0	124.5	105.4	93.6	83.6	70.2	80.3	77.0	72.7	61.4	45.2	40.7	39.6	38.7	38.0	35.9	35.8
Total, selected races/ethnicities	25.3	43.5	65.6	95.5	252.7	202.8	190.2	166.8	152.7	149.2	125.8	19.7	23.0	27.3	38.6	54.8	59.3	60.4	61.3	62.0	64.1	64.2
Black	19.8	34.6	42.9	43.5	122.8	95.3	88.7	81.5	76.8	76.0	61.4	15.5	18.3	17.9	17.6	26.6	27.9	28.2	29.9	31.2	32.7	31.3
Hispanic	2.6	5.3	15.3	34.7	98.7	77.6	73.6	60.5	55.5	53.3	44.9	2.1	2.8	6.4	14.0	21.4	22.7	23.4	22.2	22.5	22.9	22.9
Asian/Pacific Islander	0.9	1.8	4.9	12.7	17.2	15.7	14.7	11.2	10.3	9.8	9.1	0.7	1.0	2.0	5.1	3.7	4.6	4.7	4.1	4.2	4.2	4.6
Asian	—	—	—	—	14.9	13.0	12.1	9.6	8.9	8.4	7.8	—	—	—	—	3.2	3.8	3.9	3.5	3.6	3.6	4.0
Pacific Islander	—	—	—	—	2.2	2.8	2.5	1.5	1.4	1.4	1.3	—	—	—	—	0.5	0.8	0.8	0.6	0.6	0.6	0.6
American Indian/Alaska Native	1.8	1.8	2.5	4.5	5.9	4.5	4.1	3.7	3.4	3.0	2.8	1.4	1.0	1.0	1.8	1.3	1.3	1.3	1.4	1.4	1.3	1.4
Two or more races	—	—	—	—	8.1	9.7	9.2	10.0	6.8	7.0	7.6	—	—	—	—	1.8	2.8	2.9	3.7	2.8	3.0	3.9
Nonresident alien[1]	3.0	3.7	3.5	3.8	4.1	2.5	2.4	2.9	3.1	2.6	2.6	†	†	†	†	†	†	†	†	†	†	†

—Not available.
†Not applicable.
[1]Race/ethnicity not collected.
NOTE: Race categories exclude persons of Hispanic ethnicity. Because of underreporting and nonreporting of racial/ethnic data, some figures are slightly lower than corresponding data in other tables. Data through 1990 are for institutions of higher education, while later data are for degree-granting institutions. Degree-granting institutions grant associate's or higher degrees and participate in Title IV federal financial aid programs. The degree-granting classification is very similar to the earlier higher education classification, but it includes more 2-year colleges and excludes a few higher education institutions that did not grant degrees. Some data have been revised from previously published figures. Detail may not sum to totals because of rounding.
SOURCE: U.S. Department of Education, National Center for Education Statistics, Higher Education General Information Survey (HEGIS), "Fall Enrollment in Colleges and Universities" surveys, 1976 and 1980; Integrated Postsecondary Education Data System (IPEDS), "Fall Enrollment Survey" (IPEDS-EF:90); and IPEDS Spring 2001 through Spring 2019, Fall Enrollment component. (This table was prepared September 2019.)

Table 306.30. Fall enrollment of U.S. residents in degree-granting postsecondary institutions, by race/ethnicity: Selected years, 1976 through 2029

	Enrollment (in thousands)									Percentage distribution								
					Asian/Pacific Islander			American Indian/ Alaska Native	Two or more races					Asian/Pacific Islander			American Indian/ Alaska Native	Two or more races
Year	Total	White	Black	Hispanic	Total	Asian	Pacific Islander			Total	White	Black	Hispanic	Total	Asian	Pacific Islander		
1	2	3	4	5	6	7	8	9	10	11	12	13	14	15	16	17	18	19
1976	10,767	9,076	1,033	384	198	—	—	76	—	100.0	84.3	9.6	3.6	1.8	—	—	0.7	—
1980	11,782	9,833	1,107	472	286	—	—	84	—	100.0	83.5	9.4	4.0	2.4	—	—	0.7	—
1990	13,427	10,722	1,247	782	572	—	—	103	—	100.0	79.9	9.3	5.8	4.3	—	—	0.8	—
1994	13,823	10,427	1,449	1,046	774	—	—	127	—	100.0	75.4	10.5	7.6	5.6	—	—	0.9	—
1995	13,807	10,311	1,474	1,094	797	—	—	131	—	100.0	74.7	10.7	7.9	5.8	—	—	1.0	—
1996	13,901	10,264	1,506	1,166	828	—	—	138	—	100.0	73.8	10.8	8.4	6.0	—	—	1.0	—
1997	14,037	10,266	1,551	1,218	859	—	—	142	—	100.0	73.1	11.0	8.7	6.1	—	—	1.0	—
1998	14,063	10,179	1,583	1,257	900	—	—	144	—	100.0	72.4	11.3	8.9	6.4	—	—	1.0	—
1999	14,361	10,329	1,649	1,324	914	—	—	146	—	100.0	71.9	11.5	9.2	6.4	—	—	1.0	—
2000	14,784	10,462	1,730	1,462	978	—	—	151	—	100.0	70.8	11.7	9.9	6.6	—	—	1.0	—
2001	15,363	10,775	1,850	1,561	1,019	—	—	158	—	100.0	70.1	12.0	10.2	6.6	—	—	1.0	—
2002	16,021	11,140	1,979	1,662	1,074	—	—	166	—	100.0	69.5	12.4	10.4	6.7	—	—	1.0	—
2003	16,314	11,281	2,068	1,716	1,076	—	—	173	—	100.0	69.1	12.7	10.5	6.6	—	—	1.1	—
2004	16,682	11,423	2,165	1,810	1,109	—	—	176	—	100.0	68.5	13.0	10.8	6.6	—	—	1.1	—
2005	16,903	11,495	2,215	1,882	1,134	—	—	176	—	100.0	68.0	13.1	11.1	6.7	—	—	1.0	—
2006	17,158	11,568	2,280	1,964	1,165	—	—	181	—	100.0	67.4	13.3	11.4	6.8	—	—	1.1	—
2007	17,635	11,761	2,384	2,081	1,218	—	—	190	—	100.0	66.7	13.5	11.8	6.9	—	—	1.1	—
2008	18,421	12,075	2,580	2,271	1,303	—	—	193	—	100.0	65.5	14.0	12.3	7.1	—	—	1.0	—
2009	19,631	12,669	2,884	2,537	1,335	—	—	206	—	100.0	64.5	14.7	12.9	6.8	—	—	1.0	—
2010	20,312	12,721	3,039	2,749	1,282	1,218	64	196	325	100.0	62.6	15.0	13.5	6.3	6.0	0.3	1.0	1.6
2011	20,270	12,402	3,079	2,893	1,277	1,211	66	186	433	100.0	61.2	15.2	14.3	6.3	6.0	0.3	0.9	2.1
2012	19,861	11,982	2,962	2,980	1,258	1,195	64	173	505	100.0	60.3	14.9	15.0	6.3	6.0	0.3	0.9	2.5
2013	19,537	11,589	2,872	3,093	1,260	1,199	61	162	560	100.0	59.3	14.7	15.8	6.4	6.1	0.3	0.8	2.9
2014	19,291	11,239	2,793	3,192	1,272	1,214	58	153	642	100.0	58.3	14.5	16.5	6.6	6.3	0.3	0.8	3.3
2015	19,006	10,939	2,681	3,298	1,284	1,229	55	146	658	100.0	57.6	14.1	17.4	6.8	6.5	0.3	0.8	3.5
2016	18,849	10,717	2,589	3,428	1,307	1,253	53	142	666	100.0	56.9	13.7	18.2	6.9	6.7	0.3	0.8	3.5
2017	18,778	10,517	2,550	3,546	1,328	1,276	52	137	700	100.0	56.0	13.6	18.9	7.1	6.8	0.3	0.7	3.7
2018	18,654	10,301	2,493	3,645	1,353	1,302	51	134	728	100.0	55.2	13.4	19.5	7.3	7.0	0.3	0.7	3.9
2019[1]	18,736	10,385	2,549	3,626	1,314	—	—	131	731	100.0	55.4	13.6	19.4	7.0	—	—	0.7	3.9
2020[1]	18,752	10,319	2,569	3,686	1,315	—	—	131	732	100.0	55.0	13.7	19.7	7.0	—	—	0.7	3.9
2021[1]	18,776	10,267	2,585	3,738	1,323	—	—	130	733	100.0	54.7	13.8	19.9	7.0	—	—	0.7	3.9
2022[1]	18,800	10,216	2,598	3,791	1,332	—	—	129	734	100.0	54.3	13.8	20.2	7.1	—	—	0.7	3.9
2023[1]	18,838	10,166	2,616	3,850	1,343	—	—	129	735	100.0	54.0	13.9	20.4	7.1	—	—	0.7	3.9
2024[1]	18,892	10,122	2,636	3,917	1,352	—	—	128	737	100.0	53.6	14.0	20.7	7.2	—	—	0.7	3.9
2025[1]	18,947	10,079	2,657	3,988	1,357	—	—	127	739	100.0	53.2	14.0	21.0	7.2	—	—	0.7	3.9
2026[1]	19,013	10,039	2,682	4,062	1,363	—	—	126	742	100.0	52.8	14.1	21.4	7.2	—	—	0.7	3.9
2027[1]	19,033	9,969	2,703	4,129	1,365	—	—	124	743	100.0	52.4	14.2	21.7	7.2	—	—	0.7	3.9
2028[1]	19,034	9,888	2,721	4,192	1,367	—	—	123	743	100.0	51.9	14.3	22.0	7.2	—	—	0.6	3.9
2029[1]	19,029	9,807	2,738	4,252	1,367	—	—	121	742	100.0	51.5	14.4	22.3	7.2	—	—	0.6	3.9

—Not available.

[1]Projected.

NOTE: Race categories exclude persons of Hispanic ethnicity. Prior to 2010, institutions were not required to report separate data on Asians, Pacific Islanders, and students of Two or more races. Projections for Asian and Pacific Islander enrollment are not available due to the limited amount of historical data available upon which to base a projection model. Data through 1995 are for institutions of higher education, while later data are for degree-granting institutions. Degree-granting institutions grant associate's or higher degrees and participate in Title IV federal financial aid programs. The degree-granting classification is very similar to the earlier higher education classification, but it includes more 2-year colleges and excludes a few higher education institutions that did not grant degrees. Detail may not sum to totals because of rounding. Some data have been revised from previously published figures.

SOURCE: U.S. Department of Education, National Center for Education Statistics, Higher Education General Information Survey (HEGIS), "Fall Enrollment in Colleges and Universities" surveys, 1976 and 1980; Integrated Postsecondary Education Data System (IPEDS), "Fall Enrollment Survey" (IPEDS-EF:90–99); IPEDS Spring 2001 through Spring 2019, Fall Enrollment component; and Enrollment in Degree-Granting Institutions by Race/Ethnicity Projection Model, 1980 through 2029. (This table was prepared December 2019.)

Table 306.50. Total fall enrollment in degree-granting postsecondary institutions, by control and classification of institution, level of enrollment, and race/ethnicity of student: 2018

Fall enrollment

Level of enrollment and race/ethnicity of student	Total, all institutions	Public Total	Public 4-year Total	Research univ., very high[1]	Research univ., high[2]	Doctoral/research univ.[3]	Master's[4]	Baccalaureate[5]	Special focus[6]	Public 2-year	Nonprofit Total	Nonprofit 4-year Total	Research univ., very high[1]	Research univ., high[2]	Doctoral/research univ.[3]	Master's[4]	Baccalaureate[5]	Special focus[6]	Nonprofit 2-year	For-profit Total	For-profit 4-year	For-profit 2-year
1	2	3	4	5	6	7	8	9	10	11	12	13	14	15	16	17	18	19	20	21	22	23
All students, total	19,645,918	14,529,264	8,982,560	2,880,371	1,355,351	634,802	2,505,556	1,512,103	94,377	5,546,704	4,134,244	4,089,090	645,546	329,064	451,943	1,616,062	653,475	393,000	45,154	982,410	829,060	153,350
White	10,301,292	7,505,866	4,849,505	1,541,259	814,436	314,750	1,407,828	721,125	50,107	2,656,361	2,384,510	2,367,157	280,063	189,231	257,271	1,010,791	406,265	223,536	17,353	410,916	358,119	52,797
Black	2,493,306	1,711,755	969,085	195,506	152,810	99,334	328,825	182,534	10,076	742,670	494,901	476,784	40,818	31,761	62,287	196,752	100,429	44,737	18,117	286,650	243,387	43,263
Hispanic	3,645,040	3,016,367	1,561,402	397,173	186,287	132,956	425,266	410,540	9,180	1,454,965	460,431	455,701	64,562	35,197	52,751	210,252	56,833	36,106	4,730	168,242	128,042	40,200
Asian	1,302,106	994,527	652,373	311,137	64,607	37,759	144,471	83,121	11,278	342,154	266,389	265,281	88,497	23,247	30,227	67,281	21,233	34,796	1,108	41,190	34,482	6,708
Pacific Islander	50,505	33,274	18,391	4,167	1,977	1,009	5,724	5,375	139	14,883	10,602	10,440	676	609	1,067	5,438	1,579	1,071	162	6,629	5,541	1,088
American Indian/Alaska Native	133,751	105,105	54,889	9,470	8,695	2,329	16,068	10,419	7,908	50,216	19,390	18,556	1,210	918	1,806	7,955	2,905	3,762	834	9,256	7,278	1,978
Two or more races	727,863	551,241	350,422	116,354	52,998	22,608	92,487	63,743	2,232	200,819	141,180	139,548	24,177	10,837	14,517	49,901	25,517	14,599	1,632	35,442	29,495	5,947
Nonresident alien[7]	992,055	611,129	526,493	305,305	73,541	24,057	84,887	35,246	3,457	84,636	356,841	355,623	145,543	37,264	32,017	67,692	38,714	34,393	1,218	24,085	22,716	1,369
Undergraduate	16,610,235	13,049,326	7,502,622	2,187,010	1,095,720	525,972	2,153,440	1,504,994	35,486	5,546,704	2,821,653	2,776,499	309,524	213,114	273,092	1,164,431	618,808	197,530	45,154	739,256	585,906	153,350
White	8,664,500	6,680,174	4,023,813	1,180,428	657,043	254,993	1,198,358	715,752	17,239	2,656,361	1,680,715	1,663,362	139,075	131,241	160,428	736,038	382,501	114,079	17,353	303,611	250,814	52,797
Black	2,127,937	1,572,462	829,792	152,871	128,011	84,163	278,011	181,815	4,921	742,670	347,687	329,570	20,576	18,119	32,629	138,841	95,900	23,505	18,117	207,788	164,525	43,263
Hispanic	3,352,665	2,871,674	1,416,709	339,760	163,506	116,829	383,097	410,242	3,275	1,454,965	337,587	332,857	38,354	22,140	35,478	162,374	54,544	19,967	4,730	143,404	103,204	40,200
Asian	1,087,323	894,499	552,345	257,239	52,534	31,769	126,386	82,936	1,481	342,154	163,373	162,265	52,289	15,546	18,865	43,625	19,867	12,073	1,108	29,251	22,543	6,708
Pacific Islander	44,667	31,460	16,577	3,413	1,724	852	5,153	5,362	73	14,883	7,850	7,688	340	458	637	4,124	1,501	628	162	5,357	4,269	1,088
American Indian/Alaska Native	120,165	98,131	47,915	6,960	7,232	1,925	13,924	10,344	7,530	50,216	14,623	13,789	635	341	1,113	5,748	2,727	2,989	834	7,411	5,433	1,978
Two or more races	646,540	511,120	310,301	96,634	46,454	19,800	83,176	63,617	620	200,819	106,938	105,306	15,152	2,896	10,388	39,522	24,755	7,548	1,632	28,482	22,535	5,947
Nonresident alien[7]	566,638	389,806	305,170	149,705	39,216	15,641	65,335	34,926	3,110	84,636	162,880	161,662	43,103	20,172	13,554	34,159	37,013	16,741	1,218	13,952	12,583	1,369
Postbaccalaureate	3,035,683	1,479,938	1,479,938	693,361	259,631	108,830	352,116	7,109	58,891		1,312,591	1,312,591	336,022	115,950	178,851	451,631	34,667	195,470	†	243,154	243,154	†
White	1,636,792	825,692	825,692	360,831	157,393	59,757	209,470	5,373	32,868		703,795	703,795	140,988	57,990	96,843	274,753	23,764	109,457	†	107,305	107,305	†
Black	365,369	139,293	139,293	42,635	24,799	15,171	50,814	719	5,155		147,214	147,214	20,242	13,642	29,658	57,911	4,529	21,232	†	78,862	78,862	†
Hispanic	292,375	144,693	144,693	57,413	22,781	16,127	42,169	298	5,905		122,844	122,844	26,208	13,057	17,273	47,878	2,289	16,139	†	24,838	24,838	†
Asian	214,983	100,028	100,028	53,898	12,073	5,990	18,085	185	9,797		103,016	103,016	36,208	7,701	11,362	23,656	1,366	22,723	†	11,939	11,939	†
Pacific Islander	5,838	1,814	1,814	754	253	157	571	13	66		2,752	2,752	336	151	430	1,314	78	443	†	1,272	1,272	†
American Indian/Alaska Native	13,586	6,974	6,974	2,510	1,463	404	2,144	75	378		4,767	4,767	575	577	693	2,207	178	773	†	1,845	1,845	†
Two or more races	81,323	40,121	40,121	19,720	6,544	2,808	9,311	126	1,612		34,242	34,242	9,025	7,941	4,129	10,379	762	7,051	†	6,960	6,960	†
Nonresident alien[7]	425,417	221,323	221,323	155,600	34,325	8,416	19,552	320	347		193,961	193,961	102,440	17,092	18,463	33,533	1,701	17,652	†	10,133	10,133	†
Percentage distribution of U.S. resident students (excludes nonresident aliens)																						
U.S. resident students, total	100.0	100.0	100.0	100.0	100.0	100.0	100.0	100.0	100.0	100.0	100.0	100.0	100.0	100.0	100.0	100.0	100.0	100.0	100.0	100.0	100.0	100.0
White	55.2	53.9	57.3	59.9	63.5	51.5	58.2	48.8	55.1	48.6	63.1	63.4	56.0	64.8	61.3	65.3	66.1	62.3	39.5	42.9	44.4	34.7
Black	13.4	12.3	11.5	7.6	11.9	16.3	13.6	12.4	11.1	13.6	13.1	12.8	8.2	10.9	14.8	12.7	16.3	12.5	41.2	29.9	30.2	28.5
Hispanic	19.5	21.7	18.5	15.4	14.5	21.8	17.6	27.8	10.1	26.6	12.2	12.2	12.9	12.1	12.6	13.6	9.2	10.1	10.8	17.6	15.9	26.5
Asian	7.0	7.1	7.7	12.1	5.0	6.2	6.0	5.6	12.4	6.3	7.1	7.1	17.7	8.0	7.2	4.3	3.5	9.7	2.5	4.3	4.3	4.4
Pacific Islander	0.3	0.2	0.2	0.2	0.2	0.2	0.2	0.4	0.2	0.3	0.3	0.3	0.1	0.2	0.3	0.4	0.3	0.3	0.4	0.7	0.7	0.7
American Indian/Alaska Native	0.7	0.8	0.7	0.4	0.7	0.4	0.7	0.7	8.7	0.9	0.5	0.5	0.2	0.3	0.4	0.5	0.5	1.0	1.9	1.0	0.9	1.3
Two or more races	3.9	4.0	4.3	4.5	4.1	3.7	3.8	4.3	2.5	3.7	3.7	3.7	4.8	3.7	3.5	3.2	4.2	4.1	3.7	3.9	3.7	3.9
Undergraduate	100.0	100.0	100.0	100.0	100.0	100.0	100.0	100.0	100.0	100.0	100.0	100.0	100.0	100.0	100.0	100.0	100.0	100.0	100.0	100.0	100.0	100.0
White	54.0	52.8	55.9	57.9	62.2	50.0	57.4	48.7	49.1	48.6	63.2	63.6	52.2	67.0	61.8	65.1	65.7	63.1	39.5	41.9	43.7	34.7
Black	13.3	12.4	11.5	7.5	12.1	16.5	13.3	12.4	14.0	13.6	13.1	12.6	7.7	9.2	12.6	12.3	16.5	13.0	41.2	28.6	28.7	28.5
Hispanic	20.9	22.7	19.7	16.7	15.5	22.9	18.3	27.9	9.3	26.6	12.7	12.7	14.4	11.3	13.7	14.4	9.4	11.0	10.8	19.8	18.0	26.5
Asian	6.8	7.1	7.7	12.6	5.0	6.2	6.1	5.6	4.2	6.3	6.1	6.2	19.6	7.9	7.3	3.9	3.4	6.7	2.5	4.0	3.9	4.4
Pacific Islander	0.3	0.2	0.2	0.2	0.2	0.2	0.2	0.4	0.2	0.3	0.3	0.3	0.1	0.2	0.2	0.4	0.3	0.3	0.4	0.7	0.7	0.7
American Indian/Alaska Native	0.7	0.8	0.7	0.3	0.7	0.4	0.7	0.7	21.4	0.9	0.5	0.5	0.2	0.3	0.4	0.5	0.5	1.7	1.9	1.0	0.9	1.3
Two or more races	4.0	4.0	4.3	4.7	4.4	3.9	4.0	4.3	1.8	3.7	4.0	4.0	5.7	4.1	4.0	3.5	4.3	4.2	3.7	3.9	3.9	3.9

See notes at end of table.

Table 306.50. Total fall enrollment in degree-granting postsecondary institutions, by control and classification of institution, level of enrollment, and race/ethnicity of student: 2018—Continued

Level of enrollment and race/ethnicity of student	Total, all institutions	Public institutions									Nonprofit institutions									For-profit institutions		
		Total	4-year							2-year	Total	4-year							2-year	Total	4-year	2-year
			Total	Research university very high[1]	Research university high[2]	Doctoral/research university[3]	Master's[4]	Bacca-laureate[5]	Special focus[6]			Total	Research university very high[1]	Research university high[2]	Doctoral/research university[3]	Master's[4]	Bacca-laureate[5]	Special focus[6]				
1	2	3	4	5	6	7	8	9	10	11	12	13	14	15	16	17	18	19	20	21	22	23
Postbaccalaureate	100.0	100.0	100.0	100.0	100.0	100.0	100.0	100.0	100.0	†	100.0	100.0	100.0	100.0	100.0	100.0	100.0	100.0	†	100.0	100.0	†
White	62.7	65.6	65.6	67.1	69.9	59.5	63.0	79.1	58.9	†	62.9	62.9	60.4	60.5	60.4	65.7	72.1	61.6	†	46.0	46.0	†
Black	14.0	11.1	11.1	7.9	11.0	15.1	15.3	10.6	9.2	†	13.2	13.2	8.7	14.2	18.5	13.9	13.7	11.9	†	33.8	33.8	†
Hispanic	11.2	11.5	11.5	10.7	10.1	16.1	12.7	4.4	10.6	†	11.0	11.0	11.2	13.6	10.8	11.5	6.9	9.1	†	10.7	10.7	†
Asian	8.2	7.9	7.9	10.0	5.4	6.0	5.4	2.7	17.6	†	9.2	9.2	15.5	8.0	7.1	5.7	4.1	12.8	†	5.1	5.1	†
Pacific Islander	0.2	0.1	0.1	0.1	0.1	0.2	0.2	0.2	0.1	†	0.2	0.2	0.1	0.2	0.3	0.3	0.2	0.2	†	0.5	0.5	†
American Indian/Alaska Native	0.5	0.6	0.6	0.5	0.6	0.4	0.6	1.1	0.7	†	0.4	0.4	0.2	0.4	0.4	0.5	0.5	0.4	†	0.8	0.8	†
Two or more races	3.1	3.2	3.2	3.7	2.9	2.8	2.8	1.9	2.9	†	3.1	3.1	3.9	3.0	2.6	2.5	2.3	4.0	†	3.0	3.0	†

†Not applicable.

[1] Research universities with a very high level of research activity.

[2] Research universities with a high level of research activity.

[3] Institutions that award at least 20 research/scholarship doctor's degrees per year, but did not have a high level of research activity.

[4] Institutions that award at least 50 master's degrees and fewer than 20 doctor's degrees per year.

[5] Institutions that primarily emphasize undergraduate education. In addition to institutions that primarily award bachelor's degrees, also includes institutions classified as 4-year in the IPEDS system, but classified as 2-year baccalaureate/associate's colleges in the Carnegie Classification system because they primarily award associate's degrees.

[6] Four-year institutions that award degrees primarily in single fields of study, such as medicine, business, fine arts, theology, and engineering.

[7] Race/ethnicity not collected.

NOTE: Relative levels of research activity for research universities were determined by an analysis of research and development expenditures, science and engineering research staffing, and doctor's degrees conferred, by field. Further information on the research index ranking may be obtained from http://carnegieclassifications.iu.edu/. Includes imputed Carnegie classifications for institutions with missing data. Degree-granting institutions grant associate's or higher degrees and participate in Title IV federal financial aid programs. Race categories exclude persons of Hispanic ethnicity.

SOURCE: U.S. Department of Education, National Center for Education Statistics, Integrated Postsecondary Education Data System (IPEDS), Spring 2019, Fall Enrollment component. (This table was prepared September 2019.)

Table 306.60. Total fall enrollment in degree-granting postsecondary institutions, by race/ethnicity or nonresident alien status of student and state or jurisdiction: 2018

State or jurisdiction	Fall enrollment									Percentage distribution of U.S. resident students (excludes nonresident aliens)							
	Total	White	Black	Hispanic	Asian	Pacific Islander	American Indian/Alaska Native	Two or more races	Non-resident alien[1]	Total[1]	White	Black	Hispanic	Asian	Pacific Islander	American Indian/Alaska Native	Two or more races
1	2	3	4	5	6	7	8	9	10	11	12	13	14	15	16	17	18
United States	**19,645,918**	**10,301,292**	**2,493,306**	**3,645,040**	**1,302,106**	**50,505**	**133,751**	**727,863**	**992,055**	**100.0**	**55.2**	**13.4**	**19.5**	**7.0**	**0.3**	**0.7**	**3.9**
Alabama	304,182	189,523	77,604	11,758	6,086	359	1,964	7,863	9,025	100.0	64.2	26.3	4.0	2.1	0.1	0.7	2.7
Alaska	25,692	15,012	799	2,159	1,423	395	2,773	2,608	523	100.0	59.6	3.2	8.6	5.7	1.6	11.0	10.4
Arizona	581,982	282,736	70,708	146,080	22,830	2,695	13,676	23,293	19,964	100.0	50.3	12.6	26.0	4.1	0.5	2.4	4.1
Arkansas	159,738	109,342	24,358	10,758	2,868	153	1,156	6,004	5,099	100.0	70.7	15.8	7.0	1.9	0.1	0.7	3.9
California	2,712,420	737,941	165,807	1,111,638	402,035	12,388	11,164	123,529	147,918	100.0	28.8	6.5	43.3	15.7	0.5	0.4	4.8
Colorado	360,537	221,393	27,282	65,261	13,691	853	3,398	16,518	12,141	100.0	63.5	7.8	18.7	3.9	0.2	1.0	4.7
Connecticut	197,480	111,084	26,145	30,903	11,244	205	497	6,230	11,172	100.0	59.6	14.0	16.6	6.0	0.1	0.3	3.3
Delaware	60,700	33,359	12,942	5,153	2,209	82	274	1,851	4,830	100.0	59.7	23.2	9.2	4.0	0.1	0.5	3.3
District of Columbia	77,776	42,490	24,287	9,498	6,924	169	258	3,113	11,037	100.0	49.0	28.0	11.0	8.0	0.2	0.3	3.6
Florida	1,068,063	455,577	189,206	297,906	38,574	2,227	3,102	35,143	46,328	100.0	44.6	18.5	29.2	3.8	0.2	0.3	3.4
Georgia	543,443	258,145	165,611	45,310	30,610	705	1,690	16,951	24,421	100.0	49.7	31.9	8.7	5.9	0.1	0.3	3.3
Hawaii	61,855	10,088	1,223	7,397	19,080	3,561	134	16,370	4,002	100.0	17.4	2.1	12.8	33.0	6.2	0.2	28.3
Idaho	123,487	91,991	1,417	12,137	2,016	548	1,008	5,750	8,619	100.0	80.1	1.2	10.6	1.8	0.5	0.9	5.0
Illinois	738,448	385,507	92,892	142,407	52,486	998	1,594	21,046	41,518	100.0	55.3	13.3	20.4	7.5	0.1	0.2	3.0
Indiana	388,348	273,874	35,189	26,437	13,610	366	814	13,775	24,283	100.0	75.2	9.7	7.3	3.7	0.1	0.2	3.8
Iowa	254,058	185,118	21,216	19,993	7,504	500	1,295	7,052	11,380	100.0	76.3	8.7	8.2	3.1	0.2	0.5	2.9
Kansas	212,737	142,369	17,275	22,471	6,168	415	2,529	8,415	13,095	100.0	71.3	8.7	11.3	3.1	0.2	1.3	4.2
Kentucky	262,961	200,317	21,742	10,153	4,940	241	604	8,234	16,730	100.0	81.4	8.8	4.1	2.0	0.1	0.2	3.3
Louisiana	241,401	130,964	73,815	13,662	6,258	1,088	1,597	6,821	7,196	100.0	55.9	31.5	5.8	2.7	0.5	0.7	2.9
Maine	71,773	60,156	3,034	2,426	1,971	100	674	1,881	1,531	100.0	85.6	4.3	3.5	2.8	0.1	1.0	2.7
Maryland	361,442	159,405	100,270	34,735	28,122	740	1,028	14,942	22,200	100.0	47.0	29.6	10.2	8.3	0.2	0.3	4.4
Massachusetts	499,769	276,317	44,275	58,333	41,971	424	925	15,826	61,698	100.0	63.1	10.1	13.3	9.6	0.1	0.2	3.6
Michigan	541,096	373,156	62,172	29,733	23,699	496	2,995	19,200	29,645	100.0	73.0	12.2	5.8	4.6	0.1	0.6	3.8
Minnesota	408,783	266,065	61,158	24,527	23,414	639	2,951	14,632	15,397	100.0	67.6	15.5	6.2	6.0	0.2	0.8	3.7
Mississippi	169,360	94,294	61,255	4,436	2,193	118	848	3,078	3,138	100.0	56.7	36.9	2.7	1.3	0.1	0.5	1.9
Missouri	374,424	265,176	43,225	21,053	12,812	600	1,730	13,083	16,745	100.0	74.1	12.1	5.9	3.6	0.2	0.5	3.7
Montana	49,363	39,350	471	1,972	836	115	3,337	1,902	1,380	100.0	82.0	1.0	4.1	1.7	0.2	7.0	4.0
Nebraska	134,938	98,192	7,340	14,051	4,315	240	949	4,498	5,353	100.0	75.8	5.7	10.8	3.3	0.2	0.7	3.5
Nevada	117,798	49,560	9,131	33,662	12,959	1,244	839	8,123	2,280	100.0	42.9	7.9	29.1	11.2	1.1	0.7	7.0
New Hampshire	160,743	114,365	20,439	13,682	4,419	486	888	3,477	2,987	100.0	72.5	13.0	8.7	2.8	0.3	0.6	2.2
New Jersey	414,416	193,488	57,230	90,823	40,228	907	957	9,630	21,153	100.0	49.2	14.6	23.1	10.2	0.2	0.2	2.4
New Mexico	123,297	39,571	3,622	59,577	2,600	294	11,440	2,872	3,321	100.0	33.0	3.0	49.7	2.2	0.2	9.5	2.4
New York	1,250,287	582,806	168,367	227,668	124,463	2,034	4,220	32,304	108,425	100.0	51.0	14.7	19.9	10.9	0.2	0.4	2.8
North Carolina	563,710	325,076	124,282	48,178	20,998	738	6,113	18,740	19,585	100.0	59.7	22.8	8.9	3.9	0.1	1.1	3.4
North Dakota	53,286	42,233	1,813	2,065	753	72	2,211	1,756	2,383	100.0	83.0	3.6	4.1	1.5	0.1	4.3	3.4
Ohio	644,962	464,721	74,176	29,645	19,798	568	1,698	22,790	31,566	100.0	75.8	12.1	4.8	3.2	0.1	0.3	3.7
Oklahoma	195,943	112,252	15,450	19,755	6,063	305	13,664	18,955	9,499	100.0	60.2	8.3	10.6	3.3	0.2	7.3	10.2
Oregon	228,140	146,451	6,856	31,669	13,656	1,500	2,372	14,518	11,118	100.0	67.5	3.2	14.6	6.3	0.7	1.1	6.7
Pennsylvania	700,329	458,096	75,929	53,217	41,514	687	1,395	22,450	47,041	100.0	70.1	11.6	8.1	6.4	0.1	0.2	3.4
Rhode Island	80,868	51,812	6,017	11,112	3,892	71	263	3,087	4,614	100.0	67.9	7.9	14.6	5.1	0.1	0.3	4.0
South Carolina	240,533	151,642	57,654	12,355	4,534	259	860	7,927	5,302	100.0	64.5	24.5	5.3	1.9	0.1	0.4	3.4
South Dakota	53,365	42,674	1,987	1,933	723	100	2,777	1,355	1,816	100.0	82.8	3.9	3.7	1.4	0.2	5.4	2.6
Tennessee	322,115	218,471	58,592	16,040	8,872	447	971	10,144	8,578	100.0	69.7	18.7	5.1	2.8	0.1	0.3	3.2
Texas	1,643,542	583,816	202,622	632,198	103,772	2,287	6,137	45,550	67,160	100.0	37.0	12.9	40.1	6.6	0.1	0.4	2.9
Utah	359,772	267,973	18,045	37,868	10,220	2,381	2,532	13,595	7,158	100.0	76.0	5.1	10.7	2.9	0.7	0.7	3.9

See notes at end of table.

Table 306.60. Total fall enrollment in degree-granting postsecondary institutions, by race/ethnicity or nonresident alien status of student and state or jurisdiction: 2018—Continued

State or jurisdiction	Fall enrollment									Percentage distribution of U.S. resident students (excludes nonresident aliens)							
	Total	White	Black	Hispanic	Asian	Pacific Islander	American Indian/Alaska Native	Two or more races	Non-resident alien[1]	Total	White	Black	Hispanic	Asian	Pacific Islander	American Indian/Alaska Native	Two or more races
1	2	3	4	5	6	7	8	9	10	11	12	13	14	15	16	17	18
Vermont	42,914	33,826	1,651	2,463	1,230	45	161	1,839	1,699	100.0	82.1	4.0	6.0	3.0	0.1	0.4	4.5
Virginia	552,041	311,741	106,163	49,896	37,429	1,246	2,020	23,947	19,599	100.0	58.5	19.9	9.4	7.0	0.2	0.4	4.5
Washington	367,056	206,696	16,769	49,965	36,232	2,414	3,858	28,178	22,944	100.0	60.1	4.9	14.5	10.5	0.7	1.1	8.2
West Virginia	140,103	104,759	13,786	9,279	2,493	575	571	4,727	3,913	100.0	76.9	10.1	6.8	1.8	0.4	0.4	3.5
Wisconsin	336,409	253,936	18,357	24,989	13,954	293	2,303	10,152	12,425	100.0	78.4	5.7	7.7	4.3	0.1	0.7	3.1
Wyoming	32,510	26,265	405	2,987	301	57	458	1,123	914	100.0	83.1	1.3	9.5	1.0	0.2	1.4	3.6
U.S. Service Academies	15,523	10,121	1,245	1,667	1,114	75	79	1,015	207	100.0	66.1	8.1	10.9	7.3	0.5	0.5	6.6
Other jurisdictions	**212,565**	**828**	**2,164**	**197,303**	**3,224**	**8,001**	**167**	**167**	**711**	**100.0**	**0.4**	**1.0**	**93.1**	**1.5**	**3.8**	**0.1**	**0.1**
American Samoa	1,037	1	0	1	8	928	0	0	99	100.0	0.1	0.0	0.1	0.9	98.9	0.0	0.0
Federated States of Micronesia	1,931	0	0	0	0	1,931	0	0	0	100.0	0.0	0.0	0.0	#	100.0	0.0	0.0
Guam	5,888	155	45	34	2,607	2,990	8	2	47	100.0	2.7	0.8	0.6	44.6	51.2	0.1	#
Marshall Islands	1,119	1	0	0	5	1,113	0	0	0	100.0	0.1	0.0	0.0	0.4	99.5	0.0	0.0
Northern Marianas	1,194	12	4	5	490	531	0	71	81	100.0	1.1	0.4	0.4	44.0	47.7	0.0	6.4
Palau	497	1	0	0	9	487	0	0	0	100.0	0.2	0.0	0.0	1.8	98.0	0.0	0.0
Puerto Rico	198,915	527	633	197,061	91	20	156	75	352	100.0	0.3	0.3	99.2	0.0	#	0.1	#
U.S. Virgin Islands	1,984	131	1,482	202	14	1	3	19	132	100.0	7.1	80.0	10.9	0.8	0.1	0.2	1.0

#Rounds to zero.
[1]Race/ethnicity not collected.
NOTE: Race categories exclude persons of Hispanic ethnicity. Degree-granting institutions grant associate's or higher degrees and participate in Title IV federal financial aid programs. Detail may not sum to totals because of rounding.

SOURCE: U.S. Department of Education, National Center for Education Statistics, Integrated Postsecondary Education Data System (IPEDS), Spring 2019, Fall Enrollment component. (This table was prepared September 2019.)

Table 307.10. Full-time-equivalent fall enrollment in degree-granting postsecondary institutions, by control and level of institution: 1967 through 2029

Year	All institutions Total	4-year	2-year	Public institutions Total	4-year	2-year	Private institutions Total	4-year Total	Nonprofit	For-profit	2-year Total	Nonprofit	For-profit
1	2	3	4	5	6	7	8	9	10	11	12	13	14
1967	5,499,360	4,448,302	1,051,058	3,777,701	2,850,432	927,269	1,721,659	1,597,870	—	—	123,789	—	—
1968	5,977,768	4,729,522	1,248,246	4,248,639	3,128,057	1,120,582	1,729,129	1,601,465	—	—	127,664	—	—
1969	6,333,357	4,899,034	1,434,323	4,577,353	3,259,323	1,318,030	1,756,004	1,639,711	—	—	116,293	—	—
1970	6,737,819	5,145,422	1,592,397	4,953,144	3,468,569	1,484,575	1,784,675	1,676,853	—	—	107,822	—	—
1971	7,148,558	5,357,647	1,790,911	5,344,402	3,660,626	1,683,776	1,804,156	1,697,021	—	—	107,135	—	—
1972	7,253,757	5,406,833	1,846,924	5,452,854	3,706,238	1,746,616	1,800,903	1,700,595	—	—	100,308	—	—
1973	7,453,463	5,439,230	2,014,233	5,629,563	3,721,037	1,908,526	1,823,900	1,718,193	—	—	105,707	—	—
1974	7,805,452	5,606,247	2,199,205	5,944,799	3,847,543	2,097,256	1,860,653	1,758,704	—	—	101,949	—	—
1975	8,479,698	5,900,408	2,579,290	6,522,319	4,056,502	2,465,817	1,957,379	1,843,906	—	—	113,473	—	—
1976	8,312,502	5,848,001	2,464,501	6,349,903	3,998,450	2,351,453	1,962,599	1,849,551	—	—	113,048	—	—
1977	8,415,339	5,935,076	2,480,263	6,396,476	4,039,071	2,357,405	2,018,863	1,896,005	—	—	122,858	—	—
1978	8,348,482	5,932,357	2,416,125	6,279,199	3,996,126	2,283,073	2,069,283	1,936,231	—	—	133,052	—	—
1979	8,487,317	6,016,072	2,471,245	6,392,617	4,059,304	2,333,313	2,094,700	1,956,768	—	—	137,932	—	—
1980	8,819,013	6,161,372	2,657,641	6,642,294	4,158,267	2,484,027	2,176,719	2,003,105	—	—	173,614[1]	—	—
1981	9,014,521	6,249,847	2,764,674	6,781,300	4,208,506	2,572,794	2,233,221	2,041,341	—	—	191,880[1]	—	—
1982	9,091,648	6,248,923	2,842,725	6,850,589	4,220,648	2,629,941	2,241,059	2,028,275	—	—	212,784[1]	—	—
1983	9,166,398	6,325,222	2,841,176	6,881,479	4,265,807	2,615,672	2,284,919	2,059,415	—	—	225,504	—	—
1984	8,951,695	6,292,711	2,658,984	6,684,664	4,237,895	2,446,769	2,267,031	2,054,816	—	—	212,215	—	—
1985	8,943,433	6,294,339	2,649,094	6,667,781	4,239,622	2,428,159	2,275,652	2,054,717	—	—	220,935	—	—
1986	9,064,165	6,360,325	2,703,842	6,778,045	4,295,494	2,482,551	2,286,122	2,064,831	—	—	221,291[2]	—	—
1987	9,229,736	6,486,504	2,743,230	6,937,690	4,395,728	2,541,961	2,292,045	2,090,776	—	—	201,269[2]	—	—
1988	9,464,271	6,664,146	2,800,125	7,096,905	4,505,774	2,591,131	2,367,366	2,158,372	—	—	208,994	—	—
1989	9,780,881	6,813,602	2,967,279	7,371,590	4,619,828	2,751,762	2,409,291	2,193,774	—	—	215,517	—	—
1990	9,983,436	6,968,008	3,015,428	7,557,982	4,740,049	2,817,933	2,425,454	2,227,959	2,177,668	50,291	197,495	72,785	124,710
1991	10,360,606	7,081,454	3,279,152	7,862,845	4,795,704	3,067,141	2,497,761	2,285,750	2,223,463	62,287	212,011	72,545	139,466
1992	10,436,776	7,129,379	3,307,397	7,911,701	4,797,884	3,113,817	2,525,075	2,331,495	2,267,373	64,122	193,580	66,647	126,933
1993	10,351,415	7,120,921	3,230,494	7,812,394	4,765,983	3,046,411	2,539,021	2,354,938	2,282,643	72,295	184,083	70,469	113,614
1994	10,348,072	7,137,341	3,210,731	7,784,396	4,749,524	3,034,872	2,563,676	2,387,817	2,301,063	86,754	175,859	69,578	106,281
1995	10,334,956	7,172,844	3,162,112	7,751,815	4,757,223	2,994,592	2,583,141	2,415,621	2,328,730	86,891	167,520	62,416	105,104
1996	10,481,886	7,234,541	3,247,345	7,794,895	4,767,117	3,027,778	2,686,991	2,467,424	2,353,561	113,863	219,567	63,954	155,613
1997	10,615,028	7,338,794	3,276,234	7,869,764	4,813,849	3,055,915	2,745,264	2,524,945	2,389,627	135,318	220,319	61,761	158,558
1998	10,698,775	7,467,828	3,230,947	7,880,135	4,868,857	3,011,278	2,818,640	2,598,971	2,436,188	162,783	219,669	56,834	162,835
1999	10,974,519	7,634,247	3,340,272	8,059,240	4,949,851	3,109,389	2,915,279	2,684,396	2,488,140	196,256	230,883	53,956	176,927
2000	11,267,025	7,795,139	3,471,886	8,266,932	5,025,588	3,241,344	3,000,093	2,769,551	2,549,676	219,875	230,542	51,503	179,039
2001	11,765,945	8,087,980	3,677,965	8,639,154	5,194,035	3,445,119	3,126,791	2,893,945	2,612,833	281,112	232,846	41,037	191,809
2002	12,331,319	8,439,064	3,892,255	9,061,411	5,406,283	3,655,128	3,269,908	3,032,781	2,699,702	333,079	237,127	40,110	197,017
2003	12,687,597	8,744,188	3,943,409	9,240,724	5,557,680	3,683,044	3,446,873	3,186,508	2,776,850	409,658	260,365	36,815	223,550
2004	13,000,994	9,018,024	3,982,970	9,348,081	5,640,650	3,707,431	3,652,913	3,377,374	2,837,251	540,123	275,539	34,202	241,337
2005	13,200,790	9,261,634	3,939,156	9,390,216	5,728,327	3,661,889	3,810,574	3,533,307	2,878,354	654,953	277,267	34,729	242,538
2006	13,401,696	9,456,480	3,945,216	9,502,028	5,824,962	3,677,066	3,899,668	3,631,518	2,936,261	695,257	268,150	31,203	236,947
2007	13,786,735	9,768,388	4,018,347	9,744,001	5,992,611	3,751,390	4,042,734	3,775,777	2,993,901	781,876	266,957	26,140	240,817
2008	14,377,990	10,153,074	4,224,916	10,061,076	6,138,686	3,922,390	4,316,914	4,014,388	3,058,910	955,478	302,526	28,072	274,454
2009	15,379,473	10,695,816	4,683,657	10,746,637	6,452,414	4,294,223	4,632,836	4,243,402	3,153,294	1,090,108	389,434	27,964	361,470
2010	15,947,474	11,129,239	4,818,235	11,018,756	6,635,799	4,382,957	4,928,718	4,493,440	3,235,149	1,258,291	435,278	26,920	408,358
2011	15,892,792	11,261,845	4,630,947	10,954,754	6,734,116	4,220,638	4,938,038	4,527,729	3,285,711	1,242,018	410,309	34,267	376,042
2012	15,593,434	11,229,774	4,363,660	10,781,798	6,764,184	4,017,614	4,811,636	4,465,590	3,309,242	1,156,348	346,046	32,684	313,362
2013	15,410,058	11,183,239	4,226,819	10,697,939	6,790,930	3,907,009	4,712,119	4,392,309	3,337,799	1,054,510	319,810	27,313	292,497
2014	15,263,179	11,238,618	4,024,561	10,624,163	6,891,984	3,732,179	4,639,016	4,346,634	3,363,101	983,533	292,382	25,808	266,574
2015	15,078,504	11,226,353	3,852,151	10,569,574	6,970,121	3,599,453	4,508,930	4,256,232	3,399,283	856,949	252,698	41,579	211,119
2016	14,937,939	11,356,540	3,581,399	10,572,028	7,221,134	3,350,894	4,365,911	4,135,406	3,410,337	725,069	230,505	43,900	186,605
2017	14,883,617	11,404,002	3,479,615	10,568,658	7,309,343	3,259,315	4,314,959	4,094,659	3,435,813	658,846	220,300	43,992	176,308
2018	14,785,824	11,453,643	3,332,181	10,522,337	7,376,852	3,145,485	4,263,487	4,076,791	3,475,852	600,939	186,696	40,824	145,872
2019[3]	14,834,000	11,490,000	3,345,000	10,557,000	7,400,000	3,157,000	4,277,000	4,090,000	—	—	187,000	—	—
2020[3]	14,841,000	11,493,000	3,348,000	10,563,000	7,402,000	3,161,000	4,278,000	4,091,000	—	—	187,000	—	—
2021[3]	14,853,000	11,499,000	3,354,000	10,573,000	7,406,000	3,166,000	4,280,000	4,093,000	—	—	187,000	—	—
2022[3]	14,869,000	11,510,000	3,359,000	10,585,000	7,413,000	3,172,000	4,284,000	4,097,000	—	—	187,000	—	—
2023[3]	14,898,000	11,531,000	3,367,000	10,606,000	7,427,000	3,180,000	4,292,000	4,104,000	—	—	188,000	—	—
2024[3]	14,943,000	11,564,000	3,378,000	10,638,000	7,448,000	3,190,000	4,304,000	4,116,000	—	—	188,000	—	—
2025[3]	14,994,000	11,605,000	3,390,000	10,675,000	7,474,000	3,201,000	4,319,000	4,131,000	—	—	189,000	—	—
2026[3]	15,051,000	11,648,000	3,403,000	10,715,000	7,502,000	3,213,000	4,336,000	4,146,000	—	—	190,000	—	—
2027[3]	15,064,000	11,657,000	3,407,000	10,725,000	7,508,000	3,218,000	4,339,000	4,149,000	—	—	190,000	—	—
2028[3]	15,061,000	11,652,000	3,409,000	10,724,000	7,505,000	3,219,000	4,337,000	4,147,000	—	—	190,000	—	—
2029[3]	15,053,000	11,644,000	3,409,000	10,720,000	7,500,000	3,220,000	4,333,000	4,144,000	—	—	189,000	—	—

—Not available.
[1]Large increases are due to the addition of schools accredited by the Accrediting Commission of Career Schools and Colleges of Technology.
[2]Because of imputation techniques, data are not consistent with figures for other years.
[3]Projected.
NOTE: Full-time-equivalent enrollment is the number of full-time students enrolled, plus the full-time equivalent of the part-time students. Data through 1995 are for institutions of higher education, while later data are for degree-granting institutions. Degree-granting institutions grant associate's or higher degrees and participate in Title IV federal financial aid programs. The degree-granting classification is very similar to the earlier higher education classification, but it includes more 2-year colleges and excludes a few higher education institutions that did not grant degrees. Some data have been revised from previously published figures. Detail may not sum to totals because of rounding.
SOURCE: U.S. Department of Education, National Center for Education Statistics, Higher Education General Information Survey (HEGIS), "Fall Enrollment in Colleges and Universities" surveys, 1967 through 1985; Integrated Postsecondary Education Data System (IPEDS), "Fall Enrollment Survey" (IPEDS-EF:86–99); IPEDS Spring 2001 through Spring 2019, Fall Enrollment component; and Enrollment in Degree-Granting Institutions Projection Model, 2000 through 2029. (This table was prepared December 2019.)

Table 309.10. Residence and migration of all first-time degree/certificate-seeking undergraduates in degree-granting postsecondary institutions, by state or jurisdiction: Fall 2018

State or jurisdiction	Total first-time enrollment in institutions located in the state	State residents enrolled in institutions		Ratio of in-state students		Migration of students		
		In any state[1]	In their home state	To first-time enrollment (col. 4/col. 2)	To residents enrolled in any state (col. 4/col. 3)	Out of state (col. 3 - col. 4)	Into state[2] (col. 2 - col. 4)	Net (col. 8 - col. 7)
1	2	3	4	5	6	7	8	9
United States	2,885,818	2,789,820	2,256,031	0.78	0.81	533,789	629,787	95,998
Alabama	48,346	40,342	34,612	0.72	0.86	5,730	13,734	8,004
Alaska	2,931	4,700	2,710	0.92	0.58	1,990	221	-1,769
Arizona	61,748	49,967	43,463	0.70	0.87	6,504	18,285	11,781
Arkansas	26,567	23,751	20,318	0.76	0.86	3,433	6,249	2,816
California	387,767	388,386	343,780	0.89	0.89	44,606	43,987	-619
Colorado	45,827	43,935	32,886	0.72	0.75	11,049	12,941	1,892
Connecticut	31,656	36,024	20,703	0.65	0.57	15,321	10,953	-4,368
Delaware	9,879	8,508	5,818	0.59	0.68	2,690	4,061	1,371
District of Columbia	10,506	3,394	804	0.08	0.24	2,590	9,702	7,112
Florida	161,033	153,191	133,087	0.83	0.87	20,104	27,946	7,842
Georgia	87,518	90,864	72,194	0.82	0.79	18,670	15,324	-3,346
Hawaii	8,645	10,485	6,369	0.74	0.61	4,116	2,276	-1,840
Idaho	14,874	12,158	8,873	0.60	0.73	3,285	6,001	2,716
Illinois	92,486	112,391	75,859	0.82	0.67	36,532	16,627	-19,905
Indiana	64,865	53,937	46,372	0.71	0.86	7,565	18,493	10,928
Iowa	35,591	26,548	22,993	0.65	0.87	3,555	12,598	9,043
Kansas	30,960	26,183	21,993	0.71	0.84	4,190	8,967	4,777
Kentucky	38,634	36,361	31,081	0.80	0.85	5,280	7,553	2,273
Louisiana	40,876	39,813	34,017	0.83	0.85	5,796	6,859	1,063
Maine	11,665	10,336	7,323	0.63	0.71	3,013	4,342	1,329
Maryland	44,708	51,799	34,466	0.77	0.67	17,333	10,242	-7,091
Massachusetts	71,899	64,276	42,809	0.60	0.67	21,467	29,090	7,623
Michigan	81,937	81,404	70,743	0.86	0.87	10,661	11,194	533
Minnesota	44,218	49,147	34,348	0.78	0.70	14,799	9,870	-4,929
Mississippi	31,041	27,150	24,234	0.78	0.89	2,916	6,807	3,891
Missouri	50,900	48,758	38,764	0.76	0.80	9,994	12,136	2,142
Montana	8,511	7,021	5,395	0.63	0.77	1,626	3,116	1,490
Nebraska	18,258	16,809	13,710	0.75	0.82	3,099	4,548	1,449
Nevada	18,143	20,302	16,000	0.88	0.79	4,302	2,143	-2,159
New Hampshire	20,398	11,075	6,081	0.30	0.55	4,994	14,317	9,323
New Jersey	65,246	93,505	58,925	0.90	0.63	34,580	6,321	-28,259
New Mexico	16,654	16,424	13,509	0.81	0.82	2,915	3,145	230
New York	188,267	179,355	145,909	0.78	0.81	33,446	42,358	8,912
North Carolina	88,920	84,647	72,906	0.82	0.86	11,741	16,014	4,273
North Dakota	8,368	5,776	4,248	0.51	0.74	1,528	4,120	2,592
Ohio	107,591	94,972	80,385	0.75	0.85	14,587	27,206	12,619
Oklahoma	33,781	30,070	26,016	0.77	0.87	4,054	7,765	3,711
Oregon	32,046	28,434	22,951	0.72	0.81	5,483	9,095	3,612
Pennsylvania	118,558	105,198	84,300	0.71	0.80	20,898	34,258	13,360
Rhode Island	14,959	8,960	6,120	0.41	0.68	2,840	8,839	5,999
South Carolina	46,053	40,353	34,602	0.75	0.86	5,751	11,451	5,700
South Dakota	8,646	7,011	5,305	0.61	0.76	1,706	3,341	1,635
Tennessee	57,576	55,310	46,023	0.80	0.83	9,287	11,553	2,266
Texas	244,190	257,478	226,101	0.93	0.88	31,377	18,089	-13,288
Utah	40,979	26,119	23,677	0.58	0.91	2,442	17,302	14,860
Vermont	7,249	4,467	2,298	0.32	0.51	2,169	4,951	2,782
Virginia	79,615	74,433	60,400	0.76	0.81	14,033	19,215	5,182
Washington	48,363	50,797	39,109	0.81	0.77	11,688	9,254	-2,434
West Virginia	17,106	12,092	10,328	0.60	0.85	1,764	6,778	5,014
Wisconsin	50,357	47,194	37,723	0.75	0.80	9,471	12,634	3,163
Wyoming	4,828	4,065	3,118	0.65	0.77	947	1,710	763
U.S. Service Academies	4,079	†	273[3]	0.07	†	-273	3,806	4,079
State unknown[4]	†	14,145	†	†	†	14,145	†	-14,145
Other jurisdictions	37,759	39,601	37,377	0.99	0.94	2,224	382	-1,842
American Samoa	309	368	309	1.00	0.84	59	0	-59
Federated States of Micronesia	698	858	698	1.00	0.81	160	0	-160
Guam	1,093	1,279	1,041	0.95	0.81	238	52	-186
Marshall Islands	336	353	332	0.99	0.94	21	4	-17
Northern Marianas	343	410	320	0.93	0.78	90	23	-67
Palau	121	124	104	0.86	0.84	20	17	-3
Puerto Rico	34,539	35,547	34,267	0.99	0.96	1,280	272	-1,008
U.S. Virgin Islands	320	662	306	0.96	0.46	356	14	-342
Foreign countries	†	84,907	†	†	†	84,907	†	-84,907
Residence unknown	†	9,249	†	†	†	9,249	†	-9,249

†Not applicable.
[1]Students residing in a particular state when admitted to an institution anywhere—either in their home state or another state.
[2]Includes students coming to U.S. institutions from foreign countries and other jurisdictions.
[3]Students whose residence is in the same state as the service academy.
[4]Institution unable to determine student's home state.

NOTE: Includes all first-time postsecondary students enrolled at reporting institutions. Degree-granting institutions grant associate's or higher degrees and participate in Title IV federal financial aid programs.
SOURCE: U.S. Department of Education, National Center for Education Statistics, Integrated Postsecondary Education Data System (IPEDS), Spring 2019, Fall Enrollment component. (This table was prepared March 2020.)

Table 309.20. Residence and migration of all first-time degree/certificate-seeking undergraduates in degree-granting postsecondary institutions who graduated from high school in the previous 12 months, by state or jurisdiction: Fall 2018

State or jurisdiction	Total first-time enrollment in institutions located in the state	State residents enrolled in institutions		Ratio of in-state students		Migration of students		
		In any state[1]	In their home state	To first-time enrollment (col. 4/col. 2)	To residents enrolled in any state (col. 4/col. 3)	Out of state (col. 3 - col. 4)	Into state[2] (col. 2 - col. 4)	Net (col. 8 - col. 7)
1	2	3	4	5	6	7	8	9
United States	**2,264,873**	**2,207,429**	**1,766,132**	**0.78**	**0.80**	**441,297**	**498,741**	**57,444**
Alabama	40,011	32,112	28,042	0.70	0.87	4,070	11,969	7,899
Alaska	1,925	3,192	1,771	0.92	0.55	1,421	154	-1,267
Arizona	41,986	34,558	29,520	0.70	0.85	5,038	12,466	7,428
Arkansas	23,279	19,771	17,447	0.75	0.88	2,324	5,832	3,508
California	273,792	284,532	246,241	0.90	0.87	38,291	27,551	-10,740
Colorado	34,133	33,982	24,494	0.72	0.72	9,488	9,639	151
Connecticut	26,924	31,268	17,078	0.63	0.55	14,190	9,846	-4,344
Delaware	8,222	6,883	4,587	0.56	0.67	2,296	3,635	1,339
District of Columbia	8,467	2,652	503	0.06	0.19	2,149	7,964	5,815
Florida	118,172	117,499	101,298	0.86	0.86	16,201	16,874	673
Georgia	70,378	70,631	57,157	0.81	0.81	13,474	13,221	-253
Hawaii	6,505	8,412	4,811	0.74	0.57	3,601	1,694	-1,907
Idaho	11,473	9,111	6,663	0.58	0.73	2,448	4,810	2,362
Illinois	69,888	89,817	56,545	0.81	0.63	33,272	13,343	-19,929
Indiana	56,505	46,001	40,009	0.71	0.87	5,992	16,496	10,504
Iowa	30,534	23,113	20,045	0.66	0.87	3,068	10,489	7,421
Kansas	25,623	21,965	18,486	0.72	0.84	3,479	7,137	3,658
Kentucky	32,673	29,722	25,888	0.79	0.87	3,834	6,785	2,951
Louisiana	32,981	30,984	26,967	0.82	0.87	4,017	6,014	1,997
Maine	9,698	8,440	5,911	0.61	0.70	2,529	3,787	1,258
Maryland	33,736	40,997	25,843	0.77	0.63	15,154	7,893	-7,261
Massachusetts	61,097	54,508	35,041	0.57	0.64	19,467	26,056	6,589
Michigan	68,493	66,904	58,664	0.86	0.88	8,240	9,829	1,589
Minnesota	37,133	42,189	28,640	0.77	0.68	13,549	8,493	-5,056
Mississippi	27,829	23,244	21,520	0.77	0.93	1,724	6,309	4,585
Missouri	42,166	40,611	32,291	0.77	0.80	8,320	9,875	1,555
Montana	6,722	5,225	4,026	0.60	0.77	1,199	2,696	1,497
Nebraska	16,402	15,022	12,281	0.75	0.82	2,741	4,121	1,380
Nevada	13,291	14,586	11,397	0.86	0.78	3,189	1,894	-1,295
New Hampshire	10,604	9,336	4,820	0.45	0.52	4,516	5,784	1,268
New Jersey	49,685	76,325	44,486	0.90	0.58	31,839	5,199	-26,640
New Mexico	12,551	12,652	10,394	0.83	0.82	2,258	2,157	-101
New York	154,710	148,490	118,767	0.77	0.80	29,723	35,943	6,220
North Carolina	73,708	68,137	59,507	0.81	0.87	8,630	14,201	5,571
North Dakota	7,361	4,735	3,588	0.49	0.76	1,147	3,773	2,626
Ohio	84,130	77,436	65,746	0.78	0.85	11,690	18,384	6,694
Oklahoma	27,850	23,968	21,011	0.75	0.88	2,957	6,839	3,882
Oregon	23,448	20,358	15,947	0.68	0.78	4,411	7,501	3,090
Pennsylvania	100,139	85,303	68,147	0.68	0.80	17,156	31,992	14,836
Rhode Island	13,651	7,707	5,208	0.38	0.68	2,499	8,443	5,944
South Carolina	38,672	32,212	28,362	0.73	0.88	3,850	10,310	6,460
South Dakota	7,555	5,907	4,464	0.59	0.76	1,443	3,091	1,648
Tennessee	48,738	46,182	38,723	0.79	0.84	7,459	10,015	2,556
Texas	188,158	200,738	175,583	0.93	0.87	25,155	12,575	-12,580
Utah	24,364	18,362	16,639	0.68	0.91	1,723	7,725	6,002
Vermont	6,204	3,679	1,767	0.28	0.48	1,912	4,437	2,525
Virginia	65,454	62,248	50,627	0.77	0.81	11,621	14,827	3,206
Washington	36,252	37,480	28,079	0.77	0.75	9,401	8,173	-1,228
West Virginia	13,189	9,570	8,427	0.64	0.88	1,143	4,762	3,619
Wisconsin	41,485	38,202	29,925	0.72	0.78	8,277	11,560	3,283
Wyoming	4,050	3,291	2,558	0.63	0.78	733	1,492	759
U.S. Service Academies	2,877	†	191[3]	0.07	†	-191	2,686	2,877
State unknown[4]	†	7,180	†	†	†	7,180	†	-7,180
Other jurisdictions	**30,519**	**32,163**	**30,332**	**0.99**	**0.94**	**1,831**	**187**	**-1,644**
American Samoa	254	302	254	1.00	0.84	48	0	-48
Federated States of Micronesia	274	318	274	1.00	0.86	44	0	-44
Guam	735	896	694	0.94	0.77	202	41	-161
Marshall Islands	312	327	310	0.99	0.95	17	2	-15
Northern Marianas	254	319	240	0.94	0.75	79	14	-65
Palau	94	106	88	0.94	0.83	18	6	-12
Puerto Rico	28,368	29,365	28,253	1.00	0.96	1,112	115	-997
U.S. Virgin Islands	228	530	219	0.96	0.41	311	9	-302
Foreign countries	†	55,798	†	†	†	55,798	†	-55,798
Residence unknown	†	2	†	†	†	2	†	-2

†Not applicable.
[1]Students residing in a particular state when admitted to an institution anywhere—either in their home state or another state.
[2]Includes students coming to U.S. institutions from foreign countries and other jurisdictions.
[3]Students whose residence is in the same state as the service academy.
[4]Institution unable to determine student's home state.

NOTE: Includes all first-time postsecondary students who graduated from high school in the previous 12 months and were enrolled at reporting institutions. Degree-granting institutions grant associate's or higher degrees and participate in Title IV federal financial aid programs.
SOURCE: U.S. Department of Education, National Center for Education Statistics, Integrated Postsecondary Education Data System (IPEDS), Spring 2019, Fall Enrollment component. (This table was prepared March 2020.)

Table 309.30. Residence and migration of all first-time degree/certificate-seeking undergraduates in 4-year degree-granting postsecondary institutions who graduated from high school in the previous 12 months, by state or jurisdiction: Fall 2018

| State or jurisdiction | Total first-time enrollment in institutions located in the state | State residents enrolled in institutions | | Ratio of in-state students | | Migration of students | | |
		In any state[1]	In their home state	To first-time enrollment (col. 4/col. 2)	To residents enrolled in any state (col. 4/col. 3)	Out of state (col. 3 - col. 4)	Into state[2] (col. 2 - col. 4)	Net (col. 8 - col. 7)
1	2	3	4	5	6	7	8	9
United States	**1,667,223**	**1,614,718**	**1,193,561**	**0.72**	**0.74**	**421,157**	**473,662**	**52,505**
Alabama	26,723	18,979	15,365	0.57	0.81	3,614	11,358	7,744
Alaska	1,858	3,029	1,704	0.92	0.56	1,325	154	-1,171
Arizona	29,086	21,693	16,919	0.58	0.78	4,774	12,167	7,393
Arkansas	17,298	13,648	11,628	0.67	0.85	2,020	5,670	3,650
California	161,378	174,616	136,992	0.85	0.78	37,624	24,386	-13,238
Colorado	30,521	30,172	21,291	0.70	0.71	8,881	9,230	349
Connecticut	21,195	25,413	11,388	0.54	0.45	14,025	9,807	-4,218
Delaware	8,181	6,797	4,569	0.56	0.67	2,228	3,612	1,384
District of Columbia	8,461	2,520	499	0.06	0.20	2,021	7,962	5,941
Florida	114,005	112,397	97,202	0.85	0.86	15,195	16,803	1,608
Georgia	59,654	60,124	47,436	0.80	0.79	12,688	12,218	-470
Hawaii	4,129	6,005	2,542	0.62	0.42	3,463	1,587	-1,876
Idaho	9,371	6,952	4,716	0.50	0.68	2,236	4,655	2,419
Illinois	46,485	65,869	33,470	0.72	0.51	32,399	13,015	-19,384
Indiana	47,845	37,198	31,600	0.66	0.85	5,598	16,245	10,647
Iowa	20,112	13,667	10,809	0.54	0.79	2,858	9,303	6,445
Kansas	15,561	13,610	10,329	0.66	0.76	3,281	5,232	1,951
Kentucky	23,573	20,649	17,033	0.72	0.82	3,616	6,540	2,924
Louisiana	25,916	23,706	20,108	0.78	0.85	3,598	5,808	2,210
Maine	7,537	6,374	3,887	0.52	0.61	2,487	3,650	1,163
Maryland	19,679	27,629	12,749	0.65	0.46	14,880	6,930	-7,950
Massachusetts	51,505	44,877	25,630	0.50	0.57	19,247	25,875	6,628
Michigan	53,212	51,563	43,764	0.82	0.85	7,799	9,448	1,649
Minnesota	25,443	30,855	17,991	0.71	0.58	12,864	7,452	-5,412
Mississippi	12,608	8,472	6,855	0.54	0.81	1,617	5,753	4,136
Missouri	27,823	25,909	18,270	0.66	0.71	7,639	9,553	1,914
Montana	5,869	4,239	3,250	0.55	0.77	989	2,619	1,630
Nebraska	12,154	10,747	8,395	0.69	0.78	2,352	3,759	1,407
Nevada	12,934	13,996	11,041	0.85	0.79	2,955	1,893	-1,062
New Hampshire	8,821	7,479	3,151	0.36	0.42	4,328	5,670	1,342
New Jersey	33,070	59,429	28,006	0.85	0.47	31,423	5,064	-26,359
New Mexico	6,570	6,974	4,950	0.75	0.71	2,024	1,620	-404
New York	116,581	110,958	81,653	0.70	0.74	29,305	34,928	5,623
North Carolina	51,659	46,239	37,910	0.73	0.82	8,329	13,749	5,420
North Dakota	6,318	3,764	2,933	0.46	0.78	831	3,385	2,554
Ohio	70,973	64,998	53,694	0.76	0.83	11,304	17,279	5,975
Oklahoma	19,433	15,741	13,239	0.68	0.84	2,502	6,194	3,692
Oregon	15,802	13,106	8,816	0.56	0.67	4,290	6,986	2,696
Pennsylvania	84,622	69,612	53,107	0.63	0.76	16,505	31,515	15,010
Rhode Island	10,990	5,084	2,618	0.24	0.51	2,466	8,372	5,906
South Carolina	25,969	19,912	16,259	0.63	0.82	3,653	9,710	6,057
South Dakota	6,214	4,636	3,370	0.54	0.73	1,266	2,844	1,578
Tennessee	31,721	29,459	22,276	0.70	0.76	7,183	9,445	2,262
Texas	117,983	131,482	107,372	0.91	0.82	24,110	10,611	-13,499
Utah	21,920	15,816	14,304	0.65	0.90	1,512	7,616	6,104
Vermont	5,863	3,274	1,443	0.25	0.44	1,831	4,420	2,589
Virginia	45,368	42,809	31,544	0.70	0.74	11,265	13,824	2,559
Washington	34,320	35,208	26,204	0.76	0.74	9,004	8,116	-888
West Virginia	11,550	7,811	6,880	0.60	0.88	931	4,670	3,739
Wisconsin	36,719	33,230	25,377	0.69	0.76	7,853	11,342	3,489
Wyoming	1,764	1,497	832	0.47	0.56	665	932	267
U.S. Service Academies	2,877	†	191[3]	0.07	†	-191	2,686	2,877
State unknown[4]	†	4,495	†	†	†	4,495	†	-4,495
Other jurisdictions	**27,174**	**28,704**	**27,014**	**0.99**	**0.94**	**1,690**	**160**	**-1,530**
American Samoa	254	287	254	1.00	0.89	33	0	-33
Federated States of Micronesia	†	39	†	†	†	39	0	-39
Guam	461	620	420	0.91	0.68	200	41	-159
Marshall Islands	312	322	310	†	†	12	2	-10
Northern Marianas	254	316	240	0.94	0.76	76	14	-62
Palau	†	16	†	†	†	16	0	-16
Puerto Rico	25,665	26,579	25,571	1.00	0.96	1,008	94	-914
U.S. Virgin Islands	228	525	219	0.96	0.42	306	9	-297
Foreign countries	†	50,973	†	†	†	50,973	†	-50,973
Residence unknown	†	2	†	†	†	2	†	-2

†Not applicable.
[1]Students residing in a particular state when admitted to an institution anywhere—either in their home state or another state.
[2]Includes students coming to U.S. institutions from foreign countries and other jurisdictions.
[3]Students whose residence is in the same state as the service academy.
[4]Institution unable to determine student's home state.

NOTE: Includes all first-time postsecondary students who graduated from high school in the previous 12 months and were enrolled at reporting institutions. Degree-granting institutions grant associate's or higher degrees and participate in Title IV federal financial aid programs. SOURCE: U.S. Department of Education, National Center for Education Statistics, Integrated Postsecondary Education Data System (IPEDS), Spring 2019, Fall Enrollment component. (This table was prepared March 2020.)

Table 310.10. Number of U.S. students studying abroad and percentage distribution, by sex, race/ethnicity, and other selected characteristics: Selected years, 2000–01 through 2017–18

Sex, race/ethnicity, and other selected characteristics	2000–01	2007–08	2008–09	2009–10	2010–11	2011–12	2012–13	2013–14	2014–15	2015–16	2016–17	2017–18	From 2007–08 to 2017–18
1	2	3	4	5	6	7	8	9	10	11	12	13	14
	Number of students												Percentage change in number of students
Total	154,168	262,416	260,327	270,604	273,996	283,332	289,408	304,467	313,415	325,339	332,727	341,751	30.2
	Percentage distribution of students												Percentage-point change in distribution of students
Sex	100.0	100.0	100.0	100.0	100.0	100.0	100.0	100.0	100.0	100.0	100.0	100.0	†
Male	35.0	34.9	35.8	36.5	35.6	35.2	34.7	34.7	33.4	33.5	32.7	33.0	-1.9
Female	65.0	65.1	64.2	63.5	64.4	64.8	65.3	65.3	66.6	66.5	67.3	67.0	1.9
Race/ethnicity	100.0	100.0	100.0	100.0	100.0	100.0	100.0	100.0	100.0	100.0	100.0	100.0	†
White	84.3	81.8	80.5	78.7	77.8	76.4	76.3	74.3	72.9	71.6	70.8	70.0	-11.8
Black	3.5	4.0	4.2	4.7	4.8	5.3	5.3	5.6	5.6	5.9	6.1	6.1	2.1
Hispanic	5.4	5.9	6.0	6.4	6.9	7.6	7.6	8.3	8.8	9.7	10.2	10.6	4.7
Asian/Pacific Islander	5.4	6.6	7.3	7.9	7.9	7.7	7.3	7.7	8.1	8.4	8.2	8.4	1.8
American Indian/Alaska Native	0.5	0.5	0.5	0.5	0.5	0.5	0.5	0.5	0.5	0.5	0.4	0.5	#
Two or more races	0.9	1.2	1.6	1.9	2.1	2.5	3.0	3.6	4.1	3.9	4.3	4.4	3.2
Academic level	100.0	100.0	100.0	100.0	100.0	100.0	100.0	100.0	100.0	100.0	100.0	100.0	†
Associate's	0.9	2.2	1.1	0.1	0.2	1.1	1.1	1.7	1.8	1.7	1.7	1.7	-0.5
Freshman	3.1	3.5	3.4	3.5	3.3	3.3	3.8	3.9	3.9	3.6	4.0	4.2	0.7
Sophomore	14.0	13.1	13.9	13.2	12.6	13.0	13.7	13.1	13.1	12.7	13.2	12.8	-0.3
Junior	38.9	35.9	36.8	35.8	35.8	36.0	34.7	33.9	33.1	32.9	33.0	33.0	-2.9
Senior	20.0	21.3	21.6	21.8	23.4	24.4	24.7	25.3	26.4	27.7	27.4	28.2	6.9
Bachelor's, unspecified	13.5	13.4	11.3	11.0	10.3	8.4	8.4	9.1	9.3	9.1	8.6	7.8	-5.6
Master's or higher	8.3	10.5	11.8	13.6	13.5	13.5	13.5	12.7	12.1	12.1	12.3	12.1	1.6
Other academic level	1.1	0.1	#	1.0	0.9	0.3	0.1	0.3	0.3	0.2	0.2	0.2	0.1
Host region	100.0	100.0	100.0	100.0	100.0	100.0	100.0	100.0	100.0	100.0	100.0	100.0	†
Sub-Saharan Africa[1]	2.5	3.6	4.2	4.2	4.3	4.5	4.6	4.4	3.4	3.9	4.0	4.2	0.6
Asia[2]	6.0	11.1	11.4	12.0	11.7	12.4	12.4	11.9	11.4	11.1	11.6	11.2	0.1
Europe[3]	63.3	56.3	54.5	53.5	54.6	53.3	53.3	53.3	54.5	54.4	54.4	54.9	-1.4
Latin America[4]	14.5	15.3	15.4	15.0	14.6	15.8	15.7	16.2	16.0	16.3	15.5	14.9	-0.4
Middle East and North Africa[1,3]	1.6	2.2	2.5	3.1	2.6	2.5	2.2	2.1	2.2	1.9	2.1	2.1	-0.1
North America[4,5]	0.7	0.4	0.5	0.7	0.5	0.6	0.5	0.5	0.5	0.6	0.5	0.5	0.1
Oceania	6.0	5.3	5.5	5.0	4.8	4.5	4.0	3.9	4.0	4.2	4.4	4.3	-1.0
Multiple destinations	5.6	5.7	6.0	6.5	6.8	6.4	7.3	7.7	7.9	7.6	7.5	7.9	2.2
Duration of stay	100.0	100.0	100.0	100.0	100.0	100.0	100.0	100.0	100.0	100.0	100.0	100.0	†
Summer term	33.7	38.1	35.8	37.8	37.7	37.1	37.8	38.1	39.0	38.0	38.5	38.5	0.4
One semester	38.5	35.5	37.3	35.8	34.5	35.0	33.6	31.9	31.8	31.9	30.7	30.3	-5.2
8 weeks or less during academic year	7.4	11.0	11.7	11.9	13.3	14.4	15.3	16.5	16.7	17.4	18.8	19.0	8.0
January term	7.0	7.2	7.0	6.9	7.1	7.0	7.1	7.5	7.4	7.4	7.1	7.0	-0.2
Academic year	7.3	4.1	4.1	3.8	3.7	3.2	3.1	2.9	2.5	2.3	2.2	2.2	-1.9
One quarter	4.1	3.4	3.3	3.1	3.0	2.5	2.4	2.4	2.2	2.3	2.2	2.4	-1.0
Two quarters	0.6	0.6	0.5	0.4	0.5	0.4	0.3	0.6	0.3	0.3	0.2	0.2	-0.4
Calendar year	0.6	0.1	0.1	0.1	0.1	0.1	0.1	0.1	0.1	0.1	0.1	0.1	#
Other	0.8	#	0.2	0.1	0.1	0.3	0.3	#	0.1	0.4	0.2	0.3	0.3

†Not applicable.
#Rounds to zero.
[1]North Africa was combined with the Middle East to create the "Middle East and North Africa" category as of 2011–12, and the former "Africa" category was replaced by "Sub-Saharan Africa" (which excludes North Africa). Data for years prior to 2011–12 have been revised for comparability.
[2]Asia excludes the Middle Eastern countries (Bahrain, Iran, Iraq, Israel, Jordan, Kuwait, Lebanon, Oman, the Palestinian Territories, Qatar, Saudi Arabia, Syria, the United Arab Emirates, and Yemen).

[3]Cyprus and Turkey were classified as being in the Middle East prior to 2004–05 but in Europe for 2004–05 and later years. Data for 2000–01 have been revised for comparability.
[4]Mexico and Central America are included in Latin America, not in North America.
[5]Includes Antarctica from 2002–03 onward.
NOTE: Detail may not sum to totals because of rounding. Some data have been revised from previously published figures. Race categories exclude persons of Hispanic ethnicity.
SOURCE: Institute of International Education, *Open Doors: Report on International Educational Exchange*, 2019. (This table was prepared February 2020.)

Table 310.20. Foreign students enrolled in institutions of higher education in the United States, by continent, region, and selected countries of origin: Selected years, 1980–81 through 2018–19

Continent, region, and selected countries of origin	1980–81		1985–86		1990–91		1995–96		2000–01		2005–06		2010–11		2015–16		2018–19	
	Number	Percent	Number	Percent	Number	Percent	Number	Percent	Number	Percent	Number	Percent	Number	Percent	Number	Percent	Number	Percent
1	2	3	4	5	6	7	8	9	10	11	12	13	14	15	16	17	18	19
Total	311,880	100.0	343,780	100.0	407,272	100.0	453,787	100.0	547,873	100.0	564,766	100.0	723,249	100.0	1,043,839	100.0	1,095,299	100.0
Sub-Saharan Africa[1]	30,870	9.9	28,210	8.2	19,262	4.7	17,422	3.8	29,033	5.3	32,538	5.8	31,470	4.4	35,364	3.4	40,290	3.7
East Africa	6,260	2.0	6,730	2.0	7,592	1.9	7,596	1.7	13,516	2.5	13,635	2.4	8,863	1.2	7,690	0.7	9,227	0.8
Central Africa	1,130	0.4	1,540	0.4	1,647	0.4	1,346	0.3	1,859	0.3	2,825	0.5	2,831	0.4	3,311	0.3	3,325	0.3
Southern Africa	1,480	0.5	2,360	0.7	2,835	0.7	2,657	0.6	3,304	0.6	2,232	0.4	5,330	0.7	6,263	0.6	6,315	0.6
West Africa	22,000	7.1	17,580	5.1	7,178	1.8	5,818	1.3	10,346	1.9	13,846	2.5	14,446	2.0	18,100	1.7	21,423	2.0
Nigeria	17,350	5.6	13,710	4.0	3,714	0.9	2,093	0.5	3,820	0.7	6,192	1.1	7,148	1.0	10,674	1.0	13,423	1.2
Asia	94,640	30.3	156,830	45.6	229,825	56.4	259,893	57.3	302,058	55.1	327,785	58.0	461,790	63.8	689,525	66.1	768,260	70.1
East Asia	51,650	16.6	80,720	23.5	146,017	35.9	166,717	36.7	189,371	34.6	197,576	35.0	286,925	39.7	439,702	42.1	472,085	43.1
China	2,770	0.9	13,980	4.1	39,597	9.7	39,613	8.7	59,939	10.9	62,582	11.1	157,558	21.8	328,547	31.5	369,548	33.7
Hong Kong	9,660	3.1	10,710	3.1	12,625	3.1	12,018	2.6	7,627	1.4	7,849	1.4	8,136	1.1	7,923	0.8	6,917	0.6
Japan	13,500	4.3	13,360	3.9	36,611	9.0	45,531	10.0	46,497	8.5	38,712	6.9	21,290	2.9	19,060	1.8	18,105	1.7
South Korea	6,150	2.0	18,660	5.4	33,362	8.2	36,231	8.0	45,685	8.3	59,022	10.5	73,351	10.1	61,007	5.8	52,250	4.8
Taiwan	19,460	6.2	23,770	6.9	33,531	8.2	32,702	7.2	28,566	5.2	27,876	4.9	24,818	3.4	21,127	2.0	23,369	2.1
South and Central Asia	14,540	4.7	25,800	7.5	42,366	10.4	45,401	10.0	71,765	13.1	94,965	16.8	128,845	17.8	195,135	18.7	238,621	21.8
Bangladesh	1,180	0.4	1,930	0.6	2,533	0.6	3,360	0.7	4,114	0.8	2,581	0.5	2,873	0.4	6,513	0.6	8,249	0.8
India	9,250	3.0	16,070	4.7	28,857	7.1	31,743	7.0	54,664	10.0	76,503	13.5	103,895	14.4	165,918	15.9	202,014	18.4
Nepal	250	0.1	390	0.1	670	0.2	1,219	0.3	2,618	0.5	6,061	1.1	10,301	1.4	9,662	0.9	13,229	1.2
Pakistan	2,990	1.0	5,440	1.6	7,725	1.9	6,427	1.4	6,948	1.3	5,759	1.0	5,045	0.7	6,141	0.6	7,957	0.7
Southeast Asia	28,450	9.1	50,310	14.6	41,441	10.2	47,774	10.5	40,916	7.5	35,244	6.2	46,020	6.4	54,688	5.2	57,554	5.3
Indonesia	3,250	1.0	8,210	2.4	9,524	2.3	12,820	2.8	11,625	2.1	7,575	1.3	6,942	1.0	8,727	0.8	8,356	0.8
Malaysia	6,010	1.9	23,020	6.7	13,606	3.3	14,015	3.1	7,795	1.4	5,515	1.0	6,735	0.9	7,834	0.8	7,709	0.7
Singapore	1,320	0.4	3,930	1.1	4,495	1.1	4,098	0.9	4,166	0.8	3,909	0.7	4,316	0.6	4,865	0.5	4,632	0.4
Thailand	6,550	2.1	6,940	2.0	7,092	1.7	12,165	2.7	11,187	2.0	8,765	1.6	8,236	1.1	7,113	0.7	6,503	0.6
Vietnam	6,490	2.1	3,270	1.0	1,396	0.3	922	0.2	2,022	0.4	4,597	0.8	14,888	2.1	21,403	2.1	24,392	2.2
Europe[2]	28,650	9.2	38,910	11.3	55,422	13.6	76,855	16.9	93,784	17.1	84,697	15.0	84,296	11.7	91,915	8.8	90,996	8.3
France	2,570	0.8	3,680	1.1	5,633	1.4	5,710	1.3	7,273	1.3	6,640	1.2	8,098	1.1	8,764	0.8	8,716	0.8
Germany[3]	3,310	1.1	4,730	1.4	7,003	1.7	9,017	2.0	10,128	1.8	8,829	1.6	9,458	1.3	10,145	1.0	9,191	0.8
Italy	1,250	0.4	1,890	0.5	2,393	0.6	2,780	0.6	3,490	0.6	3,224	0.6	4,308	0.6	5,155	0.5	6,114	0.6
Russia[4]	630	0.2	83	#	1,206	0.3	5,589	1.2	6,858	1.3	4,801	0.9	4,692	0.6	5,444	0.5	5,292	0.5
Spain	950	0.3	1,740	0.5	4,304	1.1	4,809	1.1	4,156	0.8	3,455	0.6	4,330	0.6	6,640	0.6	7,262	0.7
Sweden	1,020	0.3	1,400	0.4	2,029	0.5	3,889	0.9	4,598	0.8	3,212	0.6	3,236	0.4	4,297	0.4	3,460	0.3
Turkey[2]	2,600	0.8	2,460	0.7	4,078	1.0	7,678	1.7	10,983	2.0	11,622	2.1	12,184	1.7	10,691	1.0	10,159	0.9
United Kingdom	4,440	1.4	5,940	1.7	7,298	1.8	7,799	1.7	8,139	1.5	8,274	1.5	8,947	1.2	11,599	1.1	11,146	1.0
Latin America	49,810	16.0	54,480	13.2	47,318	11.6	47,253	10.4	63,634	11.6	64,769	11.5	64,169	8.9	84,908	8.1	80,962	7.4
Caribbean	10,650	3.4	11,100	3.2	12,349	3.0	10,737	2.4	14,423	2.6	13,855	2.5	11,644	1.6	11,042	1.1	11,065	1.0
Central America	12,970	4.2	12,740	3.7	15,949	3.9	14,220	3.1	16,764	3.1	19,709	3.5	20,361	2.8	24,983	2.4	23,998	2.2
Mexico	6,730	2.2	5,460	1.6	6,739	1.6	8,687	1.9	10,670	1.9	13,931	2.5	13,713	1.9	16,733	1.6	15,229	1.4
South America	26,190	8.4	21,640	6.3	19,019	4.7	22,296	4.9	32,447	5.9	31,205	5.5	32,164	4.4	48,883	4.7	45,899	4.2
Brazil	2,870	0.9	2,840	0.8	3,898	1.0	5,497	1.2	8,846	1.6	7,009	1.2	8,777	1.2	19,370	1.9	16,059	1.5
Colombia	3,930	1.3	4,010	1.2	3,183	0.8	3,462	0.8	6,765	1.2	6,835	1.2	6,456	0.9	7,815	0.7	8,060	0.7
Venezuela	11,750	3.8	7,040	2.0	2,894	0.7	4,456	1.0	5,217	1.0	4,792	0.8	5,491	0.8	8,267	0.8	7,760	0.7
Middle East and North Africa[1]	88,700	28.4	54,100	15.7	32,177	7.9	24,488	5.4	28,842	5.3	21,576	3.8	47,963	6.6	108,227	10.4	81,126	7.4
Middle East[2]	81,390	26.1	48,120	14.0	27,636	6.8	21,066	4.6	23,658	4.3	17,806	3.2	42,543	5.9	100,926	9.7	74,165	6.8
Iran	47,550	15.2	14,210	4.1	6,262	1.5	2,628	0.6	1,844	0.3	2,420	0.4	5,626	0.8	12,269	1.2	12,142	1.1
Kuwait	2,990	1.0	3,810	1.1	1,624	0.4	3,035	0.7	3,045	0.6	1,703	0.3	2,998	0.4	9,772	0.9	9,195	0.8
Saudi Arabia	10,440	3.3	6,900	2.0	3,584	0.9	4,191	0.9	5,273	1.0	3,448	0.6	22,704	3.1	61,287	5.9	37,080	3.4
North Africa[1]	7,310	2.3	5,980	1.7	4,541	1.1	3,422	0.8	5,184	0.9	3,770	0.7	5,420	0.7	7,301	0.7	6,961	0.6
Egypt	1,860	0.6	2,270	0.7	1,777	0.4	1,490	0.3	2,255	0.4	1,509	0.3	2,181	0.3	3,442	0.3	3,675	0.3
North America[5]	14,790	4.7	16,030	4.7	18,949	4.7	23,644	5.2	25,888	4.7	28,699	5.1	27,941	3.9	26,973	2.6	26,122	2.4
Canada	14,320	4.6	15,410	4.5	18,350	4.5	23,005	5.1	25,279	4.6	28,202	5.0	27,546	3.8	26,973	2.6	26,122	2.4
Oceania	4,180	1.3	4,030	1.2	4,230	1.0	4,202	0.9	4,624	0.8	4,702	0.8	5,610	0.8	6,917	0.7	7,542	0.7
Australia	1,530	0.5	1,530	0.4	1,906	0.5	2,244	0.5	2,645	0.5	2,806	0.5	3,777	0.5	4,752	0.5	4,930	0.5
Unidentified[6]	240	0.1	190	0.1	89	#	30	#	10	#	#	#	10	#	10	#	1	#

#Rounds to zero.

[1]North Africa was combined with the Middle East to create the "Middle East and North Africa" category as of 2011–12, and the former "Africa" category was replaced by "Sub-Saharan Africa" (which excludes North Africa). Data for years prior to 2011–12 have been revised for comparability.

[2]Cyprus and Turkey were classified as being in the Middle East prior to 2004–05 but in Europe for 2004–05 and later years. Data for years prior to 2004–05 have been revised for comparability.

[3]Data for 1980–81 and 1985–86 are for West Germany (Federal Republic of Germany before unification).

[4]Data for 1980–81, 1985–86, and 1990–91 are for the former U.S.S.R.

[5]Excludes Mexico and Central America, which are included in Latin America.

[6]Place of origin unknown or undeclared.

NOTE: Includes foreign students enrolled in American Samoa, Guam, Puerto Rico, and the U.S. Virgin Islands. Totals and subtotals include other countries not shown separately. Region totals may not sum to continent totals because some continent totals include students who are not classified by country or region. Data are for "nonimmigrants" (i.e., students who have not migrated to the United States). Detail may not sum to totals because of rounding.

SOURCE: Institute of International Education, Open Doors: Report on International Educational Exchange, selected years, 1981 through 2019. (This table was prepared February 2020.)

Table 311.10. Number and percentage distribution of students enrolled in postsecondary institutions, by level, disability status, and selected student characteristics: 2015–16

[Standard errors appear in parentheses]

Selected student characteristic	Undergraduate						Postbaccalaureate					
	All students		Students with disabilities[1]		Students without disabilities		All students		Students with disabilities[1]		Students without disabilities	
1	2		3		4		5		6		7	
Number of students (in thousands)	19,308	(—)	3,755	(—)	15,554	(—)	3,547	(—)	423	(—)	3,124	(—)
Percentage distribution of students												
Total	100.0	(†)	19.4	(0.21)	80.6	(0.21)	100.0	(†)	11.9	(0.45)	88.1	(0.45)
Sex												
Male	100.0	(†)	19.2	(0.33)	80.8	(0.33)	100.0	(†)	9.9	(0.57)	90.1	(0.57)
Female	100.0	(†)	19.6	(0.26)	80.4	(0.26)	100.0	(†)	13.3	(0.57)	86.7	(0.57)
Race/ethnicity of student												
White	100.0	(†)	20.8	(0.31)	79.2	(0.31)	100.0	(†)	13.0	(0.59)	87.0	(0.59)
Black	100.0	(†)	17.2	(0.50)	82.8	(0.50)	100.0	(†)	10.3	(0.94)	89.7	(0.94)
Hispanic	100.0	(†)	18.3	(0.47)	81.7	(0.47)	100.0	(†)	14.3	(1.53)	85.7	(1.53)
Asian	100.0	(†)	15.2	(0.69)	84.8	(0.69)	100.0	(†)	6.2	(0.88)	93.8	(0.88)
Pacific Islander	100.0	(†)	23.6	(4.44)	76.4	(4.44)	100.0	(†)	14.9 !	(6.07)	85.1	(6.07)
American Indian/Alaska Native	100.0	(†)	27.8	(2.71)	72.2	(2.71)	100.0	(†)	11.8 !	(4.60)	88.2	(4.60)
Two or more races	100.0	(†)	22.1	(1.25)	77.9	(1.25)	100.0	(†)	19.7	(3.61)	80.3	(3.61)
Age												
15 to 23	100.0	(†)	17.6	(0.27)	82.4	(0.27)	100.0	(†)	8.1	(1.13)	91.9	(1.13)
24 to 29	100.0	(†)	21.6	(0.55)	78.4	(0.55)	100.0	(†)	11.3	(0.67)	88.7	(0.67)
30 or older	100.0	(†)	22.6	(0.48)	77.4	(0.48)	100.0	(†)	13.5	(0.66)	86.5	(0.66)
Attendance status[2]												
Full-time, full-year	100.0	(†)	17.3	(0.28)	82.7	(0.28)	100.0	(†)	12.0	(0.67)	88.0	(0.67)
Part-time or part-year	100.0	(†)	20.8	(0.28)	79.2	(0.28)	100.0	(†)	11.9	(0.57)	88.1	(0.57)
Student housing status												
On-campus	100.0	(†)	15.8	(0.49)	84.2	(0.49)	—	(†)	—	(†)	—	(†)
Off-campus	100.0	(†)	20.6	(0.31)	79.4	(0.31)	—	(†)	—	(†)	—	(†)
With parents or relatives	100.0	(†)	19.5	(0.45)	80.5	(0.45)	—	(†)	—	(†)	—	(†)
Attended more than one institution	100.0	(†)	18.7	(0.55)	81.3	(0.55)	—	(†)	—	(†)	—	(†)
Dependency status												
Dependent	100.0	(†)	17.2	(0.28)	82.8	(0.28)	—	(†)	—	(†)	—	(†)
Independent, unmarried	100.0	(†)	23.9	(0.55)	76.1	(0.55)	100.0	(†)	11.5	(0.61)	88.5	(0.61)
Independent, married	100.0	(†)	20.5	(1.07)	79.5	(1.07)	100.0	(†)	10.3	(1.12)	89.7	(1.12)
Independent with dependents	100.0	(†)	20.3	(0.41)	79.7	(0.41)	100.0	(†)	13.4	(0.74)	86.6	(0.74)
Veteran status												
Veteran	100.0	(†)	25.8	(0.98)	74.2	(0.98)	100.0	(†)	17.1	(1.09)	82.9	(1.09)
Not veteran	100.0	(†)	19.1	(0.22)	80.9	(0.22)	100.0	(†)	11.6	(0.47)	88.4	(0.47)
Field of study												
Business/management	100.0	(†)	17.7	(0.46)	82.3	(0.46)	100.0	(†)	9.9	(0.97)	90.1	(0.97)
Education	100.0	(†)	17.9	(0.92)	82.1	(0.92)	100.0	(†)	12.5	(1.25)	87.5	(1.25)
Engineering/computer science/mathematics	100.0	(†)	19.6	(0.75)	80.4	(0.75)	100.0	(†)	6.8	(0.90)	93.2	(0.90)
Health	100.0	(†)	18.3	(0.40)	81.7	(0.40)	100.0	(†)	12.2	(0.90)	87.8	(0.90)
Humanities	100.0	(†)	21.5	(0.60)	78.5	(0.60)	100.0	(†)	14.1	(1.72)	85.9	(1.72)
Law	—	(†)	—	(†)	—	(†)	100.0	(†)	15.0	(2.33)	85.0	(2.33)
Life/physical sciences	100.0	(†)	17.9	(0.74)	82.1	(0.74)	100.0	(†)	11.6	(1.81)	88.4	(1.81)
Social/behavioral sciences	100.0	(†)	21.8	(0.82)	78.2	(0.82)	100.0	(†)	17.5	(1.90)	82.5	(1.90)
Vocational/technical	100.0	(†)	21.6	(1.36)	78.4	(1.36)	—	(†)	—	(†)	—	(†)
Undeclared	100.0	(†)	21.7	(1.55)	78.3	(1.55)	—	(†)	—	(†)	—	(†)
Other	100.0	(†)	20.2	(0.64)	79.8	(0.64)	100.0	(†)	12.5	(1.29)	87.5	(1.29)

—Not available.
†Not applicable.
!Interpret data with caution. The coefficient of variation (CV) for this estimate is between 30 and 50 percent.
[1]Students with disabilities are those who reported having deafness or serious difficulty hearing; blindness or serious difficulty seeing; serious difficulty concentrating, remembering, or making decisions because of a physical, mental, or emotional condition; or serious difficulty walking or climbing stairs. For 2015–16, the question about difficulty concentrating, remembering, or making decisions was expanded to include examples of relevant conditions. Specifically, students were instructed to "consider conditions including, but not limited to, a serious learning disability, depression, ADD, or ADHD." The percentage of students reporting difficulty concentrating, remembering, or making decisions was 17 percent in 2015–16 (after the examples were added) and 8 percent in 2011–12 (before the examples were added). Due

to addition of the examples, estimates of the percentage of students with this type of disability in 2015–16 and of the overall percentage of students with disabilities in 2015–16 cannot be compared to estimates of the percentages in earlier years.
[2]Full-time, full-year includes students enrolled full time for 9 or more months. Part-time or part-year includes students enrolled part time for 9 or more months and students enrolled less than 9 months either part time or full time.
NOTE: Data are based on a sample survey of students who enrolled at any time during the school year. Data exclude students attending institutions in Puerto Rico. Detail may not sum to totals because of rounding. Race categories exclude persons of Hispanic ethnicity.
SOURCE: U.S. Department of Education, National Center for Education Statistics, 2015–16 National Postsecondary Student Aid Study (NPSAS:16). (This table was prepared May 2018.)

Table 311.15. Number and percentage of students enrolled in degree-granting postsecondary institutions, by distance education participation, location of student, level of enrollment, and control and level of institution: Fall 2017 and fall 2018

Year, level of enrollment, and control and level of institution	Number of students — Total	No distance education courses	Taking any distance education course(s) — Total, any distance education course(s)	At least one, but not all, of student's courses	Exclusively distance education courses, by location of student — Total	Same state	Different state	State not known	Outside of the United States	Location unknown	Percent of students — Total	No distance education courses	Total, any distance education course(s)	At least one, but not all, of student's courses	Exclusively distance education courses — Total	Same state	Different state	State not known	Outside of the United States	Location unknown
1	2	3	4	5	6	7	8	9	10	11	12	13	14	15	16	17	18	19	20	21
Fall 2017																				
All students, total	19,778,151	13,155,348	6,622,803	3,515,659	3,107,144	1,775,555	1,251,709	15,777	45,368	18,735	100.0	66.5	33.5	17.8	15.7	9.0	6.3	0.1	0.2	0.1
Public	14,571,739	9,907,335	4,664,404	3,002,916	1,661,488	1,394,179	225,502	11,534	17,749	12,524	100.0	68.0	32.0	20.6	11.4	9.6	1.5	0.1	0.1	0.1
Private	5,206,412	3,248,013	1,958,399	512,743	1,445,656	381,376	1,026,207	4,243	27,619	6,211	100.0	62.4	37.6	9.8	27.8	7.3	19.7	0.1	0.5	0.1
Nonprofit	4,108,489	2,929,755	1,178,734	390,579	788,155	273,133	491,664	3,141	17,292	2,925	100.0	71.3	28.7	9.5	19.2	6.6	12.0	0.1	0.4	0.1
For-profit	1,097,923	318,258	779,665	122,164	657,501	108,243	534,543	1,102	10,327	3,286	100.0	29.0	71.0	11.1	59.9	9.9	48.7	0.1	0.9	0.3
Fall 2018																				
All students, total	19,645,918	12,713,844	6,932,074	3,674,087	3,257,987	1,869,652	1,293,454	17,083	44,321	33,477	100.0	64.7	35.3	18.7	16.6	9.5	6.6	0.1	0.2	0.2
4-year	13,900,710	8,941,162	4,959,548	2,506,759	2,452,789	1,144,147	1,238,866	13,504	40,619	15,653	100.0	64.3	35.7	18.0	17.6	8.2	8.9	0.1	0.3	0.1
2-year	5,745,208	3,772,682	1,972,526	1,167,328	805,198	725,505	54,588	3,579	3,702	17,824	100.0	65.7	34.3	20.3	14.0	12.6	1.0	0.1	0.1	0.3
Public	14,529,264	9,569,412	4,959,852	3,153,470	1,806,382	1,475,262	271,659	11,794	18,583	29,084	100.0	65.9	34.1	21.7	12.4	10.2	1.9	0.1	0.1	0.2
4-year	8,982,560	5,945,224	3,037,336	2,005,490	1,031,846	755,127	242,105	8,215	14,997	11,402	100.0	66.2	33.8	22.3	11.5	8.4	2.7	0.1	0.2	0.1
2-year	5,546,704	3,624,188	1,922,516	1,147,980	774,536	720,135	29,554	3,579	3,586	17,682	100.0	65.3	34.7	20.7	14.0	13.0	0.5	0.1	0.1	0.3
Private	5,116,654	3,144,432	1,972,222	520,617	1,451,605	394,390	1,021,795	5,289	25,738	4,393	100.0	61.5	38.5	10.2	28.4	7.7	20.0	0.1	0.5	0.1
Nonprofit	4,134,244	2,878,717	1,255,527	418,048	837,479	288,963	525,951	3,705	14,838	4,022	100.0	69.6	30.4	10.1	20.3	7.0	12.7	0.1	0.4	0.1
4-year	4,089,090	2,857,653	1,231,437	414,132	817,305	286,033	508,712	3,705	14,834	4,021	100.0	69.9	30.1	10.1	20.0	7.0	12.4	0.1	0.4	0.1
2-year	45,154	21,064	24,090	3,916	20,174	2,930	17,239	0	4	1	100.0	46.6	53.4	8.7	44.7	6.5	38.2	0.0	#	#
For-profit	982,410	265,715	716,695	102,569	614,126	105,427	495,844	1,584	10,900	371	100.0	27.0	73.0	10.4	62.5	10.7	50.5	0.2	1.1	0.0
4-year	829,060	138,285	690,775	87,137	603,638	102,987	488,049	1,584	10,788	230	100.0	16.7	83.3	10.5	72.8	12.4	58.9	0.2	1.3	0.0
2-year	153,350	127,430	25,920	15,432	10,488	2,440	7,795	0	112	141	100.0	83.1	16.9	10.1	6.8	1.6	5.1	0.0	0.1	0.1
Undergraduate	16,610,235	10,885,526	5,724,709	3,399,567	2,325,142	1,464,038	798,815	9,641	24,188	28,460	100.0	65.5	34.5	20.5	14.0	8.8	4.8	0.1	0.1	0.2
4-year	10,865,027	7,112,844	3,752,183	2,232,239	1,519,944	738,533	744,227	6,062	20,486	10,636	100.0	65.5	34.5	20.5	14.0	6.8	6.8	0.1	0.2	0.1
2-year	5,745,208	3,772,682	1,972,526	1,167,328	805,198	725,505	54,588	3,579	3,702	17,824	100.0	65.7	34.3	20.3	14.0	12.6	1.0	0.1	0.1	0.3
Public	13,049,326	8,598,151	4,451,175	3,008,133	1,443,042	1,243,404	155,170	6,914	10,746	26,808	100.0	65.9	34.1	23.1	11.1	9.5	1.2	#	0.1	0.2
4-year	7,502,622	4,973,963	2,528,659	1,860,153	668,506	523,269	125,616	3,335	7,160	9,126	100.0	66.3	33.7	24.8	8.9	7.0	1.7	#	0.1	0.1
2-year	5,546,704	3,624,188	1,922,516	1,147,980	774,536	720,135	29,554	3,579	3,586	17,682	100.0	65.3	34.7	20.7	14.0	13.0	0.5	0.1	0.1	0.3
Private	3,560,909	2,287,375	1,273,534	391,434	882,100	220,634	643,645	2,727	13,442	1,652	100.0	64.2	35.8	11.0	24.8	6.2	18.1	0.1	0.4	0.1
Nonprofit	2,821,653	2,044,170	777,483	298,740	478,743	141,490	325,964	1,416	8,527	1,346	100.0	72.4	27.6	10.6	17.0	5.0	11.6	0.1	0.3	0.1
4-year	2,776,499	2,023,106	753,393	294,824	458,569	138,560	308,725	1,416	8,523	1,345	100.0	72.9	27.1	10.6	16.5	5.0	11.1	0.1	0.3	0.1
2-year	45,154	21,064	24,090	3,916	20,174	2,930	17,239	0	4	1	100.0	46.6	53.4	8.7	44.7	6.5	38.2	0.0	#	#
For-profit	739,256	243,205	496,051	92,694	403,357	79,144	317,681	1,311	4,915	306	100.0	32.9	67.1	12.5	54.6	10.7	43.0	0.2	0.7	0.2
4-year	585,906	115,775	470,131	77,262	392,869	76,704	309,886	1,311	4,803	165	100.0	19.8	80.2	13.2	67.1	13.1	52.9	0.2	0.8	0.0
2-year	153,350	127,430	25,920	15,432	10,488	2,440	7,795	0	112	141	100.0	83.1	16.9	10.1	6.8	1.6	5.1	0.0	0.1	0.1
Postbaccalaureate	3,035,683	1,828,318	1,207,365	274,520	932,845	405,614	494,639	7,442	20,133	5,017	100.0	60.2	39.8	9.0	30.7	13.4	16.3	0.2	0.7	0.2
Public	1,479,938	971,261	508,677	145,337	363,340	231,858	116,489	4,880	7,837	2,276	100.0	65.6	34.4	9.8	24.6	15.7	7.9	0.3	0.5	0.2
Private	1,555,745	857,057	698,688	129,183	569,505	173,756	378,150	2,562	12,296	2,741	100.0	55.1	44.9	8.3	36.6	11.2	24.3	0.2	0.8	0.2
Nonprofit	1,312,591	834,547	478,044	119,308	358,736	147,473	199,987	2,289	6,311	2,676	100.0	63.6	36.4	9.1	27.3	11.2	15.2	0.2	0.5	0.2
For-profit	243,154	22,510	220,644	9,875	210,769	26,283	178,163	273	5,985	65	100.0	9.3	90.7	4.1	86.7	10.8	73.3	0.1	2.5	#

#Rounds to zero.

NOTE: Degree-granting institutions grant associate's or higher degrees and participate in Title IV federal financial aid programs. Some data have been revised from previously published figures.

SOURCE: U.S. Department of Education, National Center for Education Statistics, Integrated Postsecondary Education Data System (IPEDS), Spring 2018 and Spring 2019, Fall Enrollment component. (This table was prepared December 2019.)

Table 311.22. Number and percentage of undergraduate students enrolled in distance education or online classes and degree programs, by selected characteristics: Selected years, 2003–04 through 2015–16

[Standard errors appear in parentheses]

Selected characteristic	2003–04 Total, any distance education classes	2003–04 Entire degree program through distance education[1]	2007–08 Total, any distance education classes	2007–08 Entire degree program through distance education[1]	2011–12 Total, any online classes	2011–12 Entire degree program is online[1]	2015–16 Total, all students (in thousands)	2015–16 Number taking any online classes (in thousands)	2015–16 Total, any online classes (percent)	2015–16 Entire degree program is online[1] (percent)
1	2	3	4	5	6	7	8	9	10	11
Total	15.6 (0.29)	4.9 (0.17)	20.6 (0.23)	3.8 (0.16)	32.0 (0.33)	6.5 (0.18)	19,308	8,319	43.1 (0.31)	10.8 (0.21)
Sex										
Male	13.6 (0.31)	4.3 (0.19)	18.8 (0.31)	3.4 (0.16)	28.5 (0.45)	4.9 (0.24)	8,406	3,340	39.7 (0.42)	9.2 (0.27)
Female	17.0 (0.40)	5.4 (0.23)	21.9 (0.28)	4.2 (0.22)	34.5 (0.39)	7.7 (0.21)	10,903	4,979	45.7 (0.42)	12.1 (0.28)
Race/ethnicity										
White	16.2 (0.33)	5.0 (0.19)	21.9 (0.29)	3.9 (0.19)	33.5 (0.41)	6.8 (0.21)	10,276	4,671	45.5 (0.39)	11.1 (0.27)
Black	14.9 (0.59)	4.9 (0.37)	19.9 (0.66)	5.1 (0.48)	32.7 (0.70)	9.1 (0.56)	3,006	1,278	42.5 (0.72)	14.9 (0.47)
Hispanic	13.4 (0.54)	4.1 (0.27)	16.5 (0.53)	2.7 (0.23)	27.9 (0.57)	4.3 (0.24)	3,723	1,431	38.4 (0.68)	7.7 (0.32)
Asian	14.0 (0.92)	5.2 (0.58)	18.1 (0.86)	2.9 (0.40)	26.0 (1.06)	2.9 (0.35)	1,399	544	38.9 (1.10)	7.8 (0.63)
Pacific Islander	19.1 (2.37)	6.9 (1.69)	17.0 (1.89)	1.2 ! (0.53)	29.9 (3.18)	3.1 ! (1.29)	83	35	42.2 (4.02)	12.0 (2.44)
American Indian/Alaska Native	15.5 (1.85)	6.2 (1.41)	21.9 (2.41)	1.8 ! (0.55)	32.6 (2.56)	7.0 (1.43)	160	76	47.5 (3.08)	12.2 (1.71)
Two or more races	16.5 (1.33)	5.1 (1.16)	20.4 (1.08)	3.6 (0.86)	30.6 (1.48)	5.5 (0.69)	661	283	42.8 (1.39)	10.4 (0.89)
Age										
15 to 23	11.7 (0.26)	3.1 (0.13)	15.2 (0.22)	1.4 (0.09)	26.5 (0.36)	3.2 (0.13)	11,368	4,157	36.6 (0.38)	3.5 (0.13)
24 to 29	18.4 (0.46)	6.7 (0.41)	25.7 (0.56)	5.6 (0.45)	36.5 (0.67)	8.0 (0.41)	3,536	1,793	50.7 (0.69)	17.5 (0.52)
30 or older	22.4 (0.65)	8.3 (0.42)	30.0 (0.55)	9.0 (0.40)	40.9 (0.64)	13.0 (0.50)	4,404	2,369	53.8 (0.58)	24.9 (0.58)
Attendance status										
Full-time, full-year[2]	12.7 (0.32)	3.8 (0.20)	16.7 (0.33)	3.2 (0.29)	28.8 (0.41)	6.5 (0.20)	7,239	2,789	38.5 (0.44)	6.0 (0.28)
Part-time only, for only part of year	18.7 (0.46)	6.9 (0.32)	24.8 (0.39)	5.2 (0.22)	35.3 (0.62)	7.4 (0.38)	5,059	2,398	47.4 (0.62)	14.7 (0.44)
Mixed attendance status[3]	17.4 (0.53)	4.7 (0.23)	22.5 (0.42)	2.9 (0.20)	35.0 (0.62)	5.0 (0.28)	7,010	3,131	44.7 (0.47)	13.2 (0.38)
Undergraduate field of study										
Business/management	18.7 (0.58)	7.0 (0.43)	24.2 (0.55)	6.4 (0.45)	39.3 (0.75)	11.4 (0.45)	2,973	1,525	51.3 (0.72)	17.0 (0.67)
Computer/information science	19.5 (0.96)	7.2 (0.71)	26.9 (1.53)	8.4 (1.17)	40.8 (1.37)	9.8 (0.81)	852	415	48.6 (1.60)	16.1 (1.10)
Education	17.1 (0.89)	4.6 (0.45)	22.8 (0.81)	3.2 (0.33)	33.8 (1.17)	6.4 (0.59)	841	384	45.7 (1.35)	9.7 (0.81)
Engineering	12.1 (0.83)	3.3 (0.40)	16.1 (0.77)	2.3 (0.36)	23.2 (0.93)	2.3 (0.48)	1,140	380	33.3 (0.91)	5.1 (0.51)
Health	17.4 (0.48)	5.6 (0.30)	21.9 (0.60)	4.2 (0.33)	33.3 (0.67)	6.7 (0.43)	3,438	1,547	45.0 (0.72)	13.3 (0.53)
Humanities	14.0 (0.53)	3.9 (0.26)	19.7 (0.53)	2.6 (0.22)	30.8 (0.65)	4.1 (0.33)	3,083	1,274	41.3 (0.66)	7.8 (0.40)
Life sciences	11.0 (0.81)	2.7 (0.39)	15.8 (0.68)	1.8 (0.21)	26.7 (0.92)	3.3 (0.37)	1,413	540	38.2 (0.91)	5.0 (0.53)
Mathematics	12.8 (2.48)	3.8 ! (1.42)	15.1 (2.51)	‡ (†)	20.4 (3.02)	2.2 ! (1.05)	118	50	42.2 (3.98)	9.7 (2.80)
Physical sciences	9.8 (2.02)	0.9 ! (0.41)	12.8 (1.56)	0.3 ! (0.16)	22.1 (1.93)	1.2 ! (0.46)	214	70	32.8 (2.45)	2.0 ! (0.67)
Social/behavioral sciences	12.5 (0.63)	3.4 (0.33)	17.1 (0.68)	2.3 (0.31)	31.8 (0.93)	7.0 (0.48)	1,323	556	42.0 (1.05)	9.1 (0.54)
Vocational/technical	13.1 (0.96)	4.2 (0.60)	18.5 (1.26)	3.3 (0.50)	22.3 (1.54)	2.8 (0.59)	594	188	31.7 (1.67)	6.0 (0.75)
Undeclared/no major	15.0 (0.61)	4.6 (0.34)	20.5 (0.56)	3.1 (0.45)	27.6 (1.16)	5.2 (0.81)	449	148	33.0 (1.71)	9.5 (1.12)
Other	14.4 (0.68)	4.3 (0.29)	19.0 (0.69)	3.9 (0.38)	30.5 (0.83)	6.9 (0.50)	2,279	983	43.1 (0.93)	11.4 (0.55)
Had job during academic year[4]										
Yes	16.8 (0.34)	5.5 (0.22)	22.2 (0.25)	4.2 (0.16)	36.2 (0.42)	7.6 (0.24)	11,812	5,563	47.1 (0.39)	12.9 (0.28)
No	11.9 (0.32)	3.3 (0.17)	15.8 (0.37)	2.8 (0.25)	24.9 (0.42)	4.8 (0.20)	7,496	2,756	36.8 (0.44)	7.6 (0.25)
Dependency status										
Dependent	11.1 (0.24)	2.9 (0.13)	14.4 (0.24)	1.0 (0.08)	25.5 (0.36)	2.7 (0.12)	9,772	3,428	35.1 (0.37)	1.9 (0.10)
Independent, no dependents, not married[5]	15.6 (0.50)	5.1 (0.37)	23.6 (0.56)	4.8 (0.30)	33.6 (0.64)	6.7 (0.33)	3,978	1,840	46.2 (0.69)	14.9 (0.45)
Independent, no dependents, married	19.6 (0.78)	6.9 (0.52)	28.6 (0.96)	7.2 (0.84)	37.4 (1.22)	10.1 (0.72)	953	528	55.4 (1.30)	20.8 (1.09)
Independent, with dependents, not married[5]	20.5 (0.70)	6.9 (0.49)	25.3 (0.61)	7.4 (0.52)	38.2 (0.67)	10.7 (0.45)	2,618	1,375	52.5 (0.80)	22.9 (0.74)
Independent, with dependents, married	25.1 (0.79)	9.7 (0.53)	32.9 (0.71)	9.4 (0.51)	44.9 (0.92)	14.7 (0.75)	1,987	1,148	57.8 (0.89)	27.1 (0.84)
Control and level of institution										
Public	16.2 (0.35)	4.7 (0.18)	21.5 (0.25)	2.7 (0.11)	33.2 (0.39)	4.0 (0.16)	14,491	6,362	43.9 (0.37)	6.3 (0.21)
4-year	13.5 (0.54)	3.8 (0.23)	18.4 (0.41)	2.2 (0.19)	32.7 (0.51)	4.3 (0.24)	6,786	2,956	43.6 (0.50)	6.1 (0.40)
2-year	18.2 (0.43)	5.4 (0.25)	23.9 (0.33)	3.1 (0.16)	33.9 (0.54)	3.8 (0.24)	7,640	3,400	44.5 (0.58)	6.6 (0.25)
Less-than-2-year	11.8 (1.19)	3.0 (0.66)	8.1 (1.66)	1.9 ! (0.73)	11.3 (2.24)	‡ (†)	66	6	9.4 (1.89)	‡ (†)
Private nonprofit	12.3 (0.79)	4.1 (0.46)	14.3 (0.43)	2.9 (0.23)	21.0 (0.85)	4.5 (0.57)	2,955	1,060	35.9 (0.68)	17.8 (0.54)
4-year	12.3 (0.83)	4.1 (0.48)	14.2 (0.44)	2.8 (0.23)	21.3 (0.87)	4.6 (0.59)	2,857	1,033	36.2 (0.65)	17.7 (0.47)
2-year	11.2 (2.20)	3.1 ! (1.11)	19.4 (2.30)	5.9 (1.02)	12.7 (3.26)	0.5 ! (0.22)	95	26	27.5 ! (8.33)	21.2 ! (8.99)
Less-than-2-year	17.2 (2.63)	8.1 (1.35)	15.6 ! (4.69)	2.7 (0.66)	13.6 ! (5.68)	# (†)	4	1	28.6 (1.46)	17.0 (2.97)
Private for-profit	15.3 (1.08)	8.6 (1.06)	21.7 (1.18)	12.8 (1.24)	35.5 (0.83)	21.6 (0.82)	1,861	896	48.1 (0.94)	33.5 (1.22)
4-year	26.3 (2.25)	15.6 (2.26)	29.1 (1.95)	19.1 (1.92)	53.0 (1.26)	33.3 (1.30)	1,102	816	74.0 (1.38)	55.0 (1.96)
2-year	12.1 (1.64)	6.3 (1.25)	17.6 (1.49)	8.0 (1.34)	8.4 (1.28)	2.9 ! (1.01)	420	59	14.1 (1.05)	3.0 (0.46)
Less-than-2-year	5.4 (0.26)	1.9 (0.13)	6.2 (0.40)	1.8 (0.28)	3.9 (0.77)	‡ (†)	340	21	6.2 (0.70)	1.1 (0.22)

†Not applicable.
#Rounds to zero.
!Interpret data with caution. The coefficient of variation (CV) for this estimate is between 30 and 50 percent.
‡Reporting standards not met. Either there are too few cases for a reliable estimate or the coefficient of variation (CV) is 50 percent or greater.
[1]Excludes students not in a degree or certificate program.
[2]Includes only students enrolled full-time for a full academic year (defined as 9 or more months).
[3]Includes students enrolled part-time for a full academic year, as well as, students enrolled full-time, but for only part of an academic year.
[4]Excludes work study/assistantships.
[5]Includes separated.

NOTE: In 2011–12 and 2015–16, students were asked whether they took classes that were taught entirely online and, if so, whether their entire degree program was online. In 2003–04 and 2007–08, students were asked about distance education, which was defined in 2007–08 as "primarily delivered using live, interactive audio or videoconferencing, pre-recorded instructional videos, webcasts, CD-ROM, or DVD, or computer-based systems delivered over the Internet." The 2003–04 definition was very similar, with only minor differences in wording. In both years, distance education did not include correspondence courses. Data exclude students attending institutions in Puerto Rico. Detail may not sum to totals because of rounding. Race categories exclude persons of Hispanic ethnicity.
SOURCE: U.S. Department of Education, National Center for Education Statistics, 2003–04, 2007–08, 2011–12, and 2015–16 National Postsecondary Student Aid Study (NPSAS:04, NPSAS:08, NPSAS:12, and NPSAS:16). (This table was prepared May 2018.)

Table 311.32. Number and percentage of graduate students enrolled in distance education or online classes and degree programs, by selected characteristics: Selected years, 2003–04 through 2015–16

[Standard errors appear in parentheses]

Selected characteristic	Percent of graduate students taking distance education classes						2015–16			
	2003–04		2007–08		2011–12		Number of graduate students (in thousands)		Percent of graduate students taking online classes	
	Total, any distance education classes	Entire degree program through distance education[1]	Total, any distance education classes	Entire degree program through distance education[1]	Total, any online classes	Entire degree program is online[1]	Total, all graduate students	Number taking any online classes	Total, any online classes	Entire degree program is online[1]
1	2	3	4	5	6	7	8	9	10	11
Total	16.5 (0.76)	6.1 (0.58)	22.8 (0.76)	9.5 (0.68)	36.0 (0.74)	18.2 (0.63)	3,547	1,617	45.6 (0.72)	27.3 (0.75)
Sex										
Male	15.4 (1.17)	4.9 (0.74)	20.6 (1.17)	7.8 (1.07)	31.5 (1.17)	15.9 (1.06)	1,446	591	40.8 (0.95)	24.6 (1.02)
Female	17.3 (1.00)	7.0 (0.74)	24.2 (0.99)	10.6 (0.77)	39.0 (0.97)	19.8 (0.78)	2,101	1,026	48.9 (0.91)	29.3 (0.85)
Race/ethnicity										
White	17.7 (0.88)	6.7 (0.74)	23.6 (0.99)	9.6 (0.95)	36.9 (0.98)	18.2 (0.88)	2,105	942	44.8 (0.93)	26.0 (0.90)
Black	19.2 (2.44)	7.5 (1.72)	25.8 (2.94)	11.5 (2.11)	48.8 (2.12)	31.4 (1.66)	504	315	62.5 (2.22)	45.3 (2.17)
Hispanic	13.1 (1.81)	5.0 (1.26)	23.7 (3.09)	9.4 ! (2.85)	34.6 (2.73)	17.9 (2.53)	326	161	49.5 (2.03)	31.2 (2.12)
Asian	9.4 (1.40)	3.0 ! (1.01)	12.8 (1.10)	4.5 (0.68)	19.4 (1.67)	6.0 (1.13)	500	138	27.5 (1.71)	10.8 (1.33)
Pacific Islander	‡ (†)	‡ (†)	31.1 ! (9.43)	13.5 ! (6.20)	44.2 (11.10)	‡ (†)	8	5	64.1 (11.99)	33.4 ! (11.23)
American Indian/Alaska Native	8.7 ! (3.54)	‡ (†)	16.7 ! (6.78)	‡ (†)	55.1 (12.39)	43.4 ! (15.26)	17	8	43.9 (9.31)	33.1 (7.59)
Two or more races	17.1 (4.46)	4.8 ! (2.33)	27.7 ! (8.38)	21.3 ! (9.56)	40.4 (4.24)	18.4 (3.84)	88	49	55.6 (4.48)	33.8 (4.20)
Age										
15 to 23	11.1 (1.73)	3.7 (0.77)	16.6 (2.64)	1.6 (0.40)	19.5 (1.45)	4.3 (0.76)	466	130	27.9 (1.82)	8.0 (1.32)
24 to 29	13.6 (0.82)	3.6 (0.43)	16.1 (0.79)	5.7 (0.54)	30.8 (1.05)	14.4 (0.91)	1,387	525	37.8 (0.96)	16.8 (0.87)
30 or older	20.2 (1.21)	9.0 (1.06)	29.5 (1.39)	14.5 (1.31)	44.3 (1.21)	24.9 (1.01)	1,695	962	56.8 (1.02)	41.6 (1.00)
Attendance status										
Full-time, full-year[2]	12.0 (1.00)	3.4 (0.72)	16.4 (1.35)	6.5 (1.24)	31.7 (1.16)	17.4 (0.98)	1,279	408	31.9 (0.96)	15.2 (0.81)
Part-time only, for only part of year	20.0 (1.01)	8.8 (0.97)	28.1 (1.17)	13.3 (1.07)	41.0 (1.21)	19.5 (1.21)	850	453	53.3 (1.54)	36.7 (1.72)
Mixed attendance status[3]	15.6 (1.89)	4.1 (0.71)	23.6 (2.15)	6.8 (0.95)	36.9 (1.98)	17.9 (1.66)	1,418	756	53.3 (1.09)	33.1 (1.06)
Graduate field of study										
Business/management	22.6 (2.30)	10.3 (1.98)	27.6 (2.90)	13.9 (2.68)	40.0 (2.09)	25.1 (1.82)	592	320	54.1 (1.65)	36.7 (1.84)
Education	20.7 (1.74)	8.2 (1.29)	28.3 (1.67)	9.9 (1.36)	48.9 (1.65)	23.7 (1.47)	605	352	58.2 (1.73)	34.3 (1.82)
Health	12.6 (1.23)	3.9 (0.79)	22.0 (1.59)	8.9 (1.33)	36.5 (1.42)	16.5 (1.00)	694	325	46.8 (1.58)	26.6 (1.45)
Humanities	12.9 (2.43)	2.9 ! (0.87)	15.7 (1.72)	3.1 (0.65)	28.1 (3.13)	12.1 (2.88)	281	99	35.3 (2.76)	18.2 (2.32)
Law	5.6 (1.15)	‡ (†)	6.1 (0.87)	1.7 ! (0.54)	10.3 (1.46)	2.5 (0.65)	132	21	15.9 (2.09)	8.0 (1.63)
Life and physical sciences	— (†)	— (†)	— (†)	— (†)	13.9 (1.49)	5.3 (1.21)	197	39	19.9 (2.06)	9.1 (1.77)
Life sciences	12.4 (2.51)	6.9 ! (2.14)	14.0 (2.15)	4.3 (1.14)	— (†)	— (†)	—	—	— (†)	— (†)
Mathematics, engineering, and computer science	12.0 (2.03)	4.6 ! (1.48)	19.7 (3.06)	9.4 ! (2.96)	25.5 (1.78)	13.3 (1.42)	374	135	36.0 (1.87)	19.9 (1.56)
Social/behavioral sciences	8.5 (1.42)	3.4 ! (1.11)	21.3 (3.66)	12.7 (3.68)	36.6 (2.22)	21.7 (1.89)	245	112	45.7 (2.98)	29.0 (3.28)
Other[4]	19.0 (1.56)	4.6 (1.08)	22.2 (1.49)	9.4 (1.49)	38.6 (2.03)	19.2 (2.29)	427	214	50.2 (2.00)	32.7 (2.14)
Had job during academic year[5]										
Yes	19.6 (0.97)	7.7 (0.78)	27.2 (0.89)	11.9 (0.79)	43.7 (0.91)	24.1 (0.79)	2,354	1,274	54.1 (0.90)	34.4 (0.98)
No	9.0 (0.81)	2.7 (0.41)	10.0 (1.36)	2.8 ! (1.27)	19.9 (1.12)	6.2 (0.78)	1,193	342	28.7 (1.08)	13.5 (0.75)
Dependency status										
Dependent	— (†)	— (†)	— (†)	— (†)	— (†)	— (†)	—	—	— (†)	— (†)
Independent, no dependents, not married[6]	12.1 (0.75)	3.7 (0.39)	16.6 (0.90)	5.2 (0.59)	28.1 (0.88)	11.8 (0.67)	1,901	674	35.5 (0.90)	16.9 (0.86)
Independent, no dependents, married	15.5 (1.22)	5.0 (0.77)	22.3 (1.67)	10.1 (1.56)	36.1 (1.75)	19.5 (1.64)	503	247	49.1 (1.78)	27.6 (1.53)
Independent, with dependents, not married[6]	21.3 (3.18)	9.4 (2.21)	26.8 (3.23)	10.8 (1.86)	52.0 (2.49)	32.5 (2.54)	312	198	63.5 (2.06)	45.7 (2.05)
Independent, with dependents, married	24.2 (1.72)	10.8 (1.46)	34.2 (1.76)	17.5 (2.14)	45.6 (1.60)	25.1 (1.52)	831	498	59.9 (1.48)	44.4 (1.52)
Control of institution										
Public	15.2 (0.68)	4.8 (0.39)	23.1 (0.99)	8.9 (0.95)	32.8 (0.93)	11.8 (0.69)	1,665	708	42.5 (0.99)	21.2 (1.07)
Private nonprofit	16.3 (1.25)	6.7 (1.03)	18.5 (0.74)	6.0 (0.41)	28.5 (1.16)	12.3 (1.03)	1,514	618	40.8 (1.17)	23.7 (1.11)
Private for-profit	35.3 (8.12)	18.6 ! (6.64)	41.6 (5.47)	29.9 (5.89)	74.1 (2.09)	62.5 (2.49)	368	290	78.9 (1.26)	68.5 (1.99)

—Not available.
†Not applicable.
!Interpret data with caution. The coefficient of variation (CV) for this estimate is between 30 and 50 percent.
‡Reporting standards not met. Either there are too few cases for a reliable estimate or the coefficient of variation (CV) is 50 percent or greater.
[1]Excludes students not in a degree or certificate program.
[2]Includes only students enrolled full time for a full academic year (defined as 9 or more months).
[3]Includes students enrolled part time for a full academic year as well as students enrolled full time, but for only part of an academic year.
[4]Includes students who are not in a degree program or have not declared a major. For 2003–04 and 2007–08, includes physical sciences.
[5]Excludes work study/assistantships.

[6]Includes separated.
NOTE: In 2011–12 and 2015–16, students were asked whether they took classes that were taught entirely online and, if so, whether their entire degree program was online. In 2003–04 and 2007–08, students were asked about distance education, which was defined in 2007–08 as "primarily delivered using live, interactive audio or videoconferencing, prerecorded instructional videos, webcasts, CD-ROM, or DVD, or computer-based systems delivered over the Internet." The 2003–04 definition was very similar, with only minor differences in wording. In both years, distance education did not include correspondence courses. Data exclude students attending institutions in Puerto Rico. Detail may not sum to totals because of rounding. Race categories exclude persons of Hispanic ethnicity.
SOURCE: U.S. Department of Education, National Center for Education Statistics, 2003–04, 2007–08, 2011–12, and 2015–16 National Postsecondary Student Aid Study (NPSAS:04, NPSAS:08, NPSAS:12, and NPSAS:16). (This table was prepared May 2018.)

Table 311.33. Selected statistics for degree-granting postsecondary institutions that primarily offer online programs, by control of institution and selected characteristics: Fall 2018 and 2017–18

Selected characteristic	All institutions	Primarily online institutions[1]					Other institutions[1]			
		Total	Percent of all institutions	Public	Nonprofit	For-profit	Total	Public	Nonprofit	For-profit
1	2	3	4	5	6	7	8	9	10	11
Number of institutions, fall 2018[2]	**4,034**	**104**	**2.6**	**17**	**32**	**55**	**3,930**	**1,617**	**1,632**	**681**
Fall 2018 enrollment										
Total enrollment	19,645,918	881,945	4.5	130,418	303,849	447,678	18,763,973	14,398,846	3,830,395	534,732
Full-time	11,991,721	454,761	3.8	31,279	187,749	235,733	11,536,960	8,237,541	2,938,381	361,038
Males	5,338,934	145,697	2.7	10,976	58,691	76,030	5,193,237	3,776,965	1,279,150	137,122
Females	6,652,787	309,064	4.6	20,303	129,058	159,703	6,343,723	4,460,576	1,659,231	223,916
Part-time	7,654,197	427,184	5.6	99,139	116,100	211,945	7,227,013	6,161,305	892,014	173,694
Males	3,103,728	154,507	5.0	38,286	45,247	70,974	2,949,221	2,565,244	339,429	44,548
Females	4,550,469	272,677	6.0	60,853	70,853	140,971	4,277,792	3,596,061	552,585	129,146
Undergraduate	16,610,235	624,794	3.8	102,421	237,944	284,429	15,985,441	12,946,905	2,583,709	454,827
Full-time	10,267,135	331,362	3.2	23,615	146,080	161,667	9,935,773	7,428,023	2,175,353	332,397
Part-time	6,343,100	293,432	4.6	78,806	91,864	122,762	6,049,668	5,518,882	408,356	122,430
Postbaccalaureate	3,035,683	257,151	8.5	27,997	65,905	163,249	2,778,532	1,451,941	1,246,686	79,905
Full-time	1,724,586	123,399	7.2	7,664	41,669	74,066	1,601,187	809,518	763,028	28,641
Part-time	1,311,097	133,752	10.2	20,333	24,236	89,183	1,177,345	642,423	483,658	51,264
White	10,301,292	487,253	4.7	79,082	194,791	213,380	9,814,039	7,426,784	2,189,719	197,536
Black	2,493,306	220,472	8.8	19,624	55,253	145,595	2,272,834	1,692,131	439,648	141,055
Hispanic	3,645,040	98,856	2.7	19,368	30,333	49,155	3,546,184	2,996,999	430,098	119,087
Asian	1,302,106	26,344	2.0	4,873	8,501	12,970	1,275,762	989,654	257,888	28,220
Pacific Islander	50,505	4,852	9.6	621	1,479	2,752	45,653	32,653	9,123	3,877
American Indian/Alaska Native	133,751	7,090	5.3	1,033	2,106	3,951	126,661	104,072	17,284	5,305
Two or more races	727,863	30,784	4.2	5,035	10,546	15,203	697,079	546,206	130,634	20,239
Nonresident alien	992,055	6,294	0.6	782	840	4,672	985,761	610,347	356,001	19,413
4-year institutions	13,900,710	844,796	6.1	115,883	284,956	443,957	13,055,914	8,866,677	3,804,134	385,103
Full-time	9,880,953	433,180	4.4	29,302	169,884	233,994	9,447,773	6,307,676	2,918,266	221,831
Part-time	4,019,757	411,616	10.2	86,581	115,072	209,963	3,608,141	2,559,001	885,868	163,272
2-year institutions	5,745,208	37,149	0.6	14,535	18,893	3,721	5,708,059	5,532,169	26,261	149,629
Full-time	2,110,768	21,581	1.0	1,977	17,865	1,739	2,089,187	1,929,865	20,115	139,207
Part-time	3,634,440	15,568	0.4	12,558	1,028	1,982	3,618,872	3,602,304	6,146	10,422
Degrees conferred, 2017–18										
Associate's	1,011,487	30,096	3.0	3,165	10,965	15,966	981,391	882,705	45,222	53,464
Males	398,600	10,456	2.6	1,611	2,115	6,730	388,144	352,801	17,220	18,123
Females	612,887	19,640	3.2	1,554	8,850	9,236	593,247	529,904	28,002	35,341
Bachelor's	1,980,644	97,836	4.9	13,946	30,487	53,403	1,882,808	1,297,042	540,668	45,098
Males	844,960	35,068	4.2	5,374	9,987	19,707	809,892	569,146	223,683	17,063
Females	1,135,684	62,768	5.5	8,572	20,500	33,696	1,072,916	727,896	316,985	28,035
Master's	820,102	69,099	8.4	8,550	20,508	40,041	751,003	375,379	351,578	24,046
Males	326,870	21,840	6.7	3,103	6,920	11,817	305,030	156,207	140,972	7,851
Females	493,232	47,259	9.6	5,447	13,588	28,224	445,973	219,172	210,606	16,195
Doctor's[3]	184,074	4,700	2.6	171	257	4,272	179,374	92,684	83,631	3,059
Males	85,568	1,572	1.8	58	57	1,457	83,996	44,463	38,440	1,093
Females	98,506	3,128	3.2	113	200	2,815	95,378	48,221	45,191	1,966
First-time students' graduation and retention rates from first institution attended										
Among full-time bachelor's degree-seekers starting at 4-year institutions in 2012, percent earning bachelor's degree										
Within 4 years after start	43.7	11.6	†	29.9	32.3	6.9	44.0	38.8	55.4	24.5
Within 5 years after start	58.7	16.7	†	41.5	37.7	11.6	59.0	56.7	65.0	28.7
Within 6 years after start	62.4	18.2	†	44.8	38.8	13.1	62.7	61.2	67.3	30.4
Among full-time degree/certificate-seekers starting at 2-year institutions in 2015, percent completing credential within 150 percent of normal time	32.6	62.6	†	14.9	63.7	46.2	31.3	27.0	57.9	61.6
Among degree-seekers starting in 2017, percent returning in 2018										
Full-time entrants	75.6	61.8	†	73.2	73.2	37.3	75.7	74.3	81.1	66.5
Part-time entrants	45.2	42.4	†	44.2	43.6	39.7	45.3	45.5	42.7	41.3

†Not applicable.
[1]Primarily online institutions have more than 90 percent of students enrolled in exclusively distance education courses in the fall term. Other institutions may offer distance education courses without being primarily online institutions.
[2]Includes only institutions reporting enrollment data in fall 2018.
[3]Includes Ph.D., Ed.D., and comparable degrees at the doctoral level, as well as such degrees as M.D., D.D.S., and law degrees that were classified as first-professional degrees prior to 2010–11.

NOTE: Degree-granting institutions grant associate's or higher degrees and participate in Title IV federal financial aid programs. Race categories exclude persons of Hispanic ethnicity.
SOURCE: U.S. Department of Education, National Center for Education Statistics, Integrated Postsecondary Education Data System (IPEDS), Spring 2019, Fall Enrollment component; IPEDS, Fall 2018, Completions component; and IPEDS, Winter 2018–19, Graduation Rates component. (This table was prepared February 2020.)

Table 311.40. Percentage of first-year undergraduate students who reported taking remedial education courses, by selected student and institution characteristics: Selected years, 2003–04 through 2015–16

[Standard errors appear in parentheses]

	2003–04 first-year undergraduates[1] who took any remedial courses		2007–08 first-year undergraduates[1] who took any remedial courses		2011–12 first-year undergraduates[1] who took any remedial courses		2015–16 first-year undergraduates[1]					
								Students who took any remedial courses			Percent who took specific remedial courses in 2015–16	
Selected student or institution characteristic	Ever	In 2003–04	Ever	In 2007–08	Ever	In 2011–12	Total number of students[2] (in thousands)	Percent who ever took	Number who took in 2015–16 (in thousands)	Percent who took in 2015–16	Mathematics	Reading/writing
1	2	3	4	5	6	7	8	9	10	11	12	13
Total	34.8 (0.36)	19.2 (0.30)	36.2 (0.38)	20.0 (0.35)	32.6 (0.42)	19.7 (0.36)	7,706	43.0 (0.58)	1,482	19.2 (0.43)	14.0 (0.36)	8.8 (0.28)
Sex												
Male	33.0 (0.53)	18.4 (0.46)	33.0 (0.53)	19.3 (0.51)	30.8 (0.61)	19.9 (0.55)	3,364	40.7 (0.82)	643	19.1 (0.67)	13.9 (0.58)	8.5 (0.38)
Female	36.2 (0.54)	19.8 (0.39)	38.7 (0.51)	20.6 (0.46)	34.0 (0.52)	19.7 (0.46)	4,342	44.8 (0.66)	839	19.3 (0.50)	14.1 (0.41)	8.9 (0.36)
Race/ethnicity												
White	31.7 (0.42)	17.8 (0.35)	31.3 (0.46)	17.7 (0.41)	29.4 (0.51)	17.7 (0.47)	3,683	38.3 (0.76)	620	16.8 (0.48)	12.6 (0.42)	7.0 (0.33)
Black	41.2 (1.00)	22.4 (0.76)	45.1 (0.99)	24.4 (0.86)	37.6 (0.89)	22.2 (0.75)	1,419	48.7 (1.05)	292	20.6 (0.78)	15.0 (0.74)	10.2 (0.62)
Hispanic	38.5 (0.91)	21.5 (0.72)	43.7 (1.12)	23.3 (0.84)	35.8 (0.99)	22.4 (0.81)	1,726	47.7 (0.97)	397	23.0 (0.98)	16.7 (0.82)	10.7 (0.60)
Asian	39.6 (1.72)	17.6 (1.56)	38.9 (2.05)	20.0 (1.90)	37.6 (2.25)	23.0 (1.75)	490	45.4 (1.83)	97	19.8 (1.48)	13.9 (1.28)	10.4 (1.11)
Pacific Islander	40.8 (5.11)	22.4 (4.55)	39.9 (4.63)	19.1 (3.90)	33.4 (5.16)	15.2 (3.50)	37	43.7 (6.07)	‡	21.8 (5.04)	12.0 ! (3.73)	10.6 ! (4.44)
American Indian/Alaska Native	44.8 (4.34)	23.7 (3.10)	47.9 (4.66)	29.7 (3.88)	34.9 (4.11)	19.8 (2.79)	79	50.1 (5.64)	19	23.8 (4.98)	12.0 (3.30)	13.9 (4.10)
Two or more races	33.9 (2.02)	20.9 (1.80)	32.3 (2.29)	20.4 (2.06)	29.8 (2.02)	19.0 (1.68)	271	41.1 (2.28)	49	18.1 (1.79)	12.8 (1.55)	8.4 (1.35)
Other	31.1 (2.78)	17.3 (2.34)	35.2 (6.00)	21.7 (5.11)	— (†)	— (†)	—	— (†)	—	— (†)	— (†)	— (†)
Age												
15 to 23	33.7 (0.41)	21.5 (0.39)	34.5 (0.46)	22.0 (0.43)	31.0 (0.49)	21.1 (0.38)	4,678	41.0 (0.70)	912	19.5 (0.52)	14.5 (0.46)	9.8 (0.37)
24 to 29	35.0 (0.99)	16.0 (0.78)	39.7 (0.98)	19.5 (0.86)	34.4 (1.12)	17.2 (0.91)	1,332	47.4 (1.17)	252	18.9 (0.94)	13.9 (0.82)	6.6 (0.52)
30 or older	37.6 (0.87)	15.6 (0.52)	38.1 (0.84)	15.2 (0.68)	35.4 (0.94)	18.4 (0.82)	1,696	45.1 (1.06)	318	18.8 (0.81)	13.0 (0.66)	7.5 (0.56)
Attendance status												
Full-time, full-year[3]	31.4 (0.45)	19.1 (0.37)	31.4 (0.52)	19.4 (0.46)	28.1 (0.48)	17.6 (0.41)	3,254	36.7 (0.78)	550	16.9 (0.58)	12.5 (0.48)	8.5 (0.43)
Part-time only, for only part of year	37.5 (0.65)	17.9 (0.51)	39.8 (0.71)	19.0 (0.59)	37.4 (0.81)	21.3 (0.78)	3,033	47.7 (0.92)	616	20.3 (0.74)	14.5 (0.63)	8.1 (0.46)
Mixed attendance status[4]	41.1 (0.97)	23.7 (0.85)	42.6 (0.98)	26.3 (0.93)	37.0 (0.95)	23.4 (0.74)	1,419	47.4 (0.97)	316	22.2 (0.83)	16.4 (0.69)	10.8 (0.59)
Student housing status												
On-campus	24.5 (0.70)	16.8 (0.56)	23.2 (0.84)	17.1 (0.76)	17.9 (0.78)	14.1 (0.67)	921	24.7 (1.26)	120	13.0 (0.89)	9.7 (0.82)	6.8 (0.64)
Off-campus	35.9 (0.58)	17.0 (0.40)	37.2 (0.57)	17.8 (0.49)	34.0 (0.65)	19.6 (0.63)	3,810	45.9 (0.78)	720	18.9 (0.58)	13.6 (0.50)	8.2 (0.39)
With parents or relatives	37.9 (0.59)	24.5 (0.61)	39.6 (0.78)	25.2 (0.66)	35.3 (0.78)	22.2 (0.61)	2,293	47.6 (1.04)	545	23.7 (0.79)	17.7 (0.69)	11.2 (0.51)
Attended more than one institution	36.5 (1.18)	18.3 (0.98)	36.1 (1.11)	20.2 (0.97)	32.7 (1.09)	17.0 (0.95)	682	36.0 (1.07)	97	14.2 (0.81)	9.9 (0.59)	6.4 (0.49)
Dependency status												
Dependent	33.4 (0.45)	22.1 (0.41)	34.4 (0.51)	22.8 (0.46)	31.2 (0.53)	22.0 (0.42)	3,843	39.5 (0.77)	749	19.5 (0.55)	14.4 (0.50)	9.7 (0.41)
Independent	36.4 (0.61)	16.1 (0.39)	38.1 (0.59)	17.1 (0.51)	33.9 (0.57)	17.6 (0.52)	3,863	46.5 (0.76)	732	19.0 (0.55)	13.7 (0.47)	7.8 (0.36)
Veteran status												
Veteran	35.9 (2.33)	13.2 (1.52)	35.8 (2.36)	17.1 (2.08)	31.4 (2.21)	17.4 (1.74)	363	43.9 (2.08)	62	17.1 (1.53)	12.2 (1.38)	6.7 (0.99)
Not veteran	34.8 (0.38)	19.4 (0.31)	36.2 (0.38)	20.1 (0.36)	32.7 (0.42)	19.8 (0.37)	7,343	43.0 (0.58)	1,420	19.3 (0.43)	14.1 (0.37)	8.9 (0.30)
Field of study[5]												
Business/management	36.4 (1.00)	19.6 (0.97)	37.0 (1.13)	21.7 (1.06)	32.7 (1.11)	19.8 (0.85)	996	42.6 (1.37)	182	18.2 (0.95)	13.8 (0.86)	9.2 (0.70)
Computer science	33.7 (1.59)	19.2 (1.39)	34.7 (2.28)	19.8 (1.77)	29.3 (1.69)	17.4 (1.40)	329	41.0 (2.14)	64	19.4 (1.78)	14.8 (1.58)	8.9 (1.24)
Education	41.5 (1.61)	23.1 (1.14)	40.3 (1.90)	23.0 (1.48)	36.0 (1.84)	21.6 (1.53)	289	46.6 (2.33)	64	22.1 (1.91)	18.2 (1.81)	8.8 (1.37)
Engineering	30.9 (1.79)	16.6 (1.41)	33.0 (1.81)	19.0 (1.57)	33.1 (1.63)	20.9 (1.63)	394	38.6 (2.02)	70	17.8 (1.66)	13.7 (1.54)	9.0 (1.11)
Health	37.0 (0.83)	19.7 (0.68)	38.6 (2.49)	18.9 (1.88)	34.6 (0.74)	18.8 (0.70)	1,531	46.5 (1.09)	293	19.1 (0.87)	14.7 (0.75)	9.2 (0.68)
Humanities	34.0 (1.29)	18.8 (0.94)	31.2 (1.94)	20.5 (1.77)	26.7 (1.71)	17.9 (1.11)	1,421	46.8 (1.13)	292	20.5 (0.97)	14.4 (0.84)	8.2 (0.64)
Life sciences	31.2 (1.81)	19.7 (1.72)	31.2 (6.21)	20.5 (8.64)	27.7 (1.87)	17.9 (1.11)	386	36.4 (2.03)	69	18.0 (1.56)	14.0 (1.53)	8.2 (1.16)
Mathematics	23.0 (5.55)	11.0 ! (4.43)	41.1 (4.31)	15.6 ! (5.20)	14.3 ! (4.57)	8.4 ! (2.81)	29	36.4 (7.45)	‡	13.2 ! (4.85)	12.1 ! (4.68)	‡ (†)
Physical sciences	24.0 (4.39)	12.9 (3.49)	24.5 (2.16)	15.7 ! (3.92)	29.2 (4.72)	24.7 (4.59)	62	37.2 (6.96)	‡	15.4 (3.50)	9.2 (2.47)	7.6 (2.27)
Social/behavioral sciences	33.2 (2.08)	13.2 (1.57)	35.0 (1.93)	23.4 (1.94)	24.7 (1.94)	19.8 (1.38)	341	42.4 (2.23)	66	19.2 (1.61)	13.9 (1.40)	9.6 (1.30)
Vocational/technical	38.5 (2.11)	18.3 (1.60)	31.1 (1.78)	15.7 (1.78)	26.9 (2.10)	15.7 (1.59)	336	33.0 (2.32)	51	15.3 (1.64)	11.3 (1.41)	8.4 (1.16)
Undeclared	33.6 (0.67)	19.2 (0.59)	35.8 (1.29)	20.0 (1.14)	31.8 (1.86)	22.0 (1.86)	297	45.0 (2.56)	77	25.8 (2.15)	18.4 (1.97)	11.6 (1.57)
Other	33.3 (1.49)	18.0 (1.06)	34.6 (1.23)	18.5 (0.97)	29.3 (0.94)	16.7 (0.77)	930	42.6 (1.36)	174	18.7 (1.01)	12.8 (0.94)	8.0 (0.67)

See notes at end of table.

Table 311.40. Percentage of first-year undergraduate students who reported taking remedial education courses, by selected student and institution characteristics: Selected years, 2003–04 through 2015–16—Continued

[Standard errors appear in parentheses]

Selected student or institution characteristic	Percent of 2003–04 first-year undergraduates[1] who took any remedial courses		Percent of 2007–08 first-year undergraduates[1] who took any remedial courses		Percent of 2011–12 first-year undergraduates[1] who took any remedial courses		2015–16 first-year undergraduates[1]					
							Total number of students[2] (in thousands)	Students who took any remedial courses			Percent who took specific remedial courses in 2015–16	
	Ever	In 2003–04	Ever	In 2007–08	Ever	In 2011–12		Percent who ever took	Percent who took in 2015–16 (in thousands)	Percent who took in 2015–16	Mathematics	Reading/writing
1	2	3	4	5	6	7	8	9	10	11	12	13
Control and level of institution												
Public less-than-2-year	30.6 (1.85)	10.9 (1.09)	31.9 (1.99)	9.0 (0.89)	30.2 (6.13)	12.2 ! (3.86)	55	33.0 (3.85)	‡	10.9 (1.54)	8.4 (1.61)	6.9 (0.93)
Public 2-year	41.4 (0.59)	23.0 (0.47)	41.8 (3.54)	23.7 (0.48)	40.3 (0.67)	25.6 (0.64)	4,275	52.5 (0.76)	1,082	25.3 (0.63)	18.6 (0.53)	10.8 (0.42)
Public 4-year nondoctorate	34.2 (1.77)	21.4 (1.12)	38.9 (1.24)	25.4 (1.14)	37.8 (2.12)	24.3 (1.30)	692	44.4 (1.92)	125	18.1 (1.28)	13.9 (1.09)	7.8 (0.77)
Public 4-year doctorate	25.7 (1.11)	16.3 (0.64)	25.0 (1.03)	17.8 (0.86)	21.9 (0.84)	15.6 (0.80)	819	26.2 (1.35)	96	11.7 (0.93)	9.0 (0.75)	5.7 (0.72)
Private nonprofit less-than-4-year	31.3 (2.06)	12.9 (1.89)	30.3 (3.75)	10.2 (2.81)	22.3 (4.25)	9.4 ! (3.42)	76	23.7 (1.86)	4	5.7 ! (2.02)	5.1 ! (2.05)	4.1 ! (2.06)
Private nonprofit 4-year nondoctorate	26.0 (1.16)	14.7 (0.78)	25.5 (1.74)	16.6 (1.46)	24.4 (1.66)	15.3 (1.23)	344	28.3 (1.88)	39	11.3 (0.93)	7.6 (0.91)	6.7 (0.71)
Private nonprofit 4-year doctorate	18.3 (1.67)	11.6 (1.39)	22.1 (1.70)	12.6 (1.38)	14.6 (1.85)	9.6 (1.24)	396	21.8 (1.71)	36	9.2 (1.07)	5.0 (0.97)	6.2 (0.93)
Private for-profit less-than-2-year	24.1 (0.50)	7.8 (0.23)	26.5 (1.02)	5.5 (0.51)	16.7 (0.74)	3.8 (0.56)	288	25.0 (1.10)	12	4.2 (0.69)	2.5 (0.49)	2.0 (0.50)
Private for-profit 2 years or more	25.4 (1.63)	11.7 (1.04)	28.8 (1.46)	11.3 (1.20)	20.9 (0.74)	8.2 (0.37)	761	33.9 (1.61)	82	10.7 (0.70)	7.5 (0.58)	6.7 (0.54)

—Not available.
†Not applicable.
‡Reporting standards not met.
!Interpret data with caution. The coefficient of variation (CV) for this estimate is between 30 and 50 percent. The coefficient of variation (CV) for this estimate is 50 percent or greater.
[1]First-year student status was determined by accumulation of credits. Students attending postsecondary education part time, or not completing the credit accumulation requirements for second-year status, could be considered first-year students for more than one year.
[2]Numbers may not equal those reported in other tables, since these data are based on a sample survey of students who enrolled at any time during the academic year.
[3]Includes only students enrolled full time for a full academic year (defined as 9 or more months).

[4]Includes students enrolled part time for a full academic year as well as students enrolled full time, but for only part of an academic year.
[5]Excludes students not in a degree or certificate program.
NOTE: Percentages of students who took remedial courses are based on student reports. Data exclude students attending institutions in Puerto Rico. Detail may not sum to totals because of survey item nonresponse and rounding. Race categories exclude persons of Hispanic ethnicity.
SOURCE: U.S. Department of Education, National Center for Education Statistics, 2003–04, 2007–08, 2011–12, and 2015–16 National Postsecondary Student Aid Study (NPSAS:04, NPSAS:08, NPSAS:12, and NPSAS:16). (This table was prepared June 2018.)

Table 311.60. Enrollment in postsecondary education, by level of enrollment, level of institution, student age, and major field of study: 2015–16

[Standard errors appear in parentheses]

Major field of study[1]	All students Total (in thousands)	All students — Under 25	All students — 25 to 35	All students — Over 35	Undergraduate: 2-year and less-than-2-year institutions[2] Total (in thousands)	2-year — Under 25	2-year — 25 to 35	2-year — Over 35	Undergraduate: 4-year institutions Total (in thousands)	4-year — Under 25	4-year — 25 to 35	4-year — Over 35	Post-baccalaureate Total (in thousands)
1	2	3	4	5	6	7	8	9	10	11	12	13	14
Total	**19,308**	63.3 (0.32)	23.3 (0.26)	13.4 (0.23)	**9,650**	57.2 (0.56)	26.9 (0.45)	15.9 (0.37)	**9,658**	69.3 (0.40)	19.8 (0.32)	10.9 (0.26)	**3,547**
Agriculture and related sciences	159	74.8 (3.22)	16.5 (2.56)	8.6 (1.91)	78	60.1 (5.38)	24.9 (4.62)	15.0 (3.49)	81	88.9 (2.10)	8.6 (1.72)	2.5 ! (0.99)	17
Anthropology	48	70.3 (5.64)	19.6 (5.01)	10.1 ! (4.77)	12	59.7 (17.51)	‡ (†)	‡ (†)	36	73.8 (5.28)	18.6 (4.93)	7.6 ! (3.42)	11
Architecture and related services	58	80.5 (4.08)	11.7 (3.14)	7.7 ! (3.50)	16	71.2 (8.57)	‡ (†)	14.9 ! (7.32)	42	84.1 (4.48)	10.9 ! (3.30)	‡ (†)	23
Area, ethnic, and gender studies	38	76.5 (5.27)	10.1 ! (3.05)	13.4 ! (4.93)	11	68.8 (13.23)	‡ (†)	‡ (†)	27	79.6 (4.89)	12.1 ! (3.74)	8.2 ! (3.74)	10
Biological and biomedical sciences	686	87.3 (1.03)	10.4 (0.88)	2.4 (0.52)	203	80.0 (2.03)	14.6 (1.56)	5.3 (1.59)	484	90.3 (1.05)	8.6 (1.01)	1.1 (0.30)	106
Business, management, and marketing	2,973	59.1 (0.79)	24.7 (0.61)	16.2 (0.56)	1,190	55.1 (1.61)	26.7 (1.34)	18.2 (0.94)	1,783	61.7 (1.00)	23.4 (0.75)	14.9 (0.71)	592
Communication and journalism	370	85.5 (1.23)	10.9 (1.11)	3.6 (0.56)	84	77.7 (3.16)	17.2 (2.84)	5.1 (1.39)	286	87.8 (1.30)	9.1 (1.14)	3.1 (0.67)	40
Communications technologies/technicians	97	68.9 (3.18)	20.8 (2.93)	10.2 (1.99)	50	63.0 (5.03)	23.5 (4.80)	13.5 (3.15)	47	75.1 (3.65)	18.0 (3.31)	6.8 ! (2.12)	‡
Computer and information sciences	852	53.0 (1.46)	29.5 (1.26)	17.4 (1.00)	396	50.8 (2.24)	28.6 (2.06)	20.6 (1.67)	456	55.0 (1.76)	30.3 (1.43)	14.7 (1.13)	131
Construction trades	85	41.6 (4.62)	41.5 (5.45)	16.9 (4.22)	74	40.2 (4.84)	41.3 (5.58)	18.5 (4.59)	11	50.6 (14.55)	43.0 ! (15.65)	‡ (†)	‡
Criminology	35	76.8 (4.92)	19.6 (4.64)	‡ (†)	9	70.1 (9.57)	26.6 ! (9.21)	‡ (†)	26	79.0 (5.99)	17.2 ! (5.55)	‡ (†)	‡
Economics	113	91.7 (2.13)	8.2 (2.11)	‡ (†)	17	76.8 (9.97)	23.2 ! (9.96)	‡ (†)	96	94.4 (1.44)	5.5 (1.41)	‡ (†)	16
Education	841	66.6 (1.16)	20.5 (0.96)	12.8 (0.90)	365	56.6 (2.21)	26.7 (1.81)	16.7 (1.75)	475	74.4 (1.25)	15.8 (1.12)	9.9 (0.90)	605
Engineering	799	82.6 (0.98)	13.2 (0.84)	4.2 (0.46)	244	70.9 (2.22)	21.8 (2.05)	7.3 (1.02)	555	87.7 (0.99)	9.5 (0.81)	2.8 (0.47)	188
Engineering technologies/technicians	341	49.0 (2.33)	31.8 (2.08)	19.2 (1.89)	222	46.5 (3.21)	32.0 (2.78)	21.5 (2.63)	120	53.5 (3.36)	31.3 (3.46)	15.2 (2.41)	26
English language and literature/letters	199	72.6 (4.22)	15.8 (1.93)	11.6 (3.23)	60	51.5 (9.53)	18.4 (3.70)	30.1 (7.76)	138	81.9 (2.55)	14.7 (2.31)	3.4 ! (1.06)	40
Family and consumer/human sciences	193	61.3 (2.83)	20.5 (1.93)	18.2 (2.31)	99	52.1 (4.35)	23.8 (3.25)	24.1 (3.89)	94	71.1 (3.12)	17.0 (2.35)	11.9 (2.47)	12
Foreign languages and literatures	84	74.8 (3.95)	15.9 (3.40)	9.3 (2.50)	28	58.7 (8.24)	25.4 (7.04)	15.9 ! (6.35)	55	83.0 (3.78)	11.1 ! (3.40)	5.9 ! (1.94)	11
Geography	20	61.6 (8.55)	22.4 ! (6.76)	16.0 (5.71)	‡	‡ (†)	‡ (†)	‡ (†)	13	63.2 (7.94)	29.7 (8.31)	7.1 ! (2.78)	‡
Health professions and related sciences	3,438	50.0 (0.68)	32.0 (0.52)	18.0 (0.52)	2,067	48.0 (0.86)	33.7 (0.72)	18.3 (0.66)	1,371	53.0 (1.14)	29.5 (0.85)	17.5 (0.83)	694
History	112	71.8 (2.97)	21.0 (3.06)	7.2 (1.81)	27	70.5 (7.07)	27.3 (7.19)	2.2 ! (1.01)	85	72.2 (3.05)	19.0 (2.93)	8.8 (2.28)	25
International relations and affairs	38	89.2 (3.32)	9.2 ! (2.99)	‡ (†)	‡	‡ (†)	‡ (†)	‡ (†)	33	87.5 (3.71)	10.7 ! (3.39)	‡ (†)	12
Legal professions and studies	128	47.6 (3.84)	25.0 (2.84)	27.4 (3.80)	64	47.0 (5.95)	22.9 (4.54)	30.2 (6.45)	64	48.2 (5.31)	27.2 (3.43)	24.6 (5.15)	132
Liberal arts, sciences and humanities	1,915	66.4 (0.86)	21.6 (0.83)	12.0 (0.64)	1,426	64.7 (1.12)	23.0 (1.06)	12.2 (0.74)	490	71.3 (1.35)	17.5 (1.37)	11.2 (1.24)	31
Library science	‡	‡ (†)	‡ (†)	‡ (†)	‡	‡ (†)	‡ (†)	‡ (†)	‡	‡ (†)	‡ (†)	‡ (†)	11
Mathematics and statistics	118	83.5 (2.55)	13.0 (2.20)	3.5 ! (1.39)	35	78.2 (6.66)	14.8 ! (5.35)	‡ (†)	83	85.7 (2.42)	12.3 (2.37)	2.0 ! (0.79)	29
Mechanic and repair technologies	272	54.2 (2.77)	28.7 (1.93)	17.1 (2.00)	240	54.8 (2.94)	27.9 (2.02)	17.3 (2.19)	32	50.0 (9.84)	34.6 (8.02)	15.4 ! (4.90)	‡
Military technologies	‡	‡ (†)	‡ (†)	‡ (†)	‡	‡ (†)	‡ (†)	‡ (†)	‡	‡ (†)	‡ (†)	‡ (†)	‡
Multi/interdisciplinary studies	259	66.8 (2.32)	22.2 (1.87)	11.1 (1.62)	117	63.9 (3.61)	25.5 (3.10)	10.6 (2.07)	142	69.2 (2.77)	19.4 (2.26)	11.4 (2.34)	29
Natural resources and conservation	97	73.0 (3.38)	23.5 (3.47)	3.5 ! (1.07)	29	73.6 (5.57)	20.8 (5.23)	5.6 ! (2.61)	68	72.7 (4.13)	24.6 (4.31)	2.6 ! (1.24)	17
Parks, recreation, and fitness studies	302	84.7 (1.69)	11.7 (1.43)	3.6 (0.93)	98	75.9 (3.76)	15.5 (2.84)	8.6 ! (2.65)	204	88.9 (1.58)	9.9 (1.56)	1.2 (0.36)	26
Personal and culinary services	305	54.3 (2.18)	31.3 (1.78)	14.4 (1.49)	261	54.3 (2.36)	32.2 (1.97)	13.5 (1.66)	44	54.3 (4.94)	26.1 (3.76)	19.6 (3.63)	‡
Philosophy and religious studies	56	58.5 (7.65)	19.6 (4.71)	21.9 ! (7.00)	8	30.3 (11.32)	‡ (†)	‡ (†)	48	54.8 (8.39)	20.7 (5.36)	24.5 ! (7.93)	19
Physical sciences	214	82.1 (1.21)	14.7 (1.97)	3.3 (0.93)	76	75.1 (4.42)	19.8 (3.57)	5.0 ! (2.24)	139	85.9 (2.41)	11.9 (2.29)	2.3 ! (0.74)	46
Political science and government	144	85.7 (1.87)	10.5 (1.68)	3.7 (1.11)	28	86.0 (4.13)	8.7 ! (3.26)	5.3 ! (2.26)	116	85.6 (2.14)	11.0 (1.96)	3.4 ! (1.23)	25
Precision production	102	49.4 (4.74)	30.8 (4.57)	19.8 (3.37)	89	49.2 (5.31)	34.4 (4.84)	16.4 (3.00)	‡	‡ (†)	‡ (†)	‡ (†)	‡
Psychology	684	70.8 (1.41)	20.3 (1.27)	8.9 (0.79)	207	68.2 (2.96)	22.6 (2.84)	9.2 (1.46)	477	71.9 (1.59)	19.3 (1.41)	8.8 (0.89)	169
Public administration and social services	231	51.3 (2.58)	26.2 (2.23)	22.5 (1.77)	90	47.9 (4.91)	32.0 (4.06)	20.0 (2.61)	141	53.5 (2.56)	22.5 (2.28)	24.0 (2.28)	138
Science technologies/technicians	29	57.5 (7.71)	26.2 (6.66)	16.4 (4.50)	23	62.5 (8.59)	23.5 (7.40)	14.0 ! (5.26)	‡	‡ (†)	‡ (†)	‡ (†)	‡
Security and protective services	726	63.4 (1.38)	23.8 (1.13)	12.8 (0.96)	395	63.1 (1.97)	24.7 (1.77)	12.2 (1.50)	331	63.8 (1.75)	22.7 (1.31)	13.5 (1.27)	47

See notes at end of table.

Table 311.60.   Enrollment in postsecondary education, by level of enrollment, level of institution, student age, and major field of study: 2015–16—Continued

[Standard errors appear in parentheses]

Major field of study[1]	All students				Undergraduate									Post-baccalaureate
					2-year and less-than-2-year institutions[2]				4-year institutions				
	Total (in thousands)	Percentage distribution, by age			Total (in thousands)	Percentage distribution, by age			Total (in thousands)	Percentage distribution, by age			Total (in thousands)
		Under 25	25 to 35	Over 35		Under 25	25 to 35	Over 35		Under 25	25 to 35	Over 35	
1	2	3	4	5	6	7	8	9	10	11	12	13	14
Social sciences, other	85	62.5 (4.62)	20.6 (4.01)	16.9 (3.27)	52	55.9 (6.83)	22.7 (6.28)	21.4 (5.12)	34	72.7 (5.43)	17.4 (4.31)	9.9 ! (3.15)	5
Sociology	147	67.6 (2.97)	23.5 (3.08)	8.8 (1.53)	51	53.7 (6.80)	36.8 (7.05)	9.5 (2.84)	97	75.0 (2.80)	16.6 (2.36)	8.4 (1.67)	12
Theology and religious vocations	46	55.5 (8.71)	16.1 (3.77)	28.4 ! (9.31)	‡	‡ (†)	‡ (†)	‡ (†)	43	53.8 (9.05)	16.1 (3.97)	30.1 ! (9.66)	73
Transportation and materials moving	72	53.5 (5.59)	28.9 (6.36)	17.7 (4.22)	45	44.8 (6.85)	34.8 (8.85)	20.4 ! (7.16)	27	68.0 (5.41)	18.9 (5.20)	13.1 (2.80)	‡
Visual and performing arts	745	75.4 (1.14)	17.9 (1.09)	6.7 (0.71)	283	69.9 (2.12)	20.3 (1.81)	9.8 (1.56)	462	78.8 (1.32)	16.4 (1.36)	4.8 (0.58)	72
Undecided	449	70.4 (1.99)	17.4 (1.60)	12.2 (1.47)	274	66.0 (2.58)	20.1 (2.25)	13.9 (2.08)	175	77.3 (2.62)	13.2 (1.88)	9.5 (1.77)	†

†Not applicable.
!Interpret data with caution. The coefficient of variation (CV) for this estimate is between 30 and 50 percent.
‡Reporting standards not met. Either there are too few cases for a reliable estimate or the coefficient of variation (CV) is 50 percent or greater.
[1]For undergraduate students, the field of study categories include students who had already declared a major as well as students who had decided on, but not yet declared, an intended major. The "Undecided" category consists of undergraduate students who had neither declared nor decided on a major.

[2]Also includes students attending more than one institution.
NOTE: Because of different survey editing and processing procedures, enrollment data in this table may differ from those appearing in other tables. Includes students who enrolled at any time during the 2015–16 academic year. Data exclude Puerto Rico. Data have been revised from previously published figures. Detail may not sum to totals because of rounding.
SOURCE: U.S. Department of Education, National Center for Education Statistics, 2015–16 National Postsecondary Student Aid Study (NPSAS:16). (This table was prepared May 2018.)

Table 312.10. Enrollment of the 120 largest degree-granting college and university campuses, by selected characteristics and institution: Fall 2018

Institution	State	Rank[1]	Control[2]	Level	Total enroll-ment	Institution	State	Rank[1]	Control[2]	Level	Total enroll-ment
1	2	3	4	5	6	1	2	3	4	5	6
Western Governors University	UT	1	PrivNp	4-year	121,437	Capella University	MN	61	PrivFp	4-year	37,171
Southern New Hampshire University	NH	2	PrivNp	4-year	104,068	University of Colorado, Boulder	CO	62	Public	4-year	36,681
University of Phoenix, Arizona	AZ	3	PrivFp	4-year	95,777	University of California, Irvine	CA	63	Public	4-year	36,032
Grand Canyon University	AZ	4	PrivFp	4-year	90,253	North Carolina State University at Raleigh	NC	64	Public	4-year	35,479
Liberty University	VA	5	PrivNp	4-year	79,152	Kennesaw State University	GA	65	Public	4-year	35,420
Lone Star College System	TX	6	Public	2-year	73,499	East Los Angeles College	CA	66	Public	2-year	35,403
Ivy Tech Community College	IN	7	Public	2-year	72,006	San Jose State University	CA	67	Public	4-year	35,400
Texas A & M University, College Station	TX	8	Public	4-year	68,679	San Diego State University	CA	68	Public	4-year	35,303
University of Central Florida	FL	9	Public	4-year	68,475	Iowa State University	IA	69	Public	4-year	34,992
Ohio State University, Main Campus	OH	10	Public	4-year	61,170	University of South Carolina, Columbia	SC	70	Public	4-year	34,795
University of Maryland, University College	MD	11	Public	4-year	60,603	Ashford University	CA	71	PrivFp	4-year	34,710
Florida International University	FL	12	Public	4-year	57,942	Virginia Polytechnic Institute and State University	VA	72	Public	4-year	34,683
Houston Community College	TX	13	Public	2-year	57,200	Boston University	MA	73	PrivNp	4-year	34,657
Miami Dade College	FL	14	Public	4-year	54,973	Brigham Young University, Provo	UT	74	PrivNp	4-year	34,499
University of Florida	FL	15	Public	4-year	52,218	Georgia State University	GA	75	Public	4-year	34,316
New York University	NY	16	PrivNp	4-year	51,847	College of Southern Nevada	NV	76	Public	4-year	34,169
University of Texas at Austin	TX	17	Public	4-year	51,832	Collin County Community College District	TX	77	Public	2-year	33,668
Arizona State University, Tempe	AZ	18	Public	4-year	51,585	Colorado State University, Fort Collins	CO	78	Public	4-year	33,478
Tarrant County College District	TX	19	Public	2-year	51,100	University of Utah	UT	79	Public	4-year	33,023
Northern Virginia Community College	VA	20	Public	2-year	50,929	Georgia Institute of Technology, Main Campus	GA	80	Public	4-year	32,723
University of Minnesota, Twin Cities	MN	21	Public	4-year	50,734	University of Texas at San Antonio	TX	81	Public	4-year	32,264
Walden University	MN	22	PrivFp	4-year	50,360	San Jacinto Community College	TX	82	Public	2-year	32,137
Michigan State University	MI	23	Public	4-year	50,351	South Texas College	TX	83	Public	4-year	31,949
Rutgers University, New Brunswick	NJ	24	Public	4-year	50,254	California State University, Sacramento	CA	84	Public	4-year	31,902
University of Illinois at Urbana-Champaign	IL	25	Public	4-year	49,702	Palm Beach State College	FL	85	Public	4-year	31,816
University of Texas at Arlington	TX	26	Public	4-year	47,899	University of Illinois at Chicago	IL	86	Public	4-year	31,683
University of Washington, Seattle Campus	WA	27	Public	4-year	47,400	University of Iowa	IA	87	Public	4-year	31,656
University of Southern California	CA	28	PrivNp	4-year	47,310	Harvard University	MA	88	PrivNp	4-year	31,566
Pennsylvania State University, Main Campus	PA	29	Public	4-year	46,810	University at Buffalo	NY	89	Public	4-year	31,503
University of Michigan, Ann Arbor	MI	30	Public	4-year	46,716	Washington State University	WA	90	Public	4-year	31,478
Valencia College	FL	31	Public	4-year	46,521	American River College	CA	91	Public	2-year	31,366
University of Houston	TX	32	Public	4-year	46,324	Columbia University in the City of New York	NY	92	PrivNp	4-year	31,077
American Public University System	WV	33	PrivFp	4-year	46,088	Northern Arizona University	AZ	93	Public	4-year	31,066
University of California, Los Angeles	CA	34	Public	4-year	44,537	Oregon State University	OR	94	Public	4-year	30,986
Purdue University, Main Campus	IN	35	Public	4-year	44,474	Louisiana State U. and Agricultural & Mechanical	LA	95	Public	4-year	30,983
University of Arizona	AZ	36	Public	4-year	44,097	Virginia Commonwealth University	VA	96	Public	4-year	30,697
University of South Florida, Main Campus	FL	37	Public	4-year	43,846	University of Massachusetts, Amherst	MA	97	Public	4-year	30,593
Indiana University, Bloomington	IN	38	Public	4-year	43,503	Purdue University Global, Davenport Campus	IA	98	Public	4-year	30,512
University of Wisconsin, Madison	WI	39	Public	4-year	43,463	University of Nevada, Las Vegas	NV	99	Public	4-year	30,457
University of California, Berkeley	CA	40	Public	4-year	42,501	Auburn University	AL	100	Public	4-year	30,440
Brigham Young University, Idaho	ID	41	PrivNp	4-year	42,341	University of North Carolina at Chapel Hill	NC	101	Public	4-year	30,011
University of Maryland, College Park	MD	42	Public	4-year	41,200	Excelsior College	NY	102	PrivNp	4-year	30,008
Florida State University	FL	43	Public	4-year	41,005	University of Missouri, Columbia	MO	103	Public	4-year	29,843
Austin Community College District	TX	44	Public	4-year	40,799	San Francisco State University	CA	104	Public	4-year	29,778
Broward College	FL	45	Public	4-year	40,784	Florida Atlantic University	FL	105	Public	4-year	29,772
California State University, Fullerton	CA	46	Public	4-year	40,280	University of North Carolina at Charlotte	NC	106	Public	4-year	29,710
California State University, Northridge	CA	47	Public	4-year	40,212	Indiana University-Purdue University, Indianapolis	IN	107	Public	4-year	29,579
Utah Valley University	UT	48	Public	4-year	39,931	Mount San Antonio College	CA	108	Public	2-year	29,346
Temple University	PA	49	Public	4-year	39,740	Saint Petersburg College	FL	109	Public	4-year	29,183
University of Georgia	GA	50	Public	4-year	38,652	University of Kentucky	KY	110	Public	4-year	29,182
Texas State University	TX	51	Public	4-year	38,644	Salt Lake Community College	UT	111	Public	2-year	29,156
Arizona State University, Skysong	AZ	52	Public	4-year	38,540	University of Tennessee, Knoxville	TN	112	Public	4-year	28,894
University of Alabama	AL	53	Public	4-year	38,390	El Paso Community College	TX	113	Public	2-year	28,819
University of North Texas	TX	54	Public	4-year	38,241	Santa Monica College	CA	114	Public	4-year	28,800
Texas Tech University	TX	55	Public	4-year	38,209	University of Texas at Dallas	TX	115	Public	4-year	28,755
University of California, Davis	CA	56	Public	4-year	38,167	East Carolina University	NC	116	Public	4-year	28,718
University of California, San Diego	CA	57	Public	4-year	37,887	University of Pittsburgh, Pittsburgh Campus	PA	117	Public	4-year	28,673
University of Cincinnati, Main Campus	OH	58	Public	4-year	37,886	University of Texas, Rio Grande Valley	TX	118	Public	4-year	28,644
California State University, Long Beach	CA	59	Public	4-year	37,466	University of Oklahoma, Norman Campus	OK	119	Public	4-year	28,564
George Mason University	VA	60	Public	4-year	37,316	Ohio University, Main Campus	OH	120	Public	4-year	28,480

[1]College and university campuses ranked by fall 2018 enrollment data.
[2]"PrivNp" stands for private nonprofit. "PrivFp" stands for private for-profit.
NOTE: Degree-granting institutions grant associate's or higher degrees and participate in Title IV federal financial aid programs. Includes enrollment in online and distance education.

SOURCE: U.S. Department of Education, National Center for Education Statistics, Integrated Postsecondary Education Data System (IPEDS), Spring 2019, Fall Enrollment component. (This table was prepared April 2020.)

Table 312.50. Fall enrollment and degrees conferred in degree-granting tribally controlled postsecondary institutions, by state and institution: Selected years, fall 2000 through fall 2018, and 2016–17 and 2017–18

State and institution	Level and control[1]	Total fall enrollment 2000 Total	2000 Total American Indian/ Alaska Native	2000 Percent American Indian/ Alaska Native	2005	2010	2015	2016	2017	2018 Total	2018 Total American Indian/ Alaska Native	2018 Percent American Indian/ Alaska Native	Degrees awarded to American Indians/Alaska Natives Associate's 2015–16	Associate's 2017–18	Bachelor's 2016–17	Bachelor's 2017–18
1	2	3	4	5	6	7	8	9	10	11	12	13	14	15	16	17
Tribally controlled institutions	†	13,680	11,459	83.8	17,167	21,179	17,089	16,822	16,621	16,190	12,705	78.5	1,135	1,248	341	376
Alaska																
Ilisagvik College	1	322	174	54.0	278	288	193	188	111	335	210	62.7	7	16	0	0
Arizona																
Diné College	1	1,712	1,645	96.1	1,825	2,033	1,490	1,396	1,465	1,519	1,497	98.6	129	138	10	28
Tohono O'odham Community College	2	—	—	—	270	207	212	276	400	459	393	85.6	17	21	†	†
Kansas																
Haskell Indian Nations University	1	918	918	100.0	918	958	799	820	806	733	733	100.0	93	114	102	93
Michigan																
Bay Mills Community College	2	360	228	63.3	406	607	541	467	448	477	267	56.0	21	39	†	†
Keweenaw Bay Ojibwa Community College	2	—	—	—	—	—	102	104	98	84	57	67.9	6	9	†	†
Saginaw Chippewa Tribal College	2	—	—	—	123	153	116	141	154	140	104	74.3	15	21	†	†
Minnesota																
Fond du Lac Tribal and Community College	2	999	221	22.1	1,981	2,339	2,227	2,101	1,946	1,982	118	6.0	22	29	†	†
Leech Lake Tribal College	2	240	228	95.0	189	235	348	286	181	173	147	85.0	39	36	†	†
White Earth Tribal and Community College	4	—	—	—	61	117	68	77	90	106	93	87.7	9	5	†	†
Montana																
Aaniiih Nakoda College	2	295	266	90.2	175	214	219	149	122	150	125	83.3	28	29	†	†
Blackfeet Community College	4	299	288	96.3	485	473	442	425	375	305	284	93.1	71	43	†	†
Chief Dull Knife College	2	461	365	79.2	554	433	218	168	186	196	176	89.8	20	22	†	†
Fort Peck Community College	2	400	338	84.5	408	452	321	385	358	305	250	82.0	20	23	†	†
Little Big Horn College	2	320	303	94.7	259	380	248	225	243	255	250	98.0	21	29	†	†
Salish Kootenai College	3	1,042	881	84.5	1,142	1,158	784	859	809	720	539	74.9	55	48	30	35
Stone Child College	1	38	38	100.0	344	332	540	544	554	444	424	95.5	17	20	0	0
Nebraska																
Little Priest Tribal College	2	141	121	85.8	109	148	132	132	141	130	113	86.9	10	10	†	†
Nebraska Indian Community College	2	170	146	85.9	107	177	158	175	180	200	185	92.5	4	10	†	†
New Mexico																
Institute of American Indian and Alaska Native Culture and Arts Development	1	139	139	100.0	113	313	493	582	659	589	409	69.4	4	1	19	17
Navajo Technical University	1	841	841	100.0	333	1,019	1,686	1,675	1,875	1,600	1,555	97.2	48	78	22	40
Southwestern Indian Polytechnic Institute	2	304	304	100.0	614	531	402	307	300	367	367	100.0	71	70	†	†
North Dakota																
Cankdeska Cikana Community College	2	9	8	88.9	198	220	188	178	242	178	157	88.2	22	10	†	†
Nueta Hidatsa Sahnish College	1	50	47	94.0	241	215	229	268	228	198	163	82.3	6	10	1	8
Sitting Bull College	1	22	20	90.9	287	314	261	282	317	273	247	90.5	23	20	6	6
Turtle Mountain Community College	3	686	608	88.6	615	969	555	584	567	573	550	96.0	62	110	9	7
United Tribes Technical College	3	204	186	91.2	885	600	391	483	315	429	392	91.4	25	44	18	13
Oklahoma																
College of the Muscogee Nation	2	—	—	—	—	—	202	213	227	217	190	87.6	26	39	†	†
South Dakota																
Oglala Lakota College	1	1,174	1,077	91.7	1,302	1,830	1,366	1,301	1,246	1,300	1,227	94.4	70	48	53	61
Sinte Gleska University	3	900	757	84.1	1,123	2,473	581	568	581	583	524	89.9	28	34	19	16
Sisseton Wahpeton College	2	250	192	76.8	290	261	132	142	197	167	131	78.4	9	11	†	†
Washington																
Northwest Indian College	1	524	440	84.0	495	626	641	579	544	535	450	84.1	86	71	47	47
Wisconsin																
College of the Menominee Nation	3	371	283	76.3	532	615	433	394	285	237	198	83.5	27	21	5	5
Lac Courte Oreilles Ojibwa Community College	2	489	397	81.2	505	489	371	288	305	231	180	77.9	24	19	†	†

—Not available.
†Not applicable.
[1]1 = 4-year public; 2 = 2-year public; 3 = 4-year private nonprofit; and 4 = 2-year private nonprofit.
NOTE: This table only includes institutions that were in operation during the 2018–19 academic year. They are all members of the American Indian Higher Education Consortium and, with few exceptions, are tribally controlled and located on reservations. Degree-granting institutions grant associate's or higher degrees and participate in Title IV federal financial aid programs. Totals include persons of other racial/ethnic groups not separately identified. Some data have been revised from previously published figures.
SOURCE: U.S. Department of Education, National Center for Education Statistics, Integrated Postsecondary Education Data System (IPEDS), Spring 2001 through Spring 2019, Fall Enrollment component; and Fall 2017 and Fall 2018, Completions component. (This table was prepared September 2019.)

Table 313.10. Fall enrollment, degrees conferred, and expenditures in degree-granting historically Black colleges and universities, by institution: 2017, 2018, and 2017–18

Institution	State	Level and control[1]	Total enrollment, fall 2018[2]	Enrollment, fall 2018		Full-time-equivalent enrollment, fall 2018	Degrees conferred, 2017–18				Total expenditures, 2017–18 (in thousands of current dollars)[4]
				Total	Black enrollment		Associate's	Bachelor's	Master's	Doctor's[3]	
1	2	3	4	5	6	7	8	9	10	11	12
Total	†	†	298,134	291,767	223,163	251,390	5,465	32,639	7,697	2,518	$7,966,186
Alabama A&M University[5]	AL	1	6,001	6,106	5,701	5,726	0	507	332	8	148,803
Alabama State University	AL	1	4,760	4,413	4,067	4,118	0	650	144	32	148,377
Bishop State Community College	AL	2	3,233	2,860	1,796	1,907	275	†	†	†	32,081
Gadsden State Community College	AL	2	4,979	4,736	850	3,117	642	†	†	†	50,921
H. Councill Trenholm State Technical College	AL	2	1,845	1,855	1,267	1,181	178	†	†	†	21,972
J.F. Drake State Community and Technical College	AL	2	752	831	432	486	64	†	†	†	10,863
Lawson State Community College	AL	2	3,248	3,274	2,653	2,192	316	†	†	†	50,318
Miles College	AL	3	1,650	1,550	1,470	1,501	0	295	0	0	30,916
Oakwood University	AL	3	1,711	1,636	1,391	1,555	4	306	5	0	54,786
Selma University	AL	3	324	317	308	264	13	20	4	0	4,007
Shelton State Community College	AL	2	4,607	4,350	1,667	2,771	535	†	†	†	42,421
Stillman College	AL	3	677	797	750	714	0	72	0	0	14,207
Talladega College	AL	3	782	1,212	1,042	1,138	0	128	0	0	14,708
Tuskegee University[5]	AL	3	3,289	3,026	2,771	2,953	0	423	86	67	122,619
Arkansas Baptist College	AR	3	593	525	472	486	41	30	0	0	14,820
Philander Smith College	AR	3	891	1,000	935	973	0	89	0	0	21,513
Shorter College	AR	4	521	569	323	425	30	†	†	†	5,409
University of Arkansas at Pine Bluff[5]	AR	1	2,612	2,579	2,318	2,405	9	377	34	1	80,292
Delaware State University[5]	DE	1	4,352	4,586	3,235	4,247	0	613	101	21	143,128
Howard University	DC	3	9,392	9,139	7,676	8,747	0	1,232	313	504	791,820
University of the District of Columbia[5]	DC	1	4,247	4,244	2,735	2,967	172	338	114	0	158,530
Bethune-Cookman University	FL	3	4,143	3,773	3,408	3,673	0	508	63	0	97,091
Edward Waters College	FL	3	3,443	2,906	1,803	1,703	0	121	0	0	24,685
Florida A&M University[5]	FL	1	9,913	10,021	8,254	9,151	40	1,258	303	340	290,819
Florida Memorial University	FL	3	1,250	1,189	874	1,126	0	214	25	0	35,256
Albany State University	GA	1	6,615	6,371	4,822	5,168	648	481	138	0	113,575
Clark Atlanta University	GA	3	3,992	3,911	3,673	3,732	0	411	233	30	98,282
Fort Valley State University[5]	GA	1	2,752	2,776	2,537	2,522	0	334	112	0	78,548
Interdenominational Theological Center	GA	3	295	293	288	182	0	0	38	28	7,546
Morehouse College	GA	3	2,202	2,206	2,106	2,170	0	398	0	0	87,802
Morehouse School of Medicine	GA	3	520	542	415	528	0	0	46	83	165,187
Paine College	GA	3	426	469	442	447	0	74	0	0	13,830
Savannah State University	GA	1	4,429	4,077	3,297	3,698	41	548	69	0	102,918
Spelman College	GA	3	2,137	2,171	2,107	2,142	0	446	0	0	99,659
Kentucky State University[5]	KY	1	1,926	1,778	963	1,389	52	222	57	6	67,996
Simmons College of Kentucky	KY	3	216	210	202	178	16	10	0	0	3,273
Dillard University	LA	3	1,290	1,309	1,272	1,257	0	220	0	0	45,815
Grambling State University	LA	1	5,191	5,205	4,758	4,511	1	551	215	10	91,270
Southern University and A&M College[5]	LA	1	6,118	6,693	6,191	5,851	0	736	297	14	138,156
Southern University at New Orleans	LA	1	2,546	2,356	2,202	1,949	17	296	167	0	39,063
Southern University at Shreveport	LA	2	3,088	2,651	2,419	1,894	207	†	†	†	31,499
Xavier University of Louisiana	LA	3	3,044	3,231	2,408	3,139	0	299	32	165	115,404
Bowie State University	MD	1	6,148	6,320	5,278	5,441	0	781	245	8	121,201
Coppin State University	MD	1	2,893	2,738	2,211	2,219	0	399	74	6	89,373
Morgan State University	MD	1	7,747	7,712	6,141	7,168	0	1,153	268	54	244,280
University of Maryland, Eastern Shore[5]	MD	1	3,490	3,193	2,181	2,908	0	482	52	100	118,011
Alcorn State University[5]	MS	1	3,716	3,658	3,345	3,257	16	450	151	0	89,836
Coahoma Community College	MS	2	1,954	1,895	1,777	1,540	287	†	†	†	34,137
Hinds Community College, Utica Campus	MS	2	688	646	621	615	114	0	0	0	—
Jackson State University	MS	1	8,558	7,250	6,504	6,203	0	1,109	374	75	192,155
Mississippi Valley State University	MS	1	2,385	2,285	2,191	1,888	0	302	109	0	51,506
Rust College	MS	3	860	846	820	794	5	110	0	0	17,107
Tougaloo College	MS	3	809	736	719	716	0	130	7	0	24,780
Harris-Stowe State University	MO	1	1,442	1,716	1,488	1,526	0	176	0	0	35,290
Lincoln University[5]	MO	1	2,619	2,478	1,191	2,029	72	289	48	0	52,840
Bennett College	NC	3	493	534	488	491	0	72	0	0	15,621
Elizabeth City State University	NC	1	1,411	1,677	1,213	1,530	0	245	17	0	62,244
Fayetteville State University	NC	1	6,226	6,318	3,871	5,189	0	1,004	160	8	122,105
Johnson C. Smith University	NC	3	1,483	1,565	1,448	1,525	0	206	37	0	43,393
Livingstone College	NC	3	1,150	1,148	1,083	1,143	10	157	0	0	30,461
North Carolina A&T State University[5]	NC	1	11,877	12,142	9,724	11,111	0	1,662	423	57	288,219
North Carolina Central University	NC	1	8,097	8,207	6,248	7,204	0	1,026	467	134	208,311
Saint Augustine's College	NC	3	974	767	711	757	0	121	0	0	30,191
Shaw University	NC	3	1,660	1,411	1,054	1,349	0	179	28	0	42,219
Winston-Salem State University	NC	1	5,098	5,190	3,897	4,719	0	999	99	40	141,832
Central State University	OH	1	1,784	2,099	1,943	2,057	0	211	0	0	60,652
Wilberforce University	OH	3	627	672	662	612	0	66	7	0	15,479
Langston University[5]	OK	1	2,219	2,119	1,645	1,945	13	242	62	14	59,768
Cheyney University of Pennsylvania	PA	1	755	466	392	446	0	152	24	0	27,338
Lincoln University	PA	1	2,266	2,376	2,121	2,241	0	260	126	0	58,979

See notes at end of table.

Table 313.10. Fall enrollment, degrees conferred, and expenditures in degree-granting historically Black colleges and universities, by institution: 2017, 2018, and 2017–18—Continued

Institution	State	Level and control[1]	Total enrollment, fall 2018[2]	Enrollment, fall 2018		Full-time-equivalent enrollment, fall 2018	Degrees conferred, 2017–18				Total expenditures, 2017–18 (in thousands of current dollars)[4]
				Total	Black enrollment		Associate's	Bachelor's	Master's	Doctor's[3]	
1	2	3	4	5	6	7	8	9	10	11	12
Allen University	SC	3	590	743	724	709	0	59	0	0	15,485
Benedict College	SC	3	2,090	2,165	2,032	2,134	0	248	0	0	50,115
Claflin University	SC	3	2,129	2,172	2,022	2,101	0	310	32	0	51,419
Clinton College	SC	3	170	193	183	193	9	11	0	0	4,192
Denmark Technical College	SC	2	523	489	397	329	52	†	†	†	10,393
Morris College	SC	3	747	649	635	639	0	117	0	0	18,485
South Carolina State University[5]	SC	1	2,942	3,022	2,858	2,638	0	310	83	11	88,257
Voorhees College	SC	3	475	491	471	484	0	65	0	0	13,348
American Baptist College	TN	3	115	123	121	108	2	32	0	0	4,266
Fisk University	TN	3	701	780	690	762	0	132	9	0	28,687
Lane College	TN	3	1,420	1,232	1,207	1,203	0	171	0	0	24,731
Le Moyne-Owen College	TN	3	863	885	865	810	0	106	0	0	15,806
Meharry Medical College	TN	3	826	828	682	828	0	0	57	159	147,926
Tennessee State University[5]	TN	1	8,177	7,774	5,341	6,474	67	1,085	374	74	197,131
Huston-Tillotson University	TX	3	1,102	1,119	719	1,068	33	210	4	0	21,401
Jarvis Christian College	TX	3	909	964	791	939	11	77	0	0	18,224
Paul Quinn College	TX	3	519	550	438	532	0	41	0	0	11,410
Prairie View A&M University[5]	TX	1	9,219	9,516	7,932	8,844	0	1,104	393	13	245,322
Saint Philip's College	TX	2	12,050	11,590	1,103	4,925	1,242	†	†	†	80,787
Southwestern Christian College	TX	3	159	87	81	83	25	2	0	0	4,473
Texas College	TX	3	983	1,042	864	1,032	21	84	0	0	16,206
Texas Southern University	TX	1	10,237	9,732	7,624	8,689	0	974	360	312	212,216
Wiley College	TX	3	1,323	1,003	821	926	1	224	0	0	25,289
Hampton University	VA	3	4,618	4,321	4,043	4,156	3	594	150	91	183,386
Norfolk State University	VA	1	5,305	5,204	4,456	4,781	2	729	213	12	158,619
Virginia State University[5]	VA	1	4,713	4,385	3,123	4,193	0	731	126	13	145,558
Virginia Union University	VA	3	1,674	1,552	1,490	1,459	0	204	92	16	37,953
Virginia University of Lynchburg	VA	3	307	298	292	274	35	12	5	12	4,370
Bluefield State College	WV	1	1,379	1,275	95	1,102	113	226	0	0	21,039
West Virginia State University[5]	WV	1	3,879	3,692	314	2,498	0	370	32	0	46,809
University of the Virgin Islands[5]	VI	1	2,170	1,984	1,482	1,571	31	221	61	0	75,370

—Not available.

†Not applicable.

[1] 1 = 4-year public; 2 = 2-year public; 3 = 4-year private nonprofit; and 4 = 2-year private nonprofit.

[2] Total fall 2017 enrollment includes enrollment at Concordia College in Alabama. This institution closed in 2018 and therefore does not appear in this table.

[3] Includes Ph.D., Ed.D., and comparable degrees at the doctoral level, as well as such degrees as M.D., D.D.S., and law degrees that were classified as first-professional degrees prior to 2010–11.

[4] Includes private and some public institutions reporting total expenses and deductions under Financial Accounting Standards Board (FASB) reporting standards and public institutions reporting total expenses and deductions under Governmental Accounting Standards Board (GASB) 34/35 reporting standards.

[5] Land-grant institution.

NOTE: Degree-granting institutions grant associate's or higher degrees and participate in Title IV federal financial aid programs. Excludes historically Black colleges and universities that are not participating in Title IV programs. Historically Black colleges and universities are degree-granting institutions established prior to 1964 with the principal mission of educating Black Americans. Federal regulations, 20 U.S. Code, Section 1061 (2), allow for certain exceptions to the founding date. Totals include persons of other racial/ethnic groups not separately identified. Detail may not sum to totals because of rounding.

SOURCE: U.S. Department of Education, National Center for Education Statistics, Integrated Postsecondary Education Data System (IPEDS), Fall 2018, Completions component; Spring 2018 and Spring 2019, Fall Enrollment component; and Spring 2019, Finance component. (This table was prepared November 2019.)

Table 313.20. Fall enrollment in degree-granting historically Black colleges and universities, by sex of student and level and control of institution: Selected years, 1976 through 2018

Year	Total enrollment	Males	Females	4-year	2-year	Public Total	Public 4-year	Public 2-year	Private Total	Private 4-year	Private 2-year
1	2	3	4	5	6	7	8	9	10	11	12
						All students					
1976	222,613	104,669	117,944	206,676	15,937	156,836	143,528	13,308	65,777	63,148	2,629
1980	233,557	106,387	127,170	218,009	15,548	168,217	155,085	13,132	65,340	62,924	2,416
1982	228,371	104,897	123,474	212,017	16,354	165,871	151,472	14,399	62,500	60,545	1,955
1984	227,519	102,823	124,696	212,844	14,675	164,116	151,289	12,827	63,403	61,555	1,848
1986	223,275	97,523	125,752	207,231	16,044	162,048	147,631	14,417	61,227	59,600	1,627
1988	239,755	100,561	139,194	223,250	16,505	173,672	158,606	15,066	66,083	64,644	1,439
1990	257,152	105,157	151,995	240,497	16,655	187,046	171,969	15,077	70,106	68,528	1,578
1992	279,541	114,622	164,919	261,089	18,452	204,966	188,143	16,823	74,575	72,946	1,629
1993	282,856	116,397	166,459	262,430	20,426	208,197	189,032	19,165	74,659	73,398	1,261
1994	280,071	114,006	166,065	259,997	20,074	206,520	187,735	18,785	73,551	72,262	1,289
1995	278,725	112,637	166,088	259,409	19,316	204,726	186,278	18,448	73,999	73,131	868
1996	273,018	109,498	163,520	253,654	19,364	200,569	182,063	18,506	72,449	71,591	858
1997	269,167	106,865	162,302	248,860	20,307	194,674	175,297	19,377	74,493	73,563	930
1998	273,472	108,752	164,720	248,931	24,541	198,603	174,776	23,827	74,869	74,155	714
1999	274,321	108,301	166,020	249,156	25,165	199,826	175,364	24,462	74,495	73,792	703
2000	275,680	108,164	167,516	250,710	24,970	199,725	175,404	24,321	75,955	75,306	649
2001	289,985	112,874	177,111	260,547	29,438	210,083	181,346	28,737	79,902	79,201	701
2002	299,041	115,466	183,575	269,020	30,021	218,433	189,183	29,250	80,608	79,837	771
2003	306,727	117,795	188,932	274,326	32,401	228,096	196,077	32,019	78,631	78,249	382
2004	308,939	118,129	190,810	276,136	32,803	231,179	198,810	32,369	77,760	77,326	434
2005	311,768	120,023	191,745	272,666	39,102	235,875	197,200	38,675	75,893	75,466	427
2006	308,774	118,865	189,909	272,770	36,004	234,505	198,676	35,829	74,269	74,094	175
2007	306,742	118,672	188,070	270,554	36,188	234,034	197,939	36,095	72,708	72,615	93
2008	313,491	121,874	191,617	274,568	38,923	235,824	197,025	38,799	77,667	77,543	124
2009	322,860	125,728	197,132	280,133	42,727	246,595	204,016	42,579	76,265	76,117	148
2010	326,614	127,437	199,177	283,099	43,515	249,146	205,774	43,372	77,468	77,325	143
2011	323,648	126,160	197,488	281,150	42,498	246,685	204,363	42,322	76,963	76,787	176
2012	312,438	121,719	190,719	273,033	39,405	237,782	198,568	39,214	74,656	74,465	191
2013	303,191	119,299	183,892	264,454	38,737	230,325	191,918	38,407	72,866	72,536	330
2014	294,316	115,837	178,479	256,936	37,380	222,876	185,899	36,977	71,440	71,037	403
2015	293,304	115,818	177,486	256,295	37,009	221,276	184,503	36,773	72,028	71,792	236
2016	292,083	114,705	177,378	254,839	37,244	220,292	183,494	36,798	71,791	71,345	446
2017	298,134	115,316	182,818	260,646	37,488	225,181	188,214	36,967	72,953	72,432	521
2018	291,767	110,853	180,914	256,021	35,746	220,910	185,733	35,177	70,857	70,288	569
						Black students					
1976	190,305	84,492	105,813	179,848	10,457	129,770	121,851	7,919	60,535	57,997	2,538
1980	190,989	81,818	109,171	181,237	9,752	131,661	124,236	7,425	59,328	57,001	2,327
1982	182,639	78,874	103,765	171,942	10,697	126,368	117,562	8,806	56,271	54,380	1,891
1984	180,803	76,819	103,984	171,401	9,402	124,445	116,845	7,600	56,358	54,556	1,802
1986	178,628	74,276	104,352	167,971	10,657	123,555	114,502	9,053	55,073	53,469	1,604
1988	194,151	78,268	115,883	183,402	10,749	133,786	124,438	9,348	60,365	58,964	1,401
1990	208,682	82,897	125,785	198,237	10,445	144,204	134,924	9,280	64,478	63,313	1,165
1992	228,963	91,949	137,014	217,614	11,349	159,585	149,754	9,831	69,378	67,860	1,518
1993	231,198	93,110	138,088	219,431	11,767	161,444	150,867	10,577	69,754	68,564	1,190
1994	230,162	91,908	138,254	218,565	11,597	161,098	150,682	10,416	69,064	67,883	1,181
1995	229,418	91,132	138,286	218,379	11,039	159,925	149,661	10,264	69,493	68,718	775
1996	224,201	88,306	135,895	213,309	10,892	156,851	146,753	10,098	67,350	66,556	794
1997	222,331	86,641	135,690	210,741	11,590	153,039	142,326	10,713	69,292	68,415	877
1998	223,745	87,163	136,582	211,822	11,923	154,244	142,985	11,259	69,501	68,837	664
1999	226,592	87,987	138,605	213,779	12,813	156,292	144,166	12,126	70,300	69,613	687
2000	227,239	87,319	139,920	215,172	12,067	156,706	145,277	11,429	70,533	69,895	638
2001	238,638	90,718	147,920	224,417	14,221	164,354	150,831	13,523	74,284	73,586	698
2002	247,292	93,538	153,754	231,834	15,458	172,203	157,507	14,696	75,089	74,327	762
2003	253,257	95,703	157,554	236,753	16,504	180,104	163,977	16,127	73,153	72,776	377
2004	257,545	96,750	160,795	241,030	16,515	184,708	168,619	16,089	72,837	72,411	426
2005	256,584	96,891	159,693	238,030	18,554	186,047	167,916	18,131	70,537	70,114	423
2006	255,144	96,507	158,637	238,440	16,704	185,894	169,365	16,529	69,250	69,075	175
2007	253,241	96,214	157,027	236,571	16,670	185,170	168,592	16,578	68,071	67,979	92
2008	258,402	98,633	159,769	240,132	18,270	186,446	168,299	18,147	71,956	71,833	123
2009	264,092	100,590	163,502	243,956	20,136	194,088	174,099	19,989	70,004	69,857	147
2010	265,908	101,605	164,303	245,158	20,750	193,840	173,233	20,607	72,068	71,925	143
2011	263,435	100,526	162,909	242,881	20,554	192,042	171,664	20,378	71,393	71,217	176
2012	251,527	96,079	155,448	232,897	18,630	183,018	164,578	18,440	68,509	68,319	190
2013	241,485	92,491	148,994	223,491	17,994	175,308	157,640	17,668	66,177	65,851	326
2014	231,889	88,469	143,420	214,631	17,258	167,246	150,383	16,863	64,643	64,248	395
2015	228,062	86,857	141,205	211,698	16,364	163,508	147,376	16,132	64,554	64,322	232
2016	223,512	84,153	139,359	207,379	16,133	160,053	144,176	15,877	63,459	63,203	256
2017	226,847	83,917	142,930	210,664	16,183	162,703	146,804	15,899	64,144	63,860	284
2018	223,163	81,055	142,108	207,858	15,305	160,871	145,889	14,982	62,292	61,969	323

NOTE: Historically Black colleges and universities are degree-granting institutions established prior to 1964 with the principal mission of educating Black Americans. Federal regulations, 20 U.S. Code, Section 1061 (2), allow for certain exceptions to the founding date. Data through 1995 are for institutions of higher education, while later data are for degree-granting institutions. Degree-granting institutions grant associate's or higher degrees and participate in Title IV federal financial aid programs. The degree-granting classification is very similar to the earlier higher education classification, but it includes more 2-year colleges and excludes a few higher education institutions that did not grant degrees. Some data have been revised from previously published figures.

SOURCE: U.S. Department of Education, National Center for Education Statistics, Higher Education General Information Survey (HEGIS), "Fall Enrollment in Colleges and Universities," 1976 through 1985 surveys; Integrated Postsecondary Education Data System (IPEDS), "Fall Enrollment Survey" (IPEDS-EF:86–99); and IPEDS Spring 2001 through Spring 2019, Fall Enrollment component. (This table was prepared November 2019.)

Table 313.30. Selected statistics on degree-granting historically Black colleges and universities, by control and level of institution: Selected years, 1990 through 2018

Selected statistics	Total	Public			Private		
		Total	4-year	2-year	Total	4-year	2-year
1	2	3	4	5	6	7	8
Number of institutions, fall 2017	**101**	**51**	**40**	**11**	**50**	**49**	**1**
Fall enrollment							
Total enrollment, fall 1990	257,152	187,046	171,969	15,077	70,106	68,528	1,578
Males	105,157	76,541	70,220	6,321	28,616	28,054	562
Males, Black	82,897	57,255	54,041	3,214	25,642	25,198	444
Females	151,995	110,505	101,749	8,756	41,490	40,474	1,016
Females, Black	125,785	86,949	80,883	6,066	38,836	38,115	721
Total enrollment, fall 2000	275,680	199,725	175,404	24,321	75,955	75,306	649
Males	108,164	78,186	68,322	9,864	29,978	29,771	207
Males, Black	87,319	60,029	56,017	4,012	27,290	27,085	205
Females	167,516	121,539	107,082	14,457	45,977	45,535	442
Females, Black	139,920	96,677	89,260	7,417	43,243	42,810	433
Total enrollment, fall 2010	326,614	249,146	205,774	43,372	77,468	77,325	143
Males	127,437	95,883	78,528	17,355	31,554	31,482	72
Males, Black	101,605	72,629	65,512	7,117	28,976	28,904	72
Females	199,177	153,263	127,246	26,017	45,914	45,843	71
Females, Black	164,303	121,211	107,721	13,490	43,092	43,021	71
Total enrollment, fall 2018	291,767	220,910	185,733	35,177	70,857	70,288	569
Males	110,853	83,015	68,415	14,600	27,838	27,530	308
Males, Black	81,055	57,283	51,863	5,420	23,772	23,634	138
Females	180,914	137,895	117,318	20,577	43,019	42,758	261
Females, Black	142,108	103,588	94,026	9,562	38,520	38,335	185
Full-time enrollment, fall 2018	227,415	163,126	149,356	13,770	64,289	63,958	331
Males	87,026	62,050	55,954	6,096	24,976	24,806	170
Females	140,389	101,076	93,402	7,674	39,313	39,152	161
Part-time enrollment, fall 2018	64,352	57,784	36,377	21,407	6,568	6,330	238
Males	23,827	20,965	12,461	8,504	2,862	2,724	138
Females	40,525	36,819	23,916	12,903	3,706	3,606	100
Degrees conferred, 2017–18							
Associate's	5,465	5,206	1,294	3,912	259	229	30
Males	1,909	1,794	320	1,474	115	106	9
Males, Black	716	619	135	484	97	88	9
Females	3,556	3,412	974	2,438	144	123	21
Females, Black	1,658	1,523	456	1,067	135	114	21
Bachelor's	32,639	23,603	23,603	†	9,036	9,036	†
Males	11,952	8,715	8,715	†	3,237	3,237	†
Males, Black	9,083	6,292	6,292	†	2,791	2,791	†
Females	20,687	14,888	14,888	†	5,799	5,799	†
Females, Black	17,193	11,924	11,924	†	5,269	5,269	†
Master's	7,697	6,424	6,424	†	1,273	1,273	†
Males	2,449	2,011	2,011	†	438	438	†
Males, Black	1,591	1,261	1,261	†	330	330	†
Females	5,248	4,413	4,413	†	835	835	†
Females, Black	3,836	3,153	3,153	†	683	683	†
Doctor's[1]	2,518	1,363	1,363	†	1,155	1,155	†
Males	975	538	538	†	437	437	†
Males, Black	519	256	256	†	263	263	†
Females	1,543	825	825	†	718	718	†
Females, Black	1,036	535	535	†	501	501	†
Financial statistics, 2017–18[2]	In thousands of current dollars						
Total revenue	$8,673,522	$5,408,362	$5,039,982	$368,380	$3,265,159	$3,258,836	$6,323
Student tuition and fees	1,939,022	1,008,241	966,772	41,469	930,781	926,978	3,803
Federal government[3]	2,007,472	1,290,761	1,162,948	127,813	716,711	715,530	1,180
State governments	1,989,311	1,892,318	1,763,450	128,868	96,993	96,993	0
Local governments	115,050	79,745	35,774	43,971	35,305	34,848	457
Private gifts and grants[4]	478,947	203,192	190,642	12,550	275,755	275,427	328
Investment return (gain or loss)	455,325	62,397	61,683	714	392,928	392,928	0
Auxiliary (essentially self-supporting) enterprises	977,002	613,770	607,247	6,523	363,232	362,678	554
Hospitals and other sources	711,392	257,938	251,467	6,472	453,454	453,454	0
Total expenditures	7,966,186	5,181,127	4,815,735	365,392	2,785,059	2,779,649	5,409
Instruction	2,301,598	1,589,122	1,442,240	146,882	712,476	710,741	1,735
Research	487,564	326,112	326,112	0	161,452	161,452	0
Academic support	662,825	462,427	431,000	31,427	200,398	199,976	423
Institutional support	1,416,307	757,939	693,358	64,581	658,369	656,278	2,090
Auxiliary (essentially self-supporting) enterprises	1,121,950	802,029	795,308	6,721	319,921	318,958	963
Other expenditures	1,975,941	1,243,498	1,127,717	115,781	732,443	732,245	198

†Not applicable.
[1]Includes Ph.D., Ed.D., and comparable degrees at the doctoral level, as well as such degrees as M.D., D.D.S., and law degrees that were classified as first-professional degrees prior to 2010–11.
[2]Totals (column 2) of public and private institutions together are approximate because reporting is based on two different survey forms with different accounting concepts. Included are data reported by public institutions using the Governmental Accounting Standards Board (GASB) form as well as data reported by private and some public institutions using the Financial Accounting Standards Board (FASB) form.
[3]Includes independent operations.
[4]Includes contributions from affiliated entities.
NOTE: Degree-granting institutions grant associate's or higher degrees and participate in Title IV federal financial aid programs. Historically Black colleges and universities are degree-granting institutions established prior to 1964 with the principal mission of educating Black Americans. Federal regulations, 20 U.S. Code, Section 1061 (2), allow for certain exceptions to the founding date. Federal, state, and local governments revenue includes appropriations, grants, and contracts. Totals include persons of other racial/ethnic groups not separately identified. Detail may not sum to totals because of rounding. SOURCE: U.S. Department of Education, National Center for Education Statistics, Integrated Postsecondary Education Data System (IPEDS), "Fall Enrollment Survey" (IPEDS-EF:90); IPEDS Spring 2001, Spring 2011, and Spring 2019, Fall Enrollment component; IPEDS Spring 2019, Finance component; and IPEDS Fall 2018, Finance component; and IPEDS Fall 2018, Completions component. (This table was prepared November 2019.)

Table 314.10. Total and full-time-equivalent (FTE) staff and FTE student/FTE staff ratios in postsecondary institutions participating in Title IV aid programs, by degree-granting status, control of institution, and primary occupation: Fall 1999, fall 2009, and fall 2018

Degree-granting status, control of institution, and primary occupation	Fall 1999				Fall 2009				Fall 2018			
	Total		Full-time-equivalent (FTE)		Total		Full-time-equivalent (FTE)		Total		Full-time-equivalent (FTE)	
	Number	Percent	Total	FTE students per FTE staff	Number	Percent	Total	FTE students per FTE staff	Number	Percent	Total	FTE students per FTE staff
1	2	3	4	5	6	7	8	9	10	11	12	13
All Title IV institutions[1]												
	2,964,535	100.0	2,299,290	4.9	3,795,744	100.0	2,885,823	5.5	3,983,860	100.0	3,054,431	4.9
Faculty (instruction/research/ public service)	1,072,202	36.2	765,284	14.8	1,476,716	38.9	992,148	16.0	1,573,995	39.5	1,090,567	13.8
Graduate assistants	242,525	8.2	80,842	139.8	343,204	9.0	114,401	138.6	382,715	9.6	127,572	118.3
Other staff	1,649,808	55.7	1,453,164	7.8	1,975,824	52.1	1,779,273	8.9	2,027,150	50.9	1,836,293	8.2
Degree-granting institutions[2] **Total**	2,902,479	100.0	2,252,050	4.9	3,724,661	100.0	2,829,757	5.4	3,923,374	100.0	3,007,701	4.9
Faculty (instruction/research/ public service)	1,037,529	35.7	741,426	14.8	1,439,074	38.6	965,793	15.9	1,542,613	39.3	1,068,950	13.8
Graduate assistants	240,995	8.3	80,332	136.6	343,204	9.2	114,401	134.4	382,715	9.8	127,572	115.9
Other staff	1,623,955	56.0	1,430,292	7.7	1,942,383	52.1	1,749,563	8.8	1,998,046	50.9	1,811,179	8.2
Public	1,999,704	100.0	1,524,881	5.3	2,442,693	100.0	1,832,312	5.9	2,586,155	100.0	1,962,958	5.4
Faculty (instruction/research/ public service)	718,585	35.9	511,400	15.8	913,788	37.4	623,675	17.2	980,835	37.9	688,784	15.3
Graduate assistants	201,611	10.1	67,204	119.9	275,878	11.3	91,959	116.9	299,271	11.6	99,757	105.5
Other staff	1,079,508	54.0	946,277	8.5	1,253,027	51.3	1,116,678	9.6	1,306,049	50.5	1,174,418	9.0
Private nonprofit	847,615	100.0	688,914	3.7	1,074,042	100.0	856,067	3.7	1,221,378	100.0	969,106	3.6
Faculty (instruction/research/ public service)	288,663	34.1	213,130	11.9	408,382	38.0	287,116	11.1	491,014	40.2	346,152	10.2
Graduate assistants	37,421	4.4	12,474	203.8	67,057	6.2	22,352	142.3	83,077	6.8	27,692	127.0
Other staff	521,531	61.5	463,310	5.5	598,603	55.7	546,599	5.8	647,287	53.0	595,262	5.9
Private for-profit	55,160	100.0	38,255	9.8	207,926	100.0	141,378	10.3	115,841	100.0	75,636	9.9
Faculty (instruction/research/ public service)	30,281	54.9	16,896	22.1	116,904	56.2	55,002	26.4	70,764	61.1	34,015	22.0
Graduate assistants	1,963	3.6	654	570.3	269	0.1	90	16,188.6	367	0.3	122	6,104.7
Other staff	22,916	41.5	20,705	18.0	90,753	43.6	86,286	16.8	44,710	38.6	41,499	18.0
Non-degree-granting institutions[3] **Total**	62,056	100.0	47,239	6.9	71,083	100.0	56,066	8.5	60,486	100.0	46,731	6.4
Faculty (instruction/research/ public service)	34,673	55.9	23,858	13.7	37,642	53.0	26,355	18.1	31,382	51.9	21,617	13.9
Graduate assistants	1,530	2.5	510	641.0	0	0.0	0	†	0	0.0	0	†
Other staff	25,853	41.7	22,872	14.3	33,441	47.0	29,710	16.1	29,104	48.1	25,114	12.0
Public	29,220	100.0	21,583	5.8	21,599	100.0	15,728	6.0	22,262	100.0	16,182	4.6
Faculty (instruction/research/ public service)	18,085	61.9	12,040	10.4	13,266	61.4	8,510	11.0	11,815	53.1	7,473	10.0
Graduate assistants	487	1.7	162	774.0	0	0.0	0	†	0	0.0	0	†
Other staff	10,648	36.4	9,380	13.4	8,333	38.6	7,218	13.0	10,447	46.9	8,709	8.6
Private nonprofit	4,712	100.0	3,677	6.4	5,087	100.0	4,141	5.7	3,052	100.0	2,419	5.2
Faculty (instruction/research/ public service)	2,365	50.2	1,674	14.0	2,442	48.0	1,834	12.8	1,473	48.3	1,085	11.6
Graduate assistants	78	1.7	26	902.1	0	0.0	0	†	0	0.0	0	†
Other staff	2,269	48.2	1,976	11.9	2,645	52.0	2,307	10.2	1,579	51.7	1,334	9.4
Private for-profit	28,124	100.0	21,980	8.1	44,397	100.0	36,197	9.9	35,172	100.0	28,129	7.6
Faculty (instruction/research/ public service)	14,223	50.6	10,143	17.5	21,934	49.4	16,011	22.5	18,094	51.4	13,059	16.3
Graduate assistants	965	3.4	322	552.8	0	0.0	0	†	0	0.0	0	†
Other staff	12,936	46.0	11,515	15.4	22,463	50.6	20,186	17.8	17,078	48.6	15,071	14.2

†Not applicable.
[1]Includes degree-granting and non-degree-granting institutions.
[2]Degree-granting institutions grant associate's or higher degrees and participate in Title IV federal financial aid programs.
[3]Data are for institutions that did not offer accredited 4-year or 2-year degree programs, but were participating in Title IV federal financial aid programs. Includes some institutions transitioning to higher level program offerings, though still classified at a lower level.
NOTE: Full-time-equivalent staff is the full-time staff, plus the full-time equivalent of the part-time staff. Data for 2009 and 2018 include institutions with fewer than 15 full-time employees; these institutions did not report staff data prior to 2007. By definition, all graduate assistants are part time. Detail may not sum to totals because of rounding.
SOURCE: U.S. Department of Education, National Center for Education Statistics, Integrated Postsecondary Education Data System (IPEDS), "Fall Enrollment Survey" (IPEDS-EF:99) and "Fall Staff Survey" (IPEDS-S:99); IPEDS Spring 2010 and Spring 2019, Fall Enrollment component; IPEDS Winter 2009–10, Human Resources Component, Fall Staff Section; and IPEDS Spring 2019, Human Resources component, Fall Staff section. (This table was prepared November 2019.)

Table 314.20. Employees in degree-granting postsecondary institutions, by sex, employment status, control and level of institution, and primary occupation: Selected years, fall 1991 through fall 2018

Sex, employment status, control and level of institution, and primary occupation	1991	1995	1999	2001	2003	2005	2007	2009	2011	2013	2015	2016	2017	2018	Percent change, 2007 to 2018
1	2	3	4	5	6	7	8	9	10	11	12	13	14	15	16
All institutions	2,545,235	2,662,075	2,902,479	3,083,353	3,187,907	3,379,087	3,561,730	3,724,661	3,841,819	3,896,053	3,914,284	3,906,240	3,916,658	3,923,374	10.2
Executive/administrative/managerial	144,755	147,445	160,793	152,038	184,913	196,324	217,039	230,438	238,677	(¹)	(¹)	(¹)	(¹)	(¹)	†
Faculty (instruction/research/public service)	826,252	931,706	1,037,529	1,113,183	1,173,593	1,290,426	1,371,587	1,439,074	1,524,469	1,545,381	1,552,256	1,546,081	1,545,653	1,542,613	12.5
Graduate assistants	197,751	215,909	240,995	261,136	292,061	317,141	329,001	343,204	355,916	363,416	366,868	375,204	377,049	382,715	16.3
Other	1,376,477	1,367,015	1,463,162	1,556,996	1,537,340	1,575,196	1,644,103	1,711,945	1,722,757	1,987,256	1,995,160	1,984,955	1,993,956	1,998,046	†
Males	1,227,591	1,274,676	1,375,114	1,451,773	1,496,867	1,581,498	1,650,641	1,710,021	1,754,919	1,772,803	1,776,928	1,775,229	1,774,403	1,767,361	7.1
Executive/administrative/managerial	85,423	82,127	84,425	79,348	91,604	95,223	102,066	106,842	109,336	(¹)	(¹)	(¹)	(¹)	(¹)	†
Faculty (instruction/research/public service)	525,599	562,893	608,007	644,514	663,723	714,453	744,047	761,002	789,567	791,971	789,405	783,495	778,873	771,594	3.7
Graduate assistants	119,125	123,962	133,066	142,120	156,881	167,529	173,128	181,328	188,305	191,501	193,202	196,170	196,014	196,792	13.7
Other	497,444	505,694	549,616	585,791	584,659	604,293	631,400	660,849	667,711	789,331	794,321	795,564	799,516	798,975	†
Females	1,317,644	1,387,399	1,527,365	1,631,580	1,691,040	1,797,589	1,911,089	2,014,640	2,086,900	2,123,250	2,137,356	2,131,011	2,142,255	2,156,013	12.8
Executive/administrative/managerial	59,332	65,318	76,368	72,690	93,309	101,101	114,973	123,596	129,341	(¹)	(¹)	(¹)	(¹)	(¹)	†
Faculty (instruction/research/public service)	300,653	368,813	429,522	468,669	509,870	575,973	627,540	678,072	734,902	753,410	762,851	762,586	766,780	771,019	22.9
Graduate assistants	78,626	91,947	107,929	119,016	135,180	149,612	155,873	161,876	167,611	171,915	173,666	179,034	181,035	185,923	19.3
Other	879,033	861,321	913,546	971,205	952,681	970,903	1,012,703	1,051,096	1,055,046	1,197,925	1,200,839	1,189,391	1,194,440	1,199,071	†
Full-time	1,812,912	1,801,371	1,926,836	2,043,208	2,083,142	2,179,864	2,281,516	2,382,305	2,435,988	2,472,434	2,507,787	2,506,784	2,531,496	2,549,864	11.8
Executive/administrative/managerial	139,116	140,990	154,584	146,523	178,691	190,078	209,812	222,143	231,559	(¹)	(¹)	(¹)	(¹)	(¹)	†
Faculty (instruction/research/public service)	535,623	550,822	593,375	617,868	630,092	675,624	703,757	729,152	762,114	791,378	807,109	813,978	822,513	832,119	18.2
Other	1,138,173	1,109,559	1,178,877	1,278,817	1,274,359	1,314,162	1,367,947	1,431,010	1,442,315	1,681,056	1,700,678	1,692,806	1,708,983	1,717,745	†
Part-time	732,323	860,704	975,643	1,040,145	1,104,765	1,199,223	1,280,214	1,342,356	1,405,831	1,423,619	1,406,497	1,399,456	1,385,162	1,373,510	7.3
Executive/administrative/managerial	5,639	6,455	6,209	5,515	6,222	6,246	7,227	8,295	7,118	(¹)	(¹)	(¹)	(¹)	(¹)	†
Faculty (instruction/research/public service)	290,629	380,884	444,154	495,315	543,501	614,802	667,830	709,922	762,355	754,003	745,147	732,103	723,140	710,494	6.4
Graduate assistants	197,751	215,909	240,995	261,136	292,061	317,141	329,001	343,204	355,916	363,416	366,868	375,204	377,049	382,715	16.3
Other	238,304	257,456	284,285	278,179	262,981	261,034	276,156	280,935	280,442	306,200	294,482	292,149	284,973	280,301	†
Public 4-year	1,341,914	1,383,476	1,474,830	1,558,576	1,569,870	1,656,709	1,742,370	1,804,332	1,843,314	1,884,854	1,925,674	1,966,008	1,989,365	2,019,697	15.9
Executive/administrative/managerial	63,674	60,590	64,479	60,245	70,397	74,241	81,162	84,214	84,918	(¹)	(¹)	(¹)	(¹)	(¹)	†
Faculty (instruction/research/public service)	358,376	384,399	418,500	438,459	450,123	486,691	518,930	539,946	575,024	601,126	622,283	646,584	656,145	670,734	29.3
Graduate assistants	144,344	178,342	196,802	218,260	239,600	257,578	266,451	275,878	285,905	287,839	291,770	293,954	295,389	299,254	12.3
Other	775,520	760,145	795,049	841,612	809,750	838,199	875,827	904,294	896,867	995,889	1,011,621	1,025,470	1,037,831	1,049,709	†
Private 4-year	734,509	770,004	865,434	912,924	988,895	1,073,764	1,158,196	1,230,409	1,297,376	1,318,760	1,323,899	1,308,587	1,313,901	1,306,916	12.8
Executive/administrative/managerial	57,148	62,314	70,082	65,739	84,306	90,415	102,906	111,616	118,220	(¹)	(¹)	(¹)	(¹)	(¹)	†
Faculty (instruction/research/public service)	232,893	262,660	300,756	325,713	364,166	430,305	473,455	498,403	540,018	550,512	558,262	550,073	552,998	545,790	15.3
Graduate assistants	23,989	33,853	38,757	41,611	52,101	59,147	62,550	67,326	70,011	75,537	75,079	81,241	81,638	83,433	33.4
Other	420,479	411,177	455,839	479,861	488,322	493,897	519,285	553,064	569,127	692,711	690,558	677,273	679,265	677,693	†
Public 2-year	441,414	482,454	524,874	578,394	593,466	610,978	619,455	638,361	642,455	642,430	622,754	591,066	577,387	566,458	-8.6
Executive/administrative/managerial	20,772	21,806	21,699	22,566	25,872	26,770	27,363	27,827	27,562	(¹)	(¹)	(¹)	(¹)	(¹)	†
Faculty (instruction/research/public service)	222,532	272,434	300,085	332,665	341,643	354,497	357,596	373,842	378,535	367,608	348,708	327,655	316,544	310,101	-13.3
Graduate assistants	29,216	3,401	4,809	1,215	323	374	0	0	0	13	13	9	15	17	†
Other	168,894	184,813	198,281	221,948	225,628	229,337	234,496	236,692	236,358	274,809	274,033	263,402	260,828	256,340	†
Private 2-year	27,398	26,141	37,341	33,459	35,676	37,636	41,709	51,559	58,674	50,009	41,957	40,579	36,005	30,303	-27.3
Executive/administrative/managerial	3,161	2,735	4,533	3,488	4,338	4,898	5,608	6,781	7,977	(¹)	(¹)	(¹)	(¹)	(¹)	†
Faculty (instruction/research/public service)	12,451	12,213	18,188	16,346	17,661	18,933	21,606	26,883	30,292	26,135	23,003	21,769	19,966	15,988	-26.0
Graduate assistants	202	313	627	50	37	42	0	0	0	27	6	11	11	†	
Other	11,584	10,880	13,993	13,575	13,640	13,763	14,495	17,895	20,405	23,847	18,948	18,810	16,032	14,304	†

†Not applicable.
¹Included in other. Primary occupations were reclassified as of fall 2013; only the faculty and graduate assistant categories are comparable with data from earlier years.
NOTE: Data through 1995 are for institutions of higher education, while later data are for degree-granting institutions. Degree-granting institutions grant associate's or higher degrees and participate in Title IV federal financial aid programs. The degree-granting classification is very similar to the earlier higher education classification, but it includes more 2-year colleges and excludes a few higher education institutions that did not grant degrees. Beginning in 2007, includes institutions with fewer than 15 full-time employees; these institutions did not report staff data prior to 2007. By definition, all graduate assistants are part time. Some data have been revised from previously published figures.
SOURCE: U.S. Department of Education, National Center for Education Statistics, Integrated Postsecondary Education Data System (IPEDS), "Fall Staff Survey" (IPEDS-S:91–99); IPEDS Winter 2001–02 through Winter 2011–12, Human Resources component, Fall Staff section; and IPEDS Spring 2014 through Spring 2019, Human Resources component, Fall Staff section. (This table was prepared November 2019.)

Table 314.30. Employees in degree-granting postsecondary institutions, by employment status, sex, control and level of institution, and primary occupation: Fall 2018

Control and level of institution and primary occupation	Full-time and part-time					Full-time				Part-time		
	Total		Males	Females		Total		Males	Females	Total	Males	Females
	Number	Percentage distribution		Number	Percent of all employees	Number	Percent of all employees					
1	2	3	4	5	6	7	8	9	10	11	12	13
All institutions	**3,923,374**	**100.0**	**1,767,361**	**2,156,013**	**55.0**	**2,549,864**	**65.0**	**1,134,999**	**1,414,865**	**1,373,510**	**632,362**	**741,148**
Faculty (instruction/research/public service)	1,542,613	39.3	771,594	771,019	50.0	832,119	53.9	443,589	388,530	710,494	328,005	382,489
Instruction	1,422,754	36.3	705,729	717,025	50.4	731,543	51.4	387,144	344,399	691,211	318,585	372,626
Research	90,489	2.3	51,730	38,759	42.8	78,656	86.9	45,574	33,082	11,833	6,156	5,677
Public service	29,370	0.7	14,135	15,235	51.9	21,920	74.6	10,871	11,049	7,450	3,264	4,186
Graduate assistants	382,715	9.8	196,792	185,923	48.6	†	†	†	†	382,715	196,792	185,923
Librarians, curators, and archivists	41,495	1.1	12,354	29,141	70.2	34,892	84.1	10,558	24,334	6,603	1,796	4,807
Student and academic affairs and other education services	182,831	4.7	58,059	124,772	68.2	125,264	68.5	36,404	88,860	57,567	21,655	35,912
Management	262,919	6.7	113,505	149,414	56.8	255,881	97.3	110,690	145,191	7,038	2,815	4,223
Business and financial operations	219,793	5.6	59,552	160,241	72.9	206,333	93.9	55,957	150,376	13,460	3,595	9,865
Computer, engineering, and science	238,073	6.1	143,457	94,616	39.7	219,241	92.1	134,978	84,263	18,832	8,479	10,353
Community, social service, legal, arts, design, entertainment, sports, and media	185,765	4.7	83,114	102,651	55.3	151,033	81.3	66,137	84,896	34,732	16,977	17,755
Healthcare practitioners and technicians	111,076	2.8	32,561	78,515	70.7	93,426	84.1	28,029	65,397	17,650	4,532	13,118
Service occupations	242,151	6.2	139,252	102,899	42.5	202,902	83.8	117,976	84,926	39,249	21,276	17,973
Sales and related occupations	12,534	0.3	4,375	8,159	65.1	10,142	80.9	3,677	6,465	2,392	698	1,694
Office and administrative support	409,591	10.4	70,126	339,465	82.9	334,256	81.6	49,814	284,442	75,335	20,312	55,023
Natural resources, construction, and maintenance	73,098	1.9	67,276	5,822	8.0	69,197	94.7	64,483	4,714	3,901	2,793	1,108
Production, transportation, and material moving	18,720	0.5	15,344	3,376	18.0	15,178	81.1	12,707	2,471	3,542	2,637	905
Public 4-year	**2,019,697**	**100.0**	**928,516**	**1,091,181**	**54.0**	**1,375,487**	**68.1**	**626,530**	**748,957**	**644,210**	**301,986**	**342,224**
Faculty (instruction/research/public service)	670,734	33.2	348,778	321,956	48.0	441,689	65.9	242,451	199,238	229,045	106,327	122,718
Instruction	598,731	29.6	309,476	289,255	48.3	381,191	63.7	209,002	172,189	217,540	100,474	117,066
Research	55,798	2.8	31,528	24,270	43.5	46,746	83.8	26,833	19,913	9,052	4,695	4,357
Public service	16,205	0.8	7,774	8,431	52.0	13,752	84.9	6,616	7,136	2,453	1,158	1,295
Graduate assistants	299,254	14.8	153,396	145,858	48.7	†	†	†	†	299,254	153,396	145,858
Librarians, curators, and archivists	18,673	0.9	5,773	12,900	69.1	16,756	89.7	5,200	11,556	1,917	573	1,344
Student and academic affairs and other education services	73,163	3.6	22,574	50,589	69.1	56,281	76.9	16,405	39,876	16,882	6,169	10,713
Management	120,750	6.0	53,726	67,024	55.5	117,237	97.1	52,303	64,934	3,513	1,423	2,090
Business and financial operations	131,507	6.5	35,761	95,746	72.8	122,648	93.3	33,304	89,344	8,859	2,457	6,402
Computer, engineering, and science	146,914	7.3	88,391	58,523	39.8	135,210	92.0	83,465	51,745	11,704	4,926	6,778
Community, social service, legal, arts, design, entertainment, sports, and media	89,703	4.4	37,834	51,869	57.8	77,786	86.7	32,739	45,047	11,917	5,095	6,822
Healthcare practitioners and technicians	73,591	3.6	21,995	51,596	70.1	63,836	86.7	19,898	43,938	9,755	2,097	7,658
Service occupations	129,155	6.4	70,221	58,934	45.6	112,711	87.3	62,103	50,608	16,444	8,118	8,326
Sales and related occupations	3,080	0.2	1,158	1,922	62.4	2,197	71.3	893	1,304	883	265	618
Office and administrative support	202,560	10.0	34,127	168,433	83.2	172,393	85.1	25,819	146,574	30,167	8,308	21,859
Natural resources, construction, and maintenance	48,166	2.4	44,459	3,707	7.7	45,935	95.4	42,823	3,112	2,231	1,636	595
Production, transportation, and material moving	12,447	0.6	10,323	2,124	17.1	10,808	86.8	9,127	1,681	1,639	1,196	443
Public 2-year	**566,458**	**100.0**	**239,775**	**326,683**	**57.7**	**275,873**	**48.7**	**111,582**	**164,291**	**290,585**	**128,193**	**162,392**
Faculty (instruction/research/public service)	310,101	54.7	140,989	169,112	54.5	101,069	32.6	45,209	55,860	209,032	95,780	113,252
Instruction	306,576	54.1	139,675	166,901	54.4	100,515	32.8	45,018	55,497	206,061	94,657	111,404
Research	111	#	37	74	66.7	97	87.4	32	65	14	5	9
Public service	3,414	0.6	1,277	2,137	62.6	457	13.4	159	298	2,957	1,118	1,839
Graduate assistants	17	#	14	3	17.6	†	†	†	†	17	14	3
Librarians, curators, and archivists	5,493	1.0	1,266	4,227	77.0	3,499	63.7	823	2,676	1,994	443	1,551
Student and academic affairs and other education services	49,475	8.7	17,295	32,180	65.0	21,736	43.9	6,351	15,385	27,739	10,944	16,795
Management	31,923	5.6	13,009	18,914	59.2	30,855	96.7	12,580	18,275	1,068	429	639
Business and financial operations	16,290	2.9	4,182	12,108	74.3	14,591	89.6	3,693	10,898	1,699	489	1,210
Computer, engineering, and science	15,604	2.8	10,477	5,127	32.9	13,199	84.6	9,019	4,180	2,405	1,458	947
Community, social service, legal, arts, design, entertainment, sports, and media	23,427	4.1	8,902	14,525	62.0	16,016	68.4	5,671	10,345	7,411	3,231	4,180
Healthcare practitioners and technicians	1,525	0.3	530	995	65.2	714	46.8	293	421	811	237	574
Service occupations	32,546	5.7	22,514	10,032	30.8	22,836	70.2	16,381	6,455	9,710	6,133	3,577
Sales and related occupations	1,668	0.3	446	1,222	73.3	955	57.3	260	695	713	186	527
Office and administrative support	71,332	12.6	13,862	57,470	80.6	44,565	62.5	5,905	38,660	26,767	7,957	18,810
Natural resources, construction, and maintenance	5,774	1.0	5,285	489	8.5	5,113	88.6	4,807	306	661	478	183
Production, transportation, and material moving	1,283	0.2	1,004	279	21.7	725	56.5	590	135	558	414	144
Private nonprofit 4-year	**1,213,723**	**100.0**	**550,090**	**663,633**	**54.7**	**837,644**	**69.0**	**373,602**	**464,042**	**376,079**	**176,488**	**199,591**
Faculty (instruction/research/public service)	487,473	40.2	250,732	236,741	48.6	272,084	55.8	148,331	123,753	215,389	102,401	112,988
Instruction	443,271	36.5	225,541	217,730	49.1	232,640	52.5	125,558	107,082	210,631	99,983	110,648
Research	34,518	2.8	20,138	14,380	41.7	31,761	92.0	18,687	13,074	2,757	1,451	1,306
Public service	9,684	0.8	5,053	4,631	47.8	7,683	79.3	4,086	3,597	2,001	967	1,034
Graduate assistants	83,066	6.8	43,245	39,821	47.9	†	†	†	†	83,066	43,245	39,821
Librarians, curators, and archivists	16,369	1.3	5,088	11,281	68.9	14,021	85.7	4,397	9,624	2,348	691	1,657
Student and academic affairs and other education services	48,961	4.0	14,844	34,117	69.7	37,145	75.9	10,775	26,370	11,816	4,069	7,747
Management	100,279	8.3	42,628	57,651	57.5	98,030	97.8	41,738	56,292	2,249	890	1,359
Business and financial operations	67,656	5.6	18,363	49,293	72.9	64,955	96.0	17,754	47,201	2,701	609	2,092
Computer, engineering, and science	73,558	6.1	43,061	30,497	41.5	68,937	93.7	41,044	27,893	4,621	2,017	2,604
Community, social service, legal, arts, design, entertainment, sports, and media	69,310	5.7	34,987	34,323	49.5	54,420	78.5	26,608	27,812	14,890	8,379	6,511
Healthcare practitioners and technicians	35,662	2.9	9,922	25,740	72.2	28,685	80.4	7,751	20,934	6,977	2,171	4,806
Service occupations	78,169	6.4	45,023	33,146	42.4	65,822	84.2	38,507	27,315	12,347	6,516	5,831
Sales and related occupations	3,485	0.3	1,199	2,286	65.6	2,854	81.9	1,015	1,839	631	184	447
Office and administrative support	126,274	10.4	20,018	106,256	84.1	109,430	86.7	16,291	93,139	16,844	3,727	13,117
Natural resources, construction, and maintenance	18,640	1.5	17,098	1,542	8.3	17,728	95.1	16,492	1,236	912	606	306
Production, transportation, and material moving	4,821	0.4	3,882	939	19.5	3,533	73.3	2,899	634	1,288	983	305

See notes at end of table.

Table 314.30. Employees in degree-granting postsecondary institutions, by employment status, sex, control and level of institution, and primary occupation: Fall 2018—Continued

Control and level of institution and primary occupation	Full-time and part-time					Full-time				Part-time		
	Total			Females		Total						
	Number	Percentage distribution	Males	Number	Percent of all employees	Number	Percent of all employees	Males	Females	Total	Males	Females
1	2	3	4	5	6	7	8	9	10	11	12	13
Private nonprofit 2-year	**7,655**	**100.0**	**2,874**	**4,781**	**62.5**	**5,326**	**69.6**	**1,879**	**3,447**	**2,329**	**995**	**1,334**
Faculty (instruction/research/public service)	3,541	46.3	1,415	2,126	60.0	1,637	46.2	598	1,039	1,904	817	1,087
Instruction	3,518	46.0	1,405	2,113	60.1	1,618	46.0	591	1,027	1,900	814	1,086
Research	8	0.1	2	6	75.0	8	100.0	2	6	0	0	0
Public service	15	0.2	8	7	46.7	11	73.3	5	6	4	3	1
Graduate assistants	11	0.1	7	4	36.4	†	†	†	†	11	7	4
Librarians, curators, and archivists	101	1.3	21	80	79.2	68	67.3	16	52	33	5	28
Student and academic affairs and other education services	1,408	18.4	423	985	70.0	1,339	95.1	397	942	69	26	43
Management	763	10.0	333	430	56.4	744	97.5	321	423	19	12	7
Business and financial operations	202	2.6	61	141	69.8	188	93.1	60	128	14	1	13
Computer, engineering, and science	137	1.8	106	31	22.6	130	94.9	102	28	7	4	3
Community, social service, legal, arts, design, entertainment, sports, and media	224	2.9	119	105	46.9	178	79.5	90	88	46	29	17
Healthcare practitioners and technicians	30	0.4	5	25	83.3	7	23.3	1	6	23	4	19
Service occupations	195	2.5	138	57	29.2	113	57.9	77	36	82	61	21
Sales and related occupations	485	6.3	130	355	73.2	479	98.8	128	351	6	2	4
Office and administrative support	509	6.6	75	434	85.3	405	79.6	57	348	104	18	86
Natural resources, construction, and maintenance	46	0.6	39	7	15.2	38	82.6	32	6	8	7	1
Production, transportation, and material moving	3	#	2	1	33.3	0	0.0	0	0	3	2	1
Private for-profit 4-year	**93,193**	**100.0**	**37,920**	**55,273**	**59.3**	**41,783**	**44.8**	**16,362**	**25,421**	**51,410**	**21,558**	**29,852**
Faculty (instruction/research/public service)	58,317	62.6	24,789	33,528	57.5	10,514	18.0	4,728	5,786	47,803	20,061	27,742
Instruction	58,261	62.5	24,760	33,501	57.5	10,489	18.0	4,716	5,773	47,772	20,044	27,728
Research	19	#	10	9	47.4	13	68.4	7	6	6	3	3
Public service	37	#	19	18	48.6	12	32.4	5	7	25	14	11
Graduate assistants	367	0.4	130	237	64.6	†	†	†	†	367	130	237
Librarians, curators, and archivists	685	0.7	160	525	76.6	442	64.5	98	344	243	62	181
Student and academic affairs and other education services	7,852	8.4	2,430	5,422	69.1	7,021	89.4	2,051	4,970	831	379	452
Management	6,827	7.3	2,868	3,959	58.0	6,701	98.2	2,824	3,877	126	44	82
Business and financial operations	3,174	3.4	953	2,221	70.0	3,070	96.7	927	2,143	104	26	78
Computer, engineering, and science	1,664	1.8	1,244	420	25.2	1,597	96.0	1,195	402	67	49	18
Community, social service, legal, arts, design, entertainment, sports, and media	2,881	3.1	1,185	1,696	58.9	2,491	86.5	973	1,518	390	212	178
Healthcare practitioners and technicians	195	0.2	79	116	59.5	151	77.4	68	83	44	11	33
Service occupations	1,679	1.8	1,103	576	34.3	1,220	72.7	783	437	459	320	139
Sales and related occupations	2,622	2.8	1,013	1,609	61.4	2,567	97.9	990	1,577	55	23	32
Office and administrative support	6,476	6.9	1,590	4,886	75.4	5,633	87.0	1,405	4,228	843	185	658
Natural resources, construction, and maintenance	299	0.3	253	46	15.4	269	90.0	233	36	30	20	10
Production, transportation, and material moving	155	0.2	123	32	20.6	107	69.0	87	20	48	36	12
Private for-profit 2-year	**22,648**	**100.0**	**8,186**	**14,462**	**63.9**	**13,751**	**60.7**	**5,044**	**8,707**	**8,897**	**3,142**	**5,755**
Faculty (instruction/research/public service)	12,447	55.0	4,891	7,556	60.7	5,126	41.2	2,272	2,854	7,321	2,619	4,702
Instruction	12,397	54.7	4,872	7,525	60.7	5,090	41.1	2,259	2,831	7,307	2,613	4,694
Research	35	0.2	15	20	57.1	31	88.6	13	18	4	2	2
Public service	15	0.1	4	11	73.3	5	33.3	0	5	10	4	6
Graduate assistants	0	0.0	0	0	†	†	†	†	†	†	†	†
Librarians, curators, and archivists	174	0.8	46	128	73.6	106	60.9	24	82	68	22	46
Student and academic affairs and other education services	1,972	8.7	493	1,479	75.0	1,742	88.3	425	1,317	230	68	162
Management	2,377	10.5	941	1,436	60.4	2,314	97.3	924	1,390	63	17	46
Business and financial operations	964	4.3	232	732	75.9	881	91.4	219	662	83	13	70
Computer, engineering, and science	196	0.9	178	18	9.2	168	85.7	153	15	28	25	3
Community, social service, legal, arts, design, entertainment, sports, and media	220	1.0	87	133	60.5	142	64.5	56	86	78	31	47
Healthcare practitioners and technicians	73	0.3	30	43	58.9	33	45.2	18	15	40	12	28
Service occupations	407	1.8	253	154	37.8	200	49.1	125	75	207	128	79
Sales and related occupations	1,194	5.3	429	765	64.1	1,090	91.3	391	699	104	38	66
Office and administrative support	2,440	10.8	454	1,986	81.4	1,830	75.0	337	1,493	610	117	493
Natural resources, construction, and maintenance	173	0.8	142	31	17.9	114	65.9	96	18	59	46	13
Production, transportation, and material moving	11	#	10	1	9.1	5	45.5	4	1	6	6	0

†Not applicable.
#Rounds to zero.
NOTE: Degree-granting institutions grant associate's or higher degrees and participate in Title IV federal financial aid programs. By definition, all graduate assistants are part time. Detail may not sum to totals because of rounding.

SOURCE: U.S. Department of Education, National Center for Education Statistics, Integrated Postsecondary Education Data System (IPEDS), Spring 2019, Human Resources component, Fall Staff section. (This table was prepared November 2019.)

Table 314.40. Employees in degree-granting postsecondary institutions, by race/ethnicity, sex, employment status, control and level of institution, and primary occupation: Fall 2018

Sex, employment status, control and level of institution, and primary occupation	Total	White	Black, Hispanic, Asian, Pacific Islander, American Indian/Alaska Native, and Two or more races								Race/ethnicity unknown	Non-resident alien[2]
			Total	Percent[1]	Black	Hispanic	Asian	Pacific Islander	American Indian/ Alaska Native	Two or more races		
1	2	3	4	5	6	7	8	9	10	11	12	13
All institutions	3,923,374	2,538,970	1,010,232	28.5	374,765	302,227	254,088	7,612	19,809	51,731	168,573	205,599
Faculty (instruction/research/public service)	1,542,613	1,073,453	331,525	23.6	105,380	80,673	119,559	2,730	6,882	16,301	79,247	58,388
Instruction	1,422,754	1,012,627	304,470	23.1	101,054	75,389	103,858	2,623	6,550	14,996	74,084	31,573
Research	90,489	40,698	19,585	32.5	2,085	3,677	12,586	74	192	971	4,241	25,965
Public service	29,370	20,128	7,470	27.1	2,241	1,607	3,115	33	140	334	922	850
Graduate assistants	382,715	169,629	74,343	30.5	16,104	22,516	26,629	390	958	7,746	21,196	117,547
Librarians, curators, and archivists	41,495	31,342	8,725	21.8	3,122	2,513	2,143	86	251	610	1,122	306
Student and academic affairs and other education services	182,831	118,910	54,889	31.6	23,435	18,569	7,954	523	1,418	2,990	6,827	2,205
Management	262,919	194,842	60,062	23.6	27,340	16,979	10,960	481	1,275	3,027	6,798	1,217
Business and financial operations	219,793	146,393	64,356	30.5	24,228	20,245	15,106	478	1,122	3,177	7,229	1,815
Computer, engineering, and science	238,073	153,234	63,483	29.3	15,195	16,955	26,585	383	1,059	3,306	7,860	13,496
Community, social service, legal, arts, design, entertainment, sports, and media	185,765	130,773	46,581	26.3	21,308	14,854	5,842	548	995	3,034	7,073	1,338
Healthcare practitioners and technicians	111,076	68,935	33,008	32.4	11,324	8,522	11,349	146	363	1,304	5,960	3,173
Service occupations	242,151	125,555	104,809	45.5	52,478	38,034	8,896	665	1,956	2,780	9,525	2,262
Sales and related occupations	12,534	7,411	4,482	37.7	2,121	1,535	437	54	80	255	593	48
Office and administrative support	409,591	253,887	140,440	35.6	62,168	51,635	16,659	938	2,687	6,353	11,896	3,368
Natural resources, construction, and maintenance	73,098	52,662	17,525	25.0	7,566	7,136	1,421	146	613	643	2,537	374
Production, transportation, and material moving	18,720	11,944	6,004	33.5	2,996	2,061	548	44	150	205	710	62
Males	1,767,361	1,147,368	417,368	26.7	139,863	125,201	120,109	3,323	8,367	20,505	79,816	122,809
Faculty (instruction/research/public service)	771,594	539,503	156,992	22.5	41,524	39,229	64,848	1,304	3,187	6,900	38,990	36,109
Instruction	705,729	507,351	143,407	22.0	39,901	36,789	56,071	1,254	3,052	6,340	36,345	18,626
Research	51,730	22,325	10,204	31.4	834	1,693	7,151	33	79	414	2,212	16,989
Public service	14,135	9,827	3,381	25.6	789	747	1,626	17	56	146	433	494
Graduate assistants	196,792	81,144	33,714	29.4	6,071	10,167	13,535	157	389	3,395	10,720	71,214
Librarians, curators, and archivists	12,354	9,412	2,450	20.7	765	857	562	38	59	169	379	113
Student and academic affairs and other education services	58,059	37,601	17,082	31.2	6,997	5,985	2,525	209	464	902	2,346	1,030
Management	113,505	86,797	22,985	20.9	9,816	6,600	4,660	190	534	1,185	3,119	604
Business and financial operations	59,552	41,058	15,620	27.6	5,425	5,233	3,742	124	284	812	2,236	638
Computer, engineering, and science	143,457	95,875	34,593	26.5	8,169	10,019	13,571	257	629	1,948	4,809	8,180
Community, social service, legal, arts, design, entertainment, sports, and media	83,114	59,792	19,167	24.3	9,672	5,634	2,035	263	401	1,162	3,531	624
Healthcare practitioners and technicians	32,561	18,855	9,723	34.0	2,530	2,463	4,224	51	99	356	2,340	1,643
Service occupations	139,252	76,199	56,443	42.6	28,826	19,803	4,711	383	1,177	1,543	5,502	1,108
Sales and related occupations	4,375	2,589	1,535	37.2	702	571	140	17	20	85	228	23
Office and administrative support	70,126	39,541	26,656	40.3	10,527	10,341	3,850	162	448	1,328	2,704	1,225
Natural resources, construction, and maintenance	67,276	49,034	15,684	24.2	6,589	6,595	1,247	132	556	565	2,312	246
Production, transportation, and material moving	15,344	9,968	4,724	32.2	2,250	1,704	459	36	120	155	600	52
Females	2,156,013	1,391,602	592,864	29.9	234,902	177,026	133,979	4,289	11,442	31,226	88,757	82,790
Faculty (instruction/research/public service)	771,019	533,950	174,533	24.6	63,856	41,444	54,711	1,426	3,695	9,401	40,257	22,279
Instruction	717,025	505,276	161,063	24.2	61,153	38,600	47,787	1,369	3,498	8,656	37,739	12,947
Research	38,759	18,373	9,381	33.8	1,251	1,984	5,435	41	113	557	2,029	8,976
Public service	15,235	10,301	4,089	28.4	1,452	860	1,489	16	84	188	489	356
Graduate assistants	185,923	88,485	40,629	31.5	10,033	12,349	13,094	233	569	4,351	10,476	46,333
Librarians, curators, and archivists	29,141	21,930	6,275	22.2	2,357	1,656	1,581	48	192	441	743	193
Student and academic affairs and other education services	124,772	81,309	37,807	31.7	16,438	12,584	5,429	314	954	2,088	4,481	1,175
Management	149,414	108,045	37,077	25.5	17,524	10,379	6,300	291	741	1,842	3,679	613
Business and financial operations	160,241	105,335	48,736	31.6	18,803	15,012	11,364	354	838	2,365	4,993	1,177
Computer, engineering, and science	94,616	57,359	28,890	33.5	7,026	6,936	13,014	126	430	1,358	3,051	5,316
Community, social service, legal, arts, design, entertainment, sports, and media	102,651	70,981	27,414	27.9	11,636	9,220	3,807	285	594	1,872	3,542	714
Healthcare practitioners and technicians	78,515	50,080	23,285	31.7	8,794	6,059	7,125	95	264	948	3,620	1,530
Service occupations	102,899	49,356	48,366	49.5	23,652	18,231	4,185	282	779	1,237	4,023	1,154
Sales and related occupations	8,159	4,822	2,947	37.9	1,419	964	297	37	60	170	365	25
Office and administrative support	339,465	214,346	113,784	34.7	51,641	41,294	12,809	776	2,239	5,025	9,192	2,143
Natural resources, construction, and maintenance	5,822	3,628	1,841	33.7	977	541	174	14	57	78	225	128
Production, transportation, and material moving	3,376	1,976	1,280	39.3	746	357	89	8	30	50	110	10
Full-time	2,549,864	1,690,962	706,413	29.5	264,700	212,024	179,106	5,109	13,644	31,830	79,339	73,150
Faculty (instruction/research/public service)	832,119	572,586	184,941	24.4	45,748	41,403	84,806	1,229	3,413	8,342	25,180	49,412
Instruction	731,543	523,251	162,191	23.7	42,659	37,009	70,952	1,142	3,163	7,266	21,231	24,870
Research	78,656	34,282	17,260	33.5	1,810	3,158	11,255	62	148	827	3,327	23,787
Public service	21,920	15,053	5,490	26.7	1,279	1,236	2,599	25	102	249	622	755
Graduate assistants	†	†	†	†	†	†	†	†	†	†	†	†
Librarians, curators, and archivists	34,892	26,659	7,142	21.1	2,481	2,081	1,792	74	198	516	832	259
Student and academic affairs and other education services	125,264	81,694	38,463	32.0	16,708	12,570	5,541	410	1,030	2,204	3,819	1,288
Management	255,881	189,546	58,668	23.6	26,751	16,639	10,634	471	1,246	2,927	6,500	1,167
Business and financial operations	206,333	136,834	61,265	30.9	23,267	19,250	14,277	424	1,041	3,006	6,601	1,633
Computer, engineering, and science	219,241	141,576	58,322	29.2	13,888	15,326	24,763	351	966	3,028	7,052	12,291
Community, social service, legal, arts, design, entertainment, sports, and media	151,033	106,128	38,923	26.8	17,796	12,448	4,920	462	822	2,475	4,920	1,062
Healthcare practitioners and technicians	93,426	57,131	28,672	33.4	9,983	7,544	9,567	127	306	1,145	5,253	2,370
Service occupations	202,902	102,886	91,155	47.0	45,427	33,468	7,824	564	1,628	2,244	7,062	1,799
Sales and related occupations	10,142	5,892	3,864	39.6	1,881	1,348	342	49	66	178	371	15
Office and administrative support	334,256	210,161	113,407	35.0	51,309	41,228	12,825	782	2,223	5,040	9,137	1,551
Natural resources, construction, and maintenance	69,197	50,177	16,620	24.9	7,106	6,882	1,340	133	579	580	2,148	252
Production, transportation, and material moving	15,178	9,692	4,971	33.9	2,355	1,837	475	33	126	145	464	51

See notes at end of table.

Table 314.40. Employees in degree-granting postsecondary institutions, by race/ethnicity, sex, employment status, control and level of institution, and primary occupation: Fall 2018—Continued

Sex, employment status, control and level of institution, and primary occupation	Total	White	Black, Hispanic, Asian, Pacific Islander, American Indian/Alaska Native, and Two or more races								Race/ ethnicity unknown	Non- resident alien[2]
			Total	Percent[1]	Black	Hispanic	Asian	Pacific Islander	American Indian/ Alaska Native	Two or more races		
1	2	3	4	5	6	7	8	9	10	11	12	13
Part-time	1,373,510	848,008	303,819	26.4	110,065	90,203	74,982	2,503	6,165	19,901	89,234	132,449
Faculty (instruction/research/public service)	710,494	500,867	146,584	22.6	59,632	39,270	34,753	1,501	3,469	7,959	54,067	8,976
Instruction	691,211	489,376	142,279	22.5	58,395	38,380	32,906	1,481	3,387	7,730	52,853	6,703
Research	11,833	6,416	2,325	26.6	275	519	1,331	12	44	144	914	2,178
Public service	7,450	5,075	1,980	28.1	962	371	516	8	38	85	300	95
Graduate assistants	382,715	169,629	74,343	30.5	16,104	22,516	26,629	390	958	7,746	21,196	117,547
Librarians, curators, and archivists	6,603	4,683	1,583	25.3	641	432	351	12	53	94	290	47
Student and academic affairs and other education services	57,567	37,216	16,426	30.6	6,727	5,999	2,413	113	388	786	3,008	917
Management	7,038	5,296	1,394	20.8	589	340	326	10	29	100	298	50
Business and financial operations	13,460	9,559	3,091	24.4	961	995	829	54	81	171	628	182
Computer, engineering, and science	18,832	11,658	5,161	30.7	1,307	1,629	1,822	32	93	278	808	1,205
Community, social service, legal, arts, design, entertainment, sports, and media	34,732	24,645	7,658	23.7	3,512	2,406	922	86	173	559	2,153	276
Healthcare practitioners and technicians	17,650	11,804	4,336	26.9	1,341	978	1,782	19	57	159	707	803
Service occupations	39,249	22,669	13,654	37.6	7,051	4,566	1,072	101	328	536	2,463	463
Sales and related occupations	2,392	1,519	618	28.9	240	187	95	5	14	77	222	33
Office and administrative support	75,335	43,726	27,033	38.2	10,859	10,407	3,834	156	464	1,313	2,759	1,817
Natural resources, construction, and maintenance	3,901	2,485	905	26.7	460	254	81	13	34	63	389	122
Production, transportation, and material moving	3,542	2,252	1,033	31.4	641	224	73	11	24	60	246	11
Public 4-year	2,019,697	1,271,357	520,427	29.0	180,723	156,344	142,988	3,081	10,546	26,745	81,476	146,437
Faculty (instruction/research/public service)	670,734	456,349	147,608	24.4	37,684	35,608	63,872	818	3,031	6,595	30,339	36,438
Instruction	598,731	418,326	133,031	24.1	35,644	32,535	55,395	745	2,817	5,895	26,688	20,686
Research	55,798	26,081	11,438	30.5	1,159	2,340	7,188	54	138	559	3,111	15,168
Public service	16,205	11,942	3,139	20.8	881	733	1,289	19	76	141	540	584
Graduate assistants	299,254	134,555	57,111	29.8	12,632	18,062	19,307	313	830	5,967	15,381	92,207
Librarians, curators, and archivists	18,673	13,969	4,074	22.6	1,370	1,269	961	23	141	310	476	154
Student and academic affairs and other education services	73,163	47,301	22,095	31.8	9,045	7,545	3,513	212	623	1,157	2,641	1,126
Management	120,750	89,740	27,634	23.5	12,789	7,630	5,068	150	669	1,328	2,703	673
Business and financial operations	131,507	87,493	38,641	30.6	13,923	12,322	9,529	245	728	1,894	4,195	1,178
Computer, engineering, and science	146,914	96,476	36,753	27.6	8,112	9,960	15,840	207	623	2,011	4,830	8,855
Community, social service, legal, arts, design, entertainment, sports, and media	89,703	61,676	23,968	28.0	10,629	7,953	3,083	251	542	1,510	3,338	721
Healthcare practitioners and technicians	73,591	46,297	20,950	31.2	7,597	4,972	7,196	69	270	846	4,679	1,665
Service occupations	129,155	65,295	57,408	46.8	28,990	20,004	5,450	301	1,101	1,562	5,149	1,303
Sales and related occupations	3,080	2,005	824	29.1	295	327	113	13	21	55	221	30
Office and administrative support	202,560	127,251	68,207	34.9	30,961	24,767	7,724	363	1,438	2,954	5,302	1,800
Natural resources, construction, and maintenance	48,166	35,026	11,168	24.2	4,816	4,448	946	91	427	440	1,731	241
Production, transportation, and material moving	12,447	7,924	3,986	33.5	1,880	1,477	386	25	102	116	491	46
Public 2-year	566,458	390,344	153,540	28.2	65,032	53,444	22,861	1,497	4,502	6,204	18,439	4,135
Faculty (instruction/research/public service)	310,101	229,890	66,391	22.4	27,270	20,314	13,145	758	1,945	2,959	11,727	2,093
Instruction	306,576	227,685	65,244	22.3	26,510	20,110	13,050	755	1,901	2,918	11,626	2,021
Research	111	75	34	31.2	9	9	10	0	6	0	1	1
Public service	3,414	2,130	1,113	34.3	751	195	85	3	38	41	100	71
Graduate assistants	17	9	3	25.0	0	2	1	0	0	0	2	3
Librarians, curators, and archivists	5,493	3,983	1,369	25.6	572	450	232	17	51	47	117	24
Student and academic affairs and other education services	49,475	31,525	16,164	33.9	6,768	6,188	1,862	137	542	667	1,546	240
Management	31,923	22,709	8,451	27.1	4,378	2,626	828	58	261	300	658	105
Business and financial operations	16,290	10,106	5,675	36.0	2,541	2,009	772	35	147	171	405	104
Computer, engineering, and science	15,604	10,498	4,634	30.6	1,463	1,656	1,106	45	147	217	340	132
Community, social service, legal, arts, design, entertainment, sports, and media	23,427	15,013	7,631	33.7	3,767	2,606	665	74	212	307	681	102
Healthcare practitioners and technicians	1,525	1,146	276	19.4	99	95	42	2	21	17	100	3
Service occupations	32,546	17,609	13,559	43.5	6,693	5,218	840	95	377	336	1,015	363
Sales and related occupations	1,668	1,254	385	23.5	154	134	52	3	22	20	26	3
Office and administrative support	71,332	41,728	27,021	39.3	10,479	11,367	3,156	254	667	1,098	1,656	927
Natural resources, construction, and maintenance	5,774	4,046	1,575	28.0	663	640	128	13	86	45	117	36
Production, transportation, and material moving	1,283	828	406	32.9	185	139	32	6	24	20	49	0
Private nonprofit 4-year	1,213,723	805,080	294,591	26.8	110,046	80,099	82,011	2,576	3,974	15,885	59,300	54,752
Faculty (instruction/research/public service)	487,473	342,456	95,274	21.8	29,389	19,592	38,799	920	1,467	5,107	29,999	19,744
Instruction	443,271	321,913	84,005	20.7	27,882	17,593	31,692	889	1,399	4,550	28,600	8,753
Research	34,518	14,510	8,084	35.8	913	1,323	5,375	20	46	407	1,128	10,796
Public service	9,684	6,033	3,185	34.6	594	676	1,732	11	22	150	271	195
Graduate assistants	83,066	34,899	17,098	32.9	3,414	4,427	7,289	75	127	1,766	5,752	25,317
Librarians, curators, and archivists	16,369	12,736	3,023	19.2	1,090	700	905	42	53	233	485	125
Student and academic affairs and other education services	48,961	34,116	11,943	25.9	5,549	3,216	2,025	108	183	862	2,075	827
Management	100,279	75,669	21,142	21.8	8,985	5,803	4,596	234	300	1,224	3,042	426
Business and financial operations	67,656	46,154	18,502	28.6	7,273	5,317	4,504	187	204	1,017	2,476	524
Computer, engineering, and science	73,558	45,067	21,452	32.2	5,467	5,115	9,437	122	276	1,035	2,598	4,441
Community, social service, legal, arts, design, entertainment, sports, and media	69,310	52,022	13,839	21.0	6,446	3,908	1,949	215	221	1,100	2,936	513
Healthcare practitioners and technicians	35,662	21,326	11,672	35.4	3,595	3,443	4,065	75	69	425	1,159	1,505
Service occupations	78,169	41,692	32,633	43.9	16,304	12,261	2,539	260	455	814	3,250	594
Sales and related occupations	3,485	2,366	976	29.2	371	385	122	12	9	77	130	13
Office and administrative support	126,274	80,106	40,988	33.8	19,211	13,657	5,330	275	493	2,022	4,570	610
Natural resources, construction, and maintenance	18,640	13,359	4,520	25.3	2,040	1,862	338	40	94	146	664	97
Production, transportation, and material moving	4,821	3,112	1,529	32.9	912	413	113	11	23	57	164	16

See notes at end of table.

Table 314.40. Employees in degree-granting postsecondary institutions, by race/ethnicity, sex, employment status, control and level of institution, and primary occupation: Fall 2018—Continued

Sex, employment status, control and level of institution, and primary occupation	Total	White	Black, Hispanic, Asian, Pacific Islander, American Indian/Alaska Native, and Two or more races								Race/ ethnicity unknown	Non- resident alien[2]
			Total	Percent[1]	Black	Hispanic	Asian	Pacific Islander	American Indian/ Alaska Native	Two or more races		
1	2	3	4	5	6	7	8	9	10	11	12	13
Private nonprofit 2-year	**7,655**	**4,654**	**2,645**	**36.2**	**1,579**	**630**	**152**	**8**	**161**	**115**	**344**	**12**
Faculty (instruction/research/public service)	3,541	2,437	967	28.4	610	168	69	3	64	53	128	9
Instruction	3,518	2,425	956	28.3	605	168	69	3	59	52	128	9
Research	8	6	2	25.0	0	0	0	0	1	1	0	0
Public service	15	6	9	60.0	5	0	0	0	4	0	0	0
Graduate assistants	11	8	0	0.0	0	0	0	0	0	0	1	2
Librarians, curators, and archivists	101	81	18	18.2	9	3	1	0	4	1	2	0
Student and academic affairs and other education services	1,408	588	728	55.3	428	220	26	1	24	29	92	0
Management	763	525	206	28.2	110	50	21	3	17	5	31	1
Business and financial operations	202	125	72	36.5	30	17	9	0	10	6	5	0
Computer, engineering, and science	137	92	35	27.6	10	11	8	0	4	2	10	0
Community, social service, legal, arts, design, entertainment, sports, and media	224	176	48	21.4	29	14	0	0	3	2	0	0
Healthcare practitioners and technicians	30	28	2	6.7	2	0	0	0	0	0	0	0
Service occupations	195	105	90	46.2	53	23	0	0	13	1	0	0
Sales and related occupations	485	140	287	67.2	195	71	9	1	0	11	58	0
Office and administrative support	509	321	176	35.4	95	47	9	0	20	5	12	0
Natural resources, construction, and maintenance	46	26	15	36.6	7	6	0	0	2	0	5	0
Production, transportation, and material moving	3	2	1	33.3	1	0	0	0	0	0	0	0
Private for-profit 4-year	**93,193**	**55,159**	**29,630**	**34.9**	**13,213**	**8,517**	**5,013**	**339**	**499**	**2,049**	**8,193**	**211**
Faculty (instruction/research/public service)	58,317	35,127	16,594	32.1	8,221	3,694	3,027	181	318	1,153	6,529	67
Instruction	58,261	35,099	16,567	32.1	8,212	3,693	3,012	181	318	1,151	6,528	67
Research	19	12	7	36.8	0	1	6	0	0	0	0	0
Public service	37	16	20	55.6	9	0	9	0	0	2	1	0
Graduate assistants	367	158	131	45.3	58	25	32	2	1	13	60	18
Librarians, curators, and archivists	685	452	190	29.6	60	68	38	4	2	18	40	3
Student and academic affairs and other education services	7,852	4,330	3,102	41.7	1,302	1,052	445	54	38	211	414	6
Management	6,827	4,761	1,752	26.9	669	582	345	22	19	115	303	11
Business and financial operations	3,174	2,025	1,034	33.8	333	372	234	9	17	69	110	5
Computer, engineering, and science	1,664	984	540	35.4	123	185	183	6	6	37	73	67
Community, social service, legal, arts, design, entertainment, sports, and media	2,881	1,810	960	34.7	398	306	136	8	13	99	109	2
Healthcare practitioners and technicians	195	101	76	42.9	12	8	37	0	3	16	18	0
Service occupations	1,679	647	929	58.9	358	451	57	8	9	46	102	1
Sales and related occupations	2,622	1,162	1,347	53.7	776	372	104	12	19	64	111	2
Office and administrative support	6,476	3,405	2,740	44.6	876	1,236	356	29	50	193	302	29
Natural resources, construction, and maintenance	299	121	162	57.2	11	137	2	2	3	7	16	0
Production, transportation, and material moving	155	76	73	49.0	16	29	17	2	1	8	6	0
Private for-profit 2-year	**22,648**	**12,376**	**9,399**	**43.2**	**4,172**	**3,193**	**1,063**	**111**	**127**	**733**	**821**	**52**
Faculty (instruction/research/public service)	12,447	7,194	4,691	39.5	2,206	1,297	647	50	57	434	525	37
Instruction	12,397	7,179	4,667	39.4	2,201	1,290	640	50	56	430	514	37
Research	35	14	20	58.8	4	4	7	0	1	4	1	0
Public service	15	1	4	80.0	1	3	0	0	0	0	10	0
Graduate assistants	0	0	0	†	0	0	0	0	0	0	0	0
Librarians, curators, and archivists	174	121	51	29.7	21	23	6	0	0	1	2	0
Student and academic affairs and other education services	1,972	1,050	857	44.9	343	348	83	11	8	64	59	6
Management	2,377	1,438	877	37.9	409	288	102	14	9	55	61	1
Business and financial operations	964	490	432	46.9	128	208	58	2	16	20	38	4
Computer, engineering, and science	196	117	69	37.1	20	28	11	3	3	4	9	1
Community, social service, legal, arts, design, entertainment, sports, and media	220	76	135	64.0	39	67	9	0	4	16	9	0
Healthcare practitioners and technicians	73	37	32	46.4	19	4	9	0	0	0	4	0
Service occupations	407	207	190	47.9	80	77	10	1	1	21	9	1
Sales and related occupations	1,194	484	663	57.8	330	246	37	13	9	28	47	0
Office and administrative support	2,440	1,076	1,308	54.9	546	561	84	17	19	81	54	2
Natural resources, construction, and maintenance	173	84	85	50.3	29	43	7	0	1	5	4	0
Production, transportation, and material moving	11	2	9	81.8	2	3	0	0	0	4	0	0

†Not applicable.
[1]Combined total of staff who were Black, Hispanic, Asian, Pacific Islander, American Indian/Alaska Native, and of Two or more races as a percentage of total staff, excluding race/ethnicity unknown and nonresident alien.
[2]Race/ethnicity not collected.

NOTE: Degree-granting institutions grant associate's or higher degrees and participate in Title IV federal financial aid programs. By definition, all graduate assistants are part time. Race categories exclude persons of Hispanic ethnicity.
SOURCE: U.S. Department of Education, National Center for Education Statistics, Integrated Postsecondary Education Data System (IPEDS), Spring 2019, Human Resources component, Fall Staff section. (This table was prepared November 2019.)

Table 315.10. Number of faculty in degree-granting postsecondary institutions, by employment status, sex, control, and level of institution: Selected years, fall 1970 through fall 2018

| | | Employment status | | | Sex | | | Control | | | | Level | |
| | | | | | | | | | Private | | | | |
Year	Total	Full-time	Part-time	Percent full-time	Males	Females	Percent female	Public	Total	Nonprofit	For-profit	4-year	2-year
1	2	3	4	5	6	7	8	9	10	11	12	13	14
1970	474,000	369,000	104,000	77.8	—	—	—	314,000	160,000	—	—	382,000	92,000
1971[1]	492,000	379,000	113,000	77.0	—	—	—	333,000	159,000	—	—	387,000	105,000
1972	500,000	380,000	120,000	76.0	—	—	—	343,000	157,000	—	—	384,000	116,000
1973[1]	527,000	389,000	138,000	73.8	—	—	—	365,000	162,000	—	—	401,000	126,000
1974[1]	567,000	406,000	161,000	71.6	—	—	—	397,000	170,000	—	—	427,000	140,000
1975[1]	628,000	440,000	188,000	70.1	—	—	—	443,000	185,000	—	—	467,000	161,000
1976	633,000	434,000	199,000	68.6	—	—	—	449,000	184,000	—	—	467,000	166,000
1977	678,000	448,000	230,000	66.1	—	—	—	492,000	186,000	—	—	485,000	193,000
1979[1]	675,000	445,000	230,000	65.9	—	—	—	488,000	187,000	—	—	494,000	182,000
1980[1]	686,000	450,000	236,000	65.6	—	—	—	495,000	191,000	—	—	494,000	192,000
1981	705,000	461,000	244,000	65.4	—	—	—	509,000	196,000	—	—	493,000	212,000
1982[1]	710,000	462,000	248,000	65.1	—	—	—	506,000	204,000	—	—	493,000	217,000
1983	724,000	471,000	254,000	65.1	—	—	—	512,000	212,000	—	—	504,000	220,000
1984[1]	717,000	462,000	255,000	64.4	—	—	—	505,000	212,000	—	—	504,000	213,000
1985[1]	715,000	459,000	256,000	64.2	—	—	—	503,000	212,000	—	—	504,000	211,000
1986[1]	722,000	459,000	263,000	63.6	—	—	—	510,000	212,000	—	—	506,000	216,000
1987[2]	793,070	523,420	269,650	66.0	529,413	263,657	33.2	552,749	240,321	—	—	547,505	245,565
1989[2]	824,220	524,426	299,794	63.6	534,254	289,966	35.2	577,298	246,922	—	—	583,700	240,520
1991[2]	826,252	535,623	290,629	64.8	525,599	300,653	36.4	580,908	245,344	236,066	9,278	591,269	234,983
1993[2]	915,474	545,706	369,768	59.6	561,123	354,351	38.7	650,434	265,040	254,130	10,910	625,969	289,505
1995[2]	931,706	550,822	380,884	59.1	562,893	368,813	39.6	656,833	274,873	260,900	13,973	647,059	284,647
1997[2]	989,813	568,719	421,094	57.5	587,420	402,393	40.7	694,560	295,253	271,257	23,996	682,650	307,163
1999[2]	1,037,529	593,375	444,154	57.2	608,007	429,522	41.4	718,585	318,944	288,663	30,281	719,256	318,273
2001[2]	1,113,183	617,868	495,315	55.5	644,514	468,669	42.1	771,124	342,059	306,487	35,572	764,172	349,011
2003[2]	1,173,593	630,092	543,501	53.7	663,723	509,870	43.4	791,766	381,827	330,097	51,730	814,289	359,304
2005[2]	1,290,426	675,624	614,802	52.4	714,453	575,973	44.6	841,188	449,238	361,523	87,715	916,996	373,430
2007[2]	1,371,587	703,757	667,830	51.3	744,047	627,540	45.8	876,526	495,061	386,688	108,373	992,385	379,202
2009[2]	1,439,074	729,152	709,922	50.7	761,002	678,072	47.1	913,788	525,286	408,382	116,904	1,038,349	400,725
2011[2]	1,524,469	762,114	762,355	50.0	789,567	734,902	48.2	954,159	570,310	432,630	137,680	1,115,642	408,827
2013[2]	1,545,381	791,378	754,003	51.2	791,971	753,410	48.8	968,734	576,647	449,072	127,575	1,151,638	393,743
2015[2]	1,552,256	807,109	745,147	52.0	789,405	762,851	49.1	970,991	581,265	472,638	108,627	1,180,545	371,711
2016[2]	1,546,081	813,978	732,103	52.6	783,495	762,586	49.3	974,239	571,842	476,872	94,970	1,196,657	349,424
2017[2]	1,545,653	822,513	723,140	53.2	778,873	766,780	49.6	972,689	572,964	486,761	86,203	1,209,143	336,510
2018[2]	1,542,613	832,119	710,494	53.9	771,594	771,019	50.0	980,835	561,778	491,014	70,764	1,216,524	326,089

—Not available.

[1]Estimated on the basis of enrollment. For methodological details on estimates, see National Center for Education Statistics, *Projections of Education Statistics to 2000*.

[2]Because of revised survey methods, data are not directly comparable with figures for years prior to 1987.

NOTE: Includes faculty members with the title of professor, associate professor, assistant professor, instructor, lecturer, assisting professor, adjunct professor, or interim professor (or the equivalent). Excluded are graduate students with titles such as graduate or teaching fellow who assist senior faculty. Data through 1995 are for institutions of higher education, while later data are for degree-granting institutions. Degree-granting institutions grant associate's or higher degrees and participate in Title IV federal financial aid programs. The degree-granting classification is very similar to the earlier higher education classification, but it includes more 2-year colleges and excludes a few higher education institutions that did not grant degrees. Beginning in 2007, includes institutions with fewer than 15 full-time employees; these institutions did not report staff data prior to 2007. Some data have been revised from previously published figures. Detail may not sum to totals because of rounding.
SOURCE: U.S. Department of Education, National Center for Education Statistics, Higher Education General Information Survey (HEGIS), *Employees in Institutions of Higher Education*, 1970 and 1972, and "Staff Survey" 1976; *Projections of Education Statistics to 2000*; Integrated Postsecondary Education Data System (IPEDS), "Fall Staff Survey" (IPEDS-S:87–99); IPEDS Winter 2001–02 through Winter 2011–12, Human Resources component, Fall Staff section; IPEDS Spring 2014 and Spring 2016 through Spring 2019, Human Resources component, Fall Staff section; and U.S. Equal Employment Opportunity Commission, Higher Education Staff Information Survey (EEO-6), 1977, 1981, and 1983. (This table was prepared November 2019.)

Table 315.20. Full-time faculty in degree-granting postsecondary institutions, by race/ethnicity, sex, and academic rank: Fall 2015, fall 2017, and fall 2018

Year, sex, and academic rank	Total	White	Black, Hispanic, Asian, Pacific Islander, American Indian/Alaska Native, and Two or more races									Race/ethnicity unknown	Non-resident alien[2]
			Total	Percent[1]	Black	Hispanic	Asian/Pacific Islander			American Indian/ Alaska Native	Two or more races		
							Total	Asian	Pacific Islander				
1	2	3	4	5	6	7	8	9	10	11	12	13	14
2015[3]													
Total	**807,109**	**575,752**	**167,372**	**22.5**	**44,106**	**35,811**	**77,456**	**76,298**	**1,158**	**3,530**	**6,469**	**22,359**	**41,626**
Professors	182,388	147,095	31,171	17.5	6,731	5,957	16,938	16,734	204	599	946	2,486	1,636
Associate professors	158,082	116,754	35,132	23.1	9,090	6,978	17,285	17,067	218	608	1,171	3,070	3,126
Assistant professors	173,409	115,226	40,251	25.9	10,874	7,634	19,432	19,132	300	639	1,672	6,577	11,355
Instructors	99,915	73,052	21,673	22.9	7,264	6,890	5,696	5,467	229	862	961	3,563	1,627
Lecturers	40,894	30,488	7,635	20.0	2,074	2,367	2,690	2,653	37	142	362	1,256	1,515
Other faculty	152,421	93,137	31,510	25.3	8,073	5,985	15,415	15,245	170	680	1,357	5,407	22,367
2017[3]													
Total	**822,513**	**574,364**	**179,251**	**23.8**	**45,461**	**39,190**	**83,516**	**82,316**	**1,200**	**3,477**	**7,607**	**23,467**	**45,431**
Professors	184,428	145,927	33,971	18.9	6,936	6,535	18,817	18,624	193	633	1,050	2,714	1,816
Associate professors	157,975	115,065	36,527	24.1	9,157	7,253	18,269	18,033	236	573	1,275	3,308	3,075
Assistant professors	179,051	115,830	43,727	27.4	11,507	8,571	20,993	20,713	280	631	2,025	6,876	12,618
Instructors	98,673	70,967	22,469	24.0	7,048	7,431	6,019	5,787	232	851	1,120	3,378	1,859
Lecturers	43,222	32,031	8,121	20.2	1,994	2,708	2,760	2,722	38	160	499	1,493	1,577
Other faculty	159,164	94,544	34,436	26.7	8,819	6,692	16,658	16,437	221	629	1,638	5,698	24,486
Males	441,472	307,287	92,804	23.2	19,432	19,732	48,424	47,835	589	1,693	3,523	12,422	28,959
Professors	123,867	97,492	23,146	19.2	4,127	4,115	13,895	13,767	128	381	628	1,874	1,355
Associate professors	86,222	62,422	19,927	24.2	4,300	3,908	10,808	10,694	114	269	642	1,937	1,936
Assistant professors	86,236	54,432	20,503	27.4	4,345	4,111	10,905	10,772	133	295	847	3,556	7,745
Instructors	42,843	31,031	9,348	23.2	2,577	3,298	2,554	2,455	99	429	490	1,472	992
Lecturers	19,219	14,396	3,318	18.7	847	1,154	1,061	1,043	18	60	196	699	806
Other faculty	83,085	47,514	16,562	25.8	3,236	3,146	9,201	9,104	97	259	720	2,884	16,125
Females	381,041	267,077	86,447	24.5	26,029	19,458	35,092	34,481	611	1,784	4,084	11,045	16,472
Professors	60,561	48,435	10,825	18.3	2,809	2,420	4,922	4,857	65	252	422	840	461
Associate professors	71,753	52,643	16,600	24.0	4,857	3,345	7,461	7,339	122	304	633	1,371	1,139
Assistant professors	92,815	61,398	23,224	27.4	7,162	4,460	10,088	9,941	147	336	1,178	3,320	4,873
Instructors	55,830	39,936	13,121	24.7	4,471	4,133	3,465	3,332	133	422	630	1,906	867
Lecturers	24,003	17,635	4,803	21.4	1,147	1,554	1,699	1,679	20	100	303	794	771
Other faculty	76,079	47,030	17,874	27.5	5,583	3,546	7,457	7,333	124	370	918	2,814	8,361
2018[3]													
Total	**832,119**	**572,586**	**184,941**	**24.4**	**45,748**	**41,403**	**86,035**	**84,806**	**1,229**	**3,413**	**8,342**	**25,180**	**49,412**
Professors	185,758	145,207	35,404	19.6	7,005	6,826	19,729	19,529	200	606	1,238	3,107	2,040
Associate professors	159,135	114,804	37,463	24.6	9,196	7,684	18,696	18,451	245	578	1,309	3,686	3,182
Assistant professors	181,239	115,381	44,822	28.0	11,628	8,913	21,408	21,137	271	663	2,210	7,591	13,445
Instructors	98,798	70,171	23,327	24.9	7,225	7,885	6,165	5,885	280	786	1,266	3,480	1,820
Lecturers	44,969	32,808	8,790	21.1	2,120	2,986	2,975	2,936	39	162	547	1,594	1,777
Other faculty	162,220	94,215	35,135	27.2	8,574	7,109	17,062	16,868	194	618	1,772	5,722	27,148
Males	443,589	304,009	94,801	23.8	19,351	20,621	49,507	48,872	635	1,617	3,705	13,352	31,427
Professors	123,569	96,178	23,736	19.8	4,091	4,222	14,401	14,271	130	351	671	2,109	1,546
Associate professors	86,082	61,665	20,259	24.7	4,282	4,117	10,963	10,831	132	279	618	2,171	1,987
Assistant professors	86,493	53,673	20,748	27.9	4,334	4,227	10,987	10,851	136	295	905	3,798	8,274
Instructors	42,923	30,679	9,642	23.9	2,616	3,497	2,624	2,501	123	384	521	1,605	997
Lecturers	19,891	14,637	3,577	19.6	904	1,247	1,164	1,147	17	56	206	772	905
Other faculty	84,631	47,177	16,839	26.3	3,124	3,311	9,368	9,271	97	252	784	2,897	17,718
Females	388,530	268,577	90,140	25.1	26,397	20,782	36,528	35,934	594	1,796	4,637	11,828	17,985
Professors	62,189	49,029	11,668	19.2	2,914	2,604	5,328	5,258	70	255	567	998	494
Associate professors	73,053	53,139	17,204	24.5	4,914	3,567	7,733	7,620	113	299	691	1,515	1,195
Assistant professors	94,746	61,708	24,074	28.1	7,294	4,686	10,421	10,286	135	368	1,305	3,793	5,171
Instructors	55,875	39,492	13,685	25.7	4,609	4,388	3,541	3,384	157	402	745	1,875	823
Lecturers	25,078	18,171	5,213	22.3	1,216	1,739	1,811	1,789	22	106	341	822	872
Other faculty	77,589	47,038	18,296	28.0	5,450	3,798	7,694	7,597	97	366	988	2,825	9,430

[1]Combined total of faculty who were Black, Hispanic, Asian, Pacific Islander, American Indian/Alaska Native, and of Two or more races as a percentage of total faculty, excluding race/ethnicity unknown and nonresident alien.
[2]Race/ethnicity not collected.
[3]Only instructional faculty were classified by academic rank. Primarily research and primarily public service faculty, as well as faculty without ranks, appear under "other faculty."

NOTE: Degree-granting institutions grant associate's or higher degrees and participate in Title IV federal financial aid programs. Race categories exclude persons of Hispanic ethnicity. Some data have been revised from previously published figures.
SOURCE: U.S. Department of Education, National Center for Education Statistics, Integrated Postsecondary Education Data System (IPEDS), Spring 2016 through Spring 2019 Human Resources component, Fall Staff section. (This table was prepared November 2019.)

Table 316.10. Average salary of full-time instructional faculty on 9-month contracts in degree-granting postsecondary institutions, by academic rank, control and level of institution, and sex: Selected years, 1970–71 through 2018–19

Sex and academic year	All faculty	Academic rank						Public institutions			Private institutions		
		Professor	Associate professor	Assistant professor	Instructor	Lecturer	No rank	Total	4-year	2-year	Total	4-year	2-year
1	2	3	4	5	6	7	8	9	10	11	12	13	14
							Current dollars						
Total													
1970–71	$12,710	$17,958	$13,563	$11,176	$9,360	$11,196	$12,333	$12,953	$13,121	$12,644	$11,619	$11,824	$8,664
1975–76	16,659	22,649	17,065	13,986	13,672	12,906	15,196	16,942	17,400	15,820	15,921	16,116	10,901
1980–81	23,302	30,753	23,214	18,901	15,178	17,301	22,334	23,745	24,373	22,177	22,093	22,325	15,065
1982–83	27,196	35,540	26,921	22,056	17,601	20,072	25,557	27,488	28,293	25,567	26,393	26,691	16,595
1984–85	30,447	39,743	29,945	24,668	20,230	22,334	27,683	30,646	31,764	27,864	29,910	30,247	18,510
1985–86	32,392	42,268	31,787	26,277	20,918	23,770	29,088	32,750	34,033	29,590	31,402	31,732	19,436
1987–88	35,897	47,040	35,231	29,110	22,728	25,977	31,532	36,231	37,840	32,209	35,049	35,346	21,867
1989–90	40,133	52,810	39,392	32,689	25,030	28,990	34,559	40,416	42,365	35,516	39,464	39,817	24,601
1990–91	42,165	55,540	41,414	34,434	26,332	30,097	36,395	42,317	44,510	37,055	41,788	42,224	24,088
1991–92	43,851	57,433	42,929	35,745	30,916	30,456	37,783	43,641	45,638	38,959	44,376	44,793	25,673
1992–93	44,714	58,788	43,945	36,625	28,499	30,543	37,771	44,197	46,515	38,935	45,985	46,427	26,105
1993–94	46,364	60,649	45,278	37,630	28,828	32,729	40,584	45,920	48,019	41,040	47,465	47,880	28,435
1994–95	47,811	62,709	46,713	38,756	29,665	33,198	41,227	47,432	49,738	42,101	48,741	49,379	25,613
1995–96	49,309	64,540	47,966	39,696	30,344	34,136	42,996	48,837	51,172	43,295	50,466	50,819	31,915
1996–97	50,829	66,659	49,307	40,687	31,193	34,962	44,200	50,303	52,718	44,584	52,112	52,443	32,628
1997–98	52,335	68,731	50,828	41,830	32,449	35,484	45,268	51,638	54,114	45,919	54,039	54,379	33,592
1998–99	54,097	71,322	52,576	43,348	33,819	36,819	46,250	53,319	55,948	47,285	55,981	56,284	34,821
1999–2000	55,888	74,410	54,524	44,978	34,918	38,194	47,389	55,011	57,950	48,240	58,013	58,323	35,925
2001–02	59,742	80,792	58,724	48,796	46,959	41,798	46,569	58,524	62,013	50,837	62,818	63,088	33,139
2002–03	61,330	83,466	60,471	50,552	48,304	42,622	46,338	60,014	63,486	52,330	64,533	64,814	34,826
2003–04	62,579	85,333	61,746	51,798	49,065	43,648	47,725	60,874	64,340	53,076	66,666	66,932	36,322
2004–05	64,234	88,158	63,558	53,308	49,730	44,514	48,942	62,346	66,053	53,932	68,755	68,995	37,329
2005–06	66,172	91,208	65,714	55,106	50,883	45,896	50,425	64,158	67,951	55,405	71,016	71,263	38,549
2006–07	68,479	94,649	68,056	57,079	53,272	47,306	52,180	66,443	70,287	57,459	73,358	73,575	41,138
2007–08	71,101	98,595	70,830	59,293	55,356	49,389	54,377	68,988	72,852	59,672	76,169	76,378	43,402
2008–09	73,587	102,336	73,445	61,544	56,918	51,316	56,408	71,236	75,244	61,432	79,191	79,454	43,542
2009–10	74,620	103,682	74,125	62,245	57,791	52,185	56,803	72,178	76,147	62,264	80,379	80,597	44,748
2010–11	75,481	104,961	75,107	63,136	58,003	52,584	56,549	72,715	76,857	62,359	81,897	82,098	45,146
2011–12	76,567	107,090	76,177	64,011	58,350	53,359	56,898	73,496	77,843	62,553	83,540	83,701	47,805
2012–13	77,278	108,074	77,029	64,673	57,674	53,072	58,752	73,877	78,012	62,907	84,932	85,096	44,978
2013–14	78,733	109,998	78,693	66,093	58,240	54,566	59,161	75,491	79,897	63,714	86,178	86,390	44,598
2014–15	80,157	112,825	80,335	67,589	59,208	55,335	58,305	76,811	81,372	64,116	87,605	88,212	38,168
2015–16	82,224	115,539	82,147	69,378	60,911	57,306	60,341	78,869	83,389	66,018	89,867	90,309	31,296
2016–17	84,737	119,159	84,244	71,748	63,613	58,770	61,785	81,392	85,803	67,664	92,458	92,642	53,017
2017–18	86,870	122,069	86,130	73,474	65,176	60,816	62,748	83,433	87,900	68,723	94,819	94,941	57,030
2018–19	88,703	124,671	87,841	75,102	67,789	62,542	63,153	85,148	89,641	70,404	96,962	97,115	54,452
Males													
1975–76	17,414	22,902	17,209	14,174	14,430	13,579	15,761	17,661	18,121	16,339	16,784	16,946	11,378
1980–81	24,499	31,082	23,451	19,227	15,545	18,281	23,170	24,873	25,509	22,965	23,493	23,669	16,075
1982–83	28,664	35,956	27,262	22,586	18,160	21,225	26,541	28,851	29,661	26,524	28,159	28,380	17,346
1984–85	32,182	40,269	30,392	25,330	21,159	23,557	28,670	32,240	33,344	28,891	32,028	32,278	19,460
1985–86	34,294	42,833	32,273	27,094	21,693	25,238	30,267	34,528	35,786	30,758	33,656	33,900	20,412
1987–88	38,112	47,735	35,823	30,086	23,645	27,652	32,747	38,314	39,898	33,477	37,603	37,817	22,641
1989–90	42,763	53,650	40,131	33,781	25,933	31,162	35,980	42,959	44,834	37,081	42,312	42,595	25,218
1990–91	45,065	56,549	42,239	35,636	27,388	32,398	38,036	45,084	47,168	38,787	45,019	45,319	25,937
1991–92	46,848	58,494	43,814	36,969	33,359	32,843	39,422	46,483	48,401	40,811	47,733	48,042	26,825
1992–93	47,866	59,972	44,855	37,842	29,583	32,512	39,365	47,175	49,392	40,725	49,518	49,837	27,402
1993–94	49,579	61,857	46,229	38,794	29,815	34,796	42,251	48,956	50,989	42,938	51,076	51,397	30,783
1994–95	51,228	64,046	47,705	39,923	30,528	35,082	43,103	50,629	52,874	44,020	52,653	53,036	29,639
1995–96	52,814	65,949	49,037	40,858	30,940	36,135	44,624	52,163	54,448	45,209	54,364	54,649	33,301
1996–97	54,465	68,214	50,457	41,864	31,738	36,932	45,688	53,737	56,162	46,393	56,185	56,453	34,736
1997–98	56,115	70,468	52,041	43,017	33,070	37,481	46,822	55,191	57,744	47,690	58,293	58,576	36,157
1998–99	58,048	73,260	53,830	44,650	34,741	38,976	47,610	57,038	59,805	48,961	60,392	60,641	38,040
1999–2000	60,084	76,478	55,939	46,414	35,854	40,202	48,788	58,984	62,030	50,033	62,631	62,905	38,636
2001–02	64,320	83,356	60,300	50,518	48,844	44,519	48,049	62,835	66,577	52,360	67,871	68,100	33,395
2002–03	66,126	86,191	62,226	52,441	50,272	45,469	47,412	64,564	68,322	53,962	69,726	69,976	34,291
2003–04	67,485	88,262	63,466	53,649	50,985	46,214	48,973	65,476	69,248	54,623	72,021	72,250	35,604
2004–05	69,337	91,290	65,394	55,215	51,380	46,929	50,102	67,130	71,145	55,398	74,318	74,540	34,970
2005–06	71,569	94,733	67,654	57,099	52,519	48,256	51,811	69,191	73,353	56,858	76,941	77,143	38,215
2006–07	74,050	98,348	70,077	59,090	55,051	49,487	53,701	71,659	75,890	58,960	79,428	79,599	41,196
2007–08	76,957	102,605	72,943	61,374	57,134	51,795	56,170	74,394	78,671	61,189	82,734	82,903	42,995
2008–09	79,718	106,743	75,633	63,710	58,812	53,935	58,404	76,897	81,394	62,868	86,033	86,231	43,871
2009–10	80,881	108,225	76,400	64,451	59,793	54,947	58,647	77,948	82,423	63,697	87,382	87,546	44,500
2010–11	81,873	109,656	77,429	65,391	59,851	55,457	58,392	78,609	83,279	63,745	89,000	89,160	44,542
2011–12	83,150	112,066	78,560	66,303	60,066	56,367	58,807	79,544	84,444	63,918	90,840	90,976	45,250
2012–13	83,979	113,311	79,423	67,085	59,350	55,759	61,086	80,016	84,700	64,282	92,385	92,530	42,906
2013–14	85,545	115,466	81,178	68,492	59,777	57,218	61,511	81,703	86,646	65,076	93,898	94,065	44,277
2014–15	87,199	118,573	82,954	70,260	60,707	58,441	60,310	83,291	88,393	65,513	95,455	96,041	37,389
2015–16	89,361	121,535	84,781	72,272	62,390	60,428	62,468	85,367	90,464	67,352	98,016	98,466	30,050
2016–17	92,068	125,303	86,943	74,929	65,282	61,466	64,456	88,083	93,062	68,943	100,859	101,034	51,866
2017–18	94,444	128,467	88,936	76,816	67,177	63,623	65,005	90,319	95,363	69,908	103,606	103,694	61,840
2018–19	96,369	131,403	90,721	78,575	69,903	65,504	64,992	92,098	97,208	71,606	105,915	106,072	52,171

See notes at end of table.

Table 316.10. Average salary of full-time instructional faculty on 9-month contracts in degree-granting postsecondary institutions, by academic rank, control and level of institution, and sex: Selected years, 1970–71 through 2018–19–Continued

Sex and academic year	All faculty	Academic rank						Public institutions			Private institutions		
		Professor	Associate professor	Assistant professor	Instructor	Lecturer	No rank	Total	4-year	2-year	Total	4-year	2-year
1	2	3	4	5	6	7	8	9	10	11	12	13	14
Females													
1975–76	14,308	20,308	16,364	13,522	12,572	11,901	14,094	14,762	14,758	14,769	13,030	13,231	10,201
1980–81	19,996	27,959	22,295	18,302	14,854	16,168	20,843	20,673	20,608	20,778	18,073	18,326	13,892
1982–83	23,261	32,221	25,738	21,130	17,102	18,830	23,855	23,892	23,876	23,917	21,451	21,785	15,845
1984–85	25,941	35,824	28,517	23,575	19,362	21,004	26,050	26,566	26,813	26,172	24,186	24,560	17,575
1985–86	27,576	38,252	30,300	24,966	20,237	22,273	27,171	28,299	28,680	27,693	25,523	25,889	18,504
1987–88	30,499	42,371	33,528	27,600	21,962	24,370	29,605	31,215	31,820	30,228	28,621	28,946	21,215
1989–90	34,183	47,663	37,469	31,090	24,320	26,995	32,528	34,796	35,704	33,307	32,650	33,010	24,002
1990–91	35,881	49,728	39,329	32,724	25,534	28,111	34,179	36,459	37,573	34,720	34,359	34,898	22,585
1991–92	37,534	51,621	40,766	34,063	28,873	28,550	35,622	37,800	38,634	36,517	36,828	37,309	24,683
1992–93	38,385	52,755	41,861	35,032	27,700	28,922	35,792	38,356	39,470	36,710	38,460	38,987	25,068
1993–94	40,058	54,746	43,178	36,169	28,136	31,048	38,474	40,118	41,031	38,707	39,902	40,378	26,142
1994–95	41,369	56,555	44,626	37,352	29,072	31,677	38,967	41,548	42,663	39,812	40,908	41,815	22,851
1995–96	42,871	58,318	45,803	38,345	29,940	32,584	41,085	42,871	43,986	41,086	42,871	43,236	30,671
1996–97	44,325	60,160	47,101	39,350	30,819	33,415	42,474	44,306	45,402	42,531	44,374	44,726	30,661
1997–98	45,775	61,965	48,597	40,504	32,011	33,918	43,491	45,648	46,709	43,943	46,106	46,466	30,995
1998–99	47,421	64,236	50,347	41,894	33,152	35,115	44,723	47,247	48,355	45,457	47,874	48,204	31,524
1999–2000	48,997	67,079	52,091	43,367	34,228	36,607	45,865	48,714	50,168	46,340	49,737	50,052	32,951
2001–02	52,662	72,542	56,186	46,824	45,262	39,538	45,003	52,123	53,895	49,290	54,149	54,434	32,921
2002–03	54,105	75,028	57,716	48,380	46,573	40,265	45,251	53,435	55,121	50,717	55,881	56,158	35,296
2003–04	55,378	76,652	59,095	49,689	47,404	41,536	46,519	54,408	56,117	51,591	57,921	58,192	36,896
2004–05	56,926	79,160	60,809	51,154	48,351	42,455	47,860	55,780	57,714	52,566	59,919	60,143	39,291
2005–06	58,665	81,514	62,860	52,901	49,533	43,934	49,172	57,462	59,437	54,082	61,830	62,092	38,786
2006–07	60,926	84,857	65,131	54,909	51,828	45,505	50,814	59,677	61,713	56,121	64,194	64,428	41,099
2007–08	63,357	88,340	67,823	57,102	53,929	47,410	52,809	62,138	64,223	58,346	66,538	66,755	43,670
2008–09	65,662	91,528	70,393	59,291	55,431	49,184	54,663	64,230	66,391	60,195	69,375	69,668	43,344
2009–10	66,647	92,830	71,017	59,997	56,239	49,957	55,206	65,139	67,276	61,047	70,507	70,746	44,892
2010–11	67,473	94,041	72,003	60,888	56,566	50,270	54,985	65,632	67,935	61,193	72,091	72,306	45,518
2011–12	68,468	95,845	73,057	61,763	57,013	50,994	55,299	66,368	68,897	61,417	73,629	73,788	49,382
2012–13	69,124	96,563	73,966	62,321	56,361	50,963	56,777	66,703	69,083	61,774	74,987	75,149	46,407
2013–14	70,589	98,374	75,592	63,782	57,043	52,497	57,196	68,335	71,059	62,597	76,127	76,358	44,789
2014–15	71,792	100,783	77,115	65,009	58,020	52,901	56,616	69,384	72,288	62,971	77,504	78,089	38,841
2015–16	73,850	103,364	78,977	66,603	59,726	54,825	58,562	71,493	74,378	64,924	79,549	79,959	32,495
2016–17	76,199	106,881	81,037	68,701	62,277	56,601	59,568	73,826	76,696	66,616	81,976	82,146	53,866
2017–18	78,153	109,605	82,814	70,316	63,595	58,575	60,902	75,716	78,689	67,755	84,065	84,201	54,319
2018–19	79,995	111,945	84,488	71,856	66,103	60,188	61,616	77,450	80,437	69,425	86,179	86,311	56,267
				Constant 2018–19 dollars[1]									
Total													
1970–71	$81,030	$114,489	$86,474	$71,253	$59,673	$71,381	$78,631	$82,585	$83,656	$80,612	$74,074	$75,386	$55,238
1975–76	76,077	103,435	77,934	63,872	62,440	58,939	69,398	77,372	79,463	72,246	72,708	73,601	49,782
1980–81	68,129	89,913	67,871	55,261	44,376	50,583	65,299	69,424	71,260	64,840	64,594	65,272	44,046
1982–83	70,177	91,708	69,467	56,914	45,418	51,794	65,948	70,931	73,008	65,974	68,105	68,874	42,822
1984–85	72,908	95,168	71,706	59,070	48,442	53,481	66,289	73,384	76,062	66,723	71,622	72,429	44,324
1985–86	75,391	98,377	73,983	61,159	48,686	55,324	67,701	76,225	79,211	68,870	73,087	73,855	45,237
1987–88	78,483	102,845	77,026	63,644	49,690	56,793	68,940	79,213	82,730	70,419	76,628	77,278	47,808
1989–90	80,050	105,336	78,573	65,203	49,926	57,825	68,931	80,615	84,502	70,842	78,715	79,421	49,070
1990–91	79,745	105,039	78,323	65,123	49,800	56,921	68,832	80,032	84,179	70,079	79,031	79,856	45,556
1991–92	80,358	105,246	78,668	65,504	56,654	55,810	69,238	79,973	83,632	71,393	81,319	82,083	47,046
1992–93	79,457	104,466	78,090	65,083	50,643	54,275	67,119	78,538	82,657	69,188	81,715	82,502	46,389
1993–94	80,310	105,053	78,427	65,181	49,934	56,690	70,297	79,540	83,176	71,086	82,216	82,934	49,253
1994–95	80,508	105,593	78,659	65,260	49,951	55,901	69,421	79,869	83,752	70,893	82,073	83,148	43,129
1995–96	80,832	105,799	78,629	65,073	49,743	55,958	70,482	80,058	83,886	70,973	82,728	83,307	52,318
1996–97	81,012	106,242	78,586	64,847	49,716	55,722	70,447	80,173	84,022	71,058	83,056	83,584	52,003
1997–98	81,950	107,625	79,590	65,500	50,811	55,564	70,884	80,858	84,737	71,904	84,619	85,151	52,600
1998–99	83,267	109,781	80,926	66,723	52,055	56,672	71,190	82,070	86,116	72,782	86,168	86,634	53,597
1999–2000	83,611	111,321	81,570	67,290	52,239	57,140	70,896	82,299	86,695	72,170	86,790	87,254	53,745
2001–02	84,912	114,831	83,466	69,354	66,744	59,409	66,189	83,181	88,140	72,256	89,284	89,669	47,101
2002–03	85,295	116,081	84,100	70,306	67,179	59,277	64,445	83,465	88,294	72,779	89,750	90,141	48,434
2003–04	85,169	116,137	84,035	70,496	66,776	59,404	64,953	82,849	87,566	72,236	90,731	91,093	49,433
2004–05	84,868	116,477	83,974	70,432	65,704	58,813	64,663	82,372	87,270	71,256	90,841	91,158	49,320
2005–06	84,221	116,085	83,638	70,136	64,761	58,414	64,178	81,658	86,485	70,517	90,386	90,701	49,063
2006–07	84,960	117,428	84,436	70,817	66,093	58,691	64,738	82,434	87,202	71,287	91,013	91,282	51,039
2007–08	85,061	117,953	84,737	70,934	66,225	59,086	65,053	82,533	87,156	71,388	91,124	91,374	51,924
2008–09	86,823	120,743	86,656	72,613	67,155	60,547	66,554	84,050	88,778	72,482	93,435	93,745	51,373
2009–10	87,198	121,158	86,619	72,737	67,532	60,982	66,378	84,345	88,982	72,760	93,928	94,182	52,291
2010–11	86,468	120,239	86,040	72,326	66,446	60,238	64,780	83,299	88,044	71,436	93,818	94,048	51,717
2011–12	85,215	119,186	84,781	71,241	64,941	59,386	63,325	81,797	86,635	69,618	92,976	93,155	53,205
2012–13	84,599	118,311	84,326	70,799	63,137	58,100	64,318	80,875	85,402	68,866	92,978	93,158	49,239
2013–14	84,866	118,566	84,822	71,241	62,777	58,816	63,769	81,372	86,121	68,677	92,891	93,119	48,072
2014–15	85,776	120,735	85,967	72,327	63,358	59,214	62,393	82,195	87,076	68,611	93,746	94,396	40,844
2015–16	87,399	122,811	87,317	73,744	64,744	60,912	64,138	83,832	88,636	70,172	95,523	95,992	33,265
2016–17	88,443	124,370	87,928	74,886	66,395	61,340	64,487	84,952	89,556	70,624	96,501	96,693	55,336
2017–18	88,670	124,599	87,915	74,996	66,526	62,077	64,049	85,162	89,721	70,147	96,784	96,909	58,212
2018–19	88,703	124,671	87,841	75,102	67,789	62,542	63,153	85,148	89,641	70,404	96,962	97,115	54,452

See notes at end of table.

Table 316.10. Average salary of full-time instructional faculty on 9-month contracts in degree-granting postsecondary institutions, by academic rank, control and level of institution, and sex: Selected years, 1970–71 through 2018–19—Continued

Sex and academic year	All faculty	Academic rank						Public institutions			Private institutions		
		Professor	Associate professor	Assistant professor	Instructor	Lecturer	No rank	Total	4-year	2-year	Total	4-year	2-year
1	2	3	4	5	6	7	8	9	10	11	12	13	14
Males													
1975–76	79,525	104,589	78,589	64,732	65,899	62,013	71,977	80,656	82,754	74,620	76,651	77,388	51,960
1980–81	71,628	90,875	68,564	56,215	45,449	53,449	67,743	72,722	74,581	67,143	68,687	69,202	46,999
1982–83	73,965	92,781	70,347	58,281	46,860	54,769	68,487	74,448	76,538	68,443	72,662	73,232	44,760
1984–85	77,063	96,428	72,776	60,655	50,667	56,409	68,653	77,201	79,845	69,182	76,694	77,292	46,599
1985–86	79,818	99,692	75,114	63,060	50,490	58,741	70,445	80,363	83,291	71,588	78,333	78,901	47,508
1987–88	83,324	104,363	78,321	65,779	51,695	60,457	71,595	83,767	87,230	73,192	82,212	82,680	49,501
1989–90	85,297	107,012	80,046	67,380	51,726	62,156	71,767	85,687	89,428	73,964	84,398	84,960	50,301
1990–91	85,229	106,947	79,883	67,395	51,798	61,272	71,935	85,265	89,205	73,355	85,142	85,709	49,052
1991–92	85,850	107,190	80,290	67,745	61,131	60,186	72,241	85,181	88,696	74,787	87,471	88,037	49,157
1992–93	85,057	106,571	79,709	67,245	52,569	57,774	69,952	83,830	87,771	72,368	87,994	88,561	48,693
1993–94	85,877	107,144	80,075	67,196	51,644	60,271	73,184	84,798	88,320	74,374	88,471	89,027	53,321
1994–95	86,262	107,846	80,329	67,225	51,405	59,074	72,581	85,253	89,032	74,124	88,661	89,306	49,909
1995–96	86,577	108,109	80,386	66,977	50,720	59,235	73,152	85,509	89,256	74,110	89,117	89,585	54,590
1996–97	86,806	108,720	80,418	66,723	50,584	58,862	72,818	85,646	89,511	73,941	89,548	89,974	55,362
1997–98	87,870	110,344	81,490	67,359	51,784	58,691	73,317	86,423	90,420	74,677	91,280	91,724	56,618
1998–99	89,349	112,765	82,856	68,726	53,475	59,992	73,283	87,795	92,054	75,363	92,957	93,340	58,553
1999–2000	89,888	114,414	83,687	69,437	53,639	60,144	72,989	88,242	92,800	74,852	93,699	94,108	57,801
2001–02	91,420	118,475	85,705	71,802	69,422	63,276	68,294	89,308	94,627	74,421	96,466	96,791	47,465
2002–03	91,966	119,871	86,541	72,932	69,916	63,236	65,939	89,793	95,019	75,048	96,971	97,320	47,690
2003–04	91,845	120,123	86,377	73,015	69,389	62,896	66,652	89,111	94,245	74,341	98,020	98,330	48,457
2004–05	91,610	120,614	86,400	72,952	67,884	62,004	66,196	88,694	93,999	73,193	98,191	98,485	46,203
2005–06	91,090	120,572	86,107	72,673	66,844	61,418	65,943	88,063	93,361	72,366	97,927	98,184	48,639
2006–07	91,871	122,018	86,943	73,311	68,300	61,397	66,625	88,905	94,155	73,150	98,543	98,756	51,111
2007–08	92,066	122,751	87,265	73,425	68,351	61,964	67,198	89,001	94,117	73,203	98,978	99,180	51,437
2008–09	94,057	125,942	89,236	75,169	69,391	63,636	68,909	90,728	96,034	74,176	101,508	101,741	51,762
2009–10	94,515	126,468	89,278	75,315	69,871	64,209	68,532	91,086	96,316	74,434	102,111	102,303	52,001
2010–11	93,790	125,618	88,699	74,909	68,563	63,529	66,891	90,051	95,401	73,024	101,955	102,138	51,026
2011–12	92,542	124,723	87,433	73,792	66,850	62,733	65,449	88,529	93,982	71,138	101,100	101,251	50,361
2012–13	91,934	124,045	86,946	73,440	64,972	61,041	66,872	87,596	92,723	70,372	101,136	101,295	46,971
2013–14	92,209	124,460	87,501	73,827	64,433	61,675	66,302	88,067	93,395	70,145	101,212	101,392	47,725
2014–15	93,311	126,884	88,769	75,185	64,963	62,538	64,537	89,129	94,590	70,105	102,146	102,773	40,010
2015–16	94,984	129,184	90,116	76,821	66,316	64,230	66,399	90,740	96,157	71,590	104,185	104,662	31,941
2016–17	96,094	130,783	90,746	78,205	68,137	64,154	67,274	91,935	97,132	71,958	105,270	105,452	54,134
2017–18	96,401	131,129	90,779	78,408	68,569	64,941	66,352	92,191	97,339	71,357	105,753	105,843	63,121
2018–19	96,369	131,403	90,721	78,575	69,903	65,504	64,992	92,098	97,208	71,606	105,915	106,072	52,171
Females													
1975–76	65,340	92,743	74,731	61,752	57,413	54,348	64,365	67,418	67,400	67,447	59,508	60,423	46,584
1980–81	58,463	81,745	65,185	53,510	43,429	47,271	60,939	60,442	60,252	60,749	52,841	53,580	40,616
1982–83	60,023	83,144	66,415	54,524	44,130	48,589	61,556	61,651	61,610	61,716	55,353	56,214	40,887
1984–85	62,118	85,784	68,286	56,452	46,364	50,296	62,379	63,615	64,206	62,671	57,915	58,811	42,085
1985–86	64,182	89,030	70,522	58,108	47,101	51,840	63,240	65,865	66,752	64,455	59,404	60,256	43,067
1987–88	66,681	92,637	73,303	60,343	48,016	53,281	64,726	68,246	69,569	66,088	62,575	63,285	46,383
1989–90	68,182	95,069	74,736	62,012	48,509	53,846	64,882	69,406	71,217	66,435	65,124	65,843	47,875
1990–91	67,858	94,048	74,381	61,889	48,291	53,165	64,640	68,953	71,060	65,664	64,980	66,000	42,714
1991–92	68,781	94,596	74,704	62,421	52,910	52,318	65,278	69,269	70,797	66,918	67,487	68,369	45,232
1992–93	68,210	93,747	74,387	62,253	49,224	51,395	63,602	68,158	70,138	65,234	68,344	60,280	44,546
1993–94	69,387	94,828	74,790	62,649	48,736	53,780	66,642	69,489	71,070	67,046	69,116	69,940	45,281
1994–95	69,661	95,231	75,145	62,896	48,954	53,339	65,615	69,961	71,839	67,038	68,884	70,411	38,479
1995–96	70,277	95,599	75,084	62,859	49,080	53,414	67,349	70,277	72,105	67,352	70,278	70,876	50,279
1996–97	70,645	95,883	75,070	62,716	49,120	53,257	67,696	70,614	72,362	67,786	70,723	71,285	48,868
1997–98	71,678	97,029	76,098	63,424	50,126	53,111	68,101	71,479	73,140	68,810	72,197	72,761	48,535
1998–99	72,991	98,874	77,496	64,484	51,029	54,050	68,838	72,724	74,429	69,968	73,690	74,197	48,522
1999–2000	73,301	100,353	77,930	64,879	51,206	54,766	68,616	72,878	75,053	69,327	74,409	74,880	49,296
2001–02	74,849	103,105	79,859	66,552	64,331	56,195	63,963	74,083	76,603	70,056	76,963	77,369	46,791
2002–03	75,246	104,346	80,270	67,284	64,772	55,999	62,933	74,315	76,660	70,535	77,717	78,103	49,089
2003–04	75,368	104,322	80,428	67,626	64,516	56,530	63,312	74,048	76,375	70,215	78,830	79,198	50,215
2004–05	75,212	104,588	80,342	67,586	63,882	56,093	63,233	73,698	76,253	69,452	79,166	79,462	51,912
2005–06	74,666	103,747	80,005	67,330	63,044	55,917	62,584	73,135	75,648	68,834	78,695	79,028	49,365
2006–07	75,589	105,280	80,806	68,124	64,301	56,457	63,043	74,040	76,565	69,628	79,643	79,933	50,991
2007–08	75,796	105,685	81,139	68,314	64,518	56,718	63,178	74,338	76,832	69,802	79,602	79,862	52,245
2008–09	77,472	107,991	83,054	69,955	65,401	58,031	64,495	75,783	78,333	71,023	81,853	82,199	51,140
2009–10	77,881	108,478	82,987	70,110	65,719	58,378	64,511	76,119	78,616	71,337	82,391	82,671	52,459
2010–11	77,295	107,730	82,484	69,751	64,799	57,588	62,988	75,185	77,824	70,100	82,584	82,830	52,144
2011–12	76,202	106,671	81,308	68,739	63,453	56,754	61,545	73,864	76,679	68,354	81,945	82,112	54,960
2012–13	75,672	105,710	80,973	68,225	61,700	55,791	62,156	73,022	75,627	67,626	82,090	82,268	50,803
2013–14	76,088	106,036	81,480	68,751	61,486	56,586	61,651	73,658	76,594	67,472	82,056	82,305	48,278
2014–15	76,825	107,848	82,521	69,566	62,088	56,609	60,584	74,248	77,355	67,385	82,937	83,563	41,564
2015–16	78,497	109,869	83,948	70,795	63,485	58,275	62,247	75,992	79,059	69,010	84,555	84,991	34,540
2016–17	79,532	111,555	84,581	71,706	65,000	59,076	62,173	77,055	80,050	69,529	85,561	85,739	56,221
2017–18	79,773	111,876	84,530	71,774	64,913	59,789	62,164	77,285	80,319	69,159	85,807	85,946	55,445
2018–19	79,995	111,945	84,488	71,856	66,103	60,188	61,616	77,450	80,437	69,425	86,179	86,311	56,267

[1]Constant dollars based on the Consumer Price Index, prepared by the Bureau of Labor Statistics, U.S. Department of Labor, adjusted to an academic-year basis.
NOTE: Data exclude instructional faculty at medical schools. Data through 1995–96 are for institutions of higher education, while later data are for degree-granting institutions. Degree-granting institutions grant associate's or higher degrees and participate in Title IV federal financial aid programs. Data for 1987–88 and later years include imputations for nonrespondent institutions. Some data have been revised from previously published figures.

SOURCE: U.S. Department of Education, National Center for Education Statistics, Higher Education General Information Survey (HEGIS), "Faculty Salaries, Tenure, and Fringe Benefits" surveys, 1970–71 through 1985–86; Integrated Postsecondary Education Data System (IPEDS), "Salaries, Tenure, and Fringe Benefits of Full-Time Instructional Faculty Survey" (IPEDS-SA:87–99); and IPEDS, Winter 2001–02 through Winter 2011–12 and Spring 2013 through Spring 2019, Human Resources component, Salaries section. (This table was prepared November 2019.)

Table 316.20. Average salary of full-time instructional faculty on 9-month contracts in degree-granting postsecondary institutions, by academic rank, sex, and control and level of institution: Selected years, 1999–2000 through 2018–19

Academic year, control and level of institution	Constant 2018–19 dollars[1] All faculty, total	Current dollars												
		All faculty			Academic rank									
					Professor			Associate professor			Assistant professor	Instructor	Lecturer	No academic rank
		Total	Males	Females	Total	Males	Females	Total	Males	Females				
1	2	3	4	5	6	7	8	9	10	11	12	13	14	15
1999–2000														
All institutions	$83,611	$55,888	$60,084	$48,997	$74,410	$76,478	$67,079	$54,524	$55,939	$52,091	$44,978	$34,918	$38,194	$47,389
Public	82,299	55,011	58,984	48,714	72,475	74,501	65,568	54,641	55,992	52,305	45,285	35,007	37,403	47,990
4-year	86,695	57,950	62,030	50,168	75,204	76,530	69,619	55,681	56,776	53,599	45,822	33,528	37,261	40,579
Doctoral[2]	93,133	62,253	66,882	52,287	81,182	82,445	74,653	57,744	58,999	55,156	48,190	33,345	38,883	39,350
Master's[3]	78,951	52,773	55,565	48,235	66,588	67,128	64,863	53,048	53,686	51,977	43,396	33,214	34,448	43,052
Other 4-year	71,611	47,867	49,829	44,577	60,360	60,748	59,052	49,567	50,133	48,548	42,306	35,754	36,088	38,330
2-year	72,170	48,240	50,033	46,340	57,806	59,441	55,501	48,056	49,425	46,711	41,984	37,634	40,061	48,233
Nonprofit	87,027	58,172	62,788	49,881	78,512	80,557	70,609	54,300	55,836	51,687	44,423	34,670	40,761	41,415
4-year	87,406	58,425	63,028	50,117	78,604	80,622	70,774	54,388	55,898	51,809	44,502	34,813	40,783	41,761
Doctoral[2]	107,525	71,873	77,214	59,586	95,182	96,768	87,342	62,503	63,951	59,536	52,134	39,721	42,693	45,887
Master's[3]	74,610	49,871	52,642	45,718	62,539	63,603	59,353	50,176	51,470	48,165	41,447	33,991	37,923	44,153
Other 4-year	69,979	46,776	48,847	43,544	60,200	60,757	58,364	46,822	47,135	46,365	38,775	31,574	33,058	35,120
2-year	56,226	37,583	39,933	34,733	39,454	38,431	40,571	36,349	37,342	35,608	31,818	27,696	25,965	40,373
For-profit	44,198	29,543	30,023	28,942	45,505	44,248	49,693	48,469	53,548	43,389	33,043	29,894	‡	27,958
2009–10														
All institutions	87,198	74,620	80,881	66,647	103,682	108,225	92,830	74,125	76,400	71,017	62,245	57,791	52,185	56,803
Public	84,345	72,178	77,948	65,139	99,208	103,746	88,815	73,379	75,687	70,256	62,160	59,310	50,228	55,864
4-year	88,982	76,147	82,423	67,276	103,948	107,191	95,048	75,251	77,282	72,298	63,442	46,028	50,104	54,005
Doctoral[2]	95,647	81,850	89,186	70,307	113,063	115,829	103,793	78,539	80,830	74,963	66,902	44,406	50,313	53,135
Master's[3]	79,746	68,243	71,574	64,239	87,917	88,929	85,883	70,332	71,340	69,036	59,396	44,422	49,746	55,765
Other 4-year	71,519	61,202	63,678	58,349	76,448	79,143	72,073	65,003	66,297	63,338	55,055	54,050	49,432	54,487
2-year	72,760	62,264	63,697	61,047	72,377	74,423	70,429	60,632	61,565	59,852	54,161	65,503	53,548	56,239
Nonprofit	94,171	80,587	87,600	70,676	112,146	116,401	101,119	75,565	77,764	72,502	62,395	47,842	57,508	62,242
4-year	94,347	80,738	87,720	70,834	112,252	116,472	101,290	75,664	77,827	72,642	62,465	47,885	57,520	62,542
Doctoral[2]	111,574	95,480	104,514	80,888	134,776	138,354	123,283	85,864	88,699	81,499	71,973	53,825	58,932	66,634
Master's[3]	76,863	65,776	68,776	62,128	82,516	84,062	79,452	66,524	67,508	65,309	55,469	45,305	53,637	60,591
Other 4-year	75,506	64,614	67,178	61,326	84,869	85,528	83,480	64,747	64,949	64,478	53,130	42,145	52,422	52,775
2-year	53,440	45,731	44,417	46,529	53,063	55,046	51,310	45,768	45,863	45,717	42,706	46,010	32,393	43,562
For-profit	64,087	54,842	56,689	52,925	79,574	81,765	75,817	71,376	72,429	70,199	66,027	41,742	‡	53,705
2017–18														
All institutions	88,670	86,870	94,444	78,153	122,069	128,467	109,605	86,130	88,936	82,814	73,474	65,176	60,816	62,748
Public	85,162	83,433	90,319	75,716	115,675	121,960	103,855	85,030	87,868	81,670	73,503	66,561	58,433	60,605
4-year	89,721	87,900	95,363	78,689	122,122	126,856	111,746	87,498	89,986	84,359	75,507	58,699	58,372	61,519
Doctoral[2]	96,259	94,305	102,935	82,930	132,004	136,342	121,379	91,828	94,614	88,200	79,942	53,367	59,479	60,723
Master's[3]	76,795	75,236	78,724	71,382	96,212	97,611	93,833	78,316	79,301	77,145	67,252	49,820	55,529	58,318
Other 4-year	70,607	69,173	70,967	67,421	80,794	83,274	77,490	70,240	71,706	68,646	61,212	74,216	52,801	62,706
2-year	70,147	68,723	69,908	67,755	79,170	80,694	77,865	67,430	68,273	66,795	60,343	72,741	60,610	60,167
Nonprofit	97,168	95,195	103,979	84,411	134,378	140,602	121,408	88,307	91,064	85,057	73,531	58,117	68,198	75,680
4-year	97,257	95,282	104,059	84,492	134,437	140,638	121,497	88,323	91,076	85,075	73,566	58,237	68,205	75,824
Doctoral[2]	113,020	110,726	122,121	95,349	160,179	166,375	144,995	99,148	102,838	94,590	84,103	63,983	69,754	81,783
Master's[3]	76,138	74,593	77,835	71,075	92,484	93,658	90,537	74,409	75,698	72,958	63,298	53,927	62,123	75,222
Other 4-year	76,563	75,008	77,176	72,641	98,505	98,427	98,635	75,740	75,898	75,568	61,552	48,098	63,604	59,277
2-year	58,221	57,039	54,468	58,676	70,019	71,602	68,984	72,127	71,674	72,362	54,995	50,491	62,508	52,523
For-profit	57,318	56,155	59,043	53,543	70,020	69,939	70,218	65,084	62,200	67,616	53,762	49,334	‡	57,206
2018–19														
All institutions	88,703	88,703	96,369	79,995	124,671	131,403	111,945	87,841	90,721	84,488	75,102	67,789	62,542	63,153
Public	85,148	85,148	92,098	77,450	117,969	124,480	106,060	86,469	89,441	83,006	75,061	69,162	59,871	61,467
4-year	89,641	89,641	97,208	80,437	124,169	129,276	113,465	89,025	91,662	85,753	77,107	60,529	59,834	61,870
Doctoral[2]	95,942	95,942	104,629	84,700	134,213	138,903	123,296	93,266	96,135	89,578	81,563	54,719	60,750	62,179
Master's[3]	76,321	76,321	79,871	72,439	97,246	98,841	94,604	79,107	80,215	77,829	68,215	50,896	56,853	56,557
Other 4-year	70,858	70,858	72,706	69,088	81,276	84,316	77,514	72,126	73,849	70,335	62,406	77,157	54,627	62,577
2-year	70,404	70,404	71,606	69,425	80,480	81,994	79,180	68,067	68,680	67,611	60,956	75,441	61,278	61,275
Nonprofit	97,338	97,338	106,353	86,474	137,539	144,262	123,986	90,503	93,211	87,354	75,213	60,132	70,481	76,366
4-year	97,447	97,447	106,459	86,570	137,587	144,299	124,045	90,523	93,226	87,376	75,251	60,374	70,501	76,569
Doctoral[2]	112,794	112,794	124,378	97,525	163,299	169,943	147,610	101,284	104,875	96,946	86,034	66,825	72,311	81,379
Master's[3]	75,367	75,367	78,459	72,054	92,990	94,243	90,993	75,515	76,821	74,049	64,279	54,067	63,482	76,307
Other 4-year	76,487	76,487	78,890	73,936	100,460	100,635	100,182	77,412	77,643	77,162	62,770	49,352	64,320	61,071
2-year	57,120	57,120	54,179	59,181	77,990	75,217	80,234	76,058	73,806	76,991	57,190	46,528	59,064	54,550
For-profit	53,692	53,692	53,816	53,553	82,216	84,096	79,253	72,399	71,922	72,834	65,524	61,083	82,871	44,335

‡Reporting standards not met (too few cases).
[1]Constant dollars based on the Consumer Price Index, prepared by the Bureau of Labor Statistics, U.S. Department of Labor, adjusted to an academic-year basis.
[2]Institutions that awarded 20 or more doctor's degrees during the previous academic year.
[3]Institutions that awarded 20 or more master's degrees, but less than 20 doctor's degrees, during the previous academic year. This definition differs from the definition of master's institutions that is used in some *Digest* tables that present postsecondary finance data.

NOTE: Data exclude instructional faculty at medical schools. Degree-granting institutions grant associate's or higher degrees and participate in Title IV federal financial aid programs. Some data have been revised from previously published figures.
SOURCE: U.S. Department of Education, National Center for Education Statistics, Integrated Postsecondary Education Data System (IPEDS), "Salaries, Tenure, and Fringe Benefits of Full-Time Instructional Faculty Survey" (IPEDS-SA:99); and IPEDS, Winter 2009–10, Spring 2018, and Spring 2019, Human Resources component, Salaries section. (This table was prepared November 2019.)

Table 316.30. Average salary of full-time instructional faculty on 9-month contracts in degree-granting postsecondary institutions, by control and level of institution and state or jurisdiction: 2018–19

[In current dollars]

State or jurisdiction	All insti-tutions	Public institutions						Nonprofit institutions						For-profit insti-tutions
		Total	4-year institutions				2-year	Total	4-year institutions				2-year	
			Total	Doctoral[1]	Master's[2]	Other			Total	Doctoral[1]	Master's[2]	Other		
1	2	3	4	5	6	7	8	9	10	11	12	13	14	15
United States	$88,703	$85,148	$89,641	$95,942	$76,321	$70,858	$70,404	$97,338	$97,447	$112,794	$75,367	$76,487	$57,120	$53,692
Alabama	73,892	76,153	82,523	87,030	67,788	†	56,046	59,473	59,473	64,032	51,251	56,563	†	66,321
Alaska	81,258	82,350	82,350	85,871	80,408	†	†	54,804	54,776	†	54,776	†	55,106	†
Arizona	86,878	87,562	91,434	92,499	84,373	51,429	75,774	76,004	76,004	†	76,004	†	†	69,139
Arkansas	63,583	64,092	69,771	75,132	58,079	62,110	46,908	60,731	60,760	66,175	64,630	56,901	56,927	†
California	109,371	107,450	113,518	124,260	89,765	100,951	96,416	116,271	116,271	125,713	86,593	107,407	†	78,026
Colorado	85,512	84,218	86,808	94,760	63,813	64,189	58,228	93,307	93,307	95,360	88,867	†	†	52,575
Connecticut	107,248	94,380	99,571	110,044	88,482	†	76,987	119,082	119,082	126,266	92,376	87,925	†	93,049
Delaware	105,103	105,831	105,831	112,746	†	70,754	†	73,575	76,679	†	76,679	†	60,714	‡
District of Columbia	115,372	83,712	83,712	143,504	76,695	†	†	117,754	117,754	118,087	76,837	†	†	72,060
Florida	82,728	81,901	82,351	96,182	80,302	60,767	60,530	85,314	85,314	97,046	76,818	66,449	†	47,728
Georgia	78,218	76,684	78,017	83,759	62,325	58,983	48,700	83,669	83,897	105,122	71,417	63,259	74,961	53,257
Hawaii	92,066	93,852	101,893	104,939	†	80,566	76,092	79,474	79,474	†	76,438	113,483	†	†
Idaho	69,774	70,205	73,572	75,293	†	55,921	56,131	64,536	64,536	58,681	†	69,499	†	†
Illinois	93,330	85,996	89,931	92,948	75,549	†	78,928	102,805	102,853	120,598	72,204	65,738	52,817	61,339
Indiana	84,101	83,888	89,052	95,646	68,852	53,069	50,839	84,523	84,523	96,083	66,668	70,168	†	†
Iowa	78,834	85,361	95,342	95,342	†	†	62,148	67,766	67,766	74,069	61,064	69,618	†	47,400
Kansas	70,493	73,337	80,161	85,028	64,394	†	56,420	52,935	52,935	55,198	56,614	46,651	†	†
Kentucky	68,514	70,156	76,008	77,858	57,088	†	52,135	62,129	62,129	66,242	55,072	67,632	†	†
Louisiana	70,111	65,833	71,292	80,203	58,696	53,091	45,262	88,344	88,344	94,979	60,053	52,146	†	†
Maine	80,266	74,073	78,653	83,844	63,879	64,458	58,663	88,465	88,653	69,418	57,518	101,547	59,714	†
Maryland	85,635	84,622	89,415	91,922	77,518	†	75,021	88,980	88,980	102,224	74,276	71,745	†	68,722
Massachusetts	112,141	89,950	97,295	104,909	84,239	†	66,164	122,612	122,616	135,715	97,377	96,010	‡	†
Michigan	94,098	97,490	99,824	102,466	81,216	81,876	82,986	71,706	71,706	92,595	70,347	66,607	†	†
Minnesota	83,875	86,259	93,541	107,095	81,131	66,067	72,612	78,517	78,558	77,051	70,483	82,719	39,147	†
Mississippi	62,811	62,897	70,387	73,043	57,060	†	52,000	61,895	61,895	66,812	73,842	44,588	†	66,406
Missouri	77,741	71,761	75,769	84,393	63,142	†	59,229	87,487	87,487	102,883	66,113	57,372	†	70,587
Montana	67,356	70,891	73,818	79,165	62,103	55,955	50,541	48,185	52,829	†	54,770	51,540	19,102	†
Nebraska	78,724	80,878	85,080	91,660	67,015	†	62,348	71,423	71,423	88,428	60,138	58,369	†	†
Nevada	86,920	86,936	86,936	94,254	†	73,064	†	78,922	78,922	‡	75,153	†	†	†
New Hampshire	99,666	91,918	97,833	107,879	81,376	86,524	67,223	110,282	110,282	151,186	73,577	75,882	†	†
New Jersey	109,290	105,646	113,212	114,387	107,508	†	77,802	118,043	118,043	133,590	86,989	75,976	†	47,838
New Mexico	68,015	67,968	73,692	79,724	63,697	50,155	54,281	69,321	69,321	†	69,321	†	†	‡
New York	100,116	89,939	94,158	109,000	87,074	76,926	80,591	110,324	110,401	120,468	83,498	91,751	74,311	32,266
North Carolina	80,384	76,047	87,134	90,736	73,652	74,259	52,332	91,946	92,261	114,336	62,777	66,258	42,156	69,724
North Dakota	70,099	71,372	73,066	80,997	60,300	53,745	58,228	58,573	58,573	65,711	†	52,476	†	†
Ohio	82,517	85,652	89,711	92,721	60,947	71,151	67,227	76,009	76,033	82,760	67,807	73,841	38,750	52,935
Oklahoma	69,602	68,926	73,417	80,692	62,644	49,601	49,942	72,641	72,641	84,449	61,677	39,807	†	47,743
Oregon	81,965	82,613	86,583	90,928	67,682	68,618	74,108	79,690	79,690	81,513	59,044	82,408	†	†
Pennsylvania	94,446	91,562	95,507	103,726	88,122	76,231	66,538	97,395	97,783	111,061	73,930	87,191	58,185	65,139
Rhode Island	101,815	82,037	87,541	94,465	73,070	†	62,179	115,224	115,224	143,426	93,540	†	†	†
South Carolina	70,530	72,922	82,126	95,713	69,639	62,144	50,093	61,262	61,370	67,269	62,679	56,839	54,598	85,949
South Dakota	66,146	67,919	70,116	71,599	70,130	51,717	58,490	57,038	57,038	†	58,371	47,743	†	†
Tennessee	79,423	74,886	81,011	83,488	71,093	†	54,383	89,209	89,209	108,571	67,216	51,752	†	62,658
Texas	82,383	80,147	87,608	92,277	70,029	59,898	62,140	93,080	93,171	106,557	71,423	58,708	38,602	41,630
Utah	78,986	78,672	80,572	93,980	71,013	62,928	59,680	84,893	84,893	114,059	76,370	†	†	‡
Vermont	82,642	83,320	83,320	92,534	60,336	57,874	†	82,019	82,019	†	84,976	55,726	†	†
Virginia	85,083	87,337	92,550	96,225	72,864	76,232	64,269	77,580	77,580	86,742	58,179	66,823	†	52,885
Washington	84,110	84,946	86,387	103,758	85,680	65,680	64,460	81,044	81,044	87,552	66,500	79,105	†	83,252
West Virginia	66,772	68,500	71,462	79,844	59,915	57,514	49,589	52,397	52,397	56,711	49,888	51,193	†	†
Wisconsin	79,637	81,433	82,140	90,995	63,582	95,928	79,600	72,322	72,322	79,641	67,029	67,740	†	†
Wyoming	76,182	76,182	90,173	90,173	†	†	59,268	†	†	†	†	†	†	†
U.S. Service Academies	109,778	109,778	109,778	†	†	109,778	†	†	†	†	†	†	†	†
Other jurisdictions	60,987	64,575	68,770	70,847	76,258	55,570	31,877	53,066	53,066	60,481	50,584	37,846	†	25,857
American Samoa	29,068	29,068	29,068	†	†	29,068	†	†	†	†	†	†	†	†
Federated States of Micronesia	25,272	25,272	†	†	†	†	25,272	†	†	†	†	†	†	†
Guam	66,511	66,511	69,979	†	69,979	†	57,347	†	†	†	†	†	†	†
Marshall Islands	†	†	†	†	†	†	†	†	†	†	†	†	†	†
Northern Marianas	51,249	51,249	51,249	†	†	51,249	†	†	†	†	†	†	†	†
Palau	20,492	20,492	†	†	†	†	20,492	†	†	†	†	†	†	†
Puerto Rico	62,761	68,400	70,311	70,847	79,149	59,601	26,460	53,066	53,066	60,481	50,584	37,846	†	25,857
U.S. Virgin Islands	71,002	71,002	71,002	†	71,002	†	†	†	†	†	†	†	†	†

†Not applicable.
‡Reporting standards not met (too few cases).
[1]Institutions that awarded 20 or more doctor's degrees during the previous academic year.
[2]Institutions that awarded 20 or more master's degrees, but less than 20 doctor's degrees, during the previous academic year. This definition differs from the definition of master's institutions that is used in some *Digest* tables that present postsecondary finance data.

NOTE: Data exclude instructional faculty at medical schools. Degree-granting institutions grant associate's or higher degrees and participate in Title IV federal financial aid programs. Data include imputations for nonrespondent institutions.
SOURCE: U.S. Department of Education, National Center for Education Statistics, Integrated Postsecondary Education Data System (IPEDS), Spring 2019, Human Resources component, Salaries section. (This table was prepared November 2019.)

Table 316.50. Average salary of full-time instructional faculty on 9-month contracts in 4-year degree-granting postsecondary institutions, by control and classification of institution, academic rank of faculty, and state or jurisdiction: 2018–19

[In current dollars]

State or jurisdiction	Public doctoral[1]			Public master's[2]			Nonprofit doctoral[1]			Nonprofit master's[2]		
	Professor	Associate professor	Assistant professor	Professor	Associate professor	Assistant professor	Professor	Associate professor	Assistant professor	Professor	Associate professor	Assistant professor
1	2	3	4	5	6	7	8	9	10	11	12	13
United States	**$134,213**	**$93,266**	**$81,563**	**$97,246**	**$79,107**	**$68,215**	**$163,299**	**$101,284**	**$86,034**	**$92,990**	**$75,515**	**$64,279**
Alabama	129,750	90,765	76,975	86,003	71,112	61,776	101,006	73,957	43,630	56,331	54,653	47,333
Alaska	105,822	87,480	73,678	103,252	85,404	69,466	†	†	†	66,703	54,168	47,985
Arizona	133,813	97,421	82,188	151,796	97,068	75,853	†	†	†	111,636	73,181	69,390
Arkansas	108,093	80,003	71,898	73,755	65,397	56,673	80,697	67,932	60,202	72,755	65,253	58,805
California	165,791	112,818	95,132	110,072	94,554	83,845	174,220	110,813	94,711	103,941	83,724	71,910
Colorado	127,627	95,433	85,068	82,461	67,849	61,549	135,739	99,919	81,711	118,742	88,746	70,507
Connecticut	150,560	102,214	82,889	103,734	83,742	69,843	190,700	99,116	89,948	123,581	99,133	80,452
Delaware	152,773	104,784	90,995	†	†	†	†	†	†	96,922	79,494	71,504
District of Columbia	164,016	125,544	100,439	104,672	75,415	62,622	171,141	109,987	92,214	88,364	77,221	72,547
Florida	134,226	94,696	83,881	113,039	88,358	70,224	132,585	93,721	78,223	99,003	82,558	68,448
Georgia	117,492	84,748	74,968	77,078	63,318	58,577	148,156	94,825	82,132	80,827	62,670	56,005
Hawaii	134,748	99,617	87,964	†	†	†	†	†	†	91,545	79,176	73,324
Idaho	98,097	78,886	71,918	†	†	†	66,436	58,161	52,460	†	†	†
Illinois	128,284	90,100	84,185	98,001	78,465	69,196	185,577	106,316	94,023	86,676	73,579	62,376
Indiana	133,964	93,902	81,862	88,585	73,216	65,818	143,362	93,238	76,156	83,561	69,580	56,680
Iowa	130,245	91,946	81,117	†	†	†	89,991	73,681	59,603	72,497	61,294	55,582
Kansas	115,255	82,198	70,886	78,994	67,937	61,103	68,002	54,060	51,286	65,117	60,699	52,080
Kentucky	107,575	77,915	68,460	70,258	61,946	51,697	79,507	65,348	55,613	64,390	55,801	50,840
Louisiana	113,129	78,869	75,292	76,937	62,823	57,263	134,310	84,670	90,386	68,830	58,399	56,034
Maine	108,777	86,779	69,464	78,160	65,284	53,303	94,505	77,861	64,276	67,245	58,671	53,035
Maryland	130,926	94,503	80,256	93,166	76,577	69,919	157,104	109,428	95,845	85,558	72,006	64,409
Massachusetts	145,572	107,333	90,632	101,791	80,494	68,225	194,058	116,725	102,673	125,001	93,769	78,981
Michigan	138,714	96,301	84,281	97,578	82,814	74,118	114,007	91,123	76,845	80,814	70,599	62,441
Minnesota	138,384	98,468	88,672	97,654	81,574	69,308	101,476	77,541	65,099	80,487	67,721	61,061
Mississippi	101,987	79,369	70,520	69,118	63,313	55,108	84,834	67,390	58,465	98,568	69,051	60,494
Missouri	111,473	79,785	72,994	79,329	65,921	58,259	148,326	93,357	80,099	83,333	68,473	58,723
Montana	97,127	75,365	69,075	74,738	67,695	58,247	†	†	†	66,750	53,402	50,413
Nebraska	121,964	89,440	87,131	83,027	66,927	55,434	119,865	88,131	70,997	67,259	62,013	55,416
Nevada	133,361	97,595	82,420	†	†	†	†	†	†	‡	‡	‡
New Hampshire	134,951	106,519	86,399	97,126	79,873	67,190	198,177	123,727	101,527	93,536	74,055	67,738
New Jersey	158,393	109,725	88,230	127,843	102,044	83,936	198,777	107,817	95,243	107,717	93,139	70,235
New Mexico	104,648	76,441	73,215	81,828	67,610	58,114	†	†	†	‡	58,998	46,909
New York	141,102	102,036	86,544	112,097	87,609	74,193	171,248	109,522	90,310	102,383	82,539	72,534
North Carolina	128,728	87,984	80,004	93,500	76,295	69,005	166,605	99,825	81,087	74,556	64,891	58,856
North Dakota	107,334	82,124	71,451	79,182	64,981	54,512	69,443	74,154	60,961	†	†	†
Ohio	126,030	91,074	80,913	75,607	63,092	53,948	113,899	82,155	74,264	80,497	67,710	58,600
Oklahoma	110,488	80,704	75,205	81,090	65,596	57,881	103,407	78,411	77,347	72,406	60,687	55,267
Oregon	128,787	96,026	84,047	84,789	69,433	55,846	104,454	81,888	67,037	68,635	58,908	53,005
Pennsylvania	145,409	100,169	81,737	112,206	91,293	72,296	161,783	99,770	87,384	92,401	74,425	64,417
Rhode Island	123,929	92,025	85,831	83,318	73,013	63,047	186,408	124,143	101,455	120,777	90,287	77,002
South Carolina	135,110	95,422	87,370	88,520	72,603	63,222	71,675	66,449	62,810	77,883	64,073	55,568
South Dakota	96,468	77,456	71,796	92,669	72,601	65,556	†	†	†	69,357	58,622	55,430
Tennessee	114,699	83,983	72,556	88,115	72,159	64,245	152,613	95,727	81,279	83,606	67,963	58,015
Texas	135,495	93,713	80,710	92,342	77,284	67,511	148,198	99,258	89,140	87,593	73,988	62,810
Utah	126,152	90,798	81,633	91,653	74,575	67,092	156,795	110,530	76,368	88,971	74,151	66,622
Vermont	122,428	96,557	79,789	70,181	56,615	49,204	†	†	†	108,411	78,386	72,830
Virginia	135,195	94,081	80,299	89,489	74,613	66,064	116,740	85,324	67,565	74,914	57,604	53,189
Washington	138,980	101,663	93,164	109,446	92,466	80,557	116,109	87,935	71,750	82,048	68,045	64,389
West Virginia	102,535	80,001	69,932	71,043	62,592	55,614	67,748	58,829	53,661	59,860	54,836	46,324
Wisconsin	120,677	82,397	79,570	74,079	63,894	64,445	108,493	82,935	73,888	81,867	67,962	59,741
Wyoming	123,387	86,994	81,558	†	†	†	†	†	†	†	†	†
U.S. Service Academies	†	†	†	†	†	†	†	†	†	†	†	†
Other jurisdictions	**83,092**	**70,144**	**54,303**	**85,605**	**73,054**	**58,787**	**78,036**	**60,374**	**51,444**	**71,747**	**60,408**	**48,338**
American Samoa	†	†	†	†	†	†	†	†	†	†	†	†
Federated States of Micronesia	†	†	†	†	†	†	†	†	†	†	†	†
Guam	†	†	†	92,939	74,686	56,253	†	†	†	†	†	†
Marshall Islands	†	†	†	†	†	†	†	†	†	†	†	†
Northern Marianas	†	†	†	†	†	†	†	†	†	†	†	†
Palau	†	†	†	†	†	†	†	†	†	†	†	†
Puerto Rico	83,092	70,144	54,303	84,388	72,112	56,700	78,036	60,374	51,444	71,747	60,408	48,338
U.S. Virgin Islands	†	†	†	93,336	73,742	63,835	†	†	†	†	†	†

†Not applicable.
‡Reporting standards not met (too few cases).
[1]Institutions that awarded 20 or more doctor's degrees during the previous academic year.
[2]Institutions that awarded 20 or more master's degrees, but less than 20 doctor's degrees, during the previous academic year. This definition differs from the definition of master's institutions that is used in some *Digest* tables that present postsecondary finance data.

NOTE: Data exclude instructional faculty at medical schools. Degree-granting institutions grant associate's or higher degrees and participate in Title IV federal financial aid programs. Data include imputations for nonrespondent institutions.
SOURCE: U.S. Department of Education, National Center for Education Statistics, Integrated Postsecondary Education Data System (IPEDS), Spring 2019, Human Resources component, Salaries section. (This table was prepared November 2019.)

Table 316.80. Percentage of degree-granting postsecondary institutions with a tenure system and percentage of full-time faculty with tenure at these institutions, by control and level of institution and selected characteristics of faculty: Selected years, 1993–94 through 2018–19

Selected characteristic and academic year	All insti- tutions	Public institutions						Nonprofit institutions						For-profit insti- tutions
		Total	4-year institutions				2-year	Total	4-year institutions				2-year	
			Total	Doctoral[1]	Master's[2]	Other			Total	Doctoral[1]	Master's[2]	Other		
1	2	3	4	5	6	7	8	9	10	11	12	13	14	15
Percent of institutions with a tenure system														
1993–94	62.6	73.6	92.6	100.0	98.3	76.4	62.1	62.0	66.3	90.5	76.5	58.3	26.1	7.8
1999–2000	55.0	72.8	94.6	100.0	95.5	86.3	60.3	59.0	63.4	81.2	72.6	54.9	14.0	4.0
2003–04	52.7	71.3	90.9	100.0	98.0	70.9	59.4	57.9	61.2	86.6	71.6	49.5	14.4	3.6
2005–06	50.9	71.5	90.9	99.5	98.0	71.6	59.4	56.5	59.8	85.1	67.1	49.2	11.5	2.0
2007–08	49.5	70.7	91.0	100.0	98.6	70.1	57.4	57.5	60.2	81.3	64.2	45.4	13.0	1.4
2009–10	47.8	71.2	90.9	99.6	98.5	71.3	57.7	57.1	59.5	80.6	64.4	44.6	12.9	1.5
2011–12	45.3	71.6	90.8	99.6	98.5	70.5	57.8	55.6	58.6	79.5	64.0	42.7	8.0	1.3
2013–14	49.3	74.6	95.8	99.6	98.1	86.6	58.9	59.7	61.8	79.6	63.2	49.0	12.5	1.2
2015–16	51.9	74.8	95.2	99.6	97.6	85.7	58.9	57.7	60.6	79.8	60.8	47.0	7.5	1.3
2016–17	54.4	74.6	94.6	99.6	97.2	85.0	58.0	58.8	61.5	79.3	61.1	48.8	9.2	1.5
2017–18	55.1	74.7	94.6	99.6	96.8	86.2	57.7	58.3	60.6	80.2	59.4	46.9	7.8	1.6
2018–19	57.4	74.3	93.6	99.3	97.5	82.4	57.5	58.8	60.8	78.7	58.2	49.0	8.8	1.3
Faculty with tenure at institutions with a tenure system														
Percent of all full-time faculty[3]														
1993–94	56.2	58.9	56.3	54.5	60.5	51.1	69.9	49.5	49.5	47.6	51.8	50.4	47.9	33.8
1999–2000	53.7	55.9	53.2	50.4	59.1	54.7	67.7	48.2	48.1	43.4	52.3	53.5	59.7	77.4
2003–04	50.4	53.0	50.2	48.9	52.9	51.2	65.2	44.6	44.6	40.1	48.7	51.9	47.7	69.2
2005–06	49.6	51.5	48.7	47.2	52.3	49.1	64.1	45.1	45.1	40.7	49.1	52.5	45.2	69.3
2007–08	48.8	50.5	47.8	45.9	52.7	49.5	63.6	44.7	44.7	41.0	50.5	53.1	41.3	51.3
2009–10	48.7	50.6	47.8	45.7	53.6	51.3	64.1	44.3	44.3	40.4	50.5	54.1	38.5	51.0
2011–12	48.5	50.7	48.0	45.8	54.3	53.4	64.7	43.7	43.7	39.7	50.7	54.3	31.4	31.0
2013–14	48.3	50.4	47.3	44.9	55.4	52.2	67.2	43.8	43.8	39.5	51.7	55.9	31.5	19.8
2015–16	47.2	49.3	46.6	44.2	54.7	53.5	65.0	42.8	42.8	38.6	51.6	55.6	33.9	17.0
2016–17	46.4	48.2	45.8	43.3	53.4	56.9	63.6	42.4	42.4	38.3	51.1	55.4	32.2	17.2
2017–18	45.5	47.3	44.8	42.3	52.7	56.1	63.2	41.8	41.8	37.9	50.7	55.0	27.2	17.6
2018–19	45.1	46.9	44.5	42.2	52.8	54.7	62.8	41.4	41.4	37.6	50.0	55.2	28.9	12.8
Percent of full-time instructional faculty only														
2017–18														
Total	48.0	49.7	47.4	45.5	52.9	56.1	63.2	44.4	44.4	41.2	50.7	55.0	27.2	17.6
Male	54.0	55.5	54.2	52.8	58.8	59.4	65.5	50.8	50.9	48.2	56.4	60.5	32.9	20.1
Female	40.8	42.8	39.1	35.9	46.4	52.8	61.3	36.4	36.5	32.0	44.7	49.0	24.0	15.3
Professor	89.6	90.7	90.7	88.9	98.2	96.2	90.6	87.5	87.5	85.0	92.7	95.9	60.9	70.7
Male	90.1	91.3	91.3	89.8	98.1	96.5	91.6	87.9	87.9	85.9	92.7	95.9	77.8	74.5
Female	88.5	89.5	89.4	86.5	98.3	95.7	89.8	86.6	86.6	82.7	92.8	95.9	50.0	65.7
Associate professor	75.0	78.3	78.5	75.5	89.6	86.4	75.1	68.6	68.6	62.5	77.7	87.6	52.7	41.5
Male	75.5	79.1	79.2	76.4	89.8	86.3	77.4	68.6	68.6	63.0	77.7	86.7	71.4	37.5
Female	74.3	77.3	77.8	74.3	89.4	86.5	73.3	68.6	68.7	61.8	77.8	88.6	46.3	45.5
Assistant professor	5.1	6.5	3.5	1.3	8.3	21.8	43.9	2.5	2.5	1.7	5.4	2.8	†	†
Male	5.0	6.3	3.5	1.3	8.6	22.7	47.0	2.6	2.6	1.7	5.7	3.3	†	†
Female	5.2	6.8	3.6	1.4	8.0	21.0	41.7	2.4	2.4	1.6	5.2	2.4	†	†
Instructor	25.6	31.4	9.6	0.6	1.5	45.3	55.5	0.3	0.3	0.2	0.4	1.1	†	3.6
Lecturer	1.7	2.2	1.6	1.0	3.2	5.7	28.2	0.2	0.2	0.1	‡	1.7	†	†
No academic rank	28.4	35.6	21.3	1.2	6.9	56.5	65.3	4.8	4.6	2.1	21.0	1.5	41.4	†
2018–19														
Total	47.5	49.2	47.0	45.2	53.0	54.7	62.8	43.9	43.9	40.8	50.0	55.2	28.9	12.8
Male	53.5	55.0	53.7	52.5	58.7	57.6	65.3	50.4	50.5	47.9	55.7	60.9	30.1	14.8
Female	40.5	42.5	38.9	35.9	46.8	51.9	60.8	36.0	36.0	31.8	44.0	49.2	28.1	10.8
Professor	89.4	90.5	90.5	88.8	98.3	95.1	90.0	87.3	87.3	84.7	92.4	96.5	60.9	61.0
Male	90.1	91.2	91.2	89.8	98.4	95.4	91.2	87.8	87.8	85.8	92.5	96.6	75.0	70.6
Female	88.0	89.0	89.0	86.3	98.2	94.6	89.0	86.1	86.1	82.2	92.1	96.2	53.3	48.0
Associate professor	74.5	77.8	78.0	75.2	89.5	84.7	74.7	68.2	68.2	62.1	77.8	88.0	56.9	49.1
Male	75.3	78.8	78.9	76.4	89.6	85.4	76.8	68.4	68.4	62.8	78.4	86.7	66.7	42.3
Female	73.6	76.5	76.9	73.6	89.3	83.9	73.0	68.0	68.0	61.2	77.2	89.5	53.5	55.6
Assistant professor	4.9	6.3	3.3	1.3	7.8	21.3	44.8	2.3	2.3	1.5	4.9	3.3	†	†
Male	4.7	6.0	3.2	1.2	7.9	22.5	47.6	2.4	2.4	1.6	5.0	3.9	†	†
Female	5.0	6.6	3.4	1.4	7.7	20.2	42.7	2.2	2.2	1.4	4.9	2.8	†	†
Instructor	24.9	30.7	9.1	0.6	2.4	41.5	54.6	0.3	0.3	0.1	0.4	1.5	†	2.3
Lecturer	1.7	2.2	1.6	1.0	3.7	5.6	28.9	0.1	0.1	0.1	‡	1.1	†	†
No academic rank	28.3	35.4	21.0	1.2	3.6	56.6	68.2	4.5	4.3	1.6	24.2	1.5	48.3	†

†Not applicable.
‡Reporting standards not met (too few cases).
[1]Institutions that awarded 20 or more doctor's degrees during the previous academic year.
[2]Institutions that awarded 20 or more master's degrees, but less than 20 doctor's degrees, during the previous academic year.
[3]Includes instructional, research, and public service faculty.

NOTE: Degree-granting institutions grant associate's or higher degrees and participate in Title IV federal financial aid programs. Data include imputations for nonrespondent institutions. Some data have been revised from previously published figures.
SOURCE: U.S. Department of Education, National Center for Education Statistics, Integrated Postsecondary Education Data System (IPEDS), "Fall Staff Survey" (IPEDS-S:93–99); and IPEDS Winter 2003–04 through Winter 2011–12 and Spring 2014 through Spring 2019, Human Resources component, Fall Staff section. (This table was prepared November 2019.)

Table 317.10. Degree-granting postsecondary institutions, by control and level of institution: Selected years, 1949–50 through 2018–19

Year	All institutions Total	4-year	2-year	Public Total	4-year	2-year	Private Total	4-year, total	2-year, total	Nonprofit Total	4-year	2-year	For-profit Total	4-year	2-year
1	2	3	4	5	6	7	8	9	10	11	12	13	14	15	16
Excluding branch campuses															
1949–50	1,851	1,327	524	641	344	297	1,210	983	227	—	—	—	—	—	—
1959–60	2,004	1,422	582	695	367	328	1,309	1,055	254	—	—	—	—	—	—
1969–70	2,525	1,639	886	1,060	426	634	1,465	1,213	252	—	—	—	—	—	—
1979–80	2,975	1,863	1,112	1,310	464	846	1,665	1,399	266	—	—	—	—	—	—
1980–81	3,056	1,861	1,195	1,334	465	869	1,722	1,396	326[1]	—	—	—	—	—	—
1981–82	3,083	1,883	1,200	1,340	471	869	1,743	1,412	331[1]	—	—	—	—	—	—
1982–83	3,111	1,887	1,224	1,336	472	864	1,775	1,415	360[1]	—	—	—	—	—	—
1983–84	3,117	1,914	1,203	1,325	474	851	1,792	1,440	352	—	—	—	—	—	—
1984–85	3,146	1,911	1,235	1,329	461	868	1,817	1,450	367	—	—	—	—	—	—
1985–86	3,155	1,915	1,240	1,326	461	865	1,829	1,454	375	—	—	—	—	—	—
Including branch campuses															
1974–75	3,004	1,866	1,138	1,433	537	896	1,571	1,329	242	—	—	—	—	—	—
1975–76	3,026	1,898	1,128	1,442	545	897	1,584	1,353	231	—	—	—	—	—	—
1976–77	3,046	1,913	1,133	1,455	550	905	1,591	1,363	228	1,536	1,348	188	55	15	40
1977–78	3,095	1,938	1,157	1,473	552	921	1,622	1,386	236	—	—	—	—	—	—
1978–79	3,134	1,941	1,193	1,474	550	924	1,660	1,391	269	1,564	1,376	188	96	15	81
1979–80	3,152	1,957	1,195	1,475	549	926	1,677	1,408	269	—	—	—	—	—	—
1980–81	3,231	1,957	1,274	1,497	552	945	1,734	1,405	329[1]	1,569	1,387	182	165	18	147
1981–82	3,253	1,979	1,274	1,498	558	940	1,755	1,421	334[1]	—	—	—	—	—	—
1982–83	3,280	1,984	1,296	1,493	560	933	1,787	1,424	363[1]	—	—	—	—	—	—
1983–84	3,284	2,013	1,271	1,481	565	916	1,803	1,448	355	—	—	—	—	—	—
1984–85	3,331	2,025	1,306	1,501	566	935	1,830	1,459	371	1,616	1,430	186	214	29	185
1985–86	3,340	2,029	1,311	1,498	566	932	1,842	1,463	379	—	—	—	—	—	—
1986–87	3,406	2,070	1,336	1,533	573	960	1,873	1,497	376	1,635	1,462	173	238	35	203
1987–88	3,587	2,135	1,452	1,591	599	992	1,996	1,536	460	1,673	1,487	186	323	49	274
1988–89	3,565	2,129	1,436	1,582	598	984	1,983	1,531	452	1,658	1,478	180	325	53	272
1989–90	3,535	2,127	1,408	1,563	595	968	1,972	1,532	440	1,656	1,479	177	316	53	263
1990–91	3,559	2,141	1,418	1,567	595	972	1,992	1,546	446	1,649	1,482	167	343	64	279
1991–92	3,601	2,157	1,444	1,598	599	999	2,003	1,558	445	1,662	1,486	176	341	72	269
1992–93	3,638	2,169	1,469	1,624	600	1,024	2,014	1,569	445	1,672	1,493	179	342	76	266
1993–94	3,632	2,190	1,442	1,625	604	1,021	2,007	1,586	421	1,687	1,506	181	320	80	240
1994–95	3,688	2,215	1,473	1,641	605	1,036	2,047	1,610	437	1,702	1,510	192	345	100	245
1995–96	3,706	2,244	1,462	1,655	608	1,047	2,051	1,636	415	1,706	1,519	187	345	117	228
1996–97	4,009	2,267	1,742	1,702	614	1,088	2,307	1,653	654	1,693	1,509	184	614	144	470
1997–98	4,064	2,309	1,755	1,707	615	1,092	2,357	1,694	663	1,707	1,528	179	650	166	484
1998–99	4,048	2,335	1,713	1,681	612	1,069	2,367	1,723	644	1,695	1,531	164	672	192	480
1999–2000	4,084	2,363	1,721	1,682	614	1,068	2,402	1,749	653	1,681	1,531	150	721	218	503
2000–01	4,182	2,450	1,732	1,698	622	1,076	2,484	1,828	656	1,695	1,551	144	789	277	512
2001–02	4,197	2,487	1,710	1,713	628	1,085	2,484	1,859	625	1,676	1,541	135	808	318	490
2002–03	4,168	2,466	1,702	1,712	631	1,081	2,456	1,835	621	1,665	1,538	127	791	297	494
2003–04	4,236	2,530	1,706	1,720	634	1,086	2,516	1,896	620	1,664	1,546	118	852	350	502
2004–05	4,216	2,533	1,683	1,700	639	1,061	2,516	1,894	622	1,637	1,525	112	879	369	510
2005–06	4,276	2,582	1,694	1,693	640	1,053	2,583	1,942	641	1,647	1,534	113	936	408	528
2006–07	4,314	2,629	1,685	1,688	643	1,045	2,626	1,986	640	1,640	1,533	107	986	453	533
2007–08	4,352	2,675	1,677	1,685	653	1,032	2,667	2,022	645	1,624	1,532	92	1,043	490	553
2008–09	4,409	2,719	1,690	1,676	652	1,024	2,733	2,067	666	1,629	1,537	92	1,104	530	574
2009–10	4,495	2,774	1,721	1,672	672	1,000	2,823	2,102	721	1,624	1,539	85	1,199	563	636
2010–11	4,599	2,870	1,729	1,656	678	978	2,943	2,192	751	1,630	1,543	87	1,313	649	664
2011–12	4,706	2,968	1,738	1,649	682	967	3,057	2,286	771	1,653	1,553	100	1,404	733	671
2012–13	4,726	3,026	1,700	1,623	689	934	3,103	2,337	766	1,652	1,555	97	1,451	782	669
2013–14	4,724	3,039	1,685	1,625	691	934	3,099	2,348	751	1,675	1,587	88	1,424	761	663
2014–15	4,627	3,011	1,616	1,621	701	920	3,006	2,310	696	1,672	1,584	88	1,334	726	608
2015–16	4,583	3,004	1,579	1,620	710	910	2,963	2,294	669	1,701	1,594	107	1,262	700	562
2016–17	4,360	2,832	1,528	1,623	737	886	2,737	2,095	642	1,682	1,581	101	1,055	514	541
2017–18	4,313	2,828	1,485	1,626	750	876	2,687	2,078	609	1,689	1,590	99	998	488	510
2018–19	4,042	2,703	1,339	1,636	768	868	2,406	1,935	471	1,664	1,577	87	742	358	384

—Not available.
[1]Large increases are due to the addition of schools accredited by the Accrediting Commission of Career Schools and Colleges of Technology.
NOTE: Data through 1995–96 are for institutions of higher education, while later data are for degree-granting institutions. Degree-granting institutions grant associate's or higher degrees and participate in Title IV federal financial aid programs. Changes in counts of institutions over time are partly affected by increasing or decreasing numbers of institutions submitting separate data for branch campuses.

SOURCE: U.S. Department of Education, National Center for Education Statistics, *Education Directory, Colleges and Universities*, 1949–50 through 1965–66; Higher Education General Information Survey (HEGIS), "Institutional Characteristics of Colleges and Universities" surveys, 1966–67 through 1985–86; Integrated Postsecondary Education Data System (IPEDS), "Institutional Characteristics Survey"(IPEDS-IC:86–99); and IPEDS Fall 2000 through Fall 2018, Institutional Characteristics component. (This table was prepared September 2019.)

Table 317.20. Degree-granting postsecondary institutions, by control and classification of institution and state or jurisdiction: 2018–19

State or jurisdiction	Total	All public institutions	Public 4-year institutions							Public 2-year	All nonprofit institutions	Nonprofit 4-year institutions							Nonprofit 2-year	For-profit institutions		
			Total	Research university, very high[1]	Research university, high[2]	Doctoral/research university[3]	Master's[4]	Baccalaureate[5]	Special focus[6]			Total	Research university, very high[1]	Research university, high[2]	Doctoral/research university[3]	Master's[4]	Baccalaureate[5]	Special focus[6]		Total	4-year	2-year
1	2	3	4	5	6	7	8	9	10	11	12	13	14	15	16	17	18	19	20	21	22	23
United States	4,042	1,636	768	81	74	38	271	250	54	868	1,664	1,577	34	30	53	407	458	595	87	742	358	384
Alabama	62	38	14	1	4	0	8	1	0	24	20	20	0	0	0	4	11	5	0	4	3	1
Alaska	8	4	4	0	1	0	2	1	0	0	3	2	0	0	0	1	0	1	1	1	0	1
Arizona	71	29	9	2	1	2	2	1	1	20	12	12	0	0	0	2	3	7	0	30	15	15
Arkansas	53	33	11	1	0	1	6	2	1	22	18	14	0	0	0	2	9	3	4	2	1	1
California	420	151	49	8	2	3	18	16	2	102	148	143	3	1	9	30	24	76	5	121	67	54
Colorado	70	28	19	2	3	0	6	8	0	9	14	12	0	0	0	3	3	6	2	28	14	14
Connecticut	41	22	10	1	0	0	4	5	0	12	17	17	1	0	1	8	4	3	0	2	2	0
Delaware	8	3	3	2	0	0	1	0	0	0	4	3	0	0	0	1	1	1	1	1	0	1
District of Columbia	18	2	2	0	0	1	1	0	0	0	12	12	2	0	1	2	0	7	0	4	3	1
Florida	181	43	42	5	1	1	5	30	0	1	65	58	1	2	1	14	17	23	7	73	30	43
Georgia	111	50	27	3	1	4	8	10	1	23	37	33	1	0	1	4	18	9	4	24	9	15
Hawaii	18	10	4	1	0	2	1	0	0	6	5	5	0	0	0	2	3	0	0	3	0	3
Idaho	15	8	4	0	1	2	1	0	0	4	6	6	0	0	0	1	3	2	0	1	0	1
Illinois	157	60	12	2	3	0	7	0	0	48	80	78	2	2	4	19	15	36	2	17	10	7
Indiana	75	16	15	2	2	1	7	3	0	1	43	42	1	0	1	11	17	12	1	16	4	12
Iowa	61	24	8	2	0	0	2	4	0	16	34	34	0	0	0	9	15	10	0	3	2	1
Kansas	64	33	8	2	1	0	4	1	0	25	24	24	0	0	0	6	13	5	0	7	5	2
Kentucky	59	24	8	2	0	0	5	1	0	16	25	25	0	0	2	7	13	3	0	10	5	5
Louisiana	56	32	8	1	2	0	4	1	0	24	15	12	1	0	0	3	4	4	3	9	1	8
Maine	31	17	10	0	1	0	1	8	0	7	13	12	0	0	0	4	6	2	1	1	0	1
Maryland	53	30	14	1	1	2	7	2	1	16	20	20	1	0	0	6	4	9	0	3	1	2
Massachusetts	111	30	14	1	1	0	7	3	2	16	77	75	7	1	4	17	17	29	2	4	2	2
Michigan	94	46	22	3	3	2	6	7	1	24	40	40	0	0	1	10	13	16	0	8	3	5
Minnesota	88	44	12	1	0	2	6	2	1	32	34	33	0	0	1	8	11	13	1	10	8	2
Mississippi	36	23	8	2	2	0	4	0	0	15	9	9	0	0	0	3	4	2	0	4	1	3
Missouri	101	28	14	1	2	0	6	5	0	14	54	52	1	0	2	13	11	25	2	19	9	10
Montana	23	17	7	1	0	0	4	1	1	10	5	4	0	0	0	1	3	0	1	1	0	1
Nebraska	39	18	9	0	2	0	4	2	1	9	17	16	0	0	0	6	5	5	1	4	2	2
Nevada	23	7	7	1	1	0	2	2	1	0	5	4	0	0	0	1	0	3	1	11	6	5
New Hampshire	25	13	6	0	1	0	2	2	1	7	12	11	0	1	0	5	4	1	1	0	0	0
New Jersey	83	32	13	1	2	0	8	0	2	19	38	37	1	0	2	10	2	22	1	13	9	4
New Mexico	39	28	9	1	1	0	4	1	2	19	3	3	0	0	0	2	1	0	0	8	5	3
New York	295	79	43	1	4	1	23	10	4	36	183	169	5	5	7	35	26	91	14	33	19	14
North Carolina	136	75	17	4	1	0	8	4	0	58	49	48	1	0	1	10	24	12	1	12	8	4
North Dakota	20	14	9	0	1	0	2	4	2	5	5	5	0	0	0	1	1	3	0	1	1	0
Ohio	169	60	36	2	7	1	1	22	3	24	72	68	1	1	2	20	22	22	4	37	11	26
Oklahoma	49	30	17	1	1	0	8	5	2	13	14	13	0	0	0	6	4	3	1	5	2	3
Oregon	55	26	9	1	1	1	3	2	1	17	25	24	0	0	0	6	6	12	1	4	2	2
Pennsylvania	220	63	45	2	0	1	16	23	3	18	116	105	2	3	4	32	34	30	11	41	6	35
Rhode Island	13	3	2	1	0	0	1	0	0	1	10	10	1	0	0	5	1	3	0	0	0	0
South Carolina	67	33	13	2	2	0	4	4	1	20	23	22	0	0	0	8	13	1	1	11	4	7
South Dakota	22	12	7	0	1	0	4	0	2	5	7	7	0	0	0	2	2	3	0	3	3	0
Tennessee	88	23	10	1	1	0	2	5	1	13	46	43	1	1	3	13	11	14	3	19	10	9
Texas	242	109	49	7	4	8	5	16	9	60	70	65	1	3	1	18	18	24	5	63	29	34
Utah	30	8	7	1	1	0	3	2	0	1	11	10	0	1	0	3	3	3	1	11	10	1

See notes at end of table.

Table 317.20. Degree-granting postsecondary institutions, by control and classification of institution and state or jurisdiction: 2018–19—Continued

State or jurisdiction	Total	All public institutions	Public 4-year institutions — Total	Research university, very high[1]	Research university, high[2]	Doctoral/research university[3]	Master's[4]	Baccalaureate[5]	Special focus[6]	Public 2-year	All nonprofit institutions	Nonprofit 4-year — Total	Research university, very high[1]	Research university, high[2]	Doctoral/research university[3]	Master's[4]	Baccalaureate[5]	Special focus[6]	Nonprofit 2-year	For-profit Total	For-profit 4-year	For-profit 2-year
1	2	3	4	5	6	7	8	9	10	11	12	13	14	15	16	17	18	19	20	21	22	23
Vermont	22	5	4	0	1	0	1	2	0	1	16	16	0	0	0	6	8	2	0	1	1	0
Virginia	115	41	17	4	2	0	7	2	2	24	42	40	0	0	3	6	16	15	2	32	18	14
Washington	74	43	36	2	0	0	6	27	1	7	22	20	0	0	1	10	4	5	2	9	6	3
West Virginia	42	22	13	1	0	0	3	8	1	9	10	10	0	0	0	3	4	3	0	10	4	6
Wisconsin	75	34	17	2	0	0	9	6	0	17	34	34	0	0	2	10	12	9	0	7	5	2
Wyoming	9	8	1	0	1	0	0	0	0	7	0	0	0	0	0	0	0	0	0	1	0	1
U.S. Service Academies	5	5	5	0	0	0	0	5	0	0	†	†	†	†	†	†	†	†	†	†	†	†
Other jurisdictions	**96**	**26**	**19**	**0**	**1**	**0**	**3**	**12**	**3**	**7**	**49**	**47**	**0**	**0**	**3**	**13**	**13**	**18**	**2**	**21**	**11**	**10**
American Samoa	1	1	1	0	0	0	0	1	0	0	0	0	0	0	0	0	0	0	0	0	0	0
Federated States of Micronesia	1	1	0	0	0	0	0	0	0	1	0	0	0	0	0	0	0	0	0	0	0	0
Guam	3	2	1	0	0	0	1	0	0	1	1	1	0	0	0	1	0	0	0	0	0	0
Marshall Islands	1	1	1	0	0	0	0	1	0	0	0	0	0	0	0	0	0	0	0	0	0	0
Northern Marianas	1	1	1	0	0	0	0	1	0	0	0	0	0	0	0	0	0	0	0	0	0	0
Palau	1	1	0	0	0	0	0	0	0	1	0	0	0	0	0	0	0	0	0	0	0	0
Puerto Rico	87	18	14	0	1	0	1	9	3	4	48	46	0	0	3	13	13	17	2	21	11	10
U.S. Virgin Islands	1	1	1	0	0	0	1	0	0	0	0	0	0	0	0	0	0	0	0	0	0	0

†Not applicable.

[1]Research universities with a very high level of research activity.

[2]Research universities with a high level of research activity.

[3]Institutions that award at least 20 research/scholarship doctor's degrees per year, but did not have a high level of research activity.

[4]Institutions that award at least 50 master's degrees and fewer than 20 doctor's degrees per year.

[5]Institutions that primarily emphasize undergraduate education. In addition to institutions that primarily award bachelor's degrees, also includes institutions classified as 4-year in the IPEDS system, but classified as 2-year baccalaureate/associate's colleges in the Carnegie Classification system because they primarily award associate's degrees.

[6]Four-year institutions that award degrees primarily in single fields of study, such as medicine, business, fine arts, theology, and engineering.

NOTE: Branch campuses are counted as separate institutions. Relative levels of research activity for research universities were determined by an analysis of research and development expenditures, science and engineering research staffing, and doctor's degrees conferred, by field. Further information on the research index ranking may be obtained from http://carnegieclassifications.iu.edu/. Degree-granting institutions grant associate's or higher degrees and participate in Title IV federal financial aid programs.

SOURCE: U.S. Department of Education, National Center for Education Statistics, Integrated Postsecondary Education Data System (IPEDS), Fall 2018, Institutional Characteristics component. (This table was prepared September 2019.)

Table 317.40. Number of degree-granting postsecondary institutions and enrollment in these institutions, by enrollment size, control, and classification of institution: Fall 2018

Control and classification of institution	Total	Number of institutions, by enrollment size of institution[1]								
	Total	Under 200	200 to 499	500 to 999	1,000 to 2,499	2,500 to 4,999	5,000 to 9,999	10,000 to 19,999	20,000 to 29,999	30,000 or more
1	2	3	4	5	6	7	8	9	10	11
Total	**4,034**	**601**	**491**	**469**	**826**	**603**	**483**	**339**	**120**	**102**
Research university, very high[2]	115	0	0	0	1	0	4	21	32	57
Research university, high[3]	104	0	0	0	1	3	23	46	23	8
Doctoral/research university[4]	100	0	0	3	7	17	24	31	10	8
Master's[5]	727	15	15	32	175	208	169	87	14	12
Baccalaureate[6]	810	56	95	150	306	110	48	31	6	8
Special-focus[7] 4-year	842	332	195	150	107	42	10	5	1	0
2-year	1,336	198	186	134	229	223	205	118	34	9
Public	1,634	18	46	75	303	351	373	278	105	85
Research university, very high[2]	81	0	0	0	0	0	1	3	25	52
Research university, high[3]	74	0	0	0	0	0	11	35	21	7
Doctoral/research university[4]	38	0	0	0	1	1	6	19	8	3
Master's[5]	271	0	1	0	19	57	102	74	11	7
Baccalaureate[6]	249	2	12	23	63	62	44	30	6	7
Special-focus[7] 4-year	54	3	10	12	14	11	4	0	0	0
Arts, music, or design	2	0	0	0	2	0	0	0	0	0
Business and management	0	0	0	0	0	0	0	0	0	0
Engineering and other technology-related	1	0	0	0	0	1	0	0	0	0
Law	6	0	3	2	1	0	0	0	0	0
Medical schools and centers	27	2	0	6	6	10	3	0	0	0
Other health professions	6	0	3	1	2	0	0	0	0	0
Tribal colleges	11	1	4	3	3	0	0	0	0	0
Other special focus	1	0	0	0	0	0	1	0	0	0
2-year	867	13	23	40	206	220	205	117	34	9
High transfer institutions[8]	335	1	6	8	60	67	99	66	21	7
Mixed transfer/career and technical institutions[9]	297	0	2	14	79	77	72	39	12	2
High career and technical institutions[10]	211	2	5	17	64	76	34	12	1	0
Special-focus[7] 2-year	24	10	10	1	3	0	0	0	0	0
Health professions	4	1	2	0	1	0	0	0	0	0
Tribal colleges	17	9	7	0	1	0	0	0	0	0
Other programs	3	0	1	1	1	0	0	0	0	0
Private nonprofit	1,664	332	229	236	463	229	97	56	11	11
Research university, very high[2]	34	0	0	0	1	0	3	18	7	5
Research university, high[3]	30	0	0	0	1	3	12	11	2	1
Doctoral/research university[4]	53	0	0	2	6	15	16	11	2	1
Master's[5]	407	5	7	25	149	148	58	12	0	3
Baccalaureate[6]	458	27	49	104	234	41	2	0	0	1
Special-focus[7] 4-year	595	261	140	93	70	22	6	3	0	0
Arts, music, or design	56	14	13	13	12	1	2	1	0	0
Business and management	18	3	3	4	4	4	0	0	0	0
Engineering and other technology-related	6	1	1	2	1	0	0	1	0	0
Faith-related	306	197	75	23	7	3	1	0	0	0
Law	21	4	5	8	4	0	0	0	0	0
Medical schools and centers	29	0	3	5	12	8	1	0	0	0
Other health professions	132	32	35	31	28	4	1	1	0	0
Tribal colleges	5	0	2	3	0	0	0	0	0	0
Other special focus	22	10	3	4	2	2	1	0	0	0
2-year	87	39	33	12	2	0	0	1	0	0
High transfer institutions[8]	9	1	2	6	0	0	0	0	0	0
Mixed transfer/career and technical institutions[9]	3	0	1	0	2	0	0	0	0	0
High career and technical institutions[10]	13	5	7	1	0	0	0	0	0	0
Special-focus[7] 2-year	62	33	23	5	0	0	0	1	0	0
Health professions	26	14	8	3	0	0	0	1	0	0
Tribal colleges	2	1	1	0	0	0	0	0	0	0
Other programs	34	18	14	2	0	0	0	0	0	0
Private for-profit	736	251	216	158	60	23	13	5	4	6
Doctoral/research university[4]	9	0	0	1	0	1	2	1	0	4
Master's[5]	49	10	7	7	7	3	9	1	3	2
Baccalaureate[6]	103	27	34	23	9	7	2	1	0	0
Special-focus[7] 4-year	193	68	45	45	23	9	0	2	1	0
Arts, music, or design	35	18	4	5	6	1	0	1	0	0
Business and management	40	14	12	5	4	4	0	1	0	0
Engineering and other technology-related	6	1	2	3	0	0	0	0	0	0
Law	3	0	2	1	0	0	0	0	0	0
Medical schools and centers	2	1	0	1	0	0	0	0	0	0
Other health professions	103	33	23	29	13	4	0	0	1	0
Other special focus	4	1	2	1	0	0	0	0	0	0
2-year	382	146	130	82	21	3	0	0	0	0
High transfer institutions[8]	2	1	1	0	0	0	0	0	0	0
Mixed transfer/career and technical institutions[9]	3	1	1	0	0	1	0	0	0	0
High career and technical institutions[10]	99	39	30	23	6	1	0	0	0	0
Special-focus[7] 2-year	278	105	98	59	15	1	0	0	0	0
Health professions	195	66	77	45	6	1	0	0	0	0
Other programs	83	39	21	14	9	0	0	0	0	0

See notes at end of table.

Table 317.40. Number of degree-granting postsecondary institutions and enrollment in these institutions, by enrollment size, control, and classification of institution: Fall 2018—Continued

Control and classification of institution	Enrollment, by enrollment size of institution								
	Total	Under 200	200 to 499	500 to 999	1,000 to 2,499	2,500 to 4,999	5,000 to 9,999	10,000 to 19,999	20,000 to 29,999	30,000 or more
1	12	13	14	15	16	17	18	19	20	21
Total	**19,645,918**	**61,138**	**164,206**	**340,741**	**1,389,917**	**2,157,608**	**3,450,612**	**4,662,627**	**2,942,992**	**4,476,077**
Research university, very high[2]	3,525,917	0	0	0	2,233	0	29,339	310,571	818,710	2,365,064
Research university, high[3]	1,684,415	0	0	0	1,882	12,825	176,363	657,586	564,696	271,063
Doctoral/research university[4]	1,387,413	0	0	2,421	13,991	66,976	188,315	405,255	243,502	466,953
Master's[5]	4,385,674	1,689	5,382	26,258	323,948	744,931	1,172,468	1,169,629	329,032	612,337
Baccalaureate[6]	2,262,858	7,034	34,095	111,263	489,265	374,923	337,084	429,148	156,694	323,352
Special-focus[7] 4-year	654,433	32,325	61,752	105,065	164,028	139,339	64,832	59,463	27,629	0
2-year	5,745,208	20,090	62,977	95,734	394,570	818,614	1,482,211	1,630,975	802,729	437,308
Public	14,529,264	2,641	16,585	58,438	531,245	1,282,056	2,681,084	3,855,036	2,588,423	3,513,756
Research university, very high[2]	2,880,371	0	0	0	0	0	8,041	55,354	648,369	2,168,607
Research university, high[3]	1,355,351	0	0	0	0	0	88,971	510,189	519,627	236,564
Doctoral/research university[4]	634,802	0	0	0	2,220	3,193	52,566	263,153	199,430	114,240
Master's[5]	2,505,556	0	401	0	39,100	215,690	714,708	998,057	261,574	276,026
Baccalaureate[6]	1,512,103	291	4,790	17,026	106,207	221,303	308,580	416,201	156,694	281,011
Special-focus[7] 4-year	94,377	407	3,522	8,918	21,232	34,291	26,007	0	0	0
Arts, music, or design	3,129	0	0	0	3,129	0	0	0	0	0
Business and management	0	0	0	0	0	0	0	0	0	0
Engineering and other technology-related	2,654	0	0	0	0	2,654	0	0	0	0
Law	2,946	0	742	1,202	1,002	0	0	0	0	0
Medical schools and centers	64,823	209	0	5,326	10,456	31,637	17,195	0	0	0
Other health professions	4,010	0	1,251	533	2,226	0	0	0	0	0
Tribal colleges	8,003	198	1,529	1,857	4,419	0	0	0	0	0
Other special focus	8,812	0	0	0	0	0	8,812	0	0	0
2-year	5,546,704	1,943	7,872	32,494	362,486	807,579	1,482,211	1,612,082	802,729	437,308
High transfer institutions[8]	2,841,075	186	2,125	6,361	109,875	246,965	714,959	938,848	488,591	333,165
Mixed transfer/career and technical institutions[9]	1,867,650	0	892	11,733	134,796	278,244	526,262	521,287	290,293	104,143
High career and technical institutions[10]	825,934	226	1,926	13,713	110,917	282,370	240,990	151,947	23,845	0
Special-focus[7] 2-year	12,045	1,531	2,929	687	6,898	0	0	0	0	0
Health professions	3,171	170	560	0	2,441	0	0	0	0	0
Tribal colleges	5,377	1,361	2,034	0	1,982	0	0	0	0	0
Other programs	3,497	0	335	687	2,475	0	0	0	0	0
Private nonprofit	4,134,244	33,800	75,957	172,037	767,922	793,921	677,532	745,631	259,482	607,962
Research university, very high[2]	645,546	0	0	0	2,233	0	21,298	255,217	170,341	196,457
Research university, high[3]	329,064	0	0	0	1,882	12,825	87,392	147,397	45,069	34,499
Doctoral/research university[4]	451,943	0	0	1,914	11,771	60,003	123,464	131,567	44,072	79,152
Master's[5]	1,616,062	526	2,685	20,143	271,040	519,863	392,084	154,208	0	255,513
Baccalaureate[6]	653,475	3,552	18,090	77,621	370,151	127,251	14,469	0	0	42,341
Special-focus[7] 4-year	393,000	25,820	44,565	63,956	107,506	73,979	38,825	38,349	0	0
Arts, music, or design	64,501	1,482	4,294	8,935	20,087	3,639	11,978	14,086	0	0
Business and management	25,729	294	1,003	2,554	7,309	14,569	0	0	0	0
Engineering and other technology-related	18,177	104	390	1,373	2,142	0	0	14,168	0	0
Faith-related	85,207	19,061	22,597	15,036	13,219	8,639	6,655	0	0	0
Law	12,732	540	1,703	5,936	4,553	0	0	0	0	0
Medical schools and centers	58,596	0	951	3,422	17,840	28,597	7,786	0	0	0
Other health professions	105,701	3,438	11,986	21,853	39,737	11,528	7,064	10,095	0	0
Tribal colleges	2,542	0	666	1,876	0	0	0	0	0	0
Other special focus	19,815	901	975	2,971	2,619	7,007	5,342	0	0	0
2-year	45,154	3,902	10,617	8,403	3,339	0	0	18,893	0	0
High transfer institutions[8]	4,884	75	662	4,147	0	0	0	0	0	0
Mixed transfer/career and technical institutions[9]	3,645	0	306	0	3,339	0	0	0	0	0
High career and technical institutions[10]	3,876	566	2,407	903	0	0	0	0	0	0
Special-focus[7] 2-year	32,749	3,261	7,242	3,353	0	0	0	18,893	0	0
Health professions	24,843	1,624	2,472	1,854	0	0	0	18,893	0	0
Tribal colleges	411	106	305	0	0	0	0	0	0	0
Other programs	7,495	1,531	4,465	1,499	0	0	0	0	0	0
Private for-profit	982,410	24,697	71,664	110,266	90,750	81,631	91,996	61,960	95,087	354,359
Doctoral/research university[4]	300,668	0	0	507	0	3,780	12,285	10,535	0	273,561
Master's[5]	264,056	1,163	2,296	6,115	13,808	9,378	65,676	17,364	67,458	80,798
Baccalaureate[6]	97,280	3,191	11,215	16,616	12,907	26,369	14,035	12,947	0	0
Special-focus[7] 4-year	167,056	6,098	13,665	32,191	35,290	31,069	0	21,114	27,629	0
Arts, music, or design	29,412	1,613	1,169	3,225	8,399	4,390	0	10,616	0	0
Business and management	37,459	1,000	3,678	3,528	5,723	13,032	0	10,498	0	0
Engineering and other technology-related	3,088	134	633	2,321	0	0	0	0	0	0
Law	1,218	0	591	627	0	0	0	0	0	0
Medical schools and centers	1,049	97	0	952	0	0	0	0	0	0
Other health professions	93,286	3,181	6,929	20,732	21,168	13,647	0	0	27,629	0
Other special focus	1,544	73	665	806	0	0	0	0	0	0
2-year	153,350	14,245	44,488	54,837	28,745	11,035	0	0	0	0
High transfer institutions[8]	414	56	358	0	0	0	0	0	0	0
Mixed transfer/career and technical institutions[9]	4,877	115	406	0	0	4,356	0	0	0	0
High career and technical institutions[10]	41,651	4,795	10,614	15,280	7,462	3,500	0	0	0	0
Special-focus[7] 2-year	106,408	9,279	33,110	39,557	21,283	3,179	0	0	0	0
Health professions	72,250	5,918	26,551	29,061	7,541	3,179	0	0	0	0
Other programs	34,158	3,361	6,559	10,496	13,742	0	0	0	0	0

See notes at end of table.

Table 317.40. **Number of degree-granting postsecondary institutions and enrollment in these institutions, by enrollment size, control, and classification of institution: Fall 2017—Continued**

[1]Excludes institutions with no enrollment reported separately from the enrollment of an associated main campus.

[2]Research universities with a very high level of research activity.

[3]Research universities with a high level of research activity.

[4]Institutions that award at least 20 research/scholarship doctor's degrees per year, but did not have a high level of research activity.

[5]Institutions that award at least 50 master's degrees and fewer than 20 doctor's degrees per year.

[6]Institutions that primarily emphasize undergraduate education. In addition to institutions that primarily award bachelor's degrees, also includes institutions classified as 4-year in the IPEDS system, but classified as 2-year baccalaureate/associate's colleges in the Carnegie Classification system because they primarily award associate's degrees.

[7]Institutions that award degrees primarily in single fields of study, such as medicine, business, fine arts, theology, and engineering.

[8]Institutions that award less than 30 percent of their awards in career and technical programs.

[9]Institutions that award 30 to 49 percent of their awards in career and technical programs.

[10]Institutions that award 50 percent or more of their awards in career and technical programs.

NOTE: Degree-granting institutions grant associate's or higher degrees and participate in Title IV federal financial aid programs. Relative levels of research activity for research universities were determined by an analysis of research and development expenditures, science and engineering research staffing, and doctor's degrees conferred, by field. Further information on the research index ranking may be obtained from http://carnegieclassifications.iu.edu/.

SOURCE: U.S. Department of Education, National Center for Education Statistics, Integrated Postsecondary Education Data System (IPEDS), Spring 2019, Fall Enrollment component. (This table was prepared September 2019.)

Table 317.50. Number of degree-granting postsecondary institutions that have closed, by control and level of institution: 1969–70 through 2018–19

Year	All institutions			Public			Private								
							Total			Nonprofit			For-profit		
	Total	4-year	2-year	Total	4-year	2-year	Total	4-year	2-year	Total	4-year	2-year	Total	4-year	2-year
1	2	3	4	5	6	7	8	9	10	11	12	13	14	15	16
1969–70	24	10	14	5	1	4	19	9	10	—	—	—	—	—	—
1970–71	35	10	25	11	0	11	24	10	14	—	—	—	—	—	—
1971–72	14	5	9	3	0	3	11	5	6	—	—	—	—	—	—
1972–73	21	12	9	4	0	4	17	12	5	—	—	—	—	—	—
1973–74	20	12	8	1	0	1	19	12	7	—	—	—	—	—	—
1974–75	18	13	5	4	0	4	14	13	1	—	—	—	—	—	—
1975–76	9	7	2	2	1	1	7	6	1	—	—	—	—	—	—
1976–77	9	6	3	0	0	0	9	6	3	—	—	—	—	—	—
1977–78	12	9	3	0	0	0	12	9	3	—	—	—	—	—	—
1978–79	9	4	5	0	0	0	9	4	5	—	—	—	—	—	—
1979–80	6	5	1	0	0	0	6	5	1	—	—	—	—	—	—
1980–81	4	3	1	0	0	0	4	3	1	—	—	—	—	—	—
1981–82	7	6	1	0	0	0	7	6	1	—	—	—	—	—	—
1982–83	7	4	3	0	0	0	7	4	3	—	—	—	—	—	—
1983–84	5	5	0	1	1	0	4	4	0	—	—	—	—	—	—
1984–85	4	4	0	0	0	0	4	4	0	—	—	—	—	—	—
1985–86	12	8	4	1	1	0	11	7	4	—	—	—	—	—	—
1986–87 and 1987–88	26	19	7	1	0	1	25	19	6	—	—	—	—	—	—
1988–89	14	6	8	0	0	0	14	6	8	—	—	—	—	—	—
1989–90	19	8	11	0	0	0	19	8	11	—	—	—	—	—	—
1990–91	18	6	12	0	0	0	18	6	12	7	5	2	11	1	10
1991–92	26	8	18	1	0	1	25	8	17	8	7	1	17	1	16
1992–93	23	6	17	0	0	0	23	6	17	6	5	1	17	1	16
1993–94	38	11	27	1	0	1	37	11	26	13	10	3	24	1	23
1994–95	15	8	7	2	0	2	13	8	5	8	7	1	5	1	4
1995–96	21	8	13	1	1	0	20	7	13	9	7	2	11	0	11
1996–97	36	13	23	2	0	2	34	13	21	14	10	4	20	3	17
1997–98	5	0	5	0	0	0	5	0	5	1	0	1	4	0	4
1998–99	7	1	6	1	0	1	6	1	5	2	0	2	4	1	3
1999–2000	16	3	13	3	0	3	13	3	10	8	3	5	5	0	5
2000–01	14	9	5	0	0	0	14	9	5	8	8	0	6	1	5
2001–02	14	2	12	0	0	0	14	2	12	1	1	0	13	1	12
2002–03	13	7	6	0	0	0	13	7	6	6	6	0	7	1	6
2003–04	12	5	7	0	0	0	12	5	7	8	5	3	4	0	4
2004–05	3	1	2	0	0	0	3	1	2	1	1	0	2	0	2
2005–06	11	6	5	1	1	0	10	5	5	5	4	1	5	1	4
2006–07	13	4	9	0	0	0	13	4	9	6	4	2	7	0	7
2007–08	26	10	16	0	0	0	26	10	16	9	6	3	17	4	13
2008–09	16	6	10	0	0	0	16	6	10	6	5	1	10	1	9
2009–10	17	11	6	0	0	0	17	11	6	9	9	0	8	2	6
2010–11	20	9	11	0	0	0	20	9	11	7	6	1	13	3	10
2011–12	10	5	5	4	0	4	6	5	1	2	2	0	4	3	1
2012–13	21	3	18	1	1	0	20	2	18	4	2	2	16	0	16
2013–14	20	8	12	1	1	0	19	7	12	4	3	1	15	4	11
2014–15	54	7	47	0	0	0	54	7	47	5	3	2	49	4	45
2015–16	66	24	42	0	0	0	66	24	42	8	5	3	58	19	39
2016–17	112	65	47	0	0	0	112	65	47	20	12	8	92	53	39
2017–18	86	39	47	1	0	1	85	39	46	17	12	5	68	27	41
2018–19	236	111	125	0	0	0	236	111	125	30	15	15	206	96	110

—Not available.
NOTE: This table indicates the year by which the institution no longer operated (generally it closed at the end of or during the prior year). Data through 1995–96 are for institutions of higher education, while later data are for degree-granting institutions. Degree-granting institutions grant associate's or higher degrees and participate in Title IV federal financial aid programs. The degree-granting classification is very similar to the earlier higher education classification, but it includes more 2-year colleges and excludes a few higher education institutions that did not grant degrees.

SOURCE: U.S. Department of Education, National Center for Education Statistics, *Education Directory, Higher Education*, 1969–70 through 1974–75; *Education Directory, Colleges and Universities*, 1975–76 through 1985–86; *1982–83 Supplement to the Education Directory, Colleges and Universities*; Integrated Postsecondary Education Data System (IPEDS), "Institutional Characteristics Survey" (IPEDS-IC:86–99); and IPEDS Fall 2000 through Fall 2018, Institutional Characteristics component. (This table was prepared April 2020.)

Table 318.10. Degrees conferred by postsecondary institutions, by level of degree and sex of student: Selected years, 1869–70 through 2029–30

Year	Associate's degrees				Bachelor's degrees				Master's degrees				Doctor's degrees[1]			
	Total	Males	Females	Percent female	Total	Males	Females	Percent female	Total	Males	Females	Percent female	Total	Males	Females	Percent female
1	2	3	4	5	6	7	8	9	10	11	12	13	14	15	16	17
1869–70	—	—	—	—	9,371[2]	7,993[2]	1,378[2]	14.7	0	0	0	—	1	1	0	0.0
1879–80	—	—	—	—	12,896[2]	10,411[2]	2,485[2]	19.3	879	868	11	1.3	54	51	3	5.6
1889–90	—	—	—	—	15,539[2]	12,857[2]	2,682[2]	17.3	1,015	821	194	19.1	149	147	2	1.3
1899–1900	—	—	—	—	27,410[2]	22,173[2]	5,237[2]	19.1	1,583	1,280	303	19.1	382	359	23	6.0
1909–10	—	—	—	—	37,199[2]	28,762[2]	8,437[2]	22.7	2,113	1,555	558	26.4	443	399	44	9.9
1919–20	—	—	—	—	48,622[2]	31,980[2]	16,642[2]	34.2	4,279	2,985	1,294	30.2	615	522	93	15.1
1929–30	—	—	—	—	122,484[2]	73,615[2]	48,869[2]	39.9	14,969	8,925	6,044	40.4	2,299	1,946	353	15.4
1939–40	—	—	—	—	186,500[2]	109,546[2]	76,954[2]	41.3	26,731	16,508	10,223	38.2	3,290	2,861	429	13.0
1949–50	—	—	—	—	432,058[2]	328,841[2]	103,217[2]	23.9	58,183	41,220	16,963	29.2	6,420	5,804	616	9.6
1959–60	—	—	—	—	392,440[2]	254,063[2]	138,377[2]	35.3	74,435	50,898	23,537	31.6	9,829	8,801	1,028	10.5
1969–70	206,023	117,432	88,591	43.0	792,316	451,097	341,219	43.1	213,589	130,799	82,790	38.8	59,486	53,792	5,694	9.6
1979–80	400,910	183,737	217,173	54.2	929,417	473,611	455,806	49.0	305,196	156,882	148,314	48.6	95,631	69,526	26,105	27.3
1980–81	416,377	188,638	227,739	54.7	935,140	469,883	465,257	49.8	302,637	152,979	149,658	49.5	98,016	69,567	28,449	29.0
1981–82	434,526	196,944	237,582	54.7	952,998	473,364	479,634	50.3	302,447	151,349	151,098	50.0	97,838	68,630	29,208	29.9
1982–83	449,620	203,991	245,629	54.6	969,510	479,140	490,370	50.6	296,415	150,092	146,323	49.4	99,335	67,757	31,578	31.8
1983–84	452,240	202,704	249,536	55.2	974,309	482,319	491,990	50.5	291,141	149,268	141,873	48.7	100,799	67,769	33,030	32.8
1984–85	454,712	202,932	251,780	55.4	979,477	482,528	496,949	50.7	293,472	149,276	144,196	49.1	100,785	66,269	34,516	34.2
1985–86	446,047	196,166	249,881	56.0	987,823	485,923	501,900	50.8	295,850	149,373	146,477	49.5	100,280	65,215	35,065	35.0
1986–87	436,304	190,839	245,465	56.3	991,264	480,782	510,482	51.5	296,530	147,063	149,467	50.4	98,477	62,790	35,687	36.2
1987–88	435,085	190,047	245,038	56.3	994,829	477,203	517,626	52.0	305,783	150,243	155,540	50.9	99,139	63,019	36,120	36.4
1988–89	436,764	186,316	250,448	57.3	1,018,755	483,346	535,409	52.6	316,626	153,993	162,633	51.4	100,571	63,055	37,516	37.3
1989–90	455,102	191,195	263,907	58.0	1,051,344	491,696	559,648	53.2	330,152	158,052	172,100	52.1	103,508	63,963	39,545	38.2
1990–91	481,720	198,634	283,086	58.8	1,094,538	504,045	590,493	53.9	342,863	160,842	182,021	53.1	105,547	64,242	41,305	39.1
1991–92	504,231	207,481	296,750	58.9	1,136,553	520,811	615,742	54.2	358,089	165,867	192,222	53.7	109,554	66,603	42,951	39.2
1992–93	514,756	211,964	302,792	58.8	1,165,178	532,881	632,297	54.3	375,032	173,354	201,678	53.8	112,072	67,130	44,942	40.1
1993–94	530,632	215,261	315,371	59.4	1,169,275	532,422	636,853	54.5	393,037	180,571	212,466	54.1	112,636	66,773	45,863	40.7
1994–95	539,691	218,352	321,339	59.5	1,160,134	526,131	634,003	54.6	403,609	183,043	220,566	54.6	114,266	67,324	46,942	41.1
1995–96	555,216	219,514	335,702	60.5	1,164,792	522,454	642,338	55.1	412,180	183,481	228,699	55.5	115,507	67,189	48,318	41.8
1996–97	571,226	223,948	347,278	60.8	1,172,879	520,515	652,364	55.6	425,260	185,270	239,990	56.4	118,747	68,387	50,360	42.4
1997–98	558,555	217,613	340,942	61.0	1,184,406	519,956	664,450	56.1	436,037	188,718	247,319	56.7	118,735	67,232	51,503	43.4
1998–99	564,984	220,508	344,476	61.0	1,202,239	519,961	682,278	56.8	446,038	190,230	255,808	57.4	116,700	65,340	51,360	44.0
1999–2000	564,933	224,721	340,212	60.2	1,237,875	530,367	707,508	57.2	463,185	196,129	267,056	57.7	118,736	64,930	53,806	45.3
2000–01	578,865	231,645	347,220	60.0	1,244,171	531,840	712,331	57.3	473,502	197,770	275,732	58.2	119,585	64,171	55,414	46.3
2001–02	595,133	238,109	357,024	60.0	1,291,900	549,816	742,084	57.4	487,313	202,604	284,709	58.4	119,663	62,731	56,932	47.6
2002–03	634,016	253,451	380,565	60.0	1,348,811	573,258	775,553	57.5	518,699	215,172	303,527	58.5	121,579	62,730	58,849	48.4
2003–04	665,301	260,033	405,268	60.9	1,399,542	595,425	804,117	57.5	564,272	233,056	331,216	58.7	126,087	63,981	62,106	49.3
2004–05	696,660	267,536	429,124	61.6	1,439,264	613,000	826,264	57.4	580,151	237,155	342,996	59.1	134,387	67,257	67,130	50.0
2005–06	713,315	270,139	443,176	62.1	1,485,104	630,502	854,602	57.5	599,862	241,701	358,161	59.7	138,056	68,912	69,144	50.1
2006–07	727,616	275,034	452,582	62.2	1,524,729	649,816	874,913	57.4	610,703	242,213	368,490	60.3	144,694	71,311	73,383	50.7
2007–08	750,166	282,695	467,471	62.3	1,563,734	668,184	895,550	57.3	630,844	250,203	380,641	60.3	149,190	73,340	75,850	50.8
2008–09	787,243	298,066	489,177	62.1	1,601,399	685,422	915,977	57.2	662,082	263,515	398,567	60.2	154,564	75,674	78,890	51.0
2009–10	848,856	322,747	526,109	62.0	1,649,919	706,660	943,259	57.2	693,313	275,317	417,996	60.3	158,590	76,610	81,980	51.7
2010–11	943,506	361,408	582,098	61.7	1,716,053	734,159	981,894	57.2	730,922	291,680	439,242	60.1	163,827	79,672	84,155	51.4
2011–12	1,021,718	393,479	628,239	61.5	1,792,163	765,772	1,026,391	57.3	755,967	302,484	453,483	60.0	170,217	82,670	87,547	51.4
2012–13	1,007,427	389,195	618,232	61.4	1,840,381	787,408	1,052,973	57.2	751,718	301,552	450,166	59.9	175,026	85,080	89,946	51.4
2013–14	1,005,155	391,474	613,681	61.1	1,870,150	801,905	1,068,245	57.1	754,582	302,846	451,736	59.9	177,587	85,585	92,002	51.8
2014–15	1,014,341	396,782	617,559	60.9	1,894,969	812,693	1,082,276	57.1	758,804	306,615	452,189	59.6	178,548	84,922	93,626	52.4
2015–16	1,008,228	392,084	616,144	61.1	1,920,750	821,746	1,099,004	57.2	785,757	320,574	465,183	59.2	178,134	84,240	93,894	52.7
2016–17	1,005,687	394,147	611,540	60.8	1,956,114	836,021	1,120,093	57.3	804,542	326,857	477,685	59.4	181,357	84,649	96,708	53.3
2017–18	1,011,487	398,600	612,887	60.6	1,980,644	844,960	1,135,684	57.3	820,102	326,870	493,232	60.1	184,074	85,568	98,506	53.5
2018–19[3]	977,000	381,000	596,000	61.0	1,989,000	843,000	1,146,000	57.6	829,000	326,000	502,000	60.6	186,000	85,000	100,000	54.1
2019–20[3]	981,000	382,000	599,000	61.0	1,996,000	846,000	1,151,000	57.6	832,000	327,000	505,000	60.7	186,000	86,000	101,000	54.1
2020–21[3]	983,000	383,000	600,000	61.1	1,998,000	846,000	1,152,000	57.7	833,000	327,000	506,000	60.7	187,000	86,000	101,000	54.1
2021–22[3]	986,000	384,000	602,000	61.1	2,000,000	846,000	1,154,000	57.7	835,000	328,000	507,000	60.7	187,000	86,000	101,000	54.1
2022–23[3]	989,000	385,000	604,000	61.1	2,002,000	847,000	1,156,000	57.7	836,000	328,000	508,000	60.7	187,000	86,000	101,000	54.2
2023–24[3]	992,000	386,000	606,000	61.1	2,007,000	848,000	1,158,000	57.7	838,000	329,000	509,000	60.7	188,000	86,000	102,000	54.2
2024–25[3]	995,000	387,000	608,000	61.1	2,013,000	851,000	1,162,000	57.7	841,000	330,000	511,000	60.7	188,000	86,000	102,000	54.2
2025–26[3]	998,000	389,000	610,000	61.1	2,020,000	854,000	1,166,000	57.7	844,000	331,000	513,000	60.7	189,000	87,000	102,000	54.2
2026–27[3]	1,002,000	390,000	612,000	61.1	2,027,000	857,000	1,170,000	57.7	847,000	333,000	514,000	60.7	190,000	87,000	103,000	54.2
2027–28[3]	1,005,000	391,000	613,000	61.1	2,030,000	858,000	1,171,000	57.7	849,000	333,000	515,000	60.7	190,000	87,000	103,000	54.2
2028–29[3]	1,006,000	392,000	614,000	61.1	2,030,000	858,000	1,171,000	57.7	849,000	333,000	516,000	60.7	190,000	87,000	103,000	54.2
2029–30[3]	1,007,000	392,000	615,000	61.1	2,029,000	858,000	1,171,000	57.7	849,000	334,000	516,000	60.7	190,000	87,000	103,000	54.2

—Not available.

[1]Includes Ph.D., Ed.D., and comparable degrees at the doctoral level. Includes most degrees that were classified as first-professional prior to 2010–11, such as M.D., D.D.S., and law degrees.

[2]Includes some degrees classified as master's or doctor's degrees in later years.

[3]Projected.

NOTE: Data through 1994–95 are for institutions of higher education, while later data are for degree-granting institutions. Degree-granting institutions grant associate's or higher degrees and participate in Title IV federal financial aid programs. Some data have been revised from previously published figures. Detail may not sum to totals because of rounding. SOURCE: U.S. Department of Education, National Center for Education Statistics, *Earned Degrees Conferred*, 1869–70 through 1964–65; Higher Education General Information Survey (HEGIS), "Degrees and Other Formal Awards Conferred" surveys, 1965–66 through 1985–86; Integrated Postsecondary Education Data System (IPEDS), "Completions Survey" (IPEDS-C:87–99); IPEDS Fall 2000 through Fall 2018, Completions component; and Degrees Conferred Projection Model, 1980–81 through 2029–30. (This table was prepared December 2019.)

Table 318.20. Bachelor's, master's, and doctor's degrees conferred by postsecondary institutions, by field of study: Selected years, 1970–71 through 2017–18

[Standard errors appear in parentheses]

Degree and year	Number of degrees conferred								Percentage distribution of degrees conferred							
	Total degrees	Humanities[1]	Social and behavioral sciences[2]	Natural sciences and mathematics[3]	Computer sciences and engineering[4]	Education	Business	Other fields[5]	Total degrees	Humanities[1]	Social and behavioral sciences[2]	Natural sciences and mathematics[3]	Computer sciences and engineering[4]	Education	Business	Other fields[5]
1	2	3	4	5	6	7	8	9	10	11	12	13	14	15	16	17
Bachelor's degrees																
1970–71	839,730	143,549	193,511	81,916	52,570	176,307	115,396	76,481	100.0	17.1	23.0	9.8	6.3	21.0	13.7	9.1
1975–76	925,746	150,736	176,674	91,596	52,328	154,437	143,171	156,804	100.0	16.3	19.1	9.9	5.7	16.7	15.5	16.9
1980–81	935,140	134,139	141,581	78,092	90,476	108,074	200,521	182,257	100.0	14.3	15.1	8.4	9.7	11.6	21.4	19.5
1985–86	987,823	132,891	134,468	76,228	139,459	87,147	236,700	180,930	100.0	13.5	13.6	7.7	14.1	8.8	24.0	18.3
1990–91	1,094,538	172,485	183,762	70,209	104,910	110,807	249,165	203,200	100.0	15.8	16.8	6.4	9.6	10.1	22.8	18.6
1995–96	1,164,792	193,404	199,895	93,443	102,503	105,384	226,623	243,540	100.0	16.6	17.2	8.0	8.8	9.0	19.5	20.9
2000–01	1,244,171	214,107	201,681	89,772	117,011	105,458	263,515	252,627	100.0	17.2	16.2	7.2	9.4	8.5	21.2	20.3
2005–06	1,485,104	261,666	249,600	105,883	129,108	107,235	318,043	313,569	100.0	17.6	16.8	7.1	8.7	7.2	21.4	21.1
2010–11	1,716,053	288,446	278,075	131,871	136,163	104,008	365,133	412,357	100.0	16.8	16.2	7.7	7.9	6.1	21.3	24.0
2014–15	1,894,969	280,956	284,544	161,800	174,691	91,596	363,741	537,641	100.0	14.8	15.0	8.5	9.2	4.8	19.2	28.4
2015–16	1,920,750	274,513	278,658	167,055	188,350	87,221	371,690	553,263	100.0	14.3	14.5	8.7	9.8	4.5	19.4	28.8
2016–17	1,956,114	270,931	275,956	172,115	205,206	85,130	381,109	565,667	100.0	13.9	14.1	8.8	10.5	4.4	19.5	28.9
2017–18	1,980,644	268,554	276,399	175,461	220,281	82,621	386,201	571,127	100.0	13.6	14.0	8.9	11.1	4.2	19.5	28.8
Master's degrees																
1970–71	235,564	34,510	22,256	17,152	18,535	87,666	26,490	28,955	100.0	14.6	9.4	7.3	7.9	37.2	11.2	12.3
1975–76	317,477	37,079	26,120	15,742	19,403	126,061	42,592	50,480	100.0	11.7	8.2	5.0	6.1	39.7	13.4	15.9
1980–81	302,637	35,130	22,168	13,579	21,434	96,713	57,888	55,725	100.0	11.6	7.3	4.5	7.1	32.0	19.1	18.4
1985–86	295,850	34,834	20,409	14,055	30,216	74,816	66,676	54,844	100.0	11.8	6.9	4.8	10.2	25.3	22.5	18.5
1990–91	342,863	35,984	23,582	13,664	34,774	87,352	78,255	69,252	100.0	10.5	6.9	4.0	10.1	25.5	22.8	20.2
1995–96	412,180	40,795	30,164	16,154	39,422	104,936	93,554	87,155	100.0	9.9	7.3	3.9	9.6	25.5	22.7	21.1
2000–01	473,502	40,625	30,330	15,360	44,098	127,829	115,602	99,658	100.0	8.6	6.4	3.2	9.3	27.0	24.4	21.0
2005–06	599,862	49,590	37,143	19,575	50,581	174,622	146,396	121,955	100.0	8.3	6.2	3.3	8.4	29.1	24.4	20.3
2010–11	730,922	57,160	46,147	23,576	62,695	185,127	187,178	169,039	100.0	7.8	6.3	3.2	8.6	25.3	25.6	23.1
2014–15	758,804	59,181	47,305	29,344	82,916	146,581	185,236	208,241	100.0	7.8	6.2	3.9	10.9	19.3	24.4	27.4
2015–16	785,757	59,067	47,506	31,299	97,843	145,792	186,835	217,415	100.0	7.5	6.0	4.0	12.5	18.6	23.8	27.7
2016–17	804,542	57,895	47,543	32,500	106,782	145,624	187,412	226,786	100.0	7.2	5.9	4.0	13.3	18.1	23.3	28.2
2017–18	820,102	59,088	47,725	34,819	105,436	146,367	192,184	234,483	100.0	7.2	5.8	4.2	12.9	17.8	23.4	28.6
Doctor's degrees[6]																
1970–71	64,998	4,402	5,804	9,126	3,816	6,041	774	35,035	100.0	6.8	8.9	14.0	5.9	9.3	1.2	53.9
1975–76	91,007	5,461	7,314	7,591	3,118	7,202	906	59,415	100.0	6.0	8.0	8.3	3.4	7.9	1.0	65.3
1980–81	98,016	4,827	6,698	7,473	2,860	7,279	808	68,071	100.0	4.9	6.8	7.6	2.9	7.4	0.8	69.4
1985–86	100,280	4,648	6,548	7,668	3,800	6,610	923	70,083	100.0	4.6	6.5	7.6	3.8	6.6	0.9	69.9
1990–91	105,547	4,858	6,944	9,378	6,006	6,189	1,185	70,987	100.0	4.6	6.6	8.9	5.7	5.9	1.1	67.3
1995–96	115,507	6,356	7,901	10,997	7,223	6,246	1,366	75,418	100.0	5.5	6.8	9.5	6.3	5.4	1.2	65.3
2000–01	119,585	6,466	9,021	10,190	6,315	6,284	1,180	80,129	100.0	5.4	7.5	8.5	5.3	5.3	1.0	67.0
2005–06	138,056	6,628	8,835	12,097	8,734	7,584	1,711	92,467	100.0	4.8	6.4	8.8	6.3	5.5	1.2	67.0
2010–11	163,827	8,359	10,241	14,574	10,013	9,642	2,286	108,712	100.0	5.1	6.3	8.9	6.1	5.9	1.4	66.4
2014–15	178,548	8,391	11,411	15,677	12,360	11,772	3,116	115,821	100.0	4.7	6.4	8.8	6.9	6.6	1.7	64.9
2015–16	178,134	8,324	11,246	15,851	12,387	11,838	3,325	115,163	100.0	4.7	6.3	8.9	7.0	6.6	1.9	64.6
2016–17	181,357	8,120	11,408	16,039	12,505	12,692	3,328	117,265	100.0	4.5	6.3	8.8	6.9	7.0	1.8	64.7
2017–18	184,074	8,336	10,951	16,413	13,046	12,780	3,338	119,210	100.0	4.5	5.9	8.9	7.1	6.9	1.8	64.8

[1]Includes degrees in Area, ethnic, cultural, gender, and group studies; English language and literature/letters; Foreign languages, literatures, and linguistics; Liberal arts and sciences, general studies, and humanities; Multi/interdisciplinary studies; Philosophy and religious studies; Theology and religious vocations; and Visual and performing arts.
[2]Includes Psychology: Social sciences; and History.
[3]Includes Biological and biomedical sciences; Mathematics and statistics; and Physical sciences and science technologies.
[4]Includes Computer and information sciences; Engineering; and Engineering technologies.
[5]Includes Agriculture and natural resources; Architecture and related services; Communication, journalism, and related programs; Communications technologies; Family and consumer sciences/human sciences; Health professions and related programs; Homeland security, law enforcement, and firefighting; Legal professions and studies; Library science; Military technologies and applied sciences; Parks, recreation, leisure, and fitness studies; Precision production; Public administration and social services; Transportation and materials moving; and Not classified by field of study.
[6]Includes Ph.D., Ed.D., and comparable degrees at the doctoral level. Includes most degrees that were classified as first-professional prior to 2010–11, such as M.D., D.D.S., and law degrees.

NOTE: Data are for postsecondary institutions participating in Title IV federal financial aid programs. Data in this table are based on the 2010 Classification of Instructional Programs. The figures for earlier years have been reclassified when necessary to make them conform to the new taxonomy. To facilitate trend comparisons, certain aggregations have been made of the degree fields as reported in the Integrated Postsecondary Education Data System (IPEDS): "Agriculture and natural resources" includes Agriculture, agriculture operations, and related sciences and Natural resources and conservation; "Business" includes Business, management, marketing, and related support services and Personal and culinary services; and "Engineering technologies" includes Engineering technologies and engineering-related fields, Construction trades, and Mechanic and repair technologies/technicians. Detail may not sum to totals because of rounding. Some data have been revised from previously published figures.
SOURCE: U.S. Department of Education, National Center for Education Statistics, Higher Education General Information Survey (HEGIS), "Degrees and Other Formal Awards Conferred" surveys, 1970–71 through 1985–86; Integrated Postsecondary Education Data System (IPEDS), "Completions Survey" (IPEDS-C:91–96); and IPEDS Fall 2001 through Fall 2018, Completions component. (This table was prepared February 2020.)

Table 318.30. Bachelor's, master's, and doctor's degrees conferred by postsecondary institutions, by sex of student and discipline division: 2017–18

Discipline division	Bachelor's degrees			Master's degrees			Doctor's degrees[1]		
	Total	Males	Females	Total	Males	Females	Total	Males	Females
1	2	3	4	5	6	7	8	9	10
All fields, total	**1,980,644**	**844,960**	**1,135,684**	**820,102**	**326,870**	**493,232**	**184,074**	**85,568**	**98,506**
Agriculture and natural resources	39,314	18,202	21,112	6,967	2,997	3,970	1,496	798	698
Agriculture, agriculture operations, and related sciences	20,215	9,003	11,212	2,856	1,247	1,609	886	488	398
Agriculture, general	2,194	1,096	1,098	301	120	181	14	11	3
Agricultural business and management, general	1,124	745	379	66	40	26	1	0	1
Agribusiness/agricultural business operations	2,195	1,362	833	43	21	22	0	0	0
Agricultural economics	1,531	1,046	485	336	175	161	131	80	51
Farm/farm and ranch management	171	129	42	6	5	1	0	0	0
Agricultural/farm supplies retailing and wholesaling	1	0	1	0	0	0	0	0	0
Agricultural business technology	36	20	16	2	1	1	0	0	0
Agricultural business and management, other	81	42	39	8	2	6	0	0	0
Agricultural mechanization, general	336	310	26	1	0	1	0	0	0
Agricultural mechanics and equipment/machine technology	0	0	0	0	0	0	0	0	0
Agricultural production operations, general	81	43	38	7	3	4	0	0	0
Animal/livestock husbandry and production	193	54	139	1	0	1	0	0	0
Aquaculture	58	39	19	41	26	15	12	8	4
Crop production	75	61	14	0	0	0	0	0	0
Dairy husbandry and production	2	0	2	0	0	0	0	0	0
Horse husbandry/equine science and management	159	9	150	7	0	7	0	0	0
Agroecology and sustainable agriculture	211	108	103	73	25	48	13	7	6
Viticulture and enology	132	67	65	0	0	0	0	0	0
Agricultural and food products processing	103	56	47	0	0	0	0	0	0
Animal training	23	5	18	0	0	0	0	0	0
Equestrian/equine studies	302	14	288	0	0	0	0	0	0
Agricultural and domestic animal services, other	1	0	1	0	0	0	0	0	0
Applied horticulture/horticultural operations, general	87	33	54	7	5	2	5	3	2
Ornamental horticulture	28	16	12	6	4	2	6	4	2
Landscaping and groundskeeping	132	96	36	2	0	2	0	0	0
Plant nursery operations and management	2	1	1	0	0	0	0	0	0
Turf and turfgrass management	94	90	4	4	4	0	0	0	0
Floriculture/floristry operations and management	1	1	0	0	0	0	0	0	0
Applied horticulture/horticultural business services, other	32	22	10	0	0	0	0	0	0
International agriculture	54	16	38	54	14	40	0	0	0
Agricultural and extension education services	67	29	38	94	23	71	15	8	7
Agricultural communication/journalism	422	72	350	27	4	23	0	0	0
Agricultural public services, other	53	22	31	5	1	4	0	0	0
Animal sciences, general	5,890	1,184	4,706	414	137	277	166	82	84
Agricultural animal breeding	0	0	0	4	0	4	1	0	1
Animal health	2	1	1	1	0	1	0	0	0
Animal nutrition	0	0	0	0	0	0	3	0	3
Dairy science	153	60	93	33	9	24	5	2	3
Livestock management	3	1	2	2	0	2	0	0	0
Poultry science	103	46	57	17	10	7	17	8	9
Animal sciences, other	79	11	68	4	1	3	0	0	0
Food science	1,318	388	930	451	139	312	140	55	85
Food technology and processing	13	5	8	10	5	5	7	3	4
Food science and technology, other	74	42	32	29	13	16	0	0	0
Plant sciences, general	531	327	204	87	58	29	46	29	17
Agronomy and crop science	704	485	219	276	173	103	110	72	38
Horticultural science	485	251	234	137	68	69	38	25	13
Agricultural and horticultural plant breeding	6	3	3	25	15	10	28	22	6
Plant protection and integrated pest management	109	90	19	28	21	7	7	3	4
Range science and management	110	62	48	37	18	19	14	8	6
Plant sciences, other	32	21	11	61	30	31	42	24	18
Soil science and agronomy, general	190	132	58	91	53	38	55	31	24
Soil chemistry and physics	38	33	5	1	1	0	0	0	0
Soil sciences, other	38	18	20	8	4	4	4	2	2
Agriculture, agriculture operations, and related sciences, other	356	239	117	49	19	30	6	1	5
Natural resources and conservation	19,099	9,199	9,900	4,111	1,750	2,361	610	310	300
Natural resources/conservation, general	1,377	660	717	581	238	343	100	51	49
Environmental studies	6,532	2,752	3,780	1,199	492	707	110	45	65
Environmental science	6,697	3,166	3,531	899	375	524	168	91	77
Natural resources conservation and research, other	130	67	63	79	38	41	25	11	14
Natural resources management and policy	695	399	296	497	191	306	25	11	14
Natural resource economics	73	41	32	8	3	5	1	0	1
Water, wetlands, and marine resources management	77	39	38	171	61	110	1	1	0
Land use planning and management/development	66	54	12	44	20	24	1	1	0
Natural resource recreation and tourism	53	33	20	62	29	33	1	0	1
Natural resources law enforcement and protective services	31	25	6	0	0	0	0	0	0
Natural resources management and policy, other	253	154	99	25	9	16	0	0	0
Fishing and fisheries sciences and management	357	196	161	41	19	22	17	10	7
Forestry, general	521	373	148	136	75	61	39	24	15
Forest sciences and biology	192	157	35	122	70	52	50	24	26
Forest management/forest resources management	166	136	30	36	21	15	5	4	1
Urban forestry	20	5	15	13	8	5	4	2	2
Wood science and wood products/pulp and paper technology	78	58	20	12	9	3	9	4	5
Forest resources production and management	5	4	1	8	4	4	8	6	2
Forest technology/technician	0	0	0	0	0	0	0	0	0
Forestry, other	76	53	23	6	4	2	8	5	3
Wildlife, fish, and wildlands science and management	1,564	741	823	157	80	77	36	20	16
Natural resources and conservation, other	136	86	50	15	4	11	2	0	2

See notes at end of table.

Table 318.30. Bachelor's, master's, and doctor's degrees conferred by postsecondary institutions, by sex of student and discipline division: 2017–18—Continued

Discipline division	Bachelor's degrees			Master's degrees			Doctor's degrees[1]		
	Total	Males	Females	Total	Males	Females	Total	Males	Females
1	2	3	4	5	6	7	8	9	10
Architecture and related services	8,464	4,474	3,990	7,317	3,516	3,801	250	136	114
Architecture	4,511	2,422	2,089	2,609	1,385	1,224	117	70	47
City/urban, community and regional planning	825	492	333	1,667	733	934	101	52	49
Environmental design/architecture	521	288	233	91	31	60	11	5	6
Interior architecture	425	38	387	144	20	124	0	0	0
Landscape architecture	720	394	326	524	194	330	3	1	2
Architectural history and criticism, general	80	38	42	28	11	17	2	0	2
Architectural technology/technician	128	77	51	9	4	5	0	0	0
Architectural and building sciences/technology	986	575	411	1,907	917	990	16	8	8
Real estate development	60	49	11	292	203	89	0	0	0
Architecture and related services, other	208	101	107	46	18	28	0	0	0
Area, ethnic, cultural, gender, and group studies	7,717	2,118	5,599	1,673	565	1,108	335	116	219
African studies	94	18	76	44	17	27	14	5	9
American/United States studies/civilization	958	368	590	220	60	160	88	40	48
Asian studies/civilization	679	294	385	84	40	44	0	0	0
East Asian studies	281	115	166	165	69	96	25	9	16
Russian, Central European, East European and Eurasian studies	41	16	25	29	11	18	0	0	0
European studies/civilization	48	14	34	19	12	7	0	0	0
Latin American studies	305	101	204	168	65	103	3	0	3
Near and Middle Eastern studies	143	50	93	159	75	84	33	17	16
Pacific Area/Pacific Rim studies	17	8	9	2	0	2	0	0	0
Russian studies	70	31	39	39	21	18	0	0	0
Scandinavian studies	11	7	4	4	2	2	1	0	1
South Asian studies	4	2	2	10	4	6	4	3	1
Southeast Asian studies	0	0	0	6	4	2	0	0	0
Western European studies	8	2	6	33	18	15	0	0	0
Canadian studies	1	0	1	4	4	0	0	0	0
Slavic studies	5	1	4	5	3	2	3	1	2
Ural-Altaic and Central Asian studies	6	3	3	4	4	0	2	0	2
Regional studies (U.S., Canadian, foreign)	16	7	9	14	5	9	3	1	2
Chinese studies	45	23	22	9	4	5	0	0	0
French studies	49	10	39	16	4	12	8	2	6
German studies	43	19	24	6	2	4	7	3	4
Italian studies	32	8	24	17	3	14	2	0	2
Japanese studies	57	26	31	4	3	1	0	0	0
Korean studies	0	0	0	0	0	0	0	0	0
Spanish and Iberian studies	19	5	14	0	0	0	0	0	0
Irish studies	0	0	0	4	0	4	0	0	0
Latin American and Caribbean studies	37	14	23	14	2	12	0	0	0
Area studies, other	612	202	410	51	19	32	8	5	3
Ethnic studies	181	45	136	7	0	7	5	1	4
African-American/Black studies	677	210	467	72	25	47	39	12	27
American Indian/Native American studies	212	80	132	69	24	45	10	2	8
Hispanic-American, Puerto Rican, and Mexican-American/Chicano studies	420	94	326	41	11	30	13	6	7
Asian-American studies	82	34	48	8	2	6	0	0	0
Women's studies	1,459	100	1,359	187	20	167	21	2	19
Gay/lesbian studies	7	0	7	0	0	0	0	0	0
Folklore studies	10	2	8	19	4	15	7	0	7
Disability studies	32	3	29	36	3	33	7	0	7
Deaf studies	236	36	200	4	1	3	0	0	0
Ethnic, cultural minority, gender, and group studies, other	820	170	650	100	24	76	32	7	25
Biological and biomedical sciences	118,663	44,852	73,811	17,180	7,028	10,152	8,222	3,829	4,393
Biology/biological sciences, general	73,983	26,686	47,297	3,579	1,409	2,170	1,036	485	551
Biomedical sciences, general	4,460	1,749	2,711	2,532	1,111	1,421	628	287	341
Biochemistry	8,861	4,287	4,574	321	160	161	521	274	247
Biophysics	167	109	58	26	17	9	102	67	35
Molecular biology	841	353	488	193	88	105	162	66	96
Molecular biochemistry	398	202	196	95	37	58	59	32	27
Molecular biophysics	0	0	0	1	0	1	14	14	0
Structural biology	0	0	0	0	0	0	0	0	0
Radiation biology/radiobiology	5	0	5	10	9	1	6	4	2
Biochemistry and molecular biology	1,051	482	569	125	49	76	147	66	81
Biochemistry, biophysics and molecular biology, other	219	95	124	22	12	10	34	14	20
Botany/plant biology	231	111	120	93	47	46	109	59	50
Plant pathology/phytopathology	17	5	12	68	35	33	81	42	39
Plant physiology	0	0	0	5	2	3	9	5	4
Plant molecular biology	0	0	0	2	2	0	13	7	6
Botany/plant biology, other	30	13	17	8	4	4	9	4	5
Cell/cellular biology and histology	371	180	191	45	15	30	136	55	81
Anatomy	482	169	313	235	107	128	38	14	24
Developmental biology and embryology	48	18	30	5	2	3	47	21	26
Cell/cellular and molecular biology	2,773	1,184	1,589	192	86	106	420	207	213
Cell biology and anatomy	15	9	6	34	12	22	35	22	13
Cell/cellular biology and anatomical sciences, other	100	33	67	144	64	80	115	59	56
Microbiology, general	2,024	874	1,150	177	61	116	198	82	116
Medical microbiology and bacteriology	398	152	246	205	68	137	131	52	79
Virology	0	0	0	1	1	0	13	7	6
Parasitology	0	0	0	0	0	0	0	0	0
Immunology	0	0	0	90	36	54	143	68	75
Microbiology and immunology	137	61	76	74	26	48	75	33	42
Microbiological sciences and immunology, other	131	56	75	38	16	22	62	26	36
Zoology/animal biology	1,568	471	1,097	87	38	49	87	35	52
Entomology	98	41	57	137	65	72	112	64	48
Animal physiology	124	46	78	30	15	15	19	11	8
Animal behavior and ethology	146	22	124	29	3	26	9	3	6

See notes at end of table.

Table 318.30. Bachelor's, master's, and doctor's degrees conferred by postsecondary institutions, by sex of student and discipline division: 2017–18—Continued

Discipline division	Bachelor's degrees			Master's degrees			Doctor's degrees[1]		
	Total	Males	Females	Total	Males	Females	Total	Males	Females
1	2	3	4	5	6	7	8	9	10
Wildlife biology	450	163	287	9	5	4	3	1	2
Zoology/animal biology, other	2	1	1	14	5	9	7	4	3
Genetics, general	359	107	252	58	24	34	138	53	85
Molecular genetics	212	62	150	16	6	10	83	40	43
Animal genetics	36	9	27	0	0	0	18	5	13
Plant genetics	6	3	3	4	3	1	15	8	7
Human/medical genetics	0	0	0	184	33	151	89	35	54
Genome sciences/genomics	7	2	5	11	3	8	31	13	18
Genetics, other	0	0	0	1	0	1	19	12	7
Physiology, general	1,593	637	956	812	387	425	146	79	67
Molecular physiology	0	0	0	0	0	0	37	16	21
Cell physiology	3	0	3	25	10	15	29	11	18
Endocrinology	0	0	0	2	0	2	9	2	7
Reproductive biology	0	0	0	25	7	18	3	0	3
Cardiovascular science	0	0	0	7	2	5	7	6	1
Exercise physiology	3,879	1,658	2,221	531	219	312	86	51	35
Vision science/physiological optics	97	17	80	40	12	28	16	7	9
Pathology/experimental pathology	22	3	19	105	39	66	176	77	99
Oncology and cancer biology	0	0	0	25	6	19	130	70	60
Physiology, pathology, and related sciences, other	59	14	45	20	5	15	7	6	1
Pharmacology	78	39	39	226	115	111	210	100	110
Molecular pharmacology	0	0	0	5	1	4	57	27	30
Neuropharmacology	0	0	0	32	19	13	0	0	0
Toxicology	63	18	45	55	21	34	71	28	43
Molecular toxicology	0	0	0	0	0	0	1	1	0
Environmental toxicology	22	8	14	46	19	27	41	16	25
Pharmacology and toxicology	68	31	37	102	36	66	55	22	33
Pharmacology and toxicology, other	0	0	0	0	0	0	0	0	0
Biometry/biometrics	31	18	13	34	20	14	11	6	5
Biostatistics	30	8	22	718	284	434	206	98	108
Bioinformatics	284	163	121	420	221	199	119	81	38
Computational biology	40	20	20	30	17	13	49	28	21
Biomathematics, bioinformatics, and computational biology, other	38	11	27	65	42	23	22	16	6
Biotechnology	844	399	445	1,344	557	787	15	9	6
Ecology	715	280	435	159	65	94	172	78	94
Marine biology and biological oceanography	1,357	418	939	244	63	181	75	33	42
Evolutionary biology	103	29	74	22	9	13	33	18	15
Aquatic biology/limnology	91	52	39	9	4	5	0	0	0
Environmental biology	337	140	197	42	14	28	16	8	8
Population biology	0	0	0	8	3	5	8	3	5
Conservation biology	141	49	92	91	29	62	12	6	6
Systematic biology/biological systematics	0	0	0	4	1	3	11	7	4
Epidemiology	23	5	18	1,400	399	1,001	359	95	264
Ecology and evolutionary biology	452	164	288	57	21	36	94	48	46
Ecology, evolution, systematics and population biology, other	194	83	111	26	14	12	41	22	19
Molecular medicine	0	0	0	16	3	13	34	16	18
Neuroscience	6,191	2,110	4,081	243	95	148	618	272	346
Neurobiology and anatomy	834	327	507	11	2	9	54	17	37
Neurobiology and behavior	139	40	99	33	10	23	15	10	5
Neurobiology and neurosciences, other	44	11	33	0	0	0	5	4	1
Biological and biomedical sciences, other	1,141	345	796	1,246	581	665	199	79	120
Business, management, marketing, and personal and culinary services	386,201	204,839	181,362	192,184	99,860	92,324	3,338	1,926	1,412
Business, management, marketing, and related support services	385,400	204,563	180,837	192,154	99,855	92,299	3,338	1,926	1,412
Business/commerce, general	25,128	13,342	11,786	9,402	5,576	3,826	249	149	100
Business administration and management, general	138,905	74,085	64,820	106,000	58,051	47,949	2,003	1,217	786
Purchasing, procurement/acquisitions and contracts management	655	388	267	409	211	198	3	3	0
Logistics, materials, and supply chain management	5,494	3,679	1,815	959	638	321	2	1	1
Office management and supervision	430	175	255	62	31	31	0	0	0
Operations management and supervision	3,005	1,940	1,065	544	326	218	9	5	4
Nonprofit/public/organizational management	386	112	274	1,860	553	1,307	5	3	2
Customer service management	57	18	39	2	0	2	0	0	0
E-commerce/electronic commerce	99	42	57	41	26	15	0	0	0
Transportation/mobility management	167	108	59	147	117	30	4	4	0
Research and development management	8	5	3	164	60	104	0	0	0
Project management	601	361	240	1,018	555	463	8	4	4
Retail management	306	49	257	97	3	94	0	0	0
Organizational leadership	3,946	1,900	2,046	5,605	2,437	3,168	366	177	189
Business administration, management and operations, other	8,466	3,984	4,482	5,704	2,778	2,926	48	22	26
Accounting	50,128	24,316	25,812	19,637	8,737	10,900	36	16	20
Accounting technology/technician and bookkeeping	200	115	85	0	0	0	0	0	0
Auditing	31	10	21	126	53	73	0	0	0
Accounting and finance	818	477	341	868	370	498	0	0	0
Accounting and business/management	968	415	553	400	195	205	0	0	0
Accounting and related services, other	142	79	63	207	91	116	2	1	1
Administrative assistant and secretarial science, general	57	21	36	0	0	0	0	0	0
Executive assistant/executive secretary	0	0	0	0	0	0	0	0	0
Business/office automation/technology/data entry	29	9	20	0	0	0	0	0	0
General office occupations and clerical services	0	0	0	0	0	0	0	0	0
Parts, warehousing, and inventory management operations	0	0	0	0	0	0	0	0	0
Traffic, customs, and transportation clerk/technician	47	31	16	0	0	0	0	0	0
Business operations support and secretarial services, other	0	0	0	0	0	0	0	0	0
Business/corporate communications	937	324	613	72	18	54	0	0	0
Business/managerial economics	5,535	3,632	1,903	250	155	95	53	33	20
Entrepreneurship/entrepreneurial studies	2,600	1,664	936	680	357	323	11	7	4
Franchising and franchise operations	2	1	1	0	0	0	0	0	0
Small business administration/management	165	82	83	9	6	3	0	0	0

See notes at end of table.

Table 318.30. Bachelor's, master's, and doctor's degrees conferred by postsecondary institutions, by sex of student and discipline division: 2017–18—Continued

Discipline division	Bachelor's degrees			Master's degrees			Doctor's degrees[1]		
	Total	Males	Females	Total	Males	Females	Total	Males	Females
1	2	3	4	5	6	7	8	9	10
Entrepreneurial and small business operations, other	91	54	37	92	29	63	1	0	1
Finance, general	39,479	27,985	11,494	5,648	3,429	2,219	33	22	11
Banking and financial support services	494	316	178	34	15	19	0	0	0
Financial planning and services	480	335	145	222	134	88	12	7	5
International finance	3	1	2	26	16	10	0	0	0
Investments and securities	64	54	10	149	100	49	0	0	0
Public finance	16	12	4	12	9	3	0	0	0
Finance and financial management services, other	198	136	62	128	81	47	0	0	0
Hospitality administration/management, general	7,522	2,233	5,289	544	168	376	29	13	16
Tourism and travel services management	684	198	486	108	38	70	2	1	1
Hotel/motel administration/management	1,677	543	1,134	106	41	65	7	3	4
Restaurant/food services management	738	296	442	1	1	0	0	0	0
Resort management	258	104	154	0	0	0	0	0	0
Meeting and event planning	618	51	567	6	3	3	0	0	0
Casino management	0	0	0	0	0	0	0	0	0
Hotel, motel, and restaurant management	48	20	28	0	0	0	0	0	0
Hospitality administration/management, other	383	142	241	72	33	39	1	0	1
Human resources management/personnel administration, general	6,850	1,862	4,988	4,700	1,181	3,519	44	18	26
Labor and industrial relations	974	448	526	728	246	482	8	6	2
Organizational behavior studies	2,276	966	1,310	1,292	482	810	153	71	82
Labor studies	53	21	32	17	9	8	0	0	0
Human resources development	724	139	585	978	249	729	34	18	16
Human resources management and services, other	349	69	280	1,128	392	736	0	0	0
International business/trade/commerce	5,698	2,694	3,004	1,960	1,047	913	29	13	16
Management information systems, general	8,335	6,006	2,329	1,760	1,171	589	28	16	12
Information resources management	236	159	77	668	486	182	29	21	8
Knowledge management	43	23	20	199	106	93	0	0	0
Management information systems and services, other	141	73	68	164	99	65	0	0	0
Management science, general	3,556	2,119	1,437	4,689	2,615	2,074	46	31	15
Business statistics	412	249	163	1,143	631	512	0	0	0
Actuarial science	1,440	852	588	550	319	231	0	0	0
Management sciences and quantitative methods, other	708	452	256	2,902	1,605	1,297	9	6	3
Marketing/marketing management, general	37,010	17,036	19,974	1,969	679	1,290	32	15	17
Marketing research	28	13	15	140	64	76	2	1	1
International marketing	206	49	157	493	206	287	2	1	1
Marketing, other	755	370	385	277	80	197	4	0	4
Real estate	977	735	242	1,039	764	275	0	0	0
Taxation	9	8	1	1,619	807	812	0	0	0
Insurance	1,138	738	400	115	58	57	0	0	0
Sales, distribution, and marketing operations, general	1,549	829	720	557	151	406	3	1	2
Merchandising and buying operations	0	0	0	7	0	7	0	0	0
Retailing and retail operations	387	87	300	3	0	3	0	0	0
Selling skills and sales operations	341	225	116	0	0	0	0	0	0
General merchandising/sales/related marketing operations, other	94	24	70	3	2	1	0	0	0
Fashion merchandising	2,649	156	2,493	67	6	61	0	0	0
Apparel and accessories marketing operations	40	6	34	50	5	45	0	0	0
Tourism and travel services marketing operations	29	11	18	0	0	0	0	0	0
Tourism promotion operations	1	1	0	0	0	0	0	0	0
Vehicle and vehicle parts and accessories marketing operations	68	55	13	0	0	0	0	0	0
Business and personal/financial services marketing operations	0	0	0	0	0	0	0	0	0
Special products marketing operations	202	83	119	14	5	9	0	0	0
Hospitality and recreation marketing operations	78	65	13	0	0	0	0	0	0
Specialized merchandising/sales/related marketing operations, other	133	41	92	52	23	29	0	0	0
Construction management	2,274	2,056	218	425	308	117	6	6	0
Telecommunications management	0	0	0	24	16	8	0	0	0
Business/management/marketing/related support services, other	3,572	1,999	1,573	1,011	602	409	25	14	11
Personal and culinary services	801	276	525	30	5	25	0	0	0
Funeral service and mortuary science, general	137	42	95	0	0	0	0	0	0
Funeral direction/service	44	16	28	0	0	0	0	0	0
Cosmetology/cosmetologist, general	0	0	0	0	0	0	0	0	0
Cooking and related culinary arts, general	0	0	0	0	0	0	0	0	0
Baking and pastry arts/baker/pastry chef	79	11	68	0	0	0	0	0	0
Culinary arts/chef training	324	114	210	0	0	0	0	0	0
Restaurant, culinary, and catering management/manager	111	57	54	0	0	0	0	0	0
Food service, waiter/waitress, and dining room management	0	0	0	0	0	0	0	0	0
Culinary science/culinology	57	24	33	0	0	0	0	0	0
Culinary arts and related services, other	49	12	37	30	5	25	0	0	0
Personal and culinary services, other	0	0	0	0	0	0	0	0	0
Communication and communications technologies	96,521	34,187	62,334	10,772	3,187	7,585	666	252	414
Communication, journalism, and related programs	92,290	31,811	60,479	10,243	2,923	7,320	666	252	414
Communication, general	9,540	3,045	6,495	994	291	703	71	16	55
Speech communication and rhetoric	32,804	11,421	21,383	1,812	564	1,248	303	109	194
Mass communication/media studies	9,218	3,331	5,887	932	272	660	139	61	78
Communication and media studies, other	1,707	591	1,116	547	155	392	48	23	25
Journalism	11,049	3,574	7,475	1,095	332	763	39	14	25
Broadcast journalism	815	365	450	24	8	16	0	0	0
Photojournalism	101	23	78	18	7	11	0	0	0
Journalism, other	738	195	543	456	109	347	0	0	0
Radio and television	4,618	2,459	2,159	150	54	96	13	6	7
Digital communication and media/multimedia	4,186	1,805	2,381	1,226	439	787	30	17	13
Radio, television, and digital communication, other	871	469	402	15	7	8	0	0	0
Public relations, advertising, and applied communication	2,397	578	1,819	394	85	309	0	0	0
Organizational communication, general	1,478	442	1,036	319	78	241	0	0	0
Public relations/image management	4,971	977	3,994	561	137	424	0	0	0
Advertising	4,451	1,443	3,008	213	46	167	6	0	6

See notes at end of table.

Table 318.30. Bachelor's, master's, and doctor's degrees conferred by postsecondary institutions, by sex of student and discipline division: 2017–18—Continued

Discipline division	Bachelor's degrees			Master's degrees			Doctor's degrees[1]		
	Total	Males	Females	Total	Males	Females	Total	Males	Females
1	2	3	4	5	6	7	8	9	10
Political communication	80	26	54	43	17	26	0	0	0
Health communication	128	22	106	163	22	141	4	1	3
Sports communication	258	184	74	57	34	23	0	0	0
International and intercultural communication	115	35	80	141	35	106	0	0	0
Technical and scientific communication	48	24	24	24	7	17	8	3	5
Public relations, advertising and applied communication, other	1,558	349	1,209	244	71	173	0	0	0
Publishing	13	3	10	203	19	184	0	0	0
Communication, journalism, and related programs, other	1,146	450	696	612	134	478	5	2	3
Communications technologies/technicians and support services	4,231	2,376	1,855	529	264	265	0	0	0
Communications technology/technician	281	234	47	17	8	9	0	0	0
Photographic and film/video technology/technician and assistant	70	43	27	0	0	0	0	0	0
Radio and television broadcasting technology/technician	372	196	176	75	32	43	0	0	0
Recording arts technology/technician	438	361	77	54	35	19	0	0	0
Audiovisual communications technologies/technicians, other	161	144	17	0	0	0	0	0	0
Graphic communications, general	422	156	266	33	8	25	0	0	0
Printing management	92	25	67	0	0	0	0	0	0
Prepress/desktop publishing and digital imaging design	55	21	34	0	0	0	0	0	0
Animation/interactive technology/video graphics/special effects	2,081	1,081	1,000	341	174	167	0	0	0
Graphic and printing equipment operator, general production	17	7	10	0	0	0	0	0	0
Printing press operator	14	7	7	0	0	0	0	0	0
Graphic communications, other	110	44	66	0	0	0	0	0	0
Communications technologies/technicians and support services, other	118	57	61	9	7	2	0	0	0
Computer and information sciences and support services	79,598	63,704	15,894	46,468	31,397	15,071	2,017	1,580	437
Computer and information sciences, general	20,707	17,024	3,683	11,217	7,948	3,269	648	508	140
Artificial intelligence	11	11	0	204	152	52	31	25	6
Information technology	10,054	8,022	2,032	4,988	2,940	2,048	57	43	14
Informatics	1,268	909	359	498	273	225	24	14	10
Computer and information sciences, other	529	418	111	222	133	89	12	6	6
Computer programming/programmer, general	918	796	122	40	29	11	5	5	0
Computer programming, specific applications	386	334	52	31	29	2	0	0	0
Computer programming, vendor/product certification	27	21	6	0	0	0	0	0	0
Computer programming, other	44	40	4	38	24	14	0	0	0
Data processing and data processing technology/technician	136	110	26	11	8	3	0	0	0
Information science/studies	8,047	6,030	2,017	6,856	4,177	2,679	164	89	75
Computer systems analysis/analyst	1,070	847	223	692	438	254	2	2	0
Data entry/microcomputer applications, general	0	0	0	20	12	8	0	0	0
Computer science	26,313	21,497	4,816	12,483	8,885	3,598	1,003	835	168
Web page, digital/multimedia and information resources design	1,217	549	668	556	231	325	0	0	0
Data modeling/warehousing and database administration	130	94	36	766	460	306	0	0	0
Computer graphics	721	390	331	285	124	161	0	0	0
Modeling, virtual environments and simulation	346	287	59	141	101	40	0	0	0
Computer software and media applications, other	262	180	82	194	130	64	1	1	0
Computer systems networking and telecommunications	1,352	1,139	213	726	528	198	3	1	2
Network and system administration/administrator	392	357	35	66	35	31	0	0	0
System, networking, and LAN/WAN management/manager	194	171	23	26	19	7	0	0	0
Computer and information systems security/information assurance	3,813	3,204	609	4,926	3,780	1,146	43	35	8
Web/multimedia management and webmaster	145	98	47	5	2	3	0	0	0
Information technology project management	555	449	106	397	236	161	1	1	0
Computer support specialist	5	5	0	0	0	0	0	0	0
Computer/information tech. services admin. and management, other	771	591	180	813	537	276	0	0	0
Computer and information sciences and support services, other	185	131	54	267	166	101	23	15	8
Education	82,621	15,167	67,454	146,367	32,871	113,496	12,780	4,112	8,668
Education, general	3,611	590	3,021	20,231	4,372	15,859	2,565	747	1,818
Bilingual and multilingual education	147	7	140	322	56	266	10	2	8
Multicultural education	2	0	2	100	21	79	13	4	9
Indian/Native American education	0	0	0	0	0	0	0	0	0
Bilingual, multilingual, and multicultural education, other	0	0	0	85	7	78	3	0	3
Curriculum and instruction	31	8	23	14,713	2,666	12,047	1,374	322	1,052
Educational leadership and administration, general	316	13	303	18,500	6,031	12,469	4,677	1,720	2,957
Administration of special education	0	0	0	66	6	60	11	2	9
Adult and continuing education administration	0	0	0	369	96	273	48	14	34
Educational, instructional, and curriculum supervision	36	5	31	1,281	319	962	103	25	78
Higher education/higher education administration	0	0	0	3,133	961	2,172	643	231	412
Community college education	0	0	0	62	17	45	191	78	113
Elementary and middle school administration/principalship	120	7	113	732	299	433	12	2	10
Secondary school administration/principalship	2	0	2	293	140	153	3	3	0
Urban education and leadership	79	26	53	384	97	287	77	21	56
Superintendency and educational system administration	0	0	0	462	177	285	135	38	97
Educational administration and supervision, other	0	0	0	1,247	374	873	397	135	262
Educational/instructional technology	62	27	35	5,176	1,404	3,772	177	69	108
Educational evaluation and research	0	0	0	96	37	59	144	44	100
Educational statistics and research methods	0	0	0	94	39	55	45	17	28
Educational assessment, testing, and measurement	0	0	0	64	5	59	12	3	9
Learning sciences	370	50	320	99	21	78	10	3	7
Educational assessment, evaluation, and research, other	14	1	13	128	37	91	30	7	23
International and comparative education	47	8	39	313	39	274	11	5	6
Social and philosophical foundations of education	20	2	18	333	89	244	130	48	82
Special education and teaching, general	6,197	656	5,541	11,666	1,884	9,782	197	47	150
Education/teaching of individuals with hearing impairments/deafness	76	2	74	132	7	125	6	3	3
Education/teaching of the gifted and talented	0	0	0	312	35	277	1	0	1
Education/teaching of individuals with emotional disturbances	33	3	30	80	18	62	11	1	10
Education/teaching of individuals with mental retardation	112	16	96	44	8	36	3	2	1
Education/teaching of individuals with multiple disabilities	111	8	103	263	44	219	0	0	0
Education/teaching of individuals with orthopedic/physical health impairments	2	0	2	0	0	0	4	0	4
Education/teaching of individuals with vision impairments/blindness	8	2	6	126	20	106	0	0	0

See notes at end of table.

Table 318.30. Bachelor's, master's, and doctor's degrees conferred by postsecondary institutions, by sex of student and discipline division: 2017–18—Continued

Discipline division	Bachelor's degrees			Master's degrees			Doctor's degrees[1]		
	Total	Males	Females	Total	Males	Females	Total	Males	Females
1	2	3	4	5	6	7	8	9	10
Education/teaching of individuals with specific learning disabilities	151	11	140	272	31	241	0	0	0
Education/teaching of individuals with speech/language impairments	143	8	135	301	10	291	0	0	0
Education/teaching of individuals with autism	6	0	6	1,071	103	968	0	0	0
Education/teaching of individuals who are developmentally delayed	20	1	19	171	23	148	0	0	0
Education/teaching of individuals in early childhood special educ. programs	589	34	555	1,051	39	1,012	0	0	0
Education/teaching of individuals in elementary special educ. programs	450	32	418	980	122	858	0	0	0
Education/teaching of individuals in jr. high/middle school special educ. programs	39	4	35	42	9	33	0	0	0
Education/teaching of individuals in secondary special educ. programs	21	2	19	481	129	352	0	0	0
Special education and teaching, other	373	26	347	674	126	548	15	1	14
Counselor education/school counseling and guidance services	3	0	3	11,033	1,893	9,140	323	78	245
College student counseling and personnel services	0	0	0	1,148	299	849	57	18	39
Student counseling and personnel services, other	0	0	0	235	42	193	5	2	3
Adult and continuing education and teaching	28	9	19	976	289	687	113	42	71
Elementary education and teaching	27,484	2,230	25,254	7,619	906	6,713	23	5	18
Junior high/intermediate/middle school education and teaching	2,147	571	1,576	682	180	502	0	0	0
Secondary education and teaching	3,055	1,213	1,842	5,298	2,019	3,279	15	5	10
Teacher education, multiple levels	1,405	176	1,229	3,994	977	3,017	6	2	4
Montessori teacher education	4	0	4	201	12	189	0	0	0
Waldorf/Steiner teacher education	0	0	0	0	0	0	0	0	0
Kindergarten/preschool education and teaching	904	39	865	201	12	189	10	2	8
Early childhood education and teaching	12,179	458	11,721	3,029	115	2,914	17	0	17
Teacher education and prof. dev., specific levels and methods, other	162	22	140	3,522	824	2,698	94	27	67
Agricultural teacher education	645	190	455	245	60	185	32	8	24
Art teacher education	879	92	787	639	113	526	32	5	27
Business teacher education	144	69	75	68	31	37	0	0	0
Driver and safety teacher education	0	0	0	23	17	6	0	0	0
English/language arts teacher education	1,717	351	1,366	727	184	543	16	7	9
Foreign language teacher education	73	11	62	192	38	154	9	4	5
Health teacher education	1,134	316	818	297	87	210	26	4	22
Family and consumer sciences/home economics teacher education	239	18	221	71	1	70	1	0	1
Technology teacher education/industrial arts teacher education	259	214	45	353	156	197	4	3	1
Sales and marketing operations/marketing and dist. teacher educ.	13	7	6	0	0	0	0	0	0
Mathematics teacher education	1,382	387	995	1,418	421	997	51	25	26
Music teacher education	3,122	1,272	1,850	1,078	428	650	87	48	39
Physical education teaching and coaching	6,537	3,617	2,920	1,574	932	642	40	24	16
Reading teacher education	25	1	24	5,437	280	5,157	102	15	87
Science teacher education/general science teacher education	423	151	272	828	272	556	59	23	36
Social science teacher education	396	224	172	119	69	50	0	0	0
Social studies teacher education	1,028	622	406	417	241	176	2	1	1
Technical teacher education	157	66	91	139	62	77	39	10	29
Trade and industrial teacher education	501	286	215	193	86	107	19	6	13
Computer teacher education	62	8	54	135	48	87	0	0	0
Biology teacher education	288	99	189	283	73	210	1	1	0
Chemistry teacher education	74	34	40	83	35	48	0	0	0
Drama and dance teacher education	108	11	97	66	8	58	0	0	0
French language teacher education	19	5	14	19	5	14	0	0	0
German language teacher education	4	0	4	1	0	1	0	0	0
Health occupations teacher education	4	0	4	159	10	149	43	2	41
History teacher education	469	263	206	82	43	39	0	0	0
Physics teacher education	36	23	13	54	32	22	2	0	2
Spanish language teacher education	208	42	166	142	41	101	0	0	0
Speech teacher education	13	5	8	30	5	25	7	1	6
Geography teacher education	0	0	0	1	0	1	0	0	0
Latin teacher education	2	1	1	4	3	1	0	0	0
School librarian/library media specialist	0	0	0	253	20	233	0	0	0
Psychology teacher education	4	0	4	0	0	0	0	0	0
Earth science teacher education	29	11	18	51	21	30	2	1	1
Environmental education	1	0	1	80	18	62	1	1	0
Teacher education and prof. dev., specific subject areas, other	163	52	111	1,389	307	1,082	42	10	32
Teaching English as a second/foreign language/ESL language instructor	283	55	228	3,427	681	2,746	38	15	23
Teaching English or French as a second or foreign language, other	13	5	8	17	2	15	0	0	0
Teacher assistant/aide	4	1	3	0	0	0	0	0	0
Adult literacy tutor/instructor	0	0	0	16	1	15	0	0	0
Education, other	1,604	391	1,213	2,370	554	1,816	404	123	281
Engineering and engineering technologies	140,683	111,171	29,512	58,968	43,627	15,341	11,029	8,331	2,698
Engineering	121,956	94,847	27,109	51,721	38,496	13,225	10,817	8,180	2,637
Engineering, general	2,673	2,025	648	2,730	2,068	662	443	340	103
Pre-engineering	27	22	5	0	0	0	0	0	0
Aerospace, aeronautical and astronautical engineering	4,132	3,557	575	1,620	1,351	269	348	306	42
Agricultural engineering	1,170	712	458	207	124	83	153	94	59
Architectural engineering	660	433	227	148	99	49	9	5	4
Bioengineering and biomedical engineering	7,416	4,009	3,407	2,831	1,604	1,227	1,091	653	438
Ceramic sciences and engineering	81	49	32	16	14	2	14	12	2
Chemical engineering	11,384	7,443	3,941	1,875	1,196	679	986	688	298
Chemical and biomolecular engineering	158	95	63	43	30	13	24	18	6
Chemical engineering, other	0	0	0	2	2	0	0	0	0
Civil engineering, general	13,836	10,305	3,531	5,336	3,791	1,545	1,027	726	301
Geotechnical and geoenvironmental engineering	0	0	0	2	2	0	0	0	0
Structural engineering	160	120	40	250	172	78	8	6	2
Transportation and highway engineering	9	9	0	97	67	30	11	7	4
Water resources engineering	16	10	6	56	32	24	6	1	5
Civil engineering, other	18	14	4	55	41	14	4	4	0
Computer engineering, general	8,266	7,225	1,041	2,826	2,106	720	376	295	81
Computer hardware engineering	0	0	0	43	33	10	0	0	0
Computer software engineering	1,309	1,122	187	1,698	1,128	570	7	5	2
Computer engineering, other	25	23	2	78	63	15	5	4	1
Electrical and electronics engineering	16,694	14,296	2,398	11,144	8,526	2,618	2,295	1,896	399

See notes at end of table.

Table 318.30. Bachelor's, master's, and doctor's degrees conferred by postsecondary institutions, by sex of student and discipline division: 2017–18—Continued

Discipline division	Bachelor's degrees			Master's degrees			Doctor's degrees[1]		
	Total	Males	Females	Total	Males	Females	Total	Males	Females
1	2	3	4	5	6	7	8	9	10
Laser and optical engineering	63	44	19	41	35	6	17	15	2
Telecommunications engineering	5	5	0	201	137	64	2	2	0
Electrical, electronics and communications engineering, other	139	116	23	128	101	27	13	10	3
Engineering mechanics	119	96	23	99	87	12	80	65	15
Engineering physics/applied physics	676	545	131	106	78	28	90	67	23
Engineering science	553	374	179	321	227	94	114	85	29
Environmental/environmental health engineering	1,578	822	756	945	501	444	165	85	80
Materials engineering	1,522	1,050	472	1,162	837	325	708	512	196
Mechanical engineering	35,182	30,150	5,032	8,150	7,019	1,131	1,586	1,346	240
Metallurgical engineering	162	107	55	35	23	12	20	16	4
Mining and mineral engineering	253	217	36	99	77	22	20	18	2
Naval architecture and marine engineering	453	392	61	35	29	6	7	6	1
Nuclear engineering	535	451	84	247	211	36	181	154	27
Ocean engineering	194	138	56	70	53	17	16	13	3
Petroleum engineering	2,151	1,786	365	515	429	86	134	108	26
Systems engineering	755	529	226	1,808	1,331	477	108	73	35
Textile sciences and engineering	254	68	186	80	28	52	25	11	14
Polymer/plastics engineering	164	123	41	106	70	36	61	44	17
Construction engineering	521	443	78	331	244	87	1	1	0
Forest engineering	39	35	4	0	0	0	0	0	0
Industrial engineering	5,538	3,703	1,835	3,235	2,458	777	330	246	84
Manufacturing engineering	484	411	73	331	258	73	13	12	1
Operations research	466	277	189	774	461	313	81	60	21
Surveying engineering	43	39	4	6	5	1	2	1	1
Geological/geophysical engineering	275	172	103	137	102	35	18	15	3
Paper science and engineering	23	22	1	10	7	3	6	4	2
Electromechanical engineering	35	30	5	0	0	0	3	3	0
Mechatronics, robotics, and automation engineering	271	234	37	272	227	45	30	26	4
Biochemical engineering	107	50	57	13	9	4	0	0	0
Engineering chemistry	5	3	2	0	0	0	0	0	0
Biological/biosystems engineering	363	184	179	21	13	8	16	10	6
Engineering, other	994	762	232	1,386	990	396	163	112	51
Engineering technologies/construction trades/mechanics and repairers	18,727	16,324	2,403	7,247	5,131	2,116	212	151	61
Engineering technologies and engineering-related fields	18,228	15,861	2,367	7,246	5,131	2,115	212	151	61
Engineering technology, general	1,520	1,376	144	331	221	110	12	8	4
Architectural engineering technology/technician	331	272	59	18	9	9	0	0	0
Civil engineering technology/technician	527	461	66	0	0	0	0	0	0
Electrical/electronic/communications eng. technology/technician	1,368	1,247	121	16	14	2	0	0	0
Laser and optical technology/technician	0	0	0	0	0	0	0	0	0
Telecommunications technology/technician	51	44	7	186	141	45	0	0	0
Electrical/electronic eng. technologies/technicians, other	199	175	24	13	10	3	0	0	0
Biomedical technology/technician	55	44	11	5	4	1	3	0	3
Electromechanical technology/electromechanical eng. technology	141	132	9	6	6	0	0	0	0
Instrumentation technology/technician	35	34	1	0	0	0	0	0	0
Robotics technology/technician	34	32	2	12	9	3	0	0	0
Automation engineer technology/technician	128	119	9	0	0	0	0	0	0
Electromechanical/instrumentation and maintenance technol./tech.	15	11	4	0	0	0	0	0	0
Heating, ventilation, air conditioning and refrig. eng. technol./tech.	1	1	0	0	0	0	0	0	0
Energy management and systems technology/technician	116	96	20	102	87	15	0	0	0
Solar energy technology/technician	0	0	0	15	11	4	0	0	0
Water quality/wastewater treatment management/recycling technol./tech.	1	1	0	0	0	0	0	0	0
Environmental engineering technology/environmental technology	135	92	43	83	41	42	0	0	0
Hazardous materials management and waste technology/technician	1	1	0	0	0	0	0	0	0
Environmental control technologies/technicians, other	6	3	3	25	17	8	0	0	0
Plastics and polymer engineering technology/technician	106	89	17	5	5	0	0	0	0
Industrial technology/technician	1,754	1,554	200	379	260	119	15	13	2
Manufacturing engineering technology/technician	676	617	59	86	70	16	0	0	0
Welding engineering technology/technician	19	18	1	0	0	0	0	0	0
Industrial production technologies/technicians, other	250	212	38	7	2	5	0	0	0
Occupational safety and health technology/technician	1,576	1,290	286	592	443	149	4	4	0
Quality control technology/technician	5	4	1	62	34	28	0	0	0
Industrial safety technology/technician	196	157	39	20	17	3	0	0	0
Quality control and safety technologies/technicians, other	36	35	1	11	3	8	0	0	0
Aeronautical/aerospace engineering technology/technician	204	174	30	43	36	7	0	0	0
Automotive engineering technology/technician	365	343	22	97	94	3	2	1	1
Mechanical engineering/mechanical technology/technician	1,954	1,810	144	17	7	10	0	0	0
Mechanical engineering related technologies/technicians, other	256	240	16	0	0	0	0	0	0
Mining technology/technician	1	1	0	0	0	0	0	0	0
Petroleum technology/technician	61	53	8	0	0	0	0	0	0
Mining and petroleum technologies/technicians, other	0	0	0	0	0	0	0	0	0
Construction engineering technology/technician	2,148	1,936	212	181	133	48	1	1	0
Surveying technology/surveying	170	155	15	7	6	1	7	5	2
Hydraulics and fluid power technology/technician	0	0	0	0	0	0	0	0	0
Engineering-related technologies, other	12	9	3	0	0	0	0	0	0
Computer engineering technology/technician	588	537	51	0	0	0	0	0	0
Computer technology/computer systems technology	245	218	27	354	257	97	1	0	1
Computer hardware technology/technician	0	0	0	0	0	0	0	0	0
Computer software technology/technician	57	46	11	0	0	0	2	2	0
Computer engineering technologies/technicians, other	42	40	2	0	0	0	0	0	0
Drafting and design technologies/technicians, general	114	51	63	58	10	48	0	0	0
CAD/CADD drafting and/or design technology/technician	169	130	39	62	40	22	1	0	1
Architectural drafting and architectural CAD/CADD	25	20	5	34	21	13	0	0	0
Civil drafting and civil engineering CAD/CADD	4	3	1	0	0	0	0	0	0
Mechanical drafting and mechanical drafting CAD/CADD	30	21	9	0	0	0	0	0	0
Drafting/design engineering technologies/technicians, other	25	21	4	0	0	0	0	0	0
Nuclear engineering technology/technician	175	162	13	1	1	0	0	0	0

See notes at end of table.

Table 318.30. Bachelor's, master's, and doctor's degrees conferred by postsecondary institutions, by sex of student and discipline division: 2017–18—Continued

Discipline division	Bachelor's degrees			Master's degrees			Doctor's degrees[1]		
	Total	Males	Females	Total	Males	Females	Total	Males	Females
1	2	3	4	5	6	7	8	9	10
Engineering/industrial management	1,100	862	238	4,014	2,855	1,159	134	100	34
Engineering design	2	1	1	77	43	34	2	2	0
Packaging science	390	223	167	38	23	15	2	0	2
Engineering-related fields, other	117	80	37	18	11	7	11	4	7
Nanotechnology	21	13	8	63	49	14	15	11	4
Engineering tech. and engineering-related fields, other	671	595	76	208	141	67	0	0	0
Construction trades	151	130	21	0	0	0	0	0	0
Construction trades, general	0	0	0	0	0	0	0	0	0
Mason/masonry	0	0	0	0	0	0	0	0	0
Electrician	0	0	0	0	0	0	0	0	0
Building/property maintenance	0	0	0	0	0	0	0	0	0
Building/construction site management/manager	151	130	21	0	0	0	0	0	0
Building construction technology	0	0	0	0	0	0	0	0	0
Building/construction finishing, mgmt., and inspection, other	0	0	0	0	0	0	0	0	0
Construction trades, other	0	0	0	0	0	0	0	0	0
Mechanic and repair technologies/technicians	348	333	15	1	0	1	0	0	0
Communications systems installation and repair technology	0	0	0	0	0	0	0	0	0
Industrial electronics technology/technician	3	3	0	0	0	0	0	0	0
Heating, air conditioning, ventilation and refrig. main. technician	0	0	0	0	0	0	0	0	0
Heavy equipment maintenance technology/technician	20	20	0	0	0	0	0	0	0
Autobody/collision and repair technology/technician	0	0	0	0	0	0	0	0	0
Automobile/automotive mechanics technology/technician	43	42	1	0	0	0	0	0	0
Diesel mechanics technology/technician	39	36	3	0	0	0	0	0	0
Airframe mechanics and aircraft maintenance technology/technician	36	31	5	0	0	0	0	0	0
Aircraft powerplant technology/technician	117	115	2	1	0	1	0	0	0
Avionics maintenance technology/technician	88	84	4	0	0	0	0	0	0
Vehicle maintenance and repair technologies, other	2	2	0	0	0	0	0	0	0
English language and literature/letters	40,002	11,680	28,322	8,300	2,640	5,660	1,295	512	783
English language and literature, general	32,098	9,139	22,959	4,367	1,283	3,084	1,107	445	662
Writing, general	590	153	437	66	9	57	0	0	0
Creative writing	2,829	874	1,955	2,994	1,091	1,903	16	8	8
Professional, technical, business, and scientific writing	657	212	445	317	91	226	30	14	16
Rhetoric and composition	2,612	895	1,717	153	47	106	107	33	74
Rhetoric and composition/writing studies, other	241	119	122	128	47	81	4	1	3
General literature	244	60	184	20	10	10	0	0	0
American literature (United States)	16	7	9	8	0	8	0	0	0
English literature (British and Commonwealth)	179	52	127	84	22	62	7	4	3
Children's and adolescent literature	1	0	1	15	0	15	0	0	0
Literature, other	9	1	8	5	0	5	0	0	0
English language and literature/letters, other	526	168	358	143	40	103	24	7	17
Family and consumer sciences/human sciences	24,349	2,947	21,402	3,308	467	2,841	274	63	211
Work and family studies	0	0	0	0	0	0	0	0	0
Family and consumer sciences/human sciences, general	3,484	413	3,071	542	121	421	50	17	33
Business family and consumer sciences/human sciences	162	64	98	13	8	5	2	0	2
Family and consumer sciences/human sciences communication	14	2	12	0	0	0	0	0	0
Consumer merchandising/retailing management	177	30	147	26	4	22	1	0	1
Family and consumer sciences/human sciences business services, other	9	1	8	0	0	0	0	0	0
Family resource management studies, general	886	263	623	236	49	187	1	1	0
Consumer economics	144	64	80	0	0	0	0	0	0
Consumer services and advocacy	23	4	19	0	0	0	0	0	0
Family and consumer economics and related services, other	308	28	280	5	1	4	14	6	8
Foods, nutrition, and wellness studies, general	2,379	458	1,921	571	68	503	31	6	25
Human nutrition	396	86	310	412	55	357	13	4	9
Food service systems administration/management	783	273	510	4	1	3	0	0	0
Foods, nutrition, and related services, other	30	11	19	44	7	37	0	0	0
Housing and human environments, general	98	29	69	37	14	23	6	3	3
Facilities planning and management	46	43	3	3	3	0	0	0	0
Housing and human environments, other	2	0	2	0	0	0	0	0	0
Human development and family studies, general	8,499	684	7,815	622	55	567	108	19	89
Adult development and aging	6	2	4	90	9	81	2	0	2
Family systems	514	53	461	33	1	32	6	2	4
Child development	1,569	57	1,512	187	12	175	9	2	7
Family and community services	1,098	122	976	232	26	206	10	1	9
Child care and support services management	445	20	425	75	2	73	0	0	0
Child care provider/assistant	36	0	36	2	0	2	0	0	0
Developmental services worker	0	0	0	0	0	0	0	0	0
Human development, family studies, and related services, other	580	33	547	48	9	39	7	1	6
Apparel and textiles, general	2,092	158	1,934	42	7	35	12	0	12
Apparel and textile manufacture	98	9	89	2	0	2	0	0	0
Textile science	4	0	4	0	0	0	1	0	1
Apparel and textile marketing management	388	33	355	66	10	56	1	1	0
Fashion and fabric consultant	31	1	30	0	0	0	0	0	0
Apparel and textiles, other	14	2	12	7	1	6	0	0	0
Family and consumer sciences/human sciences, other	34	4	30	9	4	5	0	0	0
Foreign languages, literatures, and linguistics	16,958	5,288	11,670	3,261	1,084	2,177	1,213	507	706
Foreign languages and literatures, general	1,627	511	1,116	243	85	158	28	9	19
Linguistics	2,040	619	1,421	543	188	355	243	92	151
Language interpretation and translation	39	7	32	227	49	178	5	3	2
Comparative literature	671	219	452	159	61	98	151	61	90
Applied linguistics	35	8	27	88	25	63	0	0	0
Linguistic/comparative/related language studies and serv., other	230	75	155	27	13	14	14	3	11
African languages, literatures, and linguistics	2	1	1	4	2	2	0	0	0
East Asian languages, literatures, and linguistics, general	152	62	90	88	33	55	36	14	22

See notes at end of table.

Table 318.30. Bachelor's, master's, and doctor's degrees conferred by postsecondary institutions, by sex of student and discipline division: 2017–18—Continued

Discipline division	Bachelor's degrees			Master's degrees			Doctor's degrees[1]		
	Total	Males	Females	Total	Males	Females	Total	Males	Females
1	2	3	4	5	6	7	8	9	10
Chinese language and literature	466	221	245	46	8	38	11	4	7
Japanese language and literature	560	262	298	20	7	13	6	2	4
Korean language and literature	55	21	34	6	2	4	2	0	2
East Asian languages, literatures, and linguistics, other	60	33	27	17	7	10	24	10	14
Slavic languages, literatures, and linguistics, general	35	12	23	44	20	24	20	7	13
Russian language and literature	296	157	139	10	2	8	3	2	1
Polish language and literature	3	0	3	0	0	0	0	0	0
Germanic languages, literatures, and linguistics, general	63	30	33	23	12	11	21	10	11
German language and literature	697	343	354	77	29	48	42	21	21
Scandinavian languages, literatures, and linguistics	14	5	9	2	0	2	4	2	2
Danish language and literature	0	0	0	0	0	0	0	0	0
Dutch/Flemish language and literature	0	0	0	0	0	0	0	0	0
Norwegian language and literature	6	3	3	0	0	0	0	0	0
Swedish language and literature	0	0	0	0	0	0	0	0	0
Germanic languages, literatures, and linguistics, other	13	6	7	0	0	0	0	0	0
Modern Greek language and literature	0	0	0	0	0	0	0	0	0
South Asian languages, literatures, and linguistics, general	2	2	0	1	0	1	2	2	0
Sanskrit and classical Indian languages, literatures, and linguistics	0	0	0	0	0	0	0	0	0
Iranian languages, literatures, and linguistics	6	4	2	0	0	0	0	0	0
Romance languages, literatures, and linguistics, general	130	42	88	74	22	52	39	12	27
French language and literature	1,438	348	1,090	277	76	201	86	21	65
Italian language and literature	145	47	98	36	12	24	22	7	15
Portuguese language and literature	28	13	15	9	3	6	6	3	3
Spanish language and literature	6,011	1,554	4,457	731	217	514	209	91	118
Hispanic and Latin American languages, lit., and linguistics, general	138	35	103	23	11	12	16	9	7
Romance languages, literatures, and linguistics, other	45	8	37	51	19	32	39	22	17
American Indian/Native American languages, literatures, and linguistics	2	0	2	10	4	6	0	0	0
Middle/Near Eastern and Semitic languages, lit., and linguistics, general	16	9	7	22	11	11	26	16	10
Arabic language and literature	153	67	86	6	4	2	2	1	1
Hebrew language and literature	4	2	2	10	4	6	4	2	2
Ancient Near Eastern and biblical languages, lit., and linguistics	16	7	9	19	13	6	6	6	0
Middle/Near Eastern and Semitic languages, lit., and linguistics, other	43	23	20	33	18	15	27	17	10
Classics and classical languages, lit., and linguistics, general	818	346	472	189	85	104	90	46	44
Ancient/classical Greek language and literature	18	6	12	1	1	0	0	0	0
Latin language and literature	47	19	28	18	9	9	1	1	0
Classics and classical languages, lit., and linguistics, other	23	14	9	14	9	5	0	0	0
Celtic languages, literatures, and linguistics	0	0	0	2	0	2	0	0	0
Filipino/Tagalog language and literature	8	6	2	0	0	0	0	0	0
Turkish language and literature	0	0	0	0	0	0	0	0	0
Uralic languages, literatures, and linguistics	1	1	0	0	0	0	0	0	0
American sign language (ASL)	156	19	137	25	7	18	0	0	0
Linguistics of ASL and other sign languages	0	0	0	13	2	11	1	0	1
Sign language interpretation and translation	419	48	371	40	7	33	5	1	4
American sign language, other	3	0	3	0	0	0	0	0	0
Foreign languages, literatures, and linguistics, other	224	73	151	33	7	26	22	10	12
Health professions and related programs	244,909	38,022	206,887	125,216	22,768	102,448	80,305	32,494	47,811
Health and wellness, general	15,559	3,702	11,857	919	266	653	265	103	162
Chiropractic	0	0	0	0	0	0	2,503	1,436	1,067
Communication sciences and disorders, general	4,748	228	4,520	1,740	90	1,650	38	10	28
Audiology/audiologist	205	11	194	141	13	128	698	84	614
Speech-language pathology/pathologist	1,379	42	1,337	3,896	173	3,723	44	3	41
Audiology/audiologist and speech-language pathology/pathologist	4,611	201	4,410	2,682	121	2,561	234	40	194
Communication disorders sciences and services, other	78	2	76	89	3	86	8	3	5
Dentistry	0	0	0	0	0	0	6,441	3,258	3,183
Dental clinical sciences, general	0	0	0	306	151	155	11	6	5
Advanced general dentistry	0	0	0	28	19	9	0	0	0
Oral biology and oral maxillofacial pathology	0	0	0	120	66	54	19	9	10
Dental public health and education	0	0	0	7	1	6	5	3	2
Dental materials	0	0	0	0	0	0	0	0	0
Endodontics/endodontology	0	0	0	35	25	10	1	1	0
Oral/maxillofacial surgery	0	0	0	0	0	0	0	0	0
Orthodontics/orthodontology	0	0	0	103	52	51	0	0	0
Pediatric dentistry/pedodontics	0	0	0	27	6	21	0	0	0
Periodontics/periodontology	0	0	0	31	18	13	1	0	1
Prosthodontics/prosthodontology	0	0	0	26	18	8	4	2	2
Advanced/graduate dentistry and oral sciences, other	0	0	0	79	35	44	9	2	7
Dental assisting/assistant	3	0	3	0	0	0	0	0	0
Dental hygiene/hygienist	2,410	100	2,310	92	4	88	0	0	0
Dental laboratory technology/technician	6	0	6	0	0	0	0	0	0
Dental services and allied professions, other	14	0	14	7	2	5	0	0	0
Health/health care administration/management	11,963	2,427	9,536	10,067	2,808	7,259	225	73	152
Hospital and health care facilities administration/management	2,440	319	2,121	1,397	381	1,016	2	0	2
Health unit manager/ward supervisor	0	0	0	1	0	1	0	0	0
Medical office management/administration	3	0	3	0	0	0	0	0	0
Health information/medical records administration/administrator	1,508	267	1,241	495	142	353	0	0	0
Health information/medical records technology/technician	60	20	40	47	16	31	0	0	0
Medical office assistant/specialist	5	0	5	0	0	0	0	0	0
Medical/health management and clinical assistant/specialist	69	8	61	2	0	2	0	0	0
Medical staff services technology/technician	0	0	0	0	0	0	0	0	0
Long term care administration/management	145	13	132	9	1	8	0	0	0
Clinical research coordinator	9	1	8	93	21	72	0	0	0
Health and medical administrative services, other	748	120	628	272	79	193	8	3	5
Medical/clinical assistant	9	0	9	35	8	27	0	0	0
Occupational therapist assistant	9	2	7	30	4	26	0	0	0
Pharmacy technician/assistant	0	0	0	0	0	0	0	0	0
Physical therapy technician/assistant	45	14	31	0	0	0	0	0	0
Veterinary/animal health technology/technician and vet. assistant	441	33	408	0	0	0	0	0	0

See notes at end of table.

Table 318.30. Bachelor's, master's, and doctor's degrees conferred by postsecondary institutions, by sex of student and discipline division: 2017–18—Continued

Discipline division	Bachelor's degrees			Master's degrees			Doctor's degrees[1]		
	Total	Males	Females	Total	Males	Females	Total	Males	Females
1	2	3	4	5	6	7	8	9	10
Anesthesiologist assistant	0	0	0	207	104	103	0	0	0
Emergency care attendant (EMT ambulance)	2	1	1	0	0	0	0	0	0
Pathology/pathologist assistant	12	5	7	77	19	58	0	0	0
Respiratory therapy technician/assistant	17	3	14	0	0	0	0	0	0
Radiologist assistant	0	0	0	4	2	2	0	0	0
Speech-language pathology assistant	21	1	20	0	0	0	0	0	0
Allied health and medical assisting services, other	297	75	222	136	34	102	0	0	0
Cardiovascular technology/technologist	98	26	72	23	15	8	0	0	0
Electrocardiograph technology/technician	0	0	0	0	0	0	0	0	0
Electroneurodiagnostic/electroencephalographic technology/technologist	6	1	5	0	0	0	0	0	0
Emergency medical technology/technician (EMT paramedic)	299	208	91	13	6	7	0	0	0
Nuclear medical technology/technologist	255	74	181	10	5	5	0	0	0
Perfusion technology/perfusionist	8	6	2	74	35	39	0	0	0
Medical radiologic technology/science radiation therapist	1,195	236	959	83	36	47	1	0	1
Respiratory care therapy/therapist	1,332	391	941	70	27	43	0	0	0
Surgical technology/technologist	20	5	15	0	0	0	0	0	0
Diagnostic medical sonography/sonographer and ultrasound technician	752	95	657	9	1	8	0	0	0
Radiologic technology/science radiographer	1,441	356	1,085	85	35	50	1	1	0
Physician assistant	580	155	425	8,527	2,253	6,274	16	10	6
Athletic training/trainer	3,958	1,432	2,526	991	385	606	80	32	48
Gene/genetic therapy	14	10	4	0	0	0	1	1	0
Cardiopulmonary technology/technologist	19	2	17	0	0	0	0	0	0
Radiation protection/health physics technician	16	4	12	6	4	2	0	0	0
Polysomnography	3	2	1	0	0	0	0	0	0
Magnetic resonance imaging (MRI) technology/technician	38	13	25	6	3	3	0	0	0
Allied health diagnostic/intervention/treatment professions, other	549	150	399	55	19	36	73	14	59
Blood bank technology specialist	0	0	0	13	1	12	0	0	0
Cytotechnology/cytotechnologist	32	14	18	11	6	5	0	0	0
Hematology technology/technician	0	0	0	5	2	3	0	0	0
Clinical/medical laboratory technician	187	54	133	0	0	0	0	0	0
Clinical laboratory science/medical technology/technologist	2,924	749	2,175	260	68	192	0	0	0
Histologic technology/histotechnologist	20	2	18	5	1	4	0	0	0
Histologic technician	11	4	7	0	0	0	0	0	0
Cytogenetics/genetics/clinical genetics technology/technologist	37	15	22	14	5	9	0	0	0
Clinical/medical laboratory science and allied professions, other	536	136	400	110	27	83	7	5	2
Pre-dentistry studies	17	6	11	0	0	0	0	0	0
Pre-medicine/pre-medical studies	917	345	572	63	26	37	0	0	0
Pre-pharmacy studies	27	12	15	0	0	0	0	0	0
Pre-veterinary studies	440	60	380	1	0	1	0	0	0
Pre-nursing studies	19	1	18	0	0	0	0	0	0
Pre-occupational therapy studies	69	5	64	0	0	0	0	0	0
Pre-optometry studies	2	1	1	0	0	0	0	0	0
Pre-physical therapy studies	259	107	152	0	0	0	0	0	0
Health/medical preparatory programs, other	1,774	495	1,279	230	103	127	0	0	0
Medicine	0	0	0	0	0	0	19,142	10,049	9,093
Medical scientist	0	0	0	584	276	308	38	15	23
Substance abuse/addiction counseling	461	99	362	420	114	306	2	1	1
Psychiatric/mental health services technician	269	50	219	0	0	0	3	0	3
Clinical/medical social work	200	32	168	962	137	825	9	2	7
Community health services/liaison/counseling	1,628	297	1,331	215	36	179	9	0	9
Marriage and family therapy/counseling	39	8	31	2,751	429	2,322	137	34	103
Clinical pastoral counseling/patient counseling	0	0	0	109	39	70	6	1	5
Psychoanalysis and psychotherapy	0	0	0	10	4	6	6	2	4
Mental health counseling/counselor	12	2	10	5,545	917	4,628	25	4	21
Genetic counseling/counselor	0	0	0	172	13	159	0	0	0
Mental and social health services and allied professions, other	451	60	391	1,688	331	1,357	30	4	26
Optometry	0	0	0	0	0	0	1,623	531	1,092
Ophthalmic technician/technologist	2	1	1	0	0	0	0	0	0
Orthoptics/orthoptist	0	0	0	0	0	0	0	0	0
Ophthalmic/optometric support services/allied professions, other	6	1	5	22	6	16	6	3	3
Osteopathic medicine/osteopathy	0	0	0	0	0	0	6,392	3,611	2,781
Pharmacy	834	311	523	3	2	1	14,926	5,629	9,297
Pharmacy admin. and pharmacy policy and regulatory affairs	0	0	0	483	152	331	17	7	10
Pharmaceutics and drug design	131	53	78	151	63	88	197	109	88
Medicinal and pharmaceutical chemistry	19	11	8	54	24	30	94	51	43
Natural products chemistry and pharmacognosy	0	0	0	0	0	0	4	2	2
Clinical and industrial drug development	37	4	33	130	47	83	5	3	2
Pharmacoeconomics/pharmaceutical economics	0	0	0	57	25	32	39	19	20
Clinical, hospital, and managed care pharmacy	0	0	0	12	6	6	0	0	0
Industrial and physical pharmacy and cosmetic sciences	10	0	10	60	24	36	0	0	0
Pharmaceutical sciences	1,007	374	633	254	110	144	175	96	79
Pharmaceutical marketing and management	63	33	30	12	4	8	0	0	0
Pharmacy, pharmaceutical sciences, and administration, other	634	226	408	237	60	177	26	13	13
Podiatric medicine/podiatry	0	0	0	0	0	0	543	341	202
Public health, general	6,656	1,274	5,382	10,059	2,480	7,579	479	136	343
Environmental health	307	134	173	624	211	413	104	42	62
Health/medical physics	46	23	23	133	92	41	44	33	11
Occupational health and industrial hygiene	184	140	44	56	34	22	3	2	1
Public health education and promotion	3,032	599	2,433	938	130	808	57	5	52
Community health and preventive medicine	1,802	322	1,480	258	54	204	19	1	18
Maternal and child health	34	0	34	104	3	101	15	1	14
International public health/international health	160	37	123	490	109	381	21	7	14
Health services administration	1,198	179	1,019	1,015	355	660	16	5	11
Behavioral aspects of health	307	59	248	68	8	60	28	9	19
Public health, other	1,424	323	1,101	931	216	715	103	27	76
Art therapy/therapist	210	3	207	448	24	424	8	1	7
Dance therapy/therapist	0	0	0	60	2	58	0	0	0

See notes at end of table.

Table 318.30. Bachelor's, master's, and doctor's degrees conferred by postsecondary institutions, by sex of student and discipline division: 2017–18—Continued

Discipline division	Bachelor's degrees			Master's degrees			Doctor's degrees[1]		
	Total	Males	Females	Total	Males	Females	Total	Males	Females
1	2	3	4	5	6	7	8	9	10
Music therapy/therapist	456	67	389	137	28	109	1	0	1
Occupational therapy/therapist	835	61	774	6,871	743	6,128	895	76	819
Orthotist/prosthetist	8	4	4	238	117	121	0	0	0
Physical therapy/therapist	286	87	199	59	17	42	11,872	4,406	7,466
Therapeutic recreation/recreational therapy	838	102	736	64	10	54	0	0	0
Vocational rehabilitation counseling/counselor	320	57	263	904	175	729	29	10	19
Kinesiotherapy/kinesiotherapist	98	42	56	44	18	26	0	0	0
Assistive/augmentative technology and rehabilitation engineering	0	0	0	67	8	59	2	0	2
Animal-assisted therapy	36	2	34	0	0	0	0	0	0
Rehabilitation science	899	152	747	152	43	109	68	27	41
Rehabilitation and therapeutic professions, other	603	144	459	275	57	218	41	8	33
Veterinary medicine	0	0	0	0	0	0	3,169	632	2,537
Veterinary sciences/veterinary clinical sciences, general	28	6	22	178	42	136	74	26	48
Veterinary physiology	0	0	0	0	0	0	2	1	1
Veterinary microbiology and immunobiology	40	12	28	3	0	3	9	6	3
Veterinary pathology and pathobiology	0	0	0	14	3	11	56	26	30
Large animal/food animal/equine surgery and medicine	0	0	0	1	0	1	1	0	1
Small/companion animal surgery and medicine	0	0	0	5	1	4	0	0	0
Comparative and laboratory animal medicine	0	0	0	44	8	36	0	0	0
Veterinary preventive medicine epidemiology/public health	0	0	0	18	7	11	0	0	0
Veterinary infectious diseases	0	0	0	15	3	12	7	3	4
Medical illustration/medical illustrator	44	5	39	38	4	34	0	0	0
Medical informatics	166	44	122	1,079	391	688	46	20	26
Medical illustration and informatics, other	0	0	0	38	10	28	0	0	0
Dietetics/dietitian	2,712	341	2,371	497	44	453	3	1	2
Clinical nutrition/nutritionist	201	21	180	599	76	523	9	2	7
Dietetic technician	0	0	0	0	0	0	0	0	0
Dietitian assistant	111	32	79	0	0	0	0	0	0
Dietetics and clinical nutrition services, other	222	41	181	135	12	123	19	3	16
Bioethics/medical ethics	29	9	20	369	130	239	41	13	28
Alternative and complementary medicine and medical systems, general	134	19	115	12	1	11	0	0	0
Acupuncture and oriental medicine	28	8	20	1,227	329	898	542	174	368
Traditional Chinese medicine and Chinese herbology	0	0	0	164	43	121	23	7	16
Naturopathic medicine/naturopathy	0	0	0	0	0	0	322	70	252
Ayurvedic medicine/Ayurveda	0	0	0	21	5	16	0	0	0
Holistic health	180	28	152	35	4	31	0	0	0
Alternative and complementary medicine and medical systems, other	54	6	48	29	1	28	0	0	0
Direct entry midwifery	23	0	23	15	0	15	0	0	0
Alternative and complementary medical support services, other	0	0	0	69	3	66	0	0	0
Massage therapy/therapeutic massage	31	5	26	0	0	0	0	0	0
Asian bodywork therapy	0	0	0	0	0	0	0	0	0
Somatic bodywork and related therapeutic services, other	0	0	0	0	0	0	0	0	0
Movement therapy and movement education	55	19	36	28	2	26	3	2	1
Yoga teacher training/Yoga therapy	2	1	1	24	2	22	0	0	0
Herbalism/herbalist	10	2	8	9	0	9	0	0	0
Energy and biologically based therapies, other	0	0	0	0	0	0	0	0	0
Registered nursing/registered nurse	139,952	17,459	122,493	16,620	1,932	14,688	1,011	122	889
Nursing administration	796	96	700	7,131	745	6,386	318	35	283
Adult health nurse/nursing	275	46	229	1,427	193	1,234	48	3	45
Nurse anesthetist	0	0	0	1,328	568	760	496	205	291
Family practice nurse/nursing	288	34	254	12,723	1,592	11,131	513	63	450
Maternal/child health and neonatal nurse/nursing	0	0	0	179	7	172	10	2	8
Nurse midwife/nursing midwifery	0	0	0	438	1	437	4	0	4
Nursing science	1,234	141	1,093	1,623	167	1,456	882	89	793
Pediatric nurse/nursing	0	0	0	419	15	404	12	2	10
Psychiatric/mental health nurse/nursing	0	0	0	359	78	281	36	3	33
Public health/community nurse/nursing	435	44	391	279	20	259	4	2	2
Perioperative/operating room and surgical nurse/nursing	0	0	0	136	10	126	0	0	0
Clinical nurse specialist	13	2	11	376	39	337	35	5	30
Critical care nursing	0	0	0	414	80	334	11	1	10
Occupational and environmental health nursing	0	0	0	36	9	27	9	1	8
Emergency room/trauma nursing	0	0	0	22	7	15	0	0	0
Nursing education	22	1	21	1,610	124	1,486	115	8	107
Nursing practice	786	84	702	307	40	267	4,131	485	3,646
Palliative care nursing	0	0	0	5	1	4	2	0	2
Clinical nurse leader	66	4	62	418	48	370	0	0	0
Geriatric nurse/nursing	0	0	0	294	36	258	3	0	3
Women's health nurse/nursing	0	0	0	163	0	163	0	0	0
Reg. nursing, nursing admin., nursing research and clinical nursing, other	1,969	250	1,719	1,512	178	1,334	278	23	255
Licensed practical/vocational nurse training	0	0	0	0	0	0	0	0	0
Practical nursing, vocational nursing and nursing assistants, other	7	3	4	0	0	0	0	0	0
Health professions and related clinical sciences, other	4,784	1,119	3,665	941	259	682	107	37	70
Homeland security, law enforcement, firefighting and related prot. services	58,114	30,481	27,633	10,293	5,276	5,017	150	58	92
Corrections	414	175	239	7	3	4	0	0	0
Criminal justice/law enforcement administration	15,629	8,059	7,570	2,495	1,252	1,243	40	18	22
Criminal justice/safety studies	30,513	15,293	15,220	3,216	1,336	1,880	78	28	50
Forensic science and technology	1,551	431	1,120	549	140	409	3	0	3
Criminal justice/police science	2,925	1,603	1,322	50	9	41	6	3	3
Security and loss prevention services	4	2	2	32	17	15	0	0	0
Juvenile corrections	24	9	15	10	4	6	2	0	2
Criminalistics and criminal science	174	41	133	12	3	9	1	0	1
Securities services administration/management	474	366	108	174	134	40	0	0	0
Corrections administration	113	61	52	6	4	2	0	0	0
Law enforcement investigation and interviewing	0	0	0	59	26	33	0	0	0
Cyber/computer forensics and counterterrorism	362	285	77	513	328	185	0	0	0
Financial forensics and fraud investigation	109	40	69	152	52	100	0	0	0

See notes at end of table.

Table 318.30. Bachelor's, master's, and doctor's degrees conferred by postsecondary institutions, by sex of student and discipline division: 2017–18—Continued

Discipline division	Bachelor's degrees			Master's degrees			Doctor's degrees[1]		
	Total	Males	Females	Total	Males	Females	Total	Males	Females
1	2	3	4	5	6	7	8	9	10
Law enforcement intelligence analysis	18	8	10	10	3	7	0	0	0
Critical incident response/special police operations	0	0	0	0	0	0	0	0	0
Protective services operations	1	1	0	0	0	0	0	0	0
Corrections and criminal justice, other	1,371	613	758	424	176	248	0	0	0
Fire prevention and safety technology/technician	170	151	19	9	7	2	0	0	0
Fire services administration	859	813	46	65	41	24	3	0	3
Fire science/firefighting	363	326	37	6	5	1	0	0	0
Fire/arson investigation and prevention	55	36	19	0	0	0	0	0	0
Fire protection, other	40	33	7	17	17	0	0	0	0
Homeland security	972	715	257	757	530	227	4	3	1
Crisis/emergency/disaster management	956	734	222	768	519	249	9	3	6
Critical infrastructure protection	96	74	22	415	304	111	0	0	0
Terrorism and counterterrorism operations	4	3	1	15	11	4	0	0	0
Homeland security, other	91	69	22	19	11	8	0	0	0
Homeland sec., law enforcement, firefighting and related prot. serv., other	826	540	286	513	344	169	4	3	1
Legal professions and studies	4,239	1,340	2,899	9,177	4,110	5,067	34,544	17,383	17,161
Pre-law studies	231	109	122	36	16	20	0	0	0
Legal studies, general	2,098	742	1,356	264	96	168	9	1	8
Law	0	0	0	0	0	0	34,128	17,161	16,967
Advanced legal research/studies, general	69	31	38	2,241	990	1,251	228	125	103
Programs for foreign lawyers	0	0	0	1,757	794	963	9	3	6
American/U.S. law/legal studies/jurisprudence	88	29	59	474	209	265	20	13	7
Banking, corporate, finance, and securities law	0	0	0	271	125	146	0	0	0
Comparative law	0	0	0	49	29	20	0	0	0
Energy, environment, and natural resources law	16	12	4	198	103	95	2	2	0
Health law	0	0	0	292	84	208	2	0	2
International law and legal studies	1	0	1	486	207	279	9	6	3
International business, trade, and tax law	0	0	0	256	123	133	0	0	0
Tax law/taxation	0	0	0	795	485	310	1	0	1
Intellectual property law	0	0	0	111	45	66	0	0	0
Legal research and advanced professional studies, other	0	0	0	895	403	492	29	23	6
Legal administrative assistant/secretary	10	3	7	11	8	3	0	0	0
Legal assistant/paralegal	1,271	261	1,010	99	16	83	0	0	0
Court reporting/court reporter	4	0	4	0	0	0	0	0	0
Legal support services, other	5	1	4	6	4	2	0	0	0
Legal professions and studies, other	446	152	294	936	373	563	107	49	58
Liberal arts and sciences, general studies and humanities	44,262	15,966	28,296	2,473	880	1,593	93	35	58
Liberal arts and sciences/liberal studies	24,179	7,786	16,393	1,514	580	934	19	7	12
General studies	14,268	5,930	8,338	179	59	120	2	0	2
Humanities/humanistic studies	1,804	610	1,194	487	162	325	65	27	38
Liberal arts and sciences, general studies and humanities, other	4,011	1,640	2,371	293	79	214	7	1	6
Library science	81	7	74	4,953	856	4,097	54	16	38
Library and information science	81	7	74	4,665	814	3,851	54	16	38
Children and youth library services	0	0	0	18	1	17	0	0	0
Archives/archival administration	0	0	0	144	25	119	0	0	0
Library science, other	0	0	0	126	16	110	0	0	0
Mathematics and statistics	25,256	14,541	10,715	10,443	5,959	4,484	2,010	1,448	562
Mathematics, general	17,944	10,225	7,719	2,707	1,684	1,023	1,176	909	267
Analysis and functional analysis	4	3	1	0	0	0	0	0	0
Topology and foundations	0	0	0	0	0	0	1	1	0
Mathematics, other	349	189	160	30	15	15	18	9	9
Applied mathematics, general	2,494	1,561	933	1,040	634	406	241	167	74
Computational mathematics	205	143	62	9	5	4	28	19	9
Computational and applied mathematics	261	160	101	229	127	102	15	8	7
Financial mathematics	361	216	145	2,886	1,589	1,297	18	14	4
Mathematical biology	34	12	22	0	0	0	0	0	0
Applied mathematics, other	210	127	83	8	4	4	11	10	1
Statistics, general	2,560	1,417	1,143	3,181	1,695	1,486	456	279	177
Mathematical statistics and probability	216	118	98	168	92	76	14	11	3
Mathematics and statistics	116	77	39	86	52	34	1	0	1
Statistics, other	196	126	70	58	37	21	4	1	3
Mathematics and statistics, other	306	167	139	41	25	16	27	20	7
Military technologies and applied sciences	655	533	122	355	265	90	0	0	0
Intelligence, general	360	294	66	58	30	28	0	0	0
Strategic intelligence	4	3	1	44	30	14	0	0	0
Signal/geospatial intelligence	13	8	5	2	2	0	0	0	0
Cyber/electronic operations and warfare	93	76	17	236	190	46	0	0	0
Intelligence, command control and information operations, other	0	0	0	0	0	0	0	0	0
Military applied sciences, other	73	68	5	0	0	0	0	0	0
Aerospace ground equipment technology	3	3	0	0	0	0	0	0	0
Air and space operations technology	24	19	5	0	0	0	0	0	0
Military systems and maintenance technology, other	0	0	0	0	0	0	0	0	0
Military technologies and applied sciences, other	85	62	23	15	13	2	0	0	0
Multi/interdisciplinary studies	51,909	17,573	34,336	10,175	3,677	6,498	850	345	505
Multi/interdisciplinary studies, general	5,175	1,998	3,177	141	55	86	3	1	2
Biological and physical sciences	2,207	866	1,341	450	185	265	68	33	35
Peace studies and conflict resolution	483	157	326	457	151	306	27	13	14
Systems science and theory	339	208	131	225	115	110	17	9	8
Mathematics and computer science	663	514	149	118	75	43	15	13	2
Biopsychology	147	33	114	3	1	2	3	0	3
Gerontology	287	29	258	485	87	398	24	4	20
Historic preservation and conservation	86	16	70	199	54	145	1	0	1

See notes at end of table.

Table 318.30. Bachelor's, master's, and doctor's degrees conferred by postsecondary institutions, by sex of student and discipline division: 2017–18—Continued

Discipline division	Bachelor's degrees			Master's degrees			Doctor's degrees[1]		
	Total	Males	Females	Total	Males	Females	Total	Males	Females
1	2	3	4	5	6	7	8	9	10
Cultural resource management and policy analysis	0	0	0	37	12	25	0	0	0
Historic preservation and conservation, other	2	1	1	12	4	8	0	0	0
Medieval and renaissance studies	15	8	7	27	7	20	10	5	5
Museology/museum studies	20	6	14	579	85	494	0	0	0
Science, technology and society	824	423	401	132	49	83	24	11	13
Accounting and computer science	8	3	5	5	2	3	0	0	0
Behavioral sciences	3,190	613	2,577	327	61	266	31	8	23
Natural sciences	554	193	361	58	20	38	13	6	7
Nutrition sciences	3,380	574	2,806	1,219	150	1,069	186	38	148
International/global studies	5,810	2,031	3,779	1,141	567	574	2	0	2
Holocaust and related studies	9	3	6	34	15	19	0	0	0
Ancient studies/civilization	89	36	53	5	3	2	16	6	10
Classical, ancient Mediterranean/Near Eastern studies/archaeology	71	26	45	4	2	2	2	0	2
Intercultural/multicultural and diversity studies	158	27	131	117	43	74	4	4	0
Cognitive science	1,575	611	964	109	46	63	36	22	14
Cultural studies/critical theory and analysis	124	40	84	46	12	34	4	1	3
Human biology	1,015	256	759	0	0	0	0	0	0
Dispute resolution	0	0	0	299	96	203	35	16	19
Maritime studies	10	3	7	5	4	1	0	0	0
Computational science	47	33	14	510	364	146	25	20	5
Human computer interaction	603	496	107	402	191	211	11	5	6
Marine sciences	118	38	80	79	29	50	19	7	12
Sustainability studies	510	211	299	788	295	493	9	5	4
Multi/interdisciplinary studies, other	24,390	8,120	16,270	2,162	897	1,265	265	118	147
Parks, recreation, leisure, and fitness studies	53,883	27,558	26,325	9,005	5,104	3,901	298	157	141
Parks, recreation and leisure studies	2,937	1,318	1,619	173	73	100	14	3	11
Parks, recreation and leisure facilities management	3,133	1,416	1,717	404	197	207	22	13	9
Golf course operation and grounds management	7	6	1	0	0	0	0	0	0
Parks, recreation and leisure facilities management, other	6	6	0	0	0	0	0	0	0
Health and physical education/fitness, general	10,475	5,123	5,352	1,150	635	515	33	13	20
Sport and fitness administration/management	10,248	7,472	2,776	4,390	2,775	1,615	32	15	17
Kinesiology and exercise science	25,376	11,245	14,131	2,580	1,279	1,301	160	97	63
Physical fitness technician	104	67	37	15	7	8	0	0	0
Sports studies	199	145	54	87	42	45	5	5	0
Health and physical education/fitness, other	1,091	579	512	153	77	76	25	5	20
Outdoor education	143	86	57	35	10	25	0	0	0
Parks, recreation, leisure, and fitness studies, other	164	95	69	18	9	9	7	6	1
Philosophy and religious studies	9,603	5,935	3,668	1,692	1,110	582	768	532	236
Philosophy and religious studies, general	109	80	29	7	6	1	27	16	11
Philosophy	5,644	3,756	1,888	713	529	184	458	341	117
Logic	3	2	1	4	2	2	9	7	2
Ethics	49	11	38	50	23	27	0	0	0
Applied and professional ethics	16	8	8	18	10	8	0	0	0
Philosophy, other	235	134	101	8	5	3	0	0	0
Religion/religious studies	2,779	1,536	1,243	470	272	198	243	147	96
Buddhist studies	0	0	0	4	2	2	1	1	0
Christian studies	303	204	99	204	141	63	0	0	0
Hindu studies	0	0	0	0	0	0	0	0	0
Islamic studies	8	4	4	17	9	8	1	1	0
Jewish/Judaic studies	213	50	163	89	34	55	11	9	2
Religion/religious studies, other	67	30	37	41	22	19	8	6	2
Philosophy and religious studies, other	177	120	57	67	55	12	10	4	6
Physical sciences and science technologies	31,542	18,938	12,604	7,196	4,492	2,704	6,181	4,074	2,107
Physical sciences	31,003	18,628	12,375	7,131	4,470	2,661	6,178	4,073	2,105
Physical sciences	274	143	131	49	30	19	21	14	7
Astronomy	323	210	113	90	63	27	120	71	49
Astrophysics	209	134	75	27	19	8	60	43	17
Planetary astronomy and science	13	6	7	12	6	6	22	9	13
Astronomy and astrophysics, other	46	33	13	16	7	9	9	6	3
Atmospheric sciences and meteorology, general	502	328	174	219	133	86	154	94	60
Atmospheric chemistry and climatology	9	5	4	0	0	0	0	0	0
Atmospheric physics and dynamics	0	0	0	1	0	1	1	1	0
Meteorology	184	124	60	16	12	4	17	12	5
Atmospheric sciences and meteorology, other	19	11	8	2	2	0	2	1	1
Chemistry, general	14,040	6,999	7,041	2,256	1,246	1,010	2,809	1,712	1,097
Analytical chemistry	11	2	9	28	16	12	5	3	2
Inorganic chemistry	0	0	0	1	0	1	1	0	1
Organic chemistry	0	0	0	0	0	0	11	8	3
Physical chemistry	0	0	0	0	0	0	3	3	0
Polymer chemistry	1	1	0	63	38	25	52	38	14
Chemical physics	32	23	9	6	4	2	17	11	6
Environmental chemistry	7	5	2	3	1	2	9	3	6
Forensic chemistry	171	33	138	6	2	4	0	0	0
Theoretical chemistry	7	4	3	0	0	0	2	2	0
Chemistry, other	468	217	251	25	9	16	42	24	18
Geology/earth science, general	5,699	3,537	2,162	1,306	748	558	462	258	204
Geochemistry	23	17	6	5	3	2	8	5	3
Geophysics and seismology	175	110	65	99	60	39	70	38	32
Paleontology	16	12	4	4	3	1	0	0	0
Hydrology and water resources science	32	20	12	85	42	43	22	11	11
Geochemistry and petrology	0	0	0	0	0	0	0	0	0
Oceanography, chemical and physical	181	75	106	153	67	86	111	49	62
Geological and earth sciences/geosciences, other	576	333	243	161	106	55	86	53	33
Physics, general	7,211	5,712	1,499	1,886	1,441	445	1,734	1,365	369
Atomic/molecular physics	2	0	2	11	7	4	8	7	1

See notes at end of table.

Table 318.30. Bachelor's, master's, and doctor's degrees conferred by postsecondary institutions, by sex of student and discipline division: 2017–18—Continued

Discipline division	Bachelor's degrees			Master's degrees			Doctor's degrees[1]		
	Total	Males	Females	Total	Males	Females	Total	Males	Females
1	2	3	4	5	6	7	8	9	10
Elementary particle physics	0	0	0	0	0	0	2	2	0
Nuclear physics	1	0	1	1	1	0	1	1	0
Optics/optical sciences	52	36	16	97	81	16	55	38	17
Condensed matter and materials physics	3	2	1	3	2	1	6	6	0
Acoustics	15	12	3	32	26	6	9	7	2
Theoretical and mathematical physics	14	12	2	0	0	0	1	1	0
Physics, other	217	176	41	119	96	23	63	50	13
Materials science	163	98	65	234	159	75	149	100	49
Materials chemistry	4	3	1	7	3	4	8	5	3
Materials sciences, other	0	0	0	3	2	1	5	4	1
Physical sciences, other	303	195	108	105	35	70	21	18	3
Science technologies/technicians	539	310	229	65	22	43	3	1	2
Science technologies/technicians, general	47	44	3	7	0	7	0	0	0
Biology technician/biotechnology laboratory technician	43	19	24	0	0	0	3	1	2
Nuclear/nuclear power technology/technician	16	13	3	0	0	0	0	0	0
Nuclear and industrial radiologic technologies/technicians, other	0	0	0	0	0	0	0	0	0
Chemical technology/technician	0	0	0	0	0	0	0	0	0
Physical science technologies/technicians, other	0	0	0	0	0	0	0	0	0
Science technologies/technicians, other	433	234	199	58	22	36	0	0	0
Precision production	45	19	26	11	5	6	0	0	0
Tool and die technology/technician	0	0	0	0	0	0	0	0	0
Welding technology/welder	2	2	0	0	0	0	0	0	0
Furniture design and manufacturing	43	17	26	11	5	6	0	0	0
Psychology	116,432	24,578	91,854	27,841	5,526	22,315	6,275	1,649	4,626
Psychology, general	103,801	21,944	81,857	6,306	1,521	4,785	1,735	515	1,220
Cognitive psychology and psycholinguistics	150	36	114	26	5	21	19	7	12
Comparative psychology	0	0	0	14	3	11	0	0	0
Developmental and child psychology	552	51	501	313	26	287	44	6	38
Experimental psychology	1,920	468	1,452	274	94	180	192	84	108
Personality psychology	12	3	9	8	2	6	6	1	5
Physiological psychology/psychobiology	1,191	325	866	42	11	31	16	7	9
Social psychology	1,039	225	814	36	11	25	43	19	24
Psychometrics and quantitative psychology	1	1	0	18	2	16	7	1	6
Psychopharmacology	0	0	0	43	15	28	0	0	0
Research and experimental psychology, other	4,432	940	3,492	195	67	128	192	76	116
Clinical psychology	206	30	176	2,388	431	1,957	2,202	476	1,726
Community psychology	368	72	296	218	34	184	50	9	41
Counseling psychology	422	69	353	8,054	1,470	6,584	400	101	299
Industrial and organizational psychology	168	37	131	1,360	417	943	174	60	114
School psychology	1	0	1	1,811	261	1,550	353	68	285
Educational psychology	113	9	104	1,255	219	1,036	347	100	247
Clinical child psychology	0	0	0	21	1	20	25	5	20
Environmental psychology	0	0	0	9	5	4	1	0	1
Geropsychology	0	0	0	2	0	2	1	0	1
Health/medical psychology	98	18	80	8	3	5	30	7	23
Family psychology	15	2	13	65	11	54	0	0	0
Forensic psychology	583	107	476	775	116	659	94	15	79
Applied psychology	842	160	682	415	107	308	33	12	21
Applied behavior analysis	220	39	181	1,869	237	1,632	97	25	72
Clinical, counseling and applied psychology, other	58	13	45	299	59	240	42	11	31
Psychology, other	240	29	211	2,017	398	1,619	172	44	128
Public administration and social service professions	35,629	6,127	29,502	46,294	10,692	35,602	1,157	399	758
Human services, general	6,938	952	5,986	1,299	176	1,123	48	7	41
Community organization and advocacy	1,688	345	1,343	311	98	213	6	2	4
Public administration	3,093	1,548	1,545	12,173	5,095	7,078	300	153	147
Public policy analysis, general	1,678	718	960	2,693	1,184	1,509	199	83	116
Education policy analysis	0	0	0	63	13	50	11	4	7
Health policy analysis	81	13	68	85	26	59	18	4	14
International policy analysis	14	2	12	12	7	5	4	2	2
Public policy analysis, other	0	0	0	80	26	54	8	4	4
Social work	21,698	2,456	19,242	29,127	3,949	25,178	520	121	399
Youth services/administration	88	13	75	92	12	80	0	0	0
Social work, other	33	4	29	111	17	94	0	0	0
Public administration and social service professions, other	318	76	242	248	89	159	43	19	24
Social sciences and history	159,967	79,628	80,339	19,884	9,832	10,052	4,676	2,475	2,201
Social sciences	136,585	65,758	70,827	16,612	8,062	8,550	3,765	1,983	1,782
Social sciences, general	6,486	2,435	4,051	637	210	427	22	10	12
Research methodology and quantitative methods	0	0	0	54	29	25	2	2	0
Anthropology	8,227	2,221	6,006	1,094	325	769	519	175	344
Physical and biological anthropology	31	7	24	29	4	25	3	1	2
Medical anthropology	67	13	54	7	2	5	1	0	1
Cultural anthropology	43	14	29	14	2	12	10	2	8
Anthropology, other	60	13	47	36	10	26	7	0	7
Archeology	167	58	109	47	14	33	33	11	22
Criminology	7,677	3,472	4,205	721	236	485	54	22	32
Demography and population studies	0	0	0	47	20	27	20	6	14
Economics, general	29,275	20,389	8,886	1,713	1,058	655	770	521	249
Applied economics	326	205	121	309	182	127	31	18	13
Econometrics and quantitative economics	4,669	2,936	1,733	1,625	982	643	369	266	103
Development economics and international development	293	65	228	302	108	194	18	11	7
International economics	397	152	245	39	21	18	2	1	1
Economics, other	367	231	136	110	69	41	5	2	3
Geography	3,723	2,278	1,445	617	354	263	229	122	107
Geographic information science and cartography	588	438	150	563	341	222	19	14	5

See notes at end of table.

Table 318.30. Bachelor's, master's, and doctor's degrees conferred by postsecondary institutions, by sex of student and discipline division: 2017–18—Continued

Discipline division	Bachelor's degrees			Master's degrees			Doctor's degrees[1]		
	Total	Males	Females	Total	Males	Females	Total	Males	Females
1	2	3	4	5	6	7	8	9	10
Geography, other	156	87	69	60	37	23	5	4	1
International relations and affairs	8,392	3,282	5,110	4,134	2,062	2,072	77	39	38
National security policy studies	74	62	12	194	129	65	0	0	0
International relations and national security studies, other	117	67	50	175	95	80	1	1	0
Political science and government, general	33,845	17,762	16,083	1,567	836	731	774	459	315
American government and politics (United States)	148	95	53	178	117	61	0	0	0
Political economy	214	115	99	10	3	7	0	0	0
Political science and government, other	761	401	360	99	60	39	15	6	9
Sociology	27,294	7,780	19,514	1,411	501	910	687	253	434
Urban studies/affairs	951	414	537	345	136	209	47	24	23
Sociology and anthropology	443	104	339	2	0	2	0	0	0
Rural sociology	28	8	20	0	0	0	0	0	0
Social sciences, other	1,766	654	1,112	473	119	354	45	13	32
History	23,382	13,870	9,512	3,272	1,770	1,502	911	492	419
History, general	22,752	13,526	9,226	2,913	1,553	1,360	856	468	388
American history (United States)	50	30	20	57	30	27	1	1	0
European history	21	16	5	0	0	0	0	0	0
History and philosophy of science and technology	100	47	53	30	15	15	27	10	17
Public/applied history	50	21	29	93	33	60	4	1	3
Asian history	1	1	0	0	0	0	0	0	0
Military history	71	62	9	108	95	13	0	0	0
History, other	337	167	170	71	44	27	23	12	11
Theology and religious vocations	9,521	6,601	2,920	13,828	9,023	4,805	2,023	1,476	547
Bible/biblical studies	1,984	1,315	669	725	506	219	39	36	3
Missions/missionary studies and missiology	579	215	364	398	238	160	100	84	16
Religious education	764	361	403	550	239	311	63	44	19
Religious/sacred music	276	144	132	77	43	34	13	8	5
Theology/theological studies	976	667	309	3,972	2,585	1,387	430	321	109
Divinity/ministry	406	304	102	5,236	3,654	1,582	501	365	136
Pre-theology/pre-ministerial studies	169	142	27	10	10	0	0	0	0
Rabbinical studies	3	3	0	96	58	38	9	9	0
Talmudic studies	2,269	2,213	56	502	501	1	26	26	0
Theological and ministerial studies, other	415	249	166	689	417	272	339	253	86
Pastoral studies/counseling	471	327	144	603	267	336	187	127	60
Youth ministry	469	274	195	42	18	24	0	0	0
Urban ministry	16	7	9	38	18	20	26	14	12
Women's ministry	7	0	7	4	0	4	0	0	0
Lay ministry	168	86	82	119	60	59	10	7	3
Pastoral counseling and specialized ministries, other	173	91	82	164	65	99	19	16	3
Theology and religious vocations, other	376	203	173	603	344	259	261	166	95
Transportation and materials moving	4,924	4,282	642	815	657	158	16	13	3
Aeronautics/aviation/aerospace science and technology, general	2,596	2,264	332	556	472	84	11	8	3
Airline/commercial/professional pilot and flight crew	708	643	65	0	0	0	0	0	0
Aviation/airway management and operations	880	728	152	224	156	68	5	5	0
Air traffic controller	89	74	15	0	0	0	0	0	0
Flight instructor	10	9	1	0	0	0	0	0	0
Air transportation, other	36	34	2	29	23	6	0	0	0
Marine science/merchant marine officer	602	528	74	0	0	0	0	0	0
Transportation and materials moving, other	3	2	1	6	6	0	0	0	0
Visual and performing arts	88,582	34,202	54,380	17,686	7,399	10,287	1,759	852	907
Visual and performing arts, general	1,538	539	999	134	46	88	13	8	5
Digital arts	1,445	769	676	238	137	101	3	3	0
Crafts/craft design, folk art and artisanry	118	30	88	22	8	14	0	0	0
Dance, general	2,269	258	2,011	226	42	184	10	1	9
Ballet	49	7	42	0	0	0	0	0	0
Dance, other	56	2	54	0	0	0	3	0	3
Design and visual communications, general	2,786	861	1,925	390	141	249	4	2	2
Commercial and advertising art	988	339	649	39	12	27	0	0	0
Industrial and product design	1,656	917	739	224	108	116	0	0	0
Commercial photography	138	37	101	3	0	3	0	0	0
Fashion/apparel design	1,870	186	1,684	153	20	133	1	0	1
Interior design	2,433	234	2,199	299	46	253	0	0	0
Graphic design	4,488	1,520	2,968	165	48	117	0	0	0
Illustration	1,891	530	1,361	159	53	106	0	0	0
Game and interactive media design	1,231	894	337	121	69	52	3	3	0
Design and applied arts, other	715	251	464	278	99	179	3	0	3
Drama and dramatics/theatre arts, general	8,464	3,041	5,423	997	396	601	76	29	47
Technical theatre/theatre design and technology	541	194	347	176	67	109	0	0	0
Playwriting and screenwriting	313	154	159	354	159	195	0	0	0
Theatre literature, history and criticism	36	9	27	7	3	4	9	5	4
Acting	998	363	635	189	89	100	0	0	0
Directing and theatrical production	117	33	84	84	42	42	0	0	0
Musical theatre	592	214	378	18	5	13	0	0	0
Costume design	19	4	15	5	0	5	0	0	0
Dramatic/theatre arts and stagecraft, other	597	252	345	66	28	38	4	0	4
Film/cinema/video studies	3,600	1,997	1,603	560	294	266	30	14	16
Cinematography and film/video production	4,583	2,717	1,866	1,056	545	511	6	4	2
Photography	1,252	409	843	259	114	145	0	0	0
Documentary production	12	7	5	46	22	24	0	0	0
Film/video and photographic arts, other	897	507	390	56	14	42	5	4	1
Art/art studies, general	10,413	3,078	7,335	713	248	465	3	0	3
Fine/studio arts, general	8,943	2,575	6,368	1,394	522	872	3	3	0
Art history, criticism and conservation	2,269	339	1,930	849	128	721	200	46	154
Drawing	260	75	185	25	7	18	0	0	0

See notes at end of table.

Table 318.30. Bachelor's, master's, and doctor's degrees conferred by postsecondary institutions, by sex of student and discipline division: 2017–18—Continued

Discipline division	Bachelor's degrees			Master's degrees			Doctor's degrees[1]		
	Total	Males	Females	Total	Males	Females	Total	Males	Females
1	2	3	4	5	6	7	8	9	10
Intermedia/multimedia	773	411	362	41	22	19	1	1	0
Painting	578	160	418	142	46	96	0	0	0
Sculpture	191	58	133	50	19	31	0	0	0
Printmaking	121	30	91	33	10	23	0	0	0
Ceramic arts and ceramics	99	30	69	46	18	28	0	0	0
Fiber, textile and weaving arts	153	12	141	43	3	40	0	0	0
Metal and jewelry arts	109	21	88	56	7	49	0	0	0
Fine arts and art studies, other	579	189	390	287	85	202	4	0	4
Music, general	7,318	3,917	3,401	1,830	955	875	580	313	267
Music history, literature, and theory	118	66	52	42	23	19	9	4	5
Music performance, general	4,031	2,168	1,863	2,195	1,129	1,066	469	226	243
Music theory and composition	564	427	137	324	216	108	70	52	18
Musicology and ethnomusicology	59	35	24	75	32	43	48	22	26
Conducting	5	3	2	184	133	51	35	23	12
Keyboard instruments	159	58	101	262	86	176	46	22	24
Voice and opera	294	90	204	294	81	213	17	7	10
Jazz/jazz studies	330	278	52	183	155	28	22	22	0
Stringed instruments	189	81	108	247	96	151	13	10	3
Music pedagogy	66	27	39	92	39	53	12	5	7
Music technology	640	529	111	120	100	20	3	2	1
Brass instruments	35	32	3	50	43	7	1	1	0
Woodwind instruments	47	22	25	71	36	35	8	1	7
Percussion instruments	12	9	3	16	11	5	0	0	0
Music, other	1,163	739	424	265	157	108	21	15	6
Arts, entertainment, and media management, general	486	213	273	299	61	238	0	0	0
Fine and studio arts management	624	154	470	576	94	482	7	1	6
Music management	1,531	824	707	49	21	28	0	0	0
Theatre/theatre arts management	173	41	132	49	16	33	0	0	0
Arts, entertainment, and media management, other	130	64	66	229	127	102	0	0	0
Visual and performing arts, other	428	172	256	231	66	165	20	6	14
Not classified by field of study	0	0	0	0	0	0	0	0	0

[1]Includes Ph.D., Ed.D., and comparable degrees at the doctoral level. Includes most degrees that were classified as first-professional prior to 2010–11, such as M.D., D.D.S., and law degrees.
NOTE: Data are for postsecondary institutions participating in Title IV federal financial aid programs. Aggregations by field of study derived from the Classification of Instructional Programs developed by the National Center for Education Statistics.

SOURCE: U.S. Department of Education, National Center for Education Statistics, Integrated Postsecondary Education Data System (IPEDS), Fall 2018, Completions component. (This table was prepared September 2019.)

Table 318.40. Degrees/certificates conferred by postsecondary institutions, by control of institution and level of degree/certificate: 1970–71 through 2017–18

Year	Public — Certificates below the associate's	Public — Associate's degrees	Public — Bachelor's degrees	Public — Master's degrees	Public — Doctor's degrees[1]	Private Total — Certificates below the associate's	Private Total — Associate's degrees	Private Total — Bachelor's degrees	Private Total — Master's degrees	Private Total — Doctor's degrees[1]	Nonprofit — Certificates below the associate's	Nonprofit — Associate's degrees	Nonprofit — Bachelor's degrees	Nonprofit — Master's degrees	Nonprofit — Doctor's degrees[1]	For-profit — Certificates below the associate's	For-profit — Associate's degrees	For-profit — Bachelor's degrees	For-profit — Master's degrees	For-profit — Doctor's degrees[1]
1	2	3	4	5	6	7	8	9	10	11	12	13	14	15	16	17	18	19	20	21
1970–71	—	215,645	557,996	151,603	36,927	—	36,666	281,734	83,961	28,071	—	—	—	—	—	—	—	—	—	—
1971–72	—	255,218	599,615	167,075	40,297	—	36,796	287,658	90,126	30,909	—	—	—	—	—	—	—	—	—	—
1972–73	—	278,132	630,899	174,405	44,229	—	38,042	291,463	94,249	35,283	—	—	—	—	—	—	—	—	—	—
1973–74	—	303,188	651,544	184,632	45,018	—	40,736	294,232	97,442	37,573	—	—	—	—	—	—	—	—	—	—
1974–75	—	318,474	634,785	193,804	45,788	—	41,697	288,148	103,741	39,116	—	—	—	—	—	—	—	—	—	—
1975–76	—	345,006	635,161	206,298	47,517	—	46,448	290,585	111,179	43,490	—	—	—	—	—	—	—	—	—	—
1976–77	—	355,650	630,463	208,901	47,573	—	50,727	289,086	114,124	44,157	—	—	—	—	—	—	—	—	—	—
1977–78	—	358,874	627,903	202,099	47,553	—	53,372	293,301	115,888	44,792	—	—	—	—	—	—	—	—	—	—
1978–79	—	346,808	621,666	192,016	48,602	—	55,894	299,724	115,670	46,369	—	—	—	—	—	—	—	—	—	—
1979–80	—	344,536	624,084	187,499	48,550	—	56,374	305,333	117,697	47,081	—	—	—	—	—	—	—	—	—	—
1980–81	—	352,391	626,452	184,384	50,023	—	63,986[2]	308,688	118,253	47,993	—	—	—	—	—	—	—	—	—	—
1981–82	—	366,732	636,475	182,295	50,500	—	67,794[2]	316,523	120,152	47,338	—	—	—	—	—	—	—	—	—	—
1982–83	—	377,817	646,317	176,246	50,943	—	71,803[2]	323,193	120,169	48,392	—	—	—	—	—	—	—	—	—	—
1983–84	—	379,249	646,013	170,693	50,727	—	72,991	328,296	120,448	50,072	—	—	—	—	—	—	—	—	—	—
1984–85	—	377,625	652,246	170,000	51,489	—	77,087	327,231	123,472	49,296	—	—	—	—	—	—	—	—	—	—
1985–86	—	369,052	658,586	169,903	51,001	—	76,995	329,237	125,947	49,279	—	—	—	—	—	—	—	—	—	—
1986–87	—	358,811	659,260	167,797	51,216	—	77,493	332,004	128,733	47,261	—	—	—	—	—	—	—	—	—	—
1987–88	—	354,180	658,491	173,778	51,641	—	80,905	336,338	132,005	47,498	—	—	—	—	—	—	—	—	—	—
1988–89	—	357,001	675,675	179,109	51,963	—	79,763	343,080	137,517	48,608	—	—	—	—	—	—	—	—	—	—
1989–90	—	375,635	700,015	186,104	53,451	—	79,467	351,329	144,048	50,057	—	42,497	344,569	142,681	49,655	—	36,970	6,760	1,367	402
1990–91	—	398,055	724,062	193,057	55,235	—	83,665	370,476	149,806	50,312	—	45,821	360,634	146,161	49,841	—	37,844	9,842	3,645	471
1991–92	—	420,265	759,475	203,398	56,186	—	83,966	377,078	154,691	53,368	—	45,700	370,718	153,291	52,830	—	38,266	6,360	1,400	538
1992–93	—	430,321	785,112	213,843	57,020	—	84,435	380,066	161,189	55,052	—	47,713	373,346	159,562	54,399	—	36,722	6,720	1,627	653
1993–94	—	444,373	789,148	221,428	58,366	—	86,259	380,127	171,609	54,247	—	48,493	371,561	168,718	53,502	—	37,766	8,566	2,891	768
1994–95	—	451,539	776,670	224,152	58,788	—	88,152	383,464	179,457	55,478	—	48,643	373,454	176,485	54,675	—	39,509	10,010	2,972	803
1995–96	307,358	454,291	774,070	227,179	59,398	313,311	100,925	390,722	185,001	56,109	34,259	50,678	379,916	181,142	55,506	279,052	50,247	10,806	3,859	603
1996–97	326,687	465,494	776,677	233,237	61,081	272,237	105,732	396,202	192,023	57,666	35,560	49,168	384,086	186,963	56,864	236,677	56,564	12,116	5,060	802
1997–98	305,910	455,084	784,296	235,922	60,948	246,571	103,471	400,110	200,115	57,787	32,166	47,525	386,455	194,048	57,089	214,405	55,846	13,655	6,067	698
1998–99	304,294	452,616	792,392	238,954	60,028	251,589	112,368	409,847	207,084	56,672	29,402	47,757	394,749	198,481	55,663	222,187	64,611	15,098	8,603	1,009
1999–2000	294,912	448,446	810,855	243,157	60,655	263,217	116,487	427,020	220,028	58,081	28,580	46,337	406,958	209,720	56,972	234,637	70,150	20,062	10,308	1,109
2000–01	309,624	456,487	812,438	246,054	60,820	242,879	122,378	431,733	227,448	58,765	29,336	45,711	408,701	215,815	57,722	213,543	76,667	23,032	11,633	1,043
2001–02	319,291	471,660	841,180	249,820	61,061	264,957	123,473	450,720	237,493	58,602	32,904	45,761	424,322	223,229	57,707	232,053	77,712	26,398	14,264	895
2002–03	355,727	498,279	875,596	265,643	61,611	290,698	135,737	473,215	253,056	59,968	36,926	46,183	442,060	238,069	58,894	253,772	89,554	31,155	14,987	1,074
2003–04	364,053	524,875	905,718	285,138	64,205	323,734	140,426	493,824	279,134	61,882	35,316	45,759	451,518	250,894	60,447	288,418	94,667	42,306	28,240	1,435
2004–05	370,683	547,519	932,443	291,505	67,511	340,190	149,141	506,821	288,646	66,876	35,968	45,344	457,963	253,564	65,278	304,222	103,797	48,858	35,082	1,598
2005–06	370,570	557,366	955,370	293,535	70,036	344,220	155,949	529,734	306,327	68,020	35,909	46,459	467,697	261,203	66,066	308,311	109,490	62,037	45,124	1,954
2006–07	389,244	566,219	975,903	292,073	73,087	339,071	161,397	548,826	318,630	71,607	34,195	43,790	478,053	267,694	69,241	304,876	117,607	70,773	50,936	2,366
2007–08	399,741	578,661	996,769	300,019	75,551	348,613	171,505	566,965	330,825	73,639	33,915	45,014	491,016	275,971	70,473	314,698	126,491	75,949	54,854	3,166
2008–09	428,849	596,391	1,020,521	308,215	77,270	375,771	190,852	580,878	353,867	77,294	31,939	46,930	496,353	290,401	73,583	343,832	143,922	84,525	63,466	3,711
2009–10	472,428	640,265	1,049,179	322,389	78,805	463,291	208,591	600,740	370,924	79,785	35,652	46,673	503,264	300,053	75,172	427,639	161,918	97,476	70,871	4,613
2010–11	519,711	696,884	1,088,722	339,420	82,013	510,766	246,622	627,331	391,502	81,814	36,534	51,967	512,821	313,317	76,595	474,232	194,655	114,510	78,185	5,219
2011–12	525,264	756,484	1,131,885	349,349	84,730	463,797	265,234	660,278	406,618	85,487	32,856	54,347	526,022	325,175	79,498	430,941	210,887	134,256	81,443	5,989
2012–13	545,446	772,978	1,163,616	346,751	86,411	421,768	234,449	676,765	404,967	88,615	30,913	55,651	535,958	327,013	81,543	390,855	178,798	140,807	77,954	7,072
2013–14	576,468	794,925	1,186,742	346,238	88,911	392,810	210,230	683,408	408,344	88,676	30,738	53,127	544,253	333,539	80,894	362,072	157,103	139,155	74,805	7,782
2014–15	602,904	822,218	1,209,464	351,216	90,252	358,242	192,123	685,505	407,588	88,296	46,090	58,613	553,543	336,181	80,093	312,152	133,510	131,962	71,407	8,203
2015–16	615,137	848,081	1,240,423	364,619	90,030	324,154	160,147	680,327	421,138	88,104	40,010	56,595	560,834	350,790	80,067	284,144	103,552	119,493	70,348	8,037
2016–17	631,076	861,570	1,275,610	374,160	91,532	314,947	143,717	680,504	430,382	89,825	35,281	56,487	566,607	360,437	81,550	279,666	87,230	113,897	69,945	8,275
2017–18	671,880	885,870	1,310,988	383,929	92,855	282,858	125,617	669,656	436,173	91,219	25,789	56,187	571,155	372,086	83,888	257,069	69,430	98,501	64,087	7,331

—Not available.

[1] Includes Ph.D., Ed.D., and comparable degrees at the doctoral level. Includes most degrees that were classified as first-professional prior to 2010–11, such as M.D., D.D.S., and law degrees.

[2] Part of the increase is due to the addition of schools accredited by the Accrediting Commission of Career Schools and Colleges of Technology.

NOTE: Data are for postsecondary institutions participating in Title IV federal financial aid programs. Some data have been revised from previously published figures.

SOURCE: U.S. Department of Education, National Center for Education Statistics, Higher Education General Information Survey (HEGIS), "Degrees and Other Formal Awards Conferred" surveys, 1970–71 through 1985–86; Integrated Postsecondary Education Data System (IPEDS), "Completions Survey" (IPEDS-C:87–99); and IPEDS Fall 2000 through Fall 2018, Completions component. (This table was prepared November 2019.)

Table 318.50. Degrees conferred by postsecondary institutions, by control of institution, level of degree, and field of study: 2017–18

Field of study	All institutions				Public institutions				Private nonprofit institutions				Private for-profit institutions			
	Associate's degrees	Bachelor's degrees	Master's degrees	Doctor's degrees[1]	Associate's degrees	Bachelor's degrees	Master's degrees	Doctor's degrees[1]	Associate's degrees	Bachelor's degrees	Master's degrees	Doctor's degrees[1]	Associate's degrees	Bachelor's degrees	Master's degrees	Doctor's degrees[1]
1	2	3	4	5	6	7	8	9	10	11	12	13	14	15	16	17
All fields, total	1,011,487	1,980,644	820,102	184,074	885,870	1,310,988	383,929	92,855	56,187	571,155	372,086	83,888	69,430	98,501	64,087	7,331
Agriculture and natural resources	8,076	39,314	6,967	1,496	7,799	32,962	5,392	1,378	267	5,708	1,475	118	10	644	100	0
Architecture and related services	539	8,464	7,317	250	511	6,024	4,339	180	27	2,360	2,945	70	1	80	33	0
Area, ethnic, cultural, gender, and group studies	559	7,717	1,673	335	549	5,280	989	204	10	2,437	684	131	0	0	0	0
Biological and biomedical sciences	6,390	118,663	17,180	8,222	6,272	82,654	9,642	5,499	115	35,710	7,514	2,723	3	299	24	0
Business	117,782	386,201	192,184	3,338	94,654	238,673	75,163	1,111	9,494	116,498	96,141	936	13,634	31,030	20,880	1,291
Communication, journalism, and related programs	7,785	92,290	10,243	666	7,658	67,292	4,290	530	71	24,226	5,672	136	56	772	281	0
Communications technologies	4,197	4,231	529	0	3,495	1,606	43	0	77	1,555	342	0	625	1,070	144	0
Computer and information sciences	31,479	79,598	46,468	2,017	26,080	52,555	24,150	1,308	1,588	20,156	19,825	624	3,811	6,887	2,493	85
Construction trades	5,277	151	0	0	4,574	151	0	0	204	0	0	0	499	0	0	0
Education	16,182	82,621	146,367	12,780	14,783	56,931	72,924	6,278	617	22,924	63,055	5,141	782	2,766	10,388	1,361
Engineering	6,408	121,956	51,721	10,817	6,276	96,656	34,574	7,904	31	25,188	17,110	2,913	101	112	37	0
Engineering technologies and engineering-related fields[2]	26,745	18,228	7,246	212	23,740	14,591	3,583	89	1,307	1,986	3,112	123	1,698	1,651	551	0
English language and literature/letters	3,133	40,002	8,300	1,295	3,027	27,549	4,713	958	8	11,907	3,467	337	98	546	120	0
Family and consumer sciences/human sciences	8,854	24,349	3,308	274	8,336	19,618	2,155	233	264	4,121	964	36	254	610	189	5
Foreign languages, literatures, and linguistics	2,607	16,958	3,261	1,213	2,594	12,292	2,277	800	13	4,636	984	413	0	30	0	0
Health professions and related programs	181,056	244,909	125,216	80,305	126,226	135,750	48,713	38,652	21,742	79,069	57,688	38,712	33,088	30,090	18,815	2,941
Homeland security, law enforcement, and firefighting	35,276	58,114	10,293	150	30,139	36,634	4,714	96	1,347	13,929	3,884	20	3,790	7,551	1,695	34
Legal professions and studies	6,237	4,239	9,177	34,544	4,623	2,582	2,472	12,953	449	1,311	6,616	21,093	1,165	346	89	498
Liberal arts and sciences, general studies, and humanities	397,926	44,262	2,473	93	386,151	31,309	1,283	36	10,281	12,771	1,148	47	1,494	182	42	10
Library science	156	81	4,953	54	156	54	4,171	49	0	0	782	5	0	27	0	0
Mathematics and statistics	4,135	25,256	10,443	2,010	4,129	17,390	6,078	1,504	6	7,845	4,365	506	0	21	0	0
Mechanic and repair technologies/technicians	21,295	348	1	0	14,715	198	0	0	2,161	150	1	0	4,419	0	0	0
Military technologies and applied sciences	1,226	655	355	0	1,180	175	57	0	0	392	290	0	46	88	8	0
Multi/interdisciplinary studies	31,068	51,909	10,175	850	30,155	37,041	5,461	570	433	11,545	4,271	280	480	3,323	443	0
Parks, recreation, leisure, and fitness studies	5,095	53,883	9,005	298	4,636	39,994	5,854	254	193	13,214	3,000	40	266	675	151	4
Philosophy and religious studies	1,049	9,603	1,692	768	371	4,287	527	292	678	5,268	1,165	476	0	48	0	0
Physical sciences and science technologies	10,116	31,542	7,196	6,181	10,042	22,820	5,324	4,479	74	8,722	1,872	1,702	0	0	0	0
Precision production	5,333	45	0	0	4,823	1	0	0	179	44	11	0	331	0	0	0
Psychology	12,489	116,432	27,841	6,275	12,095	81,526	9,250	2,577	383	33,420	14,873	2,856	11	1,486	3,718	842
Public administration and social services	7,136	35,629	46,294	1,157	5,516	23,902	27,763	573	1,198	9,344	16,825	352	422	2,383	1,706	232
Social sciences and history	23,683	159,967	19,884	4,676	23,570	110,767	10,409	3,063	86	48,395	8,978	1,594	27	805	497	19
Social sciences	21,545	136,585	16,612	3,765	21,495	94,879	8,313	2,486	50	41,148	8,012	1,260	0	558	287	19
History	2,138	23,382	3,272	911	2,075	15,888	2,096	577	36	7,247	966	334	27	247	210	0
Theology and religious vocations	1,435	9,521	13,828	2,023	0	0	0	0	1,435	9,256	13,668	2,014	0	265	160	9
Transportation and materials moving	1,610	4,924	815	16	1,147	2,802	151	1	412	2,118	664	15	51	4	0	0
Visual and performing arts	19,153	88,582	17,686	1,759	15,848	48,922	7,468	1,284	1,037	34,950	8,695	475	2,268	4,710	1,523	0

[1]Includes Ph.D., Ed.D., and comparable degrees at the doctoral level, as well as such degrees as M.D., D.D.S., and law degrees that were classified as first-professional degrees prior to 2010–11.
[2]Excludes "Construction trades" and "Mechanic and repair technologies/technicians," which are listed separately.
NOTE: Data are for degree-granting postsecondary institutions, which are institutions that grant associate's or higher degrees and participate in Title IV federal financial aid programs. To facilitate trend comparisons, certain aggregations have been made of the degree fields as reported in the Integrated Postsecondary Education Data System (IPEDS): "Agriculture and natural resources" includes Agriculture, Agriculture operations, and related sciences and Natural resources and conservation; and "Business" includes Business, management, marketing, and related support services and Personal and culinary services.
SOURCE: U.S. Department of Education, National Center for Education Statistics, Integrated Postsecondary Education Data System (IPEDS), Fall 2018, Completions component. (This table was prepared February 2020.)

Table 318.60. Number of postsecondary institutions conferring degrees, by control of institution, level of degree, and field of study: 2017–18

Field of study	All institutions				Public institutions				Private nonprofit institutions				Private for-profit institutions			
	Associate's degrees	Bachelor's degrees	Master's degrees	Doctor's degrees[1]	Associate's degrees	Bachelor's degrees	Master's degrees	Doctor's degrees[1]	Associate's degrees	Bachelor's degrees	Master's degrees	Doctor's degrees[1]	Associate's degrees	Bachelor's degrees	Master's degrees	Doctor's degrees[1]
1	2	3	4	5	6	7	8	9	10	11	12	13	14	15	16	17
All fields, total	**2,457**	**2,335**	**1,884**	**1,011**	**1,242**	**712**	**557**	**364**	**635**	**1,326**	**1,151**	**599**	**580**	**297**	**176**	**48**
Agriculture and natural resources	515	799	241	106	490	355	184	95	23	438	56	11	2	6	1	0
Architecture and related services	75	198	160	41	70	120	105	30	4	74	53	11	1	4	2	0
Area, ethnic, cultural, gender, and group studies	75	475	150	60	70	241	102	39	5	234	48	21	0	0	0	0
Biological and biomedical sciences	307	1,378	522	268	289	544	351	183	17	829	170	85	0	5	1	0
Business	1,598	1,791	1,238	212	1,085	635	458	111	260	954	658	89	253	202	122	12
Communication, journalism, and related programs	309	1,186	361	78	286	472	228	61	16	688	129	17	7	26	4	0
Communications technologies	304	153	22	0	282	55	7	0	7	77	13	0	15	21	2	0
Computer and information sciences	1,177	1,352	553	176	920	554	315	120	86	669	182	52	171	129	56	4
Construction trades	357	6	0	0	326	6	0	0	13	0	0	0	18	0	0	0
Education	694	1,244	1,162	449	615	491	477	249	62	732	636	188	17	21	49	12
Engineering	405	566	337	219	382	304	224	158	16	254	110	61	7	8	3	0
Engineering technologies and engineering-related fields[2]	920	344	182	25	834	241	122	14	37	77	56	11	49	26	4	0
English language and literature/letters	213	1,329	499	151	204	521	324	104	6	801	174	47	3	7	1	0
Family and consumer sciences/human sciences	499	355	166	52	476	207	114	39	16	139	48	12	7	9	4	1
Foreign languages, literatures, and linguistics	201	871	226	99	196	398	165	67	5	472	61	32	0	1	0	0
Health professions and related programs	1,700	1,514	1,116	601	1,055	582	430	268	237	751	582	303	408	181	104	30
Homeland security, law enforcement, and firefighting	1,072	958	334	34	869	384	187	27	98	448	125	4	105	126	22	3
Legal professions and studies	520	246	173	213	384	92	71	87	42	121	97	119	94	33	5	7
Liberal arts and sciences, general studies, and humanities	1,390	896	165	18	1,092	382	89	7	290	508	74	10	8	6	2	1
Library science	29	6	63	10	29	5	51	8	0	0	12	2	0	1	0	0
Mathematics and statistics	230	1,200	356	179	226	507	264	128	4	692	92	51	0	1	0	0
Mechanic and repair technologies/technicians	696	18	1	0	628	11	0	0	20	7	1	0	48	0	0	0
Military technologies and applied sciences	11	20	12	0	8	6	3	0	0	10	7	0	3	4	2	0
Multi/interdisciplinary studies	414	1,009	405	133	383	418	230	94	27	569	170	39	4	22	5	0
Parks, recreation, leisure, and fitness studies	329	883	317	53	302	359	219	45	15	516	97	7	12	8	1	1
Philosophy and religious studies	96	892	229	117	74	314	93	58	22	577	136	59	0	1	0	0
Physical sciences and science technologies	377	1,112	329	221	365	490	244	155	12	622	85	66	0	0	0	0
Precision production	410	6	2	0	389	1	0	0	9	5	2	0	12	0	0	0
Psychology	260	1,455	698	324	233	547	348	168	26	885	337	147	0	23	13	9
Public administration and social services	356	810	557	135	309	380	322	88	33	409	205	45	14	21	30	2
Social sciences and history	298	1,366	469	194	278	535	317	137	19	816	147	56	1	15	5	1
Social sciences	276	1,277	403	183	262	520	268	128	14	744	130	54	0	13	5	1
History	179	1,230	345	142	170	498	270	98	8	727	74	44	1	5	1	5
Theology and religious vocations	121	417	367	158	0	0	0	0	121	416	366	154	0	1	1	4
Transportation and materials moving	107	89	15	4	92	56	8	1	10	31	7	3	5	2	0	0
Visual and performing arts	719	1,399	472	113	603	505	262	75	54	832	200	38	62	62	10	0

[1] Includes Ph.D., Ed.D., and comparable degrees at the doctoral level, as well as such degrees as M.D., D.D.S., and law degrees that were classified as first-professional degrees prior to 2010–11.
[2] Excludes "Construction trades" and "Mechanic and repair technologies/technicians," which are listed separately.
NOTE: Data are for degree-granting postsecondary institutions, which are institutions that grant associate's or higher degrees and participate in Title IV federal financial aid programs. To facilitate trend comparisons, certain aggregations have been made of the degree fields as reported in the Integrated Postsecondary Education Data System (IPEDS): "Agriculture and natural resources" includes Agriculture, agriculture operations, and related sciences and Natural resources and conservation; and "Business" includes Business, management, marketing, and related support services and Personal and culinary services.
SOURCE: U.S. Department of Education, National Center for Education Statistics, Integrated Postsecondary Education Data System (IPEDS), Fall 2018, Completions component. (This table was prepared February 2020.)

Table 319.10. Degrees conferred by postsecondary institutions, by control of institution, level of degree, and state or jurisdiction: 2017–18

State or jurisdiction	Public				Private nonprofit				Private for-profit			
	Associate's degrees	Bachelor's degrees	Master's degrees	Doctor's degrees[1]	Associate's degrees	Bachelor's degrees	Master's degrees	Doctor's degrees[1]	Associate's degrees	Bachelor's degrees	Master's degrees	Doctor's degrees[1]
1	2	3	4	5	6	7	8	9	10	11	12	13
United States	885,870	1,310,988	383,929	92,855	56,187	571,155	372,086	83,888	69,430	98,501	64,087	7,331
Alabama	9,914	25,353	10,175	1,965	234	3,786	925	682	2,152	3,359	2,019	16
Alaska	1,172	1,876	561	57	11	47	67	4	38	0	0	0
Arizona	19,383	31,505	9,986	2,106	189	827	630	852	8,192	24,863	16,319	667
Arkansas	8,628	13,667	5,495	951	391	2,534	526	87	42	14	21	0
California	159,087	160,876	32,775	7,167	1,980	40,715	38,768	9,976	9,822	15,221	8,939	2,569
Colorado	10,341	26,788	9,006	1,934	411	4,133	3,742	603	2,599	4,628	1,941	388
Connecticut	5,237	11,497	3,421	730	843	10,502	7,801	1,469	204	828	189	0
Delaware	1,979	4,828	1,039	334	129	2,522	3,222	163	13	35	20	0
District of Columbia	172	338	114	64	218	8,684	11,744	3,340	268	587	949	0
Florida	74,651	75,432	19,009	5,130	12,409	22,365	13,685	3,948	5,971	7,048	2,059	194
Georgia	16,581	39,776	12,184	2,695	869	10,318	5,028	1,939	1,429	2,443	2,526	233
Hawaii	3,823	4,693	1,035	513	407	1,577	498	0	23	188	52	0
Idaho	3,581	6,648	1,860	362	1,676	5,664	195	23	127	0	0	0
Illinois	34,422	32,948	13,142	3,123	942	31,243	25,153	5,439	2,419	11,419	5,230	245
Indiana	11,185	33,171	10,336	2,723	1,521	14,491	5,524	1,295	440	102	37	0
Iowa	12,805	17,079	5,365	1,601	337	9,609	2,734	1,349	213	597	133	0
Kansas	9,564	15,922	5,662	1,481	296	3,736	1,412	190	834	648	454	0
Kentucky	10,383	19,086	5,665	1,735	294	4,609	4,598	567	1,162	566	308	93
Louisiana	5,782	19,031	5,557	1,553	270	3,466	2,037	853	500	0	0	0
Maine	2,487	4,388	845	140	111	3,185	1,380	529	97	0	0	0
Maryland	16,780	28,253	11,840	2,141	3	6,062	8,825	932	182	255	236	0
Massachusetts	11,251	21,932	6,436	841	1,222	39,614	34,721	7,618	172	232	91	0
Michigan	24,338	48,140	17,205	4,626	2,248	12,394	4,353	1,163	189	176	69	0
Minnesota	15,279	21,555	5,466	1,736	674	10,955	5,777	1,108	1,270	4,641	13,870	2,337
Mississippi	13,576	13,482	3,415	1,113	58	2,306	1,713	277	85	8	18	0
Missouri	12,351	23,039	7,401	1,760	2,925	17,801	13,170	3,310	498	402	87	0
Montana	2,056	5,101	1,226	437	132	788	82	0	10	0	0	0
Nebraska	4,478	9,089	3,017	794	170	5,270	2,626	869	55	15	0	0
Nevada	5,558	8,589	1,818	536	64	499	316	504	511	341	59	0
New Hampshire	2,109	5,377	1,124	168	2,081	11,821	8,413	296	0	0	0	0
New Jersey	21,280	33,368	9,950	2,291	325	10,208	7,243	969	1,561	795	159	0
New Mexico	9,661	8,558	2,935	671	0	166	276	0	228	161	36	0
New York	52,244	66,533	18,763	3,177	6,932	70,921	54,804	11,640	6,484	3,654	1,488	1
North Carolina	31,738	40,484	11,955	2,744	908	14,838	6,422	2,310	852	631	432	0
North Dakota	1,983	5,844	1,381	500	171	728	388	122	164	8	0	0
Ohio	24,778	49,982	15,929	4,513	3,131	21,166	8,201	1,548	2,487	513	112	3
Oklahoma	10,201	17,424	5,314	1,350	183	3,892	1,538	270	395	46	0	0
Oregon	13,825	18,431	4,613	1,071	34	5,257	3,510	1,151	381	17	70	0
Pennsylvania	17,157	48,815	13,117	3,442	3,335	42,405	26,281	7,078	3,214	609	172	0
Rhode Island	1,944	4,781	831	275	1,586	7,528	2,348	487	0	0	0	0
South Carolina	9,966	19,759	4,992	1,563	316	6,247	1,083	180	305	311	235	140
South Dakota	2,039	4,702	1,301	447	66	1,042	440	3	145	247	9	4
Tennessee	11,997	22,544	5,589	1,959	785	12,382	5,736	1,976	1,076	449	257	172
Texas	88,326	112,806	43,154	8,702	1,593	20,903	11,158	2,524	4,367	1,958	714	36
Utah	12,035	16,584	4,088	863	1,306	23,907	12,424	224	642	346	117	195
Vermont	873	3,380	479	228	154	3,190	1,988	147	55	60	0	0
Virginia	18,331	37,866	11,712	3,409	1,610	17,223	11,051	2,046	3,571	3,620	1,762	37
Washington	30,385	26,990	6,555	2,007	119	6,954	3,466	737	489	278	68	1
West Virginia	3,485	9,345	2,770	1,015	110	1,472	374	116	2,930	6,131	2,809	0
Wisconsin	11,794	27,731	5,816	1,850	408	9,203	3,690	975	507	51	21	0
Wyoming	2,875	2,127	501	262	0	0	0	0	60	0	0	0
U.S. Service Academies	0	3,475	4	0	†	†	†	†	†	†	†	†
Other jurisdictions	2,501	7,966	948	510	3,489	10,972	3,994	714	2,844	2,028	577	109
American Samoa	215	10	0	0	0	0	0	0	0	0	0	0
Federated States of Micronesia	284	0	0	0	0	0	0	0	0	0	0	0
Guam	283	485	110	0	7	13	0	0	0	0	0	0
Marshall Islands	118	0	0	0	0	0	0	0	0	0	0	0
Northern Marianas	195	47	0	0	0	0	0	0	0	0	0	0
Palau	114	0	0	0	0	0	0	0	0	0	0	0
Puerto Rico	1,261	7,203	777	510	3,482	10,959	3,994	714	2,844	2,028	577	109
U.S. Virgin Islands	31	221	61	0	0	0	0	0	0	0	0	0

†Not applicable.
[1]Includes Ph.D., Ed.D., and comparable degrees at the doctoral level. Includes most degrees classified as first-professional prior to 2010–11, such as M.D., D.D.S., and law degrees.

NOTE: Data are for postsecondary institutions participating in Title IV federal financial aid programs.
SOURCE: U.S. Department of Education, National Center for Education Statistics, Integrated Postsecondary Education Data System (IPEDS), Fall 2018, Completions component. (This table was prepared May 2020.)

Table 319.20. Degrees conferred by postsecondary institutions, by level of degree and state or jurisdiction: 2015–16 through 2017–18

State or jurisdiction	2015–16				2016–17				2017–18			
	Associate's degrees	Bachelor's degrees	Master's degrees	Doctor's degrees[1]	Associate's degrees	Bachelor's degrees	Master's degrees	Doctor's degrees[1]	Associate's degrees	Bachelor's degrees	Master's degrees	Doctor's degrees[1]
1	2	3	4	5	6	7	8	9	10	11	12	13
United States	1,008,228	1,920,750	785,757	178,134	1,005,687	1,956,114	804,542	181,357	1,011,487	1,980,644	820,102	184,074
Alabama	12,882	31,123	12,074	2,432	13,042	31,912	12,753	2,585	12,300	32,498	13,119	2,663
Alaska	1,372	1,957	670	53	1,353	2,006	633	59	1,221	1,923	628	61
Arizona	33,564	56,625	27,353	3,607	30,019	56,385	26,274	3,565	27,764	57,195	26,935	3,625
Arkansas	8,767	16,019	5,277	1,041	8,600	16,107	6,149	1,022	9,061	16,215	6,042	1,038
California	143,571	203,797	77,468	18,820	151,343	211,947	79,142	19,336	170,889	216,812	80,482	19,712
Colorado	14,027	33,580	14,934	2,969	13,523	34,590	14,812	2,899	13,351	35,549	14,689	2,925
Connecticut	7,320	22,721	10,829	2,052	6,908	23,365	11,391	2,234	6,284	22,827	11,411	2,199
Delaware	2,064	6,988	3,903	418	2,091	6,873	3,938	418	2,121	7,385	4,281	497
District of Columbia	603	9,337	11,512	3,496	727	9,519	12,059	3,443	658	9,609	12,807	3,404
Florida	93,341	101,876	33,785	9,098	92,755	103,726	34,928	9,274	93,031	104,845	34,753	9,272
Georgia	19,815	50,827	18,557	4,751	19,342	51,997	18,956	4,863	18,879	52,537	19,738	4,867
Hawaii	4,571	6,922	1,917	527	4,452	6,812	1,733	537	4,253	6,458	1,585	513
Idaho	5,588	11,424	1,860	413	5,310	11,759	1,916	372	5,384	12,312	2,055	385
Illinois	40,410	75,716	42,129	8,860	39,728	76,093	43,774	8,866	37,783	75,610	43,525	8,807
Indiana	14,703	47,614	14,841	3,609	14,436	47,964	15,648	3,905	13,146	47,764	15,897	4,018
Iowa	15,639	27,761	8,341	2,721	15,189	27,702	8,315	2,851	13,355	27,285	8,232	2,950
Kansas	11,008	20,249	7,480	1,578	10,692	20,092	7,627	1,634	10,694	20,306	7,528	1,671
Kentucky	12,276	23,221	9,503	2,143	12,350	23,752	9,702	2,164	11,839	24,261	10,571	2,395
Louisiana	7,396	22,602	7,508	2,554	6,931	22,542	7,367	2,471	6,552	22,497	7,594	2,406
Maine	3,103	7,652	2,237	571	2,864	7,688	2,231	670	2,695	7,573	2,225	669
Maryland	17,003	33,883	18,829	2,821	16,877	34,150	19,505	2,840	16,965	34,570	20,901	3,073
Massachusetts	13,776	61,053	38,391	8,475	13,367	61,712	39,039	8,253	12,645	61,778	41,248	8,459
Michigan	29,787	60,305	21,675	5,576	28,283	61,341	22,060	5,640	26,775	60,710	21,627	5,789
Minnesota	19,526	36,588	23,884	5,433	17,927	36,795	24,465	5,346	17,223	37,151	25,113	5,181
Mississippi	13,759	14,702	5,029	1,344	13,497	15,219	5,176	1,421	13,719	15,796	5,146	1,390
Missouri	18,305	41,447	22,162	4,700	17,278	41,207	22,670	5,077	15,774	41,242	20,658	5,070
Montana	2,339	6,011	1,196	430	2,244	5,994	1,211	489	2,198	5,889	1,308	437
Nebraska	5,144	14,301	5,506	1,699	5,067	14,133	5,972	1,607	4,703	14,374	5,643	1,663
Nevada	6,097	8,638	2,229	1,016	6,169	8,944	2,187	1,091	6,133	9,429	2,193	1,040
New Hampshire	3,076	12,527	6,960	468	3,699	14,869	7,634	432	4,190	17,198	9,537	464
New Jersey	23,845	42,464	16,970	2,987	23,421	43,720	17,079	3,147	23,166	44,371	17,352	3,260
New Mexico	9,435	9,183	3,212	656	10,457	9,207	3,308	651	9,889	8,885	3,247	671
New York	66,966	139,136	71,571	14,668	65,436	139,738	73,163	14,292	65,660	141,108	75,055	14,818
North Carolina	32,108	53,537	18,162	4,607	33,887	54,947	18,662	5,138	33,498	55,953	18,809	5,054
North Dakota	2,222	6,298	1,625	569	2,349	6,427	1,682	554	2,318	6,580	1,769	622
Ohio	31,494	70,052	24,213	6,046	31,374	71,631	24,922	6,013	30,396	71,661	24,242	6,064
Oklahoma	12,027	21,024	6,576	1,662	11,561	21,297	6,735	1,713	10,779	21,362	6,852	1,620
Oregon	12,955	22,614	10,024	1,973	13,161	23,400	9,093	2,123	14,240	23,705	8,193	2,222
Pennsylvania	25,877	92,353	36,940	10,077	24,398	92,757	38,079	10,426	23,706	91,829	39,570	10,520
Rhode Island	3,291	11,989	2,676	716	3,353	12,180	2,942	744	3,530	12,309	3,179	762
South Carolina	11,517	25,107	6,068	1,892	11,259	25,831	6,193	1,825	10,587	26,317	6,310	1,883
South Dakota	2,236	6,040	1,538	437	2,319	6,068	1,563	395	2,250	5,991	1,750	454
Tennessee	13,225	35,255	11,841	3,670	13,538	35,801	12,180	3,981	13,858	35,375	11,502	4,107
Texas	86,838	126,128	52,585	10,978	91,644	130,818	53,047	11,072	94,286	135,667	55,026	11,262
Utah	13,367	34,118	11,081	1,263	13,778	36,862	13,354	1,277	13,983	40,837	16,629	1,282
Vermont	1,176	6,222	2,251	347	1,056	6,428	2,486	352	1,082	6,630	2,467	375
Virginia	25,123	58,642	24,665	5,258	24,187	58,563	24,658	5,455	23,512	58,709	24,525	5,492
Washington	30,591	33,598	9,750	2,591	30,217	34,218	10,090	2,642	30,993	34,222	10,089	2,745
West Virginia	6,479	16,519	6,244	1,160	6,456	16,344	6,330	1,233	6,525	16,948	5,953	1,131
Wisconsin	13,854	37,493	9,298	2,686	13,008	37,075	9,229	2,728	12,709	36,985	9,527	2,825
Wyoming	2,770	2,164	425	216	2,765	2,207	475	232	2,935	2,127	501	262
U.S. Service Academies	0	3,348	3	0	0	3,400	5	0	0	3,475	4	0
Other jurisdictions	9,635	21,422	5,642	1,476	8,979	17,080	5,424	1,143	8,834	20,966	5,519	1,333
American Samoa	216	17	0	0	220	8	0	0	215	10	0	0
Federated States of Micronesia	281	0	0	0	241	0	0	0	284	0	0	0
Guam	253	470	112	0	263	456	121	0	290	498	110	0
Marshall Islands	86	0	0	0	103	0	0	0	118	0	0	0
Northern Marianas	120	34	0	0	140	30	0	0	195	47	0	0
Palau	63	0	0	0	102	0	0	0	114	0	0	0
Puerto Rico	8,572	20,684	5,486	1,476	7,874	16,358	5,255	1,143	7,587	20,190	5,348	1,333
U.S. Virgin Islands	44	217	44	0	36	228	48	0	31	221	61	0

[1]Includes Ph.D., Ed.D., and comparable degrees at the doctoral level. Includes most degrees classified as first-professional prior to 2010–11, such as M.D., D.D.S., and law degrees.
NOTE: Data are for postsecondary institutions participating in Title IV federal financial aid programs. Some data have been revised from previously published figures.

SOURCE: U.S. Department of Education, National Center for Education Statistics, Integrated Postsecondary Education Data System (IPEDS), Fall 2016 through Fall 2018, Completions component. (This table was prepared May 2020.)

Table 320.10. Certificates below the associate's degree level conferred by postsecondary institutions, by length of curriculum, sex of student, institution level and control, and field of study: 2017–18

	Less-than-1-year certificates								1- to less-than-4-year certificates							
	Sex			Institution level		Institution control			Sex			Institution level		Institution control		
Field of study	Total	Males	Females	Non-degree-granting (less-than-2-year)[1]	Degree-granting (2-year and 4-year)	Public	Nonprofit	For-profit	Total	Males	Females	Non-degree-granting (less-than-2-year)[1]	Degree-granting (2-year and 4-year)	Public	Nonprofit	For-profit
1	2	3	4	5	6	7	8	9	10	11	12	13	14	15	16	17
Total	518,424	247,426	270,998	97,192	421,232	406,906	9,378	102,140	436,314	172,758	263,556	139,093	297,221	264,974	16,411	154,929
Agriculture and natural resources	4,777	2,844	1,933	84	4,693	4,597	41	139	2,628	1,693	935	142	2,486	2,412	95	121
Agriculture, agriculture operations, and related sciences	3,635	2,209	1,426	84	3,551	3,531	28	76	2,388	1,524	864	141	2,247	2,178	89	121
Natural resources and conservation	1,142	635	507	0	1,142	1,066	13	63	240	169	71	1	239	234	6	0
Architecture and related services	259	166	93	0	259	245	14	0	97	58	39	0	97	96	0	1
Area, ethnic, cultural, gender, and group studies	862	185	677	0	862	857	5	0	101	25	76	0	101	75	26	0
Biological and biomedical sciences	593	203	390	9	584	575	9	9	213	74	139	100	113	177	36	0
Business, management, marketing, and support services	70,106	26,734	43,372	2,051	68,055	63,437	958	5,711	21,589	6,631	14,958	1,971	19,618	19,492	820	1,277
Accounting and related services	11,782	3,459	8,323	408	11,374	11,046	136	600	4,939	1,249	3,690	506	4,433	4,540	294	105
Business/commerce, general	2,788	1,183	1,605	2	2,786	2,786	1	1	1,604	761	843	0	1,604	1,581	1	22
Business administration, management, and operations	22,387	9,379	13,008	49	22,338	20,537	131	1,719	5,430	1,952	3,478	89	5,341	5,369	22	39
Management information systems and services	607	424	183	28	579	474	133	0	121	88	33	39	82	113	0	8
Business operations support and assistant services	9,004	2,834	6,170	1,053	7,951	8,013	7	984	4,831	865	3,966	1,260	3,571	3,690	186	955
Business and management, other	23,538	9,455	14,083	513	23,025	20,581	550	2,407	4,664	1,716	2,948	77	4,587	4,199	317	148
Communication, journalism, and related programs	3,960	1,829	2,131	909	3,051	2,561	46	1,353	1,022	557	465	518	504	592	16	414
Communications technologies	3,286	2,188	1,098	502	2,784	2,591	4	691	2,600	1,893	707	1,224	1,376	1,479	26	1,095
Computer and information sciences and support services	31,968	24,305	7,663	2,243	29,725	27,459	420	4,089	9,500	7,492	2,008	2,100	7,400	8,107	146	1,247
Construction trades	14,576	13,715	861	2,437	12,139	12,637	526	1,413	12,626	12,037	589	3,737	8,889	9,668	566	2,392
Education	8,855	890	7,965	48	8,807	7,919	430	506	3,863	499	3,364	58	3,805	2,834	772	257
Engineering	1,057	833	224	192	865	907	4	146	396	330	66	170	226	368	28	0
Engineering technologies and engineering-related fields[2]	22,883	19,687	3,196	1,960	20,923	20,857	98	1,928	13,491	11,963	1,528	2,009	11,482	10,340	459	2,692
English language and literature/letters	962	299	663	239	723	713	142	107	450	166	284	78	372	136	35	279
Family and consumer sciences/human sciences	18,456	1,224	17,232	932	17,524	18,256	64	136	4,044	172	3,872	366	3,678	3,989	41	14
Foreign languages, literatures, and linguistics	2,104	454	1,650	8	2,096	1,939	164	1	674	136	538	2	672	664	10	0
Health professions and related programs	144,958	29,424	115,534	34,099	110,859	103,317	2,778	38,863	138,699	18,785	119,914	45,424	93,275	64,347	8,113	66,239
Dental assisting	5,896	461	5,435	1,617	4,279	1,433	268	4,195	9,970	820	9,150	3,590	6,380	4,027	213	5,730
Emergency medical technician (EMT paramedic)	18,423	11,400	7,023	1,213	17,210	17,980	99	344	5,814	4,279	1,535	428	5,386	5,480	121	213
Clinical/medical lab science	9,775	1,341	8,434	2,477	7,298	6,943	226	2,606	1,787	422	1,365	238	1,549	632	463	692
Medical assisting	10,651	738	9,913	4,849	5,802	2,791	12	7,848	37,767	2,979	34,788	14,530	23,237	6,319	1,876	29,572
Pharmacy assisting	2,626	535	2,091	1,177	1,449	1,276	42	1,308	3,934	822	3,112	1,253	2,681	1,476	200	2,258
Other allied health assisting	7,287	2,463	4,824	1,416	5,871	5,316	1	1,970	2,002	197	1,805	567	1,435	1,122	164	716
Nursing and patient care assistant	40,599	4,917	35,682	8,015	32,584	35,819	524	4,256	892	122	770	304	588	453	0	439
Practical nursing	5,135	647	4,488	526	4,609	4,770	7	358	40,597	4,155	36,442	13,585	27,012	27,996	1,040	11,561
Nursing, registered nurse and other	1,384	178	1,206	0	1,384	1,378	6	0	2,287	295	1,992	1,448	839	816	1,273	198
Health sciences, other	43,182	6,744	36,438	12,809	30,373	25,611	1,593	15,978	33,649	4,694	28,955	9,481	24,168	16,026	2,763	14,860
Homeland security, law enforcement, and firefighting	34,156	25,542	8,614	2,036	32,120	32,952	467	737	7,531	4,959	2,572	488	7,043	6,848	72	611
Criminal justice and corrections	20,714	13,547	7,167	1,058	19,656	19,752	359	603	6,401	3,959	2,442	432	5,969	5,768	22	611
Fire control and safety	12,508	11,457	1,051	932	11,576	12,491	4	13	997	908	89	56	941	997	0	0
Homeland security and related protective services, other	934	538	396	46	888	709	104	121	133	92	41	0	133	83	50	0
Legal professions and studies	1,943	379	1,564	23	1,920	1,428	242	273	2,368	399	1,969	236	2,132	1,968	203	197
Liberal arts and sciences, general studies, and humanities	3,883	1,416	2,467	0	3,883	3,881	2	0	65,701	26,091	39,610	0	65,701	65,616	85	0
Library science	216	48	168	0	216	216	0	0	44	9	35	0	44	40	4	0
Mathematics and statistics	270	203	67	0	270	262	8	0	67	48	19	0	67	57	10	0
Mechanic and repair technologies/technicians	39,191	37,024	2,167	3,637	35,554	36,715	294	2,182	45,047	42,831	2,216	17,574	27,473	24,082	1,071	19,894
Military technologies and applied sciences	47	40	7	0	47	33	0	14	10	9	1	7	3	7	3	0
Multi/interdisciplinary studies	2,423	939	1,484	0	2,423	2,126	89	208	1,683	878	805	0	1,683	1,680	3	0

See notes at end of table.

Table 320.10. Certificates below the associate's degree level conferred by postsecondary institutions, by length of curriculum, sex of student, institution level and control, and field of study: 2017–18—Continued

Field of study	Less-than-1-year certificates								1- to less-than-4-year certificates							
	Sex			Institution level		Institution control			Total	Sex		Institution level		Institution control		
	Total	Males	Females	Non-degree-granting (less-than-2-year)[1]	Degree-granting (2-year and 4-year)[1]	Public	Nonprofit	For-profit		Males	Females	Non-degree-granting (less-than-2-year)[1]	Degree-granting (2-year and 4-year)	Public	Nonprofit	For-profit
1	2	3	4	5	6	7	8	9	10	11	12	13	14	15	16	17
Parks, recreation, leisure, and fitness studies studies	1,756	838	918	414	1,342	1,333	0	423	422	224	198	83	339	271	15	136
Personal and culinary services	42,209	5,342	36,867	31,388	10,821	11,346	373	30,490	67,528	10,561	56,967	55,068	12,460	13,357	745	53,426
Philosophy and religious studies	100	52	48	0	100	68	32	0	48	21	27	0	48	18	30	0
Physical sciences and science technologies	1,535	787	748	56	1,479	1,535	0	0	1,243	790	453	27	1,216	1,216	0	27
Physical sciences	276	166	110	0	276	276	0	0	28	19	9	0	28	28	0	0
Science technologies/technicians	1,259	621	638	56	1,203	1,259	0	0	1,215	771	444	27	1,188	1,188	0	27
Precision production	30,505	28,476	2,029	4,408	26,097	26,478	353	3,674	18,660	17,482	1,178	6,101	12,559	14,357	1,130	3,173
Psychology	201	27	174	0	201	178	23	0	95	26	69	0	95	93	2	0
Public administration and social services	2,233	436	1,797	0	2,233	1,820	48	365	810	126	684	0	810	728	39	43
Social sciences and history	1,588	742	846	3	1,585	1,496	92	0	496	263	233	0	496	395	101	0
Social sciences	1,538	728	810	3	1,535	1,447	91	0	485	257	228	0	485	384	101	0
History	50	14	36	0	50	49	1	0	11	6	5	0	11	11	0	0
Theology and religious vocations	260	125	135	0	260	0	252	8	895	363	532	320	575	0	895	0
Transportation and materials moving	18,741	16,612	2,129	8,546	10,195	9,618	737	8,386	1,063	978	85	346	717	695	20	348
Visual and performing arts	7,505	3,418	4,087	968	6,537	6,554	663	288	10,610	4,189	6,421	944	9,666	8,770	794	1,046
Fine and studio arts	862	281	581	618	244	241	525	96	6,187	2,273	3,914	79	6,108	6,081	34	72
Music and dance	377	234	143	0	377	312	7	58	427	230	197	89	338	140	129	158
Visual and performing arts, other[3]	6,266	2,903	3,363	350	5,916	6,001	131	134	3,996	1,686	2,310	776	3,220	2,549	631	816

[1]Non-degree-granting institutions do not offer accredited 4-year or 2-year programs for degrees at the associate's or higher level, but they may include institutions offering programs 2 years or longer in duration for lower level awards.

[2]Excludes "Construction trades" and "Mechanic and repair technologies/technicians," which are listed separately.

[3]Includes design and applied arts, drama and theatre arts, film and photographic arts, and all other arts not included under "Fine and studio arts" or "Music and dance."

NOTE: Data are for postsecondary institutions participating in Title IV federal financial aid programs. Degree-granting institutions grant degrees at the associate's or higher level, while non-degree-granting institutions grant only awards below that level.
SOURCE: U.S. Department of Education, National Center for Education Statistics, Integrated Postsecondary Education Data System (IPEDS), Fall 2018, Completions component. (This table was prepared May 2020.)

Table 320.20. Certificates below the associate's degree level conferred by postsecondary institutions, by race/ethnicity and sex of student: 1998–99 through 2017–18

Year and sex	Number of certificates conferred to U.S. citizens, permanent residents, and nonresident aliens								Percentage distribution of certificates conferred to U.S. citizens and permanent residents						
	Total	White	Black	Hispanic	Asian/Pacific Islander	American Indian/Alaska Native	Two or more races	Non-resident alien	Total	White	Black	Hispanic	Asian/Pacific Islander	American Indian/Alaska Native	Two or more races
1	2	3	4	5	6	7	8	9	10	11	12	13	14	15	16
Total															
1998–99	555,883	345,359	92,800	76,833	27,920	7,510	—	5,461	100.0	62.7	16.9	14.0	5.1	1.4	—
1999–2000	558,129	337,546	97,329	81,132	29,361	6,966	—	5,795	100.0	61.1	17.6	14.7	5.3	1.3	—
2000–01	552,503	333,478	99,397	78,528	28,123	6,598	—	6,379	100.0	61.1	18.2	14.4	5.1	1.2	—
2001–02	584,248	352,559	106,647	83,950	27,490	7,430	—	6,172	100.0	61.0	18.4	14.5	4.8	1.3	—
2002–03	646,425	382,289	120,582	95,499	32,981	8,117	—	6,957	100.0	59.8	18.9	14.9	5.2	1.3	—
2003–04	687,787	402,989	129,891	107,216	32,819	8,375	—	6,497	100.0	59.2	19.1	15.7	4.8	1.2	—
2004–05	710,873	415,670	133,601	114,089	32,783	8,150	—	6,580	100.0	59.0	19.0	16.2	4.7	1.2	—
2005–06	714,790	411,919	135,387	118,728	33,848	8,393	—	6,515	100.0	58.2	19.1	16.8	4.8	1.2	—
2006–07	728,315	420,199	139,796	119,375	32,963	8,781	—	7,201	100.0	58.3	19.4	16.6	4.6	1.2	—
2007–08	748,354	429,670	144,982	122,406	35,791	8,548	—	6,957	100.0	58.0	19.6	16.5	4.8	1.2	—
2008–09	804,620	450,562	161,487	138,301	37,941	9,485	—	6,844	100.0	56.5	20.2	17.3	4.8	1.2	—
2009–10	935,719	511,186	191,657	172,015	41,407	12,003	—	7,451	100.0	55.1	20.6	18.5	4.5	1.3	—
2010–11	1,030,477	557,595	207,693	187,433	44,294	11,204	14,999	7,259	100.0	54.5	20.3	18.3	4.3	1.1	1.5
2011–12	989,061	535,621	190,253	187,014	43,048	10,638	14,140	8,347	100.0	54.6	19.4	19.1	4.4	1.1	1.4
2012–13	967,214	524,000	177,006	186,248	44,196	10,824	17,642	7,298	100.0	54.6	18.4	19.4	4.6	1.1	1.8
2013–14	969,278	523,015	177,860	185,677	43,800	10,817	19,971	8,138	100.0	54.4	18.5	19.3	4.6	1.1	2.1
2014–15	961,146	512,077	174,828	187,943	44,707	11,084	21,681	8,826	100.0	53.8	18.4	19.7	4.7	1.2	2.3
2015–16	939,291	496,717	162,367	192,977	43,923	10,558	23,222	9,527	100.0	53.4	17.5	20.8	4.7	1.1	2.5
2016–17	946,023	493,302	159,209	202,731	44,886	10,911	24,710	10,274	100.0	52.7	17.0	21.7	4.8	1.2	2.6
2017–18	954,738	495,461	150,779	212,099	47,088	10,998	26,882	11,431	100.0	52.5	16.0	22.5	5.0	1.2	2.8
Males															
1998–99	219,872	144,735	29,875	27,719	11,742	3,061	—	2,740	100.0	66.7	13.8	12.8	5.4	1.4	—
1999–2000	226,110	143,634	33,792	30,337	13,082	2,862	—	2,403	100.0	64.2	15.1	13.6	5.8	1.3	—
2000–01	223,951	143,144	34,381	28,685	12,072	2,719	—	2,950	100.0	64.8	15.6	13.0	5.5	1.2	—
2001–02	235,275	152,226	36,482	29,749	10,938	3,226	—	2,654	100.0	65.4	15.7	12.8	4.7	1.4	—
2002–03	254,238	161,001	40,080	33,925	12,930	3,506	—	2,796	100.0	64.0	15.9	13.5	5.1	1.4	—
2003–04	257,138	161,684	40,809	36,157	12,713	3,135	—	2,640	100.0	63.5	16.0	14.2	5.0	1.2	—
2004–05	259,261	161,126	41,644	38,297	12,448	3,068	—	2,678	100.0	62.8	16.2	14.9	4.9	1.2	—
2005–06	259,413	158,719	41,847	40,682	12,575	3,214	—	2,376	100.0	61.7	16.3	15.8	4.9	1.3	—
2006–07	269,470	164,856	44,862	40,932	12,621	3,524	—	2,675	100.0	61.8	16.8	15.3	4.7	1.3	—
2007–08	283,102	172,438	48,013	43,076	13,460	3,431	—	2,684	100.0	61.5	17.1	15.4	4.8	1.2	—
2008–09	302,449	179,813	53,879	47,860	14,427	3,856	—	2,614	100.0	60.0	18.0	16.0	4.8	1.3	—
2009–10	355,381	205,404	65,487	60,771	15,940	5,067	—	2,712	100.0	58.2	18.6	17.2	4.5	1.4	—
2010–11	391,676	223,755	71,867	66,514	16,944	4,760	4,884	2,952	100.0	57.6	18.5	17.1	4.4	1.2	1.3
2011–12	374,086	213,833	65,224	65,838	16,180	4,507	4,952	3,552	100.0	57.7	17.6	17.8	4.4	1.2	1.3
2012–13	375,928	215,432	61,668	67,377	17,352	4,446	6,511	3,142	100.0	57.8	16.5	18.1	4.7	1.2	1.7
2013–14	390,795	223,180	65,595	68,821	17,280	4,731	7,781	3,407	100.0	57.6	16.9	17.8	4.5	1.2	2.0
2014–15	394,707	222,413	64,574	72,020	18,132	4,848	8,836	3,884	100.0	56.9	16.5	18.4	4.6	1.2	2.3
2015–16	396,834	223,269	60,835	76,483	17,667	4,613	9,622	4,345	100.0	56.9	15.5	19.5	4.5	1.2	2.5
2016–17	405,430	225,423	60,124	81,767	18,034	4,969	10,307	4,806	100.0	56.3	15.0	20.4	4.5	1.2	2.6
2017–18	420,184	231,999	58,064	88,597	19,832	4,987	11,436	5,269	100.0	55.9	14.0	21.4	4.8	1.2	2.8
Females															
1998–99	336,011	200,624	62,925	49,114	16,178	4,449	—	2,721	100.0	60.2	18.9	14.7	4.9	1.3	—
1999–2000	332,019	193,912	63,537	50,795	16,279	4,104	—	3,392	100.0	59.0	19.3	15.5	5.0	1.2	—
2000–01	328,552	190,334	65,016	49,843	16,051	3,879	—	3,429	100.0	58.5	20.0	15.3	4.9	1.2	—
2001–02	348,973	200,333	70,165	54,201	16,552	4,204	—	3,518	100.0	58.0	20.3	15.7	4.8	1.2	—
2002–03	392,187	221,288	80,502	61,574	20,051	4,611	—	4,161	100.0	57.0	20.7	15.9	5.2	1.2	—
2003–04	430,649	241,305	89,082	71,059	20,106	5,240	—	3,857	100.0	56.5	20.9	16.6	4.7	1.2	—
2004–05	451,612	254,544	91,957	75,792	20,335	5,082	—	3,902	100.0	56.9	20.5	16.9	4.5	1.1	—
2005–06	455,377	253,200	93,540	78,046	21,273	5,179	—	4,139	100.0	56.1	20.7	17.3	4.7	1.1	—
2006–07	458,845	255,343	94,934	78,443	20,342	5,257	—	4,526	100.0	56.2	20.9	17.3	4.5	1.2	—
2007–08	465,252	257,232	96,969	79,330	22,331	5,117	—	4,273	100.0	55.8	21.0	17.2	4.8	1.1	—
2008–09	502,171	270,749	107,608	90,441	23,514	5,629	—	4,230	100.0	54.4	21.6	18.2	4.7	1.1	—
2009–10	580,338	305,782	126,170	111,244	25,467	6,936	—	4,739	100.0	53.1	21.9	19.3	4.4	1.2	—
2010–11	638,801	333,840	135,826	120,919	27,350	6,444	10,115	4,307	100.0	52.6	21.4	19.1	4.3	1.0	1.6
2011–12	614,975	321,788	125,029	121,176	26,868	6,131	9,188	4,795	100.0	52.7	20.5	19.9	4.4	1.0	1.5
2012–13	591,286	308,568	115,338	118,871	26,844	6,378	11,131	4,156	100.0	52.6	19.6	20.2	4.6	1.1	1.9
2013–14	578,483	299,835	112,265	116,856	26,520	6,086	12,190	4,731	100.0	52.3	19.6	20.4	4.6	1.1	2.1
2014–15	566,439	289,664	110,254	115,923	26,575	6,236	12,845	4,942	100.0	51.6	19.6	20.6	4.7	1.1	2.3
2015–16	542,457	273,448	101,532	116,494	26,256	5,945	13,600	5,182	100.0	50.9	18.9	21.7	4.9	1.1	2.5
2016–17	540,593	267,879	99,085	120,964	26,852	5,942	14,403	5,468	100.0	50.1	18.5	22.6	5.0	1.1	2.7
2017–18	534,554	263,462	92,715	123,502	27,256	6,011	15,446	6,162	100.0	49.9	17.5	23.4	5.2	1.1	2.9

—Not available.
NOTE: Includes less-than-1-year awards and 1- to less-than-4-year awards (excluding associate's degrees) conferred by postsecondary institutions participating in Title IV federal financial aid programs. Race categories exclude persons of Hispanic ethnicity. Reported racial/ethnic distributions of students by level of degree, field of degree, and sex were used to estimate race/ethnicity for students whose race/ethnicity was not reported.

Some data have been revised from previously published figures. Detail may not sum to totals because of rounding.
SOURCE: U.S. Department of Education, National Center for Education Statistics, Integrated Postsecondary Education Data System (IPEDS), "Completions Survey" (IPEDS-C:99); and IPEDS Fall 2000 through Fall 2018, Completions component. (This table was prepared October 2019.)

Table 321.10. Associate's degrees conferred by postsecondary institutions, by sex of student and discipline division: 2007–08 through 2017–18

Discipline division	2007–08	2008–09	2009–10	2010–11	2011–12	2012–13	2013–14	2014–15	2015–16	2016–17	2017–18 Total	2017–18 Males	2017–18 Females
1	2	3	4	5	6	7	8	9	10	11	12	13	14
Total	**750,166**	**787,243**	**848,856**	**943,506**	**1,021,718**	**1,007,427**	**1,005,155**	**1,014,341**	**1,008,228**	**1,005,687**	**1,011,487**	**398,600**	**612,887**
Agriculture and natural resources	5,738	5,724	5,852	6,430	7,068	6,826	7,057	7,693	7,858	8,208	8,076	4,834	3,242
Agriculture, agriculture operations, and related sciences	4,554	4,525	4,615	4,925	5,400	5,227	5,420	5,975	6,158	6,439	6,306	3,659	2,647
Natural resources and conservation	1,184	1,199	1,237	1,505	1,668	1,599	1,637	1,718	1,700	1,769	1,770	1,175	595
Architecture and related services	568	605	553	569	593	468	425	491	478	503	539	358	181
Area, ethnic, cultural, gender, and group studies	169	174	199	209	194	271	363	382	419	420	559	230	329
Biological and biomedical sciences	2,200	2,337	2,664	3,276	3,834	4,185	4,557	4,883	5,266	5,550	6,390	2,072	4,318
Business	121,221	127,882	133,265	139,994	143,390	134,114	129,957	132,374	128,259	122,252	117,782	47,418	70,364
Business, management, marketing, and support services	104,631	111,524	116,798	121,735	123,014	114,842	113,056	113,681	110,036	108,376	105,751	43,015	62,736
Accounting and related services	15,963	16,707	17,925	20,180	20,270	18,061	17,400	16,080	14,790	13,760	13,013	3,798	9,215
Business/commerce, general	12,496	13,100	14,553	15,083	17,301	17,211	17,372	18,235	18,087	18,293	17,060	7,491	9,569
Business administration, management, and operations	47,910	52,938	46,086	46,253	45,879	49,816	50,121	52,668	52,758	53,930	55,382	25,198	30,184
Management information systems and services	1,232	1,103	1,221	1,244	1,164	1,085	1,176	987	935	953	920	646	274
Business operations support and assistant services	7,838	7,550	7,399	8,259	8,977	7,986	7,331	6,570	5,871	5,141	4,617	473	4,144
Business and management, other	19,192	20,126	29,614	30,716	29,423	20,683	19,656	19,141	17,595	16,299	14,759	5,409	9,350
Personal and culinary services	16,590	16,358	16,467	18,259	20,376	19,272	16,901	18,693	18,223	13,876	12,031	4,403	7,628
Communication, journalism, and related programs	2,620	2,722	2,841	3,051	3,495	4,299	4,970	6,034	6,759	7,379	7,785	3,269	4,516
Communications technologies	4,268	4,805	4,418	4,209	5,004	5,028	4,713	4,628	4,569	4,307	4,197	2,782	1,415
Computer and information sciences and support services	28,298	29,912	32,351	37,689	41,250	38,954	37,646	36,420	30,571	31,171	31,479	25,236	6,243
Construction trades	4,309	4,252	4,684	5,402	5,750	5,038	4,837	4,643	4,699	5,308	5,277	4,968	309
Education	13,111	14,123	17,346	20,460	20,762	18,744	17,605	17,178	17,032	16,603	16,182	1,843	14,339
Engineering	2,279	2,170	2,508	2,825	3,382	3,732	4,306	4,875	5,278	5,915	6,408	5,334	1,074
Engineering technologies and engineering-related fields[1]	29,359	30,441	31,883	35,519	36,642	33,752	31,792	31,958	27,243	27,021	26,745	22,899	3,846
English language and literature/letters	1,402	1,534	1,658	2,019	2,137	2,089	2,082	2,324	2,551	2,870	3,133	1,049	2,084
Family and consumer sciences/human sciences	8,614	9,035	9,515	8,532	9,506	8,996	8,669	8,750	8,930	8,871	8,854	400	8,454
Foreign languages, literatures, and linguistics	1,258	1,630	1,683	1,888	1,980	2,131	2,284	2,102	2,208	2,363	2,607	625	1,982
Health professions and related programs	155,794	165,015	177,321	202,920	219,491	214,040	208,885	200,018	191,442	186,312	181,056	29,483	151,573
Dental assisting	6,642	6,574	7,063	7,498	7,790	7,823	7,988	7,762	7,584	7,397	7,073	361	6,712
Emergency medical technician (EMT paramedic)	2,140	2,270	2,413	2,895	3,352	3,520	3,521	3,456	3,380	3,453	3,410	2,306	1,104
Clinical/medical lab science	2,316	2,538	2,621	2,811	3,240	3,387	3,517	3,143	3,186	3,062	3,051	722	2,329
Medical and other health assisting	24,291	25,858	29,776	39,277	46,950	41,921	39,126	36,813	34,749	32,297	28,723	4,611	24,112
Nursing and patient care assistant	329	385	1	33	36	35	38	50	52	56	100	11	89
Practical nursing	1,417	1,299	1,973	2,069	2,366	2,361	2,230	1,858	1,404	1,420	1,105	99	1,006
Nursing, registered nurse and other	73,398	77,922	81,281	83,023	84,569	86,380	86,435	82,953	78,577	77,083	77,674	11,217	66,457
Health sciences, other	45,261	48,169	52,193	65,314	71,188	68,613	66,030	63,983	62,510	61,544	59,920	10,156	49,764
Homeland security, law enforcement, and firefighting	29,485	33,012	37,154	44,922	51,318	48,460	45,771	43,041	39,930	37,362	35,276	19,997	15,279
Criminal justice and corrections	25,471	28,998	32,648	40,022	45,971	42,785	40,297	37,820	35,122	32,589	30,463	15,713	14,750
Fire control and safety	3,949	3,947	4,307	4,603	4,779	4,910	4,649	4,525	4,241	4,191	4,287	3,916	371
Homeland security and related protective services, other	65	67	199	297	568	765	825	696	567	582	526	368	158
Legal professions and studies	9,464	9,062	9,999	11,619	12,315	11,862	10,502	9,095	8,017	6,904	6,237	1,011	5,226
Liberal arts and sciences, general studies, and humanities	253,990	263,947	284,954	306,674	336,938	344,171	353,946	367,852	381,202	386,746	397,926	151,028	246,898
Library science	117	116	112	160	159	181	194	170	146	158	156	21	135
Mathematics and statistics	855	933	1,051	1,644	1,529	1,801	2,148	2,697	3,027	3,454	4,135	2,880	1,255
Mechanic and repair technologies/technicians	15,518	16,059	16,326	19,969	20,715	20,487	20,100	19,984	20,543	20,821	21,295	19,846	1,449
Military technologies and applied sciences	851	721	668	856	986	1,002	1,084	1,229	1,047	1,093	1,226	946	280
Multi/interdisciplinary studies	16,247	15,472	17,279	23,729	27,263	27,407	28,167	29,139	30,482	30,780	31,068	13,002	18,066
Parks, recreation, leisure, and fitness studies	1,345	1,587	2,006	2,366	3,123	3,455	4,383	4,669	4,771	5,037	5,095	2,758	2,337
Philosophy and religious studies	458	193	256	283	308	326	435	697	814	1,002	1,049	640	409
Physical sciences and science technologies	3,394	3,650	4,141	5,078	5,827	6,376	6,916	7,568	8,484	9,223	10,116	5,927	4,189
Physical sciences	1,979	2,196	2,378	3,148	3,652	4,083	4,518	5,040	5,528	5,838	6,688	3,908	2,780
Science technologies/technicians	1,415	1,454	1,763	1,930	2,175	2,293	2,398	2,528	2,956	3,385	3,428	2,019	1,409
Precision production	1,967	2,127	2,794	3,254	3,320	3,345	3,903	4,382	4,794	5,251	5,333	4,967	366
Psychology	2,411	3,957	6,582	3,866	4,717	6,122	7,604	8,780	10,603	11,283	12,489	2,921	9,568
Public administration and social services	4,194	4,177	4,522	7,472	9,222	8,788	8,914	8,436	7,988	7,591	7,136	1,003	6,133
Social sciences and history	7,812	9,157	10,649	12,772	14,132	15,668	16,554	17,916	20,056	21,392	23,683	8,849	14,834
Social sciences	7,358	8,670	10,108	12,072	13,321	14,749	15,473	16,631	18,451	19,636	21,545	7,516	14,029
History	454	487	541	700	811	919	1,081	1,285	1,605	1,756	2,138	1,333	805
Theology and religious vocations	582	676	613	758	839	881	944	1,135	1,089	1,546	1,435	786	649
Transportation and materials moving	1,550	1,430	1,444	1,698	2,098	2,119	2,102	1,810	1,497	1,547	1,610	1,394	216
Visual and performing arts	18,704	18,606	19,565	21,394	22,431	22,309	21,340	20,988	20,176	19,444	19,153	7,824	11,329
Fine and studio arts	1,706	2,019	2,277	2,414	2,339	2,541	2,699	2,866	3,082	3,315	3,766	1,260	2,506
Music and dance	1,317	1,152	1,335	1,356	1,683	1,743	1,715	1,886	1,989	1,993	2,313	1,456	857
Visual and performing arts, other[2]	15,681	15,435	15,953	17,624	18,409	18,025	16,926	16,236	15,105	14,136	13,074	5,108	7,966
Not classified by field of study	14	0	0	0	0	0	0	0	0	0	0	0	0

[1]Excludes "Construction trades" and "Mechanic and repair technologies/technicians," which are listed separately.
[2]Includes design and applied arts, drama and theatre arts, film and photographic arts, and all other arts not included under "Fine and studio arts" or "Music and dance."
NOTE: Data are for postsecondary institutions participating in Title IV federal financial aid programs. Some data have been revised from previously published figures.

SOURCE: U.S. Department of Education, National Center for Education Statistics, Integrated Postsecondary Education Data System (IPEDS), Fall 2008 through Fall 2018, Completions component. (This table was prepared August 2019.)

Table 321.20. Associate's degrees conferred by postsecondary institutions, by race/ethnicity and sex of student: Selected years, 1976–77 through 2017–18

Year and sex	Number of degrees conferred to U.S. citizens, permanent residents, and nonresident aliens								Percentage distribution of degrees conferred to U.S. citizens and permanent residents						
	Total	White	Black	Hispanic	Asian/ Pacific Islander	American Indian/ Alaska Native	Two or more races[1]	Non-resident alien	Total	White	Black	Hispanic	Asian/ Pacific Islander	American Indian/ Alaska Native	Two or more races[1]
1	2	3	4	5	6	7	8	9	10	11	12	13	14	15	16
Total															
1976–77[2]	404,956	342,290	33,159	16,636	7,044	2,498	—	3,329	100.0	85.2	8.3	4.1	1.8	0.6	—
1980–81[3]	410,174	339,167	35,330	17,800	8,650	2,584	—	6,643	100.0	84.0	8.8	4.4	2.1	0.6	—
1990–91	481,720	391,264	38,835	25,540	15,257	3,871	—	6,953	100.0	82.4	8.2	5.4	3.2	0.8	—
1999–2000	564,933	408,822	60,208	51,563	27,778	6,474	—	10,088	100.0	73.7	10.9	9.3	5.0	1.2	—
2000–01	578,865	411,075	63,855	57,288	28,463	6,623	—	11,561	100.0	72.5	11.3	10.1	5.0	1.2	—
2003–04	665,301	456,047	81,183	72,270	33,149	8,119	—	14,533	100.0	70.1	12.5	11.1	5.1	1.2	—
2004–05	696,660	475,513	86,402	78,557	33,669	8,435	—	14,084	100.0	69.7	12.7	11.5	4.9	1.2	—
2005–06	713,315	485,481	89,813	80,870	35,215	8,555	—	13,381	100.0	69.4	12.8	11.6	5.0	1.2	—
2006–07	727,616	491,333	91,440	85,275	37,243	8,579	—	13,746	100.0	68.8	12.8	11.9	5.2	1.2	—
2007–08	750,166	501,467	95,566	91,289	38,848	8,827	—	14,169	100.0	68.1	13.0	12.4	5.3	1.2	—
2008–09	787,243	521,834	101,631	98,408	41,364	8,823	—	15,183	100.0	67.6	13.2	12.7	5.4	1.1	—
2009–10	848,856	552,376	113,867	112,403	44,026	10,101	—	16,083	100.0	66.3	13.7	13.5	5.3	1.2	—
2010–11	943,506	604,745	129,044	126,297	45,489	10,180	11,126	16,625	100.0	65.2	13.9	13.6	4.9	1.1	1.2
2011–12	1,021,718	635,755	142,512	151,807	48,861	10,738	14,858	17,187	100.0	63.3	14.2	15.1	4.9	1.1	1.5
2012–13	1,007,427	617,308	135,892	157,989	49,474	10,546	19,383	16,835	100.0	62.3	13.7	15.9	5.0	1.1	2.0
2013–14	1,005,155	601,959	134,621	168,106	50,368	10,338	22,695	17,068	100.0	60.9	13.6	17.0	5.1	1.0	2.3
2014–15	1,014,341	590,616	137,920	180,598	51,767	9,996	25,505	17,939	100.0	59.3	13.8	18.1	5.2	1.0	2.6
2015–16	1,008,228	566,622	134,012	196,044	53,753	9,490	28,933	19,374	100.0	57.3	13.6	19.8	5.4	1.0	2.9
2016–17	1,005,687	551,057	129,880	209,159	55,814	9,265	29,603	20,909	100.0	56.0	13.2	21.2	5.7	0.9	3.0
2017–18	1,011,487	536,256	125,517	225,462	58,952	9,285	32,971	23,044	100.0	54.3	12.7	22.8	6.0	0.9	3.3
Males															
1976–77[2]	209,672	178,236	15,330	9,105	3,630	1,216	—	2,155	100.0	85.9	7.4	4.4	1.7	0.6	—
1980–81[3]	183,819	151,242	14,290	8,327	4,557	1,108	—	4,295	100.0	84.2	8.0	4.6	2.5	0.6	—
1990–91	198,634	161,858	14,143	10,738	7,164	1,439	—	3,292	100.0	82.9	7.2	5.5	3.7	0.7	—
1999–2000	224,721	164,317	20,968	20,947	12,009	2,222	—	4,258	100.0	74.5	9.5	9.5	5.4	1.0	—
2000–01	231,645	166,322	22,147	23,350	12,339	2,294	—	5,193	100.0	73.4	9.8	10.3	5.4	1.0	—
2003–04	260,033	183,819	25,961	27,828	13,907	2,740	—	5,778	100.0	72.3	10.2	10.9	5.5	1.1	—
2004–05	267,536	188,569	27,151	29,658	13,802	2,774	—	5,582	100.0	72.0	10.4	11.3	5.3	1.1	—
2005–06	270,139	190,174	27,618	30,043	14,227	2,777	—	5,300	100.0	71.8	10.4	11.3	5.4	1.0	—
2006–07	275,034	191,487	28,251	31,609	15,502	2,872	—	5,313	100.0	71.0	10.5	11.7	5.7	1.1	—
2007–08	282,695	194,354	29,984	33,852	15,941	2,989	—	5,575	100.0	70.1	10.8	12.2	5.8	1.1	—
2008–09	298,066	202,670	32,004	36,919	17,305	3,075	—	6,093	100.0	69.4	11.0	12.6	5.9	1.1	—
2009–10	322,747	215,977	36,148	42,210	18,268	3,555	—	6,589	100.0	68.3	11.4	13.4	5.8	1.1	—
2010–11	361,408	238,012	41,649	47,911	19,085	3,727	4,197	6,827	100.0	67.1	11.7	13.5	5.4	1.1	1.2
2011–12	393,479	251,964	46,377	57,926	20,537	3,924	5,569	7,182	100.0	65.2	12.0	15.0	5.3	1.0	1.4
2012–13	389,195	243,868	45,458	60,536	21,223	3,638	7,434	7,038	100.0	63.8	11.9	15.8	5.6	1.0	1.9
2013–14	391,474	239,289	45,868	64,658	21,824	3,682	8,969	7,184	100.0	62.3	11.9	16.8	5.7	1.0	2.3
2014–15	396,782	236,381	47,393	69,291	22,377	3,590	9,997	7,753	100.0	60.8	12.2	17.8	5.8	0.9	2.6
2015–16	392,084	226,142	44,777	74,531	23,426	3,335	11,251	8,622	100.0	59.0	11.7	19.4	6.1	0.9	2.9
2016–17	394,147	223,637	43,170	78,470	24,459	3,370	11,678	9,363	100.0	58.1	11.2	20.4	6.4	0.9	3.0
2017–18	398,600	219,372	41,820	84,868	25,736	3,366	12,958	10,480	100.0	56.5	10.8	21.9	6.6	0.9	3.3
Females															
1976–77[2]	195,284	164,054	17,829	7,531	3,414	1,282	—	1,174	100.0	84.5	9.2	3.9	1.8	0.7	—
1980–81[3]	226,355	187,925	21,040	9,473	4,093	1,476	—	2,348	100.0	83.9	9.4	4.2	1.8	0.7	—
1990–91	283,086	229,406	24,692	14,802	8,093	2,432	—	3,661	100.0	82.1	8.8	5.3	2.9	0.9	—
1999–2000	340,212	244,505	39,240	30,616	15,769	4,252	—	5,830	100.0	73.1	11.7	9.2	4.7	1.3	—
2000–01	347,220	244,753	41,708	33,938	16,124	4,329	—	6,368	100.0	71.8	12.2	10.0	4.7	1.3	—
2003–04	405,268	272,228	55,222	44,442	19,242	5,379	—	8,755	100.0	68.7	13.9	11.2	4.9	1.4	—
2004–05	429,124	286,944	59,251	48,899	19,867	5,661	—	8,502	100.0	68.2	14.1	11.6	4.7	1.3	—
2005–06	443,176	295,307	62,195	50,827	20,988	5,778	—	8,081	100.0	67.9	14.3	11.7	4.8	1.3	—
2006–07	452,582	299,846	63,189	53,666	21,741	5,707	—	8,433	100.0	67.5	14.2	12.1	4.9	1.3	—
2007–08	467,471	307,113	65,582	57,437	22,907	5,838	—	8,594	100.0	66.9	14.3	12.5	5.0	1.3	—
2008–09	489,177	319,164	69,627	61,489	24,059	5,748	—	9,090	100.0	66.5	14.5	12.8	5.0	1.2	—
2009–10	526,109	336,399	77,719	70,193	25,758	6,546	—	9,494	100.0	65.1	15.0	13.6	5.0	1.3	—
2010–11	582,098	366,733	87,395	78,386	26,404	6,453	6,929	9,798	100.0	64.1	15.3	13.7	4.6	1.1	1.2
2011–12	628,239	383,791	96,135	93,881	28,324	6,814	9,289	10,005	100.0	62.1	15.5	15.2	4.6	1.1	1.5
2012–13	618,232	373,440	90,434	97,453	28,251	6,908	11,949	9,797	100.0	61.4	14.9	16.0	4.6	1.1	2.0
2013–14	613,681	362,670	88,753	103,448	28,544	6,656	13,726	9,884	100.0	60.1	14.7	17.1	4.7	1.1	2.3
2014–15	617,559	354,235	90,527	111,307	29,390	6,406	15,508	10,186	100.0	58.3	14.9	18.3	4.8	1.1	2.6
2015–16	616,144	340,480	89,235	121,513	30,327	6,155	17,682	10,752	100.0	56.2	14.7	20.1	5.0	1.0	2.9
2016–17	611,540	327,420	86,710	130,689	31,355	5,895	17,925	11,546	100.0	54.6	14.5	21.8	5.2	1.0	3.0
2017–18	612,887	316,884	83,697	140,594	33,216	5,919	20,013	12,564	100.0	52.8	13.9	23.4	5.5	1.0	3.3

—Not available.
[1]For years prior to 2010–11, the survey did not yet include the "Two or more races" category, and each student could be counted in only one race category.
[2]Excludes 1,170 males and 251 females whose racial/ethnic group was not available.
[3]Excludes 4,819 males and 1,384 females whose racial/ethnic group was not available.
NOTE: Data are for postsecondary institutions participating in Title IV federal financial aid programs. Race categories exclude persons of Hispanic ethnicity. For 1989–90 and later years, reported racial/ethnic distributions of students by level of degree, field of degree,

and sex were used to estimate race/ethnicity for students whose race/ethnicity was not reported. Detail may not sum to totals because of rounding. Some data have been revised from previously published figures.
SOURCE: U.S. Department of Education, National Center for Education Statistics, Higher Education General Information Survey (HEGIS), "Degrees and Other Formal Awards Conferred" surveys, 1976–77 and 1980–81; Integrated Postsecondary Education Data System (IPEDS), "Completions Survey" (IPEDS-C:90–99); and IPEDS Fall 2000 through Fall 2018, Completions component. (This table was prepared October 2019.)

Table 321.30. Associate's degrees conferred by postsecondary institutions, by race/ethnicity and field of study: 2016–17 and 2017–18

Field of study	2016–17										2017–18									
	Total	White	Black	Hispanic	Asian/Pacific Islander Total	Asian	Pacific Islander	American Indian/Alaska Native	Two or more races	Nonresident alien	Total	White	Black	Hispanic	Asian/Pacific Islander Total	Asian	Pacific Islander	American Indian/Alaska Native	Two or more races	Nonresident alien
1	2	3	4	5	6	7	8	9	10	11	12	13	14	15	16	17	18	19	20	21
All fields, total	1,005,687	551,057	129,880	209,159	55,814	52,633	3,181	9,265	29,603	20,909	1,011,487	536,266	125,517	225,462	58,952	55,840	3,112	9,285	32,971	23,044
Agriculture and natural resources[2]	8,208	7,189	127	524	65	56	9	107	153	43	8,076	6,988	126	578	73	61	12	108	158	45
Architecture and related services	503	195	26	211	31	31	0	1	17	22	539	204	24	222	56	55	1	6	9	18
Area, ethnic, cultural, gender, and group studies	420	115	47	118	30	19	11	66	37	7	559	122	67	177	38	38	0	81	67	7
Biological and biomedical sciences	5,550	2,213	473	1,783	682	670	12	66	194	139	6,390	2,401	501	2,173	842	811	31	65	225	183
Business[2]	122,252	61,949	18,952	23,190	8,966	8,539	427	1,205	3,430	4,560	117,782	58,058	17,186	23,443	9,190	8,805	385	1,243	3,618	5,044
Communication, journalism, and related programs	7,379	3,036	857	2,433	541	519	22	39	276	197	7,785	3,073	764	2,781	573	546	27	27	365	202
Communications technologies	4,307	2,385	662	780	169	161	8	31	154	126	4,197	2,207	627	884	177	170	7	31	162	109
Computer and information sciences	31,171	18,464	4,038	4,279	2,390	2,281	109	269	947	784	31,479	18,014	3,971	4,521	2,640	2,542	98	277	981	1,075
Construction trades	5,308	3,666	519	507	275	230	45	125	198	24	5,277	3,889	367	530	197	175	22	99	171	24
Education	16,603	9,254	2,444	3,582	400	359	41	365	397	161	16,182	8,677	2,298	3,885	396	366	30	335	408	183
Engineering	5,915	3,162	407	1,204	589	582	7	48	152	353	6,408	3,323	476	1,304	651	635	16	35	191	428
Engineering technologies and engineering-related fields[1]	27,021	18,689	2,688	3,296	1,001	920	81	257	645	445	26,745	18,479	2,422	3,448	1,097	1,031	66	254	660	385
English language and literature/letters	2,870	1,154	200	1,110	219	214	5	12	124	51	3,133	1,197	190	1,345	208	201	7	15	137	41
Family and consumer sciences/human sciences	8,871	3,767	1,499	2,791	411	392	19	93	187	123	8,854	3,606	1,351	3,035	431	410	21	99	193	139
Foreign languages, literatures, and linguistics	2,363	1,026	106	991	92	88	4	10	84	54	2,607	1,079	106	1,164	108	105	3	14	100	36
Health professions and related programs	186,312	115,554	27,392	26,827	9,130	8,536	594	1,760	4,487	1,162	181,056	109,919	26,293	27,809	9,265	8,649	616	1,641	4,905	1,224
Homeland security, law enforcement, and firefighting	37,362	18,629	5,476	10,837	1,060	924	136	314	881	165	35,276	16,992	4,725	10,991	1,039	932	107	355	957	217
Legal professions and studies	6,904	4,023	1,072	1,350	160	141	19	64	175	60	6,237	3,376	958	1,290	275	257	18	47	182	109
Liberal arts and sciences, general studies, and humanities	386,746	208,757	49,492	85,562	18,684	17,555	1,129	3,145	12,277	8,829	397,926	208,180	49,958	93,087	19,665	18,510	1,155	3,228	14,064	9,744
Library science	158	109	10	25	7	7	0	2	5	0	156	107	7	25	10	10	0	5	2	0
Mathematics and statistics	3,454	1,221	108	1,149	629	615	14	15	121	211	4,135	1,312	119	1,456	798	788	10	23	167	260
Mechanic and repair technologies/technicians	20,821	13,817	1,828	3,469	700	608	92	268	522	217	21,295	13,856	1,659	3,878	787	692	95	278	623	214
Military technologies and applied sciences	1,093	702	144	141	50	43	7	11	45	0	1,226	756	166	211	58	52	6	9	26	0
Multi/interdisciplinary studies	30,780	13,961	2,416	8,875	3,643	3,567	76	153	1,096	636	31,068	12,859	2,206	9,947	3,973	3,884	89	173	1,239	671
Parks, recreation, leisure, and fitness studies	5,037	2,242	489	1,606	394	366	28	38	188	80	5,095	1,928	489	1,852	462	438	24	53	214	97
Philosophy and religious studies	1,002	719	78	123	31	29	2	4	23	24	1,049	720	59	176	31	28	3	2	23	38
Physical sciences and science technologies	9,223	4,226	942	2,136	1,036	1,011	25	73	312	498	10,116	4,314	1,014	2,613	1,208	1,185	23	84	371	512
Precision production	5,251	3,970	256	663	140	125	15	81	129	12	5,333	4,013	238	674	169	164	5	73	149	17
Psychology	11,283	3,758	864	5,085	891	844	47	117	445	123	12,489	3,928	924	5,938	937	908	29	106	494	162
Public administration and social services	7,591	3,420	2,206	1,475	121	99	22	140	191	38	7,136	2,991	2,238	1,410	133	111	22	139	193	32
Social sciences and history	21,392	7,467	1,715	8,635	1,973	1,870	103	209	913	480	23,683	7,902	1,868	9,914	2,120	1,996	124	221	1,033	625
Social sciences	19,636	6,586	1,661	7,983	1,894	1,795	99	199	841	472	21,545	6,923	1,807	9,050	2,017	1,897	120	198	937	613
History	1,756	881	54	652	79	75	4	10	72	8	2,138	979	61	864	103	99	4	23	96	12
Theology and religious vocations	1,546	1,071	288	98	29	27	2	16	29	15	1,435	976	271	96	20	15	5	15	30	12
Transportation and materials moving	1,547	948	116	230	107	91	16	10	51	85	1,610	1,014	110	236	78	70	8	14	49	109
Visual and performing arts	19,444	10,205	1,943	4,074	1,168	1,114	54	151	718	1,185	19,153	9,796	1,739	4,369	1,239	1,202	37	122	801	1,087
Other and not classified	0	0	0	0	0	0	0	0	0	0	0	0	0	0	0	0	0	0	0	0

[1]Excludes "Construction trades" and "Mechanic and repair technologies/technicians," which are listed separately.
NOTE: Data are for postsecondary institutions participating in Title IV federal financial aid programs. Race categories exclude persons of Hispanic ethnicity. Reported racial/ethnic distributions of students by level of degree, field of degree, and sex were used to estimate race/ethnicity for students whose race/ethnicity was not reported. To facilitate trend comparisons, certain aggregations have been made of the degree fields as reported in the Integrated Postsecondary Education Data System

[2]"Agriculture and natural resources" includes Agriculture, agriculture operations, and related sciences and Natural resources and conservation; and "Business" includes Business management, marketing, and related support services and Personal and culinary services. Some data have been revised from previously published figures.
SOURCE: U.S. Department of Education, National Center for Education Statistics, Integrated Postsecondary Education Data System (IPEDS), Fall 2017 and Fall 2018, Completions component. (This table was prepared October 2019.)

Table 322.10. Bachelor's degrees conferred by postsecondary institutions, by field of study: Selected years, 1970–71 through 2017–18

Field of study	1970–71	1975–76	1980–81	1985–86	1990–91	1995–96	2000–01	2005–06	2007–08	2009–10	2010–11	2011–12	2012–13	2013–14	2014–15	2015–16	2016–17	2017–18
1	2	3	4	5	6	7	8	9	10	11	12	13	14	15	16	17	18	19
Total	**839,730**	**925,746**	**935,140**	**987,823**	**1,094,538**	**1,164,792**	**1,244,171**	**1,485,104**	**1,563,734**	**1,649,919**	**1,716,053**	**1,792,163**	**1,840,381**	**1,870,150**	**1,894,969**	**1,920,750**	**1,956,114**	**1,980,644**
Agriculture and natural resources	12,672	19,402	21,886	16,823	13,124	21,425	23,370	23,052	24,125	26,343	28,630	30,972	33,592	35,125	36,278	36,995	37,734	39,314
Architecture and related services	5,570	9,146	9,455	9,119	9,781	8,352	8,480	9,515	9,809	10,051	9,831	9,727	9,757	9,149	9,090	8,825	8,579	8,464
Area, ethnic, cultural, gender, and group studies	2,579	3,577	2,887	3,021	4,776	5,633	6,160	7,878	8,453	8,620	8,955	9,228	8,850	8,275	7,783	7,840	7,720	7,717
Biological and biomedical sciences	35,705	54,154	43,078	38,395	39,482	61,014	60,576	70,602	79,869	86,391	89,984	95,850	100,291	104,657	109,904	113,794	116,768	118,663
Business	115,396	143,171	200,521	236,700	249,165	226,623	263,515	318,043	335,495	358,119	365,133	367,235	360,887	358,132	363,741	371,690	381,109	386,201
Communication, journalism, and related programs	10,324	20,045	29,428	41,666	51,650	47,320	58,013	73,658	76,400	81,280	83,231	83,771	84,818	87,612	90,658	92,551	93,794	92,290
Communications technologies	478	1,237	1,854	1,479	1,397	853	1,178	2,987	4,654	4,782	4,858	4,983	4,987	4,991	5,135	4,824	4,615	4,231
Computer and information sciences	2,388	5,652	15,121	42,337	25,159	24,506	44,142	47,702	38,523	39,593	43,066	47,406	50,961	55,271	59,586	64,402	71,416	79,598
Education	176,307	154,437	108,074	87,147	110,807	105,384	105,458	107,235	102,849	101,287	104,008	105,656	104,698	98,838	91,596	87,221	85,130	82,621
Engineering	45,034	38,733	63,642	77,391	62,448	62,168	58,209	66,841	68,404	72,657	76,356	81,371	85,987	92,169	97,852	106,789	115,671	121,956
Engineering technologies	5,148	7,943	11,713	19,731	17,303	15,829	14,660	14,565	15,278	16,078	16,741	17,283	17,010	16,807	17,253	17,159	18,119	18,727
English language and literature/letters	63,914	41,452	31,922	34,083	51,064	49,928	50,569	55,094	55,001	53,229	52,754	53,765	52,401	50,464	45,851	42,797	41,314	40,002
Family and consumer sciences/human sciences	11,167	17,409	18,370	13,847	13,920	14,353	16,421	20,775	21,880	21,832	22,438	23,441	23,930	24,689	24,584	25,080	25,389	25,256
Foreign languages, literatures, and linguistics	20,988	17,068	11,638	11,550	13,937	14,832	16,128	19,393	20,976	21,507	21,705	21,756	21,647	20,332	19,493	18,436	17,643	16,958
Health professions and related programs	25,223	53,885	63,665	65,309	59,875	86,087	75,933	91,973	111,548	129,623	143,463	163,675	181,149	198,777	216,228	228,907	237,979	244,909
Homeland security, law enforcement, and firefighting	2,045	12,507	13,707	12,704	16,806	24,810	25,211	35,319	40,297	43,613	47,600	54,091	60,264	62,416	62,723	61,159	59,553	58,114
Legal professions and studies	545	531	776	1,223	1,827	2,123	1,991	3,302	3,771	3,886	4,429	4,595	4,425	4,513	4,420	4,243	4,272	4,239
Liberal arts and sciences, general studies, and humanities	7,481	18,855	21,643	21,336	30,526	33,997	37,962	44,898	46,882	46,963	46,717	46,961	46,790	45,281	43,649	43,669	44,103	44,262
Library science	1,013	843	375	155	90	58	52	76	68	85	96	95	102	127	99	85	99	81
Mathematics and statistics	24,801	15,984	11,078	16,122	14,393	12,713	11,171	14,760	15,169	16,029	17,182	18,841	20,449	20,987	21,854	22,778	24,075	25,256
Military technologies and applied sciences	357	952	42	255	183	7	21	33	39	56	64	86	105	185	276	358	469	655
Multi/interdisciplinary studies	6,324	13,709	12,986	13,754	17,774	26,885	26,478	30,583	34,172	37,717	42,473	45,717	47,658	45,651	47,556	48,833	49,631	51,909
Parks, recreation, leisure, and fitness studies	1,621	5,182	5,729	4,623	4,315	12,974	17,948	25,489	29,908	33,332	35,934	38,998	42,628	46,047	49,008	50,912	53,292	53,883
Philosophy and religious studies	8,149	8,447	6,776	6,396	7,423	7,541	8,717	11,980	12,259	12,503	12,830	12,645	12,792	11,999	11,071	10,155	9,711	9,603
Physical sciences and science technologies	21,410	21,458	23,936	21,711	16,334	19,716	18,025	20,521	22,164	23,381	24,705	26,664	28,053	29,307	30,042	30,483	31,272	31,542
Precision production	0	0	0	2	2	12	31	55	33	33	43	37	36	37	48	51	32	45
Psychology	38,187	50,278	41,068	40,628	58,655	73,416	73,645	88,132	92,592	97,215	100,906	109,099	114,446	117,312	117,573	117,447	116,859	116,432
Public administration and social services	5,466	15,440	16,707	11,887	14,350	19,849	19,447	21,986	23,523	25,421	26,799	29,695	31,950	33,483	34,364	34,433	35,461	35,629
Social sciences and history	155,324	126,396	100,513	93,840	125,107	126,479	128,036	161,468	167,321	172,782	177,169	178,534	177,767	173,132	166,971	161,211	159,097	159,967
Theology and religious vocations	3,720	5,490	5,808	5,510	4,799	5,292	6,945	8,548	8,992	8,719	9,073	9,304	9,385	9,642	9,713	9,804	9,518	9,521
Transportation and materials moving	0	225	263	1,838	2,622	3,561	3,748	5,849	5,202	4,998	4,941	4,876	4,661	4,588	4,730	4,531	4,708	4,924
Visual and performing arts	30,394	42,138	40,479	37,241	42,186	49,296	61,148	83,292	87,731	91,798	93,939	95,806	97,799	97,414	95,840	92,979	91,291	88,582
Not classified by field of study	0	0	0	0	13,258	1,756	783	0	377	0	0	0	0	0	0	0	0	0

NOTE: Data are for postsecondary institutions participating in Title IV federal financial aid programs. The new Classification of Instructional Programs was initiated in 2009–10. The figures for earlier years have been reclassified when necessary to make them conform to the new taxonomy. To facilitate trend comparisons, certain aggregations have been made of the degree fields as reported in the Integrated Postsecondary Education Data System (IPEDS): "Agriculture and natural resources" includes Agriculture, agriculture operations, and related sciences and Natural resources and conservation; "Business" includes Business, management, marketing, and related support services and Personal and culinary services; and "Engineering technologies" includes Engineering technologies and engineering-related fields, Construction trades, and Mechanic and repair technologies/technicians. Some data have been revised from previously published figures.
SOURCE: U.S. Department of Education, National Center for Education Statistics, Higher Education General Information Survey (HEGIS), "Degrees and Other Formal Awards Conferred" surveys, 1970–71 through 1985–86; Integrated Postsecondary Education Data System (IPEDS), "Completions Survey" (IPEDS-C:91–99); and IPEDS Fall 2000 through Fall 2018, Completions component. (This table was prepared November 2019.)

Table 322.20. Bachelor's degrees conferred by postsecondary institutions, by race/ethnicity and sex of student: Selected years, 1976–77 through 2017–18

Year and sex	Number of degrees conferred to U.S. citizens, permanent residents, and nonresident aliens								Percentage distribution of degrees conferred to U.S. citizens and permanent residents						
	Total	White	Black	Hispanic	Asian/ Pacific Islander	American Indian/ Alaska Native	Two or more races[1]	Non-resident alien	Total	White	Black	Hispanic	Asian/ Pacific Islander	American Indian/ Alaska Native	Two or more races[1]
1	2	3	4	5	6	7	8	9	10	11	12	13	14	15	16
Total															
1976–77[2]	917,900	807,688	58,636	18,743	13,793	3,326	—	15,714	100.0	89.5	6.5	2.1	1.5	0.4	—
1980–81[3]	934,800	807,319	60,673	21,832	18,794	3,593	—	22,589	100.0	88.5	6.7	2.4	2.1	0.4	—
1990–91	1,094,538	914,093	66,375	37,342	42,529	4,583	—	29,616	100.0	85.8	6.2	3.5	4.0	0.4	—
1999–2000	1,237,875	929,102	108,018	75,063	77,909	8,717	—	39,066	100.0	77.5	9.0	6.3	6.5	0.7	—
2000–01	1,244,171	927,357	111,307	77,745	78,902	9,049	—	39,811	100.0	77.0	9.2	6.5	6.6	0.8	—
2003–04	1,399,542	1,026,114	131,241	94,644	92,073	10,638	—	44,832	100.0	75.7	9.7	7.0	6.8	0.8	—
2004–05	1,439,264	1,049,141	136,122	101,124	97,209	10,307	—	45,361	100.0	75.3	9.8	7.3	7.0	0.7	—
2005–06	1,485,104	1,075,471	142,405	107,575	102,371	10,938	—	46,344	100.0	74.7	9.9	7.5	7.1	0.8	—
2006–07	1,524,729	1,100,308	146,767	114,962	105,287	11,463	—	45,942	100.0	74.4	9.9	7.8	7.1	0.8	—
2007–08	1,563,734	1,123,246	152,627	122,770	109,117	11,509	—	44,405	100.0	73.9	10.0	8.1	7.2	0.8	—
2008–09	1,601,399	1,144,628	156,603	129,473	112,581	12,221	—	45,893	100.0	73.6	10.1	8.3	7.2	0.8	—
2009–10	1,649,919	1,167,322	164,789	140,426	117,391	12,405	—	47,586	100.0	72.9	10.3	8.8	7.3	0.8	—
2010–11	1,716,053	1,182,690	172,731	154,450	121,118	11,935	20,589	52,540	100.0	71.1	10.4	9.3	7.3	0.7	1.2
2011–12	1,792,163	1,212,417	185,916	169,736	126,177	11,498	27,234	59,185	100.0	70.0	10.7	9.8	7.3	0.7	1.6
2012–13	1,840,381	1,221,908	191,233	186,677	130,129	11,432	34,128	64,874	100.0	68.8	10.8	10.5	7.3	0.6	1.9
2013–14	1,870,150	1,218,998	191,437	202,425	131,662	10,784	45,422	69,422	100.0	67.7	10.6	11.2	7.3	0.6	2.5
2014–15	1,894,969	1,210,071	192,829	218,098	133,916	10,202	54,215	75,638	100.0	66.5	10.6	12.0	7.4	0.6	3.0
2015–16	1,920,750	1,197,323	194,408	235,190	138,257	9,735	61,584	84,253	100.0	65.2	10.6	12.8	7.5	0.5	3.4
2016–17	1,956,114	1,195,977	196,338	252,203	144,093	9,589	66,532	91,382	100.0	64.1	10.5	13.5	7.7	0.5	3.6
2017–18	1,980,644	1,189,619	195,014	267,065	150,999	9,157	70,553	98,237	100.0	63.2	10.4	14.2	8.0	0.5	3.7
Males															
1976–77[2]	494,424	438,161	25,147	10,318	7,638	1,804	—	11,356	100.0	90.7	5.2	2.1	1.6	0.4	—
1980–81[3]	469,625	406,173	24,511	10,810	10,107	1,700	—	16,324	100.0	89.6	5.4	2.4	2.2	0.4	—
1990–91	504,045	421,290	24,800	16,598	21,203	1,938	—	18,216	100.0	86.7	5.1	3.4	4.4	0.4	—
1999–2000	530,367	402,954	37,029	30,304	35,853	3,463	—	20,764	100.0	79.1	7.3	5.9	7.0	0.7	—
2000–01	531,840	401,780	38,103	31,368	35,865	3,700	—	21,024	100.0	78.7	7.5	6.1	7.0	0.7	—
2003–04	595,425	445,483	43,851	37,288	41,360	4,244	—	23,199	100.0	77.9	7.7	6.5	7.2	0.7	—
2004–05	613,000	456,592	45,810	39,490	43,711	4,143	—	23,254	100.0	77.4	7.8	6.7	7.4	0.7	—
2005–06	630,502	467,397	48,073	41,805	45,803	4,202	—	23,222	100.0	77.0	7.9	6.9	7.5	0.7	—
2006–07	649,816	480,747	49,715	44,761	47,577	4,508	—	22,508	100.0	76.6	7.9	7.1	7.6	0.7	—
2007–08	668,184	492,360	52,298	47,797	49,535	4,523	—	21,671	100.0	76.2	8.1	7.4	7.7	0.7	—
2008–09	685,422	503,396	53,465	50,596	50,773	4,849	—	22,343	100.0	75.9	8.1	7.6	7.7	0.7	—
2009–10	706,660	513,711	56,136	55,139	53,365	4,879	—	23,430	100.0	75.2	8.2	8.1	7.8	0.7	—
2010–11	734,159	519,992	59,015	60,869	55,321	4,798	8,028	26,136	100.0	73.4	8.3	8.6	7.8	0.7	1.1
2011–12	765,772	532,463	63,736	67,083	57,521	4,476	10,945	29,548	100.0	72.3	8.7	9.1	7.8	0.6	1.5
2012–13	787,408	535,358	67,351	74,067	59,806	4,611	13,834	32,381	100.0	70.9	8.9	9.8	7.9	0.6	1.8
2013–14	801,905	536,009	68,290	80,312	59,844	4,171	18,137	35,142	100.0	69.9	8.9	10.5	7.8	0.5	2.4
2014–15	812,693	530,418	69,316	86,881	61,080	4,061	22,245	38,692	100.0	68.5	9.0	11.2	7.9	0.5	2.9
2015–16	821,746	522,834	69,847	92,989	63,182	3,822	25,157	43,915	100.0	67.2	9.0	12.0	8.1	0.5	3.2
2016–17	836,021	521,359	70,568	99,344	65,405	3,731	27,089	48,525	100.0	66.2	9.0	12.6	8.3	0.5	3.4
2017–18	844,960	516,621	70,316	104,926	68,196	3,506	28,868	52,527	100.0	65.2	8.9	13.2	8.6	0.4	3.6
Females															
1976–77[2]	423,476	369,527	33,489	8,425	6,155	1,522	—	4,358	100.0	88.2	8.0	2.0	1.5	0.4	—
1980–81[3]	465,175	401,146	36,162	11,022	8,687	1,893	—	6,265	100.0	87.4	7.9	2.4	1.9	0.4	—
1990–91	590,493	492,803	41,575	20,744	21,326	2,645	—	11,400	100.0	85.1	7.2	3.6	3.7	0.5	—
1999–2000	707,508	526,148	70,989	44,759	42,056	5,254	—	18,302	100.0	76.3	10.3	6.5	6.1	0.8	—
2000–01	712,331	525,577	73,204	46,377	43,037	5,349	—	18,787	100.0	75.8	10.6	6.7	6.2	0.8	—
2003–04	804,117	580,631	87,390	57,356	50,713	6,394	—	21,633	100.0	74.2	11.2	7.3	6.5	0.8	—
2004–05	826,264	592,549	90,312	61,634	53,498	6,164	—	22,107	100.0	73.7	11.2	7.7	6.7	0.8	—
2005–06	854,602	608,074	94,332	65,770	56,568	6,736	—	23,122	100.0	73.1	11.3	7.9	6.8	0.8	—
2006–07	874,913	619,561	97,052	70,201	57,710	6,955	—	23,434	100.0	72.8	11.4	8.2	6.8	0.8	—
2007–08	895,550	630,886	100,329	74,973	59,642	6,986	—	22,734	100.0	72.3	11.5	8.6	6.8	0.8	—
2008–09	915,977	641,232	103,138	78,877	61,808	7,372	—	23,550	100.0	71.9	11.6	8.8	6.9	0.8	—
2009–10	943,259	653,611	108,653	85,287	64,026	7,526	—	24,156	100.0	71.1	11.8	9.3	7.0	0.8	—
2010–11	981,894	662,698	113,716	93,581	65,797	7,137	12,561	26,404	100.0	69.4	11.9	9.8	6.9	0.7	1.3
2011–12	1,026,391	679,954	122,180	102,653	68,656	7,022	16,289	29,637	100.0	68.2	12.3	10.3	6.9	0.7	1.6
2012–13	1,052,973	686,550	123,882	112,610	70,323	6,821	20,294	32,493	100.0	67.3	12.1	11.0	6.9	0.7	2.0
2013–14	1,068,245	682,989	123,147	122,113	71,818	6,613	27,285	34,280	100.0	66.1	11.9	11.8	6.9	0.6	2.6
2014–15	1,082,276	679,653	123,513	131,217	72,836	6,141	31,970	36,946	100.0	65.0	11.8	12.6	7.0	0.6	3.1
2015–16	1,099,004	674,489	124,561	142,201	75,075	5,913	36,427	40,338	100.0	63.7	11.8	13.4	7.1	0.6	3.4
2016–17	1,120,093	674,618	125,770	152,859	78,688	5,858	39,443	42,857	100.0	62.6	11.7	14.2	7.3	0.5	3.7
2017–18	1,135,684	672,998	124,698	162,139	82,803	5,651	41,685	45,710	100.0	61.7	11.4	14.9	7.6	0.5	3.8

—Not available.

[1]For years prior to 2010–11, the survey did not yet include the "Two or more races" category, and each student could be counted in only one race category.
[2]Excludes 1,121 males and 528 females whose racial/ethnic group was not available.
[3]Excludes 258 males and 82 females whose racial/ethnic group was not available.
NOTE: Data are for postsecondary institutions participating in Title IV federal financial aid programs. Race categories exclude persons of Hispanic ethnicity. For 1989–90 and later years, reported racial/ethnic distributions of students by level of degree, field of degree,

and sex were used to estimate race/ethnicity for students whose race/ethnicity was not reported. Detail may not sum to totals because of rounding. Some data have been revised from previously published figures.
SOURCE: U.S. Department of Education, National Center for Education Statistics, Higher Education General Information Survey (HEGIS), "Degrees and Other Formal Awards Conferred" surveys, 1976–77 and 1980–81; Integrated Postsecondary Education Data System (IPEDS), "Completions Survey" (IPEDS-C:90–99); and IPEDS Fall 2000 through Fall 2018, Completions component. (This table was prepared October 2019.)

Table 322.30. Bachelor's degrees conferred by postsecondary institutions, by race/ethnicity and field of study: 2016–17 and 2017–18

Field of study	Total	White	Black	Hispanic	Asian/Pacific Islander Total	Asian	Pacific Islander	American Indian/Alaska Native	Two or more races	Nonresident alien	Total	White	Black	Hispanic	Asian/Pacific Islander Total	Asian	Pacific Islander	American Indian/Alaska Native	Two or more races	Nonresident alien
					2016–17										2017–18					
1	2	3	4	5	6	7	8	9	10	11	12	13	14	15	16	17	18	19	20	21
All fields, total	1,956,114	1,195,977	196,338	252,203	144,093	139,541	4,552	9,589	66,532	91,382	1,980,644	1,189,619	195,014	267,065	150,999	146,648	4,351	9,157	70,553	98,237
Agriculture and natural resources	37,734	29,586	1,180	3,196	1,383	1,317	66	250	1,235	904	39,314	30,377	1,201	3,481	1,479	1,412	67	273	1,445	1,058
Architecture and related services	8,579	4,631	466	1,356	744	721	23	23	271	1,088	8,464	4,520	439	1,296	693	684	9	23	320	1,173
Area, ethnic, cultural, gender, and group studies	7,720	3,169	1,145	1,701	700	662	38	163	519	323	7,717	3,118	1,143	1,739	643	621	22	187	516	371
Biological and biomedical sciences	116,768	66,728	9,335	14,138	17,923	17,691	232	455	4,688	3,501	118,663	66,377	9,313	15,416	18,286	18,048	238	448	5,019	3,804
Business	381,109	228,592	38,206	45,607	28,037	27,090	947	1,792	10,579	28,296	386,201	229,344	37,425	48,804	28,579	27,724	855	1,748	11,573	28,728
Communication, journalism, and related programs	93,794	58,712	11,155	12,502	3,806	3,621	185	297	3,778	3,544	94,290	57,024	10,781	12,823	3,936	3,766	170	298	3,797	3,631
Communications technologies	4,615	2,586	626	647	278	259	19	24	200	254	4,231	2,352	575	573	295	283	12	22	171	243
Computer and information sciences	71,416	39,485	6,391	7,234	10,426	10,239	187	268	2,470	5,142	79,598	42,080	6,862	8,084	12,609	12,444	165	262	2,905	6,796
Construction trades	153	103	1	43	1	1	0	0	2	3	151	98	2	41	3	2	1	0	0	7
Education	85,130	64,694	6,289	8,280	2,273	2,135	138	552	2,143	899	82,621	61,794	6,130	8,642	2,350	2,221	129	501	2,210	994
Engineering	115,671	70,006	4,505	11,875	13,368	13,207	161	301	3,820	11,796	121,956	72,484	4,836	12,777	14,080	13,909	171	360	4,138	13,281
Engineering technologies and engineering-related fields[1]	17,667	11,766	1,522	1,709	778	749	29	119	440	1,333	18,228	11,959	1,536	1,833	836	795	41	118	485	1,461
English language and literature/letters	41,314	28,421	3,260	5,353	1,803	1,740	63	185	1,718	574	40,002	27,105	3,210	5,538	1,718	1,659	59	156	1,720	555
Family and consumer sciences/human sciences	25,080	15,306	3,221	3,620	1,388	1,338	50	133	891	521	24,349	14,536	3,088	3,676	1,472	1,414	58	116	901	560
Foreign languages, literatures, and linguistics	17,643	10,274	859	4,074	1,071	1,051	20	48	781	536	16,958	9,788	813	3,849	1,063	1,043	20	40	772	633
Health professions and related programs	237,979	155,642	27,359	26,378	18,289	17,532	757	1,199	6,457	2,655	244,909	158,507	27,908	28,279	19,136	18,346	790	1,162	7,095	2,822
Homeland security, law enforcement, and firefighting	59,553	31,286	11,539	12,161	1,696	1,465	231	440	1,828	603	58,114	30,316	11,036	12,122	1,719	1,504	215	370	1,845	706
Legal professions and studies	4,272	2,387	659	779	201	194	7	39	155	52	4,239	2,341	669	746	220	209	11	30	169	64
Liberal arts and sciences, general studies, and humanities	44,103	26,946	6,684	6,131	1,605	1,463	142	360	1,550	827	44,262	25,942	6,943	6,622	1,665	1,549	116	365	1,750	975
Library science	99	80	7	4	1	0	1	2	5	0	81	65	5	8	0	0	0	0	3	0
Mathematics and statistics	24,075	13,190	1,022	2,321	2,620	2,598	22	59	772	4,091	25,256	13,294	1,059	2,506	3,116	3,075	41	63	816	4,402
Mechanic and repair technologies/technicians	299	213	25	25	11	11	0	4	9	12	348	262	18	23	10	10	0	8	14	13
Military technologies and applied sciences	469	351	39	40	14	12	2	4	14	7	655	486	44	59	17	16	1	5	32	12
Multi/interdisciplinary studies	49,631	28,160	6,391	7,944	3,404	3,281	123	269	1,990	1,473	51,909	28,627	6,570	8,744	3,777	3,663	114	267	2,141	1,783
Parks, recreation, leisure, and fitness studies	53,292	34,485	6,219	6,582	2,557	2,434	123	323	2,072	1,054	53,883	33,899	6,524	7,171	2,845	2,720	125	253	2,122	1,069
Philosophy and religious studies	9,711	6,454	791	1,124	571	554	17	40	421	310	9,603	6,278	729	1,227	590	570	20	40	420	319
Physical sciences and science technologies	31,272	20,449	1,653	3,119	2,934	2,901	33	126	1,200	1,791	31,542	20,007	1,688	3,419	3,004	2,947	57	143	1,322	1,959
Precision production	32	24	1	2	4	3	1	0	0	1	45	30	0	2	4	4	0	0	3	6
Psychology	116,859	65,183	14,809	20,787	7,814	7,520	294	633	4,585	3,048	116,432	63,253	14,382	22,435	7,782	7,547	235	563	4,757	3,260
Public administration and social services	35,461	19,015	7,662	5,824	1,106	1,003	103	287	1,140	427	35,629	18,783	7,516	6,185	1,243	1,129	114	282	1,174	446
Social sciences and history	159,097	90,382	15,206	25,064	11,177	10,861	316	728	6,372	10,168	159,967	89,641	14,880	26,056	11,566	11,240	326	616	6,471	10,737
Social sciences	135,043	72,594	13,902	22,119	10,420	10,139	281	591	5,537	9,880	136,585	72,584	13,630	22,958	10,829	10,535	294	513	5,665	10,406
History	24,054	17,788	1,304	2,945	757	722	35	137	835	288	23,382	17,057	1,250	3,098	737	705	32	103	806	331
Theology and religious vocations	9,518	7,488	806	561	240	223	17	45	161	217	9,521	7,511	713	574	263	245	18	32	216	212
Transportation and materials moving	4,708	3,304	280	355	205	187	18	25	201	338	4,924	3,355	294	441	253	237	16	32	147	402
Visual and performing arts	91,291	56,879	7,025	11,667	5,665	5,478	187	396	4,065	5,594	88,582	54,066	6,682	11,874	5,747	5,612	135	374	4,084	5,755
Other and not classified	0	0	0	0	0	0	0	0	0	0	0	0	0	0	0	0	0	0	0	0

[1]Excludes "Construction trades" and "Mechanic and repair technologies/technicians," which are listed separately.

NOTE: Data are for postsecondary institutions participating in Title IV federal financial aid programs. Race categories exclude persons of Hispanic ethnicity. Reported racial/ethnic distributions of students by level of degree, field of study, and sex were used to estimate race/ethnicity for students whose race/ethnicity was not reported. To facilitate trend comparisons, certain aggregations have been made of the degree fields as reported in the Integrated Postsecondary Education Data System

(IPEDS): "Agriculture and natural resources" includes Agriculture, agriculture operations, and related sciences and Natural resources and conservation; and "Business" includes Business management, marketing, and related support services and Personal and culinary services. Some data have been revised from previously published figures.
SOURCE: U.S. Department of Education, National Center for Education Statistics, Integrated Postsecondary Education Data System (IPEDS), Fall 2017 and Fall 2018, Completions component. (This table was prepared October 2019.)

Table 323.10. Master's degrees conferred by postsecondary institutions, by field of study: Selected years, 1970–71 through 2017–18

Field of study	1970–71	1975–76	1980–81	1985–86	1990–91	1995–96	2000–01	2005–06	2007–08	2009–10	2010–11	2011–12	2012–13	2013–14	2014–15	2015–16	2016–17	2017–18
1	2	3	4	5	6	7	8	9	10	11	12	13	14	15	16	17	18	19
Total	235,564	317,477	302,637	295,850	342,863	412,180	473,502	599,862	630,844	693,313	730,922	755,967	751,718	754,582	758,804	785,757	804,542	820,102
Agriculture and natural resources	2,457	3,340	4,003	3,801	3,295	4,551	4,272	4,653	4,682	5,215	5,766	6,390	6,336	6,544	6,426	6,702	6,843	6,967
Architecture and related services	1,705	3,215	3,153	3,260	3,490	3,993	4,302	5,743	6,059	7,280	7,788	8,448	8,095	8,048	8,006	7,991	7,883	7,317
Area, ethnic, cultural, gender, and group studies	1,032	993	802	915	1,233	1,652	1,555	2,080	1,778	1,775	1,913	1,947	1,897	1,844	1,847	1,767	1,717	1,673
Biological and biomedical sciences	5,625	6,457	5,766	5,064	4,834	6,593	7,017	8,783	9,691	10,730	11,324	12,419	13,300	13,964	14,655	15,717	16,282	17,180
Business	26,490	42,592	57,888	66,676	78,255	93,554	115,602	146,396	155,804	177,748	187,178	191,606	188,617	189,364	185,236	186,835	187,412	192,184
Communication, journalism, and related programs	1,770	2,961	2,896	3,500	4,123	5,080	5,218	7,106	6,916	7,630	8,302	9,005	8,760	9,353	9,581	9,676	10,119	10,243
Communications technologies	86	165	209	308	204	481	427	521	631	463	502	497	577	577	554	491	539	529
Computer and information sciences	1,588	2,603	4,218	8,070	9,324	10,579	16,911	17,195	17,096	17,955	19,516	20,925	22,782	24,514	31,475	40,130	46,553	46,468
Education	87,666	126,061	96,713	74,816	87,352	104,936	127,829	174,622	175,880	182,165	185,127	179,047	164,652	154,655	146,581	145,792	145,624	146,367
Engineering	16,813	16,472	16,893	21,529	24,454	26,789	25,174	30,845	31,559	35,133	38,664	40,323	40,420	42,376	46,117	51,646	52,826	51,721
Engineering technologies	134	328	323	617	996	2,054	2,013	2,541	2,884	4,258	4,515	4,793	4,908	4,967	5,324	6,067	7,403	7,247
English language and literature/letters	10,441	8,599	5,742	5,335	6,784	7,657	6,763	8,845	9,142	9,202	9,475	9,938	9,755	9,294	8,928	8,581	8,244	8,300
Family and consumer sciences/human sciences	1,452	2,179	2,570	2,011	1,541	1,712	1,838	1,983	2,199	2,592	2,918	3,155	3,255	3,082	3,148	3,228	3,295	3,308
Foreign languages, literatures, and linguistics	5,480	4,432	2,934	2,690	3,049	3,443	3,035	3,539	3,564	3,756	3,727	3,827	3,708	3,482	3,566	3,407	3,271	3,261
Health professions and related programs	5,330	12,164	16,176	18,603	21,354	33,920	43,623	51,492	58,147	69,112	75,571	84,355	90,933	97,416	103,052	110,350	119,242	125,216
Homeland security, law enforcement, and firefighting	194	1,197	1,538	1,074	1,108	1,812	2,514	4,277	5,779	6,717	7,433	8,420	8,868	9,310	9,643	9,775	10,209	10,293
Legal professions and studies	955	1,442	1,832	1,924	2,057	2,751	3,829	4,453	4,823	5,767	6,475	6,614	7,013	7,654	7,924	8,181	8,674	9,177
Liberal arts and sciences, general studies, and humanities	885	2,633	2,375	1,586	2,213	2,778	3,193	3,702	3,797	3,822	3,997	3,792	3,264	3,002	2,794	2,598	2,485	2,473
Library science	7,001	8,037	4,859	3,564	4,763	5,099	4,727	6,448	7,169	7,448	7,729	7,443	6,983	5,840	5,259	4,926	4,843	4,953
Mathematics and statistics	5,191	3,857	2,567	3,131	3,549	3,651	3,209	4,729	4,993	5,639	5,866	6,246	6,957	7,273	7,589	8,451	9,082	10,443
Military technologies and applied sciences	2	0	43	83	0	136	0	0	3	0	0	29	32	29	71	152	274	355
Multi/interdisciplinary studies	924	1,283	2,356	2,869	2,079	2,713	3,413	4,396	5,166	5,947	6,762	7,746	7,953	8,120	8,100	8,554	9,264	10,175
Parks, recreation, leisure, and fitness studies	218	571	643	570	483	1,684	2,354	3,994	4,443	5,617	6,546	7,047	7,139	7,609	7,654	8,268	8,651	9,005
Philosophy and religious studies	1,326	1,358	1,231	1,193	1,471	1,363	1,386	1,739	1,879	2,045	1,839	2,003	1,934	2,095	1,912	1,756	1,704	1,692
Physical sciences and science technologies	6,336	5,428	5,246	5,860	5,281	5,910	5,134	6,063	6,058	6,066	6,386	6,911	7,014	6,984	7,100	7,131	7,136	7,196
Precision production	0	0	0	0	0	8	2	0	3	10	5	11	9	15	4	10	14	11
Psychology	5,717	10,167	10,223	9,845	11,349	15,152	16,539	19,775	21,420	23,763	25,062	27,052	27,787	27,926	26,772	27,645	27,539	27,841
Public administration and social services	7,785	15,209	17,803	15,692	17,905	24,229	25,268	30,492	32,962	35,740	38,614	41,737	43,591	44,508	45,948	46,754	45,361	46,294
Social sciences and history	16,539	15,953	11,945	10,564	12,233	15,012	13,791	17,368	18,496	20,234	21,085	21,591	21,591	21,497	20,533	19,861	20,004	19,884
Theology and religious vocations	7,747	8,964	11,061	11,826	10,498	10,909	9,876	11,758	12,578	12,848	13,170	13,341	14,275	14,128	14,278	14,352	13,694	13,828
Transportation and materials moving	0	0	0	0	406	919	756	784	992	1,074	1,390	1,702	1,444	1,243	971	911	839	815
Visual and performing arts	6,675	8,817	8,629	8,420	8,657	10,280	11,404	13,531	14,170	15,562	16,277	17,307	17,869	17,869	17,756	18,052	17,516	17,686
Not classified by field of study	0	0	0	0	8,523	780	528	0	84	0	0	0	0	0	0	0	0	0

NOTE: Data are for postsecondary institutions participating in Title IV federal financial aid programs. The figures for earlier years have been reclassified when necessary to make them conform to the new taxonomy. To facilitate trend comparisons, certain aggregations have been made of the degree fields as reported in the Integrated Postsecondary Education Data System (IPEDS): "Agriculture and natural resources" includes Agriculture, agriculture operations, and related sciences and Natural resources and conservation; "Business" includes Business, management, marketing, and related support services and Personal and culinary services; and "Engineering technologies" includes Engineering technologies and engineering-related fields, Construction trades, and Mechanic and repair technologies/technicians. Some data have been revised from previously published figures.
SOURCE: U.S. Department of Education, National Center for Education Statistics, Higher Education General Information Survey (HEGIS), "Degrees and Other Formal Awards Conferred" surveys, 1970–71 through 1985–86; Integrated Postsecondary Education Data System (IPEDS), "Completions Survey" (IPEDS-C:91–99); and IPEDS Fall 2000 through Fall 2018, Completions component. (This table was prepared November 2019.)

Table 323.20. Master's degrees conferred by postsecondary institutions, by race/ethnicity and sex of student: Selected years, 1976–77 through 2017–18

	Number of degrees conferred to U.S. citizens, permanent residents, and nonresident aliens								Percentage distribution of degrees conferred to U.S. citizens and permanent residents						
Year and sex	Total	White	Black	Hispanic	Asian/ Pacific Islander	American Indian/ Alaska Native	Two or more races[1]	Non-resident alien	Total	White	Black	Hispanic	Asian/ Pacific Islander	American Indian/ Alaska Native	Two or more races[1]
1	2	3	4	5	6	7	8	9	10	11	12	13	14	15	16
Total															
1976–77[2]	322,463	271,402	21,252	6,136	5,127	1,018	—	17,528	100.0	89.0	7.0	2.0	1.7	0.3	—
1980–81[3]	301,081	247,475	17,436	6,534	6,348	1,044	—	22,244	100.0	88.8	6.3	2.3	2.3	0.4	—
1990–91	342,863	265,927	17,023	8,981	11,869	1,189	—	37,874	100.0	87.2	5.6	2.9	3.9	0.4	—
1999–2000	463,185	324,990	36,606	19,379	23,523	2,263	—	56,424	100.0	79.9	9.0	4.8	5.8	0.6	—
2000–01	473,502	324,211	38,853	21,661	24,544	2,496	—	61,737	100.0	78.7	9.4	5.3	6.0	0.6	—
2003–04	564,272	373,448	51,402	29,806	31,202	3,206	—	75,208	100.0	76.4	10.5	6.1	6.4	0.7	—
2004–05	580,151	383,246	55,330	31,639	33,042	3,310	—	73,584	100.0	75.7	10.9	6.2	6.5	0.7	—
2005–06	599,862	397,519	59,822	32,578	34,302	3,519	—	72,122	100.0	75.3	11.3	6.2	6.5	0.7	—
2006–07	610,703	403,623	63,439	34,962	36,420	3,590	—	68,669	100.0	74.5	11.7	6.5	6.7	0.7	—
2007–08	630,844	413,348	65,912	36,899	37,743	3,775	—	73,167	100.0	74.1	11.8	6.6	6.8	0.7	—
2008–09	662,082	427,713	70,772	39,567	40,510	3,777	—	79,743	100.0	73.4	12.2	6.8	7.0	0.6	—
2009–10	693,313	445,158	76,472	43,603	42,520	3,965	—	81,595	100.0	72.8	12.5	7.1	7.0	0.6	—
2010–11	730,922	462,922	80,742	46,823	43,482	3,946	6,597	86,410	100.0	71.8	12.5	7.3	6.7	0.6	1.0
2011–12	755,967	470,822	86,007	50,994	45,379	3,681	9,823	89,261	100.0	70.6	12.9	7.6	6.8	0.6	1.5
2012–13	751,718	455,896	87,989	52,991	44,906	3,693	11,794	94,449	100.0	69.4	13.4	8.1	6.8	0.6	1.8
2013–14	754,582	444,771	88,606	55,962	44,533	3,512	13,417	103,781	100.0	68.3	13.6	8.6	6.8	0.5	2.1
2014–15	758,804	433,096	87,288	58,752	44,489	3,410	14,628	117,141	100.0	67.5	13.6	9.2	6.9	0.5	2.3
2015–16	785,757	431,885	88,786	63,060	45,921	3,538	16,589	135,978	100.0	66.5	13.7	9.7	7.1	0.5	2.6
2016–17	804,542	433,638	89,577	67,026	47,810	3,397	17,674	145,420	100.0	65.8	13.6	10.2	7.3	0.5	2.7
2017–18	820,102	439,051	91,273	72,470	50,091	3,318	18,850	145,049	100.0	65.0	13.5	10.7	7.4	0.5	2.8
Males															
1976–77[2]	172,703	144,042	7,970	3,328	3,128	565	—	13,670	100.0	90.6	5.0	2.1	2.0	0.4	—
1980–81[3]	151,602	120,927	6,418	3,155	3,830	507	—	16,765	100.0	89.7	4.8	2.3	2.8	0.4	—
1990–91	160,842	117,993	6,201	4,017	6,765	495	—	25,371	100.0	87.1	4.6	3.0	5.0	0.4	—
1999–2000	196,129	131,221	11,642	7,738	11,299	845	—	33,384	100.0	80.6	7.2	4.8	6.9	0.5	—
2000–01	197,770	128,516	11,878	8,371	11,561	925	—	36,519	100.0	79.7	7.4	5.2	7.2	0.6	—
2003–04	233,056	146,369	15,027	10,929	14,551	1,137	—	45,043	100.0	77.9	8.0	5.8	7.7	0.6	—
2004–05	237,155	150,076	16,136	11,501	15,238	1,167	—	43,037	100.0	77.3	8.3	5.9	7.8	0.6	—
2005–06	241,701	153,696	17,388	11,738	16,037	1,253	—	41,589	100.0	76.8	8.7	5.9	8.0	0.6	—
2006–07	242,213	154,250	18,340	12,471	16,689	1,275	—	39,188	100.0	76.0	9.0	6.1	8.2	0.6	—
2007–08	250,203	157,622	18,759	13,166	17,480	1,294	—	41,882	100.0	75.7	9.0	6.3	8.4	0.6	—
2008–09	263,515	162,863	20,146	14,314	18,865	1,349	—	45,978	100.0	74.9	9.3	6.6	8.7	0.6	—
2009–10	275,317	170,243	22,121	15,554	19,423	1,419	—	46,557	100.0	74.4	9.7	6.8	8.5	0.6	—
2010–11	291,680	177,786	23,746	17,183	19,918	1,409	2,540	49,098	100.0	73.3	9.8	7.1	8.2	0.6	1.0
2011–12	302,484	183,222	25,284	18,633	20,751	1,298	3,518	49,778	100.0	72.5	10.0	7.4	8.2	0.5	1.4
2012–13	301,552	177,208	26,417	19,441	20,456	1,280	4,472	52,278	100.0	71.1	10.6	7.8	8.2	0.5	1.8
2013–14	302,846	173,303	26,608	20,565	19,955	1,219	4,890	56,306	100.0	70.3	10.8	8.3	8.1	0.5	2.0
2014–15	306,615	168,151	26,295	21,384	19,577	1,223	5,438	64,547	100.0	69.5	10.9	8.8	8.1	0.5	2.2
2015–16	320,574	166,161	27,024	22,749	20,071	1,229	6,129	77,211	100.0	68.3	11.1	9.3	8.2	0.5	2.5
2016–17	326,857	164,734	26,978	23,749	20,693	1,151	6,453	83,099	100.0	67.6	11.1	9.7	8.5	0.5	2.6
2017–18	326,870	164,714	27,552	25,255	21,273	1,076	6,658	80,342	100.0	66.8	11.2	10.2	8.6	0.4	2.7
Females															
1976–77[2]	149,760	127,360	13,282	2,808	1,999	453	—	3,858	100.0	87.3	9.1	1.9	1.4	0.3	—
1980–81[3]	149,479	126,548	11,018	3,379	2,518	537	—	5,479	100.0	87.9	7.7	2.3	1.7	0.4	—
1990–91	182,021	147,934	10,822	4,964	5,104	694	—	12,503	100.0	87.3	6.4	2.9	3.0	0.4	—
1999–2000	267,056	193,769	24,964	11,641	12,224	1,418	—	23,040	100.0	79.4	10.2	4.8	5.0	0.6	—
2000–01	275,732	195,695	26,975	13,290	12,983	1,571	—	25,218	100.0	78.1	10.8	5.3	5.2	0.6	—
2003–04	331,216	227,079	36,375	18,877	16,651	2,069	—	30,165	100.0	75.4	12.1	6.3	5.5	0.7	—
2004–05	342,996	233,170	39,194	20,138	17,804	2,143	—	30,547	100.0	74.6	12.5	6.4	5.7	0.7	—
2005–06	358,161	243,823	42,434	20,840	18,265	2,266	—	30,533	100.0	74.4	13.0	6.4	5.6	0.7	—
2006–07	368,490	249,373	45,099	22,491	19,731	2,315	—	29,481	100.0	73.6	13.3	6.6	5.8	0.7	—
2007–08	380,641	255,726	47,153	23,733	20,263	2,481	—	31,285	100.0	73.2	13.5	6.8	5.8	0.7	—
2008–09	398,567	264,850	50,626	25,253	21,645	2,428	—	33,765	100.0	72.6	13.9	6.9	5.9	0.7	—
2009–10	417,996	274,915	54,351	28,049	23,097	2,546	—	35,038	100.0	71.8	14.2	7.3	6.0	0.7	—
2010–11	439,242	285,136	56,996	29,640	23,564	2,537	4,057	37,312	100.0	70.9	14.2	7.4	5.9	0.6	1.0
2011–12	453,483	287,600	60,723	32,361	24,628	2,383	6,305	39,483	100.0	69.5	14.7	7.8	5.9	0.6	1.5
2012–13	450,166	278,688	61,572	33,550	24,450	2,413	7,322	42,171	100.0	68.3	15.1	8.2	6.0	0.6	1.8
2013–14	451,736	271,468	61,998	35,397	24,578	2,293	8,527	47,475	100.0	67.2	15.3	8.8	6.1	0.6	2.1
2014–15	452,189	264,945	60,993	37,368	24,912	2,187	9,190	52,594	100.0	66.3	15.3	9.4	6.2	0.5	2.3
2015–16	465,183	265,724	61,762	40,311	25,850	2,309	10,460	58,767	100.0	65.4	15.2	9.9	6.4	0.6	2.6
2016–17	477,685	268,904	62,599	43,277	27,117	2,246	11,221	62,321	100.0	64.7	15.1	10.4	6.5	0.5	2.7
2017–18	493,232	274,337	63,721	47,215	28,818	2,242	12,192	64,707	100.0	64.0	14.9	11.0	6.7	0.5	2.8

—Not available.
[1]For years prior to 2010–11, the survey did not yet include the "Two or more races" category, and each student could be counted in only one race category.
[2]Excludes 387 males and 175 females whose racial/ethnic group was not available.
[3]Excludes 1,377 males and 179 females whose racial/ethnic group was not available.
NOTE: Data are for postsecondary institutions participating in Title IV federal financial aid programs. Race categories exclude persons of Hispanic ethnicity. For 1989–90 and later years, reported racial/ethnic distributions of students by level of degree, field of degree,

and sex were used to estimate race/ethnicity for students whose race/ethnicity was not reported. Detail may not sum to totals because of rounding. Some data have been revised from previously published figures.
SOURCE: U.S. Department of Education, National Center for Education Statistics, Higher Education General Information Survey (HEGIS), "Degrees and Other Formal Awards Conferred" surveys, 1976–77 and 1980–81; Integrated Postsecondary Education Data System (IPEDS), "Completions Survey" (IPEDS-C:90–99); and IPEDS Fall 2000 through Fall 2018, Completions component. (This table was prepared October 2019.)

Table 323.30. Master's degrees conferred by postsecondary institutions, by race/ethnicity and field of study: 2016–17 and 2017–18

Field of study	2016–17 Total	White	Black	Hispanic	Asian/Pacific Islander Total	Asian	Pacific Islander	American Indian/Alaska Native	Two or more races	Non-resident alien	2017–18 Total	White	Black	Hispanic	Asian/Pacific Islander Total	Asian	Pacific Islander	American Indian/Alaska Native	Two or more races	Non-resident alien
	2	3	4	5	6	7	8	9	10	11	12	13	14	15	16	17	18	19	20	21
All fields, total	804,542	433,638	89,577	67,026	47,810	46,225	1,585	3,397	17,674	145,420	820,102	439,051	91,273	72,470	50,091	48,480	1,611	3,318	18,850	145,049
Agriculture and natural resources	6,843	4,615	245	392	221	214	7	34	185	1,151	6,967	4,651	249	420	235	225	10	39	185	1,188
Architecture and related services	7,883	3,630	332	700	443	435	8	25	169	2,584	7,317	3,236	338	639	430	421	9	18	179	2,477
Area, ethnic, cultural, gender, and group studies	1,717	765	165	222	129	121	8	69	64	303	1,673	715	172	255	81	80	1	67	74	309
Biological and biomedical sciences	16,282	8,504	1,198	1,287	2,162	2,146	16	43	495	2,593	17,180	8,865	1,336	1,410	2,352	2,334	18	33	514	2,670
Business	187,412	94,277	25,669	15,354	13,874	13,409	465	737	3,752	33,749	192,184	96,470	25,642	16,292	14,455	14,008	447	745	4,088	34,492
Communication, journalism, and related programs	10,119	5,116	1,349	939	380	370	10	38	304	1,993	10,243	5,039	1,438	1,028	336	325	11	32	314	2,056
Communications technologies	539	197	27	29	33	33	0	3	0	242	529	159	33	38	31	29	2	7	7	259
Computer and information sciences	46,553	8,664	2,345	1,275	3,587	3,538	49	78	531	30,073	46,468	9,411	2,601	1,492	3,484	3,441	43	53	609	28,818
Construction trades	—	—	—	—	—	—	—	—	—	—	—	—	—	—	—	—	—	—	—	—
Education	145,624	101,795	15,955	15,098	4,562	4,291	271	709	3,069	4,436	146,367	101,246	15,958	16,223	4,870	4,573	297	687	3,238	4,145
Engineering	52,826	14,861	1,147	2,137	3,743	3,701	39	67	697	30,177	51,721	15,186	1,142	2,253	3,727	3,698	29	64	767	28,582
Engineering technologies and engineering-related fields[1]	7,403	2,324	394	253	295	290	6	28	82	4,026	7,246	2,418	384	330	313	309	4	16	91	3,694
English language and literature/letters	8,244	6,107	484	699	275	270	6	57	270	351	8,300	6,020	581	709	257	253	4	47	310	376
Family and consumer sciences/human sciences	3,295	2,025	498	318	123	116	13	15	82	228	3,308	2,018	488	326	133	127	6	14	88	241
Foreign languages, literatures, and linguistics	3,271	1,547	81	532	96	96	0	9	95	911	3,261	1,540	75	569	131	127	4	6	68	872
Health professions and related programs	119,242	76,101	15,905	9,725	9,627	9,313	314	588	2,831	4,465	125,216	78,737	16,508	10,946	10,596	10,240	356	596	3,043	4,790
Homeland security, law enforcement, and firefighting	10,209	5,728	2,438	1,160	293	252	41	65	286	239	10,293	5,773	2,412	1,200	308	265	43	69	321	210
Legal professions and studies	8,674	2,083	699	494	325	320	6	61	92	4,919	9,177	2,208	753	574	315	306	9	81	139	5,107
Liberal arts and sciences, general studies, and humanities	2,485	1,668	287	257	63	59	4	25	62	123	2,473	1,585	316	232	73	71	2	30	81	156
Library science	4,843	3,824	256	389	131	125	6	24	146	73	4,953	3,881	240	446	133	128	5	18	154	81
Mathematics and statistics	9,082	2,777	187	309	663	658	5	5	132	5,009	10,443	2,965	188	363	720	716	4	4	124	6,079
Mechanic and repair technologies/technicians	0	0	0	0	0	0	0	0	0	0	1	1	0	0	0	0	0	0	0	0
Military technologies and applied sciences	274	158	67	15	5	5	0	0	3	26	355	198	75	29	16	15	1	3	9	25
Multi/interdisciplinary studies	9,264	5,158	902	811	515	506	10	45	297	1,535	10,175	5,495	934	928	647	631	16	41	294	1,836
Parks, recreation, leisure, and fitness studies	8,651	5,824	1,183	691	202	179	23	31	287	433	9,005	5,974	1,242	747	205	185	20	45	279	513
Philosophy and religious studies	1,704	1,148	116	144	80	79	1	4	40	172	1,692	1,144	130	141	77	74	3	6	44	150
Physical sciences and science technologies	7,136	3,855	186	394	380	374	6	14	159	2,148	7,196	3,879	197	443	414	406	8	11	193	2,059
Precision production	14	4	0	0	1	1	0	0	0	9	11	4	0	1	2	2	0	0	0	4
Psychology	27,539	16,974	3,788	3,461	1,199	1,108	91	150	897	1,070	27,841	16,707	3,907	3,777	1,286	1,206	80	145	928	1,091
Public administration and social services	45,361	24,289	8,755	6,203	1,892	1,781	111	285	1,295	2,642	46,294	24,602	9,023	6,621	1,842	1,738	104	289	1,366	2,551
Social sciences and history	20,004	10,942	1,430	1,713	892	872	20	74	546	4,407	19,884	10,588	1,456	1,820	844	826	18	60	566	4,550
Social sciences	16,569	8,205	1,312	1,447	827	808	19	63	446	4,269	16,612	8,012	1,313	1,544	786	771	15	50	484	4,423
History	3,435	2,737	118	266	65	64	1	11	100	138	3,272	2,576	143	276	58	55	3	10	82	127
Theology and religious vocations	13,694	8,774	2,237	691	708	685	23	54	243	987	13,828	8,624	2,215	766	808	778	30	45	271	1,099
Transportation and materials moving	839	547	98	43	35	33	2	4	43	69	815	507	71	72	35	33	2	6	32	92
Visual and performing arts	17,516	9,357	1,154	1,291	863	845	24	56	512	4,277	17,686	9,205	1,169	1,380	935	910	25	46	474	4,477
Other and not classified	—	—	—	—	—	—	—	—	—	—	—	—	—	—	—	—	—	—	—	—

[1]Excludes "Construction trades" and "Mechanic and repair technologies/technicians," which are listed separately.

NOTE: Data are for postsecondary institutions participating in Title IV federal financial aid programs. Race categories exclude persons of Hispanic ethnicity. Reported racial/ethnic distributions of students by level of degree, field of degree, and sex were used to estimate race/ethnicity for students whose race/ethnicity was not reported. To facilitate trend comparisons, certain aggregations have been made of the degree fields as reported in the Integrated Postsecondary Education Data System (IPEDS). "Agriculture and natural resources" includes Agriculture, agriculture operations, and related sciences and Natural resources and conservation; and "Business" includes Business management, marketing, and related support services and Personal and culinary services. Some data have been revised from previously published figures.

SOURCE: U.S. Department of Education, National Center for Education Statistics, Integrated Postsecondary Education Data System (IPEDS), Fall 2017 and Fall 2018, Completions component. (This table was prepared October 2019.)

Table 324.10. Doctor's degrees conferred by postsecondary institutions, by field of study: Selected years, 1970–71 through 2017–18

Field of study	1970–71	1975–76	1980–81	1985–86	1990–91	1995–96	2000–01	2005–06	2007–08	2009–10	2010–11	2011–12	2012–13	2013–14	2014–15	2015–16	2016–17	2017–18
1	2	3	4	5	6	7	8	9	10	11	12	13	14	15	16	17	18	19
Total	**64,998**	**91,007**	**98,016**	**100,280**	**105,547**	**115,507**	**119,585**	**138,056**	**149,190**	**158,590**	**163,827**	**170,217**	**175,026**	**177,587**	**178,548**	**178,134**	**181,357**	**184,074**
Agriculture and natural resources	1,086	928	1,067	1,158	1,185	1,259	1,127	1,194	1,261	1,149	1,246	1,333	1,411	1,407	1,561	1,526	1,561	1,496
Architecture and related services	36	82	93	73	135	141	153	201	199	210	205	255	247	247	272	245	291	250
Area, ethnic, cultural, gender, and group studies	143	186	161	156	159	183	216	226	270	253	278	302	291	336	312	323	349	335
Biological and biomedical sciences	3,603	3,347	3,640	3,405	4,152	5,250	5,225	6,162	7,398	7,672	7,693	7,935	7,939	8,302	8,053	7,939	8,087	8,222
Business	774	906	808	923	1,185	1,366	1,180	1,711	2,084	2,249	2,286	2,538	2,828	3,039	3,116	3,325	3,328	3,338
Communication, journalism, and related programs	145	196	171	212	259	338	368	461	489	570	577	563	612	611	644	629	615	666
Communications technologies	0	8	11	6	13	7	2	3	7	3	1	4	0	3	0	4	0	0
Computer and information sciences	128	244	252	344	676	869	768	1,416	1,697	1,599	1,588	1,698	1,834	1,982	1,998	1,989	1,982	2,017
Education	6,041	7,202	7,279	6,610	6,189	6,246	6,284	7,584	8,496	9,237	9,642	10,118	10,572	10,929	11,772	11,838	12,692	12,780
Engineering	3,687	2,872	2,598	3,444	5,316	6,304	5,485	7,243	7,929	7,706	8,369	8,722	9,356	10,010	10,239	10,265	10,371	10,817
Engineering technologies	1	2	10	12	14	50	62	75	55	67	56	134	111	107	123	133	152	212
English language and literature/letters	1,554	1,514	1,040	895	1,056	1,395	1,330	1,254	1,262	1,334	1,344	1,427	1,377	1,393	1,418	1,402	1,347	1,295
Family and consumer sciences/human sciences	123	178	247	307	229	375	354	340	323	296	320	325	351	335	335	374	317	274
Foreign languages, literatures, and linguistics	1,084	1,245	931	768	889	1,020	1,078	1,074	1,078	1,091	1,158	1,231	1,304	1,230	1,243	1,278	1,168	1,213
Health professions and related programs	15,988	25,267	29,595	31,922	29,842	32,678	39,019	45,677	51,655	57,750	60,221	62,097	64,192	67,447	71,004	73,687	77,693	80,305
Homeland security, law enforcement, and firefighting	1	9	21	21	28	38	44	80	88	106	131	117	147	152	193	205	177	150
Legal professions and studies	17,441	32,369	36,391	35,898	38,035	39,919	38,190	43,569	43,699	44,627	44,853	46,836	47,246	44,169	40,329	37,034	35,123	34,544
Liberal arts and sciences, general studies, and humanities	32	162	121	90	70	75	102	84	76	96	95	93	98	90	96	105	95	93
Library science	39	71	71	62	56	53	58	44	64	64	50	60	50	52	44	54	42	54
Mathematics and statistics	1,199	856	728	742	978	1,158	997	1,293	1,360	1,596	1,586	1,669	1,823	1,863	1,801	1,855	1,925	2,010
Multi/interdisciplinary studies	101	156	236	352	306	549	512	600	660	631	660	727	730	769	840	849	854	850
Parks, recreation, leisure, and fitness studies	2	15	42	39	28	104	177	194	228	266	257	288	295	317	311	331	319	298
Philosophy and religious studies	555	556	411	480	464	550	600	578	635	667	804	778	794	698	762	750	741	768
Physical sciences and science technologies	4,324	3,388	3,105	3,521	4,248	4,589	3,968	4,642	4,995	5,065	5,295	5,370	5,514	5,806	5,823	6,057	6,027	6,181
Psychology	2,144	3,157	3,576	3,593	3,932	4,141	5,091	4,921	5,296	5,540	5,851	5,936	6,326	6,634	6,583	6,540	6,702	6,275
Public administration and social services	174	292	362	382	430	499	574	704	760	838	851	890	979	1,047	1,123	1,066	1,116	1,157
Social sciences and history	3,660	4,157	3,122	2,955	3,012	3,760	3,930	3,914	4,058	4,238	4,390	4,597	4,610	4,724	4,828	4,706	4,706	4,676
Theology and religious vocations	312	1,022	1,273	1,185	1,076	1,517	1,461	1,429	1,615	2,071	2,374	2,446	2,174	2,103	1,927	1,808	1,792	2,023
Transportation and materials moving	0	0	0	3	0	0	0	0	0	0	0	0	1	7	5	8	11	16
Visual and performing arts	621	620	654	722	838	1,067	1,167	1,383	1,453	1,599	1,646	1,728	1,814	1,778	1,793	1,809	1,774	1,759
Not classified by field of study	0	0	0	0	747	0	63	0	0	0	0	0	0	0	0	0	0	0

NOTE: Data are for postsecondary institutions participating in Title IV federal financial aid programs. Includes Ph.D., Ed.D., and comparable degrees at the doctoral level, as well as such degrees as M.D., D.D.S., and law degrees that were classified as first-professional degrees prior to 2010–11. The new Classification of Instructional Programs was initiated in 2009–10. The figures for earlier years have been reclassified when necessary to make them conform to the new taxonomy. To facilitate trend comparisons, certain aggregations have been made of the degree fields as reported in the Integrated Postsecondary Education Data System (IPEDS). "Agriculture and natural resources" includes Agriculture, agriculture operations, and related sciences and Natural resources and conservation; "Business" includes Business, management, marketing, and related support services and Personal and culinary services; and "Engineering technologies" includes Engineering technologies and engineering-related fields, Construction trades, and Mechanic and repair technologies/technicians. Some data have been revised from previously published figures.

SOURCE: U.S. Department of Education, National Center for Education Statistics, Higher Education General Information Survey (HEGIS), "Degrees and Other Formal Awards Conferred" surveys, 1970–71 through 1985–86; Integrated Postsecondary Education Data System (IPEDS), "Completions Survey" (IPEDS-C:91–99); and IPEDS Fall 2000 through Fall 2018, Completions component. (This table was prepared November 2019.)

Table 324.20. Doctor's degrees conferred by postsecondary institutions, by race/ethnicity and sex of student: Selected years, 1976–77 through 2017–18

| Year and sex | Number of degrees conferred[1] to U.S. citizens, permanent residents, and nonresident aliens | | | | | | | | Percentage distribution of degrees conferred[1] to U.S. citizens and permanent residents | | | | | | |
	Total	White	Black	Hispanic	Asian/ Pacific Islander	American Indian/ Alaska Native	Two or more races[2]	Non-resident alien	Total	White	Black	Hispanic	Asian/ Pacific Islander	American Indian/ Alaska Native	Two or more races[2]
1	2	3	4	5	6	7	8	9	10	11	12	13	14	15	16
Total															
1976–77[3]	91,218	79,932	3,575	1,533	1,674	240	—	4,264	100.0	91.9	4.1	1.8	1.9	0.3	—
1980–81[4]	97,281	84,200	3,893	1,924	2,267	312	—	4,685	100.0	90.9	4.2	2.1	2.4	0.3	—
1990–91	105,547	81,791	4,429	3,210	5,120	356	—	10,641	100.0	86.2	4.7	3.4	5.4	0.4	—
1999–2000	118,736	82,984	7,078	5,042	10,682	708	—	12,242	100.0	77.9	6.6	4.7	10.0	0.7	—
2000–01	119,585	82,321	7,035	5,204	11,587	705	—	12,733	100.0	77.0	6.6	4.9	10.8	0.7	—
2003–04	126,087	84,695	8,089	5,795	12,371	771	—	14,366	100.0	75.8	7.2	5.2	11.1	0.7	—
2004–05	134,387	89,763	8,527	6,115	13,176	788	—	16,018	100.0	75.8	7.2	5.2	11.1	0.7	—
2005–06	138,056	91,050	8,523	6,202	13,686	929	—	17,666	100.0	75.6	7.1	5.2	11.4	0.8	—
2006–07	144,694	94,225	9,371	6,576	14,727	917	—	18,878	100.0	74.9	7.4	5.2	11.7	0.7	—
2007–08	149,190	97,701	9,451	6,933	15,170	932	—	19,003	100.0	75.0	7.3	5.3	11.7	0.7	—
2008–09	154,564	101,400	10,188	7,497	15,840	978	—	18,661	100.0	74.6	7.5	5.5	11.7	0.7	—
2009–10	158,590	104,419	10,413	8,085	16,560	952	—	18,161	100.0	74.4	7.4	5.8	11.8	0.7	—
2010–11	163,827	105,990	10,934	8,662	17,078	947	1,251	18,965	100.0	73.2	7.5	6.0	11.8	0.7	0.9
2011–12	170,217	109,365	11,794	9,223	17,896	915	1,571	19,453	100.0	72.5	7.8	6.1	11.9	0.6	1.0
2012–13	175,026	110,759	12,085	10,108	18,406	900	2,440	20,328	100.0	71.6	7.8	6.5	11.9	0.6	1.6
2013–14	177,587	110,157	12,621	10,665	19,118	861	2,966	21,199	100.0	70.4	8.1	6.8	12.2	0.6	1.9
2014–15	178,548	108,914	13,272	11,263	19,186	884	3,670	21,359	100.0	69.3	8.4	7.2	12.2	0.6	2.3
2015–16	178,134	107,235	13,377	11,781	19,614	811	3,782	21,534	100.0	68.5	8.5	7.5	12.5	0.5	2.4
2016–17	181,357	107,444	14,070	12,493	20,345	747	4,166	22,092	100.0	67.5	8.8	7.8	12.8	0.5	2.6
2017–18	184,074	107,415	14,241	13,253	20,762	707	4,497	23,199	100.0	66.8	8.9	8.2	12.9	0.4	2.8
Males															
1976–77[3]	71,709	62,977	2,338	1,216	1,311	182	—	3,685	100.0	92.6	3.4	1.8	1.9	0.3	—
1980–81[4]	68,853	59,574	2,206	1,338	1,589	223	—	3,923	100.0	91.8	3.4	2.1	2.4	0.3	—
1990–91	64,242	48,812	1,991	1,835	3,038	196	—	8,370	100.0	87.4	3.6	3.3	5.4	0.4	—
1999–2000	64,930	45,308	2,762	2,602	5,467	333	—	8,458	100.0	80.2	4.9	4.6	9.7	0.6	—
2000–01	64,171	44,131	2,655	2,564	5,759	346	—	8,716	100.0	79.6	4.8	4.6	10.4	0.6	—
2003–04	63,981	43,014	2,888	2,731	5,620	357	—	9,371	100.0	78.8	5.3	5.0	10.3	0.7	—
2004–05	67,257	44,749	2,904	2,863	5,913	370	—	10,458	100.0	78.8	5.1	5.0	10.4	0.7	—
2005–06	68,912	45,476	2,949	2,850	5,977	429	—	11,231	100.0	78.8	5.1	4.9	10.4	0.7	—
2006–07	71,311	46,215	3,223	3,037	6,449	421	—	11,966	100.0	77.9	5.4	5.1	10.9	0.7	—
2007–08	73,340	48,118	3,291	3,139	6,516	447	—	11,829	100.0	78.2	5.4	5.1	10.6	0.7	—
2008–09	75,674	49,880	3,531	3,388	6,914	460	—	11,501	100.0	77.7	5.5	5.3	10.8	0.7	—
2009–10	76,610	50,707	3,609	3,642	7,184	430	—	11,038	100.0	77.3	5.5	5.6	11.0	0.7	—
2010–11	79,672	51,688	3,838	3,990	7,545	454	557	11,600	100.0	75.9	5.6	5.9	11.1	0.7	0.8
2011–12	82,670	53,488	4,121	4,218	7,792	418	701	11,932	100.0	75.6	5.8	6.0	11.0	0.6	1.0
2012–13	85,080	54,196	4,310	4,473	8,190	400	1,085	12,426	100.0	74.6	5.9	6.2	11.3	0.6	1.5
2013–14	85,585	53,374	4,510	4,788	8,270	365	1,297	12,981	100.0	73.5	6.2	6.6	11.4	0.5	1.8
2014–15	84,922	52,069	4,464	5,011	8,330	410	1,678	12,960	100.0	72.4	6.2	7.0	11.6	0.6	2.3
2015–16	84,240	50,694	4,564	5,122	8,632	371	1,718	13,139	100.0	71.3	6.4	7.2	12.1	0.5	2.4
2016–17	84,649	50,002	4,794	5,421	8,906	307	1,780	13,439	100.0	70.2	6.7	7.6	12.5	0.4	2.5
2017–18	85,568	49,649	4,957	5,856	9,004	309	1,869	13,924	100.0	69.3	6.9	8.2	12.6	0.4	2.6
Females															
1976–77[3]	19,509	16,955	1,237	317	363	58	—	579	100.0	89.6	6.5	1.7	1.9	0.3	—
1980–81[4]	28,428	24,626	1,687	586	678	89	—	762	100.0	89.0	6.1	2.1	2.5	0.3	—
1990–91	41,305	32,979	2,438	1,375	2,082	160	—	2,271	100.0	84.5	6.2	3.5	5.3	0.4	—
1999–2000	53,806	37,676	4,316	2,440	5,215	375	—	3,784	100.0	75.3	8.6	4.9	10.4	0.7	—
2000–01	55,414	38,190	4,380	2,640	5,828	359	—	4,017	100.0	74.3	8.5	5.1	11.3	0.7	—
2003–04	62,106	41,681	5,201	3,064	6,751	414	—	4,995	100.0	73.0	9.1	5.4	11.8	0.7	—
2004–05	67,130	45,014	5,623	3,252	7,263	418	—	5,560	100.0	73.1	9.1	5.3	11.8	0.7	—
2005–06	69,144	45,574	5,574	3,352	7,709	500	—	6,435	100.0	72.7	8.9	5.3	12.3	0.8	—
2006–07	73,383	48,010	6,148	3,539	8,278	496	—	6,912	100.0	72.2	9.2	5.3	12.5	0.7	—
2007–08	75,850	49,583	6,160	3,794	8,654	485	—	7,174	100.0	72.2	9.0	5.5	12.6	0.7	—
2008–09	78,890	51,520	6,657	4,109	8,926	518	—	7,160	100.0	71.8	9.3	5.7	12.4	0.7	—
2009–10	81,980	53,712	6,804	4,443	9,376	522	—	7,123	100.0	71.8	9.1	5.9	12.5	0.7	—
2010–11	84,155	54,302	7,096	4,672	9,533	493	694	7,365	100.0	70.7	9.2	6.1	12.4	0.6	0.9
2011–12	87,547	55,877	7,673	5,005	10,104	497	870	7,521	100.0	69.8	9.6	6.3	12.6	0.6	1.1
2012–13	89,946	56,563	7,775	5,635	10,216	500	1,355	7,902	100.0	68.9	9.5	6.9	12.5	0.6	1.7
2013–14	92,002	56,783	8,111	5,877	10,848	496	1,669	8,218	100.0	67.8	9.7	7.0	12.9	0.6	2.0
2014–15	93,626	56,845	8,808	6,252	10,856	474	1,992	8,399	100.0	66.7	10.3	7.3	12.7	0.6	2.3
2015–16	93,894	56,541	8,813	6,659	10,982	440	2,064	8,395	100.0	66.1	10.3	7.8	12.8	0.5	2.4
2016–17	96,708	57,442	9,276	7,072	11,439	440	2,386	8,653	100.0	65.2	10.5	8.0	13.0	0.5	2.7
2017–18	98,506	57,766	9,284	7,397	11,758	398	2,628	9,275	100.0	64.7	10.4	8.3	13.2	0.4	2.9

—Not available.
[1]Includes Ph.D., Ed.D., and comparable degrees at the doctoral level, as well as such degrees as M.D., D.D.S., and law degrees that were classified as first-professional degrees prior to 2010–11.
[2]For years prior to 2010–11, the survey did not yet include the "Two or more races" category, and each student could be counted in only one race category.
[3]Excludes 500 males and 12 females whose racial/ethnic group was not available.
[4]Excludes 714 males and 21 females whose racial/ethnic group was not available.
NOTE: Data are for postsecondary institutions participating in Title IV federal financial aid programs. Race categories exclude persons of Hispanic ethnicity. For 1989–90 and later years, reported racial/ethnic distributions of students by level of degree, field of degree, and sex were used to estimate race/ethnicity for students whose race/ethnicity was not reported. Detail may not sum to totals because of rounding. Some data have been revised from previously published figures.
SOURCE: U.S. Department of Education, National Center for Education Statistics, Higher Education General Information Survey (HEGIS), "Degrees and Other Formal Awards Conferred" surveys, 1976–77 and 1980–81; Integrated Postsecondary Education Data System (IPEDS), "Completions Survey" (IPEDS-C:90–99); and IPEDS Fall 2000 through Fall 2018, Completions component. (This table was prepared October 2019.)

Table 324.25. Doctor's degrees conferred by postsecondary institutions, by race/ethnicity and field of study: 2016–17 and 2017–18

Field of study	2016–17 Total	White	Black	Hispanic	A/PI Total	Asian	Pacific Islander	American Indian/Alaska Native	Two or more races	Nonresident alien	2017–18 Total	White	Black	Hispanic	A/PI Total	Asian	Pacific Islander	American Indian/Alaska Native	Two or more races	Nonresident alien
	2	3	4	5	6	7	8	9	10	11	12	13	14	15	16	17	18	19	20	21
All fields, total	181,357	107,444	14,070	12,493	20,345	20,017	328	747	4,166	22,092	184,074	107,415	14,241	13,253	20,762	20,447	315	707	4,497	23,199
Agriculture and natural resources	1,561	722	49	56	51	51	0	3	20	660	1,496	726	49	52	45	43	2	5	20	599
Architecture and related services	291	103	7	15	36	33	3	1	9	120	250	81	14	13	25	24	1	1	9	107
Area, ethnic, cultural, gender, and group studies	349	153	58	42	18	18	0	4	9	65	335	139	55	35	28	26	2	13	12	53
Biological and biomedical sciences	8,087	4,246	303	467	769	758	11	25	210	2,067	8,222	4,427	322	479	733	727	6	13	179	2,069
Business	3,328	1,411	721	206	238	231	7	14	43	695	3,338	1,467	726	148	217	206	11	11	64	705
Communication, journalism, and related programs	615	357	49	30	35	35	0	2	12	130	666	385	34	19	28	27	1	3	13	184
Communications technologies	0	0	0	0	0	0	0	0	0	0	0	0	0	0	0	0	0	0	0	0
Computer and information sciences	1,982	617	85	54	116	115	1	2	19	1,089	2,017	572	76	58	122	122	0	4	27	1,158
Construction trades	0	0	0	0	0	0	0	0	0	0	0	0	0	0	0	0	0	0	0	0
Education	12,692	7,582	2,639	1,009	444	407	37	90	219	709	12,780	7,582	2,491	1,156	462	431	31	79	260	750
Engineering	10,371	3,076	187	319	749	744	5	12	117	5,911	10,817	3,190	179	303	720	720	0	11	143	6,271
Engineering technologies and engineering-related fields	152	65	13	6	11	11	0	0	0	57	212	92	33	7	20	20	0	0	3	57
English language and literature/letters[1]	1,347	994	54	97	49	47	2	10	32	111	1,295	946	65	74	64	63	1	7	25	114
Family and consumer sciences/human sciences	317	172	30	18	21	21	0	1	5	70	274	141	25	15	16	16	0	0	6	71
Foreign languages, literatures, and linguistics	1,168	604	12	121	50	50	0	4	13	364	1,213	565	20	147	49	48	1	3	21	408
Health professions and related programs	77,693	49,286	5,031	4,851	13,715	13,536	179	260	1,949	2,601	80,305	50,069	5,345	5,322	14,325	14,146	179	274	2,186	2,784
Homeland security, law enforcement, and firefighting	177	107	30	16	2	2	0	1	0	21	150	88	20	16	5	4	1	1	3	17
Legal professions and studies	35,123	23,319	3,006	3,730	2,594	2,537	57	231	1,022	1,221	34,544	22,601	3,073	3,946	2,385	2,333	52	198	1,007	1,334
Liberal arts and sciences, general studies, and humanities	95	74	3	5	4	3	1	1	3	5	93	67	3	4	4	4	0	1	2	12
Library science	42	21	4	3	4	3	1	0	3	10	54	27	4	2	6	6	0	0	1	14
Mathematics and statistics	1,925	739	22	50	138	138	0	3	30	943	2,010	753	35	62	124	122	2	1	32	1,003
Mechanic and repair technologies/technicians	0	0	0	0	0	0	0	0	0	0	0	0	0	0	0	0	0	0	0	0
Military technologies and applied sciences	0	0	0	0	0	0	0	0	0	0	0	0	0	0	0	0	0	0	0	0
Multi/interdisciplinary studies	854	462	82	40	44	44	0	5	20	201	850	462	79	51	49	47	2	4	12	193
Parks, recreation, leisure, and fitness studies	319	208	20	11	6	6	0	1	7	66	298	189	21	7	10	10	0	1	8	62
Philosophy and religious studies	741	509	42	29	31	31	0	2	18	110	768	526	57	28	23	23	0	2	12	120
Physical sciences and science technologies	6,027	2,910	110	227	327	326	1	14	85	2,354	6,181	2,910	120	226	367	359	8	9	109	2,440
Precision production	0	0	0	0	0	0	0	0	0	0	0	0	0	0	0	0	0	0	0	0
Psychology	6,702	4,525	623	597	388	373	15	25	162	382	6,275	4,231	515	576	386	380	6	30	166	371
Public administration and social services	1,116	575	238	67	54	54	0	5	26	151	1,157	596	223	75	42	40	2	9	30	182
Social sciences and history	4,706	2,564	238	259	215	211	4	19	88	1,323	4,676	2,472	218	259	247	243	4	17	96	1,367
Social sciences	3,781	1,909	197	184	189	185	4	13	71	1,218	3,765	1,827	170	190	221	218	3	15	85	1,257
History	925	655	41	75	26	26	0	6	17	105	911	645	48	69	26	25	1	2	11	110
Theology and religious vocations	1,792	950	364	71	143	140	3	4	12	248	2,023	1,070	385	90	148	146	2	6	22	302
Transportation and materials moving	11	7	0	0	0	0	0	0	0	0	16	9	2	0	2	2	0	0	0	5
Visual and performing arts	1,774	1,086	50	97	93	92	1	8	36	404	1,759	1,032	54	83	110	109	1	4	29	447
Other and not classified	0	0	0	0	0	0	0	0	0	0	0	0	0	0	0	0	0	0	0	0

[1]Excludes "Construction trades" and "Mechanic and repair technologies/technicians," which are listed separately.

NOTE: Data are for postsecondary institutions participating in Title IV federal financial aid programs. Race categories exclude persons of Hispanic ethnicity. Reported racial/ethnic distributions of students by level of degree, field of degree, and sex were used to estimate race/ethnicity for students whose race/ethnicity was not reported. To facilitate trend comparisons, certain aggregations have been made of the degree fields as reported in the Integrated Postsecondary Education Data System

(IPEDS). "Agriculture and natural resources" includes Agriculture, agriculture operations, and related sciences and Natural resources and conservation; and "Business" includes Business management, marketing, and related support services and Personal and culinary services. Some data have been revised from previously published figures.
SOURCE: U.S. Department of Education, National Center for Education Statistics, Integrated Postsecondary Education Data System (IPEDS), Fall 2017 and Fall 2018, Completions component. (This table was prepared October 2019.)

Table 324.40. Number of postsecondary institutions conferring doctor's degrees in dentistry, medicine, and law, and number of such degrees conferred, by sex of student: Selected years, 1949–50 through 2017–18

	Dentistry (D.D.S. or D.M.D.)				Medicine (M.D.)				Law (LL.B. or J.D.)			
	Number of institutions conferring degrees	Number of degrees conferred			Number of institutions conferring degrees	Number of degrees conferred			Number of institutions conferring degrees	Number of degrees conferred		
Year		Total	Males	Females		Total	Males	Females		Total	Males	Females
1	2	3	4	5	6	7	8	9	10	11	12	13
1949–50	40	2,579	2,561	18	72	5,612	5,028	584	—	—	—	—
1951–52	41	2,918	2,895	23	72	6,201	5,871	330	—	—	—	—
1953–54	42	3,102	3,063	39	73	6,712	6,377	335	—	—	—	—
1955–56	42	3,009	2,975	34	73	6,810	6,464	346	131	8,262	7,974	288
1957–58	43	3,065	3,031	34	75	6,816	6,469	347	131	9,394	9,122	272
1959–60	45	3,247	3,221	26	79	7,032	6,645	387	134	9,240	9,010	230
1961–62	46	3,183	3,166	17	81	7,138	6,749	389	134	9,364	9,091	273
1963–64	46	3,180	3,168	12	82	7,303	6,878	425	133	10,679	10,372	307
1964–65	46	3,108	3,086	22	81	7,304	6,832	472	137	11,583	11,216	367
1965–66	47	3,178	3,146	32	84	7,673	7,170	503	136	13,246	12,776	470
1967–68	48	3,422	3,375	47	85	7,944	7,318	626	138	16,454	15,805	649
1968–69	—	3,408	3,376	32	—	8,025	7,415	610	—	17,053	16,373	680
1969–70	48	3,718	3,684	34	86	8,314	7,615	699	145	14,916	14,115	801
1970–71	48	3,745	3,703	42	89	8,919	8,110	809	147	17,421	16,181	1,240
1971–72	48	3,862	3,819	43	92	9,253	8,423	830	147	21,764	20,266	1,498
1972–73	51	4,047	3,992	55	97	10,307	9,388	919	152	27,205	25,037	2,168
1973–74	52	4,440	4,355	85	99	11,356	10,093	1,263	151	29,326	25,986	3,340
1974–75	52	4,773	4,627	146	104	12,447	10,818	1,629	154	29,296	24,881	4,415
1975–76	56	5,425	5,187	238	107	13,426	11,252	2,174	166	32,293	26,085	6,208
1976–77	57	5,138	4,764	374	109	13,461	10,891	2,570	169	34,104	26,447	7,657
1977–78	57	5,189	4,623	566	109	14,279	11,210	3,069	169	34,402	25,457	8,945
1978–79	58	5,434	4,794	640	109	14,786	11,381	3,405	175	35,206	25,180	10,026
1979–80	58	5,258	4,558	700	112	14,902	11,416	3,486	179	35,647	24,893	10,754
1980–81	58	5,460	4,672	788	116	15,505	11,672	3,833	176	36,331	24,563	11,768
1981–82	59	5,282	4,467	815	119	15,814	11,867	3,947	180	35,991	23,965	12,026
1982–83	59	5,585	4,631	954	118	15,484	11,350	4,134	177	36,853	23,550	13,303
1983–84	60	5,353	4,302	1,051	119	15,813	11,359	4,454	179	37,012	23,382	13,630
1984–85	59	5,339	4,233	1,106	120	16,041	11,167	4,874	181	37,491	23,070	14,421
1985–86	59	5,046	3,907	1,139	120	15,938	11,022	4,916	181	35,844	21,874	13,970
1986–87	58	4,741	3,603	1,138	121	15,428	10,431	4,997	179	36,056	21,561	14,495
1987–88	57	4,477	3,300	1,177	122	15,358	10,278	5,080	180	35,397	21,067	14,330
1988–89	58	4,265	3,124	1,141	124	15,460	10,310	5,150	182	35,634	21,069	14,565
1989–90	57	4,100	2,834	1,266	124	15,075	9,923	5,152	182	36,485	21,079	15,406
1990–91	55	3,699	2,510	1,189	121	15,043	9,629	5,414	179	37,945	21,643	16,302
1991–92	52	3,593	2,431	1,162	120	15,243	9,796	5,447	177	38,848	22,260	16,588
1992–93	55	3,605	2,383	1,222	122	15,531	9,679	5,852	184	40,302	23,182	17,120
1993–94	53	3,787	2,330	1,457	121	15,368	9,544	5,824	185	40,044	22,826	17,218
1994–95	53	3,897	2,480	1,417	119	15,537	9,507	6,030	183	39,349	22,592	16,757
1995–96	53	3,697	2,374	1,323	119	15,341	9,061	6,280	183	39,828	22,508	17,320
1996–97	52	3,784	2,387	1,397	118	15,571	9,121	6,450	184	40,079	22,548	17,531
1997–98	53	4,032	2,490	1,542	117	15,424	9,006	6,418	185	39,331	21,876	17,455
1998–99	53	4,143	2,673	1,470	118	15.566	8,972	6,594	185	38,207	21,102	17,195
1999–2000	54	4,250	2,547	1,703	118	15,286	8,761	6,525	190	38,152	20,638	17,514
2000–01	54	4,391	2,696	1,695	118	15,403	8,728	6,675	192	37,904	19,981	17,923
2001–02	53	4,239	2,608	1,631	118	15,237	8,469	6,768	192	38,981	20,254	18,727
2002–03	53	4,345	2,654	1,691	118	15,034	8,221	6,813	194	39,067	19,916	19,151
2003–04	53	4,335	2,532	1,803	118	15,442	8,273	7,169	195	40,209	20,332	19,877
2004–05	53	4,454	2,505	1,949	120	15,461	8,151	7,310	198	43,423	22,297	21,126
2005–06	54	4,389	2,435	1,954	119	15,455	7,900	7,555	197	43,440	22,597	20,843
2006–07	55	4,596	2,548	2,048	120	15,730	7,987	7,743	200	43,485	22,777	20,708
2007–08	55	4,795	2,661	2,134	120	15,646	7,935	7,711	201	43,588	23,110	20,478
2008–09	55	4,918	2,637	2,281	120	15,987	8,164	7,823	203	44,045	23,860	20,185
2009–10	55	5,062	2,745	2,317	120	16,356	8,468	7,888	205	44,346	23,384	20,962
2010–11	55	5,071	2,764	2,307	120	16,863	8,701	8,162	206	44,421	23,481	20,940
2011–12	55	5,109	2,748	2,361	120	16,927	8,809	8,118	207	46,445	24,576	21,869
2012–13	56	5,219	2,707	2,512	122	17,264	8,976	8,288	209	46,811	25,087	21,724
2013–14	57	5,407	2,839	2,568	124	17,604	9,232	8,372	210	43,772	23,278	20,494
2014–15	60	5,816	3,030	2,786	127	18,302	9,558	8,744	212	40,024	20,810	19,214
2015–16	61	5,951	3,032	2,919	128	18,409	9,852	8,557	214	36,798	18,935	17,863
2016–17	63	6,388	3,328	3,060	131	18,698	9,834	8,864	214	34,894	17,579	17,315
2017–18	63	6,441	3,258	3,183	133	19,142	10,049	9,093	211	34,128	17,161	16,967

—Not available.
NOTE: Data are for postsecondary institutions participating in Title IV federal financial aid programs. Some data have been revised from previously published figures.
SOURCE: U.S. Department of Education, National Center for Education Statistics, *Earned Degrees Conferred*, 1949–50 through 1964–65; Higher Education General Information Survey (HEGIS), "Degrees and Other Formal Awards Conferred" surveys, 1965–66 through 1985–86; Integrated Postsecondary Education Data System (IPEDS), "Completions Survey" (IPEDS-C:87–99); and IPEDS Fall 2000 through Fall 2018, Completions component. (This table was prepared April 2020.)

Table 326.15. Percentage distribution of first-time, full-time bachelor's degree-seeking students at 4-year postsecondary institutions 6 years after entry, by completion and enrollment status at first institution attended, sex, race/ethnicity, control of institution, and percentage of applications accepted: Cohort entry years 2007 and 2012

Sex, race/ethnicity, control of institution, and percent of applications accepted	Total	Bachelor's degree	Award below bachelor's degree level	Trans-ferred out[1]	Remained enrolled	No longer enrolled, status unknown[2]	Total	Bachelor's degree	Award below bachelor's degree level	Trans-ferred out[1]	Remained enrolled	No longer enrolled, status unknown[2]
	\<--- Percentage distribution of 2007 entry cohort 6 years after entry ---\> Completed an award at first institution attended / Did not complete an award at first institution						\<--- Percentage distribution of 2012 entry cohort 6 years after entry ---\> Completed an award at first institution attended / Did not complete an award at first institution					
1	2	3	4	5	6	7	8	9	10	11	12	13
Total	100.0	59.4	0.3	9.3	2.5	28.4	100.0	62.4	0.4	12.4	2.2	22.6
Sex												
Male	100.0	56.5	0.3	9.3	3.0	30.9	100.0	59.0	0.3	12.5	2.7	25.6
Female	100.0	61.9	0.4	9.3	2.1	26.3	100.0	65.3	0.5	12.3	1.8	20.2
Race/ethnicity												
White	100.0	62.9	0.3	9.2	2.0	25.6	100.0	65.9	0.4	12.0	1.7	19.9
Black	100.0	40.7	0.3	12.9	3.5	42.6	100.0	42.4	0.4	19.0	3.0	35.3
Hispanic	100.0	52.5	0.3	9.3	4.6	33.2	100.0	56.7	0.4	12.8	3.8	26.3
Asian	100.0	70.5	0.2	7.0	3.1	19.2	100.0	75.5	0.2	7.9	2.7	13.7
Pacific Islander	100.0	49.5	0.5	3.9	4.0	42.2	100.0	49.1	1.5	10.9	2.8	35.7
American Indian/Alaska Native	100.0	40.6	0.9	12.4	3.7	42.4	100.0	40.6	1.0	15.7	3.1	39.6
Two or more races	100.0	67.8	0.2	6.1	2.8	23.0	100.0	57.7	0.4	12.7	2.4	26.8
Sex and race/ethnicity												
Male												
White	100.0	60.0	0.3	9.2	2.5	28.0	100.0	62.7	0.4	12.2	2.2	22.5
Black	100.0	35.3	0.3	12.4	3.8	48.2	100.0	36.2	0.3	18.9	3.4	41.2
Hispanic	100.0	48.6	0.3	9.4	5.3	36.5	100.0	51.9	0.4	13.4	4.5	29.9
Asian	100.0	67.1	0.1	7.6	3.8	21.4	100.0	72.4	0.1	8.6	3.4	15.4
Pacific Islander	100.0	50.0	0.3	3.5	4.3	41.8	100.0	48.0	1.4	11.1	2.6	36.9
American Indian/Alaska Native	100.0	37.3	1.0	11.6	4.1	45.9	100.0	36.6	1.1	16.1	3.3	43.0
Two or more races	100.0	64.9	0.3	6.0	3.2	25.5	100.0	53.8	0.4	12.5	2.8	30.4
Female												
White	100.0	65.4	0.4	9.1	1.6	23.5	100.0	68.6	0.5	11.8	1.4	17.7
Black	100.0	44.5	0.4	13.2	3.2	38.7	100.0	46.9	0.4	19.1	2.7	30.8
Hispanic	100.0	55.5	0.4	9.3	4.1	30.7	100.0	60.4	0.4	12.3	3.3	23.6
Asian	100.0	73.6	0.2	6.4	2.5	17.3	100.0	78.3	0.2	7.3	2.1	12.1
Pacific Islander	100.0	49.1	0.5	4.2	3.7	42.4	100.0	50.1	1.6	10.7	3.0	34.5
American Indian/Alaska Native	100.0	43.1	0.9	12.9	3.4	39.7	100.0	43.8	0.9	15.4	2.9	37.0
Two or more races	100.0	69.9	0.1	6.1	2.6	21.2	100.0	60.7	0.4	12.8	2.0	24.1
Control of institution and percent of applications accepted												
Public institutions	100.0	57.7	0.2	11.6	3.4	27.1	100.0	61.2	0.3	13.8	2.9	21.8
Open admissions	100.0	32.8	1.4	17.1	6.5	42.3	100.0	32.5	2.4	18.7	4.6	41.9
90.0 percent or more accepted	100.0	46.9	0.6	13.1	3.4	36.0	100.0	48.4	0.8	18.2	3.8	28.8
75.0 to 89.9 percent accepted	100.0	53.7	0.3	13.2	3.4	29.5	100.0	56.8	0.3	12.2	3.0	27.7
50.0 to 74.9 percent accepted	100.0	61.4	0.1	9.7	3.3	25.5	100.0	63.3	0.2	14.3	2.7	19.6
25.0 to 49.9 percent accepted	100.0	64.4	#	13.1	2.9	19.6	100.0	70.6	#	12.6	2.8	14.0
Less than 25.0 percent accepted	100.0	84.8	0.0	4.2	0.3	10.8	100.0	80.0	0.0	2.5	1.0	16.5
Information not available	100.0	49.3	0.2	17.8	4.6	28.0	100.0	45.0	0.2	20.0	5.6	29.2
Nonprofit institutions	100.0	65.3	0.4	5.2	0.8	28.2	100.0	67.2	0.4	9.9	0.8	21.7
Open admissions	100.0	38.2	2.0	8.8	2.0	48.9	100.0	39.5	2.0	11.0	1.9	45.6
90.0 percent or more accepted	100.0	48.2	1.0	10.9	1.9	37.9	100.0	46.2	1.6	15.2	2.1	34.9
75.0 to 89.9 percent accepted	100.0	59.9	0.5	5.4	0.8	33.5	100.0	63.0	0.3	13.7	0.6	22.4
50.0 to 74.9 percent accepted	100.0	62.5	0.3	6.0	0.8	30.5	100.0	64.1	0.3	10.9	0.7	24.0
25.0 to 49.9 percent accepted	100.0	76.6	0.2	3.0	0.6	19.5	100.0	74.7	0.2	7.4	0.7	16.9
Less than 25.0 percent accepted	100.0	90.6	#	2.0	0.6	6.8	100.0	92.5	0.1	1.2	0.6	5.5
Information not available	100.0	54.9	0.8	6.6	1.2	36.6	100.0	49.5	3.1	18.8	2.6	25.9
For-profit institutions	100.0	31.9	1.8	1.6	2.2	62.4	100.0	25.4	4.6	5.9	2.2	62.0
Open admissions	100.0	32.7	0.7	0.8	2.7	63.1	100.0	27.9	6.3	3.3	2.5	60.1
90.0 percent or more accepted	100.0	28.3	8.1	2.0	0.7	60.9	100.0	7.3	8.1	15.2	0.8	68.6
75.0 to 89.9 percent accepted	100.0	27.2	4.5	5.8	0.6	61.8	100.0	35.2	2.3	4.1	2.2	56.2
50.0 to 74.9 percent accepted	100.0	37.7	4.0	5.6	1.4	51.3	100.0	37.2	1.1	6.3	2.1	53.2
25.0 to 49.9 percent accepted	100.0	33.6	1.5	1.3	2.8	60.8	100.0	32.2	0.3	0.2	1.9	65.4
Less than 25.0 percent accepted	100.0	37.9	0.0	0.0	0.0	62.1	100.0	28.6	0.0	42.9	0.0	28.6
Information not available	100.0	24.9	1.2	0.1	1.9	72.0	100.0	21.2	0.5	7.1	2.8	68.4

#Rounds to zero.
[1]Transfer out data are required to be reported only by those institutions for which preparation for transfers is a substantial part of the institutional mission.
[2]Includes students who dropped out of the reporting institution and students who transferred to another institution without notifying the reporting institution.
NOTE: Data are for first-time full-time bachelor's degree-seeking students at 4-year degree-granting postsecondary institutions participating in Title IV federal financial aid programs.

Detail may not sum to totals because of rounding. Totals include data for persons whose race/ethnicity was not reported. Race categories exclude persons of Hispanic ethnicity.
SOURCE: U.S. Department of Education, National Center for Education Statistics, Integrated Postsecondary Education Data System (IPEDS), Winter 2013–14 and Winter 2018–19 Graduation Rates component; and IPEDS Fall 2007 and Fall 2012, Institutional Characteristics component. (This table was prepared October 2019.)

Table 326.25. Percentage distribution of first-time, full-time degree/certificate-seeking students at 2-year postsecondary institutions 3 years after entry, by completion and enrollment status at first institution attended, sex, race/ethnicity, and control of institution: Cohort entry years 2010 and 2015

Sex, race/ethnicity, and control of institution	Percentage distribution of 2010 entry cohort 3 years after entry							Percentage distribution of 2015 entry cohort 3 years after entry						
		Completed a program at first institution attended			Did not complete a program at first institution				Completed a program at first institution attended			Did not complete a program at first institution		
	Total	Total, any program	Program of less than 2 years	Program of 2 to 4 years	Trans-ferred out[1]	Re-mained enrolled	No longer enrolled, status un-known[2]	Total	Total, any program	Program of less than 2 years	Program of 2 to 4 years	Trans-ferred out[1]	Re-mained enrolled	No longer enrolled, status un-known[2]
1	2	3	4	5	6	7	8	9	10	11	12	13	14	15
Total	100.0	29.4	15.0	14.4	13.8	11.5	45.2	100.0	32.6	12.3	20.3	14.8	11.4	41.2
Sex														
Male	100.0	26.2	12.0	14.2	14.7	11.1	48.0	100.0	29.7	9.9	19.8	15.4	11.0	43.9
Female	100.0	32.1	17.6	14.5	13.1	11.8	42.9	100.0	35.1	14.4	20.6	14.3	11.8	38.8
Race/ethnicity														
White	100.0	29.4	12.1	17.3	15.3	11.4	43.9	100.0	34.9	10.9	24.0	16.6	10.1	38.5
Black	100.0	23.7	16.2	7.5	14.6	8.6	53.2	100.0	27.7	17.9	9.9	14.9	8.2	49.1
Hispanic	100.0	33.8	22.4	11.4	10.1	14.2	41.9	100.0	30.7	12.4	18.2	11.2	16.0	42.2
Asian	100.0	35.1	11.6	23.6	14.9	17.4	32.5	100.0	38.7	7.5	31.2	16.1	17.1	28.1
Pacific Islander	100.0	37.9	27.1	10.8	10.6	7.7	43.8	100.0	30.3	16.7	13.7	13.6	9.7	46.4
American Indian/Alaska Native	100.0	23.9	14.7	9.2	12.1	9.6	54.4	100.0	29.5	15.8	13.7	11.8	9.5	49.2
Two or more races	100.0	25.9	12.4	13.6	15.0	11.8	47.3	100.0	27.2	9.0	18.2	16.6	11.3	44.9
Sex and race/ethnicity														
Male														
White	100.0	27.5	10.9	16.6	15.7	10.5	46.2	100.0	33.1	9.6	23.5	16.7	9.4	40.8
Black	100.0	19.5	12.2	7.3	15.7	8.1	56.7	100.0	21.9	12.1	9.8	17.2	8.2	52.7
Hispanic	100.0	27.7	16.4	11.3	11.3	14.5	46.5	100.0	26.7	10.2	16.5	11.7	15.4	46.1
Asian	100.0	31.5	8.9	22.6	15.6	18.6	34.3	100.0	35.4	6.0	29.4	16.5	17.5	30.6
Pacific Islander	100.0	31.8	19.9	11.9	13.1	8.1	46.9	100.0	25.5	12.0	13.6	15.0	9.3	50.1
American Indian/Alaska Native	100.0	21.4	13.5	7.9	12.4	8.8	57.4	100.0	27.4	13.2	14.2	11.4	8.2	53.0
Two or more races	100.0	22.3	9.3	13.0	15.4	12.1	50.2	100.0	23.9	6.8	17.1	17.3	11.5	47.3
Female														
White	100.0	31.1	13.3	17.9	14.8	12.1	41.9	100.0	36.5	12.1	24.4	16.5	10.7	36.3
Black	100.0	26.7	19.1	7.6	13.7	8.9	50.7	100.0	31.9	22.0	9.9	13.3	8.3	46.6
Hispanic	100.0	38.2	26.7	11.5	9.2	13.9	38.7	100.0	33.9	14.3	19.6	10.8	16.4	38.9
Asian	100.0	38.9	14.3	24.6	14.1	16.2	30.7	100.0	42.3	9.1	33.2	15.7	16.7	25.3
Pacific Islander	100.0	43.2	33.4	9.9	8.3	7.3	41.1	100.0	34.8	21.1	13.7	12.3	10.0	42.9
American Indian/Alaska Native	100.0	26.0	15.7	10.3	11.8	10.3	51.9	100.0	31.1	17.7	13.3	12.1	10.4	46.4
Two or more races	100.0	28.9	14.8	14.0	14.6	11.6	44.9	100.0	30.1	10.9	19.1	16.0	11.1	42.9
Control of institution														
Public	100.0	19.5	3.7	15.8	17.8	14.7	48.0	100.0	27.0	4.5	22.5	17.4	13.3	42.3
Nonprofit	100.0	53.4	37.7	15.8	6.8	1.8	37.9	100.0	62.3	54.9	7.4	2.8	0.9	34.0
For-profit	100.0	62.8	53.5	9.2	0.5	0.9	35.8	100.0	61.5	52.2	9.3	0.5	1.8	36.2

[1]Transfer out data are required to be reported only by those institutions for which preparation for transfers is a substantial part of the institutional mission.
[2]Includes students who dropped out of the reporting institution and students who transferred to another institution without notifying the reporting institution.
NOTE: Data are for first-time full-time certificate/degree-seeking students at 2-year degree-granting postsecondary institutions participating in Title IV federal financial aid programs.

Detail may not sum to totals because of rounding. Totals include data for persons whose race/ethnicity was not reported. Race categories exclude persons of Hispanic ethnicity.
SOURCE: U.S. Department of Education, National Center for Education Statistics, Integrated Postsecondary Education Data System (IPEDS), Winter 2013–14 and Winter 2018–19 Graduation Rates component. (This table was prepared October 2019.)

Table 326.30. Retention of first-time degree-seeking undergraduates at degree-granting postsecondary institutions, by attendance status, level and control of institution, and percentage of applications accepted: Selected years, 2006 to 2018

Attendance status, level, control, and percent of applications accepted	First-time degree-seekers (adjusted entry cohort),[1] by entry year							Students from adjusted cohort returning in the following year							Percent of first-time undergraduates retained						
	2006	2009	2013	2014	2015	2016	2017	2007	2010	2014	2015	2016	2017	2018	2006 to 2007	2009 to 2010	2013 to 2014	2014 to 2015	2015 to 2016	2016 to 2017	2017 to 2018
1	2	3	4	5	6	7	8	9	10	11	12	13	14	15	16	17	18	19	20	21	22
Full-time students																					
All institutions	2,170,504	2,371,220	2,222,085	2,211,406	2,180,675	2,177,194	2,180,170	1,541,201	1,705,242	1,642,567	1,647,295	1,640,963	1,643,904	1,648,776	71.0	71.9	73.5	74.5	75.3	75.5	75.6
Public institutions	1,522,928	1,732,822	1,646,902	1,639,875	1,619,768	1,620,387	1,624,433	1,071,986	1,222,688	1,193,200	1,200,374	1,198,609	1,203,750	1,206,993	70.4	70.6	72.5	73.2	74.0	74.3	74.3
Nonprofit institutions	466,078	478,755	483,617	489,834	491,898	491,742	505,768	368,783	381,364	392,080	396,659	399,434	399,354	409,821	79.1	79.7	81.1	81.0	81.2	81.2	81.0
For-profit institutions	181,498	159,643	91,566	81,697	69,009	65,065	49,969	100,432	101,190	57,287	50,262	42,920	40,800	31,962	55.3	63.4	62.6	61.5	62.2	62.7	64.0
4-year institutions	1,457,745	1,452,575	1,483,526	1,501,582	1,524,088	1,534,945	1,553,162	1,114,923	1,146,534	1,194,097	1,212,464	1,231,920	1,242,850	1,257,978	76.5	78.9	80.5	80.7	80.8	81.0	81.0
Public institutions	911,509	936,840	978,041	995,110	1,018,253	1,028,968	1,041,749	711,200	745,703	790,227	807,687	825,885	836,675	846,079	78.0	79.6	80.8	81.2	81.1	81.3	81.2
Open admissions	61,832	45,458	34,706	31,477	26,888	26,639	27,498	38,383	28,675	21,547	19,618	16,689	16,671	17,278	62.1	63.1	62.1	62.3	62.1	62.1	62.8
90.0 percent or more accepted	68,835	63,453	55,188	60,160	71,117	69,603	82,664	49,274	46,280	40,116	43,559	51,533	50,537	60,453	71.6	72.9	72.7	72.4	72.5	72.6	73.1
75.0 to 89.9 percent accepted	244,177	212,573	261,763	281,422	317,658	288,854	306,567	185,457	163,639	203,517	221,245	251,113	228,127	241,826	76.0	77.0	77.7	78.6	79.1	79.0	78.9
50.0 to 74.9 percent accepted	417,093	462,554	461,551	456,622	435,275	468,321	433,808	336,021	376,021	381,607	376,587	357,438	383,791	354,792	80.6	81.3	82.7	82.5	82.1	82.0	81.8
25.0 to 49.9 percent accepted	103,118	131,241	147,849	145,622	150,981	156,438	167,075	88,908	112,209	127,595	128,568	133,668	139,838	148,465	86.2	85.5	86.3	88.3	88.5	89.4	88.9
Less than 25.0 percent accepted	7,716	14,326	15,315	14,947	15,563	15,951	22,740	7,048	13,649	14,651	14,336	14,959	15,330	21,999	91.3	95.3	95.7	95.9	96.1	96.1	96.7
Information not available	8,738	7,235	1,669	4,860	771	2,962	1,397	5,765	5,230	1,194	3,774	485	2,381	1,266	66.0	72.3	71.5	77.7	62.9	80.4	90.6
Nonprofit institutions	457,505	470,795	476,437	476,823	481,241	484,334	495,026	363,459	376,668	387,685	388,745	392,330	394,415	402,106	79.4	80.0	81.4	81.5	81.5	81.4	81.2
Open admissions	26,565	22,613	12,549	11,792	13,289	13,378	12,117	16,019	14,349	7,653	7,414	8,499	8,795	7,873	60.3	63.5	61.0	62.9	64.0	65.7	65.0
90.0 percent or more accepted	13,632	15,135	22,841	22,225	28,503	23,596	33,038	9,543	10,953	16,881	16,188	20,247	16,897	23,971	70.0	72.4	73.9	72.8	71.0	71.6	72.6
75.0 to 89.9 percent accepted	102,358	80,301	86,040	94,830	80,940	91,372	92,986	78,424	62,196	68,481	74,984	63,872	71,328	72,983	76.6	77.5	79.6	79.1	78.8	78.1	78.5
50.0 to 74.9 percent accepted	190,079	218,072	207,431	199,677	199,442	203,979	201,207	148,681	170,232	162,937	157,866	157,181	162,016	158,256	78.2	78.1	78.5	79.1	78.8	79.4	78.7
25.0 to 49.9 percent accepted	93,560	98,312	98,202	95,164	102,823	98,053	95,878	81,880	84,941	85,484	82,511	89,426	84,421	82,935	87.5	86.4	87.0	86.7	86.1	86.1	86.5
Less than 25.0 percent accepted	26,696	32,980	45,222	48,076	54,573	51,642	55,035	25,639	31,790	43,522	46,054	51,699	49,508	53,162	96.0	96.4	96.2	95.8	94.7	96.1	96.6
Information not available	4,615	3,382	4,152	5,059	1,671	2,314	4,765	3,273	2,207	2,727	3,728	1,406	1,450	2,926	70.9	65.3	65.7	73.7	84.1	62.7	61.4
For-profit institutions	88,731	44,940	29,048	29,649	24,594	21,643	16,387	40,264	24,163	16,185	16,032	13,705	11,760	9,793	45.4	53.8	55.7	54.1	55.7	54.3	59.8
Open admissions	45,240	16,826	19,206	21,732	16,511	13,943	10,036	18,720	9,260	10,053	10,827	8,270	6,706	5,490	41.4	55.0	52.3	49.8	50.1	48.1	54.7
90.0 percent or more accepted	6,285	3,722	717	591	770	1,108	803	3,454	1,311	509	308	472	559	560	55.0	35.2	71.0	52.1	61.3	50.5	69.7
75.0 to 89.9 percent accepted	3,703	3,224	2,920	5,265	3,253	1,174	2,874	2,081	1,549	1,865	3,459	2,159	885	1,839	56.2	48.0	63.9	65.7	66.4	75.4	64.0
50.0 to 74.9 percent accepted	12,845	12,061	3,690	1,489	3,000	4,577	2,344	6,536	6,839	2,472	994	1,973	3,108	1,642	50.9	56.7	67.0	66.8	65.8	67.9	70.1
25.0 to 49.9 percent accepted	18,142	6,098	419	463	1,020	672	300	8,036	3,423	293	353	802	363	240	44.3	56.1	69.9	76.2	78.6	54.0	80.0
Less than 25.0 percent accepted	0	3	0	0	0	1	0	0	0	0	0	8	0	0	†	66.7	†	†	100.0	†	†
Information not available	2,516	3,006	2,096	109	32	168	30	1,437	1,779	993	91	21	138	22	57.1	59.2	47.4	83.5	65.6	82.1	73.3
2-year institutions	712,759	918,645	738,559	709,824	656,587	642,249	627,008	426,278	558,708	448,470	434,831	409,043	401,054	390,798	59.8	60.8	60.7	61.3	62.3	62.4	62.3
Public institutions	611,419	795,982	668,861	644,765	601,515	591,419	582,684	360,786	476,985	402,973	392,687	372,724	367,075	360,914	59.0	59.9	60.2	60.9	62.0	62.1	61.9
Nonprofit institutions	8,573	7,960	7,180	13,011	10,657	7,408	10,742	5,324	4,696	4,395	7,914	7,104	4,939	7,715	62.1	59.0	61.2	60.8	66.7	66.7	71.8
For-profit institutions	92,767	114,703	62,518	52,048	44,415	43,422	33,582	60,168	77,027	41,102	34,230	29,215	29,040	22,169	64.9	67.2	65.7	65.8	65.8	66.9	66.0
Part-time students																					
All institutions	461,574	545,635	490,124	470,772	429,109	411,269	404,081	190,547	229,566	213,235	205,366	192,527	186,683	182,838	41.3	42.1	43.5	43.6	44.9	45.4	45.2
Public institutions	417,314	497,453	461,943	445,495	404,279	390,075	380,256	170,682	209,164	202,243	195,147	181,993	177,878	172,830	40.9	42.0	43.8	43.8	45.0	45.6	45.5
Nonprofit institutions	14,618	10,359	9,340	8,885	10,446	8,825	13,902	7,027	4,892	3,883	3,681	4,951	3,893	5,968	48.1	47.2	41.6	41.4	47.4	44.1	42.9
For-profit institutions	29,642	37,823	18,841	16,392	14,384	12,369	9,923	12,838	15,510	7,109	6,538	5,583	4,912	4,040	43.3	41.0	37.7	39.9	38.8	39.7	40.7
4-year institutions	81,423	72,046	49,304	46,606	48,716	46,515	50,441	37,988	32,344	22,269	21,818	23,845	22,669	24,771	46.7	44.9	45.2	46.8	48.9	48.7	49.1
Public institutions	47,377	33,327	26,473	25,833	28,096	29,746	29,470	23,337	16,944	13,862	13,917	15,374	16,029	16,158	49.3	50.8	52.4	53.9	54.7	53.9	54.8
Open admissions	19,247	8,356	5,250	4,605	4,412	5,403	4,176	8,004	3,586	2,098	1,791	1,873	2,136	1,654	41.6	42.9	40.0	38.9	42.5	39.5	39.6
90.0 percent or more accepted	3,745	4,004	2,098	1,951	2,931	2,326	2,509	1,909	1,959	1,063	880	1,382	1,013	1,089	51.0	48.9	50.7	45.1	47.2	43.6	43.4
75.0 to 89.9 percent accepted	8,969	6,493	7,424	6,663	8,722	9,007	9,649	4,196	3,268	3,964	3,591	4,972	4,925	5,324	46.8	50.3	53.4	53.9	57.0	54.7	55.2
50.0 to 74.9 percent accepted	11,599	11,254	9,042	10,343	9,815	10,729	10,891	6,766	6,053	5,065	6,107	5,654	6,458	6,630	58.3	53.8	56.0	59.0	57.6	60.2	60.9
25.0 to 49.9 percent accepted	3,373	3,046	2,553	2,040	2,112	2,103	2,177	2,223	1,982	1,617	1,395	1,433	1,392	1,413	65.9	65.1	63.3	68.4	67.9	66.2	64.9
Less than 25.0 percent accepted	65	44	51	58	48	65	58	50	35	33	49	38	57	44	76.9	79.5	64.7	84.5	79.2	87.7	75.9
Information not available	379	130	55	173	56	113	10	189	61	22	104	22	48	4	49.9	46.9	40.0	60.1	39.3	42.5	40.0

See notes at end of table.

Table 326.30. Retention of first-time degree-seeking undergraduates at degree-granting postsecondary institutions, by attendance status, level and control of institution, and percentage of applications accepted: Selected years, 2006 to 2018—Continued

Attendance status, level, control, and percent of applications accepted	First-time degree-seekers (adjusted entry cohort),[1] by entry year							Students from adjusted cohort returning in the following year							Percent of first-time undergraduates retained						
	2006	2009	2013	2014	2015	2016	2017	2007	2010	2014	2015	2016	2017	2018	2006 to 2007	2009 to 2010	2013 to 2014	2014 to 2015	2015 to 2016	2016 to 2017	2017 to 2018
1	2	3	4	5	6	7	8	9	10	11	12	13	14	15	16	17	18	19	20	21	22
Nonprofit institutions	12,861	9,599	8,501	8,093	9,666	7,962	13,356	6,054	4,491	3,448	3,322	4,612	3,553	5,758	47.1	46.8	40.6	41.0	47.6	44.6	43.1
Open admissions	5,419	3,821	2,434	1,450	1,540	1,583	1,757	2,558	1,693	848	486	673	660	758	47.2	44.3	34.8	33.5	43.7	41.7	43.1
90.0 percent or more accepted	523	393	1,159	494	3,769	1,990	911	237	199	468	204	1,882	887	566	45.3	50.6	40.4	41.3	49.9	44.6	62.1
75.0 to 89.9 percent accepted	2,459	1,164	1,332	1,903	874	938	4,522	1,047	550	622	811	422	465	1,967	42.6	47.3	46.7	42.6	48.3	49.6	43.5
50.0 to 74.9 percent accepted	3,131	3,256	1,515	2,231	1,812	2,358	1,985	1,406	1,531	701	928	839	1,018	871	44.9	47.0	46.3	41.6	46.3	43.2	43.9
25.0 to 49.9 percent accepted	853	715	606	815	866	587	1,030	452	366	305	394	381	263	430	53.0	51.2	50.3	48.3	44.0	44.8	41.7
Less than 25.0 percent accepted	112	93	115	136	640	458	99	86	78	101	123	302	238	84	76.8	83.9	87.8	90.4	47.2	52.0	84.8
Information not available	364	157	1,340	1,064	165	48	3,052	268	74	403	376	113	22	1,082	73.6	47.1	30.1	35.3	61.1	45.8	35.5
For-profit institutions	21,185	29,120	14,330	12,680	10,934	8,807	7,615	8,597	10,909	4,959	4,579	3,859	3,087	2,855	40.6	37.5	34.6	36.1	35.3	35.1	37.5
Open admissions	10,514	10,926	10,395	10,089	8,822	6,384	5,667	4,121	4,299	3,751	3,863	3,183	2,388	2,227	39.2	39.3	36.1	38.3	36.1	37.4	39.3
90.0 percent or more accepted	2,212	1,372	126	123	246	453	204	639	375	59	30	85	115	47	28.9	27.3	46.8	24.4	34.6	25.4	23.0
75.0 to 89.9 percent accepted	2,838	3,151	1,232	1,794	1,027	109	1,065	1,342	1,093	353	492	259	29	382	47.3	34.7	28.7	27.4	25.2	26.6	35.9
50.0 to 74.9 percent accepted	2,774	4,591	2,471	586	753	812	668	1,134	2,249	756	158	282	328	196	40.9	49.0	30.6	27.0	37.5	40.4	29.3
25.0 to 49.9 percent accepted	2,033	1,099	73	9	81	1,043	6	627	342	25	2	45	227	3	30.8	31.1	34.2	22.2	55.6	21.8	50.0
Less than 25.0 percent accepted	0	0	0	0	0	0	0	0	0	0	0	0	0	0	†	†	†	†	†	†	†
Information not available	814	7,981	33	79	5	6	5	734	2,551	15	34	5	0	0	90.2	32.0	45.5	43.0	100.0	0.0	0.0
2-year institutions	380,151	473,589	440,820	424,166	380,393	364,754	353,640	152,559	197,222	190,966	183,548	168,682	164,014	158,067	40.1	41.6	43.3	43.3	44.3	45.0	44.7
Public institutions	369,937	464,126	435,470	419,662	376,183	360,329	350,786	147,345	192,220	188,381	181,230	166,619	161,849	156,672	39.8	41.4	43.3	43.2	44.3	44.9	44.7
Nonprofit institutions	1,757	760	839	792	760	863	546	973	401	435	359	339	340	210	55.4	52.8	51.8	45.3	44.6	39.4	38.5
For-profit institutions	8,457	8,703	4,511	3,712	3,450	3,562	2,308	4,241	4,601	2,150	1,959	1,724	1,825	1,185	50.1	52.9	52.8	52.8	50.0	51.2	51.3

†Not applicable.

[1]Adjusted entry cohort counts exclude students who died or were totally and permanently disabled, served in the armed forces (including those called to active duty), served with a foreign aid service of the federal government (e.g., Peace Corps), or served on official church missions. For 4-year institutions, the adjusted entry cohort is based on first-time bachelor's degree-seeking students.

NOTE: Returning students data for 2-year institutions include returning students, plus students who completed their program. Some data have been revised from previously published figures.
SOURCE: U.S. Department of Education, National Center for Education Statistics, Integrated Postsecondary Education Data System (IPEDS), Spring 2008 through Spring 2018, Fall Enrollment component; and IPEDS Fall 2006 through Fall 2017, Institutional Characteristics component. (This table was prepared October 2019.)

Table 329.10 On-campus crimes, arrests, and referrals for disciplinary action at degree-granting postsecondary institutions, by location of incident, control and level of institution, and type of incident: Selected years, 2001 through 2017

Control and level of institution and type of incident	Number of incidents																
	Total, in residence halls and at other locations														2017		
	2001	2005	2006	2007	2008	2009	2010	2011	2012	2013	2014	2015	2016	Total	In residence halls	At other locations
1	2	3	4	5	6	7	8	9	10	11	12	13	14	15	16	17
All institutions																
Selected crimes against persons and property	41,596	42,710	44,492	41,829	40,296	34,054	32,097	30,407	29,766	27,236	26,818	27,532	28,376	28,873	14,671	14,202
Murder[1]	17	11	8	44	12	16	15	16	12	23	11	28	15	21	2	19
Negligent manslaughter[2]	2	2	0	3	3	0	1	1	1	0	2	2	2	3	1	2
Sex offenses—forcible[3]	2,201	2,674	2,670	2,694	2,639	2,544	2,927	3,375	4,015	4,977	6,751	8,022	8,931	10,398	7,517	2,881
Rape	—	—	—	—	—	—	—	—	—	—	4,431	5,119	5,853	6,521	5,386	1,135
Fondling	—	—	—	—	—	—	—	—	—	—	2,320	2,903	3,078	3,877	2,131	1,746
Sex offenses—nonforcible[4]	461	42	43	40	35	65	33	46	46	45	53	63	60	80	57	23
Robbery[5]	1,663	1,551	1,547	1,561	1,576	1,409	1,392	1,285	1,368	1,317	1,041	1,044	1,097	1,040	230	810
Aggravated assault[6]	2,947	2,656	2,817	2,604	2,495	2,327	2,221	2,239	2,423	2,048	2,258	2,181	2,216	699	1,517	
Burglary[7]	26,904	29,256	31,260	29,488	28,737	23,083	21,335	19,472	18,183	15,232	13,419	12,320	11,965	11,053	5,810	5,243
Motor vehicle theft[8]	6,221	5,531	5,231	4,619	4,104	3,977	3,441	3,334	3,013	2,971	2,890	3,218	3,528	3,450	26	3,424
Arson[9]	1,180	987	916	776	695	633	732	639	705	627	603	577	597	612	329	283
Weapons-, drug-, and liquor-related arrests and referrals																
Arrests[10]	40,348	49,024	50,187	50,558	50,639	50,066	51,519	54,285	52,325	46,975	44,531	40,299	39,018	37,626	18,527	19,099
Illegal weapons possession	1,073	1,316	1,316	1,318	1,190	1,077	1,112	1,023	1,023	1,018	990	1,183	1,200	1,245	317	928
Drug law violations	11,854	13,707	13,952	14,135	15,146	15,871	18,589	20,729	21,212	19,799	19,172	19,431	19,239	19,568	9,441	10,127
Liquor law violations	27,421	34,001	34,919	35,105	34,303	33,118	31,818	32,533	30,090	26,158	24,369	19,685	18,579	16,813	8,769	8,044
Referrals for disciplinary action[10]	155,201	202,816	218,040	216,600	217,526	220,987	230,269	249,694	251,402	244,985	253,315	241,687	229,589	216,379	198,302	18,077
Illegal weapons possession	1,277	1,882	1,871	1,658	1,455	1,275	1,314	1,282	1,404	1,410	1,425	1,425	1,405	1,309	923	386
Drug law violations	23,900	25,356	27,251	28,476	32,469	36,344	42,022	51,562	53,959	53,439	56,575	56,037	55,768	58,079	49,700	8,379
Liquor law violations	130,024	175,578	188,918	186,466	183,602	183,368	186,933	196,850	196,039	190,136	195,315	184,225	172,416	156,991	147,679	9,312
Public 4-year																
Selected crimes against persons and property	18,710	19,582	20,648	19,579	18,695	15,975	15,503	14,675	14,510	13,127	13,346	13,592	14,189	14,814	7,138	7,676
Murder[1]	9	4	5	42	9	8	9	10	7	10	3	13	8	12	1	11
Negligent manslaughter[2]	2	1	0	2	1	0	0	1	1	0	1	1	2	3	1	2
Sex offenses—forcible[3]	1,245	1,398	1,400	1,425	1,317	1,214	1,461	1,638	1,973	2,264	3,211	3,960	4,421	5,252	3,674	1,578
Rape	—	—	—	—	—	—	—	—	—	—	2,118	2,541	2,945	3,379	2,728	651
Fondling	—	—	—	—	—	—	—	—	—	—	1,093	1,419	1,476	1,873	946	927
Sex offenses—nonforcible[4]	207	25	15	23	12	40	15	17	17	18	28	37	30	63	49	14
Robbery[5]	584	696	680	722	750	647	662	612	657	635	550	580	590	525	125	400
Aggravated assault[6]	1,434	1,280	1,338	1,258	1,182	1,134	1,076	1,076	1,200	1,000	1,016	1,144	1,153	1,139	394	745
Burglary[7]	11,520	12,935	14,027	13,371	12,970	10,708	10,219	9,373	8,821	7,258	6,678	5,782	5,599	5,429	2,688	2,741
Motor vehicle theft[8]	3,072	2,667	2,662	2,266	2,027	1,824	1,604	1,592	1,406	1,537	1,500	1,770	2,049	2,036	8	2,028
Arson[9]	637	576	521	470	427	400	457	356	428	405	359	305	337	355	198	157
Weapons-, drug-, and liquor-related arrests and referrals																
Arrests[10]	31,077	38,051	39,900	39,570	40,607	40,780	41,992	44,891	43,155	38,073	36,249	32,717	31,606	30,062	14,455	15,607
Illegal weapons possession	692	878	859	825	759	659	669	629	621	637	619	721	759	813	226	587
Drug law violations	9,125	10,606	10,850	10,693	11,714	12,186	14,362	16,323	16,792	15,571	15,119	15,509	15,545	15,610	7,624	7,986
Liquor law violations	21,260	26,567	28,191	28,052	28,134	27,935	26,961	27,939	25,742	21,865	20,511	16,487	15,302	13,639	6,605	7,034
Referrals for disciplinary action[10]	79,152	100,211	107,289	106,148	104,585	108,756	116,029	129,667	132,363	127,155	134,310	127,315	119,009	112,112	102,052	10,060
Illegal weapons possession	678	1,097	972	867	792	669	664	610	644	604	646	569	602	530	388	142
Drug law violations	13,179	13,020	13,798	14,458	16,656	18,260	21,451	27,339	28,880	28,259	30,376	30,599	29,759	31,990	26,769	5,221
Liquor law violations	65,295	86,094	92,519	90,823	87,137	89,827	93,914	101,718	102,839	98,292	103,288	96,147	88,648	79,592	74,895	4,697
Nonprofit 4-year																
Selected crimes against persons and property	14,844	15,574	16,864	15,452	14,892	11,964	11,202	10,740	10,790	10,290	9,995	10,460	11,062	10,954	6,748	4,206
Murder[1]	5	5	3	2	1	6	5	3	2	5	5	2	4	6	0	6
Negligent manslaughter[2]	0	1	0	1	0	0	0	0	0	0	0	1	0	0	0	0
Sex offenses—forcible[3]	820	1,088	1,080	1,065	1,083	1,102	1,225	1,431	1,741	2,379	3,105	3,510	3,961	4,497	3,580	917
Rape	—	—	—	—	—	—	—	—	—	—	2,152	2,366	2,704	2,876	2,469	407
Fondling	—	—	—	—	—	—	—	—	—	—	953	1,144	1,257	1,621	1,111	510
Sex offenses—nonforcible[4]	113	6	10	8	16	11	8	13	10	12	7	15	11	8	6	2
Robbery[5]	649	500	502	460	437	366	319	320	386	373	263	280	330	352	90	262
Aggravated assault[6]	882	744	834	768	754	661	641	631	667	681	655	727	673	756	249	507
Burglary[7]	10,471	11,657	13,051	11,941	11,551	8,810	8,138	7,421	7,046	5,999	5,020	4,894	5,035	4,284	2,695	1,589
Motor vehicle theft[8]	1,471	1,248	1,077	984	859	834	641	704	711	667	754	821	836	847	7	840
Arson[9]	433	325	307	223	191	174	225	217	227	174	186	210	212	204	121	83
Weapons-, drug-, and liquor-related arrests and referrals																
Arrests[10]	6,329	7,406	6,134	6,732	6,112	5,777	5,459	5,444	5,477	5,642	4,950	4,583	4,505	4,216	2,423	1,793
Illegal weapons possession	167	150	146	178	158	148	137	129	127	131	129	168	195	188	61	127
Drug law violations	1,628	1,691	1,650	1,804	1,883	2,080	2,248	2,425	2,415	2,503	2,258	2,237	2,199	2,281	1,298	983
Liquor law violations	4,534	5,565	4,338	4,750	4,071	3,549	3,074	2,890	2,935	3,008	2,563	2,178	2,111	1,747	1,064	683
Referrals for disciplinary action[10]	71,293	96,646	103,484	103,254	105,289	103,457	104,939	110,607	110,268	109,298	110,150	105,567	102,444	95,840	89,287	6,553
Illegal weapons possession	443	590	622	545	457	358	393	417	498	535	481	569	573	535	428	107
Drug law violations	9,688	11,208	12,114	12,685	14,157	15,845	17,841	21,240	22,168	22,116	23,000	22,180	22,931	22,867	20,645	2,222
Liquor law violations	61,162	84,848	90,748	90,024	90,675	87,254	86,705	88,950	87,602	86,647	86,669	82,818	78,940	72,438	68,214	4,224

See notes at end of table.

Table 329.10 On-campus crimes, arrests, and referrals for disciplinary action at degree-granting postsecondary institutions, by location of incident, control and level of institution, and type of incident: Selected years, 2001 through 2017—Continued

Control and level of institution and type of incident	\multicolumn{16}{c}{Number of incidents}															
	\multicolumn{13}{c}{Total, in residence halls and at other locations}												\multicolumn{3}{c}{2017}		
	2001	2005	2006	2007	2008	2009	2010	2011	2012	2013	2014	2015	2016	Total	In residence halls	At other locations
1	2	3	4	5	6	7	8	9	10	11	12	13	14	15	16	17
For-profit 4-year																
Selected crimes against persons and property	505	829	641	612	574	525	561	446	364	511	442	295	293	317	130	187
Murder[1]	0	0	0	0	0	0	0	1	0	1	0	0	0	0	0	0
Negligent manslaughter[2]	0	0	0	0	0	0	0	0	0	0	0	0	0	0	0	0
Sex offenses—forcible[3]	4	4	12	12	9	9	22	26	18	18	43	34	32	56	42	14
Rape	—	—	—	—	—	—	—	—	—	—	26	11	18	33	28	5
Fondling	—	—	—	—	—	—	—	—	—	—	17	23	14	23	14	9
Sex offenses—nonforcible[4]	13	1	0	2	0	1	1	0	3	2	2	0	1	0	0	0
Robbery[5]	64	43	25	31	38	86	70	74	51	86	52	24	26	23	1	22
Aggravated assault[6]	23	59	31	31	63	43	51	36	43	58	33	27	41	32	3	29
Burglary[7]	347	607	489	446	385	299	350	249	195	276	251	162	126	147	72	75
Motor vehicle theft[8]	52	110	78	89	79	85	65	58	53	68	59	47	64	56	11	45
Arson[9]	2	5	6	1	0	2	2	2	1	2	2	1	3	3	1	2
Weapons-, drug-, and liquor-related arrests and referrals																
Arrests[10]	11	28	52	28	40	54	165	152	126	74	117	102	116	132	57	75
Illegal weapons possession	2	2	5	3	8	6	13	11	10	12	9	14	11	7	0	7
Drug law violations	4	16	14	16	14	22	66	41	49	48	68	78	83	114	54	60
Liquor law violations	5	10	33	9	18	26	86	100	67	14	40	10	22	11	3	8
Referrals for disciplinary action[10]	316	529	513	519	566	882	760	718	668	1,161	935	804	747	1,035	883	152
Illegal weapons possession	11	42	13	11	13	23	9	16	23	18	16	11	8	12	10	2
Drug law violations	92	128	138	132	159	231	221	233	254	537	403	330	298	334	241	93
Liquor law violations	213	359	362	376	394	628	530	469	391	606	516	463	441	689	632	57
Public 2-year																
Selected crimes against persons and property	6,817	5,981	5,669	5,381	5,464	4,984	4,396	4,141	3,749	3,075	2,845	3,014	2,660	2,643	628	2,015
Murder[1]	2	2	0	0	2	2	1	2	3	7	3	13	3	2	1	1
Negligent manslaughter[2]	0	0	0	0	0	0	1	0	0	0	1	0	0	0	0	0
Sex offenses—forcible[3]	118	175	167	181	210	205	210	262	263	303	385	495	492	575	209	366
Rape	—	—	—	—	—	—	—	—	—	—	132	197	176	222	153	69
Fondling	—	—	—	—	—	—	—	—	—	—	253	298	316	353	56	297
Sex offenses—nonforcible[4]	119	10	16	7	7	12	8	16	13	11	16	11	18	9	2	7
Robbery[5]	245	248	284	279	285	251	298	262	244	197	148	149	138	129	14	115
Aggravated assault[6]	545	501	546	462	401	431	409	406	437	278	305	335	281	261	52	209
Burglary[7]	4,132	3,541	3,261	3,202	3,430	2,920	2,398	2,235	1,964	1,583	1,383	1,411	1,135	1,147	342	805
Motor vehicle theft[8]	1,552	1,428	1,319	1,174	1,059	1,109	1,028	899	776	651	548	541	549	471	0	471
Arson[9]	104	76	76	76	70	54	43	59	49	45	56	59	44	49	8	41
Weapons-, drug-, and liquor-related arrests and referrals																
Arrests[10]	2,660	3,416	3,993	4,124	3,764	3,335	3,811	3,723	3,464	3,060	3,121	2,840	2,701	3,146	1,571	1,575
Illegal weapons possession	198	278	300	304	258	256	282	248	253	230	220	268	215	227	27	200
Drug law violations	989	1,326	1,378	1,563	1,490	1,507	1,866	1,892	1,885	1,588	1,671	1,568	1,373	1,505	447	1,058
Liquor law violations	1,473	1,812	2,315	2,257	2,016	1,572	1,663	1,583	1,326	1,242	1,230	1,004	1,113	1,414	1,097	317
Referrals for disciplinary action[10]	3,529	4,088	5,897	5,987	6,425	7,241	8,017	8,174	7,586	6,845	7,240	7,292	6,868	6,816	5,555	1,261
Illegal weapons possession	127	133	238	218	183	210	242	228	224	243	269	271	214	220	89	131
Drug law violations	761	819	908	1,006	1,302	1,745	2,336	2,573	2,468	2,304	2,548	2,626	2,575	2,661	1,853	808
Liquor law violations	2,641	3,736	4,751	4,763	4,940	5,286	5,439	5,373	4,894	4,298	4,423	4,395	4,079	3,935	3,613	322
Nonprofit 2-year																
Selected crimes against persons and property	248	314	250	258	272	147	120	148	107	66	64	53	57	60	25	35
Murder[1]	1	0	0	0	0	0	0	0	0	0	0	0	0	0	0	0
Negligent manslaughter[2]	0	0	0	0	1	0	0	0	0	0	0	0	0	0	0	0
Sex offenses—forcible[3]	2	8	3	9	16	8	7	11	8	4	3	11	16	13	12	1
Rape	—	—	—	—	—	—	—	—	—	—	2	1	8	9	8	1
Fondling	—	—	—	—	—	—	—	—	—	—	1	10	8	4	4	0
Sex offenses—nonforcible[4]	2	0	1	0	0	0	0	0	0	2	0	0	0	0	0	0
Robbery[5]	54	9	7	2	13	9	5	1	2	3	0	2	5	2	0	2
Aggravated assault[6]	23	22	35	52	66	5	9	53	46	13	27	7	8	12	1	11
Burglary[7]	142	266	187	178	160	120	95	74	47	41	29	27	24	20	11	9
Motor vehicle theft[8]	23	7	14	14	9	4	2	7	4	3	5	4	3	12	0	12
Arson[9]	1	2	3	3	7	1	2	2	0	0	0	2	1	1	1	0
Weapons-, drug-, and liquor-related arrests and referrals																
Arrests[10]	108	76	67	59	93	58	49	52	52	66	39	32	56	47	18	29
Illegal weapons possession	1	5	3	4	3	4	6	5	5	5	5	9	12	9	2	7
Drug law violations	21	32	34	27	33	35	18	34	31	49	28	20	21	37	16	21
Liquor law violations	86	39	30	28	57	19	25	13	16	12	6	3	23	1	0	1
Referrals for disciplinary action[10]	624	514	537	519	413	348	377	360	300	320	448	546	420	488	462	26
Illegal weapons possession	2	12	19	10	6	7	4	1	6	7	11	2	3	7	7	0
Drug law violations	91	47	74	73	85	100	105	109	103	129	155	214	163	185	165	20
Liquor law violations	531	455	444	436	322	241	268	250	191	184	282	330	254	296	290	6

See notes at end of table.

Table 329.10 On-campus crimes, arrests, and referrals for disciplinary action at degree-granting postsecondary institutions, by location of incident, control and level of institution, and type of incident: Selected years, 2001 through 2017—Continued

Control and level of institution and type of incident	Number of incidents															
	Total, in residence halls and at other locations														2017	
	2001	2005	2006	2007	2008	2009	2010	2011	2012	2013	2014	2015	2016	Total	In residence halls	At other locations
1	2	3	4	5	6	7	8	9	10	11	12	13	14	15	16	17
For-profit 2-year																
Selected crimes against persons and property	472	430	420	547	399	459	315	257	246	167	126	118	115	85	2	83
Murder[1]	0	0	0	0	0	0	0	0	0	0	0	0	0	1	0	1
Negligent manslaughter[2]	0	0	0	0	1	0	0	0	0	0	0	0	0	0	0	0
Sex offenses—forcible[3]	12	1	8	2	4	6	2	7	12	9	4	12	9	5	0	5
Rape	—	—	—	—	—	—	—	—	—	—	1	3	2	2	0	2
Fondling	—	—	—	—	—	—	—	—	—	—	3	9	7	3	0	3
Sex offenses—nonforcible[4]	7	0	1	0	0	1	1	0	3	0	0	0	0	0	0	0
Robbery[5]	67	55	49	67	53	50	38	16	28	23	28	9	8	9	0	9
Aggravated assault[6]	40	50	33	33	29	53	35	37	30	14	12	18	25	16	0	16
Burglary[7]	292	250	245	350	241	226	135	120	110	75	58	44	46	26	2	24
Motor vehicle theft[8]	51	71	81	92	71	121	101	74	63	45	24	35	27	28	0	28
Arson[9]	3	3	3	3	0	2	3	3	0	1	0	0	0	0	0	0
Weapons-, drug-, and liquor-related arrests and referrals																
Arrests[10]	163	47	41	45	23	62	43	23	51	60	55	25	34	23	3	20
Illegal weapons possession	13	3	3	4	4	4	5	1	7	3	8	3	8	1	1	0
Drug law violations	87	36	26	32	12	41	29	14	40	40	28	19	18	21	2	19
Liquor law violations	63	8	12	9	7	17	9	8	4	17	19	3	8	1	0	1
Referrals for disciplinary action[10]	287	228	320	173	248	303	147	168	217	206	232	163	101	88	63	25
Illegal weapons possession	16	8	7	7	4	8	2	10	9	3	2	3	5	5	1	4
Drug law violations	89	134	219	122	110	163	68	68	86	94	93	88	42	42	27	15
Liquor law violations	182	86	94	44	134	132	77	90	122	109	137	72	54	41	35	6

—Not available.

[1]Excludes suicides, fetal deaths, traffic fatalities, accidental deaths, and justifiable homicide (such as the killing of a felon by a law enforcement officer in the line of duty).
[2]Killing of another person through gross negligence (excludes traffic fatalities).
[3]Any sexual act directed against another person forcibly and/or against that person's will.
[4]Includes only statutory rape or incest.
[5]Taking or attempting to take anything of value using actual or threatened force or violence.
[6]Attack upon a person for the purpose of inflicting severe or aggravated bodily injury.
[7]Unlawful entry of a structure to commit a felony or theft.
[8]Theft or attempted theft of a motor vehicle.
[9]Willful or malicious burning or attempt to burn a dwelling house, public building, motor vehicle, or personal property of another.
[10]If an individual is both arrested and referred to college officials for disciplinary action for a single offense, only the arrest is counted.

NOTE: Data are for degree-granting institutions, which are institutions that grant associate's or higher degrees and participate in Title IV federal financial aid programs. Some institutions that report Clery data—specifically, non-degree-granting institutions and institutions outside of the 50 states and the District of Columbia—are excluded from this table. Crimes, arrests, and referrals include incidents involving students, staff, and on-campus guests. Excludes off-campus crimes and arrests even if they involve college students or staff. Some data have been revised from previously published figures.
SOURCE: U.S. Department of Education, Office of Postsecondary Education, Campus Safety and Security Reporting System, 2001 through 2017; and National Center for Education Statistics, Integrated Postsecondary Education Data System (IPEDS), Fall 2002 through Fall 2017, Institutional Characteristics component. (This table was prepared September 2019.)

Table 329.20 On-campus crimes, arrests, and referrals for disciplinary action per 10,000 full-time-equivalent (FTE) students at degree-granting postsecondary institutions, by whether institution has residence halls, control and level of institution, and type of incident: Selected years, 2001 through 2017

Control and level of institution and type of incident	Number of incidents per 10,000 FTE students[1]															
	Total, institutions with and without residence halls													2017		
															Institutions with residence halls	Institutions without residence halls
	2001	2005	2006	2007	2008	2009	2010	2011	2012	2013	2014	2015	2016	Total		
1	2	3	4	5	6	7	8	9	10	11	12	13	14	15	16	17
All institutions																
Selected crimes against persons and property	35.619	32.864	33.350	30.559	28.993	22.955	20.869	20.027	19.983	18.461	18.069	18.694	19.258	19.605	25.065	6.211
Murder[2]	0.015	0.008	0.006	0.032	0.009	0.011	0.010	0.011	0.008	0.016	0.007	0.019	0.010	0.014	0.018	0.005
Negligent manslaughter[3]	0.002	0.002	0.000	0.002	0.002	0.000	0.001	0.001	0.001	0.000	0.001	0.001	0.001	0.002	0.003	0.000
Sex offenses—forcible[4]	1.885	2.058	2.001	1.968	1.899	1.715	1.903	2.223	2.695	3.374	4.549	5.447	6.061	7.060	9.529	1.006
Rape	—	—	—	—	—	—	—	—	—	—	2.985	3.476	3.972	4.428	6.157	0.185
Fondling	—	—	—	—	—	—	—	—	—	—	1.563	1.971	2.089	2.633	3.371	0.821
Sex offenses—nonforcible[5]	0.395	0.032	0.032	0.029	0.025	0.044	0.021	0.030	0.031	0.031	0.036	0.043	0.041	0.054	0.068	0.021
Robbery[6]	1.424	1.193	1.160	1.140	1.134	0.950	0.905	0.846	0.918	0.893	0.701	0.709	0.745	0.706	0.820	0.427
Aggravated assault[7]	2.524	2.044	2.112	1.902	1.795	1.569	1.444	1.475	1.627	1.385	1.380	1.533	1.480	1.505	1.788	0.809
Burglary[8]	23.038	22.511	23.432	21.543	20.676	15.559	13.872	12.825	12.207	10.325	9.041	8.365	8.120	7.505	9.621	2.314
Motor vehicle theft[9]	5.327	4.256	3.921	3.375	2.953	2.681	2.237	2.196	2.023	2.014	1.947	2.185	2.394	2.343	2.682	1.510
Arson[10]	1.010	0.759	0.687	0.567	0.500	0.427	0.476	0.421	0.473	0.425	0.406	0.392	0.405	0.416	0.536	0.120
Weapons-, drug-, and liquor-related arrests and referrals																
Arrests[11]	34.550	37.722	37.619	36.936	36.435	33.748	33.497	35.755	35.127	31.841	30.004	27.362	26.481	25.549	34.570	3.419
Illegal weapons possession	0.919	1.013	0.986	0.963	0.856	0.726	0.723	0.674	0.687	0.690	0.667	0.803	0.814	0.845	0.995	0.478
Drug law violations	10.151	10.547	10.458	10.327	10.898	10.698	12.086	13.653	14.240	13.420	12.917	13.193	13.057	13.287	17.764	2.305
Liquor law violations	23.481	26.163	26.175	25.647	24.681	22.324	20.687	21.428	20.200	17.730	16.419	13.366	12.609	11.416	15.811	0.635
Referrals for disciplinary action[11]	132.899	156.060	163.438	158.241	156.511	148.959	149.716	164.460	168.772	166.056	170.675	164.100	155.818	146.925	205.702	2.741
Illegal weapons possession	1.093	1.448	1.402	1.211	1.047	0.859	0.854	0.844	0.943	0.956	0.960	0.968	0.954	0.889	1.141	0.270
Drug law violations	20.466	19.511	20.427	20.804	23.362	24.498	27.322	33.961	36.224	36.222	38.118	38.048	37.849	39.437	54.950	1.381
Liquor law violations	111.340	135.101	141.609	136.226	132.103	123.602	121.540	129.654	131.606	128.878	131.597	125.084	117.016	106.600	149.610	1.090
Public 4-year																
Selected crimes against persons and property	36.191	34.295	35.531	32.846	30.535	24.898	23.448	21.958	21.669	19.553	19.545	19.655	19.811	20.411	21.899	7.014
Murder[2]	0.017	0.007	0.009	0.070	0.015	0.012	0.014	0.015	0.010	0.015	0.004	0.019	0.011	0.017	0.017	0.014
Negligent manslaughter[3]	0.004	0.002	0.000	0.003	0.002	0.000	0.000	0.001	0.001	0.000	0.001	0.001	0.003	0.004	0.005	0.000
Sex offenses—forcible[4]	2.408	2.448	2.409	2.391	2.151	1.892	2.210	2.451	2.946	3.372	4.702	5.726	6.173	7.236	7.916	1.116
Rape	—	—	—	—	—	—	—	—	—	—	3.102	3.674	4.112	4.656	5.158	0.138
Fondling	—	—	—	—	—	—	—	—	—	—	1.601	2.052	2.061	2.581	2.759	0.978
Sex offenses—nonforcible[5]	0.400	0.044	0.026	0.039	0.020	0.062	0.023	0.025	0.025	0.027	0.041	0.054	0.042	0.087	0.093	0.028
Robbery[6]	1.130	1.219	1.170	1.211	1.225	1.008	1.001	0.916	0.981	0.946	0.805	0.839	0.824	0.723	0.761	0.386
Aggravated assault[7]	2.774	2.242	2.302	2.110	1.931	1.767	1.627	1.610	1.792	1.490	1.488	1.654	1.610	1.569	1.673	0.634
Burglary[8]	22.283	22.654	24.138	22.432	21.184	16.689	15.456	14.025	13.173	10.811	9.780	8.361	7.817	7.480	7.999	2.811
Motor vehicle theft[9]	5.942	4.671	4.581	3.802	3.311	2.843	2.426	2.382	2.100	2.289	2.197	2.560	2.861	2.805	2.913	1.833
Arson[10]	1.232	1.009	0.897	0.788	0.697	0.623	0.691	0.533	0.639	0.603	0.526	0.441	0.471	0.489	0.522	0.193
Weapons-, drug-, and liquor-related arrests and referrals																
Arrests[11]	60.113	66.641	68.660	66.384	66.324	63.558	63.512	67.169	64.447	56.711	53.086	47.311	44.128	41.420	45.437	5.264
Illegal weapons possession	1.339	1.538	1.478	1.384	1.240	1.027	1.012	0.941	0.927	0.949	0.907	1.043	1.060	1.120	1.180	0.579
Drug law violations	17.651	18.575	18.671	17.939	19.133	18.993	21.722	24.424	25.077	23.194	22.142	22.427	21.704	21.508	23.554	3.087
Liquor law violations	41.123	46.529	48.511	47.061	45.952	43.539	40.778	41.804	38.443	32.569	30.038	23.842	21.365	18.792	20.702	1.598
Referrals for disciplinary action[11]	153.104	175.506	184.622	178.077	170.820	169.503	175.490	194.017	197.669	189.403	196.696	184.108	166.160	154.470	171.440	1.722
Illegal weapons possession	1.311	1.921	1.673	1.455	1.294	1.043	1.004	0.913	0.962	0.900	0.946	0.823	0.841	0.730	0.779	0.289
Drug law violations	25.492	22.803	23.744	24.255	27.204	28.459	32.444	40.907	43.129	42.093	44.485	44.249	41.549	44.076	48.877	0.868
Liquor law violations	126.301	150.782	159.206	152.367	142.322	140.001	142.042	152.198	153.578	146.410	151.264	139.036	123.770	109.663	121.784	0.565
Nonprofit 4-year																
Selected crimes against persons and property	57.358	54.165	57.679	52.036	49.337	38.613	35.193	33.154	33.198	31.205	30.156	31.148	32.667	32.071	34.431	9.294
Murder[2]	0.019	0.017	0.010	0.007	0.003	0.019	0.016	0.009	0.006	0.015	0.015	0.006	0.012	0.018	0.019	0.000
Negligent manslaughter[3]	0.000	0.003	0.000	0.003	0.000	0.000	0.000	0.000	0.000	0.000	0.000	0.003	0.000	0.000	0.000	0.000
Sex offenses—forcible[4]	3.169	3.784	3.694	3.586	3.588	3.557	3.848	4.417	5.357	7.214	9.368	10.452	11.697	13.166	14.404	1.216
Rape	—	—	—	—	—	—	—	—	—	—	6.493	7.046	7.985	8.420	9.267	0.250
Fondling	—	—	—	—	—	—	—	—	—	—	2.875	3.407	3.712	4.746	5.138	0.967
Sex offenses—nonforcible[5]	0.437	0.021	0.034	0.027	0.053	0.036	0.025	0.040	0.031	0.036	0.021	0.045	0.032	0.023	0.026	0.000
Robbery[6]	2.508	1.739	1.717	1.549	1.448	1.181	1.002	0.988	1.188	1.131	0.793	0.834	0.975	1.031	1.063	0.717
Aggravated assault[7]	3.408	2.588	2.853	2.586	2.498	2.133	2.014	1.948	2.052	2.065	1.976	2.165	1.987	2.213	2.120	3.119
Burglary[8]	40.460	40.542	44.638	40.212	38.269	28.434	25.567	22.908	21.679	18.192	15.146	14.573	14.869	12.543	13.555	2.776
Motor vehicle theft[9]	5.684	4.340	3.684	3.314	2.846	2.692	2.014	2.173	2.188	2.023	2.275	2.445	2.469	2.480	2.591	1.403
Arson[10]	1.673	1.130	1.050	0.751	0.633	0.562	0.707	0.670	0.698	0.528	0.561	0.625	0.626	0.597	0.653	0.062

See notes at end of table.

Table 329.20 On-campus crimes, arrests, and referrals for disciplinary action per 10,000 full-time-equivalent (FTE) students at degree-granting postsecondary institutions, by whether institution has residence halls, control and level of institution, and type of incident: Selected years, 2001 through 2017—Continued

Control and level of institution and type of incident	Number of incidents per 10,000 FTE students[1]															
	Total, institutions with and without residence halls													2017		
	2001	2005	2006	2007	2008	2009	2010	2011	2012	2013	2014	2015	2016	Total	Institutions with residence halls	Institutions without residence halls
1	2	3	4	5	6	7	8	9	10	11	12	13	14	15	16	17
Weapons-, drug-, and liquor-related arrests and referrals																
Arrests[11]	24.456	25.758	20.980	22.670	20.249	18.645	17.150	16.805	16.851	17.110	14.935	13.647	13.304	12.344	13.477	1.403
Illegal weapons possession	0.645	0.522	0.499	0.599	0.523	0.478	0.430	0.398	0.391	0.397	0.389	0.500	0.576	0.550	0.598	0.094
Drug law violations	6.291	5.881	5.643	6.075	6.238	6.713	7.062	7.486	7.430	7.590	6.813	6.661	6.494	6.678	7.251	1.154
Liquor law violations	17.520	19.355	14.837	15.996	13.487	11.454	9.657	8.921	9.030	9.122	7.733	6.486	6.234	5.115	5.629	0.156
Referrals for disciplinary action[11]	275.480	336.127	353.943	347.714	348.824	333.904	329.679	341.437	339.263	331.451	332.331	314.359	302.523	280.603	308.611	10.261
Illegal weapons possession	1.712	2.052	2.127	1.835	1.514	1.155	1.235	1.287	1.532	1.622	1.451	1.694	1.692	1.566	1.725	0.031
Drug law violations	37.435	38.981	41.433	42.718	46.902	51.139	56.050	65.567	68.205	67.068	69.393	66.048	67.717	66.951	73.680	1.996
Liquor law violations	236.333	295.095	310.383	303.161	300.408	281.609	272.395	274.583	269.526	262.761	261.487	246.617	233.115	212.086	233.205	8.234
For-profit 4-year																
Selected crimes against persons and property	19.109	17.049	9.552	8.092	10.334	7.513	6.499	6.003	5.531	8.553	5.763	4.371	4.489	5.277	19.368	2.561
Murder[2]	0.000	0.000	0.000	0.000	0.000	0.000	0.000	0.013	0.000	0.017	0.000	0.000	0.000	0.000	0.000	0.000
Negligent manslaughter[3]	0.000	0.000	0.000	0.000	0.000	0.000	0.000	0.000	0.000	0.000	0.000	0.000	0.000	0.000	0.000	0.000
Sex offenses—forcible[4]	0.151	0.082	0.179	0.159	0.162	0.129	0.255	0.350	0.274	0.301	0.561	0.504	0.490	0.932	5.151	0.119
Rape	—	—	—	—	—	—	—	—	—	—	0.339	0.163	0.276	0.549	3.194	0.040
Fondling	—	—	—	—	—	—	—	—	—	—	0.222	0.341	0.215	0.383	1.957	0.079
Sex offenses—nonforcible[5]	0.492	0.021	0.000	0.026	0.000	0.014	0.012	0.000	0.046	0.033	0.026	0.000	0.015	0.000	0.000	0.000
Robbery[6]	2.422	0.884	0.373	0.410	0.684	1.231	0.811	0.996	0.775	1.440	0.678	0.356	0.398	0.383	0.515	0.357
Aggravated assault[7]	0.870	1.213	0.462	0.410	1.134	0.615	0.591	0.485	0.653	0.971	0.430	0.400	0.628	0.533	1.030	0.437
Burglary[8]	13.130	12.484	7.287	5.897	6.931	4.279	4.055	3.351	2.963	4.620	3.273	2.401	1.931	2.447	9.993	0.993
Motor vehicle theft[9]	1.968	2.262	1.162	1.177	1.422	1.216	0.753	0.781	0.805	1.138	0.769	0.696	0.981	0.932	2.369	0.655
Arson[10]	0.076	0.103	0.089	0.013	0.000	0.029	0.023	0.027	0.015	0.033	0.026	0.015	0.046	0.050	0.309	0.000
Weapons-, drug-, and liquor-related arrests and referrals																
Arrests[11]	0.416	0.576	0.775	0.370	0.720	0.773	1.911	2.046	1.915	1.239	1.526	1.511	1.777	2.197	11.847	0.338
Illegal weapons possession	0.076	0.041	0.075	0.040	0.144	0.086	0.151	0.148	0.152	0.201	0.117	0.207	0.169	0.117	0.309	0.079
Drug law violations	0.151	0.329	0.209	0.212	0.252	0.315	0.765	0.552	0.745	0.803	0.887	1.156	1.272	1.898	10.508	0.238
Liquor law violations	0.189	0.206	0.492	0.119	0.324	0.372	0.996	1.346	1.018	0.234	0.522	0.148	0.337	0.183	1.030	0.020
Referrals for disciplinary action[11]	11.957	10.880	7.645	6.862	10.190	12.623	8.804	9.663	10.150	19.433	12.191	11.914	11.446	17.230	103.125	0.675
Illegal weapons possession	0.416	0.864	0.194	0.145	0.234	0.329	0.104	0.215	0.349	0.301	0.209	0.163	0.123	0.200	1.030	0.040
Drug law violations	3.481	2.632	2.056	1.745	2.863	3.306	2.560	3.136	3.860	8.989	5.255	4.890	4.566	5.560	31.525	0.556
Liquor law violations	8.060	7.383	5.394	4.971	7.093	8.988	6.140	6.312	5.941	10.143	6.728	6.861	6.757	11.470	70.570	0.079
Public 2-year																
Selected crimes against persons and property	19.867	16.389	15.430	14.365	13.990	11.745	10.195	9.998	9.379	7.912	7.682	8.415	7.973	8.155	14.371	6.374
Murder[2]	0.006	0.005	0.000	0.000	0.005	0.005	0.002	0.005	0.008	0.018	0.008	0.036	0.009	0.006	0.014	0.004
Negligent manslaughter[3]	0.000	0.000	0.000	0.000	0.000	0.000	0.000	0.002	0.000	0.000	0.003	0.000	0.000	0.000	0.000	0.000
Sex offenses—forcible[4]	0.344	0.480	0.455	0.483	0.538	0.483	0.487	0.633	0.658	0.780	1.040	1.382	1.475	1.774	3.852	1.179
Rape	—	—	—	—	—	—	—	—	—	—	0.356	0.550	0.528	0.685	2.300	0.222
Fondling	—	—	—	—	—	—	—	—	—	—	0.683	0.832	0.947	1.089	1.552	0.957
Sex offenses—nonforcible[5]	0.347	0.027	0.044	0.019	0.018	0.028	0.019	0.039	0.033	0.028	0.043	0.031	0.054	0.028	0.028	0.028
Robbery[6]	0.714	0.680	0.773	0.745	0.730	0.591	0.691	0.633	0.610	0.507	0.400	0.416	0.414	0.398	0.374	0.405
Aggravated assault[7]	1.588	1.373	1.486	1.233	1.027	1.016	0.949	0.980	1.093	0.715	0.824	0.935	0.842	0.805	1.497	0.607
Burglary[8]	12.042	9.703	8.876	8.548	8.782	6.881	5.561	5.396	4.914	4.073	3.734	3.940	3.402	3.539	7.372	2.441
Motor vehicle theft[9]	4.523	3.913	3.590	3.134	2.712	2.613	2.384	2.171	1.941	1.675	1.480	1.511	1.645	1.453	1.039	1.572
Arson[10]	0.303	0.208	0.207	0.203	0.179	0.127	0.100	0.142	0.123	0.116	0.151	0.165	0.132	0.151	0.194	0.139
Weapons-, drug-, and liquor-related arrests and referrals																
Arrests[11]	7.752	9.360	10.868	11.009	9.638	7.859	8.838	8.989	8.666	7.874	8.427	7.930	8.095	9.706	30.030	3.886
Illegal weapons possession	0.577	0.762	0.817	0.812	0.661	0.603	0.654	0.599	0.633	0.592	0.594	0.748	0.644	0.700	1.025	0.607
Drug law violations	2.882	3.633	3.751	4.172	3.815	3.551	4.328	4.568	4.716	4.086	4.512	4.378	4.115	4.643	11.460	2.691
Liquor law violations	4.293	4.965	6.301	6.025	5.162	3.704	3.857	3.822	3.317	3.196	3.321	2.803	3.336	4.363	17.544	0.587
Referrals for disciplinary action[11]	10.284	12.846	16.051	15.983	16.451	17.063	18.592	19.735	18.979	17.613	19.549	20.360	20.585	21.030	85.420	2.588
Illegal weapons possession	0.370	0.364	0.648	0.582	0.469	0.495	0.561	0.550	0.560	0.625	0.726	0.757	0.641	0.679	1.815	0.353
Drug law violations	2.218	2.244	2.471	2.686	3.334	4.112	5.417	6.212	6.174	5.928	6.880	7.332	7.718	8.210	31.139	1.643
Liquor law violations	7.697	10.237	12.932	12.715	12.649	12.456	12.614	12.972	12.244	11.059	11.942	12.271	12.226	12.141	52.466	0.591

See notes at end of table.

Table 329.20 On-campus crimes, arrests, and referrals for disciplinary action per 10,000 full-time-equivalent (FTE) students at degree-granting postsecondary institutions, by whether institution has residence halls, control and level of institution, and type of incident: Selected years, 2001 through 2017—Continued

Control and level of institution and type of incident	2001	2005	2006	2007	2008	2009	2010	2011	2012	2013	2014	2015	2016	2017 Total	2017 Institutions with residence halls	2017 Institutions without residence halls
1	2	3	4	5	6	7	8	9	10	11	12	13	14	15	16	17
Nonprofit 2-year																
Selected crimes against persons and property	63.955	91.263	81.948	103.794	99.274	55.883	48.448	45.531	35.148	26.993	27.354	20.036	21.920	14.389	37.843	8.423
Murder[2]	0.258	0.000	0.000	0.000	0.000	0.000	0.000	0.000	0.000	0.000	0.000	0.000	0.000	0.000	0.000	0.000
Negligent manslaughter[3]	0.000	0.000	0.000	0.000	0.365	0.000	0.000	0.000	0.000	0.000	0.000	0.000	0.000	0.000	0.000	0.000
Sex offenses—forcible[4]	0.516	2.325	0.983	3.621	5.840	3.041	2.826	3.384	2.628	1.636	1.282	4.158	6.153	3.118	14.191	0.301
Rape	—	—	—	—	—	—	—	—	—	—	0.855	0.378	3.076	2.158	9.461	0.301
Fondling	—	—	—	—	—	—	—	—	—	—	0.427	3.780	3.076	0.959	4.730	0.000
Sex offenses—nonforcible[5]	0.516	0.000	0.328	0.000	0.000	0.000	0.000	0.000	0.000	0.818	0.000	0.000	0.000	0.000	0.000	0.000
Robbery[6]	13.926	2.616	2.295	0.805	4.745	3.421	2.019	0.308	0.657	1.227	0.000	0.756	1.923	0.480	0.000	0.602
Aggravated assault[7]	5.931	6.394	11.473	20.920	24.088	1.901	3.634	16.305	15.110	5.317	11.540	2.646	3.076	2.878	4.730	2.407
Burglary[8]	36.620	77.312	61.297	71.610	58.396	45.619	38.354	22.766	15.439	16.768	12.395	10.207	9.229	4.796	16.556	1.805
Motor vehicle theft[9]	5.931	2.035	4.589	5.632	3.285	1.521	0.807	2.154	1.314	1.227	2.137	1.512	1.154	2.878	1.183	3.309
Arson[10]	0.258	0.581	0.983	1.207	2.555	0.380	0.807	0.615	0.000	0.000	0.000	0.756	0.385	0.240	1.183	0.000
Weapons-, drug-, and liquor-related arrests and referrals																
Arrests[11]	27.852	22.089	21.962	23.736	33.943	22.049	19.783	15.998	17.081	26.993	16.669	12.097	21.535	11.271	37.843	4.512
Illegal weapons possession	0.258	1.453	0.983	1.609	1.095	1.521	2.422	1.538	1.642	2.045	2.137	3.402	4.615	2.158	8.278	0.602
Drug law violations	5.416	9.301	11.145	10.862	12.044	13.305	7.267	10.460	10.183	20.040	11.967	7.561	8.076	8.873	28.382	3.911
Liquor law violations	22.178	11.335	9.834	11.264	20.804	7.223	10.093	3.999	5.256	4.908	2.564	1.134	8.845	0.240	1.183	0.000
Referrals for disciplinary action[11]	160.920	149.393	176.025	208.794	150.735	132.294	152.206	110.752	98.545	130.874	191.478	206.404	161.514	117.029	570.009	1.805
Illegal weapons possession	0.516	3.488	6.228	4.023	2.190	2.661	1.615	0.308	1.971	2.863	4.701	0.756	1.154	1.679	8.278	0.000
Drug law violations	23.468	13.660	24.257	29.368	31.023	38.016	42.392	33.533	33.834	52.759	66.248	80.898	62.683	44.366	212.867	1.504
Liquor law violations	136.937	132.244	145.540	175.403	117.523	91.618	108.200	76.911	62.740	75.253	120.528	124.750	97.677	70.985	348.865	0.301
For-profit 2-year																
Selected crimes against persons and property	25.385	17.851	18.237	23.731	14.825	13.033	8.167	7.503	9.325	7.141	6.140	6.867	6.736	4.993	7.426	4.871
Murder[2]	0.000	0.000	0.000	0.000	0.000	0.000	0.000	0.000	0.000	0.000	0.000	0.000	0.000	0.059	1.238	0.000
Negligent manslaughter[3]	0.000	0.000	0.000	0.000	0.037	0.000	0.000	0.000	0.000	0.000	0.000	0.000	0.000	0.000	0.000	0.000
Sex offenses—forcible[4]	0.645	0.042	0.347	0.087	0.149	0.170	0.052	0.204	0.455	0.385	0.195	0.698	0.527	0.294	0.000	0.308
Rape	—	—	—	—	—	—	—	—	—	—	0.049	0.175	0.117	0.117	0.000	0.123
Fondling	—	—	—	—	—	—	—	—	—	—	0.146	0.524	0.410	0.176	0.000	0.185
Sex offenses—nonforcible[5]	0.376	0.000	0.043	0.000	0.000	0.028	0.026	0.000	0.114	0.000	0.000	0.000	0.000	0.000	0.000	0.000
Robbery[6]	3.603	2.283	2.128	2.907	1.969	1.420	0.985	0.467	1.061	0.983	1.364	0.524	0.469	0.529	0.000	0.555
Aggravated assault[7]	2.151	2.076	1.433	1.432	1.078	1.505	0.907	1.080	1.137	0.599	0.585	1.048	1.464	0.940	0.000	0.987
Burglary[8]	15.704	10.378	10.638	15.185	8.954	6.417	3.500	3.503	4.170	3.207	2.826	2.561	2.695	1.527	3.713	1.418
Motor vehicle theft[9]	2.743	2.947	3.517	3.991	2.638	3.436	2.619	2.160	2.388	1.924	1.170	2.037	1.582	1.645	2.475	1.603
Arson[10]	0.161	0.125	0.130	0.130	0.000	0.057	0.078	0.088	0.000	0.043	0.000	0.000	0.000	0.000	0.000	0.000
Weapons-, drug-, and liquor-related arrests and referrals																
Arrests[11]	8.766	1.951	1.780	1.952	0.855	1.760	1.115	0.671	1.933	2.565	2.680	1.455	1.992	1.351	3.713	1.233
Illegal weapons possession	0.699	0.125	0.130	0.174	0.149	0.114	0.130	0.029	0.265	0.128	0.390	0.175	0.469	0.059	1.238	0.000
Drug law violations	4.679	1.495	1.129	1.388	0.446	1.164	0.752	0.409	1.516	1.710	1.364	1.106	1.054	1.233	2.475	1.172
Liquor law violations	3.388	0.332	0.521	0.390	0.260	0.483	0.233	0.234	0.152	0.727	0.926	0.175	0.469	0.059	0.000	0.062
Referrals for disciplinary action[11]	15.435	9.465	13.894	7.506	9.215	8.603	3.811	4.905	8.225	8.808	11.305	9.486	5.916	5.169	80.446	1.418
Illegal weapons possession	0.861	0.332	0.304	0.304	0.149	0.227	0.052	0.292	0.341	0.128	0.097	0.175	0.293	0.294	3.713	0.123
Drug law violations	4.787	5.563	9.509	5.293	4.087	4.628	1.763	1.985	3.260	4.019	4.532	5.122	2.460	2.467	33.416	0.925
Liquor law violations	9.788	3.570	4.082	1.909	4.979	3.748	1.996	2.627	4.624	4.661	6.676	4.190	3.163	2.408	43.317	0.370

—Not available.
[1]Although crimes, arrests, and referrals include incidents involving students, staff, and campus guests, they are expressed as a ratio to FTE students because comprehensive FTE counts of all these groups are not available.
[2]Excludes suicides, fetal deaths, traffic fatalities, accidental deaths, and justifiable homicide (such as the killing of a felon by a law enforcement officer in the line of duty).
[3]Killing of another person through gross negligence (excludes traffic fatalities).
[4]Any sexual act directed against another person forcibly and/or against that person's will.
[5]Includes only statutory rape or incest.
[6]Taking or attempting to take anything of value using actual or threatened force or violence.
[7]Attack upon a person for the purpose of inflicting severe or aggravated bodily injury.
[8]Unlawful entry of a structure to commit a felony or theft.
[9]Theft or attempted theft of a motor vehicle.
[10]Willful or malicious burning or attempt to burn a dwelling house, public building, motor vehicle, or personal property of another.
[11]If an individual is both arrested and referred to college officials for disciplinary action for a single offense, only the arrest is counted.

NOTE: Data are for degree-granting institutions, which are institutions that grant associate's or higher degrees and participate in Title IV federal financial aid programs. Some institutions that report Clery data—specifically, non-degree-granting institutions and institutions outside of the 50 states and the District of Columbia—are excluded from this table. Crimes, arrests, and referrals include incidents involving students, staff, and on-campus guests. Excludes off-campus crimes and arrests even if they involve college students or staff. Detail may not sum to totals because of rounding. Some data have been revised from previously published figures.
SOURCE: U.S. Department of Education, Office of Postsecondary Education, Campus Safety and Security Reporting System, 2001 through 2017; and National Center for Education Statistics, Integrated Postsecondary Education Data System (IPEDS), Spring 2002 through Spring 2018; and National Center for Education Statistics, Integrated Postsecondary Education Data System (IPEDS), Spring 2001 through Spring 2018, Fall Enrollment component. (This table was prepared September 2019.)

Table 329.30. On-campus hate crimes at degree-granting postsecondary institutions, by level and control of institution, type of crime, and category of bias motivating the crime: Selected years, 2010 through 2017

Type of crime and category of bias motivating the crime[1]	Total, 2010	Total, 2012	Total, 2013	Total, 2014	Total, 2015	2016							2017						
							4-year			2-year				4-year			2-year		
						Total	Public	Non-profit	For-profit	Public	Non-profit	For-profit	Total	Public	Non-profit	For-profit	Public	Non-profit	For-profit
1	2	3	4	5	6	7	8	9	10	11	12	13	14	15	16	17	18	19	20
All on-campus hate crimes	928	784	778	794	859	1,072	483	395	7	183	0	4	958	416	405	1	136	0	0
Murder[2]	0	0	0	0	0	0	0	0	0	0	0	0	1	1	0	0	0	0	0
Sex offenses—forcible[3]	7	4	7	4	7	8	1	1	0	6	0	0	6	1	3	0	2	0	0
Race	0	1	2	1	0	1	1	0	0	0	0	0	0	0	0	0	0	0	0
Ethnicity	0	0	0	0	0	0	0	0	0	0	0	0	0	0	0	0	0	0	0
Religion	0	0	0	0	1	0	0	0	0	0	0	0	0	0	0	0	0	0	0
Sexual orientation	4	2	1	1	3	1	0	1	0	0	0	0	0	0	0	0	0	0	0
Gender	3	1	4	2	1	5	0	0	0	5	0	0	4	1	1	0	2	0	0
Gender identity	—	—	—	0	2	1	0	0	0	1	0	0	2	0	2	0	0	0	0
Disability	0	0	0	0	0	0	0	0	0	0	0	0	0	0	0	0	0	0	0
Sex offenses—nonforcible[4]	0	0	0	0	0	0	0	0	0	0	0	0	0	0	0	0	0	0	0
Robbery[5]	2	5	1	2	3	2	1	0	0	1	0	0	2	1	1	0	0	0	0
Aggravated assault[6]	17	14	7	18	18	35	26	2	0	7	0	0	15	6	3	0	6	0	0
Race	6	6	5	5	5	8	5	0	0	3	0	0	6	2	3	0	1	0	0
Ethnicity	1	0	1	4	4	15	14	0	0	1	0	0	5	1	0	0	4	0	0
Religion	1	1	0	1	0	1	1	0	0	0	0	0	1	1	0	0	0	0	0
Sexual orientation	9	5	1	7	7	8	6	1	0	1	0	0	2	2	0	0	0	0	0
Gender	0	1	0	1	1	1	0	0	0	1	0	0	0	0	0	0	0	0	0
Gender identity	—	—	—	0	1	2	0	1	0	1	0	0	0	0	0	0	0	0	0
Disability	0	1	0	0	0	0	0	0	0	0	0	0	1	0	0	0	1	0	0
Burglary[7]	11	5	4	28	4	6	0	4	0	2	0	0	3	1	2	0	1	0	0
Race	7	0	1	24	0	1	0	1	0	0	0	0	1	0	1	0	0	0	0
Ethnicity	0	0	0	0	0	0	0	0	0	0	0	0	1	0	0	0	1	0	0
Religion	0	1	1	3	0	0	0	0	0	0	0	0	0	0	0	0	0	0	0
Sexual orientation	2	0	0	1	0	2	0	2	0	0	0	0	0	0	0	0	0	0	0
Gender	1	4	2	0	0	3	0	1	0	2	0	0	1	0	1	0	0	0	0
Gender identity	—	—	—	0	4	0	0	0	0	0	0	0	0	0	0	0	0	0	0
Disability	1	0	0	0	0	0	0	0	0	0	0	0	0	0	0	0	0	0	0
Motor vehicle theft[8]	0	0	0	0	1	0	0	0	0	0	0	0	1	0	1	0	0	0	0
Arson[9]	0	0	0	1	2	2	2	0	0	0	0	0	1	1	0	0	0	0	0
Simple assault[10]	67	79	91	63	80	98	64	26	0	7	0	1	83	41	23	0	19	0	0
Race	25	36	36	14	36	42	27	13	0	2	0	0	40	18	15	0	7	0	0
Ethnicity	5	5	5	11	9	14	10	2	0	2	0	0	8	3	1	0	4	0	0
Religion	4	9	6	2	9	12	9	2	0	1	0	0	9	7	2	0	0	0	0
Sexual orientation	23	21	27	23	18	16	9	5	0	2	0	0	18	9	3	0	6	0	0
Gender	9	5	17	9	2	11	8	2	0	0	0	1	3	1	0	0	2	0	0
Gender identity	—	—	—	3	5	2	1	1	0	0	0	0	5	3	2	0	0	0	0
Disability	1	3	0	1	1	1	0	1	0	0	0	0	0	0	0	0	0	0	0
Larceny[11]	9	9	15	17	25	33	3	16	3	10	0	1	24	4	19	0	1	0	0
Race	1	2	5	5	1	12	1	5	3	2	0	1	6	1	5	0	0	0	0
Ethnicity	3	2	2	1	0	4	0	0	0	4	0	0	3	2	1	0	0	0	0
Religion	1	2	3	3	19	5	2	3	0	0	0	0	1	0	1	0	0	0	0
Sexual orientation	1	3	3	1	1	5	0	5	0	0	0	0	6	1	4	0	1	0	0
Gender	3	0	2	7	3	3	0	0	0	3	0	0	7	0	7	0	0	0	0
Gender identity	—	—	—	0	1	3	0	2	0	1	0	0	1	0	1	0	0	0	0
Disability	0	0	0	0	0	1	0	1	0	0	0	0	0	0	0	0	0	0	0
Intimidation[12]	260	265	296	339	355	425	183	169	1	70	0	2	385	191	147	0	47	0	0
Race	79	120	111	111	141	170	81	62	0	27	0	0	172	92	63	0	17	0	0
Ethnicity	17	22	49	32	37	48	19	22	0	7	0	0	45	20	19	0	6	0	0
Religion	38	28	25	35	48	67	35	22	0	10	0	0	48	26	18	0	4	0	0
Sexual orientation	87	70	68	78	77	83	32	35	1	14	0	1	66	29	25	0	12	0	0
Gender	37	21	37	63	34	28	9	16	0	3	0	0	26	11	12	0	3	0	0
Gender identity	—	—	—	13	11	20	4	11	0	4	0	1	19	9	6	0	4	0	0
Disability	2	4	6	7	7	9	3	1	0	5	0	0	9	4	4	0	1	0	0
Destruction, damage, and vandalism[13]	555	403	357	322	364	463	203	177	3	80	0	0	437	170	206	1	60	0	0
Race	257	186	147	116	151	175	82	56	1	36	0	0	186	80	78	0	28	0	0
Ethnicity	43	34	38	29	25	30	17	11	0	2	0	0	33	16	15	0	2	0	0
Religion	103	70	48	67	108	134	54	51	0	29	0	0	111	34	59	1	17	0	0
Sexual orientation	135	104	108	89	61	67	33	27	2	5	0	0	61	30	21	0	10	0	0
Gender	17	9	14	13	10	35	14	15	0	6	0	0	22	5	16	0	1	0	0
Gender identity	—	—	—	6	8	22	3	17	0	2	0	0	24	5	17	0	2	0	0
Disability	0	0	2	2	1	0	0	0	0	0	0	0	0	0	0	0	0	0	0

—Not available.
[1]Bias categories correspond to characteristics against which the bias is directed (i.e., race, ethnicity, religion, sexual orientation, gender, gender identity, or disability).
[2]Excludes suicides, fetal deaths, traffic fatalities, accidental deaths, and justifiable homicide (such as the killing of a felon by a law enforcement officer in the line of duty).
[3]Any sexual act directed against another person forcibly and/or against that person's will.
[4]Includes only statutory rape or incest.
[5]Taking or attempting to take anything of value using actual or threatened force or violence.
[6]Attack upon a person for the purpose of inflicting severe or aggravated bodily injury.
[7]Unlawful entry of a structure to commit a felony or theft.
[8]Theft or attempted theft of a motor vehicle.
[9]Willful or malicious burning or attempt to burn a dwelling house, public building, motor vehicle, or personal property of another.
[10]A physical attack by one person upon another where neither the offender displays a weapon, nor the victim suffers obvious severe or aggravated bodily injury involving apparent broken bones, loss of teeth, possible internal injury, severe laceration, or loss of consciousness.
[11]The unlawful taking, carrying, leading, or riding away of property from the possession of another.

[12]Placing another person in reasonable fear of bodily harm through the use of threatening words and/or other conduct, but without displaying a weapon or subjecting the victim to actual physical attack.
[13]Willfully or maliciously destroying, damaging, defacing, or otherwise injuring real or personal property without the consent of the owner or the person having custody or control of it.
NOTE: Data are for degree-granting institutions, which are institutions that grant associate's or higher degrees and participate in Title IV federal financial aid programs. Some institutions that report Clery data—specifically, non-degree-granting institutions and institutions outside of the 50 states and the District of Columbia—are excluded from this table. A hate crime is a criminal offense that is motivated, in whole or in part, by the perpetrator's bias against a group of people based on their race, ethnicity, religion, sexual orientation, gender, gender identity, or disability. Includes on-campus incidents involving students, staff, and on-campus guests. Excludes off-campus crimes and arrests even if they involve college students or staff. Some data have been revised from previously published figures.
SOURCE: U.S. Department of Education, Office of Postsecondary Education, Campus Safety and Security Reporting System, 2010 through 2017. (This table was prepared September 2019.)

Table 330.10. Average undergraduate tuition and fees and room and board rates charged for full-time students in degree-granting postsecondary institutions, by level and control of institution: Selected years, 1963–64 through 2018–19

Year and control of institution	Constant 2018–19 dollars[1]												Current dollars												
	Total tuition, fees, room, and board			Tuition and required fees[2]			Dormitory rooms			Board[3]			Total tuition, fees, room, and board			Tuition and required fees[2]			Dormitory rooms			Board[3]		
	All insti-tutions	4-year	2-year	All insti-tutions	4-year	2-year	All insti-tutions	4-year	2-year	All insti-tutions	4-year	2-year	All insti-tutions	4-year	2-year	All insti-tutions	4-year	2-year	All insti-tutions	4-year	2-year	All insti-tutions	4-year	2-year
1	2	3	4	5	6	7	8	9	10	11	12	13	14	15	16	17	18	19	20	21	22	23	24	25
All institutions																								
1963–64	10,248	10,561	6,368	4,174	4,538	1,406	2,319	2,288	1,717	3,756	3,736	3,244	1,248	1,286	775	508	553	171	282	279	209	457	455	395
1968–69	10,357	10,973	7,477	4,234	4,852	1,778	2,558	2,557	2,321	3,565	3,564	3,378	1,459	1,545	1,053	596	683	250	360	360	327	502	502	476
1969–70	10,460	11,227	7,304	4,325	5,062	1,659	2,610	2,627	2,326	3,524	3,537	3,319	1,560	1,674	1,089	645	755	247	389	392	347	526	528	495
1970–71	10,537	11,376	7,143	4,387	5,188	1,590	2,670	2,690	2,355	3,480	3,498	3,197	1,653	1,784	1,120	688	814	249	419	422	369	546	549	501
1971–72	10,651	11,556	7,212	4,455	5,326	1,544	2,738	2,760	2,406	3,458	3,470	3,262	1,730	1,878	1,172	724	865	251	445	448	391	562	564	530
1972–73	10,853	12,015	7,549	4,493	5,623	1,697	2,886	2,913	2,454	3,474	3,479	3,398	1,834	2,031	1,276	759	950	287	488	492	415	587	588	574
1973–74	10,337	11,392	7,379	4,322	5,348	1,784	2,691	2,715	2,334	3,324	3,329	3,260	1,903	2,097	1,358	796	985	328	495	500	430	612	613	600
1974–75	9,698	10,693	7,000	3,958	4,930	1,602	2,582	2,605	2,250	3,158	3,158	3,148	1,983	2,187	1,432	809	1,008	328	528	533	460	646	646	644
1975–76	9,605	10,754	6,729	3,786	4,901	1,357	2,598	2,631	2,165	3,221	3,222	3,207	2,103	2,355	1,473	829	1,073	297	569	576	474	705	706	702
1976–77	9,818	11,019	6,895	3,987	5,258	1,491	2,604	2,636	2,169	3,227	3,226	3,235	2,275	2,577	1,598	924	1,218	346	603	611	503	748	748	750
1977–78	9,748	11,020	6,888	3,981	5,222	1,529	2,609	2,644	2,122	3,158	3,153	3,237	2,411	2,725	1,703	984	1,291	378	645	654	525	781	780	801
1978–79	9,564	10,786	6,759	3,966	5,164	1,519	2,544	2,572	2,126	3,054	3,050	3,114	2,587	2,917	1,828	1,073	1,397	411	688	696	575	826	825	842
1979–80	9,164	10,332	6,458	3,794	4,936	1,471	2,450	2,477	2,049	2,920	2,919	2,938	2,809	3,167	1,979	1,163	1,513	451	751	759	628	895	895	900
1980–81	9,067	10,231	6,520	3,768	4,908	1,538	2,445	2,473	2,060	2,855	2,850	2,923	3,101	3,499	2,230	1,289	1,679	526	836	846	705	976	975	1,000
1981–82	9,391	10,633	6,663	3,920	5,133	1,587	2,556	2,587	2,133	2,914	2,912	2,943	3,489	3,951	2,476	1,457	1,907	590	950	961	793	1,083	1,082	1,094
1982–83	10,003	11,369	7,002	4,195	5,520	1,741	2,745	2,781	2,254	3,064	3,067	3,007	3,877	4,406	2,713	1,626	2,139	675	1,064	1,078	873	1,187	1,189	1,165
1983–84	10,369	11,812	7,103	4,436	5,832	1,817	2,849	2,892	2,280	3,084	3,089	3,006	4,167	4,747	2,854	1,783	2,344	730	1,145	1,162	916	1,239	1,242	1,208
1984–85	10,926	12,357	7,613	4,754	6,148	1,966	3,034	3,070	2,533	3,138	3,139	3,114	4,563	5,160	3,179	1,985	2,567	821	1,267	1,282	1,058	1,310	1,311	1,301
1985–86[4]	11,369	12,811	7,836	5,076	6,481	2,068	3,115	3,153	2,576	3,178	3,177	3,192	4,885	5,504	3,367	2,181	2,784	888	1,338	1,355	1,107	1,365	1,365	1,372
1986–87	11,853	13,580	7,503	5,503	6,927	2,043	3,198	3,248	2,355	3,390	3,405	3,106	5,206	5,964	3,295	2,312	3,042	897	1,405	1,427	1,034	1,489	1,495	1,364
1987–88	12,013	13,713	7,134	5,374	6,998	1,769	3,252	3,315	2,224	3,386	3,400	3,141	5,494	6,272	3,263	2,458	3,201	809	1,488	1,516	1,017	1,549	1,555	1,437
1988–89	12,264	14,055	7,467	5,554	7,256	2,047	3,291	3,362	2,267	3,420	3,437	3,153	5,869	6,725	3,573	2,658	3,472	979	1,575	1,609	1,085	1,636	1,644	1,509
1989–90	12,381	14,384	7,390	5,663	7,580	1,950	3,267	3,340	2,204	3,451	3,464	3,236	6,207	7,212	3,705	2,839	3,800	978	1,638	1,675	1,105	1,730	1,737	1,622
1990–91	12,410	14,376	7,433	5,704	7,582	2,057	3,297	3,370	2,236	3,408	3,425	3,140	6,562	7,602	3,930	3,016	4,009	1,087	1,743	1,782	1,182	1,802	1,811	1,660
1991–92	12,969	15,096	7,499	6,021	8,036	2,179	3,434	3,520	2,218	3,514	3,539	3,101	7,077	8,238	4,092	3,286	4,385	1,189	1,874	1,921	1,210	1,918	1,931	1,692
1992–93	13,243	15,562	7,477	6,250	8,444	2,267	3,445	3,538	2,204	3,548	3,580	3,006	7,452	8,758	4,207	3,517	4,752	1,276	1,939	1,991	1,240	1,996	2,015	1,692
1993–94	13,738	16,103	7,706	6,629	8,867	2,423	3,563	3,656	2,308	3,546	3,580	2,976	7,931	9,296	4,449	3,827	5,119	1,399	2,057	2,111	1,332	2,047	2,067	1,718
1994–95	13,985	16,381	7,802	6,810	9,078	2,505	3,612	3,704	2,351	3,563	3,599	2,946	8,306	9,728	4,633	4,044	5,391	1,488	2,145	2,200	1,396	2,116	2,138	1,750
1995–96	14,426	16,934	7,745	7,111	9,485	2,495	3,711	3,800	2,414	3,604	3,649	2,836	8,800	10,330	4,725	4,338	5,786	1,522	2,264	2,318	1,473	2,199	2,226	1,730
1996–97	14,672	17,278	7,802	7,274	9,752	2,459	3,770	3,860	2,427	3,628	3,667	2,916	9,206	10,841	4,895	4,564	6,118	1,543	2,365	2,422	1,522	2,276	2,301	1,830
1997–98	15,013	17,659	8,130	7,445	9,944	2,653	3,827	3,926	2,502	3,740	3,789	2,975	9,588	11,277	5,192	4,755	6,351	1,695	2,444	2,507	1,598	2,389	2,419	1,900
1998–99	15,509	18,299	8,144	7,716	10,348	2,656	3,936	4,041	2,487	3,857	3,910	3,001	10,076	11,888	5,291	5,013	6,723	1,725	2,557	2,626	1,616	2,506	2,540	1,950
1999–2000	15,604	18,475	8,108	7,812	10,533	2,585	4,018	4,115	2,650	3,774	3,827	2,873	10,430	12,349	5,420	5,222	7,040	1,728	2,686	2,751	1,771	2,523	2,558	1,920
2000–01	15,651	18,692	7,907	7,778	10,663	2,456	4,081	4,184	2,576	3,791	3,845	2,875	10,820	12,922	5,466	5,377	7,372	1,698	2,821	2,893	1,781	2,621	2,658	1,987
2001–02	16,175	19,386	8,127	8,025	11,066	2,558	4,237	4,349	2,627	3,912	3,970	2,942	11,380	13,639	5,718	5,646	7,786	1,800	2,981	3,060	1,848	2,753	2,793	2,070
2002–03	16,708	20,081	8,695	8,348	11,555	2,647	4,421	4,538	2,889	3,939	3,988	3,160	12,014	14,439	6,252	6,002	8,309	1,903	3,179	3,263	2,077	2,832	2,867	2,272
2003–04	17,629	21,103	9,125	8,993	12,288	2,959	4,572	4,693	3,005	4,064	4,122	3,161	12,953	15,505	6,705	6,608	9,029	2,174	3,359	3,448	2,208	2,986	3,028	2,322
2004–05	18,224	21,813	9,374	9,410	12,824	3,089	4,719	4,838	3,110	4,095	4,151	3,176	13,793	16,510	7,095	7,122	9,706	2,338	3,572	3,662	2,354	3,100	3,142	2,404
2005–06	18,625	22,211	9,209	9,675	13,082	3,076	4,849	4,970	3,068	4,101	4,159	3,065	14,634	17,451	7,236	7,601	10,279	2,417	3,810	3,905	2,411	3,222	3,268	2,408
2006–07	19,212	22,918	9,264	10,041	13,561	3,097	4,986	5,116	3,136	4,186	4,250	3,031	15,486	18,473	7,467	8,093	10,931	2,496	4,019	4,116	2,528	3,374	3,426	2,443
2007–08	19,413	23,166	9,137	10,145	13,704	3,010	5,041	5,164	3,151	4,228	4,298	2,975	16,227	19,364	7,637	8,480	11,455	2,516	4,213	4,317	2,634	3,534	3,593	2,487
2008–09	20,111	24,024	9,697	10,492	14,212	3,088	5,246	5,377	3,282	4,374	4,435	3,327	17,045	20,361	8,219	8,892	12,046	2,617	4,446	4,557	2,782	3,707	3,759	2,820
2009–10	20,625	24,687	9,981	10,674	14,495	3,416	5,443	5,591	3,498	4,507	4,601	3,066	17,650	21,126	8,541	9,135	12,404	2,923	4,658	4,785	2,994	3,857	3,937	2,624
2010–11	21,165	25,287	10,159	10,969	14,830	3,505	5,588	5,751	3,521	4,608	4,706	3,133	18,475	22,074	8,868	9,575	12,945	3,060	4,878	5,020	3,074	4,023	4,108	2,734
2011–12	21,593	25,610	10,402	11,328	15,105	3,611	5,659	5,814	3,563	4,605	4,691	3,229	19,401	23,011	9,347	10,179	13,572	3,244	5,085	5,224	3,201	4,138	4,215	2,901
2012–13	22,150	26,132	10,480	11,693	15,435	3,636	5,797	5,948	3,657	4,659	4,749	3,187	20,233	23,871	9,573	10,681	14,099	3,322	5,296	5,433	3,340	4,256	4,338	2,911
2013–14	22,630	26,625	10,662	11,935	15,697	3,632	5,950	6,094	3,817	4,745	4,834	3,213	20,995	24,701	9,891	11,073	14,563	3,369	5,520	5,654	3,541	4,402	4,484	2,981
2014–15	23,252	27,190	10,864	12,293	16,005	3,627	6,120	6,261	3,911	4,840	4,924	3,327	21,729	25,409	10,153	11,487	14,957	3,389	5,719	5,850	3,655	4,523	4,602	3,109
2015–16	23,851	27,777	11,062	12,608	16,309	3,626	6,287	6,423	4,091	4,955	5,046	3,345	22,439	26,132	10,407	11,862	15,343	3,412	5,915	6,043	3,849	4,662	4,747	3,147
2016–17	24,101	27,755	11,061	12,753	16,190	3,673	6,374	6,503	4,104	4,974	5,062	3,285	23,091	26,592	10,597	12,219	15,567	3,519	6,107	6,231	3,932	4,766	4,850	3,147
2017–18	24,327	27,923	10,925	12,874	16,253	3,611	6,452	6,585	4,008	5,001	5,085	3,307	23,833	27,357	10,704	12,613	15,923	3,537	6,321	6,451	3,926	4,899	4,982	3,240
2018–19	24,623	28,123	11,389	13,016	16,318	3,564	6,542	6,675	4,123	5,065	5,131	3,702	24,623	28,123	11,389	13,016	16,318	3,564	6,542	6,675	4,123	5,065	5,131	3,702

See notes at end of table.

Table 330.10. Average undergraduate tuition and fees and room and board rates charged for full-time students in degree-granting postsecondary institutions, by level and control of institution: Selected years, 1963–64 through 2018–19—Continued

Columns 2–13 are in **Constant 2018–19 dollars[1]**; columns 14–25 are in **Current dollars**. Within each, the four groupings are: Total tuition, fees, room, and board; Tuition and required fees[2]; Dormitory rooms; Board[3]; each split into All institutions / 4-year / 2-year.

Public institutions

Year and control of institution	Total TFRB, All inst (2)	4-yr (3)	2-yr (4)	Tuition & fees[2], All inst (5)	4-yr (6)	2-yr (7)	Dorm rooms, All inst (8)	4-yr (9)	2-yr (10)	Board[3], All inst (11)	4-yr (12)	2-yr (13)	Total TFRB, All inst (14)	4-yr (15)	2-yr (16)	Tuition & fees[2], All inst (17)	4-yr (18)	2-yr (19)	Dorm rooms, All inst (20)	4-yr (21)	2-yr (22)	Board[3], All inst (23)	4-yr (24)	2-yr (25)
1963–64	7,493	7,626	5,173	1,922	1,998	797	2,051	2,081	1,412	3,520	3,546	2,964	912	929	630	234	243	97	250	253	172	429	432	361
1968–69	7,893	8,116	6,270	2,095	2,279	1,207	2,372	2,393	1,974	3,426	3,443	3,089	1,112	1,143	883	295	321	170	334	337	278	482	485	435
1969–70	8,023	8,300	6,376	2,166	2,403	1,193	2,453	2,476	2,065	3,404	3,421	3,118	1,197	1,238	951	323	358	178	366	369	308	508	510	465
1970–71	8,135	8,453	6,363	2,238	2,510	1,192	2,533	2,557	2,155	3,364	3,386	3,016	1,276	1,326	998	351	394	187	397	401	338	528	531	473
1971–72	8,290	8,646	6,604	2,314	2,633	1,182	2,620	2,645	2,252	3,356	3,368	3,170	1,347	1,405	1,073	376	428	192	426	430	366	545	547	515
1972–73	8,593	9,191	7,082	2,408	2,974	1,379	2,789	2,818	2,355	3,396	3,399	3,349	1,452	1,553	1,197	407	503	233	471	476	398	574	575	566
1973–74	8,229	8,670	6,920	2,379	2,790	1,488	2,599	2,626	2,222	3,251	3,254	3,210	1,515	1,596	1,274	438	514	274	479	483	409	598	599	591
1974–75	7,634	8,052	6,548	2,113	2,506	1,355	2,470	2,500	2,073	3,051	3,046	3,120	1,561	1,647	1,339	432	512	277	505	511	424	624	623	638
1975–76	7,594	8,127	6,330	1,977	2,476	1,119	2,481	2,520	2,019	3,136	3,131	3,192	1,663	1,780	1,386	433	542	245	543	552	442	687	686	699
1976–77	7,720	8,350	6,432	2,065	2,661	1,223	2,514	2,554	2,006	3,141	3,136	3,203	1,789	1,935	1,491	479	617	283	582	592	465	728	727	742
1977–78	7,633	8,240	6,428	2,069	2,647	1,239	2,511	2,552	1,965	3,053	3,040	3,224	1,888	2,038	1,590	512	655	306	621	631	486	755	752	797
1978–79	7,371	7,930	6,252	2,007	2,543	1,210	2,421	2,455	1,948	2,943	2,932	3,094	1,994	2,145	1,691	543	688	327	655	664	527	796	793	837
1979–80	7,063	7,593	5,942	1,903	2,406	1,158	2,333	2,366	1,872	2,827	2,821	2,913	2,165	2,327	1,822	583	738	355	715	725	574	867	865	893
1980–81	6,939	7,457	5,927	1,856	2,350	1,144	2,335	2,371	1,893	2,748	2,736	2,907	2,373	2,550	2,027	635	804	391	799	811	642	940	936	994
1981–82	7,166	7,726	5,985	1,921	2,448	1,169	2,448	2,491	1,893	2,798	2,788	2,923	2,663	2,871	2,224	714	909	434	909	925	703	1,039	1,036	1,086
1982–83	7,599	8,247	6,166	2,060	2,662	1,221	2,607	2,659	1,948	2,932	2,927	2,997	2,945	3,196	2,390	798	1,031	473	1,010	1,030	755	1,136	1,134	1,162
1983–84	7,853	8,542	6,305	2,218	2,856	1,314	2,705	2,761	1,992	2,930	2,925	2,999	3,156	3,433	2,534	891	1,148	528	1,087	1,110	801	1,178	1,175	1,205
1984–85	8,161	8,816	6,722	2,325	2,940	1,398	2,864	2,914	2,205	2,973	2,962	3,119	3,408	3,682	2,807	971	1,228	584	1,196	1,217	921	1,241	1,237	1,302
1985–86[4]	8,312	8,981	6,938	2,432	3,067	1,492	2,890	2,940	2,234	2,991	2,974	3,212	3,571	3,859	2,981	1,045	1,318	641	1,242	1,263	960	1,285	1,278	1,380
1986–87	8,664	9,421	6,805	2,519	3,219	1,504	2,962	3,012	2,229	3,183	3,191	3,073	3,805	4,138	2,988	1,106	1,414	660	1,301	1,323	979	1,398	1,401	1,349
1987–88	8,855	9,627	6,702	2,664	3,361	1,543	3,013	3,082	2,061	3,178	3,184	3,098	4,050	4,403	3,066	1,218	1,537	706	1,378	1,410	943	1,454	1,456	1,417
1988–89	8,932	9,777	6,651	2,685	3,440	1,526	3,044	3,126	2,016	3,203	3,210	3,110	4,274	4,678	3,183	1,285	1,646	730	1,457	1,496	965	1,533	1,536	1,488
1989–90	8,983	9,924	6,581	2,705	3,550	1,508	3,018	3,106	1,919	3,260	3,268	3,154	4,504	4,975	3,299	1,356	1,780	756	1,513	1,557	962	1,635	1,638	1,581
1990–91	8,996	9,915	6,558	2,750	3,571	1,559	3,049	3,133	1,985	3,198	3,211	3,014	4,757	5,243	3,467	1,454	1,888	824	1,612	1,657	1,050	1,691	1,698	1,594
1991–92	9,416	10,433	6,639	2,983	3,879	1,716	3,172	3,270	1,969	3,261	3,283	2,954	5,138	5,693	3,623	1,628	2,117	936	1,731	1,785	1,074	1,780	1,792	1,612
1992–93	9,558	10,697	6,751	3,166	4,174	1,822	3,121	3,228	1,965	3,271	3,295	2,963	5,379	6,020	3,799	1,782	2,349	1,025	1,756	1,816	1,106	1,841	1,854	1,668
1993–94	9,863	11,025	6,921	3,364	4,394	1,948	3,244	3,350	2,061	3,256	3,282	2,912	5,694	6,365	3,996	1,942	2,537	1,125	1,873	1,934	1,190	1,880	1,895	1,681
1994–95	10,044	11,232	6,966	3,464	4,514	2,008	3,299	3,406	2,074	3,282	3,312	2,883	5,965	6,670	4,137	2,057	2,681	1,192	1,959	2,023	1,232	1,949	1,967	1,712
1995–96	10,255	11,498	6,912	3,572	4,668	2,032	3,373	3,477	2,125	3,311	3,353	2,755	6,256	7,014	4,217	2,179	2,848	1,239	2,057	2,121	1,297	2,020	2,045	1,681
1996–97	10,407	11,689	7,019	3,620	4,761	2,033	3,423	3,528	2,134	3,364	3,400	2,851	6,530	7,334	4,410	2,271	2,987	1,276	2,148	2,214	1,339	2,111	2,143	1,795
1997–98	10,669	12,016	7,061	3,696	4,869	2,058	3,484	3,602	2,193	3,488	3,544	2,810	6,813	7,673	4,510	2,360	3,110	1,314	2,225	2,301	1,401	2,228	2,263	1,795
1998–99	10,939	12,355	7,087	3,741	4,970	2,042	3,586	3,708	2,232	3,613	3,677	2,813	7,107	8,027	4,604	2,430	3,229	1,327	2,330	2,409	1,450	2,347	2,389	1,828
1999–2000	10,933	12,378	7,076	3,745	5,010	2,016	3,650	3,769	2,317	3,537	3,600	2,743	7,308	8,274	4,730	2,504	3,349	1,348	2,440	2,519	1,549	2,364	2,406	1,834
2000–01	10,973	12,517	7,000	3,706	5,063	1,928	3,716	3,839	2,315	3,552	3,614	2,757	7,586	8,653	4,839	2,562	3,501	1,333	2,569	2,654	1,600	2,455	2,499	1,906
2001–02	11,401	13,071	7,302	3,838	5,309	1,961	3,870	4,003	2,448	3,693	3,759	2,893	8,022	9,196	5,137	2,700	3,735	1,380	2,723	2,816	1,722	2,598	2,645	2,036
2002–03	11,824	13,612	7,790	4,037	5,627	2,063	4,075	4,212	2,717	3,712	3,772	3,010	8,502	9,787	5,601	2,903	4,046	1,483	2,930	3,029	1,954	2,669	2,712	2,164
2003–04	12,585	14,527	8,182	4,517	6,242	2,316	4,227	4,372	2,843	3,841	3,914	3,023	9,247	10,675	6,012	3,319	4,587	1,702	3,106	3,212	2,089	2,822	2,876	2,221
2004–05	13,033	15,096	8,423	4,795	6,641	2,443	4,366	4,517	2,872	3,873	3,938	3,108	9,864	11,426	6,375	3,629	5,027	1,849	3,304	3,418	2,174	2,931	2,981	2,353
2005–06	13,306	15,411	8,262	4,930	6,810	2,463	4,512	4,664	2,865	3,863	3,937	2,935	10,454	12,108	6,492	3,874	5,351	1,935	3,545	3,664	2,251	3,035	3,093	2,306
2006–07	13,711	15,880	8,456	5,089	7,030	2,503	4,661	4,812	2,988	3,961	4,038	2,965	11,051	12,799	6,815	4,102	5,666	2,017	3,757	3,878	2,408	3,192	3,255	2,390
2007–08	13,842	16,066	8,347	5,130	7,110	2,463	4,727	4,883	2,997	3,986	4,072	2,888	11,570	13,429	6,977	4,288	5,943	2,058	3,951	4,082	2,505	3,332	3,404	2,414
2008–09	14,405	16,768	8,906	5,323	7,447	2,520	4,943	5,110	3,143	4,138	4,211	3,244	12,209	14,212	7,549	4,512	6,312	2,136	4,190	4,331	2,664	3,507	3,569	2,749
2009–10	14,980	17,570	9,008	5,566	7,849	2,668	5,143	5,334	3,335	4,271	4,388	3,004	12,819	15,036	7,708	4,763	6,717	2,283	4,401	4,564	2,854	3,655	3,755	2,571
2010–11	15,540	18,237	9,255	5,814	8,170	2,796	5,322	5,535	3,385	4,405	4,532	3,073	13,566	15,919	8,079	5,075	7,132	2,441	4,646	4,832	2,955	3,845	3,956	2,683
2011–12	15,980	18,683	9,590	6,192	8,585	2,951	5,397	5,599	3,450	4,392	4,499	3,189	14,359	16,787	8,617	5,563	7,713	2,651	4,849	5,031	3,100	3,946	4,042	2,866
2012–13	16,444	19,130	9,773	6,457	8,835	3,056	5,541	5,738	3,555	4,446	4,557	3,162	15,021	17,475	8,927	5,899	8,070	2,792	5,062	5,241	3,247	4,061	4,163	2,888
2013–14	16,846	19,509	10,006	6,597	8,959	3,105	5,717	5,906	3,716	4,532	4,644	3,185	15,628	18,100	9,283	6,120	8,312	2,881	5,304	5,479	3,448	4,205	4,308	2,955
2014–15	17,323	19,938	10,257	6,817	9,142	3,162	5,890	6,075	3,808	4,616	4,721	3,287	16,188	18,632	9,585	6,370	8,543	2,955	5,504	5,677	3,559	4,313	4,412	3,072
2015–16	17,821	20,413	10,538	7,028	9,331	3,229	6,043	6,219	3,995	4,750	4,863	3,314	16,766	19,204	9,914	6,612	8,778	3,038	5,686	5,850	3,759	4,469	4,576	3,118
2016–17	17,992	20,341	10,531	7,116	9,189	3,294	6,115	6,281	3,990	4,761	4,870	3,247	17,238	19,488	10,090	6,818	8,804	3,156	5,859	6,018	3,823	4,562	4,666	3,111
2017–18	18,163	20,464	10,493	7,198	9,223	3,309	6,186	6,356	3,914	4,780	4,885	3,271	17,794	20,049	10,280	7,051	9,036	3,242	6,060	6,227	3,834	4,682	4,785	3,204
2018–19	18,383	20,598	10,950	7,250	9,212	3,313	6,290	6,459	4,055	4,843	4,927	3,581	18,383	20,598	10,950	7,250	9,212	3,313	6,290	6,459	4,055	4,843	4,927	3,581

See notes at end of table.

Table 330.10. Average undergraduate tuition and fees and room and board rates charged for full-time students in degree-granting postsecondary institutions, by level and control of institution: Selected years, 1963–64 through 2018–19—Continued

Year and control of institution	Constant 2018–19 dollars												Current dollars											
	Total tuition, fees, room, and board			Tuition and required fees[2]			Dormitory rooms			Board[3]			Total tuition, fees, room, and board			Tuition and required fees[2]			Dormitory rooms			Board[3]		
	All institutions	4-year	2-year	All institutions	4-year	2-year	All institutions	4-year	2-year	All institutions	4-year	2-year	All institutions	4-year	2-year	All institutions	4-year	2-year	All institutions	4-year	2-year	All institutions	4-year	2-year
1	2	3	4	5	6	7	8	9	10	11	12	13	14	15	16	17	18	19	20	21	22	23	24	25
Private nonprofit and for-profit institutions																								
1963–64	14,904	14,861	10,782	8,310	8,300	5,272	2,595	2,568	2,004	3,999	3,993	3,506	1,815	1,810	1,313	1,012	1,011	642	316	313	244	487	486	427
1968–69	16,481	16,731	13,321	9,821	10,063	6,788	2,869	2,872	2,776	3,792	3,795	3,756	2,321	2,356	1,876	1,383	1,417	956	404	405	391	534	534	529
1969–70	16,946	17,156	13,362	10,278	10,472	6,933	2,911	2,920	2,769	3,757	3,764	3,661	2,527	2,559	1,993	1,533	1,562	1,034	434	436	413	560	561	546
1970–71	17,399	17,561	13,408	10,736	10,879	7,070	2,948	2,959	2,767	3,715	3,724	3,570	2,729	2,754	2,103	1,684	1,706	1,109	462	464	434	583	584	560
1971–72	17,863	17,963	13,454	11,202	11,276	7,213	2,988	3,002	2,763	3,673	3,685	3,477	2,902	2,919	2,186	1,820	1,832	1,172	486	488	449	597	599	565
1972–73	17,963	18,289	13,448	11,229	11,527	7,224	3,094	3,116	2,704	3,640	3,646	3,520	3,036	3,091	2,273	1,898	1,948	1,221	523	527	457	615	616	595
1973–74	17,178	17,501	13,091	10,804	11,106	7,078	2,890	2,906	2,624	3,484	3,489	3,390	3,162	3,222	2,410	1,989	2,045	1,303	532	535	483	641	642	624
1974–75	16,568	16,647	12,670	10,352	10,418	6,685	2,826	2,830	2,758	3,389	3,398	3,227	3,388	3,404	2,591	2,117	2,130	1,367	578	579	564	693	695	660
1975–76	16,643	16,754	12,381	10,376	10,464	6,517	2,856	2,871	2,612	3,410	3,420	3,252	3,644	3,669	2,711	2,272	2,291	1,427	625	629	572	747	749	712
1976–77	16,855	17,161	12,820	10,644	10,935	6,870	2,800	2,811	2,621	3,411	3,415	3,329	3,906	3,977	2,971	2,467	2,534	1,592	649	651	607	790	791	772
1977–78	16,815	17,145	12,729	10,609	10,919	6,896	2,823	2,839	2,553	3,382	3,387	3,279	4,158	4,240	3,148	2,624	2,700	1,706	698	702	631	836	838	811
1978–79	16,691	17,043	12,532	10,602	10,936	6,769	2,802	2,814	2,589	3,287	3,292	3,174	4,514	4,609	3,389	2,867	2,958	1,831	758	761	700	889	890	858
1979–80	16,026	16,353	12,238	10,211	10,521	6,726	2,699	2,711	2,500	3,116	3,121	3,012	4,912	5,013	3,751	3,130	3,225	2,062	827	831	766	955	957	923
1980–81	15,993	16,354	12,580	10,227	10,575	7,055	2,683	2,691	2,548	3,083	3,088	2,978	5,470	5,594	4,303	3,498	3,617	2,413	918	921	871	1,054	1,056	1,019
1981–82	16,593	17,035	12,774	10,637	11,070	7,010	2,792	2,795	2,752	3,163	3,170	3,012	6,166	6,330	4,746	3,953	4,113	2,605	1,038	1,039	1,022	1,175	1,178	1,119
1982–83	17,856	18,388	13,842	11,454	11,970	7,762	3,048	3,049	3,038	3,354	3,369	3,042	6,920	7,126	5,364	4,439	4,639	3,008	1,181	1,181	1,177	1,300	1,306	1,179
1983–84	18,683	19,308	13,862	12,070	12,673	7,711	3,179	3,183	3,118	3,434	3,452	3,034	7,508	7,759	5,571	4,851	5,093	3,099	1,278	1,279	1,253	1,380	1,387	1,219
1984–85	19,641	20,236	14,854	12,726	13,304	8,345	3,414	3,415	3,410	3,500	3,517	3,099	8,202	8,451	6,203	5,315	5,556	3,485	1,426	1,426	1,424	1,462	1,469	1,294
1985–86[4]	20,678	21,478	15,156	13,473	14,245	8,546	3,616	3,623	3,491	3,590	3,610	3,119	8,885	9,228	6,512	5,789	6,121	3,672	1,553	1,557	1,500	1,542	1,551	1,340
1986–87	22,032	22,859	14,535	14,380	15,161	8,387	3,776	3,810	2,882	3,875	3,888	3,265	9,676	10,039	6,384	6,316	6,658	3,684	1,658	1,673	1,266	1,702	1,708	1,434
1987–88	22,982	23,305	15,475	15,279	15,558	9,097	3,821	3,848	3,018	3,882	3,898	3,360	10,512	10,659	7,078	6,988	7,116	4,161	1,748	1,760	1,380	1,775	1,783	1,537
1988–89	23,384	23,979	16,649	15,592	16,137	10,068	3,864	3,894	3,218	3,928	3,948	3,363	11,189	11,474	7,967	7,461	7,722	4,817	1,849	1,863	1,540	1,880	1,889	1,609
1989–90	23,972	24,502	17,294	16,251	16,748	10,365	3,836	3,859	3,317	3,885	3,895	3,612	12,018	12,284	8,670	8,147	8,396	5,196	1,923	1,935	1,663	1,948	1,953	1,811
1990–91	24,415	25,035	17,593	16,590	17,177	10,534	3,902	3,929	3,298	3,923	3,928	3,761	12,910	13,237	9,302	8,772	9,083	5,570	2,063	2,077	1,744	2,074	2,077	1,989
1991–92	25,458	26,127	17,652	17,261	17,884	10,545	4,071	4,106	3,277	4,126	4,136	3,830	13,892	14,258	9,632	9,419	9,759	5,754	2,221	2,241	1,788	2,252	2,257	2,090
1992–93	26,004	26,672	17,598	17,666	18,292	10,767	4,172	4,197	3,501	4,165	4,183	3,331	14,634	15,009	9,903	9,942	10,294	6,059	2,348	2,362	1,970	2,344	2,354	1,875
1993–94	26,840	27,547	18,025	18,312	18,971	11,034	4,313	4,341	3,580	4,216	4,235	3,412	15,496	15,904	10,406	10,572	10,952	6,370	2,490	2,506	2,067	2,434	2,445	1,970
1994–95	27,290	27,956	18,810	18,709	19,332	11,643	4,357	4,380	3,761	4,224	4,243	3,406	16,207	16,602	11,170	11,111	11,481	6,914	2,587	2,601	2,233	2,509	2,520	2,023
1995–96	28,209	28,870	18,956	19,449	20,070	11,630	4,488	4,510	3,887	4,272	4,290	3,439	17,208	17,612	11,563	11,864	12,243	7,094	2,738	2,751	2,371	2,606	2,617	2,098
1996–97	28,750	29,393	19,053	19,919	20,530	11,533	4,586	4,604	4,044	4,245	4,259	3,476	18,039	18,442	11,954	12,498	12,881	7,236	2,878	2,889	2,537	2,663	2,672	2,181
1997–98	28,994	29,861	20,233	20,044	20,895	11,688	4,625	4,642	4,185	4,325	4,324	4,360	18,516	19,070	12,921	12,801	13,344	7,464	2,954	2,964	2,672	2,762	2,761	2,785
1998–99	29,812	30,675	20,501	20,669	21,507	12,088	4,732	4,758	3,973	4,411	4,410	4,440	19,368	19,929	13,319	13,428	13,973	7,854	3,075	3,091	2,581	2,865	2,865	2,884
1999–2000	30,240	31,023	21,012	21,094	21,866	12,305	4,841	4,850	4,589	4,304	4,308	4,118	20,213	20,737	14,045	14,100	14,616	8,225	3,236	3,242	3,067	2,877	2,879	2,753
2000–01	30,916	31,614	21,563	21,698	22,378	13,115	4,892	4,907	4,348	4,326	4,330	4,100	21,373	21,856	14,907	15,000	15,470	9,067	3,382	3,392	3,006	2,991	2,993	2,834
2001–02	31,857	32,542	22,493	22,375	23,041	14,322	5,070	5,083	4,429	4,412	4,419	3,742	22,413	22,896	15,825	15,742	16,211	10,076	3,567	3,576	3,116	3,104	3,109	2,633
2002–03	32,461	33,082	24,690	22,784	23,401	14,813	5,218	5,235	4,495	4,458	4,447	5,382	23,340	23,787	17,753	16,383	16,826	10,651	3,752	3,764	3,232	3,206	3,197	3,870
2003–04	33,513	34,120	26,619	23,565	24,175	15,713	5,369	5,379	4,873	4,578	4,565	6,032	24,624	25,070	19,558	17,315	17,763	11,545	3,945	3,952	3,581	3,364	3,354	4,432
2004–05	34,110	34,695	26,817	23,985	24,580	16,016	5,520	5,513	5,913	4,604	4,602	4,888	25,817	26,260	20,297	18,154	18,604	12,122	4,178	4,173	4,475	3,485	3,483	3,700
2005–06	34,247	34,788	27,242	24,007	24,554	15,846	5,600	5,605	5,312	4,640	4,629	6,085	26,908	27,333	21,404	18,862	19,292	12,450	4,400	4,404	4,173	3,645	3,637	4,781
2006–07	35,285	35,879	25,166	24,871	25,454	15,766	5,715	5,723	5,145	4,698	4,702	4,255	28,440	28,919	20,284	20,047	20,517	12,708	4,606	4,613	4,147	3,787	3,790	3,430
2007–08	35,613	36,160	25,944	25,090	25,634	15,705	5,746	5,751	5,364	4,776	4,775	4,874	29,768	30,226	21,686	20,972	21,427	13,128	4,803	4,808	4,484	3,992	3,992	4,074
2008–09	36,298	36,850	26,810	25,456	26,004	16,007	5,929	5,936	5,372	4,913	4,909	5,431	30,764	31,232	22,723	21,575	22,040	13,567	5,025	5,031	4,553	4,164	4,161	4,603
2009–10	36,624	37,215	28,587	25,432	26,023	17,368	6,132	6,133	6,089	5,059	5,059	5,130	31,341	31,847	24,463	21,764	22,269	14,862	5,248	5,248	5,211	4,329	4,329	4,390
2010–11	36,515	37,250	26,464	25,250	25,978	15,680	6,189	6,197	5,658	5,075	5,075	5,127	31,875	32,517	23,101	22,042	22,677	13,687	5,403	5,410	4,939	4,430	4,430	4,475
2011–12	36,792	37,481	26,271	25,431	26,114	15,538	6,257	6,263	5,752	5,104	5,104	4,980	33,058	33,677	23,605	22,850	23,464	13,961	5,622	5,627	5,169	4,586	4,586	4,475
2012–13	37,750	38,394	25,567	26,212	26,846	15,490	6,383	6,390	5,723	5,155	5,158	4,354	34,483	35,071	23,355	23,943	24,523	14,149	5,831	5,837	5,228	4,709	4,712	3,977
2013–14	38,799	39,450	25,730	27,066	27,709	15,274	6,490	6,496	5,916	5,243	5,245	4,539	35,995	36,599	23,870	25,110	25,707	14,170	6,021	6,026	5,489	4,864	4,866	4,211
2014–15	40,045	40,651	26,032	28,017	28,613	15,261	6,657	6,665	5,892	5,371	5,373	4,879	37,422	37,988	24,327	26,182	26,739	14,261	6,221	6,228	5,506	5,019	5,021	4,560
2015–16	41,472	42,021	25,909	29,163	29,700	15,442	6,863	6,871	6,023	5,445	5,450	4,444	39,016	39,534	24,375	27,436	27,942	14,528	6,457	6,464	5,666	5,123	5,128	4,181
2016–17	42,712	43,279	25,976	30,211	30,765	15,227	7,003	7,011	6,209	5,499	5,503	4,540	40,922	41,465	24,888	28,945	29,476	14,589	6,710	6,717	5,949	5,268	5,273	4,350
2017–18	43,557	44,025	26,126	30,902	31,359	15,203	7,106	7,113	6,182	5,550	5,553	4,742	42,673	43,131	25,596	30,274	30,723	14,894	6,961	6,968	6,057	5,437	5,440	4,645
2018–19	44,306	44,662	28,627	31,519	31,875	15,727	7,171	7,179	5,967	5,616	5,608	6,933	44,306	44,662	28,627	31,519	31,875	15,727	7,171	7,179	5,967	5,616	5,608	6,933

See notes at end of table.

Table 330.10. Average undergraduate tuition and fees and room and board rates charged for full-time students in degree-granting postsecondary institutions, by level and control of institution: Selected years, 1963–64 through 2018–19—Continued

Year and control of institution	Constant 2018–19 dollars[1]												Current dollars											
	Total tuition, fees, room, and board			Tuition and required fees[2]			Dormitory rooms			Board[3]			Total tuition, fees, room, and board			Tuition and required fees[2]			Dormitory rooms			Board[3]		
	All institutions	4-year	2-year	All institutions	4-year	2-year	All institutions	4-year	2-year	All institutions	4-year	2-year	All institutions	4-year	2-year	All institutions	4-year	2-year	All institutions	4-year	2-year	All institutions	4-year	2-year
1	2	3	4	5	6	7	8	9	10	11	12	13	14	15	16	17	18	19	20	21	22	23	24	25
Nonprofit																								
1999–2000	31,401	31,763	17,486	22,307	22,637	10,312	4,793	4,818	3,164	4,301	4,308	4,010	20,989	21,231	11,688	14,911	15,131	6,893	3,204	3,221	2,115	2,875	2,879	2,680
2000–01	31,727	32,068	16,948	22,559	22,871	10,079	4,842	4,868	2,905	4,326	4,330	3,964	21,934	22,170	11,717	15,596	15,811	6,968	3,347	3,365	2,008	2,991	2,993	2,740
2001–02	32,804	33,056	18,435	23,367	23,599	11,550	5,025	5,038	3,275	4,412	4,419	3,610	23,080	23,257	12,970	16,440	16,604	8,126	3,536	3,544	2,304	3,104	3,109	2,540
2002–03	33,763	33,998	20,085	24,142	24,363	12,387	5,177	5,189	3,680	4,443	4,447	4,018	24,276	24,446	14,442	17,359	17,517	8,907	3,723	3,731	2,646	3,195	3,197	2,889
2003–04	34,957	35,185	21,190	25,081	25,293	13,047	5,317	5,328	3,884	4,558	4,565	4,259	25,685	25,853	15,569	18,429	18,584	9,587	3,907	3,915	2,853	3,349	3,354	3,129
2004–05	35,783	36,010	21,016	25,762	25,965	13,093	5,434	5,443	3,870	4,588	4,602	4,053	27,083	27,255	15,906	19,498	19,652	9,910	4,113	4,119	2,929	3,472	3,483	3,067
2005–06	36,299	36,518	20,783	26,178	26,387	13,132	5,492	5,502	3,839	4,629	4,629	3,811	28,520	28,692	16,329	20,568	20,732	10,318	4,315	4,323	3,017	3,637	3,637	2,994
2006–07	37,425	37,618	21,937	27,097	27,287	13,568	5,623	5,629	4,436	4,705	4,702	3,933	30,166	30,321	17,682	21,841	21,994	10,936	4,532	4,537	3,576	3,793	3,790	3,170
2007–08	38,188	38,343	22,559	27,757	27,909	14,103	5,653	5,659	4,541	4,779	4,775	3,915	31,921	32,050	18,857	23,201	23,329	11,789	4,725	4,730	3,796	3,994	3,992	3,272
2008–09	39,685	39,833	23,906	28,910	29,069	14,869	5,848	5,854	4,589	4,926	4,909	4,448	33,635	33,761	20,261	24,503	24,638	12,602	4,957	4,962	3,889	4,175	4,161	3,770
2009–10	40,806	40,949	24,254	29,676	29,839	14,766	6,046	6,051	4,810	5,084	5,059	4,678	34,920	35,042	20,756	25,396	25,535	12,636	5,173	5,178	4,116	4,351	4,329	4,004
2010–11	41,588	41,717	23,016	30,290	30,451	14,512	6,184	6,191	4,559	5,114	5,075	3,945	36,304	36,416	20,092	26,441	26,581	12,668	5,398	5,404	3,980	4,464	4,430	3,444
2011–12	41,964	42,108	25,515	30,543	30,735	15,668	6,263	6,269	4,765	5,158	5,104	5,083	37,705	37,835	22,926	27,443	27,616	14,078	5,628	5,633	4,281	4,634	4,586	4,567
2012–13	42,881	43,022	24,246	31,272	31,466	15,090	6,391	6,397	4,822	5,217	5,158	4,333	39,171	39,299	22,148	28,566	28,743	13,785	5,838	5,844	4,405	4,766	4,712	3,958
2013–14	43,802	43,903	24,793	31,983	32,146	15,093	6,507	6,512	5,166	5,312	5,245	4,533	40,636	40,731	23,001	29,671	29,823	14,003	6,037	6,042	4,793	4,928	4,866	4,206
2014–15	44,911	45,012	25,235	32,789	32,947	15,295	6,687	6,692	5,391	5,434	5,373	4,550	41,969	42,063	23,582	30,641	30,789	14,293	6,249	6,254	5,038	5,078	5,021	4,252
2015–16	45,787	45,921	25,882	33,386	33,565	15,651	6,900	6,905	5,718	5,502	5,450	4,513	43,077	43,202	24,349	31,409	31,578	14,724	6,491	6,497	5,379	5,176	5,128	4,246
2016–17	46,496	46,654	26,373	33,977	34,148	15,970	6,997	7,003	5,860	5,522	5,503	4,543	44,548	44,699	25,268	32,553	32,717	15,301	6,704	6,709	5,615	5,291	5,273	4,352
2017–18	46,961	47,100	27,079	34,294	34,448	16,116	7,095	7,099	6,141	5,572	5,553	4,823	46,008	46,144	26,530	33,598	33,748	15,789	6,951	6,955	6,016	5,459	5,440	4,725
2018–19	47,419	47,541	27,962	34,621	34,758	16,629	7,173	7,174	6,686	5,625	5,608	4,647	47,419	47,541	27,962	34,621	34,758	16,629	7,173	7,174	6,686	5,625	5,608	4,647
For-profit																								
1999–2000	24,123	24,756	23,538	13,026	12,957	13,114	6,353	6,929	5,852	4,744	4,870	4,572	16,124	16,547	15,734	8,707	8,661	8,766	4,247	4,631	3,912	3,171	3,255	3,056
2000–01	25,585	26,355	24,679	14,743	15,059	14,386	6,519	7,175	5,720	4,323	4,121	4,573	17,688	18,220	17,061	10,192	10,411	9,945	4,507	4,960	3,955	2,988	2,849	3,161
2001–02	26,403	28,103	24,101	15,435	15,733	15,108	6,580	7,670	5,087	4,388	4,700	3,905	18,576	19,772	16,956	10,860	11,069	10,629	4,629	5,396	3,579	3,087	3,307	2,748
2002–03	27,390	27,870	26,987	15,729	15,864	15,478	6,367	7,487	4,909	5,293	4,518	6,600	19,694	20,039	19,404	11,310	11,407	11,129	4,578	5,384	3,530	3,806	3,249	4,746
2003–04	29,699	29,782	30,446	16,711	16,874	16,364	6,930	7,831	5,433	6,058	5,077	8,650	21,822	21,883	22,371	12,278	12,398	12,024	5,092	5,754	3,992	4,451	3,730	6,355
2004–05	30,518	30,937	29,533	17,223	17,437	16,657	7,472	7,746	6,803	5,823	5,753	6,072	23,098	23,415	22,353	13,036	13,197	12,607	5,655	5,863	5,149	4,407	4,355	4,596
2005–06	29,983	29,560	32,672	16,847	16,946	16,493	7,745	8,253	6,079	5,390	4,361	10,100	23,557	23,225	25,670	13,237	13,315	12,959	6,085	6,485	4,776	4,235	3,426	7,935
2006–07	29,785	30,659	26,365	17,713	18,105	16,234	7,698	8,235	5,541	4,374	4,319	4,591	24,007	24,712	21,251	14,277	14,593	13,084	6,205	6,638	4,466	3,525	3,481	3,701
2007–08	29,605	30,007	28,143	17,238	17,519	15,989	7,711	8,112	5,863	4,656	4,376	6,291	24,746	25,083	23,524	14,409	14,643	13,365	6,445	6,781	4,901	3,892	3,658	5,258
2008–09	28,683	28,833	29,081	16,888	17,022	16,201	7,330	7,600	5,805	4,466	4,211	7,075	24,311	24,437	24,648	14,313	14,427	13,731	6,212	6,441	4,920	3,785	3,569	5,997
2009–10	28,184	27,911	30,351	16,394	16,090	17,682	7,294	7,400	6,641	4,496	4,421	6,027	24,118	23,885	25,973	14,029	13,769	15,132	6,242	6,332	5,683	3,847	3,783	5,158
2010–11	26,327	26,204	29,540	15,739	15,725	15,800	6,254	6,276	6,102	4,334	4,203	7,638	22,982	22,875	25,787	13,739	13,727	13,792	5,460	5,479	5,327	3,783	3,669	6,668
2011–12	25,567	25,512	26,138	15,304	15,261	15,519	6,186	6,178	6,262	4,077	4,074	4,357	22,972	22,923	23,486	13,751	13,712	13,944	5,558	5,551	5,627	3,663	3,660	3,915
2012–13	25,360	25,276	26,291	15,075	14,988	15,558	6,284	6,291	6,206	4,001	3,996	4,527	23,165	23,088	24,016	13,770	13,691	14,212	5,740	5,747	5,669	3,655	3,651	4,135
2013–14	24,939	24,842	26,242	14,863	14,782	15,302	6,255	6,246	6,349	3,820	3,813	4,591	23,137	23,047	24,346	13,789	13,714	14,196	5,803	5,795	5,891	3,544	3,538	4,260
2014–15	25,011	24,908	27,426	14,951	14,901	15,255	6,202	6,204	6,185	3,858	3,803	5,986	23,373	23,277	25,629	13,972	13,924	14,256	5,796	5,798	5,780	3,605	3,554	5,594
2015–16	25,273	25,215	25,840	15,086	15,041	15,388	6,217	6,209	6,301	3,970	3,965	4,151	23,777	23,722	24,310	14,193	14,150	14,477	5,849	5,842	5,928	3,735	3,731	3,905
2016–17	26,543	26,648	26,121	15,050	15,053	15,028	7,190	7,302	6,563	4,304	4,293	4,530	25,431	25,531	25,027	14,419	14,423	14,399	6,889	6,996	6,288	4,123	4,113	4,340
2017–18	26,797	26,951	25,584	14,973	14,982	14,908	7,418	7,565	6,229	4,406	4,404	4,447	26,253	26,404	25,065	14,669	14,677	14,606	7,268	7,411	6,102	4,317	4,315	4,357
2018–19	27,040	26,575	30,052	14,780	14,715	15,360	7,118	7,410	5,305	5,143	4,450	9,387	27,040	26,575	30,052	14,780	14,715	15,360	7,118	7,410	5,305	5,143	4,450	9,387

[1]Constant dollars based on the Consumer Price Index, prepared by the Bureau of Labor Statistics, U.S. Department of Labor, adjusted to an academic-year basis.

[2]For public institutions, in-state tuition and required fees are used.

[3]Data for 1986-87 and later years reflect a basis of 20 meals per week, while data for earlier years are for meals served 7 days a week (the number of meals per day was not specified). Because of this revision in data collection and tabulation procedures, data are not entirely comparable with figures for previous years. In particular, data on board rates are somewhat higher than in earlier years because they reflect the basis of 20 meals per week rather than meals served 7 days a week. Since many institutions serve fewer than 3 meals each day, the 1986-87 and later data reflect a more accurate accounting of total board costs.

[4]Room and board data are estimated.

NOTE: Data are for the entire academic year and are average charges for full-time students. Tuition and fees were weighted by the number of full-time-equivalent undergraduates, but were not adjusted to reflect student residency. Room and board are based on full-time students. Data through 1995-96 are for institutions of higher education, while later data are for degree-granting institutions. Degree-granting institutions grant associate's or higher degrees and participate in Title IV federal financial aid programs. The degree-granting classification is very similar to the earlier higher education classification, but it includes more 2-year colleges and excludes a few higher education institutions that did not grant degrees. Some data have been revised from previously published figures. Detail may not sum to totals because of rounding.

SOURCE: U.S. Department of Education, National Center for Education Statistics, *Projections of Education Statistics to 1986–87*; Higher Education General Information Survey (HEGIS), "Institutional Characteristics of Colleges and Universities" surveys, 1969–70 through 1985–86; "Fall Enrollment in Institutions of Higher Education" surveys, 1963 through 1985; Integrated Postsecondary Education Data System (IPEDS), "Fall Enrollment Survey" (IPEDS-EF:86–99) and "Institutional Characteristics Survey" (IPEDS-IC:86–99); IPEDS Spring 2001 through Spring 2019, Fall Enrollment component; and IPEDS Fall 2000 through Fall 2018, Institutional Characteristics component. (This table was prepared December 2019.)

Table 330.20. Average undergraduate tuition and fees and room and board rates charged for full-time students in degree-granting postsecondary institutions, by control and level of institution and state or jurisdiction: 2017–18 and 2018–19

[In current dollars]

State or jurisdiction	Public 4-year: In-state, 2017–18 Total	Tuition and required fees	In-state, 2018–19 Total	Tuition and required fees	Room	Board	Out-of-state tuition and required fees, 2018–19	Private 4-year: 2017–18 Total	Tuition and required fees	2018–19 Total	Tuition and required fees	Room	Board	Public 2-year, tuition and required fees: In-state, 2017–18	In-state, 2018–19	Out-of-state, 2018–19
1	2	3	4	5	6	7	8	9	10	11	12	13	14	15	16	17
United States	$20,049	$9,036	$20,598	$9,212	$6,459	$4,927	$26,382	$43,131	$30,723	$44,662	$31,875	$7,179	$5,608	$3,242	$3,313	$7,917
Alabama	19,673	9,827	19,982	10,138	5,543	4,301	25,782	26,165	16,321	26,195	16,119	5,005	5,071	4,403	4,770	9,612
Alaska	18,373	7,221	19,563	8,396	6,226	4,941	24,454	26,887	19,360	26,788	19,315	3,720	3,753	†	†	†
Arizona	22,629	10,557	23,105	10,666	7,199	5,240	26,383	22,939	13,487	22,419	12,711	5,330	4,378	2,152	2,161	8,516
Arkansas	17,479	8,187	17,977	8,391	5,310	4,276	20,825	30,828	22,610	31,564	23,179	4,255	4,130	3,292	3,291	4,698
California	22,075	8,014	22,664	8,118	8,147	6,399	31,423	47,411	33,485	49,860	35,524	7,976	6,360	1,268	1,271	7,849
Colorado	21,514	9,540	21,867	9,394	6,323	6,149	30,140	35,152	22,873	36,285	23,560	7,482	5,243	3,638	3,655	7,967
Connecticut	25,182	12,355	26,203	12,959	7,254	5,990	33,709	54,819	40,410	56,549	41,807	8,527	6,215	4,312	4,434	13,202
Delaware	22,371	9,999	23,447	10,607	7,661	5,179	30,405	26,928	15,096	26,709	14,758	6,032	5,920	†	†	†
District of Columbia	†	5,756	†	5,888	†	†	12,416	57,611	41,775	59,233	43,143	10,844	5,246	†	†	†
Florida	14,896	4,455	15,059	4,443	6,173	4,443	18,456	37,275	25,471	38,438	26,317	6,918	5,203	2,506	2,506	9,111
Georgia	17,705	7,206	18,003	7,319	6,346	4,337	22,751	40,377	27,777	41,520	28,839	6,955	5,726	2,901	2,916	8,038
Hawaii	21,201	9,709	21,865	9,952	6,046	5,868	31,581	28,858	16,447	29,781	17,098	5,870	6,813	3,080	3,140	8,277
Idaho	15,455	7,247	16,134	7,586	4,061	4,487	23,850	13,488	5,833	13,157	6,139	2,436	4,583	3,282	3,345	7,971
Illinois	25,089	13,971	25,469	14,259	6,087	5,122	28,522	44,943	32,389	46,552	33,454	7,530	5,568	3,891	3,966	11,480
Indiana	19,297	9,038	19,755	9,225	5,553	4,977	29,092	43,764	32,338	45,382	33,402	6,204	5,775	4,255	4,368	8,402
Iowa	18,427	8,767	20,122	9,966	5,709	4,448	24,521	37,379	27,991	43,364	33,821	4,687	4,855	4,923	5,137	6,449
Kansas	17,963	8,737	18,618	8,941	5,062	4,616	23,302	30,262	21,339	31,701	22,571	4,406	4,723	3,384	3,435	4,491
Kentucky	20,745	10,365	21,313	10,674	6,038	4,601	25,430	35,948	26,719	37,081	27,648	4,661	4,773	4,106	4,274	14,418
Louisiana	18,834	9,164	19,206	9,358	5,704	4,144	22,208	49,452	36,715	51,025	37,830	7,315	5,880	4,093	4,143	8,034
Maine	19,500	9,664	20,195	9,930	5,119	5,146	27,735	49,994	37,043	52,527	38,972	6,772	6,783	3,698	3,753	6,614
Maryland	21,176	9,288	21,895	9,521	7,057	5,317	26,883	55,685	41,859	57,222	43,141	8,180	5,901	4,090	4,225	9,990
Massachusetts	25,229	12,778	26,787	13,286	8,337	5,164	30,966	59,540	44,362	61,747	46,016	9,177	6,555	4,991	5,192	10,606
Michigan	22,665	12,435	23,376	12,888	5,262	5,226	35,844	36,660	26,961	38,074	27,936	5,096	5,043	3,469	3,582	6,372
Minnesota	20,420	11,226	20,860	11,381	5,194	4,286	22,780	42,716	32,416	43,677	33,212	5,616	4,850	5,381	5,389	5,947
Mississippi	17,718	7,980	18,391	8,340	5,887	4,164	19,942	25,774	17,625	26,352	17,953	4,352	4,046	3,183	3,262	5,709
Missouri	18,106	8,387	18,121	8,554	5,612	3,956	19,914	34,617	24,608	35,803	25,417	6,021	4,366	3,271	3,358	6,558
Montana	15,800	6,783	16,604	6,972	4,481	5,150	24,481	33,739	24,953	34,988	25,918	4,291	4,779	3,631	3,756	8,394
Nebraska	18,449	8,188	19,551	8,467	6,239	4,845	21,516	34,650	23,711	34,626	25,075	5,502	4,049	3,212	3,174	3,985
Nevada	16,810	5,920	17,503	5,845	6,039	5,619	21,125	36,163	23,261	38,130	24,423	6,711	6,996	3,075	†	†
New Hampshire	27,570	15,949	28,145	16,329	7,258	4,558	29,447	47,030	33,322	46,952	33,364	8,690	4,898	7,337	7,599	16,429
New Jersey	26,542	13,633	27,481	13,963	8,343	5,175	28,669	50,321	36,589	51,045	37,329	7,963	5,753	4,536	4,715	8,257
New Mexico	15,788	6,711	16,256	6,902	4,764	4,590	18,350	33,620	23,865	40,206	30,137	5,645	4,424	1,667	1,705	6,698
New York	22,343	7,938	23,053	8,184	9,746	5,123	22,083	53,658	39,006	55,741	40,527	9,115	6,098	5,229	5,367	9,197
North Carolina	17,343	7,354	17,302	7,174	5,766	4,362	22,968	44,058	32,149	46,268	33,990	6,350	5,928	2,499	2,504	8,655
North Dakota	15,998	7,687	16,668	8,091	3,733	4,844	15,565	22,511	15,256	22,856	15,206	3,099	4,551	4,700	4,895	9,293
Ohio	21,674	10,026	22,153	10,068	6,597	5,488	24,454	42,252	31,240	44,035	32,597	5,942	5,496	3,672	4,082	7,300
Oklahoma	16,263	7,623	16,732	7,866	4,738	4,128	21,526	35,542	26,240	37,447	27,694	4,872	4,882	3,875	4,112	9,393
Oregon	22,710	10,363	22,585	10,286	7,204	5,095	30,929	50,617	38,674	53,036	40,597	6,536	5,903	4,487	4,709	8,779
Pennsylvania	25,795	14,534	26,287	14,812	6,893	4,582	28,527	53,258	40,086	55,248	41,703	7,434	6,111	5,171	5,284	14,111
Rhode Island	24,280	12,239	24,827	12,576	7,666	4,585	29,998	54,877	40,361	57,176	42,108	8,981	6,088	4,564	4,564	12,156
South Carolina	22,132	12,579	23,113	13,013	6,241	3,859	32,174	34,423	24,932	35,174	25,621	4,811	4,743	4,502	4,728	9,874
South Dakota	16,421	8,540	16,847	8,772	3,917	4,159	12,465	32,157	24,219	31,359	23,252	4,002	4,105	6,027	6,170	5,839
Tennessee	18,951	9,574	19,713	9,789	5,205	4,719	26,068	37,162	26,939	38,571	28,080	5,885	4,607	4,148	4,287	16,582
Texas	18,271	8,645	18,779	8,678	5,553	4,548	25,031	43,868	32,484	46,268	34,476	6,580	5,213	2,209	2,259	5,920
Utah	14,174	6,557	14,389	6,731	3,554	4,104	21,557	15,377	7,536	15,804	7,852	4,002	3,950	3,781	3,843	12,206
Vermont	27,782	16,103	28,681	16,604	7,646	4,431	39,947	56,172	42,637	58,137	44,068	7,683	6,387	6,414	7,120	14,090
Virginia	23,427	12,637	24,492	13,413	6,242	4,838	34,890	33,662	23,018	34,470	23,380	5,890	5,199	5,118	5,241	11,455
Washington	18,323	6,830	19,272	7,036	6,517	5,719	29,228	48,518	36,807	50,873	38,754	6,381	5,739	4,078	4,169	5,691
West Virginia	17,803	7,619	18,461	8,016	5,603	4,842	21,996	21,321	12,361	21,892	12,513	4,505	4,874	4,077	4,276	9,834
Wisconsin	16,544	8,475	17,172	8,697	5,407	3,068	25,063	43,332	33,156	45,269	34,424	6,183	4,663	4,337	4,411	6,408
Wyoming	14,486	4,443	14,639	4,596	4,493	5,550	14,268	†	†	†	†	†	†	3,142	3,219	7,752

†Not applicable.

NOTE: Data are for the entire academic year and are average charges for full-time students. In-state tuition and fees were weighted by the number of full-time-equivalent undergraduates, but were not adjusted to reflect the number of students who were state residents. Out-of-state tuition and fees were weighted by the number of first-time freshmen attending the institution in fall 2018 from out of state. Institutional room and board rates are weighted by the number of full-time students. Degree-granting institutions grant associate's or higher degrees and participate in Title IV federal financial aid programs. Some data have been revised from previously published figures. Detail may not sum to totals because of rounding.

SOURCE: U.S. Department of Education, National Center for Education Statistics, Integrated Postsecondary Education Data System (IPEDS), Fall 2017 and Fall 2018, Institutional Characteristics component; and Spring 2018 and Spring 2019, Fall Enrollment component. (This table was prepared December 2019.)

Table 330.30. Average undergraduate tuition, fees, room, and board charges for full-time students in degree-granting postsecondary institutions, by percentile of charges and control and level of institution: Selected years, 2000–01 through 2018–19

Control and level of institution, and year	Current dollars										Constant 2018–19 dollars[1]				
	Tuition, fees, room, and board					Tuition and required fees					Tuition and required fees				
	10th per-centile	25th per-centile	Median (50th per-centile)	75th per-centile	90th per-centile	10th per-centile	25th per-centile	Median (50th per-centile)	75th per-centile	90th per-centile	10th per-centile	25th per-centile	Median (50th per-centile)	75th per-centile	90th per-centile
1	2	3	4	5	6	7	8	9	10	11	12	13	14	15	16
Public institutions[2]															
2000–01	$5,741	$6,880	$8,279	$9,617	$11,384	$612	$1,480	$2,403	$3,444	$4,583	$885	$2,141	$3,476	$4,982	$6,629
2005–06	7,700	9,623	11,348	13,543	16,264	990	2,070	3,329	5,322	6,972	1,260	2,635	4,237	6,774	8,874
2010–11	9,889	12,856	15,234	17,860	21,593	1,230	2,626	4,632	7,115	9,420	1,409	3,008	5,306	8,151	10,791
2015–16	13,215	15,947	18,648	21,735	25,180	1,632	3,456	6,452	9,326	11,948	1,735	3,673	6,858	9,913	12,700
2017–18	13,965	16,749	19,922	23,093	26,927	1,632	3,724	6,897	9,952	12,700	1,666	3,801	7,040	10,158	12,963
2018–19	14,111	17,281	20,554	23,755	27,960	1,696	3,843	7,140	10,308	13,110	1,696	3,843	7,140	10,308	13,110
Public 4-year[2]															
2000–01	6,503	7,347	8,468	9,816	11,611	2,118	2,520	3,314	4,094	5,085	3,064	3,645	4,794	5,922	7,355
2005–06	8,863	10,219	11,596	13,830	16,443	3,094	3,822	5,084	6,458	8,097	3,938	4,864	6,471	8,219	10,305
2010–11	12,048	13,604	15,823	18,419	22,191	4,336	5,091	6,779	8,689	11,029	4,967	5,832	7,766	9,954	12,634
2015–16	14,733	16,559	19,217	21,979	25,658	5,360	6,691	8,256	10,509	13,431	5,697	7,112	8,776	11,170	14,276
2017–18	15,663	17,461	20,369	23,274	27,283	4,343	6,958	8,738	10,974	14,018	4,433	7,102	8,919	11,201	14,308
2018–19	15,852	18,068	20,864	24,108	28,095	4,200	7,120	8,938	11,261	14,184	4,200	7,120	8,938	11,261	14,184
Public 2-year[2]															
2000–01	3,321	3,804	4,627	5,750	6,871	310	724	1,387	1,799	2,460	448	1,047	2,006	2,602	3,558
2005–06	4,380	4,822	6,234	7,567	8,993	691	1,109	1,920	2,589	3,100	879	1,411	2,444	3,295	3,946
2010–11	5,347	6,327	7,339	9,370	11,312	700	1,412	2,537	3,315	3,840	802	1,618	2,906	3,798	4,399
2015–16	6,474	7,503	9,337	11,854	14,978	1,182	1,514	3,077	4,115	5,032	1,256	1,609	3,271	4,374	5,349
2017–18	6,896	8,355	9,787	12,587	15,400	1,244	1,632	3,304	4,394	5,190	1,270	1,666	3,372	4,485	5,298
2018–19	7,076	8,386	10,389	12,900	15,680	1,220	1,661	3,375	4,530	5,300	1,220	1,661	3,375	4,530	5,300
Private nonprofit institutions															
2000–01	13,514	17,552	22,493	27,430	32,659	7,800	11,730	15,540	19,600	24,532	11,283	16,967	22,478	28,351	35,485
2005–06	18,243	23,258	29,497	35,918	41,707	9,981	15,375	21,070	26,265	31,690	12,703	19,569	26,817	33,429	40,334
2010–11	23,143	29,884	38,063	47,061	52,235	11,930	19,625	26,920	34,536	40,082	13,667	22,482	30,838	39,563	45,916
2015–16	25,903	36,436	45,951	57,465	63,209	11,900	23,162	32,250	42,270	48,190	12,649	24,620	34,280	44,930	51,223
2017–18	28,232	39,206	49,182	61,550	67,643	12,300	24,695	34,440	45,548	51,992	12,555	25,207	35,154	46,492	53,069
2018–19	28,314	40,449	50,968	63,838	70,091	12,132	25,122	35,160	47,280	53,425	12,132	25,122	35,160	47,280	53,425
Nonprofit 4-year															
2000–01	13,972	17,714	22,554	27,476	32,659	8,450	11,920	15,746	19,730	24,532	12,223	17,242	22,776	28,539	35,485
2005–06	18,350	23,322	29,598	36,028	41,774	10,300	15,560	21,190	26,500	31,690	13,109	19,804	26,970	33,728	40,334
2010–11	23,548	30,042	38,129	47,061	52,235	12,220	19,854	27,100	34,580	40,082	13,999	22,744	31,045	39,613	45,916
2015–16	26,315	36,537	46,094	57,465	63,209	12,240	23,748	32,400	42,288	48,190	13,010	25,243	34,439	44,949	51,223
2017–18	28,370	39,206	49,464	61,550	67,643	12,360	25,025	34,600	45,620	52,002	12,616	25,544	35,317	46,565	53,080
2018–19	28,581	40,457	51,028	63,838	70,091	12,306	25,390	35,350	47,290	53,430	12,306	25,390	35,350	47,290	53,430
Nonprofit 2-year															
2000–01	6,850	6,850	9,995	14,209	20,240	2,430	4,825	7,250	8,266	11,100	3,515	6,979	10,487	11,957	16,056
2005–06	8,030	15,680	16,830	20,829	28,643	4,218	8,640	9,940	12,270	14,472	5,368	10,997	12,651	15,617	18,419
2010–11	10,393	19,718	21,186	27,386	30,758	3,840	9,730	12,000	14,640	18,965	4,399	11,146	13,747	16,771	21,726
2015–16	22,582	23,059	25,696	31,405	53,387	4,904	10,800	14,110	17,346	22,060	5,213	11,480	14,998	18,438	23,448
2017–18	14,587	26,265	29,227	33,546	59,560	4,904	9,867	15,022	18,450	23,670	5,006	10,071	15,333	18,832	24,161
2018–19	16,334	26,181	29,520	34,694	65,073	4,593	10,439	14,539	18,971	28,432	4,593	10,439	14,539	18,971	28,432
Private for-profit institutions															
2000–01	13,396	15,778	19,403	21,400	21,845	6,900	8,202	9,644	12,090	14,600	9,981	11,864	13,950	17,488	21,119
2005–06	17,278	19,098	25,589	26,499	31,903	7,632	10,011	12,450	14,335	17,740	9,714	12,742	15,846	18,245	22,579
2010–11	16,097	16,097	17,484	26,175	31,639	10,194	10,194	13,520	15,750	18,048	11,678	11,678	15,488	18,043	20,675
2015–16	17,407	17,407	26,028	26,405	35,377	10,575	11,003	13,320	17,132	19,286	11,241	11,695	14,158	18,210	20,500
2017–18	25,281	26,226	26,226	27,253	37,319	10,935	11,330	13,794	17,002	21,331	11,162	11,565	14,080	17,354	21,773
2018–19	26,278	26,302	26,302	27,274	35,986	9,552	9,552	13,380	17,076	24,030	9,552	9,552	13,380	17,076	24,030
For-profit 4-year															
2000–01	13,396	15,818	20,417	21,400	21,400	7,206	8,305	9,675	12,800	15,090	10,423	12,013	13,995	18,515	21,827
2005–06	17,383	19,098	25,589	26,499	31,903	7,632	10,418	12,900	14,450	17,735	9,714	13,260	16,419	18,391	22,572
2010–11	16,097	16,097	17,484	26,175	31,639	10,194	10,194	13,560	16,500	18,048	11,678	11,678	15,534	18,902	20,675
2015–16	17,407	17,407	26,028	26,405	35,377	10,607	11,003	12,975	17,132	19,459	11,275	11,695	13,792	18,210	20,684
2017–18	25,281	26,226	26,226	27,253	37,319	10,935	11,330	13,516	17,002	23,204	11,162	11,565	13,796	17,354	23,685
2018–19	26,278	26,302	26,302	27,274	39,253	9,552	9,552	13,354	17,076	24,109	9,552	9,552	13,354	17,076	24,109
For-profit 2-year															
2000–01	15,778	15,778	19,403	21,845	21,845	6,025	7,365	9,644	12,000	14,255	8,715	10,653	13,950	17,358	20,620
2005–06	13,010	18,281	43,425	43,425	43,425	7,870	9,285	11,550	14,196	19,425	10,017	11,818	14,700	18,068	24,723
2010–11	23,687	23,687	25,161	25,161	25,161	10,075	12,049	13,418	15,263	17,918	11,541	13,803	15,371	17,485	20,526
2015–16	25,732	25,732	25,732	25,732	25,732	10,510	12,678	13,975	15,760	18,048	11,171	13,476	14,854	16,752	19,184
2017–18	27,356	27,356	27,356	27,356	27,356	10,880	11,580	14,220	15,743	17,614	11,105	11,820	14,515	16,069	17,979
2018–19	30,718	30,718	30,718	30,718	30,718	11,156	12,945	14,843	16,207	18,060	11,156	12,945	14,843	16,207	18,060

[1]Constant dollars based on the Consumer Price Index, prepared by the Bureau of Labor Statistics, U.S. Department of Labor, adjusted to an academic-year basis.
[2]Average undergraduate tuition and fees are based on in-state students only.
NOTE: Data are for the entire academic year and are average charges for full-time students. Student charges were weighted by the number of full-time-equivalent undergraduates, but were not adjusted to reflect student residency. Degree-granting institutions grant associate's or higher degrees and participate in Title IV federal financial aid programs. Some data have been revised from previously published figures.
SOURCE: U.S. Department of Education, National Center for Education Statistics, Integrated Postsecondary Education Data System (IPEDS), Fall 2000 through Fall 2018, Institutional Characteristics component; and Spring 2001 through Spring 2019, Fall Enrollment component. (This table was prepared December 2019.)

Table 330.40. Average total cost of attendance for first-time, full-time undergraduate students in degree-granting postsecondary institutions, by control and level of institution, living arrangement, and component of student costs: Selected years, 2010–11 through 2018–19

Level of institution, living arrangement, and component of student costs	2010–11 All institutions	2010–11 Public, in-state	2010–11 Private Non-profit	2010–11 Private For-profit	2015–16 All institutions	2015–16 Public, in-state	2015–16 Private Non-profit	2015–16 Private For-profit	2016–17 All institutions	2016–17 Public, in-state	2016–17 Private Non-profit	2016–17 Private For-profit	2017–18 All institutions	2017–18 Public, in-state	2017–18 Private Non-profit	2017–18 Private For-profit	2018–19 All institutions	2018–19 Public, in-state	2018–19 Private Non-profit	2018–19 Private For-profit
	2	3	4	5	6	7	8	9	10	11	12	13	14	15	16	17	18	19	20	21
Current dollars																				
4-year institutions																				
Average total cost, by living arrangement																				
On campus	$27,589	$20,035	$39,676	$31,897	$31,652	$23,113	$47,300	$31,546	$32,575	$23,765	$48,827	$32,416	$33,495	$24,351	$50,387	$32,876	$34,346	$24,869	$51,874	$33,219
Off campus, living with family	20,084	12,554	31,689	22,268	22,243	13,907	37,479	21,831	22,748	14,102	38,733	22,096	23,363	14,387	39,996	22,589	23,874	14,589	41,100	22,733
Off campus, not living with family	29,142	21,324	40,033	31,000	31,543	23,416	47,105	29,609	32,165	23,813	48,435	29,680	33,137	24,356	50,370	30,405	33,903	24,925	51,728	30,217
Component of student costs																				
Tuition and required fees	14,596	7,163	26,637	15,191	16,896	8,520	32,312	16,154	17,442	8,776	33,487	16,810	18,000	9,014	34,658	17,207	18,510	9,216	35,769	17,262
Books and supplies	1,223	1,196	1,221	1,522	1,255	1,267	1,241	1,149	1,263	1,277	1,247	1,101	1,269	1,281	1,257	1,102	1,272	1,283	1,258	1,148
Room, board, and other expenses																				
On campus																				
Room and board	8,912	8,497	9,455	9,304	10,526	10,078	11,186	9,669	10,826	10,369	11,497	10,005	11,174	10,720	11,851	10,032	11,486	11,011	12,194	10,244
Other	2,858	3,179	2,363	5,879	2,576	3,248	2,561	4,574	3,045	3,343	2,596	4,500	3,052	3,335	2,621	4,534	3,078	3,359	2,652	4,565
Off campus, living with family																				
Other	4,265	4,195	3,832	5,554	4,092	4,120	3,926	4,528	4,043	4,049	3,999	4,185	4,095	4,091	4,080	4,280	4,093	4,089	4,073	4,324
Off campus, not living with family																				
Room and board	8,802	8,942	8,202	8,866	9,144	9,658	8,778	7,587	9,269	9,799	8,838	7,339	9,593	10,073	9,231	7,694	9,823	10,366	9,387	7,718
Other	4,521	4,022	3,974	5,421	4,248	3,971	4,773	4,719	4,192	3,960	4,863	4,430	4,275	3,987	5,224	4,402	4,299	4,059	5,314	4,090
2-year institutions																				
Average total cost, by living arrangement																				
On campus	13,777	12,336	25,763	29,179	15,096	14,345	31,749	27,776	15,448	14,677	31,828	28,711	15,687	14,972	32,339	29,499	16,153	15,420	33,227	29,958
Off campus, living with family	8,964	7,843	18,931	19,350	9,303	8,838	22,655	20,144	9,482	8,997	22,945	20,078	9,596	9,169	23,453	20,208	9,805	9,369	23,951	20,652
Off campus, not living with family	16,389	15,153	27,458	27,366	17,405	16,911	30,901	28,663	17,804	17,310	32,068	28,282	18,162	17,710	31,996	29,206	18,722	18,256	32,935	30,072
Component of student costs																				
Tuition and required fees	3,850	2,748	13,832	13,954	3,893	3,425	17,137	14,779	4,031	3,542	17,429	14,667	4,066	3,637	17,876	14,648	4,177	3,737	18,387	15,021
Books and supplies	1,302	1,295	1,153	1,407	1,444	1,451	1,144	1,291	1,456	1,465	1,127	1,265	1,483	1,489	1,106	1,349	1,516	1,524	1,020	1,339
Room, board, and other expenses																				
On campus																				
Room and board	5,654	5,351	7,806	9,961	6,697	6,406	10,359	8,883	6,880	6,551	10,688	9,682	7,046	6,713	10,837	9,920	7,240	6,889	11,272	9,970
Other	2,971	2,941	2,973	3,857	3,062	3,062	3,108	2,822	3,081	3,119	2,585	3,096	3,092	3,132	2,520	3,582	3,220	3,270	2,548	3,628
Off campus, living with family																				
Other	3,812	3,799	3,947	3,989	3,966	3,962	4,374	4,073	3,995	3,990	4,389	4,146	4,047	4,042	4,471	4,211	4,113	4,107	4,544	4,292
Off campus, not living with family																				
Room and board	7,478	7,412	7,999	7,889	8,200	8,200	8,212	8,195	8,405	8,424	8,864	7,970	8,647	8,652	8,595	8,534	8,955	8,958	9,066	8,867
Other	3,759	3,698	4,475	4,117	3,858	3,834	4,408	4,397	3,913	3,879	4,650	4,380	3,967	3,931	4,418	4,675	4,074	4,036	4,463	4,845
Constant 2018–19 dollars[1]																				
4-year institutions																				
Average total cost, by living arrangement																				
On campus	$31,605	$22,951	$45,451	$36,539	$33,644	$24,568	$50,276	$33,532	$34,000	$24,804	$50,962	$33,834	$34,189	$24,855	$51,432	$33,557	$34,346	$24,869	$51,874	$33,219
Off campus, living with family	23,007	14,382	36,302	25,509	23,643	14,783	39,838	23,205	23,743	14,719	40,427	23,063	23,848	14,685	40,824	23,057	23,874	14,589	41,100	22,733
Off campus, not living with family	33,384	24,427	45,860	35,512	33,528	24,889	50,069	31,472	33,572	24,854	50,553	30,978	33,823	24,860	51,414	31,035	33,903	24,925	51,728	30,217
Tuition and required fees	16,721	8,206	30,514	17,403	17,959	9,056	34,345	17,171	18,205	9,160	34,951	17,546	18,373	9,201	35,377	17,563	18,510	9,216	35,769	17,262
2-year institutions																				
Average total cost, by living arrangement																				
On campus	15,782	14,131	29,513	33,426	16,046	15,247	33,747	29,524	16,124	15,391	33,220	29,967	16,012	15,283	33,010	30,110	16,153	15,420	33,227	29,958
Off campus, living with family	10,268	8,984	21,686	22,167	9,838	9,394	24,081	21,411	9,897	9,391	23,948	20,956	9,794	9,359	23,939	20,627	9,805	9,369	23,951	20,652
Off campus, not living with family	18,774	17,359	31,455	31,349	18,500	17,975	32,846	30,467	18,583	18,067	33,471	29,519	18,538	18,077	32,659	29,811	18,722	18,256	32,935	30,072
Tuition and required fees	4,410	3,148	15,845	15,985	4,138	3,641	18,216	15,709	4,207	3,697	18,191	15,309	4,150	3,713	18,247	14,952	4,177	3,737	18,387	15,021

[1]Constant dollars based on the Consumer Price Index, adjusted to an academic-year basis.
NOTE: Excludes students who previously attended another postsecondary institution or who began their studies on a part-time basis. Tuition and fees at public institutions are the lower of either in-district or in-state tuition and fees. Data illustrating the average total cost of attendance for all students are weighted by the number of students at the institution receiving Title IV aid. Detail may not sum to totals because of rounding. Some data have been revised from previously published figures.

SOURCE: U.S. Department of Education, National Center for Education Statistics, Integrated Postsecondary Education Data System (IPEDS), Spring 2011 and Winter 2015–16 through Winter 2018–19, Student Financial Aid component; and Fall 2010 through Fall 2018, Institutional Characteristics component. (This table was prepared December 2019.)

Table 330.50. Average and percentiles of graduate tuition and required fees in degree-granting postsecondary institutions, by control of institution: 1989–90 through 2018–19

			Average			Percentiles					
				Private institutions		Public institutions[1]			Nonprofit institutions		
Year	Total	Public institutions[1]	Total	Nonprofit	For-profit	25th percentile	Median (50th percentile)	75th percentile	25th percentile	Median (50th percentile)	75th percentile
1	2	3	4	5	6	7	8	9	10	11	12
					Current dollars						
1989–90	$4,135	$1,999	$7,881	—	—	—	—	—	—	—	—
1990–91	4,488	2,206	8,507	—	—	—	—	—	—	—	—
1991–92	5,116	2,524	9,592	—	—	—	—	—	—	—	—
1992–93	5,475	2,791	10,008	—	—	—	—	—	—	—	—
1993–94	5,973	3,050	10,790	—	—	—	—	—	—	—	—
1994–95	6,247	3,250	11,338	—	—	—	—	—	—	—	—
1995–96	6,741	3,449	12,083	—	—	—	—	—	—	—	—
1996–97	7,111	3,607	12,537	—	—	—	—	—	—	—	—
1997–98	7,246	3,744	12,774	—	—	—	—	—	—	—	—
1998–99	7,685	3,897	13,299	—	—	—	—	—	—	—	—
1999–2000	8,069	4,042	13,821	$14,123	$9,611	$2,640	$3,637	$5,163	$7,998	$12,870	$20,487
2000–01	8,429	4,243	14,420	14,457	13,229	2,931	3,822	5,347	8,276	13,200	21,369
2001–02	8,857	4,496	15,165	15,232	13,414	3,226	4,119	5,596	8,583	14,157	22,054
2002–03	9,226	4,842	14,983	15,676	9,644	3,395	4,452	5,927	8,690	14,140	22,700
2003–04	10,312	5,544	16,209	16,807	12,542	3,795	5,103	7,063	9,072	15,030	25,600
2004–05	11,004	6,080	16,751	17,551	13,133	4,236	5,663	7,616	9,300	16,060	26,140
2005–06	11,621	6,493	17,244	18,171	13,432	4,608	6,209	7,977	9,745	16,222	26,958
2006–07	12,312	6,894	18,109	19,034	14,421	4,909	6,594	8,341	10,346	17,057	29,118
2007–08	13,001	7,415	18,876	19,896	14,709	5,176	6,990	9,288	10,705	17,647	30,247
2008–09	13,652	7,999	19,245	20,509	14,414	5,612	7,376	9,912	11,340	18,465	30,514
2009–10	14,542	8,763	20,078	21,317	14,512	6,074	7,983	10,658	12,290	19,460	31,730
2010–11	15,017	9,238	20,397	21,993	13,811	6,550	8,788	10,937	12,510	19,586	33,215
2011–12	15,845	9,978	21,230	22,899	14,285	7,506	9,440	11,954	12,936	20,625	34,680
2012–13	16,407	10,408	21,907	23,642	14,418	7,706	9,900	12,590	12,960	21,352	36,820
2013–14	16,948	10,725	22,617	24,482	14,209	7,791	10,242	12,779	13,590	22,018	36,720
2014–15	17,385	10,979	23,263	25,168	14,264	7,914	10,428	12,829	13,868	22,170	38,948
2015–16	17,871	11,306	23,917	25,826	14,432	8,242	10,769	13,193	13,878	22,570	40,670
2016–17	18,417	11,617	24,713	26,555	14,778	8,500	11,097	13,509	13,826	22,913	42,305
2017–18	18,949	11,929	25,446	27,356	14,304	8,778	11,201	13,982	14,460	23,542	43,848
2018–19	19,314	12,171	25,929	27,776	14,208	8,875	11,495	14,331	13,990	23,138	44,667
					Constant 2018–19 dollars[2]						
1989–90	$8,248	$3,987	$15,720	—	—	—	—	—	—	—	—
1990–91	8,488	4,172	16,089	—	—	—	—	—	—	—	—
1991–92	9,375	4,625	17,577	—	—	—	—	—	—	—	—
1992–93	9,729	4,960	17,784	—	—	—	—	—	—	—	—
1993–94	10,346	5,283	18,690	—	—	—	—	—	—	—	—
1994–95	10,519	5,473	19,092	—	—	—	—	—	—	—	—
1995–96	11,050	5,654	19,807	—	—	—	—	—	—	—	—
1996–97	11,334	5,749	19,982	—	—	—	—	—	—	—	—
1997–98	11,346	5,863	20,003	—	—	—	—	—	—	—	—
1998–99	11,828	5,998	20,470	—	—	—	—	—	—	—	—
1999–2000	12,072	6,047	20,676	$21,129	$14,379	$3,950	$5,441	$7,724	$11,965	$19,254	$30,649
2000–01	12,193	6,138	20,858	20,911	19,135	4,240	5,528	7,734	11,971	19,094	30,910
2001–02	12,589	6,390	21,555	21,650	19,065	4,585	5,854	7,954	12,199	20,122	31,346
2002–03	12,831	6,733	20,837	21,802	13,413	4,722	6,192	8,243	12,086	19,665	31,570
2003–04	14,034	7,545	22,060	22,874	17,070	5,165	6,945	9,613	12,347	20,456	34,841
2004–05	14,539	8,033	22,132	23,189	17,352	5,597	7,482	10,062	12,287	21,219	34,537
2005–06	14,791	8,264	21,947	23,127	17,096	5,865	7,903	10,153	12,403	20,647	34,311
2006–07	15,275	8,553	22,467	23,615	17,892	6,090	8,181	10,348	12,836	21,162	36,126
2007–08	15,554	8,871	22,582	23,802	17,597	6,192	8,362	11,112	12,807	21,112	36,186
2008–09	16,108	9,437	22,707	24,198	17,007	6,621	8,703	11,695	13,380	21,786	36,002
2009–10	16,993	10,240	23,463	24,910	16,959	7,098	9,329	12,455	14,362	22,740	37,078
2010–11	17,203	10,583	23,366	25,195	15,821	7,503	10,067	12,529	14,331	22,437	38,050
2011–12	17,634	11,105	23,628	25,485	15,899	8,354	10,506	13,304	14,397	22,955	38,597
2012–13	17,962	11,394	23,982	25,882	15,784	8,436	10,838	13,783	14,188	23,375	40,308
2013–14	18,269	11,560	24,379	26,389	15,316	8,398	11,040	13,774	14,649	23,733	39,580
2014–15	18,603	11,749	24,894	26,932	15,264	8,469	11,159	13,728	14,840	23,724	41,678
2015–16	18,996	12,018	25,422	27,451	15,340	8,761	11,447	14,023	14,751	23,990	43,229
2016–17	19,222	12,125	25,794	27,717	15,425	8,872	11,582	14,100	14,431	23,915	44,155
2017–18	19,342	12,176	25,973	27,922	14,600	8,960	11,433	14,272	14,760	24,030	44,757
2018–19	19,314	12,171	25,929	27,776	14,208	8,875	11,495	14,331	13,990	23,138	44,667

—Not available.
[1]Data are based on in-state tuition only.
[2]Constant dollars based on the Consumer Price Index, prepared by the Bureau of Labor Statistics, U.S. Department of Labor, adjusted to an academic-year basis.
NOTE: Average graduate student tuition weighted by fall full-time-equivalent graduate enrollment. Excludes doctoral students in professional practice programs. Data through 1995–96 are for institutions of higher education, while later data are for degree-granting institutions. Degree-granting institutions grant associate's or higher degrees and participate in Title IV federal financial aid programs. The degree-granting classification is very similar

to the earlier higher education classification, but it includes more 2-year colleges and excludes a few higher education institutions that did not grant degrees. Some data have been revised from previously published figures.
SOURCE: U.S. Department of Education, National Center for Education Statistics, Integrated Postsecondary Education Data System (IPEDS), "Fall Enrollment Survey" (IPEDS-EF:89–99), "Completions Survey" (IPEDS-C:90–99), and "Institutional Characteristics Survey" (IPEDS-IC:89–99); IPEDS Fall 2000 through Fall 2018, Institutional Characteristics component; and IPEDS Spring 2001 through Spring 2019, Fall Enrollment component. (This table was prepared December 2019.)

Table 331.10. Percentage of undergraduates receiving financial aid, by type and source of aid and selected student characteristics: 2015–16

[Standard errors appear in parentheses]

Selected student characteristic	Number of undergraduates[1] (in thousands)	Any aid — Total[2]	Any aid — Federal[3]	Any aid — Nonfederal	Grants — Total	Grants — Federal	Grants — Nonfederal	Loans — Total[4]	Loans — Federal[4]	Loans — Nonfederal	Work study — Total[5]
1	2	3	4	5	6	7	8	9	10	11	12
All undergraduates	19,308	72.2 (0.22)	55.9 (0.14)	49.0 (0.31)	63.1 (0.23)	41.2 (0.11)	46.1 (0.33)	38.7 (0.11)	36.7 (0.09)	5.9 (0.11)	5.2 (0.14)
Sex											
Male	8,406	69.1 (0.38)	52.0 (0.33)	47.8 (0.41)	58.9 (0.36)	37.4 (0.31)	44.9 (0.42)	35.4 (0.27)	33.2 (0.25)	5.7 (0.17)	4.8 (0.18)
Female	10,903	74.6 (0.28)	59.0 (0.24)	49.9 (0.39)	66.3 (0.31)	44.1 (0.24)	47.1 (0.41)	41.3 (0.23)	39.3 (0.21)	6.0 (0.17)	5.5 (0.18)
Race/ethnicity											
White	10,276	71.2 (0.42)	53.5 (0.41)	49.3 (0.41)	60.0 (0.40)	34.3 (0.32)	46.0 (0.43)	40.2 (0.37)	37.8 (0.36)	7.1 (0.18)	5.6 (0.17)
Black	3,006	80.0 (0.62)	70.6 (0.71)	45.9 (0.73)	72.4 (0.68)	60.1 (0.70)	43.4 (0.74)	50.8 (0.76)	49.4 (0.76)	4.2 (0.24)	5.2 (0.34)
Hispanic	3,723	71.4 (0.66)	55.6 (0.65)	49.4 (0.75)	65.5 (0.65)	47.1 (0.60)	47.2 (0.76)	30.7 (0.62)	28.9 (0.60)	4.3 (0.26)	4.4 (0.41)
Asian	1,399	62.0 (1.09)	40.5 (1.05)	49.9 (1.11)	56.6 (1.12)	32.1 (1.06)	47.6 (1.09)	23.3 (0.85)	20.9 (0.81)	4.7 (0.41)	5.4 (0.41)
Pacific Islander	83	69.1 (3.97)	54.2 (3.95)	49.8 (4.53)	60.5 (4.50)	42.7 (3.98)	48.1 (4.50)	31.8 (3.49)	30.9 (3.44)	3.1 (0.83)	2.8 ! (1.26)
American Indian/Alaska Native	160	76.7 (3.02)	62.5 (3.34)	44.1 (3.34)	70.8 (2.93)	56.1 (3.16)	42.6 (3.00)	30.9 (2.66)	29.5 (2.64)	2.6 (0.68)	3.3 ! (1.15)
Two or more races	661	76.8 (1.50)	59.9 (1.78)	53.6 (1.46)	67.9 (1.46)	45.9 (1.59)	51.2 (1.40)	42.6 (1.59)	39.9 (1.56)	6.1 (0.65)	4.7 (0.62)
Age											
15 to 23	11,368	74.7 (0.32)	56.4 (0.26)	56.6 (0.41)	65.8 (0.33)	37.6 (0.22)	53.5 (0.43)	40.5 (0.22)	38.1 (0.22)	7.5 (0.15)	7.6 (0.19)
24 to 29	3,536	69.9 (0.63)	58.6 (0.62)	38.5 (0.60)	61.6 (0.66)	50.6 (0.61)	35.9 (0.64)	37.4 (0.53)	35.6 (0.54)	4.0 (0.24)	2.5 (0.24)
30 or older	4,404	67.4 (0.54)	52.7 (0.61)	37.8 (0.64)	57.3 (0.53)	43.0 (0.54)	35.3 (0.65)	35.2 (0.50)	33.9 (0.49)	3.1 (0.19)	1.3 (0.13)
Marital status											
Not married[6]	16,098	73.5 (0.26)	57.0 (0.17)	51.4 (0.34)	64.8 (0.27)	41.2 (0.15)	48.4 (0.36)	40.2 (0.16)	38.0 (0.15)	6.4 (0.13)	6.0 (0.16)
Married	2,940	64.7 (0.67)	49.7 (0.68)	36.8 (0.76)	53.4 (0.69)	39.6 (0.59)	34.4 (0.78)	30.2 (0.53)	28.8 (0.53)	3.0 (0.22)	1.2 (0.18)
Separated	270	75.0 (2.10)	63.6 (2.29)	38.1 (1.90)	68.8 (2.18)	59.1 (2.19)	35.9 (1.87)	41.5 (2.08)	40.6 (2.05)	3.3 (0.75)	2.0 (0.49)
Attendance status[7]											
Full-time, full-year	7,239	86.4 (0.26)	69.8 (0.33)	66.9 (0.40)	76.7 (0.31)	46.3 (0.30)	63.8 (0.41)	54.7 (0.33)	52.5 (0.34)	9.2 (0.21)	10.5 (0.26)
Part-time or part-year	12,069	63.6 (0.33)	47.6 (0.26)	38.2 (0.40)	54.9 (0.33)	38.2 (0.23)	35.5 (0.41)	29.2 (0.23)	27.1 (0.21)	3.9 (0.13)	2.0 (0.15)
Dependency status and family income											
Dependent	9,772	76.9 (0.35)	58.9 (0.28)	59.2 (0.43)	67.1 (0.35)	37.3 (0.24)	56.0 (0.45)	43.2 (0.25)	40.7 (0.24)	8.2 (0.17)	8.3 (0.21)
Less than $20,000	1,713	87.5 (0.72)	80.3 (0.72)	60.9 (0.93)	86.9 (0.75)	79.5 (0.74)	59.2 (0.93)	40.1 (0.83)	38.3 (0.81)	4.1 (0.31)	9.5 (0.50)
$20,000–$39,999	1,644	84.6 (0.75)	76.3 (0.80)	62.4 (0.98)	83.0 (0.76)	74.4 (0.81)	60.8 (0.99)	42.1 (0.81)	40.7 (0.79)	5.3 (0.42)	10.9 (0.56)
$40,000–$59,999	1,281	81.4 (0.96)	68.3 (1.04)	65.1 (1.02)	75.5 (1.00)	56.8 (0.98)	61.8 (1.03)	48.1 (1.11)	45.9 (1.09)	8.2 (0.52)	10.7 (0.65)
$60,000–$79,999	1,157	72.7 (0.98)	50.3 (1.00)	58.4 (1.09)	60.1 (1.03)	19.8 (0.78)	54.9 (1.08)	44.5 (1.04)	42.3 (0.93)	8.6 (0.54)	8.1 (0.52)
$80,000–$99,999	946	69.9 (1.20)	46.3 (1.03)	56.7 (1.26)	53.7 (1.29)	4.9 (0.51)	53.0 (1.28)	45.4 (1.02)	43.1 (0.99)	10.3 (0.67)	8.2 (0.71)
$100,000 or more	3,032	68.6 (0.72)	40.5 (0.57)	55.0 (0.70)	50.7 (0.68)	1.9 (0.17)	50.4 (0.69)	42.2 (0.56)	38.6 (0.54)	11.2 (0.38)	5.3 (0.29)
Independent	9,536	67.3 (0.34)	52.9 (0.31)	38.5 (0.47)	58.9 (0.34)	45.2 (0.29)	36.0 (0.48)	34.2 (0.26)	32.5 (0.24)	3.5 (0.14)	2.0 (0.14)
Less than $10,000	2,909	69.8 (0.64)	56.0 (0.72)	41.0 (0.76)	66.3 (0.69)	53.8 (0.72)	38.7 (0.77)	35.0 (0.58)	33.2 (0.55)	3.6 (0.23)	3.7 (0.26)
$10,000–$19,999	1,783	74.6 (0.86)	64.7 (0.94)	39.9 (0.89)	70.1 (0.90)	61.6 (0.91)	36.8 (0.87)	41.0 (0.79)	38.9 (0.75)	4.3 (0.34)	2.2 (0.24)
$20,000–$29,999	1,372	72.7 (0.96)	58.5 (1.06)	40.6 (1.08)	63.4 (0.96)	48.8 (0.98)	38.2 (1.10)	37.4 (1.04)	36.3 (1.01)	3.1 (0.31)	1.7 (0.21)
$30,000–$49,999	1,467	65.8 (1.00)	53.0 (1.09)	35.3 (1.04)	53.0 (1.02)	40.0 (1.01)	32.8 (1.03)	33.6 (0.81)	32.3 (0.80)	3.2 (0.29)	1.0 (0.24)
$50,000 or more	2,005	54.5 (0.90)	34.1 (0.82)	34.6 (0.85)	39.5 (0.82)	19.7 (0.61)	32.2 (0.86)	25.1 (0.69)	23.2 (0.69)	3.2 (0.33)	0.4 (0.09)
Housing status[8]											
School-owned	2,756	86.8 (0.49)	65.7 (0.63)	76.5 (0.61)	78.6 (0.60)	37.1 (0.62)	73.5 (0.67)	59.5 (0.63)	56.8 (0.64)	12.2 (0.51)	17.1 (0.57)
Off-campus, not with parents	9,926	70.0 (0.39)	54.6 (0.41)	43.4 (0.43)	60.3 (0.36)	42.5 (0.36)	40.3 (0.45)	37.3 (0.36)	35.2 (0.35)	5.0 (0.15)	3.2 (0.15)
With parents	4,749	66.0 (0.57)	49.8 (0.54)	44.3 (0.68)	58.9 (0.58)	39.4 (0.48)	42.0 (0.68)	26.0 (0.52)	24.2 (0.50)	3.9 (0.22)	2.7 (0.24)

! Interpret data with caution. The coefficient of variation (CV) for this estimate is between 30 and 50 percent.
[1] Numbers of undergraduates may not equal figures reported in other tables, since these data are based on a sample survey of students who enrolled at any time during the school year. Includes all postsecondary institutions.
[2] Includes students who reported they were awarded aid, but did not specify the source or type of aid.
[3] Includes Department of Veterans Affairs and Department of Defense benefits.
[4] Includes Parent Loans for Undergraduate Students (PLUS).
[5] Details on federal and nonfederal work-study participants are not available.
[6] Includes students who were single, divorced, or widowed.

[7] Full-time, full-year includes students enrolled full time for 9 or more months. Part-time or part-year includes students enrolled part time for 9 or more months and students enrolled less than 9 months either part time or full time.
[8] Excludes students attending more than one institution.
NOTE: Detail may not sum to totals because of rounding and because some students receive multiple types of aid and aid from different sources. Data include undergraduates in degree-granting and non-degree-granting institutions. Data exclude students attending institutions in Puerto Rico. Race categories exclude persons of Hispanic ethnicity.
SOURCE: U.S. Department of Education, National Center for Education Statistics, 2015–16 National Postsecondary Student Aid Study (NPSAS:16). (This table was prepared June 2018.)

Table 331.20. Full-time, first-time degree/certificate-seeking undergraduate students enrolled in degree-granting postsecondary institutions, by participation and average amount awarded in financial aid programs, and control and level of institution: 2000–01 through 2017–18

Control and level of institution, and year	Number enrolled	Number awarded financial aid	Percent awarded aid	Percent of enrolled students awarded aid				Average award for students in aid programs[1]							
								Current dollars				Constant 2018–19 dollars[2]			
				Federal grants	State/local grants	Institutional grants	Student loans[3]	Federal grants	State/local grants	Institutional grants	Student loans[3]	Federal grants	State/local grants	Institutional grants	Student loans[3]
1	2	3	4	5	6	7	8	9	10	11	12	13	14	15	16
All institutions															
2000–01	1,976,600	1,390,527	70.3	31.6	31.2	31.1	40.1	$2,486	$2,039	$4,740	$3,764	$3,597	$2,949	$6,856	$5,445
2001–02	2,050,016	1,481,592	72.3	33.3	32.5	31.5	40.7	2,739	2,057	4,918	3,970	3,893	2,924	6,990	5,643
2002–03	2,135,613	1,553,024	72.7	34.1	30.9	31.5	41.4	2,947	2,189	5,267	4,331	4,099	3,044	7,325	6,023
2003–04	2,178,517	1,610,967	73.9	34.6	31.2	31.9	43.1	2,934	2,226	5,648	4,193	3,993	3,030	7,687	5,707
2004–05	2,260,590	1,689,910	74.8	35.2	31.3	31.7	44.0	2,939	2,343	5,958	4,463	3,883	3,096	7,872	5,896
2005–06	2,309,543	1,731,315	75.0	33.7	30.8	32.7	44.6	2,959	2,441	6,213	4,831	3,766	3,107	7,908	6,149
2006–07	2,426,599	1,766,783	72.8	32.1	30.0	32.2	43.5	3,131	2,526	6,598	5,018	3,885	3,134	8,186	6,226
2007–08	2,528,579	1,911,296	75.6	35.4	30.6	33.6	45.5	3,381	2,586	6,808	6,008	4,045	3,094	8,145	7,187
2008–09	2,542,748	1,974,063	77.6	36.4	31.7	34.6	46.6	3,927	2,706	7,518	6,723	4,633	3,193	8,871	7,932
2009–10	2,855,241	2,323,706	81.4	46.2	28.6	33.3	51.2	4,693	2,771	7,693	7,019	5,485	3,238	8,990	8,202
2010–11	2,648,101	2,179,582	82.3	47.8	31.0	35.8	50.1	4,758	2,843	8,393	6,624	5,451	3,257	9,615	7,588
2011–12	2,571,120	2,140,556	83.3	47.6	30.8	37.9	51.2	4,424	2,912	8,767	6,641	4,924	3,241	9,757	7,391
2012–13	2,510,994	2,077,909	82.8	45.5	31.2	39.8	49.4	4,452	3,051	9,223	6,896	4,874	3,340	10,096	7,549
2013–14	2,505,306	2,077,487	82.9	45.3	32.2	41.4	47.3	4,533	3,101	9,603	7,015	4,886	3,342	10,351	7,562
2014–15	2,471,045	2,062,252	83.5	44.5	32.9	42.8	47.0	4,599	3,214	10,066	6,925	4,922	3,439	10,772	7,410
2015–16	2,458,068	2,031,557	82.6	42.6	32.3	44.3	45.6	4,682	3,375	10,353	6,989	4,977	3,587	11,004	7,429
2016–17	2,491,341	2,063,481	82.8	42.3	31.8	44.7	46.1	4,700	3,463	10,772	7,080	4,906	3,615	11,243	7,389
2017–18	2,463,084	2,057,247	83.5	42.6	33.6	46.6	44.4	4,926	3,684	11,236	7,082	5,028	3,760	11,469	7,228
Public															
2000–01	1,333,236	872,109	65.4	30.0	33.5	22.7	30.7	2,408	1,707	2,275	3,050	3,483	2,469	3,290	4,412
2005–06	1,510,268	1,066,041	70.6	31.1	34.8	25.1	34.2	2,926	2,226	3,162	3,866	3,724	2,834	4,024	4,921
2010–11	1,802,335	1,421,369	78.9	46.0	35.9	27.2	40.2	4,765	2,676	4,160	5,780	5,459	3,066	4,766	6,621
2013–14	1,752,745	1,410,234	80.5	44.9	37.3	32.4	39.8	4,518	2,961	4,950	6,213	4,870	3,191	5,336	6,696
2014–15	1,743,119	1,412,510	81.0	44.2	38.1	34.3	39.6	4,592	3,080	5,165	6,243	4,914	3,296	5,527	6,680
2015–16	1,747,471	1,399,831	80.1	42.2	37.2	35.6	38.1	4,636	3,238	5,322	6,316	4,928	3,441	5,657	6,713
2016–17	1,752,934	1,407,452	80.3	41.6	37.2	37.2	38.2	4,641	3,332	5,498	6,440	4,844	3,478	5,738	6,721
2017–18	1,766,003	1,438,174	81.4	42.8	38.9	38.9	37.2	4,907	3,558	5,550	6,483	5,008	3,632	5,665	6,617
4-year															
2000–01	804,793	573,430	71.3	26.6	36.5	29.6	40.7	2,569	2,068	2,616	3,212	3,716	2,991	3,784	4,646
2005–06	906,948	695,017	76.6	26.6	36.8	34.2	44.4	3,071	2,752	3,573	4,166	3,908	3,503	4,548	5,302
2010–11	1,039,126	858,424	82.6	38.9	38.2	39.6	51.5	4,983	3,469	4,634	6,127	5,709	3,974	5,309	7,019
2013–14	1,076,356	892,192	82.9	37.9	37.4	45.4	49.5	4,597	3,724	5,435	6,658	4,955	4,015	5,858	7,177
2014–15	1,095,363	915,024	83.5	37.5	37.6	47.2	49.5	4,669	3,842	5,651	6,694	4,997	4,111	6,047	7,163
2015–16	1,144,409	948,342	82.9	36.8	36.8	47.2	47.2	4,707	3,905	5,812	6,710	5,003	4,151	6,178	7,132
2016–17	1,161,684	965,117	83.1	36.4	36.5	48.9	47.1	4,723	3,996	5,995	6,837	4,930	4,170	6,258	7,136
2017–18	1,183,447	994,201	84.0	37.9	38.3	50.3	46.0	4,958	4,250	6,091	6,862	5,060	4,338	6,218	7,004
2-year															
2000–01	528,443	298,679	56.5	35.2	28.8	12.1	15.3	2,222	1,009	1,004	2,396	3,215	1,460	1,452	3,465
2005–06	603,320	371,024	61.5	38.0	31.9	11.3	16.1	2,774	1,314	1,297	2,812	3,530	1,673	1,651	3,580
2010–11	763,209	562,945	73.8	55.7	32.8	10.3	15.3	4,557	1,418	1,677	4,802	5,221	1,625	1,921	5,501
2013–14	676,389	518,042	76.6	56.0	37.1	11.8	17.5	4,432	1,736	1,983	4,772	4,778	1,871	2,137	5,144
2014–15	647,756	497,486	76.8	55.6	39.0	12.4	18.2	4,504	1,839	2,031	4,595	4,820	1,968	2,174	4,917
2015–16	603,062	451,489	74.9	52.4	38.0	13.5	20.7	4,542	2,010	2,066	4,610	4,828	2,137	2,196	4,900
2016–17	591,250	442,335	74.8	51.9	38.6	14.1	20.7	4,527	2,098	2,112	4,667	4,725	2,190	2,204	4,871
2017–18	582,556	443,973	76.2	53.0	40.0	15.9	19.4	4,832	2,211	2,064	4,656	4,932	2,257	2,107	4,753
Private nonprofit															
2000–01	439,369	363,044	82.6	28.4	31.8	68.1	57.7	2,879	2,998	7,368	4,019	4,164	4,336	10,657	5,814
2005–06	471,069	401,908	85.3	26.5	31.3	73.8	59.8	3,426	3,117	9,932	5,270	4,361	3,967	12,641	6,707
2010–11	517,831	462,840	89.4	36.4	27.7	78.4	64.3	5,076	3,556	14,324	7,296	5,815	4,073	16,409	8,358
2013–14	513,574	458,526	89.3	33.7	26.1	81.1	61.1	4,738	3,760	16,832	8,064	5,107	4,053	18,143	8,692
2014–15	535,142	479,437	89.6	35.0	24.9	78.3	60.1	4,763	3,839	17,705	7,940	5,097	4,108	18,946	8,496
2015–16	540,835	484,705	89.6	35.2	23.8	78.7	61.0	4,998	4,013	18,452	7,925	5,312	4,266	19,613	8,424
2016–17	569,122	511,634	89.9	36.9	22.6	75.7	62.3	5,097	4,125	19,299	8,010	5,320	4,305	20,143	8,360
2017–18	550,431	496,948	90.3	35.8	23.8	79.2	60.6	5,215	4,369	20,626	8,100	5,323	4,460	21,053	8,268

See notes at end of table.

Table 331.20. Full-time, first-time degree/certificate-seeking undergraduate students enrolled in degree-granting postsecondary institutions, by participation and average amount awarded in financial aid programs, and control and level of institution: 2000–01 through 2017–18—Continued

Control and level of institution, and year	Number enrolled	Number awarded financial aid	Percent awarded aid	Percent of enrolled students awarded aid — Federal grants	State/local grants	Institutional grants	Student loans[3]	Average award, Current dollars — Federal grants	State/local grants	Institutional grants	Student loans[3]	Average award, Constant 2018–19 dollars[2] — Federal grants	State/local grants	Institutional grants	Student loans[3]
1	2	3	4	5	6	7	8	9	10	11	12	13	14	15	16
4-year															
2000–01	419,499	347,638	82.9	27.4	32.2	70.1	58.1	2,930	3,001	7,458	4,000	4,239	4,342	10,788	5,786
2005–06	460,832	393,429	85.4	26.0	31.2	74.6	59.8	3,437	3,121	10,002	5,264	4,375	3,972	12,731	6,700
2010–11	504,715	451,012	89.4	35.4	27.7	79.6	64.3	5,105	3,574	14,414	7,305	5,848	4,094	16,513	8,368
2013–14	504,584	450,228	89.2	33.1	26.1	81.6	61.0	4,758	3,762	16,966	8,069	5,129	4,055	18,288	8,697
2014–15	503,662	450,897	89.5	32.6	25.9	82.3	60.9	4,830	3,838	17,835	7,994	5,169	4,107	19,086	8,554
2015–16	505,549	451,276	89.3	31.9	25.0	82.1	59.2	4,931	4,017	18,826	8,002	5,241	4,270	20,011	8,505
2016–17	508,494	454,979	89.5	31.5	24.9	82.2	59.4	4,929	4,125	19,774	8,179	5,144	4,305	20,638	8,537
2017–18	516,571	464,446	89.9	32.6	24.9	83.0	58.8	5,146	4,373	20,885	8,187	5,253	4,464	21,318	8,357
2-year															
2000–01	19,870	15,406	77.5	49.2	23.9	25.7	49.5	2,269	2,892	2,168	4,509	3,283	4,183	3,135	6,522
2005–06	10,237	8,479	82.8	51.6	36.1	38.5	55.9	3,176	2,974	3,799	5,531	4,043	3,785	4,835	7,040
2010–11	13,116	11,828	90.2	73.3	26.8	29.8	64.3	4,553	2,835	5,059	6,944	5,215	3,248	5,796	7,955
2013–14	8,990	8,298	92.3	70.6	27.3	49.5	65.5	4,216	3,618	4,346	7,818	4,544	3,899	4,685	8,427
2014–15	31,480	28,540	90.7	74.3	8.4	14.4	48.4	4,288	3,881	5,768	6,855	4,588	4,153	6,172	7,336
2015–16	35,286	33,429	94.7	81.8	7.2	30.0	85.8	5,374	3,810	3,770	7,171	5,712	4,049	4,007	7,622
2016–17	60,628	56,655	93.4	81.7	3.7	21.1	86.9	5,641	4,145	3,778	7,041	5,888	4,326	3,943	7,349
2017–18	33,860	32,502	96.0	84.1	6.3	20.0	88.5	5,624	4,130	4,235	7,220	5,740	4,215	4,323	7,369
Private for-profit															
4-year															
2000–01	203,995	155,374	76.2	49.3	15.2	6.2	63.5	2,312	2,494	1,540	5,517	3,345	3,607	2,227	7,981
2005–06	328,206	263,366	80.2	55.6	11.4	8.8	70.4	2,725	2,796	1,423	6,454	3,468	3,558	1,811	8,214
2010–11	327,935	295,373	90.1	75.7	9.0	15.5	82.0	4,494	3,028	1,884	8,064	5,148	3,469	2,158	9,238
2013–14	238,987	208,727	87.3	72.8	8.2	21.5	73.3	4,394	3,278	2,489	8,336	4,737	3,534	2,683	8,986
2014–15	192,784	170,305	88.3	73.1	8.6	20.7	76.6	4,421	3,571	3,193	7,906	4,730	3,821	3,416	8,460
2015–16	169,762	147,021	86.6	69.9	8.7	25.3	74.4	4,460	3,841	2,860	8,096	4,741	4,083	3,039	8,606
2016–17	169,285	144,395	85.3	67.9	7.6	18.9	73.6	4,354	3,490	3,319	7,871	4,544	3,642	3,464	8,215
2017–18	146,650	122,125	83.3	65.4	7.2	17.0	69.1	4,484	3,333	3,915	7,614	4,577	3,402	3,997	7,771
4-year															
2000–01	81,075	51,739	63.8	36.1	11.9	8.3	57.7	2,295	2,889	1,616	5,749	3,320	4,178	2,337	8,315
2005–06	157,705	116,237	73.7	46.8	8.9	10.9	67.2	2,490	2,945	1,641	7,046	3,170	3,748	2,089	8,968
2010–11	112,706	102,000	90.5	73.6	11.3	23.6	82.9	4,733	2,950	2,805	8,561	5,422	3,379	3,213	9,808
2013–14	90,264	80,686	89.4	72.5	10.5	34.5	78.1	4,624	3,021	3,065	8,581	4,984	3,256	3,304	9,250
2014–15	81,791	73,040	89.3	71.9	9.8	30.9	75.7	4,677	3,262	4,137	8,237	5,005	3,491	4,427	8,814
2015–16	59,269	51,636	87.1	65.5	10.9	38.5	73.4	4,641	3,715	4,128	8,413	4,933	3,949	4,388	8,942
2016–17	57,680	49,045	85.0	63.6	9.9	31.8	71.5	4,646	3,609	4,690	8,331	4,849	3,767	4,895	8,695
2017–18	52,371	43,342	82.8	62.2	9.1	30.6	65.1	4,888	3,822	4,880	8,330	4,989	3,901	4,981	8,502
2-year															
2000–01	122,920	103,635	84.3	58.0	17.3	4.8	67.3	2,319	2,314	1,453	5,387	3,355	3,347	2,101	7,792
2005–06	170,501	147,129	86.3	63.6	13.7	6.8	73.4	2,885	2,706	1,098	5,951	3,672	3,444	1,398	7,575
2010–11	215,229	193,373	89.8	76.8	7.8	11.3	81.5	4,374	3,088	875	7,799	5,011	3,538	1,002	8,934
2013–14	148,723	128,041	86.1	73.0	6.7	13.6	70.3	4,256	3,523	1,602	8,171	4,587	3,798	1,727	8,808
2014–15	110,993	97,265	87.6	74.0	7.8	13.1	77.2	4,237	3,856	1,556	7,667	4,534	4,126	1,666	8,205
2015–16	110,493	95,385	86.3	72.3	7.5	18.3	75.0	4,373	3,940	1,425	7,930	4,648	4,188	1,515	8,429
2016–17	111,605	95,350	85.4	70.1	6.4	12.2	74.6	4,217	3,394	1,464	7,643	4,401	3,542	1,528	7,978
2017–18	94,279	78,783	83.6	67.2	6.1	9.5	71.3	4,276	2,930	2,187	7,251	4,365	2,991	2,232	7,401

[1]Average amounts for students participating in indicated programs.
[2]Constant dollars based on the Consumer Price Index, prepared by the Bureau of Labor Statistics, U.S. Department of Labor, adjusted to an academic-year basis.
[3]Includes only loans made directly to students. Does not include Parent Loans for Undergraduate Students (PLUS) and other loans made directly to parents.

NOTE: Degree-granting institutions grant associate's or higher degrees and participate in Title IV federal financial aid programs. Data through 2009–10 are for students receiving aid, while later data are for students awarded aid. Students were counted as receiving aid only if they were awarded and accepted aid and their aid was also disbursed. Some data have been revised from previously published figures.
SOURCE: U.S. Department of Education, National Center for Education Statistics, Integrated Postsecondary Education Data System (IPEDS), Spring 2002 through Spring 2011 and Winter 2011–12 through Winter 2018–19, Student Financial Aid component. (This table was prepared December 2019.)

Table 331.30. Average amount of grant and scholarship aid and average net price for first-time, full-time degree/certificate-seeking students awarded Title IV aid, by control and level of institution and income level: Selected years, 2009–10 through 2017–18

Level of institution and income level	2009–10[1]				2015–16				2016–17				2017–18			
	All institutions	Public	Private		All institutions	Public	Private		All institutions	Public	Private		All institutions	Public	Private	
			Nonprofit	For-profit			Nonprofit	For-profit			Nonprofit	For-profit			Nonprofit	For-profit
1	2	3	4	5	6	7	8	9	10	11	12	13	14	15	16	17
							Current dollars									
4-year institutions																
Grant and scholarship aid[2]																
All income levels	$9,050	$5,980	$15,560	$4,420	$11,810	$7,190	$20,890	$5,920	$12,260	$7,370	$21,800	$6,170	$13,100	$7,930	$23,190	$6,510
$0 to $30,000	10,290	9,080	17,460	5,110	13,100	10,360	21,890	6,060	13,650	10,700	22,780	6,540	14,350	11,190	24,070	6,700
$30,001 to $48,000	11,170	8,330	18,710	4,530	13,980	9,810	24,570	6,460	14,460	10,130	25,720	6,020	15,280	10,630	27,130	6,970
$48,001 to $75,000	9,140	4,910	16,810	2,430	12,250	6,720	23,190	5,550	12,790	7,090	24,220	5,310	13,730	7,540	25,810	5,690
$75,001 to $110,000	7,150	2,270	14,650	1,220	10,080	3,440	20,740	4,880	10,550	3,710	21,720	4,950	11,450	4,020	23,230	5,140
$110,001 or more	6,300	1,590	11,560	1,020	9,210	2,150	17,270	4,250	9,660	2,280	18,220	5,210	10,340	2,430	19,360	5,770
Net price[3]																
All income levels	15,900	11,070	21,780	22,590	17,660	13,080	25,680	21,750	18,020	13,440	26,200	21,370	18,120	13,460	26,440	21,650
$0 to $30,000	12,570	7,720	15,970	21,770	12,690	9,170	19,450	20,720	12,660	9,260	19,610	20,080	12,730	9,300	19,860	20,660
$30,001 to $48,000	13,110	9,260	17,200	23,590	13,720	10,710	19,810	22,490	13,820	10,910	19,970	21,770	13,870	10,900	20,210	22,290
$48,001 to $75,000	16,610	13,290	20,270	26,710	17,430	14,560	22,500	24,800	17,560	14,660	22,740	25,290	17,670	14,770	22,780	24,990
$75,001 to $110,000	19,860	16,410	23,900	29,830	21,540	18,570	26,040	27,380	21,790	18,790	26,450	27,090	22,020	19,050	26,540	27,080
$110,001 or more	24,080	17,880	30,210	32,910	26,880	20,960	33,490	30,160	27,320	21,390	34,120	29,180	27,890	21,850	34,690	29,930
2-year institutions																
Grant and scholarship aid[2]																
All income levels	4,460	4,540	5,180	4,090	5,080	5,090	7,070	4,250	5,110	5,150	6,750	4,170	5,470	5,520	7,580	4,300
$0 to $30,000	5,250	5,450	5,540	4,590	6,010	6,140	6,770	4,650	6,020	6,200	6,450	4,540	6,410	6,600	7,260	4,680
$30,001 to $48,000	4,380	4,520	5,080	3,670	5,500	5,530	8,130	4,130	5,530	5,600	7,280	4,140	5,910	5,980	8,670	4,180
$48,001 to $75,000	2,240	2,250	4,150	1,960	3,330	3,290	7,850	2,790	3,480	3,430	7,730	2,940	3,700	3,670	8,310	3,040
$75,001 to $110,000	800	750	3,240	830	1,210	1,090	9,210	1,130	1,380	1,260	8,750	1,260	1,470	1,360	8,790	1,340
$110,001 or more	610	600	2,940	470	680	540	7,610	720	1,070	940	8,370	790	920	710	10,480	930
Net price[3]																
All income levels	8,930	6,290	16,270	18,360	8,500	7,050	18,180	20,640	8,800	7,200	18,830	21,110	8,670	7,060	18,400	21,180
$0 to $30,000	8,560	5,380	16,500	18,240	7,900	5,900	17,720	20,680	8,250	6,060	18,410	21,260	8,050	5,810	17,970	21,400
$30,001 to $48,000	8,720	6,330	16,620	19,070	7,640	6,610	19,480	20,990	7,920	6,680	20,160	21,430	7,690	6,550	19,600	21,500
$48,001 to $75,000	10,690	8,810	18,650	21,290	9,730	8,960	20,460	22,510	9,840	9,000	20,760	22,220	9,780	8,980	20,680	22,470
$75,001 to $110,000	12,230	10,630	20,760	23,020	12,200	11,430	22,840	24,290	12,360	11,530	21,820	24,000	12,430	11,580	23,060	24,090
$110,001 or more	12,760	10,820	20,930	24,620	13,030	12,110	27,890	25,100	12,890	11,910	29,390	25,340	13,380	12,380	29,730	24,830
							Constant 2018–19 dollars[4]									
4-year institutions																
Grant and scholarship aid[2]																
All income levels	$10,570	$6,980	$18,180	$5,160	$12,560	$7,640	$22,210	$6,290	$12,800	$7,700	$22,750	$6,440	$13,370	$8,100	$23,670	$6,650
$0 to $30,000	12,030	10,610	20,400	5,970	13,920	11,010	23,270	6,440	14,250	11,170	23,780	6,820	14,650	11,430	24,560	6,840
$30,001 to $48,000	13,050	9,740	21,870	5,290	14,860	10,420	26,110	6,860	15,090	10,570	26,850	6,280	15,600	10,850	27,690	7,120
$48,001 to $75,000	10,680	5,740	19,650	2,840	13,020	7,150	24,650	5,900	13,340	7,400	25,280	5,540	14,010	7,700	26,350	5,810
$75,001 to $110,000	8,360	2,650	17,120	1,420	10,710	3,660	22,050	5,190	11,010	3,870	22,670	5,170	11,690	4,110	23,710	5,240
$110,001 or more	7,360	1,860	13,510	1,190	9,790	2,280	18,350	4,520	10,080	2,380	19,010	5,440	10,560	2,480	19,760	5,890
Net price[3]																
All income levels	18,580	12,940	25,450	26,400	18,770	13,900	27,290	23,110	18,810	14,020	27,340	22,300	18,500	13,740	26,990	22,100
$0 to $30,000	14,690	9,020	18,670	25,440	13,480	9,750	20,680	22,030	13,210	9,670	20,470	20,960	12,990	9,500	20,270	21,090
$30,001 to $48,000	15,320	10,820	20,100	27,570	14,580	11,380	21,060	23,900	14,430	11,390	20,850	22,720	14,160	11,120	20,650	22,750
$48,001 to $75,000	19,410	15,530	23,680	31,210	18,520	15,480	23,920	26,360	18,320	15,300	23,740	26,390	18,040	15,080	23,650	25,500
$75,001 to $110,000	23,200	19,170	27,930	34,850	22,890	19,740	27,680	29,100	22,740	19,610	27,600	28,270	22,470	19,440	27,090	27,640
$110,001 or more	28,140	20,890	35,300	38,460	28,570	22,280	35,600	32,060	28,520	22,320	35,610	30,460	28,470	22,310	35,410	30,550

See notes at end of table.

Table 331.30. Average amount of grant and scholarship aid and average net price for first-time, full-time degree/certificate-seeking students awarded Title IV aid, by control and level of institution and income level: Selected years, 2009–10 through 2017–18—Continued

Level of institution and income level	2009–10[1]				2015–16				2016–17				2017–18			
	All institutions	Public	Private		All institutions	Public	Private		All institutions	Public	Private		All institutions	Public	Private	
			Nonprofit	For-profit			Nonprofit	For-profit			Nonprofit	For-profit			Nonprofit	For-profit
1	2	3	4	5	6	7	8	9	10	11	12	13	14	15	16	17
2-year institutions																
Grant and scholarship aid[2]																
All income levels																
All income levels	5,210	5,300	6,060	4,780	5,400	5,410	7,510	4,520	5,330	5,370	7,050	4,350	5,580	5,630	7,730	4,390
$0 to $30,000	6,130	6,370	6,480	5,370	6,390	6,520	7,200	4,940	6,280	6,470	6,730	4,740	6,540	6,740	7,410	4,780
$30,001 to $48,000	5,120	5,290	5,930	4,280	5,840	5,880	8,640	4,390	5,780	5,850	7,600	4,320	6,030	6,110	8,850	4,260
$48,001 to $75,000	2,620	2,630	4,860	2,290	3,540	3,500	8,340	2,960	3,630	3,590	8,070	3,060	3,770	3,740	8,480	3,110
$75,001 to $110,000	930	880	3,780	970	1,290	1,160	9,790	1,200	1,440	1,310	9,130	1,310	1,500	1,390	8,970	1,370
$110,001 or more	720	700	3,440	550	730	570	8,090	770	1,120	980	8,740	820	940	730	10,700	950
Net price[3]																
All income levels	10,430	7,350	19,020	21,450	9,030	7,500	19,330	21,930	9,190	7,520	19,660	22,030	8,850	7,200	18,780	21,620
$0 to $30,000	10,010	6,290	19,280	21,310	8,390	6,280	18,840	21,980	8,610	6,330	19,220	22,190	8,220	5,930	18,340	21,840
$30,001 to $48,000	10,190	7,400	19,430	22,280	8,120	7,030	20,700	22,310	8,270	6,980	21,040	22,370	7,850	6,690	20,010	21,950
$48,001 to $75,000	12,490	10,300	21,790	24,880	10,340	9,530	21,750	23,930	10,270	9,390	21,670	23,190	9,980	9,160	21,100	22,940
$75,001 to $110,000	14,290	12,420	24,260	26,900	12,970	12,150	24,280	25,810	12,900	12,030	22,840	25,050	12,690	11,820	23,540	24,590
$110,001 or more	14,920	12,640	24,460	28,770	13,850	12,870	29,640	26,680	13,450	12,430	30,670	26,450	13,650	12,640	30,350	25,350

[1]Data for 2009–10 are for students receiving aid, while later data are for students awarded aid. Students were counted as receiving aid only if they were awarded and accepted aid and their aid was also disbursed.
[2]Grant and scholarship aid consists of federal Title IV grants, as well as other grant or scholarship aid from the federal government, state or local governments, or institutional sources. Title IV grants include Federal Pell Grants, Federal Supplemental Educational Opportunity Grants (FSEOGs), Academic Competitiveness Grants (ACGs), National Science and Mathematics Access to Retain Talent Grants (National SMART Grants), and Teacher Education Assistance for College and Higher Education (TEACH) Grants. The average amount of grant and scholarship aid by income level was calculated based on all students who were awarded any type of Title IV aid, even those students who were awarded zero Title IV aid in the form of grants and were awarded Title IV aid only in the form of work-study aid or loan aid.
[3]Net price is the total cost of attendance minus grant and scholarship aid from the federal government, state or local governments, or institutional sources. However, average net price by income level was calculated based on all students who were awarded any type of Title IV aid, even those who were awarded zero Title IV aid in the form of grants and were awarded Title IV aid only in the form of work-study aid or loan aid.

[4]Constant dollars based on the Consumer Price Index, prepared by the Bureau of Labor Statistics, U.S. Department of Labor, adjusted to an academic-year basis.
NOTE: Excludes students who previously attended another postsecondary institution or who began their studies on a part-time basis. Includes only first-time, full-time students who paid the in-state or in-district tuition rate (if they attended public institutions) and who were awarded Title IV aid. Excludes the approximately 17 percent of students who were not awarded any Title IV aid. Title IV aid includes grant aid, work-study aid, and loan aid. Data are weighted by the number of students at the institution who were awarded Title IV aid. Totals include students for whom income data were not available. Some data have been revised from previously published figures.
SOURCE: U.S. Department of Education, National Center for Education Statistics, Integrated Postsecondary Education Data System (IPEDS), Spring 2011 and Winter 2016–17 through Winter 2018–19, Student Financial Aid component. (This table was prepared December 2019.)

Table 331.35. Percentage of full-time, full-year undergraduates receiving financial aid, and average annual amount received, by type and source of aid and selected student characteristics: Selected years, 1999–2000 through 2015–16

[Standard errors appear in parentheses. Amounts in constant 2018–19 dollars]

Year and selected student characteristic	Number enrolled¹ (in thousands)	Any aid — Percent receiving: Total³	Federal⁴	Nonfederal	Any aid — Average amount: Total³	Federal⁴	Nonfederal	Grants — Percent receiving: Total	Pell	Grants — Average amount: Total	Pell	Loans² — Percent receiving	Loans² — Average amount
1	2	3	4	5	6	7	8	9	10	11	12	13	14
1999–2000													
Total	6,145 (—)	71.9 (0.59)	56.7 (0.44)	52.3 (0.67)	$12,670 (149)	$8,930 (87)	$7,720 (142)	58.5 (0.60)	28.3 (0.43)	$7,630 (121)	$3,420 (22)	45.6 (0.44)	$9,020 (88)
Sex													
Male	2,687 (†)	69.1 (0.74)	53.9 (0.65)	49.7 (0.79)	12,640 (230)	9,040 (127)	7,760 (221)	53.9 (0.83)	24.5 (0.59)	7,600 (185)	3,350 (32)	43.8 (0.67)	9,210 (154)
Female	3,458 (†)	74.0 (0.73)	59.0 (0.62)	54.3 (0.86)	12,690 (170)	8,840 (100)	7,700 (144)	62.1 (0.75)	31.3 (0.61)	7,650 (127)	3,460 (30)	46.9 (0.64)	8,880 (110)
Race/ethnicity													
White	4,335 (†)	69.9 (0.73)	53.1 (0.59)	52.2 (0.73)	12,800 (200)	8,980 (111)	8,010 (183)	55.2 (0.70)	21.5 (0.53)	7,680 (154)	3,230 (32)	45.3 (0.61)	9,240 (120)
Black	675 (†)	88.0 (1.16)	78.6 (1.49)	54.7 (2.09)	12,430 (431)	9,290 (257)	6,630 (376)	76.2 (1.24)	55.7 (1.38)	7,160 (225)	3,670 (50)	59.2 (2.36)	8,230 (285)
Hispanic	500 (†)	77.1 (1.41)	65.6 (1.84)	53.1 (2.20)	11,580 (452)	8,380 (315)	6,450 (353)	66.7 (1.76)	45.4 (2.10)	6,920 (279)	3,570 (57)	42.7 (1.99)	8,840 (289)
Asian	372 (†)	60.3 (1.65)	47.8 (1.79)	47.9 (1.55)	13,300 (842)	8,750 (327)	8,010 (771)	53.0 (1.67)	31.7 (1.62)	8,830 (695)	3,730 (92)	33.0 (2.03)	8,480 (316)
Pacific Islander	41 (†)	62.3 (6.39)	56.0 (5.70)	48.8 (5.63)	13,070 (1,217)	7,860 (671)	7,660 (1,141)	53.1 (6.29)	31.9 (5.85)	7,840 (902)	3,360 (281)	40.7 (5.58)	9,220 (1,282)
American Indian/Alaska Native	42 (†)	81.5 (4.72)	75.0 (5.05)	61.7 (6.64)	13,050 (1,114)	8,180 (821)	7,290 (1,026)	78.7 (4.73)	50.8 (7.04)	8,000 (723)	3,790 (188)	44.6 (7.94)	8,340 (819)
Two or more races	93 (†)	75.6 (3.00)	60.6 (3.36)	57.1 (3.44)	13,330 (710)	8,560 (433)	8,560 (595)	62.0 (3.22)	34.2 (3.30)	9,030 (642)	3,580 (194)	43.8 (2.76)	8,780 (395)
Other	86 (†)	61.9 (3.54)	45.2 (3.64)	46.9 (4.04)	12,050 (1,092)	7,990 (507)	8,210 (1,084)	51.4 (4.32)	26.0 (3.70)	8,320 (878)	3,250 (243)	29.8 (4.02)	8,840 (928)
Dependency status and family income													
Dependent	4,612 (†)	70.2 (0.65)	53.4 (0.52)	53.7 (0.75)	13,110 (177)	8,590 (100)	8,600 (178)	56.2 (0.70)	21.1 (0.52)	8,330 (147)	3,180 (28)	45.6 (0.50)	8,920 (111)
Low-income⁵	990 (†)	85.4 (0.90)	78.1 (1.03)	65.2 (1.43)	13,420 (239)	8,610 (132)	7,270 (209)	82.3 (0.94)	70.4 (1.12)	8,570 (162)	3,630 (30)	50.5 (1.27)	7,530 (153)
Middle-income⁵	2,383 (†)	70.6 (0.85)	53.4 (0.79)	54.7 (1.01)	13,260 (268)	8,200 (120)	9,100 (263)	54.3 (1.00)	11.6 (0.47)	8,270 (250)	2,030 (52)	49.8 (0.80)	8,790 (128)
High-income⁵	1,238 (†)	57.3 (1.10)	33.7 (0.77)	42.6 (1.07)	12,410 (242)	9,720 (277)	9,010 (196)	38.8 (1.08)	‡ (†)	8,090 (194)	‡ (†)	33.5 (0.72)	10,970 (286)
Independent	1,533 (†)	76.9 (0.88)	66.8 (0.80)	48.1 (1.11)	11,450 (208)	9,750 (137)	4,760 (151)	65.5 (0.84)	50.0 (0.72)	5,810 (119)	3,730 (35)	45.6 (1.17)	9,310 (111)
2003–04													
Total	7,562 (—)	75.3 (0.62)	60.3 (0.49)	54.9 (0.63)	$13,290 (127)	$9,540 (82)	$7,740 (161)	62.2 (0.58)	31.4 (0.31)	$7,720 (137)	$4,140 (24)	48.6 (0.42)	$9,520 (98)
Sex													
Male	3,340 (†)	72.8 (0.89)	57.2 (0.83)	53.8 (0.78)	13,440 (167)	9,700 (112)	7,860 (177)	58.6 (0.82)	28.0 (0.62)	7,690 (155)	4,050 (37)	46.8 (0.77)	9,860 (138)
Female	4,222 (†)	77.3 (0.56)	62.7 (0.51)	55.8 (0.70)	13,170 (146)	9,420 (87)	7,650 (183)	65.0 (0.61)	34.2 (0.46)	7,740 (151)	4,210 (28)	50.0 (0.45)	9,280 (100)
Race/ethnicity													
White	5,137 (†)	73.3 (0.86)	56.3 (0.79)	55.5 (0.81)	13,240 (161)	9,510 (94)	7,880 (175)	59.0 (0.79)	23.9 (0.54)	7,540 (160)	3,940 (30)	48.4 (0.68)	9,710 (104)
Black	895 (†)	88.7 (0.90)	81.3 (1.08)	55.5 (1.68)	13,840 (298)	10,130 (202)	7,280 (270)	79.0 (1.27)	61.5 (1.64)	7,900 (249)	4,410 (38)	59.2 (1.90)	9,030 (243)
Hispanic	718 (†)	78.8 (1.09)	67.8 (1.21)	55.0 (1.32)	12,870 (280)	9,160 (174)	7,150 (278)	68.1 (1.15)	46.7 (1.17)	7,850 (200)	4,340 (61)	46.3 (1.19)	9,180 (244)
Asian	459 (†)	65.1 (1.55)	51.4 (1.46)	50.6 (1.70)	13,550 (332)	8,770 (243)	8,530 (285)	54.5 (1.74)	30.6 (1.40)	9,350 (279)	4,390 (78)	35.7 (1.28)	8,920 (317)
Pacific Islander	34 (†)	71.1 (5.10)	61.5 (4.79)	46.2 (4.95)	12,940 (1,267)	9,230 (944)	7,620 (1,235)	53.0 (5.12)	28.1 (4.85)	7,930 (834)	4,410 (310)	45.0 (5.02)	10,000 (1,149)
American Indian/Alaska Native	59 (†)	81.1 (5.18)	66.2 (6.31)	64.5 (4.42)	12,290 (849)	9,350 (493)	5,860 (1,017)	73.8 (5.79)	43.4 (4.64)	7,390 (800)	3,970 (211)	46.5 (5.70)	8,660 (572)
Two or more races	156 (†)	77.1 (2.12)	61.6 (2.12)	55.9 (2.11)	13,530 (552)	9,900 (388)	7,750 (475)	63.8 (2.18)	31.5 (2.39)	7,610 (403)	4,140 (120)	49.3 (2.34)	10,080 (524)
Other	104 (†)	72.2 (2.56)	56.6 (2.71)	53.2 (2.58)	12,340 (671)	9,280 (447)	6,870 (612)	61.7 (2.89)	35.5 (2.94)	7,090 (429)	4,230 (147)	42.9 (2.65)	9,390 (592)
Dependency status and family income													
Dependent	5,574 (†)	73.3 (0.79)	56.3 (0.68)	57.2 (0.74)	13,740 (158)	9,140 (87)	8,600 (177)	59.6 (0.74)	23.6 (0.39)	8,340 (170)	3,900 (28)	47.5 (0.62)	9,670 (110)
Low-income⁵	1,250 (†)	87.9 (0.70)	77.8 (0.80)	66.6 (1.00)	14,620 (277)	9,790 (129)	7,850 (265)	84.8 (0.80)	70.8 (0.92)	9,590 (225)	4,600 (26)	51.0 (0.91)	7,900 (178)
Middle-income⁵	2,886 (†)	72.7 (1.01)	55.4 (0.89)	58.0 (0.97)	13,450 (187)	8,560 (113)	8,690 (196)	57.2 (0.88)	14.8 (0.42)	7,690 (193)	2,440 (37)	50.4 (0.80)	9,680 (134)
High-income⁵	1,438 (†)	61.6 (0.98)	39.3 (0.82)	47.4 (0.91)	13,340 (232)	9,690 (164)	9,310 (231)	42.5 (1.02)	‡ (†)	7,930 (229)	‡ (†)	38.8 (0.83)	11,670 (204)
Independent	1,988 (†)	80.9 (0.77)	71.5 (0.79)	48.5 (0.91)	12,120 (143)	10,400 (122)	4,890 (135)	69.4 (0.79)	53.5 (0.82)	6,230 (92)	4,450 (33)	51.6 (0.85)	9,140 (122)

See notes at end of table.

Table 331.35. Percentage of full-time, full-year undergraduates receiving financial aid, and average annual amount received, by type and source of aid and selected student characteristics: Selected years, 1999–2000 through 2015–16—Continued

[Standard errors appear in parentheses. Amounts in constant 2018–19 dollars]

Year and selected student characteristic	Number enrolled[1] (in thousands)	Any aid — Percent receiving — Total[3]	Federal[4]	Nonfederal	Any aid — Average amount — Total[3]	Federal[4]	Nonfederal	Grants — Percent receiving — Total	Pell	Grants — Average amount — Total	Pell	Loans[2] — Percent receiving	Average amount
1	2	3	4	5	6	7	8	9	10	11	12	13	14
2007–08													
Total	7,527 (—)	80.1 (0.28)	63.9 (0.31)	63.7 (1.36)	$15,540 (118)	$9,780 (61)	$9,730 (106)	64.6 (0.37)	32.7 (0.29)	$8,670 (85)	$3,890 (17)	54.8 (0.32)	$11,390 (92)
Sex													
Male	3,277 (—)	77.1 (0.44)	60.0 (0.47)	61.8 (0.49)	15,650 (170)	9,930 (110)	9,890 (131)	60.8 (0.54)	27.7 (0.42)	8,740 (113)	3,840 (26)	52.1 (0.56)	11,610 (140)
Female	4,249 (—)	82.4 (0.36)	66.9 (0.42)	65.2 (0.47)	15,450 (138)	9,670 (67)	9,610 (134)	67.6 (0.47)	36.6 (0.41)	8,630 (101)	3,910 (25)	56.9 (0.43)	11,220 (103)
Race/ethnicity													
White	4,983 (—)	78.1 (0.39)	59.6 (0.44)	63.2 (0.46)	15,540 (150)	9,670 (84)	10,080 (136)	61.1 (0.51)	24.1 (0.37)	8,560 (109)	3,700 (25)	54.0 (0.45)	11,700 (117)
Black	899 (—)	92.1 (0.58)	83.9 (0.86)	67.8 (0.85)	16,220 (199)	10,730 (133)	8,750 (194)	79.6 (0.92)	61.5 (1.06)	8,500 (169)	4,140 (45)	70.3 (0.84)	10,640 (179)
Hispanic	844 (—)	84.3 (0.71)	71.8 (0.88)	65.8 (0.91)	14,760 (233)	9,360 (129)	8,690 (215)	72.0 (0.85)	50.5 (1.02)	8,400 (146)	4,000 (40)	52.0 (0.92)	11,160 (247)
Asian	489 (—)	69.5 (1.35)	53.7 (1.33)	57.6 (1.47)	15,240 (341)	8,940 (216)	10,070 (301)	57.0 (1.61)	32.2 (1.21)	10,580 (288)	4,120 (52)	38.6 (1.29)	10,430 (297)
Pacific Islander	45 (—)	81.4 (3.79)	67.3 (4.93)	64.1 (4.44)	16,220 (1,073)	10,750 (853)	9,320 (878)	69.0 (4.14)	36.1 (4.59)	7,530 (622)	3,770 (252)	53.8 (4.44)	13,360 (833)
American Indian/Alaska Native	50 (—)	85.9 (3.32)	71.3 (3.81)	61.8 (4.53)	13,130 (940)	9,210 (623)	7,630 (772)	76.3 (3.20)	48.3 (4.15)	8,010 (715)	3,930 (201)	48.7 (4.70)	9,690 (716)
Two or more races	199 (—)	83.4 (1.31)	68.1 (1.72)	67.1 (2.01)	16,570 (471)	10,300 (277)	10,150 (419)	67.9 (1.66)	37.6 (1.87)	9,890 (401)	3,990 (104)	59.1 (1.92)	10,710 (409)
Other	17 (—)	79.8 (5.18)	72.9 (5.30)	50.9 (6.42)	14,990 (1,484)	9,440 (711)	9,990 (1,393)	67.3 (5.59)	51.9 (5.87)	9,040 (1,330)	3,770 (285)	54.7 (5.64)	8,780 (888)
Dependency status and family income													
Dependent	5,675 (—)	78.0 (0.34)	59.5 (0.37)	65.1 (0.40)	16,030 (144)	9,450 (77)	10,590 (123)	62.7 (0.44)	25.2 (0.27)	9,500 (104)	3,810 (20)	51.9 (0.38)	11,630 (116)
Low-income[5]	1,203 (—)	92.3 (0.49)	85.9 (0.59)	74.9 (0.62)	16,530 (190)	9,930 (94)	8,970 (156)	89.2 (0.57)	80.9 (0.66)	10,660 (133)	4,460 (19)	56.7 (0.75)	9,000 (170)
Middle-income[5]	2,825 (—)	79.3 (0.41)	59.4 (0.50)	67.1 (0.48)	15,940 (175)	8,870 (102)	11,000 (159)	61.6 (0.57)	16.1 (0.33)	9,030 (139)	2,410 (33)	56.0 (0.50)	11,640 (132)
High-income[5]	1,647 (—)	65.5 (0.66)	40.3 (0.65)	54.4 (0.76)	15,710 (250)	10,170 (226)	11,370 (194)	45.2 (0.84)	‡ (†)	8,930 (178)	‡ (†)	41.4 (0.68)	14,240 (241)
Independent	1,851 (—)	86.4 (0.47)	77.4 (0.59)	59.6 (0.74)	14,170 (143)	10,550 (92)	6,840 (122)	70.5 (0.64)	55.8 (0.64)	6,420 (84)	4,000 (31)	63.6 (0.74)	10,780 (118)
2011–12													
Total	8,864 (—)	84.4 (0.36)	72.8 (0.51)	56.9 (0.46)	$17,260 (118)	$12,040 (84)	$10,200 (123)	72.4 (0.41)	47.1 (0.50)	$10,280 (102)	$4,920 (18)	56.7 (0.53)	$11,230 (83)
Sex													
Male	3,868 (—)	82.3 (0.50)	70.1 (0.65)	56.2 (0.61)	17,480 (187)	12,240 (121)	10,350 (193)	68.9 (0.58)	42.9 (0.60)	10,480 (166)	4,900 (27)	53.9 (0.70)	11,330 (125)
Female	4,996 (—)	86.0 (0.42)	74.9 (0.60)	57.5 (0.53)	17,090 (149)	11,900 (97)	10,080 (157)	75.1 (0.46)	50.4 (0.62)	10,130 (122)	4,940 (24)	58.8 (0.58)	11,170 (105)
Race/ethnicity[6]													
White	5,369 (—)	82.6 (0.45)	68.5 (0.63)	57.0 (0.50)	17,120 (162)	11,980 (113)	10,420 (154)	68.8 (0.50)	37.8 (0.57)	10,090 (128)	4,720 (27)	56.4 (0.67)	11,450 (110)
Black	1,209 (—)	94.0 (0.54)	90.7 (0.70)	52.8 (1.24)	17,940 (286)	13,230 (174)	9,200 (334)	84.6 (0.72)	73.5 (1.07)	9,570 (213)	5,160 (29)	71.9 (1.12)	11,120 (185)
Hispanic	1,274 (—)	88.3 (0.74)	79.1 (0.91)	60.4 (1.12)	16,400 (345)	11,340 (174)	9,130 (355)	79.9 (0.84)	62.7 (0.94)	10,330 (298)	5,110 (38)	51.2 (1.09)	10,520 (200)
Asian	603 (—)	71.4 (1.77)	58.5 (1.82)	56.4 (1.60)	18,060 (596)	10,600 (276)	11,900 (570)	63.3 (1.71)	40.8 (1.60)	13,070 (494)	5,070 (71)	38.4 (1.59)	10,560 (445)
Pacific Islander	42 (—)	82.1 (3.87)	71.5 (5.20)	55.0 (4.22)	19,830 (1,846)	13,260 (970)	12,360 (2,082)	67.3 (4.42)	44.6 (4.76)	13,310 (1,897)	5,360 (164)	50.7 (5.38)	11,970 (1,303)
American Indian/Alaska Native	67 (—)	93.0 (2.55)	86.4 (2.44)	57.1 (3.82)	16,420 (1,104)	11,110 (572)	9,940 (1,257)	85.4 (3.24)	69.5 (3.37)	10,410 (874)	4,960 (186)	62.3 (3.60)	8,910 (676)
Two or more races	301 (—)	85.8 (1.46)	76.3 (1.76)	59.6 (2.14)	18,990 (606)	12,790 (328)	10,950 (638)	73.1 (1.71)	49.4 (1.94)	11,210 (463)	5,060 (93)	59.3 (2.06)	12,120 (393)
Age													
15 to 23	6,650 (—)	82.7 (0.39)	68.6 (0.54)	62.4 (0.46)	18,020 (140)	11,640 (101)	11,090 (138)	70.9 (0.43)	39.7 (0.44)	11,510 (124)	4,890 (21)	54.0 (0.53)	11,470 (110)
24 to 29	1,048 (—)	87.5 (0.76)	83.1 (0.91)	43.4 (1.31)	15,710 (268)	13,100 (183)	6,620 (395)	76.7 (0.95)	68.6 (1.11)	7,290 (224)	4,990 (41)	61.9 (1.20)	10,800 (137)
30 or over	1,165 (—)	91.1 (0.72)	87.2 (0.80)	37.8 (1.14)	14,650 (233)	12,940 (161)	5,470 (261)	77.0 (0.90)	70.3 (1.01)	6,460 (139)	4,970 (40)	67.3 (1.08)	10,530 (136)
Marital status													
Not married[7]	7,920 (—)	84.0 (0.37)	71.6 (0.53)	59.1 (0.47)	17,680 (123)	12,010 (88)	10,520 (128)	72.5 (0.41)	45.3 (0.50)	10,700 (108)	4,940 (19)	56.4 (0.54)	11,360 (90)
Married	828 (—)	86.9 (0.90)	80.6 (1.06)	38.4 (1.18)	13,790 (283)	12,010 (198)	5,980 (373)	69.5 (1.15)	59.5 (1.28)	6,670 (208)	4,780 (52)	57.3 (1.16)	10,310 (187)
Separated	117 (—)	97.2 (1.02)	95.9 (1.25)	37.5 (2.73)	14,610 (576)	12,650 (398)	5,530 (909)	88.6 (2.00)	85.0 (2.35)	6,690 (338)	5,160 (82)	71.4 (2.68)	9,960 (350)
Dependency status and family income													
Dependent	6,141 (—)	82.3 (0.39)	67.7 (0.56)	63.3 (0.46)	18,310 (147)	11,690 (106)	11,300 (139)	69.9 (0.43)	37.0 (0.43)	11,770 (131)	4,830 (22)	54.3 (0.55)	11,620 (117)
Low-income[5]	1,361 (—)	94.2 (0.58)	90.6 (0.73)	67.9 (0.94)	18,510 (250)	11,720 (130)	10,040 (298)	93.6 (0.61)	89.2 (0.76)	12,650 (228)	5,800 (17)	56.1 (0.89)	8,960 (147)
Middle-income[5]	3,045 (—)	83.2 (0.50)	65.8 (0.68)	65.8 (0.64)	18,360 (204)	11,250 (124)	11,420 (190)	70.1 (0.59)	34.6 (0.55)	11,420 (180)	3,710 (34)	58.2 (0.70)	11,530 (142)
High-income[5]	1,735 (—)	71.3 (0.73)	47.4 (0.89)	55.4 (0.81)	18,020 (334)	12,780 (281)	12,260 (310)	50.9 (0.83)	0.4 (0.07)	11,330 (301)	3,680 (469)	46.1 (0.92)	14,370 (269)
Independent	2,723 (—)	89.2 (0.54)	84.3 (0.64)	42.5 (0.80)	15,070 (184)	12,680 (116)	6,480 (247)	78.1 (0.67)	70.0 (0.79)	7,260 (131)	5,040 (28)	62.0 (0.86)	10,470 (99)

See notes at end of table.

Table 331.35. Percentage of full-time, full-year undergraduates receiving financial aid, and average annual amount received, by type and source of aid and selected student characteristics: Selected years, 1999–2000 through 2015–16—Continued

[Standard errors appear in parentheses. Amounts in constant 2018–19 dollars]

Year and selected student characteristic	Number enrolled[1] (in thousands)	Any aid — Percent receiving — Total[3]	Federal[4]	Nonfederal	Any aid — Average amount — Total[3]	Federal[4]	Nonfederal	Grants — Percent receiving — Total[3]	Pell	Grants — Average amount — Total	Pell	Loans[2] — Percent receiving	Average amount
1	2	3	4	5	6	7	8	9	10	11	12	13	14
Housing status													
School-owned	2,219	88.2 (0.50)	72.9 (0.66)	76.3 (0.59)	24,720 (279)	13,730 (179)	15,440 (277)	78.1 (0.59)	35.9 (0.67)	16,020 (286)	4,870 (40)	65.9 (0.75)	12,690 (156)
Off-campus, not with parents	3,222	84.4 (0.63)	74.6 (0.73)	48.9 (0.73)	15,000 (188)	12,000 (125)	7,590 (192)	71.6 (0.63)	53.0 (0.77)	8,000 (137)	4,940 (30)	56.1 (0.74)	10,940 (138)
With parents	2,502	82.7 (0.69)	72.0 (0.85)	52.0 (0.86)	13,780 (186)	10,630 (109)	7,180 (215)	71.2 (0.73)	52.1 (0.87)	8,170 (157)	4,970 (35)	49.4 (0.88)	10,210 (147)
Attended more than one institution	921	79.9 (0.74)	68.2 (0.94)	51.5 (0.87)	15,540 (249)	11,880 (159)	8,380 (263)	64.9 (0.90)	40.0 (0.86)	8,700 (203)	4,780 (44)	56.3 (1.00)	10,570 (163)
2015–16													
Total	7,239	86.4 (0.26)	69.8 (0.33)	66.9 (0.40)	$19,360 (112)	$12,530 (62)	$11,940 (129)	76.7 (0.31)	44.0 (0.31)	$12,060 (98)	$4,980 (16)	54.7 (0.33)	$11,850 (80)
Sex													
Male	3,202	84.2 (0.45)	66.7 (0.56)	65.4 (0.62)	19,730 (181)	12,990 (126)	12,150 (198)	73.3 (0.52)	40.0 (0.58)	12,230 (169)	4,900 (26)	52.0 (0.51)	11,980 (141)
Female	4,037	88.3 (0.31)	72.3 (0.41)	68.1 (0.51)	19,080 (163)	12,190 (91)	11,790 (166)	79.3 (0.40)	47.2 (0.46)	11,930 (131)	5,030 (22)	56.8 (0.49)	11,750 (117)
Race/ethnicity[6]													
White	4,171	85.7 (0.42)	66.7 (0.54)	67.6 (0.52)	19,540 (161)	12,510 (95)	12,430 (184)	73.8 (0.48)	34.0 (0.49)	11,920 (132)	4,810 (27)	56.0 (0.52)	12,350 (114)
Black	935	95.5 (0.42)	88.3 (0.60)	65.9 (1.23)	20,570 (402)	14,060 (230)	10,970 (396)	88.0 (0.66)	71.8 (0.88)	11,890 (305)	5,120 (36)	70.9 (1.08)	11,370 (239)
Hispanic	1,168	89.0 (0.65)	79.5 (0.81)	67.9 (0.84)	17,920 (349)	11,680 (187)	10,360 (355)	82.4 (0.74)	59.8 (0.90)	11,580 (283)	5,070 (37)	50.1 (0.90)	10,710 (216)
Asian	618	71.3 (1.30)	49.5 (1.45)	61.1 (1.37)	19,140 (499)	11,080 (293)	13,380 (549)	65.9 (1.35)	36.4 (1.35)	14,440 (449)	5,250 (65)	31.2 (1.26)	11,160 (476)
Pacific Islander	22	90.1 (3.86)	76.0 (5.62)	71.7 (5.83)	18,300 (1,628)	12,930 (1,248)	9,300 (1,536)	83.5 (4.79)	58.5 (6.28)	10,730 (1,366)	5,250 (229)	52.9 (7.06)	12,820 (1,545)
American Indian/Alaska Native	49	92.2 (2.28)	77.4 (3.78)	64.5 (4.46)	15,740 (1,546)	10,140 (653)	10,330 (1,789)	87.5 (2.76)	61.6 (4.57)	11,220 (1,534)	4,880 (182)	37.7 (4.26)	9,400 (608)
Two or more races	277	88.6 (1.39)	70.3 (2.07)	68.5 (1.60)	19,610 (640)	12,930 (459)	12,100 (633)	79.1 (1.59)	48.0 (1.84)	12,460 (516)	5,040 (86)	53.7 (1.95)	11,650 (465)
Age													
15 to 23	5,835	85.6 (0.28)	66.3 (0.37)	70.5 (0.39)	19,850 (132)	11,800 (65)	13,000 (141)	75.9 (0.34)	38.4 (0.33)	13,200 (119)	4,940 (20)	53.0 (0.37)	12,090 (96)
24 to 29	722	89.4 (0.73)	84.0 (0.84)	53.6 (1.25)	18,010 (284)	14,820 (207)	6,820 (266)	80.7 (0.86)	69.5 (1.00)	8,140 (172)	5,030 (47)	60.4 (1.01)	11,030 (183)
30 or over	682	90.7 (0.76)	84.4 (0.90)	50.4 (1.67)	16,780 (245)	15,030 (227)	5,030 (198)	78.9 (1.02)	65.1 (1.07)	6,880 (110)	5,110 (41)	62.3 (1.15)	10,940 (140)
Marital status[7]													
Not married[7]	6,684	86.4 (0.26)	69.1 (0.34)	68.4 (0.39)	19,570 (117)	12,300 (64)	12,310 (130)	76.9 (0.31)	42.9 (0.32)	12,450 (102)	4,970 (18)	54.8 (0.34)	11,930 (87)
Married	506	86.6 (1.04)	77.8 (1.25)	48.9 (1.55)	16,750 (324)	14,950 (268)	5,870 (312)	72.4 (1.36)	56.1 (1.34)	7,050 (177)	4,910 (59)	52.0 (1.45)	10,860 (221)
Separated	48	91.4 (2.46)	87.2 (2.90)	53.2 (4.31)	17,580 (783)	15,240 (653)	5,200 (802)	87.2 (2.79)	80.9 (3.27)	8,000 (470)	5,510 (89)	67.9 (3.86)	10,740 (487)
Dependency status and family income													
Dependent	5,352	86.7 (0.30)	68.0 (0.37)	71.9 (0.41)	20,100 (135)	11,710 (68)	13,160 (145)	76.5 (0.35)	38.0 (0.35)	13,360 (123)	4,890 (23)	54.8 (0.39)	12,190 (100)
Low-income[5]	1,043	96.2 (0.40)	91.3 (0.62)	76.7 (0.92)	20,310 (308)	11,970 (158)	11,240 (301)	95.9 (0.41)	90.2 (0.65)	14,370 (261)	5,900 (16)	55.4 (0.95)	9,480 (217)
Middle-income[5]	2,691	88.2 (0.41)	71.8 (0.51)	74.5 (0.52)	19,930 (193)	11,140 (117)	12,890 (189)	78.9 (0.51)	40.5 (0.59)	12,910 (172)	4,010 (32)	58.4 (0.55)	11,720 (149)
High-income[5]	1,619	78.0 (0.71)	46.8 (0.77)	64.5 (0.79)	20,230 (306)	12,840 (226)	15,150 (325)	60.0 (0.79)	# (†)	13,300 (299)	‡ (†)	48.6 (0.75)	15,100 (285)
Independent	1,887	85.7 (0.53)	74.8 (0.63)	52.8 (0.97)	17,250 (196)	14,650 (146)	7,240 (206)	77.2 (0.62)	61.2 (0.68)	8,390 (134)	5,130 (29)	54.1 (0.74)	10,870 (106)
Housing status													
School-owned	2,089	90.4 (0.45)	69.5 (0.65)	81.2 (0.54)	26,380 (276)	13,840 (159)	17,520 (288)	82.4 (0.57)	35.9 (0.66)	17,590 (256)	4,970 (44)	63.6 (0.71)	13,380 (201)
Off-campus, not with parents	2,794	85.5 (0.47)	71.3 (0.61)	60.1 (0.72)	17,350 (167)	13,070 (120)	9,180 (167)	74.5 (0.57)	48.3 (0.66)	9,550 (120)	5,020 (25)	55.2 (0.60)	11,450 (115)
With parents	1,502	83.6 (0.64)	66.4 (0.85)	63.1 (0.93)	13,390 (232)	9,610 (158)	7,640 (183)	75.4 (0.74)	47.8 (0.84)	8,980 (165)	4,960 (38)	39.7 (0.96)	10,010 (225)
Attended more than one institution	855	84.7 (0.71)	71.6 (0.99)	60.9 (1.07)	18,060 (287)	12,440 (172)	10,490 (404)	72.2 (1.03)	43.4 (1.28)	10,730 (294)	4,870 (43)	57.5 (1.07)	11,170 (182)

—Not available.
†Not applicable.
#Rounds to zero.
‡Reporting standards not met. Either there are too few cases for a reliable estimate or the coefficient of variation (CV) is 50 percent or greater.
[1]Numbers of undergraduates may not equal figures reported in other tables, since these data are based on a sample survey of students who enrolled at any time during the academic year.
[2]Includes Parent Loans for Undergraduate Students (PLUS).
[3]Includes students who reported they were awarded aid but did not specify the source or type of aid as well as students who specified work-study, vocational rehabilitation and training, and military education assistance, which are not separately shown.
[4]Includes Department of Veterans Affairs and Department of Defense benefits.
[5]Low-income students have family incomes below the 25th percentile, middle-income students have family incomes from

the 25th to the 75th percentile, and high-income students have family incomes above the 75th percentile.
[6]The 2012 and 2016 questionnaires did not offer respondents the option of choosing an "Other" race category.
[7]Includes students who were single, divorced, or widowed.
NOTE: Full-time, full-year undergraduates are those who were enrolled full time for 9 or more months at one or more institutions. Data include undergraduates in degree-granting and non-degree-granting institutions. Constant dollars based on the Consumer Price Index, prepared by the Bureau of Labor Statistics, U.S. Department of Labor, adjusted to an academic-year basis. Detail may not sum to totals because of rounding and because some students receive multiple types of aid and aid from different sources. Data exclude Puerto Rico. Race categories exclude persons of Hispanic ethnicity. Some data have been revised from previously published figures.
SOURCE: U.S. Department of Education, National Center for Education Statistics, 1999–2000, 2003–04, 2007–08, 2011–12, and 2015–16 National Postsecondary Student Aid Study (NPSAS:2000, NPSAS:04, NPSAS:08, NPSAS:12, and NPSAS:16). (This table was prepared October 2019.)

Table 331.40. Average amount of financial aid awarded to full-time, full-year undergraduates, by type and source of aid and selected student characteristics: 2015–16

[In current dollars. Standard errors appear in parentheses]

Selected student characteristic	Any aid Total[1]	Any aid Federal[2]	Any aid Nonfederal	Grants Total	Grants Federal	Grants Nonfederal	Loans Total[3]	Loans Federal[3]	Loans Nonfederal	Work study Total[4]
1	2	3	4	5	6	7	8	9	10	11
All full-time, full-year undergraduates	$18,210 (105)	$11,790 (58)	$11,240 (121)	$11,340 (92)	$6,190 (57)	$10,220 (114)	$11,140 (75)	$9,810 (48)	$10,200 (238)	$2,430 (30)
Sex										
Male	18,560 (170)	12,220 (118)	11,430 (187)	11,510 (159)	7,040 (103)	10,440 (182)	11,270 (133)	9,910 (106)	10,460 (341)	2,450 (51)
Female	17,950 (153)	11,470 (85)	11,090 (156)	11,220 (123)	5,590 (67)	10,050 (151)	11,050 (110)	9,740 (85)	10,010 (326)	2,420 (43)
Race/ethnicity										
White	18,380 (152)	11,770 (89)	11,690 (173)	11,220 (125)	6,370 (86)	10,390 (152)	11,620 (107)	9,900 (73)	10,770 (292)	2,360 (35)
Black	19,350 (378)	13,230 (217)	10,750 (373)	11,180 (287)	5,960 (105)	9,880 (373)	10,700 (225)	10,080 (200)	8,790 (838)	2,450 (98)
Hispanic	16,860 (328)	10,990 (176)	9,750 (334)	10,890 (266)	5,950 (101)	9,100 (327)	10,080 (203)	9,250 (186)	8,630 (697)	2,620 (86)
Asian	18,010 (470)	10,420 (276)	12,580 (517)	13,590 (423)	6,080 (177)	11,900 (481)	10,500 (448)	9,300 (406)	10,120 (992)	2,540 (104)
Pacific Islander	17,220 (1,532)	12,160 (1,174)	8,750 (1,445)	10,090 (1,285)	5,940 (527)	7,990 (1,426)	12,060 (1,454)	10,810 (1,276)	‡ (†)	‡ (†)
American Indian/Alaska Native	14,810 (1,455)	9,540 (614)	9,720 (1,683)	10,560 (1,443)	6,210 (490)	9,420 (1,713)	8,840 (572)	8,450 (544)	‡ (†)	‡ (†)
Two or more races	18,450 (602)	12,170 (432)	11,390 (596)	11,730 (486)	6,630 (315)	10,450 (558)	10,960 (437)	10,060 (393)	8,590 (876)	2,590 (200)
Age										
15 to 23 years old	18,680 (124)	11,100 (61)	12,230 (132)	12,420 (112)	5,330 (51)	11,180 (124)	11,370 (91)	9,860 (57)	10,260 (251)	2,380 (30)
24 to 29 years old	16,950 (267)	13,940 (195)	6,410 (250)	7,660 (162)	8,030 (189)	5,410 (209)	10,370 (172)	9,510 (112)	10,050 (804)	2,780 (149)
30 years old or over	15,780 (231)	14,140 (213)	4,730 (187)	6,470 (104)	8,250 (230)	3,940 (159)	10,290 (132)	9,720 (120)	9,410 (598)	3,430 (257)
Marital status										
Not married[5]	18,410 (110)	11,570 (60)	11,580 (122)	11,710 (96)	5,810 (56)	10,550 (115)	11,220 (82)	9,830 (51)	10,210 (243)	2,420 (30)
Married	15,760 (305)	14,070 (252)	5,520 (294)	6,630 (167)	9,550 (293)	4,640 (256)	10,220 (208)	9,470 (150)	10,350 (911)	2,730 (214)
Separated	16,540 (737)	14,340 (615)	4,890 (754)	7,520 (442)	6,970 (428)	4,450 (757)	10,110 (458)	9,900 (435)	‡ (†)	‡ (†)
Dependency status and family income										
Dependent	18,910 (127)	11,010 (64)	12,380 (137)	12,570 (116)	5,190 (54)	11,300 (128)	11,470 (94)	9,910 (59)	10,240 (250)	2,360 (30)
Less than $20,000	19,080 (352)	11,200 (175)	10,620 (354)	13,570 (306)	5,930 (37)	10,270 (356)	8,810 (235)	8,430 (227)	6,820 (629)	2,460 (83)
$20,000–$39,999	19,360 (369)	11,090 (181)	10,850 (321)	13,420 (281)	5,400 (57)	10,390 (310)	9,160 (224)	8,520 (195)	6,320 (572)	2,510 (80)
$40,000–$59,999	19,210 (396)	10,270 (199)	11,720 (380)	12,130 (333)	3,690 (85)	10,910 (371)	10,390 (245)	9,140 (214)	8,590 (676)	2,470 (89)
$60,000–$79,999	17,730 (413)	9,700 (259)	12,380 (367)	11,360 (338)	2,740 (157)	11,350 (349)	11,150 (317)	9,600 (266)	9,580 (772)	2,250 (101)
$80,000–$99,999	18,810 (481)	11,010 (331)	12,960 (439)	11,440 (429)	6,870 (1,075)	11,320 (430)	12,900 (388)	10,600 (354)	11,270 (671)	2,240 (119)
$100,000 or more	18,910 (266)	11,800 (177)	14,080 (282)	12,420 (261)	13,760 (1,299)	12,440 (264)	13,850 (228)	11,530 (174)	12,030 (394)	2,180 (55)
Independent	16,230 (184)	13,780 (137)	6,810 (194)	7,890 (126)	7,890 (135)	6,010 (189)	10,220 (99)	9,520 (72)	9,970 (526)	2,900 (110)
Less than $10,000	17,120 (307)	13,850 (220)	8,120 (310)	9,630 (230)	7,430 (164)	7,430 (297)	10,100 (167)	9,470 (132)	10,190 (1,082)	2,890 (139)
$10,000–$19,999	15,570 (364)	13,180 (274)	5,780 (318)	7,220 (190)	6,510 (212)	5,110 (278)	9,870 (193)	9,310 (165)	8,220 (677)	2,580 (206)
$20,000–$29,999	16,520 (553)	14,180 (388)	6,120 (585)	6,810 (368)	8,440 (428)	5,320 (557)	10,400 (339)	9,700 (225)	10,690 (1,706)	3,440 (560)
$30,000–$49,999	15,780 (377)	14,210 (331)	5,140 (322)	6,290 (157)	9,770 (390)	4,000 (257)	10,420 (265)	9,580 (199)	10,320 (1,104)	2,850 (256)
$50,000 or more	14,670 (431)	13,710 (414)	6,190 (432)	5,340 (255)	10,760 (704)	4,910 (331)	10,860 (374)	9,850 (222)	10,930 (1,337)	‡ (†)
Housing status										
School-owned	24,820 (260)	13,020 (149)	16,480 (271)	16,550 (241)	5,780 (109)	15,050 (260)	12,590 (189)	10,690 (147)	11,120 (449)	2,300 (38)
Off-campus, not with parents	16,320 (157)	12,290 (113)	8,640 (157)	8,980 (113)	6,810 (98)	7,620 (146)	10,770 (108)	9,610 (89)	10,320 (372)	2,740 (75)
With parents	12,600 (219)	9,040 (148)	7,190 (172)	8,440 (155)	5,260 (81)	6,710 (166)	9,420 (212)	8,670 (202)	7,860 (442)	2,450 (96)
Attended more than one institution	17,000 (270)	11,710 (162)	9,870 (380)	10,100 (277)	6,450 (168)	9,020 (383)	10,510 (171)	9,480 (150)	9,010 (443)	2,290 (71)

†Not applicable.
‡Reporting standards not met. Either there are too few cases for a reliable estimate or the coefficient of variation (CV) is 50 percent or greater.
[1]Includes students who reported they were awarded aid, but did not specify the source or type of aid.
[2]Includes Department of Veterans Affairs and Department of Defense benefits.
[3]Includes Parent Loans for Undergraduate Students (PLUS).
[4]Details on federal and nonfederal work-study participants are not available.
[5]Includes students who were single, divorced, or widowed.
NOTE: Aid averages are for those students who received the specified type of aid. Detail may not sum to totals because of rounding and because some students receive multiple types of aid and aid from different sources. Full-time, full-year undergraduates were enrolled full time for 9 or more months at one or more institutions. Data include undergraduates in degree-granting and non-degree-granting institutions. Data exclude Puerto Rico. Race categories exclude persons of Hispanic ethnicity.
SOURCE: U.S. Department of Education, National Center for Education Statistics, 2015–16 National Postsecondary Student Aid Study (NPSAS:16). (This table was prepared June 2018.)

Table 331.50. Aid status and sources of aid for full-time and part-time undergraduates, by control and level of institution: 2011–12 and 2015–16

[Standard errors appear in parentheses]

Control and level of institution	Number of undergraduates[1] (in thousands)	Aid status (percent of students)											
		Nonaided		Source of aid									
				Any aid[2,3]		Federal[3]		State		Institutional		Other[2]	
1	2	3		4		5		6		7		8	
						2011–12							
Full-time, full-year student[4]													
All institutions	8,864	15.6	(0.36)	84.4	(0.36)	72.8	(0.51)	26.5	(0.48)	31.0	(0.45)	28.1	(0.36)
Public	5,997	19.6	(0.47)	80.4	(0.47)	68.4	(0.61)	30.2	(0.64)	22.0	(0.52)	24.3	(0.36)
4-year doctoral	2,893	16.1	(0.46)	83.9	(0.46)	70.9	(0.47)	31.2	(0.69)	32.2	(0.90)	28.1	(0.49)
Other 4-year	969	16.5	(0.93)	83.5	(0.93)	72.7	(1.34)	31.3	(1.36)	21.6	(1.32)	27.5	(0.90)
2-year	2,104	25.5	(1.03)	74.5	(1.03)	63.0	(1.24)	28.3	(1.31)	8.3	(0.54)	17.8	(0.57)
Less-than-2-year	31	28.4	(4.50)	71.6	(4.50)	67.8	(4.72)	18.2 !	(6.85)	‡	(†)	18.9	(4.08)
Private, nonprofit	1,875	8.4	(0.55)	91.6	(0.55)	76.1	(0.75)	25.3	(0.87)	73.7	(0.97)	39.6	(0.96)
4-year doctoral	990	9.6	(0.84)	90.4	(0.84)	74.3	(0.94)	23.3	(1.29)	74.5	(1.29)	38.9	(1.50)
Other 4-year	849	6.9	(0.68)	93.1	(0.68)	78.0	(1.20)	28.0	(1.24)	74.3	(1.38)	40.5	(1.08)
Less-than-4-year	36	9.8 !	(4.12)	90.2	(4.12)	78.1	(5.04)	19.5 !	(7.60)	34.5 !	(11.90)	38.4	(4.24)
Private, for-profit	992	5.2	(0.46)	94.8	(0.46)	93.1	(0.51)	6.9	(0.70)	4.8	(0.72)	29.2	(0.89)
2-year and above	859	5.4	(0.53)	94.6	(0.53)	92.8	(0.59)	7.5	(0.78)	5.4	(0.83)	30.7	(0.96)
Less-than-2-year	133	4.1	(0.75)	95.9	(0.75)	95.2	(0.79)	‡	(†)	‡	(†)	19.3	(2.30)
Part-time or part-year students[5]													
All institutions	14,192	37.9	(1.05)	62.1	(1.05)	51.1	(1.10)	14.6	(0.51)	7.3	(0.27)	16.4	(0.34)
Public	10,929	44.0	(1.18)	56.0	(1.18)	44.5	(1.22)	16.7	(0.63)	5.6	(0.24)	13.4	(0.36)
4-year doctoral	1,875	33.9	(1.04)	66.1	(1.04)	53.4	(0.81)	15.1	(0.61)	13.4	(0.87)	20.7	(0.73)
Other 4-year	1,477	40.5	(1.46)	59.5	(1.46)	49.7	(1.66)	12.0	(0.74)	6.8	(0.80)	16.9	(0.94)
2-year	7,521	47.3	(1.36)	52.7	(1.36)	41.2	(1.39)	18.0	(0.87)	3.5	(0.25)	10.9	(0.39)
Less-than-2-year	56	29.8	(4.21)	70.2	(4.21)	60.3	(4.47)	19.7	(5.84)	3.1 !	(1.37)	9.2	(2.44)
Private, nonprofit	1,135	22.6	(1.47)	77.4	(1.47)	61.0	(1.61)	13.5	(1.28)	30.2	(1.95)	28.7	(1.58)
4-year doctoral	557	24.0	(1.87)	76.0	(1.87)	57.9	(2.12)	9.5	(1.49)	30.1	(2.15)	28.1	(2.61)
Other 4-year	527	20.8	(2.42)	79.2	(2.42)	64.0	(2.54)	18.6	(2.12)	32.3	(3.36)	30.2	(2.14)
Less-than-4-year	51	25.7	(4.47)	74.3	(4.47)	64.3	(3.22)	‡	(†)	‡	(†)	18.2	(4.18)
Private, for-profit	2,128	14.6	(1.02)	85.4	(1.02)	79.7	(0.83)	4.2	(0.52)	3.7	(0.71)	25.3	(1.09)
2-year and above	1,790	14.7	(1.20)	85.3	(1.20)	78.8	(0.97)	4.2	(0.49)	3.6	(0.68)	27.0	(1.22)
Less-than-2-year	337	14.1	(1.39)	85.9	(1.39)	84.6	(1.40)	‡	(†)	‡	(†)	16.3	(1.71)
						2015–16							
Full-time, full-year students[4]													
All institutions	7,239	13.6	(0.26)	86.4	(0.26)	69.8	(0.33)	29.7	(0.44)	42.8	(0.45)	28.6	(0.36)
Public	5,023	16.0	(0.34)	84.0	(0.34)	67.7	(0.42)	34.1	(0.55)	32.7	(0.58)	25.8	(0.43)
4-year doctoral	2,849	13.3	(0.38)	86.7	(0.38)	69.4	(0.48)	34.0	(0.61)	42.8	(0.66)	29.0	(0.54)
Other 4-year	765	14.7	(0.78)	85.3	(0.78)	72.6	(0.98)	36.0	(1.61)	29.5	(1.76)	27.5	(1.39)
2-year	1,391	22.2	(0.79)	77.8	(0.79)	61.6	(0.85)	33.4	(1.07)	14.0	(1.22)	18.6	(0.77)
Less-than-2-year	19	18.0 !	(6.98)	82.0	(6.98)	67.0	(8.01)	12.5	(2.54)	23.1 !	(10.82)	9.2 !	(3.31)
Private, nonprofit	1,735	8.3	(0.48)	91.7	(0.48)	70.3	(0.61)	22.6	(0.73)	75.1	(0.82)	37.8	(0.81)
4-year doctoral	1,011	9.0	(0.62)	91.0	(0.62)	67.5	(0.89)	21.4	(0.99)	78.1	(1.07)	39.7	(1.07)
Other 4-year	684	7.1	(0.72)	92.9	(0.72)	73.7	(0.89)	25.1	(1.06)	73.7	(1.46)	36.3	(1.08)
Less-than-4-year	40	13.1	(2.20)	86.9	(2.20)	81.7	(3.76)	‡	(†)	22.3 !	(11.17)	14.0 !	(6.88)
Private, for-profit	481	7.1	(0.59)	92.9	(0.59)	89.4	(0.71)	9.5	(1.01)	30.8	(3.37)	24.3	(0.91)
2-year and above	382	6.4	(0.65)	93.6	(0.65)	89.7	(0.77)	10.2	(1.15)	36.4	(3.98)	26.8	(1.14)
Less-than-2-year	99	9.5	(1.36)	90.5	(1.36)	88.6	(1.74)	7.2	(1.84)	9.1	(2.52)	14.6	(1.55)
Part-time or part-year students[5]													
All institutions	12,069	36.4	(0.33)	63.6	(0.33)	47.6	(0.26)	18.0	(0.34)	13.9	(0.31)	17.0	(0.30)
Public	9,468	41.5	(0.39)	58.5	(0.39)	42.0	(0.30)	20.1	(0.43)	9.8	(0.27)	14.9	(0.31)
4-year doctoral	1,825	27.6	(0.74)	72.4	(0.74)	55.5	(0.71)	20.7	(0.80)	24.6	(0.75)	22.2	(0.68)
Other 4-year	1,346	39.7	(1.33)	60.3	(1.33)	44.8	(1.25)	16.9	(0.94)	12.2	(0.93)	18.2	(0.81)
2-year	6,249	45.9	(0.54)	54.1	(0.54)	37.5	(0.38)	20.7	(0.62)	4.9	(0.29)	12.1	(0.40)
Less-than-2-year	48	33.3	(7.04)	66.7	(7.04)	38.4	(2.59)	10.8	(2.31)	23.0	(5.88)	10.8	(3.21)
Private, nonprofit	1,220	21.0	(0.82)	79.0	(0.82)	58.0	(1.03)	12.5	(0.76)	32.6	(1.28)	29.2	(1.19)
4-year doctoral	622	19.9	(1.27)	80.1	(1.27)	53.5	(1.58)	11.9	(0.97)	33.9	(1.89)	34.3	(1.80)
Other 4-year	540	22.1	(0.94)	77.9	(0.94)	61.6	(1.13)	12.8	(1.03)	33.5	(1.81)	24.2	(1.38)
Less-than-4-year	58	21.8	(4.07)	78.2	(4.07)	73.2	(4.47)	15.5 !	(7.70)	10.4	(2.15)	21.4	(5.96)
Private, for-profit	1,381	15.5	(0.48)	84.5	(0.48)	77.0	(0.59)	8.4	(0.75)	25.5	(1.30)	21.2	(0.78)
2-year and above	1,140	14.5	(0.54)	85.5	(0.54)	77.5	(0.67)	9.1	(0.88)	28.9	(1.52)	22.2	(0.70)
Less-than-2-year	240	20.3	(1.47)	79.7	(1.47)	74.6	(1.55)	5.4	(1.18)	9.4	(2.57)	16.5	(3.08)

†Not applicable.
!Interpret data with caution. The coefficient of variation (CV) for this estimate is between 30 and 50 percent.
‡Reporting standards not met. The coefficient of variation (CV) for this estimate is 50 percent or greater.
[1]Numbers of undergraduates may not equal figures reported in other tables, since these data are based on a sample survey of students who enrolled at any time during the academic year.
[2]Includes students who reported that they were awarded aid but did not specify the source of the aid.
[3]Includes Department of Veterans Affairs and Department of Defense benefits.

[4]Full-time, full-year undergraduates are those who were enrolled full time for 9 or more months at one or more institutions.
[5]Part-time or part-year undergraduates include those who were enrolled part time for 9 or more months and those who were enrolled for less than 9 months either part time or full time.
NOTE: Data exclude students whose attendance status was not reported. Data include undergraduates in degree-granting and non-degree-granting institutions. Detail may not sum to totals because of rounding and because some students received multiple types of aid and aid from different sources. Data exclude Puerto Rico.
SOURCE: U.S. Department of Education, National Center for Education Statistics, 2011–12 and 2015–16 National Postsecondary Student Aid Study (NPSAS:12 and NPSAS:16). (This table was prepared July 2018.)

Table 331.60. Percentage of full-time, full-year undergraduates receiving financial aid, by type and source of aid and control and level of institution: Selected years, 1992–93 through 2015–16

[Standard errors appear in parentheses]

Control and level of institution	Any aid Total[2]	Any aid Federal[3]	Any aid Nonfederal	Grants Total	Grants Federal	Grants Nonfederal	Loans Total[4]	Loans Federal[4]	Loans Nonfederal	Work study[1] Total	Work study[1] Federal
1	2	3	4	5	6	7	8	9	10	11	12
1992–93, all institutions	**58.2** (0.50)	**45.0** (0.50)	**37.9** (0.58)	**48.3** (0.51)	**28.6** (0.47)	**34.9** (0.51)	**34.0** (0.61)	**33.1** (0.61)	**2.7** (0.22)	**10.3** (0.38)	**6.8** (0.30)
Public	52.4 (0.67)	39.8 (0.60)	32.7 (0.69)	42.8 (0.58)	27.4 (0.50)	29.6 (0.64)	27.1 (0.57)	26.3 (0.54)	2.0 (0.27)	6.8 (0.36)	4.2 (0.23)
4-year doctoral	54.0 (0.94)	39.1 (0.80)	34.7 (0.82)	42.2 (0.80)	23.6 (0.65)	31.2 (0.79)	33.1 (0.86)	32.3 (0.86)	2.4 (0.29)	7.1 (0.50)	4.3 (0.34)
Other 4-year	56.5 (1.07)	45.4 (1.19)	36.7 (1.27)	45.4 (1.29)	31.1 (1.24)	32.4 (1.32)	34.4 (0.98)	33.4 (0.93)	2.8 (0.69)	9.7 (0.77)	5.6 (0.57)
2-year	47.2 (1.93)	36.0 (1.70)	27.0 (1.62)	41.9 (1.68)	29.9 (1.43)	25.7 (1.65)	12.7 (1.23)	12.3 (1.17)	0.7 ! (0.28)	4.1 (0.79)	3.0 (0.54)
Less-than-2-year	35.4 (3.60)	31.6 (4.08)	15.7 (4.47)	30.3 (2.53)	26.6 (2.91)	13.3 ! (4.75)	3.0 ! (1.30)	3.0 ! (1.30)	‡ (†)	‡ (†)	‡ (†)
Private, nonprofit	69.5 (1.38)	52.3 (1.42)	58.9 (1.49)	62.0 (1.36)	25.8 (1.59)	55.9 (1.47)	47.6 (1.33)	45.9 (1.40)	5.1 (0.47)	22.5 (1.10)	16.1 (1.00)
4-year doctoral	63.5 (1.65)	44.3 (1.37)	54.7 (1.76)	56.0 (1.61)	17.0 (0.97)	52.7 (1.68)	41.7 (1.27)	39.8 (1.27)	6.1 (0.74)	18.9 (1.33)	13.2 (1.40)
Other 4-year	75.4 (1.91)	59.4 (2.08)	64.3 (2.46)	68.4 (2.11)	33.0 (2.79)	60.6 (2.81)	53.8 (1.88)	52.4 (1.99)	4.3 (0.80)	27.7 (1.75)	20.1 (1.58)
Less-than-4-year	70.7 (3.80)	59.5 (4.15)	44.4 (6.26)	56.6 (4.50)	40.9 (3.70)	39.2 (6.82)	43.5 (5.33)	41.7 (5.08)	2.8 ! (1.17)	4.1 ! (1.90)	2.3 ! (1.00)
Private, for-profit	77.0 (2.18)	72.0 (2.17)	16.8 (2.32)	56.2 (1.75)	49.9 (1.71)	13.6 (2.41)	55.4 (4.82)	55.1 (4.79)	2.2 ! (0.91)	1.9 ! (0.78)	0.7 ! (0.25)
2-year and above	82.2 (4.50)	76.5 (4.35)	24.1 (4.65)	50.3 (4.06)	40.5 (2.52)	21.0 (5.02)	68.5 (5.41)	68.5 (5.41)	‡ (†)	3.6 ! (1.62)	1.4 ! (0.54)
Less-than-2-year	73.2 (2.46)	68.8 (2.64)	11.5 (2.49)	60.4 (2.46)	56.7 (2.31)	8.3 ! (2.53)	46.0 (5.63)	45.4 (5.56)	1.5 ! (0.53)	‡ (†)	0.2 ! (0.09)
1999–2000, all institutions	**71.9** (0.59)	**56.7** (0.44)	**52.3** (0.67)	**58.5** (0.60)	**29.0** (0.44)	**49.0** (0.69)	**45.6** (0.44)	**44.5** (0.41)	**6.8** (0.31)	**11.6** (0.46)	**8.9** (0.36)
Public	66.9 (0.73)	51.6 (0.51)	46.4 (0.86)	52.8 (0.68)	29.3 (0.43)	43.0 (0.81)	37.9 (0.50)	36.9 (0.46)	4.4 (0.30)	7.5 (0.47)	5.6 (0.38)
4-year doctoral	71.1 (0.79)	54.4 (0.68)	49.7 (0.77)	53.3 (0.87)	25.1 (0.74)	45.6 (0.68)	49.0 (0.73)	47.9 (0.69)	5.6 (0.41)	8.7 (0.51)	6.1 (0.42)
Other 4-year	75.7 (1.29)	63.0 (1.43)	50.6 (2.13)	57.5 (1.38)	33.7 (1.53)	46.6 (2.10)	51.5 (1.66)	50.7 (1.66)	4.7 (0.45)	11.0 (1.33)	8.1 (1.12)
2-year	55.7 (1.47)	40.5 (1.08)	39.5 (1.51)	49.2 (1.34)	31.9 (0.97)	37.3 (1.49)	14.9 (0.75)	13.9 (0.62)	2.5 (0.40)	3.8 (0.69)	3.5 (0.68)
Less-than-2-year	58.4 (6.03)	45.0 (6.96)	35.0 (5.14)	48.4 (7.50)	39.7 (7.40)	26.4 (6.54)	4.7 ! (2.14)	4.7 ! (2.13)	‡ (†)	‡ (†)	# (†)
Private, nonprofit	84.0 (0.77)	67.3 (0.75)	73.5 (1.37)	74.9 (1.13)	24.2 (1.24)	71.1 (1.42)	62.6 (0.83)	61.2 (0.83)	14.2 (0.89)	25.8 (1.27)	19.8 (0.88)
4-year doctoral	79.0 (1.03)	62.7 (1.22)	71.0 (1.27)	70.4 (1.63)	20.6 (1.22)	68.2 (1.33)	60.0 (1.16)	58.4 (1.19)	16.0 (1.08)	25.7 (1.16)	21.7 (1.05)
Other 4-year	88.7 (1.08)	72.2 (1.31)	76.3 (2.29)	78.9 (1.63)	26.3 (1.80)	74.1 (1.41)	67.4 (1.41)	66.0 (1.45)	13.4 (1.20)	26.7 (2.24)	19.0 (1.55)
Less-than-4-year	77.2 (4.01)	53.3 (2.88)	64.0 (5.11)	72.7 (4.37)	37.0 (3.48)	62.5 (5.62)	27.4 (2.59)	27.3 (2.60)	3.1 (0.62)	13.7 (2.56)	10.0 (2.71)
Private, for-profit	89.9 (1.11)	87.0 (1.39)	33.4 (3.08)	63.5 (2.14)	52.9 (2.59)	26.6 (2.83)	82.7 (1.49)	82.0 (1.50)	7.8 (1.62)	2.2 (0.87)	1.9 ! (0.86)
2-year and above	88.6 (1.50)	85.7 (1.77)	37.5 (4.17)	60.8 (2.81)	47.3 (3.29)	32.6 (3.88)	82.9 (2.19)	82.2 (2.19)	6.9 (2.04)	2.9 (1.17)	2.5 ! (1.15)
Less-than-2-year	93.7 (1.32)	91.1 (1.88)	20.8 (2.75)	71.9 (2.96)	69.8 (2.97)	8.6 (2.27)	81.9 (3.65)	81.5 (3.64)	10.4 (1.93)	‡ (†)	‡ (0.18)
2007–08, all institutions	**80.1** (0.28)	**63.9** (0.31)	**63.7** (0.36)	**64.6** (0.37)	**33.1** (0.29)	**53.6** (0.41)	**54.8** (0.32)	**51.0** (0.32)	**20.5** (0.31)	**13.8** (0.29)	**10.6** (0.23)
Public	75.4 (0.33)	58.7 (0.36)	58.0 (0.39)	59.2 (0.38)	32.3 (0.29)	49.6 (0.40)	46.2 (0.34)	42.7 (0.33)	14.2 (0.25)	9.5 (0.25)	7.1 (0.22)
4-year doctoral	77.8 (0.40)	59.6 (0.48)	62.8 (0.49)	59.9 (0.55)	27.8 (0.38)	53.8 (0.53)	54.7 (0.50)	50.8 (0.50)	17.4 (0.38)	10.2 (0.35)	7.6 (0.32)
Other 4-year	82.5 (0.59)	67.6 (0.68)	62.7 (0.80)	63.2 (0.81)	35.2 (0.66)	52.7 (0.85)	57.5 (0.72)	54.4 (0.72)	16.4 (0.61)	11.5 (0.60)	8.7 (0.45)
2-year	66.9 (0.69)	51.4 (0.73)	47.5 (0.79)	55.5 (0.63)	37.3 (0.65)	41.3 (0.76)	25.5 (0.59)	22.3 (0.57)	7.8 (0.37)	7.1 (0.36)	5.5 (0.29)
Less-than-2-year	69.1 (3.87)	58.6 (3.84)	33.0 (4.74)	56.6 (3.58)	50.0 (3.97)	16.1 (2.88)	26.5 (4.79)	23.6 (4.33)	10.7 (2.75)	# (†)	# (†)
Private, nonprofit	89.5 (0.57)	71.2 (0.62)	83.2 (0.79)	80.9 (0.85)	27.4 (0.67)	77.5 (1.02)	68.1 (0.66)	64.3 (0.61)	30.4 (0.74)	32.2 (1.08)	25.0 (0.86)
4-year doctoral	85.5 (0.93)	67.1 (1.12)	79.4 (1.11)	76.5 (1.18)	23.6 (0.82)	73.6 (1.38)	64.2 (1.21)	60.0 (1.22)	29.7 (1.02)	30.3 (1.10)	24.5 (1.04)
Other 4-year	93.6 (0.74)	75.1 (1.12)	87.5 (1.06)	85.8 (1.11)	31.0 (1.18)	82.1 (1.40)	72.3 (1.18)	68.8 (1.21)	31.2 (1.06)	34.7 (1.50)	26.0 (1.45)
Less-than-4-year	92.0 (2.79)	84.4 (3.65)	61.8 (10.16)	61.3 (4.96)	45.3 (5.77)	48.2 (9.77)	60.2 (7.26)	56.8 (7.31)	26.0 ! (7.94)	5.8 (1.88)	4.7 ! (1.63)
Private, for-profit	92.6 (0.70)	86.6 (1.24)	59.8 (1.60)	65.5 (1.48)	53.0 (1.50)	25.8 (1.66)	86.5 (1.19)	81.2 (1.29)	43.1 (1.67)	1.8 (0.29)	1.6 (0.28)
2-year and above	92.4 (0.79)	84.2 (1.41)	61.7 (1.82)	64.7 (1.69)	50.7 (1.70)	27.8 (1.90)	86.4 (1.36)	81.3 (1.46)	44.1 (1.92)	2.0 (0.34)	1.8 (0.33)
Less-than-2-year	93.6 (0.82)	87.4 (1.74)	47.6 (2.52)	70.8 (2.12)	67.6 (2.14)	13.5 (2.33)	87.2 (1.70)	80.7 (2.44)	36.9 (1.61)	0.7 ! (0.27)	‡ (†)
2011–12, all institutions	**84.4** (0.36)	**72.8** (0.51)	**56.9** (0.46)	**72.4** (0.41)	**47.4** (0.50)	**52.6** (0.45)	**56.7** (0.53)	**55.5** (0.54)	**9.2** (0.22)	**11.9** (0.25)	**10.5** (0.24)
Public	80.4 (0.47)	68.4 (0.61)	53.3 (0.58)	67.3 (0.49)	46.1 (0.59)	49.7 (0.56)	48.5 (0.57)	47.4 (0.57)	6.3 (0.19)	6.9 (0.24)	6.2 (0.23)
4-year doctoral	83.9 (0.46)	70.9 (0.47)	61.2 (0.63)	67.8 (0.51)	41.1 (0.40)	56.8 (0.61)	61.6 (0.44)	60.4 (0.43)	8.6 (0.31)	8.3 (0.37)	7.4 (0.37)
Other 4-year	83.5 (0.93)	72.7 (1.34)	54.1 (1.23)	69.2 (1.09)	48.3 (1.10)	50.1 (1.32)	55.5 (1.49)	54.3 (1.51)	7.4 (0.60)	9.3 (0.70)	8.6 (0.61)
2-year	74.5 (1.03)	63.0 (1.24)	42.5 (1.14)	65.7 (1.09)	51.6 (1.30)	40.2 (1.15)	27.5 (0.99)	26.6 (1.00)	2.7 (0.24)	3.9 (0.28)	3.4 (0.28)
Less-than-2-year	71.6 (4.50)	67.8 (4.72)	33.5 (5.54)	68.6 (4.05)	63.7 (4.54)	27.2 (3.90)	20.5 (5.20)	20.2 (5.20)	‡ (†)	1.0 ! (0.46)	‡ (†)
Private, nonprofit	91.6 (0.55)	76.1 (0.75)	83.1 (0.77)	85.4 (0.77)	37.6 (0.65)	80.4 (0.85)	68.4 (0.90)	66.7 (0.88)	15.3 (0.65)	33.1 (0.85)	29.2 (0.81)
4-year doctoral	90.4 (0.84)	74.3 (0.94)	82.9 (1.13)	84.2 (1.17)	34.9 (0.80)	80.4 (1.21)	66.7 (1.08)	65.3 (1.05)	15.0 (0.92)	33.2 (1.27)	30.0 (1.26)
Other 4-year	93.1 (0.68)	78.0 (1.20)	84.2 (0.98)	87.2 (0.92)	40.3 (1.10)	81.3 (1.15)	70.7 (1.41)	68.7 (1.44)	15.8 (0.91)	33.9 (1.22)	29.1 (1.14)
Less-than-4-year	90.2 (4.12)	81.1 (5.04)	60.2 (7.07)	77.8 (6.09)	48.5 (6.54)	51.1 (8.78)	61.2 (5.71)	59.0 (7.42)	12.2 (2.62)	‡ (†)	‡ (†)
Private, for-profit	94.8 (0.46)	93.1 (0.51)	29.3 (1.05)	78.6 (0.76)	73.9 (0.82)	17.4 (0.94)	84.1 (0.85)	83.4 (0.89)	14.8 (0.75)	1.9 (0.21)	1.8 (0.20)
2-year and above	94.6 (0.53)	92.8 (0.59)	30.7 (1.16)	77.4 (0.86)	72.2 (0.92)	18.9 (1.05)	84.2 (0.85)	83.4 (0.89)	15.0 (0.82)	2.2 (0.24)	2.1 (0.23)
Less-than-2-year	95.9 (0.75)	95.2 (0.79)	20.3 (2.64)	86.2 (1.54)	85.4 (1.63)	7.5 (1.82)	83.8 (3.56)	83.0 (3.52)	13.5 (1.58)	‡ (†)	‡ (†)

See notes at end of table.

Table 331.60. Percentage of full-time, full-year undergraduates receiving financial aid, by type and source of aid and control and level of institution: Selected years, 1992–93 through 2015–16—Continued

[Standard errors appear in parentheses]

Control and level of institution	Any aid			Grants			Loans			Work study[1]	
	Total[2]	Federal[3]	Nonfederal	Total	Federal	Nonfederal	Total[4]	Federal[4]	Nonfederal	Total	Federal
1	2	3	4	5	6	7	8	9	10	11	12
2015–16, all institutions	86.4 (0.26)	69.8 (0.33)	66.9 (0.40)	76.7 (0.31)	44.7 (0.31)	63.8 (0.41)	54.7 (0.33)	52.5 (0.34)	9.2 (0.21)	10.5 (0.26)	9.1 (0.25)
Public	84.0 (0.34)	67.7 (0.42)	63.4 (0.49)	72.5 (0.40)	44.9 (0.39)	60.1 (0.49)	48.5 (0.41)	46.7 (0.41)	6.9 (0.21)	6.6 (0.25)	5.8 (0.24)
4-year doctoral	86.7 (0.38)	69.4 (0.48)	69.8 (0.53)	73.7 (0.47)	41.8 (0.39)	65.8 (0.54)	59.7 (0.43)	57.5 (0.44)	9.1 (0.31)	8.3 (0.36)	7.1 (0.35)
Other 4-year	85.3 (0.78)	72.6 (0.98)	63.3 (1.45)	71.8 (1.18)	45.9 (1.27)	59.6 (1.42)	53.2 (1.29)	51.2 (1.29)	8.3 (0.65)	5.4 (0.68)	5.2 (0.67)
2-year	77.8 (0.79)	61.6 (0.85)	50.6 (1.11)	70.3 (0.86)	50.4 (0.79)	48.9 (1.10)	23.4 (0.62)	22.6 (0.62)	1.9 (0.21)	3.8 (0.44)	3.4 (0.41)
Less-than-2-year	82.0 (6.98)	67.0 (8.01)	36.3 (10.64)	72.2 (7.51)	56.0 (7.26)	34.6 ! (11.07)	25.1 (6.39)	25.1 (6.39)	‡ (†)	‡ (†)	‡ (†)
Private, nonprofit	91.7 (0.48)	70.3 (0.61)	83.1 (0.70)	87.1 (0.59)	36.4 (0.52)	81.1 (0.76)	65.9 (0.61)	62.5 (0.60)	15.9 (0.64)	24.4 (0.82)	21.0 (0.75)
4-year doctoral	91.0 (0.62)	67.5 (0.61)	85.6 (0.84)	87.1 (0.66)	32.9 (0.62)	84.0 (0.88)	62.9 (0.85)	59.3 (0.81)	16.7 (0.87)	23.7 (1.05)	21.3 (1.03)
Other 4-year	92.9 (0.72)	73.7 (0.89)	82.2 (1.20)	87.6 (1.03)	39.3 (0.84)	80.0 (1.37)	69.8 (0.93)	66.7 (0.95)	15.1 (0.95)	26.8 (1.35)	21.7 (1.22)
Less-than-4-year	86.9 (2.20)	81.7 (3.76)	37.5 (10.42)	78.4 (3.61)	72.4 (4.87)	29.3 ! (9.48)	72.9 (5.85)	71.1 (5.79)	8.7 (2.22)	‡ (†)	‡ (†)
Private, for-profit	92.9 (0.59)	89.4 (0.71)	45.4 (2.86)	82.9 (0.97)	72.2 (0.84)	39.9 (3.14)	78.1 (0.77)	76.8 (0.81)	8.9 (0.59)	1.5 (0.23)	1.5 (0.23)
2-year and above	93.6 (0.65)	89.7 (0.77)	50.9 (3.34)	83.5 (1.10)	70.7 (0.97)	45.6 (3.68)	78.4 (0.75)	77.4 (0.79)	9.1 (0.69)	1.6 (0.28)	1.5 (0.28)
Less-than-2-year	90.5 (1.36)	88.6 (1.74)	24.4 (2.72)	80.6 (2.11)	78.0 (2.12)	18.0 (2.87)	76.9 (2.54)	74.7 (2.62)	8.1 (0.94)	‡ (†)	‡ (†)

†Not applicable.
#Rounds to zero.
!Interpret data with caution. The coefficient of variation (CV) for this estimate is between 30 and 50 percent. The coefficient of variation (CV) for this estimate is 50 percent or greater.
‡Reporting standards not met.
[1]Details on nonfederal work-study participants are not available.
[2]Includes students who reported they were awarded aid, but did not specify the source or type of aid.
[3]Includes Department of Veterans Affairs and Department of Defense benefits.

[4]Includes Parent Loans for Undergraduate Students (PLUS).
NOTE: Full-time, full-year undergraduates were enrolled full time for 9 or more months at one or more institutions. Data include undergraduates in degree-granting and non-degree-granting institutions. Detail may not sum to totals because of rounding and because some students receive multiple types of aid and aid from different sources. Data exclude Puerto Rico.
SOURCE: U.S. Department of Education, National Center for Education Statistics, 1992–93, 1999–2000, 2007–08, 2011–12, and 2015–16 National Postsecondary Student Aid Study (NPSAS:93, NPSAS:2000, NPSAS:08, NPSAS:12, and NPSAS:16). (This table was prepared June 2018.)

Table 331.70. Average amount of financial aid awarded to full-time, full-year undergraduates, by type and source of aid and control and level of institution: Selected years, 1992–93 through 2015–16

[Standard errors appear in parentheses]

Current dollars

Control and level of institution	Any aid Total[2]	Any aid Federal[3]	Any aid Nonfederal	Grants Total[4]	Grants Federal	Grants Nonfederal	Loans Total[5]	Loans Federal[5]	Loans Nonfederal	Work study[1] Total	Work study[1] Federal
1	2	3	4	5	6	7	8	9	10	11	12
1992–93, all institutions	**$5,600** (80)	**$4,320** (54)	**$3,390** (85)	**$3,520** (63)	**$2,000** (17)	**$3,250** (85)	**$3,860** (59)	**$3,750** (54)	**$2,640** (133)	**$1,360** (34)	**$1,280** (38)
Public	4,030 (39)	3,740 (40)	1,860 (34)	2,420 (28)	1,900 (18)	1,740 (34)	3,350 (42)	3,290 (40)	2,020 (133)	1,380 (48)	1,350 (52)
4-year doctoral	4,720 (60)	4,390 (49)	2,330 (55)	2,750 (45)	1,970 (26)	2,230 (55)	3,660 (46)	3,590 (43)	2,150 (142)	1,440 (57)	1,360 (55)
Other 4-year	4,240 (92)	3,850 (68)	1,710 (47)	2,430 (48)	1,960 (26)	1,530 (52)	3,200 (65)	3,120 (71)	2,150 (198)	1,240 (59)	1,260 (69)
2-year	2,720 (88)	2,640 (87)	1,170 (84)	1,940 (59)	1,760 (42)	1,120 (88)	2,500 (125)	2,530 (112)	‡ (†)	1,500 (79)	1,490 (155)
Less-than-2-year	2,250 (198)	1,950 (192)	1,100! (476)	1,930 (154)	1,760 (60)	880 (154)	3,310 (472)	3,120 (621)	‡ (†)	‡ (†)	‡ (†)
Private nonprofit	9,040 (184)	5,280 (94)	5,880 (206)	6,010 (183)	2,320 (39)	5,600 (171)	4,360 (86)	4,140 (67)	3,350 (274)	1,320 (44)	1,230 (48)
4-year doctoral	10,160 (253)	5,650 (147)	7,060 (225)	6,940 (201)	2,420 (74)	6,590 (200)	4,910 (140)	4,560 (106)	3,750 (411)	1,520 (64)	1,360 (79)
Other 4-year	8,460 (253)	5,120 (130)	5,100 (276)	5,500 (275)	2,290 (56)	4,970 (233)	4,000 (115)	3,880 (103)	2,750 (272)	1,190 (48)	1,140 (51)
2-year	‡ (†)	‡ (†)	‡ (†)	‡ (†)	‡ (†)	‡ (†)	‡ (†)	‡ (†)	‡ (†)	‡ (†)	‡ (†)
Less-than-4-year	4,910 (507)	3,980 (258)	2,490 (434)	2,890 (431)	2,140 (149)	1,940 (427)	3,520 (260)	3,410 (257)	‡ (†)	‡ (†)	‡ (†)
Private for-profit	5,460 (321)	5,130 (301)	2,590 (377)	2,290 (116)	1,950 (47)	2,320 (452)	4,910 (276)	4,840 (254)	2,410 (373)	‡ (†)	‡ (†)
2-year and above	6,670 (296)	6,110 (251)	2,820 (528)	2,780 (265)	2,060 (93)	2,670 (582)	5,590 (291)	5,480 (260)	‡ (†)	‡ (†)	‡ (†)
Less-than-2-year	4,480 (425)	4,330 (416)	2,240 (533)	2,010 (95)	1,890 (68)	1,680 (532)	4,180 (383)	4,150 (372)	‡ (†)	‡ (†)	‡ (†)
1995–96, all institutions	**$6,880** (159)	**$5,250** (61)	**$4,000** (163)	**$3,990** (138)	**$2,000** (23)	**$3,710** (162)	**$4,830** (61)	**$4,770** (58)	**$2,790** (232)	**$1,410** (40)	**$1,350** (37)
Public	5,160 (105)	4,670 (77)	2,410 (74)	2,740 (68)	1,920 (23)	2,110 (74)	4,390 (87)	4,370 (81)	2,440 (476)	1,390 (63)	1,350 (63)
4-year doctoral	6,230 (124)	5,490 (122)	3,050 (82)	3,250 (107)	1,920 (35)	2,790 (105)	4,910 (149)	4,850 (140)	2,750 (500)	1,330 (100)	1,290 (89)
Other 4-year	5,440 (235)	4,790 (166)	2,170 (81)	2,720 (91)	1,970 (25)	1,870 (60)	4,100 (139)	4,090 (137)	‡ (†)	1,450 (56)	1,380 (58)
2-year	3,130 (162)	3,110 (101)	1,530 (213)	2,020 (106)	1,900 (53)	1,100 (140)	3,140 (120)	3,210 (137)	‡ (†)	1,430 (254)	1,410 (234)
Less-than-2-year	2,440! (383)	2,040 (267)	2,120! (897)	2,190 (485)	1,650 (127)	2,360! (882)	2,870 (441)	2,870 (441)	‡ (†)	‡ (†)	‡ (†)
Private nonprofit	10,870 (388)	6,470 (137)	6,740 (331)	6,640 (312)	2,280 (75)	6,230 (305)	5,600 (128)	5,470 (126)	3,210 (328)	1,430 (52)	1,350 (45)
4-year doctoral	13,130 (727)	7,160 (176)	8,720 (735)	8,370 (674)	2,350 (63)	8,000 (641)	6,260 (188)	6,120 (160)	3,610 (933)	1,660 (84)	1,550 (63)
Other 4-year	10,220 (453)	6,310 (229)	6,040 (357)	6,090 (349)	2,280 (106)	5,590 (345)	5,340 (162)	5,220 (160)	3,300 (417)	1,320 (40)	1,250 (39)
2-year	‡ (†)	‡ (†)	‡ (†)	‡ (†)	‡ (†)	‡ (†)	‡ (†)	‡ (†)	‡ (†)	‡ (†)	‡ (†)
Less-than-4-year	5,310 (424)	4,150 (229)	3,050 (201)	3,230 (364)	2,060 (159)	2,780 (340)	4,520 (189)	4,480 (181)	‡ (241)	1,260 (81)	1,210 (241)
Private for-profit	6,150 (137)	5,540 (162)	3,010 (188)	2,470 (123)	1,940 (30)	2,350 (211)	4,940 (237)	4,920 (212)	2,300 (210)	‡ (†)	‡ (†)
2-year and above	6,850 (235)	6,110 (310)	3,340 (157)	2,880 (264)	2,010 (40)	2,860 (148)	5,330 (164)	5,250 (200)	‡ (†)	‡ (†)	‡ (†)
Less-than-2-year	5,520 (337)	5,020 (318)	2,700 (284)	2,120 (67)	1,880 (43)	1,520 (264)	4,550 (525)	4,570 (443)	2,080 (160)	‡ (†)	‡ (†)
1999–2000, all institutions	**$8,470** (100)	**$5,970** (58)	**$5,160** (95)	**$5,100** (81)	**$2,520** (19)	**$4,590** (92)	**$6,030** (59)	**$5,430** (51)	**$4,870** (155)	**$1,680** (37)	**$1,570** (39)
Public	6,140 (90)	5,260 (60)	2,990 (61)	3,520 (55)	2,490 (22)	2,630 (53)	5,180 (72)	4,870 (55)	3,820 (194)	1,720 (56)	1,630 (69)
4-year doctoral	7,410 (84)	6,180 (65)	3,840 (85)	4,170 (77)	2,530 (33)	3,480 (80)	5,620 (81)	5,300 (68)	3,850 (209)	1,780 (45)	1,680 (66)
Other 4-year	6,190 (135)	5,280 (136)	2,690 (105)	3,270 (91)	2,430 (42)	2,290 (83)	4,770 (179)	4,520 (147)	3,540 (426)	1,670 (148)	1,580 (194)
2-year	3,990 (135)	3,670 (143)	1,860 (96)	2,800 (91)	2,490 (45)	1,560 (80)	4,190 (198)	3,750 (122)	4,090 (841)	1,650 (118)	1,580 (105)
Less-than-2-year	3,490 (383)	3,050 (387)	1,900 (296)	2,930 (234)	2,410 (167)	1,750 (357)	5,090 (950)	5,040 (975)	‡ (†)	‡ (†)	‡ (†)
Private nonprofit	14,050 (307)	7,280 (104)	9,390 (238)	8,710 (235)	2,660 (52)	8,280 (218)	7,460 (117)	6,300 (93)	5,750 (211)	1,620 (41)	1,500 (33)
4-year doctoral	16,060 (359)	7,890 (149)	10,910 (326)	10,140 (302)	2,860 (81)	9,600 (283)	8,240 (156)	6,700 (131)	6,430 (237)	1,810 (51)	1,700 (51)
Other 4-year	12,930 (424)	6,930 (162)	8,480 (318)	7,880 (317)	2,530 (106)	7,490 (291)	6,910 (166)	6,020 (149)	5,070 (312)	1,490 (69)	1,330 (47)
2-year	‡ (†)	‡ (†)	‡ (†)	‡ (†)	‡ (†)	‡ (†)	‡ (†)	‡ (†)	‡ (†)	‡ (†)	‡ (†)
Less-than-4-year	7,700 (780)	5,540 (645)	4,680 (485)	5,070 (459)	2,640 (196)	4,340 (550)	6,010 (186)	5,380 (176)	5,590 (1,440)	850 (96)	850 (63)
Private for-profit	8,730 (285)	7,440 (240)	4,120 (296)	3,380 (144)	2,490 (77)	3,110 (285)	6,590 (285)	6,070 (266)	5,970 (474)	‡ (†)	‡ (†)
2-year and above	9,430 (381)	7,920 (315)	4,190 (375)	3,730 (197)	2,550 (109)	3,240 (321)	7,030 (367)	6,530 (345)	6,620 (663)	‡ (†)	‡ (†)
Less-than-2-year	6,730 (354)	6,080 (330)	3,700 (556)	2,490 (64)	2,370 (63)	1,570 (385)	5,240 (355)	4,670 (319)	4,660 (800)	‡ (†)	‡ (†)
2003–04, all institutions	**$9,760** (93)	**$7,010** (60)	**$5,690** (118)	**$5,670** (101)	**$3,230** (22)	**$4,930** (125)	**$7,000** (72)	**$6,060** (57)	**$6,100** (138)	**$1,940** (36)	**$1,790** (37)
Public	7,400 (95)	6,260 (90)	3,620 (45)	4,230 (45)	3,190 (31)	3,110 (45)	6,060 (72)	5,520 (64)	5,100 (114)	2,020 (45)	1,860 (51)
4-year doctoral	8,970 (109)	7,360 (99)	4,500 (70)	4,890 (64)	3,220 (39)	3,930 (63)	6,760 (107)	6,150 (81)	5,510 (160)	2,070 (64)	1,900 (66)
Other 4-year	7,870 (183)	6,440 (146)	3,560 (84)	4,230 (118)	3,150 (64)	2,900 (91)	5,870 (127)	5,280 (112)	5,260 (227)	1,930 (86)	1,820 (100)
2-year	4,690 (130)	4,420 (143)	2,140 (84)	3,330 (64)	3,180 (45)	1,810 (86)	4,170 (146)	3,850 (147)	3,700 (207)	2,010 (100)	1,830 (109)
Less-than-2-year	4,770 (389)	4,490 (368)	2,920 (250)	3,180 (206)	2,800 (157)	2,500 (243)	5,260 (621)	4,740 (402)	4,230 (802)	2,460! (1,180)	‡ (†)
Private nonprofit	16,250 (258)	8,480 (127)	10,270 (234)	9,620 (261)	3,390 (49)	8,860 (250)	8,800 (178)	7,040 (135)	7,430 (273)	1,810 (52)	1,670 (51)
4-year doctoral	17,650 (367)	9,000 (204)	11,590 (383)	10,660 (465)	3,460 (101)	9,950 (466)	9,790 (272)	7,600 (190)	8,220 (333)	2,120 (78)	1,980 (66)
Other 4-year	15,650 (352)	8,260 (161)	9,580 (303)	9,130 (295)	3,340 (57)	8,280 (283)	8,270 (219)	6,740 (161)	6,920 (391)	1,620 (56)	1,470 (52)
2-year	‡ (†)	‡ (†)	‡ (†)	‡ (†)	‡ (†)	‡ (†)	‡ (†)	‡ (†)	‡ (†)	‡ (†)	‡ (†)
Less-than-4-year	8,910 (647)	6,240 (375)	5,160 (534)	5,720 (459)	3,560 (333)	4,600 (607)	6,200 (584)	5,630 (470)	4,460 (774)	1,580! (549)	1,580! (557)
Private for-profit	10,480 (328)	8,550 (222)	5,070 (285)	4,300 (167)	3,230 (72)	3,880 (317)	7,640 (267)	6,580 (190)	5,730 (525)	2,660 (275)	2,730 (328)
2-year and above	11,380 (433)	9,100 (297)	5,330 (349)	4,660 (222)	3,370 (101)	4,030 (369)	8,140 (351)	6,950 (253)	6,050 (657)	2,780 (308)	2,890 (361)
Less-than-2-year	7,810 (139)	6,890 (93)	3,980 (157)	3,210 (102)	2,850 (58)	3,010 (185)	6,050 (140)	5,350 (112)	4,560 (205)	1,760 (129)	1,570 (108)

See notes at end of table.

Table 331.70. Average amount of financial aid awarded to full-time, full-year undergraduates, by type and source of aid and control and level of institution: Selected years, 1992–93 through 2015–16—Continued

[Standard errors appear in parentheses]

Control and level of institution	Any aid			Grants			Loans			Work study[1]	
	Total[2]	Federal[3]	Nonfederal	Total[4]	Federal	Nonfederal	Total[5]	Federal[5]	Nonfederal	Total	Federal
1	2	3	4	5	6	7	8	9	10	11	12
2007–08, all institutions	$12,990 (98)	$8,170 (51)	$8,130 (89)	$7,250 (71)	$3,680 (19)	$6,470 (79)	$9,520 (77)	$7,080 (56)	$7,800 (112)	$2,270 (26)	$2,160 (30)
Public	9,680 (62)	7,250 (51)	5,240 (50)	5,420 (40)	3,670 (18)	4,080 (43)	7,990 (60)	6,470 (58)	6,520 (108)	2,430 (37)	2,360 (44)
4-year doctoral	11,670 (96)	8,320 (82)	6,550 (83)	6,410 (71)	3,780 (33)	6,070 (67)	8,870 (90)	7,100 (83)	7,130 (156)	2,440 (42)	2,290 (46)
Other 4-year	10,040 (136)	7,430 (110)	5,200 (95)	5,420 (88)	3,690 (32)	4,410 (99)	7,690 (123)	6,240 (95)	6,300 (204)	2,280 (69)	2,110 (81)
2-year	5,750 (68)	5,160 (63)	2,510 (45)	3,750 (44)	3,530 (29)	2,320 (35)	5,450 (91)	4,600 (73)	4,670 (150)	2,560 (107)	2,760 (122)
Less-than-2-year	6,210 (528)	5,200 (441)	3,750 (477)	3,610 (212)	3,320 (153)	2,170! (351)	6,910 (500)	5,550 (387)	4,920 (284)	‡	‡
Private nonprofit	21,640 (307)	10,020 (158)	14,700 (221)	12,470 (186)	4,090 (51)	11,570 (176)	12,320 (207)	8,350 (164)	9,930 (224)	2,090 (35)	1,930 (35)
4-year doctoral	22,880 (388)	10,380 (192)	15,850 (289)	13,170 (250)	4,280 (82)	12,320 (231)	13,420 (253)	8,840 (213)	11,140 (351)	2,230 (52)	2,080 (55)
Other 4-year	20,620 (447)	9,720 (234)	13,710 (341)	11,880 (268)	3,920 (60)	10,940 (263)	11,330 (313)	7,920 (223)	8,750 (263)	1,970 (40)	1,780 (43)
Less-than-4-year	12,530 (1,097)	8,340 (1,134)	7,270 (1,107)	6,970 (1,588)	4,710 (935)	4,440 (1,230)	11,310 (613)	8,000 (1,208)	8,740 (1,011)	‡	‡
Private for-profit	12,890 (294)	9,160 (176)	6,990 (269)	4,050 (96)	3,200 (60)	3,720 (201)	10,260 (233)	7,040 (133)	7,340 (307)	3,650 (392)	3,840 (385)
2-year and above	13,270 (340)	9,270 (203)	7,220 (303)	4,130 (113)	3,180 (73)	3,810 (216)	10,600 (269)	7,140 (153)	7,610 (350)	3,760 (402)	3,940 (386)
Less-than-2-year	10,540 (234)	8,510 (188)	5,100 (250)	3,590 (86)	3,270 (52)	2,470 (381)	8,150 (215)	6,380 (166)	5,320 (212)	‡	‡
2011–12, all institutions	$15,510 (106)	$10,820 (75)	$9,160 (110)	$9,230 (92)	$4,580 (20)	$8,590 (115)	$10,090 (75)	$9,160 (69)	$6,980 (187)	$2,250 (48)	$2,180 (37)
Public	11,420 (93)	9,400 (71)	5,170 (75)	6,610 (62)	4,560 (22)	4,730 (75)	8,860 (87)	8,300 (81)	5,790 (237)	2,330 (60)	2,290 (60)
4-year doctoral	14,130 (125)	11,000 (106)	6,610 (108)	7,880 (101)	4,610 (27)	6,070 (112)	9,750 (112)	9,040 (109)	6,400 (289)	2,410 (80)	2,320 (79)
Other 4-year	11,730 (229)	9,800 (150)	4,920 (170)	6,440 (133)	4,650 (49)	4,410 (155)	8,790 (186)	8,210 (152)	5,630 (483)	2,020 (106)	2,050 (112)
2-year	7,120 (117)	6,740 (91)	2,480 (76)	4,910 (76)	4,460 (41)	2,320 (74)	6,200 (78)	6,060 (79)	3,380 (208)	2,460 (130)	2,460 (146)
Less-than-2-year	7,300 (989)	6,360 (1,018)	2,740 (813)	5,050 (458)	4,510 (464)	2,170! (676)	7,260 (950)	7,060 (939)	‡	‡	‡
Private nonprofit	27,250 (300)	13,300 (217)	17,870 (265)	17,780 (264)	4,710 (46)	16,720 (266)	12,550 (200)	10,930 (190)	8,460 (437)	2,150 (67)	2,050 (44)
4-year doctoral	29,080 (456)	13,700 (355)	19,410 (383)	18,370 (410)	4,690 (81)	18,260 (396)	13,120 (356)	11,420 (330)	8,700 (728)	2,280 (65)	2,220 (60)
Other 4-year	25,630 (384)	12,870 (216)	16,400 (355)	16,370 (336)	4,720 (46)	15,210 (348)	11,960 (167)	10,430 (172)	8,200 (385)	1,980 (130)	1,830 (69)
Less-than-4-year	16,190 (2,359)	12,830 (1,038)	7,610! (2,474)	7,410 (1,336)	4,870 (140)	6,670! (2,156)	11,600 (1,621)	10,330 (1,239)	8,170! (3,055)	2,750 (478)	2,790 (508)
Private for-profit	15,070 (214)	13,300 (173)	6,480 (205)	5,270 (85)	4,520 (49)	4,600 (257)	10,610 (139)	9,440 (107)	7,170 (211)	3,690 (272)	3,760 (291)
2-year and above	15,520 (219)	13,660 (181)	6,650 (218)	5,310 (85)	4,500 (40)	4,580 (267)	10,960 (151)	9,740 (117)	7,350 (222)	3,750 (281)	3,830 (299)
Less-than-2-year	12,170 (633)	10,990 (483)	5,960 (551)	5,050 (268)	4,670 (230)	4,880 (532)	8,370 (313)	7,510 (211)	5,810 (675)	‡	‡
2015–16, all institutions	$18,210 (105)	$11,790 (58)	$11,240 (121)	$11,340 (92)	$4,880 (22)	$10,220 (114)	$11,140 (75)	$9,810 (48)	$10,200 (238)	$2,430 (30)	$2,340 (31)
Public	13,420 (88)	10,330 (59)	6,740 (83)	8,050 (74)	4,840 (22)	6,100 (77)	9,750 (66)	8,920 (53)	8,160 (222)	2,550 (52)	2,430 (50)
4-year doctoral	16,060 (95)	11,870 (81)	8,140 (96)	9,380 (90)	4,750 (28)	7,390 (90)	10,580 (82)	9,650 (63)	8,260 (268)	2,500 (55)	2,400 (55)
Other 4-year	12,820 (215)	9,610 (135)	6,270 (221)	7,570 (199)	4,750 (82)	5,470 (213)	9,250 (182)	8,270 (143)	8,260 (572)	2,470 (139)	2,410 (135)
2-year	7,820 (135)	7,300 (97)	3,130 (172)	5,520 (120)	4,800 (39)	2,990 (179)	6,080 (104)	5,920 (90)	4,490 (460)	2,820 (195)	2,620 (164)
Less-than-2-year	7,230 (637)	7,110 (655)	3,200! (971)	4,690 (480)	4,130 (250)	3,120! (1,031)	7,630 (1,281)	7,630 (1,281)	‡	‡	‡
Private nonprofit	30,920 (310)	14,380 (130)	21,950 (316)	20,610 (265)	5,120 (71)	19,840 (287)	13,870 (193)	11,380 (98)	12,720 (440)	2,330 (35)	2,250 (40)
4-year doctoral	32,620 (442)	14,630 (173)	23,150 (444)	22,010 (380)	5,170 (122)	20,810 (404)	14,800 (255)	11,950 (137)	13,290 (604)	2,450 (52)	2,380 (58)
Other 4-year	29,450 (460)	14,150 (210)	20,610 (449)	19,360 (416)	5,070 (57)	18,700 (426)	12,960 (250)	10,830 (133)	12,100 (604)	2,180 (51)	2,070 (58)
Less-than-4-year	13,150 (897)	12,550 (571)	3,130! (1,333)	5,600 (469)	5,020 (121)	2,600! (994)	8,470 (624)	8,230 (577)	‡	‡	‡
Private for-profit	18,310 (376)	15,960 (330)	6,030 (415)	6,240 (147)	4,730 (55)	4,420 (316)	11,880 (222)	10,850 (191)	10,560 (653)	3,160 (395)	3,160 (407)
2-year and above	19,750 (471)	17,140 (412)	6,130 (462)	6,500 (173)	4,780 (59)	4,510 (349)	12,700 (263)	11,550 (219)	11,210 (742)	3,410 (400)	3,410 (409)
Less-than-2-year	12,580 (470)	11,380 (414)	5,290 (687)	5,190 (258)	4,550 (121)	3,510 (803)	8,680 (359)	8,090 (355)	7,750 (1,036)	‡	‡
Constant 2018–19 dollars[6]											
All institutions											
1992–93	$9,960 (142)	$7,680 (96)	$6,020 (150)	$6,260 (111)	$3,550 (30)	$5,770 (151)	$6,870 (104)	$6,670 (96)	$4,690 (236)	$2,420 (61)	$2,270 (68)
1995–96	11,270 (261)	8,600 (100)	6,560 (267)	6,540 (226)	3,280 (38)	6,080 (266)	7,920 (100)	7,820 (95)	4,570 (381)	2,310 (66)	2,100 (60)
1999–2000	12,670 (149)	8,930 (87)	7,200 (142)	7,630 (121)	3,770 (28)	6,870 (138)	9,020 (88)	8,120 (76)	7,290 (231)	2,510 (55)	2,340 (59)
2003–04	13,290 (127)	9,540 (82)	7,400 (161)	7,720 (137)	4,390 (31)	6,770 (170)	9,520 (98)	8,250 (77)	8,300 (188)	2,630 (48)	2,340 (51)
2007–08	15,540 (118)	9,780 (61)	9,730 (106)	8,670 (85)	4,400 (22)	7,740 (95)	11,390 (92)	8,470 (67)	9,330 (134)	2,710 (31)	2,580 (36)
2011–12	17,260 (118)	12,040 (84)	10,200 (123)	10,280 (102)	5,090 (22)	9,560 (128)	11,230 (83)	10,190 (77)	7,770 (208)	2,500 (53)	2,420 (41)
2015–16	19,360 (112)	12,530 (62)	11,940 (129)	12,060 (98)	5,190 (23)	10,860 (122)	11,850 (80)	10,430 (51)	10,840 (253)	2,590 (32)	2,490 (33)

†Not applicable.
‡Reporting standards not met. Either there are too few cases for a reliable estimate or the coefficient of variation (CV) is 50 percent or greater.
!Interpret data with caution. The coefficient of variation (CV) for this estimate is between 30 and 50 percent.
[1]Details on nonfederal work-study participants are not available.
[2]Details on students who reported that they were awarded aid but did not specify the source or type of aid.
[3]Includes Department of Veterans Affairs and Department of Defense benefits.
[4]Indicates all grants, scholarships, or tuition waivers received from federal, state, institutional, or private sources, including employers.
[5]Includes Parent Loans for Undergraduate Students (PLUS).
[6]Constant dollars based on the Consumer Price Index, prepared by the Bureau of Labor Statistics, U.S. Department of Labor, adjusted to a school-year basis.
NOTE: Aid averages are for those students who received the specified type of aid. Full-time, full-year students were enrolled full time for 9 or more months from July 1 through June 30. Data exclude Puerto Rico.
SOURCE: U.S. Department of Education, National Center for Education Statistics, 1992–93, 1995–96, 1999–2000, 2003–04, 2007–08, 2011–12, and 2015–16 National Postsecondary Student Aid Study (NPSAS:93, NPSAS:96, NPSAS:2000, NPSAS:04, NPSAS:08, 2011–12, and NPSAS:16). (This table was prepared October 2019.)

Table 331.90. Percentage of full-time and part-time undergraduates receiving federal aid, by aid program and control and level of institution: 2011–12 and 2015–16

[Standard errors appear in parentheses]

Control and level of institution	Number of undergraduates[1] (in thousands)	Any federal aid	Any Title IV aid	Pell	SEOG[3]	CWS[4]	Perkins[5]	Stafford[6]	PLUS[7]
1	2	3	4	5	6	7	8	9	10
2011–12									
Full-time, full-year students									
All institutions	8,864	72.8 (0.51)	71.4 (0.54)	47.1 (0.50)	9.0 (0.24)	10.5 (0.24)	4.2 (0.18)	55.1 (0.54)	9.1 (0.23)
Public	5,997	68.4 (0.61)	67.1 (0.64)	45.8 (0.59)	6.6 (0.26)	6.2 (0.23)	2.7 (0.15)	47.1 (0.57)	7.1 (0.28)
4-year doctoral	2,893	70.9 (0.47)	70.1 (0.48)	40.8 (0.39)	7.1 (0.39)	7.4 (0.37)	4.3 (0.30)	60.0 (0.43)	11.4 (0.45)
Other 4-year	969	72.7 (1.34)	71.4 (1.43)	48.1 (1.07)	6.5 (0.52)	8.6 (0.61)	2.8 (0.35)	54.0 (1.53)	8.1 (0.67)
2-year	2,104	63.0 (1.24)	61.0 (1.29)	51.4 (1.30)	5.9 (0.40)	3.4 (0.28)	0.3 (0.06)	26.5 (0.99)	1.0 (0.11)
Less-than-2-year	31	67.8 (4.72)	66.4 (5.20)	62.4 (5.04)	‡ (†)	‡ (†)	# (†)	19.7 (4.83)	‡ (†)
Private, nonprofit	1,875	76.1 (0.75)	74.9 (0.75)	37.2 (0.64)	12.2 (0.60)	29.2 (0.81)	10.6 (0.61)	66.0 (0.90)	16.5 (0.67)
4-year doctoral	990	74.3 (0.94)	73.4 (0.96)	34.5 (0.77)	11.0 (0.89)	30.0 (1.26)	13.3 (0.97)	64.4 (1.08)	16.7 (1.10)
Other 4-year	849	78.0 (1.20)	76.7 (1.17)	39.8 (1.11)	13.6 (0.74)	29.1 (1.14)	8.0 (0.69)	68.2 (1.48)	16.2 (0.76)
Less-than-4-year	36	78.1 (5.04)	74.6 (5.35)	48.5 (6.54)	13.1 ! (5.38)	‡ (†)	‡ (†)	59.0 (7.42)	13.9 (3.36)
Private, for-profit	992	93.1 (0.51)	90.4 (0.52)	73.8 (0.81)	17.8 (0.87)	1.8 (0.20)	1.4 (0.23)	83.2 (0.90)	7.1 (0.44)
2-year and above	859	92.8 (0.59)	89.7 (0.59)	72.1 (0.91)	15.7 (0.81)	2.1 (0.23)	1.6 (0.27)	83.3 (0.91)	7.3 (0.48)
Less-than-2-year	133	95.2 (0.79)	95.1 (0.80)	85.0 (1.46)	31.4 (4.40)	‡ (†)	‡ (†)	82.9 (3.51)	5.9 (0.77)
Part-time or part-year students									
All institutions	14,192	51.1 (1.10)	48.4 (1.09)	37.6 (0.85)	4.4 (0.19)	2.0 (0.12)	0.9 (0.08)	30.7 (0.44)	1.6 (0.10)
Public	10,929	44.5 (1.22)	42.4 (1.13)	33.4 (0.89)	2.6 (0.14)	1.6 (0.11)	0.5 (0.05)	22.1 (0.43)	1.0 (0.08)
Private, nonprofit	1,135	61.0 (1.61)	56.5 (1.99)	34.8 (1.51)	6.8 (0.66)	7.1 (0.76)	1.9 (0.30)	49.5 (1.57)	4.3 (0.51)
Private, for-profit	2,128	79.7 (0.83)	75.2 (1.16)	60.5 (1.09)	12.8 (0.83)	0.9 (0.14)	2.0 (0.47)	65.3 (0.47)	3.4 (0.32)
2015–16									
Full-time, full-year students									
All institutions	7,239	69.8 (0.33)	68.4 (0.34)	44.0 (0.31)	10.4 (0.22)	9.1 (0.25)	4.3 (0.17)	52.0 (0.34)	9.3 (0.18)
Public	5,023	67.7 (0.42)	66.3 (0.42)	44.3 (0.38)	8.6 (0.25)	5.8 (0.24)	3.3 (0.18)	46.3 (0.40)	7.8 (0.18)
4-year doctoral	2,849	69.4 (0.48)	68.3 (0.48)	41.3 (0.38)	9.4 (0.35)	7.1 (0.35)	4.9 (0.29)	56.9 (0.44)	11.5 (0.28)
Other 4-year	765	72.6 (0.98)	70.9 (1.05)	45.0 (1.20)	7.2 (0.54)	5.2 (0.67)	2.7 (0.49)	50.4 (1.25)	7.3 (0.49)
2-year	1,391	61.6 (0.85)	59.5 (0.86)	50.0 (0.80)	8.0 (0.51)	3.4 (0.41)	0.5 (0.08)	22.6 (0.62)	0.6 (0.10)
Less-than-2-year	19	67.0 (8.01)	64.4 (8.15)	56.0 (7.26)	3.0 ! (1.20)	‡ (†)	‡ (†)	25.1 (6.39)	‡ (†)
Private, nonprofit	1,735	70.3 (0.61)	69.6 (0.59)	35.5 (0.52)	13.9 (0.46)	21.0 (0.75)	8.2 (0.52)	61.9 (0.63)	14.0 (0.43)
4-year doctoral	1,011	67.5 (0.89)	66.8 (0.88)	31.9 (0.61)	13.2 (0.49)	21.3 (1.03)	9.0 (0.71)	58.6 (0.82)	14.2 (0.63)
Other 4-year	684	73.7 (0.89)	73.0 (0.86)	38.7 (0.81)	15.3 (0.82)	21.7 (1.22)	7.4 (0.76)	66.3 (1.00)	14.2 (0.55)
Less-than-4-year	40	81.7 (3.76)	81.0 (3.83)	72.2 (4.88)	‡ (†)	‡ (†)	‡ (†)	70.7 (5.65)	‡ (†)
Private, for-profit	481	89.4 (0.71)	86.7 (0.68)	71.9 (0.85)	15.6 (0.95)	1.5 (0.23)	0.7 (0.16)	76.5 (0.79)	8.0 (0.59)
2-year and above	382	89.7 (0.77)	86.3 (0.74)	70.4 (0.97)	16.2 (0.81)	1.5 (0.28)	0.8 (0.21)	77.2 (0.79)	7.8 (0.48)
Less-than-2-year	99	88.6 (1.74)	88.2 (1.76)	77.5 (2.19)	13.2 (3.37)	1.1 ! (0.54)	‡ (†)	73.9 (2.40)	8.8 (2.05)
Part-time or part-year students									
All institutions	12,069	47.6 (0.26)	45.4 (0.24)	35.5 (0.20)	5.9 (0.16)	1.8 (0.15)	0.8 (0.07)	27.0 (0.21)	1.4 (0.08)
Public	9,468	42.0 (0.30)	40.0 (0.28)	31.4 (0.24)	4.4 (0.16)	1.5 (0.16)	0.6 (0.05)	19.8 (0.21)	0.9 (0.07)
4-year doctoral	1,825	55.5 (0.71)	53.5 (0.73)	34.1 (0.72)	5.5 (0.37)	2.2 (0.26)	2.5 (0.26)	43.4 (0.67)	3.6 (0.32)
Other 4-year	1,346	44.8 (1.25)	42.8 (1.12)	32.9 (0.99)	3.5 (0.42)	1.1 (0.24)	0.4 (0.08)	21.9 (0.75)	1.0 (0.19)
2-year	6,249	37.5 (0.38)	35.5 (0.35)	30.3 (0.30)	4.3 (0.19)	1.4 (0.24)	# (†)	12.6 (0.15)	0.1 (0.02)
Less-than-2-year	48	38.4 (2.59)	35.2 (2.52)	30.0 (2.05)	1.9 ! (0.61)	‡ (†)	‡ (†)	12.4 (2.70)	‡ (†)
Private, nonprofit	1,220	58.0 (1.03)	55.9 (1.03)	37.7 (0.93)	8.0 (0.69)	4.7 (0.63)	2.7 (0.50)	46.7 (0.93)	3.7 (0.40)
4-year doctoral	622	53.5 (1.58)	51.4 (1.55)	32.5 (1.37)	6.5 (0.77)	4.8 (0.98)	3.5 (0.89)	44.7 (1.34)	3.4 (0.52)
Other 4-year	540	61.6 (1.13)	59.5 (1.16)	41.7 (1.18)	9.5 (1.14)	4.9 (0.79)	2.0 (0.46)	48.5 (1.12)	3.9 (0.63)
Less-than-4-year	58	73.2 (4.47)	70.2 (4.96)	56.2 (5.18)	9.0 ! (3.71)	1.1 ! (0.47)	‡ (†)	52.7 (4.60)	3.7 ! (1.39)
Private, for-profit	1,381	77.0 (0.59)	73.5 (0.53)	61.5 (0.57)	14.6 (0.76)	0.9 (0.11)	0.8 (0.19)	58.4 (0.53)	3.0 (0.28)
2-year and above	1,140	77.5 (0.67)	73.6 (0.60)	61.4 (0.60)	15.6 (0.87)	1.0 (0.12)	0.9 (0.22)	59.2 (0.47)	2.9 (0.31)
Less-than-2-year	240	74.6 (1.55)	73.1 (1.41)	61.8 (1.63)	9.9 (1.60)	0.7 ! (0.32)	‡ (†)	54.6 (2.11)	3.5 (0.63)

†Not applicable.
#Rounds to zero.
!Interpret data with caution. The coefficient of variation (CV) for this estimate is between 30 and 50 percent.
‡Reporting standards not met. The coefficient of variation (CV) for this estimate is 50 percent or greater.
[1]Numbers of undergraduates may not equal figures reported in other tables, since these data are based on a sample survey of students who enrolled at any point during the year.
[2]Refers to Title IV of the Higher Education Act.
[3]Supplemental Educational Opportunity Grants.
[4]College Work Study. Prior to October 17, 1986, private for-profit institutions were prohibited by law from spending CWS funds for on-campus work. Includes persons who participated in the program but had no earnings.

[5]Formerly National Direct Student Loans (NDSL).
[6]Formerly Guaranteed Student Loans (GSL).
[7]Parent Loans for Undergraduate Students.
NOTE: Full-time, full-year undergraduates are those who were enrolled full time for 9 or more months. Part-time or part-year undergraduates include those who were enrolled part time for 9 or more months and those who were enrolled for less than 9 months either part time or full time. Excludes students whose attendance status was not reported. Detail may not sum to totals because of rounding and because some students receive multiple types of aid and aid from different sources. Data exclude students attending institutions in Puerto Rico.
SOURCE: U.S. Department of Education, National Center for Education Statistics, 2011–12 and 2015–16 National Postsecondary Student Aid Study (NPSAS:12 and NPSAS:16). (This table was prepared June 2018.)

Table 331.95. Percentage of undergraduate degree/certificate completers who ever received loans and average cumulative amount borrowed, by degree level, selected student characteristics, and institution control: Selected years, 1999–2000 through 2015–16

[Standard errors appear in parentheses]

Degree level, selected student characteristic, and institution control	1999–2000 Loans to students — Total loans to students	1999–2000 Loans to students — Federal loan to students	1999–2000 Parent PLUS Loans[1]	2011–12 Loans to students — Total loans to students	2011–12 Loans to students — Federal loans to students	2011–12 Loans to students — Nonfederal loans	2011–12 Parent PLUS Loans[1]	2015–16 Loans to students — Total loans to students	2015–16 Loans to students — Federal loan to students	2015–16 Loans to students — Nonfederal loans	2015–16 Parent PLUS Loans[1]
1	2	3	4	5	6	7	8	9	10	11	12
				Percent of completers who ever received loans							
Total, all completers	52.5 (0.75)	50.5 (0.74)	7.2 (0.27)	61.6 (0.62)	58.6 (0.62)	24.8 (0.50)	10.5 (0.40)	61.8 (0.55)	59.7 (0.56)	10.4 (0.27)	10.3 (0.24)
Certificate below associate's level	43.5 (2.64)	39.6 (2.57)	3.3 (0.55)	66.3 (1.71)	63.8 (1.79)	23.4 (1.25)	7.9 (0.83)	67.7 (1.76)	65.9 (1.88)	9.2 (0.71)	7.2 (0.65)
Sex											
Male	39.3 (3.48)	35.9 (3.55)	3.4 (0.81)	58.0 (2.93)	55.9 (3.00)	21.5 (2.01)	8.7 (1.67)	57.4 (3.21)	55.9 (3.25)	7.7 (0.86)	8.4 (1.25)
Female	46.7 (3.12)	42.5 (2.95)	3.3 (0.68)	70.0 (1.90)	67.2 (1.96)	24.2 (1.50)	7.6 (0.93)	73.6 (1.75)	71.6 (1.87)	10.0 (0.93)	6.6 (0.76)
Institution control											
Public	27.1 (2.64)	22.2 (2.26)	0.9! (0.39)	36.2 (3.17)	31.8 (3.18)	10.5 (1.81)	1.8! (0.74)	44.6 (2.43)	43.0 (2.47)	4.3 (0.96)	3.4 (0.82)
Private nonprofit	53.2 (7.86)	49.8 (7.91)	9.8! (3.05)	76.1 (5.06)	73.3 (5.80)	23.1 (4.84)	‡ (†)	80.1 (3.50)	76.4 (4.97)	11.9 (2.42)	6.4! (2.07)
Private for-profit	86.3 (1.60)	85.0 (1.75)	8.5 (1.33)	85.9 (1.73)	84.6 (1.92)	32.2 (1.64)	12.0 (1.27)	87.5 (1.58)	85.7 (1.89)	13.3 (1.11)	11.0 (0.98)
Associate's degree	38.9 (1.59)	36.9 (1.65)	4.3 (0.54)	49.8 (1.09)	46.1 (1.03)	18.7 (0.83)	5.0 (0.44)	48.1 (1.04)	46.2 (1.04)	5.8 (0.46)	5.1 (0.42)
Sex											
Male	37.9 (2.76)	36.0 (2.82)	5.8 (1.28)	46.2 (1.75)	42.1 (1.73)	18.6 (1.05)	6.0 (0.75)	41.9 (1.48)	39.8 (1.46)	5.3 (0.72)	5.4 (0.72)
Female	39.4 (2.04)	37.4 (2.11)	3.5 (0.80)	52.3 (1.41)	48.9 (1.29)	18.9 (1.13)	4.3 (0.47)	52.5 (1.25)	50.8 (1.28)	6.1 (0.58)	4.9 (0.49)
Race/ethnicity											
White	39.5 (2.04)	37.4 (2.03)	4.5 (0.76)	49.2 (1.52)	45.7 (1.54)	19.8 (1.11)	5.0 (0.54)	50.2 (1.60)	48.4 (1.63)	6.4 (0.66)	6.1 (0.67)
Black	44.5 (4.38)	42.3 (4.26)	2.8! (1.06)	66.2 (2.62)	60.8 (2.67)	22.1 (2.06)	3.2 (0.93)	66.7 (2.41)	65.6 (2.48)	5.4 (1.03)	4.2 (0.72)
Hispanic	41.3 (5.26)	39.5 (5.00)	7.2! (2.98)	44.6 (2.34)	40.7 (2.28)	15.8 (1.60)	5.9 (1.18)	35.4 (1.89)	34.0 (1.86)	3.6 (0.70)	4.1 (0.73)
Asian	16.9! (5.79)	16.3! (5.73)	‡ (†)	26.1 (4.11)	23.0 (3.93)	9.9 (2.87)	6.1! (2.18)	26.7 (3.28)	22.1 (3.07)	6.2! (1.95)	2.5! (0.88)
Pacific Islander	‡ (†)	‡ (†)	‡ (†)	‡ (†)	‡ (†)	‡ (†)	‡ (†)	47.3 (11.14)	41.7 (11.28)	19.0! (8.22)	‡ (†)
American Indian/Alaska Native	‡ (†)	‡ (†)	‡ (†)	64.6 (11.14)	64.6 (11.14)	‡ (†)	‡ (†)	67.2 (10.02)	63.3 (10.20)	6.4! (2.55)	4.6! (1.95)
Two or more races	‡ (†)	‡ (†)	‡ (†)	52.1 (6.13)	51.5 (5.97)	21.9 (5.24)	6.2! (2.47)	47.1 (5.10)	45.5 (5.18)	‡ (†)	‡ (†)
Other[2]	‡ (†)	‡ (†)	‡ (†)	‡ (†)	‡ (†)	‡ (†)	‡ (†)	‡ (†)	‡ (†)	‡ (†)	‡ (†)
Dependency status											
Dependent	36.7 (2.91)	35.6 (2.89)	8.9 (1.38)	41.3 (1.57)	38.6 (1.54)	16.2 (1.10)	7.9 (0.79)	34.9 (1.57)	33.2 (1.50)	4.4 (0.51)	5.3 (0.59)
Independent	40.1 (1.87)	37.6 (2.04)	1.7 (0.50)	54.7 (1.39)	50.4 (1.34)	20.2 (1.01)	3.3 (0.48)	55.4 (1.29)	53.4 (1.35)	6.5 (0.65)	5.0 (0.59)
Institution control											
Public	32.6 (1.66)	30.6 (1.69)	1.9 (0.48)	42.1 (1.28)	38.1 (1.17)	14.9 (0.87)	3.2 (0.40)	40.9 (1.15)	38.8 (1.15)	4.8 (0.49)	3.9 (0.47)
Private nonprofit	45.7 (5.92)	43.0 (5.63)	11.1! (3.83)	86.9 (5.23)	84.8 (6.80)	43.2 (6.75)	12.5! (4.28)	83.9 (3.01)	83.1 (3.26)	11.9 (3.49)	9.0 (1.99)
Private for-profit	92.5 (1.29)	91.6 (1.20)	22.4 (3.49)	88.3 (1.77)	86.4 (1.87)	37.2 (1.93)	14.1 (1.63)	88.3 (1.16)	87.8 (1.15)	10.6 (0.86)	12.4 (1.02)
Bachelor's degree	62.2 (0.70)	61.0 (0.70)	10.2 (0.40)	69.0 (0.75)	66.3 (0.72)	29.8 (0.79)	15.5 (0.68)	68.9 (0.62)	66.7 (0.64)	13.8 (0.33)	14.6 (0.36)
Sex											
Male	61.4 (1.00)	60.2 (1.01)	10.6 (0.56)	67.0 (1.39)	63.9 (1.37)	29.4 (1.20)	15.1 (1.00)	65.7 (0.85)	63.3 (0.86)	13.3 (0.53)	14.8 (0.57)
Female	62.8 (0.94)	61.6 (0.92)	9.8 (0.54)	70.5 (0.94)	68.2 (0.92)	30.1 (1.04)	15.9 (0.92)	71.4 (0.71)	69.3 (0.75)	14.2 (0.44)	14.4 (0.46)
Race/ethnicity											
White	60.7 (0.87)	59.5 (0.85)	10.2 (0.45)	67.5 (0.94)	64.8 (0.92)	30.2 (1.03)	16.0 (0.87)	69.4 (0.69)	67.1 (0.70)	15.5 (0.45)	15.7 (0.44)
Black	80.5 (1.81)	80.0 (1.82)	13.9 (1.66)	84.2 (1.78)	82.0 (1.92)	33.2 (2.37)	16.9 (1.83)	84.9 (1.17)	83.8 (1.20)	10.6 (1.03)	16.7 (1.23)
Hispanic	68.7 (1.86)	67.1 (2.00)	11.7 (1.69)	71.9 (2.42)	69.2 (2.32)	30.0 (2.08)	15.1 (1.82)	66.6 (1.57)	64.7 (1.59)	10.2 (0.80)	11.8 (0.94)
Asian	50.2 (2.43)	49.0 (2.55)	4.3 (0.85)	47.2 (3.22)	42.7 (3.02)	20.5 (2.49)	7.8 (1.70)	45.1 (2.04)	41.4 (1.98)	10.6 (1.02)	8.7 (1.19)
Pacific Islander	66.7 (6.35)	66.7 (6.35)	19.1 (5.45)	61.5 (11.92)	60.2 (12.04)	19.5! (8.06)	‡ (†)	89.4 (4.56)	80.7 (8.09)	18.3! (8.05)	14.1! (5.77)
American Indian/Alaska Native	75.2 (6.58)	71.8 (6.80)	3.8! (1.73)	81.0 (3.68)	78.7 (3.94)	31.7 (4.43)	21.0 (4.63)	76.1 (5.87)	69.9 (6.68)	14.4 (4.23)	6.9! (2.22)
Two or more races	55.0 (5.12)	52.7 (5.48)	7.6 (1.95)	‡ (†)	‡ (†)	‡ (†)	‡ (†)	72.9 (2.35)	70.1 (2.60)	17.5 (2.58)	17.1 (2.01)
Other[2]	53.5 (6.22)	53.1 (6.19)	6.3! (2.25)	‡ (†)	‡ (†)	‡ (†)	‡ (†)	‡ (†)	‡ (†)	‡ (†)	‡ (†)
Dependency status											
Dependent	59.2 (0.95)	58.0 (0.92)	14.4 (0.63)	64.9 (1.09)	61.6 (1.06)	29.8 (1.02)	21.0 (0.96)	65.9 (0.69)	63.4 (0.70)	15.9 (0.43)	18.9 (0.54)
Independent	65.9 (0.92)	64.8 (0.94)	4.9 (0.34)	74.1 (1.16)	72.2 (1.13)	29.7 (1.19)	8.6 (0.76)	72.6 (0.92)	70.6 (0.97)	11.3 (0.52)	9.3 (0.50)
Institution control											
Public	60.0 (0.80)	58.8 (0.81)	8.3 (0.42)	64.1 (0.89)	61.2 (0.86)	25.9 (0.84)	13.5 (0.69)	66.4 (0.68)	64.1 (0.66)	11.7 (0.40)	13.7 (0.45)
Private nonprofit	66.2 (1.16)	65.2 (1.17)	14.1 (0.93)	73.5 (1.72)	70.7 (1.74)	34.6 (1.83)	21.5 (1.75)	69.2 (0.94)	66.7 (0.96)	17.9 (0.75)	17.0 (0.66)
Private for-profit	77.2 (4.41)	77.0 (4.45)	10.8! (3.55)	87.2 (1.62)	86.3 (1.76)	40.5 (1.76)	10.9 (1.17)	86.5 (1.95)	85.3 (2.43)	15.1 (1.16)	12.7 (1.63)

See notes at end of table.

Table 331.95. Percentage of undergraduate degree/certificate completers who ever received loans and average cumulative amount borrowed, by degree level, selected student characteristics, and institution control: Selected years, 1999–2000 through 2015–16—Continued

[Standard errors appear in parentheses]

Average cumulative loan amount for students with loans (current dollars)[3]

Degree level, selected student characteristic, and institution control	1999–2000 Total loans to students	1999–2000 Federal loan to students	1999–2000 Parent PLUS Loans[1]	2011–12 Total loans to students	2011–12 Federal loans to students	2011–12 Nonfederal loans	2011–12 Parent PLUS Loans[1]	2015–16 Total loans to students	2015–16 Federal loan to students	2015–16 Nonfederal loans	2015–16 Parent PLUS Loans[1]
1	2	3	4	5	6	7	8	9	10	11	12
Total, all completers	$14,260 (186)	$13,540 (162)	$12,630 (443)	$23,050 (285)	$19,510 (208)	$11,210 (450)	$22,990 (1,197)	$24,480 (336)	$22,520 (305)	$16,160 (439)	$27,170 (676)
Certificate below associate's level	7,790 (418)	7,150 (330)	6,850 (1,081)	13,280 (374)	11,380 (343)	6,630 (526)	8,900 (612)	15,520 (502)	14,280 (413)	12,080 (1,649)	12,920 (1,158)
Sex											
Male	8,110 (533)	7,550 (544)	8,290 (2,316)	13,370 (743)	10,970 (629)	7,540 (1,314)	10,080 (1,199)	15,380 (1,091)	13,760 (891)	14,630 (3,942)	16,320 (2,136)
Female	7,590 (492)	6,900 (373)	5,720 (941)	13,250 (393)	11,520 (357)	6,280 (510)	8,300 (775)	15,590 (476)	14,520 (423)	10,950 (1,549)	10,450 (1,172)
Institution control											
Public	7,640 (819)	7,540 (623)	†	12,420 (1,151)	11,030 (1,095)	9,410 (2,241)	‡	16,400 (1,080)	15,550 (946)	13,520! (6,105)	17,470! (6,447)
Private nonprofit	11,240 (2,280)	9,880 (1,828)	9,680 (2,443)	15,820 (2,721)	11,850 (1,463)	14,530! (6,937)	‡	17,110 (2,536)	15,840 (1,951)	11,040 (1,616)	11,110 (943)
Private for-profit	7,470 (323)	6,540 (287)	6,260 (1,604)	13,320 (345)	11,430 (329)	5,510 (338)	9,180 (650)	14,880 (434)	13,480 (326)	‡	‡
Associate's degree	9,490 (334)	8,840 (339)	7,630 (1,046)	17,160 (359)	15,130 (305)	8,370 (413)	14,830 (1,095)	18,550 (408)	18,060 (392)	9,950 (1,136)	12,980 (1,148)
Sex											
Male	9,320 (698)	8,590 (663)	7,860 (2,013)	15,950 (536)	13,930 (418)	8,090 (561)	16,000 (1,696)	17,010 (652)	16,150 (552)	13,220 (2,547)	13,500 (1,712)
Female	9,570 (436)	8,970 (384)	7,430 (803)	17,900 (535)	15,850 (447)	8,570 (621)	13,690 (1,445)	19,420 (492)	19,110 (485)	7,970 (792)	12,580 (1,338)
Race/ethnicity											
White	9,590 (480)	8,910 (433)	8,510 (1,285)	17,110 (485)	14,630 (377)	8,810 (577)	15,400 (1,429)	17,760 (533)	17,100 (486)	10,210 (1,837)	13,350 (1,638)
Black	9,500 (771)	8,590 (659)	†	19,280 (922)	17,580 (783)	9,380 (1,321)	15,050 (4,419)	22,300 (834)	21,930 (792)	9,020 (2,182)	11,310 (1,748)
Hispanic	8,840 (2,037)	9,090 (2,124)	†	15,170 (912)	14,020 (786)	6,650 (667)	12,220 (1,572)	15,970 (904)	15,590 (928)	9,340 (2,170)	12,440 (1,563)
Asian	‡	‡	†	13,580 (1,965)	13,400 (1,786)	4,640 (902)	†	16,830 (1,772)	17,720 (1,981)	‡	†
Pacific Islander	‡	‡	†	‡	‡	‡	†	‡	‡	‡	†
American Indian/Alaska Native	‡	‡	†	22,330 (3,730)	22,100 (3,720)	‡	†	18,230 (3,431)	17,830 (3,110)	‡	†
Two or more races	‡	‡	†	17,570 (1,740)	15,260 (1,453)	5,920 (1,367)	†	21,790 (2,159)	20,940 (2,134)	‡	†
Other[2]	‡	‡	†	‡	‡	‡	†	‡	‡	‡	†
Dependency status											
Dependent	8,280 (530)	7,400 (452)	8,830 (1,306)	13,240 (391)	11,200 (391)	7,090 (618)	15,520 (1,739)	12,140 (438)	11,660 (440)	8,340 (1,100)	15,470 (1,677)
Independent	10,120 (479)	9,630 (459)	‡	18,860 (420)	16,860 (420)	8,960 (534)	13,880 (1,419)	20,780 (474)	20,250 (448)	10,550 (1,504)	11,510 (1,381)
Institution control											
Public	8,060 (431)	7,360 (398)	‡	13,970 (349)	12,300 (315)	8,080 (538)	12,070 (1,154)	15,640 (511)	15,230 (494)	10,110 (1,639)	11,600 (1,490)
Private nonprofit	11,850 (1,035)	11,950 (999)	9,550 (1,804)	25,310 (2,076)	20,420 (1,564)	10,790 (2,742)	17,590 (1,854)	24,830 (1,159)	23,890 (1,239)	8,180 (2,395)	14,950 (2,567)
Private for-profit	13,440 (685)	12,540 (672)	†	24,680 (624)	21,550 (537)	‡	‡	26,420 (512)	25,340 (537)	10,220 (718)	15,740 (1,994)
Bachelor's degree	17,480 (204)	16,530 (180)	14,350 (548)	29,380 (456)	24,400 (295)	13,760 (704)	27,350 (1,613)	29,910 (402)	27,050 (384)	18,700 (432)	32,600 (796)
Sex											
Male	17,470 (247)	16,530 (232)	14,730 (784)	29,030 (666)	23,740 (451)	14,630 (1,044)	29,780 (3,015)	28,920 (477)	26,120 (429)	18,760 (800)	33,790 (1,296)
Female	17,490 (256)	16,530 (230)	14,050 (627)	29,650 (551)	24,890 (378)	13,090 (857)	25,530 (1,602)	30,610 (451)	27,710 (420)	18,650 (641)	31,660 (967)
Race/ethnicity											
White	17,370 (211)	16,390 (195)	14,720 (591)	29,060 (579)	23,690 (354)	14,050 (766)	27,450 (2,033)	30,090 (346)	26,460 (325)	20,040 (595)	34,370 (1,088)
Black	19,510 (793)	18,760 (718)	10,880 (1,006)	33,020 (1,066)	29,200 (842)	11,620 (1,662)	24,490 (4,344)	34,000 (877)	32,370 (809)	16,450 (1,555)	24,800 (2,009)
Hispanic	17,450 (821)	16,270 (626)	13,810 (1,693)	29,520 (1,584)	23,710 (825)	16,050 (2,820)	26,470 (3,900)	26,820 (774)	25,420 (725)	13,900 (1,028)	29,440 (2,070)
Asian	14,540 (619)	13,990 (545)	20,260 (4,188)	23,130 (1,259)	20,740 (1,041)	10,070 (2,255)	†	25,450 (1,094)	22,770 (882)	19,250 (2,191)	34,080 (3,962)
Pacific Islander	18,380 (1,787)	16,850 (1,222)	‡	‡	‡	‡	†	26,520 (3,981)	27,690 (3,236)	‡	†
American Indian/Alaska Native	18,770 (1,553)	18,290 (1,646)	‡	28,050 (1,731)	23,950 (1,427)	12,250 (2,067)	†	26,380 (2,659)	25,550 (2,696)	14,490 (1,605)	40,070 (3,890)
Two or more races	17,210 (1,352)	16,470 (1,229)	‡	‡	‡	‡	†	29,680 (1,097)	27,280 (940)	‡	†
Other[2]	‡	‡	†	‡	‡	‡	†	‡	‡	‡	†
Dependency status											
Dependent	16,910 (221)	15,620 (177)	15,680 (671)	26,070 (575)	20,370 (285)	14,700 (917)	28,410 (1,566)	26,760 (282)	22,450 (199)	21,340 (575)	36,790 (1,047)
Independent	18,110 (320)	17,540 (300)	9,490 (802)	33,040 (637)	28,740 (481)	12,570 (905)	24,060 (4,374)	33,340 (649)	32,010 (587)	14,230 (634)	22,420 (1,257)
Institution control											
Public	16,210 (233)	15,700 (213)	11,600 (550)	25,640 (454)	22,030 (336)	11,400 (621)	20,460 (1,080)	26,930 (278)	25,000 (235)	15,770 (611)	27,530 (990)
Private nonprofit	19,620 (373)	17,810 (313)	17,950 (810)	32,310 (1,181)	24,610 (594)	18,370 (1,698)	37,130 (3,739)	31,890 (453)	26,670 (331)	23,840 (766)	41,940 (1,853)
Private for-profit	24,040 (1,204)	23,170 (1,160)	†	40,040 (798)	34,880 (612)	‡	25,650 (2,506)	41,320 (1,592)	39,150 (1,303)	15,460 (1,060)	31,890 (2,316)

See notes at end of table.

Table 331.95. Percentage of undergraduate degree/certificate completers who ever received loans and average cumulative amount borrowed, by degree level, selected student characteristics, and institution control: Selected years, 1999–2000 through 2015–16—Continued

[Standard errors appear in parentheses]

Average cumulative loan amount for students with loans (constant 2018–19 dollars)[3,4]

Degree level, selected student characteristic, and institution control	1999–2000 Total loans to students	1999–2000 Federal loan to students	1999–2000 Parent PLUS Loans[1]	2011–12 Total loans to students	2011–12 Federal loans to students	2011–12 Nonfederal loans	2011–12 Parent PLUS Loans[1]	2015–16 Total loans to students	2015–16 Federal loans to students	2015–16 Nonfederal loans	2015–16 Parent PLUS Loans[1]
1	2	3	4	5	6	7	8	9	10	11	12
Total, all completers	$21,330 (279)	$20,250 (243)	$18,890 (662)	$25,660 (317)	$21,710 (231)	$12,480 (500)	$25,590 (1,332)	$26,020 (533)	$23,940 (324)	$17,180 (467)	$28,880 (718)
Certificate below associate's level	11,660 (626)	10,700 (494)	10,250 (1,617)	14,780 (416)	12,660 (382)	7,380 (586)	9,900 (681)	16,500 (357)	15,180 (439)	12,840 (1,753)	13,740 (1,231)
Sex											
Male	12,130 (797)	11,300 (814)	12,410 (3,465)	14,880 (827)	12,210 (700)	8,390 (1,462)	11,220 (1,335)	16,340 (1,160)	14,630 (948)	15,550 (4,190)	17,350 (2,271)
Female	11,360 (737)	10,330 (558)	8,560 (1,408)	14,740 (437)	12,830 (397)	6,990 (567)	9,230 (863)	16,570 (506)	15,430 (449)	11,640 (1,647)	11,110 (1,246)
Institution control											
Public	11,430 (1,225)	11,280 (932)	‡	13,820 (1,281)	12,280 (1,219)	10,470 (2,494)	†	17,430 (1,148)	16,530 (1,005)	14,370! (6,490)	18,570! (6,852)
Private nonprofit	16,810 (3,410)	14,780 (2,734)	14,490 (3,655)	17,610 (3,029)	13,190 (1,629)	16,170! (7,721)	10,220 (723)	18,190 (2,695)	16,830 (2,073)	14,370! (1,717)	11,810 (1,002)
Private for-profit	11,180 (484)	9,790 (429)	9,360 (2,399)	14,830 (384)	12,720 (366)	6,130 (376)	†	15,820 (461)	14,320 (346)	11,740 (1,717)	†
Associate's degree	14,190 (500)	13,230 (507)	11,420 (1,564)	19,100 (400)	16,840 (340)	9,320 (459)	16,510 (1,219)	19,720 (434)	19,200 (416)	10,570 (1,207)	13,800 (1,220)
Sex											
Male	13,940 (1,044)	12,850 (993)	11,760 (3,011)	17,750 (597)	15,500 (466)	9,000 (624)	17,800 (1,887)	18,080 (693)	17,170 (587)	14,050 (2,708)	14,350 (1,820)
Female	14,320 (653)	13,420 (575)	11,120 (1,201)	19,930 (595)	17,640 (497)	9,540 (691)	15,230 (1,609)	20,640 (523)	20,320 (516)	8,470 (842)	13,370 (1,422)
Race/ethnicity											
White	14,340 (717)	13,320 (649)	12,730 (1,922)	19,050 (1,026)	16,280 (420)	9,800 (642)	17,140 (1,591)	18,880 (567)	18,170 (516)	10,860 (1,952)	14,190 (1,741)
Black	14,210 (1,153)	12,850 (986)	‡	21,460 (1,015)	19,560 (871)	10,440 (1,470)	16,750 (4,918)	23,710 (887)	23,310 (841)	9,580 (2,319)	12,020 (1,858)
Hispanic	13,230 (3,047)	13,590 (3,178)	†	16,880 (2,187)	15,600 (875)	7,400 (743)	13,600 (1,750)	16,980 (961)	16,570 (987)	10,380 (1,763)	13,230 (1,662)
Asian	‡	‡	‡	15,110 (2,187)	14,920 (1,987)	5,160 (1,003)	†	17,890 (1,883)	18,830 (2,105)	9,930 (2,307)	‡
Pacific Islander	†	†	†	†	†	†	†	†	†	†	†
American Indian/Alaska Native	‡	‡	‡	22,330 (3,730)	22,100 (3,720)	6,590 (1,521)	†	19,370 (3,647)	18,950 (3,306)	‡	‡
Two or more races	‡	‡	†	19,560 (1,937)	16,980 (1,617)	‡	†	23,170 (2,295)	22,260 (2,269)	‡	†
Other[2]	22,260 (2,061)			†	†	†	†	†	†	†	†
Dependency status											
Dependent	12,390 (793)	11,070 (676)	13,200 (1,954)	14,740 (570)	12,460 (436)	7,900 (688)	17,280 (1,936)	12,900 (466)	12,390 (468)	8,870 (1,169)	16,440 (1,783)
Independent	15,130 (716)	14,400 (687)	‡	20,990 (525)	18,760 (468)	9,970 (594)	15,450 (1,579)	22,090 (504)	21,530 (476)	11,210 (1,599)	16,230 (1,468)
Institution control											
Public	12,060 (645)	11,020 (596)	‡	15,550 (388)	13,690 (351)	8,990 (599)	13,440 (1,285)	16,620 (544)	16,190 (525)	10,740 (1,743)	12,330 (1,584)
Private nonprofit	17,720 (1,548)	17,880 (1,495)	‡	28,170 (2,311)	22,730 (1,741)	12,010 (3,052)	19,580 (2,064)	26,390 (1,232)	25,400 (1,317)	8,690 (2,546)	15,900 (2,728)
Private for-profit	20,110 (1,025)	18,770 (1,006)	14,290 (2,698)	27,470 (695)	23,980 (598)	9,510 (540)	†	28,080 (544)	26,940 (571)	10,860 (763)	16,730 (2,120)
Bachelor's degree	26,150 (305)	24,730 (270)	21,470 (820)	32,700 (508)	27,160 (329)	15,310 (784)	30,440 (1,796)	31,790 (427)	28,760 (408)	19,870 (459)	34,650 (846)
Sex											
Male	26,130 (370)	24,730 (347)	22,040 (1,173)	32,310 (741)	26,420 (502)	16,280 (1,162)	33,140 (3,355)	30,740 (507)	27,760 (456)	19,940 (851)	35,920 (1,377)
Female	26,160 (383)	24,740 (344)	21,010 (938)	33,000 (614)	27,710 (421)	14,560 (954)	28,410 (1,783)	32,540 (479)	29,450 (446)	19,820 (682)	33,650 (1,028)
Race/ethnicity											
White	25,990 (316)	24,530 (291)	22,020 (885)	32,350 (644)	26,370 (394)	15,640 (852)	30,550 (2,262)	31,980 (367)	28,120 (346)	21,300 (633)	36,530 (1,156)
Black	29,190 (1,187)	28,060 (1,075)	16,270 (1,505)	36,740 (1,186)	32,490 (937)	12,940 (1,849)	27,260 (4,835)	36,140 (932)	34,400 (860)	17,490 (1,653)	26,370 (2,136)
Hispanic	26,110 (1,228)	24,340 (936)	22,530 (2,533)	32,850 (1,763)	26,380 (918)	17,860 (3,139)	29,460 (4,340)	28,510 (823)	27,020 (771)	14,770 (1,092)	31,290 (2,200)
Asian	21,750 (926)	20,930 (815)	30,310 (6,266)	25,750 (1,401)	23,080 (1,159)	11,210 (2,509)	23,080 (2,328)	24,200 (1,163)	24,240 (938)	20,460 (2,328)	36,230 (4,211)
Pacific Islander	‡	‡	‡	†	†	†	†	†	†	†	†
American Indian/Alaska Native	27,490 (2,673)	27,360 (2,463)	‡	‡	‡	‡	†	29,430 (3,440)	27,160 (2,866)	‡	‡
Two or more races	28,080 (2,324)	28,180 (2,324)	‡	‡	‡	‡	†	28,040 (2,826)	27,160 (2,866)	‡	42,590 (4,135)
Other[2]	26,500 (2,022)	27,650 (1,838)	‡	13,630 (1,588)	13,630 (2,301)	†	†	31,540 (1,166)	29,000 (999)	15,400 (1,706)	†
Dependency status											
Dependent	25,300 (330)	23,370 (265)	23,470 (1,004)	28,540 (505)	22,670 (318)	16,360 (1,021)	31,620 (1,743)	28,440 (300)	23,860 (212)	22,680 (611)	39,110 (1,113)
Independent	27,100 (479)	26,240 (449)	14,200 (1,200)	36,770 (709)	31,990 (535)	13,990 (1,007)	26,780 (4,868)	35,440 (690)	34,020 (624)	15,130 (674)	23,840 (1,336)
Institution control											
Public	24,250 (348)	23,490 (318)	17,350 (822)	24,520 (505)	22,770 (691)	12,690 (691)	22,770 (1,202)	26,570 (296)	26,350 (250)	16,760 (649)	29,260 (1,052)
Private nonprofit	29,350 (558)	26,650 (468)	26,850 (1,211)	35,960 (1,315)	27,390 (1,315)	20,440 (1,890)	41,320 (4,161)	33,900 (482)	28,350 (352)	25,340 (815)	44,580 (1,970)
Private for-profit	35,960 (1,801)	34,660 (1,736)	†	44,560 (888)	38,820 (888)	13,210 (1,014)	28,550 (2,789)	43,920 (1,692)	41,610 (1,386)	16,440 (1,127)	33,900 (2,462)

†Not applicable.
‡Reporting standards not met. Either there are too few cases for a reliable estimate or the coefficient of variation (CV) is 50 percent or greater.
!Interpret data with caution. The coefficient of variation (CV) for this estimate is between 30 and 50 percent.

[1]Parent PLUS Loans are taken out by parents of dependent students and are used toward the students' undergraduate education. Parent PLUS Loans were available through both the William D. Ford Federal Direct Loan Program and the Federal Family Education Loan Program (FFELP) until FFELP was discontinued in 2010. Since then, Parent PLUS Loans have been referred to as Direct PLUS Loans.

[2]The 2012 and 2016 questionnaires did not offer students the option of choosing an "Other" race category.

[3]Average loan amounts were calculated only for students who took out each type of loan (or whose parents took out a PLUS Loan on their behalf).

[4]Constant dollars based on the Consumer Price Index, prepared by the Bureau of Labor Statistics, U.S. Department of Labor, adjusted to a school-year basis.

NOTE: Race categories exclude persons of Hispanic ethnicity. Data exclude students attending institutions in Puerto Rico. Race categories exclude persons of Hispanic ethnicity.

SOURCE: U.S. Department of Education, National Center for Education Statistics, 1999–2000, 2011–12, and 2015–16 National Postsecondary Student Aid Study (NPSAS:2000, NPSAS:12, and NPSAS:16). (This table was prepared September 2019.)

Table 332.10. Amount borrowed, aid status, and sources of aid for full-time, full-year postbaccalaureate students, by level of study and control and level of institution: Selected years, 1992–93 through 2015–16

[Standard errors appear in parentheses]

Level of study, control and level of institution	Cumulative borrowing for undergraduate and graduate education[1]						Aid status (percent of students)											
	Percent who borrowed		Average amount for those who borrowed				Nonaided		Source of aid									
			Current dollars		Constant 2018–19 dollars[2]				Any aid[3]		Federal[4]		State		Institutional		Employer	
1	2		3		4		5		6		7		8		9		10	
1992–93, all institutions	—	(†)	—	(†)	—	(†)	30.7	(1.43)	69.3	(1.43)	44.3	(1.42)	6.9	(0.64)	40.6	(2.02)	5.3	(0.59)
Master's degree	—	(†)	—	(†)	—	(†)	35.5	(2.54)	64.5	(2.54)	33.8	(1.91)	5.8	(0.79)	42.4	(2.97)	8.3	(1.01)
Public	—	(†)	—	(†)	—	(†)	32.7	(2.40)	67.3	(2.40)	33.9	(2.04)	7.8	(1.10)	44.1	(2.68)	7.6	(1.24)
4-year doctoral	—	(†)	—	(†)	—	(†)	32.4	(2.59)	67.6	(2.59)	32.4	(2.23)	6.7	(0.96)	46.4	(3.19)	7.7	(1.28)
Other 4-year	—	(†)	—	(†)	—	(†)	34.6	(4.38)	65.4	(4.38)	42.5	(5.30)	14.4	(4.13)	30.5	(3.67)	6.8!	(2.66)
Private	—	(†)	—	(†)	—	(†)	39.2	(4.74)	60.8	(4.74)	33.7	(3.62)	3.2	(0.89)	40.2	(6.34)	9.4	(1.88)
4-year doctoral	—	(†)	—	(†)	—	(†)	37.4	(4.70)	62.6	(4.70)	34.2	(4.09)	2.9!	(1.00)	42.9	(6.75)	8.9	(1.88)
Other 4-year	—	(†)	—	(†)	—	(†)	50.5	(10.60)	49.5	(10.60)	30.5	(7.06)	‡	(†)	22.8!	(9.39)	‡	(†)
Doctor's degree	—	(†)	—	(†)	—	(†)	30.1	(2.32)	69.9	(2.32)	28.3	(2.14)	4.4	(0.71)	51.6	(2.70)	3.0	(0.79)
Public	—	(†)	—	(†)	—	(†)	29.9	(2.99)	70.1	(2.99)	22.3	(2.26)	6.5	(1.14)	55.5	(3.01)	3.9	(1.00)
Private	—	(†)	—	(†)	—	(†)	30.4	(3.27)	69.6	(3.27)	37.8	(3.54)	‡	(†)	45.5	(3.52)	‡	(†)
First-professional	—	(†)	—	(†)	—	(†)	22.6	(0.96)	77.4	(0.96)	68.2	(1.54)	9.9	(1.34)	37.0	(1.81)	2.3	(0.52)
Public	—	(†)	—	(†)	—	(†)	20.4	(1.02)	79.6	(1.02)	72.5	(1.29)	13.4	(1.75)	37.7	(1.67)	2.3	(0.59)
Private	—	(†)	—	(†)	—	(†)	24.6	(1.66)	75.4	(1.66)	64.2	(2.42)	6.8	(1.19)	36.4	(3.29)	2.3!	(0.70)
Other graduate	—	(†)	—	(†)	—	(†)	38.3	(6.82)	61.7	(6.82)	42.1	(4.26)	6.6	(1.81)	23.0	(4.05)	6.0!	(2.98)
1999–2000, all institutions	69.4	(0.74)	$41,920	(863)	$62,720	(1,291)	18.3	(0.66)	81.7	(0.66)	52.5	(0.76)	6.0	(0.60)	49.7	(1.03)	6.0	(0.57)
Master's degree	68.3	(1.12)	31,930	(1,097)	47,770	(1,642)	20.6	(1.15)	79.4	(1.15)	50.6	(1.23)	5.1	(0.66)	45.4	(1.61)	9.2	(1.03)
Public	63.2	(1.60)	28,070	(1,079)	42,000	(1,614)	22.3	(1.52)	77.7	(1.52)	44.8	(1.82)	7.3	(1.14)	49.8	(2.16)	7.0	(1.04)
4-year doctoral	62.5	(1.56)	27,510	(1,234)	41,160	(1,846)	20.2	(1.46)	79.8	(1.46)	43.3	(1.71)	7.0	(1.31)	54.3	(2.02)	7.3	(1.20)
Other 4-year	70.9	(6.04)	31,920	(2,822)	47,750	(4,222)	29.9	(5.08)	70.1	(5.08)	54.7	(6.88)	10.2!	(3.32)	27.4	(6.85)	5.1!	(1.79)
Private	74.4	(1.55)	35,890	(1,855)	53,700	(2,775)	18.6	(1.59)	81.4	(1.59)	57.8	(1.88)	2.5	(0.63)	40.2	(2.63)	11.8	(1.89)
4-year doctoral	73.3	(1.76)	38,420	(2,521)	57,480	(3,772)	17.1	(1.93)	82.9	(1.93)	58.3	(2.36)	2.9!	(0.90)	50.5	(3.22)	8.3	(1.31)
Other[5]	76.9	(3.74)	30,770	(1,850)	46,030	(2,768)	21.8	(2.75)	78.2	(2.75)	56.6	(4.41)	‡	(†)	18.1	(3.91)	19.1	(5.24)
Doctor's degree	56.8	(1.95)	38,990	(3,421)	58,330	(5,118)	12.0	(1.38)	88.0	(1.38)	29.6	(2.80)	2.6	(0.54)	77.4	(1.65)	5.4	(0.64)
Public	54.5	(1.92)	33,600	(1,564)	50,260	(2,340)	11.4	(1.38)	88.6	(1.38)	26.1	(1.86)	3.2	(0.75)	80.0	(1.59)	7.3	(0.88)
Private	60.5	(3.62)	46,680	(7,288)	69,830	(10,904)	13.0	(2.80)	87.0	(2.80)	35.2	(6.26)	‡	(†)	73.2	(3.22)	2.3	(0.55)
First-professional	85.1	(1.14)	60,860	(1,713)	91,040	(2,563)	13.4	(1.18)	86.6	(1.18)	77.1	(1.29)	9.9	(1.65)	41.4	(2.40)	1.7!	(0.53)
Public	86.8	(1.70)	52,790	(1,954)	78,980	(2,923)	13.8	(1.82)	86.2	(1.82)	78.3	(2.13)	12.7	(2.57)	38.9	(2.84)	1.8!	(0.87)
Private	83.6	(1.63)	67,820	(3,213)	101,460	(4,807)	13.1	(1.49)	86.9	(1.49)	76.1	(1.84)	7.5	(2.11)	43.4	(3.65)	1.7!	(0.66)
Other graduate	57.5	(3.81)	27,840	(2,036)	41,640	(3,046)	39.3	(3.68)	60.7	(3.68)	44.9	(3.72)	8.1	(2.37)	25.3	(3.22)	2.8!	(1.20)
2007–08, all institutions	71.3	(1.04)	$55,110	(993)	$65,930	(1,188)	13.1	(0.80)	86.9	(0.80)	56.6	(1.18)	3.8	(0.28)	43.9	(1.17)	11.6	(0.93)
Master's degree	71.8	(1.77)	43,250	(1,374)	51,750	(1,644)	15.6	(1.34)	84.4	(1.34)	55.5	(1.93)	2.9	(0.40)	35.5	(1.48)	16.3	(1.76)
Public	66.5	(1.79)	37,770	(1,473)	45,190	(1,762)	13.3	(1.27)	86.7	(1.27)	50.7	(1.91)	4.1	(0.83)	52.2	(2.40)	13.4	(1.49)
4-year doctoral	65.1	(1.95)	38,450	(1,644)	46,000	(1,967)	12.1	(1.34)	87.9	(1.34)	50.1	(2.07)	4.2	(0.93)	56.0	(2.62)	14.5	(1.68)
Other 4-year	77.1	(4.81)	33,440	(2,285)	40,010	(2,734)	22.7	(3.92)	77.3	(3.92)	55.6	(5.96)	‡	(†)	23.5	(4.89)	5.1!	(1.92)
Private	75.5	(2.58)	46,590	(1,974)	55,730	(2,361)	17.2	(1.96)	82.8	(1.96)	58.8	(2.81)	2.0	(0.35)	24.0	(1.59)	18.3	(2.79)
4-year doctoral	71.4	(1.85)	46,510	(1,654)	55,640	(1,979)	19.1	(1.45)	80.9	(1.45)	55.1	(1.51)	2.4	(0.50)	36.0	(2.46)	14.4	(1.17)
Other[5]	80.8	(5.13)	46,670	(3,671)	55,840	(4,392)	14.8	(3.91)	85.2	(3.91)	63.6	(5.96)	1.6	(0.43)	8.4	(1.44)	23.4	(6.23)
Doctor's degree	59.8	(1.73)	55,200	(2,108)	66,040	(2,522)	7.1	(0.88)	92.9	(0.88)	38.4	(2.18)	2.9	(0.41)	70.7	(3.03)	7.9	(0.79)
Public	52.3	(2.17)	44,190	(1,604)	52,870	(1,919)	7.9	(1.48)	92.1	(1.48)	29.7	(1.80)	3.6	(0.65)	81.1	(1.89)	7.7	(0.93)
Private	67.8	(2.41)	64,120	(3,123)	76,720	(3,737)	6.2	(1.08)	93.8	(1.08)	47.6	(3.43)	2.2!	(0.65)	59.8	(5.02)	8.0	(1.36)
First-professional	84.9	(1.29)	81,400	(1,782)	97,380	(2,131)	11.5	(1.12)	88.5	(1.12)	81.7	(1.35)	7.5	(0.83)	35.7	(1.89)	4.6	(0.75)
Public	84.4	(1.96)	73,230	(2,717)	87,600	(3,251)	11.5	(1.65)	88.5	(1.65)	81.8	(2.12)	10.6	(1.46)	34.0	(2.67)	4.9	(1.44)
Private	85.4	(1.57)	87,800	(2,183)	105,040	(2,612)	11.5	(1.46)	88.5	(1.46)	81.5	(1.67)	5.1	(0.85)	37.0	(2.56)	4.4	(0.72)
Other graduate	62.4	(6.48)	43,740	(3,904)	52,330	(4,671)	30.8	(6.54)	69.2	(6.54)	51.0	(6.62)	‡	(†)	25.5	(5.78)	6.2!	(2.33)
2011–12, all institutions	73.3	(0.90)	$74,710	(996)	$83,150	(1,109)	13.9	(0.77)	86.1	(0.77)	62.3	(0.93)	2.4	(0.34)	42.2	(1.19)	10.2	(0.48)
Master's degree	73.5	(1.45)	58,590	(1,142)	65,210	(1,271)	17.4	(1.28)	82.6	(1.28)	63.0	(1.44)	1.8	(0.35)	35.1	(1.53)	8.8	(0.70)
Public	71.8	(2.24)	50,200	(1,816)	55,870	(2,021)	16.2	(1.84)	83.8	(1.84)	58.2	(2.41)	3.7	(0.80)	45.6	(2.35)	10.3	(1.17)
4-year doctoral	70.7	(2.41)	50,620	(2,015)	56,330	(2,242)	16.3	(2.03)	83.7	(2.03)	57.0	(2.60)	4.0	(0.89)	47.1	(2.56)	10.8	(1.28)
Other 4-year	82.2	(3.71)	46,900	(2,538)	52,190	(2,825)	15.4	(4.13)	84.6	(4.13)	69.5	(5.18)	‡	(†)	31.2	(3.46)	5.9	(1.68)
Private	74.8	(1.95)	64,510	(1,456)	71,790	(1,620)	18.2	(1.80)	81.8	(1.80)	66.5	(2.13)	0.4!	(0.19)	27.5	(2.09)	7.8	(0.88)
4-year doctoral	70.1	(2.41)	67,130	(2,165)	74,710	(2,410)	19.6	(2.06)	80.4	(2.06)	59.5	(2.45)	‡	(†)	35.2	(2.96)	7.8	(1.23)
Other[5]	81.8	(3.20)	61,140	(1,816)	68,040	(2,021)	16.1	(3.09)	83.9	(3.09)	77.0	(3.66)	‡	(†)	15.9	(2.70)	7.6	(1.04)
Doctor's degree—research/ scholarship	50.5	(1.42)	65,090	(2,343)	72,450	(2,608)	6.6	(0.73)	93.4	(0.73)	27.8	(1.19)	1.5!	(0.49)	79.8	(1.27)	24.0	(1.25)
Public	47.9	(2.23)	55,500	(2,291)	61,770	(2,550)	5.9	(1.04)	94.1	(1.04)	24.2	(1.41)	2.1!	(0.78)	87.2	(1.59)	27.0	(1.93)
Private	54.0	(1.86)	76,180	(4,351)	84,790	(4,843)	7.5	(1.07)	92.5	(1.07)	32.3	(2.30)	‡	(†)	70.1	(2.28)	20.1	(1.06)
Doctor's degree—professional practice and other[6]	88.3	(0.90)	110,570	(1,848)	123,050	(2,056)	9.3	(0.88)	90.7	(0.88)	84.4	(1.03)	4.5	(0.96)	35.1	(1.66)	4.4	(0.51)
Public	88.3	(1.00)	102,220	(2,726)	113,770	(3,034)	8.9	(1.09)	91.1	(1.09)	84.4	(1.31)	8.1	(2.27)	40.6	(2.51)	5.4	(0.82)
Private	88.3	(1.28)	116,000	(2,490)	129,100	(2,771)	9.6	(1.22)	90.4	(1.22)	84.4	(1.50)	2.2	(0.53)	31.5	(2.19)	3.7	(0.62)
Other graduate	74.9	(6.28)	57,540	(5,456)	64,040	(6,072)	29.1	(6.46)	70.9	(6.46)	61.4	(7.24)	‡	(†)	16.9	(4.78)	5.5!	(2.47)

See notes at end of table.

Table 332.10. Amount borrowed, aid status, and sources of aid for full-time, full-year postbaccalaureate students, by level of study and control and level of institution: Selected years, 1992–93 through 2015–16—Continued

[Standard errors appear in parentheses]

Level of study, control and level of institution	Cumulative borrowing for undergraduate and graduate education[1]			Aid status (percent of students)						
	Percent who borrowed	Average amount for those who borrowed		Nonaided	Source of aid					
		Current dollars	Constant 2018–19 dollars[2]		Any aid[3]	Federal[4]	State	Institutional	Employer	
1	2	3	4	5	6	7	8	9	10
2015–16, all institutions	68.3 (0.93)	$80,750 (2,158)	$85,830 (2,294)	17.0 (0.82)	83.0 (0.82)	54.0 (0.89)	3.3 (0.52)	46.6 (1.25)	6.9 (0.54)
Master's degree	66.6 (1.45)	59,100 (1,608)	62,820 (1,709)	20.0 (1.17)	80.0 (1.17)	51.9 (1.48)	3.1 (0.46)	41.6 (1.62)	9.0 (0.75)
Public	63.7 (2.22)	49,450 (2,109)	52,570 (2,242)	21.6 (1.77)	78.4 (1.77)	45.0 (2.10)	5.5 (0.93)	44.4 (2.17)	6.6 (0.89)
4-year doctoral	63.1 (2.34)	49,950 (2,287)	53,090 (2,431)	21.2 (1.86)	78.8 (1.86)	44.2 (2.23)	5.4 (1.00)	46.2 (2.28)	6.6 (0.96)
Other 4-year	71.7 (3.46)	44,240 (2,997)	47,030 (3,186)	25.9 (3.22)	74.1 (3.22)	54.7 (3.65)	5.8! (1.82)	23.6 (4.31)	6.3! (2.28)
Private	69.1 (1.74)	66,890 (2,295)	71,100 (2,439)	18.5 (1.52)	81.5 (1.52)	57.9 (1.98)	1.0! (0.35)	39.1 (2.52)	11.1 (1.14)
4-year doctoral	65.3 (2.35)	67,870 (3,010)	72,140 (3,199)	20.4 (1.97)	79.6 (1.97)	54.3 (2.57)	1.2! (0.48)	39.7 (3.06)	9.2 (1.44)
Other[5]	78.4 (2.23)	64,910 (2,838)	68,990 (3,016)	14.0 (1.56)	86.0 (1.56)	66.7 (2.52)	0.7! (0.28)	37.7 (4.15)	15.8 (1.46)
Doctor's degree—research/ scholarship	52.5 (2.13)	74,510 (3,435)	79,200 (3,652)	9.9 (1.05)	90.1 (1.05)	27.9 (1.94)	1.2 (0.31)	71.9 (1.93)	6.2 (0.78)
Public	46.6 (2.93)	61,200 (4,167)	65,050 (4,429)	10.9 (1.82)	89.1 (1.82)	18.3 (2.49)	1.5 (0.44)	78.7 (2.56)	5.0 (0.90)
Private	58.2 (3.11)	84,910 (5,368)	90,250 (5,706)	8.8 (1.18)	91.2 (1.18)	37.3 (2.86)	0.9! (0.40)	65.2 (3.08)	7.4 (1.24)
Doctor's degree—professional practice and other[6]	80.3 (1.56)	121,940 (6,425)	129,610 (6,830)	14.0 (1.48)	86.0 (1.48)	73.0 (1.54)	4.6! (1.57)	45.9 (2.17)	2.3 (0.68)
Public	79.8 (2.45)	99,450 (3,685)	105,710 (3,917)	15.9 (2.29)	84.1 (2.29)	71.8 (2.26)	4.5 (1.06)	48.6 (3.18)	2.2! (0.84)
Private	80.7 (2.02)	138,370 (11,011)	147,070 (11,704)	12.6 (2.00)	87.4 (2.00)	74.0 (2.11)	‡ (†)	43.9 (2.93)	2.5! (1.04)
Other graduate	70.9 (4.84)	80,210 (8,667)	85,250 (9,213)	20.7 (3.95)	79.3 (3.95)	54.0 (5.41)	‡ (†)	28.2 (5.29)	10.7 (3.09)

—Not available.
†Not applicable.
!Interpret data with caution. The coefficient of variation (CV) for this estimate is between 30 and 50 percent.
‡Reporting standards not met. Either there are too few cases for a reliable estimate or the coefficient of variation (CV) is 50 percent or greater.
[1]Includes all loans ever taken out for both graduate and undergraduate education. Does not include Parent Loans for Undergraduate Students (PLUS) or loans from families and friends.
[2]Constant dollars based on the Consumer Price Index, prepared by the Bureau of Labor Statistics, U.S. Department of Labor, adjusted to a school-year basis.
[3]Includes students who reported they were awarded aid but did not specify the source of aid.
[4]Includes Department of Veterans Affairs and Department of Defense benefits.
[5]Includes nonprofit 4-year nondoctoral institutions and for-profit 2-year-and-above institutions.

[6]Professional practice doctor's degrees include most degrees that were classified as first-professional degrees prior to 2010–11 (such as M.D., D.D.S., and J.D.). "Other" doctor's degrees are those that are neither research/scholarship degrees nor professional practice degrees.
NOTE: Full-time, full-year students are those who were enrolled full time for 9 or more months. Excludes students whose attendance status was not reported. Total includes some students whose level of study or control of institution was unknown. Detail may not sum to totals because of rounding and because some students receive multiple types of aid and aid from different sources. Data exclude students attending institutions in Puerto Rico.
SOURCE: U.S. Department of Education, National Center for Education Statistics, 1992–93, 1999–2000, 2007–08, 2011–12, and 2015–16 National Postsecondary Student Aid Study (NPSAS:93, NPSAS:2000, NPSAS:08, NPSAS:12, and NPSAS:16). (This table was prepared October 2019.)

Table 332.45. Percentage of graduate degree completers with student loan debt and average cumulative amount owed, by level of education funded and graduate degree type, institution control, and degree program: Selected years, 1999–2000 through 2015–16

[Standard errors appear in parentheses]

Symbols: † Not applicable. ‡ Reporting standards not met.

Percentage of graduate degree completers with student loan debt

Graduate degree type, institution control, and degree program	Loans for graduate education only					Total loans (for undergraduate and graduate education)				
	1999–2000	2003–04	2007–08	2011–12	2015–16	1999–2000	2003–04	2007–08	2011–12	2015–16
	2	3	4	5	6	7	8	9	10	11
Total	44.6 (1.06)	54.6 (1.77)	54.6 (1.18)	58.6 (1.25)	54.2 (1.05)	51.3 (1.00)	60.9 (1.72)	62.9 (1.15)	64.1 (1.23)	60.5 (1.08)
Graduate degree type and institution control[1]										
Postbaccalaureate certificate	35.8 (5.12)	46.3 (7.43)	49.5 (5.02)	39.4 (4.66)	47.6 (4.18)	53.0 (4.72)	53.0 (7.02)	64.1 (4.68)	44.5 (4.53)	55.1 (3.88)
Public	33.4 (6.29)	30.1 (5.25)	45.1 (7.45)	35.5 (6.04)	39.0 (5.78)	51.2 (5.62)	39.9 (6.22)	64.5 (6.95)	41.5 (5.84)	48.7 (5.49)
Private nonprofit	32.8 (9.10)	70.3 (9.55)	54.7 (6.47)	48.0 (7.97)	53.5 (5.99)	40.4 (9.55)	73.1 (9.13)	63.8 (5.82)	50.5 (8.06)	57.8 (6.03)
Private for-profit	‡ (†)	‡ (†)	‡ (†)	‡ (†)	72.5 (4.88)	‡ (†)	‡ (†)	‡ (†)	‡ (†)	78.1 (3.99)
Master's	39.9 (1.30)	52.0 (2.10)	53.8 (1.79)	59.0 (1.50)	52.8 (1.23)	59.4 (1.19)	59.4 (2.03)	62.7 (1.45)	65.2 (1.48)	60.0 (1.28)
Public	35.6 (1.53)	41.6 (2.20)	48.4 (1.69)	53.0 (2.19)	49.1 (1.82)	50.0 (1.57)	50.0 (2.28)	59.1 (1.87)	62.1 (2.14)	57.3 (2.04)
Private nonprofit	44.1 (2.65)	60.8 (3.13)	55.2 (2.54)	60.8 (2.29)	53.0 (3.18)	67.6 (2.46)	67.6 (2.85)	63.3 (1.84)	64.6 (2.38)	59.8 (1.74)
Private for-profit	60.4 (11.61)	76.7 (10.88)	80.3 (6.41)	74.9 (4.97)	67.5 (3.45)	77.2 (10.98)	77.2 (10.76)	83.5 (6.34)	78.6 (4.86)	71.3 (2.74)
Doctor's, research	38.8 (2.92)	45.3 (2.52)	43.1 (3.12)	40.7 (2.33)	43.6 (3.45)	50.5 (3.04)	50.5 (2.28)	49.3 (3.73)	47.5 (2.44)	48.2 (3.51)
Public	34.6 (3.35)	39.6 (2.14)	38.5 (3.39)	35.3 (2.73)	32.7 (3.96)	45.7 (3.52)	45.7 (2.82)	45.0 (3.22)	42.1 (3.04)	36.7 (4.16)
Private nonprofit	46.0 (6.55)	54.5 (4.19)	51.2 (3.39)	39.9 (3.38)	46.8 (6.14)	58.3 (6.29)	58.3 (4.13)	57.2 (3.22)	48.7 (3.30)	54.2 (6.01)
Private for-profit	‡ (†)	‡ (†)	‡ (†)	95.1 (3.45)	75.8 (6.27)	‡ (†)	‡ (†)	‡ (†)	95.1 (3.45)	76.2 (6.26)
Doctor's, professional[2]	79.4 (2.82)	84.8 (2.39)	83.8 (2.09)	84.6 (1.60)	73.5 (2.43)	81.2 (2.77)	84.8 (2.39)	84.9 (1.97)	84.9 (1.65)	74.5 (2.39)
Public	83.6 (4.65)	87.2 (2.82)	82.8 (3.61)	85.9 (2.72)	74.1 (4.18)	84.7 (4.59)	87.2 (2.82)	84.3 (3.28)	85.9 (2.72)	75.9 (4.07)
Private nonprofit	76.7 (4.06)	82.8 (4.21)	84.5 (2.42)	94.1 (5.12)	71.3 (3.40)	79.0 (3.95)	82.8 (4.21)	85.4 (2.34)	84.7 (2.31)	71.9 (3.42)
Private for-profit	‡ (†)	‡ (†)	‡ (†)	‡ (†)	89.5 (1.95)	‡ (†)	‡ (†)	‡ (†)	94.1 (5.12)	90.2 (1.82)
Graduate degree program										
Postbaccalaureate certificate	35.8 (5.12)	46.3 (7.43)	49.5 (5.02)	39.4 (4.66)	47.6 (4.18)	53.0 (4.72)	53.0 (7.02)	64.1 (4.68)	44.5 (4.53)	55.1 (3.88)
Master of business administration (M.B.A.)	35.7 (2.70)	49.2 (5.05)	54.2 (3.45)	49.4 (4.63)	43.8 (3.41)	54.8 (2.78)	54.8 (4.67)	60.6 (3.29)	57.0 (4.78)	51.0 (3.34)
Master of education (any)	35.7 (2.86)	49.1 (3.14)	55.5 (3.46)	59.7 (3.55)	51.2 (2.83)	60.2 (2.86)	60.2 (3.24)	68.4 (3.13)	67.3 (3.64)	61.9 (3.21)
Other master of arts (M.A.) except in education	46.8 (4.97)	57.7 (5.07)	60.4 (4.04)	62.1 (3.53)	51.9 (4.81)	55.6 (5.09)	62.6 (5.04)	66.6 (3.76)	69.5 (3.50)	58.5 (4.42)
Other master of science (M.S.) except in education	35.9 (2.89)	40.0 (3.85)	45.8 (2.88)	53.6 (2.47)	49.5 (2.42)	41.9 (2.58)	47.1 (4.12)	53.9 (2.83)	59.3 (2.56)	56.1 (2.33)
Theology (M.Div, M.H.L., or B.D.)	‡ (†)	69.3 (4.70)	56.3 (2.65)	71.8 (2.61)	65.0 (2.65)	58.4 (3.85)	74.5 (4.33)	62.2 (2.69)	75.0 (2.55)	70.2 (2.53)
Other master's degree[3]	52.5 (4.06)	33.5 (2.01)	31.9 (2.89)	31.6 (2.22)	38.5 (3.41)	43.6 (3.37)	40.3 (2.12)	40.2 (3.52)	40.3 (2.63)	44.7 (3.55)
Ph.D. except in education	36.3 (3.02)	49.7 (4.81)	58.0 (5.68)	72.3 (3.46)	61.4 (6.82)	33.4 (6.36)	51.9 (4.75)	61.4 (5.44)	73.3 (3.33)	63.0 (6.74)
Education (any doctorate)	33.4 (6.36)	91.8 (3.02)	78.3 (4.73)	84.3 (4.12)	80.3 (4.38)	86.4 (7.18)	91.8 (3.02)	79.6 (4.81)	84.3 (4.12)	81.0 (4.34)
Medicine (M.D. or D.O.)	86.4 (7.18)	88.3 (4.13)	86.7 (5.64)	89.5 (3.54)	73.6 (6.22)	80.9 (6.47)	88.3 (4.13)	88.6 (4.54)	89.5 (3.54)	74.6 (5.94)
Other health science professional practice doctorate[4]	‡ (†)	86.8 (3.05)	87.3 (2.50)	85.6 (2.46)	68.8 (5.84)	84.6 (2.52)	86.8 (3.05)	87.3 (2.50)	86.3 (2.54)	68.8 (5.84)
Law (LL.B. or J.D.)	79.1 (6.47)	66.7 (4.99)	59.6 (4.47)	66.0 (4.09)	65.5 (7.35)	51.5 (7.46)	70.5 (4.56)	62.6 (4.47)	66.7 (4.15)	66.3 (7.42)
Other doctorate (non-Ph.D.)[5]	49.0 (7.64)	—	—	—	—	—	—	—	—	—

Average cumulative amount owed (current dollars)

Graduate degree type and institution control[1]	1999–2000	2003–04	2007–08	2011–12	2015–16	1999–2000	2003–04	2007–08	2011–12	2015–16
	2	3	4	5	6	7	8	9	10	11
Total	$33,290 ($1,197)	$39,460 ($1,440)	$43,680 ($1,014)	$59,420 ($1,257)	$70,980 ($2,155)	$37,890 ($1,168)	$45,600 ($1,516)	$51,730 ($1,001)	$73,130 ($1,339)	$82,810 ($2,127)
Postbaccalaureate certificate	21,400 (3,254)	20,900 (4,492)	31,370 (3,171)	44,240 (5,085)	54,090 (7,671)	25,550 (2,679)	29,920 (4,291)	38,640 (3,633)	60,790 (5,338)	66,550 (7,946)
Public	‡ (†)	10,310 (1,716)	32,070 (5,333)	40,370 (6,120)	43,270 (8,478)	22,760 (3,112)	19,060 (2,980)	38,680 (4,797)	57,050 (6,204)	50,130 (8,080)
Private nonprofit	‡ (†)	26,680 (5,250)	30,280 (3,870)	48,610 (8,683)	65,680 (18,039)	‡ (†)	37,770 (4,980)	38,220 (6,019)	67,960 (10,010)	80,010 (19,084)
Private for-profit	‡ (†)	‡ (†)	‡ (†)	‡ (†)	61,300 (6,394)	‡ (†)	‡ (†)	‡ (†)	‡ (†)	95,500 (8,527)
Master's	23,540 (967)	29,060 (1,145)	34,330 (1,091)	45,070 (1,252)	50,290 (1,635)	29,390 (1,109)	35,240 (1,327)	43,860 (1,168)	60,000 (1,472)	64,770 (1,688)
Public	19,720 (1,058)	24,750 (997)	31,110 (1,096)	35,620 (1,644)	42,330 (2,369)	25,570 (1,099)	31,440 (1,294)	38,750 (1,328)	49,100 (2,182)	53,470 (2,397)
Private nonprofit	27,330 (1,795)	32,280 (1,729)	38,020 (1,373)	50,740 (1,994)	56,350 (2,664)	32,730 (2,087)	37,700 (2,166)	46,790 (1,606)	71,900 (2,168)	70,590 (2,702)
Private for-profit	29,670 (3,676)	‡ (†)	33,870 (6,033)	49,510 (4,434)	62,010 (3,347)	40,920 (6,394)	‡ (†)	54,120 (6,093)	80,330 (3,704)	88,680 (4,064)
Doctor's, research	34,650 (3,721)	52,030 (3,051)	62,730 (3,664)	77,580 (2,757)	101,490 (6,346)	37,330 (3,925)	56,210 (3,211)	65,210 (3,443)	85,400 (3,289)	106,430 (6,551)
Public	28,730 (2,788)	44,450 (2,668)	51,180 (3,468)	60,440 (3,593)	84,820 (9,384)	31,740 (3,044)	48,430 (3,044)	54,020 (3,277)	63,230 (3,982)	90,510 (8,614)
Private nonprofit	42,770 (9,509)	61,310 (5,721)	78,810 (7,053)	84,410 (5,554)	89,430 (13,755)	45,330 (9,646)	66,550 (6,411)	81,360 (6,631)	85,400 (5,396)	92,370 (13,680)
Private for-profit	‡ (†)	‡ (†)	‡ (†)	‡ (†)	144,890 (7,544)	‡ (†)	‡ (†)	‡ (†)	‡ (†)	157,260 (7,749)
Doctor's, professional[2]	61,930 (2,712)	78,850 (3,858)	91,470 (2,901)	125,930 (7,663)	171,670 (9,386)	68,480 (2,993)	90,630 (4,157)	102,600 (3,184)	140,330 (3,645)	183,200 (8,520)
Public	53,470 (2,875)	66,740 (3,001)	81,450 (4,652)	132,610 (3,922)	130,750 (3,182)	60,830 (3,175)	78,030 (3,182)	91,860 (5,142)	150,210 (4,118)	140,070 (10,316)
Private nonprofit	68,930 (4,244)	89,820 (5,753)	97,530 (4,114)	114,580 (4,118)	205,050 (16,330)	74,680 (4,574)	102,330 (6,075)	109,070 (4,637)	140,070 (5,015)	217,830 (18,532)
Private for-profit	‡ (†)	‡ (†)	‡ (†)	142,550 (18,040)	167,380 (5,860)	‡ (†)	‡ (†)	‡ (†)	160,200 (21,607)	186,790 (5,877)

See notes at end of table.

Table 332.45. Percentage of graduate degree completers with student loan debt and average cumulative amount owed, by level of education funded and graduate degree type, institution control, and degree program: Selected years, 1999–2000 through 2015–16—Continued

[Standard errors appear in parentheses]

Graduate degree type, institution control, and degree program	Loans for graduate education only					Total loans (for undergraduate and graduate education)				
	1999–2000	2003–04	2007–08	2011–12	2015–16	1999–2000	2003–04	2007–08	2011–12	2015–16
1	2	3	4	5	6	7	8	9	10	11
Graduate degree program										
Postbaccalaureate certificate	21,400 (3,254)	20,900 (4,492)	31,370 (3,171)	44,240 (5,085)	54,090 (7,671)	25,550 (2,679)	29,920 (4,291)	38,640 (3,633)	60,790 (5,338)	66,550 (7,946)
Master of business administration (M.B.A.)	27,930 (2,856)	36,090 (4,254)	36,420 (3,676)	40,860 (2,884)	50,150 (3,784)	33,060 (2,437)	42,720 (4,543)	47,500 (3,012)	51,430 (3,819)	65,090 (4,175)
Master of education (any)	17,990 (1,244)	25,940 (1,449)	29,920 (1,705)	41,600 (2,509)	41,750 (3,419)	22,470 (1,627)	31,780 (1,934)	39,340 (2,543)	58,720 (3,718)	54,180 (3,409)
Other master of arts (M.A.) except in education	22,900 (1,985)	28,180 (3,721)	35,960 (3,199)	48,850 (3,553)	52,920 (5,165)	30,730 (2,913)	37,420 (3,923)	47,960 (4,166)	66,340 (5,564)	71,470 (5,044)
Other master of science (M.S.) except in education	23,000 (1,621)	29,810 (2,963)	33,610 (2,053)	45,450 (2,668)	47,950 (3,020)	31,320 (2,421)	35,150 (3,103)	42,910 (2,414)	60,900 (3,011)	61,200 (2,954)
Theology (M.Div., M.H.L., or B.D.)	‡ (†)	‡ (†)	‡ (†)	‡ (†)	‡ (†)	‡ (†)	‡ (†)	‡ (†)	‡ (†)	‡ (†)
Other master's degree[3]	26,820 (1,654)	27,150 (1,823)	40,690 (1,878)	48,960 (2,320)	57,340 (3,589)	32,950 (2,182)	32,840 (2,536)	48,820 (2,086)	62,490 (2,566)	73,730 (3,643)
Ph.D. except in education	33,870 (4,154)	41,860 (2,962)	47,950 (2,850)	66,450 (3,268)	96,750 (7,789)	33,740 (4,219)	45,080 (2,767)	49,180 (2,931)	65,070 (3,456)	97,000 (7,873)
Education (any doctorate)	‡ (†)	48,210 (9,267)	58,550 (7,140)	80,940 (6,008)	101,730 (12,692)	‡ (†)	51,590 (8,728)	60,980 (7,025)	93,820 (7,235)	109,880 (13,724)
Medicine (M.D. or D.O.)	78,660 (4,069)	108,110 (8,209)	128,260 (7,373)	166,330 (7,790)	223,060 (24,919)	87,020 (4,317)	118,690 (7,793)	135,510 (7,906)	182,610 (8,001)	241,560 (30,768)
Other health science professional practice doctorate[4]	72,470 (6,419)	79,020 (9,754)	91,750 (8,221)	133,510 (7,024)	190,310 (16,900)	80,590 (6,322)	94,870 (10,227)	108,280 (9,453)	157,690 (7,895)	198,760 (16,398)
Law (LL.B. or J.D.)	51,760 (2,207)	71,320 (3,936)	82,770 (2,640)	126,570 (5,041)	129,290 (10,279)	57,490 (2,541)	82,080 (4,463)	94,350 (3,166)	140,420 (5,883)	142,870 (10,786)
Other doctorate (non-Ph.D.)[5]	36,800 (6,987)	64,060 (5,041)	81,350 (7,115)	104,950 (5,885)	115,510 (12,106)	44,970 (6,843)	71,140 (6,520)	88,870 (7,019)	119,170 (6,600)	129,840 (11,534)
	Average cumulative amount owed (constant 2018–19 dollars)[6]									
Total	**$49,800 ($1,791)**	**$53,710 ($1,960)**	**$52,250 ($1,213)**	**$66,130 ($1,399)**	**$75,440 ($2,291)**	**$56,680 ($1,748)**	**$62,060 ($2,064)**	**$61,880 ($1,197)**	**$81,390 ($1,490)**	**$88,020 ($2,261)**
Graduate degree type and institution control[1]										
Postbaccalaureate certificate	32,020 (4,868)	28,450 (6,113)	37,530 (3,794)	49,240 (5,659)	57,490 (8,154)	38,220 (4,007)	40,720 (5,841)	46,230 (4,346)	67,650 (5,940)	70,740 (8,446)
Public	‡ (†)	14,030 (2,336)	38,370 (6,380)	44,930 (6,811)	45,990 (9,012)	34,050 (4,656)	25,940 (4,056)	46,280 (5,739)	63,490 (6,904)	53,290 (8,588)
Private nonprofit	‡ (†)	36,580 (7,145)	36,220 (4,630)	54,100 (9,664)	69,810 (19,174)	‡ (†)	51,410 (6,777)	45,720 (7,200)	75,640 (11,141)	85,040 (20,284)
Private for-profit	‡ (†)	‡ (†)	‡ (†)	‡ (†)	65,160 (6,797)	‡ (†)	‡ (†)	‡ (†)	‡ (†)	101,510 (9,064)
Master's	35,220 (1,447)	39,550 (1,559)	41,070 (1,306)	50,160 (1,393)	53,450 (1,738)	43,970 (1,659)	47,970 (1,806)	52,470 (1,397)	66,780 (1,638)	68,840 (1,794)
Public	29,500 (1,583)	33,690 (1,357)	37,220 (1,311)	39,650 (1,830)	45,000 (2,518)	38,260 (1,644)	42,790 (1,761)	46,360 (1,589)	54,650 (2,428)	56,840 (2,548)
Private nonprofit	40,880 (2,685)	43,940 (2,353)	45,490 (1,643)	56,470 (2,219)	59,900 (2,832)	48,970 (3,123)	51,310 (2,948)	55,970 (1,922)	71,960 (2,413)	75,030 (2,872)
Private for-profit	44,390 (5,499)	‡ (†)	40,520 (7,218)	55,100 (4,935)	65,910 (3,558)	61,220 (9,565)	‡ (†)	64,750 (7,290)	80,020 (4,123)	94,260 (4,319)
Doctor's, research	51,830 (5,566)	70,810 (4,152)	75,050 (4,383)	86,340 (3,069)	107,870 (6,746)	55,850 (5,872)	76,500 (4,370)	78,020 (4,119)	89,400 (3,660)	113,130 (6,963)
Public	42,980 (4,171)	60,500 (3,632)	61,230 (4,149)	67,260 (3,999)	90,150 (9,974)	47,490 (4,554)	65,920 (4,088)	64,620 (3,920)	70,370 (4,432)	96,200 (9,156)
Private nonprofit	63,980 (14,226)	83,440 (7,786)	94,290 (8,438)	93,950 (6,181)	95,060 (14,620)	67,810 (14,431)	90,580 (8,725)	97,340 (7,933)	95,040 (6,005)	98,180 (14,541)
Private for-profit	‡ (†)	‡ (†)	‡ (†)	140,150 (8,528)	154,010 (8,019)	‡ (†)	‡ (†)	‡ (†)	156,170 (8,624)	167,150 (9,056)
Doctor's, professional[2]	92,640 (4,058)	107,310 (5,251)	109,430 (3,470)	147,580 (3,417)	182,470 (9,977)	102,450 (4,477)	123,350 (5,657)	122,750 (3,809)	167,090 (4,057)	194,730 (10,966)
Public	79,990 (4,301)	90,830 (4,084)	97,440 (5,566)	127,520 (4,365)	138,980 (9,001)	91,000 (4,749)	106,190 (4,330)	109,890 (6,152)	144,910 (4,583)	148,880 (10,166)
Private nonprofit	103,130 (6,349)	122,240 (7,830)	116,680 (4,922)	158,650 (4,583)	217,950 (17,357)	111,720 (6,843)	139,270 (8,268)	130,490 (5,547)	178,300 (5,582)	231,530 (19,698)
Private for-profit	‡ (†)	‡ (†)	‡ (†)	195,760 (20,078)	177,910 (6,228)	‡ (†)	‡ (†)	‡ (†)	205,550 (24,048)	198,540 (6,247)
Graduate degree program										
Postbaccalaureate certificate	32,020 (4,868)	28,450 (6,113)	37,530 (3,794)	49,240 (5,659)	57,490 (8,154)	38,220 (4,007)	40,720 (5,841)	46,230 (4,346)	67,650 (5,940)	70,740 (8,446)
Master of business administration (M.B.A.)	41,790 (4,273)	49,120 (5,790)	43,570 (4,397)	45,480 (3,209)	53,300 (4,022)	49,450 (3,646)	58,140 (6,183)	56,830 (3,604)	57,240 (4,250)	69,180 (4,438)
Master of education (any)	26,920 (1,861)	35,300 (1,972)	35,790 (2,039)	46,300 (2,792)	44,380 (3,635)	33,610 (2,433)	43,260 (2,632)	47,060 (3,042)	65,350 (4,138)	57,590 (3,624)
Other master of arts (M.A.) except in education	34,270 (2,970)	38,350 (5,064)	43,020 (3,827)	54,370 (3,954)	56,250 (5,490)	45,980 (4,358)	50,930 (5,339)	57,370 (4,984)	73,830 (6,193)	75,970 (5,362)
Other master of science (M.S.) except in education	34,420 (2,425)	40,570 (4,033)	40,210 (2,457)	50,590 (2,969)	50,970 (3,210)	46,860 (3,622)	47,830 (4,223)	51,330 (2,888)	67,780 (3,351)	65,050 (3,140)
Theology (M.Div., M.H.L., or B.D.)	‡ (†)	‡ (†)	‡ (†)	‡ (†)	‡ (†)	‡ (†)	‡ (†)	‡ (†)	‡ (†)	‡ (†)
Other master's degree[3]	40,120 (2,474)	36,950 (2,480)	48,680 (2,247)	54,490 (2,582)	60,950 (3,815)	49,290 (3,265)	44,690 (3,452)	58,400 (2,495)	69,550 (2,856)	78,370 (3,873)
Ph.D. except in education	50,660 (6,214)	56,970 (4,031)	57,360 (3,409)	73,950 (3,637)	102,840 (8,279)	50,480 (6,311)	61,350 (3,765)	58,840 (3,507)	72,420 (3,847)	103,110 (8,368)
Education (any doctorate)	‡ (†)	65,620 (12,612)	70,050 (8,542)	90,080 (6,686)	108,130 (13,491)	‡ (†)	70,210 (11,879)	72,960 (8,404)	104,410 (8,052)	116,800 (14,588)
Medicine (M.D. or D.O.)	117,680 (6,088)	147,130 (11,173)	153,450 (8,820)	185,110 (8,669)	237,090 (26,487)	130,190 (6,459)	161,530 (10,606)	162,120 (9,458)	203,230 (8,905)	256,760 (32,704)
Other health science professional practice doctorate[4]	108,410 (9,603)	107,550 (13,275)	109,760 (9,835)	148,590 (7,817)	202,290 (17,964)	120,570 (9,457)	129,120 (13,919)	129,540 (11,309)	175,500 (8,787)	211,270 (17,430)
Law (LL.B. or J.D.)	77,440 (3,301)	97,060 (5,357)	99,020 (3,158)	140,870 (5,610)	137,430 (10,926)	86,010 (3,801)	111,720 (6,073)	112,880 (3,788)	156,280 (6,547)	151,860 (11,465)
Other doctorate (non-Ph.D.)[5]	55,050 (10,454)	87,180 (6,860)	97,320 (8,512)	116,800 (6,549)	122,780 (12,867)	67,270 (10,237)	96,820 (8,873)	106,320 (8,397)	132,630 (7,345)	138,000 (12,260)

†Not applicable.
‡Reporting standards not met. Either there are too few cases for a reliable estimate or the coefficient of variation (CV) is 50 percent or greater.
[1]Individuals who attended more than one institution for graduate studies are included in the subtotals by degree type but excluded from the detail by control of institution.
[2]Includes chiropractic, dentistry, law, medicine, optometry, pharmacy, podiatry, and veterinary medicine.
[3]Includes public administration or policy, social work, fine arts, public health, and other.
[4]Includes chiropractic, dentistry, optometry, pharmacy, podiatry, and veterinary medicine.
[5]Includes science or engineering, psychology, business or public administration, fine arts, theology, and other. Estimates for 2011–12 and 2015–16 also include "other professional practice doctoral degrees," which were not reported as a separate category in previous years.
[6]Constant dollars based on the Consumer Price Index, prepared by the Bureau of Labor Statistics, U.S. Department of Labor, adjusted to a school-year basis.

NOTE: Data refer to students who completed graduate degrees in the academic years indicated. Data are based on the principal balance (excluding interest) as of June 30th of the survey year (e.g., the 2015–16 data are based on the principal balance as of June 30, 2016). Average amounts owed were calculated only for graduate degree completers who had outstanding loans at the level of education indicated. Data include federal and private student loans, but exclude Parent PLUS loans. Direct Subsidized Loans for graduate students were discontinued after academic year 2011–12.

SOURCE: U.S. Department of Education, National Center for Education Statistics, 1999–2000, 2003–04, 2007–08, 2011–12, and 2015–16 National Postsecondary Student Aid Study (NPSAS:2000, NPSAS:04, NPSAS:08, NPSAS:12, and NPSAS:16). (This table was prepared October 2019.)

Table 333.10. Revenues of public degree-granting postsecondary institutions, by source of revenue and level of institution: Selected years, 2007–08 through 2017–18

Level of institution and year	Total revenues	Tuition and fees[1,2]	Grants and contracts			Sales and services of auxiliary enterprises[1]	Sales and services of hospitals	Independent operations	Other operating revenues[3]
			Federal[2]	State	Local and private				
1	2	3	4	5	6	7	8	9	10
					In thousands of current dollars				
All levels									
2007–08	$273,070,439	$48,068,614	$25,499,038	$7,831,049	$8,699,401	$20,487,684	$25,183,379	$1,174,836	$14,085,890
2010–11	324,473,342	60,268,927	29,821,416	7,019,420	10,110,953	23,605,640	30,998,993	1,330,334	15,758,118
2014–15	346,812,800	73,476,374	27,290,446	7,409,069	12,460,665	26,583,777	41,582,927	1,508,778	19,489,191
2015–16	364,349,979	76,603,554	27,677,857	7,779,950	12,979,361	27,585,281	45,956,104	1,537,639	20,825,325
2016–17	390,508,373	79,244,979	28,267,575	8,017,761	13,812,044	28,421,678	50,089,201	1,635,853	21,535,947
2017–18	408,855,251	81,300,494	29,529,310	8,804,327	14,187,478	28,987,897	53,558,528	1,805,852	22,699,302
4-year									
2007–08	223,530,092	40,083,063	23,500,633	5,715,188	8,106,887	18,507,688	25,183,379	1,174,836	13,112,536
2010–11	266,688,058	51,046,786	27,656,656	5,480,573	9,543,780	21,506,767	30,998,993	1,330,334	14,830,150
2014–15	290,239,686	64,152,076	25,570,548	5,578,550	11,912,198	24,830,846	41,582,927	1,508,778	18,615,218
2015–16	308,813,202	67,533,647	26,106,025	6,007,791	12,472,377	25,984,815	45,956,104	1,537,639	19,950,465
2016–17	335,175,388	70,090,665	26,800,717	6,142,106	13,304,532	26,896,786	50,089,201	1,635,853	20,640,711
2017–18	353,195,723	72,453,183	27,988,187	6,415,440	13,623,951	27,557,917	53,558,528	1,805,852	21,794,537
2-year									
2007–08	49,540,347	7,985,551	1,998,404	2,115,861	592,513	1,979,996	0	0	973,353
2010–11	57,785,284	9,222,142	2,164,760	1,538,848	567,174	2,098,872	0	0	927,968
2014–15	56,573,114	9,324,298	1,719,898	1,830,518	548,467	1,752,931	0	0	873,974
2015–16	55,536,777	9,069,907	1,571,832	1,772,158	506,984	1,600,466	0	0	874,859
2016–17	55,332,985	9,154,315	1,466,858	1,875,655	507,512	1,524,892	0	0	895,236
2017–18	55,659,527	8,847,312	1,541,123	2,388,887	563,527	1,429,979	0	0	904,764
					Percentage distribution				
All levels									
2007–08	100.00	17.60	9.34	2.87	3.19	7.50	9.22	0.43	5.16
2010–11	100.00	18.57	9.19	2.16	3.12	7.28	9.55	0.41	4.86
2014–15	100.00	21.19	7.87	2.14	3.59	7.67	11.99	0.44	5.62
2015–16	100.00	21.02	7.60	2.14	3.56	7.57	12.61	0.42	5.72
2016–17	100.00	20.29	7.24	2.05	3.54	7.28	12.83	0.42	5.51
2017–18	100.00	19.88	7.22	2.15	3.47	7.09	13.10	0.44	5.55
4-year									
2007–08	100.00	17.93	10.51	2.56	3.63	8.28	11.27	0.53	5.87
2010–11	100.00	19.14	10.37	2.06	3.58	8.06	11.62	0.50	5.56
2014–15	100.00	22.10	8.81	1.92	4.10	8.56	14.33	0.52	6.41
2015–16	100.00	21.87	8.45	1.95	4.04	8.41	14.88	0.50	6.46
2016–17	100.00	20.91	8.00	1.83	3.97	8.02	14.94	0.49	6.16
2017–18	100.00	20.51	7.92	1.82	3.86	7.80	15.16	0.51	6.17
2-year									
2007–08	100.00	16.12	4.03	4.27	1.20	4.00	0.00	0.00	1.96
2010–11	100.00	15.96	3.75	2.66	0.98	3.63	0.00	0.00	1.61
2014–15	100.00	16.48	3.04	3.24	0.97	3.10	0.00	0.00	1.54
2015–16	100.00	16.33	2.83	3.19	0.91	2.88	0.00	0.00	1.58
2016–17	100.00	16.54	2.65	3.39	0.92	2.76	0.00	0.00	1.62
2017–18	100.00	15.90	2.77	4.29	1.01	2.57	0.00	0.00	1.63
				Revenue per full-time-equivalent student in constant 2018–19 dollars[4]					
All levels									
2007–08	$32,846	$5,782	$3,067	$942	$1,046	$2,464	$3,029	$141	$1,694
2010–11	33,049	6,139	3,037	715	1,030	2,404	3,157	135	1,605
2014–15	34,223	7,251	2,693	731	1,230	2,623	4,103	149	1,923
2015–16	35,897	7,547	2,727	767	1,279	2,718	4,528	151	2,052
2016–17	37,771	7,665	2,734	775	1,336	2,749	4,845	158	2,083
2017–18	38,686	7,693	2,794	833	1,342	2,743	5,068	171	2,148
4-year									
2007–08	43,719	7,840	4,596	1,118	1,586	3,620	4,925	230	2,565
2010–11	45,104	8,633	4,678	927	1,614	3,637	5,243	225	2,508
2014–15	44,150	9,758	3,890	849	1,812	3,777	6,325	230	2,832
2015–16	46,137	10,090	3,900	898	1,863	3,882	6,866	230	2,981
2016–17	47,462	9,925	3,795	870	1,884	3,809	7,093	232	2,923
2017–18	48,321	9,912	3,829	878	1,864	3,770	7,327	247	2,982
2-year									
2007–08	15,478	2,495	624	661	185	619	0	0	304
2010–11	14,797	2,361	554	394	145	537	0	0	238
2014–15	15,891	2,619	483	514	154	492	0	0	246
2015–16	16,067	2,624	455	513	147	463	0	0	253
2016–17	16,885	2,793	448	572	155	465	0	0	273
2017–18	17,077	2,714	473	733	173	439	0	0	278

See notes at end of table.

Table 333.10. Revenues of public degree-granting postsecondary institutions, by source of revenue and level of institution: Selected years, 2007–08 through 2017–18—Continued

Level of institution and year	Nonoperating revenue									Other revenues and additions			
	Appropriations			Nonoperating grants				Investment return (gain or loss)	Other non-operating revenues	Capital appro-priations	Capital grants and gifts	Additions to per-manent endow-ments	Other
	Federal	State	Local	Federal	State	Local	Gifts						
1	11	12	13	14	15	16	17	18	19	20	21	22	23
	In thousands of current dollars												
All levels													
2007–08	$1,849,775	$68,394,962	$9,302,794	$10,045,255	$1,925,994	$177,116	$6,053,147	$5,278,656	$2,234,287	$7,575,827	$3,092,817	$1,151,300	$4,958,618
2010–11	1,946,965	63,063,322	10,023,157	24,231,846	3,404,970	228,055	6,287,358	14,215,863	6,888,955	5,645,126	3,745,699	965,007	4,913,217
2014–15	1,779,758	65,172,431	11,248,036	21,590,392	4,406,434	291,197	8,087,953	1,342,180	5,155,201	6,295,695	3,709,702	1,012,258	6,920,335
2015–16	1,666,978	67,145,689	12,213,323	20,477,681	4,861,395	417,856	8,490,640	3,926,734	5,417,126	6,467,364	3,781,347	1,130,058	7,408,716
2016–17	1,923,743	68,641,049	12,958,544	19,697,011	5,163,737	432,922	8,264,805	15,042,298	8,072,507	6,575,388	3,665,778	1,189,554	7,855,999
2017–18	2,036,103	72,891,268	13,401,408	20,903,792	5,645,582	382,323	9,099,000	16,923,007	7,408,113	6,335,749	4,010,781	1,360,786	7,584,152
4-year													
2007–08	1,776,452	53,268,648	436,856	5,194,645	1,217,818	103,824	5,781,369	4,430,479	1,773,078	5,635,746	2,764,505	1,138,323	4,624,141
2010–11	1,853,109	49,025,814	507,010	11,812,776	2,320,005	130,451	6,061,629	13,781,509	6,061,802	3,884,591	3,249,844	943,748	4,661,730
2014–15	1,675,671	51,089,552	587,588	11,329,817	2,866,382	158,091	7,767,802	1,194,597	4,464,354	4,632,561	3,383,607	998,211	6,340,310
2015–16	1,617,876	53,067,153	1,051,753	11,522,288	3,008,676	205,597	8,207,812	3,771,368	4,666,805	4,742,620	3,482,369	1,117,698	6,802,323
2016–17	1,884,327	54,721,859	1,400,806	11,399,315	3,227,298	243,196	7,995,012	14,811,646	7,230,940	4,994,288	3,307,489	1,176,695	7,181,945
2017–18	1,984,446	58,513,022	1,708,949	12,507,190	4,024,166	234,277	8,786,344	16,581,753	6,643,024	4,708,911	3,686,661	1,347,758	7,271,628
2-year													
2007–08	73,324	15,126,314	8,865,938	4,850,610	708,176	73,292	271,778	848,177	461,209	1,940,082	328,312	12,978	334,477
2010–11	93,856	14,037,508	9,516,147	12,419,069	1,084,965	97,604	225,730	434,353	827,153	1,760,535	495,855	21,258	251,487
2014–15	104,087	14,082,879	10,660,448	10,260,575	1,540,052	133,106	320,151	147,583	690,846	1,663,135	326,095	14,047	580,025
2015–16	49,102	14,078,537	11,161,570	8,955,393	1,852,719	212,259	282,827	155,366	750,321	1,724,744	298,979	12,361	606,393
2016–17	39,417	13,919,190	11,557,739	8,297,696	1,936,438	189,726	269,793	230,652	841,567	1,581,100	358,288	12,859	674,054
2017–18	51,656	14,378,246	11,692,459	8,396,602	1,621,417	148,046	312,656	341,254	765,089	1,626,839	324,120	13,028	312,524
	Percentage distribution												
All levels													
2007–08	0.68	25.05	3.41	3.68	0.71	0.06	2.22	1.93	0.82	2.77	1.13	0.42	1.82
2010–11	0.60	19.44	3.09	7.47	1.05	0.07	1.94	4.38	2.12	1.74	1.15	0.30	1.51
2014–15	0.51	18.79	3.24	6.23	1.27	0.08	2.33	0.39	1.49	1.82	1.07	0.29	2.00
2015–16	0.46	18.43	3.35	5.62	1.33	0.11	2.33	1.08	1.49	1.78	1.04	0.31	2.03
2016–17	0.49	17.58	3.32	5.04	1.32	0.11	2.12	3.85	2.07	1.68	0.94	0.30	2.01
2017–18	0.50	17.83	3.28	5.11	1.38	0.09	2.23	4.14	1.81	1.55	0.98	0.33	1.85
4-year													
2007–08	0.79	23.83	0.20	2.32	0.54	0.05	2.59	1.98	0.79	2.52	1.24	0.51	2.07
2010–11	0.69	18.38	0.19	4.43	0.87	0.05	2.27	5.17	2.27	1.46	1.22	0.35	1.75
2014–15	0.58	17.60	0.20	3.90	0.99	0.05	2.68	0.41	1.54	1.60	1.17	0.34	2.18
2015–16	0.52	17.18	0.34	3.73	0.97	0.07	2.66	1.22	1.51	1.54	1.13	0.36	2.20
2016–17	0.56	16.33	0.42	3.40	0.96	0.07	2.39	4.42	2.16	1.49	0.99	0.35	2.14
2017–18	0.56	16.57	0.48	3.54	1.14	0.07	2.49	4.69	1.88	1.33	1.04	0.38	2.06
2-year													
2007–08	0.15	30.53	17.90	9.79	1.43	0.15	0.55	1.71	0.93	3.92	0.66	0.03	0.68
2010–11	0.16	24.29	16.47	21.49	1.88	0.17	0.39	0.75	1.43	3.05	0.86	0.04	0.44
2014–15	0.18	24.89	18.84	18.14	2.72	0.24	0.57	0.26	1.22	2.94	0.58	0.02	1.03
2015–16	0.09	25.35	20.10	16.13	3.34	0.38	0.51	0.28	1.35	3.11	0.54	0.02	1.09
2016–17	0.07	25.16	20.89	15.00	3.50	0.34	0.49	0.42	1.52	2.86	0.65	0.02	1.22
2017–18	0.09	25.83	21.01	15.09	2.91	0.27	0.56	0.61	1.37	2.92	0.58	0.02	0.56
	Revenue per full-time-equivalent student in constant 2018–19 dollars[4]												
All levels													
2007–08	$222	$8,227	$1,119	$1,208	$232	$21	$728	$635	$269	$911	$372	$138	$596
2010–11	198	6,423	1,021	2,468	347	23	640	1,448	702	575	382	98	500
2014–15	176	6,431	1,110	2,131	435	29	798	132	509	621	366	100	683
2015–16	164	6,615	1,203	2,018	479	41	837	387	534	637	373	111	730
2016–17	186	6,639	1,253	1,905	499	42	799	1,455	781	636	355	115	760
2017–18	193	6,897	1,268	1,978	534	36	861	1,601	701	599	379	129	718
4-year													
2007–08	347	10,418	85	1,016	238	20	1,131	867	347	1,102	541	223	904
2010–11	313	8,292	86	1,998	392	22	1,025	2,331	1,025	657	550	160	788
2014–15	255	7,771	89	1,723	436	24	1,182	182	679	705	515	152	964
2015–16	242	7,928	157	1,721	450	31	1,226	563	697	709	520	167	1,016
2016–17	267	7,749	198	1,614	457	34	1,132	2,097	1,024	707	468	167	1,017
2017–18	271	8,005	234	1,711	551	32	1,202	2,269	909	644	504	184	995
2-year													
2007–08	23	4,726	2,770	1,515	221	23	85	265	144	606	103	4	105
2010–11	24	3,594	2,437	3,180	278	25	58	111	212	451	127	5	64
2014–15	29	3,956	2,995	2,882	433	37	90	41	194	467	92	4	163
2015–16	14	4,073	3,229	2,591	536	61	82	45	217	499	86	4	175
2016–17	12	4,248	3,527	2,532	591	58	82	70	257	482	109	4	206
2017–18	16	4,411	3,587	2,576	497	45	96	105	235	499	99	4	96

[1]After deducting discounts and allowances.

[2]Public institutions typically report Pell grants as revenues from federal grants and as allowances that reduce revenues from tuition and fees.

[3]Includes sales and services of educational activities.

[4]Constant dollars based on the Consumer Price Index, prepared by the Bureau of Labor Statistics, U.S. Department of Labor, adjusted to a school-year basis.

NOTE: Degree-granting institutions grant associate's or higher degrees and participate in Title IV federal financial aid programs. Includes data for public institutions reporting data according to either Governmental Accounting Standards Board (GASB) or Financial Accounting Standards Board (FASB) guidance. Data in this table pertain to institutions' fiscal years that end in the academic year noted. Some data have been revised from previously published figures. Detail may not sum to totals because of rounding.

SOURCE: U.S. Department of Education, National Center for Education Statistics, Integrated Postsecondary Education Data System (IPEDS), Spring 2008 through Spring 2018, Fall Enrollment component; and Spring 2009 through Spring 2019, Finance component. (This table was prepared December 2019.)

Table 333.20.　Revenues of public degree-granting postsecondary institutions, by source of revenue and state or jurisdiction: 2017–18

[In thousands of current dollars]

State or jurisdiction	Total revenues	Operating revenue							Nonoperating revenue			Other revenues and additions
		Total	Tuition and fees[1,2]	Federal grants and contracts[2]	State, local, and private grants and contracts	Sales and services of auxiliary enterprises[1]	Sales and services of hospitals	Independent operations and other[3]	Total[4]	State appropriations	Local appropriations	
1	2	3	4	5	6	7	8	9	10	11	12	13
United States	$408,855,251	$240,873,187	$81,300,494	$29,529,310	$22,991,804	$28,987,897	$53,558,528	$24,505,154	$148,690,596	$72,891,268	$13,401,408	$19,291,468
Alabama	8,716,819	6,217,058	1,989,264	714,569	271,299	572,120	2,280,790	389,016	2,234,559	1,404,166	2,917	265,202
Alaska	855,302	380,903	135,131	122,752	63,130	39,222	0	20,668	419,453	325,302	13,986	54,946
Arizona	7,078,915	3,974,707	2,435,757	571,274	293,523	454,067	0	220,086	3,010,510	745,394	890,883	93,697
Arkansas	4,396,924	2,981,845	626,140	228,792	202,433	320,765	1,231,064	372,652	1,305,929	764,581	34,966	109,150
California	63,233,502	36,323,599	8,024,339	3,701,170	4,007,661	2,448,689	12,064,599	6,077,142	24,418,114	11,563,516	4,048,931	2,491,789
Colorado	7,889,190	6,542,222	2,393,366	1,068,569	820,575	647,436	1,035,850	576,425	1,006,648	44,306	100,434	340,321
Connecticut	3,923,056	2,129,856	766,751	176,905	98,656	321,640	439,491	326,413	1,402,990	1,124,904	0	390,211
Delaware	1,425,523	962,176	525,959	137,165	83,272	162,662	0	53,117	451,405	236,699	0	11,942
District of Columbia	159,987	57,169	33,759	13,829	5,969	417	0	3,194	91,169	80,000	0	11,649
Florida	13,472,403	6,136,343	2,509,411	1,177,619	1,350,949	919,685	0	178,679	6,728,937	4,195,023	0	607,122
Georgia	9,246,194	5,337,378	2,271,578	938,347	666,834	925,084	236,420	299,115	3,567,264	2,442,075	737	341,551
Hawaii	1,846,509	793,277	259,446	305,248	90,435	100,246	0	37,901	846,279	485,153	0	206,954
Idaho	1,387,428	704,885	366,495	133,117	49,038	105,163	0	51,072	637,327	431,993	31,430	45,216
Illinois	14,459,180	6,236,993	2,458,427	798,550	386,482	859,753	835,807	897,975	8,147,020	2,282,662	1,164,980	75,167
Indiana	7,385,602	4,661,601	2,451,011	600,871	317,358	812,256	0	480,105	2,508,441	1,566,933	8,802	215,561
Iowa	7,081,669	5,121,444	1,407,655	501,295	162,970	597,416	2,040,227	411,881	1,391,815	806,471	153,442	568,411
Kansas	3,854,195	2,269,389	978,546	317,642	213,591	471,928	0	287,683	1,428,852	735,972	307,814	155,953
Kentucky	6,453,223	4,573,365	1,111,410	438,287	250,934	396,679	1,893,750	482,305	1,613,590	879,606	25,389	266,269
Louisiana	4,392,001	2,805,547	1,206,100	298,239	755,312	405,966	18,785	121,145	1,365,564	780,591	0	220,890
Maine	922,920	507,618	249,040	60,202	54,950	83,935	0	59,492	392,066	276,659	0	23,236
Maryland	7,395,279	4,198,607	1,777,871	774,498	464,032	742,916	0	439,291	2,745,123	1,754,397	415,121	451,548
Massachusetts	5,639,240	3,496,215	1,508,549	404,013	290,572	582,469	0	710,612	1,924,525	1,461,553	0	218,500
Michigan	18,552,490	12,897,848	4,376,569	1,592,860	605,115	1,230,407	4,438,744	654,152	5,215,134	1,851,003	573,630	439,508
Minnesota	5,794,811	3,158,962	1,353,065	456,774	486,453	677,439	0	185,232	2,428,356	1,395,343	0	207,493
Mississippi	4,627,187	2,962,437	738,965	350,505	223,880	370,549	1,097,356	181,182	1,478,340	900,717	73,997	186,410
Missouri	5,451,878	3,579,142	1,157,516	220,362	188,370	839,160	1,014,469	159,264	1,734,982	866,474	162,976	137,755
Montana	1,144,329	731,595	314,429	173,512	43,844	106,763	0	93,047	358,538	231,921	11,098	54,195
Nebraska	2,869,951	1,523,962	502,317	275,053	215,889	376,305	22,333	132,064	1,197,775	706,512	179,912	148,215
Nevada	1,913,800	927,392	431,319	168,216	73,255	97,199	0	157,402	853,065	610,647	0	133,344
New Hampshire	1,072,058	768,862	392,934	67,823	55,871	220,407	0	31,827	265,463	127,475	0	37,732
New Jersey	8,681,858	5,023,918	2,440,064	561,548	391,964	563,624	782,023	284,695	3,391,225	1,731,245	213,900	266,714
New Mexico	3,822,225	2,338,552	318,233	382,522	143,447	97,433	1,222,291	174,626	1,383,717	743,941	273,450	99,956
New York	18,270,637	9,154,681	2,784,447	766,020	1,362,005	719,850	3,255,196	267,163	8,435,340	5,163,444	1,032,349	680,616
North Carolina	12,279,465	5,465,160	2,056,200	992,922	309,430	1,845,806	0	260,802	6,253,077	3,916,624	250,200	561,228
North Dakota	1,183,443	746,007	330,578	140,754	59,170	108,926	0	106,579	415,376	311,308	4,707	22,060
Ohio	15,013,059	10,613,391	3,727,381	682,204	630,381	1,230,740	3,980,411	362,274	3,975,751	2,108,298	203,217	423,917
Oklahoma	4,555,584	2,965,434	1,011,723	322,787	304,899	551,231	98,766	676,028	1,407,262	702,760	64,797	182,888
Oregon	7,573,819	5,516,113	1,335,342	701,629	393,511	584,029	2,278,051	223,552	1,838,945	848,629	273,572	218,760
Pennsylvania	16,181,115	12,971,027	4,518,170	1,376,998	714,326	1,111,380	4,240,139	1,010,016	3,098,216	1,301,307	118,653	111,872
Rhode Island	887,305	548,547	306,552	71,040	31,503	109,630	0	29,822	251,985	175,942	0	86,773
South Carolina	4,994,148	3,532,139	1,681,901	422,744	493,918	541,823	0	391,752	1,324,853	649,971	75,821	137,155
South Dakota	937,110	556,120	263,673	95,715	62,603	76,735	0	57,394	299,443	201,270	0	81,548
Tennessee	4,845,600	2,383,086	1,170,821	278,557	322,859	377,189	0	233,660	2,262,071	1,310,889	0	200,444
Texas	44,583,655	18,772,861	6,038,734	2,185,617	2,697,356	1,660,613	3,013,706	3,176,834	19,780,081	6,163,142	2,189,620	6,030,712
Utah	7,261,544	5,346,507	884,630	509,073	178,024	279,888	2,209,201	1,285,691	1,568,327	942,253	0	346,710
Vermont	926,655	755,131	412,792	124,364	70,731	113,130	0	34,114	166,880	73,329	0	4,643
Virginia	11,710,707	7,705,123	2,971,140	917,166	285,935	1,477,155	1,672,286	381,440	3,508,504	1,806,299	4,104	497,080
Washington	10,679,623	7,621,928	2,072,003	1,295,707	946,454	807,479	2,008,317	491,968	2,673,494	1,528,779	0	384,202
West Virginia	1,920,743	1,290,117	635,377	134,673	220,911	243,556	0	55,601	589,591	362,646	833	41,036
Wisconsin	6,791,863	3,999,110	1,460,158	648,199	513,835	494,859	0	882,058	2,601,182	1,338,784	446,893	191,572
Wyoming	923,839	349,451	100,831	75,636	62,982	62,378	0	47,625	450,921	303,171	47,847	123,467
U.S. Service Academies	2,189,686	256,386	26,625	55,377	2,910	41,700	148,455	-18,680	1,845,125	129,186	0	88,175
Other jurisdictions	1,540,141	418,746	95,182	162,720	42,012	9,249	68,198	41,384	1,113,295	781,855	45,961	8,099
American Samoa	16,947	9,196	1,128	5,625	0	334	0	2,109	7,750	2,028	0	0
Federated States of Micronesia	19,865	11,385	1,061	2,627	4,889	1,711	0	1,095	8,480	0	0	0
Guam	146,093	63,431	16,538	31,078	2,382	2,798	0	10,636	82,515	30,491	21,722	147
Marshall Islands	15,180	7,226	625	4,326	0	894	0	1,380	7,335	3,120	0	620
Northern Marianas	20,180	11,097	2,454	8,396	0	225	0	22	9,082	5,634	0	0
Palau	9,437	4,406	2,255	1,599	0	170	0	383	5,031	2,411	0	0
Puerto Rico	1,237,067	272,288	57,590	87,820	31,505	1,615	68,198	25,561	962,439	738,172	2,119	2,340
U.S. Virgin Islands	75,372	39,717	13,532	21,249	3,235	1,503	0	198	30,663	0	22,120	4,992

[1]After deducting discounts and allowances.
[2]Public institutions typically report Pell grants as revenues from federal grants and as allowances that reduce revenues from tuition and fees.
[3]Includes sales and services of educational activities.
[4]Includes other categories not separately shown.
NOTE: Degree-granting institutions grant associate's or higher degrees and participate in Title IV federal financial aid programs. Includes data for public institutions reporting data according to either Governmental Accounting Standards Board (GASB) or Financial Accounting Standards Board (FASB) guidance. Data in this table pertain to institutions' fiscal years that end in the academic year noted. Detail may not sum to totals because of rounding.
SOURCE: U.S. Department of Education, National Center for Education Statistics, Integrated Postsecondary Education Data System (IPEDS), Spring 2019, Finance component. (This table was prepared December 2019.)

Table 333.40. Total revenue of private nonprofit degree-granting postsecondary institutions, by source of funds and level of institution: Selected years, 1999–2000 through 2017–18

Level of institution and year	Total	Student tuition and fees (net of allowances)[1]	Federal appropriations, grants, and contracts[1,2]	State and local appropriations, grants, and contracts	Private gifts, grants, and contracts		Private gifts and contributions from affiliated entities	Investment return (gain or loss)	Educational activities	Auxiliary enterprises (net of allowances)	Hospitals	Other
					Total	Private grants and contracts						
1	2	3	4	5	6	7	8	9	10	11	12	13
In thousands of current dollars												
All levels												
1999–2000	$120,625,806	$29,651,812	$12,191,827	$1,697,979	$16,488,984	—	—	$37,763,518	$2,865,606	$8,317,607	$7,208,600	$4,439,874
2004–05	140,150,716	41,394,424	19,699,204	1,957,921	16,738,916	—	—	30,431,521	3,595,559	10,823,963	10,377,808	5,131,401
2006–07	182,377,987	47,482,331	20,193,722	2,164,167	20,194,264	—	—	55,907,577	4,104,373	12,291,765	12,636,904	7,402,884
2007–08	139,261,907	50,741,273	20,204,251	2,386,121	20,991,920	—	—	6,261,553	4,848,435	12,930,918	13,298,642	7,598,794
2008–09	69,064,340	53,698,893	21,026,721	2,391,238	17,670,642	—	—	-64,204,943	4,787,360	13,579,506	14,790,231	5,324,691
2009–10	168,688,480	56,386,895	22,913,755	2,193,062	18,019,300	$4,189,574	$13,829,726	28,427,192	4,821,683	14,080,329	16,541,461	5,304,802
2010–11	207,132,349	60,069,691	24,319,663	2,165,584	22,096,853	4,379,206	17,717,647	53,574,169	4,979,595	14,797,601	17,521,091	7,608,102
2011–12	161,843,203	63,010,873	24,147,131	1,964,921	21,619,470	4,446,517	17,172,953	4,538,153	5,082,873	15,500,185	18,658,649	7,320,948
2012–13	202,042,331	65,562,231	23,710,290	1,939,417	22,335,345	4,834,258	17,501,087	38,532,782	5,530,428	15,969,232	19,011,711	9,450,894
2013–14	228,806,876	67,681,378	23,640,029	1,971,815	25,842,976	5,152,784	20,690,192	57,147,772	6,280,766	16,407,013	20,667,484	9,167,642
2014–15	200,395,534	70,181,110	24,186,839	2,113,187	26,932,309	5,520,105	21,412,204	21,274,906	6,702,519	16,883,478	23,880,282	8,240,906
2015–16	182,571,838	72,100,188	23,471,268	2,162,083	28,622,642	5,819,574	22,803,069	-2,735,211	7,042,281	17,608,294	24,107,516	10,192,778
2016–17	242,602,673	73,966,392	25,244,371	2,103,049	28,864,670	6,197,207	22,667,463	48,838,957	7,516,359	18,004,385	26,744,919	11,319,571
2017–18	248,465,960	75,871,170	26,440,108	2,165,914	30,668,285	6,574,834	24,093,451	45,451,443	7,991,521	18,326,993	29,399,644	12,150,882
4-year												
1999–2000	119,708,625	29,257,523	12,133,829	1,673,707	16,346,616	—	—	37,698,219	2,837,784	8,261,507	7,208,600	4,290,841
2004–05	139,528,763	41,045,608	19,622,002	1,931,021	16,671,017	—	—	30,408,545	3,581,869	10,784,161	10,377,808	5,106,733
2006–07	181,850,660	47,211,942	20,137,197	2,143,146	20,144,883	—	—	55,857,135	4,096,086	12,253,089	12,636,904	7,370,278
2007–08	138,760,610	50,436,622	20,143,562	2,361,744	20,938,758	—	—	6,273,767	4,837,355	12,892,828	13,298,642	7,577,331
2008–09	68,617,705	53,399,912	20,967,794	2,370,169	17,624,319	—	—	-64,172,755	4,781,845	13,542,690	14,790,231	5,313,500
2009–10	168,169,216	56,087,965	22,843,520	2,179,050	17,968,453	4,185,607	13,782,846	28,406,397	4,814,283	14,044,652	16,541,461	5,283,434
2010–11	206,473,105	59,603,541	24,260,568	2,150,124	22,057,300	4,376,381	17,680,919	53,557,782	4,975,158	14,762,888	17,521,091	7,584,652
2011–12	161,246,877	62,571,879	24,098,863	1,953,307	21,580,612	4,444,004	17,136,608	4,532,992	5,079,866	15,471,860	18,658,649	7,298,849
2012–13	201,526,648	65,213,804	23,664,427	1,925,893	22,293,530	4,831,951	17,461,579	38,519,232	5,527,564	15,939,735	19,011,711	9,430,753
2013–14	228,233,305	67,325,986	23,578,760	1,959,405	25,792,211	5,149,819	20,642,392	57,105,397	6,278,456	16,376,022	20,667,484	9,149,584
2014–15	199,546,338	69,519,464	24,127,099	2,102,335	26,895,138	5,518,411	21,376,727	21,267,202	6,696,900	16,840,357	23,880,282	8,217,562
2015–16	181,729,580	71,425,134	23,427,914	2,155,610	28,581,387	5,816,843	22,764,544	-2,736,188	7,037,367	17,562,236	24,107,516	10,168,604
2016–17	241,772,907	73,307,606	25,206,303	2,097,462	28,824,410	6,194,800	22,629,610	48,824,390	7,511,347	17,964,144	26,744,919	11,292,325
2017–18	247,644,652	75,218,369	26,404,744	2,159,775	30,615,084	6,572,718	24,042,366	45,435,307	7,986,306	18,290,555	29,399,644	12,134,868
2-year												
1999–2000	917,181	394,289	57,998	24,272	142,368	—	—	65,299	27,822	56,100	0	149,033
2004–05	621,953	348,815	77,202	26,900	67,899	—	—	22,976	13,690	39,802	0	24,668
2006–07	527,327	270,389	56,525	21,021	49,381	—	—	50,442	8,288	38,675	0	32,606
2007–08	501,297	304,651	60,689	24,377	53,162	—	—	-12,214	11,080	38,091	0	21,462
2008–09	446,635	298,981	58,927	21,069	46,323	—	—	-32,187	5,515	36,816	0	11,191
2009–10	519,264	298,930	70,235	14,012	50,847	3,967	46,880	20,795	7,400	35,677	0	21,368
2010–11	659,244	466,149	59,095	15,460	39,553	2,825	36,727	16,388	4,437	34,712	0	23,450
2011–12	596,326	438,994	48,269	11,614	38,858	2,513	36,345	5,161	3,007	28,325	0	22,099
2012–13	515,683	348,427	45,863	13,524	41,815	2,307	39,508	13,550	2,865	29,498	0	20,140
2013–14	573,571	355,392	61,269	12,409	50,766	2,965	47,800	42,376	2,311	30,991	0	18,058
2014–15	849,197	661,646	59,740	10,852	37,171	1,694	35,477	7,704	5,619	43,121	0	23,344
2015–16	842,258	675,053	43,354	6,473	41,256	2,731	38,525	976	4,913	46,058	0	24,174
2016–17	829,766	658,786	38,068	5,587	40,260	2,407	37,853	14,567	5,012	40,241	0	27,245
2017–18	821,309	652,801	35,364	6,139	53,201	2,116	51,085	16,135	5,216	36,438	0	16,014
Percentage distribution												
All levels												
1999–2000	100.00	24.58	10.11	1.41	13.67	—	—	31.31	2.38	6.90	5.98	3.68
2004–05	100.00	29.54	14.06	1.40	11.94	—	—	21.71	2.57	7.72	7.40	3.66
2006–07	100.00	26.04	11.07	1.19	11.07	—	—	30.65	2.25	6.74	6.93	4.06
2007–08	100.00	36.44	14.51	1.71	15.07	—	—	4.50	3.48	9.29	9.55	5.46
2008–09	100.00	77.75	30.45	3.46	25.59	—	—	-92.96	6.93	19.66	21.42	7.71
2009–10	100.00	33.43	13.58	1.30	10.68	2.48	8.20	16.85	2.86	8.35	9.81	3.14
2010–11	100.00	29.00	11.74	1.05	10.67	2.11	8.55	25.86	2.40	7.14	8.46	3.67
2011–12	100.00	38.93	14.92	1.21	13.36	2.75	10.61	2.80	3.14	9.58	11.53	4.52
2012–13	100.00	32.45	11.74	0.96	11.05	2.39	8.66	19.07	2.74	7.90	9.41	4.68
2013–14	100.00	29.58	10.33	0.86	11.29	2.25	9.04	24.98	2.75	7.17	9.03	4.01
2014–15	100.00	35.02	12.07	1.05	13.44	2.75	10.68	10.62	3.34	8.43	11.92	4.11
2015–16	100.00	39.49	12.86	1.18	15.68	3.19	12.49	-1.50	3.86	9.64	13.20	5.58
2016–17	100.00	30.49	10.41	0.87	11.90	2.55	9.34	20.13	3.10	7.42	11.02	4.67
2017–18	100.00	30.54	10.64	0.87	12.34	2.65	9.70	18.29	3.22	7.38	11.83	4.89
4-year												
1999–2000	100.00	24.44	10.14	1.40	13.66	—	—	31.49	2.37	6.90	6.02	3.58
2004–05	100.00	29.42	14.06	1.38	11.95	—	—	21.79	2.57	7.73	7.44	3.66
2006–07	100.00	25.96	11.07	1.18	11.08	—	—	30.72	2.25	6.74	6.95	4.05
2007–08	100.00	36.35	14.52	1.70	15.09	—	—	4.52	3.49	9.29	9.58	5.46
2008–09	100.00	77.82	30.56	3.45	25.68	—	—	-93.52	6.97	19.74	21.55	7.74
2009–10	100.00	33.35	13.58	1.30	10.68	2.49	8.20	16.89	2.86	8.35	9.84	3.14
2010–11	100.00	28.87	11.75	1.04	10.68	2.12	8.56	25.94	2.41	7.15	8.49	3.67
2011–12	100.00	38.81	14.95	1.21	13.38	2.76	10.63	2.81	3.15	9.60	11.57	4.53
2012–13	100.00	32.36	11.74	0.96	11.06	2.40	8.66	19.11	2.74	7.91	9.43	4.68
2013–14	100.00	29.50	10.33	0.86	11.30	2.26	9.04	25.02	2.75	7.18	9.06	4.01
2014–15	100.00	34.84	12.09	1.05	13.48	2.77	10.71	10.66	3.36	8.44	11.97	4.12
2015–16	100.00	39.30	12.89	1.19	15.73	3.20	12.53	-1.51	3.87	9.66	13.27	5.60
2016–17	100.00	30.32	10.43	0.87	11.92	2.56	9.36	20.19	3.11	7.43	11.06	4.67
2017–18	100.00	30.37	10.66	0.87	12.36	2.65	9.71	18.35	3.22	7.39	11.87	4.90

See notes at end of table.

Table 333.40. Total revenue of private nonprofit degree-granting postsecondary institutions, by source of funds and level of institution: Selected years, 1999–2000 through 2017–18—Continued

Level of institution and year	Total	Student tuition and fees (net of allowances)[1]	Federal appropriations, grants, and contracts[1,2]	State and local appropriations, grants, and contracts	Private gifts, grants, and contracts			Investment return (gain or loss)	Educational activities	Auxiliary enterprises (net of allowances)	Hospitals	Other
					Total	Private grants and contracts	Private gifts and contributions from affiliated entities					
1	2	3	4	5	6	7	8	9	10	11	12	13
2-year												
1999–2000	100.00	42.99	6.32	2.65	15.52	—	—	7.12	3.03	6.12	0.00	16.25
2004–05	100.00	56.08	12.41	4.33	10.92	—	—	3.69	2.20	6.40	0.00	3.97
2006–07	100.00	51.28	10.72	3.99	9.36	—	—	9.57	1.57	7.33	0.00	6.18
2007–08	100.00	60.77	12.11	4.86	10.60	—	—	-2.44	2.21	7.60	0.00	4.28
2008–09	100.00	66.94	13.19	4.72	10.37	—	—	-7.21	1.23	8.24	0.00	2.51
2009–10	100.00	57.57	13.53	2.70	9.79	0.76	9.03	4.00	1.43	6.87	0.00	4.12
2010–11	100.00	70.71	8.96	2.35	6.00	0.43	5.57	2.49	0.67	5.27	0.00	3.56
2011–12	100.00	73.62	8.09	1.95	6.52	0.42	6.09	0.87	0.50	4.75	0.00	3.71
2012–13	100.00	67.57	8.89	2.62	8.11	0.45	7.66	2.63	0.56	5.72	0.00	3.91
2013–14	100.00	61.96	10.68	2.16	8.85	0.52	8.33	7.39	0.40	5.40	0.00	3.15
2014–15	100.00	77.91	7.03	1.28	4.38	0.20	4.18	0.91	0.66	5.08	0.00	2.75
2015–16	100.00	80.15	5.15	0.77	4.90	0.32	4.57	0.12	0.58	5.47	0.00	2.87
2016–17	100.00	79.39	4.59	0.67	4.85	0.29	4.56	1.76	0.60	4.85	0.00	3.28
2017–18	100.00	79.48	4.31	0.75	6.48	0.26	6.22	1.96	0.64	4.44	0.00	1.95
				Revenue per full-time-equivalent student in constant 2018–19 dollars[3]								
All levels												
1999–2000	$71,078	$17,472	$7,184	$1,001	$9,716	—	—	$22,252	$1,689	$4,901	$4,248	$2,616
2004–05	64,531	19,060	9,070	902	7,707	—	—	14,012	1,656	4,984	4,778	2,363
2006–07	76,404	19,892	8,460	907	8,460	—	—	23,422	1,719	5,149	5,294	3,101
2007–08	54,878	19,995	7,962	940	8,272	—	—	2,467	1,911	5,096	5,241	2,994
2008–09	26,446	20,562	8,051	916	6,766	—	—	-24,585	1,833	5,200	5,663	2,039
2009–10	62,281	20,818	8,460	810	6,653	$1,547	$5,106	10,496	1,780	5,199	6,107	1,959
2010–11	72,235	20,949	8,481	755	7,706	1,527	6,179	18,683	1,737	5,160	6,110	2,653
2011–12	54,360	21,164	8,111	660	7,262	1,494	5,768	1,524	1,707	5,206	6,267	2,459
2012–13	65,994	21,415	7,745	633	7,295	1,579	5,716	12,586	1,806	5,216	6,210	3,087
2013–14	73,483	21,736	7,592	633	8,300	1,655	6,645	18,353	2,017	5,269	6,637	2,944
2014–15	62,958	22,049	7,599	664	8,461	1,734	6,727	6,684	2,106	5,304	7,502	2,589
2015–16	56,531	22,325	7,268	669	8,863	1,802	7,061	-847	2,181	5,452	7,465	3,156
2016–17	73,251	22,333	7,622	635	8,715	1,871	6,844	14,746	2,269	5,436	8,075	3,418
2017–18	73,205	22,354	7,790	638	9,036	1,937	7,099	13,391	2,355	5,400	8,662	3,580
4-year												
1999–2000	72,049	17,609	7,303	1,007	9,839	—	—	22,689	1,708	4,972	4,339	2,583
2004–05	65,025	19,129	9,145	900	7,769	—	—	14,171	1,669	5,026	4,836	2,380
2006–07	76,844	19,950	8,509	906	8,513	—	—	23,603	1,731	5,178	5,340	3,114
2007–08	55,171	20,054	8,009	939	8,325	—	—	2,494	1,923	5,126	5,288	3,013
2008–09	26,498	20,621	8,097	915	6,806	—	—	-24,781	1,847	5,230	5,712	2,052
2009–10	62,599	20,878	8,503	811	6,689	1,558	5,131	10,574	1,792	5,228	6,157	1,967
2010–11	72,778	21,009	8,551	758	7,775	1,543	6,232	18,878	1,754	5,204	6,176	2,673
2011–12	54,697	21,225	8,175	663	7,320	1,507	5,813	1,538	1,723	5,248	6,329	2,476
2012–13	66,380	21,481	7,795	634	7,343	1,592	5,752	12,688	1,821	5,250	6,262	3,106
2013–14	73,891	21,797	7,634	634	8,350	1,667	6,683	18,488	2,033	5,302	6,691	2,962
2014–15	63,531	22,133	7,681	669	8,563	1,757	6,806	6,771	2,132	5,362	7,603	2,616
2015–16	56,953	22,384	7,342	676	8,957	1,823	7,134	-858	2,205	5,504	7,555	3,187
2016–17	73,891	22,404	7,704	641	8,809	1,893	6,916	14,922	2,296	5,490	8,174	3,451
2017–18	73,841	22,428	7,873	644	9,129	1,960	7,169	13,548	2,381	5,454	8,766	3,618
2-year												
1999–2000	25,762	11,075	1,629	682	3,999	—	—	1,834	781	1,576	0	4,186
2004–05	23,864	13,384	2,962	1,032	2,605	—	—	882	525	1,527	0	947
2006–07	25,706	13,181	2,755	1,025	2,407	—	—	2,459	404	1,885	0	1,589
2007–08	22,216	13,501	2,690	1,080	2,356	—	—	-541	491	1,688	0	951
2008–09	20,292	13,584	2,677	957	2,105	—	—	-1,462	251	1,673	0	508
2009–10	23,531	13,546	3,183	635	2,304	180	2,124	942	335	1,617	0	968
2010–11	21,651	15,310	1,941	508	1,299	93	1,206	538	146	1,140	0	770
2011–12	20,391	15,011	1,651	397	1,329	86	1,243	176	103	969	0	756
2012–13	20,140	13,608	1,791	528	1,633	90	1,543	529	112	1,152	0	787
2013–14	22,970	14,233	2,454	497	2,033	119	1,914	1,697	93	1,241	0	723
2014–15	20,198	15,737	1,421	258	884	40	844	183	134	1,026	0	555
2015–16	21,767	17,446	1,120	167	1,066	71	996	25	127	1,190	0	625
2016–17	20,801	16,514	954	140	1,009	60	949	365	126	1,009	0	683
2017–18	20,355	16,179	876	152	1,319	52	1,266	400	129	903	0	397

—Not available.

[1]Private institutions typically report Pell grants as revenues from tuition and fees rather than as revenues from federal grants.

[2]Includes independent operations.

[3]Constant dollars based on the Consumer Price Index, prepared by the Bureau of Labor Statistics, U.S. Department of Labor, adjusted to a school-year basis.

NOTE: Degree-granting institutions grant associate's or higher degrees and participate in Title IV federal financial aid programs. Data in this table pertain to institutions' fiscal years that end in the academic year noted. Some data have been revised from previously published figures. Detail may not sum to totals because of rounding.

SOURCE: U.S. Department of Education, National Center for Education Statistics, Integrated Postsecondary Education Data System (IPEDS), "Fall Enrollment Survey" (IPEDS-EF:99); Spring 2001 through Spring 2007, Enrollment component; Spring 2008 through Spring 2018, Fall Enrollment component; and Spring 2001 through Spring 2019, Finance component. (This table was prepared December 2019.)

Table 333.50. Total revenue of private nonprofit degree-granting postsecondary institutions, by source of funds and classification of institution: 2017–18

Classification of institution	Total	Student tuition and fees (net of allowances)[1]	Federal appropriations, grants, and contracts[1,2]	State appropriations, grants, and contracts	Local appropriations, grants, and contracts	Private grants and contracts	Private gifts and contributions from affiliated entities	Investment return (gain or loss)	Educational activities	Auxiliary enterprises (net of allowances)	Hospitals	Other
1	2	3	4	5	6	7	8	9	10	11	12	13
In thousands of current dollars												
Total	$248,465,960	$75,871,170	$26,440,108	$1,676,697	$489,217	$6,574,834	$24,093,451	$45,451,443	$7,991,521	$18,326,993	$29,399,644	$12,150,882
4-year	247,644,652	75,218,369	26,404,744	1,671,850	487,925	6,572,718	24,042,366	45,435,307	7,986,306	18,290,555	29,399,644	12,134,868
Research university, very high[3]	127,519,521	19,589,241	20,165,663	858,374	226,256	4,337,374	11,619,637	30,437,749	5,994,725	5,427,298	20,368,962	8,494,243
Research university, high[4]	17,828,061	7,265,595	1,361,977	126,482	29,551	333,538	2,196,512	2,751,321	892,017	1,645,394	502,711	722,962
Doctoral/research[5]	11,115,848	7,304,558	294,560	105,899	3,535	52,501	725,714	960,244	53,624	1,262,889	0	352,324
Master's[6]	34,970,904	22,545,043	852,411	261,910	8,968	155,239	2,602,695	2,627,314	166,748	4,781,855	13,773	954,946
Baccalaureate[7]	27,564,073	10,398,318	635,604	103,155	4,319	259,275	4,374,179	6,651,087	161,084	4,286,562	0	690,490
Special-focus institutions[8]	28,646,245	8,115,613	3,094,529	216,031	215,297	1,434,791	2,523,629	2,007,593	718,108	886,556	8,514,198	919,902
Arts, music, or design	2,916,192	1,806,906	36,917	13,611	5,135	27,569	334,008	275,785	18,030	322,001	0	76,230
Business and management	726,431	438,264	27,161	10,049	0	3,542	60,632	82,235	5,471	91,229	0	7,848
Engineering and other technology-related	318,482	180,748	2,971	1,086	0	1,483	41,776	54,054	1,443	28,918	0	6,003
Faith related	2,228,694	631,585	46,384	2,290	311	55,994	739,305	437,937	12,151	175,748	0	126,990
Law	472,683	335,577	8,943	2,614	422	4,393	33,424	60,914	558	14,733	0	11,104
Medical schools and centers and other heath professions schools	21,262,589	4,366,610	2,811,524	180,905	199,975	1,334,393	1,241,892	1,061,734	668,261	217,274	8,514,198	665,823
Tribal colleges[9]	90,269	7,683	72,413	1,242	242	1,199	958	443	697	978	0	4,413
Other special focus	630,905	348,240	88,214	4,233	9,213	6,218	71,634	34,491	11,496	35,674	0	21,491
2-year	821,309	652,801	35,364	4,847	1,292	2,116	51,085	16,135	5,216	36,438	0	16,014
Associate's colleges	804,017	651,623	23,238	3,684	717	906	50,485	16,100	5,142	36,162	0	15,959
Tribal colleges[9]	17,292	1,178	12,126	1,163	575	1,210	600	35	73	276	0	55
Percentage distribution												
Total	100.00	30.54	10.64	0.67	0.20	2.65	9.70	18.29	3.22	7.38	11.83	4.89
4-year	100.00	30.37	10.66	0.68	0.20	2.65	9.71	18.35	3.22	7.39	11.87	4.90
Research university, very high[3]	100.00	15.36	15.81	0.67	0.18	3.40	9.11	23.87	4.70	4.26	15.97	6.66
Research university, high[4]	100.00	40.75	7.64	0.71	0.17	1.87	12.32	15.43	5.00	9.23	2.82	4.06
Doctoral/research[5]	100.00	65.71	2.65	0.95	0.03	0.47	6.53	8.64	0.48	11.36	0.00	3.17
Master's[6]	100.00	64.47	2.44	0.75	0.03	0.44	7.44	7.51	0.48	13.67	0.04	2.73
Baccalaureate[7]	100.00	37.72	2.31	0.37	0.02	0.94	15.87	24.13	0.58	15.55	0.00	2.51
Special-focus institutions[8]	100.00	28.33	10.80	0.75	0.75	5.01	8.81	7.01	2.51	3.09	29.72	3.21
Arts, music, or design	100.00	61.96	1.27	0.47	0.18	0.95	11.45	9.46	0.62	11.04	0.00	2.61
Business and management	100.00	60.33	3.74	1.38	0.00	0.49	8.35	11.32	0.75	12.56	0.00	1.08
Engineering and other technology-related	100.00	56.75	0.93	0.34	0.00	0.47	13.12	16.97	0.45	9.08	0.00	1.88
Faith related	100.00	28.34	2.08	0.10	0.01	2.51	33.17	19.65	0.55	7.89	0.00	5.70
Law	100.00	70.99	1.89	0.55	0.09	0.93	7.07	12.89	0.12	3.12	0.00	2.35
Medical schools and centers and other heath professions schools	100.00	20.54	13.22	0.85	0.94	6.28	5.84	4.99	3.14	1.02	40.04	3.13
Tribal colleges[9]	100.00	8.51	80.22	1.38	0.27	1.33	1.06	0.49	0.77	1.08	0.00	4.89
Other special focus	100.00	55.20	13.98	0.67	1.46	0.99	11.35	5.47	1.82	5.65	0.00	3.41
2-year	100.00	79.48	4.31	0.59	0.16	0.26	6.22	1.96	0.64	4.44	0.00	1.95
Associate's colleges	100.00	81.05	2.89	0.46	0.09	0.11	6.28	2.00	0.64	4.50	0.00	1.98
Tribal colleges[9]	100.00	6.81	70.13	6.73	3.33	7.00	3.47	0.20	0.42	1.60	0.00	0.32
Revenue per full-time-equivalent student in current dollars												
Total	$71,719	$21,900	$7,632	$484	$141	$1,898	$6,954	$13,119	$2,307	$5,290	$8,486	$3,507
4-year	72,342	21,973	7,713	488	143	1,920	7,023	13,273	2,333	5,343	8,588	3,545
Research university, very high[3]	221,773	34,068	35,071	1,493	393	7,543	20,208	52,935	10,426	9,439	35,424	14,773
Research university, high[4]	61,028	24,871	4,662	433	101	1,142	7,519	9,418	3,054	5,632	1,721	2,475
Doctoral/research[5]	31,512	20,708	835	300	10	149	2,057	2,722	152	3,580	0	999
Master's[6]	27,217	17,546	663	204	7	121	2,026	2,045	130	3,722	11	743
Baccalaureate[7]	46,210	17,432	1,066	173	7	435	7,333	11,150	270	7,186	0	1,158
Special-focus institutions[8]	88,963	25,204	9,610	671	669	4,456	7,837	6,235	2,230	2,753	26,441	2,857
Arts, music, or design	49,511	30,678	627	231	87	468	5,671	4,682	306	5,467	0	1,294
Business and management	30,453	18,373	1,139	421	0	148	2,542	3,447	229	3,824	0	329
Engineering and other technology-related	26,022	14,768	243	89	0	121	3,413	4,417	118	2,363	0	490
Faith related	32,957	9,340	686	34	5	828	10,932	6,476	180	2,599	0	1,878
Law	46,224	32,816	875	256	41	430	3,269	5,957	55	1,441	0	1,086
Medical schools and centers and other heath professions schools	159,165	32,687	21,046	1,354	1,497	9,989	9,296	7,948	5,002	1,626	63,735	4,984
Tribal colleges[9]	43,841	3,731	35,169	603	118	582	465	215	339	475	0	2,143
Other special focus	46,696	25,775	6,529	313	682	460	5,302	2,553	851	2,640	0	1,591
2-year	19,942	15,850	859	118	31	51	1,240	392	127	885	0	389
Associate's colleges	19,712	15,975	570	90	18	22	1,238	395	126	887	0	391
Tribal colleges[9]	43,667	2,974	30,622	2,937	1,452	3,055	1,515	88	185	698	0	140

[1]Private institutions typically report Pell grants as revenues from tuition and fees rather than as revenues from federal grants.
[2]Includes independent operations.
[3]Research universities with a very high level of research activity.
[4]Research universities with a high level of research activity.
[5]Institutions that award at least 20 research/scholarship doctor's degrees per year, but did not have high levels of research activity.
[6]Institutions that award at least 50 master's and fewer than 20 doctor's degrees per year.
[7]Institutions that primarily emphasize undergraduate education. In addition to institutions that primarily award bachelor's degrees, also includes institutions classified as 4-year in the IPEDS system, but classified as 2-year baccalaureate/associate's colleges in the Carnegie Classification system because they primarily award associate's degrees.
[8]Four-year institutions that award degrees primarily in single fields of study, such as medicine, business, fine arts, theology, and engineering.

[9]Tribally controlled colleges, which are located on reservations and are members of the American Indian Higher Education Consortium.
NOTE: Relative levels of research activity for research universities were determined by an analysis of research and development expenditures, science and engineering research staffing, and doctor's degrees conferred, by field. Further information on the Carnegie 2015 classification system used in this table may be obtained from https://carnegieclassifications.iu.edu/downloads/CCIHE2015-FactsFigures.pdf. Degree-granting institutions grant associate's or higher degrees and participate in Title IV federal financial aid programs. Data in this table pertain to institutions' fiscal years that end in the academic year noted. Detail may not sum to totals because of rounding.
SOURCE: U.S. Department of Education, National Center for Education Statistics, Integrated Postsecondary Education Data System (IPEDS), Spring 2018, Fall Enrollment component; and Spring 2019, Finance component. (This table was prepared December 2019.)

Table 333.55. Total revenue of private for-profit degree-granting postsecondary institutions, by source of funds and level of institution: Selected years, 1999–2000 through 2017–18

Level of institution and year	Total	Student tuition and fees (net of allowances)[1]	Federal appropriations, grants, and contracts[1]	State and local appropriations, grants, and contracts	Private gifts, grants, and contracts	Investment return (gain or loss)	Educational activities	Auxiliary enterprises (net of allowances)	Other
1	2	3	4	5	6	7	8	9	10
					In thousands of current dollars				
All levels									
1999–2000	$4,321,985	$3,721,032	$198,923	$71,904	$2,151	$18,537	$70,672	$156,613	$82,153
2010–11	28,285,216	25,157,459	1,583,370	157,290	31,272	32,551	402,206	542,622	378,447
2013–14	22,645,566	20,481,607	941,363	77,986	12,206	43,032	256,321	482,439	350,611
2014–15	19,665,772	17,705,922	848,223	53,217	15,935	45,317	224,389	434,253	338,516
2015–16	17,049,389	15,493,140	712,642	46,680	14,901	27,484	176,339	312,166	266,036
2016–17	15,778,912	14,427,696	520,794	40,206	12,588	41,453	203,365	247,202	285,609
2017–18	13,233,730	12,374,965	228,157	21,357	12,175	58,806	159,937	147,597	230,737
4-year									
1999–2000	2,381,042	2,050,136	103,865	39,460	1,109	10,340	33,764	102,103	40,266
2010–11	21,690,069	19,483,895	1,113,186	118,054	29,118	28,671	346,786	405,604	164,755
2013–14	17,832,352	16,188,360	709,409	51,830	10,232	36,012	222,841	395,509	218,160
2014–15	15,845,578	14,281,696	626,082	37,570	14,474	37,530	198,393	371,131	278,702
2015–16	13,575,294	12,376,301	519,399	32,097	13,708	21,959	151,174	255,030	205,627
2016–17	12,733,999	11,692,675	368,141	27,872	11,586	34,559	180,112	210,935	208,120
2017–18	10,779,287	10,190,630	111,302	12,118	11,521	51,759	138,034	121,056	142,867
2-year									
1999–2000	1,940,943	1,670,896	95,058	32,444	1,042	8,197	36,908	54,510	41,888
2010–11	6,595,147	5,673,564	470,183	39,236	2,154	3,880	55,420	137,018	213,692
2013–14	4,813,214	4,293,247	231,954	26,157	1,975	7,021	33,480	86,930	132,450
2014–15	3,820,194	3,424,226	222,141	15,647	1,461	7,787	25,996	63,122	59,814
2015–16	3,474,095	3,116,840	193,243	14,583	1,193	5,525	25,166	57,136	60,409
2016–17	3,044,913	2,735,021	152,652	12,334	1,002	6,894	23,253	36,266	77,490
2017–18	2,454,442	2,184,335	116,855	9,240	654	7,047	21,903	26,540	87,869
					Percentage distribution				
All levels									
1999–2000	100.00	86.10	4.60	1.66	0.05	0.43	1.64	3.62	1.90
2010–11	100.00	88.94	5.60	0.56	0.11	0.12	1.42	1.92	1.34
2013–14	100.00	90.44	4.16	0.34	0.05	0.19	1.13	2.13	1.55
2014–15	100.00	90.03	4.31	0.27	0.08	0.23	1.14	2.21	1.72
2015–16	100.00	90.87	4.18	0.27	0.09	0.16	1.03	1.83	1.56
2016–17	100.00	91.44	3.30	0.25	0.08	0.26	1.29	1.57	1.81
2017–18	100.00	93.51	1.72	0.16	0.09	0.44	1.21	1.12	1.74
4-year									
1999–2000	100.00	86.10	4.36	1.66	0.05	0.43	1.42	4.29	1.69
2010–11	100.00	89.83	5.13	0.54	0.13	0.13	1.60	1.87	0.76
2013–14	100.00	90.78	3.98	0.29	0.06	0.20	1.25	2.22	1.22
2014–15	100.00	90.13	3.95	0.24	0.09	0.24	1.25	2.34	1.76
2015–16	100.00	91.17	3.83	0.24	0.10	0.16	1.11	1.88	1.51
2016–17	100.00	91.82	2.89	0.22	0.09	0.27	1.41	1.66	1.63
2017–18	100.00	94.54	1.03	0.11	0.11	0.48	1.28	1.12	1.33
2-year									
1999–2000	100.00	86.09	4.90	1.67	0.05	0.42	1.90	2.81	2.16
2010–11	100.00	86.03	7.13	0.59	0.03	0.06	0.84	2.08	3.24
2013–14	100.00	89.20	4.82	0.54	0.04	0.15	0.70	1.81	2.75
2014–15	100.00	89.63	5.81	0.41	0.04	0.20	0.68	1.65	1.57
2015–16	100.00	89.72	5.56	0.42	0.03	0.16	0.72	1.64	1.74
2016–17	100.00	89.82	5.01	0.41	0.03	0.23	0.76	1.19	2.54
2017–18	100.00	89.00	4.76	0.38	0.03	0.29	0.89	1.08	3.58
					Revenue per full-time-equivalent student in constant 2018–19 dollars[2]				
All levels									
1999–2000	$16,811	$14,474	$774	$280	$8	$72	$275	$609	$320
2010–11	19,595	17,428	1,097	109	22	23	279	376	262
2013–14	23,017	20,818	957	79	12	44	261	490	356
2014–15	17,803	16,029	768	48	14	41	203	393	306
2015–16	18,326	16,653	766	50	16	30	190	336	286
2016–17	18,387	16,813	607	47	15	48	237	288	333
2017–18	17,989	16,821	310	29	17	80	217	201	314
4-year									
1999–2000	17,063	14,691	744	283	8	74	242	732	289
2010–11	19,755	17,746	1,014	108	27	26	316	369	150
2013–14	24,661	22,387	981	72	14	50	308	547	302
2014–15	17,807	16,049	704	42	16	42	223	417	313
2015–16	18,265	16,652	699	43	18	30	203	343	277
2016–17	18,364	16,863	531	40	17	50	260	304	300
2017–18	18,167	17,174	188	20	19	87	233	204	241
2-year									
1999–2000	16,513	14,215	809	276	9	70	314	464	356
2010–11	19,087	16,420	1,361	114	6	11	160	397	618
2013–14	18,460	16,465	890	100	8	27	128	333	508
2014–15	17,786	15,943	1,034	73	7	36	121	294	278
2015–16	18,568	16,658	1,033	78	6	30	134	305	323
2016–17	18,484	16,602	927	75	6	42	141	220	470
2017–18	17,247	15,349	821	65	5	50	154	186	617

[1]Private institutions typically report Pell grants as revenues from tuition and fees rather than as revenues from federal grants.
[2]Constant dollars based on the Consumer Price Index, prepared by the Bureau of Labor Statistics, U.S. Department of Labor, adjusted to a school-year basis.
NOTE: Degree-granting institutions grant associate's or higher degrees and participate in Title IV federal financial aid programs. Data in this table pertain to institutions' fiscal years that end in the academic year noted. Some data have been revised from previously published figures. Detail may not sum to totals because of rounding.

SOURCE: U.S. Department of Education, National Center for Education Statistics, Integrated Postsecondary Education Data System (IPEDS), "Fall Enrollment Survey" (IPEDS-EF:99); Spring 2011 through Spring 2018, Fall Enrollment component; and selected years, Spring 2001 through Spring 2019, Finance component. (This table was prepared December 2019.)

Table 334.10. Total expenditures of public degree-granting postsecondary institutions, by purpose of expenditure and level of institution: 2009–10 through 2017–18

Level of institution and year	Total	Instruction Total[3]	Instruction Salaries and wages	Research	Public service	Academic support	Student services	Institutional support	Auxiliary enterprises[1]	Net grant aid to students[2]	Hospitals	Independent operations	Other
1	2	3	4	5	6	7	8	9	10	11	12	13	14
						In thousands of current dollars							
All levels													
2009-10	$281,390,445	$89,237,995	$51,808,563	$32,270,072	$12,980,154	$22,788,482	$15,661,212	$27,554,886	$25,981,203	$15,494,246	$28,484,978	$1,310,925	$9,626,291
2010-11	296,862,854	93,090,749	53,586,472	33,866,656	13,426,331	23,441,698	16,276,833	29,051,411	27,649,838	17,487,275	29,980,642	1,233,264	11,358,158
2011-12	305,537,590	95,093,836	54,341,187	34,282,999	13,567,337	24,712,457	17,019,195	29,512,479	28,475,340	16,611,881	33,063,066	1,297,507	11,901,492
2012-13	311,421,148	97,716,338	55,555,358	34,634,474	13,495,240	25,725,240	17,679,256	30,850,117	29,002,556	16,227,767	34,208,788	1,320,284	10,561,112
2013-14	323,893,053	101,281,681	57,591,057	34,407,750	13,906,406	27,038,128	18,668,134	32,398,315	30,031,093	15,978,858	36,965,327	1,512,402	11,704,959
2014-15	335,630,086	105,240,912	59,348,073	35,189,410	14,105,428	28,349,420	19,545,937	33,290,396	31,011,138	15,881,788	39,887,678	1,603,180	11,524,799
2015-16	354,775,570	108,299,168	61,715,250	36,125,887	14,756,434	29,627,129	20,278,907	34,475,739	31,449,402	15,518,286	45,053,249	1,688,715	17,502,653
2016-17	371,705,042	111,838,548	63,829,915	37,352,788	15,588,815	31,088,231	21,200,127	35,967,658	33,203,335	15,370,320	49,002,994	1,712,683	19,379,543
2017-18	384,971,839	112,541,721	65,056,485	38,644,659	15,852,432	32,028,659	21,784,611	35,665,052	33,938,680	16,152,444	51,588,949	1,751,610	25,023,022
4-year													
2009-10	230,212,346	67,643,385	39,032,863	32,246,034	12,071,239	18,517,775	10,439,050	19,637,465	23,267,303	9,103,655	28,484,978	1,310,925	7,490,538
2010-11	242,591,219	70,524,278	40,420,752	33,842,288	12,497,023	19,037,101	10,918,171	20,760,495	24,856,936	10,088,873	29,980,642	1,233,264	8,852,149
2011-12	251,518,494	72,456,621	41,334,687	34,259,475	12,635,035	20,246,241	11,548,269	21,042,773	25,720,831	9,737,295	33,063,066	1,297,507	9,511,380
2012-13	257,550,418	74,836,904	42,537,154	34,613,057	12,608,770	21,150,882	12,114,278	22,151,644	26,335,976	9,823,162	34,208,788	1,320,284	8,386,673
2013-14	269,871,401	78,181,765	44,567,486	34,381,434	13,042,105	22,291,975	12,983,254	23,519,705	27,469,515	9,914,507	36,965,327	1,512,402	9,609,411
2014-15	281,198,453	81,857,112	46,260,575	35,166,043	13,257,351	23,504,976	13,595,835	24,290,848	28,543,769	10,057,062	39,887,678	1,603,180	9,434,598
2015-16	301,270,243	85,962,887	48,769,505	36,100,447	13,954,900	24,946,937	14,449,291	25,621,839	29,213,644	10,403,387	45,053,249	1,688,715	13,874,946
2016-17	317,579,534	89,338,819	50,967,703	37,324,213	14,748,258	26,371,904	15,226,010	26,688,763	31,028,018	10,631,345	49,002,994	1,712,683	15,506,527
2017-18	331,147,172	90,341,563	52,367,162	38,615,952	14,982,606	27,343,769	15,734,637	26,981,641	31,830,062	11,285,805	51,588,949	1,751,610	20,690,580
2-year													
2009-10	51,178,098	21,594,609	12,775,700	24,038	908,915	4,270,708	5,222,163	7,917,422	2,713,901	6,390,591	0	0	2,135,752
2010-11	54,271,635	22,566,471	13,165,721	24,368	929,308	4,404,597	5,358,662	8,290,916	2,792,902	7,398,402	0	0	2,506,009
2011-12	54,019,096	22,637,215	13,006,500	23,525	932,302	4,466,216	5,470,926	8,469,706	2,754,509	6,874,585	0	0	2,390,112
2012-13	53,870,729	22,879,434	13,018,204	21,417	886,446	4,574,358	5,564,978	8,698,474	2,666,580	6,404,605	0	0	2,174,439
2013-14	54,021,651	23,099,916	13,023,571	26,316	864,300	4,746,153	5,684,879	8,878,610	2,561,577	6,064,351	0	0	2,095,548
2014-15	54,431,633	23,383,800	13,087,499	23,367	848,077	4,844,444	5,950,102	8,999,548	2,467,368	5,824,726	0	0	2,090,201
2015-16	53,505,327	22,336,281	12,945,745	25,440	801,533	4,680,192	5,829,616	8,853,900	2,235,758	5,114,899	0	0	3,627,707
2016-17	54,125,509	22,499,729	12,862,211	28,574	840,557	4,716,327	5,974,117	9,278,896	2,175,317	4,738,975	0	0	3,873,016
2017-18	53,824,666	22,200,158	12,689,323	28,707	869,826	4,684,890	6,049,974	8,683,412	2,108,618	4,866,639	0	0	4,332,442
						Percentage distribution							
All levels													
2009-10	100.00	31.71	18.41	11.47	4.61	8.10	5.57	9.79	9.23	5.51	10.12	0.47	3.42
2010-11	100.00	31.36	18.05	11.41	4.52	7.90	5.48	9.79	9.31	5.89	10.10	0.42	3.83
2011-12	100.00	31.12	17.79	11.22	4.44	8.09	5.57	9.66	9.32	5.44	10.82	0.42	3.90
2012-13	100.00	31.38	17.84	11.12	4.33	8.26	5.68	9.91	9.31	5.21	10.98	0.42	3.39
2013-14	100.00	31.27	17.78	10.62	4.29	8.35	5.76	10.00	9.27	4.93	11.41	0.47	3.61
2014-15	100.00	31.36	17.68	10.48	4.20	8.45	5.82	9.92	9.24	4.73	11.88	0.48	3.43
2015-16	100.00	30.53	17.40	10.18	4.16	8.35	5.72	9.72	8.86	4.37	12.70	0.48	4.93
2016-17	100.00	30.09	17.17	10.05	4.19	8.36	5.70	9.68	8.93	4.14	13.18	0.46	5.21
2017-18	100.00	29.23	16.90	10.04	4.12	8.32	5.66	9.26	8.82	4.20	13.40	0.45	6.50
4-year													
2009-10	100.00	29.38	16.96	14.01	5.24	8.04	4.53	8.53	10.11	3.95	12.37	0.57	3.25
2010-11	100.00	29.07	16.66	13.95	5.15	7.85	4.50	8.56	10.25	4.16	12.36	0.51	3.65
2011-12	100.00	28.81	16.43	13.62	5.02	8.05	4.59	8.37	10.23	3.87	13.15	0.52	3.78
2012-13	100.00	29.06	16.52	13.44	4.90	8.21	4.70	8.60	10.23	3.81	13.28	0.51	3.26
2013-14	100.00	28.97	16.51	12.74	4.83	8.26	4.81	8.72	10.18	3.67	13.70	0.56	3.56
2014-15	100.00	29.11	16.45	12.51	4.71	8.36	4.83	8.64	10.15	3.58	14.18	0.57	3.36
2015-16	100.00	28.53	16.19	11.98	4.63	8.28	4.80	8.50	9.70	3.45	14.95	0.56	4.61
2016-17	100.00	28.13	16.05	11.75	4.64	8.30	4.79	8.40	9.77	3.35	15.43	0.54	4.88
2017-18	100.00	27.28	15.81	11.66	4.52	8.26	4.75	8.15	9.61	3.41	15.58	0.53	6.25

See notes at end of table.

Table 334.10. Total expenditures of public degree-granting postsecondary institutions, by purpose of expenditure and level of institution: 2009–10 through 2017–18—Continued

Level of institution and year	Total	Instruction		Research	Public service	Academic support	Student services	Institutional support	Auxiliary enterprises[1]	Net grant aid to students[2]	Hospitals	Independent operations	Other
		Total[3]	Salaries and wages										
1	2	3	4	5	6	7	8	9	10	11	12	13	14
2-year													
2009–10	100.00	42.20	24.96	0.05	1.78	8.34	10.20	15.47	5.30	12.49	0.00	0.00	4.17
2010–11	100.00	41.58	24.26	0.04	1.71	8.12	9.87	15.28	5.15	13.63	0.00	0.00	4.62
2011–12	100.00	41.91	24.08	0.04	1.73	8.27	10.13	15.68	5.10	12.73	0.00	0.00	4.42
2012–13	100.00	42.47	24.17	0.04	1.65	8.49	10.33	16.15	4.95	11.89	0.00	0.00	4.04
2013–14	100.00	42.76	24.11	0.05	1.60	8.79	10.52	16.44	4.74	11.23	0.00	0.00	3.88
2014–15	100.00	42.96	24.04	0.04	1.56	8.90	10.93	16.53	4.53	10.70	0.00	0.00	3.84
2015–16	100.00	41.75	24.20	0.05	1.50	8.75	10.90	16.55	4.18	9.56	0.00	0.00	6.78
2016–17	100.00	41.57	23.76	0.05	1.55	8.71	11.04	17.14	4.02	8.76	0.00	0.00	7.16
2017–18	100.00	41.25	23.58	0.05	1.62	8.70	11.24	16.13	3.92	9.04	0.00	0.00	8.05
Expenditure per full-time-equivalent student in constant 2018–19 dollars[4]													
All levels													
2009–10	$30,598	$9,704	$5,634	$3,509	$1,411	$2,478	$1,703	$2,996	$2,825	$1,685	$3,097	$143	$1,047
2010–11	30,863	9,678	5,571	3,521	1,396	2,437	1,692	3,020	2,875	1,818	3,117	128	1,181
2011–12	31,041	9,661	5,521	3,483	1,378	2,511	1,729	2,998	2,893	1,688	3,359	132	1,209
2012–13	31,620	9,922	5,641	3,517	1,370	2,612	1,795	3,132	2,945	1,648	3,473	134	1,072
2013–14	32,634	10,205	5,803	3,467	1,401	2,724	1,881	3,264	3,026	1,610	3,725	152	1,179
2014–15	33,806	10,600	5,978	3,544	1,421	2,855	1,969	3,353	3,124	1,600	4,018	161	1,161
2015–16	35,678	10,891	6,206	3,633	1,484	2,979	2,039	3,467	3,163	1,561	4,531	170	1,760
2016–17	36,697	11,041	6,302	3,688	1,539	3,069	2,093	3,551	3,278	1,517	4,838	169	1,913
2017–18	37,181	10,869	6,283	3,732	1,531	3,093	2,104	3,445	3,278	1,560	4,982	169	2,417
4-year													
2009–10	41,692	12,251	7,069	5,840	2,186	3,354	1,891	3,556	4,214	1,649	5,159	237	1,357
2010–11	41,879	12,175	6,978	5,842	2,157	3,286	1,885	3,584	4,291	1,742	5,176	213	1,528
2011–12	41,568	11,975	6,831	5,662	2,088	3,346	1,909	3,478	4,251	1,609	5,464	214	1,572
2012–13	41,683	12,112	6,884	5,602	2,041	3,423	1,961	3,585	4,262	1,590	5,536	214	1,357
2013–14	42,835	12,409	7,074	5,457	2,070	3,538	2,061	3,733	4,360	1,574	5,867	240	1,525
2014–15	43,661	12,710	7,183	5,460	2,058	3,650	2,111	3,772	4,432	1,562	6,193	249	1,465
2015–16	45,943	13,109	7,437	5,505	2,128	3,804	2,203	3,907	4,455	1,586	6,871	258	2,116
2016–17	45,903	12,913	7,367	5,395	2,132	3,812	2,201	3,858	4,485	1,537	7,083	248	2,241
2017–18	46,244	12,616	7,313	5,393	2,092	3,818	2,197	3,768	4,445	1,576	7,204	245	2,889
2-year													
2009–10	13,927	5,876	3,477	7	247	1,162	1,421	2,155	739	1,739	0	0	581
2010–11	14,185	5,898	3,441	6	243	1,151	1,401	2,167	730	1,934	0	0	655
2011–12	14,244	5,969	3,430	6	246	1,178	1,443	2,233	726	1,813	0	0	630
2012–13	14,679	6,234	3,547	6	242	1,246	1,516	2,370	727	1,745	0	0	592
2013–14	14,904	6,373	3,593	7	238	1,309	1,568	2,449	707	1,673	0	0	578
2014–15	15,607	6,705	3,752	7	243	1,389	1,706	2,580	707	1,670	0	0	599
2015–16	15,800	6,596	3,823	8	237	1,382	1,722	2,615	660	1,510	0	0	1,071
2016–17	16,859	7,008	4,006	9	262	1,469	1,861	2,890	678	1,476	0	0	1,206
2017–18	16,856	6,952	3,974	9	272	1,467	1,895	2,719	660	1,524	0	0	1,357

[1]Essentially self-supporting operations of institutions that furnish a service to students, faculty, or staff, such as residence halls and food services.
[2]Scholarship and fellowship expenses, net of discounts and allowances. Excludes the amount of discounts and allowances that were recorded as a reduction to revenues from tuition and fees and from auxiliary enterprises, such as room, board, and books.
[3]Includes other categories not separately shown.
[4]Constant dollars based on the Consumer Price Index, prepared by the Bureau of Labor Statistics, U.S. Department of Labor, adjusted to a school-year basis.

NOTE: Degree-granting institutions grant associate's or higher degrees and participate in Title IV federal financial aid programs. Includes data for public institutions reporting data according to either the Governmental Accounting Standards Board (GASB) or the Financial Accounting Standards Board (FASB) guidance. Data in this table pertain to institutions' fiscal years that end in the academic year noted. Some data have been revised from previously published figures. Detail may not sum to totals because of rounding.
SOURCE: U.S. Department of Education, National Center for Education Statistics, Integrated Postsecondary Education Data System (IPEDS), Spring 2010 through Spring 2018, Fall Enrollment component; and Spring 2011 through Spring 2019, Finance component. (This table was prepared December 2019.)

Table 334.20. Total expenditures of public degree-granting postsecondary institutions, by level of institution, purpose of expenditure, and state or jurisdiction: 2014–15 through 2017–18

[In thousands of current dollars]

State or jurisdiction	Total, 2014–15	Total, 2015–16	Total, 2016–17 All institutions	Total, 2016–17 4-year institutions	Total, 2016–17 2-year institutions	2017–18 All institutions Total[1]	2017–18 All institutions Instruction	2017–18 4-year institutions Total[1]	2017–18 4-year institutions Instruction	2017–18 2-year institutions Total[1]	2017–18 2-year institutions Instruction
1	2	3	4	5	6	7	8	9	10	11	12
United States	**$335,630,086**	**$354,775,570**	**$371,705,042**	**$317,579,534**	**$54,125,509**	**$384,971,839**	**$112,541,721**	**$331,147,172**	**$90,341,563**	**$53,824,666**	**$22,200,158**
Alabama	6,961,128	7,306,483	7,785,726	7,028,015	757,711	8,208,437	1,940,080	7,445,895	1,620,897	762,541	319,182
Alaska	850,928	868,913	839,381	839,381	0	804,290	250,159	804,290	250,159	0	0
Arizona	5,931,197	6,296,207	6,507,273	5,130,163	1,377,110	6,834,890	2,290,487	5,438,363	1,766,297	1,396,527	524,190
Arkansas	3,800,707	3,934,428	4,106,519	3,647,177	459,342	4,264,757	959,029	3,801,104	771,493	463,653	187,536
California	50,652,807	55,642,923	57,844,991	45,542,517	12,302,474	61,868,678	15,879,303	49,392,235	11,433,986	12,476,443	4,445,317
Colorado	6,109,407	6,587,748	7,781,063	7,265,477	515,585	8,445,117	2,504,779	8,053,205	2,348,433	391,913	156,346
Connecticut	3,496,698	3,662,471	3,798,052	3,277,990	520,062	3,908,139	1,169,712	3,390,801	954,605	517,338	215,107
Delaware	1,190,562	1,247,600	1,264,208	1,264,208	0	1,335,450	592,062	1,335,450	592,062	0	0
District of Columbia	139,524	147,290	141,861	141,861	0	158,530	43,712	158,530	43,712	0	0
Florida	11,511,020	11,822,548	12,415,119	12,232,102	183,017	13,163,072	4,257,666	12,972,157	4,184,349	190,915	73,318
Georgia	7,826,896	8,050,634	8,496,265	7,570,386	925,880	8,958,011	2,593,283	8,021,957	2,209,630	936,054	383,653
Hawaii	1,664,624	1,816,736	1,847,752	1,575,966	271,786	1,821,603	631,700	1,532,735	480,771	288,868	150,930
Idaho	1,203,133	1,255,012	1,306,952	1,093,158	213,794	1,359,948	500,405	1,138,288	412,685	221,660	87,720
Illinois	12,195,375	12,355,733	12,961,076	9,604,390	3,356,686	13,280,125	4,574,301	9,788,570	3,169,674	3,491,555	1,404,626
Indiana	6,372,728	6,563,583	6,805,880	6,263,480	542,399	6,949,227	2,853,632	6,414,537	2,616,663	534,691	236,969
Iowa	5,261,496	5,512,712	5,789,532	4,842,637	946,894	6,383,620	1,316,608	5,431,567	898,782	952,054	417,827
Kansas	3,451,776	3,436,560	3,498,812	2,748,778	750,035	3,709,971	1,303,424	2,940,791	1,002,698	769,180	300,726
Kentucky	5,547,286	5,873,502	6,113,027	5,541,058	571,969	6,166,575	1,343,745	5,603,907	1,117,207	562,668	226,537
Louisiana	3,910,077	3,883,693	4,108,399	3,624,253	484,147	4,133,564	1,339,865	3,680,115	1,162,909	453,449	176,955
Maine	864,068	849,532	869,566	738,682	130,885	894,187	286,390	765,817	222,965	128,370	63,424
Maryland	6,343,340	6,502,220	6,724,452	5,287,563	1,436,889	6,958,575	2,101,528	5,516,612	1,502,509	1,441,963	599,018
Massachusetts	4,758,073	5,170,474	5,246,452	4,334,984	911,468	5,411,839	1,838,525	4,500,608	1,450,023	911,231	388,502
Michigan	14,627,268	15,327,986	16,259,165	14,803,153	1,456,011	17,589,767	4,445,796	16,122,686	3,816,280	1,467,081	629,516
Minnesota	5,215,646	5,303,793	5,927,210	4,738,233	1,188,977	5,952,483	1,761,270	4,780,542	1,243,585	1,171,941	517,685
Mississippi	4,171,973	4,451,207	4,623,103	3,675,243	947,861	4,603,388	1,130,522	3,669,367	771,027	934,021	359,495
Missouri	4,904,991	5,010,347	5,175,185	4,420,785	754,400	5,202,013	1,530,046	4,452,878	1,199,662	749,134	330,384
Montana	1,022,708	1,046,082	1,101,301	987,966	113,334	1,101,233	329,145	989,266	288,907	111,967	40,239
Nebraska	2,398,348	2,450,500	2,574,085	2,146,023	428,062	2,643,655	869,695	2,196,035	671,570	447,620	198,125
Nevada	1,544,133	1,621,662	1,701,829	1,633,648	68,181	1,794,822	773,264	1,794,822	773,264	0	0
New Hampshire	973,796	997,737	989,727	842,941	146,786	1,010,063	319,221	862,491	268,420	147,572	50,801
New Jersey	7,266,925	7,473,275	7,999,108	6,680,061	1,319,047	8,645,442	2,655,631	7,270,427	2,114,350	1,375,015	541,281
New Mexico	3,454,803	3,523,749	3,786,755	3,176,827	609,928	4,134,037	838,375	3,452,140	589,589	681,897	248,785
New York	16,791,853	17,785,235	18,073,969	14,594,521	3,479,447	18,562,136	6,362,628	15,107,942	4,683,210	3,454,194	1,679,419
North Carolina	10,484,190	10,499,040	11,144,591	8,942,833	2,201,758	11,479,183	3,692,580	9,218,460	2,713,475	2,260,722	979,105
North Dakota	1,150,777	1,192,090	1,194,445	1,090,829	103,616	1,164,255	431,205	1,064,138	390,326	100,117	40,879
Ohio	12,534,515	13,257,601	14,314,104	12,875,624	1,438,480	12,433,497	3,634,154	11,475,674	3,117,620	957,822	516,534
Oklahoma	4,158,353	4,335,312	4,364,905	3,884,702	480,203	4,411,735	1,349,828	3,941,232	1,159,165	470,503	190,663
Oregon	5,843,944	7,025,969	6,949,056	5,723,589	1,225,467	7,231,394	1,662,681	6,036,895	1,187,740	1,194,499	474,941
Pennsylvania	13,046,794	13,752,080	14,340,017	13,147,338	1,192,679	14,773,798	3,867,582	13,564,163	3,344,515	1,209,635	523,067
Rhode Island	737,640	775,112	792,218	667,893	124,325	827,466	281,000	698,103	213,295	129,363	67,705
South Carolina	4,352,405	4,459,393	4,646,259	3,827,382	818,877	4,899,684	1,795,711	4,082,571	1,431,884	817,113	363,827
South Dakota	784,051	827,198	841,747	754,648	87,099	851,429	299,830	769,171	258,931	82,258	40,899
Tennessee	4,172,603	4,320,721	4,503,298	3,836,474	666,824	4,595,946	1,848,382	3,877,564	1,549,342	718,382	299,040
Texas	31,050,594	33,792,807	35,461,725	30,311,913	5,149,812	36,447,523	10,628,437	31,430,227	8,546,091	5,017,296	2,082,347
Utah	5,349,506	5,700,948	6,189,020	5,971,621	217,399	6,483,500	1,140,874	6,278,272	1,044,534	205,228	96,341
Vermont	854,406	865,326	896,401	862,131	34,270	905,945	277,083	873,832	267,204	32,112	9,879
Virginia	9,540,486	9,896,996	10,253,120	9,125,778	1,127,342	10,796,512	3,256,187	9,659,568	2,720,015	1,136,944	536,172
Washington	8,588,560	9,171,287	10,229,088	9,808,391	420,697	10,220,427	3,085,099	9,829,859	2,919,746	390,568	165,354
West Virginia	1,819,173	1,874,851	1,889,691	1,752,931	136,760	1,866,864	616,135	1,733,190	563,086	133,674	53,050
Wisconsin	6,285,882	6,566,464	6,598,862	5,367,016	1,231,846	6,538,284	2,230,861	5,293,472	1,523,866	1,244,812	706,995
Wyoming	798,626	878,588	877,311	579,425	297,886	819,916	274,028	527,813	174,282	292,104	99,746
U.S. Service Academies	1,662,286	1,805,213	1,755,387	1,755,387	0	1,966,837	584,072	1,966,837	584,072	0	0
Other jurisdictions	**1,638,670**	**1,693,441**	**987,460**	**891,071**	**96,389**	**1,798,094**	**645,709**	**1,723,072**	**618,519**	**75,022**	**27,190**
American Samoa	13,690	13,952	14,337	14,337	0	15,470	3,783	15,470	3,783	0	0
Federated States of Micronesia	18,324	20,070	20,331	0	20,331	19,435	7,227	0	0	19,435	7,227
Guam	116,302	129,640	127,294	88,902	38,392	132,066	32,586	99,617	22,487	32,449	10,099
Marshall Islands	11,382	13,731	15,022	0	15,022	15,008	2,240	15,008	2,240	0	0
Northern Marianas	19,048	16,502	17,443	17,443	0	18,358	3,968	18,358	3,968	0	0
Palau	10,209	9,425	9,621	0	9,621	8,861	3,085	0	0	8,861	3,085
Puerto Rico	1,362,861	1,406,463	701,403	688,381	13,022	1,513,526	579,668	1,499,249	572,889	14,277	6,779
U.S. Virgin Islands	86,855	83,659	82,008	82,008	0	75,370	13,152	75,370	13,152	0	0

[1]Includes other categories not separately shown.
NOTE: Degree-granting institutions grant associate's or higher degrees and participate in Title IV federal financial aid programs. Includes data for public institutions reporting data according to either the Governmental Accounting Standards Board (GASB) or the Financial Accounting Standards Board (FASB) guidance. Data in this table pertain to institutions' fiscal years that end in the academic year noted. Some data have been revised from previously published figures. Detail may not sum to totals because of rounding.
SOURCE: U.S. Department of Education, National Center for Education Statistics, Integrated Postsecondary Education Data System (IPEDS), Spring 2016 through Spring 2019, Finance component. (This table was prepared December 2019.)

Table 334.30. Total expenditures of private nonprofit degree-granting postsecondary institutions, by purpose and level of institution: Selected years, 1999–2000 through 2017–18

Level of institution and year	Total	Instruction	Research	Public service	Academic support	Student services	Institutional support	Auxiliary enterprises[1]	Net grant aid to students[2]	Hospitals	Independent operations	Other
1	2	3	4	5	6	7	8	9	10	11	12	13
					In thousands of current dollars							
All levels												
1999–2000	$80,613,037	$26,012,599	$8,381,926	$1,446,958	$6,510,951	$5,688,499	$10,585,850	$8,300,021	$1,180,882	$7,355,110	$2,753,679	$2,396,563
2004–05	110,394,127	36,258,473	12,812,857	2,000,437	9,342,064	8,191,737	14,690,328	10,944,342	1,069,591	9,180,775	4,223,779	1,679,741
2005–06	116,821,175	38,451,724	13,242,851	1,937,149	10,225,476	8,925,987	15,668,595	11,790,104	707,411	9,645,428	4,203,523	2,022,926
2006–07	124,558,591	41,224,316	13,704,450	2,036,662	10,881,954	9,591,801	16,831,560	12,449,053	728,200	10,400,055	4,680,393	2,030,146
2007–08	133,501,778	44,227,021	14,474,152	2,182,525	11,883,707	10,361,344	18,366,446	13,317,944	720,764	10,752,821	4,887,609	2,327,446
2008–09	141,363,564	46,456,178	15,264,804	2,298,520	12,585,948	11,016,097	19,403,346	13,713,701	754,752	11,930,840	5,158,480	2,780,898
2009–10	145,115,244	47,566,210	16,221,823	2,090,243	12,953,023	11,422,737	19,438,608	13,890,396	826,379	13,174,405	5,154,851	2,376,569
2010–11	152,501,429	49,759,574	17,362,082	2,255,075	13,601,137	12,198,263	20,214,683	14,460,084	759,683	14,239,347	5,376,016	2,275,486
2011–12	159,831,378	52,163,647	17,483,157	2,333,298	14,215,689	12,881,102	21,175,119	14,948,315	845,525	15,474,737	5,450,038	2,860,752
2012–13	165,515,671	54,296,267	17,597,379	2,317,116	14,924,886	13,692,561	21,766,760	15,349,949	844,435	16,726,819	5,437,783	2,561,716
2013–14	172,529,736	56,711,775	17,736,647	2,459,956	15,454,493	14,555,421	22,623,170	15,984,991	867,482	17,377,766	5,693,990	3,064,047
2014–15	181,419,541	58,769,788	18,310,027	2,636,019	15,557,155	15,421,897	23,845,927	16,358,009	887,495	20,529,450	6,063,555	3,040,219
2015–16	188,689,819	60,227,646	18,386,969	2,730,335	16,011,794	16,061,062	24,829,855	16,723,913	914,001	21,267,887	6,192,792	5,343,565
2016–17	197,171,304	62,161,805	21,059,795	2,890,409	16,261,179	16,868,202	25,517,409	17,224,876	942,542	24,090,294	5,810,625	4,344,168
2017–18	206,778,042	63,489,832	21,872,856	3,090,888	17,843,700	17,560,444	26,471,439	17,824,434	986,591	26,740,972	6,294,985	4,601,901
4-year												
1999–2000	79,699,659	25,744,199	8,376,568	1,438,544	6,476,338	5,590,978	10,398,914	8,228,409	1,162,570	7,355,110	2,752,019	2,176,011
2004–05	109,789,731	36,051,084	12,812,326	1,993,767	9,307,600	8,101,214	14,516,197	10,899,456	1,051,216	9,180,775	4,223,779	1,652,317
2005–06	116,250,621	38,235,791	13,242,277	1,927,434	10,185,584	8,854,613	15,525,499	11,745,356	698,715	9,645,428	4,203,523	1,986,402
2006–07	124,062,344	41,057,423	13,703,502	2,028,438	10,850,196	9,523,002	16,694,195	12,412,575	714,459	10,400,055	4,680,393	1,998,105
2007–08	132,965,591	44,041,854	14,473,179	2,176,544	11,847,284	10,284,649	18,218,103	13,280,036	711,180	10,752,821	4,887,609	2,292,334
2008–09	140,866,945	46,289,898	15,264,459	2,294,909	12,544,436	10,947,638	19,261,017	13,676,329	747,586	11,930,840	5,158,480	2,751,352
2009–10	144,624,598	47,400,673	16,221,238	2,085,201	12,910,113	11,353,608	19,303,251	13,855,994	819,196	13,174,405	5,154,851	2,346,068
2010–11	151,878,613	49,550,398	17,361,796	2,252,726	13,547,801	12,111,973	20,048,321	14,430,101	758,318	14,239,347	5,376,016	2,201,817
2011–12	159,245,924	51,959,761	17,482,484	2,331,249	14,164,326	12,795,619	21,024,665	14,924,702	843,453	15,474,737	5,450,038	2,794,891
2012–13	165,015,452	54,115,153	17,597,050	2,315,345	14,885,715	13,624,969	21,628,217	15,323,444	839,753	16,726,819	5,437,783	2,521,204
2013–14	171,974,051	56,513,597	17,736,254	2,458,223	15,405,771	14,462,852	22,499,365	15,953,094	863,119	17,377,766	5,693,990	3,010,020
2014–15	180,583,663	58,497,366	18,309,351	2,633,736	15,460,861	15,226,681	23,669,210	16,323,295	883,309	20,529,450	6,063,555	2,986,850
2015–16	187,829,392	59,962,885	18,386,002	2,728,006	15,907,072	15,846,653	24,654,441	16,684,252	910,455	21,267,887	6,192,792	5,288,945
2016–17	196,311,110	61,907,159	21,058,634	2,889,051	16,157,576	16,652,370	25,330,274	17,187,656	941,362	24,090,294	5,810,625	4,286,108
2017–18	205,992,273	63,268,589	21,872,111	3,089,523	17,745,371	17,345,090	26,293,205	17,794,013	985,036	26,740,972	6,294,985	4,563,379
2-year												
1999–2000	913,378	268,400	5,358	8,415	34,612	97,521	186,936	71,612	18,311	0	1,660	220,553
2004–05	604,395	207,389	532	6,670	34,464	90,523	174,131	44,886	18,375	0	0	27,425
2005–06	570,554	215,934	574	9,715	39,893	71,374	143,096	44,748	8,696	0	0	36,524
2006–07	496,247	166,893	947	8,224	31,758	68,799	137,366	36,478	13,741	0	0	32,041
2007–08	536,187	185,167	973	5,982	36,423	76,696	148,343	37,908	9,584	0	0	35,112
2008–09	496,620	166,280	345	3,612	41,511	68,459	142,330	37,372	7,165	0	0	29,546
2009–10	490,645	165,538	585	5,041	42,909	69,129	135,357	34,402	7,183	0	0	30,502
2010–11	622,815	209,176	285	2,349	53,336	86,290	166,362	29,983	1,365	0	0	73,669
2011–12	585,454	203,885	673	2,049	51,363	85,483	150,455	23,613	2,072	0	0	65,861
2012–13	500,218	181,113	329	1,771	39,171	67,591	138,543	26,505	4,682	0	0	40,512
2013–14	555,685	198,178	393	1,732	48,722	92,569	123,804	31,897	4,364	0	0	54,027
2014–15	835,878	272,422	677	2,283	96,294	195,216	176,718	34,714	4,186	0	0	53,369
2015–16	860,427	264,761	967	2,329	104,722	214,409	175,414	39,660	3,546	0	0	54,620
2016–17	860,194	254,647	1,160	1,358	103,603	215,833	187,135	37,219	1,180	0	0	58,060
2017–18	785,770	221,244	745	1,366	98,329	215,354	178,234	30,421	1,555	0	0	38,522
					Percentage distribution							
All levels												
1999–2000	100.00	32.27	10.40	1.79	8.08	7.06	13.13	10.30	1.46	9.12	3.42	2.97
2004–05	100.00	32.84	11.61	1.81	8.46	7.42	13.31	9.91	0.97	8.32	3.83	1.52
2005–06	100.00	32.92	11.34	1.66	8.75	7.64	13.41	10.09	0.61	8.26	3.60	1.73
2006–07	100.00	33.10	11.00	1.64	8.74	7.70	13.51	9.99	0.58	8.35	3.76	1.63
2007–08	100.00	33.13	10.84	1.63	8.90	7.76	13.76	9.98	0.54	8.05	3.66	1.74
2008–09	100.00	32.86	10.80	1.63	8.90	7.79	13.73	9.70	0.53	8.44	3.65	1.97
2009–10	100.00	32.78	11.18	1.44	8.93	7.87	13.40	9.57	0.57	9.08	3.55	1.64
2010–11	100.00	32.63	11.38	1.48	8.92	8.00	13.26	9.48	0.50	9.34	3.53	1.49
2011–12	100.00	32.64	10.94	1.46	8.89	8.06	13.25	9.35	0.53	9.68	3.41	1.79
2012–13	100.00	32.80	10.63	1.40	9.02	8.27	13.15	9.27	0.51	10.11	3.29	1.55
2013–14	100.00	32.87	10.28	1.43	8.96	8.44	13.11	9.27	0.50	10.07	3.30	1.78
2014–15	100.00	32.39	10.09	1.45	8.58	8.50	13.14	9.02	0.49	11.32	3.34	1.68
2015–16	100.00	31.92	9.74	1.45	8.49	8.51	13.16	8.86	0.48	11.27	3.28	2.83
2016–17	100.00	31.53	10.68	1.47	8.25	8.56	12.94	8.74	0.48	12.22	2.95	2.20
2017–18	100.00	30.70	10.58	1.49	8.63	8.49	12.80	8.62	0.48	12.93	3.04	2.23
4-year												
1999–2000	100.00	32.30	10.51	1.80	8.13	7.02	13.05	10.32	1.46	9.23	3.45	2.73
2004–05	100.00	32.84	11.67	1.82	8.48	7.38	13.22	9.93	0.96	8.36	3.85	1.50
2005–06	100.00	32.89	11.39	1.66	8.76	7.62	13.36	10.10	0.60	8.30	3.62	1.71
2006–07	100.00	33.09	11.05	1.64	8.75	7.68	13.46	10.01	0.58	8.38	3.77	1.61
2007–08	100.00	33.12	10.88	1.64	8.91	7.73	13.70	9.99	0.53	8.09	3.68	1.72
2008–09	100.00	32.86	10.84	1.63	8.91	7.77	13.67	9.71	0.53	8.47	3.66	1.95
2009–10	100.00	32.77	11.22	1.44	8.93	7.85	13.35	9.58	0.57	9.11	3.56	1.62
2010–11	100.00	32.63	11.43	1.48	8.92	7.97	13.20	9.50	0.50	9.38	3.54	1.45
2011–12	100.00	32.63	10.98	1.46	8.89	8.04	13.20	9.37	0.53	9.72	3.42	1.76
2012–13	100.00	32.79	10.66	1.40	9.02	8.26	13.11	9.29	0.51	10.14	3.30	1.53
2013–14	100.00	32.86	10.31	1.43	8.96	8.41	13.08	9.28	0.50	10.10	3.31	1.75
2014–15	100.00	32.39	10.14	1.46	8.56	8.43	13.11	9.04	0.49	11.37	3.36	1.65
2015–16	100.00	31.92	9.79	1.45	8.47	8.44	13.13	8.88	0.48	11.32	3.30	2.82
2016–17	100.00	31.54	10.73	1.47	8.23	8.48	12.90	8.76	0.48	12.27	2.96	2.18
2017–18	100.00	30.71	10.62	1.50	8.61	8.42	12.76	8.64	0.48	12.98	3.06	2.22

See notes at end of table.

Table 334.30. Total expenditures of private nonprofit degree-granting postsecondary institutions, by purpose and level of institution: Selected years, 1999–2000 through 2017–18—Continued

Level of institution and year	Total	Instruction	Research	Public service	Academic support	Student services	Institutional support	Auxiliary enterprises[1]	Net grant aid to students[2]	Hospitals	Independent operations	Other
1	2	3	4	5	6	7	8	9	10	11	12	13
2-year												
1999–2000	100.00	29.39	0.59	0.92	3.79	10.68	20.47	7.84	2.00	0.00	0.18	24.15
2004–05	100.00	34.31	0.09	1.10	5.70	14.98	28.81	7.43	3.04	0.00	0.00	4.54
2005–06	100.00	37.85	0.10	1.70	6.99	12.51	25.08	7.84	1.52	0.00	0.00	6.40
2006–07	100.00	33.63	0.19	1.66	6.40	13.86	27.68	7.35	2.77	0.00	0.00	6.46
2007–08	100.00	34.53	0.18	1.12	6.79	14.30	27.67	7.07	1.79	0.00	0.00	6.55
2008–09	100.00	33.48	0.07	0.73	8.36	13.78	28.66	7.53	1.44	0.00	0.00	5.95
2009–10	100.00	33.74	0.12	1.03	8.75	14.09	27.59	7.01	1.46	0.00	0.00	6.22
2010–11	100.00	33.59	0.05	0.38	8.56	13.85	26.71	4.81	0.22	0.00	0.00	11.83
2011–12	100.00	34.83	0.11	0.35	8.77	14.60	25.70	4.03	0.35	0.00	0.00	11.25
2012–13	100.00	36.21	0.07	0.35	7.83	13.51	27.70	5.30	0.94	0.00	0.00	8.10
2013–14	100.00	35.66	0.07	0.31	8.77	16.66	22.28	5.74	0.79	0.00	0.00	9.72
2014–15	100.00	32.59	0.08	0.27	11.52	23.35	21.14	4.15	0.50	0.00	0.00	6.38
2015–16	100.00	30.77	0.11	0.27	12.17	24.92	20.39	4.61	0.41	0.00	0.00	6.35
2016–17	100.00	29.60	0.13	0.16	12.04	25.09	21.75	4.33	0.14	0.00	0.00	6.75
2017–18	100.00	28.16	0.09	0.17	12.51	27.41	22.68	3.87	0.20	0.00	0.00	4.90
					Expenditure per full-time-equivalent student in constant 2018–19 dollars[3]							
All levels												
1999–2000	$47,501	$15,328	$4,939	$853	$3,837	$3,352	$6,238	$4,891	$696	$4,334	$1,623	$1,412
2004–05	50,830	16,695	5,900	921	4,301	3,772	6,764	5,039	492	4,227	1,945	773
2005–06	51,110	16,823	5,794	848	4,474	3,905	6,855	5,158	309	4,220	1,839	885
2006–07	52,182	17,270	5,741	853	4,559	4,018	7,051	5,215	305	4,357	1,961	850
2007–08	52,608	17,428	5,704	860	4,683	4,083	7,238	5,248	284	4,237	1,926	917
2008–09	54,130	17,789	5,845	880	4,819	4,218	7,430	5,251	289	4,568	1,975	1,065
2009–10	53,578	17,562	5,989	772	4,782	4,217	7,177	5,128	305	4,864	1,903	877
2010–11	53,183	17,353	6,055	786	4,743	4,254	7,050	5,043	265	4,966	1,875	794
2011–12	53,685	17,521	5,872	784	4,775	4,327	7,112	5,021	284	5,198	1,831	961
2012–13	54,063	17,735	5,748	757	4,875	4,472	7,110	5,014	276	5,464	1,776	837
2013–14	55,409	18,213	5,696	790	4,963	4,675	7,266	5,134	279	5,581	1,829	984
2014–15	56,997	18,464	5,752	828	4,888	4,845	7,492	5,139	279	6,450	1,905	955
2015–16	58,426	18,649	5,693	845	4,958	4,973	7,688	5,178	283	6,585	1,918	1,655
2016–17	59,534	18,769	6,359	873	4,910	5,093	7,705	5,201	285	7,274	1,754	1,312
2017–18	60,923	18,706	6,444	911	5,257	5,174	7,799	5,252	291	7,879	1,855	1,356
4-year												
1999–2000	47,969	15,495	5,042	866	3,898	3,365	6,259	4,952	700	4,427	1,656	1,310
2004–05	51,166	16,801	5,971	929	4,338	3,775	6,765	5,080	490	4,279	1,968	770
2005–06	51,413	16,910	5,857	852	4,505	3,916	6,866	5,195	309	4,266	1,859	879
2006–07	52,424	17,349	5,791	857	4,585	4,024	7,054	5,245	302	4,395	1,978	844
2007–08	52,867	17,511	5,755	865	4,710	4,089	7,244	5,280	283	4,275	1,943	911
2008–09	54,398	17,876	5,895	886	4,844	4,228	7,438	5,281	289	4,607	1,992	1,062
2009–10	53,835	17,644	6,038	776	4,806	4,226	7,185	5,158	305	4,904	1,919	873
2010–11	53,534	17,466	6,120	794	4,775	4,269	7,067	5,086	267	5,019	1,895	776
2011–12	54,019	17,626	5,930	791	4,805	4,340	7,132	5,063	286	5,249	1,849	948
2012–13	54,354	17,825	5,796	763	4,903	4,488	7,124	5,047	277	5,510	1,791	830
2013–14	55,677	18,296	5,742	796	4,988	4,682	7,284	5,165	279	5,626	1,843	974
2014–15	57,493	18,624	5,829	839	4,922	4,848	7,536	5,197	281	6,536	1,930	951
2015–16	58,865	18,792	5,762	855	4,985	4,966	7,727	5,229	285	6,665	1,941	1,658
2016–17	59,997	18,920	6,436	883	4,938	5,089	7,741	5,253	288	7,363	1,776	1,310
2017–18	61,421	18,865	6,522	921	5,291	5,172	7,840	5,306	294	7,973	1,877	1,361
2-year												
1999–2000	25,655	7,539	150	236	972	2,739	5,251	2,011	514	0	47	6,195
2004–05	23,190	7,957	20	256	1,322	3,473	6,681	1,722	705	0	0	1,052
2005–06	23,215	8,786	23	395	1,623	2,904	5,822	1,821	354	0	0	1,486
2006–07	24,191	8,136	46	401	1,548	3,354	6,696	1,778	670	0	0	1,562
2007–08	23,762	8,206	43	265	1,614	3,399	6,574	1,680	425	0	0	1,556
2008–09	22,563	7,555	16	164	1,886	3,110	6,467	1,698	326	0	0	1,342
2009–10	22,234	7,501	27	228	1,944	3,133	6,134	1,559	325	0	0	1,382
2010–11	20,455	6,870	9	77	1,752	2,834	5,464	985	45	0	0	2,419
2011–12	20,019	6,972	23	70	1,756	2,923	5,145	807	71	0	0	2,252
2012–13	19,536	7,074	13	69	1,530	2,640	5,411	1,035	183	0	0	1,582
2013–14	22,254	7,937	16	69	1,951	3,707	4,958	1,277	175	0	0	2,164
2014–15	19,881	6,479	16	54	2,290	4,643	4,203	826	100	0	0	1,269
2015–16	22,236	6,842	25	60	2,706	5,541	4,533	1,025	92	0	0	1,412
2016–17	21,563	6,383	29	34	2,597	5,410	4,691	933	30	0	0	1,455
2017–18	19,474	5,483	18	34	2,437	5,337	4,417	754	39	0	0	955

[1]Essentially self-supporting operations of institutions that furnish a service to students, faculty, or staff, such as residence halls and food services.
[2]Excludes allowances that were recorded as a reduction to revenues from tuition and fees and from auxiliary enterprises, such as room, board, and books; also excludes agency transactions, such as student awards made from contributed funds or grant funds. These exclusions account for the majority of total student grants.
[3]Constant dollars based on the Consumer Price Index, prepared by the Bureau of Labor Statistics, U.S. Department of Labor, adjusted to a school-year basis.

NOTE: Degree-granting institutions grant associate's or higher degrees and participate in Title IV federal financial aid programs. Data in this table pertain to institutions' fiscal years that end in the academic year noted. Some data have been revised from previously published figures. Detail may not sum to totals because of rounding.
SOURCE: U.S. Department of Education, National Center for Education Statistics, Integrated Postsecondary Education Data System (IPEDS), "Fall Enrollment Survey" (IPEDS-EF:99); Spring 2005 through Spring 2007, Enrollment component; Spring 2008 through Spring 2018, Fall Enrollment component; and Spring 2001 through Spring 2019, Finance component. (This table was prepared December 2019.)

Table 334.40. Total expenditures of private nonprofit degree-granting postsecondary institutions, by purpose and classification of institution: 2017–18

Classification of institution	Total	Instruction	Research	Public service	Academic support	Student services	Institutional support	Auxiliary enterprises[1]	Net grant aid to students[2]	Hospitals	Independent operations	Other
1	2	3	4	5	6	7	8	9	10	11	12	13
In thousands of current dollars												
Total	$206,778,042	$63,489,832	$21,872,856	$3,090,888	$17,843,700	$17,560,444	$26,471,439	$17,824,434	$986,591	$26,740,972	$6,294,985	$4,601,901
4-year	205,992,273	63,268,589	21,872,111	3,089,523	17,745,371	17,345,090	26,293,205	17,794,013	985,036	26,740,972	6,294,985	4,563,379
Research university, very high[3]	101,260,896	29,581,680	17,638,396	1,094,333	7,563,986	4,053,799	8,959,755	6,545,325	685,271	17,680,570	4,239,227	3,218,555
Research university, high[4]	15,062,942	5,063,970	1,408,749	259,422	2,420,869	1,264,753	2,164,286	1,792,043	34,484	499,279	82,486	72,600
Doctoral/research[5]	9,676,253	3,859,881	178,397	118,602	1,032,995	1,536,102	1,686,602	1,197,216	7,002	0	33,388	26,067
Master's[6]	31,610,369	11,872,385	254,173	234,696	3,206,398	5,493,979	6,044,947	3,894,197	114,820	28,873	124,800	341,100
Baccalaureate[7]	22,030,214	7,750,332	215,145	184,662	2,003,276	3,761,583	4,198,525	3,533,439	75,007	0	46,614	261,630
Special-focus institutions[8]	26,351,599	5,140,341	2,177,251	1,197,807	1,517,846	1,234,874	3,239,090	831,792	68,452	8,532,249	1,768,470	643,426
Arts, music, or design	2,471,665	999,416	1,091	27,551	312,765	257,447	510,317	272,625	4,626	0	48,636	37,190
Business and management	605,790	155,921	2,276	965	72,852	107,557	181,779	75,047	635	0	0	8,759
Engineering and other technology-related	259,879	111,205	3,775	0	22,563	45,229	52,512	19,028	4,081	0	0	1,487
Faith related	1,928,756	601,819	6,900	64,080	203,568	187,516	512,868	185,618	43,131	0	14,019	109,239
Law	492,177	201,053	3,342	9,373	77,201	64,758	120,779	13,437	1,394	0	0	840
Medical schools and centers and other heath professions schools	19,893,768	2,842,277	2,151,002	987,097	775,697	484,958	1,709,264	222,768	13,087	8,532,249	1,705,796	469,575
Tribal colleges[9]	88,983	24,300	2,383	6,157	5,420	13,099	21,532	1,534	742	0	0	13,817
Other special focus	610,581	204,350	6,482	102,586	47,780	74,313	130,041	41,734	757	0	19	2,520
2-year	785,770	221,244	745	1,366	98,329	215,354	178,234	30,421	1,555	0	0	38,522
Associate's colleges	770,539	217,993	19	1,060	95,733	213,901	174,135	30,072	322	0	0	37,305
Tribal colleges[9]	15,231	3,251	726	306	2,596	1,454	4,099	349	1,233	0	0	1,217
Percentage distribution												
Total	100.00	30.70	10.58	1.49	8.63	8.49	12.80	8.62	0.48	12.93	3.04	2.23
4-year	100.00	30.71	10.62	1.50	8.61	8.42	12.76	8.64	0.48	12.98	3.06	2.22
Research university, very high[3]	100.00	29.21	17.42	1.08	7.47	4.00	8.85	6.46	0.68	17.46	4.19	3.18
Research university, high[4]	100.00	33.62	9.35	1.72	16.07	8.40	14.37	11.90	0.23	3.31	0.55	0.48
Doctoral/research[5]	100.00	39.89	1.84	1.23	10.68	15.87	17.43	12.37	0.07	0.00	0.35	0.27
Master's[6]	100.00	37.56	0.80	0.74	10.14	17.38	19.12	12.32	0.36	0.09	0.39	1.08
Baccalaureate[7]	100.00	35.18	0.98	0.84	9.09	17.07	19.06	16.04	0.34	0.00	0.21	1.19
Special-focus institutions[8]	100.00	19.51	8.26	4.55	5.76	4.69	12.29	3.16	0.26	32.38	6.71	2.44
Arts, music, or design	100.00	40.43	0.04	1.11	12.65	10.42	20.65	11.03	0.19	0.00	1.97	1.50
Business and management	100.00	25.74	0.38	0.16	12.03	17.75	30.01	12.39	0.10	0.00	0.00	1.45
Engineering and other technology-related	100.00	42.79	1.45	0.00	8.68	17.40	20.21	7.32	1.57	0.00	0.00	0.57
Faith related	100.00	31.20	0.36	3.32	10.55	9.72	26.59	9.62	2.24	0.00	0.73	5.66
Law	100.00	40.85	0.68	1.90	15.69	13.16	24.54	2.73	0.28	0.00	0.00	0.17
Medical schools and centers and other heath professions schools	100.00	14.29	10.81	4.96	3.90	2.44	8.59	1.12	0.07	42.89	8.57	2.36
Tribal colleges[9]	100.00	27.31	2.68	6.92	6.09	14.72	24.20	1.72	0.83	0.00	0.00	15.53
Other special focus	100.00	33.47	1.06	16.80	7.83	12.17	21.30	6.84	0.12	0.00	#	0.41
2-year	100.00	28.16	0.09	0.17	12.51	27.41	22.68	3.87	0.20	0.00	0.00	4.90
Associate's colleges	100.00	28.29	#	0.14	12.42	27.76	22.60	3.90	0.04	0.00	0.00	4.84
Tribal colleges[9]	100.00	21.34	4.77	2.01	17.05	9.54	26.91	2.29	8.10	0.00	0.00	7.99

See notes at end of table.

Table 334.40. Total expenditures of private nonprofit degree-granting postsecondary institutions, by purpose and classification of institution: 2017–18—Continued

Classification of institution	Total	Instruction	Research	Public service	Academic support	Student services	Institutional support	Auxiliary enterprises[1]	Net grant aid to students[2]	Hospitals	Independent operations	Other
1	2	3	4	5	6	7	8	9	10	11	12	13
					Expenditure per full-time-equivalent student in current dollars							
Total	**$59,686**	**$18,326**	**$6,314**	**$892**	**$5,151**	**$5,069**	**$7,641**	**$5,145**	**$285**	**$7,719**	**$1,817**	**$1,328**
4-year												
Research university, very high[3]	60,174	18,482	6,389	903	5,184	5,067	7,681	5,198	288	7,812	1,839	1,333
Research university, high[4]	176,106	51,446	30,676	1,903	13,155	7,050	15,582	11,383	1,192	30,749	7,373	5,597
Doctoral/research[5]	51,563	17,335	4,822	888	8,287	4,329	7,409	6,134	118	1,709	282	249
Master's[6]	27,431	10,942	506	336	2,928	4,355	4,781	3,394	20	0	95	74
Baccalaureate[7]	24,602	9,240	198	183	2,495	4,276	4,705	3,031	89	22	97	265
Baccalaureate/associate's	36,932	12,993	361	310	3,358	6,306	7,039	5,924	126	0	78	439
Special-focus institutions[8]	81,837	15,964	6,762	3,720	4,714	3,835	10,059	2,583	213	26,498	5,492	1,998
Arts, music, or design	41,964	16,968	19	468	5,310	4,371	8,664	4,629	79	0	826	631
Business and management	25,396	6,536	95	40	3,054	4,509	7,620	3,146	27	0	0	367
Engineering and other technology-related	21,234	9,086	308	0	1,844	3,695	4,291	1,555	333	0	0	121
Faith related	28,521	8,899	102	948	3,010	2,773	7,584	2,745	638	0	207	1,615
Law	48,130	19,661	327	917	7,550	6,333	11,811	1,314	136	0	0	82
Medical schools and centers and other heath professions schools	148,919	21,276	16,102	7,389	5,807	3,630	12,795	1,668	98	63,870	12,769	3,515
Tribal colleges[9]	43,217	11,802	1,157	2,990	2,632	6,362	10,458	745	360	0	0	6,710
Other special focus	45,191	15,125	480	7,593	3,536	5,500	9,625	3,089	56	0	1	187
2-year												
Associate's colleges	19,079	5,372	18	33	2,387	5,229	4,328	739	38	0	0	935
Special-focus institutions	18,890	5,344	#	26	2,347	5,244	4,269	737	8	0	0	915
Tribal colleges[9]	38,461	8,209	1,834	772	6,557	3,671	10,351	880	3,114	0	0	3,073

#Rounds to zero.
[1]Essentially self-supporting operations of institutions that furnish a service to students, faculty, or staff, such as residence halls and food services.
[2]Excludes allowances that were recorded as a reduction to revenues from tuition and fees and from auxiliary enterprises, such as room, board, and books; also excludes agency transactions, such as student awards made from contributed funds or grant funds. These exclusions account for the majority of total student grants.
[3]Research universities with a very high level of research activity.
[4]Research universities with a high level of research activity.
[5]Research universities with a high level of research activity.
[6]Institutions that award at least 20 research/scholarship doctor's degrees per year, but did not have high levels of research activity.
[7]Institutions that award at least 50 master's and fewer than 20 doctor's degrees per year.
[8]Institutions that primarily emphasize undergraduate education. In addition to institutions that primarily award bachelor's degrees, also includes institutions classified as 4-year in the IPEDS system, but classified as 2-year baccalaureate/associate's degrees, also includes institutions classified as 4-year in the Carnegie Classification system because they primarily award associate's degrees.

[8]Four-year institutions that award degrees primarily in single fields of study, such as medicine, business, fine arts, theology, and engineering.
[9]Tribally controlled colleges, which are located on reservations and are members of the American Indian Higher Education Consortium.
NOTE: Relative levels of research activity for research universities were determined by an analysis of research and development expenditures, science and engineering research staffing, and doctor's degrees conferred, by field. Further information on the Carnegie 2015 classification system used in this table may be obtained from https://carnegieclassifications.iu.edu/downloads/CCIHE2015-FactsFigures.pdf. Degree-granting institutions grant associate's or higher degrees and participate in Title IV federal financial aid programs. Data in this table pertain to institutions' fiscal years that end in the academic year noted. Detail may not sum to totals because of rounding.
SOURCE: U.S. Department of Education, National Center for Education Statistics, Integrated Postsecondary Education Data System (IPEDS), Spring 2018, Fall Enrollment component; and Spring 2019, Finance component. (This table was prepared December 2019.)

Table 334.50. Total expenditures of private for-profit degree-granting postsecondary institutions, by purpose and level of institution: Selected years, 1999–2000 through 2017–18

Year and level of institution	Total	Instruction	Research and public service	Academic support, student services, and institutional support	Auxiliary enterprises[1]	Net grant aid to students[2]	Other[3]
1	2	3	4	5	6	7	8
	In thousands of current dollars						
All levels							
1999–2000	$3,846,246	$1,171,732	$24,738	$2,041,594	$144,305	$26,278	$437,599
2004–05	8,830,792	2,313,895	7,583	5,693,200	269,883	54,819	491,411
2005–06	10,208,845	2,586,870	8,445	6,575,800	276,108	66,569	695,053
2006–07	12,165,629	2,883,207	6,087	7,776,210	332,887	67,090	1,100,148
2007–08	13,939,251	3,273,627	9,695	9,299,306	421,714	82,072	852,837
2008–09	16,375,034	3,876,258	9,939	11,069,416	396,715	44,440	978,267
2009–10	19,973,034	4,759,300	13,257	13,230,271	466,040	120,032	1,384,134
2010–11	22,632,244	5,656,167	19,327	14,853,799	486,433	87,151	1,529,368
2011–12	22,713,683	5,538,070	42,657	15,111,978	489,409	54,579	1,476,991
2012–13	21,923,722	5,467,671	27,729	14,294,090	467,973	53,555	1,612,705
2013–14	20,644,593	5,536,025	16,447	13,103,182	472,204	36,569	1,480,166
2014–15	18,441,030	4,917,479	20,028	11,624,796	504,091	35,524	1,339,112
2015–16	16,000,640	4,248,320	17,453	10,081,942	399,110	25,277	1,228,537
2016–17	14,698,133	3,923,606	17,027	9,196,550	318,897	26,649	1,215,403
2017–18	12,165,398	3,304,987	19,403	7,712,011	232,192	15,417	881,389
4-year							
1999–2000	2,022,622	595,976	4,393	1,104,001	92,071	11,805	214,377
2004–05	5,989,792	1,430,196	3,513	4,110,514	180,036	38,639	226,894
2005–06	7,218,830	1,680,603	4,065	4,986,009	178,587	54,291	315,276
2006–07	8,850,759	1,856,614	4,303	5,925,855	228,624	56,930	778,433
2007–08	10,422,080	2,184,872	7,682	7,312,117	312,834	71,324	533,252
2008–09	12,409,748	2,585,133	7,629	8,893,714	276,211	33,417	613,644
2009–10	15,286,893	3,268,070	10,726	10,732,002	337,499	72,082	866,514
2010–11	17,141,926	3,925,347	15,582	12,031,073	343,319	74,921	751,684
2011–12	17,407,585	3,928,903	37,912	12,153,860	349,405	51,818	885,687
2012–13	16,759,402	3,939,227	24,432	11,377,216	359,987	46,446	1,012,095
2013–14	16,017,246	4,078,270	15,190	10,545,883	371,018	32,306	974,579
2014–15	14,628,734	3,729,921	17,904	9,617,433	334,087	33,089	896,300
2015–16	12,564,815	3,199,028	15,489	8,199,419	323,247	22,834	804,796
2016–17	11,680,961	2,995,663	15,090	7,592,227	261,821	24,039	792,122
2017–18	9,748,366	2,539,652	18,026	6,418,623	175,954	13,803	582,308
2-year							
1999–2000	1,823,624	575,756	20,345	937,593	52,234	14,473	223,223
2004–05	2,840,999	883,699	4,070	1,582,687	89,846	16,181	264,517
2005–06	2,990,015	906,267	4,381	1,589,791	97,521	12,278	379,777
2006–07	3,314,870	1,026,592	1,784	1,850,355	104,264	10,160	321,715
2007–08	3,517,171	1,088,755	2,014	1,987,189	108,880	10,747	319,586
2008–09	3,965,287	1,291,124	2,310	2,175,703	120,504	11,023	364,623
2009–10	4,686,142	1,491,230	2,531	2,498,269	128,542	47,950	517,619
2010–11	5,490,318	1,730,820	3,744	2,822,726	143,113	12,230	777,685
2011–12	5,306,098	1,609,167	4,745	2,958,118	140,004	2,761	591,304
2012–13	5,164,320	1,528,444	3,297	2,916,874	107,986	7,109	600,609
2013–14	4,627,347	1,457,755	1,257	2,557,299	101,186	4,263	505,588
2014–15	3,812,297	1,187,558	2,124	2,007,363	170,004	2,435	442,812
2015–16	3,435,825	1,049,292	1,964	1,882,523	75,863	2,443	423,740
2016–17	3,017,172	927,944	1,937	1,604,323	57,076	2,610	423,281
2017–18	2,417,033	765,335	1,377	1,293,388	56,238	1,615	299,080
	Percentage distribution						
All levels							
1999–2000	100.00	30.46	0.64	53.08	3.75	0.68	11.38
2004–05	100.00	26.20	0.09	64.47	3.06	0.62	5.56
2005–06	100.00	25.34	0.08	64.41	2.70	0.65	6.81
2006–07	100.00	23.70	0.05	63.92	2.74	0.55	9.04
2007–08	100.00	23.48	0.07	66.71	3.03	0.59	6.12
2008–09	100.00	23.67	0.06	67.60	2.42	0.27	5.97
2009–10	100.00	23.83	0.07	66.24	2.33	0.60	6.93
2010–11	100.00	24.99	0.09	65.63	2.15	0.39	6.76
2011–12	100.00	24.38	0.19	66.53	2.15	0.24	6.50
2012–13	100.00	24.94	0.13	65.20	2.13	0.24	7.36
2013–14	100.00	26.82	0.08	63.47	2.29	0.18	7.17
2014–15	100.00	26.67	0.11	63.04	2.73	0.19	7.26
2015–16	100.00	26.55	0.11	63.01	2.49	0.16	7.68
2016–17	100.00	26.69	0.12	62.57	2.17	0.18	8.27
2017–18	100.00	27.17	0.16	63.39	1.91	0.13	7.25
4-year							
1999–2000	100.00	29.47	0.22	54.58	4.55	0.58	10.60
2004–05	100.00	23.88	0.06	68.63	3.01	0.65	3.79
2005–06	100.00	23.28	0.06	69.07	2.47	0.75	4.37
2006–07	100.00	20.98	0.05	66.95	2.58	0.64	8.80
2007–08	100.00	20.96	0.07	70.16	3.00	0.68	5.12
2008–09	100.00	20.83	0.06	71.67	2.23	0.27	4.94
2009–10	100.00	21.38	0.07	70.20	2.21	0.47	5.67
2010–11	100.00	22.90	0.09	70.19	2.00	0.44	4.39
2011–12	100.00	22.57	0.22	69.82	2.01	0.30	5.09
2012–13	100.00	23.50	0.15	67.89	2.15	0.28	6.04

See notes at end of table.

Table 334.50. Total expenditures of private for-profit degree-granting postsecondary institutions, by purpose and level of institution: Selected years, 1999–2000 through 2017–18—Continued

Year and level of institution	Total	Instruction	Research and public service	Academic support, student services, and institutional support	Auxiliary enterprises[1]	Net grant aid to students[2]	Other[3]
1	2	3	4	5	6	7	8
2013–14	100.00	25.46	0.09	65.84	2.32	0.20	6.08
2014–15	100.00	25.50	0.12	65.74	2.28	0.23	6.13
2015–16	100.00	25.46	0.12	65.26	2.57	0.18	6.41
2016–17	100.00	25.65	0.13	65.00	2.24	0.21	6.78
2017–18	100.00	26.05	0.18	65.84	1.80	0.14	5.97
2-year							
1999–2000	100.00	31.57	1.12	51.41	2.86	0.79	12.24
2004–05	100.00	31.11	0.14	55.71	3.16	0.57	9.31
2005–06	100.00	30.31	0.15	53.17	3.26	0.41	12.70
2006–07	100.00	30.97	0.05	55.82	3.15	0.31	9.71
2007–08	100.00	30.96	0.06	56.50	3.10	0.31	9.09
2008–09	100.00	32.56	0.06	54.87	3.04	0.28	9.20
2009–10	100.00	31.82	0.05	53.31	2.74	1.02	11.05
2010–11	100.00	31.52	0.07	51.41	2.61	0.22	14.16
2011–12	100.00	30.33	0.09	55.75	2.64	0.05	11.14
2012–13	100.00	29.60	0.06	56.48	2.09	0.14	11.63
2013–14	100.00	31.50	0.03	55.26	2.19	0.09	10.93
2014–15	100.00	31.15	0.06	52.65	4.46	0.06	11.62
2015–16	100.00	30.54	0.06	54.79	2.21	0.07	12.33
2016–17	100.00	30.76	0.06	53.17	1.89	0.09	14.03
2017–18	100.00	31.66	0.06	53.51	2.33	0.07	12.37
	Expenditure per full-time-equivalent student in constant 2018–19 dollars[4]						
All levels							
1999–2000	$14,961	$4,558	$96	$7,941	$561	$102	$1,702
2004–05	14,805	3,879	13	9,544	452	92	824
2005–06	14,429	3,656	12	9,294	390	94	982
2006–07	15,997	3,791	8	10,225	438	88	1,447
2007–08	16,188	3,802	11	10,800	490	95	990
2008–09	15,340	3,631	9	10,369	372	42	916
2009–10	15,666	3,733	10	10,377	366	94	1,086
2010–11	15,679	3,918	13	10,290	337	60	1,060
2011–12	15,681	3,823	29	10,433	338	38	1,020
2012–13	16,962	4,230	21	11,059	362	41	1,248
2013–14	20,983	5,627	17	13,318	480	37	1,504
2014–15	16,694	4,452	18	10,524	456	32	1,212
2015–16	17,199	4,566	19	10,837	429	27	1,321
2016–17	17,128	4,572	20	10,717	372	31	1,416
2017–18	16,536	4,492	26	10,483	316	21	1,198
4-year							
1999–2000	14,494	4,271	31	7,911	660	85	1,536
2004–05	14,293	3,413	8	9,808	430	92	541
2005–06	13,870	3,229	8	9,580	343	104	606
2006–07	15,594	3,271	8	10,441	403	100	1,372
2007–08	15,797	3,312	12	11,083	474	108	808
2008–09	15,161	3,158	9	10,865	337	41	750
2009–10	15,983	3,417	11	11,220	353	75	906
2010–11	15,613	3,575	14	10,958	313	68	685
2011–12	15,462	3,490	34	10,796	310	46	787
2012–13	16,566	3,894	24	11,246	356	46	1,000
2013–14	22,151	5,640	21	14,584	513	45	1,348
2014–15	16,439	4,192	20	10,808	375	37	1,007
2015–16	16,905	4,304	21	11,032	435	31	1,083
2016–17	16,846	4,320	22	10,949	378	35	1,142
2017–18	16,429	4,280	30	10,817	297	23	981
2-year							
1999–2000	15,514	4,898	173	7,977	444	123	1,899
2004–05	16,013	4,981	23	8,921	506	91	1,491
2005–06	15,984	4,845	23	8,499	521	66	2,030
2006–07	17,180	5,321	9	9,590	540	53	1,667
2007–08	17,470	5,408	10	9,871	541	53	1,587
2008–09	15,926	5,186	9	8,739	484	44	1,464
2009–10	14,714	4,682	8	7,845	404	151	1,625
2010–11	15,890	5,009	11	8,169	414	35	2,251
2011–12	16,445	4,987	15	9,168	434	9	1,833
2012–13	18,386	5,442	12	10,385	384	25	2,138
2013–14	17,747	5,591	5	9,808	388	16	1,939
2014–15	17,750	5,529	10	9,346	792	11	2,062
2015–16	18,363	5,608	10	10,061	405	13	2,265
2016–17	18,315	5,633	12	9,739	346	16	2,569
2017–18	16,984	5,378	10	9,088	395	11	2,102

[1]Essentially self-supporting operations of institutions that furnish a service to students, faculty, or staff, such as residence halls and food services.
[2]Excludes allowances that were recorded as a reduction to revenues from tuition and fees and from auxiliary enterprises, such as room, board, and books; also excludes agency transactions, such as student awards made from contributed funds or grant funds. These exclusions account for the majority of total student grants.
[3]"Other" categories of expenditures include hospitals.
[4]Constant dollars based on the Consumer Price Index, prepared by the Bureau of Labor Statistics, U.S. Department of Labor, adjusted to a school-year basis.

NOTE: Degree-granting institutions grant associate's or higher degrees and participate in Title IV federal financial aid programs. Data in this table pertain to institutions' fiscal years that end in the academic year noted. Some data have been revised from previously published figures. Detail may not sum to totals because of rounding.
SOURCE: U.S. Department of Education, National Center for Education Statistics, Integrated Postsecondary Education Data System (IPEDS), "Fall Enrollment Survey" (IPEDS-EF:99); Spring 2005 through Spring 2007, Enrollment component; Spring 2008 through Spring 2018, Fall Enrollment component; and Spring 2001 through Spring 2019, Finance component. (This table was prepared December 2019.)

CHAPTER 4
Federal Funds for Education and Related Activities

This chapter provides information on federal support for education. The tables include detailed data on funding by specific federal agencies, funding for different levels of education and types of education-related activities, and funding for specific programs. Preceding the tables is a brief chronology of federal education legislation enacted since 1787, which provides historical context for the education funding data.

The data in this chapter primarily reflect outlays and appropriations of federal agencies. The data are compiled from budget information prepared by federal agencies. In contrast, most of the federal revenue data reported in other chapters are compiled by educational institutions or state education agencies and reported to the federal government through standardized survey forms. Tabulations based on institution- or state-reported revenue data differ substantially from federal budget reports because of numerous variations in methodology and definitions. Federal dollars are not necessarily spent by recipient institutions in the same year in which they are appropriated. In some cases, institutions cannot identify the source of federal revenues because they flow through state agencies. Some types of revenues, such as tuition and fees, are reported as revenues from students even though they may be supported by federal student aid programs. Some institutions that receive federal education funds (e.g., Department of Defense overseas and domestic schools, state education agencies, Head Start programs, and federal libraries) are not included in regular surveys, censuses, and administrative data collections conducted by the National Center for Education Statistics (NCES). Thus, the federal programs data tabulated in this chapter are not comparable with figures reported in other chapters. Readers should also be careful about comparing the data on obligations shown in table 402.10 (web only) with the data on outlays and appropriations appearing in other tables in this chapter.

Federal Education Funding

Federal on-budget funding (federal funds for education programs tied to appropriations) for education increased by 77 percent from $138.1 billion in fiscal year (FY) 2000 to $244.4 billion in FY 2019, after adjustment for inflation (table D, table 401.10, and figure 20). Federal funds in FY 2019 were higher than in FY 2000 for all major program categories. Federal funds for elementary and secondary education in FY 2019 were 34 percent higher than in FY 2000; funds for postsecondary education were 219 percent higher; funds for other education were 16 percent higher; and funds for research at educational institutions were 30 percent higher. While funding levels were higher in FY 2019 than in

FY 2000 for these major categories, changes were not consistent across the categories during this time period.

The overall increase in the federal funding level for education was smaller between FY 2010 and FY 2019 (18 percent) than between FY 2000 and FY 2010 (50 percent), after adjustment for inflation. Federal on-budget funding was higher in FY 2010 than in FY 2000 for each of the four major categories reported: postsecondary education (by 99 percent), elementary and secondary education (by 35 percent), research at educational institutions (by 34 percent), and other education (by 25 percent; table D, table 401.10, and figure 20). In contrast, federal on-budget funding was higher in FY 2019 than in FY 2010 for only one of the four categories: for postsecondary education, federal on-budget funding was 60 percent higher in FY 2019 than in FY 2010. Federal funding for the category of other education was 7 percent lower in FY 2019 than in FY 2010, after adjustment for inflation. Also, funding for research at educational institutions was 3 percent lower in FY 2019 than in FY 2010, and funding for elementary and secondary education was 1 percent lower.

Table D. Federal on-budget funding for education, by category: Selected fiscal years, 2000 through 2019

[In billions of constant fiscal year (FY) 2019 dollars]

Fiscal year	Total	Elementary/ secondary	Post-secondary	Other education	Research at educational institutions
2000	$138.1	$64.2	$33.7	$8.5	$31.7
2005	201.8	89.0	60.4	9.4	43.1
2010	206.7	86.5	67.0	10.6	42.6
2015	220.9	84.0	92.3	10.1	34.5
2016	211.6	86.8	79.2	10.2	35.5
2017[1]	249.9	85.1	118.7	10.0	36.1
2018	219.9	86.5	85.0	9.7	38.7
2019	244.4	85.9	107.5	9.9	41.2

[1]The increase in postsecondary expenditures in 2017 resulted primarily from an accounting adjustment.
NOTE: Detail may not sum to totals because of rounding.
SOURCE: U.S. Department of Education, Budget Service and National Center for Education Statistics, unpublished tabulations. U.S. Office of Management and Budget, *Budget of the U.S. Government, Appendix*, various FYs. National Science Foundation, *Federal Funds for Research and Development*, various FYs.

After adjustment for inflation, off-budget support and nonfederal funds generated by federal legislation (e.g., primarily loans for postsecondary students supported by federal appropriations) showed an increase of 135 percent between FY 2000 ($49.3 billion in FY 2019 dollars) and FY 2010 ($116.1 billion in FY 2019 dollars; table 401.10). In FY 2019, these same funds totaled $91.0 billion, reflecting a decrease of 22 percent from FY 2010. Note that total enrollment in degree-granting institutions decreased by 7 percent between fall 2010 and fall 2018 (table 303.10).

In current dollars (not adjusted for inflation), federal on-budget funds for education in FY 2018 totaled $216.1 billion (figure 21 and table 401.20). The U.S. Department of Education provided 45 percent ($96.4 billion) of this total. Funds exceeding $2.5 billion also came from the U.S. Department of Health and Human Services ($45.0 billion), the U.S. Department of Agriculture ($26.8 billion), the U.S. Department of Veterans Affairs ($14.5 billion), the U.S. Department of Defense ($7.9 billion), the National Science Foundation ($6.1 billion), the U.S. Department of Labor ($5.0 billion), the U.S. Department of Energy ($4.4 billion), and the National Aeronautics and Space Administration ($2.9 billion).

The largest program areas for elementary and secondary education in FY 2019 were Child nutrition programs (U.S. Department of Agriculture, $23.1 billion), Education for the disadvantaged (U.S. Department of Education, $16.5 billion), Special education (U.S. Department of Education, $13.5 billion), and Head Start (U.S. Department of Health and Human Services, $10.1 billion; table 401.30). The largest postsecondary programs were the Direct Loan Program (U.S. Department of Education, $36.5 billion), Student financial assistance (U.S. Department of Education, $31.6 billion), Medicare medical education benefits (U.S. Department of Health and Human Services, $14.1 billion), and the Post-9/11 GI Bill (U.S. Department of Veterans Affairs, $10.7 billion). Another program area exceeding $10 billion in FY 2019 was U.S. Department of Health and Human Services funds for research at universities and related institutions ($20.9 billion).

Chronology of Federal Education Legislation

A capsule view of the history of federal education activities is provided in the following list of selected legislation:

1787 *Northwest Ordinance* authorized land grants for the establishment of educational institutions.

1802 *An Act Fixing the Military Peace Establishment of the United States* established the U.S. Military Academy. (The U.S. Naval Academy was established in 1845 by the Secretary of the Navy.)

1862 *First Morrill Act* authorized public land grants to the states for the establishment and maintenance of agricultural and mechanical colleges.

1867 *Department of Education Act* authorized the establishment of the U.S. Department of Education.[1]

1876 *Appropriation Act*, U.S. Department of the Treasury, established the U.S. Coast Guard Academy.

1890 *Second Morrill Act* provided for monetary grants for support of instruction in the agricultural and mechanical colleges.

1911 *State Marine School Act* authorized federal funds to be used for the benefit of any nautical school in any of 11 specified seaport cities.

1917 *Smith-Hughes Act* provided for grants to states for support of vocational education.

1918 *Vocational Rehabilitation Act* provided for grants for rehabilitation through training of World War I veterans.

1920 *Smith-Bankhead Act* authorized grants to states for vocational rehabilitation programs.

1935 *Bankhead-Jones Act* (Public Law 74-182) authorized grants to states for agricultural experiment stations.

Agricultural Adjustment Act (Public Law 74-320) authorized 30 percent of the annual customs receipts to be used to encourage the exportation and domestic consumption of agricultural commodities. Commodities purchased under this authorization began to be used in school lunch programs in 1936. The National School Lunch Act of 1946 continued and expanded this assistance.

1936 *An Act to Further the Development and Maintenance of an Adequate and Well-Balanced American Merchant Marine* (Public Law 74-415) established the U.S. Merchant Marine Academy.

1937 *National Cancer Institute Act* (Public Law 75-244) established the Public Health Service fellowship program.

1941 *Amendment to Lanham Act of 1940* authorized federal aid for construction, maintenance, and operation of schools in federally impacted areas. Such assistance was continued under Public Law 815 and Public Law 874, 81st Congress, in 1950.

1943 *Vocational Rehabilitation Act* (Public Law 78-16) provided assistance to veterans with disabilities.

School Lunch Indemnity Plan (Public Law 78-129) provided funds for local lunch food purchases.

1944 *Servicemen's Readjustment Act* (Public Law 78-346), known as the GI Bill, provided assistance for the education of veterans.

Surplus Property Act (Public Law 78-457) authorized transfer of surplus property to educational institutions.

1946 *National School Lunch Act* (Public Law 79-396) authorized assistance through grants-in-aid and other means to states to assist in providing adequate foods and facilities for the establishment, maintenance, operation, and expansion of non-profit school lunch programs.

George-Barden Act (Public Law 80-402) expanded federal support of vocational education.

---

[1] The U.S. Department of Education as established in 1867 was later known as the Office of Education. In 1980, under Public Law 96-88, it became a cabinet-level department. Therefore, for purposes of consistency, it is referred to as the "U.S. Department of Education" even in those tables covering years when it was officially the Office of Education.

1948 *United States Information and Educational Exchange Act* (Public Law 80-402) provided for the interchange of people, knowledge, and skills between the United States and other countries.

1949 *Federal Property and Administrative Services Act* (Public Law 81-152) provided for donation of surplus property to educational institutions and for other public purposes.

1950 *Financial Assistance for Local Educational Agencies Affected by Federal Activities* (Public Law 81-815 and Public Law 81-874) provided assistance for construction (Public Law 815) and operation (Public Law 874) of schools in federally affected areas.

Housing Act (Public Law 81-475) authorized loans for construction of college housing facilities.

1954 *An Act for the Establishment of the United States Air Force Academy and Other Purposes* (Public Law 83-325) established the U.S. Air Force Academy.

Educational Research Act (Public Law 83-531) authorized cooperative arrangements with universities, colleges, and state educational agencies for educational research.

School Milk Program Act (Public Law 83-597) provided funds for purchase of milk for school lunch programs.

1956 *Library Services Act* (Public Law 84-597) provided grants to states for extension and improvement of rural public library services.

1957 *Practical Nurse Training Act* (Public Law 84-911) provided grants to states for practical nurse training.

1958 *National Defense Education Act* (Public Law 85-864) provided assistance to state and local school systems for instruction in science, mathematics, modern foreign languages, and other critical subjects; state statistical services; guidance, counseling, and testing services and training institutes; higher education student loans and fellowships as well as foreign language study and training; experimentation and dissemination of information on more effective use of television, motion pictures, and related media for educational purposes; and vocational education for technical occupations necessary to the national defense.

Education of Mentally Retarded Children Act (Public Law 85-926) authorized federal assistance for training teachers of the disabled.

Captioned Films for the Deaf Act (Public Law 85-905) authorized a loan service of captioned films for the deaf.

1961 *Area Redevelopment Act* (Public Law 87-27) included provisions for training or retraining of people in redevelopment areas.

1962 *Manpower Development and Training Act* (Public Law 87-415) provided training in new and improved skills for the unemployed and underemployed.

Migration and Refugee Assistance Act of 1962 (Public Law 87-510) authorized loans, advances, and grants for education and training of refugees.

1963 *Health Professions Educational Assistance Act of 1963* (Public Law 88-129) provided funds to expand teaching facilities and for loans to students in the health professions.

Vocational Education Act of 1963 (Public Law 88-210, Part A) increased federal support of vocational education schools; vocational work-study programs; and research, training, and demonstrations in vocational education.

Higher Education Facilities Act of 1963 (Public Law 88-204) authorized grants and loans for classrooms, libraries, and laboratories in public community colleges and technical institutes, as well as undergraduate and graduate facilities in other higher education institutions.

1964 *Civil Rights Act of 1964* (Public Law 88-352) authorized the Commissioner of Education to arrange for support for higher education institutions and school districts to provide inservice programs for assisting instructional staff in dealing with problems caused by desegregation.

Economic Opportunity Act of 1964 (Public Law 88-452) authorized grants for college work-study programs for students from low-income families; established a Job Corps program and authorized support for work-training programs to provide education and vocational training and work experience opportunities in welfare programs; authorized support of education and training activities and of community action programs, including Head Start, Follow Through, and Upward Bound; and authorized the establishment of Volunteers in Service to America (VISTA).

1965 *Elementary and Secondary Education Act of 1965* (Public Law 89-10) authorized grants for elementary and secondary school programs for children of low-income families; school library resources, textbooks, and other instructional materials for school children; supplementary educational centers and services; strengthening state education agencies; and educational research and research training.

Health Professions Educational Assistance Amendments of 1965 (Public Law 89-290) authorized scholarships to aid needy students in the health professions.

Higher Education Act of 1965 (Public Law 89-329) provided grants for university community service programs, college library assistance, library training and research, strengthening developing institutions, teacher training programs, and undergraduate instructional equipment. Authorized insured student loans, established a National Teacher Corps, and provided for graduate teacher training fellowships.

National Foundation on the Arts and the Humanities Act (Public Law 89-209) authorized grants and loans for projects in the creative and performing arts and for research, training, and scholarly publications in the humanities.

National Technical Institute for the Deaf Act (Public Law 89-36) provided for the establishment, construction, equipping, and operation of a residential school for postsecondary education and technical training of the deaf.

School Assistance in Disaster Areas Act (Public Law 89-313) provided for assistance to local education agencies to help meet exceptional costs resulting from a major disaster.

1966 *International Education Act* (Public Law 89-698) provided grants to higher education institutions for the establishment, strengthening, and operation of centers for research and training in international studies and the international aspects of other fields of study.

National Sea Grant College and Program Act (Public Law 89-688) authorized the establishment and operation of Sea Grant Colleges and programs by initiating and supporting programs of education and research in the various fields relating to the development of marine resources.

Adult Education Act (Public Law 89-750) authorized grants to states for the encouragement and expansion of educational programs for adults, including training of teachers of adults and demonstrations in adult education (previously part of Economic Opportunity Act of 1964).

Model Secondary School for the Deaf Act (Public Law 89-694) authorized the establishment and operation, by Gallaudet College, of a model secondary school for the deaf.

1967 *Education Professions Development Act* (Public Law 90-35) amended the Higher Education Act of 1965 for the purpose of improving the quality of teaching and to help meet critical shortages of adequately trained educational personnel.

Public Broadcasting Act of 1967 (Public Law 90-129) established a Corporation for Public Broadcasting to assume major responsibility in channeling federal funds to noncommercial radio and television stations, program production groups, and educational television networks; conduct research, demonstration, or training in matters related to noncommercial broadcasting; and award grants for construction of educational radio and television facilities.

1968 *Elementary and Secondary Education Amendments of 1968* (Public Law 90-247) modified existing programs and authorized support of regional centers for education of children with disabilities, model centers and services for deaf-blind children, recruitment of personnel and dissemination of information on education of children with disabilities; technical assistance in education to rural areas; support of dropout prevention projects; and support of bilingual education programs.

Handicapped Children's Early Education Assistance Act (Public Law 90-538) authorized preschool and early education programs for children with disabilities.

Vocational Education Amendments of 1968 (Public Law 90-576) modified existing programs and provided for a National Advisory Council on Vocational Education and collection and dissemination of information for programs administered by the Commissioner of Education.

1970 *Elementary and Secondary Education Assistance Programs, Extension* (Public Law 91-230) authorized comprehensive planning and evaluation grants to state and local education agencies; provided for the establishment of a National Commission on School Finance.

National Commission on Libraries and Information Science Act (Public Law 91-345) established a National Commission on Libraries and Information Science to effectively utilize the nation's educational resources.

Office of Education Appropriation Act (Public Law 91-380) provided emergency school assistance to desegregating local education agencies.

Environmental Education Act (Public Law 91-516) established an Office of Environmental Education to develop curriculum and initiate and maintain environmental education programs at the elementary/secondary levels; disseminate information; provide training programs for teachers and other educational, public, community, labor, and industrial leaders and employees; provide community education programs; and distribute material dealing with the environment and ecology.

Drug Abuse Education Act of 1970 (Public Law 91-527) provided for development, demonstration, and evaluation of curricula on the problems of drug abuse.

1971 *Comprehensive Health Manpower Training Act of 1971* (Public Law 92-257) amended Title VII of the Public Health Service Act, increasing and expanding provisions for health manpower training and training facilities.

1972 *Drug Abuse Office and Treatment Act of 1972* (Public Law 92-255) established a Special Action Office for Drug Abuse Prevention to provide overall planning and policy for all federal drug-abuse prevention functions; a National Advisory Council for Drug Abuse Prevention; community assistance grants for community mental health centers for treatment and rehabilitation of people with drug-abuse problems; and, in December 1974, a National Institute on Drug Abuse.

Education Amendments of 1972 (Public Law 92-318) established the Education Division in the U.S. Department of Health, Education, and Welfare and the National Institute of Education; general aid for higher education institutions; federal matching grants for state Student Incentive Grants; a National Commission on Financing Postsecondary Education; State Advisory Councils on Community Colleges; a Bureau of Occupational and Adult Education and State Grants for the design, establishment, and conduct of postsecondary occupational education; and a bureau-level Office of Indian Education. Amended current U.S. Department of Education programs to increase their effectiveness and better meet special needs. Prohibited sex bias in admission to vocational, professional, and graduate schools, and public institutions of undergraduate higher education.

1973 *Older Americans Comprehensive Services Amendment of 1973* (Public Law 93-29) made available to older citizens comprehensive programs of health, education, and social services.

Comprehensive Employment and Training Act of 1973 (Public Law 93-203) provided for employment and training opportunities for unemployed and underemployed people. Extended and expanded provisions in the Manpower Development and Training Act of 1962, Title I of the Economic Opportunity Act of 1962, Title I of the Economic Opportunity Act of 1964, and the Emergency Employment Act of 1971 as in effect prior to June 30, 1973.

1974 *Education Amendments of 1974* (Public Law 93-380) provided for the consolidation of certain programs and established a National Center for Education Statistics.

Juvenile Justice and Delinquency Prevention Act of 1974 (Public Law 93-415) provided for technical assistance, staff training, centralized research, and resources to develop and implement programs to keep students in elementary and secondary schools; and established, in the U.S. Department of Justice, a National Institute for Juvenile Justice and Delinquency Prevention.

1975 *Indian Self-Determination and Education Assistance Act* (Public Law 93-638) provided for increased participation of American Indian/Alaska Native populations in the establishment and conduct of their education programs and services.

Harry S Truman Memorial Scholarship Act (Public Law 93-642) established the Harry S Truman Scholarship Foundation and created a perpetual education scholarship fund for young Americans to prepare for and pursue careers in public service.

Education for All Handicapped Children Act (Public Law 94-142) provided that all children with disabilities have available to them a free appropriate education designed to meet their unique needs.

1976 *Educational Broadcasting Facilities and Telecommunications Demonstration Act of 1976* (Public Law 94-309) established a telecommunications demonstration program to promote the development of nonbroadcast telecommunications facilities and services for the transmission, distribution, and delivery of health, education, and public or social service information.

1977 *Youth Employment and Demonstration Projects Act of 1977* (Public Law 95-93) established a youth employment training program including, among

other activities, promotion of education-to-work transition, literacy training and bilingual training, and attainment of certificates of high school equivalency.

Career Education Incentive Act (Public Law 95-207) authorized the establishment of a career education program for elementary and secondary schools.

1978 *Tribally Controlled Community College Assistance Act of 1978* (Public Law 95-471) provided federal funds for the operation and improvement of tribally controlled community colleges for American Indian/Alaska Native students.

Middle Income Student Assistance Act (Public Law 95-566) modified the provisions for student financial assistance programs to allow middle-income as well as low-income students attending college or other postsecondary institutions to qualify for federal education assistance.

1979 *Department of Education Organization Act* (Public Law 96-88) established a U.S. Department of Education containing functions from the Education Division of the U.S. Department of Health, Education, and Welfare (HEW) along with other selected education programs from HEW, the U.S. Department of Justice, U.S. Department of Labor, and the National Science Foundation.

1980 *Asbestos School Hazard Detection and Control Act of 1980* (Public Law 96-270) established a program for inspection of schools for detection of hazardous asbestos materials and provided loans to assist educational agencies to contain or remove and replace such materials.

1981 *Education Consolidation and Improvement Act of 1981* (Part of Public Law 97-35) consolidated 42 programs into 7 programs to be funded under the elementary and secondary block grant authority.

1983 *Student Loan Consolidation and Technical Amendments Act of 1983* (Public Law 98-79) established an 8 percent interest rate for Guaranteed Student Loans and an extended Family Contribution Schedule.

Challenge Grant Amendments of 1983 (Public Law 98-95) amended Title III of the Higher Education Act of 1965 and added authorization of the Challenge Grant program. The Challenge Grant program provides funds to eligible institutions on a matching basis as an incentive to seek alternative sources of funding.

Education of the Handicapped Act Amendments of 1983 (Public Law 98-199) added the Architectural Barrier amendment (providing funds for altering existing buildings and equipment to make them accessible to those with physical disabilities) and clarified participation of children with disabilities in private schools.

1984 *Education for Economic Security Act* (Public Law 98-377) added new science and mathematics programs for elementary, secondary, and postsecondary education. The new programs included magnet schools, excellence in education, and equal access.

Carl D. Perkins Vocational Education Act (Public Law 98-524) continued federal assistance for vocational education through FY 1989. The act replaced the Vocational Education Act of 1963. It provided aid to the states to make vocational education programs accessible to all people, including disabled and disadvantaged, single parents and homemakers, and the incarcerated.

Human Services Reauthorization Act (Public Law 98-558) created a Carl D. Perkins scholarship program, a National Talented Teachers Fellowship program, a Federal Merit Scholarships program, and a Leadership in Educational Administration program.

1985 *Montgomery GI Bill—Active Duty* (Public Law 98-525) brought about a new GI Bill for individuals who initially entered active military duty on or after July 1, 1985.

Montgomery GI Bill—Selected Reserve (Public Law 98-525) established an education program for members of the Selected Reserve (which includes the National Guard) who enlist, reenlist, or extend an enlistment after June 30, 1985, for a 6-year period.

1986 *Handicapped Children's Protection Act of 1986* (Public Law 99-372) allowed parents of children with disabilities to collect attorneys' fees in cases brought under the Education of the Handicapped Act and provided that the Education of the Handicapped Act does not preempt other laws, such as Section 504 of the Rehabilitation Act.

Drug-Free Schools and Communities Act of 1986 (Part of Public Law 99-570) established programs for drug abuse education and prevention, coordinated with related community efforts and resources, through the use of federal financial assistance.

1988 *Augustus F. Hawkins-Robert T. Stafford Elementary and Secondary School Improvement Amendments of 1988* (Public Law 100-297) reauthorized through 1993 major elementary and secondary education programs, including Chapter 1, Chapter 2, Bilingual Education, Math-Science Education, Magnet Schools, Impact Aid, Indian Education, Adult Education, and other smaller education programs.

Stewart B. McKinney Homeless Assistance Amendments Act of 1988 (Public Law 100-628) extended for 2 additional years programs providing assistance to the homeless, including literacy training for homeless adults and education for homeless youths.

Tax Reform Technical Amendments (Public Law 100-647) authorized an Education Savings Bond for the purpose of postsecondary educational expenses. The bill grants tax exclusion for interest earned on regular series EE savings bonds.

1989 *Childhood Education and Development Act of 1989* (Part of Public Law 101-239) authorized the appropriations to expand Head Start programs and programs carried out under the Elementary and Secondary Education Act of 1965 to include child care services.

1990 *Excellence in Mathematics, Science and Engineering Education Act of 1990* (Public Law 101-589) created a national mathematics and science clearinghouse and created several other mathematics, science, and engineering education programs.

Student Right-To-Know and Campus Security Act (Public Law 101-542) required higher education institutions receiving federal financial assistance to provide certain information about graduation rates of student-athletes and about campus crime statistics and security policies. (The 1990 campus crime and security legislation, along with later acts that amended it, is generally referred to as "the Clery Act.")

Americans with Disabilities Act of 1990 (Public Law 101-336) prohibited discrimination against people with disabilities.

National and Community Service Act of 1990 (Public Law 101-610) increased school and college-based community service opportunities and authorized the President's Points of Light Foundation.

1991 *National Literacy Act of 1991* (Public Law 102-73) established the National Institute for Literacy, the National Institute Board, and the Interagency Task Force on Literacy. Amended various federal laws to establish and extend various literacy programs.

High-Performance Computing Act of 1991 (Public Law 102-194) directed the President to implement a National High-Performance Computing Program. Provided for (1) establishment of a National Research and Education Network; (2) standards and guidelines for high-performance networks; and (3) the responsibility of certain federal departments and agencies with regard to the Network.

Veterans' Educational Assistance Amendments of 1991 (Public Law 102-127) restored certain educational benefits available to reserve and active-duty personnel under the Montgomery GI Bill to students whose courses of studies were interrupted by the Persian Gulf War.

Civil Rights Act of 1991 (Public Law 102-166) amended the Civil Rights Act of 1964, the Age Discrimination in Employment Act of 1967, and the Americans with Disabilities Act of 1990, with regard to employment discrimination. Established the Technical Assistance Training Institute.

1992 *Ready-To-Learn Act* (Public Law 102-545) amended the General Education Provisions Act to establish Ready-To-Learn Television programs to support educational programming and related materials for preschool and elementary school children and their parents, child care providers, and educators.

1993 *Student Loan Reform Act* (Public Law 103-66) reformed the student aid process by phasing in a system of direct lending designed to provide savings for taxpayers and students. Allows students to choose among a variety of repayment options, including income contingency.

National Service Trust Act (Public Law 103-82) amended the National and Community Service Act of 1990 to establish a Corporation for National Service. In addition, provided education grants up to $4,725 per year for 2 years to people age 17 or older who perform community service before, during, or after postsecondary education.

1994 *Goals 2000: Educate America Act* (Public Law 103-227) established a new federal partnership through a system of grants to states and local communities to reform the nation's education system. The Act formalized the national education goals and established the National Education Goals Panel.

School-to-Work Opportunities Act of 1994 (Public Law 103-239) established a national framework within which states and communities can develop School-to-Work Opportunities systems to prepare young people for first jobs and continuing education. The Act also provided money to states and communities to develop a system of programs that include work-based learning, school-based learning, and connecting activities components.

Safe Schools Act of 1994 (Part of Public Law 103-227) authorized the award of competitive grants to local educational agencies with serious crime to implement violence prevention activities such as conflict resolution and peer mediation.

1996 *Contract With America: Unfunded Mandates* (Public Law 104-4) ended the imposition, in the absence of full consideration by Congress, of federal mandates on state, local, and tribal governments without adequate funding, in a manner that may displace other essential governmental priorities; and ensured that the federal government pays the costs incurred by those governments in complying with certain requirements under federal statutes and regulations.

1997 *The Taxpayer Relief Act of 1997* (Public Law 105-34) enacted the Hope Scholarship and Life-Long Learning Tax Credit provisions into law.

Emergency Student Loan Consolidation Act of 1997 (Public Law 105-78) amended the Higher Education Act of 1965 to provide for improved student loan consolidation services.

1998 *Workforce Investment Act of 1998* (Public Law 105-220) enacted the Adult Education and Family Literacy Act, and substantially revised and extended, through FY 2003, the Rehabilitation Act of 1973.

Jeanne Clery Disclosure of Campus Security Policy and Campus Crime Statistics Act (Public Law 105-244) expanded crime categories that must be reported by postsecondary institutions.

Omnibus Consolidated and Emergency Supplemental Appropriations Act, 1999 (Public Law 105-277) enacted the Reading Excellence Act, to promote the ability of children to read independently by the third grade, and earmarked funds to help states and school districts reduce class sizes in the early grades.

Charter School Expansion Act (Public Law 105-278) amended the charter school program, enacted in 1994 as Title X, Part C of the Elementary and Secondary Education Act of 1965.

Carl D. Perkins Vocational and Applied Technology Education Amendments of 1998 (Public Law 105-332) revised, in its entirety, the Carl D. Perkins Vocational and Applied Technology Education Act and reauthorized the Act through FY 2003.

Assistive Technology Act of 1998 (Public Law 105-394) replaced the Technology-Related Assistance for Individuals with Disabilities Act of 1988 with a new Act, authorized through FY 2004, to address the assistive-technology needs of individuals with disabilities.

1999 *Education Flexibility Partnership Act of 1999* (Public Law 106-25) authorized the Secretary of Education to allow all states to participate in the Education Flexibility Partnership program.

District of Columbia College Access Act of 1999 (Public Law 106-98) established a program to afford high school graduates from the District of Columbia the benefits of in-state tuition at state colleges and universities outside the District of Columbia.

2000 *The National Defense Authorization Act for Fiscal Year 2001* (Public Law 106-398) included, as Title XVIII, the Impact Aid Reauthorization Act of 2000, which extended the Impact Aid programs through FY 2003.

College Scholarship Fraud Prevention Act of 2000 (Public Law 106-420) enhanced federal penalties for offenses involving scholarship fraud; required an annual scholarship fraud report by the Attorney General, the Secretary of Education, and the Federal Trade Commission (FTC); and required the Secretary of Education, in conjunction with the FTC, to maintain a scholarship fraud awareness website.

Consolidated Appropriations Act 2001 (Public Law 106-554) created a new program of assistance for school repair and renovation and amended the Elementary and Secondary Education Act of 1965 to authorize credit enhancement initiatives to help charter schools obtain, construct, or repair facilities; reauthorized the Even Start program; and enacted the Children's Internet Protection Act.

2001 *50th Anniversary of Brown v. Board of Education* (Public Law 107-41) established a commission for the purpose of encouraging and providing for the commemoration of the 50th anniversary of the 1954 Supreme Court decision Brown v. Board of Education.

2002 *No Child Left Behind Act of 2001* (Public Law 107-110) provided for the comprehensive reauthorization of the Elementary and Secondary Education Act of 1965, incorporating specific proposals in such areas as testing, accountability, parental choice, and early reading.

Education Sciences Reform Act (Public Law 107-279) established the Institute of Education Sciences within the U.S. Department of Education to carry out a coordinated, focused agenda of high-quality research, statistics, and evaluation that is relevant to the educational challenges of the nation.

The Higher Education Relief Opportunities for Students Act of 2001 (Public Law 107-122) provided the Secretary of Education with waiver authority over student financial aid programs under Title IV of the Higher Education Act of 1965, to deal with student and family situations resulting from the September 11, 2001, terrorist attacks.

Public Law 107-139 amended Title IV of the Higher Education Act to establish fixed interest rates for student and parent borrowers.

2003 *The Higher Education Relief Opportunities for Students Act of 2003* (Public Law 108-76) provided the Secretary of Education with waiver authority over student financial aid programs under Title IV of the Higher Education Act of 1965, to deal with student and family situations resulting from wars or national emergencies.

2004 *Assistive Technology Act of 2004* (Public Law 108-364) reauthorized the Assistive Technology program, administered by the Department of Education.

Taxpayer-Teacher Protection Act of 2004 (Public Law 108-409) temporarily stopped excessive special allowance payments to certain lenders under the Federal Family Education Loan (FFEL) Program and increased the amount of loans that can be forgiven for certain borrowers who are highly qualified in mathematics, science, and special education teachers who serve in high-poverty schools for 5 years.

Individuals with Disabilities Education Improvement Act of 2004 (Public Law 108-446) provided a comprehensive reauthorization of the Individuals with Disabilities Education Act.

2005 *Student Grant Hurricane and Disaster Relief Act* (Public Law 109-67) authorized the Secretary of Education to waive certain repayment requirements for students receiving campus-based federal grant assistance if they were residing in, employed in, or attending an institution of higher education located in a major disaster area, or their attendance was interrupted because of the disaster.

Natural Disaster Student Aid Fairness Act (Public Law 109-86) authorized the Secretary of Education during FY 2006 to reallocate campus-based student aid funds to institutions of higher learning in Louisiana, Mississippi, Alabama, and Texas, or institutions that had accepted students displaced by Hurricane Katrina or Rita. The law also waived requirements for matching funds that are normally imposed on institutions and students.

Hurricane Education Recovery Act (Public Law 109-148, provision in the Defense Department Appropriations Act for FY 2006) provided funds for states affected by Hurricane Katrina to restart school operations, provide temporary emergency aid for displaced students, and assist homeless youth. The law also permitted the Secretary of Education to extend deadlines under the Individuals with Disabilities Education Act for those affected by Katrina or Rita.

2006 *Higher Education Reconciliation Act of 2005* (Public Law 109-171) made various amendments to programs of student financial assistance under Title IV of the Higher Education Act of 1965.

Public Law 109-211 reauthorized the "ED-FLEX" program (under the Education Flexibility Partnership Act of 1999), under which the Secretary of Education permits states to waive certain requirements of federal statutes and regulations if they meet certain conditions.

Carl D. Perkins Career and Technical Education Improvement Act of 2006 (Public Law 109-270) reauthorized the vocational and technical education programs under the Perkins Act through 2012.

2007 *America COMPETES Act* (or "America Creating Opportunities to Meaningfully Promote Excellence in Technology, Education, and Science Act") (Public Law 110-69) created new STEM (science, technology, engineering, and mathematics) education programs in various agencies, including the Department of Education.

College Cost Reduction and Access Act of 2007 (Public Law 110-84) reduced interest rates on student loans and made other amendments to the Higher Education Act of 1965 to make college more accessible and affordable.

Public Law 110-93 made permanent the waiver authority of the Secretary of Education with respect to student financial assistance during a war or other military operation or national emergency.

2008 *Ensuring Continued Access to Student Loans Act of 2008* (Public Law 110-227) provided various authorities to the Department of Education, among other provisions, to help ensure that college students and their parents continue to have access to loans in the tight credit market.

Higher Education Opportunity Act (Public Law 110-315) provided a comprehensive reauthorization of the Higher Education Act of 1965.

2009 *American Recovery and Reinvestment Act of 2009* (Public Law 111-5) provided about $100 billion to state education systems and supplemental appropriations for several Department of Education programs.

Public Law 111-39 made miscellaneous and technical amendments to the Higher Education Act of 1965.

2010 *Health Care and Education Reconciliation Act of 2010* (Public Law 111-152) included, as Title II, the "SAFRA Act" (also known as the "Student Aid and Fiscal Responsibility Act"). The SAFRA Act ended the federal government's role in subsidizing financial institutions that make student loans through the Federal Family Education Loan (FFEL) Program under Part B of Title IV of the Higher Education Act of 1965 (HEA), and correspondingly expanded the Federal Direct Student Loan Program administered by the Department of Education under Part D of Title IV of the HEA.

Public Law 111-226 provided an additional $10 billion to states and school districts, through an "Education Jobs Fund" modeled closely on the State Fiscal Stabilization Fund created by the 2009 Recovery Act, to hire (or avoid laying off) teachers and other educators.

2013 *The Bipartisan Student Loan Certainty Act of 2013* (Public Law 113-28) amended the Higher Education Act of 1965 (HEA) to govern the interest rates on the various categories of student loans under Title IV of the HEA.

Violence Against Women Reauthorization Act of 2013 (Public Law 113-4) amended the Clery Act, increasing the responsibility of postsecondary institutions to prevent, address, and report crimes on campus.

2014 *Workforce Innovation and Opportunity Act* (Public Law 113-128) amended the Workforce Investment Act of 1998 to strengthen the U.S. workforce development system through innovation in, and alignment and improvement of, employment, training, and education programs in the United States, and to promote individual and national economic growth, and for other purposes.

Public Law 113-174 extended the National Advisory Committee on Institutional Quality and Integrity and the Advisory Committee on Student Financial Assistance for 1 year.

2015 *Need-Based Educational Aid Act of 2015* (Public Law 114-44) amended the Improving America's Schools Act of 1994 to extend through FY 2022 the antitrust exemption that allows higher education institutions that admit all students on a need-blind basis to enter or attempt to enter into agreements among themselves regarding the administration of need-based financial aid.

STEM Education Act of 2015 (Public Law 114-59) defined STEM education to include computer science and provided for continued support for existing STEM education programs at the National Science Foundation.

Every Student Succeeds Act (Public Law 114-95) reauthorized and amended the Elementary and Secondary Education Act of 1965, incorporating provisions to expand state responsibility over schools, provide grants to charter schools, and reduce the federal test-based accountability system of the No Child Left Behind Act.

Federal Perkins Loan Program Extension Act of 2015 (Public Law 114-105) temporarily extended the Federal Perkins Loan program, allowing continued disbursement of loans to current undergraduate borrowers through September 30, 2017.

2016 *National Defense Authorization Act for Fiscal Year 2017* (Public Law 114-328) authorizes appropriations to continue assistance to local educational agencies that benefit dependents of members of the Armed Forces and Department of Defense civilian employees, including assistance to schools with significant numbers of military dependents as well as impact aid for children with severe disabilities.

2017 *Hurricanes Harvey, Irma, and Maria Education Relief Act of 2017* (Public Law 115-64) provides educational relief in areas for which the President has declared a major disaster or an emergency as a result of Hurricanes Harvey, Irma, or Maria or Tropical Storms Harvey, Irma, or Maria.

2018 *National Historic Site Boundary Modification Act of 2018* (Public Law 115-117) adjusts the boundary of the Little Rock Central High School National Historic Site in Arkansas.

Bipartisan Budget Act of 2018 (Public Law 115-123) provides disaster-relief funds for education.

National Memorial to Fallen Educators Act (Public Law 115-169) designates a National Memorial to Fallen Educators at the National Teachers Hall of Fame in Emporia, Kansas.

Strengthening Career and Technical Education for the 21st Century Act (Public Law 115-224) brings changes to the $1.2 billion annual federal investment in career and technical education (CTE).

Foundations for Evidence-Based Policymaking Act of 2018 (Public Law 115-435) establishes an Interagency Council on Evaluation Policy to assist the OMB in supporting government-wide evaluation activities and policies.

2019 *Recognizing Achievement in Classified School Employees Act* (Public Law 116-13) establishes the Recognizing Inspiring School Employees (RISE) Award Program recognizing excellence exhibited by school employees providing services to students in prekindergarten through high school.

Building Blocks of STEM Act (Public Law 116-102) modifies grant programs of the National Science Foundation that support science, technology, engineering, and mathematics, including computer science (STEM) education, particularly for underrepresented groups.

2020 *Never Again Education Act* (Public Law 116-141) authorizes the U.S. Holocaust Memorial Museum to support Holocaust education programs.

Figure 20. Federal on-budget funds for education, by level or other educational purpose: Selected years, 1965 through 2019

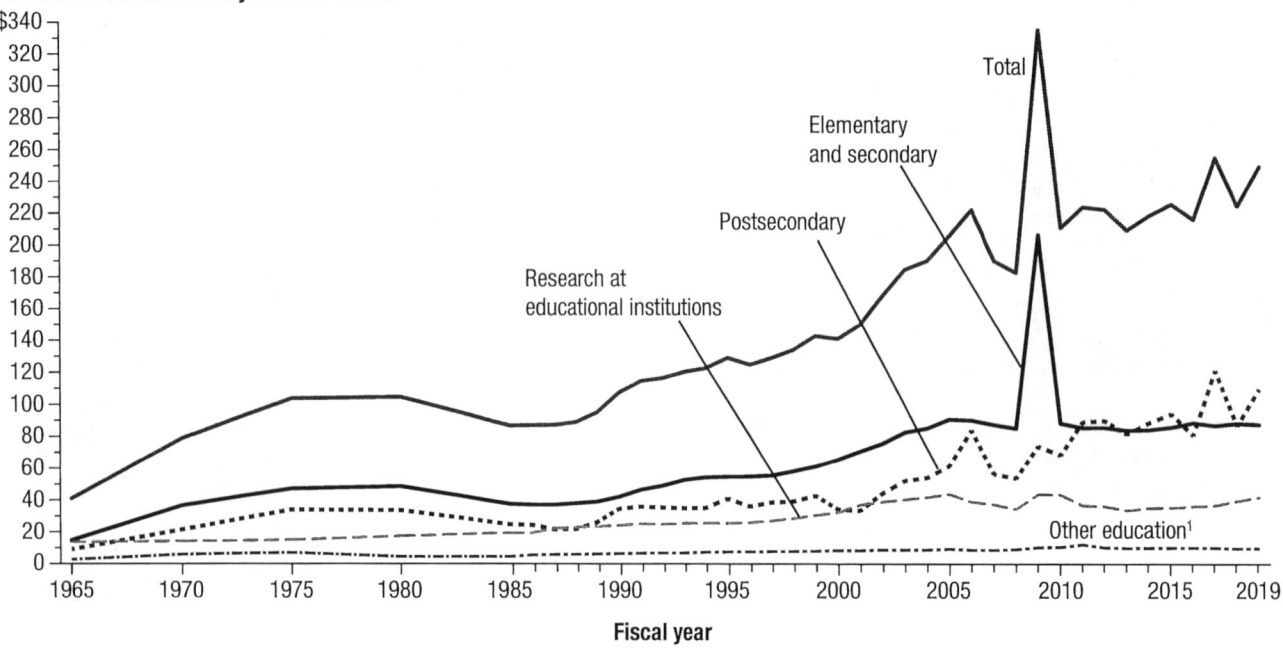

Billions of constant fiscal year 2019 dollars

[1]Other education includes libraries, museums, cultural activities, and miscellaneous research.
NOTE: On-budget funds are tied to appropriations for education programs. The increase in postsecondary expenditures in 2006 and 2017 resulted primarily from an accounting adjustment. Amounts for 2009 include funds from the American Recovery and Reinvestment Act of 2009 (ARRA). Data for research at education institutions are estimated for 2019. Constant dollars based on the Consumer Price Index, prepared by the Bureau of Labor Statistics, U.S. Department of Labor, adjusted to a school-year basis.
SOURCE: U.S. Department of Education, Budget Service, unpublished tabulations. U.S. Department of Education, National Center for Education Statistics, unpublished tabulations. U.S. Office of Management and Budget, *Budget of the U.S. Government, Appendix,* fiscal years 1967 through 2020. National Science Foundation, *Federal Funds for Research and Development,* fiscal years 1967 through 2019.

Figure 21. Percentage distribution of federal on-budget funds for education, by agency: Fiscal year 2018

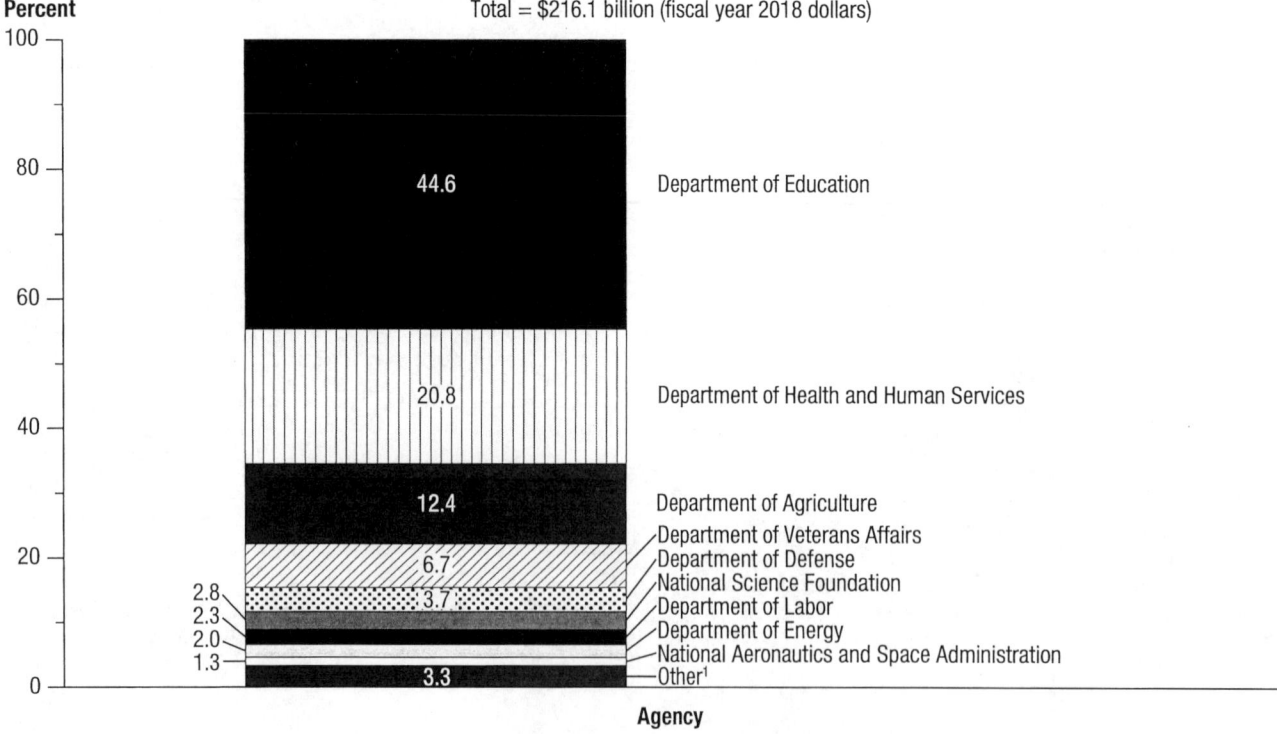

Percent   Total = $216.1 billion (fiscal year 2018 dollars)

[1]In addition to the nine agencies shown in this figure, other agencies provide smaller amounts of funding for education.
NOTE: On-budget funds are tied to federal appropriations for education programs. Graphic display was generated using unrounded data. Detail may not sum to totals because of rounding.
SOURCE: U.S. Department of Education, National Center for Education Statistics, unpublished tabulations. U.S. Office of Management and Budget, *Budget of the U.S. Government, Appendix,* fiscal year 2019. National Science Foundation, *Federal Funds for Research and Development,* fiscal year 2018.

Table 401.10. Federal support and estimated federal tax expenditures for education, by category: Selected fiscal years, 1965 through 2019

[In thousands of dollars]

Fiscal year	Total on-budget support, off-budget support, and nonfederal funds generated by federal legislation	On-budget support[1] — Total	Elementary and secondary	Post-secondary	Other education[3]	Research at educational institutions	Off-budget support — Total	Direct Loan Program[4]	Federal Family Education Loan Program[5]	Perkins Loans[6]	Income Contingent Loans[7]	Leveraging Educational Assistance Partnerships[8]	Supplemental Educational Opportunity Grants[9]	Work-Study Aid[10]	Estimated federal tax expenditures for education[2]
1	2	3	4	5	6	7	8	9	10	11	12	13	14	15	16
							Current dollars								
1965	$5,324,767	$5,331,016	$1,942,577	$1,197,511	$374,652	$1,816,276	-$6,249	†	†	$16,111	†	†	†	-$22,360	—
1970	13,318,909	12,511,079	5,830,442	3,432,277	964,719	2,283,641	807,830	†	$770,000	20,976	†	†	-$30,986	47,840	$8,605,000
1975	24,412,487	23,288,120	10,617,195	7,644,037	1,608,478	3,418,410	1,124,367	†	1,233,000	35,667	†	$20,000	-39,300	-125,000	13,320,000
1980	39,273,874	34,465,651	16,027,686	11,087,992	1,548,730	5,801,204	4,808,262	†	4,598,000	31,778	†	76,800	-8,477	110,161	19,105,000
1985	47,642,802	39,027,876	16,901,334	11,174,379	2,107,588	8,844,575	8,614,926	†	8,467,000	21,387	†	76,000	-12,961	63,500	19,040,000
1990	67,188,203	56,033,753	21,984,361	18,060,326	3,383,031	12,606,035	11,154,450	†	10,826,000	15,014	$500	59,181	127,719	126,036	18,995,000
1991	75,249,116	62,499,477	25,418,031	19,607,407	3,698,617	13,775,422	12,749,639	†	12,372,000	17,349	500	63,530	131,115	165,145	19,950,000
1992	80,151,676	66,153,112	27,926,887	20,057,407	3,991,955	14,176,863	13,998,564	†	13,568,000	17,333	542	72,000	175,656	165,033	21,010,000
1993	87,266,261	70,314,009	30,834,326	20,417,407	4,107,193	14,955,083	16,952,252	$818,540	16,524,000	29,255	†	72,429	172,023	154,545	22,630,000
1994	97,404,473	72,934,561	32,304,356	20,857,407	4,483,704	15,289,094	24,469,912	†	23,214,000	52,667	†	72,429	172,000	140,276	24,600,000
1995	102,727,958	79,149,520	33,623,809	25,128,137	4,719,655	15,677,919	23,578,438	4,615,671	18,519,000	52,667	†	63,400	181,000	146,700	26,340,000
1996	103,633,432	78,107,362	34,391,501	22,555,508	4,828,038	16,332,315	25,526,070	8,414,470	16,711,000	31,100	†	31,400	179,000	159,100	28,125,000
1997	111,760,841	82,431,845	35,478,905	24,659,425	5,021,163	17,272,352	29,328,996	9,758,696	19,163,000	52,700	†	50,000	228,200	76,400	29,540,000
1998	116,853,639	86,369,233	37,486,166	25,259,570	5,148,492	18,475,005	30,484,406	10,087,664	20,002,500	45,000	†	25,000	240,950	83,292	37,360,000
1999	123,427,861	93,153,597	39,937,911	27,941,199	5,318,020	19,956,467	30,274,264	9,805,764	20,107,000	33,300	†	25,000	255,900	47,300	—
2000	127,911,410	94,257,817	43,790,783	22,997,852	5,809,048	21,660,134	33,653,603	10,577,535	22,711,000	33,300	†	50,000	276,743	5,025	39,475,000
2001	138,337,565	102,876,476	48,530,061	22,968,278	5,880,007	25,498,130	35,461,089	10,324,341	24,694,000	25,000	†	80,000	316,655	21,093	41,460,000
2002	157,459,682	117,211,479	52,754,118	30,964,176	6,297,697	27,195,488	40,248,203	11,117,896	28,606,000	25,000	†	104,000	308,811	86,496	—
2003	178,450,390	132,374,489	59,274,219	37,499,694	6,532,502	29,068,074	46,075,901	11,742,063	33,791,000	33,000	†	103,000	304,671	102,167	—
2004	191,990,526	139,762,703	62,653,231	39,774,974	6,576,821	30,757,677	52,227,823	12,448,155	39,266,000	33,000	†	102,000	295,143	83,525	—
2005	212,926,929	156,606,678	69,029,389	46,860,566	7,297,025	33,419,698	56,320,251	12,569,446	43,284,000	0	†	101,000	305,644	60,161	—
2006[11]	234,749,825	174,795,661	70,948,229	66,057,738	7,074,484	30,715,210	59,954,164	12,175,674	47,307,000	0	†	100,000	309,608	61,882	—
2007	218,194,867	153,897,988	70,735,875	45,665,287	7,214,906	30,281,920	64,296,879	12,507,162	51,320,000	0	†	100,000	287,126	82,591	—
2008	228,598,213	152,938,889	71,272,580	44,986,271	7,882,220	28,797,817	75,659,324	17,850,773	57,296,000	0	†	98,000	281,812	132,739	—
2009[12]	376,406,421	280,097,568	172,660,784	61,885,401	8,853,694	36,697,689	96,308,853	28,857,577	66,778,000	0	†	98,000	309,058	266,218	—
2010	280,458,555	179,560,187	75,155,797	58,198,856	9,212,228	36,993,306	100,898,368	80,709,552	19,618,000	0	†	98,000	255,108	217,708	—
2011	305,352,452	195,006,154	74,538,319	77,645,852	10,804,871	32,017,112	110,346,298	109,917,342	0	0	†	0	231,480	197,476	—
2012	302,574,280	197,534,242	76,106,350	79,923,155	9,328,554	32,176,184	105,040,038	104,612,005	0	0	†	0	243,871	184,162	—
2013	290,712,525	188,644,529	75,642,514	73,479,680	9,217,187	30,305,148	102,067,996	101,729,011	0	0	†	0	192,116	146,869	—
2014	299,166,582	199,611,510	77,055,620	80,916,948	9,435,306	32,203,636	99,555,072	99,186,791	0	0	†	0	249,553	118,728	—
2015	303,379,413	207,426,048	78,909,699	86,660,617	9,464,840	32,390,891	95,953,365	95,578,878	0	0	†	0	259,745	114,742	—
2016	294,818,076	200,023,892	82,029,675	74,837,278	9,600,541	33,556,398	94,794,185	94,435,754	0	0	†	0	253,990	104,440	—
2017[11]	334,728,235	241,137,480	82,803,943	114,022,573	9,643,170	34,667,794	93,590,755	93,288,102	0	0	†	0	274,607[13]	28,046	—
2018	309,167,308	217,316,354	86,166,625	83,544,180	9,565,623	38,039,926	91,850,953	91,504,259	0	0	†	0	314,667[13]	32,027[13]	—
2019	336,598,961	245,591,373	87,085,005	107,465,117	9,872,654	41,168,597[13]	91,007,588	90,660,894	0	0	0	0	314,667[13]	32,027[13]	—
							Constant fiscal year 2019 dollars[14]								
1965	$40,196,342	$40,243,515	$14,664,395	$9,039,938	$2,828,225	$13,710,957	-$47,173	†	†	$121,621	†	†	†	-$168,794	—
1970	82,293,696	77,302,348	36,024,619	21,207,049	5,960,720	14,109,959	4,991,348	†	$4,757,608	129,605	†	†	-$191,454	295,590	$37,541,355
1975	106,505,269	101,599,951	46,320,033	33,348,926	7,017,367	14,913,625	4,905,318	†	5,379,255	155,606	†	$87,255	-171,456	-545,342	39,586,710
1980	116,720,980	102,430,944	47,633,885	32,953,237	4,602,787	17,241,034	14,290,035	†	13,665,142	94,443	†	228,248	-25,193	-327,396	41,650,335
1985	103,864,887	85,083,701	36,846,178	24,360,986	4,594,700	19,281,838	18,781,186	†	18,458,696	46,625	†	165,686	-28,256	138,435	35,712,952
1990	126,023,586	105,101,405	41,235,631	33,875,398	6,345,485	23,644,891	20,922,182	†	20,306,115	28,161	$938	111,005	239,560	236,403	34,103,183
1991	135,100,521	112,210,114	45,634,944	35,202,685	6,640,411	24,732,074	22,890,407	†	22,212,402	31,148	898	114,060	235,401	296,498	34,417,105
1992	138,275,119	114,125,242	48,178,576	34,602,400	6,886,794	24,457,473	24,149,877	†	23,407,081	29,902	935	124,212	303,036	284,710	35,204,997
1993	146,226,009	117,820,299	51,666,937	34,212,030	6,882,138	25,059,193	28,405,711	$1,347,818	27,688,119	49,021	†	121,364	288,247	258,960	37,262,805
1994	160,387,270	120,094,845	53,192,706	34,344,034	7,382,916	25,175,189	40,292,425	†	38,224,426	86,722	†	119,262	283,217	230,980	

See notes at end of table.

Table 401.10. Federal support and estimated federal tax expenditures for education, by category: Selected fiscal years, 1965 through 2019—Continued

[In thousands of dollars]

Fiscal year	Total on-budget support, off-budget support, and nonfederal funds generated by federal legislation	On-budget support[1] Total	Elementary and secondary	Post-secondary	Other education[3]	Research at educational institutions	Off-budget support and nonfederal funds generated by federal legislation Total	Off-budget support Direct Loan Program[4]	Federal Family Education Loan Program[5]	Nonfederal funds Perkins Loans[6]	Income Contingent Loans[7]	Leveraging Educational Assistance Partnerships[8]	Supplemental Educational Opportunity Grants[9]	Work-Study Aid[10]	Estimated federal tax expenditures for education[2]
1	2	3	4	5	6	7	8	9	10	11	12	13	14	15	16
1995	164,272,387	126,568,081	53,767,869	40,182,430	7,547,205	25,070,577	37,704,306	7,380,925	29,613,753	84,220	†	101,383	289,437	234,588	39,337,886
1996	162,308,026	122,329,749	53,863,088	35,325,859	7,561,549	25,579,253	39,978,277	13,178,528	26,172,340	48,708	†	49,178	280,345	249,178	41,253,033
1997	171,433,979	126,445,176	54,422,370	37,825,980	7,702,143	26,494,683	44,988,803	14,969,215	29,394,816	80,838	†	76,697	350,044	117,193	43,141,951
1998	177,762,591	131,388,451	57,025,507	38,425,903	7,832,099	28,104,942	46,374,140	15,345,772	30,428,631	68,456	†	38,031	366,543	126,707	44,937,470
1999	185,486,561	139,990,601	60,018,425	41,989,847	7,991,885	29,990,445	45,495,960	14,736,036	30,216,665	50,043	†	37,570	384,565	71,082	56,144,358
2000	187,473,097	138,148,766	64,181,866	33,706,752	8,514,019	31,746,129	49,324,331	15,502,942	33,286,328	48,806	†	73,282	405,608	7,365	57,856,449
2001	197,581,585	146,934,040	69,313,396	32,804,602	8,398,161	36,417,881	50,647,546	14,745,811	35,269,377	35,706	†	114,261	452,265	30,126	59,215,532
2002	221,479,764	164,867,415	74,202,929	43,553,615	8,858,220	38,252,651	56,612,349	15,638,219	40,236,650	35,165	†	146,284	434,368	121,664	—
2003	244,063,660	181,046,409	81,068,373	51,287,714	8,934,395	39,755,926	63,017,251	16,059,427	46,215,394	45,134	†	140,871	416,694	139,732	—
2004	255,917,755	186,299,595	83,514,924	53,018,877	8,766,710	40,999,084	69,618,160	16,593,026	52,340,430	43,988	†	135,963	393,417	111,336	—
2005	274,406,532	217,824,615	88,960,637	60,390,884	9,403,936	43,069,157	72,581,918	16,198,694	55,781,635	0	†	130,162	393,894	77,532	—
2006[11]	292,416,515	217,734,509	88,376,781	82,284,933	8,812,343	38,260,453	74,682,005	15,166,649	58,928,044	0	†	124,565	385,664	77,083	—
2007	264,476,447	186,541,478	85,739,748	55,351,407	8,745,269	36,705,055	77,934,969	15,160,072	62,205,548	0	†	121,211	348,029	100,109	—
2008	267,814,923	179,176,015	83,499,606	52,703,801	9,234,439	33,738,169	88,638,908	20,913,127	67,125,301	0	†	114,812	330,158	155,511	—
2009[12]	441,026,922	328,184,009	202,302,750	72,509,730	10,373,673	42,997,855	112,842,913	33,811,773	78,242,278	0	†	114,824	362,116	311,922	—
2010	322,844,943	206,697,558	86,514,277	66,994,591	10,604,495	42,584,195	116,147,385	92,907,384	22,582,916	0	†	112,811	293,663	250,611	—
2011	343,470,902	219,349,605	83,843,255	87,338,715	12,153,689	36,013,945	124,121,297	123,638,793	0	0	†	0	260,377	222,128	—
2012	333,709,173	217,860,516	83,937,693	88,147,247	10,288,462	35,487,114	115,848,658	115,376,580	0	0	†	0	268,965	203,112	—
2013	316,137,688	205,143,020	82,258,064	79,906,073	10,023,304	32,955,579	110,994,668	110,626,036	0	0	†	0	208,918	159,714	—
2014	320,278,415	213,697,859	82,493,344	86,627,162	10,101,144	34,476,209	106,580,556	106,186,286	0	0	†	0	267,164	127,106	—
2015	323,126,175	220,927,270	84,045,879	92,301,299	10,080,900	34,499,192	102,198,905	101,800,043	0	0	†	0	276,652	122,210	—
2016	311,929,064	211,633,106	86,790,606	79,180,769	10,157,748	35,503,982	100,295,958	99,916,724	0	0	†	0	268,732	110,502	—
2017[11]	348,373,852	250,967,752	86,179,549	118,670,847	10,036,286	36,081,070	97,406,100	97,091,109	0	0	†	0	285,802	29,189	—
2018	314,586,792	221,125,756	87,677,065	85,008,650	9,733,302	38,706,739	93,461,036	93,108,264	0	0	†	0	320,183[13]	32,588[13]	—
2019	336,598,961	245,591,373	87,085,005	107,465,117	9,872,654	41,168,597[13]	91,007,588	90,660,894	0	0	†	0	314,667[13]	32,027[13]	—

—Not available.
†Not applicable.
[1]On-budget support includes federal funds for education programs tied to appropriations. Excludes federal support for medical education benefits under Medicare in the U.S. Department of Health and Human Services prior to fiscal year (FY) 1990 because data before FY 1990 are not available. This program has existed since Medicare began but was not available as a separate budget item until FY 1990.
[2]Losses of tax revenue attributable to provisions of the federal income tax laws that allow a special exclusion, exemption, or deduction from gross income or provide a special credit, preferential rate of tax, or a deferral of tax liability affecting individual or corporate income tax liabilities.
[3]Other education includes libraries, museums, cultural activities, and miscellaneous research.
[4]The William D. Ford Federal Direct Loan Program (commonly referred to as the Direct Loan Program) provides students with the same benefits they were eligible to receive under the Federal Family Education Loan (FFEL) Program, but provides loans to students through federal capital rather than through private lenders.
[5]The Federal Family Education Loan (FFEL) Program, formerly known as the Guaranteed Student Loan Program, provided student loans guaranteed by the federal government and disbursed to borrowers. Since June 30, 2010, no new FFEL loans have been originated; all new loans are originated through the Direct Loan Program.
[6]Student loans created from institutional matching funds (since 1993, one-ninth of federal capital contributions). Excludes repayments of outstanding loans.
[7]Student loans created from institutional matching funds (one-ninth of federal contributions). This was a demonstration project that involved only 10 institutions and had unsubsidized interest rates. Program repealed in fiscal year 1992.

[8]Formerly the State Student Incentive Grant Program. Starting in fiscal year 2000, amounts under $30.0 million have required dollar-for-dollar state matching contributions, while amounts over $30.0 million have required two-to-one state matching contributions.
[9]Institutions award grants to undergraduate students, and the federal share of such grants may not exceed 75 percent of the total grant.
[10]Employer contributions to student earnings are generally one-third of federal allocation.
[11]The increases in postsecondary expenditures in 2006 and 2017 resulted primarily from accounting adjustments.
[12]All education funds from the American Recovery and Reinvestment Act of 2009 (ARRA) are included in the FY 2009 row of this table. Most of these funds had a 2-year availability, meaning that they were available for the U.S. Department of Education to obligate during FY 2009 and FY 2010.
[13]Estimated.
[14]Data adjusted by the federal budget composite deflator, as reported in the U.S. Office of Management and Budget's *Budget of the U.S. Government, Historical Tables, Fiscal Year 2021*.
NOTE: To the extent possible, federal education funds data do not represent obligations, but instead represent appropriations or (especially for earlier years) outlays. Negative amounts occur when program receipts exceed outlays. Some data have been revised from previously published figures. Detail may not sum to totals because of rounding.
SOURCE: U.S. Department of Education, National Center for Education Statistics, unpublished tabulations. U.S. Office of Management and Budget, *Budget of the U.S. Government, Appendix*, fiscal years 1967 through 2020. National Science Foundation, *Federal Funds for Research and Development*, fiscal years 1967 through 2020. (This table was prepared June 2020.)

Table 401.20. Federal on-budget funds for education, by agency: Selected fiscal years, 1970 through 2018

[In thousands of dollars]

Agency	1970[1]	1980[1]	1990	2000	2010	2012	2013	2014	2015	2016	2017	2018
	2	3	4	5	6	7	8	9	10	11	12	13
	Current dollars											
Total	$12,511,079	$34,465,612	$56,033,753	$94,257,817	$179,560,187	$197,534,242	$188,644,529	$199,611,510	$207,426,048	$200,023,892	$241,137,480	$217,316,354
Department of Education[2]	4,625,224	13,137,785	23,198,575	34,106,697	80,886,361	98,948,633	88,839,759	95,402,189	100,421,930	88,871,248	127,025,204	97,614,576
Department of Agriculture	960,910	4,562,467	6,260,843	11,080,031	19,719,460	20,578,995	22,354,763	21,739,689	23,855,189	24,712,496	25,388,830	26,763,572
Department of Commerce	13,990	135,561	53,835	114,575	303,000	205,085	235,936	275,521	272,897	272,936	310,300	383,612
Department of Defense	821,388	1,560,301	3,605,509	4,525,080	7,686,288	7,400,880	7,036,469	7,297,021	7,006,346	7,194,204	7,230,743	7,920,474
Department of Energy	551,527	1,605,558	2,561,950	3,577,004	3,402,600	2,983,055	2,941,159	3,288,681	3,484,388	3,680,701	3,690,688	4,417,406
Department of Health and Human Services	1,127,521	3,712,930	11,906,197	24,961,831	39,742,472	37,100,826	35,766,013	39,071,095	38,996,167	41,076,948	42,492,380	44,973,040
Department of Homeland Security	†	†	†	†	540,229	333,630	358,580	371,808	372,144	332,266	312,254	301,672
Department of Housing and Urban Development	114,709	5,314	118	1,400	400	300	4,500	100	1,100	500	1,200	3,000
Department of the Interior	175,555	412,657	599,948	928,939	1,008,316	939,075	873,040	944,214	947,975	1,012,768	1,011,876	1,044,119
Department of Justice	15,728	60,721	99,775	292,859	219,993	224,295	218,994	240,957	233,264	265,780	242,304	197,797
Department of Labor	424,494	1,862,738	2,511,380	4,696,100	4,845,735	4,898,863	4,729,187	4,837,010	4,827,861	5,024,580	5,018,397	5,020,641
Department of State	59,742	25,188	51,225	388,349	801,180	741,922	812,957	835,741	870,920	864,395	854,326	914,232
Department of Transportation	27,534	54,712	76,186	117,054	160,243	173,888	178,502	168,000	178,050	182,614	188,918	228,054
Department of the Treasury	18	1,247,463	41,715	83,000	†	†	†	†	†	†	†	†
Department of Veterans Affairs	1,032,918	2,351,233	757,476	1,577,374	8,795,010	10,905,455	12,616,616	13,085,173	13,517,156	13,960,336	14,423,386	14,477,963
Other agencies and programs												
ACTION	†	2,833	8,472	†	†	†	†	†	†	†	†	†
Agency for International Development	88,034	176,770	249,786	332,500	557,900	629,900	603,900	594,039	648,000	657,111	688,243	461,030
Appalachian Regional Commission	37,838	19,032	93	7,243	5,070	11,124	13,070	13,073	23,682	39,639	35,712	21,904
Barry Goldwater Scholarship and Excellence in Education Foundation	†	†	1,033	3,000	4,000	4,000	4,000	3,000	2,000	3,000	3,000	3,000
Corporation for National and Community Service	†	†	†	696,545	857,021	750,252	711,009	756,849	758,349	787,929	736,029	736,029
Environmental Protection Agency	19,446	41,083	87,481	98,900	54,700	87,200	73,700	86,100	68,600	56,600	51,500	51,400
Estimated education share of federal aid to the District of Columbia	33,019	81,847	104,940	127,127	159,670	151,381	217,160	210,732	147,424	129,091	161,031	147,483
Federal Emergency Management Agency	290	1,946	215	14,894	8,000	9,000	8,000	9,000	9,000	12,000	12,000	15,000
General Services Administration	14,775	34,800	2,883	3,000	2,000	1,200	1,500	1,000	1,000	1,000	1,000	1,000
Harry S. Truman Scholarship Foundation	†	-1,895	†	2,000	2,000	†	†	†	†	†	†	†
Institute of American Indian and Alaska Native Culture and Arts Development	†	†	†	†	†	†	†	†	†	†	†	†
Institute of Museum and Library Services	†	†	†	166,000	282,251	231,954	219,821	226,860	227,860	230,000	230,000	229,000
James Madison Memorial Fellowship Foundation	†	†	4,305	7,000	2,000	2,000	2,000	2,000	2,000	2,000	2,000	2,000
Japanese-United States Friendship Commission	†	2,294	2,299	3,000	2,000	3,700	3,700	3,000	3,000	3,000	3,000	3,000
Library of Congress	29,478	151,871	189,827	299,000	510,877	465,961	442,051	455,760	464,449	469,547	500,915	510,412
National Aeronautics and Space Administration	258,366	255,511	1,093,303	2,077,830	1,585,500	2,289,837	2,200,143	2,287,755	2,355,450	2,522,132	2,683,000	2,894,900
National Archives and Records Administration	†	†	77,397	121,879	339,000	391,500	371,022	386,630	381,730	389,073	392,956	393,960
National Commission on Libraries and Information Science	†	2,090	3,281	2,000	†	†	†	†	†	†	†	†
National Endowment for the Arts	340	5,220	5,577	10,048	14,413	16,595	13,910	15,426	13,509	14,364	14,216	13,354
National Endowment for the Humanities	8,459	142,586	141,048	100,014	142,654	136,100	114,171	117,533	120,216	121,925	104,533	93,392
National Science Foundation	295,628	808,392	1,588,891	2,955,244	5,533,530	5,534,426	5,302,011	5,476,858	5,808,512	5,735,629	5,956,118	6,109,979
Nuclear Regulatory Commission	†	32,590	42,328	12,200	14,500	8,600	5,400	9,400	8,000	8,000	5,900	6,000
Office of Economic Opportunity	1,092,410	†	†	†	†	†	†	†	†	†	†	†
Social Security Administration	669,333	1,901,000	489,814	729,036	1,281,700	1,301,800	1,300,700	1,328,700	1,327,200	1,319,900	1,294,600	1,288,700
Smithsonian Institution	2,461	5,153	5,779	25,764	28,814	28,809	29,986	28,796	29,979	27,779	27,538	28,070
U.S. Arms Control and Disarmament Agency	100	661	25	†	†	†	†	†	†	†	†	†
United States Information Agency	8,423	†	201,547	13,000	†	†	†	†	†	†	†	†
United States Institute of Peace	†	†	7,621	†	49,000	39,000	37,000	37,000	35,000	35,300	37,884	37,884
Other agencies	1,421	990	885	300	14,300	5,000	3,800	4,800	5,700	7,100	5,500	8,700

See notes at end of table.

Table 401.20. Federal on-budget funds for education, by agency: Selected fiscal years, 1970 through 2018—Continued

[In thousands of dollars]

Agency	1970[1]	1980[1]	1990	2000	2010	2012	2013	2014	2015	2016	2017	2018
1	2	3	4	5	6	7	8	9	10	11	12	13
					Constant fiscal year 2019 dollars[3]							
Total	**$77,302,348**	**$102,430,944**	**$105,101,405**	**$138,148,766**	**$206,697,558**	**$217,860,516**	**$205,143,020**	**$213,697,859**	**$220,927,270**	**$211,633,106**	**$250,967,752**	**$221,125,756**
Department of Education[2]	28,577,925	39,045,171	43,513,109	49,988,407	93,110,915	109,130,447	96,609,515	102,134,609	106,958,326	94,029,259	132,203,546	99,325,690
Department of Agriculture	5,937,186	13,559,539	11,743,340	16,239,424	22,699,710	22,696,574	24,309,868	23,273,833	25,407,907	26,146,788	26,423,838	27,232,718
Department of Commerce	86,440	402,884	100,977	167,927	348,793	226,188	256,571	294,964	290,660	288,777	322,950	390,336
Department of Defense	5,075,119	4,637,176	6,762,782	6,632,174	8,847,936	8,162,431	7,651,865	7,811,963	7,462,384	7,611,749	7,525,513	8,059,314
Department of Energy	3,407,726	4,771,679	4,805,399	5,242,628	3,916,843	3,290,011	3,198,387	3,520,759	3,711,185	3,894,326	3,841,143	4,494,840
Department of Health and Human Services	6,966,627	11,034,736	22,332,218	36,585,254	45,748,849	40,918,501	38,894,040	41,828,296	41,534,402	43,461,019	44,224,635	45,761,386
Department of Homeland Security	†	†	†	†	621,875	367,961	389,941	398,046	396,367	351,550	324,983	306,960
Department of Housing and Urban Development	708,754	15,793	221	2,052	460	331	4,894	107	1,172	529	1,249	3,053
Department of the Interior	1,084,704	1,226,406	1,125,311	1,361,497	1,160,705	1,035,705	949,394	1,010,846	1,009,678	1,071,548	1,053,126	1,062,422
Department of Justice	97,179	180,461	187,146	429,228	253,241	247,375	238,147	257,961	248,447	281,206	252,182	201,264
Department of Labor	2,622,826	5,536,011	4,710,546	6,882,829	5,578,083	5,402,956	5,142,793	5,178,352	5,142,103	5,316,202	5,222,978	5,108,649
Department of State	369,125	74,858	96,082	569,183	922,264	818,266	884,057	894,718	927,608	914,564	889,154	930,258
Department of Transportation	170,125	162,603	142,900	171,560	184,461	191,781	194,113	179,856	189,639	193,213	196,619	232,052
Department of the Treasury	111	3,707,429	78,244	121,649	†	†	†	†	†	†	†	†
Department of Veterans Affairs	6,382,102	6,987,806	1,420,783	2,311,875	10,124,221	12,027,626	13,720,041	14,008,578	14,396,979	14,770,582	15,011,373	14,731,751
Other agencies and programs												
ACTION	543,937	8,420	15,891	487,328	642,217	694,717	656,716	635,960	690,178	695,249	716,300	469,112
Agency for International Development	233,790	525,356	468,519	10,615	5,836	12,269	14,213	13,996	25,223	41,940	37,168	22,288
Appalachian Regional Commission	†	56,563	174	†	†	†	†	†	†	†	†	†
Barry Goldwater Scholarship and Excellence in Education Foundation	†	†	1,938	4,397	4,605	4,412	4,350	3,212	2,130	3,174	3,122	3,053
Corporation for National and Community Service	†	†	†	1,020,890	986,545	827,453	773,192	810,259	807,709	833,660	766,034	748,931
Environmental Protection Agency	120,151	122,098	164,086	144,953	62,967	96,173	80,146	92,176	73,065	59,885	53,599	52,301
Estimated education share of federal aid to the District of Columbia	204,015	243,247	196,834	186,323	183,801	166,958	236,152	225,603	157,020	136,583	167,596	150,068
Federal Emergency Management Agency	1,792	5,783	403	21,830	†	†	†	†	†	†	†	†
General Services Administration	91,290	103,425	†	†	†	†	†	†	†	†	†	†
Harry S. Truman Scholarship Foundation	†	-5,632	5,408	4,397	2,302	1,323	1,631	1,071	1,065	1,058	1,041	1,018
Institute of American Indian and Alaska Native Culture and Arts Development	†	†	8,075	2,931	9,209	9,926	8,700	9,635	9,586	12,696	12,489	15,263
Institute of Museum and Library Services	†	†	†	243,298	324,908	255,862	239,046	242,869	242,691	243,349	239,376	233,014
James Madison Memorial Fellowship Foundation	†	†	358	10,260	2,302	2,206	2,175	2,141	2,130	2,116	2,082	2,035
Japanese-United States Friendship Commission	†	6,818	4,312	4,397	2,302	4,081	4,024	3,212	3,195	3,174	3,122	3,053
Library of Congress	182,136	451,357	356,055	438,229	588,087	513,908	480,712	487,922	494,680	496,799	521,335	519,359
National Aeronautics and Space Administration	1,596,369	759,372	2,050,687	3,045,367	1,825,120	2,525,462	2,392,563	2,449,199	2,508,765	2,668,514	2,792,376	2,945,646
National Archives and Records Administration	†	†	145,172	178,632	390,234	431,785	403,471	413,914	406,577	411,654	408,975	400,866
National Commission on Libraries and Information Science	†	6,211	6,154	2,931	†	†	†	†	†	†	†	†
National Endowment for the Arts	2,101	15,514	10,461	14,726	16,591	18,303	15,127	16,515	14,388	15,198	14,796	13,588
National Endowment for the Humanities	52,266	423,762	264,561	146,586	164,213	150,105	124,156	125,827	128,041	129,001	108,794	95,029
National Science Foundation	1,826,600	2,402,521	2,980,252	4,331,347	6,369,826	6,103,919	5,765,715	5,863,354	6,186,584	6,068,520	6,198,926	6,217,082
Nuclear Regulatory Commission	†	96,857	79,394	17,881	16,691	9,485	5,872	10,063	8,521	8,464	6,141	6,105
Office of Economic Opportunity	6,749,686	†	†	†	†	†	†	†	†	†	†	†
Social Security Administration	4,135,615	5,649,725	918,734	1,068,510	1,475,406	1,435,755	1,414,457	1,422,465	1,413,587	1,396,506	1,347,376	1,311,290
Smithsonian Institution	15,206	15,315	10,840	37,761	33,169	31,773	32,609	30,828	31,930	29,391	28,661	28,562
U.S. Arms Control and Disarmament Agency	618	1,964	47	†	†	†	†	†	†	†	†	†
United States Information Agency	52,043	196,774	378,038	†	†	†	†	†	†	†	†	†
United States Institute of Peace	†	†	14,295	19,053	56,405	43,013	40,236	39,611	37,278	37,349	39,428	38,548
Other agencies	8,780	2,942	1,660	440	16,461	5,515	4,132	5,139	6,071	7,512	5,724	8,853

†Not applicable.

[1]Excludes federal support for medical education benefits under Medicare in the U.S. Department of Health and Human Services. Benefits are excluded because data before fiscal year (FY) 1990 are not available. This program has existed since Medicare began but was not available as a separate budget item until FY 1990.

[2]The U.S. Department of Education was created in May 1980. It formerly was the Office of Education in the U.S. Department of Health, Education, and Welfare. This table does not include education funds from the American Recovery and Reinvestment Act of 2009 (ARRA) because these funds are included only in tables that show FY 2009. Most of these funds had a 2-year availability, meaning that they were available for the Department of Education to obligate during FY 2009 and FY 2010.

[3]Data adjusted by the federal budget composite deflator, as reported in the U.S. Office of Management and Budget's Budget of the U.S. Government, Historical Tables, Fiscal Year 2021.

NOTE: To the extent possible, federal education funds data do not represent obligations but instead represent appropriations or (especially for earlier years) outlays. Negative amounts occur when program receipts exceed outlays. Some data have been revised from previously published figures. Detail may not sum to totals because of rounding.
SOURCE: U.S. Department of Education, National Center for Education Statistics, unpublished tabulations. U.S. Office of Management and Budget, Budget of the U.S. Government, Appendix; and supplemental agency budget documents, fiscal years 1972 through 2019. National Science Foundation, Federal Funds for Research and Development, fiscal years 1970 through 2018. (This table was prepared June 2020.)

Table 401.60. U.S. Department of Education appropriations for major programs, by state or jurisdiction: Fiscal year 2018

[In thousands of current dollars]

State or jurisdiction	Total	Grants for the disadvantaged[1]	Block grants to states for school improvement[2]	School assistance in federally affected areas[3]	Career/ technical and adult education[4]	Special education[5]	English language acquisition	Indian education	Student financial assistance[6]	Rehabilitation services[7]
1	2	3	4	5	6	7	8	9	10	11
Total, 50 states and D.C.[8]	**$69,286,547**	**$15,595,840**	**$3,743,760**	**$1,186,981**	**$1,758,536**	**$12,826,617**	**$673,966**	**$105,381**	**$30,200,695**	**$3,194,771**
Total, 50 states, D.C., other activities, and other jurisdictions	**71,590,817**	**16,182,167**	**3,911,343**	**1,335,964**	**1,809,553**	**13,128,968**	**737,400**	**105,381**	**31,068,488**	**3,311,553**
Alabama	1,193,338	254,363	63,549	1,974	30,005	202,667	3,728	1,336	566,202	69,514
Alaska	342,173	59,869	19,968	148,003	5,724	42,371	1,294	12,863	39,966	12,115
Arizona	1,969,266	368,734	74,578	164,024	42,056	226,541	13,282	11,330	986,694	82,027
Arkansas	754,417	164,501	42,472	223	18,110	126,934	3,621	143	354,685	43,726
California	8,701,763	2,104,943	419,338	53,020	220,209	1,375,595	150,625	5,190	4,060,756	312,087
Colorado	970,658	159,530	44,768	32,154	25,267	179,965	9,779	679	472,789	45,727
Connecticut	666,759	126,222	35,218	3,886	15,624	148,543	6,381	37	306,050	24,799
Delaware	201,839	51,938	19,587	49	6,898	41,342	1,180	0	68,397	12,449
District of Columbia	300,203	50,996	19,309	23	5,982	22,372	1,212	0	183,336	16,972
Florida	4,222,747	875,726	184,215	6,849	112,278	718,293	43,458	105	2,081,925	199,898
Georgia	2,294,667	541,965	118,390	17,902	62,588	386,016	15,269	0	1,050,201	102,336
Hawaii	263,192	52,114	19,817	40,317	7,977	45,019	3,710	0	80,030	14,208
Idaho	361,409	63,992	22,456	6,119	9,601	64,021	2,259	504	172,368	20,088
Illinois	2,818,895	681,399	154,422	14,378	63,501	565,595	24,944	217	1,198,536	115,902
Indiana	1,319,151	273,351	66,885	50	37,618	289,627	8,447	0	573,747	69,427
Iowa	685,908	99,760	32,710	175	15,878	136,616	4,167	287	362,534	33,781
Kansas	603,207	108,229	34,052	43,234	14,769	120,562	4,731	738	248,067	28,826
Kentucky	985,091	245,461	61,953	302	26,969	182,104	3,826	0	410,531	53,945
Louisiana	1,161,538	342,801	79,423	7,895	30,891	211,209	3,450	896	447,325	37,648
Maine	284,273	56,121	22,693	2,104	7,555	62,262	830	198	115,089	17,422
Maryland	1,030,919	240,867	55,041	5,343	26,640	225,012	10,890	63	421,479	45,585
Massachusetts	1,288,396	240,813	63,547	535	30,342	315,919	14,888	211	567,345	54,797
Michigan	2,075,228	496,235	131,878	4,240	53,152	444,142	12,289	1,955	816,839	114,498
Minnesota	1,094,627	172,060	50,885	23,207	23,984	214,280	9,551	4,348	543,949	52,363
Mississippi	851,482	210,779	56,229	1,855	19,627	134,057	1,493	513	382,505	44,423
Missouri	1,268,002	246,277	70,876	22,511	32,491	252,769	4,682	75	567,364	70,957
Montana	273,207	50,376	24,886	58,392	6,884	43,042	500	3,932	72,572	12,622
Nebraska	392,315	80,833	24,877	19,093	9,537	83,622	3,403	1,000	148,953	20,997
Nevada	443,819	130,625	27,543	4,731	16,998	86,688	6,642	616	149,325	20,652
New Hampshire	283,958	40,798	21,753	5	7,501	53,675	985	0	146,982	12,258
New Jersey	1,709,693	366,591	86,219	13,096	40,267	402,374	19,092	0	717,209	64,845
New Mexico	605,734	130,195	32,707	86,101	13,112	101,661	4,496	8,189	202,791	26,482
New York	4,785,047	1,224,303	274,605	46,439	99,058	855,956	56,816	2,012	2,059,314	166,546
North Carolina	2,013,543	457,392	100,106	12,606	58,403	378,199	14,468	3,680	871,820	116,869
North Dakota	193,729	39,166	20,810	26,380	5,761	34,869	530	2,677	52,091	11,445
Ohio	2,205,309	559,441	134,462	1,627	60,227	485,806	10,151	0	850,535	103,059
Oklahoma	886,007	189,664	55,925	28,541	21,729	165,278	5,350	25,932	351,227	42,360
Oregon	774,940	170,229	40,176	3,165	20,659	144,140	7,058	1,932	339,274	48,307
Pennsylvania	2,494,070	654,535	143,343	855	60,712	476,663	14,976	0	997,007	145,978
Rhode Island	272,073	53,184	19,711	1,391	7,904	49,883	1,904	0	125,490	12,606
South Carolina	1,013,660	246,590	55,338	1,262	29,390	199,326	4,376	14	408,251	69,113
South Dakota	280,609	49,290	21,012	62,598	6,103	41,184	894	4,186	83,798	11,545
Tennessee	1,351,009	311,342	72,979	2,086	37,254	265,333	6,158	0	594,830	61,027
Texas	6,220,562	1,560,775	333,829	92,312	169,214	1,136,799	113,237	450	2,560,977	252,969
Utah	778,279	83,789	27,548	7,786	17,899	129,977	4,314	1,408	470,786	34,771
Vermont	162,766	37,273	20,196	11	5,673	33,788	500	218	52,946	12,162
Virginia	1,565,352	268,436	68,908	31,338	40,334	318,597	13,232	8	744,766	79,732
Washington	1,194,972	258,176	62,700	53,439	32,617	249,758	16,708	4,440	452,097	65,037
West Virginia	474,452	98,130	30,359	0	12,150	85,516	546	0	217,521	30,230
Wisconsin	1,041,237	208,927	60,122	14,754	27,871	235,162	7,144	1,998	418,864	66,396
Wyoming	161,058	36,734	19,382	18,601	5,544	35,490	500	1,001	32,561	11,245
Other activities/jurisdictions										
Indian Tribe Set-Aside	294,265	110,284	21,132	0	14,907	102,620	5,000	0	0	40,322
Other nonstate allocations	273,283	16,190	32,791	147,895	3,069	21,000	51,378	0	0	959
American Samoa	37,985	19,323	4,288	0	549	6,990	1,122	0	4,601	1,112
Freely Associated States[9]	25,110	1,000	0	0	175	6,579	0	0	17,355	0
Guam	63,297	20,936	6,386	0	1,148	15,641	1,341	0	15,730	2,115
Northern Marianas	26,520	11,680	2,677	0	589	5,316	1,113	0	4,078	1,067
Puerto Rico	1,551,347	396,833	96,690	986	29,496	134,419	3,387	0	820,550	68,986
U.S. Virgin Islands	32,463	10,081	3,621	102	1,082	9,785	93	0	5,479	2,221

[1]Title I grants. Includes grants to local education agencies (Basic, Concentration, Targeted, and Education Finance Incentive Grants); School Improvement State Grants; State Agency Program—Migrant Education; and State Agency Program—Neglected and Delinquent Children.
[2]Title VI grants. Includes Supporting Effective Instruction State Grants; Mathematics and Science Partnerships; 21st Century Community Learning Centers; State Assessments; Rural and Low-Income Schools Program; Small, Rural School Achievement Program; and Homeless Children and Youth Education.
[3]Includes Impact Aid—Basic Support Payments; Impact Aid—Payments for Children with Disabilities; and Impact Aid—Construction.
[4]Includes Career and Technical Education State Grants; Adult Basic and Literacy Education State Grants; and English Literacy and Civics Education State Grants.
[5]Includes Special Education—Grants to States; Special Education—Preschool Grants; and Grants for Infants and Families.

[6]Includes Federal Pell Grants; Federal Supplemental Educational Opportunity Grants; Federal Work-Study; and Student Loan Program interest subsidies.
[7]Includes Vocational Rehabilitation State Grants; Client Assistance State Grants; Protection and Advocacy of Individual Rights; Supported Employment State Grants; and Independent Living Services for Older Blind Individuals.
[8]Total excludes other activities and other jurisdictions.
[9]Includes the Marshall Islands, the Federated States of Micronesia, and Palau.
NOTE: Data reflect revisions to figures in the Budget of the United States Government, Fiscal Year 2020. Detail may not sum to totals because of rounding.
SOURCE: U.S. Department of Education, Budget Service, retrieved April 13, 2020, from https://www2.ed.gov/about/overview/budget/statetables/20stbyprogram.pdf; and unpublished tabulations. (This table was prepared April 2020.)

Table 401.70. Appropriations for Title I and selected other programs under the Every Student Succeeds Act of 2015, by program and state or jurisdiction: Fiscal years 2018 and 2019

[In thousands of current dollars]

State or jurisdiction	Title I total, 2018[1]	Title I, 2019 Total[1]	Grants to local education agencies[2]	State agency programs Neglected and Delinquent	State agency programs Migrant	Assessing Achievement, 2019	Supporting Effective Instruction State Grants, 2019
1	2	3	4	5	6	7	8
Total, 50 states and D.C.[3]	**$15,595,840**	**$15,685,340**	**$15,274,571**	**$46,018**	**$364,751**	**$360,598**	**$1,967,248**
Total, 50 states, D.C., other activities, and other jurisdictions	**16,182,167**	**16,282,167**	**15,859,802**	**47,614**	**374,751**	**378,000**	**2,055,830**
Alabama	254,363	259,790	257,319	586	1,885	6,086	33,628
Alaska	59,869	62,988	45,609	415	16,964	3,506	9,857
Arizona	368,734	348,683	339,128	1,638	7,917	7,675	37,200
Arkansas	164,501	162,264	157,131	304	4,829	4,987	20,277
California	2,104,943	2,079,389	1,963,513	1,490	114,386	28,369	229,490
Colorado	159,530	153,307	145,897	561	6,849	6,596	23,292
Connecticut	126,222	132,143	131,135	1,009	0	5,139	17,930
Delaware	51,938	53,198	52,114	698	386	3,576	9,857
District of Columbia	50,996	49,171	49,085	86	0	3,317	9,857
Florida	875,726	920,110	898,113	1,513	20,483	14,954	102,439
Georgia	541,965	547,317	538,160	1,677	7,479	10,160	61,190
Hawaii	52,114	53,505	51,230	128	2,147	3,836	9,857
Idaho	63,992	63,242	58,150	627	4,385	4,281	9,857
Illinois	681,399	673,946	671,396	479	2,071	11,122	79,034
Indiana	273,351	261,819	257,161	673	3,985	7,453	36,200
Iowa	99,760	90,566	87,956	513	2,097	5,063	15,088
Kansas	108,229	109,525	100,955	205	8,365	5,001	15,906
Kentucky	245,461	238,800	231,667	1,124	6,009	5,841	31,211
Louisiana	342,801	345,523	341,692	2,040	1,790	6,056	44,060
Maine	56,121	54,277	53,336	93	847	3,721	9,857
Maryland	240,867	244,109	242,109	1,633	366	6,780	28,509
Massachusetts	240,813	255,717	252,965	1,586	1,166	6,900	34,310
Michigan	496,235	477,898	469,889	1,242	6,768	9,169	72,707
Minnesota	172,060	169,255	166,981	437	1,837	6,670	26,519
Mississippi	210,779	206,609	205,452	407	750	5,017	29,060
Missouri	246,277	251,337	248,761	1,477	1,099	6,890	35,300
Montana	50,376	50,712	48,946	254	1,511	3,647	9,857
Nebraska	80,833	84,859	77,333	438	7,088	4,332	10,015
Nevada	130,625	137,448	136,383	893	171	4,949	13,136
New Hampshire	40,798	45,295	44,616	432	247	3,752	9,857
New Jersey	366,591	370,352	366,132	1,905	2,315	8,559	45,227
New Mexico	130,195	130,918	129,745	325	848	4,386	16,431
New York	1,224,303	1,229,947	1,219,497	2,521	7,929	14,341	148,453
North Carolina	457,392	472,051	466,200	688	5,163	9,549	52,478
North Dakota	39,166	40,222	39,467	117	638	3,480	9,857
Ohio	559,441	584,102	581,146	1,034	1,921	10,355	74,458
Oklahoma	189,664	192,308	190,662	535	1,111	5,696	25,123
Oregon	170,229	170,172	145,184	1,573	23,415	5,477	19,869
Pennsylvania	654,535	641,281	630,162	1,751	9,368	10,538	76,769
Rhode Island	53,184	55,064	54,762	302	0	3,584	9,857
South Carolina	246,590	256,873	255,374	725	774	6,152	28,640
South Dakota	49,290	49,683	48,946	0	736	3,602	9,857
Tennessee	311,342	310,364	308,799	298	1,268	7,260	37,879
Texas	1,560,775	1,557,572	1,512,298	2,604	42,670	23,818	184,124
Utah	83,789	83,943	81,619	988	1,336	5,632	14,195
Vermont	37,273	37,540	36,920	126	494	3,334	9,857
Virginia	268,436	280,756	279,166	704	887	8,264	37,837
Washington	258,176	288,528	256,762	2,512	29,254	7,651	34,073
West Virginia	98,130	102,440	101,309	1,131	0	4,042	15,459
Wisconsin	208,927	208,794	207,563	481	750	6,648	31,588
Wyoming	36,734	39,632	38,596	1,036	0	3,383	9,857
Other activities/jurisdictions							
Indian Tribe Set-Aside	110,284	110,984	110,984	0	0	1,846	10,228
Other nonstate allocations	16,190	16,190	5,000	1,190	10,000	8,900	10,279
American Samoa	19,323	19,447	19,447	0	0	359	2,574
Freely Associated States[4]	1,000	1,000	1,000	0	0	0	0
Guam	20,936	21,071	21,071	0	0	809	3,817
Northern Marianas	11,680	11,755	11,755	0	0	262	1,584
Puerto Rico	396,833	406,234	405,828	406	0	4,811	57,847
U.S. Virgin Islands	10,081	10,146	10,146	0	0	416	2,252

[1]This table does not include funding for School Improvement State Grants because the Every Student Succeeds Act of 2015 did not authorize funding for these grants. For fiscal years prior to FY 2017, School Improvement State Grants had been funded under the No Child Left Behind Act of 2001.
[2]Includes Basic, Concentration, Targeted, and Education Finance Incentive Grants.
[3]Total excludes other activities and other jurisdictions.
[4]Includes the Marshall Islands, the Federated States of Micronesia, and Palau.

NOTE: Data for FY 2018 are revised from previously published figures. Estimates for FY 2019 are preliminary. Detail may not sum to totals because of rounding.
SOURCE: U.S. Department of Education, Budget Service, Elementary, Secondary, and Vocational Education Analysis Division, retrieved April 13, 2020, from https://www2.ed.gov/about/overview/budget/statetables/20stbyprogram.pdf. (This table was prepared April 2020.)

CHAPTER 5
Outcomes of Education

This chapter contains tables comparing educational attainment and workforce characteristics. The data show labor force status, income levels, and occupations of high school dropouts and high school and college graduates. Most of these tables are based on data from the U.S. Census Bureau and the U.S. Bureau of Labor Statistics. Population characteristics are provided for many of the measures to allow for comparisons among various demographic groups. While most of the tables in this chapter focus on labor market outcomes, the chapter ends with several tables on adults' attitudes, skills, and participation in continuing education.

Statistics related to outcomes of education appear in other sections of the *Digest*. Chapter 1 includes statistics on educational attainment of the entire population. Chapters 2 and 3 have more detailed data on the numbers of high school and college graduates. Chapter 3 also contains trend data on the percentage of high school completers going to college. Chapter 6 includes international comparisons of employment rates by educational attainment. In addition, data on earnings by educational attainment may be obtained from the U.S. Census Bureau's Current Population Reports, Series P-60. The U.S. Bureau of Labor Statistics has a series of publications regarding the educational characteristics of the labor force.

Further information on survey methodologies can be found in Appendix A: Guide to Sources and in the publications cited in the table source notes.

Labor Force Participation by Education Level

In 2018, *the labor force participation rate*—the percentage of people either employed or actively seeking employment—was generally higher for adults with higher levels of educational attainment than for those with less education. Among 25- to 64-year-olds, 87 percent of those with a bachelor's or higher degree participated in the labor force in 2018, compared with 72 percent of those who had completed only high school and 61 percent of those who had not completed high school (table 501.10). Within each education level, the labor force participation rate also varied by race/ethnicity. For 25- to 64-year-olds who had completed only high school, the 2018 labor force participation rate was highest for those who were Hispanic (77 percent), followed by those who were Asian (74 percent), White (72 percent), Black (69 percent), and American Indian/

Alaska Native (61 percent). The same patterns by race/ethnicity were observed for 25- to 64-year-olds who had not completed high school. For 25- to 64-year-olds with a bachelor's or higher degree in 2018, the labor force participation rate was highest for those who were Black (89 percent), followed by those who were Hispanic (88 percent), White (87 percent), and then Asian and American Indian/Alaska Native (84 and 82 percent, respectively, which were not measurably different from each other).

In 2019, the *unemployment rate*—the percentage of people in the labor force who are not employed and who have made specific efforts to find employment sometime during the prior 4 weeks—was generally higher for people with lower levels of educational attainment than for those with more education. The unemployment rate for 25- to 64-year-olds who had not completed high school was 6 percent in 2019, compared with 4 percent for those who had completed only high school and 2 percent for those with a bachelor's or higher degree (table 501.80). Among 25- to 34-year-olds, the 2019 unemployment rate was 10 percent for those who had not completed high school, 6 percent for high school completers, and 2 percent for those with a bachelor's or higher degree (table 501.80 and figure 22).

In 2019, the *employment to population ratio*—the percentage of the population that is employed—was generally higher for people with higher levels of educational attainment than for those with less education. Among 25- to 34-year-olds, for example, 87 percent of those with a bachelor's or higher degree were employed in 2019, compared with 74 percent of those who had completed only high school and 57 percent of those who had not completed high school (table 501.50 and figure 23).

The relative difficulties that high school dropouts encounter in entering the job market are highlighted by comparing the labor force participation and employment to population ratio of recent high school dropouts with those of recent high school completers who did not immediately enroll in postsecondary education. In October 2018, about 47 percent of 2017–18 high school dropouts participated in the labor force (i.e., were either employed or looking for work), which was lower than the labor force participation rate for high school completers who were not enrolled in college (74 percent; tables 504.10 and 504.20 and figure 24). Similarly, the employment to population ratio for recent high school dropouts (41 percent) was lower than that for recent high school completers who were not enrolled in college (60 percent). However, the percentage of recent high school dropouts who were unemployed (6 percent) was lower than the percentage for recent high school completers who were not enrolled in college (14 percent).

In 2019, about 7 percent of employed people age 25 and over had not completed high school and 25 percent had completed high school only (table 502.10). In contrast, about half (53 percent) of all employed people age 25 and over had a postsecondary degree (i.e., an associate's or higher degree), which included 26 percent who had a bachelor's degree and 16 percent who had a master's or higher degree.

Earnings by Education Level

Median annual earnings were generally higher for adults with higher levels of educational attainment than for those with lower levels of educational attainment. Among full-time year-round workers age 25 and over, both males and females who had more education generally earned more than their counterparts of the same sex who had less education. In 2018, for example, males whose highest level of educational attainment was a bachelor's degree earned 65 percent more than males whose highest level of attainment was high school completion, and females who had attained a bachelor's degree earned 74 percent more than females who had only completed high school (table E and table 502.20).

Among full-time year-round workers age 25 and over, the earnings of females were lower than the earnings of males overall, as well as at each education level. For example, median 2018 earnings for full-time year-round workers whose highest level of educational attainment was a bachelor's degree were 33 percent higher for males than for females. Among those who had only completed high school, median 2018 earnings were 40 percent higher for males than for females (table 502.20).

Differences in earnings by sex at the same level of education can also be seen in the changes in median annual earnings between 1995 and 2018 (adjusted for inflation). For full-time year-round workers age 25 and over who had started but not completed high school, median annual earnings in 2018 were $35,600 for males and $25,140 for females, and were not measurably different from 1995 for either group (table 502.20). Among those who had completed high school only, male and female full-time year-round workers in 2018 earned $45,580 and $32,620, respectively, reflecting constant dollar declines for both since 1995 (down 6 percent from $48,630 for males and 3 percent from $33,720 for females). In contrast, females whose highest level of attainment was a bachelor's degree saw median annual earnings that were 7 percent higher in 2018 ($56,680) than in 1995 ($52,820). This was not the case for male bachelor's degree holders. Although their earnings in 2018 ($75,150) were higher than those for female bachelor's degree holders, they were not measurably different than in 1995, after adjustment for inflation.

Table E. Median annual earnings of full-time year-round workers age 25 and over, by selected levels of educational attainment and sex: Selected years, 1995 through 2018

[In constant 2018 dollars]

Sex and year	Some high school, no completion	High school completion	Bachelor's degree
Males			
1995	$36,560	$48,630	$74,590
2000	36,590	50,020	82,150
2005	34,960	46,680	77,170
2010	33,900	46,130	73,400
2015	34,050	44,040	75,630
2018	35,600	45,580	75,150
Females			
1995	$26,080	$33,720	$52,820
2000	26,130	36,410	58,930
2005	25,880	33,800	54,220
2010	24,050	34,380	54,620
2015	24,020	33,110	54,750
2018	25,140	32,620	56,680

SOURCE: U.S. Department of Commerce, Census Bureau, Current Population Reports, Series P-60, *Money Income in the United States*, 1995 and 2000; and Current Population Survey (CPS), Annual Social and Economic Supplement, 2006, 2011, 2016, and 2019.

Earnings for Recent College Graduates

Economic returns to education differ not only by level of educational attainment, but by field of study. For 25- to 29-year-old full-time year-round workers with a bachelor's degree (i.e., workers whose earnings are most directly determined by their recent educational credentials, as opposed to job tenure), median annual earnings were $50,600 in 2018 (table 505.10 and figure 26). However, these earnings varied by degree field. For example, among the most common bachelor's degree fields,[1] median annual earnings in 2018 were over $60,000 for two fields—computer and information sciences ($70,140) and engineering and engineering-related fields ($70,890)—but below $45,000 for the fields of psychology ($41,420), education ($41,510), criminal justice and fire protection ($41,810), and fine and commercial arts ($42,520; table 505.10).

Overall, the median annual earnings of 25- to 29-year-old full-time year-round workers with a bachelor's degree did not measurably change between 2010 and 2018, after adjustment for inflation (table 505.10). However, changes in median annual earnings from 2010 to 2018 varied by degree field. For example, inflation-adjusted median annual earnings were lower in 2018 than in 2010 for those with a bachelor's degree in education (6 percent lower), health professions (5 percent lower), and social sciences (3 percent lower). There was no measurable change in inflation-adjusted median annual earnings for 25- to 29-year-old full-time year-round workers with a bachelor's degree in fine and commercial arts, business, communications and communications technologies, criminal justice and fire protection, engineering and engineering-related fields, English language and literature, natural sciences, and psychology. Earnings for workers with a bachelor's degree in computer and information sciences were 8 percent higher in 2018 than in 2010, after adjustment for inflation.

---

[1] Degree fields in which more than 200,000 25- to 29-year-olds held bachelor's degrees in 2018 were examined for this discussion.

Figure 22. Unemployment rates of persons 25 to 34 years old, by highest level of educational attainment: Selected years, 1990 through 2019

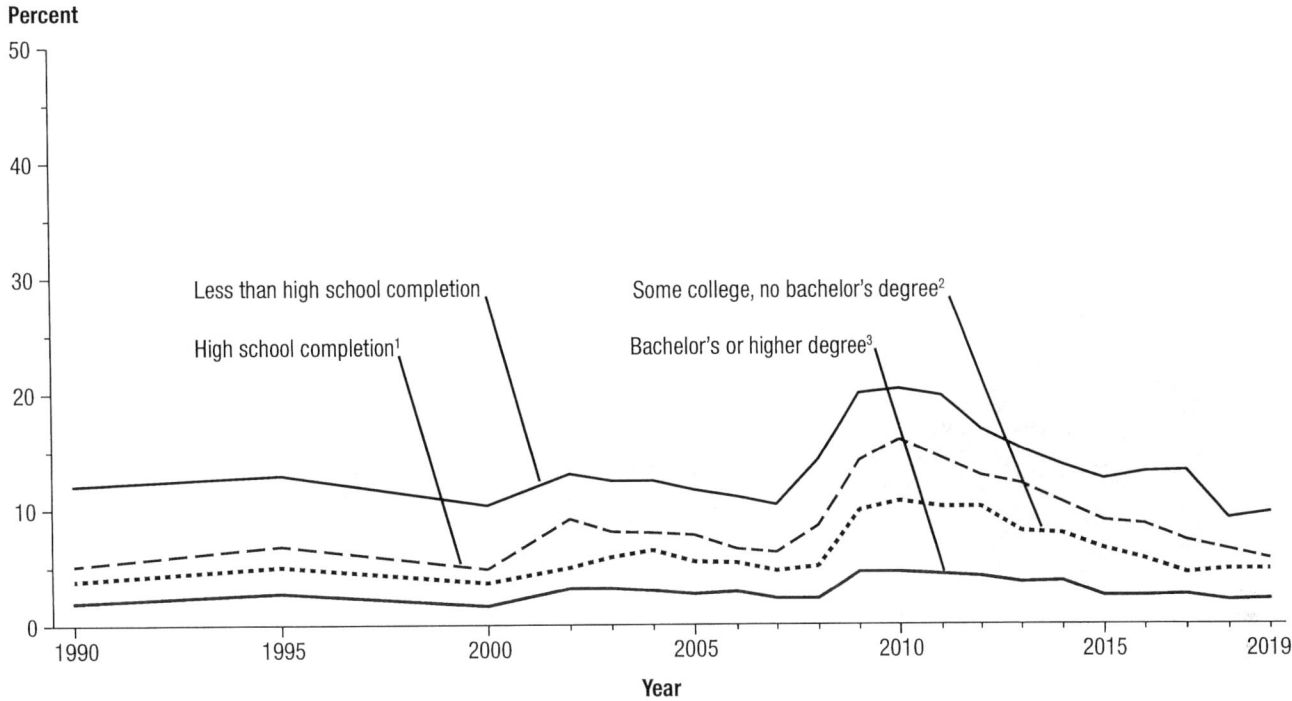

[1]Includes equivalency credentials, such as the GED credential. For 1990, includes all persons with 4 or more years of high school.
[2]Includes persons with no college degree as well as those with an associate's degree.
[3]For 1990, includes all persons with 4 or more years of college.
NOTE: Data are based on sample surveys of the noninstitutionalized population, which excludes persons living in institutions (e.g., prisons or nursing facilities); this table includes only data on the civilian population (excludes all military personnel). The unemployment rate is the percentage of persons in the civilian labor force who are not working and who made specific efforts to find employment sometime during the prior 4 weeks. The civilian labor force consists of all civilians who are employed or seeking employment.
SOURCE: U.S. Department of Commerce, Census Bureau, Current Population Survey (CPS), Annual Social and Economic Supplement, selected years, 1990 through 2019.

Figure 23. Employment to population ratios of persons 25 to 34 years old, by highest level of educational attainment: Selected years, 1990 through 2019

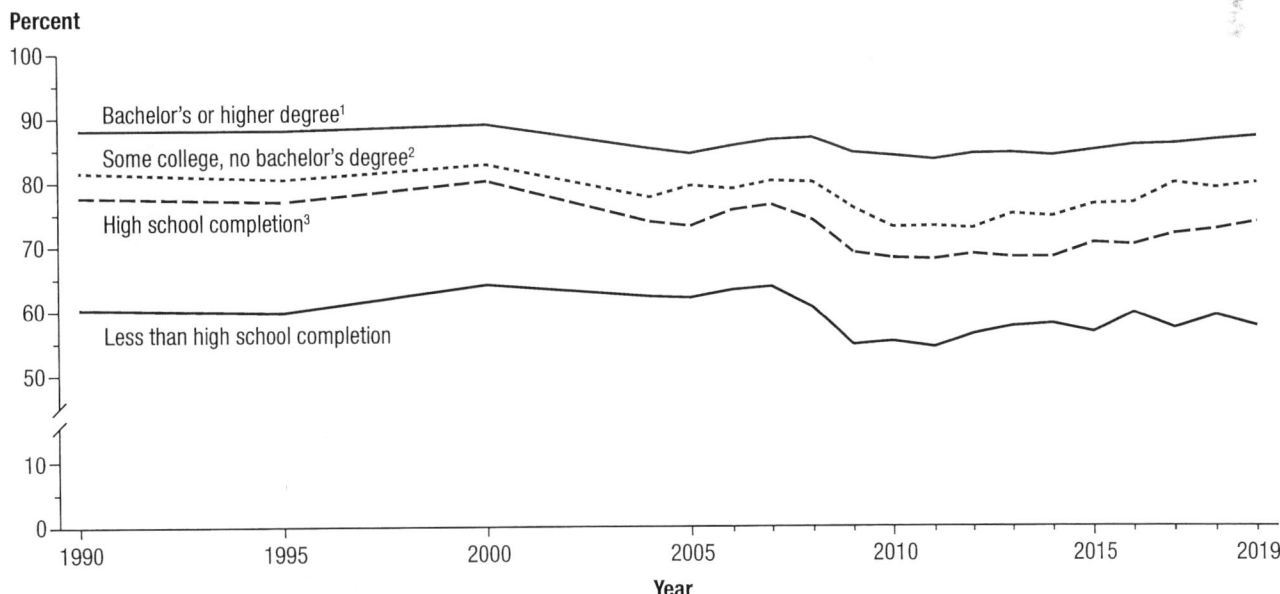

[1]For 1990, includes all persons with 4 or more years of college.
[2]Includes persons with no college degree as well as those with an associate's degree.
[3]Includes equivalency credentials, such as the GED credential. For 1990, includes all persons with 4 or more years of high school.
NOTE: Data are based on sample surveys of the noninstitutionalized population, which excludes persons living in institutions (e.g., prisons or nursing facilities); this table includes only data on the civilian population (excludes all military personnel). The employment to population ratio is the number of persons employed as a percentage of the civilian population.
SOURCE: U.S. Department of Commerce, Census Bureau, Current Population Survey (CPS), Annual Social and Economic Supplement, selected years, 1990 through 2019.

Figure 24. Percentage distribution of 2017–18 high school dropouts and high school completers not enrolled in college, by labor force status: October 2018

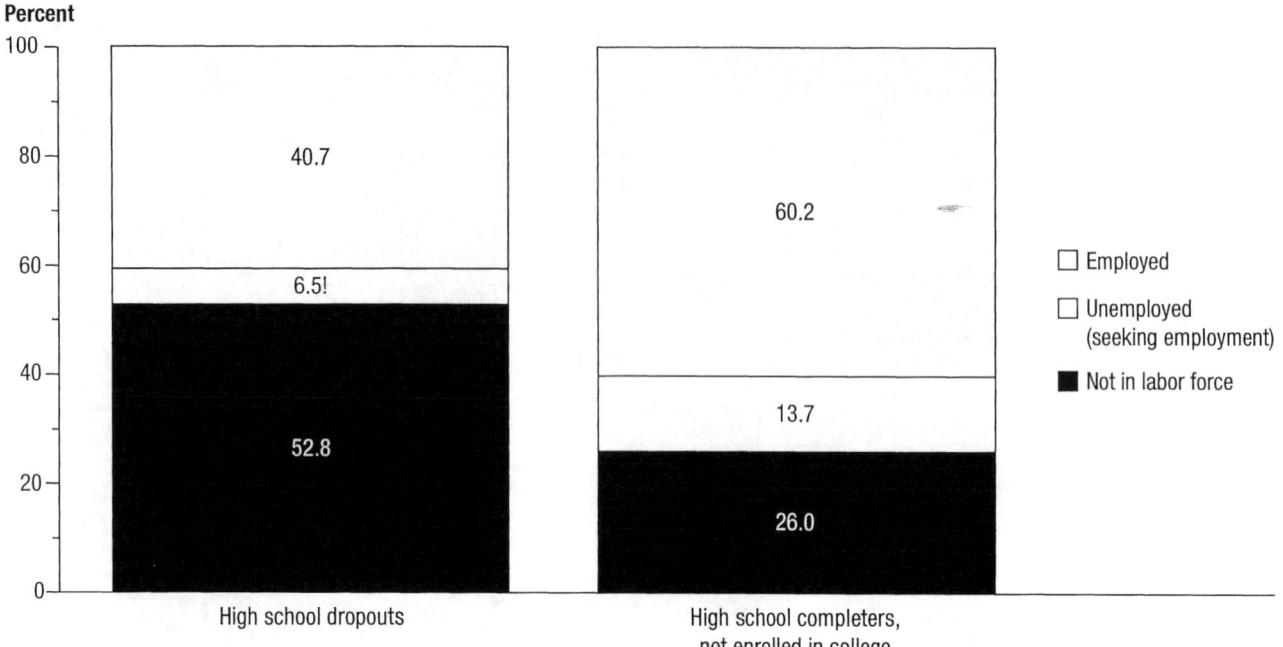

! Interpret data with caution. The coefficient of variation (CV) for this estimate is between 30 and 50 percent.
NOTE: Dropouts are those who left school in the 12-month period ending in October 2018 without completing a high school credential. Completers are those who received either a high school diploma or an equivalency credential between January and October 2018. Excludes persons in the military and persons living in institutions (e.g., prisons or nursing facilities). Estimates are for 16- to 24-year-olds only. Graphic display was generated using unrounded data. Detail may not sum to totals because of rounding.
SOURCE: U.S. Department of Commerce, Census Bureau, Current Population Survey (CPS), October 2018.

Figure 25. Median annual earnings of full-time year-round workers 25 to 34 years old, by highest level of educational attainment and sex: 2018

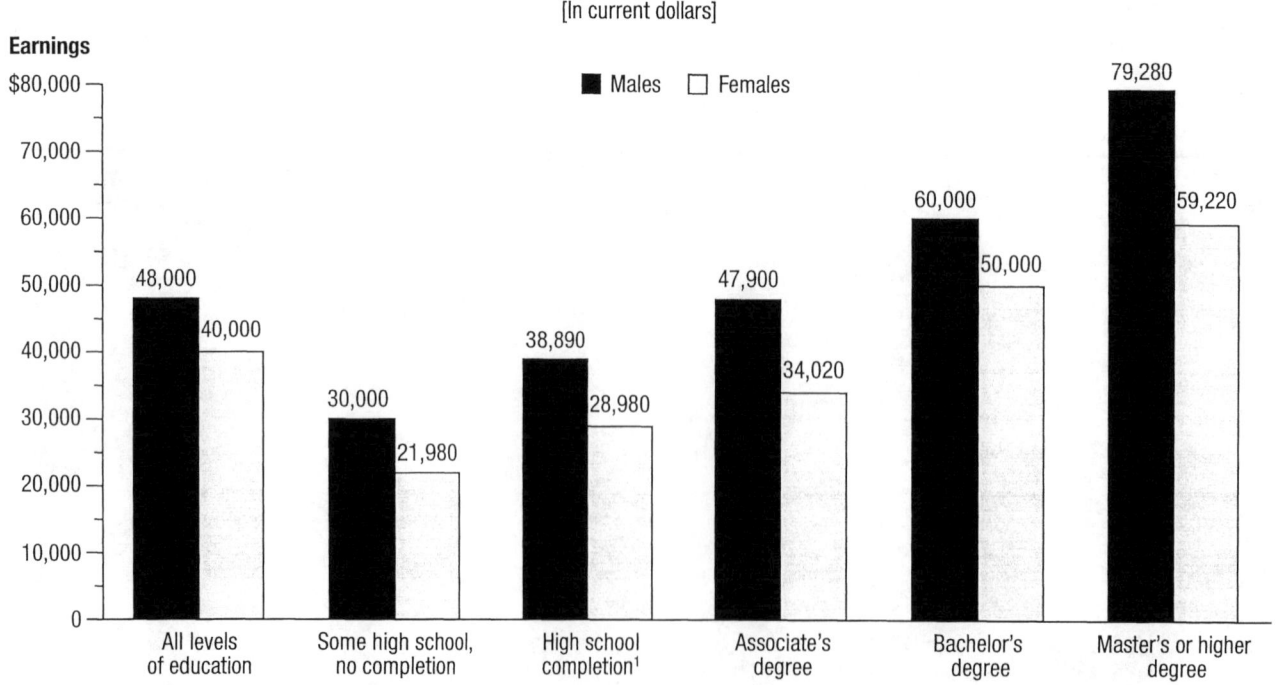

[1]Includes equivalency credentials, such as the GED credential.
SOURCE: U.S. Department of Commerce, Census Bureau, Current Population Survey (CPS), Annual Social and Economic Supplement, 2019.

Figure 26. Median annual earnings of 25- to 29-year-old bachelor's degree holders employed full time, by field of study: 2010 and 2018

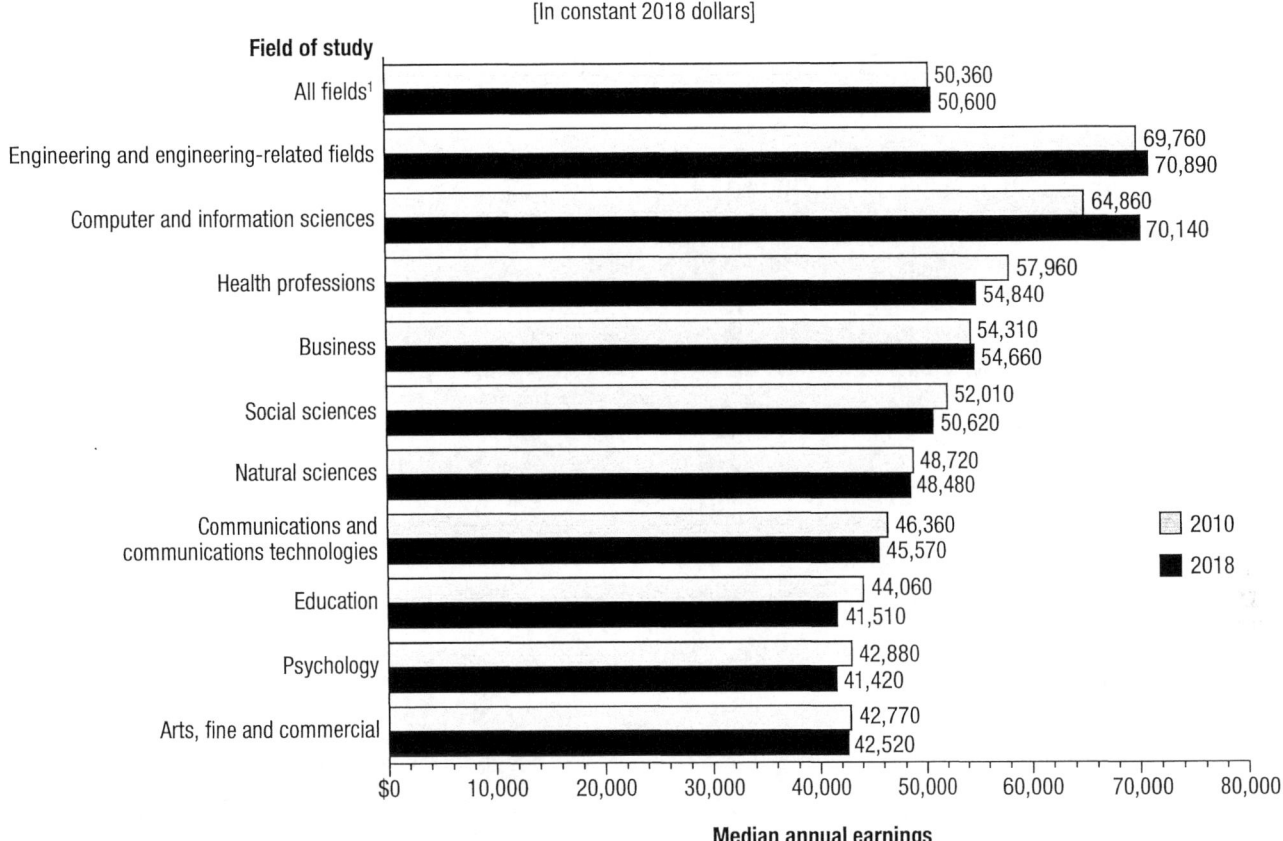

[In constant 2018 dollars]

[1]Includes graduates in other fields not separately shown.
NOTE: Constant dollars based on the Consumer Price Index, prepared by the Bureau of Labor Statistics, U.S. Department of Labor, adjusted to a school-year basis.
SOURCE: U.S. Department of Commerce, Census Bureau, 2010 and 2018 American Community Survey (ACS) Public Use Microdata Sample (PUMS) data.

Table 501.10. Labor force participation, employment, and unemployment of persons 25 to 64 years old, by sex, race/ethnicity, age group, and educational attainment: 2016, 2017, and 2018

[Standard errors appear in parentheses]

Sex, race/ethnicity, age group, and educational attainment	Labor force participation				Employment				Unemployment			
	Labor force participation rate[1]			Number of participants (in thousands)	Employment to population ratio[2]			Number employed (in thousands)	Unemployment rate[3]			Number unemployed (in thousands)
	2016	2017	2018	2018	2016	2017	2018	2018	2016	2017	2018	2018
1	2	3	4	5	6	7	8	9	10	11	12	13
All persons 25 to 64 years old, all education levels	77.3 (0.04)	77.7 (0.04)	78.1 (0.04)	132,952 (84.4)	73.7 (0.05)	74.3 (0.04)	75.0 (0.04)	127,639 (89.3)	4.7 (0.02)	4.3 (0.02)	4.0 (0.02)	5,314 (32.8)
Less than high school completion	60.2 (0.13)	59.9 (0.14)	60.8 (0.13)	11,121 (48.6)	55.0 (0.14)	55.2 (0.14)	56.3 (0.13)	10,292 (46.1)	8.7 (0.11)	8.0 (0.11)	7.5 (0.09)	829 (11.1)
High school completion[4]	72.0 (0.09)	72.2 (0.09)	72.5 (0.09)	31,727 (56.5)	68.2 (0.09)	68.6 (0.09)	68.6 (0.10)	30,048 (86.3)	5.6 (0.06)	5.6 (0.06)	5.3 (0.06)	1,679 (19.8)
Some college, no degree	77.5 (0.08)	77.8 (0.08)	78.0 (0.08)	27,109 (41.2)	73.5 (0.09)	73.7 (0.08)	74.6 (0.09)	25,917 (58.7)	5.1 (0.05)	4.7 (0.05)	4.4 (0.05)	1,193 (13.6)
Associate's degree	81.5 (0.14)	81.9 (0.14)	82.1 (0.12)	12,832 (32.6)	78.3 (0.14)	79.1 (0.12)	79.4 (0.13)	12,410 (45.3)	3.9 (0.07)	3.4 (0.08)	3.3 (0.07)	422 (8.7)
Bachelor's or higher degree	86.2 (0.06)	86.5 (0.05)	86.8 (0.05)	50,162 (137.5)	83.9 (0.07)	84.2 (0.05)	84.7 (0.05)	48,971 (134.8)	2.7 (0.03)	2.6 (0.03)	2.4 (0.03)	1,191 (14.6)
Sex												
Male, all education levels	82.6 (0.05)	82.9 (0.05)	83.3 (0.05)	70,014 (47.6)	78.7 (0.06)	79.3 (0.05)	80.0 (0.05)	67,240 (49.8)	4.7 (0.04)	4.3 (0.03)	4.0 (0.03)	2,774 (24.3)
Less than high school completion	69.4 (0.18)	69.6 (0.16)	70.2 (0.17)	7,021 (37.0)	64.0 (0.19)	64.6 (0.18)	65.7 (0.18)	6,571 (35.0)	7.7 (0.13)	7.1 (0.13)	6.4 (0.12)	450 (9.2)
High school completion[4]	77.8 (0.12)	78.1 (0.11)	78.3 (0.11)	18,636 (56.5)	72.9 (0.12)	73.7 (0.12)	74.3 (0.12)	17,676 (55.1)	6.3 (0.08)	5.5 (0.08)	5.1 (0.08)	959 (14.5)
Some college, no degree	82.8 (0.12)	83.1 (0.11)	83.3 (0.11)	14,134 (41.2)	78.7 (0.12)	79.3 (0.12)	79.8 (0.13)	13,548 (40.4)	4.9 (0.07)	4.5 (0.08)	4.1 (0.07)	586 (10.4)
Associate's degree	86.4 (0.16)	86.8 (0.16)	86.9 (0.16)	5,883 (32.6)	83.0 (0.16)	84.0 (0.18)	84.0 (0.18)	5,690 (31.8)	4.0 (0.10)	3.3 (0.10)	3.3 (0.10)	193 (6.3)
Bachelor's or higher degree	91.4 (0.07)	91.5 (0.07)	91.8 (0.06)	24,340 (71.1)	89.0 (0.09)	89.1 (0.07)	89.6 (0.09)	23,756 (70.6)	2.6 (0.05)	2.6 (0.04)	2.4 (0.04)	585 (10.1)
Female, all education levels	72.2 (0.06)	72.5 (0.06)	73.0 (0.06)	62,938 (58.1)	68.8 (0.06)	69.4 (0.06)	70.1 (0.06)	60,398 (60.2)	4.7 (0.03)	4.3 (0.04)	4.0 (0.03)	2,540 (20.3)
Less than high school completion	49.0 (0.20)	48.3 (0.25)	49.5 (0.23)	4,100 (25.5)	44.0 (0.21)	43.7 (0.23)	45.0 (0.22)	3,721 (24.0)	10.3 (0.19)	9.6 (0.22)	9.2 (0.16)	379 (7.1)
High school completion[4]	65.2 (0.14)	65.2 (0.14)	65.5 (0.14)	13,091 (49.1)	61.2 (0.16)	61.5 (0.14)	61.9 (0.14)	12,371 (50.5)	6.2 (0.09)	5.7 (0.08)	5.5 (0.08)	720 (10.5)
Some college, no degree	72.6 (0.12)	72.7 (0.11)	72.7 (0.11)	12,976 (27.6)	68.6 (0.12)	69.1 (0.14)	69.6 (0.16)	12,369 (26.8)	5.4 (0.08)	5.0 (0.08)	4.7 (0.07)	607 (9.7)
Associate's degree	77.9 (0.19)	78.3 (0.15)	78.5 (0.18)	6,949 (30.0)	74.9 (0.20)	75.5 (0.17)	75.9 (0.17)	6,720 (29.3)	3.8 (0.09)	3.6 (0.10)	3.8 (0.09)	229 (6.1)
Bachelor's or higher degree	81.8 (0.09)	82.2 (0.08)	82.6 (0.08)	25,822 (80.5)	79.5 (0.10)	80.1 (0.08)	80.6 (0.08)	25,216 (78.8)	2.8 (0.04)	2.6 (0.04)	2.3 (0.04)	606 (10.7)
Race/ethnicity												
White, all education levels	78.3 (0.05)	78.5 (0.05)	78.9 (0.05)	81,631 (54.7)	75.2 (0.05)	75.8 (0.06)	76.3 (0.06)	78,966 (60.0)	3.9 (0.03)	3.5 (0.02)	3.3 (0.03)	2,664 (23.5)
Less than high school completion	52.9 (0.27)	52.8 (0.27)	53.7 (0.25)	3,229 (26.7)	47.7 (0.28)	48.1 (0.23)	49.2 (0.23)	2,955 (25.5)	9.8 (0.24)	8.8 (0.20)	8.5 (0.22)	274 (7.4)
High school completion[4]	71.8 (0.11)	71.8 (0.11)	72.0 (0.12)	18,608 (66.7)	68.0 (0.11)	68.3 (0.11)	68.8 (0.12)	17,777 (64.4)	5.3 (0.07)	4.8 (0.07)	4.5 (0.07)	830 (13.9)
Some college, no degree	77.3 (0.10)	77.5 (0.10)	77.7 (0.12)	16,660 (48.3)	73.9 (0.10)	74.4 (0.11)	74.8 (0.13)	16,042 (47.7)	4.4 (0.06)	4.0 (0.06)	3.7 (0.05)	618 (8.7)
Associate's degree	81.7 (0.16)	81.9 (0.16)	82.0 (0.14)	8,547 (37.8)	79.0 (0.15)	79.5 (0.14)	79.8 (0.15)	8,313 (37.0)	3.3 (0.07)	2.9 (0.07)	2.7 (0.07)	234 (5.5)
Bachelor's or higher degree	86.5 (0.07)	86.8 (0.06)	87.0 (0.06)	34,587 (88.9)	84.5 (0.08)	84.9 (0.06)	85.2 (0.06)	33,879 (87.0)	2.4 (0.03)	2.2 (0.03)	2.0 (0.03)	708 (12.0)
Black, all education levels	73.4 (0.14)	73.9 (0.11)	74.4 (0.12)	15,907 (33.9)	67.3 (0.14)	68.2 (0.13)	69.1 (0.14)	14,782 (36.2)	8.2 (0.10)	7.7 (0.11)	7.1 (0.11)	1,125 (16.8)
Less than high school completion	46.9 (0.47)	47.8 (0.44)	47.9 (0.38)	1,158 (14.1)	38.6 (0.43)	39.2 (0.44)	40.3 (0.39)	974 (12.5)	17.6 (0.51)	17.9 (0.48)	15.8 (0.51)	184 (6.6)
High school completion[4]	67.9 (0.27)	68.4 (0.23)	68.7 (0.29)	4,630 (31.2)	60.8 (0.28)	61.8 (0.24)	62.6 (0.30)	4,217 (30.5)	10.5 (0.20)	9.7 (0.22)	8.9 (0.20)	413 (9.4)
Some college, no degree	77.1 (0.23)	77.0 (0.26)	77.6 (0.24)	4,129 (27.6)	71.1 (0.26)	71.1 (0.28)	72.3 (0.28)	3,846 (26.8)	7.9 (0.17)	7.6 (0.16)	6.9 (0.17)	283 (7.3)
Associate's degree	81.5 (0.36)	81.9 (0.39)	82.1 (0.37)	1,608 (18.2)	76.6 (0.39)	77.6 (0.45)	77.7 (0.40)	1,521 (17.1)	6.0 (0.27)	5.1 (0.25)	5.4 (0.25)	87 (4.3)
Bachelor's or higher degree	88.2 (0.17)	88.4 (0.20)	88.7 (0.19)	4,382 (30.1)	84.7 (0.21)	84.9 (0.20)	85.5 (0.20)	4,223 (29.7)	4.0 (0.14)	4.0 (0.13)	3.6 (0.14)	159 (6.0)
Hispanic, all education levels	77.0 (0.10)	77.4 (0.11)	78.0 (0.09)	23,215 (29.6)	72.8 (0.11)	73.8 (0.11)	74.5 (0.11)	22,178 (28.9)	5.4 (0.08)	4.8 (0.07)	4.5 (0.06)	1,037 (13.5)
Less than high school completion	69.6 (0.20)	68.9 (0.22)	69.7 (0.20)	5,837 (38.6)	65.1 (0.21)	65.0 (0.21)	66.0 (0.23)	5,525 (37.4)	6.4 (0.14)	5.7 (0.14)	5.3 (0.12)	311 (7.5)
High school completion[4]	76.1 (0.23)	76.9 (0.19)	77.1 (0.20)	6,620 (31.1)	71.7 (0.25)	73.0 (0.21)	73.2 (0.20)	6,289 (30.5)	5.8 (0.15)	5.0 (0.13)	5.0 (0.12)	331 (8.0)
Some college, no degree	80.2 (0.25)	80.6 (0.25)	80.5 (0.21)	4,438 (28.2)	76.0 (0.27)	76.7 (0.26)	76.9 (0.24)	4,241 (30.1)	5.2 (0.18)	4.8 (0.14)	4.4 (0.14)	197 (5.6)
Associate's degree	82.3 (0.40)	84.1 (0.34)	84.0 (0.34)	1,728 (17.8)	78.3 (0.43)	80.8 (0.40)	80.7 (0.34)	1,660 (17.1)	4.8 (0.23)	3.9 (0.25)	3.9 (0.17)	68 (3.0)
Bachelor's or higher degree	86.7 (0.21)	87.0 (0.20)	87.5 (0.22)	4,592 (36.8)	83.9 (0.22)	84.0 (0.24)	85.1 (0.23)	4,462 (36.2)	3.3 (0.11)	3.4 (0.11)	2.8 (0.14)	130 (4.8)
Asian, all education levels	78.4 (0.17)	78.7 (0.16)	79.9 (0.16)	8,518 (24.1)	75.4 (0.17)	75.9 (0.18)	77.3 (0.17)	8,246 (24.4)	3.7 (0.10)	3.6 (0.08)	3.2 (0.07)	272 (6.3)
Less than high school completion	64.6 (0.54)	63.0 (0.60)	65.1 (0.54)	656 (9.2)	61.5 (0.49)	60.1 (0.62)	62.0 (0.56)	625 (8.9)	4.8 (0.34)	4.6 (0.41)	4.7 (0.27)	31 (1.9)
High school completion[4]	73.6 (0.53)	73.4 (0.54)	74.3 (0.50)	1,047 (14.5)	70.2 (0.50)	70.4 (0.59)	71.6 (0.49)	1,010 (14.0)	4.7 (0.28)	4.1 (0.24)	3.6 (0.23)	38 (2.5)
Some college, no degree	76.4 (0.46)	77.9 (0.51)	78.9 (0.43)	956 (12.7)	72.9 (0.49)	74.6 (0.57)	75.9 (0.57)	919 (12.9)	4.3 (0.28)	4.3 (0.30)	3.8 (0.25)	37 (2.3)
Associate's degree	78.4 (0.65)	79.9 (0.50)	79.8 (0.54)	577 (9.3)	75.1 (0.69)	77.3 (0.53)	77.4 (0.53)	559 (9.5)	4.2 (0.38)	3.3 (0.24)	3.0 (0.31)	17 (1.7)
Bachelor's or higher degree	82.5 (0.19)	82.7 (0.21)	83.7 (0.17)	5,282 (24.5)	80.0 (0.20)	80.0 (0.22)	81.3 (0.18)	5,132 (23.7)	3.2 (0.12)	3.2 (0.10)	2.8 (0.08)	150 (4.2)

See notes at end of table.

Table 501.10. Labor force participation, employment, and unemployment of persons 25 to 64 years old, by sex, race/ethnicity, age group, and educational attainment: 2016, 2017, and 2018—Continued

[Standard errors appear in parentheses]

Sex, race/ethnicity, age group, and educational attainment	Labor force participation				Employment				Unemployment			
	Labor force participation rate[1]			Number of participants (in thousands)	Employment to population ratio[2]			Number employed (in thousands)	Unemployment rate[3]			Number unemployed (in thousands)
	2016	2017	2018	2018	2016	2017	2018	2018	2016	2017	2018	2018
1	2	3	4	5	6	7	8	9	10	11	12	13
American Indian/Alaska Native, all education levels	65.5 (0.48)	65.0 (0.52)	65.3 (0.59)	744 (10.3)	58.2 (0.51)	58.9 (0.51)	60.0 (0.57)	683 (9.8)	11.1 (0.44)	9.4 (0.40)	8.2 (0.25)	61 (2.0)
Less than high school completion	42.1 (1.29)	44.5 (1.35)	44.4 (1.43)	77 (3.2)	34.1 (1.27)	36.3 (1.35)	37.5 (1.60)	65 (3.3)	18.8 (1.51)	18.4 (1.67)	15.5 (1.62)	12 (1.2)
High school completion[4]	63.1 (0.82)	61.7 (0.82)	60.7 (1.06)	225 (5.7)	53.7 (0.86)	54.7 (0.91)	54.1 (0.98)	201 (5.4)	14.9 (0.98)	11.3 (0.84)	10.8 (0.64)	24 (1.5)
Some college, no degree	69.1 (0.94)	68.1 (0.90)	69.6 (0.89)	219 (5.5)	62.3 (1.01)	61.9 (1.03)	64.5 (1.01)	203 (5.4)	10.4 (0.98)	8.5 (0.62)	7.3 (0.66)	16 (1.5)
Associate's degree	74.8 (1.42)	72.2 (1.65)	75.7 (1.60)	80 (3.0)	69.6 (1.57)	68.6 (1.73)	71.4 (1.65)	76 (3.0)	6.9 (1.03)	5.0 (0.73)	5.6 (0.86)	5 (0.7)
Bachelor's or higher degree	82.8 (1.01)	83.0 (0.95)	82.2 (0.98)	142 (4.2)	79.3 (1.05)	78.8 (1.08)	79.9 (0.97)	138 (4.2)	4.2 (0.68)	5.1 (0.62)	2.9 (0.43)	4 (0.6)
Age group												
25 to 34, all education levels	82.2 (0.07)	82.6 (0.08)	83.2 (0.06)	37,386 (36.6)	77.3 (0.08)	78.1 (0.08)	79.0 (0.07)	35,477 (39.5)	5.9 (0.05)	5.5 (0.05)	5.1 (0.05)	1,909 (17.3)
Less than high school completion	63.8 (0.25)	63.4 (0.29)	63.4 (0.32)	2,460 (24.8)	55.9 (0.27)	55.9 (0.32)	56.4 (0.33)	2,190 (23.3)	12.3 (0.26)	11.7 (0.28)	11.0 (0.27)	269 (7.1)
High school completion[4]	76.8 (0.20)	77.2 (0.19)	77.4 (0.16)	8,411 (46.5)	69.9 (0.21)	70.9 (0.20)	71.4 (0.19)	7,760 (43.7)	9.0 (0.13)	8.2 (0.14)	7.7 (0.12)	651 (11.2)
Some college, no degree	82.6 (0.15)	82.7 (0.15)	83.5 (0.15)	8,222 (39.1)	77.2 (0.18)	77.7 (0.18)	78.8 (0.17)	7,755 (37.8)	6.6 (0.11)	6.0 (0.12)	5.7 (0.11)	467 (9.7)
Associate's degree	86.3 (0.23)	87.0 (0.19)	87.5 (0.20)	3,512 (25.0)	82.2 (0.25)	83.3 (0.21)	83.9 (0.25)	3,369 (24.9)	4.7 (0.17)	4.2 (0.16)	4.1 (0.14)	143 (5.0)
Bachelor's or higher degree	89.9 (0.10)	90.0 (0.11)	90.6 (0.09)	14,781 (58.5)	87.4 (0.11)	87.4 (0.11)	88.2 (0.10)	14,403 (57.3)	2.8 (0.05)	2.8 (0.06)	2.6 (0.06)	379 (8.4)
35 to 44, all education levels	82.3 (0.08)	82.3 (0.08)	83.0 (0.08)	34,430 (39.4)	78.4 (0.08)	78.9 (0.09)	79.7 (0.07)	33,086 (38.9)	4.7 (0.05)	4.2 (0.04)	3.9 (0.04)	1,344 (15.1)
Less than high school completion	67.8 (0.26)	66.7 (0.29)	67.5 (0.23)	3,176 (25.5)	62.1 (0.25)	61.4 (0.32)	62.4 (0.25)	2,934 (24.4)	8.4 (0.20)	7.9 (0.21)	7.6 (0.15)	242 (5.0)
High school completion[4]	77.4 (0.17)	77.5 (0.19)	78.0 (0.19)	7,511 (41.8)	72.3 (0.22)	72.9 (0.20)	73.7 (0.19)	7,094 (41.6)	6.6 (0.13)	6.0 (0.12)	5.5 (0.12)	417 (9.0)
Some college, no degree	82.4 (0.17)	82.4 (0.17)	82.8 (0.18)	6,659 (33.3)	78.1 (0.19)	78.5 (0.18)	79.2 (0.18)	6,363 (30.6)	5.3 (0.12)	4.8 (0.10)	4.5 (0.10)	297 (7.4)
Associate's degree	86.1 (0.24)	86.7 (0.22)	86.6 (0.22)	3,361 (23.2)	82.7 (0.27)	83.9 (0.26)	83.9 (0.23)	3,256 (22.8)	4.0 (0.16)	4.0 (0.14)	3.1 (0.11)	105 (3.7)
Bachelor's or higher degree	89.5 (0.08)	89.4 (0.08)	89.9 (0.09)	13,722 (48.5)	87.3 (0.09)	88.1 (0.10)	88.1 (0.10)	13,439 (48.5)	2.5 (0.05)	2.3 (0.06)	2.1 (0.05)	283 (6.5)
45 to 54, all education levels	80.2 (0.08)	80.5 (0.08)	81.0 (0.07)	33,638 (42.1)	76.8 (0.09)	77.5 (0.09)	78.1 (0.08)	32,453 (44.9)	4.1 (0.04)	3.7 (0.04)	3.5 (0.04)	1,185 (14.0)
Less than high school completion	62.7 (0.26)	62.8 (0.28)	62.8 (0.27)	3,101 (21.5)	58.1 (0.29)	58.7 (0.28)	60.2 (0.28)	2,899 (21.5)	7.4 (0.19)	6.7 (0.18)	6.5 (0.17)	202 (5.3)
High school completion[4]	75.7 (0.16)	75.9 (0.16)	76.4 (0.16)	8,363 (33.0)	71.8 (0.15)	72.4 (0.16)	73.0 (0.15)	7,997 (33.3)	5.2 (0.09)	4.6 (0.09)	4.4 (0.10)	366 (8.6)
Some college, no degree	80.6 (0.15)	81.2 (0.17)	80.9 (0.17)	6,538 (28.0)	77.3 (0.17)	78.0 (0.18)	78.0 (0.19)	6,298 (28.2)	4.2 (0.09)	4.0 (0.11)	3.7 (0.09)	240 (6.2)
Associate's degree	84.4 (0.22)	84.5 (0.19)	84.9 (0.23)	3,265 (24.0)	81.4 (0.23)	81.4 (0.21)	82.5 (0.24)	3,171 (22.4)	3.5 (0.12)	2.9 (0.11)	2.9 (0.13)	94 (4.1)
Bachelor's or higher degree	89.1 (0.10)	89.3 (0.10)	89.3 (0.09)	12,372 (47.8)	86.8 (0.11)	87.0 (0.10)	87.3 (0.10)	12,088 (46.8)	2.7 (0.05)	2.5 (0.05)	2.3 (0.05)	284 (6.3)
55 to 64, all education levels	64.3 (0.09)	64.9 (0.09)	65.0 (0.09)	27,498 (38.1)	61.8 (0.09)	62.6 (0.09)	63.0 (0.09)	26,623 (38.2)	3.8 (0.04)	3.5 (0.04)	3.2 (0.04)	876 (11.7)
Less than high school completion	46.6 (0.25)	47.4 (0.30)	48.9 (0.29)	2,385 (18.7)	43.7 (0.26)	44.7 (0.30)	46.5 (0.29)	2,269 (17.8)	6.3 (0.19)	5.7 (0.22)	4.8 (0.18)	115 (4.4)
High school completion[4]	60.0 (0.17)	60.3 (0.17)	60.2 (0.17)	7,442 (30.7)	57.5 (0.17)	58.2 (0.16)	58.3 (0.16)	7,197 (29.3)	4.2 (0.08)	3.5 (0.09)	3.3 (0.09)	245 (6.8)
Some college, no degree	64.2 (0.20)	64.8 (0.20)	64.8 (0.18)	5,691 (25.9)	61.6 (0.20)	62.4 (0.17)	62.6 (0.17)	5,501 (25.1)	4.1 (0.10)	3.7 (0.08)	3.3 (0.08)	189 (5.5)
Associate's degree	68.7 (0.31)	69.2 (0.28)	69.3 (0.29)	2,694 (20.1)	66.5 (0.31)	67.1 (0.28)	67.3 (0.29)	2,614 (20.0)	3.2 (0.12)	3.1 (0.14)	3.0 (0.12)	80 (3.3)
Bachelor's or higher degree	74.5 (0.14)	75.2 (0.15)	75.1 (0.13)	9,287 (36.6)	72.2 (0.14)	73.1 (0.15)	73.1 (0.13)	9,041 (36.0)	3.0 (0.07)	2.8 (0.07)	2.6 (0.06)	246 (5.7)

[1]Percentage of the civilian population who are employed or seeking employment.
[2]Number of persons employed as a percentage of the civilian population.
[3]The percentage of persons in the civilian labor force who are not working and who made specific efforts to find employment sometime during the prior 4 weeks.
[4]Includes equivalency credentials, such as the GED credential.

NOTE: Estimates are for the entire civilian population, including persons living in households and persons living in group quarters (e.g., college residence halls, residential treatment centers, or correctional facilities). Race categories exclude persons of Hispanic ethnicity. Totals include racial/ethnic groups not separately shown. Detail may not sum to totals because of rounding.
SOURCE: U.S. Department of Commerce, Census Bureau, American Community Survey (ACS), 2016, 2017, and 2018. (This table was prepared February 2020.)

Table 501.20. Labor force participation, employment, and unemployment of persons 16 to 24 years old who are not enrolled in school, by age group, sex, race/ethnicity, and educational attainment: 2016, 2017, and 2018

[Standard errors appear in parentheses]

Age group, sex, race/ethnicity, and educational attainment	Labor force participation rate[1] 2016	2017	2018	Number of participants (in thousands) 2018	Employment to population ratio[2] 2016	2017	2018	Number employed (in thousands) 2018	Unemployment rate[3] 2016	2017	2018	Number unemployed (in thousands) 2018
1	2	3	4	5	6	7	8	9	10	11	12	13
16 to 19 years old												
All persons, all education levels	65.6 (0.41)	65.3 (0.42)	65.6 (0.40)	1,642 (18.9)	52.2 (0.44)	52.2 (0.45)	52.6 (0.40)	1,316 (17.4)	20.0 (0.42)	20.0 (0.42)	19.8 (0.37)	325 (6.4)
Less than high school completion	48.5 (0.81)	48.4 (0.72)	48.3 (0.78)	319 (7.6)	35.4 (0.73)	35.4 (0.74)	35.2 (0.77)	233 (6.5)	27.0 (1.08)	27.0 (1.03)	27.2 (1.15)	87 (4.3)
High school completion[4]	71.9 (0.50)	70.8 (0.48)	71.3 (0.49)	1,101 (16.1)	57.0 (0.56)	57.0 (0.56)	57.8 (0.52)	893 (14.6)	19.5 (0.53)	19.5 (0.48)	19.0 (0.48)	209 (5.7)
At least some college	76.4 (1.04)	75.9 (1.18)	74.3 (1.15)	221 (5.8)	66.4 (1.17)	64.3 (1.29)	64.3 (1.12)	191 (5.3)	12.5 (1.00)	12.5 (1.11)	13.5 (0.98)	30 (2.4)
Male, all education levels	66.5 (0.50)	66.2 (0.54)	66.9 (0.54)	952 (12.8)	52.7 (0.54)	52.7 (0.61)	53.4 (0.62)	760 (13.7)	21.2 (0.52)	20.5 (0.58)	20.1 (0.61)	192 (5.3)
Less than high school completion	49.9 (0.99)	51.1 (0.99)	51.0 (1.11)	202 (6.4)	37.3 (0.98)	37.3 (0.99)	37.4 (1.11)	148 (5.7)	30.2 (1.45)	27.0 (1.41)	26.8 (1.59)	54 (3.6)
High school completion[4]	73.2 (0.66)	72.1 (0.61)	72.7 (0.67)	639 (10.4)	58.2 (0.75)	58.2 (0.73)	58.9 (0.78)	517 (10.9)	19.1 (0.67)	19.2 (0.67)	19.0 (0.74)	121 (4.5)
At least some college	76.1 (1.54)	75.0 (1.48)	74.7 (1.45)	112 (5.0)	63.5 (1.67)	63.5 (1.56)	63.9 (1.49)	95 (4.5)	16.1 (1.56)	15.3 (1.65)	14.5 (1.29)	16 (1.6)
Female, all education levels	64.6 (0.65)	64.1 (0.69)	63.8 (0.60)	690 (10.6)	51.7 (0.66)	51.7 (0.70)	51.2 (0.58)	556 (9.7)	20.8 (0.69)	19.3 (0.68)	19.4 (0.64)	134 (4.8)
Less than high school completion	46.5 (1.37)	44.4 (1.25)	44.1 (1.23)	118 (4.0)	32.4 (1.16)	32.4 (1.12)	31.0 (1.19)	85 (3.5)	33.3 (1.74)	27.0 (1.60)	27.8 (1.63)	33 (2.2)
High school completion[4]	70.2 (0.83)	69.1 (0.87)	69.4 (0.76)	463 (9.4)	55.4 (0.93)	55.4 (0.88)	56.3 (0.73)	375 (8.5)	18.7 (0.86)	19.9 (0.82)	18.9 (0.85)	87 (4.4)
At least some college	76.7 (1.49)	76.8 (1.54)	74.0 (1.73)	109 (3.7)	69.2 (1.67)	69.2 (1.68)	64.8 (1.81)	96 (3.5)	13.6 (1.30)	9.8 (1.22)	12.5 (1.45)	14 (1.7)
White, all education levels	68.3 (0.58)	69.7 (0.60)	69.2 (0.55)	825 (11.8)	57.9 (0.59)	57.9 (0.64)	57.2 (0.55)	682 (10.6)	18.6 (0.51)	16.9 (0.52)	17.3 (0.47)	142 (4.3)
Less than high school completion	49.6 (1.17)	51.3 (1.25)	51.9 (1.07)	159 (4.0)	39.3 (0.97)	39.3 (1.18)	39.0 (1.15)	120 (4.0)	30.2 (1.23)	23.5 (1.47)	24.8 (1.41)	40 (2.3)
High school completion[4]	74.9 (0.75)	75.2 (0.66)	74.5 (0.62)	552 (9.5)	62.9 (0.76)	62.4 (0.77)	62.4 (0.62)	462 (8.5)	16.2 (0.61)	16.3 (0.64)	16.3 (0.59)	90 (3.6)
At least some college	80.3 (1.19)	81.0 (1.50)	78.5 (1.50)	114 (3.9)	72.3 (1.52)	72.3 (1.61)	69.7 (1.51)	101 (3.7)	12.5 (1.24)	10.8 (1.31)	11.3 (1.15)	13 (1.4)
Black, all education levels	60.4 (0.97)	57.4 (1.14)	57.7 (1.28)	240 (7.3)	40.3 (1.11)	41.2 (1.22)	41.0 (1.21)	171 (6.5)	32.2 (1.59)	28.8 (1.29)	28.6 (1.18)	69 (3.1)
Less than high school completion	43.3 (1.95)	37.9 (1.95)	37.3 (2.03)	40 (3.0)	21.5 (1.60)	21.5 (1.73)	22.2 (1.58)	23 (2.1)	48.7 (3.61)	43.4 (3.34)	43.6 (3.15)	17 (1.8)
High school completion[4]	65.2 (1.34)	63.6 (1.41)	64.6 (1.62)	167 (6.9)	45.5 (1.64)	45.5 (1.53)	47.3 (1.65)	122 (5.9)	28.5 (1.95)	28.5 (1.52)	26.8 (1.63)	45 (3.1)
At least some college	74.3 (3.04)	69.2 (3.32)	66.2 (3.16)	33 (2.8)	56.1 (3.67)	53.2 (3.56)	53.2 (2.91)	27 (2.3)	22.8 (3.16)	19.0 (3.58)	19.6 (3.05)	7 (1.2)
Hispanic, all education levels	64.4 (0.77)	64.5 (0.68)	64.4 (0.66)	456 (8.3)	51.7 (0.81)	51.7 (0.73)	52.1 (0.80)	370 (8.3)	19.1 (0.81)	19.9 (0.75)	18.9 (0.78)	86 (3.6)
Less than high school completion	50.6 (1.47)	52.1 (1.48)	48.7 (1.52)	97 (4.4)	39.1 (1.50)	39.1 (1.45)	38.1 (1.55)	74 (3.6)	24.7 (2.03)	24.9 (1.71)	24.0 (2.15)	23 (2.5)
High school completion[4]	70.7 (0.91)	69.1 (0.76)	70.2 (0.93)	304 (7.0)	55.6 (0.93)	55.6 (0.85)	57.1 (1.02)	248 (7.0)	17.9 (0.99)	19.5 (0.93)	18.6 (0.93)	57 (2.8)
At least some college	70.8 (2.12)	73.2 (1.97)	73.0 (1.96)	54 (2.8)	64.4 (2.16)	64.4 (2.06)	64.6 (2.09)	48 (2.7)	14.1 (1.90)	12.0 (1.74)	11.6 (1.61)	6 (0.9)
Asian, all education levels	58.6 (3.14)	48.9 (3.06)	58.6 (2.86)	28 (2.0)	39.2 (3.25)	39.2 (2.96)	47.0 (3.01)	22 (1.8)	14.5 (3.17)	19.8 (3.24)	19.8 (3.33)	5 (1.0)
Less than high school completion	40.7 (5.06)	29.2 (5.42)	46.2 (5.22)	5 (0.9)	21.1 (5.41)	21.1 (5.17)	42.8 (5.32)	5 (0.9)	18.3! (6.73)	27.8! (8.64)	7.3! (2.99)	#!
High school completion[4]	64.0 (3.71)	53.8 (3.98)	63.8 (3.98)	16 (1.7)	42.7 (3.99)	42.7 (4.05)	48.4 (4.02)	13 (1.4)	11.6 (3.44)	20.6 (4.50)	7.3! (4.51)	4 (0.9)
At least some college	66.0 (6.86)	59.2 (7.23)	59.7 (6.82)	6 (1.1)	51.1 (7.22)	51.1 (7.26)	48.2 (7.57)	5 (1.0)	20.2! (7.51)	13.7! (4.97)	19.3! (8.22)	1! (0.5)
American Indian/Alaska Native, all education levels	53.6 (3.72)	52.5 (3.74)	52.6 (3.77)	16 (1.5)	39.6 (3.40)	39.6 (3.51)	38.6 (3.80)	11 (1.4)	27.3 (3.59)	24.5 (3.31)	26.6 (4.88)	4 (0.8)
Less than high school completion	30.8 (4.76)	37.2 (5.79)	43.6 (5.48)	4 (0.7)	25.3 (3.61)	25.3 (5.79)	28.8 (6.47)	3 (0.7)	41.6 (8.34)	32.1 (7.92)	33.9! (10.25)	1 (0.4)
High school completion[4]	65.4 (3.83)	62.4 (4.54)	55.8 (5.07)	10 (1.2)	48.0 (4.27)	40.4 (4.05)	40.4 (4.90)	7 (1.0)	25.0 (4.55)	23.0 (4.67)	27.6 (6.34)	3! (0.7)
At least some college	57.7 (7.60)	59.2 (9.33)	59.4 (9.12)	2 (0.4)	50.8 (7.86)	50.8 (8.91)	55.8 (8.80)	2 (0.4)	20.5! (9.95)	‡ (†)	‡ (†)	‡ (†)
20 to 24 years old												
All persons, all education levels	82.2 (0.16)	82.2 (0.16)	82.5 (0.16)	10,283 (35.8)	72.9 (0.18)	73.6 (0.19)	74.6 (0.17)	9,299 (34.0)	11.3 (0.14)	10.4 (0.13)	9.6 (0.13)	984 (13.6)
Less than high school completion	64.4 (0.55)	63.3 (0.55)	63.6 (0.54)	899 (14.3)	50.7 (0.57)	51.3 (0.59)	52.8 (0.59)	746 (13.0)	21.4 (0.56)	19.0 (0.63)	17.0 (0.61)	153 (6.0)
High school completion[4]	79.9 (0.27)	79.2 (0.27)	79.8 (0.27)	4,273 (30.7)	69.1 (0.31)	70.5 (0.29)	70.5 (0.29)	3,774 (29.3)	13.5 (0.25)	12.9 (0.20)	11.7 (0.22)	499 (9.8)
Some college, no degree	86.2 (0.29)	86.6 (0.24)	86.6 (0.24)	2,538 (22.2)	78.6 (0.35)	79.8 (0.27)	79.8 (0.31)	2,338 (21.6)	8.8 (0.24)	8.1 (0.25)	7.9 (0.22)	200 (5.8)
Associate's degree	90.9 (0.57)	90.4 (0.45)	90.3 (0.49)	585 (9.5)	85.8 (0.65)	85.7 (0.55)	85.7 (0.59)	555 (9.6)	5.6 (0.43)	4.7 (0.36)	5.1 (0.42)	30 (2.5)
Bachelor's or higher degree	93.5 (0.24)	94.0 (0.24)	93.9 (0.21)	1,987 (19.4)	88.0 (0.32)	89.0 (0.30)	89.0 (0.27)	1,885 (18.9)	5.9 (0.21)	5.8 (0.21)	5.2 (0.20)	103 (4.1)

See notes at end of table.

Table 501.20. Labor force participation, employment, and unemployment of persons 16 to 24 years old who are not enrolled in school, by age group, sex, race/ethnicity, and educational attainment: 2015, 2016, and 2018—Continued

[Standard errors appear in parentheses]

Age group, sex, race/ethnicity, and educational attainment	Labor force participation rate[1] 2016	2017	2018	Number of participants (in thousands) 2018	Employment to population ratio[2] 2016	2017	2018	Number employed (in thousands) 2018	Unemployment rate[3] 2016	2017	2018	Number unemployed (in thousands) 2018
1	2	3	4	5	6	7	8	9	10	11	12	13
Male, all education levels	83.7 (0.18)	83.9 (0.18)	84.0 (0.22)	5,603 (25.7)	73.8 (0.24)	74.5 (0.22)	75.4 (0.22)	5,031 (23.5)	11.8 (0.20)	11.1 (0.16)	10.2 (0.16)	572 (9.6)
Less than high school completion	68.2 (0.66)	67.1 (0.63)	68.3 (0.64)	580 (11.0)	54.8 (0.69)	55.0 (0.71)	57.1 (0.74)	485 (10.1)	19.8 (0.64)	18.0 (0.75)	16.4 (0.72)	95 (4.5)
High school completion[4]	82.6 (0.31)	82.5 (0.27)	82.1 (0.32)	2,550 (22.8)	71.6 (0.38)	71.8 (0.34)	72.6 (0.35)	2,253 (21.5)	13.3 (0.31)	13.0 (0.25)	11.6 (0.25)	297 (6.7)
Some college, no degree	87.9 (0.34)	88.5 (0.35)	88.8 (0.38)	1,328 (16.9)	79.8 (0.44)	81.3 (0.40)	81.6 (0.46)	1,219 (16.2)	9.2 (0.31)	8.1 (0.36)	8.2 (0.33)	109 (4.6)
Associate's degree	93.7 (0.58)	93.6 (0.56)	92.6 (0.59)	287 (6.5)	88.2 (0.85)	88.5 (0.74)	87.2 (0.75)	271 (6.3)	5.9 (0.63)	5.4 (0.53)	5.8 (0.64)	17 (1.9)
Bachelor's or higher degree	94.1 (0.36)	94.5 (0.36)	94.3 (0.35)	857 (13.5)	87.7 (0.47)	87.4 (0.50)	88.3 (0.40)	802 (12.4)	6.9 (0.35)	7.5 (0.40)	6.4 (0.33)	55 (3.1)
Female, all education levels	80.5 (0.23)	80.2 (0.23)	80.7 (0.22)	4,680 (24.0)	71.9 (0.24)	72.5 (0.27)	73.6 (0.25)	4,268 (23.5)	10.6 (0.19)	9.6 (0.19)	8.8 (0.17)	412 (8.4)
Less than high school completion	58.4 (0.93)	57.6 (0.94)	56.4 (1.03)	319 (9.0)	44.1 (0.95)	45.6 (0.88)	46.2 (0.99)	261 (7.8)	24.4 (1.04)	20.8 (0.91)	18.0 (0.96)	57 (3.6)
High school completion[4]	76.1 (0.40)	74.7 (0.44)	76.6 (0.43)	1,723 (17.0)	65.6 (0.44)	65.1 (0.46)	67.6 (0.48)	1,521 (15.9)	13.7 (0.41)	12.9 (0.33)	11.7 (0.35)	202 (6.5)
Some college, no degree	84.4 (0.42)	84.6 (0.41)	84.3 (0.37)	1,210 (12.4)	77.3 (0.52)	77.8 (0.45)	77.9 (0.41)	1,119 (12.0)	8.4 (0.36)	8.1 (0.35)	7.5 (0.34)	91 (4.3)
Associate's degree	88.6 (0.81)	87.8 (0.68)	88.3 (0.81)	298 (6.8)	83.9 (0.93)	84.2 (0.71)	84.4 (0.96)	285 (6.7)	5.3 (0.59)	4.4 (0.40)	4.4 (0.56)	13 (1.7)
Bachelor's or higher degree	93.0 (0.32)	93.7 (0.28)	93.5 (0.26)	1,131 (14.3)	88.2 (0.41)	89.5 (0.37)	89.6 (0.34)	1,083 (14.3)	5.2 (0.26)	4.5 (0.26)	4.2 (0.24)	48 (2.7)
White, all education levels	84.8 (0.20)	85.2 (0.19)	85.4 (0.20)	5,615 (25.6)	77.1 (0.25)	77.8 (0.24)	78.9 (0.20)	5,186 (25.3)	9.1 (0.18)	8.7 (0.16)	7.6 (0.15)	429 (8.6)
Less than high school completion	65.6 (0.81)	63.8 (0.87)	64.1 (0.74)	361 (7.9)	51.1 (0.96)	51.7 (0.86)	53.6 (0.77)	302 (7.2)	22.1 (1.07)	18.9 (0.85)	16.3 (0.89)	59 (3.5)
High school completion[4]	81.3 (0.36)	82.2 (0.32)	82.2 (0.33)	2,203 (18.7)	72.1 (0.40)	72.6 (0.40)	74.3 (0.36)	1,990 (18.1)	11.3 (0.30)	11.5 (0.28)	9.6 (0.26)	212 (5.9)
Some college, no degree	87.3 (0.35)	88.1 (0.27)	88.0 (0.32)	1,309 (14.4)	81.3 (0.41)	82.5 (0.34)	82.5 (0.35)	1,227 (14.3)	6.9 (0.27)	6.4 (0.28)	6.2 (0.30)	82 (4.0)
Associate's degree	93.0 (0.61)	92.2 (0.51)	91.6 (0.52)	374 (7.5)	88.6 (0.84)	88.2 (0.57)	88.4 (0.64)	361 (7.6)	5.0 (0.56)	3.9 (0.38)	3.6 (0.42)	14 (1.6)
Bachelor's or higher degree	95.0 (0.29)	95.2 (0.27)	95.5 (0.20)	1,368 (16.9)	90.4 (0.37)	90.6 (0.35)	91.2 (0.20)	1,306 (16.4)	4.9 (0.20)	4.8 (0.24)	4.5 (0.24)	62 (3.4)
Black, all education levels	77.1 (0.48)	76.0 (0.49)	75.4 (0.44)	1,419 (14.9)	62.9 (0.51)	62.2 (0.56)	62.4 (0.52)	1,175 (13.5)	18.5 (0.45)	18.2 (0.51)	17.2 (0.51)	244 (8.0)
Less than high school completion	53.5 (1.43)	51.2 (1.41)	50.3 (1.68)	121 (5.8)	33.8 (1.45)	33.8 (1.49)	33.6 (1.52)	81 (4.4)	34.1 (1.82)	34.1 (2.13)	33.3 (2.10)	40 (3.3)
High school completion[4]	76.1 (0.74)	73.7 (0.66)	72.8 (0.80)	664 (11.9)	60.0 (0.91)	58.8 (0.85)	58.7 (0.86)	535 (11.0)	21.1 (0.78)	20.2 (0.79)	19.3 (0.79)	128 (5.6)
Some college, no degree	85.9 (0.76)	84.8 (0.79)	85.5 (0.86)	424 (9.0)	74.3 (0.98)	72.5 (0.86)	74.3 (1.03)	368 (8.8)	13.5 (0.83)	14.6 (0.80)	13.1 (0.74)	56 (3.2)
Associate's degree	84.1 (2.28)	87.5 (1.87)	87.7 (1.58)	64 (3.9)	79.9 (2.48)	75.4 (2.28)	75.4 (2.57)	55 (3.8)	9.5 (1.90)	8.6 (1.78)	14.1 (2.45)	9 (1.6)
Bachelor's or higher degree	92.1 (1.05)	93.1 (0.96)	90.5 (0.99)	146 (5.8)	84.0 (1.25)	84.0 (1.44)	84.0 (1.23)	136 (5.5)	9.0 (1.01)	9.7 (1.15)	7.2 (1.04)	10 (1.6)
Hispanic, all education levels	80.6 (0.34)	80.3 (0.28)	81.3 (0.29)	2,453 (17.9)	72.6 (0.39)	72.6 (0.32)	73.7 (0.33)	2,224 (17.9)	11.6 (0.31)	9.6 (0.26)	9.3 (0.24)	228 (5.9)
Less than high school completion	69.3 (0.85)	69.6 (0.91)	69.7 (0.93)	354 (8.6)	60.1 (0.94)	60.1 (0.91)	61.4 (1.05)	312 (8.7)	13.6 (0.83)	13.6 (0.88)	11.9 (0.72)	42 (2.5)
High school completion[4]	80.6 (0.46)	78.7 (0.49)	80.7 (0.51)	1,145 (14.8)	70.5 (0.56)	70.4 (0.48)	72.2 (0.48)	1,025 (14.7)	12.6 (0.46)	10.5 (0.35)	10.5 (0.44)	121 (5.1)
Some college, no degree	85.1 (0.51)	85.6 (0.59)	85.1 (0.57)	621 (10.5)	79.1 (0.66)	79.1 (0.73)	79.4 (0.73)	576 (10.4)	9.3 (0.59)	7.5 (0.55)	7.4 (0.46)	46 (2.9)
Associate's degree	90.1 (1.09)	88.1 (1.40)	90.1 (1.12)	110 (5.2)	83.6 (1.28)	83.6 (1.66)	85.6 (1.28)	105 (5.0)	5.8 (1.01)	5.2 (0.96)	5.0 (0.80)	6 (0.9)
Bachelor's or higher degree	91.1 (0.93)	93.5 (0.66)	90.9 (0.84)	222 (6.8)	83.7 (1.15)	87.9 (0.88)	85.2 (1.08)	208 (6.6)	8.1 (0.89)	6.0 (0.67)	6.3 (0.81)	14 (1.8)
Asian, all education levels	80.1 (0.91)	81.7 (0.73)	82.6 (0.65)	351 (8.3)	72.4 (1.05)	74.8 (0.84)	76.5 (0.76)	325 (8.2)	9.6 (0.59)	8.4 (0.68)	7.4 (0.58)	26 (2.0)
Less than high school completion	67.9 (2.88)	62.7 (3.54)	67.9 (3.41)	20 (2.0)	58.9 (2.98)	55.5 (3.63)	60.9 (3.30)	17 (1.8)	13.2 (2.70)	11.5! (4.21)	10.7 (2.46)	2 (0.5)
High school completion[4]	76.1 (1.92)	76.1 (1.56)	76.5 (1.75)	74 (4.0)	68.7 (1.99)	68.7 (1.86)	69.4 (1.91)	68 (3.5)	8.9 (1.22)	10.3 (1.29)	9.2 (1.49)	7 (1.3)
Some college, no degree	77.5 (2.04)	80.2 (1.68)	80.1 (1.77)	62 (3.5)	72.8 (2.30)	75.3 (1.90)	74.5 (1.78)	57 (3.4)	11.7 (1.64)	6.1 (1.16)	7.0 (1.06)	4 (0.7)
Associate's degree	77.0 (4.25)	87.8 (3.02)	80.5 (3.76)	15 (1.5)	85.8 (4.32)	77.0 (3.23)	77.0 (4.25)	14 (1.5)	‡ (3.10)	9.8! (†)	‡ (†)	‡
Bachelor's or higher degree	86.0 (1.21)	87.5 (0.88)	88.8 (1.01)	180 (5.5)	79.9 (1.30)	82.9 (0.95)	82.9 (1.23)	168 (5.3)	7.1 (0.85)	5.3 (0.92)	6.7 (0.77)	12 (1.4)
American Indian/Alaska Native, all education levels	70.0 (1.34)	66.4 (1.59)	66.6 (1.63)	73 (3.3)	53.5 (1.57)	55.2 (1.89)	54.4 (1.74)	59 (2.9)	23.5 (1.70)	16.9 (1.75)	18.3 (1.98)	13 (1.6)
Less than high school completion	55.2 (3.79)	45.1 (4.12)	45.9 (4.69)	9 (1.2)	32.3 (3.86)	32.5 (4.44)	31.4 (4.61)	6 (1.0)	41.6 (5.16)	28.0 (5.48)	31.6 (5.87)	3 (0.6)
High school completion[4]	67.8 (2.10)	66.9 (2.03)	66.3 (2.36)	37 (2.0)	49.7 (2.24)	54.0 (2.22)	53.6 (2.42)	30 (2.2)	26.6 (2.42)	19.2 (2.62)	14.9 (2.69)	7 (1.1)
Some college, no degree	70.8 (3.00)	75.1 (3.05)	76.9 (2.83)	21 (2.0)	69.7 (3.43)	65.9 (3.00)	65.4 (3.85)	18 (1.8)	13.6 (2.55)	12.3 (2.39)	14.9 (4.09)	3 (0.9)
Associate's degree	82.9 (6.08)	76.2 (6.89)	81.6 (8.38)	2 (0.5)	82.9 (6.08)	71.7 (7.75)	69.3 (8.88)	2 (0.4)	‡ (†)	‡ (†)	15.0! (6.39)	‡
Bachelor's or higher degree	93.4 (4.37)	81.1 (7.52)	84.4 (6.83)	4 (0.6)	75.8 (8.72)	79.0 (7.85)	83.5 (6.91)	4 (0.6)	18.8! (8.63)	‡ (†)	‡ (†)	‡

†Not applicable.
#Rounds to zero.
!Interpret data with caution. The coefficient of variation (CV) for this estimate is between 30 and 50 percent.
‡Reporting standards not met. Either there are too few cases for a reliable estimate or the coefficient of variation (CV) is 50 percent or greater.
[1]Percentage of the civilian population who are employed or seeking employment.
[2]Number of persons employed as a percentage of the civilian population.
[3]The percentage of persons in the civilian labor force who are not working and who made specific efforts to find employment sometime during the prior 4 weeks.
[4]Includes equivalency credentials, such as the GED credential.
NOTE: Table excludes persons enrolled in school. Estimates are for all nonenrolled civilians in the given age range, including persons living in households and persons living in group quarters (e.g., residential treatment centers or correctional facilities). Race categories exclude persons of Hispanic ethnicity. Totals include racial/ethnic groups not separately shown. Detail may not sum to totals because of rounding.
SOURCE: U.S. Department of Commerce, Census Bureau, American Community Survey (ACS), 2016, 2017, and 2018. (This table was prepared May 2020.)

Table 501.30. Percentage and number of persons 18 to 24 years old who were neither enrolled in school nor working, by age group, high school completion status, sex, and race/ethnicity: Selected years, 2006 through 2018

[Standard errors appear in parentheses]

Age group, high school completion status, sex, and race/ethnicity	Percent who were neither enrolled in school nor working 2006	2008	2009	2010	2011	2012	2013	2014	2015	2016	2017	2018 Number (in thousands) — Total, all persons 18 to 24 years old	2018 Number (in thousands) — Neither enrolled in school nor working	2018 Percent who were neither enrolled in school nor working
1	2	3	4	5	6	7	8	9	10	11	12	13	14	15
18 to 24 years old, all persons	15.4 (0.07)	15.2 (0.08)	17.6 (0.09)	17.9 (0.09)	17.7 (0.08)	17.1 (0.08)	16.7 (0.11)	15.9 (0.09)	14.8 (0.09)	14.1 (0.09)	13.9 (0.10)	30,648 (33.6)	4,125 (28.5)	13.5 (0.09)
Male	14.5 (0.10)	14.8 (0.12)	18.1 (0.15)	18.5 (0.12)	18.3 (0.12)	17.6 (0.11)	17.1 (0.14)	16.1 (0.14)	15.2 (0.13)	14.6 (0.12)	14.3 (0.12)	15,710 (23.3)	2,180 (20.1)	13.9 (0.12)
Female	16.4 (0.12)	15.6 (0.13)	17.0 (0.12)	17.2 (0.12)	17.1 (0.11)	16.6 (0.13)	16.3 (0.14)	15.7 (0.12)	14.5 (0.13)	13.6 (0.12)	13.4 (0.13)	14,938 (18.9)	1,945 (17.8)	13.0 (0.11)
White	11.8 (0.08)	11.7 (0.11)	13.8 (0.11)	14.1 (0.10)	14.1 (0.11)	13.5 (0.12)	13.5 (0.12)	12.9 (0.09)	12.1 (0.11)	11.6 (0.12)	11.3 (0.13)	16,286 (11.5)	1,792 (15.3)	11.0 (0.09)
Black	25.3 (0.31)	25.0 (0.30)	27.3 (0.31)	28.9 (0.29)	27.4 (0.28)	27.2 (0.30)	26.2 (0.30)	24.9 (0.30)	22.6 (0.31)	20.9 (0.31)	21.6 (0.32)	4,345 (22.1)	912 (15.2)	21.0 (0.32)
Hispanic	20.9 (0.21)	20.4 (0.24)	22.8 (0.22)	22.6 (0.23)	22.0 (0.22)	21.2 (0.22)	19.8 (0.26)	18.4 (0.24)	17.5 (0.21)	16.6 (0.22)	16.1 (0.18)	6,873 (14.9)	1,065 (13.2)	15.5 (0.19)
Asian	9.1 (0.35)	7.7 (0.30)	9.9 (0.38)	9.4 (0.30)	9.0 (0.32)	8.6 (0.27)	9.0 (0.31)	8.7 (0.30)	8.2 (0.28)	7.6 (0.26)	7.4 (0.23)	1,731 (11.6)	120 (4.3)	6.9 (0.24)
Pacific Islander	19.6 (2.51)	20.3 (2.69)	21.3 (2.01)	23.8 (2.37)	23.3 (2.32)	24.2 (2.35)	24.8 (2.34)	23.7 (2.65)	16.8 (2.04)	15.5 (1.99)	19.8 (2.68)	57 (2.9)	12 (1.6)	20.8 (2.48)
American Indian/Alaska Native	30.2 (1.20)	29.0 (1.31)	34.0 (1.17)	34.3 (1.15)	33.3 (1.29)	32.7 (1.07)	33.3 (1.06)	32.1 (1.15)	31.0 (1.10)	32.0 (1.01)	29.2 (1.15)	227 (5.5)	65 (2.9)	28.7 (1.11)
Some other race	16.4 (1.79)	15.6 (1.86)	18.5 (1.99)	18.2 (2.22)	20.9 (2.26)	14.5 (1.60)	13.6 (1.73)	14.1 (1.54)	20.1 (2.07)	13.4 (1.82)	15.0 (1.64)	91 (4.9)	15 (1.7)	16.0 (1.67)
Two or more races	15.0 (0.55)	16.3 (0.56)	20.1 (0.64)	18.0 (0.63)	18.5 (0.60)	16.6 (0.55)	15.4 (0.48)	16.6 (0.52)	14.7 (0.54)	13.7 (0.49)	14.4 (0.43)	1,036 (13.3)	145 (5.4)	14.0 (0.46)
Race/ethnicity by sex														
Male														
White	11.1 (0.12)	11.3 (0.14)	14.3 (0.17)	14.9 (0.13)	14.7 (0.15)	13.9 (0.14)	13.9 (0.16)	12.9 (0.16)	12.3 (0.15)	11.9 (0.16)	11.5 (0.17)	8,372 (8.8)	937 (10.0)	11.2 (0.12)
Black	28.9 (0.42)	29.0 (0.43)	31.5 (0.44)	32.5 (0.43)	31.8 (0.37)	31.1 (0.45)	30.3 (0.44)	28.6 (0.51)	26.5 (0.41)	24.5 (0.38)	25.3 (0.52)	2,198 (14.5)	529 (10.4)	24.1 (0.40)
Hispanic	15.5 (0.31)	15.5 (0.28)	20.5 (0.32)	20.3 (0.33)	19.9 (0.29)	19.5 (0.31)	18.1 (0.30)	16.9 (0.34)	15.9 (0.27)	15.3 (0.28)	15.1 (0.23)	3,544 (11.0)	525 (9.8)	14.8 (0.27)
Asian	9.0 (0.48)	6.8 (0.42)	9.2 (0.49)	9.3 (0.43)	8.6 (0.40)	8.1 (0.40)	8.3 (0.34)	8.1 (0.40)	8.0 (0.36)	7.7 (0.36)	7.3 (0.38)	883 (8.2)	61 (2.8)	7.0 (0.32)
Pacific Islander	18.0 (3.32)	17.2 (3.43)	17.4 (2.85)	23.0 (2.89)	19.8 (2.67)	23.6 (3.79)	28.8 (2.85)	17.9 (3.23)	10.4 (1.89)	13.5 (2.56)	19.0 (3.20)	29 (2.0)	6 (1.1)	21.3 (3.43)
American Indian/Alaska Native	29.8 (1.63)	29.0 (1.63)	35.7 (1.89)	36.6 (1.77)	35.2 (1.71)	34.1 (1.50)	34.7 (1.44)	33.0 (1.68)	32.0 (1.46)	34.9 (1.81)	28.1 (1.76)	113 (3.1)	31 (1.6)	26.9 (1.24)
Some other race	15.0 (2.32)	16.1 (2.47)	19.7 (2.91)	19.0 (2.66)	18.1 (2.72)	14.8 (2.17)	16.0 (2.22)	13.0 (2.34)	21.1 (3.11)	16.6 (2.69)	14.5 (2.10)	43 (3.0)	8 (1.2)	18.2 (2.58)
Two or more races	15.4 (0.76)	16.8 (0.85)	21.8 (1.02)	19.4 (0.83)	20.5 (0.83)	18.7 (0.82)	16.1 (0.72)	16.3 (0.74)	15.7 (0.83)	15.2 (0.75)	15.3 (0.63)	526 (9.3)	82 (4.5)	15.6 (0.73)
Female														
White	12.5 (0.12)	12.0 (0.15)	13.2 (0.15)	13.4 (0.15)	13.6 (0.15)	13.0 (0.15)	13.2 (0.17)	13.0 (0.13)	11.9 (0.14)	11.3 (0.14)	11.0 (0.16)	7,914 (7.6)	855 (9.9)	10.8 (0.12)
Black	21.6 (0.43)	21.6 (0.41)	22.9 (0.42)	23.4 (0.39)	23.0 (0.36)	23.3 (0.40)	22.1 (0.39)	21.1 (0.38)	18.6 (0.37)	17.2 (0.37)	17.8 (0.36)	2,147 (12.5)	383 (9.7)	17.9 (0.45)
Hispanic	27.3 (0.33)	24.9 (0.37)	25.4 (0.33)	25.2 (0.30)	24.2 (0.34)	23.1 (0.31)	21.8 (0.40)	20.1 (0.35)	19.2 (0.31)	18.1 (0.30)	17.1 (0.29)	3,329 (9.8)	540 (9.0)	16.2 (0.26)
Asian	9.2 (0.47)	8.7 (0.42)	10.6 (0.51)	9.6 (0.41)	9.4 (0.45)	9.2 (0.41)	9.7 (0.45)	9.3 (0.43)	8.3 (0.40)	7.5 (0.38)	7.6 (0.30)	849 (8.2)	58 (3.0)	6.8 (0.35)
Pacific Islander	21.5 (3.59)	23.5 (3.68)	25.8 (3.18)	24.7 (3.17)	28.6 (3.76)	26.2 (3.11)	23.0 (3.17)	30.6 (4.17)	22.6 (3.27)	17.6 (2.77)	20.8 (3.29)	28 (3.0)	6 (1.0)	20.3 (3.35)
American Indian/Alaska Native	30.6 (1.56)	29.0 (1.76)	32.3 (1.65)	31.9 (1.51)	31.3 (1.65)	31.2 (2.42)	31.9 (2.20)	31.2 (2.36)	30.0 (1.61)	28.9 (1.46)	30.3 (1.33)	113 (3.9)	34 (2.2)	30.4 (1.65)
Some other race	18.1 (2.45)	15.1 (2.84)	17.1 (2.82)	17.5 (3.21)	23.5 (3.24)	14.1 (2.20)	11.4 (2.42)	15.3 (2.36)	19.1 (2.85)	10.2 (2.36)	10.2 (2.58)	48 (3.5)	7 (1.2)	13.9 (2.06)
Two or more races	14.6 (0.84)	15.9 (0.79)	18.3 (0.92)	16.5 (0.88)	16.7 (0.84)	14.5 (0.68)	14.7 (0.61)	16.9 (0.61)	13.8 (0.68)	12.1 (0.63)	12.1 (0.67)	510 (9.5)	63 (3.2)	12.3 (0.60)
18 and 19 years old, all persons	11.8 (0.15)	12.1 (0.14)	13.8 (0.15)	13.9 (0.16)	13.5 (0.16)	13.0 (0.15)	12.5 (0.18)	11.6 (0.15)	11.1 (0.13)	10.5 (0.16)	10.8 (0.15)	8,870 (28.7)	960 (13.5)	10.8 (0.14)
20 to 24 years old, all persons	16.9 (0.09)	16.5 (0.10)	19.1 (0.10)	19.6 (0.11)	19.4 (0.10)	18.7 (0.11)	18.3 (0.12)	17.6 (0.11)	16.3 (0.12)	15.5 (0.11)	15.1 (0.12)	21,778 (35.4)	3,166 (23.3)	14.5 (0.10)
Male	15.5 (0.13)	15.7 (0.13)	19.4 (0.17)	20.0 (0.15)	19.6 (0.16)	18.9 (0.14)	18.5 (0.16)	17.4 (0.17)	16.3 (0.17)	15.7 (0.15)	15.2 (0.15)	11,154 (23.9)	1,638 (15.7)	14.7 (0.14)
Female	18.4 (0.13)	17.4 (0.16)	18.9 (0.15)	19.2 (0.16)	19.3 (0.14)	18.5 (0.17)	18.2 (0.16)	17.7 (0.16)	16.2 (0.17)	15.3 (0.14)	15.0 (0.16)	10,624 (23.1)	1,528 (16.2)	14.4 (0.15)
White	13.0 (0.10)	12.8 (0.13)	15.2 (0.14)	15.5 (0.14)	15.6 (0.14)	14.9 (0.13)	15.0 (0.15)	14.3 (0.12)	13.4 (0.12)	12.9 (0.14)	12.5 (0.15)	11,664 (16.3)	1,386 (13.2)	11.9 (0.11)
Black	28.0 (0.37)	27.6 (0.35)	30.1 (0.34)	31.2 (0.37)	30.5 (0.33)	30.1 (0.41)	28.6 (0.37)	27.8 (0.36)	24.9 (0.38)	24.1 (0.32)	23.7 (0.39)	3,083 (18.7)	708 (12.4)	23.0 (0.36)
Hispanic	22.4 (0.25)	21.6 (0.26)	24.5 (0.26)	24.5 (0.25)	23.8 (0.25)	21.4 (0.31)	21.4 (0.31)	19.8 (0.28)	18.8 (0.26)	18.1 (0.27)	17.1 (0.22)	4,826 (15.9)	794 (11.1)	16.4 (0.23)
Asian	10.4 (0.43)	9.1 (0.38)	11.4 (0.47)	10.8 (0.38)	10.3 (0.42)	10.2 (0.32)	10.4 (0.39)	10.1 (0.40)	9.5 (0.36)	9.0 (0.35)	8.3 (0.31)	1,243 (11.2)	100 (3.5)	8.0 (0.27)
Pacific Islander	22.2 (2.95)	22.2 (2.99)	24.5 (2.60)	26.2 (2.88)	27.8 (2.88)	26.5 (2.81)	26.5 (2.59)	22.3 (3.23)	19.8 (2.44)	16.6 (2.52)	20.2 (3.23)	40 (2.7)	9 (1.4)	21.5 (3.07)
American Indian/Alaska Native	32.9 (1.54)	31.9 (1.45)	36.9 (1.32)	37.2 (1.45)	36.4 (1.49)	34.3 (1.25)	36.5 (1.37)	36.5 (1.37)	33.3 (1.41)	35.2 (1.31)	31.6 (1.52)	156 (4.8)	50 (2.1)	31.9 (1.43)
Some other race	18.0 (2.26)	16.8 (2.45)	20.5 (2.71)	18.1 (2.74)	24.7 (2.73)	13.6 (1.85)	13.9 (2.01)	15.5 (1.84)	19.6 (2.39)	14.6 (2.23)	15.0 (1.63)	66 (4.3)	11 (1.7)	16.7 (2.15)
Two or more races	16.0 (0.70)	17.8 (0.71)	23.0 (0.78)	20.9 (0.90)	21.1 (0.80)	18.2 (0.68)	17.6 (0.71)	19.1 (0.72)	16.2 (0.71)	15.0 (0.58)	16.2 (0.62)	701 (10.4)	109 (4.3)	15.6 (0.55)
Has completed high school,[1] all persons	13.1 (0.09)	12.8 (0.11)	15.3 (0.11)	15.8 (0.12)	15.9 (0.09)	15.4 (0.12)	15.2 (0.13)	14.8 (0.11)	13.7 (0.11)	13.1 (0.11)	12.9 (0.11)	20,142 (35.4)	2,497 (20.1)	12.4 (0.11)
Male	12.0 (0.14)	12.1 (0.15)	15.6 (0.17)	16.1 (0.16)	16.2 (0.15)	15.4 (0.15)	15.4 (0.16)	14.7 (0.16)	13.7 (0.15)	13.2 (0.15)	12.9 (0.13)	10,175 (25.2)	1,273 (13.9)	12.5 (0.13)
Female	14.2 (0.14)	13.5 (0.16)	14.9 (0.15)	15.4 (0.16)	15.6 (0.14)	15.2 (0.17)	15.0 (0.16)	14.9 (0.15)	13.8 (0.15)	13.0 (0.15)	12.9 (0.16)	9,967 (22.5)	1,224 (14.8)	12.3 (0.14)

See notes at end of table.

Table 501.30. Percentage and number of persons 18 to 24 years old who were neither enrolled in school nor working, by age group, high school completion status, sex, and race/ethnicity: Selected years, 2006 through 2018—Continued

[Standard errors appear in parentheses]

Age group, high school completion status, sex, and race/ethnicity	Percent who were neither enrolled in school nor working											2018 — Number (in thousands)		2018
	2006	2008	2009	2010	2011	2012	2013	2014	2015	2016	2017	Total, all persons 18 to 24 years old	Neither enrolled in school nor working	Percent who were neither enrolled in school nor working
1	2	3	4	5	6	7	8	9	10	11	12	13	14	15
White	10.5 (0.10)	10.3 (0.13)	12.6 (0.14)	12.9 (0.13)	13.0 (0.13)	12.6 (0.13)	12.8 (0.15)	12.4 (0.11)	11.5 (0.12)	11.0 (0.13)	10.7 (0.14)	11,028 (19.2)	1,125 (11.4)	10.2 (0.10)
Black	21.8 (0.41)	21.6 (0.34)	24.1 (0.35)	25.1 (0.40)	24.8 (0.32)	24.9 (0.41)	23.5 (0.38)	23.4 (0.39)	21.1 (0.40)	19.5 (0.37)	20.4 (0.38)	2,787 (18.4)	548 (10.7)	19.7 (0.35)
Hispanic	17.4 (0.26)	16.4 (0.27)	19.0 (0.27)	19.5 (0.29)	19.8 (0.25)	18.5 (0.27)	17.7 (0.32)	16.4 (0.28)	15.8 (0.25)	15.2 (0.29)	14.7 (0.23)	4,248 (15.5)	598 (9.7)	14.1 (0.22)
Asian	9.1 (0.39)	8.3 (0.40)	10.0 (0.44)	9.4 (0.37)	9.1 (0.41)	8.9 (0.32)	9.5 (0.37)	8.9 (0.37)	8.5 (0.33)	8.2 (0.35)	7.5 (0.28)	1,203 (11.0)	88 (3.3)	7.3 (0.27)
Pacific Islander	17.6 (3.08)	20.4 (3.31)	19.4 (2.61)	24.8 (3.04)	25.0 (2.82)	22.4 (2.72)	18.8 (2.67)	17.6 (3.34)	17.7 (2.36)	15.8 (2.68)	19.2 (3.40)	36 (2.4)	6 (1.1)	17.2 (2.70)
American Indian/Alaska Native	25.7 (1.67)	26.0 (1.45)	29.2 (1.45)	29.6 (1.43)	30.9 (1.71)	29.6 (1.26)	32.9 (1.52)	32.0 (1.40)	27.9 (1.56)	30.8 (1.35)	28.0 (1.47)	135 (4.4)	37 (2.2)	27.4 (1.37)
Some other race	13.7 (2.10)	14.6 (2.53)	17.8 (2.61)	14.2 (2.62)	19.6 (2.59)	12.8 (1.89)	12.2 (1.94)	11.4 (1.80)	17.9 (2.47)	11.9 (1.89)	12.4 (1.55)	62 (4.2)	9 (1.6)	15.2 (2.25)
Two or more races	12.7 (0.72)	14.0 (0.64)	19.6 (0.81)	17.7 (0.93)	17.6 (0.76)	15.6 (0.70)	14.8 (0.69)	16.7 (0.73)	13.6 (0.65)	12.9 (0.57)	14.2 (0.64)	644 (10.1)	86 (4.0)	13.4 (0.57)
Has not completed high school, all persons	41.1 (0.37)	42.8 (0.36)	47.5 (0.35)	47.8 (0.35)	47.9 (0.45)	48.2 (0.39)	46.0 (0.47)	44.8 (0.49)	42.7 (0.48)	42.6 (0.49)	41.6 (0.56)	1,636 (18.2)	668 (10.9)	40.8 (0.53)
Male	34.0 (0.48)	37.0 (0.52)	42.4 (0.47)	43.3 (0.45)	42.3 (0.51)	43.9 (0.58)	41.5 (0.60)	40.3 (0.64)	39.7 (0.55)	39.4 (0.62)	39.0 (0.64)	979 (13.7)	364 (7.8)	37.2 (0.66)
Female	52.1 (0.65)	51.5 (0.61)	55.3 (0.56)	55.0 (0.69)	56.3 (0.74)	54.5 (0.71)	52.9 (0.68)	51.4 (0.63)	47.1 (0.87)	47.6 (0.92)	45.6 (0.87)	657 (11.5)	304 (7.4)	46.3 (0.91)
White	40.0 (0.50)	42.6 (0.61)	48.1 (0.67)	49.2 (0.62)	51.0 (0.68)	48.9 (0.66)	46.4 (0.70)	44.5 (0.79)	42.7 (0.69)	43.0 (0.88)	42.4 (0.79)	636 (10.9)	262 (6.1)	41.1 (0.73)
Black	58.0 (1.10)	58.8 (1.02)	62.1 (0.76)	64.6 (0.67)	63.1 (1.00)	63.3 (0.95)	60.0 (1.02)	58.7 (0.93)	55.9 (1.13)	54.2 (1.35)	54.1 (1.41)	296 (7.6)	160 (6.0)	54.0 (1.45)
Hispanic	34.3 (0.58)	35.5 (0.59)	39.3 (0.54)	39.3 (0.56)	38.1 (0.70)	40.5 (0.79)	38.0 (0.78)	37.1 (0.82)	35.6 (0.83)	36.4 (0.83)	34.5 (0.88)	578 (11.8)	196 (6.4)	33.9 (0.96)
Asian	36.2 (2.49)	26.6 (2.48)	38.3 (2.89)	37.8 (2.66)	32.0 (2.27)	36.4 (3.09)	36.4 (3.26)	38.3 (2.73)	31.7 (2.93)	30.4 (2.63)	30.7 (2.82)	40 (3.0)	11 (1.3)	27.9 (2.53)
Pacific Islander	49.6 (9.53)	36.5 (8.89)	58.9 (7.61)	‡ (†)	48.4 (9.11)	49.2 (10.64)	‡ (†)	56.4 (8.67)	‡ (†)	23.6! (7.13)	34.4! (12.22)	4 (1.0)	‡ (†)	56.0 (11.05)
American Indian/Alaska Native	58.5 (2.96)	53.6 (3.82)	66.9 (3.65)	67.1 (3.02)	58.1 (3.66)	57.6 (3.46)	58.0 (3.15)	58.2 (2.89)	56.1 (3.29)	57.5 (3.56)	56.3 (4.03)	21 (2.0)	13 (1.6)	60.4 (4.55)
Some other race	43.2 (9.41)	29.6 (7.61)	41.1 (8.85)	39.8 (7.57)	61.6 (9.79)	29.2 (7.85)	23.5! (9.79)	‡ (†)	39.6 (11.25)	37.7 (10.56)	45.6 (7.32)	4 (0.9)	‡ (†)	42.8 (10.79)
Two or more races	48.1 (3.32)	53.0 (3.29)	56.5 (3.05)	49.4 (3.46)	56.4 (3.09)	47.1 (2.76)	49.7 (3.22)	50.8 (2.55)	55.2 (3.20)	43.1 (3.19)	43.5 (3.17)	56 (3.3)	23 (2.0)	40.2 (2.70)

†Not applicable.

‡Reporting standards not met. Either there are too few cases for a reliable estimate or the coefficient of variation (CV) is 50 percent or greater.

!Interpret data with caution. The coefficient of variation (CV) for this estimate is between 30 and 50 percent.

¹Includes completing high school through equivalency programs, such as a GED program.

NOTE: Data are based on sample surveys of the entire population in the given age range residing within the United States, including both noninstitutionalized persons (e.g., those living in households, college housing, or military housing located within the United States) and institutionalized persons (e.g., those living in prisons, nursing facilities, or other healthcare facilities). Institutionalized persons made up 1 percent of all 18- to 24-year-olds in 2018. Race categories exclude persons of Hispanic ethnicity. Detail may not sum to totals because of rounding.
SOURCE: U.S. Department of Commerce, Census Bureau, American Community Survey (ACS), 2006 through 2018. (This table was prepared December 2019.)

Table 501.40. Percentage distribution of 25- to 34-year-olds with various levels of educational attainment, by labor force status, sex, race/ethnicity, and U.S. nativity and citizenship status: 2018

[Standard errors appear in parentheses]

Sex, race/ethnicity, and U.S. nativity and citizenship status	All 25- to 34-year-olds — In labor force: Employed	Unemployed (seeking employment)	Not in labor force	Less than high school completion — In labor force: Employed	Unemployed (seeking employment)	Not in labor force	High school completion[1] — In labor force: Employed	Unemployed (seeking employment)	Not in labor force	Some college, no bachelor's degree[2] — In labor force: Employed	Unemployed (seeking employment)	Not in labor force	Bachelor's or higher degree — In labor force: Employed	Unemployed (seeking employment)	Not in labor force
1	2	3	4	5	6	7	8	9	10	11	12	13	14	15	16
Total[3]	79.0 (0.07)	4.2 (0.04)	16.8 (0.06)	56.4 (0.33)	6.9 (0.18)	36.6 (0.32)	71.4 (0.19)	6.0 (0.10)	22.6 (0.16)	80.3 (0.14)	4.4 (0.08)	15.3 (0.12)	88.2 (0.10)	2.3 (0.05)	9.4 (0.09)
Sex															
Male	82.9 (0.11)	4.5 (0.06)	12.6 (0.09)	65.9 (0.44)	6.5 (0.23)	27.6 (0.39)	77.1 (0.25)	5.9 (0.12)	17.0 (0.21)	84.7 (0.22)	4.4 (0.12)	10.9 (0.18)	91.5 (0.13)	2.6 (0.08)	5.9 (0.12)
Female	75.0 (0.10)	4.0 (0.05)	21.0 (0.10)	43.3 (0.44)	7.5 (0.30)	49.1 (0.48)	63.7 (0.28)	6.1 (0.14)	30.2 (0.27)	76.0 (0.17)	4.4 (0.10)	19.6 (0.16)	85.6 (0.14)	2.1 (0.06)	12.4 (0.14)
Race/ethnicity															
White	81.7 (0.10)	3.4 (0.05)	14.8 (0.09)	52.1 (0.63)	7.8 (0.33)	40.1 (0.58)	73.1 (0.25)	5.2 (0.16)	21.8 (0.23)	81.4 (0.18)	3.6 (0.09)	15.0 (0.16)	90.0 (0.11)	1.9 (0.06)	8.1 (0.10)
Black	72.8 (0.24)	7.6 (0.17)	19.6 (0.18)	39.3 (1.04)	11.5 (0.72)	49.2 (0.96)	64.3 (0.52)	9.6 (0.28)	26.1 (0.48)	78.9 (0.46)	7.2 (0.30)	13.9 (0.33)	88.6 (0.40)	3.8 (0.24)	7.6 (0.33)
Hispanic	76.8 (0.17)	4.4 (0.08)	18.8 (0.16)	65.6 (0.50)	4.8 (0.24)	29.6 (0.47)	73.8 (0.32)	5.1 (0.16)	21.0 (0.28)	79.9 (0.32)	4.3 (0.19)	15.7 (0.27)	87.9 (0.40)	2.7 (0.16)	9.4 (0.35)
Asian	77.7 (0.28)	3.2 (0.11)	19.2 (0.28)	61.5 (1.50)	3.5 (0.67)	34.9 (1.39)	71.9 (1.14)	4.1 (0.49)	24.0 (1.13)	76.3 (0.85)	3.6 (0.35)	20.2 (0.75)	80.0 (0.34)	2.9 (0.13)	17.1 (0.34)
Pacific Islander	75.5 (1.84)	4.0 (0.70)	20.5 (1.67)	61.1 (7.05)	‡ (†)	38.8 (7.03)	75.5 (2.81)	4.9! (1.67)	17.6 (2.56)	74.8 (3.57)	2.8! (0.95)	22.4 (3.39)	89.1 (3.29)	‡ (†)	8.9! (2.86)
American Indian/Alaska Native[4]	64.0 (0.88)	7.6 (0.48)	28.4 (1.02)	35.8 (2.93)	12.7 (1.86)	51.5 (2.65)	57.2 (1.58)	9.5 (0.97)	33.3 (1.87)	74.0 (1.41)	5.8 (0.79)	20.2 (1.31)	81.7 (2.54)	2.1! (0.75)	16.0 (2.46)
American Indian	64.9 (0.96)	7.6 (0.55)	27.5 (1.13)	39.4 (3.54)	12.5 (2.14)	48.2 (3.31)	58.7 (1.71)	9.5 (1.11)	33.6 (1.91)	73.5 (1.56)	5.8 (0.78)	20.7 (1.49)	81.8 (2.51)	2.8! (0.94)	15.3 (2.49)
Alaska Native	48.9 (4.01)	12.3 (2.85)	38.8 (3.98)	16.1! (6.05)	16.1! (7.26)	67.7 (8.45)	54.7 (5.63)	11.7 (2.86)	33.6 (5.10)	60.7 (8.38)	‡ (†)	24.7! (8.11)	87.6 (0.65)	‡ (†)	‡ (†)
Two or more races	77.9 (0.54)	5.1 (0.30)	16.9 (0.46)	48.4 (2.91)	11.8 (1.71)	39.8 (2.76)	68.6 (1.25)	7.5 (0.74)	23.9 (1.22)	77.2 (0.94)	5.1 (0.50)	17.7 (0.75)	87.6 (0.65)	3.0 (0.31)	9.4 (0.54)
Race/ethnicity by sex															
Male															
White	85.5 (0.13)	3.8 (0.07)	10.7 (0.12)	60.9 (0.75)	8.1 (0.48)	31.0 (0.68)	79.1 (0.30)	5.2 (0.16)	15.7 (0.28)	86.7 (0.22)	3.6 (0.13)	9.7 (0.20)	92.7 (0.15)	2.3 (0.08)	5.0 (0.13)
Black	70.3 (0.40)	7.8 (0.27)	21.9 (0.36)	35.7 (1.39)	9.5 (0.79)	54.9 (1.24)	62.9 (0.70)	9.5 (0.41)	27.6 (0.39)	79.1 (0.68)	7.4 (0.46)	13.5 (0.50)	88.9 (0.67)	4.4 (0.39)	6.7 (0.59)
Hispanic	84.3 (0.21)	4.3 (0.13)	11.4 (0.18)	80.1 (0.53)	4.3 (0.25)	15.7 (0.47)	82.8 (0.41)	5.0 (0.22)	12.2 (0.28)	85.2 (0.48)	4.2 (0.28)	10.6 (0.38)	91.5 (0.47)	2.9 (0.24)	5.5 (0.37)
Asian	84.8 (0.33)	3.3 (0.16)	11.9 (0.32)	73.9 (2.18)	4.8 (1.18)	21.3 (1.95)	80.0 (1.19)	4.3 (0.61)	15.7 (1.15)	80.0 (1.05)	3.9 (0.44)	16.1 (0.97)	87.8 (0.41)	2.9 (0.21)	9.4 (0.42)
Pacific Islander	83.7 (2.02)	3.0 (0.77)	13.3 (1.76)	66.6 (7.35)	‡ (†)	30.6 (6.82)	86.6 (2.90)	4.9! (1.61)	8.5! (2.64)	83.6 (4.78)	‡ (†)	14.8 (4.55)	90.4 (4.85)	‡ (†)	‡ (†)
American Indian/Alaska Native[4]	65.2 (1.20)	8.0 (0.72)	26.8 (1.33)	40.3 (4.19)	11.1 (2.19)	48.6 (3.90)	59.7 (2.18)	9.6 (1.30)	31.1 (2.28)	78.3 (1.89)	6.9 (1.25)	14.8 (1.57)	79.2 (4.30)	‡ (†)	19.3 (4.33)
American Indian	66.6 (1.40)	8.3 (0.81)	25.0 (1.45)	42.9 (4.78)	11.1 (2.68)	45.4 (4.31)	60.6 (2.40)	9.6 (2.54)	29.7 (2.34)	78.2 (2.09)	7.2 (1.38)	14.7 (1.68)	84.6 (3.54)	‡ (†)	13.4 (3.57)
Alaska Native	51.1 (5.35)	8.3 (2.11)	40.6 (5.45)	17.9! (6.36)	17.1! (5.60)	64.9 (8.34)	58.4 (7.79)	5.8 (7.22)	35.8 (7.22)	‡ (†)	‡ (†)	‡ (†)	‡ (†)	‡ (†)	‡ (†)
Two or more races	80.1 (0.72)	5.8 (0.46)	14.1 (0.62)	52.3 (3.34)	11.2 (2.15)	36.5 (3.18)	73.2 (1.68)	8.1 (1.14)	18.7 (1.51)	80.1 (1.29)	5.6 (0.79)	14.3 (1.09)	89.8 (0.92)	3.4 (0.56)	6.7 (0.82)
Female															
White	77.9 (0.14)	3.1 (0.07)	19.0 (0.14)	40.1 (0.89)	7.4 (0.45)	52.5 (0.84)	64.1 (0.36)	5.2 (0.20)	30.8 (0.37)	76.1 (0.27)	3.6 (0.11)	20.4 (0.26)	87.8 (0.17)	1.6 (0.07)	10.6 (0.17)
Black	75.2 (0.33)	7.4 (0.27)	17.4 (0.27)	44.4 (1.38)	14.4 (1.00)	41.2 (1.36)	66.0 (0.78)	9.8 (0.44)	24.2 (0.69)	77.8 (0.63)	6.9 (0.39)	15.3 (0.41)	88.3 (0.49)	3.5 (0.30)	8.2 (0.40)
Hispanic	68.7 (0.30)	4.4 (0.13)	26.9 (0.29)	45.2 (0.80)	5.5 (0.45)	49.3 (0.83)	62.1 (0.55)	5.3 (0.31)	32.5 (0.53)	75.0 (0.46)	4.4 (0.24)	20.6 (0.46)	85.1 (0.54)	2.4 (0.21)	12.5 (0.50)
Asian	71.0 (0.46)	5.1 (0.19)	23.9 (0.46)	49.2 (2.40)	2.2! (0.79)	48.5 (2.30)	60.8 (1.85)	3.8 (0.70)	35.4 (1.85)	72.5 (1.11)	3.3 (0.50)	24.2 (1.03)	73.1 (0.53)	2.9 (0.22)	24.0 (0.50)
Pacific Islander	66.8 (2.93)	7.2 (0.69)	26.0 (2.79)	30.1! (12.45)	14.6 (3.35)	54.9 (4.49)	53.8 (2.53)	9.6! (1.63)	36.3 (2.82)	66.5 (5.15)	4.3! (1.67)	29.2 (5.03)	88.3 (4.02)	‡ (†)	10.0! (3.61)
American Indian/Alaska Native[4]	62.8 (1.40)	8.3 (0.70)	28.9 (1.42)	35.2 (4.53)	13.3 (3.52)	51.5 (4.49)	56.3 (2.56)	9.9 (1.82)	34.4 (2.75)	70.4 (2.20)	4.9 (1.02)	24.7 (2.01)	83.1 (2.84)	2.6! (1.02)	14.3 (2.57)
American Indian	63.2 (1.42)	8.3 (0.72)	28.4 (1.45)	35.2 (5.35)	‡ (†)	‡ (†)	48.2 (7.29)	9.3 (5.32)	29.9! (10.82)	69.4 (2.38)	4.6 (0.93)	26.0 (2.01)	80.5 (3.25)	3.2! (1.22)	16.3 (3.10)
Alaska Native	46.5 (6.27)	16.7 (4.94)	36.8 (6.69)	‡ (†)	‡ (†)	‡ (†)	63.0 (7.29)	21.9 (5.32)	‡ (†)	54.4 (11.02)	‡ (†)	29.3! (10.82)	‡ (†)	‡ (†)	‡ (†)
Two or more races	75.8 (0.73)	4.5 (0.35)	19.7 (0.70)	41.7 (4.80)	12.8 (2.90)	45.5 (4.91)	63.0 (2.21)	6.7 (1.04)	30.3 (2.08)	74.4 (1.33)	4.6 (0.63)	21.0 (1.12)	85.7 (1.00)	2.6 (0.42)	11.7 (0.83)
Nativity															
Hispanic															
U.S.-born[5]	77.4 (0.22)	5.0 (0.11)	17.6 (0.19)	56.9 (0.81)	7.1 (0.44)	36.0 (0.76)	73.0 (0.42)	6.2 (0.22)	20.8 (0.43)	79.9 (0.39)	4.7 (0.23)	15.4 (0.32)	89.8 (0.43)	2.6 (0.19)	7.5 (0.38)
Foreign-born	75.8 (0.31)	3.2 (0.13)	20.9 (0.29)	70.6 (0.59)	3.5 (0.26)	25.9 (0.55)	75.3 (0.53)	3.3 (0.21)	21.4 (0.51)	79.9 (0.61)	3.2 (0.27)	16.9 (0.59)	83.0 (0.78)	2.7 (0.27)	14.3 (0.75)
Asian															
U.S.-born[5]	83.6 (0.48)	3.5 (0.19)	12.8 (0.44)	51.6 (3.91)	5.2! (1.99)	43.2 (3.65)	72.5 (1.58)	6.0 (0.94)	21.5 (1.50)	80.6 (1.13)	3.8 (0.48)	15.6 (1.03)	87.8 (0.52)	2.9 (0.26)	9.3 (0.47)
Foreign-born	74.6 (0.35)	3.0 (0.15)	22.5 (0.35)	64.0 (1.63)	3.1 (0.69)	32.9 (1.56)	71.6 (1.43)	3.1 (0.46)	25.3 (1.41)	72.8 (1.11)	3.4 (0.46)	23.9 (1.02)	76.2 (0.42)	2.9 (0.16)	20.9 (0.43)
Citizenship status															
U.S.-born citizen	79.7 (0.08)	4.4 (0.04)	15.9 (0.08)	49.8 (0.44)	8.7 (0.25)	41.5 (0.42)	71.0 (0.22)	6.4 (0.11)	22.5 (0.20)	80.7 (0.15)	4.4 (0.07)	14.9 (0.13)	90.3 (0.10)	2.2 (0.06)	7.5 (0.08)
Naturalized citizen	80.7 (0.35)	3.5 (0.17)	15.8 (0.34)	68.2 (1.37)	3.0 (0.44)	28.7 (1.36)	75.0 (0.86)	3.4 (0.34)	21.7 (0.63)	80.3 (0.67)	4.2 (0.33)	15.4 (0.63)	86.4 (0.50)	3.2 (0.25)	10.5 (0.50)
Noncitizen	72.6 (0.25)	3.3 (0.12)	24.1 (0.24)	68.7 (0.52)	3.8 (0.27)	27.5 (0.49)	73.3 (0.48)	3.5 (0.22)	23.2 (0.46)	73.6 (0.72)	3.8 (0.46)	22.6 (0.43)	74.3 (0.43)	2.6 (0.13)	23.2 (0.43)

†Not applicable.
!Interpret data with caution. The coefficient of variation (CV) for this estimate is between 30 and 50 percent.
‡Reporting standards not met. Either there are too few cases for a reliable estimate or the coefficient of variation (CV) is 50 percent or greater.
[1]Data are for all persons with high school completion as their highest level of education, including those with equivalency credentials, such as the GED credential.
[2]Includes persons with no college degree as well as those with an associate's degree.
[3]Total includes other racial/ethnic groups not shown separately.
[4]Includes persons reporting American Indian alone, persons reporting Alaska Native alone, and persons from American Indian and/or Alaska Native tribes specified or not specified.
[5]Includes those born in the 50 states, the District of Columbia, Puerto Rico, American Samoa, Guam, the U.S. Virgin Islands, and the Northern Marianas, as well as those born abroad to U.S.-citizen parents.
NOTE: Estimates are for the entire civilian population in the given age range, including persons living in households and persons living in group quarters (e.g., college residence halls, residential treatment centers, or correctional facilities). The labor force consists of all employed persons plus those seeking employment. Detail may not sum to totals because of rounding. Race categories exclude persons of Hispanic ethnicity.
SOURCE: U.S. Department of Commerce, Census Bureau, American Community Survey (ACS), 2018. (This table was prepared April 2020.)

Table 501.50. Employment to population ratios of persons 16 to 64 years old, by age group and highest level of educational attainment: Selected years, 1975 through 2019

[Standard errors appear in parentheses]

Age group and highest level of educational attainment	1975	1980	1985	1990	1995	2000	2005	2010	2012	2014	2015	2016	2017	2018	2019
1	2	3	4	5	6	7	8	9	10	11	12	13	14	15	16
16 to 19 years old, all education levels[1]	(†)	(†)	(†)	60.8 (2.03)	58.0 (2.13)	62.6 (2.09)	53.7 (1.40)	43.2 (1.30)	45.8 (1.43)	51.0 (1.67)	49.2 (1.36)	50.4 (1.55)	56.4 (1.57)	55.7 (1.48)	57.6 (1.37)
Less than high school completion	(†)	(†)	(†)	44.2 (3.08)	44.0 (3.13)	52.2 (3.19)	39.4 (2.01)	29.4 (1.83)	28.5 (2.05)	39.7 (2.63)	35.3 (2.03)	35.6 (2.05)	39.6 (2.27)	40.4 (2.52)	41.1 (2.39)
High school completion[2]	(†)	(†)	(†)	74.2 (2.54)	70.1 (2.99)	70.1 (2.92)	65.0 (2.04)	51.1 (1.84)	53.6 (1.90)	58.5 (2.22)	56.1 (1.83)	58.7 (2.28)	66.4 (1.96)	62.9 (1.96)	65.5 (1.87)
At least some college	(†)	(†)	(†)	76.8 (9.32)	71.6 (6.38)	78.2 (6.22)	66.6 (4.54)	57.5 (3.99)	64.3 (4.07)	60.5 (5.27)	65.7 (3.40)	69.1 (3.66)	69.6 (3.94)	70.9 (3.44)	74.7 (3.60)
20 to 24 years old, all education levels[1]	(†)	(†)	(†)	75.6 (0.90)	73.7 (0.93)	77.4 (0.93)	73.2 (0.66)	65.5 (0.72)	68.7 (0.67)	69.4 (0.74)	71.4 (0.66)	72.3 (0.59)	75.9 (0.64)	76.3 (0.59)	77.4 (0.59)
Less than high school completion	(†)	(†)	(†)	54.4 (2.29)	52.7 (2.41)	60.8 (2.43)	55.7 (1.27)	44.4 (1.95)	47.7 (1.95)	46.6 (2.62)	51.4 (2.62)	48.0 (2.08)	54.5 (2.30)	51.4 (2.25)	57.6 (2.49)
High school completion[2]	(†)	(†)	(†)	76.6 (1.26)	72.2 (1.46)	76.5 (1.46)	72.3 (0.91)	61.5 (1.01)	64.2 (0.99)	63.7 (1.31)	66.9 (1.01)	69.4 (1.03)	72.1 (1.05)	72.4 (0.94)	73.4 (0.96)
Some college, no bachelor's degree[3]	(†)	(†)	(†)	85.6 (1.69)	83.6 (1.52)	86.6 (1.49)	80.3 (1.19)	72.9 (1.27)	75.3 (1.19)	75.0 (1.29)	76.4 (1.03)	76.7 (1.02)	80.3 (0.99)	82.7 (1.07)	80.5 (1.05)
Bachelor's or higher degree	(†)	(†)	(†)	93.3 (1.57)	90.9 (1.76)	87.8 (2.07)	89.3 (1.16)	86.5 (1.37)	87.3 (1.16)	88.1 (1.47)	88.9 (1.05)	88.1 (1.12)	89.3 (1.04)	87.7 (1.28)	90.4 (1.14)
25 to 64 years old, all education levels	65.8 (0.33)	70.2 (0.30)	71.6 (0.30)	75.0 (0.29)	75.5 (0.28)	77.7 (0.27)	75.0 (0.19)	71.5 (0.19)	71.7 (0.18)	72.3 (0.26)	73.1 (0.19)	73.8 (0.18)	74.4 (0.17)	74.9 (0.18)	75.6 (0.18)
Less than high school completion	55.3 (0.62)	55.5 (0.66)	53.1 (0.74)	54.9 (0.80)	53.8 (0.85)	57.8 (0.91)	57.2 (0.51)	52.1 (0.60)	52.9 (0.60)	54.9 (0.78)	54.7 (0.58)	56.6 (0.62)	55.6 (0.65)	56.8 (0.61)	56.1 (0.58)
High school completion[2]	65.7 (0.53)	70.4 (0.48)	70.7 (0.48)	74.4 (0.46)	73.3 (0.49)	75.5 (0.49)	71.5 (0.34)	67.0 (0.36)	66.5 (0.35)	67.0 (0.44)	67.3 (0.37)	67.6 (0.39)	68.4 (0.36)	69.0 (0.36)	69.9 (0.35)
Some college, no bachelor's degree[3]	71.7 (0.86)	76.1 (0.70)	77.8 (0.66)	80.2 (0.60)	79.5 (0.51)	80.7 (0.50)	77.7 (0.33)	72.7 (0.30)	72.2 (0.30)	72.6 (0.44)	74.1 (0.32)	73.9 (0.32)	75.3 (0.30)	75.0 (0.33)	76.0 (0.31)
Bachelor's or higher degree	82.5 (0.68)	84.5 (0.55)	85.6 (0.51)	86.7 (0.47)	86.5 (0.44)	86.4 (0.42)	83.7 (0.26)	81.6 (0.24)	82.1 (0.24)	82.0 (0.34)	82.8 (0.26)	83.5 (0.23)	83.5 (0.25)	83.8 (0.27)	84.3 (0.27)
25 to 34 years old, all education levels	67.7 (0.59)	74.5 (0.49)	76.2 (0.48)	78.6 (0.47)	78.5 (0.48)	81.6 (0.49)	76.8 (0.31)	73.2 (0.34)	73.8 (0.31)	74.5 (0.43)	76.0 (0.35)	76.8 (0.38)	78.1 (0.38)	78.7 (0.35)	79.4 (0.34)
Less than high school completion	52.9 (1.43)	58.3 (1.46)	57.0 (1.54)	60.3 (1.50)	59.8 (1.59)	64.1 (1.76)	62.0 (0.95)	55.1 (0.95)	56.2 (1.14)	57.8 (1.37)	56.5 (1.11)	59.5 (1.30)	57.1 (1.36)	59.1 (1.50)	57.4 (1.41)
High school completion[2]	65.5 (0.92)	72.0 (0.81)	74.3 (0.78)	77.7 (0.74)	77.0 (0.84)	80.2 (0.91)	73.1 (0.60)	68.1 (0.72)	68.7 (0.75)	68.2 (0.73)	70.4 (0.72)	70.1 (0.79)	71.8 (0.70)	72.5 (0.73)	73.6 (0.72)
Some college, no bachelor's degree[3]	71.7 (1.33)	80.9 (1.01)	80.1 (0.97)	81.6 (0.96)	80.5 (0.87)	82.8 (0.90)	79.4 (0.54)	72.9 (0.57)	72.7 (0.68)	74.5 (0.74)	76.4 (0.60)	76.6 (0.65)	79.7 (0.54)	78.9 (0.60)	79.7 (0.57)
Bachelor's or higher degree	82.0 (1.04)	86.6 (0.82)	86.6 (0.79)	88.1 (0.76)	88.1 (0.75)	89.0 (0.73)	84.4 (0.52)	84.0 (0.49)	84.3 (0.45)	84.0 (0.59)	84.8 (0.48)	85.6 (0.49)	85.8 (0.47)	86.4 (0.46)	86.9 (0.45)
35 to 44 years old, all education levels	70.3 (0.66)	76.5 (0.58)	78.1 (0.54)	81.6 (0.48)	80.2 (0.46)	81.8 (0.45)	79.9 (0.26)	76.0 (0.30)	76.9 (0.35)	77.1 (0.40)	78.3 (0.31)	78.5 (0.33)	79.2 (0.31)	80.1 (0.30)	80.3 (0.31)
Less than high school completion	61.4 (1.31)	63.4 (1.39)	60.0 (1.58)	62.5 (1.69)	58.6 (1.66)	64.8 (1.64)	64.9 (0.93)	58.2 (1.13)	59.6 (1.13)	61.3 (1.25)	62.3 (0.84)	64.2 (1.00)	64.0 (1.01)	64.5 (1.13)	63.3 (1.11)
High school completion[2]	69.6 (1.02)	76.6 (0.90)	76.6 (0.88)	80.0 (0.80)	78.6 (0.82)	81.0 (0.79)	78.0 (0.52)	72.4 (0.64)	72.1 (0.68)	72.6 (0.80)	72.5 (0.63)	72.0 (0.76)	73.8 (0.66)	74.4 (0.68)	74.6 (0.71)
Some college, no bachelor's degree[3]	74.5 (1.74)	81.6 (1.33)	81.6 (1.15)	85.0 (0.93)	83.3 (0.81)	84.4 (0.80)	82.0 (0.48)	76.9 (0.53)	78.2 (0.61)	77.3 (0.68)	79.6 (0.53)	79.4 (0.58)	79.7 (0.63)	80.8 (0.55)	81.2 (0.58)
Bachelor's or higher degree	84.5 (1.31)	88.5 (1.00)	88.8 (0.80)	89.5 (0.72)	88.5 (0.71)	87.6 (0.74)	85.9 (0.41)	84.7 (0.39)	85.0 (0.41)	85.0 (0.57)	86.7 (0.39)	86.3 (0.39)	86.1 (0.35)	86.8 (0.37)	87.3 (0.39)
45 to 54 years old, all education levels	68.4 (0.65)	71.7 (0.65)	73.5 (0.67)	77.6 (0.62)	78.8 (0.55)	81.2 (0.50)	78.4 (0.32)	74.7 (0.35)	74.6 (0.30)	76.2 (0.43)	75.9 (0.33)	77.0 (0.36)	77.3 (0.38)	77.9 (0.34)	79.0 (0.34)
Less than high school completion	59.8 (1.14)	61.8 (1.24)	58.7 (1.52)	60.7 (1.63)	58.4 (1.79)	60.3 (1.89)	59.0 (1.04)	52.5 (1.05)	54.7 (1.06)	59.4 (1.50)	56.8 (1.16)	58.8 (1.13)	58.8 (1.22)	59.0 (1.20)	60.4 (1.20)
High school completion[2]	68.8 (1.03)	72.0 (1.02)	74.0 (1.03)	77.5 (0.97)	75.9 (1.01)	78.2 (0.95)	75.1 (0.64)	71.0 (0.65)	70.4 (0.62)	70.7 (0.84)	70.9 (0.63)	71.7 (0.68)	72.2 (0.66)	73.0 (0.67)	74.0 (0.76)
Some college, no bachelor's degree[3]	74.7 (1.81)	76.5 (1.72)	79.2 (1.63)	81.9 (1.38)	81.7 (1.03)	83.4 (0.91)	80.4 (0.57)	77.3 (0.54)	76.2 (0.53)	77.4 (0.76)	77.1 (0.60)	77.2 (0.71)	78.6 (0.61)	78.5 (0.62)	79.6 (0.58)
Bachelor's or higher degree	87.1 (1.36)	87.3 (1.21)	87.9 (1.16)	89.4 (0.97)	89.5 (0.78)	89.7 (0.71)	87.5 (0.45)	84.4 (0.45)	84.7 (0.48)	85.9 (0.54)	85.7 (0.43)	87.1 (0.44)	86.2 (0.46)	86.6 (0.48)	87.1 (0.47)
55 to 64 years old, all education levels	54.6 (0.77)	54.1 (0.73)	52.1 (0.77)	53.4 (0.81)	55.0 (0.82)	58.1 (0.79)	60.8 (0.48)	60.6 (0.41)	60.6 (0.41)	60.9 (0.52)	61.9 (0.37)	62.6 (0.37)	63.0 (0.40)	62.9 (0.38)	63.7 (0.43)
Less than high school completion	48.5 (1.11)	43.2 (1.16)	41.8 (1.29)	39.5 (1.46)	38.1 (1.67)	40.4 (1.84)	39.4 (1.13)	40.0 (1.19)	39.1 (1.08)	39.6 (1.34)	42.4 (1.12)	43.6 (1.27)	42.5 (1.07)	45.4 (1.09)	44.1 (1.22)
High school completion[2]	56.5 (1.32)	57.5 (1.19)	52.1 (1.22)	54.0 (1.29)	53.7 (1.34)	55.4 (1.34)	55.3 (0.79)	55.1 (0.71)	54.6 (0.75)	57.6 (0.90)	56.9 (0.74)	57.7 (0.75)	57.7 (0.73)	58.3 (0.72)	59.3 (0.67)
Some college, no bachelor's degree[3]	62.6 (2.48)	62.5 (2.08)	58.9 (2.21)	60.4 (2.12)	62.0 (1.74)	62.4 (1.64)	64.8 (0.90)	61.8 (0.76)	61.2 (0.70)	60.5 (0.99)	63.2 (0.68)	62.7 (0.68)	63.2 (0.70)	62.2 (0.75)	63.9 (0.74)
Bachelor's or higher degree	72.6 (2.34)	71.9 (1.96)	71.3 (1.83)	70.5 (1.79)	70.0 (1.72)	71.9 (1.49)	73.5 (0.74)	72.0 (0.65)	73.1 (0.66)	71.7 (0.90)	72.3 (0.62)	73.4 (0.60)	74.4 (0.71)	73.6 (0.65)	74.0 (0.71)

—Not available.
†Not applicable.
[1] Data for 16- to 19-year-olds and 20- to 24-year-olds exclude persons enrolled in school.
[2] Includes equivalency credentials, such as the GED credential.
[3] Includes persons with no college degree as well as those with an associate's degree.

NOTE: Data are based on sample surveys of the noninstitutionalized population, which excludes persons living in institutions (e.g., prisons or nursing facilities); this table includes only data on the civilian population (excludes all military personnel). For each age group, the employment to population ratio is the number of persons in that age group who are employed as a percentage of the civilian population in that age group. SOURCE: U.S. Department of Commerce, Census Bureau, Current Population Survey (CPS), Annual Social and Economic Supplement, selected years, 1975 through 2019. (This table was prepared October 2019.)

Table 501.80. Unemployment rates of persons 16 to 64 years old, by age group and highest level of educational attainment: Selected years, 1975 through 2019

[Standard errors appear in parentheses]

Age group and highest level of educational attainment	1975	1980	1985	1990	1995	2000	2005	2010	2012	2014	2015	2016	2017	2018	2019
1	2	3	4	5	6	7	8	9	10	11	12	13	14	15	16
16 to 19 years old, all education levels[1]	(†)	(†)	(†)	**17.0 (1.83)**	**21.0 (2.06)**	**17.2 (1.89)**	**22.8 (1.39)**	**31.9 (1.59)**	**30.6 (1.57)**	**22.9 (1.83)**	**22.5 (1.35)**	**20.2 (1.37)**	**14.8 (1.39)**	**15.4 (1.40)**	**14.5 (1.11)**
Less than high school completion	—	—	—	26.2 (3.54)	30.3 (3.67)	21.4 (3.23)	30.3 (2.34)	41.7 (3.14)	41.1 (3.01)	22.9 (3.38)	25.6 (2.67)	21.6 (2.39)	21.7 (2.91)	16.3 (2.77)	16.7 (2.57)
High school completion[2]	—	—	—	11.7 (2.05)	15.1 (2.59)	15.3 (2.54)	19.1 (2.02)	29.6 (2.08)	28.7 (2.00)	25.0 (2.32)	23.3 (1.90)	22.0 (2.00)	12.6 (1.44)	16.7 (1.92)	14.5 (1.45)
At least some college	—	—	—	(†)	12.4! (5.19)	‡	15.8 (3.54)	18.1 (3.65)	19.6 (3.83)	15.1 (4.16)	13.2 (2.96)	11.8 (2.75)	9.2 (2.59)	9.5! (3.19)	11.1 (2.79)
20 to 24 years old, all education levels[1]	(†)	(†)	(†)	**8.2 (0.63)**	**10.7 (0.72)**	**9.2 (0.70)**	**10.9 (0.48)**	**18.8 (0.66)**	**15.5 (0.55)**	**14.9 (0.70)**	**12.3 (0.53)**	**10.5 (0.53)**	**8.1 (0.43)**	**8.7 (0.48)**	**7.5 (0.43)**
Less than high school completion	—	—	—	17.4 (2.15)	19.5 (2.37)	16.6 (2.18)	18.9 (1.24)	32.3 (1.80)	27.6 (2.12)	25.3 (2.75)	19.9 (1.99)	17.3 (2.05)	16.0 (2.10)	19.5 (2.64)	15.9 (2.24)
High school completion[2]	—	—	—	7.8 (0.88)	12.0 (1.18)	10.0 (1.12)	12.0 (0.73)	22.3 (0.95)	18.3 (0.96)	18.9 (1.18)	15.8 (0.92)	12.2 (0.92)	9.7 (0.80)	11.1 (0.85)	8.8 (0.68)
Some college, no bachelor's degree[3]	—	—	(†)	4.8 (1.09)	7.3 (1.13)	5.2 (1.02)	7.3 (0.76)	14.2 (1.07)	12.7 (0.89)	12.2 (1.16)	9.6 (0.89)	9.9 (0.87)	6.4 (0.75)	5.3 (0.69)	6.7 (0.67)
Bachelor's or higher degree	—	—	(†)	3.1! (1.12)	4.1! (1.26)	5.0 (1.43)	5.4 (0.91)	7.9 (1.15)	6.0 (0.95)	6.7 (1.09)	5.1 (0.72)	4.9 (0.81)	4.7 (0.76)	5.3 (0.89)	3.3 (0.67)
25 to 64 years old, all education levels	**6.8 (0.41)**	**5.0 (0.17)**	**6.1 (0.18)**	**3.6 (0.14)**	**4.8 (0.15)**	**3.3 (0.13)**	**4.4 (0.09)**	**9.1 (0.13)**	**7.4 (0.11)**	**5.8 (0.14)**	**4.7 (0.10)**	**4.4 (0.09)**	**3.9 (0.09)**	**3.5 (0.09)**	**3.2 (0.08)**
Less than high school completion	10.5 (0.49)	8.4 (0.48)	11.4 (0.61)	7.7 (0.55)	10.0 (0.66)	7.9 (0.63)	9.0 (0.36)	16.8 (0.54)	14.3 (0.49)	10.6 (0.63)	9.2 (0.44)	8.1 (0.42)	8.3 (0.47)	6.6 (0.39)	6.5 (0.41)
High school completion[2]	6.8 (0.34)	5.1 (0.27)	6.9 (0.31)	3.8 (0.23)	5.2 (0.28)	3.8 (0.25)	5.5 (0.17)	12.1 (0.26)	9.2 (0.25)	7.4 (0.29)	6.2 (0.21)	6.1 (0.24)	5.2 (0.18)	4.7 (0.19)	4.0 (0.17)
Some college, no bachelor's degree[3]	5.5 (0.50)	4.3 (0.38)	4.7 (0.37)	3.1 (0.29)	4.5 (0.29)	3.0 (0.24)	4.2 (0.17)	8.8 (0.23)	7.9 (0.24)	6.1 (0.27)	4.9 (0.16)	4.5 (0.17)	3.8 (0.16)	3.7 (0.16)	3.5 (0.17)
Bachelor's or higher degree	2.4 (0.30)	1.9 (0.23)	2.4 (0.24)	1.7 (0.19)	2.5 (0.21)	1.5 (0.16)	2.3 (0.13)	4.7 (0.15)	4.1 (0.14)	3.4 (0.16)	2.4 (0.11)	2.4 (0.12)	2.3 (0.11)	2.2 (0.11)	1.9 (0.10)
25 to 34 years old, all education levels	**8.6 (0.41)**	**6.8 (0.32)**	**7.3 (0.33)**	**4.8 (0.27)**	**5.8 (0.30)**	**4.0 (0.27)**	**5.8 (0.18)**	**10.8 (0.28)**	**9.2 (0.26)**	**7.4 (0.30)**	**5.9 (0.20)**	**5.6 (0.22)**	**4.9 (0.20)**	**4.3 (0.17)**	**4.1 (0.19)**
Less than high school completion	17.2 (1.36)	13.7 (1.24)	15.5 (1.38)	12.0 (1.21)	12.9 (1.32)	10.3 (1.33)	11.6 (0.69)	20.3 (1.02)	16.8 (1.09)	13.7 (1.24)	12.5 (1.01)	13.1 (0.97)	13.2 (1.16)	9.1 (0.98)	9.6 (1.04)
High school completion[2]	9.4 (0.67)	7.9 (0.55)	9.1 (0.57)	5.1 (0.44)	6.8 (0.56)	4.8 (0.54)	7.7 (0.41)	15.9 (0.62)	12.8 (0.57)	10.5 (0.68)	8.9 (0.50)	8.6 (0.52)	7.2 (0.44)	6.4 (0.38)	5.6 (0.41)
Some college, no bachelor's degree[3]	6.7 (0.85)	6.0 (0.64)	5.4 (0.60)	3.8 (0.51)	5.0 (0.52)	3.6 (0.49)	5.4 (0.36)	10.6 (0.44)	7.4 (0.52)	7.8 (0.52)	6.5 (0.39)	5.6 (0.41)	4.4 (0.34)	4.7 (0.34)	4.7 (0.34)
Bachelor's or higher degree	2.9 (0.50)	2.5 (0.39)	2.8 (0.41)	1.9 (0.34)	2.7 (0.40)	1.6 (0.31)	2.6 (0.26)	4.5 (0.28)	4.1 (0.28)	3.7 (0.30)	2.4 (0.20)	2.4 (0.23)	2.5 (0.22)	2.0 (0.19)	2.1 (0.22)
35 to 44 years old, all education levels	**6.4 (0.41)**	**4.3 (0.31)**	**5.6 (0.33)**	**3.3 (0.24)**	**4.6 (0.27)**	**3.5 (0.23)**	**4.2 (0.14)**	**9.2 (0.24)**	**7.1 (0.22)**	**5.7 (0.24)**	**4.4 (0.17)**	**4.1 (0.18)**	**4.0 (0.16)**	**3.3 (0.14)**	**2.9 (0.16)**
Less than high school completion	11.2 (1.02)	9.0 (1.00)	12.4 (1.29)	8.3 (1.17)	10.5 (1.28)	8.4 (1.14)	8.7 (0.63)	17.8 (1.07)	14.1 (0.88)	11.5 (1.08)	8.4 (0.74)	6.2 (0.66)	6.9 (0.61)	5.5 (0.69)	5.7 (0.69)
High school completion[2]	5.7 (0.60)	4.2 (0.48)	6.1 (0.55)	3.7 (0.41)	5.1 (0.48)	3.9 (0.43)	5.2 (0.31)	11.9 (0.51)	9.1 (0.48)	7.4 (0.48)	6.3 (0.41)	6.6 (0.44)	5.7 (0.41)	4.9 (0.36)	4.3 (0.37)
Some college, no bachelor's degree[3]	4.6 (0.95)	3.1 (0.64)	4.8 (0.69)	2.8 (0.47)	4.7 (0.49)	3.1 (0.41)	3.9 (0.25)	9.2 (0.42)	7.4 (0.44)	6.1 (0.49)	4.5 (0.31)	4.5 (0.35)	4.4 (0.35)	4.7 (0.34)	3.1 (0.30)
Bachelor's or higher degree	2.3 (0.59)	1.6 (0.41)	2.2 (0.39)	1.6 (0.31)	2.2 (0.34)	1.8 (0.31)	2.0 (0.19)	4.6 (0.26)	3.6 (0.26)	2.8 (0.30)	2.1 (0.20)	2.0 (0.16)	2.3 (0.21)	2.0 (0.18)	1.4 (0.14)
45 to 54 years old, all education levels	**5.9 (0.39)**	**3.9 (0.32)**	**5.4 (0.39)**	**2.5 (0.26)**	**3.9 (0.29)**	**2.4 (0.22)**	**3.9 (0.16)**	**8.4 (0.22)**	**6.8 (0.18)**	**4.9 (0.24)**	**4.1 (0.15)**	**3.7 (0.17)**	**3.3 (0.17)**	**3.2 (0.16)**	**3.0 (0.16)**
Less than high school completion	8.5 (0.81)	6.6 (0.78)	10.2 (1.16)	4.7 (0.89)	7.9 (1.24)	6.1 (1.16)	7.0 (0.66)	15.6 (0.98)	13.5 (0.92)	8.0 (0.95)	8.6 (0.80)	6.6 (0.65)	6.9 (0.79)	6.5 (0.70)	5.5 (0.71)
High school completion[2]	5.6 (0.60)	3.4 (0.48)	5.4 (0.60)	2.3 (0.39)	4.0 (0.53)	2.7 (0.42)	4.6 (0.33)	11.0 (0.43)	7.8 (0.36)	6.1 (0.50)	5.2 (0.34)	5.0 (0.39)	4.3 (0.32)	3.5 (0.32)	3.3 (0.32)
Some college, no bachelor's degree[3]	4.7 (1.00)	3.0 (0.78)	3.2 (0.79)	2.6 (0.62)	3.9 (0.56)	2.4 (0.40)	3.7 (0.30)	7.6 (0.40)	6.9 (0.36)	4.8 (0.44)	4.1 (0.30)	3.4 (0.33)	2.9 (0.28)	3.3 (0.30)	3.3 (0.31)
Bachelor's or higher degree	2.0! (0.61)	1.3! (0.44)	2.1 (0.54)	1.4 (0.38)	2.4 (0.41)	1.3 (0.28)	2.5 (0.26)	4.8 (0.30)	3.2 (0.27)	3.2 (0.29)	2.2 (0.18)	2.3 (0.24)	2.1 (0.21)	2.2 (0.22)	2.1 (0.20)
55 to 64 years old, all education levels	**5.5 (0.46)**	**3.2 (0.35)**	**4.6 (0.44)**	**2.8 (0.36)**	**3.9 (0.42)**	**2.8 (0.35)**	**3.7 (0.20)**	**7.3 (0.25)**	**6.6 (0.23)**	**5.2 (0.28)**	**4.2 (0.20)**	**3.9 (0.18)**	**3.2 (0.16)**	**3.3 (0.18)**	**2.6 (0.16)**
Less than high school completion	7.1 (0.79)	5.2 (0.77)	7.1 (1.01)	3.9 (0.90)	6.7 (1.35)	5.2 (1.28)	7.5 (0.90)	10.1 (0.99)	11.5 (1.05)	8.2 (1.21)	6.9 (0.84)	6.5 (0.80)	6.0 (0.75)	5.6 (0.71)	5.6 (0.92)
High school completion[2]	5.1 (0.76)	2.7 (0.51)	4.5 (0.69)	3.0 (0.59)	3.4 (0.65)	3.1 (0.62)	4.3 (0.39)	9.3 (0.56)	7.1 (0.50)	5.6 (0.53)	4.4 (0.38)	4.1 (0.41)	3.6 (0.33)	4.0 (0.42)	2.6 (0.32)
Some college, no bachelor's degree[3]	4.1! (1.26)	2.0! (0.77)	3.0! (1.00)	2.2! (0.82)	3.2 (0.80)	2.8 (0.70)	3.5 (0.37)	7.7 (0.52)	7.1 (0.44)	5.5 (0.54)	4.3 (0.40)	4.1 (0.37)	3.2 (0.32)	3.2 (0.33)	2.6 (0.31)
Bachelor's or higher degree	1.5! (0.75)	‡	2.2! (0.70)	1.8! (0.62)	3.3 (0.79)	1.4! (0.46)	2.3 (0.30)	5.0 (0.34)	4.8 (0.38)	4.0 (0.39)	3.3 (0.30)	3.2 (0.29)	2.4 (0.24)	2.2 (0.23)	2.0 (0.21)

—Not available.
†Not applicable.
!Interpret data with caution. The coefficient of variation (CV) for this estimate is between 30 and 50 percent.
‡Reporting standards not met. The coefficient of variation (CV) for this estimate is 50 percent or greater.
[1]Data for 16- to 19-year-olds and 20- to 24-year-olds exclude persons enrolled in school.
[2]Includes equivalency credentials, such as the GED credential.
[3]Includes persons with no college degree as well as those with an associate's degree.

NOTE: Data are based on sample surveys of the noninstitutionalized population, which excludes persons living in institutions (e.g., prisons or nursing facilities); this table includes only data on the civilian population (excludes all military personnel). The unemployment rate is the percentage of persons in the civilian labor force who are not working and who made specific efforts to find employment sometime during the prior 4 weeks. The civilian labor force consists of all civilians who are employed or seeking employment.
SOURCE: U.S. Department of Commerce, Census Bureau, Current Population Survey (CPS), Annual Social and Economic Supplement, selected years, 1975 through 2019. (This table was prepared October 2019.)

Table 502.10. Occupation of employed persons 25 years old and over, by highest level of educational attainment and sex: 2018 and 2019

[Standard errors appear in parentheses]

Sex and occupation	Total employed (in thousands)	Total	Less than high school completion	High school completion (includes equivalency)	Some college, no degree	Associate's degree	Bachelor's degree	Master's or higher degree
					Percentage distribution, by highest level of educational attainment			
							College	
1	2	3	4	5	6	7	8	9
2018								
All persons	**135,851** (365.3)	100.0	7.0 (0.12)	25.1 (0.24)	15.5 (0.16)	11.1 (0.14)	25.7 (0.25)	15.5 (0.18)
Management, professional, and related	59,266 (439.8)	100.0	1.2 (0.07)	9.5 (0.21)	10.5 (0.21)	10.1 (0.20)	37.6 (0.34)	31.1 (0.32)
Management, business, and financial operations	24,827 (277.4)	100.0	2.1 (0.14)	14.2 (0.42)	13.1 (0.33)	9.1 (0.30)	39.8 (0.50)	21.6 (0.42)
Professional and related	34,439 (323.0)	100.0	0.5 (0.06)	6.1 (0.21)	8.7 (0.27)	10.8 (0.29)	36.0 (0.45)	37.9 (0.45)
Education, training, and library	9,187 (175.7)	100.0	0.6 (0.13)	5.8 (0.42)	6.7 (0.42)	5.9 (0.39)	34.4 (0.76)	46.7 (0.90)
Preschool and kindergarten teachers	604 (41.2)	100.0	1.8! (0.75)	11.3 (1.83)	15.4 (2.47)	13.9 (1.95)	40.2 (2.98)	17.3 (2.68)
Elementary and middle school teachers	3,540 (97.2)	100.0	‡ (†)	2.4 (0.44)	2.7 (0.44)	2.8 (0.41)	44.0 (1.21)	48.1 (1.34)
Secondary school teachers	1,135 (59.4)	100.0	‡ (†)	1.3! (0.51)	2.6! (0.84)	1.5! (0.59)	35.9 (2.33)	58.6 (2.37)
Special education teachers	411 (31.1)	100.0	‡ (†)	3.2! (1.04)	3.8! (1.26)	3.4! (1.28)	30.9 (3.79)	57.8 (4.07)
Postsecondary teachers	1,279 (65.8)	100.0	‡ (†)	‡ (†)	1.9 (0.55)	1.5! (0.51)	12.2 (1.63)	84.2 (1.79)
Other education, training, and library workers	2,219 (79.2)	100.0	1.8 (0.45)	15.5 (1.22)	16.0 (1.24)	13.8 (1.12)	30.1 (1.57)	22.7 (1.44)
Service occupations	20,719 (221.4)	100.0	14.6 (0.38)	37.2 (0.49)	18.4 (0.41)	12.7 (0.38)	14.2 (0.42)	2.8 (0.18)
Sales and office occupations	27,253 (268.4)	100.0	3.7 (0.18)	29.2 (0.44)	22.5 (0.40)	12.9 (0.33)	26.0 (0.47)	5.7 (0.22)
Natural resources, construction, and maintenance	12,387 (162.3)	100.0	19.4 (0.50)	42.6 (0.74)	16.3 (0.50)	11.8 (0.50)	8.4 (0.47)	1.5 (0.17)
Production, transportation, and material moving	16,226 (213.8)	100.0	14.1 (0.48)	46.7 (0.66)	18.0 (0.49)	9.4 (0.38)	9.7 (0.37)	2.2 (0.18)
Males	**72,248** (244.9)	100.0	8.4 (0.16)	27.7 (0.31)	15.5 (0.23)	9.6 (0.18)	24.5 (0.29)	14.2 (0.22)
Management, professional, and related	28,773 (280.9)	100.0	1.5 (0.11)	10.3 (0.29)	11.1 (0.32)	8.0 (0.26)	38.3 (0.44)	30.8 (0.43)
Management, business, and financial operations	13,768 (194.9)	100.0	2.6 (0.20)	15.2 (0.51)	13.3 (0.48)	7.8 (0.37)	39.6 (0.64)	21.4 (0.61)
Professional and related	15,006 (184.7)	100.0	0.5 (0.09)	5.7 (0.34)	9.0 (0.41)	8.2 (0.40)	37.1 (0.64)	39.5 (0.62)
Education, training, and library	2,526 (86.7)	100.0	0.4! (0.15)	3.6 (0.65)	6.0 (0.79)	4.2 (0.66)	31.1 (1.43)	54.7 (1.59)
Service occupations	8,790 (152.1)	100.0	14.8 (0.62)	36.4 (0.86)	18.2 (0.68)	11.5 (0.58)	16.1 (0.64)	2.9 (0.30)
Sales and office occupations	10,536 (167.7)	100.0	4.2 (0.32)	27.2 (0.66)	21.2 (0.65)	10.3 (0.50)	30.2 (0.78)	6.9 (0.38)
Natural resources, construction, and maintenance	11,814 (159.3)	100.0	19.1 (0.52)	43.3 (0.76)	16.2 (0.51)	11.9 (0.51)	8.0 (0.45)	1.4 (0.17)
Production, transportation, and material moving	12,334 (168.3)	100.0	13.2 (0.50)	47.6 (0.75)	18.4 (0.57)	9.3 (0.43)	9.4 (0.42)	2.2 (0.22)
Females	**63,603** (231.6)	100.0	5.3 (0.14)	22.2 (0.29)	15.6 (0.21)	12.8 (0.21)	27.1 (0.33)	17.0 (0.23)
Management, professional, and related	30,493 (260.9)	100.0	0.9 (0.09)	8.8 (0.27)	10.0 (0.28)	12.0 (0.27)	37.0 (0.46)	31.3 (0.40)
Management, business, and financial operations	11,059 (165.8)	100.0	1.6 (0.18)	13.0 (0.55)	12.9 (0.49)	10.7 (0.46)	40.0 (0.78)	21.9 (0.54)
Professional and related	19,434 (218.9)	100.0	0.5 (0.08)	6.4 (0.28)	8.4 (0.33)	12.8 (0.36)	35.2 (0.55)	36.7 (0.54)
Education, training, and library	6,661 (133.0)	100.0	0.7 (0.16)	6.6 (0.51)	6.9 (0.47)	6.5 (0.45)	35.6 (0.92)	43.7 (0.97)
Service occupations	11,929 (149.0)	100.0	14.5 (0.45)	37.8 (0.65)	18.6 (0.54)	13.6 (0.50)	12.8 (0.50)	2.8 (0.23)
Sales and office occupations	16,717 (196.8)	100.0	3.4 (0.21)	30.5 (0.56)	23.3 (0.47)	14.4 (0.44)	23.4 (0.57)	5.0 (0.27)
Natural resources, construction, and maintenance	573 (36.0)	100.0	24.4 (2.64)	27.2 (2.70)	17.0 (2.32)	9.9 (1.79)	17.2 (2.84)	4.3 (1.28)
Production, transportation, and material moving	3,892 (99.7)	100.0	17.0 (0.89)	44.0 (1.25)	16.8 (0.95)	9.6 (0.79)	10.5 (0.86)	2.1 (0.38)
2019								
All persons	**137,478** (347.4)	100.0	6.8 (0.11)	25.1 (0.24)	15.1 (0.17)	11.1 (0.16)	26.1 (0.23)	15.9 (0.18)
Management, professional, and related	60,087 (407.3)	100.0	1.1 (0.07)	9.3 (0.20)	9.8 (0.21)	10.0 (0.20)	38.0 (0.33)	31.7 (0.33)
Management, business, and financial operations	25,465 (298.1)	100.0	2.0 (0.14)	13.4 (0.38)	13.0 (0.38)	9.2 (0.28)	40.0 (0.50)	22.4 (0.44)
Professional and related	34,622 (302.3)	100.0	0.4 (0.05)	6.4 (0.20)	7.4 (0.23)	10.6 (0.26)	36.6 (0.40)	38.6 (0.46)
Education, training, and library	9,050 (141.0)	100.0	0.4 (0.10)	5.8 (0.37)	6.0 (0.39)	5.5 (0.41)	34.6 (0.77)	47.7 (0.85)
Preschool and kindergarten teachers	611 (41.0)	100.0	1.3! (0.57)	11.1 (2.01)	9.7 (1.73)	17.1 (2.33)	44.3 (3.18)	16.6 (2.30)
Elementary and middle school teachers	3,580 (99.7)	100.0	‡ (†)	2.4 (0.37)	2.1 (0.37)	2.3 (0.39)	41.5 (1.40)	51.4 (1.38)
Secondary school teachers	948 (51.6)	100.0	‡ (†)	1.0! (0.43)	1.4! (0.59)	0.9! (0.43)	40.1 (2.63)	56.6 (2.67)
Special education teachers	337 (30.7)	100.0	‡ (†)	‡ (†)	4.5! (1.56)	‡ (†)	37.2 (4.36)	54.8 (4.31)
Postsecondary teachers	1,281 (62.3)	100.0	‡ (†)	0.5! (0.24)	1.4! (0.54)	1.8! (0.56)	14.1 (1.63)	82.3 (1.75)
Other education, training, and library workers	2,293 (72.3)	100.0	0.9! (0.32)	15.2 (1.15)	16.0 (1.25)	12.0 (1.17)	29.9 (1.56)	26.0 (1.60)
Service occupations	20,981 (238.1)	100.0	14.3 (0.38)	37.8 (0.54)	18.7 (0.48)	12.2 (0.37)	14.0 (0.42)	3.0 (0.17)
Sales and office occupations	27,638 (251.2)	100.0	3.7 (0.20)	29.1 (0.46)	21.9 (0.41)	12.7 (0.38)	26.4 (0.45)	6.2 (0.24)
Natural resources, construction, and maintenance	12,344 (182.8)	100.0	19.2 (0.65)	43.0 (0.85)	15.6 (0.50)	12.4 (0.51)	8.7 (0.45)	1.2 (0.16)
Production, transportation, and material moving	16,428 (217.4)	100.0	13.8 (0.45)	46.1 (0.70)	17.9 (0.50)	9.9 (0.38)	10.2 (0.37)	2.1 (0.20)
Males	**72,785** (238.8)	100.0	8.3 (0.17)	27.6 (0.32)	15.0 (0.24)	9.8 (0.19)	24.9 (0.28)	14.4 (0.23)
Management, professional, and related	28,809 (288.7)	100.0	1.5 (0.11)	10.2 (0.30)	10.4 (0.34)	7.9 (0.25)	38.7 (0.44)	31.3 (0.45)
Management, business, and financial operations	14,106 (219.5)	100.0	2.5 (0.20)	14.4 (0.51)	13.4 (0.51)	8.1 (0.36)	39.7 (0.63)	22.0 (0.56)
Professional and related	14,703 (195.3)	100.0	0.5 (0.10)	6.1 (0.36)	7.4 (0.39)	7.8 (0.35)	37.8 (0.63)	40.3 (0.66)
Education, training, and library	2,356 (81.0)	100.0	‡ (†)	3.7 (0.63)	4.3 (0.66)	4.1 (0.65)	31.6 (1.46)	55.9 (1.55)
Service occupations	8,725 (153.4)	100.0	14.6 (0.58)	36.7 (0.86)	18.3 (0.75)	11.1 (0.63)	16.2 (0.70)	3.1 (0.31)
Sales and office occupations	10,778 (167.3)	100.0	4.4 (0.32)	27.0 (0.69)	20.2 (0.63)	10.9 (0.47)	30.5 (0.75)	7.0 (0.39)
Natural resources, construction, and maintenance	11,760 (176.8)	100.0	18.7 (0.65)	43.4 (0.88)	15.8 (0.52)	12.5 (0.52)	8.3 (0.44)	1.2 (0.16)
Production, transportation, and material moving	12,712 (187.2)	100.0	13.0 (0.53)	46.8 (0.77)	18.3 (0.58)	10.0 (0.43)	9.8 (0.41)	2.1 (0.22)
Females	**64,693** (240.5)	100.0	5.1 (0.13)	22.2 (0.26)	15.1 (0.22)	12.5 (0.23)	27.4 (0.31)	17.7 (0.24)
Management, professional, and related	31,278 (230.6)	100.0	0.7 (0.07)	8.6 (0.26)	9.3 (0.26)	11.9 (0.30)	37.4 (0.46)	32.1 (0.42)
Management, business, and financial operations	11,358 (169.0)	100.0	1.3 (0.16)	12.2 (0.49)	12.5 (0.54)	10.6 (0.45)	40.4 (0.75)	23.0 (0.64)
Professional and related	19,919 (198.7)	100.0	0.4 (0.06)	6.5 (0.27)	7.5 (0.26)	12.7 (0.37)	35.6 (0.55)	37.3 (0.55)
Education, training, and library	6,694 (116.4)	100.0	0.4 (0.09)	6.5 (0.47)	6.6 (0.46)	6.0 (0.46)	35.6 (0.95)	44.8 (0.96)
Service occupations	12,256 (177.4)	100.0	14.2 (0.44)	38.5 (0.68)	18.9 (0.55)	13.0 (0.47)	12.4 (0.49)	3.0 (0.23)
Sales and office occupations	16,860 (184.6)	100.0	3.3 (0.22)	30.4 (0.57)	23.0 (0.56)	13.9 (0.49)	23.8 (0.54)	5.7 (0.30)
Natural resources, construction, and maintenance	583 (39.0)	100.0	29.5 (2.91)	33.1 (2.73)	10.7 (1.85)	9.6 (1.90)	15.5 (2.67)	1.5! (0.64)
Production, transportation, and material moving	3,716 (98.7)	100.0	16.7 (0.89)	43.7 (1.22)	16.6 (0.95)	9.5 (0.75)	11.4 (0.83)	2.2 (0.38)

†Not applicable.
!Interpret data with caution. The coefficient of variation (CV) for this estimate is between 30 and 50 percent.
‡Reporting standards not met. Either there are too few cases for a reliable estimate or the coefficient of variation (CV) is 50 percent or greater.
NOTE: Data are based on sample surveys of the noninstitutionalized population, which excludes persons living in institutions (e.g., prisons or nursing facilities); this table includes only data on the civilian population (excludes all military personnel). Detail may not sum to totals because of rounding. Some data have been revised from previously published figures.
SOURCE: U.S. Department of Commerce, Census Bureau, Current Population Survey (CPS), Annual Social and Economic Supplement, 2018 and 2019. (This table was prepared February 2020.)

Table 502.20. Median annual earnings, number, and percentage of full-time year-round workers age 25 and over, by highest level of educational attainment and sex: 1990 through 2018

[Standard errors appear in parentheses]

[Current dollars]

Sex and year	Total	Elementary/secondary — Less than 9th grade	Elementary/secondary — Some high school, no completion[1]	Elementary/secondary — High school completion (includes equivalency)[2]	Some college, no degree[3]	College — Associate's degree	College — Bachelor's or higher degree[4] Total	College — Bachelor's degree[5]	College — Master's degree	College — Professional degree[4]	College — Doctor's degree
1	2	3	4	5	6	7	8	9	10	11	12
Males											
1990	$30,730 (—)	$17,390 (—)	$20,900 (—)	$26,650 (—)	$31,730 (—)	35,200[5] (†)	$42,670 (—)	$39,240 (—)	55,220 (†)	79,670[5] (†)	65,340 (†)
1995	34,550 (275)	18,350 (545)	22,190 (342)	29,510 (358)	33,880 (517)	41,950 (535)	50,480 (312)	45,270 (510)	68,320 (973)	99,410 (2,582)	80,250 (2,188)
2000	41,060 (156)	20,790 (376)	25,100 (436)	34,300 (457)	40,340 (312)	42,780 (460)	61,870 (303)	56,330 (573)	70,900 (1,506)	100,000 (20,832)	86,970 (2,446)
2001	41,620 (104)	21,360 (235)	26,210 (251)	34,720 (299)	41,050 (214)	42,860 (561)	62,220 (279)	55,930 (335)	67,280 (687)	100,000 (‡)	83,310 (3,013)
2002	41,150 (100)	20,920 (213)	25,900 (207)	33,210 (311)	40,850 (195)	42,870 (673)	61,700 (201)	56,080 (385)	70,640 (1,294)	100,000 (‡)	87,130 (2,076)
2003	41,940 (90)	21,220 (227)	26,470 (280)	35,410 (168)	41,350 (182)	44,400 (719)	62,080 (187)	56,500 (365)	71,530 (562)	100,000 (‡)	82,400 (2,528)
2004	42,090 (89)	21,660 (191)	26,280 (234)	35,730 (148)	41,900 (175)	44,400 (931)	62,800 (798)	57,220 (393)	71,530 (490)	100,000 (‡)	82,400 (2,423)
2005	43,320 (367)	22,330 (220)	27,190 (237)	36,300 (141)	42,420 (323)	47,180 (367)	66,170 (356)	60,020 (653)	75,030 (1,229)	100,000 (‡)	85,860 (3,061)
2006	45,760 (134)	22,710 (398)	27,650 (573)	37,030 (164)	43,830 (812)	47,070 (390)	66,930 (346)	60,910 (235)	75,430 (859)	100,000 (‡)	100,000 (‡)
2007	47,000 (130)	23,380 (544)	29,320 (590)	37,860 (406)	44,900 (585)	49,040 (801)	70,400 (241)	62,090 (236)	76,280 (416)	100,000 (‡)	92,090 (1,894)
2008	49,000 (339)	24,260 (631)	29,680 (458)	39,010 (399)	45,820 (276)	50,150 (344)	72,220 (236)	65,800 (388)	80,960 (468)	100,000 (‡)	100,000 (‡)
2009	49,990 (201)	23,950 (394)	28,020 (542)	39,480 (379)	47,100 (347)	50,300 (238)	71,470 (239)	62,440 (707)	79,340 (1,568)	123,240 (2,539)	100,740 (519)
2010	50,360 (93)	24,450 (597)	29,440 (684)	40,060 (237)	46,430 (348)	50,280 (245)	71,780 (267)	63,740 (1,115)	80,960 (453)	115,300 (4,891)	101,220 (653)
2011	50,950 (25)	25,220 (23)	30,420 (300)	40,450 (87)	47,070 (78)	50,930 (212)	73,850 (490)	66,200 (25)	83,030 (755)	119,470 (1,917)	100,770 (192)
2012	50,950 (144)	25,130 (440)	30,330 (430)	40,350 (194)	47,190 (407)	50,960 (329)	75,320 (565)	66,150 (570)	85,120 (1,412)	116,350 (5,632)	106,470 (4,656)
2013	51,120 (149)	26,160 (531)	30,570 (551)	40,290 (227)	47,650 (739)	51,000 (493)	76,110 (485)	67,240 (992)	86,310 (1,429)	126,730 (8,647)	105,280 (4,631)
2014	51,400 (133)	26,580 (382)	30,840 (382)	40,930 (197)	46,900 (429)	51,110 (345)	75,910 (391)	68,160 (1,282)	84,760 (1,988)	121,750 (5,986)	100,710 (852)
2015	52,310 (152)	27,160 (460)	32,140 (320)	41,570 (184)	49,670 (708)	52,070 (352)	79,320 (1,350)	71,390 (420)	86,740 (1,632)	131,190 (7,197)	102,340 (4,801)
2016	53,740 (725)	30,350 (500)	32,490 (1,237)	41,890 (180)	49,240 (784)	52,120 (462)	80,320 (446)	71,630 (383)	88,430 (2,215)	117,550 (7,311)	120,430 (4,017)
2017	55,630 (269)	31,000 (369)	34,620 (1,249)	42,440 (524)	50,850 (274)	54,700 (1,414)	81,390 (321)	71,990 (395)	91,600 (648)	127,230 (5,441)	118,450 (4,152)
2018	57,430 (442)	31,800 (420)	35,600 (406)	45,580 (300)	51,690 (291)	56,720 (598)	82,840 (1,930)	75,150 (959)	99,620 (1,750)	135,440 (10,136)	115,790 (5,892)
Females											
1990	$21,370 (—)	$12,250 (—)	$14,430 (—)	$18,320 (—)	$22,230 (—)	27,310[5] (†)	$30,380 (—)	$28,020 (—)	40,260 (†)	50,000[5] (†)	48,140 (†)
1995	24,880 (160)	13,580 (490)	15,830 (293)	20,460 (162)	24,000 (274)	31,070 (428)	35,260 (313)	32,050 (273)	50,140 (556)	58,960 (2,532)	57,080 (2,373)
2000	30,330 (138)	15,800 (327)	17,920 (434)	24,970 (236)	28,700 (364)	32,150 (307)	42,710 (439)	40,420 (284)	50,670 (735)	61,750 (3,552)	62,120 (2,999)
2001	31,360 (91)	16,690 (255)	19,310 (359)	25,300 (132)	30,420 (186)	31,630 (231)	44,780 (367)	40,990 (231)	48,890 (328)	57,020 (3,976)	65,720 (2,228)
2002	31,010 (83)	16,510 (297)	18,940 (360)	25,180 (121)	29,400 (299)	32,250 (241)	43,250 (568)	40,850 (173)	50,160 (595)	66,490 (2,421)	67,210 (2,462)
2003	31,570 (85)	16,910 (256)	19,160 (327)	26,070 (118)	30,140 (176)	33,480 (489)	45,120 (291)	41,330 (204)	51,320 (454)	75,040 (3,469)	68,880 (2,450)
2004	31,990 (80)	17,020 (241)	19,160 (319)	26,030 (116)	30,820 (135)	33,480 (489)	45,910 (229)	41,680 (172)	51,320 (263)	75,040 (2,436)	68,880 (2,450)
2005	33,080 (242)	16,140 (250)	20,130 (274)	26,290 (134)	31,400 (165)	33,940 (497)	46,950 (232)	42,170 (179)	51,410 (283)	80,460 (2,774)	66,850 (2,490)
2006	35,100 (113)	18,130 (408)	20,130 (270)	26,740 (136)	31,950 (165)	35,160 (376)	49,570 (441)	45,410 (259)	52,440 (561)	76,240 (2,488)	70,520 (1,779)
2007	36,090 (105)	18,260 (461)	20,400 (292)	27,240 (133)	32,840 (415)	36,330 (283)	50,400 (158)	45,770 (262)	55,430 (412)	71,100 (910)	68,990 (2,155)
2008	36,700 (109)	18,630 (494)	20,410 (295)	28,380 (283)	32,630 (355)	36,760 (243)	51,410 (145)	47,030 (237)	57,510 (745)	71,300 (2,859)	74,030 (2,144)
2009	37,260 (107)	18,480 (451)	21,230 (301)	29,150 (273)	34,090 (483)	37,270 (310)	51,880 (169)	46,830 (260)	61,070 (304)	83,910 (3,210)	76,580 (912)
2010	38,290 (272)	18,240 (592)	20,880 (334)	29,860 (260)	33,400 (410)	37,770 (588)	51,940 (159)	47,440 (336)	59,100 (1,021)	76,740 (2,723)	77,390 (2,174)
2011	38,910 (216)	20,100 (250)	21,110 (131)	30,010 (145)	34,590 (512)	39,290 (40)	52,140 (88)	49,110 (103)	60,720 (533)	80,720 (135)	77,460 (21)
2012	39,980 (294)	20,060 (514)	21,390 (285)	30,410 (165)	35,060 (452)	37,320 (455)	53,690 (888)	50,170 (290)	60,930 (464)	94,470 (6,655)	77,900 (3,616)
2013	40,610 (134)	19,840 (502)	22,250 (544)	30,800 (173)	35,240 (312)	37,700 (751)	55,720 (416)	50,750 (341)	61,280 (561)	85,400 (6,196)	75,090 (3,515)
2014	40,830 (151)	20,990 (279)	21,990 (322)	30,650 (151)	34,380 (891)	37,480 (591)	55,940 (333)	51,350 (230)	60,830 (442)	91,810 (8,587)	80,540 (2,875)
2015	41,680 (146)	21,050 (275)	22,670 (714)	31,250 (138)	36,140 (273)	40,190 (437)	57,220 (527)	51,680 (278)	62,380 (1,135)	82,470 (5,049)	82,310 (3,752)
2016	43,010 (617)	22,210 (485)	24,800 (562)	31,540 (152)	36,880 (273)	40,220 (362)	60,060 (483)	52,030 (257)	64,910 (1,091)	92,030 (4,468)	86,370 (4,485)
2017	44,620 (530)	22,360 (533)	25,450 (459)	32,240 (199)	36,620 (259)	40,640 (335)	60,740 (270)	52,440 (601)	68,510 (1,524)	100,180 (‡)	‡ (3,137)
2018	46,570 (204)	22,970 (1,042)	25,140 (576)	32,620 (471)	38,840 (600)	41,490 (329)	61,760 (227)	56,680 (466)	66,740 (581)	99,780 (7,090)	95,170 (5,083)

See notes at end of table.

Table 502.20. Median annual earnings, number, and percentage of full-time year-round workers age 25 and over, by highest level of educational attainment and sex: 1990 through 2018—Continued

[Standard errors appear in parentheses]

[Values shown as earnings (standard error). Columns 7–12 fall under "College"; columns 8–12 fall under "Bachelor's or higher degree[4]". Earnings are in constant 2018 dollars[7].]

Sex and year	Total	Elementary/secondary — Less than 9th grade	Some high school, no completion[1]	High school completion (includes equivalency)[2]	Some college, no degree[3]	Associate's degree	Bachelor's or higher degree — Total	Bachelor's degree[5]	Master's degree	Professional degree[4]	Doctor's degree
1	2	3	4	5	6	7	8	9	10	11	12
Males											
1990	$59,060 (—)	$33,430 (—)	$40,170 (—)	$51,220 (—)	$60,990 (—)	[e] †	$82,010 (—)	$75,410 (—)	[e] †	[e] †	[e] †
1995	56,940 (453)	30,240 (898)	36,560 (564)	48,630 (590)	55,830 (852)	58,010 (882)	83,190 (514)	74,590 (840)	90,990 (1,603)	131,280 (4,255)	107,670 (3,606)
2000	59,870 (227)	30,320 (548)	36,590 (636)	50,020 (666)	58,820 (455)	61,180 (671)	90,220 (442)	82,150 (836)	99,630 (2,196)	144,960 (30,378)	117,020 (3,567)
2001	59,020 (147)	30,290 (333)	37,170 (356)	49,240 (424)	58,210 (303)	60,660 (796)	88,240 (396)	79,320 (475)	100,550 (974)	141,810 (‡)	123,330 (4,273)
2002	57,450 (140)	29,200 (297)	36,160 (289)	46,360 (434)	57,030 (272)	59,830 (940)	86,130 (281)	78,280 (537)	93,920 (1,806)	139,600 (‡)	116,290 (2,898)
2003	57,250 (123)	28,960 (310)	36,130 (382)	48,340 (229)	56,440 (248)	58,520 (981)	84,730 (255)	77,130 (498)	96,430 (767)	136,500 (‡)	118,940 (3,451)
2004	55,950 (118)	28,790 (254)	34,930 (311)	47,490 (197)	55,700 (233)	59,030 (1,238)	83,480 (1,061)	76,070 (522)	95,090 (651)	132,940 (‡)	109,550 (3,221)
2005	55,700 (472)	28,710 (283)	34,960 (305)	46,680 (181)	54,540 (415)	60,660 (472)	85,080 (458)	77,170 (840)	96,470 (1,580)	128,580 (‡)	110,400 (3,936)
2006	57,000 (167)	28,290 (496)	34,450 (714)	46,130 (204)	54,600 (1,011)	58,630 (486)	83,370 (431)	75,870 (293)	93,960 (1,070)	124,560 (‡)	124,560 (214)
2007	56,930 (157)	28,310 (659)	35,510 (715)	45,850 (492)	54,380 (708)	58,490 (970)	85,260 (292)	75,190 (286)	92,390 (504)	121,110 (‡)	111,530 (2,294)
2008	57,150 (395)	28,290 (736)	34,610 (534)	45,500 (465)	53,440 (322)	58,490 (401)	84,220 (275)	76,740 (453)	94,430 (546)	116,630 (‡)	116,630 (‡)
2009	58,520 (235)	28,030 (461)	32,800 (634)	46,210 (444)	55,130 (406)	58,880 (279)	83,650 (280)	73,090 (828)	92,870 (1,835)	144,250 (2,972)	117,910 (607)
2010	57,990 (107)	28,160 (687)	33,900 (788)	46,130 (273)	53,470 (401)	57,900 (282)	82,660 (307)	73,400 (1,284)	93,230 (522)	132,770 (5,632)	116,560 (752)
2011	56,550 (28)	28,160 (26)	33,960 (335)	45,150 (97)	52,550 (87)	56,850 (237)	82,450 (547)	73,900 (28)	92,690 (843)	133,370 (2,140)	112,490 (214)
2012	55,730 (157)	27,490 (481)	33,170 (470)	44,130 (212)	51,610 (445)	55,740 (360)	82,380 (618)	72,350 (623)	93,090 (1,540)	127,260 (6,160)	116,440 (5,092)
2013	55,100 (161)	28,200 (572)	32,950 (594)	43,430 (245)	51,360 (797)	54,970 (531)	82,030 (523)	72,470 (1,069)	93,030 (1,540)	136,600 (9,321)	113,480 (4,992)
2014	54,520 (141)	28,200 (405)	32,710 (405)	43,420 (209)	49,740 (455)	54,210 (366)	80,520 (415)	72,300 (1,360)	89,900 (2,109)	129,150 (6,349)	106,820 (904)
2015	55,410 (161)	28,770 (487)	34,050 (339)	44,040 (195)	52,620 (750)	55,170 (373)	84,040 (1,430)	75,630 (445)	91,890 (1,729)	130,990 (7,625)	108,420 (5,086)
2016	56,230 (759)	31,760 (523)	34,000 (1,294)	43,830 (188)	51,510 (820)	54,530 (483)	84,030 (467)	74,950 (401)	92,520 (2,317)	122,990 (7,649)	126,000 (4,203)
2017	56,990 (276)	31,750 (378)	35,470 (1,280)	43,480 (537)	52,090 (281)	56,040 (1,449)	83,370 (329)	73,750 (405)	93,840 (664)	130,340 (5,574)	121,340 (4,253)
2018	57,430 (442)	31,800 (420)	35,600 (406)	45,580 (300)	51,690 (291)	56,720 (598)	82,840 (1,930)	75,150 (959)	99,620 (1,750)	135,440 (10,136)	115,790 (5,892)
Females											
1990	$41,070 (—)	$23,540 (—)	$27,730 (—)	$35,210 (—)	$42,720 (—)	[e] †	$58,380 (—)	$53,840 (—)	[e] †	[e] †	[e] †
1995	40,990 (264)	22,370 (807)	26,080 (483)	33,720 (267)	39,540 (452)	45,000 (705)	58,100 (516)	52,820 (450)	66,350 (916)	82,390 (4,172)	79,330 (3,910)
2000	44,220 (201)	23,040 (477)	26,130 (633)	36,130 (344)	41,850 (531)	45,310 (448)	62,280 (640)	58,930 (414)	73,110 (1,072)	85,970 (5,180)	83,240 (4,373)
2001	44,470 (129)	23,670 (362)	27,170 (509)	35,880 (187)	43,140 (264)	45,600 (328)	63,500 (520)	58,140 (328)	71,860 (465)	87,570 (5,639)	88,100 (3,160)
2002	43,290 (116)	23,050 (415)	26,950 (503)	35,150 (169)	41,040 (417)	44,150 (295)	60,370 (793)	57,030 (242)	68,250 (831)	79,600 (3,380)	91,750 (3,166)
2003	43,090 (116)	23,080 (349)	25,850 (446)	35,590 (161)	41,140 (240)	44,030 (329)	61,580 (397)	56,410 (278)	68,470 (620)	90,760 (4,735)	91,750 (3,361)
2004	42,530 (106)	22,630 (320)	25,470 (424)	34,600 (154)	40,970 (179)	44,510 (650)	61,040 (304)	55,410 (229)	68,220 (350)	99,760 (3,238)	91,560 (3,257)
2005	42,530 (311)	20,760 (321)	25,880 (352)	33,800 (172)	40,370 (212)	43,640 (639)	60,370 (298)	54,220 (230)	66,110 (364)	103,450 (3,567)	85,960 (3,202)
2006	43,720 (141)	22,590 (508)	25,070 (336)	33,300 (169)	39,800 (206)	43,790 (468)	61,750 (549)	56,560 (323)	65,320 (699)	94,970 (3,099)	87,840 (2,216)
2007	43,700 (127)	22,120 (558)	24,700 (354)	32,990 (161)	39,770 (503)	44,000 (343)	61,040 (191)	55,430 (317)	67,130 (499)	86,110 (1,102)	83,550 (2,610)
2008	42,800 (127)	21,730 (576)	23,800 (344)	33,100 (330)	38,050 (414)	42,870 (283)	59,960 (169)	54,850 (276)	67,080 (869)	83,150 (3,334)	86,340 (2,501)
2009	43,620 (125)	21,630 (528)	24,840 (352)	34,120 (320)	39,900 (565)	43,620 (363)	60,720 (198)	54,810 (304)	71,480 (356)	98,210 (3,757)	89,640 (1,067)
2010	44,100 (313)	21,000 (682)	24,050 (385)	34,380 (299)	38,460 (472)	43,500 (677)	59,810 (183)	54,620 (387)	68,060 (1,176)	88,370 (3,136)	89,120 (2,504)
2011	43,440 (241)	22,440 (279)	23,570 (146)	33,500 (162)	38,620 (572)	43,860 (45)	58,200 (98)	54,820 (115)	67,320 (595)	90,110 (151)	86,470 (23)
2012	43,720 (322)	21,940 (562)	23,390 (312)	33,260 (180)	38,340 (494)	40,640 (498)	58,720 (971)	54,870 (317)	66,640 (507)	103,330 (7,279)	85,200 (3,955)
2013	43,780 (144)	21,390 (541)	23,980 (586)	33,200 (186)	37,990 (336)	40,640 (810)	60,070 (448)	54,700 (368)	66,060 (605)	92,050 (6,679)	80,940 (3,789)
2014	43,310 (160)	22,270 (296)	23,320 (342)	32,510 (160)	36,460 (945)	39,750 (627)	59,340 (353)	54,460 (244)	64,520 (469)	97,390 (9,108)	85,430 (3,050)
2015	44,160 (155)	22,310 (291)	24,020 (756)	33,110 (146)	38,290 (289)	42,570 (463)	60,620 (558)	54,750 (295)	66,090 (1,242)	87,380 (5,349)	87,200 (3,975)
2016	45,000 (646)	23,240 (507)	25,950 (588)	33,000 (159)	38,590 (286)	42,080 (379)	62,240 (505)	54,440 (269)	67,910 (1,141)	96,290 (4,675)	90,360 (4,692)
2017	45,710 (543)	22,970 (546)	26,080 (470)	33,030 (204)	37,520 (265)	41,630 (343)	62,220 (277)	53,720 (616)	70,180 (1,561)	102,620 (4,935)	94,280 (3,214)
2018	46,570 (204)	22,970 (1,042)	25,140 (576)	32,620 (471)	38,840 (600)	41,490 (329)	61,760 (227)	56,680 (466)	66,740 (581)	99,780 (7,090)	95,170 (5,083)

See notes at end of table.

Table 502.20. Median annual earnings, number, and percentage of full-time year-round workers age 25 and over, by highest level of educational attainment and sex: 1990 through 2018—Continued

[Standard errors appear in parentheses]

Number of persons with earnings who worked full time, year round (in thousands). (Column 2 shows median annual earnings.)

Column groupings: columns 3–5 = Elementary/secondary; columns 7–12 = College; columns 8–12 = Bachelor's or higher degree[4].

Sex and year	Total	Less than 9th grade	Some high school, no completion[1]	High school completion (includes equivalency)[2]	Some college, no degree[3]	Associate's degree	Total	Bachelor's degree[5]	Master's degree	Professional degree	Doctor's degree
1	2	3	4	5	6	7	8	9	10	11	12
Males											
1990	44,406 (268.6)	2,250 (73.9)	3,315 (89.3)	16,394 (188.0)	9,113 (144.6)	†	13,334 (171.8)	7,569 (132.6)	3,395 (95.7)	1,208 (57.5)	853 (48.4)
1995	48,500 (306.2)	1,946 (72.8)	3,335 (94.9)	15,331 (195.6)	8,908 (152.3)	3,926 (102.8)	15,054 (194.0)	9,597 (157.8)	3,680 (92.6)	1,274 (54.8)	1,038 (49.5)
2000	54,065 (309.7)	1,968 (68.0)	3,354 (88.4)	16,834 (191.7)	9,792 (148.8)	4,729 (104.7)	17,387 (194.6)	11,395 (159.9)	3,961 (68.5)	1,298 (39.5)	1,041 (35.4)
2001	54,013 (224.8)	2,207 (51.4)	3,503 (64.5)	16,314 (135.4)	9,494 (104.9)	4,714 (74.7)	17,780 (140.9)	11,479 (114.8)	4,065 (69.4)	1,308 (39.6)	1,065 (35.8)
2002	54,108 (225.0)	2,154 (50.7)	3,680 (66.1)	16,005 (134.2)	9,603 (105.5)	4,399 (72.2)	18,267 (142.7)				
2003	54,253 (225.2)	2,209 (51.4)	3,369 (63.3)	16,285 (135.3)	9,340 (104.1)	4,696 (74.5)	18,354 (143.0)	11,846 (116.6)	4,124 (69.9)	1,348 (40.2)	1,037 (35.3)
2004	55,469 (227.0)	2,427 (53.8)	3,468 (64.2)	17,067 (138.3)	9,257 (103.6)	4,913 (76.2)	18,338 (142.9)	11,701 (115.9)	4,243 (70.9)	1,305 (39.6)	1,088 (36.1)
2005	56,717 (228.7)	2,425 (53.8)	3,652 (65.9)	17,266 (139.0)	9,532 (105.1)	5,022 (77.0)	18,820 (144.7)	12,032 (117.4)	4,275 (71.2)	1,369 (40.5)	1,144 (37.1)
2006	58,109 (230.6)	2,361 (53.8)	3,872 (67.8)	17,369 (139.4)	9,493 (104.9)	5,110 (77.4)	19,903 (148.4)	12,764 (121.6)	4,542 (73.3)	1,425 (41.3)	1,172 (37.5)
2007	58,147 (230.7)	2,142 (50.6)	3,451 (64.0)	17,224 (138.0)	9,867 (106.8)	5,244 (78.7)	20,218 (149.5)	12,962 (121.6)	4,800 (75.3)	1,332 (40.0)	1,125 (36.7)
2008	55,655 (227.2)	1,982 (48.7)	3,118 (60.9)	16,195 (135.0)	9,515 (105.0)	5,020 (77.0)	19,825 (148.1)	12,609 (120.0)	4,709 (74.6)	1,388 (40.8)	1,119 (36.7)
2009	52,445 (222.5)	1,561 (43.2)	2,795 (57.7)	15,258 (131.3)	8,609 (100.1)	4,828 (75.5)	19,395 (146.7)	12,290 (118.6)	4,575 (73.6)	1,319 (39.8)	1,212 (38.1)
2010	52,890 (223.2)	1,600 (43.8)	2,615 (55.9)	15,104 (130.7)	8,541 (99.7)	5,042 (77.2)	19,990 (148.7)	12,836 (121.1)	4,670 (74.3)	1,237 (38.5)	1,246 (38.7)
2011	54,279 (225.2)	1,848 (47.0)	2,715 (56.9)	15,335 (131.4)	8,752 (100.9)	5,206 (78.4)	20,423 (150.1)	13,013 (121.8)	4,839 (75.6)	1,300 (39.5)	1,271 (39.0)
2012	55,208 (226.6)	1,793 (46.3)	2,671 (56.4)	15,295 (131.4)	8,974 (102.1)	5,423 (80.0)	21,052 (152.2)	13,315 (123.2)	5,003 (76.9)	1,301 (39.5)	1,433 (41.4)
2013	56,703 (289.3)	1,944 (61.0)	2,910 (74.5)	16,034 (170.0)	8,960 (129.0)	5,605 (102.8)	21,249 (193.4)	13,378 (156.2)	5,146 (98.6)	1,249 (49.0)	1,476 (53.2)
2014	58,435 (256.1)	1,994 (54.0)	3,012 (66.2)	16,429 (150.3)	9,281 (114.7)	5,622 (90.0)	22,098 (172.1)	13,969 (139.3)	5,401 (88.2)	1,359 (44.6)	1,369 (44.8)
2015	59,690 (264.8)	2,008 (54.2)	2,984 (66.0)	16,286 (150.5)	9,445 (116.0)	5,907 (92.3)	23,059 (176.9)	14,469 (142.4)	5,883 (92.2)	1,256 (42.9)	1,451 (46.1)
2016	60,677 (266.4)	1,844 (52.0)	2,828 (64.2)	16,855 (153.0)	9,603 (117.0)	6,091 (93.7)	23,456 (178.3)	14,723 (143.5)	5,975 (92.9)	1,169 (41.4)	1,589 (48.2)
2017	61,794 (268.2)	1,820 (51.6)	2,931 (65.4)	16,997 (153.6)	9,629 (117.1)	6,052 (93.4)	24,365 (181.4)	15,445 (146.8)	6,065 (93.5)	1,188 (41.7)	1,667 (49.4)
2018	62,603 (392.2)	1,878 (75.1)	2,859 (92.5)	17,306 (222.7)	9,341 (165.6)	6,310 (136.8)	24,908 (263.9)	15,961 (214.3)	6,080 (134.3)	1,248 (61.3)	1,619 (69.8)
Females											
1990	28,636 (234.7)	847 (45.6)	1,861 (67.3)	11,810 (162.8)	6,462 (123.1)	†	7,655 (133.3)	4,704 (105.8)	2,268 (78.5)	421 (34.0)	283 (27.9)
1995	32,673 (268.2)	774 (46.1)	1,763 (69.3)	11,064 (168.6)	6,329 (129.5)	3,336 (94.9)	9,406 (156.3)	6,434 (130.5)	2,823 (81.2)	509 (34.7)	353 (28.9)
2000	37,762 (271.6)	930 (46.8)	1,950 (67.7)	11,789 (162.5)	7,391 (130.0)	4,118 (97.8)	11,584 (161.1)	7,899 (134.3)	3,089 (60.6)	531 (25.3)	392 (21.7)
2001	38,228 (197.0)	927 (33.4)	1,869 (47.3)	11,690 (115.8)	7,283 (92.3)	4,190 (70.5)	12,269 (118.5)	8,257 (98.1)	3,281 (62.5)	572 (26.2)	402 (22.0)
2002	38,510 (197.6)	858 (32.1)	1,841 (46.9)	11,687 (115.8)	7,354 (92.7)	4,285 (71.2)	12,484 (119.5)				
2003	38,681 (197.9)	882 (32.6)	1,739 (45.6)	11,587 (115.3)	7,341 (92.6)	4,397 (72.2)	12,735 (120.6)	8,330 (98.5)	3,376 (63.4)	567 (26.1)	462 (23.6)
2004	39,072 (198.7)	917 (33.2)	1,797 (46.4)	11,392 (114.4)	7,330 (92.6)	4,505 (73.0)	13,131 (122.4)	8,664 (100.4)	3,451 (64.0)	564 (26.0)	452 (23.3)
2005	40,021 (200.6)	902 (32.9)	1,740 (45.6)	11,419 (114.5)	7,452 (93.3)	4,751 (74.9)	13,758 (125.1)	9,074 (102.6)	3,591 (65.3)	657 (28.1)	437 (22.9)
2006	41,311 (203.2)	934 (33.5)	1,802 (46.4)	11,652 (115.6)	7,613 (94.3)	4,760 (75.0)	14,549 (128.4)	9,645 (105.7)	3,746 (66.7)	662 (28.2)	497 (24.5)
2007	42,196 (204.9)	823 (31.5)	1,649 (44.4)	11,447 (114.7)	7,916 (96.1)	4,891 (76.5)	15,469 (132.1)	9,931 (107.2)	4,389 (72.1)	666 (28.3)	484 (24.1)
2008	40,979 (202.5)	814 (31.3)	1,568 (43.3)	10,851 (111.8)	7,456 (93.3)	4,955 (76.5)	15,335 (131.6)	9,856 (106.8)	4,176 (70.3)	753 (30.1)	550 (25.7)
2009	40,376 (201.4)	776 (30.5)	1,519 (42.7)	10,467 (109.9)	7,164 (91.6)	4,924 (76.3)	15,526 (132.4)	10,066 (107.9)	4,261 (71.0)	606 (27.0)	592 (26.7)
2010	40,196 (201.0)	732 (29.7)	1,371 (40.5)	10,117 (108.1)	7,150 (91.5)	4,999 (76.8)	15,826 (133.5)	9,903 (107.0)	4,576 (73.6)	622 (27.4)	725 (29.5)
2011	40,885 (202.4)	779 (30.6)	1,380 (40.7)	10,040 (107.7)	6,989 (90.5)	5,131 (77.8)	16,566 (136.4)	10,537 (110.2)	4,700 (74.6)	635 (27.6)	694 (28.9)
2012	41,319 (203.2)	690 (28.8)	1,351 (40.3)	9,870 (106.8)	6,899 (89.9)	5,246 (78.7)	17,263 (139.0)	10,961 (112.3)	4,887 (76.0)	670 (28.4)	745 (29.9)
2013	42,021 (258.8)	788 (38.9)	1,309 (50.1)	9,990 (135.9)	7,070 (115.1)	5,253 (99.6)	17,611 (177.5)	11,124 (143.1)	4,963 (96.9)	793 (39.1)	732 (37.5)
2014	42,957 (228.5)	796 (34.2)	1,356 (44.6)	9,802 (117.7)	7,241 (101.7)	5,426 (88.4)	18,336 (158.1)	11,420 (126.6)	5,310 (87.5)	776 (33.8)	830 (34.9)
2015	44,012 (234.8)	823 (34.8)	1,308 (43.8)	9,739 (117.8)	7,525 (103.9)	5,507 (89.2)	19,109 (162.2)	11,751 (128.9)	5,562 (89.7)	784 (33.9)	1,012 (38.5)
2016	44,968 (236.9)	728 (32.7)	1,382 (45.0)	9,832 (118.3)	7,305 (102.4)	5,764 (91.2)	19,957 (165.5)	12,143 (131.0)	5,997 (93.0)	841 (35.1)	976 (37.9)
2017	45,868 (238.3)	766 (33.5)	1,341 (44.3)	9,783 (118.0)	7,004 (100.4)	5,838 (91.8)	21,136 (170.0)	12,937 (135.0)	6,308 (95.4)	805 (34.4)	1,085 (39.9)
2018	46,945 (349.3)	718 (46.5)	1,337 (63.4)	10,014 (171.3)	6,927 (143.2)	5,802 (131.2)	22,147 (250.0)	13,302 (196.5)	6,856 (142.4)	826 (49.9)	1,163 (59.2)

† Not applicable.

See notes at end of table.

Table 502.20. Median annual earnings, number, and percentage of full-time year-round workers age 25 and over, by highest level of educational attainment and sex: 1990 through 2018—Continued

[Standard errors appear in parentheses]

Percent of persons with earnings who worked full time, year round[8]

Sex and year	Total	Elementary/secondary			Some college, no degree[3]	Associate's degree	College					
		Less than 9th grade	Some high school, no completion[1]	High school completion (includes equivalency)[2]			Total	Bachelor's or higher degree[4]				
								Bachelor's degree[5]	Master's degree	Professional degree	Doctor's degree	
	2	3	4	5	6	7	8	9	10	11	12	
Males												
2000	81.7 (0.23)	69.2 (1.33)	71.8 (1.01)	80.9 (0.42)	82.2 (0.54)	86.6 (0.71)	84.8 (0.39)	85.6 (0.47)	82.8 (0.87)	85.8 (1.39)	82.5 (1.65)	
2001	80.1 (0.17)	69.7 (0.90)	70.9 (0.71)	79.4 (0.31)	80.2 (0.40)	84.1 (0.54)	83.3 (0.28)	83.6 (0.35)	82.4 (0.60)	84.6 (1.01)	82.2 (1.18)	
2002	79.4 (0.17)	70.1 (0.91)	71.3 (0.69)	77.8 (0.32)	78.8 (0.41)	81.4 (0.58)	83.9 (0.27)	84.4 (0.34)	82.2 (0.60)	85.7 (0.99)	82.8 (1.16)	
2003	79.5 (0.17)	71.5 (0.89)	70.1 (0.73)	78.7 (0.31)	78.8 (0.41)	82.1 (0.56)	83.1 (0.28)	84.0 (0.34)	81.1 (0.60)	84.4 (1.00)	80.3 (1.22)	
2004	80.0 (0.17)	74.7 (0.84)	71.2 (0.71)	79.1 (0.30)	79.3 (0.41)	83.6 (0.53)	83.0 (0.28)	83.1 (0.35)	83.1 (0.58)	83.3 (1.03)	81.7 (1.16)	
2005	80.3 (0.16)	74.0 (0.84)	73.8 (0.69)	79.5 (0.30)	80.0 (0.40)	82.5 (0.54)	82.9 (0.27)	83.0 (0.34)	82.7 (0.58)	83.7 (1.00)	82.4 (1.12)	
2006	81.1 (0.16)	73.6 (0.85)	72.9 (0.67)	79.6 (0.30)	80.1 (0.40)	85.3 (0.50)	84.7 (0.26)	85.2 (0.32)	83.5 (0.55)	85.9 (0.94)	83.4 (1.09)	
2007	80.5 (0.16)	71.1 (0.91)	70.8 (0.72)	79.4 (0.30)	79.5 (0.40)	83.3 (0.52)	84.5 (0.26)	85.1 (0.32)	83.5 (0.54)	83.1 (1.03)	83.5 (1.11)	
2008	77.0 (0.17)	66.3 (0.95)	64.6 (0.76)	74.6 (0.32)	76.5 (0.42)	79.4 (0.56)	82.6 (0.27)	83.2 (0.33)	80.9 (0.57)	82.4 (1.02)	83.1 (1.12)	
2009	73.9 (0.18)	56.2 (1.03)	61.8 (0.79)	70.1 (0.34)	73.4 (0.45)	77.9 (0.58)	80.8 (0.28)	79.9 (0.35)	82.0 (0.56)	85.1 (0.99)	81.2 (1.11)	
2010	74.8 (0.18)	58.8 (1.04)	61.6 (0.82)	71.9 (0.34)	72.9 (0.45)	78.2 (0.56)	81.4 (0.27)	81.8 (0.34)	80.0 (0.58)	81.4 (1.10)	82.2 (1.08)	
2011	76.6 (0.17)	67.2 (0.98)	64.2 (0.81)	74.2 (0.33)	75.2 (0.44)	78.0 (0.56)	82.0 (0.27)	82.1 (0.33)	82.3 (0.55)	81.6 (1.07)	81.0 (1.09)	
2012	76.5 (0.17)	65.4 (1.00)	64.4 (0.82)	74.5 (0.33)	73.7 (0.44)	78.8 (0.54)	82.1 (0.26)	82.5 (0.33)	80.8 (0.55)	84.4 (1.01)	81.4 (1.02)	
2013	78.1 (0.21)	69.3 (1.21)	68.9 (0.99)	76.5 (0.41)	76.2 (0.55)	79.6 (0.67)	82.4 (0.33)	82.6 (0.41)	82.5 (0.67)	83.2 (1.34)	79.7 (1.30)	
2014	79.2 (0.18)	72.2 (1.03)	69.4 (0.85)	78.3 (0.35)	76.7 (0.47)	79.9 (0.58)	83.3 (0.28)	83.7 (0.35)	82.7 (0.57)	83.5 (1.12)	81.2 (1.15)	
2015	79.3 (0.18)	72.2 (1.03)	71.1 (0.85)	77.7 (0.35)	77.2 (0.46)	80.6 (0.56)	83.0 (0.27)	83.5 (0.34)	82.7 (0.54)	82.1 (1.19)	80.0 (1.14)	
2016	80.1 (0.18)	72.3 (1.08)	71.5 (0.87)	78.8 (0.34)	78.4 (0.45)	81.1 (0.55)	83.4 (0.27)	83.8 (0.34)	82.8 (0.54)	82.3 (1.23)	83.5 (1.03)	
2017	80.4 (0.17)	74.3 (1.07)	72.2 (0.85)	79.5 (0.34)	79.1 (0.45)	81.8 (0.54)	83.0 (0.27)	83.1 (0.33)	82.7 (0.54)	83.7 (1.19)	82.0 (1.03)	
2018	81.1 (0.25)	75.2 (1.50)	73.1 (1.23)	80.7 (0.47)	78.7 (0.65)	82.8 (0.75)	83.4 (0.37)	84.3 (0.46)	81.7 (0.78)	85.1 (1.62)	79.7 (1.55)	
Females												
2000	64.6 (0.30)	53.5 (1.84)	56.5 (1.30)	64.1 (0.54)	65.3 (0.69)	66.6 (0.92)	66.5 (0.55)	66.7 (0.67)	64.9 (1.11)	70.6 (2.61)	71.5 (3.13)	
2001	64.3 (0.22)	54.0 (1.32)	55.5 (0.94)	63.5 (0.39)	65.1 (0.49)	65.8 (0.65)	66.6 (0.38)	66.6 (0.47)	65.6 (0.76)	70.3 (1.83)	70.9 (2.12)	
2002	64.1 (0.22)	52.6 (1.36)	55.5 (0.95)	63.2 (0.39)	65.0 (0.49)	65.6 (0.65)	66.5 (0.38)	65.9 (0.47)	66.1 (0.74)	74.3 (1.73)	73.8 (2.07)	
2003	64.4 (0.21)	56.5 (1.38)	53.8 (0.96)	64.4 (0.39)	64.2 (0.49)	65.6 (0.64)	66.4 (0.37)	65.8 (0.46)	66.3 (0.73)	72.3 (1.75)	71.9 (1.95)	
2004	64.5 (0.21)	56.3 (1.35)	56.1 (0.96)	64.5 (0.40)	64.2 (0.49)	64.6 (0.63)	66.7 (0.37)	66.3 (0.45)	66.3 (0.72)	71.5 (1.77)	71.2 (1.97)	
2005	65.3 (0.21)	56.5 (1.36)	54.5 (0.97)	65.1 (0.40)	63.5 (0.49)	67.2 (0.61)	68.2 (0.36)	68.0 (0.44)	68.3 (0.70)	71.2 (1.64)	67.3 (2.02)	
2006	66.2 (0.21)	58.5 (1.35)	56.0 (0.96)	65.6 (0.39)	65.9 (0.48)	67.3 (0.61)	68.6 (0.35)	68.4 (0.43)	67.5 (0.69)	73.6 (1.61)	74.0 (1.86)	
2007	66.7 (0.21)	56.8 (1.43)	55.3 (1.00)	65.7 (0.39)	66.7 (0.48)	67.3 (0.60)	69.3 (0.34)	68.4 (0.42)	70.6 (0.63)	74.1 (1.60)	71.2 (1.91)	
2008	64.4 (0.21)	51.6 (1.38)	52.8 (1.01)	62.4 (0.40)	64.7 (0.49)	65.5 (0.60)	67.9 (0.34)	67.8 (0.43)	66.9 (0.65)	74.0 (1.51)	70.0 (1.80)	
2009	64.3 (0.21)	52.0 (1.42)	54.5 (1.04)	62.4 (0.41)	63.9 (0.50)	64.5 (0.60)	68.0 (0.34)	68.3 (0.42)	67.5 (0.65)	66.4 (1.72)	68.3 (1.74)	
2010	64.4 (0.21)	51.7 (1.46)	52.4 (1.07)	62.6 (0.42)	63.3 (0.50)	64.3 (0.60)	68.5 (0.34)	67.7 (0.42)	68.5 (0.62)	73.9 (1.66)	76.3 (1.51)	
2011	65.0 (0.21)	52.2 (1.42)	49.1 (1.04)	63.0 (0.42)	62.9 (0.50)	66.3 (0.59)	69.6 (0.33)	69.4 (0.41)	69.0 (0.62)	72.8 (1.65)	73.6 (1.58)	
2012	64.8 (0.21)	50.0 (1.48)	51.1 (1.07)	62.3 (0.42)	61.7 (0.50)	64.7 (0.58)	70.0 (0.32)	70.6 (0.40)	68.0 (0.60)	73.2 (1.61)	73.9 (1.52)	
2013	65.6 (0.26)	56.0 (1.84)	52.3 (1.07)	63.8 (0.46)	63.4 (0.62)	65.1 (0.79)	69.6 (0.40)	70.4 (0.50)	67.4 (0.82)	73.9 (1.86)	69.4 (1.97)	
2014	66.1 (0.23)	53.5 (1.57)	54.1 (1.21)	63.6 (0.47)	64.3 (0.55)	66.5 (0.63)	70.0 (0.34)	70.3 (0.44)	69.2 (0.64)	73.8 (1.65)	68.1 (1.62)	
2015	66.3 (0.22)	54.9 (1.56)	51.5 (1.20)	64.1 (0.47)	65.4 (0.54)	65.6 (0.63)	70.1 (0.34)	70.3 (0.43)	68.3 (0.63)	75.9 (1.62)	74.5 (1.44)	
2016	67.2 (0.22)	55.4 (1.66)	56.0 (1.21)	63.7 (0.47)	65.7 (0.55)	67.7 (0.62)	71.0 (0.33)	70.6 (0.42)	71.1 (0.60)	75.8 (1.56)	71.3 (1.48)	
2017	68.0 (0.22)	57.3 (1.64)	55.1 (1.22)	64.5 (0.47)	65.5 (0.56)	68.0 (0.61)	72.2 (0.32)	71.9 (0.41)	72.4 (0.58)	75.6 (1.60)	71.8 (1.41)	
2018	68.5 (0.31)	56.3 (2.41)	56.4 (1.77)	65.8 (0.67)	65.1 (0.80)	67.8 (0.88)	72.7 (0.44)	71.9 (0.57)	73.4 (0.79)	78.3 (2.21)	73.9 (1.92)	

—Not available.
†Not applicable.
[1]Includes 1 to 3 years of high school for 1990.
[2]Includes 4 years of high school for 1990.
[3]Includes 1 to 3 years of college and associate's degrees for 1990.
[4]Includes 4 or more years of college for 1990.
[5]Includes 4 years of college for 1990.
[6]Not reported separately for 1990.

[7]Constant dollars based on the Consumer Price Index, prepared by the Bureau of Labor Statistics, U.S. Department of Labor.
[8]Data not available for 1990 and 1995.
NOTE: Detail may not sum to totals because of rounding.
SOURCE: U.S. Department of Commerce, Census Bureau, Current Population Reports, Series P-60, *Money Income of Households, Families, and Persons in the United States, Income, Poverty, and Valuation of Noncash Benefits, 1990*; Series P-60, *Money Income in the United States*, 1995 through 2002; and Current Population Survey (CPS), Annual Social and Economic Supplement, 2003 through 2019. Retrieved January 21, 2020, from https://www.census.gov/data/tables/time-series/demo/income-poverty/cps-pinc/pinc-03.html. (This table was prepared January 2020.)

Table 502.40. Annual earnings of persons 25 years old and over, by highest level of educational attainment and sex: 2018

[Standard errors appear in parentheses]

| | | Elementary/secondary | | | | | College | | | | |
| | | | | | | | Bachelor's or higher degree | | | | |
Sex and earnings	Total	Less than 9th grade	Some high school, no completion	High school completion (includes equivalency)	Some college, no degree	Associate's degree	Total	Bachelor's degree	Master's degree	Professional degree (e.g., M.D., D.D.S., or J.D.)	Doctor's degree (e.g., Ph.D., or Ed.D.)
1	2	3	4	5	6	7	8	9	10	11	12
Number of persons (in thousands)	**221,478** (438.8)	**8,603** (148.8)	**13,372** (184.1)	**62,259** (365.3)	**34,690** (286.3)	**22,738** (236.5)	**79,816** (399.8)	**49,937** (334.6)	**22,214** (233.9)	**3,136** (90.6)	**4,529** (108.6)
With earnings	145,773 (463.7)	3,774 (99.3)	6,282 (127.6)	36,668 (293.4)	22,517 (235.4)	16,173 (201.5)	60,359 (360.9)	37,449 (296.1)	16,784 (205.1)	2,521 (81.3)	3,606 (97.1)
For persons with earnings											
Percentage distribution, by total annual earnings[1]	100.0 (†)	100.0 (†)	100.0 (†)	100.0 (†)	100.0 (†)	100.0 (†)	100.0 (†)	100.0 (†)	100.0 (†)	100.0 (†)	100.0 (†)
$1 to $4,999 or loss[2]	3.5 (0.08)	5.6 (0.61)	6.2 (0.50)	3.9 (0.16)	4.5 (0.22)	3.3 (0.23)	2.6 (0.11)	2.9 (0.14)	2.5 (0.20)	1.3 (0.37)	1.8 (0.36)
$5,000 to $9,999	3.7 (0.08)	5.7 (0.61)	7.4 (0.54)	4.6 (0.18)	4.1 (0.22)	3.5 (0.23)	2.5 (0.10)	2.6 (0.13)	2.5 (0.20)	1.1! (0.33)	1.9 (0.37)
$10,000 to $14,999	4.5 (0.09)	8.3 (0.73)	9.6 (0.60)	6.1 (0.20)	5.3 (0.24)	4.5 (0.27)	2.5 (0.10)	2.8 (0.14)	2.1 (0.18)	1.6 (0.40)	1.1 (0.28)
$15,000 to $19,999	5.2 (0.09)	12.4 (0.87)	12.3 (0.67)	6.9 (0.22)	6.3 (0.26)	5.0 (0.28)	2.6 (0.11)	3.1 (0.15)	1.9 (0.17)	1.2! (0.35)	1.7 (0.35)
$20,000 to $24,999	6.8 (0.11)	17.0 (0.99)	13.7 (0.70)	9.3 (0.25)	7.9 (0.29)	7.2 (0.33)	3.5 (0.12)	4.0 (0.16)	2.8 (0.21)	2.2 (0.48)	2.4 (0.42)
$25,000 to $29,999	6.5 (0.10)	11.3 (0.84)	9.7 (0.61)	9.4 (0.25)	7.5 (0.28)	7.3 (0.33)	3.5 (0.12)	4.1 (0.17)	2.6 (0.20)	1.7 (0.41)	1.7 (0.35)
$30,000 to $34,999	7.2 (0.11)	10.3 (0.80)	8.8 (0.58)	9.8 (0.25)	8.9 (0.31)	8.3 (0.35)	4.3 (0.13)	5.3 (0.19)	2.8 (0.21)	1.5 (0.40)	2.3 (0.40)
$35,000 to $39,999	6.5 (0.10)	8.4 (0.73)	7.9 (0.55)	8.5 (0.24)	7.4 (0.28)	6.8 (0.32)	4.5 (0.14)	5.5 (0.19)	3.2 (0.22)	2.4 (0.50)	1.8 (0.36)
$40,000 to $49,999	11.3 (0.13)	8.2 (0.73)	9.6 (0.61)	12.9 (0.28)	12.5 (0.36)	13.2 (0.43)	9.7 (0.20)	10.9 (0.26)	8.7 (0.35)	4.3 (0.66)	5.5 (0.62)
$50,000 to $74,999	20.8 (0.17)	9.4 (0.77)	10.1 (0.62)	18.0 (0.33)	20.7 (0.44)	24.4 (0.55)	23.4 (0.28)	23.9 (0.36)	25.0 (0.54)	15.8 (1.18)	16.0 (0.99)
$75,000 to $99,999	10.0 (0.13)	1.7 (0.34)	3.0 (0.35)	5.9 (0.20)	8.0 (0.29)	9.2 (0.37)	14.7 (0.23)	13.9 (0.29)	16.5 (0.47)	12.3 (1.06)	16.7 (1.01)
$100,000 or more	14.1 (0.15)	1.7 (0.35)	2.1 (0.22)	4.7 (0.18)	6.9 (0.27)	7.4 (0.33)	26.3 (0.29)	21.1 (0.34)	29.3 (0.57)	54.5 (1.61)	46.9 (1.35)
Median annual earnings[1]	$44,960 (410)	$25,320 (402)	$25,280 (345)	$35,020 (376)	$37,810 (600)	$41,830 (271)	$62,140 (181)	$57,110 (373)	$70,240 (672)	$104,590 (5,439)	$92,130 (2,250)
Number of males (in thousands)	**106,695** (301.0)	**4,313** (105.7)	**6,792** (131.8)	**31,257** (258.1)	**16,591** (198.8)	**9,936** (157.4)	**37,807** (276.4)	**23,785** (231.8)	**9,621** (155.1)	**1,820** (69.2)	**2,580** (82.2)
With earnings	77,236 (322.9)	2,498 (80.9)	3,913 (100.8)	21,454 (222.1)	11,873 (170.9)	7,618 (138.9)	29,880 (253.8)	18,938 (210.6)	7,445 (137.4)	1,466 (62.2)	2,032 (73.1)
For males with earnings											
Percentage distribution, by total annual earnings[1]	100.0 (†)	100.0 (†)	100.0 (†)	100.0 (†)	100.0 (†)	100.0 (†)	100.0 (†)	100.0 (†)	100.0 (†)	100.0 (†)	100.0 (†)
$1 to $4,999 or loss[2]	2.4 (0.09)	3.7 (0.62)	5.2 (0.58)	2.7 (0.18)	2.9 (0.25)	2.0 (0.26)	1.7 (0.12)	1.8 (0.16)	1.7 (0.25)	‡ (†)	1.8 (0.48)
$5,000 to $9,999	2.5 (0.09)	3.0 (0.55)	5.6 (0.60)	2.9 (0.19)	3.0 (0.26)	2.2 (0.27)	1.7 (0.12)	1.8 (0.16)	1.8 (0.25)	‡ (†)	1.5 (0.44)
$10,000 to $14,999	3.3 (0.10)	5.6 (0.75)	6.0 (0.62)	4.3 (0.22)	3.7 (0.28)	2.8 (0.31)	2.0 (0.13)	2.2 (0.18)	1.8 (0.25)	1.2! (0.46)	1.4! (0.42)
$15,000 to $19,999	3.8 (0.11)	10.4 (1.00)	9.1 (0.75)	4.8 (0.24)	4.0 (0.29)	3.4 (0.34)	1.8 (0.13)	2.1 (0.17)	1.4 (0.22)	‡ (†)	1.6 (0.45)
$20,000 to $24,999	5.8 (0.14)	16.5 (1.21)	12.6 (0.87)	7.4 (0.29)	6.2 (0.36)	4.9 (0.40)	2.8 (0.16)	3.1 (0.21)	2.5 (0.29)	1.6! (0.54)	2.3 (0.54)
$25,000 to $29,999	5.6 (0.14)	10.8 (1.01)	9.2 (0.75)	7.9 (0.30)	6.3 (0.36)	5.1 (0.41)	2.9 (0.16)	3.6 (0.22)	2.0 (0.26)	2.1 (0.61)	1.3! (0.41)
$30,000 to $34,999	6.4 (0.14)	11.9 (1.06)	10.1 (0.79)	8.7 (0.31)	7.6 (0.40)	6.0 (0.45)	3.5 (0.17)	4.4 (0.24)	1.9 (0.26)	1.2! (0.47)	2.5 (0.56)
$35,000 to $39,999	6.2 (0.14)	10.8 (1.01)	9.2 (0.75)	8.9 (0.32)	6.5 (0.37)	5.3 (0.42)	3.5 (0.17)	4.3 (0.24)	2.5 (0.29)	1.9! (0.58)	1.3! (0.41)
$40,000 to $49,999	11.0 (0.18)	10.2 (0.99)	12.2 (0.86)	14.4 (0.39)	13.0 (0.50)	13.4 (0.64)	7.1 (0.24)	8.4 (0.33)	5.8 (0.44)	2.3 (0.64)	4.0 (0.71)
$50,000 to $74,999	22.3 (0.24)	12.8 (1.09)	13.7 (0.90)	23.1 (0.47)	24.3 (0.64)	29.4 (0.85)	21.1 (0.39)	23.5 (0.50)	18.5 (0.73)	13.6 (1.46)	13.1 (1.22)
$75,000 to $99,999	11.8 (0.19)	2.3 (0.49)	4.6 (0.55)	8.1 (0.30)	11.6 (0.48)	13.4 (0.64)	15.9 (0.34)	15.7 (0.43)	17.1 (0.71)	11.6 (1.36)	16.5 (1.34)
$100,000 or more	18.8 (0.23)	2.3 (0.49)	2.3 (0.39)	6.9 (0.28)	10.8 (0.47)	12.0 (0.61)	35.8 (0.45)	29.1 (0.54)	43.2 (0.94)	62.6 (2.06)	52.8 (1.81)
Median annual earnings[1]	$51,300 (139)	$30,020 (688)	$30,610 (352)	$40,900 (200)	$46,850 (531)	$51,730 (314)	$76,400 (396)	$67,440 (1105)	$90,010 (2,980)	$122,340 (4,971)	$101,130 (729)

See notes at end of table.

Table 502.40. Annual earnings of persons 25 years old and over, by highest level of educational attainment and sex: 2018—Continued

[Standard errors appear in parentheses]

Sex and earnings	Total	Elementary/secondary				College					
		Less than 9th grade	Some high school, no completion	High school completion (includes equivalency)	Some college, no degree	Associate's degree	Bachelor's or higher degree				
							Total	Bachelor's degree	Master's degree	Professional degree (e.g., M.D., D.D.S., or J.D.)	Doctor's degree (e.g., Ph.D. or Ed.D.)
1	2	3	4	5	6	7	8	9	10	11	12
Number of females (in thousands)	**114,783** (269.1)	**4,290** (96.7)	**6,580** (118.8)	**31,002** (236.5)	**18,099** (189.5)	**12,802** (162.3)	**42,009** (263.3)	**26,151** (221.3)	**12,593** (161.1)	**1,317** (54.1)	**1,948** (65.6)
With earnings	68,537 (296.0)	1,276 (53.2)	2,369 (72.3)	15,214 (175.5)	10,644 (149.1)	8,554 (134.6)	30,479 (235.0)	18,511 (191.4)	9,338 (140.3)	1,055 (48.4)	1,574 (59.1)
For females with earnings											
Percentage distribution, by total annual earnings[1]	100.0 (†)	100.0 (†)	100.0 (†)	100.0 (†)	100.0 (†)	100.0 (†)	100.0 (†)	100.0 (†)	100.0 (†)	100.0 (†)	100.0 (†)
$1 to $4,999 or loss[2]	4.8 (0.12)	9.4 (1.22)	7.9 (0.83)	5.6 (0.28)	6.2 (0.35)	4.3 (0.33)	3.5 (0.16)	3.9 (0.21)	3.2 (0.27)	2.4 (0.70)	1.8 (0.51)
$5,000 to $9,999	4.9 (0.12)	11.0 (1.31)	10.3 (0.94)	6.9 (0.31)	5.3 (0.33)	4.6 (0.34)	3.2 (0.15)	3.4 (0.20)	3.1 (0.27)	1.8! (0.61)	2.5 (0.59)
$10,000 to $14,999	5.9 (0.13)	13.6 (1.44)	15.6 (1.12)	8.8 (0.34)	7.0 (0.37)	6.1 (0.39)	2.9 (0.14)	3.4 (0.20)	2.3 (0.23)	2.3! (0.69)	0.8! (0.33)
$15,000 to $19,999	6.8 (0.14)	16.4 (1.55)	17.5 (1.17)	8.8 (0.34)	8.8 (0.41)	6.3 (0.39)	3.4 (0.16)	4.2 (0.22)	2.4 (0.24)	1.8! (0.61)	2.0 (0.52)
$20,000 to $24,999	8.1 (0.16)	17.9 (1.60)	15.4 (1.11)	9.9 (0.36)	9.8 (0.43)	9.2 (0.47)	4.2 (0.17)	4.9 (0.24)	3.1 (0.27)	3.0 (0.79)	2.5 (0.59)
$25,000 to $29,999	7.4 (0.15)	12.2 (1.37)	10.5 (0.94)	12.0 (0.39)	8.8 (0.41)	9.2 (0.47)	4.0 (0.17)	4.7 (0.23)	3.1 (0.27)	1.0! (0.47)	2.4 (0.57)
$30,000 to $34,999	8.0 (0.15)	7.2 (1.08)	6.6 (0.76)	11.4 (0.39)	10.3 (0.44)	10.3 (0.49)	5.0 (0.19)	6.2 (0.26)	3.6 (0.29)	2.0! (0.64)	2.0 (0.53)
$35,000 to $39,999	6.8 (0.14)	3.8 (0.80)	5.8 (0.72)	11.3 (0.38)	8.4 (0.40)	8.2 (0.44)	5.4 (0.19)	6.7 (0.27)	3.8 (0.29)	3.1 (0.80)	2.5 (0.59)
$40,000 to $49,999	11.6 (0.18)	4.3 (0.85)	5.4 (0.69)	8.1 (0.33)	12.0 (0.47)	13.1 (0.55)	12.2 (0.28)	13.5 (0.38)	10.9 (0.48)	6.9 (1.17)	7.4 (0.99)
$50,000 to $74,999	19.1 (0.22)	2.7 (0.67)	4.2 (0.62)	10.9 (0.38)	16.7 (0.54)	19.8 (0.64)	25.6 (0.37)	24.2 (0.47)	30.2 (0.71)	19.1 (1.81)	19.8 (1.50)
$75,000 to $99,999	8.0 (0.16)	‡ (†)	0.4! (0.19)	2.7 (0.20)	4.0 (0.28)	5.5 (0.37)	13.6 (0.29)	12.1 (0.36)	16.0 (0.57)	13.4 (1.57)	17.0 (1.42)
$100,000 or more	8.7 (0.16)	0.7! (0.35)	0.5! (0.21)	1.5 (0.15)	2.5 (0.23)	3.4 (0.29)	16.9 (0.32)	12.9 (0.37)	18.3 (0.60)	43.3 (2.28)	39.3 (1.84)
Median annual earnings[1]	$37,140 (168)	$19,800 (759)	$19,610 (476)	$27,200 (195)	$31,140 (205)	$34,950 (705)	$53,210 (715)	$49,010 (784)	$60,370 (423)	$82,170 (4,457)	$81,600 (2,308)

†Not applicable.
!Interpret data with caution. The coefficient of variation (CV) for this estimate is between 30 and 50 percent.
‡Reporting standards not met. Either there are too few cases for a reliable estimate or the coefficient of variation (CV) is 50 percent or greater.
[1]Excludes persons without earnings.
[2]A negative amount (a net loss) may be reported by self-employed persons.

NOTE: Data are based on sample surveys of the noninstitutionalized population, which excludes persons living in institutions (e.g., prisons or nursing facilities); data include military personnel who live in households with civilians but exclude those who live in military barracks. Detail may not sum to totals because of rounding and suppression of data that do not meet reporting standards.
SOURCE: U.S. Department of Commerce, Census Bureau, Current Population Survey (CPS), Annual Social and Economic Supplement, 2018; retrieved March 11, 2020, from https://www.census.gov/data/tables/time-series/demo/income-poverty/cps-pinc/pinc-03.html. (This table was prepared March 2020.)

Table 503.10. Percentage of high school students age 16 and over who were employed, by age group, sex, race/ethnicity, family income, nativity, and hours worked per week: Selected years, 1970 through 2017

[Standard errors appear in parentheses]

Year	Total	Age group		Sex		Race/ethnicity			Family income[1]			Nativity	
		16 and 17 years old	18 years old and over	Male	Female	White	Black	Hispanic	Low income	Middle income	High income	U.S.-born	Foreign-born
1	2	3	4	5	6	7	8	9	10	11	12	13	14
Percent employed[2]													
1970	31.9 (0.88)	30.8 (0.93)	39.7 (2.55)	35.2 (1.24)	28.3 (1.22)	— (†)	— (†)	— (†)	22.0 (2.51)	31.5 (1.12)	35.9 (1.64)	— (†)	— (†)
1975	33.2 (0.85)	32.9 (0.91)	34.9 (2.40)	35.0 (1.19)	31.2 (1.22)	38.0 (1.00)	13.9 (1.63)	21.8 (3.59)	18.4 (2.22)	31.8 (1.10)	40.4 (1.59)	— (†)	— (†)
1980	35.6 (0.87)	34.9 (0.94)	39.6 (2.28)	36.9 (1.22)	34.2 (1.24)	41.2 (1.03)	15.0 (1.64)	24.1 (3.65)	19.4 (2.10)	35.2 (1.15)	42.3 (1.59)	— (†)	— (†)
1985	31.6 (0.93)	30.8 (1.00)	36.1 (2.47)	32.1 (1.29)	31.0 (1.33)	37.9 (1.15)	15.0 (1.85)	17.6 (2.63)	14.7 (1.85)	31.0 (1.23)	41.1 (1.81)	— (†)	— (†)
1990	32.3 (0.98)	31.2 (1.08)	37.1 (2.33)	33.1 (1.37)	31.3 (1.39)	37.8 (1.24)	17.3 (2.05)	26.4 (2.86)	21.4 (2.16)	33.1 (1.29)	36.8 (1.97)	— (†)	— (†)
1995	33.6 (0.92)	32.7 (1.02)	37.5 (2.19)	33.1 (1.26)	34.2 (1.35)	40.8 (1.18)	18.0 (1.91)	22.2 (2.41)	17.4 (1.82)	34.4 (1.23)	42.1 (1.88)	34.9 (0.97)	20.1 (2.65)
2000	34.1 (0.93)	33.3 (1.03)	37.7 (2.15)	33.2 (1.28)	35.1 (1.36)	41.3 (1.20)	21.3 (2.14)	20.9 (2.18)	22.0 (2.11)	34.1 (1.22)	40.7 (1.85)	35.1 (0.99)	24.4 (2.74)
2001	32.4 (0.86)	31.1 (0.95)	37.8 (1.99)	30.6 (1.17)	34.5 (1.27)	38.9 (1.11)	18.7 (1.85)	23.6 (2.23)	21.4 (2.04)	33.3 (1.12)	36.1 (1.70)	33.3 (0.90)	23.0 (2.64)
2002	30.6 (0.84)	29.2 (0.93)	35.9 (1.92)	28.0 (1.13)	33.4 (1.24)	37.5 (1.11)	16.9 (1.81)	21.1 (1.94)	18.4 (1.83)	31.4 (1.11)	35.3 (1.64)	31.6 (0.89)	21.3 (2.34)
2003	27.0 (0.79)	25.3 (0.86)	34.6 (1.97)	26.7 (1.09)	27.3 (1.15)	33.3 (1.07)	15.2 (1.68)	18.8 (1.82)	14.3 (1.64)	27.5 (1.05)	31.8 (1.57)	28.0 (0.84)	17.7 (2.17)
2004	27.2 (0.80)	25.6 (0.87)	34.7 (2.03)	26.2 (1.09)	28.3 (1.17)	32.9 (1.08)	15.1 (1.71)	21.2 (1.92)	12.0 (1.55)	27.5 (1.05)	34.4 (1.64)	27.8 (0.85)	20.8 (2.43)
2005	26.4 (0.77)	25.2 (0.84)	32.2 (1.95)	25.3 (1.05)	27.6 (1.14)	31.8 (1.05)	13.7 (1.63)	19.4 (1.78)	14.8 (1.61)	26.9 (1.03)	31.7 (1.55)	26.8 (0.81)	21.7 (2.49)
2006	27.6 (0.79)	26.0 (0.86)	34.1 (1.87)	26.5 (1.08)	28.8 (1.16)	33.6 (1.08)	20.1 (1.85)	17.5 (1.72)	17.8 (1.72)	27.5 (1.04)	33.5 (1.59)	27.9 (0.82)	23.9 (2.64)
2007	26.2 (0.78)	24.8 (0.85)	32.2 (1.87)	25.0 (1.06)	27.6 (1.14)	31.3 (1.06)	15.1 (1.68)	21.1 (1.83)	17.3 (1.74)	25.9 (1.01)	32.1 (1.62)	26.0 (0.81)	28.5 (2.64)
2008	22.6 (0.74)	21.0 (0.80)	29.5 (1.83)	20.0 (0.99)	25.4 (1.10)	27.7 (1.04)	15.5 (1.69)	15.1 (1.54)	13.5 (1.54)	22.6 (0.96)	28.4 (1.59)	23.1 (0.78)	18.0 (2.35)
2009	17.0 (0.67)	15.2 (0.72)	23.8 (1.65)	16.0 (0.91)	18.1 (0.98)	21.5 (0.96)	10.5 (1.43)	11.9 (1.39)	9.7 (1.33)	16.3 (0.85)	23.5 (1.51)	17.0 (0.70)	16.9 (2.32)
2010	16.2 (0.55)	15.0 (0.59)	20.8 (1.52)	14.0 (0.78)	18.5 (0.86)	20.9 (0.86)	9.6 (1.28)	10.4 (1.18)	8.5 (1.01)	16.5 (0.80)	20.9 (1.31)	16.4 (0.60)	13.4 (2.20)
2011	16.9 (0.67)	16.4 (0.77)	18.7 (1.28)	14.7 (0.76)	19.4 (1.09)	22.2 (1.07)	10.2 (1.43)	11.3 (1.11)	10.2 (1.29)	17.5 (0.83)	19.6 (1.39)	17.3 (0.74)	12.4 (1.91)
2012	18.0 (0.71)	16.0 (0.75)	24.5 (1.88)	16.6 (0.83)	19.4 (1.13)	23.2 (0.97)	12.7 (2.17)	11.4 (1.23)	13.0 (1.42)	16.4 (0.88)	24.9 (1.55)	18.6 (0.76)	12.0 (2.01)
2013	17.9 (0.65)	15.8 (0.69)	24.7 (1.73)	17.6 (0.89)	18.3 (0.94)	23.3 (0.99)	11.8 (1.42)	14.0 (1.19)	9.7 (1.26)	16.9 (0.90)	25.4 (1.69)	17.8 (0.66)	19.0 (2.67)
2014	19.2 (0.70)	17.3 (0.71)	25.5 (1.63)	18.1 (0.90)	20.3 (1.03)	23.2 (1.00)	14.0 (1.65)	14.7 (1.47)	12.6 (1.52)	19.3 (0.88)	23.2 (1.54)	19.2 (0.75)	18.8 (2.20)
2015	19.0 (0.73)	17.2 (0.79)	25.8 (1.70)	18.1 (0.92)	20.0 (1.23)	22.2 (1.05)	15.0 (2.03)	15.7 (1.42)	13.7 (1.87)	18.8 (0.93)	22.3 (1.47)	19.0 (0.78)	19.2 (2.20)
2016	18.3 (0.70)	16.5 (0.79)	24.9 (1.80)	15.8 (0.88)	20.9 (1.16)	22.9 (0.95)	9.3 (1.54)	15.0 (1.38)	8.1 (1.17)	18.9 (0.98)	22.8 (1.58)	18.7 (0.77)	14.0 (2.13)
2017	20.3 (0.73)	17.7 (0.72)	29.5 (1.88)	18.1 (0.89)	22.7 (1.08)	24.8 (1.01)	15.7 (1.73)	15.9 (1.53)	13.3 (1.60)	19.9 (0.92)	25.0 (1.57)	20.4 (0.74)	19.4 (2.75)
Percent working less than 15 hours per week[3]													
1970	13.6 (0.64)	14.5 (0.71)	7.5 (1.37)	12.3 (0.85)	14.9 (0.97)	— (†)	— (†)	— (†)	9.9 (1.81)	12.6 (0.80)	16.8 (1.28)	— (†)	— (†)
1975	13.4 (0.62)	14.0 (0.67)	8.8 (1.43)	12.5 (0.82)	14.3 (0.92)	15.5 (0.75)	5.3 (1.05)	6.6! (2.15)	6.8 (1.44)	12.3 (0.78)	17.4 (1.23)	— (†)	— (†)
1980	14.0 (0.63)	14.9 (0.70)	8.9 (1.33)	13.7 (0.87)	14.2 (0.91)	16.4 (0.77)	4.6 (0.96)	9.4 (2.49)	7.7 (1.41)	13.2 (0.82)	17.7 (1.23)	— (†)	— (†)
1985	12.3 (0.65)	12.8 (0.72)	9.5 (1.51)	11.7 (0.89)	12.9 (0.96)	15.2 (0.85)	6.2 (1.25)	3.0! (1.18)	3.6 (0.97)	11.8 (0.86)	17.5 (1.40)	— (†)	— (†)
1990	11.7 (0.67)	12.9 (0.78)	6.8 (1.21)	11.3 (0.92)	12.2 (0.98)	14.7 (0.90)	6.0 (1.28)	4.8 (1.39)	5.9 (1.24)	11.5 (0.88)	15.6 (1.48)	— (†)	— (†)
1995	11.9 (0.63)	13.1 (0.73)	6.8 (1.14)	11.1 (0.84)	12.9 (0.96)	14.8 (0.85)	6.5 (1.22)	6.5 (1.42)	4.4 (0.98)	11.3 (0.82)	18.1 (1.47)	12.6 (0.68)	5.1 (1.46)
2000	11.9 (0.64)	12.9 (0.73)	7.8 (1.19)	11.2 (0.86)	12.6 (0.94)	15.4 (0.88)	6.3 (1.27)	3.7 (1.01)	5.4 (1.15)	11.3 (0.82)	16.5 (1.40)	12.6 (0.68)	5.2 (1.42)
2001	11.6 (0.59)	12.6 (0.68)	7.7 (1.10)	9.8 (0.75)	13.7 (0.91)	15.0 (0.82)	4.3 (0.96)	6.1 (1.26)	5.7 (1.15)	10.8 (0.74)	16.4 (1.31)	12.2 (0.63)	5.5 (1.43)
2002	11.1 (0.57)	12.1 (0.66)	7.2 (1.04)	9.7 (0.74)	12.7 (0.87)	15.0 (0.82)	4.5 (1.00)	3.6 (0.89)	6.0 (1.12)	10.0 (0.72)	16.1 (1.26)	11.9 (0.62)	4.1 (1.13)
2003	9.6 (0.52)	10.0 (0.59)	7.8 (1.11)	9.0 (0.70)	10.2 (0.78)	12.4 (0.75)	4.5 (0.96)	5.5 (1.06)	4.8 (1.00)	9.1 (0.67)	13.1 (1.14)	10.2 (0.57)	3.7 (1.07)
2004	10.4 (0.55)	10.9 (0.62)	8.4 (1.18)	9.9 (0.74)	11.0 (0.82)	14.0 (0.80)	4.9 (1.03)	4.4 (0.96)	3.5 (0.87)	8.5 (0.66)	18.1 (1.33)	11.0 (0.59)	5.2 (1.33)
2005	10.1 (0.53)	10.7 (0.60)	7.2 (1.08)	8.9 (0.69)	11.4 (0.81)	13.4 (0.77)	3.7 (0.89)	5.0 (0.99)	3.7 (0.85)	9.9 (0.69)	13.9 (1.16)	10.6 (0.56)	4.6 (1.26)
2006	9.9 (0.53)	10.7 (0.61)	6.4 (0.97)	8.8 (0.69)	11.0 (0.80)	12.8 (0.76)	5.2 (1.03)	4.2 (0.91)	3.7 (0.85)	9.2 (0.67)	14.7 (1.20)	10.5 (0.56)	3.0! (1.06)
2007	10.6 (0.54)	11.4 (0.63)	7.0 (1.02)	9.5 (0.72)	11.7 (0.82)	14.2 (0.80)	3.0 (0.80)	6.0 (1.06)	6.1 (1.10)	9.6 (0.68)	15.3 (1.25)	11.1 (0.58)	5.7 (1.36)
2008	9.2 (0.51)	9.9 (0.59)	6.1 (0.96)	8.1 (0.68)	10.3 (0.77)	12.4 (0.77)	3.2 (0.82)	4.1 (0.85)	3.1 (0.78)	9.1 (0.66)	13.0 (1.18)	9.6 (0.54)	4.6 (1.28)
2009	7.6 (0.47)	8.0 (0.54)	6.2 (0.94)	6.8 (0.62)	8.4 (0.71)	10.1 (0.71)	3.6 (0.86)	4.7 (0.91)	3.6 (0.83)	6.9 (0.58)	11.8 (1.15)	7.8 (0.50)	5.2 (1.38)

See notes at end of table.

Table 503.10. Percentage of high school students age 16 and over who were employed, by age group, sex, race/ethnicity, family income, nativity, and hours worked per week: Selected years, 1970 through 2017—Continued

[Standard errors appear in parentheses]

Year	Total	Age group		Sex		Race/ethnicity			Family income[1]			Nativity	
		16 and 17 years old	18 years and over	Male	Female	White	Black	Hispanic	Low income	Middle income	High income	U.S.-born	Foreign-born
1	2	3	4	5	6	7	8	9	10	11	12	13	14
2010	7.3 (0.42)	7.5 (0.49)	6.8 (0.94)	6.3 (0.50)	8.4 (0.69)	9.5 (0.65)	4.1 (0.82)	4.5 (0.79)	3.0 (0.63)	7.1 (0.54)	10.9 (1.01)	7.7 (0.45)	3.4! (1.21)
2011	7.3 (0.40)	8.1 (0.50)	4.4 (0.71)	5.8 (0.51)	9.0 (0.66)	11.0 (0.66)	2.2 (0.60)	2.7 (0.54)	3.7 (0.81)	7.0 (0.55)	10.2 (0.94)	7.7 (0.44)	2.8! (0.98)
2012	8.2 (0.46)	8.5 (0.53)	7.3 (0.95)	7.1 (0.57)	9.4 (0.73)	12.2 (0.73)	3.7 (0.92)	2.4 (0.58)	4.2 (0.89)	7.2 (0.53)	13.3 (1.27)	8.8 (0.50)	2.4! (0.75)
2013	7.9 (0.50)	8.2 (0.54)	6.8 (0.99)	6.9 (0.61)	8.9 (0.77)	12.2 (0.81)	2.6 (0.71)	3.4 (0.62)	2.9 (0.78)	7.0 (0.54)	13.1 (1.38)	8.1 (0.50)	5.5! (1.75)
2014	7.8 (0.43)	8.4 (0.49)	5.7 (0.85)	6.5 (0.54)	9.1 (0.67)	10.7 (0.67)	3.5 (0.91)	3.5 (0.65)	3.8 (0.90)	7.6 (0.57)	10.9 (1.04)	8.2 (0.46)	3.7! (1.14)
2015	8.5 (0.48)	8.7 (0.54)	7.8 (1.07)	7.8 (0.70)	9.3 (0.75)	10.9 (0.75)	7.0 (1.49)	5.3 (0.97)	5.0 (1.07)	7.7 (0.60)	12.2 (1.18)	9.1 (0.53)	3.4 (1.00)
2016	8.1 (0.48)	8.4 (0.57)	7.0 (1.12)	6.5 (0.58)	9.8 (0.85)	10.8 (0.73)	2.4! (0.81)	5.0 (0.81)	2.6 (0.70)	7.5 (0.63)	12.4 (1.18)	8.5 (0.51)	4.5 (1.33)
2017	7.7 (0.50)	7.6 (0.55)	8.0 (1.01)	6.4 (0.58)	9.2 (0.73)	10.9 (0.79)	3.3 (0.84)	3.9 (0.80)	3.3 (0.74)	6.3 (0.59)	13.1 (1.19)	8.1 (0.54)	3.1! (1.19)
Percent working 15 or more total hours per week[3]													
1970	17.5 (0.71)	15.6 (0.73)	30.8 (2.41)	22.1 (1.08)	12.6 (0.90)	— (†)	— (†)	— (†)	10.6 (1.87)	18.4 (0.93)	18.1 (1.32)	— (†)	— (†)
1975	19.2 (0.71)	18.2 (0.75)	25.7 (2.20)	21.7 (1.03)	16.4 (0.97)	21.8 (0.85)	8.3 (1.30)	14.7 (3.08)	11.3 (1.81)	19.0 (0.93)	22.1 (1.34)	— (†)	— (†)
1980	20.5 (0.73)	19.0 (0.77)	29.4 (2.12)	22.1 (1.05)	18.9 (1.02)	23.5 (0.89)	10.1 (1.39)	14.3 (2.99)	11.4 (1.69)	21.0 (0.98)	23.1 (1.36)	— (†)	— (†)
1985	18.4 (0.77)	17.2 (0.81)	25.5 (2.24)	19.5 (1.09)	17.3 (1.09)	21.7 (0.97)	8.4 (1.44)	13.7 (2.37)	10.0 (1.57)	18.4 (1.03)	22.6 (1.54)	— (†)	— (†)
1990	19.7 (0.83)	17.5 (0.88)	29.1 (2.19)	21.0 (1.19)	18.3 (1.16)	22.1 (1.06)	10.6 (1.67)	21.5 (2.66)	15.0 (1.88)	20.8 (1.11)	20.2 (1.64)	— (†)	— (†)
1995	20.5 (0.79)	18.4 (0.84)	29.7 (2.07)	20.8 (1.09)	20.2 (1.14)	24.5 (1.03)	10.9 (1.55)	15.1 (2.07)	12.7 (1.60)	21.9 (1.07)	22.5 (1.59)	21.1 (0.83)	14.9 (2.35)
2000	21.1 (0.80)	19.2 (0.86)	28.8 (2.01)	21.1 (1.11)	21.0 (1.16)	24.6 (1.05)	13.8 (1.80)	16.3 (1.98)	15.6 (1.85)	21.5 (1.06)	23.1 (1.59)	21.3 (0.84)	19.0 (2.50)
2001	19.4 (0.73)	17.1 (0.77)	28.3 (1.85)	19.6 (1.01)	19.1 (1.05)	22.2 (0.95)	13.4 (1.62)	17.0 (1.97)	14.6 (1.76)	20.9 (0.97)	18.4 (1.37)	19.6 (0.76)	16.9 (2.35)
2002	18.5 (0.71)	16.1 (0.75)	27.9 (1.80)	17.5 (0.95)	19.7 (1.04)	21.4 (0.94)	11.9 (1.57)	16.8 (1.78)	12.3 (1.55)	20.7 (0.97)	17.4 (1.30)	18.7 (0.75)	16.5 (2.12)
2003	16.4 (0.66)	14.3 (0.69)	25.9 (1.82)	16.8 (0.92)	16.0 (0.94)	19.5 (0.90)	10.4 (1.42)	13.1 (1.57)	9.1 (1.35)	17.6 (0.89)	17.7 (1.29)	16.7 (0.70)	13.6 (1.95)
2004	16.0 (0.66)	13.8 (0.68)	26.2 (1.88)	15.5 (0.90)	16.6 (0.97)	17.8 (0.88)	10.2 (1.45)	16.6 (1.75)	8.1 (1.30)	18.3 (0.91)	15.2 (1.24)	16.1 (0.69)	15.2 (2.15)
2005	15.2 (0.63)	13.4 (0.66)	23.5 (1.77)	15.5 (0.88)	14.8 (0.90)	17.0 (0.84)	9.6 (1.40)	13.6 (1.55)	10.8 (1.40)	15.9 (0.85)	16.1 (1.23)	15.1 (0.66)	16.5 (2.24)
2006	17.0 (0.66)	14.4 (0.69)	27.0 (1.75)	16.8 (0.91)	17.1 (0.96)	19.5 (0.90)	14.5 (1.63)	13.3 (1.54)	13.8 (1.55)	17.7 (0.89)	17.3 (1.27)	16.6 (0.68)	20.8 (2.51)
2007	15.0 (0.63)	12.8 (0.66)	24.2 (1.72)	14.8 (0.87)	15.2 (0.92)	16.2 (0.85)	11.4 (1.49)	14.9 (1.59)	10.9 (1.44)	15.6 (0.83)	15.8 (1.27)	14.3 (0.65)	22.2 (2.43)
2008	12.8 (0.59)	10.3 (0.60)	22.7 (1.68)	11.4 (0.79)	14.1 (0.88)	14.3 (0.82)	11.9 (1.51)	10.6 (1.32)	9.9 (1.34)	12.8 (0.77)	14.4 (1.23)	12.7 (0.62)	13.0 (2.06)
2009	8.7 (0.50)	6.4 (0.49)	17.3 (1.47)	8.4 (0.69)	9.1 (0.73)	10.4 (0.71)	6.5 (1.15)	7.2 (1.11)	5.9 (1.06)	8.9 (0.66)	9.9 (1.07)	8.4 (0.52)	11.7 (1.99)
2010	8.3 (0.45)	6.9 (0.47)	13.4 (1.24)	7.2 (0.62)	9.4 (0.70)	10.5 (0.67)	5.3 (1.01)	5.6 (0.84)	5.3 (0.88)	9.0 (0.58)	8.7 (1.16)	8.1 (0.46)	9.6 (1.83)
2011	9.0 (0.52)	7.7 (0.56)	13.6 (1.10)	8.4 (0.63)	9.8 (0.78)	10.5 (0.77)	7.4 (1.30)	8.4 (1.06)	6.3 (1.10)	10.0 (0.69)	8.5 (0.94)	9.0 (0.55)	9.6 (1.84)
2012	8.9 (0.55)	6.7 (0.51)	16.5 (1.62)	8.4 (0.62)	9.5 (0.84)	10.0 (0.69)	8.2 (1.97)	8.4 (1.04)	8.3 (1.22)	8.7 (0.68)	9.9 (1.30)	8.9 (0.59)	9.6 (1.76)
2013	9.7 (0.56)	7.3 (0.53)	17.4 (1.57)	10.3 (0.85)	9.1 (0.67)	10.6 (0.81)	9.1 (1.37)	10.6 (1.10)	6.7 (1.19)	9.7 (0.82)	11.7 (1.12)	9.4 (0.60)	13.4 (2.15)
2014	10.7 (0.55)	8.2 (0.48)	19.3 (1.49)	10.8 (0.72)	10.6 (0.81)	11.6 (0.75)	9.4 (1.52)	11.0 (1.30)	8.6 (1.34)	11.1 (0.73)	11.1 (1.25)	10.2 (0.56)	15.1 (2.12)
2015	9.7 (0.54)	7.8 (0.53)	17.2 (1.50)	9.7 (0.66)	10.5 (0.86)	10.5 (0.75)	7.3 (1.31)	9.8 (1.11)	8.2 (1.41)	10.2 (0.72)	9.7 (1.05)	9.2 (0.57)	15.0 (2.08)
2016	9.7 (0.55)	7.6 (0.58)	17.3 (1.54)	8.8 (0.65)	10.6 (0.87)	11.6 (0.79)	6.9 (1.32)	9.0 (1.16)	5.5 (1.01)	10.8 (0.72)	9.8 (1.13)	9.7 (0.60)	9.0 (1.69)
2017	11.6 (0.58)	9.1 (0.55)	20.5 (1.62)	11.0 (0.75)	12.3 (0.90)	12.4 (0.77)	12.4 (1.61)	11.6 (1.33)	9.7 (1.47)	12.7 (0.67)	10.5 (1.17)	11.3 (0.58)	15.7 (2.54)

—Not available.
†Not applicable.
!Interpret data with caution. The coefficient of variation (CV) for this estimate is between 30 and 50 percent.
[1]Low income refers to the bottom 20 percent of all family incomes; high income refers to the top 20 percent of all family incomes; and middle income refers to the 60 percent in between.
[2]Percent employed includes those who were employed but not at work during the survey week.
[3]Hours worked per week refers to the number of hours the respondent worked at all jobs during the survey week. The estimates of the percentage of high school students age 16 and over who worked less than 15 hours per week or 15 or more hours per week exclude those who were employed but not at work during the survey week. Therefore, detail may not sum to total percentage employed.
NOTE: Race categories exclude persons of Hispanic ethnicity. Totals include racial/ethnic groups not shown separately. Prior to 2010, standard errors were computed using generalized variance function methodology rather than the more precise replicate weight methodology used in later years.
SOURCE: U.S. Department of Commerce, Census Bureau, Current Population Survey (CPS), October, 1970 through 2017. (This table was prepared April 2019.)

Table 503.20. Percentage of college students 16 to 24 years old who were employed, by attendance status, hours worked per week, and control and level of institution: Selected years, October 1970 through 2017

[Standard errors appear in parentheses]

Control and level of institution and year	Full-time students				Part-time students			
	Percent employed[1]	Hours worked per week[2]			Percent employed[1]	Hours worked per week[2]		
		Less than 20 hours	20 to 34 hours	35 or more hours		Less than 20 hours	20 to 34 hours	35 or more hours
1	2	3	4	5	6	7	8	9
Total, all institutions								
1970	33.8 (0.88)	19.0 (0.73)	10.4 (0.57)	3.7 (0.35)	82.1 (1.81)	5.0 (1.03)	15.9 (1.72)	60.1 (2.31)
1975	35.3 (0.83)	18.0 (0.67)	12.0 (0.56)	4.6 (0.36)	80.8 (1.55)	6.0 (0.94)	19.4 (1.56)	52.6 (1.97)
1980	40.0 (0.84)	21.3 (0.70)	14.0 (0.59)	3.9 (0.33)	84.7 (1.38)	7.9 (1.04)	22.5 (1.60)	52.7 (1.91)
1985	44.2 (0.88)	21.7 (0.73)	17.3 (0.67)	4.3 (0.36)	85.9 (1.41)	5.7 (0.94)	26.9 (1.80)	52.2 (2.03)
1990	45.7 (0.89)	20.6 (0.73)	19.3 (0.71)	4.8 (0.38)	83.7 (1.50)	4.0 (0.80)	26.0 (1.78)	52.7 (2.03)
1991	47.2 (0.88)	20.9 (0.72)	19.8 (0.70)	5.6 (0.41)	85.9 (1.45)	8.2 (1.15)	25.4 (1.82)	51.0 (2.09)
1992	47.2 (0.87)	20.3 (0.70)	20.3 (0.70)	5.5 (0.40)	83.4 (1.50)	7.5 (1.06)	27.2 (1.79)	47.8 (2.01)
1993	46.3 (0.89)	20.8 (0.72)	19.5 (0.71)	5.1 (0.39)	84.6 (1.43)	8.5 (1.10)	31.4 (1.84)	43.7 (1.96)
1994	48.6 (0.87)	20.1 (0.70)	21.7 (0.72)	5.8 (0.41)	86.3 (1.28)	9.8 (1.10)	31.1 (1.72)	43.8 (1.84)
1995	47.2 (0.87)	19.1 (0.69)	20.3 (0.70)	6.5 (0.43)	82.9 (1.45)	8.6 (1.08)	30.4 (1.77)	42.3 (1.90)
1996	49.2 (0.88)	18.2 (0.68)	22.3 (0.74)	7.0 (0.45)	84.8 (1.47)	8.3 (1.13)	27.5 (1.83)	48.0 (2.05)
1997	47.8 (0.86)	18.3 (0.67)	21.4 (0.71)	7.4 (0.45)	84.4 (1.46)	9.4 (1.17)	26.2 (1.77)	47.7 (2.01)
1998	50.2 (0.86)	20.2 (0.69)	20.6 (0.70)	8.0 (0.47)	84.1 (1.45)	7.0 (1.01)	26.8 (1.76)	49.3 (1.98)
1999	50.4 (0.86)	19.0 (0.68)	22.3 (0.72)	7.8 (0.46)	82.3 (1.55)	6.2 (0.98)	28.8 (1.85)	45.9 (2.03)
2000	52.0 (0.86)	20.1 (0.69)	21.7 (0.71)	8.9 (0.49)	84.9 (1.38)	8.6 (1.08)	27.8 (1.73)	47.5 (1.93)
2001	47.1 (0.80)	17.4 (0.61)	20.6 (0.65)	7.9 (0.43)	84.4 (1.29)	8.0 (0.97)	25.8 (1.56)	48.9 (1.78)
2002	47.8 (0.78)	17.3 (0.59)	20.9 (0.64)	8.5 (0.44)	78.9 (1.51)	8.7 (1.04)	25.3 (1.61)	43.4 (1.84)
2003	47.7 (0.78)	17.1 (0.59)	20.7 (0.63)	8.8 (0.44)	79.0 (1.44)	7.8 (0.95)	27.2 (1.58)	42.8 (1.75)
2004	49.0 (0.76)	17.7 (0.58)	21.6 (0.62)	8.6 (0.43)	81.5 (1.44)	8.5 (1.04)	27.4 (1.66)	44.1 (1.84)
2005	49.1 (0.75)	17.8 (0.58)	21.1 (0.61)	9.0 (0.43)	85.0 (1.30)	10.2 (1.10)	27.1 (1.62)	47.1 (1.82)
2006	46.5 (0.76)	15.1 (0.55)	22.0 (0.63)	8.1 (0.42)	81.0 (1.41)	7.3 (0.94)	27.6 (1.61)	45.5 (1.80)
2007	45.5 (0.74)	15.4 (0.54)	20.7 (0.60)	8.7 (0.42)	81.2 (1.39)	6.8 (0.90)	27.2 (1.59)	45.9 (1.78)
2008	45.3 (0.72)	15.6 (0.53)	20.1 (0.58)	8.7 (0.41)	79.4 (1.51)	9.3 (1.09)	24.7 (1.61)	44.4 (1.86)
2009	40.6 (0.69)	15.6 (0.51)	17.6 (0.54)	6.2 (0.34)	76.2 (1.57)	10.1 (1.11)	27.5 (1.65)	36.9 (1.78)
2010	39.8 (1.01)	14.9 (0.57)	17.2 (0.77)	6.6 (0.46)	73.4 (2.03)	10.7 (1.24)	28.3 (1.92)	32.8 (2.19)
2011	41.3 (0.94)	15.8 (0.67)	17.4 (0.66)	7.0 (0.44)	75.5 (1.93)	9.7 (1.21)	28.4 (1.99)	35.5 (2.16)
2012	41.0 (0.83)	15.1 (0.72)	17.8 (0.71)	7.2 (0.44)	71.7 (2.07)	9.0 (1.27)	29.5 (2.09)	32.1 (2.07)
2013	39.5 (1.00)	14.0 (0.67)	18.5 (0.77)	6.6 (0.50)	75.7 (2.06)	10.5 (1.44)	28.7 (1.76)	35.4 (2.11)
2014	41.3 (0.97)	15.6 (0.69)	17.9 (0.80)	6.6 (0.48)	80.3 (1.81)	13.8 (1.58)	26.9 (2.33)	38.5 (2.36)
2015	39.5 (0.98)	15.6 (0.77)	16.1 (0.75)	6.7 (0.56)	75.3 (2.33)	10.5 (1.48)	32.2 (2.67)	31.7 (2.15)
2016	39.7 (0.99)	15.5 (0.71)	16.6 (0.72)	6.6 (0.55)	79.2 (2.18)	10.8 (1.55)	31.4 (2.35)	36.0 (2.21)
2017	41.1 (1.10)	15.6 (0.76)	17.2 (0.81)	7.1 (0.54)	82.2 (1.78)	11.0 (1.45)	34.3 (2.19)	35.8 (2.32)
Public 4-year institutions								
1990	43.0 (1.18)	19.8 (0.95)	18.6 (0.93)	3.7 (0.45)	87.4 (2.25)	4.2! (1.37)	27.9 (3.05)	54.7 (3.39)
1995	48.8 (1.16)	19.4 (0.92)	22.6 (0.97)	5.6 (0.53)	86.7 (2.08)	9.6 (1.80)	30.8 (2.83)	45.0 (3.05)
2000	50.5 (1.15)	19.1 (0.90)	21.5 (0.94)	9.0 (0.66)	87.3 (1.91)	8.5 (1.60)	26.4 (2.53)	50.9 (2.87)
2005	49.6 (0.99)	17.8 (0.76)	22.7 (0.83)	8.0 (0.54)	86.3 (1.90)	9.0 (1.58)	26.8 (2.45)	49.7 (2.76)
2010	40.8 (1.27)	15.2 (0.88)	18.0 (0.93)	6.6 (0.64)	70.4 (3.58)	10.5 (2.04)	26.9 (2.82)	32.1 (3.59)
2012	41.0 (1.13)	14.9 (0.95)	18.6 (0.99)	6.7 (0.57)	77.6 (3.20)	9.9 (2.41)	28.0 (3.44)	38.8 (3.36)
2013	40.1 (1.31)	13.9 (0.88)	19.2 (0.98)	6.6 (0.63)	78.8 (2.88)	9.8 (1.94)	26.6 (2.80)	41.1 (3.84)
2014	41.1 (1.31)	14.6 (0.91)	18.4 (0.99)	6.9 (0.69)	83.4 (2.86)	12.2 (2.61)	28.4 (3.69)	42.3 (3.81)
2015	39.5 (1.32)	14.9 (0.98)	16.5 (1.01)	6.6 (0.73)	76.9 (3.39)	10.1 (2.01)	30.4 (3.84)	34.8 (3.38)
2016	39.7 (1.27)	15.0 (0.81)	16.8 (0.95)	6.9 (0.72)	81.9 (3.00)	11.6 (2.10)	32.6 (3.67)	36.7 (3.33)
2017	39.8 (1.28)	14.7 (0.81)	16.3 (0.91)	7.4 (0.69)	85.1 (2.21)	8.8 (1.97)	37.2 (3.24)	38.0 (3.47)
Private 4-year institutions								
1990	38.1 (1.89)	24.0 (1.66)	9.9 (1.17)	3.5 (0.72)	89.9 (4.27)	‡ (†)	31.9 (6.62)	53.1 (7.09)
1995	38.6 (1.78)	21.6 (1.51)	10.7 (1.13)	4.6 (0.77)	80.1 (4.85)	14.9 (4.32)	26.8 (5.38)	36.5 (5.84)
2000	45.8 (1.88)	23.6 (1.60)	14.9 (1.34)	5.4 (0.85)	78.0 (5.36)	‡ (†)	18.5 (5.02)	52.6 (6.46)
2005	42.3 (1.64)	20.1 (1.33)	13.8 (1.15)	7.0 (0.85)	88.5 (3.32)	10.6! (3.20)	34.5 (4.94)	43.2 (5.15)
2010	35.6 (2.37)	15.7 (1.63)	12.2 (1.52)	6.0 (1.08)	78.6 (7.00)	‡ (†)	23.4! (7.49)	45.6 (9.01)
2012	40.4 (2.39)	19.9 (1.80)	12.2 (1.40)	6.7 (1.13)	84.4 (5.35)	9.5! (4.53)	33.9 (6.58)	36.9 (7.38)
2013	34.0 (2.27)	14.9 (1.55)	12.8 (1.33)	5.6 (1.13)	86.9 (4.71)	21.9 (6.40)	29.8 (7.01)	35.2 (6.56)
2014	37.8 (2.29)	18.7 (1.72)	12.0 (1.62)	5.3 (1.00)	77.1 (6.82)	12.9! (4.92)	13.5! (5.59)	50.8 (8.76)
2015	32.8 (2.49)	18.5 (1.86)	8.3 (1.40)	5.7 (1.20)	73.8 (8.30)	10.4! (4.68)	17.8! (5.73)	45.6 (8.91)
2016	34.8 (2.20)	17.2 (1.73)	11.0 (1.20)	5.4 (0.94)	75.6 (8.00)	‡ (†)	13.4! (5.72)	53.3 (8.65)
2017	37.7 (2.41)	19.7 (2.09)	12.4 (1.69)	4.7 (1.09)	78.3 (7.39)	‡ (†)	29.5 (7.41)	41.5 (9.13)
Public 2-year institutions								
1990	61.2 (1.94)	19.1 (1.57)	31.2 (1.85)	9.2 (1.15)	81.5 (2.17)	4.1 (1.12)	24.9 (2.42)	51.1 (2.80)
1995	52.9 (1.97)	15.6 (1.43)	25.3 (1.72)	10.9 (1.23)	81.1 (2.21)	6.1 (1.35)	32.5 (2.64)	40.5 (2.77)
2000	63.9 (1.79)	20.6 (1.51)	29.9 (1.71)	11.9 (1.21)	85.5 (2.09)	9.9 (1.77)	30.0 (2.72)	44.9 (2.95)
2005	54.2 (1.69)	15.6 (1.23)	24.2 (1.46)	13.4 (1.16)	82.0 (2.20)	10.8 (1.77)	25.8 (2.50)	44.8 (2.84)
2010	40.6 (1.90)	14.0 (1.20)	19.1 (1.50)	6.8 (0.78)	74.7 (2.51)	11.6 (1.93)	30.1 (2.86)	31.0 (3.08)
2012	41.2 (1.76)	12.0 (1.17)	19.8 (1.44)	8.4 (0.95)	66.1 (2.98)	8.3 (1.60)	30.0 (2.70)	26.9 (2.79)
2013	41.8 (1.89)	13.8 (1.37)	20.5 (1.55)	7.1 (1.05)	71.1 (3.02)	8.8 (1.92)	29.8 (2.85)	31.2 (3.09)
2014	45.0 (2.28)	15.9 (1.57)	21.3 (1.82)	6.9 (0.91)	77.5 (2.64)	15.2 (2.35)	28.3 (3.35)	32.4 (3.58)
2015	44.9 (2.08)	15.1 (1.44)	21.8 (1.64)	7.5 (1.08)	75.1 (3.03)	11.4 (2.54)	36.6 (3.66)	26.7 (3.20)
2016	45.6 (2.01)	15.4 (1.51)	22.4 (1.70)	7.5 (1.14)	78.2 (3.23)	10.7 (2.31)	33.0 (3.46)	33.4 (3.33)
2017	46.8 (2.30)	14.9 (1.47)	22.9 (1.91)	7.9 (1.22)	81.0 (2.85)	14.0 (2.46)	33.0 (3.47)	32.7 (3.47)

†Not applicable.

!Interpret data with caution. The coefficient of variation (CV) for this estimate is between 30 and 50 percent.

‡Reporting standards not met. Either there are too few cases for a reliable estimate or the coefficient of variation (CV) is 50 percent or greater.

[1]Includes those who were employed but not at work during the survey week.

[2]Excludes those who were employed but not at work during the survey week; therefore, detail may not sum to total percentage employed. "Hours worked per week" refers to the number of hours worked at all jobs during the survey week.

NOTE: Students were classified as full time if they were taking at least 12 hours of classes (or at least 9 hours of graduate classes) during an average school week and as part time if they were taking fewer hours. Prior to 2010, standard errors were computed using generalized variance function methodology rather than the more precise replicate weight methodology used in later years.
SOURCE: U.S. Department of Commerce, Census Bureau, Current Population Survey (CPS), October, selected years, 1970 through 2017. (This table was prepared April 2019.)

Table 504.10. Labor force status of recent high school completers, by college enrollment status, sex, and race/ethnicity: October 2016, 2017, and 2018

[Standard errors appear in parentheses]

College enrollment status, sex, and race/ethnicity	Total number of high school completers (in thousands)	Percent of high school completers — Separately for those enrolled in college vs. those not enrolled[3]	Percent of high school completers — For all high school completers	Percentage distribution of all high school completers — Employed	Percentage distribution — Unemployed (seeking employment)	Percentage distribution — Not in labor force	Labor force participation rate of all high school completers[1]	High school completers in civilian labor force, Number (in thousands) — Total, all completers in labor force	Employed	Unemployed (seeking employment)	Unemployment rate	High school completers not in labor force (in thousands)
1	2	3	4	5	6	7	8	9	10	11	12	13
2016 high school completers[4]												
Total	3,137 (102.3)	† (†)	100.0 (†)	42.3 (1.64)	6.4 (0.85)	51.3 (1.75)	48.7 (1.75)	1,526 (72.2)	1,327 (66.1)	199 (27.1)	13.1 (1.63)	1,610 (77.4)
Male	1,517 (70.6)	† (†)	48.3 (1.47)	45.2 (2.62)	8.3 (1.33)	46.6 (2.62)	53.4 (2.62)	811 (52.5)	685 (48.9)	126 (20.9)	15.5 (2.42)	706 (53.2)
Female	1,620 (66.7)	† (†)	51.7 (1.47)	39.6 (2.18)	4.6 (1.00)	55.8 (2.37)	44.2 (2.37)	716 (48.4)	642 (45.4)	‡ (†)	10.3 (2.12)	904 (53.2)
White	1,714 (66.9)	† (†)	54.6 (1.65)	47.6 (2.20)	4.6 (0.89)	47.8 (2.30)	52.2 (2.30)	895 (55.0)	816 (51.8)	79 (15.5)	8.8 (1.64)	819 (48.2)
Black	364 (35.6)	† (†)	11.6 (1.02)	41.7 (5.07)	20.4 (4.19)	37.9 (5.30)	62.1 (5.30)	226 (29.8)	152 (23.0)	‡ (†)	32.8 (6.10)	138 (23.0)
Hispanic	742 (50.8)	† (†)	23.7 (1.32)	35.5 (3.53)	4.2 (1.23)	60.3 (3.69)	39.7 (3.69)	295 (32.3)	264 (31.0)	‡ (†)	10.7 (2.95)	447 (42.8)
Enrolled in college, 2016	2,188 (93.4)	100.0 (†)	69.8 (1.64)	35.3 (1.94)	3.1 (0.63)	61.6 (2.03)	38.4 (2.03)	840 (57.2)	773 (54.3)	‡ (†)	8.0 (1.58)	1,348 (72.5)
Male	1,023 (57.8)	46.8 (1.86)	32.6 (1.36)	37.0 (3.07)	4.5 (1.06)	58.5 (3.21)	41.5 (3.21)	425 (38.0)	379 (35.8)	‡ (†)	10.8 (2.45)	599 (49.9)
Female	1,165 (66.2)	53.2 (1.86)	37.1 (1.72)	33.9 (2.56)	1.8! (0.67)	64.3 (2.64)	35.7 (2.64)	416 (40.0)	394 (38.9)	‡ (†)	5.2! (1.83)	749 (50.8)
2-year	744 (56.3)	34.0 (2.12)	23.7 (1.56)	47.0 (3.39)	4.9 (1.29)	48.2 (3.58)	51.8 (3.58)	386 (38.3)	349 (35.7)	‡ (†)	9.4 (2.38)	359 (39.1)
4-year	1,444 (76.1)	66.0 (2.12)	46.0 (1.85)	29.4 (2.20)	2.1! (0.66)	68.5 (2.27)	31.5 (2.27)	455 (40.6)	424 (39.4)	‡ (†)	6.8 (2.03)	989 (61.5)
Full-time students	1,992 (88.1)	91.0 (1.30)	63.5 (1.80)	31.7 (1.92)	2.9 (0.64)	65.4 (1.98)	34.6 (1.98)	689 (49.7)	632 (47.1)	‡ (†)	8.4 (1.79)	1,303 (70.2)
Part-time students	196 (30.1)	9.0 (1.30)	6.3 (0.91)	72.3 (7.83)	‡ (†)	22.9 (7.67)	77.1 (7.67)	151 (23.4)	142 (22.7)	‡ (†)	‡ (†)	‡ (†)
White	1,194 (59.5)	54.6 (1.93)	38.1 (1.56)	39.7 (2.63)	2.9 (0.83)	57.4 (2.72)	42.6 (2.72)	509 (41.7)	475 (40.7)	‡ (†)	6.8 (1.88)	685 (46.2)
Black	209 (31.9)	9.5 (1.36)	6.7 (0.97)	40.5 (7.07)	7.7! (2.90)	51.8 (6.96)	48.2 (6.96)	‡ (†)	‡ (†)	‡ (†)	‡ (†)	108 (21.1)
Hispanic	534 (44.6)	24.4 (1.60)	17.0 (1.22)	28.0 (3.98)	2.6! (1.09)	69.4 (4.11)	30.6 (4.11)	163 (25.3)	149 (24.2)	‡ (†)	8.5! (3.47)	371 (38.5)
Not enrolled in college, 2016	948 (56.3)	100.0 (†)	30.2 (1.64)	58.4 (2.69)	14.0 (2.17)	27.7 (2.65)	72.3 (2.65)	686 (46.2)	554 (38.6)	132 (22.5)	19.3 (2.81)	262 (30.4)
Male	493 (39.5)	52.0 (2.98)	15.7 (1.17)	62.0 (4.06)	16.2 (3.09)	21.7 (3.25)	78.3 (3.25)	386 (33.0)	306 (29.2)	80 (16.9)	20.7 (3.89)	107 (18.8)
Female	455 (40.5)	48.0 (2.98)	14.5 (1.26)	54.4 (4.02)	11.5 (3.07)	34.1 (4.23)	65.9 (4.23)	300 (33.3)	248 (28.8)	‡ (†)	17.5 (4.31)	155 (23.1)
White	520 (46.0)	54.8 (3.50)	16.6 (1.45)	65.6 (3.45)	8.5 (2.13)	25.8 (3.17)	74.2 (3.17)	386 (37.2)	341 (32.3)	‡ (†)	11.5 (2.81)	134 (20.6)
Black	156 (25.0)	16.4 (2.49)	5.0 (0.78)	43.3 (8.12)	37.4 (8.29)	19.3 (6.97)	80.7 (6.97)	126 (23.9)	‡ (†)	‡ (†)	46.4 (9.29)	‡ (†)
Hispanic	208 (27.2)	21.9 (2.60)	6.6 (0.85)	54.8 (6.14)	8.5! (3.34)	36.7 (6.30)	63.3 (6.30)	132 (21.5)	114 (20.2)	‡ (†)	13.4! (5.02)	‡ (†)
2017 high school completers[4]												
Total	2,870 (95.9)	† (†)	100.0 (†)	42.5 (1.95)	6.5 (0.88)	51.0 (1.87)	49.0 (1.87)	1,407 (72.4)	1,221 (70.4)	186 (25.7)	13.2 (1.80)	1,463 (70.8)
Male	1,345 (60.2)	† (†)	46.9 (1.58)	44.9 (2.48)	8.0 (1.40)	47.1 (2.41)	52.9 (2.41)	712 (44.4)	604 (41.8)	108 (19.4)	15.2 (2.57)	633 (43.8)
Female	1,525 (71.3)	† (†)	53.1 (1.58)	40.5 (2.71)	5.1 (1.14)	54.4 (2.73)	45.6 (2.73)	695 (51.5)	617 (49.2)	‡ (†)	11.2 (2.46)	830 (57.9)
White	1,601 (64.5)	† (†)	55.8 (1.57)	42.8 (2.41)	5.5 (1.10)	51.7 (2.37)	48.3 (2.37)	774 (49.1)	686 (47.2)	88 (18.0)	11.4 (2.24)	827 (50.3)
Black	402 (35.5)	† (†)	14.0 (1.19)	38.4 (5.44)	8.2! (2.53)	53.4 (5.14)	46.6 (5.14)	187 (25.2)	154 (24.7)	‡ (†)	17.6! (5.58)	214 (29.1)
Hispanic	597 (52.0)	† (†)	20.8 (1.62)	47.9 (4.36)	8.4 (2.34)	43.7 (4.19)	56.3 (4.19)	336 (38.4)	286 (35.9)	‡ (†)	15.0 (4.11)	261 (33.8)
Enrolled in college, 2017	1,915 (80.6)	100.0 (†)	66.7 (1.68)	35.8 (2.32)	4.1 (0.82)	60.2 (2.32)	39.8 (2.32)	763 (54.4)	685 (53.1)	‡ (†)	10.2 (2.06)	1,152 (65.9)
Male	822 (53.1)	42.9 (2.06)	28.7 (1.62)	36.8 (3.23)	4.4! (1.35)	58.8 (3.24)	41.2 (3.24)	339 (34.1)	303 (33.0)	‡ (†)	10.6! (3.20)	483 (41.3)
Female	1,093 (59.8)	57.1 (2.06)	38.1 (1.60)	35.0 (3.15)	3.8! (1.21)	61.2 (3.21)	38.8 (3.21)	424 (41.2)	382 (39.4)	‡ (†)	9.9! (3.07)	669 (51.5)
2-year	648 (45.9)	33.8 (2.11)	22.6 (1.50)	53.5 (3.75)	4.9! (1.68)	41.6 (3.66)	58.4 (3.66)	378 (33.9)	346 (33.6)	‡ (†)	8.4! (2.87)	269 (31.7)
4-year	1,267 (70.3)	66.2 (2.11)	44.2 (1.83)	26.7 (2.63)	3.6 (0.92)	69.7 (2.81)	30.3 (2.81)	384 (43.4)	338 (39.9)	‡ (†)	11.9 (2.87)	883 (57.3)
Full-time students	1,764 (80.2)	92.1 (1.23)	61.5 (1.74)	32.5 (2.37)	4.4 (0.89)	63.1 (2.39)	36.9 (2.39)	651 (51.4)	574 (49.5)	‡ (†)	11.9 (2.39)	1,113 (65.7)
Part-time students	150 (23.6)	7.9 (1.23)	5.2 (0.83)	74.0 (6.68)	‡ (†)	26.0 (6.68)	74.0 (6.68)	111 (20.8)	111 (20.8)	‡ (†)	‡ (†)	‡ (†)
White	1,106 (54.9)	57.8 (2.06)	38.5 (1.61)	35.7 (2.88)	3.2! (1.07)	61.1 (2.89)	38.9 (2.89)	431 (38.3)	395 (37.3)	‡ (†)	8.3! (2.69)	675 (46.2)
Black	239 (30.0)	12.5 (1.48)	8.3 (1.01)	28.4 (6.37)	‡ (†)	66.5 (6.66)	33.5 (6.66)	‡ (†)	‡ (†)	‡ (†)	‡ (†)	159 (25.7)
Hispanic	364 (42.4)	19.0 (1.98)	12.7 (1.40)	45.1 (5.78)	7.8! (2.69)	47.2 (5.62)	52.8 (5.62)	193 (29.5)	164 (28.4)	‡ (†)	14.7! (5.13)	172 (29.3)
Not enrolled in college, 2017	955 (57.1)	100.0 (†)	33.3 (1.68)	56.1 (3.07)	11.3 (1.94)	32.6 (2.80)	67.4 (2.80)	644 (47.4)	536 (44.4)	108 (19.2)	16.8 (2.83)	311 (32.1)
Male	523 (39.5)	54.8 (3.03)	18.2 (1.30)	57.6 (3.78)	13.8 (2.67)	28.7 (3.34)	71.3 (3.34)	373 (33.3)	301 (30.0)	‡ (†)	19.3 (3.66)	150 (20.5)
Female	432 (41.4)	45.2 (3.03)	15.1 (1.33)	54.3 (4.92)	8.4! (2.57)	37.3 (4.68)	62.7 (4.68)	271 (32.6)	235 (31.7)	‡ (†)	13.3! (4.08)	161 (25.8)
White	495 (39.4)	51.8 (2.86)	17.2 (1.26)	58.8 (4.10)	10.6 (2.51)	30.6 (3.79)	69.4 (3.79)	343 (33.2)	291 (30.4)	‡ (†)	15.3 (3.54)	151 (22.1)
Black	163 (22.6)	17.1 (2.18)	5.7 (0.80)	52.9 (7.65)	12.9! (5.02)	34.2 (7.14)	65.8 (7.14)	107 (19.2)	‡ (†)	‡ (†)	19.6! (7.46)	‡ (†)
Hispanic	233 (28.6)	24.4 (2.61)	8.1 (0.94)	52.3 (6.10)	9.4! (3.98)	38.3 (5.84)	61.7 (5.84)	144 (23.4)	122 (21.2)	‡ (†)	15.3! (6.28)	‡ (†)

See notes at end of table.

Table 504.10. Labor force status of recent high school completers, by college enrollment status, sex, and race/ethnicity: October 2016, 2017, and 2018—Continued

[Standard errors appear in parentheses]

College enrollment status, sex, and race/ethnicity	Total number of high school completers (in thousands)	Percent of high school completers — Separately for those enrolled in college vs. those not enrolled[3]	Percent of high school completers — For all high school completers	Percentage distribution of all high school completers — Employed	Percentage distribution — Unemployed (seeking employment)	Percentage distribution — Not in labor force	Labor force participation rate of all high school completers[1]	HS completers in civilian labor force[2] — Number (thousands) — Total, all completers in labor force	Number — Employed	Number — Unemployed (seeking employment)	Unemployment rate	High school completers not in labor force (in thousands)
1	2	3	4	5	6	7	8	9	10	11	12	13
2018 high school completers[4]												
Total	3,212 (94.6)	† (†)	100.0 (†)	41.2 (1.62)	6.8 (0.78)	52.0 (1.72)	48.0 (1.72)	1,541 (71.7)	1,324 (62.6)	218 (26.9)	14.1 (1.53)	1,670 (73.5)
Male	1,614 (61.2)	† (†)	50.3 (1.42)	42.7 (2.18)	6.0 (1.12)	51.3 (2.33)	48.7 (2.33)	787 (44.4)	690 (39.1)	97 (18.8)	12.3 (2.16)	827 (52.1)
Female	1,598 (69.9)	† (†)	49.7 (1.42)	39.7 (2.49)	7.6 (1.16)	52.8 (2.65)	47.2 (2.65)	755 (52.8)	634 (45.4)	121 (20.2)	16.0 (2.30)	843 (57.0)
White	1,727 (71.2)	† (†)	53.8 (1.60)	42.1 (2.23)	5.1 (0.93)	52.8 (2.20)	47.2 (2.20)	815 (50.5)	727 (47.4)	88 (16.9)	10.8 (1.93)	913 (53.8)
Black	449 (37.6)	† (†)	14.0 (1.04)	36.4 (5.04)	10.8 (2.78)	52.8 (4.94)	47.2 (4.94)	212 (26.0)	163 (24.6)	‡ (†)	23.0 (5.79)	237 (31.9)
Hispanic	727 (50.4)	† (†)	22.6 (1.45)	49.6 (3.67)	7.3 (1.74)	43.1 (3.36)	56.9 (3.36)	414 (38.4)	361 (37.3)	‡ (†)	12.8 (3.10)	313 (31.6)
Enrolled in college, 2018												
Total	2,220 (86.7)	100.0 (†)	69.1 (1.62)	32.7 (1.96)	3.7 (0.75)	63.6 (2.03)	36.4 (2.03)	808 (54.9)	726 (50.8)	‡ (†)	10.1 (1.99)	1,412 (71.1)
Male	1,080 (55.7)	48.6 (1.84)	33.6 (1.49)	33.9 (2.89)	3.4! (1.16)	62.7 (2.97)	37.3 (2.97)	403 (35.5)	366 (33.6)	‡ (†)	9.0! (3.02)	677 (50.5)
Female	1,140 (63.7)	51.4 (1.84)	35.5 (1.52)	31.6 (2.50)	4.0 (1.11)	64.5 (2.60)	35.5 (2.60)	405 (35.6)	360 (32.4)	‡ (†)	11.2 (2.97)	735 (52.8)
2-year	819 (56.0)	36.9 (2.06)	25.5 (1.54)	41.6 (3.50)	3.3! (1.25)	55.1 (3.59)	44.9 (3.59)	368 (37.8)	341 (35.4)	‡ (†)	7.3! (2.71)	451 (43.4)
4-year	1,401 (70.9)	63.1 (2.06)	43.6 (1.76)	27.5 (2.10)	3.9 (1.03)	68.6 (2.19)	31.4 (2.19)	440 (37.3)	385 (34.8)	‡ (†)	12.4 (3.11)	961 (58.4)
Full-time students	2,015 (81.8)	90.8 (1.13)	62.7 (1.58)	28.9 (1.92)	3.6 (0.77)	67.5 (2.02)	32.5 (2.02)	656 (48.1)	583 (43.5)	‡ (†)	11.1 (2.26)	1,360 (69.2)
Part-time students	205 (26.5)	9.2 (1.13)	6.4 (0.81)	69.9 (6.54)	‡ (†)	25.7 (6.41)	74.3 (6.41)	152 (24.1)	143 (23.5)	‡ (†)	‡ (†)	‡ (†)
White	1,224 (62.8)	55.1 (1.98)	38.1 (1.62)	32.9 (2.40)	3.8 (0.99)	63.2 (2.43)	36.8 (2.43)	450 (38.4)	403 (35.8)	‡ (†)	10.4 (2.61)	774 (48.7)
Black	289 (31.9)	13.0 (1.31)	9.0 (0.93)	27.3 (5.21)	‡ (†)	69.8 (5.54)	30.2 (5.54)	‡ (†)	‡ (†)	‡ (†)	‡ (†)	202 (29.6)
Hispanic	476 (42.6)	21.4 (1.73)	14.8 (1.24)	44.0 (4.72)	‡ (†)	53.2 (4.70)	46.8 (4.70)	223 (31.0)	209 (30.4)	‡ (†)	‡ (†)	253 (29.9)
Not enrolled in college, 2018												
Total	992 (57.4)	100.0 (†)	30.9 (1.62)	60.2 (2.69)	13.7 (1.82)	26.0 (2.49)	74.0 (2.49)	733 (49.0)	597 (43.4)	136 (19.7)	18.6 (2.38)	258 (28.8)
Male	534 (40.3)	53.8 (2.94)	16.6 (1.19)	60.6 (3.21)	11.3 (2.20)	28.1 (3.19)	71.9 (3.19)	384 (32.8)	324 (28.0)	‡ (†)	15.7 (2.90)	150 (20.7)
Female	458 (41.2)	46.2 (2.94)	14.2 (1.23)	59.8 (4.58)	16.6 (2.85)	23.7 (3.99)	76.3 (3.99)	349 (35.9)	273 (31.1)	76 (15.2)	21.7 (3.75)	108 (21.0)
White	503 (37.8)	50.8 (2.71)	15.7 (1.10)	64.4 (3.96)	8.1 (2.04)	27.5 (3.51)	72.5 (3.51)	365 (31.5)	324 (30.8)	‡ (†)	11.2 (2.84)	138 (21.0)
Black	159 (22.9)	16.1 (2.09)	5.0 (0.69)	52.9 (8.88)	25.2 (6.46)	21.9! (6.72)	78.1 (6.72)	124 (19.9)	‡ (†)	‡ (†)	32.2 (8.48)	‡ (†)
Hispanic	251 (30.5)	25.3 (2.60)	7.8 (0.95)	60.3 (5.67)	15.8 (4.36)	23.9 (4.71)	76.1 (4.71)	191 (26.9)	152 (25.0)	‡ (†)	20.8 (5.59)	‡ (†)

†Not applicable.
!Interpret data with caution. The coefficient of variation (CV) for this estimate is between 30 and 50 percent.
‡Reporting standards not met (too few cases for a reliable estimate).
[1]The labor force participation rate is the percentage of persons who are either employed or seeking employment.
[2]The labor force includes all employed persons plus those seeking employment. The unemployment rate is the percentage of persons in the labor force who are not working and who made specific efforts to find employment sometime during the prior 4 weeks.
[3]Column 3 does not present any percentages that apply to all high school completers. Instead, it presents one set of percentages for only those completers who were enrolled in college and a second set of percentages for only those completers who were not enrolled in college.
[4]Includes 16- to 24-year-olds who completed high school between January and October of the given year. Includes recipients of equivalency credentials as well as diploma recipients.
NOTE: Data are based on sample surveys of the civilian noninstitutionalized population, which excludes persons in the military and persons living in institutions (e.g., prisons or nursing facilities). Data are for October of a given year. Standard errors were computed using replicate weights. Totals include race categories not separately shown. Race categories exclude persons of Hispanic ethnicity. Detail may not sum to totals because of rounding.
SOURCE: U.S. Department of Commerce, Census Bureau, Current Population Survey (CPS), October 2016, 2017, and 2018. (This table was prepared February 2020.)

Table 504.20. Labor force status of recent high school dropouts, by sex and race/ethnicity: Selected years, October 1980 through 2018

[Standard errors appear in parentheses]

Year, sex, and race/ethnicity	Number of dropouts (in thousands)	Percent of all dropouts	Percentage distribution of dropouts — Employed	Unemployed (seeking employment)	Not in labor force	Labor force participation rate of dropouts[1]	Dropouts in civilian labor force[2] — Number (in thousands) Total	Unemployed (seeking employment)	Unemploy- ment rate	Dropouts not in labor force (in thousands)
1	2	3	4	5	6	7	8	9	10	11
Estimates for individual years										
All dropouts										
1980	738 (44.0)	100.0 (†)	43.8 (2.97)	20.0 (2.37)	36.2 (2.87)	63.8 (2.87)	471 (35.2)	148 (19.5)	31.4 (3.44)	267 (26.5)
1990	412 (36.0)	100.0 (†)	46.3 (4.37)	21.6 (3.57)	32.2 (4.09)	67.8 (4.09)	279 (29.7)	89 (16.6)	31.8 (4.90)	132 (20.4)
2000	515 (28.5)	100.0 (†)	48.7 (2.77)	19.2 (3.01)	32.0 (2.59)	68.0 (2.59)	350 (23.5)	99 (17.2)	28.1 (4.16)	165 (16.2)
2005	407 (35.3)	100.0 (†)	38.3 (4.22)	18.9 (3.42)	42.8 (3.32)	57.2 (4.30)	233 (26.7)	77 (15.4)	32.9 (5.42)	174 (17.9)
2010[3]	340 (29.0)	100.0 (†)	30.9 (4.24)	23.0 (4.29)	46.1 (4.78)	53.9 (4.78)	183 (21.5)	78 (16.0)	42.7 (6.67)	157 (21.9)
2017[3]	530 (42.6)	100.0 (†)	33.9 (3.53)	7.9 (2.06)	58.2 (3.66)	41.8 (3.66)	222 (23.4)	‡ (†)	18.9 (4.59)	308 (34.2)
2018[3]	527 (46.5)	100.0 (†)	40.7 (4.07)	6.5! (2.06)	52.8 (4.47)	47.2 (4.47)	249 (32.5)	‡ (†)	13.7 (4.04)	278 (33.4)
3-year moving averages[4]										
All dropouts										
1980	748 (44.3)	100.0 (†)	44.4 (1.70)	19.9 (1.38)	35.7 (1.27)	64.3 (1.64)	481 (35.6)	149 (19.9)	30.9 (1.99)	267 (20.5)
1990	413 (36.1)	100.0 (†)	43.5 (2.50)	21.5 (2.08)	35.0 (1.86)	65.0 (2.41)	268 (26.7)	89 (16.8)	33.1 (2.96)	144 (16.5)
2000	515 (41.8)	100.0 (†)	44.1 (2.33)	19.0 (1.85)	36.9 (1.75)	63.1 (2.27)	325 (33.2)	98 (18.3)	30.1 (2.72)	190 (19.7)
2005	449 (37.1)	100.0 (†)	36.8 (2.30)	17.7 (1.83)	45.5 (1.84)	54.5 (2.38)	245 (27.4)	79 (15.7)	32.5 (3.04)	205 (19.4)
2010	365 (33.4)	100.0 (†)	28.7 (2.39)	23.7 (2.26)	47.6 (2.24)	52.4 (2.64)	191 (24.2)	87 (16.4)	45.2 (3.65)	174 (17.8)
2017	523 (26.6)	100.0 (†)	36.5 (2.32)	10.1 (1.33)	53.4 (2.43)	46.6 (2.43)	244 (17.9)	53 (7.6)	21.8 (2.67)	279 (18.8)
2018	528 (33.6)	100.0 (†)	37.3 (2.85)	7.2 (1.38)	55.5 (3.02)	44.5 (3.02)	235 (19.7)	38 (7.3)	16.2 (2.92)	293 (26.5)
Sex										
Male										
1980	393 (31.6)	52.6 (1.69)	55.5 (2.31)	19.5 (1.84)	25.0 (2.01)	75.0 (2.01)	295 (27.4)	77 (14.0)	25.9 (2.35)	98 (15.8)
1990	216 (25.7)	52.3 (2.48)	50.9 (3.44)	25.2 (2.98)	23.9 (2.93)	76.1 (2.93)	164 (22.4)	55 (12.9)	33.1 (3.71)	52 (12.6)
2000	279 (30.3)	54.1 (2.30)	49.8 (3.14)	19.6 (2.49)	30.7 (2.90)	69.3 (2.90)	193 (25.2)	55 (13.4)	28.2 (3.39)	85 (16.8)
2005	254 (27.4)	56.5 (2.33)	40.0 (3.06)	19.0 (2.45)	41.0 (3.07)	59.0 (3.07)	150 (21.1)	48 (12.0)	32.2 (3.80)	104 (17.6)
2010	196 (24.1)	53.6 (2.60)	32.1 (3.32)	22.4 (2.97)	45.5 (3.54)	54.5 (3.54)	107 (17.8)	44 (11.4)	41.2 (4.74)	89 (16.3)
2017	287 (18.0)	54.9 (2.37)	41.0 (3.23)	11.2 (2.00)	47.8 (3.14)	52.2 (3.14)	150 (13.0)	32 (6.1)	21.5 (3.66)	137 (12.4)
2018	281 (20.5)	53.2 (2.96)	40.7 (3.90)	7.1 (1.88)	52.2 (3.95)	47.8 (3.95)	135 (13.4)	‡ (†)	14.9 (3.80)	147 (16.5)
Female										
1980	354 (29.1)	47.4 (1.63)	32.1 (2.21)	20.4 (1.91)	47.5 (2.37)	52.5 (2.37)	186 (21.1)	72 (13.1)	38.9 (3.19)	168 (20.0)
1990	197 (23.7)	47.7 (2.40)	35.4 (3.33)	17.4 (2.64)	47.2 (3.48)	52.8 (3.48)	104 (17.2)	34 (9.9)	33.0 (4.51)	93 (16.3)
2000	236 (27.0)	45.9 (2.23)	37.4 (3.19)	18.3 (2.55)	44.3 (3.28)	55.7 (3.28)	132 (20.1)	43 (11.6)	32.9 (4.15)	105 (18.0)
2005	196 (23.3)	43.5 (2.25)	32.6 (3.23)	16.0 (2.52)	51.4 (3.44)	48.6 (3.44)	95 (16.2)	31 (9.3)	32.9 (4.64)	101 (16.7)
2010	169 (21.7)	46.4 (2.51)	24.9 (3.20)	25.1 (3.21)	50.0 (3.70)	50.0 (3.70)	85 (15.3)	43 (10.9)	50.2 (5.23)	85 (15.3)
2017	236 (18.2)	45.1 (2.37)	30.9 (3.49)	8.8 (1.90)	60.2 (3.93)	39.8 (3.93)	94 (11.7)	‡ (†)	22.2 (4.27)	142 (14.2)
2018	247 (24.7)	46.8 (2.96)	33.5 (4.22)	7.2! (2.27)	59.3 (4.73)	40.7 (4.73)	101 (14.8)	‡ (†)	17.8 (5.04)	147 (19.2)
Race/ethnicity										
White										
1980	494 (36.0)	66.0 (1.62)	50.9 (2.11)	17.6 (1.61)	31.5 (1.52)	68.5 (1.96)	338 (29.8)	87 (15.2)	25.7 (2.24)	156 (15.7)
1990	240 (27.5)	58.0 (2.49)	51.4 (3.31)	19.3 (2.63)	29.3 (2.33)	70.7 (3.02)	170 (23.1)	46 (12.1)	27.3 (3.53)	70 (11.5)
2000	279 (30.8)	54.1 (2.34)	48.3 (3.19)	18.7 (2.50)	33.0 (2.32)	67.0 (3.00)	187 (25.2)	52 (13.4)	27.8 (3.51)	92 (13.7)
2005	215 (25.7)	48.0 (2.38)	41.6 (3.40)	14.2 (2.42)	44.2 (2.64)	55.8 (3.42)	120 (19.2)	31! (9.7)	25.5 (4.04)	95 (13.2)
2010	164 (22.4)	45.0 (2.63)	32.7 (3.70)	20.8 (3.22)	46.4 (3.04)	53.6 (3.93)	88 (16.4)	34! (10.3)	38.9 (5.28)	76 (11.8)
2017	244 (16.6)	46.6 (2.50)	46.4 (3.28)	8.6 (1.63)	45.0 (3.19)	55.0 (3.19)	134 (12.9)	‡ (†)	15.7 (2.94)	110 (9.9)
2018	231 (21.6)	43.7 (3.20)	52.9 (4.23)	5.3! (1.67)	41.7 (4.09)	58.3 (4.09)	134 (15.7)	‡ (†)	9.2! (2.84)	96 (13.1)
Black										
1980	154 (21.3)	20.6 (1.47)	21.0 (3.27)	28.3 (3.62)	50.6 (4.01)	49.4 (4.01)	76 (15.0)	44 (11.4)	57.4 (5.65)	78 (15.2)
1990	96 (18.5)	23.3 (2.27)	27.1 (4.93)	29.0 (5.04)	43.9 (5.51)	56.1 (5.51)	54 (13.8)	28! (10.0)	51.7 (7.41)	42 (12.3)
2000	102 (19.7)	19.8 (1.98)	28.0 (5.03)	22.2 (4.65)	49.8 (5.60)	50.2 (5.60)	51 (14.0)	‡ (†)	44.2 (7.85)	51 (13.9)
2005	88 (17.4)	19.5 (2.01)	21.5 (4.71)	27.7 (5.13)	50.9 (5.73)	49.1 (5.73)	43 (12.2)	‡ (†)	56.3 (8.11)	45 (12.4)
2010	70 (15.6)	19.3 (2.22)	22.4 (5.33)	30.4 (5.88)	47.2 (6.38)	52.8 (6.38)	37! (11.3)	‡ (†)	57.5 (8.69)	33! (10.7)
2017	84 (10.7)	16.1 (1.89)	24.9 (4.95)	18.2 (4.66)	56.9 (6.42)	43.1 (6.42)	36 (6.8)	‡ (†)	42.2 (8.49)	48 (8.3)
2018	85 (13.4)	16.1 (2.43)	16.6! (5.16)	16.5! (5.41)	66.9 (7.57)	33.1 (7.57)	‡ (†)	‡ (†)	‡ (†)	57 (11.6)
Hispanic										
1980	84 (18.7)	11.3 (1.36)	48.2 (6.40)	19.5 (5.07)	32.3 (5.99)	67.7 (5.99)	57 (15.4)	‡ (†)	28.8 (7.05)	27! (10.6)
1990	66 (15.3)	15.9 (1.96)	39.3 (6.56)	19.9 (5.36)	40.8 (6.60)	59.2 (6.60)	39! (11.8)	‡ (†)	33.5 (8.24)	27! (9.8)
2000	113 (20.8)	21.9 (2.06)	50.4 (5.32)	17.7 (4.06)	31.9 (4.96)	68.1 (4.96)	77 (17.1)	‡ (†)	26.0 (5.66)	36! (11.7)
2005	125 (20.8)	27.9 (2.27)	39.2 (4.68)	16.1 (3.52)	44.7 (4.77)	55.3 (4.77)	69 (15.4)	‡ (†)	29.1 (5.86)	56 (13.9)
2010	102 (18.8)	28.0 (2.52)	25.8 (4.64)	24.3 (4.55)	49.9 (5.30)	50.1 (5.30)	51 (13.3)	25! (9.3)	48.4 (7.49)	51 (13.3)
2017	149 (15.0)	28.5 (2.37)	29.1 (3.86)	8.4 (2.17)	62.5 (3.90)	37.5 (3.90)	56 (7.6)	‡ (†)	22.4 (5.53)	93 (11.5)
2018	167 (21.5)	31.7 (3.28)	29.4 (4.46)	4.9! (2.10)	65.7 (4.66)	34.3 (4.66)	57 (9.7)	‡ (†)	14.2! (5.80)	110 (17.3)

†Not applicable.
!Interpret data with caution. The coefficient of variation (CV) for this estimate is between 30 and 50 percent.
‡Reporting standards not met. Either there are too few cases for a reliable estimate or the coefficient of variation (CV) is 50 percent or greater.
[1]The labor force participation rate is the percentage of persons who are either employed or seeking employment.
[2]The labor force includes all employed persons plus those seeking employment. The unemployment rate is the percentage of persons in the labor force who are not working and who made specific efforts to find employment sometime during the prior 4 weeks.
[3]Beginning in 2010, standard errors for the individual year estimates were computed using replicate weights in order to produce more precise values. This methodology can only be used for these estimates. For all other estimates in the table, standard errors were computed using generalized variance function methodology.
[4]A 3-year moving average is the arithmetic average of the year indicated, the year immediately preceding, and the year immediately following. For example, the estimates

shown for 2000 reflect an average of 1999, 2000, and 2001. Use of a moving average increases the sample size, thereby reducing the size of sampling errors and producing more stable estimates. For the final year of available data, a 2-year moving average is used; thus, the estimates for 2018 reflect the average of 2017 and 2018.
NOTE: Data are based on sample surveys of the civilian noninstitutionalized population, which excludes persons in the military and persons living in institutions (e.g., prisons or nursing facilities). Data are for October of a given year. Dropouts are considered persons 16 to 24 years old who dropped out of school in the 12-month period ending in October of years shown. Includes dropouts from any grade, including a small number from elementary and middle schools. Totals include race categories not separately shown. Race categories exclude persons of Hispanic ethnicity. Detail may not sum to totals because of rounding.
SOURCE: U.S. Department of Commerce, Census Bureau, Current Population Survey (CPS), selected years, October 1979 through 2018. (This table was prepared February 2020.)

Table 505.10. Number, percentage distribution, unemployment rates, and median earnings of 25- to 29-year-old bachelor's degree holders and percentage of degree holders among all 25- to 29-year-olds, by field of study and science, technology, engineering, or mathematics (STEM) status of field: 2010 and 2018

[Standard errors appear in parentheses]

Field of study and STEM status of field	2010 — 25- to 29-year-old bachelor's degree holders			Median annual earnings of full-time year-round workers		Percent of all 25- to 29-year-olds with degree in specific field[1]	2018 — 25- to 29-year-old bachelor's degree holders			Median annual earnings of full-time year-round workers	Percent of all 25- to 29-year-olds with degree in specific field
	Number, in thousands	Percentage distribution	Unemployment rate for the civilian labor force	Current dollars	Constant 2018 dollars[1]		Number, in thousands	Percentage distribution	Unemployment rate for the civilian labor force	Median annual earnings of full-time year-round workers	
1	2	3	4	5	6	7	8	9	10	11	12
Total, all bachelor's degrees	6,366 (30.5)	100.0 (†)	5.6 (0.13)	$43,730 (684)	$50,360 (788)	30.5 (0.14)	8,103 (40.2)	100.0 (†)	2.9 (0.08)	$50,600 (4)	34.8 (0.16)
Agriculture	59 (2.8)	0.9 (0.04)	3.8 (0.99)	46,150 (424)	46,240 (488)	0.3 (0.01)	78 (3.9)	1.0 (0.05)	1.8! (0.72)	45,380 (1,856)	0.3 (0.02)
Architecture	47 (2.5)	0.7 (0.04)	13.8 (2.49)	44,300 (2,686)	51,020 (3,094)	0.2 (0.01)	60 (3.6)	0.7 (0.04)	1.8! (0.70)	52,170 (1,239)	0.3 (0.02)
Area, ethnic, and civilization studies	28 (1.9)	0.4 (0.03)	5.2! (1.61)	41,250 (3,100)	47,510 (3,570)	0.1 (0.01)	31 (2.2)	0.4 (0.03)	1.7! (0.77)	50,140 (1,018)	0.1 (0.01)
Arts, fine and commercial	334 (7.0)	5.3 (0.11)	6.8 (0.55)	37,140 (803)	42,770 (884)	1.6 (0.03)	440 (8.5)	5.4 (0.10)	3.7 (0.41)	42,520 (1,152)	1.9 (0.04)
Fine arts	245 (5.4)	3.8 (0.08)	6.1 (0.69)	36,170 (888)	41,650 (1,022)	1.2 (0.03)	314 (6.6)	3.9 (0.08)	3.7 (0.40)	40,500 (1,152)	1.4 (0.03)
Commercial art and graphic design	89 (3.9)	1.4 (0.06)	8.6 (1.09)	38,860 (1,799)	44,750 (2,071)	0.4 (0.02)	125 (5.2)	1.5 (0.06)	3.5 (0.86)	48,140 (1,389)	0.5 (0.02)
Business	1,252 (13.9)	19.7 (0.19)	5.5 (0.24)	47,160 (1,004)	54,310 (1,105)	6.0 (0.07)	1,432 (16.1)	17.7 (0.18)	2.8 (0.22)	54,660 (776)	6.2 (0.07)
Business, general	222 (5.5)	3.5 (0.09)	5.7 (0.66)	45,960 (1,425)	52,930 (1,642)	1.1 (0.03)	266 (5.6)	3.3 (0.07)	3.7 (0.60)	50,260 (255)	1.1 (0.02)
Accounting	194 (5.7)	3.0 (0.09)	5.8 (0.68)	50,100 (141)	57,690 (162)	0.9 (0.03)	226 (6.2)	2.8 (0.08)	2.3 (0.47)	60,000 (265)	1.0 (0.03)
Business management and administration	339 (7.2)	5.3 (0.11)	6.5 (0.57)	43,200 (1,200)	49,750 (1,382)	1.6 (0.03)	343 (8.5)	4.2 (0.10)	2.4 (0.34)	50,600 (25)	1.5 (0.04)
Marketing and marketing research	187 (5.5)	2.9 (0.08)	4.6 (0.57)	44,250 (765)	50,960 (881)	0.9 (0.03)	200 (6.1)	2.5 (0.07)	2.9 (0.57)	52,160 (1,050)	0.9 (0.03)
Finance	170 (5.5)	2.7 (0.09)	4.9 (0.61)	52,620 (1,865)	60,590 (2,148)	0.8 (0.03)	187 (6.1)	2.3 (0.07)	2.1 (0.47)	65,270 (709)	0.8 (0.03)
Management information systems and statistics	23 (1.6)	0.4 (0.03)	3.4! (1.12)	55,020 (1,939)	63,360 (2,233)	0.1 (0.01)	26 (2.0)	0.3 (0.02)	2.2! (1.00)	64,390 (3,029)	0.1 (0.01)
Business, other and medical administration	118 (3.7)	1.9 (0.06)	4.5 (0.57)	44,400 (720)	51,130 (829)	0.6 (0.02)	184 (6.1)	2.3 (0.07)	3.7 (0.74)	50,520 (73)	0.8 (0.03)
Communications and communications technologies	373 (8.2)	5.9 (0.12)	6.4 (0.45)	40,260 (18)	46,360 (20)	1.8 (0.04)	446 (8.4)	5.5 (0.11)	3.3 (0.37)	45,570 (511)	1.9 (0.04)
Computer and information science	249 (6.2)	3.9 (0.10)	5.6 (0.55)	56,320 (1,809)	64,860 (2,083)	1.2 (0.03)	310 (7.1)	3.8 (0.08)	5.6 (0.65)	70,140 (423)	1.3 (0.03)
Construction/electrical/transportation technologies	35 (2.6)	0.5 (0.04)	4.8! (1.64)	49,720 (1,595)	57,260 (1,837)	0.2 (0.01)	36 (2.4)	0.4 (0.03)	‡ (†)	59,920 (1,015)	0.2 (0.01)
Criminal justice and fire protection	140 (4.7)	2.2 (0.07)	6.2 (0.74)	39,300 (1,458)	45,250 (1,679)	0.7 (0.02)	212 (5.9)	2.6 (0.07)	3.8 (0.60)	41,810 (1,237)	0.9 (0.03)
Education	573 (8.0)	9.0 (0.12)	3.4 (0.31)	38,260 (80)	44,060 (88)	2.7 (0.04)	537 (8.4)	6.6 (0.10)	1.2 (0.19)	41,510 (506)	2.3 (0.04)
General education	151 (5.3)	2.4 (0.09)	4.7 (0.80)	39,350 (1,076)	45,310 (1,239)	0.7 (0.03)	160 (5.9)	2.0 (0.07)	1.4 (0.35)	41,260 (1,264)	0.7 (0.03)
Early childhood education	32 (2.0)	0.5 (0.03)	1.2! (0.58)	36,820 (1,808)	42,400 (2,082)	0.2 (0.01)	42 (2.6)	0.5 (0.03)	1.8! (0.80)	38,130 (736)	0.2 (0.01)
Elementary education	181 (5.0)	2.8 (0.08)	3.2 (0.53)	38,150 (938)	43,940 (1,081)	0.9 (0.02)	134 (4.2)	1.7 (0.05)	1.3 (0.36)	40,490 (72)	0.6 (0.02)
Secondary teacher education	19 (1.4)	0.3 (0.02)	2.5! (1.08)	36,140 (976)	41,620 (1,124)	0.1 (0.01)	17 (1.9)	0.2 (0.02)	‡ (†)	43,500 (1,297)	0.1 (0.01)
Education, other	190 (4.8)	3.0 (0.07)	2.9 (0.45)	38,480 (940)	44,320 (1,082)	0.9 (0.02)	184 (4.8)	2.3 (0.06)	0.9 (0.27)	43,000 (636)	0.8 (0.02)
Engineering and engineering-related fields	474 (8.8)	7.4 (0.13)	5.0 (0.41)	60,580 (748)	69,760 (823)	2.3 (0.04)	716 (12.0)	8.8 (0.14)	2.7 (0.22)	70,890 (1,237)	3.1 (0.05)
General engineering	63 (3.0)	1.0 (0.05)	4.3! (1.44)	60,100 (324)	69,210 (373)	0.3 (0.01)	91 (5.1)	1.1 (0.06)	2.4! (0.94)	68,860 (2,539)	0.4 (0.02)
Chemical engineering	28 (2.2)	0.4 (0.03)	4.4! (1.42)	65,580 (3,098)	75,520 (3,568)	0.1 (0.01)	49 (2.5)	0.6 (0.03)	3.4! (1.08)	77,750 (2,728)	0.2 (0.01)
Civil engineering	46 (2.9)	0.7 (0.05)	6.6 (1.69)	58,910 (1,276)	67,840 (1,469)	0.2 (0.01)	67 (3.4)	0.8 (0.04)	1.0! (0.47)	65,420 (647)	0.3 (0.01)
Computer engineering	45 (2.8)	0.7 (0.04)	7.1 (1.50)	65,320 (842)	75,220 (970)	0.2 (0.01)	63 (2.8)	0.8 (0.03)	1.5! (0.56)	75,730 (2,641)	0.3 (0.01)
Electrical engineering	86 (4.3)	1.3 (0.07)	5.1 (1.13)	65,060 (685)	74,920 (788)	0.4 (0.02)	118 (4.3)	1.5 (0.05)	1.9 (0.44)	78,740 (1,175)	0.5 (0.02)
Mechanical engineering	86 (3.9)	1.3 (0.06)	3.7 (0.77)	61,620 (1,428)	70,960 (1,644)	0.4 (0.02)	148 (4.7)	1.8 (0.06)	3.3 (0.64)	73,960 (1,556)	0.6 (0.02)
Engineering, other	78 (3.6)	1.2 (0.06)	4.9 (1.01)	59,850 (600)	68,930 (690)	0.4 (0.02)	129 (4.5)	1.6 (0.05)	3.0 (0.71)	70,480 (477)	0.6 (0.02)
Engineering technologies	42 (2.5)	0.7 (0.04)	4.7 (1.17)	55,890 (2,180)	64,360 (2,511)	0.2 (0.01)	51 (3.5)	0.6 (0.04)	5.2 (1.20)	60,570 (3,451)	0.2 (0.01)
English language and literature	194 (5.2)	3.0 (0.08)	7.6 (0.73)	38,100 (1,100)	43,870 (1,266)	0.9 (0.02)	208 (6.1)	2.6 (0.07)	4.4 (0.54)	44,640 (1,284)	0.9 (0.03)
Family and consumer sciences	55 (3.1)	0.9 (0.05)	3.9 (0.97)	36,060 (1,375)	41,520 (1,583)	0.3 (0.01)	76 (3.4)	0.9 (0.04)	2.7! (0.87)	40,300 (733)	0.3 (0.01)
Health professions	378 (8.2)	5.9 (0.12)	3.3 (0.39)	50,330 (20)	57,960 (22)	1.8 (0.04)	680 (10.1)	8.4 (0.13)	2.0 (0.25)	54,840 (293)	2.9 (0.04)
General medical and health services	200 (6.5)	3.1 (0.10)	3.6 (0.54)	46,290 (1,500)	53,310 (1,727)	1.0 (0.03)	342 (7.6)	4.2 (0.09)	2.3 (0.39)	50,270 (261)	1.5 (0.03)
Nursing	179 (5.5)	2.8 (0.08)	3.0 (0.57)	53,350 (1,366)	61,430 (1,573)	0.9 (0.03)	338 (6.7)	4.2 (0.09)	1.7 (0.36)	58,690 (1,423)	1.5 (0.03)
History	138 (4.5)	2.2 (0.07)	8.4 (0.77)	41,060 (1,385)	47,280 (1,595)	0.7 (0.02)	136 (4.4)	1.7 (0.05)	3.6 (0.71)	45,090 (816)	0.6 (0.02)
Liberal arts and humanities	76 (3.4)	1.2 (0.05)	7.2 (1.19)	40,130 (1,161)	46,210 (1,337)	0.4 (0.02)	89 (4.1)	1.1 (0.05)	4.6 (1.09)	40,270 (482)	0.4 (0.02)
Linguistics and comparative language and literature	68 (3.5)	1.1 (0.05)	8.6 (1.73)	38,130 (1,373)	43,910 (1,582)	0.3 (0.02)	82 (3.3)	1.0 (0.04)	3.7 (0.96)	45,370 (690)	0.4 (0.01)

See notes at end of table.

Table 505.10. Number, percentage distribution, unemployment rates, and median earnings of 25- to 29-year-old bachelor's degree holders and percentage of degree holders among all 25- to 29-year-olds, by field of study and science, technology, engineering, or mathematics (STEM) status of field: 2010 and 2018—Continued

[Standard errors appear in parentheses]

Field of study and STEM status of field	2010						2018				
	25- to 29-year-old bachelor's degree holders						25- to 29-year-old bachelor's degree holders				
	Number, in thousands	Percentage distribution	Unemployment rate for the civilian labor force	Median annual earnings of full-time year-round workers		Percent of all 25- to 29-year-olds with degree in specific field	Number, in thousands	Percentage distribution	Unemployment rate for the civilian labor force	Median annual earnings of full-time year-round workers	Percent of all 25- to 29-year-olds with degree in specific field
				Current dollars	Constant 2018 dollars[1]						
1	2	3	4	5	6	7	8	9	10	11	12
Mathematics	78 (3.8)	1.2 (0.06)	4.6 (1.04)	50,120 (781)	57,720 (899)	0.4 (0.02)	116 (4.8)	1.4 (0.06)	2.5 (0.56)	54,560 (1,483)	0.5 (0.02)
Multi/interdisciplinary studies	55 (2.6)	0.9 (0.04)	5.4 (0.96)	39,770 (922)	45,790 (1,062)	0.3 (0.01)	100 (4.3)	1.2 (0.05)	4.8 (1.11)	47,760 (1,743)	0.4 (0.02)
Natural sciences	586 (9.2)	9.2 (0.14)	5.2 (0.38)	42,300 (787)	48,720 (867)	2.8 (0.04)	833 (12.3)	10.3 (0.14)	2.7 (0.25)	48,480 (799)	3.6 (0.05)
Biology	364 (8.1)	5.7 (0.13)	4.9 (0.50)	43,300 (927)	49,870 (1,067)	1.7 (0.04)	533 (9.5)	6.6 (0.11)	2.4 (0.28)	50,450 (1,288)	2.3 (0.04)
Environmental science	42 (2.8)	0.7 (0.04)	9.7 (1.98)	39,960 (1,549)	46,020 (1,784)	0.2 (0.01)	74 (3.2)	0.9 (0.04)	2.6 (0.75)	40,570 (2,153)	0.3 (0.01)
Physical sciences	180 (4.8)	2.8 (0.08)	4.7 (0.76)	42,210 (1,545)	48,610 (1,779)	0.9 (0.02)	226 (6.4)	2.8 (0.08)	3.4 (0.54)	47,570 (1,292)	1.0 (0.03)
Physical fitness, parks, recreation and leisure	101 (3.6)	1.6 (0.06)	3.5 (0.68)	40,250 (27)	46,350 (31)	0.5 (0.02)	193 (5.3)	2.4 (0.06)	2.1 (0.42)	45,500 (1,309)	0.8 (0.02)
Philosophy and religious studies	53 (2.3)	0.8 (0.04)	7.8 (1.56)	40,280 (1,419)	46,390 (1,634)	0.3 (0.01)	44 (2.6)	0.5 (0.03)	3.1! (1.10)	48,840 (2,467)	0.2 (0.01)
Psychology	378 (7.9)	5.9 (0.12)	5.9 (0.48)	37,240 (532)	42,880 (612)	1.8 (0.04)	498 (9.3)	6.1 (0.11)	3.2 (0.33)	41,420 (972)	2.1 (0.04)
Public administration and public policy	12 (1.6)	0.2 (0.02)	‡ (†)	50,090 (6,667)	57,680 (7,677)	0.1 (0.01)	17 (1.5)	0.2 (0.02)	† (†)	49,850 (1,681)	0.1 (0.01)
Social sciences	519 (8.6)	8.2 (0.13)	6.9 (0.43)	45,160 (528)	52,010 (581)	2.5 (0.04)	574 (10.2)	7.1 (0.12)	3.1 (0.34)	50,620 (19)	2.5 (0.04)
Anthropology and archeology	33 (2.0)	0.5 (0.03)	4.5 (1.14)	37,950 (2,738)	43,700 (3,153)	0.2 (0.01)	41 (2.5)	0.5 (0.03)	1.8! (0.82)	45,230 (1,757)	0.2 (0.01)
Economics	126 (4.4)	2.0 (0.07)	8.2 (1.00)	52,380 (2,049)	60,320 (2,360)	0.6 (0.02)	152 (5.4)	1.9 (0.07)	2.3 (0.53)	64,860 (3,204)	0.7 (0.02)
Geography	15 (1.7)	0.2 (0.03)	9.2! (3.53)	43,580 (2,973)	50,190 (3,424)	0.1 (0.01)	20 (1.7)	0.2 (0.02)	† (†)	45,920 (5,315)	0.1 (0.01)
International relations	23 (2.0)	0.4 (0.03)	7.1! (2.75)	49,080 (1,756)	56,520 (2,023)	0.1 (0.01)	32 (2.5)	0.4 (0.03)	5.2 (1.46)	53,730 (3,863)	0.1 (0.01)
Political science and government	173 (4.8)	2.7 (0.08)	5.9 (0.70)	45,220 (108)	52,070 (124)	0.8 (0.02)	167 (5.2)	2.1 (0.07)	4.2 (0.89)	53,640 (1,299)	0.7 (0.02)
Sociology	116 (4.3)	1.8 (0.07)	7.6 (1.15)	38,200 (1,253)	43,990 (1,443)	0.6 (0.02)	119 (5.3)	1.5 (0.06)	2.7 (0.68)	43,140 (1,418)	0.5 (0.02)
Miscellaneous social sciences	32 (2.0)	0.5 (0.03)	5.3 (1.38)	40,250 (798)	46,350 (919)	0.2 (0.01)	42 (2.8)	0.5 (0.03)	3.1! (1.01)	40,080 (961)	0.2 (0.01)
Social work and human services	59 (2.8)	0.9 (0.04)	5.6 (1.38)	35,020 (138)	40,330 (159)	0.3 (0.01)	99 (4.8)	1.2 (0.06)	3.0 (0.71)	40,480 (431)	0.4 (0.02)
Theology and religious vocations	28 (2.0)	0.4 (0.03)	3.9! (1.88)	32,790 (1,349)	37,770 (1,553)	0.1 (0.01)	35 (2.2)	0.4 (0.03)	2.0! (0.95)	35,230 (919)	0.1 (0.01)
Other fields	26 (2.0)	0.4 (0.03)	9.0 (2.31)	36,660 (2,542)	42,220 (2,928)	0.1 (0.01)	26 (2.1)	0.3 (0.03)	5.3! (2.44)	40,250 (5,725)	0.1 (0.01)
STEM status of field[2]											
STEM field	1,345 (13.7)	21.1 (0.21)	5.0 (0.26)	53,150 (967)	61,210 (1,113)	6.4 (0.07)	1,901 (21.0)	23.5 (0.22)	3.2 (0.15)	60,760 (216)	8.2 (0.09)
Non-STEM field	5,021 (29.4)	78.9 (0.21)	5.7 (0.14)	41,660 (692)	47,970 (797)	24.0 (0.14)	6,202 (33.8)	76.5 (0.22)	2.9 (0.09)	48,560 (20)	26.7 (0.14)

†Not applicable
!Interpret data with caution. The coefficient of variation (CV) for this estimate is between 30 and 50 percent.
‡Reporting standards not met. Either there are too few cases for a reliable estimate or the coefficient of variation (CV) is 50 percent or greater.
[1]Constant dollars based on the Consumer Price Index, prepared by the Bureau of Labor Statistics, U.S. Department of Labor.
[2]STEM fields include biological and biomedical sciences, computer and information sciences, engineering and engineering technologies, mathematics and statistics, and physical sciences and science technologies.

NOTE: The first bachelor's degree major reported by respondents was used to classify their field of study, even though they were able to report a second bachelor's degree major and may possess advanced degrees in other fields. Median earnings are for full-time employees working 35 or more hours per week. Data are based on sample surveys of the entire population residing within the United States, including both noninstitutionalized persons (e.g., those living in households, college housing, or military housing located within the United States) and institutionalized persons (e.g., those living in prisons, nursing facilities, or other healthcare facilities). Detail may not sum to totals because of rounding. Some data have been revised from previously published figures.
SOURCE: U.S. Department of Commerce, Census Bureau, 2010 and 2018 American Community Survey (ACS) Public Use Microdata Sample (PUMS) data. (This table was prepared November 2019.)

Table 507.15. Average literacy and numeracy scale scores and percentage distribution of 25- to 65-year-olds, by proficiency level and selected characteristics: 2017

[Standard errors appear in parentheses]

Selected characteristic	Literacy						Numeracy					
	Average scale score[1]	Percentage distribution, by proficiency level[2]					Average scale score[1]	Percentage distribution, by proficiency level[2]				
		Below level 1	Level 1	Level 2	Level 3	Level 4/5		Below level 1	Level 1	Level 2	Level 3	Level 4/5
1	2	3	4	5	6	7	8	9	10	11	12	13
Total	271 (1.3)	4 (0.6)	15 (1.0)	33 (1.4)	34 (1.7)	14 (1.0)	255 (1.4)	9 (0.8)	20 (1.2)	33 (1.6)	27 (1.2)	10 (0.9)
Sex												
Male	270 (1.9)	5 (1.1)	15 (1.5)	32 (2.2)	33 (2.5)	15 (1.4)	259 (2.1)	10 (1.3)	18 (1.7)	31 (1.9)	28 (1.9)	14 (1.4)
Female	271 (1.4)	3 (0.5)	15 (1.3)	33 (1.7)	36 (1.8)	13 (1.2)	251 (1.6)	9 (0.8)	22 (1.4)	36 (2.2)	26 (1.7)	8 (0.9)
Age												
25 to 34	279 (2.4)	3 (0.8)	13 (1.8)	28 (2.8)	38 (3.2)	17 (2.3)	261 (2.4)	7 (1.0)	18 (1.8)	33 (2.4)	30 (2.9)	11 (2.0)
35 to 44	275 (2.3)	4 (1.0)	13 (1.7)	32 (2.6)	36 (3.3)	15 (2.0)	259 (2.2)	8 (1.1)	18 (1.9)	33 (2.4)	29 (2.4)	12 (1.8)
45 to 54	266 (2.9)	6 (1.5)	17 (2.3)	31 (2.7)	34 (2.8)	13 (1.7)	251 (3.2)	12 (1.8)	20 (2.6)	30 (2.8)	27 (2.6)	10 (1.7)
55 to 65	264 (2.1)	5 (1.1)	17 (2.1)	38 (2.9)	30 (2.7)	10 (1.3)	249 (2.4)	9 (1.4)	24 (2.4)	36 (2.9)	22 (1.8)	9 (1.3)
Race/ethnicity												
White	282 (1.5)	1! (0.4)	11 (1.2)	30 (1.8)	39 (2.1)	18 (1.4)	269 (1.5)	4 (0.7)	16 (1.6)	34 (1.8)	32 (1.5)	13 (1.1)
Black	240 (2.8)	10 (1.9)	29 (3.1)	40 (4.2)	19 (3.1)	3! (1.3)	215 (3.1)	24 (2.8)	34 (3.1)	29 (3.7)	10 (2.4)	‡ (†)
Hispanic	250 (4.8)	11 (2.6)	22 (3.0)	33 (3.7)	26 (3.8)	8 (2.1)	228 (5.4)	20 (3.4)	25 (2.9)	30 (3.8)	20 (3.5)	4! (1.8)
Asian/Pacific Islander	264 (5.1)	8! (3.2)	14! (4.6)	31 (5.3)	35 (6.2)	12! (4.6)	262 (5.2)	9! (3.5)	15! (5.5)	33 (6.2)	29 (6.9)	13! (5.5)
Other[3]	256 (4.4)	‡ (†)	16! (5.5)	47 (6.2)	29 (5.6)	‡ (†)	239 (4.9)	11! (3.8)	26 (5.9)	42 (6.7)	17 (4.8)	‡ (†)
Nativity												
Born in United States	275 (1.3)	3 (0.5)	14 (1.0)	32 (1.5)	36 (1.8)	15 (1.1)	258 (1.3)	8 (0.8)	19 (1.4)	34 (1.8)	29 (1.3)	11 (0.8)
Not born in United States	247 (4.0)	12 (2.9)	22 (3.4)	34 (3.5)	23 (3.5)	9 (2.5)	237 (4.8)	17 (2.9)	24 (3.4)	31 (3.3)	18 (3.1)	10 (2.9)
Educational attainment												
Less than high school completion[4]	220 (3.7)	17 (3.7)	39 (4.3)	33 (4.3)	10 (2.9)	‡ (†)	192 (4.7)	37 (4.3)	37 (4.9)	20 (4.0)	5! (2.0)	‡ (†)
High school completion[4]	252 (2.1)	6 (1.1)	23 (2.1)	40 (2.4)	25 (2.1)	6 (1.1)	234 (2.1)	13 (1.5)	29 (2.2)	38 (2.7)	17 (1.9)	3! (0.9)
Associate's degree	267 (3.3)	‡ (†)	13 (3.2)	43 (4.6)	36 (4.8)	6! (2.4)	251 (3.3)	5! (1.6)	24 (4.5)	40 (5.8)	25 (4.2)	5! (2.2)
Bachelor's or higher degree	295 (1.6)	‡ (†)	5 (0.9)	24 (2.0)	45 (2.5)	24 (1.9)	284 (1.9)	2! (0.6)	9 (1.1)	30 (1.9)	39 (1.8)	19 (1.8)
Employment[5]												
Full-time[6]	277 (1.6)	3 (0.8)	13 (1.3)	31 (2.1)	37 (2.4)	16 (1.3)	261 (1.9)	7 (1.2)	19 (1.4)	32 (2.0)	30 (1.6)	12 (1.1)
Part-time[7]	271 (3.1)	3! (1.2)	16 (3.0)	35 (3.5)	33 (3.2)	14 (2.5)	257 (3.2)	7 (1.7)	20 (3.0)	34 (3.4)	28 (3.4)	10 (2.1)
Unemployed	269 (6.0)	‡ (†)	15 (4.1)	35 (9.9)	30 (7.9)	15! (5.2)	251 (6.9)	10! (3.6)	21! (6.9)	36 (8.4)	22! (6.6)	10! (4.6)
Not in labor force	250 (3.2)	10 (1.6)	21 (2.5)	35 (2.8)	26 (2.7)	7 (1.6)	232 (3.5)	18 (2.5)	24 (2.9)	34 (2.9)	18 (2.2)	6 (1.3)
Annual earnings[8]												
Bottom quintile	257 (4.4)	6! (2.5)	20 (3.7)	36 (4.4)	28 (3.7)	9 (2.5)	239 (4.5)	13 (2.9)	26 (4.1)	32 (4.2)	22 (3.6)	6! (1.8)
Fourth quintile	255 (3.2)	7 (2.0)	22 (3.5)	35 (3.3)	28 (3.2)	8 (1.9)	235 (4.2)	18 (3.2)	26 (3.6)	32 (3.7)	18 (2.7)	7 (1.9)
Third quintile	271 (3.0)	‡ (†)	16 (3.0)	37 (3.9)	32 (3.3)	13 (2.3)	253 (3.1)	6! (2.1)	27 (3.5)	34 (3.4)	25 (3.5)	8 (2.2)
Second quintile	287 (2.5)	‡ (†)	7 (1.8)	28 (3.3)	46 (4.1)	17 (2.2)	273 (2.3)	2! (0.9)	12 (2.0)	37 (3.8)	38 (3.2)	11 (2.1)
Top quintile	298 (2.6)	‡ (†)	5! (1.5)	24 (3.1)	44 (4.0)	26 (3.0)	288 (3.3)	‡ (†)	9 (2.1)	28 (3.2)	39 (3.3)	22 (2.6)

†Not applicable.
!Interpret data with caution. The coefficient of variation (CV) for this estimate is between 30 and 50 percent.
‡Reporting standards not met. Either there are too few cases for a reliable estimate or the coefficient of variation (CV) is 50 percent or greater.
[1]Scale ranges from 0 to 500.
[2]Proficiency levels 4 and 5 are combined for reporting purposes. The proficiency levels correspond to the score ranges shown in parentheses: below level 1 (0–175), level 1 (176–225), level 2 (226–275), level 3 (276–325), and level 4/5 (326–500). For details about the literacy proficiency levels as well as specific examples of tasks at each level, see https://nces.ed.gov/surveys/piaac/litproficiencylevel.asp. For details about the numeracy proficiency levels as well as specific examples of tasks at each level, see https://nces.ed.gov/surveys/piaac/numproficiencylevel.asp.
[3]Includes persons of all other races and those of Two or more races.
[4]Includes completion through an equivalency program, such as a GED program.
[5]Excludes those who were employed but did not report the number of hours worked per week.
[6]Full-time employment is defined as working 35 hours or more per week.
[7]Part-time employment is defined as working less than 35 hours per week.
[8]Annual earnings were calculated based on monthly earnings, which include bonuses and self-employment income. Excludes those who reported no earnings.
NOTE: Data exclude literacy-related nonresponse. Race categories exclude persons of Hispanic ethnicity. Detail may not sum to totals because of rounding.
SOURCE: U.S. Department of Education, National Center for Education Statistics, Program for the International Assessment of Adult Competencies (PIAAC), U.S. PIAAC 2017, retrieved May 26, 2020, from the PIAAC International Data Explorer (https://nces.ed.gov/surveys/piaac/ideuspiaac/). (This table was prepared May 2020.)

Table 507.30. Participation of employed persons, 17 years old and over, in career-related adult education during the previous 12 months, by selected characteristics of participants: 1995, 1999, and 2005

[Standard errors appear in parentheses]

Characteristic of employed person	1995 Percent of adults participating in career- or job-related courses	1995 Number of career- or job-related courses taken, per employed adult	1999 Percent of adults participating in career- or job-related courses	1999 Number of career- or job-related courses taken, per employed adult	2005 Employed persons, in thousands	2005 Percent of adults participating: In career- or job-related courses[1]	2005 In apprenticeship programs	2005 In personal interest courses	2005 In informal learning activities for personal interest	2005 Number of career- or job-related courses taken[1]: In thousands	2005 Per employed adult
1	2	3	4	5	6	7	8	9	10	11	12
Total	31.1 (0.54)	0.8 (0.02)	30.5 (1.14)	0.7 (0.03)	133,386 (1,508.1)	38.8 (0.83)	1.4 (0.24)	21.8 (0.94)	73.5 (1.01)	108,443	0.8 (0.03)
Sex											
Male	29.0 (0.72)	0.7 (0.02)	28.3 (1.15)	0.6 (0.03)	71,754 (934.7)	31.7 (1.22)	2.0 (0.37)	18.5 (1.30)	73.4 (1.52)	44,512	0.6 (0.03)
Female	33.4 (0.83)	0.9 (0.03)	32.9 (1.14)	0.8 (0.03)	61,632 (1,219.3)	47.1 (1.43)	0.8 (0.23)	25.8 (1.23)	73.6 (1.37)	63,931	1.0 (0.05)
Age											
17 through 24 years old	18.6 (1.01)	0.4 (0.02)	19.1 (1.91)	0.4 (0.06)	15,027 (1,030.4)	26.4 (3.01)	3.0 ! (1.03)	25.2 (3.37)	71.4 (3.15)	8,024	0.5 (0.09)
25 through 29 years old	31.2 (1.46)	0.8 (0.05)	34.3 (2.44)	0.8 (0.08)	14,555 (918.4)	36.1 (2.94)	3.1 ! (1.12)	24.5 (3.66)	70.9 (4.49)	9,493	0.7 (0.06)
30 through 34 years old	31.6 (1.30)	0.8 (0.04)	34.4 (2.50)	0.8 (0.08)	15,250 (977.2)	41.0 (3.06)	2.7 ! (1.10)	23.7 (2.63)	74.0 (2.54)	12,681	0.8 (0.07)
35 through 39 years old	35.1 (1.02)	0.9 (0.03)	29.2 (2.15)	0.7 (0.07)	15,286 (922.4)	41.7 (4.16)	1.0 ! (0.46)	21.6 (3.15)	77.7 (3.15)	13,807	0.9 (0.14)
40 through 44 years old	36.6 (1.29)	0.9 (0.04)	36.4 (2.44)	0.8 (0.07)	18,141 (946.3)	39.8 (2.73)	‡ (†)	23.3 (2.60)	71.2 (3.15)	15,586	0.9 (0.07)
45 through 49 years old	39.6 (1.94)	1.0 (0.06)	30.4 (2.42)	0.7 (0.06)	18,149 (842.5)	45.0 (2.15)	0.7 ! (0.29)	19.0 (2.09)	73.5 (2.68)	16,809	0.9 (0.06)
50 through 54 years old	34.4 (1.69)	0.9 (0.04)	34.7 (2.57)	0.8 (0.07)	14,624 (732.1)	42.6 (2.49)	0.7 ! (0.32)	19.5 (1.92)	76.3 (2.27)	14,881	1.0 (0.10)
55 through 59 years old	26.7 (1.86)	0.7 (0.06)	30.3 (2.83)	0.6 (0.08)	10,522 (676.0)	44.7 (2.98)	‡ (†)	18.3 (1.93)	73.0 (2.95)	9,901	0.9 (0.09)
60 through 64 years old	21.1 (2.41)	0.5 (0.06)	27.2 (3.80)	0.7 (0.15)	6,021 (498.8)	38.9 (3.97)	# (†)	23.4 (3.52)	73.0 (4.22)	4,919	0.8 (0.10)
65 years old and over	13.7 (1.86)	0.4 (0.06)	20.3 (4.21)	0.4 (0.08)	5,812 (493.3)	21.6 (3.48)	# (†)	17.4 (3.13)	74.2 (3.75)	2,343	0.4 (0.07)
65 through 69	13.1 (2.28)	0.4 (0.08)	— (†)	— (†)	3,385 (415.5)	19.1 (4.05)	# (†)	20.9 (4.88)	75.4 (5.18)	1,102	0.3 (0.08)
70 and over	14.6 (2.85)	0.4 (0.09)	— (†)	— (†)	2,427 (282.3)	25.1 (5.81)	# (†)	12.6 (2.93)	72.6 (6.11)	1,241	0.5 (0.14)
Race/ethnicity											
White	33.2 (0.61)	0.8 (0.02)	32.8 (0.98)	0.6 (0.03)	94,881 (1,538.6)	41.3 (0.93)	1.2 (0.25)	22.2 (1.11)	75.3 (1.17)	82,511	0.9 (0.03)
Black	26.2 (1.46)	0.7 (0.04)	28.1 (2.34)	1.0 (0.07)	13,773 (533.2)	39.2 (3.82)	1.7 ! (0.83)	23.5 (3.04)	66.9 (3.02)	10,311	0.7 (0.11)
Hispanic	18.1 (1.00)	0.4 (0.02)	16.4 (1.83)	0.5 (0.05)	15,741 (681.1)	25.0 (2.66)	2.9 (0.85)	16.2 (2.31)	65.8 (3.39)	8,786	0.6 (0.11)
Asian	— (†)	— (†)	— (†)	— (†)	3,770 (520.7)	36.9 (7.00)	‡ (†)	32.3 (7.26)	81.1 (5.88)	2,207	0.6 (0.12)
Pacific Islander	— (†)	— (†)	— (†)	— (†)	‡ (†)	‡ (†)	‡ (†)	‡ (†)	‡ (†)	‡	‡ (†)
Asian/Pacific Islander	25.5 (2.69)	0.6 (0.07)	32.8 (4.84)	0.4 ! (0.15)	— (†)	— (†)	— (†)	— (†)	— (†)	—	— (†)
American Indian/Alaska Native	34.0 (6.32)	0.9 (0.20)	29.5 ! (11.52)	‡ (†)	3,786 (562.7)	39.1 (6.85)	‡ (†)	22.6 (6.34)	77.6 (8.40)	3,083	0.8 (0.15)
Two or more races	— (†)	— (†)	— (†)	— (†)	‡ (†)	‡ (†)	‡ (†)	‡ (†)	‡ (†)	‡	‡ (†)
Other races	25.3 (2.99)	0.7 (0.09)	— (†)	— (†)	‡ (†)	‡ (†)	— (†)	‡ (†)	‡ (†)	‡	‡ (†)
Highest level of education completed											
Less than high school completion	8.8 ! (1.05)	0.1 (0.02)	7.9 (2.29)	0.4 (0.05)	16,627 (838.2)	10.4 (2.11)	2.4 ! (0.90)	8.8 (2.01)	57.0 (3.76)	2,592	0.2 (0.03)
8th grade or less	6.1 ! (2.00)	0.1 ! (0.04)	— (†)	— (†)	5,016 (599.7)	2.7 (1.12)	‡ (†)	3.8 ! (1.71)	46.7 (7.11)	197	# (†)
9th through 12th grade, no completion	10.0 (1.27)	0.2 (0.02)	— (†)	— (†)	11,610 (792.8)	13.7 (2.99)	‡ (†)	11.0 (2.06)	61.5 (4.05)	2,396	0.2 (0.04)
High school completion	20.9 (0.79)	0.4 (0.02)	21.4 (1.45)	0.8 (0.03)	34,121 (1,147.2)	24.7 (1.76)	1.3 ! (0.46)	17.1 (1.89)	63.4 (2.55)	16,640	0.5 (0.05)
Some vocational/technical	32.3 (2.50)	0.8 (0.07)	28.7 (5.76)	0.9 (0.17)	3,744 (393.1)	48.2 (5.92)	‡ (†)	25.5 (4.61)	74.0 (5.54)	3,802	1.0 (0.17)
Some college	29.9 (0.91)	0.7 (0.03)	29.0 (1.78)	0.7 (0.06)	24,479 (1,067.7)	39.9 (2.36)	1.9 ! (0.69)	25.2 (2.50)	79.8 (2.04)	18,437	0.8 (0.05)
Associate's degree	39.2 (1.58)	1.0 (0.05)	39.7 (3.07)	0.9 (0.09)	9,943 (730.7)	50.4 (3.71)	2.3 ! (0.84)	19.1 (2.86)	78.4 (3.88)	14,224	1.4 (0.21)
Bachelor's degree	44.6 (1.33)	1.2 (0.04)	43.8 (2.01)	1.0 (0.06)	26,475 (902.7)	53.1 (1.88)	‡ (†)	29.0 (1.77)	78.7 (1.94)	28,099	1.1 (0.06)
Some graduate work (or study)	50.2 (1.63)	1.4 (0.05)	46.8 (4.17)	1.2 (0.14)	17,998 (735.4)	61.1 (2.16)	‡ (†)	28.6 (2.01)	88.8 (1.16)	24,649	1.4 (0.07)
No degree	44.3 (3.18)	1.2 (0.10)	54.2 (4.94)	1.2 (0.14)	2,125 (227.9)	53.8 (5.79)	‡ (†)	39.3 (6.05)	75.0 (5.64)	2,412	1.1 (0.16)
Master's	50.5 (1.99)	1.4 (0.06)	45.3 (2.97)	1.1 (0.11)	11,330 (614.7)	62.7 (2.98)	‡ (†)	28.2 (2.27)	90.5 (1.40)	15,394	1.4 (0.09)
Doctor's	40.4 (6.42)	1.0 (0.16)	34.4 (4.79)	0.7 (0.12)	1,600 (227.2)	49.0 (5.80)	‡ (†)	28.8 (4.76)	87.8 (4.35)	2,204	1.4 (0.36)
Professional	67.6 (3.89)	2.0 (0.15)	67.6 (6.98)	1.9 (0.31)	2,943 (382.7)	66.5 (6.39)	‡ (†)	22.1 (5.05)	92.9 (2.21)	4,639	1.6 (0.21)

See notes at end of table.

Table 507.30. Participation of employed persons, 17 years old and over, in career-related adult education during the previous 12 months, by selected characteristics of participants: 1995, 1999, and 2005—Continued

[Standard errors appear in parentheses]

Characteristic of employed person	1995		1999		2005						
	Percent of adults participating in career- or job-related courses	Number of career- or job-related courses taken, per employed adult	Percent of adults participating in career- or job-related courses	Number of career- or job-related courses taken, per employed adult	Employed persons, in thousands	Percent of adults participating				Number of career- or job-related courses taken[1]	
						In career- or job-related courses[1]	In apprenticeship programs	In personal interest courses	In informal learning activities for personal interest	In thousands	Per employed adult
1	2	3	4	5	6	7	8	9	10	11	12
Locale[2]											
City	— (†)	— (†)	— (†)	— (†)	39,283 (1,391.3)	39.6 (1.67)	2.2 (0.60)	23.1 (1.43)	74.0 (1.77)	34,327	0.9 (0.05)
Suburban	— (†)	— (†)	— (†)	— (†)	48,452 (1,555.0)	41.1 (1.87)	1.2 (0.32)	23.3 (1.38)	74.2 (1.49)	39,802	0.8 (0.04)
Town	— (†)	— (†)	— (†)	— (†)	17,616 (1,060.7)	36.0 (2.64)	‡ (†)	19.6 (2.83)	71.7 (3.02)	12,947	0.7 (0.07)
Rural	— (†)	— (†)	— (†)	— (†)	27,847 (885.2)	35.4 (2.14)	1.4! (0.58)	19.0 (2.19)	72.7 (2.22)	21,135	0.8 (0.06)
Occupation											
Executive, administrative, or managerial occupations	42.9 (1.49)	1.2 (0.05)	40.6 (2.06)	1.0 (0.07)	14,596 (707.6)	53.6 (2.79)	‡ (†)	29.5 (2.89)	77.7 (2.87)	16,567	1.1 (0.09)
Engineers, surveyors, and architects	44.2 (4.46)	1.1 (0.12)	52.1 (6.96)	1.0 (0.16)	1,987 (244.9)	56.3 (5.68)	‡ (†)	30.5 (6.36)	81.0 (4.73)	2,323	1.2 (0.16)
Natural scientists and mathematicians	59.7 (3.97)	1.7 (0.15)	46.0 (6.61)	0.8 (0.14)	4,130 (445.4)	51.5 (5.64)	‡ (†)	31.2 (4.83)	85.3 (5.44)	3,693	0.9 (0.11)
Social scientists and workers, religious workers, and lawyers	59.5 (2.61)	1.8 (0.11)	56.9 (5.66)	1.7 (0.24)	4,697 (480.9)	66.8 (4.48)	‡ (†)	28.3 (3.81)	88.6 (2.95)	7,822	1.7 (0.29)
Teachers, elementary/secondary	53.9 (2.23)	1.5 (0.08)	52.1 (3.53)	1.2 (0.11)	7,085 (568.5)	67.7 (4.16)	‡ (†)	31.5 (3.93)	83.0 (2.79)	12,233	1.7 (0.13)
Teachers, postsecondary and counselors, librarians, and archivists	41.6 (4.57)	1.0 (0.15)	35.6 (5.85)	0.7 (0.14)	2,393 (420.9)	53.1 (8.63)	‡ (†)	17.7 (4.91)	90.9 (3.97)	2,122	0.9 (0.09)
Health diagnosing and treating practitioners	68.6 (5.85)	2.0 (0.23)	65.2 (11.99)	1.5! (0.50)	978 (208.8)	78.9 (7.10)	‡ (†)	27.4! (9.60)	86.6 (5.37)	1,951	2.0 (0.25)
Registered nurses, pharmacists, dieticians, therapists, and physician's assistants	72.8 (3.02)	2.2 (0.14)	72.2 (5.04)	1.8 (0.21)	2,794 (238.8)	79.7 (4.60)	‡ (†)	29.4 (4.17)	84.3 (3.70)	4,984	1.8 (0.15)
Writers, artists, entertainers, and athletes	23.4 (2.89)	0.5 (0.07)	30.6 (6.21)	0.6 (0.18)	2,969 (405.2)	29.9 (5.69)	‡ (†)	31.8 (6.15)	88.9 (4.39)	1,865	0.6 (0.15)
Health technologists and technicians	50.0 (4.08)	1.4 (0.12)	41.8 (6.00)	1.0 (0.19)	3,060 (436.7)	70.6 (7.31)	‡ (†)	27.8 (6.48)	77.5 (6.40)	4,473	1.5 (0.18)
Technologists and technicians, except health	43.8 (2.67)	1.1 (0.10)	37.6 (4.87)	1.0 (0.15)	1,774 (336.5)	29.4 (8.10)	‡ (†)	5.3! (2.02)	75.2 (8.98)	1,015	0.6 (0.17)
Marketing and sales occupations	25.2 (1.26)	0.6 (0.03)	21.1 (2.27)	0.4 (0.06)	14,845 (971.9)	32.3 (3.17)	‡ (†)	20.8 (2.64)	70.5 (3.53)	7,724	0.5 (0.05)
Administrative support occupations, including clerical	30.8 (1.15)	0.7 (0.03)	27.4 (2.02)	0.6 (0.05)	21,167 (1,179.4)	36.1 (2.95)	0.8! (0.40)	28.2 (2.28)	72.9 (2.37)	15,443	0.7 (0.10)
Service occupations	22.6 (1.25)	0.6 (0.04)	21.0 (2.15)	0.5 (0.07)	17,180 (1,033.7)	33.7 (3.13)	1.1! (0.36)	16.2 (2.31)	69.0 (2.74)	13,029	0.8 (0.10)
Agriculture, forestry, and fishing occupations	12.4 (2.47)	0.3 (0.07)	12.2! (4.09)	0.2! (0.07)	2,522 (423.8)	22.4! (7.61)	‡ (†)	23.0! (11.03)	62.9 (11.04)	960	0.4! (0.12)
Mechanics and repairers	29.1 (2.62)	0.7 (0.08)	15.0 (3.40)	0.3 (0.09)	5,241 (521.6)	28.3 (4.47)	4.0! (1.44)	12.6 (3.24)	69.3 (4.36)	2,669	0.5 (0.09)
Construction and extractive occupations	18.6 (2.33)	0.3 (0.04)	13.2 (3.16)	0.2 (0.06)	6,827 (647.1)	12.4 (3.04)	5.3! (2.26)	7.8 (1.88)	69.0 (5.25)	2,323	0.3! (0.13)
Precision production[3]	25.6 (4.04)	0.6 (0.12)	18.3! (6.52)	0.4! (0.12)	10,483 (839.3)	23.5 (3.79)	‡ (†)	14.0 (3.34)	64.9 (3.74)	4,904	0.5 (0.07)
Production workers	14.8 (1.13)	0.3 (0.02)	23.0 (3.17)	0.5 (0.08)	— (†)	— (†)	— (†)	—	— (†)	—	— (†)

See notes at end of table.

Table 507.30. Participation of employed persons, 17 years old and over, in career-related adult education during the previous 12 months, by selected characteristics of participants: 1995, 1999, and 2005—Continued

[Standard errors appear in parentheses]

Characteristic of employed person	1995		1999		2005						
	Percent of adults participating in career- or job-related courses	Number of career- or job-related courses taken, per employed adult	Percent of adults participating in career- or job-related courses	Number of career- or job-related courses taken, per employed adult	Employed persons, in thousands	Percent of adults participating				Number of career- or job-related courses taken[1]	
						In career- or job-related courses[1]	In apprenticeship programs	In personal interest courses	In informal learning activities for personal interest	In thousands	Per employed adult
1	2	3	4	5	6	7	8	9	10	11	12
Transportation and material moving	15.8 (1.83)	0.3 (0.04)	18.4 (3.62)	0.3 (0.06)	7,858 (742.5)	15.2 (2.81)	‡ (†)	10.5 (3.10)	62.5 (5.32)	1,935	0.2 (0.05)
Handlers, equipment cleaners, helpers, and laborers	11.7 (2.77)	0.2 (0.06)	‡ (†)	‡ (†)	— (†)	— (†)	‡ (†)	— (†)	— (†)	—	— (†)
Miscellaneous occupations	38.8 (3.50)	1.0 (0.11)	14.2! (4.62)	0.3! (0.08)	801 (189.4)	17.2! (6.87)	‡ (†)	8.7! (4.31)	48.3 (13.96)	409	‡ (†)
Annual household income											
$10,000 or less	12.6 (1.31)	0.2 (0.03)	9.5! (3.09)	0.2! (0.05)	4,425 (444.8)	16.7 (4.35)	‡ (†)	26.2! (7.96)	69.7 (5.72)	1,556	0.4! (0.12)
$5,000 or less	8.7 (1.91)	0.1 (0.03)	— (†)	— (†)	1,635 (252.7)	19.1 (6.52)	‡ (†)	22.9! (7.91)	60.9 (8.84)	850	‡ (†)
$5,001 to $10,000	15.1 (1.62)	0.3 (0.04)	— (†)	— (†)	2,791 (454.1)	15.3 (5.68)	‡ (†)	28.1! (12.27)	74.8 (6.88)	706	0.3! (0.10)
$10,001 to $15,000	15.1 (1.71)	0.4 (0.04)	8.3 (1.88)	0.1 (0.03)	4,814 (633.4)	22.2 (5.77)	‡ (†)	17.3! (5.25)	64.5 (7.57)	2,189	0.5 (0.12)
$15,001 to $20,000	20.1 (1.36)	0.4 (0.03)	16.3 (2.75)	0.3 (0.05)	4,515 (398.8)	18.2 (3.09)	5.7! (2.71)	11.5 (1.96)	60.4 (5.11)	1,322	0.3 (0.05)
$20,001 to $25,000	20.4 (1.52)	0.5 (0.05)	18.8 (2.79)	0.4 (0.08)	5,593 (490.2)	23.8 (4.02)	1.1! (0.51)	13.3 (3.21)	71.5 (4.11)	2,817	0.5 (0.10)
$25,001 to $30,000	24.7 (1.34)	0.5 (0.03)	22.2 (2.73)	0.5 (0.07)	7,444 (680.4)	31.4 (4.88)	‡ (†)	16.7 (3.77)	73.5 (3.91)	4,322	0.6 (0.11)
$30,001 to $40,000	30.2 (1.13)	0.8 (0.03)	26.6 (2.82)	0.6 (0.07)	13,123 (928.5)	35.1 (3.45)	1.5! (0.65)	21.7 (3.71)	69.1 (3.55)	8,224	0.6 (0.06)
$40,001 to $50,000	34.7 (1.30)	0.8 (0.04)	32.3 (2.34)	0.7 (0.07)	13,647 (1,058.4)	31.5 (3.01)	1.8! (0.72)	20.1 (3.32)	73.5 (2.78)	10,072	0.7 (0.10)
$50,001 to $75,000	40.0 (1.18)	1.0 (0.04)	36.6 (1.86)	0.9 (0.06)	33,665 (1,430.4)	42.7 (1.80)	1.2! (0.51)	20.9 (2.10)	71.3 (2.55)	28,991	0.9 (0.06)
More than $75,000	45.2 (1.40)	1.3 (0.04)	42.5 (1.79)	1.0 (0.06)	46,160 (1,263.3)	48.1 (1.57)	1.3! (0.39)	26.0 (1.37)	79.2 (1.55)	48,951	1.1 (0.05)

—Not available.
†Not applicable.
#Rounds to zero.
!Interpret data with caution. The coefficient of variation (CV) for this estimate is between 30 and 50 percent. The coefficient of variation (CV) for this estimate is 50 percent or greater.
‡Reporting standards not met.
[1]The 2005 estimates on participation in career- or job-related courses were based on responses to multiple questions. Specifically, respondents were first asked what courses they had taken, and then whether each course was career- or job-related. In contrast, 1995 and 1999 respondents were asked a single, general question about whether they had participated in any career- or job-related courses. Therefore, 2005 results may not be comparable to results from the earlier years.

[2]Detail may not sum to totals due to missing locale information.
[3]For 2005, figures include "Production workers" occupations data.
NOTE: Data do not include persons enrolled in high school or below. Race categories exclude persons of Hispanic ethnicity. Detail may not sum to totals because of rounding.
SOURCE: U.S. Department of Education, National Center for Education Statistics, Adult Education Survey (AE-NHES:1995, AE-NHES:1999, and AE-NHES:2005) of the National Household Education Surveys Program. (This table was prepared October 2010.)

Table 507.40. Participation rate of persons, 17 years old and over, in adult education during the previous 12 months, by selected characteristics of participants: Selected years, 1991 through 2005

[Standard errors appear in parentheses]

Characteristic of participant	Percent taking any program, class, or course					Percent taking specific programs, classes, or courses, 2005						Percent doing informal learning activities for personal interest, 2005
	1991	1995	1999	2001	2005	Basic skills/General Educational Development (GED) classes	English as a second language (ESL) classes	Part-time postsecondary education[1]	Career- or job-related courses	Apprenticeship programs	Personal-interest courses	
1	2	3	4	5	6	7	8	9	10	11	12	13
Total	33.0 (0.68)	40.2 (0.48)	44.5 (0.77)	46.4 (0.55)	44.4 (0.74)	1.3 (0.22)	0.9 (0.17)	5.0 (0.29)	27.0 (0.63)	1.2 (0.18)	21.4 (0.71)	70.5 (0.79)
Sex												
Male	32.6 (1.09)	38.2 (0.65)	41.7 (1.15)	43.1 (0.83)	41.0 (1.20)	1.4 (0.41)	0.9 (0.29)	5.0 (0.44)	24.5 (0.99)	1.7 (0.31)	18.3 (1.08)	70.8 (1.10)
Female	33.2 (0.97)	42.1 (0.59)	47.1 (1.02)	49.5 (0.78)	47.5 (1.01)	1.2 (0.19)	0.9 (0.15)	5.1 (0.37)	29.2 (0.95)	0.7 (0.15)	24.2 (0.88)	70.2 (1.03)
Age												
17 to 24 years old	37.8 (1.46)	47.0 (1.12)	49.9 (2.34)	52.8 (2.04)	52.8 (2.79)	6.0 (1.48)	1.7 (0.61)	11.5 (1.34)	21.3 (2.22)	2.7 (0.76)	26.3 (2.60)	69.2 (2.54)
25 to 29 years old	40.0 (2.33)	49.6 (1.31)	56.5 (2.53)	52.9 (2.60)	51.6 (3.82)	1.8 (0.48)	3.3 (1.48)	9.1 (1.50)	29.5 (2.48)	3.2 (1.06)	20.9 (2.78)	66.8 (3.75)
30 to 34 years old	37.6 (2.88)	47.3 (1.41)	56.2 (2.57)	53.7 (2.18)	52.7 (2.52)	1.9 (0.66)	1.6 (0.64)	8.4 (1.28)	33.8 (2.71)	2.5 (0.89)	23.2 (2.23)	73.8 (2.22)
35 to 39 years old	42.1 (2.71)	47.3 (1.15)	50.1 (2.43)	54.0 (1.71)	48.6 (3.21)	0.4 (0.16)	0.7 (0.26)	6.1 (0.90)	32.6 (3.29)	0.9 (0.36)	20.7 (2.67)	75.5 (2.69)
40 to 44 years old	49.2 (3.28)	50.9 (1.15)	50.5 (2.43)	53.5 (1.88)	48.9 (2.43)	0.8 ! (0.31)	0.6 (0.23)	4.7 (0.77)	34.8 (2.30)	0.9 (0.42)	23.4 (2.29)	71.5 (2.62)
45 to 49 years old	40.0 (2.43)	48.7 (1.66)	49.8 (2.69)	55.4 (2.02)	49.0 (2.09)	‡	0.6 (0.25)	3.2 (0.48)	37.7 (1.83)	0.5 ! (0.23)	19.3 (1.88)	71.6 (2.52)
50 to 54 years old	26.8 (3.31)	42.5 (1.38)	47.2 (2.51)	51.1 (2.22)	46.6 (2.36)	‡	0.3 ! (0.15)	4.5 (0.75)	35.2 (2.25)	0.6 ! (0.28)	20.3 (1.64)	75.6 (1.89)
55 to 59 years old	29.0 (3.74)	32.2 (1.66)	38.0 (2.60)	44.1 (1.98)	42.2 (2.36)	‡	‡	1.9 (0.43)	31.9 (2.39)	‡	18.0 (1.63)	69.5 (2.56)
60 to 64 years old	17.4 (1.90)	23.7 (1.89)	31.4 (2.83)	30.8 (2.18)	37.9 (3.00)	0.9 ! (0.36)	‡	0.9 ! (0.36)	20.9 (2.07)	‡	24.1 (2.40)	71.4 (3.04)
65 to 69 years old	14.2 (2.97)	18.1 (1.46)	25.4 (2.54)	20.5 (1.74)	26.2 (2.67)	‡	‡	0.5 ! (0.22)	8.1 (1.36)	‡	20.9 (2.41)	67.6 (2.52)
70 years old and over	8.6 (1.25)	13.8 (1.09)	15.0 (1.38)	21.7 (1.37)	21.5 (1.44)	5.1 (2.17)	‡	‡	4.0 (0.78)	‡	17.9 (1.33)	62.9 (1.82)
Racial/ethnic group												
White	34.1 (0.82)	41.5 (0.54)	44.4 (0.89)	47.4 (0.59)	45.6 (0.84)	0.9 (0.23)	0.2 (0.08)	4.9 (0.35)	29.1 (0.70)	0.9 (0.17)	22.1 (0.87)	73.0 (0.92)
Black	25.9 (2.23)	37.0 (1.45)	46.3 (2.30)	43.3 (1.50)	46.4 (2.81)	1.9 (0.49)	‡	5.4 (0.97)	27.0 (2.53)	1.5 ! (0.73)	23.7 (2.11)	65.3 (2.02)
Hispanic	31.4 (2.63)	33.7 (1.18)	41.3 (2.51)	41.7 (2.28)	37.8 (2.43)	2.6 (0.72)	5.6 (1.22)	5.7 ! (1.55)	16.9 (1.72)	2.2 (0.63)	15.4 (1.75)	57.5 (2.86)
Asian	—	—	—	—	48.3 (5.39)	‡	2.6 ! (1.03)	7.6 ! (2.62)	27.2 (4.70)	‡	26.5 (5.06)	81.1 ! (4.10)
Pacific Islander	†	†	†	†	‡	‡	‡	‡	‡	‡	‡	‡
Asian/Pacific Islander	35.9 (5.55)	39.7 (2.92)	51.1 (4.63)	49.5 (3.81)	†	†	†	†	†	†	†	†
American Indian/Alaska Native	29.3 ! (11.55)	38.8 (4.85)	36.3 (9.16)	50.2 (8.28)	36.3 (10.17)	‡	‡	4.4 ! (1.82)	23.0 ! (8.51)	1.3 ! (0.59)	13.0 ! (6.16)	70.6 (9.18)
Two or more races	—	—	—	—	39.4 (4.94)	5.1 (2.17)	‡	3.2 ! (1.07)	23.8 (4.06)	‡	21.0 (4.13)	77.6 (5.28)
Highest level of education completed												
8th grade or less	7.7 (1.44)	10.0 (1.10)	14.7 (2.92)	19.7 (2.84)	15.5 (2.47)	1.9 (0.57)	4.3 (1.70)	†	1.7 ! (0.55)	†	7.3 (1.24)	38.1 (3.27)
9th through 12th grade, no completion	15.8 (2.25)	20.2 (1.38)	25.6 (2.55)	25.5 (1.53)	27.2 (2.40)	7.9 (1.69)	1.1 (0.41)	2.1 (0.57)	7.6 (1.44)	1.5 ! (0.61)	12.5 (1.53)	55.7 (2.52)
High school completion	24.1 (1.10)	30.7 (0.84)	34.8 (1.37)	33.9 (1.07)	33.0 (1.62)	0.5 ! (0.24)	0.7 ! (0.24)	2.5 (0.36)	17.2 (1.18)	1.1 (0.35)	16.8 (1.27)	63.6 (1.93)
Some vocational/technical	34.2 (3.80)	41.9 (2.16)	41.1 (3.97)	50.7 (3.51)	43.3 (4.30)	‡	‡	4.5 ! (1.06)	28.3 (3.71)	1.4 ! (0.47)	23.2 (3.09)	77.6 (3.98)
Some college	41.4 (1.67)	49.3 (0.92)	51.1 (1.76)	57.4 (1.29)	51.1 (1.79)	‡	1.1 ! (0.51)	8.6 (1.42)	28.8 (1.54)	1.4 (0.66)	26.8 (1.80)	79.8 (1.52)
Associate's degree	49.2 (5.82)	56.1 (1.85)	56.6 (2.93)	62.5 (2.15)	56.5 (3.64)	‡	0.4 ! (0.17)	6.6 (0.82)	40.8 (3.27)	1.9 ! (0.17)	20.1 (2.48)	75.9 (3.70)
Bachelor's degree	51.1 (2.46)	56.9 (1.20)	60.3 (1.84)	64.5 (1.39)	59.8 (1.56)	‡	‡	6.3 (0.86)	44.1 (1.61)	0.4 !	28.6 (1.55)	79.3 (1.72)
Some graduate work (or study)	55.1 (2.90)	59.9 (1.55)	63.6 (1.96)	68.9 (1.64)	66.3 (1.99)	‡	‡	8.7 (2.15)	49.3 (2.15)	‡	30.7 (1.77)	88.0 (1.06)
No degree	—	62.2 (2.67)	64.7 (4.39)	64.2 (3.54)	65.3 (4.84)	‡	‡	14.5 (2.55)	40.5 (4.68)	‡	38.7 (4.81)	78.2 (4.34)
Master's	—	59.1 (1.88)	65.7 (2.64)	70.7 (2.10)	67.5 (2.59)	‡	‡	8.9 (1.31)	51.4 (2.81)	‡	30.6 (2.04)	88.8 (1.33)
Doctor's	—	54.0 (6.99)	53.1 (4.73)	63.7 (3.98)	58.0 (4.94)	‡	‡	10.1 ! (3.14)	34.0 (4.53)	‡	31.4 (3.95)	90.3 (3.26)
Professional	—	65.9 (3.91)	72.5 (5.75)	72.8 (3.79)	68.2 (5.77)	‡	‡	†	59.0 (6.35)	‡	23.9 (4.35)	91.6 (2.15)
Urbanicity												
City	—	—	—	†	45.8 (1.46)	1.4 (0.31)	1.6 ! (0.38)	5.7 (0.59)	26.3 (1.24)	1.8 (0.43)	22.5 (1.10)	69.2 (1.39)
Suburban	—	—	—	†	46.9 (1.33)	0.9 (0.23)	0.4 ! (0.36)	5.8 (0.55)	29.7 (1.26)	0.9 (0.21)	23.4 (1.16)	73.4 (1.28)
Town	—	—	—	†	41.8 (2.33)	2.7 ! (1.16)	0.4 ! (0.14)	4.2 (0.87)	25.6 (1.74)	0.5 ! (0.21)	18.5 (1.96)	70.5 (2.43)
Rural	—	—	—	†	39.5 (2.04)	0.8 (0.22)	†	3.3 (0.59)	24.2 (1.38)	1.2 (0.40)	18.3 (1.76)	67.6 (1.76)
Labor force status												
In labor force	40.7 (0.96)	49.8 (0.69)	52.1 (0.94)	†	52.3 (0.93)	1.4 (0.32)	0.8 (0.19)	6.4 (0.39)	37.1 (0.83)	1.5 (0.24)	21.9 (0.91)	73.0 (0.94)
Employed	42.0 (1.00)	50.7 (0.53)	52.5 (0.96)	†	53.4 (0.94)	1.1 (0.31)	0.7 (0.20)	6.5 (0.39)	38.8 (0.83)	1.4 (0.24)	21.8 (0.94)	73.5 (1.01)
Unemployed	26.0 (3.24)	36.6 (1.91)	44.9 (4.60)	†	37.8 (4.26)	5.8 (1.60)	1.9 (0.79)	5.2 (1.37)	13.5 (2.16)	†	22.1 (3.99)	66.7 (3.80)
Not in labor force	15.7 (0.91)	21.3 (0.69)	24.9 (1.17)	†	27.6 (1.18)	1.1 (0.24)	1.3 (0.36)	2.3 (0.45)	5.7 (0.55)	0.6 ! (0.22)	20.5 (0.97)	65.2 (1.27)

See notes at end of table.

Table 507.40.   Participation rate of persons, 17 years old and over, in adult education during the previous 12 months, by selected characteristics of participants: Selected years, 1991 through 2005—Continued

[Standard errors appear in parentheses]

Characteristic of participant	Percent taking any program, class, or course					Percent taking specific programs, classes, or courses, 2005						Percent doing informal learning activities for personal interest, 2005
	1991	1995	1999	2001	2005	Basic skills/General Educational Development (GED) classes	English as a second language (ESL) classes	Part-time postsecondary education[1]	Career- or job-related courses	Apprenticeship programs	Personal-interest courses	
1	2	3	4	5	6	7	8	9	10	11	12	13
Occupation												
Executive, administrative, or managerial occupations	49.3 (3.45)	55.8 (1.92)	57.0 (2.11)	66.2 (1.61)	64.1 (2.73)	‡ (†)	‡ (†)	6.0 (1.10)	51.8 (2.82)	‡ (†)	28.8 (2.89)	78.6 (2.71)
Engineers, surveyors, and architects	62.6 (7.85)	65.5 (4.18)	79.8 (6.01)	68.1 (4.46)	71.2 (5.68)	‡ (†)	‡ (†)	9.3! (3.21)	55.6 (5.60)	‡ (†)	31.4 (6.19)	81.1 (4.63)
Natural scientists and mathematicians	48.2 (9.86)	72.3 (3.52)	60.5 (6.74)	74.0 (4.46)	69.1 (4.63)	‡ (†)	‡ (†)	9.2 (2.49)	49.6 (5.27)	‡ (†)	30.2 (4.53)	85.5 (5.16)
Social scientists and workers, religious workers, and lawyers	55.6 (6.01)	76.6 (2.61)	79.3 (4.35)	83.5 (3.05)	77.7 (4.11)	‡ (†)	‡ (†)	12.8 (3.16)	64.3 (4.42)	‡ (†)	29.2 (3.52)	89.4 (2.78)
Teachers, elementary/secondary	56.0 (4.20)	54.8 (4.64)	66.5 (5.61)	79.9 (2.95)	79.7 (2.59)	‡ (†)	‡ (†)	8.3! (3.16)	65.0 (3.99)	‡ (†)	31.7 (3.78)	83.8 (2.62)
Teachers: college, university, postsecondary institutions	45.5 (8.31)	76.7 (1.98)	78.4 (3.11)	69.4 (4.60)	61.3 (6.96)	‡ (†)	‡ (†)	‡ (†)	49.0 (8.50)	‡ (†)	19.5 (4.98)	91.7 (3.58)
Health diagnosing and treating practitioners	67.1 (13.73)	71.1 (5.78)	79.8 (9.02)	78.5 (6.38)	88.8 (5.59)	‡ (†)	‡ (†)	15.4 (2.47)	79.5 (6.59)	‡ (†)	31.9 (9.15)	84.5 (5.63)
Registered nurses, pharmacists, dieticians, therapists, and physician's assistants	59.6 (6.69)	86.7 (2.47)	85.4 (4.10)	82.7 (3.83)	85.4 (4.05)	‡ (†)	‡ (†)	7.9 (2.17)	78.2 (4.89)	‡ (†)	27.4 (3.73)	83.1 (3.92)
Writers, artists, entertainers, and athletes	42.9 (6.63)	49.9 (4.37)	50.0 (6.93)	46.8 (6.03)	52.5 (6.59)	‡ (†)	‡ (†)	5.4! (2.16)	27.8 (5.02)	‡ (†)	35.3 (6.42)	88.2 (3.89)
Health technologists and technicians	68.6 (10.03)	74.8 (3.64)	66.9 (6.16)	85.6 (3.25)	72.1 (8.37)	‡ (†)	‡ (†)	6.0! (2.11)	63.2 (8.67)	‡ (†)	24.6 (5.91)	75.6 (7.26)
Technologists and technicians, except health and engineering	53.0 (6.49)	64.3 (2.84)	59.6 (5.07)	70.2 (3.32)	33.8 (8.53)	1.7! (0.59)	‡ (†)	7.1! (3.19)	29.1 (7.68)	‡ (†)	6.2! (2.14)	76.0 (8.80)
Marketing and sales occupations	34.4 (2.38)	44.2 (1.34)	44.4 (2.73)	51.1 (2.10)	45.7 (3.00)	‡ (†)	‡ (†)	4.5 (0.88)	30.2 (2.77)	‡ (†)	21.5 (2.43)	68.9 (3.37)
Administrative support occupations, including clerical	29.9 (1.74)	51.7 (1.25)	50.1 (2.29)	58.7 (1.72)	54.6 (2.70)	1.1! (0.53)	‡ (†)	6.6 (0.98)	33.5 (2.70)	‡ (†)	27.7 (2.18)	73.8 (2.33)
Service occupations	25.2 (1.82)	46.5 (1.38)	50.9 (2.74)	49.3 (2.24)	44.7 (2.47)	1.6! (0.39)	1.9! (0.88)	6.8 (1.42)	28.5 (2.64)	1.4! (0.57)	17.5 (2.10)	65.4 (2.71)
Agriculture, forestry, and fishing occupations	14.3! (5.19)	26.4 (3.55)	34.3 (7.16)	46.4 (6.80)	44.4 (9.02)	‡ (†)	‡ (†)	‡ (†)	20.3! (6.92)	‡ (†)	21.6! (10.05)	64.0 (10.03)
Mechanics and repairers	32.1 (4.72)	47.6 (2.70)	42.2 (5.44)	35.1 (3.40)	40.1 (5.10)	‡ (†)	‡ (†)	6.0! (1.89)	27.4 (4.26)	3.8! (1.38)	12.7 (3.18)	69.3 (4.27)
Construction and extractive occupations	21.9 (3.38)	38.0 (2.45)	34.5 (4.78)	32.3 (3.19)	27.6 (3.73)	‡ (†)	1.1! (0.49)	3.2! (1.08)	12.3 (2.54)	5.2! (1.89)	11.4 (2.72)	72.3 (4.48)
Precision production[2]	31.2 (6.09)	43.0 (4.32)	38.3 (8.48)	35.1 (6.19)	33.0 (3.98)	‡ (†)	0.4! (0.16)	4.2! (1.42)	22.2 (3.41)	‡ (†)	13.3 (2.99)	63.9 (3.46)
Production workers	21.1 (2.31)	30.7 (1.29)	38.0 (3.47)	39.4 (2.82)	— (†)	— (†)	— (†)	— (†)	— (†)	— (†)	— (†)	—
Transportation, material moving	20.7 (4.69)	28.4 (2.32)	33.3 (4.25)	30.4 (3.29)	34.6 (5.27)	‡ (†)	‡ (†)	‡ (†)	14.7 (2.63)	3.2! (1.57)	11.2 (2.85)	60.8 (4.98)
Handler, equipment, cleaners, helpers, and laborers	20.8 (3.49)	25.1 (2.70)	19.6 (4.56)	18.2 (3.20)	—	— (†)	— (†)	—	—	—	— (†)	—
Miscellaneous occupations	— (†)	56.6 (3.61)	43.0 (7.98)	64.9 (7.07)	39.2 (11.25)	‡ (†)	‡ (†)	‡ (†)	15.7! (5.81)	‡ (†)	7.8! (3.63)	52.2 (12.32)
Annual household income												
$5,000 or less	13.6 (1.70)	21.3 (1.59)	21.0 (3.22)	25.1 (2.92)	35.9 (4.83)	2.4! (0.92)	1.5! (0.71)	3.6! (1.52)	13.7 (4.00)	‡ (†)	17.2 (3.59)	52.9 (4.97)
$5,001 to $10,000	17.5 (2.14)	23.9 (1.37)	24.5 (3.39)	28.0 (2.74)	29.6 (4.49)	2.4 (0.69)	0.8! (0.33)	1.7! (0.81)	8.4 (2.11)	‡ (†)	21.8 (4.75)	61.0 (3.75)
$10,001 to $15,000	22.8 (2.60)	26.7 (1.61)	22.8 (2.45)	28.6 (2.30)	25.0 (3.41)	1.0! (0.38)	‡ (†)	3.3! (1.17)	11.3 (2.52)	‡ (†)	15.5 (3.14)	58.6 (4.43)
$15,001 to $20,000	21.9 (2.35)	31.8 (1.55)	31.4 (2.75)	30.2 (2.48)	24.3 (2.54)	1.7! (0.78)	‡ (†)	3.3! (1.19)	10.1 (1.37)	‡ (†)	12.9 (2.00)	61.1 (3.17)
$20,001 to $25,000	26.7 (3.20)	31.4 (1.27)	35.8 (2.81)	35.2 (2.27)	28.2 (2.51)	‡ (†)	1.9! (0.62)	4.4 (1.26)	12.8 (2.04)	2.6! (1.20)	13.6 (1.88)	63.2 (3.11)
$25,001 to $30,000	32.1 (2.51)	37.9 (1.47)	36.7 (2.61)	38.3 (2.43)	38.6 (3.63)	1.9! (0.65)	1.3! (0.61)	6.8! (2.09)	20.2 (3.37)	1.1! (0.50)	18.4 (2.52)	71.0 (3.38)
$30,001 to $40,000	35.6 (1.84)	42.7 (0.86)	45.2 (2.05)	44.6 (1.54)	42.7 (2.65)	1.6! (0.53)	1.0! (0.49)	3.7 (0.68)	22.8 (2.27)	1.1! (0.39)	23.0 (2.49)	68.7 (2.36)
$40,001 to $50,000	44.8 (1.84)	46.8 (1.39)	47.9 (2.31)	49.1 (1.93)	41.4 (2.92)	0.4! (0.19)	‡ (†)	2.9 (0.55)	22.4 (2.00)	1.5! (0.56)	20.5 (2.47)	71.9 (2.62)
$50,001 to $75,000	46.6 (2.03)	52.0 (0.94)	55.1 (1.80)	55.7 (1.48)	47.7 (1.74)	‡ (†)	‡ (†)	5.8 (0.69)	33.0 (1.37)	0.9! (0.36)	20.5 (1.67)	70.6 (2.15)
More than $75,000	48.7 (3.15)	58.0 (1.27)	56.9 (1.66)	— (†)	— (†)	— (†)	— (†)	— (†)	— (†)	— (†)	— (†)	— (†)
$75,001 to $100,000	— (†)	— (†)	— (†)	59.7 (1.91)	56.4 (2.28)	‡ (†)	‡ (†)	7.5 (0.89)	38.6 (2.26)	1.8! (0.64)	25.3 (1.51)	75.0 (1.97)
More than $100,000	— (†)	— (†)	— (†)	59.3 (1.82)	58.4 (2.11)	‡ (†)	‡ (†)	6.1 (0.70)	39.4 (1.80)	‡ (†)	28.2 (1.62)	81.2 (1.68)

—Not available.
†Not applicable.
!Interpret data with caution. The coefficient of variation (CV) for this estimate is between 30 and 50 percent.
‡Reporting standards not met. Either there are too few cases for a reliable estimate or the coefficient of variation (CV) is 50 percent or greater.
[1]Includes college and university degree programs, post-degree certificate programs, and vocational certificate programs.

[2]For 2005, figures include "Production workers" occupations data.
NOTE: Adult education is defined as all education activities, except full-time enrollment in higher education credential programs. Data do not include persons enrolled in high school or below. Race categories exclude persons of Hispanic ethnicity.
SOURCE: U.S. Department of Education, National Center for Education Statistics, Adult Education Survey (AE-NHES:1991, AE-NHES:1995, AE-NHES:1999, and AE-NHES:2005) and Adult Education and Lifelong Learning Survey (AELL-NHES:2001) of the National Household Education Surveys Program. (This table was prepared November 2010.)

CHAPTER 6
International Comparisons of Education

This chapter offers a statistical overview of education around the world, which provides an international context for examining the condition of education in the United States. Insights and new perspectives on U.S. educational practices and outcomes have emerged by comparing them with those of other education systems. The data in this chapter are drawn from materials collected or prepared by the International Association for the Evaluation of Educational Achievement (IEA), the Organization for Economic Cooperation and Development (OECD), and the United Nations Educational, Scientific, and Cultural Organization (UNESCO). Most of the education systems that report to these agencies represent entire countries; however, some of the tables in this chapter also include data for subnational entities with separate education systems, such as Hong Kong or French-speaking Belgium. The National Center for Education Statistics (NCES) carries out a variety of activities to provide statistical data for international comparisons of education.

Basic summary data on enrollments and enrollment ratios, teachers, educational attainment, and finances are synthesized from data published by the OECD in the Online Education Database, as well as from data collected by UNESCO. Even though these tabulations are carefully prepared, international data users should be cautioned about the many problems of definition and reporting involved in the collection of data about the education systems around the world, which vary greatly in structure, organization, and practices from country to country (see the UNESCO entry at the end of Appendix A: Guide to Sources).

This chapter also presents data from international studies carried out under the aegis of IEA or OECD and supported by NCES. Three of these studies include assessments of student achievement: (1) the Trends in International Mathematics and Science Study (TIMSS), which assesses the mathematics and science knowledge and skills of fourth- and eighth-graders every 4 years; (2) the Progress in International Reading Literacy Study (PIRLS), which measures the reading knowledge and skills of fourth-graders every 5 years; and (3) the Program for International Student Assessment (PISA), which measures the reading, mathematics, and science literacy of 15-year-olds every 3 years.

This chapter mainly focuses on data for the OECD countries. All current member countries for which a given year's data are available are included in the discussion, even if they were not members of OECD in that year. Even though there are 37 current OECD countries, not all data are available for all countries in all years. Some discussions in this chapter are only based on data for 36 OECD countries. Further information on survey methodologies is in Appendix A: Guide to Sources and in the publications cited in the table source notes.

School-age Population

The percentage of the population who are of school-age (and hence eligible to attend publicly or privately supported schools) varies markedly across countries. Among the 37 OECD countries, all of which reported data to UNESCO in 2017, the percentage of the country's population made up of children ages 5 to 14 was highest in Mexico and Israel (18 percent each), followed by Colombia (17 percent) and Turkey (16 percent; *web-only table 601.30*). OECD countries with the lowest percentages of children in this age range were Italy, the Republic of Korea, Germany, and Japan (9 percent each). In the United States, 13 percent of the population was 5 to 14 years old—a higher percentage than the OECD average (12 percent) and the percentages in the majority of other OECD countries.

The percentage of the population made up of teenagers between 15 and 19 years old was highest in Mexico (9 percent). Other countries with percentages of 15- to 19-year-olds of 8 percent or higher included Colombia (9 percent) and Turkey (8 percent). Latvia and the Czech Republic (both 4 percent) had the lowest percentages of 15- to 19-year-olds among OECD countries. In the United States, 7 percent of the population was 15 to 19 years old—a higher percentage than the OECD average (6 percent).

School Enrollments

In 2017, about 1.6 billion students were enrolled in schools around the world (table 601.10). Of these students, roughly 741 million were in elementary programs, 588 million were in secondary programs, and 223 million were in postsecondary programs.

Changes in enrollment over time vary from region to region. Compared to 2000, elementary school enrollment in 2017 was 76 percent higher in Africa, 36 percent higher in Oceania, and 2 percent higher in Asia (table F, table 601.10, and figure 27). In contrast, elementary enrollment in 2017 was 9 percent lower in Central and South America (including Latin America and the Caribbean) than in 2000, and 5 percent lower in Europe. In Northern America (including Bermuda, Canada, Greenland, St. Pierre and

Miquelon, and the United States), elementary enrollment was less than 1 percent higher in 2017 than it was in 2000.

At the secondary level, enrollment in 2017 was 106 percent higher in Africa, 38 percent higher in Asia, 20 percent higher in Oceania, 13 percent higher in Central and South America, and 9 percent higher in Northern America than it was in 2000. In contrast, secondary enrollment in Europe was 18 percent lower in 2017 than it was in 2000.

At the postsecondary level, enrollment in all major areas of the world was higher in 2017 than it was in 2000. Postsecondary enrollment in 2017 was 210 percent higher in Asia, 144 percent higher in Central and South America, 141 percent higher in Africa, 61 percent higher in Oceania, 43 percent higher in Northern America, and 14 percent higher in Europe than it was in 2000.

Table F. Population and enrollment at different levels of education in major areas of the world: 2000 and 2017

[In millions]

Area of the world	Population	Enrollment		
		Elementary	Secondary	Post-secondary
World total				
2000	6,086.1	657.3	452.3	100.2
2017	7,424.2	740.9	588.4	222.7
Africa				
2000	807.2	109.4	38.4	6.2
2017	1,234.7	192.1	78.9	14.8
Asia				
2000	3,686.1	405.4	258.4	41.3
2017	4,411.8	413.6	356.2	128.1
Europe				
2000	730.4	41.7	70.5	25.5
2017	747.2	39.8	57.7	29.0
Central and South America				
2000	518.6	70.2	56.7	11.5
2017	630.9	63.6	64.2	28.0
Northern America				
2000	313.4	27.4	25.1	14.4
2017	361.5	27.5	27.4	20.6
Oceania				
2000	30.4	3.1	3.2	1.3
2017	38.0	4.3	3.9	2.1

SOURCE: United Nations Educational, Scientific, and Cultural Organization, unpublished tabulations; and U.S. Department of Commerce, Census Bureau, International Data Base.

Percent of Population Enrolled

Across OECD countries in 2017, an average of 83 percent of 3- and 4-year-olds were enrolled in preschool, with 25 of the 36 OECD countries that reported data reporting preschool enrollment rates of 80 percent or higher (table 601.35). The countries with the lowest enrollment rates of 3- and 4-year-olds were the United States (54 percent), Greece (51 percent), Switzerland (25 percent), and Turkey (23 percent).

The average enrollment rate of 5- to 14-year-olds was 98 percent across all OECD countries in 2017, with 35 OECD countries reporting enrollment rates of 93 percent or higher. In the United States, the enrollment rate for 5- to 14-year-olds was over 99 percent, which was higher than the OECD average of 98 percent.

For 15- to 19-year-olds, the percentage of the population enrolled varied more than at the elementary level because of differences in countries' educational systems as well as in the age ranges covered by their compulsory

schooling laws. Among the 36 OECD countries that reported data, 10 countries had rates of at least 90 percent while 3 countries had rates of 70 percent or lower (table 601.40). The U.S. enrollment rate for 15- to 19-year-olds was 83 percent, which was lower than the OECD average (84 percent).

It is important to note that enrollment rates for students in this age range include enrollment at both the secondary and postsecondary level. It also should be noted that the age at which students are typically eligible to graduate from secondary school and start postsecondary education varies across countries. For this reason, students in some countries need to complete the equivalent of what is a fifth year of high school in the United States to graduate from the secondary level. Likewise, students in some countries typically enroll in secondary career/technical programs at older ages than in the United States.

Across all OECD countries in 2017, a higher percentage of 17-year-olds were enrolled at the secondary level than at the postsecondary level (table 601.40). However, for 19-year-olds, 14 OECD countries had a higher percentage enrolled at the secondary level than at the postsecondary level, while in 22 countries a higher percentage were enrolled at the postsecondary level than at the secondary level. In 3 countries, the percentage of 19-year-olds enrolled at the secondary level was at least 5 times higher than the percentage enrolled at the postsecondary level. At the other end of the spectrum, in 6 countries (including the United States), the percentage of 19-year-olds enrolled at the post-secondary level was at least 5 times higher than the percentage enrolled at the secondary level.

For 20- to 29-year-olds, enrollment rates across the 36 OECD countries that reported data were much lower than for the other age ranges. Four OECD countries had enrollment rates of at least 40 percent, while 4 OECD countries had rates of 20 percent or lower. The U.S. enrollment rate for 20- to 29-year-olds was 25 percent, which was lower than the OECD average (28 percent). For just 20-year-olds, 13 OECD countries reported a secondary enrollment rate of at least 15 percent, and 4 OECD countries reported a higher enrollment rate at the secondary level than at the postsecondary level. However, for the whole 20- to 29-year-old age group, no OECD countries reported a higher enrollment rate at the secondary level than at the postsecondary level, and all secondary enrollment rates were below 15 percent (table 601.40). At the postsecondary level, only 3 OECD countries reported an enrollment rate below 15 percent for this whole age group, and 11 countries reported a rate of at least 25 percent. The U.S. postsecondary enrollment rate for 20- to 29-year-olds was 23 percent—higher than the OECD postsecondary average for this age group (22 percent). However, the overall secondary and postsecondary enroll-ment rate for 20- to 29-year-olds in the United States was below the OECD average, because about 4 percent of OECD 20- to 29-year-olds were enrolled in programs classified at the secondary level within their countries while no 20- to 29-year-olds in the United States were enrolled in programs classified as at the secondary level.

Student Achievement

Mathematics and Science at Grades 4 and 8

The 2015 Trends in International Mathematics and Science Study (TIMSS) assessed students' mathematics and science performance at grades 4 and 8. Mathematics performance was assessed in 43 countries at grade 4 and in 34 countries at grade 8. Science performance was assessed in 42 countries at grade 4 and in 34 countries at grade 8. TIMSS Advanced data were also collected by 9 countries from students in their final year of secondary school (grade 12 in the United States). At grades 4 and 8, in addition to countries, several subnational entities also participated in TIMSS as separate education systems. Examples of subnational participants include Hong Kong, the U.S. state of Florida, the Canadian provinces of Ontario and Quebec, England and Northern Ireland within the United Kingdom, and the Flemish community in Belgium. In the following paragraphs, comparisons of the United States to other countries do not include the subnational participants. Results for Florida are based on public school students only, while U.S. national results are based on both public and private school students. TIMSS is a curriculum based assessment, and the assessments of fourth- and eighth-graders measure what students have actually learned against the subject matter that is expected to be taught by the end of grades 4 and 8, as described in the TIMSS mathematics and science frameworks, which guide assessment development. TIMSS Advanced is designed to broadly align with the advanced mathematics and physics curricula in the participating countries. At all three grades, TIMSS scores are reported on a scale of 0 to 1,000, with a fixed scale centerpoint of 500. The scale centerpoint represents the mean of the overall achievement distribution in 1995. The TIMSS scale is the same in each administration; thus, a value of 500 in 2015 equals 500 in 1995.

In 2015, the average mathematics scores of U.S. fourth-graders (539) and eighth-graders (518) were higher than the TIMSS scale centerpoint of 500 (tables 602.20 and 602.30). At grade 4, the average U.S. mathematics score was higher than the average score in 30 of the 42 other countries participating at grade 4, lower than the average score in 6 countries, and not measurably different from the average score in the remaining 6 countries (table 602.20). The 6 countries that outperformed the United States in fourth-grade mathematics were Ireland, Japan, the Republic of Korea, Norway, the Russian Federation, and Singapore.

At grade 8, the average U.S. mathematics score was higher than the average score in 21 of the 33 other participating countries, lower than the average score in 5 countries, and not measurably different from the average score in the remaining 7 countries (table 602.30). The 5 countries that outperformed the United States in eighth-grade mathematics were Canada, Japan, the Republic of Korea, the Russian Federation, and Singapore.

Florida, the only U.S. state participating in the 2015 TIMSS as a separate education system, had an average mathematics score for public schools at grade 4 (546) that was higher than the TIMSS scale centerpoint but was not measurably different from the U.S. national average score in mathematics (table 602.20). At grade 8, Florida had a public school average score (493) that was not measurably different from the TIMSS scale centerpoint but was lower than the U.S. national average in mathematics (table 602.30).

In science, the average scores of both U.S. fourth-graders (546) and U.S. eighth-graders (530) were higher than the TIMSS scale centerpoint of 500 in 2015 (tables 602.20 and 602.30). The average U.S. fourth-grade science score was higher than the average score in 30 of the 41 other countries participating at grade 4, lower than the average score in 5 countries, and not measurably different from the average score in the remaining 6 countries (table 602.20). The 5 countries that outperformed the United States in fourth-grade science were Finland, Japan, the Republic of Korea, the Russian Federation, and Singapore.

At grade 8, the average U.S. science score was higher than the average score in 23 of the 33 other countries participating at grade 8, lower than the average score in 5 countries, and not measurably different from the average score in the remaining 5 countries (table 602.30). The 5 countries that outperformed the United States in eighth-grade science were Japan, the Republic of Korea, the Russian Federation, Singapore, and Slovenia.

Public schools in Florida had an average fourth-grade science score (549) that was higher than the TIMSS scale centerpoint but was not measurably different from the U.S. national average (table 602.20). At grade 8, Florida had a public school average score (508) that was not measurably different from the TIMSS scale centerpoint but was lower than the U.S. national average in science (table 602.30).

The TIMSS Advanced assessment measures the advanced mathematics and physics achievement of students in their final year of secondary school who are taking or have taken advanced courses in those two subjects (table 602.35). On TIMSS Advanced in 2015, the U.S. average advanced mathematics score (485) and physics score (437) were both lower than the TIMSS Advanced scale centerpoint of 500. However, the U.S. average scores in advanced mathematics and physics were not measurably different than the U.S. average scores in those subjects in 1995. No education systems had higher average advanced mathematics or physics scores in 2015 than in 1995, but three education systems (France, Italy, and Sweden) had lower average scores in advanced mathematics and four (France, Norway, Russian Federation, and Sweden) had lower average physics scores.

Reading Literacy at Grade 4

The Progress in International Reading Literacy Study (PIRLS) conducted international assessments of fourth-grade reading literacy in 2001, 2006, 2011, and 2016. In 2016, PIRLS participants consisted of 43 countries as well as several subnational education systems. Examples of subnational participants include Hong Kong, the Canadian provinces of Ontario and Quebec, England and Northern

Ireland within the United Kingdom, and the Flemish and French communities in Belgium. PIRLS scores are reported on a scale of 0 to 1,000, with a fixed scale centerpoint of 500.

On the 2016 PIRLS, U.S. fourth-graders had an average reading literacy score of 549 (table 602.10). The U.S. average score in 2016 was 7 points lower than in 2011 but 10 points higher than in 2006. In all 4 assessment years, the U.S. average score was higher than the PIRLS scale centerpoint.

In 2016, the average reading literacy score of fourth-graders in the United States was higher than the average score in 24 of the 42 other participating countries, lower than the average score in 7 countries, and not measurably different from the average score in the remaining 11 countries. The 7 countries that outperformed the United States on the 2016 PIRLS were Finland, Ireland, Latvia, Norway, Poland, the Russian Federation, and Singapore.

Reading, Mathematics, and Science Literacy at Age 15

The Program for International Student Assessment (PISA) assesses 15-year-old students' application of reading, mathematics, and science literacy to problems within a real-life context. In 2018, PISA assessed students in all 37 OECD countries as well as more than 40 other education systems. While data on mathematics literacy and science literacy were reported for all OECD countries, data on reading literacy were reported for only 36 countries due to data quality concerns. PISA scores are reported on a scale of 0 to 1,000.

On the 2018 PISA assessment, U.S. 15-year-olds' average score in reading literacy was 505, which was higher than the OECD average score of 487 (table 602.50). The average reading literacy score in the United States was lower than the average score in 4 other OECD countries, higher than the average score in 21 OECD countries, and not measurably different from the average score in 10 OECD countries. In all participating education systems, females outperformed males in reading literacy (table 602.40). The U.S. gender gap in reading (24 points) was not measurably different from the OECD average gap, but was smaller than the gaps in 12 other OECD countries, larger than the gaps in 2 OECD countries, and not measurably different from the gaps in 21 other OECD countries.

In mathematics literacy, U.S. 15-year-olds' average score of 478 on the 2018 PISA assessment was lower than the OECD average score of 489 (table 602.60). The average mathematics literacy score in the United States was lower than the average score in 24 other OECD countries, higher than the average score in 6 OECD countries, and not measurably different from the average score in 6 OECD countries. In 21 OECD countries, including the United States, males outperformed females in mathematics literacy; in 3 countries, females outperformed males in mathematics (table 602.40).

In science literacy, U.S. 15-year-olds' average score of 502 on the 2018 PISA assessment was higher than the OECD average score of 489 (table 602.70). The average science literacy score in the United States was lower than the average score in 6 other OECD countries, higher than the average score in 19 OECD countries, and not measurably different from the average score in 11 OECD countries. On average across OECD countries, females outperformed male students in science by 2 points. There was no measurable difference in the average science literacy scores for males and females in 22 OECD countries, including the United States. In 13 OECD countries, females outperformed males in science literacy; in 2 countries, males outperformed females in science literacy.

Educational Attainment

In 2018, the percentage of 25- to 64-year-olds who had completed high school varied among the 34 reporting OECD countries (table 603.10). The OECD country reporting the highest percentage of 25- to 64-year-olds who had completed high school was the Czech Republic (94 percent). High school completers made up more than 90 percent of 25- to 64-year-olds in 5 other OECD countries, including the United States (91 percent). The OECD countries reporting the lowest percentages of 25- to 64-year-olds who had completed high school were Turkey (40 percent) and Mexico (39 percent).

In 2018, the percentage of 25- to 64-year-olds with a postsecondary degree (i.e., any degree at the associate's level or higher) also varied among the 35 OECD countries reporting data for this level of educational attainment (table 603.20). The OECD country reporting the highest percentage of 25- to 64-year-olds with a postsecondary degree was Canada (58 percent). The countries with the next highest percentages were Japan (52 percent), Republic of Korea (49 percent), the United States and Ireland (both 47 percent). An additional 11 OECD countries reported that more than 40 percent of their 25- to 64-year-olds had a postsecondary degree. The OECD countries reporting the lowest percentages of 25- to 64-year-olds with a postsecondary degree were Turkey (21 percent), Italy (19 percent), and Mexico (18 percent).

Among younger adults (those 25 to 34 years old) in the 35 OECD countries reporting data, the percentage with a postsecondary degree also varied in 2018 (table 603.20 and figure 28). The OECD country reporting the highest percentage of younger adults with a postsecondary degree was the Republic of Korea (70 percent). Eight other OECD countries reported percentages of younger adults with a postsecondary degree that were higher than the percentage in the United States (49 percent). In contrast, 25 countries reported percentages of younger adults with a postsecondary degree that were lower than the percentage in the United States. Three OECD countries reported that under 30 percent of 25- to 34-year-olds completed postsecondary education: Colombia (29 percent), Italy (28 percent), and Mexico (23 percent).

Postsecondary Degrees Awarded, by Sex and in Science, Technology, Engineering, and Mathematics (STEM) fields

In 2017, women earned more than half of all postsecondary degrees (i.e., any degree at the associate's level or higher) in 34 of the 36 OECD countries reporting the percentage of degrees awarded to females (*web-only table 603.60*). In the United States, women earned 58 percent of all postsecondary degrees awarded. However, the percentage of degrees women earned varied by field. Thirty-six OECD countries reported data for degrees awarded in the field of education; in 34 of these countries, including the United States (79 percent), at least 70 percent of education degrees were awarded to women. In contrast, women earned less than 25 percent of degrees in the combined field of engineering, manufacturing, and construction in 16 OECD countries, including the United States. In the United States, women earned 21 percent of degrees in engineering, manufacturing, and construction.

In 2017, the percentage of bachelor's degrees awarded in science and mathematics, information technologies, and engineering fields—including natural sciences, mathematics, statistics, information and communication technologies, engineering, manufacturing, and construction—varied across OECD countries (*web-only table 603.70*). Two OECD countries awarded 30 percent or more of their bachelor's degrees in science and mathematics, information technologies, and engineering fields: Germany (35 percent) and the Republic of Korea (32 percent). Four countries awarded 16 percent or less of their bachelor's degrees in science and mathematics, information technologies, and engineering fields: Norway, Belgium, and Colombia each awarded 16 percent, and the Netherlands awarded 15 percent. The United States awarded 21 percent of its bachelor's degrees in science and mathematics, information technologies, and engineering fields, which was lower than the OECD average (23 percent).

The percentages of graduate degrees awarded in science and mathematics, information technologies, and engineering fields varied widely across OECD countries in 2017. A higher percentage of degrees in science and mathematics, information technologies, and engineering fields were awarded at the doctor's degree level than at the master's degree level in every OECD country except Japan. At the master's level, 5 OECD countries awarded 30 percent or more of their degrees in science and mathematics, information technologies, and engineering fields: Japan (43 percent), Germany (35 percent), Portugal (34 percent), Estonia (33 percent), and Sweden (31 percent). The United States awarded 17 percent of its master's degrees in science and mathematics, information technologies, and engineering fields, which was lower than the OECD average (23 percent). However, 6 OECD countries awarded less than 15 percent of their master's degrees in these fields: Iceland (13 percent), Colombia (13 percent), Israel (12 percent), Luxembourg (10 percent), Mexico (9 percent), and Chile (7 percent). At the doctoral level, 10 OECD countries awarded at least half

of their degrees in science and mathematics, information technologies, and engineering fields: France (62 percent), Israel (57 percent), Luxembourg (57 percent), Estonia (55 percent), Canada (51 percent), Chile (51 percent), Lithuania (50 percent), Sweden (50 percent), Switzerland (50 percent), and the Czech Republic (50 percent). Two OECD countries reported awarding 30 percent or less of their doctor's degrees in science and mathematics, information technologies, and engineering fields: Netherlands (30 percent) and Mexico (19 percent). The United States awarded 42 percent of its doctor's degrees in science and mathematics, information technologies, and engineering fields; this was lower than the OECD average of 43 percent.

Finances

In 2016, expenditures per full-time-equivalent (FTE) student (expressed in current U.S. dollars) varied by level of education and across OECD countries. At the combined elementary and secondary level of education, expenditures per FTE student were $13,000 in the United States, which was higher than the OECD average of $9,400 (table 605.10). In addition to the United States, 5 of the 35 other OECD countries that reported data at the combined elementary and secondary level had expenditures of at least $12,000 per FTE student: Luxembourg ($19,800), Switzerland ($15,500), Austria ($14,700), Norway ($13,800), and Belgium ($12,300). At the postsecondary level, the United States spent $30,200 per FTE student, which was higher than the OECD average of $15,500. In addition to the United States, 5 of the 33 other OECD countries that reported higher education finance data had expenditures of over $20,000 per FTE student: Luxembourg ($48,400), Sweden ($24,300), the United Kingdom ($23,800), Canada ($23,700), and Norway ($22,000). These expenditures were adjusted to U.S. dollars using the purchasing-power-parity (PPP) index. This index is considered more stable and comparable than indexes using currency exchange rates; for more information, see Appendix B: Definitions.

Total government and private expenditures on education institutions as a percentage of gross domestic product (GDP) varied across the 35 reporting OECD countries in 2016, ranging from 3.2 in Luxembourg to 6.5 percent in Norway (table 605.20 and figure 29). In the United States, total expenditures on education institutions (based on international definitions) amounted to 6.0 percent of GDP, which was higher than the OECD average (5.0 percent). A comparison of government expenditures on education institutions as a percentage of GDP shows that public investment in education ranged from 2.9 percent in Japan to 6.3 percent in Norway. In the United States, the government expenditure on education institutions as a percentage of GDP was 4.1 percent, which was higher than the OECD average government expenditure on education institutions (4.0 percent of GDP). The percentage of private expenditures on education ranged from a low of 0.1 percent in Finland, Luxembourg, and Norway to 2.3 percent in Chile and 2.4 percent in Colombia. The U.S. percentage (1.9 percent) was higher than the OECD average (0.9 percent).

Figure 27. Percentage change in enrollment, by major areas of the world and level of education: 2000 to 2017

Percent change

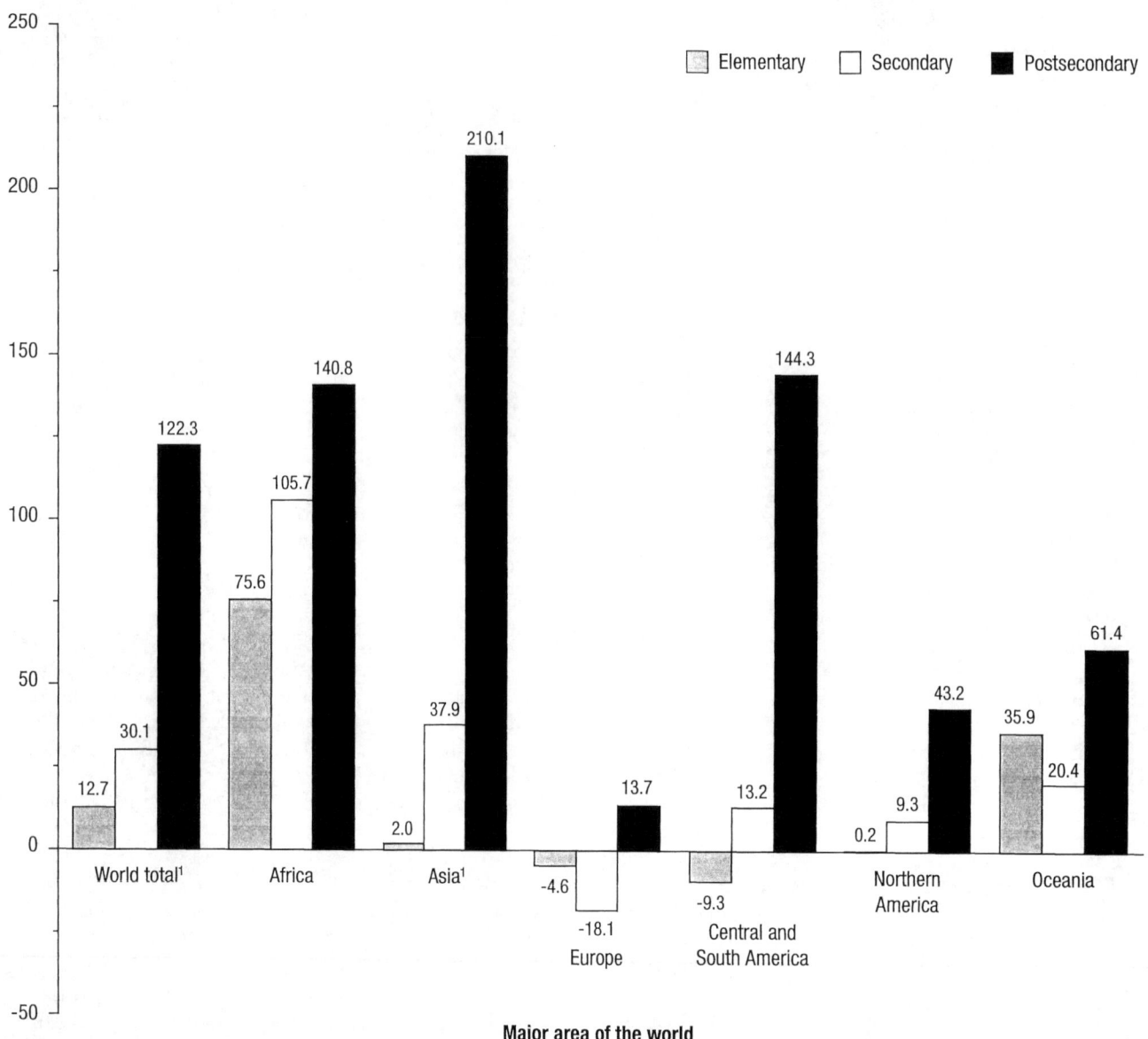

¹Enrollment data for the world total and Asia exclude Taiwan.
NOTE: Europe includes all countries of the former Union of Soviet Socialist Republics (U.S.S.R.) except Armenia, Azerbaijan, Georgia, Kazakhstan, Kyrgyzstan, Tajikistan, Turkmenistan, and Uzbekistan, which are included in Asia. Asia also includes Turkey, the Arab states (except those located in Africa), and Israel. Central and South America includes Latin America and the Caribbean. Northern America includes Bermuda, Canada, Greenland, St. Pierre and Miquelon, and the United States. Elementary level generally corresponds to grades 1–6 in the United States. Secondary level includes general education, teacher training (at the secondary level), and technical and vocational education; this level generally corresponds to grades 7–12 in the United States. Postsecondary level includes college and university enrollment and technical and vocational education beyond the secondary level. Data include imputed values for nonrespondent countries. Graphic display was generated using unrounded data.
SOURCE: United Nations Educational, Scientific, and Cultural Organization (UNESCO), unpublished tabulations; U.S. Department of Commerce, Census Bureau, International Data Base (November 2019).

Figure 28. Percentage of the population 25 to 34 years old with an associate's or higher degree, by country: 2018

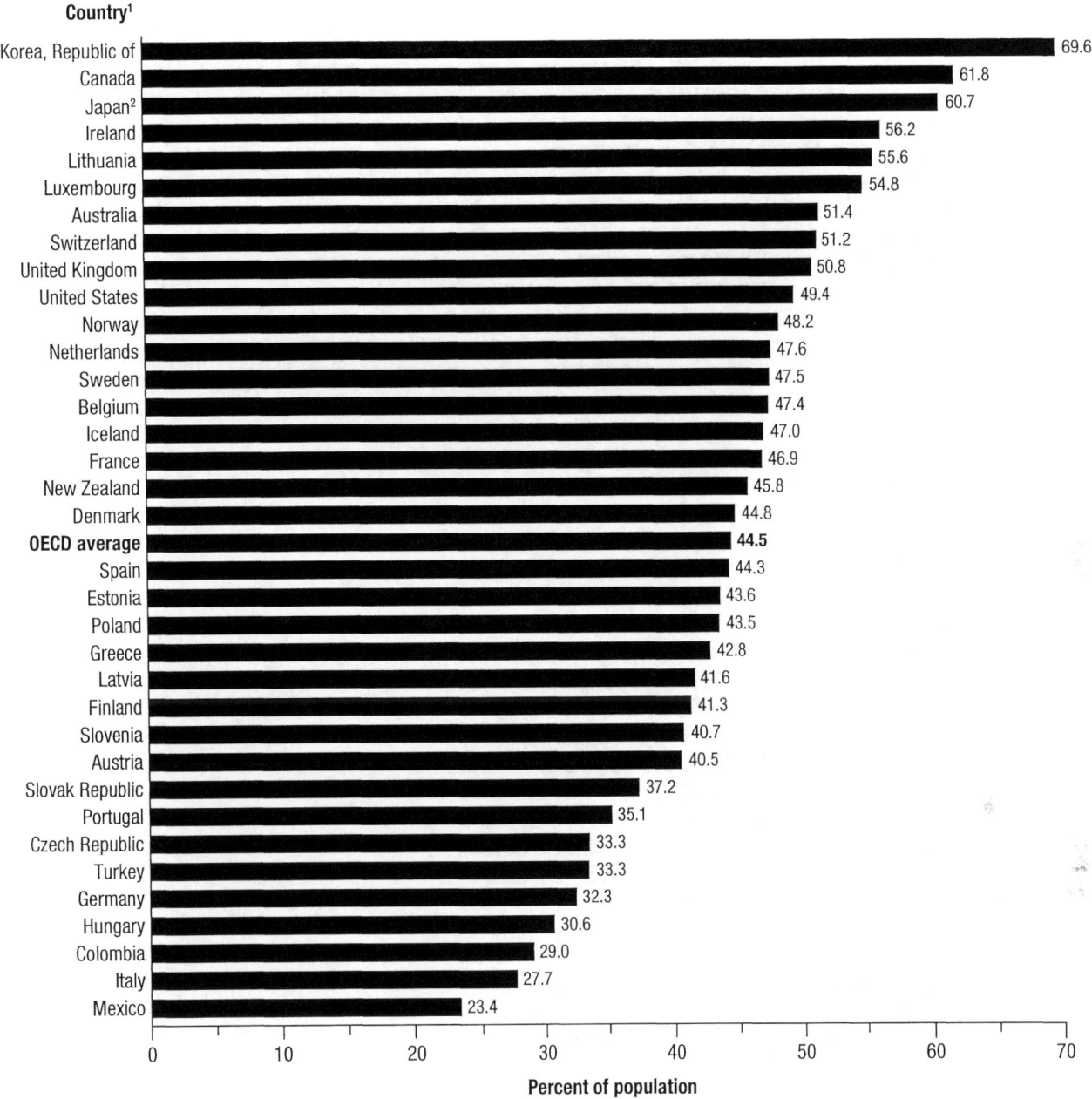

Country[1]

Country	Percent
Korea, Republic of	69.6
Canada	61.8
Japan[2]	60.7
Ireland	56.2
Lithuania	55.6
Luxembourg	54.8
Australia	51.4
Switzerland	51.2
United Kingdom	50.8
United States	49.4
Norway	48.2
Netherlands	47.6
Sweden	47.5
Belgium	47.4
Iceland	47.0
France	46.9
New Zealand	45.8
Denmark	44.8
OECD average	**44.5**
Spain	44.3
Estonia	43.6
Poland	43.5
Greece	42.8
Latvia	41.6
Finland	41.3
Slovenia	40.7
Austria	40.5
Slovak Republic	37.2
Portugal	35.1
Czech Republic	33.3
Turkey	33.3
Germany	32.3
Hungary	30.6
Colombia	29.0
Italy	27.7
Mexico	23.4

Percent of population

[1]All the countries shown in this figure are members of the Organization for Economic Cooperation and Development (OECD).
[2]Data include some upper secondary and postsecondary nontertiary awards (i.e., awards that are below the associate's degree level).
NOTE: All data in this figure were calculated using International Standard Classification of Education (ISCED) 2011. The data refer to tertiary degrees, which correspond to all degrees at the associate's level and above in the United States and include the following ISCED 2011 levels: level 5 (corresponding to the associate's degree in the United States), level 6 (bachelor's or equivalent degree), level 7 (master's or equivalent degree), and level 8 (doctoral or equivalent degree). Graphic display was generated using unrounded data.
SOURCE: Organization for Economic Cooperation and Development (OECD), Online Education Database, retrieved September 23, 2019, from http://stats.oecd.org/Index.aspx.

Figure 29. Government and private expenditures on education institutions as a percentage of gross domestic product (GDP), by OECD country: 2016

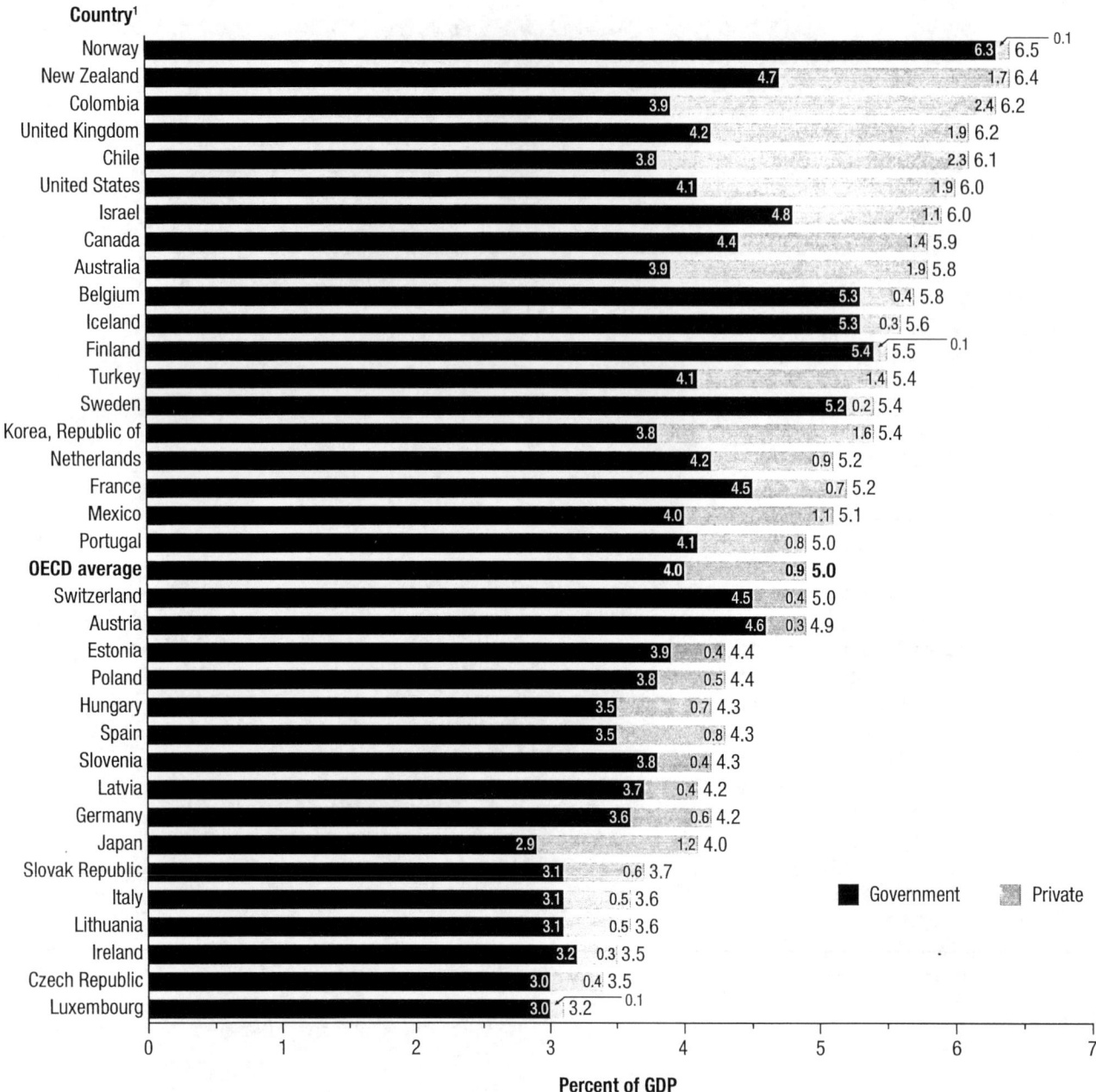

[1]All the countries shown in this figure are current members of the Organization for Economic Cooperation and Development (OECD) for which data are available.
NOTE: Includes government and private expenditures on all levels of education institutions. Government expenditures include both amounts spent directly by governments to hire education personnel and to procure other resources and amounts provided by governments to public or private institutions. Government subsidies used by households for payments to education institutions are counted as government expenditures, not private expenditures. Government expenditures may also include expenditures on education institutions from international sources. Graphic display was generated using unrounded data. Detail may not sum to totals because of rounding.
SOURCE: Organization for Economic Cooperation and Development (OECD), Online Education Database, retrieved October 14, 2019, from https://stats.oecd.org/Index.aspx.

Table 601.10. Population, school enrollment, and number of teachers, by major areas of the world and level of education: Selected years, 1980 through 2017

[In thousands]

Year and selected characteristic	World total[1,2]	Major areas of the world					
		Africa	Asia[2,3]	Europe[3]	Central and South America[4]	Northern America[4]	Oceania
1	2	3	4	5	6	7	8
1980							
Population, all ages[5]	4,445,386	479,432	2,637,685	695,225	358,579	251,929	22,534
Enrollment, all levels	872,127	77,981	495,345	134,817	98,236	60,541	5,207
Elementary[6]	525,248	61,284	333,912	47,705	56,804	22,893	2,650
Secondary[7]	296,790	14,999	148,057	70,262	36,630	24,695	2,147
Postsecondary[8]	50,089	1,697	13,375	16,850	4,802	12,954	411
Teachers, all levels	40,140	2,373	19,578	2,506	4,574	2,124	277
Elementary[6]	18,530	1,676	10,730	2,506	1,872	—	134
Secondary[7]	17,640	606	7,654	—	2,319	1,309	112
Postsecondary[8]	3,970	91	1,194	—	384	815	31
1990							
Population, all ages[5]	5,286,811	631,684	3,184,509	725,798	440,874	277,533	26,412
Enrollment, all levels	987,870	107,061	563,295	132,645	117,539	61,543	5,787
Elementary[6]	576,798	78,024	361,316	45,166	65,056	24,629	2,606
Secondary[7]	343,199	26,202	178,783	68,871	45,245	21,534	2,563
Postsecondary[8]	67,873	2,836	23,195	18,608	7,238	15,380	617
Teachers, all levels	48,299	3,692	24,655	8,403	5,763	3,938	314
Elementary[6]	22,002	2,330	12,921	2,608	2,396	1,608	139
Secondary[7]	21,204	1,222	9,949	5,795	2,764	1,340	135
Postsecondary[8]	5,093	139	1,786	—	603	991	41
2000							
Population, all ages[5]	6,086,149	807,188	3,686,112	730,427	518,614	313,388	30,421
Enrollment, all levels	1,209,810	153,961	705,119	137,729	138,384	66,968	7,649
Elementary[6]	657,303	109,430	405,399	41,721	70,188	27,435	3,131
Secondary[7]	452,347	38,373	258,416	70,480	56,728	25,117	3,233
Postsecondary[8]	100,159	6,158	41,303	25,528	11,468	14,416	1,286
Teachers, all levels	57,231	4,988	29,649	10,720	6,809	4,650	155
Elementary[6]	24,984	2,898	14,623	2,741	2,760	1,806	155
Secondary[7]	25,486	1,805	12,529	6,104	3,172	1,682	—
Postsecondary[8]	6,761	284	2,497	1,875	877	1,163	—
2010							
Population, all ages[5]	6,872,671	1,039,861	4,127,141	740,240	587,253	343,230	34,946
Enrollment, all levels	1,425,451	233,201	828,095	129,092	150,517	75,233	9,313
Elementary[6]	697,001	159,492	403,420	36,752	67,216	26,565	3,556
Secondary[7]	546,192	62,312	333,440	58,635	61,227	26,809	3,770
Postsecondary[8]	182,258	11,398	91,235	33,705	22,074	21,859	1,987
Teachers, all levels	72,158	7,642	39,858	10,560	8,141	5,464	175
Elementary[6]	28,671	4,139	16,848	2,674	2,915	1,920	175
Secondary[7]	32,336	3,030	18,172	5,471	3,549	1,898	—
Postsecondary[8]	11,151	473	4,838	2,416	1,677	1,646	—
2015							
Population, all ages[5]	7,267,035	1,177,295	4,332,060	745,332	618,928	356,273	37,147
Enrollment, all levels	1,520,616	272,401	882,390	125,478	154,879	75,254	10,215
Elementary[6]	720,012	182,505	403,333	38,365	64,615	27,094	4,101
Secondary[7]	582,977	75,814	354,683	57,466	64,042	27,063	3,909
Postsecondary[8]	217,627	14,081	124,374	29,646	26,223	21,097	2,206
Teachers, all levels	77,558	9,726	42,722	10,441	8,704	5,435	195
Elementary[6]	31,161	5,247	18,166	2,732	2,975	1,847	195
Secondary[7]	33,479	3,874	18,346	5,329	3,906	1,803	—
Postsecondary[8]	12,918	606	6,211	2,380	1,824	1,786	—
2017							
Population, all ages[5]	7,424,172	1,234,712	4,411,836	747,218	630,926	361,477	38,002
Enrollment, all levels	1,551,915	285,854	897,880	126,511	155,869	75,578	10,225
Elementary[6]	740,868	192,108	413,567	39,804	63,641	27,492	4,256
Secondary[7]	588,390	78,918	356,235	57,694	64,205	27,445	3,894
Postsecondary[8]	222,657	14,827	128,077	29,013	28,023	20,641	2,076
Teachers, all levels	79,570	10,096	44,068	10,606	8,776	5,501	202
Elementary[6]	31,676	5,492	18,273	2,821	2,982	1,906	202
Secondary[7]	34,728	3,954	19,435	5,398	3,889	1,837	—
Postsecondary[8]	13,166	649	6,359	2,388	1,905	1,759	—

—Not available.
[1]The world total includes estimations for missing data on teachers.
[2]Enrollment and teacher data for the world total and Asia exclude Taiwan.
[3]Europe includes all countries of the former Union of Soviet Socialist Republics (U.S.S.R.) except Armenia, Azerbaijan, Georgia, Kazakhstan, Kyrgyzstan, Tajikistan, Turkmenistan, and Uzbekistan, which are included in Asia. Asia also includes Turkey, the Arab states (except those located in Africa), and Israel.
[4]Central and South America includes Latin America and the Caribbean. Northern America includes Bermuda, Canada, Greenland, St. Pierre and Miquelon, and the United States.
[5]Estimate of midyear population.
[6]This level generally corresponds to grades 1–6 in the United States.
[7]Includes general education, teacher training (at the secondary level), and technical and vocational education. This level generally corresponds to grades 7–12 in the United States.

[8]Includes college and university enrollment, and technical and vocational education beyond the secondary level.
NOTE: Detail may not sum to totals because of rounding and missing teacher data. Data include imputed values for nonrespondent countries. Enrollment and teacher data exclude several island countries or territories with small populations (less than 150,000). Some data have been revised from previously published figures.
SOURCE: United Nations Educational, Scientific, and Cultural Organization (UNESCO), unpublished tabulations. U.S. Department of Commerce, Census Bureau, International Data Base, retrieved November 18, 2019, from https://www.census.gov/programs-surveys/international-programs/about/idb.html. (This table was prepared November 2019.)

Table 601.35. Percentage of 3- and 4-year-olds and 5- to 14-year-olds enrolled in school, by country: Selected years, 2000 through 2017

Country	Percent of 3- and 4-year-olds enrolled						Percent of 5- to 14-year-olds enrolled									
	2012	2013	2014	2015	2016	2017	2000	2005	2010	2011	2012	2013	2014	2015	2016	2017
1	2	3	4	5	6	7	8	9	10	11	12	13	14	15	16	17
OECD average[1]	**77.4**	**79.7**	**80.4**	**80.8**	**80.4**	**82.8**	**97.8**	**98.9**	**98.4**	**98.3**	**98.3**	**98.2**	**97.9**	**98.0**	**97.9**	**98.1**
Australia	46.9	72.1	77.3	79.2	77.0	76.3	100.0	99.2	100.1	99.8	100.2	100.6	100.8	100.9	100.5	100.2
Austria	80.6	81.4	82.2	83.7	84.2	85.0	98.2	—	97.8	98.6	98.5	98.4	98.4	98.5	97.9	98.6
Belgium	98.2	98.3	98.1	98.2	98.2	98.3	99.1	98.2[2]	97.4	98.1	98.2	98.2	98.3	98.2	98.2	98.8
Canada	—	—	—	—	—	—	97.1	—	93.5	93.4	99.9	99.9	100.2	100.7	101.6	102.1
Chile	62.0	66.6	68.5	70.5	71.0	71.5	93.6	—	96.0	96.0	96.0	96.2	96.4	96.7	96.9	97.1
Colombia	—	—	—	70.5	46.9	57.8	—	—	—	—	—	89.4	87.9	89.5	86.8	86.6
Czech Republic	70.3	70.9	76.1	81.5	84.3	83.8	99.8	100.0	98.7	98.4	98.6	98.1	97.7	97.7	97.5	97.9
Denmark	96.9	96.9	96.9	97.5	97.3	97.3	99.2	—	99.1	99.3	99.4	99.4	99.3	99.3	99.2	99.3
Estonia	88.1	89.2	88.4	88.7	89.4	89.8	—	104.3	97.2	96.7	96.4	95.6	96.5	96.4	96.6	96.7
Finland	71.3	71.4	71.1	71.5	76.1	76.7	91.6	96.7	96.8	96.9	96.8	96.8	96.7	96.5	97.2	97.2
France	100.1	100.0	99.1	100.1	100.4	100.7	99.8	99.9	99.1	99.2	99.1	99.0	98.3	99.0	99.4	99.9
Germany	94.3	94.5	94.6	95.0	93.7	93.2	99.4	95.9	98.7	98.3	98.5	99.2	98.9	98.9	98.1	98.6
Greece	—	37.3	58.7	46.6	46.8	51.0	99.8	—	—	—	—	97.1	96.0	97.7	97.3	96.9
Hungary	84.0	84.3	86.6	88.2	90.1	90.3	99.9	100.3	98.5	98.1	97.8	97.1	96.6	95.9	95.5	95.5
Iceland	—	96.4	96.6	96.9	96.7	97.2	98.5	—	—	—	—	98.5	98.6	98.7	98.9	98.9
Ireland	—	73.0	73.0	68.3	75.7	96.9	100.5	100.9	101.8	102.1	—	100.9	100.7	100.4	100.8	101.1
Israel	86.4	101.4	97.9	100.4	100.6	100.7	96.6	94.1	96.0	96.4	96.3	98.3	97.8	97.5	97.4	96.9
Italy	97.0	96.5	94.1	93.9	94.1	92.9	99.7	102.3	101.1	100.8	100.8	100.2	98.2	97.8	97.6	97.4
Japan	—	88.2	88.4	87.7	89.6	89.2	101.2	—	—	—	—	101.4	101.6	101.7	101.5	101.6
Korea, Republic of	89.1	93.6	91.4	91.5	94.9	95.5	92.3	—	99.4	98.6	98.4	98.1	98.2	98.4	97.5	96.9
Latvia	83.4	86.1	88.3	89.1	90.5	91.5	—	99.5	98.2	98.6	98.2	97.8	97.7	97.6	98.0	98.3
Lithuania	73.1	77.7	80.6	81.3	81.3	82.8	—	97.5	98.2	98.7	98.8	98.5	98.9	99.4	100.3	101.1
Luxembourg	—	85.1	83.1	80.4	80.2	82.3	95.3	—	—	—	—	97.1	97.1	97.0	97.0	96.6
Mexico	65.0	66.1	66.0	67.6	67.9	69.3	94.8	97.1	99.6	99.8	100.2	100.9	101.5	101.7	101.9	101.4
Netherlands	91.4	91.5	88.4	89.5	91.2	92.2	99.4	98.7	99.5	99.7	99.7	99.5	99.4	99.8	99.8	99.7
New Zealand	95.9	91.6	90.2	91.9	90.7	93.1	99.0	99.6	99.0	98.8	98.5	100.6	98.5	98.7	99.0	99.2
Norway	96.1	96.2	96.1	96.2	96.4	96.5	97.4	98.6	99.5	99.6	99.5	99.5	99.4	99.3	99.1	99.2
Poland	58.7	60.0	64.7	72.5	78.1	76.1	93.6	94.6	95.1	95.2	96.3	95.9	95.7	95.5	95.5	95.2
Portugal	84.9	84.2	83.6	84.6	85.2	88.2	105.2	101.8	101.6	102.2	102.1	101.2	99.7	98.9	98.3	98.3
Slovak Republic	67.5	68.1	68.9	67.7	69.1	73.3	—	97.2	95.2	94.8	94.5	94.2	93.7	93.4	93.3	93.0
Slovenia	87.1	86.7	85.8	86.1	86.8	88.1	—	96.7	97.1	97.1	97.4	97.1	97.0	97.4	97.1	97.5
Spain	96.1	96.2	96.5	96.2	96.3	97.0	104.4	100.8	98.6	98.2	97.8	97.5	97.2	97.1	97.1	97.2
Sweden	—	93.7	93.9	92.2	92.9	93.5	97.8	—	—	—	—	98.5	98.2	98.5	99.0	99.5
Switzerland	21.6	22.2	23.5	24.8	25.1	25.3	98.8	99.6	100.1	99.4	99.3	99.6	99.8	99.8	99.7	99.7
Turkey	12.0	21.7	20.0	20.8	21.1	23.3	80.2	—	—	—	—	96.3	95.9	95.8[3]	94.9[3]	96.5[3]
United Kingdom	95.1	96.3	90.7	103.3	—	109.4	98.9	100.1	100.7	98.3	96.7	98.2	98.4	98.4	—	98.3
United States	52.2	53.7	54.7	54.4	52.7	53.8	99.3	98.7	97.4	97.3	97.3	96.9	97.2	98.0	99.2	99.8
Other reporting countries																
China	—	—	—	—	—	—	79.6	—	—	—	—	—	—	—	—	—
Russian Federation	—	75.8	80.5	81.6	81.4	81.7	—	61.8	93.2	—	—	93.2	93.5	94.8	96.1	96.7

—Not available.
[1]Refers to the mean of the data values for all reporting Organization for Economic Cooperation and Development (OECD) countries, to which each country reporting data contributes equally. The average includes all current OECD countries for which a given year's data are available, even if they were not members of OECD in that year.
[2]Excludes the German-Speaking Community of Belgium.
[3]Includes 15- to 17-year-olds enrolled in primary education.
NOTE: For each country, this table shows the number of persons in each age group who are enrolled in that country as a percentage of that country's total population in the specified age group. However, some of a country's population may be enrolled in a different country, and some persons enrolled in the country may be residents of a different country. Enrollment rates may be underestimated for countries such as Luxembourg that are net exporters of students and may be overestimated for countries that are net importers. If a country enrolls many residents of other countries, the country's total population in the specified age group can be smaller than the total number enrolled, resulting in enrollment estimates exceeding 100 percent. Some data have been revised from previously published figures.
SOURCE: Organization for Economic Cooperation and Development (OECD), *Education at a Glance*, 2002; and Online Education Database, retrieved September 16, 2019, from https://stats.oecd.org/Index.aspx. (This table was prepared September 2019.)

Table 601.40. Percentage of 15- to 29-year-olds enrolled in school, by selected levels of education, age, and country: 2017

Country	All levels¹ 15–19	All levels¹ 20–29	Secondary² 15–19 Total	15	16	17	18	19	Secondary² 20–29 Total	20	Nondegree³ 15–19 Total	18	19	20	Tertiary⁴ 15–19 Total	17	18	19	Tertiary⁴ 20–29 Total	20	21	22	23 to 29
1	2	3	4	5	6	7	8	9	10	11	12	13	14	15	16	17	18	19	20	21	22	23	24
OECD average⁵	**84.5**	**28.2**	**71.8**	**97.3**	**94.8**	**88.7**	**55.5**	**24.8**	**4.5**	**12.1**	**1.4**	**2.3**	**3.7**	**3.7**	**11.1**	**1.8**	**18.5**	**34.2**	**22.5**	**39.4**	**39.2**	**35.1**	**16.4**
Australia	90.0	41.3	69.9	101.3	100.7	90.7	39.4	22.3	10.4	18.9	1.5	2.8	3.5	3.4	18.6	5.0	35.9	48.5	27.4	49.9	45.9	39.4	20.6
Austria	78.0	25.7	62.1	93.9	89.2	72.8	42.6	19.3	2.3	9.2	0.6	1.0	1.4	1.6	15.3	13.3	28.8	31.2	22.5	31.0	31.1	29.5	19.4
Belgium	95.2	31.0	74.5	99.0	99.1	97.3	50.8	27.7	6.1	13.8	1.2	2.1	3.9	4.2	19.4	1.2	40.6	53.9	22.7	56.0	51.1	41.5	12.3
Canada	77.6	21.6	59.9	101.4	99.1	81.1	21.8	7.9	1.6	4.1	†	†	†	†	17.7	3.2	36.1	43.3	20.0	43.0	40.3	32.3	12.4
Chile	80.9	29.2	64.2	93.7	95.0	90.2	35.2	11.0	1.7	4.5	†	†	†	†	16.1	0.2	30.0	48.1	27.4	52.1	47.6	42.6	19.5
Colombia	58.9	18.8	44.2	80.6	72.7	40.9	18.8	8.7	2.0	4.8	0.2	0.3	0.2	0.1	13.4	13.8	23.3	26.9	16.6	27.3	26.6	23.4	12.4
Czech Republic	90.6	23.9	85.4	98.6	97.8	94.9	88.1	48.1	2.8	14.0	†	†	†	†	5.2	0.2	1.5	24.1	21.0	41.7	41.0	37.5	14.9
Denmark	85.9	42.0	84.3	99.0	94.2	90.8	84.9	54.3	11.6	26.6	†	†	2.4	3.7	1.5	#	1.4	6.9	30.4	20.7	35.3	44.2	29.0
Estonia	88.8	25.2	82.6	97.5	96.5	94.2	88.2	36.3	4.3	15.3	0.5	0.1	#	0.1	5.6	0.2	1.0	26.5	19.0	35.1	35.4	32.0	14.3
Finland	86.5	40.8	83.4	98.7	95.7	95.0	94.7	34.9	12.6	18.9	#	#	#	#	3.0	#	1.0	13.7	27.7	26.5	35.4	39.5	25.2
France	86.4	21.9	66.3	97.2	94.1	89.0	33.5	12.1	1.5	5.4	0.3	1.0	0.6	0.5	19.2	2.8	43.5	53.1	20.1	48.6	41.2	35.6	10.9
Germany	86.8	33.6	75.4	98.1	94.0	87.9	65.3	36.8	5.7	20.5	5.3	7.9	11.3	12.6	6.1	0.6	7.9	20.2	23.0	28.3	31.0	31.0	20.4
Greece	86.5	35.8	60.6	93.4	94.1	90.1	15.6	9.2	1.7	5.2	4.9	11.0	13.8	10.3	20.8	0.9	49.3	54.4	30.8	56.2	53.3	44.1	22.5
Hungary	83.7	23.1	73.2	97.6	92.3	87.4	66.4	25.6	2.7	9.6	4.8	5.4	17.4	15.1	5.7	0.3	5.2	22.9	17.0	29.6	29.9	27.4	12.2
Iceland	87.3	34.0	86.4	99.6	95.3	90.2	81.7	66.4	10.8	29.0	#	#	0.1	0.2	0.9	#	0.3	3.9	22.5	17.2	29.3	33.1	20.9
Ireland	92.8	27.3	69.9	103.2	100.5	90.9	47.0	6.2	2.0	3.6	6.2	13.5	11.3	7.1	16.7	3.1	27.4	53.7	22.0	56.7	50.8	36.4	11.1
Israel	66.0	20.8	61.3	96.9	95.7	91.3	16.2	1.7	0.1	1.0	0.1	0.2	0.5	0.7	4.6	0.5	8.7	13.7	19.8	15.3	15.8	19.0	21.2
Italy⁶	84.8	23.8	76.4	97.6	95.0	93.2	76.7	20.1	1.4	7.0	0.2	0.8	†	†	7.5	#	3.7	33.8	21.8	39.4	38.8	33.3	15.7
Japan⁶	—	—	57.8	98.8	95.4	95.4	2.6	0.8	#	0.1	†	†	†	†	—	—	—	—	—	—	—	—	—
Korea, Republic of	87.4	29.5	58.6	101.4	99.8	93.9	9.7	0.4	#	0.1	†	†	†	†	28.7	0.6	60.9	73.7	29.5	68.9	64.5	51.4	15.8
Latvia	92.9	28.4	83.7	99.4	98.5	94.7	88.0	35.5	3.2	13.0	0.8	0.4	3.8	3.4	8.1	0.5	3.8	37.5	23.7	46.6	54.2	42.1	17.3
Lithuania	93.9	29.6	80.3	101.2	100.7	98.4	86.2	20.9	2.0	6.0	1.7	1.0	7.0	8.0	11.9	0.4	7.6	48.0	24.4	53.6	54.2	43.5	14.6
Luxembourg	76.3	13.0	75.6	95.8	88.0	82.1	71.3	43.1	5.7	24.5	#	0.0	0.2	0.3	0.6	#	0.6	2.5	6.7	6.5	10.4	10.0	5.9
Mexico	61.1	18.2	50.7	81.3	76.2	59.9	24.2	11.7	4.7	6.3	†	†	†	†	10.2	3.0	20.6	27.8	13.5	28.8	27.2	21.9	7.8
Netherlands	93.1	35.8	78.8	99.5	98.9	89.6	63.0	42.4	9.1	28.5	†	†	†	†	14.3	7.7	25.5	38.6	26.7	45.5	45.0	42.4	19.5
New Zealand	80.5	24.4	62.5	99.7	98.1	85.0	26.8	8.3	2.6	4.3	2.9	6.2	5.5	4.2	15.1	2.1	30.4	40.5	19.4	42.3	36.7	27.5	12.7
Norway	87.2	31.8	82.9	100.2	94.5	92.7	89.9	39.0	5.2	20.0	0.1	#	0.4	0.7	4.2	0.1	0.5	19.9	26.2	35.8	41.9	40.3	20.9
Poland	92.7	29.0	83.6	94.9	95.1	94.3	92.6	44.3	2.1	10.9	0.9	0.4	3.8	7.3	8.0	1.1	2.5	34.4	23.4	46.3	46.4	43.6	15.7
Portugal	88.8	23.1	74.2	98.1	97.5	96.6	51.5	25.6	3.6	11.8	0.1	0.2	0.4	0.5	13.8	0.4	29.6	39.7	19.2	42.7	38.5	32.7	11.4
Slovak Republic	83.4	18.2	76.4	97.0	92.1	87.9	75.9	33.0	1.0	5.9	1.4	2.4	4.4	2.8	5.2	0.4	3.0	21.3	16.4	32.7	33.8	31.9	10.8
Slovenia	93.4	34.2	81.8	96.7	96.3	96.2	91.4	30.1	7.7	16.7	#	†	0.1	0.1	11.4	0.0	1.2	54.7	26.5	57.7	54.2	49.7	16.5
Spain	87.1	31.6	69.7	95.8	95.9	89.6	40.4	24.2	5.7	15.2	†	#	0.1	1.3	17.1	0.1	38.9	48.5	25.6	51.0	49.6	41.5	17.3
Sweden	91.4	35.4	87.5	102.7	104.7	107.1	96.5	27.7	10.3	18.3	0.3	0.1	1.4	1.1	3.3	0.1	0.8	15.2	20.3	22.5	27.2	29.5	18.0
Switzerland	84.7	27.2	80.9	97.5	92.9	90.5	78.6	48.3	5.9	7.4	0.5	0.6	0.9	†	3.3	0.3	3.9	11.5	20.5	21.0	27.5	30.4	18.4
Turkey	72.5	40.7	60.1	92.4	88.1	79.1	31.6	9.5	4.5	7.4	†	†	†	†	12.5	0.6	19.4	42.2	36.3	50.7	50.8	47.4	30.4
United Kingdom	84.6	20.4	67.8	100.0	98.8	91.5	36.8	18.6	5.8	11.3	†	†	†	†	16.8	2.4	33.5	44.1	14.6	43.7	32.4	21.1	7.7
United States	82.9	24.6	63.3	100.9	93.3	89.8	28.4	4.6	0.0	0.0	0.8	1.6	2.3	2.2	18.7	1.2	38.2	53.7	23.3	48.9	45.0	33.9	15.5
Other reporting countries																							
China	—	—	—	—	—	—	—	—	—	—	—	—	—	—	13.6	3.9	24.9	38.6	17.6	38.7	31.0	17.2	—
Russian Federation⁷	86.7	18.1	39.2	91.6	56.7	40.5	5.3	0.9	0.4	0.6	0.2	0.6	0.4	0.2	47.1	50.7	75.2	70.1	—	56.7	48.0	36.6	9.2

—Not available.
†Not applicable.
#Rounds to zero.
¹In addition to secondary and postsecondary education, may include enrollment in International Standard Classification of Education (ISCED) 2011 level 1 (primary or elementary education).
²Refers to ISCED 2011 level 2 (lower secondary education) and level 3 (upper secondary education). Secondary education generally corresponds to grades 7–12 in the United States.
³Refers to programs classified at ISCED 2011 level 4 (postsecondary nontertiary education). Postsecondary nontertiary education generally corresponds to postsecondary vocational programs below the associate's degree level in the United States.
⁴Postsecondary degree-granting programs (tertiary education programs) correspond to all postsecondary programs leading to associate's and higher degrees in the United States. Tertiary education includes ISCED 2011 level 5 (corresponding to U.S. programs at the associate's degree level), level 6 (bachelor's or equivalent level), level 7 (master's or equivalent level), and level 8 (doctoral or equivalent level). Enrollment rates may not be directly comparable across countries due to differing definitions of tertiary education and the age at which it begins.

⁵Refers to the mean of the data values for all reporting Organization for Economic Cooperation and Development (OECD) countries, to which each country reporting data contributes equally.
⁶Enrollment data for upper secondary education (ISCED 2011 level 3) include postsecondary nontertiary enrollment (ISCED 2011 level 4).
⁷Data for postsecondary nondegree programs (ISCED 2011 level 5) include some vocational education programs at the upper secondary level (ISCED 2011 level 3).
NOTE: For each country, this table shows the number of persons at a given age who are enrolled in that country as a percentage of that country's total population at the specified age. If a country enrolls many residents of other countries, the country's total population at the specified age can be smaller than the total number enrolled, resulting in enrollment estimates exceeding 100 percent. Conversely, if a country has many residents who are enrolled outside of the country, the country's enrollment rates may be underestimated. Enrollment estimates can also be affected if population and enrollment data were collected at different times. Includes both full-time and part-time students.
SOURCE: Organization for Economic Cooperation and Development (OECD), Online Education Database, retrieved September 24, 2019, from https://stats.oecd.org/Index.aspx. (This table was prepared September 2019.)

Table 601.50. Pupil/teacher ratios in public and private elementary and secondary schools, by level of education and country: 2013 through 2017

Country	Elementary school (primary)					Junior high school (lower secondary)					Senior high school (upper secondary)				
	2013	2014	2015	2016	2017	2013	2014	2015	2016	2017	2013	2014	2015	2016	2017
1	2	3	4	5	6	7	8	9	10	11	12	13	14	15	16
OECD average[1]	**15.2**	**15.2**	**15.3**	**15.1**	**15.0**	**13.4**	**13.2**	**13.2**	**13.0**	**13.0**	**13.5**	**13.4**	**13.6**	**13.1**	**13.2**
Australia	15.6	15.6	15.4	15.2	15.1	—	—	—	—	—	12.0[2,3]	12.1	12.3[2,3]	12.1[2,3]	12.0
Austria	11.9	12.0	11.8	11.6	11.3	9.0	8.8	8.7	8.6	8.6	9.9	10.0	10.1	10.1	10.1
Belgium	12.7[4,5]	12.7	12.8	12.8	12.9	9.3	9.2	9.5	9.0	8.9	9.9	9.9	9.9	9.8	9.7
Canada	16.5[4,5]	16.6[4,5]	17.0[4,5]	16.9[4,5]	16.2	—	—	—	—	—	13.8	12.8	13.0	12.2	13.1
Chile	22.5	21.3	20.9	20.3	19.8	24.3	22.8	21.9	21.1	20.4	25.1	23.9	23.0	22.1	21.2
Colombia	25.0	24.3	23.8	24.2	23.6	26.6	26.3	26.3	26.2	26.4	22.9	21.9	23.9	25.6	25.1
Czech Republic	18.8	18.7	19.0	19.1	19.1	11.2	11.0	11.8	12.0	12.1	11.1	11.7	11.1	11.0	11.1
Denmark	—	—	—	—	—	—	—	—	—	—	—	—	—	—	—
Estonia	13.0	12.9	13.3	13.2	13.2	9.8	9.9	9.5	10.1	10.0	14.1	14.6	15.2	15.3	15.8
Finland	13.2	13.3	13.6	13.3	13.7	9.0	8.9	9.0	9.0	8.9	16.0	16.2	16.5	17.2	18.2
France	19.3	19.4	18.7[6]	19.0[6]	19.6	15.4	15.4	14.6[6]	14.2[6]	14.0	10.1	10.4	10.0[6]	11.0[6]	11.1
Germany	15.6	15.4	15.4	15.3	15.4	13.6	13.4	13.3	13.2	13.2	13.2	13.1	13.0	12.9	12.7
Greece	9.5	9.4	—	—	—	7.3	7.8	—	—	—	8.1	—	—	—	—
Hungary	10.6	11.5	11.2	11.0	10.8	10.4	10.9	10.6	10.3	10.4	12.0	12.5	11.5	11.1	11.5
Iceland	10.4	—	10.7	10.8	11.1	10.5	—	10.5	10.2	10.1	—	—	—	—	—
Ireland	16.4[6]	16.3[6]	16.2[6]	16.0[6]	15.7	13.5	12.1	11.8	11.8	11.2	13.9[6]	13.9[6]	13.9[6]	13.8[6]	13.4
Israel	15.3	15.5	15.4	15.4	15.2	11.9	11.6	11.5	11.0	11.0	10.7[6]	10.6	10.8[6]	10.9[6]	9.6
Italy	—	12.4	12.4	11.6	11.7	13.6	13.8	13.6	13.8	13.3	13.6	12.5	12.5	10.4	11.0
Japan	17.4	17.1	16.8	16.6	16.4	—	—	—	—	—	—	—	—	—	—
Korea, Republic of	17.3	16.9	16.8	16.5	16.4	17.5	16.6	15.7	14.7	14.0	15.1	14.5	14.1	13.8	13.2
Latvia	11.2	11.2	11.6	11.4	12.1	7.8	7.6	7.7	7.8	8.4	10.2	10.0	9.7	9.8	10.4
Lithuania	10.2	10.2	10.3	10.5	10.6	7.6	7.4	7.3	7.3	7.3	8.0	8.1	8.1	7.7	8.0
Luxembourg	8.8	8.9	10.7	10.5	9.0	11.2	10.9	11.0	10.7	10.9	7.1	8.9	8.0	8.0	9.2
Mexico	27.7	27.4	26.9	26.7	26.6	32.2[6]	33.0	33.6	33.9	34.0	27.3	20.6	20.0	20.0	23.0
Netherlands	16.6[6]	16.6	16.6	16.8	16.7	16.0[6]	16.2	16.0	16.1	16.1	18.6[6]	19.2[6]	18.0	17.9	18.0
New Zealand	16.4	16.4	16.5	16.6	16.9	16.4	16.2	16.3	16.4	16.6	13.3	13.1	12.8	12.6	13.0
Norway	10.3	10.3	10.4[6]	10.3[6]	10.2	9.8	9.7	9.6[6]	9.2[6]	9.4	9.8	10.9	10.3	10.2	10.1
Poland	11.1	11.0	11.1	11.4	10.7	9.9	10.4	9.7	9.6	9.5	11.0	10.3	10.3	10.2	10.0
Portugal	13.2	14.0	13.7	13.1	12.7	10.4	10.1	10.0	9.8	9.8	8.4	8.9	9.7	9.6	9.2
Slovak Republic	16.9	17.2	17.2	17.1	17.4	12.5	12.5	11.6	12.3	12.4	13.6	13.5	13.5	13.5	13.6
Slovenia	16.0	15.9	15.9	14.3	14.5	8.2	8.3	8.5	6.1	6.0	13.5	13.7	13.4	14.2	14.1
Spain	13.8	13.5	13.7	13.6	13.6	11.6	11.8	11.9	11.7	11.8	11.0	11.3	11.1	10.7	10.7
Sweden	12.7	12.7	12.8	13.1	12.8	12.0	12.2	12.3	12.4	12.2	12.8	13.8	14.4	13.7	13.7
Switzerland	13.8	13.8	15.6[6]	15.5[6]	15.3	10.9	10.8	11.9[6]	11.8[6]	11.7	—	—	—	12.3[6]	12.3[6]
Turkey	19.8	19.3	18.4	17.7	17.0	19.3	18.4	16.8	15.1	16.5	15.6	14.8	14.1	12.7	12.9
United Kingdom	20.7	19.6	18.4	16.9	16.9	18.5	15.0	14.3	14.8	15.2	18.5	16.3	26.1	16.5	17.2
United States	15.3	15.4	15.4	15.2	15.2	15.4	15.5	15.4	15.3	15.3	15.4	15.5	15.4	15.5	15.4
Other reporting countries															
Brazil	21.2	20.9	24.8	24.4	24.3	18.5	17.8	25.0	24.9	25.0	15.7	15.4	23.6	24.1	24.1
Costa Rica	13.3	13.2	12.7	12.0	11.6	14.1	14.4	14.0	12.8	13.7	13.8	14.3	13.9	12.6	13.4
Russian Federation	20.3	20.2	20.6	21.0	21.1	8.9[7]	8.8[7]	10.4[7]	10.6[7]	10.4	—	—	—	—	—

—Not available.
[1]Refers to the mean of the data values for all reporting Organization for Economic Cooperation and Development (OECD) countries, to which each country reporting data contributes equally. The average includes all current OECD countries for which a given year's data are available, even if they were not members of OECD in that year.
[2]Junior high school data are included with the senior high school data.
[3]Includes only general programs; data on vocational programs are not available.
[4]Preprimary data are included with the elementary school data.
[5]Junior high school data are included with the elementary school data.
[6]Public institutions only.
[7]Senior high school data are included with the junior high school data.

NOTE: The pupil/teacher ratio is the number of full-time-equivalent students divided by the number of full-time-equivalent teachers, including teachers for students with disabilities and other special teachers. All data in this table were calculated using International Standard Classification of Education (ISCED) 2011. In this table, elementary school corresponds to ISCED 2011 level 1 (U.S. grades 1 through 6), junior high school corresponds to ISCED 2011 level 2 (U.S. grades 7 through 9), and senior high school corresponds to ISCED 2011 level 3 (U.S. grades 10 through 12).
SOURCE: Organization for Economic Cooperation and Development (OECD), Online Education Database, retrieved March 25, 2020, from https://stats.oecd.org/Index.aspx. (This table was prepared March 2020.)

Table 602.10. Average reading literacy scale scores of fourth-graders and percentage distribution, by international benchmark level and country or other education system: Selected years, 2001 through 2016

[Standard errors appear in parentheses]

Country or other education system[1]	Average reading literacy scale score[2]								Percentage distribution, by international benchmark level (score range), 2017[3]							
	2001		2006		2011		2016		Low (400–474) and below[4]		Intermediate (475–549)		High (550–624)		Advanced (625 and above)	
1	2		3		4		5		6		7		8		9	
Scale centerpoint[2] or median percentage[5]	500	(†)	500	(†)	500	(†)	500	(†)	18	(†)	31	(†)	36	(†)	10	(†)
Australia	—	(†)	—	(†)	527	(2.2)	544	(2.5)	19	(1.0)	30	(1.0)	35	(1.0)	16	(1.0)
Austria	—	(†)	538	(2.2)	529	(2.0)	541[6]	(2.4)	16[6]	(1.1)	37[6]	(0.9)	39[6]	(1.3)	8[6]	(0.8)
Azerbaijan[7]	—	(†)	—	(†)	462[6]	(3.3)	472[8]	(4.2)	46[8]	(2.0)	36[8]	(1.5)	16[8]	(1.0)	2[8]	(0.3)
Bahrain	—	(†)	—	(†)	—	(†)	446	(2.3)	59	(1.0)	27	(0.8)	12	(0.6)	2	(0.3)
Belgium (Flemish)	—	(†)	—	(†)	—	(†)	525	(1.9)	20	(1.3)	45	(1.1)	31	(1.1)	4	(0.4)
Belgium (French)	—	(†)	500	(2.6)	506[6,9]	(2.9)	497[6]	(2.6)	35[6]	(1.4)	42[6]	(1.1)	20[6]	(1.1)	3[6]	(0.4)
Bulgaria	550	(3.8)	547	(4.4)	532	(4.1)	552	(4.2)	17	(1.6)	28	(1.3)	35	(1.3)	19	(1.3)
Canada	—	(†)	—	(†)	548[6]	(1.6)	543[6,10]	(1.8)	17[6,10]	(0.9)	33[6,10]	(0.8)	37[6,10]	(0.8)	13[6,10]	(0.7)
Chile	—	(†)	—	(†)	—	(†)	494	(2.5)	39	(1.5)	36	(1.4)	22	(1.2)	3	(0.4)
Chinese Taipei	—	(†)	535	(2.0)	553	(1.9)	559	(2.0)	10	(0.7)	31	(1.1)	44	(1.2)	14	(1.1)
Colombia	422	(4.4)	—	(†)	448	(4.1)	—	(†)	—	(†)	—	(†)	—	(†)	—	(†)
Croatia	—	(†)	—	(†)	553[6]	(1.9)	—	(†)	—	(†)	—	(†)	—	(†)	—	(†)
Czech Republic	537	(2.3)	—	(†)	545	(2.2)	543	(2.1)	15	(0.9)	36	(1.0)	39	(1.0)	10	(0.7)
Denmark	—	(†)	546	(2.3)	554[6]	(1.7)	547[6]	(2.1)	14[6]	(1.0)	34[6]	(1.0)	41[6]	(1.1)	11[6]	(1.0)
Egypt	—	(†)	—	(†)	—	(†)	330[11]	(5.6)	89[11]	(1.2)	9[11]	(1.0)	2[11]	(0.3)	‡[11]	(†)
England (United Kingdom)	553[6,9]	(3.4)	539	(2.6)	552[9]	(2.6)	559	(1.9)	14	(0.7)	28	(0.9)	37	(1.1)	20	(0.9)
Finland	—	(†)	—	(†)	568	(1.9)	566	(1.8)	9	(0.8)	29	(1.0)	44	(1.1)	18	(0.8)
France	525	(2.4)	522	(2.1)	520	(2.6)	511	(2.2)	28	(1.2)	42	(1.2)	26	(1.1)	4	(0.6)
Georgia[7]	—	(†)	471[6,10]	(3.1)	488[10]	(3.1)	488[10]	(2.8)	40[10]	(1.6)	38[10]	(1.4)	20[10]	(1.1)	2[10]	(0.4)
Germany	539	(1.9)	548	(2.2)	541	(2.2)	537	(3.2)	19	(1.4)	34	(1.0)	36	(1.1)	11	(0.8)
Hong Kong (China)	528	(3.1)	564	(2.4)	571[12]	(2.3)	569[6,9]	(2.7)	7[6,9]	(0.9)	27[6,9]	(1.4)	47[6,9]	(1.5)	18[6,9]	(1.3)
Hungary	543	(2.2)	551	(3.0)	539	(2.9)	554	(2.9)	15	(1.0)	30	(1.2)	39	(1.1)	17	(1.2)
Indonesia	—	(†)	405	(4.1)	428	(4.2)	—	(†)	—	(†)	—	(†)	—	(†)	—	(†)
Iran, Islamic Republic of	414	(4.2)	421	(3.1)	457	(2.8)	428[13]	(4.0)	63[13]	(1.3)	26[13]	(1.0)	9[13]	(0.5)	1[13]	(0.2)
Ireland	—	(†)	—	(†)	552	(2.3)	567	(2.5)	11	(0.9)	28	(1.2)	40	(1.3)	21	(1.2)
Israel	509[14]	(2.8)	512[14]	(3.3)	541[12]	(2.7)	530[12]	(2.5)	25[12]	(1.0)	29[12]	(1.0)	33[12]	(1.1)	13[12]	(0.9)
Italy	541	(2.4)	551	(2.9)	541	(2.2)	548	(2.2)	13	(1.0)	35	(1.3)	41	(1.7)	11	(0.8)
Kazakhstan	—	(†)	—	(†)	—	(†)	536	(2.5)	16	(1.5)	42	(1.3)	35	(1.4)	7	(0.8)
Kuwait	—	(†)	—	(†)	—	(†)	393[11]	(4.1)	78[11]	(1.5)	16[11]	(1.2)	5[11]	(0.8)	‡[11]	(†)
Latvia	—	(†)	—	(†)	—	(†)	558[6]	(1.7)	10[6]	(0.8)	33[6]	(1.3)	43[6]	(1.4)	14[6]	(1.0)
Lithuania	543[10]	(2.6)	537[10]	(1.6)	528[6,10]	(2.0)	548[15]	(2.6)	14[15]	(1.1)	34[15]	(1.3)	40[15]	(1.2)	12[15]	(0.9)
Macao (China)	—	(†)	—	(†)	—	(†)	546	(1.0)	14	(0.5)	36	(0.8)	41	(0.9)	10	(0.6)
Malta (Maltese)	—	(†)	—	(†)	457	(1.5)	452[6]	(1.8)	55[6]	(1.1)	32[6]	(1.1)	12[6]	(0.8)	‡[6]	(†)
Morocco	350[16]	(9.6)	323	(5.9)	310[17]	(3.9)	358[13]	(3.9)	86[13]	(0.8)	11[13]	(0.7)	3[13]	(0.4)	‡[13]	(†)
Netherlands[9]	554	(2.5)	547	(1.5)	546	(1.9)	545	(1.7)	12	(0.9)	39	(1.3)	40	(1.1)	8	(0.6)
New Zealand	529	(3.6)	532	(2.0)	531	(1.9)	523	(2.2)	27	(1.0)	32	(1.0)	30	(1.0)	11	(0.6)
Northern Ireland (United Kingdom)	—	(†)	—	(†)	558[9]	(2.4)	565	(2.2)	13	(0.8)	26	(1.0)	38	(1.0)	22	(1.4)
Norway (grade 5)[18]	—	(†)	—	(†)	—	(†)	559	(2.3)	10	(0.9)	32	(1.4)	43	(1.4)	15	(0.9)
Oman	—	(†)	—	(†)	391[19]	(2.8)	418	(3.3)	68	(1.3)	22	(0.9)	8	(0.7)	2	(0.3)
Poland	—	(†)	519	(2.4)	526	(2.1)	565	(2.1)	11	(0.7)	28	(1.1)	41	(1.1)	20	(1.1)
Portugal	—	(†)	—	(†)	541	(2.6)	528[6]	(2.3)	21[6]	(1.3)	42[6]	(1.1)	31[6]	(1.2)	7[6]	(0.9)
Qatar	—	(†)	353	(1.1)	425[6]	(3.5)	442	(1.8)	58	(1.1)	25	(1.1)	14	(0.6)	3	(0.3)
Romania	512	(4.6)	489	(5.0)	502	(4.3)	—	(†)	—	(†)	—	(†)	—	(†)	—	(†)
Russian Federation	528[6]	(4.4)	565[6]	(3.4)	568	(2.7)	581	(2.2)	6	(0.6)	23	(1.0)	44	(1.0)	26	(1.2)
Saudi Arabia	—	(†)	—	(†)	430	(4.4)	430	(4.2)	65	(1.7)	24	(1.3)	9	(1.0)	1	(0.4)
Singapore	528	(5.2)	558	(2.9)	567[6]	(3.3)	576[12]	(3.2)	11[12]	(1.0)	23[12]	(1.1)	38[12]	(1.5)	29[12]	(1.6)
Slovak Republic	518	(2.8)	531	(2.8)	535	(2.8)	535	(3.1)	19	(1.3)	33	(1.1)	37	(1.3)	10	(0.8)
Slovenia	502	(2.0)	522	(2.1)	530	(2.0)	542	(2.0)	17	(0.9)	34	(0.9)	38	(1.1)	11	(0.8)
South Africa	—	(†)	—	(†)	—	(†)	320[11]	(4.4)	92[11]	(1.0)	6[11]	(0.7)	2[11]	(0.4)	‡[11]	(†)
Spain	—	(†)	513	(2.5)	513	(2.3)	528	(1.7)	20	(1.0)	41	(0.8)	33	(0.9)	6	(0.4)
Sweden	561	(2.2)	549	(2.3)	542	(2.1)	555	(2.4)	12	(0.9)	31	(1.1)	43	(1.7)	14	(1.4)
Trinidad and Tobago	—	(†)	436	(4.9)	471	(3.8)	479	(3.3)	45	(1.7)	31	(1.3)	20	(1.1)	4	(0.5)
United Arab Emirates	—	(†)	—	(†)	439	(2.2)	450	(3.2)	57	(1.4)	23	(0.7)	15	(0.8)	5	(0.3)

See notes at end of table.

Table 602.10. Average reading literacy scale scores of fourth-graders and percentage distribution, by international benchmark level and country or other education system: Selected years, 2001 through 2016—Continued

[Standard errors appear in parentheses]

Country or other education system[1]	Average reading literacy scale score[2] 2001		2006		2011		2016		Percentage distribution, by international benchmark level (score range), 2017[3] Low (400–474) and below[4]		Intermediate (475–549)		High (550–624)		Advanced (625 and above)	
1	2		3		4		5		6		7		8		9	
United States	542[6,9]	(3.8)	540[9]	(3.5)	556[6]	(1.5)	549[9]	(3.1)	17[9]	(1.2)	31[9]	(1.1)	37[9]	(1.4)	16[9]	(1.3)
Benchmarking education systems																
Abu Dhabi (United Arab Emirates)	—	(†)	—	(†)	424	(4.7)	414	(4.7)	69	(1.7)	20	(1.1)	9	(0.9)	2	(0.4)
Alberta (Canada)	—	(†)	560[6]	(2.4)	548[6]	(2.9)	—	(†)	—	(†)	—	(†)	—	(†)	—	(†)
Andalusia (Spain)	—	(†)	—	(†)	515	(2.3)	525	(2.1)	22	(1.2)	41	(0.9)	32	(1.1)	5	(0.5)
Bueno Aires (Argentina)	—	(†)	—	(†)	—	(†)	480	(3.1)	45	(1.5)	34	(1.1)	18	(1.0)	3	(0.4)
Dubai (United Arab Emirates)	—	(†)	—	(†)	476	(2.0)	515	(1.9)	31	(0.9)	30	(0.9)	29	(0.8)	11	(0.6)
Florida (United States)[21]	—	(†)	—	(†)	569[9,14]	(2.9)	—	(†)	—	(†)	—	(†)	—	(†)	—	(†)
Madrid (Spain)	—	(†)	—	(†)	—	(†)	549[6]	(2.0)	11[6]	(0.9)	38[6]	(1.1)	42[6]	(1.1)	9[6]	(0.7)
Malta (English)	—	(†)	—	(†)	477	(1.4)	—	(†)	—	(†)	—	(†)	—	(†)	—	(†)
Moscow City (Russian Federation)	—	(†)	—	(†)	—	(†)	612	(2.2)	2	(0.3)	14	(0.9)	41	(1.2)	43	(1.5)
Norway (grade 4)[18]	499	(2.9)	498[20]	(2.6)	507[16]	(1.9)	517	(2.0)	26	(1.1)	40	(1.1)	29	(1.0)	5	(0.6)
Ontario (Canada)	548[6]	(3.3)	555[6]	(2.7)	552[6]	(2.6)	544	(3.2)	18	(1.4)	32	(1.1)	37	(1.4)	14	(1.5)
Quebec (Canada)	537	(3.0)	533	(2.8)	538	(2.1)	547[22]	(2.8)	13[22]	(1.5)	37[22]	(1.5)	39[22]	(1.6)	11[22]	(1.2)

—Not available.
†Not applicable.
‡Reporting standards not met (too few cases for a reliable estimate).
[1]Most of the education systems represent complete countries, but some represent subnational entities; examples include the Flemish and French communities of Belgium, two components of the United Kingdom (England and Northern Ireland), a few individual cities (such as Abu Dhabi within the United Arab Emirates), and the U.S. state of Florida.
[2]Progress in International Reading Literacy Study (PIRLS) scores are reported on a scale from 0 to 1,000, with the scale centerpoint set at 500 and the standard deviation set at 100.
[3]PIRLS international benchmarks group achievement into four levels, providing a way to interpret scale scores and to understand how student proficiency varies at different points on the scale. The score range for each benchmark level (i.e., the lowest and highest score in that level) is shown in parentheses. The score cut-points (i.e., lowest scores) that define the beginning of each level were selected to be as close as possible to the standard percentile cut-points (i.e., the 25th, 50th, 75th, and 90th percentiles). Descriptions of the skills associated with each level can be found at https://nces.ed.gov/surveys/pirls/pirls2016/tables/pirls2016_exhibit02.asp.
[4]This column combines students who are in the Low level (scores of 400 to 474) with students who are below the Low level (scores of less than 400).
[5]International median percentages are shown in columns 6 through 9 of this row. Half the education systems have a percentage of students equal to or higher than the international median and half have a percentage of students below the median. The median includes only the education systems shown in the top part of this table, which are members of the International Association for the Evaluation of Educational Achievement (IEA). "Benchmarking" education systems are not members of the IEA and are therefore not included in the median.
[6]National Defined Population covers 90 to 95 percent of National Target Population.
[7]Exclusion rates for Azerbaijan and Georgia are slightly underestimated as some conflict zones were not covered and no official statistics were available for 2011.
[8]In 2016, Azerbaijan expanded its sample to include students taught in Russian. All 2016 data shown in this table are based on the expanded sample and therefore are not comparable with data for previous years.
[9]Met guidelines for sample participation rates only after replacement schools were included.

[10]National Target Population does not include all of the International Target Population.
[11]Administered PIRLS Literacy instead of the standard PIRLS assessment. PIRLS Literacy is a less difficult version of PIRLS designed to assess foundational reading skills.
[12]National Defined Population covers less than 90 percent of National Target Population (but at least 77 percent).
[13]Administered both the standard PIRLS assessment and PIRLS Literacy, a less difficult version of PIRLS that is designed to assess foundational reading skills. Results are based on an average of both assessments.
[14]National Defined Population covers less than 80 percent of National Target Population.
[15]In 2016, Lithuania expanded its sample to include students taught in Polish and Russian. All 2016 data shown in this table are based on the expanded sample and therefore are not comparable with data for previous years.
[16]Nearly satisfied guidelines for sample participation rates after replacement schools were included.
[17]The TIMSS & PIRLS International Study Center has reservations about the reliability of the average achievement score because the percentage of students with achievement too low for estimation exceeds 25 percent.
[18]In PIRLS cycles prior to 2016, Norway assessed only students in grade 4, which is similar to grade 3 in many other countries because grade 1 in Norway is considered the equivalent of kindergarten rather than the first year of primary school. For PIRLS 2016, Norway started assessing students in grade 5. For purposes of comparing results across years, however, Norway also continued to collect grade 4 data in 2016. This table includes the grade 5 results in the top part of the table and the grade 4 results under "Benchmarking education systems."
[19]The TIMSS & PIRLS International Study Center has reservations about the reliability of the average achievement score because the percentage of students with achievement too low for estimation exceeds 15 percent, though it is less than 25 percent.
[20]Data are available for at least 70 percent but less than 85 percent of students.
[21]All data for Florida are based on public schools only.
[22]Did not satisfy guidelines for sample participation rates.
SOURCE: International Association for the Evaluation of Educational Achievement (IEA), Progress in International Reading Literacy Study (PIRLS), 2001, 2006, 2011, and 2016. (This table was prepared November 2017.)

Table 602.20. Average fourth-grade scores and annual instructional time in mathematics and science, by country or other education system: 2015

[Standard errors appear in parentheses]

Country or other education system[1]	Total instructional hours per year		Mathematics						Science					
			Average score[2]		Instructional time in mathematics				Average score[2]		Instructional time in science			
					Hours per year		As a percent of total instructional hours				Hours per year		As a percent of total instructional hours	
1	2		3		4		5		6		7		8	
International average[3]	888	(2.0)	500	(†)	155	(0.5)	17	(0.1)	500	(†)	76	(0.4)	9	(#)
Australia	1,014[4]	(8.4)	517	(3.1)	202[4]	(3.5)	20	(0.4)	524	(2.9)	57[4]	(1.5)	6	(0.2)
Bahrain[5]	976	(0.6)	451	(1.6)	159[4]	(2.9)	16	(0.3)	459	(2.6)	103[4]	(0.6)	11	(0.1)
Belgium (Flemish)[6]	955[4]	(11.6)	546	(2.1)	218[4]	(3.2)	23	(0.4)	512	(2.3)	—	(†)	—	(†)
Bulgaria	707[4]	(27.3)	524	(5.3)	105	(2.9)	15	(0.7)	536	(5.9)	42	(2.3)	6	(0.4)
Canada[5,6,7,8]	951	(4.1)	511	(2.3)	196[4]	(3.2)	21	(0.3)	525	(2.6)	81[4]	(2.0)	9	(0.2)
Chile	1,094[4]	(16.9)	459	(2.4)	206[9]	(6.4)	19	(0.7)	478	(2.7)	93[9]	(2.5)	9	(0.3)
Chinese Taipei	969	(14.4)	597	(1.9)	128[4]	(4.3)	13	(0.5)	555	(1.8)	91	(1.9)	9	(0.2)
Croatia	778	(21.6)	502	(1.8)	124	(1.8)	16	(0.5)	533	(2.1)	82	(1.5)	11	(0.4)
Cyprus	827[4]	(12.4)	523	(2.7)	161[4]	(5.5)	19	(0.7)	481	(2.6)	48[4]	(0.9)	6	(0.1)
Czech Republic	771	(10.4)	528	(2.2)	125	(4.1)	16	(0.6)	534	(2.4)	38	(2.0)	5	(0.3)
Denmark[5,6]	1,051[4]	(11.2)	539	(2.7)	150[9]	(3.1)	14	(0.3)	527	(2.1)	80[9]	(2.3)	8	(0.2)
England (United Kingdom)	994	(9.9)	546	(2.8)	189[4]	(4.5)	19	(0.5)	536	(2.4)	61[4]	(2.2)	6	(0.2)
Finland	737	(8.9)	535	(2.0)	115	(2.2)	16	(0.4)	554	(2.3)	82	(1.8)	11	(0.3)
France	858[4]	(8.2)	488	(2.9)	193[4]	(3.9)	22	(0.5)	487	(2.7)	56[4]	(1.8)	7	(0.2)
Georgia[8]	743[4]	(19.5)	463	(3.6)	138[4]	(2.1)	19	(0.6)	451	(3.7)	80	(1.4)	11	(0.3)
Germany	820[4]	(9.1)	522	(2.0)	147[4]	(2.0)	18	(0.3)	528	(2.4)	61[9]	(3.8)	7	(0.5)
Hong Kong[6] (China)	999	(13.1)	615	(2.9)	159	(4.7)	16	(0.5)	557	(2.9)	‡	(†)	‡	(†)
Hungary	784	(11.8)	529	(3.2)	129	(2.5)	16	(0.4)	542	(3.3)	63	(1.7)	8	(0.2)
Indonesia	1,095[4]	(20.9)	397	(3.7)	149[4]	(5.0)	14	(0.5)	397	(4.8)	116[4]	(4.0)	11	(0.4)
Iran, Islamic Republic of	645[4]	(6.4)	431	(3.2)	112[4]	(2.3)	17	(0.4)	421	(4.0)	87[4]	(3.0)	13	(0.5)
Ireland	854	(#)	547	(2.1)	165	(2.4)	19	(0.3)	529	(2.4)	32	(0.7)	4	(0.1)
Italy[5]	1,061	(20.5)	507	(2.6)	231[4]	(4.5)	22	(0.6)	516	(2.6)	76	(1.6)	7	(0.2)
Japan	903	(3.7)	593	(2.0)	151	(1.1)	17	(0.1)	569	(1.8)	91	(0.5)	10	(0.1)
Jordan	931	(14.2)	388	(3.1)	133	(3.3)	14	(0.4)	—	(†)	—	(†)	—	(†)
Kazakhstan	813	(16.2)	544	(4.5)	132	(3.8)	16	(0.6)	550	(4.4)	58	(2.9)	7	(0.4)
Korea, Republic of	712	(8.9)	608	(2.2)	100	(1.4)	14	(0.3)	589	(2.0)	76	(1.0)	11	(0.2)
Kuwait[10]	912[9]	(27.9)	353	(4.6)	128[9]	(4.4)	14	(0.6)	337	(6.2)	77[9]	(3.5)	8	(0.5)
Lithuania[5]	629	(5.5)	535	(2.5)	111	(1.6)	18	(0.3)	528	(2.5)	53	(1.0)	8	(0.2)
Morocco	1,054[4]	(18.8)	377	(3.4)	172[4]	(2.8)	16	(0.4)	352[10]	(4.7)	54[4]	(0.9)	5	(0.1)
Netherlands[6]	1,073[9]	(16.2)	530	(1.7)	‡	(†)	—	(†)	517	(2.7)	‡	(†)	—	(†)
New Zealand	923	(5.5)	491	(2.3)	163[4]	(2.3)	18	(0.3)	506	(2.7)	43[4]	(2.0)	5	(0.2)
Northern Ireland[11] (United Kingdom)	962[4]	(10.2)	570	(2.9)	215[9]	(6.5)	22	(0.7)	520	(2.2)	38[9]	(2.1)	4	(0.2)
Norway[12]	817	(8.7)	549	(2.5)	117[4]	(2.4)	14	(0.3)	538	(2.6)	59[4]	(1.7)	7	(0.2)
Oman	962[4]	(11.7)	425	(2.5)	148[9]	(4.5)	15	(0.5)	431	(3.1)	123[9]	(3.1)	13	(0.4)
Poland	752[4]	(6.9)	535	(2.1)	112[4]	(1.1)	15	(0.2)	547	(2.4)	84[4]	(1.1)	11	(0.2)
Portugal[5]	864	(8.5)	541	(2.2)	275[4]	(4.0)	32	(0.6)	508	(2.2)	111[4]	(3.8)	13	(0.5)
Qatar	1,056[4]	(16.1)	439	(3.4)	185[4]	(4.6)	18	(0.5)	436	(4.1)	125[4]	(4.4)	12	(0.5)
Russian Federation	661	(6.9)	564	(3.4)	106	(1.4)	16	(0.3)	567	(3.2)	49	(0.9)	7	(0.2)
Saudi Arabia	1,080[4]	(19.6)	383[10]	(4.1)	148[9]	(4.5)	14	(0.5)	390	(4.9)	77[4]	(3.7)	7	(0.4)
Serbia[13]	737	(16.2)	518	(3.5)	154	(1.6)	21	(0.5)	525	(3.7)	75	(3.5)	10	(0.5)
Singapore[5]	986	(#)	618	(3.8)	201	(1.6)	20	(0.2)	590	(3.7)	85	(1.4)	9	(0.1)
Slovak Republic	759	(8.1)	498	(2.5)	129	(2.1)	17	(0.3)	520	(2.6)	52	(2.0)	7	(0.3)
Slovenia	716[4]	(7.2)	520	(1.9)	144[4]	(1.2)	20	(0.3)	543	(2.4)	86[4]	(1.3)	12	(0.2)
Spain[5]	864	(10.2)	505	(2.5)	161	(2.3)	19	(0.3)	518	(2.6)	124[4]	(2.6)	14	(0.3)
Sweden[5]	839[4]	(10.6)	519	(2.8)	110[4]	(2.3)	13	(0.3)	540	(3.6)	79	(1.8)	9	(0.2)
Turkey	847	(18.0)	483	(3.1)	120	(3.3)	14	(0.5)	483	(3.3)	83	(1.7)	10	(0.3)
United Arab Emirates	1,009[4]	(4.6)	452	(2.4)	162[9]	(2.4)	16	(0.2)	451	(2.8)	111[9]	(2.1)	11	(0.2)
United States[5,6]	1,088	(9.2)	539	(2.3)	216[4]	(4.1)	20	(0.4)	546	(2.2)	100[4]	(3.7)	9	(0.3)
Benchmarking education systems														
Abu Dhabi[5] (United Arab Emirates)	1,025[4]	(11.1)	419[10]	(4.7)	163[9]	(4.5)	16	(0.5)	415	(5.6)	116[9]	(4.3)	11	(0.4)
Buenos Aires (Argentina)	951[9]	(31.3)	432	(2.9)	‡	(†)	—	(†)	418	(4.7)	‡	(†)	—	(†)
Dubai (United Arab Emirates)	996[4]	(0.4)	511	(1.4)	160[9]	(1.4)	16	(0.1)	518	(1.8)	110[4]	(1.2)	11	(0.1)
Florida[14] (United States)	1,075[4]	(21.6)	546	(4.7)	212[9]	(11.1)	20	(1.1)	549	(4.8)	105[9]	(5.8)	10	(0.6)
Ontario (Canada)	953	(6.2)	512	(2.3)	195[4]	(3.2)	20	(0.4)	530	(2.5)	88[4]	(3.1)	9	(0.3)
Quebec[15] (Canada)	910	(8.0)	536	(4.0)	221	(8.9)	24	(1.0)	525	(4.1)	43	(2.9)	5	(0.3)

—Not available.
†Not applicable.
#Rounds to zero.
‡Reporting standards not met. Either data are available for less than 50 percent of students or the coefficient of variation (CV) is 50 percent or greater.
[1]Most of the education systems represent complete countries, but some represent subnational entities; examples include the Flemish community of Belgium, two components of the United Kingdom (England and Northern Ireland), a few individual cities (such as Abu Dhabi within the United Arab Emirates), and the U.S. state of Florida.
[2]Trends in International Mathematics and Science Study (TIMSS) scores are reported on a scale from 0 to 1,000, with the scale centerpoint set at 500 and the standard deviation set at 100.
[3]The international average includes only education systems that are members of the International Association for the Evaluation of Educational Achievement (IEA), which develops and implements TIMSS at the international level. "Benchmarking" education systems are not members of the IEA and are therefore not included in the average.
[4]Data are available for at least 70 percent but less than 85 percent of students.
[5]National Defined Population covers 90 to 95 percent of National Target Population.
[6]Met guidelines for sample participation rates only after replacement schools were included.
[7]Data for Canada include only students from the provinces of Alberta, Manitoba, Newfoundland, Ontario, and Quebec.
[8]National Target Population does not include all of the International Target Population.
[9]Data are available for at least 50 percent but less than 70 percent of students.
[10]The TIMSS & PIRLS International Study Center has reservations about the reliability of the average achievement score because the percentage of students with achievement too low for estimation exceeds 15 percent, though it is less than 25 percent.

[11]Nearly satisfied guidelines for sample participation rates after replacement schools were included.
[12]Norway collected data from students in their fifth year of schooling rather than in grade 4 because year 1 in Norway is considered the equivalent of kindergarten rather than the first year of primary school.
[13]National Defined Population covers less than 90 percent of National Target Population (but at least 77 percent).
[14]U.S. state-level data are based on public school students only.
[15]Did not satisfy guidelines for sample participation rates.
NOTE: Countries and other education systems were required to draw probability samples of students who were nearing the end of their fourth year of formal schooling (counting the first year of primary school as year 1), provided that the mean age at the time of testing was at least 9.5 years. Instructional times shown in this table are actual or implemented times (as opposed to intended times prescribed by the curriculum). Principals reported total instructional hours per day and school days per year. Total instructional hours per year were calculated by multiplying the number of school days per year by the number of instructional hours per day. Teachers reported instructional hours per week in mathematics and science. Instructional hours per year in mathematics and science were calculated by dividing weekly instructional hours by the number of school days per week and then multiplying by the number of school days per year.
SOURCE: International Association for the Evaluation of Educational Achievement (IEA), Trends in International Mathematics and Science Study (TIMSS), 2015; International Results in Mathematics and Science, retrieved from Boston College, TIMSS & PIRLS International Study Center website (http://timssandpirls.bc.edu/timss2015/international-results/). (This table was prepared December 2016.)

Table 602.30. Average eighth-grade scores and annual instructional time in mathematics and science, by country or other education system: 2015

[Standard errors appear in parentheses]

Country or other education system[1]	Total instructional hours per year		Mathematics						Science					
			Average score[2]		Instructional time in mathematics				Average score[2]		Instructional time in science[3]			
					Hours per year		As a percent of total instructional hours				Hours per year		As a percent of total instructional hours	
1		2		3		4		5		6		7		8
International average[4]	**1,013**	**(2.1)**	**500**	**(†)**	**136**	**(0.5)**	**13**	**(0.1)**	**500**	**(†)**	**144**	**(0.7)**	**14**	**(0.1)**
Australia	1,011[5]	(6.3)	505	(3.1)	139[5]	(2.0)	14	(0.2)	512	(2.7)	126[6]	(1.6)	12	(0.2)
Bahrain	1,032	(1.0)	454	(1.4)	153	(2.3)	15	(0.2)	466	(2.2)	125[5]	(10.2)	12	(1.0)
Canada[7,8,9]	949[5]	(4.9)	527	(2.2)	168[5]	(2.9)	18	(0.3)	526	(2.1)	97[6]	(2.2)	10	(0.2)
Chile	1,127[5]	(18.0)	427[10]	(3.2)	192[5]	(5.8)	17	(0.6)	454	(3.1)	113[6]	(5.0)	10	(0.5)
Chinese Taipei	1,132	(9.7)	599	(2.4)	160	(2.4)	14	(0.2)	569	(2.1)	144	(2.3)	13	(0.2)
Egypt	1,099	(21.2)	392[10]	(4.1)	132	(3.3)	12	(0.4)	371	(4.3)	114	(2.9)	10	(0.3)
England (United Kingdom)	1,009[5]	(8.3)	518	(4.2)	126[5]	(3.4)	12	(0.4)	537	(3.8)	97[6]	(3.8)	10	(0.4)
Georgia[8,11]	864[5]	(16.7)	453	(3.4)	122[5]	(4.0)	14	(0.5)	443	(3.1)	241[6]	(6.8)	28	(1.0)
Hong Kong (China)	995	(11.7)	594	(4.6)	139	(3.1)	14	(0.4)	546	(3.9)	102	(2.8)	10	(0.3)
Hungary	842	(10.3)	514	(3.8)	113	(2.3)	13	(0.3)	527	(3.4)	201	(5.4)	24	(0.7)
Iran, Islamic Republic of	971	(16.9)	436[10]	(4.6)	131	(4.6)	13	(0.5)	456	(4.0)	120	(3.1)	12	(0.4)
Ireland	963[5]	(3.2)	523	(2.7)	109	(0.8)	11	(0.1)	530	(2.8)	90[5]	(0.9)	9	(0.1)
Israel[12]	1,133[5]	(15.5)	511	(4.1)	153[5]	(2.2)	14	(0.3)	507	(3.9)	129[5]	(3.5)	11	(0.3)
Italy[11]	1,047[5]	(9.6)	494	(2.5)	149	(2.9)	14	(0.3)	499	(2.4)	71[5]	(1.3)	7	(0.1)
Japan	1,036	(6.1)	586	(2.3)	106	(1.5)	10	(0.2)	571	(1.8)	131	(1.7)	13	(0.2)
Jordan	976	(12.5)	386[13]	(3.2)	132	(2.3)	14	(0.3)	426	(3.3)	131	(2.3)	13	(0.3)
Kazakhstan	933	(19.4)	528	(5.3)	129	(3.4)	14	(0.5)	533	(4.4)	239	(5.4)	26	(0.8)
Korea, Republic of	947	(6.0)	606	(2.6)	114	(1.2)	12	(0.1)	556	(2.3)	94	(2.1)	10	(0.2)
Kuwait	997[5]	(18.6)	392[10]	(4.6)	136[5]	(3.5)	14	(0.4)	411	(5.2)	117[5]	(3.0)	12	(0.4)
Lebanon	945[5]	(14.8)	442	(3.6)	158[5]	(5.0)	17	(0.6)	398	(5.3)	243[5]	(10.7)	26	(1.2)
Lithuania[11]	856	(10.2)	511	(2.8)	115	(1.7)	13	(0.3)	519	(2.8)	205	(4.2)	24	(0.6)
Malaysia	1,172[5]	(15.6)	465	(3.6)	135	(4.1)	12	(0.4)	471	(4.1)	130[5]	(4.0)	11	(0.4)
Malta	964	(0.3)	494	(1.0)	127[5]	(0.1)	13	(#)	481	(1.6)	311[5]	(1.0)	32	(0.1)
Morocco	1,364	(25.8)	384[13]	(2.3)	152[5]	(2.4)	11	(0.3)	393	(2.5)	160[5]	(4.5)	12	(0.4)
New Zealand[9]	966[5]	(6.9)	493	(3.4)	144[5]	(2.5)	15	(0.3)	513	(3.1)	133[5]	(2.5)	14	(0.3)
Norway[14]	895	(8.8)	512	(2.3)	105[5]	(2.2)	12	(0.3)	509	(2.8)	81[5]	(1.5)	9	(0.2)
Oman	980[5]	(14.5)	403[10]	(2.4)	166[6]	(2.7)	17	(0.4)	455	(2.7)	143[5]	(3.1)	15	(0.4)
Qatar	1,085[5]	(1.9)	437[10]	(3.0)	157[5]	(2.8)	14	(0.3)	457	(3.0)	155[5]	(2.6)	14	(0.2)
Russian Federation	884	(9.4)	538	(4.7)	145	(3.1)	16	(0.4)	544	(4.2)	219[5]	(2.9)	25	(0.4)
Saudi Arabia	1,112	(18.7)	368[13]	(4.6)	155[5]	(4.3)	14	(0.5)	396	(4.5)	130	(5.7)	12	(0.5)
Singapore[11]	1,065	(#)	621	(3.2)	129	(1.3)	12	(0.1)	597	(3.2)	106	(1.4)	10	(0.1)
Slovenia	867[5]	(10.3)	516	(2.1)	114[5]	(1.3)	13	(0.2)	551	(2.4)	221[5]	(4.7)	25	(0.6)
Sweden	921	(8.6)	501	(2.8)	99	(1.5)	11	(0.2)	522	(3.5)	122	(4.1)	13	(0.5)
Thailand	1,209	(6.8)	431	(4.8)	111	(1.7)	9	(0.1)	456	(4.2)	110	(1.7)	9	(0.1)
Turkey	983	(22.6)	458	(4.7)	117	(2.7)	12	(0.4)	493	(4.0)	112	(3.0)	11	(0.4)
United Arab Emirates	1,016[5]	(6.4)	465	(2.0)	159[6]	(2.7)	16	(0.3)	477	(2.3)	115[6]	(4.3)	11	(0.4)
United States[9]	1,135	(8.8)	518	(3.1)	155[5]	(3.9)	14	(0.4)	530	(2.8)	144[6]	(2.4)	13	(0.2)
Benchmarking education systems														
Abu Dhabi (United Arab Emirates)	1,024[5]	(11.0)	442	(4.7)	166[6]	(5.2)	16	(0.5)	454	(5.6)	122[6]	(6.6)	12	(0.7)
Buenos Aires[9] (Argentina)	1,164[5]	(46.7)	396[13]	(4.2)	‡	(†)	—	(†)	386	(4.2)	‡	(†)	—	(†)
Dubai (United Arab Emirates)	1,010[5]	(1.3)	512	(2.1)	152[5]	(1.7)	15	(0.2)	525	(2.0)	115[6]	(3.5)	11	(0.3)
Florida[8,15] (United States)	1,155[6]	(39.9)	493	(6.4)	146[6]	(9.0)	13	(0.9)	508	(6.0)	‡	(†)	—	(†)
Ontario (Canada)	970[5]	(6.0)	522	(2.9)	179[5]	(3.8)	18	(0.4)	524	(2.5)	91[6]	(3.3)	9	(0.3)
Quebec[16] (Canada)	906	(7.0)	543	(3.9)	149	(4.2)	16	(0.5)	530	(4.4)	98[5]	(2.7)	11	(0.3)

—Not available.
†Not applicable.
#Rounds to zero.
‡Reporting standards not met. Either data are available for less than 50 percent of the students or the coefficient of variation (CV) is 50 percent or greater.
[1]Most of the education systems represent complete countries, but some represent subnational entities; examples include two Canadian provinces (Ontario and Quebec), a component of the United Kingdom (England), the U.S. state of Florida, and a few individual cities (such as Abu Dhabi within the United Arab Emirates).
[2]Trends in International Mathematics and Science Study (TIMSS) scores are reported on a scale from 0 to 1,000, with the scale centerpoint set at 500 and the standard deviation set at 100.
[3]General/integrated science instructional time is shown for the 27 participating countries that teach science as a general or integrated subject at eighth grade. For the 10 participating countries that teach the sciences as separate subjects (biology, chemistry, etc.) at eighth grade, total instructional time across science subjects is shown.
[4]The international average includes only education systems that are members of the International Association for the Evaluation of Educational Achievement (IEA), which develops and implements TIMSS at the international level. "Benchmarking" education systems are not members of the IEA and are therefore not included in the average.
[5]Data are available for at least 70 percent but less than 85 percent of students.
[6]Data are available for at least 50 percent but less than 70 percent of students.
[7]Data for Canada include only students from the provinces of Manitoba, Newfoundland, Ontario, and Quebec.
[8]National Target Population does not include all of the International Target Population.
[9]Met guidelines for sample participation rates only after replacement schools were included.
[10]The TIMSS & PIRLS International Study Center has reservations about the reliability of the average achievement score because the percentage of students with achievement too low for estimation exceeds 15 percent, though it is less than 25 percent.

[11]National Defined Population covers 90 to 95 percent of National Target Population.
[12]National Defined Population covers less than 90 percent of National Target Population (but at least 77 percent).
[13]The TIMSS & PIRLS International Study Center has reservations about the reliability of the average achievement score because the percentage of students with achievement too low for estimation exceeds 25 percent.
[14]Norway collected data from students in their ninth year of schooling rather than in grade 8 because year 1 in Norway is considered the equivalent of kindergarten rather than the first year of primary school.
[15]U.S. state-level data are based on public school students only.
[16]Did not satisfy guidelines for sample participation rates.
NOTE: Countries and other education systems were required to draw probability samples of students who were nearing the end of their eighth year of formal schooling (counting the first year of primary school as year 1), provided that the mean age at the time of testing was at least 13.5 years. Instructional times shown in this table are actual or implemented times (as opposed to intended times prescribed by the curriculum). Principals reported total instructional hours per day and school days per day. Total instructional hours per year were calculated by multiplying the number of school days per year by the number of instructional hours per day. Teachers reported instructional hours per week in mathematics and science. Instructional hours per year in mathematics and science were calculated by dividing weekly instructional hours by the number of school days per week and then multiplying by the number of school days per year.
SOURCE: International Association for the Evaluation of Educational Achievement (IEA), Trends in International Mathematics and Science Study (TIMSS), 2015; International Results in Mathematics and Science, retrieved from Boston College, TIMSS & PIRLS International Study Center website (http://timssandpirls.bc.edu/timss2015/international-results/). (This table was prepared December 2016.)

Table 602.35. Average advanced mathematics and physics scores of high school seniors who had taken advanced courses in these subjects, seniors who had taken such courses as a percentage of their age cohort, and instructional time in such courses, by country: 2015

[Standard errors appear in parentheses]

	Advanced mathematics					Physics				
	Total instructional hours per year (includes all subjects)[1]	Average score[2]	Percent of age cohort taking advanced mathematics courses[3,4]	Instructional time in advanced mathematics		Total instructional hours per year (includes all subjects)[1]	Average score[2]	Percent of age cohort taking physics courses[3,5]	Instructional time in physics	
				Hours per year	As a percent of total instructional hours				Hours per year	As a percent of total instructional hours
Country										
1	2	3	4	5	6	7	8	9	10	11
International average[6]	**1,027** (5.8)	**500** (†)	†	**171** (1.5)	**17** (0.2)	**1,023** (6.2)	**500** (†)	†	**133** (1.8)	**13** (0.2)
France	1,340 (22.5)	463 (3.1)	21.5	222[7] (4.3)	17 (0.4)	1,340 (22.5)	373 (4.0)	21.5	116[7] (4.2)	9 (0.3)
Italy	1,036[7] (9.6)	422 (5.3)	24.5	130 (2.1)	13 (0.2)	1,018[7] (8.2)	374 (6.9)	18.2	102[7] (1.7)	10 (0.2)
Lebanon[8]	931 (11.2)	532 (3.1)	3.9	242 (7.8)	26 (0.9)	932 (11.2)	410 (4.5)	3.9	200 (3.1)	21 (0.4)
Norway	1,033[7] (19.8)	459 (4.6)	10.6	149[7] (5.7)	14 (0.6)	991[7] (14.1)	507 (4.6)	6.5	139[7] (3.0)	14 (0.4)
Portugal	1,073[7] (32.3)	482[9] (2.5)	28.5	186 (3.6)	17 (0.6)	1,046[7] (37.1)	467 (4.6)	5.1	120 (6.2)	11 (0.7)
Russian Federation (intensive courses)[10]	942[7] (14.4)	540 (7.8)	1.9	207 (4.2)	22 (0.6)	† (†)	† (†)	†	† (†)	† (†)
Russian Federation	914 (8.9)	485 (5.7)	10.1	178 (2.1)	19 (0.3)	920 (8.7)	508 (7.1)	4.9	133 (2.0)	14 (0.3)
Slovenia	902 (10.6)	460 (3.4)	34.4	131 (1.8)	15 (0.3)	902 (5.9)	531 (2.5)	7.6	115 (1.0)	13 (0.1)
Sweden	901 (12.9)	431 (4.0)	14.1	141 (4.2)	16 (0.5)	920 (13.8)	455 (5.9)	14.3	106 (3.0)	12 (0.4)
United States[8]	1,111 (13.3)	485 (5.2)	11.4	156[7] (4.3)	14 (0.4)	1,132[7] (22.5)	437 (9.7)	4.8	162[11] (13.3)	14 (1.2)

†Not applicable.

[1]Because countries may have used two different school samples—one for advanced mathematics and one for physics—the total number of instructional hours per year for a particular country may be different in column 2 (based on the advanced mathematics sample) than in column 7 (based on the physics sample).

[2]Trends in International Mathematics and Science Study (TIMSS) Advanced scores are reported on a scale from 0 to 1,000, with the scale centerpoint set at 500 and the standard deviation set at 100.

[3]Columns 4 and 9 show final-year secondary school students who have taken or are taking the specified courses as a percentage of the age cohort that corresponds to the final year of secondary school in their country. The age cohort represents the entire population of the country that is about the same age as the average age of final-year secondary students (approximately 18 or 19 years old, depending on the country). In the United States, the cohort consists of the total population of 18-year-olds. For the United States, therefore, columns 4 and 9 show the percentage of all 18-year-olds who have taken the specified courses.

[4]Includes advanced mathematics courses covering topics in geometry, algebra, and calculus. In the United States, includes Advanced Placement (AP) calculus, International Baccalaureate (IB) mathematics, and state- and school-specific calculus courses.

[5]Includes physics courses covering topics in mechanics and thermodynamics, electricity and magnetism, and wave phenomena and atomic/nuclear physics. In the United States, includes AP physics, IB physics, and state- and school-specific second-year physics courses.

[6]The international average includes only education systems that are members of the International Association for the Evaluation of Educational Achievement (IAE), which develops and implements TIMSS at the international level. All nine of the education systems that participated in TIMSS Advanced are countries that are members of IAE.

[7]Data are available for at least 70 percent but less than 85 percent of students.

[8]Did not satisfy guidelines for sample participation rates.

[9]Met guidelines for sample participation rates only after replacement schools were included.

[10]Intensive courses are advanced mathematics courses that involve 6 or more hours per week. Results for students in these courses are reported separately from the results for other students from the Russian Federation taking courses that involve 4.5 hours per week.

[11]Data are available for at least 50 percent but less than 70 percent of students.

NOTE: Countries were required to draw probability samples of students in their final year of secondary school; in the United States, samples of 12th-graders were drawn. Instructional times shown in this table are actual or implemented times (as opposed to intended times prescribed by the curriculum). Principals reported total instructional hours per day and school days per year. Total instructional hours per year were calculated by multiplying the number of school days per year by the number of instructional hours per day. Teachers reported instructional hours per week in advanced mathematics and physics. Instructional hours per year in advanced mathematics and physics were calculated by dividing weekly instructional hours by the number of school days per week and then multiplying by the number of school days per year.

SOURCE: International Association for the Evaluation of Educational Achievement (IEA), Trends in International Mathematics and Science Study (TIMSS) Advanced, 2015. (This table was prepared January 2017.)

Table 602.40. Average reading literacy, mathematics literacy, and science literacy scores of 15-year-old students, by sex and country or other education system: Selected years, 2009 through 2018

[Standard errors appear in parentheses]

Country or other education system	Reading literacy						Mathematics literacy						Science literacy					
	2009	2012	2015	2018 Total	2018 Male	2018 Female	2009	2012	2015	2018 Total	2018 Male	2018 Female	2009	2012	2015	2018 Total	2018 Male	2018 Female
1	2	3	4	5	6	7	8	9	10	11	12	13	14	15	16	17	18	19
OECD average[1]	**490 (0.5)**	**493 (0.5)**	**490 (0.5)**	**487 (0.4)**	**472 (0.5)**	**502 (0.5)**	**492 (0.5)**	**490 (0.5)**	**487 (0.4)**	**489 (0.4)**	**492 (0.5)**	**487 (0.5)**	**498 (0.5)**	**498 (0.5)**	**491 (0.4)**	**489 (0.4)**	**488 (0.5)**	**490 (0.5)**
Australia	515 (2.3)	512 (1.6)	503 (1.7)	503 (1.6)	487 (2.2)	519 (2.0)	514 (2.5)	504 (1.6)	494 (1.6)	491 (1.9)	494 (2.4)	488 (2.5)	527 (2.5)	521 (1.8)	510 (1.5)	503 (1.8)	504 (2.4)	502 (2.0)
Austria	470 (2.9)	490 (2.8)	485 (2.8)	484 (2.7)	471 (3.7)	499 (3.7)	496 (2.7)	506 (2.7)	497 (2.9)	499 (3.0)	505 (3.9)	492 (3.8)	494 (3.2)	506 (2.7)	495 (2.4)	490 (2.8)	491 (3.8)	489 (3.3)
Belgium	506 (2.3)	509 (2.3)	499 (2.4)	493 (2.3)	482 (2.9)	504 (2.8)	515 (2.3)	515 (2.1)	507 (2.4)	508 (2.3)	514 (2.9)	502 (2.7)	507 (2.5)	505 (2.2)	502 (2.3)	499 (2.2)	501 (2.6)	496 (2.6)
Canada	524 (1.5)	523 (1.9)	527 (2.3)	520 (1.8)	506 (2.1)	535 (2.0)	527 (1.6)	518 (1.8)	516 (2.3)	512 (2.4)	514 (2.5)	510 (2.7)	529 (1.6)	525 (1.9)	528 (2.1)	518 (2.2)	516 (2.5)	520 (2.1)
Chile	449 (3.1)	441 (2.9)	459 (2.6)	452 (2.6)	442 (3.4)	462 (2.9)	421 (3.1)	423 (3.1)	423 (2.5)	417 (2.4)	421 (3.3)	414 (2.7)	447 (2.9)	445 (2.9)	447 (2.4)	444 (2.4)	445 (3.2)	442 (2.6)
Colombia	413 (3.7)	403 (3.4)	425 (2.9)	412 (3.3)	407 (4.0)	417 (3.3)	381 (3.2)	376 (2.9)	390 (2.3)	391 (3.0)	401 (3.8)	381 (3.1)	402 (3.6)	399 (3.1)	416 (2.4)	413 (3.1)	420 (3.8)	407 (2.9)
Czech Republic	478 (2.9)	493 (2.9)	487 (2.6)	490 (2.5)	474 (3.1)	507 (2.9)	493 (2.8)	499 (2.9)	492 (2.4)	499 (2.5)	501 (2.9)	498 (3.2)	500 (3.0)	508 (3.0)	493 (2.3)	497 (2.5)	496 (3.2)	498 (3.1)
Denmark	495 (2.1)	496 (2.6)	500 (2.5)	501 (1.8)	486 (2.3)	516 (2.3)	503 (2.6)	500 (2.3)	511 (2.2)	509 (1.7)	511 (2.3)	507 (2.3)	499 (2.5)	498 (2.7)	502 (2.4)	493 (1.9)	492 (2.5)	493 (2.2)
Estonia	501 (2.6)	516 (2.0)	519 (2.2)	523 (1.8)	508 (2.4)	538 (2.3)	512 (2.6)	521 (2.0)	520 (2.0)	523 (1.7)	524 (2.2)	519 (2.3)	528 (2.7)	541 (1.9)	534 (2.1)	530 (1.9)	528 (2.9)	533 (2.8)
Finland	536 (2.3)	524 (2.4)	526 (2.5)	520 (2.3)	495 (2.9)	546 (2.3)	541 (2.2)	519 (1.9)	511 (2.3)	507 (2.0)	504 (2.5)	510 (2.2)	554 (2.3)	545 (2.2)	531 (2.4)	522 (2.5)	510 (2.9)	534 (2.8)
France	496 (3.4)	505 (2.8)	499 (2.5)	493 (2.3)	480 (2.8)	505 (2.8)	497 (3.1)	495 (2.5)	493 (2.1)	495 (2.3)	499 (2.7)	492 (2.8)	498 (3.6)	499 (2.6)	495 (2.1)	493 (2.2)	493 (2.7)	493 (2.7)
Germany	497 (2.7)	508 (2.8)	509 (3.0)	498 (3.0)	486 (4.2)	512 (3.2)	513 (2.9)	514 (2.9)	506 (2.9)	500 (2.6)	503 (3.0)	496 (3.1)	520 (2.8)	524 (3.0)	509 (2.7)	503 (2.9)	502 (3.2)	504 (3.3)
Greece	483 (4.3)	477 (3.3)	467 (4.3)	457 (3.6)	437 (4.2)	479 (3.7)	466 (3.9)	453 (2.5)	454 (3.8)	451 (3.1)	446 (3.9)	455 (3.1)	470 (4.0)	467 (3.1)	455 (3.9)	452 (3.1)	446 (3.9)	458 (3.6)
Hungary	494 (3.2)	488 (3.2)	470 (2.7)	476 (2.3)	463 (2.8)	489 (3.2)	490 (3.5)	477 (3.2)	477 (2.5)	481 (2.3)	486 (3.0)	477 (3.2)	503 (3.1)	494 (2.9)	477 (2.4)	481 (2.3)	484 (3.1)	479 (3.1)
Iceland	500 (1.4)	483 (1.8)	482 (2.0)	474 (1.7)	454 (2.5)	494 (2.6)	507 (1.4)	493 (1.7)	488 (2.0)	495 (2.0)	490 (2.5)	500 (2.9)	496 (1.4)	478 (2.1)	473 (1.7)	475 (1.8)	471 (2.3)	479 (2.8)
Ireland	496 (3.0)	523 (2.6)	521 (2.5)	518 (2.2)	506 (3.0)	530 (2.5)	487 (2.5)	501 (2.2)	504 (2.1)	500 (2.2)	503 (2.9)	497 (2.7)	508 (3.3)	522 (2.5)	503 (2.4)	496 (2.2)	495 (3.0)	497 (2.6)
Israel	474 (3.6)	486 (5.0)	479 (3.8)	470 (3.7)	445 (5.6)	493 (3.7)	447 (3.3)	466 (4.7)	470 (3.6)	463 (3.5)	458 (5.2)	467 (3.5)	455 (3.1)	470 (5.0)	467 (3.4)	462 (3.6)	452 (5.3)	471 (3.1)
Italy	486 (1.6)	490 (2.0)	485 (2.7)	476 (2.4)	464 (3.1)	489 (2.7)	483 (1.9)	485 (2.0)	490 (2.8)	487 (2.8)	494 (3.4)	480 (2.7)	489 (1.8)	494 (1.9)	481 (2.5)	468 (2.4)	475 (3.1)	461 (2.6)
Japan	520 (3.5)	538 (3.7)	516 (3.2)	504 (2.7)	493 (3.8)	514 (3.0)	529 (3.3)	536 (3.6)	532 (3.0)	527 (2.5)	532 (3.4)	522 (2.9)	539 (3.4)	547 (3.6)	538 (3.0)	529 (2.6)	531 (3.5)	528 (3.0)
Korea, Republic of	539 (3.5)	536 (3.9)	517 (3.5)	514 (2.9)	503 (4.0)	526 (3.6)	546 (4.0)	554 (4.6)	524 (3.7)	526 (3.1)	528 (4.1)	524 (4.0)	538 (3.4)	538 (3.7)	516 (3.1)	519 (2.8)	521 (3.9)	517 (3.6)
Latvia	484 (3.0)	489 (2.4)	488 (1.8)	479 (1.6)	462 (2.8)	495 (1.8)	482 (3.1)	491 (2.8)	482 (1.9)	496 (2.0)	500 (2.2)	493 (2.5)	494 (3.1)	502 (2.8)	490 (1.6)	487 (1.8)	483 (2.2)	491 (2.4)
Lithuania	468 (2.4)	477 (2.5)	472 (2.7)	476 (1.5)	457 (1.8)	496 (1.6)	477 (2.6)	479 (2.6)	478 (2.3)	481 (2.0)	480 (2.4)	482 (2.1)	491 (2.9)	496 (2.6)	475 (2.7)	482 (1.6)	479 (2.7)	485 (1.9)
Luxembourg	472 (1.3)	488 (1.5)	481 (1.4)	470 (1.1)	456 (1.5)	485 (1.6)	489 (1.2)	490 (1.1)	486 (1.3)	483 (1.1)	487 (1.5)	480 (1.7)	484 (1.2)	491 (1.3)	483 (1.1)	477 (1.2)	475 (1.7)	479 (1.7)
Mexico	425 (2.0)	424 (1.5)	423 (2.6)	420 (2.7)	415 (3.5)	426 (3.0)	419 (1.8)	413 (1.4)	408 (2.2)	409 (2.5)	415 (2.9)	403 (2.7)	416 (1.8)	415 (1.3)	416 (2.1)	419 (2.6)	419 (2.8)	415 (3.6)
Netherlands	508 (5.1)	511 (3.5)	503 (2.4)	485 (2.7)	470 (3.5)	499 (2.6)	526 (4.7)	523 (3.5)	512 (2.2)	519 (2.6)	520 (3.5)	519 (2.7)	522 (5.4)	522 (3.5)	509 (2.3)	503 (2.8)	499 (3.6)	508 (3.1)
New Zealand	521 (2.4)	512 (2.4)	509 (2.4)	506 (2.0)	491 (2.7)	520 (2.7)	519 (2.3)	500 (2.2)	495 (2.3)	494 (1.7)	497 (2.5)	490 (2.3)	532 (2.6)	516 (2.1)	513 (2.4)	508 (2.1)	509 (2.9)	508 (2.8)
Norway	503 (2.6)	504 (3.2)	513 (2.5)	499 (2.2)	476 (2.6)	523 (2.6)	498 (2.4)	489 (2.7)	502 (2.2)	501 (2.2)	497 (2.9)	505 (2.6)	500 (2.6)	495 (3.1)	498 (2.3)	490 (2.3)	485 (3.2)	496 (2.5)
Poland	500 (2.6)	518 (3.1)	506 (2.5)	512 (2.7)	495 (3.0)	528 (2.9)	495 (2.8)	518 (3.6)	504 (2.4)	516 (2.6)	516 (2.9)	515 (3.1)	508 (2.4)	526 (3.1)	501 (2.5)	511 (2.6)	511 (2.8)	511 (3.5)
Portugal	489 (3.1)	488 (3.8)	498 (2.7)	492 (2.4)	480 (2.8)	504 (2.4)	487 (2.9)	487 (3.8)	492 (2.5)	492 (2.6)	497 (3.0)	488 (3.1)	493 (2.9)	489 (3.7)	501 (2.4)	492 (2.8)	494 (3.0)	489 (3.3)
Slovak Republic	477 (2.5)	463 (4.2)	453 (2.8)	458 (2.2)	441 (2.7)	475 (2.7)	497 (3.1)	482 (3.4)	475 (2.7)	486 (2.6)	488 (3.2)	484 (3.2)	490 (3.0)	471 (3.6)	461 (2.6)	464 (2.3)	461 (3.0)	467 (3.0)
Slovenia	483 (1.0)	481 (1.2)	505 (1.5)	495 (1.2)	475 (1.7)	517 (1.9)	501 (1.2)	501 (1.2)	510 (1.3)	509 (1.4)	509 (1.9)	509 (1.8)	512 (1.1)	514 (1.3)	513 (1.3)	507 (1.3)	502 (2.0)	511 (1.8)
Spain	481 (2.0)	488 (1.9)	496 (2.4)	— (†)	— (†)	— (†)	483 (2.1)	484 (1.9)	486 (2.2)	481 (1.5)	485 (2.1)	478 (1.5)	488 (2.1)	496 (1.8)	493 (2.1)	483 (1.6)	484 (1.9)	482 (1.8)
Sweden	497 (2.9)	483 (3.0)	500 (3.5)	506 (3.0)	489 (3.4)	523 (3.4)	494 (2.9)	478 (2.3)	494 (3.2)	502 (2.7)	502 (3.1)	503 (3.5)	495 (2.7)	485 (3.0)	493 (3.6)	499 (3.1)	496 (3.2)	503 (3.7)
Switzerland	501 (2.4)	509 (2.6)	492 (3.0)	484 (3.1)	469 (3.2)	500 (3.2)	534 (3.3)	531 (3.0)	521 (2.9)	515 (3.0)	519 (3.0)	511 (3.5)	517 (2.8)	515 (2.7)	506 (2.9)	495 (3.0)	493 (3.3)	495 (3.1)
Turkey	464 (3.5)	475 (4.2)	428 (4.0)	466 (2.2)	453 (3.0)	478 (2.7)	445 (4.4)	448 (4.8)	420 (4.1)	454 (2.3)	456 (3.2)	451 (2.9)	454 (3.6)	463 (3.9)	425 (3.9)	468 (2.0)	465 (2.9)	472 (2.5)
United Kingdom	494 (2.3)	499 (3.5)	498 (2.8)	504 (2.6)	494 (3.2)	514 (3.1)	492 (2.4)	494 (3.3)	492 (2.5)	502 (2.6)	509 (3.1)	496 (3.0)	514 (2.5)	514 (3.4)	509 (2.6)	505 (2.6)	506 (3.1)	503 (3.2)
United States	500 (3.7)	498 (3.7)	497 (3.4)	505 (3.6)	494 (4.2)	517 (3.6)	487 (3.6)	481 (3.6)	470 (3.2)	478 (3.2)	482 (3.9)	474 (3.3)	502 (3.6)	497 (3.8)	496 (3.2)	502 (3.3)	503 (3.9)	502 (3.5)
Non-OECD education systems																		
Albania	385 (4.0)	394 (3.2)	405 (4.1)	405 (1.9)	387 (2.2)	425 (2.2)	377 (4.0)	394 (2.0)	413 (3.4)	437 (2.4)	435 (2.8)	440 (2.7)	391 (3.9)	397 (2.4)	427 (3.3)	417 (2.0)	409 (2.5)	425 (2.0)
Algeria	— (†)	— (†)	350 (3.0)	— (†)	— (†)	— (†)	— (†)	— (†)	360 (3.0)	— (†)	— (†)	— (†)	— (†)	— (†)	376 (2.6)	— (†)	— (†)	— (†)
Argentina[2]	398 (4.6)	396 (3.7)	425 (3.2)	402 (3.0)	393 (3.4)	409 (3.1)	388 (4.1)	388 (3.5)	409 (3.1)	379 (2.8)	387 (3.2)	372 (2.7)	401 (4.6)	406 (3.9)	432 (2.9)	404 (2.9)	409 (3.3)	399 (3.3)
Baku (Azerbaijan)	— (†)	— (†)	— (†)	389 (2.5)	377 (2.6)	403 (2.8)	— (†)	— (†)	— (†)	420 (2.8)	423 (3.1)	416 (3.2)	— (†)	— (†)	— (†)	398 (2.4)	395 (2.7)	400 (2.6)
Beijing, Shanghai, Jiangsu, Zhejiang (China)	— (†)	— (†)	— (†)	555 (2.7)	549 (3.1)	562 (2.8)	— (†)	— (†)	— (†)	591 (2.5)	597 (2.9)	586 (2.6)	— (†)	— (†)	— (†)	590 (2.7)	596 (2.9)	584 (2.9)

See notes at end of table.

Table 602.40. Average reading literacy, mathematics literacy, and science literacy scores of 15-year-old students, by sex and country or other education system: Selected years, 2009 through 2018—Continued

[Standard errors appear in parentheses]

Country or other education system	Reading literacy 2009	2012	2015	2018 Total	2018 Male	2018 Female	Mathematics literacy 2009	2012	2015	2018 Total	2018 Male	2018 Female	Science literacy 2009	2012	2015	2018 Total	2018 Male	2018 Female
1	2	3	4	5	6	7	8	9	10	11	12	13	14	15	16	17	18	19
Belarus	—	(†)	(†)	474 (2.4)	463 (2.8)	486 (2.8)	—	(†)	(†)	472 (2.7)	475 (3.2)	469 (3.1)	—	(†)	(†)	471 (2.4)	473 (3.0)	470 (2.8)
Bosnia and Herzegovina	—	(†)	(†)	403 (2.9)	389 (2.9)	418 (3.5)	—	(†)	(†)	406 (3.1)	408 (3.3)	405 (3.7)	—	(†)	(†)	398 (2.7)	398 (3.1)	399 (3.3)
Brazil	412 (2.7)	407 (2.0)	407 (2.8)	413 (2.1)	400 (2.5)	426 (2.2)	386 (2.4)	389 (1.9)	377 (2.9)	384 (2.0)	388 (2.6)	379 (2.0)	405 (2.4)	402 (2.1)	401 (2.3)	404 (2.1)	403 (2.5)	404 (3.0)
Brunei Darussalam	—	(†)	(†)	408 (0.9)	393 (1.2)	423 (1.2)	—	(†)	(†)	430 (1.2)	426 (1.7)	434 (1.3)	—	(†)	(†)	431 (1.2)	427 (1.6)	435 (1.6)
Bulgaria	429 (6.7)	436 (6.0)	432 (5.0)	420 (3.9)	401 (4.8)	441 (4.1)	428 (5.9)	439 (4.0)	441 (4.0)	436 (3.8)	435 (4.9)	437 (3.9)	439 (5.9)	446 (4.8)	446 (4.4)	424 (3.6)	417 (4.5)	432 (3.8)
Chinese Taipei	476 (2.9)	441 (3.5)	427 (2.6)	426 (3.4)	419 (3.1)	434 (4.3)	460 (3.1)	407 (3.5)	437 (1.7)	402 (3.3)	411 (3.1)	394 (4.5)	420 (2.1)	429 (2.9)	433 (2.5)	416 (3.3)	420 (3.0)	411 (4.3)
Costa Rica	—	485 (3.3)	487 (2.9)	479 (2.7)	462 (3.3)	495 (2.4)	460 (3.1)	471 (3.5)	437 (1.7)	464 (2.5)	469 (3.0)	460 (3.0)	475 (2.5)	491 (3.1)	475 (2.5)	472 (2.8)	470 (3.5)	474 (3.4)
Croatia	—	449 (1.2)	443 (1.7)	424 (1.4)	401 (1.8)	448 (1.8)	440 (1.1)	440 (1.1)	437 (1.7)	451 (1.4)	447 (1.9)	455 (1.7)	433 (1.4)	438 (1.2)	433 (1.4)	439 (1.4)	429 (2.1)	450 (1.9)
Cyprus	—	(†)	358 (3.1)	342 (1.0)	326 (1.1)	357 (1.9)	—	(†)	328 (2.8)	325 (2.6)	324 (3.0)	327 (2.3)	332 (2.6)	—	332 (2.6)	336 (2.5)	331 (2.1)	340 (2.7)
Dominican Republic	—	(†)	401 (3.1)	380 (2.2)	362 (2.6)	399 (2.4)	—	(†)	404 (2.8)	398 (2.6)	396 (3.3)	400 (2.6)	411 (2.4)	—	411 (2.4)	383 (2.3)	376 (2.9)	390 (2.6)
Georgia	533 (2.1)	545 (2.8)	527 (2.7)	524 (2.7)	507 (3.5)	542 (2.8)	555 (2.7)	561 (3.2)	548 (3.0)	551 (3.0)	548 (3.6)	554 (3.4)	549 (2.8)	555 (2.6)	523 (2.5)	517 (2.5)	512 (3.4)	521 (2.8)
Hong Kong (China)	402 (3.7)	396 (4.2)	397 (2.9)	371 (2.6)	358 (3.2)	383 (2.7)	371 (3.7)	375 (4.0)	386 (3.1)	379 (3.1)	374 (3.6)	383 (3.5)	383 (3.8)	382 (3.1)	403 (2.6)	396 (2.4)	393 (2.9)	399 (2.5)
Indonesia	405 (3.3)	399 (3.6)	408 (2.9)	419 (2.5)	393 (5.0)	444 (2.5)	387 (3.0)	386 (3.1)	380 (2.7)	400 (3.3)	397 (5.2)	403 (3.1)	415 (3.5)	409 (3.1)	409 (2.7)	439 (1.4)	414 (4.9)	444 (3.0)
Jordan	390 (3.1)	393 (2.7)	427 (3.4)	387 (2.9)	374 (1.7)	401 (1.6)	405 (3.7)	432 (3.1)	460 (4.3)	366 (1.9)	368 (2.0)	364 (2.0)	400 (3.1)	425 (3.0)	456 (3.7)	397 (1.7)	394 (2.0)	401 (2.1)
Kazakhstan[2]	—	(†)	347 (1.6)	353 (1.1)	340 (1.5)	366 (1.5)	—	(†)	362 (1.6)	366 (1.5)	368 (2.1)	364 (1.9)	—	(†)	378 (1.7)	365 (1.2)	362 (1.8)	368 (1.4)
Kosovo	—	(†)	347 (4.4)	353 (4.3)	338 (5.0)	366 (4.4)	—	(†)	396 (3.7)	393 (4.0)	394 (5.0)	393 (4.0)	—	(†)	386 (3.4)	384 (3.5)	381 (4.2)	386 (3.6)
Lebanon	487 (0.9)	509 (0.9)	509 (1.3)	525 (1.2)	514 (1.9)	536 (1.8)	525 (0.9)	538 (1.0)	544 (1.1)	558 (1.5)	560 (2.2)	556 (2.2)	511 (1.0)	521 (0.8)	529 (1.1)	544 (1.5)	543 (2.1)	545 (2.0)
Macao (China)	—	398 (3.3)	431 (1.8)	415 (0.9)	402 (3.1)	428 (3.3)	—	421 (1.2)	446 (3.3)	437 (2.9)	437 (3.5)	443 (3.0)	—	420 (3.0)	443 (3.0)	438 (1.5)	434 (2.1)	441 (3.2)
Malaysia[2]	—	(†)	447 (1.8)	448 (1.7)	425 (2.4)	474 (2.4)	—	(†)	479 (1.7)	472 (1.9)	466 (2.4)	478 (2.7)	—	(†)	465 (1.6)	457 (1.9)	447 (2.4)	468 (2.5)
Malta	—	(†)	416 (2.5)	424 (2.4)	404 (2.6)	445 (2.7)	—	(†)	420 (2.5)	421 (2.4)	420 (2.7)	422 (2.9)	—	(†)	428 (2.0)	428 (2.3)	423 (2.6)	434 (2.8)
Moldova, Republic of	408 (1.7)	422 (1.2)	427 (1.6)	421 (1.1)	407 (1.6)	437 (1.2)	403 (2.0)	410 (1.1)	418 (1.5)	430 (1.2)	434 (1.9)	425 (2.2)	401 (2.0)	410 (1.1)	411 (1.0)	415 (1.3)	413 (1.9)	418 (1.6)
Montenegro, Republic of	—	(†)	(†)	359 (3.3)	347 (3.4)	373 (3.5)	—	(†)	(†)	368 (3.3)	368 (3.7)	367 (3.4)	—	(†)	(†)	377 (3.2)	372 (3.1)	381 (3.3)
Morocco	—	(†)	(†)	359 (3.1)	347 (3.2)	373 (3.1)	—	(†)	(†)	368 (3.3)	368 (3.7)	367 (3.4)	—	(†)	384 (1.2)	377 (3.0)	372 (3.1)	381 (3.3)
North Macedonia	—	352 (1.4)	352 (1.4)	393 (1.1)	368 (1.5)	420 (1.7)	371 (1.3)	445 (3.8)	371 (1.3)	394 (1.6)	391 (1.9)	398 (2.1)	413 (1.4)	—	384 (1.2)	413 (1.4)	404 (2.2)	423 (2.0)
Panama	‡	—	—	377 (3.0)	370 (3.4)	384 (3.1)	‡	—	—	353 (2.7)	357 (3.4)	349 (3.0)	‡	—	—	365 (2.3)	364 (2.6)	365 (3.2)
Peru	370 (4.0)	384 (4.3)	398 (2.9)	401 (3.0)	395 (3.4)	406 (3.2)	365 (4.0)	368 (3.7)	387 (2.7)	400 (2.6)	408 (3.3)	392 (3.2)	369 (3.5)	373 (3.6)	397 (2.4)	404 (2.7)	411 (3.2)	397 (2.7)
Philippines	(†)	(†)	(†)	340 (3.3)	325 (3.4)	352 (3.5)	(†)	(†)	(†)	353 (3.5)	346 (4.0)	358 (3.7)	(†)	(†)	(†)	357 (3.2)	355 (3.4)	359 (3.7)
Qatar	372 (0.8)	388 (0.8)	402 (1.0)	407 (0.8)	375 (1.1)	440 (1.1)	368 (0.7)	376 (0.8)	402 (1.3)	414 (1.2)	402 (1.4)	426 (1.5)	379 (0.9)	384 (0.7)	418 (1.0)	419 (0.9)	400 (3.1)	439 (1.5)
Romania	424 (4.1)	438 (4.0)	434 (4.1)	428 (5.1)	411 (4.9)	445 (5.6)	427 (3.4)	445 (3.8)	444 (3.8)	430 (4.9)	432 (4.9)	427 (5.6)	428 (3.4)	439 (3.3)	426 (3.2)	426 (4.6)	425 (4.6)	426 (5.2)
Russian Federation	459 (3.3)	475 (3.0)	495 (3.1)	479 (3.1)	466 (3.2)	491 (3.3)	468 (3.3)	482 (3.0)	494 (3.1)	488 (3.0)	490 (3.2)	485 (3.0)	478 (3.3)	486 (2.9)	487 (2.9)	478 (2.9)	477 (3.0)	478 (3.2)
Saudi Arabia	(†)	(†)	(†)	399 (3.0)	373 (4.0)	427 (3.3)	(†)	(†)	(†)	373 (3.0)	367 (3.8)	380 (4.0)	(†)	(†)	(†)	386 (2.8)	372 (3.9)	401 (3.4)
Serbia, Republic of	(†)	(†)	(†)	439 (3.3)	422 (3.7)	458 (3.5)	(†)	(†)	(†)	448 (3.2)	450 (3.9)	447 (3.4)	(†)	(†)	(†)	440 (3.0)	437 (3.4)	442 (3.4)
Singapore	526 (1.1)	542 (1.4)	535 (3.3)	549 (1.6)	538 (2.0)	561 (1.9)	562 (1.4)	573 (1.3)	564 (1.5)	569 (1.6)	571 (1.6)	567 (2.3)	542 (1.4)	551 (1.5)	556 (1.2)	551 (1.5)	553 (2.0)	549 (1.9)
Thailand	421 (2.6)	441 (3.1)	409 (3.3)	393 (3.2)	372 (4.2)	411 (3.4)	419 (3.2)	427 (3.4)	415 (3.0)	419 (3.4)	410 (4.9)	426 (3.7)	425 (3.0)	444 (2.9)	421 (2.8)	426 (3.2)	415 (4.3)	435 (3.6)
Trinidad and Tobago	416 (1.2)	(†)	427 (1.5)	—	(†)	(†)	414 (1.3)	(†)	417 (1.4)	—	(†)	(†)	410 (1.2)	(†)	425 (1.4)	—	(†)	(†)
Tunisia	404 (2.9)	404 (4.5)	361 (3.1)	—	(†)	(†)	371 (3.0)	388 (3.9)	367 (3.0)	367 (3.0)	—	367 (4.0)	401 (2.7)	398 (3.5)	386 (2.1)	—	(†)	(†)
Ukraine	(†)	(†)	(†)	466 (3.1)	450 (4.2)	484 (3.6)	(†)	(†)	(†)	453 (3.6)	456 (4.3)	449 (3.9)	(†)	(†)	(†)	469 (3.3)	470 (3.9)	468 (3.6)
United Arab Emirates	—	442 (2.5)	434 (2.9)	432 (2.3)	413 (4.2)	460 (3.6)	—	434 (2.4)	427 (2.4)	435 (2.1)	430 (2.4)	439 (2.8)	—	448 (2.8)	437 (2.4)	434 (2.0)	420 (2.1)	447 (2.8)
Uruguay	426 (2.6)	411 (3.2)	437 (2.5)	427 (2.8)	415 (3.3)	438 (3.0)	427 (2.6)	409 (2.8)	418 (2.5)	418 (2.6)	422 (3.3)	414 (3.0)	427 (2.6)	416 (2.8)	435 (2.2)	426 (2.5)	428 (3.2)	424 (2.7)
Vietnam	(†)	508 (4.4)	487 (3.7)	—	(†)	(†)	(†)	511 (4.8)	495 (4.5)	—	(†)	(†)	(†)	528 (4.3)	525 (3.9)	—	(†)	(†)

—Not available.
†Not applicable.
‡Reporting standards not met.
[1]Refers to the mean of the data values for all Organization for Economic Cooperation and Development (OECD) countries, to which each country contributes equally regardless of the absolute size of the student population of each country.

[2]In 2015, coverage is too small to ensure comparability.

NOTE: Program for International Student Assessment (PISA) scores are reported on a scale from 0 to 1,000.
SOURCE: Organization for Economic Cooperation and Development (OECD), Program for International Student Assessment (PISA), selected years, 2009 through 2018; retrieved December 18, 2019, from https://pisadataexplorer.oecd.org/ide/idepisa/. (This table was prepared December 2019.)

Table 602.50. Average reading literacy scores of 15-year-old students and percentage attaining reading literacy proficiency levels, by country or other education system: 2018

[Standard errors appear in parentheses]

Country or other education system	Average reading literacy score[1]	Percentage attaining reading literacy proficiency levels[2]										
		Below level 2					At level 2	At level 3	At level 4	At or above level 5		
		Total below level 2	Below level 1c	At level 1c	At level 1b	At level 1a				Total at or above level 5	At level 5	At level 6
1	2	3	4	5	6	7	8	9	10	11	12	13
OECD average[3]	**487 (0.4)**	**22.6 (0.16)**	**0.1 (0.01)**	**1.4 (0.04)**	**6.2 (0.09)**	**15.0 (0.12)**	**23.7 (0.13)**	**26.0 (0.14)**	**18.9 (0.12)**	**8.7 (0.10)**	**7.4 (0.09)**	**1.3 (0.04)**
Australia	503 (1.6)	19.6 (0.50)	0.1!! (0.06)	1.4 (0.15)	5.6 (0.29)	12.5 (0.36)	21.1 (0.48)	25.4 (0.51)	20.9 (0.49)	13.0 (0.46)	10.3 (0.36)	2.7 (0.21)
Austria	484 (2.7)	23.6 (1.02)	#!! (†)	0.9 (0.19)	6.4 (0.57)	16.3 (0.84)	23.5 (0.83)	26.2 (0.87)	19.3 (0.78)	7.4 (0.50)	6.7 (0.47)	0.7 (0.13)
Belgium	493 (2.3)	21.3 (0.88)	0.1!! (0.05)	1.2 (0.19)	6.0 (0.43)	14.0 (0.62)	22.4 (0.66)	26.5 (0.68)	20.4 (0.71)	9.5 (0.53)	8.3 (0.49)	1.3 (0.20)
Canada	520 (1.8)	13.8 (0.49)	#!! (†)	1.2 (0.11)	3.1 (0.20)	10.0 (0.39)	20.1 (0.57)	27.2 (0.46)	24.0 (0.51)	15.0 (0.55)	12.2 (0.46)	2.8 (0.23)
Chile	452 (2.6)	31.7 (1.20)	0.1!! (0.09)	1.7 (0.24)	8.9 (0.62)	21.0 (0.90)	29.5 (0.86)	24.4 (0.86)	11.8 (0.60)	2.6 (0.30)	2.4 (0.28)	0.2! (0.07)
Colombia[4]	412 (3.3)	49.9 (1.71)	0.2! (0.08)	3.6 (0.45)	15.8 (0.93)	30.3 (1.03)	27.7 (0.99)	15.8 (0.85)	5.7 (0.55)	0.9 (0.18)	0.9 (0.18)	#!! (†)
Czech Republic	490 (2.5)	20.7 (1.12)	0.1!! (0.06)	0.7 (0.21)	5.0 (0.54)	11.9 (0.78)	25.0 (0.87)	26.9 (0.90)	19.1 (0.78)	8.2 (0.54)	7.2 (0.48)	1.1 (0.19)
Denmark	501 (1.8)	16.0 (0.68)	#!! (†)	0.5 (0.10)	3.5 (0.31)	11.9 (0.54)	23.9 (0.80)	30.1 (0.89)	21.6 (0.80)	8.4 (0.51)	7.3 (0.48)	1.1 (0.20)
Estonia	523 (1.8)	11.1 (0.59)	#!! (†)	0.3! (0.10)	2.1 (0.23)	8.7 (0.50)	21.2 (0.86)	29.9 (0.87)	24.0 (0.80)	13.9 (0.70)	11.1 (0.57)	2.8 (0.32)
Finland	520 (2.3)	13.5 (0.71)	#!! (†)	0.8 (0.16)	3.3 (0.38)	9.4 (0.57)	19.2 (0.70)	27.6 (0.81)	25.4 (0.78)	14.2 (0.72)	11.9 (0.67)	2.4 (0.33)
France	493 (2.3)	20.9 (0.74)	#!! (†)	1.1 (0.17)	5.7 (0.43)	14.0 (0.65)	22.8 (0.82)	26.6 (0.85)	20.5 (0.71)	9.2 (0.70)	8.1 (0.62)	1.1 (0.19)
Germany	498 (3.0)	20.7 (1.05)	0.1!! (0.05)	1.3 (0.26)	5.7 (0.51)	13.6 (0.84)	21.1 (0.81)	25.4 (0.75)	21.5 (0.87)	11.3 (0.69)	9.5 (0.60)	1.8 (0.23)
Greece	457 (3.6)	30.5 (1.51)	0.1!! (0.07)	2.1 (0.33)	9.3 (0.75)	19.0 (0.90)	27.3 (0.79)	25.2 (1.04)	13.3 (0.80)	3.7 (0.50)	3.3 (0.44)	0.3! (0.11)
Hungary	476 (2.3)	25.3 (0.91)	#!! (†)	1.2 (0.23)	7.0 (0.62)	17.0 (0.77)	25.2 (0.87)	26.3 (0.93)	17.5 (0.79)	5.7 (0.54)	5.2 (0.48)	0.5 (0.15)
Iceland	474 (1.7)	26.4 (0.86)	0.1!! (0.08)	2.3 (0.35)	8.0 (0.72)	15.9 (0.85)	24.6 (0.95)	25.1 (0.85)	16.9 (0.73)	7.1 (0.57)	6.2 (0.58)	0.9 (0.23)
Ireland	518 (2.2)	11.8 (0.67)	#!! (†)	0.2! (0.08)	2.1 (0.27)	9.5 (0.60)	21.7 (0.82)	30.3 (0.86)	24.1 (0.79)	12.1 (0.67)	10.3 (0.58)	1.8 (0.27)
Israel	470 (3.7)	31.1 (1.30)	0.7 (0.19)	5.0 (0.51)	10.4 (0.67)	15.0 (0.85)	19.4 (0.74)	21.6 (0.79)	17.5 (0.87)	10.4 (0.66)	8.4 (0.55)	2.0 (0.28)
Italy	476 (2.4)	23.3 (0.97)	0.1!! (0.07)	1.7 (0.27)	6.7 (0.58)	14.8 (0.71)	26.3 (0.88)	28.2 (0.94)	16.9 (0.71)	5.3 (0.48)	4.9 (0.43)	0.5 (0.13)
Japan	504 (2.7)	16.8 (0.96)	0.1!! (0.04)	0.7 (0.16)	4.1 (0.43)	12.0 (0.66)	21.9 (0.85)	28.6 (0.95)	21.9 (0.76)	10.3 (0.72)	8.6 (0.63)	1.7 (0.26)
Korea, Republic of	514 (2.9)	15.1 (0.91)	0.1!! (0.06)	1.1 (0.20)	4.3 (0.38)	9.6 (0.66)	19.6 (0.69)	27.6 (0.80)	24.6 (0.82)	13.1 (0.87)	10.8 (0.65)	2.3 (0.36)
Latvia	479 (1.6)	22.4 (0.75)	#!! (†)	0.6 (0.14)	5.2 (0.44)	16.6 (0.61)	27.4 (0.85)	28.8 (0.84)	16.6 (0.73)	4.8 (0.43)	4.4 (0.43)	0.4! (0.14)
Lithuania	476 (1.5)	24.4 (0.75)	0.1!! (0.05)	1.0 (0.20)	6.3 (0.42)	17.6 (0.59)	26.1 (0.75)	27.7 (0.74)	16.9 (0.58)	5.0 (0.37)	4.5 (0.37)	0.4 (0.11)
Luxembourg	470 (1.1)	29.3 (0.57)	0.2!! (0.09)	2.4 (0.23)	9.2 (0.44)	17.6 (0.59)	23.7 (0.67)	23.5 (0.74)	15.9 (0.62)	7.6 (0.49)	6.4 (0.44)	1.3 (0.18)
Mexico[4]	420 (2.7)	44.7 (1.33)	#!! (†)	2.5 (0.40)	13.1 (0.79)	29.1 (1.10)	31.7 (1.00)	17.5 (0.88)	5.3 (0.64)	0.8 (0.19)	0.7 (0.19)	#!! (†)
Netherlands[5]	485 (2.7)	24.1 (1.03)	0.1!! (0.08)	1.3 (0.25)	7.0 (0.59)	15.6 (0.72)	23.7 (0.81)	24.3 (1.05)	18.8 (0.84)	9.1 (0.61)	7.9 (0.57)	1.2 (0.22)
New Zealand	506 (2.0)	19.0 (0.79)	0.1!! (0.05)	1.0 (0.19)	5.2 (0.48)	12.7 (0.62)	20.8 (0.73)	24.6 (0.71)	22.5 (0.71)	13.1 (0.61)	10.7 (0.58)	2.4 (0.32)
Norway	499 (2.2)	19.3 (0.77)	0.1 (0.05)	1.7 (0.20)	5.6 (0.42)	11.9 (0.56)	21.5 (0.72)	26.4 (0.88)	21.6 (0.81)	11.3 (0.60)	9.6 (0.57)	1.6 (0.24)
Poland	512 (2.7)	14.7 (0.75)	#!! (†)	0.5 (0.14)	3.3 (0.34)	10.8 (0.65)	22.4 (0.77)	27.7 (0.79)	23.0 (0.82)	12.2 (0.84)	10.1 (0.71)	2.1 (0.34)
Portugal[6]	492 (2.4)	20.2 (0.92)	#!! (†)	0.9 (0.18)	5.0 (0.49)	14.3 (0.69)	23.3 (0.74)	28.2 (0.84)	21.0 (0.88)	7.3 (0.63)	6.5 (0.61)	0.8 (0.17)
Slovak Republic	458 (2.2)	31.4 (0.98)	0.1!! (0.08)	2.3 (0.34)	9.2 (0.68)	19.8 (0.78)	26.9 (0.91)	23.5 (0.95)	13.6 (0.69)	4.6 (0.41)	4.1 (0.36)	0.5! (0.15)
Slovenia	495 (1.2)	17.9 (0.66)	#!! (†)	0.6 (0.16)	4.3 (0.39)	12.9 (0.54)	24.5 (0.75)	29.5 (0.88)	20.3 (0.68)	7.8 (0.46)	6.8 (0.47)	1.0 (0.22)
Spain[7]	— (†)	— (†)	— (†)	— (†)	— (†)	— (†)	— (†)	— (†)	— (†)	— (†)	— (†)	— (†)
Sweden	506 (3.0)	18.4 (1.03)	0.2! (0.07)	1.5 (0.20)	5.1 (0.50)	11.6 (0.72)	20.6 (0.76)	25.5 (0.75)	22.3 (0.81)	13.3 (0.73)	10.9 (0.68)	2.4 (0.27)
Switzerland	484 (3.1)	23.6 (1.08)	0.1!! (0.06)	1.3 (0.26)	7.1 (0.59)	15.1 (0.74)	23.4 (0.95)	26.3 (0.83)	18.5 (0.76)	8.1 (0.68)	6.9 (0.64)	1.2 (0.24)
Turkey[4]	466 (2.2)	26.1 (1.05)	#!! (†)	0.7 (0.17)	6.3 (0.61)	19.1 (0.72)	30.2 (0.88)	26.9 (0.98)	13.5 (0.60)	3.3 (0.50)	3.1 (0.46)	0.2! (0.09)
United Kingdom	504 (2.6)	17.3 (0.89)	#!! (†)	0.8 (0.16)	4.2 (0.39)	12.3 (0.68)	23.0 (0.72)	27.2 (0.67)	21.0 (0.82)	11.5 (0.76)	9.5 (0.63)	2.0 (0.24)
United States[5]	505 (3.6)	19.3 (1.11)	0.1!! (0.05)	1.1 (0.25)	5.4 (0.47)	12.7 (0.76)	21.1 (0.80)	24.7 (0.77)	21.4 (0.84)	13.5 (0.86)	10.7 (0.72)	2.8 (0.36)
Non-OECD education systems												
Albania	405 (1.9)	52.2 (1.09)	0.1!! (0.08)	2.9 (0.30)	16.4 (0.73)	32.8 (0.94)	29.9 (0.78)	14.0 (0.71)	3.5 (0.36)	0.4 (0.10)	0.4 (0.10)	#!! (†)
Algeria	402 (3.0)	52.1 (1.35)	1.3 (0.23)	6.7 (0.57)	17.4 (0.73)	26.7 (0.87)	25.7 (0.82)	16.2 (0.70)	5.3 (0.46)	0.7 (0.16)	0.7 (0.15)	#!! (†)
Baku (Azerbaijan)[8]	389 (2.5)	60.4 (1.30)	0.1 (0.06)	3.7 (0.36)	19.6 (0.81)	37.0 (1.07)	28.6 (0.87)	9.2 (0.64)	1.6 (0.41)	0.1!! (0.12)	0.1!! (0.11)	#!! (†)
Beijing, Shanghai, Jiangsu, Guangdong (China)	555 (2.7)	5.2 (0.61)	#!! (†)	0.1!! (0.06)	0.7 (0.16)	4.3 (0.53)	14.3 (0.83)	27.9 (0.97)	30.8 (0.97)	21.7 (1.11)	17.5 (0.88)	4.2 (0.58)
Belarus	474 (2.4)	23.4 (1.04)	#!! (†)	0.8 (0.19)	5.8 (0.49)	16.8 (0.80)	28.7 (0.85)	28.0 (0.96)	16.0 (0.73)	3.9 (0.42)	3.7 (0.40)	0.3 (0.08)
Bosnia and Herzegovina	403 (2.9)	53.7 (1.64)	0.1!! (0.06)	2.8 (0.37)	17.5 (0.97)	33.2 (1.06)	28.8 (1.13)	14.3 (0.91)	3.0 (0.39)	0.2! (0.07)	0.2! (0.07)	# (†)
Brazil[4]	413 (0.9)	50.0 (0.90)	0.4 (0.10)	5.3 (0.40)	17.7 (0.57)	26.7 (0.66)	24.5 (0.62)	16.3 (0.60)	7.4 (0.46)	1.8 (0.24)	1.7 (0.22)	0.2! (0.06)
Brunei Darussalam	408 (0.9)	51.8 (0.61)	0.3! (0.12)	5.4 (0.32)	19.1 (0.53)	27.0 (0.74)	24.5 (0.57)	15.5 (0.51)	6.9 (0.33)	1.3 (0.22)	1.3 (0.21)	#!! (†)
Bulgaria[4]	420 (3.9)	47.1 (1.69)	0.3! (0.10)	4.6 (0.63)	17.1 (1.09)	25.1 (0.93)	24.9 (0.97)	17.3 (0.94)	8.4 (0.70)	2.3 (0.36)	2.2 (0.32)	0.2! (0.07)
Chinese Taipei	503 (2.8)	17.8 (0.81)	0.1 (0.07)	1.2 (0.19)	4.5 (0.40)	12.0 (0.59)	21.8 (0.70)	27.4 (0.80)	22.0 (0.89)	10.9 (0.81)	9.3 (0.67)	1.6 (0.31)

See notes at end of table.

Table 602.50. Average reading literacy scores of 15-year-old students and percentage attaining reading literacy proficiency levels, by country or other education system: 2018—Continued

[Standard errors appear in parentheses]

Country or other education system	Average reading literacy score[1]	Percentage attaining reading literacy proficiency levels[2]										
		Below level 2					At level 2	At level 3	At level 4	At or above level 5		
		Total below level 2	Below level 1c	At level 1c	At level 1b	At level 1a				Total at or above level 5	At level 5	At level 6
1	2	3	4	5	6	7	8	9	10	11	12	13
Costa Rica[4]	426 (3.4)	42.0 (1.62)	0.1!! (0.05)	1.8 (0.32)	11.3 (0.70)	28.9 (1.14)	32.1 (1.10)	19.4 (1.07)	5.9 (0.85)	0.6 (0.16)	0.6 (0.16)	# (†)
Croatia	479 (2.7)	21.6 (1.16)	# (†)	0.7 (0.16)	5.0 (0.53)	15.9 (0.76)	28.3 (0.86)	29.0 (1.00)	16.4 (0.82)	4.7 (0.47)	4.3 (0.45)	0.4 (0.09)
Cyprus	424 (1.4)	43.7 (0.72)	0.3! (0.09)	4.3 (0.33)	15.0 (0.58)	24.1 (0.77)	26.9 (0.70)	19.3 (0.65)	8.4 (0.39)	1.8 (0.21)	1.7 (0.21)	0.1!! (0.07)
Dominican Republic[4]	342 (2.9)	79.1 (1.29)	1.1 (0.25)	15.9 (0.91)	33.3 (1.06)	28.8 (1.01)	15.0 (0.91)	4.9 (0.54)	0.9 (0.22)	0.1!! (0.06)	0.1!! (0.06)	#!! (†)
Georgia	380 (2.2)	64.4 (1.11)	0.4! (0.13)	7.0 (0.54)	24.2 (0.91)	32.8 (0.81)	22.9 (0.82)	10.1 (0.56)	2.4 (0.31)	0.2! (0.10)	0.2! (0.10)	#!! (†)
Hong Kong (China)[5]	524 (2.7)	12.6 (0.76)	0.1!! (0.05)	0.9 (0.22)	3.5 (0.41)	8.1 (0.58)	17.8 (0.72)	27.7 (0.70)	27.1 (0.80)	14.8 (0.73)	12.5 (0.62)	2.3 (0.26)
Indonesia	371 (2.6)	69.9 (1.42)	0.2!! (0.11)	6.3 (0.65)	26.7 (1.03)	36.7 (1.11)	21.8 (0.99)	7.2 (0.77)	1.1 (0.24)	0.1!! (0.04)	0.1!! (0.04)	#!! (†)
Jordan[4]	419 (2.9)	41.2 (1.40)	1.1 (0.22)	4.0 (0.50)	11.1 (0.70)	25.0 (0.85)	33.8 (1.00)	20.5 (0.92)	4.3 (0.45)	0.3! (0.09)	0.3! (0.09)	#!! (†)
Kazakhstan	387 (1.5)	64.2 (0.73)	0.1!! (0.04)	3.5 (0.32)	22.2 (0.70)	38.4 (0.69)	23.9 (0.51)	8.9 (0.35)	2.6 (0.25)	0.4 (0.08)	0.4 (0.08)	# (†)
Kosovo	353 (1.1)	78.7 (0.65)	0.3! (0.09)	8.7 (0.57)	31.7 (0.81)	38.0 (1.00)	17.5 (0.65)	3.6 (0.35)	0.2! (0.10)	#!! (†)	(†)	#!! (†)
Lebanon	353 (4.3)	67.8 (1.52)	6.3 (0.65)	16.9 (1.03)	23.0 (0.93)	21.6 (0.84)	17.4 (0.92)	10.5 (0.68)	3.7 (0.48)	0.7 (0.16)	0.7 (0.16)	#!! (†)
Macao (China)	525 (1.2)	10.8 (0.53)	#!! (†)	0.3! (0.11)	2.2 (0.25)	8.2 (0.56)	19.4 (0.75)	29.8 (0.83)	26.1 (0.73)	13.8 (0.64)	11.7 (0.60)	2.1 (0.25)
Malaysia[4]	415 (2.9)	45.8 (1.41)	0.2! (0.09)	3.6 (0.39)	14.2 (0.77)	27.9 (0.93)	31.4 (0.95)	17.9 (0.93)	4.3 (0.56)	0.5! (0.18)	0.5! (0.18)	#!! (†)
Malta	448 (1.7)	35.9 (0.82)	0.7! (0.22)	4.8 (0.44)	11.9 (0.70)	18.5 (0.89)	23.7 (0.90)	21.7 (0.90)	13.4 (0.89)	5.3 (0.48)	4.5 (0.51)	0.9 (0.20)
Moldova, Republic of	424 (2.4)	43.0 (1.15)	0.4! (0.14)	3.9 (0.46)	13.5 (0.66)	25.2 (0.82)	28.0 (0.93)	20.8 (0.94)	7.2 (0.62)	1.0 (0.28)	1.0 (0.27)	#!! (†)
Montenegro, Republic of	421 (1.1)	44.4 (0.69)	0.1!! (0.06)	2.8 (0.27)	13.5 (0.53)	28.0 (0.68)	30.5 (0.64)	18.3 (0.56)	6.0 (0.40)	0.8 (0.22)	0.8 (0.22)	#!! (†)
Morocco[4]	359 (3.1)	73.3 (1.62)	0.3 (0.07)	8.8 (0.69)	30.8 (1.30)	33.4 (0.90)	20.6 (1.21)	5.6 (0.50)	0.5 (0.13)	#!! (†)	#!! (†)	# (†)
North Macedonia	393 (1.1)	55.1 (0.73)	1.6 (0.22)	7.3 (0.46)	18.3 (0.79)	27.9 (1.01)	26.6 (0.82)	14.4 (0.58)	3.5 (0.34)	0.3! (0.15)	0.3! (0.16)	#!! (†)
Panama[4]	377 (3.0)	64.3 (1.42)	1.0 (0.22)	8.4 (0.77)	23.4 (0.93)	31.5 (1.04)	23.0 (0.85)	9.9 (0.86)	2.6 (0.44)	0.2! (0.09)	0.2! (0.09)	#!! (†)
Peru[4]	401 (3.0)	54.3 (1.34)	0.4! (0.12)	5.5 (0.48)	19.6 (0.90)	28.9 (0.93)	25.8 (0.69)	14.3 (0.71)	4.8 (0.54)	0.8 (0.19)	0.7 (0.19)	0.1!! (†)
Philippines[4]	340 (3.3)	80.6 (1.42)	0.5 (0.14)	15.1 (0.90)	38.3 (1.06)	26.7 (0.85)	13.1 (0.74)	5.1 (0.66)	1.1 (0.30)	0.1!! (0.04)	0.1!! (0.04)	#!! (†)
Qatar	407 (0.8)	50.9 (0.43)	1.2 (0.12)	8.5 (0.30)	17.6 (0.39)	23.6 (0.49)	23.4 (0.43)	15.8 (0.36)	7.3 (0.26)	2.6 (0.16)	2.2 (0.17)	0.4 (0.08)
Romania[4]	428 (5.1)	40.8 (2.15)	0.8! (0.26)	4.3 (0.62)	12.9 (1.01)	22.8 (1.21)	28.1 (1.05)	20.9 (1.28)	8.7 (1.02)	1.4 (0.32)	1.3 (0.30)	0.1!! (0.05)
Russian Federation	479 (3.1)	22.1 (1.22)	0.1! (0.03)	1.0 (0.25)	5.6 (0.56)	15.5 (0.86)	28.1 (0.84)	28.0 (0.83)	16.4 (0.73)	5.4 (0.52)	4.8 (0.46)	0.6 (0.13)
Saudi Arabia	399 (3.0)	52.4 (1.46)	0.5 (0.16)	5.3 (0.62)	17.0 (0.87)	29.4 (0.90)	30.4 (1.06)	14.6 (0.77)	2.6 (0.31)	0.1!! (0.07)	0.1!! (0.07)	# (†)
Serbia	439 (3.3)	37.7 (1.52)	0.1!! (0.08)	2.7 (0.36)	12.2 (0.82)	22.7 (0.81)	27.8 (0.85)	21.8 (0.85)	10.1 (0.69)	2.5 (0.32)	2.4 (0.31)	0.2! (0.07)
Singapore	549 (1.6)	11.2 (0.48)	#!! (†)	0.5 (0.09)	3.0 (0.30)	7.7 (0.38)	14.2 (0.53)	22.3 (0.65)	26.4 (0.59)	25.8 (0.69)	18.5 (0.68)	7.3 (0.37)
Thailand[4]	393 (3.2)	59.5 (1.74)	0.1!! (0.05)	3.6 (0.46)	20.6 (1.11)	35.3 (1.14)	26.0 (0.97)	11.6 (0.92)	2.7 (0.43)	0.2! (0.07)	0.2! (0.07)	#!! (†)
Ukraine[4]	466 (3.5)	25.9 (1.44)	0.2! (0.08)	1.8 (0.29)	7.2 (0.69)	16.7 (0.87)	27.7 (0.81)	28.5 (0.97)	14.5 (0.82)	3.4 (0.48)	3.2 (0.44)	0.2!! (0.11)
United Arab Emirates	432 (2.3)	42.9 (0.81)	0.6 (0.09)	5.8 (0.33)	14.9 (0.49)	21.6 (0.44)	23.4 (0.53)	18.1 (0.50)	10.8 (0.55)	4.8 (0.28)	4.1 (0.28)	0.7 (0.11)
Uruguay	427 (2.8)	41.9 (1.28)	0.3! (0.10)	4.0 (0.40)	13.6 (0.76)	24.0 (0.89)	28.1 (1.10)	20.1 (0.84)	8.3 (0.69)	1.5 (0.25)	1.5 (0.24)	0.1!! (0.06)
Vietnam[9]	— (†)	— (†)	— (†)	— (†)	— (†)	— (†)	— (†)	— (†)	— (†)	— (†)	— (†)	— (†)

†Not applicable.
#Rounds to zero.
!Interpret data with caution. The coefficient of variation (CV) for this estimate is between 30 and 50 percent.
!!Interpret data with caution. Estimate could be unstable because the standard error represents more than 50 percent of the estimate.
[1]Program for International Student Assessment (PISA) scores are reported on a scale from 0 to 1,000.
[2]To reach a particular proficiency level, a student must correctly answer a majority of items at that level. Students were classified into reading literacy levels according to their scores. Exact cut scores are as follows: below level 1c (a score less than 189.33); level 1c (a score of at least 189.33 but less than 262.04); level 1b (a score of at least 262.04 but less than 334.75); level 1a (a score of at least 334.75 but less than 407.47); level 2 (a score of at least 407.47 but less than 480.18); level 3 (a score of at least 480.18 but less than 552.89); level 4 (a score of at least 552.89 but less than 625.61); level 5 (a score of at least 625.61 but less than 698.32); and level 6 (a score of at least 698.32).
[3]Refers to the mean of the data values for all Organization for Economic Cooperation and Development (OECD) countries, to which each country contributes equally, regardless of the absolute size of the student population of each country.

[4]At least 50 percent but less than 75 percent of the 15-year-old population is covered by the Program for International Student Assessment (PISA) sample.
[5]Did not meet 85 percent threshold for school participation. However, data are considered to be largely comparable with data from other countries or education systems.
[6]Did not meet 80 percent threshold for student participation. However, data are considered to be largely comparable with data from other countries or education systems.
[7]Although Spain's PISA 2018 data met international technical standards, its reading literacy data show unusual student response behaviors that prevent these data from being reported at this time.
[8]Less than 50 percent of the 15-year-old population is covered by the PISA sample.
[9]Although Vietnam participated in PISA 2018, technical problems with its data prevent results from being included in this table.
NOTE: Detail may not sum to totals because of rounding.
SOURCE: Organization for Economic Cooperation and Development (OECD), Program for International Student Assessment (PISA), 2018. (This table was prepared December 2019.)

Table 602.60. Average mathematics literacy scores of 15-year-old students and percentage attaining mathematics literacy proficiency levels, by country or other education system: 2018

[Standard errors appear in parentheses]

Country or other education system	Average mathematics literacy score[1]	Percentage attaining mathematics literacy proficiency levels[2]								
		Below level 2			At level 2	At level 3	At level 4	At or above level 5		
		Total below level 2	Below level 1	At level 1				Total at or above level 5	At level 5	At level 6
1	2	3	4	5	6	7	8	9	10	11
OECD average[3]	489 (0.4)	24.0 (0.17)	9.1 (0.12)	14.8 (0.12)	22.2 (0.14)	24.4 (0.14)	18.5 (0.12)	10.9 (0.12)	8.5 (0.10)	2.4 (0.06)
Australia	491 (1.9)	22.4 (0.68)	7.6 (0.50)	14.8 (0.53)	23.4 (0.51)	25.6 (0.51)	18.2 (0.47)	10.5 (0.54)	8.0 (0.38)	2.5 (0.28)
Austria	499 (3.0)	21.1 (1.18)	7.3 (0.66)	13.8 (0.80)	20.8 (0.95)	24.9 (0.95)	20.6 (0.82)	12.6 (0.82)	10.0 (0.67)	2.5 (0.33)
Belgium	508 (2.3)	19.7 (0.89)	6.9 (0.65)	12.8 (0.64)	18.6 (0.65)	23.8 (0.76)	22.2 (0.75)	15.7 (0.87)	12.5 (0.63)	3.2 (0.40)
Canada	512 (2.4)	16.3 (0.72)	5.0 (0.40)	11.3 (0.40)	20.8 (0.61)	25.9 (0.57)	21.7 (0.74)	15.3 (0.70)	11.3 (0.49)	4.0 (0.33)
Chile	417 (2.4)	51.9 (1.32)	24.7 (1.11)	27.2 (0.95)	25.5 (0.89)	15.6 (0.76)	5.7 (0.48)	1.2 (0.18)	1.1 (0.17)	0.1! (0.05)
Colombia[4]	391 (3.0)	65.4 (1.57)	35.5 (1.69)	29.9 (1.22)	21.1 (0.91)	10.0 (0.69)	3.1 (0.38)	0.5 (0.14)	0.5 (0.14)	(†) (†)
Czech Republic	499 (2.5)	20.4 (1.10)	6.6 (0.69)	13.8 (0.71)	22.1 (0.82)	25.2 (0.93)	19.6 (0.74)	12.7 (0.72)	9.5 (0.53)	3.1 (0.33)
Denmark	509 (1.7)	14.6 (0.64)	3.7 (0.35)	10.9 (0.58)	22.0 (0.87)	28.8 (0.84)	23.0 (0.79)	11.6 (0.70)	9.5 (0.60)	2.1 (0.31)
Estonia	523 (1.7)	10.2 (0.64)	2.1 (0.27)	8.1 (0.57)	20.8 (0.81)	29.0 (0.82)	24.6 (0.76)	15.5 (0.77)	11.8 (0.68)	3.7 (0.40)
Finland	507 (2.0)	15.0 (0.74)	3.8 (0.40)	11.1 (0.56)	22.3 (0.85)	28.9 (0.99)	22.7 (0.81)	11.1 (0.62)	9.3 (0.54)	1.8 (0.29)
France	495 (2.3)	21.3 (0.82)	8.0 (0.53)	13.2 (0.62)	21.1 (0.80)	25.6 (0.79)	21.0 (0.82)	11.0 (0.76)	9.2 (0.63)	1.8 (0.27)
Germany	500 (2.6)	21.1 (1.07)	7.6 (0.67)	13.5 (0.83)	20.7 (0.90)	24.0 (0.76)	20.8 (0.82)	13.3 (0.79)	10.5 (0.72)	2.8 (0.30)
Greece	451 (3.1)	35.8 (1.47)	15.3 (1.15)	20.5 (0.92)	26.8 (0.87)	22.5 (0.96)	11.1 (0.61)	3.7 (0.49)	3.2 (0.40)	0.5! (0.18)
Hungary	481 (2.3)	25.6 (1.01)	9.6 (0.72)	16.1 (0.82)	23.6 (0.81)	25.2 (0.99)	17.5 (0.84)	8.0 (0.69)	6.5 (0.55)	1.4 (0.26)
Iceland	495 (2.0)	20.7 (0.96)	7.4 (0.54)	13.3 (0.71)	22.0 (0.99)	26.7 (0.98)	20.2 (0.89)	10.4 (0.61)	8.5 (0.63)	1.9 (0.31)
Ireland	500 (2.2)	15.7 (0.82)	3.8 (0.48)	11.9 (0.72)	24.7 (0.79)	30.5 (0.81)	20.8 (0.81)	8.2 (0.65)	7.2 (0.60)	1.0 (0.21)
Israel	463 (3.5)	34.1 (1.40)	17.7 (1.11)	16.4 (0.80)	20.7 (0.75)	21.0 (0.83)	15.4 (0.77)	8.8 (0.79)	7.0 (0.58)	1.8 (0.27)
Italy	487 (2.8)	23.8 (1.11)	9.1 (0.77)	14.8 (0.88)	22.9 (1.02)	25.6 (0.94)	18.1 (0.79)	9.5 (0.83)	7.5 (0.59)	2.0 (0.34)
Japan	527 (2.5)	11.5 (0.76)	2.9 (0.36)	8.6 (0.56)	18.7 (0.79)	26.4 (0.88)	25.1 (0.96)	18.3 (1.06)	14.0 (0.78)	4.3 (0.54)
Korea, Republic of	526 (3.1)	15.0 (0.90)	5.4 (0.55)	9.6 (0.65)	17.3 (0.76)	23.4 (0.74)	22.9 (0.75)	21.4 (1.11)	14.4 (0.70)	6.9 (0.78)
Latvia	496 (2.0)	17.3 (1.01)	4.4 (0.48)	12.9 (0.80)	25.8 (0.92)	29.4 (1.03)	19.0 (0.80)	8.5 (0.59)	7.1 (0.54)	1.4 (0.23)
Lithuania	481 (2.0)	25.6 (0.92)	9.3 (0.61)	16.4 (0.71)	24.2 (0.72)	25.2 (0.86)	16.5 (0.80)	8.4 (0.51)	6.8 (0.49)	1.7 (0.23)
Luxembourg	483 (1.1)	27.2 (0.70)	10.9 (0.62)	16.4 (0.62)	22.6 (0.85)	22.6 (0.75)	17.7 (0.69)	10.8 (0.56)	8.6 (0.50)	2.3 (0.34)
Mexico[4]	409 (2.5)	56.2 (1.39)	26.0 (1.19)	30.3 (0.91)	26.4 (0.93)	13.1 (0.77)	3.7 (0.46)	0.5 (0.13)	0.5 (0.12)	#!! (†)
Netherlands[5]	519 (2.6)	15.8 (1.08)	4.5 (0.57)	11.2 (0.70)	19.0 (1.04)	23.2 (1.09)	23.6 (0.94)	18.4 (0.97)	14.2 (0.78)	4.3 (0.49)
New Zealand	494 (1.7)	21.8 (0.80)	7.6 (0.49)	14.2 (0.63)	22.8 (0.77)	25.0 (0.73)	18.9 (0.74)	11.6 (0.52)	8.8 (0.44)	2.7 (0.30)
Norway	501 (2.2)	18.9 (0.84)	6.5 (0.48)	12.4 (0.56)	21.8 (0.77)	26.5 (0.77)	20.6 (0.86)	12.2 (0.71)	9.8 (0.62)	2.4 (0.35)
Poland	516 (2.6)	14.7 (0.78)	4.2 (0.46)	10.5 (0.59)	20.7 (0.79)	26.5 (0.78)	22.3 (0.75)	15.8 (1.01)	11.7 (0.72)	4.1 (0.52)
Portugal[6]	492 (2.7)	23.3 (1.04)	9.3 (0.65)	14.0 (0.83)	20.9 (0.84)	24.5 (1.11)	19.7 (0.78)	11.6 (0.74)	9.1 (0.61)	2.5 (0.34)
Slovak Republic	486 (2.6)	25.1 (1.08)	10.7 (0.86)	14.4 (0.65)	21.4 (0.88)	24.2 (0.95)	18.6 (0.86)	10.7 (0.69)	8.4 (0.57)	2.3 (0.30)
Slovenia	509 (1.4)	16.4 (0.64)	4.8 (0.59)	11.7 (0.67)	21.6 (0.90)	26.4 (0.91)	22.0 (0.81)	13.6 (0.72)	10.5 (0.77)	3.1 (0.41)
Spain[7]	481 (1.5)	24.7 (0.62)	8.7 (0.42)	16.0 (0.47)	24.4 (0.43)	26.0 (0.63)	17.5 (0.47)	7.3 (0.41)	6.2 (0.32)	1.1 (0.13)
Sweden	502 (2.7)	18.8 (1.03)	6.0 (0.63)	12.8 (0.75)	21.9 (0.90)	25.7 (0.82)	21.0 (0.82)	12.6 (0.77)	10.0 (0.66)	2.6 (0.32)
Switzerland	515 (2.9)	16.8 (0.94)	4.8 (0.45)	12.0 (0.75)	19.5 (0.88)	24.4 (0.97)	22.3 (0.86)	17.0 (1.03)	12.1 (0.74)	4.9 (0.54)
Turkey[4]	454 (2.3)	36.7 (1.08)	13.8 (0.87)	22.9 (0.75)	27.3 (0.84)	20.4 (0.84)	10.9 (0.53)	4.8 (0.59)	3.9 (0.44)	0.9 (0.25)
United Kingdom	502 (2.6)	19.2 (0.90)	6.4 (0.54)	12.8 (0.63)	22.0 (0.78)	25.5 (0.68)	20.4 (0.70)	12.9 (0.79)	9.8 (0.64)	3.1 (0.36)
United States[5]	478 (3.2)	27.1 (1.38)	10.2 (0.85)	16.9 (0.90)	24.2 (0.98)	24.1 (0.96)	16.3 (0.94)	8.3 (0.80)	6.8 (0.73)	1.5 (0.29)
Non-OECD education systems										
Albania	437 (2.4)	42.4 (1.38)	16.9 (0.87)	25.5 (0.88)	28.6 (0.98)	19.3 (0.85)	7.5 (0.66)	2.3 (0.27)	2.0 (0.24)	0.3! (0.13)
Argentina	379 (2.8)	69.0 (1.31)	40.5 (1.58)	28.5 (1.04)	19.6 (0.88)	8.8 (0.65)	2.3 (0.26)	0.3 (0.09)	0.3 (0.10)	#!! (†)
Baku (Azerbaijan)[8]	420 (2.8)	50.7 (1.33)	24.7 (1.00)	26.1 (0.82)	25.2 (0.85)	15.7 (0.71)	6.4 (0.59)	2.0 (0.32)	1.7 (0.27)	0.3! (0.10)
Beijing, Shanghai, Jiangsu, Guangdong (China)	591 (2.5)	2.4 (0.38)	0.5 (0.15)	1.9 (0.30)	6.9 (0.52)	17.5 (0.78)	28.9 (0.98)	44.3 (1.34)	27.8 (0.97)	16.5 (1.15)
Belarus	472 (2.7)	29.4 (1.09)	11.4 (0.73)	18.0 (0.72)	24.7 (0.86)	23.4 (0.75)	15.2 (0.75)	7.3 (0.64)	6.1 (0.53)	1.2 (0.24)
Bosnia and Herzegovin	406 (3.1)	57.6 (1.58)	28.7 (1.35)	28.9 (1.02)	24.2 (0.90)	13.1 (0.80)	4.3 (0.47)	0.8 (0.19)	0.7 (0.19)	0.1!! (0.04)
Brazil[4]	384 (2.0)	68.1 (0.95)	41.0 (0.99)	27.1 (0.71)	18.2 (0.67)	9.3 (0.47)	3.4 (0.32)	0.9 (0.19)	0.8 (0.17)	0.1! (0.05)
Brunei Darussalam	430 (1.2)	47.9 (0.66)	22.1 (0.80)	25.7 (0.78)	24.0 (0.61)	16.2 (0.53)	8.9 (0.46)	3.0 (0.30)	2.7 (0.28)	0.4 (0.08)
Bulgaria[4]	436 (3.8)	44.4 (1.67)	21.9 (1.40)	22.5 (0.83)	23.7 (0.95)	18.2 (0.98)	9.4 (0.65)	4.2 (0.63)	3.3 (0.50)	0.9 (0.22)
Chinese Taipei	531 (2.9)	14.0 (0.75)	5.0 (0.41)	9.0 (0.51)	16.1 (0.70)	23.2 (0.80)	23.5 (0.77)	23.2 (1.13)	15.6 (0.80)	7.6 (0.76)

See notes at end of table.

Table 602.60. Average mathematics literacy scores of 15-year-old students and percentage attaining mathematics literacy proficiency levels, by country or other education system: 2018—Continued

[Standard errors appear in parentheses]

Country or other education system	Average mathematics literacy score[1]	Percentage attaining mathematics literacy proficiency levels[2]						At or above level 5		
		Total below level 2	Below level 2		At level 2	At level 3	At level 4	Total at or above level 5	At level 5	At level 6
			Below level 1	At level 1						
1	2	3	4	5	6	7	8	9	10	11
Costa Rica[4]	402 (3.3)	60.0 (1.91)	27.8 (1.28)	32.2 (1.22)	25.6 (1.23)	11.2 (1.03)	2.8 (0.55)	0.3! (0.12)	0.3! (0.12)	# (†)
Croatia	464 (2.5)	31.2 (1.27)	11.0 (0.82)	20.2 (0.83)	27.4 (0.87)	23.3 (0.80)	13.0 (0.75)	5.1 (0.53)	4.3 (0.48)	0.8 (0.20)
Cyprus	451 (1.4)	36.9 (0.71)	17.2 (0.62)	19.7 (0.66)	24.7 (0.90)	22.0 (0.85)	12.1 (0.55)	4.4 (0.39)	3.7 (0.35)	0.7 (0.15)
Dominican Republic[4]	325 (2.6)	90.6 (0.97)	69.3 (1.40)	21.3 (0.95)	7.3 (0.63)	1.8 (0.41)	0.3! (0.11)	#!! (†)	#!! (†)	# (†)
Georgia	398 (2.6)	61.1 (1.29)	33.7 (1.23)	27.3 (1.06)	21.6 (0.81)	11.9 (0.79)	4.4 (0.51)	1.0 (0.29)	0.9 (0.27)	0.1!! (0.07)
Hong Kong (China)[5]	551 (3.0)	9.2 (0.80)	2.8 (0.42)	6.4 (0.57)	13.5 (0.71)	22.1 (0.73)	26.3 (0.91)	29.0 (1.08)	19.5 (0.76)	9.5 (0.76)
Indonesia	379 (3.1)	71.9 (1.52)	40.6 (1.64)	31.3 (1.19)	18.6 (0.98)	6.8 (0.66)	2.3 (0.51)	0.5! (0.16)	0.4! (0.15)	#!! (†)
Jordan[4]	400 (3.3)	59.3 (1.61)	30.7 (1.40)	28.6 (0.85)	24.0 (0.92)	12.4 (0.83)	3.6 (0.46)	0.7! (0.22)	0.6! (0.19)	0.1!! (0.08)
Kazakhstan	423 (1.9)	49.1 (0.95)	22.3 (0.82)	26.8 (0.62)	26.6 (0.65)	16.0 (0.55)	6.3 (0.40)	1.9 (0.20)	1.6 (0.18)	0.3 (0.09)
Kosovo	366 (1.5)	76.6 (0.93)	47.0 (0.98)	29.6 (1.11)	16.5 (0.80)	5.4 (0.40)	1.4 (0.25)	0.1!! (0.09)	0.1!! (0.09)	#!! (†)
Lebanon	393 (4.0)	59.8 (1.75)	38.0 (1.68)	21.8 (1.00)	19.1 (1.08)	13.1 (0.87)	6.0 (0.54)	2.0 (0.26)	1.7 (0.25)	0.3! (0.11)
Macao (China)	558 (1.5)	5.0 (0.49)	1.0 (0.21)	4.0 (0.42)	12.3 (0.76)	24.8 (0.91)	30.3 (1.21)	27.6 (0.83)	20.0 (0.78)	7.7 (0.59)
Malaysia[4]	440 (2.9)	41.5 (1.43)	16.1 (0.89)	25.4 (0.97)	28.3 (0.86)	19.3 (0.87)	8.5 (0.68)	2.5 (0.45)	2.2 (0.39)	0.3! (0.13)
Malta	472 (1.9)	30.2 (0.98)	14.3 (0.68)	15.9 (0.81)	21.5 (1.04)	23.2 (1.09)	16.6 (0.74)	8.5 (0.66)	6.7 (0.58)	1.8 (0.28)
Moldova, Republic of	421 (2.4)	50.3 (1.11)	26.1 (0.91)	24.2 (0.87)	23.5 (0.89)	16.5 (0.66)	7.3 (0.57)	2.4 (0.40)	2.0 (0.33)	0.4! (0.15)
Montenegro, Republic of	430 (1.2)	46.2 (0.76)	19.9 (0.69)	26.3 (0.68)	27.3 (0.74)	17.9 (0.54)	6.9 (0.39)	1.8 (0.21)	1.6 (0.21)	0.2! (0.06)
Morocco[4]	368 (3.3)	75.6 (1.60)	47.1 (1.89)	28.5 (0.97)	16.9 (1.01)	6.2 (0.61)	1.2 (0.23)	0.1! (0.06)	0.1! (0.06)	#!! (†)
North Macedonia	394 (1.6)	61.0 (0.89)	35.2 (0.82)	25.8 (0.82)	21.3 (0.75)	12.1 (0.72)	4.5 (0.43)	1.1 (0.21)	1.0 (0.19)	0.1! (0.07)
Panama[4]	353 (2.7)	81.2 (1.33)	53.7 (1.42)	27.5 (0.98)	13.5 (0.80)	4.3 (0.63)	0.9 (0.24)	0.1!! (0.07)	0.1!! (0.07)	#!! (†)
Peru[4]	400 (2.6)	60.3 (1.31)	32.0 (1.16)	28.3 (0.85)	23.1 (0.85)	11.6 (0.68)	4.1 (0.46)	0.9 (0.20)	0.8 (0.19)	0.1!! (0.04)
Philippines[4]	353 (3.5)	80.7 (1.56)	54.4 (1.65)	26.3 (0.93)	13.6 (0.99)	4.7 (0.68)	0.9! (0.30)	0.1!! (0.05)	0.1!! (0.05)	#!! (†)
Qatar	414 (1.2)	53.7 (0.64)	29.7 (0.66)	24.0 (0.54)	21.9 (0.49)	14.6 (0.37)	6.9 (0.28)	2.9 (0.20)	2.4 (0.18)	0.6 (0.08)
Romania[4]	430 (4.9)	46.6 (2.26)	22.6 (2.26)	23.9 (1.17)	24.5 (1.06)	17.3 (1.06)	8.5 (0.96)	3.2 (0.60)	2.7 (0.52)	0.4! (0.16)
Russian Federation	488 (3.0)	21.6 (1.26)	6.8 (0.70)	14.9 (0.82)	25.0 (0.94)	27.5 (0.85)	17.8 (0.83)	8.1 (0.71)	6.6 (0.57)	1.5 (0.24)
Saudi Arabia	373 (3.0)	72.7 (1.48)	42.8 (1.65)	29.9 (1.00)	18.8 (1.13)	6.8 (0.57)	1.5 (0.28)	0.2! (0.09)	0.2!! (0.08)	#!! (†)
Serbia	448 (3.2)	39.7 (1.40)	18.1 (1.12)	21.6 (0.81)	24.1 (0.80)	19.2 (0.81)	11.7 (0.70)	5.2 (0.44)	4.2 (0.37)	1.0 (0.20)
Singapore	569 (1.6)	7.1 (0.40)	1.8 (0.22)	5.3 (0.41)	11.1 (0.53)	19.1 (0.66)	25.8 (0.82)	36.9 (0.84)	23.2 (0.71)	13.8 (0.75)
Thailand[4]	419 (3.4)	52.7 (1.66)	25.0 (1.28)	27.7 (1.05)	24.6 (0.97)	14.3 (0.76)	6.1 (0.68)	2.3 (0.36)	1.9 (0.32)	0.3 (0.09)
Ukraine	453 (3.6)	35.9 (1.62)	15.6 (1.16)	20.3 (0.97)	26.2 (0.97)	21.5 (1.00)	11.5 (0.75)	5.0 (0.65)	4.0 (0.47)	1.0! (0.30)
United Arab Emirates	435 (2.1)	45.5 (0.92)	24.2 (0.87)	21.3 (0.57)	21.5 (0.52)	17.2 (0.60)	10.4 (0.49)	5.4 (0.34)	4.2 (0.33)	1.2 (0.11)
Uruguay	418 (2.6)	50.7 (1.54)	24.6 (1.07)	26.1 (1.27)	26.5 (1.02)	15.8 (0.98)	6.0 (0.61)	1.0 (0.26)	1.0 (0.24)	0.1!! (0.05)
Vietnam[9]	— (†)	— (†)	— (†)	— (†)	— (†)	— (†)	— (†)	— (†)	— (†)	— (†)

—Not available.
†Not applicable.
#Rounds to zero.
!Interpret data with caution. The coefficient of variation (CV) for this estimate is between 30 and 50 percent.
!!Interpret data with caution. Estimate could be unstable because the standard error represents more than 50 percent of the estimate.
[1]Program for International Student Assessment (PISA) scores are reported on a scale from 0 to 1,000.
[2]To reach a particular proficiency level, a student must correctly answer a majority of items at that level. Students were classified into mathematics literacy levels according to their scores. Exact cut scores are as follows: below level 1 (a score less than 357.77); level 1 (a score of at least 357.77 but less than 420.07); level 2 (a score of at least 420.07 but less than 482.38); level 3 (a score of at least 482.38 but less than 544.68); level 4 (a score of at least 544.68 but less than 606.99); level 5 (a score of at least 606.99 but less than 669.30); and level 6 (a score of at least 669.30).
[3]Refers to the mean of the data values for all Organization for Economic Cooperation and Development (OECD) countries, to which each country contributes equally, regardless of the absolute size of the student population of each country.

[4]At least 50 percent but less than 75 percent of the 15-year-old population is covered by the Program for International Student Assessment (PISA) sample.
[5]Did not meet 85 percent threshold for school participation. However, data are considered to be largely comparable with data from other countries or education systems.
[6]Did not meet 80 percent threshold for student participation. However, data are considered to be largely comparable with data from other countries or education systems.
[7]Although Spain's PISA 2018 data met international technical standards, its reading literacy data show unusual student response behaviors that prevent these data from being reported at this time.
[8]Less than 50 percent of the 15-year-old population is covered by the PISA sample.
[9]Although Vietnam participated in PISA 2018, technical problems with its data prevent results from being included in this table.
NOTE: Detail may not sum to totals because of rounding.
SOURCE: Organization for Economic Cooperation and Development (OECD), Program for International Student Assessment (PISA), 2018. (This table was prepared December 2019.)

Table 602.70. Average science literacy scores of 15-year-old students and percentage attaining science literacy proficiency levels, by country or other education system: 2018

[Standard errors appear in parentheses]

Country or other education system	Average science literacy score[1]	Below level 2 — Total below level 2	Below level 2 — Below level 1b	Below level 2 — At level 1b	Below level 2 — At level 1a	At level 2	At level 3	At level 4	At or above level 5 — Total at or above level 5	At or above level 5 — At level 5	At level 6
1	2	3	4	5	6	7	8	9	10	11	12
OECD average[3]	**489 (0.4)**	**22.0 (0.16)**	**0.7 (0.03)**	**5.2 (0.08)**	**16.0 (0.13)**	**25.8 (0.14)**	**27.4 (0.15)**	**18.1 (0.13)**	**6.8 (0.09)**	**5.9 (0.08)**	**0.8 (0.03)**
Australia	503 (1.8)	18.9 (0.61)	0.6 (0.10)	4.5 (0.28)	13.7 (0.48)	23.0 (0.56)	27.5 (0.60)	21.2 (0.57)	9.5 (0.54)	7.9 (0.40)	1.6 (0.22)
Austria	490 (2.8)	21.9 (1.04)	0.6 (0.16)	4.8 (0.47)	16.5 (0.91)	25.0 (0.85)	27.6 (0.77)	19.2 (0.82)	6.3 (0.57)	5.8 (0.56)	0.5 (0.12)
Belgium	499 (2.2)	20.0 (0.86)	0.6 (0.15)	5.3 (0.48)	14.2 (0.63)	22.2 (0.75)	28.4 (0.80)	21.3 (0.69)	8.0 (0.46)	7.3 (0.41)	0.7 (0.15)
Canada	518 (2.2)	13.4 (0.55)	0.4 (0.07)	2.6 (0.20)	10.5 (0.43)	22.4 (0.57)	29.3 (0.63)	23.5 (0.66)	11.3 (0.58)	9.5 (0.46)	1.8 (0.23)
Chile	444 (2.4)	35.3 (1.23)	1.0 (0.21)	8.8 (0.67)	25.5 (1.00)	33.1 (0.98)	22.6 (0.96)	7.9 (0.56)	1.0 (0.18)	1.0 (0.18)	#!! (†)
Colombia[4]	413 (3.1)	50.4 (1.68)	2.1 (0.33)	15.3 (1.12)	33.0 (1.07)	29.6 (1.21)	15.4 (0.84)	4.2 (0.44)	0.4 (0.11)	0.4 (0.11)	# (†)
Czech Republic	497 (2.5)	18.8 (1.05)	0.4! (0.13)	3.9 (0.45)	14.5 (0.82)	25.9 (0.97)	28.7 (0.96)	19.1 (0.84)	7.5 (0.52)	6.6 (0.48)	1.0 (0.18)
Denmark	493 (1.9)	18.7 (0.74)	0.7 (0.17)	4.1 (0.34)	13.9 (0.60)	26.6 (0.70)	30.1 (0.92)	19.1 (0.81)	5.5 (0.49)	5.0 (0.48)	0.5! (0.16)
Estonia	530 (1.9)	8.8 (0.61)	0.1!! (0.06)	1.1 (0.21)	7.5 (0.55)	21.5 (0.74)	32.1 (0.90)	25.4 (0.83)	12.2 (0.55)	10.2 (0.53)	2.0 (0.24)
Finland	522 (2.5)	12.9 (0.71)	0.4 (0.12)	2.8 (0.33)	9.7 (0.55)	21.1 (0.71)	28.9 (0.84)	24.9 (0.83)	12.3 (0.68)	10.5 (0.62)	1.8 (0.34)
France	493 (2.2)	20.5 (0.77)	0.6 (0.17)	5.0 (0.42)	14.9 (0.75)	24.6 (0.89)	28.3 (0.75)	20.0 (0.88)	6.6 (0.54)	5.9 (0.50)	0.6 (0.14)
Germany	503 (2.9)	19.6 (0.98)	0.8 (0.21)	5.0 (0.52)	13.8 (0.74)	22.0 (0.95)	26.9 (0.93)	21.5 (0.99)	10.0 (0.63)	8.5 (0.58)	1.5 (0.21)
Greece	452 (3.1)	31.7 (1.47)	1.2 (0.28)	8.1 (0.75)	22.4 (0.96)	31.6 (0.93)	26.0 (1.03)	9.3 (0.65)	1.3 (0.24)	1.3 (0.23)	#!! (†)
Hungary	481 (2.3)	24.1 (0.91)	0.6! (0.22)	5.7 (0.58)	17.8 (0.86)	26.1 (0.96)	28.1 (1.03)	17.0 (0.74)	4.7 (0.54)	4.3 (0.49)	0.4 (0.11)
Iceland	475 (1.8)	25.0 (0.90)	0.5! (0.17)	5.9 (0.51)	18.6 (0.83)	28.3 (0.93)	27.7 (0.97)	15.2 (0.84)	3.8 (0.38)	3.6 (0.39)	0.2! (0.12)
Ireland	496 (2.2)	17.0 (0.81)	0.3! (0.11)	3.3 (0.35)	13.4 (0.69)	26.9 (0.90)	31.3 (0.85)	19.0 (0.70)	5.8 (0.56)	5.4 (0.51)	0.5 (0.18)
Israel	462 (3.6)	33.1 (1.40)	3.2 (0.44)	10.7 (0.74)	19.2 (0.90)	23.1 (0.87)	22.9 (0.83)	15.1 (0.78)	5.8 (0.51)	5.2 (0.43)	0.7 (0.14)
Italy	468 (2.4)	25.9 (1.04)	0.2! (0.23)	6.6 (0.55)	19.1 (0.88)	30.2 (1.00)	27.8 (1.09)	13.4 (0.73)	2.7 (0.40)	2.6 (0.37)	0.1! (0.07)
Japan	529 (2.6)	10.8 (1.04)	0.2! (0.07)	1.8 (0.26)	8.9 (0.62)	19.9 (0.78)	29.7 (1.05)	26.5 (0.94)	13.1 (0.87)	11.4 (0.70)	1.6 (0.28)
Korea, Republic of	519 (2.8)	14.2 (0.83)	0.5 (0.13)	3.1 (0.35)	10.6 (0.66)	21.0 (0.79)	28.6 (0.95)	24.5 (0.91)	11.8 (0.82)	10.0 (0.65)	1.8 (0.32)
Latvia	487 (1.8)	18.5 (0.79)	0.3! (0.10)	3.4 (0.37)	14.8 (0.68)	29.5 (0.81)	31.5 (1.09)	16.8 (0.76)	3.7 (0.38)	3.5 (0.39)	0.3! (0.11)
Lithuania	482 (1.6)	22.2 (0.85)	0.5! (0.16)	4.7 (0.40)	17.0 (0.75)	28.4 (0.83)	28.7 (0.77)	16.3 (0.60)	4.4 (0.33)	4.0 (0.34)	0.5! (0.11)
Luxembourg	477 (1.2)	26.8 (0.58)	0.8 (0.17)	6.8 (0.40)	19.2 (0.63)	25.7 (0.81)	25.6 (0.76)	16.6 (0.58)	5.4 (0.50)	4.9 (0.51)	0.5! (0.16)
Mexico[4]	419 (2.6)	46.8 (1.43)	1.0 (0.26)	11.6 (0.97)	34.2 (1.27)	33.9 (0.93)	15.5 (0.87)	3.5 (0.47)	0.3! (0.10)	0.3! (0.10)	# (†)
Netherlands[5]	503 (2.8)	20.0 (1.14)	0.9 (0.25)	4.8 (0.51)	14.4 (0.82)	22.4 (0.83)	24.9 (1.09)	22.1 (1.03)	10.6 (0.75)	9.1 (0.68)	1.5 (0.25)
New Zealand	508 (2.1)	18.0 (0.78)	0.6 (0.15)	4.3 (0.43)	13.1 (0.60)	22.0 (0.64)	26.8 (0.72)	21.8 (0.67)	11.3 (0.60)	9.5 (0.58)	1.8 (0.27)
Norway	490 (2.3)	20.8 (0.95)	1.1 (0.21)	5.7 (0.41)	14.1 (0.79)	25.0 (0.89)	28.6 (0.74)	18.7 (0.72)	6.8 (0.48)	6.1 (0.47)	0.7 (0.13)
Poland	511 (2.6)	13.8 (0.78)	0.2!! (0.11)	2.5 (0.34)	11.1 (0.67)	24.9 (0.84)	30.0 (0.97)	22.0 (0.81)	9.3 (0.81)	8.1 (0.71)	1.2 (0.25)
Portugal[6]	492 (2.8)	19.6 (1.03)	0.4 (0.13)	4.4 (0.62)	14.7 (0.75)	24.9 (0.94)	29.4 (1.01)	19.2 (0.86)	5.6 (0.57)	5.1 (0.53)	0.5! (0.15)
Slovak Republic	464 (2.3)	29.3 (1.01)	1.4 (0.25)	7.9 (0.59)	19.9 (0.74)	28.5 (0.88)	25.3 (0.76)	13.2 (0.63)	3.7 (0.38)	3.4 (0.33)	0.3! (0.11)
Slovenia	507 (1.3)	14.6 (0.65)	0.2! (0.10)	2.5 (0.29)	11.9 (0.58)	24.6 (0.79)	31.8 (1.00)	21.8 (0.87)	7.3 (0.59)	6.7 (0.55)	0.6 (0.17)
Spain[7]	483 (1.6)	21.3 (0.65)	0.6 (0.10)	4.5 (0.28)	16.2 (0.54)	28.4 (0.50)	29.4 (0.51)	16.8 (0.44)	4.2 (0.27)	3.9 (0.24)	0.3 (0.07)
Sweden	499 (3.1)	19.0 (1.06)	0.6 (0.16)	4.6 (0.52)	13.8 (0.75)	28.0 (0.69)	28.0 (0.85)	20.7 (0.93)	8.3 (0.56)	7.3 (0.52)	1.0 (0.18)
Switzerland	495 (3.0)	20.2 (0.98)	0.4! (0.14)	4.6 (0.48)	15.2 (0.75)	24.9 (0.87)	27.8 (0.94)	19.3 (1.02)	7.8 (0.74)	6.9 (0.69)	0.9 (0.17)
Turkey[4]	468 (2.0)	25.2 (1.06)	0.3! (0.12)	4.7 (0.45)	20.1 (0.81)	32.8 (0.95)	27.3 (1.02)	12.3 (0.67)	2.5 (0.46)	2.3 (0.44)	0.1!! (0.07)
United Kingdom	505 (2.6)	17.4 (0.93)	0.6 (0.15)	3.9 (0.41)	12.9 (0.65)	24.0 (0.82)	28.1 (0.76)	20.8 (0.74)	9.7 (0.61)	8.2 (0.55)	1.5 (0.22)
United States[5]	502 (3.3)	18.6 (1.16)	0.5! (0.18)	4.4 (0.54)	13.7 (0.82)	23.6 (0.86)	27.5 (0.92)	21.1 (0.93)	9.1 (0.74)	7.9 (0.73)	1.3 (0.22)
Non-OECD education systems											
Albania	417 (2.0)	47.0 (1.26)	1.5 (0.24)	11.7 (0.65)	33.7 (1.00)	34.8 (1.06)	15.1 (0.70)	2.9 (0.31)	0.2! (0.07)	0.2! (0.07)	#!! (†)
Algeria	404 (2.9)	53.5 (1.42)	4.9 (0.56)	18.2 (0.96)	30.4 (1.08)	27.0 (0.94)	15.0 (0.75)	4.1 (0.41)	0.5 (0.13)	0.5 (0.12)	#!! (†)
Baku (Azerbaijan)[8]	398 (2.4)	57.8 (1.24)	2.5 (0.30)	17.3 (0.97)	38.0 (1.02)	29.9 (0.85)	10.3 (0.75)	1.8 (0.43)	0.1! (0.05)	0.1! (0.05)	#! (†)
Beijing, Shanghai, Jiangsu, Zhejiang (China)	590 (2.7)	2.1 (0.34)	#!! (†)	0.3! (0.10)	1.8 (0.28)	8.4 (0.63)	23.4 (0.91)	34.6 (1.03)	31.5 (1.35)	24.3 (1.07)	7.2 (0.70)
Belarus	471 (2.4)	24.2 (1.17)	0.5! (0.18)	5.0 (0.51)	18.7 (0.88)	31.3 (0.85)	28.8 (0.85)	13.1 (0.81)	2.6 (0.41)	2.5 (0.38)	0.1!! (0.07)
Bosnia and Herzegovina	398 (2.7)	56.8 (1.56)	2.9 (0.41)	18.2 (0.94)	35.6 (1.01)	29.4 (1.19)	11.7 (0.87)	1.9 (0.28)	0.1!! (0.07)	0.1!! (0.07)	# (†)
Brazil[4]	404 (2.1)	55.4 (0.98)	4.0 (0.40)	19.9 (0.69)	31.4 (0.82)	25.3 (0.69)	13.9 (0.67)	4.6 (0.42)	0.8 (0.15)	0.8 (0.15)	#!! (†)
Brunei Darussalam	431 (1.2)	45.7 (0.63)	1.9 (0.28)	14.2 (0.65)	29.7 (0.77)	25.5 (0.53)	17.4 (0.49)	9.0 (0.39)	2.3 (0.28)	2.1 (0.25)	0.1!! (0.08)
Bulgaria[4]	424 (3.6)	46.5 (1.61)	3.0 (0.50)	15.3 (1.01)	28.3 (0.92)	26.7 (1.11)	17.9 (0.87)	7.4 (0.64)	1.5 (0.34)	1.4 (0.32)	0.1!! (0.06)
Chinese Taipei	516 (2.9)	15.1 (0.78)	0.7 (0.17)	3.3 (0.33)	11.2 (0.63)	21.1 (0.86)	28.5 (0.94)	23.5 (0.80)	11.7 (0.88)	10.0 (0.77)	1.6 (0.30)

See notes at end of table.

Table 602.70. Average science literacy scores of 15-year-old students and percentage attaining science literacy proficiency levels, by country or other education system: 2018—Continued

[Standard errors appear in parentheses]

Country or other education system	Average science literacy score[1]	Total below level 2	Below level 1b	At level 1b	At level 1a	At level 2	At level 3	At level 4	Total at or above level 5	At level 5	At level 6
1	2	3	4	5	6	7	8	9	10	11	12
Costa Rica[4]	416 (3.3)	47.8 (1.76)	1.3 (0.30)	12.0 (0.84)	34.5 (1.24)	34.4 (1.15)	14.9 (1.20)	2.8 (0.58)	0.1!! (0.06)	0.1!! (0.06)	# (†)
Croatia	472 (2.8)	25.4 (1.23)	0.6 (0.18)	5.6 (0.52)	19.1 (0.85)	30.0 (0.84)	26.9 (0.91)	14.2 (0.74)	3.6 (0.39)	3.3 (0.39)	0.3! (0.12)
Cyprus	439 (1.4)	39.0 (0.96)	2.0 (0.35)	11.9 (0.64)	25.0 (0.85)	28.9 (1.01)	21.4 (0.67)	9.1 (0.43)	1.6 (0.22)	1.5 (0.22)	0.1! (0.05)
Dominican Republic[4]	336 (2.5)	84.8 (1.14)	13.6 (1.01)	39.6 (1.29)	31.6 (1.31)	12.3 (0.89)	2.6 (0.42)	0.3! (0.12)	#!! (†)	#!! (†)	# (†)
Georgia	383 (2.3)	64.4 (1.20)	5.8 (0.54)	22.9 (0.94)	35.7 (0.90)	24.3 (0.93)	9.5 (0.63)	1.7 (0.28)	0.1! (0.05)	0.1! (0.05)	# (†)
Hong Kong (China)[5]	517 (2.5)	11.6 (0.76)	0.2!! (0.11)	2.4 (0.31)	8.9 (0.65)	21.7 (0.76)	33.8 (0.89)	25.0 (0.95)	7.8 (0.69)	7.1 (0.60)	0.7 (0.18)
Indonesia	396 (2.4)	60.0 (1.48)	1.8 (0.31)	16.8 (0.98)	41.4 (1.12)	29.2 (1.20)	9.2 (0.82)	1.6 (0.34)	0.1!! (0.05)	0.1!! (0.04)	#!! (†)
Jordan[4]	429 (2.9)	40.3 (1.38)	3.2 (0.44)	11.0 (0.78)	26.2 (0.90)	32.4 (1.02)	20.7 (0.88)	6.0 (0.51)	0.7 (0.17)	0.6 (0.17)	#!! (†)
Kazakhstan	397 (1.7)	60.3 (0.97)	2.2 (0.28)	17.8 (0.74)	40.3 (0.79)	26.9 (0.84)	9.9 (0.46)	2.5 (0.30)	0.4 (0.09)	0.4 (0.09)	#!! (†)
Kosovo	365 (1.2)	76.5 (0.73)	4.2 (0.42)	29.3 (0.86)	43.1 (0.97)	19.2 (0.74)	3.9 (0.35)	0.4! (0.12)	#!! (†)	#!! (†)	# (†)
Lebanon	384 (3.5)	62.3 (1.57)	8.9 (0.78)	23.6 (1.22)	29.7 (1.00)	21.8 (0.96)	11.8 (0.84)	3.6 (0.38)	0.5! (0.17)	0.5! (0.17)	#!! (†)
Macao (China)	544 (1.5)	6.0 (0.55)	0.1!! (0.07)	0.8 (0.18)	5.1 (0.52)	17.2 (0.72)	32.3 (0.97)	30.8 (0.89)	13.6 (0.55)	11.9 (0.58)	1.7 (0.30)
Malaysia[4]	438 (2.7)	36.6 (1.31)	0.7 (0.16)	8.3 (0.66)	27.6 (1.01)	35.9 (0.98)	21.5 (0.94)	5.4 (0.76)	0.6 (0.19)	0.6 (0.19)	#!! (†)
Malta	457 (1.9)	33.5 (0.93)	3.4 (0.41)	10.8 (0.70)	19.4 (0.74)	23.7 (0.87)	23.7 (0.89)	13.5 (0.70)	4.4 (0.42)	3.9 (0.42)	0.5! (0.14)
Moldova, Republic of	428 (2.3)	42.6 (1.17)	2.4 (0.28)	12.7 (0.73)	27.4 (0.86)	29.7 (0.89)	20.2 (0.84)	6.6 (0.54)	0.9 (0.21)	0.8 (0.21)	#!! (†)
Montenegro, Republic of	415 (1.3)	48.2 (0.73)	2.2 (0.32)	14.6 (0.57)	31.4 (0.79)	31.5 (0.70)	15.9 (0.59)	4.0 (0.33)	0.3! (0.11)	0.3! (0.11)	#!! (†)
Morocco[4]	377 (3.0)	69.4 (1.82)	2.6 (0.38)	26.1 (1.45)	40.7 (1.12)	24.0 (1.36)	6.1 (0.63)	0.4! (0.14)	#!! (†)	#!! (†)	#!! (†)
North Macedonia	413 (1.4)	49.5 (0.78)	4.5 (0.39)	15.5 (0.62)	29.4 (0.78)	28.2 (0.86)	16.4 (0.68)	5.2 (0.44)	0.8 (0.17)	0.8 (0.17)	#!! (†)
Panama[4]	365 (2.9)	71.3 (1.43)	10.5 (0.87)	27.3 (1.12)	33.5 (1.29)	19.7 (0.81)	7.4 (0.75)	1.5 (0.29)	0.1!! (0.06)	0.1!! (0.06)	#!! (†)
Peru[4]	404 (2.7)	54.5 (1.37)	2.7 (0.42)	17.3 (0.92)	34.5 (1.09)	29.0 (0.82)	13.2 (0.82)	3.1 (0.45)	0.2!! (0.12)	0.2!! (0.12)	#!! (†)
Philippines[4]	357 (3.2)	78.0 (1.48)	7.5 (0.78)	35.3 (1.37)	35.2 (1.15)	15.4 (0.82)	5.6 (0.73)	1.0 (0.29)	0.1!! (0.05)	0.1!! (0.05)	# (†)
Qatar	419 (0.9)	48.4 (0.50)	5.2 (0.32)	16.6 (0.44)	26.5 (0.56)	24.9 (0.47)	17.0 (0.39)	7.5 (0.29)	2.2 (0.18)	2.0 (0.18)	0.2 (0.06)
Romania[4]	426 (4.6)	43.9 (2.14)	2.9 (0.46)	13.1 (1.15)	28.0 (1.42)	29.8 (1.03)	18.9 (1.30)	6.4 (0.78)	1.0 (0.25)	0.9 (0.25)	#!! (†)
Russian Federation	478 (2.9)	21.2 (1.20)	0.4! (0.16)	4.1 (0.47)	16.7 (0.86)	31.7 (0.93)	30.0 (0.94)	14.0 (0.77)	3.1 (0.38)	2.9 (0.36)	0.2! (0.08)
Saudi Arabia	386 (2.8)	62.3 (1.49)	4.9 (0.64)	21.7 (0.98)	35.6 (0.99)	26.6 (0.99)	9.6 (0.75)	1.5 (0.26)	0.1!! (0.05)	0.1!! (0.05)	# (†)
Serbia	440 (3.0)	38.3 (1.55)	1.9 (0.31)	11.1 (0.80)	25.3 (1.03)	29.9 (0.87)	21.1 (0.87)	9.1 (0.69)	1.6 (0.21)	1.5 (0.20)	0.1! (0.04)
Singapore	551 (1.5)	9.0 (0.45)	0.2!! (0.06)	1.8 (0.21)	7.1 (0.42)	15.1 (0.69)	25.4 (0.73)	29.7 (0.74)	20.7 (0.60)	17.0 (0.55)	3.8 (0.30)
Thailand[4]	426 (3.2)	44.5 (1.52)	1.3 (0.27)	11.6 (0.82)	31.6 (1.14)	31.7 (0.91)	17.8 (1.02)	5.3 (0.71)	0.7 (0.16)	0.7 (0.16)	#!! (†)
Ukraine	469 (3.3)	26.4 (1.39)	1.0 (0.21)	6.3 (0.65)	19.2 (0.94)	30.0 (1.10)	26.7 (1.13)	13.4 (0.80)	3.5 (0.51)	3.2 (0.45)	0.3! (0.13)
United Arab Emirates	434 (2.0)	42.8 (0.87)	3.7 (0.21)	14.4 (0.50)	24.7 (0.62)	25.6 (0.52)	19.2 (0.51)	9.5 (0.52)	2.9 (0.23)	2.6 (0.21)	0.3! (0.08)
Uruguay	426 (2.5)	43.9 (1.31)	2.1 (0.36)	13.2 (0.82)	28.6 (1.02)	30.6 (0.97)	18.7 (0.91)	6.1 (0.51)	0.7 (0.16)	0.7 (0.16)	#!! (†)
Vietnam[9]	— (†)	— (†)	— (†)	— (†)	— (†)	— (†)	— (†)	— (†)	— (†)	— (†)	— (†)

—Not available.
†Not applicable.
#Rounds to zero.
!Interpret data with caution. The coefficient of variation (CV) for this estimate is between 30 and 50 percent.
!!Interpret data with caution. Estimate could be unstable because the standard error represents more than 50 percent of the estimate.

[1]Program for International Student Assessment (PISA) scores are reported on a scale from 0 to 1,000.
[2]To reach a particular proficiency level, a student must correctly answer a majority of items at that level. Students were classified into science literacy levels according to their scores. Exact cut scores are as follows: below level 1b (a score less than 260.54); level 1b (a score of at least 260.54 but less than 334.94); level 1a (a score of at least 334.94 but less than 409.54); level 2 (a score of at least 409.54 but less than 484.14); level 3 (a score of at least 484.14 but less than 558.73); level 4 (a score of at least 558.73 but less than 633.33); level 5 (a score of at least 633.33 but less than 707.93); and level 6 (a score of at least 707.93).
[3]Refers to the mean of the data values for all Organization for Economic Cooperation and Development (OECD) countries, to which each country contributes equally, regardless of the absolute size of the student population of each country.

[4]At least 50 percent but less than 75 percent of the 15-year-old population is covered by the Program for International Student Assessment (PISA) sample.
[5]Did not meet 85 percent threshold for school participation. However, data are considered to be largely comparable with data from other countries or education systems.
[6]Did not meet 80 percent threshold for student participation. However, data are considered to be largely comparable with data from other countries or education systems.
[7]Although Spain's PISA 2018 data met international technical standards, its reading literacy data show unusual student response behaviors that prevent these data from being reported at this time.
[8]Less than 50 percent of the 15-year-old population is covered by the PISA sample.
[9]Although Vietnam participated in PISA 2018, technical problems with its data prevent results from being included in this table.
NOTE: Detail may not sum to totals because of rounding.
SOURCE: Organization for Economic Cooperation and Development (OECD), Program for International Student Assessment (PISA), 2018. (This table was prepared December 2019.)

Table 603.10. Percentage of the population 25 to 64 years old who completed high school, by age group and country: Selected years, 2000 through 2018

[Standard errors appear in parentheses]

Country	2000 Total, 25 to 64	2000 25 to 34	2005 Total, 25 to 64	2005 25 to 34	2010 Total, 25 to 64	2010 25 to 34	2015 Total, 25 to 64	2015 25 to 34	2017 Total, 25 to 64	2017 25 to 34	2018 Total, 25 to 64	2018 25 to 34	2018 35 to 44	2018 45 to 54	2018 55 to 64
1	2	3	4	5	6	7	8	9	10	11	12	13	14	15	16
OECD average[1]	65.7	75.8	71.2	79.5	75.0 (0.06)	81.7 (0.12)	76.8 (0.03)	83.3 (0.07)	78.3 (0.03)	84.4 (0.06)	78.9 (0.03)	84.7 (0.06)	81.9 (0.05)	77.6 (0.05)	70.5 (0.06)
Australia	58.8	68.3	65.0	78.6	73.2	84.8 (—)	79.0 (0.25)	88.1 (0.39)	81.0 (0.23)	89.4 (0.36)	81.9 (0.23)	89.5 (0.35)	87.4 (0.39)	78.4 (0.48)	69.5 (0.56)
Austria[2]	—	—	76.9	85.6	82.4 (0.12)	87.8 (0.23)	84.6 (0.12)	90.0 (0.22)	85.0 (0.11)	88.5 (0.22)	85.3 (0.11)	88.9 (0.22)	87.7 (0.22)	85.2 (0.21)	69.5 (0.25)
Belgium	58.5	75.3	66.1	80.9	70.5	82.1	74.7 (0.19)	82.5 (0.35)	76.8 (0.15)	82.5 (0.29)	76.8 (0.15)	85.4 (0.27)	83.0 (0.27)	78.8 (0.28)	65.8 (0.31)
Canada[2,3]	80.7	88.3	85.2	90.8	88.3 (0.12)	92.1 (0.19)	90.4 (0.11)	93.3 (0.17)	91.1 (0.12)	93.5 (0.18)	91.6 (0.12)	93.9 (0.17)	94.0 (0.18)	91.9 (0.19)	86.8 (0.24)
Chile	—	—	—	—	†	†	64.9 (0.13)	83.2 (0.20)	67.4 (0.14)	85.2 (0.21)	†	†	†	†	†
Colombia	—	—	—	—	†	†	50.4 (0.08)	66.9 (0.14)	53.8 (0.08)	70.0 (0.13)	55.2 (0.08)	70.5 (0.13)	60.0 (0.16)	44.2 (0.17)	34.6 (0.17)
Czech Republic	85.9	92.4	89.9	93.9	91.9	94.2	93.2 (0.07)	93.6 (0.16)	93.8 (0.07)	94.0 (0.16)	93.9 (0.17)	93.7 (0.17)	94.9 (0.13)	95.4 (0.13)	91.0 (0.17)
Denmark	79.8	86.9	81.0	87.4	75.6	79.6	80.4 (0.17)	83.6 (0.36)	81.3 (0.18)	83.3 (0.37)	80.9 (0.14)	82.6 (0.30)	84.1 (0.28)	82.0 (0.27)	74.9 (0.29)
Estonia[2]	85.2	91.4	88.7	87.3	89.1 (0.30)	86.5 (0.73)	88.6 (0.28)	87.7 (0.60)	88.7 (0.26)	87.2 (0.57)	89.2 (0.25)	87.9 (0.57)	87.3 (0.52)	92.1 (0.42)	89.6 (0.46)
Finland[2]	73.2	86.3	78.8	89.4	83.0	90.8	87.2 (0.21)	89.5 (0.42)	88.1 (0.13)	90.2 (0.25)	89.1 (0.12)	90.5 (0.25)	92.0 (0.22)	90.1 (0.24)	84.0 (0.27)
France[2]	62.2	76.4	66.8	81.5	70.8	83.8	77.5 (0.08)	86.5 (0.15)	78.4 (0.08)	86.2 (0.15)	79.4 (0.08)	87.0 (0.15)	84.7 (0.15)	78.7 (0.15)	67.7 (0.18)
Germany	81.7	84.9	83.1	84.1	85.8	86.5	86.8 (0.06)	87.3 (0.12)	86.5 (0.05)	86.9 (0.11)	86.7 (0.05)	87.0 (0.11)	85.9 (0.12)	87.2 (0.10)	86.5 (0.10)
Greece	49.3	68.7	57.7	74.4	62.7 (0.12)	75.5 (0.22)	70.2 (0.13)	83.6 (0.24)	72.7 (0.13)	85.7 (0.24)	73.4 (0.13)	87.0 (0.24)	80.1 (0.23)	71.8 (0.24)	55.2 (0.26)
Hungary[2]	69.2	81.3	76.4	85.0	81.3	85.5	83.2 (0.10)	86.0 (0.21)	84.0 (0.11)	86.0 (0.23)	84.9 (0.11)	86.2 (0.23)	86.2 (0.20)	85.6 (0.21)	80.7 (0.22)
Iceland[2]	—	—	68.2	70.9	70.7 (0.48)	73.6 (0.91)	74.7 (0.47)	75.2 (0.96)	77.1 (0.49)	80.7 (0.98)	77.9 (0.44)	80.6 (0.89)	81.6 (0.80)	78.2 (0.85)	70.0 (0.94)
Ireland	57.3	73.0	64.5	81.1	72.8	85.6	79.8 (0.13)	90.8 (0.19)	82.0 (0.14)	91.9 (0.22)	83.2 (0.14)	92.4 (0.23)	88.8 (0.23)	80.5 (0.29)	67.5 (0.36)
Israel	—	—	78.9	85.5	82.1	88.1	85.5 (0.09)	91.2 (0.13)	87.4 (0.09)	92.4 (0.13)	†	†	†	†	†
Italy	42.1	56.4	50.1	65.9	55.2	71.0	59.9 (0.09)	74.4 (0.19)	60.9 (0.09)	74.8 (0.19)	61.7 (0.09)	75.9 (0.19)	67.5 (0.18)	56.8 (0.17)	50.2 (0.17)
Japan	—	—	—	—	—	—	—	—	—	—	—	—	—	—	—
Korea, Republic of[4]	68.2	93.2	75.6	97.3	80.9	97.9	85.8	98.3	87.6 (0.17)	98.0 (0.13)	88.2 (0.16)	97.8 (0.14)	97.8 (0.14)	92.1 (0.26)	65.4 (0.60)
Latvia	83.2	88.7	84.4	80.4	88.6 (0.23)	84.9 (0.56)	87.4 (0.23)	84.9 (0.56)	87.6 (0.22)	85.4 (0.54)	87.6 (0.23)	85.4 (0.52)	83.4 (0.55)	90.0 (0.40)	89.7 (0.38)
Lithuania	84.2	91.8	87.5	86.6	91.9 (0.14)	89.7 (0.43)	91.4 (0.16)	89.7 (0.43)	92.8 (0.14)	92.9 (0.33)	93.0 (0.14)	92.9 (0.33)	93.4 (0.39)	95.1 (0.20)	95.0 (0.20)
Luxembourg	60.9	68.2	65.9	76.5	77.7	84.5 (0.59)	74.6 (0.33)	84.5 (0.59)	76.7 (0.36)	87.3 (0.65)	77.2 (0.23)	86.9 (0.35)	80.9 (0.40)	72.3 (0.45)	65.5 (0.67)
Mexico[5]	29.1	37.1	28.2	33.7	32.1 (0.11)	38.3 (0.20)	35.7 (0.11)	45.0 (0.21)	37.7 (0.09)	48.1 (0.21)	39.1 (0.11)	50.1 (0.21)	37.9 (0.15)	34.7 (0.22)	28.8 (0.25)
Netherlands[5]	64.9	74.3	71.8	81.3	73.0	82.7	76.4	85.6	78.4 (0.09)	86.7 (0.17)	79.0 (0.08)	87.1 (0.15)	84.4 (0.15)	77.2 (0.16)	68.5 (0.17)
New Zealand	—	—	—	—	†	†	74.7 (—)	—	78.9 (0.30)	85.0 (0.55)	80.5 (0.29)	86.7 (0.51)	84.4 (0.54)	77.7 (0.59)	71.8 (0.66)
Norway[2]	79.9	89.4	77.2	83.5	80.6	83.1	82.4 (0.17)	82.4 (0.17)	82.0 (0.16)	80.7 (0.34)	82.5 (0.16)	82.2 (0.33)	84.9 (0.30)	83.1 (0.30)	79.4 (0.35)
Poland[4]	19.4	31.8	85.1	92.0	88.5	93.6	90.1	93.9	92.1 (0.07)	94.5 (0.12)	92.4 (0.07)	94.4 (0.12)	94.6 (0.12)	92.3 (0.15)	88.2 (0.15)
Portugal[2]	—	—	26.5	42.8	31.9	52.1	45.1 (0.17)	66.7 (0.39)	48.0 (0.17)	69.6 (0.39)	49.8 (0.18)	71.5 (0.41)	60.6 (0.34)	42.8 (0.32)	28.3 (0.29)
Slovak Republic	83.8	93.7	87.9	92.8	91.0	94.1	91.3 (0.25)	92.8 (0.49)	91.3 (0.26)	91.3 (0.57)	91.6 (0.25)	91.9 (0.56)	92.7 (0.49)	93.1 (0.47)	88.3 (0.52)
Slovenia[5]	74.8	85.4	80.3	91.2	83.3	91.2	86.8 (0.18)	94.1 (0.27)	87.7 (0.17)	94.4 (0.27)	88.1 (0.17)	94.3 (0.27)	93.2 (0.28)	86.6 (0.34)	79.2 (0.40)
Spain[5]	38.6	55.6	48.8	64.5	52.9	65.3	57.4 (0.08)	65.6 (0.19)	59.1 (0.08)	66.2 (0.20)	60.1 (0.08)	67.7 (0.19)	67.7 (0.16)	58.5 (0.15)	45.9 (0.16)
Sweden	77.6	87.3	83.6	90.6	86.3	90.8	82.0 (0.10)	82.3 (0.20)	83.0 (0.10)	82.7 (0.20)	83.2 (0.10)	82.7 (0.20)	84.1 (0.19)	85.7 (0.15)	80.0 (0.21)
Switzerland	83.9	89.8	85.2	89.8	85.0	89.8	87.3 (0.11)	91.0 (0.23)	87.8 (0.11)	91.9 (0.23)	88.4 (0.11)	92.9 (0.22)	89.3 (0.21)	87.2 (0.21)	84.2 (0.21)
Turkey[4]	23.3	27.7	28.1	36.8	31.2	42.2	37.0 (—)	42.2	39.3	55.5 (0.19)	40.2 (0.10)	57.2 (0.20)	42.4 (0.18)	26.7 (0.18)	23.7 (0.19)
United Kingdom[6]	62.6	66.8	66.8	73.1	75.1	82.9	79.6 (0.18)	86.2 (0.33)	81.2 (0.18)	87.5 (0.32)	79.3 (0.19)	84.9 (0.36)	84.2 (0.35)	76.1 (0.39)	71.3 (0.43)
United States[2]	87.4	88.2	87.8	86.7	89.0	88.4	89.5 (0.10)	90.5 (0.18)	90.6 (0.09)	92.1 (0.17)	90.8 (0.10)	92.4 (0.17)	90.4 (0.19)	90.2 (0.19)	90.1 (0.21)
Other reporting countries															
China[6]	—	—	—	—	24.5 (—)	—	—	—	—	—	†	†	†	†	†
Russian Federation[2]	—	—	—	—	92.8 (0.03)	92.6 (0.07)	93.7 (0.03)	93.5 (0.06)	95.2 (—)	95.4 (—)	†	†	†	†	†

—Not available.
†Not applicable.
[1] Refers to the mean of the data values for all reporting Organization for Economic Cooperation and Development (OECD) countries, to which each country reporting data contributes equally. The average includes all current OECD countries for which a given year's data are available, even if they were not members of OECD in that year. Standard errors for the OECD average were estimated by the National Center for Education Statistics (NCES).
[2] Although all data for years prior to 2015 were originally calculated using the 1997 version of the International Standard Classification of Education (ISCED), the footnoted countries revised earlier years' data to align with the 2011 version of ISCED, which is the most recent. Most of these countries revised all of their data for years prior to 2015. The exceptions are Mexico (which revised only 2005 and 2010 data) and Spain (which revised only 2010 data).
[3] All standard errors shown for Canada were calculated by Statistics Canada.
[4] For 2017 and 2018, standard errors were estimated by NCES.
[5] For 2017, standard errors were estimated by NCES.

[6] Data include some persons who completed a sufficient number of certain types of programs, any one of which individually would be classified as a program that only partially completes the high school (or upper secondary) level of education.
NOTE: The International Standard Classification of Education (ISCED) was revised in 2011. Unless otherwise noted, all data for years prior to 2015 were calculated using the previous version, ISCED 1997. ISCED 2011 was used to calculate all data for 2015 and later years. Except where otherwise noted, data in this table refer to degrees classified under ISCED 2011 as completing level 3 (upper secondary education) or comparable degrees under ISCED 1997. For more information on OECD and NCES estimation methodology used for this table, see the "Online Education Database" section of the entry for OECD in Appendix A: Guide to Sources. Some data have been revised from previously published figures.
SOURCE: Organization for Economic Cooperation and Development (OECD), Online Education Database, retrieved September 23, 2019, from https://stats.oecd.org/Index.aspx. Eurostat, unpublished tabulations on population by age group. (This table was prepared September 2019.)

Table 603.20. Percentage of the population 25 to 64 years old who attained any postsecondary degree, by age group and country: Selected years, 2000 through 2018

[Standard errors appear in parentheses]

Country	2000 Total, 25 to 64 years old	2000 25 to 34 years old	2005 Total, 25 to 64 years old	2005 25 to 34 years old	2010 Total, 25 to 64 years old	2010 25 to 34 years old	2015 Total, 25 to 64 years old	2015 25 to 34 years old	2017 Total, 25 to 64 years old	2017 25 to 34 years old	2018 Total, 25 to 64 years old	2018 25 to 34 years old	2018 35 to 44 years old	2018 45 to 54 years old	2018 55 to 64 years old
1	2	3	4	5	6	7	8	9	10	11	12	13	14	15	16
OECD average[1]	22.3	26.4	26.5	32.4	30.6 (0.07)	37.7 (0.16)	34.3 (0.04)	41.8 (0.09)	36.2 (0.04)	43.7 (0.08)	36.9 (0.04)	44.5 (0.08)	42.4 (0.08)	33.3 (0.07)	27.0 (0.07)
Australia	27.5	31.4	31.7	38.1	37.6 (—)	44.4 (—)	42.9 (0.30)	48.5 (0.60)	45.4 (0.30)	52.0 (0.59)	45.7 (0.29)	51.4 (0.57)	51.9 (0.59)	42.5 (0.58)	34.8 (0.58)
Austria[2]	—	—	24.6	30.6	27.7 (0.14)	33.9 (0.33)	30.6 (0.15)	38.6 (0.35)	32.4 (0.15)	40.3 (0.34)	32.7 (0.15)	40.5 (0.35)	37.5 (0.32)	29.6 (0.27)	23.8 (0.26)
Belgium	27.1	36.0	31.0	40.6	35.0 (—)	— (—)	43.1 (0.21)	43.1 (0.45)	40.3 (0.17)	45.7 (0.38)	40.6 (0.17)	47.4 (0.39)	45.8 (0.36)	38.8 (0.36)	30.7 (0.30)
Canada[2,3]	40.1	48.4	46.0	53.7	50.3 (0.22)	56.2 (0.43)	55.2 (0.20)	59.2 (0.37)	56.7 (0.22)	60.9 (0.40)	57.9 (0.24)	61.8 (0.41)	63.8 (0.38)	58.5 (0.38)	47.7 (0.37)
Chile	—	—	—	—	(†)	(†)	22.5 (0.11)	29.9 (0.24)	25.2 (0.13)	33.7 (0.28)	— (†)	— (†)	— (†)	— (†)	— (†)
Colombia	11.0	—	13.1	14.2	16.8 (—)	22.6 (—)	21.6 (0.07)	27.4 (0.13)	22.5 (0.07)	28.1 (0.13)	23.4 (0.07)	29.0 (0.13)	26.7 (0.14)	18.5 (0.13)	15.4 (0.13)
Czech Republic	—	11.2	13.5	14.2	— (†)	— (†)	22.2 (0.12)	31.0 (0.31)	23.9 (0.13)	33.8 (0.32)	24.3 (0.13)	33.3 (0.33)	26.7 (0.26)	18.9 (0.23)	17.3 (0.23)
Denmark	25.8	29.3	33.5	39.8	33.3 (—)	37.6 (—)	37.1 (0.21)	44.5 (0.49)	39.2 (0.22)	46.6 (0.50)	38.1 (0.18)	44.8 (0.40)	44.1 (0.39)	35.1 (0.33)	28.8 (0.30)
Estonia[2]	28.7	28.7	33.0	32.9	35.4 (0.46)	38.0 (1.03)	38.0 (0.42)	40.5 (0.89)	39.7 (0.39)	43.0 (0.85)	41.1 (0.39)	43.6 (0.87)	44.0 (0.78)	38.5 (0.75)	38.1 (0.73)
Finland[2]	32.6	38.7	34.6	37.5	38.1 (—)	39.2 (—)	42.7 (0.30)	40.5 (0.68)	44.3 (0.20)	41.3 (0.41)	45.2 (0.20)	41.3 (0.42)	51.2 (0.41)	48.6 (0.40)	40.1 (0.36)
France[2]	21.6	31.4	25.4	39.8	26.9 (—)	34.7 (—)	34.1 (0.09)	44.7 (0.22)	35.2 (0.09)	44.3 (0.22)	36.9 (0.10)	46.9 (0.23)	44.9 (0.20)	32.8 (0.18)	24.0 (0.16)
Germany	23.5	22.3	24.6	22.5	26.6 (—)	26.1 (—)	27.6 (0.07)	29.6 (0.16)	28.6 (0.07)	31.3 (0.15)	29.1 (0.07)	32.3 (0.16)	31.6 (0.16)	27.0 (0.13)	26.3 (0.13)
Greece	17.7	23.9	21.5	25.7	24.7 (0.11)	31.2 (0.24)	29.1 (0.13)	40.1 (0.32)	31.0 (0.13)	42.5 (0.34)	31.7 (0.13)	42.8 (0.35)	34.2 (0.27)	29.2 (0.24)	21.9 (0.22)
Hungary[2]	14.0	14.7	17.1	19.6	20.1 (—)	26.0 (—)	24.2 (0.12)	32.1 (0.29)	24.1 (0.12)	30.2 (0.30)	25.1 (0.13)	30.6 (0.31)	28.8 (0.27)	22.5 (0.25)	18.2 (0.21)
Iceland[2]	—	—	29.5	34.5	32.6 (0.50)	36.2 (0.99)	38.8 (0.53)	40.1 (1.08)	42.4 (0.57)	47.4 (1.24)	43.7 (0.52)	47.0 (1.12)	51.9 (1.03)	43.3 (1.02)	30.9 (0.95)
Ireland	21.6	29.8	29.1	40.7	37.6 (—)	48.3 (—)	42.8 (0.16)	52.0 (0.34)	45.7 (0.18)	53.5 (0.40)	46.9 (0.19)	56.2 (0.43)	53.8 (0.36)	42.9 (0.36)	31.2 (0.35)
Israel	—	—	43.0	42.9	45.6 (—)	44.2 (—)	48.8 (—)	45.9 (0.19)	50.9 (0.13)	48.0 (0.25)	— (†)	— (†)	— (†)	— (†)	— (†)
Italy	9.4	10.4	12.2	16.1	14.8 (—)	20.7 (—)	17.5 (0.07)	25.1 (0.19)	18.7 (0.07)	26.8 (0.20)	19.3 (0.07)	27.7 (0.20)	23.0 (0.16)	15.7 (0.12)	13.0 (0.12)
Japan[4,5]	33.6	47.8	39.9	53.2	44.8 (—)	56.7 (—)	49.5 (—)	59.6 (—)	51.4 (0.19)	60.4 (0.40)	51.9 (0.19)	60.7 (0.40)	56.3 (0.37)	49.0 (0.42)	43.0 (0.45)
Korea, Republic of[4]	23.8	36.8	31.6	50.9	39.0 (—)	61.4 (—)	45.4 (—)	68.9 (—)	47.7 (0.25)	69.8 (0.45)	49.0 (0.25)	69.6 (0.45)	64.3 (0.45)	41.9 (0.48)	23.1 (0.53)
Latvia[2]	18.2	17.3	20.3	21.7	26.9 (0.32)	34.7 (0.74)	31.6 (0.32)	39.9 (0.74)	33.9 (0.32)	41.6 (0.75)	33.9 (0.33)	41.6 (0.77)	39.6 (0.73)	29.0 (0.60)	25.9 (0.55)
Lithuania	41.8	39.7	26.5	36.9	32.4 (0.25)	46.3 (0.63)	38.7 (0.27)	54.8 (0.63)	40.3 (0.26)	55.6 (0.67)	41.7 (0.26)	55.6 (0.66)	49.7 (0.59)	33.7 (0.45)	30.1 (0.42)
Luxembourg	18.3	22.9	26.5	37.0	35.5 (—)	37.0 (—)	39.8 (0.37)	49.9 (0.82)	43.9 (0.42)	51.4 (0.98)	43.9 (0.27)	54.8 (0.52)	51.0 (0.51)	37.2 (0.49)	28.0 (0.63)
Mexico[2]	14.6	17.5	12.7	14.9	14.7 (0.08)	17.7 (0.16)	16.3 (0.08)	20.8 (0.17)	17.4 (0.09)	22.6 (0.18)	18.0 (0.09)	23.4 (0.18)	17.7 (0.17)	14.7 (0.16)	13.9 (0.19)
Netherlands[6]	23.4	26.6	30.1	35.4	32.4 (—)	40.8 (—)	35.3 (—)	45.1 (—)	37.2 (0.10)	46.6 (0.25)	38.3 (0.10)	47.6 (0.22)	44.2 (0.21)	34.1 (0.18)	29.0 (0.16)
New Zealand[6]	—	—	—	—	37.3 (—)	47.3 (—)	34.0 (0.21)	39.1 (0.45)	37.7 (0.36)	44.2 (0.76)	39.3 (0.36)	45.8 (0.75)	44.2 (0.73)	35.5 (0.68)	30.4 (0.68)
Norway[4]	—	—	32.7	40.9	37.3 (—)	47.3 (—)	42.7 (—)	48.1 (—)	43.2 (0.21)	48.3 (0.43)	43.6 (0.21)	48.2 (0.43)	48.7 (0.42)	42.0 (0.39)	34.3 (0.41)
Poland[4]	11.4	14.2	16.9	25.5	22.5 (—)	37.1 (—)	27.7 (—)	43.2 (—)	29.9 (0.11)	43.5 (0.26)	30.9 (0.12)	43.5 (0.27)	39.8 (0.25)	23.0 (0.23)	15.3 (0.17)
Portugal[2]	8.8	12.9	12.8	19.1	15.4 (—)	24.8 (—)	22.9 (0.14)	33.1 (0.39)	24.0 (0.15)	34.0 (0.42)	25.0 (0.15)	35.1 (0.44)	32.0 (0.33)	20.5 (0.26)	14.2 (0.22)
Slovak Republic	10.4	11.2	14.0	16.3	24.0 (—)	24.0 (—)	21.1 (0.36)	31.3 (0.88)	23.1 (0.38)	35.1 (0.96)	24.6 (0.39)	37.2 (1.00)	26.0 (0.82)	17.7 (0.70)	15.6 (0.58)
Slovenia[6]	15.7	19.3	20.2	24.7	23.7 (—)	34.7 (—)	30.2 (0.25)	40.8 (0.57)	34.3 (0.25)	44.6 (0.58)	32.5 (0.25)	40.7 (0.58)	40.4 (0.54)	28.8 (0.46)	21.1 (0.40)
Spain[2]	22.7	34.0	28.5	40.7	31.0 (0.08)	40.3 (0.17)	35.1 (0.08)	41.0 (0.19)	36.4 (0.08)	42.6 (0.20)	37.3 (0.08)	44.3 (0.21)	44.2 (0.16)	35.1 (0.15)	25.1 (0.14)
Sweden	30.1	33.6	29.6	37.3	33.9 (0.11)	42.4 (—)	39.8 (0.12)	46.4 (0.26)	41.9 (0.13)	47.4 (0.26)	43.3 (0.13)	47.5 (0.27)	52.3 (0.27)	39.5 (0.27)	32.6 (0.24)
Switzerland	24.2	25.6	28.8	31.0	33.9 (0.16)	37.4 (0.39)	39.8 (0.17)	46.5 (0.41)	42.6 (0.17)	50.1 (0.42)	43.7 (0.17)	51.2 (0.42)	49.5 (0.35)	40.4 (0.31)	33.6 (0.33)
Turkey[4]	8.3	8.9	10.2	12.5	13.1 (—)	17.4 (—)	18.0 (—)	27.5 (—)	20.0 (0.08)	31.6 (0.18)	20.8 (0.08)	33.3 (0.19)	20.4 (0.15)	12.4 (0.13)	10.0 (0.13)
United Kingdom	25.7	28.9	29.7	35.3	38.2 (0.15)	46.0 (0.30)	44.2 (0.23)	49.9 (0.48)	45.7 (0.23)	51.6 (0.49)	45.8 (0.24)	50.8 (0.50)	52.6 (0.48)	42.5 (0.45)	36.6 (0.45)
United States[2]	36.5	38.1	39.1	39.4	41.7 (0.15)	42.3 (0.30)	44.6 (0.16)	46.5 (0.31)	46.4 (0.16)	47.8 (0.32)	47.4 (0.16)	49.4 (0.33)	51.0 (0.32)	46.7 (0.33)	42.6 (0.34)
Other reporting countries															
China[2]	—	—	—	—	9.7 (—)	17.9 (—)	— (†)	56.3	— (0.13)	62.7	— (†)	— (†)	— (†)	— (†)	— (†)
Russian Federation[2]	—	—	—	—	50.4 (0.06)	52.5 (0.13)	52.4 (0.06)	56.3 (0.13)	— (—)	— (—)	— (†)	— (†)	— (†)	— (†)	— (†)

—Not available.
†Not applicable.

[1]Refers to the mean of the data values for all reporting Organization for Economic Cooperation and Development (OECD) countries, to which each country reporting data contributes equally. The average includes all current OECD countries for which a given year's data are available, even if they were not members of OECD in that year. Standard errors for the OECD average were estimated by the National Center for Education Statistics (NCES).

[2]Although all data for years prior to 2015 were originally calculated using the 1997 version of the International Standard Classification of Education (ISCED), the footnoted countries revised earlier years' data to align with the 2011 version of ISCED, which is the most recent. Most of these countries revised all of their data for years prior to 2015. The exceptions are Mexico (which revised only 2005 and 2010 data) and Spain (which revised only 2010 data).

[3]All standard errors shown for Canada were calculated by Statistics Canada.

[4]For 2017 and 2018, standard errors were estimated by NCES.

[5]Data for all years include some postsecondary nontertiary awards (i.e., awards that are below the associate's degree level).

[6]For 2017, standard errors were estimated by NCES.

NOTE: Data in this table include all tertiary degrees, which correspond to all degrees at the associate's level and above in the United States. The International Standard Classification of Education (ISCED) was revised in 2011. Unless otherwise noted, all data for years prior to 2015 were calculated using the previous version, ISCED 1997. ISCED 2011 was used to calculate all data for 2015 and later years. Under ISCED 2011, tertiary degrees are classified at the following levels: level 5 (corresponding to an associate's degree in the United States), level 6 (a bachelor's or equivalent degree), level 7 (a master's or equivalent degree), and level 8 (a doctoral or equivalent degree). For more information on OECD and NCES estimation methodology used for this table, see the "Online Education Database" section of the entry for OECD in Appendix A: Guide to Sources. Standard errors for 2000 and 2005 have been excluded due to limited data availability. Some data have been revised from previously published figures.
SOURCE: Organization for Economic Cooperation and Development (OECD), Online Education Database, retrieved September 23, 2019, from https://stats.oecd.org/Index.aspx. Eurostat, unpublished tabulations on population by age group. (This table was prepared September 2019.)

Table 603.30. Percentage of the population 25 to 64 years old who attained a postsecondary degree, by highest degree attained, age group, and country: 2018

[Standard errors appear in parentheses]

Country	Associate's degree (short-cycle tertiary)					Bachelor's or equivalent degree				
	Total, 25 to 64 years old	25 to 34 years old	35 to 44 years old	45 to 54 years old	55 to 64 years old	Total, 25 to 64 years old	25 to 34 years old	35 to 44 years old	45 to 54 years old	55 to 64 years old
1	2	3	4	5	6	7	8	9	10	11
OECD average[1]	**7.6** (0.02)	**7.9** (0.04)	**8.1** (0.04)	**8.1** (0.04)	**7.2** (0.04)	**17.5** (0.03)	**23.8** (0.07)	**19.7** (0.06)	**14.5** (0.05)	**11.5** (0.05)
Australia	11.8 (0.19)	10.8 (0.36)	12.5 (0.39)	13.0 (0.39)	11.1 (0.38)	25.5 (0.26)	31.0 (0.53)	28.9 (0.53)	22.4 (0.49)	18.1 (0.47)
Austria	15.1 (0.11)	15.7 (0.26)	15.4 (0.24)	15.7 (0.21)	13.3 (0.21)	3.8 (0.06)	9.6 (0.21)	3.0 (0.11)	1.8 (0.08)	1.1 (0.07)
Belgium	0.6 (0.03)	0.5 (0.06)	0.6 (0.06)	0.5 (0.05)	0.6 (0.05)	22.5 (0.15)	25.4 (0.34)	24.7 (0.31)	21.9 (0.28)	18.2 (0.25)
Canada[2,3]	26.1 (0.17)	24.8 (0.32)	27.3 (0.31)	27.6 (0.30)	24.7 (0.30)	21.6 (0.18)	26.4 (0.35)	24.2 (0.32)	20.7 (0.33)	15.1 (0.29)
Chile[2,4]	8.7 (0.09)	10.2 (0.18)	9.6 (0.18)	8.5 (0.16)	6.2 (0.15)	14.7 (0.11)	22.1 (0.24)	17.1 (0.23)	9.7 (0.17)	8.6 (0.17)
Colombia[5,6]	‡ (†)	‡ (†)	0.1 (0.02)	0.2 (0.02)	‡ (0.02)	23.4 (0.07)	29.0 (0.13)	26.2 (0.14)	18.5 (0.13)	15.4 (0.13)
Czech Republic	0.1 (0.01)	0.1 (0.02)	0.1 (0.02)	0.2 (0.16)	0.1 (0.02)	6.1 (0.07)	12.6 (0.23)	7.1 (0.15)	2.6 (0.09)	1.8 (0.08)
Denmark	5.1 (0.08)	4.6 (0.17)	5.7 (0.18)	5.6 (0.16)	4.3 (0.13)	18.5 (0.14)	21.7 (0.33)	19.6 (0.31)	16.8 (0.26)	16.0 (0.24)
Estonia	6.0 (0.19)	— (†)	5.1 (0.34)	8.2 (0.42)	11.3 (0.48)	13.1 (0.27)	26.8 (0.78)	15.2 (0.56)	6.8 (0.39)	2.0 (0.21)
Finland	11.2 (0.13)	— (†)	4.6 (0.17)	19.5 (0.31)	20.3 (0.30)	17.4 (0.15)	26.7 (0.38)	24.2 (0.35)	11.5 (0.25)	7.7 (0.20)
France	14.4 (0.07)	14.0 (0.16)	18.2 (0.16)	14.7 (0.13)	10.7 (0.12)	10.2 (0.06)	12.8 (0.15)	12.4 (0.14)	9.7 (0.11)	6.1 (0.09)
Germany	0.6 (0.01)	0.4 (0.02)	0.4 (0.02)	0.7 (0.02)	0.7 (0.03)	15.4 (0.06)	17.2 (0.13)	15.4 (0.12)	14.7 (0.10)	14.6 (0.11)
Greece	1.8 (0.04)	1.5 (0.09)	1.1 (0.06)	1.8 (0.07)	2.6 (0.08)	25.6 (0.13)	36.1 (0.34)	26.8 (0.25)	23.6 (0.23)	17.1 (0.20)
Hungary	1.3 (0.03)	2.6 (0.11)	1.4 (0.07)	0.8 (0.05)	0.4 (0.03)	12.8 (0.10)	12.8 (0.23)	15.2 (0.21)	12.0 (0.19)	10.7 (0.17)
Iceland	2.3 (0.16)	1.2 (0.24)	2.0 (0.29)	3.5 (0.38)	2.7 (0.33)	22.6 (0.44)	27.3 (1.00)	25.9 (0.90)	20.6 (0.83)	15.1 (0.74)
Ireland	6.7 (0.10)	5.3 (0.20)	7.5 (0.19)	7.3 (0.19)	6.6 (0.19)	27.4 (0.17)	35.5 (0.42)	30.6 (0.33)	24.1 (0.31)	17.1 (0.29)
Israel	14.3 (0.09)	11.9 (0.16)	14.0 (0.17)	15.5 (0.19)	16.7 (0.21)	23.3 (0.11)	28.2 (0.23)	26.5 (0.22)	19.0 (0.21)	16.7 (0.21)
Italy	# (†)	0.1 (0.01)	# (†)	# (†)	‡ (†)	4.5 (0.04)	11.5 (0.14)	4.4 (0.08)	2.2 (0.05)	1.5 (0.04)
Japan[6,7,8]	21.3 (0.16)	19.8 (0.33)	24.3 (0.32)	22.9 (0.35)	17.2 (0.35)	30.7 (0.18)	40.9 (0.40)	31.9 (0.35)	26.1 (0.37)	25.8 (0.40)
Korea, Republic of[2]	13.7 (0.17)	21.0 (0.40)	20.2 (0.37)	9.9 (0.29)	4.7 (0.27)	30.7 (0.23)	45.3 (0.48)	37.9 (0.45)	26.9 (0.43)	14.5 (0.45)
Latvia	3.6 (0.13)	7.0 (0.40)	3.9 (0.29)	2.4 (0.20)	1.1 (0.13)	16.7 (0.26)	24.0 (0.67)	21.4 (0.61)	12.8 (0.44)	8.9 (0.36)
Lithuania	† (†)	† (†)	† (†)	† (†)	† (†)	26.7 (0.23)	39.7 (0.65)	33.1 (0.56)	20.4 (0.39)	15.6 (0.33)
Luxembourg	4.4 (0.11)	3.2 (0.18)	5.1 (0.22)	4.9 (0.22)	4.7 (0.30)	14.8 (0.19)	18.8 (0.41)	16.3 (0.38)	12.3 (0.33)	10.5 (0.43)
Mexico	0.5 (0.02)	0.5 (0.03)	0.5 (0.03)	0.5 (0.03)	0.3 (0.03)	15.9 (0.08)	21.5 (0.17)	15.4 (0.16)	12.4 (0.15)	12.0 (0.18)
Netherlands	2.2 (0.03)	1.1 (0.05)	2.4 (0.06)	2.6 (0.06)	2.5 (0.06)	22.1 (0.08)	28.2 (0.20)	25.4 (0.18)	18.8 (0.14)	16.9 (0.13)
New Zealand	3.8 (0.14)	3.8 (0.29)	3.1 (0.26)	3.7 (0.27)	4.6 (0.31)	29.3 (0.33)	36.8 (0.72)	33.8 (0.70)	24.7 (0.61)	20.5 (0.60)
Norway	11.8 (0.13)	12.6 (0.28)	11.6 (0.27)	11.7 (0.25)	11.1 (0.27)	19.2 (0.16)	20.9 (0.35)	21.5 (0.35)	18.9 (0.31)	15.2 (0.31)
Poland[8]	0.1 (0.01)	‡ (†)	‡ (†)	0.2 (0.02)	0.2 (0.02)	6.8 (0.06)	12.7 (0.18)	7.5 (0.13)	3.9 (0.10)	2.4 (0.07)
Portugal	‡ (†)	‡ (†)	‡ (†)	‡ (†)	‡ (†)	6.5 (0.09)	18.2 (0.35)	4.9 (0.15)	3.1 (0.11)	2.3 (0.10)
Slovak Republic	0.3 (0.05)	‡ (†)	0.4 (0.12)	0.3! (0.10)	0.2! (0.07)	3.1 (0.16)	6.8 (0.52)	2.7 (0.30)	1.7 (0.24)	0.8 (0.15)
Slovenia	7.5 (0.14)	6.4 (0.29)	6.8 (0.28)	9.1 (0.29)	7.6 (0.26)	6.6 (0.13)	10.6 (0.36)	9.7 (0.33)	4.4 (0.21)	2.5 (0.15)
Spain	11.3 (0.05)	13.2 (0.14)	13.7 (0.11)	11.4 (0.10)	6.4 (0.08)	10.4 (0.05)	14.0 (0.14)	11.7 (0.11)	8.7 (0.09)	7.7 (0.09)
Sweden	9.8 (0.08)	10.8 (0.17)	8.5 (0.15)	9.4 (0.15)	10.3 (0.16)	17.5 (0.10)	23.2 (0.23)	20.8 (0.22)	14.5 (0.18)	10.6 (0.16)
Switzerland[9]	‡ (†)	‡ (†)	‡ (†)	‡ (†)	‡ (†)	21.5 (0.14)	27.5 (0.38)	23.5 (0.29)	19.5 (0.25)	15.6 (0.25)
Turkey[8]	5.8 (0.05)	9.2 (0.11)	5.0 (0.08)	3.6 (0.07)	4.0 (0.09)	12.8 (0.07)	21.2 (0.16)	12.6 (0.12)	7.3 (0.10)	5.1 (0.10)
United Kingdom	9.7 (0.14)	7.1 (0.26)	9.1 (0.27)	11.4 (0.29)	11.1 (0.30)	22.9 (0.20)	29.2 (0.45)	26.7 (0.42)	19.2 (0.36)	16.1 (0.35)
United States	10.7 (0.10)	10.4 (0.20)	10.6 (0.20)	11.0 (0.20)	10.9 (0.22)	23.6 (0.14)	27.6 (0.30)	24.7 (0.27)	22.0 (0.27)	19.8 (0.28)

See notes at end of table.

Table 603.30. Percentage of the population 25 to 64 years old who attained a postsecondary degree, by highest degree attained, age group, and country: 2018—Continued

[Standard errors appear in parentheses]

Country	Master's or equivalent degree					Doctoral or equivalent degree				
	Total, 25 to 64 years old	25 to 34 years old	35 to 44 years old	45 to 54 years old	55 to 64 years old	Total, 25 to 64 years old	25 to 34 years old	35 to 44 years old	45 to 54 years old	55 to 64 years old
1	12	13	14	15	16	17	18	19	20	21
OECD average[1]	**12.7** (0.03)	**14.3** (0.06)	**15.4** (0.06)	**11.5** (0.05)	**9.2** (0.05)	**1.1** (0.01)	**0.9** (0.02)	**1.5** (0.02)	**1.2** (0.02)	**1.0** (0.02)
Australia	7.2 (0.15)	8.9 (0.33)	9.3 (0.34)	5.6 (0.27)	4.3 (0.25)	1.2 (0.06)	0.7 (0.09)	1.3 (0.13)	1.5 (0.14)	1.3 (0.14)
Austria	12.7 (0.11)	14.6 (0.25)	17.4 (0.25)	10.9 (0.18)	8.4 (0.17)	1.1 (0.03)	0.6 (0.05)	1.7 (0.09)	1.2 (0.06)	1.0 (0.06)
Belgium	16.7 (0.13)	20.7 (0.31)	19.2 (0.28)	15.7 (0.25)	11.4 (0.21)	0.8 (0.03)	0.7 (0.07)	1.4 (0.09)	0.7 (0.06)	0.6 (0.05)
Canada[2,3]	10.3 (0.15)	10.5 (0.27)	12.4 (0.29)	10.2 (0.26)	8.0 (0.21)	† (†)	† (†)	† (†)	† (†)	† (†)
Chile[2,4]	1.7 (0.04)	1.5 (0.07)	2.6 (0.10)	1.6 (0.07)	1.2 (0.07)	† (†)	† (†)	† (†)	† (†)	† (†)
Colombia[5,6]	‡ (†)	20.2 (0.28)	18.4 (0.23)	15.6 (0.22)	14.7 (0.21)	‡ (†)	0.4 (0.04)	1.1 (0.06)	0.6 (0.05)	0.5 (0.04)
Czech Republic	13.1 (0.12)	17.5 (0.30)	16.6 (0.29)	11.2 (0.22)	7.7 (0.18)	0.7 (0.03)	1.0 (0.08)	2.2 (0.11)	1.5 (0.09)	0.8 (0.06)
Denmark	21.3 (0.32)	16.3 (0.65)	22.5 (0.66)	22.8 (0.65)	24.1 (0.64)	1.4 (0.07)	0.6 (0.14)	1.2 (0.17)	0.6 (0.12)	0.6 (0.11)
Estonia	15.3 (0.14)	14.2 (0.30)	20.8 (0.33)	16.1 (0.29)	10.6 (0.23)	0.7 (0.04)	0.4 (0.06)	1.6 (0.10)	1.5 (0.10)	1.4 (0.09)
Finland	17.5 (0.40)	18.1 (0.86)	22.7 (0.86)	17.6 (0.78)	10.9 (0.64)	1.3 (0.12)	0.4! (0.15)	1.3 (0.24)	1.6 (0.26)	2.2 (0.30)
France	11.4 (0.06)	19.5 (0.18)	13.1 (0.14)	7.5 (0.10)	6.3 (0.09)	0.9 (0.02)	0.6 (0.04)	1.2 (0.04)	0.9 (0.04)	0.8 (0.03)
Germany	11.7 (0.05)	13.9 (0.12)	13.9 (0.12)	10.1 (0.09)	9.7 (0.09)	1.4 (0.02)	0.8 (0.03)	1.9 (0.05)	1.5 (0.04)	1.3 (0.03)
Greece	3.7 (0.05)	5.1 (0.16)	5.4 (0.13)	2.9 (0.09)	1.6 (0.07)	0.6 (0.02)	0.1 (0.02)	0.9 (0.05)	0.9 (0.05)	0.6 (0.04)
Hungary	10.3 (0.09)	14.8 (0.24)	11.6 (0.19)	8.6 (0.17)	6.4 (0.14)	0.7 (0.03)	0.4 (0.04)	0.7 (0.05)	1.1 (0.06)	0.7 (0.05)
Iceland	17.5 (0.40)	18.1 (0.86)	22.7 (0.86)	17.6 (0.78)	10.9 (0.64)	1.3 (0.12)	0.4! (0.15)	1.3 (0.24)	1.6 (0.26)	2.2 (0.30)
Ireland	11.5 (0.12)	14.1 (0.30)	14.1 (0.25)	10.2 (0.22)	6.4 (0.19)	1.3 (0.04)	1.3 (0.10)	1.6 (0.09)	1.2 (0.08)	1.0 (0.08)
Israel	12.0 (0.08)	7.6 (0.13)	14.3 (0.17)	14.4 (0.19)	12.7 (0.18)	1.3 (0.03)	0.4 (0.07)	1.4 (0.06)	1.8 (0.07)	2.0 (0.08)
Italy	14.3 (0.07)	15.8 (0.17)	17.6 (0.14)	13.1 (0.11)	11.3 (0.11)	0.5 (0.01)	0.4 (0.03)	0.9 (0.04)	0.5 (0.02)	0.2 (0.02)
Japan[6,7,8]	‡ (†)	‡ (†)	‡ (†)	‡ (†)	‡ (†)	‡ (†)	‡ (†)	‡ (†)	‡ (†)	‡ (†)
Korea, Republic of[2]	4.7 (0.11)	3.2 (0.17)	6.2 (0.22)	5.1 (0.21)	3.8 (0.24)	† (†)	† (†)	† (†)	† (†)	† (†)
Latvia	13.3 (0.24)	10.4 (0.48)	14.0 (0.52)	13.4 (0.45)	15.4 (0.45)	0.4 (0.04)	0.3 (0.09)	0.4 (0.09)	0.4 (0.08)	0.4 (0.08)
Lithuania	14.4 (0.19)	15.4 (0.48)	15.7 (0.43)	12.7 (0.32)	13.9 (0.32)	0.6 (0.04)	0.5 (0.09)	0.8 (0.11)	0.5 (0.07)	0.6 (0.07)
Luxembourg	22.5 (0.23)	31.0 (0.48)	26.9 (0.45)	17.9 (0.39)	10.8 (0.44)	2.2 (0.08)	1.8 (0.14)	2.7 (0.16)	2.1 (0.15)	2.0 (0.20)
Mexico	1.5 (0.03)	1.3 (0.05)	1.6 (0.06)	1.7 (0.06)	1.5 (0.07)	0.1 (0.01)	# (†)	0.1 (0.01)	0.1 (0.01)	0.1 (0.02)
Netherlands	13.3 (0.07)	17.7 (0.17)	15.3 (0.15)	11.9 (0.12)	9.0 (0.10)	0.7 (0.02)	0.6 (0.03)	1.1 (0.04)	0.8 (0.03)	0.6 (0.03)
New Zealand	5.1 (0.16)	4.6 (0.31)	5.9 (0.35)	5.6 (0.33)	4.1 (0.29)	1.1 (0.08)	0.6 (0.11)	1.4 (0.17)	1.5 (0.18)	1.1 (0.15)
Norway	11.5 (0.13)	14.1 (0.30)	14.1 (0.29)	10.0 (0.24)	7.3 (0.22)	1.1 (0.04)	0.7 (0.07)	1.5 (0.10)	1.5 (0.10)	0.7 (0.07)
Poland[8]	23.5 (0.11)	30.5 (0.25)	31.3 (0.24)	18.4 (0.21)	12.3 (0.16)	0.6 (0.02)	0.3 (0.03)	0.9 (0.05)	0.6 (0.04)	0.5 (0.03)
Portugal	17.7 (0.14)	16.3 (0.34)	26.1 (0.31)	16.3 (0.24)	11.2 (0.20)	0.8 (0.03)	0.5 (0.06)	0.9 (0.07)	1.0 (0.07)	0.8 (0.06)
Slovak Republic	20.3 (0.37)	29.1 (0.94)	21.4 (0.77)	15.2 (0.66)	14.2 (0.56)	0.9 (0.09)	1.2 (0.22)	1.4 (0.22)	0.6 (0.14)	0.4 (0.10)
Slovenia	14.5 (0.19)	18.3 (0.45)	18.8 (0.43)	11.8 (0.33)	9.5 (0.29)	3.8 (0.10)	5.3 (0.26)	5.1 (0.24)	3.4 (0.18)	1.6 (0.12)
Spain	14.8 (0.06)	16.6 (0.15)	17.9 (0.13)	14.2 (0.11)	10.2 (0.10)	0.7 (0.01)	0.4 (0.03)	0.7 (0.08)	0.7 (0.03)	0.8 (0.03)
Sweden[9]	14.3 (0.09)	12.9 (0.18)	20.5 (0.21)	13.5 (0.17)	10.1 (0.16)	1.6 (0.03)	0.6 (0.04)	2.5 (0.14)	2.1 (0.07)	1.5 (0.06)
Switzerland[9]	19.0 (0.14)	21.3 (0.35)	21.8 (0.29)	17.8 (0.24)	15.1 (0.25)	3.2 (0.06)	2.4 (0.13)	4.2 (0.14)	3.1 (0.11)	2.9 (0.12)
Turkey[8]	1.8 (0.03)	2.6 (0.06)	2.3 (0.06)	0.9 (0.04)	0.6 (0.03)	0.4 (0.01)	0.2 (0.02)	0.5 (0.03)	0.5 (0.03)	0.4 (0.03)
United Kingdom	11.8 (0.15)	13.4 (0.34)	15.1 (0.34)	10.4 (0.28)	8.2 (0.26)	1.4 (0.06)	1.0 (0.10)	1.7 (0.12)	1.5 (0.11)	1.3 (0.10)
United States	11.2 (0.10)	9.7 (0.20)	13.4 (0.22)	11.7 (0.21)	10.0 (0.21)	2.0 (0.05)	1.7 (0.09)	2.3 (0.09)	2.0 (0.09)	1.9 (0.09)

—Not available.
†Not applicable.
#Rounds to zero.
!Interpret data with caution. The coefficient of variation (CV) for this estimate is between 30 and 50 percent.
‡Reporting standards not met.
[1]Refers to the mean of the data values for all reporting Organization for Economic Cooperation and Development (OECD) countries, to which each country reporting data contributes equally. Standard errors for the OECD average were estimated by the National Center for Education Statistics (NCES).
[2]Doctoral or equivalent degree data are included in columns for master's or equivalent degree.
[3]Standard errors were calculated by Statistics Canada.
[4]Data are from 2017.
[5]Associate's degree data are included in columns for bachelor's or equivalent degree.
[6]Master's or equivalent degree data are included in columns for bachelor's or equivalent degree.

[7]Associate's degree data include postsecondary nontertiary awards (i.e., awards that are below the associate's degree level).
[8]Standard errors were estimated by NCES.
[9]Associate's degree data are included in columns for bachelor's or equivalent, master's or equivalent, and doctoral or equivalent degrees.
NOTE: All data in this table were calculated using the International Standard Classification of Education (ISCED) 2011 classification of tertiary degrees. Includes degrees at ISCED 2011 level 5 (short-cycle tertiary, which corresponds to the associate's degree in the United States), level 6 (bachelor's or equivalent degree), level 7 (master's or equivalent degree), and level 8 (doctoral or equivalent degree). For more information on OECD and NCES estimation methodology, see the "Online Education Database" section of the entry for OECD in Appendix A: Guide to Sources.
SOURCE: Organization for Economic Cooperation and Development (OECD), Online Education Database, retrieved September 23, 2019, from https://stats.oecd.org/Index.aspx. Eurostat, unpublished tabulations on population by age group. (This table was prepared September 2019.)

Table 603.90. Employment to population ratios of 25- to 64-year-olds, by sex, highest level of educational attainment, and country: 2018

[Standard errors appear in parentheses]

Country	Total population, 25 to 64 years old				Male				Female			
	All levels of education	Less than high school completion	High school completion	Associate's or higher degree	All levels of education	Less than high school completion	High school completion	Associate's or higher degree	All levels of education	Less than high school completion	High school completion	Associate's or higher degree
1	2	3	4	5	6	7	8	9	10	11	12	13
OECD average[1]	76.7 (0.03)	58.9 (0.10)	76.3 (0.05)	85.4 (0.05)	83.2 (0.04)	69.2 (0.14)	83.1 (0.06)	89.9 (0.06)	70.1 (0.05)	48.0 (0.15)	68.7 (0.08)	81.4 (0.07)
Australia	77.3 (0.25)	60.1 (0.67)	77.3 (0.41)	84.1 (0.32)	83.1 (0.32)	68.9 (0.92)	83.7 (0.48)	88.6 (0.43)	71.7 (0.37)	52.0 (0.94)	68.9 (0.69)	80.5 (0.46)
Austria	77.2 (0.13)	55.3 (0.42)	77.6 (0.18)	86.3 (0.20)	82.0 (0.18)	62.9 (0.68)	81.5 (0.24)	89.3 (0.25)	72.4 (0.20)	50.6 (0.53)	73.4 (0.27)	83.1 (0.31)
Belgium	73.0 (0.16)	46.5 (0.37)	74.1 (0.25)	86.1 (0.19)	77.4 (0.21)	55.0 (0.51)	79.8 (0.32)	88.3 (0.27)	68.6 (0.23)	37.3 (0.51)	67.5 (0.39)	84.2 (0.27)
Canada	77.7 (—)	55.6 (—)	74.5 (—)	82.7 (—)	81.5 (—)	63.7 (—)	79.7 (—)	86.3 (—)	73.9 (—)	44.4 (—)	67.4 (—)	79.9 (—)
Chile[2]	72.0 (0.14)	62.4 (0.24)	71.9 (0.21)	84.5 (0.23)	85.7 (0.15)	82.1 (0.28)	85.4 (0.24)	90.9 (0.27)	60.1 (0.20)	45.2 (0.35)	59.9 (0.31)	79.1 (0.35)
Colombia	74.9 (0.07)	71.1 (0.12)	74.9 (0.12)	82.0 (0.12)	88.6 (0.08)	88.9 (0.12)	88.0 (0.13)	89.1 (0.15)	61.9 (0.11)	52.6 (0.18)	62.6 (0.19)	76.5 (0.17)
Czech Republic	82.5 (0.12)	52.2 (0.60)	83.5 (0.13)	87.3 (0.22)	90.0 (0.13)	64.0 (0.94)	90.3 (0.15)	95.1 (0.21)	74.7 (0.19)	44.1 (0.76)	75.9 (0.22)	80.3 (0.35)
Denmark	81.6 (0.14)	65.0 (0.42)	83.3 (0.21)	87.9 (0.19)	83.9 (0.17)	69.6 (0.49)	85.5 (0.24)	90.4 (0.22)	76.8 (0.26)	53.3 (0.80)	78.0 (0.41)	84.1 (0.33)
Estonia	80.4 (0.31)	65.1 (1.13)	79.9 (0.46)	85.1 (0.44)	84.1 (0.42)	69.1 (1.40)	84.4 (0.56)	90.6 (0.62)	76.8 (0.46)	57.4 (1.91)	74.0 (0.73)	81.8 (0.60)
Finland	78.4 (0.16)	54.6 (0.60)	75.7 (0.26)	86.7 (0.20)	80.3 (0.22)	61.9 (0.74)	78.4 (0.33)	89.5 (0.28)	76.4 (0.24)	42.5 (0.97)	72.2 (0.40)	84.7 (0.28)
France	73.5 (0.09)	52.9 (0.21)	73.5 (0.13)	84.9 (0.12)	77.5 (0.12)	61.1 (0.30)	77.1 (0.18)	87.9 (0.17)	69.6 (0.13)	45.5 (0.28)	69.6 (0.20)	82.5 (0.18)
Germany	81.4 (0.06)	61.0 (0.22)	82.3 (0.08)	88.9 (0.09)	85.7 (0.08)	69.5 (0.30)	85.7 (0.10)	92.1 (0.11)	77.0 (0.09)	53.5 (0.30)	79.0 (0.12)	85.0 (0.15)
Greece	62.3 (0.14)	50.4 (0.25)	60.9 (0.22)	74.1 (0.24)	73.6 (0.18)	64.5 (0.34)	74.2 (0.29)	81.0 (0.32)	51.2 (0.20)	35.5 (0.34)	47.5 (0.32)	68.0 (0.35)
Hungary	77.0 (0.13)	57.0 (0.33)	78.3 (0.16)	85.8 (0.24)	84.8 (0.15)	68.2 (0.48)	85.6 (0.18)	92.8 (0.28)	69.3 (0.19)	48.1 (0.44)	69.9 (0.26)	80.6 (0.35)
Iceland	87.0 (0.35)	76.5 (0.94)	87.1 (0.60)	92.3 (0.42)	90.2 (0.45)	82.9 (1.16)	91.2 (0.66)	94.0 (0.61)	83.7 (0.54)	68.6 (1.48)	80.5 (1.12)	91.0 (0.58)
Ireland	75.4 (0.16)	52.4 (0.45)	73.6 (0.28)	85.1 (0.20)	82.3 (0.21)	64.7 (0.57)	83.0 (0.34)	89.7 (0.26)	68.8 (0.25)	35.4 (0.66)	64.1 (0.42)	81.2 (0.30)
Israel	77.8 (0.11)	52.5 (0.36)	73.6 (0.19)	87.1 (0.12)	82.9 (0.14)	68.6 (0.48)	78.4 (0.24)	90.8 (0.16)	72.9 (0.16)	35.4 (0.49)	67.7 (0.29)	84.2 (0.18)
Italy	65.8 (0.09)	52.5 (0.15)	70.9 (0.13)	81.1 (0.17)	76.4 (0.11)	67.7 (0.19)	80.8 (0.16)	86.1 (0.24)	55.5 (0.13)	35.9 (0.20)	60.8 (0.20)	77.5 (0.24)
Japan[3]	83.1 (—)	— (—)	— (—)	85.3 (—)	91.9 (—)	— (—)	— (—)	94.6 (—)	74.2 (—)	— (—)	— (—)	76.3 (—)
Korea, Republic of	74.1 (—)	64.7 (—)	72.4 (—)	77.6 (—)	85.3 (—)	75.4 (—)	83.7 (—)	88.4 (—)	62.4 (—)	57.7 (—)	60.9 (—)	65.1 (—)
Latvia	78.2 (0.29)	62.0 (0.90)	75.1 (0.40)	89.1 (0.39)	80.3 (0.41)	66.7 (1.11)	79.8 (0.53)	90.6 (0.65)	76.3 (0.40)	53.5 (1.49)	70.0 (0.60)	88.2 (0.49)
Lithuania	80.4 (0.21)	55.1 (1.03)	75.2 (0.31)	91.0 (0.24)	81.6 (0.31)	58.2 (1.33)	78.8 (0.41)	92.6 (0.38)	79.2 (0.29)	49.8 (1.62)	70.9 (0.46)	90.1 (0.32)
Luxembourg	76.6 (0.23)	62.0 (0.58)	74.5 (0.40)	85.7 (0.29)	81.3 (0.29)	70.7 (0.75)	77.7 (0.52)	89.6 (0.36)	71.8 (0.35)	53.5 (0.87)	71.1 (0.61)	81.8 (0.45)
Mexico	68.9 (0.11)	65.1 (0.14)	71.0 (0.22)	79.7 (0.20)	89.0 (0.11)	89.2 (0.14)	89.5 (0.22)	88.0 (0.24)	51.3 (0.16)	44.3 (0.21)	55.0 (0.33)	71.6 (0.32)
Netherlands	80.5 (0.08)	62.6 (0.22)	81.2 (0.12)	89.6 (0.09)	86.2 (0.10)	74.6 (0.28)	86.3 (0.15)	92.3 (0.12)	74.8 (0.12)	50.9 (0.31)	75.7 (0.19)	87.0 (0.14)
New Zealand	83.1 (0.28)	72.1 (0.72)	83.5 (0.42)	88.1 (0.39)	89.2 (0.33)	80.3 (0.92)	90.8 (0.47)	92.1 (0.49)	77.3 (0.42)	63.9 (1.07)	75.7 (0.69)	84.8 (0.57)
Norway	81.0 (0.16)	61.5 (0.49)	80.8 (0.26)	89.1 (0.20)	83.7 (0.22)	67.4 (0.66)	84.5 (0.33)	90.4 (0.28)	78.2 (0.24)	54.6 (0.73)	76.0 (0.42)	87.9 (0.28)
Poland	74.0 (—)	43.1 (—)	70.4 (—)	88.8 (—)	81.3 (—)	54.0 (—)	80.0 (—)	93.4 (—)	66.8 (—)	31.3 (—)	59.0 (—)	85.6 (—)
Portugal	78.0 (0.15)	70.0 (0.22)	83.7 (0.27)	88.4 (0.24)	81.8 (0.20)	77.2 (0.28)	85.8 (0.38)	89.6 (0.38)	74.6 (0.21)	62.1 (0.33)	81.8 (0.39)	87.7 (0.31)
Slovak Republic	75.0 (0.39)	38.3 (1.48)	76.9 (0.46)	82.6 (0.73)	81.4 (0.51)	47.0 (2.37)	82.6 (0.58)	89.8 (0.89)	68.6 (0.59)	31.2 (1.83)	70.3 (0.72)	77.2 (1.07)
Slovenia	77.2 (0.22)	51.3 (0.75)	75.9 (0.30)	88.9 (0.29)	80.7 (0.30)	61.9 (1.09)	79.4 (0.39)	91.6 (0.41)	73.5 (0.33)	41.4 (0.99)	71.1 (0.48)	86.9 (0.41)
Spain	69.5 (0.08)	57.4 (0.13)	70.9 (0.16)	81.6 (0.11)	76.0 (0.10)	67.4 (0.17)	77.8 (0.21)	85.6 (0.15)	63.0 (0.11)	46.0 (0.19)	64.3 (0.24)	78.2 (0.16)
Sweden	84.9 (0.09)	67.0 (0.31)	86.7 (0.14)	90.2 (0.12)	87.2 (0.12)	74.1 (0.39)	89.4 (0.17)	90.9 (0.18)	82.5 (0.14)	58.6 (0.47)	83.0 (0.23)	89.6 (0.16)
Switzerland	83.2 (0.13)	68.6 (0.49)	81.7 (0.21)	88.7 (0.17)	88.4 (0.16)	76.3 (0.69)	86.9 (0.27)	92.4 (0.19)	77.9 (0.20)	62.0 (0.68)	77.0 (0.30)	84.1 (0.28)
Turkey	59.1 (—)	52.4 (—)	63.1 (—)	74.3 (—)	78.8 (—)	75.5 (—)	82.1 (—)	83.7 (—)	37.2 (—)	29.9 (—)	34.8 (—)	62.8 (—)
United Kingdom[4]	80.2 (0.19)	65.7 (0.49)	81.1 (0.32)	86.1 (0.25)	85.5 (0.24)	74.9 (0.64)	86.6 (0.40)	89.8 (0.33)	75.1 (0.28)	56.3 (0.71)	75.3 (0.49)	82.9 (0.36)
United States	74.6 (0.14)	56.8 (0.52)	70.0 (0.23)	82.2 (0.18)	80.5 (0.19)	68.8 (0.68)	76.7 (0.30)	86.9 (0.24)	68.9 (0.21)	43.2 (0.75)	62.7 (0.34)	78.2 (0.27)
Other reporting countries												
Argentina	73.1 (0.27)	64.3 (0.47)	74.2 (0.49)	81.1 (0.40)	86.3 (0.30)	81.7 (0.53)	90.5 (0.47)	88.2 (0.52)	61.3 (0.40)	45.6 (0.71)	58.9 (0.77)	76.2 (0.57)
Brazil	67.4 (0.10)	56.3 (0.14)	71.9 (0.17)	82.1 (0.21)	79.1 (0.12)	73.7 (0.17)	83.3 (0.20)	88.6 (0.27)	56.7 (0.14)	43.8 (0.20)	62.1 (0.24)	77.7 (0.29)
Costa Rica	69.6 (0.41)	65.4 (0.52)	69.8 (1.02)	80.9 (0.83)	86.1 (0.45)	85.8 (0.55)	84.4 (1.19)	88.0 (1.07)	53.5 (0.60)	44.4 (0.75)	55.9 (1.50)	74.6 (1.19)
Indonesia[2]	74.7 (—)	73.0 (—)	74.1 (—)	85.1 (—)	91.2 (—)	91.3 (—)	90.8 (—)	91.9 (—)	58.4 (—)	56.7 (—)	52.4 (—)	78.5 (—)
Russia[2]	77.5 (—)	53.6 (—)	72.6 (—)	82.8 (—)	83.7 (—)	61.5 (—)	80.2 (—)	89.3 (—)	71.9 (—)	43.6 (—)	63.1 (—)	78.3 (—)
Saudi Arabia[5]	65.6 (—)	61.9 (—)	64.5 (—)	74.0 (—)	91.7 (—)	91.0 (—)	90.9 (—)	93.9 (—)	24.0 (—)	20.4 (—)	16.3 (—)	41.2 (—)
South Africa	55.7 (0.25)	43.9 (0.48)	57.1 (0.30)	84.6 (0.63)	62.7 (0.34)	51.5 (0.69)	64.4 (0.42)	88.0 (0.82)	48.9 (0.35)	36.3 (0.64)	50.1 (0.43)	81.2 (0.93)

—Not available.
[1]Refers to the mean of the data values for all reporting Organization for Economic Cooperation and Development (OECD) countries, to which each country reporting data contributes equally.
[2]Data are for 2017 instead of 2018.
[3]Associate's or higher degree data include some persons (less than 5 percent of the total) whose highest level of education was high school completion or a postsecondary program below the associate's degree level.
[4]High school completion data include some persons (17 percent of the total in 2015) who have completed a sufficient volume and standard of programs, any one of which individually would be classified as a program that only partially completes the high school (or upper secondary) level of education.
[5]Data are for 2016 instead of 2018.
NOTE: All data in this table were calculated using International Standard Classification of Education (ISCED) 2011. High school completion refers to completion of ISCED 2011

level 3 (upper secondary education); programs classified under ISCED 2011 as only partially completing level 3 are not included in the high school completion data except where otherwise noted. In this table, persons completing ISCED 2011 level 4 are also considered to have high school completion as their highest level of educational attainment. ISCED level 4 typically corresponds to postsecondary vocational programs below the associate's degree level in the United States. Associate's or higher degrees include ISCED 2011 level 5 (corresponding to the associate's degree in the United States), level 6 (bachelor's or equivalent degree), level 7 (master's or equivalent degree), and level 8 (doctoral or equivalent degree). For each country, the employment to population ratio of 25- to 64-year-olds is the number of persons in this age group who are employed as a percentage of the total civilian population in this age group.
SOURCE: Organization for Economic Cooperation and Development (OECD), Online Education Database, retrieved March 30, 2020, from https://stats.oecd.org/Index.aspx. (This table was prepared April 2020.)

Table 604.10. Average literacy and numeracy scale scores of 25- to 65-year-olds, by sex, age group, highest level of educational attainment, and country or other education system: 2012

[Standard errors appear in parentheses]

Country or other education system[1]	Total population of 25- to 65-year-olds	Sex		Age group				Highest level of educational attainment[2]			
		Male	Female	25 to 34	35 to 44	45 to 54	55 to 65	Less than high school completion	High school completion	Associate's degree	Bachelor's or higher degree
1	2	3	4	5	6	7	8	9	10	11	12
Literacy scale score[3]											
OECD average[4]	271 (0.2)	273 (0.3)	270 (0.2)	284 (0.4)	279 (0.3)	268 (0.3)	255 (0.3)	235 (0.5)	268 (0.3)	286 (0.5)	302 (0.3)
Austria	268 (0.8)	270 (1.1)	266 (1.0)	280 (1.5)	275 (1.7)	266 (1.4)	250 (1.6)	239 (2.1)	268 (0.9)	282 (2.2)	305 (1.7)
Canada	273 (0.6)	274 (0.9)	271 (0.9)	285 (1.3)	279 (1.4)	268 (1.3)	260 (1.1)	219 (2.1)	265 (1.1)	278 (1.2)	300 (1.0)
Czech Republic	273 (1.0)	274 (1.3)	271 (1.5)	287 (1.8)	275 (2.0)	266 (1.7)	262 (2.0)	242 (3.4)	269 (1.0)	293 (4.6)	303 (2.5)
Denmark	270 (0.7)	270 (1.1)	269 (0.9)	282 (1.7)	281 (1.6)	266 (1.4)	252 (1.1)	234 (2.1)	264 (1.2)	286 (1.3)	298 (1.5)
England (UK)	274 (1.1)	275 (1.4)	273 (1.4)	280 (2.1)	279 (1.6)	271 (1.8)	265 (2.0)	241 (1.6)	273 (1.5)	283 (2.4)	302 (1.9)
Estonia	273 (0.8)	273 (1.2)	274 (0.9)	286 (1.7)	278 (1.2)	269 (1.4)	261 (1.5)	244 (2.0)	267 (1.0)	276 (1.5)	298 (1.4)
Finland	286 (0.8)	284 (1.4)	287 (1.2)	309 (1.7)	299 (2.1)	284 (1.8)	260 (1.4)	245 (2.8)	276 (1.4)	294 (1.5)	318 (1.6)
Flanders (Belgium)	274 (0.9)	277 (1.1)	270 (1.1)	291 (1.8)	282 (1.6)	272 (1.6)	255 (1.6)	232 (2.0)	265 (1.2)	294 (1.6)	313 (1.7)
France	259 (0.6)	260 (0.9)	259 (0.8)	278 (1.4)	267 (1.3)	254 (1.2)	242 (1.3)	224 (1.3)	258 (0.9)	287 (1.4)	297 (1.2)
Germany	268 (1.0)	271 (1.2)	265 (1.3)	281 (1.8)	275 (1.6)	264 (1.7)	254 (1.7)	220 (3.0)	262 (1.1)	280 (2.3)	301 (1.6)
Ireland	266 (1.0)	267 (1.3)	264 (1.2)	276 (1.5)	271 (1.8)	259 (2.1)	251 (1.8)	232 (1.8)	266 (1.5)	279 (1.9)	301 (1.7)
Italy	249 (1.1)	249 (1.6)	248 (1.4)	260 (2.2)	253 (1.9)	249 (1.8)	233 (2.2)	231 (1.6)	263 (1.3)	‡ (†)	282 (1.6)
Japan	296 (0.7)	297 (1.0)	294 (0.9)	309 (1.7)	307 (1.0)	297 (1.5)	273 (1.6)	260 (2.6)	287 (1.0)	304 (1.4)	320 (1.1)
Korea, Republic of	269 (0.6)	273 (0.9)	264 (0.9)	290 (1.2)	278 (1.2)	259 (1.4)	244 (1.4)	230 (1.7)	265 (1.0)	282 (1.4)	297 (1.3)
Netherlands	282 (0.8)	286 (1.2)	278 (1.0)	298 (2.0)	294 (1.8)	277 (1.7)	261 (1.6)	246 (1.7)	283 (1.3)	293 (3.4)	312 (1.3)
Northern Ireland (UK)	268 (2.1)	271 (2.7)	265 (2.0)	278 (2.9)	274 (2.3)	262 (2.6)	255 (3.2)	239 (2.6)	270 (2.6)	280 (3.3)	303 (2.9)
Norway	279 (0.7)	281 (1.1)	277 (1.1)	289 (1.8)	288 (1.6)	277 (1.5)	262 (1.5)	251 (1.8)	271 (1.4)	288 (3.1)	303 (1.1)
Poland	264 (0.9)	260 (1.1)	267 (1.0)	277 (1.5)	268 (1.9)	259 (1.7)	249 (1.7)	227 (2.6)	254 (1.0)	— (†)	297 (1.3)
Slovak Republic	273 (0.7)	273 (1.0)	274 (0.9)	278 (1.4)	278 (1.4)	270 (1.3)	266 (1.3)	238 (1.9)	275 (0.9)	— (†)	295 (1.4)
Spain	250 (0.8)	253 (1.1)	248 (1.2)	263 (1.5)	260 (1.3)	248 (1.5)	227 (1.9)	225 (1.3)	258 (1.4)	266 (2.1)	288 (1.3)
Sweden	278 (0.8)	280 (1.2)	276 (1.2)	290 (1.9)	287 (1.8)	276 (1.7)	262 (1.3)	238 (2.2)	277 (1.2)	294 (2.4)	309 (1.4)
United States	269 (1.1)	270 (1.3)	269 (1.4)	275 (2.0)	273 (1.8)	266 (1.7)	263 (1.5)	211 (2.7)	259 (1.4)	282 (2.8)	302 (1.7)
Non-OECD education systems											
Cyprus[5]	269 (0.9)	269 (1.3)	270 (1.1)	275 (1.7)	270 (1.5)	270 (1.7)	261 (1.6)	248 (1.9)	266 (1.2)	273 (2.0)	290 (1.5)
Russian Federation[6]	275 (3.0)	274 (3.3)	277 (3.1)	273 (4.1)	278 (3.9)	277 (3.7)	275 (3.9)	248 (7.5)	272 (4.2)	276 (2.8)	282 (3.1)
Numeracy scale score[3]											
OECD average[4]	268 (0.2)	275 (0.3)	262 (0.3)	279 (0.4)	275 (0.4)	266 (0.4)	253 (0.4)	227 (0.5)	265 (0.3)	283 (0.9)	303 (0.4)
Austria	274 (0.9)	281 (1.3)	267 (1.1)	282 (1.7)	281 (2.0)	274 (1.7)	257 (1.7)	237 (2.3)	276 (1.1)	292 (2.6)	315 (1.8)
Canada	265 (0.8)	273 (1.0)	257 (1.0)	276 (1.4)	272 (1.5)	260 (1.4)	251 (1.4)	206 (2.5)	255 (1.2)	271 (1.5)	295 (1.0)
Czech Republic	275 (1.0)	280 (1.5)	270 (1.4)	288 (1.8)	277 (1.8)	272 (2.2)	263 (2.0)	235 (3.3)	271 (1.0)	287 (6.1)	313 (2.5)
Denmark	279 (0.8)	285 (1.4)	273 (1.0)	287 (1.9)	290 (1.6)	277 (1.6)	265 (1.2)	241 (2.4)	275 (1.3)	295 (1.4)	309 (1.8)
England (UK)	263 (1.1)	270 (1.4)	256 (1.6)	267 (2.2)	269 (1.9)	259 (1.9)	257 (1.9)	226 (1.9)	262 (1.5)	271 (3.0)	295 (2.2)
Estonia	272 (0.6)	276 (1.0)	269 (0.9)	284 (1.7)	275 (1.1)	269 (1.4)	259 (1.3)	236 (1.8)	265 (0.9)	275 (1.4)	300 (1.3)
Finland	282 (0.8)	286 (1.4)	277 (1.2)	302 (2.1)	292 (2.2)	279 (2.0)	260 (1.3)	244 (2.8)	271 (1.3)	291 (1.6)	314 (1.7)
Flanders (Belgium)	280 (0.9)	289 (1.2)	271 (1.3)	295 (1.9)	289 (1.8)	280 (1.9)	260 (1.6)	235 (1.9)	272 (1.2)	300 (1.5)	323 (1.8)
France	252 (0.7)	258 (1.0)	247 (1.0)	269 (1.5)	262 (1.6)	246 (1.4)	234 (1.5)	208 (1.3)	251 (1.0)	287 (1.7)	299 (1.4)
Germany	271 (1.1)	280 (1.4)	262 (1.4)	282 (1.8)	279 (2.0)	268 (1.9)	256 (1.9)	210 (3.4)	264 (1.2)	287 (2.5)	310 (1.7)
Ireland	255 (1.0)	261 (1.4)	249 (1.3)	266 (1.7)	260 (1.7)	250 (2.1)	238 (2.3)	218 (2.2)	254 (1.6)	274 (2.1)	294 (1.9)
Italy	246 (1.1)	253 (1.6)	240 (1.4)	262 (2.3)	251 (1.9)	244 (2.0)	229 (2.2)	225 (1.5)	265 (1.5)	‡ (†)	280 (2.1)
Japan	289 (0.8)	296 (1.2)	282 (1.1)	297 (1.6)	297 (1.3)	291 (1.7)	273 (1.6)	247 (2.5)	281 (1.3)	291 (1.3)	319 (1.2)
Korea, Republic of	260 (0.7)	266 (1.0)	254 (1.1)	281 (1.4)	271 (1.5)	251 (1.4)	232 (1.7)	215 (1.9)	256 (1.0)	275 (1.6)	293 (1.5)
Netherlands	279 (0.8)	288 (1.3)	270 (1.1)	293 (1.8)	287 (2.1)	277 (1.7)	262 (1.7)	243 (1.9)	281 (1.2)	292 (3.5)	310 (1.3)
Northern Ireland (UK)	258 (1.8)	265 (2.2)	251 (2.0)	268 (2.9)	266 (2.4)	252 (2.1)	245 (3.1)	225 (2.9)	261 (2.1)	273 (3.0)	298 (2.4)
Norway	280 (0.9)	288 (1.3)	272 (1.2)	285 (2.0)	289 (1.9)	280 (1.7)	265 (1.7)	246 (2.2)	273 (1.5)	296 (3.7)	306 (1.3)
Poland	258 (1.0)	259 (1.5)	257 (1.0)	270 (1.5)	262 (2.2)	254 (2.1)	244 (1.9)	216 (3.1)	250 (1.2)	— (†)	290 (1.5)
Slovak Republic	275 (0.9)	277 (1.2)	274 (1.1)	279 (1.6)	281 (1.7)	275 (1.6)	265 (1.6)	226 (2.4)	278 (1.0)	— (†)	306 (1.5)
Spain	245 (0.7)	251 (1.1)	238 (1.1)	257 (1.3)	255 (1.3)	242 (1.6)	221 (1.7)	217 (1.3)	254 (1.5)	264 (2.4)	283 (1.3)
Sweden	279 (1.0)	286 (1.5)	272 (1.2)	288 (2.0)	286 (2.0)	276 (2.3)	268 (1.7)	237 (2.6)	277 (1.4)	297 (2.6)	311 (1.5)
United States	254 (1.2)	262 (1.3)	246 (1.5)	260 (2.2)	258 (1.9)	250 (2.1)	247 (1.8)	185 (3.1)	241 (1.5)	266 (3.1)	293 (1.7)
Non-OECD education systems											
Cyprus[5]	265 (0.9)	270 (1.2)	260 (1.3)	273 (2.0)	269 (1.6)	265 (1.8)	250 (1.8)	230 (2.3)	264 (1.4)	270 (2.1)	292 (1.6)
Russian Federation[6]	269 (2.8)	268 (3.3)	271 (3.0)	269 (4.2)	270 (3.6)	272 (3.2)	267 (3.9)	234 (8.5)	265 (4.0)	268 (2.6)	280 (3.0)

—Not available.
†Not applicable.
‡Reporting standards not met (too few cases).
[1]Most of the education systems represent complete countries, but three of them represent subnational entities: England (which is part of the United Kingdom), Flanders (which is part of Belgium), and Northern Ireland (which is part of the United Kingdom).
[2]High school completion includes International Standard Classification of Education (ISCED) 1997 levels 3 and 4, with the exception of ISCED level 3C short programs. ISCED 3C short programs do not correspond to high school completion in the United States and are included in the "less than high school completion" column in this table. The associate's degree data in this table refer to degrees classified as ISCED 1997 level 5B. The data for bachelor's or higher degree refer to degrees classified as ISCED 1997 level 5A and as level 6.
[3]Scale scores range from 0 to 500.

[4]Refers to the mean of the data values for all reporting Organization for Economic Cooperation and Development (OECD) countries and subnational education systems, to which each country or subnational education system reporting data contributes equally, with the exception of England (UK) and Northern Ireland (UK), which contribute to the mean as a combined entity, England/Northern Ireland (UK).
[5]Cyprus includes only the population under the effective control of the Government of the Republic of Cyprus. For the educational attainment data (columns 9 through 12), the item response rate for Cyprus is below 85 percent; missing data have not been explicitly accounted for.
[6]The Russian Federation does not include the population of the Moscow municipal region.
SOURCE: Organization for Economic Cooperation and Development (OECD), Program for the International Assessment of Adult Competencies (PIAAC), 2012. (This table was prepared May 2016.)

Table 604.20. Percentage distribution of 25- to 65-year-olds, by literacy proficiency level, numeracy proficiency level, selected levels of educational attainment, and country or other education system: 2012

[Standard errors appear in parentheses]

Country or other education system[1]	Total population of 25- to 65-year-olds: At or below level 1	Total population: At level 2	Total population: At level 3	Total population: At level 4 or level 5	Highest level of educational attainment[2] – High school completion: At or below level 1	High school completion: At level 2	High school completion: At level 3	High school completion: At level 4 or level 5	Bachelor's or higher degree: At or below level 1	Bachelor's or higher degree: At level 2	Bachelor's or higher degree: At level 3	Bachelor's or higher degree: At level 4 or level 5
1	2	3	4	5	6	7	8	9	10	11	12	13
	Percentage distribution, by literacy proficiency level											
OECD average[3]	**16.6 (0.15)**	**34.0 (0.21)**	**37.6 (0.21)**	**11.8 (0.13)**	**15.1 (0.23)**	**39.7 (0.34)**	**38.0 (0.33)**	**7.2 (0.18)**	**4.0 (0.16)**	**18.7 (0.35)**	**49.5 (0.45)**	**27.8 (0.40)**
Austria	16.3 (0.70)	39.0 (1.06)	36.7 (1.04)	8.0 (0.47)	14.3 (0.86)	41.9 (1.38)	37.9 (1.40)	5.9 (0.60)	2.5! (0.79)	16.8 (1.99)	52.9 (2.47)	27.8 (2.03)
Canada	17.3 (0.47)	31.9 (0.70)	36.7 (0.74)	14.2 (0.55)	18.2 (0.85)	39.0 (1.05)	35.4 (1.13)	7.5 (0.80)	5.9 (0.49)	21.3 (0.88)	44.1 (1.20)	28.7 (1.20)
Czech Republic	12.5 (0.87)	38.5 (1.87)	40.9 (1.76)	8.1 (0.77)	12.4 (1.11)	43.4 (2.34)	39.5 (1.97)	4.8 (0.73)	1.9! (0.89)	17.1 (3.16)	57.2 (3.80)	23.8 (3.21)
Denmark	16.7 (0.58)	33.9 (0.83)	39.4 (0.81)	10.0 (0.57)	16.6 (1.01)	41.7 (1.48)	36.3 (1.46)	5.4 (0.64)	5.8 (0.69)	17.0 (1.20)	51.9 (1.86)	25.2 (1.87)
England (UK)	16.1 (0.77)	32.8 (0.97)	36.7 (1.01)	14.4 (0.89)	14.4 (1.36)	35.4 (1.81)	39.2 (1.58)	11.0 (1.07)	5.5 (1.06)	18.1 (1.55)	46.2 (2.37)	30.1 (2.26)
Estonia	14.3 (0.62)	35.5 (0.68)	39.3 (0.93)	10.9 (0.67)	16.0 (0.95)	40.4 (1.11)	37.2 (1.07)	6.5 (0.65)	4.4 (0.70)	22.8 (1.42)	48.4 (1.94)	24.5 (1.65)
Finland	11.6 (0.57)	27.5 (0.90)	39.2 (0.92)	21.7 (0.61)	13.3 (0.99)	33.8 (1.65)	39.6 (1.55)	13.2 (1.03)	2.9 (0.66)	11.0 (1.23)	39.7 (2.01)	46.4 (1.74)
Flanders (Belgium)	15.8 (0.66)	32.0 (0.96)	39.4 (1.06)	12.8 (0.65)	16.7 (1.13)	41.7 (1.53)	35.9 (1.76)	5.7 (0.68)	2.1! (0.65)	10.3 (1.62)	51.1 (2.84)	36.5 (2.44)
France	23.6 (0.55)	36.6 (0.77)	32.5 (0.69)	7.3 (0.39)	20.4 (0.95)	45.2 (1.08)	31.1 (0.96)	3.4 (0.44)	5.1 (0.71)	20.2 (1.40)	52.2 (1.56)	22.5 (1.51)
Germany	18.7 (0.86)	35.3 (1.12)	35.9 (1.00)	10.2 (0.64)	19.9 (1.13)	41.6 (1.55)	32.8 (1.33)	5.7 (0.73)	4.2 (0.90)	19.1 (1.66)	50.6 (1.84)	26.2 (1.80)
Ireland	18.5 (0.87)	37.2 (0.91)	35.6 (0.89)	8.8 (0.62)	14.7 (1.18)	42.3 (1.62)	37.6 (1.78)	5.3 (0.90)	3.0 (0.71)	20.7 (1.64)	52.2 (1.96)	24.2 (1.87)
Italy	29.2 (1.18)	42.5 (1.01)	25.1 (1.01)	3.2 (0.34)	16.6 (1.30)	44.6 (1.55)	34.9 (1.77)	3.9 (0.73)	9.2 (1.27)	30.9 (2.28)	48.2 (2.63)	11.7 (1.72)
Japan	5.3 (0.43)	23.4 (0.90)	48.4 (1.06)	22.9 (0.75)	5.8 (0.78)	30.1 (1.42)	51.1 (1.45)	13.0 (1.03)	1.1! (0.35)	8.2 (0.96)	46.2 (2.06)	44.5 (1.93)
Korea, Republic of	14.9 (0.60)	39.6 (0.92)	38.5 (0.96)	6.9 (0.43)	13.0 (0.92)	48.0 (1.67)	35.4 (1.74)	3.6 (0.50)	2.1 (0.56)	22.8 (1.48)	57.6 (1.66)	17.5 (1.30)
Netherlands	13.4 (0.56)	27.5 (0.82)	41.1 (0.84)	18.0 (0.74)	8.9 (0.96)	30.9 (1.47)	46.5 (1.56)	13.8 (1.04)	2.7 (0.59)	12.7 (1.09)	47.5 (1.52)	37.0 (1.56)
Northern Ireland (UK)	18.4 (1.29)	37.0 (1.71)	34.7 (1.76)	9.9 (0.78)	13.8 (1.97)	41.1 (2.91)	37.6 (3.61)	7.5 (1.21)	3.2! (0.99)	17.8 (2.14)	51.6 (2.26)	27.5 (2.55)
Norway	12.5 (0.67)	30.1 (0.90)	42.6 (0.86)	14.9 (0.67)	13.1 (1.26)	37.7 (1.62)	41.5 (1.47)	7.7 (0.95)	4.5 (0.57)	16.3 (1.09)	50.1 (1.44)	29.0 (1.26)
Poland	20.7 (0.73)	37.5 (1.09)	32.7 (1.05)	9.0 (0.60)	24.0 (1.08)	43.6 (1.39)	28.6 (1.15)	3.8 (0.53)	4.4 (0.77)	24.5 (1.53)	48.1 (2.05)	23.0 (1.68)
Slovak Republic	11.9 (0.69)	36.7 (1.18)	44.0 (1.02)	7.4 (0.53)	8.7 (0.68)	39.2 (1.53)	46.1 (1.48)	6.0 (0.60)	2.7! (0.84)	23.3 (2.01)	57.4 (2.04)	16.6 (1.85)
Spain	29.2 (0.84)	39.1 (0.84)	27.0 (0.76)	4.8 (0.43)	21.0 (1.42)	46.1 (1.96)	29.5 (1.81)	3.5 (0.82)	5.8 (0.90)	29.3 (1.76)	50.1 (2.15)	14.8 (1.40)
Sweden	14.1 (0.71)	29.0 (1.13)	40.5 (0.99)	16.4 (0.62)	11.7 (0.96)	32.9 (1.71)	44.9 (1.83)	10.5 (0.90)	4.9 (0.64)	13.2 (1.35)	44.5 (1.78)	37.4 (1.90)
United States	19.2 (0.88)	32.8 (1.15)	35.5 (1.08)	12.5 (0.79)	22.0 (1.32)	41.7 (1.83)	30.8 (1.38)	5.5 (0.79)	3.7 (0.68)	18.9 (1.28)	49.6 (1.79)	27.8 (2.02)
Non-OECD education systems												
Cyprus[4]	14.4 (0.73)	39.7 (1.31)	38.7 (1.18)	7.1 (0.53)	14.5 (1.20)	43.1 (2.24)	37.5 (2.17)	4.8 (0.79)	4.6 (0.94)	29.9 (2.42)	49.3 (2.27)	16.2 (1.45)
Russian Federation[5]	12.9 (1.63)	34.7 (1.92)	41.5 (2.17)	10.9 (1.93)	15.0 (2.46)	35.8 (2.59)	39.9 (3.68)	9.4! (2.87)	9.8 (1.85)	31.2 (3.01)	45.3 (3.29)	13.7 (2.60)
	Percentage distribution, by numeracy proficiency level											
OECD average[3]	**19.8 (0.16)**	**33.1 (0.20)**	**34.3 (0.20)**	**12.8 (0.14)**	**18.4 (0.25)**	**38.8 (0.33)**	**34.6 (0.33)**	**8.2 (0.19)**	**5.0 (0.18)**	**19.6 (0.35)**	**45.3 (0.45)**	**30.1 (0.40)**
Austria	15.0 (0.72)	34.2 (0.96)	37.0 (1.05)	13.8 (0.66)	11.7 (0.90)	37.1 (1.27)	39.6 (1.41)	11.5 (0.88)	2.5! (0.94)	12.9 (1.90)	44.6 (2.56)	40.0 (2.33)
Canada	23.3 (0.57)	31.8 (0.65)	32.2 (0.76)	12.7 (0.50)	26.8 (1.21)	38.0 (1.25)	29.2 (1.17)	6.0 (0.58)	8.3 (0.67)	23.5 (1.12)	42.0 (1.58)	26.2 (1.23)
Czech Republic	13.2 (0.87)	35.4 (1.31)	39.9 (1.24)	11.5 (0.81)	12.7 (1.02)	40.1 (1.72)	40.7 (1.76)	6.6 (0.84)	1.1! (0.44)	13.5 (2.52)	50.0 (3.70)	35.4 (3.22)
Denmark	14.3 (0.58)	29.7 (0.78)	38.3 (0.82)	17.7 (0.56)	12.8 (1.07)	35.4 (1.41)	39.8 (1.37)	12.0 (0.95)	5.5 (0.64)	14.0 (1.36)	41.9 (1.70)	38.7 (1.91)
England (UK)	24.1 (1.04)	32.8 (1.15)	30.7 (1.08)	12.3 (0.85)	22.4 (1.43)	37.1 (1.79)	31.8 (2.03)	8.8 (1.35)	8.1 (1.61)	23.2 (1.95)	42.1 (2.07)	26.6 (1.92)
Estonia	15.0 (0.55)	36.6 (0.71)	37.4 (0.63)	11.0 (0.46)	16.5 (0.95)	42.3 (1.15)	34.6 (1.07)	6.5 (0.60)	4.2 (0.64)	21.4 (1.48)	49.0 (2.02)	25.5 (1.55)
Finland	13.5 (0.58)	29.3 (0.70)	37.5 (0.91)	19.7 (0.66)	16.4 (0.98)	35.7 (1.27)	36.0 (1.39)	11.8 (1.04)	3.3 (0.67)	13.5 (1.38)	41.9 (1.94)	41.3 (1.89)
Flanders (Belgium)	14.7 (0.68)	29.2 (0.83)	37.8 (1.03)	18.3 (0.78)	15.0 (1.04)	37.1 (1.55)	38.0 (1.57)	10.0 (1.06)	1.7! (0.63)	8.4 (1.45)	41.4 (2.45)	48.4 (2.52)
France	29.9 (0.69)	33.5 (0.79)	28.3 (0.59)	8.4 (0.37)	26.8 (1.02)	43.0 (1.16)	26.8 (0.99)	3.4 (0.42)	5.9 (0.79)	20.0 (1.13)	48.2 (1.40)	25.9 (1.37)
Germany	19.1 (0.79)	31.5 (0.91)	34.9 (0.90)	14.5 (0.68)	19.7 (1.05)	38.7 (1.30)	33.4 (1.42)	8.1 (0.74)	3.4 (0.88)	15.6 (1.65)	45.5 (1.71)	35.5 (1.86)
Ireland	25.8 (0.94)	37.7 (0.96)	28.7 (0.89)	7.8 (0.66)	23.8 (1.57)	43.6 (1.58)	28.1 (1.37)	4.5 (0.72)	5.2 (0.89)	26.8 (1.74)	46.5 (2.31)	21.5 (2.14)
Italy	32.4 (1.13)	39.0 (1.15)	24.1 (1.03)	4.6 (0.37)	17.4 (1.38)	40.7 (1.92)	35.3 (1.81)	6.6 (0.75)	11.8 (1.65)	31.7 (2.32)	42.3 (2.59)	14.2 (1.80)
Japan	8.2 (0.55)	27.7 (0.92)	44.4 (0.94)	19.7 (0.70)	8.6 (1.01)	34.0 (1.56)	46.3 (1.61)	11.0 (1.10)	1.0! (0.41)	10.4 (0.99)	45.0 (1.86)	43.5 (1.76)
Korea, Republic of	21.3 (0.64)	40.3 (0.98)	32.1 (0.89)	6.3 (0.52)	20.3 (1.14)	49.4 (1.34)	27.5 (1.40)	2.8 (0.56)	3.3 (0.67)	26.4 (1.65)	53.3 (2.00)	17.0 (1.55)
Netherlands	14.5 (0.60)	28.6 (0.85)	39.3 (1.00)	17.6 (0.72)	10.5 (1.13)	32.4 (1.78)	43.3 (1.93)	13.8 (1.10)	2.8 (0.64)	15.6 (1.14)	46.8 (1.78)	34.9 (1.78)
Northern Ireland (UK)	26.0 (1.54)	36.1 (1.36)	29.4 (1.34)	8.5 (0.74)	20.4 (2.01)	42.9 (2.24)	30.9 (2.52)	5.8 (1.19)	4.8 (1.10)	21.5 (2.20)	49.2 (2.74)	24.5 (2.32)
Norway	14.4 (0.62)	28.1 (0.89)	38.3 (0.96)	19.1 (0.73)	15.0 (1.19)	34.8 (1.58)	38.3 (1.46)	11.8 (1.24)	5.4 (0.61)	15.8 (1.07)	44.2 (1.57)	34.5 (1.46)
Poland	24.9 (0.88)	37.5 (1.03)	29.4 (1.10)	8.1 (0.63)	28.2 (1.11)	42.7 (1.52)	25.3 (1.25)	3.9 (0.62)	7.3 (1.00)	28.0 (1.77)	44.7 (2.28)	20.0 (1.63)
Slovak Republic	14.1 (0.65)	32.5 (0.96)	40.8 (1.07)	12.6 (0.72)	9.9 (0.71)	36.0 (1.21)	44.0 (1.32)	10.2 (0.93)	2.0! (0.65)	18.1 (1.58)	51.0 (2.49)	28.9 (2.12)
Spain	32.1 (0.72)	39.6 (0.97)	24.2 (0.78)	4.1 (0.37)	22.8 (1.63)	46.9 (2.07)	26.8 (1.88)	3.6 (0.73)	7.0 (0.88)	33.7 (1.85)	47.4 (2.18)	11.9 (1.35)
Sweden	15.2 (0.79)	27.9 (1.08)	37.5 (1.02)	19.4 (0.76)	13.1 (1.02)	31.5 (1.70)	40.9 (1.90)	14.5 (1.16)	4.9 (0.68)	14.0 (1.69)	40.8 (1.85)	40.2 (2.00)
United States	29.8 (0.93)	32.9 (1.05)	27.7 (0.90)	9.6 (0.66)	36.4 (1.34)	39.3 (1.69)	20.6 (1.58)	3.7 (0.67)	7.5 (0.73)	24.1 (1.56)	45.9 (1.82)	22.6 (1.82)
Non-OECD education systems												
Cyprus[4]	18.9 (0.81)	38.6 (1.17)	33.9 (1.17)	8.7 (0.62)	17.4 (1.30)	42.1 (1.93)	34.1 (1.99)	6.4 (1.08)	5.6 (0.96)	28.5 (2.07)	46.1 (2.26)	19.9 (1.62)
Russian Federation[5]	14.4 (1.66)	39.8 (1.95)	38.1 (1.74)	7.7 (1.44)	17.1 (3.00)	41.5 (3.33)	35.5 (3.59)	5.9 (1.74)	8.5 (1.59)	36.7 (2.84)	42.9 (2.56)	11.9 (2.27)

!Interpret data with caution. The coefficient of variation (CV) for this estimate is between 30 and 50 percent.
[1]Most of the education systems represent complete countries, but three of them represent subnational entities: England (which is part of the United Kingdom), Flanders (which is part of Belgium), and Northern Ireland (which is part of the United Kingdom).
[2]High school completion includes International Standard Classification of Education (ISCED) 1997 levels 3 and 4, with the exception of ISCED level 3C short programs. ISCED 3C short programs do not correspond to high school completion in the United States and are not included in the high school completion columns in this table. The data for bachelor's or higher degree refer to degrees classified as ISCED 1997 level 5A and as level 6.
[3]Refers to the mean of the data values for all reporting Organization for Economic Cooperation and Development (OECD) countries and subnational education systems, to which each country or subnational education system reporting data contributes equally, with the exception of England (UK) and Northern Ireland (UK), which contribute to the mean as a combined entity, England/Northern Ireland (UK).
[4]Cyprus includes only the population under the effective control of the Government of the Republic of Cyprus. For the educational attainment data (columns 6 through 13), the item response rate for Cyprus is below 85 percent; missing data have not been explicitly accounted for.
[5]The Russian Federation does not include the population of the Moscow municipal region.
NOTE: In this table, scores below level 1 and scores at level 1 are combined into the "at or below level 1" reporting category; scores at level 4 and scores at level 5 are combined into the "at level 4 or level 5" reporting category. For both literacy and numeracy, the proficiency-level reporting categories correspond to the score ranges shown in parentheses: at or below level 1 (0–225.9), at level 2 (226.0–275.9), at level 3 (276.0–325.9), at level 4 or level 5 (326.0–500.0).
SOURCE: Organization for Economic Cooperation and Development (OECD), Program for the International Assessment of Adult Competencies (PIAAC), 2012. (This table was prepared May 2016.)

Table 604.30. Employment rates and mean monthly earnings of 25- to 65-year-olds, by literacy proficiency level, numeracy proficiency level, and country or other education system: 2012

[Standard errors appear in parentheses]

Country or other education system[1]	Total population of 25- to 65-year-olds		Proficiency level[2]								
			At or below level 1		At level 2		At level 3		At level 4 or level 5	
	Employment rate of labor force[3]	Mean monthly earnings (in current dollars)[4]	Employment rate of labor force[3]	Mean monthly earnings (in current dollars)[4]	Employment rate of labor force[3]	Mean monthly earnings (in current dollars)[4]	Employment rate of labor force[3]	Mean monthly earnings (in current dollars)[4]	Employment rate of labor force[3]	Mean monthly earnings (in current dollars)[4]
1	2	3	4	5	6	7	8	9	10	11
Literacy										
OECD average[5]	93.7 (0.08)	$2,930 (9)	89.7 (0.36)	$2,170 (24)	93.1 (0.19)	$2,580 (16)	95.1 (0.16)	$3,140 (16)	96.4 (0.30)	$3,740 (36)
Austria	96.2 (0.38)	— (†)	92.9 (1.54)	— (†)	96.0 (0.79)	— (†)	97.2 (0.60)	— (†)	97.8 (1.28)	— (†)
Canada	95.9 (0.22)	— (†)	93.7 (0.92)	— (†)	95.4 (0.55)	— (†)	96.7 (0.46)	— (†)	97.3 (0.61)	— (†)
Czech Republic	94.2 (0.20)	1,620 (22)	91.3 (2.62)	1,320 (66)	92.6 (0.93)	1,470 (43)	95.6 (0.87)	1,720 (43)	97.7 (1.39)	2,030 (96)
Denmark	94.5 (0.38)	4,090 (28)	90.8 (1.45)	3,210 (84)	94.5 (0.75)	3,730 (53)	95.0 (0.62)	4,390 (58)	96.4 (1.44)	4,850 (139)
England (UK)	94.0 (0.08)	3,180 (43)	87.5 (1.65)	2,140 (108)	92.5 (0.91)	2,610 (91)	96.2 (0.55)	3,440 (96)	97.3 (0.79)	4,380 (151)
Estonia	93.4 (0.34)	1,750 (25)	89.5 (1.48)	1,420 (75)	92.1 (0.75)	1,560 (42)	94.5 (0.53)	1,820 (41)	97.4 (0.74)	2,260 (87)
Finland	95.5 (0.39)	3,250 (18)	92.5 (2.04)	2,670 (120)	95.3 (0.84)	2,920 (56)	95.8 (0.59)	3,330 (43)	96.1 (0.63)	3,590 (56)
Flanders (Belgium)	98.0 (0.21)	3,650 (35)	96.5 (0.93)	2,790 (106)	97.4 (0.55)	3,220 (67)	98.6 (0.40)	3,860 (69)	98.9 (0.68)	4,470 (151)
France	92.9 (0.19)	2,490 (17)	89.4 (1.08)	1,910 (39)	92.9 (0.66)	2,340 (33)	94.3 (0.64)	2,760 (33)	95.0 (1.39)	3,270 (84)
Germany	95.2 (0.40)	— (†)	91.1 (1.53)	— (†)	94.9 (0.84)	— (†)	96.3 (0.60)	— (†)	98.3 (0.73)	— (†)
Ireland	89.2 (0.53)	3,410 (52)	83.6 (1.95)	2,370 (106)	86.7 (1.12)	2,950 (68)	92.0 (1.02)	3,820 (90)	95.8 (1.36)	4,610 (206)
Italy	87.7 (0.66)	2,510 (36)	84.1 (1.91)	2,290 (103)	87.2 (1.30)	2,360 (68)	90.8 (1.34)	2,800 (75)	93.5 (3.39)	3,140 (248)
Japan	97.6 (0.22)	3,000 (37)	98.9 (1.01)	2,210 (199)	99.1 (0.63)	2,540 (84)	97.5 (0.45)	3,000 (60)	96.2 (0.83)	3,550 (100)
Korea, Republic of	96.8 (0.27)	3,000 (32)	97.4 (0.86)	2,180 (86)	97.0 (0.53)	2,820 (60)	96.7 (0.59)	3,290 (63)	95.5 (1.71)	3,960 (133)
Netherlands	95.8 (0.41)	3,490 (30)	91.5 (2.00)	2,350 (117)	94.7 (0.93)	2,930 (75)	97.0 (0.59)	3,640 (63)	96.8 (0.88)	4,230 (90)
Northern Ireland (UK)	94.7 (0.49)	2,750 (42)	90.6 (2.03)	1,820 (90)	94.4 (0.96)	2,330 (96)	95.9 (1.01)	3,070 (92)	96.0 (2.10)	3,870 (188)
Norway	97.1 (0.31)	4,090 (30)	93.6 (1.66)	2,910 (110)	96.8 (0.74)	3,630 (66)	97.6 (0.45)	4,340 (56)	98.8 (0.65)	4,850 (99)
Poland	91.9 (0.49)	1,610 (22)	88.0 (1.75)	1,260 (56)	90.8 (1.08)	1,430 (52)	93.9 (0.89)	1,780 (56)	95.5 (1.56)	2,190 (90)
Slovak Republic	90.7 (0.48)	1,570 (25)	79.6 (2.60)	1,060 (63)	90.4 (1.06)	1,380 (39)	92.5 (0.80)	1,700 (46)	93.3 (2.09)	2,110 (150)
Spain	82.7 (0.63)	2,390 (32)	75.1 (1.60)	1,910 (55)	82.5 (1.32)	2,260 (48)	87.4 (1.19)	2,680 (61)	92.1 (2.30)	3,280 (157)
Sweden	94.9 (0.44)	— (†)	85.3 (2.21)	— (†)	94.2 (1.01)	— (†)	96.3 (0.69)	— (†)	98.4 (0.73)	— (†)
United States	92.5 (0.44)	4,260 (80)	89.0 (1.53)	2,730 (150)	90.8 (1.13)	3,480 (110)	93.8 (0.85)	4,740 (148)	97.1 (0.72)	6,310 (323)
Non-OECD education systems										
Cyprus[6]	92.0 (0.64)	2,860 (38)	87.3 (2.50)	2,490 (149)	91.8 (1.22)	2,660 (73)	93.1 (1.03)	3,010 (73)	93.9 (2.04)	3,440 (197)
Russian Federation[7]	94.9 (1.02)	840 (25)	95.0 (2.53)	790 (55)	95.9 (1.48)	770 (31)	95.0 (1.33)	870 (36)	91.7 (2.82)	1,000 (61)
Numeracy										
OECD average[5]	93.7 (0.08)	$2,930 (9)	88.8 (0.36)	$2,110 (21)	93.2 (0.20)	$2,560 (16)	95.5 (0.17)	$3,180 (18)	97.0 (0.27)	$3,940 (38)
Austria	96.2 (0.38)	— (†)	92.7 (1.56)	— (†)	95.9 (0.79)	— (†)	97.0 (0.56)	— (†)	97.6 (0.88)	— (†)
Canada	95.9 (0.22)	— (†)	93.0 (0.83)	— (†)	95.7 (0.57)	— (†)	96.8 (0.54)	— (†)	98.4 (0.58)	— (†)
Czech Republic	94.2 (0.20)	1,620 (22)	87.3 (2.81)	1,280 (56)	92.8 (0.92)	1,460 (38)	95.9 (0.69)	1,690 (43)	97.9 (1.82)	2,060 (86)
Denmark	94.5 (0.38)	4,090 (28)	89.4 (1.72)	3,100 (84)	93.2 (1.02)	3,580 (66)	95.6 (0.60)	4,210 (64)	96.8 (0.77)	4,980 (98)
England (UK)	94.0 (0.08)	3,180 (43)	87.6 (1.25)	2,120 (90)	94.1 (0.83)	2,690 (81)	96.5 (0.74)	3,650 (102)	97.6 (0.87)	4,530 (179)
Estonia	93.4 (0.34)	1,750 (25)	87.6 (1.53)	1,250 (65)	92.2 (0.76)	1,520 (46)	94.9 (0.58)	1,850 (45)	98.0 (0.73)	2,470 (83)
Finland	95.5 (0.39)	3,250 (18)	90.8 (2.06)	2,510 (89)	94.9 (0.94)	2,880 (57)	96.3 (0.58)	3,320 (47)	96.8 (0.62)	3,830 (73)
Flanders (Belgium)	98.0 (0.21)	3,650 (35)	96.8 (0.99)	2,640 (96)	97.4 (0.62)	3,100 (65)	98.5 (0.39)	3,740 (57)	98.5 (0.51)	4,650 (129)
France	92.9 (0.19)	2,490 (17)	89.1 (0.87)	1,850 (31)	92.4 (0.75)	2,300 (32)	95.5 (0.84)	2,860 (37)	95.7 (1.42)	3,440 (87)
Germany	95.2 (0.40)	— (†)	89.8 (1.52)	— (†)	94.5 (0.89)	— (†)	96.4 (0.65)	— (†)	98.8 (0.58)	— (†)
Ireland	89.2 (0.53)	3,410 (52)	84.1 (1.85)	2,340 (96)	88.2 (1.12)	3,030 (85)	92.1 (1.17)	3,970 (113)	94.9 (1.77)	4,990 (281)
Italy	87.7 (0.66)	2,510 (36)	82.5 (1.91)	2,260 (105)	88.0 (1.28)	2,330 (60)	90.8 (1.28)	2,770 (84)	95.0 (2.64)	3,290 (205)
Japan	97.6 (0.22)	3,000 (37)	98.8 (0.95)	1,980 (141)	96.9 (0.83)	2,420 (85)	97.6 (0.54)	2,990 (66)	98.1 (0.64)	4,030 (99)
Korea, Republic of	96.8 (0.27)	3,000 (32)	96.4 (0.85)	2,210 (72)	96.8 (0.52)	2,880 (61)	96.9 (0.61)	3,370 (68)	97.1 (1.17)	4,040 (145)
Netherlands	95.8 (0.41)	3,490 (30)	90.1 (1.95)	2,280 (116)	95.5 (0.92)	2,900 (79)	96.9 (0.57)	3,650 (70)	97.2 (0.96)	4,470 (106)
Northern Ireland (UK)	94.7 (0.49)	2,750 (42)	91.2 (1.54)	1,810 (90)	94.5 (1.19)	2,400 (70)	96.4 (1.06)	3,230 (107)	96.0 (2.39)	3,990 (213)
Norway	97.1 (0.31)	4,090 (30)	92.9 (1.65)	2,880 (119)	96.6 (0.77)	3,480 (69)	97.9 (0.45)	4,250 (61)	98.5 (0.56)	5,110 (101)
Poland	91.9 (0.49)	1,610 (22)	86.5 (1.75)	1,260 (53)	91.8 (1.15)	1,430 (38)	94.0 (0.86)	1,800 (49)	96.4 (1.47)	2,290 (107)
Slovak Republic	90.7 (0.48)	1,570 (25)	75.3 (2.92)	1,030 (62)	89.5 (1.12)	1,320 (52)	93.4 (0.77)	1,660 (43)	94.9 (1.41)	2,090 (94)
Spain	82.7 (0.63)	2,390 (32)	74.2 (1.59)	1,830 (45)	82.7 (1.45)	2,270 (53)	88.8 (1.51)	2,800 (68)	93.3 (2.70)	3,300 (170)
Sweden	94.9 (0.44)	— (†)	86.2 (2.24)	— (†)	93.9 (1.33)	— (†)	96.5 (0.68)	— (†)	98.2 (0.63)	— (†)
United States	92.5 (0.44)	4,260 (80)	88.2 (1.36)	2,760 (94)	91.3 (1.13)	3,690 (120)	95.6 (0.92)	5,110 (157)	98.1 (0.71)	6,780 (370)
Non-OECD education systems										
Cyprus[6]	92.0 (0.64)	2,860 (38)	86.6 (2.24)	2,250 (112)	91.7 (1.26)	2,630 (75)	93.4 (1.04)	3,050 (74)	95.9 (1.57)	3,640 (163)
Russian Federation[7]	94.9 (1.02)	840 (25)	96.3 (2.04)	750 (55)	95.5 (1.41)	780 (35)	94.9 (1.53)	890 (38)	90.5 (3.89)	990 (68)

—Not available.
†Not applicable.
[1]Most of the education systems represent complete countries, but three of them represent subnational entities: England (which is part of the United Kingdom), Flanders (which is part of Belgium), and Northern Ireland (which is part of the United Kingdom).
[2]In this table, scores below level 1 and scores at level 1 are combined into the "at or below level 1" reporting category; scores at level 4 and scores at level 5 are combined into the "at level 4 or level 5" reporting category. For both literacy and numeracy, the proficiency-level reporting categories correspond to the score ranges shown in parentheses: at or below level 1 (0–225.9), at level 2 (226.0–275.9), at level 3 (276.0–325.9), at level 4 or level 5 (326.0–500.0).
[3]The employment rate is the percentage of the labor force that is employed. The labor force consists of those who are employed as well as those who are unemployed but actively looking for work.

[4]Mean monthly earnings for those who are employed. Data adjusted to U.S. dollars using the purchasing power parity (PPP) index.
[5]Refers to the mean of the data values for all reporting Organization for Economic Cooperation and Development (OECD) countries and subnational education systems, to which each country or subnational education system reporting data contributes equally, with the exception of England (UK) and Northern Ireland (UK), which contribute to the mean as a combined entity, England/Northern Ireland (UK).
[6]Cyprus includes only the population under the effective control of the Government of the Republic of Cyprus.
[7]The Russian Federation does not include the population of the Moscow municipal region.
SOURCE: Organization for Economic Cooperation and Development (OECD), Program for the International Assessment of Adult Competencies (PIAAC), 2012. (This table was prepared March 2016.)

Table 605.10. Gross domestic product per capita and expenditures on education institutions per full-time-equivalent (FTE) student, by level of education and country: Selected years, 2005 through 2016

Country	Gross domestic product per capita						Elementary and secondary education expenditures per FTE student[1]						Higher education expenditures per FTE student[1]					
	2005	2010	2013	2014	2015	2016	2005	2010	2013	2014	2015	2016	2005	2010	2013	2014	2015	2016
1	2	3	4	5	6	7	8	9	10	11	12	13	14	15	16	17	18	19
Current dollars																		
OECD average[2]	$28,300	$34,143	$38,150[3]	$39,255	$40,523	$41,721	$6,105	$8,143	$8,775	$8,996	$9,192	$9,421	$9,897	$12,811	$14,817	$15,057	$15,284	$15,532
Australia	35,571	42,812	47,761	47,639	47,351	50,263	6,891	10,321	10,318	10,319	10,743	10,506	14,172	16,320	18,253	19,494	20,299	16,170
Austria	35,025	42,018	47,937	48,814	49,954	51,637	—	—	13,391	13,454	13,939	14,679	—	—	16,900	16,868	17,565	18,332
Belgium	33,331	40,050	43,746	44,720	45,739	47,366	7,583	10,457	11,719	11,903	11,952	12,324	12,286	15,449	16,697	17,196	17,353	18,169
Canada[4,5]	36,329	40,106	44,211	45,628	44,671	45,109	—	9,946	10,635	10,747	10,459	10,681	—	—	22,242[6]	22,070[6]	21,830[6]	23,700
Chile	12,668	18,129	22,353	22,688	22,593	22,788	2,140	3,279	4,376	4,167	4,259	4,944	5,969	7,160	7,974	7,813	6,728	8,317
Colombia	8,246	10,742	12,841[3]	13,536	13,928	14,276	—	—	2,658	2,778	2,938	3,014	—	—	6,889	3,646	5,041	6,427
Czech Republic	21,907	27,555	30,496	32,265	33,701	35,234	4,051	5,763	6,639	6,887	7,122	6,980	6,572	7,954	10,308	10,490	10,963	10,009
Denmark	34,153	43,005	46,743	47,905	49,071	50,685	8,942	11,749	11,808	12,827	—	—	14,867	19,552	15,698	15,626	12,909	—
Estonia	16,466	21,552	27,450	28,937	29,260	30,895	3,706	6,213	6,897	6,436	6,685	6,914	3,838	6,750	11,798	11,965	12,909	12,909
Finland	31,993	38,737	41,293	41,463	42,213	43,730	6,638	8,826	9,659	9,769	10,044	10,045	12,332	17,172	18,018	17,875	17,625	17,541
France	30,504	35,909	39,528	40,144	40,841	42,067	7,340	8,967	9,778	9,918	9,963	10,186	11,220	15,146	16,234	16,354	16,252	16,173
Germany[4]	32,414	39,916	45,232	47,190	47,979	49,921	7,061	9,194	10,300	10,779	10,883	11,294	13,056	17,292	16,949	17,144	17,066	17,429
Greece[4]	25,577	28,148	26,098[7]	26,839[7]	26,902[7]	27,274[7]	5,354	—	6,277	6,192	6,205	6,056[6]	6,320	—	3,713	3,881	4,104	—
Hungary	17,082	21,535	24,464	25,518	26,356	26,852	3,947	—	4,642	5,552	5,985	6,899	5,522	—	10,374	8,647	8,817	11,288
Iceland	37,338	39,582	44,153	45,713	48,857	52,340	8,961[8]	8,797	9,757	10,599	11,231	11,707	9,665[8]	8,936	11,200	11,418	12,697	14,551
Ireland	40,437	43,299	47,936	51,126	69,147	70,616	6,481	9,742	9,434	9,170	8,705	9,020	10,582	10,336	12,993	13,702	13,281	13,237
Israel	24,721	28,872	34,160	34,228	35,450	37,475	4,579	5,694	7,551	7,556	—	8,365	9,952	10,054	13,955	13,453	10,651	11,153
Italy	29,938	34,685	35,885	36,071	36,836	39,045	7,103	8,162	8,840[4]	8,727[4]	9,047[4]	8,736[6]	7,274	7,392	11,303	11,439	11,321	11,589
Japan	31,668	34,994	39,008	39,183	40,406	41,138	7,452	8,882	—	—	—	10,143	13,915	—	—	—	—	19,191[8]
Korea, Republic of	24,196	30,365	32,616	33,587	35,761	37,143	—	—	—	—	—	11,762	—	—	—	—	10,269	10,486
Latvia	13,848	17,561	22,675	23,802	24,726	25,843	3,033	4,753	5,968	6,631	6,884	6,625	4,270	5,853	8,051	8,974	10,225	7,449
Lithuania	14,526	20,091	26,661	28,174	28,910	30,300	—	4,537	5,212	5,383	5,314	5,767	4,502	7,166	9,147	10,049	9,698	7,701
Luxembourg	68,141	85,515	95,246	100,934	102,817	104,702[7]	—	—	18,758	20,939	20,711	19,770	—	—	41,995[6]	45,801	49,530	48,407
Mexico	12,540	15,258	17,462	18,168	18,438	18,969[7]	2,007	2,544	2,925	3,033	3,075	3,062	6,225	8,128	7,693	8,901	8,381	7,347
Netherlands	37,625	45,041	49,243	49,233	50,302	51,340	7,760	9,890	10,995	10,674	11,026	11,121	15,411	17,600	19,588	19,234	19,402	19,513
New Zealand	25,590	31,165	36,074	37,061	37,158	38,784	—	—	8,770	9,064	9,192	9,487	—	—	14,234	15,109	15,045	14,933
Norway	47,775	57,969	67,051	66,018	60,492	58,122	9,793	12,932	14,396	14,194	14,069	13,758	—	18,854	21,179	21,009	20,558	21,993
Poland	13,898	20,789	24,423	25,298	26,529	27,406	3,181	5,579	6,608	6,824	6,798	6,892	4,774	7,213	8,423	8,793	9,778	8,977
Portugal	22,740	27,308	27,899	28,747	29,685	31,042	5,620	—	9,514[8]	9,411[8]	8,577[8]	8,945[8]	9,636	10,260	11,094[8]	11,788[8]	11,827[8]	11,014[8]
Slovak Republic	16,572	24,785	27,900	28,928	29,700	30,896	2,770	5,277	5,929	6,369	6,765	6,686	5,846	7,191	10,225	11,234	15,916	11,413
Slovenia	23,941	27,736	29,803	30,847	31,649	33,191	7,072	8,668	8,950	8,875	8,447	8,550	9,924	8,982	9,865	10,037	10,258	11,257
Spain	27,696	31,933	32,623	33,728	35,054	36,743[7]	6,329	8,363	7,753	7,814	8,230	8,594	—	13,191	12,699	12,524	12,667	12,614
Sweden	34,006	41,633	45,722	46,573	48,437	49,084	7,672	10,096	11,061	11,007	11,174	11,549	15,550	20,634	23,817	24,509	24,686	24,341
Switzerland	40,327	52,860	60,109	61,902	63,939	64,324	—	—	—	—	15,155[6]	15,506[6]	—	—	—	—	—	—
Turkey	11,796	17,232	22,205	23,983	25,728	26,330	—	—	3,478	3,835	4,062	4,505	—	—	11,076	11,212	10,412	10,519
United Kingdom	32,486	36,016	39,519	40,878	42,055	42,943	7,698	9,422	11,487	11,875	11,109	11,061	23,637	25,681	25,614	24,346	26,513	23,771
United States	44,044	48,394	53,016	54,952	56,718	57,822	9,775	11,809	11,868	12,163	12,595	13,019	—	—	27,579	29,328	30,001	30,165
Constant 2018 dollars																		
OECD average[2]	$36,996	$38,983	$40,740[3]	$41,457	$42,527	$43,394	$7,905	$9,229	$9,363	$9,503	$9,661	$9,796	$12,732	$14,522	$15,950	$15,996	$16,131	$16,209
Australia	48,571	50,475	52,284	50,883	49,825	52,222	9,410	12,168	11,295	11,022	11,304	10,915	19,351	19,241	19,981	20,821	21,359	16,800
Austria	44,581	48,857	51,625	51,738	52,476	53,765	—	—	14,422	14,260	14,643	15,284	—	—	18,200	17,878	18,452	19,087
Belgium	42,565	46,239	46,913	47,796	48,612	49,367	9,684	12,073	12,568	12,721	12,702	12,845	15,690	17,836	17,906	18,378	18,443	18,936
Canada[4,5]	45,297	45,932	48,015	48,626	47,077	46,869	—	11,391	11,550	11,454	11,022	11,098	—	—	24,156[6]	23,520[6]	23,006[6]	24,625
Chile	19,460	23,318	26,534	25,719	24,544	23,853	3,288	4,218	5,194	4,723	4,627	5,174	9,170	9,209	9,465	8,857	7,309	8,705
Colombia	14,092	14,625	16,063[3]	16,454	16,127	15,374	—	—	3,325	3,377	3,402	3,246	—	—	8,617	4,433	5,837	6,921
Czech Republic	28,526	31,206	32,343	34,102	35,510	36,873	5,274	6,526	7,041	7,279	7,504	7,305	8,558	9,008	10,932	11,088	11,552	10,475
Denmark	41,555	47,098	48,270	49,193	50,163	51,684	10,880	12,867	12,193	13,172	—	—	18,089	21,412	16,210	16,046	—	—
Estonia	24,860	25,738	29,231	30,847	31,346	33,049	5,596	7,420	7,345	6,861	7,162	7,396	5,794	8,061	12,564	12,754	13,830	13,809
Finland	39,001	43,073	42,556	42,291	43,146	44,537	8,091	9,814	9,954	9,964	10,266	10,231	15,034	19,094	18,569	18,232	18,014	17,864

See notes at end of table.

Table 605.10. Gross domestic product per capita and expenditures on education institutions per full-time-equivalent (FTE) student, by level of education and country: Selected years, 2005 through 2016—Continued

Country	Gross domestic product per capita						Elementary and secondary education expenditures per FTE student[1]						Higher education expenditures per FTE student[1]					
	2005	2010	2013	2014	2015	2016	2005	2010	2013	2014	2015	2016	2005	2010	2013	2014	2015	2016
1	2	3	4	5	6	7	8	9	10	11	12	13	14	15	16	17	18	19
France	35,794	39,084	40,973	41,400	42,103	43,288	8,613	9,760	10,136	10,229	10,271	10,482	13,166	16,485	16,827	16,866	16,754	16,643
Germany	39,000	44,405	47,609	49,224	49,791	51,552	8,496	10,228	10,842	11,244	11,294	11,663	15,710	19,237	17,840	17,883	17,711	17,998
Greece[4]	30,486	28,625	25,540[7]	26,614[7]	27,148[7]	27,752[7]	6,381	—	6,143	6,140	6,262	6,162[6]	7,532	—	3,634	3,848	4,141	—
Hungary	26,142	25,349	25,779	26,951	27,854	28,265	6,040	—	4,892	5,863	6,325	7,262	8,451	—	10,932	9,133	9,318	11,882
Iceland	69,716	49,568	48,659	49,369	51,917	54,691	16,732[8]	11,016	10,753	11,447	11,934	12,232	18,046[8]	11,191	12,344	12,331	13,492	15,204
Ireland	45,845	45,720	48,286	51,405	69,727	71,203	7,348	10,286	9,503	9,220	8,778	9,095	11,998	11,085	13,088	13,777	13,393	13,347
Israel	30,193	30,965	34,283	34,185	35,631	37,872	5,593	6,106	7,578	7,546	—	8,454	12,155	11,055	14,006	13,436	10,705	11,272
Italy	36,183	38,137	36,807	36,908	37,677	39,974	8,585	8,975	9,067[4]	8,930[4]	9,254[4]	8,943	8,791	18,259	11,593	11,704	11,579	11,864
Japan	33,111	36,738	36,941	40,019	40,945	41,735	7,792	9,325	—	—	—	10,290	14,549	—	—	—	—	19,469[8]
Korea, Republic of	32,219	34,835	34,746	35,331	37,354	38,424	—	—	—	—	—	12,167	—	—	—	—	10,726	10,848
Latvia	21,818	19,960	24,155	25,200	26,132	27,274	4,779	5,402	6,357	7,020	7,275	6,992	6,728	6,653	8,577	9,500	10,807	7,861
Lithuania	21,639	23,241	28,432	30,016	31,074	32,276	—	5,249	5,559	5,735	5,712	6,143	6,706	8,289	9,755	10,706	10,424	8,204
Luxembourg	85,936	96,731	99,753	105,049	106,504	108,142	—	—	19,646	21,792	21,454	20,419	—	—	43,982[6]	47,668	51,306	49,997
Mexico	21,275	20,838	21,340	21,345	21,089	21,100[7]	3,404	3,474	3,575	3,563	3,518	3,407	10,561	11,102	9,402	10,457	9,586	8,173
Netherlands	45,848	50,867	51,740	51,230	52,030	52,935	9,456	11,169	11,552	11,107	11,405	11,467	18,779	19,876	20,582	20,014	20,068	20,119
New Zealand	33,062	35,036	38,143	38,711	38,699	40,133	—	—	9,273	9,468	9,573	9,817	—	—	15,050	15,782	15,669	15,453
Norway	62,944	68,239	75,784	73,123	65,578	60,849	12,903	15,224	16,271	15,722	15,252	14,404	—	22,195	23,937	23,270	22,287	23,025
Poland	17,855	23,206	25,006	25,888	27,387	28,482	4,086	6,228	6,766	6,983	7,008	7,163	6,134	8,052	8,624	8,999	10,094	9,330
Portugal	27,321	30,108	28,796	29,753	30,575	31,779	6,753	—	9,819[8]	9,741[8]	8,835[8]	9,157[8]	11,577	11,312	11,450[8]	12,201[8]	12,181[8]	11,275[8]
Slovak Republic	21,449	27,845	28,710	29,791	30,685	32,088	3,585	5,929	6,101	6,559	6,990	6,945	7,566	8,079	10,522	11,569	16,444	11,853
Slovenia	30,132	30,307	30,637	31,647	32,642	34,250	8,901	9,471	9,200	9,105	8,712	8,823	—	9,814	10,141	10,297	10,580	11,617
Spain	34,305	35,187	33,530	34,719	36,265	38,089[7]	7,839	9,215	7,969	8,044	8,514	8,909	12,292	14,535	13,052	12,892	13,105	13,076
Sweden	39,826	45,202	47,810	48,787	50,764	50,941	8,985	10,962	11,566	11,530	11,711	11,985	18,211	22,403	24,905	25,674	25,872	25,262
Switzerland	41,792	52,430	60,028	61,827	64,600	65,273	—	—	—	—	15,312[6]	15,735[6]	—	—	18,090	16,823	14,508	13,601
Turkey	36,459	35,074	36,266	35,983	35,851	34,044	—	—	5,681	5,754	5,661	5,825	—	—	—	—	—	—
United Kingdom	43,369	42,372	42,658	43,504	44,578	45,069	10,276	11,085	12,399	12,638	11,776	11,609	—	—	27,648	25,910	28,104	24,948
United States	56,632	55,729	57,147	58,288	60,090	60,496	12,569	13,599	12,793	12,901	13,343	13,622	30,393	29,574	29,728	31,109	31,785	31,560

—Not available.
[1]Includes both government and private expenditures. Includes expenditures on both public and private institutions unless otherwise noted.
[2]Refers to the mean of the data values for all reporting Organization for Economic Cooperation and Development (OECD) countries, to which each country reporting data contributes equally. The average includes all current OECD countries for which a given year's data are available, even if they were not members of OECD in that year.
[3]Estimated value.
[4]Elementary and secondary education expenditures exclude postsecondary non-higher-education.
[5]Elementary and secondary education expenditures include preprimary education (for children ages 3 and older).
[6]Includes public institutions only.

[7]Provisional value; data subject to revision.
[8]Postsecondary non-higher-education included in both secondary and higher education.
NOTE: All education expenditure data in this table were calculated using International Standard Classification of Education (ISCED) 2011. Expenditures for ISCED level 4 (postsecondary non-higher-education) are included in elementary and secondary education unless otherwise noted. Data adjusted to U.S. dollars using the purchasing power parity (PPP) index. Constant dollars based on national Consumer Price Indexes, available on the OECD database cited in the SOURCE note below. Some data have been revised from previously published figures. This table includes only data that had been validated for consistency and accuracy by OECD and the relevant country as of November 20, 2019.
SOURCE: Organization for Economic Cooperation and Development (OECD), Online Education Database, retrieved November 20, 2019, from https://stats.oecd.org/Index.aspx. (This table was prepared November 2019.)

Table 605.20. Government and private expenditures on education institutions as a percentage of gross domestic product, by level of education and country: Selected years, 2005 through 2016

Country	All institutions[1]								Elementary and secondary institutions								Higher education institutions							
	Government expenditures					All expenditures, 2016			Government expenditures					All expenditures, 2016			Government expenditures					All expenditures, 2016		
	2005	2010	2013	2014	2015	Government	Private	Total	2005	2010	2013	2014	2015	Government	Private	Total	2005	2010	2013	2014	2015	Government	Private	Total
1	2	3	4	5	6	7	8	9	10	11	12	13	14	15	16	17	18	19	20	21	22	23	24	25
OECD average[2]	**4.2**	**4.4**	**4.3**	**4.3**	**4.2**	**4.0**	**0.9**	**5.0**	**3.2**	**3.4**	**3.3**	**3.3**	**3.2**	**3.1**	**0.4**	**3.5**	**1.0**	**1.0**	**1.0**	**1.0**	**1.0**	**0.9**	**0.5**	**1.5**
Australia	3.9	4.6	4.0	3.9	3.9	3.9	1.9[3]	5.8	3.2	3.8	3.3	3.2	3.2	3.2	0.7	3.9	0.7	0.8	0.7	0.7	0.8	0.8	1.2[3]	1.9
Austria	—	—	4.7	4.6	4.6	4.6	0.3	4.9	—	—	3.1	3.0	3.0	3.0	0.1	3.1	—	1.2	1.6	1.6	1.6	1.6	0.1	1.8
Belgium	—	—	5.5	5.4	5.3	5.3	0.4	5.8	—	—	4.2	4.0	4.1	4.1	0.1	4.3	1.1	1.2	1.3	1.3	1.3	1.2	0.2	1.5
Canada	4.4	5.1	4.6	4.5	4.4	4.4	1.4	5.9	3.1	3.5	3.3[4,5]	3.2[4,5]	3.2[4,5]	3.2[4,5]	0.3[4,5]	3.5[4,5]	1.3	1.6	1.3	1.2	1.2	1.2	1.1	2.3
Chile	2.8	3.2	3.5	3.3	3.3	3.8	2.3	6.1	2.5	2.7	2.6	2.5	2.6	3.0	0.6	3.6	0.3	0.5	0.8	0.9	0.7	0.8	1.7	2.5
Colombia	3.3	—	4.1	3.9	3.9	3.9	2.4	6.2	2.5	2.4	3.3	3.1	3.1	3.1	0.9	4.0	0.8	0.9	0.8	0.8	0.8	0.8	1.4	2.2
Czech Republic	3.3	3.3	3.6	3.5	3.4	3.1	0.4	3.5	2.5	2.4	2.4	2.4	2.4	2.3	0.2	2.5	0.8	0.9	0.9	0.9	0.9	0.7	0.2	0.9
Denmark	5.9	6.2	6.0	6.2	6.2	5.9	0.5	6.4	4.4	4.6	4.4	4.7	4.6	4.4	0.3	4.6	1.6	1.7	1.5	1.6	1.6	1.4	0.1	1.5
Estonia	3.9	3.9	4.1	4.0	4.1	3.9	0.4	4.4	2.6	2.6	2.6	2.6	2.7	2.7	0.2	2.9	0.8	1.0	1.2	1.4	1.3	1.2	0.2	1.5
Finland	5.6	6.4	6.0	5.6	5.6	5.4	0.1	5.5	3.8	4.0	3.9	3.9	4.0	3.8	#	3.9	1.6	1.8	1.7	1.7	1.6	1.5	0.1	1.7
France	4.6	4.8	4.7	4.6	4.5	4.5	0.7	5.2	3.5	3.6	3.4	3.4	3.4	3.4	0.3	3.7	1.1	1.2	1.1	1.1	1.1	1.1	0.3	1.4
Germany	3.7	3.9	3.7	3.7	3.6	3.6	0.6	4.2	2.8	2.9	2.7	2.7	2.6	2.6	0.4	3.0	0.9	1.0	1.0	1.0	1.0	1.0	0.2	1.2
Greece	3.9	3.6	3.3	3.3	3.4	3.2	0.1	3.2	2.5	2.8	2.7	2.7	2.6	2.6	0.1	2.7	1.4	1.0	0.6	0.6	0.7	0.6	#	0.7
Hungary	4.1	3.6	3.1	3.3	3.2	3.5	0.7	4.3	2.7	2.7	2.3	2.7	2.7	2.9	0.2	3.2	0.8	0.8	0.6	0.7	0.6	0.7	0.4	1.1
Iceland	6.1	5.4	5.3	5.5	5.4	5.3	0.3	5.6	5.0	4.4	4.2	4.3	4.3	4.1	0.2	4.3	1.1	1.0	0.8	1.0	1.1	1.1	0.1	1.3
Ireland	4.0	5.4	4.7	4.3	3.1	3.2	0.3	3.5	3.1	4.3	3.8	3.5	2.5	2.6	0.1	2.7	0.9	1.2	0.9	0.8	0.6	0.6	0.2	0.8
Israel	4.4	4.5	4.9	4.8	4.9	4.8	1.1	6.0	3.5	3.7	4.0	4.0	4.0	4.0	0.5	4.5	0.8	0.8	0.9	0.8	0.9	0.8	0.6	1.4
Italy	3.6	3.6	3.5	3.4	3.4	3.1	0.5	3.6	2.9	3.0	2.8	2.8	2.8	2.6	0.1	2.7	0.6	0.6	0.6	0.6	0.6	0.5	0.3	0.9
Japan[6]	2.9	3.2	—	—	—	2.9	1.2	4.0	2.5	2.7	—	—	—	2.4	0.2	2.7	0.5	0.5	—	—	—	0.4	1.0	1.4
Korea, Republic of	—	—	—	—	—	3.8	1.6	5.4	—	—	—	—	—	3.1	0.6	3.7	—	—	—	—	0.7	0.7	1.1	1.7
Latvia	3.9	4.0	3.9	4.3	4.3	3.7	0.4	4.2	3.1	3.2	3.0	3.2	3.3	3.0	0.1	3.1	0.8	0.7	0.8	1.0	1.1	0.7	0.3	1.0
Lithuania	3.9	4.4	3.8	3.7	3.4	3.1	0.5	3.6	3.0	3.3	2.8	2.8	2.8	2.4	0.1	2.5	0.8	1.1	1.2	1.2	1.1	0.7	0.3	1.1
Luxembourg	—	—	3.3	3.4	3.3	3.0	0.1	3.2	—	—	2.8	2.9	2.8	2.6	0.1	2.8	—	—	0.5	0.5	0.5	0.4	0.0	0.5
Mexico	4.0	4.2	4.1	4.2	4.2	4.0	1.1	5.1	3.2	3.5	3.2	3.2	3.2	3.0	0.7	3.7	0.8	0.9	0.8	1.0	1.0	0.9	0.4	1.4
Netherlands	4.1	4.4	4.1	4.3	4.3	4.2	0.9	5.2	3.1	3.3	3.3	3.2	3.1	3.1	0.4	3.5	1.0	1.1	1.2	1.2	1.2	1.1	0.5	1.7
New Zealand	—	—	5.0	4.9	4.9	4.7	1.7	6.4	—	—	4.0	3.9	3.9	3.9	0.8	4.7	—	—	0.9	0.9	0.9	0.9	0.9	1.7
Norway	6.6	6.4	5.0	6.1	6.3	6.3	0.1	6.5	4.9	4.4	4.0	4.5	4.6	4.6	#	4.6	1.7	1.6	1.5	1.6	1.6	1.8	0.1	1.9
Poland	4.8	4.4	4.1	4.1	4.0	3.8	0.5	4.4	3.6	3.4	3.1	3.0	2.9	2.9	0.3	3.2	0.8	1.0	1.1	1.0	1.1	0.9	0.2	1.2
Portugal[6]	4.4	4.6	4.5	4.4	4.1	4.1	0.8	5.0	3.5	3.7	3.8	3.6	3.4	3.4	0.4	3.8	0.7	1.0	0.7	0.8	0.7	0.7	0.4	1.2
Slovak Republic	3.1	3.3	3.2	3.3	3.8	3.1	0.6	3.7	2.4	2.6	2.4	2.5	2.5	2.4	0.3	2.7	0.7	0.9	0.7	0.8	0.7	0.7	0.3	1.0
Slovenia	3.5	4.0	4.3	4.1	3.8	3.8	0.4	4.3	2.6	2.4	3.3	3.2	3.0	2.9	0.3	3.2	0.9	1.0	1.0	0.9	0.8	0.8	0.1	1.0
Spain	3.5	4.0	3.6	3.5	3.5	3.5	0.8	4.3	2.7	2.9	2.7	2.6	2.7	2.6	0.4	3.1	0.8	1.0	0.9	1.0	0.8	0.8	0.4	1.2
Sweden	5.3	5.2	5.2	5.1	5.0	5.2	0.2	5.4	4.0	3.8	3.7	3.7	3.6	3.8	†	3.8	1.3	1.4	1.5	1.4	1.4	1.4	0.2	1.6
Switzerland	4.7	4.4	4.6	4.6	4.5	4.5	0.4	5.0	3.5	4.0	3.7	3.7	3.6	3.3	0.4	3.7	1.3	1.2	1.2	1.3	1.3	1.3	0.2	1.6
Turkey	2.7	3.3	3.9	3.9	3.8	4.1	1.4	5.4	1.9	2.4	2.5	2.6	2.5	2.7	0.9	3.5	0.7	0.9	0.7	0.8	0.7	1.4	0.5	1.9
United Kingdom	—	—	4.7	4.7	4.4	4.2	1.9	6.2	—	—	4.1	4.2	3.9	3.7	0.7	4.4	—	—	0.6	0.5	0.5	0.5	1.2	1.7
United States	—	—	4.2	4.1	4.1	4.1	1.9	6.0	—	—	3.2	3.2	3.2	3.2	0.3	3.5	—	—	0.9	0.9	0.9	0.9	1.6	2.5
Other reporting countries																								
Russian Federation	—	2.7	2.9	2.8	2.6	2.6	0.5	3.1	—	1.8	2.0	1.9	1.8	1.9	0.1	2.0	—	0.9	0.8	0.8	0.7	0.7	0.4	1.1

—Not available.
†Not applicable.
#Rounds to zero.
[1]Includes expenditures that could not be reported by level of education.
[2]Refers to the mean of the data values for all reporting Organization for Economic Cooperation and Development (OECD) countries, to which each country reporting data contributes equally. The average includes all current OECD countries for which a given year's data are available, even if they were not members of OECD in that year.
[3]Includes expenditures on education institutions from international sources.
[4]Includes preprimary education.
[5]Excludes postsecondary non-higher-education.
[6]Postsecondary non-higher-education included in both secondary and higher education.

NOTE: Government expenditures on education include both amounts spent directly by governments to hire education personnel and to procure other resources and amounts provided by governments to public or private institutions. Types of expenditures may include direct expenditures, research and development activities, ancillary expenditures, and capital expenditures. Government expenditures may also include subsidies to households for payments to education institutions. Private expenditures exclude government subsidies that are used for payments to education institutions. All data in this table were calculated using International Standard Classification of Education (ISCED) 2011. Expenditures for ISCED level 4 (postsecondary non-higher-education) are included in elementary and secondary education unless otherwise noted. Detail may not sum to totals because of rounding. Some data have been revised from previously published figures. This table includes only data that had been validated for consistency and accuracy by OECD and the relevant country as of October 14, 2019.
SOURCE: Organization for Economic Cooperation and Development (OECD), Online Education Database, retrieved October 14, 2019, from https://stats.oecd.org/Index.aspx. (This table was prepared October 2019.)

CHAPTER 7
Libraries and Use of Technology

This chapter presents statistics on access to and use of computers and the Internet among children and adults of various racial/ethnic groups, age groups, educational attainment levels, and income levels. These tables are based on data from the U.S. Census Bureau. Other chapters also provide information on use of computers and technology. Chapter 2 includes tables on use of computers and the Internet by elementary and secondary students and schools. Chapter 3 includes tables on distance and online education at the postsecondary level.

This chapter also includes tables on elementary and secondary school libraries, college and university libraries (including institution-level information for the 60 largest college libraries in the country), and public libraries. It contains data on library collections, staff, and expenditures, as well as library usage. The tables on libraries in educational institutions are based on National Center for Education Statistics (NCES) data, while the table on public libraries is based on Institute of Museum and Library Services data.

Computer and Internet Use

Access to Computers and Other Devices

Ninety-eight percent of all 3- to 18-year-old children had some type of computer or smartphone in their household in 2018 (table 702.10). A higher percentage of 3- to 18-year-old children lived in a household with a smartphone (95 percent) than in a household with a desktop or laptop (83 percent) or in a household with a tablet or other portable wireless computer (78 percent).

The percentages of children ages 3 to 18 with various types of devices in their household differed by race/ethnicity in 2018 (table 702.10). For example, 94 percent of Asian children had a desktop or laptop in their household, compared with 90 percent of White children, 87 percent of children of Two or more races, 74 percent of Hispanic children, 72 percent of Black children, 71 percent of Pacific Islander children, and 63 percent of American Indian/Alaska Native children. The percentages of children who lived in a household with a smartphone were higher for Asian children (98 percent), children of Two or more races (97 percent), and White children (96 percent) than for Hispanic children (94 percent), Black children (93 percent), Pacific Islander children (91 percent), and American Indian/Alaska Native children (86 percent).

In 2018, the percentages of children ages 3 to 18 who lived in households with desktops or laptops, smartphones, and tablets or other portable wireless computers were higher for those with higher family incomes than for those with lower family incomes (table 702.10). For example, the percentage of children living in a household with a desktop or laptop computer was highest for children with family incomes of over $100,000 (96 percent) and lowest for children with family incomes of less than $10,000 (56 percent). The percentages of children who lived in a household with a smartphone and who lived in a household with a tablet or other portable wireless computer were also highest for children with family incomes of over $100,000 (98 and 92 percent, respectively) and lowest for children with family incomes of less than $10,000 (88 and 53 percent, respectively).

In 2018, the percentages of children who lived in households with various types of computers were higher for children whose parent(s) had higher levels of educational attainment than for those whose parent(s) had lower levels of educational attainment (table 702.10 and figure 30). For example, the percentage of children with a desktop or laptop in their household was higher for those who had a parent with a bachelor's or higher degree (97 percent) than for those whose parent(s)'s highest level of education was an associate's degree (90 percent), some college (82 percent), a high school diploma or equivalent (69 percent), and less than high school (55 percent). Also, the percentage of children with a smartphone in their household was higher for those who had a parent with a bachelor's or higher degree (98 percent) than for those whose parent(s)'s highest level of education was an associate's degree (97 percent), some college (96 percent), a high school diploma or equivalent (93 percent), and less than high school (88 percent).

Children's Internet Access by Household Characteristics

In 2018, about 88 percent of 3- to 18-year-olds had access to the Internet in their household through a desktop or laptop, tablet, or some other type of computer and 6 percent had internet access in their household only through a smartphone (*web-only table 702.12*). The remaining 6 percent of 3- to 18-year-olds had no access to the Internet in their household. These percentages varied by parental education, family income, and race/ethnicity. For example, the percentage of children with access to the Internet through a desktop, laptop, or tablet in their household was higher for those who had a parent with a bachelor's or higher degree (98 percent) than for those whose parent(s)'s highest level of education was an associate's degree (93 percent), some college (88 percent), a high school diploma or equivalent (78 percent), and less than high school (65 percent). Similarly, higher levels of family income were positively associated with having access to the Internet through a desktop or laptop within the household. For example, the percentage of 3- to 18-year-olds living in a household with access to the Internet through a desktop, laptop, or tablet was highest for children with family incomes of over $100,000 (97 percent) and lowest for children with family incomes of less than $10,000 (65 percent). Also, the percentages of 3- to 18-year-olds who were Asian (96 percent), White (93 percent), and of Two or more races (92 percent) who lived in households with internet access through a desktop, laptop, or tablet were higher than the percentages for Hispanic children (81 percent), Black children (79 percent), Pacific Islander children (76 percent), or American Indian/Alaska Native children (70 percent).

The percentage of 3- to 18-year-olds who did not have access to the Internet was inversely related to family income in 2018 (*web-only table 702.12*). For example, the percentage of 3- to 18-year-olds living in a household without access to the Internet was higher for those with family incomes of less than $10,000 (18 percent) than for those with family incomes of over $100,000 (2 percent). Also, the percentage of 3- to 18-year-olds without access to the Internet was lower for those who had a parent with a bachelor's or higher degree (1 percent) than for those whose parent(s)'s highest level of education was an associate's degree (4 percent), some college (6 percent), a high school diploma or equivalent (10 percent), or less than high school (18 percent). In addition, lower percentages of 3- to 18-year-olds who were Asian (2 percent), of Two or more races (3 percent), and White (4 percent) had no access to the Internet in their households than 3- to 18-year-olds who were Hispanic (9 percent), Black (10 percent), Pacific Islander (13 percent), or American Indian/Alaska Native (20 percent).

Internet Usage at All Ages

Seventy-eight percent of the U.S. population age 3 and older used the Internet in 2017, up from 70 percent in 2011 (table 702.30). While this overall percentage of internet users was 8 percentage points higher in 2017 than in 2011, this pattern was not consistent across age groups. For example, there was no measurable change in the percentage of 15- to 18-year-olds using the Internet (85 percent in both years). The percentage of internet users among 19- to 24-year-olds was 2 percentage points higher in 2017 (85 percent) than in 2011 (83 percent). In contrast, there were larger increases in internet use among the younger and older age groups. The percentage of internet users

among 3- and 4-year-olds nearly doubled from 2011 (26 percent) to 2017 (51 percent), and the percentage of users among 5- to 10-year-olds was 18 percentage points higher (69 percent in 2017 vs. 51 percent in 2011). Among the older age groups, the internet use rate for 60- to 69-year-olds was 76 percent in 2017, compared to 64 percent in 2011. These increases resulted in a reduction of the gaps in internet use between different age groups. For example, the gap in the percentage of 5- to 10-year-olds and 15- to 18-year-olds using the Internet fell from 34 percentage points in 2011 to 16 percentage points in 2017. Similarly, the gap between the internet use of 25- to 29-year-olds and 60- to 69-year-olds fell from 17 percentage points in 2011 to 10 percentage points in 2017.

Internet usage differed by various demographic characteristics in 2017 (table 702.30 and figure 31). For example, the percentage of internet users was higher for persons age 3 and over who were of Two or more races (82 percent), White (80 percent), and Asian (79 percent) than for those who were Black (73 percent) and Hispanic (72 percent). The percentage of internet users who were American Indian/Alaska Native (63 percent) was lower than the percentages for all other racial/ethnic groups. The percentage of the population age 3 and over who used the Internet was generally higher for those with higher family incomes than for those with lower family incomes. For example, about 86 percent of persons with family incomes of $100,000 or more used the Internet, compared with 68 percent of persons with family incomes of $20,000 to $29,999. Among persons age 25 and over, the percentage of internet users tended to be higher for those with higher levels of educational attainment. For example, the percentage of persons age 25 and over who used the Internet was higher for those whose highest level of education was a bachelor's or higher degree (89 percent) than for those whose highest level of education was an associate's degree (86 percent), some college (83 percent), a high school diploma or equivalent (70 percent), and less than high school (51 percent).

Similar to the patterns observed for decreased gaps in internet use between young children and older teens and between young adults and older adults between 2011 and 2017, there were also decreases in gaps among other demographic groups (table 702.30). The difference between the percentage of internet users among White and Black persons 3 years old and over was smaller in 2017 (7 percentage points) than in 2011 (15 percentage points). The difference in use between White and Hispanic persons in this age group was also lower in 2017 (8 percentage points) than in 2011 (21 percentage points). The gap between the internet use in families with incomes below $10,000 and above $100,000 was also lower in 2017 (23 percentage points) than in 2011 (38 percentage points). Similarly, the difference in the percentage of internet users among those 25 and over with a bachelor's or higher degree and those who had not completed high school was lower in 2017 (37 percentage points) than in 2011 (58 percentage points).

Libraries

Among public schools that had a library in 2011–12, the average number of library staff per school was 1.8, including 0.9 certified library/media specialists (*web-only table 701.10*). On average, public school libraries had larger numbers of books on a per student basis in 2011–12 (2,188 per 100 students) than in 1999–2000 (1,803 per 100 students), 2003–04 (1,891 per 100 students), and 2007–08 (2,015 per 100 students). In 2011–12, public elementary school libraries had larger holdings on a per student basis than did public secondary school libraries (2,570 books per 100 students, compared with 1,474 books per 100 students).

In 2017–18, there were libraries at 92 percent of degree-granting postsecondary institutions overall, including 95 percent of public institutions, 96 percent of private nonprofit institutions, and 76 percent of private for-profit institutions (table 701.40). The calculations of library operating expenditures and number of books per full-time-equivalent (FTE) student in the following paragraph include both institutions with libraries and those without libraries.

At degree-granting postsecondary institutions, library operating expenditures per FTE student were 25 percent lower in 2011–12 than in 2001–02, after adjustment for inflation (table 701.40). Library operating expenditures per FTE student then increased by 16 percent from 2011–12 to 2017–18. The net result of these changes was that operating expenditures per FTE student were 13 percent lower in 2017–18 than in 2001–02. In 2017–18, library operating expenditures per FTE student averaged $559 (in current dollars) across all degree-granting institutions. The amount varied widely by institution control. However, library operating expenditures averaged $464 per FTE student attending a public institution in 2017–18, compared with $961 per FTE student attending a private nonprofit institution and $87 per FTE student attending a private for-profit institution. In 2017–18, the average number of books (including physical and electronic books) per FTE student also differed for public institutions (85 books), private nonprofit institutions (191 books), and private for-profit institutions (95 books). Across all degree-granting institutions, the average number of books per FTE student in 2017–18 was 110.

In 2017, there were 9,045 public libraries in the United States with a total of 715 million books and serial volumes (table 701.60). The annual number of visits per capita—that is, per resident of the areas served by the libraries—was 4.2, the annual number of reference transactions per capita was 0.8, and the annual number of uses of public-access internet computers per capita was 0.8.

Figure 30. Percentage of children ages 3 to 18 living in households with a computer, by parents' highest level of educational attainment and type of computer: 2018

Parents' highest level of educational attainment[1]

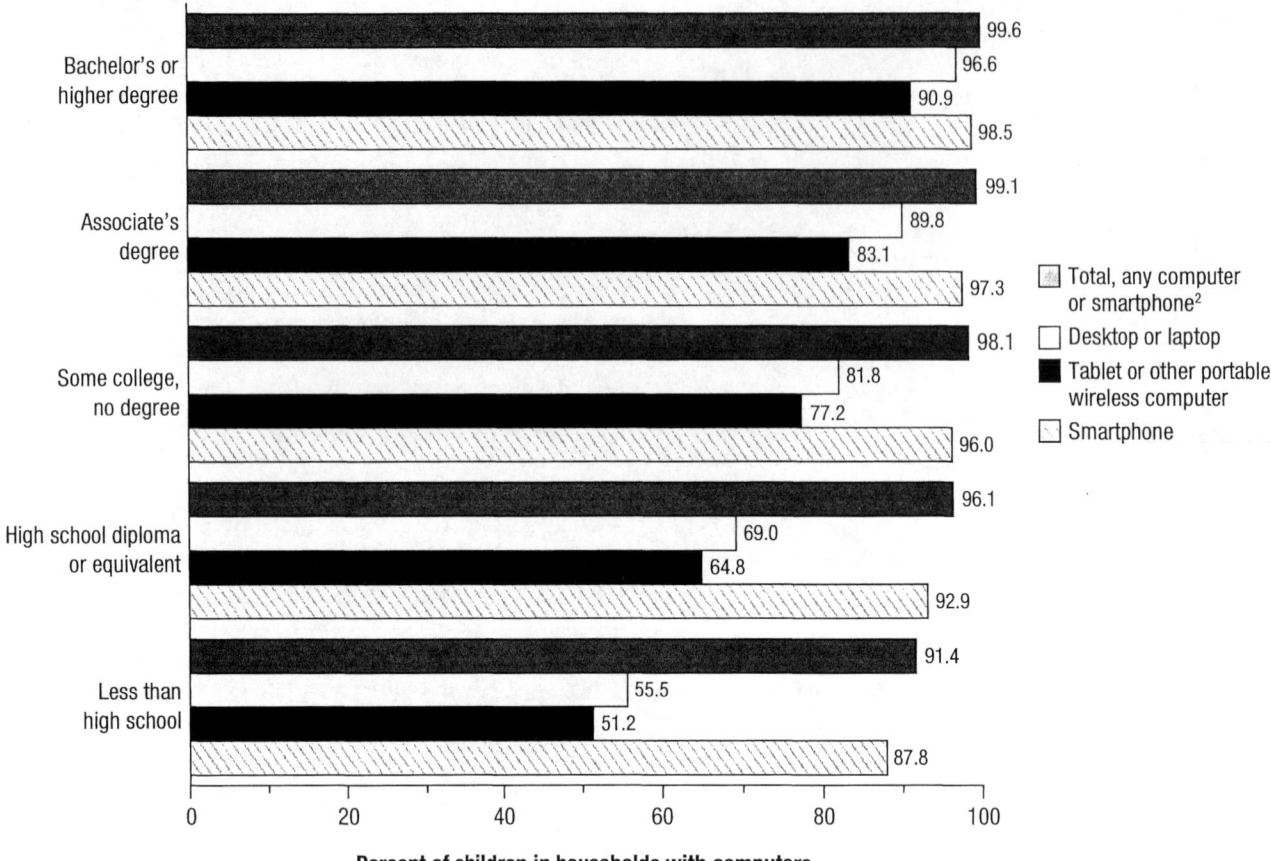

Percent of children in households with computers

[1]Highest level of educational attainment of any parent residing with the child (including adoptive parents and stepparents).
[2]Each household that had one or more computers or devices was counted only once in the total, regardless of the number and types of computers or devices reported. Total includes a small percentage (less than 1 percent) of children whose households had "some other type of computer" not listed in the survey questions.
NOTE: Data are based on all children living in households with their parents. Percentages refer to children whose household members owned or used at home the specified computers or devices. Graphic display was generated using unrounded data.
SOURCE: U.S. Department of Commerce, Census Bureau, American Community Survey (ACS), 2018.

Figure 31. Percentage of persons age 25 and over who used the Internet anywhere, at home, and at the workplace, by highest level of educational attainment: 2011 and 2017

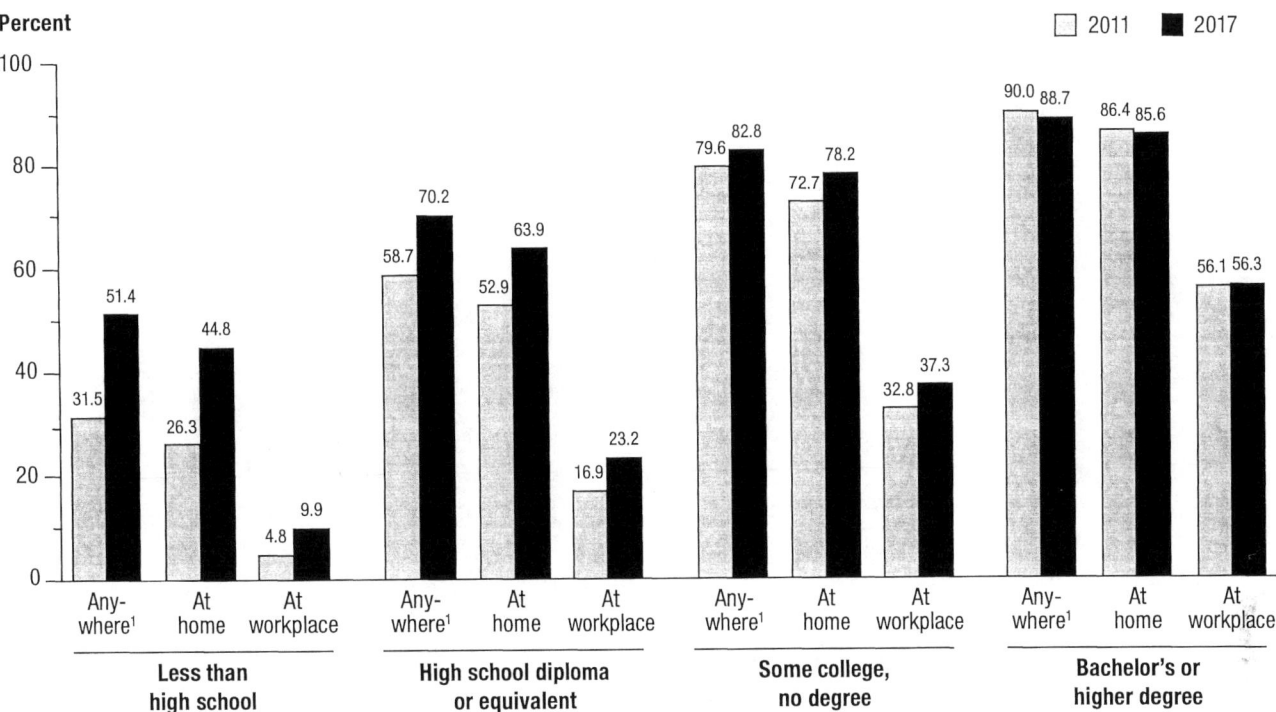

Highest level of educational attainment and location of internet use

[1]Includes all persons who use the Internet at any location.
NOTE: Data are based on sample surveys of the civilian noninstitutionalized population, which excludes persons in the military and persons living in institutions (e.g., prisons or nursing facilities).
SOURCE: U.S. Department of Commerce, Census Bureau, Current Population Survey (CPS), July 2011 and November 2017.

Table 701.15. Number and percentage of public schools with libraries/media centers and average number of staff per library/media center, by staff type and employment status and school level, enrollment size, and locale: 2015–16

[Standard errors appear in parentheses]

School level, enrollment size, and locale	Schools with libraries/ media centers				Average number of staff per library/media center								
					Librarians or library media specialists				Library media center instructional aides				Library media center noninstructional aides			
	Number		Percent		Full time		Part time		Full time		Part time		Full time		Part time	
1	2		3		4		5		6		7		8		9	
Total, all public schools[1]	**82,300**	**(440)**	**91.0**	**(0.43)**	**0.7**	**(0.01)**	**0.2**	**(0.01)**	**0.3**	**(0.01)**	**0.1**	**(0.01)**	**0.1**	**(#)**	**0.1**	**(#)**
Elementary schools	**59,500**	**(350)**	**95.4**	**(0.39)**	**0.6**	**(0.01)**	**0.2**	**(0.01)**	**0.3**	**(0.01)**	**0.1**	**(0.01)**	**0.1**	**(#)**	**0.1**	**(0.01)**
Enrollment size																
Less than 150 students	3,200	(300)	81.4	(3.88)	0.2	(0.03)	0.4	(0.05)	0.1!	(0.03)	0.2	(0.04)	‡	(†)	0.1!	(0.03)
150 to 499 students	28,700	(560)	95.1	(0.49)	0.6	(0.01)	0.3	(0.01)	0.2	(0.01)	0.2	(0.01)	0.1	(0.01)	0.1	(0.01)
500 to 749 students	18,600	(480)	97.8	(0.42)	0.7	(0.01)	0.2	(0.01)	0.3	(0.02)	0.1	(0.01)	0.1	(0.01)	0.1	(0.01)
750 or more students	9,000	(340)	97.8	(0.61)	0.8	(0.02)	0.2	(0.02)	0.3	(0.02)	0.1	(0.02)	0.1	(0.02)	0.1	(0.01)
Locale																
City	16,500	(210)	92.0	(0.92)	0.6	(0.02)	0.2	(0.02)	0.2	(0.02)	0.1	(0.01)	0.1	(0.01)	0.1	(0.01)
Suburban	21,100	(190)	97.0	(0.60)	0.7	(0.02)	0.2	(0.02)	0.2	(0.01)	0.2	(0.01)	0.1	(0.01)	0.1	(0.01)
Town	7,600	(280)	97.1	(0.69)	0.6	(0.02)	0.2	(0.02)	0.3	(0.02)	0.1	(0.02)	0.1	(0.01)	0.1	(0.01)
Rural	14,300	(320)	96.4	(0.82)	0.6	(0.02)	0.2	(0.02)	0.3	(0.02)	0.1	(0.02)	#	(†)	0.1	(0.01)
Secondary schools	**16,300**	**(410)**	**82.0**	**(1.46)**	**0.8**	**(0.02)**	**0.1**	**(0.01)**	**0.3**	**(0.02)**	**0.1**	**(0.01)**	**0.2**	**(0.01)**	**0.1**	**(0.01)**
Enrollment size																
Less than 150 students	1,400	(200)	46.0	(5.28)	0.2	(0.06)	0.2	(0.05)	‡	(†)	‡	(†)	‡	(†)	‡	(†)
150 to 499 students	4,600	(260)	77.4	(2.60)	0.6	(0.04)	0.2	(0.03)	0.2	(0.02)	0.1	(0.02)	0.1	(0.02)	0.1	(0.01)
500 to 749 students	2,600	(180)	89.6	(2.22)	0.8	(0.04)	0.2	(0.03)	0.2	(0.03)	0.2	(0.04)	0.1	(0.02)	0.1	(0.02)
750 or more students	7,600	(290)	96.5	(0.81)	1.1	(0.02)	0.1	(0.01)	0.4	(0.03)	0.1	(0.02)	0.3	(0.02)	0.1	(0.01)
Locale																
City	4,200	(220)	79.2	(2.51)	0.8	(0.04)	0.1	(0.02)	0.2	(0.03)	0.1	(0.01)	0.2	(0.03)	#	(†)
Suburban	4,800	(210)	80.9	(2.84)	1.0	(0.03)	0.1	(0.02)	0.3	(0.04)	0.1	(0.03)	0.2	(0.03)	0.1	(0.02)
Town	2,900	(180)	82.9	(3.24)	0.8	(0.03)	0.2	(0.03)	0.3	(0.03)	0.1	(0.02)	0.2	(0.03)	0.1	(0.02)
Rural	4,400	(230)	85.6	(2.42)	0.8	(0.04)	0.2	(0.03)	0.3	(0.03)	0.1	(0.02)	0.1	(0.02)	#	(†)

†Not applicable.
#Rounds to zero.
!Interpret data with caution. The coefficient of variation (CV) for this estimate is between 30 and 50 percent.
‡Reporting standards not met. Either there are too few cases for a reliable estimate or the coefficient of variation (CV) is 50 percent or greater.

[1]Total includes combined elementary/secondary schools, which are not separately shown.
NOTE: Detail may not sum to totals because of rounding.
SOURCE: U.S. Department of Education, National Center for Education Statistics, National Teacher and Principal Survey (NTPS), "Public School Data File," 2015–16. (This table was prepared May 2018.)

Table 701.40. Collections, staff, and operating expenditures of degree-granting postsecondary institution libraries: Selected years, 1991–92 through 2016–17

Collections, staff, and operating expenditures	1991–92	2001–02	2011–12	2014–15	2015–16 Total	2015–16 Public	2015–16 Private nonprofit	2015–16 Private for-profit	2016–17 Total	2016–17 Public	2016–17 Private nonprofit	2016–17 Private for-profit
1	2	3	4	5	6	7	8	9	10	11	12	13
Number of libraries	3,274	3,568	3,793	4,134	3,999	1,558	1,611	830	3,944	1,559	1,612	773
Percentage of institutions with libraries	—	85.0	80.6	90.2	91.7	96.0	95.8	78.7	91.4	95.9	95.4	77.5
Number of circulation transactions (in thousands)	—	189,248	154,409	917,510	778,357	450,032	229,091	99,235	768,383	473,808	211,565	83,010
Physical transactions (includes serials)	—	—	—	81,182	67,796	41,240	25,504	1,053	58,244	34,691	22,855	699
Electronic transactions (does not include serials)	—	—	—	836,328	710,561	408,792	203,587	98,182	710,139	439,117	188,710	82,311
Number of circulation transactions per full-time-equivalent (FTE) student	—	16	10	60	52	43	67	93	51	45	61	91
Enrollment (in thousands)												
Total enrollment[1]	14,359	15,928	20,994	20,209	19,988	14,573	4,066	1,349	19,847	14,586	4,079	1,182
Full-time-equivalent (FTE) enrollment[1]	10,361	11,766	15,886	15,263	15,079	10,570	3,441	1,068	14,938	10,572	3,454	912
Collections (in thousands)												
Total number of physical and electronic materials (books, media, and databases)	—	—	—	2,128,233	1,985,142	1,078,659	716,292	190,191	2,209,958	1,188,603	839,164	182,191
Number of books	—	—	—	1,711,851	1,573,341	854,394	594,267	124,681	1,651,471	888,869	640,484	122,118
Physical books	—	—	—	1,036,223	824,767	508,288	312,466	4,013	799,263	485,998	309,346	3,918
Electronic books	—	10,318	252,599	675,629	748,575	346,106	281,801	120,668	852,208	402,871	331,138	118,200
Number of media (includes audiovisual materials)	—	—	—	411,822	410,274	223,725	121,376	65,172	557,541	299,421	198,393	59,727
Physical media	—	—	—	253,826	190,049	135,924	53,580	545	194,634	130,051	64,135	448
Electronic media	—	—	—	157,996	220,225	87,801	67,797	64,627	362,907	169,370	134,258	59,279
Number of databases (electronic only)	—	—	—	4,560	1,527	540	649	338	946	313	288	345
Number of volumes at end of year	749,429	954,030	1,099,951	—	—	—	—	—	—	—	—	—
Number of volumes added during year	20,982	24,574	27,605	—	—	—	—	—	—	—	—	—
Number of serials at end of year[2]	6,966	9,855	—	—	222,010	124,399	75,307	22,303	290,224	112,429	85,801	91,994
Microform units at end of year	—	1,143,678	1,044,521	—	—	—	—	—	—	—	—	—
Number of volumes per full-time-equivalent (FTE) student	72	81	69	—	—	—	—	—	—	—	—	—
Number of books per full-time-equivalent (FTE) student	—	—	—	112	104	81	173	117	111	84	185	134
Full-time-equivalent (FTE) library staff												
Total staff in regular positions[3]	67,166	69,526	65,242	—	—	—	—	—	—	—	—	—
Librarians and professional staff	26,341	32,053	34,423	—	—	—	—	—	—	—	—	—
Other paid staff	40,421	37,473	30,819	—	—	—	—	—	—	—	—	—
Contributed services	404	—	—	—	—	—	—	—	—	—	—	—
Student assistants	29,075	25,305	20,509	—	—	—	—	—	—	—	—	—
FTE student enrollment per FTE staff member	154	169	243	—	—	—	—	—	—	—	—	—
Library operating expenditures[4]												
Total operating expenditures (in thousands of current dollars)	$3,648,654	$5,416,716	$7,008,114	$7,957,153	$8,085,556	$4,749,633	$3,248,421	$87,502	$8,233,469	$4,835,333	$3,312,472	$85,664
Salaries and wages[5]	1,889,368	2,753,404	3,443,831	3,422,050	3,455,940	2,127,768	1,290,595	37,577	3,499,591	2,168,144	1,295,935	35,512
Fringe benefits	—	—	—	745,195	759,363	467,031	288,499	3,833	780,980	486,278	290,912	3,789
Computer hardware/software	—	155,791	143,660	—	—	—	—	—	—	—	—	—
Bibliographic utilities/networks/consortia	—	92,242	123,650	—	—	—	—	—	—	—	—	—
Information resources	1,240,419	1,990,989	2,790,039	3,016,495	3,083,854	1,753,092	1,292,472	38,290	3,126,353	1,766,804	1,322,388	37,161
Books, serial backfiles, and other materials	—	—	—	604,100	614,389	312,052	297,454	4,883	606,196	298,142	304,108	3,947
Books and serial backfiles—paper	—	563,007	503,851	—	—	—	—	—	—	—	—	—
Books and serial backfiles—electronic	—	44,792	180,570	—	—	—	—	—	—	—	—	—
Audiovisual materials	23,879	37,041	37,022	—	—	—	—	—	—	—	—	—
Ongoing commitments to subscriptions	—	—	—	2,217,573	2,287,252	1,338,496	918,941	29,816	2,349,849	1,375,453	943,571	30,824
Current serials—paper	—	926,105	487,265	—	—	—	—	—	—	—	—	—
Current serials—electronic	—	297,657	1,436,671	—	—	—	—	—	—	—	—	—
Preservation	43,126	46,499	26,838	32,339	42,353	27,142	15,095	115	28,459	14,642	13,740	78
Other materials/services expenditures	—	—	—	162,484	139,860	75,401	60,982	3,477	141,848	78,567	60,969	2,312
Document delivery/interlibrary loan	—	22,913	32,490	—	—	—	—	—	—	—	—	—
Other collection expenditures	1,173,414	52,976	85,334	—	—	—	—	—	—	—	—	—
Other library operating expenditures	518,867	424,290	506,934	773,413	786,399	401,743	376,854	7,802	826,546	414,106	403,237	9,202
Operating expenditures per full-time-equivalent (FTE) student												
In current dollars	352	460	441	521	536	449	944	82	551	457	959	94
In constant 2017–18 dollars[6]	632	641	481	547	558	468	983	85	564	468	981	96
Information resource expenditures per FTE student												
In current dollars	120	169	176	198	205	166	376	36	209	167	383	41
In constant 2017–18 dollars[6]	215	236	191	207	213	173	391	37	214	171	391	42
Operating expenditures (percentage distribution)	100.0	100.0	100.0	100.0	100.0	100.0	100.0	100.0	100.0	100.0	100.0	100.0
Salaries and wages[5]	51.8	50.8	49.1	43.0	42.7	44.8	39.7	42.9	42.5	44.8	39.1	41.5
Fringe benefits	—	—	—	9.4	9.4	9.8	8.9	4.4	9.5	10.1	8.8	4.4
Preservation	1.2	0.9	0.4	0.4	0.5	0.6	0.5	0.1	0.3	0.3	0.4	0.1
Information resources	32.8	35.9	39.4	37.5	37.6	36.3	39.3	43.6	37.6	36.2	39.5	43.3
Other[7]	14.2	12.4	11.0	9.7	9.7	8.5	11.6	8.9	10.0	8.6	12.2	10.7
Library operating expenditures as a percent of total institutional expenditures for educational and general purposes	3.0	—	—	—	—	—	—	—	—	—	—	—

—Not available.

[1]Fall enrollment for the academic year specified.

[2]For 2001–02 and later years, includes electronic serials. If a single title comes in both paper and electronic formats, it counts as two serials.

[3]Excludes student assistants.

[4]Excludes capital outlay. Expenditure data are reported only by degree-granting institutions with total expenditures over $100,000.

[5]Includes student hourly wages.

[6]Constant dollars based on the Consumer Price Index, prepared by the Bureau of Labor Statistics, U.S. Department of Labor, adjusted to a school-year basis.

[7]Includes computer hardware/software, bibliographic utilities/networks/consortia, and "other library operating expenditures" not individually listed.

NOTE: Data through 1995 are for institutions of higher education, while later data are for degree-granting institutions. Degree-granting institutions grant associate's or higher degrees and participate in Title IV federal financial aid programs. The degree-granting classification is very similar to the earlier higher education classification, but it includes more 2-year colleges and excludes a few higher education institutions that did not grant degrees. Detail may not sum to totals because of rounding.

SOURCE: U.S. Department of Education, National Center for Education Statistics, Integrated Postsecondary Education Data System (IPEDS), "Academic Libraries Survey" (IPEDS-L:92) and "Fall Enrollment Survey" (IPEDS-EF:92); Academic Libraries Survey (ALS), 2000 through 2012; IPEDS Spring 2015 through Spring 2017, Fall Enrollment component; and IPEDS Spring 2015 through Spring 2017, Academic Libraries component. (This table was prepared July 2019.)

Table 701.60. Number of public libraries, number of books and serial volumes, and per capita usage of selected library services per year, by state: Fiscal years 2015 and 2016

State	Number of public libraries[1]		Number of books and serial volumes				Per capita[2] usage of selected services per year							
			In thousands		Per capita[2]		Number of library visits[3]		Circulation (number of materials lent)		Reference transactions[4]		Uses of public-access internet computers	
	2015	2016	2015	2016	2015	2016	2015	2016	2015	2016	2015	2016	2015	2016
1	2	3	4	5	6	7	8	9	10	11	12	13	14	15
United States	9,068	9,057	750,249	732,240	2.4	2.4	4.5	4.4	7.3	7.2	0.8	0.8	1.0	0.9
Alabama	219	219	9,227	9,007	2.0	2.0	3.5	3.4	4.3	4.3	0.9	0.9	0.9	0.8
Alaska	80	71	2,354	2,048	3.6	3.2	4.8	5.4	6.9	7.4	0.5	0.7	1.2	0.9
Arizona	90	90	8,196	7,663	1.2	1.1	3.9	3.7	6.5	6.6	0.6	0.9	1.1	1.0
Arkansas	58	59	6,371	5,722	2.4	2.3	3.9	4.0	5.4	5.2	0.9	0.8	0.7	0.6
California	184	184	63,676	62,770	1.6	1.6	4.2	4.0	5.6	5.4	0.5	0.6	0.8	0.8
Colorado	113	114	9,943	10,526	1.9	2.0	6.1	6.0	12.0	11.8	0.7	0.8	1.4	1.2
Connecticut	182	182	13,577	13,103	4.0	4.0	6.1	6.0	8.3	8.1	0.9	1.0	1.2	1.2
Delaware	21	21	1,646	1,532	1.8	1.6	4.4	4.4	6.5	6.6	0.5	0.5	0.7	0.7
District of Columbia	1	1	1,863	1,863	2.8	2.7	6.2	5.8	6.0	6.5	1.2	1.2	1.7	1.4
Florida	80	80	30,794	29,261	1.6	1.5	3.7	3.5	5.7	5.5	1.2	1.2	0.8	0.8
Georgia	63	63	16,522	16,839	1.6	1.6	2.8	2.7	3.6	3.7	0.7	0.8	1.1	1.2
Hawaii	1	1	3,197	2,967	2.3	2.1	3.5	3.1	4.5	4.4	0.4	0.5	0.5	0.6
Idaho	102	102	4,342	4,289	3.2	3.1	6.3	6.2	11.4	10.9	0.9	0.8	1.4	1.2
Illinois	622	621	42,366	40,487	3.6	3.4	6.0	5.7	9.5	9.1	0.9	0.9	1.2	1.1
Indiana	237	236	23,210	22,693	3.8	3.7	5.7	5.5	12.7	12.2	0.7	0.7	1.1	1.1
Iowa	534	534	11,934	11,749	3.9	3.9	5.9	5.9	8.9	8.8	0.6	0.6	1.0	1.0
Kansas	320	321	9,113	8,972	3.6	3.6	5.6	5.5	10.0	9.9	0.8	0.8	1.2	1.2
Kentucky	119	119	9,171	9,051	2.1	2.1	4.2	4.1	6.9	6.8	1.0	1.0	1.0	1.0
Louisiana	68	68	11,833	11,746	2.5	2.5	4.3	4.3	4.5	4.6	1.1	1.1	1.1	1.1
Maine	228	227	5,981	5,903	5.2	5.2	5.8	5.9	7.7	7.6	0.6	0.6	1.0	0.9
Maryland	24	24	11,922	10,459	2.0	1.8	4.8	4.6	9.9	9.8	1.4	1.5	1.0	0.9
Massachusetts	368	368	30,857	30,276	4.6	4.5	6.1	6.1	9.2	9.3	0.7	0.7	1.0	0.9
Michigan	392	396	31,818	29,473	3.2	3.0	4.9	4.8	8.3	7.9	0.9	0.9	1.0	1.0
Minnesota	137	137	14,363	14,339	2.6	2.6	4.4	4.4	9.6	9.3	0.7	0.7	0.9	0.9
Mississippi	52	52	5,704	5,599	1.9	1.9	3.0	3.0	2.6	2.5	0.5	0.5	0.8	0.8
Missouri	149	147	16,288	16,019	3.0	2.9	5.2	4.9	10.0	9.8	0.6	0.6	1.1	1.0
Montana	82	82	2,622	2,627	2.7	2.7	4.3	4.4	6.1	6.1	0.5	0.5	1.2	1.2
Nebraska	247	237	5,733	5,555	3.7	3.6	5.3	5.1	8.2	8.2	0.5	0.5	1.3	1.2
Nevada	22	22	4,116	4,149	1.4	1.4	3.5	3.4	7.3	6.9	0.5	0.5	0.9	0.9
New Hampshire	219	222	5,818	5,619	5.0	4.4	6.4	5.5	8.6	7.9	0.7	0.8	0.8	0.6
New Jersey	282	282	27,177	26,513	3.1	3.1	5.0	4.9	6.4	6.3	0.8	0.8	1.0	1.0
New Mexico	87	88	4,232	4,128	2.6	2.5	4.5	4.4	5.5	5.7	0.6	0.9	1.2	1.1
New York	756	756	69,313	68,858	3.6	3.6	5.4	5.3	6.9	6.8	1.4	1.4	1.1	0.9
North Carolina	80	81	16,021	15,584	1.6	1.6	3.6	3.3	5.2	5.0	0.6	0.7	0.7	0.7
North Dakota	72	74	2,173	2,173	3.2	3.2	3.3	3.3	5.9	6.3	0.7	0.8	0.9	0.9
Ohio	251	251	41,024	40,060	3.6	3.5	6.8	6.4	15.9	16.0	1.6	1.6	1.7	1.4
Oklahoma	119	119	7,093	7,351	2.2	2.3	4.2	4.1	6.9	7.0	0.6	0.6	1.1	1.1
Oregon	131	131	9,805	9,497	2.6	2.7	5.5	5.8	15.0	15.5	0.6	0.6	1.0	1.0
Pennsylvania	455	454	25,298	24,617	2.0	2.0	3.6	3.6	5.2	5.1	0.6	0.6	0.6	0.6
Rhode Island	48	48	4,241	3,561	4.0	3.4	5.6	5.5	6.4	6.1	0.6	0.6	1.2	1.0
South Carolina	42	42	9,108	8,962	2.0	1.9	3.7	3.4	5.7	5.4	0.6	0.6	0.9	0.8
South Dakota	112	112	2,768	2,755	3.7	3.6	4.9	4.9	7.6	7.8	0.5	0.6	1.5	1.4
Tennessee	185	186	11,722	11,648	1.8	1.8	3.0	2.9	4.1	4.1	0.5	0.5	0.8	0.7
Texas	549	544	39,660	39,600	1.5	1.6	2.7	2.8	4.2	4.6	0.5	0.5	0.6	0.6
Utah	72	72	6,627	6,494	2.3	2.2	6.0	5.4	12.6	12.0	0.9	1.0	1.0	0.9
Vermont	159	162	2,791	2,586	4.8	4.7	6.2	6.3	7.4	7.6	0.8	0.9	1.1	1.0
Virginia	91	92	17,210	17,097	2.1	2.1	4.6	4.3	8.8	8.2	0.8	0.8	0.9	0.9
Washington	62	62	13,261	12,825	1.9	1.8	5.7	5.5	12.0	12.1	0.5	0.6	1.3	1.1
West Virginia	97	97	5,005	4,917	2.7	2.7	2.9	2.8	3.4	3.5	0.3	0.3	0.5	0.5
Wisconsin	381	381	18,781	18,401	3.3	3.2	5.5	5.5	10.1	9.9	0.7	0.7	1.0	0.9
Wyoming	23	23	2,384	2,311	4.1	3.9	6.1	6.0	8.4	8.2	0.7	0.8	1.5	1.5

[1]Refers to the number of administrative entities that are legally established under local or state law to provide public library service to the population of a local jurisdiction. A public library (administrative entity) may have a single outlet that provides direct service to the public, or it may have multiple service outlets. In 2015, a total of 16,560 stationary service outlets (8,891 central libraries and 7,669 branch libraries) were open to the public; 647 additional service outlets were bookmobiles. In 2016, a total of 16,568 stationary service outlets (8,884 central libraries and 7,684 branch libraries) were open to the public; 659 additional service outlets were bookmobiles.
[2]Per capita (or per person) data are based on unduplicated populations of the areas served by public libraries.

[3]Includes only the number of physical visits (entering the library for any purpose). The survey does not collect data on the number of online visits.
[4]A reference transaction is an information contact that involves the knowledge, use, recommendations, interpretation, or instruction in the use of one or more information sources by a member of the library staff.
NOTE: Data include imputations for nonresponse. Detail may not sum to totals because of rounding.
SOURCE: Institute of Museum and Library Services, Public Libraries Survey, fiscal years 2015 and 2016, retrieved June 26, 2018, from https://www.imls.gov/research/public_libraries_in_the_united_states_survey.aspx. (This table was prepared June 2018.)

Table 702.10. Percentage of children ages 3 to 18 living in households with a computer, by type of computer and selected child and family characteristics: Selected years, 2010 through 2017

[Standard errors appear in parentheses]

Selected child or family characteristic	2010 Total, any computer or smartphone	2013 Total, any computer or smartphone	2015 Total, any computer or smartphone	2016 Total, any computer or smartphone[1]	2016 Desktop, laptop, tablet, or other portable wireless computer — Total[1]	2016 Desktop or laptop	2016 Tablet or other portable wireless computer	2016 Smartphone	2017 Total, any computer or smartphone[1]	2017 Desktop, laptop, tablet, or other portable wireless computer — Total[1]	2017 Desktop or laptop	2017 Tablet or other portable wireless computer	2017 Smartphone
1	2	3	4	5	6	7	8	9	10	11	12	13	14
Total	85.3 (0.37)	92.6 (0.08)	94.5 (0.06)	96.6 (0.05)	89.5 (0.09)	83.3 (0.13)	73.7 (0.15)	90.9 (0.05)	97.3 (0.04)	89.9 (0.11)	83.3 (0.13)	77.9 (0.16)	94.3 (0.05)
Sex													
Male	85.0 (0.44)	92.5 (0.08)	94.4 (0.07)	96.5 (0.06)	89.4 (0.11)	83.1 (0.14)	73.4 (0.17)	90.8 (0.07)	97.3 (0.05)	89.8 (0.12)	83.2 (0.14)	77.7 (0.18)	94.3 (0.06)
Female	85.5 (0.45)	92.6 (0.10)	94.5 (0.07)	96.7 (0.05)	89.6 (0.11)	83.4 (0.14)	74.1 (0.17)	91.0 (0.07)	97.4 (0.05)	90.0 (0.11)	83.4 (0.14)	78.0 (0.17)	94.4 (0.06)
Race/ethnicity													
White	92.4 (0.34)	95.9 (0.07)	97.0 (0.06)	97.9 (0.05)	94.2 (0.09)	90.1 (0.12)	79.8 (0.16)	92.1 (0.08)	98.2 (0.04)	94.3 (0.08)	89.9 (0.12)	84.3 (0.15)	95.6 (0.06)
Black	72.8 (1.30)	87.1 (0.25)	90.2 (0.21)	94.0 (0.20)	81.4 (0.28)	72.3 (0.31)	63.1 (0.36)	87.8 (0.22)	94.9 (0.16)	82.1 (0.32)	72.0 (0.36)	66.9 (0.39)	90.8 (0.20)
Hispanic	74.3 (0.90)	87.2 (0.20)	90.7 (0.16)	94.8 (0.12)	82.5 (0.22)	73.0 (0.25)	65.2 (0.24)	89.4 (0.16)	96.5 (0.10)	83.6 (0.23)	73.8 (0.26)	68.8 (0.30)	93.2 (0.14)
Asian	93.5 (1.18)	97.9 (0.20)	98.3 (0.14)	98.9 (0.11)	97.0 (0.18)	94.8 (0.23)	80.8 (0.34)	93.7 (0.25)	98.9 (0.12)	96.6 (0.19)	94.0 (0.24)	85.1 (0.38)	96.9 (0.18)
Pacific Islander	83.9 (7.10)	87.8 (2.10)	90.9 (1.55)	94.3 (1.50)	77.8 (2.31)	69.3 (2.56)	60.7 (2.71)	85.9 (2.21)	94.0 (1.37)	81.7 (2.28)	72.6 (2.64)	64.3 (3.30)	90.2 (1.66)
American Indian/Alaska Native	72.4 (4.70)	79.0 (0.73)	83.7 (0.82)	87.3 (0.62)	75.6 (0.81)	64.7 (1.01)	61.1 (1.04)	80.3 (0.73)	90.2 (0.61)	75.4 (0.84)	64.7 (0.96)	61.9 (1.03)	84.4 (0.76)
Two or more races	85.2 (2.09)	95.8 (0.19)	97.1 (0.18)	98.5 (0.12)	92.9 (0.28)	86.8 (0.37)	79.3 (0.44)	93.0 (0.25)	98.7 (0.11)	93.1 (0.25)	87.0 (0.35)	83.8 (0.39)	96.1 (0.19)
Age													
3 and 4	81.0 (0.76)	90.4 (0.15)	93.1 (0.15)	96.0 (0.10)	86.6 (0.22)	79.0 (0.24)	71.5 (0.27)	91.2 (0.13)	96.9 (0.08)	87.4 (0.19)	79.1 (0.24)	75.8 (0.26)	94.3 (0.11)
5 to 10	83.9 (0.52)	91.8 (0.09)	93.8 (0.09)	96.2 (0.06)	88.3 (0.12)	80.8 (0.16)	74.0 (0.16)	90.6 (0.07)	97.2 (0.06)	89.1 (0.13)	81.0 (0.14)	78.5 (0.18)	94.1 (0.07)
11 to 14	87.3 (0.59)	93.5 (0.10)	95.1 (0.08)	96.9 (0.07)	90.8 (0.12)	85.4 (0.15)	75.4 (0.18)	90.8 (0.10)	97.5 (0.06)	91.1 (0.13)	85.2 (0.17)	79.3 (0.19)	94.4 (0.09)
15 to 18	87.7 (0.49)	93.9 (0.10)	95.4 (0.08)	97.2 (0.06)	91.3 (0.11)	87.0 (0.14)	72.8 (0.21)	91.3 (0.10)	97.6 (0.06)	91.2 (0.15)	86.7 (0.16)	76.6 (0.21)	94.5 (0.08)
Metropolitan status[2]													
Metropolitan[3]	85.7 (0.40)	—	—	—	—	—	—	—	—	—	—	—	—
Nonmetropolitan[4]	82.8 (0.94)	—	—	—	—	—	—	—	—	—	—	—	—
Highest level of education attained by either parent[5]													
Less than high school	57.0 (1.77)	75.7 (0.40)	81.3 (0.35)	87.9 (0.27)	67.4 (0.34)	54.1 (0.38)	48.5 (0.37)	80.8 (0.30)	90.4 (0.28)	68.4 (0.44)	54.8 (0.43)	50.8 (0.43)	85.0 (0.33)
High school diploma or equivalent	76.1 (0.91)	87.3 (0.22)	90.2 (0.18)	94.1 (0.13)	80.6 (0.26)	69.6 (0.30)	61.4 (0.26)	87.4 (0.17)	95.3 (0.12)	81.3 (0.24)	69.2 (0.29)	65.1 (0.28)	90.9 (0.13)
Some college	88.7 (0.73)	94.3 (0.13)	95.8 (0.12)	97.5 (0.09)	90.5 (0.15)	83.0 (0.21)	73.3 (0.27)	92.4 (0.13)	98.1 (0.07)	90.5 (0.18)	82.0 (0.22)	77.1 (0.25)	95.4 (0.10)
Associate's degree	91.5 (0.67)	96.7 (0.14)	97.7 (0.12)	98.7 (0.08)	94.9 (0.18)	90.1 (0.24)	79.4 (0.27)	93.9 (0.16)	98.9 (0.07)	94.9 (0.19)	89.9 (0.19)	83.4 (0.27)	96.5 (0.12)
Bachelor's degree	95.9 (0.40)	98.6 (0.06)	99.0 (0.05)	99.6 (0.05)	98.0 (0.10)	95.9 (0.08)	86.6 (0.17)	94.9 (0.10)	99.5 (0.06)	97.8 (0.08)	95.5 (0.11)	91.2 (0.23)	96.5 (0.14)
Bachelor's or higher degree	96.8 (0.28)	99.0 (0.06)	99.0 (0.09)	99.4 (0.04)	97.0 (0.07)	95.0 (0.08)	85.1 (0.17)	94.7 (0.10)	99.4 (0.07)	97.8 (0.05)	95.3 (0.13)	89.9 (0.17)	96.3 (0.08)
Master's or higher degree	98.0 (0.35)	99.4 (0.04)	99.5 (0.04)	99.7 (0.03)	98.3 (0.06)	98.3 (0.08)	88.4 (0.17)	95.0 (0.12)	99.5 (0.05)	98.2 (0.05)	98.0 (0.07)	94.2 (0.13)	97.8 (0.07)
Family income (in current dollars)													
Less than $10,000	53.9 (1.90)	76.4 (0.40)	82.1 (0.42)	87.7 (0.40)	67.1 (0.52)	54.5 (0.50)	49.0 (0.49)	79.5 (0.44)	90.3 (0.29)	68.3 (0.52)	55.1 (0.55)	52.8 (0.57)	84.5 (0.37)
$10,000 to $19,999	68.4 (1.35)	81.2 (0.34)	85.7 (0.31)	90.6 (0.26)	72.4 (0.44)	59.3 (0.44)	52.7 (0.45)	82.7 (0.33)	92.5 (0.24)	73.0 (0.48)	59.4 (0.48)	55.7 (0.51)	86.8 (0.28)
$20,000 to $29,999	75.4 (1.34)	86.9 (0.32)	89.2 (0.29)	93.8 (0.25)	79.0 (0.40)	67.3 (0.40)	58.6 (0.43)	86.4 (0.31)	94.9 (0.16)	78.9 (0.41)	67.2 (0.39)	61.6 (0.45)	90.3 (0.23)
$30,000 to $39,999	84.9 (1.05)	90.6 (0.22)	92.8 (0.23)	95.4 (0.20)	83.7 (0.38)	74.2 (0.47)	64.0 (0.44)	88.7 (0.27)	96.2 (0.16)	84.6 (0.32)	73.6 (0.36)	67.2 (0.42)	91.9 (0.20)
$40,000 to $49,999	91.1 (0.98)	93.3 (0.22)	94.2 (0.26)	96.5 (0.16)	86.5 (0.28)	80.0 (0.36)	69.3 (0.36)	90.2 (0.25)	97.1 (0.17)	87.8 (0.30)	78.8 (0.36)	71.9 (0.38)	93.2 (0.20)
$50,000 to $74,999	92.4 (0.71)	95.7 (0.12)	96.6 (0.09)	97.9 (0.08)	92.6 (0.18)	86.0 (0.24)	75.5 (0.28)	92.2 (0.15)	98.2 (0.07)	92.2 (0.17)	85.4 (0.22)	78.2 (0.26)	95.1 (0.11)
$75,000 to $99,999	95.2 (0.59)	97.5 (0.12)	98.0 (0.08)	98.6 (0.08)	95.9 (0.13)	92.2 (0.19)	81.0 (0.29)	93.6 (0.14)	98.9 (0.09)	95.5 (0.11)	91.2 (0.23)	84.7 (0.29)	96.5 (0.14)
$100,000 or more	98.3 (0.29)	99.0 (0.04)	99.1 (0.04)	99.4 (0.04)	98.4 (0.06)	96.7 (0.08)	87.7 (0.13)	95.2 (0.09)	99.4 (0.03)	98.4 (0.06)	96.6 (0.08)	92.0 (0.11)	97.8 (0.05)
$100,000 to $149,999	98.3 (0.44)	98.8 (0.06)	98.8 (0.07)	99.2 (0.07)	97.8 (0.10)	95.7 (0.13)	85.5 (0.21)	94.8 (0.13)	99.3 (0.05)	97.8 (0.08)	95.3 (0.13)	89.9 (0.17)	97.8 (0.08)
$150,000 or more	98.8 (0.36)	99.3 (0.05)	99.4 (0.05)	99.6 (0.04)	99.0 (0.05)	98.1 (0.08)	90.0 (0.16)	95.7 (0.11)	99.5 (0.03)	98.9 (0.06)	98.0 (0.07)	94.2 (0.13)	98.6 (0.06)

—Not available.
†Not applicable.
[1]Households indicating they had the types of computers/devices listed in more than one survey question were counted only once in the total. Therefore, the total is less than the sum of the categories. In addition to the types of computers/devices specified, the total includes a small percentage (less than 1 percent) of children whose households had "some other type of computer" not listed in the survey questions.
[2]Children living in areas whose metropolitan status was not identified are excluded from this analysis. In 2010, less than 1 percent of children ages 3 to 18 lived in an area with nonidentified metropolitan status.
[3]Refers to metropolitan statistical areas, which contain at least one urbanized area with a population of 50,000 or more.
[4]Refers to areas that are outside of metropolitan statistical areas.
[5]Highest education level of any parent residing with the child (including an adoptive or stepparent). Includes only children who resided with at least one of their parents.

NOTE: Data are based on children in households and exclude children living in institutions (e.g., prisons or nursing facilities). The surveys asked about "computers" or "types of computer" (including smartphones) in the household. Percentages refer to children whose household members owned or used at home any computers/devices listed in the survey questions or "some other type of computer" that was not listed. Estimates for 2010 may not be comparable to those for later years because the 2010 estimates are based on the Current Population Survey, while those for later years are based on the American Community Survey (ACS). Estimates for 2016 and 2017 may not be comparable to those for 2013 and 2015 because the wording of the ACS computer questions was revised as of 2016. Race categories exclude persons of Hispanic ethnicity.
SOURCE: U.S. Department of Commerce, Census Bureau, Current Population Survey (CPS), October 2010; and American Community Survey (ACS), 2013, 2015, 2016, and 2017. (This table was prepared January 2019.)

Table 702.30.   Percentage of persons age 3 and over who use the Internet anywhere and who use the Internet at selected locations, by selected characteristics: 2011 and 2017

[Standard errors appear in parentheses]

Selected characteristic	Percent using the Internet, 2011								Percent using the Internet, 2017							
	Anywhere[1]		At home		At school		At workplace		Anywhere[1]		At home		At school		At workplace	
1	2		3		4		5		6		7		8		9	
Total	**69.7**	**(0.22)**	**64.1**	**(0.24)**	**17.6**	**(0.17)**	**23.9**	**(0.15)**	**77.7**	**(0.24)**	**71.9**	**(0.25)**	**15.6**	**(0.14)**	**29.2**	**(0.17)**
Sex																
Male	69.4	(0.26)	64.0	(0.28)	17.1	(0.20)	24.8	(0.19)	77.5	(0.27)	71.5	(0.27)	15.4	(0.17)	30.1	(0.23)
Female	70.1	(0.23)	64.1	(0.26)	18.0	(0.19)	23.1	(0.19)	77.9	(0.26)	72.2	(0.29)	15.7	(0.17)	28.3	(0.20)
Race/ethnicity																
White	75.0	(0.25)	70.5	(0.27)	16.9	(0.18)	28.0	(0.20)	80.2	(0.27)	75.2	(0.29)	14.0	(0.18)	33.1	(0.21)
Black	60.2	(0.67)	51.0	(0.77)	18.8	(0.49)	16.6	(0.40)	73.4	(0.54)	65.3	(0.64)	16.0	(0.40)	23.6	(0.49)
Hispanic	54.4	(0.66)	46.6	(0.72)	18.2	(0.41)	13.3	(0.35)	72.1	(0.59)	64.5	(0.62)	18.6	(0.34)	19.4	(0.34)
Asian	73.6	(0.83)	70.8	(0.91)	18.9	(0.63)	26.9	(0.75)	79.4	(0.98)	74.9	(0.99)	17.3	(0.63)	33.3	(0.77)
Pacific Islander	67.3	(3.76)	60.6	(4.16)	18.3	(2.54)	23.3	(2.95)	75.9	(3.85)	70.9	(3.83)	14.3	(2.13)	30.2	(3.17)
American Indian/Alaska Native	59.7	(2.62)	49.4	(3.47)	18.3	(1.69)	14.6	(1.31)	62.7	(2.27)	51.5	(2.41)	13.9	(1.41)	17.6	(1.54)
Two or more races	72.6	(1.26)	64.2	(1.41)	27.3	(1.30)	17.1	(0.98)	82.5	(1.13)	76.5	(1.30)	31.0	(1.32)	23.8	(1.03)
Age																
3 and 4	25.9	(0.85)	24.1	(0.85)	10.0	(0.57)	†	(†)	51.0	(1.18)	45.1	(1.16)	14.8	(0.83)	†	(†)
5 to 10	51.3	(0.63)	47.1	(0.66)	33.7	(0.59)	†	(†)	69.3	(0.68)	57.5	(0.70)	44.2	(0.67)	†	(†)
11 to 14	73.0	(0.73)	66.6	(0.78)	55.8	(0.81)	†	(†)	77.0	(0.71)	68.0	(0.75)	56.1	(0.87)	†	(†)
15 to 18	85.2	(0.54)	76.9	(0.61)	62.4	(0.70)	3.2	(0.23)	84.9	(0.58)	77.6	(0.71)	59.6	(0.74)	4.8	(0.28)
19 to 24	83.1	(0.53)	73.5	(0.69)	39.0	(0.72)	18.9	(0.42)	85.3	(0.55)	79.3	(0.62)	32.2	(0.74)	28.2	(0.56)
25 to 29	81.5	(0.55)	72.8	(0.64)	12.8	(0.42)	38.4	(0.71)	85.6	(0.52)	81.4	(0.60)	11.1	(0.41)	47.6	(0.72)
30 to 39	80.9	(0.39)	74.4	(0.42)	9.3	(0.29)	42.3	(0.43)	85.5	(0.42)	80.7	(0.46)	5.8	(0.24)	49.4	(0.47)
40 to 49	79.6	(0.40)	74.6	(0.45)	7.6	(0.23)	42.8	(0.43)	84.9	(0.43)	80.2	(0.48)	4.5	(0.21)	49.7	(0.50)
50 to 59	71.9	(0.44)	67.3	(0.46)	5.1	(0.22)	36.0	(0.43)	79.7	(0.40)	73.9	(0.45)	2.3	(0.13)	44.3	(0.44)
60 to 69	64.4	(0.54)	60.3	(0.56)	3.3	(0.20)	19.9	(0.38)	75.8	(0.43)	70.4	(0.46)	1.5	(0.13)	26.2	(0.42)
70 or older	38.5	(0.55)	35.0	(0.56)	0.9	(0.10)	3.9	(0.20)	57.1	(0.52)	53.6	(0.56)	0.7	(0.09)	6.4	(0.24)
Highest level of education attained by persons age 25 and over																
Less than high school	31.5	(0.58)	26.3	(0.57)	1.2	(0.15)	4.8	(0.28)	51.4	(0.72)	44.8	(0.73)	1.8	(0.19)	9.9	(0.45)
High school diploma or equivalent	58.7	(0.38)	52.9	(0.38)	1.9	(0.10)	16.9	(0.28)	70.2	(0.41)	63.9	(0.44)	1.9	(0.12)	23.2	(0.33)
Some college	79.6	(0.42)	72.7	(0.42)	7.7	(0.26)	32.8	(0.47)	82.8	(0.43)	78.2	(0.46)	4.8	(0.21)	37.3	(0.51)
Associate's degree	82.6	(0.48)	76.4	(0.52)	7.3	(0.34)	39.9	(0.60)	85.5	(0.45)	80.7	(0.52)	4.0	(0.26)	44.5	(0.66)
Bachelor's or higher degree	90.0	(0.22)	86.4	(0.26)	12.1	(0.27)	56.1	(0.34)	88.7	(0.27)	85.6	(0.31)	5.7	(0.18)	56.3	(0.37)
Bachelor's degree	89.1	(0.28)	85.2	(0.31)	9.6	(0.31)	53.1	(0.41)	87.8	(0.31)	84.5	(0.37)	5.2	(0.21)	53.9	(0.48)
Master's or higher degree	91.6	(0.32)	88.6	(0.39)	16.6	(0.48)	61.5	(0.58)	90.4	(0.41)	87.5	(0.45)	6.7	(0.30)	60.6	(0.55)
Metropolitan status[2]																
Metropolitan[3]	71.0	(0.24)	65.5	(0.27)	18.0	(0.18)	25.0	(0.18)	78.5	(0.25)	72.8	(0.26)	15.8	(0.16)	30.0	(0.20)
Nonmetropolitan[4]	62.8	(0.69)	55.9	(0.71)	15.2	(0.38)	18.5	(0.42)	72.9	(0.67)	65.4	(0.70)	14.1	(0.41)	23.9	(0.50)
Family income (in current dollars)																
Less than $10,000	48.9	(0.82)	36.5	(0.89)	15.3	(0.56)	6.3	(0.36)	62.8	(1.07)	52.7	(1.12)	17.0	(0.82)	9.4	(0.51)
$10,000 to $19,999	48.2	(0.67)	38.7	(0.70)	13.1	(0.43)	7.8	(0.29)	59.7	(0.86)	51.4	(0.82)	12.7	(0.53)	10.2	(0.37)
$20,000 to $29,999	55.6	(0.62)	47.5	(0.69)	13.4	(0.38)	11.4	(0.32)	67.7	(0.71)	59.9	(0.76)	13.4	(0.50)	15.2	(0.43)
$30,000 to $39,999	62.0	(0.70)	54.8	(0.73)	15.2	(0.44)	15.8	(0.39)	71.3	(0.70)	64.3	(0.69)	13.5	(0.45)	19.9	(0.45)
$40,000 to $49,999	70.3	(0.72)	64.8	(0.76)	16.2	(0.48)	21.3	(0.47)	78.0	(0.72)	72.2	(0.79)	14.0	(0.48)	24.7	(0.60)
$50,000 to $74,999	77.6	(0.43)	73.8	(0.47)	18.0	(0.36)	27.8	(0.40)	81.4	(0.44)	75.8	(0.49)	14.4	(0.34)	30.7	(0.38)
$75,000 to $99,999	83.6	(0.37)	80.6	(0.42)	20.9	(0.48)	36.0	(0.47)	84.8	(0.51)	80.3	(0.54)	16.7	(0.47)	37.2	(0.51)
$100,000 or more	86.6	(0.36)	84.5	(0.43)	23.2	(0.39)	42.5	(0.41)	86.3	(0.35)	82.3	(0.39)	18.5	(0.28)	43.9	(0.33)
$100,000 to $149,999	86.9	(0.45)	84.7	(0.50)	23.1	(0.48)	41.3	(0.56)	85.7	(0.47)	81.5	(0.52)	17.7	(0.40)	42.0	(0.47)
$150,000 or more	86.2	(0.54)	84.2	(0.66)	23.4	(0.61)	44.1	(0.61)	87.0	(0.54)	83.2	(0.57)	19.5	(0.44)	46.1	(0.50)

†Not applicable.
[1]Includes all persons who use the Internet at any location.
[2]Persons living in areas whose metropolitan status was not identified are excluded from this analysis. In 2011 and 2017, less than 1 percent of persons lived in an area with non-identified metropolitan status.
[3]Refers to metropolitan statistical areas, which contain at least one urbanized area with a population of 50,000 or more.

[4]Refers to areas that are outside of metropolitan statistical areas.
NOTE: Data are based on sample surveys of the civilian noninstitutionalized population, which excludes persons in the military and persons living in institutions (e.g., prisons or nursing facilities). Race categories exclude persons of Hispanic ethnicity.
SOURCE: U.S. Department of Commerce, Census Bureau, Current Population Survey (CPS), July 2011 and November 2017. (This table was prepared March 2019.)

APPENDIX A
Guide to Sources

The information presented in the *Digest of Education Statistics* was obtained from many sources, including federal and state agencies, private research organizations, and professional associations. The data were collected using many research methods, including surveys of a universe (such as all colleges) or of a sample, compilations of administrative records, and statistical projections. Brief descriptions of the information sources, data collections, and data collection methods that were used to produce this report are presented below, grouped by sponsoring organization. Additional details about many of these and other data sets can be found on the U.S. Department of Education's Data Inventory website (https://datainventory.ed.gov/).

National Center for Education Statistics (NCES)

Baccalaureate and Beyond Longitudinal Study

The Baccalaureate and Beyond Longitudinal Study (B&B) is based on the National Postsecondary Student Aid Study (NPSAS) and provides information concerning education and work experience after completing a bachelor's degree. A special emphasis of B&B is on those entering the teaching profession. B&B provides cross-sectional information 1 year after bachelor's degree completion (comparable to the information that was provided in the Recent College Graduates study), while at the same time providing longitudinal data concerning entry into and progress through graduate-level education and the workforce, income, and debt repayment. This information has not been available through follow-ups involving high school cohorts or even college-entry cohorts, because these cohorts have limited numbers who actually complete a bachelor's degree and continue their graduate education. Also, these cohorts are not representative of all bachelor's degree recipients.

The first B&B followed NPSAS baccalaureate degree completers for a 10-year period after completion, beginning with NPSAS:93. About 11,000 students who completed their degrees in the 1992–93 academic year were included in the first B&B cohort (B&B:93). The first follow-up of this cohort (B&B:93/94) occurred 1 year later. In addition to collecting student data, B&B:93/94 collected postsecondary transcripts covering the undergraduate period, which provided complete information on progress and persistence at the undergraduate level. The second follow-up of this cohort (B&B:93/97) took place in spring 1997 and gathered information on employment history, family formation, and enrollment in graduate programs. The third follow-up (B&B:93/03) occurred in 2003 and provided information concerning graduate study and long-term employment experiences after degree completion.

The second B&B cohort (B&B:2000), which was associated with NPSAS:2000, included 11,700 students who completed their degrees in the 1999–2000 academic year. The first and only follow-up survey of this cohort was conducted in 2001 (B&B:2000/01) and focused on time to degree completion, participation in postbaccalaureate education and employment, and the activities of newly qualified teachers.

The third B&B cohort (B&B:08), which is associated with NPSAS:08, included 18,000 students who completed their degrees in the 2007–08 academic year. The first follow-up took place in 2009 (B&B:08/09), and the second follow-up took place in 2012 (B&B:08/12). The report *Baccalaureate and Beyond: A First Look at the Employment Experiences and Lives of College Graduates, 4 Years On (B&B:08/12)* (NCES 2014-141) presents findings based on data from the second follow-up. It examines bachelor's degree recipients' labor market experiences and enrollment in additional postsecondary degree programs through the 4th year after graduation. In addition, 2008/12 *Baccalaureate and Beyond Longitudinal Study (B&B:08/12) Data File Documentation* (NCES 2015-141) describes the universe, methods, and data collection procedures used in the second follow-up. A third and final follow-up (B&B:08/18) to the third B&B cohort was conducted in 2018 and early 2019.

Further information on B&B may be obtained from

Aurora D'Amico
Longitudinal Surveys Branch
Sample Surveys Division
National Center for Education Statistics
550 12th Street SW
Washington, DC 20202
aurora.damico@ed.gov
https://nces.ed.gov/surveys/b&b

Beginning Postsecondary Students Longitudinal Study

The Beginning Postsecondary Students Longitudinal Study (BPS) provides information on persistence, progress, and attainment for 6 years after initial time of entry into postsecondary education. BPS includes traditional and nontraditional (e.g., older) students and is representative of all beginning students in postsecondary education in a given year. Initially, these individuals are surveyed in the National Postsecondary Student Aid Study (NPSAS) during the year in which they first begin their postsecondary education. These same students are surveyed again 2 and 5 years later through the BPS. By starting with a cohort that has already entered postsecondary education and following it for 6 years, the BPS can determine the extent to which students who start postsecondary education at various ages differ in their progress, persistence, and attainment, as well as their entry into the workforce. The first BPS was conducted in 1989–90, with follow-ups in 1992 (BPS:90/92) and 1994 (BPS:90/94). The second BPS was conducted in 1995–96, with follow-ups in 1998 (BPS:96/98) and 2001 (BPS:96/01). The third BPS was conducted in 2003–04, with follow-ups in 2006 (BPS:04/06) and 2009 (BPS:04/09).

The fourth BPS was conducted in 2012, with follow-ups in 2014 (BPS:12/14) and 2017 (BPS:12/17). In the base year, 1,690 institutions were sampled, of which all were confirmed eligible to participate. In addition, 128,120 students were sampled, and 123,600 were eligible to participate in the NPSAS:12 study. In the first follow-up (BPS:12/14), of the 35,540 eligible NPSAS:12 sample students, 24,770 responded, for an unweighted student response rate of 70 percent and a weighted response rate of 68 percent.

Further information on BPS may be obtained from

Aurora D'Amico
David Richards
Longitudinal Surveys Branch
Sample Surveys Division
National Center for Education Statistics
550 12th Street SW
Washington, DC 20202
aurora.damico@ed.gov
david.richards@ed.gov
https://nces.ed.gov/surveys/bps/

Common Core of Data

The Common Core of Data (CCD) is NCES's primary database on public elementary and secondary education in the United States. It is a comprehensive, annual, national statistical database of all public elementary and secondary schools and school districts containing data designed to be comparable across all states. This database can be used to select samples for other NCES surveys and provide basic information and descriptive statistics on public elementary and secondary schools and schooling in general.

The CCD collects statistical information annually from approximately 100,000 public elementary and secondary schools and approximately 18,000 public school districts (including supervisory unions and regional education service agencies) in the 50 states, the District of Columbia, the Department of Defense Education Activity (DoDEA), the Bureau of Indian Education (BIE), Puerto Rico, American Samoa, Guam, the Northern Mariana Islands, and the U.S. Virgin Islands. Three categories of information are collected in the CCD survey: general descriptive information on schools and school districts, data on students and staff, and fiscal data. The general school and district descriptive information includes name, address, and phone number; the data on students and staff include selected demographic characteristics; and the fiscal data pertain to revenues and current expenditures.

The EDFacts data collection system is the primary collection tool for the CCD. NCES works collaboratively with the U.S. Department of Education's Performance Information Management Service to develop the CCD collection procedures and data definitions. Coordinators from state education agencies (SEAs) submit the CCD data at different levels (school, agency, and state) to the EDFacts collection system. Prior to submitting CCD files to EDFacts, SEAs must collect and compile information from their respective local education agencies (LEAs) through established administrative records systems within their state or jurisdiction.

Once SEAs have completed their submissions, the CCD survey staff analyzes and verifies the data for quality assurance. Even though the CCD is a universe collection and thus not subject to sampling errors, nonsampling errors can occur. The two potential sources of nonsampling errors are nonresponse and inaccurate reporting. NCES attempts to minimize nonsampling errors through the use of annual training of SEA coordinators, extensive quality reviews, and survey editing procedures. In addition, each year SEAs are given the opportunity to revise their state-level aggregates from the previous survey cycle.

The NCES Education Demographic and Geographic Estimate (EDGE) program develops annually updated point locations (latitude and longitude) for public elementary and secondary schools included in the CCD database. The estimated location of schools and agency administrative offices is primarily derived from the physical address reported in the CCD directory files. The NCES EDGE program collaborates with the U.S. Census Bureau's EDGE Branch to develop point locations for schools reported in the annual CCD directory file. For more information about NCES school point data, please see https://nces.ed.gov/programs/edge/Geographic/SchoolLocations.

The CCD survey consists of five components: The Public Elementary/Secondary School Universe Survey, the Local Education Agency (School District) Universe Survey, the State Nonfiscal Survey of Public Elementary/Secondary Education, the National Public Education Financial Survey (NPEFS), and the School District Finance Survey (F-33).

Public Elementary/Secondary School Universe Survey

The Public Elementary/Secondary School Universe Survey includes all U.S. public schools providing education services to prekindergarten, kindergarten, grade 1–13, and ungraded students.

The Public Elementary/Secondary School Universe Survey includes data for variables such as NCES school ID number, state school ID number, name of the school, name of the agency that operates the school, mailing address, physical location address, phone number, school type, operational status, county number, county name, full-time-equivalent (FTE) classroom teacher count, low/high grade span offered, school level, students eligible for free lunch, students eligible for reduced-price lunch, total students eligible for free and reduced-price lunch, and student totals and detail (by grade, by race/ethnicity, and by sex). The survey also contains flags indicating whether a school is Title I targeted assistance eligible, Title I schoolwide eligible, a magnet school, a charter school, a shared-time school, or a BIE school, as well as which grades are offered at the school.

Local Education Agency (School District) Universe Survey

The coverage of the Local Education Agency Universe Survey includes all school districts and administrative units providing education services to prekindergarten, kindergarten, grade 1–13, and ungraded students.

The Local Education Agency Universe Survey includes the following variables: NCES agency ID number, state agency ID number, agency name, phone number, mailing address, physical location address, agency type code, supervisory union number, American National Standards Institute (ANSI) state and county code, county name, core based statistical area (CBSA), metropolitan/micropolitan code, metropolitan status code, locale code, congressional district, operational status code, BIE agency status, low/high grade span offered, agency charter status, number of schools, number of full-time-equivalent teachers, number of ungraded students, number of PK–13 students, number of special education/Individualized Education Program students, number of English language learner students, instructional staff fields, support staff fields, and LEA charter status.

State Nonfiscal Survey of Public Elementary/Secondary Education

The State Nonfiscal Survey of Public Elementary/Secondary Education provides state-level, aggregate information about students and staff in public elementary and secondary education. This survey covers public school student membership by grade, race/ethnicity, and state or jurisdiction and covers number of staff in public schools by category and state or jurisdiction. Beginning with the 2006–07 school year, the number of diploma recipients and other high school completers were no longer included in the State Nonfiscal Survey of Public Elementary/Secondary Education File. These data were published in the public-use CCD State Dropout and Completion Data File.

National Public Education Financial Survey

The purpose of the National Public Education Financial Survey (NPEFS) is to provide state-level aggregate data on revenues and expenditures for public elementary and secondary education. The data collected are useful to (1) chief officers of state education agencies; (2) policymakers in the executive and legislative branches of federal and state governments; (3) education policy and public policy researchers; (4) the press; and (5) citizens interested in information about education finance.

Data for NPEFS are collected from SEAs in the 50 states, the District of Columbia, Puerto Rico, American Samoa, Guam, the Northern Mariana Islands, and the U.S. Virgin Islands. The data file is organized by state or jurisdiction and contains revenue data by funding source; expenditure data by function (the activity being supported by the expenditure) and object (the category of expenditure); average daily attendance data; and total student membership data from the CCD State Nonfiscal Survey of Public Elementary/Secondary Education.

School District Finance Survey

The purpose of the School District Finance Survey (F-33) is to provide finance data for all LEAs that provide free public elementary and secondary education in the United States. National and state totals are not included (national- and state-level figures are presented, however, in the National Public Education Financial Survey).

NCES partners with the U.S. Census Bureau in the collection of school district finance data. The Census Bureau distributes Census Form F-33, Annual Survey of School System Finances, to all SEAs, and representatives from the SEAs collect and edit data from their LEAs and submit data to the Census Bureau. The Census Bureau then produces two data files: one for distribution and reporting by NCES and the other for distribution and reporting by the Census Bureau. The files include variables for revenues by source, expenditures by function and object, indebtedness, assets, and student membership counts, as well as identification variables.

The coverage of the F-33 survey is different from the coverage of the NPEFS survey, as NPEFS includes special state-run and federal-run school districts that are not included in the F-33. In addition, variation in data availability between the two surveys may occur in cases where some data are available at the state level but not at the district level, and this might result in state-aggregated district totals from F-33 differing from the state totals in NPEFS. When states submit NPEFS and F-33 data in their own financial accounting formats instead of the NCES-requested format, variation in the state procedures may result in variation in the data. In these instances, Census Bureau analysts design and implement a crosswalk system to conform state-formatted data to the format for variables in the F-33. Also, differences between the two surveys in the reporting of expenditures for similar data items can occur when there are differences in the methodology that the state respondents use to crosswalk their NPEFS or F-33 data.

Finally, the imputation and editing processes and procedures of the two surveys can vary. For further detail on imputations and data editing in the F-33 and NPEFS surveys, please see the FY 17 NCES F-33 (Cornman, Ampadu, and Hanak 2020 [NCES 2020-304]) and NPEFS (Cornman et al. 2019 [NCES 2020-302]) survey documentation.

The following text table lists the CCD file versions used in the current edition of the *Digest of Education Statistics*:

Table G. Common Core of Data (CCD) file versions used in the current edition of the *Digest of Education Statistics*: 1986–87 through 2017–18

Year	State Nonfiscal Survey of Public Elementary and Secondary Education	NCES CCD State Dropout and Completion Data	National Public Education Financial Survey	Local Education Agency Universe Survey	School District Finance Survey	Public Elementary/ Secondary School Universe File
1986–87 (FY 1987)	v.1c	†	v.1b–Revised	v.1	†	v.1
1987–88 (FY 1988)	v.1c	†	v.1b–Revised	v.1	†	v.1
1988–89 (FY 1989)	v.1c	†	v.1b–Revised	v.1	†	v.1
1989–90 (FY 1990)	v.1c	†	v.1b–Revised	v.1	v.1a–Final[1]	v.1
1990–91 (FY 1991)	v.1c	†	v.1b–Revised	v.1	†	v.1
1991–92 (FY 1992)	v.1c	†	v.1b–Revised	v.1	v.1a–Final[1]	Revised
1992–93 (FY 1993)	v.1c	†	v.1b–Revised	v.1	†	v.1
1993–94 (FY 1994)	v.1b	†	v.1b–Revised	v.1	†	Revised
1994–95 (FY 1995)	v.1b	†	v.1b–Revised	Revised	v.1d–Revised[1]	Revised
1995–96 (FY 1996)	v.1b	†	v.1b–Revised	v.1	v.1b–Revised[1]	v.1
1996–97 (FY 1997)	v.1c	†	v.1b–Revised	v.1	v.1a–Final[1]	v.1
1997–98 (FY 1998)	v.1c	†	v.1b–Revised	v.1	v.1e–Revised[1]	v.1
1998–99 (FY 1999)	v.1b	†	v.1b–Revised	v.1c	v.1c–Revised[1]	v.1c
1999–2000 (FY 2000)	v.1b	†	v.1b–Revised	v.1b	v.1d–Revised[1]	v.1b
2000–01 (FY 2001)	v.1c	†	v.1b–Revised	v.1a	v.1d–Revised[1]	v.1a
2001–02 (FY 2002)	v.1c	†	v.1c–Revised	v.1a	v.1c–Revised[1]	v.1a
2002–03 (FY 2003)	v.1b	†	v.1b–Revised	v.1a	v.1b–Revised[1]	v.1a
2003–04 (FY 2004)	v.1b	†	v.1b–Revised	v.1b	v.1b–Revised[1]	v.1a
2004–05 (FY 2005)	v.1f	†	v.1b–Revised	v.1c	v.1c–Revised[1]	v.1b
2005–06 (FY 2006)	v.1b	v.1b	v.1b–Revised	v.1a	v.1a–Final[1]	v.1a
2006–07 (FY 2007)	v.1c	v.1a	v.1b–Revised	v.1c	v.1a–Final[1]	v.1c
2007–08 (FY 2008)	v.1b	v.1a	v.1b–Revised	v.1b	v.1a–Final[1]	v.1b
2008–09 (FY 2009)	v.1c	v.1a	v.1b–Revised	v.1a	v.1a–Final[1]	v.1b
2009–10 (FY 2010)	v.1b	v.1a	v.2a–Final	v.2a	v.1a–Provisional[1]	v.2a
2010–11 (FY 2011)	v.1a	v.1a–Provisional[1]	v.2a–Final	v.2a	v.1a–Provisional[1]	v.2a
2011–12 (FY 2012)	v.1a	v.1a–Preliminary	v.2a–Final	v.1a	v.1a–Provisional	v.1a
2012–13 (FY 2013)	v.1a	—	v.2a–Final	v.1a	v.1a–Provisional	v.1a
2013–14 (FY 2014)	v.1a	—	v.2a–Final	v.1a	v.1a–Provisional	v.1a
2014–15 (FY 2015)	v.1a	—	v.2a–Final	v.1a	v.1a–Provisional	v.1a
2015–16 (FY 2016)	v.1a	—	v.2a–Final	v.1a	v.1a–Provisional	v.2a
2016–17 (FY 2017)	v.1a	—	v.1a–Provisional	v.1a	v.1a–Provisional	v.1a
2017–18 (FY 2018)	v.1a	—	—	v.1a	—	v.1a

—Not available.
†Not applicable. Survey not conducted.
[1]Data not used in current edition of *Digest of Education Statistics*.
NOTE: Preliminary data have been edited but are subject to further NCES quality control procedures. Provisional data have undergone all NCES data quality control procedures. NCES releases a final data file after a publication using provisional data has been released.

If NCES receives revised data from states or discovers errors in the final data file, a revised data file is released.
SOURCE: U.S. Department of Education, National Center for Education Statistics, Common Core of Data (CCD), retrieved April 30, 2020, from https://nces.ed.gov/ccd/ccddata.asp. (This table was prepared April 2020.)

Further information on the nonfiscal CCD data may be obtained from

Chen-Su Chen
Elementary and Secondary Branch
Administrative Data Division
National Center for Education Statistics
550 12th Street SW
Washington, DC 20202
chen-su.chen@ed.gov
https://nces.ed.gov/ccd

Further information on the fiscal CCD data may be obtained from

Stephen Cornman
Elementary and Secondary Branch
Administrative Data Division
National Center for Education Statistics
550 12th Street SW
Washington, DC 20202
stephen.cornman@ed.gov
https://nces.ed.gov/ccd

Early Childhood Longitudinal Study, Birth Cohort

The Early Childhood Longitudinal Study, Birth Cohort (ECLS-B) was designed to provide policymakers, researchers, child care providers, teachers, and parents with nationally representative information about children's early learning experiences and their transition to child care and school. From the time the ECLS-B children were infants until they entered kindergarten, their cognitive and physical development was measured using standardized assessments, and information about their care and learning experiences at home, in early care and education settings, and at school was collected through interviews with adults in the children's lives.

Data were collected from a sample of about 14,000 children born in the United States in 2001, representing a population of approximately 4 million. The children participating in the study came from diverse socioeconomic and racial/ ethnic backgrounds, with oversamples of Chinese, other Asian and Pacific Islander, and American Indian/Alaska Native children. There were also oversamples of twins and of children born with moderately low and very low birthweight. Children, their parents (including nonresident and resident fathers), their child care and early education providers, and their kindergarten teachers provided information on children's cognitive, social, emotional, and physical development. Information was also collected about the children's experiences across multiple settings (e.g., home, child care, and school).

Information about the ECLS-B children was collected when they were approximately 9 months old (2001–02), 2 years old (2003–04), and 4 years old/preschool age (2005–06). Additionally, in fall 2006, data were collected from all participating sample children, approximately 75 percent of whom were in kindergarten or higher. In fall 2007, data were collected from the approximately 25 percent of participating sample children who had not yet entered kindergarten or higher in the previous collection, as well as children who were repeating kindergarten in the 2007–08 school year.

In every round of data collection, children participated in assessment activities and parent respondents (usually the mothers of the children) were asked about themselves, their families, and their children. Resident fathers were asked about themselves and their role in the ECLS-B children's lives in the 9-month, 2-year, and preschool collections. Similar information was collected from nonresident biological fathers in the 9-month and 2-year collections. In addition, beginning when the children were 2 years old, their child care and early education providers were asked to provide information about their own experience and training and their setting's learning environment. At 2 years and at preschool, observations were conducted in the regular nonparental care and education arrangements of a subsample of children in order to obtain information about the quality of

the arrangements. When the ECLS-B children were in kindergarten, their teachers were asked to provide information about the children's early learning experiences and their school and classroom environments. Also, the before- and after-school care and education providers of children in kindergarten were asked to provide information about their own experience, their training, and their setting's learning environment. School-level data, taken from other NCES datasets (the Common Core of Data and the Private School Universe Survey), and residential ZIP codes collected at each wave are also available.

Further information on the ECLS-B may be obtained from

Gail Mulligan
Jill McCarroll
Longitudinal Surveys Branch
Sample Surveys Division
National Center for Education Statistics
550 12th Street SW
Washington, DC 20202
ecls@ed.gov
https://nces.ed.gov/ecls/birth.asp

Early Childhood Longitudinal Study, Kindergarten Class of 1998–99

The Early Childhood Longitudinal Study, Kindergarten Class of 1998–99 (ECLS-K) was designed to provide detailed information on children's school experiences throughout elementary school and into middle school. The study began in fall 1998. A nationally representative sample of about 21,300 children enrolled in 940 kindergarten programs during the 1998–99 school year was selected to participate in the ECLS-K. The children attended both public and private kindergartens and full- and part-day programs. The sample included children from different racial/ethnic and socioeconomic backgrounds and oversamples of Asian and Pacific Islander children and private school kindergartners.

In the kindergarten year (1998–99), base-year data were collected in the fall and spring. In the first-grade year (1999–2000), data were collected again in the fall and spring. In the 3rd-grade (2002), 5th-grade (2004), and 8th-grade (2007) years, data were collected in the spring. The fall 1999 collection drew from a 30 percent subsample of schools; all other collections drew from the full sample of schools.

From kindergarten through 5th grade, the ECLS-K included a direct child cognitive assessment that was administered one on one with each child in the study. The assessment used a computer-assisted personal interview (CAPI) approach and a two-stage adaptive testing methodology. In the 8th grade, a two-stage adaptive paper-and-pencil assessment was administered in small groups. In kindergarten and first grade, the assessment included three cognitive domains: reading, mathematics, and general knowledge. General knowledge was replaced by science in the 3rd, 5th, and 8th grades. Children's height and weight were measured at each data collection point, and a direct measure of children's psychomotor development was administered in the fall of the kindergarten year only. In addition to these measures, the ECLS-K collected information about children's social skills and academic achievement through teacher reports in every grade and through student reports in the 3rd, 5th, and 8th grades.

A computer-assisted telephone interview with the children's parents/guardians was conducted at each data collection point. Parents/guardians were asked to provide key information about the children in the ECLS-K sample on subjects such as family structure (e.g., household members and composition), family demographics (e.g., family members' age, relation to the child being studied, and race/ethnicity), parent involvement, home educational activities (e.g., reading to the child), child health, parental education and employment status, and the social skills and behaviors of their children.

Data on the schools that children attended and their classrooms were collected through self-administered questionnaires completed by school administrators and classroom teachers. Administrators provided information about their schools' populations, programs, and policies. At the classroom level, data were collected from teachers on the composition of the classroom, teaching practices, curriculum, and teacher qualifications and experience. In addition, special education teachers and related services staff provided reports on the services received by children with an Individualized Education Program (IEP).

Further information on the ECLS-K may be obtained from

Gail Mulligan
Jill McCarroll
Longitudinal Surveys Branch
Sample Surveys Division
National Center for Education Statistics
550 12th Street SW
Washington, DC 20202
ecls@ed.gov
https://nces.ed.gov/ecls/kindergarten.asp

Early Childhood Longitudinal Study, Kindergarten Class of 2010–11

The Early Childhood Longitudinal Study, Kindergarten Class of 2010–11 (ECLS-K:2011) provides detailed information on the school achievement and experiences of students throughout their elementary school years. The students who participated in the ECLS-K:2011 were followed longitudinally from the kindergarten year (the 2010–11 school year) through spring 2016, when most of them were expected to be in 5th grade. This sample of students was designed to be nationally representative of all students who were enrolled in kindergarten or who were of kindergarten age and being educated in an ungraded classroom or school in the United States in the 2010–11 school year, including those in public and private schools, those who attended full-day and part-day programs, those who were in kindergarten for the first time, and those who were kindergarten repeaters. Students who attended early learning centers or institutions that offered education only through kindergarten were included in the study sample and represented in the cohort if those institutions were included in NCES's Common Core of Data or Private School Survey universe collections.

The ECLS-K:2011 placed emphasis on measuring students' experiences within multiple contexts and development in multiple domains. The design of the study included the collection of information from the students, their parents/guardians, their teachers, and their schools. Information was also collected from their before- and after-school care providers in the kindergarten year.

A nationally representative sample of approximately 18,170 children from about 1,310 schools participated in the base-year administration of the ECLS-K:2011 in the 2010–11 school year. The sample included children from different racial/ethnic and socioeconomic backgrounds. Asian/Pacific Islander students were oversampled to ensure that the sample included enough students of this race/ethnicity to make accurate estimates for the group as a whole. Nine data collections were conducted: fall and spring of the children's kindergarten year (the base year), fall 2011 and spring 2012 (the 1st-grade year), fall 2012 and spring 2013 (the 2nd-grade year), spring 2014 (the 3rd-grade year), spring 2015 (the 4th-grade year), and spring 2016 (the 5th-grade year). Although the study refers to later rounds of data collection by the grade the majority of children were expected to be in (that is, the modal grade for children who were in kindergarten in the 2010–11 school year), children were included in subsequent data collections regardless of their grade level.

A total of approximately 780 of the 1,310 originally sampled schools participated during the base year of the study. This translates to a weighted unit response rate (weighted by the base weight) of 63 percent for the base year. In the base year, the weighted child assessment unit response rate was 87 percent for the fall data collection and 85 percent for the spring collection, and the weighted parent unit response rate was 74 percent for the fall collection and 67 percent for the spring collection.

Fall and spring data collections were conducted in the 2011–12 school year, when the majority of the children were in the 1st grade. The fall collection was conducted within a 33 percent subsample of the full base-year sample, and the spring collection was conducted within the full base-year sample. The weighted child assessment unit response rate was 89 percent for the fall data collection and 88 percent for the spring collection, and the weighted parent unit response rate was 87 percent for the fall data collection and 76 percent for the spring data collection.

In the 2012–13 data collection (when the majority of the children were in the 2nd grade) the weighted child assessment unit response rate was 84.0 percent in the fall and 83.4 percent in the spring. In the 2014 spring data collection (when the majority of the children were in the 3rd grade), the weighted child assessment unit response rate was 79.9 percent. In the 2015 spring data collection (when the majority of the children were in the 4th grade), the weighted child assessment unit response rate was 77.3 percent; in the 2016 spring data collection (when the majority of the children were in the 5th grade), the weighted child assessment unit response rate was 72.4 percent.

Further information on ECLS-K:2011 may be obtained from

Gail Mulligan
Jill McCarroll
Longitudinal Surveys Branch
Sample Surveys Division
National Center for Education Statistics
550 12th Street SW
Washington, DC 20202
ecls@ed.gov
https://nces.ed.gov/ecls/kindergarten2011.asp

Education Longitudinal Study of 2002

The Education Longitudinal Study of 2002 (ELS:2002) is a longitudinal survey that is monitoring the transitions of a national probability sample of 10th-graders in public, Catholic, and other private schools. Survey waves follow both students and high school dropouts and monitor the transition of the cohort to postsecondary education, the labor force, and family formation.

In the base year of the study, of 1,200 eligible contacted schools, 750 participated, for an overall weighted school participation rate of approximately 68 percent (62 percent unweighted). Of 17,600 selected eligible students, 15,400 participated, for an overall weighted student response rate of approximately 87 percent. (School and student weighted response rates reflect use of the base weight [design weight] and do not include nonresponse adjustments.) Information for the study is obtained not just from students and their school records, but also from the students' parents, their teachers, their librarians, and the administrators of their schools.

The first follow-up was conducted in 2004, when most sample members were high school seniors. Base-year students who remained in their base schools were resurveyed and tested in mathematics. Sample freshening was conducted to make the study representative of spring 2004 high school seniors nationwide. Students who were not still at their base schools were all administered a questionnaire. The first follow-up weighted student response rate was 89 percent.

The second follow-up, conducted in 2006, continued to follow the sample of students into postsecondary education, the workforce, or both. The weighted student response rate for this follow-up was 82 percent. The third follow-up, which had a weighted student response rate of 78 percent, was conducted in 2012; the data were released in January 2014.

The postsecondary transcript data collection was conducted in 2013–14. Postsecondary transcripts were requested for each of the ELS:2002 sample members who reported attending a postsecondary institution in the Integrated Postsecondary Education Data System (IPEDS). Transcripts were obtained for 11,623 of 12,549 eligible sample members for a weighted response rate of 77 percent. For more information on the postsecondary transcript data collection, see *Education Longitudinal Study of 2002 (ELS:2002): A First Look at the Postsecondary Transcripts of 2002 High School Sophomores* (NCES 2015-034).

Further information on ELS:2002 may be obtained from

Elise Christopher
Longitudinal Surveys Branch
Sample Surveys Division
National Center for Education Statistics
550 12th Street SW
Washington, DC 20202
elise.christopher@ed.gov
https://nces.ed.gov/surveys/els2002/

Fast Response Survey System

The Fast Response Survey System (FRSS) was established in 1975 to collect issue-oriented data quickly, with a minimal burden on respondents. The FRSS, whose surveys collect and report data on key education issues at the elementary and secondary levels, was designed to meet the data needs of U.S. Department of Education analysts, planners, and decisionmakers when information could not be collected quickly through NCES's large recurring surveys. Findings from FRSS surveys have been included in congressional reports, testimony to congressional subcommittees, NCES reports, and other U.S. Department of Education reports. The findings are also often used by state and local education officials.

Data collected through FRSS surveys are representative at the national level, drawing from a sample that is appropriate for each study. The FRSS collects data from state education agencies and national samples of other educational organizations and participants, including local education agencies, public and private elementary and secondary schools, elementary and secondary school teachers and principals, and public libraries and school libraries. To ensure a minimal burden on respondents, the surveys are generally limited to three pages of questions, with a response burden of about 30 minutes per respondent. Sample sizes are relatively small (usually about 1,000 to 1,500 respondents per survey) so that data collection can be completed quickly.

Further information on the FRSS may be obtained from

Chris Chapman
Sample Surveys Division
National Center for Education Statistics
550 12th Street SW
Washington, DC 20202
chris.chapman@ed.gov
https://nces.ed.gov/surveys/frss/

Condition of Public School Facilities in the United States

Condition of America's Public School Facilities: 1999 (NCES 2000-032) is a report that presents national data about the condition of public schools in 1999. It provides results from the survey "Condition of Public School Facilities, 1999" (FRSS 73), which was conducted by NCES using its Fast Response Survey System (FRSS). The survey collected information about the condition of school facilities and the costs of bringing them into good condition; school plans for repairs, renovations, and replacements; the age of public schools; and overcrowding and practices used to address overcrowding. The results presented in this report are based on questionnaire data for 900 public elementary and secondary schools in the United States. The responses were weighted to produce national estimates that represent all regular public schools in the United States.

In 2013, NCES conducted "Condition of Public School Facilities: 2012–13" (FRSS 105), an FRSS survey covering most of the same topics. The First Look report *Condition of America's Public School Facilities: 2012–13* (NCES 2014-022) is based on results from this FRSS survey.

Further information on these FRSS reports and surveys may be obtained from

Chris Chapman
Sample Surveys Division
National Center for Education Statistics
550 12th Street SW
Washington, DC 20202
chris.chapman@ed.gov
https://nces.ed.gov/surveys/frss/

Public School Principals Report on Their School Facilities: Fall 2005

This report (NCES 2007-007) presents information on the extent of the match between the enrollment and the capacity of school buildings, environmental factors that can affect the use of classrooms and school buildings, the extent and ways in which schools use portable buildings and the reasons for using them, the availability of dedicated rooms for particular subject areas (such as science labs or music rooms), and the cleanliness and maintenance of student restrooms.

Results from the FRSS survey "Public School Principals' Perceptions of Their School Facilities: Fall 2005" (FRSS 88) form the basis of the report. The survey was mailed to school principals, who were asked to complete it themselves. The sample included 1,205 public schools in the 50 states and the District of Columbia. The sample was selected from the 2002–03 Common Core of Data (CCD) Public Elementary/Secondary School Universe File, the most current available at the time of selection. Of the 1,205 schools surveyed, 47 were determined to be ineligible. Of the remaining 1,158 schools, responses were received from 1,045. Data have been weighted to yield national estimates

of public elementary/secondary schools. The unweighted response rate was 90 percent, and the weighted response rate was 91 percent.

Further information on this report may be obtained from

Chris Chapman
Sample Surveys Division
National Center for Education Statistics
550 12th Street SW
Washington, DC 20202
chris.chapman@ed.gov
https://nces.ed.gov/surveys/frss/

Internet Access in U.S. Public Schools and Classrooms: 1994–2005

This report (NCES 2007-020) is based on data collected in the FRSS survey "Internet Access in U.S. Public Schools, Fall 2005" (FRSS 90). The survey was designed to assess the federal government's commitment to assist every school and classroom in connecting to the Internet by the year 2000.

In 1994, NCES began surveying approximately 1,000 public schools each year regarding their access to the Internet, access in classrooms, and, since 1996, their type of internet connections. Later administrations of this survey were expanded to cover emerging issues. The 2003 survey (FRSS 86) was designed to update the questions in the 2002 survey (FRSS 83) and covered the following topics: school connectivity, student access to computers and the Internet, school websites, technologies and procedures to prevent student access to inappropriate websites, and teacher professional development on how to incorporate the Internet into the curriculum.

In 2005, respondents were asked about the number of instructional computers with access to the Internet, the types of internet connections, the technologies and procedures used to prevent student access to inappropriate material on the Internet, and the availability of handheld and laptop computers for students and teachers. Respondents also provided information on teacher professional development in integrating the use of the Internet into the curriculum and using the Internet to provide opportunities and information for teaching and learning.

Use of Educational Technology in Public Schools

In 2008, the NCES survey on educational technology use in public schools was redesigned and expanded to a set of three surveys (i.e., a school-level, a district-level, and a teacher-level survey). The three surveys provide complementary information and together cover a broader range of topics than would be possible with one survey alone. The set of surveys collected data on availability and use of a range of educational technology resources, such as district and school networks, computers, devices that enhance the capabilities of computers for instruction, and computer software. They also collected information on leadership and staff support for educational technology within districts and schools.

Educational Technology in U.S. Public Schools: Fall 2008 (NCES 2010-034) is based on the school-level survey, "Education Technology in U.S. Public Schools: Fall 2008" (FRSS 92); *Educational Technology in Public School Districts: Fall 2008* (NCES 2010-003) is based on the district-level school technology survey, "Educational Technology in Public School Districts, Fall 2008" (FRSS 93); and *Teachers' Use of Educational Technology in U.S. Public Schools: 2009* (NCES 2010-040) is based on the teacher-level school technology survey, "Teachers' Use of Educational Technology in U.S. Public Schools, 2009" (FRSS 95).

Further information on internet access and technology use in public schools and classrooms may be obtained from

Chris Chapman
Sample Surveys Division
National Center for Education Statistics
550 12th Street SW
Washington, DC 20202
chris.chapman@ed.gov
https://nces.ed.gov/surveys/frss/

Distance Education for Public Elementary and Secondary School Students

The report *Technology-Based Distance Education Courses for Public Elementary and Secondary School Students: 2002–03 and 2004–05* (NCES 2008-008) presented data collected in the FRSS survey "Distance Education Courses for Public Elementary and Secondary School Students, 2004–05" (FRSS 89, 2005). The report included national estimates of the prevalence and characteristics of technology-based distance education courses in public schools nationwide in school year 2004–05. The report also compared those data with the baseline data that were collected in the FRSS survey "Distance Education Courses for Public Elementary and Secondary School Students: 2002–03" (FRSS 84, 2003) and provided longitudinal analysis of change in the districts that responded to both the 2002–03 and 2004–05 surveys.

Distance education courses were defined as credit-granting courses offered to elementary and secondary school students enrolled in the district in which the teacher and student were in different locations. These courses could be delivered via audio, video (live or prerecorded), or Internet or other computer technologies.

Distance Education Courses for Public Elementary and Secondary School Students: 2009–10 (NCES 2012–008) presents national estimates about student enrollment in distance education courses in public school districts. The estimates are based on a district survey, "Distance Education Courses for Public Elementary and Secondary School Students: 2009–10" (FRSS 98, 2010), about distance education courses offered by the district or by any of the schools in the district during the 12-month 2009–10 school year. Distance education courses were defined as courses offered to elementary and secondary school students regularly

enrolled in the district that were (1) credit granting; (2) technology delivered; and (3) had the instructor in a different location than the students and/or had course content developed in, or delivered from, a different location than that of the students.

Further information on FRSS reports on distance education may be obtained from

Chris Chapman
Sample Surveys Division
National Center for Education Statistics
550 12th Street SW
Washington, DC 20202
chris.chapman@ed.gov
https://nces.ed.gov/surveys/frss

School Safety and Discipline

The FRSS survey "School Safety and Discipline: 2013–14" (FRSS 106, 2014) collected nationally representative data on public school safety and discipline for the 2013–14 school year. The topics covered included specific safety and discipline plans and practices, training for classroom teachers and aides related to school safety and discipline issues, security personnel, frequency of specific discipline problems, and number of incidents of various offenses.

The survey was mailed to approximately 1,600 regular public schools in the 50 states and the District of Columbia. Recipients were informed that the survey was designed to be completed by the person most knowledgeable about safety and discipline at the school. The unweighted survey response rate was 86 percent, and the weighted response rate using the initial base weights was 85 percent. The survey weights were adjusted for questionnaire/unit nonresponse, and the data were then weighted to yield national estimates that represent all eligible regular public schools in the United States. The report *Public School Safety and Discipline: 2013–14* (NCES 2015-051) presents selected findings from the survey.

Further information on this FRSS survey may be obtained from

Chris Chapman
Sample Surveys Division
National Center for Education Statistics
550 12th Street SW
Washington, DC 20202
chris.chapman@ed.gov
https://nces.ed.gov/surveys/frss

Career and Technical Education in Public Schools

The FRSS survey "Career and Technical Education Programs in Public School Districts" (FRSS 108, 2017) collected nationally representative data on career and technical education (CTE) programs. CTE programs were defined as sequences of courses at the high school level that provide students with the academic and technical knowledge and skills needed to prepare for further education and careers in current or emerging professions. Districts were instructed to include all CTE programs that the district offers to high school students, including programs provided by the district or by other entities (such as an area/regional CTE center, a consortium of districts, or a community or technical college).

The survey was mailed to approximately 1,800 regular public school districts with high school grades in the United States (the 50 states and the District of Columbia). The survey was to be completed by the person in the district most knowledgeable about career and technical education programs for high school students. The unweighted survey response rate was 87 percent, and the weighted response rate using the initial base weights was 86 percent. The survey weights were adjusted for questionnaire/unit nonresponse, and the data were then weighted to yield national estimates that represent all eligible public school districts with high schools in the United States. The report *Career and Technical Education Programs in Public School Districts: 2016–17: First Look* (NCES 2018-028) presents selected findings from the survey.

Further information on this FRSS survey may be obtained from

Chris Chapman
Sample Surveys Division
National Center for Education Statistics
550 12th Street SW
Washington, DC 20202
chris.chapman@ed.gov
https://nces.ed.gov/surveys/frss

Federal Support for Education

NCES prepares an annual compilation of federal funds for education for the *Digest of Education Statistics*. Data for U.S. Department of Education programs come from the U.S. Department of Education budget office. Budget offices of other federal agencies provide information for all other federal program support except for research funds, which are obligations reported by the National Science Foundation in *Federal Funds for Research and Development*. Some data are based on reports from the federal agencies contacted and the *Budget of the United States Government*, and some data are estimated.

Except for money spent on research, outlays are used to report program funds to the extent possible. Some *Digest of Education Statistics* tables report program funds as obligations, as noted in the title of the table. Some federal program funds not commonly recognized as education assistance are also included in the totals reported. For example, portions of federal funds paid to some states and counties as shared revenues resulting from the sale of timber and minerals from public lands have been estimated as funds used for education purposes. Parts of the funds received by states (in 1980) and localities (from 1972 to 1986) under the General Revenue Sharing Program are also included, as are portions of federal funds received by the District of Columbia.

The share of federal funds assigned to education for the District of Columbia is assumed to be equal to the share of the city's general fund expenditures for each level of education.

For the job training programs conducted by the Department of Labor, only estimated sums spent on classroom training have been reported as educational program support.

During the 1970s, the Office of Management and Budget (OMB) prepared an annual analysis of federal education program support. These were published in the *Budget of the United States Government, Special Analyses*. The information presented in this report is not, however, a continuation of the OMB series. A number of differences in the two series should be noted. OMB required all federal agencies to report outlays for education-related programs using a standardized form, thereby assuring agency compliance in reporting. The scope of education programs reported in the *Digest of Education Statistics* differs from the scope of programs reported in the OMB reports. Off-budget items such as the annual volume of guaranteed student loans were not included in OMB's reports. Finally, while some mention is made of an annual estimate of federal tax expenditures, OMB did not include them in its annual analysis of federal education support. Estimated federal tax expenditures for education are the difference between current federal tax receipts and what these receipts would be without existing education deductions to income allowed by federal tax provisions.

Further information on federal support for education may be obtained from

Cristobal de Brey
Annual Reports and Information Staff
National Center for Education Statistics
550 12th Street SW
Washington, DC 20202
cristobal.debrey@ed.gov
https://nces.ed.gov/surveys/AnnualReports/federal.asp

High School and Beyond Longitudinal Study

The High School and Beyond Longitudinal Study (HS&B) is a nationally representative sample survey of individuals who were high school sophomores and seniors in 1980. As a large-scale, longitudinal survey, its primary purpose is to observe the educational and occupational plans and activities of young people as they pass through the American educational system and take on their adult roles. The study contributes to the understanding of the development of young adults and the factors that determine individual education and career outcomes. The availability of these longitudinal data encourages research in such areas as the strength of secondary school curricula, the quality and effectiveness of secondary and postsecondary schooling, the demand for postsecondary education, problems of financing postsecondary education, and the adequacy of postsecondary alternatives open to high school students.

The HS&B survey gathered data on the education, work, and family experiences of young adults for the pivotal years during and immediately following high school. The student questionnaire covered school experiences, activities, attitudes, plans, selected background characteristics, and language proficiency. Parents were asked about their educational aspirations for their children and plans for how their postsecondary education would be financed. Teachers were surveyed regarding their assessments of their students' futures. The survey also collected detailed information, from complete high school transcripts, on courses taken and grades achieved.

The base-year survey (conducted in 1980) was a probability sample of 1,015 high schools with a target number of 36 sophomores and 36 seniors in each school. A total of 58,270 students participated in the base-year survey. Substitutions were made for nonparticipating schools—but not for students—in those strata where it was possible. Overall, 1,120 schools were selected in the original sample and 810 of these schools participated in the survey. An additional 200 schools were drawn in a replacement sample. Student refusals and absences resulted in an 82 percent completion rate for the survey.

Several small groups in the population were oversampled to allow for special study of certain types of schools and students. Students completed questionnaires and took a battery of cognitive tests. In addition, a sample of parents of sophomores and seniors (about 3,600 for each cohort) was surveyed.

The first HS&B follow-up activities took place in spring 1982. The sample for the first follow-up survey included approximately 30,000 individuals who were sophomores in 1980. The completion rate for sample members eligible for on-campus survey administration was about 96 percent. About 89 percent of the students who left school between the base-year and first follow-up surveys (e.g., dropouts, transfer students, and early graduates) completed the first follow-up sophomore questionnaire.

As part of the first follow-up survey of HS&B, transcripts were requested in fall 1982 for an 18,150-member subsample of the sophomore cohort. Of the 15,940 transcripts actually obtained, 12,120 transcripts represented students who had graduated in 1982 and thus were eligible for use in the overall curriculum analysis presented in this publication. All courses in each transcript were assigned a 6-digit code based on the Classification of Secondary School Courses (a coding system developed to standardize course descriptions; see https://nces.ed.gov/surveys/hst/courses.asp). Credits earned in each course are expressed in Carnegie units. (The Carnegie unit is a standard of measurement that represents one credit for the completion of a 1-year course. To receive credit for a course, the student must have received a passing grade—"pass," "D," or higher.) Students who transferred from public to private schools or from private to public schools between their sophomore and senior years were eliminated from public/private analyses.

In designing the senior cohort first follow-up survey, one of the goals was to reduce the size of the retained sample while still keeping sufficient numbers of various racial/ethnic groups to allow important policy analyses. A total of about 11,230 of the 12,000 individuals subsampled (93.6 percent) completed the questionnaire. Information was obtained about the respondents' school and employment experiences, family status, and attitudes and plans.

The samples for the second follow-up, which took place in spring 1984, consisted of about 12,000 members of the senior cohort and about 15,000 members of the sophomore cohort. The completion rate for the senior cohort was 91 percent, and the completion rate for the sophomore cohort was 92 percent.

HS&B third follow-up data collection activities were performed in spring 1986. Both the sophomore and senior cohort samples for this round of data collection were the same as those used for the second follow-up survey. The completion rates for the sophomore and senior cohort samples were 91 percent and 88 percent, respectively.

HS&B fourth follow-up data collection activities were performed in 1992 but only covered the 1980 sophomore class. These activities included examining aspects of these students' early adult years, such as enrollment in postsecondary education, experience in the labor market, marriage and child rearing, and voting behavior. In the postsecondary transcript update conducted in 1993, transcripts were collected based on student reports of enrollment in postsecondary education.

An NCES series of technical reports and data file user's manuals, available electronically, provides additional information on the survey methodology.

Further information on HS&B may be obtained from

Aurora D'Amico
Longitudinal Surveys Branch
Sample Surveys Division
National Center for Education Statistics
550 12th Street SW
Washington, DC 20202
aurora.damico@ed.gov
https://nces.ed.gov/surveys/hsb/

High School Longitudinal Study of 2009

The High School Longitudinal Study of 2009 (HSLS:09) is a nationally representative, longitudinal study of approximately 21,000 9th-grade students in 944 schools who will be followed through their secondary and postsecondary years. The study focuses on understanding students' trajectories from the beginning of high school into postsecondary education, the workforce, and beyond. The HSLS:09 questionnaire is focused on, but not limited to, information on science, technology, engineering, and mathematics (STEM) education and careers. It is designed to provide data on mathematics and science education, the changing high school environment, and postsecondary education. This study features a new student assessment in algebra skills, reasoning, and problem solving and includes surveys of students, their parents, math and science teachers, and school administrators, as well as a new survey of school counselors.

The HSLS:09 base year took place in the 2009–10 school year, with a randomly selected sample of fall-term 9th-graders in more than 900 public and private high schools that had both a 9th and an 11th grade. Students took a mathematics assessment and survey online. Students' parents, principals, and mathematics and science teachers and the school's lead counselor completed surveys on the phone or online.

The HSLS:09 student questionnaire includes interest and motivation items for measuring key factors predicting choice of postsecondary paths, including majors and eventual careers. This study explores the roles of different factors in the development of a student's commitment to attend college and then take the steps necessary to succeed in college (the right courses, courses in specific sequences, etc.). Questionnaires in this study have asked more questions of students and parents regarding reasons for selecting specific colleges (e.g., academic programs, financial aid and access prices, and campus environment).

The first follow-up of HSLS:09 occurred in spring 2012, when most sample members were in the 11th grade. A between-round postsecondary status update survey took place in the spring of students' expected graduation year (2013). It asked respondents about college applications, acceptances, and rejections, as well as their actual college choices. In fall 2013 and spring 2014, high school transcripts were collected and coded.

A full second follow-up took place in 2016, when most sample members were 3 years beyond high school graduation. Additional follow-ups are planned, to at least age 30.

Further information on HSLS:09 may be obtained from

Elise Christopher
Longitudinal Surveys Branch
Sample Surveys Division
National Center for Education Statistics
550 12th Street SW
Washington, DC 20202
hsls09@ed.gov
https://nces.ed.gov/surveys/hsls09/

High School Transcript Studies

High school transcript studies have been conducted since 1982 in conjunction with major NCES data collections. The studies collect information that is contained in a student's high school record—courses taken while attending secondary school, information on credits earned, when specific courses were taken, and final grades.

A high school transcript study was conducted in 2004 as part of the Education Longitudinal Study of 2002 (ELS:2002/2004). A total of 1,550 schools participated in the request for transcripts, for an unweighted participation rate of approximately 79 percent. Transcript information

was received on 14,920 members of the student sample (not just graduates), for an unweighted response rate of 91 percent.

Similar studies were conducted on the coursetaking patterns of 1982, 1987, 1990, 1992, 1994, 1998, 2000, 2005, and 2009 high school graduates. The 1982 data are based on approximately 12,000 transcripts collected by the High School and Beyond Longitudinal Study (HS&B). The 1987 data are based on approximately 25,000 transcripts from 430 schools obtained as part of the 1987 NAEP High School Transcript Study, a scope comparable to that of the NAEP transcript studies conducted in 1990, 1994, 1998, and 2000. The 1992 data are based on approximately 15,000 transcripts collected by the National Education Longitudinal Study of 1988 (NELS:88/92). The 2005 data, from the 2005 NAEP High School Transcript Study, come from a sample of over 26,000 transcripts from 640 public schools and 80 private schools. The 2009 data are from the 2009 NAEP High School Transcript Study, which collected transcripts from a nationally representative sample of 37,700 high school graduates from about 610 public schools and 130 private schools.

Because the 1982 HS&B transcript study used a different method for identifying students with disabilities than was used in NAEP transcript studies after 1982, and in order to make the statistical summaries as comparable as possible, all the counts and percentages in this report are restricted to students whose records indicate that they had not participated in a special education program. This restriction lowers the number of 1990 graduates represented in the tables to 20,870.

Further information on NAEP high school transcript studies may be obtained from

Linda Hamilton
International Assessment Branch
Assessments Division
National Center for Education Statistics
550 12th Street SW
Washington, DC 20202
linda.hamilton@ed.gov
https://nces.ed.gov/surveys/hst/

Integrated Postsecondary Education Data System

IPEDS consists of 12 interrelated survey components that provide information on postsecondary institutions and academic libraries at these institutions, student enrollment, student financial aid, programs offered, retention and graduation rates, degrees and certificates conferred, and the human and financial resources involved in the provision of institutionally based postsecondary education. Prior to 2000, the IPEDS survey had the following subject-matter components: Institutional Characteristics; Total Institutional Activity (these data were moved to the Institutional Characteristics component in 1990–91, then to the Fall Enrollment component in 2000–01); Fall Enrollment; Fall Staff; Salaries,

Tenure, and Fringe Benefits of Full-Time Faculty; Completions; Finance; Academic Libraries (in 2000, the Academic Libraries component separated from the IPEDS collection); and Graduation Rates. Since 2000, IPEDS survey components occurring in a particular collection year have been organized into three seasonal collection periods: fall, winter, and spring. The Institutional Characteristics and Completions components first took place during the fall 2000 collection. The Employees by Assigned Position (EAP); Salaries, Tenure, and Fringe Benefits of Full-Time Faculty; and Fall Staff components first took place during the winter 2001–02 collection. The Fall Enrollment, Student Financial Aid, Finance, and Graduation Rates components first took place during the spring 2001 collection. In the winter 2005–06 data collection, the EAP; Fall Staff; and Salaries, Tenure, and Fringe Benefits of Full-Time Faculty components were merged into the Human Resources component. During the 2007–08 collection year, the Fall Enrollment component was broken into two components: 12-month Enrollment (taking place in the fall collection) and Fall Enrollment (taking place in the spring collection). In the 2011–12 IPEDS data collection year, the Student Financial Aid component was moved to the winter data collection to aid in the timing of the net price of attendance calculations displayed on the College Navigator (https://nces.ed.gov/collegenavigator/). In the 2012–13 IPEDS data collection year, the Human Resources component was moved from the winter data collection to the spring data collection, and in the 2013–14 data collection year, the Graduation Rates and Graduation Rates 200 Percent components were moved from the spring data collection to the winter data collection. In the 2014–15 data collection year, a new component (Admissions) was added to IPEDS and a former IPEDS component (Academic Libraries) was reintegrated into IPEDS. The Admissions component, created out of admissions data contained in the fall data collection's Institutional Characteristics component, was made a part of the winter data collection. The Academic Libraries component, after having been conducted as a survey independent of IPEDS between 2000 and 2012, was reintegrated into IPEDS as part of the spring data collection. Finally, in the 2015–16 data collection year, the Outcome Measures survey component was added to IPEDS.

Beginning in 2008–09, the first-professional degree category was combined with the doctor's degree category. However, some degrees formerly identified as first-professional that take more than 2 full-time-equivalent academic years to complete, such as those in Theology (M.Div., M.H.L./Rav), are included in the master's degree category. Doctor's degrees were broken out into three distinct categories: research/scholarship, professional practice, and other doctor's degrees.

The collection of race/ethnicity data also changed in 2008–09. IPEDS now collects a count of students who identify as Hispanic and counts of non-Hispanic students who identify with each race category. The "Asian" race category is now separate from the "Native Hawaiian or Other Pacific Islander" category, and a new category of "Two or more races" has been added.

The degree-granting institutions portion of IPEDS is a census of colleges that award associate's or higher degrees and are eligible to participate in Title IV financial aid programs. Prior to 1993, data from technical and vocational institutions were collected through a sample survey. Beginning in 1993, all data are gathered in a census of all postsecondary institutions. Beginning in 1997, the survey was restricted to institutions participating in Title IV programs. The tabulations developed for editions of the *Digest of Education Statistics* from 1993 forward are based on lists of all institutions and are not subject to sampling errors.

The classification of institutions offering college and university education changed as of 1996. Prior to 1996, institutions that either had courses leading to an associate's or higher degree or that had courses accepted for credit toward those degrees were considered higher education institutions. Higher education institutions were accredited by an agency or association that was recognized by the U.S. Department of Education or were recognized directly by the Secretary of Education. The newer standard includes institutions that award associate's or higher degrees and that are eligible to participate in Title IV federal financial aid programs. Tables that contain any data according to this standard are titled "degree-granting" institutions. Time-series tables may contain data from both series, and they are noted accordingly. The impact of this change on data collected in 1996 was not large. For example, tables on faculty salaries and benefits were affected only to a small extent. Also, degrees awarded at the bachelor's level or higher were not heavily affected. The largest impact was on private 2-year college enrollment. In contrast, most of the data on public 4-year colleges were affected to a minimal extent. The impact on enrollment in public 2-year colleges was noticeable in certain states, such as Arizona, Arkansas, Georgia, Louisiana, and Washington, but was relatively small at the national level. Overall, total enrollment for all institutions was about one-half of 1 percent higher in 1996 for degree-granting institutions than for higher education institutions.

Prior to the establishment of IPEDS in 1986, the Higher Education General Information Survey (HEGIS) acquired and maintained statistical data on the characteristics and operations of higher education institutions. Implemented in 1966, HEGIS was an annual universe survey of institutions accredited at the college level by an agency recognized by the Secretary of the U.S. Department of Education. These institutions were listed in NCES's *Education Directory, Colleges and Universities*.

HEGIS surveys collected information on institutional characteristics, faculty salaries, finances, libraries, fall enrollment, student residence and migration, and earned degrees. Since these surveys, like IPEDS, were distributed to all higher education institutions, the data presented are not subject to sampling error. However, they are subject to nonsampling error, the sources of which varied with the survey instrument.

The NCES Taskforce for IPEDS Redesign recognized that there were issues related to the consistency of data definitions as well as the accuracy, reliability, and validity of other quality measures within and across surveys. The IPEDS redesign in 2000 provided institution-specific web-based data forms. While the new system shortened data processing time and provided better data consistency, it did not address the accuracy of the data provided by institutions.

Beginning in 2003–04 with the Prior Year Data Revision System, prior-year data have been available to institutions entering current data. This allows institutions to make changes to their prior-year entries either by adjusting the data or by providing missing data. These revisions allow the evaluation of the data's accuracy by looking at the changes made.

NCES conducted a study (NCES 2005-175) of the 2002–03 data that were revised in 2003–04 to determine the accuracy of the imputations, track the institutions that submitted revised data, and analyze the revised data they submitted. When institutions made changes to their data, NCES accepted that the revised data were the most accurate, correct, and "true" data. The data were analyzed for the number and type of institutions making changes, the type of changes, the magnitude of the changes, and the impact on published data.

Because NCES imputes for missing data, imputation procedures were also addressed by the Redesign Taskforce. For the 2003–04 assessment, differences between revised values and values that were imputed in the original files were compared (i.e., revised value minus imputed value). These differences were then used to provide an assessment of the effectiveness of imputation procedures. The size of the differences also provides an indication of the accuracy of imputation procedures. To assess the overall impact of changes on aggregate IPEDS estimates, published tables for each component were reconstructed using the revised 2002–03 data. These reconstructed tables were then compared to the published tables to determine the magnitude of aggregate bias and the direction of this bias. The aggregate bias analysis revealed that, generally, differences between originally published estimates and revised estimates were small.

Since the 2000–01 data collection year, IPEDS data collections have been web based. Data have been provided by "keyholders," institutional representatives appointed by campus chief executives, who are responsible for ensuring that survey data submitted by the institution are correct and complete. Because Title IV institutions are the primary focus of IPEDS and because these institutions are required to respond to IPEDS, response rates for Title IV institutions have been high (data on specific components are cited below). More details on the accuracy and reliability of IPEDS data can be found in the *Integrated Postsecondary Education Data System Data Quality Study* (NCES 2005-175).

Further information on IPEDS may be obtained from

Samuel Barbett
Postsecondary Branch
Administrative Data Division
National Center for Education Statistics
550 12th Street SW
Washington, DC 20202
samuel.barbett@ed.gov
https://nces.ed.gov/ipeds/

Fall (12-month Enrollment)

The 12-month period during which data are collected is July 1 through June 30. Data are collected by race/ethnicity, gender, and level of study (undergraduate or postbaccalaureate) and include unduplicated headcounts and instructional activity (contact or credit hours). These data are also used to calculate a full-time-equivalent (FTE) enrollment based on instructional activity. FTE enrollment is useful for gauging the size of the educational enterprise at the institution. Prior to the 2007–08 IPEDS data collection, the data collected in the 12-month Enrollment component were part of the Fall Enrollment component, which is conducted during the spring data collection period. However, to improve the timeliness of the data, a separate 12-month Enrollment survey component was developed in 2007. These data are now collected in the fall for the previous academic year. The response rate for the 12-month Enrollment component of the fall 2018 data collection was nearly 100 percent. Data from 2 of the 6,274 Title IV institutions that were expected to respond to this component were imputed due to unit nonresponse.

Further information on the IPEDS 12-month Enrollment component may be obtained from

Tara Lawley
Postsecondary Branch
Administrative Data Division
National Center for Education Statistics
550 12th Street SW
Washington, DC 20202
tara.lawley@ed.gov
https://nces.ed.gov/ipeds/

Fall (Completions)

The Completions component collects data on the number of students who complete a postsecondary education program (completers) and the number of postsecondary awards earned (completions). This component was part of the HEGIS series throughout its existence. However, the degree classification taxonomy was revised in 1970–71, 1982–83, 1991–92, 2002–03, and 2009–10. Collection of degree data has been maintained through IPEDS.

Degrees-conferred trend tables arranged by the 2009–10 classification are included in the *Digest of Education Statistics* to provide consistent data from 1970–71 through the most recent year. Data in this edition on associate's and other formal awards below the baccalaureate degree, by field of study, cannot be made comparable with figures from years prior to 1982–83. The nonresponse rate does not appear to be a significant source of nonsampling error for this component. The response rate over the years has been high; for the fall 2018 Completions component, the response rate rounded to 100 percent. Data from 1 of the 6,281 Title IV institutions that were expected to respond to this component were imputed due to unit nonresponse.

Further information on the IPEDS Completions component may be obtained from

Tara Lawley
Postsecondary Branch
Administrative Data Division
National Center for Education Statistics
550 12th Street SW
Washington, DC 20202
tara.lawley@ed.gov
https://nces.ed.gov/ipeds/

Fall (Institutional Characteristics)

This survey collects the basic information necessary to classify institutions, including control, level, and types of programs offered, as well as information on tuition, fees, and room and board charges. Beginning in 2000, the survey collected institutional pricing data from institutions with first-time, full-time, degree/certificate-seeking undergraduate students. Unduplicated full-year enrollment counts and instructional activity are now collected in the 12-month Enrollment survey. Beginning in 2008–09, the student financial aid data collected include greater detail.

In the fall 2018 data collection, the response rate for Title IV entities on the Institutional Characteristics component was 100 percent. Of the 6,353 Title IV entities that were expected to respond to this component, all provided data.

Further information on the IPEDS Institutional Characteristics component may be obtained from

Moussa Ezzeddine
Postsecondary Branch
Administrative Data Division
National Center for Education Statistics
550 12th Street SW
Washington, DC 20202
moussa.ezzeddine@ed.gov
https://nces.ed.gov/ipeds/

Winter (Student Financial Aid)

This component was part of the spring data collection from IPEDS data collection years 2000–01 to 2010–11, but it moved to the winter data collection starting with the 2011–12 IPEDS data collection year. This move assists with the timing of the net price of attendance calculations displayed on College Navigator (https://nces.ed.gov/collegenavigator/).

Financial aid data are collected for undergraduate students. Data are collected regarding federal grants, state and local government grants, institutional grants, and loans. The collected data include the number of students receiving each type of financial assistance and the average amount of aid received by type of aid. Beginning in 2008–09, student financial aid data collected includes greater detail on types of aid offered.

In the winter 2018–19 data collection, the Student Financial Aid component collected data about financial aid awarded to undergraduate students, with particular emphasis on full-time, first-time degree/certificate-seeking undergraduate students awarded financial aid for the 2017–18 academic year. In addition, the component collected data on undergraduate and graduate students receiving benefits for veterans and members of the military service. Finally, student counts and awarded aid amounts were collected to calculate the net price of attendance for two subsets of full-time, first-time degree/certificate-seeking undergraduate students: those awarded any grant aid, and those awarded Title IV aid.

The response rate for the Student Financial Aid component in 2018–19 was nearly 100 percent. Of the 6,202 Title IV institutions that were expected to respond, responses were missing for 8 institutions, and these missing data were imputed.

Further information on the IPEDS Student Financial Aid component may be obtained from

Tara Lawley
Postsecondary Branch
Administrative Data Division
National Center for Education Statistics
550 12th Street SW
Washington, DC 20202
tara.lawley@ed.gov
https://nces.ed.gov/ipeds/

Winter (Graduation Rates and Graduation Rates 200 Percent)

In IPEDS data collection years 2012–13 and earlier, the Graduation Rates and Graduation Rates 200 Percent components were collected during the spring collection. In the IPEDS 2013–14 data collection year, however, the Graduation Rates and Graduation Rates 200 Percent collections were moved to the winter data collection.

The 2018–19 Graduation Rates component collected counts of full-time, first-time degree/certificate-seeking undergraduate students beginning their postsecondary education in the specified cohort year and their completion status as of 150 percent of normal program completion time at the same institution where the students started. If 150 percent of normal program completion time extended beyond August 31, 2018, the counts as of that date were collected. Four-year institutions used 2012 as the cohort year, while less-than-4-year institutions used 2015 as the cohort year. Four-year institutions also report for full-time, first-time bachelor's degree-seeking undergraduate students.

Starting with the 2016–17 Graduation Rates component, two new subcohort groups—students who received Pell Grants and students who received a subsidized Direct loan and did not receive Pell Grants—were added.

Of the 5,596 institutions that were expected to respond to the Graduation Rates component, responses were missing for 7 institutions, and these missing data were imputed.

The 2018–19 Graduation Rates 200 Percent component was designed to combine information reported in a prior collection via the Graduation Rates component with current information about the same cohort of students. From previously collected data, the following counts were obtained: the number of students entering the institution as full-time, first-time degree/certificate-seeking students in a cohort year; the number of students in this cohort completing within 100 and 150 percent of normal program completion time; and the number of cohort exclusions (such as students who left for military service). Then the number of additional cohort exclusions and additional program completers between 151 and 200 percent of normal program completion time was collected. Four-year institutions reported on bachelor's or equivalent degree-seeking students and used cohort year 2010 as the reference period, while less-than-4-year institutions reported on all students in the cohort and used cohort year 2014 as the reference period. Of the 5,203 institutions that were expected to respond to the Graduation Rates 200 Percent component, responses were missing for 4 institutions, and these missing data were imputed.

Further information on the IPEDS Graduation Rates and Graduation Rates 200 Percent components may be obtained from

Andrew Mary
Postsecondary Branch
Administrative Data Division
National Center for Education Statistics
550 12th Street SW
Washington, DC 20202
andrew.mary@ed.gov
https://nces.ed.gov/ipeds/

Winter (Admissions)

In the 2014–15 survey year, an Admissions component was added to the winter data collection. This component was created out of the admissions data that had previously been a part of the fall Institutional Characteristics component. Situating these data in a new component in the winter collection enables all institutions to report data for the most recent fall period.

The Admissions component collects information about the selection process for entering first-time degree/certificate-seeking undergraduate students. Data obtained from institutions include admissions considerations (e.g., secondary school records, admission test scores),

the number of first-time degree/certificate-seeking undergraduate students who applied, the number admitted, and the number enrolled. Admissions data were collected only from institutions that do not have an open admissions policy for entering first-time students. Data collected for the IPEDS winter 2018–19 Admissions component relate to individuals applying to be admitted during the fall of the 2018–19 academic year (the fall 2018 reporting period). Of the 2,021 Title IV institutions that were expected to respond to the Admissions component, all responded.

Further information on the IPEDS Admissions component may be obtained from

Moussa Ezzeddine
Postsecondary Branch
Administrative Data Division
National Center for Education Statistics
550 12th Street SW
Washington, DC 20202
moussa.ezzeddine@ed.gov
https://nces.ed.gov/ipeds/

Winter (Outcome Measures)

First administered in the winter 2015–16 data collection, the Outcome Measures component is designed to provide measures of student success for traditional college students, as well as for nontraditional college students, including those who are part-time students and transfers.

In the winter 2015–16 data collection, the Outcome Measures component collected data from 2- and 4-year degree-granting institutions on the award and enrollment status for these four cohorts of degree/certificate-seeking undergraduates:

- First-time, full-time entering students;
- First-time, part-time entering students;
- Non-first-time (or "transfer-in"), full-time entering students; and
- Non-first-time, part-time entering students.

Since the 2017–18 collection, two new subcohort groups—students who received Pell Grants and students who did not receive Pell Grants—have been added to each of the four main cohorts in the Outcome Measures component, resulting in a total of eight undergraduate subcohorts.

The cohorts that were a part of the winter 2018–19 data collection consisted of all entering students who began their studies between July 1, 2010, and June 30, 2011. Student completion status was collected as of August 31 at 4 years, 6 years, and 8 years after students entered the institution (e.g., 4-year completion status was measured on August 31, 2014). For students within the cohorts who did not receive a degree or certificate, the Outcome Measures component collected the enrollment status as of 8 years after they entered the reporting institution (August 31, 2018).

The response rate for the Outcome Measures component of the winter 2018–19 collection was nearly 100 percent. Of the 3,752 institutions that were expected to respond, 4 responses were missing, and these data were imputed.

Further information on the IPEDS Outcome Measures component may be obtained from

Tara Lawley
Postsecondary Branch
Administrative Data Division
National Center for Education Statistics
550 12th Street SW
Washington, DC 20202
tara.lawley@ed.gov
https://nces.ed.gov/ipeds/

Spring (Academic Libraries)

From 1966 to 1988, the Academic Libraries Survey was conducted on a 3-year cycle as part of HEGIS. From 1988 to 1998, the survey was a part of IPEDS and conducted on a 2-year cycle. It remained on a 2-year cycle from 2000 to 2012, but during that period it was conducted independently of IPEDS. In 2014, the survey was reincorporated into IPEDS as the Academic Libraries component, with data collection occurring annually.

The Academic Libraries component collects information from degree-granting institutions on library collections, circulations, expenses, and services. Institutions answer two screening questions in the IPEDS Institutional Characteristics component to determine whether they should also respond to the Academic Libraries component. The component consists of two sections. In section I, all degree-granting institutions with annual library expenses greater than $0 and/ or access to a library collection report information on collections, circulations, and interlibrary loan services. In section II, all degree-granting institutions with annual library expenses greater than or equal to $100,000 report the information reported in section I, as well as information on library expenses.

Of the 4,082 institutions that were expected to respond to the Academic Libraries component in the IPEDS spring 2019 data collection, 2 responses were missing, and these data were imputed.

Further information on the IPEDS Academic Libraries component may be obtained from

Samuel Barbett
Postsecondary Branch
Administrative Data Division
National Center for Education Statistics
550 12th Street SW
Washington, DC 20202
samuel.barbett@ed.gov
https://nces.ed.gov/ipeds/

Spring (Fall Enrollment)

This survey has been part of the HEGIS and IPEDS series since 1966. Response rates have been relatively high, generally exceeding 85 percent. Beginning in 2000, with web-based data collection, higher response rates were attained. In the spring 2019 data collection, in which the Fall Enrollment component covered student enrollment in fall 2018, the response rate was greater than 99 percent. Of the 6,267 institutions that were expected to respond, 6 institutions did not respond, and these data were imputed.

Beginning with the fall 1986 survey and the introduction of IPEDS (see above), a redesign of the survey resulted in the collection of data by race/ethnicity, gender, level of study (i.e., undergraduate and graduate), and attendance status (i.e., full-time and part-time). Other aspects of the survey include allowing (in alternating years) for the collection of age and residence data. The Fall Enrollment component also collects data on first-time retention rates, student-to-faculty ratios, and student enrollment in distance education courses. Finally, in even-numbered years, 4-year institutions provide enrollment data by level of study, race/ethnicity, and gender for nine selected fields of study or Classification of Instructional Programs (CIP) codes. (The CIP is a taxonomic coding scheme that contains titles and descriptions of primarily postsecondary instructional programs.)

Beginning in 2000, the survey collected instructional activity and unduplicated headcount data, which are needed to compute a standardized, full-time-equivalent (FTE) enrollment statistic for the entire academic year. As of 2007–08, the timeliness of the instructional activity data has been improved by collecting these data in the fall as part of the 12-month Enrollment component instead of in the spring as part of the Fall Enrollment component.

Further information on the IPEDS Fall Enrollment component may be obtained from

Tara Lawley
Postsecondary Branch
Administrative Data Division
National Center for Education Statistics
550 12th Street SW
Washington, DC 20202
tara.lawley@ed.gov
https://nces.ed.gov/ipeds/

Spring (Finance)

This survey was part of the HEGIS series and has been continued under IPEDS. Substantial changes were made in the financial survey instruments in fiscal year (FY) 1976, FY 1982, FY 1987, FY 1997, and FY 2002. While these changes were significant, a considerable effort has been made in this report to present only comparable information on trends and to note inconsistencies. The FY 1976 survey instrument contained numerous revisions to earlier survey forms, which made direct comparisons of line items very difficult. Beginning in FY 1982, Pell Grant data were collected in the categories of federal restricted grant and contract revenues and restricted scholarship and fellowship expenditures. The introduction of IPEDS in the FY 1987 survey included several important changes to the survey instrument and data processing procedures. Beginning in FY 1997, data for private institutions were collected using new financial concepts consistent with Financial Accounting Standards Board (FASB) reporting standards, which provide a more comprehensive view of college finance activities. The data for public institutions continued to be collected using the older survey form. The data for public and private institutions were no longer comparable and, as a result, no longer presented together in analysis tables. In FY 2001, public institutions had the option of either continuing to report using Government Accounting Standards Board (GASB) standards or using the new FASB reporting standards. Beginning in FY 2002, public institutions could use either the original GASB standards, the FASB standards, or the new GASB Statement 35 standards (GASB35). Beginning in FY 2004, public institutions could no longer submit survey forms based on the original GASB standards. Beginning in FY 2008, public institutions could submit their GASB survey forms using a revised structure that was modified for better comparability with the IPEDS FASB finance forms, or the institutions could use the structure of the prior forms used from FY 2004 to FY 2007. Similarly, in FY 2008, private nonprofit institutions and public institutions using the FASB form were given an opportunity to report using the forms that had been modified to improve comparability with the GASB forms, or they could use forms with a structure that was consistent with the prior years. In FY 2010, the use of the forms with the older structure was discontinued, and all institutions used either the GASB or FASB forms that had been modified for comparability. Also, in FY 2010, a new series of forms was introduced for non-degree-granting institutions that included versions for for-profit, FASB, and GASB reporting institutions. From FY 2000 through FY 2013, private for-profit institutions used a version of the FASB form with much less detail than the FASB form used by private nonprofit institutions. As of FY 2014, however, private for-profit institutions have been required to report the same level of detail as private nonprofit institutions.

Possible sources of nonsampling error in the financial statistics include nonresponse, imputation, and misclassification. The unweighted response rate has been about 85 to 90 percent for most of the years these data appeared in the *Digest of Education Statistics*; however, in more recent years, response rates have been much higher because Title IV institutions are required to respond. Since 2002, the IPEDS data collection has been a full-scale web-based collection, which has improved the quality and timeliness of the data. For example, the ability of IPEDS to tailor online data entry forms for each institution based on characteristics such as institutional control, level of institution, and calendar system and the institutions' ability to submit their data online are aspects of full-scale web-based collections that have improved response.

The response rate for the FY 2018 Finance component was greater than 99 percent: Of the 6,339 institutions and administrative offices that were expected to respond, 10 did not respond, and these missing data were imputed.

Further information on the IPEDS Finance component may be obtained from

Samuel Barbett
Postsecondary Branch
Administrative Data Division
National Center for Education Statistics
550 12th Street SW
Washington, DC 20202
samuel.barbett@ed.gov
https://nces.ed.gov/ipeds/

Spring (Human Resources)

The Human Resources component was part of the IPEDS winter data collection from data collection years 2000–01 to 2011–12. For the 2012–13 data collection year, the Human Resources component was moved to the spring 2013 data collection in order to give institutions more time to prepare their survey responses.

IPEDS Collection Years, 2012–13 to Present

In 2012–13, new occupational categories replaced the primary function/occupational activity categories previously used in the IPEDS Human Resources component. This change was required in order to align the IPEDS Human Resources categories with the 2010 Standard Occupational Classification (SOC) system. In tandem with the change in 2012–13 from using primary function/occupational activity categories to using the new occupational categories, the sections making up the IPEDS Human Resources component (which previously had been Employees by Assigned Position, Fall Staff, and Salaries) were changed to Full-Time Instructional Staff, Full-Time Noninstructional Staff, Salaries, Part-Time Staff, and New Hires.

The webpages "Archived Changes—Changes to IPEDS Data Collections, 2012–13" (https://nces.ed.gov/ipeds/ InsidePages/ArchivedChanges?year=2012-13) and "2012–13 IPEDS Human Resources (HR) Occupational Categories Compared with 2011–12 IPEDS HR Primary Function/Occupational Activity Categories" (https://nces.ed.gov/ipeds/ resource/download/IPEDS_HR_2012-13_compared_to_ IPEDS_HR_2011-12.pdf) provide information on the redesign of the IPEDS Human Resources component initiated in the 2012–13 data collection year.

In 2018, an update to the Standard Occupational Classification (SOC) system was released. As a consequence, revisions were made to the occupational categories in the Human Resources component in the IPEDS spring 2019 data collection. These revisions are described on the webpage "Resources for Implementing Changes to the IPEDS Human Resources (HR) Survey Component Due to Updated 2018 Standard Occupational Classification (SOC) System" (https://nces.ed.gov/ipeds/report-your-data/taxono mies-standard-occupational-classification-soc-codes).

In the IPEDS spring 2019 data collection, the response rate for the Human Resources component was greater than 99 percent. Of the 6,339 institutions and administrative offices that were expected to respond, 7 institutions did not respond, and these missing data were imputed.

IPEDS Collection Years Prior to 2012–13

In collection years before 2001–02, IPEDS conducted a Fall Staff survey and a Salaries survey; in the 2001–02 collection year, the Employees by Assigned Position (EAP) survey was added to IPEDS. In the 2005–06 collection year, these three surveys became sections of the IPEDS "Human Resources" component.

Data gathered by the EAP section categorized all employees by full- or part-time status, faculty status, and primary function/occupational activity. Institutions with M.D. or D.O. programs were required to report their medical school employees separately. A response to the EAP was required of all 6,858 Title IV institutions and administrative offices in the United States and other jurisdictions for winter 2008–09, and 6,845, or 99.8 percent unweighted, responded. Of the 6,970 Title IV institutions and administrative offices required to respond to the winter 2009–10 EAP, 6,964, or 99.9 percent, responded. Of the 7,256 Title IV institutions and administrative offices required to respond to the EAP for winter 2010–11, about 99.9 percent responded. In the original winter 2010–11 data collection, 7,252 responded to the EAP and data for the 4 nonrespondents were imputed; the next year, 1 of the nonrespondents whose data were imputed submitted a revision.

The main functions/occupational activities of the EAP section were primarily instruction, instruction combined with research and/or public service, primarily research, primarily public service, executive/administrative/managerial, other professionals (support/service), graduate assistants, technical and paraprofessionals, clerical and secretarial, skilled crafts, and service/maintenance.

All full-time instructional faculty classified in the EAP full-time nonmedical school part as either (1) primarily instruction or (2) instruction combined with research and/or public service were included in the Salaries section, unless they were exempt (i.e., unless they contributed their services, were employed on an ad hoc or occasional basis, or worked strictly in hospitals associated with medical schools).

The Fall Staff section categorized all staff on the institution's payroll as of November 1 of the collection year by employment status (full time or part time), primary function/occupational activity, gender, and race/ethnicity. Title IV institutions and administrative offices were only required to respond to the Fall Staff section in odd-numbered reporting years, so they were not required to respond during the 2008–09 Human Resources data collection. However, of the 6,858 Title IV institutions and administrative offices in the United States and other jurisdictions, 3,295, or 48.0 percent unweighted, did provide data in the Fall Staff section that

year. During the 2009–10 Human Resources data collection, when all 6,970 Title IV institutions and administrative offices were required to respond to the Fall Staff section, 6,964, or 99.9 percent, did so. A response to the Fall Staff section of the 2010–11 Human Resources collection was optional, and 3,364 Title IV institutions and administrative offices responded that year (a response rate of 46.3 percent).

The Salaries section collected data for full-time instructional faculty (except those in medical schools in the EAP section, described above) on the institution's payroll as of November 1 of the collection year by contract length/teaching period, gender, and academic rank. The reporting of data by faculty status in the Salaries section was required from 4-year degree-granting institutions and above only. Salary outlays and fringe benefits were also collected for full-time instructional staff on 9/10- and 11/12-month contracts/teaching periods. This section was applicable to degree-granting institutions unless exempt (i.e., unless they met one of the following exclusions: all instructional faculty were part time, all contributed their services, all were in the military, or all taught preclinical or clinical medicine).

Between 1966–67 and 1985–86, this survey differed from other HEGIS surveys in that imputations were not made for nonrespondents. Thus, there is some possibility that the salary averages presented in this report may differ from the results of a complete enumeration of all colleges and universities. Beginning with the surveys for 1987–88, the IPEDS data tabulation procedures included imputations for survey nonrespondents. The unweighted response rate for the 2008–09 Salaries survey section was 99.9 percent. The response rate for the 2009–10 Salaries section was 100.0 percent (4,453 of the 4,455 required institutions responded), and the response rate for 2010–11 was 99.9 percent (4,561 of the 4,565 required institutions responded). Imputation methods for the 2010–11 Salaries survey section are discussed in *Employees in Postsecondary Institutions, Fall 2010, and Salaries of Full-Time Instructional Staff, 2010–11* (https://nces.ed.gov/pubs2012/2012276.pdf).

Further information on the Human Resources component may be obtained from

Samuel Barbett
Postsecondary Branch
Administrative Data Division
National Center for Education Statistics
550 12th Street SW
Washington, DC 20202
samuel.barbett@ed.gov
https://nces.ed.gov/ipeds/

Library Statistics

In the past, NCES collected library data through the Public Libraries Survey (PLS), the State Library Agencies (StLA) Survey, the Academic Libraries Survey (ALS), and the Library Media Centers (LMC) Survey. On October 1,

2007, the administration of the Public Libraries Survey (PLS) and the State Library Agencies (StLA) Survey was transferred to the Institute of Museum and Library Services (IMLS) (see below).

NCES administered the Academic Libraries Survey (ALS) on a 3-year cycle between 1966 and 1988. From 1988 through 1999, ALS was a component of the Integrated Post-secondary Education Data System (IPEDS) and was on a 2-year cycle. Beginning in the year 2000, ALS began collecting data independent of the IPEDS data collection while remaining on a 2-year cycle. ALS provided data on approximately 3,700 academic libraries. In aggregate, these data provided an overview of the status of academic libraries nationally and statewide. The survey collected data on the libraries in the entire universe of degree-granting institutions. Beginning with the collection of FY 2000 data, ALS changed to web-based data collection. ALS produced descriptive statistics on academic libraries in postsecondary institutions in the 50 states, the District of Columbia, and the outlying areas. *Academic Libraries: 2012* (NCES 2014-038) presented tabulations for the 2012 survey. In 2014, ALS was reincorporated into the IPEDS collection. Since then, it has been collected annually, as the Academic Libraries component, in the IPEDS spring data collection.

School library data were collected on the School and Principal Surveys of the 1990–91 Schools and Staffing Survey (SASS). The School Library Media Centers (LMC) Survey became a component of SASS with the 1993–94 administration of the survey. Thus, readers should refer to the section on the Schools and Staffing Survey, below, regarding data on school libraries. Data for the 2011–12 LMC Survey are available on the NCES website at https://nces.ed.gov/surveys/sass/index.asp.

Further information on library statistics may be obtained from

Tara Lawley
Postsecondary Branch
Administrative Data Division
National Center for Education Statistics
550 12th Street SW
Washington, DC 20202
tara.lawley@ed.gov
https://nces.ed.gov/surveys/libraries/

National Adult Literacy Survey

The National Adult Literacy Survey (NALS), funded by the U.S. Department of Education and 12 states, was created in 1992 as a new measure of literacy. The aim of the survey was to profile the English literacy of adults in the United States based on their performance across a wide array of tasks that reflect the types of materials and demands they encounter in their daily lives.

To gather information on adults' literacy skills, trained staff interviewed a nationally representative sample of nearly 13,600 individuals ages 16 and over during the first

8 months of 1992. These participants had been randomly selected to represent the adult population in the country as a whole. Black and Hispanic households were oversampled to ensure reliable estimates of literacy proficiencies and to permit analyses of the performance of these subpopulations. In addition, some 1,100 inmates from 80 federal and state prisons were interviewed to gather information on the proficiencies of the prison population. In total, nearly 26,000 adults were surveyed.

Each survey participant was asked to spend approximately an hour responding to a series of diverse literacy tasks, as well as to questions about his or her demographic characteristics, educational background, reading practices, and other areas related to literacy. Based on their responses to the survey tasks, adults received proficiency scores along three scales that reflect varying degrees of skill in prose, document, and quantitative literacy. The results of the 1992 survey were first published in *Adult Literacy in America: A First Look at the Findings of the National Adult Literacy Survey* (NCES 93-275), in September 1993. See the section on the National Assessment of Adult Literacy (below) for information on later adult literacy surveys.

Further information on NALS may be obtained from

Emmanuel Sikali
Reporting and Dissemination Branch
Assessments Division
National Center for Education Statistics
550 12th Street SW
Washington, DC 20202
emmanuel.sikali@ed.gov
https://nces.ed.gov/naal/nals_products.asp

National Assessment of Adult Literacy

The 2003 National Assessment of Adult Literacy (NAAL) was conducted to measure both English literacy and health literacy. The assessment was administered to 19,000 adults (including 1,200 prison inmates) age 16 and over in all 50 states and the District of Columbia. Components of the assessment included a background questionnaire; a prison component that assesses the literacy skills of adults in federal and state prisons; the State Assessment of Adult Literacy (SAAL), a voluntary survey given in conjunction with NAAL; a health literacy component; the Fluency Addition to NAAL (FAN), an oral reading assessment; and the Adult Literacy Supplemental Assessment (ALSA). ALSA is an alternative to the main NAAL for those with very low scores on seven core screening questions. NAAL assesses literacy directly through the completion of tasks that covered quantitative literacy, document literacy, and prose literacy. Results were reported using the following achievement levels: *Below Basic, Basic, Intermediate*, and *Proficien* .

Results from NAAL and NALS can be compared. NALS offers a snapshot of the condition of literacy of the U.S.

population as a whole and among key population subgroups in 1992. NAAL provides a picture of adult literacy skills in 2003, revealing changes in literacy over the intervening decade.

Further information on NAAL may be obtained from

Emmanuel Sikali
Reporting and Dissemination Branch
Assessments Division
National Center for Education Statistics
550 12th Street SW
Washington, DC 20202
emmanuel.sikali@ed.gov
https://nces.ed.gov/naal/

National Assessment of Educational Progress

The National Assessment of Educational Progress (NAEP) is a series of cross-sectional studies initially implemented in 1969 to assess the educational achievement of U.S. students and monitor changes in those achievements. In the main national NAEP, a nationally representative sample of students is assessed at grades 4, 8, and 12 in various academic subjects. The assessment is based on frameworks developed by the National Assessment Governing Board (NAGB). It includes both multiple-choice items and constructed-response items (those requiring written answers). Results are reported in two ways: by average score and by achievement level. Average scores are reported for the nation, for participating states and jurisdictions, and for subgroups of the population. Percentages of students performing at or above three achievement levels (*Basic*, *Proficien*, and *Advanced*) are also reported for these groups.

Main NAEP Assessments

From 1990 until 2001, main NAEP was conducted for states and other jurisdictions that chose to participate. In 2002, under the provisions of the No Child Left Behind Act of 2001, all states began to participate in main NAEP, and an aggregate of all state samples replaced the separate national sample. (School district-level assessments—under the Trial Urban District Assessment [TUDA] program—also began in 2002.)

Results are available for the mathematics assessments administered in 1990, 1992, 1996, 2000, 2003, 2005, 2007, 2009, 2011, 2013, 2015, 2017, and 2019. In 2005, NAGB called for the development of a new mathematics framework. The revisions made to the mathematics framework for the 2005 assessment were intended to reflect recent curricular emphases and better assess the specific objectives for students at each grade level.

The revised mathematics framework focuses on two dimensions: mathematical content and cognitive demand. By considering these two dimensions for each item in the assessment, the framework ensures that NAEP assesses an appropriate balance of content, as well as a variety of ways of knowing and doing mathematics.

Since the 2005 changes to the mathematics framework were minimal for grades 4 and 8, comparisons over time can be made between assessments conducted before and after the framework's implementation for these grades. The changes that the 2005 framework made to the grade 12 assessment, however, were too drastic to allow grade 12 results from before and after implementation to be directly compared. These changes included adding more questions on algebra, data analysis, and probability to reflect changes in high school mathematics standards and coursework; merging the measurement and geometry content areas; and changing the reporting scale from 0–500 to 0–300. For more information regarding the 2005 mathematics framework revisions, see https://nces.ed.gov/nationsreportcard/mathematics/frameworkcomparison.asp.

Results are available for the reading assessments administered in 1992, 1994, 1998, 2000, 2002, 2003, 2005, 2007, 2009, 2011, 2013, 2015, 2017, and 2019. In 2009, a new framework was developed for the 4th-, 8th-, and 12th-grade NAEP reading assessments.

Both a content alignment study and a reading trend, or bridge, study were conducted to determine whether the new reading assessment was comparable to the prior assessment. Overall, the results of the special analyses suggested that the assessments were similar in terms of their item and scale characteristics and the results they produced for important demographic groups of students. Thus, it was determined that the results of the 2009 reading assessment could still be compared to those from earlier assessment years, thereby maintaining the trend lines first established in 1992. For more information regarding the 2009 reading framework revisions, see https://nces.ed.gov/nationsreportcard/reading/whatmeasure.asp.

In spring 2013, NAEP released results from the NAEP 2012 economics assessment in *The Nation's Report Card: Economics 2012* (NCES 2013-453). First administered in 2006, the NAEP economics assessment measures 12th-graders' understanding of a wide range of topics in three main content areas: market economy, national economy, and international economy. The 2012 assessment is based on a nationally representative sample of nearly 11,000 students in the 12th grade.

In *The Nation's Report Card: A First Look—2013 Mathematics and Reading* (NCES 2014-451), NAEP released the results of the 2013 mathematics and reading assessments. Results can also be accessed using the interactive graphics and downloadable data available at the online Nation's Report Card website (https://nationsreportcard.gov/reading_math_2013/).

The Nation's Report Card: A First Look—2013 Mathematics and Reading Trial Urban District Assessment (NCES 2014-466) provides the results of the 2013 mathematics and reading TUDA, which measured the reading and mathematics progress of 4th- and 8th-graders from 21 urban school districts. Results from the 2013 mathematics and reading

TUDA can also be accessed using the interactive graphics and downloadable data available at the online TUDA website (https://nationsreportcard.gov/reading_math_tuda_2013/).

The online interactive report *The Nation's Report Card: 2014 U.S. History, Geography, and Civics at Grade 8* (NCES 2015-112) provides grade 8 results for the 2014 NAEP U.S. history, geography, and civics assessments. Trend results for previous assessment years in these three subjects, as well as information on school and student participation rates and sample tasks and student responses, are also presented.

In 2014, the first administration of the NAEP Technology and Engineering Literacy (TEL) Assessment asked 8th-graders to respond to questions aimed at assessing their knowledge and skill in understanding technological principles, solving technology and engineering-related problems, and using technology to communicate and collaborate. The online report *The Nation's Report Card: Technology and Engineering Literacy* (NCES 2016-119) presents national results for 8th-graders on the TEL assessment.

The Nation's Report Card: 2015 Mathematics and Reading Assessments (NCES 2015-136) is an online interactive report that presents national and state results for 4th- and 8th-graders on the NAEP 2015 mathematics and reading assessments. The report also presents TUDA results in mathematics and reading for 4th- and 8th-graders. The online interactive report *The Nation's Report Card: 2015 Mathematics and Reading at Grade 12* (NCES 2016-018) presents grade 12 results from the NAEP 2015 mathematics and reading assessments.

Results from the 2015 NAEP science assessment are presented in the online report *The Nation's Report Card: 2015 Science at Grades 4, 8, and 12* (NCES 2016-162). The assessment measures the knowledge of 4th-, 8th-, and 12th-graders in the content areas of physical science, life science, and Earth and space sciences, as well as their understanding of four science practices (identifying science principles, using science principles, using scientific inquiry, and using technological design). National results are reported for grades 4, 8, and 12, and results from 46 participating states and one jurisdiction are reported for grades 4 and 8. Since a new NAEP science framework was introduced in 2009, results from the 2015 science assessment can be compared to results from the 2009 and 2011 science assessments, but cannot be compared to the science assessments conducted prior to 2009.

As a consequence of NAEP's transition from paper-based assessments to technology-based assessments, data were needed regarding students' access to and familiarity with technology, at home and at school. The Computer Access and Familiarity Study (CAFS) was designed to fulfill this need. CAFS was conducted as part of the main administration of the 2015 NAEP. A subset of the grade 4, 8, and 12 students who took the main NAEP were chosen to take the additional CAFS questionnaire. The main 2015 NAEP was administered in a paper-and-pencil format to some students and a digital-based format to others, and CAFS participants were given questionnaires in the same format as their NAEP questionnaires.

The online Highlights report *2017 NAEP Mathematics and Reading Assessments: Highlighted Results at Grades 4 and 8 for the Nation, States, and Districts* (NCES 2018-037) presents an overview of results from the NAEP 2017 mathematics and reading reports. Highlighted results include key findings for the nation, states/jurisdictions, and 27 districts that participated in the Trial Urban District Assessment (TUDA) in mathematics and reading at grades 4 and 8.

Results from the NAEP 2018 TEL Assessment are contained in the online report *The Nation's Report Card: Highlighted Results for the 2018 Technology and Engineering Literacy (TEL) Assessment at Grade 8* (NCES 2019-068). The digitally based assessment (participants took the assessment via laptop) was taken by approximately 15,400 eighth-graders from about 600 schools across the nation. Results were reported in terms of average scale scores (on a 0 to 300 scale) and in relation to the NAEP achievement levels NAEP Basic, NAEP Proficient, and NAEP Advanced.

The online reports *2019 NAEP Reading Assessment: Highlighted Results at Grades 4 and 8 for the Nation, States, and Districts and 2019 NAEP Mathematics Assessment: Highlighted Results at Grades 4 and 8 for the Nation, States, and Districts* (NCES 2020-012) present overviews of results from the NAEP 2019 reading and mathematics reports. Highlighted results include key findings for the nation, states/jurisdictions, and 27 districts that participated in the Trial Urban District Assessment (TUDA) in mathematics and reading at grades 4 and 8.

NAEP Long-Term Trend Assessments

In addition to conducting the main assessments, NAEP also conducts the long-term trend assessments. Long-term trend assessments provide an opportunity to observe educational progress in reading and mathematics of 9-, 13-, and 17-year-olds since the early 1970s. The long-term trend reading assessment measures students' reading comprehension skills using an array of passages that vary by text types and length. The assessment was designed to measure students' ability to locate specific information in the text provided; make inferences across a passage to provide an explanation; and identify the main idea in the text.

The NAEP long-term trend assessment in mathematics measures knowledge of mathematical facts; ability to carry out computations using paper and pencil; knowledge of basic formulas, such as those applied in geometric settings; and ability to apply mathematics to skills of daily life, such as those involving time and money.

The Nation's Report Card: Trends in Academic Progress 2012 (NCES 2013-456) provides the results of 12 long-term trend reading assessments dating back to 1971 and 11 long-term trend mathematics assessments dating back to 1973.

Further information on NAEP may be obtained from

Daniel McGrath
Reporting and Dissemination Branch
Assessments Division
National Center for Education Statistics
550 12th Street SW
Washington, DC 20202
daniel.mcgrath@ed.gov
https://nces.ed.gov/nationsreportcard

National Education Longitudinal Study of 1988

The National Education Longitudinal Study of 1988 (NELS:88) was the third major secondary school student longitudinal study conducted by NCES. The two studies that preceded NELS:88—the National Longitudinal Study of the High School Class of 1972 (NLS:72) and the High School and Beyond Longitudinal Study (HS&B) in 1980—surveyed high school seniors (and sophomores in HS&B) through high school, postsecondary education, and work and family formation experiences. Unlike its predecessors, NELS:88 began with a cohort of 8th-grade students. In 1988, some 25,000 8th-graders, their parents, their teachers, and their school principals were surveyed. Follow-ups were conducted in 1990 and 1992, when a majority of these students were in the 10th and 12th grades, respectively, and then 2 years after their scheduled high school graduation, in 1994. A fourth follow-up was conducted in 2000.

NELS:88 was designed to provide trend data about critical transitions experienced by young people as they develop, attend school, and embark on their careers. It complements and strengthens state and local efforts by furnishing new information on how school policies, teacher practices, and family involvement affect student educational outcomes (i.e., academic achievement, persistence in school, and participation in postsecondary education). For the base year, NELS:88 included a multifaceted student questionnaire, four cognitive tests, a parent questionnaire, a teacher questionnaire, and a school questionnaire.

In 1990, when most of the students were in 10th grade, students, their teachers, and their school principals, as well as school dropouts, were surveyed. (Parents were not surveyed in the 1990 follow-up.) In 1992, when most of the students were in 12th grade, the second follow-up conducted surveys of students, dropouts, parents, teachers, and school principals. Also, information from the students' transcripts was collected. The 1994 survey data were collected when most sample members had completed high school. The primary goals of the 1994 survey were (1) to provide data for trend comparisons with NLS:72 and HS&B; (2) to address issues of employment and postsecondary access and choice; and (3) to ascertain how many dropouts had returned to school and by what route. The 2000 follow-up examined the educational and labor market outcomes of the 1988 cohort at a time of transition. Most had been out of high school for 8 years; many had completed their postsecondary educations, were embarking on first or even second careers, and were starting families. For those who had attended postsecondary institutions after high school, student transcript data were collected from the institutions attended.

Further information on NELS:88 may be obtained from

Elise Christopher
Longitudinal Surveys Branch
Sample Surveys Division
National Center for Education Statistics
550 12th Street SW
Washington, DC 20202
elise.christopher@ed.gov
https://nces.ed.gov/surveys/nels88

National Household Education Surveys Program

The National Household Education Surveys Program (NHES) is a data collection system that is designed to address a wide range of education-related issues. Surveys have been conducted in 1991, 1993, 1995, 1996, 1999, 2001, 2003, 2005, 2007, 2012, and 2016. NHES targets specific populations for detailed data collection. It is intended to provide more detailed data on the topics and populations of interest than are collected through supplements to other household surveys.

The 2007 and earlier administrations of NHES used a random-digit-dial sample of landline phones and computer-assisted telephone interviewing to conduct interviews. However, due to declining response rates for all telephone surveys and the increase in households that only or mostly use a cell phone instead of a landline, the data collection method was changed to an address-based sample survey for NHES:2012. Because of this change in survey mode, readers should use caution when comparing NHES:2012 estimates to those of prior NHES administrations.

The topics addressed by NHES:1991 were early childhood education and adult education. About 60,000 households were screened for NHES:1991. In the Early Childhood Education Survey, about 14,000 parents/guardians of 3- to 8-year-olds completed interviews about their children's early educational experiences. Included in this component were participation in nonparental care/education; care arrangements and school; and family, household, and child characteristics. In the NHES:1991 Adult Education Survey, about 9,800 people 16 years of age and over, identified as having participated in an adult education activity in the previous 12 months, were questioned about their activities. Data were collected on programs and up to four courses, including the subject matter, duration, sponsorship, purpose, and cost. Information on the household and the adult's background and current employment was also collected.

In NHES:1993, nearly 64,000 households were screened. Approximately 11,000 parents of 3- to 7-year-olds completed interviews for the School Readiness Survey. Topics included the developmental characteristics of preschoolers; school adjustment and teacher feedback to parents for kindergartners and primary students; center-based program participation; early school experiences; home activities with family members; and health status. In the School Safety and Discipline Survey, about 12,700 parents of children in grades 3 to 12 and about 6,500 youth in grades 6 to 12 were interviewed about their school experiences. Topics included the school learning environment, discipline policy, safety at school, victimization, the availability and use of alcohol/drugs, and alcohol/drug education. Peer norms for behavior in school and substance use were also included in this topical component. Extensive family and household background information was collected, as well as characteristics of the school attended by the child.

In NHES:1995, the Early Childhood Program Participation Survey and the Adult Education Survey were similar to those fielded in 1991. In the Early Childhood component, about 14,000 parents of children from birth to 3rd grade were interviewed out of 16,000 sampled, for a completion rate of 90.4 percent. In the Adult Education Survey, about 24,000 adults were sampled and 82.3 percent (20,000) completed the interview.

NHES:1996 covered parent and family involvement in education and civic involvement. Data on homeschooling and school choice also were collected. The 1996 survey screened about 56,000 households. For the Parent and Family Involvement in Education Survey, nearly 21,000 parents of children in grades 3 to 12 were interviewed. For the Civic Involvement Survey, about 8,000 youth in grades 6 to 12, about 9,000 parents, and about 2,000 adults were interviewed. The 1996 survey also addressed public library use. Adults in almost 55,000 households were interviewed to support state-level estimates of household public library use.

NHES:1999 collected end-of-decade estimates of key indicators from the surveys conducted throughout the 1990s. Approximately 60,000 households were screened for a total of about 31,000 interviews with parents of children from birth through grade 12 (including about 6,900 infants, toddlers, and preschoolers) and adults age 16 or older not enrolled in grade 12 or below. Key indicators included participation of children in nonparental care and early childhood programs, school experiences, parent/family involvement in education at home and at school, youth community service activities, plans for future education, and adult participation in educational activities and community service.

NHES:2001 included two surveys that were largely repeats of similar surveys included in earlier NHES collections. The Early Childhood Program Participation Survey was similar in content to the Early Childhood Program Participation Survey fielded as part of NHES:1995, and the

Adult Education and Lifelong Learning Survey was similar in content to the Adult Education Survey of NHES:1995. The Before- and After-School Programs and Activities Survey, while containing items fielded in earlier NHES collections, had a number of new items that collected information about what school-age children were doing during the time they spent in child care or in other activities, what parents were looking for in care arrangements and activities, and parent evaluations of care arrangements and activities. Parents of approximately 6,700 children from birth through age 6 who were not yet in kindergarten completed Early Childhood Program Participation Survey interviews. Nearly 10,900 adults completed Adult Education and Lifelong Learning Survey interviews, and parents of nearly 9,600 children in kindergarten through grade 8 completed Before- and After-School Programs and Activities Survey interviews.

NHES:2003 included two surveys: the Parent and Family Involvement in Education Survey and the Adult Education for Work-Related Reasons Survey (the first administration). Whereas previous adult education surveys were more general in scope, this survey had a narrower focus on occupation-related adult education programs. It collected in-depth information about training and education in which adults participated specifically for work-related reasons, either to prepare for work or a career or to maintain or improve work-related skills and knowledge they already had. The Parent and Family Involvement Survey expanded on the first survey fielded on this topic in 1996. In 2003, screeners were completed with 32,050 households. About 12,700 of the 16,000 sampled adults completed the Adult Education for Work-Related Reasons Survey, for a weighted response rate of 76 percent. For the Parent and Family Involvement in Education Survey, interviews were completed by the parents of about 12,400 of the 14,900 sampled children in kindergarten through grade 12, yielding a weighted unit response rate of 83 percent.

NHES:2005 included surveys that covered adult education, early childhood program participation, and after-school programs and activities. Data were collected from about 8,900 adults for the Adult Education Survey, from parents of about 7,200 children for the Early Childhood Program Participation Survey, and from parents of nearly 11,700 children for the After-School Programs and Activities Survey. These surveys were substantially similar to the surveys conducted in 2001, with the exceptions that the Adult Education Survey addressed a new topic—informal learning activities for personal interest—and the Early Childhood Program Participation Survey and After-School Programs and Activities Survey did not collect information about before-school care for school-age children.

NHES:2007 fielded the Parent and Family Involvement in Education Survey and the School Readiness Survey. These surveys were similar in design and content to surveys included in the 2003 and 1993 collections, respectively. New features added to the Parent and Family Involvement

Survey were questions about supplemental education services provided by schools and school districts (including use of and satisfaction with such services), as well as questions that would efficiently identify the school attended by the sampled students. New features added to the School Readiness Survey were questions that collected details about TV programs watched by the sampled children. For the Parent and Family Involvement Survey, interviews were completed with parents of 10,680 sampled children in kindergarten through grade 12, including 10,370 students enrolled in public or private schools and 310 homeschooled children. For the School Readiness Survey, interviews were completed with parents of 2,630 sampled children ages 3 to 6 and not yet in kindergarten. Parents who were interviewed about children in kindergarten through 2nd grade for the Parent and Family Involvement Survey were also asked some questions about these children's school readiness.

NHES:2012 included the Parent and Family Involvement in Education Survey and the Early Childhood Program Participation Survey. The Parent and Family Involvement in Education Survey gathered data on students age 20 or younger who were enrolled in kindergarten through grade 12 or who were homeschooled at equivalent grade levels. Survey questions that pertained to students enrolled in kindergarten through grade 12 requested information on various aspects of parent involvement in education (such as help with homework, family activities, and parent involvement at school) and survey questions pertaining to homeschooled students requested information on the student's homeschooling experiences, the sources of the curriculum, and the reasons for homeschooling.

The 2012 Parent and Family Involvement in Education Survey questionnaires were completed for 17,563 (397 homeschooled and 17,166 enrolled) children, for a weighted unit response rate of 78.4 percent. The overall estimated unit response rate (the product of the screener unit response rate of 73.8 percent and the Parent and Family Involvement in Education Survey unit response rate) was 57.8 percent.

The 2012 Early Childhood Program Participation Survey collected data on the early care and education arrangements and early learning of children from birth through the age of 5 who were not yet enrolled in kindergarten. Questionnaires were completed for 7,893 children, for a weighted unit response rate of 78.7 percent. The overall estimated weighted unit response rate (the product of the screener weighted unit response rate of 73.8 percent and the Early Childhood Program Participation Survey unit weighted response rate) was 58.1 percent.

NHES:2016 used a nationally representative address-based sample covering the 50 states and the District of Columbia. The 2016 administration of NHES included a screener survey and three topical surveys: The Parent and Family Involvement in Education Survey, the Early Childhood Program Participation Survey, and the Adult Training and Education Survey. The screener survey questionnaire identified households with children under age 20 and adults ages 16 to 65. A total of 206,000 households were selected based on this screener, and the screener response rate was 66.4 percent. All sampled households received initial contact by mail. Although the majority of respondents completed paper questionnaires, a small sample of cases was part of a web experiment with mailed invitations to complete the survey online.

The 2016 Parent and Family Involvement in Education Survey, like its predecessor in 2012, gathered data about students age 20 or under who were enrolled in kindergarten through grade 12 or who were being homeschooled for the equivalent grades. The 2016 survey's questions also covered aspects of parental involvement in education similar to those in the 2012 survey. The total number of completed questionnaires in the 2016 survey was 14,075 (13,523 enrolled and 552 homeschooled children), representing a population of 53.2 million students either homeschooled or enrolled in a public or private school in 2015–16. The survey's weighted unit response rate was 74.3 percent, and the overall response rate was 49.3 percent.

The 2016 Early Childhood Program Participation Survey collected data about children from birth through age 6 who were not yet enrolled in kindergarten. The survey asked about children's participation in relative care, nonrelative care, and center-based care arrangements. It also requested information such as the main reason for choosing care, factors that were important to parents when choosing a care arrangement, the primary barriers to finding satisfactory care, activities the family does with the child, and what the child is learning. Questionnaires were completed for 5,844 children, representing a population of 21.4 million children from birth through age 6 who were not yet enrolled in kindergarten. The Early Childhood Program Participation Survey weighted unit response rate was 73.4 percent and the overall estimated weighted unit response rate (the product of the screener weighted unit response rate and the Early Childhood Program Participation Survey weighted unit response rate) was 48.7 percent.

The third topical survey of NHES:2016 was a new NHES survey, the Adult Training and Education Survey. The survey collected information from noninstitutionalized adults ages 16 to 65 not enrolled in high school—it also collected information from adults living at residential addresses associated with educational institutions such as colleges (thus, it collected information from enrolled college students). One of the main goals of the Adult Training and Education Survey is to capture the prevalence of nondegree credentials, including estimates of adults with occupational certifications or licenses, as well as to capture the prevalence of postsecondary educational certificates. A further goal is to learn more about work experience programs. The survey's data, when weighted, were nationally representative of noninstitutionalized adults ages 16 to 65, not enrolled in grades 12 or below. The total number of completed questionnaires was 47,744, representing a population of 196.3 million. The survey had a weighted response rate of 73.1 percent and an overall response rate of 48.5 percent.

Data for the three topical surveys in the 2016 administration of NHES are available in *Parent and Family*

Involvement in Education: Results From the National Household Education Surveys Program of 2016 (NCES 2017-102); *Early Childhood Program Participation, Results From the National Household Education Surveys Program of 2016* (NCES 2017-101); and *Adult Training and Education: Results From the National Household Education Surveys Program of 2016* (NCES 2017-103rev). In addition, public-use data for the three 2016 surveys are available at https://nces.ed.gov/nhes/dataproducts.asp.

Further information on NHES may be obtained from

Sarah Grady
Andrew Zukerberg
Sample Surveys Division
National Center for Education Statistics
550 12th Street SW
Washington, DC 20202
sarah.grady@ed.gov
andrew.zukerberg@ed.gov
https://nces.ed.gov/nhes/

National Longitudinal Study of the High School Class of 1972

The National Longitudinal Study of the High School Class of 1972 (NLS:72) began with the collection of base-year survey data from a sample of about 19,000 high school seniors in the spring of 1972. In each of the years 1973, 1974, 1976, 1979, and 1986, a follow-up survey of these students was conducted. NLS:72 was designed to provide the education community with information on the transitions of young adults from high school through postsecondary education and the workplace.

In addition to the follow-ups, a number of supplemental data collection efforts were made. For example, a Post-secondary Education Transcript Study (PETS) was conducted in 1984; in 1986, the fifth follow-up included a supplement for those who became teachers.

The sample design for NLS:72 was a stratified, two-stage probability sample of 12th-grade students from all schools, public and private, in the 50 states and the District of Columbia during the 1971–72 school year. During the first stage of sampling, about 1,070 schools were selected for participation in the base-year survey. As many as 18 students were selected at random from each of the sample schools. The sizes of both the school and student samples were increased during the first follow-up survey. Beginning with the first follow-up and continuing through the fourth follow-up, about 1,300 schools participated in the survey and slightly fewer than 23,500 students were sampled. The unweighted response rates for each of the different rounds of data collection were 80 percent or higher.

Sample retention rates across the survey years were quite high. For example, of the individuals responding to the base-year questionnaire, the percentages who responded to the first, second, third, and fourth follow-up questionnaires were about 94, 93, 89, and 83 percent, respectively. The fifth follow-up took its sample from students who had participated in at least one of the prior surveys. In all, 91.7 percent of participants had responded to at least five of the six surveys, and 62.1 percent had responded to all six.

Further information on NLS:72 may be obtained from

Aurora D'Amico
Longitudinal Surveys Branch
Sample Surveys Division
National Center for Education Statistics
550 12th Street SW
Washington, DC 20202
aurora.damico@ed.gov
https://nces.ed.gov/surveys/nls72/

National Postsecondary Student Aid Study

The National Postsecondary Student Aid Study (NPSAS) is a comprehensive nationwide study of how students and their families pay for postsecondary education. Data gathered from the study are used to help guide future federal student financial aid policy. The study is conducted with nationally representative samples of undergraduates, graduates, and first-professional students in the 50 states, the District of Columbia, and Puerto Rico, including students attending less-than-2-year institutions, community colleges, and 4-year colleges and universities. Participants include both students who receive financial aid and those who do not. Since NPSAS identifies nationally representative samples of student subpopulations of interest to policymakers and obtains baseline data for longitudinal study of these subpopulations, data from the study provide the base-year sample for the Beginning Postsecondary Students Longitudinal Study (BPS) and the Baccalaureate and Beyond Longitudinal Study (B&B).

Originally, NPSAS was conducted every 3 years. Beginning with the 1999–2000 study (NPSAS:2000), NPSAS has been conducted every 4 years. NPSAS:08 included a new set of instrument items to obtain baseline measures of the awareness of two new federal grants introduced in 2006: the Academic Competitiveness Grant (ACG) and the National Science and Mathematics Access to Retain Talent (SMART) grant.

The first NPSAS (NPSAS:87) was conducted during the 1986–87 school year. Data were gathered from about 1,100 colleges, universities, and other postsecondary institutions; 60,000 students; and 14,000 parents. These data provided information on the cost of postsecondary education, the distribution of financial aid, and the characteristics of both aided and nonaided students and their families.

NPSAS:90 included a stratified sample of approximately 69,000 eligible students (about 47,000 of whom were undergraduates) from about 1,100 institutions. For each of the students included in the NPSAS sample, there were up to three sources of data. First, institution registration and financial aid records were extracted. Second, a Computer Assisted

Telephone Interview (CATI) designed for each student was conducted. Finally, a CATI designed for the parents or guardians of a subsample of students was conducted. The purpose of the parent survey was to obtain detailed information on the family and economic characteristics of dependent students who did not receive financial aid, especially first-time, first-year students. In keeping with this purpose, parents of financially independent students who were over 30 years of age and parents of graduate/first-professional students were excluded from the sample. Data from these three sources were synthesized into a single system with an overall response rate of 89 percent.

For NPSAS:93, information on 77,000 undergraduates and graduate students enrolled during the school year was collected at 1,000 postsecondary institutions. The sample included students who were enrolled at any time between July 1, 1992, and June 30, 1993. About 66,000 students and a subsample of their parents were interviewed by telephone. NPSAS:96 contained information on more than 48,000 undergraduate and graduate students from about 1,000 postsecondary institutions who were enrolled at any time during the 1995–96 school year. NPSAS:2000 included nearly 62,000 students (50,000 undergraduates and almost 12,000 graduate students) from 1,000 postsecondary institutions. NPSAS:04 collected data on about 80,000 undergraduates and 11,000 graduate students from 1,400 postsecondary institutions. For NPSAS:08, about 114,000 undergraduate students and 14,000 graduate students who were enrolled in postsecondary education during the 2007–08 school year were selected from more than 1,730 postsecondary institutions.

NPSAS:12 sampled about 95,000 undergraduates and 16,000 graduate students from approximately 1,500 postsecondary institutions.

NPSAS:16 sampled about 89,000 undergraduate and 24,000 graduate students attending approximately 1,800 Title IV eligible postsecondary institutions in the 50 states, the District of Columbia, and Puerto Rico. The sample represents approximately 20 million undergraduate and 4 million graduate students enrolled in postsecondary education at Title IV eligible institutions at any time between July 1, 2015, and June 30, 2016. Public access to the data is available online through PowerStats (http://nces.ed.gov/datalab/).

Further information on NPSAS may be obtained from

Aurora D'Amico
Tracy Hunt-White
Longitudinal Surveys Branch
Sample Surveys Division
National Center for Education Statistics
550 12th Street SW
Washington, DC 20202
aurora.damico@ed.gov
tracy.hunt-white@ed.gov
https://nces.ed.gov/surveys/npsas/

National Study of Postsecondary Faculty

The National Study of Postsecondary Faculty (NSOPF) was designed to provide data about faculty to postsecondary researchers, planners, and policymakers. NSOPF is the most comprehensive study of faculty in postsecondary education institutions ever undertaken.

The first cycle of NSOPF (NSOPF:88) was conducted by NCES with support from the National Endowment for the Humanities (NEH) in 1987–88 with a sample of 480 colleges and universities, over 3,000 department chairpersons, and over 11,000 instructional faculty. The second cycle of NSOPF (NSOPF:93) was conducted by NCES with support from NEH and the National Science Foundation in 1992–93. NSOPF:93 was limited to surveys of institutions and faculty, but with a substantially expanded sample of 970 colleges and universities and 31,350 faculty and instructional staff. The third cycle, NSPOF:99, included 960 degree-granting postsecondary institutions and approximately 18,000 faculty and instructional staff. The fourth cycle of NSOPF was conducted in 2003–04 and included 1,080 degree-granting postsecondary institutions and approximately 26,000 faculty and instructional staff.

There are no plans to repeat the study. Rather, NCES plans to provide technical assistance to state postsecondary data systems and to encourage the development of robust connections between faculty and student data systems so that key questions concerning faculty, instruction, and student outcomes—such as persistence and completion—can be addressed.

Further information on NSOPF may be obtained from

Aurora D'Amico
Longitudinal Surveys Branch
Sample Surveys Division
National Center for Education Statistics
550 12th Street SW
Washington, DC 20202
aurora.damico@ed.gov
https://nces.ed.gov/surveys/nsopf/

National Teacher and Principal Survey

The National Teacher and Principal Survey (NTPS) is a set of related questionnaires that collect descriptive data on the context of elementary and secondary education. Data reported by schools, principals, and teachers provide a variety of statistics on the condition of education in the United States that may be used by policymakers and the general public. The NTPS system covers a wide range of topics, including teacher demand, teacher and principal characteristics, teachers' and principals' perceptions of school climate and problems in their schools, teacher and principal compensation, general conditions in schools, and basic characteristics of the student population.

The NTPS is a redesign of the Schools and Staffing Survey (SASS), which was conducted from the 1987–88 school year to the 2011–12 school year. Although the NTPS maintains the SASS survey's focus on schools, teachers, and administrators, the NTPS has a different structure and sample than SASS. In addition, whereas SASS operated on a 4-year survey cycle, the NTPS operates on a 2- or 3-year survey cycle. The NTPS universe of schools is confined to the 50 states plus the District of Columbia. It excludes the Department of Defense dependents schools overseas, schools in U.S. territories overseas, and CCD schools that do not offer teacher-provided classroom instruction in grades 1–12 or the ungraded equivalent. Bureau of Indian Education schools are included in the NTPS universe, but these schools were not oversampled and the data do not support separate BIE estimates.

The NTPS includes three key components: school questionnaires, principal questionnaires, and teacher questionnaires. NTPS data are collected by the U.S. Census Bureau through mail and online questionnaires with telephone and in-person field follow-up. The school and principal questionnaires were sent to sampled schools, and the teacher questionnaire was sent to a sample of teachers working at sampled schools.

The school questionnaire asks knowledgeable school staff members about grades offered, student attendance and enrollment, staffing patterns, teaching vacancies, programs and services offered, curriculum, and community service requirements. In addition, basic information is collected about the school year, including the beginning time of students' school days and the length of the school year.

The principal questionnaire collects information about principal/school head demographic characteristics, training, experience, salary, goals for the school, and judgments about school working conditions and climate. Information is also obtained on professional development opportunities for teachers and principals, teacher performance, barriers to dismissal of underperforming teachers, school climate and safety, parent/guardian participation in school events, and attitudes about educational goals and school governance.

The teacher questionnaire collects data from teachers about their current teaching assignment, workload, education history, and perceptions and attitudes about teaching. Questions are also asked about teacher preparation, induction, organization of classes, computers, and professional development.

The NTPS was first conducted during the 2015–16 school year. The school sample for the 2015–16 NTPS was based on an adjusted public school universe file from the 2013–14 Common Core of Data (CCD), a database of all the nation's public school districts and public schools. Schools outside of the United States, schools that teach only prekindergarten, kindergarten, or postsecondary students, and administrative units that do not offer teacher-provided classroom instruction were deleted from the CCD frame prior to sampling for NTPS. Public schools that closed in school year 2013–14 or were not yet opened were not included. Prior to stratification and sampling, CCD schools were collapsed to match the NTPS definition of a school. (The NTPS definition of a school is the same as the SASS definition of a school—an institution or part of an institution that provides classroom instruction to students, has one or more teachers to provide instruction, serves students in one or more of grades 1–12 or the ungraded equivalent, and is located in one or more buildings apart from a private home.)

In the 2015–16 NTPS, the school sample consisted of about 8,300 public schools; the principal sample consisted of about 8,300 public school principals; and the teacher sample consisted of about 50,000 public school teachers. Weighted unit response rates were 72.5 percent for the school survey, 71.8 percent for the principal survey, and 67.8 percent for the teacher survey.

Whereas the 2015–16 NTPS covered only schools, teachers, and principals in the public sector, the 2017–18 NTPS covered schools, teachers, and principals in both the public and private sectors. In the 2017–18 NTPS, all principals associated with sampled public and private schools were also included in the sample. Teachers associated with a selected school were sampled from a list of teachers that was provided by the school, collected from school websites, or purchased from a vendor. The selected samples included about 10,600 traditional and charter public schools and their principals, 60,000 public school teachers, 4,000 private schools and their principals, and 9,600 private school teachers.

Weighted unit response rates for the 2017–18 NTPS were 72.5 percent for the public school survey and 64.5 percent for the private school survey, 70.2 percent for the public school principal survey and 62.6 percent for the private school principal survey, and 76.9 percent for the public school teacher survey and 75.9 percent for the private school teacher survey.

General information on NTPS and electronic copies of the questionnaires are available at the NTPS home page (https://nces.ed.gov/surveys/ntps).

For additional information about the NTPS program, please contact

Maura Spiegelman
Cross-Sectional Surveys Branch
Sample Surveys Division
National Center for Education Statistics
550 12th Street SW
Washington, DC 20202
maura.spiegelman@ed.gov
https://nces.ed.gov/surveys/ntps/

Principal Follow-Up Survey

The Principal Follow-up Survey (PFS), originally a component of the Schools and Staffing Survey (SASS) and currently a component of the National Teacher and Principal Survey (NTPS), was created in order to provide attrition rates for principals in K–12 schools. It assesses, from one year to the year following, how many principals are principals at the same school, how many are principals at a different school, and how many are no longer working as principals.

The 2012–13 PFS sample consisted of schools who had returned a completed 2011–12 SASS principal questionnaire. Schools that had returned the completed SASS questionnaire were mailed the 2012–13 PFS form in March 2013. The 2012–13 PFS sample included about 7,500 public schools and 1,700 private schools; it was made up of only one survey item and had a response rate of nearly 100 percent.

The 2016–17 PFS sample consisted of schools who had returned a completed 2015–16 NTPS principal questionnaire. Schools that had returned the completed NTPS questionnaire were mailed the 2016–17 PFS form in March 2017. The 2016–17 PFS sample included about 5,700 public schools. (The 2016–17 PFS did not include private schools because these schools were not included in the 2015–16 NTPS.) The survey was made up of only one item and had a response rate of about 95 percent.

Further information on the PFS may be obtained from

Julia Merlin
Cross-Sectional Surveys Branch
Sample Surveys Division
National Center for Education Statistics
550 12th Street SW
Washington, DC 20202
julia.merlin@ed.gov
https://nces.ed.gov/surveys/ntps/overview.
 asp?OverviewType=6

Private School Universe Survey

The purposes of the Private School Universe Survey (PSS) data collection activities are (1) to build an accurate and complete list of private schools to serve as a sampling frame for NCES sample surveys of private schools and (2) to report data on the total number of private schools, teachers, and students in the survey universe. Since its inception in 1989, the survey has been conducted every 2 years. Selected findings from the 2017–18 PSS are presented in the First Look report *Characteristics of Private Schools in the United States: Results From the 2017–18 Private School Universe Survey* (NCES 2019-071).

The PSS produces data similar to that of the Common Core of Data for public schools, and can be used for public-private comparisons. The data are useful for a variety of policy- and research-relevant issues, such as the growth of religiously affiliated schools, the number of private high school graduates, the length of the school year for various private schools, and the number of private school students and teachers.

The target population for this universe survey is all private schools in the United States that meet the PSS criteria of a private school (i.e., the private school is an institution that provides instruction for any of grades K through 12, has one or more teachers to give instruction, is not administered by a public agency, and is not operated in a private home).

The survey universe is composed of schools identified from a variety of sources. The main source is a list frame initially developed for the 1989–90 PSS. The list is updated regularly by matching it with lists provided by nationwide private school associations, state departments of education, and other national guides and sources that list private schools. The other source is an area frame search in approximately 124 geographic areas, conducted by the U.S. Census Bureau.

Of the 40,302 schools included in the 2009–10 sample, 10,229 were considered as out-of-scope (not eligible for the PSS). Those not responding numbered 1,856, and those responding numbered 28,217. The unweighted response rate for the 2009–10 PSS survey was 93.8 percent.

Of the 39,325 schools included in the 2011–12 sample, 10,030 cases were considered as out-of-scope (not eligible for the PSS). A total of 26,983 private schools completed a PSS interview (15.8 percent completed online), while 2,312 schools refused to participate, resulting in an unweighted response rate of 92.1 percent.

There were 40,298 schools in the 2013–14 sample; of these, 10,659 were considered as out-of-scope (not eligible for the PSS). A total of 24,566 private schools completed a PSS interview (34.1 percent completed online), while 5,073 schools refused to participate, resulting in an unweighted response rate of 82.9 percent.

The 2015–16 PSS included 42,389 schools, of which 12,754 were considered as out-of-scope (not eligible for the PSS). A total of 22,428 private schools completed a PSS interview and 7,207 schools failed to respond, which resulted in an unweighted response rate of 75.7 percent.

Of the 43,384 schools included in the 2017–18 sample, 15,272 cases were considered as out-of-scope (not eligible for the PSS). A total of 22,895 private schools completed a PSS interview, while 5,217 schools refused to participate, resulting in an unweighted response rate of 81.4 percent.

Further information on the PSS may be obtained from

Steve Broughman
Cross-Sectional Surveys Branch
Sample Surveys Division
National Center for Education Statistics
550 12th Street SW
Washington, DC 20202
stephen.broughman@ed.gov
https://nces.ed.gov/surveys/pss/

Projections of Education Statistics

Since 1964, NCES has published projections of key statistics for elementary and secondary schools and higher education institutions. The latest report is *Projections of Education Statistics to 2028* (NCES 2020-024). The *Projections of Education Statistics* series provides national data for elementary and secondary enrollment, high school graduates, elementary and secondary teachers, expenditures for public elementary and secondary education, enrollment in postsecondary degree-granting institutions, and postsecondary degrees conferred. The report also provides state-level projections for public elementary and secondary enrollment and public high school graduates. These models are described in the report's appendix on projection methodology.

Differences between the reported and projected values are, of course, almost inevitable. In *Projections of Education Statistics to 2028*, an evaluation of past projections revealed that, at the elementary and secondary levels, projections of public school enrollments have been quite accurate: mean absolute percentage differences for enrollment in public schools ranged from 0.3 to 1.2 percent for projections from 1 to 5 years in the future, while those for teachers in public schools were 3.0 percent or less. At the higher education level, projections of enrollment have been fairly accurate: mean absolute percentage differences were reported as 5.9 percent or less for projections from 1 to 5 years into the future in *Projections of Education Statistics to 2026* (NCES 2018-019). (*Projections of Education Statistics to 2027* and *Projections of Education Statistics to 2028* did not report mean absolute percentage errors for institutions at the higher educational level because enrollment projections were calculated using a new model.)

Further information on *Projections of Education Statistics* may be obtained from

William Hussar
Annual Reports and Information Staff
National Center for Education Statistics
550 12th Street SW
Washington, DC 20202
william.hussar@ed.gov
https://nces.ed.gov/pubs2020/2020024.pdf

Recent College Graduates Study

Between 1976 and 1991, NCES conducted periodic surveys of baccalaureate and master's degree recipients 1 year after graduation with the Recent College Graduates (RCG) Study. The RCG Study—which was replaced by the Baccalaureate and Beyond Longitudinal Study (B&B) in 1993 (see listing above)—concentrated on those graduates entering the teaching profession. The study linked respondents' major field of study with outcomes such as whether the respondent entered the labor force or was seeking additional education. Labor force data collected included employment status (unemployed, employed part time, or employed full time), occupation, salary, career potential, relation to major field of study, and need for a college degree. To obtain accurate results on teachers, NCES oversampled graduates with a major in education. The last two studies oversampled education majors and increased the sampling of graduates with majors in other fields.

For each of the selected institutions, a list of graduates by major field of study was obtained, and a sample of graduates was drawn by major field of study. Graduates in certain major fields of study (e.g., education, mathematics, and physical sciences) were sampled at higher rates than were graduates in other fields. Roughly 1 year after graduation, the sample of graduates was located, contacted by mail or telephone, and asked to respond to the questionnaire.

The locating process was more detailed than that in most surveys. Nonresponse rates were directly related to the time, effort, and resources used in locating graduates, rather than to graduates' refusals to participate. Despite the difficulties in locating graduates, RCG response rates are comparable to studies that do not face problems locating their sample membership.

The 1976 study of 1974–75 college graduates was the first, and smallest, of the series. The sample consisted of about 210 institutions, of which 200 (96 percent) responded. Of the approximately 5,850 graduates in the sample, 4,350 responded, for a response rate of 79 percent.

The 1981 study was somewhat larger than the 1976 study, covering about 300 institutions and 15,850 graduates. Responses were obtained from 280 institutions, for an institutional response rate of 95 percent, and from 9,310 graduates (about 720 others were found not to meet eligibility requirements), for a response rate of 74 percent.

The 1985 study sampled about 400 colleges and 18,740 graduates, of whom 17,850 were found to be eligible. Responses were obtained from 13,200 graduates, for a response rate of 78 percent. The response rate for colleges was 98 percent. The 1987 study sampled 21,960 graduates. Responses were received from 16,880, for a response rate of nearly 80 percent.

The 1991 study sampled about 18,140 graduates of 400 bachelor's and master's degree-granting institutions, including 16,170 bachelor's degree recipients and 1,960 master's degree recipients receiving diplomas between July 1, 1989, and June 30, 1990. Random samples of graduates were selected from lists stratified by field of study. Graduates in education, mathematics, and the physical sciences were sampled at a higher rate, as were graduates of various racial/ethnic groups, to provide a sufficient number of these graduates for analysis purposes. The graduates included in the sample were selected in proportion to the institution's number of graduates. The unweighted institutional response rate was 95 percent, and the unweighted graduate response rate was 83 percent.

Further information on the RCG Study may be obtained from

Aurora D'Amico
Longitudinal Surveys Branch
Sample Surveys Division
National Center for Education Statistics
550 12th Street SW
Washington, DC 20202
aurora.damico@ed.gov
https://nces.ed.gov/surveys/b&b/

School Survey on Crime and Safety

The School Survey on Crime and Safety (SSOCS) is the only recurring federal survey that collects detailed information on the incidence, frequency, seriousness, and nature of violence affecting students and school personnel, as well as other indicators of school safety from the schools' perspective. SSOCS is conducted by the National Center for Education Statistics (NCES) within the U.S. Department of Education and collected by the U.S. Census Bureau. Data from this collection can be used to examine the relationship between school characteristics and violent and serious violent crimes in primary, middle, high, and combined schools. In addition, data from SSOCS can be used to assess what crime prevention programs, practices, and policies are used by schools. SSOCS has been conducted in school years 1999–2000, 2003–04, 2005–06, 2007–08, 2009–10, 2015–16, and 2017–18.

The sampling frame for SSOCS:2018 was constructed using the 2014–15 CCD Public Elementary/Secondary School Universe data file. The sampling frame was restricted to regular public schools, charter schools, and schools with partial or total magnet programs in the 50 states and the District of Columbia. It excluded special education schools, vocational schools, alternative schools, virtual schools, newly closed schools, home schools, ungraded schools, schools with a highest grade of kindergarten or lower, Department of Defense Education Activity schools, and Bureau of Indian Education schools, as well as schools in Puerto Rico, American Samoa, the Northern Marianas, Guam, and the U.S. Virgin Islands.

The SSOCS:2018 universe totaled 82,300 schools. The SSOCS:2018 findings were based on a nationally representative, stratified, random sample of 4,803 U.S. public schools. Data collection for SSOCS:2018 began on February 20, 2018, and continued through July 18, 2018. Although SSOCS has historically been conducted by mail with telephone and e-mail follow-up, the 2018 survey administration experimented with an online questionnaire. The survey also experimented with offering a $10 cash incentive to a subset of sampled schools. A total of 2,762 primary, middle, high, and combined schools provided complete SSOCS:2018 questionnaires, yielding a weighted response rate of 62 percent.

Further information about SSOCS may be obtained from

Rachel Hansen
Cross-Sectional Surveys Branch
Sample Surveys Division
National Center for Education Statistics
550 12th Street SW
Washington, DC 20202
rachel.hansen@ed.gov
https://nces.ed.gov/surveys/ssocs/

Schools and Staffing Survey

The Schools and Staffing Survey (SASS) was a set of related questionnaires that collected descriptive data on the context of public and private elementary and secondary education. Data reported by districts, schools, principals, and teachers provided a variety of statistics on the condition of education in the United States that may be used by policymakers and the general public. The SASS system covered a wide range of topics, including teacher demand, teacher and principal characteristics, teachers' and principals' perceptions of school climate and problems in their schools, teacher and principal compensation, district hiring and retention practices, general conditions in schools, and basic characteristics of the student population.

SASS data were collected through a mail questionnaire with telephone and in-person field follow-up. SASS was conducted by the Census Bureau for NCES beginning with the first administration of the survey, which was conducted during the 1987–88 school year. Subsequent SASS administrations were conducted in 1990–91, 1993–94, 1999–2000, 2003–04, 2007–08, and 2011–12. It was succeeded by the National Teacher and Principal Survey (NTPS), which was first conducted in the 2015–16 school year.

SASS was designed to produce national, regional, and state estimates for public elementary and secondary schools, school districts, principals, teachers, and school library media centers and national and regional estimates for public charter schools, as well as principals, teachers, and school library media centers within these schools. For private schools, the sample supported national, regional, and affiliation estimates for schools, principals, and teachers.

From its inception, SASS had four core components: school questionnaires, teacher questionnaires, principal questionnaires, and school district (prior to 1999–2000, "teacher demand and shortage") questionnaires. A fifth component, school library media center questionnaires, was introduced in the 1993–94 administration and was included in every subsequent administration of SASS. School library data were also collected in the 1990–91 administration of the survey through the school and principal questionnaires.

School questionnaires used in SASS included the Public and Private School Questionnaires; teacher questionnaires included the Public and Private School Teacher Questionnaires; principal questionnaires included the Public and Private School Principal (or School Administrator) Questionnaires; and school district questionnaires included the School District (or Teacher Demand and Shortage) Questionnaires.

Although the four core questionnaires and the school library media questionnaires remained relatively stable over the various administrations of SASS, the survey was changed to accommodate emerging issues in elementary and secondary education. Some questionnaire items were added, some were deleted, and some were reworded.

During the 1990–91 SASS cycle, NCES worked with the Office of Indian Education to add an Indian School Questionnaire to SASS, and it remained a part of SASS through 2007–08. The Indian School Questionnaire explored the same school-level issues that the Public and Private School Questionnaires explored, allowing comparisons among the three types of schools. The 1990–91, 1993–94, 1999–2000, 2003–04, and 2007–08 administrations of SASS obtained data on Bureau of Indian Education (BIE) schools (schools funded or operated by the BIE), but the 2011–12 administration did not obtain BIE data. SASS estimates for all survey years presented in this report exclude BIE schools, and as a result, estimates in this report may differ from those in previously published reports.

School library media center questionnaires were administered in public, private, and BIE schools as part of the 1993–94 and 1999–2000 SASS. During the 2003–04 administration of SASS, only library media centers in public schools were surveyed, and in 2007–08 only library media centers in public schools and BIE and BIE-funded schools were surveyed. The 2011–12 survey collected data only on school library media centers in traditional public schools and in public charter schools. School library questions focused on facilities, services and policies, staffing, technology, information literacy, collections and expenditures, and media equipment. New or revised topics included access to online licensed databases, resource availability, and additional elements on information literacy. The Student Records and Library Media Specialist/Librarian Questionnaires were administered only in 1993–94.

As part of the 1999–2000 SASS, the Charter School Questionnaire was sent to the universe of charter schools in operation in 1998–99. In 2003–04 and in subsequent administrations of SASS, there was no separate questionnaire for charter schools—charter schools were included in the public school sample instead. Another change in the 2003–04 administration of SASS was a revised data collection procedure using a primary in-person contact within the school intended to reduce the field follow-up phase.

The SASS teacher surveys collected information on the characteristics of teachers, such as their age, race/ethnicity, years of teaching experience, average number of hours per week spent on teaching activities, base salary, average class size, and highest degree earned. These teacher-reported data may be combined with related information on their school's characteristics, such as school type (e.g., public traditional, public charter, Catholic, private other religious, and private nonsectarian), community type, and school enrollment size. The teacher questionnaires also asked for information on teacher opinions regarding the school and teaching environment. In 1993–94, about 53,000 public school teachers and 10,400 private school teachers were sampled. In 1999–2000, about 56,300 public school teachers, 4,400 public charter school teachers, and 10,800 private school teachers were sampled. In 2003–04, about 52,500 public school teachers and 10,000 private school teachers were sampled. In 2007–08, about 48,400 public school teachers and 8,200 private school teachers were sampled. In 2011–12, about 51,100 public school teachers and 7,100 private school teachers were sampled. Weighted overall response rates in 2011–12 were 61.8 percent for public school teachers and 50.1 percent for private school teachers.

The SASS principal surveys focused on such topics as age, race/ethnicity, sex, average annual salary, years of experience, highest degree attained, perceived influence on decisions made at the school, and hours spent per week on all school activities. These data on principals can be placed in the context of other SASS data, such as the type of the principal's school (e.g., public traditional, public charter, Catholic, other religious, or nonsectarian), enrollment, and percentage of students eligible for free or reduced price lunch. In 2003–04, about 10,200 public school principals were sampled, and in 2007–08, about 9,800 public school principals were sampled. In 2011–12, about 11,000 public school principals and 3,000 private school principals were sampled. Weighted response rates in 2011–12 for public school principals and private school principals were 72.7 percent and 64.7 percent, respectively.

The SASS 2011–12 sample of schools was confined to the 50 states and the District of Columbia and excluded the other jurisdictions, the Department of Defense overseas schools, the BIE schools, and schools that did not offer teacher-provided classroom instruction in grades 1–12 or the ungraded equivalent. The SASS 2011–12 sample included 10,250 traditional public schools, 750 public charter schools, and 3,000 private schools.

The public school sample for the 2011–12 SASS was based on an adjusted public school universe file from the 2009–10 Common Core of Data, a database of all the nation's public school districts and public schools. The private school sample for the 2011–12 SASS was selected from the 2009–10 Private School Universe Survey (PSS), as updated for the 2011–12 PSS. This update collected membership lists from private school associations and religious denominations, as well as private school lists from state education departments. The 2011–12 SASS private school frame was further augmented by the inclusion of additional schools that were identified through the 2009–10 PSS area frame data collection.

The NCES data product 2011–12 Schools and Staffing Survey (SASS) Restricted-Use Data Files (NCES 2014-356) contains eight files (Public School District, Public School Principal, Public School, Public School Teacher, Public School Library Media Center, Private School Principal, Private School, and Private School Teacher) in multiple formats. It also contains a six-volume User's Manual, which includes a codebook for each file. (Information on how to obtain a restricted-use data license is located at https://nces.ed.gov/pubsearch/licenses.asp.)

Further information on SASS may be obtained from

Maura Spiegelman
Cross-Sectional Surveys Branch
Sample Surveys Division
National Center for Education Statistics
550 12th Street SW
Washington, DC 20202
maura.spiegelman@ed.gov
https://nces.ed.gov/surveys/sass/

Teacher Follow-Up Survey

The Teacher Follow-Up Survey (TFS) is a follow-up survey of selected elementary and secondary school teachers who participate in the NCES Schools and Staffing Survey (SASS). Its purpose is to determine how many teachers remain at the same school, move to another school, or leave the profession in the year following a SASS administration. It is administered to elementary and secondary teachers in the 50 states and the District of Columbia. The TFS uses two questionnaires, one for teachers who left teaching since the previous SASS administration and another for those who are still teaching either in the same school as last year or in a different school. The objective of the TFS is to focus on the characteristics of each group in order to answer questions about teacher mobility and attrition.

The 2008–09 TFS is different from any previous TFS administration in that it also serves as the second wave of a longitudinal study of first-year teachers. Because of this, the 2008–09 TFS consists of four questionnaires. Two are for respondents who were first-year public school teachers in the 2007–08 SASS and two are for the remainder of the sample.

The 2012–13 TFS sample was made up of teachers who had taken the 2011–12 SASS survey. The 2012–13 TFS sample contained about 5,800 public school teachers and 1,200 private school teachers. The weighted overall response rate using the initial basic weight for private school teachers was notably low (39.7 percent), resulting in a decision to exclude private school teachers from the 2012–13 TFS data files. The weighted overall response rate for public school teachers was 49.9 percent (50.3 percent for current and 45.6 percent for former teachers). Additional information about the 2012–13 TFS, including the analysis of unit nonresponse bias, is available in the First Look report *Teacher Attrition and Mobility: Results From the 2012–13 Teacher Follow-up Survey* (NCES 2014-077).

Further information on the TFS may be obtained from

Julia Merlin
Cross-Sectional Surveys Branch
Sample Surveys Division
National Center for Education Statistics
550 12th Street SW
Washington, DC 20202
julia.merlin@ed.gov
https://nces.ed.gov/surveys/sass/

Other U.S. Department of Education Agencies and Programs

EDFacts Data Governance Board

The EDFacts Initiative

EDFacts is a centralized data collection through which state education agencies (SEAs) submit PK–12 education data to the U.S. Department of Education (ED). All data in EDFacts are organized into "data groups" and reported to ED using defined file specifications. Depending on the data group, SEAs may submit aggregate counts for the state as a whole or detailed counts for individual schools or school districts. EDFacts does not collect student-level records. The entities that are required to report EDFacts data vary by data group but may include the 50 states, the District of Columbia, the Department of Defense Education Activity, the Bureau of Indian Education, Puerto Rico, American Samoa, Guam, the Northern Mariana Islands, and the U.S. Virgin Islands. More information about EDFacts file specifications and data groups can be found at https://www2.ed.gov/about/inits/ed/edfacts/index.html.

EDFacts is a universe collection and is not subject to sampling error, although nonsampling errors such as nonresponse and inaccurate reporting may occur. The U.S. Department of Education attempts to minimize nonsampling errors by training data submission coordinators and reviewing the quality of state data submissions. However, anomalies may still be present in the data.

Differences in state data collection systems may limit the comparability of EDFacts data across states and across time. To build EDFacts files, SEAs rely on data that were reported by their schools and school districts. The systems used to collect these data are evolving rapidly and differ from state to state.

In some cases, EDFacts data may not align with data reported on SEA websites. States may update their websites on schedules different from those they use to report data to ED. Furthermore, ED may use methods for protecting the privacy of individuals represented within the data that could be different from the methods used by an individual state.

EDFacts data on homeless students enrolled in public schools are collected in data group 655 within file 118. EDFacts data on English language learners enrolled in public schools are collected in data group 678 within file 141. EDFacts four-year adjusted cohort graduation rate (ACGR) data are collected in data group 696 within file 151. EDFacts data on students in incidents involving firearms are collected in data group 596 within file 086. EDFacts data on students being removed from school due to disciplinary action are collected in data group 523 within file 030. EDFacts collects these data groups on behalf of the Office of Elementary and Secondary Education.

For more information about ED*Facts*, please contact

Ross Santy
Administrative Data Division
National Center for Education Statistics
U.S. Department of Education
550 12th Street SW
Washington, DC 20202
ross.santy@ed.gov
https://www2.ed.gov/about/inits/ed/edfacts/index.html

National Center for Special Education Research

The National Center for Special Education Research (NCSER) was created as part of the reauthorization of the Individuals with Disabilities Education Act (IDEA). NCSER sponsors a program of special education research designed to expand the knowledge and understanding of infants, toddlers, and children with disabilities. NCSER funds programs of research that address its mission. In order to determine which programs work, as well as how, why, and in what settings they work, NCSER sponsors research on the needs of infants, toddlers, and children with disabilities and evaluates the effectiveness of services provided through IDEA.

Further information on NCSER may be obtained from

Joan McLaughlin
Commissioner
National Center for Special Education Research
550 12th Street SW
Washington, DC 20202
joan.mclaughlin@ed.gov
https://ies.ed.gov/ncser/

The National Longitudinal Transition Study-2

Funded by NCSER, the National Longitudinal Transition Study-2 (NLTS-2) was a follow-up of the original National Longitudinal Transition Study conducted from 1985 through 1993. NLTS-2 began in 2001 with a sample of students who received special education services, were ages 13 through 16, and were in at least 7th grade on December 1, 2000. The study was designed to provide a national picture of these youths' experiences and achievements as they transition into adulthood. Data were collected from parents, youth, and schools by survey, telephone interviews, student assessments, and transcripts.

NLTS-2 was designed to align with the original NLTS by including many of the same questions and data items, thus allowing comparisons between the NLTS and NLTS-2 youths' experiences. NLTS-2 also included items that have been collected in other national databases to permit comparisons between NLTS-2 youth and the general youth population. Information was collected over five waves, beginning in 2001 and ending in 2009.

Further information on NLTS-2 may be obtained from

Jacquelyn Buckley
Office of the Commissioner
National Center for Special Education Research
550 12th Street SW
Washington, DC 20202
jacquelyn.buckley@ed.gov
https://nlts2.sri.com/

Office for Civil Right

Civil Rights Data Collection

The U.S. Department of Education's Office for Civil Rights (OCR) has surveyed the nation's public elementary and secondary schools since 1968. The survey was first known as the OCR Elementary and Secondary School (E&S) Survey; in 2004, it was renamed the Civil Rights Data Collection (CRDC). The survey collects data on school discipline, access to and participation in high-level mathematics and science courses, teacher characteristics, school finances, and other school characteristics. These data are reported by race/ethnicity, sex, and disability.

Data in the survey are collected pursuant to 34 C.F.R. Section 100.6(b) of the U.S. Department of Education regulation implementing Title VI of the Civil Rights Act of 1964. The requirements are also incorporated by reference in Department regulations implementing Title IX of the Education Amendments of 1972, Section 504 of the Rehabilitation Act of 1973, and the Age Discrimination Act of 1975. School, district, state, and national data are currently available. Data from individual public schools and districts are used to generate national and state data.

The CRDC has generally been conducted biennially in each of the 50 states plus the District of Columbia. The 2009–10 CRDC was collected from a sample of approximately 7,000 school districts and over 72,000 schools in those districts. It was made up of two parts: part 1 contained beginning-of-year "snapshot" data and part 2 contained cumulative, or end-of-year, data.

The 2011–12, 2013–14, and 2015–16 CRDC were surveys of all public school schools and school districts in the nation. The 2011–12 survey collected data from approximately 16,500 school districts and 97,000 schools, the 2013–14 survey collected data from approximately 16,800 school districts and 95,500 schools, and the 2015–16 survey collected data from 17,400 school districts and 96,400 schools.

The CRDC web page (https://www2.ed.gov/about/offices/list/ocr/data.html) contains, among other information, survey forms, lists of data elements, and lists of questions and answers pertaining to the 2009–10 through 2015–16 CRDC surveys.

Further information on the Civil Rights Data Collection may be obtained from

Office for Civil Rights
U.S. Department of Education
400 Maryland Avenue SW
Washington, DC 20202
OCR@ed.gov
https://www2.ed.gov/about/offices/list/ocr/data.html

Office of Federal Student Aid

Cohort Default Rate Database

A school's cohort default rate is the percentage of the school's borrowers who enter repayment on certain Federal Family Education Loan (FFEL) program or William D. Ford Federal Direct Loan (Direct Loan) program loans during a particular federal fiscal year and default within the cohort default period. The 2-year cohort default period is the period that begins on October 1 of the fiscal year when the borrower enters repayment and ends on September 30 of the following fiscal year. The 3-year cohort default period is the period that begins on October 1 of the fiscal year when the borrower enters repayment and ends on September 30 of second fiscal year following the fiscal year in which the borrower entered repayment.

The Office of Federal Student Aid's cohort default rate database can be accessed at https://nslds.ed.gov/nslds/nslds_SA/defaultmanagement/search_cohortCY2016.cfm.

Further information about cohort default rates produced by the Office of Federal Student Aid may be obtained from

https://www2.ed.gov/offices/OSFAP/defaultmanagement/
    schooltyperates.pdf
https://www2.ed.gov/offices/OSFAP/defaultmanagement/
    cdr.html
https://ifap.ed.gov/dm/finalcdrg

Office of Special Education Programs

Annual Report to Congress on the Implementation of the Individuals with Disabilities Education Act

The Individuals with Disabilities Education Act (IDEA) is a law ensuring services to children with disabilities throughout the nation. IDEA governs how states and public agencies provide early intervention, special education, and related services to more than 6.9 million eligible infants, toddlers, children, and youth with disabilities.

IDEA, formerly the Education of the Handicapped Act (EHA), requires the Secretary of Education to transmit, on an annual basis, a report to Congress describing the progress made in serving the nation's children with disabilities. This annual report contains information on children served by public schools under the provisions of Part B of IDEA and on children served in state-operated programs for persons with disabilities under Chapter I of the Elementary and Secondary Education Act.

Statistics on children receiving special education and related services in various settings and school personnel providing such services are reported in an annual submission of data to the Office of Special Education Programs (OSEP) by the 50 states, the District of Columbia, the Bureau of Indian Education schools, Puerto Rico, American Samoa, Guam, the Northern Mariana Islands, the U.S. Virgin Islands, the Federated States of Micronesia, Palau, and the Marshall Islands. The child count information is based on the number of children with disabilities receiving special education and related services on December 1 of each year. Count information is available from https://ideadata.org/.

Since all participants in programs for persons with disabilities are reported to OSEP, the data are not subject to sampling error. However, nonsampling error can arise from a variety of sources. Some states only produce counts of students receiving special education services by disability category because Part B of the IDEA requires it. In those states that typically produce counts of students receiving special education services by disability category without regard to IDEA requirements, definitions and labeling practices vary.

Further information on this annual report to Congress may be obtained from

Office of Special Education Programs
Office of Special Education and Rehabilitative Services
U.S. Department of Education
400 Maryland Avenue SW
Washington, DC 20202
https://www2.ed.gov/about/reports/annual/osep/index.html
https://sites.ed.gov/idea/
https://ideadata.org/

Office of Caree , Technical, and Adult Education, Division of Adult Education and Literacy

Enrollment Data for State-Administered Adult Education Programs

The Division of Adult Education and Literacy (DAEL) promotes programs that help American adults get the basic skills they need to be productive workers, family members, and citizens. The major areas of support are Adult Basic Education, Adult Secondary Education, and English Language Acquisition. These programs emphasize basic skills such as reading, writing, math, English language competency, and problem solving. Each year, DAEL reports enrollment numbers in state-administered adult education programs for these major areas of support for all 50 states, the District of Columbia, American Samoa, the Federated States of Micronesia, Guam, the Marshall Islands, the Northern Mariana Islands, Palau, Puerto Rico, and the U.S. Virgin Islands.

Further information on DAEL may be obtained from

Office of Career, Technical, and Adult Education
Division of Adult Education and Literacy
U.S. Department of Education
400 Maryland Avenue SW
Washington, DC 20202
https://www2.ed.gov/about/offices/list/ovae/pi/AdultEd/
    index.html
https://www2.ed.gov/about/offices/list/ovae/pi/AdultEd/
    facts-figures.html

Other Governmental Agencies and Programs

Bureau of Economic Analysis

National Income and Product Accounts

The National Income and Product Accounts (NIPAs), produced by the Bureau of Economic Analysis, are a set of economic accounts that provide information on the value and composition of output produced in the United States during a given period. NIPAs represent measures of economic activity in the United States, including production, income distribution, and personal savings. NIPAs also include data on employee compensation and wages. These estimations were first calculated in the early 1930s to help the government design economic policies to combat the Great Depression. Most of the NIPA series are published quarterly, with annual reviews of estimates from the three most recent years conducted in the summer.

Revisions to the NIPAs have been made over the years to create a more comprehensive economic picture of the United States. For example, in 1976, consumption of fixed capital (CFC) estimates shifted to a current-cost basis. In 1991, NIPAs began to use gross domestic product (GDP) instead of gross national product (GNP) as the primary measure of U.S. production. (At that time, virtually all other countries were already using GDP as their primary measure of production.) In the 2003 comprehensive revision, a more complete and accurate measure of insurance services was adopted. The incorporation of a new classification system for personal consumption expenditures (PCE) was among the changes contained in the 2009 comprehensive revision. The comprehensive revision of 2013 included the treatment of research and development expenditures by business, government, and nonprofit institutions serving households as fixed investment. The 2017 annual update of the NIPA accounts contained estimates that reflected the incorporation of newly available and revised source data and the adoption of improved estimating methods. Information on the 2018 comprehensive update of the NIPA accounts and the 2019 annual update of the NIPA accounts can be accessed at https://www.bea.gov/information-previous-updates-nipa-accounts.

NIPAs are slowly being integrated with other federal account systems, such as the federal account system of the Bureau of Labor Statistics.

Further information on NIPAs may be obtained from

U.S. Department of Commerce
Bureau of Economic Analysis
https://www.bea.gov/

Bureau of Labor Statistics

Consumer Price Indexes

The Consumer Price Index (CPI) represents changes in prices of all goods and services purchased for consumption by urban households. Indexes are available for two population groups: a CPI for All Urban Consumers (CPI-U) and a CPI for Urban Wage Earners and Clerical Workers (CPI-W). Unless otherwise specified, data in this report are adjusted for inflation using the CPI-U. These values are generally adjusted to a school-year basis by averaging the July through June figures. Price indexes are available for the United States, the 4 Census regions, 9 Census divisions, 2 size of city classes, cross-classifications of regions and size-classes, and 23 local areas. The major uses of the CPI include as an economic indicator, as a deflator of other economic series, and as a means of adjusting income.

Also available is the Consumer Price Index research series using current methods (CPI-U-RS), which presents an estimate of the CPI-U from 1978 to the present that incorporates most of the improvements that the Bureau of Labor Statistics has made over that time span into the entire series. The historical price index series of the CPI-U does not reflect these changes, though these changes do make the present and future CPI more accurate. The limitations of the CPI-U-RS include considerable uncertainty surrounding the magnitude of the adjustments and the several improvements in the CPI that have not been incorporated into the CPI-U-RS for various reasons. Nonetheless, the CPI-U-RS can serve as a valuable proxy for researchers needing a historical estimate of inflation using current methods. This series has not been used in NCES tables.

Further information on consumer price indexes may be obtained from

Bureau of Labor Statistics
U.S. Department of Labor
2 Massachusetts Avenue NE
Washington, DC 20212
https://www.bls.gov/cpi/

Employment and Unemployment Surveys

Statistics on the employment and unemployment status of the population and related data are compiled by the Bureau of Labor Statistics (BLS) using data from the Current Population Survey (CPS) (see below) and other surveys. The CPS, a monthly household survey conducted by the U.S. Census Bureau for the Bureau of Labor Statistics, provides a comprehensive body of information on the employment and unemployment experience of the nation's population, classified by age, sex, race, and various other characteristics.

Further information on unemployment surveys may be obtained from

Bureau of Labor Statistics
U.S. Department of Labor
2 Massachusetts Avenue NE
Washington, DC 20212
cpsinfo@bls.gov
https://www.bls.gov/bls/employment.htm

Census Bureau

American Community Survey

The Census Bureau introduced the American Community Survey (ACS) in 1996. Fully implemented in 2005, it provides a large monthly sample of demographic, socioeconomic, and housing data comparable in content to the Long Forms of the Decennial Census up to and including the 2000 long form. Aggregated over time, these data serve as a replacement for the Long Form of the Decennial Census. The survey includes questions mandated by federal law, federal regulations, and court decisions.

Since 2011, the survey has been mailed to approximately 295,000 addresses in the United States and Puerto Rico each month, or about 3.5 million addresses annually. A larger proportion of addresses in small governmental units (e.g., American Indian reservations, small counties, and towns) also receive the survey. The monthly sample size is designed to approximate the ratio used in the 2000 Census, which requires more intensive distribution in these areas. The ACS covers the U.S. resident population, which includes the entire civilian, noninstitutionalized population; incarcerated persons; institutionalized persons; and the active-duty military who are in the United States. In 2006, the ACS began collecting data from the population living in group quarters. Institutionalized group quarters include adult and juvenile correctional facilities, nursing facilities, and other health care facilities. Noninstitutionalized group quarters include college and university housing, military barracks, and other noninstitutional facilities such as workers and religious group quarters and temporary shelters for the homeless.

National-level data from the ACS are available from 2000 onward. The ACS produces 1-year estimates for jurisdictions with populations of 65,000 and over and 5-year estimates for jurisdictions with smaller populations. The 1-year estimates for 2018 used data collected between January 1, 2018, and December 31, 2018, and the 5-year estimates for 2014–2018 used data collected between January 1, 2014, and December 31, 2018. The ACS produced 3-year estimates (for jurisdictions with populations of 20,000 or over) for the periods 2005–2007, 2006–2008, 2007–2009, 2008–2010, 2009–2011, 2010–2012, and 2011–2013. Three-year estimates for these periods will continue to be available to data users, but no further 3-year estimates will be produced.

Further information about the ACS is available at https://www.census.gov/programs-surveys/acs/.

Annual Survey of State and Local Government Finances

The Census Bureau conducts an Annual Survey of State and Local Government Finances as authorized by law under Title 13, United States Code, Section 182. Periodic surveys of government finances have been conducted since 1902 and have been conducted annually since 1952. This survey covers the entire range of government finance activities: revenue, expenditure, debt, and assets. Revenues and expenditures comprise actual receipts and payments of a government and its agencies, including government-operated enterprises, utilities, and public trust funds. The expenditure-reporting categories comprise all amounts of money paid out by a government and its agencies, with the exception of amounts for debt retirement and for loan, investment, agency, and private trust transactions.

State government finances are based primarily on the Census Bureau Annual Survey of State and Local Government Finances. Census Bureau analysts compile figures from official records and reports of the state governments for most of the state financial data. States differ in the ways in which they administer activities; they may fund such activities directly, or they may disburse the money to a lower level government or government agency. Therefore, caution is advised when attempting to make a direct comparison between states regarding their state fiscal aid data.

The sample of local governments is drawn from the periodic Census of Governments (which is conducted in years ending in "2" and "7") and consists of certain local governments sampled with certainty plus a sample below the certainty level. Finance data for all school districts are collected on an annual basis and released through the NCES Common Core of Data system. A new sample is usually selected every 5 years (in years ending in "4" and "9").

The statistics in Government Finances that are based wholly or partly on data from the sample are subject to sampling error. State government finance data are not subject to sampling error. Estimates of major U.S. totals for local governments are subject to a computed sampling variability of less than one-half of 1 percent. The estimates are also subject to the inaccuracies in classification, response, and processing that would occur if a complete census had been conducted under the same conditions as the sample.

Further information on government finances may be obtained from

Governments Division
Census Bureau
U.S. Department of Commerce
4600 Silver Hill Road
Washington, DC 20233
https://www.census.gov/econ/overview/go0400.html

Local government
ewd.local.finance@census.gov

State government
govs.statefinance@census.gov
https://www.census.gov/govs/

Census of Population—Education in the United States

Some NCES tables are based on a part of the decennial census that consisted of questions asked of a 1 in 6 sample of people and housing units in the United States. This sample asked more detailed questions about income, occupation, and housing costs, as well as questions about general demographic information. This decennial census "long form" has been discontinued and has been replaced by the American Community Survey (ACS).

School enrollment. People classified as enrolled in school reported attending a "regular" public or private school or college. They were asked whether the institution they attended was public or private and what level of school they were enrolled in.

Educational attainment. Data for educational attainment were tabulated for people ages 15 and over and classified according to the highest grade completed or the highest degree received. Instructions were also given to include the level of the previous grade attended or the highest degree received for people currently enrolled in school.

Poverty status. To determine poverty status, answers to income questions were used to make comparisons to the appropriate poverty threshold. All people except those who were institutionalized, people in military group quarters and college dormitories, and unrelated people under age 15 were considered. If the total income of each family or unrelated individual in the sample was below the corresponding cutoff, that family or individual was classified as "below the poverty level."

Further information on the 1990 and 2000 Census of Population may be obtained from

Population Division
Census Bureau
U.S. Department of Commerce
4600 Silver Hill Road
Washington, DC 20233
https://www.census.gov/main/www/cen1990.html
https://www.census.gov/main/www/cen2000.html

Current Population Survey

The Current Population Survey (CPS) is a monthly survey of about 50,000 households conducted by the U.S. Census Bureau for the Bureau of Labor Statistics. The CPS is the primary source of labor force statistics on the U.S. population. In addition, supplemental questionnaires are used to provide further information about the U.S. population. The March supplement (also known as the Annual Social and Economic [ASEC] supplement) contains detailed questions on topics such as income, employment, and educational attainment; additional questions, such as items on disabilities, have also been included. In the July supplement, items on computer and internet use are the principal focus. The October supplement also contains some questions about computer and internet use, but most of its questions relate to school enrollment and school characteristics.

CPS samples are initially selected based on results from the decennial census and are periodically updated to reflect new housing construction. The current sample design for the main CPS, last revised in July 2015, includes about 70,000 households. Each month, about 50,000 of the 70,000 households are interviewed. Information is obtained each month from those in the household who are 15 years of age and over, and demographic data are collected for children 0–14 years of age. In addition, supplemental questions regarding school enrollment are asked about eligible household members age 3 and over in the October CPS supplement.

In January 1992, the CPS educational attainment variable was changed. The "Highest grade attended" and "Year completed" questions were replaced by the question "What is the highest level of school...has completed or the highest degree...has received?" Thus, for example, while the old questions elicited data for those who completed more than 4 years of high school, the new question elicited data for those who were high school completers, i.e., those who graduated from high school with a diploma as well as those who completed high school through equivalency programs, such as a GED program.

A major redesign of the CPS was implemented in January 1994 to improve the quality of the data collected. Survey questions were revised, new questions were added, and computer-assisted interviewing methods were used for the survey data collection. Further information about the redesign is available in *Current Population Survey, October 1995: (School Enrollment Supplement) Technical Documentation* at https://www.census.gov/prod/techdoc/cps/cpsoct95.pdf.

Caution should be used when comparing data from 2012 through 2019 (which reflect 2010 Census-based controls) with data from 2002 through 2011 (which reflect 2000 Census-based controls) and with data from 2001 and earlier (which reflect population controls based on the 1990 and earlier Censuses). Changes in population controls generally have relatively little impact on summary measures such as means, medians, and percentage distributions; they can, however, have a significant impact on population counts. For example, use of 2010 Census-based controls results in about a 0.2 percent increase from the 2000 Census-based controls in the civilian noninstitutionalized population and in the number of families and households. Thus, estimates of levels for data collected in 2012 and later years will differ from those for earlier years by more than what could be attributed to actual changes in the population. These differences could be disproportionately greater for certain subpopulation groups than for the total population.

Beginning in 2003, the race/ethnicity questions were expanded. Information on people of Two or more races were included, and the Asian and Pacific Islander race category was split into two categories—Asian and Native Hawaiian or Other Pacific Islander. In addition, questions were reworded to make it clear that self-reported data on race/ethnicity should reflect the race/ethnicity with which the responder identifies, rather than what may be written in official documentation.

The estimation procedure employed for monthly CPS data involves inflating weighted sample results to independent estimates of characteristics of the civilian noninstitutional population in the United States by age, sex, and race. These independent estimates are based on statistics from decennial censuses; statistics on births, deaths, immigration, and emigration; and statistics on the population in the armed services. Generalized standard error tables are provided in the Current Population Reports; methods for deriving standard errors can be found within the CPS technical documentation at https://www.census.gov/programs-surveys/cps/technical-documentation/complete.html. The CPS data are subject to both nonsampling and sampling errors.

Standard errors were estimated using the generalized variance function prior to 2005 for March CPS data and prior to 2010 for October CPS data. The generalized variance function is a simple model that expresses the variance as a function of the expected value of a survey estimate. Standard errors were estimated using replicate weight methodology beginning in 2005 for March CPS data and beginning in 2010 for October CPS data. Those interested in using CPS household-level supplement replicate weights to calculate variances may refer to *Estimating Current Population Survey (CPS) Household-Level Supplement Variances Using Replicate Weights* at https://www.nber.org/cps/HH-level_Use_of_the_Public_Use_Replicate_Weight_File.doc.

Further information on the CPS may be obtained from

Associate Directorate for Demographic Programs—Survey Operations
Census Bureau
U.S. Department of Commerce
4600 Silver Hill Road
Washington, DC 20233
(301) 763-3806
dsd.cps@census.gov
https://www.census.gov/programs-surveys/cps.html

Computer and Internet Use

The Current Population Survey (CPS) has been conducting supplemental data collections regarding computer use since 1984. In 1997, these supplemental data collections were expanded to include data on internet access. More recently, data regarding computer and internet use were collected in October 2010, July 2011, October 2012, July 2013, July 2015, and November 2017.

In the July 2011, 2013, and 2015 supplements, as well as in the November 2017 supplement, the sole focus was on computer and internet use. In the October 2010 and 2012 supplements questions on school enrollment were the principal focus, and questions on computer and internet use were less prominent. Measurable differences in estimates taken from these supplements across years could reflect actual changes in the population; however, differences could also reflect any unknown bias from major changes in the questionnaire over time due to rapidly changing technology. In addition, data may vary slightly due to seasonal variations in data collection between the July, October, and November supplements. Therefore, caution should be used when making year-to-year comparisons of CPS computer and internet use estimates.

The most recent computer and internet use supplement, conducted in November 2017, collected household information from all eligible CPS households, as well as information from individual household members age 3 and over. Information was collected about the household's computer and internet use and the household member's use of the Internet from any location in the past year. Additionally, information was gathered regarding a randomly selected household respondent's use of the Internet.

For the November 2017 basic CPS, the household-level nonresponse rate was 14.3 percent. The person-level nonresponse rate for the computer and internet use supplement was an additional 23.0 percent. Since one rate is a person-level rate and the other a household-level rate, the rates cannot be combined to derive an overall rate.

Further information on the CPS Computer and Internet Use Supplement may be obtained from

Associate Directorate for Demographic Programs—Survey Operations
Census Bureau
U.S. Department of Commerce
4600 Silver Hill Road
Washington, DC 20233
(301) 763-3806
dsd.cps@census.gov
https://www.census.gov/programs-surveys/cps.html

Dropouts

Each October, the Current Population Survey (CPS) includes supplemental questions on the enrollment status of the population age 3 years and over as part of the monthly basic survey on labor force participation. In addition to gathering the information on school enrollment, with the limitations on accuracy as noted below under "School Enrollment," the survey data permit calculations of dropout rates. Both status and event dropout rates are tabulated from the October CPS. Event rates describe the proportion of students who leave school each year without completing a high school program. Status rates provide cumulative data on dropouts among all young adults within a specified age range. Status rates are higher than event rates because they include all dropouts ages 16 through 24, regardless of when they last attended school.

In addition to other survey limitations, dropout rates may be affected by survey coverage and exclusion of the institutionalized population. The incarcerated population has increased and has a high dropout rate. Dropout rates for the total population might be higher than those for the noninstitutionalized population if the prison and jail populations were included in the dropout rate calculations. On the other hand, if military personnel, who tend to be high school graduates, were included, it might offset some or all of the impact from the theoretical inclusion of the jail and prison populations. Tables on status dropout rates based on the American Community Survey do include the institutionalized population and are also included in the *Digest of Education Statistics*.

Another area of concern with tabulations involving young people in household surveys is the relatively low coverage ratio compared to older age groups. CPS undercoverage results from missed housing units and missed people within sample households. Overall CPS undercoverage for October 2018 is estimated to be about 11 percent.

CPS coverage varies with age, sex, and race. Generally, coverage is larger for females than for males and larger for non-Blacks than for Blacks. This differential coverage is a general problem for most household-based surveys. Further information on CPS methodology may be found in the technical documentation at https://www.census.gov/programs-surveys/cps/technical-documentation.html. Tables on status

dropout rates based on the American Community Survey do include the institutionalized population and are also included in the *Digest of Education Statistics*.

Further information on the calculation of dropouts and dropout rates may be obtained from the *Trends in High School Dropout and Completion Rates in the United States* report at https://nces.ed.gov/programs/dropout/index.asp or by contacting

Cristobal de Brey
Annual Reports and Information Staff
National Center for Education Statistics
550 12th Street SW
Washington, DC 20202
cristobal.debrey@ed.gov

Educational Attainment

Reports documenting educational attainment are produced by the Census Bureau using the March Current Population Survey (CPS) supplement (Annual Social and Economic supplement [ASEC]). Currently, the ASEC supplement consists of approximately 50,000 interviewed households. Both recent and earlier editions of *Educational Attainment in the United States* may be downloaded at https://www.census.gov/topics/education/educational-attainment/data/tables.All.html.

In 2014, the CPS ASEC included redesigned questions on income (specifically retirement income) and health insurance coverage, which were followed, in the 2015 CPS ASEC, by changes to allow spouses and unmarried partners to specifically identify as opposite- or same-sex. Beginning with the 2019 CPS ASEC, the Census Bureau used a modified processing system that improved procedures for imputing income and health insurance variables. The Census Bureau analyzed the impact of the use of the new processing system by comparing its use with the use of the legacy processing system on income, poverty, and health insurance coverage data from 2017 ASEC files. The Census Bureau found that differences in the overall poverty rate and household income resulting from the use of the new processing system compared to the legacy processing system were not statistically significant, although there were differences for some demographic groups. Use of the new processing system caused the supplemental poverty rate (https://www.census.gov/topics/income-poverty/supplemental-poverty-measure.html) to decrease overall and for most demographic groups. The Census Bureau attributed the decrease to improvements in the new processing system's imputation of medical-out-of-pocket expenses, housing subsidies, and school lunch receipts. More information on these changes can be found at https://www.census.gov/newsroom/blogs/research-matters/2019/09/cps-asec.html.

In addition to the general constraints of CPS, some data indicate that the respondents have a tendency to overestimate the educational level of members of their household. Some inaccuracy is due to a lack of the respondent's knowledge of the exact educational attainment of each household member and the hesitancy to acknowledge anything less than a high school education.

Further information on educational attainment data from CPS may be obtained from

Associate Directorate for Demographic Programs—Survey Operations
Census Bureau
U.S. Department of Commerce
4600 Silver Hill Road
Washington, DC 20233
(301) 763-3806
dsd.cps@census.gov
https://www2.census.gov/programs-surveys/cps/techdocs/cpsmar19.pdf

School Enrollment

Each October, the Current Population Survey (CPS) includes supplemental questions on the enrollment status of the population age 3 years and over. Currently, the October supplement consists of approximately 50,000 interviewed households, the same households interviewed in the basic Current Population Survey. The primary sources of non-sampling variability in the responses to the supplement are those inherent in the main survey instrument. The question of current enrollment may not be answered accurately for various reasons. Some respondents may not know current grade information for every student in the household, a problem especially prevalent for households with members in college or in nursery school. Confusion over college credits or hours taken by a student may make it difficult to determine the year in which the student is enrolled. Problems may occur with the definition of nursery school (a group or class organized to provide educational experiences for children) where respondents' interpretations of "educational experiences" vary.

For the October 2018 basic CPS, the household-level nonresponse rate was 15.2 percent. The person-level nonresponse rate for the school enrollment supplement was an additional 9.2 percent. Since the basic CPS nonresponse rate is a household-level rate and the school enrollment supplement nonresponse rate is a person-level rate, these rates cannot be combined to derive an overall nonresponse rate. Nonresponding households may have more or fewer persons than interviewed ones, so combining these rates may lead to an under- or overestimate of the true overall nonresponse rate for persons for the school enrollment supplement.

Although the principal focus of the October supplement is school enrollment, in some years the supplement has included additional questions on other topics. In 2010 and 2012, for example, the October supplement included additional questions on computer and internet use.

Further information on CPS methodology may be obtained from https://www.census.gov/programs-surveys/cps.html.

Further information on the CPS School Enrollment Supplement may be obtained from

Associate Directorate for Demographic Programs—Survey Operations
Census Bureau
U.S. Department of Commerce
4600 Silver Hill Road
Washington, DC 20233
(301) 763-3806
dsd.cps@census.gov
https://www.census.gov/programs-surveys/cps.html

Decennial Census, Population Estimates, and Population Projections

The decennial census is a universe survey mandated by the U.S. Constitution. It is a questionnaire sent to every household in the country every 10 years, and it is composed of seven questions about the household and its members (name, sex, age, relationship, Hispanic origin, race, and whether the housing unit is owned or rented). The Census Bureau also produces annual estimates of the resident population by demographic characteristics (age, sex, race, and Hispanic origin) for the nation, states, and counties, as well as national and state projections for the resident population. (Historical data and other information about the annual estimates produced by Census may be found at the Population Estimates Program web page: https://www.census.gov/programs-surveys/popest.html.) The reference date for population estimates is July 1 of the given year. With each new issue of July 1 estimates, the Census Bureau revises estimates for each year back to the last census. Previously published estimates are superseded and archived.

Census respondents self-report race and ethnicity. The race questions on the 1990 and 2000 censuses differed in some significant ways. In 1990, the respondent was instructed to select the one race "that the respondent considers himself/herself to be," whereas in 2000, the respondent could select one or more races that the person considered himself or herself to be. American Indian, Eskimo, and Aleut were three separate race categories in 1990; in 2000, the American Indian and Alaska Native categories were combined, with an option to write in a tribal affiliation. This write-in option was provided only for the American Indian category in 1990. There was a combined Asian and Pacific Islander race category in 1990, but the groups were separated into two categories in 2000.

The census question on ethnicity asks whether the respondent is of Hispanic origin, regardless of the race option(s) selected; thus, persons of Hispanic origin may be of any race. In the 2000 census, respondents were first asked, "Is this person Spanish/Hispanic/Latino?" and then given the following options: No, not Spanish/Hispanic/Latino; Yes, Puerto Rican; Yes, Mexican, Mexican American, Chicano; Yes, Cuban; and Yes, other Spanish/Hispanic/Latino (with space to print the specific group). In the 2010 census, respondents were asked "Is this person of Hispanic, Latino, or Spanish origin?" The options given were No, not of Hispanic, Latino, or Spanish origin; Yes, Mexican, Mexican Am., Chicano; Yes, Puerto Rican; Yes, Cuban; and Yes, another Hispanic, Latino, or Spanish origin—along with instructions to print "Argentinean, Colombian, Dominican, Nicaraguan, Salvadoran, Spaniard, and so on" in a specific box.

The 2000 and 2010 censuses each asked the respondent "What is this person's race?" and allowed the respondent to select one or more options. The options provided were largely the same in both the 2000 and 2010 censuses: White; Black, African American, or Negro; American Indian or Alaska Native (with space to print the name of enrolled or principal tribe); Asian Indian; Japanese; Native Hawaiian; Chinese; Korean; Guamanian or Chamorro; Filipino; Vietnamese; Samoan; Other Asian; Other Pacific Islander; and Some other race. The last three options included space to print the specific race. Two significant differences between the 2000 and 2010 census questions on race were that no race examples were provided for the "Other Asian" and "Other Pacific Islander" responses in 2000, whereas the race examples of "Hmong, Laotian, Thai, Pakistani, Cambodian, and so on" and "Fijian, Tongan, and so on," were provided for the "Other Asian" and "Other Pacific Islander" responses, respectively, in 2010.

The census population estimates program modified the enumerated population from the 2010 census to produce the population estimates base for 2010 and onward. As part of the modification, the Census Bureau recoded the "Some other race" responses from the 2010 census to one or more of the five OMB race categories used in the estimates program (for more information, see https://www.census.gov/programs-surveys/popest/technical-documentation/methodology.html).

Further information on the decennial census may be obtained from

https://www.census.gov/.

Small Area Income and Poverty Estimates

Small Area Income and Poverty Estimates (SAIPE) are produced for school districts, counties, and states. The main objective of this program is to provide updated estimates of income and poverty statistics for the administration of federal programs and the allocation of federal funds to local jurisdictions. Estimates for 2018 were released in December 2019. These estimates combine data from administrative records, postcensal population estimates, and the decennial census with direct estimates from the American Community Survey to provide consistent and reliable single-year estimates. These model-based single-year estimates are more reflective of current conditions than multiyear survey estimates.

Further information on the SAIPE program may be obtained from

Small Area Estimates Branch
Census Bureau
U.S. Department of Commerce
sehsd.saipe@census.gov
https://www.census.gov/programs-surveys/saipe/about/contact.html

Centers for Disease Control and Prevention

Morbidity and Mortality Weekly Report: Summary of Notifiable Diseases

The Summary of Notifiable Diseases, a publication of the Morbidity and Mortality Weekly Report (MMWR), contains the official statistics, in tabular and graphical form, for the reported occurrence of nationally notifiable infectious diseases in the United States. These statistics are collected and compiled from reports sent by U.S. state and territory, New York City, and District of Columbia health departments to the National Notifiable Diseases Surveillance System (NNDSS), which is operated by the Centers for Disease Control and Prevention (CDC) in collaboration with the Council of State and Territorial Epidemiologists.

For more information on the MMWR: Summary of Notifiable Diseases, see https://www.cdc.gov/mmwr/mmwr_nd/.

National Vital Statistics System

The National Vital Statistics System (NVSS) is the method by which data on vital events—births, deaths, marriages, divorces, and fetal deaths—are provided to the National Center for Health Statistics (NCHS), part of the Centers for Disease Control and Prevention (CDC). The data are provided to NCHS through the Vital Statistics Cooperative Program (VSCP). In 1984 and earlier years, the VSCP included varying numbers of states that provided data based on a 100 percent sample of their birth certificates. Data for states not in the VSCP were based on a 50 percent sample of birth certificates filed in those states. Population data used to compile birth rates are based on special estimation procedures and are not actual counts.

Race and Hispanic ethnicity are reported separately in the NVSS. Data are available for non-Hispanic Whites and non-Hispanic Blacks for 1990 and later; however, for 1980 and 1985, data for Whites and Blacks may include persons of Hispanic ethnicity. For all years, Asian/Pacific Islander and American Indian/Alaska Native categories include persons of Hispanic ethnicity.

For more information on the NCHS and the NVSS, see https://www.cdc.gov/nchs/nvss/index.htm.

School-Associated Violent Death Surveillance System

The School-Associated Violent Death Surveillance System (SAVD-SS) was developed by the Centers for Disease Control and Prevention (CDC) in conjunction with the U.S. Department of Education and the U.S. Department of Justice. The system contains descriptive data on all school-associated violent deaths in the United States, including homicides, suicides, and legal intervention deaths where the fatal injury occurred on the campus of a functioning elementary or secondary school; while the victim was on the way to or from regular sessions at such a school; or while attending or on the way to or from an official school-sponsored event. Victims of such incidents include students as well as nonstudents (e.g., students' parents, community residents, and school staff). SAVD-SS includes data on the school, event, victim(s), and offender(s). These data are used to describe the epidemiology of school-associated violent deaths, identify common features of these deaths, estimate the rate of school-associated violent deaths in the United States, and identify potential risk factors for these deaths. The CDC has collected SAVD-SS data from July 1, 1992, to the present.

SAVD-SS uses a three-step process to identify and collect data on school-associated violent deaths. First, cases are identified through a systematic search of the LexisNexis newspaper and media database. Second, law enforcement officials from the office that investigated the death(s) are contacted to confirm the details of the case and to determine if the event meets the case definition. Third, once a case is confirmed, a copy of the full law enforcement report is requested for each case. Finally, in previous data years whenever possible, interviews were conducted with law enforcement and/or school officials familiar with cases to obtain contextual information about the incidents. However, interviews are no longer conducted as a part of SAVD-SS protocol. Information regarding the fatal incident is abstracted from law enforcement reports and includes the location of injury, context of injury (while classes were being held, during break, etc.), motives for injury, method of injury, and relationship, school, and community circumstances that may have been related to the incident (e.g., relationship problems with family members, school disciplinary issues, gang-related activity in the community). Information obtained on victim(s) and offender(s) includes demographics, contextual information about the event (date/time, alcohol or drug use, number of persons involved), types and origins of weapons, criminal history, psychological risk factors, school-related problems, extracurricular activities, and family history, including structure and stressors. For specific SAVD studies, school-level data for schools where incidents occur are obtained through the Common Core of Data survey of the National Center for Education Statistics and include school demographics,

locale (e.g., urban, suburban, rural), grade levels offered by the school, Title I eligibility, and percentage of students eligible for free/reduced-price lunch, among other variables.

All data years are flagged as preliminary. For some recent cases, the law enforcement reports have not yet been received. The details learned during data abstraction from law enforcement reports can occasionally change the classification of a case. Also, new cases may be identified because of the expansion of the scope of the media files used for case identification. However, cases not identified during earlier data years may be discovered at a later date as a result of newly published media articles describing the incident. Finally, other cases may occasionally be identified while the law enforcement and school interviews are being conducted to verify known cases.

Further information on SAVD-SS may be obtained from

Kristin Holland
Principal Investigator and Lead Behavioral Scientist
School-Associated Violent Death Surveillance System
Division of Violence Prevention
National Center for Injury Control and Prevention
Centers for Disease Control and Prevention
1600 Clifton Road
Atlanta, GA 30329
kholland@cdc.gov

Web-Based Injury Statistics Query and Reporting System Fatal

Web-Based Injury Statistics Query and Reporting System (WISQARS) Fatal is an interactive online database that provides mortality data related to injury. The mortality data reported in WISQARS Fatal come from death certificate data reported to the National Center for Health Statistics (NCHS), Centers for Disease Control and Prevention (CDC). Data include causes of death reported by attending physicians, medical examiners, and coroners and demographic information about decedents reported by funeral directors, who obtain that information from family members and other informants. NCHS collects, compiles, verifies, and prepares these data for release to the public. The data provide information about unintentional injury, homicide, and suicide as leading causes of death, how common these causes of death are, and whom they affect. These data are intended for a broad audience—the public, the media, public health practitioners and researchers, and public health officials—to increase their knowledge of injury.

WISQARS Fatal mortality reports provide tables of the total numbers of injury-related deaths and the death rates per 100,000 U.S. population. The reports list deaths according to cause (mechanism) and intent (manner) of injury by state, race, Hispanic origin, sex, and age groupings.

Further information on WISQARS Fatal may be obtained from

National Center for Injury Prevention and Control
Centers for Disease Control and Prevention
1600 Clifton Road
Atlanta, GA 30329
https://wwwn.cdc.gov/dcs/ContactUs/Form
https://www.cdc.gov/injury/wisqars/fatal_help/data_
   sources.html

Youth Risk Behavior Surveillance System

The Youth Risk Behavior Surveillance System (YRBSS) is an epidemiological surveillance system developed by the Centers for Disease Control and Prevention (CDC) to monitor the prevalence of youth behaviors that most influence health. The YRBSS focuses on priority health-risk behaviors established during youth that result in the most significant mortality, morbidity, disability, and social problems during both youth and adulthood. The YRBSS includes a national school-based Youth Risk Behavior Survey (YRBS), as well as surveys conducted in states, territories, tribes, and large urban school districts.

The national YRBS uses a three-stage cluster sampling design to produce a nationally representative sample of students in grades 9–12 in the United States. In each survey, the target population consisted of all public and private school students in grades 9–12 in the 50 states and the District of Columbia. The first-stage sampling frame included selecting primary sampling units (PSUs) from strata formed on the basis of urbanization and the relative percentage of Black and Hispanic students in the PSU. These PSUs are either counties; subareas of large counties; or groups of smaller, adjacent counties. At the second stage, schools were selected with probability proportional to school enrollment size.

The final stage of sampling consisted of randomly selecting, in each chosen school and in each of grades 9–12, one or two classrooms from either a required subject, such as English or social studies, or a required period, such as homeroom or second period. All students in selected classes are eligible to participate. In surveys conducted before 2013, three strategies were used to oversample Black and Hispanic students: (1) larger sampling rates were used to select PSUs that are in high-Black and high-Hispanic strata; (2) a modified measure of size was used that increased the probability of selecting schools with a disproportionately high minority enrollment; and (3) two classes per grade, rather than one, were selected in schools with a high percentage of Black or Hispanic enrollment. In 2013, 2015, and 2017, only selection of two classes per grade was needed to achieve an adequate precision with minimum variance. Approximately 16,300 students participated in the 1993 survey; 10,900 students participated in 1995; 16,300 students participated in 1997; 15,300 students participated in 1999; 13,600 students

participated in 2001; 15,200 students participated in 2003; 13,900 participated in 2005; 14,000 participated in 2007; 16,400 participated in 2009; 15,400 participated in 2011; 13,600 participated in 2013; 15,600 participated in 2015; and 14,800 participated in 2017.

The overall response rate was 70 percent for the 1993 survey, 60 percent for the 1995 survey, 69 percent for the 1997 survey, 66 percent in 1999, 63 percent in 2001, 67 percent in 2003, 67 percent in 2005, 68 percent in 2007, 71 percent in 2009, 71 percent in 2011, 68 percent in 2013, 60 percent in 2015, and 60 percent in 2017. NCES standards call for response rates of 85 percent or greater for cross-sectional surveys, and bias analyses are required by NCES when that percentage is not achieved. For YRBS data, a full nonresponse bias analysis has not been done because the data necessary to do the analysis are not available. A school nonresponse bias analysis, however, was done for the 2017 survey. This analysis found some evidence of potential bias by school type and school poverty level, but concluded that the bias had little impact on the overall estimates and would be further reduced by weight adjustment. The weights were developed to adjust for nonresponse and the oversampling of Black and Hispanic students in the sample. The final weights were constructed so that only weighted proportions of students (not weighted counts of students) in each grade matched national population projections.

State-level data were downloaded from the Youth Online: Comprehensive Results web page (https://nccd.cdc.gov/ Youthonline/App/Default.aspx). Each state and district school-based YRBS employs a two-stage, cluster sample design to produce representative samples of students in grades 9–12 in their jurisdiction. All except one state sample (South Dakota), and all district samples, include only public schools, and each district sample includes only schools in the funded school district (e.g., San Diego Unified School District) rather than in the entire city (e.g., greater San Diego area).

In the first sampling stage in all except a few states and districts, schools are selected with probability proportional to school enrollment size. In the second sampling stage, intact classes of a required subject or intact classes during a required period (e.g., second period) are selected randomly. All students in sampled classes are eligible to participate. Certain states and districts modify these procedures to meet their individual needs. For example, in a given state or district, all schools, rather than a sample of schools, might be selected to participate. State and local surveys that have a scientifically selected sample, appropriate documentation, and an overall response rate greater than or equal to 60 percent are weighted. The overall response rate reflects the school response rate multiplied by the student response rate. These three criteria are used to ensure that the data from those surveys can be considered representative of students in grades 9–12 in that jurisdiction. A weight is applied to each record to adjust for student nonresponse and the distribution of students by grade, sex, and race/ethnicity in each jurisdiction. Therefore, weighted estimates are representative of all students in grades 9–12 attending schools in each jurisdiction. Surveys that do not have an overall response rate of greater than or equal to 60 percent and that do not have appropriate documentation are not weighted and are not included in this report.

In the 2017 YRBS, 39 states and 21 large urban districts had weighted data. It should be noted that not all of the districts that had weighted data were located in a state that had weighted data. For example, Georgia was not one of the 39 states that had weighted data, but the state contained one of the 21 districts that did (DeKalb County, GA). (For information on the location of the districts, please see https://www.cdc.gov/healthyyouth/data/yrbs/participation.htm.) In sites with weighted data, the student sample sizes for the state and district YRBS ranged from 805 to 51,807. School response rates ranged from 68 to 100 percent, student response rates ranged from 67 to 90 percent, and overall response rates ranged from 60 to 89 percent.

Readers should note that reports of these data published by the CDC and in this report do not include percentages for which the denominator includes fewer than 100 unweighted cases.

In 1999, in accordance with changes to the Office of Management and Budget's standards for the classification of federal data on race and ethnicity, the YRBS item on race/ethnicity was modified. The version of the race and ethnicity question used in 1993, 1995, and 1997 was

How do you describe yourself?
    a. White—not Hispanic
    b. Black—not Hispanic
    c. Hispanic or Latino
    d. Asian or Pacific Islander
    e. American Indian or Alaska Native
    f. Other

The version used in 1999, 2001, and 2003, as well as in the 2005 state and local district surveys was

How do you describe yourself? (Select one or more responses.)
    a. American Indian or Alaska Native
    b. Asian
    c. Black or African American
    d. Hispanic or Latino
    e. Native Hawaiian or Other Pacific Islander
    f. White

In the 2005 national survey and in all 2007, 2009, 2011, 2013, 2015, and 2017 surveys, race/ethnicity was computed from two questions: (1) "Are you Hispanic or Latino?" (response options were "Yes" and "No"), and (2) "What is your race?" (response options were "American Indian or Alaska Native," "Asian," "Black or African American," "Native Hawaiian or Other Pacific Islander," or "White"). For the second question, students could select more than one response option. For this report, students were classified as "Hispanic" if they answered "Yes" to the first question, regardless of how they answered the second question. Students who answered "No" to the first question and selected more than one race/ethnicity in the second category were classified as "More than one race." Students who answered "No" to the first question and selected only one race/ethnicity were classified as that race/ethnicity. Race/ethnicity was classified as missing for students who did not answer the first question and for students who answered "No" to the first question but did not answer the second question.

CDC has conducted two studies to understand the effect of changing the race/ethnicity item on the YRBS. Brener, Kann, and McManus (*Public Opinion Quarterly*, 67:227–226, 2003) found that allowing students to select more than one response to a single race/ethnicity question on the YRBS had only a minimal effect on reported race/ethnicity among high school students. Eaton, Brener, Kann, and Pittman (*Journal of Adolescent Health, 41*: 488–494, 2007) found that self-reported race/ethnicity was similar regardless of whether the single-question or a two-question format was used.

Further information on the YRBSS may be obtained from

Nancy Brener
Division of Adolescent and School Health
National Center for HIV/AIDS, Viral Hepatitis, STD, and TB Prevention
Centers for Disease Control and Prevention
1600 Clifton Road
Atlanta, GA 30329
nad1@cdc.gov
http://www.cdc.gov/yrbs

Department of Defense

Defense Manpower Data Center

The Statistical Information Analysis Division of the Defense Manpower Data Center (DMDC) maintains the largest archive of personnel, manpower, and training data in the Department of Defense (DoD). The DMDC's statistical activities include the personnel survey program, an enlistment testing program to support screening of military applicants, and a client support program to provide statistical support to the Office of the Secretary of Defense. The DMDC collects DoD contract information in support of national economic tables and the Small Business Competitiveness Demonstration Program; it also produces statistics on DoD purchases from educational and nonprofit institutions and from state and local governments.

For more information on the DMDC, see https://www.dmdc.osd.mil/appj/dwp/index.jsp.

Department of Justice

Bureau of Justice Statistics

A division of the U.S. Department of Justice Office of Justice Programs, the Bureau of Justice Statistics (BJS) collects, analyzes, publishes, and disseminates statistical information on crime, criminal offenders, victims of crime, and the operations of the justice system at all levels of government and internationally. It also provides technical and financial support to state governments for development of criminal justice statistics and information systems on crime and justice.

For information on the BJS, see https://www.bjs.gov/.

National Crime Victimization Survey

The National Crime Victimization Survey (NCVS), administered for the U.S. Bureau of Justice Statistics (BJS) by the U.S. Census Bureau, is the nation's primary source of information on crime and the victims of crime. Initiated in 1972 and redesigned in 1992 and 2016, the NCVS collects detailed information on the frequency and nature of the crimes of rape, sexual assault, robbery, aggravated and simple assault, theft, household burglary, and motor vehicle theft experienced by Americans and American households each year. The survey measures both crimes reported to the police and crimes not reported to the police.

NCVS estimates presented may differ from those in previous published reports. This is because a small number of victimizations, referred to as series victimizations, are included using a new counting strategy. High-frequency repeat victimizations, or series victimizations, are six or more similar but separate victimizations that occur with such frequency that the victim is unable to recall each individual event or describe each event in detail. As part of ongoing research efforts associated with the redesign of the NCVS, BJS investigated ways to include high-frequency repeat victimizations, or series victimizations, in estimates of criminal victimization. Including series victimizations results in more accurate estimates of victimization. BJS has decided to include series victimizations using the victim's estimates of the number of times the victimizations occurred over the past 6 months, capping the number of victimizations within each series at a maximum of 10. This strategy for counting series victimizations balances the desire to estimate national rates and account for the experiences of persons who have been subjected to repeat victimizations against the desire to minimize the estimation errors that can occur when repeat victimizations are reported. Including series victimizations in national rates results in rather large increases in the level of violent victimization; however, trends in violence are generally similar regardless of whether series victimizations are included. For more information on the new counting strategy and supporting research, see *Methods for Counting High-Frequency Repeat Victimizations in the National Crime Victimization Survey* at https://www.bjs.gov/content/pub/pdf/mchfrv.pdf.

Readers should note that in 2003, in accordance with changes to the Office of Management and Budget's standards for the classification of federal data on race and ethnicity, the NCVS item on race/ethnicity was modified. A question on Hispanic origin is now followed by a new question on race. The new question about race allows the respondent to choose more than one race and delineates Asian as a separate category from Native Hawaiian or Other Pacific Islander. An analysis conducted by the Demographic Surveys Division at the U.S. Census Bureau showed that the new race question had very little impact on the aggregate racial distribution of the NCVS respondents, with one exception: There was a 1.6 percentage point decrease in the percentage of respondents who reported themselves as White. Due to changes in race/ethnicity categories, comparisons of race/ethnicity across years should be made with caution.

Every 10 years, the NCVS sample is redesigned to reflect changes in the population. In the 2006 NCVS, changes in the sample design and survey methodology affected the survey's estimates. Caution should be used when comparing the 2006 estimates to estimates of other years. For more information on the 2006 NCVS data, see *Criminal Victimization, 2006*, at https://www.bjs.gov/content/pub/pdf/cv06.pdf; the NCVS 2006 technical notes, at https://bjs.ojp.usdoj.gov/content/pub/pdf/cv06tn.pdf; and *Criminal Victimization, 2007*, at https://bjs.ojp.usdoj.gov/content/pub/pdf/cv07.pdf. Due to a sample increase and redesign in 2016, victimization estimates among youth were not comparable to estimates for other years and are not available in this report. For more information on the redesign, see https://www.bjs.gov/content/pub/pdf/cv16re.pdf.

The number of NCVS-eligible households in the 2018 sample was approximately 208,000. Households were selected using a stratified, multistage cluster design. In the first stage, the primary sampling units (PSUs), consisting of counties or groups of counties, were selected. In the second stage, smaller areas, called Enumeration Districts (EDs), were selected from each sampled PSU. Finally, from selected EDs, clusters of four households, called segments, were selected for interview. At each stage, the selection was done proportionate to population size in order to create a self-weighting sample. The final sample was augmented to account for households constructed after the decennial census. Within each sampled household, the U.S. Census Bureau interviewer attempts to interview all household members age 12 and over to determine whether they had been victimized by the measured crimes during the 6 months preceding the interview.

The first NCVS interview with a housing unit is conducted in person. Subsequent interviews are conducted by telephone, if possible. All persons age 12 and older are interviewed every 6 months. Households remain in the sample for 3 years and are interviewed seven times at 6-month intervals. Since the survey's inception, the initial interview at each sample unit has been used only to bound future interviews to establish a time frame to avoid duplication of crimes uncovered in these subsequent interviews. Beginning in 2006, data from the initial interview have been adjusted to account for the effects of bounding and have been included in the survey estimates. After a household has been interviewed its seventh time, it is replaced by a new sample household. In 2018, the household response rate was about 73 percent, and the completion rate for persons within households was about 82 percent. Weights were developed to permit estimates for the total U.S. population 12 years and older. For more information on the 2018 NCVS, see https://www.bjs.gov/content/pub/pdf/cv18.pdf.

Further information on the NCVS may be obtained from

Barbara A. Oudekerk
Victimization Statistics Branch
Bureau of Justice Statistics
barbara.a.oudekerk@usdoj.gov
https://www.bjs.gov/

School Crime Supplement

Created as a supplement to the NCVS and codesigned by the National Center for Education Statistics and Bureau of Justice Statistics, the School Crime Supplement (SCS) survey has been conducted in 1989, 1995, and biennially since 1999 to collect additional information about school-related victimizations on a national level. This report includes data from the 1995, 1999, 2001, 2003, 2005, 2007, 2009, 2011, 2013, 2015, and 2017 collections. The 1989 data are not included in this report as a result of methodological changes to the NCVS and SCS. The SCS was designed to assist policymakers, as well as academic researchers and practitioners at federal, state, and local levels, to make informed decisions concerning crime in schools. The survey asks students a number of key questions about their experiences with and perceptions of crime and violence that occurred inside their school, on school grounds, on the school bus, or on the way to or from school. Students are asked additional questions about security measures used by their school, students' participation in after-school activities, students' perceptions of school rules, the presence of weapons and gangs in school, the presence of hate-related words and graffiti in school, student reports of bullying and reports of rejection at school, and the availability of drugs and alcohol in school. Students are also asked attitudinal questions relating to fear of victimization and avoidance behavior at school.

The SCS survey was conducted for a 6-month period from January through June in all households selected for the NCVS (see discussion above for information about the NCVS sampling design and changes to the race/ethnicity variable beginning in 2003). Within these households, the eligible respondents for the SCS were those household members who had attended school at any time during the 6 months preceding the interview, were enrolled in grades 6–12, and were not homeschooled. In 2007, the questionnaire was changed and household members who attended school sometime during the school year of the interview were included. The age range of students covered in this report is 12–18 years of age. Eligible respondents were asked the supplemental questions in the SCS only after completing their entire NCVS interview. It should be noted that the first

or unbounded NCVS interview has always been included in analysis of the SCS data and may result in the reporting of events outside of the requested reference period.

The prevalence of victimization for 1995, 1999, 2001, 2003, 2005, 2007, 2009, 2011, 2013, 2015, and 2017 was calculated by using NCVS incident variables appended to the SCS data files of the same year. The NCVS type of crime variable was used in the SCS to classify student victimizations into the categories "serious violent," "violent," and "theft." The NCVS variables asking where the incident happened (at school) and what the victim was doing when it happened (attending school or on the way to or from school) were used to ascertain whether the incident happened at school. Only incidents that occurred inside the United States are included.

In 2001, the SCS survey instrument was modified. In 1995 and 1999, "at school" had been defined for respondents as meaning in the school building, on the school grounds, or on a school bus. In 2001, the definition of at "school" was changed to mean in the school building, on school property, on a school bus, or going to and from school. The change to the definition of "at school" in the 2001 questionnaire was made in order to render the definition there consistent with the definition as it is constructed in the NCVS. This change to the definition of "at school" has been retained in subsequent SCS collections. Cognitive interviews conducted by the U.S. Census Bureau on the 1999 SCS suggested that modifications to the definition of "at school" would not have a substantial impact on the estimates.

Shown in table H, below, are the number of students participating, household completion rates, student completion rates, and overall unit response rates in the SCS from 1995 to 2017:

Table H. Student participation in the School Crime Supplement (SCS) by number participating, household completion rate, student completion rate, and overall unit response rate: Selected years, 1995 to 2017

SCS collection year	Number participating	Household completion rate (percent)	Student completion rate (percent)	Overall unit response rate (percent)[1]
1995	9,700	95	78	74
1999	8,400	94	78	73
2001	8,400	93	77	72
2003	7,200	92	70	64
2005	6,300	91	62	56
2007	5,600	90	58	53
2009	5,000	92	56	51
2011	6,500	91	63	57
2013	5,700	86	60	51
2015	5,500	82	58	48
2017	7,100	76	52	40

[1]The overall unit response rate is calculated by multiplying the household completion rate by the student completion rate. Prior to 2011, overall SCS unit response rates were unweighted; starting in 2011, overall SCS unit response rates are weighted.
SOURCE: U.S. Department of Justice, Bureau of Justice Statistics, School Crime Supplement (SCS) to the National Crime Victimization Survey, 1995 through 2017.

There are two types of nonresponse: unit and item nonresponse. NCES requires that any stage of data collection within a survey that has a unit base-weighted response rate of less than 85 percent be evaluated for the potential magnitude of unit nonresponse bias before the data or any analysis using the data may be released (NCES Statistical

Standards, 2002, at https://nces.ed.gov/statprog/2002/std4_4.asp). Due to the low unit response rate in 2005, 2007, 2009, 2011, 2013, 2015, and 2017, a unit nonresponse bias analysis was done. Unit response rates indicate how many sampled units have completed interviews. Because interviews with students could only be completed after households had responded to the NCVS, the unit completion rate for the SCS reflects both the household interview completion rate and the student interview completion rate. Nonresponse can greatly affect the strength and application of survey data by leading to an increase in variance as a result of a reduction in the actual size of the sample and can produce bias if the nonrespondents have characteristics of interest that are different from the respondents. In order for response bias to occur, respondents must have different response rates and responses to particular survey variables. The magnitude of unit nonresponse bias is determined by the response rate and the differences between respondents and nonrespondents on key survey variables. Although the bias analysis cannot measure response bias since the SCS is a sample survey and it is not known how the population would have responded, the SCS sampling frame has several key student or school characteristic variables for which data are known for respondents and nonrespondents: sex, age, race/ethnicity, household income, region, and urbanicity, all of which are associated with student victimization. To the extent that there are differential responses by respondents in these groups, nonresponse bias is a concern.

In 2005, the analysis of unit nonresponse bias found evidence of bias for the race, household income, and urbanicity variables. White (non-Hispanic) and Other (non-Hispanic) respondents had higher response rates than Black (non-Hispanic) and Hispanic respondents. Respondents from households with an income of $35,000–$49,999 and $50,000 or more had higher response rates than those from households with incomes of less than $7,500, $7,500–$14,999, $15,000–$24,999, and $25,000–$34,999. Respondents who live in urban areas had lower response rates than those who live in rural or suburban areas. Although the extent of nonresponse bias cannot be determined, weighting adjustments, which corrected for differential response rates, should have reduced the problem.

In 2007, the analysis of unit nonresponse bias found evidence of bias by the race/ethnicity and household income variables. Hispanic respondents had lower response rates than respondents of other races/ethnicities. Respondents from households with an income of $25,000 or more had higher response rates than those from households with incomes of less than $25,000. However, when responding students are compared to the eligible NCVS sample, there were no measurable differences between the responding students and the eligible students, suggesting that the nonresponse bias has little impact on the overall estimates.

In 2009, the analysis of unit nonresponse bias found evidence of potential bias for the race/ethnicity and urbanicity variables. White students and students of other races/ethnicities had higher response rates than did Black and Hispanic respondents. Respondents from households located in rural areas had higher response rates than those from households located in urban areas. However, when responding students are compared to the eligible NCVS sample, there were no measurable differences between the responding students and the eligible students, suggesting that the nonresponse bias has little impact on the overall estimates.

In 2011, the analysis of unit nonresponse bias found evidence of potential bias for the age variable. Respondents 12 to 17 years old had higher response rates than did 18-year-old respondents in the NCVS and SCS interviews. Weighting the data adjusts for unequal selection probabilities and for the effects of nonresponse. The weighting adjustments that correct for differential response rates are created by region, age, race, and sex, and should have reduced the effect of nonresponse.

In 2013, the analysis of unit nonresponse bias found evidence of potential bias for the age, region, and Hispanic origin variables in the NCVS interview response. Within the SCS portion of the data, only the age and region variables showed significant unit nonresponse bias. Further analysis indicated that only the age 14 and the west region categories showed positive response biases that were significantly different from some of the other categories within the age and region variables. Based on the analysis, nonresponse bias seems to have little impact on the SCS results. In 2015, the analysis of unit nonresponse bias found evidence of potential bias for age, race, Hispanic origin, urbanicity, and region in the NCVS interview response. For the SCS interview, the age, race, urbanicity, and region variables showed significant unit nonresponse bias. The age 14 group and rural areas showed positive response biases that were significantly different from other categories within the age and urbanicity variables. The northeast region and Asian race group showed negative response biases that were significantly different from other categories within the region and race variables. These results provide evidence that these subgroups may have a nonresponse bias associated with them. In 2017, the analysis of unit nonresponse bias found that the race/ethnicity and census region variables showed significant differences in response rates between different race/ethnicity and census region subgroups. Respondent and nonrespondent distributions were significantly different for the race/ethnicity subgroup only. However, after using weights adjusted for person nonresponse, there was no evidence that these response differences introduced nonresponse bias in the final victimization estimates. Response rates for SCS survey items in all survey years were high—typically over 95 percent of all eligible respondents, meaning there is little potential for item nonresponse bias for most items in the survey. The weighted data permit inferences about the eligible student population who were enrolled in schools in all SCS data years.

Further information about the SCS may be obtained from

Rachel Hansen
Cross-Sectional Surveys Branch
Sample Surveys Division
National Center for Education Statistics
550 12th Street SW
Washington, DC 20202
rachel.hansen@ed.gov
https://nces.ed.gov/programs/crime/

Federal Bureau of Investigation

The Federal Bureau of Investigation (FBI) collects statistics on crimes from law enforcement agencies throughout the country through the Uniform Crime Reporting (UCR) Program. The UCR Program was conceived in 1929 by the International Association of Chiefs of Police to meet a need for reliable, uniform crime statistics for the nation. In 1930, the FBI was tasked with collecting, publishing, and archiving those statistics. Today, several annual statistical publications, such as the comprehensive *Crime in the United States* (CIUS), are produced from data provided by over 18,000 law enforcement agencies across the United States. CIUS is an annual publication in which the FBI compiles the volume and rate of crime offenses for the nation, the states, and individual agencies. This report also includes arrest, clearance, and law enforcement employee data.

For more information on the UCR Program, see https://ucr.fbi.gov/ucr.

Studies of Active Shooter Incidents

The Investigative Assistance for Violent Crimes Act of 2012, which was signed into law in 2013, authorizes the attorney general, upon the request of an appropriate state or local law enforcement official, to "assist in the investigation of violent acts and shootings occurring in a place of public use and in the investigation of mass killings and attempted mass killings." The attorney general delegated this responsibility to the FBI.

In 2014, the FBI initiated studies of active shooter incidents in order to advance the understanding of these incidents and provide law enforcement agencies with data that can inform efforts toward preventing, preparing for, responding to, and recovering from them.

Data on active shooter incidents at educational institutions come from FBI reports. Recent reports include *Active Shooter Incidents in the United States in 2016 and 2017*, *Active Shooter Incidents in the United States in 2018*, and *Active Shooter Incidents in the United States in 2019*, which can be accessed at https://www.fbi.gov/about/partnerships/office-of-partner-engagement/active-shooter-resources.

Further information about FBI resources on active shooter incidents may be obtained from

Active Shooter Resources
Office of Partner Engagement
Federal Bureau of Investigation
U.S. Department of Justice
935 Pennsylvania Avenue NW
Washington, DC 20535
https://www.fbi.gov/about/partnerships/office-of-partner-engagement/active-shooter-resources

Supplementary Homicide Reports

Supplementary Homicide Reports (SHR) are a part of the Uniform Crime Reporting (UCR) program of the Federal Bureau of Investigation (FBI). These reports provide incident-level information on criminal homicides, including situation type (e.g., number of victims, number of offenders, and whether offenders are known); the age, sex, and race of victims and offenders; the weapon used; circumstances of the incident; and the relationship of the victim to the offender. The data are provided monthly to the FBI by local law enforcement agencies participating in the UCR program. The data include murders and nonnegligent manslaughters in the United States; thus, negligent manslaughters and justifiable homicides have been eliminated from the data.

About 90 percent of homicides are included in the SHR program. However, adjustments can be made to the weights to correct for missing victim reports. Estimates from the SHR program used in this report were generated by the Bureau of Justice Statistics (BJS).

Further information on the SHR program may be obtained from

Criminal Justice Information Services Division
Federal Bureau of Investigation
Module D3
1000 Custer Hollow Road
Clarksburg, WV 26306
(304) 625-4995
crimestatsinfo@fbi.gov

Institute of Museum and Library Services

On October 1, 2007, the administration of the Public Libraries Survey (PLS) and the State Library Agencies (StLA) Survey was transferred from the National Center for Education Statistics to the Institute of Museum and Library Services (IMLS).

IMLS Library Statistics

Public library statistics are collected annually using the PLS and disseminated annually through the Federal-State Cooperative System (FSCS) for Public Library Data. Descriptive statistics are produced for over 9,000 public libraries. The PLS includes information about staffing; operating income and expenditures; type of governance; type of administrative structure; size of collection; and service measures such as reference transactions, public service hours, interlibrary loans, circulation, and library visits. In the FSCS, respondents supply the information electronically, and data are edited and tabulated in machine-readable form.

PLS respondents are public libraries identified by state administrative library agencies in the 50 states, the District of Columbia, and certain U.S. territories. At the state level, FSCS is administered by State Data Coordinators, who are appointed by the chief officer of each state library agency. The State Data Coordinator collects the requested data from local public libraries. The 50 states, District of Columbia, and territories submit data for individual public libraries, which are aggregated to state and national levels.

Further information on these library surveys can be obtained from

Institute of Museum and Library Services
955 L'Enfant Plaza North SW
Washington, DC 20024-2135
https://www.imls.gov/
https://www.imls.gov/research-evaluation/data-collection/
    public-libraries-survey

National Institute on Drug Abuse

Monitoring the Future survey

The National Institute on Drug Abuse of the U.S. Department of Health and Human Services is the primary supporter of the long-term national study "Monitoring the Future: A Continuing Study of American Youth," conducted by the University of Michigan Institute for Social Research. One component of this national sample survey deals with student drug abuse, and its results have been published annually since 1975.

In this study, 8th-, 10th-, and 12th-graders complete self-administered questionnaires given to them in their classrooms by University of Michigan personnel (12th-graders have participated since the beginning of the study, and 8th- and 10th-graders began participating in 1991). The 8th- and 10th-grade surveys are anonymous, while the 12th-grade survey is confidential. In addition, beginning with the class of 1976, a randomly selected sample from each senior class has been followed in the years after high school on a continuing basis.

The annual sample for each grade is made up of roughly 16,000 students in 133 public and private schools, for a total of about 50,000 students in 420 public and private secondary schools. In 2019, the survey involved about 42,500 8th-, 10th-, and 12th-graders in 396 public and private secondary schools nationwide.

Understandably, there is some reluctance to admit illegal activities. In addition, students who are out of school on the day of the survey are nonrespondents, and the survey does not include high school dropouts. The inclusion of absentees and dropouts would tend to increase the proportion of individuals who had used drugs. A 1983 study found that the inclusion of absentees could increase some of the drug usage estimates by as much as 2.7 percentage points. (Details on that study and its methodology were published in *Drug Use Among American High School Students, College Students, and Other Young Adults*, by L.D. Johnston, P.M. O'Malley, and J.G. Bachman, available from the National Clearinghouse on Drug Abuse Information, 5600 Fishers Lane, Rockville, MD 20857.)

The first published results of the 2019 survey were presented in *Monitoring the Future, National Results on Drug Use, 1975–2019: Overview, Key Findings on Adolescent Drug Use*, at https://www.drugabuse.gov/drug-topics/trends-statistics/monitoring-future.

Further information on the Monitoring the Future drug abuse survey may be obtained from

National Institute on Drug Abuse
Division of Epidemiology, Services and Prevention
    Research
6001 Executive Boulevard
Rockville, MD 20852
mtfinformation@umich.edu
https://www.drugabuse.gov/drug-topics/trends-statistics/
    monitoring-future

National Science Foundation

Survey of Federal Funds for Research and Development

The annual Survey of Federal Funds for Research and Development is the primary source of information about federal funding for research and development in the United States. It is used by policymakers in the executive and legislative branches of the federal government in determining policies, laws, and regulations affecting science; it is also used by those who follow science trends in every sector of the economy, including university administrators and professors, economic and political analysts, research and development managers inside and outside the government, the science press, and leading members of the science community in the United States and around the world.

The survey's target population consists of the federal agencies that conduct research and development programs, excluding the CIA. The federal agencies in the sampling frame are those identified from information in the President's budget submitted to Congress.

In the survey cycle for fiscal years 2018–19, a total of 32 federal agencies (15 federal departments and 17 independent agencies) reported research and development data. Because multiple subdivisions of some federal departments completed the survey, there were 82 agency-level respondents: 5 federal departments, 60 agencies within another 10 federal departments, and 17 independent agencies.

Federal funds data are for the fiscal year just completed and the current fiscal year. Actual data are collected for the year just completed; estimates are obtained for the current fiscal year.

The data are collected and managed online; this system was designed to help improve survey reporting by offering respondents direct online reporting and editing.

There is no known unit or item nonresponse, so no weighting or imputation methods are used; NCES assumes a blank field is zero for estimation purposes. The information included in this survey has been stable since fiscal year 1973, when federal obligations for research to universities and colleges by agency and detailed science and engineering fields were added to the survey.

Further information on federal funds for research and development may be obtained from

Christopher Pece
Project Officer
Research and Development Statistics Program
National Center for Science and Engineering Statistics
National Science Foundation
2415 Eisenhower Avenue
Alexandria, VA 22314
cpece@nsf.gov
https://www.nsf.gov/statistics/srvyfedfunds/

Survey of Earned Doctorates

The Survey of Earned Doctorates (SED) has collected basic statistics from the universe of doctoral recipients in the United States each year since 1957. It is sponsored by the National Center for Science and Engineering Statistics (NCSES) within the National Science Foundation (NSF) and by three other federal agencies: the National Institutes of Health, U.S. Department of Education, and National Endowment for the Humanities.

With the assistance of institutional coordinators at each doctorate-awarding institution, a survey form or web link is distributed to each person completing the requirements for a research doctorate. Of the 55,195 persons granted a research doctorate in 2018, 92.1 percent completed the survey. The survey questionnaire obtained information on sex, race/ethnicity, marital status, citizenship, disabilities, specialty field of doctorate, educational institutions attended, financial support, education debt, postgraduation plans, and educational attainment of parents.

Further information on the Survey of Earned Doctorates may be obtained from

Kelly Kang
Project Officer
Human Resources Statistics Program
National Center for Science and Engineering Statistics
National Science Foundation
2415 Eisenhower Avenue
Alexandria, VA 22314
kkang@nsf.gov
https://www.nsf.gov/statistics/srvydoctorates/

Survey of Graduate Students and Postdoctorates in Science and Engineering

The Survey of Graduate Students and Postdoctorates in Science and Engineering, also known as the graduate student survey (GSS), is an annual survey of all U.S. academic institutions granting research-based master's degrees or doctorates in science, engineering, or selected health fields. Sponsored by the National Science Foundation and the National Institutes of Health, the survey collects counts of enrolled graduate students, postdoctoral researchers, and other doctorate-holding nonfaculty researchers at these institutions by demographics and other characteristics, such as source of financial support. Results are used to assess shifts in graduate enrollment, shifts in postdoctoral researcher and nonfaculty researcher appointments, and trends in financial support.

Data collection for the 2018 GSS began in fall 2018. The 2018 survey universe included 19,592 units at 715 academic institutions in the United States that granted research-based master's degrees or doctorates in science, engineering, or selected health fields.

New procedures to improve coverage of GSS-eligible units were introduced in the 2007 survey cycle and were continued in subsequent cycles. Increased emphasis was given to updating the unit list by providing an exhaustive list of GSS-eligible programs within existing GSS fields. In previous years, only a representative list was provided for each GSS field, which may have resulted in not reporting all eligible units. The set of GSS-eligible fields was also modified. Due to these changes, data for 2007 and later years are not directly comparable with data from previous years.

More recently, the survey universe was modified in 2014 to include 151 new institutions and exclude 2 for-profit institutions; these changes were the result of a comprehensive frame evaluation study conducted from 2010 to 2013 and the annual frame evaluation conducted in the 2013–14 cycle. In 2015 and 2016, some institutions became newly eligible for GSS, some became ineligible, some changed GSS degree-granting status, and some merged. As a result of these changes, the total number of institutions included in the GSS increased from 706 in 2014 to 714 in 2016. And although it decreased to 703 in 2017 (due to the fact that institutions that became ineligible that year outnumbered institutions that were added) the number of institutions included in the GSS reached 715 in 2018.

Further information on the Survey of Graduate Students and Postdoctorates in Science and Engineering may be obtained from

Mike Yamaner
Project Officer
Human Resources Statistics Program
National Center for Science and Engineering Statistics
National Science Foundation
2415 Eisenhower Avenue
Alexandria, VA 22314
myamaner@nsf.gov
https://www.nsf.gov/statistics/srvygradpostdoc/

Substance Abuse and Mental Health Services Administration

National Survey on Drug Use and Health

Conducted by the federal government since 1971 (and annually since 1991), the National Survey on Drug Use and Health (NSDUH) is a survey of the civilian, noninstitutionalized population of the United States age 12 or older. It is the primary source of information on the prevalence, patterns, and consequences of alcohol, tobacco, and illegal drug use and abuse. The survey collects data by administering questionnaires to a representative sample of the population (since 1999, the NSDUH interview has been carried out using computer-assisted interviewing). NSDUH collects information from residents of households, noninstitutional group quarters, and civilians living on military bases. The main results of the NSDUH present national estimates of rates of use, numbers of users, and other measures related to illicit drugs, alcohol, and tobacco products.

Prior to 2002, the survey was called the National Household Survey on Drug Abuse (NHSDA). The 2002 update of the survey's name coincided with improvements to the survey. In light of these improvements, NSDUH data from 2002 and later should not be compared with NHSDA data from 2001 and earlier as a method of assessing changes in substance use over time.

The 2005 NSDUH was the first in a coordinated 5-year sample design providing estimates for all 50 states and the District of Columbia for the years 2005 through 2009. Because the 2005 design enables estimates to be developed by state, states may be viewed as the first level of stratification, as well as a reporting variable.

In the 2018 NSDUH, screening was completed at 141,879 addresses, and 67,791 completed interviews were obtained: 16,852 interviews from adolescents ages 12 to 17 and 50,939 interviews from adults age 18 and over. Weighted response rates for household screening and for interviewing were 73.3 and 66.6 percent, respectively, for an overall response rate of 48.8 percent for persons age 12 and over. The weighted interview response rates were 73.9 percent for adolescents and 65.8 percent for adults.

Further information on the NSDUH may be obtained from

SAMHSA
Center for Behavioral Health Statistics and Quality
5600 Fishers Lane
Rockville, MD 20857
https://www.samhsa.gov/data/

Other Organization Sources

ACT

ACT assessment

The ACT assessment is designed to measure educational development in the areas of English, mathematics, social studies, and natural sciences. The assessment is taken by college-bound high school students. The test results are used to predict how well students might perform in college.

Prior to the 1984–85 school year, national norms were based on a 10 percent sample of the students taking the test. Since then, national norms have been based on the test scores of all students taking the test. Beginning with 1984–85, these norms have been based on the most recent ACT scores available from students scheduled to graduate in the spring of the year. Duplicate test records are no longer used to produce national figures.

Separate ACT standard scores are computed for English, mathematics, science reasoning, and, as of October 1989, reading. ACT standard scores are reported for each subject area on a scale from 1 to 36. In 2019, the national composite score (the simple average of the four ACT standard scores) was 20.7, with a standard deviation of 5.9. The tests emphasize reasoning, analysis, problem solving, and the integration of learning from various sources, as well as the application of these proficiencies to the kinds of tasks college students are expected to perform.

Further information on the ACT may be obtained from

ACT
500 ACT Drive
Iowa City, IA 52243
(319) 337-1270
https://www.act.org/

The College Board

Advanced Placement Exam

The Advanced Placement (AP) program is a curriculum sponsored by the College Board that offers high school students the opportunity to take college-level courses in a high school setting. A student taking an AP course in high school can earn college credit for participation by attaining a certain minimum score on the AP exam in that subject area.

The AP program offers 38 courses and exams. In most cases, the College Board does not require students to take an AP course before taking an AP exam. AP exams are given in the first two weeks in May. Most of the exams take 2 to 3 hours to complete. The scores for all AP exams range from 1 to 5, with 5 being the highest score.

SAT

The Admissions Testing Program of the College Board is made up of a number of college admissions tests, including the Preliminary Scholastic Assessment Test (PSAT) and the Scholastic Assessment Test, now known as the SAT. High school students participate in the testing program as sophomores, juniors, or seniors—some more than once during these three years. If they have taken the tests more than once, only the most recent scores are tabulated. The PSAT and SAT report subscores in the areas of mathematics and verbal ability.

Each year, approximately 2 million students take the SAT examination. The current version of the SAT, which includes an optional writing component among other content, format, and scoring changes, was first administered in March 2016.

Further information on AP and the SAT may be obtained from

The College Board National Office
250 Vesey Street
New York, NY 10281
https://www.collegeboard.org/

Commonfund Institute

Higher Education Price Index

Commonfund Institute took over management of the Higher Education Price Index (HEPI) in 2005 from Research Associates of Washington, which originated the index in 1961. HEPI is an inflation index designed specifically to track the main cost drivers in higher education. It measures the average relative level of prices in a fixed basket of goods and services purchased each year by colleges and universities through current fund educational and general expenditures, excluding research.

The main components of HEPI are faculty salaries; administrative salaries; clerical salaries; service employee salaries; fringe benefits; miscellaneous services; supplies and materials; and utilities. These represent the major items purchased for current operations by colleges and universities. Prices for these items are obtained from salary surveys conducted by the American Association of University Professors, the College and University Professional Association for Human Resources, and the Bureau of Labor Statistics (BLS), as well as from price series for components of BLS's Consumer Price Index (CPI), Employment Cost Index (ECI), and Producer Price Index (PPI).

HEPI measures price levels from a designated reference year in which budget weights are assigned. This base year is FY 1983 and is assigned a price value of 100.0 for index compilation. An index value of 115.0, for example, represents a 15 percent price increase over 1983 values.

Further information on HEPI may be obtained from

Commonfund Institute
15 Old Danbury Road
Wilton, CT 06897
https://www.commonfund.org/institute

Council for Advancement and Support of Education

Voluntary Support of Education survey

The Voluntary Support of Education (VSE) survey has collected data on fundraising at public and private colleges and universities (as well as a sample of precollege institutions) in the United States since 1957. The Council for Aid to Education (CAE) managed the survey from 1957 to 2017. The Council for Advancement and Support of Education (CASE) currently manages the survey, after having acquired it from CAE in 2018. CASE is a global nonprofit membership association of educational institutions that helps develop the communities of professional practice that build institutional resilience and success in challenging times. The communities include staff engaged in alumni relations, advancement services, communications, fundraising, government relations, marketing, and student recruitment.

The VSE survey is conducted online, and all accredited higher education institutions are eligible to participate. The number of U.S. higher education participants in 2018 was 929, a number that represented about one-fourth of colleges and universities in the United States but raised about 80 percent of total voluntary support of U.S. higher education institutions in the 2017–18 academic fiscal year.

The "Voluntary Support of Education Data & Research Findings" page (https://www.case.org/resources/voluntary-support-education-data-research-findings) on the CASE website provides information and the latest research briefs on the VSE survey. The AMAtlas Data Miner (https://www.case.org/resources/amatlas-data-miner) makes available, by subscription, 20 years of VSE survey data from approximately 1,000 public and private U.S. higher education institutions and a select group of private precollege institutions.

Further information on the VSE survey may be obtained from

Council for Advancement and Support of Education
1307 New York Avenue NW
Suite 100
Washington, DC 20005-4701
https://www.case.org/resources/voluntary-support-
    education-data-research-findings

Council of Chief State School Officer

State Education Indicators

The Council of Chief State School Officers (CCSSO) is a nonpartisan, nationwide, nonprofit organization of the public officials who head departments of public education in the 50 states, the District of Columbia, the Department of Defense Education Activity, the Bureau of Indian Education, Puerto Rico, American Samoa, Guam, the Northern Mariana Islands, and the U.S. Virgin Islands. The CCSSO State Education Indicators project (http://programs.ccsso.org/projects/State_Education_Indicators/) provides leadership in developing a system of state-by-state indicators of the condition of K–12 education. Indicator activities include collecting and reporting statistical indicators by state, tracking state policy changes, assisting with accountability systems, and conducting analysis of trends in education. *Key State Education Policies on PK–12 Education* is one of the publications issued by the State Education Indicators project. It is intended to inform policymakers and educators about the current status of key education policies that define and shape elementary and secondary education in the nation's public schools. State education staff reported on current policies through a survey, and CCSSO staff collected additional assessment information through state websites.

Further information on CCSSO publications may be obtained from

State Education Indicators Program
Standards, Assessment, and Accountability
Council of Chief State School Officers
1 Massachusetts Avenue NW
Suite 700
Washington, DC 20001
https://ccsso.org/

Editorial Projects in Education

Education Week

Editorial Projects in Education is an independent, nonprofit publisher of *Education Week* and other print and online products on K–12 education.

Further information on Editorial Projects in Education publications may be obtained from

Editorial Projects in Education
6935 Arlington Road
Bethesda, MD 20814
https://www.edweek.org/info/about/

Education Commission of the States

StateNotes

Education Commission of the States (ECS) regularly issues compilations, comparisons, and summaries of state policies—enacted or pending—on a number of education issues, including high school graduation requirements and school term information. ECS monitors state education activities for changes in education policies and updates ECS state information accordingly.

Further information on ECS StateNotes may be obtained from

Education Commission of the States
700 Broadway, #810
Denver, CO 80203
ecs@ecs.org
https://www.ecs.org/

GED Testing Service

GED Testing Service is a joint venture, begun in 2011, between the American Council on Education (ACE) and Pearson. A GED credential documents high school-level academic skills. The test was first administered to World War II veterans in 1942 and was subsequently administered to civilians beginning in 1947. The first four generations of the GED test were the original GED test released in 1942, the 1978 series, the 1988 series, and the 2002 series. In 2014, a new test was implemented. A comparison of the 2014 GED test and the 2002 series test is available at https://files.eric.ed.gov/fulltext/ED578900.pdf. Additional information about the various GED test series is available at https://ged.com/score_scale/.

It is important to note that attempting to make comparisons in GED testing across jurisdictions is problematic, since each jurisdiction manages its own GED testing program. Thus, each jurisdiction develops its own policies, and these policies are reflected in a jurisdiction's testing program outcomes (its pass rates, for instance).

Further information on the GED may be obtained from

GED Testing Service
1850 M Street NW
Washington, DC 20036
https://ged.com/

Graduate Record Examinations Board

GRE tests

Graduate Record Examinations (GRE) tests are taken by individuals applying to graduate or professional school. GRE offers two types of tests, the GRE General Test and Subject Tests. The GRE General Test, which is mainly taken via computer, measures verbal, quantitative, and analytical writing skills. The analytical writing section (which replaced the analytical reasoning section on the GRE General Test in 2002) consists of two analytical writing tasks. The Subject Tests measure achievement in biochemistry, cell and molecular biology, biology, chemistry, literature in English, mathematics, physics, and psychology. Each graduate institution (or institution division) determines which GRE tests are required for admission.

Individuals may take GRE tests more than once. Score reports only reflect scores earned within the past 5-year period.

Further information on the GRE may be obtained from

GRE-ETS
Educational Testing Service
P.O. Box 6000
Princeton, NJ 08541
https://www.ets.org/gre

Institute of International Education

Open Doors

Each year, the Institute of International Education (IIE) conducts a survey of the number of foreign students studying in American colleges and universities and U.S. students studying abroad. The results of these surveys are reported in the publication *Open Doors*. All of the regionally accredited institutions in NCES's Integrated Postsecondary Education Data System (IPEDS) are surveyed by IIE. The foreign student enrollment data presented in the *Digest of Education Statistics* are drawn from IIE surveys that ask U.S. institutions for information on enrollment of foreign students, as well as student characteristics such as country of origin. For the 2017–18 survey, 62 percent of the 2,812 institutions surveyed reported data. For 2018–19, 61 percent of the 2,796 institutions surveyed reported data.

Surveys on the flows of U.S. college students studying abroad have been conducted since 1985–86. Surveys are sent to U.S. institutions asking them to provide information on the number and characteristics of the students to whom they awarded credit for study abroad during the previous academic year. For the 2016–17 academic year, data were obtained from 1,242, or 68 percent, of the 1,830 institutions surveyed; for the 2017–18 academic year, data were obtained from 1,218, or 67 percent, of the 1,828 institutions surveyed.

Additional information may be obtained from the publication *Open Doors* or by contacting

Institute of International Education
809 United Nations Plaza
New York, NY 10017
(212) 883-8200
opendoors@iie.org
https://www.iie.org/en/Research-and-Insights/Open-Doors

International Association for the Evaluation of Educational Achievement

The International Association for the Evaluation of Educational Achievement (IEA) is composed of governmental research centers and national research institutions around the world whose aim is to investigate education problems common among countries. Since its inception in 1958, the IEA has conducted more than 30 research studies of cross-national achievement. The regular cycle of studies encompasses learning in basic school subjects. Examples are the Trends in International Mathematics and Science Study (TIMSS) and the Progress in International Reading Literacy Study (PIRLS). IEA projects also include studies of particular interest to IEA members, such as the TIMSS 1999 Video Study of Mathematics and Science Teaching, the Civic Education Study, and studies on information technology in education.

The international bodies that coordinate international assessments vary in the labels they apply to participating education systems, most of which are countries. IEA differentiates between IEA members, which IEA refers to as "countries" in all cases, and "benchmarking participants." IEA members include countries such as the United States and Ireland, as well as subnational entities such as England and Scotland (which are both part of the United Kingdom), the Flemish community of Belgium, and Hong Kong (a Special Administrative Region of China). IEA benchmarking participants are all subnational entities and include Canadian provinces, U.S. states, and Dubai in the United Arab Emirates (among others). Benchmarking participants, like the participating countries, are given the opportunity to assess the comparative international standing of their students' achievement and to view their curriculum and instruction in an international context.

Some IEA studies, such as TIMSS and PIRLS, include an assessment portion, as well as contextual questionnaires for collecting information about students' home and school experiences. The TIMSS and PIRLS scales, including the scale averages and standard deviations, are designed to remain constant from assessment to assessment so that education systems (including countries and subnational education systems) can compare their scores over time as well as compare their scores directly with the scores of other education systems. Although each scale was created to have a mean of 500 and a standard deviation of 100, the subject matter and the level of difficulty of items necessarily differ by grade, subject, and domain/dimension. Therefore, direct comparisons between scores across grades, subjects, and different domain/dimension types should not be made.

Further information on the International Association for the Evaluation of Educational Achievement may be obtained from https://www.iea.nl/.

Trends in International Mathematics and Science Study

The Trends in International Mathematics and Science Study (TIMSS, formerly known as the Third International Mathematics and Science Study) provides data on the mathematics and science achievement of U.S. 4th- and 8th-graders compared with that of their peers in other countries. TIMSS collects information through mathematics and science assessments and questionnaires. The questionnaires request information to help provide a context for student performance. They focus on such topics as students' attitudes and beliefs about learning mathematics and science, what students do as part of their mathematics and science lessons, students' completion of homework, and their lives both in and outside of school; teachers' perceptions of their preparedness for teaching mathematics and science, teaching assignments, class size and organization, instructional content and practices, collaboration with other teachers, and participation in professional development activities; and principals' viewpoints on policy and budget responsibilities, curriculum and instruction issues, and student behavior. The questionnaires also elicit information on the organization of schools and courses. The assessments and questionnaires are designed to specifications in a guiding framework. The TIMSS framework describes the mathematics and science content to be assessed and provides grade-specific objectives, an overview of the assessment design, and guidelines for item development.

TIMSS is on a 4-year cycle. Data collections occurred in 1995, 1999 (8th grade only), 2003, 2007, 2011, and 2015. TIMSS 2015 consisted of assessments in 4th-grade mathematics; numeracy (a less difficult version of 4th-grade mathematics, newly developed for 2015); 8th-grade mathematics; 4th-grade science; and 8th-grade science. Students in Bahrain, Indonesia, Iran, Kuwait, Jordan, Morocco, and South Africa as well as Buenos Aires participated in the 4th-grade mathematics assessment through the numeracy assessment. In addition, TIMSS 2015 included the third administration of TIMSS Advanced since 1995. TIMSS

Advanced is an international comparative study that measures the advanced mathematics and physics achievement of students in their final year of secondary school (the equivalent of 12th grade in the United States) who are taking or have taken advanced courses. The TIMSS 2015 survey also collected policy-relevant information about students, curriculum emphasis, technology use, and teacher preparation and training.

Progress in International Reading Literacy Study

The Progress in International Reading Literacy Study (PIRLS) provides data on the reading literacy of U.S. 4th-graders compared with that of their peers in other countries. PIRLS is on a 5-year cycle: PIRLS data collections have been conducted in 2001, 2006, 2011, and 2016. In 2016, a total of 58 education systems, including both IEA members and IEA benchmarking participants, participated in the survey. Sixteen of the education systems participating in PIRLS also participated in ePIRLS, an innovative, computer-based assessment of online reading designed to measure students' approaches to informational reading in an online environment.

PIRLS collects information through a reading literacy assessment and questionnaires that help to provide a context for student performance. Questionnaires are administered to collect information about students' home and school experiences in learning to read. A student questionnaire addresses students' attitudes toward reading and their reading habits. In addition, questionnaires are given to students' teachers and school principals in order to gather information about students' school experiences in developing reading literacy. In countries other than the United States, a parent questionnaire is also administered. The assessments and questionnaires are designed to specifications in a guiding framework. The PIRLS framework describes the reading content to be assessed and provides objectives specific to 4th grade, an overview of the assessment design, and guidelines for item development.

TIMSS and PIRLS Sampling and Response Rates

2016 PIRLS

As is done in all participating countries and other education systems, representative samples of students in the United States are selected. The sample design that was employed by PIRLS in 2016 is generally referred to as a two-stage stratified cluster sample. In the first stage of sampling, individual schools were selected with a probability proportionate to size (PPS) approach, which means that the probability is proportional to the estimated number of students enrolled in the target grade. In the second stage of sampling, intact classrooms were selected within sampled schools.

PIRLS guidelines call for a minimum of 150 schools to be sampled, with a minimum of 4,000 students assessed for each participating education system. The basic sample design of one classroom per school was designed to yield a total sample of approximately 4,500 students per population. About 4,400 U.S. students participated in PIRLS in 2016, joining 319,000 other student participants around the world. Accommodations were not provided for students with disabilities or students who were unable to read or speak the language of the test. These students were excluded from the sample. The IEA requirement is that the overall exclusion rate, of which exclusions of schools and students are a part, should not exceed more than 5 percent of the national desired target population.

In order to minimize the potential for response biases, the IEA developed participation or response rate standards that apply to all participating education systems and govern whether or not an education system's data are included in the TIMSS or PIRLS international datasets and the way in which its statistics are presented in the international reports. These standards were set using composites of response rates at the school, classroom, and student and teacher levels. Response rates were calculated with and without the inclusion of substitute schools that were selected to replace schools refusing to participate. In the 2016 PIRLS administered in the United States, the unweighted school response rate was 76 percent, and the weighted school response rate was 75 percent. All schools selected for PIRLS were also asked to participate in ePIRLS. The unweighted school response rate for ePIRLS in the final sample with replacement schools was 89.0 percent and the weighted response rate was 89.1 percent. The weighted and unweighted student response rates for PIRLS were both 94 percent. The weighted and unweighted student response rates for ePIRLS were both 90 percent.

2015 TIMSS and TIMSS Advanced

TIMSS 2015 was administered between March and May of 2015 in the United States. The U.S. sample was randomly selected and weighted to be representative of the nation. In order to reliably and accurately represent the performance of each country, international guidelines required that countries sample at least 150 schools and at least 4,000 students per grade (countries with small class sizes of fewer than 30 students per school were directed to consider sampling more schools, more classrooms per school, or both, to meet the minimum target of 4,000 tested students). In the United States, a total of 250 schools and 10,029 students participated in the grade 4 TIMSS survey, and 246 schools and 10,221 students participated in the grade 8 TIMSS (these figures do not include the participation of the state of Florida as a subnational education system, which was separate from and additional to its participation in the U.S. national sample).

TIMSS Advanced, also administered between March and May of 2015 in the United States, required participating

countries and other education systems to draw probability samples of students in their final year of secondary school—ISCED Level 3—who were taking or had taken courses in advanced mathematics or who were taking or had taken courses in physics. International guidelines for TIMSS Advanced called for a minimum of 120 schools to be sampled, with a minimum of 3,600 students assessed per subject. In the United States, a total of 241 schools and 2,954 students participated in advanced mathematics, and 165 schools and 2,932 students participated in physics.

In TIMSS 2015, the weighted school response rate for the United States was 77 percent for grade 4 before the use of substitute schools (schools substituted for originally sampled schools that refused to participate) and 85 percent with the inclusion of substitute schools. For grade 8, the weighted school response rate before the use of substitute schools was 78 percent, and it was 84 percent with the inclusion of substitute schools. The weighted student response rate was 96 percent for grade 4 and 94 percent for grade 8.

In TIMSS Advanced 2015, the weighted school response rate for the United States for advanced mathematics was 72 percent before the use of substitute schools and 76 percent with the inclusion of substitute schools. The weighted school response rate for the United States for physics was 65 percent before the use of substitute schools and 68 percent with the inclusion of substitute schools. The weighted student response rate was 87 percent for advanced mathematics and 85 percent for physics. Student response rates are based on a combined total of students from both sampled and substitute schools.

Further information on the TIMSS study may be obtained from

Stephen Provasnik
International Assessment Branch
Assessments Division
National Center for Education Statistics
550 12th Street SW
Washington, DC 20202
(202) 245-6442
stephen.provasnik@ed.gov
https://nces.ed.gov/timss/
https://www.iea.nl/studies/iea/timss

Further information on the PIRLS study may be obtained from

Sheila Thompson
International Assessment Branch
Assessments Division
National Center for Education Statistics
550 12th Street SW
Washington, DC 20202
(202) 245-8330
sheila.thompson@ed.gov
https://nces.ed.gov/surveys/pirls/
https://www.iea.nl/studies/iea/pirls

National Association of State Directors of Teacher Education and Certificatio

NASDTEC Manual/KnowledgeBase

The National Association of State Directors of Teacher Education and Certification (NASDTEC) was organized in 1928 to represent professional standards boards and commissions and state departments of education that are responsible for the preparation, licensure, and discipline of educational personnel. Currently, NASDTEC's membership includes all 50 states, the District of Columbia, the U.S. Department of Defense Education Activity, U.S. territories, and Canadian provinces and territories.

The NASDTEC Manual on the Preparation and Certification of Educational Personnel was printed between 1984 and 2004, when it was replaced by an online publication, KnowledgeBase (https://www.nasdtec.net/page/AdditionalMaps?&hhsearchterms=%22knowledgebase%22). KnowledgeBase is an expanded version of the Manual and is recognized as a comprehensive source of state-by-state information pertaining to the preparation, certification, and fitness of teachers and other school personnel in the United States and Canada.

Further information on KnowledgeBase may be obtained from

Phillip S. Rogers
Executive Director
NASDTEC
1629 K Street NW
Suite 300
Washington, DC 20006
philrogers@nasdtec.com
https://www.nasdtec.net/default.aspx

National Catholic Educational Association

The United States Catholic Elementary and Secondary Schools

The National Catholic Educational Association (NCEA) has been providing leadership and service to Catholic education since 1904. NCEA began to publish *United States Catholic Elementary and Secondary Schools: Annual Statistical Report on Schools` Enrollment and Staffin* in 1970 in order to fill a need for educational data on the private sector. The report is based on data gathered by all of the archdiocesan and diocesan offices of education in the United States. These data enable NCEA to present information on school enrollment patterns, regional geographic trends, types and locations of schools, student and staffing demographic characteristics, and student participation in selected education programs.

Further information on *United States Catholic Elementary and Secondary Schools: Annual Statistical Report on Schools, Enrollment and Staffing* may be obtained from

Sister Dale McDonald, PBVM
National Catholic Educational Association
1005 North Glebe Road
Suite 525
Arlington, VA 22201
mcdonald@ncea.org
https://www.ncea.org/

National Education Association

Estimates of School Statistics

The National Education Association (NEA) publishes *Estimates of School Statistics* annually as part of the report *Rankings of the States & Estimates of School Statistics*. *Estimates of School Statistics* presents projections of public school enrollment, employment and personnel compensation, and finances, as reported by individual state departments of education. The state-level data in these estimates allow broad assessments of trends in the above areas. These data should be looked at with the understanding that the state-level data do not necessarily reflect the varying conditions within a state on education issues.

Data in *Estimates of School Statistics* are provided by state and District of Columbia departments of education and by other, mostly governmental, sources. Surveys are sent to state departments of education requesting estimated data for the current year and revisions to 4 years of historical data, as necessary. NEA submits current-year estimates of education statistics to each state's department of education for verification or revision each year. Estimates are also generated using regression analyses; these regression-generated figures are only used in the report in cases where a state does not provide current data.

Further information on *Estimates of School Statistics* may be obtained from

NEA Rankings & Estimates Team—NEA Research
1201 16th Street NW
Washington, DC 20036
http://www.nea.org

Organization for Economic Cooperation and Development

The Organization for Economic Cooperation and Development (OECD) publishes analyses of national policies and survey data in education, training, and economics in OECD and partner countries. Newer studies include student survey data on financial literacy and on digital literacy.

Education at a Glance

To highlight current education issues and create a set of comparative education indicators that represent key features of education systems, OECD initiated the Indicators of Education Systems (INES) project and charged the Centre for Educational Research and Innovation (CERI) with developing the cross-national indicators for it. The development of these indicators involved representatives of the OECD countries and the OECD Secretariat. Improvements in data quality and comparability among OECD countries have resulted from the country-to-country interaction sponsored through the INES project. The most recent publication in this series is *Education at a Glance 2020: OECD Indicators*.

Education at a Glance 2020 features data on the 37 OECD countries (Australia, Austria, Belgium, Canada, Chile, Colombia, the Czech Republic, Denmark, Estonia, Finland, France, Germany, Greece, Hungary, Iceland, Ireland, Israel, Italy, Japan, the Republic of Korea, Latvia, Lithuania, Luxembourg, Mexico, the Netherlands, New Zealand, Norway, Poland, Portugal, the Slovak Republic, Slovenia, Spain, Sweden, Switzerland, Turkey, the United Kingdom, and the United States) and a number of partner countries, including Argentina, Brazil, China, Costa Rica, India, Indonesia, the Russian Federation, Saudi Arabia, and South Africa.

The *OECD Handbook for Internationally Comparative Education Statistics` Concepts` Standards` Definitions and Classification* (https://www.oecd.org/publications/oecd-handbook-for-internationally-comparative-education-statistics-9789264279889-en.htm) provides countries with specific guidance on how to prepare information for OECD education surveys; facilitates countries' understanding of OECD indicators and their use in policy analysis; and provides a reference for collecting and assimilating educational data. Chapter 6 of the *OECD Handbook for Internationally Comparative Education Statistics* contains a discussion of data quality issues. Users should examine footnotes carefully to recognize some of the data limitations.

Further information on international education statistics may be obtained from

Andreas Schleicher
Director for the Directorate of Education and Skills and
    Special Advisor on Education Policy to the OECD's
    Secretary General
OECD Directorate for Education and Skills
2, rue André Pascal
75775 Paris Cedex 16
France
andreas.schleicher@oecd.org
https://www.oecd.org/

Online Education Database (OECD.Stat)

The statistical online platform of the OECD, OECD.Stat, allows users to access OECD's databases for OECD member countries and selected nonmember economies. A user can build tables using selected variables and customizable table layouts, extract and download data, and view metadata on methodology and sources.

Data for educational attainment in this report are pulled directly from OECD.Stat. (Information on these data can be found in chapter A, indicator A1, of annex 3 in *Education at a Glance 2019* and accessed at https://read.oecd-ilibrary.org/education/education-at-a-glance-2019_d138983d-en#page1.) However, to support statistical testing for NCES publications, standard errors for some countries had to be estimated and therefore may not be included on OECD.Stat. Standard errors for 2017 and 2018 for Poland, Turkey, and the Republic of Korea; for 2017 for the Netherlands and Slovenia; and for the 2017 and 2018 postsecondary data for Japan were estimated by NCES using a simple random sample assumption. These standard errors are likely to be lower than standard errors that take into account complex sample designs. Lastly, NCES estimated the standard errors for the OECD average using the sum of squares technique.

OECD.Stat can be accessed at https://stats.oecd.org/. A user's guide for OECD.Stat can be accessed at https://stats.oecd.org/Content/themes/OECD/static/help/WBOS%20User%20Guide%20(EN).pdf.

Program for International Student Assessment

The Program for International Student Assessment (PISA) is a system of international assessments organized by the Organization for Economic Cooperation and Development (OECD), an intergovernmental organization of industrialized countries, that focuses on 15-year-olds' capabilities in reading literacy, mathematics literacy, and science literacy. PISA also includes measures of general, or cross-curricular, competencies such as learning strategies. PISA emphasizes functional skills that students have acquired as they near the end of compulsory schooling.

PISA is a 2-hour exam. Assessment items include a combination of multiple-choice questions and open-ended questions that require students to develop their own response. PISA scores are reported on a scale that ranges from 0 to 1,000, with the OECD mean set at 500 and a standard deviation set at 100. In each education system, the assessment is translated into the primary language of instruction; in the United States, all materials are written in English.

Forty-three education systems participated in the 2000 PISA; 41 education systems participated in 2003; 57 (30 OECD member countries and 27 nonmember countries or education systems) participated in 2006; and 65 (34 OECD member countries and 31 nonmember countries or education systems) participated in 2009. (An additional nine education systems administered the 2009 PISA in 2010.) In PISA 2012, 65 education systems (34 OECD member countries and 31 nonmember countries or education systems), as well as the states of Connecticut, Florida, and Massachusetts, participated. In the 2015 PISA, 70 education systems (35 OECD member countries and 35 nonmember countries or education systems), as well as the states of Massachusetts and North Carolina and the territory of Puerto Rico, participated. In PISA 2018, 79 education systems (37 OECD member countries and 42 nonmember countries or education systems) participated.

To implement PISA, each of the participating education systems scientifically draws a nationally representative sample of 15-year-olds, regardless of grade level. In the 2018 PISA, there were 162 participating schools and 4,811 participating students. The overall weighted school response rate was 76 percent, and the overall weighted student response rate was 85 percent.

The intent of PISA reporting is to provide an overall description of performance in reading literacy, mathematics literacy, and science literacy every 3 years, and to provide a more detailed look at each domain in the years when it is the major focus. These cycles will allow education systems to compare changes in trends for each of the three subject areas over time. In the first cycle, PISA 2000, reading literacy was the major focus, occupying roughly two-thirds of assessment time. For 2003, PISA focused on mathematics literacy as well as the ability of students to solve problems in real-life settings. In 2006, PISA focused on science literacy; in 2009, it focused on reading literacy again; and in 2012, it focused on mathematics literacy. PISA 2015 focused on science, as it did in 2006. PISA 2018 focused on reading, as it did in 2009; it also offered an optional assessment of financial literacy, administered by the United States.

Further information on PISA may be obtained from

Samantha Burg
International Assessment Branch
Assessments Division
National Center for Education Statistics
550 12th Street SW
Washington, DC 20202
samantha.burg@ed.gov
https://nces.ed.gov/surveys/pisa/

Program for the International Assessment of Adult Competencies

The Program for the International Assessment of Adult Competencies (PIAAC) is a cyclical, large-scale study that aims to assess and compare the broad range of basic skills and competencies of adults around the world. Developed under the auspices of the Organization for Economic Cooperation and Development (OECD), it is the most comprehensive international survey of adult skills ever undertaken. Adults were surveyed in 24 participating countries in 2012 and in an additional 9 countries in 2014.

PIAAC focuses on what are deemed basic cognitive and workplace skills necessary to adults' successful participation in 21st-century society and in the global economy. Skills assessed include literacy, numeracy, problem solving in technology-rich environments, and basic reading skills. PIAAC measures the relationships between these skills and other characteristics such as individuals' educational background, workplace experiences, and occupational attainment. PIAAC was administered on laptop computers or in paper-and-pencil format. In the United States, the background questionnaire was administered in both English and Spanish, and the cognitive assessment was administered only in English.

The 2012 PIAAC assessment for the United States included a nationally representative probability sample of households. This household sample was selected on the basis of a four-stage, stratified area sample: (1) primary sampling units (PSUs) consisting of counties or groups of contiguous counties; (2) secondary sampling units (referred to as segments) consisting of area blocks; (3) housing units containing households; and (4) eligible persons within households. Person-level data were collected through a screener, a background questionnaire, and the assessment.

Based on the screener data, 6,100 U.S. respondents ages 16 to 65 were selected to complete the 2012 background questionnaire and the assessment; 4,898 actually completed the background questionnaire. Of the 1,202 respondents who did not complete the background questionnaire, 112 were unable to do so because of a literacy-related barrier—either the inability to communicate in English or Spanish or a mental disability. Twenty others were unable to complete the questionnaire due to technical problems. The final response rate for the background questionnaire, which included respondents who completed it and respondents who were unable to complete it because of a language problem or mental disability, was 82.2 percent weighted. The overall person-weighted response rate for the household sample—the product of the component response rates—was 70.3 percent.

The 2014 PIAAC supplement repeated the 2012 administration of PIAAC to an additional sample of U.S. adults in order to enhance the 2012 sample. It included a sample of participants from different households in the PSUs from the 2012 sample.

In the U.S. PIAAC 2017 assessment, the sample design had two core objectives: (i) to ensure a nationally representative sample of the U.S. adult population 16 to 74 years old, and (ii) to have coverage of different types of counties that would be sufficient, when combined with previous samples, to produce indirect small area county-level estimates and state-level estimates. This was accomplished through a four-stage area sample, consisting of 80 primary sampling units, 698 secondary sampling units, 8,576 dwelling units, and 4,769 sampled persons, resulting in 3,660 respondents to the survey. The final response rate for the background questionnaire was 76.3 percent weighted. The overall person-weighted response rate for the household sample was 56.0 percent.

Key to PIAAC's value is its collaborative and international nature. In the United States, NCES has consulted extensively with the Department of Labor in the development of the survey, and staff from both agencies are co-representatives of the United States in PIAAC's international governing body. Internationally, PIAAC has been developed through the collaboration of OECD staff and participating countries' representatives from their ministries or departments of education and labor. Through this cooperative effort, all participating countries follow the quality assurance guidelines set by the OECD consortium and closely follow all agreed-upon standards set for survey design, assessment implementation, and reporting of results.

Further information on PIAAC may be obtained from

Holly Xie
International Assessment Branch
Assessments Division
National Center for Education Statistics
550 12th Street SW
Washington, DC 20202
holly.xie@ed.gov
https://nces.ed.gov/surveys/piaac/
https://www.oecd.org/skills/piaac/

United Nations Educational, Scientific, and Cultural Organizatio

Statistical Yearbook and Global Education Digest

The United Nations Educational, Scientific, and Cultural Organization (UNESCO) conducts annual surveys of education statistics of its member countries. Data from official surveys are supplemented by information obtained by UNESCO through other publications and sources. Each year, more than 200 countries reply to the UNESCO surveys. In some cases, estimates are made by UNESCO for particular items, such as world and continent totals. While great efforts are made to make them as comparable as possible, the data still reflect the vast differences among the countries of the world in the structure of education. While there is some agreement about the reporting of primary and secondary data, tertiary-level data (i.e., post-secondary education data) present numerous substantive problems. Some countries report only university enrollment, while other countries report all postsecondary enrollment, including enrollment in vocational and technical schools and correspondence programs. A very high proportion of some countries' tertiary-level students attend institutions in other countries. The member countries that provide data to UNESCO are responsible for their validity. Thus, data for particular countries are subject to nonsampling error as well as possible sampling error. Users should examine footnotes carefully to recognize some of the data limitations. UNESCO publishes the data in reports such as the *Statistical Yearbook* and the *Global Education Digest*.

Further information on the *Statistical Yearbook* and the *Global Education Digest* may be obtained from

UNESCO Institute for Statistics
C.P. 6128 Succursale Centre-Ville
Montreal, Quebec, H3C 3J7
Canada
http://uis.unesco.org/
https://en.unesco.org/
http://www.ungei.org/resources/1612_2645.html

APPENDIX B
Definitions

Academic support This category of college expenditures includes expenditures for support services that are an integral part of the institution's primary missions of instruction, research, or public service. It also includes expenditures for libraries, galleries, audio/visual services, academic computing support, ancillary support, academic administration, personnel development, and course and curriculum development.

Achievement gap See Gap.

Achievement levels, NAEP Specific achievement levels for each subject area and grade to provide a context for interpreting student performance. At this time they are being used on a trial basis.

> ***NAEP Basic***—denotes partial mastery of the knowledge and skills that are fundamental for proficient work at a given grade.

> ***NAEP Proficient***—represents solid academic performance. Students reaching this level have demonstrated competency over challenging subject matter.

> ***NAEP Advanced***—signifies superior performance.

Achievement test An examination that measures the extent to which a person has acquired certain information or mastered certain skills, usually as a result of specific instruction.

ACT The ACT (formerly the American College Testing Program) assessment program measures educational development and readiness to pursue college-level coursework in English, mathematics, natural science, and social studies. Student performance on the tests does not reflect innate ability and is influenced by a student's educational preparedness.

Adjusted Cohort Graduation Rate (ACGR) The number of students who graduate in 4 years with a regular high school diploma divided by the number of students who form the adjusted cohort for the graduating class. From the beginning of 9th grade (or the earliest high school grade), students who are entering that grade for the first time form a cohort that is "adjusted" by adding any students who subsequently transfer into the cohort and subtracting any students who subsequently transfer out, emigrate to another country, or die.

Administrative support staff Staff whose activities are concerned with support of teaching and administrative duties of the office of the principal or department chairpersons, including clerical staff and secretaries.

Advanced Placement (AP) A program of tertiary-level courses and examinations, taught by specially qualified teachers, that provides opportunities for secondary school students to earn undergraduate credits for university courses. The schools and teachers offering AP programs must meet College Board requirements and are monitored by the College Board.

Agriculture Courses designed to improve competencies in agricultural occupations. Included is the study of agricultural production, supplies, mechanization and products, agricultural science, forestry, and related services.

Alternative school A public elementary/secondary school that serves students whose needs cannot be met in a regular, special education, or vocational school; may provide nontraditional education; and may serve as an adjunct to a regular school. Although alternative schools fall outside the categories of regular, special education, and vocational education, they may provide similar services or curriculum. Some examples of alternative schools are schools for potential dropouts; residential treatment centers for substance abuse (if they provide elementary or secondary education); schools for chronic truants; and schools for students with behavioral problems.

Appropriation (federal funds) Budget authority provided through the congressional appropriation process that permits federal agencies to incur obligations and to make payments.

Appropriation (institutional revenues) An amount (other than a grant or contract) received from or made available to an institution through an act of a legislative body.

Associate's degree A degree granted for the successful completion of a sub-baccalaureate program of studies, usually requiring at least 2 years (or equivalent) of full-time college-level study. This includes degrees granted in a cooperative or work-study program.

Autism See Disabilities, children with.

Autocorrelation Correlation of the error terms from different observations of the same variable. Also called Serial correlation.

Auxiliary enterprises This category includes those essentially self-supporting operations which exist to furnish a service to students, faculty, or staff, and which charge a fee that is directly related to, although not necessarily equal to, the cost of the service. Examples are residence halls, food services, college stores, and intercollegiate athletics.

Average daily attendance (ADA) The aggregate attendance of a school during a reporting period (normally a school year) divided by the number of days school is in session during this period. Only days on which the pupils are under the guidance and direction of teachers should be considered days in session.

Average daily membership (ADM) The aggregate membership of a school during a reporting period (normally a school year) divided by the number of days school is in session during this period. Only days on which the pupils are under the guidance and direction of teachers should be considered as days in session. The ADM for groups of schools having varying lengths of terms is the average of the ADMs obtained for the individual schools. Membership includes all pupils who are enrolled, even if they do not actually attend.

Averaged freshman graduation rate (AFGR) A measure of the percentage of the incoming high school freshman class that graduates 4 years later. It is calculated by taking the number of graduates with a regular diploma and dividing that number by the estimated count of incoming freshman 4 years earlier, as reported through the NCES Common Core of Data (CCD). The estimated count of incoming freshman is the sum of the number of 8th-graders 5 years earlier, the number of 9th-graders 4 years earlier (when current seniors were freshman), and the number of 10th-graders 3 years earlier, divided by 3. The purpose of this averaging is to account for the high rate of grade retention in the freshman year, which adds 9th-grade repeaters from the previous year to the number of students in the incoming freshman class each year. Ungraded students are allocated to individual grades proportional to each state's enrollment in those grades. The AFGR treats students who transfer out of a school or district in the same way as it treats students from that school or district who drop out.

Bachelor's degree A degree granted for the successful completion of a baccalaureate program of studies, usually requiring at least 4 years (or equivalent) of full-time college-level study. This includes degrees granted in a cooperative or work-study program.

Books Nonperiodical printed publications bound in hard or soft covers, or in loose-leaf format, of at least 49 pages, exclusive of the cover pages; juvenile nonperiodical publications of any length found in hard or soft covers.

Breusch-Godfrey serial correlation LM test A statistic testing the independence of errors in least-squares regression against alternatives of first-order and higher degrees of serial correlation. The test belongs to a class of asymptotic tests known as the Lagrange multiplier (LM) tests.

Budget authority (BA) Authority provided by law to enter into obligations that will result in immediate or future outlays. It may be classified by the period of availability (1-year, multiple-year, no-year), by the timing of congressional action (current or permanent), or by the manner of determining the amount available (definite or indefinite).

Business Program of instruction that prepares individuals for a variety of activities in planning, organizing, directing, and controlling business office systems and procedures.

Capital outlay Funds for the acquisition of land and buildings; building construction, remodeling, and additions; the initial installation or extension of service systems and other built-in equipment; and site improvement. The category also encompasses architectural and engineering services, including the development of blueprints.

Career/technical education (CTE) In high school, encompasses occupational education, which teaches skills required in specific occupations or occupational clusters, as well as nonoccupational CTE, which includes family and consumer sciences education (i.e., courses that prepare students for roles outside the paid labor market) and general labor market preparation (i.e., courses that teach general employment skills such as word processing and introductory technology skills).

Carnegie unit The number of credits a secondary student received for a course taken every day, one period per day, for a full year; a factor used to standardize all credits indicated on secondary school transcripts across studies.

Catholic school A private school over which a Roman Catholic church group exercises some control or provides some form of subsidy. Catholic schools for the most part include those operated or supported by a parish, a group of parishes, a diocese, or a Catholic religious order.

Central cities The largest cities, with 50,000 or more inhabitants, in a Metropolitan Statistical Area (MSA). Additional cities within the metropolitan area can also be classified as "central cities" if they meet certain employment, population, and employment/residence ratio requirements.

Certificate A formal award certifying the satisfactory completion of a postsecondary education program. Certificates can be awarded at any level of postsecondary education and include awards below the associate's degree level.

Charter school See Public charter school.

City location See Locale codes.

Class size The membership of a class at a given date.

Classification of Instructional Programs (CIP) The CIP is a taxonomic coding scheme that contains titles and descriptions of primarily postsecondary instructional programs. It was developed to facilitate NCES's collection and reporting of postsecondary degree completions by major field of study using standard classifications that capture the majority of reportable program activity. It was originally published in 1980 and was revised in 1985, 1990, 2000, and 2010.

Classification of Secondary School Courses (CSSC) A modification of the Classification of Instructional Programs used for classifying high school courses. The CSSC contains over 2,200 course codes that help compare the thousands of high school transcripts collected from different schools.

Classroom teacher A staff member assigned the professional activities of instructing pupils in self-contained classes or courses, or in classroom situations; usually expressed in full-time equivalents.

Coefficient of variation (CV) Represents the ratio of the standard error to the estimate. For example, a CV of 30 percent indicates that the standard error of the estimate is equal to 30 percent of the estimate's value. The CV is used to compare the amount of variation relative to the magnitude of the estimate. A CV of 30 percent or greater indicates that an estimate should be interpreted with caution. A CV of 50 percent or greater should result in the estimate being suppressed. For a discussion of standard errors, see Appendix A: Guide to Sources.

Cohort A group of individuals who have a statistical factor in common, for example, year of birth.

Cohort-component method A method for estimating and projecting a population that is distinguished by its ability to preserve knowledge of an age distribution of a population (which may be of a single sex, race, and Hispanic origin) over time.

College A postsecondary school that offers general or liberal arts education, usually leading to an associate's, bachelor's, master's, or doctor's degree. Junior colleges and community colleges are included under this terminology.

Combined school A school that encompasses instruction at both the elementary and the secondary levels; includes schools starting with grade 6 or below and ending with grade 9 or above.

Combined school (2007–08 and 2011–12 Schools and Staffing Survey; 2015–16 and 2017–18 National Teacher and Principal Survey) A school with at least one grade lower than 7 and at least one grade higher than 8; schools with only ungraded classes are included with combined schools.

Combined Statistical Area (CSA) A combination of Core Based Statistical Areas (see below), each of which contains a core with a substantial population nucleus as well as adjacent communities having a high degree of economic and social integration with that core. A CSA is a region with social and economic ties as measured by commuting, but at lower levels than are found within each component area. CSAs represent larger regions that reflect broader social and economic interactions, such as wholesaling, commodity distribution, and weekend recreation activities.

Computer science A group of instructional programs that describes computer and information sciences, including computer programming, data processing, and information systems.

Constant dollars Dollar amounts that have been adjusted by means of price and cost indexes to eliminate inflationary factors and allow direct comparison across years.

Consumer Price Index (CPI) This price index measures the average change in the cost of a fixed market basket of goods and services purchased by consumers. Indexes vary for specific areas or regions, periods of time, major groups of consumer expenditures, and population groups. The CPI reflects spending patterns for two population groups: (1) all urban consumers and urban wage earners and (2) clerical workers. CPIs are calculated for both the calendar year and the school year using the U.S. All Items CPI for All Urban Consumers (CPI-U). The calendar year CPI is the same as the annual CPI-U. The school year CPI is calculated by adding the monthly CPI-U figures, beginning with July of the first year and ending with June of the following year, and then dividing that figure by 12.

Consumption That portion of income that is spent on the purchase of goods and services rather than being saved.

Control of institutions A classification of institutions of elementary/secondary or postsecondary education by whether the institution is operated by publicly elected or appointed officials and derives its primary support from public funds (public control) or is operated by privately elected or appointed officials and derives its major source of funds from private sources (private control).

Core Based Statistical Area (CBSA) A population nucleus and the nearby communities having a high degree of economic and social integration with that nucleus. Each CBSA includes at least one urban area of 10,000 or more people and one or more counties. In addition to a "central county" (or counties), additional "outlying counties" are included in the CBSA if they meet specified requirements of commuting to or from the central counties.

Credit The unit of value, awarded for the successful completion of certain courses, intended to indicate the quantity of course instruction in relation to the total requirements for a diploma, certificate, or degree. Credits are frequently expressed in terms such as "Carnegie units," "semester credit hours," and "quarter credit hours."

Current dollars Dollar amounts that have not been adjusted to compensate for inflation.

Current expenditures (elementary/secondary) The expenditures for operating local public schools, excluding capital outlay and interest on school debt. These expenditures include such items as salaries for school personnel, benefits, student transportation, school books and materials, and energy costs. Beginning in 1980–81, expenditures for state administration are excluded.

>   **Instruction expenditures** Includes expenditures for activities related to the interaction between teacher and students. Includes salaries and benefits for teachers and instructional aides, textbooks, supplies, and purchased services such as instruction via television, webinars, and other online instruction. Also included are tuition expenditures to other local education agencies.

>   **Administration expenditures** Includes expenditures for school administration (i.e., the office of the principal, full-time department chairpersons, and graduation expenses), general administration (the superintendent and board of education and their immediate staff), and other support services expenditures.

>   **Transportation** Includes expenditures for vehicle operation, monitoring, and vehicle servicing and maintenance.

>   **Food services** Includes all expenditures associated with providing food to students and staff in a school or school district. The services include preparing and serving regular and incidental meals or snacks in connection with school activities, as well as the delivery of food to schools.

>   **Enterprise operations** Includes expenditures for activities that are financed, at least in part, by user charges, similar to a private business. These include operations funded by sales of products or services, together with amounts for direct program support made by state education agencies for local school districts.

Current expenditures per pupil in average daily attendance Current expenditures for the regular school term divided by the average daily attendance of full-time pupils (or full-time equivalency of pupils) during the term. See also Current expenditures and Average daily attendance.

Current-fund expenditures (postsecondary education) Money spent to meet current operating costs, including salaries, wages, utilities, student services, public services, research libraries, scholarships and fellowships, auxiliary enterprises, hospitals, and independent operations; excludes loans, capital expenditures, and investments.

Current-fund revenues (postsecondary education) Money received during the current fiscal year from revenue that can be used to pay obligations currently due, and surpluses reappropriated for the current.

Deaf-blindness See Disabilities, children with.

Default rate The percentage of loans that are in delinquency and have not been repaid according to the terms of the loan. According to the federal government, a federal student loan is in default if there has been no payment on the loan in 270 days. The U.S. Department of Education calculates a 3-year cohort default rate, which is the percentage of students who entered repayment in a given fiscal year (from October 1 to September 30) and then defaulted within the following 2 fiscal years. For example, the 3-year cohort default rate for fiscal year (FY) 2009 is the percentage of borrowers who entered repayment during FY 2009 (any time from October 1, 2008, through September 30, 2009) and who defaulted by the end of FY 2011 (September 30, 2011).

Degree An award conferred by a college, university, or other postsecondary education institution as official recognition for the successful completion of a program of studies. Refers specifically to associate's or higher degrees conferred by degree-granting institutions. See also Associate's degree, Bachelor's degree, Master's degree, and Doctor's degree.

Degree/certificate-seeking student A student enrolled in courses for credit and recognized by the institution as seeking a degree, certificate, or other formal award. High school students also enrolled in postsecondary courses for credit are not considered degree/certificate-seeking. See also Degree and Certificate.

Degree-granting institutions Postsecondary institutions that are eligible for Title IV federal financial aid programs and grant an associate's or higher degree. For an institution to be eligible to participate in Title IV financial aid programs, it must offer a program of at least 300 clock hours in length, have accreditation recognized by the U.S. Department of Education, have been in business for at least 2 years, and have signed a participation agreement with the Department.

Degrees of freedom The number of free or linearly independent sample observations used in the calculation of a statistic. In a time series regression with t time periods and k independent variables including a constant term, there would be t minus k degrees of freedom.

Department of Defense (DoD) dependents schools Schools that are operated by the Department of Defense Education Activity (a civilian agency of the U.S. Department of Defense) and provide comprehensive prekindergarten through 12th-grade educational programs on military installations both within the United States and overseas.

Dependency status A designation of whether postsecondary students are financially dependent on their parents or financially independent of their parents. Undergraduates are assumed to be dependent unless they meet one of the following criteria: are age 24 or older, are married or have legal dependents other than a spouse, are veterans, are orphans or wards of the court, or provide documentation that they self-supporting.

Dependent variable A mathematical variable whose value is determined by that of one or more other variables in a function. In regression analysis, when a random variable, y, is expressed as a function of variables $x1$, $x2$, ...xk, plus a stochastic term, then y is known as the "dependent variable."

Developmental delay See Disabilities, children with.

Direct Loan Program The William D. Ford Federal Direct Loan (Direct Loan) Program, established in 2010, is the largest federal student loan program. Direct Loans can be awarded to undergraduate students, with either the interest subsidized (based on need) or unsubsidized; to parents of undergraduate students; or to graduate students. The U.S. Department of Education is the lender for these loans.

Disabilities, children with Those children evaluated as having any of the following impairments and who, by reason thereof, receive special education and related services under the Individuals with Disabilities Education Act (IDEA) according to an Individualized Education Program (IEP), Individualized Family Service Plan (IFSP), or a services plan. There are local variations in the determination of disability conditions, and not all states use all reporting categories.

> *Autism* Having a developmental disability significantly affecting verbal and nonverbal communication and social interaction, generally evident before age 3, that adversely affects educational performance. Other characteristics often associated with autism are engagement in repetitive activities and stereotyped movements, resistance to environmental change or change in daily routines, and unusual responses to sensory experiences. A child is not considered autistic if the child's educational performance is adversely affected primarily because of an emotional disturbance.

> *Deaf-blindness* Having concomitant hearing and visual impairments that cause such severe communication and other developmental and educational problems that the student cannot be accommodated in special education programs solely for deaf or blind students.

Developmental delay Having developmental delays, as defined at the state level, and as measured by appropriate diagnostic instruments and procedures in one or more of the following cognitive areas: physical development, cognitive development, communication development, social or emotional development, or adaptive development. Applies only to 3- through 9-year-old children.

Emotional disturbance Exhibiting one or more of the following characteristics over a long period of time, to a marked degree, and adversely affecting educational performance: an inability to learn that cannot be explained by intellectual, sensory, or health factors; an inability to build or maintain satisfactory interpersonal relationships with peers and teachers; inappropriate types of behavior or feelings under normal circumstances; a general pervasive mood of unhappiness or depression; or a tendency to develop physical symptoms or fears associated with personal or school problems. This term does not include children who are socially maladjusted, unless they also display one or more of the listed characteristics.

Hearing impairment Having a hearing impairment, whether permanent or fluctuating, that adversely affects the student's educational performance. Also reported in this category is deafness, a hearing impairment so severe that the student is impaired in processing linguistic information through hearing (with or without amplification).

Intellectual disability Having significantly subaverage general intellectual functioning, existing concurrently with defects in adaptive behavior and manifested during the developmental period, that adversely affects the child's educational performance.

Multiple disabilities Having concomitant impairments (such as intellectually disabled-blind, intellectually disabled-orthopedically impaired, etc.), the combination of which causes such severe educational problems that the student cannot be accommodated in special education programs solely for one of the impairments. This term does not include deaf-blind students.

Orthopedic impairment Having a severe orthopedic impairment that adversely affects a student's educational performance. The term includes impairment resulting from congenital anomaly, disease, or other causes.

Other health impairment Having limited strength, vitality, or alertness due to chronic or acute health problems—such as a heart condition, tuberculosis, rheumatic fever, nephritis, asthma, sickle cell anemia, hemophilia, epilepsy, lead poisoning, leukemia, or diabetes—that adversely affect the student's educational performance.

Specific learning disability Having a disorder in one or more of the basic psychological processes involved in understanding or in using spoken or written language, which may manifest itself in an imperfect ability to listen, think, speak, read, write, spell, or do mathematical calculations. The term includes such conditions as perceptual disabilities, brain injury, minimal brain dysfunction, dyslexia, and developmental aphasia. The term does not include children who have learning problems that are primarily the result of visual, hearing, motor, or intellectual disabilities, or of environmental, cultural, or economic disadvantage.

Speech or language impairment Having a communication disorder, such as stuttering, impaired articulation, language impairment, or voice impairment, that adversely affects the student's educational performance.

Traumatic brain injury Having an acquired injury to the brain caused by an external physical force, resulting in total or partial functional disability or psychosocial impairment or both, that adversely affects the student's educational performance. The term applies to open or closed head injuries resulting in impairments in one or more areas, such as cognition; language; memory; attention; reasoning; abstract thinking; judgment; problem-solving; sensory, perceptual, and motor abilities; psychosocial behavior; physical functions; information processing; and speech. The term does not apply to brain injuries that are congenital or degenerative or to brain injuries induced by birth trauma.

Visual impairment Having a visual impairment that, even with correction, adversely affects the student's educational performance. The term includes partially seeing and blind children.

Discipline divisions Degree programs that include breakouts to the 6-digit level of the Classification of Instructional Programs (CIP). See also Fields of study.

Disposable personal income Current income received by people less their contributions for social insurance, personal tax, and nontax payments. It is the income available to people for spending and saving. Nontax payments include passport fees, fines and penalties, donations, and tuitions and fees paid to schools and hospitals operated mainly by the government. See also Personal income.

Distance education Education that uses one or more technologies to deliver instruction to students who are separated from the instructor and to support regular and substantive interaction between the students and the instructor synchronously or asynchronously. Technologies used for instruction may include the following: Internet; one-way and two-way transmissions through open broadcasts, closed circuit, cable, microwave, broadband lines, fiber optics, and satellite or wireless communication devices; audio conferencing; and DVDs and CD-ROMs, if used in a course in conjunction with the technologies listed above.

Doctor's degree (also referred to as doctoral degree) The highest award a student can earn for graduate study. Includes such degrees as the Doctor of Education (Ed.D.); Doctor of Juridical Science (S.J.D.); Doctor of Public Health (Dr.P.H.);

and Doctor of Philosophy (Ph.D.) in any field, such as agronomy, food technology, education, engineering, public administration, ophthalmology, or radiology. The doctor's degree classification encompasses three main subcategories—research/scholarship degrees, professional practice degrees, and other degrees—which are described below.

> ***Doctor's degree—research/scholarship*** A Ph.D. or other doctor's degree that requires advanced work beyond the master's level, including the preparation and defense of a dissertation based on original research, or the planning and execution of an original project demonstrating substantial artistic or scholarly achievement. Examples of this type of degree may include the following and others, as designated by the awarding institution: the Ed.D. (in education), D.M.A. (in musical arts), D.B.A. (in business administration), D.Sc. (in science), D.A. (in arts), or D.M (in medicine).

> ***Doctor's degree—professional practice*** A doctor's degree that is conferred upon completion of a program providing the knowledge and skills for the recognition, credential, or license required for professional practice. The degree is awarded after a period of study such that the total time to the degree, including both preprofessional and professional preparation, equals at least 6 full-time-equivalent academic years. Some doctor's degrees of this type were formerly classified as first-professional degrees. Examples of this type of degree may include the following and others, as designated by the awarding institution: the D.C. or D.C.M. (in chiropractic); D.D.S. or D.M.D. (in dentistry); L.L.B. or J.D. (in law); M.D. (in medicine); O.D. (in optometry); D.O. (in osteopathic medicine); Pharm.D. (in pharmacy); D.P.M., Pod.D., or D.P. (in podiatry); or D.V.M. (in veterinary medicine).

> ***Doctor's degree—other*** A doctor's degree that does not meet the definition of either a doctor's degree—research/scholarship or a doctor's degree—professional practice.

Double exponential smoothing A method that takes a single smoothed average component of demand and smoothes it a second time to allow for estimation of a trend effect.

Dropout The term is used to describe both the event of leaving school before completing high school and the status of an individual who is not in school and who is not a high school completer. High school completers include both graduates of school programs as well as those completing high school through equivalency programs such as the GED program. Transferring from a public school to a private school, for example, is not regarded as a dropout event. A person who drops out of school may later return and graduate but is called a "dropout" at the time he or she leaves school. Measures to describe these behaviors include the event dropout rate (or the closely related school persistence rate), the status dropout rate, and the high school completion rate.

Durbin-Watson statistic A statistic testing the independence of errors in least squares regression against the alternative of first-order serial correlation. The statistic is a simple linear transformation of the first-order serial correlation of residuals and, although its distribution is unknown, it is tested by bounding statistics that follow R. L. Anderson's distribution.

Early childhood school Early childhood program schools serve students in prekindergarten, kindergarten, transitional (or readiness) kindergarten, and/or transitional first (or prefirst) grade.

Econometrics The quantitative examination of economic trends and relationships using statistical techniques, and the development, examination, and refinement of those techniques.

Education specialist/professional diploma A certificate of advanced graduate studies that advance educators in their instructional and leadership skills beyond a master's degree level of competence.

Educational and general expenditures The sum of current funds expenditures on instruction, research, public service, academic support, student services, institutional support, operation and maintenance of plant, and awards from restricted and unrestricted funds.

Educational attainment The highest grade of regular school attended and completed.

Educational attainment (Current Population Survey) This measure uses March CPS data to estimate the percentage of civilian, noninstitutionalized people who have achieved certain levels of educational attainment. Estimates of educational attainment do not differentiate between those who graduated from public schools, those who graduated from private schools, and those who earned a GED; these estimates also include individuals who earned their credential or completed their highest level of education outside of the United States.

1972–1991 During this period, an individual's educational attainment was considered to be his or her last fully completed year of school. Individuals who completed 12 years of schooling were deemed to be high school graduates, as were those who began but did not complete the first year of college. Respondents who completed 16 or more years of schooling were counted as college graduates.

1992–present Beginning in 1992, CPS asked respondents to report their highest level of school completed or their highest degree received. This change means that some data collected before 1992 are not strictly comparable with data collected from 1992 onward and that care

must be taken when making comparisons across years. The revised survey question emphasizes credentials received rather than the last grade level attended or completed. The new categories include the following:

- High school graduate, high school diploma, or the equivalent (e.g., GED)
- Some college but no degree
- Associate's degree in college, occupational/vocational program
- Associate's degree in college, academic program (e.g., A.A., A.S., A.A.S.)
- Bachelor's degree (e.g., B.A., A.B., B.S.)
- Master's degree (e.g., M.A., M.S., M.Eng., M.Ed., M.S.W., M.B.A.)
- Professional school degree (e.g., M.D., D.D.S., D.V.M., LL.B., J.D.)
- Doctor's degree (e.g., Ph.D., Ed.D.)

Elementary education/programs Learning experiences concerned with the knowledge, skills, appreciations, attitudes, and behavioral characteristics that are considered to be needed by all pupils in terms of their awareness of life within our culture and the world of work, and that normally may be achieved during the elementary school years (usually kindergarten through grade 8 or kindergarten through grade 6), as defined by applicable state laws and regulations.

Elementary school A school classified as elementary by state and local practice and composed of any span of grades not above grade 8.

Elementary/secondary school Includes only schools that are part of state and local school systems, and also most nonprofit private elementary/secondary schools, both religiously affiliated and nonsectarian. Includes regular, alternative, vocational, and special education schools. U.S. totals exclude federal schools for American Indians, and federal schools on military posts and other federal installations.

Emotional disturbance See Disabilities, children with.

Employees in degree-granting institutions Persons employed by degree-granting institutions, who are classified into the following occupational categories in this publication:

Executive/administrative/managerial staff Employees whose assignments require management of the institution or of a customarily recognized department or subdivision thereof. These employees perform work that is directly related to management policies or general business operations and that requires them to exercise discretion and independent judgment.

Faculty (instruction/research/public service) Employees whose principal activities are for the purpose of providing instruction or teaching, research, or public service. These employees may hold such titles as professor, associate professor, assistant professor, instructor, or lecturer. Graduate assistants are not included in this category. The aggregated "faculty (instruction/research/public service)" category includes faculty reported in four separate Integrated Postsecondary Education System (IPEDS) occupational categories: "primarily instruction," "research," "public service," and "instruction combined with research and/or public service." These categories are based on the types of assignments that employees formally spend the majority of their time doing. "Instruction combined with research and/or public service" includes those who provide instruction but "for whom it is not possible to differentiate between instruction or teaching, research, and public service because each of these functions is an integral component of their regular assignment." For purposes of presentation in the *Digest of Education Statistics*, "instruction" faculty include those reported in the "instruction combined with research and/or public service" category as well as those reported in the "primarily instruction" category.

Graduate assistants Graduate-level students who are employed on a part-time basis for the primary purpose of assisting in classroom or laboratory instruction or in the conduct of research.

Nonprofessional staff Employees whose primary activities can be classified as one of the following: technical and paraprofessional work (which generally requires less formal training and experience than required for professional status); clerical and secretarial work; skilled crafts work; or service/maintenance work.

Other professional staff Employees who perform academic support, student service, and institutional support and who need either a degree at the bachelor's or higher level or experience of such kind and amount as to provide a comparable background.

Professional staff Employees who are classified as executive/administrative/managerial staff, faculty, graduate assistants, or other professional staff.

Employment Includes civilian, noninstitutional people who (1) worked during any part of the survey week as paid employees; worked in their own business, profession, or farm; or worked 15 hours or more as unpaid workers in a family-owned enterprise; or (2) were not working but had jobs or businesses from which they were temporarily absent due to illness, bad weather, vacation, labor-management dispute, or personal reasons whether or not they were seeking another job.

Employment (Current Population Survey) According to the October Current Population Survey (CPS), employed persons are persons age 16 or older who, during the reference week, (1) did any work at all (at least 1 hour) as paid employees or (2) were not working but had jobs or businesses from which they were temporarily absent because of vacation, illness, bad weather, child care problems, maternity or paternity leave, labor-management dispute, job training, or other family or personal reasons, whether or not they were paid for the time off or were seeking other jobs.

Employment status A classification of individuals as employed (either full or part time), unemployed (looking for work or on layoff), or not in the labor force (due to being retired, having unpaid employment, or some other reason).

Endowment A trust fund set aside to provide a perpetual source of revenue from the proceeds of the endowment investments. Endowment funds are often created by donations from benefactors of an institution, who may designate the use of the endowment revenue. Normally, institutions or their representatives manage the investments, but they are not permitted to spend the endowment fund itself, only the proceeds from the investments. Typical uses of endowments would be an endowed chair for a particular department or for a scholarship fund. Endowment totals tabulated in this book also include funds functioning as endowments, such as funds left over from the previous year and placed with the endowment investments by the institution. These funds may be withdrawn by the institution and spent as current funds at any time. Endowments are evaluated by two different measures, book value and market value. Book value is the purchase price of the endowment investment. Market value is the current worth of the endowment investment. Thus, the book value of a stock held in an endowment fund would be the purchase price of the stock. The market value of the stock would be its selling price as of a given day.

Engineering Instructional programs that describe the mathematical and natural science knowledge gained by study, experience, and practice and applied with judgment to develop ways to utilize the materials and forces of nature economically. Includes programs that prepare individuals to support and assist engineers and similar professionals.

English A group of instructional programs that describes the English language arts, including composition, creative writing, and the study of literature.

English language learner (ELL) An individual who, due to any of the reasons listed below, has sufficient difficulty speaking, reading, writing, or understanding the English language to be denied the opportunity to learn successfully in classrooms where the language of instruction is English or to participate fully in the larger U.S. society. Such an individual (1) was not born in the United States or has a native language other than English; (2) comes from environments where a language other than English is dominant; or (3) is an American Indian or Alaska Native and comes from environments where a language other than English has had a significant impact on the individual's level of English language proficiency.

Enrollment The total number of students registered in a given school unit at a given time, generally in the fall of a year. At the postsecondary level, separate counts are also available for full-time and part-time students, as well as full-time-equivalent enrollment. See also Full-time enrollment, Full-time-equivalent (FTE) enrollment, and Part-time enrollment.

Estimate A numerical value obtained from a statistical sample and assigned to a population parameter. The particular value yielded by an estimator in a given set of circumstances or the rule by which such particular values are calculated.

Estimating equation An equation involving observed quantities and an unknown that serves to estimate the latter.

Estimation Estimation is concerned with inference about the numerical value of unknown population values from incomplete data, such as a sample. If a single figure is calculated for each unknown parameter, the process is called point estimation. If an interval is calculated within which the parameter is likely, in some sense, to lie, the process is called interval estimation.

Executive/administrative/managerial staff See Employees in degree-granting institutions.

Expenditures, Total For elementary/secondary schools, these include all charges for current outlays plus capital outlays and interest on school debt. For degree-granting institutions, these include current outlays plus capital outlays. For government, these include charges net of recoveries and other correcting transactions other than for retirement of debt, investment in securities, extension of credit, or as agency transactions. Government expenditures include only external transactions, such as the provision of perquisites or other payments in kind. Aggregates for groups of governments exclude intergovernmental transactions among the governments.

Expenditures per pupil Charges incurred for a particular period of time divided by a student unit of measure, such as average daily attendance or fall enrollment.

Exponential smoothing A method used in time series analysis to smooth or to predict a series. There are various forms, but all are based on the supposition that more remote history has less importance than more recent history.

Expulsion Removing a student from his or her regular school for an extended length of time or permanently for disciplinary purposes.

Extracurricular activities Activities that are not part of the required curriculum and that take place outside of the regular course of study. They include both school-sponsored (e.g., varsity athletics, drama, and debate clubs) and community-sponsored (e.g., hobby clubs and youth organizations like the Junior Chamber of Commerce or Boy Scouts) activities.

Faculty (instruction/research/public service) See Employees in degree-granting institutions.

Family A group of two or more people (one of whom is the householder) related by birth, marriage, or adoption and residing together. All such people (including related subfamily members) are considered as members of one family.

Family income Includes all monetary income from all sources (including jobs, businesses, interest, rent, and Social Security payments) over a 12-month period. The income of nonrelatives living in the household is excluded, but the income of all family members age 15 or older (age 14 or older in years prior to 1989), including those temporarily living outside of the household, is included. In the October Current Population Survey, family income is determined from a single question asked of the household respondent.

Federal funds Amounts collected and used by the federal government for the general purposes of the government. The major federal fund is the general fund, which is derived from general taxes and borrowing. Other types of federal fund accounts include special funds (earmarked for a specific purpose other than a business-like activity), public enterprise funds (earmarked for a business-like activity conducted primarily with the public), and intragovernmental funds (earmarked for a business-like activity conducted primarily within the government).

Federal sources (postsecondary degree-granting institutions) Includes federal appropriations, grants, and contracts, and federally funded research and development centers (FFRDCs). Federally subsidized student loans are not included.

Fields of study The primary field of concentration in postsecondary certificates and degrees. In the Integrated Postsecondary Education Data System (IPEDS), refers to degree programs that are broken out only to the 2-digit level of the Classification of Instructional Programs (CIP). See also Discipline divisions.

Financial aid Grants, loans, assistantships, scholarships, fellowships, tuition waivers, tuition discounts, veteran's benefits, employer aid (tuition reimbursement), and other monies (other than from relatives or friends) provided to students to help them meet expenses. Except where designated, includes Title IV subsidized and unsubsidized loans made directly to students.

First-order serial correlation When errors in one time period are correlated directly with errors in the ensuing time period.

First-professional degree NCES no longer uses this classification. Most degrees formerly classified as first-professional (such as M.D., D.D.S., Pharm.D., D.V.M., and J.D.) are now classified as doctor's degrees—professional practice. However, master's of divinity degrees are now classified as master's degrees.

First-time student (undergraduate) A student who has no prior postsecondary experience (except as noted below) attending any institution for the first time at the undergraduate level. Includes students enrolled in the fall term who attended college for the first time in the prior summer term, and students who entered with advanced standing (college credits earned before graduation from high school).

Fiscal year A period of 12 months for which accounting records are compiled. Institutions and states may designate their own accounting period, though most states use a July 1 through June 30 accounting year. The yearly accounting period for the federal government begins on October 1 and ends on the following September 30. The fiscal year is designated by the calendar year in which it ends; e.g., fiscal year 2006 begins on October 1, 2005, and ends on September 30, 2006. (From fiscal year 1844 to fiscal year 1976, the federal fiscal year began on July 1 and ended on the following June 30.)

Forecast An estimate of the future based on rational study and analysis of available pertinent data, as opposed to subjective prediction.

Forecasting Assessing the magnitude that a quantity will assume at some future point in time, as distinct from "estimation," which attempts to assess the magnitude of an already existent quantity.

Foreign languages A group of instructional programs that describes the structure and use of language that is common or indigenous to people of a given community or nation, geographical area, or set of cultural traditions. Programs cover such features as sound, literature, syntax, phonology, semantics, sentences, prose, and verse, as well as the development of skills and attitudes used in communicating and evaluating thoughts and feelings through oral and written language.

For-profit institution A private institution in which the individual(s) or agency in control receives compensation other than wages, rent, or other expenses for the assumption of risk.

Free or reduced-price lunch See National School Lunch Program.

Full-time enrollment The number of students enrolled in postsecondary education courses with total credit load equal to at least 75 percent of the normal full-time course load. At the undergraduate level, full-time enrollment typically includes students who have a credit load of 12 or more semester or quarter credits. At the postbaccalaureate level, full-time enrollment includes students who typically have a credit load of 9 or more semester or quarter credits, as well as other students who are considered full time by their institutions.

Full-time-equivalent (FTE) enrollment For postsecondary institutions, enrollment of full-time students, plus the full-time equivalent of part-time students. The full-time equivalent of the part-time students is estimated using different factors depending on the type and control of institution and level of student.

Full-time-equivalent (FTE) staff Full-time staff, plus the full-time equivalent of the part-time staff.

Full-time-equivalent teacher See Instructional staff.

Full-time instructional faculty Those members of the instruction/research staff who are employed full time as defined by the institution, including faculty with released time for research and faculty on sabbatical leave. Full-time counts exclude faculty who are employed to teach less than two semesters, three quarters, two trimesters, or two 4-month sessions; replacements for faculty on sabbatical leave or those on leave without pay; faculty for preclinical and clinical medicine; faculty who are donating their services; faculty who are members of military organizations and paid on a different pay scale than civilian employees; those academic officers whose primary duties are administrative; and graduate students who assist in the instruction of courses.

Full-time worker In educational institutions, an employee whose position requires being on the job on school days throughout the school year for at least the number of hours the schools are in session. For higher education, a member of an educational institution's staff who is employed full time, as defined by the institution.

Function A mathematical correspondence that assigns exactly one element of one set to each element of the same or another set. A variable that depends on and varies with another.

Functional form A mathematical statement of the relationship among the variables in a model.

Gap Occurs when an outcome—for example, average test score or level of educational attainment—is higher for one group than for another group, and the difference between the two groups' outcomes is statistically significant.

GED certificate An award that is received following successful completion of the GED test. The GED program—sponsored by the GED Testing Service (a joint venture of the American Council on Education and Pearson)—enables individuals to demonstrate that they have acquired a level of learning comparable to that of high school graduates. See also High school equivalency certificate.

GED program Academic instruction to prepare people to take the high school equivalency examination. Formerly known as the General Educational Development program. See also GED recipient.

GED recipient A person who has obtained certification of high school equivalency by meeting state requirements and passing an approved exam, which is intended to provide an appraisal of the person's achievement or performance in the broad subject matter areas usually required for high school graduation.

General administration support services Includes salary, benefits, supplies, and contractual fees for boards of education staff and executive administration. Excludes state administration.

General program A program of studies designed to prepare students for the common activities of a citizen, family member, and worker. A general program of studies may include instruction in both academic and vocational areas.

Geographic region One of the four regions of the United States used by the U.S. Census Bureau, as follows:

Northeast
Connecticut (CT)
Maine (ME)
Massachusetts (MA)
New Hampshire (NH)
New Jersey (NJ)
New York (NY)
Pennsylvania (PA)
Rhode Island (RI)
Vermont (VT)

Midwest
Illinois (IL)
Indiana (IN)
Iowa (IA)
Kansas (KS)
Michigan (MI)
Minnesota (MN)
Missouri (MO)
Nebraska (NE)
North Dakota (ND)
Ohio (OH)
South Dakota (SD)
Wisconsin (WI)

South
Alabama (AL)
Arkansas (AR)
Delaware (DE)
District of Columbia (DC)
Florida (FL)
Georgia (GA)
Kentucky (KY)
Louisiana (LA)
Maryland (MD)
Mississippi (MS)
North Carolina (NC)
Oklahoma (OK)
South Carolina (SC)
Tennessee (TN)
Texas (TX)
Virginia (VA)
West Virginia (WV)

West
Alaska (AK)
Arizona (AZ)
California (CA)
Colorado (CO)
Hawaii (HI)
Idaho (ID)
Montana (MT)
Nevada (NV)
New Mexico (NM)
Oregon (OR)
Utah (UT)
Washington (WA)
Wyoming (WY)

Government appropriation An amount (other than a grant or contract) received from or made available to an institution through an act of a legislative body.

Government grant or contract Revenues received by a postsecondary institution from a government agency for a specific research project or other program. Examples are research projects, training programs, and student financial assistance.

Graduate An individual who has received formal recognition for the successful completion of a prescribed program of studies.

Graduate assistants See Employees in degree-granting institutions.

Graduate enrollment The number of students who are working toward a master's or doctor's degree and students who are in postbaccalaureate classes but not in degree programs.

Graduate Record Examination (GRE) Multiple-choice examinations administered by the Educational Testing Service and taken by college students who intend to attend certain graduate schools. There are two types of testing available: (1) the general exam which measures critical thinking, analytical writing, verbal reasoning, and quantitative reasoning skills, and (2) the subject test which is offered in eight specific subjects and gauges undergraduate achievement in a specific field. The subject tests are intended for those who have majored in or have extensive background in that specific area.

Graduation Formal recognition given to an individual for the successful completion of a prescribed program of studies.

Gross domestic product (GDP) The total national output of goods and services valued at market prices. GDP can be viewed in terms of expenditure categories that include purchases of goods and services by consumers and government, gross private domestic investment, and net exports of goods and services. The goods and services included are largely those bought for final use (excluding illegal transactions) in the market economy. A number of inclusions, however, represent imputed values, the most important of which is rental value of owner-occupied housing.

Group quarters Living arrangements where people live or stay in a group situation that is owned or managed by an entity or organization providing housing and/or services for the residents. Group quarters include such places as college residence halls, residential treatment centers, skilled nursing facilities, group homes, military barracks, correctional facilities, and workers' dormitories.

Noninstitutionalized group quarters Include college and university housing, military quarters, facilities for workers and religious groups, and temporary shelters for the homeless.

Institutionalized group quarters Include adult and juvenile correctional facilities, nursing facilities, and other health care facilities.

Handicapped See Disabilities, children with.

Head Start A local public or private nonprofit or for-profit entity authorized by the Department of Health and Human Services' Administration for Children and Families to operate a Head Start program to serve children age 3 to compulsory school age, pursuant to section 641(b) and (d) of the Head Start Act.

Hearing impairment See Disabilities, children with.

High school A secondary school offering the final years of high school work necessary for graduation. A high school is usually either a 3-year school that includes grades 10, 11, and 12 or a 4-year school that includes grades 9, 10, 11, and 12.

High school (2007–08 Schools and Staffing Survey) A school with no grade lower than 7 and at least one grade higher than 8.

High school completer An individual who has been awarded a high school diploma or an equivalent credential, including a GED certificate.

High school diploma A formal document regulated by the state certifying the successful completion of a prescribed secondary school program of studies. In some states or communities, high school diplomas are differentiated by type, such as an academic diploma, a general diploma, or a vocational diploma.

High school equivalency certificate A formal document certifying that an individual has met the state requirements for high school graduation equivalency by obtaining satisfactory scores on an approved examination and meeting other performance requirements (if any) set by a state education agency or other appropriate body. One particular version of this certificate is the GED test. The GED test is a comprehensive test used primarily to appraise the educational development of students who have not completed their formal high school education and who may earn a high school equivalency certificate by achieving satisfactory scores. GEDs are awarded by the states or other agencies, and the test is developed and distributed by the GED Testing Service (a joint venture of the American Council on Education and Pearson).

High school program A program of studies designed to prepare students for employment and postsecondary education. Three types of programs are often distinguished—academic, vocational, and general. An academic program is designed to prepare students for continued study at a college or university. A vocational program is designed to prepare students for employment in one or more semiskilled, skilled, or technical occupations. A general program is designed to provide students with the understanding and competence to function effectively in a free society and usually represents a mixture of academic and vocational components.

Higher education Study beyond secondary school at an institution that offers programs terminating in an associate's, bachelor's, or higher degree.

Higher education institutions (basic classification and Carnegie classification) See Postsecondary institutions (basic classification by level) and Postsecondary institutions (Carnegie classification of degree-granting institutions).

Higher Education Price Index A price index that measures average changes in the prices of goods and services purchased by colleges and universities through current-fund education and general expenditures (excluding expenditures for sponsored research and auxiliary enterprises).

Historically black colleges and universities Accredited higher education institutions established prior to 1964 with the principal mission of educating Black Americans. Federal regulations (20 USC 1061 (2)) allow for certain exceptions of the founding date.

Hours worked per week According to the October Current Population Survey, the number of hours a respondent worked in all jobs in the week prior to the survey interview.

Household All the people who occupy a housing unit. A house, an apartment, a mobile home, a group of rooms, or a single room is regarded as a housing unit when it is occupied or intended for occupancy as separate living quarters, that is, when the occupants do not live and eat with any other people in the structure, and there is direct access from the outside or through a common hall.

Housing unit A house, an apartment, a mobile home, a group of rooms, or a single room that is occupied as separate living quarters.

Income tax Taxes levied on net income, that is, on gross income less certain deductions permitted by law. These taxes can be levied on individuals or on corporations or unincorporated businesses where the income is taxed distinctly from individual income.

Independent operations A group of self-supporting activities under control of a college or university. For purposes of financial surveys conducted by the National Center for Education Statistics, this category is composed principally of federally funded research and development centers (FFRDC).

Independent variable In regression analysis, a random variable, y, is expressed as a function of variables $x1$, $x2$, ... xk, plus a stochastic term; the x's are known as "independent variables."

Individuals with Disabilities Education Act (IDEA) IDEA is a federal law enacted in 1990 and reauthorized in 1997 and 2004. IDEA requires services to children with disabilities throughout the nation. IDEA governs how states and public agencies provide early intervention, special education, and related services to eligible infants, toddlers, children, and youth with disabilities. Infants and toddlers with disabilities (birth–age 2) and their families receive early intervention services under IDEA, Part C. Children and youth (ages 3–21) receive special education and related services under IDEA, Part B.

Inflation A rise in the general level of prices of goods and services in an economy over a period of time, which generally corresponds to a decline in the real value of money or a loss of purchasing power. See also Constant dollars and Purchasing Power Parity indexes.

Institutional support The category of higher education expenditures that includes day-to-day operational support for colleges, excluding expenditures for physical plant operations. Examples of institutional support include general administrative services, executive direction and planning, legal and fiscal operations, and community relations.

Instruction (colleges and universities) That functional category including expenditures of the colleges, schools, departments, and other instructional divisions of higher education institutions and expenditures for departmental research and public service that are not separately budgeted; includes expenditures for both credit and noncredit activities. Excludes expenditures for academic administration where the primary function is administration (e.g., academic deans).

Instruction (elementary and secondary) Instruction encompasses all activities dealing directly with the interaction between teachers and students. Teaching may be provided for students in a school classroom, in another location such as a home or hospital, and in other learning situations such as those involving co-curricular activities. Instruction may be provided through some other approved medium, such as the Internet, television, radio, telephone, and correspondence.

Instructional staff Full-time-equivalent number of positions, not the number of different individuals occupying the positions during the school year. In local schools, includes all public elementary and secondary (junior and senior high) day-school positions that are in the nature of teaching or in the improvement of the teaching-learning situation; includes consultants or supervisors of instruction, principals, teachers, guidance personnel, librarians, psychological personnel, and other instructional staff, and excludes administrative staff, attendance personnel, clerical personnel, and junior college staff.

Instructional support services Includes salary, benefits, supplies, and contractual fees for staff providing instructional improvement, educational media (library and audiovisual), and other instructional support services.

Intellectual disability See Disabilities, children with.

Interest on debt Includes expenditures for long-term debt service interest payments (i.e., those longer than 1 year).

International baccalaureate (IB) A recognized international program of primary, middle, and secondary studies leading to the International Baccalaureate (IB) Diploma. This diploma (or certificate) is recognized in Europe and elsewhere as qualifying holders for direct access to university studies. Schools offering the IB program are approved by the International Baccalaureate Organization (IBO) and their regional office and may use IBO instructional materials, local school materials, or a combination.

International finance data Include data on public and private expenditures for educational institutions. Educational institutions directly provide instructional programs (i.e., teaching) to individuals in an organized group setting or through distance education. Business enterprises or other institutions that provide short-term courses of training or instruction to individuals on a "one-to-one" basis are not included. Where noted, international finance data may also include publicly subsidized spending on education-related purchases, such as school books, living costs, and transportation.

Public expenditures Corresponds to the nonrepayable current and capital expenditures of all levels of the government directly related to education. Expenditures that are not directly related to education (e.g., cultures, sports, youth activities) are, in principle, not included. Expenditures on education by other ministries or equivalent institutions (e.g., Health and Agriculture) are included. Public subsidies for students' living expenses are excluded to ensure international comparability of the data.

Private expenditures Refers to expenditures funded by private sources (i.e., households and other private entities). "Households" means students and their families. "Other private entities" includes private business firms and nonprofit organizations, including religious organizations, charitable organizations, and business and labor associations. Private expenditures are composed of school fees, the cost of materials (such as textbooks and teaching equipment), transportation costs (if organized by the school), the cost of meals (if provided by the school), boarding fees, and expenditures by employers on initial vocational training.

Current expenditures Includes final consumption expenditures (e.g., compensation of employees, consumption of intermediate goods and services, consumption of fixed capital, and military expenditures); property income paid; subsidies; and other current transfers paid.

Capital expenditures Includes spending to acquire and improve fixed capital assets, land, intangible assets, government stocks, and nonmilitary, nonfinancial assets, as well as spending to finance net capital transfers.

International Standard Classification of Education (ISCED) Used to compare educational systems in different countries. ISCED is the standard used by many countries to report education statistics to the United Nations Educational,

Scientific, and Cultural Organization (UNESCO) and the Organization for Economic Cooperation and Development (OECD). ISCED was revised in 2011.

ISCED 2011 ISCED 2011 divides educational systems into the following nine categories, based on eight levels of education.

ISCED Level 0 Education preceding the first level (early childhood education) includes early childhood programs that target children below the age of entry into primary education.

ISCED Level 01 Early childhood educational development programs are generally designed for children younger than 3 years.

ISCED Level 02 Preprimary education preceding the first level usually begins at age 3, 4, or 5 (sometimes earlier) and lasts from 1 to 3 years, when it is provided. In the United States, this level includes nursery school and kindergarten.

ISCED Level 1 Education at the first level (primary or elementary education) usually begins at age 5, 6, or 7 and continues for about 4 to 6 years. For the United States, the first level starts with 1st grade and ends with 6th grade.

ISCED Level 2 Education at the second level (lower secondary education) typically begins at about age 11 or 12 and continues for about 2 to 6 years. For the United States, the second level starts with 7th grade and typically ends with 9th grade. Education at the lower secondary level continues the basic programs of the first level, although teaching is typically more subject focused, often using more specialized teachers who conduct classes in their field of specialization. The main criterion for distinguishing lower secondary education from primary education is whether programs begin to be organized in a more subject-oriented pattern, using more specialized teachers conducting classes in their field of specialization. If there is no clear breakpoint for this organizational change, lower secondary education is considered to begin at the end of 6 years of primary education. In countries with no clear division between lower secondary and upper secondary education, and where lower secondary education lasts for more than 3 years, only the first 3 years following primary education are counted as lower secondary education.

ISCED Level 3 Education at the third level (upper secondary education) typically begins at age 15 or 16 and lasts for approximately 3 years. In the United States, the third level starts with 10th grade and ends with 12th grade. Upper secondary education is the final stage of secondary education in most OECD countries. Instruction is often organized along subject-matter lines, in contrast to the lower secondary level, and teachers typically must have a higher-level, or more subject-specific, qualification. There are substantial differences in the typical duration of programs both across and between countries, ranging from 2 to 5 years of schooling. The main criteria for classifications are (1) national boundaries between lower and upper secondary education and (2) admission into educational programs, which usually requires the completion of lower secondary education or a combination of basic education and life experience that demonstrates the ability to handle the subject matter in upper secondary schools. Includes programs designed to review the content of third level programs, such as preparatory courses for tertiary education entrance examinations, and programs leading to a qualification equivalent to upper secondary general education.

ISCED Level 4 Education at the fourth level (postsecondary nontertiary education) straddles the boundary between secondary and postsecondary education. This program of study, which is primarily vocational in nature, is generally taken after the completion of secondary school and typically lasts from 6 months to 2 years. Although the content of these programs may not be significantly more advanced than upper secondary programs, these programs serve to broaden the knowledge of participants who have already gained an upper secondary qualification.

ISCED Level 5 Education at the fifth level (short-cycle tertiary education) is noticeably more complex than in upper secondary programs giving access to this level. Programs at the fifth level typically provide practically based, occupationally specific content and prepare students to enter the labor market. However, the fifth level may also provide a pathway to other tertiary education programs (the sixth or seventh level). Short cycle-tertiary programs last for at least 2 years, and usually for no more than 3. In the United States, this level includes associate's degrees.

ISCED Level 6 Education at the sixth level (bachelor's or equivalent level) is longer and usually more theoretically oriented than programs at the fifth level, but may include practical components. Entry into these programs normally requires the completion of a third or fourth level program. They typically have a duration of 3 to 4 years of full-time study. Programs at the sixth level do not necessarily require the preparation of a substantive thesis or dissertation.

ISCED Level 7 Education at the seventh level (master's or equivalent level) has significantly more complex and specialized content than programs at the sixth level. The content at the seventh level is often designed to provide participants with advanced academic and/or professional knowledge, skills, and competencies, leading to a second degree or equivalent qualification. Programs at this level may have a substantial research component but do not yet lead to the award of a doctoral qualification. In the United States, this level includes professional degrees such as J.D., M.D., and D.D.S., as well as master's degrees.

ISCED Level 8 Education at the eighth level (doctoral or equivalent level) is provided in graduate and professional schools that generally require a university degree or diploma as a minimum condition for admission. Programs at this level lead to the award of an advanced, postgraduate degree, such as a Ph.D. The theoretical duration of these programs is 3 years of full-time enrollment in most countries (for a cumulative total of at least 7 years at the tertiary level), although the length of the actual enrollment is often longer. Programs at this level are devoted to advanced study and original research.

ISCED 1997 ISCED 1997 divides educational systems into the following seven categories, based on six levels of education.

ISCED Level 0 Education preceding the first level (early childhood education) usually begins at age 3, 4, or 5 (sometimes earlier) and lasts from 1 to 3 years, when it is provided. In the United States, this level includes nursery school and kindergarten.

ISCED Level 1 Education at the first level (primary or elementary education) usually begins at age 5, 6, or 7 and continues for about 4 to 6 years. For the United States, the first level starts with 1st grade and ends with 6th grade.

ISCED Level 2 Education at the second level (lower secondary education) typically begins at about age 11 or 12 and continues for about 2 to 6 years. For the United States, the second level starts with 7th grade and typically ends with 9th grade. Education at the lower secondary level continues the basic programs of the first level, although teaching is typically more subject focused, often using more specialized teachers who conduct classes in their field of specialization. The main criterion for distinguishing lower secondary education from primary education is whether programs begin to be organized in a more subject-oriented pattern, using more specialized teachers conducting classes in their field of specialization. If there is no clear breakpoint for this organizational change, lower secondary education is considered to begin at the end of 6 years of primary education. In countries with no clear division between lower secondary and upper secondary education, and where lower secondary education lasts for more than 3 years, only the first 3 years following primary education are counted as lower secondary education.

ISCED Level 3 Education at the third level (upper secondary education) typically begins at age 15 or 16 and lasts for approximately 3 years. In the United States, the third level starts with 10th grade and ends with 12th grade. Upper secondary education is the final stage of secondary education in most OECD countries. Instruction is often organized along subject-matter lines, in contrast to the lower secondary level, and teachers typically must have a higher-level, or more subject-specific, qualification. There are substantial differences in the typical duration of programs both across and between countries, ranging from 2 to 5 years of schooling. The main criteria for classifications are (1) national boundaries between lower and upper secondary education and (2) admission into educational programs, which usually requires the completion of lower secondary education or a combination of basic education and life experience that demonstrates the ability to handle the subject matter in upper secondary schools.

ISCED Level 4 Education at the fourth level (post-secondary nontertiary education) straddles the boundary between secondary and postsecondary education. This program of study, which is primarily vocational in nature, is generally taken after the completion of secondary school and typically lasts from 6 months to 2 years. Although the content of these programs may not be significantly more advanced than upper secondary programs, these programs serve to broaden the knowledge of participants who have already gained an upper secondary qualification.

ISCED Level 5 Education at the fifth level (first stage of tertiary education) includes programs with more advanced content than those offered at the two previous levels. Entry into programs at the fifth level normally requires successful completion of either of the two previous levels.

ISCED Level 5A Tertiary-type A programs provide an education that is largely theoretical and is intended to provide sufficient qualifications for gaining entry into advanced research programs and professions with high skill requirements. Entry into these programs normally requires the successful completion of an upper secondary education; admission is competitive in most cases. The minimum cumulative theoretical duration at this level is 3 years of full-time enrollment. In the United States, tertiary-type A programs include first university programs that last approximately 4 years and lead to the award of a bachelor's degree and second university programs that lead to a master's degree or a first-professional degree such as an M.D., a J.D., or a D.V.M.

ISCED Level 5B Tertiary-type B programs are typically shorter than tertiary-type A programs and focus on practical, technical, or occupational skills for direct entry into the labor market, although they may cover some theoretical foundations in the respective programs. They have a minimum duration of 2 years of full-time enrollment at the tertiary level. In the United States, such programs are often provided at community colleges and lead to an associate's degree.

ISCED Level 6 Education at the sixth level (advanced research qualification) is provided in graduate and professional schools that generally require a university degree or diploma as a minimum condition for admission. Programs at this level lead to the award of an advanced, postgraduate degree, such as a Ph.D. The theoretical duration of these programs is 3 years of full-time enrollment in most countries (for a cumulative total of at least 7 years at levels five and six), although the length of the actual enrollment is often longer. Programs at this level are devoted to advanced study and original research.

Interpolation See Linear interpolation.

Junior high school A separately organized and administered secondary school intermediate between the elementary and senior high schools. A junior high school is usually either a 3-year school that includes grades 7, 8, and 9 or a 2-year school that includes grades 7 and 8.

Labor force People employed (either full time or part time) as civilians, unemployed but looking for work, or in the armed services during the survey week. The "civilian labor force" comprises all civilians classified as employed or unemployed. See also Unemployed.

Lag An event occurring at time $t + k$ $(k > 0)$ is said to lag behind an event occurring at time t, the extent of the lag being k. An event occurring k time periods before another may be regarded as having a negative lag.

Land-grant colleges The First Morrill Act of 1862 facilitated the establishment of colleges through grants of land or funds in lieu of land. The Second Morrill Act in 1890 provided for money grants and for the establishment of land-grant colleges and universities for Black Americans in those states with dual systems of higher education.

Lead time When forecasting a statistic, the number of time periods since the last time period of actual data for that statistic used in producing the forecast.

Level of school A classification of elementary/secondary schools by instructional level. Includes elementary schools, secondary schools, and combined elementary and secondary schools. See also Elementary school, Secondary school, and Combined school.

Limited English proficient Refers to an individual who was not born in the United States and whose native language is a language other than English, or who comes from an environment where a language other than English has had a significant impact on the individual's level of English language proficiency. It may also refer to an individual who is migratory, whose native language is a language other than English, and who comes from an environment where a language other than English is dominant; and whose difficulties in speaking, reading, writing, or understanding the English language may be sufficient to deny the individual the ability to meet the state's proficient level of achievement on state assessments as specified under the Every Student Succeeds Act (2015), the ability to successfully achieve in classrooms where the language of instruction is English, or the opportunity to participate fully in society. See also English language learner.

Linear interpolation A method that allows the prediction of an unknown value if any two particular values on the same scale are known and the rate of change is assumed constant.

Local basic administrative unit See School district.

Local education agency (LEA) See School district.

Locale codes A classification system to describe a type of location. The "Metro-Centric" locale codes, developed in the 1980s, classified locations based on their proximity to a Metropolitan Statistical Area (MSA) and their population size and density. In 2006, the "Urban-Centric" locale codes were introduced. These locale codes are based on an address's proximity to an urbanized area. For more information, see https://nces.ed.gov/ccd/CCDLocaleCodeDistrict.asp.

Pre-2006 Metro-Centric Locale Codes (used in *Digest of Education Statistics* tables that reference "urbanicity"). The eight urbanicity subcategories are often collapsed into three major categories—urban, suburban, and rural—as shown below.

Urban

Large City: A central city of a consolidated metropolitan statistical area (CMSA) or MSA, with the city having a population greater than or equal to 250,000.

Mid-size City: A central city of a CMSA or MSA, with the city having a population less than 250,000.

Suburban

Urban Fringe of a Large City: Any territory within a CMSA or MSA of a Large City and defined as urban by the Census Bureau.

Urban Fringe of a Mid-size City: Any territory within a CMSA or MSA of a Mid-size City and defined as urban by the Census Bureau.

Rural (not within a CMSA or MSA)

Large Town: An incorporated place or Census-designated place with a population greater than or equal to 25,000 and located outside a CMSA or MSA.

Small Town: An incorporated place or Census-designated place with a population less than 25,000 and greater than or equal to 2,500 and located outside a CMSA or MSA.

Rural, Outside MSA: Any territory designated as rural by the Census Bureau that is outside a CMSA or MSA of a Large or Mid-size City.

Rural, Inside MSA: Any territory designated as rural by the Census Bureau that is within a CMSA or MSA of a Large or Mid-size City.

2006 Urban-Centric Locale Codes (used in *Digest of Education Statistics* tables that reference "locale"). The 12 locale subcategories are often collapsed into 4 major categories—city, suburban, town, and rural—as shown below.

City

City, Large: Territory inside an urbanized area and inside a principal city with population of 250,000 or more.

City, Midsize: Territory inside an urbanized area and inside a principal city with population less than 250,000 and greater than or equal to 100,000.

City, Small: Territory inside an urbanized area and inside a principal city with population less than 100,000.

Suburban

Suburb, Large: Territory outside a principal city and inside an urbanized area with population of 250,000 or more.

Suburb, Midsize: Territory outside a principal city and inside an urbanized area with population less than 250,000 and greater than or equal to 100,000.

Suburb, Small: Territory outside a principal city and inside an urbanized area with population less than 100,000.

Town

Town, Fringe: Territory inside an urban cluster that is less than or equal to 10 miles from an urbanized area.

Town, Distant: Territory inside an urban cluster that is more than 10 miles and less than or equal to 35 miles from an urbanized area.

Town, Remote: Territory inside an urban cluster that is more than 35 miles from an urbanized area.

Rural

Rural, Fringe: Census-defined rural territory that is less than or equal to 5 miles from an urbanized area, as well as rural territory that is less than or equal to 2.5 miles from an urban cluster.

Rural, Distant: Census-defined rural territory that is more than 5 miles but less than or equal to 25 miles from an urbanized area, as well as rural territory that is more than 2.5 miles but less than or equal to 10 miles from an urban cluster.

Rural, Remote: Census-defined rural territory that is more than 25 miles from an urbanized area and is also more than 10 miles from an urban cluster.

Magnet school or program A special school or program designed to reduce, prevent, or eliminate racial isolation and/or to provide an academic or social focus on a particular theme.

Mandatory transfer A transfer of current funds that must be made in order to fulfill a binding legal obligation of a postsecondary institution. Included under mandatory transfers are debt service provisions relating to academic and administrative buildings, including (1) amounts set aside for debt retirement and interest and (2) required provisions for renewal and replacement of buildings to the extent these are not financed from other funds.

Margin of error The range of potential true or actual values for a sample survey estimate. The margin of error depends on several factors such as the amount of variation in the responses, the size and representativeness of the sample, and the size of the subgroup for which the estimate is computed. The magnitude of the margin of error is represented by the standard error of the estimate.

Master's degree A degree awarded for successful completion of a program generally requiring 1 or 2 years of full-time college-level study beyond the bachelor's degree. One type of master's degree, including the Master of Arts degree, or M.A., and the Master of Science degree, or M.S., is awarded in the liberal arts and sciences for advanced scholarship in a subject field or discipline and demonstrated ability to perform scholarly research. A second type of master's degree is awarded for the completion of a professionally oriented program, for example, an M.Ed. in education, an M.B.A. in business administration, an M.F.A. in fine arts, an M.M. in music, an M.S.W. in social work, and an M.P.A. in public administration. Some master's degrees—such as divinity degrees (M.Div. or M.H.L./Rav), which were formerly classified as "first-professional"—may require more than 2 years of full-time study beyond the bachelor's degree.

Mathematics A group of instructional programs that describes the science of numbers and their operations, interrelations, combinations, generalizations, and abstractions and of space configurations and their structure, measurement, transformations, and generalizations.

Mean absolute percentage error (MAPE) The average value of the absolute value of errors expressed in percentage terms.

Mean test score The score obtained by dividing the sum of the scores of all individuals in a group by the number of individuals in that group for which scores are available.

Median earnings The amount that divides the income distribution into two equal groups, half having income above that amount and half having income below that amount. Earnings include all wage and salary income. Unlike mean earnings, median earnings either do not change or change very little in response to extreme observations.

Middle school A school with no grade lower than 5 and no grade higher than 8.

Migration Geographic mobility involving a change of usual residence between clearly defined geographic units, that is, between counties, states, or regions.

Minimum-competency testing Measuring the acquisition of competence or skills to or beyond a certain specified standard.

Model A system of postulates, data, and inferences presented as a mathematical description of a phenomenon, such as an actual system or process. The actual phenomenon is represented by the model in order to explain, predict, and control it.

Montessori school A school that provides instruction using Montessori teaching methods.

Multiple disabilities See Disabilities, children with.

National Assessment of Educational Progress (NAEP) See Appendix A: Guide to Sources.

National School Lunch Program Established by President Truman in 1946, the program is a federally assisted meal program operated in public and private nonprofit schools and residential child care centers. To be eligible for free lunch, a student must be from a household with an income at or below 130 percent of the federal poverty guideline; to be eligible for reduced-price lunch, a student must be from a household with an income between 130 percent and 185 percent of the federal poverty guideline.

Newly qualified teachers People who (1) first became eligible for a teaching license during the period of the study referenced or who were teaching at the time of survey, but were not certified or eligible for a teaching license; and (2) had never held full-time, regular teaching positions (as opposed to substitute) prior to completing the requirements for the degree that brought them into the survey.

Non-degree-granting institutions Postsecondary institutions that participate in Title IV federal financial aid programs but do not offer accredited 4-year or 2-year degree programs. Includes some institutions transitioning to higher level program offerings, though still classified at a lower level.

Nonprofessional staff See Employees in degree-granting institutions.

Nonprofit institution See Private institution.

Nonresident alien A person who is not a citizen or national of the United States and who is in this country on a visa or temporary basis and does not have the right to remain indefinitely.

Nonsectarian school Nonsectarian schools do not have a religious orientation or purpose and are categorized as regular, special program emphasis, or special education schools. See also Regular school, Special program emphasis school, and Special education school.

Nonsupervisory instructional staff People such as curriculum specialists, counselors, librarians, remedial specialists, and others possessing education certification, but not responsible for day-to-day teaching of the same group of pupils.

Nursery school An instructional program for groups of children during the year or years preceding kindergarten, which provides educational experiences under the direction of teachers. See also Prekindergarten and Preschool.

Obligations Amounts of orders placed, contracts awarded, services received, or similar legally binding commitments made by federal agencies during a given period that will require outlays during the same or some future period.

Occupied housing unit Separate living quarters with occupants currently inhabiting the unit. See also Housing unit.

Off-budget federal entities Organizational entities, federally owned in whole or in part, whose transactions belong in the budget under current budget accounting concepts, but that have been excluded from the budget totals under provisions of law. An example of an off-budget federal entity is the Federal Financing Bank, which provides student loans under the Direct Loan Program.

On-budget funding Federal funding for education programs that is tied to appropriations. On-budget funding does not include the Direct Loan Program, under which student loans are provided by the Federal Financing Bank, an off-budget federal entity. See also Off-budget federal entities.

Operation and maintenance services Includes salary, benefits, supplies, and contractual fees for supervision of operations and maintenance, operating buildings (heating, lighting, ventilating, repair, and replacement), care and upkeep of grounds and equipment, vehicle operations and maintenance (other than student transportation), security, and other operations and maintenance services.

Ordinary least squares (OLS) The estimator that minimizes the sum of squared residuals.

Organization for Economic Cooperation and Development (OECD) An intergovernmental organization of industrialized countries that serves as a forum for member countries to cooperate in research and policy development on social and economic topics of common interest. In addition to member countries, partner countries contribute to the OECD's work in a sustained and comprehensive manner.

Orthopedic impairment See Disabilities, children with.

Other health impairment See Disabilities, children with.

Other professional staff See Employees in degree-granting institutions.

Other religious school Other religious schools have a religious orientation or purpose, but are not Roman Catholic. Other religious schools are categorized according to religious association membership as Conservative Christian, other affiliated, or unaffiliated.

Other support services Includes salary, benefits, supplies, and contractual fees for business support services, central support services, and other support services not otherwise classified.

Other support services staff All staff not reported in other categories. This group includes media personnel, social workers, bus drivers, security, cafeteria workers, and other staff.

Outlays The value of checks issued, interest accrued on the public debt, or other payments made, net of refunds and reimbursements.

Parameter A quantity that describes a statistical population.

Part-time enrollment The number of students enrolled in postsecondary education courses with a total credit load less than 75 percent of the normal full-time credit load. At the undergraduate level, part-time enrollment typically includes students who have a credit load of less than 12 semester or quarter credits. At the postbaccalaureate level, part-time enrollment typically includes students who have a credit load of less than 9 semester or quarter credits.

Pass-through transaction A payment that a postsecondary institution applies directly to a student's account. The payment "passes through" the institution for the student's benefit. Most private institutions treat Pell grants as pass-through transactions. At these institutions, any Pell grant funds that are applied to a student's tuition are reported as tuition revenues. In contrast, the vast majority of public institutions report Pell grants both as federal revenues and as allowances that reduce tuition revenues.

Personal income Current income received by people from all sources, minus their personal contributions for social insurance. Classified as "people" are individuals (including owners of unincorporated firms), nonprofit institutions serving individuals, private trust funds, and private noninsured welfare funds. Personal income includes transfers (payments not resulting from current production) from government and business such as social security benefits and military pensions, but excludes transfers among people.

Physical plant assets Includes the values of land, buildings, and equipment owned, rented, or utilized by colleges. Does not include those plant values that are a part of endowment or other capital fund investments in real estate; excludes construction in progress.

Postbaccalaureate certificate An award that requires completion of an organized program of study beyond the bachelor's. It is designed for persons who have completed a bachelor's degree, but does not meet the requirements of a master's degree.

Postbaccalaureate enrollment The number of students working toward advanced degrees and of students enrolled in graduate-level classes but not enrolled in degree programs. See also Graduate enrollment.

Postsecondary education The provision of formal instructional programs with a curriculum designed primarily for students who have completed the requirements for a high school diploma or equivalent. This includes programs of an academic, vocational, and continuing professional education purpose, and excludes avocational and adult basic education programs.

Postsecondary institutions (basic classification by level)

   4-year institution An institution offering at least a 4-year program of college-level studies wholly or principally creditable toward a baccalaureate degree.

   2-year institution An institution offering at least a 2-year program of college-level studies that terminates in an associate degree or is principally creditable toward a baccalaureate degree. Data prior to 1996 include some institutions that have a less-than-2-year program, but were designated as higher education institutions in the Higher Education General Information Survey.

   Less-than-2-year institution An institution that offers programs of less than 2 years' duration below the baccalaureate level. Includes occupational and vocational schools with programs that do not exceed 1,800 contact hours.

Postsecondary institutions (2005 Carnegie classification of degree-granting institutions)

   Doctorate-granting Characterized by a significant level and breadth of activity in commitment to doctoral-level education as measured by the number of doctorate recipients and the diversity in doctoral-level program offerings. These institutions are assigned to one of the three subcategories listed below based on level of research activity (for more information on the research activity index used to assign institutions to the subcategories, see http://carnegieclassifications.iu.edu/):

   Research university, very high Characterized by a very high level of research activity.

   Research university, high Characterized by a high level of research activity.

   Doctoral/research university Awarding at least 20 doctor's degrees per year, but not having a high level of research activity.

Master's Characterized by diverse postbaccalaureate programs but not engaged in significant doctoral-level education.

Baccalaureate Characterized by primary emphasis on general undergraduate, baccalaureate-level education. Not significantly engaged in postbaccalaureate education.

Special focus Baccalaureate or postbaccalaureate institution emphasizing one area (plus closely related specialties), such as business or engineering. The programmatic emphasis is measured by the percentage of degrees granted in the program area.

Associate's Institutions conferring at least 90 percent of their degrees and awards for work below the bachelor's level. In NCES tables, excludes all institutions offering any 4-year programs leading to a bachelor's degree.

Tribal Colleges and universities that are members of the American Indian Higher Education Consortium, as identified in IPEDS Institutional Characteristics.

Poverty (official measure) The U.S. Census Bureau uses a set of money income thresholds that vary by family size and composition. A family, along with each individual in it, is considered poor if the family's total income is less than that family's threshold. The poverty thresholds do not vary geographically and are adjusted annually for inflation using the Consumer Price Index. The official poverty definition counts money income before taxes and does not include capital gains and noncash benefits (such as public housing, Medicaid, and food stamps). See also Supplemental Poverty Measure (SPM).

Prekindergarten Preprimary education for children typically ages 3–4 who have not yet entered kindergarten. It may offer a program of general education or special education and may be part of a collaborative effort with Head Start.

Preschool An instructional program enrolling children generally younger than 5 years of age and organized to provide children with educational experiences under professionally qualified teachers during the year or years immediately preceding kindergarten (or prior to entry into elementary school when there is no kindergarten). See also Nursery school and Prekindergarten.

Primary school A school with at least one grade lower than 5 and no grade higher than 8.

Private institution An institution that is controlled by an individual or agency other than a state, a subdivision of a state, or the federal government; that is usually supported primarily by other than public funds; and the operation of whose program rests with other than publicly elected or appointed officials.

Private nonprofit institution An institution in which the individual(s) or agency in control receives no compensation other than wages, rent, or other expenses for the assumption of risk. These include both independent nonprofit institutions and those affiliated with a religious organization.

Private for-profit institution An institution in which the individual(s) or agency in control receives compensation other than wages, rent, or other expenses for the assumption of risk (e.g., proprietary schools).

Private school Private elementary/secondary schools surveyed by the Private School Universe Survey (PSS) are assigned to one of three major categories of religious orientation (Catholic, other religious, or nonsectarian) and, within each major category, one of three subcategories based on the school's religious affiliation provided by respondents.

Catholic Schools categorized according to governance, provided by Catholic school respondents, into (i) parochial, (ii) diocesan, and (iii) private Catholic schools.

Other religious Schools that have a religious orientation or purpose but are not Roman Catholic. Other religious schools are categorized according to religious association membership, provided by respondents, into (i) Conservative Christian, (ii) other affiliated, and (iii) unaffiliated schools. Conservative Christian schools are those "Other religious" schools with membership in at least one of four associations: Accelerated Christian Education, American Association of Christian Schools, Association of Christian Schools International, and Oral Roberts University Education Fellowship. Affiliated schools are those "Other religious" schools not classified as Conservative Christian with membership in at least 1 of 11 associations—Association of Christian Teachers and Schools, Christian Schools International, Evangelical Lutheran Education Association, Friends Council on Education, General Conference of the Seventh-Day Adventist Church, Islamic School League of America, National Association of Episcopal Schools, National Christian School Association, National Society for Hebrew Day Schools, Solomon Schechter Day Schools, and Southern Baptist Association of Christian Schools— or indicating membership in "other religious school associations." Unaffiliated schools are those "Other religious" schools that have a religious orientation or purpose but are not classified as Conservative Christian or affiliated.

Nonsectarian Schools that do not have a religious orientation or purpose and are categorized according to program emphasis, provided by respondents, into (i) regular, (ii) special emphasis, and (iii) special education schools. Regular schools are those that have a regular elementary/ secondary or early childhood program emphasis. Special emphasis schools are those that have a Montessori, vocational/technical, alternative, or special program emphasis. Special education schools are those that have a special education program emphasis.

Professional staff See Employees in degree-granting institutions.

Program for International Student Assessment (PISA) See Appendix A: Guide to Sources.

Projection In relation to a time series, an estimate of future values based on a current trend.

Property tax The sum of money collected from a tax levied against the value of property.

Proprietary (for profit) institution A private institution in which the individual(s) or agency in control receives compensation other than wages, rent, or other expenses for the assumption of risk.

Public charter school A school providing free public elementary and/or secondary education to eligible students under a specific charter granted by the state legislature or other authority, and designated by such authority to be a charter school.

Public school or institution A school or institution controlled and operated by publicly elected or appointed officials and deriving its primary support from public funds.

Pupil/teacher ratio The enrollment of pupils at a given period of time, divided by the full-time-equivalent number of classroom teachers serving these pupils during the same period.

Purchasing Power Parity (PPP) indexes PPP exchange rates, or indexes, are the currency exchange rates that equalize the purchasing power of different currencies, meaning that when a given sum of money is converted into different currencies at the PPP exchange rates, it will buy the same basket of goods and services in all countries. PPP indexes are the rates of currency conversion that eliminate the difference in price levels among countries. Thus, when expenditures on gross domestic product (GDP) for different countries are converted into a common currency by means of PPP indexes, they are expressed at the same set of international prices, so that comparisons among countries reflect only differences in the volume of goods and services purchased.

R^2 The coefficient of determination; the square of the correlation coefficient between the dependent variable and its ordinary least squares (OLS) estimate.

Racial/ethnic group Classification indicating general racial or ethnic heritage. Race/ethnicity data are based on the Hispanic ethnic category and the race categories listed below (five single-race categories, plus the Two or more races category). Race categories exclude persons of Hispanic ethnicity unless otherwise noted.

White A person having origins in any of the original peoples of Europe, the Middle East, or North Africa.

Black or African American A person having origins in any of the black racial groups of Africa. Used interchangeably with the shortened term *Black*.

Hispanic or Latino A person of Cuban, Mexican, Puerto Rican, South or Central American, or other Spanish culture or origin, regardless of race. Used interchangeably with the shortened term *Hispanic*.

Asian A person having origins in any of the original peoples of the Far East, Southeast Asia, or the Indian subcontinent, including, for example, Cambodia, China, India, Japan, Korea, Malaysia, Pakistan, the Philippine Islands, Thailand, and Vietnam. Prior to 2010–11, the Common Core of Data (CCD) combined Asian and Pacific Islander categories.

Native Hawaiian or Other Pacific Islander A person having origins in any of the original peoples of Hawaii, Guam, Samoa, or other Pacific Islands. Prior to 2010–11, the Common Core of Data (CCD) combined Asian and Pacific Islander categories. Used interchangeably with the shortened term *Pacific Islander*.

American Indian or Alaska Native A person having origins in any of the original peoples of North and South America (including Central America), and who maintains tribal affiliation or community attachment.

Two or more races A person identifying himself or herself as of two or more of the following race groups: White, Black, Asian, Native Hawaiian or Other Pacific Islander, or American Indian or Alaska Native. Some, but not all, reporting districts use this category. "Two or more races" was introduced in the 2000 Census and became a regular category for data collection in the Current Population Survey in 2003. The category is sometimes excluded from a historical series of data with constant categories. It is sometimes included within the category "Other."

Region See Geographic region.

Regression analysis A statistical technique for investigating and modeling the relationship between variables.

Regular school An elementary/secondary or charter school providing instruction and education services that does not focus primarily on special education, vocational/technical education, or alternative education.

Related children Related children in a family include own children and all other children in the household who are related to the householder by birth, marriage, or adoption.

Remedial education Instruction for a student lacking those reading, writing, or math skills necessary to perform college-level work at the level required by the attended institution.

Resident population Includes civilian population and armed forces personnel residing within the United States; excludes armed forces personnel residing overseas.

Retention in grade Retaining a student in the same grade from one school year to the next.

Retention rate A measure of the rate at which students persist in their educational program at an institution, expressed as a percentage. For 4-year institutions, this is the percentage of first-time bachelor's (or equivalent) degree-seeking undergraduates from the previous fall who are again enrolled in the current fall. For all other institutions, this is the percentage of first-time degree/certificate-seeking students from the previous fall who either re-enrolled or successfully completed their program by the current fall.

Revenue All funds received from external sources, net of refunds, and correcting transactions. Noncash transactions, such as receipt of services, commodities, or other receipts in kind are excluded, as are funds received from the issuance of debt, liquidation of investments, and nonroutine sale of property.

Revenue receipts Additions to assets that do not incur an obligation that must be met at some future date and do not represent exchanges of property for money. Assets must be available for expenditures.

Rho A measure of the correlation coefficient between errors in time period t and time period t minus 1.

Rural location See Locale codes.

Salary The total amount regularly paid or stipulated to be paid to an individual, before deductions, for personal services rendered while on the payroll of a business or organization.

Sales and services Revenues derived from the sales of goods or services that are incidental to the conduct of instruction, research, or public service. Examples include film rentals, scientific and literary publications, testing services, university presses, and dairy products.

Sales tax Tax imposed upon the sale and consumption of goods and services. It can be imposed either as a general tax on the retail price of all goods and services sold or as a tax on the sale of selected goods and services.

SAT An examination administered by the Educational Testing Service and used to predict the facility with which an individual will progress in learning college-level academic subjects. It was formerly called the Scholastic Assessment Test.

Scholarships and fellowships This category of college expenditures applies only to money given in the form of outright grants and trainee stipends to individuals enrolled in formal coursework, either for credit or not. Aid to students

in the form of tuition or fee remissions is included. College work-study funds are excluded and are reported under the program in which the student is working.

School A division of the school system consisting of students in one or more grades or other identifiable groups and organized to give instruction of a defined type. One school may share a building with another school or one school may be housed in several buildings. Excludes schools that have closed or are planned for the future.

School administration support services Includes salary, benefits, supplies, and contractual fees for the office of the principal, full-time department chairpersons, and graduation expenses.

School climate The social system and culture of the school, including the organizational structure of the school and values and expectations within it.

School district An education agency at the local level that exists primarily to operate public schools or to contract for public school services. Synonyms are "local basic administrative unit" and "local education agency."

Science The body of related courses concerned with knowledge of the physical and biological world and with the processes of discovering and validating this knowledge.

Secondary enrollment The total number of students registered in a school beginning with the next grade following an elementary or middle school (usually 7, 8, or 9) and ending with or below grade 12 at a given time.

Secondary instructional level The general level of instruction provided for pupils in secondary schools (generally covering grades 7 through 12 or 9 through 12) and any instruction of a comparable nature and difficulty provided for adults and youth beyond the age of compulsory school attendance.

Secondary school A school comprising any span of grades beginning with the next grade following an elementary or middle school (usually 7, 8, or 9) and ending with or below grade 12. Both junior high schools and senior high schools are included.

Senior high school A secondary school offering the final years of high school work necessary for graduation.

Serial correlation Correlation of the error terms from different observations of the same variable. Also called Autocorrelation.

Serial volumes Publications issued in successive parts, usually at regular intervals, and as a rule, intended to be continued indefinitely. Serials include periodicals, newspapers, annuals, memoirs, proceedings, and transactions of societies.

Social studies A group of instructional programs that describes the substantive portions of behavior, past and present activities, interactions, and organizations of people associated together for religious, benevolent, cultural, scientific, political, patriotic, or other purposes.

Socioeconomic status (SES) The SES index is a composite of often equally weighted, standardized components, such as parental education and occupations, and family income. The terms high, middle, and low SES refer to ranges of the weighted SES composite index distribution.

Special education Direct instructional activities or special learning experiences designed primarily for students identified as having exceptionalities in one or more aspects of the cognitive process or as being underachievers in relation to general level or model of their overall abilities. Such services usually are directed at students with the following conditions: (1) physically disabled; (2) emotionally disabled; (3) culturally different, including compensatory education; (4) intellectually disabled; and (5) students with learning disabilities. Programs for the mentally gifted and talented are also included in some special education programs. See also Disabilities, children with.

Special education school A public elementary/secondary school that focuses primarily on special education for children with disabilities and that adapts curriculum, materials, or instruction for students served. See also Disabilities, children with.

Special program emphasis school A science/mathematics school, a performing arts high school, a foreign language immersion school, and a talented/gifted school are examples of schools that offer a special program emphasis.

Specific learning disability See Disabilities, children with.

Speech or language impairment See Disabilities, children with.

Standard error of estimate An expression for the standard deviation of the observed values about a regression line. An estimate of the variation likely to be encountered in making predictions from the regression equation.

Standardized test A test composed of a systematic sampling of behavior, administered and scored according to specific instructions, capable of being interpreted in terms of adequate norms, and for which there are data on reliability and validity.

Standardized test performance The weighted distributions of composite scores from standardized tests used to group students according to performance.

Status dropout rate The percentage of individuals within a given age range who are not enrolled in school and lack a high school credential, regardless of when they dropped out.

Status dropout rate (Current Population Survey) The percentage of civilian, noninstitutionalized young people ages 16–24 who are not in school and have not earned a high school credential (either a diploma or equivalency credential such as a GED certificate). The numerator of the status dropout rate for a given year is the number of individuals ages 16–24 who, as of October of that year, have not completed a high school credential and are not currently enrolled in school. The denominator is the total number of individuals ages 16–24 in the United States in October of that year. Status dropout rates count the following individuals as dropouts: those who never attended school and immigrants who did not complete the equivalent of a high school education in their home country.

Status dropout rate (American Community Survey) Similar to the status dropout rate (Current Population Survey), except that institutionalized persons, incarcerated persons, and active-duty military personnel living in barracks in the United States may be included in this calculation.

STEM fields Science, Technology, Engineering, and Mathematics (STEM) fields of study that are considered to be of particular relevance to advanced societies. In current *Digest of Education Statistics* tables, STEM fields include biological and biomedical sciences, computer and information sciences, engineering and engineering technologies, mathematics and statistics, and physical sciences and science technologies. STEM occupations include computer scientists and mathematicians; engineers; life and physical scientists; and managers of STEM activities.

Student An individual for whom instruction is provided in an educational program under the jurisdiction of a school, school system, or other education institution. No distinction is made between the terms "student" and "pupil," though "student" may refer to one receiving instruction at any level while "pupil" refers only to one attending school at the elementary or secondary level. A student may receive instruction in a school facility or in another location, such as at home or in a hospital. Instruction may be provided by direct student-teacher interaction or by some other approved medium such as television, radio, telephone, and correspondence.

Student membership Student membership is an annual headcount of students enrolled in school on October 1 or the school day closest to that date. The Common Core of Data (CCD) allows a student to be reported for only a single school or agency. For example, a vocational school (identified as a "shared time" school) may provide classes for students from a number of districts and show no membership.

Student support services Includes salary, benefits, supplies, and contractual fees for staff providing attendance and social work, guidance, health, psychological services, speech pathology, audiology, and other support to students.

Study abroad population U.S. citizens and permanent residents, enrolled for a degree at an accredited higher education institution in the United States, who received academic credit for study abroad from their home institutions upon their return. Students studying abroad without receiving academic credit are not included, nor are U.S. students enrolled for a degree overseas.

Suburban location See Locale codes.

Supervisory staff Principals, assistant principals, and supervisors of instruction; does not include superintendents or assistant superintendents.

Supplemental Poverty Measure (SPM) An alternative measure of poverty that supplements the U.S. Census Bureau's official poverty measure by adding to family income the value of benefits—including nutritional assistance, housing subsidies, and home energy assistance—from many government programs designed to assist those with low incomes, subtracting taxes and necessary expenses such as child care costs (for working families) and out-of-pocket medical expenses, and adjusting poverty thresholds for geographic differences in housing costs. See also Poverty (official measure).

Suspension Temporarily removing a student from his or her regular classroom (an in-school suspension) or from his or her regular school (an out-of-school suspension), generally for disciplinary purposes.

Tax base The collective value of objects, assets, and income components against which a tax is levied.

Tax expenditures Losses of tax revenue attributable to provisions of the federal income tax laws that allow a special exclusion, exemption, or deduction from gross income or provide a special credit, preferential rate of tax, or a deferral of tax liability affecting individual or corporate income tax liabilities.

Teacher see Instructional staff.

Technical education A program of vocational instruction that ordinarily includes the study of the sciences and mathematics underlying a technology, as well as the methods, skills, and materials commonly used and the services performed in the technology. Technical education prepares individuals for positions—such as draftsman or lab technician—in the occupational area between the skilled craftsman and the professional person.

Three-year moving average An arithmetic average of the year indicated, the year immediately preceding, and the year immediately following. Use of a 3-year moving average increases the sample size, thereby reducing the size of

sampling errors and producing more stable estimates.

Time series A set of ordered observations on a quantitative characteristic of an individual or collective phenomenon taken at different points in time. Usually the observations are successive and equally spaced in time.

Time series analysis The branch of quantitative forecasting in which data for one variable are examined for patterns of trend, seasonality, and cycle.

Title I school A school designated under appropriate state and federal regulations as a high-poverty school that is eligible for participation in programs authorized by Title I of the Reauthorization of the Elementary and Secondary Education Act, P.L. 107-110 (https://www2.ed.gov/policy/elsec/leg/esea02/pg1.html).

Title IV Refers to a section of the Higher Education Act of 1965 that covers the administration of the federal student financial aid program.

Title IV eligible institution A postsecondary institution that meets the criteria for participating in federal student financial aid programs. An eligible institution must be any of the following: (1) an institution of higher education (with public or private, nonprofit control), (2) a proprietary institution (with private for-profit control), and (3) a postsecondary vocational institution (with public or private, nonprofit control). In addition, it must have acceptable legal authorization, acceptable accreditation and admission standards, eligible academic program(s), administrative capability, and financial responsibility.

Total expenditure per pupil in average daily attendance Includes all expenditures allocable to per pupil costs divided by average daily attendance. These allocable expenditures include current expenditures for regular school programs, interest on school debt, and capital outlay. Beginning in 1980–81, expenditures for state administration are excluded and expenditures for other programs (summer schools and designated subsidies for community colleges and private schools) are included.

Town location See Locale codes.

Traditional public school Publicly funded schools other than public charter schools. See also Public charter school and Public school or institution.

Transcript An official list of all courses taken by a student at a school or college showing the final grade received for each course, with definitions of the various grades given at the institution.

Traumatic brain injury See Disabilities, children with.

Tribal colleges and universities An institutional

classification developed by the Andrew W. Carnegie Foundation for the Advancement of Teaching. Tribal colleges and universities, with few exceptions, are tribally controlled and located on reservations. They are all members of the American Indian Higher Education Consortium.

Trust funds Amounts collected and used by the federal government for carrying out specific purposes and programs according to terms of a trust agreement or statute, such as the Social Security and unemployment trust funds. Trust fund receipts that are not anticipated to be used in the immediate future are generally invested in interest-bearing government securities and earn interest for the trust fund.

Tuition and fees A payment or charge for instruction or compensation for services, privileges, or the use of equipment, books, or other goods. Tuition may be charged per term, per course, or per credit.

Type of school A classification of public elementary and secondary schools that includes the following categories: regular schools, special education schools, vocational schools, and alternative schools. See also Regular school, Special education school, Vocational school, and Alternative school. "School type" can also refer to whether the public school attended by a student was assigned to the student by the school district or chosen by the student's family in a district that allows school choice.

Unadjusted dollars See Current dollars.

Unclassified students Students who are not candidates for a degree or other formal award, although they are taking higher education courses for credit in regular classes with other students.

Undergraduate students Students registered at an institution of postsecondary education who are working in a baccalaureate degree program or other formal program below the baccalaureate, such as an associate's degree or a vocational or technical program.

Unemployed Civilians who had no employment but were available for work and (1) had engaged in any specific job-seeking activity within the past 4 weeks; (2) were waiting to be called back to a job from which they had been laid off; or (3) were waiting to report to a new wage or salary job within 30 days.

Ungraded student (elementary/secondary) A student who has been assigned to a school or program that does not have standard grade designations.

Urban location See Locale codes.

U.S. resident A citizen or national, or a person who has been admitted as a legal immigrant for the purpose of obtaining permanent resident alien status.

U.S. Service Academies These higher education institutions are controlled by the U.S. Department of Defense and the U.S. Department of Transportation. The five institutions counted in the NCES surveys of degree-granting institutions include: the U.S. Air Force Academy, U.S. Coast Guard Academy, U.S. Merchant Marine Academy, U.S. Military Academy, and the U.S. Naval Academy.

Variable A quantity that may assume any one of a set of values.

Visual and performing arts A group of instructional programs that generally describes the historic development, aesthetic qualities, and creative processes of the visual and performing arts.

Visual impairment See Disabilities, children with.

Vocational education Organized educational programs, services, and activities that are directly related to the preparation of individuals for paid or unpaid employment, or for additional preparation for a career, requiring other than a baccalaureate or advanced degree.

Vocational school A public school that focuses primarily on providing formal preparation for semiskilled, skilled, technical, or professional occupations for high school-age students who have opted to develop or expand their employment opportunities, often in lieu of preparing for college entry.

Women's colleges A college or university identified by the Women's College Coalition as a women's college.

Years out In forecasting by year, the number of years since the last year of actual data for that statistic used in producing the forecast.